# PSYCHOLOGY

## IN CONTEXT

### 3rd Edition

Stephen M. Kosslyn
**Harvard University**

Robin Rosenberg

Boston    New York    San Francisco

Mexico City    Montreal    Toronto    London    Madrid    Munich    Paris

Hong Kong    Singapore    Tokyo    Cape Town    Sydney

*To David, Nathaniel, and Justin,*
*for showing us how psychology really works.*

Editor-in-Chief: Susan Hartman
Series Editorial Assistant: Therese Felser
Senior Development Editor: Cheryl deJong-Lambert
Marketing Manager: Pamela Laskey
Managing Editor: Michael Granger
Editorial Production Service: Lifland et al., Bookmakers—Jane Hoover
Composition Buyer: Linda Cox
Manufacturing Buyer: Megan Cochran
Electronic Composition: Modern Graphics, Inc.
Interior Design: Gina Hagen
Photo Researcher: Imagequest—Sarah Evertson
Cover Administrator: Linda Knowles

For related titles and support materials, visit our online catalog at www.ablongman.com.

Between the time website information is gathered and then published, it is not unusual for some sites to have closed. Also, the transcription of URLs can result in typographical errors. The publisher would appreciate notification where these errors occur so that they may be corrected in subsequent editions.

**Library of Congress Cataloging-in-Publication Data**

Kosslyn, Stephen Michael
   Psychology in context / Stephen M. Kosslyn, Robin Rosenberg.—
3rd ed.
      p. cm.
   Includes bibliographical references and indexes.
   ISBN 0-205-45614-6
   1. Psychology—Textbooks. I. Rosenberg, Robin S. II. Title.

BF121.K59 2006
150—dc22

                                        2005058901

# BRIEF CONTENTS

**1**  **PSYCHOLOGY:** Yesterday and Today  2

**2**  **THE RESEARCH PROCESS:** How We Find Things Out  36

**3**  **THE BIOLOGY OF MIND AND BEHAVIOR:** The Brain in Action  76

**4**  **SENSATION AND PERCEPTION:** How the World Enters the Mind  132

**5**  **CONSCIOUSNESS:** Focus on Awareness  188

**6**  **LEARNING**  232

**7**  **MEMORY:** Living With Yesterday  276

**8**  **LANGUAGE AND THINKING:** What Humans Do Best  324

**9**  **TYPES OF INTELLIGENCE:** What Does It Mean To Be Smart?  378

**10**  **EMOTION AND MOTIVATION:** Feeling and Striving  426

**11**  **PERSONALITY:** Vive la Différence!  480

**12**  **PSYCHOLOGY OVER THE LIFE SPAN:** Growing Up, Growing Older, Growing Wiser  528

**13**  **STRESS, HEALTH, AND COPING**  586

**14**  **PSYCHOLOGICAL DISORDERS:** More Than Everyday Problems  628

**15**  **TREATMENT:** Healing Actions, Healing Words  684

**16**  **SOCIAL PSYCHOLOGY:** Meeting of the Minds  732

**References**  R-1
**Glossary**  G-1
**Name Index**  NI-1
**Subject Index**  SI-1

# CONTENTS

Preface    xvii
Integrated Coverage of Gender and Cross-Cultural Issues    xxxiv
About the Authors    1

## CHAPTER 1

## PSYCHOLOGY: Yesterday and Today    2

**THE SCIENCE OF PSYCHOLOGY: Getting to Know You**    4
What Is Psychology?    4
Levels of Analysis: The Complete Psychology    5
   *Three Levels of Analysis in Psychology • All Together Now • Levels of Analysis in Action: Examining Racial Prejudice*

**PSYCHOLOGY THEN AND NOW: The Evolution of a Science**    10
Early Days: Beginning to Map Mental Processes and Behavior    11
   *Structuralism • Functionalism • Gestalt Psychology*
Psychodynamic Theory: More Than Meets the Eye    14
Behaviorism: The Power of the Environment    15
Humanistic Psychology    16
The Cognitive Revolution    17
Evolutionary Psychology    18
The State of the Union: Psychology Today    21

**THE PSYCHOLOGICAL WAY: What Today's Psychologists Do**    22
Clinical and Counseling Psychology: A Healing Profession    22
Academic Psychology: Teaching and Research    24
Applied Psychology: Better Living Through Psychology    25
The Changing Face of Psychology    27

**ETHICS: Doing It Right**    29

**ETHICS IN RESEARCH**    29
   *Research With People: Human Guinea Pigs? • Research With Animals*
Ethics in Clinical Practice    30
New Frontiers: Neuroethics    32

**REVIEW AND REMEMBER!**    33

## CHAPTER 2

## THE RESEARCH PROCESS: How We Find Things Out    36

**THE SCIENTIFIC METHOD: Designed to Be Valid**    38
Step 1: Specifying a Problem    38
Step 2: Observing Events    38
Step 3: Forming a Hypothesis    39
Step 4: Testing the Hypothesis    39
Step 5: Formulating a Theory    40
Step 6: Testing the Theory    40

**THE PSYCHOLOGIST'S TOOLBOX: Techniques of Scientific Research**    42
Descriptive Research: Just the Facts, Ma'am    42
   *Naturalistic Observation • Case Studies • Surveys*

Correlational Research: Do Birds of a Feather Flock Together?    44
Experimental Research: Manipulating and Measuring    45
   *Independent and Dependent Variables • Experimental and Control Groups and Conditions • Quasi-Experimental Design*
Be a Critical Consumer of Psychology    49
   *Reliability: Count on It! • Validity: What Does It Really Mean? •*

Bias: Playing With Loaded Dice • Experimenter Expectancy
Effects: Making It Happen • Psychology and
Pseudopsychology: What's Flaky and What Isn't?

**STATISTICS: Measuring Reality**    54
Descriptive Statistics: Telling It Like It Is    55
  Data • Frequency Distributions • Measures of Central
  Tendency • Measures of Variability • Relative Standing
Inferential Statistics: Sorting the Wheat From the Chaff    58
  Correlation: The Relationship Between Two Variables •
  Samples and Populations • Meta-Analysis
Lying With Statistics: When Good Numbers Go Bad    61

Selective Reporting • Lying with Graphs
Looking at Levels:  Graph Design for the Human Mind    65

**HOW TO THINK ABOUT RESEARCH STUDIES**    66
Reading Research Reports: The QALMRI Method    67
  Q Stands for the Question • A Stands for Alternatives •
  L Stands for the Logic of the Study • M Stands for the
  Method • R Stands for the Results • I Stands for Inferences
Writing Your Own Research Papers    00
  Understanding Research:  When Does Mental Practice
  Improve Later Performance?    70
**REVIEW AND REMEMBER!**    73

CHAPTER 3

# THE BIOLOGY OF MIND AND BEHAVIOR:  The Brain in Action    76

**BRAIN CIRCUITS: Making Connections**    78
The Neuron: A Powerful Computer    78
  Structure of a Neuron: The Ins and Outs • Neural Impulses:
  The Brain in Action
Neurotransmitters and Neuromodulators: Bridging the Gap  82
  Chemical Messages: Signals and Modulators • Receptors:
  On the Receiving End • Unbalanced Brain: Coping
  With Bad Chemicals
Glial Cells: More Than the Neurons' Helpmates    86
  Neurons and Glia: A Mutually Giving Relationship •
  Glial Networks: Another Way to Think and Feel?

**THE NERVOUS SYSTEM: An Orchestra With
  Many Members**    88
The Peripheral Nervous System: A Moving Story    88
  The Autonomic Nervous System • The Sensory–Somatic
  Nervous System
The Central Nervous System: Reflex and Reflection    90
  The Visible Brain: Lobes and Landmarks • Structure and
  Function: No Dotted Lines

**SPOTLIGHT ON THE BRAIN: How It Divides
  and Conquers**    94
The Cerebral Cortex: The Seat of the Mind    94
  Occipital Lobes: Looking Good • Temporal Lobes: Up to
  Their Ears in Work • Parietal Lobes: Inner Space • Frontal
  Lobes: Leaders of the Pack

The Dual Brain: Thinking
With Both Barrels
97
  Split-Brain Research:
  A Deep Disconnect
  Understanding Research:  The Hemispheric Interpreter    98
  Hemispheric Specialization: Not Just for the
  Deeply Disconnected
Beneath the Cortex: The Inner Brain    100
  Thalamus: Crossroads of the Brain • Hypothalamus:
  Thermostat and More • Hippocampus: Remember It •
  Amygdala: Inner Feelings • Basal Ganglia: More Than
  Habit-Forming • Brainstem: The Brain's Wakeup Call •
  Cerebellum: Walking Tall
The Neuroendocrine and Neuroimmune Systems: More
  Brain–Body Connections    104
  The Neuroendocrine System: It's Hormonal! • The
  Neuroimmune System: How the Brain Fights Disease
Looking at Levels:  The Musical Brain    106

**PROBING THE BRAIN**    109
The Damaged Brain: What's Missing?    109
Recording Techniques: The Music of the Cells    109
Neuroimaging: Picturing the Living Brain    111
  Visualizing Brain Structure • Visualizing Brain Function
Stimulation: Tickling the Neurons    114

**GENES, BRAIN, AND ENVIRONMENT: The Brain in the World**   115

**Genes as Blueprints: Born to Be Wild?**   115
   *Genetic Programs: The Genes Matter • Tuning Genetic Programs: The Environment Matters • Genes and Environment: A Single System • Environment and Genes: A Two-Way Street*

**Behavioral Genetics**   122

   *Heritability: Not Inheritability • Twin Studies: Only Shared Genes? • Adoption Studies: Separating Genes and Environment?*

**Evolution and the Brain: The Best of All Possible Brains?**   123
   *Natural Selection: Reproduction of the Fittest • Not Just Natural Selection: Accidents Do Happen*

**REVIEW AND REMEMBER!**   127

# CHAPTER 4

## SENSATION AND PERCEPTION: How the World Enters the Mind   132

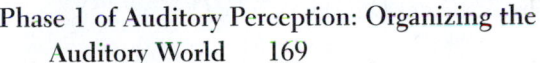

**VISION: Window on the World**   134

**Visual Sensation: More Than Meets the Eye**   135
   *Psychophysics: A World of Experience • How Do Objects Enter the Mind? Let There Be Light • The Brain's Eye: More Than a Camera • Color Vision: Mixing and Matching • Visual Problems: Distorted Windows on the World*

**Phase 1 of Visual Perception: Organizing the World**   144
   *Perceptual Organization: Seeing the Forest Through the Trees • Perceptual Constancies: Stabilizing the World • Knowing the Distance*

**Phase 2 of Visual Perception: Recognition and Identification**   150
   *Knowing More Than You Can See • Informed Perception: The Active Viewer • Coding Space in the Brain: More Than One Way to Identify "Where"*

   **Understanding Research:  Two Ways to Specify Spatial Relations**   154

**Combining What and Where: Faces and Gazes**   155
   *Identifying Faces: A Special Brain System? • Identifying Gaze Direction: Where's Something Important?*

**Attention: The Gateway to Awareness**   157
   *Pop-Out: What Grabs Attention? • Active Searching: Not Just What Grabs Attention • Limits of Attention • Seeing Without Awareness*

**Looking at Levels:  The Essential Features of Good Looks**   163

**HEARING**   165

**Auditory Sensation: If a Tree Falls but Nobody Hears It, Is There a Sound?**   165

   *Sound Waves: Being Pressured • The Brain's Ear: More Than a Microphone • Deafness: Hear Today, Gone Tomorrow*

**Phase 1 of Auditory Perception: Organizing the Auditory World**   169
   *Sorting Out Sounds: From One, Many • Locating Sounds: Why Two Ears Are Better Than One*

**Phase 2 of Auditory Perception: Recognition and Identification**   171
   *More Than Meets the Ear • Hearing Without Awareness • Music: Hearing for Pleasure*

**SENSING AND PERCEIVING IN OTHER WAYS**   174

**Smell: A Nose for News?**   174
   *Distinguishing Odors: Lock and Key • Olfaction Gone Awry: Is It Safe to Cook Without Smell? • Pheromones: Another Kind of Scents?*

**Taste: The Mouth Has It**   177
   *Sweet, Sour, Salty, Bitter • Taste and Smell*

**Somasthetic Senses: Not Just Skin Deep**   179
   *Kinesthetic Sense: A Moving Sense • Vestibular Sense: Being Oriented • Touch: Feeling Well • Temperature • Pain*

**Other Senses**   181
   *Magnetic Sense: Only for the Birds? • Extrasensory Perception (ESP)*

**REVIEW AND REMEMBER!**   183

# CHAPTER 5

# CONSCIOUSNESS: Focus on Awareness   188

**THE NATURE OF CONSCIOUSNESS**   190
Functions of Consciousness   190
The Experience of Consciousness   191
Altered States of Consciousness   191

**TO SLEEP, PERCHANCE TO DREAM**   193
Stages of Sleep: Working Through the Night   193
*Stage 1 • Stage 2 • Stages 3 and 4 • REM Sleep • Sleep Cycles*
Sleep Deprivation: Is Less Just as Good?   196
*REM Rebound • Sleep Deprivation: What Happens When You Skimp on Sleep • The Effects of All-Nighters*
Understanding Research: Sleep Deprivation Lite   197
The Function of Sleep   199
*Evolutionary Theory • Restorative Theory • Facilitating Learning*
Dream On   200
*What Triggers Particular Dreams? • Why Do We Dream?*
The Brain Asleep   202
*The Chemistry of Sleep: Ups and Downs • Circadian Rhythms*
Troubled Sleep   205
*Night Terrors: Not Your Usual Nightmares • Narcolepsy: Asleep at the Drop of a Hat • Insomnia • Sleep Apnea*
Looking at Levels: Recovery From Jet Lag   208

**HYPNOSIS AND MEDITATION**   209
What Is Hypnosis?   210
Individual Differences: Who Is Hypnotizable?   211
Hypnosis: Role Play or Brain State?   212
*Trance Theory • Sociocognitive Theory • Evidence From Neuroimaging*
Hypnosis as a Tool: Practical Applications   213
Hypnosis as Possession Trance   214
Meditation   214
*Types of Meditation • Benefits of Meditation • Meditation and the Body: More Than a Pause That Refreshes • Meditation Versus Relaxation • The Biology of Meditation*

**DRUGS AND ALCOHOL**   218
Substance Use and Abuse   218
Depressants: Focus on Alcohol   220
*Biological Effects of Alcohol • Psychological Effects of Alcohol • Chronic Abuse: More Than a Bad Habit • Other Depressants*
Stimulants: Focus on Cocaine   224
*Crack • Other Stimulants*
Narcotic Analgesics: Focus on Heroin   226
Hallucinogens: Focus on LSD   227
*A Creativity Boost? • Other Hallucinogens*

**REVIEW AND REMEMBER!**   229

# CHAPTER 6

# LEARNING   232

**CLASSICAL CONDITIONING**   235
Pavlov's Experiments   235
*The Three Phases of Classical Conditioning • Variations of the Procedure*
Classical Conditioning: How It Works   237
*Conditioned Emotions: Getting a Gut Response • Preparedness and Contrapreparedness • Extinction and Spontaneous Recovery in Classical Conditioning: Gone Today, Here Tomorrow • Generalization and Discrimination in Classical Conditioning: Seen One, Seen 'Em All? • Cognition and the Conditioned Stimulus*
Dissecting Conditioning: Mechanisms   242
*Learning to Be Afraid • Learning When to Blink*
Classical Conditioning Applied   244

*Drug Use and Abuse • Therapy Techniques • Advertising • Food and Taste Aversion*

**Understanding Research:** The Discovery of Taste Aversion   246
*Conditioning and Chemotherapy • Conditioning the Immune System*

**OPERANT CONDITIONING**   250

The Roots of Operant Conditioning: Its Discovery and How It Works   251
*Thorndike's Puzzle Box • The Skinner Box*

Principles of Operant Conditioning   252
*Reinforcement: Getting Your Just Desserts • Punishment • Primary and Secondary Reinforcers • Immediate Versus Delayed Reinforcement*

Beyond Basic Reinforcement   258
*Generalization and Discrimination in Operant Conditioning • Extinction and Spontaneous Recovery in Operant*

*Conditioning: Gone Today, Back Tomorrow • Building Complicated Behaviors: Shaping Up • Reinforcement Schedules: An Hourly or a Piece-Rate Wage?*

The Operant Brain   262
*Operant Conditioning: A Multifaceted Process • Classical Conditioning Versus Operant Conditioning: Are They Really Different?*

**Looking at Levels:** Facial Expressions as Reinforcement and Punishment   265

**COGNITIVE AND SOCIAL LEARNING**   267

Cognitive Learning   267

Insight Learning: Seeing the Connection   268

Observational Learning: To See Is to Know   269

Learning From Models   271
*"Do as I Do" • "Television Made Me Do It"*

**REVIEW AND REMEMBER!**   274

# CHAPTER 7

## MEMORY: LIVING WITH YESTERDAY   276

**ENCODING INFORMATION INTO MEMORY: Time and Space Are of the Essence**   278

Types of Memory Stores   279
*Sensory Memory: Lingering Sensations • Short-Term Memory: The Contents of Consciousness • Long-Term Memory: Records of Experience*

Making Memories   283
*Coding: Packaged to Store • Consolidation and Reconsolidation • Variations in Processing: Why "Thinking It Through" Is a Good Idea • Emotionally Charged Memories*

**STORING INFORMATION: Not Just One LTM**   290

Modality-Specific Memories: The Multimedia Brain   291

Semantic Versus Episodic Memory   291

Explicit Versus Implicit Memories: Not Just the Facts, Ma'am   292
*Classically Conditioned Responses • Nonassociative Learning • Habits • Skills: Automatic Versus Controlled Processing • Priming*

Biological Foundations of Memory   296
*Specialized Brain Areas • Linking Up New Connections • Genes and Memory • Stressed Memories*

**Looking at Levels:** Autobiographical Memory   299

**RETRIEVING INFORMATION FROM MEMORY: More Than Reactivating the Past**   301

The Act of Remembering: Reconstructing Buried Cities   301

Recognition Versus Recall   302

**Understanding Research:** A Better Police Lineup   303
*The Role of Cues: Hints on Where to Dig • Supplying Your Own Cues*

**FACT, FICTION, AND FORGETTING: When Memory Goes Wrong**   307

False Memories   307
*Implanting Memories • Distinguishing Fact From Fiction*

Forgetting: Many Ways to Lose It   310
*Encoding Failure: Lost in Translation • Decay: Fade Away • Interference: Tangled Up in Memory • Intentional Forgetting: Out of Mind, Out of Sight • Amnesia: Not Just Forgetting to Remember*

Repressed Memories: Real or Imagined?   313

**IMPROVING MEMORY: Tricks and Tools**   315

Enhancing Encoding: New Habits and Special Tricks   315

    *Organize It! • Process It! • Mnemonic Tricks: Going the Extra Mile*

Enhancing Memory Retrieval: Knowing Where and How to Dig   319

**REVIEW AND REMEMBER!**   321

CHAPTER 8

# LANGUAGE AND THINKING: What Humans Do Best   324

**LANGUAGE: More Than Meaningful Sounds**   326

The Essentials: What Makes Language Language?   326

    *Phonology: Some Say "ToMAYto" • Syntax: The Rules of the Road • Semantics: The Meaning Is the Message • Pragmatics: Being Indirect*

    Understanding Research:  Untangling Ambiguity During Comprehension   333

Language Development: Out of the Mouths of Babes   335

    *How Is Language Acquired? • Foundations of Language: Organizing the Linguistic World • Getting the Words • Grammar: Not From School • Biological Bases of Language Development*

Other Ways to Communicate: Are They Language?   342

    *Nonverbal Communication • Sign Language • Gesture: Is It Just for Show? • Aping Language*

Bilingualism: A Window of Opportunity?   344

**MEANS OF THOUGHT: Words, Images, Concepts**   346

Words: Inner Speech and Spoken Thoughts   347

    *Putting Thoughts Into Words • Does Language Shape Thought?*

Mental Imagery: Perception Without Sensation   348

    *Mental Space • The Visualizing Brain • Limitations of Mental Images as Vehicles of Thought*

Concepts: Neither Images nor Words   352

    *Prototypes: An Ostrich Is a Bad Bird • How Are Concepts Organized? • Concepts in the Brain*

**PROBLEM SOLVING**   356

Solving Problems: More Than Inspiration   357

    *Solving the Representation Problem: It's All in How You Look at It • Algorithms and Heuristics: Getting From Here to There • Solving Problems by Analogy: Comparing Features • Sudden Solutions • Cognitive Control*

Expertise: Why Hard Work Pays Off   362

Artificial Intelligence   364

Overcoming Obstacles to Problem Solving   365

**LOGIC, REASONING, AND DECISION MAKING**   366

Are People Logical?   367

    *How People Reason • Logical Errors • Framing Decisions*

Heuristics and Biases: Cognitive Illusions?   369

    *Representativeness • Availability*

Emotions and Decision Making: Having a Hunch   371

Looking at Levels:  The Ultimatum Game   372

**REVIEW AND REMEMBER!**   375

CHAPTER 9

# TYPES OF INTELLIGENCE: What Does It Mean to Be Smart?   378

**MEASURING INTELLIGENCE: What Is IQ?**   380

A Brief History of Intelligence Testing   381

    *Binet and Simon: Testing to Help • Terman and Wechsler: Tests for Everyone*

Scoring IQ Tests: Measuring the Mind   383

*Interpreting IQ Scores: Standardized Samples and Norming •*
*Reliability and Validity*

**IQ and Achievement: IQ in the Real World**   384

### ANALYZING INTELLIGENCE: One Ability or Many?   385

**Psychometric Approaches: IQ, g, and Specialized Abilities**   386

*Spearman's g Factor • Thurstone's Primary Mental Abilities •
Cattell and Horn's Fluid and Crystallized Intelligences •
Carroll's Three-Stratum Theory of Cognitive Ability • The g
Factor and Specific Abilities in the Real World*

**Emotional Intelligence: Knowing Feelings**   391

**Multiple Intelligences: More Than One Way to Shine?**   392

*Gardner's Theory of Multiple Intelligences: Something
for Everyone • Sternberg's Analytic, Practical, and
Creative Intelligences*

### WHAT MAKES US SMART? Nature and Nurture   395

**The Machinery of Intelligence**   396

*Brain Size and Intelligence: Is Bigger Always Better? •
Speed: Of the Essence? • Working Memory: Juggling
More Balls*

**Smart Genes, Smart Environment: A Single System**   399

*Genetic Effects: How Important Are Genes for Intelligence? •
Environmental Effects: More Real Than Apparent?*

**Group Differences in Intelligence**   404

*Within-Group Versus Between-Group Differences • Race
Differences • Sex Differences*

**Boosting IQ: Pumping Up the Mind's Muscle**   409

*The Flynn Effect: Another Reason to Appreciate Being
Young • Accidentally Making Kids Smarter:
The Pygmalion Effect • Intelligence Enhancement
Programs: Mental Workouts*

Looking at Levels:  Stereotype Threat   412

### DIVERSITY IN INTELLIGENCE   414

**Mental Retardation: People With Special Needs**   414

*Genetic Influences: When Good Genes Go Bad •
Environmental Influences: Bad Luck, Bad Behavior*

**The Gifted**   416

**Creative Smarts**   417

*Creative Thinking: Not Just Inspiration • What Makes a
Person Creative? • Enhancing Creativity*

Understanding Research:  Constrained Creativity   421

### REVIEW AND REMEMBER!   423

CHAPTER 10

## EMOTION AND MOTIVATION: Feeling and Striving   426

### EMOTION: I Feel, Therefore I Am   429

**Types of Emotion: What Can You Feel?**   429

*Basic Emotions • Separate But Equal Emotions*

**What Causes Emotions?**   432

*Theories of Emotion: Brain, Body, and World • Physiological
Profiles: Are Emotions Just Bodily Responses? • Cognitive
Interpretation • Fear: The Amygdala and You • Positive
Emotions: More Than Feeling Good*

**Expressing Emotions: Letting It All Hang Out?**   440

*Culture and Emotional Expression: Rules of the Mode*

Understanding Research:  Culture and Emoting   441

*Body Language: Broadcasting Feelings • Emotion Regulation*

**Perceiving Emotions: A Form of Mind Reading**   444

*Reading Cues • Perceiving by Imitating: Making the
Match • Individual Differences in Emotion Perception*

Looking at Levels:  Lie Detection   446

### MOTIVATION AND REWARD: More Than Feeling Good   449

**Getting Motivated: Sources
and Theories of
Motivation**   449

*Instincts: My Genes Made Me Do It • Drives and
Homeostasis: Staying in Balance • Arousal Theory:
Avoiding Boredom, Avoiding Overload • Incentives and
Reward: Happy Expectations • Learned Helplessness:
Unhappy Expectations*

**Needs and Wants: The Stick and the Carrot**   453

*Is There More Than One Type of Reward? • Types of Needs:
No Shortage of Shortages • Regulatory Fit • Achievement in
Individualist Versus Collectivist Cultures*

**Hunger and Eating: Not Just About Fueling
the Body**   458

Eating Behavior: The Hungry Mind in the Hungry Body   459
  *Is Being Hungry the Opposite of Being Full? • Appetite: A Moving Target • Why Does It Taste Good?*
Overeating: When Enough Is Not Enough   462
  *Set Point: Your Normal Weight • Obesity*
Dieting   465

**SEX: Not Just About Having Babies**   466
Sexual Behavior: A Many-Splendored Thing   467
  *Sexual Responses: Step by Step • The Role of Hormones: Do Chemicals Dictate Behavior?*

Sexual Stimuli   470
  *Mating Preferences*
Sexual Orientation: More Than a Choice   472
  *The Biology of Homosexuality • The Environment and Homosexuality*
What's Normal?   474
  *Cultural Variations: Experience Counts • Sexual Dysfunction: When Good Things Go Wrong • Atypical Sexual Behavior • Homophobia*

**REVIEW AND REMEMBER!**   477

CHAPTER 11

# PERSONALITY: Vive la Différence!   480

**PERSONALITY: Historical Perspectives**   482
Freud's Theory: The Dynamic Personality   482
  *The Structure of Personality • Personality Development: Avoiding Arrest • Defense Mechanisms: Protecting the Self • Freud's Followers • Critiquing Freudian Theory: Is It Science?*
Humanistic Psychology: Thinking Positively   487
  *Abraham Maslow • Carl Rogers*

**WHAT EXACTLY IS PERSONALITY?**   489
Personality: Traits and Situations   489
  *The Power of the Situation • Interactions Between Situation and Personality*
Factors of Personality: The Big Five? Three? More?   491
Measuring Personality: Is Grumpy Really Grumpy?   493
  *Interviews • Observation • Inventories: Check This • Projective Tests: Faces in the Clouds*

**BIOLOGY'S INFLUENCES ON PERSONALITY**   497
Temperament: Waxing Hot or Cold   497
  *Shyness: The Wallflower Temperament • Sensation Seeking: What's New?*
Biologically Based Theories of Personality   499
  *Behavioral Activation and Inhibition Systems • Eysenck's Theory • Cloninger's Theory • Zuckerman's Theory • Comparing the Biologically Based Theories*
Genes and Personality: Born to Be Mild?   504

Understanding Research: The Minnesota Study of Twins Reared Apart   504
  *Heritability of Personality • Heritability of Specific Behaviors • Genes and the Family Environment • How Do Genes Exert Their Influence?*

**LEARNING AND THE COGNITIVE ELEMENTS OF PERSONALITY**   509
Learning to Have Personality: Genes Are Not Destiny   509
The Sociocognitive View of Personality: You Are What You Expect   510
  *Expectancies • Self-Efficacy • Reciprocal Determinism*

**SOCIOCULTURAL INFLUENCES ON PERSONALITY**   513
Birth Order: Are You Number One?   513
Sex Differences in Personality: Nature and Nurture   515
  *Sociocultural Explanations • Biological Explanations*
Culture and Personality   517
  *Personality Changes Within a Culture, Over Time: The Times They Are A-Changin' • Consistent Personality Differences Across Cultures: Different Strokes for Different Countries • Understanding Cultural Differences in Personality: How Do Differences Arise?*
Looking at Levels: Attachment   520

**REVIEW AND REMEMBER!**   525

# CHAPTER 12

## PSYCHOLOGY OVER THE LIFE SPAN: Growing Up, Growing Older, Growing Wiser   528

**IN THE BEGINNING: From Conception to Birth**   530

Prenatal Development: Nature and Nurture From the Start   530

*From Zygote to Birth: Getting a Start in Life • Learning and Behavior in the Womb • Teratogens: Negative Environmental Events • Positive Environmental Events: The Earliest Head Start*

Understanding Research:  Stimulating the Unborn   536

The Newborn: A Work in Progress   537

*Sensory Capacities • Reflexes • Temperament: Instant Personality*

**INFANCY AND CHILDHOOD: Taking Off**   541

Physical and Motor Development: Getting Control   541

Perceptual and Cognitive Development: Extended Horizons   543

*Perceptual Development: Opening Windows on the World • Long-Term Memory Development: Living Beyond the Here and Now • Stages of Cognitive Development: Piaget's Theory • The Child's Concepts: Beyond Piaget • Information Processing and Neural Development • Vygotsky's Sociocultural Theory: Outside/Inside*

Social and Emotional Development: The Child in the World   554

*Attachment: More Than Dependency • Is Daycare Bad for Children? • Self-Concept and Identity: The Growing Self • Gender Identity and Gender Roles • Moral Development: The Right Stuff*

**ADOLESCENCE: Between Two Worlds**   562

Physical Development: In Puberty's Wake   562

Cognitive Development: Getting It All Together   564

*More Reasoned Reasoning? • Adolescent Egocentrism: It's All in Your Point of View*

Social and Emotional Development: New Rules, New Roles   565

*"Storm and Stress": Raging Hormones? • Evolving Peer Relationships • Teenage Pregnancy*

**ADULTHOOD AND AGING: The Continuously Changing Self**   568

Becoming an Adult   569

The Changing Body: What's Inevitable, What's Not   569

*Learning to Live With Aging • Why Do We Age?*

Perception and Cognition in Adulthood: Taking the Good With the Bad   570

*Perception: Through a Glass Darkly? • Memory: Difficulties in Digging It Out • Intelligence and Specific Abilities: Different Strokes for Different Folks*

Social and Emotional Development During Adulthood   575

*Theories of Psychosocial Stages in Adulthood • Continued Personality Development • Mature Emotions • Adult Relationships: Stable Changes*

Death and Dying   578

Looking at Levels:  Keeping the Aging Brain Sharp   580

**REVIEW AND REMEMBER!**   582


# CHAPTER 13

## STRESS, HEALTH, AND COPING   586

**WHAT IS STRESS?**   588

Stress: The Big Picture   588

The Biology of Stress   589

*The Alarm Phase: Fight or Flight • The Resistance Phase • The Exhaustion Phase • From Stressor to Allostatic Load: Multiple Stressors and Their Time Course • When Stressed, Women May Tend and Befriend*

It's How You Think of It: Interpreting Stimuli as Stressors    592
   *Appraisal: Stressors in the Eyes of the Beholder •*
   *Perceived Control*
Sources of Stress    595
   *Internal Conflict • Life Hassles • Work- and Economic-*
   *Related Factors • Hostility*

**STRESS, DISEASE, AND HEALTH**    601
The Immune System: Catching Cold    602
Cancer    603
Heart Disease    603
   *How Stress Affects the Heart • Stress, Emotions, and Heart*
   *Disease • Lifestyle Can Make a Difference*
Health-Impairing Behaviors    605
   *Why Do We Engage in Health-Impairing Behaviors? •*
   *Changing Health-Impairing Behaviors • Moving Through the*
   *Stages: The Shifting Pros and Cons*

**STRATEGIES FOR COPING**    609
Coping Strategies: Approaches and Tactics    609
   *Problem-Focused and Emotion-Focused Coping*
Understanding Research:  Emotional Disclosure
  and Health    611
   *Thought Suppression • Humor: Is Laughter the Best*
   *Medicine? • Aggression: Coping Gone Awry*
Personality and Coping    616
   *The Healthy Personality: Control, Commitment, Challenge •*
   *Optimism and Pessimism: Look on the Bright Side • Avoiders*
   *Versus Nonavoiders • Genes and Coping*
Coping and Social Support    619
   *Enacted Social Support • Perceived Social Support*
Mind–Body Interventions    621
   *The Effects of Mind–Body Interventions • The Placebo Effect*
   *as a Mind–Body Intervention*
Gender, Culture, and Coping    622
   *Gender Differences in Coping • Cultural Differences*
   *in Coping*
Looking at Levels:  Voodoo Death    624

**REVIEW AND REMEMBER!**    626

CHAPTER 14

# PSYCHOLOGICAL DISORDERS:
## More Than Everyday Problems    628

**IDENTIFYING PSYCHOLOGICAL DISORDERS:**
**What's Abnormal?**    630
Defining Abnormality    630
   *Distress • Impairment • Danger • Cultural and Social*
   *Influences*
Explaining Abnormality    632
   *The Brain: Genes, Neurotransmitters, and Brain Structure*
   *and Function • The Person: Behaviors, Thoughts and Biases,*
   *and Emotions • The Group: Social and Cultural Factors*
Categorizing Disorders: Is a Rose Still a Rose by Any Other
  Name?    635
   *History of the DSM • Disadvantages and Advantages of the*
   *DSM*

**MOOD DISORDERS**    638
Major Depressive Disorder: Not Just Feeling Blue    638
  Understanding Research:  Symptoms of Depression in China
   and the United States    640
Bipolar Disorder: Going to Extremes    642
Explaining Mood Disorders    643
   *Level of the Brain in*
   *Mood Disorders •*
   *Level of the Person in*
   *Mood Disorders •*
   *Level of the Group in*
   *Mood Disorders • Interacting Levels: Depression Is as*
   *Depression Does*

**ANXIETY DISORDERS**    648
Panic Disorder    648
   *Level of the Brain in Panic Disorder • Level of the*
   *Person in Panic Disorder • Level of the Group in*
   *Panic Disorder*
Phobias: Social and Specific    651
   *Level of the Brain in Phobias • Level of the Person in Phobias*
   *• Level of the Group in Phobias*
Obsessive-Compulsive Disorder (OCD)    653
   *Level of the Brain in OCD • Level of the Person in OCD •*
   *Level of the Group in OCD*
Posttraumatic Stress Disorder (PTSD)    655

*Level of the Brain in PTSD • Level of the Person in PTSD • Level of the Group in PTSD • Interacting Levels: Individual Differences in Responses to Trauma*

**SCHIZOPHRENIA**   659

**Symptoms: What Schizophrenia Looks Like**   660
*Positive Symptoms • Negative Symptoms • Diagnosing Schizophrenia*

**Subtypes of Schizophrenia**   661

**Why Does This Happen to Some People, But Not Others?**   662
*Level of the Brain in Schizophrenia • Level of the Person in Schizophrenia • Level of the Group in Schizophrenia • Interacting Levels in Schizophrenia*

**OTHER AXIS I DISORDERS: Dissociative and Eating Disorders**   667

**Dissociative Disorders**   668

*Dissociative Amnesia and Dissociative Fugue • Dissociative Identity Disorder*

**Eating Disorders: You Are How You Eat?**   670
*Anorexia Nervosa: You Can Be Too Thin • Bulimia Nervosa • Explaining Eating Disorders*

**Looking at Levels:** Binge Eating   674

**PERSONALITY DISORDERS**   675

**Axis II Personality Disorders**   676

**Antisocial Personality Disorder**   677

**Understanding Antisocial Personality Disorder**   678
*Level of the Brain in Antisocial Personality Disorder • Level of the Person in Antisocial Personality Disorder • Level of the Group in Antisocial Personality Disorder • Interacting Levels in Antisocial Personality Disorder*

**A CAUTIONARY NOTE ABOUT DIAGNOSIS**   680

**REVIEW AND REMEMBER!**   680

CHAPTER **15**

# TREATMENT:
# Healing Actions, Healing Words   684

**HISTORICAL INFLUENCES ON PSYCHOTHERAPY: Insight-Oriented Therapies**   686

**Psychodynamic Therapy: Origins in Psychoanalysis**   686
*Theory of Psychodynamic Therapy • Techniques of Psychodynamic Therapy*

**Humanistic Therapy: Client-Centered Therapy**   689
*Theory of Client-Centered Therapy • Techniques of Client-Centered Therapy*

**Evaluating Insight-Oriented Therapies**   690

**COGNITIVE–BEHAVIOR THERAPY**   692

**Behavior Therapy and Its Techniques**   692
*Theory of Behavior Therapy • Techniques of Behavior Therapy*

**Cognitive Therapy and Techniques: It's the Thought That Counts**   697
*Theory of Cognitive Therapy • Techniques of Cognitive Therapy*

**Cognitive–Behavior Therapy**   700

**BIOMEDICAL THERAPIES**   702

**Psychopharmacology**   702

*Schizophrenia and Other Psychotic Disorders • Mood Disorders • Anxiety Disorders*

**Electroconvulsive Therapy**   705

**Transcranial Magnetic Stimulation**   706

**OTHER FORMS OF TREATMENT**   707

**Modalities: When Two or More Isn't a Crowd**   707
*Group Therapy • Family Therapy • Self-Help Therapies*

**Innovations in Psychotherapy**   710
*Psychotherapy Integration: Mixing and Matching • Managed Care and Psychotherapy • Time and Therapy: Therapy Protocols and Brief Therapy • Technology and Therapy: High-Tech Treatment*

**Prevention: Sometimes Worth More Than a Pound of Cure**   713

**WHICH THERAPY WORKS BEST?**   715

**Issues in Psychotherapy Research**   715

*Positive Change in Therapy: The Healing Powers • Comparing Therapy Approaches and the Allegiance Effect • What's an Appropriate Control Group? • Reducing Confounds • Randomized Controlled Trials*

**Understanding Research:** For OCD: CBT Plus Medication, Without Exclusion  721

*Which Treatment Works Best for Which Disorder? • Therapy, Medication, or Both? • Treatment for an Ethnically Diverse Population*

How to Pick a Therapist and a Type of Therapy  726

**Looking at Levels:** Treating Obsessive-Compulsive Disorder  727

**REVIEW AND REMEMBER!**  729

## CHAPTER 16

# SOCIAL PSYCHOLOGY: Meeting of the Minds  732

**SOCIAL COGNITION: Thinking About People**  734

Making an Impression  734

*Thin Slices Are Enough • Halo and Primacy Effects • Self-Fulfilling Prophecy • Impression Management*

Attitudes and Behavior: Feeling and Doing  738

*Attitudes and Cognitions • Predicting Behavior • Behavior Affects Attitudes • Assessing Attitudes Directly and Indirectly • Cognitive Dissonance • Attitude Change: Persuasion • Social Cognitive Neuroscience*

Stereotypes: Seen One, Seen 'Em All  746

*Stereotypes Affect Attention, Cognition, and Behavior • Cognition and Prejudice*

**Understanding Research:** How Stereotypes Can Prime Behavior  748

*Processes Perpetuating Unconscious Prejudice • Discrimination • Why Does Prejudice Exist? • Changing Prejudice: Easier Said Than Done*

Attributions: Making Sense of Events  755

*What Is the Cause? • Taking Shortcuts: Attributional Biases*

**SOCIAL BEHAVIOR: Interacting With People**  758

Relationships: Having a Date, Having a Partner  759

*Liking: To Like or Not to Like • Loving: How Do I Love Thee? • Making Love Last • Mating Preferences: Your Cave or Mine?*

Social Organization: Group Rules, Group Roles  764

*Norms: The Rules of the Group • Roles and Status • When Roles Become Reality: The Stanford Prison Experiment*

Yielding to Others: Going Along With the Group  768

*Conformity and Independence: Doing What's Expected • Compliance: Doing What You're Asked • Obedience: Doing as You're Told*

Performance in Groups: Working Together  774

*Decision Making in Groups: Paths to a Decision • Social Loafing and Social Compensation • Social Facilitation: Everybody Loves an Audience*

Helping Behavior: Helping Others  776

*Prosocial Behavior • Bystander Intervention*

**Looking at Levels:** Cults  780

**A FINAL WORD: Ethics and Social Psychology**  781

**REVIEW AND REMEMBER!**  782

*References*  R-1
*Glossary*  G-1
*Name Index*  NI-1
*Subject Index*  SI-1
*Credits*  C-1

# PREFACE

How can we write a book that engages students and provides them with an *integrated* introduction to the field of psychology? That is what we asked each other as we began writing this textbook. One of us is a cognitive neuroscientist and the other a clinical psychologist. In writing collaboratively, we began to see how our different areas of psychology were dovetailing. Our teaching experience convinced us that the different areas of psychology really are facets of the same whole—and we were inspired to try to bring this view to a larger audience. We also wanted to show students how to apply the results of psychological research to make learning and remembering easier—not just for this course, but for any course, from economics to art history, and for the demands of life in general. In this edition, we continue to pursue our goal of presenting an integrated view of psychology, and we've tried to make the textbook even more accessible for students—to help them better understand and retain the material they read and to help them identify gaps in their understanding.

## Our Vision: Psychology in Context

Our vision has always been a textbook that better integrates the field of psychology. We do this by exploring how psychology can be viewed in terms of psychological events that occur in the context of other sorts of psychological events. The key to this approach is the idea that psychology can best be understood in terms of events that occur at different *levels of analysis*, a concept widely used in psychology and other sciences and in the real world. This approach leads us to focus on events in the brain (biological factors), the person (beliefs, desires and feelings), and the group (social, cultural and environmental factors). We stress that not only do all of these events occur in the physical world, where we are bathed with specific stimuli and behave in accordance with certain goals, but they also are constantly interacting.

One central idea of this book is that events at any two of the levels of analysis serve as the context for events at the remaining level. To understand fully events in the brain, we must also consider what's going on at the levels of the person and the group; by the same token, to understand events at the level of the person, we must consider the context of the brain and the group; and to understand events at the level of the group, we must consider the context of the brain and the person. No one level has a special status or is most important; any level can be the focus of our interest, leading the other levels to serve as the context. So important is this idea that we changed the title of this book—to stress that events at all three levels are always occurring and that events at any two levels serve as the context for understanding events at the third level.

For example, our brains are affected by our beliefs (just think of how worrying can make our bodies become tense, which is a direct result of events in the brain), and our social interactions both shape and are affected by our beliefs. In fact, as we discuss in this book, social interactions can actually cause the genes in our brain cells to operate differently. All psychological phenomena—from group interactions to psychological disorders, memory, and creativity—can best be understood by considering events at all three levels and how they interact, both with the world and with each other.

This view of psychology is exciting because it offers a way to organize a diverse range of theories and discoveries. The different areas of psychology are interconnected, although they are not often presented this way in textbooks. We wrote this book because no other textbook, in our opinion, was able to succeed in connecting the diverse areas of psychology.

# Greater Emphasis on the Science of Psychology

In the second edition of this book, we added a chapter on research methods (Chapter 2). Given our emphasis on the science of psychology, we decided that students really needed to see this material in one place. This chapter describes the scientific method, types of studies that psychologists typically conduct, and fundamental concepts of statistics. In addition, we describe a novel way to conceptualize and analyze research. The QALMRI method relies on clearly understanding the Question the research study asks, the Alternative answers that are considered, and the Logic that is applied to distinguish among the possible answers, as well as the Method, the Results, and the Inferences that can be drawn from the results. We use this method in Chapter 2 to take a detailed look at a specific study, and we continue to use it in each of the subsequent chapters in this book; in fact, in each chapter, we use the method to examine one study in detail, in an updated feature called Understanding Research.

In the third edition, we have continued to update and increase our coverage of relevant, cutting-edge scientific advances and their influences on the field of psychology. We also pride ourselves on providing the most comprehensive and yet accessible coverage of neuroscience for the introductory psychology student. Moreover, we put the neuroscience solidly in a *psychological context*; we don't describe facts about the brain for their own sake, but rather show how such facts illuminate psychology. We show how findings about the brain are best understood in the context of the person and the group.

## UNDERSTANDING RESEARCH

### Constrained Creativity

**QUESTION:** Many people believe that truly creative thought requires freedom, but others have argued that creativity thrives when there is a great deal of structure. When a problem is specified precisely and the approach is made very clear, is it easier to be creative?

**ALTERNATIVES:** (1) Structure can facilitate creativity. (2) Structure can inhibit creativity. (3) Structure makes no difference.

**LOGIC:** Goldenberg and colleagues (1999) programmed a computer to engage in the most extreme form of structured thinking: following an algorithm, a step-by-step set of rules. If such structure facilitates creativity, then the computer should be able to produce creative solutions—perhaps more of them than humans who are not working within such a strict structure.

**METHOD:** The researchers first studied effective advertisements and noticed that they seemed to rely on a few simple ideas (which are involved in creativity in general; Boden, 2000). For instance, many involved replacing properties of one thing with those of another: An ad for Bally shoes, for example, suggested that the shoes gave wearers a sense of freedom by showing clouds or an inviting island in the shape of a shoe; the sense of freedom conveyed by the clouds and the island was intended to transfer to the shoes. After being armed with such rules, the computer was asked to describe ads for specific products in order to convey certain messages; its suggestions were then compared to those from humans (who were not in the ad business).

# Text Organization

Most psychology textbooks have anywhere from 16 to 22 chapters; ours has 16. Market research has shown that when using textbooks with more than 16 chapters, introductory psychology instructors often end up either either skipping chapters or parts of a chapter in the interest of time or requiring students to read multiple chapters per week. Neither option is ideal, and both are likely to result in only a superficial grasp of the field as a whole. Introductory psychology is intended to be a survey of the entire field, and we believe that a book with 16 chapters allows students to sample all the areas of psychology. We have carefully chosen core and cutting-edge concepts, theories, and findings, to give students a thorough understanding of the field.

# Enhanced Pedagogical Features

Within each chapter of the third edition, we have chunked the material into smaller and thus easier-to-retain units of information to help students more readily learn it. This means an increased number of headings at all levels. Furthermore, the headings themselves are written to provide concise overviews of the material covered in the text sections, which allows students to use these headings both as a roadmap to the chapter and as an aid while studying. For easier studying and remembering, we have also grouped appropriate material into bulleted or numbered lists. In addition, the running foot of each right-hand page of a spread lists all the major sections within the chapter. The section in which material on that page is included is highlighted in red, so students are never lost—they see where they are, where they've been, and what lies ahead.

## Chapter Story

We begin each chapter with a story about a person or group. The story is then elaborated on throughout the chapter, providing a framework for the chapter's discussion of relevant psychological theories and research. These stories serve several purposes. They allow students to see how the psychological material covered in the chapter might apply to people outside of a psychological laboratory. They also make the

CHAPTER 9

# TYPES OF INTELLIGENCE: WHAT DOES IT MEAN TO BE SMART?

oanne (J. K.) Rowling's books about the young wizard Harry Potter have catapulted her into the role of international superstar and made her one of the world's wealthiest people. These books are chock full of clever plot twists and novel ideas. For example, the long-dead people in the portraits hanging on the walls throughout Harry's school not only talk, but develop relationships with each other. Photographs are not the inanimate tracings of remembered events, but instead are living entities, whose subjects come and go. Rowling got the idea for Harry Potter in a flash, and she knew from the start that she would write a seven-book series. She took 5 years to plan the series in detail, working out the plots for each of the novels. When she writes each book, "I know what and who's coming when, and it can feel like greeting old friends" (Fraser, 2000, p. 39). Think of it! What does it take to work out the details of seven novels in advance? Especially when you must not only attend to the usual ingredients of story-telling (the characters, the plot, and so on), but also need to create (and keep consistent) a whole new world?

At an early age, it was clear that Joanne Rowling had something special. To hear her tell it, "I was the epitome of a bookish child—short and squat, thick National Health glasses, living in a world of complete daydreams, wrote stories endlessly and occasionally came out of the fog to bully my poor sister and force her to listen to my stories and play the games I'd just invented. . . . I always felt I had to achieve, my hand always had to be the first to go up, I always had to be right" (Smith, 2001, p. 45). She proved more than adept at making up long and complex stories and was extraordinarily inventive. Foreshadowing her later interests, as a child, she made up games of wizards and witches, devising spells and concocting strange brews.

379

material more interesting and applicable to students' lives, thus facilitating learning and remembering. In addition, each story integrates the various topics addressed within a chapter, creating a coherent thematic whole to further enhance students' understanding. Finally, the story itself provides retrieval cues to help students remember the material.

In the third edition, we have introduced two new stories: The story in Chapter 9 (Types of Intelligence) traces the life of J. K. Rowling, the creative mind behind the wizard Harry Potter, and that in Chapter 10 (Emotion and Motivation) follows Mahatma Gandhi on his long journey of peaceful activism for social justice. As students learn more about Rowling or Gandhi (or any of the other people in the chapter stories) over the course of a chapter, they also learn more about psychological findings and principles and their applications. Because students are likely to remember the biographical information about these interesting individuals, they will also remember a lot about the content of the chapter. The chapter story is referred to or continued at the beginning of each section. This fosters integration with the rest of the chapter and introduces each section's topic in an applied context.

## Looking at Levels

Within each chapter, we take one aspect of the content—a theory or a psychological phenomenon—and consider it from the three levels of analysis: the brain, the person, and the group, as well as the interactions among events at each level. For instance, in Chapter 11 (Personality), we examine the concept of attachment from the level of the brain (what happens biologically and how attachment might be linked to temperament), the person (how feelings of attachment affect a person's sense of security and self-worth), and the group (how attachment style, which begins as a social event between infant and primary caretaker, in turn, influences an individual's interactions with other people throughout life). Each Looking at Levels feature serves to integrate knowledge about the brain, personal beliefs, desires, and feelings, and group interactions. Moreover, we show how events at each level can be the point of focus, with events at the other two levels serving as the context; we show that no one level of analysis is the most important, and no one level alone is sufficient to understand psychological phenomena. We integrate these diverse types of knowledge within each chapter, rather than relegating such information to one or two separate chapters. The Looking at Levels features also forge bridges that reach across chapters, leading to more effective learning and remembering.

## LOOKING AT LEVELS

### Attachment

In our closest relationships, we develop deep attachments to other people. However, people differ in their *attachment style*—their way of relating to significant others. Before we can analyze the nature of attachment, we must consider some key facts about it. One crucial finding is that an adult's attachment style with a partner stems from the way that the adult interacted with his or her parent (or

## Test Yourself

At the end of each major section, the fully revised Test Yourself feature asks general content questions that students should be able to answer based on a careful reading of the material. In the third edition, these are multiple-choice questions, whose answers appear upside-down at the end of each set. This format should help students quickly identify which concepts they've mastered and which topics will need more of their attention before they move on.

### Test Yourself

1. A young girl has an IQ of 50 and functions well socially. Her mother was nearly 50 years old when the girl was born. What is the most likely cause of her mental retardation?
   a. fragile X syndrome      c. autism
   b. Down syndrome           d. fetal alcohol syndrome
2. A gifted individual has an IQ
   a. the same as that of a normal person.
   b. between 150 and 180, according to the most common definition.
   c. at least 2 standard deviations above the mean, 130.
   d. over 200, if the person is truly gifted, but otherwise over 180.
3. Creative people are very likely to
   a. be the offspring of noncreative people.
   b. be chronically depressed.
   c. have a low IQ.
   d. be flexible in their thinking.
4. Research on enhancing creativity has found that it
   a. can never be enhanced.
   b. is predominantly genetic.
   c. can be enhanced.
   d. cannot be studied scientifically.

#### Answers

1.b 2.c 3.d 4.c

# Think It Through!

Critical thinking questions—called Think It Through!—are also provided for each major section of the chapter, immediately following the Test Yourself content-check questions. The Think It Through! questions ask students to apply the material to real-world settings or to the chapter-opening story, requiring them to think deeply about the material. Such active processing enhances memory. And the location of these questions encourages students to immediately apply and analyze the information they have just acquired.

## Think It Through!

The eugenics movement seeks to improve the human species by encouraging those with extremely low IQ scores not to have children. What do you think of this idea? Do you think it is useful to define people as mentally retarded or gifted? Why or why not?

Is creativity always desirable? What would the world be like if everyone were supercreative, always trying to change things? In what circumstances might creativity be more of a drawback than a benefit? Do you think all phases of the creative process rely equally on intelligence? If not, are there ways in which people of differing intelligence might best work together to be creative?

# Understanding Research

Certain basic elements are included in all research reports. In the Understanding Research features, we discuss and illustrate these elements, to help students as they read and interpret published research studies and as they write up their own research. In each chapter, we walk students through a selected research study so that they can understand the content in greater depth and learn to think critically about research. In the third edition, each Understanding Research feature is followed by a Think Critically! question set, which asks students to reflect on how best to interpret the research results.

# Review and Remember!

We have fully revised the end-of-chapter review elements to help students further grasp and consolidate what they have learned. The new two-column format allows students to review key concepts from each major section and to note their own questions, mnemonics, and content reminders.

**SUMMARY:** A section-by-section outline of the chapter's material is provided in the left-hand column of each Review and Remember! section. These outlines highlight key points that students should know after a thorough reading of the material. They help consolidate the core material even further into memory.

**YOUR NOTES:** In the right-hand column of the Review and Remember! section, students are encouraged to write their own thoughts, questions, and mnemonics, as well as study tips for each chapter. A sprinkling of sample notes is provided in each chapter.

## REVIEW AND REMEMBER!

### Summary

### I. Measuring Intelligence: What Is IQ?

**A.** The most common measure of intelligence is the score on an intelligence test, called the intelligence quotient, or IQ. IQ scores are a composite of many different underlying abilities, and the same IQ score can arise from different mixtures of relative strengths and weaknesses.

**B.** The most common IQ tests, the Wechsler Adult Intelligence Scale (WAIS) and the Wechsler Intelligence Scale for Children (WISC), consist of two sets of subtests, one that assesses verbal performance and one that assesses non-verbal performance.

**C.** When first devised, IQ was a measure of mental age compared to chronological age. Today, IQ scores are based on standardized norms for large samples, which are updated periodically so that the mean score on the WAIS or the WISC is always 100 and a standard deviation is 15.

**D.** Scores on IQ tests are positively correlated with achievement in school and on the job; they are also correlated with many aspects of success in life, such as staying out of prison or having an enduring marriage.

### Your Notes

I.

A.

B.

C. *IQ now based on norms: 100 = average; 15 = one standard deviation*

D.

**KEY TERMS:** Each end-of-chapter review also contains a list of key terms, including page references, to aid students in mastering key psychological vocabulary. The key terms are highlighted in the text, and their definitions are provided in a marginal glossary that runs throughout each chapter, as well as in an alphabetized end-of-book glossary.

## Hands On Features

In most chapters we have included at least one demonstration of psychological phenomena for students to try alone or with others. The brief exercises will (1) provide students with another way to learn about the phenomenon—experiencing, not merely reading about it; (2) make the material more vivid, thereby enhancing students' attention and memory; and (3) put psychological principles into a concrete context, showing students that the principles really can affect how we think, feel, and behave.

The mini demonstrations include:

Introspection (p. 12)
Simulated participation in a research study (pp. 49–50)
Measured neural conduction time (p. 81)
Transduction in the retina (p. 138)
Finding your blind spot (p. 139)
Dark adaptation (p. 139)
Seeing afterimages (p. 142)
Ambiguous figures (p. 146)
Motion cues (p. 149)
Recognition and identification (pp. 151–152)
Pop-out (p. 158)
The Stroop Effect (p. 160)
Supertaster test (p. 178)
Kinesthetic sense (p. 179)
Meditation (pp. 215–216)
Mental image and classical conditioning (p. 242)
Chunking (p. 280)
Lincoln's head on a penny (p. 283)
Modality-specific memory (p. 291)

False memory (pp. 307–308)
Interactive images (p. 317)
Method of loci (p. 317)
Pegword systems (p. 318)
Rhyming words (p. 318)
Building mnemonics (p. 318)
Memory enhancing techniques (pp. 319–320)
Discovering syntax (pp. 328-329)
Mental imagery (pp. 349–350)
Prototypes (p. 353)
The hiking monk problem (p. 357)
The candle problem (p. 358)
Wason and Johnson-Laird's card task (p. 368)
Mental models (p. 367)
Representativeness (pp. 369–370)
Prochaska self-test (p. 606–607)
Suicide misconceptions self-test (p. 641)
Progressive muscle relaxation (p. 694)
Cognitive dissonance (p. 742)
Asch experiment (pp. 769–770)

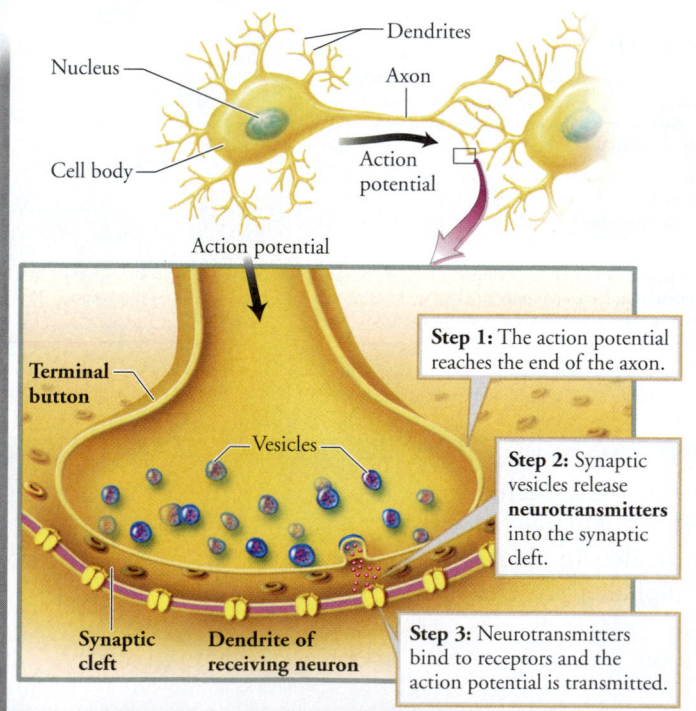

# New!
# Enhanced Art Program and Graphics Display

The third edition includes an entirely new art program that features high-quality and appropriately colorized images. The style and color schemes are carried throughout the book, so students don't encounter a hand-rendered fuchsia brain on one page and a grainy green brain photograph on another. Scrupulous adherence to one art style should help students develop and reinforce their own consistent mental images of important content material.

Many illustrations continue to highlight, in step-by-step fashion, some of the most important studies covered in the book. Examples are a study on alcohol and sexual aggression (p. 222), Watson's famous experiment with Little Albert (p. 239), Bandura's Bobo doll experiment (p. 270), Schachter and Singer's experiment on cognitive influences on emotion (p. 436), and Festinger's and Carlsmith's cognitive dissonance study (p. 742). These visual presentations not only complement the in-text descriptions, they enhance learning in several ways:

- The panels walk students through each study, allowing them to understand its details more fully.
- The clear, uncomplicated illustrations use perceptual principles to convey information effectively (these principles are described in detail in Kosslyn, 1994a, in press).
- This dual-mode format promotes both verbal and visual learning; students can recall either the words in the text or the illustrations when they remember the study.
- Working through these illustrations leads to active processing—and better remembering.

We have also added many new photos to illustrate particularly important or interesting facts or research findings. The photo captions convey information pertinent to the section, and the photos themselves are hooks that students can use to anchor their understanding of the material.

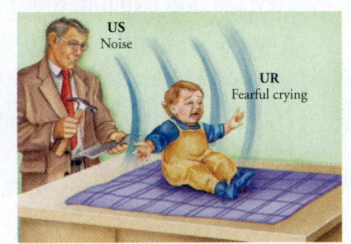

Initially, Little Albert did not show a fear of animals, but he did exhibit fear if a loud noise was made behind his back (a hammer striking a steel bar).

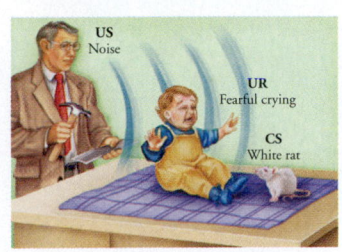

Then the researchers presented a white rat (CS) and made the loud noise (US).

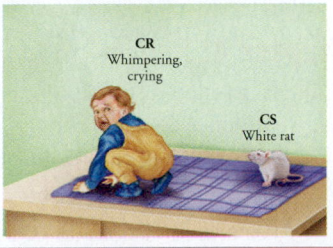

After five presentations of the CS and US, Albert developed a phobia of rats—he began whimpering and withdrawing (the conditioned emotional response) and trying to avoid the rat. After two more presentations of the CS and US, he immediately began crying on seeing the rat. "He ... fell over on his left side, raised himself ... and began to crawl away so rapidly that he was caught with difficulty before reaching the edge of the table" (Watson & Rayner, 1920, p. 5).

# What's New in the Third Edition?

Every chapter is full of discussion of cutting-edge research, accessibly presented with engaging real-world examples that make the material relevant and interesting to readers. Examples of the key changes in the third edition are listed below by chapter.

## Chapter 1: Psychology: Yesterday and Today

- Revised and expanded explanation of the unique levels-of-analysis approach
- Clear definition and discussion of psychodynamic theory
- Expanded discussion of cognitive neuroscience, which continues to draw on the skill of Tiger Woods to illustrate the concept
- Two new sections, entitled "The State of the Union: Psychology Today" and "The Changing Face of Psychology," to highlight new developments in the field and the increasing role of women
- New illustrations showing the jobs held by graduates with a B.A. in psychology and their job satisfaction
- Discussion of the burgeoning field of neuroethics in a new section called "New Frontiers: Neuroethics"
- 13 new citations of references

## Chapter 2: The Research Process: How We Find Things Out

- New text and illustrations to explain the steps of the scientific method
- Revised table summarizing the different research methods used in psychology
- 3 new citations of references

## Chapter 3: The Biology of Mind and Behavior: The Brain in Action

- Expanded coverage of glial cells and how they work in conjunction with neurons
- New section on the components of the sensory-somatic nervous system
- Revised discussion of the central nervous system

- Revised and expanded discussion of how the different parts of the brain work together
- Expanded discussion of the neuroimmune system and how the brain helps fight disease
- Revised Looking at Levels feature, "The Musical Brain"
- New photos to illustrate key concepts
- Discussion of magnetoencephalography (MEG) and its uses
- Discussion of new research in genetics and its relationship to the mind and behavior
- New coverage of knockout and knockin mice
- New figure illustrating how features of the environment can select among variations of characteristics, called natural selection
- 75 new citations of references

## Chapter 4: Sensation and Perception: How the World Enters the Mind

- Expanded discussion of color vision, newly formatted to make it easier for students to understand
- Reorganization of the section on visual perception for improved readability and understanding
- Expanded discussion of bottom-up and top-down processing
- New section, "Combining What and Where: Faces and Gazes," discussing how the two visual pathways work together
- New discussion of decibels, with an illustration to clarify the concept
- New illustration of dichotic listening
- Expanded discussion of pheromones and the behavior they elicit
- 101 new citations of references

## Chapter 5: Consciousness: Focus on Awareness

- Revised introduction to the nature of consciousness
- New and revised figures, tables, and photos to highlight key concepts
- New Understanding Research feature, "Sleep Deprivation Lite"
- New table outlining different theories of why we dream
- Discussion of new research findings related to sleep apnea
- Expansion of the Looking at Levels feature, "Recovery from Jet Lag," including a new table with methods of combating jet lag
- Expanded discussion of the ways in which hypnosis can help with pain management
- Revised section on the biology of meditation
- New table summarizing the psychological effects of alcohol
- Discussion of MDMA (also known as ecstasy or "e")
- 92 new citations of references

## Chapter 6: Learning

- Explanation of how sensitization occurs
- Division of the main section on classical conditioning into smaller units for improved readability and understanding
- New photos and figures to highlight key concepts
- Extended coverage of taste aversion in the Understanding Research feature, "The Discovery of Taste Aversion"
- New coverage on conditioning and chemotherapy
- Revised discussion of operant conditioning
- Discussion of additional research findings regarding delayed reinforcement

- Expanded discussion of observational learning
- Revised Looking at Levels feature, "Facial Expressions as Reinforcement and Punishment"
- Discussion of the actor-critic model of learning and its biological bases
- 70 new citations of references

## Chapter 7: Memory: Living With Yesterday

- Revised chapter organization and introduction
- Revised coverage of types of memory stores
- Revised discussion of how we make memories
- New photos, tables, and figures to illustrate key concepts
- New section about automatic versus controlled processing
- New discussion of brain specialization
- Expanded discussion of stress and its effect on memory
- Revised coverage of memory retrieval
- New section about hypnosis and memory
- Discussion of new research findings related to false memories
- New section about intentional forgetting
- Expanded coverage of amnesia
- Expanded coverage of repressed memories
- Revised section on tools and tricks that aid memory
- 77 new citations of references

## Chapter 8: Language and Thinking: What Humans Do Best

- Expanded coverage of language development with a new introduction to the section
- Discussion of latest research on the role of environment in language acquisition in the section titled "Enriching Environments"
- New illustrations and tables to demonstrate key concepts
- Expanded discussion of the neural bases of recollection
- Expanded discussion of prototypes
- Discussion of new research on the relationship between studying and GPA
- Expanded coverage of inductive and deductive reasoning
- Expanded coverage of the availability heuristic
- New Looking at Levels feature, "The Ultimatum Game"
- 61 new citations of references

## Chapter 9: Types of Intelligence: What Does It Mean to Be Smart?

- New opening story about J. K. Rowling
- Reorganization of some of the key concepts
- Expanded coverage of factor analysis
- Expanded discussion of fluid and crystallized intelligences
- New figures and tables to demonstrate key concepts
- Detailed discussion of Carroll's Three-Stratum Theory of Cognitive Ability
- Revised discussion of IQ and specific abilities in the real world
- Two new subsections, "The Importance of Having a Good Personality" and "The Importance of Analyzing the Tasks"

- Revised and expanded discussion of the role of working memory in intelligence
- Expanded discussion of twins and the effects of the prenatal environment
- Revised and expanded discussion of group differences in intelligence
- Expanded coverage of biological factors and sex differences in intelligence
- New Looking at Levels feature, "Stereotype Threat"
- 139 new citations of references

## Chapter 10: Emotion and Motivation: Feeling and Striving

- New opening story featuring Mahatma Gandhi
- Expanded discussion of theories of emotion
- Expanded discussion of fear
- Revised discussion of happiness
- New section, "Positive Psychology: More Than a State of Mind"
- Revised discussion of body language
- Expanded information on emotions and the brain
- New section, "Perceiving Emotions: A Form of Mind Reading," discussing cues that help us interpret emotions, such as body language, tone of voice, and facial expressions
- Expanded Looking at Levels feature, "Lie Detection"
- New introduction to the section on motivation and reward
- New section dealing with regulatory fit
- Expanded section on dieting, with a new table on popular diets and the key concerns physicians have with them
- New discussion of androgen insensitivity syndrome
- 95 new citations of references

## Chapter 11: Personality: Vive la Différence!

- New chapter organization
- Revised treatment of personality traits
- Reorganization of the discussion of the effect of situation on personality
- Expanded discussion of personality dimensions (superfactors)
- New sections, "Sensation Seeking," "Biologically Based Theories of Personality," and "Behavioral Activation and Inhibition Systems"
- Revised discussion of Eysenck's theory
- Expanded discussion of Cloninger's and Zuckerman's theories of personality
- New introduction to genes and their influence on personality
- Expanded discussion of the sociocognitive aspects of personality
- Expanded coverage of the relationship between culture and personality
- New Looking at Levels feature, "Attachment"
- 74 new citations of references

## Chapter 12: Psychology Over the Life Span: Growing Up, Growing Older, Growing Wiser

- New chapter organization
- New discussion of maturation
- Expanded discussion of the effects of teratogens on a fetus
- Expanded discussion of the effect of a positive environment on a fetus

- Expanded coverage of sensory perception in babies
- Revised discussion of brain development and memory
- Expanded discussion of changes in information processing with cognitive development
- Expanded discussion of attachment
- Expanded section on gender roles
- Expanded coverage of adolescent cognitive development
- New introduction to the section titled "Becoming an Adult"
- Discussion of the less differentiated brain in the section about adult development
- Expanded coverage on the aging brain
- 125 new citations of references

## Chapter 13: Stress, Health, and Coping

- New section, "From Stressor to Allostatic Load: Multiple Stressors and Their Time Course"
- New section on cognitive appraisal of stimuli
- Revised and expanded coverage of coping strategies
- Expanded discussion of optimism and pessimism
- Expanded coverage of social support
- New introduction to mind–body interventions
- Revised Looking at Levels feature, "Voodoo Death"
- 125 new citations of references

## Chapter 14: Psychological Disorders: More Than Everyday Problems

- Increased emphasis on looking at psychological disorders from the three levels of brain, person, and group, as well as on considering how events at the different levels interact
- Expanded discussion of the advantages and disadvantages of the *DSM*
- Revised discussion of major depressive disorder
- Reorganization of the section "Explaining Mood Disorders" for improved readability and understanding
- Revised discussion of how events at the various levels interact with each other to lead to depression
- Revised coverage of phobias, obsessive-compulsive disorder, and posttraumatic stress disorder
- Revised and reorganized discussion of schizophrenia and its subtypes
- Expanded discussion of how eating disorders can be explained at the level of the person
- Expanded cautionary note about the diagnosis of psychological disorders
- 86 new citations of references

## Chapter 15: Treatment: Healing Actions, Healing Words

- New chapter organization
- New introduction, with information about historical influences on psychotherapy
- New section, "Evaluating Insight-Oriented Therapies"
- Expanded section, "Techniques Based on Classical Conditioning"
- Expanded and revised coverage of psychopharmacology
- New coverage of how the placebo effect can lessen depression

- Revised discussion of self-help treatments
- Expanded discussion of therapy protocols
- Revised discussion of the use of technology in psychotherapy
- New discussion of research methods, including appropriate control groups, potential confounds, and randomized controlled trials
- New Looking at Levels feature, "Treating Obsessive-Compulsive Disorder"
- 104 new citations of references

**Chapter 16:** Social Psychology: Meeting of the Minds
- Expanded information on the self-fulfilling prophecy
- Revised discussion of direct versus indirect methods of assessing attitudes
- Expanded discussion of persuasion
- Expanded coverage of social cognitive neuroscience
- Expanded discussion of prejudice and the ways it influences behavior
- 79 new citations of references

# Instructor and Student Resources

*Psychology in Context, Third Edition,* is accompanied by the following teaching and learning tools.

## Instructor Supplements

### NEW! *PSYCHOLOGY IN CONTEXT,* INSTRUCTOR'S CLASSROOM KIT AND CD-ROM, VOLUMES I AND II

Our unparalleled classroom kit includes every instructional aid an introductory psychology professor needs to excel in the classroom. We have made our resources even easier to use by placing all of our print supplements in two convenient volumes. Organized by chapter, each volume contains the Instructor's Manual, Test Bank, Grade Aid Study Guide, and slides from the PowerPoint presentation. Electronic versions of the Instructor's Manual, Test Bank, PowerPoint presentation, images from the text, and video clips, all searchable by key terms, are made easily accessible to instructors on the accompanying Classroom Kit CD-ROMs.

- **Instructor's Manual** Written and updated for this edition by Marcia J. McKinley of Mount St. Mary's University, this robust teaching resource can be used by first-time or experienced instructors. Included are numerous handouts, detailed chapter outlines, lecture material, suggested reading and video sources, teaching objectives, and classroom activities and demonstrations.

- **Test Bank** Featuring more than 100 questions per chapter, the Test Bank includes multiple-choice, true/false, short answer, and essay items, each coded with difficulty rating, page references, and answer justifications. The test-writing team includes Rose Marie Ward of Miami University of Ohio, Michael McGuire of Washburn University, Robert Sorrells of Central Washington University, and Kristin Vickers of Ryerson University. The Test Bank is also available in TestGen 5.5 computerized version, for use in personalizing tests.

- **PowerPoint<sup>TM</sup> Presentation** The PowerPoint presentation for *Psychology in Context* includes images and key topics from the textbook and a link to the companion Web site for corresponding activities. The PowerPoint presentation is included on the Instructor's Classroom Kit CD-ROM and can also be downloaded from the Instructor Resource Center at www.ablongman.com/kosslyn3e.

**MYPSYCHLAB** This interactive and instructive multimedia resource can be used to supplement a traditional lecture course or to administer a course entirely online. It is an all-inclusive tool, a text-specific e-book plus multimedia tutorials, audio, video, simulations, animations, and controlled assessment to completely engage students and reinforce learning. Fully customizable and easy to use, MyPsychLab meets the individual teaching and learning needs of every instructor and every student. Visit the site at www.mypsychlab.com.

**NEW! PRINTED APPENDIX ON INDUSTRIAL/ORGANIZATIONAL PSYCHOLOGY** Available for the first time with this edition, this appendix provides students with a valuable overview of the growing field of industrial and organizational (I/O) psychology. In this guide, students can see how the psychological concepts presented in the textbook are applied in the real world in any professional workplace. Regardless of the careers students pursue, they may be affected by the work of I/O psychologists, in anything from the description of a position they wish to obtain to the interview and evaluation processes to the way the work environment is designed.

**INSIGHTS INTO PSYCHOLOGY VIDEO OR DVD, VOLS. I–IV** These video programs include two or three short clips per topic, covering such topics as animal research, parapsychology, health and stress, Alzheimer's disease, bilingual education, genetics and IQ, and much more. A Video Guide containing critical thinking questions accompanies each video. Also available on DVD.

**THE BLOCKBUSTER APPROACH: A GUIDE TO TEACHING INTRODUCTORY PSYCHOLOGY WITH VIDEO** The Blockbuster Approach is a unique print resource for instructors who enjoy enhancing their classroom presentations with films. With heavy coverage of general, abnormal, social, and developmental psychology, this guide suggests a wide range of films to use in class and provides questions for reflection and other pedagogical tools to make the classroom use of film more effective.

**NEW! INTERACTIVE LECTURE QUESTIONS FOR CLICKERS** These lecture questions will jump-start exciting classroom discussions.

**ALLYN AND BACON DIGITAL MEDIA ARCHIVE FOR PSYCHOLOGY, 5.0** This comprehensive source includes still images, audio clips, web links, animation and video clips. Highlights include classic experimental psychology footage from Stanley Milgrim's *Invitation to Social Psychology*, biology animations, and more—with coverage of such topics as eating disorders, aggression, therapy, intelligence, and sensation and perception.

**INTRODUCTION TO PSYCHOLOGY TRANSPARENCY PACKAGE** The Transparency Kit includes approximately 230 full-color acetates to enhance classroom lecture and discussion—including images from all of Allyn and Bacon's introductory psychology texts.

**COURSE MANAGEMENT** Use these preloaded, customizable, content and assessment items to teach your online courses. Available in CourseCompass, Blackboard, and WebCT formats.

## Student Supplements

**MYPSYCHLAB, STUDENT VERSION** This interactive and instructive multimedia resource is an all-inclusive tool, a text-specific e-book plus multimedia tutorials, audio, video, simulations, animations, and controlled assessment to completely engage users and reinforce learning. Easy to use, MyPsychLab meets the individual learning needs of every student. Visit the site at www.mypsychlab.com.

### Tutor Center One-on-One Tutoring!—Now Included in MyPsychLab or Available for Separate Purchase  www.ablongman.com/tutorcenter/psych

A support service that's available when you need it! Qualified tutors will answer questions about material in the text. The Tutor Center is open during peak study hours—in the late afternoon and evenings, 5–12 p.m. (EST), Sunday through Thursday during the academic calendar.

### Research Navigator™—Now Included in MyPsychLab or Available for Separate Purchase  www.ablongman.com/researchnavigator

The easiest way to start a research assignment or research paper. Research Navigator™ helps you quickly and efficiently make the most of your research time and write better papers. The program provides extensive help with the research process and includes three exclusive databases of credible and reliable source material: EBSCO's ContentSelect Academic Journal Database, *The New York Times* Search by Subject Archive, and Allyn and Bacon's "Best of the Web" Link Library.

### Grade Aid Study Guide with Practice Tests—Now included in MyPsychLab or available for Separate Purchase

Developed by Marcia J. McKinley at Mount St. Mary's College, this is a comprehensive and interactive study guide. Each chapter includes: "Before You Read," with a brief chapter summary and chapter learning objectives; "As You Read," a collection of demonstrations, activities, and exercises; "After You Read," containing three short practice quizzes and one comprehensive practice test; "When You Have Finished," with Web links for further information and crossword puzzles using key terms from the text. An appendix includes answers to all practice tests and crossword puzzles.

# ACKNOWLEDGMENTS

We want to give a heartfelt thanks to the many reviewers who read earlier versions of one or more chapters, sometimes the entire book, and helped shape this third edition. This is by far a better book for their efforts.

Nancy Adler, University of California, San Francisco

Michael Todd Allen, University of Northern Colorado

Marlene Behrmann, Carnegie Mellon University

Bernard J. Baars, The Neurosciences Institute

Lisa Feldman Barrett, Boston College

Sara C. Broaders, Northwestern University

Ekaterina V. Burdo, Wright State School of Professional Psychology

Howard Casey Cromwell, Bowling Green State University

Charles S. Carver, University of Miami

Patrick Cavanagh, Harvard University

KinHo Chan, Hartwick College

Jonathan D. Cohen, Princeton University

Virginia Ann Cylke, Sweet Briar College

Richard J. Davidson, University of Wisconsin, Madison

Mark Davis, University of West Alabama

Pamela Davis-Kean, University of Michigan

Douglas R. Detterman, Case Western Reserve University

Wendy Domjan, University of Texas, Austin

Dale V. Doty, Monroe Community College

Nicholas Epley, University of Chicago

Joseph R. Ferrari, DePaul University

Albert M. Galaburda, Harvard Medical School

Peter Gerhardstein, Binghamton University

David T. Hall, Baton Rouge Community College

Argye Hillis, Johns Hopkins School of Medicine

Herman Huber, College of Saint Elizabeth

Alan E. Kazdin, Yale University School of Medicine

Andrea Rittman Lassiter, Minnesota State University, Mankato

Angela Lipsitz, Northern Kentucky University

Jon K. Maner, Florida State University

Michele Mathis, University of North Carolina, Wilmington

Stuart McKelvie, Bishop's University

Richard J. McNally, Harvard University

Steven E. Meier, University of Idaho

Robin K. Morgan, Indiana University Southeast

Eric S. Murphy, University of Alaska, Anchorage

Lynn Nadel, University of Arizona

Margaret Nauta, Illinois State University

Jason Nier, Connecticut College

Matthew K. Nock, Harvard University

Kevin Ochsner, Columbia University

Kathy R. Phillippi-Immel, University of Wisconsin, Fox Valley

Brad Pinter, Pennsylvania State University, Altoona

Robert Plomin, Institute of Psychiatry, London

Frank J. Provenzano, Greenville Technical College

Scott Rauch, Harvard Medical School

Patricia Sampson, University of Maryland, Eastern Shore

Lisa M. Shin, Tufts University

Jennifer Siciliani, University of Missouri, St. Louis

William C. Spears, Louisiana State University

Larry R. Squire, University of California, San Diego

Robert Stickgold, Harvard Medical School

Lisa Valentino, Seminole Community College

Tor Wager, Columbia University

J. Celeste Walley-Jean, Spelman College

Daniel T. Willingham, University of Virginia

Karen L. Yanowitz, Arkansas State University

Marvin Zuckerman, University of Delaware

We also want to thank the reviewers who helped shape previous editions: They helped create the foundation on which this new edition is built. Their comments were invaluable. (Note that the institution given below as the affiliation for each reviewer was accurate at the time of the review; some affiliations may have changed since then.)

## Second Edition Reviewers

Joel Alesancer, Western Oregon University

Mark Bardgett, Northern Kentucky University

Mark Baxter, Harvard University

Marlene Behrmann, Carnegie Mellon University

Joseph Bilotta, Western Kentucky University

Sarah Bing, University of Maryland, Eastern Shore

Galen Bodenhausen, Northwestern University

Douglas Cody Brooks, Denison University

Greg Buchanan, Beloit College

Michelle Butler, U.S. Air Force Academy

Laura Cartensen, Stanford University

Patrick Cavanagh, Harvard University

Paul Costa, National Institute of Aging, NIH

Joseph Davis, San Diego State University

Perri Bruen, York College

Lorin Elias, University of Saskatchewan

Delbert Ellsworth, Elizabethtown College

Merrill Garrett, University of Arizona

Michael Garza, Brookhaven College

Peter Gerhardstein, State University of New York–Binghamton

Harvey Ginsburg, Southwest Texas State University

Jordan Grafman, National Institute of Neurological Disorders and Strokes

Dana Gross, St. Olaf College

Larry Hawk, State University of New York–Buffalo

Julie Hoigaard, University of California–Irvine

Dan Horn, University of Michigan

Stephen Hoyer, Pittsburgh State University

Kathy Immel, University of Wisconsin–Fox Valley

Alan Kazdin, Yale University

Melvyn King, State University of New York–Cortland

Joseph LeDoux, New York University

Matthew Lieberman, University of California, Los Angeles

Serry Loch, Paradise Valley Community College

Linda Lockwood, Metropolitan State College

Eric Loken, University of Pittsburgh

Michal Markham, Florida International University

Bruce McEwen, Rockefeller University

Marcia McKinley, Mount St. Mary's College

Marisa McLeod, Santa Fe Community College

Richard McNally, Harvard University

Todd D. Nelxon, California State University

Jacqueline Pope-Tarrence, Western Kentucky University

Beth Post, University of California, Davis

Celia Reaves, Monroe Community College

Gregory Robinson-Riegler, University of St. Thomas

Bennett Schwartz, Florida International University

Alan Searleman, St. Lawerence University

Paul Shinkman, University of North Carlina–Chapel Hill

Larry Squire, Veterans Affairs Medical Center, San Diego

Robert Stickgold, Harvard Medical School

Irene Valchos-Weber, Indiana University

John Wiebe, University of Texas, El Paso

# First Edition Reviewers

Sharon Akimoto, Carleton College

Jeff Anastasi, Francis Marion University

Joe Bean, Shorter College

James Benedict, James Madison University

James F. Calhoun, University of Georgia

Brad Carothers, Evergreen Valley College

James Carroll, Central Michigan University

M. D. Casey, St. Mary's College of Maryland

Dave Christian, University of Idaho

George A. Cicala, University of Delaware

Gerald S. Clack, Loyola University of New Orleans

Verne C. Cox, University of Texas, Arlington

Nancy Dickson, Tennessee Technical College

William O. Dwyer, University of Memphis

Valeri Farmer-Dougan, Illinois State University

William Ford, Bucks County Community College

Mary Gauvain, University of California, Riverside

Dan Gilbert, Harvard University

Peter Graf, University of British Columbia

Peter Gram, Pensacola Junior College

Karl Haberlandt, Trinity College

Richard Hackman, Harvard University

Richard Haier, University of California, Irvine

Marjorie Hardy, Eckerd College

Bruce Henderson, Western Carolina University

James Hilton, University of Michigan

Rich Ingram, San Diego State University

John H. Krantz, Hanover College

Richard Lippa, California State University, Fresno

Walter J. Lonner, Western Washington University

Michael Markham, Florida International University

Pam McAuslan, University of Michigan, Dearborn

David G. McDonald, University of Missouri

Rafael Mendez, Bronx Community College

Sarah Murray, Kwantlen University College

Paul Ngo, Saint Norbert College

Thomas R. Oswald, Northern Iowa Area Community College

Carol Pandey, Los Angeles Pierce College

Robert J. Pellegrini, San Jose State University

Dorothy C. Piontkowski, San Francisco State University

Brad Redburn, Johnson County Community College

Cheryl Rickabaugh, University of Redlands

Alan Salo, University of Maine, Presque Isle

Jim Schirillo, Wake Forest University

Michael Scoles, University of Central Arkansas

Michal Shaughnessy, Eastern New Mexico University

Nancy Simpson, Trident Technical College

Linda J. Skinner, Middle Tennessee State University

Michael Spiegler, Providence College

Don Stanley, North Harris College

Bruce B. Svare, State University of New York at Albany

Thomas Thielan, College of St. Catherine

Paul E. Turner, Lipscomb University

Lori Van Wallendael, University of North Carolina, Charlotte

Frank J. Vattano, Colorado State Univesity

Rich Velayo, Pace University

Rich Wesp, East Stroudsburg University

We also profited enormously from conversations with our friends and colleagues, particularly Nalini Ambady, Mahzarin Banaji, Mark Baxter, Alain Berthoz, John Cacioppo, David Caplan, Alfonso Caramazza, Patrick Cavanagh, Verne Caviness, Christopher Chabris, Jonathan Cohen, Suzanne Corkin, Francis Crick, Richard Davidson, Susan Edbril, Jeffrey Epstein, Michael Friedman, Al Galaburda, Giorgio Gain, Jeremy Gray, Anne Harrington, Marc Hauser, Kenneth Hugdahl, Steven Hyman, Jerome Kagan, Julian Keenan, Denis Le Bihan, Fred Mast, Amy Mayer, Richard McNally, Merrill Mead-Fox, Ken Nakayama, Kevin O'Regan, Alvaro Pascual-Leone, Steven Pinker, Susan Pollak, Scott Rauch, Kim Rawlins, Melissa Robbins, Robert Rose, Steven Rosenberg, Margaret Ross, Daniel Schacter, Jeanne Serafin, Lisa Shin, Dan Simons, Edward E. Smith, Elizabeth Spelke, David Spiegel, Larry Squire, Eve van Cauter, Laura Weisberg, and Edgar Zurif. We thank Maya and Alain Berthoz, Maryvonne Carafatan and Michel Denis, Christiane and Denis Le Bihan, Josette and Jacques Lautrey, Bernard Mazoyer, and Nathalie Tzurio-Mazoyer for their hospitality during our year in France, which made it possible and enjoyable to work productively there. We also thank the staff at the Collège de France for their help, in too many ways to list. And to our parents (Bunny, Stanley, Rhoda, and the late Duke) and our children (Nathaniel, David, and Justin), a huge thanks for your patience with our work-filled weekends and evenings, and for your love, support, and good humor. You have sustained us.

Other people have been instrumental in making the first draft of this book, and thus this third edition, a reality. These include Andrea Volfova (for her good-humored assistance and incisive comments), Jennifer Shepard, Bill Thompson, David Hurvitz, Steve Stose, Cinthia Guzman, Nicole Rosenberg, and Deborah Bell for their patience and willingness to help us dig out references and check facts, especially via long-distance communication during the year we were in France. The idea for the book developed over years of working with the Sophomore Tutors and Assistant to the Head Tutor, Shawn Harriman, at Harvard University, and we want to thank them all; helping them grapple with the concepts of levels of analysis led us to make this book clearer. We are particularly indebted to two of the tutors, Laurie Santos and Jason Mitchell, who read an early draft of the book and offered copious and wise comments. Finally, we wish to thank Christopher Brunt, an undergraduate who used the first edition of the book and spotted an ambiguity in one of the figures; we fixed the figure and appreciate his feedback. Dr. Suzanne M. Delaney, Dr. James H. Geer, and students Katherine Geier and June Ha took the time to share with us ways in which the second edition could be improved, and we greatly appreciate their observations and suggestions. We welcome with open arms feedback from all who read this book and have ideas about how to improve it.

Last but definitely not least, we want to thank the crew at Allyn and Bacon for their vision, support, good humor, and patience. Many special thanks to Karon Bowers, who, as Executive Editor for Psychology, initiated this revision before becoming the Editor-in-Chief for Communication, and to Susan Hartman, who has since taken the helm as Editor-in-Chief for Psychology; Pamela Laskey, Executive Marketing Manager, whose vision and enthusiasm for the book inspired us; Michael Granger, Production Manager, whose diligence and great eye made this edition look so good; Jane Hoover, copy editor extraordinaire, whose eagle eye and depth of processing of our words continually impress us; Sharon Geary, Director of Development, for reading first pages so carefully; Lara Torsky and Deb Hanlon, the editorial assistants who facilitated many important projects, including the commissioning of all the reviews; Jennifer Trebby, Associate Development Editor, and Kristin Vickers, for the many hours they spent on the all new Test Yourself questions, and editorial intern Mekea Harvey, who helped put some vital, final pieces of this project together. We also thank Editorial Director Jason Jordon, for his good listening abilities and creative solutions; Roth Wilkofsky, President of Allyn and Bacon/Longman, for his support and understanding; Sandi Kirschner, President of Addison Wesley Higher Education, and Bill Barke, CEO of Addison Wesley Higher Education, for their continuing support and participation in the project. Finally, and most importantly, our development editors on this edition, who have given so much of themselves to this project: Lisa McLellan, Senior Development Editor, who expertly and patiently guided the second edition of this text and labored through the critical early stages of this edition before departing for her own labor and motherhood, and Cheryl de Jong-Lambert, Senior Development Editor, who gallantly stepped into the breach with energy, patience, and great ideas. Thank you all.

Interest in gender and cultural diversity issues remains an important theme in modern psychology. These topics are treated throughout the text in an integrated fashion.

# Integrated Coverage of Gender Issues

Women in history of psychology, 28
Sex differences in color perceptions, 141
Sex differences in color blindness, 142–143
Sex differences in detecting odors, 175
Female pheromones and male attraction, 176–177
Sex differences in sensitivity to touch, 179
Possession trance in the Comoros, 214
Sex differences in drinking, 220
Alcohol and sexual aggression, 222
Sex differences in remembering emotional stimuli, 289
Sex differences when processing phonemes, 328
Women and emotional intelligence, 392
Sex differences in intelligence, 407–408
Sex differences in nonverbal behavior, 442–443
Sex differences in sexual response, 468
Sex differences in hormones, 468–470
Sex differences in sexual stimuli, 470
Mating preferences, 471–472, 762–763
Sexual orientation, 472–474

Sexual dysfunction for men and women, 474–475
Homophobia, 475–476
Freud's sex differences in psychosexual development, 484–485
Gender differences in personality, 515–517
Gender identity, 557–558
Sex differences in moral development, 559–560
Gender role development, 558–559
Sex differences in pubertal development, 562–563
Peer relationships, 567
Menopause, 570
Sex differences in grieving, 579
Stress and women, 590
Sex differences in hostility, 600
Gender differences in aggression, 614
Gender and coping, 622–623
Sex differences in prevalence of depression, 645–646
Sex differences in onset of schizophrenia, 661
Sex differences in prevalence of eating disorders, 671–672

# Integrated Coverage of Cross-Cultural Issues

Cultural universality, 19
Cross-cultural differences in drawing, 148–149
Perception of physical beauty and culture, 163–164
Possession trance in the Comoros, 214
Meditation and religion, 215
Behavior modification in nutrition in the Philippines, 258
Cultural differences in memory, 287
Cultural differences when processing phonemes, 327
Linguistic relativity hypothesis, 347–348
Group differences in intelligence, 404–405
Bias in intelligence testing, 406
Race and basic emotions, 429–431
Cultural differences in happiness, 439–440
Emotional expression and culture, 441–442
Achievement in individualist versus collectivist cultures, 457–458
Food preferences (taste) and culture, 461
Sexual behavior and culture, 474

Culture and personality, 517–520
Cognitive development and culture, 551–552
Teenage pregnancy and culture, 567–568
Death and culture, 579
Psychoneuroimmunology and culture, 602
Coping and culture, 622–623
Abnormal behavior and culture, 632, 634–635
Depression in China and the United States, 640–641
Depression and culture, 640–641
Khmer refugees and panic attacks, 650
Schizophrenia and culture, 666
Eating disorders and culture, 673–674
Treatment and culture, 726
Implicit attitudes, 740–741
Cognition, prejudice, and culture, 748
Attraction and culture, 760
Conformity and culture, 769–770

# ABOUT THE AUTHORS

## Stephen M. Kosslyn

Stephen M. Kosslyn is Chair of the Psychology Department and John Lindsley Professor of Psychology in Memory of William James at Harvard University, as well as Associate Psychologist in the Department of Neurology at Massachusetts General Hospital. He received his B.A. from UCLA and his Ph.D. from Stanford University, both in psychology. His research has focused primarily on the nature of visual mental imagery and visual communication, and he has published six books and over 250 papers on these topics. For ten years he was "head tutor," supervising graduate students teaching year-long introductory psychology courses using levels of analysis. While actively engaged with writing and academic pursuits, Dr. Kosslyn is currently on the editorial boards of many professional journals.

## Robin S. Rosenberg

Robin S. Rosenberg is a clinical psychologist in private practice and has taught psychology at Lesley University and Harvard University. She is certified in clinical hypnosis and is a member of the Academy for Eating Disorders. She received her B.A. in psychology from New York University, and her M.A. and Ph.D. in clinical psychology from the University of Maryland, College Park. Dr. Rosenberg did her clinical internship at Massachusetts Mental Health Center, had a postdoctoral fellowship at Harvard Community Health Plan, and was on the staff at Newton-Wellesley Hospital's Outpatient Services. Dr. Rosenberg specializes in treating people with eating disorders, depression, and anxiety.

# CHAPTER 1

# PSYCHOLOGY: YESTERDAY AND TODAY

On a balmy April day in 2002, a young man was playing golf. Nothing unusual about that. But when this young man sank his final putt, the watching crowd let out a roar, and he looked for his parents and embraced them, fighting back tears. The occasion was the PGA Masters Tournament, and the young man was Tiger Woods.

Think of the magnitude of his victory: At 26, Woods was the youngest three-time winner of the Masters. And golf's reigning champion, in a sport that had long been effectively closed to all but Whites, was of Asian, Black, White, and Native American ancestry. Tiger Woods dominated the sport of golf like no one before him or perhaps to come—all at a very young age. Before he came on the scene, golf was truly "the White man's sport," and the only place for a minority was as a caddy. After he burst into our collective awareness, he not only opened the sport to minorities, but also brought it into the mainstream—golf courses nationwide have become more crowded since Woods's rise to prominence.

If you could discern and explain the factors that led to Tiger Woods's meteoric rise to fame, you would be a very insightful psychologist.

But where would you begin? You could look at Woods's hand-eye coordination, his concentration and focus, and his ability to judge distances and calculate factors of wind, temperature, and humidity.

You could look at his personality—his reaction to racist hate mail (as a college student at Stanford University, he even kept one particularly vile letter taped to his wall), his religious beliefs (he was raised in his mother's faith, Buddhism), his demeanor during play, and his discipline in training.

You could look at his relationships with the social world around him—his family, his competitors, his fans.

Is this psychology? Indeed it is. Psychologists ask and, in scientific ways, attempt to answer questions about why and how people think, feel, and behave as they do. Because we are all human and so have much in common, sometimes the answers are universal. But we are also, like snowflakes, all different, and psychology helps to explain our uniqueness. Psychology is about mental processes and behavior, both exceptional and ordinary. In this chapter, we show you how to look at and answer such questions by methods used in current research and (because the inquiry into what makes us tick has a history) how psychologists over the past century have approached these questions.

# THE SCIENCE OF PSYCHOLOGY:
## Getting to Know You

Virtually everything any of us does, thinks, or feels falls within the sphere of psychology. You are dealing with the subject matter of psychology when you watch people interacting in a classroom or at a party, or notice that a friend is in a really terrible mood. The field of psychology aims to understand what is at work when you daydream as you watch the clouds drift by, when you have trouble recalling someone's name, even when you're asleep.

## What Is Psychology?

Although it may seem complex and wide-ranging, the field you are studying in this textbook can be defined in one simple sentence: **Psychology** *is the science of mental processes and behavior*. Let's look at the key words in this definition.

First, *science*: From the Latin *scire*, "to know," science avoids mere opinions, intuitions, and guesses and instead strives to nail down facts—to *know* them—by using objective evidence to answer questions like these: What makes the sun shine? Why does garlic make your breath smell strong? How is Tiger Woods able to direct his swings so superbly? A scientist uses logic to reason about the possible causes of a phenomenon and then tests the resulting ideas by collecting additional facts, which will either support the ideas or refute them, and thus nudge the scientist further along the road to the answer.

Second, *mental processes*: **Mental processes** are what your brain is doing not only when you engage in "thinking" activities such as storing memories, recognizing objects, and using language, but also when you feel depressed, jump for joy, or savor the experience of being in love. How can we find objective facts about mental processes, which are hidden and internal? One way, which has a long history in psychology, is to work backward, observing what people do and inferring from outward signs what is going on "inside." Another, as new as the latest technological advances in neuroscience, is to use brain-scanning techniques to take pictures of the living brain that show its physical changes as it works.

Third, *behavior*: By **behavior**, we mean the outwardly observable acts of a person, either alone or in a group. Behavior consists of physical movements, voluntary or involuntary, of the limbs, facial muscles, or other parts of the body. A particular behavior is often preceded by mental processes, such as a perception of the current situation (how far the golf ball must travel) and a decision about what to do next (how forcefully to swing the club). A behavior may also be governed by the relationship between the individual and a group. Tiger Woods might not have performed the way he did in 2002 had he been playing in 1920, when many in the crowd would not have wanted a non-White person to win. So there are layers upon layers: An individual's mental processes affect his or her behavior, and these processes are affected by the surrounding group (the members of which, in turn, have their own individual mental processes and behaviors).

When you think about a friend's "psychology," you might wonder about his or her motivations ("Why would she say such a thing?"), knowledge ("What does she know

**Psychology:** The science of mental processes and behavior.

**Mental processes:** What the brain does when a person stores, recalls, or uses information or has specific feelings.

**Behavior:** The outwardly observable acts of an individual, alone or in a group.

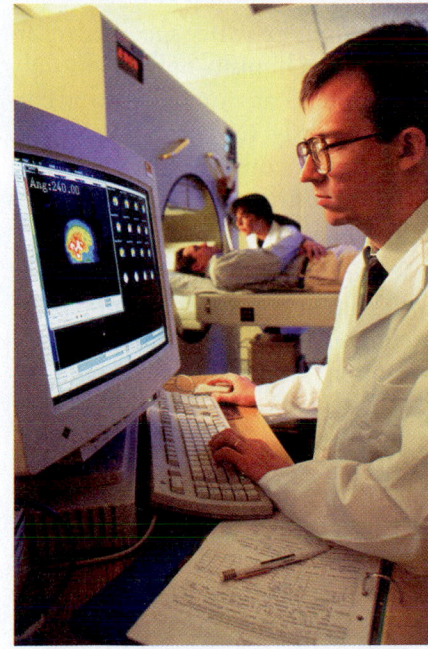
Science

Mental Processes

Behavior

that led her to make that decision?"), or goals ("What is she trying to accomplish by acting like that?"). In all cases, you are trying to *describe* (such as by inferring what your friend knows or believes) and *explain* (such as by inferring your friend's motivations) your friend's mental processes and behavior. Most people try to describe and explain other people's psychology on the basis of "common sense" or generalizations they've heard (such as the idea that some people are grouchy in the morning). The field of psychology is dedicated to helping us understand each other by using the tools of science. But more than that, psychology's goals are not simply to describe and explain mental processes and behavior, but also to *predict* and *control* them. As an individual, you'd probably like to be able to predict what kind of person would make a good spouse for you or which politician would make sound decisions in crisis situations. As a society, we all would greatly benefit by knowing how people learn most effectively, how to control addictive and destructive behaviors, and how to cure mental illness.

# Levels of Analysis: The Complete Psychology

The areas you might explore to answer questions about Tiger Woods's success—his coordination and focus, his beliefs and attitudes, his relationships with his parents and his audience—can be understood in terms of three types of events, each of which provides a field for analysis. Think for a moment about a computer. How can we understand what it does?

1. First, we can ponder the machine itself. The computer is a *mechanism*. One event causes another. You enter a "Save" command, it saves a file to a disk; you enter a "Print" command, it sends the file to the printer, and so forth. Each input triggers

a specific event, cause and effect. The computer program is like a mental process; it specifies the steps the mechanism takes in particular circumstances.

2. Second, we can ask about the *content* of the computer—the specific information it contains and what's being done to it. The mechanism behaves exactly the same way if you type a research paper, a love letter, or directions to a barbecue. Nevertheless, the differences in content obviously matter a great deal. The content relies on the mechanism (for instance, if the computer is not turned on, you cannot type in any content), but the mechanism and content are not the same.

3. Third, we can hook the computer into a network. We now focus on how different computers *affect each other and the network itself*. What happens when you type in a query to Google? Your computer (both the mechanism and the particular content you type) interacts with others that relay the query and finally send back information in response.

These so-called *levels of analysis* (to rely on the most accepted and widely used terminology) build on one another, with each level adding something new to our understanding of computing. Specifically, the content relies on the mechanism (as anyone knows who has tried to use a computer with a broken hard drive or malfunctioning power supply), and the network depends on both the content (such as the particular commands or requests you enter) and the mechanism (a functioning computer).

Do we really need to consider these three levels of analysis? To see why we do, suppose you log onto the internet and your computer suddenly freezes. Why? It could be that your hard drive has crashed (mechanism); or perhaps you entered an invalid command (content); or perhaps the network itself is down (network). To consider all of the possible reasons for your computer's malfunction, you need to contemplate disruptions at each level of analysis.

Now let's see how this analogy applies to humans.

## Three Levels of Analysis in Psychology

At any moment in Tiger Woods's day, or yours, events are happening at the same three levels we just considered in our computer analogy. Considering psychological phenomena from these three levels reveals much that would be hidden were we to look at only one level.

In humans, the *mechanism* is the brain and all of the biological factors that affect it. At this **level of the brain**, psychologists consider not only the activity of the brain but also the structure and properties of the organ itself—brain cells and their connections, the chemical soup in which they exist (including the hormones that alter the way the brain operates), and the genes that give rise to them. At the level of the brain, a psychologist might want to design an experiment to study how Tiger Woods can adjust the force of his swing so exquisitely well for driving, chipping, and putting and might speculate that the parts of his brain that control hand-eye coordination are especially well developed.

At the next level, consider how we use the information that our brains store and process. At this **level of the person**, psychologists focus on the *content* of mental processes, not just the internal mechanics that are the focus at the level of the brain. Unlike the level of the brain, we no longer talk about the characteristics of brain areas or how they operate to process information; rather, we talk about mental con-

**Level of the brain:** Events that involve the structure and properties of the organ itself—brain cells and their connections, the chemical soup in which they exist, and the genes.

**Level of the person:** Events that involve the nature of beliefs, desires, and feelings—the *content* of the mind, not just its internal mechanics.

tents such as beliefs (including ideas, explanations, expectations), desires (such as hopes, goals, needs), and feelings (fears, guilts, attractions, and the like). Although the brain is the locus and vehicle for content, the two are not the same—any more than a computer and a love letter written on it are the same. Rather, the brain is in many ways a canvas on which life's experiences are painted. Just as we can discuss how aspects of a canvas (such as its texture) allow us to paint, we can discuss how the brain supports mental contents. But just as we can talk about the picture itself (a portrait, a landscape, and so on), we can talk about mental contents. To do so, we must shift to another level of analysis. At the level of the person, a psychologist who is studying Tiger Woods might want to investigate the factors—among them, possibly, his Buddhist faith—behind the strong sense of inner calm he displays under pressure.

And third, just as computers in a network affect each other, people affect one another. "No man is an island," the poet John Donne wrote. We all live in *social environments* that vary over time and space and that are populated by our friends and professors, our parents, the other viewers in a movie theater, the other drivers on a busy highway. Our lives are intertwined with other people's lives, and from birth to old age, we take our cues from other people around us. The relationships that arise within groups make them more than simply collections of individuals. Psychologists not only study isolated individuals, but also investigate the mental processes and behavior of members of groups. Members of street gangs and political parties both have distinct identities based on shared beliefs and practices that are passed on to new members as *culture*, which has been defined as the "language, beliefs, values, norms, behaviors, and even material objects that are passed from one generation to the next" (Henslin, 1999). Thus, at the **level of the group**, psychologists consider the ways that collections of people (as few as two, as many as a society) shape individual mental processes and behavior. At the level of the group, a psychologist might want to examine the role of a supportive and enthusiastic audience in helping Tiger Woods birdie instead of bogey.

Events that occur at every level of analysis—brain, person, and group—are intimately tied to conditions in the physical world. All our mental processes and behaviors take place within and are influenced by a specific *physical environment*. A windy day at the golf course changes the way Tiger Woods plays a shot. The group is only part of the world; to understand the events at each level of analysis, we must always relate them to the physical world that surrounds all of us.

## All Together Now

Many people seem delighted to discover that their brains are not in fact computers. We noted above that the computer acts the same way when it is used to write a love letter or directions to someone's house. The human brain does not. When you feel an emotion (at the level of the person), that experience is accompanied by changes in how your brain operates (Davidson, 2004; Sheehan et al., 2004). In humans, unlike computers, events at the different levels are constantly interacting. For example, as you sit in a lecture hall, the signals among your brain cells that enable you to understand the lecture, and the new connections among your brain cells that enable you to remember it, are happening because you decided to take the course (perhaps because you need it to graduate): That is, events at the level of the person (your interests or perhaps knowledge of your school's requirements) are affecting events at the level of the brain. But, as you listen to the lecture, your neighbor's knuckle cracking is really getting to

Level of the group: Events that involve relationships between people (such as love, competition, and cooperation), relationships among groups, and culture. Events at the level of the group are one aspect of the environment; the other aspect is the physical environment itself (the time, temperature, and other physical stimuli).

you, and you're finding it hard to concentrate: Events at the level of the group are affecting events at the level of the brain. Because you really want to hear this stuff, you're wondering how to get your neighbor to cut it out, and you decide to shoot a few dirty looks his way: Events at the level of the person are affecting events at the level of the group (which, as we've seen, affect events at the level of the brain). And all of this is going on within the physical environment of the room, where the sunlight that had seemed warm and welcoming is now pretty hot, and you're getting drowsy, and you're *really* irritated, and you finally change your seat. . . . And round and round. Events at the three levels of analysis, in a specific physical context, are constantly changing and influencing one another. To understand fully what's going on in any life situation, you need to look at all three.

The concept of levels of analysis has long held a central role in science in general (Anderson, 1998; Nagel, 1979; Schaffner, 1967) and in the field of psychology in particular (Fodor, 1968, 1983; Kosslyn & Koenig, 1995; Looren de Jong, 1996; Marr, 1982; Putnam, 1973; Saha, 2004), and for good reason: This view of psychology not only allows you to see how different types of theories and discoveries illuminate the same phenomena, but it also lets you see how these theories and discoveries are interconnected—and thus how the field of psychology as a whole emerges from them.

## Levels of Analysis in Action: Examining Racial Prejudice

To help you grasp the crucial and central idea of levels of analysis, let's see how it helps us gain insight into a topic that touches each of our lives—namely, racial prejudice. At first glance, you might think that prejudice is based on a set of attitudes (in other words, overall evaluations) and those attitudes guide behavior (Durrheim & Dixon, 2004). However, this idea was challenged in the 1930s by the psychologist Richard La Piere (1934), who traveled the United States with a young Chinese couple. They stayed in 67 paid lodgings and ate in 184 restaurants and cafés. Six months after each visit, La Piere sent a questionnaire to those establishments inquiring whether they would accept Chinese people as customers. More than 90% of the proprietors said no. Yet on their trip La Piere and his companions were refused only once. This disparity did not arise because they engaged in behavior that provoked anti-Chinese sentiments, leading to negative views 6 months after their visit. Rather, stated attitudes do not necessarily predict behavior. In this case, the actual social interaction overrode how the people who ran the establishments felt. Our culture imposes certain rules of behavior, and these rules can sway us.

But this is not to say that attitudes have nothing to do with racial prejudice. For example, Dovidio, Kawakami, and Gaertner (2002) wanted to discover whether attitudes about race predicted how Whites actually behaved toward Blacks. To study this issue, they asked a number of students (who were all White) to discuss specific topics (for instance, dating) with other students, one at a time; sometimes the other student was Black, sometimes White. These interactions were video- and audio-taped, and later were rated by observers for both *nonverbal* friendliness (such as smiling and holding eye contact, which were considered to be unconscious, spontaneous behaviors) and *verbal* friendliness (the content of what was said, which was considered to be conscious, deliberative behavior).

The researchers wanted to predict these forms of behavior with measures of the White participants' attitudes towards Blacks. They collected two such measures. In one, they asked the participants to indicate directly (on a questionnaire) how they felt about Blacks—their conscious (self-aware) attitude. In the other, they used an indirect measure (based on measuring time to make decisions) to assess unconscious (not self-aware) attitudes (in Chapter 16, we will learn more about how such indirect measures work).

Did the participants' attitudes about Blacks predict their actual behavior toward the Black students? Yes and no. Their *conscious* attitudes, as measured by the questionnaire, predicted how *verbally* friendly they behaved toward the Black students, but not their nonverbal friendliness. In contrast, their unconscious attitudes (as measured by their response times) predicted *nonverbal* friendliness, but not verbal friendliness. The authors believe that the attitudes expressed on the questionnaire predict "deliberative behaviors," where the participants are aware of what they are doing, and the unconscious measures predict spontaneous behaviors.

What about the level of the brain—can knowing about the brain help us to understand the roots of racial prejudice? Absolutely. Here's an example of one study. Researchers used brain scanning to monitor how strongly one part of the brain, the amygdala (which we will discuss in Chapter 3), was activated while White participants viewed unfamiliar and familiar Black and White faces (Phelps et al., 2000). The amygdala is automatically activated when you are afraid (see Chapter 10). In this study, the researchers obtained a measure of the participants' unconscious prejudice against Blacks. They found that the amygdala was more strongly activated by viewing Black faces, compared to White faces, in people who had strong negative unconscious attitudes about Blacks. But this isn't all the researchers discovered: They did not find this relation between amygdala activation and scores of unconscious prejudice for the faces of *familiar* Black celebrities, such as Michael Jordan. These findings make sense if the amygdala is registering fear or other negative feelings in general, not just about race. These findings suggest that racial prejudice might have its roots—at least in part—in fear of the unfamiliar.

In short, we need to consider events at all three levels of analysis if we want to understand how people behave toward members of other races. Social conventions, including politeness, affect such behavior. And so do attitudes, with conscious and unconscious attitudes affecting different aspects of behavior. And so does the brain; in fact, unconscious attitudes in turn may reflect the way key parts of the brain respond. But more than this, we can see how events at these different levels *interact*. Social conventions may more easily affect deliberative behaviors that are controlled by your conscious attitudes than spontaneous behaviors that are unconsciously motivated. And these spontaneous behaviors in turn may arise from specific brain processes—the automatic nature of which explains why it is so difficult to control some of our behaviors consciously. By studying events at all three levels we can attain a much more thorough and deep understanding of prejudice than we could if we stuck to only one level. And by considering how these events interact, we may come to understand why some aspects of prejudice are more difficult to change than others—but also may see how even these aspects (such as those based on unfamiliarity and fear) might ultimately be changed.

In each of the rest of the chapters of this book, we will consider one aspect of psychology in detail, showing how it is illuminated when we investigate events at the three levels of analysis and their interactions. Moreover, we shall draw on the different levels continually as we encounter different aspects of the field throughout the book. The fact that interactions of events at the different levels of analysis are always present is one thread that holds the different areas of psychology together, that makes the field more than a collection of separate topics.

1. What is psychology?
   a. the scientific analysis of behavior
   b. the science of behavior and mental processes
   c. an exploration of human feelings
   d. the scientific study of the brain
2. At which level of analysis can Tiger Woods's golfing ability be best explained?
   a. the level of the brain
   b. the level of the person
   c. the level of the group
   d. All three levels are needed to explain behavior adequately.
3. Prejudice seems to be influenced by many factors, including social conventions and people's attitudes. Even brain structures play a role in prejudice. Looking at prejudice from the level of the person involves
   a. examining people's attitudes.
   b. looking at social conventions.
   c. mapping brain structures.
   d. looking at the history of prejudice in a specific culture.
4. Advantages to using a levels-of-analysis approach in psychology are
   a. learning how different theories shed light on the same event.
   b. seeing how various theories are interconnected.
   c. developing a richer and more comprehensive understanding of human behavior.
   d. All of these are advantages to using a levels-of-analysis approach.

## Answers

1.b 2.d 3.a 4.d

NOTE: Once you feel comfortable with the Test Yourself questions in this chapter, visit the book's Web site at www.ablongman.com/kosslyn3e for additional study questions.

## Think It Through!

In your own life, can you identify instances where events at the different levels of analysis were clearly at work? How would you react if it could be shown conclusively that all criminals have an abnormal structure in a certain part of their brains? If this were true, what should we do with this knowledge? Or, what if it could be shown that criminals have perfectly normal brains, but they all had weak parents who didn't give them enough discipline when they were children? Neither of these single-perspective views is likely to be correct, but what if one level of analysis turns out to be more important than the others?

# PSYCHOLOGY THEN AND NOW:
## The Evolution of a Science

How do you think psychologists 50 or 100 years ago might have interpreted Tiger Woods's performance? Would they have focused on the same things that psychologists do today? One hallmark of the sciences is that rather than casting aside earlier findings, researchers use them as stepping stones to the next set of discoveries. Reviewing how psychology has developed over time helps us understand where we are today. In the century or so during which psychology has taken shape as a formal discipline, the issues under investigation have changed, the emphasis has shifted from one level of analysis to another, and events at each level have often been viewed as operating separately or occurring in isolation.

In one form or another, psychology has probably always been with us. People have apparently always been curious about why they and others think, feel, and behave the way they do. In contrast, the history of psychology as a scientific field is relatively brief, spanning little more than a century. The roots of psychology lie in *philosophy* (the use of logic and speculation to understand the nature of reality, experience, and values) on the one hand and *physiology* (the study of the biological workings of the body, including the brain) on the other. From philosophy, psychology borrowed theories of the nature of mental processes and behavior. For example, the 17th-century French philosopher René Descartes focused attention on the distinction between mind and body and the relation between the two (still a focus of considerable debate). John Locke, a 17th-century English philosopher (and friend of Sir Isaac Newton), stressed that all human knowledge arises from experience of the world and from reflection about it. Locke argued that we only know about the world via how it is represented in the mind. From physiology, psychologists learned to recognize the role of the brain in giving rise to mental processes and behavior and acquired tools to investigate these processes. These twin influences of philosophy and physiology remain in force today, shaped and sharpened by developments over time.

**Structuralism:** The school of psychology that sought to identify the basic elements of experience and to describe the rules and circumstances under which these elements combine to form mental *structures*.

# Early Days: Beginning to Map Mental Processes and Behavior

The earliest scientific psychologists were not much interested in why we behave as we do. Instead, these pioneers typically focused their efforts on understanding the operation of perception (the ways in which we sense the world), memory, and problem solving—events at what we now think of as the level of the brain. But even at the beginning, psychologists focused on events at several levels of analysis.

## Structuralism

Wilhelm Wundt (1832–1920), usually considered the founder of scientific psychology, set up the first psychology laboratory in 1879 in Leipzig, Germany. The work of Wundt and his colleagues led to **structuralism**, the first formal movement in psychology. The structuralists sought to identify the "building blocks" of consciousness (*consciousness* is the state of being aware). Part of Wundt's research led him to characterize two types of elements of consciousness. The first comprised sensations, which arise from the eyes, ears, and other sense organs; the second consisted of feelings, such as fear, anger, and love. The goal of structuralism was to describe the rules that determine how particular sensations or feelings may occur at the same time or in sequence, combining in various ways into mental *structures*. Edward Titchener (1867–1927), an American student of Wundt, broadened the structuralist approach to apply it to the nature of concepts and thinking in general.

Margaret Floy Washburn was not only Edward Titchener's first graduate student to receive a Ph.D., but was also the first woman to earn a Ph.D. in psychology (1894, Cornell).

Wilhelm Wundt (the man with the long gray beard standing behind one table) in his laboratory.

The structuralists developed and tested their theories partly with objective techniques, such as measures of the time it takes to respond to different sensations. Their primary research tool, however, was **introspection**, which means literally "looking within." Here is an example of introspection: Try to recall how many windows and doors are in your parents' living room. Are you aware of "seeing" the room in a mental image, of scanning along the walls and counting the windows and doors? Introspection is the technique of noticing your mental processes as, or immediately after, they occur. Insofar as the structuralists' theories were about the structure of consciousness, they addressed the mechanisms of mental processes—and hence considered events at the level of the brain. But they also considered the contents of consciousness itself, at the level of the person.

Had the structuralists been asked to analyze Tiger Woods's golf success—how, for example, he perceives distances, fairway terrain, and wind direction—they probably would have trained him to use introspection to describe his mental processes. By 1913, however, another German scientist, Oswald Külpe, had discovered that not all mental processes are accompanied by mental imagery. In fact, if you asked Tiger Woods how he manages to swing a golf club so well, he probably wouldn't be able to tell you. Contemporary researchers have discovered that as our expertise in a skill increases, we are less able to use introspection to describe it.

Let's say that although you are able to use mental imagery as a tool to recall the numbers of windows and doors in your parents' living room, your best friend doesn't seem to be able to do the same. How could you prove that mental images actually exist and objects can indeed be visualized? For the early psychologists, this was the core of the problem. Barring the ability to read minds, there was no way to resolve disagreements about the mental processes that introspection revealed. If the only evidence you gather cannot be verified, you cannot establish the evidence as fact. This is precisely what happened when the structuralists tried to use introspection as a scientific tool. Their observations could not be objectively repeated with the same results, and thus their theorizing based on introspective reports fell apart.

## Functionalism

Rather than trying to chart the elements of mental processes, the adherents of **functionalism** sought to understand how our minds help us to adapt to the world around us—in short, to *function* in it (Boring, 1950). Whereas the structuralists asked *what* mental processes are and *how* they operate, the functionalists wanted to know *why* humans think, feel, and behave as we do. The functionalists had less interest in events at the level of the brain than did the structuralists and greater interest in events at the level of the group. The functionalists, many of whom were Americans, shared the urge to gather knowledge that could be put to immediate use. Sitting in a room introspecting simply didn't seem worthwhile to them. The functionalists' interest lay in the methods by which people learn and in how goals and beliefs are shaped by environments. As such, their interests spanned the levels of the person and the group.

The functionalists were strongly influenced by Charles Darwin (1809–1882), whose theory of evolution by natural selection stressed that some individual organisms

Introspection: The process of "looking within."

Functionalism: The school of psychology that sought to understand how the mind helps individuals *function*, or adapt to the world.

in every species, from ants to oaks, possess characteristics that enable them to survive and reproduce more fruitfully than others. The phrase "survival of the fittest," often quoted in relation to natural selection, doesn't quite capture the key idea. (For one thing, these days "the fittest" implies the muscle-bound star of the health club, whereas in Darwin's time it meant something "fit for" or "suited to" its situation.) The idea of natural selection is that certain inborn characteristics make particular individuals more fit for their environments, enabling them to have more offspring that survive, and those in turn have more offspring, and so on, until the characteristics that led the original individuals to flourish are spread through the whole population. Darwin called the inborn characteristics that help an organism survive and produce many offspring *adaptations*. (Chapter 3 covers Darwin's theory more fully.)

The functionalists sought to apply knowledge of psychology and helped to improve education in the United States.

The functionalists applied Darwin's theory to mental characteristics. For example, William James (1842–1910), who set up the first psychology laboratory in the United States at Harvard University, studied the ways in which consciousness helps an individual survive and adapt to an environment. The functionalists likely would have tried to discover how Tiger Woods's goals and beliefs enable him to press on in the face of adversity, such as losing an important match or receiving hate mail.

The functionalists made several enduring contributions to psychology. Their emphasis on Darwin's theory of natural selection and its link between humans and non-human animals led them to theorize that human psychology is related to the psychology of animals. This insight meant that the observation of animals could provide clues to human behavior. The functionalists' focus on social issues, such as improving methods of education, also spawned research that continues today.

## Gestalt Psychology

Although their work began in earnest nearly 50 years later, the Gestalt psychologists, like the structuralists, were interested in consciousness, particularly as it arises during perception (and thus, they too focused on events at the levels of the brain and the person). But instead of trying to dissect the elements of experience, **Gestalt psychology**—taking its name from the German word *Gestalt*, which means "whole"—emphasized the overall patterns of thoughts or experience. Based in Germany, Max Wertheimer (1880–1943) and other scientists noted that much of the content of our thoughts comes from what we perceive and, further, from inborn tendencies to structure what we see in certain ways.

Have you ever glanced up to see a flock of birds heading south for the winter? If so, you probably didn't pay attention to each individual bird but instead focused on the flock. In Gestalt terms, the flock was a *perceptual unit*, a whole formed from individual parts. The Gestalt psychologists developed over 100 perceptual laws, or principles, that describe how our eyes and brains organize the world. For example, both because the birds are near one another (the law of proximity) and because they are moving in the same direction (the law of common fate), we perceive them as a single unit. Gestaltists believed that such principles are a result of the most basic workings of the brain and that they affect how we all think. Most of the Gestalt principles illustrate the dictum that "the whole is more than the sum of its parts." When you see the birds in flight, the flock has a size and shape that cannot be predicted from the size and shape

Gestalt psychology: An approach to understanding mental processes that focuses on the idea that the whole is more than the sum of its parts.

We do not see isolated individual musicians, but a marching band. In the words of the Gestalt psychologists, "the whole is more than the sum of its parts."

of the birds viewed one at a time. To Gestalt psychologists, just as the flock is an entity that is more than a collection of individual birds, our patterns of thought are more than the simple sum of individual images or ideas. Gestaltists would want to know how Tiger Woods can take in the overall layout of each hole, or even an 18-hole course, and plan his strategy accordingly.

Today the study of perception is no longer the province of Gestalt psychology alone but rather a central focus of psychology, as well it should be. Perception is, after all, our gateway to the world; if our perceptions are not accurate, our corresponding thoughts and feelings will be based on a distorted view of reality. The research of the Gestaltists addressed how the brain works, and today Gestaltism has become integrated into studies of the brain itself.

# Psychodynamic Theory: More Than Meets the Eye

Sigmund Freud (1856–1939), a Viennese physician specializing in neurology (the study and treatment of diseases of the brain and nervous system), developed a detailed and subtle theory of how thoughts and feelings affect our actions. We consider Freud and theorists who followed in his footsteps in Chapter 11; here we touch briefly on key points of his theory.

Freud stressed the notion that the mind is not a single thing, but in fact has separate components. Moreover, some of these mental processes are **unconscious**; that is, they are outside our awareness and beyond our ability to bring to awareness at will. Freud believed that we have many unconscious sexual, and sometimes aggressive, urges. Moreover, Freud also believed that a child absorbs his or her parents' and culture's moral standards, which then censor the child's (and, later, the adult's) goals and motivations. Thus, he argued, we often find our urges unacceptable and so keep them in check, hidden in the unconscious. According to Freud, these unconscious urges build up until, eventually and inevitably, they demand release as thoughts, feelings, or actions.

Freud developed what has since been called a **psychodynamic theory**. From the Greek words *psyche*, or "mind," and *dynamo*, meaning "power," the term refers to the continual push-and-pull interaction among conscious and unconscious forces. Freud believed that it was these interactions that produced abnormal behaviors, such as obsessively washing one's hands until they crack and bleed. According to Freud, such hand washing might be traced to unacceptable unconscious sexual or aggressive impulses bubbling up to consciousness (the "dirt" perceived on the hands) and that washing symbolically serves to remove the "dirt." What would followers of psychodynamic theory say about Tiger Woods? A Freudian would probably ask Woods about his earliest memories and experiences and try with him to analyze the unconscious urges that led to his intense interest in golf. This theory addresses mental processes and behavior at all three levels of analysis: The theory of mental mechanisms is at the level of the brain, but an individual's experience affects events at the level of the person, and the

**Unconscious:** Outside conscious awareness and not able to be brought to consciousness at will.

**Psychodynamic theory:** A theory of how thoughts and feelings affect behavior; refers to the continual push-and-pull interaction among conscious and unconscious forces.

nature of one's upbringing is to be understood at the level of the group. Freud developed an extraordinarily ambitious theory, which attempted to reach into all corners of human thought, feeling, and behavior.

Others modified Freud's theory in various ways, for example, by de-emphasizing sex in favor of other sources of unconscious conflicts; Alfred Adler (1870–1937), for instance, stressed the role of feelings of inferiority. Psychodynamic theories have attracted many passionate followers. Rather than deriving from objective scientific studies, however, their guiding principles rest primarily on subjective interpretations of what people say and do. Moreover, psychodynamic theory became so intricate and complicated that it could usually explain any given observation or research result as easily as the opposite result, and thus became impossible to test—obviously a serious drawback.

Nevertheless, the key idea of psychodynamic theory—that behavior is driven by a collection of mental processes—had a crucial influence on later theories. In addition, the idea that some mental processes are hidden from conscious awareness has proven invaluable, as has the focus on the level of the person. Furthermore, psychodynamic theory focused attention on novel kinds of observations, such as the interpretation of slips-of-the-tongue and the analysis of dreams. These observations sparked much subsequent research. Psychodynamic theory led to entirely new approaches to treating psychological problems, which have since been modified and refined (see Chapter 14). For instance, Freud's theory led to psychoanalysis, in which a therapist listens to a patient talk about his or her childhood, relationships, and dreams, and attempts to help the patient understand the unconscious basis of his or her thoughts, feelings, and behavior.

Sigmund Freud, the father of psychodynamic theory.

# Behaviorism: The Power of the Environment

By the early part of the 20th century, a new generation of psychologists calling themselves behaviorists began to question a key assumption shared by their predecessors, that psychologists should study hidden mental processes. Because they found the theories of mental processes so difficult to pin down, American psychologists such as Edward Lee Thorndike (1874–1949), John B. Watson (1878–1958), and Clark L. Hull (1884–1952) rejected the idea that psychology should focus on these unseen phenomena. Instead, these followers of **behaviorism** concluded that psychology should concentrate on understanding directly observable behavior.

Some behaviorists were willing to talk about internal stimuli such as motivation, but only those stimuli that were directly reflected in behavior (such as running quickly to catch a bus). Later behaviorists, among them B. F. Skinner (1904–1990), acknowledged that mental processes probably exist, but argued that it was not useful for psychology to focus on them. Instead, Skinner and his followers held that to understand behavior, we should study behavior. For instance, rather than trying to study the nature of "affection" so as to understand why someone treats dogs well ("affection" being an unobservable mental process), these behaviorists would look at when and how a person approaches dogs, protects them from harm, pets them, and otherwise treats them well. Such a scientific investigation would be aimed at discovering how particular responses came to be associated with the stimulus of perceiving a dog. Because of their concern with the content of the stimulus–stimulus and stimulus–response associations, the behaviorists focus on events at the level of the person.

The behaviorists have had many important insights, among them the fact that responses usually produce consequences, either negative or positive, which in turn affect how the organism responds the next time it encounters the same stimulus. Say you put money in a vending machine (a response to the stimulus of seeing the machine) and

Behaviorism: The school of psychology that focuses on how a specific stimulus (object, person, or event) evokes a specific response (behavior in reaction to the stimulus).

**"Stimulus, response! Stimulus, response! Don't you ever *think*?"**

the machine dispenses a tasty candy bar; chances are good that you will repeat the behavior in the future. If, on the other hand, the machine serves up a stale candy bar with a torn wrapper, you will be less inclined to use this or another machine like it again (see Chapter 6 for a detailed discussion of how consequences affect learning).

How might the behaviorists explain Tiger Woods's success? A key idea in behaviorism is *reinforcement*, any consequence that results from a given behavior and strengthens or supports the behavior. A reward, such as payment for a job, is a common type of reinforcement. If the consequence of a behavior is reinforcing, we are likely to repeat the behavior. Conversely, if a behavior produces an undesirable outcome ("punishment"), we are less likely to do it again. From his earliest days, Tiger Woods received an extraordinary amount of reinforcement for playing well, at first from his father and then from an increasingly larger affirming public. It was this reinforcement, the behaviorists would argue, that spurred him to repeat those acts that brought desirable consequences, while shunning behaviors (including ineffective golfing techniques) that did not help him play well.

The behaviorists have developed many principles that describe the conditions in which specific stimuli lead to specific responses, many of which have stood up well in later investigations (as you will see in Chapter 6). For example, they found that individuals respond more frequently when the desirable outcomes are intermittent than when those "rewards" occur every time. Thus, Tiger Woods might be more likely to keep practicing putting if he were sinking only some of the balls than if every one he tapped rolled right into the hole. Contemporary behaviorists often develop theories (sometimes derived from economics) to describe how humans and other animals choose which responses to make to sets of competing stimuli (Grafen, 2002; Herrnstein, 1990).

The behaviorists' emphasis on controlled, objective observation has had a deep and lasting impact on psychology. Today, even studies of mental processes must conform to the level of rigor established by the behaviorists. Behaviorist insights also have improved psychotherapy and education. On the other hand, as we will see, many of the behaviorists' objections to the study of mental processes have been refuted by subsequent research.

# Humanistic Psychology

Partly as a reaction to the theories of the Freudians and behaviorists, which viewed people as driven either by the content of their mental processes or by external stimuli, a new school of psychological thought emerged in the late 1950s and early 1960s. According to **humanistic psychology**, people have positive values, free will, and deep inner creativity, which in combination allow them to choose life-fulfilling paths to personal growth. The humanistic approach (focused on the level of the person) rests on the ideas that the "client" (no longer the "patient" as in psychodynamic approaches) must be respected as equal to the therapist and that each person has dignity and self-worth.

Psychologists such as Carl Rogers (1902–1987) and Abraham Maslow (1908–1970) developed therapies based on the humanistic approach. Rogers's *client-centered ther-*

Humanistic psychology: The school of psychology that assumes people have positive values, free will, and deep inner creativity, the combination of which leads them to choose life-fulfilling paths to personal growth.

*apy* incorporated Maslow's theory that people have an urge to *self-actualize*—that is, to develop to their fullest potentials—and that, given the right environment, this development will in time occur. Rather than serving as an expert in a position of authority, the client-centered therapist provides a "mirror" in the form of an unconditionally supportive and positive environment. How might humanistic psychologists explain Tiger Woods's success? No doubt they would point to him as someone who is striving to reach his full potential. They might question, however, whether in the long run his intense focus on golf will prove entirely satisfying, especially if he ignores other aspects of life.

Although humanistic psychology never had the impact that the other schools had, it is important in part because it represented a renewed interest in mental processes. This school continues to attract followers today, but it is not a major force in the field. Nevertheless, many of the therapies now in use reflect the influence of humanistic thinking (as we discuss in Chapter 15).

**Cognitive psychology:** The approach in psychology that attempts to characterize how information is stored and operated on internally.

# The Cognitive Revolution

The tension between approaches—on the one hand, structuralism, functionalism, and psychodynamic psychology, which studied unobservable mental processes, and on the other hand, behaviorism, which considered only directly observable behavior—was resolved by a new arrival on the scene, the computer. The computer led to the *cognitive revolution* of the late 1950s and early 1960s; its proponents looked to the computer as a model for the way human mental processes work. This movement came into full flower in the mid-1970s, led by, among others, psychologists/computer scientists Herbert A. Simon and Alan Newell (Simon went on to win a Nobel Prize, in part for this work) and linguist Noam Chomsky. (Gardner [1985] provides a detailed history of the cognitive revolution.)

We saw earlier in the chapter how useful computer metaphors can be, but the cognitive revolution focused not on the levels of analysis we have discussed, but rather solely on a new way to conceive of mental processes. This perspective gave birth to **cognitive psychology**, which attempts to characterize the nature of human *information processing*, that is, the way information is stored and operated

Computers provided a new way to conceptualize mental processes and to develop detailed theories about them.

on internally (Neisser, 1967). In this view, mental processes are like computer software (programs), and the brain is like the hardware (the machine itself). Cognitive psychologists focus on mechanism, not content, but they believe that just as different types of software can be discussed without ever considering how the hardware works, mental processes can be discussed without referring to the structure of the brain.

Computers showed, once and for all, why it is important that there be a science of the unobservable events that take place in the head, not just a science of directly observable behavior. Consider, for example, how you might react if your word-processing program produced *italics* whenever you entered the command for **boldface**. Noticing the software's "behavior" would be only the first step in fixing this error: You would need to dig deeper in

order to find out where the program had gone wrong. This would involve seeing what internal events are triggered by the command and how those events affect what the machine does. So, too, for people. If somebody is acting odd, we must go beyond the essential step of noticing the unusual behavior; we also need to think about what is happening inside and consider what is causing the problem. Indeed, the cognitive revolution led to new ways of conceptualizing and treating mental disorders, such as depression. For example, Albert Ellis (b. 1913) and Aaron Beck (b. 1921) claimed that people's distressing feelings or symptoms are caused by irrational and distorted ways of thinking about their interactions with others, themselves, and their surroundings. Beck showed that symptoms such as anxiety and depression could be addressed by attacking these problems in thinking.

Cognitive psychology defined many of the questions that are still being pursued in psychology, such as how information is stored and manipulated when we perform a particular task, and it continues to develop subtle experimental methods to study hidden mental processes. Principles of cognitive psychology have been used to compare abilities across cultures, in part to sort out which aspects of our psychologies arise from inherent properties of the brain (common to all people) and which are a product of our particular social experiences (Cole, 1996; Cole et al., 1997).

The theories and research methods developed by cognitive psychologists have also proven crucial in the recent development of **cognitive neuroscience**, which blends cognitive psychology and neuroscience (the study of the brain). Cognitive neuroscientists argue that "the mind is what the brain does" (Gazzaniga, 2004; Kosslyn & Koenig, 1995) and hope to discover the nature, organization, and operation of mental processes by studying the brain. One of the goals of cognitive neuroscience is to distinguish among different sorts of mental processes. For example, after Tiger Woods began to lose consistently, he was asked how he felt—and was upbeat in his response. It seems unlikely that this is how he actually felt, but he may have believed he had to "put on a happy face" and try to deceive the reporters. Researchers have found that the particular mental processes used in deception depend on whether a person draws on previously rehearsed and memorized stories or on new stories made up on the spot; brain scanning has revealed that there is more than one way to tell a lie, with separate neural systems being used in the different sorts of lying—which in turn differ from the neural systems used when one tells the truth (Ganis et al., 2003). This is one of the most exciting areas of psychology today, in part because brain-scanning technologies have allowed us, for the first time in history, to observe human brains at work.

The cognitive neuroscience approach considers events at the three levels of analysis, but with a primary focus on the brain. Cognitive neuroscientists seeking to explain Tiger Woods's golfing achievements would likely investigate how different parts of his brain function while he plays golf, looking to discover the way his brain processes information. For example, how does the visual input he receives standing at the tee allow him to judge distance to the pin? They would also compare Woods's brain function with that of less accomplished golfers and would even program computers to mimic the way his brain works during play.

# Evolutionary Psychology

Cognitive neuroscience: A blending of cognitive psychology and neuroscience (the study of the brain) that aims to specify how the brain stores and processes information.

One of the most recent developments in the field, evolutionary psychology, first made its appearance in the late 1980s. This school of thought has a heritage—with a twist—in the work of the functionalists and their emphasis on Darwin's theory of natural

Probably the best source of evidence for theories in evolutionary psychology is *cultural universals*, instances of the same practices occurring in all cultures.

selection. Central to **evolutionary psychology** is the idea that certain cognitive strategies and goals are so important that natural selection has built them into our brains. But instead of proposing that evolution has selected any specific behaviors as such (as earlier evolutionary theorists, including Charles Darwin himself, believed), these theorists believe that general cognitive strategies (such as using deception to achieve one's goals) and certain goals (such as finding attractive mates) are inborn. This approach addresses events at all three levels of analysis and is currently being developed by researchers such as Lida Cosmides and John Tooby (1996), David Buss (1994, 1999), and Steven Pinker (1994, 1997) and reviewed by others (Barkow et al., 1992; Plotkin, 1994, 1997; Schmitt, 2002). For example, these theorists claim that we have the ability to lie because our ancestors who could lie had an advantage: They could trick their naïve companions into giving up resources. These more devious ancestors had more children who survived than did their non-lying contemporaries, and their lying children had more children, and so on, until the ability to lie was inborn in all members of our species. Notice that lying is not a specific behavior; it is a strategy that can be expressed by many behaviors, all of them deceitful.

How can you test a theory about the history of human psychology? Fossils will tell you little. Instead, some researchers seek evidence for evolutionary developments in contemporary humans. Probably the best source of evidence for theories in evolutionary psychology is *cultural universality*, instances of the same practice occurring in all cultures. If people even in remote areas with very different cultures show the same tendencies, it is likely that the tendencies are not the result of learning. In fact, people in all cultures have been found to share certain concepts and practices, including lying, telling stories, gossiping, using proper names, expressing emotions with facial expressions, fearing snakes, dancing, making music, giving gifts, making medicines; the list goes on and on (Brown, 1991). Being human is more than having a certain type of body and brain; it is also having a certain type of mind that works in certain ways.

Evolutionary psychologists also compare human abilities with those of animals, particularly nonhuman primates (Hauser, 1996). For example, by studying the way animals communicate, researchers try to infer which abilities formed the basis of

**Evolutionary psychology:** The approach in psychology that assumes that certain cognitive strategies and goals are so important that natural selection has built them into our brains.

human language. By studying animals, researchers hope to discover the abilities of our common ancestors and, from those data, develop theories about the way those abilities may have been refined over the course of evolution. When asked about what might underlie Tiger Woods's achievements, an evolutionary psychologist might note that although our species did not evolve to play golf, the abilities that arose via natural selection for hunting game and avoiding predators can also be used in other ways—in playing sports, for example.

But evidence of the universality of certain behaviors among humans or of shared abilities in nonhuman animals and humans does not tell us *why* those characteristics are present. Are they really adaptations? Evolutionary theories are notoriously difficult to test because we don't know what our ancestors were like and how they evolved. Just because we are born with certain tendencies and characteristics does not mean that these are evolutionarily selected adaptations. As Stephen Jay Gould and Richard Lewontin (1979) pointed out, at least some of our modern characteristics are simply by-products of other characteristics that were in fact selected. Your nose evolved to warm air and detect odors; and once you have a nose, you can use it to hold up your eyeglasses. But just as nobody would claim that the nose evolved to hold up glasses, nobody should claim that all the current functions of the brain resulted from natural selection.

The various schools of psychological thought are summarized in Table 1.1.

| TABLE 1.1 | Schools of Psychological Thought | |
|---|---|---|
| **Name** | **Landmark Events** | **Key Ideas** |
| **Structuralism** | Wundt founds first psychology laboratory, 1879. | Use introspection to discover the elements of mental processes and rules for combining them. |
| **Functionalism** | James's *Principles of Psychology*, published 1890. | Study why thoughts, feelings, and behavior occur, how they are adaptive. |
| **Gestalt psychology** | Wertheimer's paper on perceived movement, 1912. | Focus on overall patterns of thoughts or experience; "the whole is more than the sum of its parts." |
| **Psychodynamic theory** | Freud publishes *The Ego and the Id*, 1927. | Conflicts among conscious and unconscious forces underlie many thoughts, feelings, and behaviors. |
| **Behaviorism** | Watson's paper *Psychology as the Behaviorist Views It*, 1913; Skinner's *The Behavior of Organisms*, 1938. | Behavior is the appropriate focus of psychology, and it can be understood by studying stimuli, responses, and the consequences of responses. |
| **Humanistic psychology** | Maslow publishes *Motivation and Personality*, 1954. | Nonscientific approach; belief that people have positive values, free will, and deep inner creativity. |
| **Cognitive psychology** | Neisser's book *Cognitive Psychology* gives the "school" its name, 1967. | Mental processes are like information processing in a computer. |
| **Cognitive neuroscience** | First issue of the *Journal of Cognitive Neuroscience* appears, 1989. | "The mind is what the brain does." |
| **Evolutionary psychology** | Barkow, Cosmides, and Tooby edit *The Adapted Mind*, 1992. | Mental strategies and goals are often inborn, the result of natural selection. |

Note: Dates prior to Maslow based on Boring (1950).

# The State of the Union: Psychology Today

Although schools of psychology gave rise to other schools over time, the original schools did not simply fade away. Rather than being replaced by their descendents, the parent schools often continued to develop and produce new and important discoveries. Moreover, the different schools began to influence each other. Today we have a rich mix of different sorts of psychology, which are cross-fertilizing and interacting with one another in fascinating ways. For example, techniques in cognitive neuroscience (most notably brain scanning) are being used to test hypotheses about the effects of social context on reasoning and to test behaviorist principles about stimulus–response relations (Blakemore et al., 2004), and research in cognitive psychology is having an impact on many questions that motivated the functionalists, particularly in the area of improving methods of education (Kozhevnikov et al., in press). In addition, behaviorist techniques have been used to train animals to respond only to certain visual patterns, which then has allowed scientists to discover how interactions among individual brain cells give rise to some of the Gestalt laws of organization (Merchant et al., 2003). Moreover, psychodynamic theory has influenced questions being asked in cognitive psychology and cognitive neuroscience, such as those concerning the nature of forgetting (Anderson et al., 2004). Similarly, evolutionary psychology is making intriguing points of contact with modern behaviorist theories, most notably regarding the idea that behaviors may obey economic laws (for example, by maximizing gain while minimizing expended effort).

All of these varied approaches to psychology not only co-exist but feed off one another. The result is that we are learning about mental processes and behavior at an ever-increasing clip. If you are interested in psychology, these arc truly exciting times in which to live!

# Test Yourself

1. Which of the early schools of psychology was most influenced by the theory of Charles Darwin?
   a. structuralism
   b. functionalism
   c. Gestalt psychology
   d. behaviorism

2. The early schools of psychology disagreed on the proper realm of psychological study. Structuralism was concerned with _____, whereas psychodynamic theory was concerned largely with _____.
   a. evolution; conscious behavior
   b. conscious experience; unconscious events
   c. behavior only; evolution
   d. unconscious experience; perception

3. Cognitive and behavioral psychologists disagree over the terms used in psychological explanations. This disagreement revolves around the difference between
   a. humans and animals.
   b. adults and infants.
   c. mental processes and behaviors.
   d. structural processes and functional processes.

4. What has happened to the different schools of psychological thought?
   a. They have all been replaced by one dominant school of thought.
   b. They have all disappeared.
   c. They have continued to develop and influence each other.
   d. They were replaced by cognitive neuroscience.

## Answers

1. b 2. b 3. c 4. c

If Tiger Woods were to be studied by adherents of a single school of psychological thought, which one would be least likely to produce useful insights? Most likely? When asked to account for his remarkable skill, Woods professes to have no conscious knowledge about how he plays so well. How would this report affect the approaches taken by the different schools?

Which school of psychology is most interesting to you? Can you think of any ways in which combining ideas or approaches from the different schools might be helpful?

# THE PSYCHOLOGICAL WAY:
## What Today's Psychologists Do

If you read that Tiger Woods had seen a psychologist, would you think that he had a personal problem, or that he was suffering from too much stress? Neither guess is necessarily true; psychologists do much more than help people cope with their problems. As the field of psychology developed, different schools of thought focused on different aspects of mental processes and behavior; their varying influences are felt in what today's psychologists do. And just what is that?

Here we consider three major types of psychologists: those who help people deal with personal problems or stress, those who teach and usually also study the science of mental processes and behavior, and those who seek to solve specific practical problems, such as helping athletes perform better.

## Clinical and Counseling Psychology: A Healing Profession

Andrea is a **clinical psychologist** who specializes in treating people with eating disorders. Many of Andrea's clients have a disorder called *anorexia nervosa*, characterized by refusal to maintain a healthy weight. Others, who have a disorder called *bulimia nervosa*, eat and then force themselves to vomit or take laxatives immediately afterward. Andrea sees such patients once or twice a week, for 50 minutes per session. During these sessions, Andrea's job is usually to discover why behaviors that are so destructive in the long run seem so desirable to the patient in the short run. She then helps her patients phase out the destructive behaviors and replace them with more adaptive behaviors—for instance, responding to anxiety after eating by taking a quick walk around the block instead of vomiting. Depending on the setting in which Andrea works (probably a private office, clinic, or hospital), she will spend varying portions of her day with patients; meeting with other psychologists to discuss how to be more helpful to patients; supervising psychotherapists in training; going out into the community, perhaps lecturing about eating disorders at high school assemblies; and doing paperwork, including writing notes on each patient, submitting forms to insurance companies for

Clinical psychologist: The type of psychologist who provides psychotherapy and is trained to administer and interpret psychological tests.

payment, and reading professional publications to keep up with new findings and techniques.

Andrea has been trained to provide **psychotherapy**, which involves helping clients learn to change so that they can cope with troublesome thoughts, feelings, and behaviors. She also administers and interprets psychological tests, which can help in diagnosis and in planning the appropriate treatment. *Clinical neuropsychologists* are clinical psychologists who work specifically with tests designed to diagnose the effects of brain damage on thoughts, feelings, and behavior and to indicate which parts of the brain are impaired following trauma. Other clinical psychologists work with organizations, such as corporations, to help groups function more effectively; for example, a psychologist might advise a company about reducing stress among workers in a

There are many kinds of psychotherapy, and different training prepares therapists in different ways. Psychiatrists, for example, typically would not treat families, but clinical psychologists and social workers—as well as other mental health professionals—might.

particular unit or might teach relaxation techniques to all employees. Some clinical psychologists have a Ph.D. (doctor of philosophy) degree, awarded by a university psychology department; these graduate programs teach students not only how to do psychotherapy and psychological testing, but also how to conduct and interpret psychological research. Other clinical psychologists have a Psy.D. (doctor of psychology), a graduate degree from a program with less emphasis on research. In some states, clinical psychologists can obtain additional training and be granted the right to prescribe drugs (the first state to grant this privilege was New Mexico, in 2002).

If Andrea had been trained as a **counseling psychologist**, she would have learned to help people deal with issues we all face, such as choosing a career, marrying, raising a family, and performing at work. Counseling psychologists often provide career counseling and vocational testing to help people decide which occupations best suit their interests and abilities. These professionals sometimes provide psychotherapy, but they may have a more limited knowledge of therapeutic techniques than do clinical psychologists. They may have a Ph.D. (often from a program that specifically trains people in this area) or often an Ed.D. (doctor of education) degree from a school of education.

Andrea could also have become a **psychiatrist**. If she had gone this route, her training and area of competence would have differed from those of the other mental health professionals. First, as a physician with an M.D. (doctor of medicine) degree, a psychiatrist has extensive medical training and can prescribe drugs, whereas, in general, psychologists cannot. Second, as a medical doctor, a psychiatrist (unlike a clinical psychologist) has typically not been trained to interpret and understand psychological research or psychological testing.

There are two other types of clinical mental health practitioners who are not psychologists. Her interest in clinical work might have led Andrea to choose either of those professions: social work or psychiatric nursing. If she had earned an M.S.W. (master of social work) degree, as a **social worker**, she would typically focus on using psychotherapy to help families and individuals, and she also would teach clients how to use the social service systems in their communities. A **psychiatric nurse** holds a master's degree (M.S.N., master of science in nursing) as well as a certificate of clinical specialization (C.S.) in psychiatric nursing. A psychiatric nurse provides psychotherapy, usually in a hospital or clinic or in private practice, and works closely with medical doctors to monitor and administer medications; in some cases, a psychiatric nurse can prescribe medications.

**Psychotherapy:** The process of helping clients learn to change so they can cope with troublesome thoughts, feelings, and behaviors.

**Counseling psychologist:** The type of psychologist who is trained to help people with issues that naturally arise during the course of life.

**Psychiatrist:** A physician who focuses on mental disorders; unlike psychologists, psychiatrists can prescribe drugs, but they are not trained to administer and interpret psychological tests, nor are they trained to interpret and understand psychological research.

**Social worker:** A mental health professional who uses psychotherapy to help families (and individuals) and teaches clients to use the social service systems in their communities.

**Psychiatric nurse:** A nurse with a master's degree and a clinical specialization in psychiatric nursing who provides psychotherapy and works with medical doctors to monitor and administer medications.

# Academic Psychology: Teaching and Research

Developmental psychologists often take special care to prevent their presence from affecting the child's behavior in any way.

James is a professor of psychology at a large state university. Most mornings he prepares lectures, which he delivers three times a week. He also has morning office hours, when students can come by to ask questions about their program of courses in the department or their progress in one of James's classes. Once a week at noon he has a committee meeting; this week the committee on computer technology is discussing how best to structure the department computer network. His afternoons are taken up mostly with research. If he worked at a smaller college, he might spend more time teaching and less time on research; alternatively, if he worked at a hospital, he might spend the lion's share of his time doing research and very little time teaching. In fact, if John worked in a research institute (perhaps affiliated with a medical school), he might not teach at all, but instead would make discoveries that others could teach; if he worked in a small college, he might not do research, but instead would dedicate himself to teaching the accumulated knowledge of the science of psychology. James's specialty is *developmental psychology*, the study of how thinking, feeling, and behaving develop with age and experience. His research work takes place at a laboratory preschool at the university, where he and his assistants are testing the ways children become attached to objects such as dolls and blankets. James also must find time to write papers for publication in professional journals, and he regularly writes grant proposals requesting funding for his research, so that he can pay students to help him test the children in his studies. He also writes letters of recommendation, grades papers and tests, and reads journal articles to keep up with current research in his and related fields. James tries to eat lunch with colleagues at least twice a week to keep up-to-date on departmental events and the work going on at the university in other areas of psychology.

Although the activities of most **academic psychologists** are similar in that most teach and many also conduct research, the kinds of teaching and research vary widely. Different types of academic psychologists focus on different types of questions. For example, if James had become a *cognitive psychologist* (one who studies thinking, memory, and related topics), he might ask, "How is Tiger Woods able to hit the ball with the appropriate force in the correct direction?" but not, "What is the role of the audience at a major golf tournament, and would it have been different 50 years ago?" If he had become a *social psychologist* (one who studies how people think and feel about themselves and other people and how groups function), he might ask the second question, but not the first. And in neither case would he ask, "What aspects of Tiger Woods's character help him deal with the extreme stress he faces?" That question would interest a *personality psychologist* (one who studies individual differences in preferences and inclinations).

Because psychology is a science, it rests on objective tests of its theories and ideas. It is through research that psychologists learn how to diagnose people's problems and how to cure them; it is through research that they determine what kind of career will make good use of a particular person's talents; it is through research that they discover how to present material so that students can understand and remember it most effectively. Theories about such issues can come from anywhere, but there is no way to know whether an idea is right or wrong except by testing it scientifically, through research.

Academic psychologist: The type of psychologist who focuses on teaching and conducting research.

There are at least as many different types of academic psychologists as there are separate sections in this book. In fact, this book represents a harvest of their research. Thousands of researchers are working on the topics covered in each chapter, and it is their efforts that allow a book like this one to be written.

# Applied Psychology: Better Living Through Psychology

Maria works in the software development department of a high-tech company; she is a *human factors psychologist*, a professional who works to improve products so that people can use them more intuitively and effectively. Maria begins her day by testing several versions of menus to be used with a computer program under development. She wants to know which commands the software users will expect to find listed under the headings on the menu bar at the top of the screen. She has designed a study in which she asks people to find specific commands and records through the computer where they look for the commands and how long it takes to find them. Maria often has lunch in the company cafeteria, but today she is eating at her desk, studying the results from the morning's testing session. Puzzled by what she sees, Maria suddenly realizes that the way she has labeled the commands is affecting how people think of them. She quickly begins to set up another series of tests on the computer. After lunch, she attends a talk by a visiting scientist about his latest research, some of which may prove useful in her project: The subject is the nature of memory, and she takes careful notes. Afterward, she has a weekly meeting of the project team. Today the person who is designing the screen icons reports that he has run into difficulty; he describes the problem to the team, and various members ask questions and make suggestions. After this meeting, Maria goes to her office and works for an hour on a written progress report, then spends another hour on an article she is writing for a technical journal.

**Applied psychologists** use the principles and theories of psychology in practical areas such as education, industry, and marketing. An applied psychologist may have a Ph.D. or, sometimes, only a master's degree in an area of psychology (in North America, a master's degree typically requires two years of postgraduate study instead of the four to six for a Ph.D.). Applied psychologists not only work on improving products and procedures but also conduct research aimed at solving specific practical problems. Working in applied psychology, a *developmental psychologist* may be employed by or consult with the product development department of a toy company. Using her knowledge of children, she can help design toys that will be appropriate for particular age levels; she then brings children to a playroom at the company to see how they play with the new toys. A *physiological psychologist* studies the brain and brain–body interactions and may work at a company that makes drugs or brain-scanning machines. A *social psychologist* may help lawyers decide which potential jurors should be rejected. A *personality psychologist* may design a new test to help select suitable personnel for a job. An *industrial/organizational (I/O) psychologist* focuses on using psychology in the workplace; he or she might help an employer create a more comfortable and effective work environment so as to increase worker productivity or might redesign work spaces to promote more effective employee communication. A *sport psychologist* works with athletes to help them improve their performances, by helping them learn to concentrate better, deal with stress, and practice

Applied psychologists have many roles, one of which is to help attorneys decide which potential jurors are likely to be sympathetic or hostile to the defendant.

Applied psychologist: The type of psychologist who studies how to improve products and procedures and conducts research to help solve specific practical problems.

**FIGURE 1.1**

**Percentages of Psychologists Working in Different Specialty Areas**

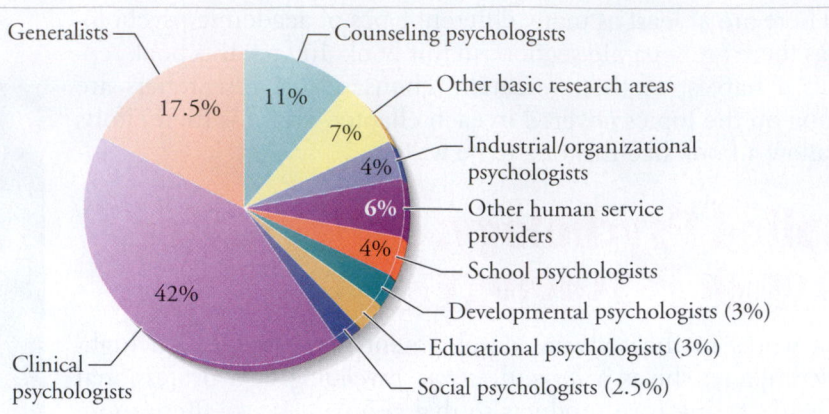

more efficiently (Tiger Woods consults a sport psychologist). An *educational* or *school psychologist* works with educators (and sometimes families), devising ways to improve the cognitive, emotional, and social development of children at school.

The relative numbers of the various types of psychologists are presented in Figure 1.1, and their occupations are summarized in Table 1.2. In addition, Figure 1.2 identifies the types of jobs people with B.A. degrees in psychology hold, and Figure 1.3 shows that most of the people who are employed with B.A. degrees in psychology are satisfied with their work situation.

| TABLE 1.2 | **What Psychologists Do** |
|---|---|
| **Clinical psychologist** | Administers and interprets psychological tests; provides psychotherapy. |
| **Clinical neuropsychologist** | Diagnoses effects of brain damage on thoughts, feelings, and behavior, and diagnoses the locus of damage. |
| **Counseling psychologist** | Helps people with issues that arise during everyday life (career, marriage, family, work). |
| **Developmental psychologist** | Researches and teaches the development of mental processes and behavior with age and experience. |
| **Cognitive psychologist** | Researches and teaches the nature of thinking, memory, and related aspects of mental processes. |
| **Social psychologist** | Researches and teaches how people think and feel about themselves and other people, and how groups function. |
| **Personality psychologist** | Researches and teaches individual differences in preferences and inclinations. |
| **Physiological psychologist** | Researches and teaches the nature of the brain and brain/body interactions. |
| **Human factors psychologist** | Applies psychology to improve products. |
| **Industrial/organizational psychologist** | Applies psychology in the workplace. |
| **Sport psychologist** | Applies psychology to improve athletic performance. |
| **Educational or school psychologist** | Applies psychology to improve cognitive, emotional, and social development of schoolchildren. |

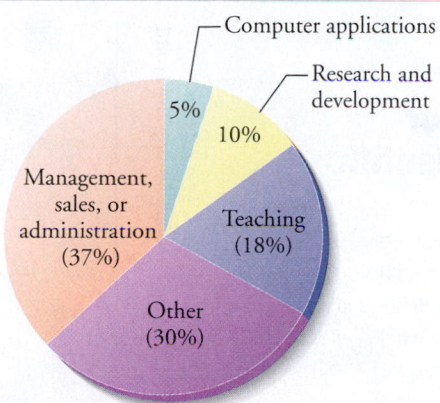

**FIGURE 1.2**

## Primary Work Activity of Psychology Majors with the B.A. Degree

Psychology majors work in a wide variety of professions after graduation.

# The Changing Face of Psychology

You may have noticed a lack of female names when we reviewed the history of psychology, and for good reason. In earlier times, few opportunities were available for women to make major contributions to this field; however, even in spite of the barriers of those days, a few women did make their mark on psychology, such as Margaret Floy Washburn, who was Edward Titchener's first student to earn a Ph.D. (in 1894), and Mary Whiton Calkins, the first woman to become president of the American Psychological Association (in 1905).

As shown in Figure 1.4 (p. 28), the situation is changing—increasing numbers of women, such as Anne Treisman, Ursula Bellugi, Susan Carey, and Elizabeth Spelke, are making major contributions in all areas of psychology (we will review fruits of their labors in the pages to come). In fact, in the last major survey (National Science Foundation, 2001), fully 77% of college graduates with psychology majors were women. Thus, we can expect to see increasing representation of women in the field at large.

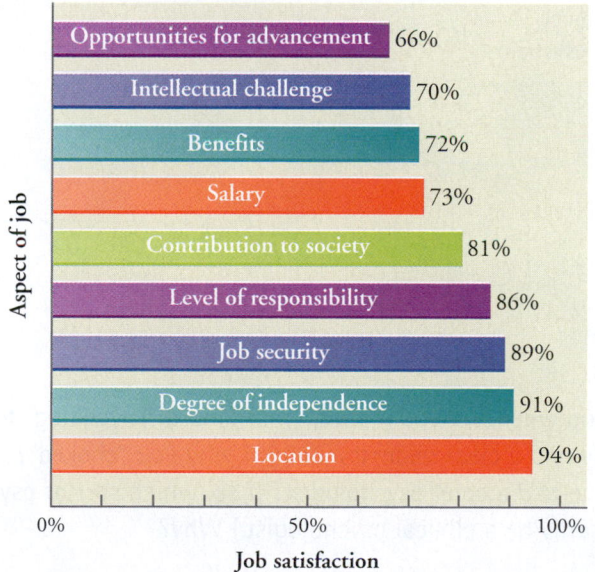

**FIGURE 1.3**

## Job Satisfaction Among Those Who Have a B.A. in Psychology

Percentages of people holding B.A. degrees in psychology who reported being very satisfied or somewhat satisfied with specific aspects of their jobs.

Mary Whiton Calkins, the first woman president of the American Psychological Association (1905).

**FIGURE 1.4**

## Women Winning the APA Award for Distinguished Scientific Contributions

Women are playing an increasingly prominent role in scientific psychology. In 1997, two-thirds of all Ph.D. degrees in psychology were earned by women (American Psychological Association, www.apa.org/pi/wpo/wapa/final.html).

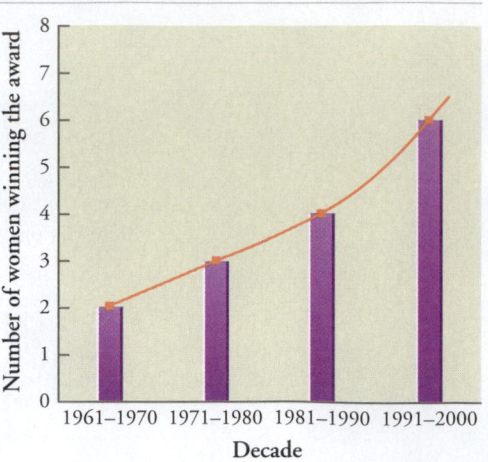

# Test Yourself

1. Which type of psychologist would be most interested in helping toy companies design safe and age-appropriate products?
   a. clinical psychologist
   b. academic psychologist
   c. applied psychologist
   d. counseling psychologist

2. Which type of psychologist would be most interested in studying and dealing with personal mental health issues?
   a. clinical or counseling psychologist
   b. academic psychologist
   c. applied psychologist
   d. Psychologists would not be interested in this subject.

3. The difference between a clinical and a counseling psychologist lies in
   a. the type of problems they help people with.
   b. the type of training they have had.
   c. the extent of their therapeutic expertise.
   d. All of these are differences between the two types of psychologist.

4. Which one of the following questions is *not* a potential focus of study for an academic psychologist?
   a. How does Tiger Woods calculate distance, loft, and club speed to hit a perfect wedge shot?
   b. How is Tiger Woods's performance influenced by pressure and crowd response?
   c. How much protein does Tiger Woods need?
   d. How does Tiger Woods's brain respond differently to social and nonsocial stimuli?

# Answers

1.c 2.a 3.d 4.c

# Think It Through!

If you were an athlete who began to freeze up whenever you played, what kind of psychologist would you consult? Would your choice be different if you already had a clear understanding of why you "choked"?

Would the President be more effective if he had a chief psychologist? If so, which sort of psychologist would be most helpful? (Don't assume it would necessarily be a clinical psychologist.) Why?

# ETHICS: Doing It Right

Let's say that Tiger Woods wants to learn how to overcome pain so that he can practice hard even when he is hurt, but that practicing when injured might cause long-term damage to his body. Would it be ethical for a sport psychologist to teach Woods—or anyone else—techniques for continuing to work out even in the presence of damaging pain? Or, what if Woods developed a "block" that impaired his playing? Would it be ethical for a therapist to treat him with new, unproven techniques?

## Ethics in Research

Following World War II, people were horrified to learn that the Nazis had performed ghastly experiments on human beings. The war trials in Nuremberg led directly to the first set of rules, subscribed to by many nations, outlawing those sorts of experiments (in Chapter 2, we will consider in detail the kinds of research methods psychologists use).

Sometimes the actions of psychologists also call for a set of rules, especially when participants' rights conflict with a research method or clinical treatment. Certain methods are obviously unethical: no psychologist would cause people who participate in experiments to become addicted to drugs to see how easily they can overcome the addiction or beat people to help them overcome a psychological problem. But many research situations are not so clear-cut.

## Research With People: Human Guinea Pigs?

In 1996, some New York psychiatrists were tapping the spines of severely depressed teenagers at regular intervals in order to see whether the presence of certain chemicals in the spinal fluid could predict which particular teens would attempt suicide. As required by law, the youths' parents had given permission for the researchers to draw the fluids. However, this study was one of at least ten that a court ruling brought to a screeching halt on December 5, 1996 (*New York Times*, page A1). The New York State Appeals Court found that the existing rules for the treatment of children and mentally ill people in experimental settings were unconstitutional because they did not properly protect these participants from abuse by researchers. However, the researchers claimed that without these studies they would never be able to develop the most effective drugs for treating serious impairments, some of which might lead to suicide. Do the potential benefits of such studies outweigh the pain they cause?

New York was more lax in its policies than many other states. California, Connecticut, Massachusetts, and Illinois do not allow researchers to conduct experiments in which the gain is not outweighed by the pain or experiments that have risks but do not benefit participants directly, unless the participants themselves (not someone else for them) provide **informed consent**. Informed consent means that before agreeing to take part, potential participants in a study must be told what they will be asked to do and must be advised of the possible risks and benefits of the procedure. They are also told that they can withdraw from the study at any time without being penalized. Only after an individual clearly understands this information and gives consent by signature can he or she take part in a study. But not all states have such rules, and there are no general federal laws that regulate all research with human participants.

Informed consent: The requirement that a potential participant in a study be told what he or she will be asked to do and be advised of possible risks and benefits of the study before agreeing to take part.

Nevertheless, a study that uses funds from the U.S. government or from most private funding sources must be approved by an institutional review board (IRB) at the university, hospital, or other institution that sponsors or hosts the study. The IRB monitors all research projects at that institution, not just those of psychologists. An IRB usually includes not only scientists but also physicians, clergy, and representatives from the local community. The IRB considers the potential risks and benefits of each research study and decides whether the study can be performed. These risks and benefits are considered from all three levels of analysis: Effects on the brain (for example, of drugs), the person (for example, through imparting false beliefs), and the group (for example, from embarrassment or humiliation). In many universities and hospitals, researchers are asked to discuss their proposed studies with the board, to explain in more detail what they are doing and why.

Concerns about the ethical treatment of human participants lead most IRBs to insist that participants be **debriefed**, that is, interviewed after the study about their experience. The purpose of debriefing is to ensure that participants are having no negative reactions as a result of their participation and that they have understood the purposes of the study. Deceiving participants with false or misleading information is allowable only when the participants will not be harmed and the knowledge gained clearly outweighs the use of dishonesty.

In large parts of India, animals are not eaten (some are even considered sacred). Many in that culture may believe that animal research is not appropriate.

## Research With Animals

Animals are studied in some types of psychological research, particularly studies that focus on understanding the brain. Animals, of course, can't give informed consent, don't volunteer, and can't decide to withdraw from the study if they get nervous or uncomfortable. But this doesn't mean that animals lack protection. Animal studies, like human ones, must have the stamp of approval of an IRB. The IRB makes sure the animals are housed properly (in cages that are large enough and cleaned often enough) and that they are not mistreated. Researchers are not allowed to cause animals pain unless that is explicitly what is being studied—and even then, they must justify in detail the potential benefits to humans (and possibly to animals, by advancing veterinary medicine) of inflicting the pain.

Is it ethical to test animals at all? This is not an easy question to answer. Researchers who study animals argue that their research is ethical. They point out that although there are substitutes for eating meat and wearing leather, there is no substitute for the use of animals in certain kinds of research. So, if the culture allows the use of animals for food and clothing, it is not clear why animals should not be studied in laboratories if the animals do not suffer and the findings produce important knowledge. This is not a cut-and-dried issue, however, and thoughtful people disagree. As brain-scanning technologies improve (see Chapter 3), the need for some types of animal studies of the brain may diminish.

## Ethics in Clinical Practice

Imagine a Dr. Smith who has developed a new type of therapy that she claims is particularly effective for patients who are afraid of some social situations, such as public speaking or meeting strangers. You are a therapist who has a patient struggling with such difficulties and not responding to conventional therapy. You haven't been trained in Smith therapy, but you want to help your patient. Should you try this therapy?

According to the American Psychological Association guidelines (see Table 1.3), the answer is clear: No. If you have not been trained appropriately or are not learning the therapy under supervision, you have no business delivering it.

This sort of ethical decision is relatively straightforward. But the process of psychotherapy sometimes requires careful stepping through emotional and ethical minefields. Psychologists are bound by their states' laws of confidentiality and may not communicate about a patient without specific permission from the patient, except in certain extreme cases, as when a life or (in some states) property is at stake. Therapists have gone to jail rather than reveal personal information about their patients. Indeed, difficult cases sometimes cause new laws to be written. A patient at the University of California told a psychologist at the student health center that he wanted to kill someone and named the person. The campus police were told; they interviewed the patient and let him go. The patient then killed his targeted victim. The dead woman's parents sued the university for "failure to warn." The case eventually wound its way to California's highest court. One issue was whether the therapist had the right to divulge confidential information from therapy sessions. The court ruled that a therapist is obligated to use reasonable care to protect a potential victim. More specifically, in California (and in most other states now), if a patient has told his or her psychologist that he or she plans to harm a specific other person, and the psychologist has reason to believe the patient can and will follow through with that plan, the psychologist must take steps to protect the targeted person from harm, even though doing so may violate the patient's confidentiality. Similar guidelines apply to cases of potential suicide.

Further, a therapist cannot engage in sexual relations with a patient or mistreat a patient physically or emotionally. The American Psychological Association has developed many detailed ethical guidelines based on the principles listed in Table 1.3.

| TABLE 1.3 | **General Ethical Principles and Code of Conduct for Psychologists** |
| --- | --- |
| **Principle A: Beneficence and Nonmaleficence** | "Psychologists strive to benefit those with whom they work and take care to do no harm. . . . Because psychologists' scientific and professional judgments and actions may affect the lives of others, they are alert to and guard against personal, financial, social, organizational, or political factors that might lead to misuse of their influence." |
| **Principle B: Fidelity and Responsibility** | "Psychologists uphold professional standards of conduct, clarify their professional roles and obligations, accept appropriate responsibility for their behavior, and seek to manage conflicts of interest that could lead to exploitation or harm." |
| **Principle C: Integrity** | "Psychologists seek to promote accuracy, honesty, and truthfulness in the science, teaching, and practice of psychology. In these activities psychologists do not steal, cheat, or engage in fraud, subterfuge, or intentional misrepresentation of fact. Psychologists strive to keep their promises and to avoid unwise or unclear commitments." |
| **Principle D: Justice** | "Psychologists recognize that fairness and justice entitle all persons to access to and benefit from the contributions of psychology and to equal quality in the processes, procedures, and services being conducted by psychologists." |
| **Principle E: Respect for People's Rights and Dignity** | "Psychologists respect the dignity and worth of all people, and the rights of individuals to privacy, confidentiality, and self-determination. . . . Psychologists are aware of and respect cultural, individual, and role differences, including those based on age, gender, gender identity, race, ethnicity, culture, national origin, religion, sexual orientation, disability, language, and socioeconomic status and consider these factors when working with members of such groups." |

Note: This is a direct quote with portions abridged; a complete description can be found at http://www.apa.org/ethics/code2002.html.

# New Frontiers: Neuroethics

As research in psychology continues to progress at an increasing pace, new issues have emerged that would have been only in the realm of science fiction a few years ago. To address one set of these issues, a new branch of ethics, called *neuroethics*, is focusing on the possible dangers and benefits of research on the brain. Still in its infancy, this field is already a hotbed of debate (a recent Google search on "neuroethics" turned up more than 4,600 hits). So far, however, neuroethicists have more questions than answers. For example, Is it ethical to use brain-altering drugs to force prisoners to be docile? To scan people's brains to discover whether they are telling the truth? To require young children to take medication that makes them pay attention better in school?

Some scholars have been particularly concerned about the use of neuroscience to predict and control individual behavior (see Markus, 2002). For example, suppose that the brains of murderers could be shown conclusively to have a distinctive characteristic (perhaps one region that is much smaller than normal). Should we then scan people's brains and watch them carefully if they have this characteristic? Should this characteristic be used as a criterion for parole for prisoners? Or, what about using pictures of people's brains as reasons to, or not to, hire them for specific jobs? What if brain scanning of fetuses could predict whether children would have certain talents—would this be a good thing to know?

The Center for Cognitive Liberty and Ethics (www.cognitiveliberty.org) asserts that two fundamental principles should form the core of neuroethics: First, individuals should never be forced to use technologies or drugs that interact with their brains. Second, individuals should not be prohibited from using such technologies or drugs if they so desire, provided that such use would not lead them to harm others.

# Test Yourself

1. An institutional review board (IRB) would be interested in whether human research participants were
   a. told about potential risks and benefits of a study.
   b. debriefed after the study.
   c. both told about risks and benefits of a study and debriefed after it.
   d. recruited from the local area.

2. An IRB would be interested in whether animal research participants were
   a. housed and treated properly.
   b. voluntary participants in the study.
   c. thinking or not thinking.
   d. conscious or not conscious.

3. In many states, it is ethical and legal for clinical and counseling psychologists to
   a. administer therapy they are not trained for.
   b. violate client confidentiality when a credible specific threat against any person is made.
   c. administer drugs they believe will help their clients.
   d. mistreat a client in order to help the person.

4. The recent emergence of the field of neuroethics indicates that
   a. ethical questions will become less important as technology advances.
   b. ethical questions will not affect modern psychology.
   c. as technologies progress, more ethical questions will arise concerning the use of these technologies.
   d. psychology cannot be both scientific and ethical.

## Answers

1.c  2.a  3.b  4.c

# Think It Through!

Would it be ethical to study Tiger Woods as if he were some kind of guinea pig? How about asking him to try out a new way to relieve stress, which you are convinced is better than anything else available but for which you have no evidence to back up your intuitions?

Imagine you are an academic psychologist doing research on whether sugar makes chimps more active and less able to perform certain tasks. So far, your student who is helping with the research has found that sugar clearly leads to increased activity and difficulty with cognitive tasks requiring concentration. A new student joins the research team, and she tells you that the animals appear to be agitated, have difficulty sleeping, and, at times, appear to be in pain. The study is otherwise going well. What should you do? When you write up the study for publication, how will you address this issue?

# REVIEW AND REMEMBER!

## Summary

### I. The Science of Psychology: Getting to Know You

**A.** Psychology is the science of mental processes and behavior.

**B.** The goals of psychology are to describe, explain, predict, and control mental processes and behavior.

**C.** Psychology can best be understood by studying events at different levels of analysis: the levels of the brain, the person, and the group.

**D.** The level of the brain consists of the activity of certain brain systems, structural differences in people's brains, and effects of various genes and chemicals (such as hormones) on mental processes and behavior.

**E.** The level of the person comprises the contents of mental processes, not just the mechanisms that give rise to them. The contents of our memories, beliefs, goals, and feelings are part and parcel of who we are.

**F.** The level of the group encompasses all our social interactions, including those that reflect our particular culture.

**G.** Events at the different levels are interdependent and are always interacting.

### II. Psychology Then and Now: The Evolution of a Science

**A.** Psychology began as the study of mental processes, such as those that underlie perception, memory, and reasoning.

**B.** The structuralists tried to understand such processes; their goal was to identify the elements of consciousness and the rules by which these elements are

## Your Notes

I.

A.

B.

C.

D. The brain: mechanism

E. The person: contents of mental processes

F. The group: social environment

G.

II.

A.

B.

combined into mental structures. One of the primary methods of the structuralists was introspection ("looking within"), which turned out to be unreliable and not always valid.

**C.** The functionalists rejected the goal of identifying mental processes and how they operated in favor of seeking explanations for thoughts, feelings, and behaviors. The functionalists were interested in how mental processes adapt to help people survive in the natural world.

**D.** In contrast, the Gestalt psychologists also reacted against the structuralists, but they were more disturbed by the emphasis on breaking mental processes into distinct elements. The Gestaltists studied the way the brain organizes material into overall patterns, both in perception and in thinking.

**E.** Freud and his colleagues shifted the focus to events at the level of the person (and, to some extent, the level of the group). Psychodynamic theories are concerned largely with the operation of unconscious mental processes and primitive impulses (often related to sex) in dictating what we think, feel, and do.

**F.** The behaviorists rejected the assumption that psychology should focus on mental processes; they favored sticking with what could be seen—stimuli, responses, and the consequences of responses.

**G.** The humanists, in part reacting against Freud's theory, were interested in developing treatments of psychological problems that relied on respect for individuals and their potentials.

**H.** Elements of the various schools of psychological thought came together in cognitive psychology, which began by thinking of the mind as analogous to a computer program; in this view, mental processing is information processing.

**I.** Cognitive neuroscientists study the relation between events at all three levels of analysis, with an emphasis on how the brain gives rise to thoughts, feelings, and behaviors.

**J.** Evolutionary psychology views many cognitive strategies and goals as adaptations that are the results of natural selection.

## III. The Psychological Way: What Today's Psychologists Do

**A.** The three general types of psychologists are distinguished by their training, work settings, and types of work.

**B.** Clinical and counseling psychologists administer and interpret psychological tests, provide psychotherapy, offer career and vocational counseling, and help people with specific psychological problems.

**C.** Academic psychologists teach and do research, in addition to helping to run their universities, colleges, or institutions.

**D.** Applied psychologists use the findings and theories of psychology to solve practical problems.

## IV. Ethics: Doing It Right

**A.** Research with humans or nonhuman animals at universities, hospitals, and most industrial settings requires approval from an institutional review board (IRB).

*C.*

*D. Perceptual unit is flock rather than individual birds.*

*E.*

*F.*

*G.*

*H.*

*I.*

*J.*

*III.*

*A.*

*B.*

*C.*

*D.*

*IV.*

*A.*

**B.** For research with humans, the IRB will insist that the researchers obtain informed consent, which means providing in advance information about the possible risks and benefits of participation.

**C.** The IRB will also require debriefing, which is an interview after the study to ensure that the participant had no negative reactions and did, in fact, understand the purpose of the study.

**D.** The IRB will not allow deception of participants, unless the deception is harmless and absolutely necessary.

**E.** For research with animals, the IRB requires that the animals be treated well (for example, housed in clean cages) and that pain be inflicted only if that is what is being studied and if it is justified by the benefits from the research.

**F.** In clinical practice, psychotherapists have clear ethical guidelines to follow, which include maintaining confidentiality unless a specific other person (or, in some states, property) is clearly in danger or suicide is an imminent concern.

**G.** In addition, therapists cannot use techniques that they have not been trained to use or engage in inappropriate personal behavior with patients.

**H.** Neuroethics focuses on ethical issues that are emerging from the ability to monitor and alter brain function.

NOTE: Once you feel that you understand the material in this chapter, visit the book's Web site at www.ablongman.com/kosslyn3e to test your knowledge with additional study questions.

*B.*

*C.*

*D.*

*E.*

*F.*

*G.*

*H.*

# Key Terms

academic psychologist, p. 24
applied psychologist, p. 25
behavior, p. 4
behaviorism, p. 15
clinical psychologist, p. 22
cognitive neuroscience, p. 18
cognitive psychology, p. 17
counseling psychologist, p. 23
debriefing, p. 30

evolutionary psychology, p. 19
functionalism, p. 12
Gestalt psychology, p. 13
humanistic psychology, p. 16
informed consent, p. 29
introspection, p. 12
level of the brain, p. 6
level of the group, p. 7
level of the person, p. 6

mental processes, p. 4
psychiatric nurse, p. 23
psychiatrist, p. 23
psychodynamic theory, p. 14
psychology, p. 4
psychotherapy, p. 23
social worker, p. 23
structuralism, p. 11
unconscious, p. 14

# CHAPTER 2

# THE RESEARCH PROCESS: HOW WE FIND THINGS OUT

In 1984, President Ronald Reagan gave his official blessing to a daring project, building a permanent inhabited space station. A key part of President Reagan's vision was that the space station should be built and staffed by people from many different countries. His vision came to pass, and the International Space Station (ISS) is in place some 250 miles above earth. The ISS is a mammoth structure, comparable in size and scope to the pyramids of ancient Egypt. The station spans a distance greater than a football field and weighs over 1 million pounds. Its solar panels spread over almost an acre, and it will cost at least $90 billion.

The ISS is not just a technological marvel, it is also a testament to our very human ability to cooperate and interact effectively. The project is particularly impressive because it was initiated by 16 countries—including former enemies, notably the United States and Russia.

In the first phase of the program (which began in 1995), American and Russian astronauts lived and worked together on the Russian space station *Mir*. These experiences taught astronauts and earth-bound scientists about living and working in space and, equally important, also built cooperation and trust between the astronauts themselves and the respective organizations back on earth.

Astronauts living on the ISS not only observe the earth, but also experiment with new ways to manufacture materials, to make drugs, and to study diseases ranging from osteoporosis to cancer. But more than that, the science of psychology is playing a key role in discovering the best ways for people to live and function in space. The ISS experience will reveal new facets of human mental processes and behavior, both when people are alone and when they are part of a group. How can we learn such things from the ISS, or from events in any other context? Through science. In this chapter, we see how the science of psychology can be used to learn about the brain, the person, and the group.

# THE SCIENTIFIC METHOD:
## Designed to Be Valid

On November 2, 2000, the first astronauts moved into the ISS. They moved into just one small part of the station, which provided the bare minimum in basic facilities. Among these basic essentials were a treadmill and an exercise bike. These pieces of equipment are not luxury items, but absolute necessities: Astronauts must exercise to retain their bone density and muscles. The trouble is (as too many of we earth-bound couch potatoes know only too well) that the benefits of exercising occur later, whereas the benefits of coping with the press of immediate events occurs right now—and thus it's sometimes difficult to be motivated to exercise. A substitute has been proposed: Simply vibrating the bones appears to prevent calcium loss. But could this procedure also disrupt the astronauts' concentration? Perhaps make it difficult for them to sleep?

How could we find out whether the new vibration treatment might have unintended consequences, for example, by affecting the quality of sleep (either as the procedure was conducted or afterward)? Psychology is a science because it relies on a specific type of method of inquiry, and this method, in principle, allows psychologists to discover characteristics that predict human behavior.

The **scientific method** is a way to gather facts that will lead to the formulation and validation of a theory. It involves *specifying a problem, systematically observing events, forming a hypothesis of the relation between variables, collecting new observations to test the hypothesis, using such evidence to formulate and support a theory, and finally, testing the theory*. Let's take a closer look at the scientific method, one step at a time.

## Step 1: Specifying a Problem

What do we mean by "specifying a problem"? Science tries to answer questions, any one of which may be rephrased as a "problem." Despite the way the word is often used in ordinary conversation, a problem is not necessarily bad: It is simply a question you want to answer or a puzzle you want to solve. A scientist might notice what seems to be a consistent pattern, for example, and wonder if it reflects a connection or a coincidence. A scientist might reflect on the fact that all humans must sleep, which might lead her to wonder whether weightlessness could disrupt astronauts' normal sleeping—and if so, whether that might affect their performance. This, then, would be the specific problem: Will weightlessness affect astronauts' sleep patterns and performance?

## Step 2: Observing Events

After the problem is specified, it is investigated by "systematically observing events." Scientists are not content to rely on impressions or interpretations. They want to know the facts, as free from any particular notions of their significance as possible. Facts are established by collecting **data**, which are numerical measurements or careful observations of a phenomenon. Properly collected data can be obtained again in a **replication**

Scientific method: The scientific method involves specifying a problem, systematically observing events, forming a hypothesis of the relation between variables, collecting new observations to test the hypothesis, using such evidence to formulate and support a theory, and finally testing the theory.

Data: Objective observations.

Replication: Collecting the same observations or measurements and finding the same results as were found previously.

of a study; that is, they can be collected again by the original investigator or someone else. Scientists often prefer quantitative data (numerical measurements), such as how long a person sleeps normally versus how long he or she sleeps during weightlessness or how many items on a list a person can learn in a given time. In addition to collecting numerical data, scientists rely on systematic observations, which simply document that a certain event occurs. But unless the data include numbers, it is often difficult to sort the observation from the interpretation. The data are just the facts, ma'am, nothing but the facts—when data are collected, the interpretation must be set aside, saved for later.

What do we mean by "events"? An event in the scientific sense is the occurrence of a particular phenomenon. Scientists study two kinds of events: those that are themselves directly observable (such as how long someone sleeps) and those that, like thoughts, motivations, or emotions, can only be inferred. For example, if we notice that astronauts yawn more frequently than normal, this might suggest that they are sleepy (an inferred internal state).

But observations are just the beginning; they typically can be interpreted in more than one way. For example, perhaps astronauts yawn so often because repetitive work is boring.

# Step 3: Forming a Hypothesis

What about "forming a hypothesis of the relation between variables"? First, by the term **variable**, researchers mean an aspect of a situation that is liable to change (or, in other words, that can vary); more precisely, a variable is a characteristic of a substance, quantity, or entity that is measurable. A **hypothesis** is a tentative idea that might explain a set of observations. For example, the ISS does not have normal patterns of "day" and "night," and thus astronauts do not sleep when it gets dark outside. Rather, they may get wrapped up in what they are doing and forget how much time has passed since they last slept. Do they actually sleep less than normal? If so, we could then ask whether losing sleep interferes with learning. To ensure optimal performance on the ISS, it's important to know whether astronauts are in fact sleep-deprived, and if so, whether lack of sleep impairs learning and thus memory; memory lapses that would lead to harmless mishaps on earth could lead to disaster in space. This hypothesis comes down to the assertion that there's a connection between two variables—amount of sleep and effectiveness of learning. However, before you urge the ISS astronauts to force themselves to sleep 8 hours in 24, you ought to test the hypothesis to find out whether it's correct.

# Step 4: Testing the Hypothesis

Thus, you must go about "collecting new observations to test the hypothesis." The first thing you need to do is create operational definitions of the key concepts, which makes them concrete enough to test. An **operational definition** specifies a variable by indicating how it is measured or manipulated. In this example, "not sleeping" might be defined as having stayed continuously awake for 24 hours, and "learning" might be defined as retaining memory for material that was studied earlier in the day. Are there rigorous studies that focus on memory following a sleepless night? Yes, and researchers have found that staying up all night does disrupt memory for information learned that day (Graves et al., 2001; Stickgold et al., 2000). In fact, memory for verbal material is impaired even when people do sleep but their sleep patterns are disrupted because they've had to wake up intermittently (Ficca et al., 2000). A

**Variable:** An aspect of a situation that can vary, or change; specifically, a characteristic of a substance, quantity, or entity that is measurable.

**Hypothesis:** A tentative idea that might explain a set of observations.

**Operational definition:** A definition of a variable that specifies how it is measured or manipulated.

FIGURE 2.1 **The Scientific Method**

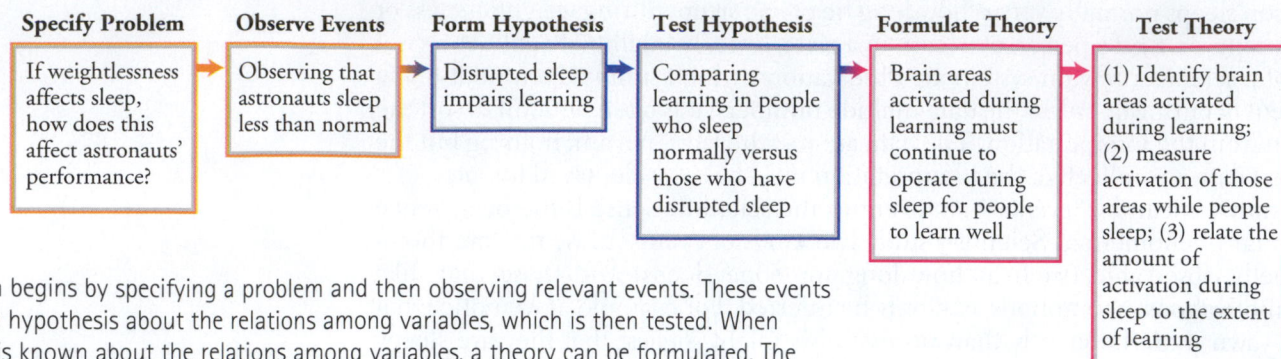

Research begins by specifying a problem and then observing relevant events. These events lead to a hypothesis about the relations among variables, which is then tested. When enough is known about the relations among variables, a theory can be formulated. The theory in turn produces predictions, which are new hypotheses and are in turn tested. If these theory-based hypotheses are confirmed, the theory is supported; if they fail to bear fruit, then the theory must be altered and the whole process repeated.

typical study has two groups: In one, participants learn some information, such as a list of words. These people then sleep normally, and their memory is tested the next day. Participants in a second group learn the same material (and learn it as well) as the participants in the first group, but then stay up all night or are allowed to sleep only intermittently and are tested the next day. The hypothesis is that participants will have better memory if they were allowed to sleep normally.

## Step 5: Formulating a Theory

Now consider "using such evidence to formulate and support a theory." A **theory** consists of an interlocking set of concepts or principles that explains a set of observations. A theory does not appear out of thin air; rather, a theory is formulated on the basis of empirical findings that were obtained before the theory existed. Unlike a hypothesis, a theory is not a tentative idea and doesn't focus on possible relationships among variables. Instead, theories are rooted in an established web of facts and concepts and focus on the *reasons* for established relationships among variables. In our example, the notion that people will fail to store information in memory if they don't sleep normally is a hypothesis, not a theory. A theory might explain that sleep is necessary for learning because: (1) specific brain areas are activated when we learn during the day; and (2) those areas must continue to operate for a specific period of time while we sleep in order to store the information acquired during the day. Hypotheses and theories both produce **predictions**, which are new hypotheses. These hypotheses are expectations about specific events that should occur in particular circumstances if the original theory is correct. The new hypotheses can then be put to the test.

## Step 6: Testing the Theory

**Theory:** An interlocking set of concepts or principles that explain a set of observations.

**Prediction:** An expectation about specific events that should occur in particular circumstances if the theory or hypothesis is correct.

Finally, what do we mean by "testing the theory"? The history of science is littered with theories that turned out to be wrong. Researchers evaluate a theory by testing its predictions. As illustrated in Figure 2.1, once a theory has been formulated, it plays a key role in the process of formulating hypotheses. Each prediction of the theory is in fact a new hypothesis to be tested. For example, in one study researchers scanned the brains of people as they learned sequences of responses, and then scanned their brains again while they slept that night. Brain areas that were active during learning continued to be active during sleep. Moreover, these areas were more active during sleep in the people who had learned the responses that day than in others who had not (Maquet et al., 2000). Each time a theory makes a correct prediction, the theory is supported, and each time it fails to make a correct prediction, the theory is weakened. If enough of its predictions are unsupported, the theory must be rejected and the data explained in some other way. A good theory is *falsifiable*; that is, it makes predictions it cannot "squirm out of." A falsifiable theory can be rejected if the predictions are not confirmed. Part of the problem with astrology, for example, is that its predictions are so vague and general that they are difficult to disprove.

# Test Yourself

1. In the scientific method, specifying a problem involves
   a. collecting data.
   b. posing questions about the phenomenon.
   c. defining the variables.
   d. analyzing data.

2. Psychologists study two types of events: directly observable behaviors, such as the frequency of an astronaut's yawns, and other events, such as the astronaut's mental state (sleepy or not). The second type of events are
   a. only imagined to happen.
   b. inferred from the behaviors.
   c. unrelated to the behaviors.
   d. easier to study.

3. When forming and testing hypotheses, scientists must specify how the key concepts will be measured or manipulated. This kind of specification is a(n)
   a. operational definition.
   b. hypothesis.
   c. hypothetical definition.
   d. variable definition.

4. Once a theory is developed, it is used to make predictions about certain events. These predictions become
   a. new theories.
   b. operational definitions.
   c. new hypotheses.
   d. testing variables.

## Answers

NOTE: Once you feel comfortable with the Test Yourself questions in this chapter, visit the book's Web site at www.ablongman.com/kosslyn3e for additional study questions.

# Think It Through!

Think of five questions about the way being cooped up with six other people for months on end could change relationships (imagine that there are four men and three women in total). Can each one of your questions be answered using the scientific method? Why or why not? What are the limits of the scientific method for studying psychology? Are there any? If you think that there are such limits, what other methods could you use to study such aspects of mental processes and behavior?

# THE PSYCHOLOGIST'S TOOLBOX:
## Techniques of Scientific Research

Life on the ISS is not like life on earth. The beginning of the day isn't signaled by the dawn's early light, and your morning shower is more likely to be a sponge bath. Drinking from a glass is a challenge; a wrong nudge, and a glob of liquid floats up into your face—or, worse yet, escapes and drifts toward sensitive equipment mounted on a nearby wall or ceiling. And forget about sleeping in a bed. Instead, you crawl into a special sleeping bag that is anchored to a wall, and tie your arms down before nodding off. But perhaps the most striking differences from life as we usually experience it are social. The ISS will only house seven people. How will they get along as time goes on? How should living quarters be designed to ensure enough privacy, to "give them some space"—but at the same time promote social support? How should daily wake/sleep schedules be synchronized for the different crew members? And how many of the crew should be men, how many women? Would it be best if most of the crew were married couples? The questions go on and on. How can we answer them? Although all sound psychological investigations rely on the scientific method, the different areas of psychology often pose and answer questions differently. Psychologists use a variety of research tools, each with its own advantages and disadvantages.

## Descriptive Research: Just the Facts, Ma'am

Some scientists observe animals in the wilds of Africa; others observe sea life in the depths of the ocean; and others observe humans in their natural habitats.

Although the scientific method is always described in terms of testing hypotheses, this isn't quite the whole story. Not all research is sparked by specific hypotheses. Some research is devoted simply to describing "things as they are." It's no accident that "observing events" is a key part of the scientific method: Theorizing without facts is a little like cooking without ingredients.

### Naturalistic Observation

For the scientist, facts are *not* intuitions, impressions, or anecdotes. Essential to the scientific method is careful, systematic, and unbiased observation that can be repeated by others, and some researchers specialize in collecting such data from real-world settings. For example, researchers observed caregivers interacting with young children, and noted that the caregivers changed their language and speech patterns, using short sentences and speaking in a high pitch. This modified way of speaking is known as *child-directed speech* (Morgan & Demuth, 1996; Snow, 1991, 1999).

Although naturalistic observation is an essential part of science, it is only a first step. The discovery of child-directed speech does not tell us whether caregivers use it in order to help children understand them, or to entertain them, or simply to imitate other caregivers they have heard. It is difficult to test specific interpretations of a finding using only naturalistic observation (although not impossible, as any astronomer will tell you). The problem is that to test your hypothesis, you must seek out a specific situation where nature has set the relevant variables in just the right way. In science, observing an event typically is only the first step.

## Case Studies

Sometimes nature or human affairs produce unique situations, which change an independent variable in a novel way. A **case study** focuses on a single instance of a situation, examining it in detail. For example, a researcher might study a single astronaut, looking closely at her life and circumstances in an effort to formulate hypotheses about the psychological underpinnings that allow someone to succeed in this profession. Many neuropsychologists study individual brain-damaged patients in depth to discover which abilities are "knocked out" following certain types of damage (in Chapter 3, you will read about a young soldier who, after suffering brain injury, had bizarre visual impairments). A psychologist who studies abnormal behavior might study a reported case of multiple personalities to discover whether there's anything to the idea (books such as *Sybil* and *The Three Faces of Eve* describe such cases in great detail); a cognitive psychologist may investigate how an unusually gifted memory expert is able to retain huge amounts of information almost perfectly; a personality psychologist might study in detail how astronauts remain motivated through years and years of hard work with no guarantee that they will ever fly into space.

However, we must always be cautious about generalizing from a single case; that is, we must be careful in assuming that the findings in the case study extend to all other similar cases. Any particular person may be unusual for many reasons and so may not be at all representative of people in general.

Brain damage following an accident can cause someone to fail to name fruits and vegetables while still able to name other objects (Hart et al., 1985). A case study would examine such a person in detail, documenting precisely what sorts of things could and could not be named.

## Surveys

A **survey** is a set of questions put to a number of participants about their beliefs, attitudes, preferences, or activities. Surveys are a relatively inexpensive way to collect a lot of data fairly quickly, and they are popular among psychologists who study personality and social interactions. Surveys provide data that can be used to formulate or test a hypothesis. However, the value of surveys is limited by what people are capable of reporting accurately. You could use a survey to ask people how they feel about the government's using tax dollars to build the ISS, but not to ask people how their brains work or to ask them to report subtle behaviors, such as body language, that they may engage in unconsciously. Moreover, even if they are capable of answering, people may not always respond honestly; as we note in Chapter 11, this is especially a problem when the survey touches on sensitive personal issues, such as sex. And even if people do respond honestly, what they say does not always reflect what they do. We cite a classic example in Chapter 1, reported in 1934 by La Piere, in which restaurant managers were asked whether they would serve Chinese people; although most said they would not, when Chinese people actually came to their restaurants, virtually all served them without question. Finally, not everyone who is asked to respond does, in fact, fill in the survey. Because a particular factor (such as income or age) may incline some people, but not others, to respond, it is difficult to know whether the responses obtained are actually representative of the whole group that the survey was designed to assess.

Case study: A scientific study that focuses on a single instance of a situation, examining it in detail.

Survey: A set of questions, typically about beliefs, attitudes, preferences, or activities.

Survey questions have to be carefully worded so that they don't lead the respondents to answer in a certain way and yet still get at the data of interest. Similarly, the nature of the response scale (for example, the range of values presented) affects what people say, as does the order in which questions are asked (Schwarz, 1999).

Researchers have found that the lower the level of a chemical called monoamine oxidase (MAO) in the blood, the more the person will tend to seek out thrilling activities (such as sky diving and bungee jumping; Zuckerman, 1995). Thus, there is a negative correlation between the two measures: As MAO levels go down, thrill seeking goes up. But we don't know whether MAO level causes the behavior or vice versa—or whether some other chemical, personality trait, or social factor causes the levels of both MAO and thrill seeking to vary together.

Correlation coefficient (or *correlation*): An index of how closely interrelated two sets of measured variables are, which ranges from −1.0 to +1.0. The higher the correlation (in either direction), the better we can predict the value of one type of measurement when given the value of the other.

# Correlational Research: Do Birds of a Feather Flock Together?

Researchers use another method to study the relations among variables, a method that relies on the idea of correlation. A correlation is a relationship in which changes in the measurements of one variable are accompanied by changes in the measurements of another variable. Moreover, the correlation examines whether the magnitudes of the changes in one variable are accompanied by correspondingly sized changes in the magnitudes of another variable. For example, taller people tend to be heavier than smaller people (and given the cost of rocketing each pound into space, shorter, lighter people might have an edge over taller, heavier people in pursuing a career as an astronaut). A **correlation coefficient** (often simply called a *correlation*) is an index of how closely related two measured variables are. Figure 2.2 illustrates three predicted correlations between variables.

In Figure 2.2a, we see a positive correlation, a relationship in which increases in one variable (height) are accompanied by increases in another (weight); a positive correlation is indicated by a correlation value that falls between 0 and 1.0. In Figure 2.2b, we see a negative correlation, a relationship, in which increases in one variable (age) are accompanied by decreases in another (health); a negative correlation is indicated by a correlation value that is between 0 and −1.0. Finally, in Figure 2.2c, we see a zero correlation, which indicates no relationship between the two variables (height and aggressiveness); they do not vary together. The closer the correlation is to 1.0 or −1.0, the stronger the relationship; visually, the more tightly the data points cluster around the line, the higher the correlation.

Correlational research involves measuring at least two things about each of a number of individuals or groups (or measuring the same individuals or groups at a number of different times), and looking at the way one set of measurements goes up or down in tandem with another set of measurements; correlations always compare one pair of measurements at a time. The main advantage of correlational research is that it allows researchers to compare variables that cannot be manipulated directly. The main disadvantage is that correlations indicate only that two variables tend to vary together, not that one *causes* the other. For example, evidence suggests a small correlation between poor eyesight and intelligence (Belkin & Rosner, 1987; Miller, 1992; Williams et al., 1988), but poor eyesight doesn't cause someone to be smarter! Similarly, researchers have found that weightlessness disrupts spatial orientation (such as awareness of the position of your body) and that these effects may be related to space motion sickness (Young et al., 1993). Does motion sickness disrupt spatial orientation, or does impaired spatial orientation produce motion sickness? Or, does some other variable—such as abnormal head movements—produce both effects? Given only the correlation between problems in spatial orientation and the occurrence of motion sickness, you can't say. Remember: *Correlation does not imply causation.*

**FIGURE 2.2** **Strength of Correlation**

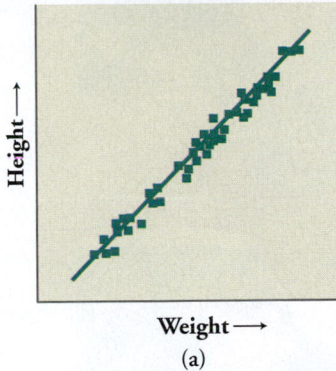

POSITIVE CORRELATION
BETWEEN 0 AND 1.0

(a)

Here, increases in one variable (height) are accompanied by increases in another (weight); this is a positive correlation, indicated by a correlation value that falls between 0 and 1.0.

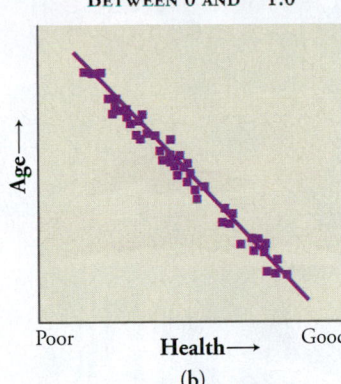

NEGATIVE CORRELATION
BETWEEN 0 AND −1.0

(b)

Here, increases in one variable (age) are accompanied by decreases in another (health); this is a negative correlation, indicated by a correlation value that is between 0 and −1.0.

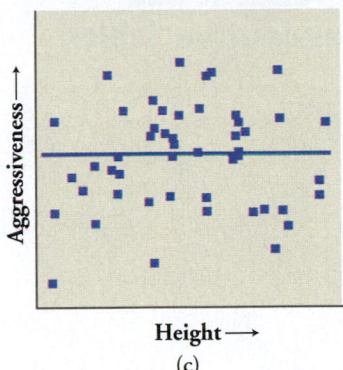

ZERO CORRELATION

(c)

A zero correlation indicates no relationship between the two variables, height and aggressiveness here; they do not vary together. The closer the correlation is to 1.0 or −1.0, the stronger the relationship; visually, the more tightly the data points cluster around the line, the higher the correlation.

# Experimental Research: Manipulating and Measuring

Much psychological research relies on conducting *experiments*, controlled situations in which variables are manipulated. Experiments provide the strongest way to test a hypothesis, in that they can provide evidence that one event causes another.

## Independent and Dependent Variables

The variables in a situation—for example, "amount of sleep" and "memory performance"—are the aspects of the situation that can vary. In an experiment, the investigator deliberately alters one aspect of a situation, which is called the **independent variable**, and measures another, called the **dependent variable**. In other words, in an experiment, the value of the dependent variable depends on the value of the independent variable. In our sleeplessness and memory example in the previous section, whether or not participants slept was the independent variable (it was deliberately varied), and memory performance was the dependent variable (it was measured); see Figure 2.3 (p. 46). By examining the link between independent and dependent variables, a researcher hopes to discover exactly which factor is causing an **effect**, which is the difference in the dependent variable that results from a change in the independent variable. In the sleeplessness and memory example, the effect is the degree to which memory is better following sleep than it is following a sleepless night.

Once researchers have found a relation between two variables, they need to test that relation to rule out other possible explanations for it; only by eliminating other

**Independent variable:** The aspect of the situation that is intentionally varied while another aspect is measured.

**Dependent variable:** The aspect of the situation that is measured as an independent variable is changed; the value of the dependent variable depends on the independent variable.

**Effect:** The difference in the dependent variable that is due to the changes in the independent variable.

**FIGURE 2.3**

## Relationship Between Independent and Dependent Variables

The independent variable is what is manipulated—in this example, whether or not participants slept. The dependent variable, what is measured, is in this case memory performance the next day.

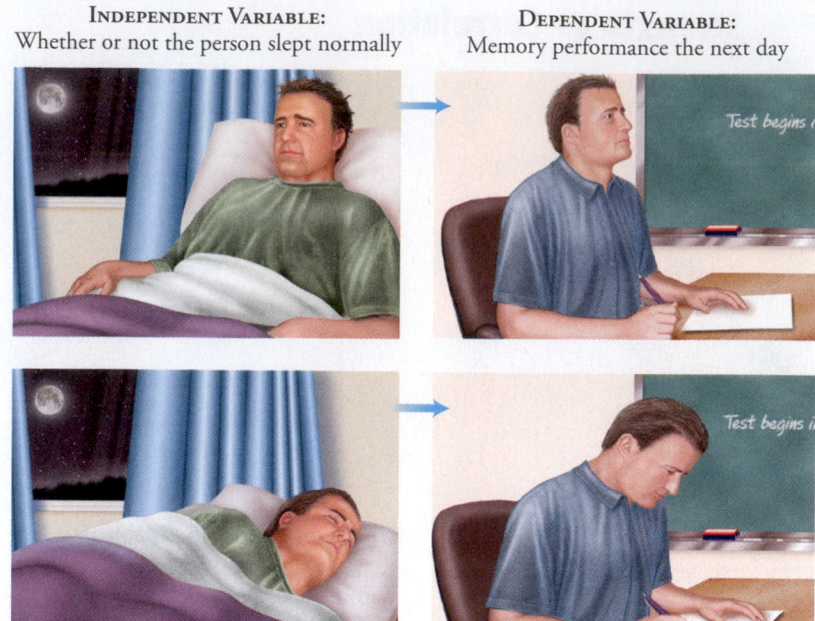

**INDEPENDENT VARIABLE:**
Whether or not the person slept normally

**DEPENDENT VARIABLE:**
Memory performance the next day

Test begins in

Test begins in

possibilities can we know whether a hypothesized relation is correct. Say we had tested only one group, the one that was kept awake. The fact that these students failed to recall many words would not necessarily show that sleep is critical for learning. Why? Perhaps the test was too difficult and, even in the best of circumstances, the participants wouldn't have been able to remember much. Or perhaps the testing situation created a lot of anxiety, and that's what interfered with learning. A **confound**, or *confounding variable*, is another possible aspect of the situation (such as the anxiety that accompanies a test) that has become entangled with the aspects that the researcher has chosen to vary. Confounds thus lead to results that are ambiguous, that do not have a clear-cut interpretation (see Figure 2.4).

### Experimental and Control Groups and Conditions

One way to disentangle confounds is to use a control group. The **experimental group** receives the complete *treatment*, that is, the complete procedure that defines the experiment. A **control group** is treated identically to the experimental group except with regard to the one variable that is the focus of study; a good control group holds constant—or controls—all of the variables in the experimental group except the one of interest. In experiments on the role of sleep in learning, the experimental group doesn't sleep; the control group does. If the kinds of people assigned to the two groups differ markedly, say, in age, gender, or learning ability (or any combination of the three), those factors could be confounds that would mask a clear reading of the experiment's results; any difference in the groups' performance could have been caused by any of those elements. For instance, if the sleepless group happened to include more people who were elderly than the control group, the researchers should not conclude that sleeplessness led the experimental group to forget—perhaps aging can make people learn less effectively in general. In a properly conducted experiment, therefore, the researchers rely on **random assignment**: Participants are assigned randomly, that is, by

Confound (or *confounding variable*): An independent variable that varies along with the ones of interest, and could be the actual basis for what you are measuring.

Experimental group: A group that receives the complete procedure that defines the experiment.

Control group: A group that is treated exactly the same way as the experimental group, except that the one aspect of the situation being studied is not manipulated for this group. The control group holds constant—"controls"—all of the variables in the experimental group except the one of interest.

Random assignment: The technique of assigning participants randomly, that is, by chance, to the experimental and the control groups, so that no biases can sneak into the composition of the groups.

**FIGURE 2.4**

## Confounding Variables in Everyday Life

Professor Jones has made a startling observation: Students with poor posture are more intelligent than those who stand up straight. He plans to alert the college admissions office to this finding, and urge them to require applicants to supply full-body photos. But is it intelligence that accompanies poor posture? Perhaps a strong motivation to do well leads to more intense poring over books, with hunched posture. Or is it that shy people both tend to hunch and to be more comfortable spending time alone studying? Can you think of other possible confounding variables that should make Professor Jones take pause?

chance, to the experimental and the control groups, so that no confounds can sneak into the composition of the groups.

Similarly, you can use an **experimental condition** and a **control condition**, either for a group of people or a single person. Instead of testing a separate control group, you test the same group another time, keeping everything the same as in the experimental condition except for the single independent variable of interest. For example, you could test the same people twice, once when they were allowed to sleep normally after studying the words and once when they were kept awake. (Indeed, you can test them four times, twice while on earth and then twice while on the ISS; this experiment would allow you to discover whether sleep has the same effects on memory during weightlessness as it does normally.) To avoid confounding the order of testing with the condition (experimental versus control), you would test half the participants in the control condition before testing them in the experimental condition and would test the other half of the participants in the experimental condition before testing them in the control condition.

## Quasi-Experimental Design

One element of a true experiment is that the participants are assigned randomly to the different groups. But in the real world, it is not always possible or desirable to achieve randomness, and so sometimes research designs must be quasi-experimental (*quasi* means "as if" in Latin). A *quasi-experimental design* includes independent and dependent variables and assesses the effects of different values of the independent variable on what is measured. However, participants are not randomly assigned to conditions, and the conditions typically are selected from naturally occurring variations in situations (not created by the investigator's manipulating the independent variable). For instance, let's say that you want to discover whether the effects of sleep on learning are different for people of different ages, and so you decide to test four groups of people: teenagers, college students, middle-aged people, and elderly people. Obviously

**Experimental condition:** A part of a study in which the participant receives the complete procedure that defines the experiment. Usually this is accompanied by a control condition, with the same participants receiving both experimental and control conditions.

**Control condition:** A condition administered to the same participants who receive the experimental condition; this effectively makes the participants both the experimental and the control group.

you cannot assign people to the different age groups randomly. Rather, you select groups from what nature has provided. When composing the groups, you should control for as many variables—such as health and education level—as you can in order to make the groups as similar as possible. Similarly, if you want to track changes over time (for example, in astronauts' memory abilities after they return from a stint in the ISS), it is not possible to assign people randomly to the groups as time goes by because you are taking measurements only from people you have measured before. In these examples, participants are not assigned randomly to groups, and such quasi-experiments rely on comparing multiple groups or multiple sets of measurements, attempting to eliminate potential confounds as much as possible. Unfortunately, because the groups can never be perfectly equated on all characteristics, you can never be certain exactly what differences among groups are responsible for the observed results. The conclusions you draw from quasi-experiments cannot be as strong as those from genuine experiments.

Table 2.1 summarizes the basic research methods used in psychology, along with their relative strengths and weaknesses. When thinking about the various methods, keep in mind that even though experiments are the most rigorous, they cannot always be performed—particularly if you are interested in studying large groups or if it is

**TABLE 2.1**     **Summary of Research Methods**

| Method | Key Characteristic(s) | Advantage(s) | Disadvantage(s) |
|---|---|---|---|
| Naturalistic observation | Observed events are carefully documented. | Forms the foundation for additional research by documenting the existence of an event or situation | Cannot control for confounded variables or change the variables to discover the critical factor in a particular mental process or behavior |
| Case study | A single instance of a situation is analyzed in depth. | Can provide in-depth understanding of the particular situation | Cannot assume that the findings extend to all other similar cases |
| Survey | A number of participants answer specific questions. | Relatively inexpensive way to collect a lot of data fairly quickly | Limited by how the questions are stated and by what people can and are willing to report |
| Correlational research | Relations among different variables are documented. | Allows comparison of variables that cannot be manipulated directly | Cannot infer causation |
| Experimental design | Participants are assigned randomly to groups, and the effects of manipulating one or more independent variables on a dependent variable are studied. | Allows rigorous control of variables; is able to establish causal relations between independent and dependent variables | Not all phenomena can be studied in controlled laboratory experiments (in part, because not all characteristics can be manipulated). |
| Quasi-experimental design | Similar to an experiment but participants are not assigned to groups randomly and conditions are often selected, not created. | Allows the study of real-world phenomena that cannot be studied in experiments | Cannot control relevant aspects of the independent variables |

difficult (or unethical) to manipulate the variables. For instance, let's say you want to answer this question: Do people who need minimal sleep make better astronauts? Not only is there a problem in randomly assigning participants to long-sleep and minimal-sleep groups, but you also can't simply declare that someone is an astronaut. In this case, not even a quasi-experiment is possible. For studying a question like this, one of the other approaches would be appropriate. In addition, keep in mind that different combinations of the methods are often used. For example, observational methods are used as part of correlational research, and observational, correlational, or experimental research can be conducted with single individuals (case studies).

# Be a Critical Consumer of Psychology

No research technique is always used perfectly, so you must be a critical consumer of all science, including the science of psychology. Metaphorically speaking, there are no good psychologists on salt-free diets—we take everything with at least a grain of salt! But this doesn't mean that you should be cynical, doubting everything you hear or read. Rather, whenever you read a report of a psychological finding in a newspaper, a journal article, or a book (including this one), look for aspects of the study that could lead to alternative explanations. You already know about the possibility of confounds; here are a few other issues that can cloud the interpretation of studies.

## Reliability: Count on It!

Not all data are created equal; some are better than others. One way to evaluate data is in terms of reliability. **Reliability** means consistency. A reliable car is one you can count on to behave consistently, starting even on cold mornings and not dropping random parts on the highway. A reliable set of measurements is one that can be replicated, that is, obtained again if the study is repeated. When you read about the results of a study, find out whether they have been replicated; if so, then you can have greater confidence that the measurements were reliable.

## Validity: What Does It Really Mean?

Something is said to be valid if it is what it claims to be; a valid driver's license, for example, is one that was, in fact, issued by the state and has not expired (and thus does confer the right to drive). In science, **validity** means that a method provides a true measure of what it is supposed to measure. A study may be reliable but not valid, or vice versa. Table 2.2 (p. 50) lists four of the major types of validity (Carmines & Zeller, 1979).

To understand the concept of validity, let's see what it's like to be a participant in a study. So, before reading further, try this exercise. Table 2.3 (p. 50) contains a list of words. Decide whether the first word names a living object or a nonliving one (circle the word "living" at the right if it is living; otherwise move to the next word); then decide whether the second word begins with the letter t (circle the words "begins with t" if it does; otherwise move to the next word); then decide whether the third word names a living or a nonliving object, whether the fourth word begins with the letter t, and so on, alternating judgments as you go down the list. Please do this now.

When you have finished marking the list, take out a piece of paper and (without looking!) write down as many of the words as you can. How many words from the list were you able to remember?

Reliability: Data are reliable if the same results are obtained when the measurements are repeated.

Validity: A measure is valid if it does in fact measure what it is supposed to measure.

## TABLE 2.2 Four Major Types of Validity

| Type | Description | Example |
|------|-------------|---------|
| Face validity | Design and procedure appear to assess the variables of interest. | Sample essay as part of an entrance exam for journalism school. |
| Content validity | Measures assess all aspects of phenomenon of interest. | Test of knowledge of research methods that covers all methods. |
| Criterion validity | A measure or procedure is comparable to a different, valid measure or procedure. | A paper-and-pencil test of leadership ability correlates highly with poll results of leadership of actual leaders. |
| Construct validity | Measures assess variables specified by a theory. | A theory defines "fatigue" in terms of lack of alertness, and the measure assesses this lack. |

## TABLE 2.3 What's in a Word?

Circle the word or phrase on the right if the word on the left has the named property; otherwise, move on to the next word. After you finish the list, read on.

| | | | | |
|---|---|---|---|---|
| salmon | living | | trout | living |
| tortoise | begins with *t* | | donkey | begins with *t* |
| airplane | living | | teapot | living |
| toad | begins with *t* | | house | begins with *t* |
| guitar | living | | table | living |
| goat | begins with *t* | | terrain | begins with *t* |
| truck | living | | tiger | living |
| automobile | begins with *t* | | rosebush | begins with *t* |
| snake | living | | bacteria | living |
| tent | begins with *t* | | carpet | begins with *t* |
| toast | living | | staple | living |
| television | begins with *t* | | tricycle | begins with *t* |
| wagon | living | | lawn | living |
| tarantula | begins with *t* | | ocean | begins with *t* |
| toadstool | living | | tuna | living |
| elephant | begins with *t* | | terrier | begins with *t* |

The standard result from this kind of study is that people will remember more words after making a living/nonliving judgment than after making a t/non-t judgment (for example, see Craik & Tulving, 1975). This result is usually interpreted to mean that the more we think about (or "process") the material, as we must in order to make the living/nonliving decision, the better we remember it; for the t words, we only need to look at the first letter, not think about the named object at all. In fact, if we are forced to think about something in detail but don't consciously try to learn it, we end up remembering it about as well as if we did try to learn it (we discuss this curiosity more in Chapter 7).

Does this demonstration of differences in memory following differences in judgment really support this interpretation? What if you remembered the words you judged as living/nonliving better because you had to read the whole word to make the required judgment, but you only looked at the first letter of the other words to decide whether they began with t? If this were the case, your better memory of words in the living/nonliving category would have nothing to do with "thinking about it more." Therefore, the experiment would not be valid—it would not be measuring what the investigator designed it to measure.

When you read a result, always try to think of as many interpretations for it as you can; you may be surprised at how easy this can be. And, if you can think of an alternative interpretation, see whether you can think of a control group or condition that would allow you to tell who was right, you or the authors of the study.

## Bias: Playing With Loaded Dice

Sometimes beliefs, expectations, or habits alter how participants in a study respond or affect how a researcher sets up or conducts a study, thereby influencing its outcome. This leaning toward a particular result, whether conscious or unconscious, is called **bias**, and it can take many forms. One form of bias is **response bias**, in which people have a tendency to respond in a particular way regardless of their actual knowledge or beliefs. For example, many people tend to say "yes" more than "no," particularly in some Asian cultures (such as that of Japan). This sort of bias toward responding in "acceptable" ways is a devilish problem for survey research. For example, consider the difference between these two versions of a question: "Do you support research on the ISS?" versus "Do you support research on the ISS, which is intended in part to cure cancer and other diseases?" Given the way the second question is phrased, you would be hard-pressed to say "no." Another form of bias is **sampling bias**, which occurs when the participants or items are not chosen at random but instead are selected so that an attribute is over- or underrepresented—which leads to a confound. For example, say you wanted to know the average heights of male and females, and you went to shopping malls to measure people. What if you measured the males outside a toy store (and so were likely to be measuring little boys), but measured the women outside a fashion outlet for tall people (and so were likely to find especially tall women)? Or, what if the words in the living/nonliving category in Table 2.3 were interesting words such as "centipede" and "boomerang," and the words in the t/non-t category were bland words such as "toe" and "broom"? Or, perhaps the living/nonliving words were more emotionally charged than the t/non-t words, or were more familiar. What if only language majors were tested, or only people who read a lot and have terrific vocabularies? Could we assume that all people would respond the same way? Take another look at Table 2.3; can you spot any potential sampling bias?

Sampling bias isn't just something that sometimes spoils otherwise good studies. Do you remember the U.S. Presidential election of 2000? Albert Gore and George W.

**Bias:** When beliefs, expectations, or habits alter how participants in a study respond or affect how a researcher sets up or conducts a study, thereby influencing its outcome.

**Response bias:** A tendency to respond in a particular way regardless of respondents' actual knowledge or beliefs.

**Sampling bias:** A bias that occurs when the participants or items are not chosen at random, but instead are chosen so that one attribute is over- or underrepresented.

Bush were in a dead heat, and the election came down to the tally in a few counties in Florida. Based on surveys of voters exiting their polling places, the TV commentators predicted that Gore would be the winner. What led them astray? Sampling bias. The news organizations that conducted the surveys did not ask absentee voters how they cast their ballots. In such a close election, this was an important factor because the absentee voters included many members of the armed services, who tend to be Republicans. Thus, sampling only from those who voted on election day produced a biased view of how the entire population voted—and the TV commentators had to eat their words.

## Experimenter Expectancy Effects: Making It Happen

Clever Hans, a horse that lived in Germany in the early 1890s, apparently could add (Rosenthal, 1976). When a questioner (one of several) called out two numbers to add, for example, "6 plus 4," Hans would tap out the correct answer with his hoof. Was Hans a genius horse? Was he psychic? No. Despite appearances, Hans wasn't really adding. He seemed to be able to add, and even to spell out words (with one tap for the letter a, and an additional tap for each letter in the alphabet), but he responded only if his questioner stood in his line of sight and knew the answer. The questioner, who expected Hans to begin tapping, always looked at Hans's feet right after asking the question—thereby cuing Hans to start tapping. When Hans had tapped out the right number, the questioner always looked up—cuing Hans to stop tapping. Although, in fact, Hans could neither add nor spell, he was a pretty bright horse: He was not trained to do this; he "figured it out" on his own.

The cues offered by Hans's questioners were completely unintentional; they had no wish to mislead (and, in fact, some of them were probably doubters). But unintentional cues such as these lead to **experimenter expectancy effects**, which occur when an investigator's expectations lead him or her (consciously or unconsciously) to treat participants in a way that encourages them to produce the expected results. Such effects can occur in all types of research, from experiments to surveys—in all cases, the investigator can provide cues that influence how participants behave. For instance, if you were polling voters about their choice for President, your own views could color what they say; if you smile whenever they mention your candidate and frown when they mention the other candidate, they may try to please you by saying what they think (perhaps unconsciously) you want to hear.

At least for experiments, it's clear how to guarantee that experimenter expectancy effects won't occur: In a **double-blind design**, not only is the participant "blind" to (unaware of) the predictions of the study and hence unable consciously or unconsciously to serve up the expected results, but the experimenter is also "blind" to the condition assigned to the participant and thus is unable to induce the expected results. What would have happened if a questioner of Clever Hans had not known the answer to the question?

## Psychology and Pseudopsychology: What's Flaky and What Isn't?

Are you a fire sign? Do you believe that your Zodiac sign matters? So many people apparently do that the home page for *Yahoo!* will automatically provide your daily horoscope. But astrology—along with palm reading and tea-leaf reading, and all their relatives—is not a branch of psychology; it is pseudopsychology. **Pseudopsychology** is superstition or unsupported opinion pretending to be science. Pseudopsychology is not just "bad psychology," which rests on poorly documented observations or badly designed studies and, therefore, has questionable foundations. Pseudopsychology is not

**Experimenter expectancy effects:** Effects that occur when an investigator's expectations lead him or her (consciously or unconsciously) to treat participants in a way that encourages them to produce the expected results.

**Double-blind design:** The participant is "blind" to (unaware of) the predictions of the study (and so cannot consciously or unconsciously produce the predicted results), and the experimenter is "blind" to the condition assigned to the participant (and so experimenter expectancy effects cannot produce the predicted results).

**Pseudopsychology:** Theories or statements that at first glance look like psychology, but are in fact superstition or unsupported opinion pretending to be science.

Dogbert (Dilbert's dog) is thinking scientifically about astrology. He proposes a relationship among seasonal differences in diet, sunlight, and other factors and personality characteristics. These variables can be quantified, and their relationships tested. If these hypotheses are not supported by the data but Dogbert believes in astrology nevertheless, he's crossed the line into pseudopsychology.

psychology at all. It may look and sound like psychology, but it is not science. Unfortunately, advice to be found in some self-help books falls into this category. For instance, at one point we were told that screaming would "let it all out," and so was good for us—but there was absolutely no evidence that such screams did any more than annoy the neighbors. (This is why it is a good idea to check whether the advice dispensed in a self-help book you are contemplating buying is supported by research.)

Appearances can be misleading. Consider extrasensory perception (ESP). Is this pseudopsychology? ESP refers to a collection of mental abilities that do not rely on the ordinary senses or abilities. Telepathy, for instance, is the ability to read minds. This sounds not only wonderful but magical. No wonder people are fascinated by the possibility that they, too, may have latent, untapped, extraordinary abilities. The evidence that such abilities really exist is shaky, as discussed in Chapter 4. But the mere fact that many experiments on ESP have come up empty does not mean that the experiments themselves are bad or "unscientific." One can conduct a perfectly good experiment, guarding against confounds, bias, and expectancy effects, even on ESP. Such research is not necessarily pseudopsychology.

Let's say you want to study telepathy. You might arrange to test pairs of participants, with one member of each pair acting as "sender" and the other as "receiver." Both the sender and receiver would look at hands of playing cards that contained the same four cards. The sender would focus on one card (say, an ace) and would "send" the receiver a mental image of the chosen card. The receiver's job would be to guess which card the sender is focusing on. By chance alone, with only four cards to choose from, the receiver would guess right about 25% of the time. So the question is, can the receiver do better than mere guesswork? In this study, you would measure the percentage of times the receiver picks the right card, and compare this to what you would expect from guessing alone.

But wait! What if the sender, like the questioners of Clever Hans, provided visible cues (accidentally or on purpose) that have nothing to do with ESP, perhaps smiling when "sending" an ace, grimacing when "sending" a two. A better experiment would have sender and receiver in different rooms (or better yet, have one on the ISS and another here on earth), thus controlling for such possible confounds. Furthermore, what if people have an unconscious bias to prefer red over black cards, which leads both sender and receiver to select them more often than would be dictated by chance? This difficulty can be countered by including a control condition, in which a receiver guesses cards when the sender is not actually sending. Such guesses will reveal response biases (such as a preference for red cards), which exist independently of messages sent via ESP.

Whether ESP can be considered a valid, reliable phenomenon will depend on the results of such studies. If they conclusively show that there is nothing to it, then people who claim to have ESP or to understand it will be trying to sell a bill of goods—and will be engaging in pseudopsychology. But as long as proper studies are under way, we cannot dismiss them as pseudopsychology.

1. Which of the following is *not* a method used in descriptive research?
   a. naturalistic observation   c. survey
   b. case study                 d. experiment
2. The strength of a correlational relationship is indicated by
   a. whether the correlation is positive or negative.
   b. the absolute magnitude of the correlation (how close it is to $-1$ or $+1$).
   c. the number of variables in the equation.
   d. the direction of the line.
3. In an experimental design, the variable that is manipulated is the _____, and the variable that is measured is the _____.
   a. dependent variable; independent variable
   b. independent variable; dependent variable
   c. control variable; confounding variable

d. confounding variable; independent variable
4. To help reduce experimenter expectancy effects, a double-blind design ensures that the experimenter is
   a. unaware of the hypotheses and predictions of the study.
   b. unaware of the outcome of the study.
   c. unaware of the conditions to which participants are assigned.
   d. aware of all experimental conditions.

## Answers

## Think It Through!

If you wanted to know whether a particular astronaut's upbringing played a crucial role in leading her to become an astronaut, how would you go about studying this? Don't assume that it has to be a case study. Which specific questions would you ask? What are the best methods for answering them?

What characteristics and qualities do you think an astronaut should have? Do you think psychologists should prevent anyone from entering astronaut training who does not have these characteristics and qualities? Why and why not?

# STATISTICS: Measuring Reality

Like Rome or the pyramids, the ISS couldn't be built in a day. This limitation also applies to the astronauts' functioning as a team. Only over time, largely by evaluating current practices and trying to improve them, will researchers discover how best to help astronauts work together smoothly. Over time, researchers will collect various measures of mental processes and performance, such as the rate of human error when operating machines, levels of stress, sleep quality, and memory ability. **Statistics** are numbers that summarize or indicate differences or patterns of differences in measurements. Statistics from the crew of the ISS will be used to guide planners of future missions to outer space, such as the manned mission to Mars.

Mark Twain, borrowing a line from Benjamin Disraeli (Best, 2001), once said that there are three kinds of lies: "Lies, damn lies, and statistics." The point is that statistics can be used to obscure the facts as easily as to illuminate them. For instance, although the divorce rate in the United States is about 50%, this does not necessarily mean that

Statistics: Numbers that summarize or indicate differences or patterns of differences in measurements.

out of 10 couples only 5 will stay married. If 3 of the 10 couples divorce and remarry, and all 3 of those second marriages end in divorce, that makes 6 divorces out of 13 marriages; and if one of those ex-partners remarries a third time and divorces again, the count becomes 14 marriages and 7 divorces: This is a 50% divorce rate, even though 7 of the original 10 couples stayed married from the start. To understand and evaluate reports of psychological research, whether surveys in newspapers or television or formal research reports in scientific publications, you need to know a few basics about statistics.

In trying to assess the success of his company's new ad campaign, Dilbert is searching for statistical evidence of success, rather than relying on people's intuitions.

# Descriptive Statistics: Telling It Like It Is

There are two major types of statistics: One type describes or summarizes data, whereas the other indicates which differences or patterns in the data are worthy of attention. This is the distinction between descriptive statistics and inferential statistics. **Descriptive statistics** are concise ways of summarizing properties of sets of numbers. You're already familiar with such statistics: They are what you see plotted in bar graphs and pie charts, and presented in tables. But descriptive statistics are not limited to figures and tables. For example, in financial news, the Dow Jones Industrial Average is a descriptive statistic, as is the unemployment rate.

You already know a lot about descriptive statistics, but you may not be aware you know it—and you may not be familiar with the technical vocabulary scientists use to discuss such statistics. This section provides a review of the essential points of descriptive statistics.

## Data

As we noted earlier, data are numerical measurements or careful observations of a phenomenon. In other words, in an experiment or quasi-experiment, data are the various measured or observed values of the dependent variable. Examples of dependent variables used in psychological research are response time (how fast it takes to press a button after perceiving a stimulus), scores on an intelligence test, and ratings of fatigue or the severity of depression.

To understand properties of data, let's consider an example. Astronauts face long hours and grueling work as a normal part of their job and might put to good use a safe medication that could boost memory (particularly if it countered the effects of losing sleep). But before we would recommend taking such a drug, we would want to know whether it really is more effective than a **placebo**, a medically inactive substance, such as a sugar pill. If the drug works as promised, it would be in great demand—for instance, by language-learning schools, Wall Street firms, and countless students. To test whether the drug is effective, you ask people to learn a set of words either after taking the drug or, on another day, after taking a placebo. You are interested in whether the participants can later recall more words if they've taken your drug than if they've taken the placebo; the condition, drug versus placebo, is the independent variable, and the number of words recalled is the dependent variable. Half of the participants get the

Descriptive statistics: Concise ways of summarizing properties of sets of numbers.

Placebo: A medically inactive substance that is presented as though it has medicinal effects.

| TABLE 2.4 | Fictional Participant Data From Drug and Placebo Conditions | |
| --- | --- | --- |
| **Number of Words Remembered** | | |
| **Placebo** | | **Memory drug** |
| 15 | | 27 |
| 12 | | 34 |
| 18 | | 21 |
| 21 | | 17 |
| 22 | | 31 |
| 38 | | 47 |
| 28 | | 31 |
| 15 | | 23 |
| 14 | | 40 |
| 17 | | 19 |

drug first, and half get an identical-looking and -tasting placebo first. You've put the pills in coded envelopes so that your assistant doesn't know when she's giving the drug versus the placebo (nor do the participants because you've used a double-blind procedure). The comparison would be expressed as the number of words remembered following the drug minus the number following the placebo. The data (scores) from 10 participants are shown in Table 2.4.

## Frequency Distributions

Frequency distributions indicate the number of each type of case that was observed in a set of data. For example, a frequency distribution could indicate how many participants recalled 0 words, 1 word, 2 words, and so on, up to the total of 50 possible words, after taking the drug versus after taking the placebo. Another example of a frequency distribution would be one that indicated the number of men versus women in each state who favored building the ISS. If you worked for a company that manufactured key components of the ISS (earning a hefty portion of that $90 billion price tag), you could use such data to decide how to spend your advertising budget to promote the ISS: You could target the regions of the country where people were skeptical about the project, or you could write your ads to appeal to men or to women (or both, as the polling data indicated).

If you look at the feet of everyone you know, you'll notice a few very small or very large feet, but most will be an intermediate size. The same is true for many psychological qualities, such as scores on intelligence or personality tests.

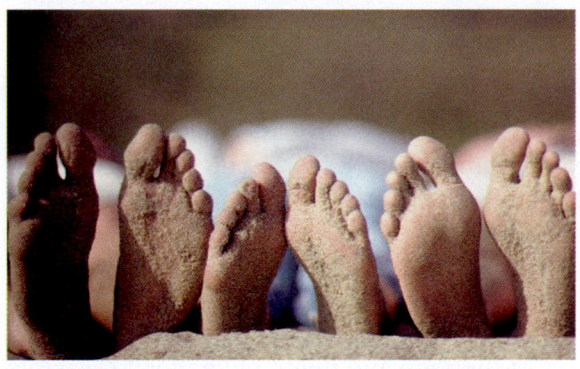

## Measures of Central Tendency

When individual measurements are directly presented, they are considered **raw data**; Table 2.4 presents raw data. Descriptive statistics are used to summarize characteristics of a set of such data. Transforming raw data into statistical terms makes the data useful, allowing researchers to discover and illustrate the relationships among the values or scores. One important type of descriptive statistic is the **central tendency** of the data: the clustering of the most characteristic values, or scores, for a particular group. Central tendency can be expressed three ways. The most common, and probably the one with which you are most familiar, is the arithmetic average, or **mean**, of the scores or values. You calculate a mean by adding up the values in the set of measurements, then dividing that sum by the total number of entries you summed. In Table 2.4, the mean for the placebo condition is 20 words remembered, and the mean for the drug condition is 29 words remembered.

A second way to specify central tendency is the **median**, which is the score that is the midpoint of the set of values; half the values fall above the median, and half fall

**Raw data:** Individual measurements, taken directly from the situation being studied.

**Central tendency:** The clustering of the most characteristic values, or scores, for a particular group.

**Mean:** The arithmetic average.

**Median:** The score that is the midpoint of the set of values; half the values fall above the median, and half fall below the median.

**Mode:** The value that appears most frequently in the set of data.

below the median. It is easier to find the median if the data are arranged in order, as shown in Table 2.5. The median in the placebo condition is 17.5, halfway between 17 and 18, the fifth and sixth ordered scores. In the drug condition, the median is 29.0, halfway between the fifth and sixth ordered scores of 27 and 31.

A third measure of central tendency is the **mode**, the value that appears most frequently in the set of measurements. The mode can be any value, from the highest to the lowest. The mode in Table 2.5 is 15 for the placebo condition and 31 for the drug condition.

The mean is the measure of central tendency that is most sensitive to extreme values or scores; if there are a few values at the extreme end of the scale, the mean will change much more than the median (which often will not change at all). The mode does not generally change in response to an extreme score. For example, if you changed the last score in Table 2.5 in the placebo condition from 38 to 100, the mean would change from 20 to 26.2, but the median and mode would remain the same. When a set of data has many scores near one extreme value and away from the center, it is said to have a *skewed distribution*. When a set of data has a skewed distribution, the median is often a more appropriate measure of central tendency than the mean.

However, the three measures of central tendency generally yield similar results; this is especially likely as the number of measurements or observations (data points) becomes larger and the data follow a normal distribution. The **normal distribution** is the familiar bell-shaped curve, in which most data points (values or scores) fall in the middle range of the scale and data points are increasingly less frequent as they taper off symmetrically toward the extremes (see Figure 2.5). Normal distributions occur many places in nature. For example, look at stone stairs in a very old building: You can usually see that they are worn more deeply in the center and less toward the sides. (If the building isn't

| TABLE 2.5 | **Fictional Data From Drug and Placebo Conditions, Arranged in Order** | |
|---|---|
| Number of Words Remembered | |
| **Placebo condition** | **Memory drug condition** |
| 12 | 17 |
| 14 | 19 |
| 15 | 21 |
| 15 | 23 |
| 17 | 27 |
| – – – Median 17.5 | – – – Median 29.0 |
| 18 | 31 |
| 21 | 31 |
| 22 | 34 |
| 28 | 40 |
| 38 | 47 |
| Mean* = 20 | Mean* = 29 |
| Mode† = 15 | Mode† = 31 |

*Mean = The arithmetic average.
†Mode = The value that appears most frequently.

**Normal distribution:** The familiar bell-shaped curve, in which most values fall in the midrange of the scale and scores are increasingly less frequent as they taper off symmetrically toward the extremes.

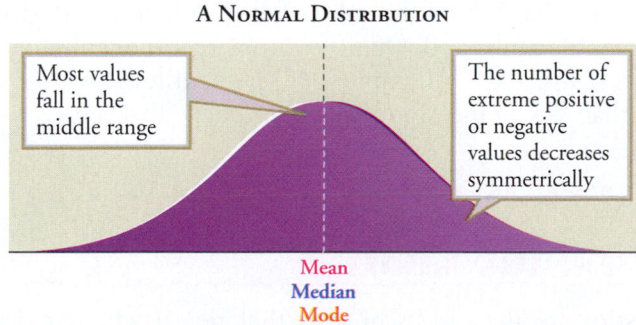

A NORMAL DISTRIBUTION

Most values fall in the middle range

The number of extreme positive or negative values decreases symmetrically

Mean
Median
Mode

**FIGURE 2.5**

## The Normal Distribution

The height of the normal curve indicates the number of values that occur at that position along the scale measured on the horizontal axis. In the normal distribution, most values fall in the middle range, with the number of extreme positive and extreme negative values decreasing symmetrically toward the right and the left.

You've probably heard a news announcer say that "Exit polling indicates that it's a dead heat! Smith has 51% and Jones has 49%, with a margin of error of 4%." The margin of error—usually called a *confidence interval*—specifies the range of values within which the mean is likely to fall.

old enough, you will see the beginnings of a normal curve, which over the generations will become deeper in the center until it resembles the shape of the bell curve in Figure 2.5 upside down.)

## Measures of Variability

Whereas measures of central tendency convey information about the most common values or scores, measures of variability convey information about the spread of the scores. The **range** is the difference obtained when you subtract the smallest score from the largest, the simplest measure of variability. For the data in Table 2.5, for example, the range of scores in the placebo condition is 38 − 12, or 26. The range of scores for the drug condition is 47 − 17, or 30. But the range does not tell you how variable the scores are in general.

Another method of assessing variability is the **standard deviation**, which is a kind of "average variability" in a set of measurements. In Chapter 9, you will see how important the standard deviation is for understanding intelligence. For values that are normally distributed, the standard deviation will tell you the percentage of values that fall at different points on the distribution. For instance, about 68% of values fall between 1 standard deviation below the mean and 1 standard deviation above the mean. And about 95% of the values fall between 2 standard deviations below the mean and 2 standard deviations above the mean. For example, if the placebo condition had a standard deviation of 7.46 words (for simplicity's sake, we'll round this down to 7 words) and a mean of 20 words, then roughly 68% of the participants in this condition will remember somewhere between 13 and 27 words (20 − 7 to 20 + 7). At 2 standard deviations from the mean, roughly 95% of participants will remember between about 6 and 34 words.

## Relative Standing

Sometimes you want to know where a particular score stands relative to other scores. For example, college admissions officers want to know how an applicant's SAT scores stand relative to other applicants' scores. One way to convey this information is in terms of measures of variability. You could specify how many standard deviations a score is from the mean. However, this isn't very useful if you are interested in the specific number or percentage of scores or values that fall above or below a particular one. Another way of conveying information about a value relative to other values in a set of measurements is to use a **percentile rank**: the percentage of data that have values at or below the particular value. If a value is assigned a percentile rank of 50, for example, that instantly tells you that 50% of the values fall at or below that particular score; the median has a percentile rank of 50. Quartiles are percentile ranks that divide the set of scores into fourths (25th, 50th, 75th, and 100th percentiles); a score that is at the third quartile signifies that 75% of the group falls at or below that score.

**Range:** The difference obtained when you subtract the smallest score from the largest, the simplest measure of variability.

**Standard deviation:** A kind of "average variability" in a set of measurements.

**Percentile rank:** The percentage of data that have values at or below a particular value.

**Inferential statistics:** The results of tests that reveal whether differences or patterns in measurements reflect true differences or patterns versus just chance variations.

# Inferential Statistics: Sorting the Wheat From the Chaff

**Inferential statistics** are the results of tests that reveal whether differences or patterns in measurements reflect true differences or just chance variations. The goal of the most common type of inferential statistics used in psychology is to reject the *null hypothesis*, which is the hypothesis that there is no difference between means. It's a logic of "innocent until proven guilty," where "innocent" means that two sets of measures don't actually differ (even if by chance they may sometimes appear to differ). For instance, if you toss a coin 10 times and it lands heads up 7 times, instead of the 5 you would expect purely by chance, does this mean that it is a "trick coin" or an edge is worn away, or could this outcome also arise from just chance? Inferential statistics seek to address this question of whether patterns in a set of data are random or instead reflect a true underlying phenomenon. A correlation is an example of an inferential statistic; if the correlation is high enough (we will discuss what "high enough" means shortly), it tells you that the scores on one variable do in fact vary systematically with the scores on another variable.

## Correlation: The Relationship Between Two Variables

As we've just noted, the correlation indicates whether two variables are related to each other. That is, is a change in one variable accompanied by a change in another?

Correlations and other types of inferential statistics may or may not be **statistically significant**. What does "significant" mean? In statistics, it does not mean "important." Rather, it means that the measured relationship is not simply due to chance. If you correlate any two randomly selected sets of measurements, it is likely that the correlation will not be precisely zero. Say you correlated a measure of happiness with height and found a correlation of $-.12$. Should you pay attention to this correlation, developing a grand theory to explain it? The size of a correlation needed for statistical significance—to be taken as more than just chance variation—depends on the number of pairs of values analyzed (each represented by a data point, as in Figure 2.2, p. 45). As a general rule, the more observations (pairs of values) considered when computing the correlation, the smaller the magnitude of the correlation needs to be to achieve statistical significance. Why? Imagine that you were randomly throwing darts into a rectangular corkboard on the wall. It is possible that the first few on the left would be lower than those on the right. But as you tossed more and more darts, those initial quirks would be balanced out by quirks later in the process—so after 100 darts, there would no longer be any discernible pattern. In addition, the more observations you have, the less influence extreme values will have. The larger the difference between two averages, which is referred to as the *effect size*, and the larger the number of observations that went into those measures, the more significant a result will be. Statistical significance is expressed in terms of the probability ($p$) that a value (such as the size of a correlation) could be due to chance. Psychologists generally view a finding as "statistically significant" if it has no more than a 5% probability of occurring by chance.

## Samples and Populations

Back to the memory-enhancing drug study. Did the drug work? If you had included every person on the planet as a participant, all you would need to do is look at the descriptive statistics. Either the drug resulted in more learning than the placebo, or it didn't. But such all-inclusive testing just isn't practical. Virtually all research in psychology relies on studying data from a **sample**—a group drawn from a population—and the goal is to generalize from the findings obtained with the sample to the larger **population**, the group from which the sample is drawn. Inferential statistics let you infer that the difference found in your sample does in fact reflect a difference in the corresponding population.

Here's a simple example: You are impressed by astronaut Sally Ride's memory and want to know whether astronauts in general tend to have better memories than the population as a whole (you theorize that to be a successful astronaut you need to

**Statistical significance:** The conclusion that the measured relationship is not simply due to chance.

**Sample:** A group that is drawn from a larger population and measured or observed.

**Population:** The entire set of relevant people or animals.

No matter how you assigned these six pears to two groups, the groups would not weigh exactly the same. Inferential statistics allows you to know whether observed differences are just due to the luck of the draw when the samples were taken or instead reflect actual differences between the populations from which the samples were drawn.

remember many facts and procedures). To find out, you send memory tests to current and former astronauts all over the world and include stamped, self-addressed return envelopes. No luck—these people are very busy and don't have time to take your test. So you travel to Houston and get permission to visit the astronauts at NASA headquarters. By some miracle, you are actually able to induce 10 astronauts to take your test. You will next need to compare them with 10 non-astronauts selected to be as similar as possible to your sample of astronauts—same ages, education levels, gender, and even the same level of fitness. If you then compare the two groups, you will probably find a difference in memory performance.

But now consider this: If you had data from 20 people, all of whom were astronauts, and you arbitrarily assigned them to two groups of 10, you probably would also find a difference in the mean memory scores for these arbitrarily formed groups! This difference would arise because of how you happened to assign the people to groups. No matter how you did it, the groups would probably have different average memory performance. Only if you had a large number of people would assigning them arbitrarily to two equal-sized groups be likely to result in groups that had nearly identical scores. When you have enough data, people who happen to have unusually good or poor memories will be assigned equally often to each group, on average, and thus their disproportionate contributions will cancel out.

**Sampling error** produces differences that arise from the luck of the draw, not because two samples are in fact representative of different populations. In this example, if differences in memory scores between astronauts and non-astronauts are due to sampling error, this means that the two groups are not actually different. When you compare astronauts and non-astronauts, the problem is to know for sure whether any difference between them is "real"—reflecting actual differences between the two populations in general—or is due to sampling error. (There are statistical tests that can indicate whether a difference between two groups is due to sampling error or reflects a real difference, but details about such inferential tests are beyond the scope of this section.)

## Meta-Analysis

Science is a communal effort. Usually many people are studying the same phenomenon, each one painting additional strokes onto an emerging picture. **Meta-analysis** is a technique that allows researchers to combine results from different studies. This is particularly useful when results have been mixed, with some studies showing an effect and some not. Meta-analysis can determine whether there is a relationship among variables that transcends any one study, a strand that cuts across the entire range of findings.

Sometimes results that are not evident in any individual study become obvious in a meta-analysis. Why? Studies almost always involve observing or testing a sample from the population; if a sample is relatively small, the luck of the draw could obscure an overall difference that actually exists in the population. For example, if you stopped the first two males and first two females you saw on the street and measured their heights, the females might actually be taller than the males. The problem of variation in samples is particularly severe when the difference of interest—the effect—is not great. If men averaged 8 feet tall and women 4 feet tall, small samples would not be a problem; you would quickly figure out the usual height difference between men and women. But if men averaged 5 feet 10 inches and women averaged 5 feet 9 inches (and the

**Sampling error:** Any difference that arises from the luck of the draw, due to nonrandom sampling from a population, not because two samples are in fact representative of different populations.

**Meta-analysis:** A statistical technique that allows researchers to combine results from different studies, which can determine whether there is a relationship among variables that transcends any one study.

standard deviation was a few inches), you would need to measure many men and women before you were assured of finding the difference. Meta-analysis is a way of combining the samples from many studies, which allows you to detect even subtle differences or relations among variables (Rosenthal, 1991).

# Lying With Statistics: When Good Numbers Go Bad

Statistics can be used or misused. In a famous book entitled *How to Lie with Statistics*, Derrell Huff (1954) demonstrated many ways that people use statistics to distort the pattern of results. Joel Best (2001) has followed in this tradition. Such books play a valuable role in inoculating people against deceptive techniques, and some of their key points are summarized here. Be on the lookout for these manipulations whenever you see statistics.

## Selective Reporting

Because different types of statistics convey different information, the same data can be manipulated to "say" different things. Look at Figure 2.6 and Table 2.6 (p. 62), which present fictitious data for the results of a new type of therapy for people with acrophobia—a fear of heights (obviously a crucial problem to overcome for aspiring astronauts). Before the therapy, participants reported, on average, 9 symptoms of acrophobia; that is, before treatment, the mean number of symptoms was 9. After the therapy, the mean number of symptoms was 4.85, the median was 3.5, and the mode was 10. Proponents of the new therapy make the following claims: On average, symptoms decreased by almost half (based on the mean), and more than 50% of participants had substantial symptom reduction (based on the median). Opponents, however, convey the data differently. A spokeswoman from the pharmaceutical company that manufactures a medication to treat acrophobia makes several counterclaims when she promotes the superiority of her company's medication: The number of symptoms most frequently reported was 10, which shows that the therapy actually made people more symptomatic (based on the mode). Also, the therapy achieved

**FIGURE 2.6**  **Number of Symptoms After Therapy for Acrophobia**

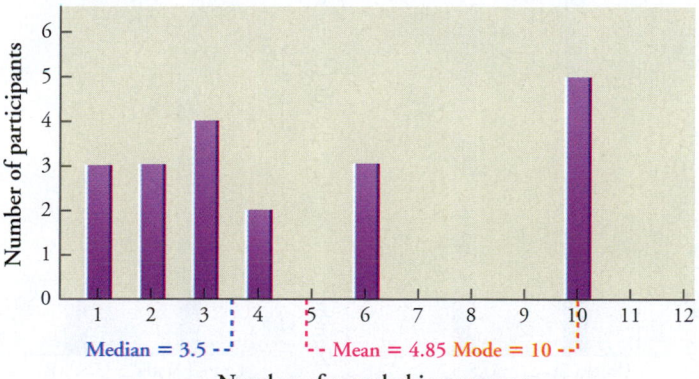

How effective is this therapy? The answer depends on which measure—mean, median, or mode—is used as the measure of central tendency for these data.

| TABLE 2.6 | **Fictional Results of Therapy for Acrophobia** |
|---|---|

Mean number of symptoms after therapy for acrophobia

= Total number of symptoms ÷ Total number of participants

= 1 + 1 + 1 + 2 + 2 + 2 + 3 + 3 + 3 + 3 + 4
+ 4 + 6 + 6 + 6 + 10 + 10 + 10 + 10 + 10

= 97 ÷ 20 = 4.85

Median = 3.5

Mode = 10

mixed results, as indicated by the fact that the number of symptoms after treatment ranged from 1 to 10.

As you can see, both supporters and detractors of the new treatment are correct. They are just presenting different aspects of the data. Thus, when hearing or reading about research or survey results, you should ask these questions before taking the results too seriously:

1. What is the distribution of the results? If they are normally distributed, the measures of central tendency will be similar to each other. If they are skewed, the measures of central tendency will convey different information, and the one presented will be the one that conveys the information the reporter wants you to know about. Do the other measures of central tendency paint a different picture of the results?

2. How variable are the data? What does it mean if the results vary a lot rather than a little?

## Lying With Graphs

Many results are presented in graph form. Graphs work largely because of a single principle: *More is more* (Kosslyn, 1994a). Taller bars, higher lines, or bigger wedges stand for greater amounts than do shorter bars, lower lines, or smaller wedges. Our tendency to see more on the page as standing for a bigger amount or effect can lead us astray if graphs are constructed to deceive. Be alert to the following tricks.

**SHORTENING THE *Y* (VERTICAL) AXIS TO EXAGGERATE A DIFFERENCE**   As you can see by comparing the right-hand graph in Figure 2.7 with the left-hand one, starting the Y axis at a high value and devoting that axis to a small part of the scale make what is in fact a small difference look like a large one. If a difference is statistically significant, it should

**FIGURE 2.7**

The left-hand graph presents the actual numbers in a neutral way; the right-hand graph exaggerates the difference.

## Shortening the *Y* Axis Can Mislead

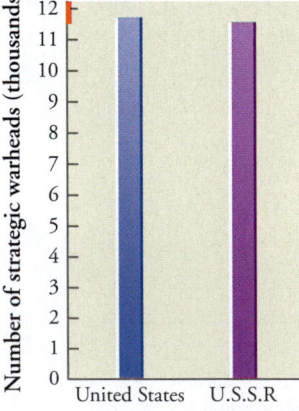
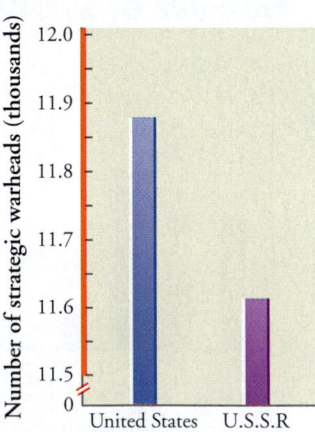

FIGURE 2.8

## Lengthening the *Y* Axis Can Mislead

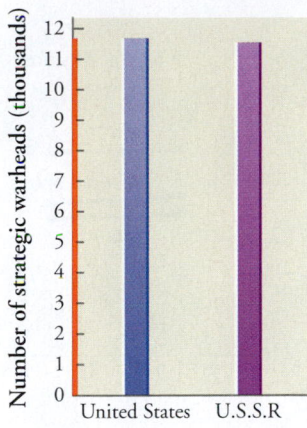 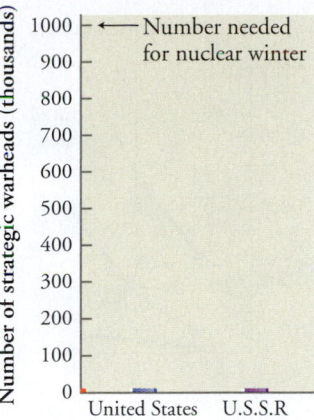

The left-hand graph presents the actual numbers in a neutral way; the right-hand graph minimizes the difference.

look that way (and thus shortening the axis may be appropriate). But if it's not, then shortening the axis to exaggerate the difference is deception.

**USING AN INAPPROPRIATELY LARGE RANGE OF VALUES TO MINIMIZE A DIFFERENCE**   The flip side of the coin is illustrated in Figure 2.8, in which a difference is made to appear smaller by using a large range in values on the Y axis.

**USING THREE-DIMENSIONAL GRAPHICS TO EXAGGERATE SIZE**   As shown in Figure 2.9, a graphic designer can take advantage of our tendency to impose size constancy (see Chapter 4), so that a bar that is farther away will be seen as much larger than a bar that is closer. Even if an actual difference exists, this technique can exaggerate its magnitude.

**FIGURE 2.9**   ## Perceived Distance Can Exaggerate Bar Size

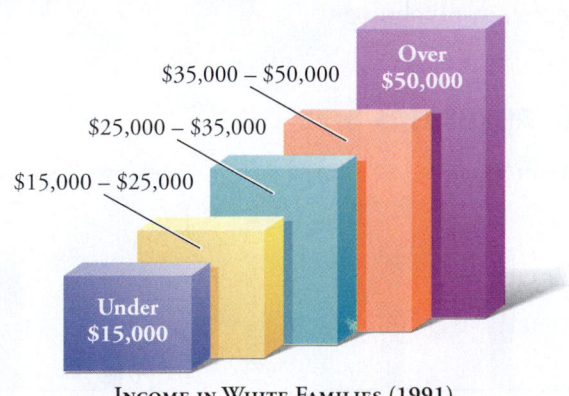

Size constancy leads us to see the bars that are farther away as larger than they are, thereby exaggerating a difference.

INCOME IN WHITE FAMILIES (1991)

## FIGURE 2.10 Transforming Data Can Distort the Conclusions

The left-hand graph shows the actual dollar figures, and the right-hand graph shows the percent change. Clearly, the message conveyed by the two graphs is different. Which one is "more honest" depends on the purpose for which the graph is used.

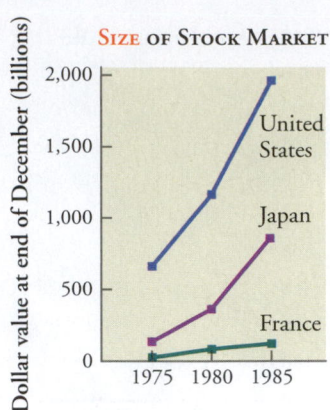

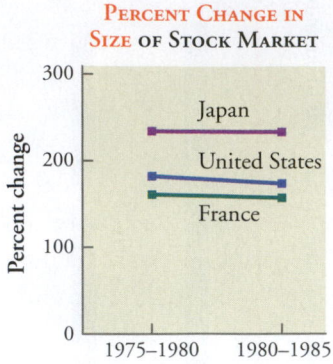

**TRANSFORMING THE DATA BEFORE PLOTTING**   Compare the two graphs of Figure 2.10. The one on the left shows the size of the stock market in three countries over 3 years, the other graph shows the percent change over two 5-year periods. If you saw only the second graph, you wouldn't realize that the increases in the U.S. stock market were actually much greater than those in Japan. If the user is trying to sell Japanese stocks, you can guess which graphic display will be preferred.

**CHANGING WIDTH ALONG WITH HEIGHT**   As Figure 2.11 demonstrates, our visual system does not register height and width separately, but rather we see them simultaneously, as specifying area. So changing the width of bars in a graph along with the height gives the impression of a much larger amount of increase than is conveyed by changing height alone.

In short, you can see that there is nothing magical or mysterious about statistics or how they are represented visually. Whenever you see a graph in the newspaper, you are seeing statistics; when you hear that a poll is accurate to "plus or minus 3 points," that's the spread within which the mean is likely to occur if you look at other samples. The crucial ideas are that there are measures of central tendency (mean, median, and mode), measures of variability (such as range and standard deviation), and statistical tests that tell you the likelihood that a measured difference is due to chance alone. What you've learned here is enough to enable you to read and understand many reports of original research in psychology.

## FIGURE 2.11 Changing Width With Height Exaggerates Size

Expanding the bar width along with the height conveys the impression that more quantity is being presented than increasing the height alone signals.

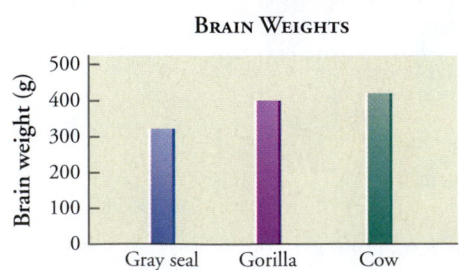

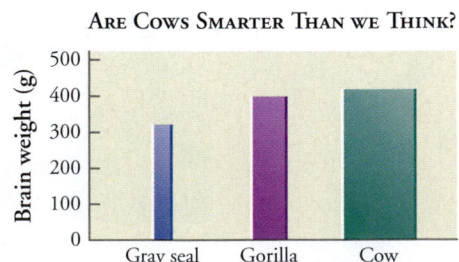

# LOOKING AT LEVELS
## Graph Design for the Human Mind

Astronauts on the ISS have to monitor many sources of data, both from the experiments they conduct and to ensure that the space station functions effectively. Graphs are a way to convey a lot of information without overwhelming the user. But what kind of graph should be used? It depends on what message needs to be conveyed. For example, Jeffrey Zacks and Barbara Tversky (1999) found that bar graphs are better than line graphs when you need to make or illustrate comparisons between discrete data points (such as specific numbers of Democratic versus Republican voters who support the space program), whereas line graphs are better when you need to understand or illustrate trends (such as changes in the numbers of Democratic and Republican supporters in different parts of the United States over time). Bars end at discrete locations, and thus it's easy to compare data points simply by comparing the heights of the bars. In contrast, bars are not as useful for conveying trends because the reader needs mentally to connect the tops of bars, creating a line in order to determine visually whether there is a trend. Hence, if that's what you want to convey, it's better to give the reader the line in the first place. But if the reader needs to compare discrete data points, a line isn't so good: Now the reader must "mentally break down" the line into specific points, which requires effort (Kosslyn, 1994a; in press).

Think about this finding from the levels-of-analysis perspective: When designing a graph, you need to respect the way the human perceptual and conceptual systems work (level of the brain). If you choose an inappropriate graph, you will force the reader to work hard to understand your message—which he or she may not be willing to do. But that's not all there is to it. Researchers who focus on the level of the group argue that people use graphs not only to communicate, but also to impress others. "For example, the use of gratuitous graphics [for example, adding the third dimension] may allow presenters to demonstrate their mastery of state-of-the-art technology, or their 'professionalism'; they may demonstrate the extra effort they have put into setting up the presentation or show their care about the contentment of their audience. Thus, social considerations in organizations are likely to promote self-presentation behavior in the context of information presentation" (Tractinsky & Meyer, 1999; p. 401; material in square brackets added for clarification).

In addition, researchers have studied events at the level of the person, such as the qualities of graphs that presenters prefer. One finding is that a presenter's preferences depend in part on the quality of the data. Tractinsky and Meyer (1999) asked participants to choose a display to present data; they found that participants preferred visually elaborate three-dimensional graphs when the graphs were presenting bad results. Why might this be? Perhaps because the graph obscures the data? Or perhaps because a fancy graph might partly compensate for poor results?

As usual, events at the three levels interact: Depending on the graph you choose for a specific purpose, you will affect the readers (level of the group) more effectively if the readers do not have to work hard to understand the display (level of the brain), and the particular message (level of the person) may not only influence the type of graph you choose but also how motivated the readers are to understand it. Not only do events at the different levels interact, but also these events *themselves* often must be understood at the different levels. For example, what occurs in the brain when someone is "impressed"? Trying to impress someone is clearly a social event, but it relies on events at the other levels of analysis. Similarly, "communication" is more than a social event—it also involves conveying content to readers (level of the person) and, ultimately, engaging their brains. Any psychological event can be understood fully only by considering it from all three levels.

# Test Yourself

1. One way to describe a set of data is to use certain values, such as the average score, the most common score, or the middle score. These values are measures of
   a. spread.
   b. outliers.
   c. frequency.
   d. central tendency.

2. The measure of central tendency most affected by the presence of extreme values is the
   a. mean.
   b. median.
   c. mode.
   d. frequency.

3. Which of the following cannot be used to describe the spread of values in a distribution of data?
   a. the range
   b. the standard deviation
   c. measures of variability
   d. the mean

4. In an experimental study, when the inferential statistics indicate that the experimental group's scores differed significantly from the control group's scores, you can conclude that
   a. the difference between the groups can be attributed to chance.
   b. the difference between the groups can be attributed to the treatment.
   c. there are no differences between the groups.
   d. the difference between the groups arises from the individual differences among the participants.

## Answers

# Think It Through!

Aspiring astronauts take a variety of psychological tests. If the values of the mean, median, and mode are not the same for a set of astronauts' test scores, which measure should you take most seriously? To what extent does this depend on the purposes to which you will put these data, and to what extent should your confidence reflect properties of the measures themselves? Would it matter how many scores you have?

People sometimes claim "garbage in, garbage out": If the data you begin with are no good, you won't be able to use them to draw inferences. This generalization is sometimes applied to meta-analyses, which often include studies that have flaws. Should all meta-analyses include only "perfect" studies? (Do such studies exist?) What if the flawed studies are flawed in different ways, so that the flaws are not correlated with the outcomes?

# HOW TO THINK ABOUT RESEARCH STUDIES

Large amounts of data have been reported from studies of human performance in space. Unfortunately, many of these research reports are not as easy to understand as they should be. If a piece of research is going to have an impact (for example, on the design of a future space station or the planning of an expedition to another planet), it must be read and understood. You will find it useful to approach reading—and writing—research reports armed with the *QALMRI method*. This method ties directly into the steps of the scientific method itself, which we discussed earlier, and is a vehicle for understanding the meaning of a research study in the literature—and for reporting your own research. This method will help you become clear about what question is being asked, how the researchers have tried to answer it, and whether the results really do support the preferred answer (the hypothesis).

# Reading Research Reports: The QALMRI Method

When you read a research report, try to identify the following components.

## *Q* Stands for the Question

All research begins with a question, and the point of the research is to answer it.

The first few paragraphs of the General Introduction should tell the reader what question the research study addresses. In addition, the context provided by the General Introduction's review of previous studies should explain why the question is important, why anybody should care about answering it. In some cases, the question is important for practical reasons; in others, it is important as a way to test a theory (and, in some cases, it is important for both practical and theoretical reasons, as in our example with a placebo). The General Introduction should provide the general context, explaining the reasons why the question is worthy of consideration.

## *A* Stands for Alternatives

A good report describes at least two possible answers to the question and explains why both are plausible. After describing the question that is being addressed, the General Introduction should explain what alternatives are being considered. When reading the General Introduction, identify the question and then the alternative answers that are considered by the study. If the alternatives are not spelled out, try to figure out for yourself what they might be; if the study is simply seeking to confirm a theory's prediction, try to get a sense of whether other theories (or just common sense) would make the same prediction. If all of the theories make the same prediction, it probably isn't worth testing.

## *L* Stands for the Logic of the Study

The goal of a study is to discriminate among the alternatives, and the logic is the general idea behind the study—the way the study will distinguish among the alternatives. The logic is typically explained toward the end of the General Introduction and has the following structure: *If* alternative 1 (and not the other alternatives) is correct, then when a particular variable is manipulated, the participant's behavior should change in a specific way. For example, the logic of the memory-enhancing study described earlier was: "If the drug enhances memory (and the placebo doesn't), then people should recall more test words after taking the drug than after taking the placebo."

## *M* Stands for the Method

The details of what the researcher did are found in the Method section. The Method section has the following parts:

**PARTICIPANTS:** Look to see how the participants were selected. Are they a representative sample of the population of interest? If a study was conducted to make a recommendation for a particular type of people (such as men and women in their early 20s), then the participants should be as similar to that group as possible. If no particular population is specified, then the sample should be representative of the population in general. If the study involves more than one group, they should be equivalent on important variables, such as age and education. Depending on the study, variables such as level of depression, number and type of medications used previously, or experience in large, noisy brain-scanning machines can be relevant. Try to think of all possible confounds that could make the groups different in ways that might affect the study's outcome.

**MATERIALS:** If questionnaires are used in the study, they should have been shown to be valid (that is, they should measure what they are supposed to measure). And they should be reliable (that is, they should produce consistent results). In addition, materials used in different parts of the study should not differ except as required to answer the research question.

**APPARATUS:** The apparatus delivers stimuli or defines the experimental situation. If a computer is used, the research report should describe exactly how it presented the stimuli. It also should describe in detail any other physical props that were used. Think about how the apparatus looked to the participants and whether it could have distracted them or allowed them to pick up inappropriate cues.

**PROCEDURE:** The procedure is the step-by-step process that the researchers follow to carry out the study. Try to picture yourself in the study. A good procedure should be described so well that you could replicate the study, doing exactly the same thing as the original investigators. Were participants given appropriate instructions (clear, but not leading them on)? Was it clear that the participants did in fact understand the instructions? Could the investigators have unintentionally treated participants in different groups differently?

## *R* Stands for the Results

The outcome of the study is described in detail in the Results section. What happened? First, look for measures of central tendency (means, medians, modes) and some measure of the sampling variability (commonly, standard deviations). The actual results—what the researchers found—are descriptive, and often are presented in a graph or table. Second, not all differences and patterns in the results should be taken seriously; some differences are simply quirks due to chance. Inferential statistics should be reported to indicate which patterns of variation are unlikely to have arisen due to chance. Look for the $p$ values that document differences; if the $p$ value is .05 or less (the 5% criterion mentioned earlier), you can be reasonably certain that the difference found in the sample reflects an actual difference in the population as a whole.

## *I* Stands for Inferences

The payoff of a study is the inferences that can be drawn about the alternative answers to the question being asked, given the results that were obtained. Decide whether the researchers convincingly answered the question they posed at the outset. The Discussion section usually contains the inferences the researchers want to draw from their results. If the study was well designed (the logic sound and the method rigorous), the results should allow you to eliminate at least one of the alternatives, and ideally should be most consistent with only one of the alternatives.

At this point, take a step back and think about potential confounds that could have led to the results. Were any alternative explanations not ruled out? For example, perhaps participants in different groups were treated differently by the investigators, or perhaps they were tested at different times of day or at different periods in the semester (closer or farther from anxiety-inducing exams). And consider any loose ends—what else would you want to know about the phenomena?

In sum, the QALMRI method helps you focus on the "big picture": What a study is about, why it's important, and what the results actually mean. When you read a report in the literature, figure out exactly what question the researchers wanted to answer and what alternative answers they've considered. Can you think of others? Always be on the lookout for potential alternative explanations. Look for features of the study that limit how well its results can be generalized; for example, can you assume that the results necessarily apply to people of other ages, races, or cultures? Be sure to read the footnotes. The single most important bit of advice you need to remember about reading a research report is to be an active reader: Think about what the researchers are claiming—and about whether it makes sense.

# Writing Your Own Research Papers

The same principles apply to writing your own research papers. Write the Introduction so that the reader clearly understands the question you are addressing and why it is important. Your question can be important because it is an extension of previous research (which you summarize in the Introduction), or because you've spotted a hole in the literature and aim to fill it by supplying new information, or because you've identified a variable that might invalidate a previous study (and want to find out whether those researchers did in fact overlook something crucial). When you review other studies and theories in the published literature, only include those that help you explain why your question is worth considering, that put it in context. Abraham Lincoln was once asked how long a man's legs should be, and he replied, "Long enough to reach the ground." The same principle applies to Introductions: Don't include any more or less material than you need to put your question in context.

The Introduction should also explain the alternative possible answers you will consider—including, in most cases, your "favorite" one, which is called "the hypothesis." You need to explain why each alternative is plausible, usually by referring to previously published findings and theories. Finally, the Introduction should end with a clear statement of the logic of your study, the basic idea underlying what you did.

In the Method section, be sure to include enough detail to allow another researcher to repeat exactly what you did. Explain what sort of participants were tested, and how you ensured that participants in different groups were comparable in terms of important variables. In addition, you need to describe the materials in detail, and you also need to describe the apparatus and the procedure in precise terms.

In the Results section, first present results that bear directly on the question and alternative answers. The results that address the question being asked are most important—even if they are not as striking as some of the other findings. If your Introduction is clear, the reader is focused like a laser beam on the question you are asking and is waiting to find out which alternative answer is supported by the results. Don't keep the reader in suspense; present the results that speak to the question at the outset of the Results section. These results should be measures of central tendency and variability, which are often best presented in a graph; you should also present inferential statistics along with the results, so the reader will know which differences to take seriously. After you present these results, present anything else that you may have found.

Finally, in the Discussion section, return to the question and alternative answers, and discuss exactly what you can infer from your results. Have you shown that some of the alternatives must be discarded? Is only one viable? What should future research focus on to propel the field even further ahead?

When writing a research report, always put yourself in the place of an intelligent reader. If a report has been written clearly, the reader will glide through it effortlessly, understanding what the researcher intended to convey, why the research was conducted in a particular way, what the discoveries were, and why the report is interesting and important.

# UNDERSTANDING RESEARCH

## When Does Mental Practice Improve Later Performance?

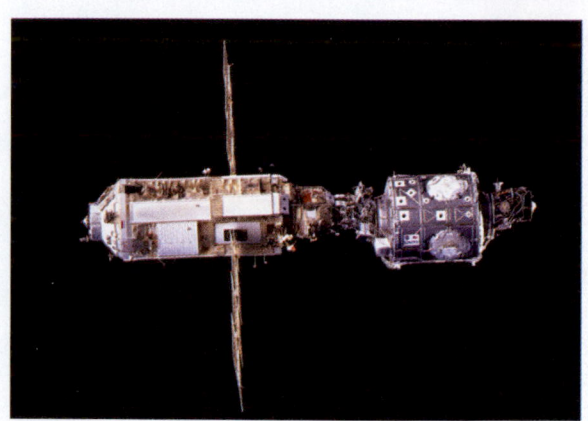

One glance at the International Space Station from the outside makes it clear why astronauts would get a lot out of mentally practicing sports—there just isn't much room on board for the real thing.

In each chapter from now on, we will examine one study in detail, using the QALMRI method. In this chapter, let's look at *mental practice*, the ability to rehearse an activity mentally, without actually making any movements. Mental practice is particularly interesting in the context of the ISS. Mission planners give astronauts "leisure time," and on earth most astronauts would use at least some of this time to play tennis, golf, or some other sport. Unfortunately, few of these sports can be played on the ISS—balls don't bounce properly in weightless environments, and there really isn't room to run around (it would jeopardize delicate equipment, even if there were room). Does this mean that the astronauts must resign themselves to getting rusty at their favorite sports? Perhaps not. Perhaps they can practice mentally, which would preserve—or even improve—their game. For example, many golfers claim that when they are off the course, they can practice by imagining themselves whacking the ball straight down the fairway or out of the sand trap. Players regularly claim that the mental practice improves their game. Well, maybe. The only way we can find out whether mental practice really works is by conducting a scientific study, and many such studies have been reported. Let's now consider one of them.

**QUESTION:** Can mental practice change subsequent golf putting? Woolfolk, Parrish, and Murphy (1985) asked whether mentally rehearsing golf putts can help as well as hurt subsequent performance.

**ALTERNATIVES:** (1) Mental practice improves putting when participants imagine successfully tapping the ball into the hole, but it actually hurts performance when they imagine tapping the ball so that it misses the hole. (2) Mental practice might always improve putting. (3) It might not have any effect at all.

**LOGIC:** If alternative 1 is correct and the other alternatives are not, then when people imagine rehearsing the right kind of movements for a successful putt, their performance should later improve—but if they imagine rehearsing the wrong kinds of movements, their performance should actually get worse.

**METHOD:** The researchers first asked 30 college students to putt golf balls into a hole and assessed how well they could do so. After performing 20 putts (from 8.5 feet away), equal numbers of students of comparable skill were randomly assigned to each group. The researchers then gave each group different instructions for mental rehearsal. They asked students in the *positive imagery group* to imagine making a "gentle but firm backswing" and then seeing the ball "rolling, rolling, right into the cup" (p. 338). Students in the *negative imagery group* received the identical instructions but were told to imagine the ball "rolling, rolling, toward the cup, but at the last second narrowly missing." Finally, they asked students in the *control group* to imagine putting, with no specific instructions about how to imagine the ball. The students then followed the instructions given to their group. After this, the researchers again asked the students to do actual putting and again assessed how well they could do it.

**RESULTS:** As shown in Figure 2.12, the students in the positive imagery group performed about 30% better after mental practice than they had when tested initially. In contrast, students in the negative imagery group actually got worse, scoring about 21% poorer than they had earlier. Finally, students in the control group improved a bit (by about 10%).

**INFERENCES:** The authors concluded that mental practice depends on the specific movements you imagine. If the movements are appropriate, mental practice will help later performance—but if the movements are not appropriate, mental practice will actually hurt later performance. Many other studies have found that mental practice improves subsequent performance (Doheny, 1993; Driskell et al., 1994; Druckman & Swets, 1988; Prather, 1973; Vieilledent et al., 2003; White & Hardy, 1995), and the present results begin to suggest why it might work.

**FIGURE 2.12** **Effects of Mental Practice on Putting Performance**

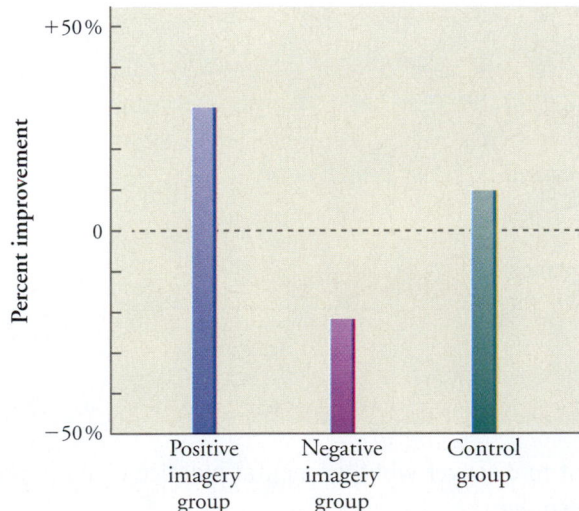

Results of Woolfolk, Parrish, and Murphy (1985), showing that mentally practicing putting improves actual performance.

You might wonder whether the results of the study of mental practice and putting performance occurred not because of differences in the images, but because the students in the positive imagery group were more relaxed than those in the negative imagery group. Or perhaps the students in the negative group found it frustrating to keep missing the hole, and thus stopped practicing altogether. Or perhaps at the time of the second actual testing, students in the negative imagery group thought the experimenter expected poorer performance, and so "threw the game" and performed more poorly than they could have. Each of these alternative explanations could be tested.

How can you be sure that results from a study of mental practice of golf apply to other sports? Do you think that everyone would benefit equally from mental practice? What characteristics might distinguish people who would benefit a lot from mental practice from those who would get little from it?

# Test Yourself

1. Based on the QALMRI method, the research question for the study of mental practice and putting performance was
   a. Does mental rehearsal of putting improve all forms of performance?
   b. Does mental rehearsal of putting hurt putting performance?
   c. Does mental rehearsal of putting affect its performance?
   d. Does mental imagery lead to relaxation?
2. In the study of mental practice and putting, the students were divided into three groups, and each group was given different instructions. In which aspect(s) of the QALMRI method would you specify this feature of the study?
   a. the alternatives  c. the method
   b. the logic  d. both logic and method
3. A potential problem with the inferences drawn in the study of mental practice of putting is that
   a. differences among the groups may not be uniquely caused by differences in the mental images.
   b. the inferences conflict with other research results.
   c. the positive imagery group showed improved performance.
   d. the negative imagery group performed worse than the others.

4. The best reason for using the QALMRI method to think about research studies is that it allows you to
   a. compare all relevant studies.
   b. see the big picture and be an active reader.
   c. study research results to prepare for an exam.
   d. replicate the studies.

## Answers

1. c 2. d 3. a 4. b

# Think It Through!

Pick your favorite hobby and design an experiment to discover whether mental practice could improve your performance. Use the QALMRI framework to describe the study.

# REVIEW AND REMEMBER!

## Summary

### I. The Scientific Method: Designed to Be Valid
The science of psychology relies on the scientific method, which involves specifying a problem, systematically observing events, forming a hypothesis of the relation between variables, collecting new observations to test the hypothesis, using such data to formulate and support a theory, and testing the theory.

*I.*

### II. The Psychologist's Toolbox: Techniques of Scientific Research

*II.*

**A.** Psychologists test hypotheses and look for relations among variables using a variety of tools, including descriptive (naturalistic observation, case studies, and surveys), correlational, and experimental research methods.

*A.*

**B.** Naturalistic observation involves careful observation and documentation of events.

*B.*

**C.** Case studies are detailed investigations of a single instance of a situation (the detailed exploration of an astronaut's training would be a case study).

*C.*

**D.** In surveys, participants are asked to answer sets of specific questions.

*D.*

**E.** In correlational studies, the relationship between the values of pairs of variables is assessed, showing how the values of one go up or down as the values of the other increase (but not showing that changes in the values of one variable *cause* changes in the other).

*E. Correlation ≠ causation*

**F.** In an experiment, the effect of manipulating one or more independent variables on the value of a dependent variable is measured, and participants are assigned randomly to experimental or control groups.

*F.*

**G.** Quasi-experiments are like experiments but participants are not assigned randomly to groups.

*G.*

**H.** When reading reports of research results, you should be alert for the following: (1) evidence that the data are reliable, (2) evidence that the data are valid, (3) possible contamination from confounding variables, (4) biases, including the tendency to respond in particular ways to everything (response bias) and the nonrandom selection of participants or experimental materials (sampling bias), and (5) experimenter expectancy effects.

*H.*

**I.** Pseudopsychology differs from psychology not necessarily in its content, but in how its findings are supported by data.

*I.*

### III. Statistics: Measuring Reality

*III.*

**A.** Descriptive statistics characterize observations by specifying measures of central tendency and variability.

*A.*

**B.** Measures of central tendency include the mean (which is the arithmetic average of the values or scores), the median (which is the value for which half the other

*B.*

values are higher and half lower), and the mode (which is the most frequently occurring value of the set).

**C.** Measures of variability include the range (which is the difference between the highest and lowest score) and the standard deviation (which is a measure of "average spread" from the mean).

**D.** Different descriptive statistics indicate the frequency of different scores and the standing of any one score relative to the others (for example, in terms of quartiles or deciles).

**E.** Inferential statistics tell us which differences among values or patterns (such as increasing or decreasing trends) in the data should be taken seriously. Inferential statistics rely on assigning a probability that a difference or a pattern could have arisen purely due to chance. Generally speaking, if that probability is less than 5%, the result is considered "statistically significant."

**F.** A sample is the group you measure, which is drawn from a larger population; the goal is to use the sample to draw inferences about the population in general.

**G.** A correlation indicates whether one set of measurements tends to vary along with another set.

**H.** A meta-analysis identifies trends or patterns that are present across many studies.

**I.** Inferential statistics can be used deceptively, largely because of selective reporting.

**J.** Graphs can be constructed to bias viewers' interpretation, by either appropriately emphasizing the actual results (statistically significant differences or patterns in the data) or inappropriately emphasizing nonsignificant results.

## IV. How to Think About Research Studies

One way to think about the relation between theory and data is the QALMRI method.

**A.** *Q* stands for the *question*, what the study is about and why it is important.

**B.** *A* stands for *alternative answers* to that question, which the study is designed to discriminate among.

**C.** *L* stands for the *logic* of the study, the basic idea that will allow the researchers to discriminate among the alternatives.

**D.** *M* stands for the *method*, the details of exactly what was done in the study.

**E.** *R* stands for the *results*, which include both descriptive and inferential statistics.

**F.** *I* stands for *inferences* that can be drawn from the results, indicating which alternatives can be eliminated and which receive support.

NOTE: Once you feel that you understand the material in this chapter, visit the book's Web site at www.ablongman.com/kosslyn3e to test your knowledge with additional study questions.

*Margin notes:*

*C.*

*D.*

*E. Think of coin-tossing example.*

*F.*

*G.*

*H.*

*I.*

*J.*

*IV. QALMRI: Questions lead to Inferences*

*A.*

*B.*

*C.*

*D.*

*E.*

*F.*

# Key Terms

bias, p. 51
case study, p. 43
central tendency, p. 56
confound, p. 46
control condition, p. 47
control group, p. 46
correlation coefficient, p. 44
data, p. 38
dependent variable, p. 45
descriptive statistics, p. 55
double-blind design, p. 52
effect, p. 45
experimental condition, p. 47
experimental group, p. 46
experimenter expectancy effects, p. 52
hypothesis, p. 39

independent variable, p. 45
inferential statistics, p. 58
mean, p. 56
median, p. 56
meta-analysis, p. 60
mode, p. 57
normal distribution, p. 57
operational definition, p. 39
percentile rank, p. 58
placebo, p. 55
population, p. 59
prediction, p. 40
pseudopsychology, p. 52
random assignment, p. 46
range, p. 58
raw data, p. 56

reliability, p. 49
replication, p. 38
response bias, p. 51
sample, p. 59
sampling bias, p. 51
sampling error, p. 60
scientific method, p. 38
standard deviation, p. 58
statistical significance, p. 59
statistics, p. 54
survey, p. 43
theory, p. 40
validity, p. 49
variable, p. 39

# CHAPTER 3

# THE BIOLOGY OF MIND AND BEHAVIOR: THE BRAIN IN ACTION

A s the hard jets of water massaged the 25-year-old soldier while he showered, colorless and odorless fumes of carbon monoxide, which are known to cause brain damage, slowly seeped into the stall. Unaware that he was gradually being poisoned, the soldier continued his routine until he eventually passed out.

After the soldier was discovered and revived, doctors examined him. The young man could get around with ease, but he presented a host of bizarre symptoms. He was unable to name objects by sight, but as soon as he touched them, he could say what they were. He could identify things by smell and sound, he could name colors or identify a color named by someone else by pointing to it, and he had no difficulty recognizing familiar people when they spoke. But he couldn't identify these same people by sight alone. In fact, when he looked at his own face in the mirror, he thought he was looking at his doctor. When he was shown a rubber eraser, he identified it as "a small ball"; when shown a safety pin, he said it was "like a watch or nail clipper." When the doctors asked the soldier to inspect a picture of a nude woman and show where her eyes were, he pointed to her breasts (Benson & Greenberg, 1969).

Clearly, something was wrong with the young soldier's vision, but the problem had nothing to do with his eyes; it had to do with his brain. He couldn't acquire knowledge by way of his sense of sight. Why? Though he retained some aspects of his vision, he had lost others—he seemed unable to recognize what he clearly could see. The fumes the soldier had inhaled had affected his brain, but how? What, exactly, had gone wrong? To consider these questions, you need to understand essential facts about how the brain works.

As you have seen, events at the level of the brain can influence many aspects of behavior, in ways not immediately apparent. If you broke your hand, you would have trouble holding a pencil: The effect of the accident would be direct and mechanical. If you were in any doubt before your mishap about the role of muscle and bone in grasping and holding, you would be in no doubt afterwards, when those abilities would be distinctly impaired because muscles were torn and bones fractured. But, although it is a physical organ like muscle and bone, the brain is unique: It is also a *psychological* organ, ultimately responsible for our moods of despair and elation, our sense of well-being and our sense that something's wrong, our perception of the outside world and our awareness of its meaning. The effects of damage to the brain are no less real than those of a broken hand, but the path by which they arise is less obvious (indeed, until recently was unobservable). It is this path, through a thicket of sometimes difficult names and processes, that we must trace if we are to gain a meaningful understanding of who we are and why we behave as we do.

So, how does it work, this mysterious brain? What is it made up of; what are its building blocks? Can we ever see the brain at work? How could we find out exactly which parts of the soldier's brain were damaged? Do all of our brains respond the same way to the same environmental influences? Or, do different people, with different genetic makeups and life experiences, respond differently? Let's start finding out.

# BRAIN CIRCUITS: Making Connections

The carbon monoxide fumes that the soldier breathed interfered with his brain's ability to use oxygen, causing him to pass out. Unfortunately, he inhaled enough of these fumes that some brain cells probably died; ordinarily, brain cells begin to succumb after a few minutes without oxygen. But just saying that brain cells "died" isn't much of an explanation—that would be a little like saying that a building fell down because its molecules were rearranged. Why did the death of those cells have the effects it did?

## The Neuron: A Powerful Computer

The brain is "the psychological organ"; it gives rise to the mind, that is, to mental processes (such as perception, memory, and language) and mental experiences. The brain is arguably the most complex object in the known universe, and to begin to grasp its general outlines, we start small (with brain cells) and then move to large (brain structures). We could easily write a book about each of these topics; we present here just what you will need to know to understand material in the remainder of this book (for example, the actions of drugs that treat psychological disorders).

All brain activity hinges on the workings of brain cells, or **neurons** (Kandel et al., 2000). There are three types of neurons. Some, the **sensory neurons**, respond to input from the senses; others, the **motor neurons**, send signals to muscles to control movement; finally, **interneurons** stand between the neurons that register what's out there and those that control movement—or they stand between other interneurons. Most of the neurons in the brain are interneurons, and most interneurons are connected to yet other interneurons.

Neurons differ in their size, shape, and function. Some major types of neurons are shown in Figure 3.1. Just as stone can be used to build either a hut or a palace, the same neural building blocks can make up very different brains. For example, most mammals, from horses to humans, largely share the same types of neurons.

Neurons would not be much good if they did not affect other neurons or the rest of the body—how useful would the Internet be if only one computer were connected to it? **Brain circuits** are sets of neurons that affect one another. When one neuron in a circuit is triggered by another neuron, it in turn triggers others, and so on, causing a chain reaction. Neurons often receive and put together many inputs at the same time. The result can be the awareness that a sumptuous dessert is on the table, a command to the muscles to turn up the volume of a stereo, a sudden memory of an assignment due yesterday, a flash of feeling for an attractive classmate—anything we perceive, think, feel, or do.

## Structure of a Neuron: The Ins and Outs

To understand psychological events, you need to know a few facts about the structure of the neuron. As you can see in Figure 3.2 (p. 80), each neuron has certain parts.

The central part of a neuron is called the **cell body**. Like all cells, it has a nucleus, which regulates the cell's functions, and a **cell membrane**, which is the skin of the cell.

Neuron: A cell that receives signals from other neurons or sense organs, processes these signals, and sends the signals to other neurons, muscles, or organs; the basic unit of the nervous system.

Sensory neuron: A neuron that responds to input from sense organs.

Motor neuron: A neuron that sends signals to muscles to control movement.

Interneuron: A neuron that is connected to other neurons, not to sense organs or muscles.

Brain circuit: A set of neurons that affect one another.

Cell body: The central part of a neuron (or other cell), which contains the nucleus.

Cell membrane: The skin of a cell.

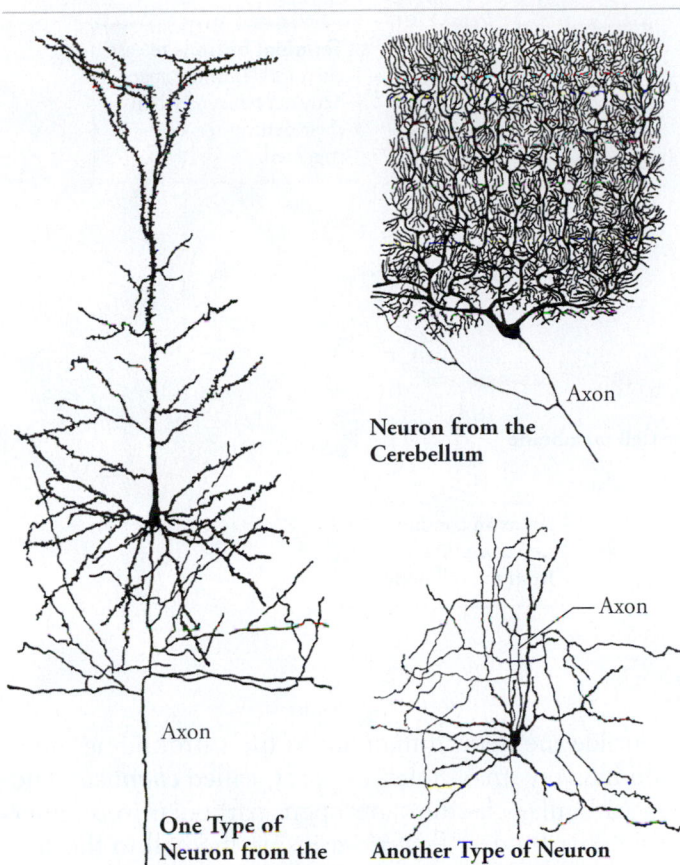

## FIGURE 3.1

## Examples of Types of Neurons

Neurons come in many shapes and sizes. Researchers are still discovering the ways in which the differences among such cells affect their functioning.

**Neuron from the Cerebellum**

Axon

**One Type of Neuron from the Cerebral Cortex**

Axon

**Another Type of Neuron from the Cerebral Cortex**

Axon

The sending end of the neuron is the **axon**, the long, cablelike structure extending from the cell body, along which signals travel to other neurons, muscles, or bodily organs. Although each neuron has only a single axon, most axons divide into many branches, called *terminals,* so that a neuron can send a message to more than one place at a time. At the ends of the terminals are **terminal buttons**, little knoblike structures that release chemicals into the space between neurons when the neuron has been triggered. Most neurons communicate this way, releasing chemicals that affect other neurons, usually at their receiving end. (A few neurons, such as some of those in the eye, communicate directly via electrical impulses, but this direct electrical communication is rare.)

Each neuron has only one sending end—that is, only one axon—but a neuron may have many receiving ends. These are the **dendrites**; their name is derived from the Greek word *dendron,* meaning "tree," which makes sense when you look at their shape (see Figure 3.1). The dendrites receive messages from the axons of other neurons. Although axons sometimes connect directly to the cell body of another neuron, the connection is usually made from axon to dendrite.

## Neural Impulses: The Brain in Action

Neurons are not always firing. When at rest, they maintain a negative charge within; this negative charge is called the **resting potential**. This potential arises because of how ions are distributed inside and outside the cell; **ions** are atoms that are positively or negatively charged. During rest, more positively charged ions (called *cations,* and consisting mostly of sodium ions) are outside the neuron than inside it, and more negatively

**Axon:** The sending end of the neuron; the long cablelike structure extending from the cell body.

**Terminal button:** A structure at the end of a branch of an axon that, when the neuron is triggered, releases chemicals into the space between neurons.

**Dendrite:** The treelike part of a neuron that receives messages from the axons of other neurons.

**Resting potential:** The negative charge within a neuron when it is at rest.

**Ion:** An atom that has a positive or negative charge.

FIGURE 3.2

## Major Parts of a Neuron

A neuron has many parts. The major ones are labeled here, but much of the action occurs internally where a complex dance of chemicals occurs.

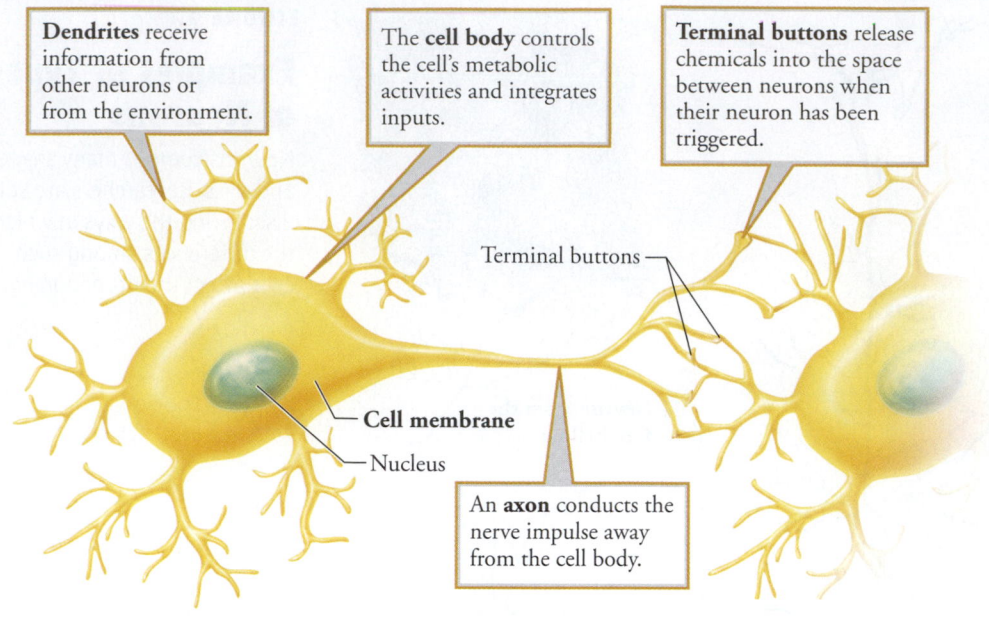

**Dendrites** receive information from other neurons or from the environment.

The **cell body** controls the cell's metabolic activities and integrates inputs.

**Terminal buttons** release chemicals into the space between neurons when their neuron has been triggered.

Terminal buttons

**Cell membrane**

Nucleus

An **axon** conducts the nerve impulse away from the cell body.

charged ions (called *anions*) are inside the neuron than are in the surrounding fluid. The membrane covering the axon has very small holes, or pores, called *channels*. The channels open and close: When particular channels are open, particular ions either flow into the cell from the surrounding fluid or flow from inside the cell to the surrounding fluid. When a neuron receives enough stimulation from other neurons (when a specific *threshold* is exceeded), some of the channels in the cell membrane open, allowing a complex exchange of ions that changes the charge in the axon. This exchange works its way down to the end of the axon, finally causing the terminal buttons to release chemicals that will affect other neurons. When this occurs, the neuron is said to "fire." The shifting change in charge that moves down the axon is known as an **action potential**. This process, the basis of the neural communication that permits us to live in the world and respond to it, is illustrated in Figure 3.3.

Notice that the action potential obeys an **all-or-none law**. If enough stimulation reaches the neuron, it fires. In other words, the sequence of shifting charges sends the action potential all the way down the axon, releasing chemicals from the terminal buttons. Either the action potential occurs or it doesn't. Many neurons can fire hundreds of times a second because chemical reactions reset them so that they can fire again if they receive adequate stimulation.

Nevertheless, neurons require a measurable amount of time to work; to convince yourself that this is so, gather some friends and try the simple exercise described in Figure 3.4 (developed by Rozin & Jonides, 1977).

Neurons would operate substantially more slowly were it not for the fact that most axons are covered with **myelin**, a fatty substance that helps impulses travel down the axon more efficiently. Myelin is a bit like the insulation around copper wires, which allows them to transmit current more effectively. *Multiple sclerosis (MS)* is one of several disorders that illustrates the importance of myelin. In MS, the myelin has deteriorated, which makes impulses "stumble" as they move down the axon. People with MS experience impaired sensation in their limbs, loss of vision, and paralysis (Zajicek, 2004). Could myelin loss have caused the young soldier's problem? Probably not: His visual problem was selective, whereas myelin loss creates overall problems in seeing.

**Action potential:** The shifting change in charge that moves down the axon.

**All-or-none law:** States that if the neuron is sufficiently stimulated, it fires, sending the action potential all the way down the axon and releasing chemicals from the terminal buttons; either the action potential occurs or it doesn't.

**Myelin:** A fatty substance that helps impulses travel down the axon more efficiently.

## FIGURE 3.3  Ion Flow That Produces an Action Potential

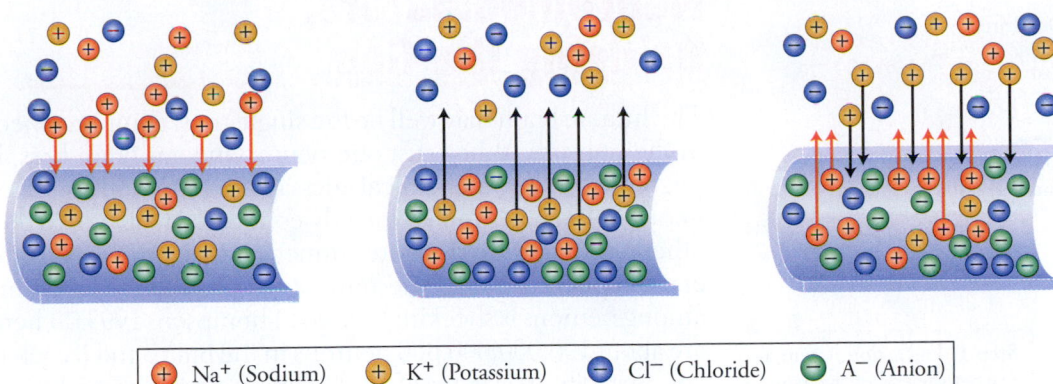

| | | | |
|---|---|---|---|
| ⊕ Na⁺ (Sodium) | ⊕ K⁺ (Potassium) | ⊖ Cl⁻ (Chloride) | ⊖ A⁻ (Anion) |

$Na^+$ channels open after the neuron is stimulated, and $Na^+$ ions rush into the cell; the inside of the cell then becomes positively charged. (Note: Ions are not drawn to scale, but relative proportions are correct.)

The $Na^+$ channels close, $K^+$ channels briefly open, and $K^+$ ions go outside the cell. (The $K^+$ ions are pushed out because of the addition of the positively charged $Na^+$ ions.)

After this, $Na^+$ pumps actively push $Na^+$ ions back outside and $K^+$ ions are drawn inside, until the inside and outside concentrations are returned to their original levels.

When the ion exchanges reach the end of the axon, they cause chemicals to be released from the terminal buttons.

Direction of action potential

Chemicals released

## FIGURE 3.4  Measuring Neural Conduction Time

In the fastest neurons, impulses travel only about 120 meters per second, compared with 300,000,000 meters per second for the speed of light. Even compared with the impulses traveling in a computer, our neurons are extremely slow. You can actually measure the speed of neural processing. Here's how.

Sit in a row with some friends, with each person using his or her left hand to grasp the ankle of the person on his or her left. The person at the head of the line, the leader, says "Go" and starts a stopwatch at the same time he or she squeezes the ankle of the person to his or her left; as soon as that person feels the squeeze, he or she squeezes the ankle of the next person to the left; and so on. When the last person feels the squeeze, he or she says "Done." The leader records the time.

Now repeat the exercise, but each of you should grasp not the ankle but the shoulder of the person to your left. Less time is required for the squeezes to make their way down the row when shoulders are squeezed than when ankles are squeezed. Why? Because the impulses have farther to travel when the ankle is squeezed. By subtracting the difference in times and estimating the average distance from ankle to shoulder for each person you can actually estimate neural transmission time! This exercise should be done several times, first ankle, then shoulder, then shoulder, and then ankle; this procedure helps to control for the effects of practice in general.

FIGURE 3.5 **The Synapse**

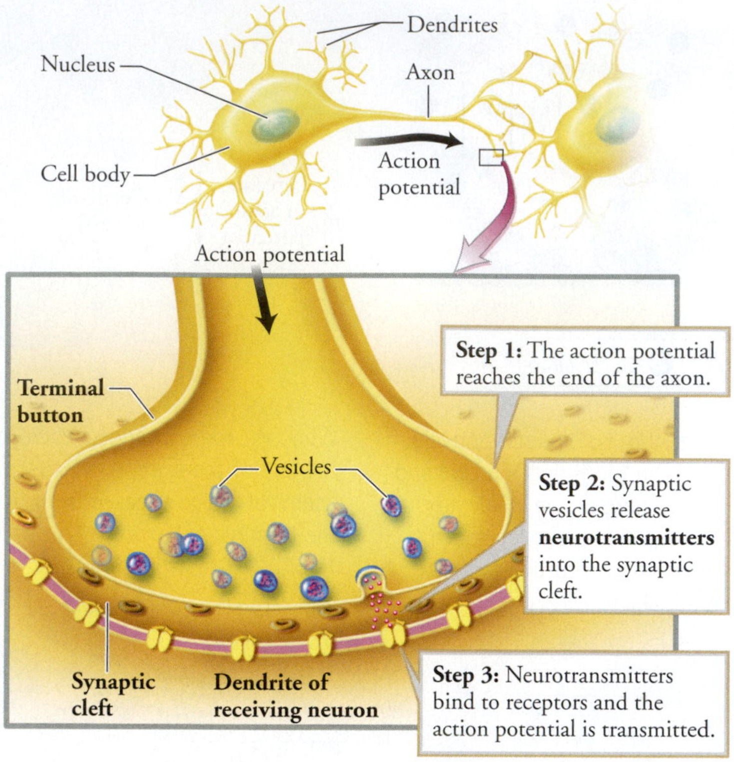

Impulses cross between neurons at the synapse. Chemicals released at the terminal buttons cross the synaptic cleft, where they bind to receptors and trigger events in the receiving neuron.

**Step 1:** The action potential reaches the end of the axon.

**Step 2:** Synaptic vesicles release **neurotransmitters** into the synaptic cleft.

**Step 3:** Neurotransmitters bind to receptors and the action potential is transmitted.

Synapse: The place where an axon of one neuron can send signals to the membrane (on a dendrite or cell body) of another neuron.

Synaptic cleft: The gap between the axon of one neuron and the membrane of another, across which communication occurs.

Neurotransmitter: A chemical that carries a signal from the terminal button on one neuron to the dendrite or cell body of another.

Neuromodulator: A chemical that alters the effect of a neurotransmitter.

Endogenous cannabinoids: Neuromodulators released by the receiving neuron that then influence the activity of the sending neuron.

# Neurotransmitters and Neuromodulators: Bridging the Gap

The human brain may well be the single most complex object in the universe. When just one neuron in your brain fires, it might be sending a chemical message to thousands of other neurons. Each neuron is typically connected to about 10,000 others (and some neurons are connected to up to 100,000 others; Shepherd, 1999). The number of possible connections among neurons is shockingly large (Thompson, 1993). There are about 100,000,000,000 neurons in the brain, and if each is connected to an average of 10,000 others (varying which ones are connected in all combinations), the numbers of ways your neurons can be "linked up" becomes . . . well, astronomical!

How do neurons actually communicate? What are the connections between them like? The site where communication between neurons occurs is the **synapse**, where an axon of one neuron sends a signal to the membrane of another neuron. The sending and receiving neurons do not actually touch each other, but rather are separated by a gap called the **synaptic cleft**, shown in Figure 3.5.

## Chemical Messages: Signals and Modulators

As their name suggests, the chemicals that carry signals, crossing from the terminal buttons across the synaptic clefts, are the **neurotransmitters**. Other chemicals, called **neuromodulators** alter the effects of the neurotransmitters. Here's an analogy: Imagine that you are using a pair of tin cans with a string between them as a walkie-talkie. When you speak into one can and your friend holds the other up to her ear, sound waves transmit the message. The gap from your mouth to one of the cans, and from the other can to her ear, is crossed by these waves, which carry the message. Neurotransmitters play the same role as the sound waves, allowing the message to cross the gap. In contrast to the neurotransmitters, neuromodulators would produce the effect of tightening or loosening the string connecting the cans. When the string is drawn tight, the message is transmitted more effectively from one can to the other; when it is slackened, the sound must be louder to be heard.

Other substances (which are not, strictly speaking, called neuromodulators) can affect what happens at the gap itself, for example, by affecting how quickly the neurotransmitters are removed from the synaptic cleft. Imagine that the room holding the linked tin cans has very thin air, with fewer molecules to vibrate. In this case, a louder sound would be needed to cause the bottoms of the tin cans to vibrate. On the other hand, if the air pressure were greater, a softer sound could convey the signal.

Researchers have discovered many substances that act as neurotransmitters or neuromodulators in the brain, including some unexpected ones such as nitric oxide and carbon monoxide (Barañano et al., 2001). Table 3.1 summarizes key properties of the major neurotransmitter substances.

Not all neuromodulators are released at terminal buttons. Notably, **endogenous cannabinoids** are chemicals released by the *receiving* neuron that then influence the ac-

TABLE 3.1

# Major Neurotransmitter Substances

Summary of the most important neurotransmitters and neuromodulators, distinguishing features, major associated disorders, and typical drugs that modulate their effects. The disorders are discussed in later chapters of this book. A question mark indicates that the substance may be involved in the disorder, but conclusive evidence has yet to be obtained.

| Name | Distinguishing Features | Related Disorders and Symptoms | Drugs That Alter |
|---|---|---|---|
| Acetylcholine (ACh) | Transmitter at the neuromuscular junction (causes muscles to contract); memory; used in autonomic nervous system | Alzheimer's disease, delusions (shortage); convulsions, spasms, tremors (excess) | Physostigmine (increases, used to treat Alzheimer's disease); scopolamine (blocks) |
| Dopamine (DA) | Motivation, reward, movement, thought, learning | Parkinson's disease, depression, attention deficit/hyperactivity disorder (ADHD) (shortage); aggression, schizophrenia (excess) | Amphetamine, cocaine (causes release); chlorpromazine (blocks at receptors); methylphenidate (Ritalin, blocks reuptake) |
| Noradrenaline (NA) (Norepinephrine, NE) | Dreaming, attention | Depression, fatigue, distractability (shortage); anxiety, headache, schizophrenia (excess) | Tricyclic antidepressants such as Elavil (keep more available at the synapse) |
| Adrenaline (Epinephrine) | Orientation towards stimuli | Depression, Alzheimer's disease (?) (shortage); arousal or apprehension (excess) | Amphetamine, cocaine (mimic effects) |
| Serotonin (5-Hydroxytryptamine; 5HT) | Primary inhibitory neurotransmitter regulating mood, sleep | Obsessive-compulsive disorder, insomnia, depression (shortage); sleepiness, lack of motivation (excess) | Fluoxetine (Prozac), tricyclic antidepressants (keep more present at the synapse) |
| Glutamate | Most widely used fast excitatory neurotransmitter; memory formation; pain | Amyotrophic lateral sclerosis (ALS—Lou Gehrig's disease) (shortage); neurodegeneration, stroke, interferes with learning (excess) | Phencyclidine (PCP), dextromethorphan (block glutamate) |
| GABA (Gamma-amino butyric acid) | Inhibits sending neuron | Anxiety, panic (?), epilepsy, Huntington's disease (shortage); sluggish, unmotivated (excess) | Sedatives (such as phenobarbital), alcohol, benzodiazepines (such as Valium, Halcion) mimic effects |
| Beta-endorphin | Inhibits acetylcholine and glutamate at the receiving neuron; blocks pain, alters mood | Pain sensitivity, immune problems (shortage); numb to pain (excess) | Naxalone (blocks effects of); opiates (mimic effects of) |
| Endogenous cannabinoids | Memory, attention, emotion, movement control, appetite | Chronic pain (shortage); memory and attention problems, eating disorders, schizophrenia (?) (excess) | R141716A (blocks effects of); THC (mimics effects of) |

tivity of the *sending* neuron (Wilson & Nicoll, 2002). This signaling system is one of the most important in the brain; cannabinoids affect precise locations on neurons, which allows them to fine-tune activity underlying learning, memory, pain perception, and attention (Katona et al., 2000; Kreitzer & Regehr, 2001b; Sanudo-Pena et al., 2000). Endogenous cannabinoids work by subtly dampening down sending neurons (Katona et al., 2001; Kreitzer & Regehr, 2001a; Kreitzer et al., 2002; Manning et al., 2001; Wilson &

Nicoll, 2001; Wilson et al., 2001). Marijuana contains cannabinoids, but it affects neurons indiscriminately and promiscuously and thereby overwhelms our exquisitely tuned neural systems—which in turn disrupts memory and attention, as well as other cognitive functions (Ashton, 2001; Schneider & Koch, 2002). As Barinaga (2001) put it, the chemicals introduced by marijuana eliminate the fine-tuned "local activity patterns . . . just as spilling a bottle of ink across a page obliterates any words written there" (p. 2531).

## Receptors: On the Receiving End

What do the neurotransmitters do once they cross the gap? That depends. Each neuron has **receptors**, specialized sites on the dendrites or cell bodies that respond to specific neurotransmitters or neuromodulators. The receptor sites are the places where "messenger molecules" of the released chemicals—neurotransmitters or neuromodulators—attach themselves. A good analogy here is an ordinary lock set: The lock is the receptor, which is opened by the keylike action of a particular neurotransmitter or neuromodulator.

When neurotransmitters or neuromodulators become attached to receptors, they are said to *bind* (see Figure 3.6). After binding, they can have one of two general types of effects. They can be *excitatory*, making the receiving neuron more likely to fire an action potential, or they can be *inhibitory*, making the receiving neuron less easily triggered. Because the typical axon divides into many branches and each neuron has many dendrites, there are many binding sites; thus, the neuron can receive thousands of different inputs from different sending neurons at the same time. The exciting and inhibiting inputs to each receiving neuron add up or cancel one another out, and their sum determines whether and when the neuron fires an action potential down its axon.

Each particular neuron produces a small number of transmitters or modulators, and each neuron can have many types of receptors. The same neurotransmitter or neuromodulator can have very different effects, depending on which receptors are present. Dopamine, for instance, is often considered to be a neurotransmitter that is involved in motivation and reward. However, dopamine can function as a neurotransmitter in one context (for example, in the retina) and a neuromodulator in another context (for example, in the frontal parts of the brain). In fact, the same neurotransmitter can have opposite effects on a neuron depending on which type of receptor accepts it, and the same chemical that can act as a neurotransmitter (sending a signal) in one context can act as a neuromodulator (altering a signal) in another (Dowling, 1992). For example, acetylcholine (ACh) can act as a neurotransmitter to slow down the heart, and can also function as a neuromodulator to help us store new memories. Thus, the distinction between neurotransmitters and neuromodulators has become blurred in recent years. In this book, the term *neurotransmitter substance* often covers both sorts of chemicals, since they often affect neurons in complex ways. We will encounter these substances repeatedly throughout the book, particularly when we consider the factors contributing to mental illness.

Not all of a given neurotransmitter released by the terminal buttons is taken up by receptors; some of it remains in the gap. Special chemical reactions are required to reabsorb—or **reuptake**—the excess neurotransmitter back into the *vesicles* (which store neurotransmitters) of the sending neuron.

## Unbalanced Brain: Coping With Bad Chemicals

By piecing together the story of how neurons communicate, scientists are not only developing a clear picture of how the brain works but are also learning how its functioning can go awry and how they can use drugs to repair it. Drugs that affect the way the brain works either increase or decrease the effectiveness of neural activity. Some of these

**Receptor:** A site on a dendrite or cell body where a messenger molecule attaches itself; like a lock that is opened by one key, a receptor receives only one type of neurotransmitter or neuromodulator.

**Reuptake:** The process by which surplus neurotransmitter is reabsorbed back into the sending neuron so that the neuron can effectively fire again.

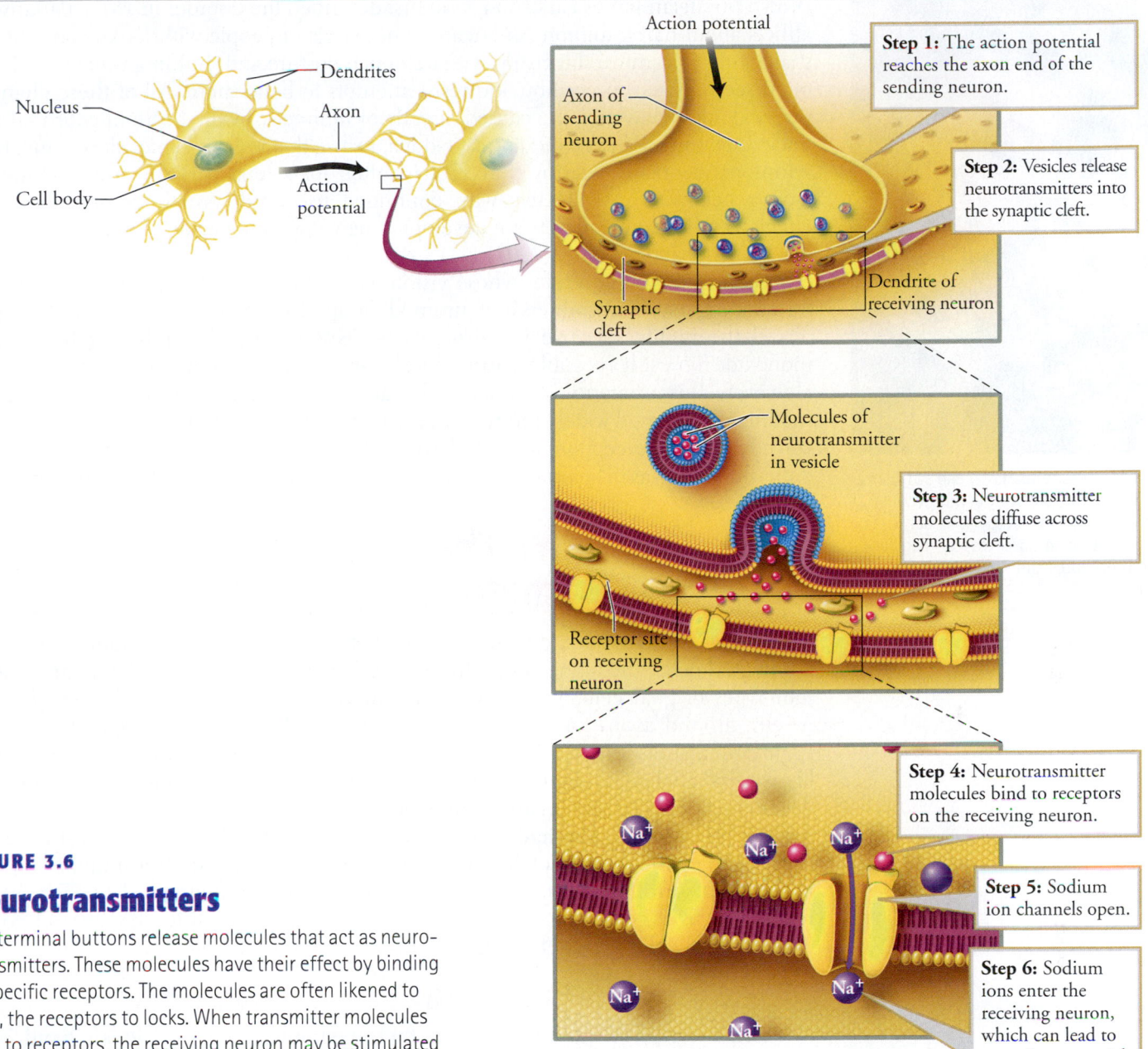

**FIGURE 3.6**

# Neurotransmitters

The terminal buttons release molecules that act as neurotransmitters. These molecules have their effect by binding to specific receptors. The molecules are often likened to keys, the receptors to locks. When transmitter molecules bind to receptors, the receiving neuron may be stimulated or inhibited.

**Image labels:**

Action potential

Nucleus

Dendrites

Axon

Cell body

Action potential

Axon of sending neuron

**Step 1:** The action potential reaches the axon end of the sending neuron.

**Step 2:** Vesicles release neurotransmitters into the synaptic cleft.

Synaptic cleft

Dendrite of receiving neuron

Molecules of neurotransmitter in vesicle

**Step 3:** Neurotransmitter molecules diffuse across synaptic cleft.

Receptor site on receiving neuron

**Step 4:** Neurotransmitter molecules bind to receptors on the receiving neuron.

**Step 5:** Sodium ion channels open.

**Step 6:** Sodium ions enter the receiving neuron, which can lead to an action potential.

Na⁺

---

drugs are **agonists**, which mimic the effects of a neurotransmitter substance by activating a particular type of receptor. Other drugs may actually increase the amount of a neurotransmitter, sometimes by slowing down its reuptake. Depression, for example, is currently treated by several types of drugs that affect neurotransmitters, including **selective serotonin-reuptake inhibitors (SSRIs)**, which block the reuptake of the neurotransmitter serotonin. (Prozac, Zoloft, and Paxil are all SSRIs.) Still other drugs interfere with the effect of a neurotransmitter. Some of these drugs are **antagonists**, which block a particular receptor. (As a memory aid, think of an "antagonist" at a party who is "blocking you" from meeting a charmer across the room.)

The connection between neurotransmitter substances and behavior is also evident in the devastating effects of *Parkinson's disease,* a classic brain disorder. Named after the

**Agonist:** A chemical that mimics the effects of a neurotransmitter by activating a type of receptor.

**Selective serotonin-reuptake inhibitor (SSRI):** A chemical that blocks the reuptake of the neurotransmitter serotonin.

**Antagonist:** A chemical that interferes with the effect of a neurotransmitter (often by blocking a receptor).

Parkinson's disease apparently can strike anyone and can interfere with a wide variety of careers. However, as actor Michael J. Fox showed, at least in some cases, medical or surgical procedures can help keep symptoms in check.

British physician James Parkinson, who first described the disorder in 1817, Parkinson's afflicts about half a million Americans. The hands of people with Parkinson's disease shake; they may move sluggishly, with a stooped posture and shuffling walk; their limbs often seem frozen in position and resist attempts to bend them. All of these changes, physical and behavioral, are caused directly or indirectly by the death of cells that produce dopamine. When patients take L-dopa, a drug that helps produce dopamine, their symptoms decrease (Marini et al., 2003), often for a long period of time. However, L-dopa becomes less effective with continued use (and sometimes produces side-effects), and thus researchers are developing new dopamine agonists to treat this disorder (Barone, 2003; Jenner, 2002).

Could the young soldier whose vision was so strangely disrupted have had malfunctioning neurotransmitters or neuromodulators? Could such a disturbance have produced the highly selective impairments he experienced after inhaling the carbon monoxide fumes? It's possible, if just the right combinations of chemicals were disrupted. However, this scenario is unlikely. Because most neurotransmitters and neuromodulators are used widely throughout the brain, not solely in the parts of the brain involved in visual perception, we would expect their disruption to create more widespread difficulties, such as in hearing, understanding language, walking, and other functions.

# Glial Cells: More Than the Neurons' Helpmates

The average human brain contains about 100 billion neurons, plus about ten times as many **glial cells** (the name comes from the Greek word for "glue"). There are at least four types of glial cells; two of the most important are *Schwann cells*, which wrap myelin around axons for insulation of nerves outside the brain or spinal cord (see Figure 3.7), and *astrocytes*, found in the brain and spinal cord. Researchers have long known that glial cells help neurons to form appropriate connections while the brain is developing during gestation and childhood, and thereafter participate in the "care and feeding" of neurons. The traditional view was that glial cells physically cushion neurons, clean up the remains of dead neurons, dispose of extra neurotransmitters and ions in the fluid surrounding neurons, and provide nutrients to neurons. This view is correct, as far as it goes. But recent research has revealed that this view doesn't go far enough; glial cells are much more than just the neurons' helpmates.

## Neurons and Glia: A Mutually Giving Relationship

Neurons and glial cells influence each other in complex ways. On the one hand, neurons have synapses not just with other neurons, but also with glial cells—and they stimulate glial cells to release specific chemicals. On the other hand, glial cells can directly regulate how strongly one neuron affects another. Astrocytes and Schwann cells surround synapses (in nerves in the body and in the brain, respectively) and alter how much neurotransmitter is released from neurons. In addition, astrocytes can actually release the neurotransmitter glutamate, which directly stimulates neurons (Parpura & Haydon, 2000). Researchers now believe that glial cells might coordinate the activity of vast networks of neurons.

In addition, glial cells can prod neurons to form additional synapses (Pfrieger, 2002). Although neurons can form synapses even in the absence of glial cells, they form about seven times as many when glial cells are present (Ullian et al., 2001). How does this work? You've probably heard that cholesterol is a bad thing, but all generalizations have their limits: It turns out that astrocytes produce a type of cholesterol that stimulates neurons to produce more synapses (Mauch et al., 2001).

**Glial cell:** A type of cell that surrounds neurons, influences the communication among neurons, and generally helps in the "care and feeding" of neurons.

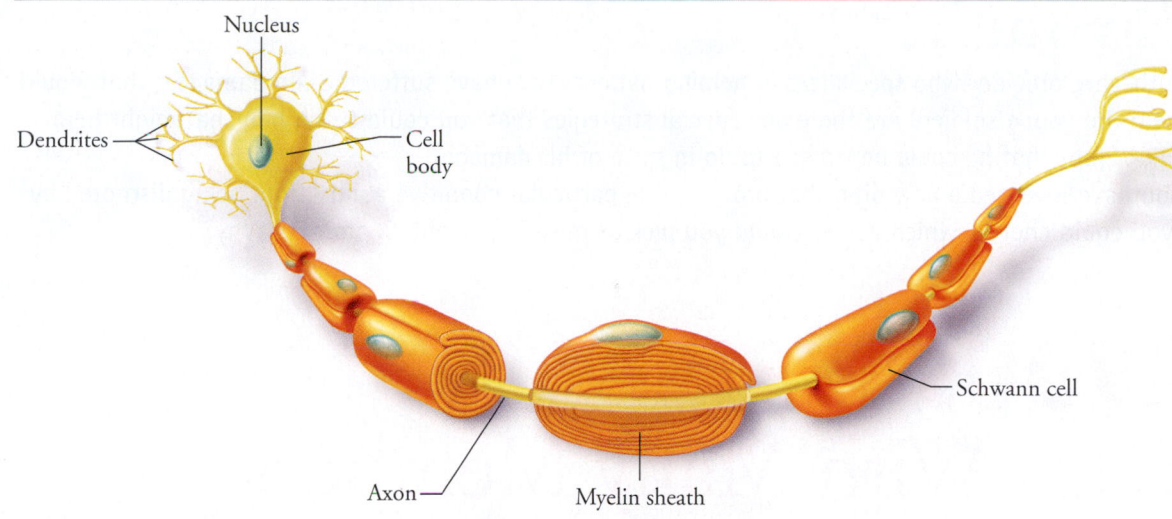

**FIGURE 3.7**

## Schwann Cells

The glial cells called Schwann cells wrap around neurons' axons, insulating them with a sheath of myelin.

Labels: Nucleus, Dendrites, Cell body, Schwann cell, Axon, Myelin sheath

## Glial Networks: Another Way to Think and Feel?

Glial cells do not produce action potentials; you will never hear about a glial cell "firing." Instead, these cells communicate by passing chemicals directly through their walls to adjoining glia or by releasing into brain fluid molecules that affect both neurons and other glia. Chemicals released by one glial cell can induce other glial cells to release chemicals, and so on, "like ripples on a pond" (Fields & Stevens-Graham, 2002). Researchers do not yet understand exactly what these networks do, but they have found that glia are important in a remarkably wide range of brain functions. For example, they play a role in the perception of pain and may act as a bridge between the brain and the immune system (Watkins et al., 2001); they may be important for memory (Lonky, 2003); they may underlie some of the effects of aging on the brain (Blalock et al., 2003); and they may be involved in emotion and its disorders (Harrison, 2002), possibly even in major mental illness (Cotter et al., 2001).

Research on glia is an exciting part of psychology; it promises to deepen our understanding not only of how the brain works, but also of why it may go awry—and how to put it back on track.

# Test Yourself

1. Sensory neurons are to motor neurons as
   a. input is to output.
   b. output is to input.
   c. slow is to fast.
   d. big is to small.
2. A signal moving from one neuron to another travels through the cells' parts in this order:
   a. dendrite, axon, synapse, cell body.
   b. cell body, axon, synapse, dendrite.
   c. dendrite, cell body, synapse, axon.
   d. synapse, axon, dendrite, cell body.
3. When a neuron fires, the action potential involves
   a. movement of ions across the cell membrane.
   b. movement of proteins across the cell membrane.
   c. production of complex sugars.
   d. metabolism of fatty amino acids.

4. Which of the following is *not* true of glial cells?
   a. Glial cells can cause neurons to form additional synapses.
   b. Glial cells do not produce action potentials, but rather release molecules directly into brain fluid and thus affect neurons and other glial cells.
   c. Glial cells affect one and only one neuron at a time.
   d. There are ten times more glial cells than neurons.

# Answers

1.a 2.b 3.a 4.c

NOTE: Once you feel comfortable with the Test Yourself questions in this chapter, visit the book's Web site at www.ablongman.com/kosslyn3e for additional study questions.

# Think It Through!

Say you are a health-care provider who specializes in helping patients who have suffered brain damage. What would you try to do to help the young soldier? Are there any special strategies that you could teach him that might help him? Can you think of jobs that he could be trained to do in spite of his damage?

Imagine that you have invented a new drug that protects one particular cognitive ability from being disrupted by brain damage. If you could choose, which ability would you pick as most important to protect? Why?

# THE NERVOUS SYSTEM:
## An Orchestra With Many Members

Consider some additional problems experienced by the young soldier who was poisoned while taking a shower. When researchers showed him a blue page on which white letters were printed, he thought he was looking at a "beach scene"—the blue was water and the white letters were "people seen on the beach from an airplane." He could visually pick out objects when they were placed in front of him, but only if they were of a similar color and size. His doctors found that he could be trained to name a few everyday objects by sight as children are taught to recognize words by sight on *Sesame Street* without actually reading them, but this training broke down when the color or size of the objects changed. The young man learned to name a red toothbrush as "toothbrush," but he couldn't properly name a green toothbrush, and when he was shown a red pencil, he called it "my toothbrush."

The results of the entire series of tests made it clear that the soldier could see and understand color and size, but not shape. He had *some* sense of shape, though; he didn't call the pencil a "shoe" or a "basketball" but a "toothbrush." To understand what had gone wrong in the soldier's brain, we need to go beyond the essentials of how neurons work and how they affect each other via neurotransmitters and neuromodulators. You are ready to examine how neurons work within different brain structures and how their functioning can break down. To understand the root causes of the soldier's problems, you need to know what the different parts of the nervous system do.

The nervous system has two parts: the peripheral nervous system and the central nervous system. We will start with the simpler peripheral nervous system, which is crucial for getting information into and out of the brain.

## The Peripheral Nervous System: A Moving Story

The **peripheral nervous system (PNS)** links the brain to the organs of the body. As shown in Figure 3.8, the PNS has two parts: the autonomic nervous system and the sensory-somatic nervous system.

## The Autonomic Nervous System

The **autonomic nervous system (ANS)** controls the smooth muscles in the body and some glandular functions. Smooth muscles, so called because they look smooth under

Peripheral nervous system (PNS): The autonomic nervous system and the sensory-somatic nervous system.

Autonomic nervous system (ANS): Controls the smooth muscles in the body, some glandular functions, and many of the body's self-regulating activities, such as digestion and circulation.

FIGURE 3.8

# Major Parts of the Nervous System

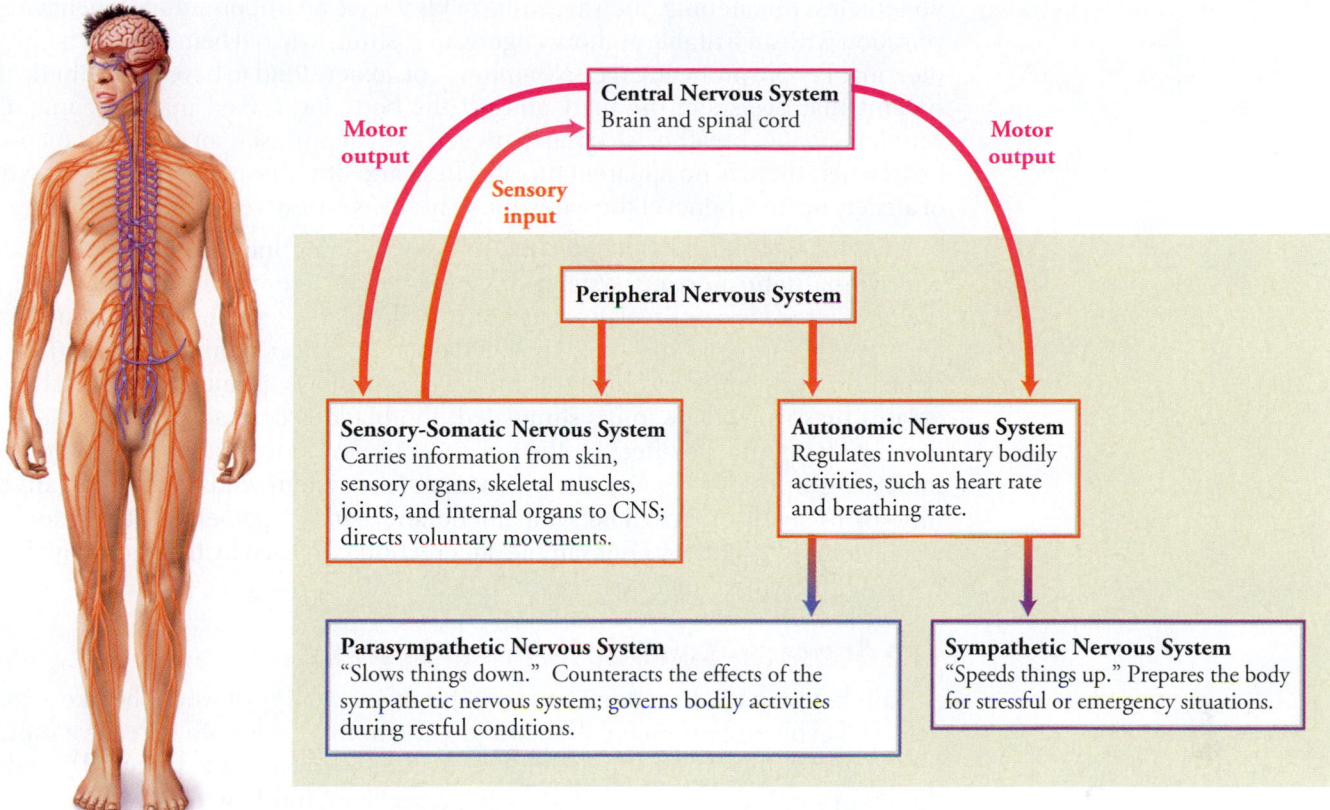

The peripheral nervous system (PNS) comprises the sensory-somatic nervous system (SSNS) and the autonomic nervous system (ANS). The two major branches of the ANS are the sympathetic and parasympathetic nervous systems. In general, the sympathetic nervous system prepares the body to fight or flee, and the parasympathetic dampens down the sympathetic nervous system.

a microscope, are found in the heart, blood vessels, stomach lining, and intestines. Many of the activities that the ANS controls, such as digestion and circulation, are self-regulating and are usually not under conscious control (Goldstein, 2000). The ANS has two branches—which are often referred to as "nervous systems" in their own right—the sympathetic and parasympathetic nervous systems.

**THE SYMPATHETIC BRANCH OF THE ANS**  The **sympathetic nervous system** readies an animal (including you and the authors) to cope with an emergency. This system usually comes into play in response to a threat in the environment, perhaps a near-accident when you are driving in heavy traffic. The sympathetic system speeds up the heart, increases the breathing rate to provide more oxygen, dilates the pupils for greater light sensitivity and thus sharper vision, produces a small amount of sweat (giving your hand a better grip), decreases salivation, inhibits stomach activity, and relaxes the bladder. If your heart is pounding and your palms are sweaty, but your mouth is dry, it's a good bet that your sympathetic system has kicked in. The overall effect of these changes is to prepare your body to react—to fight or to flee. More oxygen flows into your muscles, your vision is improved, and the rest of your body is ready to support physical exertion.

Sympathetic nervous system: Part of the ANS that readies an animal to fight or to flee by speeding up the heart, increasing breathing rate to deliver more oxygen, dilating the pupils, producing sweat, decreasing salivation, inhibiting activity in the stomach, and relaxing the bladder.

Fight-or-flight situations are not the only conditions that activate the sympathetic nervous system. This system also operates in circumstances that may be less extreme but nonetheless threatening, such as getting ready to give an important speech, having a conversation with an irritable authority figure, or rushing to avoid being late for an important meeting. People prone to excessive amounts of anxiety tend to have sympathetic nervous systems that overshoot the mark and get the body too revved up. They might hyperventilate (that is, breathe in too much oxygen), sweat profusely, or experience a pounding heart when there is no apparent threat. These and other unpleasant physical symptoms of anxiety occur whenever the sympathetic nervous system responds too strongly.

**THE PARASYMPATHETIC BRANCH OF THE ANS**   The other branch of the ANS is called the **parasympathetic nervous system**; this system lies, figuratively, "next to" the sympathetic system (*para* is Greek for "next to" or "alongside") and tends to counteract its effects (see Figure 3.8). The sympathetic system speeds things up, and the parasympathetic system slows them down. Heart rate slows, pupils contract, salivation increases massively, digestion is stimulated, the bladder contracts. Whereas the sympathetic system tends to affect all the organs at the same time and can be thought of as increasing arousal in general, the parasympathetic system tends to affect organs one at a time or in small groups. The sympathetic and parasympathetic systems don't always work against each other. For example, an erection is caused by the parasympathetic system, but the sympathetic system controls ejaculation.

## The Sensory–Somatic Nervous System

A brain living in a vat wouldn't be of much use to anyone—it would be like a computer with no keyboard or monitor. To do its job, the brain needs both to receive inputs from the body and the outside world and to be able to act on these inputs. To understand the brain's job, then, you must see what it receives and how it in turn can move the body. The other part of the PNS is the **sensory-somatic nervous system (SSNS)**. This system includes the input–output connections themselves: neurons in our sensory organs (such as the eyes and ears) that convey information to the brain, as well as neurons that trigger muscles and glands.

**CRANIAL NERVES**   The SSNS includes the 12 *cranial nerves*, so named because they connect to the brain through holes in the cranium, the part of the skull that encloses the brain. These nerves control specific muscles, and also receive information from sense organs. Damage to a cranial nerve can cut off key inputs or outputs from the brain. If you weren't wearing a seat belt in an automobile accident, for example, your head might slam into the steering wheel. This could cause your brain to slosh forward and scrape along the underside of your skull. The scraping could disrupt the functioning of your olfactory nerves, and thus impair your ability to smell. This may not sound like a severe problem, but as you will see in the following chapter, smell plays a major role in taste—and food would never taste the same again.

**THE SKELETAL SYSTEM**   The SSNS also includes the **skeletal system**, which consists of nerves that are attached to muscles that can be triggered voluntarily; these muscles are also known as striated muscles because under a microscope they appear "striated," or striped. If you clench your fist and "make a muscle," you are using this system.

## The Central Nervous System: Reflex and Reflection

The largest conduit for information going to and from the brain is the **spinal cord**, the flexible rope of nerves that runs inside the backbone, or *spinal column*. In fact, so intimately connected is the spinal cord to the brain that the two together are called the **central nervous system (CNS)**. At each of 31 places, spinal nerves emerge from the spinal cord in pairs, one on the left and one on the right. Through these nerves, the spinal cord plays a key role in sending the brain's commands to the body (along the front side of the cord) and, in turn, allowing the brain to register information about the state of the body (along the rear side of the cord). The spinal cord also allows us, through our sense of touch, to gain information about the world.

The spinal cord isn't simply a set of cables that relays commands and information between brain and body. The spinal cord itself can initiate some aspects of our behavior, such as reflexes. A **reflex** is an automatic response to an event, an action that does not require thought. Even a simple reflex requires hundreds of neurons. How do reflexes work? When sensory neurons in the skin detect a sharp thorn, for example, they send signals that stimulate sensory neurons in the spinal cord. These neurons in turn are connected to interneurons in the spinal cord, as shown in Figure 3.9. When you jerk away from something that pricks you, interneurons have sent signals to motor neurons, which then cause the muscles to jerk, pulling your finger away from the source of pain. This arrangement allows you to respond immediately, bypassing the brain—it wouldn't be efficient or safe to have to think through what to do every time you encountered a noxious stimulus.

If the point of reflexes is to get things done in a hurry, why aren't the sensory neurons directly connected to motor neurons? Why the intermediary? Because interneurons provide a particular benefit: They allow the brain to send signals to *prevent* a reflex response. Perhaps you are handing a beautiful red rose to a good friend as a gift and accidentally prick your finger. Instead of flinging the rose away, you grit your teeth and continue to hold it. You are able to do this because the part of your brain that is involved in formulating goals and intentions knows not to flub this gesture and sends a signal to the interneurons to stop the motor neurons from firing.

## The Visible Brain: Lobes and Landmarks

To understand the range of human abilities, you need to turn to the other part of the central nervous system, the brain itself. Imagine that you could see through someone's hair and scalp, even through the skull itself. The first thing you would see under the skull are the **meninges**, three protective layered membranes that cover the brain (*meningitis* is an inflammation of these membranes). Under this lies a network of blood vessels on the surface of the brain itself. Viewing the brain from above—looking down through the top of the head—you can see that the brain is divided into two halves, left and right, separated by a deep fissure down the middle. Each half-brain is called a **cerebral hemisphere** (*cerebrum* is Latin for "brain") because each is shaped roughly like half a sphere. Curiously, each hemisphere receives information from, and controls the muscles of, the opposite side of the body. For example, if you are right-handed, your left hemisphere controls your hand as you write.

Each hemisphere is divided into four major parts, or **lobes**: the *occipital* lobe, at the back of the brain; the *temporal* lobe, which lies below the temples, in front of the ears, where sideburns begin to grow down; the *parietal* lobe, in the upper rear portion of the brain, above the occipital lobe; and the *frontal* lobe, behind the forehead (see Figure 3.10, p. 92; we shall discuss the functions of the cortex covering the lobes in the following section). The two halves of the brain are connected by the **corpus callosum**, which contains somewhere between 250 and 300 million nerve

**FIGURE 3.9**   **Reflexes**

**Step 1**: A stimulus initiates a pain sensation.

**Step 2**: Sensory messages are carried to the spinal cord by sensory neurons.

**Step 3**: Interneurons integrate information from sensory neurons and stimulate the appropriate motor neurons.

**Step 4**: Motor neurons stimulate the appropriate muscles.

**Step 5**: Leg muscles contract, causing them to lift the foot off the glass.

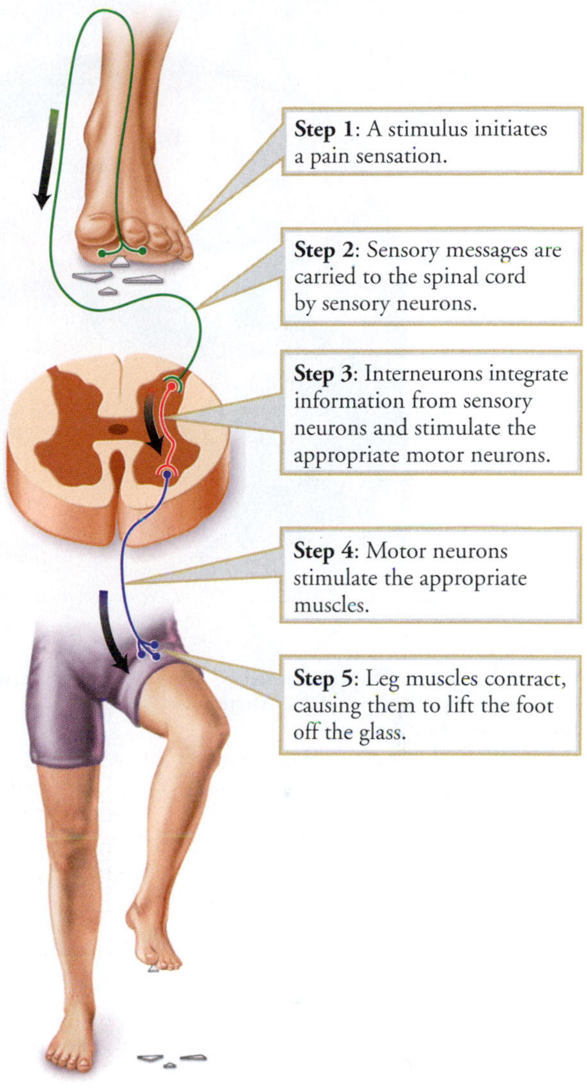

A simple reflex circuit allows the spinal cord to produce reflexive behavior without involving the brain. However, in some circumstances the brain can inhibit reflexes by stimulating interneurons.

Central nervous system (CNS): The spinal cord and the brain.

Reflex: An automatic response to an event.

Meninges: Membranes that cover the brain.

Cerebral hemisphere: A left or right half-brain, shaped roughly like half a sphere.

Lobes: The four major parts of each cerebral hemisphere—occipital, temporal, parietal, and frontal.

Corpus callosum: The large band of nerve fibers that connects the two halves of the brain.

FIGURE 3.10 **The Lobes of the Brain**

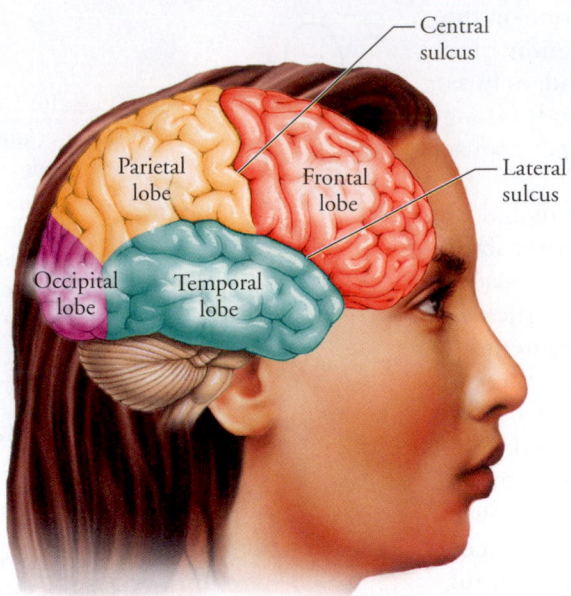

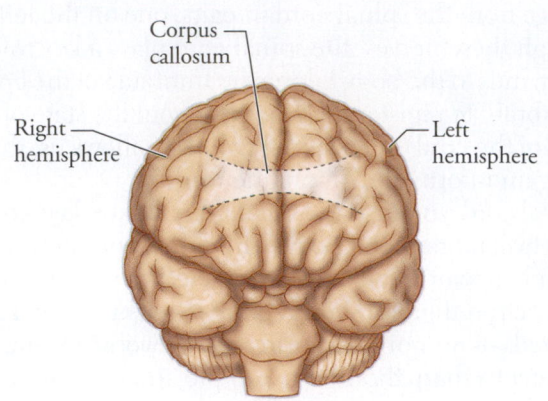

**FRONTAL VIEW**

The brain is divided into four major lobes—occipital, temporal, parietal, and frontal. These lobes are named after the bones that cover them. The same major sulci (creases) and gyri (bulges) are evident on most brains.

---

**Cerebral cortex:** The convoluted pinkish-gray outer layer of the brain, where most mental processes take place.

**Sulcus:** A crease in the cerebral cortex.

**Gyrus:** A bulge between sulci in the cerebral cortex.

**Ventricle:** A hollow area in the center of the brain that stores fluid.

**Subcortical structures:** Parts of the brain located under the cerebral cortex and beneath the ventricles.

Most of your brain is water; the average brain weighs about 3 pounds, but if the water were removed, it would weigh only 10 ounces. This material (which includes proteins and fats, as well as various types of ions) comprises the parts of the neurons, glial cells, and everything else that gives the brain a structure.

fibers (some other smaller connections exist between the two halves of the brain, but they are less important).

Now, peer deeper. Immediately under the network of blood vessels on the surface of the brain is the convoluted, pinkish-gray outer layer of the brain itself: This is the **cerebral cortex** (*cortex* means "rind" or "shell" in Latin). This is where most of the brain's mental processes take place. Although the cerebral cortex is only about 2 millimeters thick, it is brimming with the cell bodies of neurons, giving the cortex its characteristic color and its nickname, "gray matter." Looking directly at the surface of the brain, you can see that the cortex has many creases and bulges, as shown in Figure 3.10. The creases are called **sulci** (the singular is *sulcus*), and the areas that bulge up between the sulci are the **gyri** (singular, *gyrus*). The cortex, so vital to our functioning, is crumpled up so that more of it can be stuffed into the skull.

Now peel back the cortex and look beneath it. Here you see lots of white fibers packed together. This material is actually myelinated axons, mostly from the neurons in the cortex; it is white because that is the color of the fatty white myelin insulation that surrounds the axons, and, not surprisingly, these fibers are called "white matter." Below the white matter, in the very center of the brain, are hollow areas, called **ventricles**, where fluid is stored (the same fluid surrounds the spinal cord, within the core of the spinal column). On either side and beneath the ventricles are the **subcortical** ("under the cortex") **structures** of the inner brain; these contain gray matter and are very similar to structures in the brains of many nonhuman animals.

## Structure and Function: No Dotted Lines

You've probably seen porcelain models like the one appearing on the next page. These beguiling heads show the presumed locations of mental faculties, as identified by the *phrenologists* (led in the late 18th century by the Austrian anatomist Franz Joseph Gall, later joined by J. G. Spurzheim). The phrenologists practiced their profession by measuring the sizes of bumps on the head, which led them to infer the relative sizes of the underlying brain areas—and from there, to diagnose the relative strengths and weaknesses of the faculties presumably housed in those areas. The phrenologists were misguided in many ways; for example, bumps on the skull do not reflect underlying brain size, and the characteristics that they localized to single brain areas (such as secretiveness, hope, and parental love) in fact arise from the joint action of many brain areas working together. Nevertheless, the phrenologists had two important insights: First, they focused on the outer surface of the brain, whereas their predecessors had incorrectly focused on the interior regions of the brain. Second, they realized that many parts of the brain have distinct specializations.

So far we've considered the structure, or physical makeup, of the brain. But what do the various parts of the brain do? It's one thing to say what parts of the brain don't do (produce hope, for example), but quite another to figure out what they do in fact accomplish. Let's first consider an analogy, a bike: You can point to its parts and discuss their physical structures (for example, a chain connects a metal gear to the back wheel), and you can discuss how the parts work (what the chain does). So too with the brain: You can point to and discuss various physical parts of the brain, and you can describe how parts of the brain function—both individually and working together.

Already, though, there is a problem. When it comes to its functioning, the brain isn't like the diagram of a cow in a butcher's shop; there are no dotted lines to show the different cuts of beef, the distinct regions that do different things. But in spite of the missing dotted lines, there are physical hints we can use to identify the brain's functional parts. Think of two stone walls; from a distance they may look the same—same height, same color. But as you move up close, you can see that they are different, both because they are made up of different kinds of stones and because the stones are arranged differently. Similarly, under the microscope, parts of the brain appear to be different because they contain different types of neurons and these cells are organized differently. Brain areas that differ in terms of the arrangement of their neurons often turn out to have distinct functions.

In addition, normal human brains do have certain major physical landmarks that help us to recognize parts that carry out different functions. Particular sulci and gyri, the creases and bulges in the cerebral cortex, for example, consist of groups of neurons with well-defined functions. Unlike the creases and bulges that occur randomly when you crumple up a sheet of paper, some sulci and gyri occur for a reason. There are major connections between areas that tend to work together, and as the brain develops and the cortex expands, these firm connections force the cortex to fold in certain ways (Van Essen, 1997).

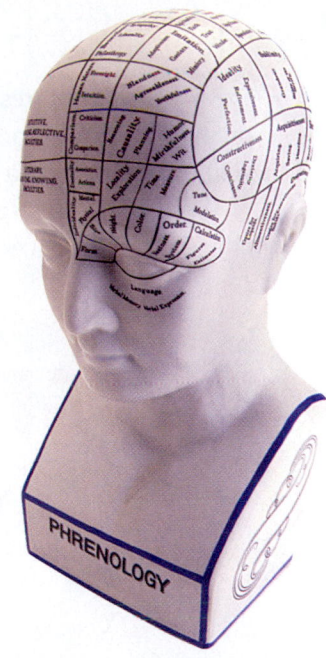

The phrenologists believed that particular faculties were housed in specific brain areas, as shown here. Although they were incorrect about the faculties, the idea that different parts of the brain are specialized for different functions is correct.

# Test Yourself

1. As you run from a bear, your _____ nervous system is active; when (if) you finally stop and rest, your _____ nervous system becomes active.
   a. central; peripheral
   b. sympathetic; parasympathetic
   c. peripheral; sympathetic
   d. parasympathetic; central
2. The cranial nerves are so named because they
   a. connect to the brain through holes in the skull.
   b. convey information only to the cranium.
   c. register input only from sensory organs on the head (eyes, ears, nose, etc.).
   d. do all of the above.

3. Reflexes are automatic responses to certain events. However, even though they are automatic, they can often be controlled. Such control depends crucially on
   a. sensory neurons.       c. motor neurons.
   b. interneurons.          d. noxious stimuli.
4. The creases on the surface of the brain are the _____, and the areas that bulge up between them are the _____.
   a. ventricles; lobes      c. gyri; sulci
   b. lobes; ventricles      d. sulci; gyri

## Answers

1. b 2. a 3. b 4. d

The fight-or-flight response was no doubt useful to our ancestors. Is it necessarily as useful to us today? Do you think it would be a good idea if we could voluntarily dampen down the autonomic nervous system? Do you think it would be a good idea if we could voluntarily amplify its activity, at least in selected situations?

If you could choose some thoughts or feelings to be reflexive responses to specific stimuli, what would they be and why?

# SPOTLIGHT ON THE BRAIN:
## How It Divides and Conquers

Testing revealed that the soldier did not have a problem with his PNS. His cranial nerves all functioned properly, and the impulses delivered by his eyes were sent on to his brain. His problem was more subtle and could be diagnosed only by considering the specific jobs performed by different parts of the brain. Even an ability such as vision, which intuitively might seem to be a single thing, is performed by a set of brain structures, not a single structure. The brain is a master at the strategy of divide-and-conquer; it takes all complex activities and breaks them into a set of relatively simple tasks, and a different brain structure usually tackles each task. The soldier's problem reflected damage to only some of the parts of the brain, which disrupted only some of the overall processing required to identify objects by sight. To understand what went wrong after his accident, we need to delve into the brain in more detail, marveling at how it divides and conquers the challenges of daily life.

## The Cerebral Cortex: The Seat of the Mind

The cortex of each of the four lobes of the brain serves different functions, but always remember that the lobes do not function in isolation; they usually work in concert with one another.

### Occipital Lobes: Looking Good

The **occipital lobes** are concerned entirely with different aspects of vision, and most of the fibers from the eyes lead to these lobes. (Brewer et al., 2002; Simos, 2001). If somebody were to hit you in the back of the head with a brick (an experiment we do not recommend), the "stars" you would likely see would appear because of the impact on this area. The occipital lobes contain many separate areas that work together to specify visual properties such as shape, color, and motion. Damage to these lobes results in partial or complete blindness. Because each half of the brain receives sensory information from the opposite side, if a surgeon has to remove the left occipital lobe (perhaps to take out a brain tumor), the patient will not be able to see things to his or her right side when looking ahead.

Because some of the neurons in the occipital cortex are highly active, they require more oxygen than other neurons—which makes them particularly vulnerable to poisoning by carbon monoxide. Carbon monoxide displaces oxygen but cannot be used in metabolism; thus, if someone breathes enough carbon monoxide, neurons in the oc-

**Occipital lobe:** The brain lobe at the back of the head; concerned entirely with different aspects of vision.

cipital lobe are suffocated to death. However, not all the neurons typically die, and thus the unfortunate person is not completely blind but rather has highly degraded vision. Our young soldier probably suffered damage to the occipital lobes, perhaps in addition to injury to other parts of the brain. Such damage often affects visual perception, making the entire world seem fuzzy and making it difficult to organize information. Still, this probably does not sufficiently explain all of the soldier's vision problems; if this were all there was to it, why would he confuse white letters with sunbathers on the beach?

## Temporal Lobes: Up to Their Ears in Work

The **temporal lobes**, which lie in front of the ears and roughly where sideburns start, play a key role in processing sound, entering new information into memory, storing visual memories, and comprehending language (Hart et al., 2003; Sekiyama et al., 2003; Witter et al., 2002). The soldier may have had damage in either one or both temporal lobes, or in the connections from the occipital lobes to the temporal lobes. If the connections were damaged, only a small amount of information might reach the part of the temporal lobes where visual memories of shapes are stored and compared to visual input (allowing you to recognize stimuli). This diagnosis would go a long way toward explaining his problem. For example, in order to see a letter, he would have to look at one segment at a time (a vertical line, then a curved line, and so on), which isn't good enough to recognize the shape of a letter as whole. The world might look to the soldier like the images in Figure 3.11.

**FIGURE 3.11** **Shattered Vision**

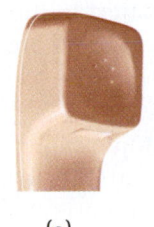 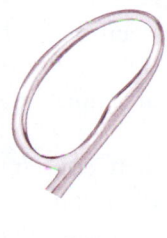  

(a)  (b)  (c)  (d)

Answers: a. telephone receiver b. scissors handle c. table leg d. baseball hat

Some forms of brain damage may lead the victims to be aware of only small fragments of objects at a time, as shown here. If all you were aware of were fragments of an object, how easily do you think you could identify it? To get a sense of what such a deficit would be like, try to identify these common objects when all you have to go on are individual parts.

## Parietal Lobes: Inner Space

When you recall where you left your keys, how to drive to a friend's house, or what's over your left shoulder, your **parietal lobes** are at work (Siegel et al., 2003). Right now, your parietal lobes are playing a role in allowing you to define the distance between your face and the book and to shift attention to each of these words; they are even helping control your eye movements. The parietal lobes are also involved when you do arithmetic. Albert Einstein (1945) claimed that he reasoned by imagining objects in space, which is interesting in light of the fact that his parietal lobes were found to be about 15% larger than normal (Witelson et al., 1999). His unusual parietal lobes may have contributed to his genius.

Part of each parietal lobe, right behind the central sulcus (see Figure 3.12, p. 96), is the **somatosensory strip**. This area registers sensation on your body. In fact, sensations from each part of your body are registered in a specific section of this strip of

**Temporal lobe:** The brain lobe under the temples, in front of the ears, where sideburns begin to grow down; among its many functions are visual memory and hearing.

**Parietal lobe:** The brain lobe across the top part of the brain behind the ears, which is involved in registering spatial location, attention, and motor control.

**Somatosensory strip:** The brain area, located immediately behind the central sulcus, that registers sensation on the body and is organized by body part.

FIGURE 3.12

# The Organization of the Somatosensory Strip

The somatosensory strip is organized so that different parts of the body are registered by adjacent portions of cortex; the size of the body part indicates the amount of brain tissue dedicated to that part.

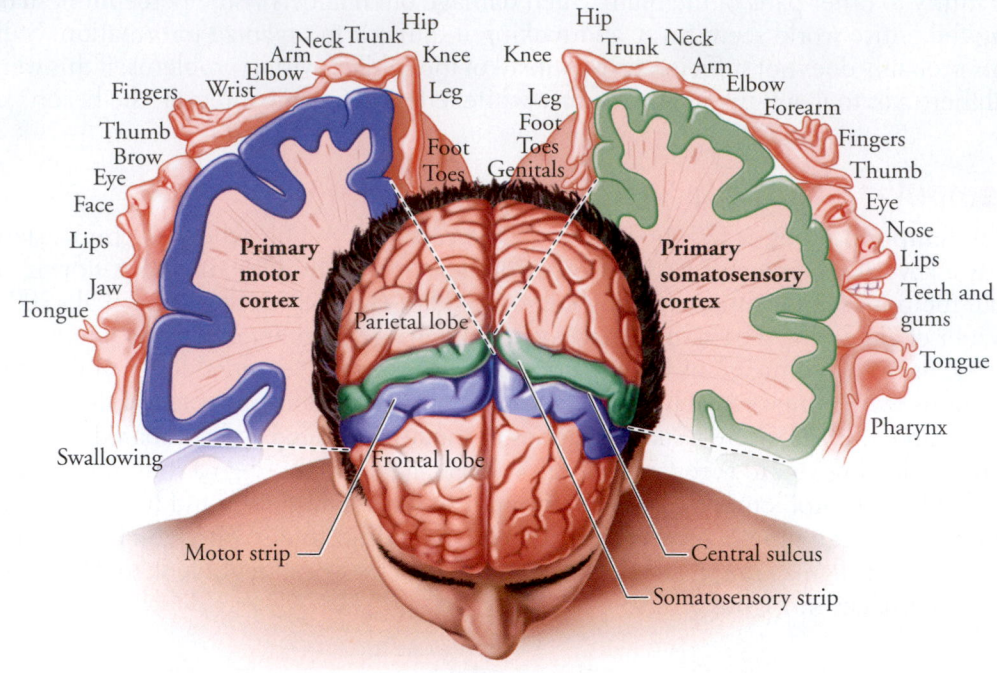

cortex. Tickling your toes, for example, activates neurons in the cortex next to the area devoted to stimulation from your ankle, as you can see in Figure 3.12. Larger areas of the cortex correspond to areas of the body that are more sensitive (notice the amount of space devoted to lips and hands).

The parietal lobes also play a role in consciousness, a topic explored in depth in Chapter 5. Patients who suffer damage to a parietal lobe may exhibit a curious deficit known as *unilateral visual neglect*. They aren't blind, but they typically ignore (that is, they "neglect") everything on the side opposite that of the damage—if the damage is in the right parietal lobe, they ignore everything on their left side (see Figure 3.13). When they shave, for instance, they shave only half the face; when they dress, they put clothes on only half the body (pulling their shirt over only one arm, pants over only one leg). Many of these patients also have *anosognosia*, a lack of awareness that anything is wrong. Indeed, in one case, a doctor showed such a patient her neglected arm and asked her what it was. The patient replied that the doctor had a third arm; she thought that her own arm was part of the doctor's body (Gerstmann, 1942, p. 892); similar cases are not uncommon (Aglioti et al., 1996; Yamadori, 1997).

FIGURE 3.13

# Unilateral Visual Neglect

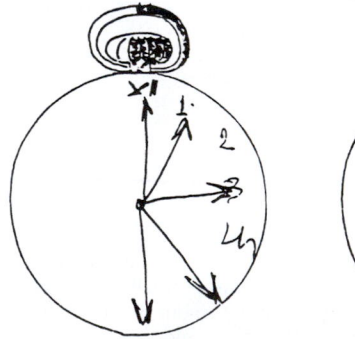 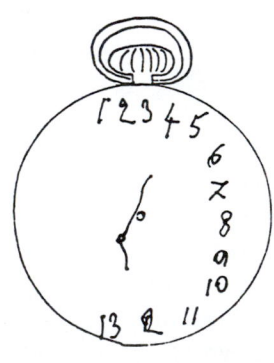

When patients who suffered from left-sided unilateral visual neglect are asked to draw a clock, they ignore the left side and try to cram all the numbers into the side to which they pay attention. Here are drawings from two such patients.

## Frontal Lobes: Leaders of the Pack

Probably the most dramatic difference between the appearance of a human brain and a monkey brain is how much the human brain bulges out in front. The size and development of the **frontal lobes**, in conjunction with their plentiful connections to other areas, are features of the brain that make us uniquely human (Goldberg, 2001). The frontal lobes are critically involved in speech, the search for specific memories, reasoning (including the use of memory in reasoning), and emotions. These crucial lobes also contain the **motor strip** (also called the *primary motor cortex*), which is located in the gyrus immediately in front of the central sulcus. The motor strip controls fine movements and, just like the somatosensory strip, is organized in terms of parts of the body. Relatively large areas of this strip of cortex are dedicated to those parts of the body that we control with precision, such as the hands and mouth.

Hints about the functions of the frontal lobes, as well as other parts of the brain, have emerged from studies of patients with brain damage. Phineas Gage, the foreman of a gang of workers building a railroad in Vermont late in the 19th century, is perhaps the most famous case of a patient with damage to the frontal lobes. Gage's unfortunate loss was psychology's gain, as researchers were able to observe the consequences of damage to this vital area of the brain. The story began when Gage became distracted as he was packing blasting powder into a hole in a rock. When the metal bar he was using to pack in the powder accidentally hit the rock, it created a spark, which set off the powder. The metal bar, like a spear shot from a cannon, went right through the front part of his head, flew high in the air, and landed about 30 meters behind him. Miraculously, Gage lived, but he was a changed man. Previously, he had been responsible and organized; he now led a disorderly life. He couldn't stick to any decision; he had little self-control, and his formerly decent language became laced with profanity (Macmillan, 1986, 1992). Like Phineas Gage, other people with damage to the frontal regions of the brain have difficulty reasoning, may have trouble controlling their emotions and may have changed personalities.

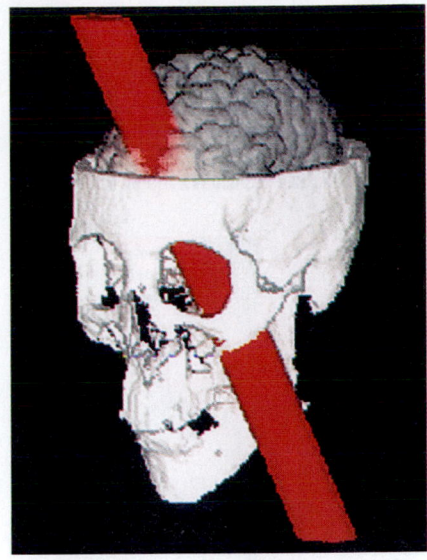

A computer-reconstructed picture of the path taken by the metal bar as it passed through Phineas Gage's skull.

# The Dual Brain: Thinking With Both Barrels

The cortices of the two cerebral hemispheres, left and right, play distinct roles in cognition. What do the hemispheres do differently?

## Split-Brain Research: A Deep Disconnect

The most compelling evidence to date that the two half-brains perform distinct functions has come from looking at the effects of severing the connection between the two hemispheres. When this is done, neuronal impulses no longer pass from one hemisphere to the other. Patients who have undergone this surgery are called **split-brain patients** (Zaidel & Iacoboni, 2003). Why would such drastic surgery be performed? This procedure has been used to help patients with severe, otherwise untreatable epilepsy. *Epilepsy* is a disease that causes massive uncontrolled neuronal firing in parts of the brain, leading to bodily convulsions; in severe form, it prevents sufferers from leading a normal life. When the epilepsy engages the entire brain and is so severe that drugs cannot control it, surgeons may cut the corpus callosum. This operation prevents the spasm that originates in one hemisphere from reaching the other hemisphere, and thus the whole brain does not become involved in the convulsions—and their severity is thereby lessened.

Although it is easy to see how cutting the corpus callosum would decrease the severity of epileptic convulsions, the full effects of this procedure on mental processes cannot be understood without discussing vision. As shown in Figure 3.14 (p. 98), the left half of each eye is connected directly to the left hemisphere, but not to the right hemisphere; similarly, the right half of each eye is connected directly, and only, to the right hemisphere. (Note, it's not that the left eye is connected only to the left hemisphere, and the right only to the right.) Thus, if you stare straight ahead, objects to the left are seen first by the right brain, and those to the right are

**Frontal lobe:** The brain lobe located behind the forehead; the seat of planning, memory search, motor control, and reasoning, as well as numerous other functions.

**Motor strip:** The brain area, located immediately in front of the central sulcus, that controls fine movements and is organized by body part; also called *primary motor cortex.*

**Split-brain patient:** A person whose corpus callosum has been severed for medical reasons, so that neuronal impulses no longer pass from one hemisphere to the other.

FIGURE 3.14

## The Eyes, Optic Nerves, and Cerebral Hemispheres

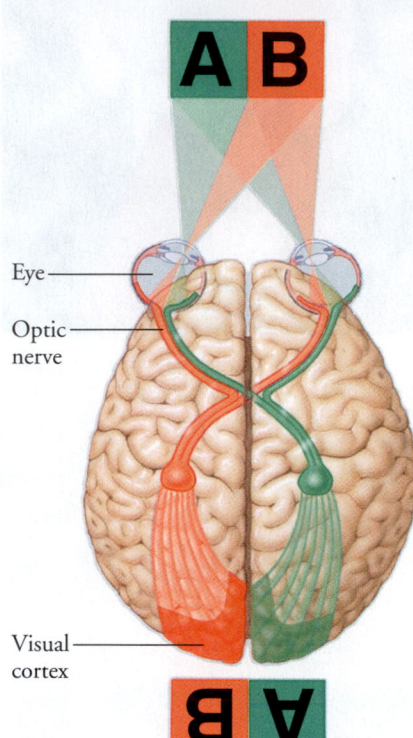

The inside, rearmost parts of the eyes are actually parts of the brain pushed forward during development; the left half of each eye is connected only to the left cerebral hemisphere, whereas the right half of each eye is connected only to the right cerebral hemisphere.

seen first by the left brain. If the corpus callosum is cut, the input stays in the hemisphere that receives the information; in normal people, it also crosses over to the other hemisphere.

# UNDERSTANDING RESEARCH

## The Hemispheric Interpreter

What are the practical effects of the division of the brain into two hemispheres? Gazzaniga and LeDoux (1979) reported a classic study of a split-brain patient, illustrated in Figure 3.15.

**QUESTION:** Does the left hemisphere construct stories to "fill in gaps" in its knowledge?

**ALTERNATIVES:** (1) The left hemisphere constructs stories to fill in the gaps in its knowledge; (2) the left hemisphere does not construct stories to fill in the gaps in its knowledge.

**LOGIC:** If the left hemisphere, which usually controls speech, makes up stories, then when a split-brain patient is asked about choices made by the right hemisphere (to which the left hemisphere is not privy because the hemispheres have been surgically disconnected), the patient should try to incorporate these choices into an interpretation consistent with what the left hemisphere knows.

**METHOD:** When researchers ask a split-brain patient to stare directly ahead and then present pictures or words to the patient's left or right side (fast enough so that the participant can't move his or her eyes to look directly at them), the stimulus will be directed into a single cerebral hemisphere. Gazzaniga and LeDoux presented a picture of a snow scene to the right hemisphere and, at the same time, a picture of a chicken's claw to the left hemisphere. The patient was then shown several other pictures and asked to choose which of them was implied by the stimulus. The patient used his right hand (controlled by the left hemisphere) to select a picture of a chicken and his left hand (controlled by the right hemisphere) to select a picture of a shovel. The investigators then asked the patient what he had seen and why he had made the selections.

**RESULTS:** The patient reported: "I saw a claw and I picked a chicken." Because the left hemisphere controls almost all of speech, it described what the left hemisphere saw. The patient continued: "And you have to clean out the chicken shed with a shovel." The left hemisphere did not actually know that the right hemisphere had seen a snow scene, so it made up a story.

**INFERENCES:** The left hemisphere, in right-handed people (and in most left-handed people), not only controls most aspects of language but also plays a crucial role in interpreting the world, in making up stories, and in many forms of reasoning (Gazzaniga, 1995; LeDoux et al., 1977).

## THINK CRITICALLY!

What about the rest of us, who don't have split brains? Do these results necessarily apply to us? We are all human, but could the disease that eventually required the surgery also have altered how the brain functions in these patients? Or could the brain function differently after the two sides were separated? Does it make sense that all reasoning would rely on information in only one half of the brain? If you were designing a brain, why might you (or might not you) design the separate halves to have separate functions?

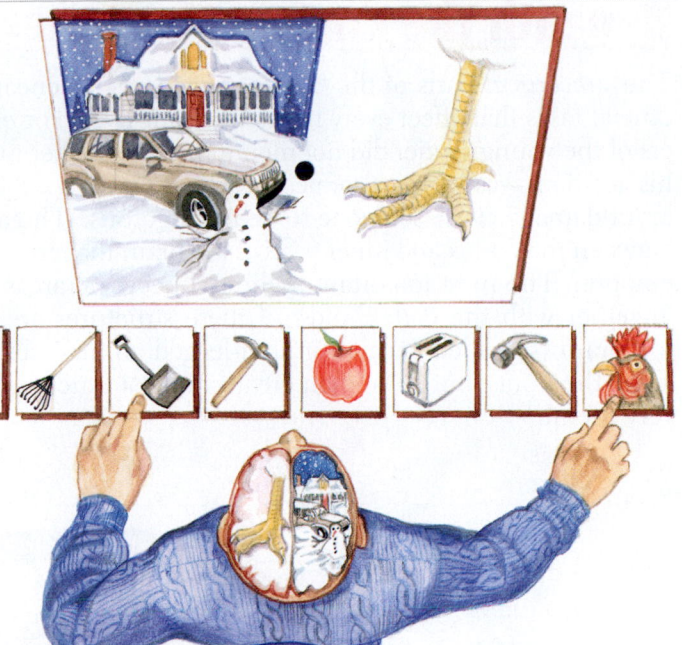

**FIGURE 3.15**

## Gazzaniga and LeDoux Experiment

The right hemisphere of split-brain patients is capable of understanding and responding to simple stimuli, but not speaking about them. Thus, the left hemisphere will sometimes make up stories to explain actions controlled by the right hemisphere.

## Hemispheric Specialization: Not Just for the Deeply Disconnected

The methods used to study split-brain patients can also be used to study brain function in people whose corpus callosum is intact. In such people, information sent first to one hemisphere moves quickly to the other—but this takes a measurable amount of time, and it is possible that the information is of slightly poorer quality after it has crossed to the other hemisphere (Springer & Deutsch, 1994). Normal participants will make a judgment faster if information is delivered initially to the hemisphere that is better at making that kind of judgment (Hellige, 1993; Hellige & Sergent, 1986; Hugdahl & Davidson, 2003).

It's often said that the left brain is analytical and verbal, whereas the right brain is intuitive and perceptual. In fact, these generalizations must be made with caution. For example, the left brain is actually better than the right at some types of perception (such as determining whether one object is above or below another; Hellige & Michimata, 1989; Kosslyn et al., 1989; Laeng et al., 2003), and the right brain is better than the left at some aspects of language (such as making the pitch of the voice rise at the end of a question or understanding humor; Bihrle et al., 1986; Brownell et al., 1984; Ellis & Young, 1987). Moreover, the abilities of the two hemispheres often differ only in degree, not in kind (Hellige, 1993; Hugdahl & Davidson, 2003). A major exception to this generalization is language. As you will see in Chapter 8, many aspects of language are carried out by a single hemisphere, usually the left.

The young soldier with difficulties in visual recognition could have suffered a functional deficit in his right hemisphere that prevented him from being able to see the overall shapes of objects. The right temporal lobe, in particular, appears to play a key role in recognizing overall shapes (Ivry & Robertson, 1998). After such damage, he would have had to rely on his left hemisphere, which tends to register details only, not overall shape.

# Beneath the Cortex: The Inner Brain

The *subcortical* parts of the brain, situated deep beneath the cortex, carry out many crucial tasks that affect every moment of our lives. For example, although the examiners of the young soldier did not mention it, the soldier probably became lethargic after his accident—as is typical of people who have suffered brain damage. But why would brain damage cause someone to be less vigorous? The answer lies in the connections between the cortex and inner parts of the brain that are concerned with motivation and emotion. The most important of these subcortical areas are illustrated in Figure 3.16. Together with the cortex, most of these structures are considered to be part of the **forebrain** (so called because in four-legged animals such as cats and rats, these areas are at the front); but given their great variety of function, this traditional category is not very useful.

**FIGURE 3.16**

## Key Subcortical Brain Areas

Many of the parts of the brain needed for day-to-day living are located beneath the cortex, such as those illustrated here.

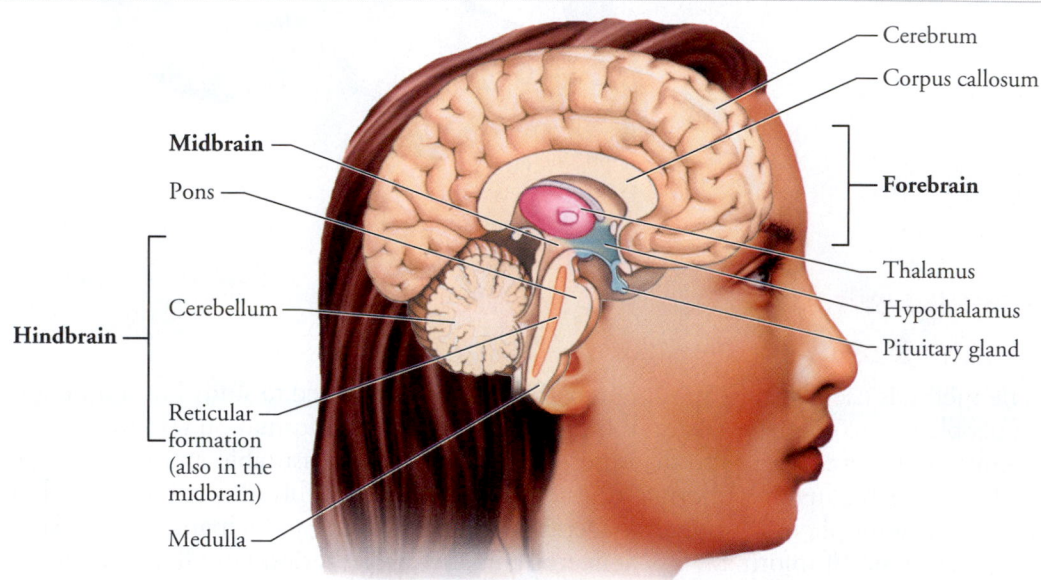

## Thalamus: Crossroads of the Brain

The **thalamus** is often compared with a switching center but could also be likened to an airline hub where planes converge and then take off for far-flung destinations. The sensory systems, such as vision and hearing, and the motor systems that control muscles have neural connections to the thalamus, which routes their signals to other parts of the brain. The intricate connections of the thalamus appear to explain a puzzling phenomenon reported by patients who have had a limb amputated. These people sometimes have the sensation that the limb is still there; they feel a *phantom limb*. K. D. Davis and her colleagues (1998) studied such patients and found that mild electrical stimulation of the thalamus produced sensations that seemed to come from the missing limb. Moreover, phantom limb sensations can be painful, and mild electrical stimulation of the thalamus has been found to relieve the pain.

The thalamus is also involved in attention; as a matter of fact, at this very second, your thalamus is allowing you to fix your attention on each word you read. The thalamus is also involved in sleep control. The thalamus plays such a critical role in daily

**Forebrain:** The cortex, thalamus, limbic system, and basal ganglia.

**Thalamus:** A subcortical structure that receives inputs from sensory and motor systems and plays a crucial role in attention; often thought of as a switching center.

life that if it is badly damaged, the patient will die, even if the cortex remains untouched. Partial damage to the young soldier's thalamus might account for some of the symptoms the doctors observed.

## Hypothalamus: Thermostat and More

The **hypothalamus** sits under the thalamus, as illustrated in Figure 3.17. The small size of this structure shouldn't fool you: It is absolutely critical for controlling many bodily functions, such as eating and drinking; keeping body temperature, blood pressure, and heart rate within the proper limits; and governing sexual behavior (Swaab, 2003). The hypothalamus also regulates hormones, such as those that prepare an animal to fight or to flee when confronted by danger. If visual recognition is impaired, as in the case of our young soldier, the hypothalamus would not receive the information it needs to function properly. If confronted by an enemy in the field, the soldier would not be able to register the information required to cause the right chemicals to flow into his bloodstream to marshal the body's resources for fight or flight.

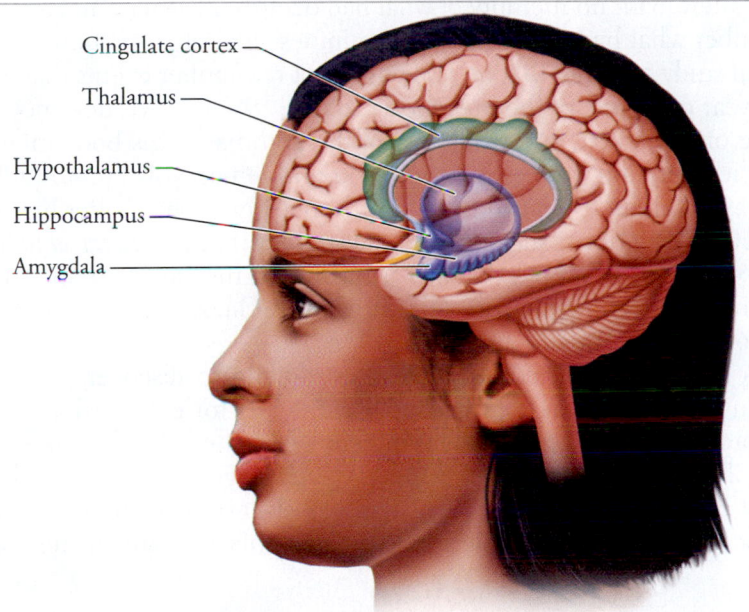

Cingulate cortex
Thalamus
Hypothalamus
Hippocampus
Amygdala

**FIGURE 3.17**

## The Limbic System

These are the key structures that make up the limbic system, which plays a role in emotions and other psychological events.

Like the thalamus, the hypothalamus consists of clusters of neurons. Some of these can produce pain if stimulated by electrical current; others produce hunger or thirst; still others produce pleasure. In a now-famous experiment with rats, James Olds and his student Peter Milner (1954) electrically stimulated part of a rat's hypothalamus whenever it pressed a bar. The rodent found the electrical reward of pressing the bar so enticing that it continued to press it for hours. Stimulated this way, rats would press the bar thousands of times an hour; if given a choice of two bars to press—one producing food and the other, electrical stimulation—the rats consistently "chose" to press the bar for electrical stimulation (Valenstein, 1973). As a result of this well-documented finding (German & Bowden; 1974; Koob, 1999; Robbins & Everitt, 1999), this hypothalamic area has sometimes been called the "pleasure center."

Hypothalamus: A brain structure that sits under the thalamus and plays a central role in controlling eating and drinking and in regulating the body's temperature, blood pressure, and heart rate.

Just how accurate the term "pleasure center" is has been brought into question, however. The effect observed by Olds and Milner could reflect a compulsion, such as the familiar "try-to-eat-just-one-salted-peanut" effect. Or it could have something to do within learning to press the bar. In fact, experiments with humans about to have brain surgery have yielded no evidence suggesting that stimulating the hypothalamus produces pure pleasure (LeDoux, 1996). At least at present, it is premature to think of any part of the hypothalamus as a "pleasure center" in the brain.

## Hippocampus: Remember It

The **hippocampus** is a structure that looks something like a seahorse (at least to some people), and hence its name, from the Greek *hippokampos*, a mythological "seahorse" monster. This structure plays a key role in allowing us to enter new information into the brain's memory banks (Gluck & Myers, 2000; Squire & Schacter, 2002). The role of the hippocampus was vividly illustrated by the case of H.M., who had his hippocampus (and nearby brain structures) removed in an effort to control his epilepsy. After the operation, his doctors noticed something unexpected: H.M. could no longer learn new facts (Milner et al., 1968). His memory for events that occurred a year or so before the operation seemed normal, but he was stuck at that stage of his life. Each day began truly anew, with no memory of what had occurred earlier—in fact, he could not even remember what had happened a few minutes ago, let alone hours or days. Later, more careful study revealed that he also could not remember events that had occurred within the year or so before the operation (Squire, 1987). H.M. does not seem particularly aware of his deficit, and when one of the authors of this book interviewed him years after the operation, he was in good spirits and remarkably comfortable with himself. When asked about the meanings of words that were coined after his operation, he gamely offered definitions, suggesting, for example, that a *jacuzzi* is a "new kind of dance." He didn't seem to notice what was missing in his life. (Perhaps this is a case of the left hemisphere telling stories to fill in gaps, as Gazzaniga and LeDoux noted in their study of a split-brain patient.)

Patients such as H.M. led researchers eventually to discover that although the hippocampus itself does not contain stored memories for extended amounts of time, it triggers processes that store new information elsewhere in the brain (as we shall discuss in Chapter 7). If the young soldier had damage to the occipital or temporal systems that register visual input, these areas would not feed the proper information to the hippocampus—and thus he would not be able to store in memory the stimuli he saw.

## Amygdala: Inner Feelings

The **amygdala** is an almond-shaped structure (its name means "almond" in ancient Greek) near the hippocampus. The amygdala plays a special role in emotions such as fear and anger (Morris & Dolan, 2002) and even affects whether one can read emotions in facial expressions (Adolphs et al., 1996). The hypothalamus and amygdala play crucial roles as bridges between the CNS and the PNS. Indeed, both are key components of the **limbic system**, shown in Figure 3.17. The limbic system has long been thought of as being involved in the basics of emotion and motivation: fighting, fleeing, feeding, and sex. But each of the structures in this "system" is now known to have distinct roles that do not involve these functions (for example, the hippocampus is crucially important in storing new memories); further, other brain structures, outside this

Hippocampus: A subcortical structure that plays a key role in allowing new information to be stored in the brain's memory banks.

Amygdala: A subcortical structure that plays a special role in fear and is involved in other sorts of emotions, such as anger.

Limbic system: A set of brain areas, including the hippocampus, amygdala, and other areas, that have long been thought of as being involved in fighting, fleeing, feeding, and sex.

set, also play a role in emotion. For these reasons, some researchers regard the very concept of a "limbic system" as out of date (LeDoux, 1996).

## Basal Ganglia: More Than Habit-Forming

The **basal ganglia**, positioned on the outer sides of the thalami, are involved in planning and producing movement (Iansek & Porter, 1980). People with Parkinson's disease often have abnormal basal ganglia; the functioning of these structures depends crucially on dopamine.

The basal ganglia also play a critical role in a particular type of learning: forming a habit. When you learn to put your foot on the brake automatically at a red light, the basal ganglia are busy connecting the stimulus (the light) with your response (moving your foot). As discussed in Chapters 6 and 7, this system is distinct from the one used to learn facts (the one, that, presumably, is at work right now, as you read this page). In addition, the *nucleus accumbens*, which is sometimes considered part of the basal ganglia, plays a crucial role in the brain's response to reward (Hall et al., 2001; Tzschentke & Schmidt, 2000) and its anticipation of reward (Knutson et al., 2001; Pagnoni et al., 2002). Indeed, drugs such as cocaine, amphetamines, and alcohol have their effects in part because they engage the nucleus accumbens (Dackis & O'Brien, 2001; Robbins & Everitt, 1999; Vinar, 2001). The neurotransmitter dopamine is central to the operation of this structure.

## Brainstem: The Brain's Wakeup Call

As illustrated in Figure 3.16, at the base of the brain are structures that feed into, and receive information from, the spinal cord. These structures are often collectively called the **brainstem**. The **medulla**, at the lowest part of the lower brainstem (see Figure 3.16), is important in the automatic control of breathing, swallowing, and blood circulation. The brainstem also contains a number of small structures, together called the **reticular formation**, which has two main parts. The "ascending" part, the *reticular activating system (RAS)*, plays a key role in keeping you awake and making you perk up when something interesting happens. The RAS produces neuromodulators (as do several other specialized structures deep in the brain) that affect the operation of many other parts of the brain. Neurons of the RAS have long axons that reach into other parts of the brain and alter the functioning of distant neurons. The soldier would have been sluggish following damage to these structures. The "descending" part of the reticular formation receives input from the hypothalamus and plays a key role in producing autonomic nervous system reactions. It is also involved in conducting impulses from muscles not under voluntary control to those under voluntary control (such as those used in swallowing and speech).

The **pons** is a bridge (*pons* is Latin for "bridge") connecting the brainstem and the cerebellum; it is involved with a variety of functions, ranging from sleep to control of muscles used to form facial expressions.

## Cerebellum: Walking Tall

The **cerebellum** is concerned in part with physical coordination. If your cerebellum were damaged, you might walk oddly and have trouble standing normally and keeping an upright posture. If you ever see an aging prizefighter, look at his walk. Too many blows to the head may have damaged his cerebellum, leading to a condition aptly

**Basal ganglia:** Subcortical structures that play a role in planning and producing movement.

**Brainstem:** The set of neural structures at the base of the brain, including the medulla and pons.

**Medulla:** The lowest part of the lower brainstem, which plays a central role in automatic control of breathing, swallowing, and blood circulation.

**Reticular formation:** Two-part structure in the brainstem; the "ascending" part plays a key role in keeping a person awake and alert; the "descending" part is important in producing autonomic nervous system reactions.

**Pons:** A bridge between the brainstem and the cerebellum that plays a role in functions ranging from sleep to control of facial muscles.

**Cerebellum:** A large structure at the base of the brain that is concerned in part with physical coordination, estimating time, and paying attention.

described as being "punch-drunk." In addition, however, damage to some parts of the cerebellum might disrupt your ability to estimate time or to pay attention properly (Ivry & Spencer, 2004). The surface area of the cerebellum is nearly the same as that of the entire cerebral cortex, and hence it will not be surprising if this structure turns out to be involved in many cognitive functions (Manto & Pandolfo, 2001). The medulla, pons, cerebellum, and parts of the reticular formation are often grouped together as the **hindbrain** because they lie at the rear end of the brain of a four-legged animal; the other brainstem structures form the **midbrain**, which lies between the hindbrain and the forebrain.

# The Neuroendocrine and Neuroimmune Systems: More Brain–Body Connections

Some of the subcortical structures we just considered play another important role: They allow the brain to communicate with the body. The brain has a total of four mechanisms for influencing the body, and these in turn provide feedback, affecting the brain itself.

- *Skeletal system.* As you now know, the sensory-somatic nervous system affects the body by moving muscles voluntarily, via the skeletal system.
- *Autonomic nervous system.* The brain can influence the ANS, which—among other things—regulates involuntary muscles (such as those in the heart).
- *Hormones.* In addition, the brain produces hormones and controls the production of hormones elsewhere in the body.
- *Immune responses.* Finally, the brain affects our immune systems, making us more or less able to fight off the onslaught of disease.

Let's consider these last two mechanisms now, which rely in part on the deep brain structures just discussed.

## The Neuroendocrine System: It's Hormonal!

Some structures in the brain affect the body by producing (or causing to be produced) certain chemicals. For example, something happens during puberty that changes a child's body into an adult's and changes the child's behavior as well. Charming boys and sweet girls may become sullen and rebellious, moody and impulsive. That "something" is hormones. **Hormones** are chemicals that are produced by glands and can act as neuromodulators. The CNS hooks into the **neuroendocrine system**, which makes hormones that affect many functions. The CNS not only regulates this system, but also receives information from it—which in turn alters the way the CNS operates.

Figure 3.18 shows the locations of the major *endocrine glands*; endocrine glands secrete substances into the bloodstream, as opposed to other glands, such as sweat glands, that excrete substances outside the body. Some hormones affect sexual development and functioning. Among these, **testosterone** causes boys to develop facial hair and other external sexual characteristics, as well as to build up muscle, and **estrogen** causes girls to develop breasts and is involved in the menstrual cycle. Some hormones affect the levels of salt and sugar in the blood, and others help the body cope with stressful situations. The outer layer of the adrenal glands produces **cortisol**, which helps the body cope with the extra energy demands of stress by breaking down protein and fat and converting them to sugar; the sugar provides energy

**Hindbrain:** The medulla, pons, cerebellum, and parts of the reticular formation.

**Midbrain:** Brainstem structures that lie between forebrain and hindbrain, including parts of the reticular formation.

**Hormone:** A chemical that is produced by a gland and can act as a neuromodulator.

**Neuroendocrine system:** The system, regulated by the CNS, that makes hormones that affect many bodily functions and that also provides the CNS with information.

**Testosterone:** The hormone that causes males to develop facial hair and other sex characteristics and to build up muscle volume.

**Estrogen:** The hormone that causes breasts to develop and is involved in the menstrual cycle.

**Cortisol:** A hormone produced by the outer layer of the adrenal glands that helps the body cope with the extra energy demands of stress by breaking down and converting protein and fat to sugar.

to the body, increases blood flow, and allows the person to respond more vigorously and for a longer period of time. Cortisol production is triggered even by the sight of angry faces (van Honk et al., 2000).

A part of the brain called the **pituitary gland** is particularly interesting because its hormones actually control the other endocrine glands; for this reason, it has sometimes been called the "master gland." But, master or not, this gland is still controlled by the brain, primarily via connections from the hypothalamus. If information from the world isn't interpreted properly by the young soldier's cortex, it won't have the normal effect on the hypothalamus, which in turn will not produce the normal hormonal response.

## The Neuroimmune System: How the Brain Fights Disease

The brain also helps our bodies fight disease. In particular, the hypothalamus, the pituitary gland, and the adrenal glands form the **hypothalamic-pituitary-adrenal (HPA) axis**, which allows us to respond effectively to infections; this system is so important that we would soon die without it. When bacteria or viruses are first detected by cells in your body, an *acute phase response* is triggered. A key part of this response is that the affected cells release *cytokines*, a type of protein that sends messages within the immune system and to the CNS. These cytokines in turn signal the brain, which then mobilizes the HPA axis (Webster & Sternberg, 2004). Specifically, neurons within one part of the hypothalamus, the *paraventricular nucleus*, interact with neurons in the brainstem (Buller, 2003) and produce a particular hormone—corticotropin-releasing hormone (CRH). This hormone then causes the pituitary gland to release another hormone—adrenocorticotropin hormone (ACTH). ACTH then circulates in the blood and causes the adrenal glands to produce cortisol (see Figure 3.19, p. 106). Cortisol, in addition to its role in the stress response (discussed in the previous section), disrupts the mechanisms that cause inflammation (Adcock, 2000; Webster et al., 2002). The hypothalamus also reacts to infection by stimulating the production of white blood cells (Hefco et al., 2004). Moreover, the ANS and the PNS also affect the immune system and interact with the HPA axis (Elenkov et al., 2000; Shigenobu, 2001).

At this point, you may be wondering why all of this is relevant to psychology. Here's why: Psychological stress and pain also activate the HPA axis; in fact, the brain can regulate the adrenal glands via neural connections (Bornstein & Chrousos, 1999). Crucially, stress is often "in the mind of the beholder"; what counts as stress for you (for instance, being put on a roller coaster) might actually be fun for someone else. Mental processes interpret a situation, and the result affects the immune system. In fact, the brain's reaction to a situation can disrupt the optimal functioning of the HPA axis, making the person more vulnerable to disease. It's true: Being stressed-out makes you more likely to catch a cold (Glaser & Kiecolt-Glaser, 1998) and more vulnerable to bacterial infections (Bailey et al., 2003). Your body affects your mind, and vice versa.

**FIGURE 3.18   The Major Endocrine Glands**

The locations of major endocrine glands in the body.

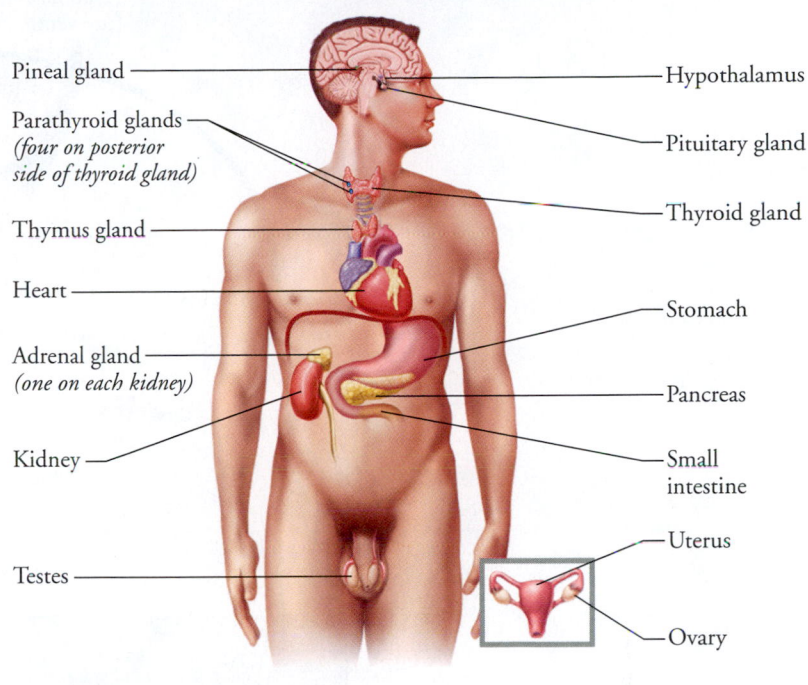

Pineal gland — Hypothalamus — Parathyroid glands (*four on posterior side of thyroid gland*) — Pituitary gland — Thyroid gland — Thymus gland — Heart — Stomach — Adrenal gland (*one on each kidney*) — Pancreas — Kidney — Small intestine — Uterus — Testes — Ovary

Pituitary gland: The "master gland" that regulates other glands but is itself controlled by the brain, primarily via connections from the hypothalamus.

Hypothalamic-pituitary-adrenal (HPA) axis: The hypothalamus, pituitary gland, and adrenal glands, which work together to fight off infection.

**FIGURE 3.19**

**The HPA Axis**

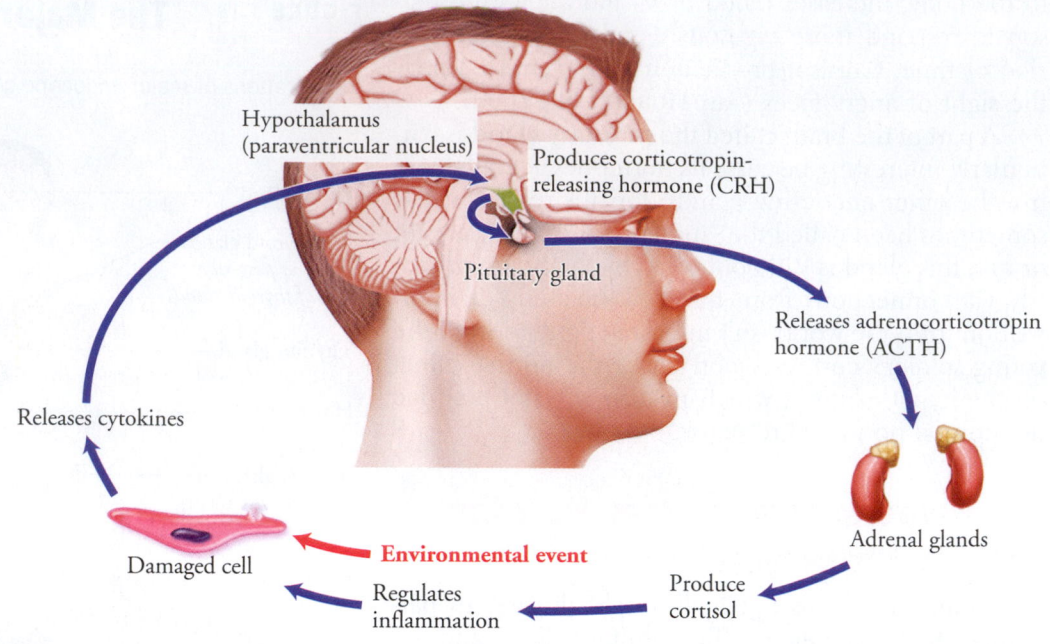

Hypothalamus
(paraventricular nucleus)

Produces corticotropin-
releasing hormone (CRH)

Pituitary gland

Releases adrenocorticotropin
hormone (ACTH)

Releases cytokines

Damaged cell

**Environmental event**

Regulates
inflammation

Produce
cortisol

Adrenal glands

# LOOKING AT LEVELS

## The Musical Brain

All human cultures have music. Does this imply that music is deeply embedded in the human brain, and we can understand everything interesting about it simply by looking at the brain? Not at all! As usual, we need to consider events at the different levels of analysis and how they interact.

First, the brain. Just as there is no single "language center" or "vision center," there is no single "music center" in the brain. Rather, a large network of different brain areas is activated when people listen to or play music (Baeck, 2002). Areas in both hemispheres of the brain pitch in; the right hemisphere is not the seat of music, as is sometimes assumed in the popular press. In fact, a set of areas spanning much of the brain is activated when people play or simply imagine hearing music. Meister and colleagues (2004) monitored brain activity while music students either played the right-hand piano part of a classical music piece or simply imagined playing the piece while keeping still. These researchers found very similar activation in a large part of the frontal and parietal lobes (in both hemispheres) during both actual playing and imagery. But only during actual playing was primary motor cortex activated, and the posterior parietal lobes were more active during actual playing (which reflects their role in programming movements).

Different parts of the activated network of brain areas play different roles. For example, damage to the superior temporal lobes, which process sound, can prevent patients from distinguishing consonant from dissonant sounds (Peretz et al., 2001). Damage to the left temporal-parietal region can disrupt rhythm while leaving perception and production of melody intact (Di Pietro et al., 2004). Other researchers (Griffiths et al., 2004) found that damage to the amygdala and a related brain area (the *insula*) led a patient to lose his emotional reactions to music; pieces that previously had sent a "shiver down his spine" no longer did so. In fact, normal people vary in how good they are at different aspects of music processing. At one extreme, some people have *amusia*—they are "tone deaf." Such people have a selective problem with discriminating pitch; they can detect time changes as well as people without this disorder (Hyde & Peretz, 2004; Peretz & Hyde, 2003). At the other extreme, some people have *absolute pitch* (also called *perfect pitch*), which is the ability to identify a particular note by itself, not simply in relation to other notes (Krumhansl, 1991, 2000).

Even if there's no single music center, is music special in terms of mental processing? On the one hand, music does rely on some neural machinery that differs from that used for language; brain damage can disrupt a person's ability to talk, while leaving his or her ability to sing virtually intact (Warren et al., 2003). On the other hand, music does share processing with various other abilities. For example, people who have strong musical ability also tend to have strong spatial ability (Brochard et al., 2004; Cupchik et al., 2001); musical training hones the ability to hear pitch variations in language (Schön et al., 2004); and there is considerable overlap of the neural networks activated while people listen to music and while they engage in nonmusical tasks that require memory, attention, and comprehension (Janata et al., 2002). Like most abilities, music draws partly on specialized processing and partly on processing that is also used when we exercise other abilities.

Music also affects events at the level of the person. For example, music can reduce arousal (Pelletier, 2004) and can even calm people who have experienced trauma and help them to be better oriented to events around them (Baker, 2001). It can also improve the mood of people who have had brain damage (Magee & Davidson, 2002). Although playing music does relax people, which in turn can improve their feelings of well-being (Winkelman, 2003), that's not all there is to it; listening to music they like can actually energize older people (Hirokawa, 2004). However, these effects depend in part on the nature of the music. One study, for example, found that listening to Mozart relaxed people more than did listening to New Age music (Smith & Joyce, 2004).

Further, music has powerful effects at the level of the group. Perhaps the most impressive of such effects occur in the context of *music therapy*, which uses structured musical exercises to help people improve their emotional state and daily functioning (Wigram et al., 2002). Music therapy is not just sitting around listening to music; rather, a therapist organizes exercises for the patient, based on the patient's background, preferences, and goals. Moreover, the therapist evaluates how well the patient responds and adjusts the therapy accordingly. Music therapy can include creating new music, producing music (singing and playing instruments), and listening and responding to music. Music therapy has been used to help people not only to relax and express their emotions, but also to improve their attention spans, manage pain, and develop new ways to communicate with others. Researchers have shown that music therapy can even help people with severe problems. For example, patients with multiple sclerosis report having higher self-esteem and being less anxious and depressed after music therapy (Schmid & Aldridge, 2004), and such therapy can help patients with brain damage to interact socially (Wheeler et al., 2003). Music therapy apparently has also reduced the severity of episodes among epileptics (Sidorenko, 2000).

Finally, events at the different levels clearly interact when it comes to making music. For example, if you are motivated (level of the person) to play music, perhaps because a teacher inspired you (level of the group), this activity will actually change your brain! Researchers have examined how playing music may change the brain. Part of the motor strip in the right half of the brain controls the fingers of the left hand, and this part of the brain is larger in orchestra members who play stringed instruments than in nonmusicians (Elber et al., 1995; Münte et al., 2001; Schlaug et al., 1995). In fact, professional keyboard players have more gray matter in auditory and visual-spatial areas than do either amateur musicians or nonmusicians (Gaser & Schlaug, 2003)—and the more people practice, the larger the relevant areas tend to be. Moreover, such differences are not restricted to variations in size: Conductors of professional orchestras actually become better able to localize sounds in the periphery, those heard from the "corner of the ear," so to speak (Münte et al., 2001). Furthermore, when you learn a particular instrument, your brain develops to allow you to hear its particular tonal quality (Pantev et al., 2001). Apparently, brain areas that are used often grow larger and come to function more effectively, probably because of the formation of additional connections among neurons.

Consider these findings from the levels perspective: The size and functionality of brain areas—the physical structure and workings of your brain—depend in part on what you do. If you have musical talent and interest (characteristics at the level of the person) and have the opportunity to develop musical ability, your brain can be altered by the experience. And if your playing is smiled upon by others (the level of the group), you will be even more motivated to continue practicing—further changing your brain. And, once your brain is altered, your playing may improve—leading to more praise from others.

# Test Yourself

1. Which of the following is not a route through which the brain affects the body?
   a. skeletal system    c. neuroendrocrine system
   b. digestive system    d. immune system

2. You see a ball (A), and then you hear children's voices (B). Your attention is drawn to your left, where you notice the children coming toward you to retrieve the ball (C). Which of your cerebral lobes is most active during each of these events?
   a. (A) parietal; (B) occipital; (C) temporal
   b. (A) parietal; (B) temporal; (C) occipital
   c. (A) occipital; (B) temporal; (C) parietal
   d. (A) occipital; (B) parietal; (C) temporal

3. In the Gazzaniga and LeDoux study described in the Understanding Research section, the participants were split-brain patients. How would a participant with an intact corpus callosum most likely respond to the experimental situation?
   a. The new participant would respond in the same way as the split-brain participants.
   b. The new participant would not need to make up a story since the participant's left hemisphere would know what the right hemisphere saw.
   c. It would depend on which hemisphere controlled language for the new participant.
   d. It is impossible to know how the new participant would respond.

4. Which of the following associations is correct?
   a. amygdala—fear    c. hypothalamus—memory
   b. hippocampus—eating    d. thalamus—drinking

## Answers

1. b 2. c 3. b 4. a

# Think It Through!

Clearly, the organization of the brain has a lot to do with why brain damage produces one disorder and not another. It is possible that some parts of the brain receive information that is not available to the parts that control language. If so, can you think of types of behaviors that might reveal that the information was "in there"?

Can you think of a way by which you could have tried to find out whether the soldier had a problem with attention or whether his paying attention to a small area was just a strategy? That is, perhaps he believed that by focusing on details he would see better, and thus he did so even though he was in fact able to pay attention to overall shapes. What difference, if any, would it make whether his problem was due to a faulty strategy or to something that was not under his control?

More careful examination of the soldier might have suggested that his problem was not confined to visual processing. What would you think if it could be shown that his personality was particularly unemotional? What if he had little interest in eating or sex?

# PROBING THE BRAIN

Having toured the major parts of the brain and noted their major functions, you can make a pretty good guess about what areas of the brain were damaged when the soldier suffered carbon monoxide poisoning. We cannot know for sure, given the limitations of the tests available at the time of his accident, in 1966. Today, however, doctors can obtain impressive high-quality images of a living brain. These images can show damage to particular brain structures and can record brain activity, or the disruption of it, in specific areas.

## The Damaged Brain: What's Missing?

The first evidence that different parts of the brain do different things came from *natural experiments*, accidents in which people suffered damage to the brain. Such damage typically produces a region of impaired tissue, called a **lesion**. The most frequent source of damage is a **stroke**, which occurs when blood, with its life-sustaining nutrients and oxygen, fails to reach part of the brain (usually because a clot clogs up a crucial blood vessel) causing neurons in the affected area to die. In such cases, researchers study the patients, seeking to learn which specific abilities are disrupted independently of others when particular brain structures are damaged.

Although natural experiments can offer important clues about brain functioning, they have several serious limitations. Most important, natural experiments are rarely very neat. The damage caused by a stroke, for example, can extend over a large part of the brain, affecting more than one area and disrupting more than one function. This can make it difficult to relate the disruption in a particular function to the operation of a specific part of the brain. Also, stroke victims are usually older people, and often they have not led healthy lives (they've smoked, eaten high-cholesterol foods, not exercised); thus, they are not a representative sample of the population as a whole.

Such drawbacks led some researchers to turn to *lesioning studies*. In these experiments, researchers remove specific parts of the brains of animals and observe the consequences on behavior. But, because animals are not people, we must be cautious in generalizing from animal brains to human brains.

Although strokes are a more common cause of brain damage, some people have suffered such damage from riding on roller coasters. One woman had trouble remembering things she just heard, could no longer see clearly, and even blacked out sporadically (S. Gilbert, 2002). A few people have died after such injuries (Brasiek & Roberts, 2002).

## Recording Techniques: The Music of the Cells

Rather than having to rely on the indirect evidence supplied by damaged brains, researchers can now make use of several methods to record the activity of normal brains. Neurons are never totally "off" (they maintain a baseline level of firing even when you sleep or are resting), but their rate of firing depends on what the brain is doing. Neurons that are used in a given task fire more frequently than those not involved in its performance, and this activity can be recorded.

To some extent, brain activity can be measured by making an electromagnetic recording. In one version of this technique, a machine called an **electroencephalograph (EEG)** records electrical current produced by the brain, as shown in Figure 3.20 (p. 110). When neurons fire, they produce electrical fields. When many neurons are firing together, these fields can be detected by electrodes (small metal disks that pick up electrical activity) placed on the scalp. Researchers can record electrical activity in response to a particular stimulus, or they can record the activity over time; the result is a

Lesion: A region of impaired tissue.

Stroke: A source of brain damage that occurs when blood (with its life-giving nutrients and oxygen) fails to reach part of the brain, causing neurons in that area to die.

Electroencephalograph (EEG): A machine that records electrical current produced by the brain.

FIGURE 3.20    **The Electroencephalograph**

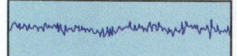 Relaxed/rest

Task performance

The top image shows an EEG during relaxed rest, whereas the bottom image shows an EEG during performance of a task; clearly, the brain is more active when an individual is performing a task than when he or she is relaxed.

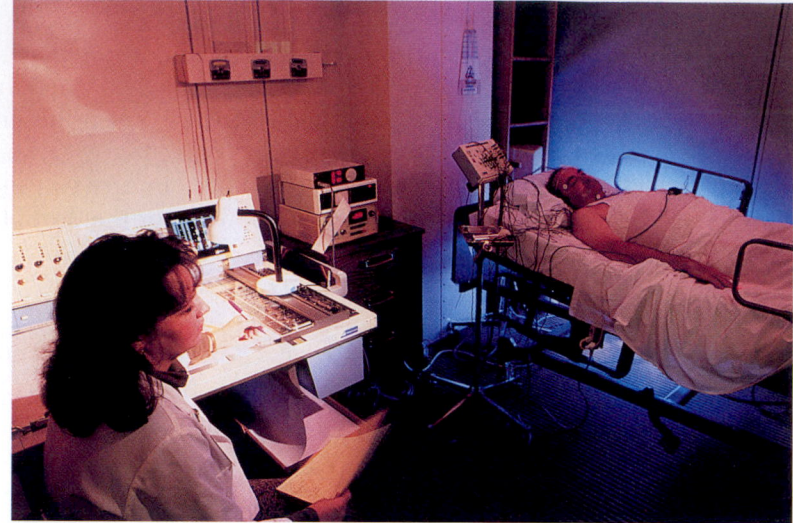

This equipment allows researchers to record electrical activity on the scalp, which reflects electrical activity in the brain.

tracing of the "brain waves" of electrical fluctuation called an **electroencephalogram** (see Figure 3.20). Psychologists have used this technique to learn much about the brain. It is through EEGs, for example, that they learned that people go through distinct stages of sleep marked by different types of brain activity (see Chapter 5 for a detailed discussion of these stages).

Although EEGs have shed light on brain activity, particularly the time course of changes, the technique poses a major problem: The electrodes placed on the scalp cannot detect the precise locations of the electrical currents in the brain. The electrical current is distorted when it passes through the skull, and it also travels across the surface of the brain and the scalp. The situation is like seeing an image in a hall of mirrors; you know *when* it occurs, but not *where* it comes from. Another, more recent, technique, **magnetoencephalography (MEG)**, avoids some of these difficulties by recording magnetic waves, which are not distorted as they pass through the skull and do not travel across the scalp. Just as running a current through a wire produces a magnetic field, neural firings produce a magnetic field. Very fast changes in neural firing can be detected with this technique. However, many neurons must be lined up the same way to produce a detectable magnetic field, and thus this technique is not sensitive to activity in all parts of the brain. In addition, neither EEG nor MEG is very sensitive to subcortical activity.

Researchers can monitor activity in specific locations by recording neural activity directly. In this technique, called *single-cell recording*, tiny probes called **microelectrodes** can be placed in individual cells in the brain and used to record the firing rates of neurons. A typical microelectrode is at most only 1/10 as wide as a human hair (and some are only 1/100 as wide!). Usually researchers hook up the wires from microelectrodes to amplifiers and speakers rather than to a screen, so they can hear neuronal activity (as clicking sounds) rather than watch a monitor; their eyes are then free to guide the placement of the electrodes. Microelectrodes are sometimes put in human brains before brain surgery in order to find out what a part of the brain does before it is cut. Studies with microelectrodes have yielded some fascinating results. For example,

**Electroencephalogram:** A recording from the scalp of electrical activity in the brain over time, which produces a tracing of pulses at different frequencies.

**Magnetoencephalography (MEG):** A technique for assessing brain activity that relies on recording magnetic waves from the outside of the head.

**Microelectrode:** A tiny probe inserted into the brain to record the electrical activity of individual neurons.

when people look at words, some neurons respond to specific words but not others (Heit et al., 1988). However, single-cell recording also has its limitations. In some ways it is like looking at a picture though a pinhole in a piece of paper that covers it. This technique fails to indicate how large collections of neurons in the brain work together.

# Neuroimaging: Picturing the Living Brain

Today, if you had an emergency like the young soldier's, you would probably be rushed to a hospital and immediately have your brain scanned. Your doctors would order the procedure to determine both the structural damage (which areas were physically affected) and the functional deficits (which areas were performing below par). Because they yield an actual picture of neuronal structure and function, scanning techniques are referred to as **neuroimaging**. It is fair to say that neuroimaging techniques have transformed psychology, allowing researchers to answer questions that were hopelessly out of reach before the mid-1980s (Cabeza & Nyberg, 2000; Cappa & Grafman, 2004; Poldrak & Wagner, 2004; Posner & Raichle, 1994).

## Visualizing Brain Structure

The oldest neuroimaging techniques involve taking pictures of brain structures using X rays. The invention of the computer allowed scientists to construct machines for **computer-assisted tomography (CT,** formerly **CAT)**. In this technique, a series of X rays builds up a three-dimensional image, slice by slice (*tomography* comes from a Greek word meaning "section"). More recently, **magnetic resonance imaging (MRI)** makes use of the magnetic properties of different atoms to take even sharper pictures of the structures of the brain. To understand how MRI works, think of how an opera singer can hit a note that will break a glass. This happens because the glass resonates with the sound waves so that it shakes at the same frequency as the note—

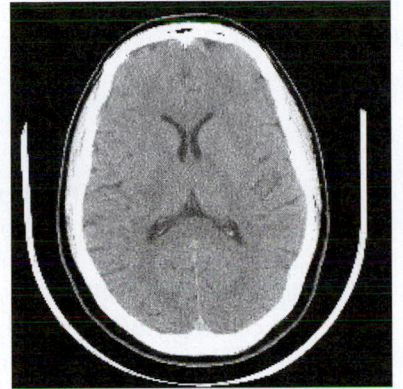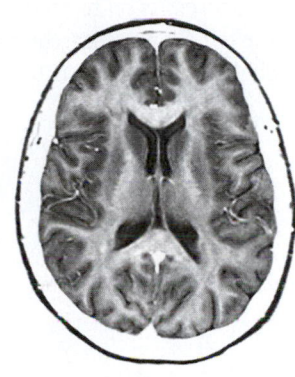

On the left, a computer-assisted tomography (CT) scan, and on the right, a magnetic resonance imaging (MRI) scan. MRI provides much higher resolution images of structures of the brain.

shakes so hard that it shatters. Different materials resonate to different frequencies; the note that cracks a thin glass may not be the same as one that cracks a thicker, leaded glass. Similarly, different atoms in the brain resonate to different frequencies of magnetic fields. In MRI, a background magnetic field lines up all the atoms in the brain (or whatever organ is being scanned). A second magnetic field, oriented differently from the background field, is turned on and off many times a second; at certain pulse rates, particular atoms resonate and line up with this second field. When the second field is turned off, the atoms that were lined up with it swing back to align with the background field. As they swing back, they create a signal that can be picked up and converted into an image. The image shows the presence or absence of the substance of interest; in the brain, MRI often assesses the density of water in a region, which differs for gray versus white matter.

## Visualizing Brain Function

CT scans and MRIs give amazing views of the physical structure of the living brain; but for images that reflect the brain in action, researchers need other types of brain scans, those that track the amount of blood, oxygen, or nutrients moving to particular parts of the brain. When you take a shower or wash a load of laundry, water is drawn

Neuroimaging: Brain-scanning techniques that produce a picture of the structure or functioning of neurons.

Computer-assisted tomography (CT, **formerly** CAT): A neuroimaging technique that produces a three-dimensional image of brain structures using X rays.

Magnetic resonance imaging (MRI): A technique that uses magnetic properties of atoms to take sharp pictures of the structures of the brain.

FIGURE 3.21

## Positron Emission Tomography

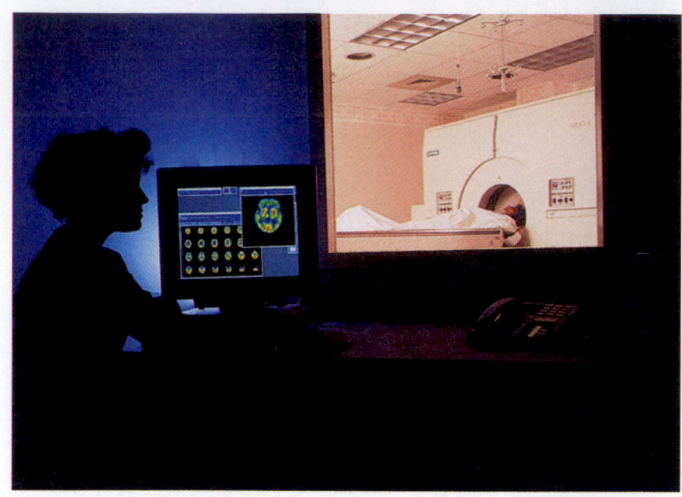

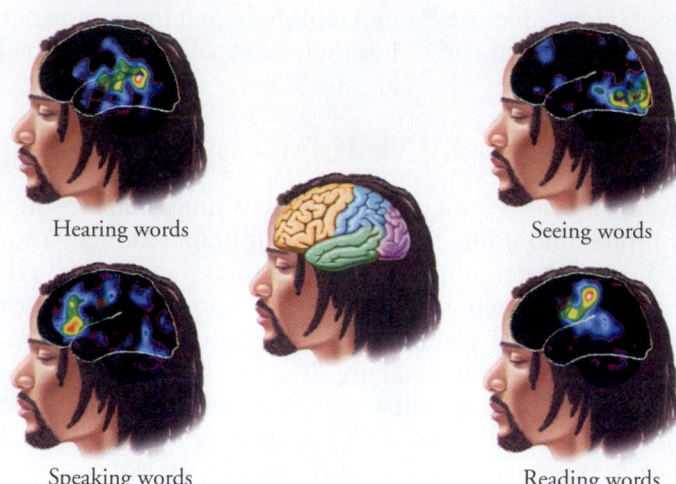

Hearing words

Seeing words

Speaking words

Reading words

A positron emission tomography (PET) machine like that shown on the left allows researchers to observe brain activity while participants perform various tasks.

Brighter colors indicate regions of greater blood flow in the brain while the participant performed a particular task.

into the plumbing pipes from the water main. Similarly, when a part of the brain is working, it draws more blood. This fact was dramatically demonstrated by the case of Walter K (as described by Posner & Raichle, 1994). After a brain operation accidentally altered the shape of the bone over the back of his head, he noticed an odd humming noise coming from inside his head, which he thought became louder when he was using his eyes. His physician, John Fulton, took Walter's report seriously. He listened carefully to the back of Walter K's head when his eyes were opened and when they were closed. Fulton too heard the sound, which became louder when Walter was looking carefully at something; the noise did not occur when Walter was listening carefully, or when he was smelling tobacco or vanilla. Fulton measured the sound coming from his patient's head and demonstrated conclusively that when Walter was looking carefully at something (for example, when he was reading a newspaper), the noise level increased. Why? Because the back of the brain is used in vision, and the noise, audible after the bone structure at the back of Walter's head changed, was the sound of the blood moving into the occipital lobe whenever it was needed for visual tasks.

One of the most important techniques for measuring blood flow or energy consumption in the brain is **positron emission tomography (PET)**. Small amounts of radiation are introduced into the blood, which is then taken up into different brain areas in proportion to how hard the neurons in each area are working (see Figure 3.21). The amount of radiation emitted at different parts of the head is recorded, and a computer uses this information to build three-dimensional images of the brain. In order to ensure that the amount of radiation falls well within safe limits, only small amounts are used — which thus limits how sensitive the technique can be. However, PET is still the only good method for charting the locations and amounts of specific neurotransmitters in the living human brain. The main drawbacks of this technique are that it requires producing and using radioactive substances, it takes at least 40 seconds or so of brain activity to collect enough data to build up an image, and it can cost as much as $2,000 to test a single person.

Positron emission tomography (PET): A neuroimaging technique that uses small amounts of radiation to track blood flow or energy consumption in the brain.

Probably the most popular type of neuroimaging today is **functional magnetic resonance imaging (fMRI)**. The most common sort of fMRI reveals function by detecting the amount of oxygen that is being brought to a particular place in the brain while a person performs a task. When a part of the brain is working hard, the blood that is drawn in brings with it more oxygen than can be used right away; so oxygen in that area piles up. The iron in the red blood cells carrying oxygen affects the surrounding water differently than the iron in the red blood cells that no longer have oxygen. The most common form of fMRI uses this difference to detect the regions where oxygen is piling up, which indicates where more brain activity is occurring (Heeger & Ress, 2002). Unlike PET, fMRI does not require the introduction of radioactivity into the brain. Moreover, it is possible to build an image of events that occur in only a few seconds. However, this technique is not as simple to use as it may seem. For one thing, the brain is never completely "off," and thus fMRI can't be used simply to show what brain areas are active while someone performs a task (such as looking at faces or solving problems). Instead, fMRI studies must compare how performing one task alters brain processing *relative* to what happens during some other task. In many fMRI studies, the comparison is between a test task and rest. One problem here is that researchers really don't know what's going on in the brain during rest. For example, what if both men and women tend to daydream during rest, but daydream about different things (for instance, the men often think about sports, the women about their friends)—and the content of their thoughts alters brain processing? If so, then comparing brain activity that arises during another task (for example, looking at faces) to that during rest might suggest that the task is performed differently by men and women. But men and women could have the identical brain responses to the task, and it's the comparison state—rest—that's different. A major challenge in contemporary fMRI studies is to devise proper comparison tasks. Additional drawbacks of this technique are that the MRI machines are noisy and require the participant to lie very still, often within a narrow tube, a situation some people find uncomfortable. Finally, because the most common sort of fMRI assesses blood flow, it is limited by how quickly blood flow adjusts to changes in neural activation, which is a matter of seconds (somewhere between 2 and 6); moreover, the fact that the technique tracks blood flow also limits the spatial resolution of the technique, or how small a region it can monitor actively.

Researchers have also employed MRI in another way: *magnetic resonance spectroscopy* (MRS) assesses not blood flow, but rather the concentration of specific chemicals—such as neurotransmitters—in different portions of the brain (Shen & Rothman, 2002). This technique may prove especially useful in studying how mental disorders change the brain.

The most recent technique for visualizing brain activity is *optical imaging*, which relies on shining lasers through the skull. These lasers are very weak, but use frequencies of light (near infrared) to which the skull is transparent. It turns out that blood with oxygen in it absorbs different frequencies of light than does blood in which the oxygen has been consumed. Thus, by observing how much light of different frequencies is reflected back from the brain, researchers can track blood flow (Hochman, 2000; Hoshi et al., 2000; Villringer & Chance, 1997). This technique is called *near infrared spectroscopy (NIRS)* or, when a map of activation is created, *diffuse optical tomography (DOT)*. Optical imaging measures blood flow in the brain, and thus has the same limitations as fMRI: It can only register changes over (at best) 2–6 seconds, and it has limited spatial resolution. A variant of this technique, called *event-related optical signal (EROS)*, observes how light is scattered following cellular changes that arise when neurons fire (Gratton & Fabiani, 2001a, 2001b); this variant can potentially assess very fast changes in neural activity (those occurring in well under a second). Because only

Functional magnetic resonance imaging (fMRI): A type of MRI that usually detects the amount of oxygen being brought to a particular place in the brain while a task is performed.

extremely weak lasers are employed, optical imaging can be used to study even young infants. The technique is inexpensive and relatively portable, as well as silent and safe. The major drawbacks at present are that the spatial resolution typically is poor, and only the cortex can be imaged—and not in its entirety.

It is worth emphasizing that *all* of the neuroimaging techniques we have discussed suffer from a fundamental problem: They produce evidence for *correlations* between performing a task and activation of a specific brain region. They do not establish that activated brain regions play a *causal* role in producing the behavior. To make this connection, we must turn to other techniques.

## Stimulation: Tickling the Neurons

To come closer to discovering how neuronal activity actually gives rise to thoughts, feelings and behavior, researchers can also stimulate neurons and observe the results. Two kinds of stimulation studies have been used to find out what parts of the human brain do.

In one technique, mild electricity is delivered to parts of the participant's brain, and the person is then asked to report what he or she experiences. Wilder Penfield and his colleagues (Penfield & Perot, 1963; Penfield & Rasmussen, 1950) pioneered this method with patients who were about to undergo brain operations. Penfield reported that people experience different images, memories, and feelings depending on the area in the brain that is stimulated. A problem with this method, however, is that researchers cannot be sure whether actual memories are activated or whether the participants are making up stories. In other stimulation studies, instead of asking for reports, researchers observe which activities are disrupted when current is applied (Ojemann, 1983; Ojemann et al., 1989). However, even this method is limited because stimulating particular neurons can lead to the activation of remote neurons, and these other neurons could produce the observed effects. Nevertheless, recent advances in *microstimulation* of nonhuman animals have allowed researchers to alter the activity of a few neurons at a time and observe the direct consequences on an animal's perceptions, decisions, and actions (Cohen & Newsome, 2004).

In another recently developed method, **transcranial magnetic stimulation (TMS)**, researchers stimulate the brain by putting a wire coil on a person's head and discharging a large current through the coil, thus creating a magnetic field. This magnetic field is so strong that it causes a large cluster of neurons within it to fire. Using this technique, researchers can make a person's fingers move by shifting the coil over the parts of the brain that control the fingers (in the motor strip) and producing on/off magnetic pulses (Pascual-Leone et al., 1997; Pascual-Leone et al., 1998; Walsh & Pascual-Leone, 2003). Similarly, if such pulses are directed to the occipital lobe, perception can be temporarily impaired (Walsh & Pascual-Leone, 2003). This technique can show that a brain area plays a causal role in the performance of a particular task, as opposed to merely being stimulated by some other area that is actually doing the work. However, it is not always clear exactly which neurons have been affected by TMS.

In closing this section, we need to emphasize that each of these techniques has different strengths and weaknesses. As you've seen, some techniques can detect neural responding in well under a second but cannot pinpoint where the responding originates, and vice versa for other techniques; some techniques establish correlations among far-flung parts of the brain and behavior but cannot establish causal relations, whereas other techniques establish causal relations between specific individual brain regions and behavior but have limited scope; some are expensive, and some are relatively inexpensive. Recognizing these tradeoffs, researchers are increasingly

Transcranial magnetic stimulation (TMS): A technique where the brain is stimulated from outside by putting a wire coil on a person's head and delivering a magnetic pulse. The magnetic fields are so strong that they make neurons under the coil fire.

using combinations of techniques, taking advantage of the strengths of each while compensating for their weaknesses. For example, PET scanning has revealed that the occipital lobe of the brain is activated even when people visualize with their eyes closed, and TMS has shown that this brain activity plays a causal role in mental imagery; when the occipital lobe is temporarily disrupted, so is the ability to visualize (Kosslyn et al., 1999).

## Test Yourself

1. Information obtained from brain-damaged patients is often supplemented with information obtained from animal surgeries called
   a. stroke studies.
   b. neuroimaging studies.
   c. lesioning studies.
   d. single-cell recordings.

2. Unlike EEGs and MEGs, which typically result in visual recordings, single-cell recordings are often used to produce
   a. sounds.
   b. magnetic fields.
   c. colored maps.
   d. music.

3. The neuroimaging techniques MRI and CT look at _____, whereas fMRI and PET look at _____.
   a. blood and oxygen flow; the physical structures of the brain
   b. the physical structures of the brain; blood and oxygen flow
   c. neurons' energy use; each neuron's output
   d. cortical features; subcortical features

4. Two kinds of stimulation studies have been used to find out what different parts of the human brain do. One technique utilizes electricity, and the other utilizes
   a. blood flow.
   b. oxygen flow.
   c. sodium usage.
   d. magnetic fields.

## Answers

## Think It Through!

Dr. Scannering has invented an improved type of brain-scanning technique, which shines very dim lasers through your head and projects an image of brain activity as it is happening. His machine will be sold for less than the price of a personal computer, is very portable, and is easy to use. What would you do with such a machine? What uses can you think of for education or psychotherapy?

# GENES, BRAIN, AND ENVIRONMENT:
## The Brain in the World

Why was the brain of the young soldier vulnerable to such damage from carbon monoxide fumes? Could he have done anything in advance to prepare his brain to survive such an event? Could he have done anything after the accident to speed his recovery? Let's consider the factors of environment and heredity that shape our brains so that they operate in particular ways and not in others, and the degree to which parts of the brain can change their functions if need be.

## Genes as Blueprints: Born to Be Wild?

Our genes affect us from the instant of conception and continue to affect us at every phase of our lives. The story of genetics begins in 1866, when Gregor Mendel, an

FIGURE 3.22 **The Secret of DNA**

What, exactly, is a gene? Let's begin with a chromosome, which is a tightly coiled molecule of deoxyribonucleic acid, or DNA, contained in the nucleus of all cells. Every cell of the human body (except for sex cells) has 23 pairs of chromosomes. The two strands in the DNA molecule are linked sequences of bases that are bridged by pairs of four types of bases. The base adenine (A) always hooks up with thymine (T), and guanine (G) always hooks up with cytosine (C). Thus, if the helix is unzipped down the middle, extra bases floating about will hook up correctly to form two complete copies of the original molecule. This is how this amazing molecule is able to reproduce itself.

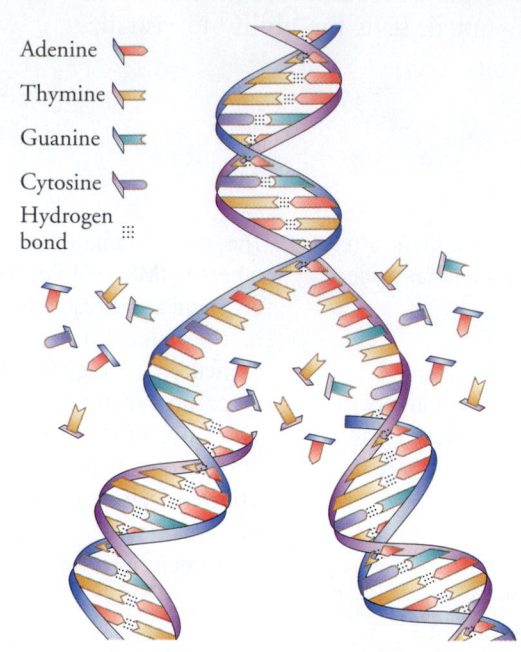

Adenine
Thymine
Guanine
Cytosine
Hydrogen bond

The particular ordering of pairs of bases codes genes; a gene is a segment along the strand of DNA that directs the sequencing of amino acids as they bond to form a protein or an enzyme (which is a type of protein that facilitates chemical reactions). Everything else in our bodies (including our brains) is derived from these molecules.

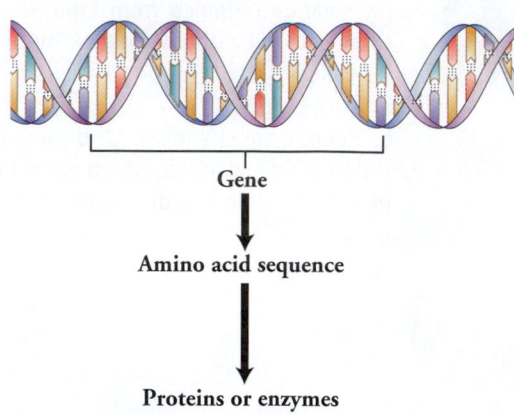

Gene

↓

Amino acid sequence

↓

Proteins or enzymes

---

Augustinian monk living in what is now the Czech Republic, wrote one of the fundamental papers in all science. In it he formulated the core ideas of what is now known as **Mendelian inheritance**, the transmission of characteristics by individual elements of inheritance, each acting separately. Two ideas are key: (1) For each trait, an offspring inherits an "element" from each parent; and (2) in some cases, one of the elements dominates the other, and that is the one whose effect is apparent. If an element is not dominant, it is recessive: The effect of a recessive element is evident only when the offspring receives two copies of it, one from each parent. Mendel, through careful experimentation and record-keeping, traced these patterns of inheritance for a number of organisms (such as pea plants), but he never knew their mechanism. That great biochemical discovery, that the mysterious "elements" are genes, was not made until the early part of the 20th century. Figure 3.22 illustrates the **deoxyribonucleic acid**, or **DNA**, molecule that contains our genes. A **gene** is a stretch of DNA that produces a specific protein (which may be an enzyme). Figure 3.23 illustrates cases where the corresponding genes in a pair of chromosomes are the same (*homozygous*) and where they are different (*heterozygous*).

In his pea plants, Mendel studied traits, such as the seeds' skin texture and color; each trait, he observed, could appear in different "flavors," such as smooth or wrinkled, yellow or green. Thus, a gene for a trait can have different forms, called *alleles*. To inherit attached ear lobes or flat feet, for example, you need to receive the appropriate recessive allele from each of your parents. The sum total of your particular set of genes is your **genotype**. In contrast, the **phenotype** is the observable structure and behavior of an organism.

**Mendelian inheritance:** The transmission of characteristics by individual elements of inheritance (genes), each acting separately.

**Deoxyribonucleic acid, or DNA:** The molecule that contains genes.

**Gene:** A stretch of DNA that produces a specific protein.

**Genotype:** The genetic code within an organism.

**Phenotype:** The observable structure and behavior of an organism.

## FIGURE 3.23 Homozygous and Heterozygous Genotypes

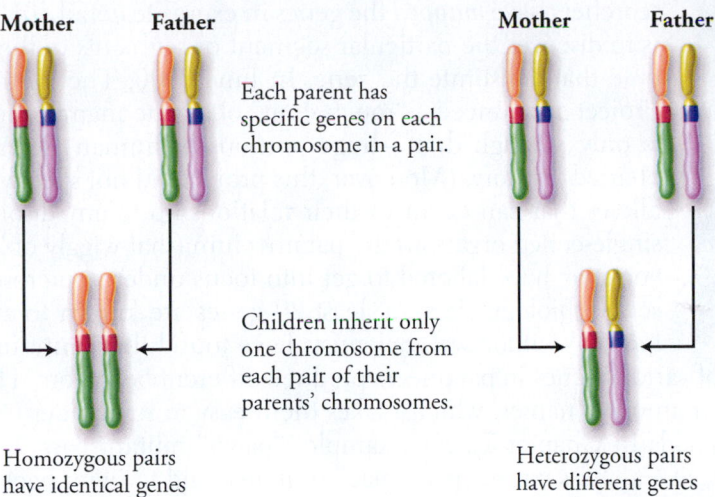

Mother  Father

Each parent has specific genes on each chromosome in a pair.

Children inherit only one chromosome from each pair of their parents' chromosomes.

Homozygous pairs have identical genes on each chromosome.

Mother  Father

Heterozygous pairs have different genes on each chromosome.

For all but the sex chromosomes, for each gene on one chromosome there is a corresponding gene on the other member of the pair. Homozygous genes are the same on both chromosomes of the pair; heterozygous genes are different.

Many genes express their effects only in combination with other genes. When this occurs, we see quantitative variations in characteristics, such as differences in height or intelligence, not qualitative variations, such as attached versus unattached ear lobes. In general, when a characteristic varies continuously over some range, it reflects **complex inheritance**, the joint action of combinations of genes working together, rather than Mendelian inheritance, which describes the effects of individual elements of inheritance (Plomin & DeFries, 1998; Plomin et al., 2003).

## Genetic Programs: The Genes Matter

Did you ever wonder which came first, the chicken or the egg? The answer is now clear: the egg. A mutation modified the genes of an ancestor of the chicken, and these genes produced a novel egg—which, when hatched, developed into a novel bird, the chicken we all know and love. Genes not only produce obvious traits—such as eye color, height, and other physical features—but also, by affecting our brains, affect our behavior. That this is so is clear if you think about other animals. Consider dogs, for example. According to Plomin and his colleagues (1997), over history, humans bred many kinds of dogs to behave in certain ways. Terriers were bred to crawl down holes and flush out small animals, Labrador retrievers to carry game such as ducks in their mouths, and so on. It is apparent that breeds of dogs differ in their intelligence and temperament, and yet all are members of the same species; they can interbreed. The variations among the different breeds are due to their genes.

As we shall see repeatedly throughout this book, genetics is not of academic interest only. Genes not only affect who and what we are, but also can make us vulnerable to certain diseases. For example, researchers in Iceland have discovered an allele for a certain gene that makes a person vulnerable to having a stroke. People who have this gene are five times more likely than those who don't to suffer a stroke—which means that having this gene is a bigger risk factor than having high cholesterol, smoking, or having high blood pressure (Wade, 2002).

**Complex inheritance:** The joint action of combinations of genes working together.

The far-reaching power of relatively small genetic differences can be seen dramatically by comparing chimpanzees with humans: About 99% of the genetic material in both species is identical (Wildman et al., 2002).

**MAPPING THE GENES** How are researchers exploring the link between genes and behavior? In some organisms, such as yeast, researchers have *mapped* the genes in exquisite detail. To "map" a gene is to discover the particular segment or segments of the DNA molecule that constitute the gene. In June 2000, The Human Genome Project announced a "rough draft" of a gene map for humans, but it is only a rough draft—huge portions of human DNA remain uncharted territory. (Moreover, this project did not specify the range of alleles that can occur or their relationship to any disorders.) In the single-celled organism the paramecium (that wiggly oblong creature you may have labored to get into focus under a microscope in high school biology class), at least 20 genes are known to affect one behavior—withdrawal. Scientists have found that **mutations**, or physical changes, of various genes in paramecia produce different behaviors. The mutations are often given amusing names, which makes them easy to remember (we talk about such memory aids in Chapter 7). For example, "pawn" mutant paramecia can only swim forward, like a chess pawn; "paranoiac" mutants tend to swim backward (apparently wary of everything in front of them); and "sluggish" mutants are, well, sluggish.

The degree of understanding scientists have achieved concerning the way genes affect behavior is staggering. Consider a startling result reported in late 1996 by Ryner and her colleagues. These researchers identified a single gene that can change the sexual behavior of fruit flies. Usually, fruit flies engage in a "courtship dance" before they mate. The male follows the female, uses his forelegs to tap her body, produces a "song" by vibrating his wings, then licks her genitals, curls his abdomen, and tries to mate with her (Ferveur et al., 1995; Hall, 1994 [cited in Ryner et al., 1996]). By altering one gene, scientists produced male fruit flies that performed this courtship dance for other males. In fact, when a group of males with this gene were together, they lined up in a long chain, each male both being courted by and courting other males. The gene that controls this behavior affects only about 500 of the 100,000 neurons in the insect's head. A small genetic change, affecting a relatively small number of neurons, had a big effect. The affected neurons apparently coordinate many other neurons, which in turn produce the behavior.

**KNOCKOUT AND KNOCKIN MICE** Genetic studies have also been done with mice. Today it is commonplace for researchers to create new strains of mice by altering their genes. One such alteration involves removing a particular gene, creating **knockout mice**. A gene is knocked out when a part of the genetic code has been snipped away, deleting all (or crucial parts) of the gene so that it is disabled. The basic idea is that if a gene is used in a particular function, then knocking out the gene should create a deficit in that function. For example, Lijam and colleagues (1997) deleted a single gene in mice, which corresponded to one in fruit flies that has been dubbed "disheveled." In fruit flies, eliminating this gene causes the larvae to develop oddly along the head-to-tail axis, which makes them look disheveled. To the researchers' surprise, mice without this gene looked perfectly normal, but their social behavior was not at all normal. When normal mice are housed in the same cage, the dominant mouse usually trims away the whiskers and facial hair of the others—but the mutant mice don't follow this practice. Normal mice tend to sleep congenially in a huddled mass, but the mutants were scattered about the cage. And the mutants also had trouble building the normal kind of nests for sleeping. In addition, the mutants had trouble with *sensorimotor gating*, which is the ability to focus on some stimuli while ignoring others. Of great interest is the fact that certain disorders in humans, such as autism, have similar symptoms. Thus, researchers are exploring the possibility that a similar human gene plays a role in such disorders.

**Mutation:** A physical change in a gene.

**Knockout mice:** Mice in which part of the genetic code has been snipped away, deleting all (or crucial parts) of a gene so that it is disabled.

Researchers also use another technique to study the role of genes in affecting the brain and behavior. This one relies on creating **knockin mice**, in which a gene is added or substituted for one already there. (The gene is introduced in the embryo.) The new gene expresses (produces) a different substance or results in different amounts of some substance. For example, in one study mice were given a gene that made their hippocampus vulnerable to *excitotoxic injury* (Zhu et al., 1999). Such injury occurs when too much glutamate is present. (Curiously, glutamate is not only the most common neurotransmitter in the brain, but it is also toxic to neurons if too much of it is present.) The gene the mice were given has been linked to Alzheimer's disease, which causes memory problems. Thus, the researchers were interested in the effects of this gene on the hippocampus (part of the brain critical for memory). And, in fact, the gene did cause damage to neurons in the hippocampus. However, the study had an interesting twist. The researchers knew that putting mice on a diet could extend their life spans and protect them from various disorders (Sohal & Weindruch, 1996); could it also mitigate the effects of the new gene? When mice were fed only every other day, the bad effects of the gene were counteracted. This study suggests that food intake could play a role in regulating Alzheimer's disease.

As marvelous as all of this sounds, there is a fundamental problem with using knockout and knockin mice to discover the function of a specific gene: The missing or introduced gene may in some way cause the other genes to function in novel ways. By analogy, if a dog had an accident and one of its front legs had to be removed, the other three legs wouldn't continue to function as they had before; the dog might now get around with a kind of hop, and the remaining front leg would become much stronger (see Figure 3.24). Similarly, if an animal is born missing a gene, the remaining genes might compensate in subtle and complex ways. By the same token, an added gene might cause other genes to function differently; by analogy, if you've broken a leg, a crutch will help you get around, but does so by making you use your intact leg in a new way (as attested by the sore leg muscles you'll get when you first start using the crutch). To get around this problem, scientists have created *inducible knockouts*, animals in which the genetic code has been altered so that the animal develops normally, but a specific chemical can activate or deactivate (depending on the alteration) a particular gene (Nestler et al., 2001). This technique allows a mutation to make its presence felt in a normal adult animal and to affect only a specific region of the brain (such as one small part of the hippocampus).

## Tuning Genetic Programs: The Environment Matters

When it comes to physical, mental, and behavioral characteristics, what you see is not necessarily what you get in the genes: The phenotype may not simply be a read-out of the underlying genotype. There can be no question that genes play a major role in shaping our abilities, but it is critical to point out that genes *cannot* program the structure of the brain entirely in advance. Your brain contained far more connections at birth than it does now. As you interacted with the environment, certain neural connections were used over and over again, while others were used hardly at all. Connections between neurons in parts of the brain that are used frequently are retained, while others, which are not used frequently, are pruned away (Huttenlocher, 2002). **Pruning** is a process whereby certain neural connections are eliminated (Cowan et al., 1984; Huttenlocher, 2002): As the saying goes, "Use it or lose it." The genes define the range of possibilities for brain circuits, but interactions with the environment lead some connections to persist and others to disappear.

FIGURE 3.24

## Many Systems Are Compensatory

If a dog had an accident and one of its front legs had to be removed, the other three legs would compensate. The dog might now hop from place to place, and the remaining front leg would grow much stronger. Similarly, if an animal is born missing a gene, the remaining genes may compensate in subtle and complex ways.

Knockin mice: Mice in which a new gene has been added or substituted for one already there.

Pruning: A process whereby certain connections among neurons are eliminated.

**Plasticity:** The brain's ability to be molded by experience.

Pruning is only one of the ways in which your brain changes as you experience the world. Such changes are part and parcel of the brain's **plasticity**, its ability to change with experience. (Like plastic, the brain can be molded by external forces.) Connections are also added. In fact, researchers have found that if rats are raised in enriched environments, with lots of toys and things to do, their brains actually become heavier than those of rats raised in average environments. The additional weight comes about in part because more blood flows to the cortex (Jones & Greenough, 1996) and in part because new connections are formed (Black et al., 1998; Comery et al., 1995; Diamond et al., 1972; Greenough & Chang, 1985; Greenough et al., 1987; Nelson, 1999; Turner & Greenough, 1985). The environment not only helps to select among connections established by the genes; it can also cause new connections to form.

In fact, even adult brains are capable of dramatic reorganization. If a finger is lost or immobilized, the part of the brain that used to register its input is soon taken over by inputs from other fingers (Merzenich et al., 1983a, 1983b; additional evidence is provided by Ramachandran, 1993; Ramachandran et al., 1992; Xerri et al., 1999). Moreover, if two fingers are surgically connected, the brain regions that register them start to function as a unit, but this unit splits up if the fingers are then surgically separated (Clark et al., 1988; Das & Gilbert, 1995; Kaas, 1995; Mogilner et al., 1993; Wang et al., 1995). We also now know that adult brains can create new neurons, at least in some regions (Gould et al., 1999; Kempermann et al., 2004).

Plasticity is most evident in four circumstances: (1) during infancy and childhood, when the brain is being shaped by interactions with the environment; (2) when the body changes, so that the sensory input changes; (3) when we learn something new, or store new information; and (4) as compensation after brain damage—even healthy portions of the young soldier's brain probably changed after his injury but, unfortunately, not as much as they probably would have if he had still been a child (Payne & Lomber, 2001).

Thus, genes are not destiny; they don't fix our characteristics forevermore. The genes determine the range of what is possible (humans can't grow wings), but within those limits interactions with the environment can alter both the structure and the function of the brain.

## Genes and Environment: A Single System

How do interactions with the environment alter the brain? Some people think of genes as blueprints for the body, providing the instructions on how to build organs, but this notion captures only part of the genes' role. For one thing, rather than being filed away in a dusty drawer once their instructions have been followed, many genes keep working throughout your life. Their action is the reason some people go bald, others develop high cholesterol, and still others get varicose veins. Even more important, genes are not simply time bombs that are set at birth and ready to explode at the proper hour. Many genes change their operation constantly, sometimes producing proteins and sometimes not. Psychiatrist Steven Hyman (personal communication) suggested the following illuminating example: Say you want bigger biceps, and so you go to the gym and start lifting weights. After the first week, all you have to show for your time and sweat is aching arms. But, after a few weeks, the muscles begin to firm up and soon may even begin to bulge. What has happened? When you first lifted weights, you actually damaged the muscles, and the damage caused the release of certain chemicals. Those chemicals then—and this is the important part—*turned on* genes in the muscle cells. Here, "turned on" means that the proteins coded by the genes were produced. These proteins were used to build up the damaged muscles. If the damage stops, so do the chemicals that signal the genes to turn on, and the genes will no longer produce those

Some songbirds learn the songs of their particular species only by hearing other birds sing them. Mello and colleagues (1992) showed that the process of learning a song begins when certain genes are turned on as the bird first hears the song, which in turn regulates the effects of other genes that actually produce the learning.

extra proteins. So, you need to lift increasingly heavier weights to keep building more muscle. No pain, no gain.

The important point to remember is that many genes are constantly being turned on and off, as needed, to produce specific substances. As you read this, for example, terminal buttons of some of your axons are releasing neurotransmitters that enable you to understand the printed words. Genes are turned on to replenish the buttons' supply of neurotransmitters. Similarly, genes regulate the flow of neuromodulators, and they also initiate new connections among cells during learning of new material.

Just as interacting with the environment by lifting weights can lead to bulging muscles, interacting with the environment in various ways can set your brain to operate more or less efficiently. And depending on how your brain is working, you behave differently. By regulating the brain, genes affect behavior.

It is commonplace today for scientists to stress that both genes and environment are important. This is true, but, stated in that way, it misses the mark. Genes and environment cannot really be considered as separate factors; they are instead *different aspects of a single system*. In much the same way as you can focus separately on the brushstrokes, perspective, composition, and colors of a painting, you can discuss genes and the environment as discrete entities. But, as with a painting, to appreciate the "whole picture," you must consider genes and environment together (Gottlieb, 1998).

If you lift heavy weights, you will damage your arm muscles, which in turn causes the release of certain chemicals that *turn on* genes in the muscle cells. These genes then produce proteins, which build up the muscles. Dwayne (The Rock) Johnson has managed to turn on many of these genes, but all of us turn on genes in our brains when we expend mental effort.

## Environment and Genes: A Two-Way Street

Genes can affect the environment, and the environment can affect the genes. Remember, we are talking about a single system here. Plomin and colleagues (1997), Scarr and McCartney (1983), and others distinguish three ways that genes and environment interact. First, **passive interaction** occurs when genetically shaped tendencies of parents or siblings produce an environment that is passively received by the child. An example: Parents with higher intelligence tend to read more, and thus have more books in the house. Given that parents with higher intelligence tend to have children with higher intelligence, this means that children with higher intelligence will tend to be born into environments with more books (Plomin, 1995). Second, **evocative** (or **reactive**) **interaction** occurs when genetically influenced characteristics draw out behaviors from other people. We might call this the "blondes have more fun" effect. Having blonde hair is (often, anyway) a genetic trait, one that can elicit varying responses. Some people react

**Passive interaction:** Occurs when genetically shaped tendencies of parents or siblings produce an environment that is passively received by the child.

**Evocative (or reactive) interaction:** Occurs when genetically influenced characteristics draw out behaviors from other people.

Passive interaction

Evocative interaction

Active interaction

Men with a particular gene (for which they can be tested) are likely to become alcoholics if they drink at all (Goedde & Agarwal, 1987). Having this gene presents no downside, however, for men who obey the norms of a strict Muslim or Mormon culture, in which alcohol is forbidden. Genes are merely one element in a larger system, which includes the environment.

to blondes more positively than they do to brunettes. Others, however, may think blondes are less substantial people than are brunettes. Third, genes and environment interact when people deliberately choose to put themselves in specific situations and aggressively avoid others. Such **active interaction** occurs when people choose, partly based on genetic tendencies, to put themselves in situations that are comfortable for them or to avoid situations that are uncomfortable (or to modify existing situations in ways that make them comfortable for existing genetic tendencies). A timid person, for instance, may avoid loud parties and amusement parks, instead seeking out peaceful settings and quiet pastimes.

# Behavioral Genetics

Researchers in the field of **behavioral genetics** try to determine the extent to which the differences among people's behaviors and abilities are due to their different genetic makeups or to differences in their environments. The environment varies at different times and places, so this is a difficult question indeed. Throughout this book, we talk about the relative contributions of genes and the environment to differences in mental processes or behavior. Here we need to stress a crucial point: Any conclusions about the relative contributions of genes and environment can apply only to the specific circumstances in which they were measured. You've just seen that genes are turned on in different circumstances, and, depending on which genes are turned on in a given environment, the brain will work more or less effectively. Statements about relative contributions of genes and environments, therefore, apply only to the situation at hand and may have no bearing on different circumstances.

## Heritability, Not Inheritability

Researchers in behavioral genetics focus on estimating the heritability of various characteristics, ranging from intelligence to personality, as they occur in specific environments. **Heritability** is a potentially confusing term. It does not indicate the amount of a characteristic or trait that is inherited, but rather how much of the *variability* in that characteristic in a population is due to genetics. Height in Western countries is about 90% heritable. This statement means that 90% of the variability among the heights of people in these countries is genetically determined, not that *your* height was determined 90% by your genes and 10% by your environment. In fact, the possible differences in height owing to diet may actually be greater than the differences owing to genes; but *in a specific environment* (for example, one in which diet is constant), heritability indicates the contribution of the genes to variations. If the environment were different, the heritability might be different, too.

## Twin Studies: Only Shared Genes?

At first glance, the simplest way to study whether variability in a characteristic is inherited might seem to involve comparing the characteristics of parents and their children. But this method doesn't sort out the effects of genes and the environment. On the one hand, parents and kids share a common household, which could *increase* the correlation. But factors such as different ages and occupations, and the likelihood that parents and children spend much of their days in different environments, could

**Active interaction:** Occurs when people choose, partly based on genetic tendencies, to put themselves in specific situations and to avoid others.

**Behavioral genetics:** The field in which researchers attempt to determine the extent to which the differences among people are due to their genes or to the environment.

**Heritability:** The degree to which variability in a characteristic is due to genetics.

*decrease* the correlation. Because of these confounding variables, we can gain greater insight by studying brothers and sisters who are about the same age. But, because even small age differences can make a big difference in certain environments (such as school), it is best to study twins, people who are exactly the same age.

**Twin studies** compare the two types of twins, identical and fraternal. Identical twins start life when a single, fertilized egg divides in two; these twins are **monozygotic** (like many scientific terms, this comes from Greek: *monos*, meaning "single," and *zygotos*, meaning "yoked," as occurs when a sperm and egg are joined). Monozygotic twins have identical genes. In contrast, fraternal twins grow from two separate eggs that are fertilized by two different sperm; these twins are **dizygotic**. Fraternal twins share only as many genes as any other pair of brothers or sisters—on average, half. By comparing identical twins and fraternal twins, we get a good idea of the contribution of the genes, if we assume that the environment is the same for members of both sets of twins. Such studies have shown that the amount of gray matter in the brain (where neural cell bodies exist) is very similar in identical twins, which suggests that the amount of gray matter is, in part, under genetic control (Thompson et al., 2001; summarized and commented on by Plomin & Kosslyn, 2001). This similarity is particularly pronounced in the frontal lobes and in a part of the temporal lobe involved in language comprehension. So what? Well, the amount of such gray matter is correlated with scores on intelligence tests—and (as we will see in Chapter 9) identical twins tend to have similar levels of intelligence, perhaps for this reason.

About 90% of the *variation* in height is controlled by the genes, and thus height is about 90% heritable. Heritability estimates assume that the environment is constant; if the environment varies (perhaps by providing a better or poorer diet), environmental factors can overshadow even very high heritability.

## Adoption Studies: Separating Genes and Environment?

An even better way to gather evidence for the relative contributions of genes and environment is to compare characteristics of children adopted at birth to those of their adoptive parents or siblings versus their biological parents or siblings. Called an **adoption study**, this type of investigation is particularly powerful when twins who have been separated at birth, or shortly thereafter, grow up in different environments. Even in these cases, however, it is difficult to separate genetic from environmental influences. If the twins are cute, for instance, caregivers in both households will treat them differently than if they look tough and fearless; if they are smart and curious, both sets of parents may be inclined to buy books and read to them. So findings from studies of twins separated at birth are fascinating, but even they don't allow us to separate genetic from environmental effects with confidence. The best we can say is that genes contribute a certain amount to differences among people in particular environments, and that environments contribute a certain amount to such differences when people have particular genes.

## Evolution and the Brain: The Best of All Possible Brains?

The loss of consciousness and brain damage suffered by the young soldier occurred because he breathed toxic fumes and was deprived of oxygen. However, not all species

**Twin study:** A study that compares identical and fraternal twins to determine the relative contribution of genes to variability in a behavior or characteristic.

**Monozygotic:** From the same egg and having identical genes.

**Dizygotic:** From different eggs and sharing only as many genes as any pair of brothers or sisters—on average, half.

**Adoption study:** A study in which characteristics of children adopted at birth are compared to those of their adoptive parents or siblings versus their biological parents or siblings (often twins). These studies often focus on comparisons of twins who were raised in the same versus different households.

would be affected by that situation the way this member of our human species was. Sperm whales, for instance, do just fine if they take a breath every 75 minutes or so. Why don't our brains give us this extra protection? This question leads to thoughts about **evolution**, the gene-based changes in the characteristics of members of a species over successive generations.

## Natural Selection: Reproduction of the Fittest

A major driving force of evolution is **natural selection**, which was first described in detail in 1858 by Charles Darwin and, independently, by Alfred Russel Wallace. Inherited characteristics that contribute to survival in an environment are those that will come to be widespread in a population. Why? Because the individuals with those characteristics are the ones that live long enough to have many offspring. In turn, those offspring, equipped with the favorable characteristics inherited from their parents, will survive to have more offspring. In this way, the "selection" of the survivors is made by "nature." An inherited characteristic that results from such selection is called an **adaptation**. The oft-used phrase "survival of the fittest" is perhaps unfortunate; the key point is that some characteristics lead some organisms to have more offspring, who in turn have more offspring, and so on—until their inheritable characteristics are spread throughout the population. Plomin and colleagues (1997) point out that the principle might better have been expressed as "reproduction of the fittest."

Darwin saw this pattern in a brilliant insight; but where are the genes in the story? Nowhere. Genes were not discovered until the early part of the 20th century, and not discovered to correspond to DNA until 1953. Darwin never knew that the mechanism for the transmission of traits from one generation to the next is the gene. Today, we would say that natural selection depends on the fact that there is variation in the genes carried by members of a population, and if a gene allows an organism to have more offspring that survive (and they have more offspring, and so on), eventually more of that particular gene will be present in the population.

Evolution via natural selection tends to mold the characteristics of a group of organisms to the requirements of their environment. If a certain animal lives near the North Pole, those individuals with warm fur will tend to have more babies that survive, and those individuals that are white (and thus harder for predators to spot in the snow) will tend to have more babies that survive. If these characteristics are useful enough in that environment, eventually the species as a whole will have warm white fur.

Here's a contemporary analogy of the way natural selection works. There were two Chinese brothers; one settled in Louisiana and the other in Ohio. They both opened Chinese restaurants and began with identical menus. After the first month, the brother in Louisiana noticed that his blander dishes were not selling well, so he dropped them from the menu; in Ohio, they were doing fine, so they remained. In Louisiana, the chef one day accidentally knocked a jar of chili powder into a pot of chicken he was simmering. He found he liked the taste, so this new dish became the special of the day. It sold so well that it became a standard on the menu. Hearing the tale, the brother up north in Ohio tried the chili dish, but it didn't sell well. This chef bought a lot of corn, which was on sale. He tried adding it to a traditional dish and called it the special of the day. The Ohio chef wasn't trying to achieve a particular taste, he was just experimenting. That corn dish did not sell well, and so was dropped. But when he added corn to another recipe, the result was an instant hit. Both chefs continued with new elements in their cooking, with varying degrees of success on different occasions. As shown in Figure 3.25, after two years, the brothers' menus had little in common.

**Evolution:** Gene-based changes in the characteristics of members of a species over successive generations.

**Natural selection:** Changes in the frequency of genes in a population that arise because genes allow an organism to have more offspring that survive.

**Adaptation:** A characteristic that increases an organism's fitness for an environment.

**FIGURE 3.25**

# The Menu Model of Natural Selection

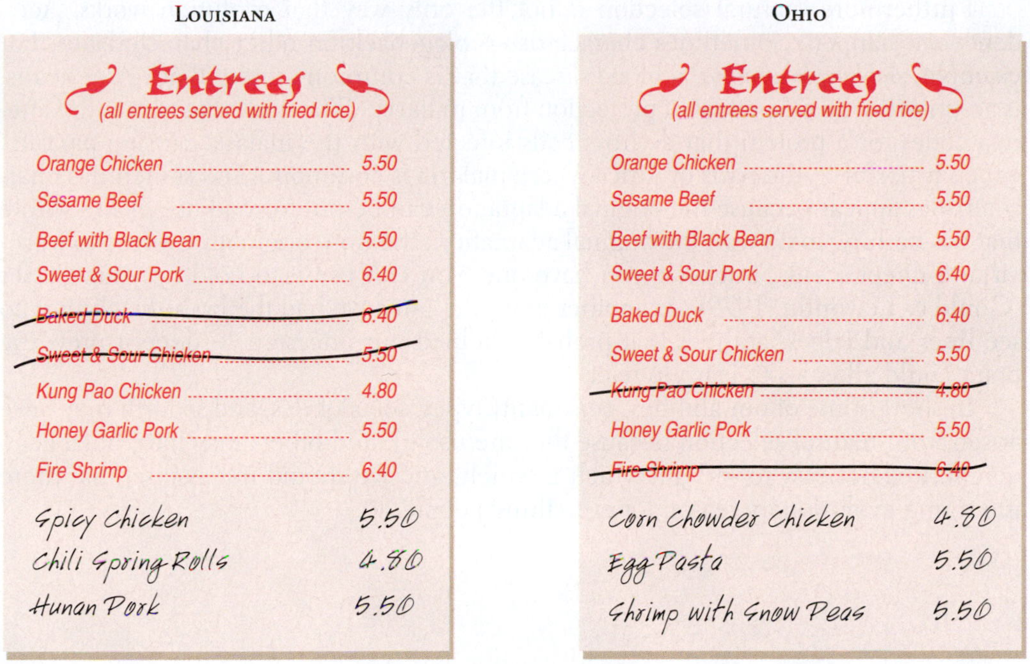

LOUISIANA

### Entrees
*(all entrees served with fried rice)*

| | |
|---|---|
| Orange Chicken | 5.50 |
| Sesame Beef | 5.50 |
| Beef with Black Bean | 5.50 |
| Sweet & Sour Pork | 6.40 |
| ~~Baked Duck~~ | ~~6.40~~ |
| ~~Sweet & Sour Chicken~~ | ~~5.50~~ |
| Kung Pao Chicken | 4.80 |
| Honey Garlic Pork | 5.50 |
| Fire Shrimp | 6.40 |
| Spicy Chicken | 5.50 |
| Chili Spring Rolls | 4.80 |
| Hunan Pork | 5.50 |

OHIO

### Entrees
*(all entrees served with fried rice)*

| | |
|---|---|
| Orange Chicken | 5.50 |
| Sesame Beef | 5.50 |
| Beef with Black Bean | 5.50 |
| Sweet & Sour Pork | 6.40 |
| Baked Duck | 6.40 |
| Sweet & Sour Chicken | 5.50 |
| ~~Kung Pao Chicken~~ | ~~4.80~~ |
| Honey Garlic Pork | 5.50 |
| ~~Fire Shrimp~~ | ~~6.40~~ |
| Corn Chowder Chicken | 4.80 |
| Egg Pasta | 5.50 |
| Shrimp with Snow Peas | 5.50 |

Evolution by natural selection is illustrated when accidental variations change the menus, and features of the environment (the diners' tastes, in this metaphor) "select" some of these changes. In living beings, over generations such selection results in changes in genes.

Two important principles of evolution are illustrated here. First, the "environment"—the hungry restaurant patrons—"selected" different aspects of the menus: The southerners, for example, apparently liked spicy food better than did the patrons in Ohio. Second, variation is at the heart of the process. Without the accidents and substitutions, the process would not have worked—the menus would not have evolved over time. Natural selection in the evolution of the two menus depended on random variation, which provided the "options" that proved more or less adaptive.

The same is true in the evolution of species, but in this case the "menu" is the set of genes different organisms possess. Genes that lead an organism to have offspring who have still more offspring stay on the menu, and those that do not lead to this result eventually get dropped.

So, back to the question of the sperm whale and breathing. If our ancestors had had to go for long periods without breathing in order to survive, then only those who could do so would have survived and had offspring—and we lucky descendants would have inherited this ability. And the story of our young soldier might have had a happier ending.

## Not Just Natural Selection: Accidents Do Happen

A word of warning: Always exercise caution when trying to use the idea of natural selection to explain our present-day characteristics. Just because a characteristic exists doesn't mean that it is an adaptation to the environment or that it is the result of natural selection. Natural selection may or may not be the reason, for example, why some people are more prone than others to alcoholism. For one thing, as human brains and bodies evolved, the environment also changed: People created not only furniture, houses, and cities, but also automobiles, guns, computers, and candy. Our brains may not be ideally suited for what they are doing now.

Furthermore, natural selection is not the only way that evolution works. Accidents can happen. Sometimes characteristics piggyback on other characteristics. For example, *sickle-cell anemia*, a blood disease that is common among Black Americans, is an unfortunate side-effect of protection from malaria. (The gene that causes the anemia codes for a protein that destroys cells infected with the malaria-causing parasite, which is useful in the parts of Africa where malaria is common.) And sometimes characteristics appear because the original adaptation can be put to good use in a new role that has nothing to do with the original adaptation; the nose originally evolved to warm air and direct scents, but once you have one, you can use it to hold up your glasses (Gould & Lewontin, 1979). As another example, once we had the brain machinery to see lines and edges, abilities that probably helped our ancestors to discern prey, the brain could allow us to learn to read.

In short, some of our abilities, personality types, social styles, and so forth may have arisen from natural selection because they are useful, and others may have been accidental. It is not easy to sort out which is which, and we should not assume that there is a sound evolutionary reason for everything people do.

# Test Yourself

1. Genes do not produce behavior directly. Instead, they produce
   a. DNA.
   b. RNA.
   c. proteins.
   d. neurons.

2. When researchers remove, add, or modify genes in fruit flies and mice, they are trying to
   a. map their genes.
   b. produce better animals.
   c. understand the link between genes and the environment.
   d. understand the link between genes and behavior.

3. In which of the following circumstances is brain plasticity *not* evident?
   a. during infancy
   b. when sensory input remains constant
   c. when we learn or store something new
   d. when neural connections are being pruned

4. Researchers in the field of behavioral genetics try to determine the extent to which the differences among people are due to their different genetic makeups or to differences in their
   a. brains.
   b. environments.
   c. behavior.
   d. personalities.

## Answers

1. c 2. d 3. b 4. b

# Think It Through!

Did natural selection change the human brain so that it is vulnerable to damage such as that sustained by the soldier's brain? Does it make sense that different areas of the brain are responsible for vision versus hearing and language? Which parts of the human brain would you expect to find in other animals, and why?

Can you think of any human abilities that seem likely to be adaptations? How about abilities that could be evolutionary accidents? How could you tell whether a characteristic is present because of natural selection?

# REVIEW AND REMEMBER!

## Summary

You've seen ample evidence that carbon monoxide fumes damaged the soldier's brain—but exactly how? We could narrow down our explanation for his problems to the following three aspects of brain function: First, many—but not all—neurons in the occipital lobes died because of a lack of oxygen and nutrients. This damage caused him to have fuzzy vision. Second, the parietal lobes, thalamus, or some other area used in attention was also damaged so that he had a narrow range of attention and thus could not perceive the context in which a shape appears. Hence, he only saw small details. Third, alternatively, or perhaps additionally, he only saw small details because the temporal lobe in his right hemisphere was damaged, an area that typically registers overall shapes; or, possibly, the connections to the right temporal lobe from the occipital lobes were damaged. But his left hemisphere, particularly his left frontal lobe, apparently was intact enough to allow him to make up a story based on what he saw, allowing him to try to make sense of the stimulus. Thus, he saw details in isolation and tried to think what they might be.

## I. Brain Circuits: Making Connections

**A.** The neuron is the key building block of the brain. The cell body receives inputs from the dendrites (or, sometimes, directly from axons of other neurons) and sends its output via the axon (which is connected to the dendrites of other neurons or, in some cases, their cell bodies).

**B.** The axon is covered with myelin, a fatty insulating material, that makes neural transmission more efficient. The axon branches into separate terminals. The terminal buttons at the end of the terminals contain chemical substances that are released by an action potential. These substances are either neurotransmitters or neuromodulators.

**C.** Neurotransmitters cross the synaptic cleft (the gap between the end of the axon and the receiving neuron) to affect another neuron. Neuromodulators can be released into this space, or they can be distributed more diffusely in the fluid surrounding neurons. Both neurotransmitters and neuromodulators affect receptors, which are like locks that are opened by the right key. Once opened, the receptor causes a chain of events inside the neuron.

**D.** When the total input to a neuron is sufficiently excitatory, the neuron "fires"— that is, chemical reactions work their way down the axon. After a neuron has fired, surplus neurotransmitter is reabsorbed back into the cells. Some drugs block this reuptake mechanism.

**E.** Some neuromodulators are not released from terminal buttons. Endogenous cannabinoids, for example, are released by the receiving neuron and inhibit sending neurons.

**F.** Glial cells not only control the creation of synapses and support neurons, but also help to regulate neurotransmitters and can affect neurons directly. Moreover, glial cells themselves may play a role in information processing.

## Your Notes

I.

A. Each neuron—only one sending end (an axon) but many receiving ends (dendrites)

B.

C.

D.

E.

F.

## II. The Nervous System: An Orchestra With Many Members

**A.** The nervous system has two major parts: the peripheral nervous system (PNS) and the central nervous system (CNS).

**B.** The PNS consists of the autonomic nervous system (ANS) and the sensory-somatic nervous system (SSNS). The ANS is in turn divided into the sympathetic and parasympathetic nervous systems, the first of which is critically involved in the "fight or flight" response. The SSNS consists of the cranial nerves, which reach the brain through openings in the skull, and the skeletal system, which connects to muscles that can be moved voluntarily.

**C.** The CNS consists of the spinal cord and the brain itself. In addition to sending commands from the brain to the body and passing along sensory input to the brain, the spinal cord also is responsible for some reflexes. Reflexes depend on the action of interneurons, neurons that hook up to other neurons.

**D.** The brain itself is organized into lobes and is covered by the cortex, a thin layer of neurons.

**E.** The cortex contains many bulges (gyri) and creases (sulci), which allows a lot of cortex to be crammed into a relatively small space.

## III. Spotlight on the Brain: How It Divides and Conquers

**A.** The four major lobes in each hemisphere are the occipital, temporal, parietal, and frontal. The occipital lobe processes visual input. The temporal lobe is the seat of visual memories and is also involved in language comprehension, hearing, storing new memories, and some aspects of consciousness. The parietal lobe registers size, three-dimensionality, and location in space, and is also involved in attention, arithmetic, motor control, and consciousness; it includes the somatosensory strip, which registers sensation from parts of the body. The frontal lobe is involved in speech production, searching for memories, reasoning (and using memory to help in reasoning), fine motor control (governed by the motor strip), and making decisions.

**B.** Each lobe is duplicated, one on the left and one on the right. The left hemisphere, which plays a larger role in language, appears to be critical to the ability to invent stories to make sense of the world. The right hemisphere plays a larger role than the left in recognizing overall shapes and in some nonverbal functions.

**C.** Split-brain patients have had the two brain hemispheres surgically disconnected, through severing of the corpus callosum. This rare surgery is done only for medical reasons.

**D.** Under the cortex, many subcortical areas play crucial roles in the brain's function. The thalamus manages connections to and from distinct parts of the brain; the hypothalamus plays a crucial role in regulating hormones, which is important for its role in controlling bodily functions such as eating, drinking, and sex; the hippocampus is involved in the storage of new memories; and the amygdala plays a role in fear and other emotions.

**E.** The hippocampus, amygdala, and other structures constitute the limbic system, which is involved in fighting, fleeing, feeding, and sex.

---

II.

A.

B. *Sympathetic increases arousal.*
   *Parasympathetic reduces arousal.*

C.

D.

E.

III.

A.

B.

C.

D.

E.

**F.** The basal ganglia are used in planning and producing movements, as well as in learning new habits. The brainstem contains structures involved in alertness, sleep, and arousal; and the cerebellum is involved in motor control, timing, and attention.

**G.** The neuroendocrine system produces hormones, which not only affect the body but also affect the brain itself (by, for example, altering moods).

**H.** The neuroimmune system produces substances that affect our immunity to infection.

## IV. Probing the Brain

**A.** The earliest method used to discover what the various parts of the brain do involved observing the effects of brain damage on behavior. Such natural experiments led scientists to investigate the effects of lesioning parts of animal brains.

**B.** Scientists can record electrical activity produced by the firing of neurons while people and animals perform specific tasks, using either electrodes on the scalp or tiny electrodes placed in neurons; they find more vigorous activity in areas involved in the task than in those that are not involved. Researchers can also record magnetic fields produced by neurons when they fire.

**C.** Neurons can be electrically or magnetically stimulated (using transcranial magnetic stimulation, or TMS) to fire and the effects on behavior observed.

**D.** Various neuroimaging techniques include the following: computer-assisted tomography (CT), which uses X rays to obtain images of the structures of the brain; magnetic resonance imaging (MRI), which makes use of magnetic fields to produce very sharp pictures of the brain; positron emission tomography (PET), which relies on small amounts of radioactivity to track blood flow or energy consumption in the brain; functional magnetic resonance imaging (fMRI), which uses changes in the magnetic properties of blood when oxygen is bound to red blood cells to track blood in the brain as a person performs a task but can also be used to track various chemicals in the brain; and optical imaging, which tracks changes in how much light of different frequencies is absorbed or reflected by the brain while a person performs a task.

## V. Genes, Brain, and Environment: The Brain in the World

**A.** Individual genes can affect the brain and behavior (via Mendelian inheritance), or sets of genes working together can have these effects (via complex inheritance). Genes cannot be considered in isolation. The genes lay down the basic structure of the brain, but the environment can mold both its structure and its function.

**B.** Genes influence how people and other animals respond to environmental effects. The effects of genes can be studied with knockout mice (which have a gene removed) or knockin mice (which have a gene replaced or a new one added).

**C.** During brain development, the environment affects brain structure and function by pruning connections that are not working well; it also causes the brain to form new connections in response to new stimuli.

*Right margin notes:*

F.

G.

H.

IV.

A.

B.

C.

D. CT, MRI: brain structure
 PET, fMRI, optical imaging: brain activity

V.

A.

B.

C.

**D.** The genes place limits on what is possible (for example, people can't grow wings), and even small genetic changes can sometimes exert significant effects on the brain, mental processes, and behavior.

**E.** However, many of your genes are under the control of the environment, and are turned on and off depending on what you are doing; specific genes cause the manufacture of neurotransmitters or neuromodulators and can even cause neurons to hook up in new ways.

**F.** Behavioral genetics attempts to discover how much of the variability in a behavior or ability is due to the genes versus the environment, but such estimates apply only to the environment in which the behavior or ability is measured.

**G.** The relative contributions of genes and environment are sometimes investigated by comparing twins (identical versus fraternal) and by studying people who have been adopted.

**H.** We have our present sets of genes because of evolution, partly as a consequence of natural selection (genes are retained in the population when they produce characteristics that lead to more surviving offspring who in turn have surviving offspring) and partly as a consequence of accidents.

**I.** Our brains and bodies were not designed for all that we use them for today, and hence it is not surprising that in some cases we are vulnerable to properties of the environment (such as sweets, drugs, and the opportunity to drive too fast).

NOTE: Once you feel that you understand the material in this chapter, visit the book's Web site at www.ablongman.com/kosslyn3e to test your knowledge with additional study questions.

## Key Terms

action potential, p. 80
active interaction, p. 122
adaptation, p. 124
adoption study, p. 123
agonist, p. 85
all-or-none law, p. 80
amygdala, p. 102
antagonist, p. 85
autonomic nervous system (ANS), p. 88
axon, p. 79
basal ganglia, p. 103
behavioral genetics, p. 122
brain circuit, p. 78
brainstem, p. 103
cell body, p. 78
cell membrane, p. 78
central nervous system (CNS), p. 91

cerebellum, p. 103
cerebral cortex, p. 92
cerebral hemisphere, p. 91
complex inheritance, p. 117
computer-assisted tomography (CT, formerly CAT), p. 111
corpus callosum, p. 91
cortisol, p. 104
dendrite, p. 79
deoxyribonucleic acid, DNA, p. 116
dizygotic, p. 123
electroencephalogram, p. 110
electroencephalograph (EEG), p. 109
endogenous cannabinoids, p. 82
estrogen, p. 104
evocative (or reactive) interaction, p. 121
evolution, p. 124

forebrain, p. 100
frontal lobe, p. 96
functional magnetic resonance imaging (fMRI), p. 113
gene, p. 116
genotype, p. 116
glial cell, p. 86
gyrus, p. 92
heritability, p. 122
hindbrain, p. 104
hippocampus, p. 102
hormone, p. 104
hypothalamic-pituitary-adrenal (HPA) axis, p. 105
hypothalamus, p. 101
interneuron, p. 78
ion, p. 79
knockin mice, p. 119

knockout mice, p. 118

lesion, p. 109

limbic system, p. 102

lobes, p. 91

magnetic resonance imaging (MRI), p. 111

magnetoencephalography, p. 110

medulla, p. 103

Mendelian inheritance, p. 116

meninges, p. 91

microelectrode, p. 110

midbrain, p. 104

monozygotic, p. 123

motor neuron, p. 78

motor strip, p. 97

mutation, p. 118

myelin, p. 80

natural selection, p. 124

neuroendocrine system, p. 104

neuroimaging, p. 111

neuromodulator, p. 82

neuron, p. 78

neurotransmitter, p. 82

occipital lobe, p. 94

parasympathetic nervous system, p. 90

parietal lobe, p. 95

passive interaction, p. 121

peripheral nervous system (PNS), p. 88

phenotype, p. 116

pituitary gland, p. 105

plasticity, p. 120

pons, p. 103

positron emission tomography (PET), p. 112

pruning, p. 119

receptor, p. 84

reflex, p. 91

resting potential, p. 79

reticular formation, p. 103

reuptake, p. 84

selective serotonin-reuptake inhibitor (SSRI), p. 85

sensory neuron, p. 78

sensory-somatic nervous system (SSNS), p. 90

skeletal system, p. 90

somatosensory strip, p. 95

spinal cord, p. 90

split-brain patient, p. 97

stroke, p. 109

subcortical structures, p. 92

sulcus, p. 92

sympathetic nervous system, 89

synapse, p. 82

synaptic cleft, p. 82

temporal lobe, p. 95

terminal button, p. 79

testosterone, p. 104

thalamus, p. 100

transcranial magnetic stimulation (TMS), p. 114

twin study, p. 123

ventricle, p. 92

# CHAPTER 4

# SENSATION AND PERCEPTION: HOW THE WORLD ENTERS THE MIND

T he Mexican painter Frida Kahlo (1907–1954) did not simply paint what she saw—she painted what she felt and understood. Kahlo's style of painting is classified as *surrealist* because she took liberties in portraying what her eyes registered, distorting objects in order to reveal the feelings, desires, and longings that welled within her as she perceived the world (Lowe, 1995). Kahlo's painting *The Two Fridas* (p. 134) is an example of this surrealism. The painting uses an "X-ray" view to show her broken heart, which of course cannot literally be seen. Kahlo often injected her physical and emotional pain into her paintings.

As an adult, Kahlo was an old hand at managing pain. She contracted polio at the age of 6, which left her right leg thin and weak. During childhood, Kahlo embarked on an intensive program of exercise and athletics to help that leg recover its strength. When she was 18 years old, she was in a horrendous bus accident. She spent a month in a cast in the hospital, and most of the next year in bed. Kahlo's mother had a special easel made so that Kahlo could pass the hours in bed painting (a mirror was rigged up above her bed so that she could be her own model). Thus began Kahlo's painting career; about a third of her paintings are self-portraits.

Four years after the accident, Kahlo married the famed Mexican mural painter Diego Rivera. They shared passions for politics, art, music, Mexican culture, and food. Kahlo took great pleasure in learning to cook Rivera's favorite dishes. Their relationship gave her great joy, but also great pain; Rivera was often unfaithful to her. They divorced, and then remarried each other about a year later. Shortly after divorce proceedings began, Frida painted her first large painting, *The Two Fridas*, which shows the Frida that Rivera loved (on the right) and the one that he no longer loved (this is the Frida with a broken heart, losing blood through a ruptured artery). Kahlo's artistic triumphs included exhibitions of her work in galleries in New York City and Paris. Her work has become even more popular now than it was during her lifetime.

Frida Kahlo was a person who delighted in her senses: She loved watching Rivera paint his giant murals; she enjoyed hearing the songs of street musicians in the local plaza; she reveled in the smells and tastes of Mexican food; she took pleasure in her husband's caresses. The act of sensing and perceiving stimuli of any kind, whether a song, a color-soaked canvas, or a soft caress, encompasses a remarkable series of events

Kahlo's label as a surrealist painter comes, in part, from her use of "X-ray" images, allowing the viewer to see what cannot normally be perceived. This painting, *The Two Fridas*, was painted in 1939 as Kahlo was getting divorced from Diego Rivera; the Frida on the left is, literally, heartbroken.

at the levels of the brain, the person, and the social group, all happening within the context of the physical world. The processes of sensation and perception lie at the root of our experience of being alive, serving as the foundation for most of what we know and do. If we cannot sense the world, then for all practical purposes it does not exist for us; if we sense it incorrectly, our world will be bent and distorted. To understand mental processes and behavior, therefore, we must understand how our senses allow us to make contact with the world.

Despite Kahlo's medical problems, her fundamental ability to receive and interpret the array of colors, shapes, sounds, and other sensations that whirled around her remained intact. How do our brains register that something is "out there"? And what of the other senses through which we register this amazing world—how do we smell, and hear, and taste; how are we able to be aware of our bodies? And, is there a perception beyond these—a perception that is literally "extra-sensory"—that some, if not all, of us possess? To a psychologist, the investigation of these questions provides fruitful clues in the search for knowledge of human mental processes and behavior.

# VISION: Window on the World

Frida Kahlo learned new ways to see the world from her father, Guillermo Kahlo, who was a photographer. Frida worked as his assistant, retouching, developing, and coloring his photographs (Zamora, 1990). In her youth, Kahlo accompanied her father (who was the first official photographer of Mexico's architectural heritage) on a trip around Mexico, photographing local architecture. Her father worked carefully when choosing camera angles and tried to take best advantage of lighting effects (Herrera, 1983). Moreover, her father was an amateur painter. Kahlo's experiences watching her father as both photographer and painter no doubt led her to develop skills that would later serve her in good stead, when she herself took up the brush to become a professional painter. Could such experiences literally have changed the way Kahlo saw?

Visual perception is not accomplished in one fell swoop, but in two broad phases. First, visual sensations are evoked by an object or event. Psychologists define **sensation** as the registration of properties of an object or event that occurs when a type of receptor (such as those at the back of the eye, in the ear, on the skin) is stimulated. Sensations arise when enough physical energy strikes a sense organ, so that receptor cells send neural impulses to the brain. As discussed in Chapter 3, receptors in general are like locks, which are opened by the appropriate key; for sensory receptors, the appropriate physical energy or molecule serves as the key. In the study of vision, the entire cell that responds to physical stimulation is called a *receptor*, not just the parts that register the input. It is the signals sent by these receptors that cause you to become aware of the outside world. Visual sensation arises in the eye and in the first parts of the brain that register visual input.

Second, you actually perceive the stimulus; **perception** occurs when you've organized and interpreted the sensory input as signaling a particular object or event.

**Sensation:** The awareness of properties of an object or event that occurs when a type of receptor (such as those at the back of the eye, in the ear, on the skin) is stimulated.

**Perception:** The act of organizing and interpreting sensory input as signaling a particular object or event.

Perception itself relies on two phases of processing (Marr, 1982; Nakayama et al., 1995):

1. *Organization into coherent units*. You don't see isolated blobs and lines, you see surfaces and objects. At the outset, you must organize patches of color, texture, edges, and other basic visual elements into coherent units, which usually correspond to surfaces and objects, such as the haystacks in a Monet painting. As part of this process, you need to register the sizes and locations of objects.

2. *Identifying what and where*. But these surfaces and objects don't have meaning; they are just surfaces and forms. The processes that organize the input are a prelude to the final task of perception, which is to recognize and identify what you see, to realize you are seeing a haystack and not a honeycomb. In addition to identifying what the object is, you need to identify where in space the object is—so you can get into your car when it's parked, but avoid cars when crossing the street.

The impressionists tried to present the changing effects of light and color in nature. The 19th-century French impressionist Claude Monet produced a series of paintings of haystacks in a field as day wore on to evening, and from season to season. Through his use of color, and the merging of subject (the "figure") and background (the "ground"), Monet tried to paint in a way that would replicate the process by which people actually see.

# Visual Sensation: More Than Meets the Eye

In everyday experience, you may think you have direct contact with the world—but you don't. You know the world only as it is filtered through your senses, and your senses are not always accurate. Your senses are your windows on the world, but sometimes the glass is not entirely transparent. The examples in Figure 4.1 show how far off base your perception can be.

Scientists have developed careful methods for discovering the relation between what's actually out there and what we sense and perceive; this field is known as psychophysics, and we explore its concepts and methods next.

## Psychophysics: A World of Experience

Well over a hundred years ago, scientists began trying to discover the relation between the properties of events in the world and people's sensations and perceptions of them. German scientist Gustav Theodor Fechner (1801–1887) founded the field of **psychophysics**, which studies the relation between physical events and the corresponding experience of those events. Researchers in psychophysics made a series of discoveries, which apply to all the senses.

Psychophysics: The study of the relation between physical events and the corresponding experience of those events.

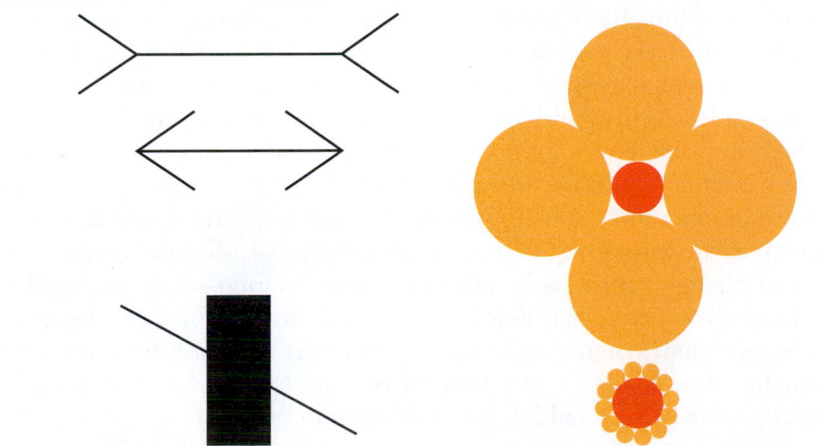

**FIGURE 4.1**

## Visual Illusions

The visual system is not like a camera that accurately captures the world, as illustrated by these visual illusions. The two lines with the arrow heads and tails are in fact the same length; the diagonal line that cuts across the vertical bar is straight, not jagged; and the circles in the center of the two "flowers" are actually the same size.

Threshold: The point at which stimulation is strong enough to be noticed.

Absolute threshold: The smallest amount of a stimulus needed in order to detect that the stimulus is present.

Just-noticeable difference (JND): The size of the difference in a stimulus property needed for the observer to notice that a change has occurred.

Weber's law: The rule that a constant percentage of a magnitude change is necessary to detect a difference.

Signal detection theory: A theory explaining why people detect signals independently of bias; the theory is based on the idea that signals are always embedded in noise, and thus the challenge is to distinguish signal from noise.

Sensitivity: In signal detection theory, the threshold level for distinguishing between a stimulus and noise; the lower the threshold, the greater the sensitivity.

Bias: In signal detection theory, a person's willingness to report noticing a stimulus.

**THRESHOLDS: "OVER THE TOP"** Have you ever wondered how far away something can be and still be seen, or how low you can turn down the sound before it becomes inaudible? Much as you cross a doorway when going from one room to the next, stimuli cross a **threshold** when a physical event becomes strong enough to be noticed. An **absolute threshold** is the smallest amount of a stimulus needed in order to notice that the stimulus is present at all. The absolute threshold is defined as the magnitude of the stimulus needed to make it noticeable to the observer half the time. In establishing absolute thresholds, you are distinguishing between the background and the stimulus, and the stimulus must have enough of its defining quality that you are, in fact, able to notice it. If a warning light isn't bright enough, you won't notice that it's on—which could be a serious deficiency if the light is meant to indicate that your car's radiator is about to boil over.

Sometimes you don't need simply to detect the presence of a stimulus, but rather to distinguish among stimuli. For example, suppose Kahlo were painting while the sun was setting; at what point would she notice that it had gotten darker in the room, and she should either adjust the way she was painting patterns of light or call it quits for the day? A **just-noticeable difference (JND)** is the size of the difference in a stimulus property (such as the brightness of light) needed for the observer to notice a difference. A JND is a kind of threshold. The change in light level might be so slight that sometimes you notice it, and sometimes you don't. This change would be defined as a JND if you noticed the difference half the time.

The size of a JND depends on the overall magnitude of the stimulus. If you are a thin person, a weight gain of 5 pounds would probably be noticeable at a glance, but if you are on the hefty side, a 5-pound gain might not be detected by anyone but you. Similarly, turning up the light the same amount is much more noticeable when the dimmer starts at a low setting than when it starts at a high setting. Why is this? Psychophysicists have an answer. **Weber's law** (named after another German researcher, Ernst Weber) states that a constant percentage of a magnitude change is necessary to detect a difference. So, the greater the magnitude of the light (or the thickness of the waist, or the volume of the sound), the greater the extra amount must be to be noticed. Weber's law is remarkably accurate except for very large or very small magnitudes of stimuli.

**DETECTING SIGNALS: NOTICING NEEDLES IN HAYSTACKS** In World War II, radar operators sometimes "saw" airplanes that did not exist and sometimes missed airplanes that did. The simple fact that people make these kinds of errors led to a new way of thinking about thresholds. **Signal detection theory** seeks to explain why people detect signals in some situations but miss them in others. The key idea is that signals are always embedded in noise, and thus the challenge is to distinguish signal from noise. Noise, in this case, refers to other events that could be mistaken for the stimulus. Two key concepts explain how signals are detected or missed: sensitivity and bias. Greater **sensitivity** means a lower threshold for distinguishing between a stimulus (the "signal") and the background (the "noise"). For example, on a radar screen, the signal dots indicating enemy aircraft would not need to be very large or bright compared with the noise composed of random-appearing specks. **Bias** is the willingness to report noticing a stimulus (such as the willingness of a radar operator to risk identifying random specks as aircraft). You change your bias by adjusting your *criterion*—how strong the signal needs to be before you say you've detected it. Sensitivity and bias can be assessed by comparing the occasions when people *say* a stimulus is or is not present with the occasions when the stimulus is *in fact* present or not (Figure 4.2; Busemeyer, 2004; Green & Swets, 1966; MacDonald & Balakrishnan, in press).

**FIGURE 4.2**

## Signal Detection Outcomes

| Signal? | Reported Signal? Yes | Reported Signal? No |
|---|---|---|
| Yes | Hit | Miss |
| No | False alarm | Correct rejection |

Four types of responses are possible when a person is asked to report whether a signal was present. Signal detection theory uses the relative frequencies of these reports to compute a measure of how sensitive an observer is to a signal and a measure of how willing the observer is to report the signal.

# How Do Objects Enter the Mind?
# Let There Be Light

What is the bridge from objects in the world to images in the mind (the connection between the "physics" and "psycho" of visual psychophysics)? The Greek philosopher Plato, who some 2,400 years ago theorized about many aspects of existence, psychological and otherwise, offered an interesting explanation of how humans see. Plato believed that the eyes produce rays that illuminate objects and that these rays are the basis of sight. Plato was no fool, and he was reasoning based on what he perceived. He isn't the only intelligent person to come to the wrong conclusions based on observable facts: Surveys of college students reveal that a surprisingly high proportion of them—fully one third—believe the same thing! The percentage of students accepting this explanation actually doubled (to 67%) when participants were shown a computer-graphic illustration of the concept (Winer & Cottrell, 1996; Winer et al., 1996). Furthermore, two thirds of the college students who believe in such rays also believe that a person whose rays fail will go blind (Winer et al., 1996). These misconceptions are remarkably difficult to change (Gregg et al., 2001; Winer et al., 2002, 2003).

Christopher Columbus had an intuitive grasp of signal detection theory. He offered a reward to the first sailor to spot land, but then sailors started mistaking low clouds for land. The reward not only increased sensitivity, but lowered the criterion. To adjust the criterion, Columbus announced that sailors who made false sightings would forfeit the reward. Columbus applied this higher criterion to himself, and didn't wake the crew on the night he first saw a glimmer of light on a distant island.

To set the record straight, there are no rays that shine from your eyes; in fact, essentially the process works the other way. Rather than producing rays, the eye registers light that is reflected from, or is produced by, objects in the line of sight. Similarly, the ear registers vibrations of air, and the skin responds to an object when pressure from it stimulates nerves.

Light is a form of electromagnetic radiation. All of us swim in a sea of electromagnetic radiation. This sea has waves: some large, some small, some that come in rapid succession, some spaced far apart. The height of a wave is its **amplitude**, and the number of waves arriving each second is the **frequency**. With higher frequency, the peaks of the waves arrive more often. When more peaks arrive per second, there is less distance between them, and hence the light is said to have a shorter **wavelength**. The distance between waves is measured in *nanometers*, or millionths of a meter. In the electromagnetic spectrum, which ranges from the terrifically long alternating currents and radio waves to the very short gamma rays and X rays, there is a narrow band of radiation perceived as visible light. An almost uncountable number of colors are conveyed in this light; the traditional seven we readily distinguish are red, orange, yellow, green, blue, indigo, and violet. The lower frequencies (and longer wavelengths—more nanometers) are toward the red end of the spectrum; the higher frequencies (and shorter wavelengths) are toward the violet end, as illustrated in Figure 4.3, which also illustrates the properties of light.

**Amplitude:** The height of the peaks in a light wave.

**Frequency:** The number of waves per second that move past a given point.

**Wavelength:** The distance between the arrival of peaks of a light wave (measured in nanometers); shorter wavelengths correspond to higher frequencies.

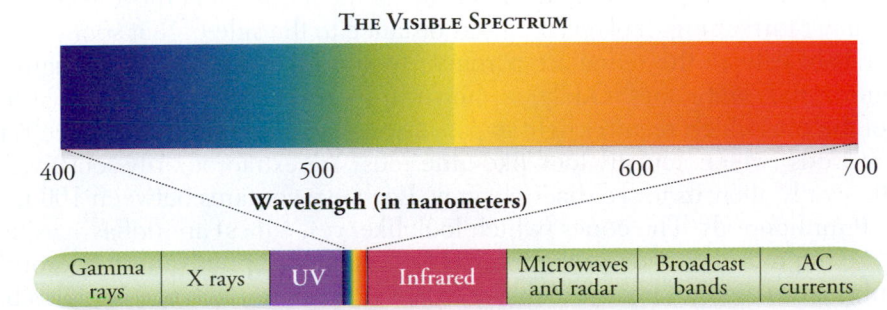

THE VISIBLE SPECTRUM

400    500    600    700
**Wavelength (in nanometers)**

| Gamma rays | X rays | UV | Infrared | Microwaves and radar | Broadcast bands | AC currents |

**FIGURE 4.3**

## The Range of Electromagnetic Radiation

Note that only a small portion of the range comprises visible light and that the hue depends on the wavelength.

**Transduction:** The process whereby physical energy is converted by a sensory neuron into neural impulses.

**Pupil:** The opening in the eye through which light passes.

**Iris:** The circular muscle that adjusts the size of the pupil.

**Cornea:** The transparent covering over the eye, which serves partly to focus the light onto the back of the eye.

**Accommodation:** Occurs when muscles adjust the shape of the lens so that it focuses light on the retina from objects at different distances.

**Retina:** A sheet of tissue at the back of the eye containing cells that convert light to neural impulses.

**Fovea:** The small, central region of the retina with the highest density of cones and the highest resolution.

**Rods:** Rod-shaped retinal cells that are very sensitive to light but register only shades of gray.

**Cones:** Cone-shaped retinal cells that respond most strongly to one of three wavelengths of light; the combined outputs from cones that are most sensitive to different wavelengths play a key role in producing color vision.

# The Brain's Eye: More Than a Camera

The eye converts the electromagnetic energy that is light into nerve impulses; this conversion process is called **transduction**. As illustrated in Figure 4.4, light enters the eye through an opening called the **pupil**. Surrounding the pupil is a circular muscle called the **iris**. The iris changes the size of the pupil to let in more or less light. The light is focused mostly by the **cornea**, the transparent covering over the iris and pupil, and then focused even more by the lens. Unlike a camera lens, the lens in a human eye flexes. In fact, muscles can adjust the lens into a more or less round shape to focus light from objects that are different distances away. **Accommodation**, the automatic adjustment of the eye for seeing at particular distances, occurs when muscles change the shape of the lens so that it focuses light on the retina from near or far away objects. The world appears sharp and clear because we are constantly moving our eyes, and what we choose to look at can quickly be brought into focus. With age, the lens thickens and becomes less flexible (Fatt & Weissman, 1992), often causing older people to have trouble seeing nearer objects, such as reading material.

**FIGURE 4.4**

## Anatomy of the Eye

The many parts of the eye either focus an image on the retina or convert light into neural impulses that are sent to the brain.

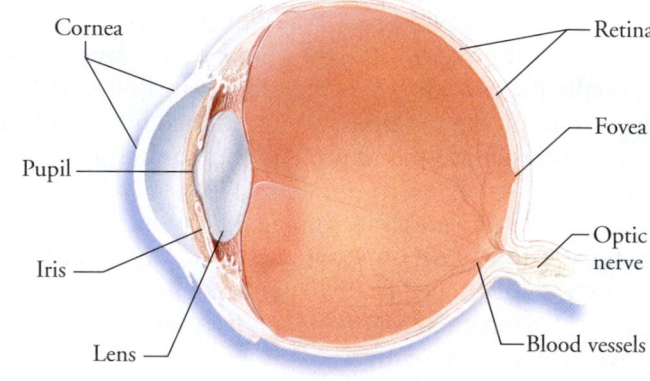

Cornea · Retina · Fovea · Pupil · Iris · Optic nerve · Lens · Blood vessels

When it comes to foveas, some animals have it all over us humans; some types of birds, for example, have two foveas. Next time you are annoyed at a noisy pigeon, appreciate the fact that it can focus to the side and ahead at the same time.

**TRANSDUCTION: FROM PHOTONS TO NEURONS** The critical step in the transduction process occurs at the **retina**, a sheet of tissue at the back of the eye that is about as thick as a piece of paper (Wässle, 2004). The central part of the retina contains densely packed cells that transform light to nerve impulses, and this region—called the **fovea**—gives us the sharpest images. We are not usually aware of how fuzzy our world looks. Most of the time we notice only the images that strike the fovea, which are sharp and clear, but much of what we see is in fact not very sharply focused. Take a moment to look up and focus on a single spot on the other side of the room; don't move your eyes, and notice how blurry things look even a short distance to the side of that spot.

Two kinds of cells in the retina are particularly important for converting light to nerve impulses: rods and cones. Oddly, as shown in Figure 4.5, these cells are at the very back of the eye, which requires light to pass through various other types of cells to reach them. **Rods** (which actually look like little rods) are extraordinarily sensitive to light, but they only allow us to see shades of gray. Each eye contains between 100 million and 120 million rods. The **cones** (which look like, yes, cones) are not as sensitive to light as are the rods, but each of the three types of cones responds most vigorously to a particular wavelength of light, which allows us to see color. Each eye contains between 5 million and 6 million cones (Beatty, 1995; Dowling, 1992). The cones are densest near the fovea, and the rods are everywhere within the retina except in the fovea. In very dim light, there isn't enough light for the less light-sensitive cones to work, so night vision is based on the firing of the rods alone. That is why a red apple looks black and an orange cat looks gray under a moonlit night sky.

The axons from retinal cells in each eye are gathered into a single large cord called the **optic nerve**, which is about as thick as your little finger. There are no rods or cones at the place where the optic nerve exits the retina, which causes a "blind spot" in what you can see laid out in front of you. Because the brain completes patterns that fall across this blind spot, you are not aware of it as you look around every day. Look at Figure 4.6, though, and you can "see" where your blind spot is.

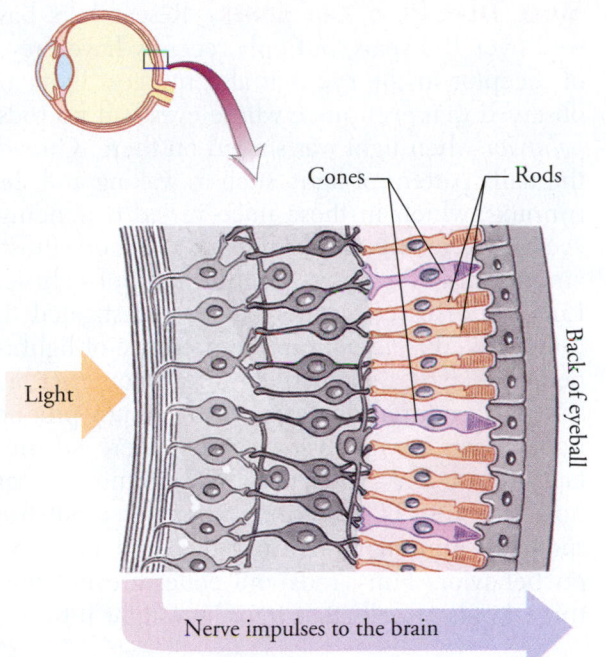

**FIGURE 4.5**

## Rods and Cones

Two types of cells in the retina convert light into nerve impulses that produce visual sensations. The rods allow us to see with less light, but not in color; the cones allow us to see colors but are not as light-sensitive as the rods.

Cones — Rods

Light

Back of eyeball

Nerve impulses to the brain

---

**FIGURE 4.6**   **Finding Your Blind Spot**

X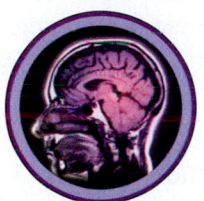

Cover your left eye and stare at the X with your right eye. Now slowly bring the book closer to you, continuing to focus on the X. When the picture on the right disappears, you have found your right eye's blind spot.

---

**DARK ADAPTATION**   When you first enter a darkened theater, you can't see a thing. You may have noticed, though, that the risk of tripping or bumping into someone is a lot less if you wait even a brief time, because you soon can see much better. In fact, after about 30 minutes in the dark, you are about 100,000 times more sensitive to light than you are during full daylight. In ideal conditions, the rods can respond when they receive a single photon, the smallest unit of light. This process is called **dark adaptation**. Part of the increased sensitivity to what light there is arises because your pupil enlarges when you are in darkness; in fact, it can expand to let in about 16 times as much light as enters in full daylight. In addition, the rods actually become more sensitive as your eyes remain in the dark because your genes cause the production of a crucial chemical, called *rhodopsin*, that responds to light. Here's a hint: Because of the way the rods are arranged on the retina, if you want to see best at night, look slightly to the side of what you want to examine.

Optic nerve:  The large bundle of nerve fibers carrying impulses from the retina into the brain.

Dark adaptation:  The process whereby exposure to darkness causes the eyes to become more sensitive, allowing for better vision in the dark.

**MORE THAN RODS AND CONES** Researchers have known about rods and cones for well over 100 years, but only recently have they discovered evidence for a third kind of receptor in the eye that also registers light. Freedman and her colleagues (1999) observed that even mice whose eyes had no rods or cones still shifted their *circadian behavior* when light was shined on them. Circadian behavior is behavior that follows the daily pattern of light, such as waking and sleeping; in this case, the behavior was running, which in these mice varied depending on the time of day. But when the eyes were removed, the mice no longer adjusted their "running schedule" to the amount of light. Thus, the third kind of light-sensitive receptor must be in the eyes. Lucas and his colleagues (1999) investigated the decrease in production of a hormone called *melatonin* in the presence of light (melatonin is the hormone that some people take as a supplement to overcome jet lag). Even mice without rods or cones showed a normal decrease in melatonin production when placed in light. Clearly, light affects the brain even when there are no rod or cone sensory cells. And, in fact, Berson and colleagues (2002) found that certain *ganglion cells* (which also function as a kind of gathering station for input from rods and cones) in the retina respond to illumination in just the right ways to explain the observed effects of light on behavior. Thus, rods and cones are not the whole story: We have not two, but three kinds of cells that transduce light into neural impulses.

## Color Vision: Mixing and Matching

How can you tell whether an apple is ripe? One way is to look at its color. Color also plays a key role in our appreciation of beauty in art, nature, and people. Kahlo associated certain colors with objects or feelings; for instance, she associated yellow with madness, sickness, and fear, and a reddish purple with liveliness (Herrera, 1983). Color is not just a "luxury feature" of vision; for one thing, color helps us make the fundamental distinction between shadows that are cast by objects versus variations in how light is reflected from objects (Kingdom et al., 2004).

One of the remarkable aspects of human vision, which makes painting and appreciation of painting such rich experiences, is the huge range of colors that people can use and see. Indeed, colors vary in three separate ways.

- *Hue*. As noted earlier when we considered the electromagnetic spectrum, different wavelengths of light produce sensations of different colors. This aspect of color—whether it looks red, blue, and so on—is called *hue*.
- *Saturation*. The purity of the input (the amount of white that's mixed in with the color) produces the perception of *saturation*, that is, how deep the color appears.
- *Lightness*. The amplitude of the light waves produces the perception of *lightness* or (if the object, such as a TV or computer screen, produces light) *brightness*—how much light is present.

Different combinations of values on these three dimensions produce the incredibly rich palette of human color vision, which is more varied than that used by any painter. Given the large number of ways that color can vary, you might think that complicated processes underlie our ability to see these visual properties—and you would be right. Color arises through the operation of two distinct types of processes.

**COLOR MIXING** At one point in the study of color vision, there was a debate about how humans can see such a large range of colors. One camp took its lead from observations reported by Thomas Young and Hermann von Helmholtz in the 19th century. This approach focused on phenomena such as the mixing of colors to produce new colors (for example, mixing yellow and blue paint produces green). These researchers, arguing by analogy, believed that the brain registers color by combining responses to separate wavelengths. In particular, they argued that the eye contains three kinds of color sensors, each most sensitive to a particular range of wavelengths: long, medium, and short. This view was therefore called the **trichromatic theory of color vision**.

This theory turns out to be essentially correct, but it describes processing at only some places in the eye and brain. Consistent with trichromatic theory, our perception of hue arises because most of us possess three different types of cones. One type of cone is most responsive to light in the wavelength seen as a shade of yellowish red, another to light in the wavelength seen as green, and another to light in the wavelength seen as bluish violet (Reid, 1999). The trick is that at least two of the three types of cones usually respond to any wavelength of visible light, but to different degrees (De Valois & De Valois, 1975, 1993). And here's the important part: The *mixture* of the three types of response signals is different for each of a huge range of wavelengths, and it is this mixture that is the crucial signal to the brain. The brain responds to the mixture, not the outputs from individual cones. Color television operates on this principle. Stare very closely at a color TV screen, and you will see little bubbles of three colors. Stand back, and a wide range of colors appears. Why? Because your eyes and your brain respond differently, depending on the mixture of wavelengths produced by clusters of these bubbles.

As if this weren't complicated enough, there's one more twist we must discuss, which concerns the difference between what you see on a TV screen versus what you see when you mix paints (see Figure 4.7). On the one hand, when you see a TV screen, each of the different wavelengths directly affects your cones. Thus, if red, green, and blue are mixed in an image, stimulating all your cones, you will see white. In this case, the hues of each contributing color are *added* together. On the other hand, when you see paints, you see the light that is *reflected* from the paints—and not all the light may be reflected. What you see is what is not *absorbed* by the paints; a yellow paint, for example, absorbs all wavelengths except that underlying our perception of yellow. This wavelength is reflected, not absorbed, and so it reaches your eyes. When you mix paints, the wavelengths absorbed by each type of paint contribute to what is absorbed by the mixture. So if you mixed red, green, and blue you would see black: The combination of paints absorbs all the visible wavelengths that give rise to the perception of hue. In this case, the hues of each contributing color are *subtracted* from the end result.

Genetic research has shown that some women possess not three, but four types of cones. As you might expect, these women see color differently from the rest of us. For example, they see more bands in a rainbow than people who have only three sorts of cones (Jameson et al., 2001). These differences in color vision arise from the same sort of mixing that underlies trichromatic theory, and thus the key ideas of that theory are correct even if—for some people—outputs from an additional type of cone are thrown into the mix.

**FIGURE 4.7** **Mixing Color**

EMITTED LIGHT          REFLECTED LIGHT

The results of mixing color depend on whether the light being perceived is emitted or reflected. When the light is emitted, from a TV screen, for example, the wavelengths of each contributing hue are added; when the light is reflected, the wavelengths of each contributing hue are subtracted.

**A COLOR TUG-OF-WAR?** The other camp in the debate about how we see hue followed the lead of German physician Ewald Hering, who worked at the end of the 19th century and the beginning of the 20th. Hering noticed that some colors cannot be mixed: You can't make reddish-green (it becomes mud) or yellowish-blue (it becomes green).

Trichromatic theory of color vision: The theory that color vision arises from the combinations of neural impulses from three different kinds of sensors, each of which responds maximally to a different wavelength.

## FIGURE 4.8   Seeing Afterimages

 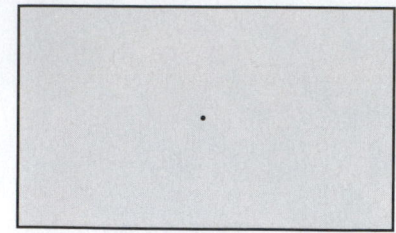

Does this flag look strange to you? Stare at the dot in the center for about 60 seconds in a bright light, and then look at the blank space. You should see a brilliant afterimage of Old Glory, with red and white stripes and a blue field.

This and similar observations led Hering to develop the **opponent process theory of color vision**, which states that the presence of one color of certain pairs (red/green, yellow/blue, and black/white) inhibits the perception of the other color.

And, in fact, researchers discovered that the mixtures of responses of the cones is not the whole story of color vision. If this were all there were to it, we should be able to see all mixtures of colors—but, as Hering originally observed, we can't. As the opponent process theory predicts, there's another factor, too, which will become apparent when you take a look at the strangely colored flag in Figure 4.8. Stare at the flag, and then look at the space to its right; you should see an **afterimage**, an image left behind by a previous perception. Furthermore, the flag should look normal in the afterimage, not strangely colored as it is printed on the page. Why are the colors of afterimages different from those of the object? You need to understand more about color vision to answer that question. A key fact is that the cones feed into special types of cells in the retina and the lateral geniculate nucleus of the brain (part of the thalamus): red/green, yellow/blue, and black/white **opponent cells**. These cells are set up to pit the colors in each pair against each other: When you gaze at a lovely green lime, for example, your opponent cells are making it difficult for you to see the red of a delicious apple. This is the sort of effect Hering predicted, and his ideas have since been developed in more detail (Hurvich & Jameson, 1957; Nayatani, 2001, 2003). This opponent process helps you to distinguish among colors that have similar wavelengths, such as green and yellow.

This mechanism explains why you can't see greenish-red or yellowish-blue: Seeing one member of a pair inhibits seeing the other. It also explains why you see afterimages like the one illustrated by staring at Figure 4.8. An afterimage occurs when one member of a pair of opponent cells inhibits the other (for example, green inhibits red), and then releases it. In the process, the previously inhibited hue (red) temporarily overshoots the mark, creating an afterimage. Think of this like a jack-in-the box: The head is stuffed into the box (which is like one color being inhibited by its opponent color), and when the box is opened, the head springs up higher than its resting height (which is like the inhibited color over-responding when released by its opponent color).

Much of the work of color vision is actually accomplished in the retina and the thalamus, but the cortex plays a key role in integrating the various signals from cones and opponent cells into a single perception (Chatterjee & Callaway, 2003; Gegenfurtner & Kiper, 2003; Reid, 1999).

**COLOR BLINDNESS**   People who have **color blindness** are either unable to distinguish two or more hues from each other (while still being able to distinguish among other hues) or, in more serious cases, unable to see hue at all. Most color blindness is present from birth. Depending on the specific group, as many as 8% of European men but less than 0.5% of European women are born color-blind (Reid, 1999). Rather than being completely insensitive to hue, most color-blind people are unable to distinguish red from green. Researchers have found that people with the most common type of color blindness possess genes that produce similar pigments in their cones (Neitz et al., 1996), and thus the cones do not respond to wavelengths as they should—leading two hues to appear the same. A small number of people (roughly 2% of males, and a very small number of females) are actually missing a type of cone. Even more severe deficits occur when more than one type of cone is affected (Reid, 1999). Researchers have

**Opponent process theory of color vision:** The theory that if a color is present, it causes cells that register it to inhibit the perception of the complementary color (such as red versus green).

**Afterimage:** The image left behind by a previous perception.

**Opponent cells:** Cells that pit the colors in a pair, most notably blue/yellow or red/green, against each other.

**Color blindness:** An inability, either acquired (by brain damage) or inherited, to perceive certain hues.

People with normal color vision see the crayons as shown on the left. People with the most common form of color blindness—inability to distinguish red from green—would see the crayons as shown on the right. Before traffic lights were arranged with red always on the top, not being able to see colors made driving hazardous for people with red/green color blindness. In what other ways would such a disorder affect your life?

identified specific genes that lead to color blindness (Tanabe et al., 2001) and have even shown that specific genes only cause color blindness when they appear in specific places on a chromosome (Hayashi et al., 2001).

Some people only become color blind after a particular part of their brains is damaged. In monkeys, visual area 4 (or V4) plays a major role in processing color (Zeki, 1993); similarly, a "color area" is activated in human brains when color is perceived (Chao & Martin, 1999; Lueck et al., 1989). If this area is damaged, the ability to see hue is lost (Cole et al., 2003). In Oliver Sacks's book *An Anthropologist on Mars* (1995), a color-blind artist describes how hard it is for him to eat certain foods, particularly red foods (such as apples and tomatoes), which appear to him to be a repulsive deep black. Nevertheless, in spite of not being able to experience color, at least some of these unfortunate people can still use wavelength variation to track moving objects and even to see shape; this remarkable ability appears to arise from the functioning of the color-opponent system (Cole et al., 2003).

## Visual Problems: Distorted Windows on the World

Precisely because the visual system is so complicated, it does not always work perfectly. It is estimated that less than a third of the world's population has perfect vision (Seuling, 1986). Problems in the visual system affect both absolute and relative thresholds and also can distort the stimuli reaching the retina.

- *Myopia*, or nearsightedness, causes people to have difficulty focusing on distant objects. As shown in Figure 4.9 (p. 144), myopia is usually caused by an eyeball that is too long to focus the image on the retina properly. This problem, which in the United States affects about one in five people, can be corrected by external lenses, either eyeglasses or contact lenses, that focus the image correctly on the retina. Moreover, laser surgery often can correct the lens of the eye itself. Time spent reading is correlated with myopia (see Young, 1981), but remember, correlation does not imply causation!

- *Hypermetropia*, or farsightness, causes people to have difficulty focusing on near objects. Such farsightedness usually results from an eyeball that is too short, or a lens that is too thin, to allow the image to focus on the retina properly. By the way, it is possible to be nearsighted in one eye and farsighted in the other, as was the case with President James Buchanan. This condition purportedly led him to tilt his head so that he could see better when he was talking to someone (Seuling, 1978).

- *Astigmatism* is a defect in the curvature of the cornea or lens, causing blurriness. Astigmatism, like nearsightedness and farsightedness, can be corrected with eyeglasses (and sometimes with contact lenses).

**FIGURE 4.9**   **Sources of Vision Difficulties**

In normal vision, an image in focused on the retina. Depending on how the lens of the eye focuses light onto the retina, the image can be distorted in different ways. External lenses can bend the light in a way that compensates for the distortions in the lens of the eye, allowing light to be focused properly on the retina.

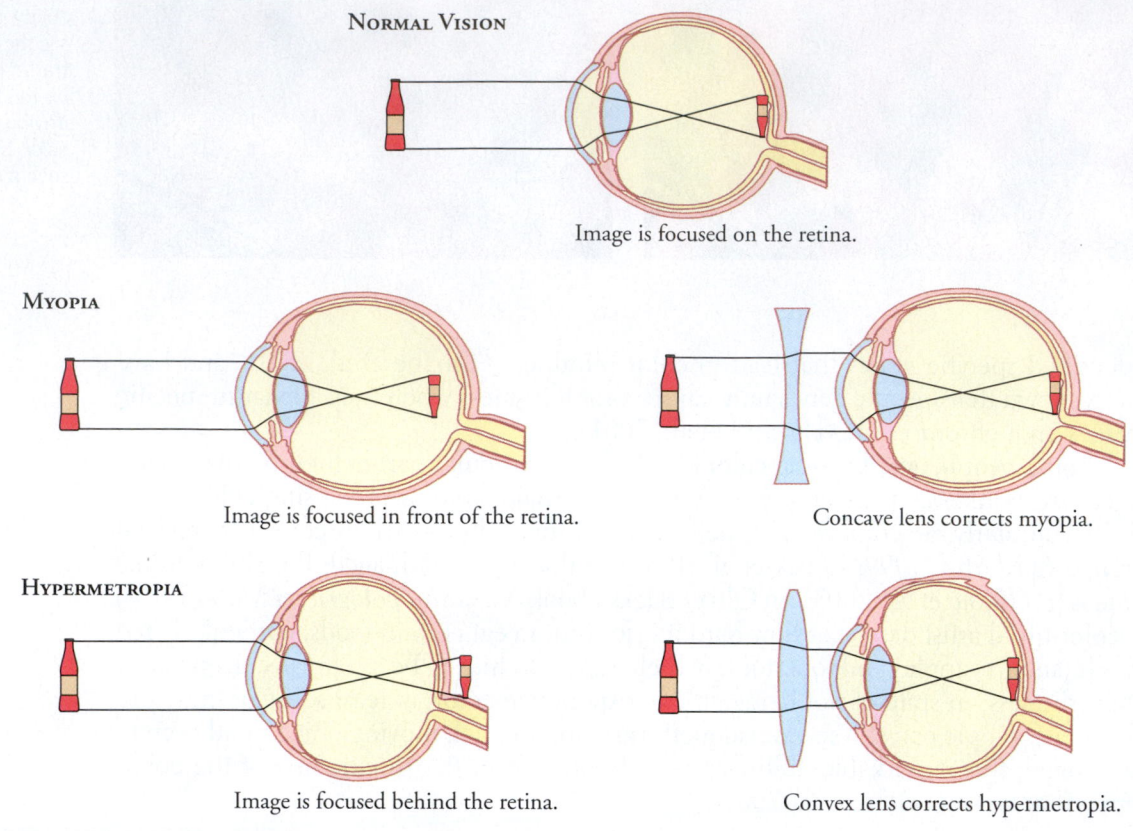

NORMAL VISION

Image is focused on the retina.

MYOPIA

Image is focused in front of the retina.

Concave lens corrects myopia.

HYPERMETROPIA

Image is focused behind the retina.

Convex lens corrects hypermetropia.

Can you see which animals are present? The coloring of the horses blends nicely with the background. Why might animals look like their surroundings?

- A *cataract* is a cloudy part of the lens of the eye, which can cause serious visual problems, including blurred vision, distorted images, sensitivity to light and glare, and outright blindness (Congdon et al., 2003). About 70% of Americans over age 75 have (or have had) a cataract. Cataracts are responsible for at least half of all incidents of blindness (Riordan-Eva, 1992). Surgery can correct cataracts, by removing the lens and replacing it with a substitute lens.

- *Macular degeneration.* The *macula* is a small region surrounding, and including, the fovea. We are able to see objects with high resolution in the center of the visual field courtesy of receptors in the macula. Smoking not only can cause cataracts, but also can cause the macula to degenerate—which causes irreversible blindness in the center of the visual field (DeBlack, 2003; Kelly et al., 2004).

# Phase 1 of Visual Perception: Organizing the World

Although it seems that we perceive what we see in, literally, the blink of an eye, a large number of mental steps actually occur between the moment a pattern of light strikes your eyes and the time you recognize and identify an object. At each step, different areas of the brain are crucial (Conner, 2002; Grill-Spector et al., 1998; Husain & Jackson, 2001; Olson, 2001; Sheinberg & Logothetis, 2001). We can divide the steps of visual perception into two phases (Treue, 2003). In Phase 1, the outputs from sensory processing are organized; in Phase 2, these organized units are recognized and identified. In this section, we consider Phase 1, the first step of visual perception after a stimulus has been sensed.

Take a glance at Figure 4.10. You have no trouble seeing the sailboats, the building, and so forth. Now take a closer look. Like pictures in a comic book, this painting is composed entirely of colored dots; no lines indicate the edges of objects or their parts. Nevertheless, you see separate objects and their parts. How? You effortlessly and unconsciously group the dots into patterns. In fact, this sort of processing is the first step of all visual perception; the edges of most objects are not specified by continuous sharp lines that set the object apart, as in a line drawing. Instead, just as you group the dots in the painting, you group the outputs from sensory processes (Marr, 1982; Nakayama et al., 1995). A crucial goal of this processing is to separate figure from ground. The **figure** is a set of characteristics (such as shape, color, and texture) that corresponds to an object, whereas the **ground** is the background, which must be distinguished in order to pick out any figure. When figure and ground are similar, the figure is said to be *camouflaged*. Animals in the desert and jungle, as well as armies the world over, have long taken advantage of this property of the perceptual system.

**FIGURE 4.10**   **Inserting Edges**

Even though this painting has no lines indicating the edges of objects and their parts, we readily see them. Why? Because we organize the elements—colored dots, in this case—into perceptual groups.

## Perceptual Organization: Seeing the Forest Through the Trees

Separating figure from ground involves organizing regions into shapes that are likely to correspond to objects or their parts. A critical part of this process is taking fragmentary outputs from sensory processing and organizing them into edges. David H. Hubel and Torsten N. Wiesel received the Nobel Prize in 1981 for discovering that neurons in the first part of the cortex to process visual input (the *primary visual cortex*, in the occipital lobe) are arranged into columns, and the neurons in each column fire selectively to sections of edges that have a specific orientation. These columns are in turn arranged into sets that are driven by input from either the left eye or the right eye, and these sets are arranged into a *hypercolumn*. The neurons in each hypercolumn respond to input from a single spot on the retina (Hubel & Wiesel, 1962, 1974). In addition, hypercolumns in the visual areas of the occipital lobe are *topographically organized*—that is, the pattern falling on the retina is spatially laid out on the cortex (Engel et al., 1997; Tootell et al., 1982). This arrangement helps the brain to delineate the edges of objects.

Figure: In perception, a set of characteristics (such as shape, color, texture) that corresponds to an object.

Ground: In perception, the background, which must be distinguished in order to pick out figures.

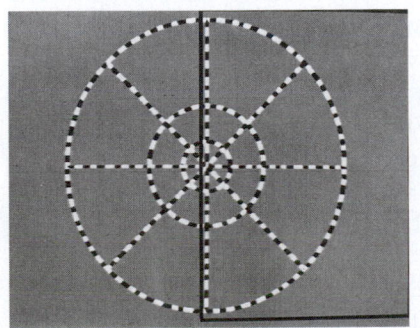 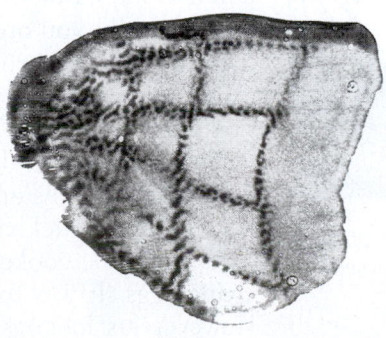

Tootell and colleagues (1982) produced this remarkable illustration of topographic organization in the monkey brain. The animal looked at the figure on the left while radioactive sugar was being ingested by the brain cells. The dark lines on the right show which brain cells in the primary visual cortex were working hardest when the animal viewed the figure (shown here is the left-hemisphere area, which processed the right side of the display). The spatial structure of the figure is evident on the surface of the brain.

**Gestalt laws of organization:** A set of rules describing the circumstances—such as proximity, good continuation, similarity, closure, and good form—under which marks will be grouped into perceptual units.

**GESTALT LAWS OF ORGANIZATION** We often view objects when they are partly covered by other objects. (Look around the room right now: What do you actually see?) Nevertheless, even when you view an object behind a bush, you don't see isolated lines, dots, and so on, but rather overall patterns. How are fragments of edges and other visual features (such as patches of color) forged into patterns? Gestalt psychologists, who were introduced briefly in Chapter 1, discovered a set of laws that describe how the brain organizes the input from the eyes (Koffka, 1935; Wertheimer, 1923). The most important of these **Gestalt laws of organization** follow:

- *Proximity*: Marks that are near one another tend to be grouped together. So, for example, we see XXX XXX as two groups and XX XX XX as three groups, even though both sets have the same total number of X marks.

- *Continuity* (also called *good continuation*): Marks that fall along a smooth curve or a straight line tend to be grouped together. So, for example, we see _ _ _ _ as a single line, not four separate dashes; and we see _ _ _ _ - - - - as two separate lines because all eight of the dashes do not fall on the same plane.

- *Similarity*: Marks that look alike tend to be grouped together. So, for example, we see XXXxxx as two groups. Whether the elements are the same or different colors also affects similarity; this is another reason color vision is so important.

- *Closure*: We tend to close any gaps in a figure, so a circle with a small section missing will still be seen as a circle.

- *Good Form*: Marks that form a single shape tend to be grouped together. So, for example, we see [ ] as a single shape, but not [ _ .

Additional laws have been added since the time of the Gestalt psychologists (who began their work in 1912). For example, Palmer (1992b) has shown that marks occurring in a common region tend to be grouped together. Moreover, the mental processes involved in perceptual grouping are becoming better understood (Kimchi & Razpurker-Apfeld, 2004), as are the details of how the brain actually works to organize the visual world (Grossberg et al., 1997; Kovacs, 1996; von der Heydt & Peterhans, 1989). As with a painting or a piece of music, in which form and color, harmony and rhythm, are at work simultaneously, so too with perceptual processing: Many different cues are used at the same time to separate figure from ground.

**FIGURE 4.11** ## Ambiguous Figures

In the left panel, you can see either two silhouetted faces or a vase, depending on what you pay attention to as the figure; in the right panel, you can see an old or a young woman, depending on how you organize the figure.

**AMBIGUOUS FIGURES** Sometimes a figure can be organized and perceived in more than one way. Figure 4.11 shows two classic *ambiguous figures*. Certain artists—for instance, Dutch illustrator Maurits Escher and Belgian surrealist René Magritte—were intrigued by how the mind actively organizes the visual world. As these figures show, sometimes you can voluntarily organize visual patterns in different ways. But, even when you organize such patterns automatically, you organize them not only on the basis of their physical properties but also as a result of learning. For example, have you ever thought about becoming a professional "chicken sexer"? Before you dismiss this possible career path out of hand, consider the fact that even during the Great Depression members of this profession prospered. Why? Chicken farmers didn't want to send female chickens to be cooked in someone's pot—they were for laying eggs. It was the males who were sent to market. However, just looking at the pattern of bumps and indentations on a baby chick's bottom, it's very difficult to distinguish a male from a female. Traditionally, experts required years of practice before they could make this distinction accurately. Biederman and Shiffrar (1987) analyzed the problem and were able to teach people to make the discrimination by observing whether a particular part of the chick's bottom was convex versus concave or flat. However, even after training, these participants were not the same as the experts. The participants in the study had to look carefully and think about exactly what they were trying to do. Experts can identify a chick's sex with extraordinary accuracy after glancing at the chick for half a second, without even being aware of what they are doing. After extensive practice, the visual system becomes tuned so that you can automatically organize what you see in a new way (Crist et al., 2001; Olson & Chun, 2002; Vuilleumier & Sagiv, 2001).

## Perceptual Constancies: Stabilizing the World

Imagine strapping a camera onto your head and making a videotape as you walk. What do you think the pictures would look like? The images striking your eyes change wildly depending on your viewpoint, but the objective world you relate to seems stable. Objects in the world appear to keep their shapes, their sizes, their colors, and so on, even when you view them in very different positions or circumstances. **Perceptual constancy** is the perception of the characteristics of objects (such as their shapes and colors) as the same even though the sensory information striking the eyes changes.

- **Size constancy** occurs when you see an object (such as a car) as the same actual size even when it is at different distances, so that its image (as in a photograph) has different sizes. Because Kahlo did not strive to paint things as they actually appear, she did not always try to convey size constancy. For example, in *Self-Portrait with Cropped Hair*, Kahlo's long strands of hair do not get smaller and thinner as they recede in the distance, as they should be painted to suggest size constancy. Because their length and thickness stay constant, the viewer probably sees some of the strands as floating in the air rather than being farther in the distance (Herrera, 1983).

- **Shape constancy** occurs when you see an object as the same shape, even when you view it from different angles (again, so that its image in a photograph would be different). This stabilization occurs not in the eyes, but in the brain, and is fundamental to the ability to recognize objects and know how to interact with them.

- **Color constancy** occurs when you see colors as constant (green as green, red as red, and so on) even when the lighting changes. When Kahlo painted in her studio or bedroom, the lighting conditions were different than they are in a gallery (perhaps the light bounced off green foliage in one setting but not the other). Nevertheless, the painting will appear to have the same colors in the different conditions. Color constancy arises in part because of experience; when monkeys are raised in light of only a single hue, their color constancy is later severely impaired (Sugita, 2004). Color constancy may occur because we see the lightest thing in a scene as white and everything else relative to that color (Land, 1959, 1977, 1983).

## Knowing the Distance

Because the world is three-dimensional, we need to register distances; this is necessary to appreciate how parts of an object are arranged, as well as to reach for things and navigate among them properly. This requirement poses an interesting problem: Our eyes project images onto the two- dimensional surface of our retinas, but we need to see objects in three dimensions. Given that our eyes capture images in only two dimensions, how is it that we see in three? Once again, the answer lies with the brain, which uses different types of cues to derive three dimensions from the two-dimensional images on the retinas.

**Perceptual constancy:** The perception of characteristics that occurs when an object or quality (such as shape or color) looks the same even though the sensory information striking the eyes changes.

**Size constancy:** Seeing an object as being the same size when viewed at different distances.

**Shape constancy:** Seeing objects as having the same shape even when the image on the retina changes.

**Color constancy:** Seeing objects as having the same color in different viewing situations.

## FIGURE 4.12    Retinal Disparity

In this type of retinal disparity, the eyes converge to fixate on an object (point B in the diagram), so that its image falls on the fovea of each eye. Slightly different images are projected into each of your eyes when you see objects at different distances in front of or behind the object you are fixating on; the brain uses the differences in these images to infer how far away objects are.

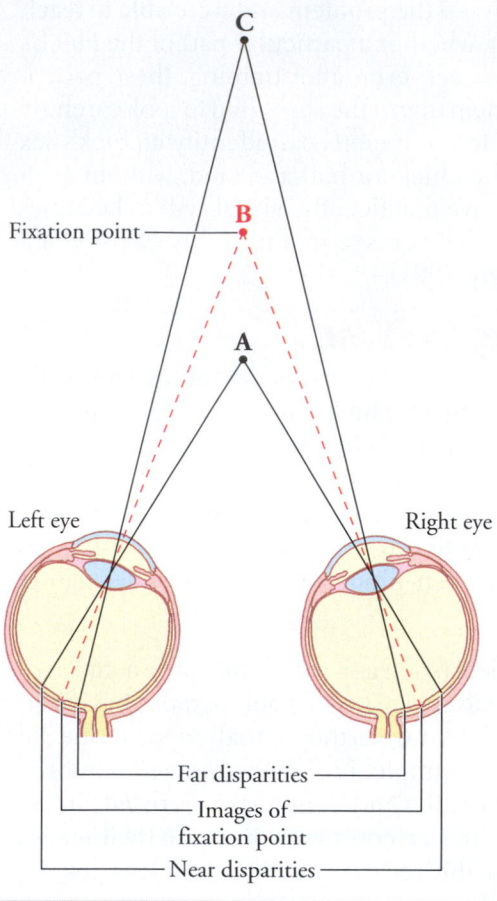

Fixation point —

Left eye          Right eye

Far disparities
Images of fixation point
Near disparities

**STATIC CUES** Static ("unmoving") information plays a large role in allowing us to determine how far away something is. **Binocular cues** arise from both eyes working together. Because your eyes are separated, they need to cross in order to focus on an object (so that the same image appears on the central, high-resolution fovea in each eye). The degree to which you cross your eyes is called **convergence**, and this is one cue you use to determine distance—the more crossed your eyes, the closer the object; for example, hold a finger 2 inches from your eyes and notice how crossed they are, and compare this to when you hold your finger at arm's length. In addition, your brain uses slight differences in the images striking each of your eyes to assess the distance of an object. When you cross your eyes to focus on an object, the images of other objects—those in front of or behind the one you are focused on—fall on slightly different parts of the retinas of the two eyes. This difference between the images on the two eyes is called **retinal disparity** (also called *binocular disparity*), and the brain uses the amount of disparity to determine which objects are in front of and which are behind others (Julesz, 1971; Pinker, 1997, pp. 220–233). Figure 4.12 illustrates an example of retinal disparity; this cue also provides information when objects are off to the side, and you are fixated elsewhere. This cue only works up to about 10 feet; after that, the disparity is too small for the brain to detect.

**Monocular** (or "one-eyed") **static cues** for distance can be picked up with one eye, and operate even for far distances. Monocular static cues are used effectively by artists (even surrealists such as Frida Kahlo) to create the illusion of distance. One of these cues is the **texture gradient**, a progressive change in the texture of an object. Gibson (1966) described the way texture gradients signal distance. Look at the brick street in the photograph (or, for that matter, such a street in reality). The bricks that are closer to you, the observer, give rise to larger images (they are larger in the photograph) and you use this cue to determine distance.

In drawing pictures, artists also use *linear perspective*, or *foreshortening*, making the parts of objects that are farther away from the viewer smaller on the paper. Artists also use *atmospheric perspective* to convey distance, taking advantage of the fact that vapor and dust in the air scatter the light, which makes far objects look hazy. You also infer distance if one object partially covers another, indicating that the obscured object is behind the other and thus farther away; this relation is called an *occlusion cue*. And if the base of an object appears higher on the horizon than the base of another object, you take that as a cue that the higher one is farther away. Figure 4.13 provides a good example of the power of these monocular cues.

However, the way such cues are depicted in drawings sometimes relies on cultural conventions, which must be learned (Leibowitz, 1971). For instance, in some rural

Notice the relative sizes and spacing of the bricks in this example of a texture gradient, one cue that the street is receding into the distance.

## FIGURE 4.13

## Size Constancy

Even though you know that the two white bars on the rails are in fact the same size, the one that appears farther away also appears larger. This figure is interesting because it violates size constancy: To be seen as the same size when it is farther away, an object needs to cover a smaller area of the picture (or visual field); when objects cover the same area of a picture (or visual field), our visual system assumes that the one appearing further away is larger.

parts of Africa, children's books are very rare, and thus it is not surprising that these children may not initially understand all depth and perspective cues in drawings (Liddell, 1997). Young children in rural Africa sometimes describe shading cues on faces as blemishes, and they may say that trees are on top of a house when the trees are drawn off in the distance, behind the house (Liddell, 1997). The actual drawing cues are ambiguous, and only after learning the conventions can you know what they are supposed to convey. Such problems in interpretation disappear with age, education, and experience. A number of cross-cultural studies have shown that people must learn how to interpret some cues in drawings (Crago & Crago, 1983; Duncan et al., 1973; Liddell, 1997; Nodelmann, 1988).

**MOTION CUES** Motion cues specify the distance of an object on the basis of its movement, and these cues work as well with one eye as with two. In fact, motion cues are so effective that Wesley Walker, blind in one eye from birth, could catch a football well enough to be the star wide receiver for the New York Jets football team (in fact, he played for them for 13 years). To notice a motion cue, try this: Hold up this book and move your head back and forth as you look at it. Note how the images of objects behind the book seem to shift. As you shift your head to the left, the distant objects seem to move to the left; as you shift to the right, they shift to the right. Now focus on the background, still holding the book, and move your head back and forth; note how the image of the book seems to shift. This time the object you aren't focusing on, the book, seems to shift in the opposite direction to the way you move your head! Objects closer than the one on which you are fixated on seem to move in the opposite direction to your movements, whereas those farther away than the fixation point seem to move in the same direction. And, depending on the distance, the objects will seem to shift at different speeds. This difference in shifting provides information about relative distance, a cue called *motion parallax*. Motion parallax is particularly important when you are moving, and thus it is unfortunate that alcohol intoxication disrupts the brain mechanisms for this sort

The woman on the left is actually taller than the boy on the right. How is this possible? The woman is farther away, but this special Ames room has been constructed to eliminate the usual monocular depth cues.

**Binocular cues:** Cues to the distance of an object that arise from both eyes working together.

**Convergence:** The degree to which the eyes are crossed when a person fixates on an object.

**Retinal disparity (also called *binocular disparity*):** The difference between the images striking the retinas of the two eyes.

**Monocular static cues:** Information that specifies the distance of an object that can be picked up with one eye without movement of the object or eye.

**Texture gradient:** Progressive change in texture that signals distance.

**Motion cues:** Information that specifies the distance of an object on the basis of its movement.

FIGURE 4.14

## Depth Cues

Depth perception depends on both binocular and monocular cues.

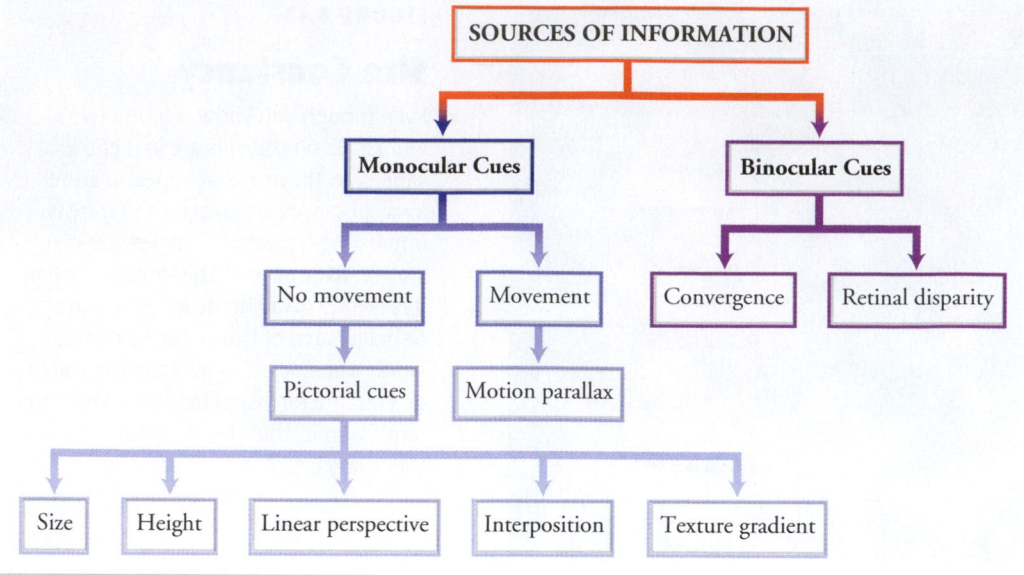

of depth perception; at least some alcohol-related driving accidents may be traced to this problem (Nawrot et al., 2004). Figure 4.14 summarizes monocular and binocular depth cues.

**DETECTING MOVEMENT: CHANGING PLACES** Motion not only helps you perceive depth, but also signals that an object is changing position relative to you—and as any driver or pedestrian will tell you, perceiving an object's movements is important in its own right. You use several types of cues to perceive movement. For example, if you are moving directly toward an object, it seems to expand symmetrically around its center and thus loom closer. Likewise, if you are moving toward its right side, that side will loom closer than the other. When silent movies were first shown to the public, the movement of an on-screen train rushing toward viewers was so startling that many moviegoers panicked and fled the theaters (Seuling, 1976). Only after they had experienced watching moving objects on a screen could they distinguish between the usual motion cues and the bogus cues in films (which are a kind of illusion called the *phi phenomenon*; see Figure 4.15), and be able to relax and enjoy the show. Such learning was necessary because these cues are ordinarily so important. In fact, neuroimaging research with humans has revealed that special areas in the brain detect this kind of motion (Tootell et al., 1997; Zeki, 1978, 1993). Also, studies of brain-damaged patients have documented the role of particular brain areas for processing motion. For example, one patient could not pour tea into a cup: She would see the tea suddenly appear, not continuously flow; instead of motion, she saw a series of static images (Zihl et al., 1983).

**FIGURE 4.15** ## Phi Phenomenon

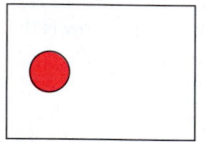  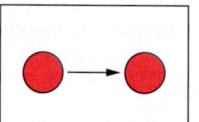

Movies are produced by a series of still photos, presented very rapidly in sequence. Why do we see movement, when there really isn't any? This sort of *apparent motion* arises from the *phi phenomenon*, a particular kind of illusion. When a stimulus appears in one location (such as in the left panel), disappears, and then appears in another location (as in the center panel), we will see it as having moved if the timing is just right (the farther the distance between locations, the greater the amount of time between removing the first stimulus and presenting the second). The phi phenomenon can produce the appearance of motion that is indistinguishable from real motion (Gregory & Harris, 1984; Shioiri et al., 2000; Wertheimer, 1912).

# Phase 2 of Visual Perception: Recognition and Identification

Vision is more than organizing the world into shapes and knowing where they are, of course. If Phase 1 processing were all there was to it, how would you know whether something was good to approach (such as a useful tool or a tasty sweet) or necessary to avoid (such as a dangerous animal or an angry boss)? To answer such questions we need to turn to the processes involved in Phase 2 of visual perception. These processes accomplish two major goals:

- *Identify shapes.* You need to assign meaning to the shapes you see.
- *Identify spatial relations.* You need to identify the spatial relations among objects (Kosslyn, 1994b; James et al., 2003; Ullman, 1996).

These two goals are attained by separate mechanisms in the brain. From the results of experiments conducted with monkeys, Ungerleider and Mishkin (1982) described two major neural pathways, which they dubbed the *what* (properties of objects) and *where* (spatial properties) *pathways* (Figure 4.16). Subsequent research has backed up this distinction (Tsao et al., 2003). Further evidence for the existence of these distinct mechanisms comes from studies of humans who have suffered brain damage. Damage in the bottom parts of the temporal lobes impairs the patient's ability to recognize objects by sight, and damage in the back parts of the parietal lobes impairs the patient's ability to register locations (Lê et al., 2002; Levine, 1982; Riddoch et al., 2004; James et al., 2003). Moreover, these separate brain areas have been found to be activated during neuroimaging studies in which normal people are asked to distinguish shapes or locations (Bar et al., 2001; Bly & Kosslyn, 1997; Flas et al., 2002; Grill-Spector, 2003; Haxby et al., 1991, 1994, 2001; Kohler et al., 1995; Rao et al., 2003; Ungerleider & Haxby, 1994). The operation of these two distinct types of processes is evident even during infancy (Mareschal & Johnson, 2003). The two pathways come together in the frontal lobes, where information about an object's identity and position is used to make decisions (Ng et al., 2001; Rao et al., 1997).

Before reading on, take a moment to pick a card from Figure 4.17; we will return to these cards shortly.

## Knowing More Than You Can See

When you see an apple, the processes that underlie visual sensation respond to basic characteristics of the input, such as the wavelengths of light and changes in lightness that may signal the presence of edges. The outputs from these processes are then organized in the first phases of perceptual processing to indicate a red, shiny object of a certain shape and size that is at a certain distance. But nothing in this information tells you that inside this object are seeds and, maybe, a worm. For you to know these things, the final phases of perceptual processing must occur, which allow the visual input to activate information you've stored in memory from your prior experience. To interpret what you see, you need to compare the input to stored information. If the input matches something you've stored in memory, that information can be applied to the present case (and that's how you know that an apple *may* have a worm inside, even if you can't see one *this time*). If the object is *recognized*, it seems familiar; if it is *identified*, you know additional facts about it.

Objects are sometimes recognized as collections of parts. Irving Biederman and his colleagues (Biederman, 1987; Hummel & Biederman, 1992) have suggested that objects are represented in the brain as collections of simple shapes, with each shape

**FIGURE 4.16** **Two Visual Pathways**

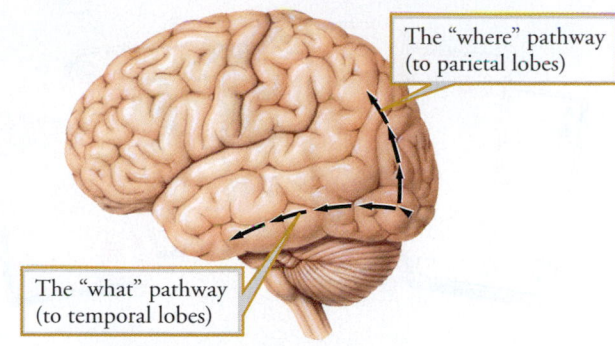

Visual input flows along two major pathways in the brain. The "where" pathway going up to the parietal lobes is concerned with spatial properties (such as an object's location) whereas the "what" pathway going down to the temporal lobes is concerned with properties of objects (such as their shape and color).

**FIGURE 4.17** **Pick a Card, Any Card**

Look at this display and pick out a card. Then turn the page, look at Figure 4.18, and read that caption.

FIGURE 4.18

## Is Only Your Card Missing?

Look at this display only after you have picked out a card in the display on the previous page. After you have picked out a card, look for it here. Did we remove the card you were thinking of? At first glance, it probably appears that we have removed only that card and left the others alone. Magic? No. Your brain coded the suits and values of the cards separately, and you only see them combined properly when you pay attention to them (Arguin et al., 1994; Treisman & Schmidt, 1982). Thus, if you only paid attention to one particular card, you will notice its absence. As for the other cards, you will notice only the values and suits, not their combinations. Fortunately, some basic features, such as color and orientation, are automatically bound together when they are superimposed (Holcombe & Cavanagh, 2001).

representing a part of the object, such as the head, neck, body, and legs of a dog. It is clear that we can see parts of objects individually (Hoffman & Richards, 1984). But take a look at the two photographs of Britney Spears (see page 156), and then turn the book around so that you can see the photos right-side up. It should also be clear that we do not always recognize or identify objects in terms of their individual parts. If that were the case, we wouldn't need to turn the book over to see how weird one of the photos is. Rather, we usually focus on the overall views of shapes, and look for details only if we need them (Cave & Kosslyn, 1993). When we do look at individual features, however, they may not always be properly combined, as demonstrated in Figure 4.18.

## Informed Perception: The Active Viewer

The progression from sensation, to organization, to recognition and identification may seem to indicate a simple sequential process, but more is happening. So far, we've been discussing **bottom-up processing**, which is initiated by the stimulus. Bottom-up processing operates like a row of standing dominoes: When the neural equivalent of the first domino is tripped by the light impulses reaching your eye (or the sound vibrations reaching your ear), other neural signals are successively tripped, like falling dominoes, until you've understood what you're seeing (or hearing). As shown in Figure 4.19, bottom-up processing can sometimes trigger additional sensory experiences, as well as comprehension. In contrast, **top-down processing** is guided by knowledge, expectation, or belief. For example, go back to those ambiguous figures in Figure 4.11. Can you intentionally see the two faces or the vase? Top-down processing allows you to impose what you want to see on what is actually out there. In most cases, top-down processing does not change how you see an object, but instead just makes it easier to organize or interpret it; expecting to see a particular object makes it easier to see it (van Zoest & Donk, 2004).

Bottom-up and top-down processes often are in play at the same time (Corbetta & Shulman, 2002; Humphreys et al., 1997; Kosslyn & Koenig, 1995). Here's how it works. If you turn on the TV to a random channel, you will be able to understand what appears on the screen even if it's a complete surprise: The processing is bottom up, from the stimulus alone, unaided by any expectation you might have. Your eyes and ears register what's there, and your brain processes the resulting signals. However, after the first few moments of watching this randomly selected channel, even if you seem to be just another vegetating couch potato, you are in fact actively anticipating what will appear next and using this information to help you see. Now you are engaging in top-down processing, which occurs when you use your knowledge of what to expect to help you look for specific characteristics and fill in missing parts of the stimulus. You can experience top-down processing at work if the TV image is really blurry and you use the sound track to provide clues to what's in the picture. For example, if the sound track makes it clear that

FIGURE 4.19

## Synesthesia

 Usual appearance

 Appearance to person with synesthesia

Bottom-up processing can sometimes produce remarkably complex experiences. For example, perhaps as many as 1 in 2,000 people experience *synesthesia*, where they simultaneously experience more than one perception when given certain stimuli (the term is from the Greek *syn*, which means "union," and *aisthises*, which means "of the senses"). Many of these people see letters, digits, and words that are in fact printed in black, as in the top row, as if they were printed in colors, as in the second row. The neural bases of this phenomenon are just now coming to be understood (Rich & Mattingley, 2002).

two people are about to kiss, you will be able to make out the outlines of the faces more easily. Such top-down processing is often used to help you integrate what you see with what you hear (Ernst & Bülthoff, 2004).

Top-down processing can alter the mechanisms used in bottom-up processing (Corbetta & Shulman, 2002; Humphreys et al., 1997; Kosslyn, 1994b). In a study by Delk and Fillenbaum (1965), for example, participants were shown stimuli that were all cut from the same orangish-red cardboard, including objects that are normally red (an apple and a valentine heart) and objects that are not normally red (a mushroom and a bell). The participants were to adjust the color of a display until they thought it matched the color of the cutouts. Apparently, the knowledge of the usual color of the objects affected how participants saw the actual color; when asked to match the color of the normally red objects, they consistently selected a redder color than the one they chose to match the color of the mushroom and the bell.

Your **perceptual set** is the sum of your assumptions and beliefs that lead you to expect to perceive certain objects or characteristics in particular contexts. For example, when the bottom light on a stoplight is illuminated, you will see it as green even if it is in fact a bluish green. People often use context to form such *perceptual expectancies*, perceptions dependent on previous experience (Palmer, 1992a). Cues in the current context are often used to guide top-down processing during perception (Chun, 2000).

## Coding Space in the Brain: More Than One Way to Identify "Where"

We have so far been focusing on the "what" pathway, but researchers have also studied the final phases of perceptual processing in the "where" pathway. The goal of this processing is to use the sum total of the distance cues (discussed earlier) to identify the distance and direction of objects, either relative to yourself or relative to other objects. Kosslyn (1987) proposed that the brain uses two different ways to code spatial relations. To get a rough sense of the idea, think of the difference between a list of directions and a map. The list relies on *categorical spatial relations*, which code relative positions with categories such as "above" or "left of" or "beside." Like all categories, these group together a set of specific examples (Laeng et al., 2002). For instance, take the simplest list of directions: Say that a friend asks you to go through the door into her bedroom and get her backpack, which she tells you is to the right of the bed. "Right of" is a categorical relation; it doesn't indicate a particular, specific spot, but instead gives you a whole group of possible locations—anywhere to the right of the bed, as shown in Figure 4.20.

However, categorical spatial relations are useless for the other main tasks of vision: navigation and reaching (Goodale & Milner, 1992; Milner & Goodale, 1995). Knowing that the backpack is "to the right of" (a categorical spatial relation) the bed will not allow you to walk right over to it. For instance, imagine that the electricity went out and the room was pitch black; if all you knew was that the backpack was to the right of the bed, you would have to creep carefully around, feeling your way until you happened upon it. For navigation and reaching, you need precise information about the distance and direction of objects. In contrast to categorical spatial relations, *coordinate spatial relations* specify continuous distances from your body or another

**Bottom-up processing:** Processing that is initiated by stimulus input.

**Top-down processing:** Processing that is guided by knowledge, expectation, or belief.

**Perceptual set:** The sum of your assumptions and beliefs that lead you to expect to perceive certain objects or characteristics in particular contexts.

**FIGURE 4.20** **Coding Space**

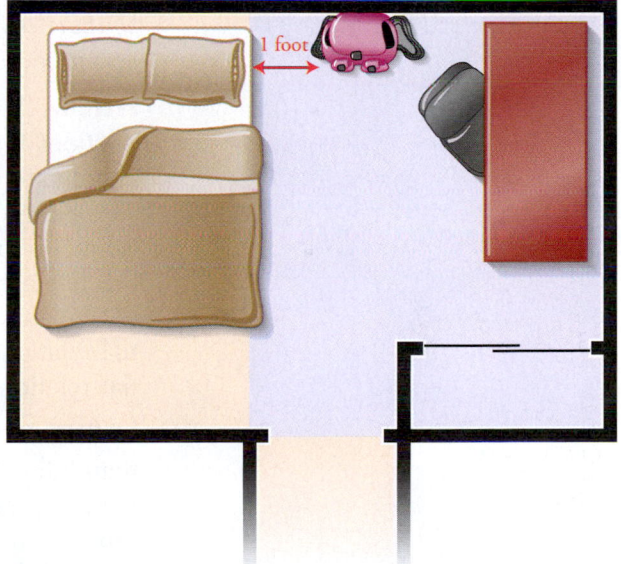

A categorical spatial relation could be used to specify that the backpack is "to the right of" the bed, which would indicate that it could be in any of the light blue region. A coordinate spatial relation would indicate that the backpack is 1 foot to the right of the back, right-hand corner of the bed, which specifies a particular spot on the floor (shown by the red arrow). Categorical and coordinate spatial relations are useful for different purposes.

object that serves as an "origin" of a coordinate space. For example, your friend might tell you that the backpack is a foot away from the right-hand corner of the head of the bed (see Figure 4.20, p. 153). Knowing this, you could find it easily, even in the dark; as soon as you felt your way to the right-hand side of the bed, you would know exactly where to find the backpack.

How can we tell whether the brain does in fact use these two different ways to identify spatial relations? Kosslyn (1987) proposed that the left cerebral hemisphere may be better at identifying categorical spatial relations, which are easily named by a word or two (and thus are compatible with the left hemisphere's facility at labeling). In contrast, he proposed that the right hemisphere may be better at identifying coordinate spatial relations, which are essential for navigation (and the right hemisphere typically is better at this ability; De Renzi, 1982). If one hemisphere is better at identifying categorical spatial relations and the other hemisphere is better at identifying coordinate spatial relations, then the two kinds of spatial relations must be distinct—if they were in fact the same thing, then they should be processed the same way. Although much research has supported this hypothesis (for example, Banich & Federmeier, 1999; Chabris & Kosslyn, 1998; Christman, 2002; Hellige & Michimata, 1989; Kosslyn et al., 1989; Laeng et al., 2002; Okubo & Michimata, 2002, 2004), a particularly strong test was reported by Slotnick and his colleagues (2001).

# UNDERSTANDING RESEARCH

## Two Ways to Specify Spatial Relations

**QUESTION:** Do the cerebral hemispheres differ in their abilities to specify categorical versus coordinate spatial relations?

**ALTERNATIVES:** (1) Yes, the left hemisphere is better at specifying categorical spatial relations than the right hemisphere, but the right hemisphere is better at specifying coordinate spatial relations than the left. (2) Yes, the right hemisphere is better at specifying categorical spatial relations than the left hemisphere, but the left hemisphere is better at specifying coordinate spatial relations than the right. (3) No, the left hemisphere is, in general, better at specifying all types of spatial relations. (4) No, the right hemisphere is, in general, better at specifying all types of spatial relations. (5) No, the hemispheres are equally good at specifying all types of spatial relations.

**LOGIC:** If the left hemisphere is better at specifying categorical spatial relations than is the right, then when the left hemisphere is temporarily deactivated (for medical reasons), the patient should be impaired while evaluating categorical spatial relations more than when the right hemisphere is deactivated. In contrast, if the right hemisphere is better at specifying coordinate spatial relations than is the left, then the opposite result should occur when each hemisphere is temporarily deactivated.

**METHOD:** The researchers (Slotnick et al., 2001) took advantage of a technique that allowed them temporarily to anesthetize one hemisphere at a time. They tested 134 participants who were about to have brain surgery (and thus it was important to know in advance which mental processes were carried out by specific brain regions). The researchers injected sodium amobarbital into the major artery (the carotid) that provides blood to one or the other of the cerebral hemispheres, which temporarily anesthetizes it. They then presented two categorical tasks and three coordinate tasks. For example, one categorical task required participants to decide whether a dot was on or off a blob in a line drawing, and one coordinate task required participants to decide whether a plus and minus sign were less than 2 inches apart. The researchers recorded the number of errors.

**RESULTS:** Deactivating the left hemisphere caused patients to make more errors in the categorical tasks than did deactivating the right hemisphere. In contrast, for a difficult coordinate task, deactivating the right hemisphere caused patients to make more errors than deactivating the left hemisphere. However, for easy coordinate tasks (where the differences in the to-be-discriminated distances were very distinct), the participants made comparable numbers of errors when either hemisphere was deactivated.

**INFERENCES:** When the task was challenging, the left hemisphere was better at specifying categorical spatial relations, whereas the right was better at specifying coordinate spatial relations. The fact that the hemispheres differed in this way is important because if there were only a single way to code spatial relations, either one hemisphere would always be better than the other or there would be no difference between them. The observed differences between the hemispheres shows that the brain can in fact code spatial relations in at least two ways. But why did this difference only emerge when the participants had to make difficult discriminations? One possibility is that when a distance discrimination is easy enough, you can quickly form a category to capture it (such as "1 versus 2 inches")—and thus either type of spatial relation can be used, and either hemisphere can perform the task.

## THINK CRITICALLY!

What can studying a brain that is missing the contribution of an entire hemisphere tell us about the normal brain? What problems might you have in interpreting results from such a study? The technique used in the study by Slotnick and colleagues has some advantages over lesioning studies (discussed in Chapter 3); does it have any disadvantages? Why can't people form categories easily for all discriminations? Are the stimuli used here truly representative of categorical and coordinate spatial relations that people deal with in daily life?

# Combining What and Where: Faces and Gazes

Many of Kahlo's paintings feature complex arrangements of objects, where both shape and location are crucial. As such paintings illustrate, perceiving many (if not most) complex stimuli requires a rich interplay between the two major visual pathways, which register "what" (shape and other properties of objects) and "where" (spatial properties). Faces are a good example of such complex stimuli; they are so important that our brains have evolved not only to identify them easily, but also to make use of facial cues, such as the direction in which another person is gazing.

## Identifying Faces: A Special Brain System?

Brain damage causes some patients to lose the ability to identify faces. When first reported, this deficit (called *prosopagnosia*) appeared strikingly specific; such patients could identify all manner of common objects and events, but not faces. This finding made sense from an evolutionary perspective—faces are so important to us that the brain may have evolved a specific mechanism just for them. However, before

Faces are important for many social animals. Researchers discovered that even sheep have specialized brain circuits for faces, and these animals can remember at least 50 other sheep faces for at least two years (Kendrick et al., 2001).

Once people become very good at distinguishing among these "greebles," part of the brain that responds to faces also responds to these objects.

long, researchers discovered that patients with prosopagnosia typically also have problems whenever they must identify a specific instance of a type of object (for example, your wallet or watch versus another person's wallet or watch; Barton et al., 2004). This finding muddied the waters. Are faces special or not? Much neuroimaging has now addressed this issue.

Nancy Kanwisher and her colleagues (1997, 1998; Tong et al., 2000) asked people to look at faces while their brains were scanned using fMRI. The researchers identified a portion of the underside of the temporal lobe (part of the "what" system) that was activated more strongly by faces than by pictures of houses or hands—or by scrambled or upside-down faces. These results led the researchers to dub this area the *fusiform face area (FFA)*, and to infer that it is specialized for recognizing faces in particular. However, other researchers, notably Isabel Gauthier and Michael Tarr, asked whether this area is really used not just for faces, but more generally to make fine distinctions among similar-but-highly-familiar objects. To test this idea, they showed bird and car experts sets of birds and cars, and found that the FFA was activated when these people saw objects in their field of expertise (Gauthier et al., 2000). In addition, these researchers created novel, computer-generated objects, called *greebles*, and trained people to become very good at distinguishing among them—and sure enough, greebles activated the FFA (Gauthier et al., 1999).

However, other researchers have found that the FFA is activated more strongly by faces than by butterflies, even when viewed by experts (Rhodes et al., 2004). Faces may in fact hold a special place in the brain's processing, but perhaps only because we have so much practice distinguishing among them, from the very beginnings of life (Hann et al., 2002; Tarr & Gauthier, 2000). In addition, faces may differ from butterflies or other objects in that we both view them as overall wholes (Gauthier & Tarr, 2002) and also look at their specific features. For example, removing eyebrows from pictures of familiar faces severely disrupts how well people can identify the people; in fact, removing eyebrows hurts identification even more than removing the eyes (Sadr et al., 2003). When we use features to identify faces, we rely not only on the "what" system to identify the shape, but also on the "where" system, which specifies the locations of specific parts; and in fact, prosopagnosic patients have deficits in the relevant kind of spatial processing (Barton et al., 2004). The dual role of the overall pattern and the specific

Look at these faces, and then turn the book and look at them right side up. One explanation for the peculiar lapse in noticing the parts is that when you view the entire face, you are attending to a single pattern—but to see the parts in detail, you need to attend to smaller pieces of the whole. Notice that if you focus on each part, you can see that some are upside down. But when you focus on the entire face, you see the overall pattern, not a collection of parts.

 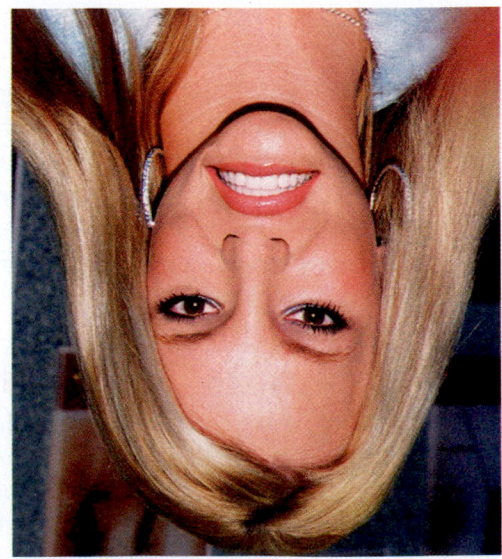

features is nicely illustrated by the upside-down photos of Britney Spears. Much complex identification relies on an interplay between the two major visual pathways.

### Identifying Gaze Direction: Where's Something Important?

The integration of the jobs of the two major visual pathways ("what" and "where") is also illustrated by the ways in which we use information about faces (Kingstone et al., 2000). When we see either a person's gaze fixated in one direction or a person's face turned toward a specific place, we look there, too. Although we shift our attention unconsciously (Friesen & Kingstone, 1998), such orienting is not a reflex, but rather depends on the kind of voluntary control that is the job of the frontal lobes; damage to these structures disrupts using face orientation or gaze direction to allocate attention (Vecera & Rizzo, 2004). Nevertheless, we may automatically pay attention to the direction of another person's gaze, even if we choose not to act on it.

The fact that our attention is drawn to where someone else looks affects us in several ways. For example, participants remember pictures of faces better if the gaze was direct than if it was averted (Mason et al., 2004). In addition, the ability to read emotion appears to rely, in part, on gaze: Adams and Kleck (2003) found that people could read "approach" emotions, such as joy, more easily when an observed face was looking directly at the observer than when the gaze was averted—but the opposite was true for "avoidance" emotions, such as fear.

## Attention: The Gateway to Awareness

In order to recognize and identify an object or event, you need to engage in Phase 2 perceptual processing. What determines which stimuli are given such treatment? **Attention** is the act of focusing on particular information, which allows that information to be processed more fully than information that is not attended to. For instance, if you are a movie buff, you might be fully absorbed by the latest Hollywood release—noticing every detail of how the cameras are used, of the lighting, and of other cinematic features. In order to soak up such details, you need to pay attention to the images themselves. If you are paying close attention, you will notice things that flit right by other people, such as rapid changes in camera angle. Research has shown that paying attention increases sensitivity to the attended events (Nakayama & Mackeben, 1989; Yeshurun & Carrasco, 1998, 1999). **Selective attention** allows you to pick out a particular characteristic, object, or event. For instance, you could be looking specifically for the ways that lighting is used, and thus tune yourself for this characteristic.

We are aware only of what we pay attention to. Although we focus here on visual attention, we stress that attention operates in virtually all domains of human thought and feeling, not only in visual perception; you can pay attention to a particular instrument in a band, a nuance of a word, a feeling, a taste, a particular place, or the feeling of a ladybug walking over the back of your hand. We pay attention to something for one of two reasons.

### Pop-Out: What Grabs Attention?

One reason we pay attention is that something about an event grabs us, such as a sudden change in illumination or movement. Certain qualities or features of displays, such as advertisements, automatically (via bottom-up processing) leap out—a phenomenon psychologists refer to as **pop-out**. For example, look at the left panel

**Attention:** The act of focusing on particular information, which allows it to be processed more fully than what is not attended to.

**Selective attention:** The process of picking out a particular quality, object, or event for relatively detailed analysis.

**Pop-out:** Phenomenon that occurs when a stimulus is sufficiently different from the ones around it that it is immediately evident.

## FIGURE 4.21 — Pop-Out Versus Search

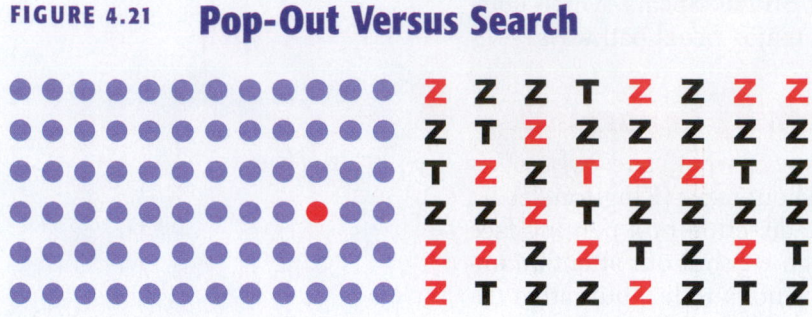

As shown in the left panel, basic features, such as color, are registered without the need for an item-by-item search. Is there a red T in the right panel? To find a combination of features, such as the arrangements of segments or a shape with a particular color, you must search the items one at a time.

of Figure 4.21. Is a red dot present? The red dot appears to pop out; it is immediately evident without your having to search for it. Attention is immediately drawn to this "odd man out." In general, pop-out occurs when objects differ in their fundamental qualities, such as size for vision or frequency for hearing (you immediately hear a high-pitched flute in a band if all the other instruments are playing low notes). Pop-out relies on the outputs of Phase 1 processes that organize figures; separate features (such as color and orientation) are detected by the same process, and thus having more than a single pop-out dimension does not make the odd-man-out much—if any—easier to detect than having a single distinctive feature (Krummenacher et al., 2002; Monnier, 2003).

## Active Searching: Not Just What Grabs Attention

The other reason we pay attention is that we are actively searching for a particular characteristic, object, or event (via top-down processing). Have you ever wondered whether you have actually glimpsed a friend in a crowd, or heard a familiar voice in an unexpected context? In many situations, your initial perception of an event may not be very clear, and you need a "second look" or "second hear." In these cases, your first suspicions of what you might have perceived guide top-down processes to collect more information in a very efficient way: You search for distinctive characteristics, such as the shape of a particular haircut, or the pitch of a certain voice. Or, have you ever waited for a friend and anticipated her appearance with every passing stranger? *Vigilance* occurs when you are anticipating a particular event and thus maintain attention as you wait for it, which also relies on your ability to focus your attention voluntarily.

This voluntary type of attention is distinct from the sort that arises when a particular characteristic of a stimulus grabs your attention. We know this is so in part because the two types of attention are accomplished by different parts of the brain. In the case of a sudden change in the environment, such as a bright light or a quick movement, the superior colliculus (a small subcortical structure) acts in a way somewhat like a reflex, shifting attention automatically to that event. Moreover, a brain region standing between the right temporal and parietal lobes and another region in the lower right frontal lobe are used in bottom-up processing (Corbetta & Shulman, 2002). In contrast, none of these areas underlie the voluntary shifts of attention that occur while you are searching for something or someone (or remaining vigilant); instead, the frontal eye fields (in the frontal lobes; Corbetta & Shulman, 2002; Kosslyn & Koenig, 1995; Paus, 1996) and regions of the parietal lobes are active (Hopf & Mangun, 2000; Intriligator & Cavanagh, 2001; Rosen et al., 1999; Shulman et al., 2003; Synder et al., 2000).

In addition, the two types of attention operate differently. In contrast to what happens with pop-out, when you are searching for an object that is not distinct from the others around it, you must look at each possible candidate one at a time. Treisman and her colleagues (Treisman & Gormican, 1988; Treisman & Souther, 1985) demonstrated how this works in an experiment like the one illustrated in Figure 4.21. The more letters there are in a display like the one in the right panel, the longer it takes to find a target. With enough letters, people end up searching the display one item at a time. Moreover, if you are engaged in another activity that requires attention, such as counting backwards from a specific digit, visual search is more difficult (Han & Kim, 2004); it's a little like rubbing your stomach clockwise with one hand while simultaneously rubbing the top of your head counterclockwise with the other hand—competition for attention makes both tasks harder. Pop-out and searching are distinct activities that arise from distinct areas of the brain. Using magnetic pulses to disrupt the parietal lobe, researchers found that while the ability to search for arrangements of features was impaired, the ability to experience pop-out was not (Ashbridge et al., 1997).

Attention is not a product of the brain alone but, like all other psychological events, it arises from the joint action of events at the different levels of analysis. What determines whether or not you will take that second look? That decision is influenced by what you believe (level of the person), which in part depends on your previous interactions with other people and your knowledge of the surrounding culture (level of the group). If you thought you saw a good friend, your attention would be engaged more fully than if you thought you saw a casual acquaintance. Similarly, if you are walking down the street and catch a glimpse of a dollar bill on the sidewalk, it will engage your attention differently than will a scrap of paper; but a young child, who doesn't know about the value of money, may react to the two stimuli the same way. Because of her experience with pain, Kahlo might have noticed a guest grimacing in pain, whereas Rivera might have "seen" the same thing but not paid attention to it. Prior experiences can govern how attention works.

## Limits of Attention

Consider three limits on attention.

- *One task at a time*. We cannot pay attention to more than one task at the same instant. If we must perform two tasks that require attention, such as talking on a cell phone and driving during a hailstorm, we must divide our attention. **Divided attention** occurs when you shift back and forth between different stimuli or tasks. Divided attention usually has a cost: You will perform one—or both—of the tasks more poorly than you would if you concentrated on one task alone (Han & Humphreys, 2002; Rodriguez et al., 2002). This problem may arise either because additional processes in the frontal lobes must be brought to bear when you shift attention back and forth (Nagahama et al., 2001) or because the same mechanisms are being used in competing tasks.

  However, if the tasks are different enough, so that they can be accomplished by different mechanisms, they won't interfere as much with each other (Bonnel et al., 2001). Moreover, if the tasks or signals don't compete with each other, but instead lead to the same response, you might actually do better when you have to pay attention to two tasks or two signals at once (Beilock et al., 2002). For example, the *redundant signal effect* occurs when you are asked to respond as soon as you perceive a signal: If you are given two signals at once instead of one, you will respond more quickly. This effect occurs even if one member of the pair of visual signals is so dim you are not consciously aware of seeing it (Savazzi & Marzi, 2002).

- *Limited region of space*. We can focus our attention only within a limited region of space, but with practice we can learn to allocate our attention over

Divided attention: The process of shifting focus back and forth between different stimuli or tasks.

## FIGURE 4.22

## The Stroop Effect

| | |
|---|---|
| GREEN | RED |
| RED | BLUE |
| BLUE | GREEN |
| BLACK | BLACK |
| BLUE | GREEN |
| RED | BLUE |
| GREEN | BLACK |
| BLACK | RED |
| RED | BLUE |
| BLUE | GREEN |

In 1935, John Ridley Stroop published a classic paper describing what is now known as the Stroop effect. Name the color of the ink used to print each word in the left column (not the color named by the word); then do the same for the words in the right column. Which is easier? You cannot help both seeing the color and reading the word and, when the meaning of the word is different from the color of the ink, you experience interference.

differently shaped regions of space (such as a vertical or horizontal rectangle; Panagopoulos et al., 2004). Moreover, if objects are moving, we can focus on them only when they move below a certain speed (Verstraten et al., 2000). For example, Intriligator and Cavanagh (2001) found that humans can focus on a particular dot when 60 or fewer dots are placed within the central 30-degree region of the visual field (in vision research, the size of a region of space is specified in degrees; if you hold your thumb out at arm's length and look at it with one eye, it spans about 2 degrees); any more dots than 60 in that region, and the participants could not focus on an individual dot. Your ability to select one thing to pay attention to is much coarser than your ability to discriminate among fine visual details.

- *Filtering.* Attention is also limited in its ability to filter out information. Figure 4.22 illustrates a classic example of such a limit of attention: the *Stroop effect.* If you are asked to pay attention only to the color of the ink (and not the word itself), and say this color aloud, you will nevertheless have trouble if the word names another color; if the meaning of the word is different from the color of the ink, you experience interference when you try to name the color of the ink. Bottom-up processes lead you to read the meaning of the word, and attention cannot simply turn off such processes (do you think it would be a good idea to be able to do so?).

## Seeing Without Awareness

Some people who suffer strokes that leave them blind can nevertheless report accurately when spots of light are presented—and will even know where they are. These people have no awareness of seeing the dots but rather simply "know" when they are present. Similarly, animals with damage to the visual cortex in the occipital lobe may appear to be blind at all other times, but when they are lowered onto a surface, they stick out their legs to support themselves at just the right point; some of these animals can avoid obstacles when walking, even though the primary visual cortex has been removed (Cowey & Stoerig, 1995). Such behavior has been called *blindsight* (Weiskrantz, 1986). Multiple pathways from the eye lead to many places in the brain (Felleman & Van Essen, 1991; Zeki, 1978, 1993), and some of these pathways can function even though they do not pass through brain areas that give rise to conscious experience. Thus, even when the areas crucial for consciousness, or connections from these areas, are damaged, some visual function persists.

**SUBLIMINAL PERCEPTION: SEEING MORE THAN YOU KNOW** Our brains can respond when we see an object even if we are not aware of seeing it. Marcel (1983) took advantage of the discovery that presenting a word makes it easier for people to read a subsequent word that has a related meaning; this kind of carryover effect is one type of *priming.* Marcel and his collaborators found that priming occurs even when the first word is presented so quickly that people are not aware of having seen it (see Figure 4.23; Bar & Biederman, 1998, and Kunde, 2004, confirm these results). Perception of events outside awareness is called *subliminal perception.* After many years of unreliable findings, researchers have not only documented that subliminal perception exists, but they are even tracking down the brain events responsible for this effect (Kolb & Braun, 1995; Luck et al., 1996).

**FORMS OF TRANSIENT BLINDNESS: SEEING LESS THAN YOU KNOW** However, let's not overstate the case. More often than not, instead of perceiving more than you are aware

FIGURE 4.23 **One Demonstration of Subliminal Perception**

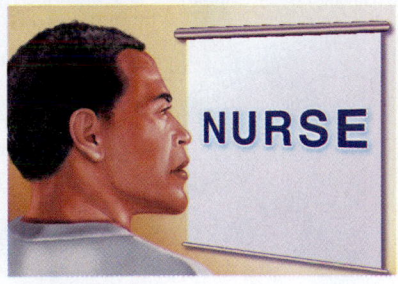 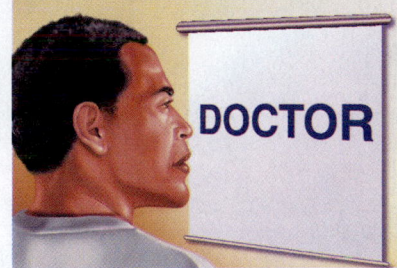 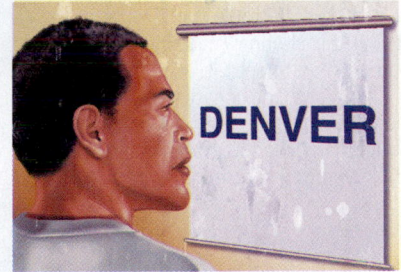

A word can be presented so briefly that the viewer has no awareness of having seen it.

After the initial word, "Nurse" in this case, a second word is presented, long enough to be seen clearly. The second word is either related to the first one, such as "Doctor," or unrelated, such as "Denver." If the two words are related, participants can read the second one more easily.

of, you are actually perceiving less than you think. For example, have you ever seen paintings of a galloping horse where the front legs are extended ahead, and the rear ones extended behind, as shown in Figure 4.24? Until the late 19th century, most people believed that this is how horses ran. In fact, it took one of the first uses of stop-action photography to convince people otherwise—and even this wasn't initially enough: In 1878, Eadweard Muybridge took a series of stop-action photographs of a running horse that clearly showed that one foot was always on the ground. So strong were people's beliefs about what they thought they saw when watching a horse gallop that they rejected Muybridge's first set of photographs, and he had to restage the event with witnesses from the press on hand to verify that the cameras were working properly (Sullivan, 1999). A large body of research shows that people can perceive with high accuracy only those stimuli to which they pay attention. Conversely, people are remarkably bad at noticing even large changes in stimuli if they are not paying attention to the relevant parts. In fact, we suffer from *change blindness*, not seeing even large alterations of features as scenes change over time (O'Regan, 1992; Simons, 2000; Simons & Ambinder, 2005; Simons & Levin, 1997).

**FIGURE 4.24**

## Belief Can Sometimes Substitute for Perception

People sometimes think that they see horses gallop with all four legs off the ground, extended out front and behind (left panel)—but in fact, horses always have at least one foot tucked under the body (right panel).

The two versions of these scenes were alternated every 640 milliseconds. In the pair of photos on the left, the railing changes, which is not of central interest. People had a difficult time noticing this change, requiring 16.2 alternations on average to spot it. In the pair of photos on the right, the location of the helicopter changes, which is of central interest. People noticed this change after only 4.0 alternations, on average (from Rensink et al., 1997).

A bird in the hand is worth two in the the bush. Did you notice anything odd about the sentence you just read? Many people miss the repeated "the"; in fact, this is said to be the hardest error for a proofreader to catch. Kanwisher (1987, 1991) has dubbed this effect **repetition blindness**, and she and many others (such as Morris & Harris, 2004) have shown that people will fail to see a second example of an object if it occurs soon after the first instance. (A similar effect, called *repetition deafness*, occurs in hearing; Soto-Faraco & Spence, 2001.) A related phenomenon is the **attentional blink**, in which attention is lost for a certain time immediately following a stimulus to which attention was paid. In contrast to repetition blindness, the attentional blink can occur for a different stimulus, not necessarily a second instance of the same or a closely related one, and the effect may actually be larger for stimuli that occur a few items after the one attended to (Arnell & Jolicoeur, 1999; Chun, 1997; Jolicoeur, 1998; Luck et al., 1996; Raymond et al., 1992). Proofreaders and copyeditors experience this unfortunate phenomenon all the time, missing obvious errors that happen to fall in the wake of a large error or a string of errors. Repetition blindness appears to result because the stimuli are not registered as individual events, but simply as a "type" of event (Kanwisher, 1987), whereas the attentional blink may occur because the act of registering information in detail may "lock up" certain neural processes for a brief period (within about a half-second of seeing the first stimulus), during which attention cannot easily be reengaged (Fell et al., 2002). The attentional blink can occur even when two stimuli are presented to the separated cerebral hemispheres of a split-brain patient (see Chapter 3), which shows that the effect arises very soon after visual input begins to be processed. (Giesbrecht & Kingstone, 2004). Nevertheless, the attentional blink reflects in part interference in later phases of perceptual processing (Christmann & Leuthold, 2004; Vogel & Luck, 2002).

**Repetition blindness:** The inability to see the second occurrence of a stimulus that appears twice in succession.

**Attentional blink:** A rebound period in which a person cannot pay attention to one thing after having just paid attention to another.

# LOOKING AT LEVELS
## The Essential Features of Good Looks

As any painter can tell you, vision is used for more than identifying objects and registering their locations. Through the visual system, we also perceive what we call "beauty," including physical attractiveness. In fact, a specific part of the frontal lobe (the medial orbital frontal cortex, OFC, which is in the midline, behind the eyes), is activated when people look at attractive faces—and is even more strongly activated when an attractive face is smiling (O'Doherty et al., 2003). This finding is intriguing because the OFC is thought to specify the "reward value" of stimuli. However, we know that some rewards (such as food) are innate, whereas other rewards are learned (such as money). Is the perception of attractiveness entirely inborn? To answer this, let's begin by considering exactly which features of faces are perceived to be attractive:

- *Smooth skin*. Smooth, even-colored skin is perceived as more attractive than coarser, uneven skin (Fink et al., 2001).
- *Symmetry*. Symmetrical faces tend to be perceived as attractive and as healthy (Reis & Zaidel, 2001).
- *Makeup*. Makeup has been shown to enhance attractiveness of female faces (Osborn, 1996), especially makeup that darkens the region around the eyes and the mouth; however, such makeup yields precisely the opposite reaction when applied to male faces (Russell, 2003).
- *Female hormones*. Faces that show the effects of female hormones (such as a relatively small chin, full lips, and high cheekbones) are perceived as attractive. David Perrett and his colleagues (1998) asked Asian people (Japanese in Japan) and Caucasians (Scots in Scotland) to choose the most attractive faces from a set of photographs, some of which had been altered to emphasize features that reflect high levels of male or female hormones. The researchers found that both national groups preferred women's faces with a female "hormone enhanced" look to average faces. In addition, both sets of participants found even *male* faces more attractive if they showed effects of *female* hormones. Faces that showed effects of high levels of male hormones were rated as having high "perceived dominance," as being older, and as having less warmth, emotionality, honesty, and cooperativeness (as well as other attributes). Apparently, the effects of female hormones not only made faces look younger but also softened these negative perceptions.

All of these variables may reflect inborn preferences, and hence reflect events at the level of the brain. However, the correlations between people's preferences explain at most only about 25% of the differences among these preferences, and thus other factors must be at work (Thornhill & Gangestad, 1999). In fact, even the variables noted above can be modified by learning. For example, take that effect of female hormones: It was in fact larger for female faces within each participant's own population, a finding that was interpreted as indicating that this is a learned preference. The results of such learning operate at the level of the person, but the process of the learning itself relies on events at the level of the group. Moreover, what's perceived as attractive in one society may not be the same as what's perceived as attractive in another (Jones, 1996). At the level of the group, values and tastes develop and are taught, either

Facial images of Caucasian and Japanese females and males were "feminized" and "masculinized" 50% in shape. Which face do you prefer? In general, faces that reflect effects of female sex hormones are seen as more attractive.

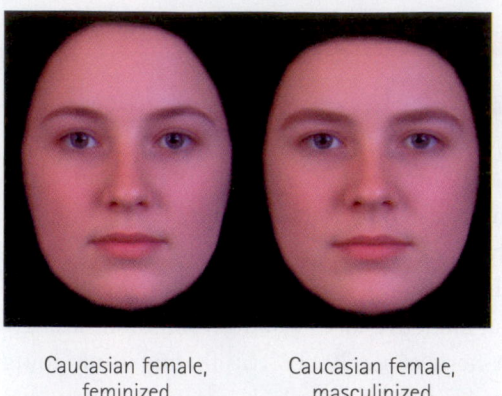

Caucasian female, feminized     Caucasian female, masculinized

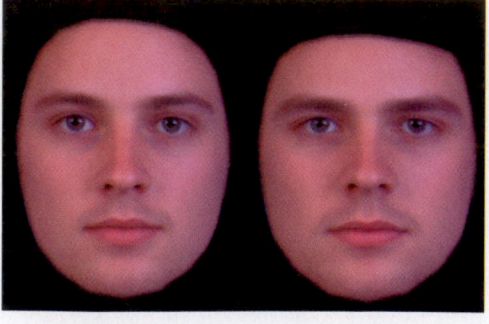

Caucasian male, feminized     Caucasian male, masculinized

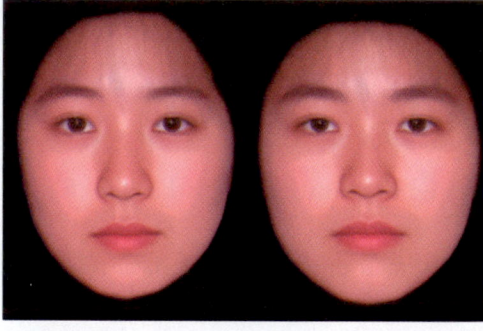

Japanese female, feminized     Japanese female, masculinized

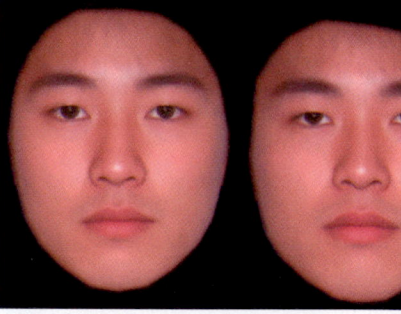

Japanese male, feminized     Japanese male, masculinized

explicitly (via instruction) or implicitly (via example) to the individual members of the group. These standards may evolve for different reasons.

In addition, faces are only part of the attractiveness story. For example, people find bodies with a specific weight for a specific height most attractive; but even here, learning is required to register this cue accurately when bodies are seen from different points of view (level of the person; Tovée & Cornelissen, 2001). Moreover, the preferred body shape varies in different cultures, and even subcultures (level of the group; Wetsman & Marlowe, 1999; Yu & Shepard, 1998)—as you might suspect from the art of Ruebens, whose roly-poly models would never find work on today's fashion runways. For example, Ford and Beach (1951) considered what people in over 200 cultures looked at when evaluating attractiveness and found that different cultures focused on different parts and characteristics of the body (such as the size of the pelvis, pudginess, and height). Moreover, posture—which may differ even between countries such as Italy and the United States—plays a role in judgments of attractiveness (Osborn, 1996).

As usual, events at the different levels interact. Once you evaluate someone as beautiful, various expectations and beliefs come to mind. Just as once you've identified an object as an apple, you know it has seeds inside, once you classify a person as attractive, you believe that he or she is likely to be kind, nurturing, and sensitive, and to have other positive attributes as well (Dion et al., 1972). Such information then affects how you interact with the person, which in turn can lead to new learning, perhaps influencing you to develop a more specialized category.

# Test Yourself

1. Transduction in vision has occurred when
   a. light is converted by the rods and cones into neural impulses.
   b. light has entered the lens.
   c. neural impulses have reached the occipital lobe.
   d. consciousness is present.
2. Which theory of color vision is based on cells that excite and inhibit complementary colors?
   a. trichromatic theory
   b. opponent process theory
   c. afterimage theory
   d. transduction theory
3. As you walk around, the pattern of sensory stimulation on your retina due to objects in your visual field changes, but your perceptions of the features of the objects do not change. This stabilization of the perceptual scene is due to
   a. figure ground distinction.
   b. movement of the eyes.
   c. genetic processes.
   d. perceptual constancy.
4. Because events at different levels of analysis interact, group-based standards of beauty can influence top-down processing at the level of the person by
   a. establishing beliefs about beauty that direct a person's attention.
   b. changing a person's brain to favor certain faces.
   c. creating group archetypes of beauty.
   d. conflicting with a person's perceptions.

## Answers

1.a 2.b 3.d 4.a

NOTE: Once you feel comfortable with the Test Yourself questions in this chapter, visit the book's Web site at www.ablongman.com/kosslyn3e for additional study questions.

## Think It Through!

Do you think "boosted" or enhanced sensory sensitivities would be an advantage or a disadvantage? (What if you could see the dirt in the pores on a friend's face across the room?) In what ways would such superabilities be a benefit? A drawback? What if you were able to adjust your sensory sensitivity and bias at will? Would such abilities help an artist such as Frida Kahlo? In what kinds of situations would this power be desirable?

What do you think would happen if you had been born blind and suddenly had vision at age 50? Such cases have been studied in depth (Gregory, 1974; Sacks, 1995), and even though light was being properly transduced in the eyes, these people failed to realize they were viewing a human face (that of the person who took off their bandages) until the person spoke. Why? If you had to help such a person adjust after the sight-giving operation, what would you do? Why might part of your training involve attention?

# HEARING

According to Diego Rivera's daughter, Kahlo loved whistles. They were sold in stands in the market: "They came in various sizes and made different sounds. She used them to call for [the different house staff], and she created quite a stir when she did" (Rivera & Colle, 1994, p. 100). How is it that Kahlo (and everyone else nearby whose hearing was intact) could *hear* the sounds of the whistles? And how could she (and we) notice that different whistles made different sounds?

## Auditory Sensation: If a Tree Falls but Nobody Hears It, Is There a Sound?

We know that rays don't emanate from our eyes when we see. Now for a trick question: Do you think that sound waves emanate from our ears when we hear? In 1978, researchers found that when a click is presented to someone, the ear soon produces

Pitch: How high or low a sound seems; higher frequencies of pressure waves produce the experience of higher pitches.

Loudness: The strength of a sound; pressure waves with greater amplitude produce the experience of louder sound.

Decibel (dB): A measure of loudness on a base-10 logarithmic scale; the threshold for hearing is set at 0dB.

an echo (Kemp, 1978). Not long after this discovery, researchers (Kemp, 1979; Zurek, 1981, 1985; Zwicker & Schloth, 1984) found that even when a person isn't hearing a particular stimulus, the ear sometimes actually makes a sound. In fact, about 40% of normal people emit a detectable soft humming sound from their ears, of which they are unaware. In some cases, the humming is loud enough that other people can hear it. These sounds are not like the natural sonar used by whales, sound waves bouncing off objects and returning to the ear. These sounds play no role in hearing. They are probably caused by feedback from the brain to the ear; feedback (not the sounds produced by it) helps us hear slight differences in sounds (Pickles, 1988; Zurek, 1985). As in vision, there are many feedback connections between areas of the brain that process sound, and between these areas and the ear (Felleman & Van Essen, 1991). This is not the only similarity between hearing and seeing, as we see in the following section.

## Sound Waves: Being Pressured

Like vision, auditory processing occurs in two major phases: sensation and perception. And, like vision, perception itself can be divided into processes used at the beginning and at the end. Hearing begins with the sensation of sound. Sound usually arises when something vibrates, creating waves of moving air that enter our ears. Sound can arise when any type of molecules—gas, liquid, or solid—move and create pressure waves. Thus, we can hear when we are surrounded by either air or water or when we put an ear to the ground, to a wall, or to another solid object. An old (but true) cliché of Western movies is listening with an ear pressed to a rail to hear whether a train is approaching. But movies sometimes get it wrong. In outer space—where there are no molecules to be moved—we could not hear anything; the loud explosion of the demolished Death Star in the original *Star Wars* movie would in fact have been silent as the grave.

These pressure waves go up, and then down, repeatedly; each complete up-and-down movement is called a *cycle*. Like light waves, sound waves have both frequency and amplitude. We usually hear variations in frequency as differences in **pitch**—how high or low the sound seems—and we hear variations in amplitude as differences in **loudness**. (It probably is no coincidence that people are most sensitive to the frequencies of a baby's cry, around 2,000–5,000 hertz; a hertz, or Hz, is the number of cycles per second.) Loudness is measured in decibels; a **decibel (dB)** is a measure of sound on a base-10 logarithmic scale (the log scale is used because we can hear an enormous range of volume). The threshold for hearing is set at 0 dB. A sound 10 times louder than the threshold sound is 10 dB; a sound 100 times louder than threshold level is 20 dB; a sound 1,000 times louder is 30 dB (the scale is based on powers of 10, so the number of zeros is indicated by the first digit in the dB measurement; a sound 10,000 times louder than threshold is 40 dB—four zeros). Figure 4.25 presents the loudness levels of some common sounds. Any sound over about 85 dB can impair your hearing if you listen to it for 8 hours straight; a sound over 140 dB can damage your hearing after a single exposure—and 160 dB will break your eardrum on the spot (National Institute for Occupational Safety and Health, 1998). The same psychophysical concepts that apply to vision, such as thresholds, JNDs, and so on, also apply to hearing and are measured in comparable ways.

**FIGURE 4.25** **Decibel Levels**

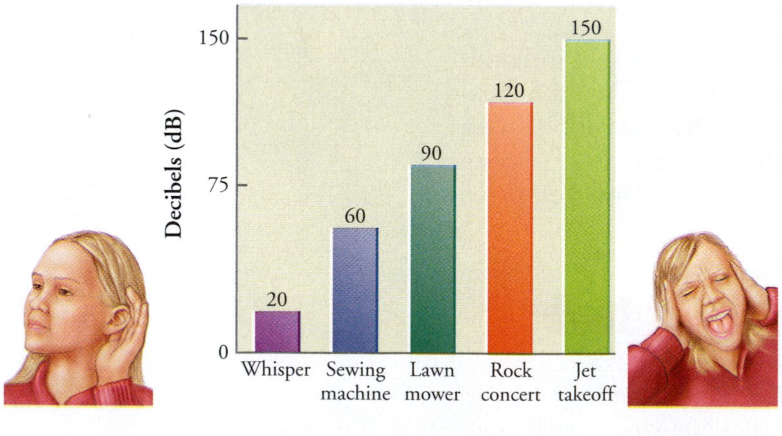


Sound is measured in terms of decibels (dB), which rely on a base-10 logarithmic scale. Any sound over 85 dB will damage hearing after 8 hours.

A question often asked in beginning philosophy classes is this: If a tree falls in the forest but nobody hears it, is there a sound? The answer is now clear: No. Sound is *caused* by waves of molecules (a physical event), but the waves themselves are not sound. Sound is a psychological event and hence depends on a nervous system to transduce the physical energy of the waves to nerve impulses. Without a brain to register the transduced physical energy, there can be no sound. The situation is exactly analogous to the relationships of wavelength to hue and of amplitude to lightness. Physical properties *lead* to psychological events, but they are not the events themselves. The discipline of psychophysics charts the relationship between physical events and our experiences of them.

## The Brain's Ear: More Than a Microphone

The anatomy of the ear is illustrated in Figure 4.26. The ear has three parts: the outer ear, middle ear, and inner ear. The eardrum (the *tympanic membrane*) stretches across the inside end of the auditory canal, and everything between the eardrum and the auditory nerve is designed to convert movements of the eardrum to nerve impulses that are sent to the brain. Specifically, waves move the eardrum, which in turn moves three bones in the middle ear (the hammer, anvil, and stirrup; incidentally, these are the smallest bones in the human body). If you hear a loud sound, the muscles in the ear reflexively tighten, which protects against damage (Borg & Counter, 1989). These muscles also contract when you talk, which protects you from hurting your own ears. Such protection is necessary because the ear is amazingly sensitive: We can hear a sound when the eardrum is moved less than 1 billionth of an inch (Green, 1976). The three bones of the middle ear not only transfer but also amplify the vibration and cause the *basilar membrane* (which is inside the cochlea, as shown in Figure 4.26) to vibrate. The basilar membrane is where different frequencies of sound are coded into varying nerve impulses. Hairs sticking up from cells lining the basilar membrane are moved by

**FIGURE 4.26** **Anatomy of the Ear**

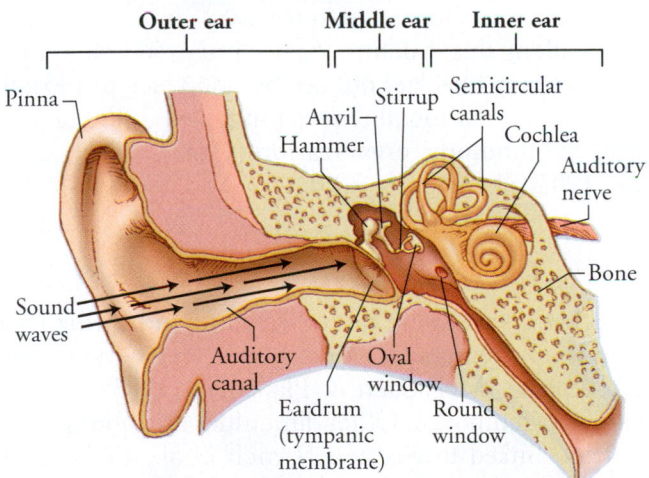
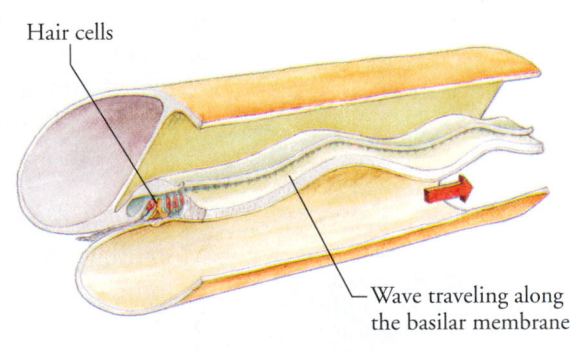

The major parts of the outer ear, middle ear, and inner ear. The semicircular canals have no role in hearing; they help us keep our balance.

If you unwound the cochlea and looked into it (as shown here), you would see the basilar membrane with its hair cells.

FIGURE 4.27 **Place Coding of Sound Frequency**

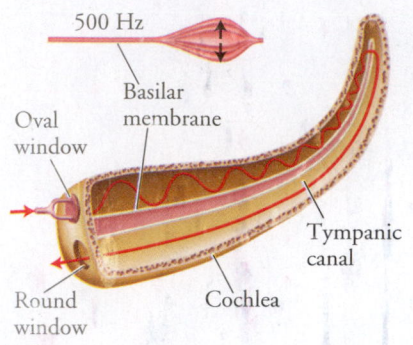
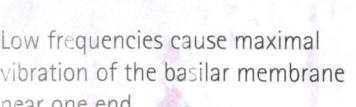
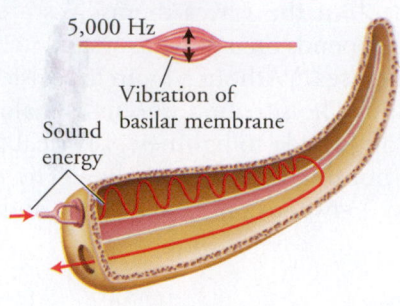
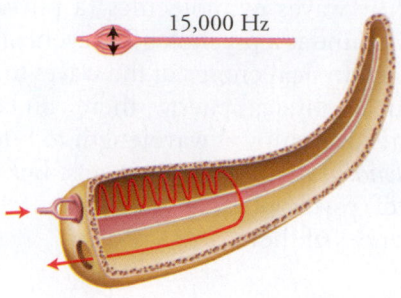

Low frequencies cause maximal vibration of the basilar membrane near one end.

Medium frequencies cause maximal vibration of the basilar membrane near the middle.

High frequencies cause maximal vibration of the basilar membrane near the other end.

the vibrations and trigger nerve impulses, which are then sent to the brain. These **hair cells** function in hearing the same way rods and cones do in vision; they produce the initial nerve impulses.

There are two main theories about the way the basilar membrane converts pressure waves to perceived sound. **Frequency theory** holds that higher frequencies produce greater neural firing. This theory cannot explain the full extent of our ability to hear: Neurons can fire only about 1,000 times a second at most, so how is it that we can hear sounds produced by much higher frequencies (Gelfand, 1981)? According to **place theory**, different frequencies activate different places along the basilar membrane, as shown in Figure 4.27. This theory appears to be correct, at least for most frequencies; it is possible, however, that the rate of vibration does help us hear relatively low tones.

As in vision, a number of brain areas working together allow us to sense sound. The first part of the cortex to receive auditory information, the *primary auditory cortex*, is spatially organized. Researchers have shown that as the pitch of sound changes, activity shifts to different locations along this structure. Again, just as in vision, in which the pattern of activation on the eye is in turn laid out on the brain (see p. 145), the spatial arrangement of vibration on the basilar membrane is mimicked in the brain. This sort of spatial arrangement is called **tonotopic organization** (Cansino et al., 2003; Clarey et al., 1992; Romani et al., 1982; Zhang et al., 2001).

## Deafness: Hear Today, Gone Tomorrow

More than 28 million Americans have some sort of difficulty in hearing (Soli, 1994). In some cases, the problem is only temporary. For example, some drugs, including aspirin, can dull a person's hearing (McFadden & Plattsmier, 1983); fortunately, the dulling effects of aspirin are only temporary. Other difficulties are more serious. In fact, over 30 genes have now been linked to deafness (Lynch et al., 1997), and thus we shouldn't be surprised to find that there are different forms of deafness, and that some forms of deafness are inherited. Lynch and colleagues studied the deaf descendants of a deaf man who was born in 1713 and found that they inherited a particular mutated gene. This gene plays a crucial role in stiffening the hairs in the inner ear, and, because of the mutation, the hair cells fail to function properly. Not all forms of deafness are genetic, however.

**Hair cells:** The cells with stiff hairs along the basilar membrane of the inner ear that, when moved, produce nerve impulses that are sent to the brain; these cells are the auditory equivalent of rods and cones.

**Frequency theory:** The theory that higher frequencies produce higher rates of neural firing.

**Place theory:** The theory that different frequencies activate different places along the basilar membrane.

**Tonotopic organization:** The use of distance along a strip of cortex to represent differences in pitch.

- *Nerve deafness.* **Nerve deafness** typically occurs when the hair cells are destroyed by loud sounds—and once a hair cell is destroyed, it is gone forever. A rock band heard at close range can produce sounds loud enough to cause this sort of damage. Nerve deafness may affect only certain frequencies; in those instances, a hearing aid can amplify the remaining frequencies, and hearing can be improved. Many researchers believe that a surgical procedure will soon be developed to make an end run around a damaged ear and allow auditory input to stimulate the auditory cortex directly (Ubell, 1995).

- *Tinnitus.* **Tinnitus** is a constant ringing or noise in the ears (McFadden, 1982), which can interfere with hearing other sounds.

- *Conduction deafness.* **Conduction deafness** can result from any accident or other cause that impairs the functioning of the external ear or middle ear. A broken eardrum, for example, can cause conduction deafness.

One study found that almost a third of a group of college students who went regularly to a dance club featuring loud music exhibited permanent hearing loss for high-frequency sounds (Hartman, 1982).

It is worth noting that if someone becomes deaf as a child, devices are now available that stimulate the auditory nerve directly—and after 3 years allow more than 75% of deaf children to understand substantial amounts of spoken language (Niparko & Blankenhorn, 2003). In addition, other senses can sometimes eventually compensate, at least in part, for loss of hearing. Catalan-Ahumeda and colleagues (1993), Neville and colleagues (1983), Wolf and Thatcher (1990), and others have found increased activation in the visual cortex of deaf people, and by adolescence, deaf individuals can focus visual attention in many tasks better than can hearing people (particularly when they have to attend to something not currently being focused on; Loke & Song, 1991; Neville, 1988, 1990; Neville & Lawson, 1987; Proksch & Bavelier, 2002). This is another example of the brain's plasticity (see Chapter 3; Bavelier & Neville, 2002). However, not all aspects of vision adjust; for example, the deaf are no better than hearing people in detecting differences in the speed of moving objects (Brozinsky & Bavelier, 2004). Many findings (such as those of Brozinksy & Bavelier, 2004, and Colmenero et al., 2004) suggest that many specific visual compensations of the deaf reflect practice in using sign language.

# Phase 1 of Auditory Perception: Organizing the Auditory World

In the last year of Kahlo's life, a Mexican gallery had the first-ever one-woman show of her work. The organizers scheduled a grand party on the show's opening night. Everyone wondered whether Kahlo would appear, but doubted it because she had been bedridden for some time. Friends, patrons, and well-wishers crowded into the gallery, waiting to see whether she would arrive. In the distance they heard a siren, which got louder and louder, and finally an ambulance pulled up in front of the gallery. The ambulance staff carried Kahlo, and the four poster bed on which she lay, out of the ambulance and into the gallery where everyone was waiting. On any other opening night, the patrons probably would not have paid much attention to the sound of a siren, but on this night they waited eagerly as they heard the sound growing louder. The processes engaged during the first phases of auditory perception allow us to organize sounds as coming from distinct objects and to locate the sources of sounds. Like vision, we can divide the steps of auditory perception into

**Nerve deafness:** A type of deafness that typically occurs when the hair cells are destroyed by loud sounds.

**Tinnitus:** A form of hearing impairment signaled by a constant ringing or noise in the ears.

**Conduction deafness:** A type of deafness caused by a physical impairment of the external or middle ear.

two main phases. In Phase 1, the outputs from sensory processing are organized; in Phase 2, these organized units are recognized and identified, or are used to guide movement (as occurs when you locate and turn your head to watch a particular member of a band play). In this section, we consider Phase 1, the first task of auditory perception after a stimulus has been sensed.

## Sorting Out Sounds: From One, Many

In daily life, a complex jumble of many sounds usually assaults our ears, not individual sounds one at a time. To make sense of what we hear, we first need to sort out individual sounds (Carlyon, 2004). As in vision, we need to distinguish figure from ground. Bregman (1990, 1993) calls this process *auditory scene analysis*, which relies on organization very much like what occurs in vision. Indeed, the Gestalt laws apply here, too. For example, people organize sounds partly based on similarity (for example, grouping sounds with the same pitch) and good continuation (grouping the same pitch continued over time). Recognizing and identifying speech relies crucially on auditory scene analysis because the actual stimulus is continuous, with no indication of breaks to delineate the beginnings and endings of words, and yet to communicate, people must identify individual words. This is the **speech-segmentation problem**. By analogy, *thisproblemisliketheoneyouarenowsolving* in vision.

In vision, we see continuous variations in the frequency of light not as continuous variations in hue, but rather as a set of distinct colors. Similarly, we hear speech sounds as distinct categories. This **categorical perception** groups a range of different sounds (such as those spoken by males, females, or children missing their front teeth) into the same categories, and it does so quickly and automatically (Jacobsen et al., 2004). Such processing produces categories with remarkably sharp boundaries. For example, if a computer is programmed to vary the time between the start of a syllable (the consonant being pronounced, such as b) and the "voiced" part of the syllable (the sound of the vowel being pronounced, such as a), we will hear "ba" if the voiced part starts from 0 to around 25 thousandths of a second after the consonant starts; but if the voiced part starts after a longer interval, we will hear "pa." There is very little intermediate ground; we hear one or the other (Eimas & Corbit, 1973). Infants (Dehaene-Lambertz & Pena, 2001), as well as monkeys, chinchillas, and various other animals (Kuhl, 1989; Moody et al., 1990), show categorical perception, which suggests that the perceptual system itself does this work—not the language systems of our various cultures. Indeed, the common ancestor of monkeys, chinchillas, and humans may have evolved many of the "building blocks" that were later incorporated into speech.

## Locating Sounds: Why Two Ears Are Better Than One

In vision, our brains use slight differences in the images striking the two eyes to assess the distance of an object. Similarly, hearing makes use of differences in the stimuli reaching the two ears to assess the distance of a sound source (Yost & Dye, 1991). Three kinds of differences are particularly important.

- *Difference in phase.* Sound waves reach the two ears at slightly different phases, that is, at slightly different points in the wave cycle. The difference in phase at the two ears is particularly useful for detecting the source of relatively low-frequency sounds, which arise from longer waves (Gulick et al., 1989).

- *Difference in loudness.* A difference in loudness at the two ears is also used as a cue. In addition to all of their other functions, our heads are useful because they block

**Speech-segmentation problem:** The problem of organizing a continuous stream of speech into separate parts that correspond to individual words.

**Categorical perception:** Identifying sounds as belonging to distinct categories that correspond to the basic units of speech.

sound, and thus the amplitude of sound waves is smaller when it reaches the ear on the side of the head away from the sound source. This cue is particularly effective for high-frequency sounds.

- *Onset difference.* A sound wave will reach the two ears at slightly different times; this onset difference is tiny, but the brain uses it effectively.

As in vision, we use many different cues to assess where an object is. Some cues depend on only one ear, not two. Consider three such cues. First, the simple loudness of a sound: Especially for familiar objects, we can use volume as an indicator of distance. If an ambulance is approaching, we can get a good sense of how far away it is from its sound. Second, the way our external ears are crinkled bends sound waves in different ways; these variations help us detect the location of the sound source (Moore, 1982). Third, by moving our heads and bodies, we can compare the relative volume of a sound from different vantage points, which helps us locate its source.

Bats and barn owls are adept at using sound to localize objects (Konishi, 1993; Suga, 1990). The structure of the barn owl's face has developed in a way to direct sound to its ears; this maximizes location cues. Bats produce sounds, and then listen for the echoes coming back. The echoes are precise enough for the bat to discern the shapes of even small objects (Simmons & Chen, 1989).

# Phase 2 of Auditory Perception: Recognition and Identification

Phase 2 of auditory perception allows us to use sound in many ways. In addition to interpreting speech and music, we also recognize that the snap of a green bean indicates freshness, that a knock on a door means someone wants to come in, that a cat's mewing may mean she wants to be fed. As in vision, sounds become meaningful when they are matched to information already stored in memory, which is the job of Phase 2 of auditory perceptual processing.

## More Than Meets the Ear

Kahlo's biography recounts an incident when Kahlo and Rivera were to meet outside a movie theatre, but crowds prevented them from seeing each other. In trying to find each other, "Diego whistled the first bar of the *Internationale*. From somewhere in the crowd came the second; it was unmistakably Frida. After this, the task no doubt seemed easier, and the whistling continued until the couple found each other" (Herrera, 1983, p. 308). Why would hearing the whistle over the noise of the crowd seem easier once they knew to listen for their whistled tune? Just as in vision, you can adjust your criterion for "detecting a signal," and this adjustment will be based on what you expect to hear. But also, as in vision, what you expect to hear actually influences what you do hear. A demonstration of such an effect was reported by Warren and Warren (1970), who asked people to listen to a tape-recorded sentence after part of a word had been replaced with the sound of a cough. Although part of the word was actually missing, all the participants claimed that they actually heard the entire word and denied that the cough covered part of it. In fact, the listeners were not exactly sure at what point the cough occurred. This effect, more obvious for words in sentences than for words standing alone, is called the *phonemic restoration effect* (a phoneme is the smallest segment of spoken speech, such as "ba" or "da"). This filling-in effect occurs not only with speech sounds but also with musical instruments. In fact, if you see someone bowing the strings of a cello at the same time as you hear the strings being plucked, the sight is enough to distort the sound you hear (Saldana & Rosenblum, 1993). Neuroimaging studies have shown that vision can modify how sound is processed in the brain (Thesen et al., 2004).

## FIGURE 4.28 Dichotic Listening

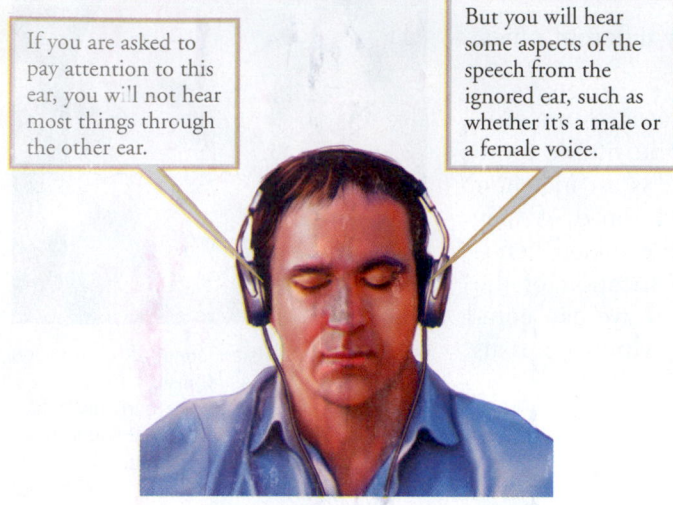

If you are asked to pay attention to this ear, you will not hear most things through the other ear.

But you will hear some aspects of the speech from the ignored ear, such as whether it's a male or a female voice.

Dichotic listening occurs when different messages are provided to the two ears, and the person is asked to listen only to one. Even so, some information from the ignored ear is processed.

## Hearing Without Awareness

As happens with vision, we pick up some auditory information without being aware of it. Perhaps the most common experience of perception without awareness is the **cocktail party phenomenon**. At an event like a large party, you may not be aware of other people's conversation until someone mentions your name—which you hear immediately (Cherry, 1953; Conway et al., 2001). But in order to become aware of the sound of your name, you must have been tracking the conversation all along (using bottom-up processing); you simply were not aware of the conversation until that important word was spoken. In experiments she performed as an undergraduate, Treisman (1964a, 1964b) showed that when people listen to stimuli presented separately to the two ears (through headphones) and are instructed to listen to only one ear, a procedure known as **dichotic listening** (Hugdahl, 2001), they still register some information—such as whether the voice is male or female—from the ignored ear (see Figure 4.28). To ensure that participants listen to only one voice, they often are asked to repeat it aloud—a practice known as *shadowing*.

This discovery spawned an industry that proclaimed that people can learn in their sleep, simply by playing tapes (purchased at low, low discount prices). Unfortunately, it turns out that unless a person is paying attention, not much gets through. And even when information does get through, it is retained very briefly; when tested hours later, people remember virtually none of the information presented outside their awareness (Greenwald et al., 1991).

## Music: Hearing for Pleasure

Phase 2 auditory perception not only allows us to recognize and identify objects, and to know where they are located, but also evokes an emotional reaction. This fact is exploited by music.

**CULTURAL CREATIONS** Music is a part of virtually all cultures; in some, its importance is so great that governments have occasionally regulated what constitutes music itself. In the former Soviet Union, for example, some chords were labeled decadent and were actually outlawed. Closer to home, in North Carolina, singing out of tune was at one time a prosecutable offense (Seuling, 1975). Aside from these cultural curiosities, however, the existence of music depends on the fact that the brain registers sounds relative to one another, not in isolation (Krumhansl, 2000). For example, when you double a frequency, you hear the same note but an *octave* higher (an octave in Western music is eight consecutive notes). The continuous variation in frequency between octaves is divided into distinct intervals, which form a *scale*. The nature of scales varies in different cultures. The Western scale relies on 12 half-steps for each octave, compared with more than 50 in Indian music. Nevertheless, all humans hear notes an octave apart as more similar than consecutive notes. This is another example of the way in which the physical nature of a stimulus differs from its psychological experience. Indeed, we can hear two different sequences of notes (which have different physical frequencies) as the same, provided that the notes are separated by the same intervals. However, not all people can recognize or remember musical steps equally well. Interestingly, identical twins have very similar abilities to

**Cocktail party phenomenon:** The effect of not being aware of other people's conversations until your name is mentioned, and then suddenly hearing it.

**Dichotic listening:** A procedure in which participants hear stimuli presented separately to the two ears (through headphones) and are instructed to listen only to sounds presented to one ear.

In all cultures, people hear notes separated by an octave as more similar than consecutive notes. Some aspects of music arise from the nature of the ear and brain, whereas others—such as the way the scale is divided—vary from culture to culture.

recognize incorrect notes in familiar popular tunes, which (when compared with the less similar abilities of fraternal twins) led researchers to conclude that genetic differences are responsible for at least 70% of the variation in this ability (Drayna et al., 2001).

Within a given culture, the ease of identifying the notes in a scale depends partly on whether a person has **absolute pitch**, the striking ability to identify a particular note by itself, not simply in relation to other notes (Krumhansl, 1991, 2000). Studies have shown that Americans with absolute pitch identify the intervals in a standard Western scale better if an instrument is "in tune" (that is, the notes are set to the correct absolute frequencies) than if it is a bit out of tune; people without absolute pitch do not show such a difference (Miyazaki, 1993). Many people with absolute pitch developed the ability during childhood (Krumhansl, 1991, 2000; Takeuchi & Hulse, 1993). People with absolute pitch have an unusually large *planum temporale*, a part of the auditory cortex that lies on the top part of the temporal lobe, near the back (see Chapter 3; Schlaug et al., 1995)—but research has yet to establish whether this is a cause or an effect of having this ability.

**MUSIC IMAGERY AND THE MUSICAL MIND**  Beethoven was stone deaf when he wrote much of his greatest music. How is this possible? Auditory mental imagery allowed him to hear music with his "mind's ear" as he was composing it. Right now, decide whether the first three notes of "Three Blind Mice" go up or down; to do this, you probably "heard" the tune in your head—you evoked auditory imagery. Auditory imagery arises when brain areas that are used in hearing are activated from stored memories (Halpern, 1988; Zatorre & Halpern, 1993). Imagery can occur even when the sense organs are damaged (for example, if the hair cells die). What Beethoven heard in his mind's ear would probably have been very similar to what he would have heard carried by sound waves had he not been deaf. Moreover, imagining making the movements involved in playing a piece of piano music evokes much the same pattern of brain activation that is found when people actually play the piece (Meister et al., 2004).

Absolute pitch: The ability to identify a particular note by itself, not simply in relation to other notes.

# Test Yourself

1. Sound and light are similar in their wave properties. Which qualities of light are similar to the sound qualities of pitch and loudness?
   a. frequency and amplitude
   b. color and hue
   c. brightness and color
   d. wavelength and waveform
2. We see different wavelengths of light as different colors, and similarly, we hear speech sounds in distinct categories. This phenomenon in speech perception is called
   a. conduction.
   b. categorical perception.
   c. wave analysis.
   d. dichotic listening.
3. In experiments like those of Treisman (1964), participants hear different things in each ear and are asked to attend to one or the other ear. This task is called
   a. feature detection.
   b. dichotic listening.
   c. cocktail party effect.
   d. "yes, dear" effect.
4. Top-down processing in hearing, like that in vision, helps us make sense out of what we hear by
   a. generating expectations about what we are hearing.
   b. organizing what we hear into distinct categories.
   c. filling in masked or missing sounds.
   d. doing all of the above.

## Answers

1.a 2.b 3.b 4.d

# Think It Through!

Will wearing a motorcycle helmet affect your ability to recognize sounds and your ability to localize them to the same extent? Why or why not? If one side of the helmet were made of thicker plastic than the other, which sound cues would be most affected?

Do you think that the way a musician looks or behaves when he or she is performing could influence the way the music sounds? How could this occur?

# SENSING AND PERCEIVING IN OTHER WAYS

Left to his own devices, Rivera did not bathe frequently—and Kahlo was not fond of his body odor. She bought him bath toys in hopes that they would motivate him to bathe more often (apparently she was successful). Kahlo's sense of smell wasn't the only other sense of which she was keenly aware; she was very aware of tastes. During several lengthy visits to the United States, Kahlo consistently complained about the blandness of American food (although she did like applesauce and American cheese). Kahlo was also aware of the senses in her body; unfortunately, she experienced much pain, and gangrene in her right foot led to its eventual amputation. What have researchers discovered about these and other senses?

## Smell: A Nose for News?

**Chemical senses:** Taste and smell, which rely on sensing the presence of specific chemicals.

Smell and taste are often grouped together as the **chemical senses** because both, unlike the other senses, rely on registering the presence of specific chemicals. People differ widely in their sense of smell, or *olfaction*. Some people are 20 times more sensitive to odors than are other people (Rabin & Cain, 1986); Kahlo may simply have had a better sense of smell than Rivera, and hence was more sensitive to the odor when he hadn't bathed. Most people are remarkably poor at identifying odors, even though they often think they are good at it (de Wijk et al., 1995). Cain (1979) found that people could correctly identify only about half of 80 common scents; although we may know that an odor is familiar—that is, we recognize it—we may be unable to identify it. In general, women are better than men at detecting many types of odors (Cain, 1982). Women are particularly sensitive to smell when they are ovulating—unless they take birth control pills, in which case their abilities do not fluctuate over the course of the month (Caruso et al., 2001; Grillo et al., 2001). In addition, younger adults are better at detecting odors than either children (up to 14 years old) or middle-aged adults (between 40 and 50 years old) (Cain & Gent, 1991; de Wijk & Cain, 1994; Murphy, 1986). For many of the years of her marriage, Kahlo was probably at the peak of her olfactory sensitivity.

## Distinguishing Odors: Lock and Key

The best theory of odor detection can be described using the lock-and-key metaphor. Molecules have different shapes, and the olfactory receptors are built so that only molecules with particular shapes will fit in particular places on the receptors (see Figure 4.29). The molecules are like keys, and the receptors like locks. When the right-shaped molecule arrives at a particular receptor, it sends a signal to the brain, and we sense the odor. Just as there is not a single type of cone for each color we can see, there is not a single receptor for each odor we can smell (see Figure 4.30, p. 176); rather, the overall pattern of receptor activity signals a particular odor (Freeman, 1991; Friedrich, 2004; Hallem et al., 2004). Two Americans, Linda Buck and Richard Axel, won the Nobel Prize in 2004 for their work in identifying the genes that produce the individual odor receptors. They found that about 1,000 different genes (which is about 3% of the total that we have) are devoted to this task.

Two major neural pathways send signals about odor into the brain. One, passing through the thalamus, is particularly involved in memory; the other, connected to the limbic system, is particularly involved in emotions. Moreover, neuroimaging studies have shown that the right cerebral hemisphere plays a special role in memory for odors, and the left cerebral hemisphere plays a special role in emotional responses (Royet & Plailly, 2004). The two hemispheres are connected by massive numbers of fibers, and these connections explain why odors often tap emotionally charged memories—remember the way you felt when you unexpectedly smelled an old girlfriend's perfume or a boyfriend's aftershave?

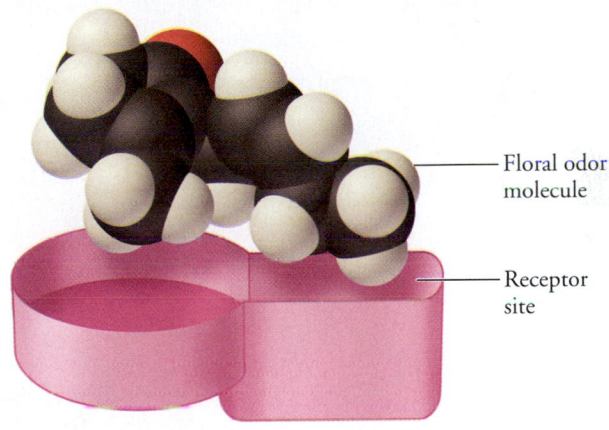

**FIGURE 4.29** **Lock-and-Key Mechanism of Smell**

Floral odor molecule

Receptor site

The shape of a molecule is like a key, and the shape of the corresponding receptor is like a lock. But when this key fits in this lock, the result is not a door opening but instead a neural signal sent to the brain—which gives rise to the experience of smell.

## Olfaction Gone Awry: Is It Safe to Cook Without Smell?

Have you ever wished you could not smell? Maybe that would be a relief once in a while, but losing your sense of smell completely is not a good idea. Smell serves to signal the presence of noxious substances; our brains are wired so that odors can quickly activate the fight-or-flight response. It would not be wise to ask a friend who has no sense of smell to cook dinner on a regular basis: Smell is often the only signal that meat

## FIGURE 4.30   The Olfactory System

Depending on which olfactory receptor cells are stimulated, different messages are sent to the olfactory bulb, the first part of the brain to process such signals.

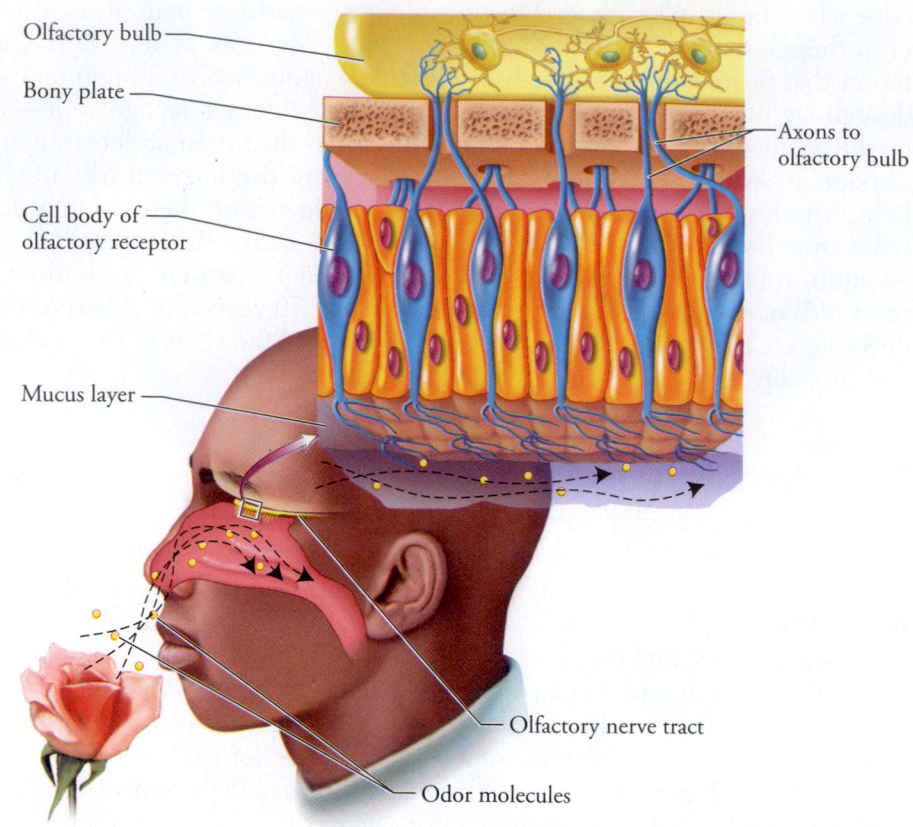

Olfactory bulb

Bony plate

Cell body of olfactory receptor

Mucus layer

Axons to olfactory bulb

Olfactory nerve tract

Odor molecules

or other food is spoiled. Relatively few people have no olfactory sense, a deficit that can arise from brain damage or a virus (Doty et al., 1991).

## Pheromones: Another Kind of Scents?

Airborne chemicals released by female animals in heat arouse the male of the species. These are an example of **pheromones**, chemical substances that serve as a means of communication. Like hormones, they modulate the functions of various organs, including the brain. Unlike hormones, pheromones are released *outside* the body, in urine and sweat. The most famous example of effects of pheromones in humans was discovered by Martha McClintock (1971). She originally found that female roommates tend to synchronize their menstrual cycles and, along with Kathleen Stern (Stern & McClintock, 1998), has since found that this effect depends on certain pheromones reaching the nose (Russell et al., 1980, report consistent results). The receptors that are triggered by pheromones are accessed via the nose, and odors sometimes accompany these chemicals.

Much to the delight of perfume manufacturers over the world, studies have recently shown that female pheromones can attract men. In one study (McCoy & Pitino, 2002), university women began by recording seven social/sexual behaviors for two weeks (the

Pheromones: Chemicals that function like hormones but are released outside the body (in urine and sweat).

baseline period), and then mixed a substance into their perfume and continued to record those behaviors; the substance was either a clear, odorless pheromone or an identically appearing but medically inactive substance (a placebo, for the control group). The study used a double-blind design; neither the investigator nor the participant knew whether a given participant received the pheromone or placebo. Participants who wore perfume containing the pheromone reported having more petting (which included affectionate behavior in general), sexual intercourse, sleeping next to a partner, and formal dates—but did not report that more men had approached them or that they had more informal dates or an increase in masturbation. As shown in Figure 4.31, many more of the group receiving the pheromone reported increases in three or more of the four behaviors that were affected. All four of the affected types of behaviors require intimate interaction with someone else, whereas none of the other three do.

However, before male readers start to bemoan the uneven advantage female pheromones might confer, they will be interested to learn that another substance (derived from the human sex steroid compound 4,16-androstadien-3-one, known as AND, for short) not only increases positive mood and decreases negative mood in women, but also appears to arouse them—while at the same time apparently relaxing men (Bensafi et al, 2004). Although this substance had such effects only at high concentrations, it might have a future role in male colognes or after-shave lotions. If this finding and those about female pheromones hold up with repeated testing, do you think that people who use such substances should warn their dates?

## FIGURE 4.31 Increased Sexual Behavior With Pheromone Perfume

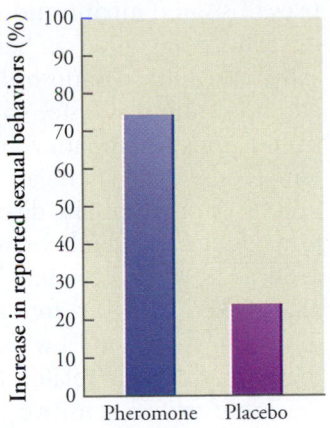

The percentages of people who reported increases in at least three of the four types of sexual behavior assessed by McCoy and Pitino (2002); members of one group wore a perfume that contained a pheromone, and members of the other wore a perfume that contained a placebo.

*Taste buds:* Microscopic structures on the bumps on the tongue surface, at the back of the throat, and inside the cheeks; the four types of taste buds are sensitive to sweet, sour, salty, and bitter tastes.

# Taste: The Mouth Has It

When scientists discuss taste, they are talking about sensing via receptors located solely in the mouth. **Taste buds** (see Figure 4.32) are microscopic structures mounted on the sides of the little bumps you can see on your tongue in a mirror. You have taste buds in other places in your mouth as well, such as the back of the throat and inside the cheeks (Smith & Frank, 1993). Your taste buds die and are replaced, on average, every 10 days (McLaughlin & Margolskee, 1994). Humans have more taste buds than some species, such as chickens, but fewer than others; some fish have taste buds spread all over their skin (Pfaffmann, 1978). Children have more sensitive taste buds than adults, and thus flavors are presumably stronger for them than for adults—which may account for children's notoriously strong likes and dislikes of foods. Nevertheless, even adults can be remarkably sensitive to slight differences in taste. When wine tasters speak of wine as having a flavor of mushrooms or cloves, they may not be speaking metaphorically. Depending on the composition of the soil in which the vines grow, grapes acquire different tastes.

## FIGURE 4.32 Taste Buds on the Tongue

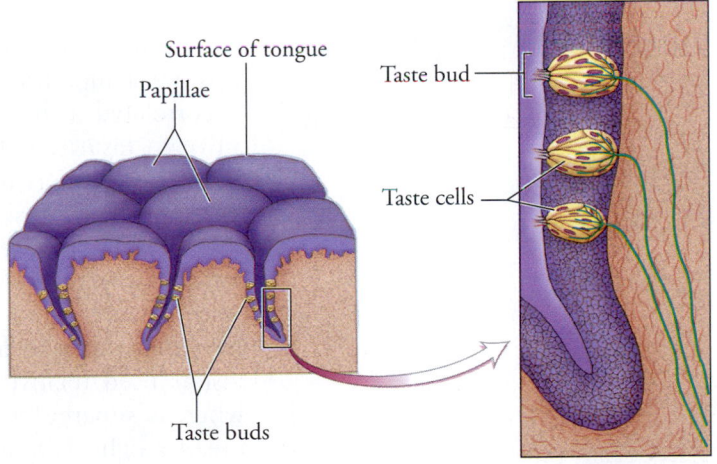

Surface of tongue
Papillae
Taste bud
Taste cells
Taste buds

The taste buds on the tongue line the sides of the *papillae*, the visible bumps.

## Sweet, Sour, Salty, Bitter

You've seen how a wide range of colors arises from three types of cones and how patterns of odors arise from the combinations of receptors being activated. The brain uses this same mixing-and-matching trick for taste. Traditionally, the tastes of all foods have been regarded as being made up of combinations of four tastes: sweet, sour, salty, and bitter (Bartoshuk & Beauchamp, 1994; Scott & Plata-Salaman, 1991). In addition, another taste, called *umami*, has been identified. This taste is stimulated by the most abundant amino acid, glutamate, which is present in many high-protein foods (such as meat and seafood). Pure glutamate produces this taste, just as pure salt produces its distinctive tang. The umami taste is registered by two additional detectors, both of which respond to monosodium glutamate (MSG)—often used as a "taste enhancer" in Chinese restaurants (Chaudhari et al., 2000; Ruiz et al., 2003). Moreover, free nerve endings in the mouth appear to be irritated by spicy foods (Lawless, 1984), which provides another source of information about taste, one that is not directly related to the taste buds. Different parts of the mouth and tongue are more or less sensitive to different tastes; you can detect bitter flavors best in the back of your mouth (Shallenberger, 1993). However, these different sensitivities are a matter of degree: All kinds of taste buds are found in most locations on the tongue. Curiously, there is a "taste hole" in the middle of the tongue, an area where there are no taste buds at all.

Sensitivities not only vary over the tongue, but among people. In fact, the population can be divided into three categories: nontasters (about 25%), medium tasters (about 50%), and supertasters (about 25%; Bartoshuk et al., 1998). Are you a supertaster? If you take a bite of broccoli or dark chocolate, does it seem so bitter that your mouth puckers up and you wish you could wash the stuff down with a sip of water? Does ice cream taste cloyingly sweet? If you responded yes, you may well be a supertaster. To find out for sure, you can do the following little study on yourself: First, find a magnifying glass, buy some blue food coloring, and punch a 7-millimeter-wide hole in a piece of paper. Next, dab some of the food coloring on the tip of your tongue. Although your tongue will become a fetching shade of blue, the tiny bumps that hold the taste buds will continue to be pink. Following this, put the paper over your tongue so that you can just see the tip through the hole. Now, use the magnifying glass to count the number of pink bumps. If you are a nontaster, you'll find 15 or fewer bumps; if you are medium taster, between 15 and 35; and if you are a supertaster, you'll have over 35 bumps. The number of bumps you have is correlated with the number of your taste buds, which make you more or less sensitive to taste sensations; your genetics determine the number of bumps and taste buds. Researchers often use a simpler way to sort people into the three categories, based on their sensitivity to the chemical *6-n-propylthiouracil*, called PROP for short; the threshold for detecting the taste of PROP neatly distinguishes among the three kinds of tasters (Bartoshuk et al., 1998; Drewnowski et al., 2001; Prescott et al., 2004). And the three groups of tasters differ not only in their sensitivity to taste, but also in how they describe foods; for example, when asked to evaluate dairy products, nontasters used relative few, simple terms to describe tastes (such as sweet and sour), whereas supertasters used a more complex set of terms (such as grainy, gritty, and creamy light; Kirkmeyer & Tepper, 2003).

For the most part, you cannot taste something unless it can be at least partially dissolved by your saliva (Seuling, 1986); that is why you can't taste a marble. However, an exception to this principle can occur if the stimulus changes the temperature of your tongue. For example, warming the front edge of your tongue can lead you to taste sweetness, but cooling this region can lead you to taste saltiness or sweetness. Moreover, changing temperature produces different tastes on different parts of the tongue (Cruz & Green, 2000). Finally, the tongue is sensitive to texture, which influences the way we experience different foods. In fact, the tongue is so sensitive that it is now being used to help blind people see! Researchers have devised machines that translate visual forms into patterns of stimulation on the tongue, and blind people can interpret these patterns to "see" rough outlines of objects (Sampaio et al., 2001).

## Taste and Smell

Most people think that the flavor of food arises from its taste (Rozin, 1982), but in fact much of what we think of as taste is actually smell, or a combination of smell and taste. For example, aspartame (NutraSweet) tastes sweeter if you are simultaneously smelling vanilla (Sakai et al., 2001). In rats, the two types of information converge on a region of the frontal lobes that is critical for the perception of flavor (Schul et al., 1996). Next time you have a stuffy nose, notice the flavor of your food, or lack thereof—particularly when you close your eyes and eliminate top-down processing to fill in your perception of the flavor. Researchers have found that people have a much harder time detecting most flavors when smell is blocked (Hyman et al., 1979). Kahlo might like the idea of not being able to smell her husband's body odor, but not smelling at all would ruin the taste of everything from chocolate to chili peppers.

# Somasthetic Senses: Not Just Skin Deep

The traditional five senses—sight, hearing, smell, taste, and touch—were listed and described by Aristotle more than 2,000 years ago. It would be a sad commentary on the value of science if we couldn't do better after all this time. Today, we are able to argue that there are at least nine senses, perhaps ten: sight, hearing, smell, taste, and then a collection of five (or six) senses that together are called **somasthetic senses**. These senses all have to do with perceiving the body and its position in space: kinesthetic sense (awareness of where the limbs are and how they move), vestibular sense (sense of balance), touch, temperature sensitivity, and pain. There may be a sixth somasthetic sense, magnetic sense. And, finally, some researchers have argued that there is possibly an eleventh sense: extrasensory perception, or ESP (also sometimes called psi).

## Kinesthetic Sense: A Moving Sense

Read this, and then close your eyes and hold out your left arm in an odd position. Now, keeping your left arm in place, touch your left hand with your right hand. You shouldn't have any trouble doing this because you know where your hands are without having to see them. You know because of your **kinesthetic sense**, which registers the movement and position of the limbs. Two types of specialized cells sense this information: One type is in the tendons (the material that connects muscles to bones) and is triggered by tension; the other is in the muscles themselves and is triggered by whether the muscle is stretched out or contracted (Pinel, 1993).

Somasthetic senses: Senses that have to do with perceiving the body and its position in space—specifically, kinesthetic sense, vestibular sense, touch, temperature sensitivity, pain sense, and possibly magnetic sense.

Kinesthetic sense: The sense that registers the movement and position of the limbs.

The vestibular and kinesthetic senses often work together. These people would be out of a job (or worse) if either sense failed. The vestibular sense lets them know how their bodies are oriented relative to gravity, and the kinesthetic sense lets them know where their limbs are relative to their bodies.

## Vestibular Sense: Being Oriented

The inner ear is used not only for hearing, but also for balance. The **vestibular sense**, which provides information about how your body is oriented relative to gravity, relies on an organ in the inner ear that contains three *semicircular canals* (illustrated in Figure 4.26, on p. 167). If these structures are disrupted, say by infection or injury (or by spending too much time in weightlessness in outer space, as happens to astronauts), people have a difficult time keeping their balance.

## Touch: Feeling Well

Here's another trick question: What's your body's largest organ? The lungs? The intestines? The answer is the skin. As well as protecting our bodies from the environment (such as dirt, germs, flying objects, changes in temperature), making crucial vitamins, and triggering the release of various hormones, the skin is also a massive sensory organ. Millions of receptors in the skin produce impulses when stimulated in specific ways. Moreover, the same mechanism used by the other senses is at work here: It is the particular combination of receptors being stimulated that produces a specific sensation. The mix-and-match principle is at work here, too: We can feel many more types of sensations than we have types of receptors. Receptors in the skin in different parts of the body send impulses to different parts of the somatosensory cortex (see Chapter 3); in general, the more cortex devoted to a particular area of the skin, the more sensitive that area is (Weinstein, 1968).

Women tend to be more sensitive to touch than are men (Weinstein, 1968). Moreover, women are especially sensitive (relative to men) on some parts of their bodies, such as their backs and stomachs.

## Temperature

The skin has separate systems for registering hot and cold; indeed, there are distinct spots on your skin that register *only* hot or *only* cold. These spots are about 1 millimeter across (Hensel, 1982). If a cold spot is stimulated, you will feel a sensation of cold even if the stimulus is something hot. This phenomenon is called **paradoxical cold**. People are not very good at telling exactly where a hot or cold stimulus is located, particularly if it is near the skin but not touching it (Cain, 1973).

## Pain

Despite the discomfort, even the agony, pain brings, the inability to feel pain is even worse in the long run than the inability to smell odors. Sternbach (1978) described children who could not feel pain normally and who picked off the skin around their nostrils and bit off their fingers because they didn't notice what they were doing. Pain serves to warn us of impending danger, and it is crucial to survival.

The sensation of pain arises primarily when two different kinds of nerves are stimulated. These nerves have fibers that differ in size and in the speed with which they transmit impulses. Thus, we can feel **double pain**: The first phase, of sharp pain, occurs at the time of the injury; it is followed by a dull pain. The two kinds of pain arise from different fibers sending their messages at different speeds (Rollman, 1991).

**Vestibular sense:** The sense that provides information about the body's orientation relative to gravity.

**Paradoxical cold:** The sensation of cold that occurs when certain nerves in the skin are stimulated by something hot.

**Double pain:** The sensation that occurs when an injury first causes a sharp pain, and later a dull pain; the two kinds of pain arise from different fibers sending their messages at different speeds.

One of the ways we deal with pain is by producing substances in our brains, called **endorphins**, that have painkilling effects. Some drugs, such as morphine, bind to the same receptors that accept endorphins, which explains how those drugs can act as painkillers (Cailliet, 1993). However, pain involves more than simple bottom-up processing. In fact, a placebo—which relies on your belief that a medically inert substance in fact has medicinal value—activates some of the same brain structures as do drugs such as morphine (Petrovic et al., 2002). In addition, although the parts of the brain that are activated when we feel pain are distinct from the parts that are activated when we *anticipate* feeling pain, the two sets of areas are very close (Ploghaus et al., 1999), which suggests that anticipating pain could interact with the real thing. And, in fact, top-down processing can directly inhibit the interneurons that regulate the input of pain signals to the brain (Gagliese & Katz, 2000; Melzack & Wall, 1982; Wall, 2000). This mechanism, called **gate control**, may explain how hypnosis can influence pain (Kihlstrom, 1985); indeed, hypnosis can selectively alter our experience of the unpleasantness of pain without affecting how intense it feels. Hypnosis thus may alter processing in only some of the brain areas that register pain (Rainville et al., 1997). Inhibitory impulses from the brain to neurons that send signals from the body may also occur when pain is reduced by a *counter-irritant*—a painful stimulus elsewhere in the body (Willer et al., 1990).

People differ widely in the amount of pain they can withstand; Rollman and Harris (1987) found that some people could put up with as much as eight times as much pain as others. And women at certain phases of the menstrual cycle have a lower threshold for pain (Hapidou & De Catanzaro, 1988). MacGregor and colleagues (1997) found that the threshold for pressure-based pain was highly correlated among twins, but this correlation was equally high for both identical and fraternal twins. Because identical twins share all their genes, but fraternal twins share only half their genes, the finding of the same correlation suggests that there is no substantial genetic component to pain thresholds. Instead, this correlation is more likely a result of common family environment.

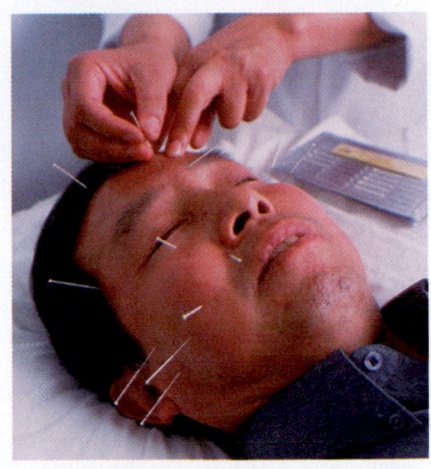

Acupuncture, the placing of small needles to treat pain, may work because the needles are a counter-irritant; this idea makes sense according to the gate control theory of pain (Carlsson & Sjoelund, 2001; Chapman & Nakamura, 1999).

# Other Senses

Two additional senses are more controversial. One of these—magnetic sense—may not exist in humans, and one—extrasensory perception—may not exist at all.

## Magnetic Sense: Only for the Birds?

Many birds migrate long distances each year, guided in part by the magnetic field of the earth. Tiny bits of iron found in crucial neurons of these birds apparently play a role in this sense (Gould, 1998; Kirschvink et al., 2001). Researchers have not only documented that at least some mammals (in particular, mole rats) also have this ability, but they have zeroed in on the crucial part of the brain that underlies it (a subcortical structure called the *superior colliculus*; Nemec et al., 2001). There is evidence that humans have a weak form of this sense (Baker, 1980), but the phenomenon has not yet been studied in enough detail to conclude with certainty that we all possess it. Magnetic fields have been shown to disrupt spatial learning in mice, at least for brief periods of time (Levine & Bluni, 1994). This is a sobering finding because the magnetic fields used in these studies were weaker than those commonly used in magnetic resonance imaging (MRI) machines.

**Endorphins:** Painkilling chemicals produced naturally in the brain.

**Gate control (of pain):** The top-down inhibition of interneurons that regulate the input of pain signals to the brain.

## Extrasensory Perception (ESP)

The ability to perceive and know things without using the ordinary senses is often referred to as **extrasensory perception (ESP)**, but also sometimes called *anomalous cognition* or *psi*. Many forms of ESP have been asserted, including *telepathy*, the ability to send and transmit thoughts directly, mind to mind; *clairvoyance*, the ability to know about events directly, without using the ordinary senses or reading someone else's mind; and *precognition*, the ability to foretell future events. In addition, *psychokinesis* (PK), the ability to move objects directly, not by manipulating them physically, has also been reported (this ability does not derive from ESP proper, since it does not involve perception or knowing). Louisa and Joseph Rhine are often credited with beginning the scientific study of ESP and PK (J. B. Rhine, 1934; L. E. Rhine, 1967), and many experiments have been conducted in an effort to demonstrate the existence of the different forms of ESP (for example, Bem & Honorton, 1994; Haraldsson & Houtkooper, 1992). Many ESP experiments use the *Ganzfeld procedure*: Participants wear either half a ping-pong ball over each eye or tight-fitting translucent glasses that allow only a blur to be seen; at the same time, they hear a dull hiss through headphones (Bem & Honorton, 1994; Haraldsson & Gissurarson, 1987). This procedure shuts off competing stimuli and thus, supposedly, increases the participant's sensitivity to ESP signals. Another person, sealed in a different room, tries to project an image of a particular card or scene to the participant, who later is asked to pick out the image from a set of alternatives.

Some researchers have argued that the results from some of these experiments suggest that the "recipient" can pick out the image "transmitted by the sender" more accurately than expected by chance (Bem & Honorton, 1994; Rosenthal, 1986). Nevertheless, most psychologists are skeptical about ESP and PK, for at least the four following reasons (Alcock, 1987, provides additional ones):

- *Failure to replicate.* The effects of ESP and PK studies are difficult to repeat. For example, it wasn't long after Bem and Honorton (1994) claimed finally to have discovered how to produce reliable telepathy before Milton and Wiseman (1999a, 1999b) reported failures to replicate. To be fair, some ESP researchers have argued that such failures to replicate occur because the phenomena depend on personality, details of the setting, and other variables (Brugger et al., 1990; Honorton, 1997; Watt & Morris, 1995). But as more such qualifications are added, the harder it becomes to disprove the claims, and the field is thus nudged further away from science.

- *Lack of brain mechanism.* It is not known how the brain could possibly produce or pick up ESP signals or produce PK signals.

- *Lack of signals.* No "ESP signals" have been measured, and it is not known what form these signals might take. For example, physical energy (such as magnetic or electrical waves) typically declines in strength with increasing distance from the source, but there is no hint that the same is true for ESP or PK signals.

- *Alternative explanations.* Finally, there is the specter of alternative explanations, which rely on known facts about mental processing and behavior. Although many recent ESP studies are well-designed, many still leave open possible avenues for the influence of other factors (of the sort discussed in Chapter 2).

In spite of many years of hard work by many dedicated scientists, this field remains highly controversial (Bem & Honorton, 1994; Child, 1985; Thalbourne, 1989).

Extrasensory perception (ESP): The ability to perceive and know things without using the ordinary senses.

# Test Yourself

1. Smell and taste rely on sensing the presence of certain molecules and therefore are called _____ senses.
   a. chemical
   b. physical
   c. virtual
   d. detection
2. The lock-and-key theory of olfaction states that
   a. only certain smells can unlock memory.
   b. odors are locks and olfactory receptors are keys.
   c. humans have only two kinds of receptors for olfaction.
   d. molecules with different shapes fit only into certain olfactory receptors.
3. If a person lost her vestibular sense, you would expect that she would
   a. not know where her hands were.
   b. have a difficult time keeping her balance.
   c. be hot and cold at the same time.
   d. not be able to taste or smell.
4. Some evidence that top-down processing affects the experience of pain comes from the use of hypnosis for pain control. What mechanism underlies this effect?
   a. endorphin production
   b. gate control mechanism
   c. pain receptor inhibition
   d. pain location transduction

## Answers

1.a 2.d 3.b 4.b

# Think It Through!

Say your uncle is a food fanatic, loving every morsel and seeking out only the best. Should you recommend that he blow his nose before each meal and not waste his money going to fancy restaurants when he has a bad cold? Why or why not?

Should researchers spend time studying ESP instead of studying the nature of learning, reasoning, or the traditional five senses? What are the potential pros and cons of studying ESP rather than abilities that clearly are used by everyone every day?

# REVIEW AND REMEMBER!

## Summary

### I. Vision: Window on the World

**A.** Sensation is the immediate registration of basic properties of an object or event, such as its color, whereas perception is the organization and interpretation of the sensory input as signaling a particular object or event.

**B.** You detect sensory stimuli when they exceed some threshold, but the level of that threshold depends in part on how hard you try to detect the stimuli. In addition, you can adjust your criteria so that you are more or less willing to guess.

**C.** Vision begins with light, which consists of physical energy of certain wavelengths.

## Your Notes

*I.*

*A. Sensation=registration*
   *Perception=organization + interpretation*

*B.*

*C.*

**D.** The retina, a thin sheet of tissue at the back of the eye, contains types of cells that convert light to nerve impulses. These signals are sent to the brain and initiate the processes of visual sensation and perception.

**D.**

**E.** Rods are sensitive to light but do not register color, whereas cones register color but are not as sensitive to light. Ganglion cells also transduce physical energy into neural signals, but these signals do not produce an image of the stimulus.

*E. Rods: sensitive, no color*
*Cones: color, less sensitive*

**F.** The operation of the three types of cones (each tuned to be most sensitive to a different wavelength of light), in combination with the opponent cells, underlies our ability to see color.

*F.*

**G.** The trichromatic theory of color vision focused on the ways that responses to different wavelengths of light are combined, whereas the opponent process theory focused on the ways that different colors can inhibit perception of other colors.

*G.*

**H.** Visual perception can be divided into two phases. The first takes the outputs from sensory processing and organizes them into sets of perceptual units that correspond to objects and surfaces.

*H.*

**I.** The Gestalt laws of organization (such as similarity, proximity, good continuation, good form, and closure) describe how the visual system organizes lines, dots, and other elements into perceptual units.

*I.*

**J.** The distance, size, and shape of figures are also specified in ways that do not vary when the object is seen from different viewpoints.

*J.*

**K.** The second phase of visual perception involves making the input meaningful.

*K.*

**L.** "What" and "where" are identified by separate neural pathways during the second phase of visual perception. In the "what" pathway, the input is matched to information already stored in memory, which allows you to know more about the stimulus than you can see at the time. In the "where" pathway, locations are coded, using either spatial categories or spatial coordinates.

*L.*

**M.** Perception relies on a combination of bottom-up processes, which are initiated by properties of the stimuli affecting receptors, and top-down processes, which are guided by knowledge, expectation, or belief.

*M.*

**N.** Perception of complex stimuli, such as faces, may require an interplay between information from the "what" and "where" pathways. The brain may be specialized to perceive faces, but such specialization may develop with experience in distinguishing among them.

*N.*

**O.** Attention can be guided both by stimulus properties (bottom-up) and by personal knowledge, expectation, and belief (top-down). Shifting the focus of attention usually allows us to detect stimuli more easily.

*O.*

**P.** When simple features are embedded in other simple features (like a red light in a sea of green lights), the stimulus "pops out" and attention is not necessary for easy detection.

*P.*

**Q.** Finally, some information can be identified outside visual awareness.

*Q.*

## II. Hearing

**A.** Auditory sensation arises when you register sound waves—pressure waves that move molecules (usually in air, but also in liquids and solids).

**B.** Sounds differ in pitch (which reflects variations in frequency) and loudness (which reflects variations in amplitude).

**C.** For most frequencies, the ear uses the position of maximal activity on the basilar membrane to specify the frequency, but for low frequencies the rate of vibration of the basilar membrane may also indicate frequency.

**D.** Hair cells along the basilar membrane, when stimulated, produce nerve impulses, which are sent to the brain. Hair cells that respond to specific frequencies can be impaired by exposure to loud sounds.

**E.** The primary auditory area (the first cortical area to receive auditory input) is a strip where the location of activation depends on the frequency of the sound.

**F.** Auditory perception begins with processes that organize sound into units and specify the locations of those units in space. Sounds are organized using Gestalt principles (such as similarity in pitch) and are localized using a combination of cues that rely on the two ears (differences in the phase, loudness, and arrival times) and cues that rely only on a single ear (loudness, distortions resulting from the shape of the outer ear, and changes in loudness resulting from movement).

**G.** Auditory perception occurs when input matches information stored in memory. Top-down processing can actually fill in missing sounds, as occurs in the phonemic restoration effect.

**H.** Not only can you understand speech sounds by accessing the appropriate stored memories, you can also understand environmental sounds (such as the meaning of a siren) and music.

**I.** Some people can identify specific pitches, but most people identify only relative differences among pitches.

## III. Sensing and Perceiving in Other Ways

**A.** The senses of smell and taste are considered to be the chemical senses because they detect the presence of particular molecules.

**B.** Both smell and taste involve mechanisms in which the right molecule triggers a specific receptor, which in turn sends neural signals to the brain. Both smell and taste rely on combinations of receptors being activated.

**C.** Pheromones can influence some types of emotional reactions and sexual behavior.

**D.** Instead of the traditional five senses, you have at least nine, and possibly ten: In addition to sight, hearing, smell, taste, and touch, you have a kinesthetic sense, a vestibular sense, temperature sensitivity, the ability to feel pain, and possibly a magnetic sense.

II.

A.

B. Frequency → pitch
    Amplitude → loudness

C.

D.

E.

F.

G.

H.

I.

III.

A. For smell and taste, chemicals trigger receptors.

B.

C.

D.

**E.** These additional senses all inform you about the state of your body (where limbs are located, how the body is positioned or located, what is touching you or otherwise affecting your skin).

**F.** Each part of the skin is mapped out on the somatosensory cortex, with the amount of brain surface reflecting the relative sensitivity in that region.

**G.** Pain is registered by two different systems, which can produce the feeling of double pain. Top-down processing can affect interneurons involved in pain, allowing your beliefs and desires to affect the degree to which you feel pain.

**H.** Finally, some researchers have argued that an eleventh sense, extrasensory perception (ESP), exists. However, the evidence for ESP is shaky, and there has yet to be a reliable demonstration that any form of it actually exists.

NOTE: Once you feel that you understand the material in this chapter, visit the book's Web site at www.ablongman.com/kosslyn3e to test your knowledge with additional study questions.

*E.*

*F.*

*G.*

*H.*

# Key Terms

absolute pitch, p. 173
absolute threshold, p. 136
accommodation, p. 138
afterimage, p. 142
amplitude, p. 137
attention, p. 157
attentional blink, p. 162
bias, p. 136
binocular cues, p. 148
bottom-up processing, p. 152
categorical perception, p. 170
chemical senses, p. 174
cocktail party phenomenon, p. 172
color blindness, p. 142
color constancy, p. 147
conduction deafness, p. 169
cones, p. 138
convergence, p. 148
cornea, p. 138
dark adaptation, p. 139

decibel (dB), p. 166
dichotic listening, p. 172
divided attention, p. 159
double pain, p. 180
endorphins, p. 181
extrasensory perception (ESP), p. 182
figure, p. 145
fovea, p. 138
frequency, p. 137
frequency theory, p. 168
gate control, p. 181
Gestalt laws of organization, p. 146
ground, p. 145
hair cells, p. 168
iris, p. 138
just-noticeable difference (JND), p. 136
kinesthetic sense, p. 179
loudness, p. 166

monocular static cues, p. 148
motion cues, p. 149
nerve deafness, p. 169
opponent cells, p. 142
opponent process theory of color vision, p. 142
optic nerve, p. 139
paradoxical cold, p. 180
perception, p. 134
perceptual constancy, p. 147
perceptual set, p. 153
pheromones, p. 176
pitch, p. 166
place theory, p. 168
pop-out, p. 157
psychophysics, p. 135
pupil, p. 138
repetition blindness, p. 162
retina, p. 138
retinal disparity, p. 148

rods, p. 138
selective attention, p. 157
sensation, p. 134
sensitivity, p. 136
shape constancy, p. 147
signal detection theory, p. 136
size constancy, p. 147
somasthetic senses, p. 179

speech-segmentation problem,
   p. 170
taste buds, p. 177
texture gradient, p. 148
threshold, p. 136
tinnitus, p. 169
tonotopic organization, p. 168
top-down processing, p. 152

transduction, p. 138
trichromatic theory of color vision,
   p. 141
vestibular sense, p. 180
wavelength, p. 137
Weber's law, p. 136

# CHAPTER 5

# CONSCIOUSNESS: FOCUS ON AWARENESS

onsider Lewis Carroll's classic tale *Alice's Adventures in Wonderland* through a psychologist's looking glass, and you may see it in a new light—not as a charming children's story but as a reflection on different levels and states of consciousness. Let's take a look at the story. A young girl, Alice, tumbles down a rabbit's burrow and finds herself in a fantastic, topsy-turvy world. There, animals speak English, regularly become invisible (and reappear), and wear waistcoats with pocket watches. Alice finds things to eat and drink, but they make her grow and shrink. Although she understands the *words* that the strange inhabitants say to her, rarely do their *statements* make sense. And, beyond all this, at times she feels not quite herself:

> "Dear, dear! How queer everything is to-day! And yesterday things went on just as usual. I wonder if I've been changed in the night? Let me think: was I the same when I got up this morning? I almost think I can remember feeling a little different. But if I'm not the same, the next question is, Who in the world am I? Ah, THAT'S the great puzzle!" (Carroll, 1992, p. 15)

One of Alice's disconcerting experiences in Wonderland is the often-changing size of her body—an experience that might occur with hypnosis. Might odd experiences like Alice's be the result of a meditative state? Do our heroine's experiences parallel those of a drug- or alcohol-induced state? Following Alice's adventures may help us explore the shifting awareness of ourselves and the world around us that is part of what makes us uniquely human. Such shifts in awareness highlight changes in consciousness.

# THE NATURE OF CONSCIOUSNESS

Alice's situation immediately reveals one aspect of the nature of consciousness: It is a private, subjective experience, and one that can change so dramatically—from one moment to the next—that you may sometimes wonder, as Alice did, whether you are still the same person. Suppose you work intently for 10 solid hours in a windowless room, reading by the yellowish artificial light of a desk lamp. Finally finished with your research, you stumble out into the bright sunlight, dazed and disoriented. You feel distinctly different from the way you felt just hours before, when you were rested and full of vigor. This difference in feeling, like Alice's, is a difference in consciousness.

Why should psychologists care about consciousness? For one thing, our sense of the world and ourselves emerges from consciousness. **Consciousness** refers to our ongoing awareness of our own thoughts, sensations, feelings—our very existence. So a full understanding of what it is to be a person requires that we understand consciousness. William James (1890) argued that a "stream of consciousness" fills each moment of our waking lives (and even some of our non-waking moments); this stream of consciousness is "a teaming multiplicity of objects and relations," where individual sensations are crammed together and are often difficult to distinguish. Francis Crick, codiscoverer of DNA and subsequently a major theorist and researcher on the nature of consciousness, was asked by one of us what he meant by the term *consciousness*. He suggested the following exercise: "Hold both hands in front of you, but with one closer to you. Now look at the front one; now look at the back one. See how the front one seems different when you are focusing on the back one? That's what consciousness is all about." "Oh," his questioner remarked, "so consciousness is just attention!" "No," Crick replied with a tinge of amused annoyance, having no doubt heard similar responses before. "Consciousness is enriched by attention, but attention is not necessary for it." Crick and Koch (1998) develop this idea in detail and suggest that particular portions of the frontal lobes are crucial for consciousness.

Many researchers and thinkers have grappled with the concept of consciousness. Consciousness isn't just about neurons; it necessarily involves subjective experience (Searle, 2000). The problem of consciousness breaks down into two parts—the "easy problem" and the "hard problem" (Chalmers, 1996). The easy problem involves figuring out the nature of the mental processes that are associated with consciousness, such as those used when we visually distinguish an apple from a tomato or realize that we've forgotten to pick up a bottle of milk on the way home ("easy" is a relative term!); measuring response times (to chart the timing of mental events), asking people to provide judgments of subjective qualities (such as how vivid mental images seem), and using neuroimaging can help to illuminate the nature of such processes. In contrast, the hard problem is figuring out the nature of consciousness itself, the nature of subjective experience, and how brain mechanisms give rise to consciousness. The easy problem is (relatively) easy because scientists already have tools for addressing it; the hard problem is hard not only because it is difficult to devise rigorous ways to study the raw stuff of experience, but also because it isn't clear how to conceptualize a theory of experience. Nevertheless, some researchers have begun to make progress even on this problem, using sophisticated types of introspection to study the nature of experience itself (Natsoulas, 2001; Varela & Shear, 1999).

## Functions of Consciousness

Theories of the functions of consciousness abound. One influential theory suggests that consciousness plays a key role in allowing us to bring information together in

**Consciousness:** A person's awareness of his or her own existence, sensations, and cognitions.

novel ways (Baars, 2002). For example, the first time you drive a new route, you are likely to be aware of every turn, every stoplight, every landmark. But after a dozen trips, chances are you no longer notice them. (It can be surprisingly difficult to describe a familiar route to someone who's never taken it before.) What has changed? On your initial journey, new experiences required you to coordinate input and output in novel ways. But, as the experiences became habitual, the new connections you established between input and output allowed you to drive without the need to respond to stimuli that were no longer novel. Even after a hundred trips, however, if you unexpectedly found a tree lying in the road, your sudden consciousness of it would direct you to make the necessary response—and step on the brakes!

Other researchers argue that consciousness serves to bind our enormously complex perceptual and mental processes into a single coherent whole (Crick, 1994; Llinas et al., 1994; Singer, 1998; von der Malsburg, 2002). Still others focus on the idea that consciousness lets us know whether perceptual and mental processes are fitting together correctly (Kosslyn, 1992; Mangan, 2001). Yet other researchers emphasize that consciousness plays a key role in self-awareness (Keenan et al., 2001), which in turn can help us control our emotions (Silvia, 2002).

Although driving can sometimes seem effortless for experienced drivers, unexpected or novel stimuli can direct attention in particular ways—changing the awareness of the experience of driving.

# The Experience of Consciousness

One way to regard consciousness, in some ways an intuitive view, is as a single, central, internal lightbulb illuminating the mind. Philosopher Daniel Dennett (1991), however, argues against such a single "consciousness center." His view is supported by recent studies indicating that different parts of the brain appear to be involved in the experience of consciousness. Depending on exactly what a person is aware of at a given time, different parts of the brain "light up" as they are activated (Alkire et al., 1998; Barbur et al., 1993; Bottini et al., 1995; Kosslyn, 1994b; Leopold & Logothetis, 1996; Vanni et al., 1996). But not all brain areas that are active when a person performs a task contribute directly to the experience of consciousness. In particular, consciousness apparently does not arise from activity in those parts of the brain that first register perceptual information, such as the primary visual cortex or primary auditory cortex (Crick & Koch, 1995, 1998). Instead, consciousness appears to rely on a number of areas in the brain (such as the right parietal lobe and the frontal lobes) involved in the interpretation and integration of information (Bisiach & Luzzatti, 1978; Gazzaniga, 1995; Keenan et al., 2001).

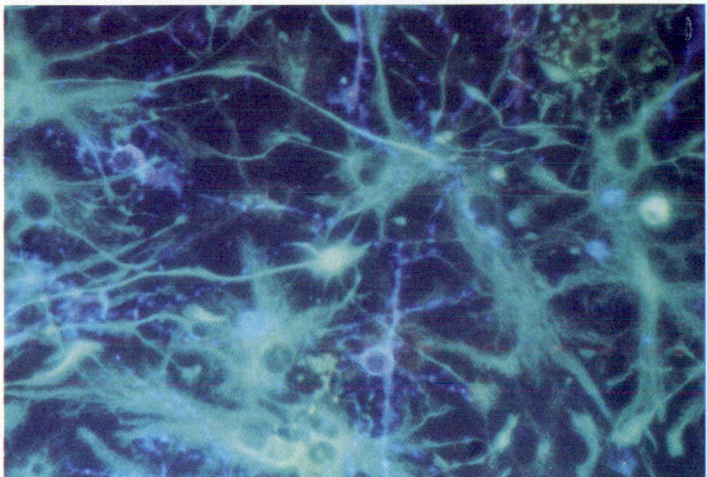

Edelman and Tononi (2000) argue that only complex, highly integrated patterns of neural activity give rise to consciousness.

# Altered States of Consciousness

The fact that many different brain areas contribute to consciousness helps to explain why consciousness is multifaceted and fluid, and why, at times, you experience yourself or the world very differently from the way you do ordinarily, in **normal consciousness** (also called *waking consciousness*). These **altered states of consciousness (ASC)** may be natural states, such as sleeping, dreaming, hypnosis, and meditation, or they may be induced by substances such as drugs and alcohol.

Normal consciousness: State of awareness that occurs during the usual waking state; also called *waking consciousness*.

Altered state of consciousness (ASC): State of awareness that is other than the normal waking state.

In many cultures, inducing an altered state of consciousness is a socially acceptable, and sometimes even mandated, ritual. The members of some cultures, for example, enter into altered states through apparent communication with spirits or souls of deceased people. Others, such as certain Native American tribes, use hallucinogenic mushrooms and other drugs as the route to altered consciousness. Such practices are often considered sacred (Bourguignon, 1973). In Bourguignon's study of 488 societies, 90% had at least one "institutionalized," or culturally approved, altered state. One such state is that experienced by a group of religious women in Trinidad. For one week, the women enter a period of "mourning," spending much of the time lying down, often in darkness and isolation. They also engage in praying, chanting, and singing. During the week, the women experience lifelike hallucinations (mental images so vivid that they seem real) and revelations about their spiritual lives (Ward, 1994). These same practices (periods of isolation accompanied by praying and chanting) are used by members of many cultures who seek to attain altered states of consciousness.

Although consciousness is a state we all experience, its definition can be tricky to pin down. The story of Alice and her experiences provides a springboard for an exploration of the nature of consciousness and its various facets. For example: Alice's adventures, we learn at the end of Carroll's book, have been only a dream.

# Test Yourself

1. The main difference between the easy and the hard problems about consciousness is that
   a. the hard problem involves understanding animal consciousness.
   b. the easy problem is simply philosophical.
   c. psychologists have devised tools for studying the easy problem.
   d. psychologists have clearly conceptualized the hard problem.

2. Which one of the following is not considered a potential function of consciousness?
   a. to bind together cognitive processes
   b. to bring together information in novel ways
   c. to keep our heart and lungs functioning
   d. for self-awareness and control of our emotions

3. Philosopher Daniel Dennett believes that consciousness does not arise in a single place in the mind. This idea is supported by
   a. studies indicating that different parts of the brain appear to be involved in the experience of consciousness.
   b. research indicating that consciousness is like a central lightbulb illuminating the mind.
   c. studies of animal consciousness.
   d. DNA evidence.

4. Examples of altered states of consciousness include
   a. meditation.
   b. sleep.
   c. hypnosis.
   d. All of these are altered states of consciousness.

## Answers

1. c 2. c 3. a 4. d

NOTE: Once you feel comfortable with the Test Yourself questions in this chapter, visit the book's Web site at www.ablongman.com/kosslyn3e for additional study questions.

# Think It Through!

Imagine that you were the only person who had consciousness. Would this make any difference in your social interactions? Do you think a computer could ever become conscious? Let's say that it told you so; would you believe it? How could you tell if it really was conscious? In fact, how can you tell if anyone else is conscious?

Do you think consciousness is an all-or-none condition (conscious versus unconscious) or is a continuum? In either case, do you think animals have consciousness? In what ways might their consciousness be like ours? In what ways different?

# TO SLEEP, PERCHANCE TO DREAM

Alice's story begins with an apparent change of consciousness on a hot afternoon:

> Alice was beginning to get very tired of sitting by her sister on the bank, and of having nothing to do, so she was considering in her own mind (as well as she could, for the hot day made her feel very sleepy and stupid), whether the pleasure of making a daisy-chain would be worth the trouble of getting up and picking the daisies, when suddenly a White Rabbit with pink eyes ran close by her. (Carroll, 1992, p. 7)

It certainly appears that Alice is about to fall asleep, and perhaps by the end of the paragraph she has. As Alice's story closes, a crowd of the odd characters she met in Wonderland

> . . . rose up into the air, and came flying down upon her: she gave a little scream, half of fright and half of anger, and tried to beat them off, and found herself lying on the bank, with her head in the lap of her sister, who was gently brushing away some dead leaves that had fluttered down from the trees upon her face. . . .
>
> "Oh, I've had such a curious dream!" said Alice, and she told her sister, as well as she could remember them, all these strange Adventures of hers that you have just been reading about; and when she had finished, her sister kissed her, and said, "It WAS a curious dream, dear, certainly: but now run in to your tea; it's getting late." So Alice got up and ran off, thinking while she ran, as well she might, what a wonderful dream it had been. (pp. 97–98)

## Stages of Sleep: Working Through the Night

Sleep is perhaps the most obvious example of an altered state of consciousness. Some people think that sleep is a single state, and you are either asleep or awake. Until the invention of the electroencephalograph (EEG; see Chapter 3) in 1928, that is what scientists used to think as well (Hobson, 1995). With the use of this new technology, they learned that **sleep**, a natural experience during which normal consciousness is suspended, is not a single state. By using EEGs to record brain activity during sleep, researchers discovered several different types of sleep, which occur in five stages during the night. Everyone proceeds through these stages, but people differ in how much time they spend in each stage (Anch et al., 1988).

### Stage 1

This initial sleep stage, lasting approximately 5 minutes and sometimes described as **hypnogogic sleep**, marks the transition from relaxed wakefulness to sleep. In Stage 1 sleep, your breathing becomes deeper and more regular, and the EEG registers brain waves that are less regular and of lower amplitude than those that mark the waking state (see Figure 5.1, p. 194). You can be awakened relatively easily from Stage 1 sleep, and if you are, you do not feel as if you have been asleep at all. In this stage, you may experience a gentle falling or floating sensation, or your body may jerk suddenly and rather violently in a movement called a *hypnic jerk*.

### Stage 2

Once you are clearly asleep, your EEG pattern begins to record *sleep spindles*—brief bursts of brain activity (see Figure 5.1)—and single high-amplitude waves. You are now more relaxed and less responsive to your environment, although still relatively easy to awaken. But if you are awakened during Stage 2, you will most likely report that you have been asleep. This phase lasts for approximately 20 minutes.

Sleep: The naturally recurrent experience during which normal consciousness is suspended.

Hypnogogic sleep: The initial stage of sleep, which lasts about 5 minutes and can include the sensation of gentle falling or floating or a sudden jerking of the body.

FIGURE 5.1 **Brain Waves During the Stages of Sleep**

Recordings show that brain waves differ in both amplitude (the height of the wave) and frequency (how often they occur). By examining individuals' EEG patterns when asleep, which differ from their EEG patterns when awake, researchers have identified five phases of sleep, each with its own unique EEG pattern.

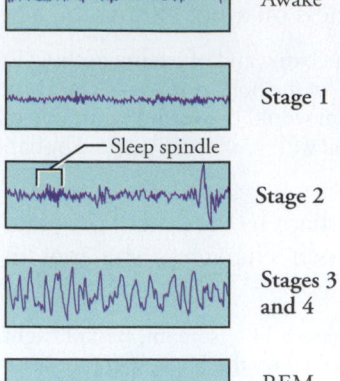

Awake

Stage 1

— Sleep spindle

Stage 2

Stages 3 and 4

REM sleep

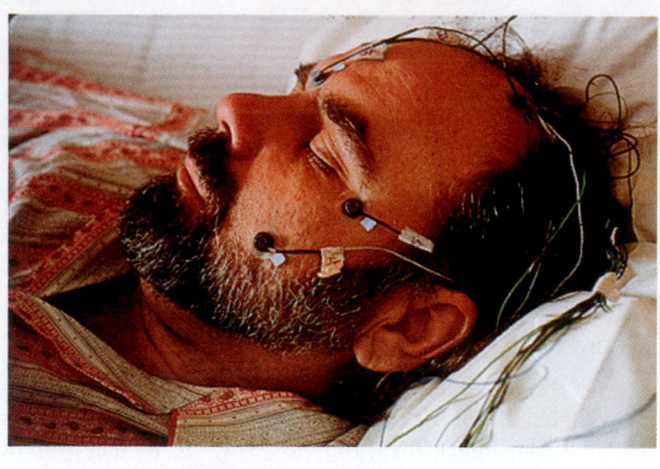

## Stages 3 and 4

Stages 3 and 4 are sometimes referred to collectively as *slow-wave sleep* (SWS) because your brain produces *delta waves*—recorded as slow, high-amplitude waves on an EEG; notice in Figure 5.1 how the waves of Stages 3 and 4 are higher and more spread out compared to those of wakefulness and Stages 1 and 2. In Stage 3, 20–50% of EEG-recorded brain activity is in the form of delta waves; in Stage 4, the proportion is greater than 50%. In Stage 3, your heart rate and body temperature decrease, and you are no longer easily awakened. By the time you reach Stage 4, you are in a very deep sleep indeed, so deep that attempts by a friend (or an alarm clock) to wake you won't readily succeed. If you do wake up directly from this stage, you are likely to be briefly disoriented. During Stage 4 sleep, your heart rate, blood pressure, breathing, and body temperature slow down; all are at their lowest ebb.

## REM Sleep

About an hour after going to sleep, you begin to reverse the sleep cycle, going from Stage 4 through Stages 3 and 2. Instead of going all the way to Stage 1, though, you now enter a state of *rapid eye movement (REM)* under the lids, and, as shown in Figure 5.1, your EEG registers marked brain activity—similar to when you are awake. It is in this stage of sleep that you are likely to have dreams vivid enough to remember. During **REM sleep**, your breathing and heart rate are fast and irregular, and your genitals may show signs of arousal (men may have an erection; women may have increased genital blood flow and vaginal lubrication). These events occur in REM sleep regardless of the content of the sleeper's dreams, unless a dream is particularly anxiety-provoking, in which case the genitals may not be aroused (Karacan et al., 1966). During REM sleep, your muscles are relaxed and unresponsive; in fact, your voluntary muscles (except those in your eyes) are so paralyzed that you could not physically enact the behaviors in your dreams. However, your involuntary muscles continue to move (which allows your respiratory, vascular, and other systems to keep working).

## Sleep Cycles

After a period of REM sleep, you go through at least some of the other stages, and then return to REM, as shown in Figure 5.2. Each cycle takes about 90 minutes and occurs

REM sleep: Stage of sleep characterized by rapid eye movements and marked brain activity.

four or five times each night. However, the time you spend in each stage varies over the course of the night, with slow-wave sleep occurring predominantly in the early hours of sleep and REM sleep occurring primarily in the later hours of sleep.

Sleep also varies over the course of a lifetime. The phrase "I slept like a baby" turns out to have more truth to it than most of us realize. Infants sleep longer than adults (13–16 hours per night in the first year; see Figure 5.3) and have a higher percentage of REM sleep. They often enter REM immediately after falling asleep and change stages often. With age, the pattern of sleep stages changes; when you enter your 40s, the amount of time spent in deep, slow-wave sleep begins to decrease (Van Cauter et al., 2000). With less slow-wave activity, your sleep is shallower and more fragmented, you wake more easily, and the sleep you do get is less satisfying (Hobson, 1995; Klerman et al., 2004). As you move from middle age to older adulthood, the amounts of lighter sleep (Stages 1 and 2) and REM sleep also decrease (Van Cauter et al., 2000). With increasing age, changes in the sleep cycle and in the production of hormones involved in the sleep process make restful sleep less common (Center for the Advancement of Health, 1998; Klinkenborg, 1997). As the quality of sleep declines, so does its restorative effect on the cardiovascular and endocrine systems.

Suppose you share a bed with someone. Do you affect each other's sleep cycles? Yes. Because most people who share a bed go to sleep at around the same time, they are likely to enter REM sleep at about the same time during the night. And if one partner is tossing and turning, the other is less likely to fall asleep until the first one does (Hobson, 1995). Thus, bed partners tend to dream together—although not necessarily about each other.

**FIGURE 5.2** **The March of Sleep Cycles**

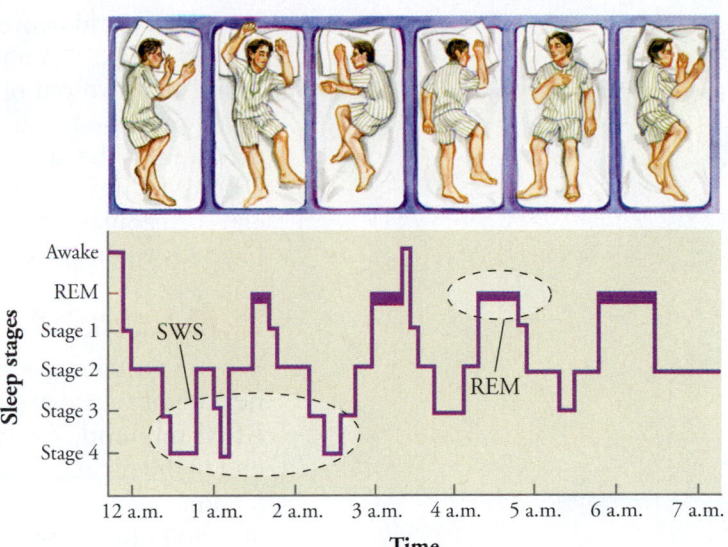

During the earlier part of the night, more time is spent in Stages 3 and 4, but later in the night, REM periods lengthen and Stages 3 and 4 shorten, eventually disappearing.

**FIGURE 5.3** **Proportion of REM Sleep Over a Lifetime**

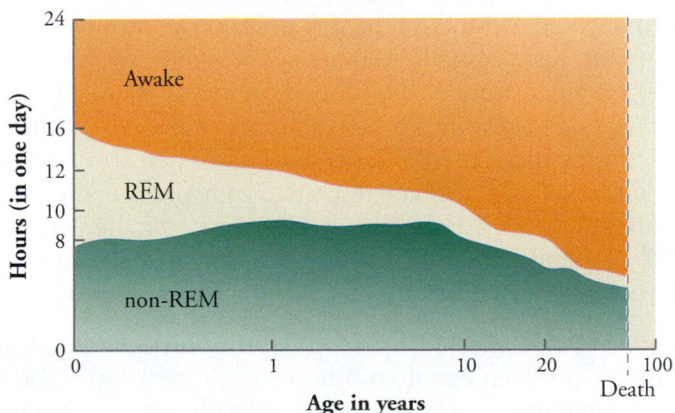

As we get older, we spend less time sleeping overall and less time in REM sleep.

"WHEN I GROW UP I'D LIKE TO BE LIKE YOU, EXCEPT I DON'T KNOW IF I COULD SLEEP THAT MUCH."

Is this cartoon based on fact? How can we understand Dennis's comment if we know that children sleep more than adults, and *much* more than older adults?

# Sleep Deprivation: Is Less Just as Good?

In today's world of overscheduled lives and 10-hour workdays, can anyone claim to be getting a natural amount of sleep? A 2002 survey by the National Sleep Foundation found that two out of three adults are not getting enough sleep (defined as approximately 8 hours), and one of those three gets less than 6 hours each night. Even children under the age of 11 are not getting enough sleep (National Sleep Foundation, 2004). Falling asleep in a dull class *may* signal sleep deprivation: "boredom doesn't cause sleepiness, it merely unmasks it" (Dement, as cited in Brody, 1998). What else happens when you don't get enough sleep, or miss a night's sleep entirely?

## REM Rebound

When you don't get enough REM sleep on a given night, a higher percentage of the next night's sleep will be REM sleep (Brunner et al., 1990); this phenomenon is called **REM rebound**. You can become REM deprived by not getting enough sleep at either end of the night (going to bed late or waking up early) or by using alcohol or sleep medications (depressants), which suppress REM sleep. If these substances are used habitually and then discontinued, REM rebound dreams can be so vivid, bizarre, and generally unpleasant that people resume using these substances to fall asleep, and to suppress dreaming as well. Some people who have been deeply traumatized (victims of rape or assault, for example) cite disturbing dreams or nightmares as a reason for using alcohol or drugs before sleep (Inman et al., 1990).

## Sleep Deprivation: What Happens When You Skimp on Sleep?

If you have ever stayed up late, say, studying or partying, and then awakened early the next morning, you have probably experienced sleep deprivation. In fact, you may be sleep deprived right now. If so, you have company: 40% of adults claim to be so sleepy during the day that daily activities are affected (National Sleep Foundation, 2002). In trying to determine the function of sleep, a common research method is to interfere with participants' sleep in some way and see what the effects might be. What happens as a result of sleep deprivation? Young adults who volunteered for a sleep deprivation study were allowed to sleep for only 5 hours each night, for a total of 7 nights. After 3 nights of restricted sleep, volunteers complained of cognitive, physical, and emotional difficulties.

**ATTENTION AND PERFORMANCE DROP**   Cognitive and physical difficulties that result from sleep deprivation involve problems in sustaining attention and in performing visual-motor tasks. Performance on a visual-motor task declined after only 2 nights of restricted sleep. Visual-motor tasks usually require participants to concentrate on detecting a change in a particular stimulus, and then to respond as quickly as they can after they perceive the change by pressing a button (Dinges et al., 1997). Although you may be able to perform simple, brief mental tasks normally when sleep deprived, if a task requires sustained attention and a motor response, your performance will suffer. Driving a car is an example of such a task. In fact, in a survey by the National Sleep Foundation (1998), 25% of the respondents reported that they had at some time fallen asleep at the wheel; sleepy drivers account for at least 100,000 car crashes each year.

**EMOTIONS FLARE**   Moods are also affected by sleep deprivation (Dinges et al., 1997; Monk et al., 1997). Those who sleep less than 6 hours each weekday night are more likely to report being impatient or aggravated when faced with common minor frustrations such as being stuck in traffic or having to wait in line, and they are more dissatisfied with life in general (National Sleep Foundation, 2002).

Some students may stay up all night before an exam or a paper is due, but not without a cost. Sleep deprivation decreases immune system functioning and temporarily impairs some cognitive abilities, such as maintaining prolonged attention.

REM rebound: The higher percentage of REM sleep that occurs following a night lacking the normal amount of REM.

**THE BODY SUFFERS**  The loss of even one night's sleep can lead to increases in the next day's level of cortisol (Leproult, Copinschi, et al., 1997). As mentioned in Chapter 3 (and discussed in more detail in Chapter 13), cortisol helps the body meet the increased demands imposed by stress. However, sleep deprivation can lead to a change in cortisol level that, in turn, alters other biological functions, such as decreasing immune system functioning (Kiecolt-Glaser et al., 1995) and creating an increased risk for diabetes.

**LEARNING DECREASES**  Sleep deprivation is also associated with deficits in learning in two ways. First, chronically increased cortisol levels can cause memory deficits (Sapolsky, 1996). Second, as we shall see in more detail later, REM and NREM sleep facilitate the learning of information that was encountered during the day (Walker & Stickgold, 2004).

## The Effects of All-Nighters

And, what about a series of all-nighters, when you get no sleep at all, as might occur during finals period? Getting no sleep can interfere with certain types of learning, such as making perceptual discriminations, but naps can help (Cajochen et al., 2004; Mednick et al., 2003). As for pulling all-nighters throughout exam periods, results from volunteers who have gone without sleep for long stretches (finally sleeping after staying awake anywhere from 4 to 11 days) show profound psychological changes, such as hallucinations, feelings of losing control or going crazy, anxiety, and paranoia (Coren, 1996). Moreover, going without sleep alters the normal daily patterns of changes in temperature, metabolism, and hormone secretions (Leproult, Van Reeth, et al., 1997). These changes are also seen in adult rats that are forced to stay awake. Within 2 weeks, they show major negative bodily changes. In fact, despite eating two and a half times their usual amount, they begin to lose weight. Moreover, their temperature does not stay in the normal range, and they die within 21 days (Rechtschaffen et al., 1983). Even rats deprived only of REM sleep (they are awakened each time they enter the REM stage) experience temperature regulation changes, but these changes are less extreme (Shaw et al., 1998). Results of a PET study found a different pattern of brain activation when sleep-deprived human participants were learning verbal material than when non–sleep-deprived participants were learning the material, which may reflect an attempt to compensate for the brain changes induced by sleep deprivation (Drummond et al., 2000).

Thus, sleep deprivation affects us in at least four important psychological areas: attention, physical performance, mood, and learning.

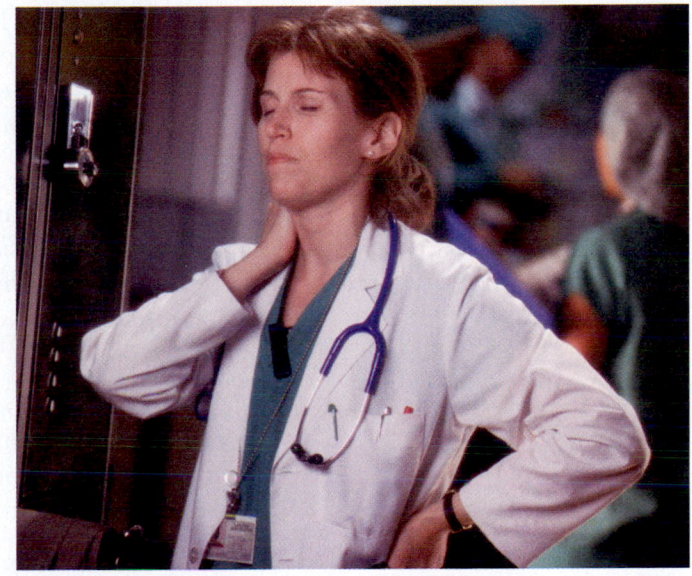

There is increasing recognition that requiring medical interns and residents to stay awake for days and nights of round-the-clock duties can have detrimental effects on their cognitive processes (Landrigan et al., 2004; Lockley et al., 2004) and even cause them to be more likely to have car accidents (Barger et al., 2005). In response, some states are restricting the number of consecutive hours doctors can work.

# UNDERSTANDING RESEARCH

## Sleep Deprivation Lite

Suppose it is midterm time or finals week: Over the next few days, you have about 7 hours more work to do than you can fit in—and therefore you must cut back on your sleep. Should you stay up all night one night to cram in as much extra work as you can, or should you sleep a couple of hours less each night over the next several nights? Christopher Drake, Timothy Roehrs, and colleagues (2001) conducted a study that may inform your choice.

**QUESTION:** Is losing sleep in one fell swoop (as occurs during an all-nighter) worse than losing the same amount of sleep a bit at a time, spread out over several nights?

**ALTERNATIVES:** (1) Losing sleep all at once is *worse* than losing the same amount of sleep a bit at a time, spread out over several nights. (2) Losing sleep all at once is *better* than losing the same amount of sleep a bit at a time, spread out over several nights. (3) Losing sleep all at once is *about the same as* losing the same amount of sleep a bit at a time, spread out over several nights.

**LOGIC:** If losing sleep all at once does indeed differ from losing the same amount of sleep a bit at a time, spread out over several nights, then the effects of a sleep loss should be worse after losing a lot of sleep at once than after losing the same amount of sleep gradually, over several nights.

**METHOD:** Twelve participants between the ages of 21 and 35 took part in each of four sleep conditions. The *control condition* involved no sleep loss, and participants spent 8 hours in bed (from 11 p.m. to 7 a.m.) for four nights.

Each of the three remaining conditions involved 8 hours of sleep loss, but the researchers varied the rate at which participants were sleep deprived:

- *slow sleep loss condition*, where participants spent 6 hours in bed (from 1 a.m. to 7 a.m.) for four nights;
- *intermediate sleep loss condition*, where participants spent 4 hours in bed (from 3 a.m. to 7 a.m.) for two nights; and
- *rapid sleep loss condition*, where participants spent no time in bed (an all-nighter) for one night.

On the nights before and after each condition, participants spent 8 hours in bed, and the conditions were 1–2 weeks apart. Participants completed tests of fatigue and of several abilities, including memory, psychomotor reaction time, attention, and concentration.

**RESULTS:** The key results were the measures taken after a total of 8 hours of sleep deprivation. The results were clear-cut: Rapid sleep loss (the all-nighter) disrupted alertness, memory, and reaction time much more than did the same amount of sleep loss spread out over time. Moreover, as shown in Figure 5.4, the faster the rate of sleep loss, the greater the impairment. Losing a couple of hours sleep per night (slow sleep loss) led to the least overall impairment.

**INFERENCES:** The researchers inferred from their results that people adapt best to losing only 2 hours per night (slow sleep loss); the participants clearly had the least impairments during that condition. Based on this and other sleep deprivation studies, the researchers propose that sleeping less than 6 hours *nightly* leads to significant cumulative impairment. If you need more hours for studying during midterms or finals weeks, sleep at least 6 hours per night; less than that and you won't be at your best in daily functioning—or when you take that exam.

## THINK CRITICALLY!

How do the results of this study compare with your own experiences with not getting enough sleep? Although participants spent 0, 4, 6, or 8 hours *in bed*, why might time in bed not have been the best way of to determine how much sleep they received? What method would you suggest as an alternative?

**FIGURE 5.4** **Adverse Effects of Different Rates of Sleep Loss**

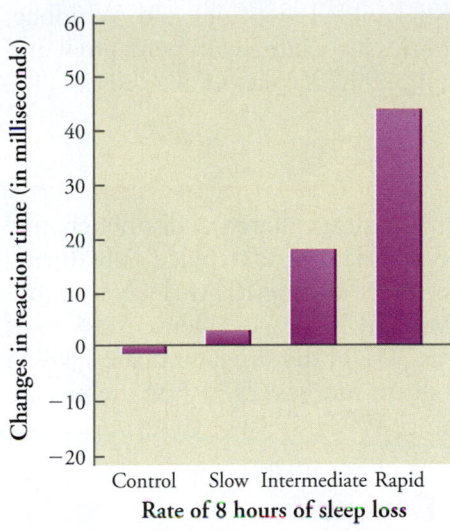 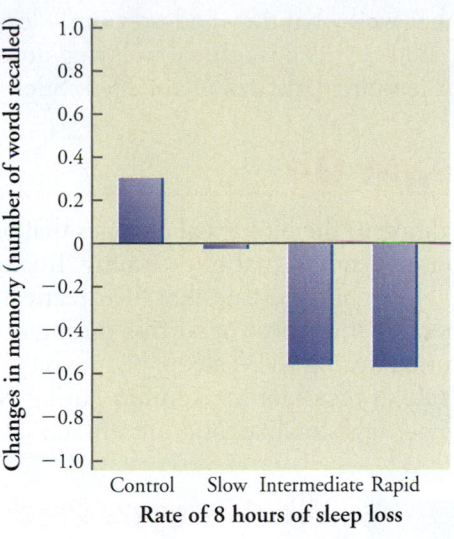 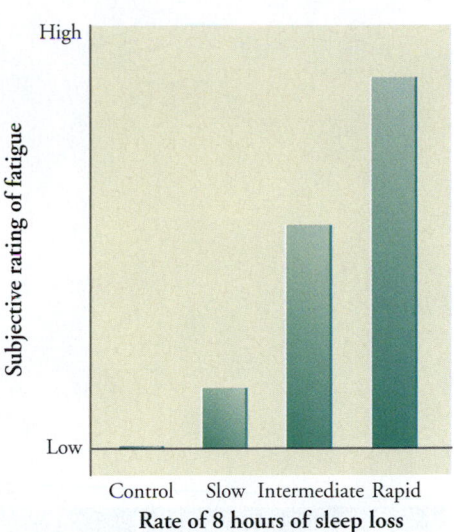

The faster the rate of sleep loss, the slower is reaction time, the fewer are the number of words recalled, and the greater is the subjective sense of fatigue.

# The Function of Sleep

We know that doing without sleep has adverse effects on attention, mood, and performance. But why do we sleep? What purpose or purposes does it serve? Research on sleep is beginning to piece together answers to these questions.

## Evolutionary Theory

One theory of the function of sleep is that it provided an evolutionary advantage—it kept our ancestors metaphorically off the streets and out of trouble. That is, sleeping removes us from potential life-threatening conflicts with predatory animals at night, when humans do not have the advantage of night vision. (Note, however, that we are also more vulnerable to prey while asleep, which is a clear disadvantage.) Another, perhaps more plausible, evolutionary account is that sleep (and its associated biological changes) allows energy conservation because the body's temperature lowers and caloric demands decline. Although interesting, such theories at present must be regarded as speculation.

## Restorative Theory

Another theory of the function of sleep is that sleep helps the body repair the wear and tear from the day's events (Hobson, 1989). Support for this view comes from research on sleep deprivation and the adverse effects of lack of sleep mentioned earlier.

## Facilitating Learning

Yet another theory about the function of sleep is that it facilitates the learning of material encountered during the day (Walker & Stickgold, 2004). In studies where participants were asked to discriminate among different visual stimuli, both slow-wave sleep in the first quarter of the night and REM sleep in the last quarter of the night were crucial for visual learning: Participants deprived of these phases of sleep did not remember well what they had previously learned (Stickgold, 1998; Stickgold, Whidbee, et al., 2000). Sleep is critical in laying down memories associated with perceptual and motor learning (Atienza et al., 2004; Stickgold et al., 2002; Walker et al., 2003).

# Dream On

In addition to the biological changes that occur during sleep, there is a distinct change in consciousness—that of dreaming. It is *not* true that dreams take place only during REM sleep, but it *is* true that the dreams that take place during REM sleep are more memorable than those occurring during non-REM (NREM) stages (Dement, 1974). If awakened during REM sleep, people recall dreams 78% of the time, compared with a 50% rate of recall for awakenings during NREM sleep; moreover, NREM dreams are less vivid, less storylike, and less emotional (Farthing, 1992; Nielsen, 2000).

## What Triggers Particular Dreams?

Although dreams may seem bizarre, disjointed, and nonsensical, their content is not necessarily totally random. President Gerald Ford once spoke the lines "Thank you. Thank you. Thank you." in his sleep. He later told his wife, Betty, that he had dreamed he was in a receiving line (Seuling, 1978). By awakening dreamers at different stages of sleep and asking them about their dreams, or asking people to keep "dream diaries" at their bedsides, researchers have learned that certain types of dreams appear to be related to events occurring during the day (Hauri, 1970). Often these reflect the short-term lack of particular stimuli: Water-deprived people dream of drinking (Bokert, 1968), for example, and people socially isolated for a day dream of being with other people (Wood, 1963). Long-term deprivation seems to have a different effect, however: For individuals chronically deprived of an experience or stimulus, there is eventually a decrease in dreams related to the missing element (Newton, 1970).

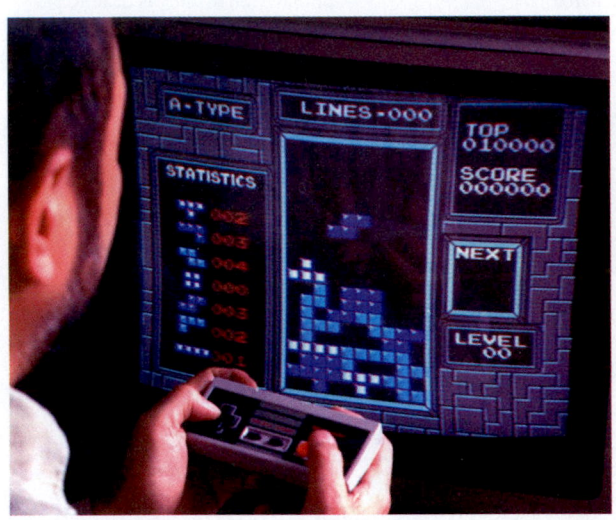

Dreams that occur right after you drift off to sleep may reflect events that occurred just before sleep: One study found that people who learned to play the computer game *Tetris* found themselves dreaming of elements of that game at the beginning of their sleep (Stickgold, Malia, et al., 2000).

Dreams may also provide an opportunity to solve personal problems: When participants thought about a moderately distressing but solvable personal problem right before sleep, they considered the problem more solvable when they awoke than did participants in a control group, who did not think about their problem right before sleep (White & Taytroe, 2003). In particular, REM sleep may facilitate such problem solving (Walker et al., 2002).

## Why Do We Dream?

Dreams can offer us a pleasant respite from the daily grind, bring us terror in the form of a nightmare, or leave us puzzled about their confusing or curious content.

What function does dreaming serve?

**FREUD: WISH FULFILLMENT**   Researchers and nonresearchers alike have long sought to know why we dream. The first modern dream theory was proposed by Sigmund Freud. Freud (1900/1958), convinced that dream content originates in the unconscious—outside our conscious awareness—dubbed dreams the "royal road to the unconscious." Further, he believed that dreams allow us to fulfill unconscious desires. Such *wish fulfillment* may not always be apparent from the **manifest content** of a dream, that is, its obvious, memorable content. We have to dig to find the **latent content** of the dream,

Manifest content: The obvious, memorable content of a dream.

Latent content: The symbolic content and meaning of a dream.

its symbolic content and meaning, which, according to Freud, might reflect sexual or aggressive themes associated with an inner conflict. In this view, the manifest content of Alice's dream includes her specific adventures in Wonderland; the latent content, according to Freud, might reflect her underlying anxiety about the integrity of her body in general and about her sexuality in particular (Schilder, 1938). Although Freud's theory of the unconscious origin of the content of dreams has yet to be supported by solid, objective evidence, the idea of dream interpretation has both ancient appeal and current fascination—witness the large number of dream interpretation books and Web sites on the Internet. Can someone interpret your dreams? Although dream interpretation can be interesting and fun, it is unclear that any meaning inferred from the content of dreams is accurate.

Research suggests, however, that Freud may have been on to something with one aspect of his dream theory: If we try *not* to think about someone before we go to sleep, that person is more likely to appear in our dreams than if we didn't try to suppress thoughts of him or her (Wegner et al., 2004). That is, although the content of our dreams may not reflect our unconscious *desires*, the content may reflect mental processes that happen outside of conscious awareness.

**ACTIVATION-SYNTHESIS HYPOTHESIS** Freudians find dreams brimming over with meaningful, albeit disguised, content. The opposite view is at the heart of the **activation-synthesis hypothesis**, which contends that dreams arise from random bursts of nerve cell activity. These bursts may affect brain cells involved in hearing and seeing, as well as storing information, and the brain's response is to try to make sense of the hodgepodge of stimuli (Hobson & McCarley, 1977); however, the dreams do not disguise meaning, as Freud suggested (Goode, 1999). The brain synthesizes the sensory images and activates stored information to create the experience of a dream. This theory would explain why dreams sometimes seem so bizarre and unrelated: Stickgold and colleagues (1994) asked people to write down their dreams and then literally cut their reports in half. They asked other people to reassemble each dream, deciding which half came first. This proved a very difficult task, a result that is understandable if dreams are merely attempts to interpret random activity and have no cohesive story line.

**EDITING VERSUS STRENGTHENING NEURAL CONNECTIONS** As part of his effort to understand consciousness, Francis Crick also investigated dreams, which he believed are used to edit out unnecessary or accidental brain connections formed during the day (Crick & Mitchison, 1983, 1986). Other theories of dreaming focus on the reverse notion: that dreams are used to *strengthen* useful connections. This view is supported by a study by Karni and colleagues (1994). Participants learned to discriminate between two visual stimuli before falling asleep; those who slept normally improved their performance on the task when tested the following morning. But participants who were awakened when they entered REM sleep did not improve when tested in the morning. In contrast, participants who slept but were deprived of slow-wave, Stage 4 sleep showed normal learning—which suggests that REM sleep is crucial for cementing in memory certain kinds of information gleaned during the day. However, as we noted in our earlier discussion about sleep deprivation, more recent research suggests that such memories do not absolutely depend on REM; at least in some circumstances, slow-wave sleep may play a role (Stickgold, 1998; Stickgold, Whidbee, et al., 2000). It may be that REM sleep—and the dreaming associated with it—is particularly important for perceptual memories, and slow-wave sleep is important for other sorts of memory, but at present this remains an area for further research.

**GOALS/DESIRES AND AROUSAL/INHIBITION** The largest and most systematic study of the neurological bases of dreaming was reported by Solms (1997), of the London Hospital Medical College. Solms interviewed more than 350 stroke patients about the changed

Activation-synthesis hypothesis: The theory that dreams arise from random bursts of nerve cell activity, which may affect brain cells involved in hearing and seeing; the brain attempts to make sense of this hodgepodge of stimuli, resulting in the experience of dreams.

In some societies, such as the Maya, telling dreams to others can provide a way to communicate feelings or solve problems (Degarrod, 1990; Tedlock, 1992).

| TABLE 5.1 | Why Do We Dream? |
| --- | --- |

**Purpose of Dreaming**

*Wish fulfillment* of unconscious desires (Freud)

Attempts to *synthesize* and make sense of effects of random bursts of neural *activity* during sleep (Hobson and McCarley)

*Changing neural connections*:

- *Editing out* unneeded neural connections (Crick)
- *Strengthening* useful neural connections (Karni)

*Arousal of motivation-related brain structures*, leading to dreams associated with needs, goals, and desires (Solms)

nature of their dreams after their strokes. Consistent with the idea that consciousness arises from many parts of the brain, Solms found that dreaming was affected by damage to any number of brain areas. Perhaps Solms's most intriguing discovery was that dreaming stopped completely if a patient had damage that disconnected parts of the frontal cortex from the brainstem and the limbic system. These connections coordinate brain areas involved in curiosity, interest, and alert involvement with goals in the world (Panksepp, 1985, cited in Solms, 1997). Solms speculates that dreaming may occur in response to any type of arousal that activates brain structures involved in motivation (Goode, 1999). Alternatively, the damage that disconnected frontal cortex from brainstem and limbic system may have disrupted the brain's storage and integration of memories related to needs, goals, and desires. In either case, the inhibiting mechanisms of sleep prevent us from acting on these memories, emotions, or desires, which may lead the brain thus to convert them into symbolic hallucinations.

In sum, although we cannot yet definitively answer *why* we dream, we do know something about *how* we dream. We know that dreaming is a neurological process, involving brain activity. We don't know whether dreams represent deep desires and conflicts, random bursts of nerve cell activity, the editing of unneeded neural connections, or the strengthening of neural connections. But it is interesting that all of these theories, despite their differences, agree that in some way the day's events, or the neural connections they instigate, affect dreams. These hypotheses about the purpose of dreaming are summarized in Table 5.1.

# The Brain Asleep

We spend about one third of our lives asleep. During that time, our brains and bodies are working away, responding to outside stimuli such as light and dark, and releasing fluctuating levels of neurotransmitters and hormones. These chemical changes are crucial to our daily functioning.

## The Chemistry of Sleep: Ups and Downs

When you are in slow-wave sleep, the brain cells that release the neurotransmitter acetylcholine are inhibited, but when you are in REM sleep, they are activated (Hobson et al., 2000; McCarley & Hobson, 1975). Your dreams of walking, flying, or falling may occur because of the increased acetylcholine during REM, which activates the motor and visual areas of your brain and may cause you to dream of a wild roller-coaster ride or other types of motion (Hobson, 1995). Moreover, the cells in parts of your brainstem that release other neurotransmitters, specifically serotonin and norepinephrine, are most active when you are awake. Sleeping pills work in part by blocking production of these two "wake-up" neurotransmitters (Garcia-Arraras & Pappenheimer, 1983).

The hormone melatonin, which is secreted by the pineal gland, plays a role in promoting sleep. The body normally begins secreting melatonin around dusk, tapering off production at dawn; this cycle appears to be regulated, at least in part, by a recently discovered type of light receptor in the eye (Brainard et al., 2001; see Chapter 4). A person who takes melatonin in pill form may soon feel drowsy and, if undisturbed, may fall asleep within half an hour. Unlike other sleep aids, melatonin appears to induce a natural sleep, with the appropriate amounts and timing of REM and NREM sleep (Zhdanova & Wurtman, 1996). Some have argued that taking melatonin at the right times can help a traveler overcome jet lag, especially when traveling east (Beaumont et al., 2004; Herxheimer & Petrie, 2002; Takahashi et al., 2002).

## Circadian Rhythms

Our brain activity and internal chemistry dance in time to the daily cycling of light and dark in a pattern called **circadian rhythms** (*circadian* means "about a day"). Daily fluctuations governed by circadian rhythms occur with blood pressure, pulse rate, body temperature, blood sugar level, hormone levels, and metabolism (see Figure 5.5 for circadian variations in several variables). Every one of us has an internal clock that coordinates these fluctuations; this clock is regulated by a small part of the hypothalamus just above the optic chiasm, called the **suprachiasmatic nucleus (SCN)**, which is illustrated in Figure 5.6 (p. 204). Through photoreceptors in the retina, the SCN registers changes in light, which lead it to produce hormones that set the body's clock and regulate various bodily functions (Berson et al., 2002). Researchers have found a gene in mice that is responsible for the regulation of their daily clocks; tissues in the eyes and the SCN generate the signals that cue the mouse's brain as to when to sleep and when to awaken (Antoch et al., 1997). The rudiments of circadian rhythms appear in human infants as early as 1 week after birth (McGraw et al., 1999). The circadian clock is even responsible for the length of time between heart beats (Hu et al., 2004).

What happens to the human sleep–wake cycle in the absence of external cues of dark and light (except for electric light, which can be turned on and off at will) and cultural cues such as clocks? Volunteers who have lived this way as part of a research project ended up living a 24.9-hour day. In a variant of this study, in which only subdued lighting was provided, with no opportunity for stronger reading light, participants were more likely to have a 24.2-hour day (Czeisler et al., 1999).

But what about people who are completely blind and cannot detect light at all? As with the people who had no external cues, but could turn lights on and off and so create a structure to their day, completely blind people show evidence of a 24.9-hour day, with 76% of the blind people studied reporting difficulty falling asleep at their usual bedtimes, based on a 24-hour day (Coren, 1996; Miles et al., 1977). Thus, the 24-hour schedule, so ingrained in us by the daily rotation of the earth, is not hard-wired into our brains, but instead is maintained by exposure to light–dark cycles, whether natural or artificial, and by cues from mechanical instruments such as clocks and radios.

**WORKING AGAINST YOUR RHYTHMS** Even within the 24-hour day, however, not everyone prefers to wake up or go to sleep at the same time. As you have no doubt noticed, some people are energetic and alert early in the morning, whereas others do

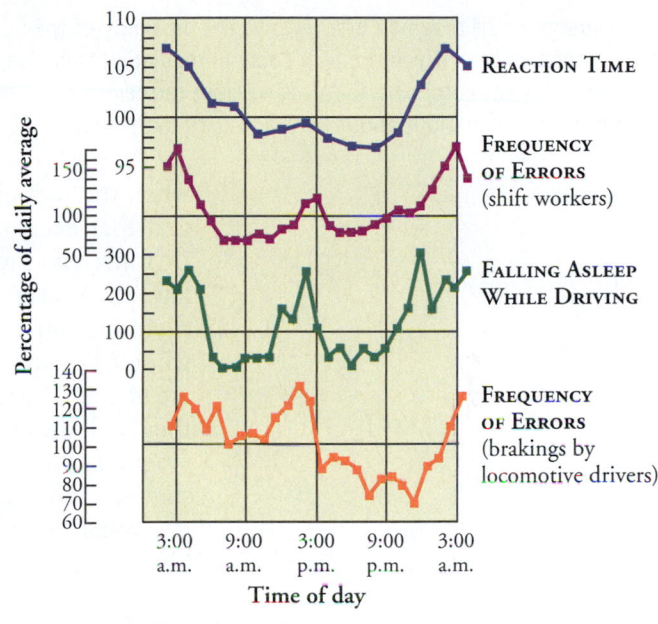

**FIGURE 5.5** **Circadian Variation of Several Variables**

In addition to the variables graphed here, body temperature and subjective alertness vary as a function of circadian rhythms.

Circadian rhythms: The body's daily fluctuations in response to the cycle of dark and light, which occur with blood pressure, pulse rate, body temperature, blood sugar level, hormone levels, and metabolism.

Suprachiasmatic nucleus (SCN): A small part of the hypothalamus just above the optic chiasm that registers changes in light, leading to production of hormones that regulate various bodily functions.

## FIGURE 5.6 The Suprachiasmatic Nucleus (SCN) and the Optic Chiasm

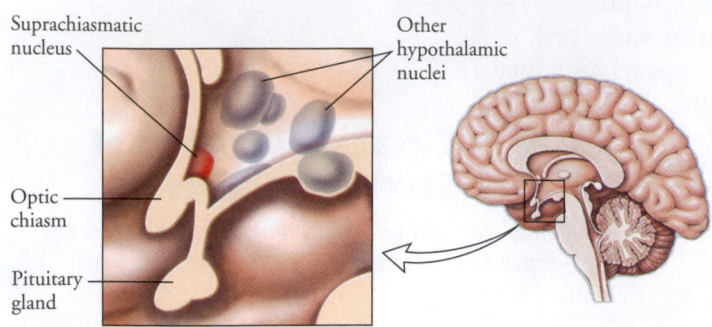

Suprachiasmatic nucleus

Other hypothalamic nuclei

Optic chiasm

Pituitary gland

This illustration of a human brain shows the proximity of the SCN to the optic chiasm. Given the SCN's role in regulating circadian rhythms, it is not surprising that it is so close to the optic chiasm, which relays visual input about light and dark to the brain.

not perk up until late morning or afternoon. People differ in the timing of their circadian rhythms: Morning people, or "larks," experience peak body temperature, alertness, and efficiency in the morning; evening people, or "owls," peak at night (Luce, 1971). Normally you are not aware of your circadian rhythms until you try to function well at your nonpeak time. If you're a night owl, for example, how do you feel when faced with a 9:00 a.m. class? Flying across time zones is bound to make you aware of your own circadian rhythms, especially if it's a long trip. Regardless of the time of day that finds you most alert, however, most people have a late-afternoon dip in energy level. More industrial and traffic accidents occur between 1:00 and 4:00 p.m. than at any other time of day (Klinkenborg, 1997). Rest breaks can help counter fatigue and enhance performance (Tucker, 2003).

Are you grouchy on a Monday morning? If so, it might be more than simply "waking up on the wrong side of the bed." Boivin and colleagues (1997), who studied mood and circadian rhythms, found that bad moods occurred during times of day when the participants' circadian clocks said they should be asleep. These results suggest that even minor alterations in sleep schedules, relative to individual circadian rhythms, can have a noticeable effect on mood after awakening. Thus, if you go to bed later and sleep later on weekends, you may be adversely altering your circadian rhythms. You are, in a sense, putting yourself in another time zone for the weekend, so when Monday morning rolls around, you are hit with jet lag. Even fifth grade children are affected by having to wake up earlier to go to school. Regardless of how much sleep they had, those children who had to be in school by 7:10 a.m. reported more daytime fatigue and poorer attention and concentration at school than those whose school day started at 8:00 a.m. (Epstein et al., 1998).

What can you do if your schedule conflicts with your natural circadian tendencies? One remedy is to sleep on a disciplined schedule 7 days a week. If, as in the case of jet lag, that isn't possible, try exposing yourself to plenty of light on Monday mornings; this may help reset your internal clock.

Many cultures have a rest time in the afternoon, perhaps related to the dip in energy during that part of the day that is part of our circadian rhythms.

### SHIFT WORK: WORK AT NIGHT, SLEEP ALL DAY

Can work schedules affect sleep? Just ask people who have worked the swing shift (4:00 p.m. to midnight) or the graveyard shift (midnight to 8:00 a.m.)—a group that includes up to 20% of American workers (Klinkenborg, 1997). Some jobs even involve daily changes in the shift worked. Working during hours when you would normally be asleep can cause an increase in accidents, insomnia, and medical and psychological difficulties (Garbarino et al., 2002; Ohayon et al., 2002). The near-meltdown at the Three Mile Island nuclear power facility occurred after workers were placed on the night shift following six weeks of constant rotation; during their disastrous shift, they did not notice several warning indicators (Moore-Ede, 1982).

Researchers studying the effects of shift work typically have found that it is easier to switch to progressively later shifts (from the night to the day shift, and from the day to the evening shift) than to move in the opposite direction (although not all studies have found this; Cruz et al., 2003). In general, people differ in their ability to adjust to such schedule changes, or even to daylight savings time (Valdez et al., 2003); those with a greater range of body temperatures in their circadian cycles have an easier time (Reinberg et al., 1983). If your work involves swing or graveyard shifts, one way to minimize the negative effects on your circadian rhythms is to have very bright lights while at work (Boivin & James, 2002a) and to wear dark sunglasses on the way home in the morning (Crowley et al., 2003). For those on the graveyard shift, an afternoon nap may help (Macchi et al., 2002). When possible, try not to stay on these shifts for more than 3 days (Knauth, 1997). This way, your sleep won't be disrupted by being on the night shift for extended periods of time, and you can still socialize with family and friends regularly. In addition, shift operators at an industrial plant who took planned naps of up to an hour while at work were more vigilant after the naps, and they viewed the naps as having improved their overall quality of life (Bonnefond et al., 2001).

One study found that drivers in sleep-related auto accidents were more likely to work multiple jobs or night shifts or have unusual work schedules than were drivers involved in non–sleep-related auto accidents or people not involved in such accidents (Stutts et al., 2003).

## Troubled Sleep

When a young girl like Alice falls asleep in the middle of the day, the reason is often simply drowsiness. In some instances, however, the cause may be a sleep disorder. Too much sleep, too little sleep, and odd variations in the timing and quality of sleep can disturb our needed rest and, therefore, our bodily and psychological functioning (see Table 5.2). Sleep disorders stem from a number of causes, in particular, hereditary, environmental, and physical problems.

### Night Terrors: Not Your Usual Nightmare

Most common among boys 3 to 7 years old, **night terrors** are vivid and frightening experiences. Night terrors occur in Stages 3 and 4, usually in the first third of a night's sleep. During a night terror, the child may sit bolt upright, screaming and sweating, and may be impossible to wake. In the morning, the child usually has no memory of the terrors, not even that they happened. For parents, however, the memory of their terrified child, eyes open and wild with fear, unresponsive to their attempts to comfort and help, is apt to linger.

Fortunately, night terrors usually subside as the child grows older. No one knows why they occur, although genetics plays a part: Night terrors can run in families. Night terrors are qualitatively different from **nightmares**, which are essentially dreams with strong negative emotion. Nightmares often take place during morning REM sleep; the dreamer can be roused during a nightmare and generally retains at least some memory of it.

| TABLE 5.2 | Sleep Disorders |
|---|---|
| **Disorder** | **Main Symptom(s)** |
| **Night terrors** | Vivid, frightening experiences; the dreamer cannot be woken and does not remember the terrors. |
| **Nightmares** | Dreams with negative emotion; they may be remembered the next day. |
| **Narcolepsy** | Sudden attacks of extreme drowsiness and possibly sleep. |
| **Insomnia** | Difficulty getting to sleep, difficulty staying asleep, or awakening too early. |
| **Sleep apnea** | Brief, temporary cessation of breathing during sleep for up to 70 seconds, following a period of difficult breathing accompanied by snoring; the sleeper then startles into a lighter state of sleep and may have no memory of these events and may not feel rested after sleeping. |

**Night terrors:** Vivid and frightening experiences while sleeping; the sleeper may appear to be awake during the experience but has no memory of it the following day.

**Nightmare:** A dream with strong negative emotion.

## Narcolepsy: Asleep at the Drop of a Hat

At the March Hare's tea party in Wonderland, Alice meets a Dormouse who is always falling asleep; occasionally he wakes, says something, then drifts off again.

"Wake up, Dormouse!" And they pinched it on both sides at once.

The Dormouse slowly opened his eyes. "I wasn't asleep," he said in a hoarse, feeble voice: "I heard every word you fellows were saying."

"Tell us a story!" said the March Hare.

"Yes, please do!" pleaded Alice.

"And be quick about it," added the Hatter, "or you'll be asleep again before it's done." (Carroll, 1992, p. 58)

The Dormouse could be suffering from **narcolepsy**. This sleep disorder causes sudden attacks of extreme drowsiness so powerful that the person with narcolepsy finds it almost impossible *not* to fall asleep, typically for 10–20 minute spells (American Psychiatric Association, 2000). Once asleep, people with narcolepsy often enter REM sleep almost immediately. The overwhelming drowsiness sufferers experience may be triggered by a large meal or intense emotions, but it can occur at any time—even while driving. An abnormality in the neurons involving the neurotransmitter *orexin* (also referred to as *hypocretin*) appears to cause narcolepsy (Mignot, 2001; Peyron et al., 2000; Siegel, 2004; Thannickal et al., 2003). Psychological treatment aimed at changing behavior is often recommended, and stimulant medication may also be prescribed (Guilleminault et al., 1976); as orexin's role in narcolepsy is uncovered more fully, treatments involving orexin-based medication may be more effective than stimulants (Tuller, 2002). Like some other sleep disorders, narcolepsy tends to run in families, a sign that the disorder has a genetic component.

## Insomnia

At the opposite end of the sleep spectrum from narcolepsy is a sleep disorder that may be more familiar to you, especially if you find it hard to get a good night's sleep. **Insomnia** is characterized by repeated difficulty falling asleep or staying asleep or waking too early. If you suffer from this disorder, you are certainly not alone. Half the adults in the United States experience occasional insomnia. Temporary insomnia may be related to environmental factors such as stress related to family, school, or work (Bastien et al., 2004), which can cause increased sympathetic nervous system activity and can make sleep difficult. When sleep does not occur rapidly, the stressed person becomes frustrated. The frustration serves to increase arousal, compounding the problem.

If you have insomnia, lying in bed should only be associated with actually going to sleep, not with watching television or reading when you are unable to fall asleep. The man in the photograph should sit in a chair or sofa while watching television if he can't sleep.

For many Americans, insomnia is a way of life. Chronic insomnia may stem from other disorders, such as anxiety and depression, as you will see in Chapter 14. Sleeping pills (barbiturates) are the most common, but not necessarily the most effective, treatment for insomnia. They not only suppress needed REM sleep but also are addictive. Moreover, people develop tolerance to this medication, requiring larger and larger dosages to get the same effect.

What can you do if you have trouble sleeping? The following nonmedical techniques may help (Hobson, 1995; Lacks & Morin, 1992; Maas, 1998):

- *Restrict your sleeping* hours to the same nightly pattern. When living in the White House, both Martha and George Washington went to bed promptly at 9:00 p.m. each evening (Seuling, 1978). The Washingtons were on to something: Keep reg-

**Narcolepsy:** Sudden attacks of extreme drowsiness.

**Insomnia:** Repeated difficulty falling asleep, difficulty staying asleep, or waking up too early.

ular sleeping hours. Avoid sleeping late in the morning, napping longer than an hour, or going to bed earlier than usual, all of which will throw you off schedule, creating even more sleep difficulties later. And try to get up at the same time every day, even on weekends or days off.

- *Control* bedtime stimuli so that things normally associated with sleep are associated only with sleep, not with the frustration of insomnia. Use your bed only for sleep or sex (don't read or watch TV in bed). If you can't fall asleep within 10 minutes, get out of bed and do something else.

- *Avoid ingesting substances with stimulant properties.* Don't smoke cigarettes or drink beverages with alcohol or caffeine in the evening. Alcohol may cause initial drowsiness, but it has a "rebound effect" that leaves many people wide awake in the middle of the night. Don't drink water close to bedtime; getting up to use the bathroom can lead to poor sleep.

- *Consider meditation or progressive muscle relaxation.* Either technique can be helpful (see Chapter 15). Regular aerobic exercise four times a week may be a long-term solution, but it can take up to 16 weeks for the effect on insomnia to kick in (King et al., 1997).

These techniques are often part of psychological treatment of insomnia, which focuses on the sleep-related thoughts and behaviors that can contribute to insomnia (Bastien, Morin, et al., 2004); such techniques can be more effective than sleep medication (Jacobs et al., 2004).

## Sleep Apnea

Snoring can be a nuisance to those sharing a room with a snorer, but it can also be a sign of a more troublesome problem. **Sleep apnea** is a disorder characterized by a temporary cessation of breathing during sleep, usually preceded by a period of difficult breathing accompanied by loud snoring. Breathing may stop for up to 70 seconds, startling the sleeper into a lighter state of sleep. This ailment, which affects 12 million Americans (National Heart, Lung, & Blood Institute, 2003), can produce many such events each hour, preventing restful sleep. Perhaps this explains the results of a research study of medical students who snore versus those who do not: 13% of nonsnorers failed their exams, compared with 42% of frequent snorers (Ficker et al., 1999). If the snorers had sleep apnea, they would not function as well because of their troubled sleep.

Sleep apnea results when muscles at the base of the throat relax and consequently block the airway. In obese patients, weight loss can help reduce the obstruction, although normal-weight people also can have sleep apnea. Sleep apnea can lead to heart problems, so treatment is essential. A device called *Continuous Positive Airway Pressure (CPAP)* can assist a person's breathing during sleep; alternatively, surgery is sometimes recommended. In addition, recent research suggests that a complex interplay of heart rate, functioning of parts of the nervous system, and breathing may also influence sleep apnea: Men with heart problems and implanted pacemakers who also had sleep apnea found that their apnea symptoms improved when their pacemakers increased the number of heartbeats by 15 per minute (Garrigue et al., 2002). Researchers hypothesized that because sleep apnea disrupts sleep, it should also impair memory and other cognitive abilities. To test this hypothesis, they studied the effects that surgically removing the airway obstruction had on learning, memory, and decision making in 53 people who had this disorder. They administered tests of cognitive abilities before surgery and 6 months after surgery. Happily, surgery did lead to better learning, memory, and decision-making abilities. Moreover, the researchers found that the more effective the

**Sleep apnea:** A disorder characterized by a temporary cessation of breathing during sleep, usually preceded by a period of difficult breathing accompanied by loud snoring.

treatment was in eliminating the apnea, the larger the improvement in these abilities (Dahloef et al., 2002).

Those with undiagnosed sleep apnea may take barbiturates to get a good night's sleep—this is unfortunate because barbiturates seriously compound the problem by depressing the central nervous system, interfering with the normal reflex to begin breathing again.

# LOOKING AT LEVELS
## Recovery From Jet Lag

If you ever doubted that sleep, or its disruption, has an effect on consciousness, one good case of jet lag will convince you otherwise. *Jet lag* is that tired, grouchy, disoriented feeling you get after flying across different time zones. If you leave California on a 2:00 p.m. nonstop flight, after about 6 hours in the air (assuming the plane is on schedule) you will arrive in Boston, where it is about 11:00 p.m. local time—time for bed. But your body ignores the 3-hour difference between the Pacific and Eastern time zones and experiences the time as 8:00 p.m. You are nowhere near ready to go to sleep. And, come morning in Boston, your body will want to continue sleeping when the alarm says it is time to get up. Bodily changes, including altered hormonal and neurotransmitter activity, occur when your circadian rhythms are out of synch with the new time zone's physical and social cues. For example, your cortisol level, which usually decreases before bedtime, is still high, and even if you do manage to get to sleep at what your body considers an early hour, the high level of cortisol is likely to lead to shallow and fragmented sleep (Center for the Advancement of Health, 1998). It may take several days—or a bit longer—for your circadian rhythms to resynchronize entirely (Herxheimer & Waterhouse, 2003; Valdez et al., 2003).

How can you make a speedy recovery from jet lag? At the level of the brain, exposing yourself to light in the new time zone is thought to help reset the SCN in the hypothalamus, changing the levels of sleep- and wake-related hormones to suit the new time zone (Boivin & James, 2002b; Cassone et al., 1993). Taking melatonin at the proper dosage and times can also help shift circadian rhythms and alleviate jet lag (Herxheimer & Petrie, 2002; Takahashi et al., 2002).

At the level of the person, motivation affects how easily people can adjust to jet lag (Bloom & Lazerson, 1988; Lieberman, 2003); there are specific actions travelers can take to lessen jet lag (see Table 5.3), but these require effort and thus motivation. For instance, not everyone is willing to stay awake when tired (or wake up in the morning when the body feels as if it is the middle of the night). In addition, exercise or activity can help shift circadian rhythms (Van Cauter & Turek, 2000). At the level of the group, adjusting to the new time zone's environmental and social cues for meal times and bedtime, called *zeitgebers* (literally, "time givers" in German), facilitates the resetting of your biological clock (Van Cauter & Turek, 2000).

Events at the different levels interact. Suppose you have flown east all night, leaving New York at 8:00 p.m. and arriving in London

| TABLE 5.3 | Actions to Minimize Jet Lag: The Importance of Light |
| --- | --- |

After traveling westward:

- Stay awake during daylight hours.
- Sleep when the sun goes down.

After traveling eastward:

- Try to stay awake, but avoid bright light in the morning.
- In the afternoon, try to be outdoors as much as possible.

After traveling in *either* direction:

- Eat (moderately) during usual mealtimes.
- Exercise.

6 hours later (7:00 a.m., UK time); further, you are meeting an old friend as soon as you arrive (which is the middle of the night to your body). You may be reasonably motivated to stay awake so that you can enjoy your reunion over breakfast. But if no one is meeting you and you have no particular plans for the day, it may not seem worth the effort to ignore the activity of your neurotransmitters and hormones and try to stay awake.

## Test Yourself

1. As you descend into deep sleep, what happens to the pattern of your brain waves?
   a. The amplitudes stay constant, and the frequencies stay constant.
   b. The amplitudes increase (become higher), and frequencies decrease (become slower).
   c. The amplitudes decrease (become lower), and frequencies increase (become faster).
   d. The amplitudes increase while the frequencies stay constant.

2. Brain activity during REM sleep is unusual in that the
   a. brain becomes less active while the muscles become more active.
   b. brain waves continue to slow down while the mind becomes active.
   c. brain waves stay the same, but muscle activity increases.
   d. brain becomes more active while the muscles become less active.

3. In the activation-synthesis hypothesis, the activation is _____, and the synthesis is _____.
   a. the experience of the dream; the random bursts of nerve cell activity
   b. latent content; manifest content
   c. the random bursts of nerve cell activity; the experience of the dream
   d. manifest content; latent content

4. A difference between night terrors and nightmares is that
   a. night terrors occur during REM sleep and nightmares do not.
   b. nightmares occur during REM sleep and night terrors do not.
   c. night terrors are less vivid and frightening than nightmares.
   d. There are no differences between night terrors and nightmares.

## Answers

1.b 2.d 3.c 4.b

## Think It Through!

While trying to finish two papers, Antonio pulled two all-nighters in a row during finals week. It is the morning after the second sleepless night, and he has a final exam. What is his mental and physical state likely to be when he walks into the examination room? Which areas of functioning are likely to be impaired, and which are likely to remain undisturbed? What can you predict about the length and type of sleep Antonio will have when he finally sleeps?

# HYPNOSIS AND MEDITATION

When Alice fell down the rabbit hole, her descent seemed endless; she kept tumbling so long she thought she might be nearing the center of the earth. Although this feeling could have been a result of Stage 1 sleep at the beginning of Alice's nap, it's also somewhat similar to the sensations associated with one method of entering a hypnotic trance. In this technique, participants are asked to imagine gradually descending an elevator or staircase, becoming more deeply relaxed (and hypnotized) as they go lower and lower.

# What Is Hypnosis?

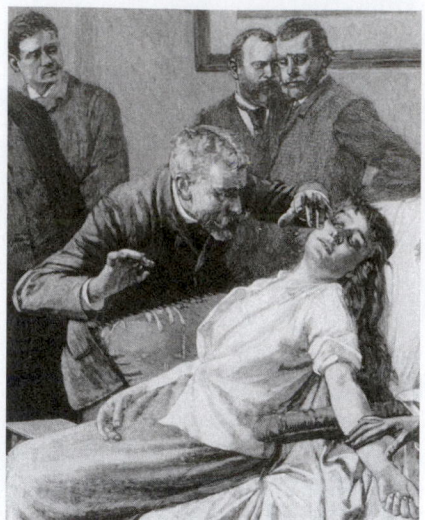

Franz Mesmer's technique of "manipulating bodily fluids" by repeatedly passing his hands near participants' skin successfully induced a hypnotic trance. Benjamin Franklin was part of a committee that used the scientific method to evaluate whether Mesmer's technique had the biological effect on patients that he claimed for it—that it unblocked electromagnetic forces in the body. The committee found Mesmer's theory to be unfounded.

When you think of hypnosis, you may imagine a stage hypnotist speaking in a soft monotone, instructing a volunteer from the audience to look at a shiny pocket watch as it swings back and forth. The volunteer's eyelids grow heavier and heavier; he feels sleepier and sleepier. . . . Then, presto, he is hypnotized. At the hypnotist's suggestion, he will happily strut like a chicken, lie rigid between two chairs, or do the hula. Hypnosis as theatrical entertainment is rare. In fact, those whom the savvy hypnotist picks from the audience are highly hypnotizable, unlike some 90% of the U.S. population (Hilgard, 1965).

Scientific interest in hypnosis began in earnest in the 18th century when Franz Mesmer claimed to be able to heal people by unblocking their bodies' flow of electromagnetism. Although his healing technique seemed effective, his theories about how it worked did not stand up to scientific inquiry (Winter, 1998). Scientists are still trying to understand exactly how hypnosis confers its effects. **Hypnosis** is characterized by a focused awareness on vivid, imagined experiences and a decreased awareness of the external environment. The state is brought on by **hypnotic induction**, a process in which the participant is encouraged to relax and focus his or her awareness in a particular way, often with closed eyes.

Once you enter a **trance state**, an altered state of consciousness in which your awareness of the external environment is diminished, the hypnotist suggests that you focus your attention or alter your perception or behavior in some particular way, as illustrated in Figure 5.7. There are at least two hallmarks of a trance state. One is **generalized reality orientation fading**, or, more simply, a tuning out of external reality. As this occurs, you have a heightened awareness of inner reality, your own imaginings and perceptions, and you experience this reality more vividly than in a daydream. Another hallmark of a trance state is the operation of **trance logic**, an uncritical acceptance of incongruous, illogical events, without being distracted by their impossibility. For instance, if you were instructed to imagine a place where you can feel safe and extremely relaxed, you might imagine a gazebo under a waterfall or a beach colony on the moon. This kind of image would come to you without your thinking twice about how such a place could exist or how safe it would really be.

Although these and other changes in awareness can occur because the hypnotist suggests them, they can also occur, with or without the hypnotist's suggestion, because of your expectations of the hypnotic situation (Kirsch & Lynn, 1999). People who expect their limbs to feel heavier during a trance have that experience, whereas people who don't expect their bodies to feel different do not, unless specifically directed to do so by the hypnotist. The hypnotist may also give you a **posthypnotic suggestion**, a suggestion for specific changes in perception, mood, or behavior that will occur *after* you leave the hypnotic state (see Figure 5.7, lower left). Consider a study on hypnotic alteration of perception (Raz; 2002): Half the participants were highly hypnotizable, and half were less hypnotizable. All participants were given the Stroop color naming task (see Chapter 4), both in the normal fashion and with a posthypnotic suggestion that the words themselves would appear meaningless, like characters in a foreign language. After the suggestion, highly hypnotizable participants were able to ignore the meaning of the word and name the color of the ink with which it was printed more quickly, and with fewer errors, than less hypnotizable participants. When there was no hypnotic suggestion, the speed of color naming by the two groups was similar.

People who are highly hypnotizable do not even have to be in the same room with the hypnotist to become hypnotized. A hypnotist on television once suggested to a vol-

**Hypnosis:** A state of mind characterized by a focused awareness on vivid, imagined experiences and decreased awareness of the external environment.

**Hypnotic induction:** The procedure used to attain a hypnotic trance state.

**Trance state:** A hypnotically induced altered state of consciousness in which awareness of the external environment is diminished.

**Generalized reality orientation fading:** A tuning out of external reality during hypnosis.

**Trance logic:** An uncritical acceptance of incongruous, illogical events during a hypnotic trance.

**Posthypnotic suggestion:** A suggestion regarding a change in perception, mood, or behavior that will occur *after* leaving the hypnotic state.

FIGURE 5.7

# Examples of Hypnotic Alterations in Perception, Mood, Memory, and Behavior

ALTERED PERCEPTION: The hypnotist says, "Imagine water splashing on your skin. Notice the sensation on your skin, the warmth of the water."

ALTERED MOOD: The hypnotist says, "While lying by the waterfall, you will feel very relaxed and peaceful."

ALTERED MEMORY: The hypnotist says, "You will still remember the experience of the fire, but the fear and anxiety about it will become less and less over time."

ALTERED BEHAVIOR: The hypnotist says, "Imagine magnets in the palms of your hands, pulling the hands toward each other."

unteer in the studio that the volunteer's arm would become numb; a highly hypnotizable TV viewer also became hypnotized. She lost feeling in her hand and did not come out of the trance state until she smelled the burning flesh of her own hand, which had been resting on the stove near an open flame (Kennedy, 1979).

# Individual Differences: Who Is Hypnotizable?

Some people are more hypnotizable than others (see Figure 5.8, p. 212), and some people are better at particular aspects of hypnosis than others. For example, some people can create extremely vivid visual images, whereas others are better at creating auditory, olfactory, or kinesthetic effects. Even those who are not very hypnotizable can go into a trance state if motivated strongly enough (Rossi & Cheek, 1988). In Western cultures, hypnotizability appears to peak before adolescence and decline during the middle adulthood years. In contrast, in non-Western cultures, the ability to go into a trance state is often valued and encouraged throughout the life span, and thus does not diminish (Ward, 1994).

FIGURE 5.8

## The Distribution of Hypnotizability

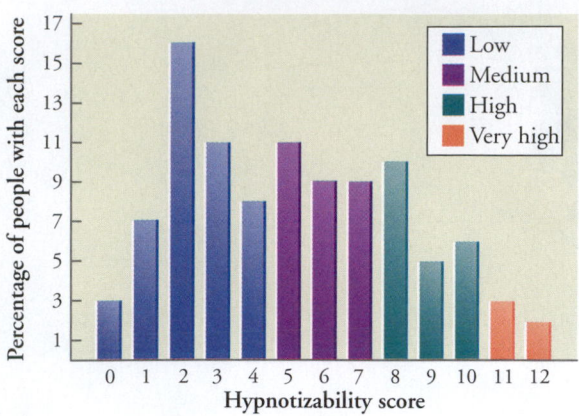

Not everyone is equally hypnotizable, and only a small percentage of people are *very* hypnotizable.

Hypnotizability is not highly correlated with biological indicators such as heart rate (Ray et al., 2000) or with personality characteristics, such as shyness, emotionality, or thrill seeking. **Absorption**, or the capacity to concentrate totally on material outside oneself, is moderately correlated with hypnotizability (Council et al., 1996; Kirsch & Council, 1992; Lichtenberg et al., 2004; Tellegen & Atkinson, 1974). Some people seem better able to lose their awareness of themselves than others; these people become deeply engrossed when watching a movie or reading a book. People who are highly hypnotizable also appear to be better able to sustain attention and filter out extraneous stimuli (Crawford, 1994; Lyons & Crawford, 1997; Woody & Bowers, 1994). In highly hypnotizable individuals, absorption may account for brief hypnotic experiences that can occur when driving on a highway for a long time or when watching a fire in a fireplace. Hypnosis also appears to be modestly related to *openness to experience*, a willingness to experience new things. People with posttraumatic stress disorder also appear to be more hypnotizable (Spiegel & Cardeña, 1991).

# Hypnosis: Role Play or Brain State?

Do people really enter an altered state of consciousness during a trance? Or, are they behaving the way they think people should behave when hypnotized? Psychologists have debated two major theories of how hypnosis works, and recent neuroimaging results help sort out these theories.

## Trance Theory

One view, trance theory, focuses on the cognitive changes that occur during a trance (Conn & Conn, 1967; Hilgard, 1992). According to **trance theory**, someone in a trance state due to hypnosis in fact experiences an altered state of consciousness, one characterized by increased susceptibility and responsiveness to suggestions. As a result, the person is dissociated, or separated, from his or her normal level of awareness (that is, consciousness). When, for instance, people are successfully hypnotized for relief of pain, while in the trance they report that they feel no pain. If, however, they are asked to write about their experience while in the trance, some people *do* report experiencing pain. This "inner" experience has been attributed to the **hidden observer**, a part of the self that experiences (and can record) what the entranced part of the self does not consciously experience (Hilgard, 1992; Hilgard et al., 1978).

## Sociocognitive Theory

Whereas trance theory suggests that hypnosis occurs because the trance state does in fact induce an altered state of consciousness, **sociocognitive theory** (Barber, 1969; Barber et al., 1974; Coe, 1978; Kirsch, 1999; Sarbin & Coe, 1972) focuses on the social context in which hypnosis takes place and the motivation to attend and respond to the suggestions of the hyponotist. In this view, the behavioral and experiential changes associated with a trance state result from the hypnotized person's expectations of that state rather than from a true trance. According to this view, the person in a trance enacts the role of a hypnotized person as he or she understands it, which leads to behaviors and experiences believed to be produced by hypnosis (Wagstaff, 1999). Thus, volunteers who are appropriately motivated can perform hypnotic feats even if they are not hypnotized.

**Absorption:** The capacity to concentrate totally on external material.

**Trance theory:** The view that a person in a trance experiences an altered, dissociated state of consciousness characterized by increasing susceptibility and responsiveness to suggestions.

**Hidden observer:** A part of the self that experiences (and can record) what the part of the self involved in a hypnotic trance does not consciously experience.

**Sociocognitive theory (of hypnosis):** The view that a person in a trance voluntarily enacts the role of a hypnotized person as he or she understands it, which leads to behaviors and experiences believed to be produced by hypnosis.

## Evidence From Neuroimaging

The sociocognitive theory stresses that hypnosis alters a person's performance (behavior), not necessarily his or her consciousness, and thus does not presume a special cognitive state with distinctive changes in brain activity. Such a distinct internal state would be more in keeping with trance theory. Thus, important information about the nature of hypnosis can come from studies of the brain.

Studies done in the 1980s that recorded electrical current on the scalp found that hypnosis does alter brain events (Barabasz & Lonsdale, 1983; Spiegel et al., 1985, 1989), and more recent PET studies indicate that hypnosis changes specific brain states (Baer et al., 1990; Crawford et al., 1993; Sabourin et al., 1990–1991). However, most of the neurological changes observed during a hypnotic trance can be explained as arising from the *actions*, either actual or imagined, that people perform in hypnosis. To isolate the source of neurological changes more precisely, Kosslyn and colleagues (2000) showed that when highly hypnotizable people in a trance are told to view a pattern in color, a brain area that processes color is activated even if the pattern shown to them is actually in shades of gray. Similarly, when these people are told to see a pattern as shades of gray, the color-processing area is deactivated, even if the pattern is brightly colored. Hypnosis not only turned on or off this color area in accordance with what a person was experiencing (even when the corresponding stimulus was not actually presented), but also overrode the actual perceptual input. Clearly, hypnosis is not simply role playing or motivated behavior; people cannot intentionally alter brain processing in these particular ways. However, research has yet to uncover biological changes that are specific to hypnosis that occur during all of the different types of tasks performed while in trance (Kallio & Revonsuo, 2003).

## Hypnosis as a Tool: Practical Applications

Hypnosis is much more than a stage trick; it has many therapeutic applications, including the treatment of anxiety, compulsive habit behaviors (such as smoking or hair pulling), certain medical conditions (such as asthma and warts), and stress-related problems (such as high blood pressure). Hypnosis has even been used to treat a particular complication during pregnancy. A study examined the use of hypnosis with 100 women pregnant with babies in the breech (feet first) position. One group was hypnotized and given the suggestion to relax bodily tensions and let nature take its course; another group did not receive hypnosis. The babies of 81% of the hypnotized women changed position to head first, compared with only 48% of the control group (Mehl, 1994).

Before the widespread availability of chemical anesthetics, hypnosis was used for the relief of pain (Winter, 1998). Pain can be controlled by top-down processing that directly inhibits the interneurons that regulate the input of pain signals to the brain (see Chapter 4; De Benedittis, 2003); hypnosis is a particularly good way to affect this processing. During surgical procedures, patients who received hypnosis-induced relaxation and analgesia for pain reported experiencing less pain and needed less pain medication during the surgery, and the surgery was completed sooner, compared to those receiving empathic attention or no special treatment (Lang et al., 2000). Under hypnosis, a surgical patient might be led to experience an icy-cold numbness in the area where an incision will be made (Rossi & Cheek, 1988). Another use of hypnosis is to create imagined *analgesia*, or insensitivity to pain (Hilgard & Hilgard, 1994). For instance, one method used to treat headaches calls for the person in a trance first to create **glove anesthesia** (Barber & Adrian, 1982)—that is, to

**Glove anesthesia:** Hypnotically induced lack of feeling in the hand.

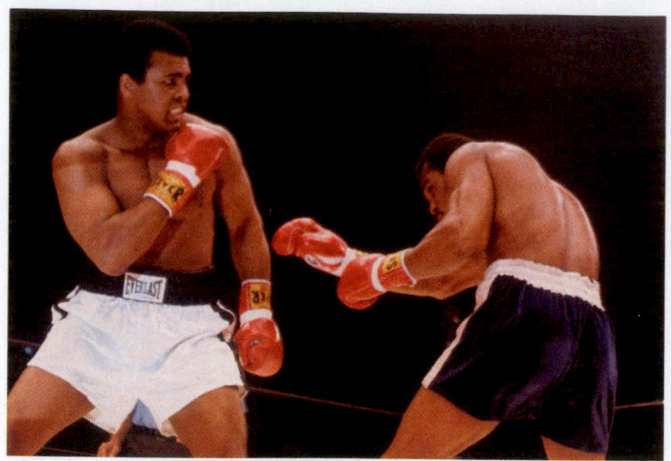

As part of his boxing training, Ken Norton used hypnosis before his match against Muhammed Ali (Spiegel, 1999). During that match, he broke Ali's jaw. Can hypnosis help athletes perform feats they would otherwise be unable to accomplish? No, but it can help them feel less anxious and free of distractions during competition, and it can help alleviate pain.

anesthetize the hand through hypnotic suggestion. Once this is accomplished, the patient touches the painful part of the head with the anesthetized hand, transferring, by suggestion, the anesthetic effect to the head.

Hypnosis is also used to induce relaxation before surgery, to lessen pain, and to speed healing (Forgione, 1988; Ginandes et al., 2003; Harandi et al., 2004; Lang et al., 2000); presurgical hypnosis also alleviates tension and the fear of pain, both of which can worsen the *experience* of pain. Thus, in addition to altering the sensation of pain itself, hypnosis can reduce pain by changing the way the sensation of pain is interpreted (Feldman, 2004). Hypnosis is used for pain control in many circumstances today—in the dentist's chair, the operating room, during childbirth, and at home and work (Chaves, 1989; Hilgard & Hilgard, 1994; Mehl-Madrona, 2004).

Many athletes work with a hypnosis consultant to enhance performance through hypnotic and posthypnotic suggestions. Will a basketball player make more baskets or block more shots because of a hypnotic suggestion? Research findings reveal that hypnosis does not improve athletic performance directly but that it can help decrease anxiety, and thereby increase the athlete's focus; hypnosis also provides an opportunity for mental practice of athletic skills, a known benefit (Druckman & Bjork, 1994).

## Hypnosis as Possession Trance

Hypnosis appears in different guises in different cultures. In a study by Bourguignon (1973), for example, people in over half of the 488 societies surveyed practiced possession trance. In this form of hypnosis, the body of the person in a trance is said to be "taken over" by a spirit. On emerging from the possession trance, the person may be unable to recall the experience. However, after experiencing a trance, people report feelings of well-being and rejuvenation, along with a decrease in distressing physical or psychological symptoms (Ward, 1994).

In societies in which possession trance is practiced, trance behaviors are learned and are governed by implicit cultural rules. In the Comoros, off Madagascar, for instance, a wife is normally subservient to her husband. She may be regularly possessed by a male spirit, however, who speaks "man to man" with her husband about her. This spirit dispenses advice and information that the wife would not otherwise be able to share because of the tightly defined cultural roles that constrain marital behavior (Boddy, 1992).

Research may be able to throw light on the question of whether possession trance differs from simply pretending to be possessed. Researchers were able to discover a biological hallmark of such trance: Those in a possession trance had higher levels of noradrenaline and endorphins in their blood than did control participants who performed the same movements but were not in the trance state (Kawai et al., 2001).

## Meditation

In the last pages of *Alice's Adventures in Wonderland*, after Alice awakens from her dream and goes home for her tea, her sister remains behind under the tree. As she watches the setting sun and thinks about Alice's adventures, she too begins to dream, after a fashion, of the characters in Wonderland:

So she sat on, with closed eyes, and half believed herself in Wonderland, though she knew she had but to open them again, and all would change to dull reality—the grass would be only rustling in the wind, and the pool rippling to the waving of the reeds—the rattling teacups would change to tinkling sheep-bells, and the Queen's shrill cries to the voice of the shepherd boy—and the sneeze of the baby, the shriek of the Gryphon, and all the other queer noises, would change (she knew) to the confused clamor of the busy farm-yard—while the lowing of the cattle in the distance would take the place of the Mock Turtle's heavy sobs. (Carroll, 1992, pp. 98–99)

Might Alice's sister be in a meditative state—or simply a relaxed state of mind?

## Types of Meditation

**Meditation** is an altered state of consciousness characterized by a sense of deep relaxation and *loss* of self-awareness, in contrast to hypnosis, which is characterized by on-going self-awareness. Nevertheless, meditation and hypnosis do share similar elements. Both forms of altered consciousness involve increased, focused awareness of a particular stimulus. In hypnosis, this stimulus may be the hypnotist's voice. In meditation, the stimulus can be an object in the environment (such as a flower or a geometric pattern called a *mandala*), a rhythmic physical motion of the body (such as breathing), or a *mantra* (a chant or phrase that the meditator repeats). Whereas the person in a hypnotic trance often uses focused attention imaginatively and creatively, the meditator focuses attention on a single stimulus during the meditation period with the goal of clearing his or her awareness of other thoughts and sensations. Meditators sometimes experience a "relaxed, blissful, and wakeful state" (Jevning et al., 1992, p. 415).

A mandala is a complex circular geometric design used to facilitate meditation.

Prayer can be a form of meditation, as seen in the Buddhist and Hindu traditions. Other religions also incorporate meditative elements. For instance, Christians might focus attention on the cross, a verse of Scripture, or a mental image of Christ in a meditative manner. Rosary beads can be thought of as a meditative aid, helping to maintain the focus on prayer. In Judaism, the Torah may serve as the object of meditation, and many Orthodox Jews sway rhythmically while praying.

There are a number of other forms of meditation (Ornstein, 1986), all of which involve focused attention on an unchanging or repetitive stimulus. If you wanted to explore **concentrative meditation**, you would try to concentrate on one stimulus alone, disregarding everything else around you. Yoga and transcendental meditation (TM) are examples of this type of meditation. In **opening-up meditation**, a more advanced form of concentrative attention, you would focus narrowly on a stimulus and then try to broaden your focus to encompass your entire surroundings, almost as if you were merging with your environment. Both types of meditation bring about an altered sense of awareness or consciousness. **Mindfulness meditation** (also known as *awareness meditation*) often involves a combination of the concentrative and opening-up forms (Smith, 2004). Using this technique, you would try to maintain a "floating" state of consciousness, one that allows you to focus on whatever is most prominent at the moment. Whatever comes into your awareness—a physical sensation, sound, or thought—is what you focus on in a meditative way, fully aware of the stimulus but not judging it. In this way, everything around you can become part of your meditation.

For a sense of what a beginning meditator may experience, try the following exercise: Set a timer or alarm clock for 5 minutes and focus your attention on the word *one*. Close your eyes and try to clear your mind of distracting thoughts, sounds, smells, and sensations in your body; just focus on *one*. At the end of the 5 minutes, you may find that you have experienced a type of concentrative meditation. Another way to induce a meditative experience is to look at and focus on a crack in the ceiling or some other spot or object, even the photograph of the mandala. As you do,

**Meditation:** An altered state of consciousness characterized by a sense of deep relaxation and loss of self-awareness.

**Concentrative meditation:** A form of meditation in which the meditator restricts attention and concentrates on one stimulus while disregarding everything else.

**Opening-up meditation:** A form of meditation in which the meditator focuses on a stimulus but also broadens that focus to encompass the whole of his or her surroundings.

**Mindfulness meditation:** A combination of concentrative and opening-up meditation in which the meditator focuses on whatever is most prominent at the moment; also known as *awareness meditation*.

try to maintain your focus on the object, letting distracting thoughts or sensations pass, and continually refocusing on your awareness of the crack or other stimulus. These suggested exercises may show you why meditation can be challenging for beginners; many people find themselves distracted by other thoughts or sensations and find it difficult to maintain their focus on the chosen stimulus. With practice, however, this type of focused attention becomes easier, and increasingly the meditator experiences the positive benefits of meditation.

## Benefits of Meditation

What are the benefits of meditation? Studies suggest that regular meditation can affect a wide variety of psychological and medical symptoms; it can:

- reduce tension and anxiety (Carrington, 1977; Gross et al., 2004; Grossman et al., 2004);
- decrease levels of stress (MacLean et al., 1997) and of excessive preoccupation with a given topic (Ramel et al., 2004);
- lower anxiety in patients preparing for surgery (Domar et al., 1987);
- decrease cardiac measures such as blood pressure (Barnes et al., 2001);
- facilitate treatment for the skin condition psoriasis (Kabat-Zinn et al., 1998); and
- increase the body's ability to fight infection (Davidson et al., 2003).

## Meditation and the Body: More Than a Pause That Refreshes

One of the documented benefits of meditation is that it quickly induces a state of deep restfulness. By meditating for only 20–30 minutes, a meditator can decrease his or her oxygen consumption to a level usually achieved only after 6–7 hours of sleep (Wallace et al., 1971); meditation also decreases heart and respiration rates (Allison, 1970; Solberg, Ekeberg, et al., 2004; Wallace, 1970). A meta-analysis of studies comparing regular meditators with non-meditators revealed lower levels of respiration, heart rate, and other biological measures in those who meditated (Dillbeck & Orme-Johnson, 1987). But recall from Chapter 2 that correlation does not imply causation. The two groups may have differed in other ways. Why might some people begin to meditate, and others not? Why might some who began meditation stick with it, and others not?

## Meditation Versus Relaxation

Can you achieve the benefits of meditation simply by relaxing? Research has yielded contradictory findings. Relaxation training uses a number of techniques to alleviate muscle and emotional tension and bring about a relaxed physical and mental state. Some researchers have found that the benefits of meditation can be obtained through relaxation training or even simply by resting (D. S. Holmes, 1984). Moreover, other researchers (Morse et al., 1977; Shapiro, 1982) have found no differences in skin conductance (which increases with anxiety-produced sweat), pulse, or respiration among meditators, those using self-hypnosis for relaxation, and those using a muscle relaxation technique. But another study, which examined the differences between meditation and relaxation training in college students, found that meditation was more effective than relaxation training in achieving a "sense of relaxation" (Janowiak, 1994). Other studies, some of them done by researchers at the Maharishi School of Management (Alexander et al., 1994a, 1994b), found that transcendental meditation was more effective than relaxation or other forms of meditation in reducing arousal. In sum, many, though not all, studies have shown that meditation alters heart rate, respiration rate, and arousal more effectively than does relaxation training. Studies have also shown that, compared with other forms of relaxation, meditation appears to provide an enhanced experience of relaxation.

## The Biology of Meditation

EEG recordings taken during a meditative state sometimes resemble those taken during sleep, with shifts between different levels of brain activity (Pagano et al., 1976). In fact, deep relaxation appears to occur during at least some phases of meditation, but such relaxation differs both from resting with closed eyes and from the hypnotic state (Jevning et al., 1992; Wallace, 1970; Wallace et al., 1971). In spite of superficial commonalities with sleep and hypnosis, meditation is widely considered to be a distinct state of consciousness, although not all researchers agree with this view (Pagano et al., 1976).

Meditation has been documented to affect the meditator's biology in various ways. For example, one study found that after 3 months of meditating, participants had higher levels of melatonin (the sleep-related hormone that affects circadian rhythms, discussed earlier) in their blood (Harinath et al., 2004); although the exact nature of the relationship between melatonin and meditation has yet to be revealed, similar findings were reported in another study (Solberg, Holen, et al., 2004).

Other researchers found that the neurons in the brains of long-term meditators tend to fire in synchrony, even during the normal waking state, but especially so during meditation (Davidson et al., 2003). However, these researchers found such synchrony at very high frequencies of neural firing, whereas other researchers found that meditation induces synchronized neural activity at much lower frequencies (Hebert & Tan, 2004). The difference in results may hinge on the type of meditation the participants were practicing. In the first case, the meditators strove to achieve a state of "unconditional loving-kindness," described as "unrestricted readiness and availability to help living beings" (Lutz et al., 2004, p. 16369). In contrast, in the second study, the meditators repeated a meaningless mantra (sound) to themselves and focused their attention on it. Why would such a difference affect the brain? This is cutting-edge research, and researchers have yet to discover how meditation affects the brain in specific ways, or why different forms of meditation might have different effects.

## Test Yourself

1. Which of the following statements about hypnosis is true?
   a. The majority of people are very hypnotizable.
   b. People with a tendency toward high absorption are not very hypnotizable.
   c. People with posttraumatic stress disorder appear to be more hypnotizable.
   d. People with low heart rates are easier to hypnotize.
2. Evidence from neuroimaging studies has shown that hypnosis
   a. can change certain brain areas not normally under conscious control.
   b. is really no more than active role playing.
   c. results in higher motivation for hypnotized individuals.
   d. is not directly related to brain functioning.
3. It is likely that the altered state of consciousness known as possession trance
   a. has little or no effect on the brain.
   b. increases blood levels of noradrenaline and endorphins.
   c. is faked or acted out for cultural purposes only.
   d. is not actually a state of consciousness.
4. Concentrative meditation is to opening-up meditation as
   a. expanding is to focusing.
   c. active is to passive.
   b. focusing is to expanding.
   d. passive is to active.

## Answers

1.c 2.a 3.b 4.b

# Think It Through!

Anna disliked her smoking habit and had been trying to quit for a year. Because her own efforts had failed, she decided to see a hypnotist. Can she be certain that the hypnotist will be able to hypnotize her successfully? How might the hypnotist use hypnosis to help her quit? If hypnosis helps her to quit smoking, how might the sociocognitive theory account for Anna's experience? If Anna smoked when she was stressed, might meditation help her stop smoking? Explain.

# DRUGS AND ALCOHOL

Midway through Alice's adventures in Wonderland, she shrinks to a height of about 3 inches and longs to be taller. She meets a talking caterpillar, who suggests that she eat some of a nearby mushroom, remarking that one side of the mushroom would make her larger, the other side smaller.

> "And now which is which?" she said to herself, and nibbled a little of the right-hand bit to try the effect. The next moment she felt a violent blow underneath her chin: it had struck her foot!
>
> She was a good deal frightened by this very sudden change, but she felt that there was no time to be lost, as she was shrinking rapidly; so she set to work at once to eat some of the other bit. Her chin was pressed so closely against her foot, that there was hardly room to open her mouth; but she did it at last, and managed to swallow a morsel of the left-hand bit.
>
> "Come, my head's free at last!" said Alice in a tone of delight, which changed into alarm in another moment, when she found that her shoulders were nowhere to be found: all she could see, when she looked down, was an immense length of neck, which seemed to rise like a stalk out of a sea of green leaves that lay far below her. (Carroll, 1992, pp. 41–42)

Many of the odd things that happen to Alice on her travels in Wonderland occur after she has eaten or drunk something. In addition to the results of nibbling that famous mushroom, she drank from a bottle labeled "DRINK ME" and shrank; she ate cakes labeled "EAT ME" and grew. Could changes such as those experienced by Alice be produced by the use of stimulants, depressants, or other chemical substances?

Although neither drugs nor alcohol can actually cause our bodies to change shape the way Alice's did, they can alter our perceptions, mood, thoughts, and behavior. So far, we've discussed natural ways of altering consciousness such as hypnosis and meditation, methods that rely solely on the abilities that reside within a person. But it's also possible to alter consciousness through external means, with the use of various psychoactive substances. These substances, which can be ingested, injected, or inhaled, affect the user's thoughts, feelings, and behaviors. Some substances—marijuana, tobacco, cocaine, and alcohol, certain types of mushrooms, and caffeine—can be found in nature and have long been used to alter consciousness, often in the context of religious ceremonies (Bourguignon, 1973). More recently, synthetically produced substances such as amphetamines, LSD, PCP, and barbiturates have also been used as consciousness-altering agents.

## Substance Use and Abuse

A woman drinks heavily, but only over the weekend, and she never misses work because of it. Is she an alcoholic? How about the man who smokes marijuana at the end of the day to feel relaxed, or the student who downs four cups of caffeinated coffee each evening while studying? Have these people crossed some biological or psychological

---

**TABLE 5.4**

## The Seven Symptoms of Substance Dependence

1. Tolerance.

2. Withdrawal.

3. Larger amounts of substance taken over a longer period of time than intended.

4. Unsuccessful efforts or a persistent desire to decrease or control the substance use.

5. Much time spent in obtaining the substance, using it, or recovering from its effects.

6. Important work, social, or recreational activities given up as a result of the substance.

7. Despite knowledge of recurrent or ongoing physical or psychological problems caused or exacerbated by the substance, continued use of substance.

line between use and abuse? The American Psychiatric Association (2000) has developed three main criteria for **substance abuse**:

1. a pattern of substance use that leads to significant distress or difficulty functioning in major areas of life (for instance, at home, work, or school, or in relationships);

2. substance use that occurs in dangerous situations (for instance, while or before driving a car); or

3. substance use that leads to legal difficulties.

**Substance dependence** results from chronic abuse. It is characterized by seven symptoms (see Table 5.4), the two most important of which are tolerance and withdrawal (American Psychiatric Association, 2000). **Tolerance** is the condition, resulting from repeated use, in which the same amount of a substance produces a diminished effect (thus, more of the substance is required to achieve the same effect). Tolerance typically occurs with the use of alcohol, barbiturates, amphetamines, and opiates such as morphine and heroin. *Withdrawal* is the cessation of the use of a substance; **withdrawal symptoms** are the uncomfortable or life-threatening effects that may be experienced during withdrawal. Substance abuse presents costs to society as a whole as well as to the individual: In the United States the costs related to crime, drug treatment, medical care, social welfare programs, and time lost from work total an estimated $67 billion per year (National Institute on Drug Abuse, 2003).

The various types of psychoactive drugs and their key properties are listed in Table 5.5.

**Substance abuse:** Drug or alcohol use that causes distress or trouble with functioning in major areas of life, occurs in dangerous situations, or leads to legal difficulties.

**Substance dependence:** Chronic substance abuse that is characterized by seven symptoms, the two most important being tolerance and withdrawal.

**Tolerance:** The condition of requiring more of a substance to achieve the same effect (because the usual amount provides a diminished response).

**Withdrawal symptoms:** The onset of uncomfortable or life-threatening effects when the use of a substance is stopped.

| TABLE 5.5 | **Psychoactive Substances: Their Biological Actions and Effects** | | | |
|---|---|---|---|---|
| **Type of Drug** | **Example** | **Biological Action** | **Main Effects** | **Tolerance/ Withdrawal Symptoms** |
| Depressants | Alcohol Barbiturates | Depress the central nervous system. | Decrease behavioral activity, anxiety, and awareness; impair cognition and judgment. | Yes / Yes |
| Stimulants | Amphetamines Cocaine MDMA | Stimulate the central nervous system. | Increase behavioral activity and arousal; create a perception of heightened physical and mental abilities. | Yes / Yes |
| Narcotic analgesics | Heroin | Depresses the central nervous system. | Dulls pain and creates an experience of euphoria and relaxation; with chronic use, the body stops producing endorphins. | Yes / Yes |
| Hallucinogens | LSD | Alters serotonergic functioning. | Hallucinations and perceptual alterations; the user's expectations shape the drug experience. | Yes / No |
| | Marijuana | Affects neurons in the hippocampus involved in learning, memory, and integrating sensory experiences. | | For heavy users only: Yes / Yes |

# Depressants: Focus on Alcohol

The **depressants**, also called *sedative-hypnotic drugs*, include barbiturates, alcohol, and antianxiety drugs such as Valium. Drugs in this category depress the central nervous system and thus tend to slow a person down, decreasing the user's behavioral activity and level of awareness. Because of its prevalence and the fact that so much is known about its effects, we focus at length on alcohol in the section.

Approximately 60% of adults in the United States reported that they drank alcohol within the previous year (Centers for Disease Control and Prevention, 2003); 8% of adults in the United States (17 million people) are considered to have either alcohol abuse or dependence (Grant et al., 2004). The younger people are when they start drinking, the more likely they are to develop an alcohol disorder (Grant & Dawson, 1997). *Binge drinking*, defined as four or more drinks per episode, occurs on some college campuses, in some states more than others. College students in California are less likely to be binge drinkers than their counterparts across the nation, perhaps because California students are older on average and more likely to be married (Wechsler et al., 1997), and thus presumably more mature. Men are more likely than women to be binge drinkers (Centers for Disease Control and Prevention, 2003; Schulenberg et al., 1996); women at women's colleges tend to binge drink less than do their female counterparts at coeducational colleges (Dowdall et al., 1998). Binge drinking is likely to occur in contexts in which the object is to get drunk (Schulenberg et al., 1996). People who engage in binge drinking are also at risk for other alcohol-related behaviors, such as driving while their functioning is impaired (Wechsler et al., 1998) or having unprotected sexual intercourse or more sexual activity than planned (Center for Addiction and Substance Abuse at Columbia University, 2002).

## Biological Effects of Alcohol

Alcohol is classified as a depressant because it depresses the nervous system through its inhibiting effect on excitatory neurotransmitters. Alcohol changes the structure of the neuron's cell membrane, altering neural transmission (Goldstein, 1994; Grilly, 1994). But depressants such as alcohol can also inhibit the action of inhibitory neurons, so some neurons fire that otherwise would be inhibited. Thus, in addition to depressing some neural activity, depressants also activate neurons that otherwise would not fire. This phenomenon is called **disinhibition**.

Although it takes about an hour for alcohol to be fully absorbed into the blood (as measured by blood alcohol levels), drinkers can feel an effect within a few minutes. The effects of alcohol depend on the dosage. At low doses, alcohol can cause a sense of decreased awareness and increased relaxation, and the drinker may become talkative or outgoing. At moderate doses, the drinker experiences slowed reaction time and impaired judgment—which is why drinking and driving shouldn't mix. Unfortunately, drinking and driving do sometimes mix. For example, one study that assessed the rates of drinking and driving in 27 countries found that the United States ranked the highest; among college students in the United States, 43% of men and 28% of women reported that in the previous year they had driven after drinking too much (Steptoe et al., 2004).

At higher doses, alcohol impairs cognition, self-control, and self-restraint, and the drinker may become emotionally unstable or overly aggressive. "Barroom brawls" often occur because a drunk patron misconstrues a casual remark that otherwise might have passed unnoticed. As the effects of the alcohol take hold, the drinker's responses are more likely to be out of proportion to the situation. At very high doses, the drinker can have a diminished sense of cold, pain, and discomfort (which is why some people drink

People's expectations of what will happen to them as a result of drinking alcohol can affect their behavior (Kirsch & Lynn, 1999).

**Depressants:** A class of substances, including barbiturates, alcohol, and antianxiety drugs, that depress the central nervous system, decreasing the user's behavioral activity and level of awareness; also called *sedative-hypnotic drugs*.

**Disinhibition:** The inhibition of inhibitory neurons, which makes other neurons (the ones that are usually inhibited) more likely to fire and which usually occurs as a result of depressant use.

when in pain). At these high doses, alcohol causes dilation of the peripheral blood vessels, which increases the amount of blood circulating through the skin and makes the drinker both feel warmer and lose heat faster. Thus, heavy drinking in the cold increases the chance of hypothermia (that is, decreased body temperature) and frostbite. Such high doses can bring on respiratory arrest, coma, or death.

## Psychological Effects of Alcohol

Knowing that mental processes arise from brain function, you won't be surprised to know that the biological effects of alcohol disrupt cognition, emotion and behavior. Such disruptions impair the abilities to think abstractly, conceptualize information, notice situational cues, and interpret ambiguous social situations. More complex effects include *inhibitory conflict*—difficulty inhibiting a behavior that would normally not be expressed when sober—and increased aggression.

**INHIBITORY CONFLICT**   Steele and Southwick (1985) conducted a meta-analysis of the effects of alcohol on social behavior, specifically in "high-conflict" and "low-conflict" situations. The type of conflict considered here is within the person, between two opposing desires. Specifically, Steele and Southwick wanted to see whether the use of alcohol changes the way people behave when they experience such internal conflict. They found a pattern of what they called **inhibitory conflict**: If a person in a high-conflict situation was sober, his or her response was "both strongly instigated and inhibited"; that is, the person would both want to act and not want to act. A person might very much want to engage in a particular behavior, but the consequences (moral, legal, social, or personal) were great enough to inhibit it. After drinking enough alcohol, however, the same person would not restrain his or her behavior. And the more alcohol consumed, the greater the likelihood of engaging in the behavior despite societal or other sanctions. When the conflict level was low, it was still possible to inhibit the behavior; only in high-conflict situations was inhibition overcome by alcohol. This finding explains how date rape can happen: When sober, a man might want to have sexual relations but be inhibited from using force. But under the influence of alcohol, he might be more likely to act—in a high-conflict, sexually charged situation, he might have difficulty attending to the consequences that would otherwise cause him to inhibit such aggressive behavior.

Steele and his colleagues also looked at the effect of alcohol on conflict in helping situations (Steele et al., 1985). After doing tedious and boring paperwork for 30 minutes, participants in the study were asked whether they would agree to do more of the same, without additional pay, while waiting for the investigator to arrange for their payment. Some participants were given an alcoholic drink before the request for additional help, and some were given water. Some participants received more pressure to help (high-conflict), and some were asked simply if they would mind helping but were not pressured by personal appeal (low-conflict). In the low-conflict situation, alcohol had no effect, and participants were able to inhibit themselves from continuing the boring task. In the high-conflict situation, alcohol affected participants' ability to inhibit their response, and they were more likely to agree to help. This result is consistent with the earlier findings: Alcohol made it more difficult for participants to inhibit their responses in the high-conflict situation. This set of findings may explain why, after drinking some alcohol, people might have a harder time saying no to a sexual proposition in high-conflict circumstances, such as the conflict between the desire for sexual intimacy and the simultaneous wish (for either moral or personal reasons) to delay a sexual encounter. One solution is to abstain from alcohol if a high-conflict situation is likely to occur.

**Inhibitory conflict:** An internal response when a behavior is both strongly instigated and inhibited.

Alcohol myopia can make a drinker incorrectly interpret someone else's clenched fist as a threatening aggressive act, rather than as an indicator of that person's nervousness or anxiety.

**Alcohol myopia:** The disproportionate influence of immediate experience on behavior and emotion due to the effects of alcohol use.

**ALCOHOL MYOPIA** The results of many studies have shown that the use of alcohol facilitates aggressive behavior (Bushman & Cooper, 1990). You have already seen one path for increased aggression with alcohol use: Alcohol can make it difficult to inhibit behavior in a high-conflict situation. Aggression can also result from misreading a situation, as in the barroom brawl example. Alcohol impairs the ability to abstract and conceptualize information (Pihl et al., 2003; Tarter et al., 1971) and to notice many situational cues (Washburne, 1956). This impairment results in **alcohol myopia**, "a state of shortsightedness in which superficially understood, immediate aspects of experience have a disproportionate influence on behavior and emotion" (Steele & Josephs, 1990, p. 923). Thus, stimuli that elicit aggression (such as someone's clenched fists or a date's refusal to have sexual intercourse) loom larger than stimuli that must be abstracted or require more thought (such as considerations that the aggressive behavior may be immoral, illegal, or unnecessary). Drinking also makes it more difficult to process ambiguous social situations, such as occasions when someone's words and body language are contradictory. For example, suppose friends have gone out drinking and all are now quite drunk. One of them might announce that he is sick, but laugh about it. The others might not understand that their friend really *is* sick and needs medical care.

**ALCOHOL AND SEXUAL AGGRESSION** Noting the fact that more than 50% of on-campus date rapes occur when men are under the influence of alcohol (Muehlenhard & Linton, 1987; Ouimette, 1997), Johnson and colleagues (2000) set out to determine ex-

---

**FIGURE 5.9**  **Alcohol and Sexual Aggression**

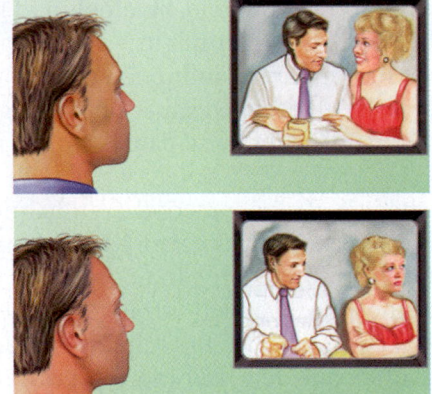

Male participants were assigned to one of four alcohol consumption groups: moderate alcohol intake, low alcohol intake, placebo alcohol intake (alcohol rubbed on the rim of glasses holding nonalcoholic drinks), and control group (drank ice water). The three alcohol groups did not know the strength of their drinks.

Half of each group of men watched a video about a blind date in which the woman was very friendly; the other half of each group watched a video about a blind date in which the woman was unresponsive and cold.

*Regardless of alcohol intake*, the participants who watched the unresponsive date were not very accepting of the idea of sexual aggression by the man, and attributed any responsibility for aggression to *him*. In contrast, there was clear alcohol myopia in those who watched the friendly date: The more alcohol they drank, the more the men accepted the idea of sexual aggression toward the woman, and the more they attributed any aggression by the man as being the *woman's* responsibility (Johnson et al., 2000).

actly how drinking might be involved. They asked male volunteers to drink different levels of alcohol, then watch one of two videos of a woman on a blind date. In one video, she exhibited friendly, cordial behavior; in the other, she was unresponsive. The men were then asked how acceptable it would be for a man to be sexually aggressive toward his date (see Figure 5.9). Among the men who viewed the video with the unresponsive woman, alcohol intake made no difference in the men's answers. However, alcohol intake did make a difference for the men who viewed the video of the friendly woman: Those men who had more to drink thought that sexual aggression toward a friendly date was acceptable. The alcohol impaired the men's ability to understand that the friendliness the woman showed did not mean that it was acceptable for a man to force her to have sex. To reason about this social situation appropriately, a person needs to be able conceptualize and engage in abstract thinking—and such functions are compromised by drinking alcohol.

Another study found that college women were more likely to be victimized when drinking, compared to when they had not been drinking (Parks & Fals-Stewart, 2004); other studies support this finding, with some college men indicating that they try to get women drunk in order to have sex with them (Carr & VanDeusen, 2004). The effects of drinking may cut two ways in dating situations: Not only does alcohol make the man more inclined to force himself on his date, but the woman may not be able to pick up the early warning signs, to understand the initial indicators of her date's unwelcome inclinations. Table 5.6 provides a summary of the psychological effects of alcohol.

## Chronic Abuse: More Than a Bad Habit

Alcoholics come from all socioeconomic classes. Historically, more males than females have become alcoholics, and this pattern continues today, although the gap is narrowing (C. B. Nelson et al., 1998). Almost all cultures recognize that drinking can create both tolerance and withdrawal symptoms, although problematic alcohol use is defined differently in different cultures (Gureje et al., 1997). Chronic alcohol abuse can cause severe memory deficits, even **blackouts**, periods of time for which the alcoholic has no memory of events that occurred while he or she was intoxicated. The chronic alcoholic often experiences difficulty with abstract reasoning, problem solving, and perceptual motor functions. It has been difficult for researchers to sort out to what degree these memory deficits are caused by the action of the alcohol itself or by the malnutrition that often accompanies alcoholism. Alcohol is highly caloric but contains very little in the way of nutrients; consequently, many heavy drinkers are inadequately nourished.

What does a hangover indicate? That the body is experiencing alcohol withdrawal (Cicero, 1978). This explains why drinking more alcohol will make hangover symptoms recede: After taking in large quantities of alcohol, your body needs more of it; otherwise, uncomfortable symptoms develop. Withdrawal symptoms for a heavy drinker include weakness, tremor, anxiety, and increased blood pressure, pulse rate, and respiration rate. Extremely heavy drinkers can experience convulsions and delirium tremens (the DTs), irritability, headaches, fever, agitation, confusion, and visual hallucinations; these typically begin within 4 days of stopping drinking (Romach & Sellers, 1991).

**TABLE 5.6**

## Summary of the Psychological Effects of Alcohol

Alcohol use can lead to:

- Difficulties in abstract thinking

- Impaired ability to conceptualize information

- Problems noticing situational cues

- Poor processing of ambiguous social situations

- Inhibitory conflict

- Alcohol myopia

- Increased aggression

Different cultures have different social norms about what constitutes appropriate and inappropriate drinking. Moreover, in many cultures, people do not drink to "get drunk" but drink as part of sharing a meal and talking together.

Blackout: A period of time for which an alcoholic has no memory of events that transpired while he or she was intoxicated.

If you drink alcohol, answer these questions to see whether your drinking is problematic:

- Do you have a hangover the morning after drinking?
- Do you need to drink more now than you did 6 months ago to get the same feeling?
- Have you tried unsuccessfully to cut back on your alcohol intake?
- Have you ever had an accident during or after drinking?
- Do you spend a fair amount of money on alcohol?
- Have you missed work, class, or social obligations because of drinking or its after-effects?
- Do you find yourself thinking about drinking or counting the time until it's a "decent hour" to have a drink?
- Have you had blackouts while drunk?

If you answered yes to any of these questions (particularly the first two, concerning tolerance and withdrawal), then you may have a problem with alcohol. You should seek more information from your doctor, a counselor, or Alcoholics Anonymous.

## Other Depressants

Barbiturates, including Amytal, Nembutal, and Seconal, mimic the effects of alcohol in that they depress the central nervous system. Barbiturates cause sedation and drowsiness and are therefore usually prescribed to aid sleep or to reduce anxiety, but they can be lethal when combined with alcohol. In higher doses, barbiturates cause slurred speech, dizziness, poor judgment, and irritability. Users will develop both tolerance and withdrawal symptoms: Withdrawal may be accompanied by agitation and restlessness, hallucinations, and delirium tremens. Sedation and drowsiness are also effects of benzodiazepines (such as Ativan, Xanax, and Valium, sometimes prescribed because they can reduce symptoms of anxiety). Because benzodiazepines are less habit-forming than barbiturates, the former are more frequently prescribed for sleep problems. (Arana & Rosenbaum, 2000)

# Stimulants: Focus on Cocaine

In contrast to depressants, **stimulants** excite the central nervous system, stimulating behavioral activity and heightened arousal. Low doses of amphetamines and cocaine can lead to a perception of increased physical and mental energy, diminished hunger, and a sense of invulnerability. Because "coming down" from this state is a disappointment, stimulant users often want to repeat the experience and so are at risk for continued drug use. Of all drugs, stimulants are the most likely to induce dependence.

Cocaine is commonly inhaled in its powdered form, and it has a local anesthetic effect. The user has an enhanced sense of physical and mental capacity and a simultaneous loss of appetite. Chronic users develop paranoia, teeth grinding, and repetitive behaviors and may also experience disturbances in the visual field, such as seeing snow, or the feeling that insects ("cocaine bugs") are crawling on the skin. This latter sensation arises from the spontaneous firing of sensory neurons, caused by the cocaine.

Cocaine exerts its effects by inhibiting the reuptake of dopamine and norepinephrine (Figure 5.10). The increased presence of these neurotransmitters in the

**Stimulants:** A class of substances that excite the central nervous system, leading to increases in behavioral activity and heightened arousal.

synaptic cleft leads to a pleasurable, even euphoric, feeling. With continued use of cocaine, the drug becomes the main trigger for activation of the reward system, leading other sources of pleasure, such as food or sex, to have little or no effect (National Institute on Drug Abuse, 1998). When cocaine and alcohol are taken together, the human liver (which metabolizes the substances) creates a third substance, called *cocaethylene*, which intensifies cocaine's effects while at the same time increasing the risk of sudden death (National Institute on Drug Abuse, 2004).

## Crack

Cocaine in crystalline form, known as **crack**, is usually smoked in a pipe ("freebasing") or rolled into a cigarette. Crack is faster acting and more intense in its effect than is cocaine powder inhaled through the nostrils; however, because its effects last for only a few minutes, the user tends to take greater amounts of crack than of powdered cocaine. Crack cocaine has more potential for abuse and dependence (Cone, 1995). The user experiences a feeling of euphoria, perceived clarity of thought, and increased energy. Crack increases heart rate and blood pressure and constricts blood vessels—a potentially lethal combination. After the drug wears off, the user experiences a massive "crash," with intense depression and intense craving for more crack. Both cocaine and crack can create strong dependence, particularly if injected or smoked. The user can develop tolerance; with crack, the development of tolerance is particularly swift. Sudden death can occur even in healthy people who use the drug only occasionally.

## Other Stimulants

**Amphetamines** are synthetic stimulants such as Benzedrine and Dexedrine; they are usually taken in pill form or injected. With high doses, the user can suffer *amphetamine psychosis*, which is similar to paranoid schizophrenia (discussed in Chapter 14); symptoms include delusions, hallucinations, and paranoia. Chronic use of amphetamines stimulates violent behaviors (Leccese, 1991) and can cause long-term neural changes associated with impaired memory and motor coordination (Volkow et al., 2001).

The stimulant *MDMA* (also known as ecstasy, or "e") causes the neurotransmitter serotonin, and to a lesser extent, dopamine, to be released from certain neurons (Colado et al., 2004; Green et al., 1995). Research on animals indicates that MDMA, used even once, can permanently damage neurons that release serotonin, affecting memory, learning, sleep, and appetite (Fischer et al., 1995). Studies (Jacobsen et al., 2004; Wareing et al., 2004) with humans have not yet been able to discern MDMA's unique effects on cognition, emotion, and behavior because these studies are generally correlational or quasiexperimental (see Chapter 2); such research designs do not lend themselves to eliminating confounds, such as the effects of other drugs that are taken along with MDMA (Green, 2004). Researchers have struggled

### FIGURE 5.10

## Action of Stimulants on Neurotransmitters

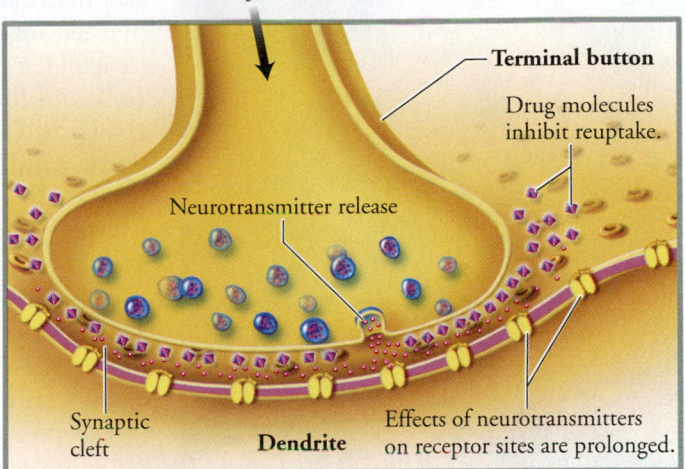

Cocaine and other stimulants create their stimulating effects by blocking reuptake—that is, by preventing the normal reabsorption into the terminal button—of some norepinephrine and dopamine molecules at the synaptic cleft. The net effect is that more of these neurotransmitters remain in the synaptic cleft.

Crack:  Cocaine in crystalline form, usually smoked in a pipe (free-basing) or rolled into a cigarette.

Amphetamines:  Synthetic stimulants.

Caffeine and nicotine are both stimulants, and people who regularly smoke or drink may experience tolerance and, when they skip their usual coffee or cigarette, symptoms of withdrawal.

mightily to sort out MDMA's effects on humans not only because users tend to take multiple drugs (Schifano, 2004), but also because MDMA pills may—unbeknownst to the user—also contain other substances. There is some evidence that cognitive impairments, as well as anxiety, depression, and other psychological symptoms, may in fact be due to the combined effects of MDMA and marijuana (Dafters et al., 2004; Daumann et al., 2004). Research suggests that too high a dose of MDMA, or its combination with other substances, can be fatal (Schifano, 2004). Some individuals' bodies do not metabolize the drug well, and these people may be at greater risk for a lethal effect (Ramamoorthy et al. 2002). Many of the side effects that occur with other stimulants also occur with MDMA.

Finally, *caffeine* and *nicotine* are also stimulants. Caffeine is present in coffee, tea, chocolate, and colas, among other beverages and foods. It causes increased alertness, raises pulse and heart rate, and can produce insomnia, restlessness, and ringing in the ears. There is some degree of tolerance, and chronic users will experience withdrawal headaches if they miss their customary morning coffee. Nicotine, present in cigarettes and tobacco in any form, can cause increased alertness and relaxation, as well as irritability, increased blood pressure, stomach pains, dizziness, emphysema, and heart disease. Nicotine works by triggering the release of several neurotransmitters that lead to a pleasurable sensation. Nicotine is addictive, causing some level of tolerance, as well as withdrawal symptoms when its use is stopped.

## Narcotic Analgesics: Focus on Heroin

Certain drugs, including heroin, morphine, codeine, Percodan, Demerol, Vicodin, and Oxycodone, are called **narcotic analgesics** because they are strongly addictive drugs that dull the senses and provide analgesia; that is, they relieve pain. These drugs affect certain endorphin receptors (see Chapter 4). Generally, drugs of this type are prescribed to relieve pain, severe diarrhea, protracted coughing, and troubled sleep. Heroin, an illegal drug, is one of the stronger narcotic analgesics. Like morphine, from which it is derived, heroin is an **opiate** (or *opioid*), produced from the opium poppy.

Heroin can bring about a feeling of relaxation and euphoria, but these effects are very short-term and are followed by negative changes in mood and behavior. Like other opiates, heroin is a central nervous system depressant, causing a slowing of neural activity in brainstem areas responsible for respiration and coughing, as well as in other areas of the brain. When heroin is in the body, the user's pupils may constrict and he or she may experience slower breathing and lethargy. Tolerance and withdrawal symptoms occur, with the latter usually involving periods of yawning, chills, hot flashes, restlessness, diarrhea, and goose bumps on the skin, followed by up to 12 hours of sleep.

In the brain, heroin and other opiates work by activating the dopamine-based reward system and also by binding to the opioid receptors, where the body's endorphins (opioids produced in the body) usually bind. This creates a negative feedback loop, leading the body to decrease its production of endorphins, and leaving the heroin user without natural means to relieve pain. Thus, more heroin is needed to achieve the analgesic effect. When the user tries to quit, endorphins do not kick in to alleviate the withdrawal symptoms, thus heightening the discomfort—and making it difficult to quit.

**Narcotic analgesics:** A class of strongly addictive drugs, such as heroin, that relieve pain.

**Opiate:** A narcotic, such as morphine, derived from the opium poppy.

**Hallucinogen:** A substance that induces hallucinations.

**Flashback:** A hallucination that recurs without the use of a drug.

# Hallucinogens: Focus on LSD

A **hallucinogen** is a substance that induces the perceptual experiences known as hallucinations. Although Alice's imaginings of Wonderland were a dream, other people, such as the 1960s rock group Jefferson Airplane in their song "White Rabbit," inferred that Alice's experiences stemmed from a hallucinogenic drug. Hallucinogens include mescaline, peyote, psilocybin, lysergic acid diethylamide (LSD), phencyclidine (PCP), ketamine ("Special K"), and marijuana. In general, all but marijuana can cause visual hallucinations at moderate dosages; much higher dosages are needed before marijuana will do so.

LSD is a synthetic substance that produces perceptual alterations. Exactly how LSD works is not well understood, but it is known to alter the functioning of the serotonin system. Users commonly experience visual hallucinations, which often include geometric shapes, vivid colors, and violent movement. At higher doses, geometric shapes give way to quickly changing meaningful objects. Users may feel as if they are becoming part of whatever they observe. Auditory hallucinations include hearing invented foreign languages or symphonies. These symptoms may last several hours, and the user's expectations can shape the experience induced by LSD.

Alice wanted to be smaller and hoped to find a "book of rules for shutting people up like telescopes" (Carroll, 1992, p. 31). Instead, she found a bottle (labeled DRINK ME) and, after drinking it, said, "What a curious feeling! . . . I must be shutting up like a telescope" (p. 31). This scene illustrates the effect of a user's *expectations* on his or her experience. Alice was hoping to find a way to shut herself up like a telescope, and that is just what she experienced after drinking the liquid. User expectations play a large role in the emotional tone of the LSD experience.

## A Creativity Boost?

Although some people report that they feel more creative as a result of taking LSD, research does not support this subjective experience of increased creativity (Dusek & Girdano, 1980). Actually, LSD can produce frightening experiences ("bad trips"), which may be caused by a change in dose, mood, expectations, and environment. A user may panic during a bad trip and need to be "talked down," repeatedly reminded that the frightening experience is in fact a drug-induced state that will wear off. Occasionally, suicide or murder takes place in the course of a user's hallucination. Hallucinations can recur without use of the drug; these spontaneous, perhaps alarming, **flashbacks** can happen weeks, even years, afterward and can be triggered by entering a dark environment (Abraham, 1983).

## Other Hallucinogens

The most commonly used hallucinogen in America is marijuana (National Institute on Drug Abuse, 2004), whose active ingredient is tetrahydrocannabinol (THC), which is chemically similar to the naturally occurring neurotransmitters in the body called *cannabinoids* (such as anandamide). There are receptors for cannabinoid molecules throughout the body and brain, including in the hippocampus (see Chapter 3) and brain areas involved in concentration, time and sensory perception, pleasure, and movement control; cannabinoids can affect learning and memory, appetite, and pain, and they can modulate other neurotransmitters (Gruber et al., 2003; Wilson & Nicoll, 2001). The effects of marijuana depend on the user's mood, expectations, and environment: If alone, the user may experience drowsiness and go to sleep; if with others, the user may feel euphoric; some people may experience anxiety and panic after using the substance (Dannon et al., 2004; Patel et al., in press). The effects of the drug can be subtle, including perceptual alterations in which sights and sounds seem more vivid. Distortions of space and time are also common, and perceptual motor skills may be impaired, making driving unsafe (Petersen,

For people with glaucoma or certain other medical problems and those undergoing nausea-inducing chemotherapy, marijuana can ease some of the effects. Such medical uses of marijuana are convincing some people that the drug should be legalized, at least for appropriate medical uses. Not everyone agrees with this position.

1977, 1979; Sterling-Smith, 1976). Although marijuana is less powerful than most other hallucinogens, every year approximately 230,000 Americans attend treatment centers in an effort to stop using it (National Admissions to Substance Abuse Treatment Services, 2001). Long-term use of marijuana can lead to withdrawal symptoms (Haney et al., 1999).

The substance *ketamine*, similar to PCP, is legally used as an anesthetic for animals. Use by humans can induce hallucinations, anesthesia, and stimulation of the cardiovascular and respiratory systems. Ketamine use is also associated with violence, a loss of contact with reality, and impaired thinking (White & Ryan, 1996). Users are likely to develop tolerance and dependence.

# Test Yourself

1. All of the following are signs of substance dependence *except*
   a. tolerance.
   b. withdrawal.
   c. use of the substance in dangerous situations.
   d. the desire to control use of the substance.
2. Alcohol sometimes increases neural activity rather than decreases it. This is because of the
   a. stimulant effects of alcohol.
   b. inhibition of inhibitory neurons.
   c. activation of the limbic system.
   d. group's expectations.
3. Narcotics such as heroin are difficult to quit using because
   a. they are socially reinforcing.
   b. the user craves bigger and bigger highs.
   c. the effects become more and more pronounced with use.
   d. they block the user's natural opioids, resulting in discomfort if use is discontinued.

4. Hallucinogenic drugs affect consciousness by
   a. mimicking or affecting the functioning of neurotransmitters.
   b. affecting all levels of processing.
   c. stimulating the peripheral nervous system.
   d. inducing expectations and false beliefs.

# Answers

1.d 2.b 3.d 4.a

# Think It Through!

A male, approximately 20 years old, was brought into the emergency room. He had been found in a local park, threatening passersby and muttering about bugs crawling on his skin. After waiting in the emergency room for an hour, he became extremely depressed and agitated. Assuming that he had no medical disorder other than drug use, what class of drug and what specific substance had he most likely taken? Suppose he hadn't complained of bugs but had trouble walking in a straight line and was slow to understand questions asked of him. What class of substance might be responsible for his actions? What specific substance?

In your opinion, did Alice exhibit symptoms only of dreaming? If not, what specific experiences lead you to suggest alternative hypotheses?

# REVIEW AND REMEMBER!

## Summary

### I. The Nature of Consciousness

**A.** Consciousness is an ongoing awareness of our own thoughts, sensations, and feelings.

**B.** Theories about the function of consciousness posit that it brings together information in novel ways, binds perceptual and mental processes together into a coherent whole, alerts the individual when perceptual and mental processes fit together correctly, or enables self-awareness.

**C.** Different parts of the brain are involved in the experience of consciousness, depending on the exact nature of what the individual is aware of. Brain areas involved in the interpretation and integration of information are particularly active, however.

**D.** Altered states of consciousness can arise by natural means (such as sleeping, dreaming, hypnosis, and meditation) or be induced by drugs or alcohol.

**E.** In some cultures, individuals use particular rituals to induce altered states of consciousness.

### II. To Sleep, Perchance to Dream

**A.** There are five stages of sleep: Stages 1 through 4 (NREM sleep) and REM sleep, in which memorable, vivid dreams occur. REM rebound—a higher proportion of REM sleep—occurs on the night following deprivation of REM sleep.

**B.** Lack of adequate sleep impairs performance on tasks that require vigilance and attention. Sleep deprivation also adversely affects mood and cortisol level (which, in turn, can affect learning and memory).

**C.** Three general theories have been proposed to explain the function of sleep: the evolutionary theory (where sleep provides an evolutionary advantage, perhaps by minimizing contact with predatory animals awake at night or by conserving energy), the restorative theory (where the body repairs itself from the wear and tear of the day), and the idea that sleep facilitates learning.

**D.** The content of dreams can be affected by certain types of events before sleep, such as thirst and the lack of social interaction.

**E.** Although researchers do not yet know with certainty why we dream, various theorists have proposed that dreams represent unconscious desires (Freud), random bursts of nerve cell activity (Hobson and McCarley), the elimination of unneeded connections in the brain (Crick and Mitchison), the strengthening of needed brain connections (Karni), or an interplay of goals with desires and arousal with inhibition (Solms).

**F.** During NREM sleep, acetylcholine release is inhibited, whereas acetylcholine is released during REM sleep. Brainstem cells that release other neurotransmitters

**Your Notes**

I.

A.

B.

C.

D.

E. Praying, chanting, singing

II.

A. Stages 3 & 4 = slow-wave sleep (deep)

B.

C.

D.

E.

F.

are less active during sleep. The hormone melatonin helps promote sleep; melatonin release is partly regulated by a light receptor in the eye.

**G.** Circadian rhythms govern blood pressure, pulse rate, body temperature, blood sugar level, hormone levels, and metabolism. The SCN governs circadian rhythms. The natural circadian rhythm is slightly longer than the 24-hour day. Jet lag and shift work can put people's schedules in opposition to their circadian rhythms, leading to increased likelihood of poor mood and attention, accidents, insomnia and fatigue.

*G.*

**H.** Some sleep disorders, such as night terrors and narcolepsy, have a genetic basis; others, such as insomnia and sleep apnea, may have physical causes. Some instances of insomnia, such as those related to jet lag and shift work, have environmental causes.

*H.*

## III. Hypnosis and Meditation

*III.*

**A.** Hypnosis involves a tuning out of the external environment and increased attention and openness to suggestion. Aspects of consciousness that characterize hypnosis are generalized reality orientation fading and trance logic. Hypnotizability varies from person to person.

*A. Can alter perception, mood, memory, and behavior*

**B.** There are two theories that explain how people behave when hypnotized: trance theory and sociocognitive theory.

*B.*

**C.** Recent neuroimaging results indicate that hypnosis is not simply role playing, but in fact corresponds to a distinct brain state.

*C.*

**D.** Hypnosis has been used to treat a variety of psychological and medical disorders, including pain.

*D.*

**E.** Meditation, which focuses awareness on a single stimulus, generally brings a subjective sense of well-being and relaxation, along with such biological changes as decreased heart and respiratory rates and shifting EEG patterns of brain activity.

*E.*

**F.** There are three main types of meditation: concentrative, opening-up, and mindfulness.

*F.*

## IV. Drugs and Alcohol

*IV. See summaries in Tables 5.4 & 5.5.*

**A.** Chronic substance abuse leads to substance dependence, whose main characteristics are tolerance and withdrawal.

*A.*

**B.** Depressants such as alcohol depress the central nervous system and can create an altered state of consciousness through disinhibition, decreased awareness, and an increased sense of relaxation. Disinhibition may make it difficult for the user to inhibit (or stop) behaviors in high-conflict situations that he or she would otherwise be able to prevent, and thus alcohol can promote aggressive behavior.

*B.*

**C.** Chronic alcohol abuse can lead to blackouts, as well as tolerance and withdrawal symptoms.

*C.*

**D.** Stimulants excite the central nervous system, leading to increases in behavioral activity, heightened arousal, perceptions of increased physical and mental energy, diminished hunger, and a sense of invulnerability.

*D.*

**E.** The user of a stimulant will "crash" after the drug wears off, become depressed and irritable, and crave more of the drug. Chronic use of some stimulants (such as amphetamines and cocaine) can cause paranoia and violent behavior.

**F.** Narcotics such as heroin act as analgesics and also produce a sense of euphoria and relaxation; they are central nervous system depressants.

**G.** Users of narcotics experience tolerance and extremely uncomfortable withdrawal symptoms; chronic use of a narcotic can suppress the body's production of endorphins.

**H.** Even moderate doses of hallucinogens (except marijuana) can cause visual hallucinations and perceptual alterations of other senses.

**I.** The altered state of consciousness produced by a hallucinogen is influenced by the user's mood and expectations. Marijuana users may experience euphoria and relaxation. Flashbacks can occur after LSD use.

NOTE: Once you feel that you understand the material in this chapter, visit the book's Web site at www.ablongman.com/kosslyn3e to test your knowledge with additional study questions.

*E.*

*F.*

*G.*

*H.*

*I.*

# Key Terms

absorption, p. 212
activation-synthesis hypothesis, p. 201
alcohol myopia, p. 222
altered state of consciousness (ASC), p. 191
amphetamines, p. 225
blackout, p. 223
circadian rhythms, p. 203
concentrative meditation, p. 215
consciousness, p. 190
crack, p. 225
depressants, p. 220
disinhibition, p. 220
flashback, p. 227
generalized reality orientation fading, p. 210
glove anesthesia, p. 213

hallucinogen, p. 227
hidden observer, p. 212
hypnogogic sleep, p. 193
hypnosis, p. 210
hypnotic induction, p. 210
inhibitory conflict, p. 221
insomnia, p. 206
latent content, p. 200
manifest content, p. 200
meditation, p. 215
mindfulness meditation, p. 215
narcolepsy, p. 206
narcotic analgesic, p. 226
night terror, p. 205
nightmare, p. 205
normal consciousness, p. 191
opening-up meditation, p. 215

opiate, p. 226
posthypnotic suggestion, p. 210
REM rebound, p. 196
REM sleep, p. 194
sleep, p. 193
sleep apnea, p. 207
sociocognitive theory (of hypnosis), p. 212
stimulants, p. 224
substance abuse, p. 219
substance dependence, p. 219
suprachiasmatic nucleus (SCN), p. 203
tolerance, p. 219
trance logic, p. 210
trance state, p. 210
trance theory, p. 212
withdrawal symptoms, p. 219

# LEARNING

Jackie Chan, actor, director, martial arts choreographer, and stuntman, begins his autobiography, *I Am Jackie Chan* (Chan & Yang, 1999), at the moment he is 45 years old and about to jump from the 21st floor of an office building in Rotterdam, the Netherlands, for his movie *Who Am I?* The stuntmen on the film had only done the jump from the 16th floor, and Chan never asks his stuntmen to do stunts that he himself would not do. Jackie Chan did, in fact, jump from the 21st floor and land safely.

Chan had begun kung fu training in early childhood: His father woke him up each morning before sunrise and required him to work out for hours as the sun rose progressively higher into the sky. His father came from a long line of Chinese warriors and believed that "pain gives you discipline. Discipline is at the root of manhood. And so, to be a real man, one must suffer as much as possible" (Chan & Yang, 1999, p. 10).

Chan's early childhood years were spent living in the French embassy in Hong Kong, where his father was the cook and his mother the housekeeper and laundress; the ambassador's youngest daughter was his friend, and he spent all day at home. When Chan was around 6 years old, he went to 1st grade, but had a hard time sitting still in the classroom. He was always making jokes and getting into trouble, often being forced to stand in the hallway, holding a desk over his head. Chan writes in his autobiography: "Sometimes I'd have to wear a sign around my neck, explaining the nature of my crime. Like, 'This is a noisy, ill behaved boy.' Or, 'This boy lost all of his books.' Or, 'This boy has not done his homework.' Sometimes it would just say, in a couple of [Chinese] characters, 'Useless!' " Chan describes standing out in the hall as "peaceful." "And, if no one was looking," he says, "I'd gently put the desk down, lean against the wall, and catch a few winks. Learning how to sleep standing up was probably the most useful thing school ever taught me" (p. 16).

Jackie Chan found the process of learning to read and write tedious, boring, and difficult. He was not promoted to 2nd grade and did not return to school the following year, remaining at home all day with his parents. Shortly thereafter, his parents brought him to visit Yu Jim-Yuen's Chinese Drama Academy, a residential school that trained students in the ancient art of Chinese opera. However, this school was not like any acting or martial arts school with which you might be familiar. In fact, schools like this no longer exist in Hong Kong because the training methods are now considered abusive, with the children rising at 5 a.m., training in martial arts, singing, and drama, for more than 12 hours, then doing chores and perhaps receiving a couple of hours of traditional "school" a few evenings a week. The children went to sleep at midnight, on the hard wooden floor with only a blanket, in the same room in which they trained during the day. Their "day" was 19 hours long, 365 days each year. School discipline included being hit repeatedly with a cane, often past the point where blood was drawn.

Jackie Chan has undertaken many dangerous stunts in his career. Why does he put himself at such risk (so great, in fact, that no insurance company will provide insurance on his films!)? According to Chan, the answer is that he wants to please his fans; their approval is very important to him. Both Chan's ability to make the type of films he does and the fact that the audience's approval is important to him reflect the capacity to learn—to learn skills and goals toward which to strive.

To learn is to discover, and the need to discover compels us from birth to the end of our days. Learning helps us both to survive and to realize our deepest dreams. It underlies virtually all of our behavior: what we eat and the way we eat it, how we dress, how we acquire the knowledge contained in books like this one, and how we live in a society with other people. And yet not all learning is positive in its results: Sometimes we "learn" to do things that either may not be good for us (as when Chan does his own death-defying stunts) or may not be what we wished to learn (as when Chan came to live out his father's view that manhood equals suffering). We can learn to do things that hurt as well as help.

Whereas many fields focus on the content of what people learn (historians, for example, add to their knowledge by finding out more facts about history), psychologists interested in the field of learning focus on the *process* of learning as well as the content. How does learning occur? To discover this, researchers have investigated both humans and animals, and, in this chapter, we look at some of the principles their research has revealed.

What did Chan learn from Master Yu Jim-Yuen's beatings? How did he learn to do martial arts so successfully? How did the audience's response to his early movies influence Chan's subsequent movies and his public behavior? Psychologists attempt to answer questions like these, in part, through theories of learning.

Psychologists define **learning** as a relatively long-term change in behavior that results from experience. When, for example, you have mastered tying your shoelaces, you will likely be able to secure your shoes properly for the rest of your life. This durability is true of all learned behavior, in virtually every domain of life, from riding a bicycle to participating in a conversation.

But, what about the following case? Suppose you watch someone write your name in Chinese characters: Having seen it done, can you claim that you have learned how to do it? What if you are able to duplicate the characters successfully? Can you legitimately say that you have learned to write your name in Chinese?

In the first instance, unless you have a photographic memory and excellent drawing ability, the answer is probably no. Merely watching someone do something complex and unfamiliar on a single occasion is usually not enough to allow you to learn it. In the second instance, even if you copy the characters correctly, the answer is still likely to be no. Just performing an action once is not enough; unless you can do it repeatedly and without assistance, you cannot claim that you have really learned to do it. You may have learned some elements of the task, but not the entire pattern, and so you cannot claim to have mastered it.

Learning can take place in a variety of ways. The simplest form of learning is *nonassociative learning*, which occurs when repeated exposure to a stimulus alters an organism's responsiveness; **habituation** occurs when repeated exposure decreases responsiveness. For instance, if you are walking in a city and hear a car horn honk

**Learning:** A relatively permanent change in behavior that results from experience.

**Habituation:** The learning that occurs when repeated exposure to a stimulus decreases an organism's responsiveness to the stimulus.

nearby, you may well be startled; if other horns chime, you will not startle as much (if at all). Here's another example: When a wild animal, such as an elk, comes into contact with a human hiker (who does not scare the elk or try to harm it), that elk will habituate to humans; the next time a peaceful hiker comes by, the elk will likely allow the hiker to come even closer before it runs away.

When repeated exposure to a stimulus *increases* responsiveness, *sensitization* occurs. For example, suppose you are trying to go to sleep and your neighbor is playing music relatively quietly (you may not have even noticed). All of a sudden, his stereo blasts for a few seconds, then quiets down to the same level it was before. You now notice the music—at this quiet level—more than you did originally. You are sensitized to it.

Many other types of learning are by association—relating one object or event with another object or event. This general phenomenon is what psychologists call *associative learning*. This chapter will explore different types of learning. For all types, the criterion for learning is that we demonstrate a relatively long-term change brought about by experience.

Let's begin by exploring the model of associative learning investigated not quite a hundred years ago—classical conditioning.

# CLASSICAL CONDITIONING

Unfortunately, Chan's early life was filled with adversity, often in the form of physical punishment. Within a few weeks of living at the Chinese Drama Academy, Chan received his first caning:

> Master pushed me down to the ground and told me to lie flat on my belly. I closed my eyes and gritted my teeth. I felt my pants being roughly drawn down to my knees, as my belly and thigh collapsed on the polished wooden floor. Then a whistle and a crack, a sound that I registered in my brain just a flash before the pain raged from my buttock up my spine. (Chan &Yang, 1999, p. 38)

That whistling sound came to elicit fear in Chan; *elicit* means that the response (fear) is drawn out of the organism (in this case, Chan). When a student received a caning (in front of the rest of the students), the entire class would cringe on hearing the sound. This fear response (and the cringe) is a complex example of classical conditioning.

In its simplest form, **classical conditioning** is a type of learning in which a neutral stimulus becomes associated, or paired, with a stimulus that causes a reflexive behavior and, in time, is sufficient to produce that behavior.

In Chan's case, the whistling sound of the fast-moving cane became paired with the extreme pain of the beating, thereby eliciting the fear and the cringe. The simplest example of the way classical conditioning works is found in the famous experiments that established the principle: the work of Pavlov and his dogs.

## Pavlov's Experiments

Classical conditioning is also sometimes called *Pavlovian conditioning* because Ivan Pavlov (1849–1936), a Russian physiologist, was the first person to investigate systematically the variables associated with classical conditioning. Pavlov's work on conditioning began by accident. As part of his work on the digestive processes, which won him a Nobel Prize, Pavlov studied salivation in dogs. To measure the amount of saliva that dogs produced when given meat powder (food), Pavlov collected the saliva in

**Classical conditioning:** A type of learning that occurs when a neutral stimulus becomes paired (associated) with a stimulus that causes a reflexive behavior and, in time, is sufficient to produce that behavior.

FIGURE 6.1

## Pavlov's Apparatus for Measuring Salivation

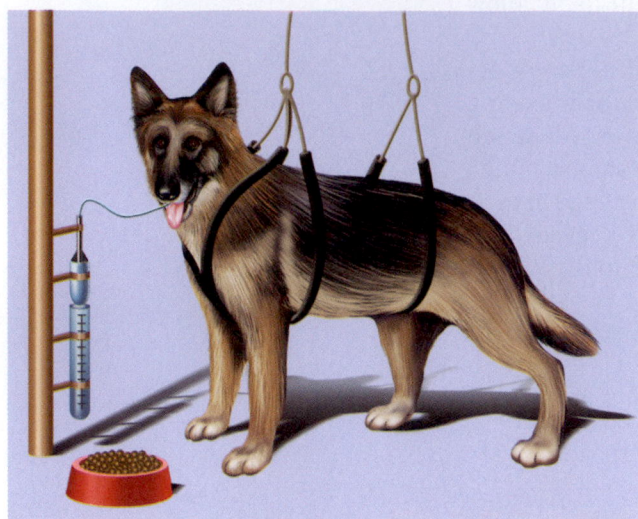

Ivan Pavlov started out measuring saliva production in dogs as part of his research on the digestive system. He went on to use this same saliva collection technique with his investigations into classical conditioning.

tubes attached to the dogs' salivary glands (see Figure 6.1). Pavlov and his colleagues noticed that even though salivation usually occurs during rather than before eating, his dogs were salivating before they were fed: They would salivate simply on seeing their food bowls or on hearing the feeder's footsteps.

### The Three Phases of Classical Conditioning

Intrigued, Pavlov pursued the issue with more experiments. His basic method is still in use today (see Figure 6.2). Pavlov would sound a tone on a tuning fork just before the food was brought into the dogs' room. After hearing the pairing of the tone with the food several times, the dogs would salivate on hearing the tone alone. Because food by itself elicits salivation, Pavlov considered the food the **unconditioned stimulus (US)**—that is, a stimulus that elicits an automatic response that does not depend on prior learning. The dogs' salivation is termed the **unconditioned response (UR)**, the reflexive or automatic response elicited by a US. The UR does not require learning, but it does depend on certain circumstances. For example, if an animal has just eaten and is full, it will not salivate when presented with food. In Pavlov's experiment, the tone is the **conditioned stimulus (CS)**—that is, an originally neutral stimulus that acquires significance through pairing(s) with a US. After hearing the tuning fork a number of times before they were fed, the dogs began to associate the tone with food. Thereafter, whenever the dogs heard the tone, even when presented by itself, they salivated. Salivation in response to the tone alone is thus a **conditioned response (CR)**, a response that depends (is conditional) on pairings of the CS with a US (Pavlov, 1927). Not surprisingly, psychologists call the initial learning of the conditioned response **acquisition**.

### Variations of the Procedure

In an attempt to discover what factors might affect the process of conditioning, Pavlov and researchers after him altered the variables involved in creating a conditioned response. Initially, researchers thought that to create a conditioned response, the US (the food) must immediately follow the CS (the tone) in a procedure called *forward conditioning*, which occurs when the CS begins before the US begins. There are two types of forward conditioning. One is *delayed conditioning*, when the CS occurs both before and during the presentation of the US (see Figure 6.3); an example with Pavlov's dogs would be when the tone sounds before and during the presentation of the food. The other type of forward conditioning is **trace conditioning**, when the presentation of the CS ends before the presentation of the US begins (Figure 6.3). A trace conditioning procedure used on Pavlov's dogs would occur if the food was not presented until the tone had already sounded and stopped. Trace conditioning thus requires that the animal remember the CS, and in general trace conditioning is most effective if there is a very short interval of time between the CS and US (such as 0.5 second). If the food were presented 30 minutes after the tone, conditioning would be weak, if it occurred at all.

Pavlov also tried the reverse order, called *backward pairing*, where the US comes first, followed quickly by the CS (Figure 6.3): He fed the dogs first and presented the tone 10, 5, or 1 second later. He found no conditioning; the dogs did not salivate when hearing the tone after eating the food. Although Pavlov did not achieve backward con-

**Unconditioned stimulus (US):** A stimulus that elicits an automatic response (UR), without requiring prior learning.

**Unconditioned response (UR):** The reflexive response elicited by a particular stimulus.

**Conditioned stimulus (CS):** An originally neutral stimulus that acquires significance through pairings with an unconditioned stimulus (US).

**Conditioned response (CR):** A response that depends, or is conditional, on pairings of the conditioned stimulus with an unconditioned stimulus; once learned, the conditioned response occurs when the conditioned stimulus is presented alone.

**Acquisition:** In classical conditioning, the initial learning of the conditioned response (CR).

**Trace conditioning:** A type of forward classical conditioning where the presentation of the conditioned stimulus (CS) ends before the presentation of the unconditioned stimulus (US) begins.

ditioning with his dogs, other researchers have since found that such conditioning can occur in some animals (Chang et al., 2003). Presenting the US and CS simultaneously, called *simultaneous conditioning* (Figure 6.3), does not usually lead to a conditioned response (Hall, 1984), although such conditioning is possible (Albert & Ayres, 1997; Barnet et al., 1991). Generally, in order for conditioning to occur, the US (food, in this example) should follow the CS (tone) immediately; however, there are exceptions, including certain food aversions, in which there may be a longer interval between the presentation of conditioned and unconditioned stimuli. As we will see, a food aversion is one of the rare examples where strong conditioning can occur when there is a long interval between the presentation of the CS and the US.

# Classical Conditioning: How It Works

Researchers studying classical conditioning have discovered a good deal about how organisms (human or otherwise) engage in this form of learning. Some conditioned responses remain with us all of our lives; others fade and even disappear altogether.

Another Russian researcher, Vladimir Bechterev (1857–1927), also conducted conditioning experiments. Here the US was a shock, and the UR was a dog's withdrawal of its foot. When a neutral stimulus such as a bell (CS) was paired with the shock, the dog learned to withdraw its foot (CR) after the bell but before the shock, thus successfully learning to avoid pain. Bechterev's findings

### FIGURE 6.3

## Variations of the Classical Conditioning Procedure

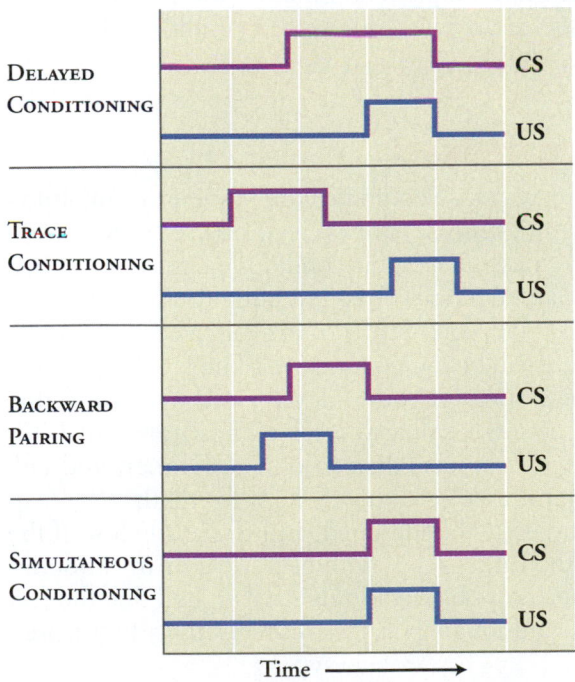

The sequence and timing of the presentation of the CS and US can vary: delayed conditioning, trace conditioning, backward pairing, and simultaneous conditioning. Delayed conditioning is generally effective, as is trace conditioning if there is a brief interval between CS and US presentation. Although backward and simultaneous conditioning can occur, they are not generally effective.

### FIGURE 6.2

## The Three Phases of Classical Conditioning

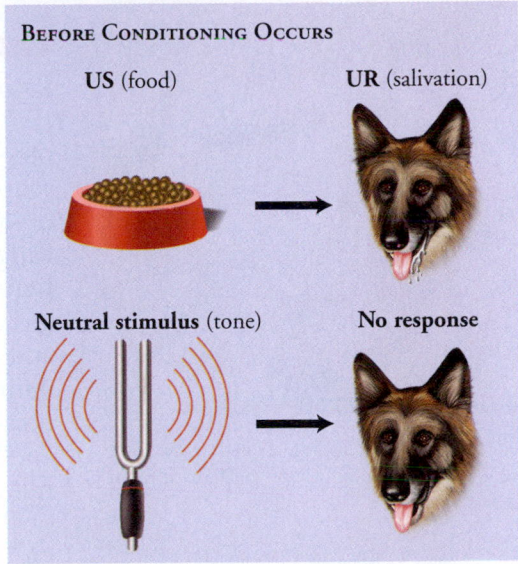

Before conditioning occurs, the CS does not lead to a conditioned response, but the US does.

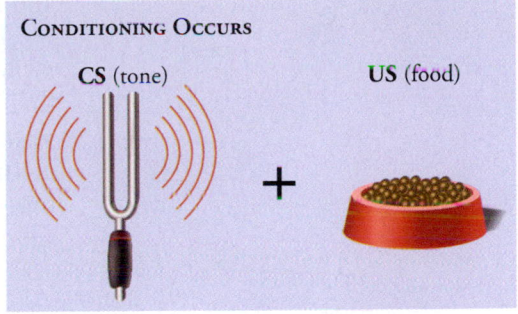

Then the CS is paired with the US—here, the tone is sounded and then the food is presented.

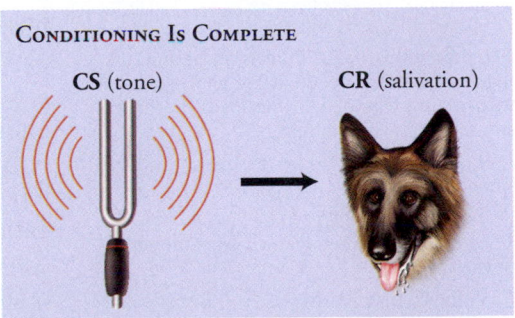

Classical conditioning is complete when the CS elicits the conditioned response—here, the dog salivates after hearing the tone.

were an important extension of Pavlov's work in that he extended the conditioned response to motor reflexes. Bechterev also established the basis for **avoidance learning** (Viney, 1993)—classical conditioning with a CS and an unpleasant US that leads the organism to try to avoid the CS.

## Conditioned Emotions: Getting a Gut Response

If you saw a cane like the one used to beat students at the Chinese Drama Academy leaning against a chair, chances are that it would not make you cringe or show any other signs of fear. The cane is a *neutral* stimulus. However, for Jackie Chan and his schoolmates, the cane that Master Yu held in his hand was no longer a neutral object or stimulus. Repeated beatings with it created a specific type of conditioned response called a **conditioned emotional response (CER)**—an emotionally charged conditioned response elicited by a previously neutral stimulus.

A landmark study by John B. Watson, the founder of behaviorism (see Chapter 1), and his assistant Rosalie Rayner (Watson & Rayner, 1920) illustrates how classical conditioning can produce a straightforward conditioned emotional response of fear, and how fear can lead to a **phobia**, an irrational fear of a specific object or situation. Watson and Rayner classically conditioned fear and then a phobia in an 11-month-old infant—Albert B.—whom they called "Little Albert" (see Figure 6.4). Through the use of classical conditioning, Watson and Rayner created in Albert a fear of rats; on seeing a white rat, Albert would cry and exhibit signs of fearfulness. This study could not be done today because of the rigorous ethical principles that now govern psychological research (see Chapter 1) but did not exist at the time the study was undertaken. Neither Watson nor Rayner followed up on what happened to Albert after the study because the boy and his mother moved away.

Inadvertent classical conditioning can occur in people with certain kinds of heart problems who have a device, called a *defibrillator*, implanted under their skin. When their heartbeat gets too fast, the device emits an electric shock that causes the heart to resume beating normally. However, the shock can be quite an uncomfortable and alarming jolt for the device wearer. The more frequent and intense the shocks are, the more likely the wearer is to develop severe anxiety—due to the conditioned fear response to the shocks (Godemann et al., 2001).

## Preparedness and Contrapreparedness

Although it was initially thought that any response could be conditioned by any stimulus (Kimble, 1981), this supposition is not entirely true. Organisms seem to have a **biological preparedness**, a built-in readiness for certain conditioned stimuli to elicit particular conditioned responses (Domjan et al., 2004), so less conditioning (training) is necessary to produce learning. For instance, you may learn to avoid a certain kind of cheese if the first time you eat that variety you become nauseated. The fact that it takes only one pairing of the cheese and the nausea for you to develop an aversion to that food is an example of biological preparedness. Similarly, research has shown that it is easier to condition a fear response to some objects than to others. Öhman and colleagues (1976) used pictures as the CS and shock as the US. They found that the fear-related response of sweaty hands is more easily conditioned, and less easily lost, if the CS is a picture of a snake or a spider than if it is a picture of flowers or mushrooms. Snakes, rats, and the dark are typical objects of phobias. Some have argued that the fear response to these makes sense from an evolutionary perspective—sensitivity to the pres-

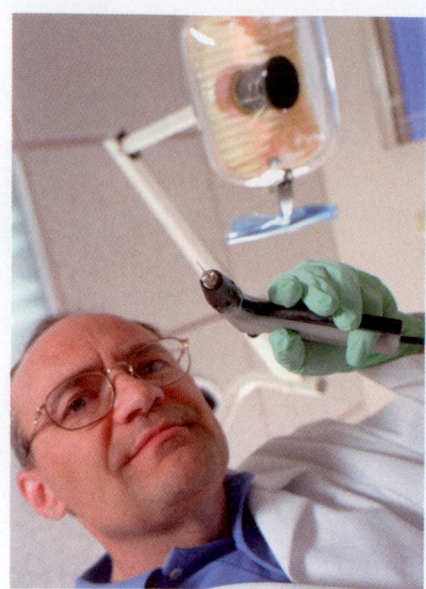

Does avoidance learning explain why some people put off going to the dentist for many years?

**Avoidance learning:** In classical conditioning, learning that occurs when a CS is paired with an unpleasant US that leads the organism to try to avoid the CS.

**Conditioned emotional response (CER):** An emotional response elicited by a previously neutral stimulus.

**Phobia:** An irrational fear of a specific object or situation.

**Biological preparedness:** A built-in readiness for certain conditioned stimuli to elicit particular conditioned responses, so less conditioning (training) is necessary to produce learning.

FIGURE 6.4

# Classical Conditioning of a Phobia: Little Albert

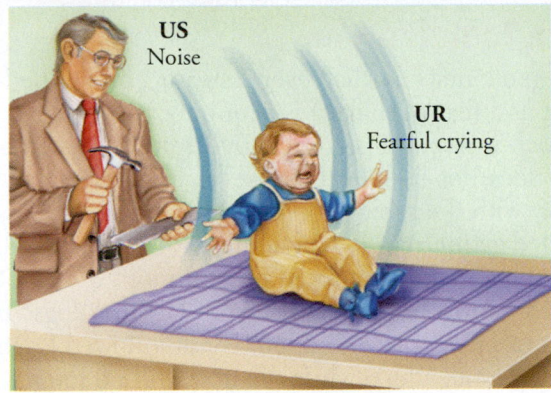

**US** Noise

**UR** Fearful crying

Initially, Little Albert did not show a fear of animals, but he did exhibit fear if a loud noise was made behind his back (a hammer striking a steel bar).

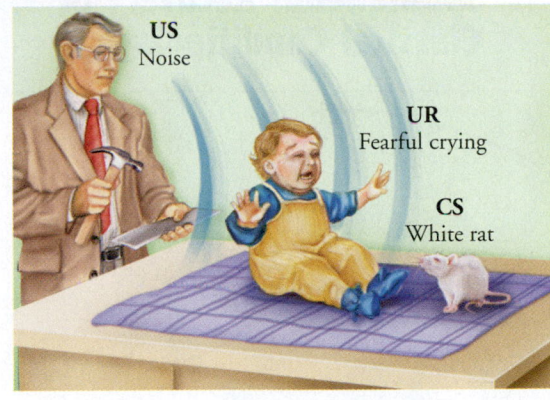

**US** Noise

**UR** Fearful crying

**CS** White rat

Then the researchers presented a white rat (CS) and made the loud noise (US).

**CR** Whimpering, crying

**CS** White rat

After five presentations of the CS and US, Albert developed a phobia of rats—he began whimpering and withdrawing (the conditioned emotional response) and trying to avoid the rat. After two more presentations of the CS and US, he immediately began crying on seeing the rat. "He . . . fell over on his left side, raised himself . . . and began to crawl away so rapidly that he was caught with difficulty before reaching the edge of the table" (Watson & Rayner, 1920, p. 5).

---

ence of such possibly dangerous elements in the environment could help an organism survive (Seligman, 1971).

**Contrapreparedness** is a built-in disinclination (or even an inability) for certain conditioned stimuli to elicit particular conditioned responses. For example, Marks (1969) described a patient he was treating as an adult. When this woman was 10 years old, she was on a car trip and had to go to the bathroom. Her father pulled off the road so that she could relieve herself in a ditch. As she stepped out of the car, she saw a snake in the ditch—and at that moment her brother accidentally slammed the door on her hand. At 43, she was still deathly afraid of snakes, but she was not afraid of car doors, which had actually done the damage. Similarly, Bregman (1934) failed—with 15 different infants—to replicate Watson and Rayner's experiment when, instead of a rat as the CS, she used various inanimate objects, such as wooden blocks and pieces of cloth. There was no evidence of conditioning when the US was a loud noise and the CS was an inanimate object. These two examples highlight the point that certain stimuli, such as a car door and a wooden block, do not make successful conditioned stimuli.

**Contrapreparedness:** A built-in disinclination (or even an inability) for certain conditioned stimuli to elicit particular conditioned responses.

**FIGURE 6.5**

## Acquisition, Extinction, and Spontaneous Recovery in Classical Conditioning

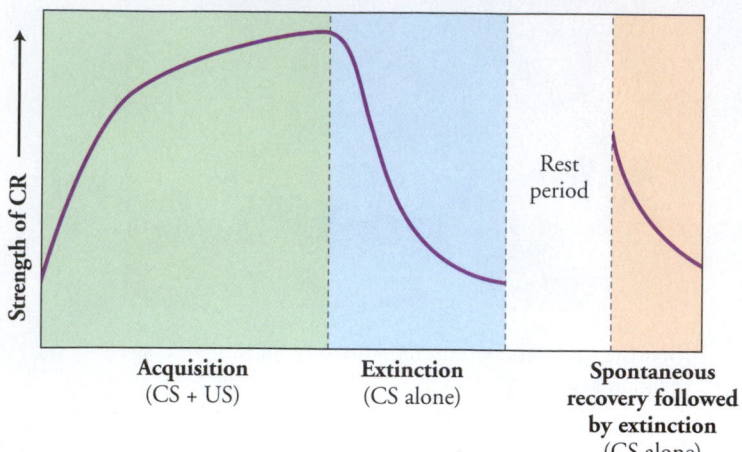

When the CS and US are paired, the organism quickly acquires the CR (left panel). However, when the CS occurs without the US, the CR quickly weakens (blue panel). After a rest period, the CR returns in response to the CS alone, but this is followed by extinction (right panel).

## Extinction and Spontaneous Recovery in Classical Conditioning: Gone Today, Here Tomorrow

The good news is that even after a conditioned response (such as a fear of snakes) is acquired, it is possible to diminish such a response significantly in the presence of the CS. This does not happen because of forgetting, which occurs simply with the passage of time. Rather, the process involved is called **extinction**, in which the CR is gradually eliminated, or *extinguished*, by repeated presentations of the CS without the US. How would this work with Pavlov's dogs? If the tone continues to be presented, but is not followed by the presentation of food, after a while the dogs will no longer salivate at the tone: The CR will be extinguished. This process is graphed in Figure 6.5.

However, after a conditioned response has been extinguished and the animal does not encounter the CS for some period of time (in an experiment, referred to as a "rest period"), when the CS is later presented, it will again elicit the CR—although sometimes not as strongly as before extinction. This event is called **spontaneous recovery** (see Figure 6.5). Let's go back to those dogs: As just noted, after the tone has been presented several times without any food forthcoming, the dogs' salivation response will be extinguished, and they will stop salivating to the tone alone. However, if the tone is not presented for a period of time before it is presented again, the previously learned conditioned response of salivation will return on simply hearing the tone. The dogs have spontaneous recovery of the response, but they may not salivate as much as they did when they were first classically conditioned to the tone.

Once classical conditioning has occurred, the connection between the CS and the US apparently never completely vanishes. After extinction occurs, the organism can be retrained so that the CS again elicits the conditioned response; in this case, learning takes place more quickly than it did during the original training period. It is much easier to condition again, after extinction, than it is to condition in the first place.

In his work on extinction and spontaneous recovery, Bouton (1993, 1994, 2000) showed that what occurs during extinction is not the forgetting of old learning, but rather the production of new learning that exists along with the old learning and interferes with the previous classically conditioned response (Bouton, 2002). Thus, according to Bouton's work, if Little Albert's fear of rats had been extinguished (that is, if the rat had been presented without the loud noise often enough that it failed to elicit the CR), Albert's association between the rat and the noise would *not* have disappeared, but rather new learning would have occurred "on top of" his previous learning. Thus, the CS (rat) would no longer signal that the US (noise) was about to occur, at least not in that context—not in Watson's testing room (Bouton, 2000).

## Generalization and Discrimination in Classical Conditioning: Seen One, Seen 'Em All?

Watson and Rayner wrote that, 5 days after the conditioning of Little Albert, a rabbit, a dog, a fur coat, cotton, and a Santa Claus mask all elicited the conditioned response of fear in him. This is an example of **stimulus generalization**, a tendency for the condi-

**Extinction:** In classical conditioning, the process by which a CR comes to be eliminated through repeated presentations of the CS without the presence of the US.

**Spontaneous recovery:** In classical conditioning, the event that occurs when the CS again elicits the CR after extinction has occurred.

**Stimulus generalization:** A tendency for the CR to be elicited by neutral stimuli that are like, but not identical to, the CS; in other words, the response generalizes to similar stimuli.

tioned response to be elicited by neutral stimuli that are like, but not identical to, the conditioned stimulus; in other words, the response generalizes to similar stimuli. Moreover, because of a *generalization gradient*, the more closely the new stimulus resembles the original CS, the stronger the response. Stimulus generalization can be helpful for survival because often a dangerous stimulus may not occur in exactly the same form the next time. Without stimulus generalization, we might not know to be afraid of lions as well as tigers.

In addition to stimulus generalization, organisms are also able to distinguish, or discriminate, among stimuli similar to the CS and to respond only to the actual CS; this ability is called **stimulus discrimination**. Stimulus discrimination can be extremely helpful for survival; consider that one type of mushroom may be poisonous, but another type is food. If Albert had been shown a pile of cotton balls without a loud noise occurring (but continued to be presented with a rat paired with the loud noise), only the rat would have elicited fear. Albert would have been able to discriminate between the two similar stimuli.

Classical conditioning can account for the learning of more complex behaviors through *higher order conditioning*: Once conditioning has occurred, the CS (now referred to as $CS_1$) acts as if it were a US when it is paired with a new CS (referred to as $CS_2$). For Pavlov's dogs, once the original conditioning occurred, another stimulus, such as a black square, could be paired with the tone (see Figure 6.6). After a number of pairings, the presentation of the black square alone would lead to the salivation response, although the response would not be as strong as it was originally, to the tone. An example of higher order conditioning with Little Albert would be if a cane ($CS_2$) was presented immediately before the white rat ($CS_1$). With enough pairings, Albert would likely become afraid of the cane as well.

## Cognition and the Conditioned Stimulus

Although strict behaviorists might not agree that thoughts play a role in classical conditioning, research suggests otherwise (see Chapter 1 for an explanation of behaviorism). The context in which classical conditioning occurs and the expectations that arise following classical conditioning influence the learning (Hollis, 1997; Kirsch, Lynn et al., 2004). For example, Rescorla (1967) presented rats with a tone (CS) immediately before delivering a shock (US); these rats quickly learned a fear response to the tone. However, another group of rats heard the tone and were shocked, but sometimes the tone was presented after the shock. As Pavlov had found years earlier, backward pairing does not produce conditioning (see Figure 6.3): This group did not come to fear the tone.

Apparently, the CS provides information by signaling the upcoming US (and therefore UR), and conditioning occurs because the animal is learning that relationship: Our current understanding is that the CS is a signal that the US will occur, at least in the particular context in which the conditioning took place. Even a placebo's effect can involve cognitive elements: The placebo signals the probability of a future event, and thus the animal (which can be a human) comes to *expect*—consciously or not—that the placebo will lead to a particular response (Kirsch, 2004; Stewart-Williams & Podd, 2004).

Kamin (1969) provided more evidence that mental processes lie between stimulus and response during conditioning. He conditioned rats by pairing a tone with a brief shock; the rats developed a conditioned fear response to the tone. But when he added a second CS by turning on a light with the tone, the rats did not develop a conditioned fear response to the light alone. Kamin hypothesized that the original pairing of tone and shock was blocking new learning. The light did not add new information and was

**FIGURE 6.6** ## Higher Order Conditioning

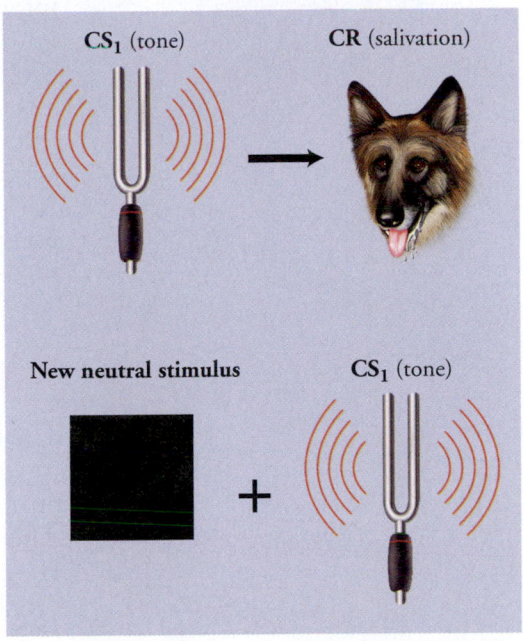

Once classical conditioning to the CS (a tone, labeled $CS_1$ here) occurs, a new neutral stimulus is paired with $CS_1$. Here the new stimulus is a black square.

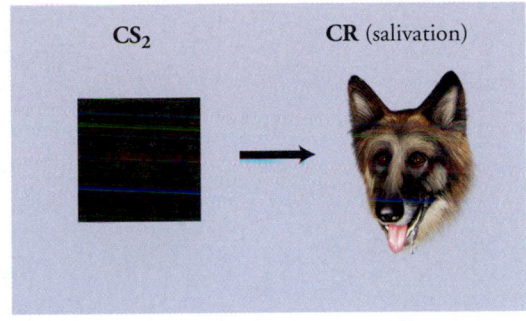

With repeated pairings, the new stimulus ($CS_2$) will elicit the CR (salivation), although it will likely be weaker than the response to $CS_1$.

**Stimulus discrimination:** The ability to distinguish among stimuli similar to the CS and to respond only to the actual CS.

therefore of no consequence and not worth their attention. The tone was enough of a signal, and the rats didn't seem to view the light as a signal. Thus, Kamin concluded that classical conditioning takes place only if the pairing of CS and US provides useful information about the likelihood of occurrence of the US.

In keeping with this way of interpreting conditioning, researchers have found that even a mental image of an object—what you see in your "mind's eye" when you visualize something—can play a role in classical conditioning, either as a CS or a US. For instance, imagining food can lead to salivation in humans (Dadds et al., 1997): Visualize the most scrumptious dessert you've ever eaten (was it a banana split? baked Alaska? ice cream drowning in chocolate sauce?). Imagine it in vivid detail. If the image is vivid enough, you may start salivating—the image is an unconditioned stimulus, the salivation is an unconditioned response.

# Dissecting Conditioning: Mechanisms

The brain generally operates by a divide-and-conquer approach: Different neural structures confer different aspects of an ability. Classical conditioning is no exception. Not only are different neural structures used in different aspects of conditioning, but also different sorts of classical conditioning rely in part on different regions of the brain. Here we will consider fear conditioning (the best understood type) in detail, but also briefly see key differences with eye-blink conditioning and other sorts.

## Learning to Be Afraid

Consider the case of a driver who has been honked at by a huge truck as it roars by and has barely missed being crushed. At the time of the incident, the driver experienced fear. As a result of this close encounter, when he later hears the sound of a horn and sees a truck drive by, he feels a twinge of fear—even if that truck in fact poses no danger. Such conditioned responses are acquired via the joint actions of the following neural mechanisms.

1. *The information registers in the brain.* When the driver later hears the sound of a horn and sees a truck drive by, the images and sounds are processed in the visual cortex and the auditory cortex, respectively. Multiple brain pathways, including direct connections from the thalamus, carry this information to the amygdala (Shi & Davis, 2001). In humans, conditioning can sensitize the perceptual pathways that register a stimulus (Cheng et al., 2003; Pizzagalli et al., 2003), so that we can recognize the CS more easily.

2. *The amygdala reacts.* After the information is registered, a specific part of the amygdala—the basolateral nucleus—reacts to the sounds and sights and plays a crucial role in storing the stimulus-response associations that underlie fear: In experimental studies with animals, it has been shown that if this particular part of the amygdala is removed, animals cannot learn that a shock will soon follow a tone (Cardinal et al,, 2002); in addition, studies have shown that certain genes are activated in this part of the amygdala during fear conditioning (Scicli et al., 2004), and that such conditioning is disrupted when substances that inactivate this region are injected into it (Huff & Rudy, 2004).

3. *The hippocampus helps store associations with context.* The hippocampus allows us to associate a conditioned stimulus with a particular context (such as the place where that truck barreled by the driver; Bast et al., 2003; Hall et al., 2001; Trivedi

& Coover, 2004;); the hippocampus is especially important when we don't make an effort to associate an event and its context, but instead pick up this information in passing (O'Reilly & Rudy, 2000, 2001). In fact, if the action of the neurotransmitter acetylcholine is disrupted in the hippocampus, animals do not learn to associate a specific context with an impending shock (Gale et al., 2001). In addition, the hippocampus is especially important during trace conditioning, where there is a lag between the disappearance of the CS and the appearance of the US (Clark et al., 2002). As we shall see in Chapter 7, the hippocampus plays a special role in memory—which is crucial in trace conditioning.

4. *The central nucleus of the amygdala kicks in.* Next, another part of the amygdala, the central nucleus, triggers the behaviors that *express* fear and conditioned fear— for example, wincing when an 18-wheeler rumbles by (Cardinal et al., 2002). When this part of the amygdala is removed in animals, the movements, autonomic responses, and other signs of fear are not produced.

5. *Other parts of the brain contribute to the outward display of fear.* Finally, yet other parts of the brain play a role in actually producing the behaviors that accompany fear. For example, Maschke and colleagues (2002) presented tones followed by electric shocks to humans, and they found that normal people were soon conditioned—their heart rate slowed down when they heard the tone (a decreased heart rate is related to "freezing" behavior seen in other animals—which may conserve energy and reflect focused attention). But this behavior was not induced in patients who had suffered damage to the cerebellum, which suggests that this part of the brain is important for regulating heart rate in a conditioned fear response.

6. *Sets of neurons become linked.* The result of conditioning is that sets of neurons become linked. With the honking truck, conditioning causes brain cells that register the stimulus to fire in tandem with cells in the amygdala that trigger the fear response. Activity in the two sets of neurons becomes hooked together, so that whenever the stimulus occurs, the amygdala automatically triggers the response. A crucial finding is that this linked activity never disappears entirely: Even after conditioning has been extinguished, linked neural activity remains, making it very easy for an animal (or person) to relearn a conditioned response. Indeed, extinction depends on the active suppression of the response, which is accomplished in part by the frontal lobe's inhibiting the amygdala (LeDoux, 1995, 1996; Morgan et al., 2003).

In one study, some rats were allowed to exercise and others were not. Both groups then heard tones, which were followed by shocks. The rats that exercised showed stronger conditioning to the particular context in which the shocks occurred. Why? Exercise enhances the functioning of the hippocampus and, in so doing, makes rats better able to distinguish the context in which a shock was delivered (Baruch et al., 2004).

## Learning When to Blink

Have you ever heard a gun being fired at close range? If you have, you may have noticed that you blinked. And after this experience, simply seeing someone nearby on the verge of pulling the trigger may cause you to blink. Such eye-blink conditioning has been studied extensively, usually by using a tone (the CS) to signal an air puff to the eye (the US), which in turn evokes a blink (the UR). After conditioning, the tone alone will produce a blink (which is now a CR). Such conditioning has been shown to rely partly on neural structures different from those that underlie fear conditioning. For example, eye-blink conditioning relies on the cerebellum not just to express behavior, but also to form and store the conditioned associations themselves. Humans with brain damage to the cerebellum do not learn the association of tone and air puff as well as normal people do (Gerwig et al., 2003).

However, as we saw with fear conditioning, eye-blink conditioning does not arise from the actions of a single brain structure; the hippocampus, basal ganglia, and amygdala (among other brain structures) also contribute (Christian & Thompson, 2003). In fact, different parts of the cerebellum play different roles in eye-blink conditioning (Bao et al., 2000; Thompson et al., 1997).

Eye-blink conditioning may not be as inherently interesting as fear conditioning (learned fear is more important in daily life), but researchers have used eye-blink conditioning to study more general issues. For example, it is known that eye blinks are not as easily conditioned in old rats as in young rats. Researchers hypothesized that antioxidants in the diet can enhance brain function, and particularly that of the cerebellum. To investigate this idea, they fed elderly rats spinach-enriched chow, which was high in antioxidants. And sure enough, the rats that ate their spinach acquired eye-blink conditioning faster than did elderly rats that ate a normal diet (Cartford et al., 2002). Popeye the sailor was onto something!

Finally, yet other brain areas may be crucial for other sorts of conditioning. For example, the anterior cingulate cortex may play a key role in the conditioning of pain (Kung et al., 2003) and in discriminating among stimuli (Cardinal et al., 2003).

In short, classical conditioning is a complex activity, which relies on many different neural structures working together. Moreover, different forms of conditioning rely, to some degree, on different parts of the brain.

# Classical Conditioning Applied

If the investigation of classical conditioning had ended with the study of dogs' salivation, the great psychological importance of this kind of learning might not have been recognized. But other studies of classical conditioning showed that emotional responses, such as the fear response, can be conditioned, and emotional responses exert a powerful effect on people's lives. If a friend slaps you hard on the back every time you see him, you are likely to wince even as he lifts his arm to begin his greeting, and in time classical conditioning will affect how you feel about him. Classical conditioning can play a role in the effectiveness of medicines, in the operation of our immune systems, and in other aspects of health and illness (as you will see in Chapter 13). Even without our awareness, it contributes to our feelings about events and objects, including ourselves (Baccus et al., 2004; Bunce et al., 1999; Núñez & de Vincente, 2004), and to our sexual interests (Lalumiere & Quinsey, 1998).

## Drug Use and Abuse

Classical conditioning plays a role in deaths caused by drug overdoses. A user who generally takes a drug in a particular setting—the bathroom, for instance—develops a conditioned response to that place (Siegel, 1988; Siegel et al., 2000; Siegel & Ramos, 2002). Here's what happens. Because of classical conditioning, as soon as the user walks into the bathroom, his or her body begins to compensate for the influx of drug that is soon to come—a *conditioned compensatory response* (Siegel & Ramos, 2002). This conditioned response is the body's attempt to counteract, or dampen, the effect of the drug. When the user takes the drug in a new setting, perhaps a friend's living room, this conditioned response does not occur. Because there is no conditioned response to the new setting, the user's body does not try to counteract the effect of the drug. The net result is a higher effective dose of the drug than the user can tolerate, leading to an overdose.

Similarly, classical conditioning also helps explain why people addicted to cocaine experience drug cravings merely from handling money (Hamilton et al., 1998). Part of the experience of using cocaine is buying it, often just before using it. Thus, handling money becomes a CS. In the same way, among cigarette smokers certain environmental stimuli can elicit a desire for a cigarette (Lazev et al., 1999), and virtual reality simulations of opioid-related cues can elicit a craving for the drug in opioid addicts (Kuntze et al., 2001). So, classical conditioning explains why some smokers automatically reach for a cigarette when they get a phone call or have a cup of coffee, often without realizing what is happening.

## Therapy Techniques

Classical conditioning also serves as the basis for a number of psychotherapy techniques, including systematic desensitization, which has been used to treat phobias (this therapeutic technique and others are discussed in more detail in Chapter 15). (According to classical conditioning principles, phobias are conditioned emotional responses.) *Systematic desensitization* is the structured and repeated presentation of a feared conditioned stimulus in circumstances designed to reduce anxiety. Systematic desensitization works to extinguish the phobic response by teaching people to be relaxed in the presence of the feared object or situation, such as an elevator for those with an elevator phobia. With systematic desensitization, the CS no longer elicits the CR (fear); extinction has occurred.

## Advertising

John B. Watson revolutionized the advertising industry when he formalized its use of behavioral principles while working for an ad agency. For instance, the use of "sex appeal" to sell products stems from Watson's ideas. Sex isn't the only unconditioned stimulus that can work to produce a desired response; Razran (1940) did a study showing that political slogans (CS), when paired with the eating of food (US), were viewed more favorably by partici-

pants. Classical conditioning continues to be used in advertising to promote consumers' positive attitudes about products (Grossman & Till, 1998; Kim et al., 1998; Till & Priluck, 2000). This is referred to as *evaluative conditioning*: The goal is to change your liking, or evaluation, of the conditioned stimulus—the product the advertisers want you to buy (De Houwer et al., 2001).

Through the obvious sex appeal of this man and woman, Polo Sport® is trying to get you to buy its swimwear. If you find the ad to have sex appeal, then classical conditioning principles suggest that your mild arousal or pleasure on seeing the ad (and thereafter on seeing the product itself, following its pairing with the attractive couple) would lead you to buy the product.

## Food and Taste Aversion

When animals or people have an unpleasant experience during or after they eat or even just taste a particular food (leading them to try to avoid that food), they may develop a **food** or **taste aversion**. This type of classical conditioning usually involves learning after only a single experience of the CS-US pairing. Generally, the US is a nausea- or vomiting-inducing agent, and the CS is a previously neutral stimulus that was paired with it, such as the sight or smell of the food. The UR is nausea or vomiting, and so is the CR.

If you have ever had food poisoning, you may have developed a classically conditioned food aversion. A likely scenario is that the food that made you sick had some unhealthy and unwanted ingredient, such as salmonella bacteria. The bacteria are the US, and the ensuing nausea and vomiting are the UR. If the salmonella was in your dinner of broiled trout, trout might become a CS for you; whenever you eat it (or perhaps another fish similarly prepared), you become nauseated (the CR). Rather than put yourself through this experience, you are likely to avoid eating broiled trout, and a food aversion is born.

**Food aversion (taste aversion):** A classically conditioned avoidance of a certain food or taste.

# UNDERSTANDING RESEARCH

## The Discovery of Taste Aversion

Garcia and Koelling (1966) accidentally discovered the existence of taste aversion when studying the effects of radiation on rats. The rats were exposed to high enough doses of radiation that they became sick. The researchers noticed that the rats drank less water from the plastic water bottle in the radiation chamber than from the glass water bottle in their "home" cage. Although this preference could have been due to many factors, it turned out that the water in the plastic bottle had a slightly different taste, thanks to the plastic, than did the water in the glass bottle. The researchers shifted their focus to discover why the rats drank less from the plastic than the glass bottle.

**QUESTION:** Was classical conditioning at work? Did the taste of the water in the plastic bottle, through its association with the radiation-induced nausea, become a conditioned stimulus, leading to a conditioned taste aversion?

**ALTERNATIVES:** (1) Garcia and Koelling's preferred alternative (that is, their hypothesis) was that nausea would lead the rats to avoid drinking water that had an unusual taste; there's a biological connection between ingestion of substances and bodily reactions, which makes such conditioning relatively likely. According to this hypothesis, the radiation was the US, the taste of the water from the plastic bottle was the CS, getting sick (nauseated) was the UR, and the taste aversion was the CR (see Figure 6.7). (2) Any type of negative stimulation (such as an electric shock), not just nausea, would lead the rats to avoid drinking water that had an unusual taste. (3) The original finding was due to chance; if another group of rats were subjected to the same procedure, the rats would drink equivalent amounts of water from the different types of water bottles.

**LOGIC:** If taste aversion is specifically linked to bodily discomfort, then pairing a taste with such discomfort should condition the animal to avoid the taste. Moreover, if taste bears a special relationship to bodily discomfort, then it should be easier to condition gustatory taste stimuli than visual and auditory stimuli to such bodily discomfort. Finally, as a control, if the visual and auditory cues are salient enough, they should become conditioned to the foot shock—which would show that their failure to be conditioned to nausea did not occur because the animals failed to notice these cues.

**METHOD:** By repeating the original experiment (and adding other elements to rule out the second possibility), Garcia and Koelling would be able to determine whether the rats' response in the original study was a result of classical conditioning of a taste aversion, a result of classical conditioning to an aversive stimulus, or a quirk due to chance. Rats were placed in cages with bottles of water. Drinking from one bottle caused flashes of light and a clicking noise. Drinking from the other bottle did not produce any of these effects. The cage was capable of giving shocks to the rodents' feet. During the first phase of this experiment, half of the rats drank water from the bottle that produced flashes of light and a clicking noise; the researchers thus referred to the water in this condition as bright-noisy water. Note that these visual (flashing light) and auditory (clicking sound) stimuli are novel. The other half of the rats drank water that was sweet (due to the addition of saccharin), but

**FIGURE 6.7** **Taste Aversion Conditioning**

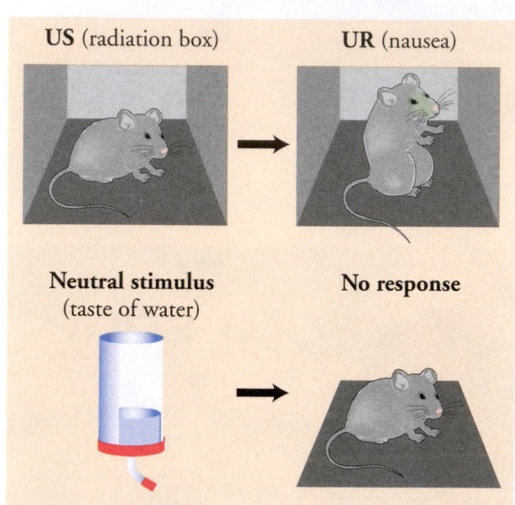

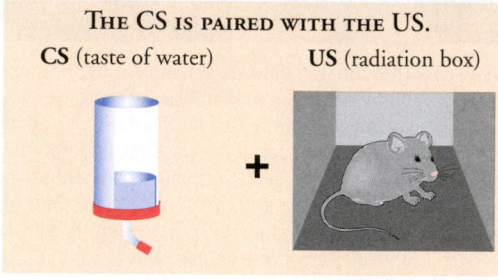

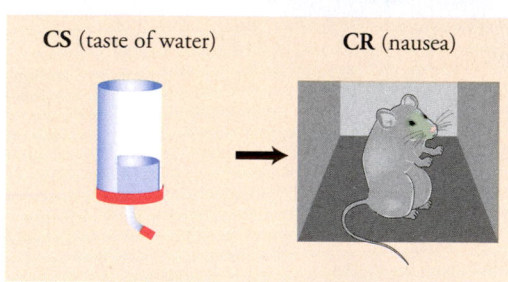

Did Garcia and Koelling (1966) inadvertently create a classically conditioned taste aversion, where the US was the radiation, the CS was the taste of water in the plastic bottle in the radiation chamber, the UR was the rat getting nauseated, and the CR was the rat's taste aversion?

neither bright nor noisy; in this condition, the rats were exposed to a novel gustatory stimulus (saccharin taste).

In the second phase of the experiment, half of each of these two groups had their feet shocked after drinking water. The other half of each group were exposed to radiation (as was originally done) or were given lithium chloride (a compound that causes nausea) after drinking water. In the final phase of the experiment, the rats were allowed to drink, and researchers noted which type of water each group would, and would *not*, drink; that is, did any of the groups of rats develop a conditioned taste aversion?

**RESULTS:** The results are summarized in Table 6.1.

---

**TABLE 6.1** **Results of Garcia and Koelling's Experiment**

The rats that previously drank bright-noisy water and had been shocked would not drink this type of water again, although they would drink sweet water. And those who drank bright-noisy water but had nausea induced did not avoid any type of water. Those who drank sweet water followed by nausea would not drink sweet water again, although they would drink bright-noisy water. Those who drank sweet water followed by shock did not avoid either type of water.

| Type of Water | Type of Aversive Stimulus | |
|---|---|---|
| | **Received shock** | **Received radiation/ lithium chloride** |
| **Bright-noisy water**  | Avoided bright-noisy water, but not sweet water | No evidence of classical conditioning |
| **Sweet water**  | No evidence of classical conditioning | Avoided sweet water, but not bright-noisy water |

---

**INFERENCES:** A taste aversion could be conditioned to a gustatory stimulus (the sweet water), but not to visual and auditory stimuli (lights and noise). However, the visual and auditory stimuli could not be conditioned to a gustatory stimulus (which shows that there was something special about the relation between taste and nausea), but those stimuli could be conditioned to shock (which shows that the animals did notice these cues, and that they could serve as a CS). No matter how the researchers manipulated the visual and auditory stimuli, they could not elicit a conditioned response of nausea. Thus, taste aversion can only be conditioned to appropriate stimuli—tastes. More generally, not all stimuli can be conditioned to elicit a given response.

## THINK CRITICALLY!

Why might it have been easier for Garcia and Koelling to condition a taste aversion to a gustatory stimulus rather than to visual or auditory stimuli? Can you think of an evolutionary explanation for this effect?

Garcia and Koelling's research led to another important discovery. (As often occurs in science, following up on a curious result can lead to unexpected but interesting and important discoveries.) Continuing with experiments on conditioned taste aversion, Garcia and colleagues (1966) found that rats avoided the novel-tasting water even if the nausea didn't occur until several hours after that water was presented. This further research showed that, at least in this case, the US doesn't need to come immediately after the CS.

These findings on taste aversion stirred considerable controversy because they described exceptions to the "rules" of classical conditioning. Taste aversion can lead to a more generalized response; just the sight of the food can elicit a conditioned response. President Ulysses S. Grant, a soldier who had seen the carnage of the Civil War, became nauseated at just the sight of rare meat (Seuling, 1978). Classically conditioned taste aversion is the mechanism behind the use of Antabuse to treat alcoholism. Antabuse is a medicine that causes violent nausea and vomiting when mixed with alcohol. If an alcoholic takes Antabuse and then drinks alcohol, he or she will vomit. If the drug achieves its larger purpose, the alcoholic will then develop a taste aversion to alcohol. Unfortunately, Antabuse has not been as successful as was originally hoped; those who were having difficulty refraining from drinking tended to stop taking their Antabuse so that they could drink without getting sick. If Antabuse is used consistently, it does decrease how often alcoholics drink, but it does not increase the likelihood of total abstinence (Fuller et al., 1986; Sereny et al., 1986). More recent findings suggest that if the person taking Antabuse is regularly supervised when taking it, thereby ensuring that the person actually takes it, then Antabuse is more effective at decreasing the amount of alcohol consumed (Brewer et al., 2000; Chick, Gough et al., 1992). This may explain why married alcoholics whose spouses help ensure that Antabuse is taken at regular intervals have the best success with it (Azrin et al., 1982).

Classical conditioning is adaptive, whether it involves an animal's (including a human's) ability to learn which foods are poisonous or which animals or objects in the environment (such as predators or guns) to fear and avoid. The more readily an organism learns these associations, the more likely that organism is to survive. Learned food aversions based on one exposure can be particularly adaptive: Animals who readily learn what not to eat will probably live longer and have more offspring.

## Conditioning and Chemotherapy

Cancer patients undergoing chemotherapy may experience intense nausea and vomiting as side effects of the treatment. But some patients develop *anticipatory nausea*, a classically conditioned response to chemotherapy triggered by a previously neutral CS (Burish & Carey, 1986; Carey & Burish, 1988; Davey, 1992). Such a stimulus might be as innocuous as a florist's shop seen en route to the hospital. For others undergoing chemotherapy, just thinking about the hospital where the treatment is received can produce nausea (Redd et al., 1993).

What is happening? The activity of neurons that feed into the patient's immune and autonomic nervous systems, stimulated by the US (the chemotherapeutic drugs) that induces the UR (nausea), becomes paired with the activity of neurons that register certain sights or sounds, for example, the sight of the florist shop, which becomes the CS. After enough such pairings, the two groups of neurons become functionally connected, and activity in one group triggers activity in the other (producing a CR).

However, some patients are more likely than others to develop anticipatory nausea. Some people are generally more reactive than others; that is, they have a tendency toward a stronger autonomic response to given levels of stimulation. Such people who become chemotherapy patients are more likely to develop anticipatory nausea (Kvale & Hugdahl, 1994), which can lead to a sense of helplessness and can cause them to stop the treatment altogether (Siegel & Longo, 1981). Fortunately, behavioral interventions such as relaxation training can help control anticipatory nausea, as can antinausea medications (Vasterling et al., 1993).

## Conditioning the Immune System

Suppose you worked day and night for a week, hardly taking the time to eat or sleep, and so severely weakened your immune system that you became very sick. During that exhausting work-filled week, you spent all of your waking hours with a laptop computer on your bed, which is covered by a bright red bedspread. Do you think that, after your recovery, simply sitting on that same bedspread could cause your immune system to weaken? Ader and his colleagues (Ader, 1976; Ader & Cohen, 1975) have shown that this kind of conditioning does in fact happen in rats. Ader and Cohen paired saccharin-flavored water with injections of cyclophosphamide, a drug given to organ transplant donors that suppresses the immune system and has a side effect of nausea. Ader had intended to use this drug not for its immune-suppressing qualities, but as a way to induce nausea in a study of taste aversion. He wanted to see how long the taste aversion would last once injections of cyclophosphamide stopped, but the rats continued to drink sweet water (the CS).

A few rats died on day 45 of the experiment, and more died over the next several days. Ader was confused; he had done similar experiments before with a different nausea-inducing drug and none of those animals had died. He eventually showed that the taste of the sweetened water was triggering not just the nausea, but a suppression of the immune system (as the actual drug would do), causing the eventual death of the rodents. Each time the rats drank the sweetened water, their immune systems were weakened—even without the immune-suppressing drug! The taste of the saccharin-sweetened water was acting as a CS, and the sweetened water was in essence a placebo. The rats' bodies responded to the CS as if it were cyclophosphamide.

Ader's accidental discovery and his follow-up studies were noteworthy for two reasons: First, they showed that the placebo effect could be induced in animals, not just humans; second, they showed that the organism doesn't have to believe that the placebo has medicinal properties in order to produce a placebo response. Although Ader and Cohen could not ask the rats what they believed would happen when they drank the sweet water, we have no reason to think that they "believed" it would impair their immune systems (Dienstfrey, 1991). Ader and Cohen have reported a number of follow-up studies, all trying to rule out other explanations of their results, and their hypothesis about the conditioning of the immune system has stood up well. Indeed, another study with rats showed that the immune response could be boosted by conditioning (Gorcynski, cited in Dienstfrey, 1991). There is evidence that the placebo effect may be a conditioned immune response that occurs in humans (Voudouris et al., 1985).

Classical conditioning explains why some people undergoing chemotherapy develop anticipatory nausea: Previously neutral stimuli—such as the sight of a florist shop on the way to the hospital—after being paired with nausea-inducing chemotherapy, can come to elicit nausea. Fortunately, treatments exist to prevent or minimize such conditioning.

# Test Yourself

1. Which of the following is true of Pavlov's experiments and most other classical conditioning procedures?
   a. The US and the CS are the same or very similar.
   b. The US and the UR must be learned.
   c. The UR and the CR are always very different.
   d. The UR and the CR are the same or very similar.

2. Imagine that your dog drools every time you open the refrigerator door. If you wanted to extinguish this behavior using classical conditioning principles, you could
   a. give the dog food from the refrigerator only occasionally.
   b. give the dog something from the refrigerator if it barks.
   c. repeatedly open the refrigerator door without ever giving the dog food.
   d. reward the dog with some food that you store in the bathroom.

3. Garcia and Koelling's use of bright-noisy water versus tasty water demonstrated that
   a. any stimulus can be conditioned to any response.
   b. there are certain constraints on what stimuli can be conditioned.
   c. only very strong stimuli can be conditioned.
   d. taste aversion does not apply to classical conditioning.

4. When a chemotherapy patient becomes nauseous at the sight of the hospital, the hospital has become the
   a. UR.          c. US.
   b. CR.          d. CS.

## Answers

NOTE: Once you feel comfortable with the Test Yourself questions in this chapter, visit the book's Web site at www.ablongman.com/kosslyn3e for additional study questions.

# Think It Through!

Dog obedience classes suggest that the following procedure will train a dog to stop barking. When the dog starts to bark, squirt water (from a water bottle) into its face. Right before you squirt, say, "Don't bark!" The dog startles because of the water and stops barking. Is this classical conditioning? If so, identify the US, CS, UR, and CR. If not, why not? What learning process has occurred if the dog stops barking only when you give the command in a particular tone of voice?

# OPERANT CONDITIONING

Classical conditioning is not the only way that Jackie Chan learned. At times Master Yu would give some of the students special rewards—extra food or a meal in a restaurant—or special punishments. Chan's classmates were also sources of rewards and punishments: Younger classmate Yuen Baio (who later acted in several of Chan's films) was a friend, providing support, camaraderie, and sometimes snacks from his parents' weekly gift of food. Moreover, Chan was honored with the most powerful reward at the school—a much desired place in the Seven Little Fortunes, a troupe of seven students who performed nightly in front of a paying audience (the income from the performances, however, went to Master Yu to pay for the running of the school).

How did the food treats come to be such a powerful force in Chan's life? And, how did the possibility of being picked to perform in the Seven Little Fortunes exert such a powerful influence on Chan and the other students, motivating them to practice even harder and more intensely than they otherwise would have? The answer might lie in another kind of learning, **operant conditioning**, the process whereby a behavior becomes associated with its consequences.

**Operant conditioning:** The process by which a behavior becomes associated with its consequences.

# The Roots of Operant Conditioning: Its Discovery and How It Works

If your behavior is followed by a positive consequence, you are more likely to repeat that behavior in the future; if it is followed by a negative consequence, you are less likely to repeat it. For instance, suppose you are swamped with schoolwork, and the day before a paper is due, you ask the professor for an extension (the behavior). If the professor gives you an extension (positive consequence), you will probably be more likely to ask for an extension in the future. In contrast, should the professor refuse you and get angry (negative consequence), you will probably be less likely to ask for an extension in the future. This basic observation about behaviors and their consequences underlies the mechanism of operant conditioning. Unlike classical conditioning, in which the organism is largely passive, operant conditioning requires the organism to "operate" in the world, to do something. Operant conditioning is also called *instrumental conditioning*, because behavior is required to produce the effect. Whereas classical conditioning usually involves involuntary reflexes, such as cringing in response to hearing the whistling of a cane whipping through the air, operant conditioning usually involves voluntary, non-reflexive behavior, such as singing a song, assuming a kung fu stance, or eating with chopsticks or a fork.

## Thorndike's Puzzle Box

At about the same time that Pavlov was working with his dogs, American psychologist Edward L. Thorndike (1874–1949) was investigating a different kind of learning. Thorndike created a puzzle box, a cage with a latched door that a cat could open by pressing down on a pedal inside the cage (see Figure 6.8). Food was placed outside the cage door. Although the cat took a while to get around to pressing down the pedal, once it did (and the door opened), the cat was quicker to press the pedal in its subsequent sessions in the box: It had learned that pressing the pedal opened the door and enabled it to get the food (see Figure 6.9). Thorndike called this type of learning "trial-and-error learning." His finding led to his famous formulation of the **Law of Effect** (Thorndike, 1927), which lies at the heart of operant conditioning: Actions that subsequently lead to a "satisfying state of affairs" are more likely to be repeated (Thorndike, 1949, p. 14).

## The Skinner Box

B. F. Skinner (1904–1990), the 20th century's foremost proponent of behaviorism, is important in the history of psychology not only because he most fully developed the

**FIGURE 6.8** **Thorndike's Puzzle Box**

Thorndike placed a hungry cat inside the box and a piece of fish just outside the door, within the cat's sight. The cat tried many behaviors to get out of the box and to the fish, but only pressing the pedal would open the door. Eventually, the cat pressed the pedal, and the door opened. When the cat was put back inside the box, it pressed the pedal more quickly, improving each time.

**FIGURE 6.9** **The Phases of Operant Conditioning**

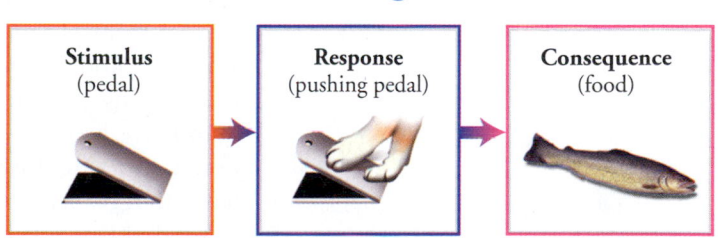

Unlike classical conditioning, operant conditioning requires the organism to produce the desired behavior (the response). That behavior is then followed by a positive or negative consequence.

Law of Effect: Actions that subsequently lead to a "satisfying state of affairs" are more likely to be repeated.

## FIGURE 6.10 Skinner Box and Cumulative Recorder

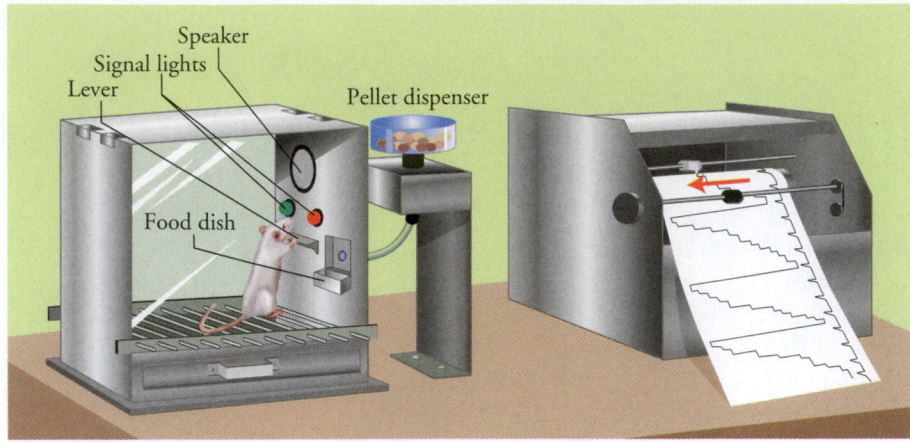

In a Skinner box, a hungry rat presses a lever (or a pigeon pecks a key). As with Thorndike's cat, the rat will emit random behaviors, eventually pressing the lever, causing a food pellet (reinforcement) to come down the chute into the food dish, increasing the likelihood of the response in the future. The rat presses the lever again, and another food pellet appears. It presses the lever (and eats) more frequently—it has learned that pressing the lever will be followed by the appearance of a food pellet. On the outside of the box is a cumulative recorder, a device that records each lever press and the time interval between presses.

concept of operant conditioning, but also because he showed how conditioning could explain much of our daily behavior. Working mostly with pigeons and wanting to minimize his handling of the birds, he developed an apparatus that is now often referred to as a *Skinner box*. The box (see Figure 6.10) could both feed the animals and record the frequency of their responses, making it easy to quantify the responses (this enormously helpful feature was, in fact, an unintended bonus of the box's design; Skinner, 1956). If a rat is put in a Skinner box, it learns to associate pressing the lever or bar with the likelihood of a food pellet's appearing. Here, the lever is the stimulus, pressing the lever is the response, or behavior, and receiving the food pellet is the consequence.

# Principles of Operant Conditioning

Operant conditioning involves an association between a stimulus, the response to the stimulus (a behavior), and its consequence. (In classical conditioning, the association is between a neutral stimulus and an unconditioned stimulus.) Operant conditioning relies on **reinforcement**, the process by which consequences lead to an increase in the likelihood that the response will occur again. To be most effective, the reinforcement should be contingent on a desired response. Not surprisingly, this relationship between the response and the consequence is called **response contingency**; it occurs when a consequence is dependent on the organism's producing the desired behavior. In contrast to the responses that are elicited in classical conditioning, responses in operant conditioning are *emitted*; the responses are voluntarily produced.

An example of operant conditioning occurred in Chan's life when, as a young adult, he and many other martial arts experts were seeking work as stuntmen in the Hong Kong film industry. There were more junior (young, inexperienced) stuntmen than there were jobs, and Chan desperately needed the work in order to pay his bills. One day, a director wanted a stunt done; it was deemed so unsafe by the stunt coordinator that he refused to have any of his stuntmen do it. Chan volunteered to do it, figuring that this was the only way he'd be likely to get work. He did the dangerous stunt (twice) and *did* get more jobs after that—he shifted from being a junior stuntman to a full-fledged stuntman with regular work. What Chan learned from this experience was that trying very dangerous stunts (behavior) would get him work (the reinforcement).

A **reinforcer** is an object or event that comes after a response and that strengthens the likelihood of its recurrence. In Thorndike's puzzle box and in the Skinner box, the reinforcer, or consequence, is food. Which reinforcer works best for people? The answer to this question is tricky: What one person considers a "reward" might leave another person cold. Reinforcement, therefore, is in the eyes of the recipient. For instance, for one person, a night at the ballet might be a wonderful reinforcer for doing well on a test. To another, a night at the ballet might seem like punishment.

Reinforcement: The process by which consequences lead to an increase in the likelihood that the response will occur again.

Response contingency: The relationship that occurs when a consequence is dependent on the organism's emitting the desired behavior.

Reinforcer: An object or event that comes after a response and that changes the likelihood of its recurrence.

As an illustration of this fact about reinforcers, consider an account Chan provides of the filming of his first *Rush Hour* movie, when he was already considered a "star" in America:

> The studio [spared] nothing to make me feel like I'm a star. I have a beautiful rented mansion, a luxurious trailer on the set, a personal trainer, and a car standing by at all times. Even my stunt-men have their own private rooms. In my Hong Kong movies, we squeeze together, share what we have to, and eat lunch together, all out of the same big pot. I do everything and anything I want to—I'm the director, the producer, the cameraman, the prop guy, the janitor. Anything. Here, they won't let me do anything except act. They won't even let me stand around so they can check the lighting—they have a stand-in, my height, my color, wearing my clothes, come in, and they check the lighting off of him while I sit in my trailer. (Chan &Yang, 1999, p. 303)

The producers apparently thought that this "star treatment" would reinforce Chan for acting in American movies—but in fact he didn't like it and was itching to be more involved between scenes.

Parents who give stickers to their child for good behavior might conclude that behavioral programs don't work if the child makes no effort to win the stickers. They'd be wrong: The problem is that their child doesn't view stickers as a reward. The parents simply need to find a reinforcer that will work, increasing the likelihood that their child will repeat a particular behavior. For instance, when we were toilet training our children, we used reinforcers whenever they tried to use the potty. We had asked each child to name a reinforcer, and one of our children requested black olives. This is a reminder that the proof is in the pudding—the degree to which an object or event is a reinforcer is determined by its effect on the individual organism. Just calling something a reinforcer doesn't make it so.

Like classical conditioning, operant conditioning involves cognitive processing. Simply telling people about the contingency between a behavior and reinforcement can lead to behavior change (Kirsch, Lynn et al., 2004), as occurs when parents or teachers explain sticker programs to children or when supervisors announce upcoming opportunities for employees to earn bonuses through improved performance.

## Reinforcement: Getting Your Just Desserts

There are two types of reinforcement, positive and negative. In **positive reinforcement**, a desired reinforcer is presented after a response, thereby increasing the likelihood of a recurrence of that response (see the first row in Figure 6.11, p. 254). The food for Thorndike's cat and black olives for our toddler are examples of positive reinforcement. Food is the usual positive reinforcer for animals; for humans, toys, money, and intangibles such as praise and attention can also be positive reinforcers, as was Jackie Chan's acceptance into the Seven Little Fortunes. Chan also describes how, when he was about 6 years old, using kung fu against other kids could produce positive reinforcement: He would fight other kids who were "stupid enough to get in my way. . . . I found out quickly that fighting was fun—when you won anyway—and it soon became one of my favorite hobbies, next to eating" (p. 12).

Sometimes we inadvertently reinforce certain behaviors by paying them too much attention (positive reinforcement); this can happen when patients with coronary heart disease receive attention when talking about their symptoms, which leads them to talk even more about their symptoms (Itkowitz et al., 2003). Scolding children is another example: If the only time a child receives any attention at all is when he or she misbehaves, then even "bad attention," such as a scolding, can be a positive reinforcer. Chan did not view having to stand outside his 1st-grade classroom with a sign around his neck as punishment for his classroom antics. Therefore, he did not

**Positive reinforcement:** Occurs when a desired reinforcer is presented after a behavior, thereby increasing the likelihood of a recurrence of that behavior.

FIGURE 6.11

## Positive and Negative Reinforcement and Punishment

Chan's behavior (a correct landing from a flying side kick) is positively reinforced; after he does the behavior correctly, he receives a treat.

In contrast, the same behavior is negatively reinforced: the Master has a frown as Chan is going into the move (an aversive stimulus), but the aversive stimulus is removed when Chan lands from the flying side kick correctly. The Master's goal is the same in both examples—to maximize the likelihood that the behavior (a perfect flying side kick landing) will occur again.

Chan's behavior (falling when landing from a flying side kick) is being positively punished: The Master gives an unpleasant consequence (a caning) so as to minimize the likelihood that the behavior (an incorrect flying side kick landing) will occur again.

Chan's behavior (falling when landing from a flying side kick) is being negatively punished: The Master removes a pleasant event (his smile at Jackie) so as to minimize the likelihood that the behavior (an incorrect flying side kick landing) will occur again.

### POSITIVE REINFORCEMENT

### NEGATIVE REINFORCEMENT

### POSITIVE PUNISHMENT

### NEGATIVE PUNISHMENT

learn what his teachers wanted him to learn. In the workplace, increased pay can be reinforcing for some people, whereas increased recognition or flexible hours are more likely to be reinforcing for others (Rynes et al., 2005). Again, reinforcement is particular to each individual.

In contrast, **negative reinforcement** is the removal of an unpleasant event or circumstance following a behavior, thereby increasing the probability of the behavior's occurring again (see Figure 6.11, second row). If a rat is being mildly shocked in its cage, and the shocks stop when it presses a bar, then bar pressing is negatively reinforced. Or consider the student whose neighbor is blaring music, song after blasting song. This unpleasant event ends when the student knocks on the neighbor's door and asks the neighbor to turn down the volume—and the neighbor complies. Asking to have the volume lowered has been negatively reinforced. Yet another example of negative reinforcement in action is when people use substances, such as alcohol, to decrease their anxiety (Hohlstein et al., 1998; Samoluk & Stewart, 1998); because it reduces the aversive state of anxiousness, using alcohol is negatively reinforced.

Negative reinforcement is sometimes referred to as *escape conditioning*, because the organism has learned to perform a behavior that decreases or stops an aversive stimulus (thereby escaping from the aversive stimulus). Imagine that your bedroom window overlooks an area where trash barrels are placed for pickup by a garbage truck. You've just moved in and find that early one Saturday morning, as you are catching up on much needed sleep, you awaken to the sound of glass bottles and other trash being compacted in the rear of the truck. Several minutes go by, and still the noise continues. You stuff wads of tissue in your ears to muffle the sound, put a pillow over your head, and go back to sleep. Putting tissue in your ears (and the pillow over your head) is negatively reinforced because it stops an aversive stimulus (the noise of the garbage truck). You have performed a behavior that allows to you "escape" the aversive situation. After a few weeks of this, you are likely to experience *avoidance learning*: You avoid the unpleasant stimulus altogether by making sure to shut your windows and wear sound-filtering ear plugs when you go to sleep Friday night.

Both positive and negative reinforcement are described as reinforcing because they increase the likelihood that a behavior will be repeated. (See Figure 6.12.) Negative reinforcement is *not* the same thing as punishment. Let's see why.

## Punishment

A punishment is an unpleasant stimulus or event that occurs as a consequence of a behavior. Punishment *decreases* the probability of the recurrence of a behavior, in contrast to reinforcement (both positive and negative), which *increases* the likelihood of recurrence. Although punishment is commonly confused with negative reinforcement, they are not the same: Punishment decreases the probability of a recurrence of a behavior; negative reinforcement increases the probability of a recurrence of a behavior by removing an unpleasant event or circumstance after the desired behavior (see Figure 6.13).

Just as there are positive and negative forms of reinforcement, there are also positive and negative forms of punishment. **Positive punishment** occurs when a behavior leads to an undesired consequence, thereby decreasing the probability that the behavior will occur again (see Figure 6.11, third row). For example, a student may be positively punished with a failing grade for not spending a lot of effort writing a term paper. If this punishment is effective, she will be less likely to blow off the paper next time. **Negative punishment** is the removal of a pleasant event or circumstance following a behavior, thereby decreasing the probability that the behavior will occur again (see Figure 6.11, fourth row). Consider a boy who misbehaves: His parents negatively punish him by temporarily taking away his MP3 player.

Chan and his classmates were required to do handstands for at least half an hour at a time, despite distressing physical experiences as a result of remaining upside down

**FIGURE 6.12**

## Positive Reinforcement and Negative Reinforcement

This couple has been positively reinforced for buying a lottery ticket—they have received a large amount of money.

The nonsmoker has been negatively reinforced for pointing out the "No smoking" sign to the smoker—the aversive cigarette smoke disappears.

Negative reinforcement: Occurs when an unpleasant event or circumstance that follows a behavior is removed, thereby increasing the likelihood of a recurrence of the behavior.

Positive punishment: Occurs when a behavior leads to an undesired consequence, thereby decreasing the likelihood of a recurrence of that behavior.

Negative punishment: Occurs when a behavior leads to the removal of a pleasant event or circumstance, thereby decreasing the likelihood of a recurrence of the behavior.

**FIGURE 6.13**

## Negative Reinforcement Versus Punishment

The boy performed the exact same behavior in both these cases, but the consequences of his behavior are different. With negative reinforcement, he is more likely to repeat the behavior. In contrast, with punishment, he is less likely to repeat the behavior.

**NEGATIVE REINFORCEMENT**

Wow, what a surprise! It's nice of you to have cleaned the kitchen—and without my asking. How about if you don't have to do any more chores this week?

**PUNISHMENT**

I didn't ask you to clean the kitchen, did I? Now I won't be able to find things when I need them. You're grounded the rest of the weekend, young man!

for so long: "after fifteen minutes, our arms would grow limp, our blood would rush to our heads, and our stomachs would begin to turn flip-flops. But we couldn't show any weakness at all. A limb that moved would receive a whack from the master's rattan cane" (p. 43). This was an example of positive punishment: Moving a limb led to a whack of the cane.

Punishment is most effective if it has three characteristics:

- *Punishment should be swift*, occurring immediately after the undesired behavior. The old threat "Wait till you get home!" undermines the effectiveness of the punishment.

- *Punishment must be consistent.* The undesired behavior must be punished each and every time it occurs. If the behavior is punished only sporadically, the person or animal doesn't effectively learn that the behavior will be followed by punishment, and so doesn't decrease the frequency of the behavior as consistently.

- *Punishment should be aversive* but not so aversive as to create problems such as high levels of fear or anxiety, injury, or new, undesired behaviors.

We must note several cautionary points about the use of punishment. First, although punishment may decrease the frequency of a behavior, it doesn't eliminate the capacity to engage in that behavior. Your little sister may learn not to push you because your mother will punish her, but she may continue to push her classmates at school because the behavior has not been punished in that context. She has learned not to push when she will be punished for it. Moreover, sometimes people are able to avoid punishment, but continue to exhibit the response, as when your little sister figures out that if she hits you, but then apologizes, she will not get punished.

Second, physical punishment, such as a spanking, may actually increase aggressive behavior in the person on the receiving end (Haapasalo & Pokela, 1999; Straus, 2000; Straus et al., 1997). Although punishment provides an opportunity for operant learning, seeing others use physical violence also creates an opportunity for learning by watching the behavior of others. Such learning could account for the finding that abusive parents (and physically aggressive juvenile delinquents) tend to come from abusive families (Conger et al., 2003; Kwong et al., 2003; Straus & Gelles, 1980; Straus & McCord, 1998).

A third problem created by punishment is that, through classical conditioning, the one being punished may come to fear the one doing the punishing. This may happen even if the punishment is infrequent. If the punishment is severe, a single instance may be enough for the person being punished to learn to live in fear of the punisher, as Chan and his classmates lived in fear of Master Yu. Constantly living in fear can make people and animals chronically stressed, and it can lead to depression (Pine et al., 2001).

Punishment alone hasn't been found to be as effective as punishment used in combination with reinforcement. This is because punishment doesn't convey information about what behavior should be exhibited in place of the undesired, punished behavior. Consider a preschool-age boy who draws on the wall. You don't want him to ruin the wallpaper so they punish him, and he learns not to draw on the wall. But, at a later time, when he's feeling creative, he might draw on the floor or the door instead. However, if you punish him for wall or floor drawing and then provide him with paper and reinforce him for drawing on the paper, he can be artistically creative without inviting punishment. Because of the disadvantages of punishment, many training programs for parents emphasize positive reinforcement for good behavior; if children don't feel their parents are noticing and appreciating their efforts at good behavior, the incentive to keep it up may diminish.

## Primary and Secondary Reinforcers

There are different levels of reinforcers: **Primary reinforcers** are events or objects that are inherently reinforcing (such as food, water, and relief from pain). At the Chinese Drama Academy, the children barely had enough to eat, and food became a much sought-out and fought-after item. Master Yu rewarded the Seven Little Fortunes with a trip to a restaurant after a particularly good performance. **Secondary reinforcers**, such as attention, praise, money, a good grade, and a promotion, are learned reinforcers and do not inherently satisfy a physical need. The theme park Sea World uses food as a primary reinforcer for its dolphins. It also uses secondary reinforcers such as squirting the dolphins' faces with water. Secondary reinforcers are generally not instinctually satisfying.

When Chan was at the Academy, his secondary reinforcers included being picked to be part of a troupe performing in public and the kind words or deeds of a schoolmate. In his adult life, Chan received very powerful secondary reinforcers for making movies that were his own creation: 4.2 million Hong Kong dollars and control over how the movies were made—the new studio would not require him to get their final approval over budgets or ideas.

**Behavior modification** is a technique that brings about therapeutic change in behavior through the use of secondary reinforcers. Programs involving mentally retarded children and adults, psychiatric patients, and prisoners have made use of secondary reinforcement. Participants in such programs earn "tokens" that can be traded for candy or for privileges such as going out for a walk or watching a particular TV show. Such tokens have also been used to reward children for desired behavior change; the tokens can be exchanged for the secondary reinforcer of watching television or playing computer games (Jason & Fries, 2004). Some behavior modification programs provide reinforcement when an interval of time has passed *without an unwanted behavior* (Conyers et al., 2003). Behavior modification techniques using secondary reinforcement have also been used in the workplace; when employees received bonus vouchers for arriving at work on time, management found a significant reduction in tardiness (Hermann et al., 1973).

Simply punishing someone does not provide that person with appropriate alternative behaviors. This mother clearly states an appropriate alternative to biting someone when angry—using words to express feelings.

**Primary reinforcer:** An event or object, such as food, water, or relief from pain, that is inherently reinforcing.

**Secondary reinforcer:** An event or object, such as attention, praise, money, a good grade, or a promotion, that is reinforcing but that does not inherently satisfy a physical need.

**Behavior modification:** A technique that brings about therapeutic change in behavior through the use of secondary reinforcers.

Choosing a delayed reinforcement over an immediate one has its advantages, but the choice is not necessarily easy. A dieter trying to obtain the delayed reinforcement of looking and feeling better sacrifices immediate reinforcement (ice cream, now!) for future personal benefits. But immediate reinforcement can be very powerful, and often difficult to reject in favor of some future good. At some point, the dieter may yield to the satisfaction of eating the ice cream, or even just a normal-sized portion of dinner, instead of making yet another sacrifice for the sake of eventual slimness.

An unusual use of behavior modification with secondary reinforcers was undertaken by researchers in the rural Philippines who wanted to improve nutrition among poor children (Guthrie et al., 1982). The study was designed to discover whether reinforcement would modify mothers' nutritional care of their children more than would simply giving the mothers information about health and nutrition for children. All of the mothers were given appropriate information. Then the health clinic provided different forms of reinforcement that were contingent on increases in the children's heights and weights. Three different villages participated in the study. In one, the reinforcement was a ticket in a clinic lottery in which the prize was food; the reinforcer used in the second village was a photograph of the child. The third village was a control group, and these people received no reinforcement for height or weight gains. One year later, children in the two villages that received reinforcement grew more and had less malnutrition than did those in the third village; no differences were observed between the first and second village.

## Immediate Versus Delayed Reinforcement

The interval of time between behavior and its consequence can affect operant conditioning. In the Skinner box, for instance, if the rat receives a food pellet immediately after pressing the bar, it is receiving **immediate reinforcement**, reinforcement given immediately after the desired behavior. If the food pellet doesn't appear immediately but comes, say, 30 seconds later, the rat is receiving **delayed reinforcement**. With delayed reinforcement, the rat has some difficulty learning that bar pressing is followed by food. After pressing the bar but before receiving reinforcement, the rat may have sniffed some other section of the cage, scratched its ear, or done any number of things. It would be hard for the rat to "figure out" which behavior had produced the pellet.

Humans often work hard for delayed reinforcement. We practice kicking the soccer ball into the goal so that we'll be able to score at the next game; we study hard in college to get into graduate school or to land a good job; we put in extra hours at work to get a promotion, raise, or bonus; we push our bodies to the limit of what's possible to please an audience or receive a medal. Walter Mischel and his colleagues (1989) found that among the 4-year-olds they studied, those who would pass up a small reward now for a big one tomorrow became more socially competent and were more likely to be high achievers during adolescence.

Chan experienced a long-delayed reinforcement: Once his acting career began, he had two wishes. One was to be part of a Hollywood "opening night" ceremony, with plush ropes to keep fans back. The other wish was to put his handprints next to his "star" outside Grauman's Chinese Theatre in Los Angeles. He had been working and hoping for that reward for more than 10 years, with two previous Hollywood films, without success. After years of work, he achieved both goals.

## Beyond Basic Reinforcement

Operant conditioning can play a powerful role in people's lives. To see how, let's look at ways in which conditioning can be more than simply learning to respond when reinforcement is likely to result.

## Generalization and Discrimination in Operant Conditioning

Just as in classical conditioning, animals (including humans) can generalize and discriminate during operant conditioning. Thus, in operant conditioning, **generalization** is the ability to emit a learned behavior in response to a similar stimulus. When a child

Immediate reinforcement: Reinforcement given immediately after the desired behavior is exhibited.

Delayed reinforcement: Reinforcement given some period of time after the desired behavior is exhibited.

Generalization: The ability to emit a learned behavior in response to a similar stimulus.

has a runny nose, most parents teach her to wipe her nose on a tissue. She may then generalize the learned behavior of wiping her nose and begin to wipe it on similar stimuli: any available soft surface—her sleeve, her parent's shirt, her pillow.

**Discrimination** is the ability to engage in a learned behavior in response to a particular stimulus (wiping a runny nose on a tissue or handkerchief) but not in response to a similar one (wiping a runny nose on a shirt sleeve). The child's parents could help her make this discrimination by reinforcing her every time she wipes her nose with tissues or handkerchiefs (making sure they are readily available), and by not reinforcing her when she wipes her nose on her sleeve or on theirs.

Discrimination depends on the ability to distinguish among the different situations in which a stimulus may occur. Animals can be trained to press a bar to get food only if a tone is sounding, or only if they hear a high tone (not a low or medium tone). A **discriminative stimulus** is the cue that tells the organism whether a specific response will lead to the expected reinforcement. Experienced drivers react to a red light without thinking, automatically putting a foot on the brake pedal. In this situation, the red light is the stimulus, stopping the car is the response, and the reinforcement (negative, in this case) is avoiding a dangerous situation. But people don't stomp their right feet if they encounter a red light while walking on the sidewalk. Driving a car is the discriminative stimulus that cues the response to move the right foot.

## Extinction and Spontaneous Recovery in Operant Conditioning: Gone Today, Back Tomorrow

Have you ever lost money in a vending machine? If so, does this sequence of behaviors sound familiar? You deposit coins in the machine and press the button for your selection because you have learned that the reinforcement (the food) will come down the chute. When you press the button and no food appears, you press the button again. You then have a burst of pressing the button several times (and maybe a few other buttons for good measure), and only after these responses fail to make the machine deliver the goods do you give up. As this example shows, when someone has learned a behavior through operant conditioning (putting money in a vending machine) and the reinforcement stops (the food doesn't appear), initially there is an increase in responding. After this initial burst of behavior, the response fades. This is how **extinction** works in operant conditioning.

As with classical conditioning, the original response isn't lost through extinction; what happens is that new, opposing learning takes place. In the vending machine example, the opposing learning is that dropping coins in the slot does not lead to the appearance of food. As with classical conditioning, **spontaneous recovery** occurs: If a period of time follows extinction, the old behavior will reappear. So if you don't use that vending machine for a month, you might very well put money in it again, expecting it to dispense your bag of chips.

## Building Complicated Behaviors: Shaping Up

Many complex behaviors are not learned all at one time, but rather are acquired gradually. Moreover, complex behaviors may often be built on previously learned behaviors. How do the animal trainers at Sea World train the dolphins to do a high jump? The dolphins don't naturally do it, so they can't be reinforced for that behavior.

**Shaping** is the gradual process of reinforcing an organism for behavior that gets closer and closer to the behavior you ultimately wish to produce. It is the method that helps train dolphins to do high jumps (see Figure 6.14), and it is also the method by which Jackie Chan learned kung fu: The complex behaviors were gradually shaped,

Discrimination: The ability to engage in a learned behavior in response to a particular stimulus but not in response to a similar one.

Discriminative stimulus: The cue that tells the organism whether a specific response will lead to the expected reinforcement.

Extinction: In operant conditioning, the fading out of a response following an initial burst of that behavior after the withdrawal of reinforcement.

Spontaneous recovery: In operant conditioning, the process by which an old response reappears if there is a period of time after extinction.

Shaping: The gradual process of reinforcing an organism for behavior that gets closer to the desired behavior.

**FIGURE 6.14**

## Shaping Dolphins at Sea World

At Sea World, training dolphins to jump requires a number of phases, each getting closer to the final goal.

First the dolphin receives reinforcement (a food treat) after touching a target on the surface of the water.

The target is raised slightly out of the water. When the dolphin touches the target, it receives food.

The target continues to be raised until eventually the dolphin's body must come out of the water for it to touch the target. The dolphin receives a treat for doing so.

first by his father when he was very young, and later by Master Yu. Shaping is used when the desired response is not one that the organism would emit in the normal course of events. The process of shaping must be done in phases, nudging the organism closer and closer to the desired response. The final desired behavior is considered as a series of smaller behaviors, which become increasingly similar to the desired behavior; these smaller behaviors are called **successive approximations**. One study found that shaping procedures could train people with profound mental retardation to choose larger, but delayed reinforcement rather than smaller, immediate reinforcement. This ability to delay reinforcement is thought to be a central feature of exercising self-control (Dixon et al., 2003).

## Reinforcement Schedules: An Hourly or a Piece-Rate Wage?

Skinner's work highlighted a critical element that can change the frequency of an organism's response: the schedule on which the reinforcement is delivered (Staddon & Ceruti, 2003). Reinforcement can be given every time a desired response occurs, or it can be given less frequently. When an organism is reinforced for each desired response, it is receiving **continuous reinforcement**. When reinforcement does not occur after every response, but only intermittently, the organism is receiving **partial reinforcement**. Initial learning is slower with partial reinforcement than with continuous reinforcement. For this reason, when shaping a new behavior, it is best to use continuous reinforcement until the desired behavior is stable. Thus, Sea

**Successive approximations:** The series of smaller behaviors involved in shaping a complex behavior.

**Continuous reinforcement:** Reinforcement given for each desired response.

**Partial reinforcement:** Reinforcement given only intermittently.

World trainers reward a dolphin every time it touches the target on the surface of the water. An advantage of a partial reinforcement schedule, however, is that it is more resistant to extinction: The organism learns that it won't receive reinforcement after each response, so it doesn't stop doing the behavior right away when no reinforcement is given. Some partial reinforcement schedules, called **interval schedules**, are based on time; reinforcement is given for responses after a specified interval of time. Other schedules, called **ratio schedules**, are based on a specified number of the desired responses; reinforcement is given after that number of responses is emitted.

**FIXED INTERVAL SCHEDULE**   On a **fixed interval schedule**, the organism receives reinforcement for a response emitted after a fixed interval of time. In a Skinner box, a rat on a fixed interval schedule of 10 minutes would receive reinforcement for the first bar press that occurs 10 minutes after the previous reinforcement was given, but not during that 10 minutes, regardless of how many times it pressed the bar. The same applies for the next 10-minute interval: The rat would receive a food pellet only for the first bar press after 10 minutes since the last reinforcement. With animals on a fixed interval schedule, the frequency of desired behavior tends to slow down right after reinforcement and pick up again right before reinforcement. A study break after every hour of studying is reinforcement on a fixed interval schedule. So is a weekly paycheck: No matter how hard you work, you will not get an additional paycheck that week. However, companies recognize that the fixed interval schedule is not necessarily the best way to reward employees, and promotions are not always available nor desirable to award. As shown in Figure 6.15 (p. 262), responses to a fixed interval schedule produce a scalloped pattern on the graph of cumulative responses.

**VARIABLE INTERVAL SCHEDULE**   In **variable interval schedules**, the interval is an average over time. If a rat were reinforced for its first response after 8 minutes, then after another response 12 minutes later, then 13 minutes later, then 7 minutes later, it would be on a variable interval schedule of 10 minutes. If you took a study break after approximately an hour of studying, but sometimes after 45 minutes, sometimes after an hour and 15 minutes, sometimes after half an hour, sometimes after an hour and a half, the average would be every hour, and so you would be on a variable interval 60-minute schedule. In animals, this kind of schedule creates consistent although somewhat slow responding (see Figure 6.15).

**FIXED RATIO SCHEDULE**   Fixed ratio schedules provide reinforcement after a fixed number of responses. If an animal is on a "fixed ratio 10" schedule, it receives a food pellet after its 10th bar

Interval schedule: Partial reinforcement schedule based on time.

Ratio schedule: Partial reinforcement schedule based on a specified number of emitted responses.

Fixed interval schedule: Reinforcement schedule in which reinforcement is given for a response emitted after a fixed interval of time.

Variable interval schedule: Reinforcement schedule in which reinforcement is given for a response emitted after a variable interval of time.

Fixed ratio schedule: Reinforcement schedule in which reinforcement is given after a fixed number of responses.

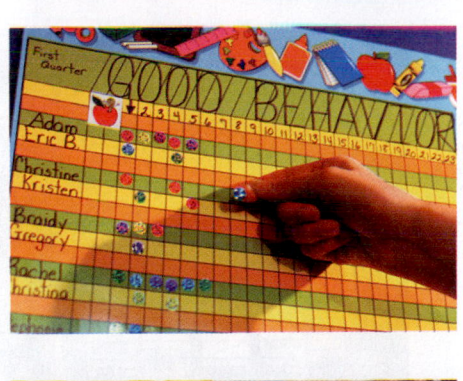

As a reward for working hard all week, these students see a movie every Friday afternoon; they have put themselves on a fixed interval schedule.

Although this teacher intends to put the appropriate star on each child's sticker chart each day, she sometimes forgets until the next day—reinforcing each child's targeted behavior on a variable interval schedule.

The fixed ratio schedule is the schedule used to pay those doing piecework: Workers receive money for a certain number of pieces, in this case, for a certain number of tee shirts. This schedule often has the highest responding rate but can be exhausting for the workers.

## FIGURE 6.15  Schedules of Reinforcement

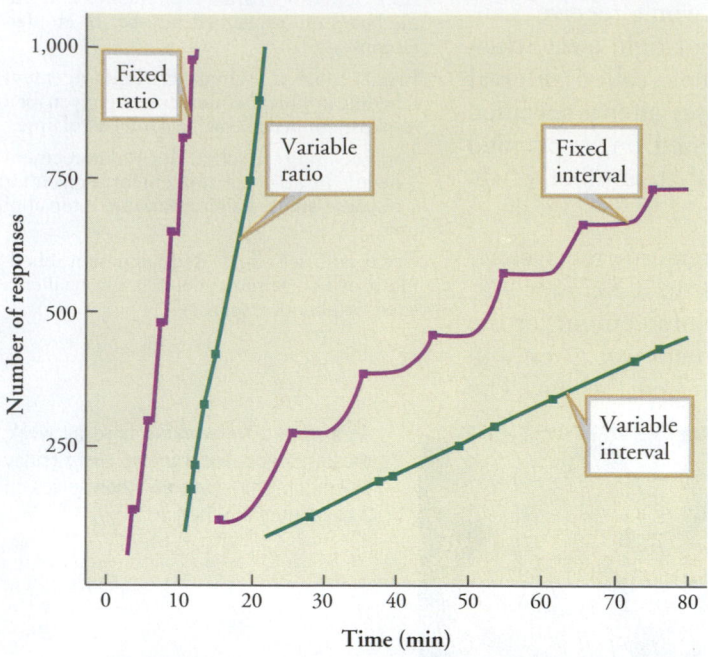

Research findings are mixed with regard to the degree of correspondence between rodents' and humans' cumulative frequencies on the four different schedules of reinforcement. These graphs show the response patterns for rodents. Some studies with humans have found similar patterns of responding (Higgens and Morris, 1984); others have not (Lowe, 1979; Matthews et al., 1977). For both humans and rodents, however, variable reinforcement schedules induce a more consistent rate of responding than do fixed reinforcement schedules.

The variable ratio reinforcement schedule, often referred to as the gambling reinforcement schedule, is the most resistant to extinction. If you were playing a slot machine and didn't hit the jackpot, how long would you need to play before you might think there was a problem with the machine?

**Variable ratio schedule:** Reinforcement schedule in which reinforcement is given after a variable number of responses.

press, then again after another 10, and so on. Factory piecework is paid on a fixed ratio schedule; for example, in the garment industry, workers may be paid a certain amount for every 10 completed articles of clothing. When responses on this schedule are graphed, they assume a steplike pattern (see Figure 6.15): There is a high rate of response until reinforcement is delivered, then a lull, followed by a high rate of response until the next reinforcement, and so on. This schedule has a higher rate of responding than a fixed interval schedule. For this reason, piecework can be exhausting, whether the work is inputting data (being paid for every 100 lines of data entered), sewing garments, or assembling machinery. On a fixed ratio schedule, workers have a good reason not to take breaks (they will not be paid for that time), but as people work long hours without breaks, efficiency and accuracy decline (Proctor & Van Zandt, 1994).

**VARIABLE RATIO SCHEDULE**   Variable ratio schedules present reinforcement at a variable rate. If reinforcement occurs on average after every 10th response, reinforcement could be presented after 5, 18, 4, and 13 responses, or it could presented after 24, 1, 10, and 5 responses. You never really know when the reinforcement will come. This type of schedule is often called the "gambling reinforcement schedule" because most gambling relies on such unpredictable reinforcement. Slot machines hit the jackpot on a variable ratio reinforcement schedule. If you play long enough (and spend enough money), eventually you will win; unfortunately, you might spend years, and tens of thousands of dollars, trying to hit the jackpot. The variable ratio schedule is the most resistant to extinction (which is part of the reason some people get hooked on gambling). Because you don't know exactly when you will be reinforced (but expect that eventually reinforcement will come), you keep responding. Animals on a variable ratio schedule tend to respond frequently, consistently, and without long pauses, and this kind of schedule tends to get the highest response rate; for example, Skinner (1953) found that when he shifted to reinforcing a pigeon on a variable, infrequent schedule, the pigeon continued to peck at a disk 150,000 times without reinforcement, as if still expecting reinforcement! Commission sales jobs are based on the same principle: The hope of an eventual sale (and therefore reinforcement in the form of the resulting commission) keeps salespeople pushing their wares.

## The Operant Brain

Until recently, learning theorists ignored the role of the brain in operant conditioning, focusing instead on overt behaviors. It has become clear, however, that an understanding of how the brain works can shed considerable light on this fundamental process (Montague et al., 2004).

## Operant Conditioning: A Multifaceted Process

The action of the neurotransmitter dopamine lies at the core of a new approach to understanding the neural events that underlie the learning of associations between stimuli, responses, and the consequences of making responses. At one point, researchers believed that dopamine was the brain's way of cementing the effects of being rewarded. However, although neurons that produce dopamine have been found to be active when an animal is rewarded, dopamine is not necessary for appreciating the value of a stimulus. For example, when dopamine is blocked, hungry animals do not walk across a cage to eat; when they are brought to the food, however, they eat as much as animals that have normal amounts of dopamine (Berridge & Robinson, 1998; Cannon & Bseikri, 2004; Ikemoto & Panksepp, 1996). Rather than simply signaling the presence of reward, dopamine helps you adjust and organize your behavior so that you can achieve your goals.

How does dopamine work to accomplish this? According to the most recent theories of how reinforcement alters behavior, animals plan their behaviors in advance in order to achieve certain goals, and dopamine signals the disparity between what an animal expected to happen as a result of a behavior and what actually occurred. Specifically, a burst of activity in dopamine-producing neurons (in the midbrain) signals that an outcome was better than expected whereas a pause in activity of these neurons signals that an outcome was worse than expected (Fiorillo, 2004; Hollerman & Schultz, 1998; Waelti et al., 2001).

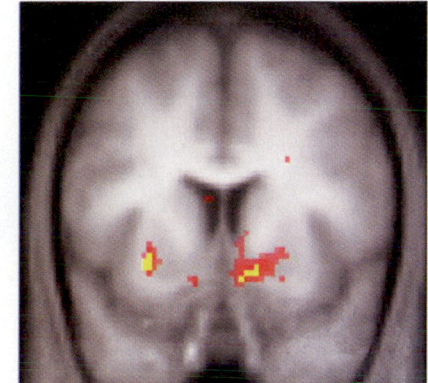

One theory suggests that such learning relies on the joint action of an internal "critic" and an internal "actor" (Sutton & Barto, 1998). Dopamine signals the "critic" with information about the disparity between expected and obtained reinforcement, and this information is then used by the "actor" to adjust the associations between stimulus, behavior, and likely reinforcement—which then affects future behavior in similar situations (Montague et al., 2004). And, in fact, there is evidence from neuroimaging that different brain areas carry out these "critic" and "actor" functions during learning by humans. In one study, people either chose one of two patterns and then learned from the outcome which one was more likely to signal a sip of tasty juice or passively watched as a computer chose one of the two patterns and then learned which one predicted the treat (O'Doherty et al., 2004). The researchers observed which brain areas responded when expectations for reward were violated. In both conditions, a brain area near the bottom of the basal ganglia was activated (see upper image); this area relies on dopamine and appears to be involved in the "critic" function. But only when the participants made an active choice was another portion of this structure, near the top, activated (see lower image); this area also relies on dopamine and appears to be involved in the "actor" function. In addition, other studies have shown that a third part of the basal ganglia, nestled near the "actor" area, is activated in proportion to the size of the reward a person expects (Knutson et al., 2001). This makes sense: In order to have one's expectations dashed down or ratcheted up by the "critic" signal, one must have clear expectations in the first place.

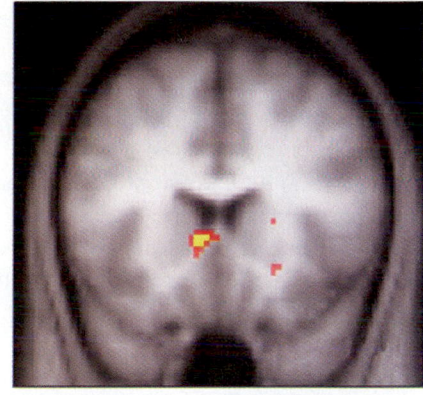

These slices of the brain, as seen from behind, are from an experiment by O'Doherty and colleagues (2004). The image on the top shows the area of the brain activated when participants' expectations of a pleasant consequence were violated, whether those expectations developed from observation or through direct action. The image on the bottom shows the area of the brain activated only when expectations were violated after participants took direct action to obtain a pleasant consequence. The two areas correspond to the "critic" and the "actor," respectively.

Many other parts of the brain are also involved in operant conditioning (Cardinal et al., 2002). For instance, the hippocampus plays an important role in allowing you to learn cues that signal the appropriate context for a behavior. As mentioned earlier, when you walk down a street, you don't stomp your right foot every time you see a red light. The hippocampus is especially important when you learn the context of a behavior unintentionally, by experiencing it but not noting it (O'Reilly & Rudy, 2000, 2001). One piece of evidence for this role of the hippocampus relies on the fact that it requires the neurotransmitter acetylcholine to function, and scopolamine is an antagonist for this neurotransmitter—in other words, it blocks the functioning of acetylcholine. Animals that are given scopolamine can't learn which stimuli should be grouped together as a signal for a particular response (Mishkin & Appenzeller, 1987). In addition, several parts of the frontal lobes are involved in operant learning; some parts store representations of goals and expectations (Braver & Cohen, 2000), other parts are involved in representing the emotion associated with an event (Gallagher et al., 1999), and the anterior cingulate cortex monitors the relationship between how you expect to perform and your actual performance, signaling when you've made an error or are in danger of making an error (Yeung et al., 2004).

Thus, at the level of the brain, operant conditioning is an exceedingly complex process that relies on interactions among many brain areas and the activity of different neurotransmitters that affect these areas in intricate and subtle ways.

## Classical Conditioning Versus Operant Conditioning: Are They Really Different?

You may have already noticed that the hippocampus plays a role in storing information about context in both classical conditioning and operant conditioning. And, noticing this, you may have wondered what else the two kinds of learning have in common. Table 6.2 presents a comparison. As you can see, both classical and operant conditioning involve extinction and spontaneous recovery, generalization, and discrimination. In both types of conditioning, response acquisition is affected by moderating factors, especially time (in classical conditioning, the length of time between CS and US; in operant conditioning, the length of time before reinforcement, which can be immediate or delayed). Also, for both types of conditioning, biological factors influence how easily certain behaviors can be learned.

| TABLE 6.2 | **Classical and Operant Conditioning Compared** | |
|---|---|---|
| | **Classical Conditioning** | **Operant Conditioning** |
| **Similarities** | ■ Learning is based on an association between the unconditioned stimulus and the conditioned stimulus. | ■ Learning is based on an association between response and reinforcement. |
| | ■ Avoidance learning. | ■ Avoidance learning. |
| | ■ Extinction. | ■ Extinction. |
| | ■ Spontaneous recovery. | ■ Spontaneous recovery. |
| | ■ Stimulus generalization. | ■ Generalization. |
| | ■ Stimulus discrimination. | ■ Discrimination. |
| | ■ Moderating factors can affect learning. | ■ Moderating factors can affect learning. |
| **Differences** | ■ The organism is passive. | ■ The organism is active, "operating" on the world. |
| | ■ Responses are reflexes (limited number of possible responses). | ■ Responses are voluntary behaviors (limitless possible responses). |
| | ■ Responses are elicited. | ■ Responses are emitted. |
| | ■ "Reinforcement" is unrelated to learning the association. | ■ Reinforcement is contingent on the desired response. |

Noting these similarities, some researchers have debated whether these two types of conditioning are really so distinct after all. Perhaps they are just different procedures toward a similar end. Indeed, their differences are not so clear cut. Some studies, for example, show that voluntary movements can be shaped via classical conditioning (Brown & Jenkins, 1968). Similarly, involuntary responses, such as learning to control tense jaw muscles to decrease facial pain, can be operantly conditioned (Dohrmann & Laskin, 1978). However, the fact that the same ends can be reached with either type of conditioning does not imply that the means to those ends are the same. After all, bats, birds, and helicopters fly, but they do so in different ways.

Perhaps the best evidence that the two kinds of conditioning are truly different is that different neural systems are used in each. Although the debate over distinguishing between classical and operant conditioning continues, recent research on the brain appears to discount the position that they are fundamentally the same. Not only do classical and operant conditioning draw on different neural mechanisms, but also classical conditioning relies on different brain structures, depending on the response being conditioned. For example, whereas classical conditioning of fear draws on the amygdala (LeDoux, 1996), classical conditioning of eye blinks relies heavily on the cerebellum (Christian & Thompson, 2003). In contrast, operant conditioning relies on neither of these brain structures, using instead the dopamine-based "reward system" (Montague et al., 2004; Robbins & Everitt, 1998). By providing evidence that different neural systems are used in the two types of conditioning, studies of the brain show that the two are essentially different.

# LOOKING AT LEVELS

## Facial Expressions as Reinforcement and Punishment

Like most people, you've probably said or done something while with a family member or friend and had that person respond with a smile or a frown. Do you think that person's smile or frown affected your behavior? Recent research suggests that other people's facial expressions can act as reinforcement or punishment (as shown in Figure 6.11, where the Master's expression serves as reinforcement or punishment). Let's look at this finding from the different levels of analysis:

First, Kringelbach and colleagues (2001) asked participants to discriminate one visual stimulus from another and found that different brain areas in the orbitofrontal cortex were active when participants' performance led to an angry face (positive punishment) rather than a happy face (positive reinforcement). Perceiving different facial expressions affects the brain in different ways. Moreover, the state of the brain affects how well we perceive faces. For instance, one study found that volunteers who took diazepam (a common antianxiety medication) were less accurate in recognizing facial emotions than those who took a placebo (Coupland et al., 2003). Thus, someone taking such a drug may be less subject to the reinforcing and punishing effects of other people's expressions.

But events in the brain are not enough to explain the effects that perceiving others' facial expressions have on behavior. We must also consider events at the level of the person. For example, some people may not perceive facial expressions as accurately as others, which would affect the reinforcing and punishing effects of the expressions. In one study, researchers found that depressed patients were less likely to correctly identify mildly happy faces as happy and less likely to discriminate between mildly sad, neutral, and mildly happy faces (Surguladze et al., 2004). Thus, people with depression may be potentially deprived of positive reinforcement when others respond with mildly happy expressions. And being less sensitive to facial expressions—and thus less responsive to them—can change the interpersonal dynamic between people (level of the group) because the facial expressions don't have their desired effect.

In fact, a smile or frown can clearly alter events at the level of the group. For example, positive and negative facial expressions can affect interaction between romantic partners: An experiment by Heisel and Mongrain (2004) required couples to complete a conflict resolution task. The number of women's negative expressions during the task predicted increases in their partners' poor mood and anxiety. Also at the level of the group, many (J. A. Hall, 1978; Hall & Matsumoto, 2004), but not all (Rahman et al., 2004), studies find that women are better than men at reading facial expressions. Might this difference cause women to find smiles more reinforcing and angry faces more punishing than do men?

Also at the level of the group, Hugenberg and Bodenhausen (2003) found that White participants were more inclined to perceive anger in Black faces than in White faces. We can wonder whether people who are more likely to perceive anger in Black faces would be more likely to feel punished (by the facial expression) and to respond, in turn, to that "punishment."

Again, events at these three levels interact. For example, we cannot understand how communication among people affects the reinforcing or punishing value of facial expressions without understanding how the brain influences such communication, nor can we understand individual differences without considering their impact on the group.

# Test Yourself

1. In classical conditioning, a learned behavior is determined by its antecedents, but in operant conditioning, a learned behavior is determined by the
   a. stimuli.
   b. responses.
   c. consequences.
   d. mind.

2. Someone's smile in response to your behavior can influence whether you either repeat or inhibit that behavior in the future. If you inhibit the behavior, then the smile was probably
   a. positive reinforcement.
   b. negative reinforcement.
   c. positive punishment.
   d. negative punishment.

3. In a series of successive approximations to shape a rat to press a lever, what would likely be the first behavior to be reinforced?
   a. pressing the lever
   b. turning toward the lever
   c. running from the lever
   d. turning away from the lever

4. Once complex behaviors are learned, they can be maintained using different schedules of reinforcement. Which type of schedule produces the highest response rate?
   a. variable schedule
   b. fixed schedule
   c. ratio schedule
   d. interval schedule

## Answers

# Think It Through!

You are babysitting a little girl one evening, and her parents have explicitly instructed you not to give her any more food. She whines for cookies, you say no, and she has a temper tantrum. What should you suspect about how her parents have handled her requests for after-dinner snacks in the past? If you want her to stop carrying on, what two different operant conditioning procedures could you use to try to change her behavior? (Physical or emotional violence, threats of cruelty, and yelling are not options.) Which technique do you think will be the most effective? Why? Which techniques were most effectively used by Master Yu?

# COGNITIVE AND SOCIAL LEARNING

Jackie Chan's first huge film success came with the film *Project A*, a pirate movie that deviated from the previously accepted formula for kung fu movies. It broke box office records in Asia. Prior to *Project A*, films starring the martial arts expert and actor Bruce Lee were all the rage, and the hero he portrayed was always a "noble" man, avenging some injustice. Chan broke the mold by having the hero of *Project A* be just a regular guy. But to understand Chan's success, we need to look beyond classical and operant conditioning to consider how he figured out what kind of movies he should make and how he learned to make them. When Chan was first given the opportunity to star in films and coordinate the stunts, he also began watching directors and film editors, observing what they did, how and why they included certain scenes and deleted others from the finished film. Chan's behavior was not being changed primarily through classical or operant conditioning, but through cognitive and social learning. Similarly, he learned how to do dangerous stunts, in part, by watching others.

## Cognitive Learning

The learning we have discussed so far focuses on behavior. In classical conditioning, the learned behavior is the conditioned response (CR); in operant conditioning, the learned behavior is the reinforced response. But even these types of learning involve the storing of new information, which guides the behavior. **Cognitive learning** is the acquisition of information that is often not immediately acted on but is stored for later use. Information acquired through cognitive learning may be used in planning, evaluating, and other forms of thinking, without producing any behavior—only, perhaps, more information to be stored. Learning how to add is an example of cognitive learning, as is learning the names of the 50 states or the meaning of a new word. You are engaged in cognitive learning right now.

These people are engaged in cognitive learning: They are storing information—directions—that they will use later.

Examples of Chan's cognitive learning include learning what underlies a successful kung fu movie and learning how to incorporate stunts into such a film. "I think that a lot of the success of *Project A* was the result of the three of us [Chan, Samo Hung, and Yuen Baio—fellow students at the Academy when they were younger] working as one. On the other hand, *Project A* was also the first film in which I did something that has since become my signature: The really, really, really dangerous stunt . . . the thrill of high risk. No blue screen and computer special effects. No stunt doubles. Real action. Real danger. And sometimes, real and terrible injury" (Chan & Yang, 1999, p. 283).

Illustrating the fact that cognitive learning is more than simple associations between stimuli and responses, Tolman and Honzik (1930a, 1930b) conducted a series of classic studies with rats. One group of rats was put in a maze that led to a food box, thus receiving a food reward for completing the maze (top panel of Figure 6.16, p. 268). The other group was also put in the maze but received no reinforcement; the rats were simply removed from the maze after a certain amount of time. Sometimes routes were blocked, and the rats had to find a different way to the end. The first group of rats, those that were rewarded with food, quickly increased their speed in the maze and decreased the number of mistakes; the speed and accuracy of the unrewarded second group did not particularly improve. This finding was consistent with what behaviorists would predict. However, when rats in the second group received a food reward on the 11th day, their

**Cognitive learning:** The acquisition of information that often is not immediately acted on but is stored for later use.

## FIGURE 6.16

## Tolman and Honzik's Discovery of Latent Learning

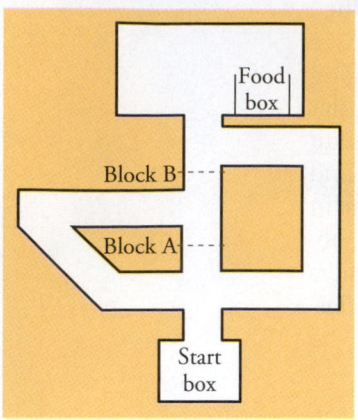

Three routes of differing lengths wind from start to finish. If two points along the most direct route are blocked, it is still possible to get to the end.

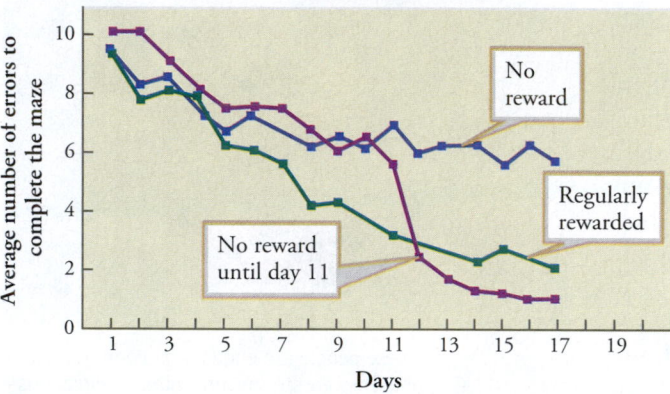

Rats that were rewarded for getting to the end of the maze made fewer "navigational" errors than rats that were not rewarded. Once rewarded (on day 11), the previously unrewarded rats made fewer mistakes than regularly reinforced rats, illustrating that the unrewarded rats had learned the spatial arrangement of the maze but did not apply that knowledge until reinforced.

**Latent learning:** Learning that occurs without behavioral signs.

**Insight learning:** Learning that occurs when a person or animal suddenly grasps what something means and incorporates that new knowledge into old knowledge.

speed increased and their errors decreased, both dramatically (Figure 6.16, bottom panel). It appears that these rats had learned how to run the maze quickly and correctly before the 11th day, but had no reason to do so.

Learning that occurs without behavioral signs is called **latent learning**. Tolman reasoned that the unreinforced rats, in their wanderings around the maze, had developed a *cognitive map* of the maze, storing information about its spatial layout. However, they did not use the map until they were motivated to do so by the reinforcement. Tolman's results, and the concept of latent learning, remind us of the important distinction between learning something and performing it. Researchers now know that latent learning depends on the hippocampus (Myers et al., 2000), which is generally used when information about new events is stored (Schacter, 1996). Note that although latent learning is a form of cognitive learning, not all cognitive learning is latent learning—you can rehearse to-be-memorized words aloud and otherwise produce observable behaviors when acquiring new information.

The study of learning focuses on the acquisition of information; in contrast, the study of memory focuses on the retention of information. By its very nature, cognitive learning relies crucially on how information is stored in memory, and most of the recent research on this topic (explored in the next chapter) focuses on the way information is stored in memory.

# Insight Learning: Seeing the Connection

**Insight learning** consists of suddenly grasping what something means and incorporating that new knowledge into old knowledge. It is based on the phenomenon known as the "ah-ha experience," the triumphal moment when an idea becomes crystal clear. By its very nature, insight learning, unlike other types of learning, is accompanied by a sudden flash of awareness that one has learned. Drawing on his experience with past films, Chan uses insight learning frequently on the set when choreographing martial arts sequences. He looks around at the items on the set right before filming a scene and gets insight into how those objects can be used in the scene:

A garden rake can be used to pull out someone's legs or to vault up to a ledge, can be spun like a staff or swung like a club. A rope becomes a whip, a restraining device, a tangling net. A barrel, a ladder, a chain-link fence—all can be thrown together in a dozen different ways, and until I'm actually there with my stunt team, weaving the scene together, I don't know which way will look best on screen. (Chan & Yang, 1999, p. 302)

The most famous psychological experiments regarding insight learning were done by Wolfgang Köhler (1887–1967), a German Gestalt psychologist. Köhler (1925/1956) put a chimpanzee named Sultan in a cage; outside the cage, and out of reach, Köhler put fruit. Also outside the cage and out of reach, but closer than the fruit, he placed a long stick. Inside the cage, Köhler placed a short stick. Initially, Sultan showed signs of frustration as he tried to reach the food. Then he stopped. He seemed suddenly to have an insight into how to snag the fruit: He used the short stick to get the long one, and then capture the fruit. In another study, Köhler put bananas in the cage but high, out of Sultan's reach. Also in the cage were stacks of boxes. At first, Sultan tried to jump up to grab the bananas. Eventually, he looked around at the objects in the cage and again appeared to have a flash of insight; he saw that stacking the boxes and climbing on them would enable him to reach the bananas.

In another instance of opportunity for insight learning, Sultan is faced with a variant of the two-stick solution to help him retrieve food that is out of reach. Here, there are four sticks of different lengths.

# Observational Learning: To See Is to Know

Piaget (1962) described a situation in which one of his daughters watched another child have a dramatic temper tantrum, complete with writhing on the floor and howling. His daughter also saw the other child's parents react with concern. Days later, his daughter tried out this behavior, presumably to see whether she would be given the attention she thought a tantrum deserved. She did not have to engage in the behavior immediately after observing it in order to learn it. Everyone, like Piaget's daughter, has had the experience of watching someone else's behavior and then being able to reproduce it. The behavior is probably voluntary (and thus not the result of classical conditioning) and may not have been reinforced (and thus not the result of operant conditioning), but it was learned nonetheless. A group of psychologists, led by Albert Bandura, developed *social learning theory*, which emphasizes the fact that much learning occurs in a social context. This kind of learning, which results simply from watching others and does not depend on reinforcement, is called **observational learning**. Observational learning helps people learn how to behave in their families (Thorn & Gilbert, 1998) and in their cultures: By watching others, we learn how to greet people, eat, laugh, tell jokes. Observational learning has helped you figure out how to behave in your classes and on campus. Do you remember your first few days at college? By watching others, you learned how people talked to each other, what clothes were "fashionable," and how to interact with instructors.

Observational learning influenced Chan's behavior: At a basic level, he learned how to do kung fu and acrobatics largely by watching others, and then practiced. (Kung fu or acrobatics would be very difficult to learn from a book!) Later in his career, Chan learned to direct and edit through years of watching others direct and edit.

Observational learning: Learning that occurs through watching others, not through reinforcement.

Observational learning explains why people may not make an effort to get to meetings on time: They see that latecomers do not suffer any negative consequences.

Bandura focused much of his work on *modeling*, a process in which someone learns new behaviors through observing other people. These other people function as models, presenting a behavior to be imitated. With modeling, you observe others' behaviors, and then none, some, or all of these behaviors may be learned and repeated, or modified. In one of Bandura's famous studies involving a Bobo doll, an inflated vinyl doll that pops back up when punched (Figure 6.17; Bandura et al., 1961), children were divided into three groups: One group watched an adult beating up a Bobo doll, one group watched an adult ignoring the Bobo doll, and the third didn't see an adult at all. After being mildly frustrated by being placed in a room with toys, but not being allowed to play with some of them, all of the children were then placed in another room with many toys, including a Bobo doll. Children who had observed the adult behaving aggressively with Bobo were themselves more aggressive. Similar studies have found similar results, including the observation that watching aggression by a live person has more of an impact than does watching a video of a person exhibiting the same behaviors. In turn, a realistic video has more of an impact than does a cartoon version of the same behaviors (Bandura et al., 1963).

**FIGURE 6.17** ## Bandura's Study on Observational Learning

Three groups of children were tested; the groups differed only in the first part of the study.

Children in one group watched an adult abuse a Bobo doll, for example, by slamming it with a mallet, kicking it, and yelling at it.

Children in a second group watched adults play with Tinkertoys and ignore the Bobo doll.

Children in a third group never saw a model (an adult) in the playroom.

In the second part of the study, all of the children played in a room with a variety of toys, including Bobo.

Children in the first group tended to imitate what they had seen, mistreating the doll (and inventing new ways to abuse it) and being more aggressive with the other toys in the room.

Children who observed the adult ignoring the Bobo doll were even less aggressive toward it than were children in the control group!

# Learning From Models

Learning from models has many advantages over other sorts of learning. By learning from models, you can avoid going through all the steps that learning usually requires and go directly to the end product.

## "Do as I Do"

Observational learning can produce both desired and undesired learning. Models may say one thing and do another, and the observer learns both, saying what the model said and doing what the model did (Rice & Grusec, 1975; Rushton, 1975). If you are surrounded by positive models, you have the opportunity to learn a lot of positive behaviors; but if you don't have that opportunity, you may find it difficult to learn certain "skills." If adults in a family have trouble holding jobs, become explosively angry, exhibit little patience, and treat others rudely, it can be harder for the children to learn the skills involved in maintaining a job, effectively controlling anger, managing impatience and frustration, and treating others kindly. On a more positive note, Bandura and colleagues (1967) conducted a study in which preschool children who were afraid of dogs observed another child who had no fear of dogs. During eight sessions, as prearranged, the model, on each successive occasion, played more closely with a dog and for a longer time. Fearful children who watched the model play with the dog had significantly more "approach" behaviors (those oriented toward the dog) than did a control group of fearful children who did not observe the model.

Both modeling and operant conditioning are involved in learning about culture and gender. You may learn how to behave by observing others, but whether you'll actually perform those behaviors depends, in part, on the consequences that occur when you first try.

Chan recounts how he learned to minimize the number of beatings he received after arriving at the Academy: "I quickly learned to watch the other children carefully. Whenever they stood up, I stood up. If they sat down, I sat down. Whatever they said, I said, and whatever they did, I did . . . it made it less likely that Master would single me out for punishment" (Chan & Yang, 1999, p. 40).

To further understand the way modeling and operant conditioning together help children learn about culture, imagine the following family interaction in a culture that has different expectations of what constitutes appropriate play for girls and boys. A boy observes his older sister asking her parents for a new doll and sees that they buy it for her. He then asks his parents for a doll for himself and is severely punished. His request was prompted by modeling, but because it resulted in punishment, he is unlikely to make that request again. Similarly, 9th and 10th graders were more likely to get involved in community activities if their parents were involved or if their parents reinforced them for minor involvement (Fletcher et al., 2000).

Researchers have discovered that several characteristics of models can make learning through observation more effective (Bandura, 1977a, 1986). Not surprisingly, the more you pay attention to the model, the more you learn. You are more likely to pay attention if the model is an expert, is good looking, has high status, or is socially powerful (Brewer & Wann, 1998). Perhaps intuitively realizing the importance of models for children's learning through observation, and recognizing the high-status position of his office, cigar enthusiast President William McKinley refused to be photographed with a cigar (Seuling, 1978). However, tobacco companies are using the same principles toward other ends, through product placement in films—showing actors smoking on screen. Unfortunately, research suggests that such use of observational learning has some success: 9- to 15-year-olds watching films with more incidents of smoking were

Observational learning occurs frequently in everyday life: An apprentice spends large amounts of time observing a master before ever doing anything more than handing over a tool. How-to videos ranging from cooking to bike repair may be more effective than how-to books because they allow the viewer to see the desired behavior. Observational learning is the way we learn first languages, form standards of judgment, and even discover ways to solve many types of problems (Bandura, 1986).

more likely to try smoking themselves (Sargent et al., 2001). We know that children learn by observing others, and powerful, high-status models such as presidents, athletes, or celebrities are likely to be more influential.

Children are not the only ones who learn through observation. Consider a study (Merlo & Schotter, 2003) that had college students play a complex game, where the best strategy was not immediately obvious. Players competed for small payoffs; behind each player was another participant who simply observed the player's moves and decisions. At the end of the tournament, each player and observer were independently given the opportunity to play again for a larger payoff. Observers were more likely to play better, perhaps because they had been able to discern patterns that were more difficult for players—caught up in the moment—to see. In addition, those observers who had the good fortune to watch better players tended to play better themselves than those who observed worse players, which suggests that observing someone who is good at their craft will help the observer to perform better. Negotiation skills can also be learned well through observation (Nadler et al., 2003).

## "Television Made Me Do It"

We learn from models by seeing which of their responses are reinforced and which are punished. We are then able to make predictions about the reactions that our behaviors will provoke. This pattern of learning is one of the reasons parents and others have become increasingly concerned about the amount and type of violence, foul language, and sexuality portrayed on television, movies, and computer and video games. A large, year-long study of violence on television found not only that 57% of programs contained some violence, but also that the perpetrators of violence in those programs received no punishment 73% of the time. Moreover, in almost half of the violent interactions, no harm came to the victim, and 58% of the victims showed no pain. Only 4% of violent programs included any emphasis on alternative, nonviolent solutions to problems (Farhi, 1996). From an observational learning perspective, this is disconcerting because children watching TV learn from the bulk of shows portraying violence that there are no negative consequences for the violent person.

Further support for television's role in children's aggression comes from a study that randomly assigned 3rd and 4th graders either to a classroom curriculum aimed at reducing television, videotape, and video game use or to a control group. Children in the "reduction" group were reported by peers and parents to be less physically and verbally aggressive than were children in the control group (Robinson et al., 2001).

Since Bandura's work on modeling, his findings have been replicated many times over, not only with TV shows and films, but also with video and computer games (Anderson, Berkowitz, et al., 2003; Clapp, 1988; Gentile et al., 2004; Huesmann & Eron, 1986). The establishment of a rating system for TV programs grew out of this body of psychological research. Many studies have been designed to identify which aspects of violence on television lead observers to behave violently later. The results suggest that age, time spent watching television, identification with the TV character, and the portrayal of violence all influence behavior (Clapp, 1988; Huesmann et al., 2003; Smith, 1993). Table 6.3 notes several spe-

---

**TABLE 6.3** **Modeling Aggressive Behavior: The Portrayal of Violence**

The ways in which violence is portrayed on television can heighten its influence (Comstock & Paik, 1991; Huesmann et al., 2003). Viewers are more likely to act aggressively in the following cases.

- The television perpetrator is rewarded (or at least not punished) for the violent behavior.

- The violence is portrayed as justified.

- Aspects of the violent situation could possibly occur in real life.

- The perpetrator is seen as similar to the viewer.

- The violence does not appear disgusting.

- No critical commentary occurs during or after the portrayals of violence.

- The violence appears real.

- The violence is not interrupted by humor (as it is in parody films).

cific aspects of the way violence is portrayed that can affect whether the aggressive behavior is modeled.

Smoking and aggression are not the only behaviors that may be modeled from television. On situation comedy shows, significantly more negative comments are made about and to overweight (as compared to underweight) women, and these comments are often followed by audience laughter (providing reinforcement for such comments; Fouts & Burggraf, 2000). Although it may not be sitcom writers' intention to "teach" such behavior, modeling and operant conditioning nonetheless lead at least some people to learn these behaviors.

Not all modeling from the media need be negative. Positive, nonviolent programs (such as *Sesame Street* and *Mr. Rogers' Neighborhood*) promote nonviolent observational learning: Preschool children who watched these programs were more likely to exhibit positive, helpful behaviors than were children who did not watch them (Forge & Phemister, 1987).

# Test Yourself

1. Tolman ran two groups of rats through a maze a number of times, but rewarded only one group. When he began to reinforce the rats in the second group also, they performed as well as the others. It appears that the second group of rats learned the maze, but did not exhibit what they learned until they were reinforced. This is an example of
   a. secondary reinforcement.
   b. insight learning.
   c. observational learning.
   d. latent learning.

2. Kohler's chimp had a sudden flash of awareness when confronted with a difficult problem. Such an "ah-ha experience" is the result of
   a. latent learning.
   b. insight learning.
   c. observational learning.
   d. modeling.

3. In Bandura's study with the Bobo doll, the children were strongly influenced by observing the behavior of an adult. What would have made the children's observational learning even more effective?
   a. if the model had high social status
   b. if the model frowned when hitting the doll
   c. if the children paid less attention to the model
   d. if the children had never seen a Bobo doll before

4. The main difference between cognitive learning and operant conditioning is that
   a. operant conditioning only works with nonhuman animals.
   b. cognitive learning does not require reinforcement.
   c. cognitive learning is a human phenomenon.
   d. There are no significant differences between cognitive learning and operant conditioning.

## Answers

1.d 2.b 3.a 4.b

# Think It Through!

Curare is a drug that so totally paralyzes an animal that a heart-lung machine is necessary to keep it alive. Although the animal can't move, it can perceive and remember normally. Imagine showing a person who has been given curare how to open a simple combination lock on a box to obtain the $1,000 inside. When the effect of the curare has worn off and the person is able to move normally, will he or she know how to open the lock to get the reward? Why or why not?

# REVIEW AND REMEMBER!

## Summary

### I. Classical Conditioning

**A.** Classical conditioning, which was first investigated systematically by Ivan Pavlov, has four basic elements:

**1.** The unconditioned stimulus (US), such as food, reflexively elicits an unconditioned response.

**2.** The unconditioned response (UR), such as salivation, is automatically elicited by a US.

**3.** The pairing of a conditioned stimulus (CS), such as a tone, with a US, such as food, elicits a conditioned response (CR), such as salivation. (Note that salivation can be either a conditioned or an unconditioned response, depending on the stimulus that elicits it.)

**4.** The presentation of the CS alone then elicits the UR (the tone presented alone elicits the response of salivation now as a CR).

**B.** A conditioned emotional response is involved in the development of fear and phobias, as shown by Watson and Rayner in the case of Little Albert.

**C.** Extinction is the unpairing of the CS and US; spontaneous recovery is the return of a classically conditioned response after a rest period following extinction.

**D.** In stimulus generalization, a similar, but not identical, stimulus elicits the CR.

**E.** In stimulus discrimination, the organism learns to distinguish among similar stimuli so that only a particular stimulus elicits the CR.

**F.** Classical conditioning is involved in certain bodily responses to drug abuse, certain therapy techniques, certain types of advertising, and the acquisition of food or taste aversions.

### II. Operant Conditioning

**A.** Operant conditioning is the process whereby a behavior (usually a voluntary one) becomes associated with the consequences of performing that behavior. Operant conditioning thus has three basic elements: stimulus, response, and consequence.

**B.** Both negative and positive reinforcement increase the probability of the recurrence of a behavior.

**C.** Both positive and negative punishment decrease the probability of the recurrence of a behavior.

**D.** Reinforcers can be primary or secondary.

**E.** Extinction, spontaneous recovery, generalization, and discrimination all occur in operant conditioning.

**F.** Shaping makes it possible to learn, by successive approximations, behaviors that would otherwise not be emitted.

**Your Notes**

I.

A. See Figure 6.2.

1.

2.

3.

4.

B.

C.

D.

E.

F.

II.

A.

B.

C.

D. Primary—inherently reinforcing
Secondary—not inherently reinforcing

E.

F.

**G.** Reinforcement schedules can be continuous or partial; if partial, reinforcement may be given for responses after an interval of time (interval schedule) or after a set number of responses (ratio schedule). For both these types of schedules, reinforcement can be given on a fixed or variable basis.

## III. Cognitive and Social Learning

**A.** Cognitive learning involves the acquisition of information that may be used in planning, evaluating, and other forms of thinking, but that is not necessarily acted on immediately.

**B.** Latent learning, learning that occurs without behavioral signs, and insight learning, suddenly grasping what something means and incorporating that new knowledge into old knowledge, are examples of cognitive learning.

**C.** Observational learning is learning by watching the behavior of others. The more you pay attention to the model, the more you are likely to learn.

**D.** Children may learn to behave aggressively from watching violent TV shows.

NOTE: Once you feel that you understand the material in this chapter, visit the book's Web site at www.ablongman.com/kosslyn3e to test your knowledge with additional study questions.

*G.*

*III.*

*A. Remember Tolman and Honzik's rats.*

*B.*

*C.*

*D.*

# Key Terms

acquisition, p. 236
avoidance learning, p. 238
behavior modification, p. 257
biological preparedness, p. 238
classical conditioning, p. 235
cognitive learning, p. 267
conditioned emotional response (CER), p. 238
conditioned response (CR), p. 236
conditioned stimulus (CS), p. 236
continuous reinforcement, p. 260
contrapreparedness, p. 239
delayed reinforcement, p. 258
discrimination, p. 259
discriminative stimulus, p. 259
extinction (in classical conditioning), p. 240
extinction (in operant conditioning), p. 259

fixed interval schedule, p. 261
fixed ratio schedule, p. 261
food aversion (taste aversion), p. 245
generalization, p. 258
habituation, p. 234
immediate reinforcement, p. 258
insight learning, p. 268
interval schedule, p. 261
latent learning, p. 268
Law of Effect, p. 251
learning, p. 234
negative punishment, p. 255
negative reinforcement, p. 255
observational learning, p. 269
operant conditioning, p. 250
partial reinforcement, p. 260
phobia, p. 238
positive punishment, p. 255
positive reinforcement, p. 253

primary reinforcer, p. 257
ratio schedule, p. 261
reinforcement, p. 252
reinforcer, p. 252
response contingency, p. 252
secondary reinforcer, p. 257
shaping, p. 259
spontaneous recovery (in classical conditioning), p. 240
spontaneous recovery (in operant conditioning), p. 259
stimulus discrimination, p. 241
stimulus generalization, p. 240
successive approximations, p. 260
trace conditioning, p. 236
unconditioned response (UR), p. 236
unconditioned stimulus (US), p. 236
variable interval schedule, p. 261
variable ratio schedule, p. 262

# CHAPTER 7

The Mind
OF A
Mnemonist

A LITTLE
BOOK
ABOUT A
VAST
MEMORY

A. R. LURIA

WITH A NEW FOREWORD BY

Jerome S. Bruner

# MEMORY:
## LIVING WITH YESTERDAY

A Latvian newspaper reporter, known simply as "S." (short for S. V. Shereshevskii), had an almost superhuman memory. Each morning the editor of his newspaper would describe the day's stories and assignments, often providing addresses and details about the information the reporters needed to track down. The editor noticed that S. never took notes and initially thought that S. was simply not paying attention. When he called S. on the carpet for this apparent negligence, he was shocked to discover that S. could repeat back the entire briefing, word-perfect. When the editor quizzed S. about his memory, S. was surprised; he assumed that everyone could accurately remember what they had heard and seen. The editor suggested that S. visit the noted Russian psychologist Alexander Luria, who then studied him over the course of almost 30 years.

Luria soon discovered that S.'s memory "for all practical purposes was inexhaustible" (Luria, 1968/1987, p. 3). S. could memorize a list of words or numbers of any length, and could recall it backward or forward equally easily! In fact, if given an item from the list, he could recall which items came immediately before it or after it. He generally made no errors. Moreover, he performed as well when he was tested years later, recalling perfectly not only the list itself but also when he learned it, where he and the examiner had been sitting, and even what the examiner had been wearing at the time.

Luria focused on unlocking the secrets behind S.'s formidable abilities. The results of this massive project are summarized in Luria's celebrated monograph *The Mind of a Mnemonist: A Little Book about a Vast Memory*. Luria found that S. recalled objects, events, words, and numbers by using mental imagery. His mental imagery was rich and complex: ". . . I recognize a word not only by the images it evokes but by a whole complex of feelings that image arouses. . . . Usually I experience a word's taste and weight, and I don't have to make an effort to remember it—the word seems to recall itself" (p. 28).

Sounds were accompanied by images of colored lines, puffs, splotches and splashes, and these visual images could later remind him of the sound. Moreover, S. used associations between images and concepts, which allowed the images to stand for other things. For example, "When I hear the word *green*, a green flowerpot appears. . . . Even numbers remind me of images. Take the number 1. This is a proud, well-built man; 2 is a high-spirited woman; 3 a gloomy person (why, I don't know) . . . 8 a very stout woman—a sack within a sack" (p. 31). S. could recall items in any order because he placed images along a scene and could imagine "seeing" the imaged objects in any order. For example, "I put the image of the pencil near a fence . . . the one down the street, you know" (p. 36).

S.'s ability may sound like a dream come true, especially to a student slaving away to memorize the contents of several textbooks. In fact, as attractive as S.'s abilities seem, they had a dark side: Unlike normal people, S. could not stop himself from thinking about a flood of associations that were triggered by commonplace stimuli, which could overwhelm him when he tried to read. Moreover, he could not understand poetry, metaphors, or abstract principles (such as those used in science), which always called to mind specific concrete images. A better memory is not necessarily an unmixed blessing.

As we shall see, S. was extraordinary but not supernatural. In fact, you can learn many of the tricks he used and put them to good end. S.'s memory, like yours, relied on three fundamental types of processing: **Encoding** is the process of organizing and transforming incoming information so that it can be entered into memory, either to be stored or to be compared with previously stored information. S. was a master at this process. **Storage** is the process of retaining information in memory. As we shall see, the mechanisms involved in storing information continue to operate for years after you've learned a fact. **Retrieval** is the process of digging information out of memory. For example, have you ever seen someone you know you've met before, but at first can't recall her name? In this situation, you get to experience the process of retrieval at work, as you struggle to bring the name to mind. S. never had such struggles, in part because his encoding and storage processing was so efficient that he could virtually always locate the information he sought in memory.

# ENCODING INFORMATION INTO MEMORY:
## Time and Space Are of the Essence

**Encoding:** The process of organizing and transforming incoming information so that it can be entered into memory, either to be stored or to be compared with previously stored information.

**Storage:** The process of retaining information in memory.

**Retrieval:** The process of accessing information stored in memory.

As he learned to use his memory, S. became a master at organizing information so that he could later remember it quickly. A key part of this activity was transforming what he was given to make it memorable. For example, when given a complex (and meaningless) mathematical formula to recall, he generated a story that described each term. The first term was N, which he recalled by thinking of a gentleman named Neiman; the next symbol was a dot (indicating multiplication), which he thought of as a small hole where Neiman had jabbed his cane in the ground; next came a square-root sign, which he converted to Neiman's looking up at a tree that had that shape; and so on (Luria, 1968/1987, p. 49).

Such fancy mental gymnastics were useful for S. because they helped him encode new information into memory. In this section, we begin at the beginning, and consider how information is encoded into memory.

# Types of Memory Stores

S.'s tricks required him to use different sorts of memories. Until someone asks for your address, chances are you aren't consciously aware of it—or even that you have one. But, once you are asked, the information is at your mental finger tips. This difference, between memories we are aware of holding and those we are not, is one sign that different types of "memory stores" are at work. A **memory store** is a set of neurons that serves to retain information over time.

Although we sometimes talk as if our "hands remember" how to shoot baskets and our "fingers remember" how to play the guitar, all memories are stored in the brain. We can distinguish among three types of memory stores, which differ in the time span over which they operate and in the amount of information they can hold (Shiffrin, 1999). These three types of structures are known as *sensory*, *short-term*, and *long-term memory stores*. The fundamental distinctions among these types of memories were first characterized in detail by Atkinson and Shiffrin (1968, 1971) and Waugh and Norman (1965), as illustrated in Figure 7.1.

## Sensory Memory: Lingering Sensations

Have you ever looked at scenery rushing past the window of a moving car and noticed that although you see literally miles and miles of landscape slipping by you, your images of the trees, signs, and telephone poles are fleeting, leaving your awareness almost as soon as you notice them? But the images linger for an instant, and even this very brief retention requires a form of memory. These rapidly fading images occur in **sensory memory (SM)**, which holds a large amount of perceptual input for a very brief time, typically less than 1 second. Sensory memory happens automatically, without effort (via bottom-up processes; see Chapter 4); sensory memory arises because of the temporary activation of perceptual areas of your brain by the stimulus.

George Sperling (1960) reported an experiment, now regarded as a classic, that demonstrated this fleeting sensory memory in vision (the visual form of SM is called *iconic memory*). When shown sets of many letters or digits very briefly, people can report only a handful afterward (see Figure 7.2). However, they claim that they can remember all the items immediately after the display is removed, but then the memory fades too quickly to "read off" all of them during recall. Sperling was able to demonstrate that this claim was, in fact, correct. He briefly showed participants rows of items, more than they could remember, and presented one of several different tones, which corresponded to specific rows. If a tone sounded *immediately* after the

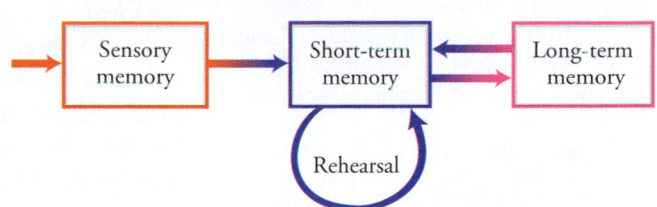

**FIGURE 7.1** **The Three-Stage Model of Memory**

The three-stage model emerged from research by Atkinson and Shiffrin (1968, 1971) and Waugh and Norman (1965). This model not only identified distinct types of memory stores, but also specified how information flows among them. Later research showed that information can, in fact, move to long-term memory without necessarily passing through short-term memory, and that rehearsal—repeating items over and over—only helps memorization if people think about the information (counter to what was initially claimed). Nevertheless, this model provided the framework for subsequent studies and theories of memory.

**Memory store:** A set of neurons that serves to retain information over time.

**Sensory memory (SM):** A memory store that holds a large amount of perceptual input for a very brief time, typically less than 1 second.

**FIGURE 7.2** **The Sperling Study**

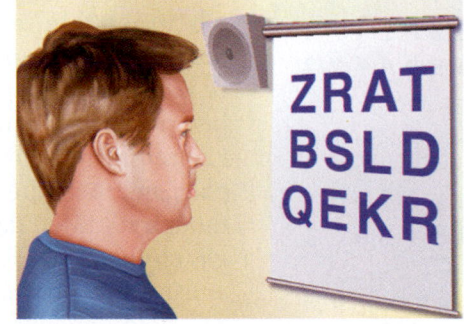

Participants saw sets of letters arranged in three rows. When the letters were flashed very quickly (for less than 0.25 second), people were able to report around 4 or 5 letters, even though they recalled seeing more.

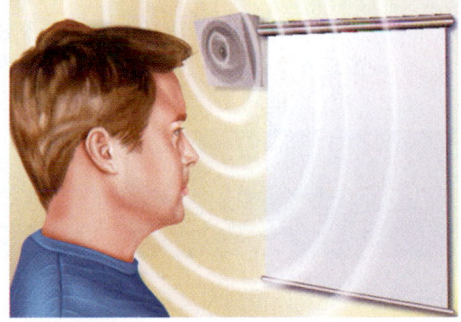

In another part of the study, a high, medium, or low tone was presented immediately *after* the rows of letters were flashed. Participants reported the top row if the tone was high, the middle row if it was medium, and the bottom row if it was low. They could report the appropriate row almost perfectly, showing that they had briefly stored more than they could report aloud.

**Short-term memory (STM) (also called immediate memory):** A memory store that holds relatively little information (typically 5 to 9 items) for only a few seconds (but perhaps as long as 30 seconds).

**Rehearsal:** The process of repeating information over and over to retain it in STM.

**Chunk:** A unit of information, such as a digit, letter, or word.

**Working memory (WM):** The system that includes two specialized STMs (auditory loop and visuospatial sketchpad) and a central executive that operates on information in them to plan, reason, or solve a problem.

items were presented, the participants were able to report the corresponding row almost perfectly. Because the tonal cue was presented *after* the items were removed, the participants had to have retained some memory of all of the rows in order to perform so well. Moreover, if the cue was presented a mere second after the items were removed, performance dropped dramatically. This finding shows that iconic memory stores a large amount of information but that it fades very quickly. The sense of a fleeting memory after the stimulus has ceased holds true for hearing as well. For example, you can continue to hear the sound of a voice that has stopped speaking for the brief time it is still in auditory sensory memory (Cherry, 1953; the auditory form of SM is called *echoic memory*).

## Short-Term Memory: The Contents of Consciousness

Whereas sensory memory retains information for the briefest of time and cannot be prolonged, **short-term memory (STM**, also called *immediate memory*) holds information for several seconds and can be prolonged voluntarily (typically for about 30 seconds). When you see something you want to remember (such as the numbers on the license plate of a car involved in an accident), you can hold this information in STM by **rehearsal**, repeating the information over and over. When you dash from telephone book to telephone, repeating like a mantra the number you've just looked up, you are rehearsing. Also in contrast to SM, which can hold a large amount of information, STM holds only a handful of separate pieces of information. For instance, do you think you would be able to keep in your STM a phone number that was 20 digits long? STM overload. In fact, the lengths of telephone numbers and license plates were determined with our STM limits in mind. You are conscious only of information stored in STM. The very fact that you are aware of information is a sure sign that the information is in STM.

### FIGURE 7.3  Chunking in Action

| A | E |
|---|---|
| 7 9 1 2 | 5 1 8 6 1 9 2 4 |
| 8 9 8 9 | 7 7 7 5 5 5 8 8 |

| B | F |
|---|---|
| 1 4 2 5 9 | 9 6 5 2 4 6 3 7 9 |
| 2 2 4 4 1 | 2 2 2 2 7 7 7 7 1 |

| C | G |
|---|---|
| 9 1 3 9 2 6 | 1 3 8 5 2 6 2 1 7 4 |
| 4 2 4 2 4 2 | 3 3 5 5 9 9 4 4 2 2 |

| D | H |
|---|---|
| 6 4 1 7 6 2 8 | 7 2 5 8 3 1 8 4 3 2 1 6 |
| 3 3 3 8 8 5 5 | 2 2 5 5 8 8 1 1 6 6 3 3 |

Read the first row in box A, left to right, and then look up from the book and say it aloud. Check to see whether you could recall all the digits. Then read the second row in box A, left to right, and do the same. Work your way down the table, and keep going until you can't recall either of the two equal-length rows in a pair perfectly. You should find that for the shorter rows, you can remember both rows with equal ease. But for the longer ones, the second row in each pair is easier to remember than the first one. Now that you know about chunking, you know why: It's not the number of digits, it's the number of chunks that's important—and the second row of each pair is easier to organize into fewer chunks.

**HOW MUCH CAN YOU HOLD IN MIND?**   How much information can we keep in our awareness at one time—in other words, how much information can STM hold? Miller (1956) argued that STM can hold only about 7 plus-or-minus 2 (that is, from 5 to 9) "chunks" at once, but more recent research suggests that the number is more like 4 (Cowan, 2001). A **chunk** is a unit of information, such as a digit, letter, or word. Generally speaking, STM can handle somewhere between 5 and 9 items (organized into about 4 chunks); this is why telephone and license plate numbers are fairly easy to remember; for example, even though it's three digits, you will organize the area code as a single chunk. The definition of a chunk is not precise, however, and research has shown that the amount of information STM can hold depends on the types of material and the individual's experience with them (Baddeley, 1994; Broadbent, 1971; Mandler, 1967). For instance, a word is usually treated as a chunk, but you can store more one-syllable words than five-syllable ones. To get a sense of the importance of chunking, try the exercise in Figure 7.3.

**WORKING MEMORY: THE THINKING PERSON'S MEMORY**   When S. was asked to memorize a set of meaningless sounds, he would organize the information in clever ways. Researchers soon realized that rehearsal is only one process at work in STM; you operate on information in STM. Whenever you reason something out—as you do, for example, during the game Scrabble, when you mentally rearrange letters to see whether you can form words—you are using STM (Zhang & Zhu, 2001). The notion that information in STM is used in various ways led researchers to expand the conception of how this type of memory works, which led to the theory of **working memory (WM)**. The theory of WM is an advance over the original theory of STM in three ways: First, the original conception of STM specified only one type of process (rehearsal) that operated on stored information, whereas the theory of WM includes processes that interpret and transform information more generally (Baddeley, 1986; Cohen, Peristein, et al., 1997; D'Esposito et al., 1995; Smith, 2000; Smith & Jonides, 1999).

Second, as shown in Figure 7.4, the theory of WM more finely characterizes how information is stored in STM; specifically, we now know that STM includes distinct stores, which retain different kinds of information (Jonides et al., 2005). Baddeley (1986, 1992) distinguishes between an STM that holds verbally produced sounds, which he calls the *articulatory loop,* and another STM that holds visual and spatial information, which he calls the *visuospatial sketchpad.* The articulatory loop is like a continuous-play loop on a tape recorder, on which the sound impulses fade when the tape isn't being played; you need to rehearse repeatedly to continue to store sounds in the articulatory loop. In contrast, the visuospatial sketchpad is like a notepad with patterns drawn in fading ink; it briefly retains mental images of the locations of objects (Logie, 1986; Logie & Baddeley, 1990; Logie & Marchetti, 1991; Quinn, 1991). Both types of STM are temporary stores of the information you are working on; depending on what you are doing, you add and delete sounds from the taped loop or you sketch and revise diagrams on the pad. The fact that these STMs are distinct is demonstrated not only by the finding that different neural patterns of activation occur when they are used (Raemae et al., 2001; Smith, 2000), but also by the finding that the functioning of the visuospatial sketchpad is more strongly influenced by genetics than is that of the articulatory loop (Ando et al., 2001).

Third, the theory of WM includes a function known as the **central executive**, which operates on information in one or another of the two STMs to plan, reason, or solve a problem. That is, WM's central executive uses the articulatory loop and the visuospatial sketchpad to help you do different sorts of reasoning (Garden et al., 2002). The central executive is at work when you plan what you will say on a first date or when you think about what you would like to do tomorrow. This function of WM relies in large measure on a part of the frontal lobes that is crucially involved in managing information in order to carry out specific plans (Passingham & Sakai, 2004). WM is so important that it is sobering to learn that people who regularly used the club drug ecstasy (also known as "e"; see Chapter 5) show impairments in this kind of memory for up to 2 years after they've sworn off the drug (Morgan et al., 2002).

## Long-Term Memory: Records of Experience

Rehearsal is important in part because it is one way in which we move information into a third type of memory store, **long-term memory (LTM)**. (But, as we shall see, rehearsal is not the only way to transfer information into LTM.) LTM holds a huge amount of information for a very long time, from hours to years. LTM stores the information that underlies the meanings of pictures, words, and objects, as well as your memories of everything you've ever done or learned. As we noted earlier, until you are asked for your address, you are not directly aware of that information; it has to move from LTM into STM before you are conscious of it. As an analogy, think of the difference between storing a file on your hard drive versus entering it into RAM, or random-access memory, the

### FIGURE 7.4

## Working Memory

Working memory (WM) is a system that involves a central executive and two specialized short-term memory (STM) stores: one that holds pronounceable sounds (the articulatory loop) and one that holds visual or spatial patterns (the visuospatial sketchpad).

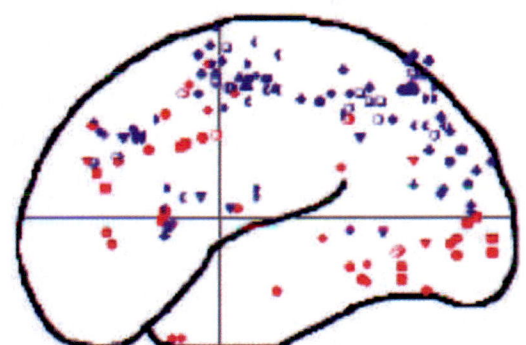

During tasks involving working memory, both the frontal lobes and perceptual areas of the brain are often activated. Different sets of areas are activated by different types of working memory tasks. The areas indicated by blue spots were activated when participants had to hold locations in mind, whereas the areas indicated by red spots were activated when participants had to hold shapes in mind (Smith, 2000).

**Central executive:** The set of processes that operates on information in one or another of two specialized STMs; part of working memory.

**Long-term memory (LTM):** A memory store that holds a huge amount of information for a long time (from hours to years).

active memory in a computer. Once information is saved on the hard drive, it can be stored indefinitely; it will not be disrupted if the power fails. If information faded rapidly from RAM (instead of being lost instantly if you close a file without clicking on "Save"), the difference between typing words into RAM and saving them on the hard drive would be much like the difference between memories held in STM versus those stored in LTM.

**HOW MUCH CAN YOU STORE FOR LONG DURATIONS?** The storage capability of LTM is so large that some researchers question whether it has a limit. Shepard (1967), for example, investigated the capacity of LTM by showing people more than 600 pictures (photographs, colored prints, and illustrations), mostly from magazines, and then testing for recognition. Pairing pictures seen in the first round with new, previously unseen ones, Shepard asked his participants to pick out those they had been shown in the first part of the study. He found that the participants could recognize over 99% of the images correctly 2 hours after seeing them, and 87% a week later. This remarkable degree of retention occurred even though the participants had spent an average of only 5.9 seconds looking at each picture. In another classic study, Standing and colleagues (1970) found that when tested an hour later, participants retained memory for at least 90% of over 2,500 pictures that they had studied for 10 seconds each. Furthermore, after looking at 1,100 pictures for 5 seconds each and then being tested 30 minutes later, the participants recognized an astonishing 97%.

**INFORMATION FLOW BETWEEN STM AND LTM: A TWO-WAY STREET** Information not only goes from STM to LTM, but often moves in the other direction, from LTM to STM. In fact, the contents of working memory are typically drawn from LTM, not SM. For example, when you wrestle with a difficult decision, you draw on the fruits of your previous experiences—which are stored in LTM. Indeed, in order for a stimulus to be meaningful, information in LTM must have been activated because that is where meaning is stored. And most information in STM is *meaningful*: That is, you don't see the squiggle 6 as a curved line but as a recognizable number that conveys meaning; similarly, without conscious thought, you see the letter pattern WORD as a recognizable word. (Remember the Stroop effect, described in Chapter 4: You can't ignore the meaning of color words when you try to report the color of the ink used to print them.) So, when you look up a telephone number, you must first access LTM in order to know how to pronounce the numbers and then keep them in STM as you prepare to make the call. Hence, LTM plays a central role in perception: You recognize and identify an object only after the appropriate information is activated in LTM.

**DISTINGUISHING BETWEEN STM AND LTM** The distinction between STM and LTM matters in everyday life, sometimes a great deal. If you see the license number of a car that has just hit a cyclist but then quickly lose that information from STM, it is gone forever. But, if the information has moved into LTM, you should be able to retrieve it.

Evidence for distinct short-term and long-term memory stores has been provided by many studies. The earliest of these took place over 100 years ago, when German philosopher and pioneering memory researcher Hermann Ebbinghaus (1850–1909) undertook a series of experiments to discover the factors that affect memory. Although he didn't realize it at the time, Ebbinghaus's findings were the first solid evidence that STM and LTM are distinct and operate differently. Here's what he did: To see how well he could memorize letters, digits, and *nonsense syllables* (such as *cac, rit,* and the like, which are not words but can be pronounced), Ebbinghaus (1885) wrote out a set of these stimuli, each on its own card. He then studied them, one at a time, and later on, assessed how many he could recall. Ebbinghaus found—as many researchers have since confirmed—

that the first and last items studied were more easily remembered than those in the middle. The left-hand graph in Figure 7.5 (called the *memory curve*) illustrates this **serial position effect**, which consists of superior memory for the items at the beginning and end of a list ("serial position" refers to the order of the items in the sequence). The increased memory for the first few stimuli is called the **primacy effect**; the increased memory for the last few stimuli is the **recency effect**.

Primacy and recency effects are evidence that STM and LTM rely on distinct stores. To see how, we need to look at additional findings. First, researchers have found that presenting items to be learned in rapid succession reduces the primacy—but, crucially, not the recency—effect; as the right-hand graph in Figure 7.5 shows, memory is still enhanced for the later items, but not for those learned early (Davelaar et al., 2005; Glanzer & Cunitz, 1966). The simple fact that the time between items affects only one part of the memory curve is evidence that both parts cannot arise from the same mental processes. Why does reducing the presentation time affect only the primacy effect? The primacy effect occurs because we have more time to think about the earlier items than the later ones, and thus the earlier ones are more likely to be stored in LTM. By rehearsing information in STM for those early items, we stretch out the time we have available for storing it in LTM and, in general, the more time we have to rehearse information, the more likely we are to store it effectively in LTM. If a list is presented quickly, the retention advantage of storing material in LTM is lost for the early items; but because STM is not affected, the items learned last are still available.

Researchers have also been able to disrupt the memory curve in the opposite way. Counting backward out loud immediately after the last item of a list is presented disrupts the recency effect (see Figure 7.5) but not the primacy effect (Glanzer & Cunitz, 1966). Why? The recency effect occurs because the last few items are still in STM and thus can be recalled immediately (when told to recall a list, people typically start with the last few items, as if they are retrieving these items before the information stored temporarily in STM is lost). Counting backward disrupts information in STM, thus disrupting the recency effect. But counting backward does not affect the information in LTM any more than unplugging a computer affects what is stored on the hard drive. The different effects of presentation rate and the interference of backward counting indicate that different memory stores are used.

# Making Memories

Look at Figure 7.6. Do you remember which way Abraham Lincoln faces on a penny? Most people don't. Unless you've had reason to pay attention to this feature and encode it, you probably didn't store this information explicitly. In this section, we examine what it means to "store" information in memory and then look at several factors that determine whether this storage will occur.

## FIGURE 7.5 The Serial Position Effect

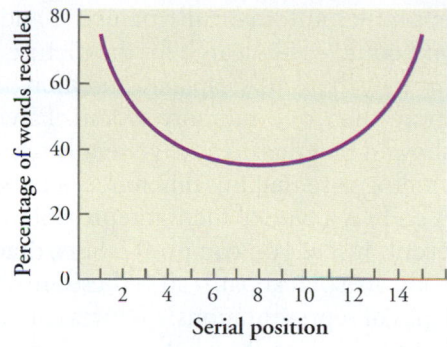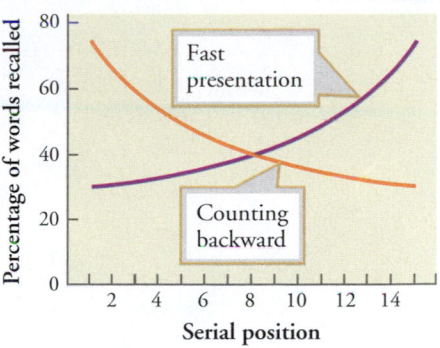

Memory is typically better for the first few and last few items in a set, producing the memory curve shown on the left. Less time between items reduces memory for the first few items, whereas counting backward impairs memory for the last few items. These different effects are evidence that different memory stores are involved for the two kinds of memories.

**Serial position effect:** Having superior memory for the items at the beginning and at the end of a list ("serial position" refers to the order of the items in the sequence).

**Primacy effect:** Increased memory for the first few stimuli in a set.

**Recency effect:** Increased memory for the last few stimuli in a set.

## FIGURE 7.6

## Which Coin Is Correct?

Nickerson and Adams (1979) found that people perform poorly when asked to choose the correct image of a coin from a set of choices. Because we need only to distinguish pennies from other coins, not to notice which way Abe faces, we do not encode the profile information very well.

# Coding: Packaged to Store

How convenient it would be if every time you scanned a picture into a computer, the computer automatically named it and stored a brief description. With such a feature, you could easily search for the picture (by its name or its characteristics). As it happens, humans have this capacity and then some. In fact, we often register information using more than one memory system. Paivio and his collaborators (Paivio, 1971) not only showed that pictures are generally remembered better than words, but also made a convincing case that this difference occurs because pictures can be stored using *dual codes*. A **code** is a type of mental representation, an internal "re-presentation" of a stimulus or event. Just as you can print letters, draw pictures, or write the dots and dashes of Morse code on a blackboard (all of these are different representations), your brain can use many types of representations. Pictures can be stored with both a visual and a verbal code; that is, you can describe what you see in words as well as store it visually, so you can later recall it in your mind's eye. Research shows that illustrations improve memory for text (Levie & Lentz, 1982; Levin et al., 1987), particularly if the picture appears before the text.

**CREATING VERBAL AND VISUAL CODES**   As part of the encoding process, you can create new codes for storing material. For example, you can verbally describe visually perceived objects, creating a *verbal code*, or you can visualize verbally described information, creating a *visual code*. By creating and storing a verbal code when you perceive information, you don't need to use visual parts of the brain when later recalling the information. Thus, when people were asked to name from memory the colors of objects such as fire trucks and tractors that were shown to them in black-and-white drawings, the "color areas" of the brain were not activated (Chao & Martin, 1999). In this study, participants claimed not to use visual mental imagery; the associations apparently were stored verbally, and thus it was not necessary to access modality-specific memories, which would be stored in the perceptual areas that originally registered the information.

**CODING IN THE BRAIN**   Portions of the frontal lobes are often active when people encode new information, an indication that organizational processing is at work (Buckner et al., 1999; Kelley et al., 1998). Indeed, the degree of activation of the frontal lobes when information is studied predicts how well it will be remembered later (Brewer et al., 1998; Wagner et al., 1998).

# Consolidation and Reconsolidation

If you were ever in a play, you probably found that although you knew your lines well for the performances, a week or two after the last performance you had almost forgotten them. What happened? And how is this process of learning lines for a play different from remembering facts about your hometown, which don't evaporate even if you don't think about them for months on end?

**CONSOLIDATION: LODGED IN MEMORY**   Consider the following metaphor: Say you want to remember a path you are supposed to take in a few days. Someone shows it to you on a lawn, and, to remember it, you walk the path over and over, repeatedly tracing its shape. This is a metaphor for *dynamic memory*; if it is not continually active, it is lost. But, if you stick with a repeated route long enough, the path you're tracing becomes worn, and grass no longer covers it; this kind of memory is called *structural memory*, and, like the worn path, it no longer depends on continuing activity. When memories are stored in a dynamic form, they depend on continuing neural activity; when they are stored in a structural form, they no longer require ongoing activity to be maintained. The process of wearing a bare pathway in a lawn, of storing a memory as a new structure, is called **consolidation**. One goal of this book's Test Yourself and Review and Remember! sections is to help you accomplish just this process.

Code: A type of mental representation, an internal "re-presentation" (such as in words or images) of a stimulus or event.

Consolidation: The process of converting information stored dynamically in LTM into a structural change in the brain.

Many studies have shown that memories are initially stored in LTM in a dynamic form and are consolidated only after considerable amounts of time (McGaugh, 2000; Squire et al., 2001). For example, patients with major depression who receive electro-convulsive therapy—consisting of powerful jolts of electricity to the head (see Chapter 15)—experience disruption of memory for recent events, even those that are no longer in STM; however, these patients' memory for older information is unaffected (McGaugh & Herz, 1972). The hippocampus and related brain areas are crucial for consolidating memories of facts and events (Squire et al., 2001), but after consolidation they are no longer necessary for many types of memory (Corkin, 2002). Consolidation occurs not only for facts and events, but also for memories of sequences of movements; such consolidation involves multiple stages (Walker, Brakefield, et al., 2003) and uses a different set of brain areas than does consolidation of factual memories (Brashers-Krug et al., 1996).

In general, memories are well along the way to being consolidated after a couple of years. However, this process is remarkably complex, and it may continue for much longer (Manns et al., 2003). In fact, the process of consolidation may occur over such a long stretch of time that some memories may never be consolidated completely (Meeter & Murre, 2004).

**RECONSOLIDATION: CAN RECALL MAKE MEMORIES FRAGILE?**  Have you ever wished that you could change a memory? Discoveries in numerous laboratories may suggest that such wishes may—for better or worse—someday be more than idle fantasy. In spite of the evidence that memories become increasingly consolidated over time, researchers have discovered that the simple act of recalling information can cause memories to become vulnerable to change—and to be retained, the information must be *reconsolidated*, restabilized as a stored structure. Here's a metaphor: When you encode information in the first place, it is as if you have assembled pieces into a puzzle, which you then set down on a shelf. When you later retrieve the information, you need to lift that puzzle, which puts it in danger of coming undone; before putting it back on the shelf, you have to nudge the pieces, and perhaps even reassemble parts of it (but this sort of reconsolidation is far different from consolidation, which was required to assemble the puzzle from scratch in the first place). Researchers have shown that reconsolidation is not just consolidation all over again (Alberini, 2004); notably, different proteins are critical for consolidation after information is initially encoded and for reconsolidation after a memory is activated (Lee et al., 2004).

An understanding of the nature of reconsolidation might play a crucial role in developing new ways to treat victims of trauma, who harbor memories that do them harm virtually every day. For example, researchers discovered that particular proteins must be produced in the brain immediately after information is recalled in order to reconsolidate the memory of it. Animals forget conditioned fear stimuli if the protein-synthesis inhibitor anisomycin is injected into the amygdala shortly after the memory of a feared stimulus is activated—but this drug does not affect that memory if it is given when the information has not been recently activated (Nader et al., 2000).

However, reconsolidation is not necessary every time stored information is activated (Biedenkapp & Rudy, 2004; Hernandez & Kelley, 2004). In fact, following avoidance learning (Chapter 6), anisomycin injected into the amygdala, hippocampus, or related cortex did not disrupt subsequent memory of the conditioned response (Cammarota et al., 2004).

Why is reconsolidation necessary some times but not others? One possibility is that the more directly memories are involved in controlling behavior, as when an animal runs to avoid a shock that follows a tone, the less likely they are to need to be reconsolidated after having been activated (Eisenberg et al., 2003). In addition, the length of time information has been retained in memory, the nature of the task, the degree to which the information was effectively stored and subsequently consolidated, the correspondence

**Depth of processing:** The number and complexity of the operations involved in processing information, expressed in a continuum from shallow to deep.

between what is expected and what actually occurs (Pedreira et al. 2004), and various other factors could affect the need for reconsolidation (Alberini, 2004).

## Variations in Processing: Why "Thinking It Through" Is a Good Idea

If you want to remember the material in this book, you should do the Test Yourself and Think It Through! exercises at the end of each section and fill in the right-hand column of Review and Remember! at the end of each chapter. These features of the book have been designed to take advantage of a fundamental fact about memory: The more you think through information, the better you will remember its meaning. This finding has been interpreted in two ways, in terms of depth of processing and breadth of processing.

**DEPTH OF PROCESSING: THE VIRTUE OF "GETTING TO THE BOTTOM OF IT"** Craik and Lockhart (1972) hypothesized that memory improves with greater **depth of processing**, which consists of the number and complexity of the operations used when you process information. They argue that the greater the depth of processing when you first encode information, the greater the likelihood of remembering it later. Craik and Tulving (1975) reported a particularly effective demonstration of this effect, illustrated in Figure 7.7. They asked participants to view a list of 60 words, telling them that the experiment was a study of perception and "speed of reaction." On seeing each word, the participants were asked a question about it. Three types of questions were posed (but only one for any particular word, randomly interspersed): The first type of question required participants simply to look at the appearance of the word (to decide whether it was printed in capital letters), which did not require accessing detailed information stored in memory; the second led them to access stored information about the sound of the word (for example, to decide whether it rhymes with "train"), requiring a bit more processing; and the third made them access complex semantic information (for example, to decide whether the word would fit into the sentence "The girl placed the _____ on the table"), requiring the most processing. Following this exercise, the participants were unexpectedly asked to recognize as many words from the list as they could in a new list of 180 words (containing the 60 original words and 120 new words).

**FIGURE 7.7** **Depth of Processing in Action**

 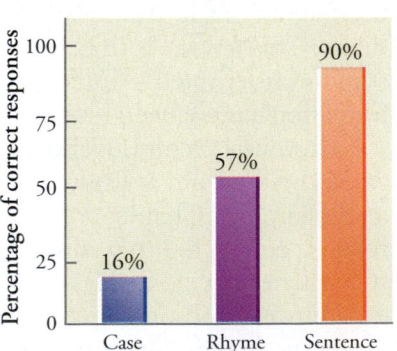

Craik and Tulving (1975) found that the more participants had to process each word (left), the better was their subsequent memory for it (right).

Craik and Tulving found that the greater the depth of processing required to answer the question, the more likely participants were to recognize the word.

A counterintuitive twist from such research is that people learn better when material includes "desirable difficulty" (Bjork, 1994; McDaniel & Einstein, 2005). A certain level of difficulty stimulates processing, and as we just saw, increased processing tends to improve memory. In addition, making a task more difficult helps memory the most when the increased difficulty leads the person to add a new sort of processing (such as seeking relations among items) that the original task did not require (McDaniel & Einstein, 2005). That said, material must not be so difficult as to be impossible to understand, and the person must be motivated to expend the extra effort.

What you pay attention to plays a key role in what is encoded into memory. However, the effect is not solely a matter of the depth of processing involved: If you are shown words and asked which ones rhyme with "train" (which forces you to pay attention to the sounds of the words), you later will recall the *sounds* of the words better than if you were initially asked to decide which words name living versus nonliving objects. But the reverse effect occurs if you are shown words and asked later to recall their *meanings*; in this case, your later recall will be better if you initially judge whether the words named living versus nonliving objects than if you initially evaluated their sounds. The most effective processing is tailored to the reasons the material is being learned (Fisher & Craik, 1977; Morris et al., 1977; Moscovitch & Craik, 1976). Practice on one task will help you perform another to the extent that the two tasks require similar processing. In particular, you will be able to remember information more easily if you use the same type of processing when you try to retrieve it as you did when you originally studied it; this is the principle of **transfer appropriate processing** (Morris et al., 1977; Rajaram et al., 1998).

**BREADTH OF PROCESSING: THE VIRTUE OF "REACHING OUT"** Information is encoded more effectively if it is *organized and integrated* into what you already know, thus engaging greater **breadth of processing**. Encoding that involves great breadth of processing is called **elaborative encoding** (Bradshaw & Anderson, 1982; Craik & Tulving, 1975). Perhaps the most dramatic demonstration of the benefits of elaborative encoding involved an undergraduate, S.F., who after a few months' practice could repeat lists of over 80 random digits (Chase & Ericsson, 1981). This is many, many more digits than can be held in STM, so how could he do it? S.F. was on the track team and was familiar with the times for various segments of races; thus, he was able to convert the numbers on the list into times, data with which he had associations. The digits 2145, for example, might be the times (with two digits each) needed to run two segments of a particular course. But in spite of his spectacular memory for numbers, S.F. was no better than average with letters. His memory, in general, had not improved over the months of practice with lists of numbers, only his tricks for organizing and integrating information about numbers.

The ability to organize and integrate explains why people in non-Western cultures recall stories better if the contents are familiar than if they are novel (Harris et al., 1992), and why Japanese abacus experts can remember 15 digits forward or backward but have only average memory for fruit names (Hatano & Osawa, 1983). The effects of organizing and integrating information also explain another of Ebbinghaus's discoveries—that you can remember better if you study in small chunks of time, spread out over time. This kind of *distributed practice* is superior to studying all in one session, which is called *massed practice* (but you might know it better as "cramming"). For example, Bahrick and Phelps (1987) showed that distributed practice helps people recall new words in Spanish much better than does massed practice. Each time you study material, you have an opportunity to think of different things that are associated with it, which provides more "hooks"

**Transfer appropriate processing:** Processing used to retrieve material that is the same type as was used when it was originally studied, which improves memory retrieval.

**Breadth of processing:** Processing that organizes and integrates information into previously stored information, often by making associations.

**Elaborative encoding:** Encoding that involves great breadth of processing.

Cramming is a good way to learn material for an exam, right? Wrong. Research has shown that people remember material much better if they rely on *distributed practice*, which takes place over a period of time, than if they rely on *massed practice*, which is crammed into one or two intense sessions.

FIGURE 7.8

## Hierarchical Organization

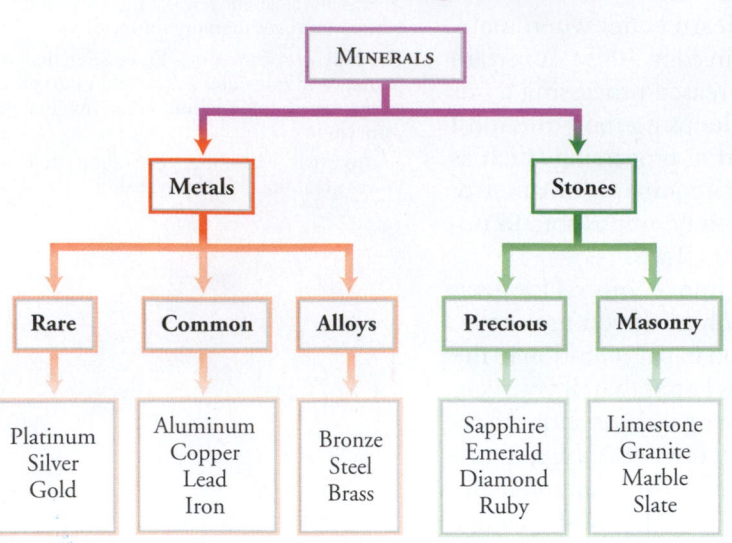

Bower and colleagues (1969) asked participants to learn lists of words that named objects in different categories. For some of the people, the words were presented in random order; for others, they were arranged hierarchically, as shown here. The participants who had the diagram to help them organize the list remembered over three times as many words.

into your previously stored knowledge. And the more hooks, the more likely you will be able to store it effectively.

The power of effective organization is illustrated in Figure 7.8. Indeed, people in Western cultures spontaneously organize newly presented words into categories, and later recall words in the same category before moving on to words from another category (Bousfield, 1953). However, in order to do this, the categories must be noticed; thus, it's a big help if they are presented explicitly.

One of the most remarkable discoveries in the study of memory is that it barely matters how much or how hard you *try* to learn something; what matters is how well you integrate and organize the material. Bower (1972) describes experiments in which participants were asked to form a mental image connecting each pair of words in a list (for example, pairing *car* and *desk* by imagining a desk strapped to the roof of a car). In one part of the study, the participants were told to use the image to memorize the pairs of words; this kind of learning, in which you *try* to learn something, is called **intentional learning**. In another part of the study, the participants were told simply to rate the vividness of the image, and they did not try to learn the pairs of words; learning that occurs without intention is called **incidental learning**. The interesting finding was that participants who were told to rate the images did as well at recalling word pairs as those who were told to memorize them. But, this is not to say that motivation and effort aren't important. In fact, the effort that went into organizing the objects into an image appears to have helped the participants learn, even without a specific instruction. This effect has been found repeatedly, with different kinds of learning tasks (J. R. Anderson, 2000; Hyde & Jenkins, 1973).

## Emotionally Charged Memories

S.'s memory was so good that the scientists who studied him found that there was no point in performing their usual memory experiments with him; such experiments typically are aimed at discovering the factors that lead to better or worse memory. For most of us, the amount that we remember depends on specific aspects of the situation, and one important aspect is emotion: People store emotionally charged information better than they do neutral information. Bradley and colleagues (1992) showed people slides with positive, negative, and neutral images—for example, an attractive nude young man hugging an attractive nude young woman, a burned body, a table lamp. The participants later remembered the arousing stimuli, both positive and negative, better than the neutral ones.

**WHY DOES EMOTION BOOST MEMORY?**  Cahill and McGaugh and colleagues (Cahill et al., 1994) have begun to answer this question in detail. They showed people photographs that illustrated a story. For some participants, the photos were all described in a neutral way ("While walking along, the boy sees some wrecked cars in a junkyard, which he finds interesting."); for others, the photos at the beginning and end were described in a neutral way, but those in the middle were described as depicting a bloody accident ("While crossing the road, the boy is caught in a terrible accident which critically injures him."). An hour before seeing the photos, half of each set of participants were given a placebo, a medically inactive sugar pill; the other half were given a drug (propranolol) that blocks the action of noradrenaline (a neurotransmitter). A week

Intentional learning: Learning that occurs as a result of trying to learn.
Incidental learning: Learning that occurs without intention.

later, all of the participants were given surprise memory tests. As expected, the group that received the sugar pill showed better memory for the pictures that had an emotional context, but the group that received the noradrenaline blocker failed to show this memory boost for emotional material.

Why does emotion cause more noradrenaline to be produced, which in turn causes enhanced memory encoding? Cahill and McGaugh thought that the boost in memory for emotional material reflects the activity of the amygdala, which is known to play a key role in emotion. Their hypothesis was that the amygdala, when activated, somehow enhances the operation of the hippocampus (perhaps via the plentiful direct connections between the two structures) as it encodes new information into memory. To test this idea, Cahill and his colleagues (1996) used PET scanning to examine the relation between activity in the amygdala and the degree to which people could recall emotionally arousing or neutral film clips. The amount of activity in the right amygdala when the participants viewed the clips later predicted remarkably well how many clips they could recall. Thus, the enhanced memory for emotional material relies on the activation of the amygdala, which in turn influences the hippocampus.

**FLASHBULB MEMORIES** A special case of an emotionally charged memory is a **flashbulb memory**, an unusually vivid and accurate memory of a dramatic event. It is as if a flashbulb in the mind goes off at key moments, creating instant records of the events. Perhaps you have such a memory for the moment you heard about the planes crashing into the World Trade Center towers on September 11, 2001. Brown and Kulik (1977) coined the term "flashbulb memory" and conducted the first studies of the phenomena. They polled people about a number of events, counting the recollections as flashbulb memories if respondents claimed to remember details about where they were when they learned of the event, who told them about it, and how they or others felt at the time. Most of the people these researchers polled at the time had flashbulb memories of President John F. Kennedy's assassination. In contrast, although three quarters of the Black Americans interviewed had flashbulb memories for the assassination of Martin Luther King, Jr., fewer than one third of the White interviewees had such memories. Brown and Kulik suggested that only events that have important consequences for a person are stored as flashbulb memories. Neisser and Harsch (1992) studied college students' memories of the crash of the space shuttle *Challenger*, interviewing them within a day of the accident and again 2 1/2 years later. They found that although people may be very confident of their flashbulb memories, these memories often become distorted over time. Moreover, this distortion becomes progressively worse with the passage of time (Schmolck et al., 2000). In fact, when researchers compared memories of a recent everyday event with those for the events of September 11, 2001 (memories initially recorded on September 12 of that year), they found that participants forgot the two events at comparable rates over time. Nevertheless, the participants' ratings of how vivid their memories were, and of how strongly they believed that the memories were accurate, did not change for their memories of September 11th, but did diminish over time for the everyday memories. Although people believed that their flashbulb memories were more accurate, they weren't (Talarico & Rubin, 2003).

Would it have been a good idea to begin this chapter with a more emotionally charged opening story, perhaps discussing a horrible accident that S. had witnessed? Making the story more memorable in this way could have distracted you from remembering the other contents of the story—and perhaps even of the chapter itself! When people are shown a set of neutral stimuli and then a highly emotionally charged stimulus, not only do they recall the emotional one best, but they also tend to forget the stimuli that came immediately before and after this arousing one. This disruptive effect, called the *von Restorf effect*, occurs with any attention-grabbing stimulus, not

Women remember emotional stimuli better than men, in part because emotion boosts the brain's memory circuits more effectively in women than in men (Canli et al., 2001). It is also possible, however, that socialization has led women to pay closer attention to emotion—and thus to encode circumstances surrounding it more effectively.

**Flashbulb memory:** An unusually vivid and accurate memory of a dramatic event.

just those that are emotionally charged. Apparently, people are so busy thinking about the noticeable stimulus that those occurring earlier and later are not encoded into LTM. Memory for items after the attention-grabbing stimulus is sometimes disrupted more severely than memory for items that came before it (Schmidt, 2002), especially when all the items are visual and not likely to be named and rehearsed.

# Test Yourself

1. Sperling was able to demonstrate that sensory memory holds a
   a. small amount of information for a very long period of time.
   b. large amount of top-down information for a brief period of time.
   c. large amount of perceptual information for a brief period of time.
   d. small amount of perceptual information for a very long period of time.

2. According to Baddeley's model of working memory, if you are rehearsing someone's phone number over and over in your head, you are utilizing the
   a. articulatory loop.          c. central executive alone.
   b. visuospatial sketchpad.     d. rehearsal module.

3. How effectively you encode new information into memory depends on all of the following *except*
   a. how hard you try to learn the new information.
   b. how the information relates to your current knowledge.
   c. thinking about your associations with the information.
   d. thinking about the complex properties of the information.

4. Making a memory is more than just putting information into a memory store. How the information is processed is also very important. Which of the following associations is correct?
   a. breadth of processing: the number of the operations used to process information
   b. depth of processing: elaborative encoding
   c. distributed practice: processing a lot of information all at once
   d. transfer appropriate processing: using very different types of processing for encoding and retrieval

## Answers

NOTE: Once you feel comfortable with the Test Yourself questions in this chapter, visit the book's Web site at www.ablongman.com/kosslyn3e for additional study questions.

# Think It Through!

At first glance, the fact that memories require time to consolidate may appear to be a disadvantage. Can you think of any advantages to having to wait a while before memories are consolidated?

Why does it make sense that we have better memory for emotional events? Would this help us make decisions or lead our lives in effective ways? Can you think of ways in which this feature of memory is a drawback? Why do you think people are so confident about their flashbulb memories?

# STORING INFORMATION:
## Not Just One LTM

S. relied heavily on mental images, but also used words and phrases as memory jogs. He eventually became a professional stage performer, and people paid to see him demonstrate his amazing memory. As part of his act, he asked audience members to produce any list or set of phrases, and he would memorize them. The audiences often tried to trip him up by giving him meaningless words or phrases. When given such verbal material to memorize, S. found it best to "break the words or meaningless phrases down into their component parts and try to attach meaning to an individual syllable by linking it up with some association" (Luria, 1968/1987, p. 43). These associations often relied on verbal knowledge, both about the meaning of words and their sounds. Unlike the single general-purpose hard drive on a computer, LTM is divided into specialized parts, as if—to continue the analogy—it has different drives for different sensory modalities (such as vision and audition), verbal information, and motor activities. S. clearly relied on many different sorts of information—and so do the rest of us. In this section, we consider these different sorts of information that are stored in memory.

## Modality-Specific Memories: The Multimedia Brain

The fact that memory is not a single capacity becomes especially clear when we look closely at how different kinds of information are stored in LTM. For example, note what seems to happen when you decide which is the darker green, a pine tree or a frozen pea, or, as you were asked in Chapter 4, whether the first three notes of "Three Blind Mice" go up or down. When answering such questions, most people report recalling visual or auditory memories, "seeing" a tree and a pea, "hearing" the nursery song. S. was superb at using these kinds of memories. In fact, virtually all of his memories were rooted in images of one sort or another; even when he used elaborate verbal associations or stories, they eventually led to specific mental images. As we saw in the discussion of perception in Chapter 4, our brains store visual memories so that we may recognize previously seen objects, auditory memories to recognize environmental sounds and melodies, olfactory memories to recognize previously encountered scents (Gottfried & Dolan, 2003), and so on. These **modality-specific memory stores** retain input from a single sense or processing system (Fuster, 1997; Karni & Sagi, 1993; Squire, 1987; Squire & Kandel, 1999; Ungerleider, 1995). In addition to visual, auditory, and olfactory memory stores, we have separate memory stores for touch, movement, and language. Interestingly, nearly everyone finds visual memories easier to recall than verbal memories. If you have a vivid mental image of an event, your chances of accurately remembering the event increase (Brewer, 1988; Dewhurst & Conway, 1994). S.'s reliance on images may have been an accident of how his brain functioned, but it clearly helped his memory.

## Semantic Versus Episodic Memory

In each kind of modality-specific memory store in LTM, you can retain two types of information. **Semantic memories** are memories of the meanings of words (a pine is an evergreen tree with long needles), concepts (heat moves from a warmer object to a cooler one), and general facts about the world (the original 13 American colonies were established by the British). For the most part, you don't remember when, where, or how you learned this kind of information. Information in semantic memory is organized into *semantic memory networks*, of the sort illustrated in Figure 7.9 on p. 292 (Collins & Loftus, 1975; Lindsay & Norman, 1977).

In contrast, **episodic memories** are memories of events that are associated with a particular time, place, and circumstance (when, where, and how); in other words, episodic memories provide a *context*. The meaning of the word *memory* is no doubt firmly implanted in your semantic memory, whereas the time and place you first began to read this book are probably in your episodic memory. At first, a new word may be entered in both ways, but after you use it for a while you probably don't remember when, where, or how you learned its meaning. However, even though the episodic memory may be gone, the word's meaning is retained in semantic memory. Neuroimaging studies have provided

**Modality-specific memory stores:** Memory stores that retain input from a single sense, such as vision or audition, or from a specific processing system, such as language.

**Semantic memories:** Memories of the meanings of words, concepts, and general facts about the world.

**Episodic memories:** Memories of events that are associated with a particular context—a time, place, and circumstance.

## FIGURE 7.9

## Structure of Semantic Memory Networks

Semantic memory is organized so that activating a concept tends to activate other concepts that are associated with it. In this diagram, the boxed words stand for concepts and the lines stand for associative links between them. Semantic memory not only contains different sorts of concepts—such as objects, living things, and characteristics—but also different sorts of associations among them—such as whether one thing is an example of a category or has specific characteristics.

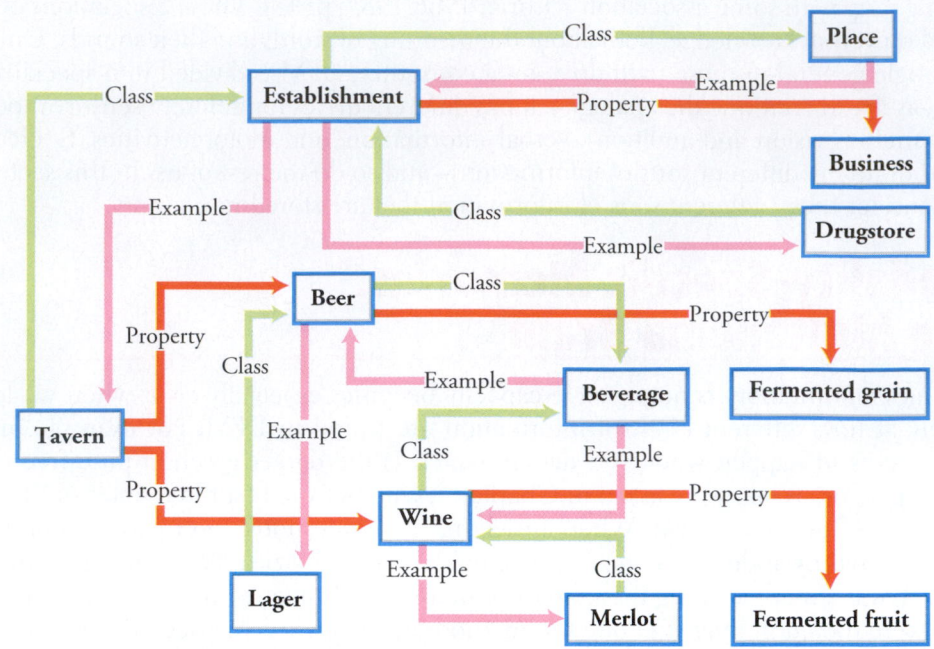

evidence that semantic and episodic memories are distinct. The frontal lobes, for instance, play a key role in looking up stored information (Hasegawa et al., 1998). However, many researchers have found that the left frontal lobe tends to be activated more than the right when we recall semantic memories, but the opposite is true when we recall episodic memories. If the two types of memories were the same, the same parts of the brain should generally access both (Cabeza & Nyberg, 1997; Nyberg et al., 1996; Shallice et al., 1994).

# Explicit Versus Implicit Memories: Not Just the Facts, Ma'am

When you consciously think about a previous experience, you are recalling an **explicit** (also called a **declarative**) **memory** (Squire, 2004). Verbal and visual memories are explicit if you can call them to mind in words or images (as you did with the pine tree and the pea). Episodic and semantic memories are explicit memories. Explicit memories are what is stored after cognitive learning occurs (see Chapter 6). When explicit memories are activated, they can be operated on in WM: You can think about the recalled information in different ways and for different purposes, and build on it with new ideas.

But think of how exhausting it would be if every time you met a friend, you had to try consciously to recall everything you knew about how people interact socially before you could have a conversation. The reason you don't have to go through such a tedious process is that you are guided through the world by **implicit** (also called **nondeclarative**) **memories**, memories that you are unaware of having but that nonetheless predispose you to behave in certain ways in the presence of specific stimuli or that make it easier to repeat an action you performed previously (Roediger & McDermott, 1993; Schacter, 1987, 1996; Squire, 2004). Unlike explicit memories, implicit memories cannot be voluntarily called to mind—that is, brought into WM and thus into awareness.

Explicit (or declarative) memories: Memories that can be retrieved at will and represented in STM; verbal and visual memories are explicit if they can be called to mind as words or images.

Implicit (or nondeclarative) memories: Memories that cannot be voluntarily called to mind, but nevertheless influence behavior or thinking.

The first hint that memory can be either explicit or implicit arose from the dreadful accidental consequences of a brain operation. H.M., whom you met in Chapter 3, suffered before his surgery from such a severe case of epilepsy that nothing could control his body-wracking convulsions. Finally, in 1953, at age 27, he underwent surgery to remove his hippocampus (and related parts of the brain in the front, inside part of the temporal lobe; Corkin, 2002). His doctors, whom H.M. had met many times, were pleased that the operation lessened his epileptic symptoms, but they were bewildered when he seemed not to recognize them. He could not remember ever having met them, and every time he saw them, he introduced himself and shook hands. To discover just how thorough this memory loss was, one of the doctors is said to have repeated an experiment first reported by Claparède in 1911: The doctor concealed a pin in his hand and gave H.M. a jab at the handshake. The next day, H.M. again behaved as if he had never seen the doctor before, but, as he reached out to shake hands, he hesitated and pulled his hand back. Even though he had no conscious memory of the doctor, his actions indicated that he had learned something about him. H.M. had acquired a type of implicit memory (Hugdahl, 1995a).

You can voluntarily recall explicit memories, such as a particularly important birthday, but you cannot voluntarily recall implicit memories, such as how to ride a bike. Implicit memories guide much of our behavior, freeing up the mental processes that underlie consciousness to focus on novel or particularly important stimuli or events.

Implicit memories are of five major types: classically conditioned responses, memories formed through nonassociative learning, habits, skills, and priming.

## Classically Conditioned Responses

The first type of implicit memory is classically conditioned responses. For example, if you burned your feet when walking barefoot on a particular pier during the summer, you probably would shy away from walking on that pier barefoot in the future. You aren't necessarily consciously aware of the association and may not even be able to explain your aversion to the pier (see Chapter 6; Hugdahl, 1995b).

## Nonassociative Learning

In addition to conditioned responses acquired through associative learning, implicit memories are also formed through nonassociative learning. For example, during habituation, a behavior changes after a stimulus is repeated over and over (see Chapter 6).

## Habits

Another type of implicit memory is habits (which are sometimes called *procedural memories*). A **habit**, as the term is defined by memory researchers, is a well-learned response that is carried out automatically (without conscious thought) when the appropriate stimulus is present. Habits include the entire gamut of automatic behaviors we engage in every day. When you see a red light, you automatically lift your foot from the accelerator, shift it left, and press it on the brake (we hope!); if you think something is automatic, that's a give-away that the action is being guided by implicit memory. Even S., who relied so strongly on mental images (which are explicit memories), must have relied heavily on implicit memories. For example, S. could play the violin, and such ability is stored as implicit memories. An example of the amnesiac patient H.M.'s implicit memory was revealed by the working of habit. When one of the authors of this book examined him some years ago, H.M. was using a walker because he had slipped on the ice and injured himself. The walker was made of aluminum tubes, and several operations were needed to fold it properly for storage. H.M. did not remember falling

**Habit:** A well-learned response that is carried out automatically (without conscious thought) when the appropriate stimulus is present.

## FIGURE 7.10 Basal Ganglia and Cerebellum

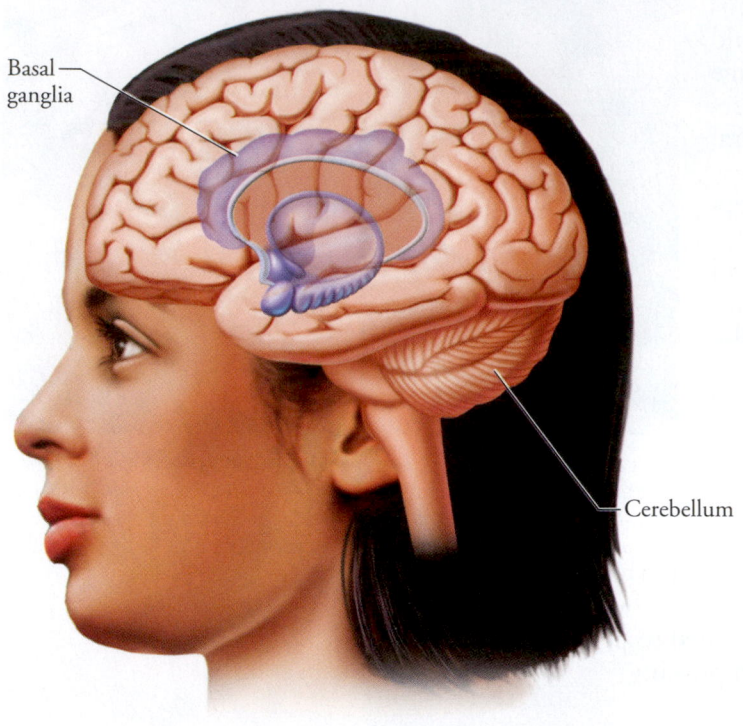

Basal ganglia

Cerebellum

The basal ganglia and cerebellum are particularly important in carrying out many automatic activities.

on the ice (which would have been an explicit memory), but he could fold and unfold the walker more quickly than the examiner could—thanks to the habit learned through using the device. He clearly had acquired a new implicit memory, even though he had no idea how he had come to need the walker in the first place. The intact ability to learn new habits, but not new episodic memories, is evidence that implicit and explicit memories are distinct from each other.

### Skills: Automatic Versus Controlled Processing

A *skill* is like a habit, but more flexible: Skills are sets of behaviors that can be applied to a variety of stimuli within a domain, such as riding a bike. Once you've learned how to ride a bike, you coordinate balancing, pedaling, and steering—not to mention looking where you are going! When you first begin to acquire a skill, you rely on controlled processing. **Controlled processing** requires paying attention to each step of an action, and using working memory to coordinate the steps. Do you remember when you first learned to ride a bike (or drive a car)? It was exhausting! Controlled processing relies heavily on the frontal lobes, in part on the anterior cingulate cortex—which monitors what you are doing and signals when you've strayed from your plan (Yeung et al., 2004). In contrast, after you've become highly practiced, you can perform the action without such painstaking control. Instead, you rely on **automatic processing**, which is processing that allows you to carry out a sequence of steps without having to pay attention to each one or to the relations between the steps. Many forms of automatic processing rely in part on the basal ganglia and cerebellum, illustrated in Figure 7.10. According to Schneider and Chein (2003), automatic processes are distinguished from controlled processes by seven characteristics, as summarized in Table 7.1.

### Priming

The fifth major type of implicit memory is **priming**, the effect that occurs when having just performed a task (such as recognizing a particular object) makes it easier to perform the same or an associated task more easily in the future (Schacter, 1987, 1996). For example, if you just saw an ant on the floor, you would be primed to see other ants and, thus primed, you would notice them in places where you might previously have missed them (such as on dark surfaces). Priming occurs when a preexisting memory or combination of memories is activated and the activation lingers. Priming that makes the same information more easily accessed in the future is called **repetition priming** (this is the kind of priming that enables you to see more ants). Many studies have shown that you can recognize a word or picture more quickly if you have seen it before than if it is novel. Such priming can be very long-lasting; for example, Cave (1997) found that people could name previously seen pictures faster when shown them again 48 weeks after the initial, single viewing. Your first exposure to the stimulus "greases the wheels" for your later reaction to it; in fact, after priming with a familiar object, the brain areas that perform the task work less

**Controlled processing:** Processing that requires paying attention to each step of an action and using working memory (WM) to coordinate the steps.

**Automatic processing:** Processing that allows you to carry out a sequence of steps without having to pay attention to each one or to the relations between the steps.

**Priming:** The result of having just performed a task that facilitates repeating the same or an associated task.

**Repetition priming:** Priming that makes the same information more easily accessed in the future.

TABLE 7.1

## Automatic Processes Versus Controlled Processes

| Characteristics of Automatic Processes Not Shared by Controlled Processes | Example Involving an Automatic Process |
| --- | --- |
| Become automatic only after extended training | Reading aloud written words |
| Occur without awareness and two or more can take place simultaneously | Driving (for an experienced driver) and understanding speech (in a highly familiar language) |
| Operate effectively even when the maximal amount of effort is required | Driving during rush hour in a very busy city |
| Work effectively even when a person is stressed | Reading street signs when rushing a pregnant friend to a hospital to give birth |
| Difficult to alter through changes in expectations, beliefs, and goals | Not reading a word when trying to see its color in a Stroop task |
| Difficult to adjust via learning | Changing a tennis swing after having played for many years |
| Depend on the importance of a stimulus, not its context | Putting the right foot on the car brake when you see a red light, even very late at night on a deserted road |

hard when repeating it than they did initially (Gabrieli et al., 1995, 1996; Henson et al., 2000; Schacter & Badgaiyan, 2001; Squire et al., 1992).

Priming is clearly different from explicit memory. For one thing, priming occurs even in brain-damaged patients who cannot store new explicit memories (Cave & Squire, 1992; Guillery et al., 2001; Schacter, 1987; Squire & Kandel, 1999; Verfaellie et al., 2001). Priming is also different from habits. Some brain-damaged patients can learn motor tasks but don't show priming; other patients show the opposite pattern (Butters et al., 1990; Salmon & Butters, 1995). These results demonstrate that more than one type of implicit memory exists. S. apparently was easily primed by perceptual information (sights and sounds set up images that, later, were easily triggered), but this says nothing about how well he could acquire skills.

The different major types of long-term memories are summarized in Figure 7.11.

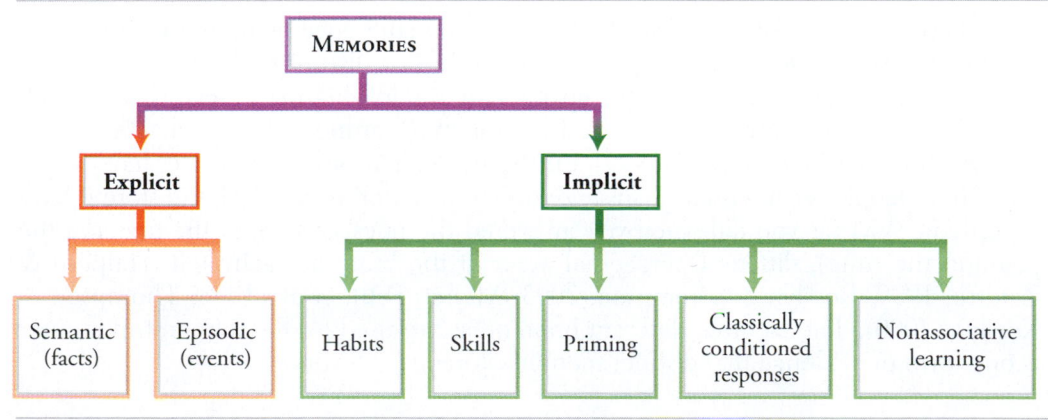

**FIGURE 7.11**

## Types of Memories

Not only are there many types of memories, as shown here, but also each type can occur in multiple stimulus modalities (visual, auditory, and so on).

# Biological Foundations of Memory

The next time someone complains that they have a bad memory, you now know to wonder, What sort of memory? Short-term or long-term? Which modalities? Explicit or implicit? Surprisingly, in most cases, the different types of memory operate independently of one another. Evidence is emerging that different parts of the brain and even different genes underlie the various types of memory, serving to demonstrate further that these types are in fact distinct.

## Specialized Brain Areas

Most of the distinctions we have drawn between different types of memories are also supported by differences in the way the brain encodes or stores information. Here we consider two major distinctions: that between habits and explicit memories, and that between memories in different modalities.

**HABITS VERSUS EXPLICIT MEMORIES** We know that habits are stored differently from explicit memories because different brain systems underlie the two types of memory. First, consider the neural bases of explicit memories. Explicit memories cannot form unless the hippocampus and the nearby areas that feed into the hippocampus and receive information from it are functional (Sperling, 2001; Spiers et al., 2001). The removal of the hippocampus (in monkeys) disrupts memory for facts (Mishkin, 1982; Squire, 1987, 1992; Squire & Kandel, 1999; Zola et al., 2000), and brain-scanning studies have shown that the hippocampus and nearby parts of the cortex are activated when people learn and remember information (Dolan & Fletcher, 1997; Schacter, 1996; Schacter & Wagner, 1999; Squire et al., 1992). Moreover, many researchers believe that the hippocampus plays a special role in memory for space and spatial context (Best et al., 2001; Nadel & Hardt, 2004; O'Keefe & Nadel, 1978). Differences in how effectively these brain areas operate could explain in part why S. has such a better memory than most of us: Researchers have found that people who had more active hippocampi when they studied words later recognized more of the words (Brewer et al., 1998; Wagner et al., 1998). Perhaps S. had a particularly active hippocampus. Second, in contrast to explicit memories, habits can be acquired by animals and humans (remember H.M.) even when the hippocampus and nearby cortex are not functional (Squire, 1987, 1992; Squire & Kandel, 1999). In fact, another circuit that bypasses the hippocampus allows us to learn habits (Mishkin & Appenzeller, 1987). Moreover, other brain structures, such as the cerebellum and basal ganglia, are crucial for habits but don't play a major role in memory for facts—which again is evidence that the two kinds of memory are different (Poldrack, Clark, et al., 2001).

**MEMORIES IN THE MULTIMODAL BRAIN** Different modality-specific memories are stored separately. Damage to particular parts of the brain can disrupt each of these types of LTM (visual, auditory, and so forth) separately while leaving the others intact, which indicates that the information is stored separately (Gardner, 1975; Schacter, 1996; Squire, 1987; Squire & Kandel, 1999). Furthermore, neuroimaging studies have found that when people recall visual versus auditory information from LTM and store it temporarily in WM (as you did when you answered the questions about the tree and the pea and the tune), different perceptual areas of the brain are activated (Halpern & Zatorre, 1999; Kosslyn & Thompson, 2003; Mellet, Petit, et al., 1998; Thompson & Kosslyn, 2000). The fact that different brain areas are used for the different memories is one form of evidence that distinct memory stores are at work.

## Linking Up New Connections

But how is information actually stored in the different brain areas? Hard disks rely on changing the magnetic state of tiny particles, but this obviously isn't how the brain works. Instead, storage in the brain apparently depends on how connections among neurons are formed and strengthened. Many researchers believe that new information is stored in LTM when a sending neuron releases a particular neurotransmitter (glutamate) at the same time that the receiving neuron reaches a specific voltage level. When these two events occur at the same time, the neurotransmitter activates a special receptor, called the *NMDA receptor* (for N-methyl-D-aspartate). NMDA activation causes the receiving neuron to change so that the sending neuron needs to send less neurotransmitter to get the same effect in the future. This change, called **long-term potentiation (LTP)**, essentially strengthens the connection between the sending and receiving neurons. According to this view, depending on which connections among neurons are altered, different types of memories are stored (Baudry & Lynch, 2001; Blair et al., 2001; Borroni et al., 2000; Geinisman, 2000; Villarreal et al., 2002).

## Genes and Memory

Like virtually all other aspects of our psychologies, our genes have something to say about how memory works.

**KNOCKOUT MICE AND BLINKING RABBITS**   How could we tell whether different genes affect different aspects of memory? One answer comes from the study of *knockout mice*, so named because a particular gene has been "knocked out" (see Chapter 3). However, tracing the connection between a missing gene and a specific behavior it normally affects is easier said than done. For example, early investigators thought they had found that knocking out particular genes disrupted a mouse's ability to remember the location of a concealed platform in a pool of water (the mice wanted to swim to the platform so that they could rest, and hence were motivated to remember where it was; Morris, 1984). However, in one such study, Huerta and colleagues (1996) observed that the mice without the "remembering" gene weren't lost; they just wouldn't swim. When the researchers tickled the mice's hind feet, the animals swam and learned where the platform was located as quickly as normal mice. Their inability to find the platform wasn't caused by poor memory but by a lessened motivation to swim. (We have to wonder whether the researchers may have stumbled on a laziness gene!) One moral of this story is that removing a given gene can have multiple effects, which can cause the animal to do poorly on a test for any number of reasons (Gerlai, 1996).

In spite of these confounded results in early experiments, subsequent research with knockout mice revealed that certain genes do influence memory, but their effects are limited to specific types of memories. In one set of studies (McHugh et al., 1996; Tsien et al., 1996) a *control sequence*, which turns specific genes on and off, was inserted into the DNA of mice. This control sequence turns off the gene of interest only after the mouse matures, and thus the gene will stop working in an otherwise normal adult mouse (this was an *inducible knockout*, as discussed in Chapter 3). Researchers were able to eliminate the functioning of a gene that affects a single part of the hippocampus. Thereafter, these animals did not show general problems, such as a lack of enthusiasm for swimming, but they did exhibit difficulty remembering locations. Without the gene, the environmental event—trying to remember the location of a submerged platform—could not turn on the mechanism that allows memories to be stored in the brain. However, the knockout mice were not totally clueless in memory tasks. They did

Long-term potentiation (LTP): A receiving neuron's increased sensitivity to input from a sending neuron, resulting from previous activation.

retain some information, and hence this part of the hippocampus alone cannot be responsible for all memory.

Another way to study the effects of genes on memory is to observe which proteins are produced during a task. Specific genes produce specific proteins, and thus researchers can infer which genes were recently active by tracking their signature proteins. In one such study, Cavallaro and colleagues (2001) studied rabbits that were conditioned to blink their eyes when they heard a tone (see Chapter 6 for a discussion of classical conditioning). The most interesting result was that many genes decreased their production of proteins during conditioning; only a relatively few genes (for example, those that affected the cerebellum and hippocampus) were activated. (Allowing the results of learning to be retained, which is what memory is all about.) Clearly, memory is a precise process, which involves intricate fine-tuning of that most marvelously complex of organs, the brain.

**GENES AND MEMORY VARIATION**   The human genome project has identified human genes that play a role in memory. For example, the apolipoprotein E (apo E) gene is present in many people who develop Alzheimer's disease, which devastates memory. But this gene does more than disrupt memory; versions (different alleles) of it also affect how well the normal brain can store information. For instance, Hubacek and colleagues (2001) found that one version of this gene tends to be present more often in people who have higher education than in people who dropped out of school by age 15, and vice versa for another version of this gene.

## Stressed Memories

When you are stressed, your brain sends signals to your body to prepare it for a fight-or-flight response. One of these signals increases the production of the hormone cortisol (see Chapter 3), which converts protein and fat into sugar, readying the body for rapid action. However, cortisol is a two-edged sword. Sapolsky and his colleagues have shown that in rats and baboons long-term exposure to cortisol actually kills neurons in the hippocampus (McEwen, 1997; Sapolsky, 1992). And the loss of hippocampal neurons disrupts memory.

Sapolsky studied a troop of baboons in Africa. The baboons had a well-defined social order, with some members of the troop being "on top" (getting the first choice of food, mates, and shelter), and others "on the bottom." Those on the bottom were found to have higher levels of cortisol in their blood; their social circumstances put them in a state of near-constant stress. When Sapolsky examined the brains of some of the baboons that died, he found that those near the bottom of the social order had smaller hippocampi than those higher up that were not continually stressed. And this sad state of affairs is not limited to baboons. MRI studies of the brains of people who have undergone prolonged stress during combat have shown that they have smaller hippocampi than people who were spared these experiences (Bremner et al., 1993). Similar results have been reported for victims of childhood sexual abuse who are diagnosed with posttraumatic stress disorder (PTSD; Bremner et al., 2003). Fortunately, in humans, the effects of stress on the hippocampus may be reversed if the environment changes (McEwen, 1997), and not all people who undergo stress fall prey to these effects (Pederson et al., 2004; Vythilingam et al., 2004).

In addition to disrupting the function of the hippocampus, at least some forms of stress may also disrupt other brain areas involved in storing and retrieving memories—including parts of the frontal lobe and amygdala. Researchers have found that when stress hormones disrupt LTP in the hippocampus, they also disrupt LTP in a pathway connecting the amygdala and frontal lobes (Maroun & Richter-Levin, 2003). High levels of stress hormones may disrupt the processes specifically involved in memory retrieval (Roozendaal, 2003).

# LOOKING AT LEVELS
## Autobiographical Memory

What is your first memory? How about your first memory of today? Episodic memories of events of your own life are called *autobiographical memories* (Conway & Rubin, 1993). Such memories require a kind of "time travel," where you put yourself back into a particular moment in your past, and relive what you experienced at that time. To understand autobiographical memories, we must consider events at each of the three levels of analysis and their interactions.

Let's start with the brain. Are autobiographical memories different from other kinds of memories? When you reflected on those events in your own life, did you experience mental images? Did you have emotional reactions? Such characteristics might suggest that memories of events that occurred in your own life might be different from memories of events that you observed happening to someone else—and research findings support this suggestion. In one study, researchers asked participants (undergraduate students) to take photos of specific locations on campus, asking different students to photograph different places. They later brought the participants into the laboratory and showed each student some of the photos taken by others. The researchers later scanned (using fMRI) the students' brains while they looked at mixed sets of photos and decided which photos they themselves had taken (based on the memory of having done so), which had been taken by others but seen in the laboratory, and which had not been previously seen. The medial prefrontal area involved in "self-referencing" was activated more strongly by the photos that corresponded to autobiographical memories than by the other photos, as were visual regions, the hippocampus, and regions near the hippocampus (Cabeza et al., 2004). Consistent with such findings, other researchers have found that brain damage can affect people's memories of famous people and events while not affecting their own autobiographical memories (Joubert et al., 2003). From these and similar studies, it is clear that autobiographical memory holds a special place not just in our lives, but also in our brains (Greenberg & Rubin, 2003; Levine, 2004).

Studies of the brain have done more than simply show that autobiographical memories are different from other types of memories. Research at this level of analysis has also shown that autobiographical memories can be divided into two types, episodic and semantic. Specifically, Brian Levine and his colleagues (2004) asked participants to keep a record over the course of several months, tape recording both descriptions of specific events they experienced and facts they observed about the world (which correspond to episodic and semantic autobiographical memories, respectively). Later, the participants listened to these recordings while their brains were scanned using fMRI. The tape recordings would presumably trigger the corresponding memories, and in fact, the brain responded differently to descriptions of experienced events and observed facts about the world. Although both types of autobiographical memories activated the left anterior medial prefrontal cortex, memories of experienced events activated this area more strongly than did memories of observed facts; this is interesting because this area has been repeatedly shown to be activated during "self-referencing," when people reflect on their own characteristics (Johnson et al., 2002; Kelley et al., 2002; Macrae et al., 2004). In addition, other brain areas were activated only during the experience-of-event condition and others only during the observation-of-fact condition. Clearly, the two kinds of autobiographical memories are distinct.

Autobiographical memories also depend on, and are affected by, events at the level of the person. What would be left if all of your autobiographical memories were erased? A large part of our personal identity hinges on our memories—memories not only of what we've done and what we know, but also of who we are. Researchers have documented this claim by showing that when people with Alzheimer's disease lose autobiographical memories, this loss is linked to distinct changes on questionnaire measures of the "self concept." Based on their results, these researchers suggest that autobiographical memories of childhood and early adulthood (which they define as the age range 16–25) are especially critical for self-identity (Addis & Tippett, 2004).

In addition, numerous events at the level of the person affect which autobiographical memories you will recall and how you will feel about them. Notably, if you felt good about an event at the time you experienced it, you are more likely to be able to recall it later. In one study, for example, people were tested on their memory for the O. J. Simpson trial. If a participant was happy about the verdict, he or she was later more likely to be able to recall details of the event (Levine & Bluck, 2004). And how you feel about autobiographical information is not determined solely by how you felt when you experienced the event—your feelings are also affected by the strategy you use during recall. In one study (Libby et al., 2005), participants were asked to recall "past social awkwardness" by taking a first-person perspective (that is, a participant's own viewpoint) or a third-person perspective (of an outside observer). Recalling events from the third-person perspective led participants to believe that they had changed more since the events had taken place. The third-person perspective apparently led participants to seek evidence that they had changed—and those who seek, often will find.

Moreover, your personal characteristics also affect the recall of autobiographical material. For example, people who are anxious in social situations tend to recall more negative and shameful autobiographical memories than do people who are not socially anxious (Field et al., 2004). And people who are inclined to feel gratitude for things others have done for them tend to be biased to recall more positive than negative events from their past (Watkins et al., 2004). Finally, the flip side of the last finding has been reported: People generally are biased to forget negative affect associated with events more quickly than they forget positive affect—unless they are mildly depressed, in which case, this bias can evaporate (Walker, Skowronski, & Thompson, 2003; Walker, Skowronski, Gibbons, et al., 2003).

And, of course, events at the level of the group affect autobiographical memories. We are immersed in social events just as a fish is immersed in water—and like the fish, we may not be aware of the many and varied ways that such events shape our memories. Most notably, the cultures in which we live play an important role in how we remember events about our lives. For example, when Americans and Chinese were asked to recall memories of their lives, the Americans recalled more unique, one-time events than did the Chinese and reported more details of the roles they personally played in the events as well as their emotional reactions. On the other hand, the Chinese recalled more social events and downplayed their own roles while emphasizing the social interactions surrounding events (Wang & Conway, 2004).

In addition, studies have shown that the emotional impact of remembered autobiographical events can be softened if people talk about these events—and this is especially the case if you have a sympathetic listener who agrees with you (Pasupathi, 2003).

Finally, effects at the different levels interact. For example, we already noted that people tend to forget negative affect associated with autobiographical memories more quickly than they forget positive affect. This effect is enhanced for memories that are frequently discussed with others—and this effect is even larger if you talk to many different types of people, such as friends, teachers, acquaintances, and strangers (Skowronski & Walker, 2004; Skowronski et al., 2004). The social factors that influence a person's decision to talk about autobiographical memories not only affect events at the level of the person, but also alter the way the brain functions at that moment.

# Test Yourself

1. Your memory of your breakfast today is _____, whereas your memory of the formula for the area of a circle is _____.
   a. a semantic memory; an episodic memory
   b. a working memory; a semantic memory
   c. an episodic memory; a semantic memory
   d. a working memory; an episodic memory
2. Knowing that semantic and episodic memories are different types of memories is an example of an explicit memory. Which of the following pieces of knowledge is the best example of an implicit memory?
   a. the name of Baddeley's theory about a form of memory
   b. the lyrics to your favorite rock hit after you've heard it one time
   c. your memory of a very familiar route you drive
   d. the definition of implicit memory
3. The knockout mice and blinking rabbits demonstrate not only that genes play a role in memory, but also that
   a. there is only one type of memory.
   b. different types of memory may rely on distinct mechanisms.
   c. environment is not important in memory, but genes are crucial.
   d. genes do not interact with the environment.
4. In Sapolsky's experiment, the stressed baboons had poorer memories than the less stressed baboons. At the level of the brain, this was due to (remember Chapter 3)
   a. the social pressure applied by dominant baboons.
   b. an impaired hippocampus.
   c. individual differences among the baboons.
   d. a smaller average brain size.

## Answers

1. c  2. c  3. b  4. b

# Think It Through!

S. was extraordinarily good at storing images. If he relied on this sort of storage alone, what sorts of material might be difficult for him to understand? Can you think of reasons why it makes sense that someone can be extraordinary with regard to only some types of memory? If a new drug were created that would improve one sort of memory, which sort of memory would you most prefer to improve?

# RETRIEVING INFORMATION FROM MEMORY:
## More Than Reactivating the Past

S. was not simply adept at readying material to be memorized; he was also expert at later digging out material from memory. No matter how well he encoded it and retained it in memory, the information would have been useless if he couldn't later retrieve it. In this section, we explore the process of retrieving information from memory.

## The Act of Remembering:
## Reconstructing Buried Cities

It is tempting to think of memory as a collection of file drawers that contain assorted documents, all neat and complete in labeled folders, so, when we need to recall something, we simply open a drawer and take out what we need. But memory doesn't work this way. When we open that file drawer, we don't find well-organized folders, but instead a bunch of partially torn pages that are not necessarily in order. Remembering is in many ways similar to the work archaeologists do when they find fragments of buildings, walls, furniture, and pottery and reconstruct from them a long-buried city; they fit the pieces together in a way that makes sense, and they fill in the missing parts (Neisser, 1967). We store in episodic memory only bits and pieces of a given event, and we use information from episodic memories of similar situations and from semantic memories of general facts about the world to fit the pieces together and fill in the gaps.

The fragmentary nature of memory is revealed in the *tip-of-the-tongue phenomenon*. Have you ever had the feeling that you know a word but just can't remember it? Brown and McNeill (1966) studied this phenomenon by reading definitions of relatively rare words to participants and asking them to recall the words being defined. As expected, people often "knew they knew it" but couldn't quite summon up the entire word. Instead, they recalled only some of the aspects of a word, such as its relative length and perhaps even its first syllable. We don't store words as unitary wholes but as collections of various aspects and characteristics—which we can sometimes recall individually.

## Recognition Versus Recall

All remembering involves tapping into the right fragments of information stored in long-term memory. We remember information in two ways. **Recall** is the intentional bringing to mind of explicit information or, put more technically, the transfer of explicit information from LTM to STM. Once information is in STM, you are aware of it and can communicate it. **Recognition** occurs when you match an encoded stimulus to one that has been stored in memory. When you match the input stimulus to a stored memory, you not only know that the stimulus is familiar, but also may have access to stored associations; for example, you may know that the stimulus occurred in a particular context, such as on a list (as used by memory researchers, the term *recognition* also implies identification; see Chapter 4). A *recognition test* occurs when you are given a set of stimuli and asked to pick out the ones you previously were given. Essay tests demand recall; the essay writer must retrieve facts from memory. Multiple-choice tests call for recognition; the test-taker must recognize the correct answer among the options.

All else being equal, tests that require you to recognize information are easier than tests that demand recall. But recognition can become difficult if you must discriminate between similar choices. The more similar the choices, the harder it is to recognize the correct one. Similar objects or concepts have more characteristics in common than do dissimilar ones. If the choices are dissimilar, you can pick out the correct one on the basis of just a few stored features. But if the choices are similar, you must have encoded the object or concept in great detail in order to recognize the correct answer. Professors who want to make devilishly hard multiple-choice tests put this principle to work. If the alternative answers for each question have very similar meanings, the test-taker must know more details than if the choices are very different. In general, the more distinctive properties of a stimulus you have stored in memory, the better you can recognize it.

Of course, you do not always know in advance which details you will need to remember. Suppose S. witnessed a theft and later was asked to pick the thief from a police lineup. S., unlike the rest of us, typically remembered exactly what he saw. In the lineup, suppose both the thief and another man in the group of six are tall, a bit overweight, and have brown hair. The major difference between them is that the thief has a scar on his left cheek. S. would have probably noticed and remembered the thief's scar and would be able to identify him. But the rest of us might not have encoded this detail at the time, and thus would be hard pressed to identify the culprit. Both recognition and recall rely on activating collections of fragments stored in LTM. If the appropriate fragments are not present, you cannot distinguish among similar alternatives, and you will have difficulty recalling information.

**Recall:** The act of intentionally bringing explicit information to awareness, which requires transferring the information from LTM to STM.

**Recognition:** The act of encoding an input and matching it to a stored representation.

# UNDERSTANDING RESEARCH

## A Better Police Lineup

You've probably seen police lineups on TV shows or in movies: A group of suspects is standing against a wall and a witness (usually behind a one-way mirror) picks out the culprit. If entertainment holds true to reality, you won't be seeing such scenes much longer. One of the great success stories of psychological research on memory resulted in a better way to have witnesses evaluate suspects (Steblay et al., 2001; Wells et al., 2000). The classic study was reported by Lindsay and Wells (1985).

**QUESTION:** After a witness has viewed a crime and is asked to identify the perpetrator, which is better: showing a set of suspects at the same time, or showing the suspects one at a time?

**ALTERNATIVES:** (1) Simultaneous presentation could be better because it allows witnesses to notice and compare subtle characteristics. (2) Sequential presentation could be better because it doesn't encourage witnesses to pick out the choice that is most like the person's memory of the actual criminal (even if it isn't identical). (3) Both methods could be about the same, with the advantages of one being matched by the advantages of the other.

**LOGIC:** If one method is better than the other, then participants should make fewer false identifications and the same number or more correct identifications when that method is used.

**METHOD:** In preparation for this study, the investigators assembled four sets of photographs. Two sets included the culprit and five other similar men; one of these sets included each of the six men mounted on a separate card, and the other included all six photos mounted together on a single large card. The other two sets were the same as the initial two except that the photo of the culprit was removed (and replaced with one of a similar looking person).

The 240 undergraduate participants did not know the purpose of the study in advance. Each participant was seated in a room (alone or in pairs), and the experimenter then left briefly "to get some forms." Thirty seconds later a confederate, acting as a criminal, came in, rifled several drawers and cupboards, and finally took a calculator and left the room. The experimenter then returned and announced that the thief was a confederate and the "crime" was staged. The participants were then told the purpose of the study (to study eyewitness accuracy), and they signed an informed consent form. Approximately 5 minutes after the "crime," each participant was randomly assigned to receive one of the four sets of photographs. Two groups of participants received the photos mounted together and were asked to select the culprit. The other two groups received the individual photos, shown one at a time in sequence, and were asked to say "yes" or "no" to each one.

**RESULTS:** When the actual culprit's photo was not present, participants made many more errors (falsely selecting one of the alternatives) when the six photographs were presented at the same time than when they were presented sequentially. Thirty-five percent of the witnesses fingered an innocent person in a simultaneous lineup compared to only 18.3% who viewed a sequential lineup. When the culprit's photo was present, accuracy rates were comparable in the two presentation conditions.

**INFERENCES:** When the photos are presented together, the participants look for the one that is most similar to the person they saw commit the crime; when the photos are presented one at a time, they judge each on its own merits, not relative to the others. These findings, and those that followed this classic study, were so compelling that police departments are now changing their standard lineup procedures (Kolata & Peterson, 2001).

## THINK CRITICALLY!

The sets of choices offered in this study were all photos of relatively similar-looking men. Do you think this was a good idea? Do you think witnesses always remember enough about what they see to narrow down the choices? What do you think would have happened if the choices were more dissimilar? Before you advised police departments across the country to revise their lineup procedures, what else would you want to know about this study and the later studies?

### The Role of Cues: Hints on Where to Dig

How does an archaeologist know where to dig to find the right bits of pottery to reconstruct a water jug? A logical place to start might be in the ruins of a kitchen. The archaeologist digs, finds bits of a typical kitchen floor from the period, and then is encouraged to continue digging in the same area. Similarly, a good cue directs you to key stored fragments, which then allow you to remember. **Cues** are stimuli that help you remember; they are reminders of an event.

**Cues:** Stimuli that trigger or enhance remembering; reminders.

**THE ANATOMY OF A GOOD RETRIEVAL CUE**   Imagine running into an acquaintance in a bookstore and trying to remember his name. You might recall that when you met him, he reminded you of someone else with the same name who had a similar hairline. Here the hairline is a cue, reminding you of your friend Sam and allowing you to greet this new Sam by name. S. at first memorized entire images but soon discovered that he was better off just remembering a specific "abbreviated or symbolic version" of the object. For example, when hearing the word "horseman," he would remember an image of a foot in a spur instead of a man on horseback. He tried "to single out one detail [he would] need in order to remember a word" (Luria, 1968/1987, p. 42). The fragments he recalled were good retrieval cues for the words. Whereas a man on horseback might bring to mind many associations (to statues, battles, historical figures, horse races, and so forth), a good retrieval cue narrows down the possibilities. Perhaps even more important, as illustrated in Figure 7.12 (Barclay et al., 1974), a helpful cue matches fragments of information stored in LTM.

**THE ENCODING SPECIFICITY PRINCIPLE**   Godden and Baddeley (1975) dramatically illustrated the role of cues in an ingenious experiment. They asked deep-sea divers to learn a list of words either when they were underwater or when they were on land. These researchers then tested half the divers in the same setting where they had learned the list, and the other half in the other setting. The results showed that the participants re-

**FIGURE 7.12**   **What Makes Something a Good Cue?**

 The man lifted the piano.

 Something heavy

 The man tuned the piano.

 Something with a nice sound

Participants were asked to memorize two sets of sentences. (What sort of mental images come to mind when you read the examples at the left?) The participants then received cues intended to help them recall the word *piano*. The top cue on the right would be more effective if the participant read the top sentence, and the bottom cue on the right would be more effective for the bottom sentence.

membered more words if they were tested in the environment in which they had originally learned the words. The significance of this finding is that when we learn, we are learning not only the material, but also the general setting and other incidental events that occur at the same time. And these events can later help cue us to recall the information (Flexser & Tulving, 1978; Koutstaal & Schacter, 1997; Parker & Gellatly, 1997; Smith & Vela, 2001). The idea that memory is better when people are given cues that were present during learning is called the *encoding specificity principle* (Tulving, 1983; Tulving & Thomson, 1973). So, if at all possible, study as much as you can in circumstances similar to those of the testing room—if there won't be music playing during the test, don't study while listening to music.

When participants were cued verbally to recall an event while at the same time smelling a common odor, the memory was more emotional than when no odor was present (Herz & Schooler, 2002).

## Supplying Your Own Cues

Some cues are internally generated.

### STATE-DEPENDENT RETRIEVAL: THE RIGHT FRAME OF MIND HELPS

We remember information better if we are in the same mood or psychological state (such as being hungry or sleepy) when we try to remember it as when we first learned it. If you were hungry when you studied material, you will remember it better if you are hungry at the time of recall than if you are stuffed. This can be a sobering thought if you are preparing for an exam: If you drink alcohol while studying, you will later recall the information better if you are drinking when you try to remember it. This effect is called **state-dependent retrieval** (Eich, 1989): Information is better remembered if recall is attempted in the same psychological state as when the information was first encoded. A closely related effect occurs with mood: If you are in a happy mood at the time you learn something, you may remember it better when you are feeling happy than when you are feeling sad (Bower, 1981, 1992). The effects of mood are not always very strong, however, and they can be overshadowed by other factors, such as how well the information is organized (Eich, 1995). Neither your psychological state nor your mood appears to be a very powerful retrieval cue.

As shown in Godden and Baddeley's study of divers, the properties of the environment in which you learn something become associated with that information in memory and can also serve as retrieval cues. If you are not in the original environment when you want to remember particular information, try to "supply the environment yourself" by visualizing it; memory is improved when you can mentally supply cues from the original setting in which the material was learned (Smith, 1988). If you lose your keys or wallet, retrace your steps in your mind's eye, if not in reality. This retracing puts you in the same environment as when you last saw the missing item, so that you are more likely to remember where you left it.

### HYPERMNESIA: PERSISTENCE HELPS

Cues can also arise when you remember information associated with a sought memory. Psychologists were surprised to discover that if they showed people pictures and then asked them to recall the names of the pictures over and over, after a while recall improved, even though the participants were not given feedback or other additional cues. If at first you don't remember, try, try again. Improved memory over time, without feedback, is called **hypermnesia** (Erdelyi, 1984; Payne, 1987). Hypermnesia probably occurs because you remember different aspects of the information each time you try to recall it, and each bit that is remembered is then used as a retrieval cue. Some of these self-supplied cues will be effective, and thus you remember pictures better as you keep trying to remember them. So, if at first you cannot recall someone's name, don't give up. Eventually you may hit on the memory of a retrieval cue, such as the shape of a hairline, which in turn will allow you to

State-dependent retrieval: Recall that is better if it occurs in the same psychological state that was present when the information was first encoded.

Hypermnesia: Memory that improves over time without feedback, particularly with repeated attempts to recall.

People who feel better about themselves in general recall more positive memories, even when they are in a bad mood, than do people who do not have a high self-regard. Both groups, however, are in a better mood after they've recalled positive memories (Setliff & Marmurek, 2002).

remember the name. Unlike S.—who almost never had this problem—when the rest of us cannot recall at first, we are well advised to try and try again.

**HYPNOSIS AND MEMORY** S. had very vivid mental images, which apparently allowed him to recall information with ease. If someone hypnotized you and told you that your images were especially vivid, would that boost your recall? Possibly. Hypnosis sometimes improves memory of prior events. In 1976 in Chowchilla, California, a school bus was hijacked, all of the children within kidnapped. The bus and all those inside were buried and held for ransom. When freed, the bus driver remembered the car driven by the assailants but no other details. In a hypnotic trance, he was able to recall the car's license plate, which ultimately led to the arrest of the kidnappers.

In many—if not most—cases, however, hypnosis increases people's confidence in their recollections but not their accuracy (Sheehan, 1988; Worthington, 1979; see Chapter 5). Indeed, studies have found no overall differences in accuracy of memory between witnesses who were hypnotized and those who were interviewed using techniques based on cognitive strategies such as those summarized earlier (Geiselman et al., 1985). In addition, hypnosis may actually lead people to believe that suggested events happened, rather than simply help them to recall actual events (e.g., Barber, 1997; Bryant & Barnier, 1999; Green et al., 1998). Thus, after hypnosis you might not, in fact, recall better than before, but you would probably be more confident that you did. Recognizing these problems, courts in many states will not consider testimony based on recall during hypnosis.

# Test Yourself

1. Recognition is usually easier than recall, but it becomes more difficult when the choices are
   a. very different.      c. very similar.
   b. humorous.            d. limited to only two.
2. Based on the idea of state-dependent retrieval, which of the following should produce the most reliable memory?
   a. encoding when you are sad and recalling when you are sad
   b. encoding when you are happy and recalling when you are sad
   c. encoding when you are sad and recalling when you are happy
   d. encoding when you are excited and recalling when you are calm

3. Godden and Baddeley's study of divers found that when the learning conditions matched the recall conditions, the divers' memory improved. This finding reflects
   a. hypermnesia.
   b. code effect learning.
   c. the serial position effect (but only the recency portion of the curve).
   d. the encoding specificity principle.
4. As you learned in Chapter 5, hypnosis increases people's confidence in their memories, but not the accuracy of those memories. This leads to a problem with hypnotizing eyewitnesses because
   a. people will not change their minds once they have been hypnotized.
   b. hypnotized people will always tell the truth.
   c. hypnosis has been found to alter consciousness in ways that harm memory.
   d. false memories and confidence in them can be inadvertently implanted.

## Answers

1.c 2.a 3.d 4.d

# Think It Through!

Can you think of any advantages to storing fragments and later reconstructing memories as opposed to storing mental photographs or other complete sets of information? We generally find recognition easier than recall; can you think of any way to convert a recall task into a recognition task? Can you think of any ways to help you generate what might turn out to be useful cues?

# FACT, FICTION, AND FORGETTING:
## When Memory Goes Wrong

S. had a near-perfect memory. When he made an error, it almost always was a "defect of perception," a result of the specific images he formed. For instance, he once forgot the word "egg" in a long list. He reported, "I had put it up against a white wall and it blended in with the background. How could I possibly spot a white egg up against a white wall?" (Luria, 1968/1987, p. 36). His memory was so good that he had a problem many of us might envy: He could not forget even when he wanted to. This became a problem when he performed on stage because material from a previous session could spring to mind unbidden, confusing him about the current list. He initially tried to imagine erasing the blackboard, or burning sheets of paper on which the information had been written, but he could just as easily imagine undoing these acts or seeing the writing on the charred embers—and thus the memories persisted. Finally, S. realized that the key to forgetting was simple: He just had to want the information not to appear, and if he did not think about it, it would not return. For S., this technique worked. Was S. like the rest of us in how his memories competed with each other? Could, for the rest of us, such interference cause losses and failures of memory? How accurate are our memories?

## False Memories

Not everything we remember actually happened. **False memories** are memories of events or situations that did not, in fact, occur. An extreme example of this sort of "memory" is illustrated in Figure 7.13.

### Implanting Memories

Deese (1959) and Roediger and McDermott (1995) showed that people regularly make errors of the sort illustrated by Figures 7.14 and 7.15. (If you weren't fooled, read the list of words to a friend and wait 5 minutes before testing him or her; this will increase the likelihood of an error.) We associate the idea of "sweet" with all of the words listed, so its representation in LTM becomes activated and associated with the context of the list, and we misremember having seen it. Here is the critical point: In general, we do not necessarily remember what actually happened but rather what we *experience* as having happened.

Lest you think that misremembering only occurs when associated material is stored, consider this disturbing study reported by psychologist Elizabeth Loftus (1993). In a study with a pair of brothers, she asked the older brother to tell his younger, 14-year-old brother about the time the younger brother had been lost in a shopping mall when he was 5 years old. This story was told as if it were fact, but it was entirely fiction. The youngster later gave every indication of having genuine memories of the event, adding rich detail to the story he had been told. For example, the boy claimed to remember the flannel shirt worn by the old man who found him, his feelings at the time, and the scolding he later received from his mother. When this study was repeated with many participants, about one quarter of them fell victim to the implanting of such false memories (Loftus & Pickrell, 1995). Moreover, these participants clung steadfastly to

**FIGURE 7.13**

### Memories of Alien Abduction

Some people claim to remember being abducted by space aliens. Such people display the same bodily reactions when asked to remember the abduction as when they imagine more mundane stressful events; people who do not report memories of abduction do not react as strongly when asked to imagine an alien abduction (McNally et al., 2004). Does this mean that the memories of alien abduction are genuine?

**FIGURE 7.14**

### False Memory

Please read this list of words. Now go to Figure 7.15 on page 308.

| | |
|---|---|
| candy | caramel |
| soda pop | chocolate |
| honey | cake |
| pie | icing |
| fudge | cookie |
| cotton candy | |

**False memories:** Memories of events or situations that did not, in fact, occur.

A twin sometimes has a false memory of an event that actually occurred to the other twin, such as being sent home from school for wearing a skirt that was too short. The same thing can happen (although less frequently) to non-twin siblings who are close in age, and even among same-sex friends (Sheen et al., 2001). Roediger and his colleagues (2001) describe a kind of "social contagion," where one person's recounting of memories can lead another to adopt them.

**FIGURE 7.15**

## True or False?

Did all of these words, including *candy*, *chocolate*, and *sweet*, appear on the list you read on page 307? Are you sure? In fact, the word *sweet* does not appear. If you think it did, you are not alone; most people do. This exercise shows how easily a false memory can be implanted in your brain.

| | |
|---|---|
| candy | chocolate |
| soda pop | cake |
| honey | sweet |
| pie | icing |
| fudge | cookie |
| cotton candy | |

their false memories, refusing even on debriefing to believe that they had been artificially created.

Similar results have been obtained many times (Loftus, 2004). Lindsay and colleagues (2004) reported especially striking results, finding that fully 65.2% of their participants could be led to believe that they had put Slime (a gooey concoction sold as a toy) in their teacher's desk when they were in first or second grade. These researchers combined the usual memory-inducing suggestions (of the sort used by Loftus) with showing the participants an actual photo of their class, which boosted the number of false memories to record levels (perhaps because they were able to imagine a plausible scenario more concretely). And there was no doubt that the participants came to harbor false memories; the participants often expressed surprise and shock upon learning the truth after the study, saying things such as "No way! I remember it! That is so weird!" and "If you didn't tell me it was a false event, I would have left here thinking I did this" (p. 153). However, some false memories are easier to create than others. Pezdek and colleagues (1997) found that whereas some participants did acquire false memories of being lost in a shopping mall, none acquired false memories of having been given a rectal enema during childhood. People may have an intuitive grasp of the role of emotion in memory, which leads us to know that we would be sure to remember such an incident if it had actually happened. (The ethics of carrying out such studies might be an interesting topic for discussion.)

Distortions of memory can be implanted in very simple ways. In a now-classic experiment, Loftus and colleagues (1978) asked people to watch a series of slides that showed a red Datsun stopping at a stop sign and then proceeding into an accident. The participants were then asked either "Did another car pass the red Datsun while it was stopped at the stop sign?" or "Did another car pass the red Datsun while it was stopped at the yield sign?" The questions differed only by a single word, "stop" or "yield." Loftus and her colleagues found that many more people who had been asked the "yield" version of the question later mistakenly recalled that a yield sign had been present. In this case, the question itself interfered with memory. Loftus initially speculated that the misleading question erased the accurate memory; later evidence suggests that the original memory was still present but difficult to access after the misleading question was presented (McCloskey & Zaragoza, 1985). In addition, at least some false memories may reflect how willing people are to agree that they had encountered a previous stimulus (a difference in *criterion*, using the language of signal detection theory—see Chapter 4; Hekkanen & McEvoy, 2002).

These kinds of memory errors have direct practical—and often quite serious—implications. After a crime is committed, for instance, witnesses are interviewed by the police, read newspaper stories about the crime, perhaps see TV reports. This information can interfere with actual memories. Moreover, during a trial, the way a question is asked can influence a witness's faith in his or her recollection, or even change the testimony altogether. Lest you think that such findings are merely of academic interest, reflect on the fact that several years ago the 100th person, Larry Mayes of Indiana, was released from prison because DNA evidence proved that he was innocent; these people were almost invariably convicted because witnesses had faulty memories (Loftus, 2004).

## Distinguishing Fact From Fiction

Does any aspect of false memories distinguish them from real memories? Daniel Schacter and his colleagues (1996) performed the "sweet" experiment, using similar words, while the participants' brains were being scanned. The participants were then asked which words were on the list and which words were merely implied by those listed. The hippocampus, which plays a key role in encoding new information into memory, was activated both when participants recognized actual words listed *and* when they identified associated words not on the original list. Crucially, when words actually on the list were correctly recognized, brain areas in the temporal and parietal lobes that register the sound and meaning of spoken words also were activated. In contrast, these areas were *not* active when people encountered words not on the list. Apparently, the construction of memory activates the representations of the perceptual qualities of stored words. Because the false words were not actually heard when the original list was read, this information was not activated. This cue of a "missing perception" may not be used all the time, but it clearly operates in many situations (Johnson et al., 1997).

The same principle applies to remembering a real versus an imagined event. Johnson and her colleagues (Johnson & Raye, 1981; Johnson et al., 1993) found that people often confuse actually having seen something with merely having imagined seeing it (which may be the basis of some false memories; Garry & Polaschek, 2000). Indeed, Dobson and Markham (1993) found that people who experience vivid mental images are more likely to confuse having read a description of an event with having seen it (similar findings have also been reported by Eberman & McKelvie, 2002). S., once again, is an extreme example; his "vivid images broke down the boundary between the real and the imaginary" (Luria, 1968/1987, p. 144). He commented, "To me there's no great difference between the things I imagine and what exists in reality" (p. 146).

**Reality monitoring** is the ongoing awareness of the perceptual and other properties that distinguish real from imagined stimuli. Reality monitoring can be improved greatly if people are led to pay attention to the context in which stimuli occur (Lindsay & Johnson, 1989). Mather and colleagues (1997) and Schacter and colleagues (Norman & Schacter, 1997; Schacter et al., 2001) found that when people are asked to pay attention to the amount of perceptual detail in their memories (as would occur if they tried to notice the texture of objects, other nearby objects, and shadows), they are better able to distinguish actual memories from false memories. In fact, people generally experience fewer false memories for visual material than auditory material (Cleary & Greene, 2002; Kellogg, 2001). However, there is a limit to how well people can use such cues to distinguish real from false memories; false memories produced in the "sweet" experiment, for example, are remarkably persistent, even when people are warned in advance about the possibility of such memories (McDermott & Roediger, 1998). However, not all people fail to take advantage of such advance warning: People who have more effective working memories can use advance warning much better than those with less effective working memories (Watson et al., 2005).

When S. was a reporter, he often interviewed people—and never took notes. Let's say that S. remembered that Mrs. Borsht had mentioned that a burglar wore a checked

Remember when you shook Mickey's hand during a childhood trip to Disneyland? Even if this never happened, seeing an advertisement that leads you to imagine this happy event will later make you more confident that this event actually occurred. Researchers found the same held true even when an ad led participants to imagine that they had shaken hands with Bugs Bunny at Disneyland, which could never have happened (Bugs is not a Disney character)—and thus the ad could not have activated an actual memory (Braun et al., 2002).

Reality monitoring: An ongoing awareness of the perceptual and other properties that distinguish real from imagined stimuli.

shirt. But later it turned out that it wasn't Mrs. Borsht at all; another witness had provided that news. This would have been an example of **source amnesia**, a failure to remember the source of information. Patients who have suffered frontal lobe damage sometimes have an extreme version of this impairment; they generally cannot remember who said what, or when and where they heard it. But, even people without brain damage can experience source amnesia; all it requires is forgetting the source of information in episodic memory (Schacter, 1996). In spite of the fact that S. apparently never had this difficulty, such problems are surprisingly common; indeed, some cases of unintentional plagiarism may be a result of source amnesia (Marsh et al., 1997; Schacter, 1999). In general, false memories are not always easy to distinguish from actual ones.

**Ebbinghaus's Forgetting Curve**

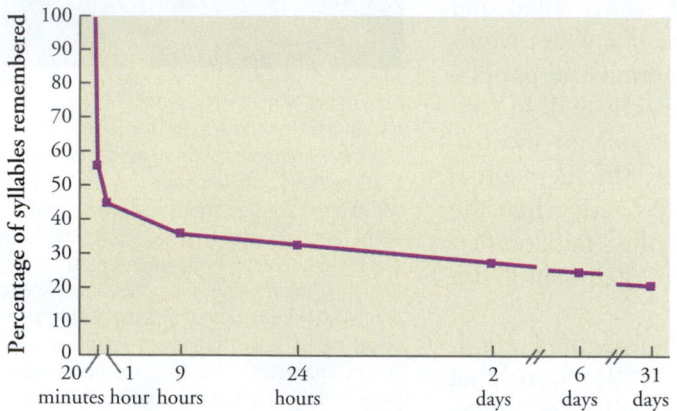

Elapsed time between learning syllables and memory test

The forgetting curve shows that information becomes harder to recall over time, but that most forgetting occurs relatively soon after learning.

# Forgetting: Many Ways to Lose It

Once S. stored information in memory, it apparently was there for good; his recall was as accurate years later as it was immediately after learning. As first shown in 1885 by Hermann Ebbinghaus, the rest of us recall recent events better than more distant ones, and most forgetting occurs soon after learning. However, as time goes on, people lose less and less additional information from memory (Wixted & Ebbesen, 1991, 1997). Ebbinghaus discovered the **forgetting curve**, illustrated in Figure 7.16, which shows the rate at which information is forgotten over time.

## Encoding Failure: Lost in Translation

Why do people lose information from memory? Sometimes the information was not well encoded in the first place. Remember the path traced over and over again through the grass? If the walker abandons the path before it is completely worn through to bare dirt, the pattern of the path is not stored structurally. Similarly, you must not "abandon" information— you must actively think about it if it is to be encoded effectively in LTM. An **encoding failure** results if you do not process information well enough to begin consolidation (Schacter, 1999).

An encoding failure causes information to be lost shortly after learning, which may be one reason for the sharp drop at the beginning of the forgetting curve. But, even if information is properly encoded, it can be lost later. Why? For many years, memory researchers hotly debated the fate of information that was once stored but then forgotten. One camp argued that once memories are gone, they are gone forever. The memory decays and disappears, just as invisible ink fades until nothing is left. The other camp claimed that the memories themselves are intact but cannot be "found." The ink hasn't faded, but the message has been misfiled. In fact, both camps had put their finger on important aspects of forgetting.

**Source amnesia:** A failure to remember the source of information.

**Forgetting curve:** A graphic representation of the rate at which information is forgotten over time: Recent events are recalled better than more distant ones, but most forgetting occurs soon after learning.

**Encoding failure:** A failure to process to-be-remembered information well enough to begin consolidation.

**Decay:** The fading away of memories with time because the relevant connections between neurons are lost.

## Decay: Fade Away

The invisible ink theory proposes that memories **decay**; that is, they degrade with time. The relevant connections between neurons are lost. What evidence supports this theory? In the sea slug, *Aplysia*, which has a relatively simple nervous system, it has been possible to document that the strength of the connections between neurons established by learning fades away over time (Baily & Chen, 1989). If human neurons are similar, as seems likely, memories may in fact decay over time. Indeed, researchers have produced evidence not only that certain genes promote stronger connections among neurons, but also that other genes prevent such connections and, hence, block memory (Abel et al., 1998). When these "memory suppressor genes" are turned on, they could cause the decay of connections that store memories.

Evidence refuting the decay theory seemed to come from dramatic findings described by Penfield (1955). Before performing brain surgery, neurosurgeons such as Penfield sometimes put small electrodes on the exposed cortex of awake patients and stimulated neurons electrically. A few patients reported vivid images and memories of long-forgotten events. For example, on having a particular area of the brain stimulated, one patient said, "Yes, sir, I think I heard a mother calling her little boy somewhere. It seemed something that happened years ago." However, at least some of these reports may not have been memories but images created on the spot (Squire, 1987; Squire & Kandel, 1999). There is no strong evidence that all memories stay stored forever. In fact, these oft-cited results occurred for only a minority of patients, and later work failed to reveal compelling evidence that memories are stored permanently.

# Interference: Tangled Up in Memory

The view that a mix-up in memory often explains forgetting has long been supported by strong direct evidence. If every summer you work with a group of kids as a camp counselor, you will find that learning the names of the current crop impairs your memory of the names of last year's campers. This is an example of interference. **Interference** is the disruption of the ability to remember one piece of information by the presence of other information. Two types of interference can plague your memories: retroactive and proactive.

**Retroactive interference** is interference that disrupts memory for something learned earlier. Learning the names of the new campers can interfere with your memory of the names of the previous group. **Proactive interference** is interference by something already learned that makes it difficult to learn something new. Your having learned the names of previous groups of kids may interfere with your learning the names on this summer's roster, particularly if some of the new names are similar to old ones.

Why does interference occur? The capacity of LTM is not the problem. You are not overloading a "memory-for-people" box in your brain; some politicians, after all, can remember the names of thousands of people with little or no difficulty. Interference probably occurs because the retrieval cues for various memories are similar, and thus a given cue may call up the wrong memory. The more similar the already-known and to-be-remembered information, the more interference you get (Adams, 1967).

The first president of Stanford University, David Starr Jordan, apparently worried that he might eventually fill up his memory if he learned too much. (But you shouldn't worry; we now know that the capacity of LTM is so vast that it hasn't yet even been measured.) President Jordan was an ichthyologist, an expert on fish who knew the names and habits of thousands of underwater species. At the beginning of each year he met the new students and politely smiled as they were introduced, but ignored their names. One bold student asked President Jordan if he had heard the name clearly, and then repeated it. Jordan listened and realized that he had now learned the student's name. He slapped himself on the forehead and exclaimed, "Drat, there goes another fish!"

# Intentional Forgetting: Out of Mind, Out of Sight

Given that interference is one reason we forget, you might wonder whether you could improve your memory by getting rid of useless information that might interfere with important facts. Was S. onto something when he tried to clear his clut-

**Interference:** The disruption of the ability to remember one piece of information by the presence of other information.

**Retroactive interference:** Interference that occurs when new learning impairs memory for something learned earlier.

**Proactive interference:** Interference that occurs when previous knowledge makes it difficult to learn something new.

tered mind by willing himself to forget unneeded information? Can we intentionally forget? Psychologists have studied this question by asking participants to learn a list of words or other stimuli, and then telling them to forget the list. Later the participants are given a surprise memory test, and their memory for the list is compared to that when they (or other people) were not told to forget it. Robert Bjork (1972) found that people have trouble later recalling information they were told to forget.

However, such information is not truly forgotten if it was successfully encoded; rather, it becomes not easily accessible (Bjork & Bjork, 2003). Indeed, when participants were asked to keep specific information out of mind, their frontal lobes became more active *and* their hippocampi became less active than when they were not trying to do this (Anderson et al., 2004). In contrast, if you decide not to remember something immediately after you perceive it, your left frontal lobe will not work as hard to encode it as it does when you try to remember (Reber et al., 2002). Clearly, the frontal lobes have a lot to do with the memory strategies we use, including those involved in trying to forget.

## Amnesia: Not Just Forgetting to Remember

Even S., if he received a strong blow to the head, might not recall anything that had happened to him after that incident. Why? Neither normal decay nor interference accounts for such unusual losses of memory. Instead, such memory failure is an example of **amnesia**, a loss of memory over an entire time span, typically resulting from brain damage caused by accident, infection, or stroke. Amnesia is not like normal forgetting, which affects only some of the material learned during a given period. Moreover, there are two broad sorts of amnesia: *Organic amnesia* arises after the brain has been damaged, by stroke, injury (including during surgery), or disease; *functional amnesia* typically arises after psychological trauma (Kritchevsky, Chang & Squire, 2004), and there is no obvious problem in the brain itself (although changes in the brain ultimately must underlie even this variety). In spite of its usefulness as a plot twist in novels and TV dramas, functional amnesia is very rare—and you would be wise to take the portrayals of amnesia in movies with more than a single grain of salt. For example, Baxendale (2004, p. 1480) notes, "*50 First Dates* maintains a venerable movie tradition of portraying an amnesiac syndrome that bears no relation to any known neurological or psychiatric condition." Moreover, other events portrayed in such movies—such as a second bump on the head hitting a "reset button" and curing the amnesia—have no basis in fact. (However, Baxendale notes that the main character in *Momento* and Dory the fish in *Finding Nemo* both do a reasonable job of portraying known forms of amnesia.) Functional amnesia is particularly difficult to study because, at least in some cases, it may in fact be *malingering*, intentional faking of the disorder.

Drew Barrymore, as the lead character in the movie *50 First Dates*, appears to suffer from retrograde amnesia. If so, this would be a very unusual case—most such patients cannot retain information for an entire day, as she was able to do.

Organic amnesia often seems to affect episodic memories while leaving semantic memories almost entirely intact (Warrington & McCarthy, 1988). Most people who have an accident that causes organic amnesia have no idea what they were doing immediately before the accident, but they can remember semantic information such as their names and birth dates. However, such selective forgetting reflects not the distinction between episodic and semantic memory, but instead the fact that most information in semantic memory was learned long ago—and hence is fully consolidated. Episodic memories of long-ago events are not disrupted by amnesia (Bayley et al., 2003). However, organic amnesia sometimes has the opposite effect, impairing mostly seman-

**Amnesia:** A loss of memory over an entire time span, resulting from brain damage caused by accident, infection, or stroke.

tic memories. For example, De Renzi and colleagues (1987) report a patient who forgot the meanings of words and most characteristics of common objects. Nevertheless, she remembered details about key events in her life, such as her wedding and her father's illness. Researchers have found that semantic memories are more likely to be impaired by amnesia if they are recent (for example, memories for new words that have entered everyday usage, such as "Segway" for the lawnmower-like scooter; Manns et al., 2003).

Amnesia may be retrograde or anterograde (Mayes & Downes, 1997; Parkin, 1987). **Retrograde amnesia** disrupts previous memories (Fast & Fujiwara, 2001). This is the sort of amnesia often popularized in soap operas and movies. Most of us are affected by a special form of retrograde amnesia called *infantile amnesia* or *childhood amnesia* (Newcombe et al., 2000): We don't remember much about our early childhood experiences, although some people apparently do remember very significant events (such as the birth of a sibling) that occurred when they were less than 2 years old (Eacott & Crawley, 1999). **Anterograde amnesia** leaves already consolidated memories intact but prevents the learning of new facts. It affects all explicit memories—that is, memories of facts that can be brought to consciousness voluntarily—and produces massive encoding failure. Its manifestation is well presented in an old joke: A man runs into a doctor's office, screaming, "Doc! I've lost my memory!" The doctor asks him, "When did this happen?" The man looks at him, puzzled, and says, "When did what happen?" However, it is no joke for people with anterograde amnesia, who live as if frozen in the present moment of time. H.M. had a form of anterograde amnesia.

What happens in the brain to produce amnesia? Often, as in the case of H.M., the cause involves damage to the hippocampus or its connections to or from other parts of the brain (Spiers et al., 2001). In addition, sometimes amnesia can result when areas of the cortex that serve as memory stores become degraded. As noted earlier, all memories are a result of changes in the interactions among neurons, and most neurons involved in memory are in the cortex. In cases of Alzheimer's disease, the amnesia typically begins with small memory deficits, which become progressively worse. In the later stages of the disease, people with Alzheimer's cannot remember who they are, where they are, or who their relatives and friends are. Alzheimer's disease not only affects the hippocampus but also degrades other parts of the brain that serve as memory stores. Depending on which other parts of the brain are affected, Alzheimer's patients can have greater amnesia for one form of information or another; for example, some patients have worse spatial memory than verbal memory, and others show the opposite pattern (Albert et al., 1990).

One possible treatment for Alzheimer's disease may come from a surprising source: tea. Both green tea and black tea may enhance memory (Okello et al., 2004). Both beverages inhibit the enzyme acetylcholinesterase (AChE) from breaking down acetylcholine, which plays a key role in storing new memories. Patients with Alzheimer's disease have low levels of acetylcholine, which suggests that the active ingredient in tea may someday help treat this disease.

Approximately 4.5 million Americans are afflicted with Alzheimer's disease and some experts estimate that this disease will affect over 13 million Americans by 2050 (Hebert et al., 2003). But not everybody is equally susceptible. In one study, nuns who had better linguistic ability, as judged from autobiographical essays they wrote in their 20s, were less likely than nuns with poorer linguistic ability to develop Alzheimer's disease (Snowdon et al., 2000).

**Retrograde amnesia:** Amnesia that disrupts previous memories.

**Anterograde amnesia:** Amnesia that leaves consolidated memories intact but prevents new learning.

**Repressed memories:** Real memories that have been pushed out of consciousness because they are emotionally threatening.

# Repressed Memories: Real or Imagined?

Recent years have witnessed many dramatic reports of suddenly recollected memories. Some people claim to have suddenly remembered that they were sexually molested by their parents decades before, when they were no more than 3 years old. One person claimed that as a child he had been strapped to the back of a dolphin as part of a bizarre devil worship ritual. Are these false memories, or are they **repressed memories**, real memories that have been pushed out of consciousness because they are emotionally threatening, as Freud believed? (When repressed information is later recalled, this is called a *recovered memory*.) Whether or not repressed memories exist is perhaps the most heated issue in memory research today (Fivush & Edwards, 2004; Madill & Holch, 2004; McNally, 2003, 2004; Ost, 2003; Pope, 1996; Rubin, 1996; Wessel & Wright, 2004).

On the one hand, there are plenty of examples where recovered memories turned out to be false, ranging from a memory of having been abducted by space aliens (McNally & Clancy, in press) to one about someone's having committed murder. For example, Eileen Franklin-Lipsker suddenly remembered that her godfather raped Veronica Cascio and her father then murdered Ms. Cascio. However, her father's attorneys discovered that the semen found on the victim could not have come from either her godfather or her father, and that her father was definitely at a union meeting when the murder was committed (Curtius, 1996).

On the other hand, there is also evidence that traumatic memories can truly be repressed. For example, Williams (1994) interviewed 129 women 17 years after each had been admitted during her childhood to a hospital emergency room for treatment of sexual abuse. Thirty-eight percent of the women had no memory of an event of sexual abuse; in fact, 12% claimed that they had never been abused. These results suggest that some people may forget traumatic memories. Could this finding simply reflect infantile amnesia, the forgetting of events that occurred in early childhood? Not likely, for two reasons: First, whereas 55% of the women who had been 3 years old or younger at the time of abuse had no recall, fully 62% of those who were between 4 and 6 years old at the time had no recall; if the forgetting were due to infantile amnesia, the women abused at a younger age should have had the poorer recall. Second, more of the women who were abused by someone they knew, as determined from independent evidence, claimed to have forgotten the incident than did the women who were abused by a stranger. Again, this difference should not have occurred if the forgetting simply reflected infantile amnesia. Indeed, a review of 28 studies of memory for childhood sexual abuse found robust evidence that such memories can be forgotten and later recalled (Scheflin & Brown, 1996). In some cases, people who suddenly remembered being abused as children then proceeded to track down the evidence for the event (Schacter, 1996).

There is a mystery here. As noted earlier, highly charged, emotional information is typically remembered *better* than neutral information. So, why should this particular kind of emotionally charged information be recalled poorly, or forgotten for decades? Schacter (1996) suggests that, in these cases of forgetting, the person has not really unconsciously pushed the memories out of awareness. Instead, it is as if the individual were "someone else" during the abuse and thus has few retrieval cues for later accessing the memories. Nevertheless, the memories may be stored and may, under some circumstances and with appropriate cues, be retrieved. If so, it seems that people sometimes forget emotionally charged events, but after long periods of time, they can come to remember them. Clancy and colleagues (2000) found that people who experience recovered memories of childhood abuse are more likely to mistakenly remember words such as "sweet" when asked to remember a previously presented list of words naming sweet things, as in the experiment discussed earlier. This finding might suggest that these people are unusually sensitive to stored fragments of information. Leavitt (1997) has shown that people who recover such memories are not especially prone to making up information when given suggestions, which indicates that they are not simply more likely to form false memories.

1. From the classic Loftus experiment on implanting a false memory and subsequent studies, researchers have concluded that a false memory
   a. completely replaces the original memory.
   b. cannot be induced.
   c. can be extremely compelling.
   d. is really a kind of social role-playing.

2. Based on what you have learned about memory, S.'s memory was
   a. no different from most people's memory.
   b. based on the same principles as everyone's memory.
   c. stronger than most people's memory but followed the same forgetting curve.
   d. lacking in all reality monitoring.

3. Retrograde interference and retrograde amnesia disrupt _____ memories, whereas proactive interference and antero-grade amnesia disrupt _____ memories.
   a. previous; new
   b. new; previous
   c. repressed; explicit
   d. implicit; explicit

4. Source amnesia is relatively _____ and likely has to do with the functioning of the _____ lobes.
   a. rare; temporal
   b. common; frontal
   c. common; parietal
   d. rare; parietal

## Answers

1.c 2.b 3.a 4.b

# Think It Through!

If effective methods for implanting false memories are demonstrated conclusively, should they be outlawed? In general, or only in certain circumstances (such as their being used by advertisers who want you to "remember" how much you like their products)? Can you think of any circumstances under which implanting a false memory might be a good idea? Explain. Can you think of anything about having amnesia that might be an advantage in some way?

# IMPROVING MEMORY:
## Tricks and Tools

No matter how hard you try, you probably will never develop a memory as good as S.'s. He apparently was born with something special, which he later learned to cultivate. However, you can use what you've learned in this chapter about the mechanics of memory to improve both your storage and later retrieval of information. Among normal people, the crucial difference between having a "good" memory and a "bad" one lies largely in the strategies used when storing and retrieving information. The fact that memory is so dependent on such strategies explains why it has among the lowest heritabilities (see Chapter 3) of all specific cognitive abilities. Even if a number of people in your family have fabulous memories, their gifts probably won't help you much, if at all (Nichols, 1978).

## Enhancing Encoding: New Habits and Special Tricks

One way to improve your memory is to learn to encode information effectively. If you encode the information, you've won half the battle. The research results you've read about in this chapter show that you can improve your memory for information if you train yourself to engage in the following activities when you study.

## Organize It!

In order to make a habit of improving your memory, you should *organize* material so that you *integrate* it, making connections between what you want to remember and what you already know.

**CHUNK IT!** The first part of the organizational process requires you to form chunks, to organize the material into units. If an orange is so large that you cannot get your mouth around it, you'll pull it apart into bite-size pieces. So too with to-be-learned material. Figure out the individual facts and ideas; it is much easier to take in information after you have divided the material into easily digestible morsels. Each chapter in this book is organized into chunks by means of appropriate subheadings and paragraph breaks.

**MAKE IT HIERARCHICAL!** After you identify the units of material, the key is to organize them in such a way that they are tightly bound to each other. If you succeed in this, then when you recall one fact, the others will follow. As you've seen, *hierarchical organization*, as in the experiment by Bower and colleagues (1969; summarized in Fig. 7.8), is an especially effective way to improve learning and memory. For example, you might memorize the errands you need to do by organizing your tasks in the same way you organize your trip: Break the trip down into separate segments and then organize the events in each segment separately. Think about which tasks need to be done at one end of town, or in one part of the store, which need to be done at another specific location, and so on. The key is to think of ways to organize the material hierarchically, so that the big task breaks down into smaller ones, which themselves may break down into yet smaller ones; the goal is to group together relatively small sets of material. This book's end-of-chapter summaries are intended to help you see the hierarchical organization of the material.

## Process It!

Organization is often only the first step to improved memory; how you process that organized information makes a big differences.

**THINK IT THROUGH!** To be sure that you understand material (such as that presented in this book), the principles of *depth and breadth of processing* imply that you need to think about the meanings and implications of facts and ideas. For instance, you can think of ways in which facts are similar and different. (Remember those compare-and-contrast essays you had to do in high school? They weren't such a bad idea.) In addition, you should think of examples that demonstrate statements made in the text (or, conversely, think of examples that seem to refute these statements).

**TRANSFER IT!** In order to succeed on tests, you should try to find out what kind of test the instructor will give: If it is an essay test, you would be better off figuring out the connections between the various facts you have read and asking yourself "why" questions about them (Pressley et al., 1995); this sort of studying will be much more helpful than simple memorization, both for success on the test and for lasting understanding. For a multiple-choice or true-false test, however, simple memorization might do as well as the more complicated strategies designed to integrate and organize the material, but even here you probably will retain more of the relevant information if you process it deeply so that you understand it well.

**DISTRIBUTE PRACTICE!** Just as two thin coats of paint are better than one thick coat, you will remember better if you study in distributed sessions—repeatedly, in relatively short sessions, spread out over time. Each time you study, you encode new retrieval cues and you have more chances to integrate the information into what you already know—and both factors will improve later memory. Moreover, the encoding specificity principle suggests that you study in conditions similar to what you will experience when you take the test.

Mnemonic devices: Strategies that improve memory, typically by using effective organization and integration.

## Mnemonic Tricks: Going the Extra Mile

In addition to developing new habits of thinking and studying, you can improve your memory by using many of the same tricks S. developed. These tricks will improve your memory—perhaps dramatically so. A recent search on "memory AND improvement" in the on-line bookstore Amazon came up with over 200 books—all of which provide tips on how to improve your memory, and many of which emphasize memory tricks. The use of **mnemonic devices**, or strategies that improve memory (*mnemonic* is derived from the Greek word for "memory"), requires extra effort, but is often well worth it: These mnemonics can easily double your recall. Using mnemonic devices not only helps you learn something in the first place, but, should you forget it, you will be able to relearn it more effectively.

### VISUALIZE INTERACTING OBJECTS: IMAGES THAT PLAY TOGETHER, STAY TOGETHER
Probably the single most effective mnemonic device is the use of *interactive images*. As discussed earlier, forming images of objects interacting will improve memory even without any effort to learn the material (Bower, 1972; Paivio, 1971). Such interacting images can help you remember the sequences of events in a history class, the associations between meanings and sounds for foreign vocabulary, and most other types of associations. For example, if you want to learn someone's first name, visualize someone else you already know who has the same name, and imagine that person interacting with your new acquaintance in some way. You might envision them hugging, or arguing, or shaking hands. Later, when you see the new person, you can recall this image, and thus the name.

### VISUALIZE "IN LOCATION": PUTTING OBJECTS IN THEIR PLACE
A related mnemonic device was discovered by the ancient Greek orator Simonides. He was attending a banquet one evening when he was called out of the room to receive a message. Shortly after he left, the ceiling collapsed, mangling the guests' bodies so badly that they were difficult to identify. When asked who had been at the feast, Simonides realized that he could remember easily if he visualized each person sitting at the table. This led him to develop a technique now called the *method of loci* (*loci*, the plural of *locus*, means "places" in Latin). To use this method, first memorize a set of locations. For example, you could walk through your house and memorize 12 distinct places, such as the front door, the computer desk, the potted plant near the big window, and so on. Later, when you want to memorize a list of objects, such as those on a shopping list, or a list of foreign language words you need to memorize, you can imagine walking through your house and placing an image of one object in each location. For instance, you might visualize a lightbulb leaning against the front door, a box of tissues on the computer desk, a can of coffee beside the plant, and so on. When you want to recall the list, all you need to do is visualize the scene and walk through it, "looking" to see what object is at each place.

To use the method of loci, pick out a set of locations in your house, and visualize each to-be-remembered object in a different location as you mentally walk through the house. To recall, later repeat this mental walk and "see" what's in each location.

However, not just any image will do. We can learn a lesson from S., who discovered some properties of effective images: "I know that I have to be on guard if I'm not to overlook something. What I do now is to make my images larger. Take the word *egg* I told you about before. It was so easy to lose sight of it; now I make it a larger image, and when I lean it up against the wall of a building, I see to it that the place is lit up by having a street lamp nearby . . . I don't put things in dark passageways any more. . . . Much better if there's some light around, it's easier to spot then" (Luria, 1968/1987, p. 41).

**PEG IT: NUMBERED IMAGES** The *pegword system* is similar to the method of loci, except that instead of places, you first memorize a set of objects in order. For example, you might memorize a list of rhymes, such as "One is a bun, two is a shoe, three is a tree, four is a door," and so on. Then you can treat the names of the memorized objects (bun, shoe, tree, and door) in the same way as the locations in the method of loci. You could associate the first item on your grocery list, for example, with a bun, the second with a shoe, and so on. In this case, when you want to remember the list, you remember each of the pegwords (*bun* and so on) in order and "see" what is associated with it. This method can be used to memorize all manner of lists, including those that you often find in tables in a textbook.

When Henry Roediger (1980) asked people to use different mnemonic devices to remember sets of words, he found that these three methods—interactive imagery, the method of loci, and the pegword system—were the most effective. However, as you know, there are many types of memory, and people differ in how well they can use various techniques. You might find some other mnemonic devices more useful.

**TRY OTHER MNEMONIC DEVICES** We can use many different sorts of tricks to improve our memories, not just the three discussed so far. For example, rhyming words provide a simple method for keeping concepts straight. For instance, the rhyme "rhyming priming rhyming" might help you remember that priming makes the same processing (like the same word repeated) easier to repeat in the future.

*Acronyms* are pronounceable words made from the first letters of the important words in a phrase, such as NOW for National Organization for Women; *initialisms* are made up of the initial letters but are usually not pronounceable words, such as LSU for Louisiana State University. Initialisms may be easier to make up for most situations; the idea in both cases is to create a single unit that can be unpacked as a set of cues for something more complicated.

In short, the key to mnemonics is figuring out a way to organize information so that you can link something new with something you already know. For example, to remember that *mnemonic* means "a memory aid," think of trying to remember something by putting a name on it: putting a NEM-ON-IC.

You can use mnemonics for material throughout this book, setting up mental connections or associations from one thing to another, perhaps with the use of imagery. For example, to remember that the word *suppression* means "voluntarily forcing unwanted thoughts back into the unconscious," you might visualize SUPerman PRESSing down demons that are bursting out of someone's head, shoving them back inside. When you form the image, you need to remember that the first part of Superman's name and what he's doing (pressing) are critical, so make sure that the S on his cape is very vivid and visible and that he is clearly pressing with his hands. Showing you a drawing of such a scene would work almost as well, but challenging you to make up your own image has the added advantage of forcing you to process the information more thoroughly, which in and of itself improves memory.

In addition, you can remember information by stringing it into a story. For example, if you wanted to remember that Freud came before the cognitivists, you can make up a story in which Freud wishes he had a computer to help him bill his patients but gets depressed when he realizes it hasn't been invented yet. Making the story a bit silly or whimsical may actually help memory (McDaniel & Einstein, 1986; McDaniel et al., 1995) and certainly makes it more fun to think about!

One of the fundamental facts about learning is that you will learn better if you are actively involved. Instead of just reading, try to find connections across areas, try to think of your own mnemonics. You won't go wrong if you simply form a visual image, make up an association, invent a rhyme or a joke. You will be better off if you try to be an active learner. Although such studying involves more time and energy in the first place, you'll need less studying to brush up on the material before a final exam—and in general will be less likely to forget the material.

# Enhancing Memory Retrieval: Knowing Where and How to Dig

S.'s ability to remember what he saw and heard was so good that he didn't need to notice patterns in the stimuli. For example, memorizing a table of numbers that were arranged in order was no easier for him than memorizing a table of random numbers. For us, however, once we notice such a pattern, we can store it—which will help us later to reconstruct the material. However, sometimes we need to remember things that we didn't expect to need or didn't have the opportunity to store effectively. Police officers are regularly faced with the effect of this unexpected demand on witnesses' memories. The need for accurate witness statements has been one impetus for developing methods to help people remember after the fact. Fisher and colleagues (Fisher & Geiselman, 1992; Fisher et al., 1989) used the results of laboratory studies to develop a method to help witnesses and victims of crimes recall what actually happened. Detectives trained in using their method were able to lead witnesses to recall 63% more information than was obtained with the standard police interview format. This method made use of the following memory principles and techniques:

- *Remember the context.* Recall is better when you mentally reinstate the environment in which information was learned. If you want to remember something, try to think of where you were when you learned it, what the weather was like, how you felt at the time, and so on.
- *Focus.* Searching for information in LTM requires effort and is easily disrupted by other stimuli. To remember well, focus on the task, shutting out distractions.
- *Keep trying.* The more times you try to remember something, the more likely you are eventually to retrieve it (Roediger & Thorpe, 1978).
- *Seize fragments.* If you cannot recall something immediately, try to think of characteristics of the information sought. Fisher and colleagues, in their 1989 study, advised detectives that if a witness could not remember a criminal's name, he or she should try to remember its length, first syllable, ethnic origin, and so on. These bits of information can serve as retrieval cues.
- *Structure the environment.* For certain kinds of memory retrieval, you can arrange your environment in such a way that you are reminded about what to remember. In other words, use external cues as mnemonic devices. If you are prone to forgetting your backpack, leave it by the door; if you forget to check the weather forecast before you leave home in the morning, put an umbrella on the door handle. A clever use of external cues was developed by historian Alistair Cooke, who hit on an ingenious way to remember where he shelved his books. He had a large number of books on the United States and its regions, but he couldn't always recall the author of a particular book. Arranging the books alphabetically by state didn't work because he couldn't decide where to put books about regions, such as the Rocky Mountains. The system that finally worked was simple: He arranged the books about western regions on the left, eastern regions on the

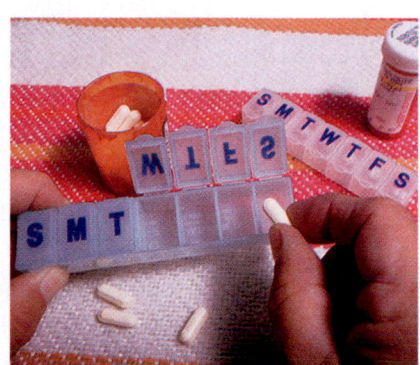

Arranging your world properly can aid memory. In this case, the pill holder makes it easy to recall whether or not you've taken your medication each day.

right, northern regions at the top, and southern regions at the bottom. The location in the bookcase mirrored the location in the country, and his problem was solved—all he had to do was look in the right place on his bookcase "map" (Morris, 1979).

If you can find a method for improving retrieval that is fun and easy and that works for you, you are more likely to use it, and benefit by it. As in the case of mnemonic devices, try various methods and see which suits you.

# Test Yourself!

1. The method of loci and the pegword system differ in the associations you make with the new material to be remembered. Loci are _____, and pegwords are _____.
   a. lists of words; numbered words
   b. vivid images; interactive schemas
   c. places; a set of objects
   d. lists of words; places
2. Mnemonics work to improve memory because
   a. rote processing improves memory automatically.
   b. active organization and integration improve memory.
   c. memory is linear and thus is reinforced by repetitive practice.
   d. Mnemonics have not been found to improve memory.
3. Fisher and colleagues found that if people cannot readily remember some information, it may help if they
   a. recall characteristics of the information or the context of the event.
   b. think about completely different information, but avoid using mental imagery.
   c. concentrate extremely hard on what preceded the event, and then put this aside—allowing incubation to work its magic.
   d. activate the right hemisphere.

4. Knowing where and how to dig for memories improves recall. What does this indicate about human memory?
   a. Memory is structured and organized.
   b. Memory is biological, and the type of input has little effect on recall.
   c. Forgetting is a function of time, not of the presence of retrieval cues.
   d. Memory is an interesting phenomenon, but has little to do with our survival.

## Answers

1.c 2.b 3.a 4.a

# Think It Through!

Suppose a friend of the family is to be the principal of a new high school in your area. She's mentioned wanting to help students learn and remember more effectively. She asks your opinion. Do you think memory improvement techniques should be taught in school? If so, in which courses? Can you think of any reason not to teach such techniques? Why do you think that many people don't use memory improvement techniques, even after they've discovered for themselves how effective these techniques are?

Would you use the same memory aids to study for a multiple-choice test and an essay exam? What would be different about your methods?

If you were setting up a class to teach executives how to improve their memories, what would you need to know about your clients' daily activities? What would you include in your curriculum?

How could you help police detectives determine which witnesses were remembering details about crimes more accurately? What new retrieval cues could you suggest that might be effective?

# REVIEW AND REMEMBER!

## Summary

### I. Encoding Information Into Memory: Time and Space Are of the Essence

**A.** Encoding is the act of organizing and transforming incoming information so that it can be entered into memory. Effective encoding depends in part on what is perceived to be important.

**B.** There are three types of memory stores: sensory memory (SM), short-term memory (STM), and long-term memory (LTM). The memory stores differ in the amount of information they can retain and how long they can retain it.

**C.** Working memory (WM) is the use of STM to reason or to solve problems. Working memory involves specialized STMs (the articulatory loop and the visuospatial sketchpad) and a central executive, which is a set of processes that manipulates information in these temporary storage structures.

**D.** Memory is improved as more time is spent thinking about the material to be stored and how it relates to current knowledge. Memory is most effective if the learner focuses on the properties of the material that will be relevant later. Depth of processing involves thinking about the more complex properties of objects.

**E.** Elaborative encoding involves thinking of relations and associations of material to be stored. It takes time to consolidate information to be stored, converting it from a dynamic form to a structural form.

**F.** Strong emotion typically amplifies memory, not diminishes it.

**G.** Flashbulb memories are unusually vivid and accurate. Although people may be very confident of these memories, they become progressively more distorted over time.

### II. Storing Information: Not Just One LTM

**A.** There are multiple types of LTMs, which store information for different sensory modalities, such as visual and auditory.

**B.** Some of the information in LTM is semantic, pertaining to the meanings of words, concepts, and facts about the world. Other information stored in LTM is episodic, pertaining to events that occurred at a specific time, place, and circumstance.

**C.** Some memories in LTM are explicit (stored so that the information can be retrieved voluntarily). Other memories in LTM are implicit (stored as tendencies to process information in specific ways). Implicit memories include classical conditioned responses, responses learned through nonassociative learning (as occurs in habituation), habits (automatic responses to appropriate stimuli), skills, and priming (which makes it easier to repeat a process in the future).

**D.** All memories arise when neurons change their patterns of interaction, so that new connections are formed or previous connections become strengthened. Long-term potentiation (LTP) is one mechanism whereby new memories are stored.

---

| Your Notes |
| --- |
| I. |
| A. |
| B. |
| C. WM = STMs + central executive |
| D. |
| E. |
| F. |
| G. |
| II. |
| A. |
| B. |
| C. |
| D. LTP strengthens neural connections. |

**E.** The process of storing new memories depends on the actions of specific genes.

**F.** Stress can impair memory, in part because it increases production of the hormone cortisol, which in turn impairs the functioning of the hippocampus.

## III. Retrieving Information From Memory: More Than Reactivating the Past

**A.** Memory retrieval depends on a constructive process; you must retrieve the right pottery fragments to build the right jug. Recognition is often easier than recall, but the ease of recognition depends on the choices you must distinguish among; the more attributes the choices have in common, the harder it is to distinguish among them.

**B.** Effective retrieval depends on having cues, or reminders, that match part of what is in memory, allowing you to reconstruct the rest.

**C.** Hypnosis typically does not improve memory retrieval.

## IV. Fact, Fiction, and Forgetting: When Memory Goes Wrong

**A.** False memories occur when a person stores information about an event that did not happen, or that did not happen in the way that is "remembered." False memories may not include information about the perceptual features of the stimuli involved, which may allow the person to distinguish them from actual memories. Reality monitoring can be used to check for perceptual features in memory.

**B.** Forgetting occurs in various ways: Encoding failure prevents information from being stored. Decay results when neural connections are weakened to the point where they are no longer functional. Interference (either retroactive or proactive) prevents the digging out of stored information.

**C.** Intentional forgetting, which can be effective, relies in part on the operation of the frontal lobes.

**D.** Memories may be difficult to recall because the stored information may not match later retrieval cues.

**E.** In contrast to ordinary forgetting, amnesia wipes out explicit memory for a span of time, not just isolated aspects of memories.

**F.** Memories of abuse may sometimes be "repressed" if the person was "someone else" when experiencing the abuse.

## V. Improving Memory: Tricks and Tools

**A.** Organizing information via chunking or hierarchical organization can make the information easier to remember.

**B.** Extensive processing of information, especially through distributed practice, aids memory.

**C.** Some mnemonic devices that can help you store information effectively include interactive images, the method of loci, the pegword system, rhyming words, and acronyms and initialisms. Mental imagery is generally very effective when it is used to organize information in a meaningful way.

*Margin notes:*

*E.*

*F.*

*III.*

*A.*

*B.*

*C.*

*IV.*

*A.*

*B.*

*C.*

*D.*

*E. Amnesia: loss of memories covering some time period*

*F.*

*V.*

*A.*

*B.*

*C.*

**D.** Several tricks have been shown to help people dig out information previously stored in LTM. One technique is to provide effective retrieval cues by having people think about where they were and how they felt at the time. Another major factor is effort: It is important to focus and keep trying. If information is still difficult to recall, then people are asked to try to recall its characteristics or associated information (which in turn can serve as retrieval cues). Finally, sometimes just arranging external cues as reminders can be helpful.

NOTE: Once you feel that you understand the material in this chapter, visit the book's Web site at www.ablongman.com/kosslyn3e to test your knowledge with additional study questions.

## Key Terms

amnesia, p. 312
anterograde amnesia, p. 313
automatic processing, p. 294
breadth of processing, p. 287
central executive, p. 281
chunk, p. 280
code, p. 284
consolidation, p. 284
controlled processing, p. 294
cues, p. 304
decay, p. 310
depth of processing, p. 286
elaborative encoding, p. 287
encoding, p. 278
encoding failure, p. 310
episodic memories, p. 291
explicit (or declarative) memories, p. 292
false memories, p. 307

flashbulb memory, p. 289
forgetting curve, p. 310
habit, p. 293
hypermnesia, p. 305
implicit (or nondeclarative) memories, p. 292
incidental learning, p. 288
intentional learning, p. 288
interference, p. 311
long-term memory (LTM), p. 281
long-term potentiation (LTP), p. 297
memory store, p. 279
mnemonic devices, p. 317
modality-specific memory stores, p. 291
primacy effect, p. 283
priming, p. 294
proactive interference, p. 311
reality monitoring, p. 309
recall, p. 302

recency effect, p. 283
recognition, p. 302
rehearsal, p. 280
repetition priming, p. 294
repressed memories, p. 313
retrieval, p. 278
retroactive interference, p. 311
retrograde amnesia, p. 313
semantic memories, p. 291
sensory memory (SM), p. 279
serial position effect, p. 283
short-term memory (STM), p. 280
source amnesia, p. 310
state-dependent retrieval, p. 305
storage, p. 278
transfer appropriate processing, p. 287
working memory (WM), p. 281

# CHAPTER 8

# LANGUAGE AND THINKING: WHAT HUMANS DO BEST

A lbert Einstein had one of the most remarkable minds in history. He didn't simply revolutionize physics, he changed the way the human species looks at the world. Einstein is often thought of today as he was in his later years—a saintly figure, patient and benevolent, his head framed by a white halo of hair. However, as a young man, he had a rebellious streak. He hated his experiences in the rigid and authoritarian German schools (experiences so alienating that he renounced his German citizenship when he was 17 years old and remained stateless until he was granted Swiss citizenship 5 years later). Einstein's father wanted him to have a practical career, and so insisted that young Albert apply to study electrical engineering. He failed the entrance exam, probably intentionally. He did attend university, but he regularly missed classes—staying home either to play his violin or to study physics on his own. When he did show up, he managed to annoy so many of his teachers that they shunned him after graduation, and he had great difficulty finding a job. Indeed, because of these personal characteristics, Einstein held only temporary teaching positions until he was 23 years old, when a friend's father helped him land an entry-level job at the Swiss patent office. He worked in the patent office for 7 years.

Even though he was cut off from universities and good libraries, Einstein later recounted that he was very lucky to be working in the patent office at that point in his life (Clark, 1971). In those days in Switzerland, hopeful inventors had to supply physical models along with their patent applications. Einstein became adept at studying such models and drawings, discerning the underlying principles; his job was to rewrite the often vague and muddled descriptions, cleaning them up so that they could be protected by law. Einstein learned to abstract clear-cut principles that explained how devices worked. He later noted that this was good training for discerning the laws of nature. In his spare time, he thought long and hard about the fundamental properties of the universe, and he published a series of papers that shook the world.

In general, Einstein's work was marked by "out of the box" thinking, by enormous intellectual flexibility. He did not accept the common wisdom of the day, but instead was comfortable breaking all the rules. He correctly reasoned not only that light waves are bent when they pass near a strong source of gravity (such as a star), but also that time isn't constant and that light transfers mass. Moreover, he put together what had previously been viewed as distinctly different—for example, showing how mass and energy are in fact different facets of the same thing.

Einstein's insights often arose only after years of thought and intense work. For example, he labored for 10 years to produce his famous Special Theory of Relativity (which showed why the laws of physics apply only in the context of specific frames of reference, except that the speed of light is always constant). But don't think of Einstein as a kind of supercomputer, working through problems methodically and systematically, a step at a time. Einstein's methods of thinking often resembled those of an artist. He said, "When I examine myself and my methods of thought, I come to the conclusion that the gift of fantasy has meant more to me than my talent for absorbing positive knowledge" (Clark, 1971, p. 88).

What is thinking? How do people solve problems and reach decisions? Can you learn to think more effectively? In this chapter, we consider some of the most fundamental ways in which we humans tower over the other animals—namely, in our thinking and language.

# LANGUAGE: More Than Meaningful Sounds

Albert Einstein did not begin to talk until he was 3 years old, and he wasn't entirely fluent even by the time he was 9 (Clark, 1971, p. 10). His language skills were so poor that his parents worried that he might be mentally retarded! Nevertheless, he eventually learned to speak not only his native German, but also French and English. However, he mixed German with his French, and his English, learned later in life, never became fluent—as countless satirists have noted, he made grammatical mistakes and had a heavy German accent. If we judged him by his language alone, we wouldn't be impressed. Clearly, using language to communicate relies on at least some abilities that are not used in reasoning and problem solving.

## The Essentials: What Makes Language Language?

Language accomplishes its role in communication via a two-pronged process of sending and receiving. **Language production** is the ability to speak or otherwise use words, phrases, and sentences to convey information. Perhaps the most remarkable thing about language production is that it is *generative*. We create, or generate, new sentences all the time; we don't simply retrieve and repeat stored sentences. The number of new sentences we can produce is astounding. Psychologist Steven Pinker (1994, p. 86) estimates that we would need at least 100 trillion years to memorize all the sen-

Language production: The ability to speak or otherwise use words, phrases, and sentences to convey information.

tences any one of us can possibly produce. **Language comprehension** is the ability to understand the message conveyed by words, phrases, and sentences. We humans are endowed with the extraordinary ability to comprehend even fragments of speech, mispronounced words, and scrambled syntax. For example, you can probably extract the general meaning from the following: "Me speech badly with grammar, but words use appropriately." We can understand the speech of the very young, speech flavored with foreign or regional accents, and lisping speech, even though the actual sounds made in each of these cases are very different. Even Albert Einstein, who spoke French and English with difficulty, could make himself understood in those languages. To put things in perspective, even today's most sophisticated speech recognition devices can decode only a fraction of what a competent 5-year-old can do effortlessly.

So, if language involves a process of sending and receiving information, what about a dog that whines when it is hungry, barks to go for a walk, and sits when told to? In fact, the Takara Company of Japan has developed a device (smaller than a credit card) that "translates" your dog's barks, yelps, whines, and growls into emotions, supposedly allowing you to know when she's lonely, hungry, and so on (Associated Press, 2001). Your pet can send and receive information, all right, but is it using language? The intuitive answer is no, and the intuitive answer is right—there's more to language than that (Pinker & Jackendoff, 2005). Language units are built from simple building blocks that can be combined in many ways, but only according to specific rules. Four types of units, and the rules for combining them, distinguish language from other communicative sounds such as whines. These units and rules provide the key to both language production and language comprehension, and—as shown in Figure 8.1—they make up the phonology, syntax, semantics, and pragmatics of a language. Let's look at each of these aspects of language in turn.

**FIGURE 8.1** **The Four Aspects of Language**

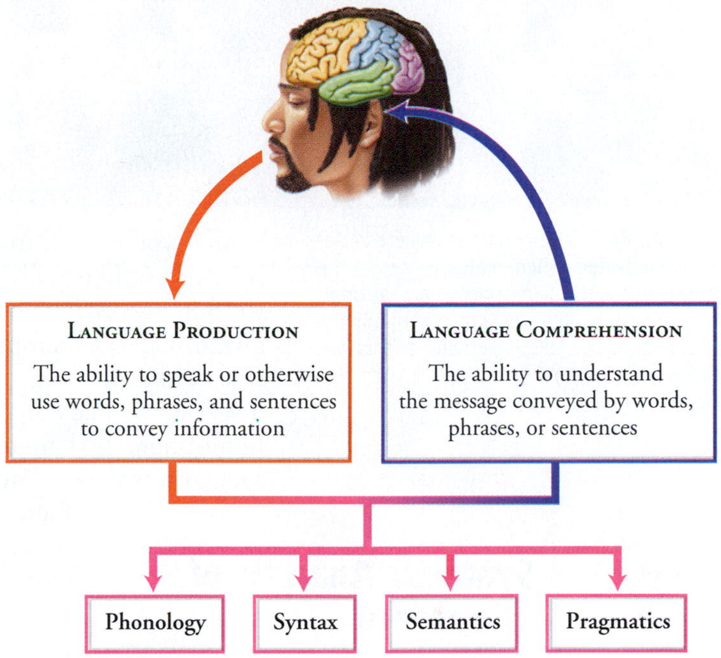

| LANGUAGE PRODUCTION | LANGUAGE COMPREHENSION |
| --- | --- |
| The ability to speak or otherwise use words, phrases, and sentences to convey information | The ability to understand the message conveyed by words, phrases, or sentences |

| Phonology | Syntax | Semantics | Pragmatics |
| --- | --- | --- | --- |

Both the sending (production) and receiving (comprehension) aspects of language rely on the interplay of phonology, syntax, semantics, and pragmatics.

## Phonology: Some Say "ToMAYto"

**Phonology** is the structure of the sounds of the words in a language. Linguists Roman Jakobson and Morris Halle (1956) provided evidence that the sounds of any language are built up from sets of **phonemes**, which are the basic building blocks of speech sounds (Halle, 1990). The words *boy* and *toy* differ in one phoneme.

Humans can produce about 100 phonemes, but no single language uses all 100; English, for instance, uses about 45. Back-of-the-throat, soft French *r*'s do not exist in the world of hard American *r*'s, and Japanese has no *r*'s at all. One of the reasons French is difficult to learn for people who learned English as their native tongue is that the two languages use some different phonemes (such as those for *r* and *u*).

In English, some sounds in each word are accented (given extra emphasis). Some people say "toMAYto," and others say "toMAHto," but in both cases the second syllable is stressed. Some other languages do not usually stress only one of the syllables in a word. In French, for example, each sound typically is given equal emphasis. Linguist Lisa Selkirk (personal communication, 2002) suggests that this difference explains why French rock and roll often sounds bland: French rock artists can't synchronize the "beats" in the language with the rhythm of the music.

**Language comprehension:** The ability to understand the message conveyed by words, phrases, and sentences.

**Phonology:** The structure of the sounds that can be used to produce words in a language.

**Phoneme:** The basic building block of speech sounds.

Curiously, the left cerebral hemisphere is primarily activated when males process phonemes, but both hemispheres are strongly activated when females process phonemes (Shaywitz et al., 1995); perhaps this is one reason females tend to be better with language than males (Halpern, 1997).

The ability to produce phonemes clearly depends on your having heard others say them. In fact, when deaf children are given *cochlear implants*—devices that directly stimulate the part of the inner ear that sends neural impulses to the brain—they not only can hear, but can also learn to speak more clearly. Four years after the operation, at least 90% of the syllables each participant spoke could be understood, whereas prior to the operation only one child could be understood at least 10% of the time (Blamey et al., 2001).

The process of organizing sounds into phonemes isn't just a matter of how good your hearing is; it also depends on your knowledge of language. You use knowledge about which words are likely to appear in a given context to narrow down the possible words you are hearing (Farrar et al., 2001; Pecher, 2001). For example, if you hear "Would you like to sit on this __air?" you can fill in the missing part of the final word. Even though the sound "air" by itself could equally well be part of "hair," "lair," or even "snare," you know that you wouldn't be invited to sit on one of these things! In addition, your experience with language shapes which parts of your brain respond to speech (Hsieh et al., 2001). When researchers sped up speech (but kept the pitch constant, so that the altered speech didn't sound like chipmunks squeaking), language parts of the brain in the left cerebral hemisphere had increasingly more activation as the speech grew faster, until the speech was so fast that it was incomprehensible, at which point the activation level in these language areas decreased (Poldrack et al., 2001). Clearly, our brains have learned to detect speech per se and to treat speech sounds differently from other types of sounds (Phillips et al., 2000).

## Syntax: The Rules of the Road

Every language has building blocks of sound and rules for cementing them together into words. Similarly, all languages include rules for how words can be organized into sentences. Sentences in any language contain an internal structure, an acceptable arrangement of words called **syntax**. The syntax of a sentence is determined by a set of rules for combining different categories of words, such as nouns, verbs, and adjectives. For example, in English, this is not an acceptable sentence: "Kicked girl ball the blue." The basic units of syntax are parts of speech, not the individual words that fall into each category. A sentence in English needs a noun phrase (which must at a minimum have a noun—a word that names a person, place, or thing) and a verb phrase (at a minimum a single verb—a word that describes an action or a state of being). Thus, the shortest possible sentence in English has only three letters: "I am." An analysis of the syntactic structure of a sentence is shown in Figure 8.2.

Ask a friend to help you perform the following experiment, which should help you understand the syntactic structures that underlie sentences: At night, turn on the lights and shut all the blinds in a room. Read aloud from any book. Ask your friend to turn off the lights at some random point. You should find that you can keep saying the words leading up to the next major syntactic boundary (usually indicated by a verb, a conjunction, or a comma, period, or other

**FIGURE 8.2**

## Syntactic Analysis of a Sentence

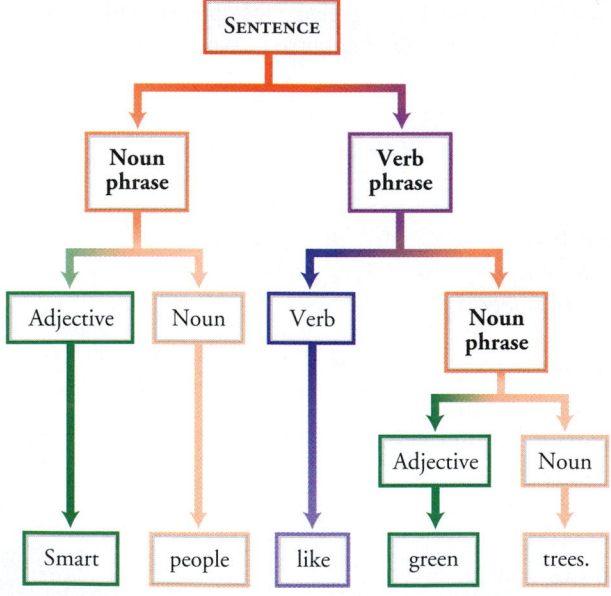

The syntactic structure of a sentence specifies the relations among words that belong to different syntactic categories such as nouns, verbs, and adjectives. All sentences have a noun phrase and a verb phrase.

punctuation mark). Fluent readers take in entire parts of the syntactic structure, one part at a time—and you can usually identify those units by seeing what you've already taken in, when the lights are turned off.

**INTERPRETING SYNTAX**   Moreover, we tend to interpret syntax in the simplest way. For example, read the following sentence and notice how you interpret each word when you first encounter it: "The model embraced the designer and the photographer laughed." When you first read the noun phrase "the photographer," did you assume that it referred to one of the things that was embraced, or that it was the subject of a new clause? If you are like the participants in a study reported by Hoeks and colleagues (2002), you probably initially assumed that the model embraced the photographer, along with the designer. And then you were thrown off when you read "laughed." People automatically try to organize sentences so that there is only one topic—the model embracing, for instance—and try not to impose two topics, such as the model embracing and the photographer laughing.

**BRAIN MECHANISMS OF SYNTAX**   The effects of brain damage on language reveal that its production and comprehension involve a system of mechanisms, not simply stored associations among words (Shelton & Caramazza, 1999). Patients with brain damage that disrupts language are said to have **aphasia** (Moore & Conway, 2004). In 1861, French anthropologist and neuroanatomist Paul Broca described how damage to the left frontal lobe—in an area later named *Broca's area*—disrupts speech much more than comprehension; this disorder is now called **Broca's aphasia**. These patients often produce long pauses between words and leave out function words, such as *of*, *if*, and *but*. For example, Goodglass (1976, p. 278) describes such a patient, who said, "And, er Wednesday . . . nine o'clock. And er Thursday, ten o'clock . . . doctors. Two doctors . . . and ah . . . teeth. . . ."

A little more than a decade after Broca's discovery, Carl Wernicke, a German neurologist, reported that damage to the back parts of the left temporal lobe has the reverse effect, disrupting comprehension more than production; this area was later named *Wernicke's area* (see Figure 8.3), and this disorder is now called **Wernicke's aphasia**. These patients not only have difficulty comprehending, but also produce "empty speech," which doesn't make sense. For example, when asked about the kind of work he did before being hospitalized, one such patient said, "Never, now mista oyge I wanna tell you this happened when happened when he rent" (Kertesz, 1981, p. 73, as cited in Carlson, 1994, p. 517). Part of the problem may have been that this patient didn't understand the request, but he clearly had trouble producing coherent speech. When patients are tested within 24 hours of having a stroke, researchers have found that the longer Wernicke's area requires to become activated (measured using fMRI) as the patients try to comprehend words, the more severe their language problems will be (Hillis et al., 2001).

However, even though production and comprehension rely on largely different mechanisms, the effects of brain damage demonstrate that both activities rely on at least some of the same processes. Damage to Broca's area and related brain areas can produce difficulties not only in forming sentences with correct syntax, but also in understanding syntactic relations (Caramazza & Zurif, 1976; Grodzinsky, 1986; Zurif, 1995, 2000; Zurif et al., 1972). Moreover, PET and fMRI studies have shown that Broca's area is activated when people must comprehend sentences with especially complex syntax (Stromswold et al., 1996; Wartenburger et al., 2004). Thus, Broca's area is involved in the use of syntax in both production and comprehension. Comprehension, however, being more completely tied to the meanings of words, may be less disrupted than production when the interpretation of syntax is impaired.

**Syntax:** The internal structure of a sentence, determined by a set of rules (grammar) for combining different parts of speech into acceptable arrangements.

**Aphasia:** A disruption of language caused by brain damage.

**Broca's aphasia:** Problems with producing language following brain damage (typically to the left frontal lobe).

**Wernicke's aphasia:** Problems with comprehending language following brain damage (typically to the left posterior temporal lobe).

**FIGURE 8.3**

## Major Language Areas of the Brain

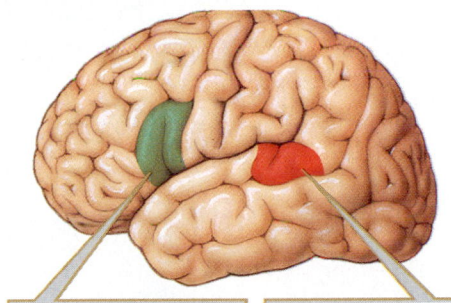

Broca's area is involved in the use of syntax to produce and understand sentences.

Wernicke's area is involved in speech comprehension.

Traditionally, Broca's area has been identified with speech production and Wernicke's area with speech comprehension, but we now know that Broca's area is involved in the use of syntax to understand sentences (Stromswold et al., 1996).

At least some of the neural machinery of language found in humans is shared by other species. MRI scans were taken of the brains of 20 chimpanzees, 5 baboons, and 2 gorillas. All of these great apes had more cortex in the left hemisphere than in the right in a region that corresponds to Broca's area in humans (Cantalupo & Hopkins, 2001).

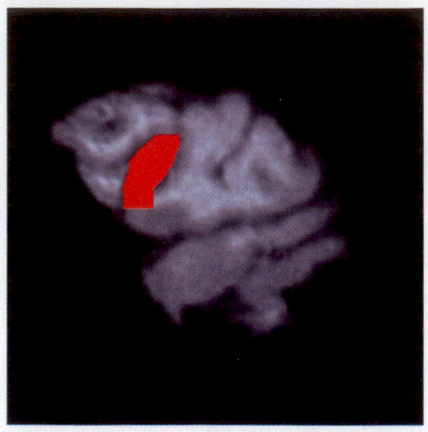

# Semantics: The Meaning Is the Message

Language is, of course, more than sounds and sentence structures (Pinker & Jackendoff, 2005). To do its job, language must convey meaning. The **semantics** of a word or sentence is its meaning. Just as the sounds of words are represented by smaller elements (phonemes) and the syntactic aspects of a sentence are represented by its elements (parts of speech), semantics is represented by **morphemes**, the smallest units of *meaning* in a language. The word *wet* includes but a single morpheme, but the meanings of many words are determined by more than one morpheme. Prefixes and suffixes are obvious examples of morphemes used in combination with other morphemes. For example, adding the morpheme *-ing* to a verb, as in *walking, talking,* or *flirting,* creates a word expressing a continuing state, whereas adding the morpheme *-ed* to a verb indicates a completed state. Just as the other elements of language are combined according to rules, so, too, with combining morphemes. We cannot add *-ing* at the front of a word, or *mis-* (another morpheme) to the end. Ambiguous words (words with more than one meaning) have more than one set of morphemes; thus, *park* as in "park the car" has different morphemes than does *park* meaning "place with benches and pigeons." Many jokes rely on the fact that words can have more than one meaning. For example, "Energizer Bunny arrested—charged with battery."

**HOW IS MEANING ASSIGNED?**   Meanings are often assigned arbitrarily to different sounds or written words; *dog* (both the combination of sounds and the written set of letters) could easily have been assigned to that feline we keep as a pet and *cat* to the animal that likes to gnaw on bones and slippers. Specific events in the past have a lot to do with how particular words have come to have their meanings. For example, early medieval Scandinavian warriors wore bearskin shirts, for which the Old Norwegian word was *berserkr*; the ferocity of the Vikings' frenzied attacks in battle thus led to the English expression "going berserk." Of more recent vintage is the word *bedlam*, which since the 16th century has meant "chaos and confusion"; its origins are in the name of the Hospital of St. Mary of Bethlehem in London ("bedlam" is a shortened version of Bethlehem), where "lunatics" were confined. Sometimes the meanings of words seem to reveal deeper aspects of a culture: The Chinese character for *crisis* is composed of two other characters, one signifying "risk" and the other "opportunity."

**HOW DOES SEMANTICS DIFFER FROM SYNTAX?**   The meaning of a sentence and its syntax are to a large extent distinct. For example, Chomsky (1957) pointed out that the sentence "Colorless green ideas sleep furiously" has an acceptable English syntax but is meaningless. On the other hand, "Fastly dinner eat, ballgame soon start" has the opposite properties: It is syntactically incorrect but understandable. The wise alien Yoda of the *Star Wars* movies often uttered such sentences, probably in part to remind the audience that he was not an ordinary person. Nevertheless, although syntax and semantics are distinct, they do interact; for example, sentences are easier to understand when named objects appear in the same order in the sentence as they do in the corresponding event (O'Grady & Lee, 2005).

Semantics: The meaning of a word or sentence.
Morpheme: The smallest unit of meaning in a language.

**How Does Semantics Differ From Phonology?** That semantics, understanding what words and sentences mean, is distinct from phonology, understanding sounds as signaling certain words, was demonstrated convincingly by Damasio and her collaborators (1996), who used PET scanning to show that different brain areas are involved in processing the sounds of words versus their meanings. (Devlin and others, 2003, and D'Arcy and collaborators, 2004, also describe brain areas that respond differently during the two types of processing.) Damasio and colleagues also found that a third brain area literally bridged the meaning and sound regions; this third area may serve to cross-reference representations of sounds and meanings.

**How Does Semantics Allow Us to Express Assertions?** Just as morphemes are combined into representations of the meanings of words, the representations of words in turn are combined into *propositions*. **Propositional representations** are mental sentences that unambiguously express the meanings of assertions. The same sets of words can express different propositions, depending on how they are organized (see Figure 8.4).

**Propositional representation:** A mental sentence that expresses the unambiguous meaning of an assertion.

## FIGURE 8.4 The Same Words Can Express Different Propositions

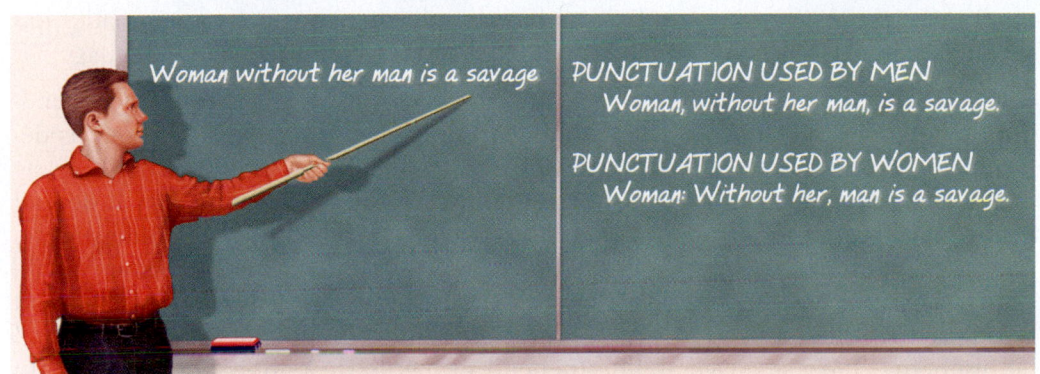

To understand the nature of propositional representation, consider this anecdote: An English professor wrote the words "Woman without her man is a savage" on the blackboard and directed his students to punctuate the sentence. The men and women used different punctuation; as you see, the punctuation organizes the words in different ways to express different propositions.

Propositional representations are not the same thing as sentences in a language such as English. Most importantly, propositional representations cannot be ambiguous; a propositional representation specifies the meaning that underlies the particular sense of a statement. Many studies have shown that people typically store not the literal words used in sentences, but rather the propositions that specify the meaning. For example, Sachs (1967) had participants in a study listen to paragraphs and then tested their memories for specific sentences. The participants had to indicate whether each test sentence had been presented in a paragraph as stated or was an altered version of one that had been presented. The participants remembered the meanings of sentences well, but not the particular wordings (Bransford and Franks, 1971, report comparable results).

## Pragmatics: Being Indirect

At least in German, Einstein was perfectly able to understand the semantics of words (he understood morphemes and how they are combined into words) and sentences (he understood how the meanings of words are combined into phrases and sentences and their underlying propositional representations); but he sometimes failed at another aspect of meaning. Utterances have not only a literal meaning but also an *implied* meaning. For example, Einstein once sat through a series of vicious attacks on his theory of relativity by Nazis, who claimed the theory was part of a plot to disrupt the proper thought processes of the German people (Clark, 1971). Einstein laughed and apparently had a great time listening to the diatribes, oblivious to the barely concealed threats beneath them. The **pragmatics** of a language is concerned with the way the words and sentences imply meaning. Have you ever asked a 13-year-old, "Do you know where the restroom is?" and got back the response "Yes"? This question can be interpreted literally, as an inquiry about your knowledge of, say, the layout of a large building, or indirectly, as a request for directions. In some contexts, as when parents are dropping off their children at an auditorium by themselves, the question might really be meant literally. But in most instances, we would understand that the questioner has a need for the facilities. This understanding depends on our grasp of pragmatics, which often involves knowledge of the world as well as of the particular language and its specific conventions about how to communicate (Grice, 1975; Lindblom, 2001).

Although some aspects of pragmatics depend on being able to hear and understand the meaning of rising or falling pitch in a sentence, as in spoken questions, pragmatics is pervasive in linguistic communication—even in reading (Kintsch, 1998). Pragmatics depends critically on our ability to draw correct inferences. The fact that we humans can draw the correct inferences quickly and seemingly without effort obscures how difficult these processes really are. Indeed, the complexity of our use of pragmatics has stymied attempts to create computer programs that can truly understand language.

**UNDERSTANDING METAPHORS AND HUMOR** Pragmatics plays a key role in understanding metaphors; a *metaphor* is a direct comparison of two things in which one is described as being the other (Bowdle & Gentner, 2005; Gentner & Bowdle, 2001). To say that somebody's lawyer is a shark means that the attorney is vicious—but it doesn't mean that he or she can breathe under water or has pebbly skin. To understand a metaphor, we actively inhibit the irrelevant aspects of the meaning (Glucksberg et al., 2001). The fact that understanding metaphors involves different mechanisms than those used for other aspects of language is attested to by the role of the right cerebral hemisphere. Other language abilities depend primarily (in right-handed people) on the left hemisphere, but the ability to understand metaphors, as well as humor, depends crucially on the brain's right hemisphere. Patients who have suffered damage to the right hemisphere might understand a metaphorical statement such as "Can you lend me a hand" as asking literally for a hand on a platter. Indeed, in normal people, the right hemisphere is particularly active (as measured by PET) when they are interpreting metaphors (Bottini et al., 1994).

The role of the right hemisphere in the comprehension of humor was documented by Brownell and his colleagues (1990; Bihrle et al., 1986; Brownell et al., 1983, 1995), who told jokes to brain-damaged patients and asked them to select the appropriate punch line from a few choices. Here is an example: "A woman is taking a shower. All of a sudden, her doorbell rings. She yells, 'Who's there?' and a man answers, 'Blind man.' Well, she's a charitable lady, so she runs out of the shower naked and opens the door." At this point, the patient is asked to select the appropriate punch line from five choices:

1. The man says, "Can you spare a little change for a blind man?"

2. The man says, "My seeing eye dog is 10 years old."

3. The man says, "I really enjoy going to the symphony."

4. The blind man throws a pie in the woman's face.

5. The man says, "Where should I put these blinds, lady?"

The patients with damage to the right hemisphere preferred the unexpected and somewhat slapstick ending, choice 4.

Pragmatics: The way in which words and sentences in a language convey meaning indirectly, by implying rather than asserting.

Rinalidi and colleagues (2004) showed that patients with damage to the right cerebral hemisphere not only make more errors when comprehending metaphors than do patients with damage to the left hemisphere, but also are particularly prone to make errors when the metaphors involve spatial information. This finding may suggest that mental imagery is sometimes used to understand such metaphors. However, other studies have shown that patients with left-hemisphere damage have more difficulty than do patients with right-hemisphere damage in other aspects of pragmatics, such as producing the proper emphasis when they speak (for example, by raising pitch at the end of a question; Gandour & Baum, 2001). Pragmatics is not a single process, and different aspects of pragmatics rely on different parts of the brain.

**RESOLVING AMBIGUITY**  It's worth underscoring that the various aspects of language interact and are not entirely independent. We've already seen that although speech production and comprehension at first may seem entirely different, they actually draw on many of the same mechanisms. Similarly, we learn phonological production through phonological perception, and the mechanisms that produce syntactically correct utterances also help us comprehend them. Moreover, the semantic representations that underlie our ability to speak coherently also allow us to comprehend; propositional representations express ideas, both our own (which we can express by speaking) and those of others (which we have decoded from their speech). Finally, we use the principles of pragmatics both when producing speech (guiding our patterns of intonation and use of metaphor and humor) and when comprehending speech.

However, there is one special problem that arises in comprehension but is not present in production: How do we resolve ambiguity? When we speak, we know which meaning of an ambiguous word we intend, but meaning often isn't so clear when we comprehend. Let's look next at a classic study that revealed how we sort out the proper meanings of ambiguous words during comprehension.

Patients with left-hemisphere damage that disrupted their ability to comprehend speech nevertheless could detect lies better than normal people (Etcoff et al., 2000). Apparently, the meanings of words can obscure other telltale features of deception, such as changes in intonation or facial expression.

# UNDERSTANDING RESEARCH

## Untangling Ambiguity During Comprehension

Comprehension poses a particularly difficult problem because words are sometimes ambiguous.

**QUESTION:** How do we know which meaning of a word is appropriate in a given situation?

**ALTERNATIVES:** (1) We could understand all the possible meanings simultaneously and use context to select the right one. (2) We could use context to select the right one from the outset.

**LOGIC:** The logic Swinney (1979) used to distinguish between these two alternatives had three steps:

1. He used semantic priming, which occurs when understanding one word makes it easier to read a second word with a related meaning. For example, in a typical semantic priming study, you would first hear a word (such as "doctor") and would then be asked to decide whether a set of letters (such as "nurse" versus "runse") spell a word. When the letters do in fact spell a word, you can make this decision faster when that word is related to the first one you heard than when it is unrelated; for instance, if you heard "doctor," you could then decide that "nurse" is a word faster than you could decide that "house" is a word (Meyer & Schvaneveldt, 1971).

2. Swinney reasoned that if all meanings of ambiguous words are activated, then people should be primed to make judgments about related words for each of the meanings.

3. He also reasoned if the irrelevant meanings are "deactivated" after having been initially active, then priming of irrelevant meanings should be evident for only a very brief time after an ambiguous word is presented.

**METHOD:** The participants wore headphones and heard statements such as "Rumor has it that, for years, the government building had been plagued with problems. The man was not surprised when he found several spiders, roaches, and other bugs in the corner of his room." Shortly after hearing a key word from a sentence they heard, such as "bugs" in this example, the participants decided whether a set of letters spelled a word; half the time it did (e.g., "spy"), and half the time it didn't (e.g., "syp"). Each of the real words that was presented was either related to the key word in the sentence (such as "ant," which is related to one meaning of the word "bugs"), related to another meaning of that word (e.g., "spy"), or unrelated ("sew"). The participants simply decided, as quickly and accurately as possible, whether the set of letters was a word. Finally, Swinney varied the interval between the last spoken word and the string of letters, in order to examine the strength of priming over time.

**RESULTS:** When the string of letters was presented within about a half-second after the ambiguous key word, both meanings of the word were equally primed: Participants could decide that "ant" and "spy" were words faster than they could decide that "sew" was a word. However, after a longer interval had passed, the relevant word, "ant" in this example, was still primed, but now the word related to the irrelevant meaning, "spy," was no longer primed.

**INFERENCES:** Both meanings of ambiguous words are activated as soon as a word is heard, but context very quickly dampens down all but the relevant meaning. Researchers have developed detailed models for how such inhibition could occur (Plaut et al., 1996). Moreover, later research showed that this principle operates in other domains. In particular, if you speak two languages, when you name a pictured object in one language, you initially also activate its name in the other (Colome, 2001).

## THINK CRITICALLY!

If the results of Swinney's study had been different, and the two alternative meanings were not equally primed, could you conclude that the context had dampened down one meaning in advance? What if one meaning is more frequently associated with the word, and thus that meaning is primed more strongly? Can you think of a way to discover

When the sound "port" is heard, both meanings—the wine and the harbor scene—are activated, but the context in which the word is used (such as "The fisherman couldn't wait to see the port") very quickly helps us to determine meaning.

whether one meaning of an ambiguous word is generally primed more strongly? (Hint: What could you learn by repeating the experiment without context, showing the ambiguous words individually?)

Swinney also included a condition in which an unambiguous word (such as "insect") was presented, which primed only the related word ("ant," not "spy"). What could this condition tell you?

# Language Development: Out of the Mouths of Babes

One of the hallmarks of language is that normal human children will pick up the language being spoken around them, without needing to be taught. As kids, we are linguistic sponges. But what do we learn, and how do we absorb it?

## How Is Language Acquired?

Why do people in France grow up speaking French, people in Japan grow up speaking Japanese, and people in Greece grow up speaking Greek? At first glance, the answer might seem obvious: They are taught by their parents and teachers, and they also absorb language from their peers. But the process is not so simple and straightforward; there has long been a debate about how language is acquired, and three different camps have emerged.

**BEHAVIORIST THEORIES** Behaviorists, following the lead of B. F. Skinner, believe that language is entirely the result of learning. According to this theory, children acquire words and combinations of words through imitation; such utterances then are reinforced, and thus language is learned according to the same principles of learning that apply to all other materials (see Chapter 6). For example, a baby might repeat the sound "dog" that her father makes when a dog is nearby; her utterance elicits a huge smile from her father, who then points at the dog. The smile is the reinforcement for making the sound when that stimulus is present—which then increases the probability that the sound will be repeated the next time a canine comes into sight. This theory is rooted in the school of philosophy known as **empiricism**, which takes the view that all knowledge derives from experience. Although this theory led psychologists to observe carefully the specific circumstances under which children acquire language, it is plagued with problems. For example, based solely on what a baby hears, there isn't enough information to learn the rules of grammar (Pinker, 1994). Moreover, this theory falters when it must explain how even young children produce novel sentences, which have not been previously imitated or reinforced.

**NATIVIST THEORIES** In contrast, many linguists believe that the crucial aspects of language are innate (inborn), not learned. This theory is rooted in the school of philosophy known as **nativism**, which takes the view that people are born with some knowledge. Linguist Noam Chomsky (1972) has championed the nativist approach to language acquisition, theorizing that we are all born with an internal **language acquisition device (LAD)**, which contains a set of grammatical rules common to all languages. According to Chomsky, we don't actually *learn* the grammar of a language. Rather, we *discover* which particular human language is being spoken around us, and our LAD "tunes" our built-in set of rules so that we can speak that language. This theory allows us to understand how children acquire language even when the input stimuli are not sufficient to specify all the rules. However, this theory of language acquisition is not specified in enough detail to be thoroughly evaluated (Bohannon & Bonvillian, 2001).

**Empiricism (approach to language):** The approach that views language as entirely the result of learning.

**Nativism (approach to language):** The view that people are born with some knowledge.

**Language acquisition device (LAD):** An innate mechanism, hypothesized by Chomsky, that contains the grammatical rules common to all languages and allows language acquisition.

**INTERACTIONIST THEORIES** Interactionist theories call on both learning and innate knowledge to explain how language is acquired. These theories hold that language acquisition relies on social events that draw on relatively general cognitive abilities, such as those used in motor control and perception (Dick et al., 2001; Dominey & Dodane, 2004; Elman et al., 1996). However, even these theorists assume that at least some language abilities are built in, part of our genetic heritage. There are many interactionist theories, which vary in the relative emphasis placed on social versus cognitive factors as well as in the relative emphasis placed on general versus language-specific innate abilities. These theories have the virtues of being testable and of having led to studies that uncovered diverse facts (Aslin et al., 1999; R. S. Chapman, 2000; Tager-Flusberg, 2001). However, as yet no general consensus on a final form of such a theory has been reached.

## Foundations of Language: Organizing the Linguistic World

The fact that virtually all normal humans come to speak a language, even without formal instruction, is evidence that there is something special about the way our brains are constructed that allows us to acquire and use language; we humans are innately gifted with the ability to acquire language. But this doesn't mean that we acquire language all at once; many genetically influenced characteristics do not appear full blown at birth (for example, consider baldness). Language ability develops in an orderly progression.

To help the child learn language, caregivers (typically, in Western culture, mothers) intuitively adjust their speech so that the baby receives clear messages. The language that caregivers use to talk to babies, dubbed **child-directed speech (CDS)**, is characterized by short sentences with clear pauses between phrases, careful enunciation, and exaggerated intonation that is spoken in a high-pitched voice (Bornstein et al., 1992; Cameron-Faulkner et al., 2003; Cooper et al., 1997; Fernald et al., 1989). A similar pattern has been observed in the sign language caregivers use to communicate with deaf infants: They make signs more slowly, often repeat a sign, and use exaggerated movements (Masataka, 1996); babies attend more closely to such signing than to the more rapid, fluent signing used between adults. People often make similar adjustments when they talk to foreigners who do not speak their language well. In all cases, the adjustments are intended to make it easier for the one being addressed to understand what is being communicated.

Infants are surprisingly sophisticated in their ability to encode spoken sounds. Although adults have difficulty hearing distinctions in spoken sounds that are not used in their language (for instance, English speakers often have trouble distinguishing between two slightly different "wah" sounds used in French), babies have no such difficulty (Jusczyk, 1995). At 2–3 months old, infants can register in less than half a second that a syllable has been changed ("ga" to "ba"; Dehaene-Lambertz & Dehaene, 1994). However, after about 6 months of age, they start to ignore distinctions among sounds that are not used in the language spoken around them (Kuhl et al., 1992). At around 8 months, infants can use patterns of sound regularity to identify individual words, even when the actual sounds run together into a single continuous stream (Saffran, 2001). Moreover, by 14 months, infants pay attention to different sound distinctions in different tasks: When they are required to distinguish between speech sounds, they are sensitive to differences in the sounds that they ignore when they are learning to pair words with particular objects (Stager & Werker, 1997).

The ability of infants to discriminate and organize sounds outstrips their ability to produce them. All babies, even deaf ones, begin by babbling at around 6 months of age

**Child-directed speech (CDS):** Speech by caregivers to babies that relies on short sentences with clear pauses, careful enunciation, exaggerated intonation, and a high-pitched voice.

(Stoel-Gammon & Otomo, 1986). Initial babbling includes the sounds made in all human languages. However, as the child is exposed to speaking adults, the range of sounds narrows; at about 1 year, the child's babbling begins to have adultlike intonation patterns (Levitt & Wang, 1991). Deaf children do not develop the more advanced types of babbling, but, if they are exposed to sign language, their hand and arm motions develop in corresponding ways—beginning with a wide range of motions and eventually narrowing down to those used in the sign language they see around them (Petitto & Marentette, 1991). The first words children in all languages say grow directly out of their babbles, such as "ma-ma" and "da-da."

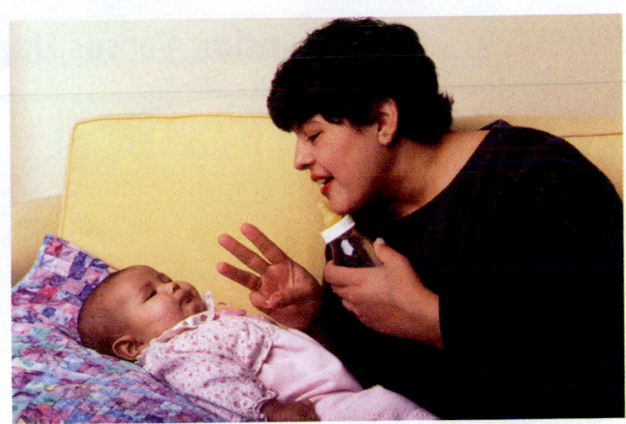

Sign language resembles spoken language in crucial ways. For example, when communicating with infants, speakers or signers slow down and exaggerate their vocalizations or their hand and arm movements in order to communicate more clearly.

## Getting the Words

Most children begin to speak when they are about a year old. Two-year-olds can learn words even when the object or action being named is not present (Akhtar & Tomasello, 1996). By the time they are 6 years old, children know approximately 10,000 words (Anglin, 1993). The rate of learning differs for boys and girls, however, as shown in Figure 8.5. Children begin by understanding words far in advance of their ability to say them. Indeed, they can understand about 50 words at about 13 months of age but cannot say this many words until about 18 months (Menyuk et al., 1995). Studies of brain activity in children, as measured by electrical activity on the scalp, have shown that when they are just beginning to learn words (at about 13 to 17 months), brain activity is widely distributed over both cerebral hemispheres. In contrast, at 20 months, adultlike patterns of activation are found in the temporal and parietal areas of the left cerebral hemisphere (Mills et al., 1997). Such findings suggest that the brain is changing as language is learned or that maturational changes in the brain facilitate language learning, or—as seems most likely (Mills et al., 1997)—that both events occur.

**LEARNING WORD MEANINGS** Even 3-year-olds can often learn words, or facts about objects, after hearing them only a single time (Carey, 1978; Markson & Bloom, 1997). Which words children learn first depends partly on their culture; in Vietnam, children learn the respectful pronouns used to refer to elders before learning the words for many objects (Nelson, 1981). However, rather than learning the exact meanings of words in one fell swoop, children sometimes make **overextensions**, using words overly broadly when referring to new objects or situations. They might use "dog" to refer to a dog and a cat and a horse, and even a sawhorse. This makes sense if their initial idea of the meaning of "dog" is anything with four legs. With learning, they discover which features—in the case of a dog, more than just four-leggedness—restrict the appropriate use of the word (Clark, 1983, 1993). Overextensions may sometimes occur simply because the child has trouble recalling the appropriate word and apparently uses the next best one instead. Children sometimes also make **underextensions**, using words too narrowly. For example, a child may use "animal" to refer only to dogs. This may occur because an adult uses a superordinate term (such as "animal") when referring to a typical member of the category (a dog), and the child does not experience the term being used more broadly for less typical members of the category (Kay & Anglin, 1982; White, 1982). However, as knowledge of distinctions within a domain (such as dinosaurs) increases, both children and adults tend to make more underextensions and fewer overextensions (Johnson &

**FIGURE 8.5**

## The Number of New Words Understood During the First 2 Years of Life

Notice the difference in comprehension rates for boys and girls.

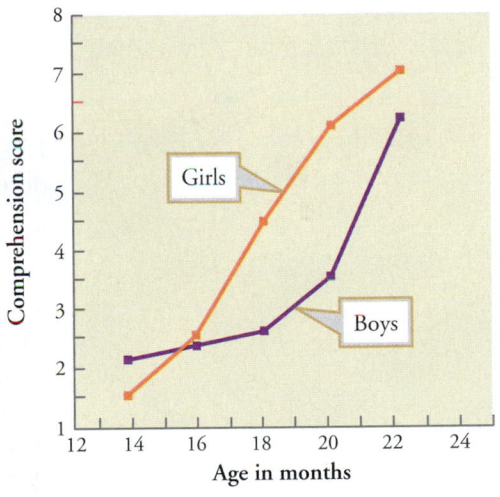

Overextension: An overly broad use of a word to refer to a new object or situation.

Underextension: An overly narrow use of a word to refer to a new object or situation.

**FIGURE 8.6**

## Overextension Versus Underextension

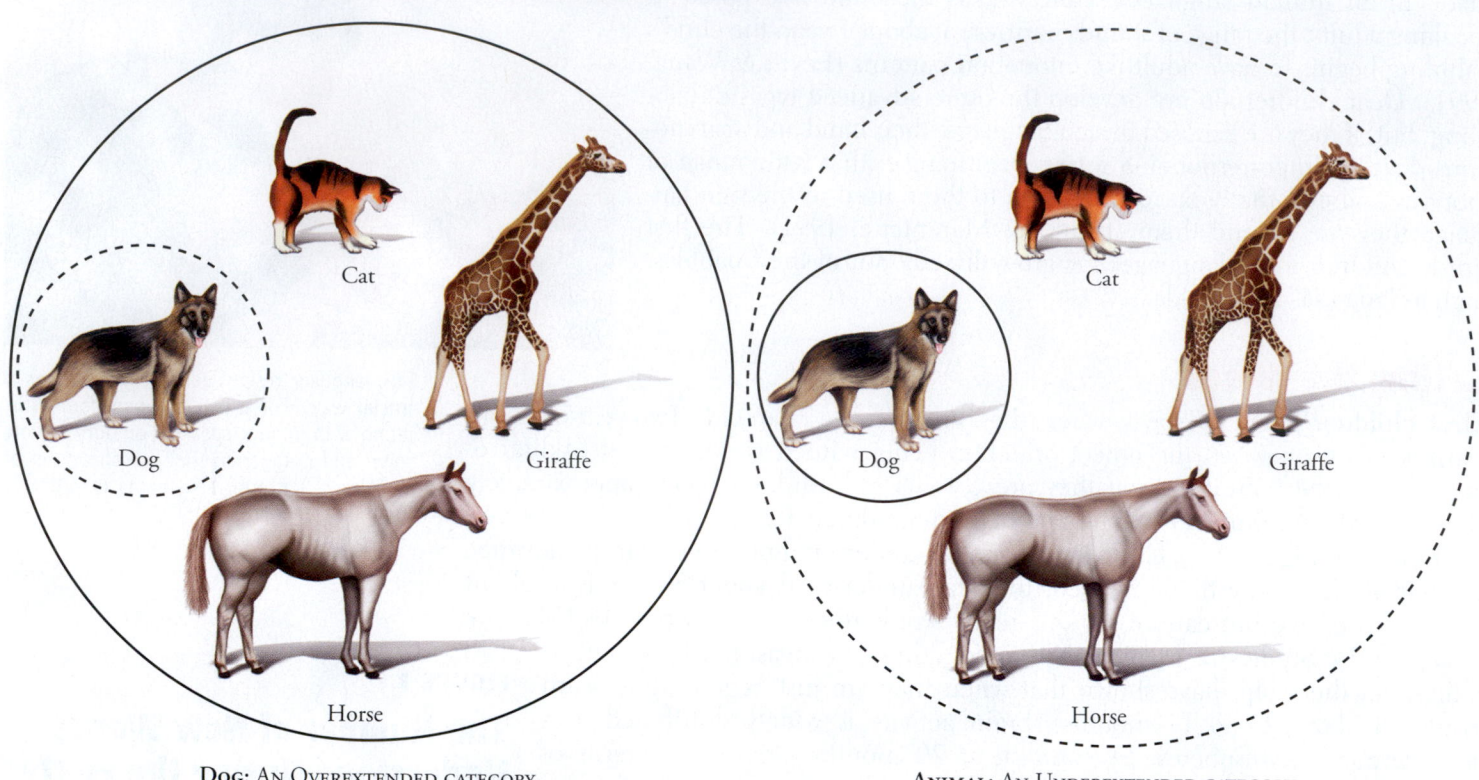

**Dog: An Overextended Category**          **Animal: An Underextended Category**

Overextension occurs when a word is used more broadly than it should be, such as calling all animals "dog" (left); underextension occurs when a word that names a broad category is used more narrowly, as when "animal" refers only to dogs (right).

Eilers, 1998). Figure 8.6 illustrates the difference between overextensions and underextensions.

**ENRICHING ENVIRONMENTS**    In order to learn new words and their meanings, children must be exposed to the words in context. In a landmark study of the relation between the linguistic environment and the acquisition of vocabulary, Betty Hart and Todd Risley (1995/2002, 1999) recorded verbal interactions (for 1 hour per month) between parents and children from the time the children were about 10 months old until they were 3 years of age. They studied three types of families, in which the parents were professionals, working class, or on welfare. Children in all three types of families began speaking at the same age, but acquired different numbers of words—and the disparity in the sizes of their vocabularies grew increasingly greater with age. By age 3, the children differed dramatically in size of vocabulary: approximately 1,100 words for the children of the professionals, 750 for the children of working-class parents, and just over 500 for the children in welfare families. What happened? One answer is straightforward: The three groups of children were exposed to vastly different amounts of language, hearing an average of 2,153, 1,251, and 606 words per hour in the professional, working-class, and welfare families, respectively. Extrapolating from these data, the children of professionals heard about 11 million words in 4 years, compared to 6 million for the children of working-class parents, and only 3 million for the children in welfare families.

Hart and Risley also found that the sheer number of words spoken was not all there was to it; they discovered that they could account for the differences in vocabulary by reference to the following five factors:

- the number of different words used in talking to the child;
- the parent's being encouraging, responding positively and not issuing prohibitions;
- a high information content, the parents talked about specific events and things;
- the children were asked their opinions and given choices;
- the parents listened to the children and responded to what they said instead of just making requests or demands.

In fact, when these factors were combined into a single measure, it accounted for a remarkable 61% of the variability in verbal expressiveness, even when the children were 9 and 10 years old! However, as exciting as these results may seem, we must be cautious: Only 13 professional, 23 working-class, and 6 welfare families were studied. Nevertheless, later research has tended to provide support for Hart and Risley's conclusions (Locke & Ginsborg, 2003; Snow et al., 1998, 2001).

People with dyslexia have difficulty with both writing and reading. With extensive training in listening to speech and dividing the continuous stream into separate words, many reading-impaired children have dramatically improved their reading abilities, presumably because they have learned to store separate representations of words in memory (Merzenich et al., 1996; Tallal et al., 1996).

## Grammar: Not From School

The heart of any language is its **grammar**, the set of rules that allow users of the language to combine words into an infinite number of acceptable sentences. Traditionally, the term *grammar* has referred to syntax and some aspects of semantics (including those aspects of word meaning that must be in agreement in a sentence, such as using a plural verb with a plural subject). However, some researchers argue that the concept of grammar should be extended to include features of all aspects of language except pragmatics (and treating pragmatics as part of grammar has been discussed by some; Hu, 1990, 1995; Payne, 1992). By looking at the patterns of sounds to which babies became habituated, Marcus and colleagues (1999) showed that even 7-month-old babies have the capacity to abstract grammarlike rules. However, it is at around 2 years of age that children start putting words together into the simplest sentences, two-word utterances such as "Go dog." These utterances are often called **telegraphic speech** because, like the telegrams of days gone by and the text messages people send to cell phones today, they pack a lot of information into a few choice words (Bochner & Jones, 2003). By about 3 years of age, children who speak English start to use sentences that follow the sequence subject–verb–object ("Dog chase cat"). Words such as *the*, *a*, and *of* are left out. The particular sequence of the parts of speech depends on the language being learned, but all children at this stage start to make sentences with words in the appropriate order (de Villiers & de Villiers, 1992).

Adults do not teach grammatical rules to children, or even systematically correct grammatical errors (de Villiers & de Villiers, 1992; Pinker, 1994), but even 4-year-olds acquire such rules. Berko (1958) showed that most children of this age generalize

**Grammar:** The set of rules that determines how words can be organized into an infinite number of acceptable sentences in a language.

**Telegraphic speech:** Speech that packs a lot of information into a few words, typically omitting words such as *the*, *a*, and *of*.

grammatical rules. This is true even when sentences contain nonsense words. For example, a child is given this problem:

This is a wug. Now there is another one. Now there are two _____.

When asked for the missing word, most 4-year-olds have no trouble saying "wugs."

Most verbs in a language are *regular*, following an easily derived rule for changes in tense—*play* becomes *played*, *work* becomes *worked*. But the most frequently used verbs in a language are often *irregular*—for example, *eat* becomes *ate*. Children may start off using irregular verbs properly, but then begin to make mistakes such as *runned* instead of *ran*. These **overregularization errors**, mistakes caused by the misapplication of the rule for regular verb formation, occur because once a child has learned the rule, he or she begins to apply it systematically, even when it is inappropriate (Pinker, 1999). The same thing happens with plurals; a child who could use *feet* correctly last week may suddenly start saying, "Mommy, my feets are tired."

The 5-year-old's language is in most ways like that of the adults in the community. Indeed, subtle testing is required to observe ways in which the language ability of 7-year-olds is less than complete. By such testing, Carol Chomsky (1969) has shown that 7-year-olds may confuse the meanings of statements such as "Please *tell* Sally" and "Please *ask* Sally"; but, remarkably, even 3-year-olds understand that "I need a pencil" is a request, not a statement, and respond appropriately (Garvey, 1974). Subtle pragmatics and conversational skills emerge between the ages of 5 and 9—for example, learning to change the topic by gradually, not suddenly, altering the direction of the conversation (Wanska & Bedrosian, 1985, 1986).

The major milestones of language acquisition are shown in the timeline in Figure 8.7.

## FIGURE 8.7 Major Milestones in Language Acquisition

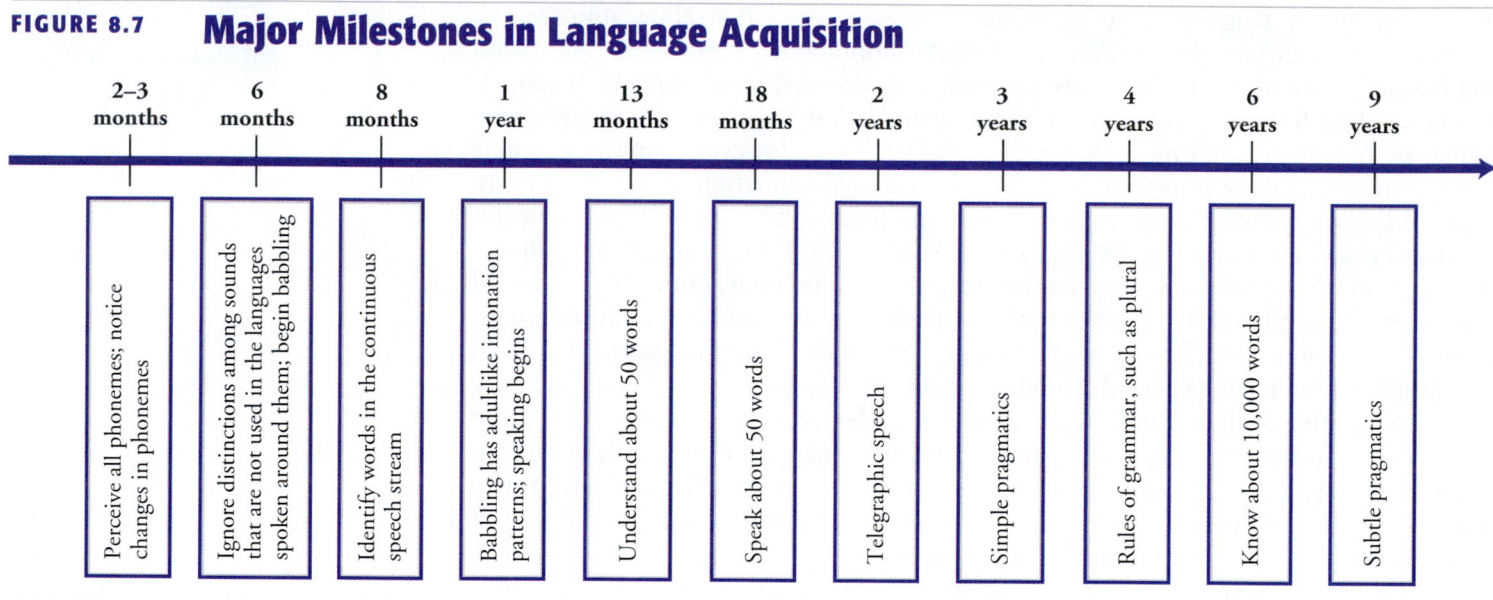

Language acquisition typically progresses through a series of orderly steps, as illustrated here.

## Biological Bases of Language Development

What is special about the human brain that leads all normal people to develop language? We consider two possibilities: Not only might the brain be "ready" to acquire language during a phase of normal development, but such a capacity might directly reflect the action of a specific gene or genes.

**IS THERE A CRITICAL PERIOD FOR ACQUIRING LANGUAGE?** Throughout history, there have been reports of children who grew up in the wild, never exposed to human language. Reports of such feral children include the story of Romulus and Remus, the legendary founders of Rome, who supposedly were abandoned as children and raised by a wolf; the fictional account of Tarzan, who was raised by apes in Edgar Rice Burroughs's novel; and the true account of Victor, the Wild Boy of Aveyron. This boy was found naked and filthy in the woods near Paris, France, in 1799; he bit and scratched those who annoyed him and generally acted more like a wild animal than a human. He was incapable of speech, making only animal-like sounds (Ball, 1971; Lane, 1976; Pinker, 1994). Real-life cases like this one provide a key test of the theory that language can only be learned during a narrow window of time called the **critical period**. This theory holds that the brain is "set" for the development of language (or other abilities) at a particular point, and trying to acquire the ability either earlier or later is fruitless. Critical periods are different from **sensitive periods**, which define time windows when learning (or some other process) is *easiest* but are not the only times when the learning can occur (Knudsen, 2004). Lennenberg (1967) claimed that language had to be learned prior to puberty, during the period when the two halves of the brain were becoming fully specialized; if language was not learned before this, he believed, it would never be learned well (see also Grimshaw et al., 1998).

Although the Wild Boy of Aveyron and other such children did have language difficulties, it is impossible to know whether they were mentally deficient to begin with; that may even be why they were abandoned. However, more recently, scientists have been able to study similar children in detail. Consider, for example, the dreadful case of a girl called Genie, whose deranged parents locked her up, nearly immobilized, in a back room from the age of 20 months until she was slightly over 13 years old (Curtiss, 1977, 1989; Rymer, 1993). Genie was not allowed any contact with other people, was not talked to, and was punished if she made any sounds. She was not intellectually slow, nor had she had difficulty beginning to speak as a toddler. After she was discovered, she received intensive training in language, with mixed success. Genie was able to learn many words and eventually had reasonably good language comprehension, so there doesn't seem to be a critical period for acquiring all aspects of language. But she was never able to grasp the rules of grammar fully, and thus there does seem to be a critical period for acquiring grammar (Grimshaw et al., 1998; Pinker, 1994).

The existence of a critical period for grammar explains why brain damage has much greater long-term effects on language when it occurs in adults than in children. Bates and her colleagues (1997) studied language acquisition in 53 infants and preschoolers with brain damage and concluded that, if parts of the brain that seem innately predisposed to be devoted to language functions are damaged in young children, other parts can take over these functions. Indeed, if the entire left half of a young child's cortex, including the areas normally used in language, has to be removed because of disease or injury, the child will nevertheless learn language. In fact, such children can sometimes learn language so well that careful testing is necessary to detect deficits (e.g., Aram et al., 1992; Bishop, 1983; Vargha-Khadem et al., 1991). In contrast, it is very difficult for an adult to recover language abilities following brain damage that produces aphasia.

**IS THERE A LANGUAGE GENE?** If you think about what makes humans special, different from other animals, language probably comes to mind immediately. We are

**Critical period:** A narrow window of time when a certain type of learning is possible.

**Sensitive period:** A window of time when a particular type of learning is *easiest*, but not the only time it can occur.

the talking animal. Some researchers have claimed that we humans have special genes for language. The best evidence for this claim involves two phases of research. First, researchers (Gopnik 1990, 1997, 1999; Gopnik & Crago, 1991) have found families in which many members have a disorder called **specific language impairment**. These people have trouble understanding grammar and complex words, those made up of many morphemes, such as *predisposing*. Pinker (1994) describes in vivid detail the anxiety that people with specific language impairment experience, even in common social interactions, because they worry about their difficulties using language. Basing their conclusions on results from many types of tests, Pinker (1994) and others have argued that this disorder is not caused by general cognitive difficulties or an overall lack of intelligence—hence the name *specific* language impairment. This disorder has been identified in speakers of English, Greek, French, and Japanese, even though these languages convey information very differently.

Second, having established a very specific disorder of language, the next step is to link it to the genes. There is evidence for a genetic contribution to specific language impairment. The disorder is more likely to occur in both twins in identical sets (who have the same genes) than in both twins in fraternal sets (who share only half their genes). Moreover, language difficulties in general often run in families (Plomin, 2001). In fact, a gene has been identified that is associated with specific language impairment (Lai et al., 2001), but it remains to be seen whether this gene also affects other aspects of cognition. Communication disorders in general—that is, impairments in the ability to express ideas in words and understand others when they do—are about 80% heritable (that is, about 80% of the variability in these disorders can be explained by variation in the genes; Bishop et al., 1995; Lewis & Thompson, 1992); stuttering, for example, is in part genetic (Ambrose et al., 1993; Kidd, 1993).

Does all of this mean that there is a single gene for language? Probably not (Gilger, 1995). As you are discovering, language is a complex phenomenon, and it is as unlikely that it is controlled by one gene as it is that a bakery would use a single ingredient in a cake. Baking a cake requires not only multiple ingredients, but also utensils and an oven and the means to make it hot and to time the baking process. An intricate system of things and events is involved in baking cakes and in using language. In either case, knocking out a link in the process disrupts the end result: No flour or liquid, no source of heat, no timing—any one of these failures means no cake. Similarly, language involves many key factors, any one of which may be affected by a different gene or genes. Indeed, many language disorders involve many different facets of language (Ahmed et al., 2001a, 2001b; Botting & Conti-Ramsden, 2001; Vargha-Khadem et al., 1995).

# Other Ways to Communicate: Are They Language?

True language must have phonology, syntax, semantics, and pragmatics. Think about these four aspects as you read the following. Which of these types of communication do you think truly qualify as language?

## Nonverbal Communication

In ancient Egypt, law courts met in the dark so that the judges could not see the accused, the accuser, or the witnesses (Seuling, 1988) and thus would not be swayed by their demeanors. People are remarkably good at **nonverbal communication**, such as interpretation of facial expressions and body language (Ambady & Rosenthal, 1992, 1993). Although women are generally better than men at decoding nonverbal behaviors (Rosip & Hall, 2004), men apparently can register unspoken signs of anger better than women (Coats & Feldman, 1996). Furthermore, men and women differ in their characteristic nonverbal behavior. Hall (1978) performed a meta-analysis of studies of nonverbal behavior and found that men tend to be more restless (for instance, they had more frequent leg movements) and more expansive (as signaled by leaving their legs open) than women, but women tend to be more expressive, as evidenced by their gestures (Gallaher, 1992). These conclusions are consistent with the finding that women are more expressive than men when watching emotional films (Kring & Gordon, 1998).

But is such nonverbal communication language? Consider again the four criteria: phonology, syntax, semantics, and pragmatics. Nonverbal communication does not have a set of perceptual units like phonemes that are combined according to particular rules to form new units. Instead, it consists of a set of specific physical signs and gestures. In addition, these specific signs cannot be combined in novel ways to create brand-new meaningful expressions. For instance, if you arch your eyebrows, open your mouth, and scrunch up your nose, people may think you're weird, but they won't read a distinct message. Nonverbal communication lacks the generative power that comes from having a true grammar; whereas language can convey an infinite number of messages, nonverbal communication lends itself to a relatively small set of messages. Finally, no clear distinction separates the literal from the implied meaning of nonverbal cues. Although nonverbal communication *is* communication, whose importance we should not underestimate, it is not truly language.

## Sign Language

One of the most remarkable things about language is that any normal person will develop it without being formally taught (Pinker, 1994). This is true for people in all cultures, including the culture of the deaf. Deaf children who are raised by speaking parents who do not sign will spontaneously invent their own sign languages (Goldin-Meadow & Mylander, 1998). Sign languages are not like the motions you might make when playing charades. Rather, the gestures specify the manual equivalent of phonemes, small units that are combined to make appropriate perceptual signals. Symbols for individual words are combined according to syntactic, semantic, and pragmatic rules (Emmorey, 1993; Klima & Bellugi, 1979). Just as there are different spoken languages, there are different sign languages: American Sign Language (ASL), for example, is not understandable to someone who uses British Sign Language (BSL), and vice versa.

One indication that sign language is a true language is that brain damage can disrupt it in ways that parallel the impairments of spoken language in hearing people (Bellugi et al., 1993; Gordon, 2004; Poizner et al., 1987; Poizner & Kegl, 1992). Damage in the same brain areas results in corresponding effects in hearing speakers and deaf signers. For example, damage to Broca's area, in the left frontal lobe, can cause both speakers and signers to have trouble using grammar when producing and comprehending sentences (Gordon, 2004; Poizner et al., 1987). In addition, just as with spoken language, there is a critical period for acquiring ASL. In fact, the right cerebral hemisphere is only activated when people who learned ASL before puberty

**Nonverbal communication:** Facial expressions and body language that allow others to infer an individual's internal mental state.

Even though a teacher's gestures might occasionally be distracting, they are actually helping that person explain material more clearly by freeing up cognitive capacity. Note that gesturing in this way isn't sign language: Such gesturing only supplements spoken language; sign language is a true language.

use it; in someone who learned ASL after puberty, the right hemisphere is not activated when signing is used (Newman et al., 2002).

## Gesture: Is It Just for Show?

The gestures hearing people make when they talk are not sign language. But they do enhance communication, partly because they lighten the cognitive load of the speaker. For example, in one study, researchers asked participants to explain a math problem while they were also trying to remember a list of words or letters. Both children and adults later remembered more of the material on the list if they had used gestures while explaining the math problem (Goldin-Meadow et al., 2001). Gestures apparently took some of the load off of processes used in verbal explanation, freeing up more cognitive resources for memorization. Such gesturing is not learned: Even people blind from birth gesture as they talk (and make gestures similar to those used by sighted people); they even gesture when they know that they are talking to another blind person (Iverson & Goldin-Meadow, 1998, 2001). Gestures can supplement information conveyed in speech (Alibali et al., 1999; Singer & Goldin-Meadow, 2005), but they are not in themselves a distinct language.

Some nonhuman primates can be trained to understand the meaning of symbols, such as these pieces of plastic, and to arrange them to form simple sentences. But is this true language?

## Aping Language

In evolutionary terms, chimpanzees are very close to humans: We have about 99% of our genes in common with chimps. Nevertheless, no one has succeeded in teaching a chimpanzee or other nonhuman primate to talk. Some heroic researchers have gone so far as to raise a chimp as though it were a child, but even then the animal did not learn to speak (Kellogg & Kellogg, 1933). More recent studies have told much the same story (Terrace et al., 1976; Terrace, 1979). Because part of the problem seems to be that the throat cannot make the sounds of speech, some researchers have tried to teach chimps sign language (Gardner & Gardner, 1969; Terrace, 1979) or how to use arbitrary symbols such as cut-out plastic shapes or computer icons to communicate (Greenfield & Savage-Rumbaugh, 1990; Savage-Rumbaugh et al., 1986). With both sign language and arbitrary shapes, chimps can in fact be taught to string symbols together to make "sentences," but Terrace (1979) found that the chimps usually were simply imitating sequences they had previously seen and could not learn rules for reordering the signs to produce novel sentences. Nevertheless, members of one species of chimp, the pygmy chimpanzee, have spontaneously created new statements using symbols (Greenfield & Savage-Rumbaugh, 1990), and at least some researchers believe that certain nonhuman primates are capable of using true language (Fouts & Mills, 1997). However, other researchers note that nonhuman primates do not use pragmatics much (if at all) when communicating (Tomasello, 2004) and only humans spontaneously invent language (Pinker, 1994).

# Bilingualism: A Window of Opportunity?

All normal people learn a language, and most of the people in the world learn a second language at some point in life (Fabbro, 2001). Is learning a second language the same as learning a first one? Using fMRI, Kim and his colleagues (1997) scanned the brains of two groups of bilingual people while the participants thought about what they had done the previous day, using each of their two languages in turn. One group had learned their second language as young children, the other as adults. Wernicke's area, involved in comprehension, was activated in the same way with both languages and in both groups. But Broca's area showed a different pattern: If the participants had learned the second language as young children, the same part of Broca's area displayed activity for both the first and the second languages. If they had learned the second language after childhood, however, activity for that language appeared in a different part of the left frontal lobe—in a part used in working memory. One theory is that if you learn grammar early enough, it becomes procedural memories, which are mediated in part by subcortical structures; if you don't learn grammar early enough, it is stored as explicit memories—which you need to think about to recall (Ullman, 2001). In any case, second (and third) languages rely primarily on the left hemisphere, as do first languages (Paradis, 1990, 1992).

Different languages may rely to differing degrees on specific cognitive processes (such as working memory) and may incorporate more or less complex phonology, syntax, and semantics. Thus, brain damage can have varying effects on different languages, even if the same underlying process is disrupted (Paradis, 2001). Indeed, Paradis and Goldblum (1989) describe a patient who had been fluent in French, Malagasy, and Gujariti prior to brain surgery; after the surgery, only Gujariti was impaired (in spite of the fact that the patient had learned both Gujariti and Malagasy as an infant). Curiously, 8 months after the surgery, the patient regained his ability to speak Gujariti, but could no longer speak Malagasy well! French, learned during school (and the only language in which he could read and write) remained intact. After 2 years, he regained complete mastery of all of his languages.

In spite of the fact that languages learned as an adult generally are not as well learned as those acquired during childhood, it is remarkably easy to learn some aspects of second languages. Dupuy and Krashen (1993) asked third-semester college students who were taking French to read five scenes from a script of a French movie, after having seen the first five scenes to get the story line. The scenes that were read contained many highly colloquial words that the students were unlikely to have seen or heard before. A surprise vocabulary test after reading showed that participants were learning almost five words per hour, without trying! This rate is remarkably close to the learning rates of children who are reading in their native languages.

Unfortunately, as you might expect from knowing that there is a critical period in childhood for learning grammar, it is not so easy to learn the grammar of a second language as an adult. In addition, it is not easy to learn the sound pattern of a second language after childhood. Indeed, the vast majority of people who learn a second language after puberty will make grammatical errors and will speak with an accent. However, some people can learn to pronounce words in another language almost flawlessly (Marinova-Todd et al., 2000; Snow, 2002).

In addition, "one-size teaching" of second languages may not fit all: Loori (2005) found that when learning English as a second language, males preferred using logical and mathematical thinking, whereas females preferred learning activities that relied on self-reflection. In general, the more formal education you have and the younger you are when you start, the better you will be at learning a second language (Hakuta et al., 2003). People differ greatly (perhaps even genetically?) in how easily they can acquire second languages.

1. A patient with Broca's aphasia has problems primarily with _____, while a patient with Wernicke's aphasia has problems with _____.
   a. production of speech; comprehension of speech
   b. comprehension of speech; production of speech
   c. semantic processing; syntactic processing
   d. pragmatic processing; semantic processing

2. The sentence "Wise alien Yoda is" has
   a. correct syntax, but incorrect phonology.
   b. incorrect syntax, but is understandable.
   c. incorrect syntax and incorrect phonology.
   d. incorrect syntax and no meaning.

3. When children start to understand that utterances can have both literal and implied meanings, they are beginning to understand the _____ of language.
   a. syntax
   b. morphology
   c. grammar
   d. pragmatics

4. Semantic priming experiments like that of Swinney (1979) have demonstrated that different meanings of ambiguous words are
   a. simultaneously activated and remain activated indefinitely.
   b. activated after context reveals them.
   c. simultaneously activated, but with emphasis on the dominant meaning from the moment the sentence is understood.
   d. simultaneously activated, but context quickly dampens the irrelevant meaning.

## Answers

1.a 2.b 3.d 4.d

NOTE: Once you feel comfortable with the Test Yourself questions in this chapter, visit the book's Web site at www.ablongman.com/kosslyn3e for additional study questions.

# Think It Through!

Would it be technically correct to say that Einstein could speak French and English? In these languages, his phonology and grammar were faulty, and he never mastered the pragmatics of any language. Is there a difference between speaking a language imperfectly and not speaking it at all? At what point would you decide that a person's command of one or more of the aspects of language was so poor that you would no longer say that he or she could use language? Can you think of a way to decide when a student studying a new language has reached the point of "speaking the language"?

Some forms of representation play critical roles in pragmatics. Consider this joke: A man showed up for work one day with huge bandages over each ear. A coworker asked him what happened. He replied, "I was ironing and was lost in thought. The phone rang, and without thinking I lifted my hand to answer it." The coworker was aghast, but then asked, "But what about the other ear?" "Oh," he replied, "then I had to call the doctor." This is a visual joke, and people who do not form mental images well don't seem to get it. Can you think of other such jokes?

# MEANS OF THOUGHT:
## Words, Images, Concepts

Einstein was a theoretical physicist. He didn't perform experiments; he didn't collect new data. Instead, he tried to put together known facts and to synthesize specialized principles into larger and simpler overarching theories. At first glance, these abilities and skills might suggest that Einstein reasoned at a very abstract level, using complex mathematical symbols to manipulate arcane ideas. But Einstein denied thinking in that way. Instead, he said that he relied on mental imagery, playing with images of objects and events, "seeing" what would happen in certain circumstances. In fact, the initial insight that led to his Special Theory of Relativity came when he imagined himself chasing a beam of light, matching its speed, and "seeing" what it would look like. He reported, "Conventional words or other signs have to be sought for laboriously only in a secondary stage, when the mentioned associative play is sufficiently established and can be reproduced at will" (Einstein, 1945, pp. 142–143).

Thinking involves manipulating information in your head. Sometimes it involves solving problems; sometimes it involves simply determining what is implied by or associated with the information at hand. We do think partly by using language, but this isn't always the case. In fact, as Einstein noted, language may come into play rather late in the thinking game. Both inner speech ("talk" we direct to ourselves) and images are manipulated in working memory, and thus they play a key role in thinking (as discussed in Chapter 7, working memory operates on stored information to allow us to perform a task). However, although language and images help us to think, they cannot themselves be the only means by which we think. To see why, let's consider each in turn, and then look at another way in which information is specified in the mind.

# Words: Inner Speech and Spoken Thoughts

Many people, if asked, would say that they think with words. And, at first glance, that seems plausible: After all, to communicate with someone, we usually have to express ourselves in words, so why not use words when thinking?

## Putting Thoughts Into Words

There are at least three problems with the idea that thinking is just talking to yourself, as was claimed by the founder of behaviorism, John B. Watson (1913):

1. If this were true, why would you ever have trouble "putting a thought into words"? If thoughts were already formed in language, expressing them in language should be child's play.

2. Words are often ambiguous, but thoughts are not. If you are thinking about "the port," you don't wonder whether you are thinking about a wine or a harbor.

3. Anyone who has owned a dog or a cat has sensed that at least some animals can think, and yet they don't use language. In fact, there is ample evidence that many animals can not only think, but can also solve problems—remember Köhler's work with the chimpanzee Sultan, discussed in Chapter 6.

## Does Language Shape Thought?

Even if thought is not the silent equivalent of talking to yourself, many people have been fascinated by the possibility that our perceptions and thoughts are shaped by the particular language we speak. This idea, known as the **linguistic relativity hypothesis**, was championed by Benjamin Lee Whorf (1956). For example, some have suggested that because the Inuit of northern Canada have many words for the different types of snow they recognize, they can see and think about subtle differences in snow better than speakers of English can, with their paltry single word for the white stuff. If this idea is correct, then people who speak languages with lots of color words should be able to perceive more distinctions among colors than people who speak languages with few such words. Rosch (1973, 1975) tested this idea by studying the Dani, a remote tribe living in Papua New Guinea. The Dani use only two words for color, corresponding to *light* and *dark*. However, they perceive variations in color and are able to learn

Linguistic relativity hypothesis: The idea that perceptions and thoughts are shaped by language, and thus people who speak different languages think differently.

Even though the Dani have only two words for color, *light* and *dark,* they can perceive and learn shades of color as easily as people who speak languages with many terms for color.

shades of color as readily as people who speak languages with words that label many colors.

Nevertheless, even if language does not entirely determine how we can think, it does influence some aspects of thought and memory. For example, Roberson and colleagues (2004) found that linguistic distinctions affect how well people can remember shades of color. They studied speakers of the Himba language of Africa; this language makes fewer distinctions among colors than does English. For instance, red, orange and pink are named with the same word. The Himba speakers made memory errors when they had to recall different colors that were named with the same word in Himba; in contrast, English speakers performed better in naming those colors, because their language helped them to draw the necessary distinctions. In addition, in some cases, we appear to use words as a crutch to help us think, particularly when working memory is involved. In such circumstances, we often perform relatively slow, step-by-step reasoning—for example, memorizing a series of directions and recalling them one at a time, holding them in working memory long enough to turn the right way and continue to the next landmark. In addition, language can enhance memory. For example, you can remember the shapes of clouds better if you come up with a distinctive characterization for each (such as "a rabbit sticking out of a tube" or "a face without a chin") than if you use a single label for them all (Ellis, 1973). In addition, the written version of a language may affect thought. For example, speakers of English tend to think of time as if it were horizontal, but speakers of Mandarin Chinese think of time as if it were vertical ("Wednesday is lower than Tuesday"; Boroditsky, 2001). However, the existence of relationships among language, memory, and perception does not imply that language determines the nature of our thoughts.

# Mental Imagery: Perception Without Sensation

If language is not the basis of thinking, what might be? Virtually all the great thinkers who applied themselves to this question in the past, including Plato and Aristotle, and later John Locke and other British philosophers, identified thought with a stream of mental images (Kosslyn, 1980). **Mental images** are representations like those that arise during perception, but they arise from stored information rather than from immediate sensory input. Visual mental images give rise to the experience of "seeing with the mind's eye," an experience you probably will have if someone asks you, for example, whether the Statue of Liberty holds the torch in her left or right hand. To "get" some jokes you need to form an image, for example: "Corduroy pillows are making headlines." (Hint: think about what your cheek would look like if you slept on a corduroy pillow all night.) Auditory mental images give rise to the experience of "hearing with the mind's ear," as is likely to happen if you try to decide whether the first three notes of "Row, Row, Row Your Boat" change in pitch. Because visual imagery is the most common form of imagery (Kosslyn et al., 1990, 2001, in press; McKellar, 1965), we focus on it here.

## Mental Space

**Mental images:** Representations like those that arise during perception, but based on stored information rather than on immediate sensory input.

There are many types of mental images (Kosslyn, 1994b); the most common seems to occur in a kind of "mental space." This space has three properties: spatial extent, limited size, and grain (the equivalent of resolution on the screen of a TV or computer monitor). Let's investigate these properties in turn.

**SPATIAL EXTENT**   First, visualize your living room, and count the number of windows. Does it feel as if you are scanning the walls? As illustrated in Figure 8.8, the greater the extent of your scan, the longer it takes to do the job; these results show that when you visualize something, its mental representation has a definite *spatial extent* (Denis & Kosslyn, 1999).

**LIMITED SIZE**   Second, how large can an object in a mental image be? When you mentally counted the windows in your living room, you scanned across each wall one by one because you couldn't "see" all four walls at once; you have only a limited field of view in a mental image. Now imagine you are walking toward an elephant, mentally staring at the center of its body. Imagine walking closer and closer to it, keeping your mental gaze fixed on its center. Most people doing this exercise report that when they are at a certain distance from the elephant, its edges seem to blur, to "overflow" their field of vision—that is, their mental space. Note the distance at which the edges of the elephant seem to blur. Now try the same exercise with a rabbit. Fixate on its center, and imagine seeing it loom up as you get closer and closer to it. When you imagine walking toward the rabbit, can you get closer to it than you could to the elephant before the edges seem to blur? When this study was done carefully, the larger the object,

**FIGURE 8.8**   ## Scanning Visual Mental Images

Participants memorized a map like this one, paying special attention to the locations of the seven objects.

Later, the participants were asked to close their eyes and focus on one location (such as the hut) and then to scan to another named location if it was on the map; they were to press one button if they found the second object and another if they could not (and the time was recorded). Participants scanned between every possible pair of objects.

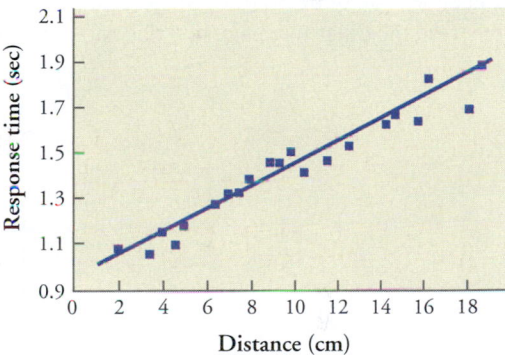

Even though their eyes were closed, the farther the participants had to scan from the first object to the second, the longer it took.

FIGURE 8.9

## Manipulating Objects in Images

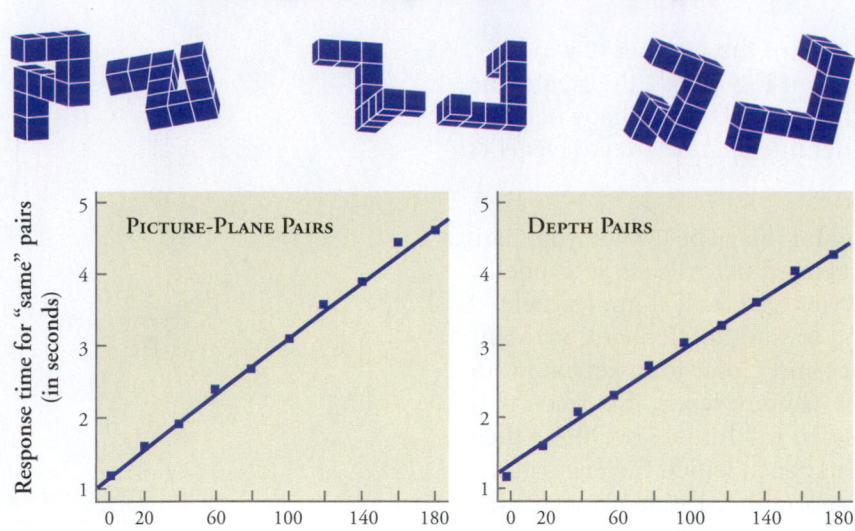

Are the objects in each pair the same or mirror images of each other? To answer the question, people mentally rotate one object of each pair until it lines up with the other. The time to make the decision increases the farther you must rotate an object mentally. It is as if the mental images were the actual objects, requiring more time the farther they have to be moved. Notice that in trying to answer the question, the pair at the far left must be rotated like the hands of a clock, not in the dimension of depth (they are said to be rotated in the "picture plane"), whereas the other two pairs must be rotated in depth.

the farther away it seemed to be in the mental image when it began to overflow (Kosslyn, 1978). This result is as expected if mental space has a *limited size*: Bigger objects must be "seen" from farther away to fit within it.

**GRAIN**  Third, try this: Imagine stretching out your arm and looking at a butterfly perched on your fingertip. Can you see the color of its head? Many people find that they have to "zoom in" mentally to answer that question. Now move the butterfly to your palm and gently bring it to within 10 inches from your eyes; this time, zooming probably isn't necessary to "see" its head. Studies have shown that people require more time to "see" properties of objects that are visualized at small sizes than those visualized at larger sizes (Kosslyn, 1975, 1976). It is as if the imagery space has a *grain*. If you look at a TV screen close up, you will see that the picture is made up of many small dots. The dots form the grain of the screen; if an object is too small, there will not be enough dots to define the details, and thus the details will be blurred.

In short, objects in images have many of the properties of actual objects; thus, images can "stand in" for objects. You can think about an absent object by visualizing it. Moreover, as shown in Figure 8.9, you can manipulate objects in images in much the same way as you manipulate actual objects.

## The Visualizing Brain

Visual images rely on most—as much as 90%—of the same parts of the brain as are used in visual perception (Ganis et al., 2004; Kosslyn et al., 2001), and we can understand the properties of mental imagery in part because images arise in brain areas used in vision.

The scans in the top row are from the front parts of the brain. It is evident from these scans that activation was virtually identical in imagery and perception, even though the participants had their eyes closed during imagery. The scans in the bottom row are from the back parts of the brain. As is evident, these parts of the brain were more strongly activated during perception than during imagery. The greater activation during perception may be one way we know whether we are seeing or imaging.

**Perception**

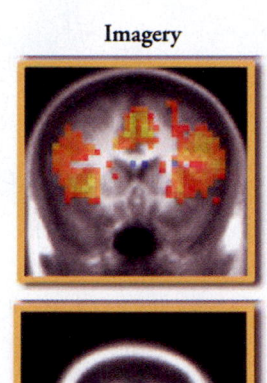

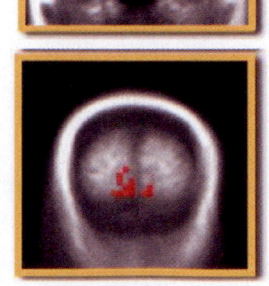

**Imagery**

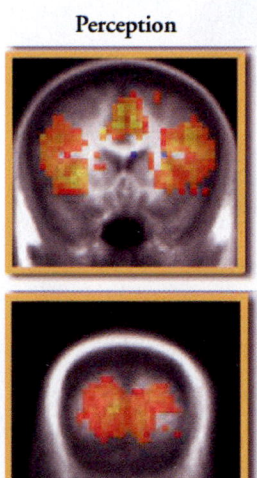

**Perception – Imagery**

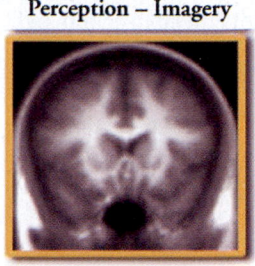

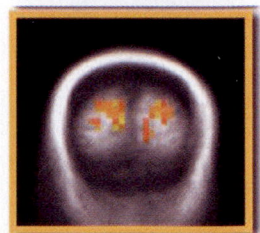

**UNDERSTANDING SPATIAL EXTENT**   How can we explain the fact that objects in images have spatial extent? Many of the areas of the brain that process visual input are organized so that images on the retina are laid out on the cortex in what are called *topographically organized areas* (from the Greek *topos*, "place"). As shown in Chapter 4 (see p. 145), there are literally "pictures in the brain" in these areas. Many researchers have found that when people visualize with their eyes closed, these areas are active (Kosslyn & Thompson, 2003; Kosslyn et al., 1995, 1999, 2001; LeBihan et al., 1993). Moreover, if these areas are temporarily impaired by the effect of strong magnetic pulses, visual mental imagery is disrupted (Kosslyn et al., 1999).

**UNDERSTANDING LIMITS ON SIZE**   Let's consider why there are limits on the spatial extent of objects in images, why they seem to overflow if they loom too large. The brain needed to evolve only to process input from the eyes, and we don't see behind our heads. Objects in images overflow at about the same size that actual objects seem to become blurred in perception (Kosslyn, 1978). Like TV or computer screens, topographically organized areas have definite boundaries, and images cannot extend beyond them. Of course, these areas do not function literally as screens: No hidden observer in the brain looks at them—rather, the areas organize and process signals, which are sent to other areas in the brain.

**UNDERSTANDING GRAIN**   Characteristics of topographically organized brain areas can also explain why images have grain. The neurons in topographically organized visual areas of the brain attempt to inhibit the activity of nearby neurons. During mental imagery, these neurons are not very strongly activated (Ganis et al., 2004), and thus when each neuron receives inhibitory input from many other nearby neurons, it may not be able to resist. If so, then some neurons would become deactivated, which would blur fine details (Kosslyn et al., in press).

Other types of images, such as the sense you have of where things are around you at any given moment, do not depict surfaces but rather specify locations; such spatial images, which even blind people can have, do not activate topographically organized areas of the brain (Mellet et al., 1998). In addition, in at least some tasks for some people, it is possible that images arise on the basis of memories that were originally formed by topographically organized areas but that no longer rely on such areas (Behrmann, 2000). Finally, we can manipulate objects in images by imagining that we physically manipulate them, which actually engages parts of the brain involved in physical movement (Grèzes & Decety, 2001; Jeannerod & Frak, 1999; Kosslyn et al., 1998; Lamm et al., 2001; Wraga et al., 2003). In all of these cases, key properties of mental imagery arise from the fact that it relies on brain mechanisms used for other purposes, specifically perception and movement control.

## Limitations of Mental Images as Vehicles of Thought

But images have limitations that prevent them from being the only tools of the mind, even in combination with words. For one thing, images cannot represent abstract concepts. Take justice, for example. How would you represent "justice" with an image? You might choose a blindfolded woman holding a pair of scales. But how would you know if that image represented the familiar statue or was supposed to stand for the abstract concept of justice? Another problem is that images are often ambiguous. An image of a box seen from the side could just as easily be an image of that side alone, detached from the box. Furthermore, not everybody can produce good images; perhaps 2% of the population have poor visual imagery (McKellar, 1965). Yet another problem is, how do you "decide" which images to form? Some other process must pick out which images are likely to be useful. Like language, imagery can contribute to our thought processes, and like language, it cannot be the only means by which we think.

# Concepts: Neither Images nor Words

A **concept** is a grouping of a set of objects (which may include living things) or events (which can specify relations between things, such as "falling" or "on"). A concept is an unambiguous internal representation that may be abstract (such as the concept of truth or justice). Concepts may be *expressed* by images and words, but they are not the same as either (Kosslyn, 1980; Pinker, 1994). Thought arises from the manipulation of concepts, but words and images are used to express thoughts and further expand on them in working memory. Words and images play much the same role that a notepad does when you are planning a shopping trip; they not only help you work through and organize your thoughts, but also provide a way to store them.

The oldest idea of the nature of concepts was proposed by Aristotle in the 4th century B.C. According to this view, a concept can be defined by a set of features. For example, for the concept "bird" the features might be "wings, feathers, a beak, and the ability to fly." The features not only describe perceivable characteristics (such as wings and beak), but also specify appropriate activities (such as flight). A modern adaptation of this view is to assume that such features are actually stored and constitute the representation of the concept. In this case, the morphemes that underlie the meaning of the word *bird* would capture each of the defining properties. Some concepts are captured by the meanings of words, but others require a phrase or two to be fully expressed. Like the meanings of words, concepts are unambiguous.

## Prototypes: An Ostrich Is a Bad Bird

According to Aristotelian theories, the features that underlie our representation of a concept must be both necessary and sufficient. A *necessary* feature is one that all members of the group must have; a *sufficient* feature is one that is enough—that "suffices"—to put an entity into a given category (having feathers is a sufficient feature for "birdness"; if it has feathers, it's a bird). A **category** is a grouping in which the members are specific cases of a more general type. But Aristotle's formula doesn't always work: Although "the ability to fly" is a feature of birds, it is also a feature of insects and bats; but they're not birds, so flying is not sufficient for "birdness." And an ostrich is a bird, but it can't fly, so flying is not a necessary feature of birds.

In addition, adapting Aristotle's notion to a theory of how concepts are represented leads us to make wrong predictions. For example, according to this theory of how concepts are specified, if an object has the required properties, it is a member of the concept, period; all members of a concept have equally good standing. But Rosch (1978) showed that some objects are actually "better" members of their concept category than others. How good an example of its category an object is depends on its **typicality**—that is, how representative it is of that type of thing. As illustrated in Figure 8.10, people name objects that are typical members of a concept category faster than objects that are not typical members. Typicality affects not only the time it takes you to identify an object, but also your confidence in naming the object as an example of a specific concept (Garrard et al., 2001; Smith & Medin, 1981).

**PROTOTYPICAL OBJECTS** Most responses related to how typical an object is for a category can be explained if a concept corresponds to a set of features that describe the **prototype** of the category—that is, its most typical member—but only a *percentage* of those features need to be present in any particular member. That is, the more features that apply above the bare minimum, the faster you can name the object—and more prototypical members of a concept have more such distinguishing features (Rips et al.,

**FIGURE 8.10**

## Name These Animals

Research has shown that you will name the animal in the center most readily; and, in fact, the mutt is most typical for the category "dog."

1973). Thus, people take longer to name ostriches as birds because fewer bird features apply to them (they cannot fly; they are not the size of the standard bird); on the other hand, robins are named faster because more of the features of birds, in general, apply to them.

If you want to impress your friends, ask them to participate in a "mind reading" exercise. Pick a category that has a well-defined prototype, for example "vegetables." And then say, "Quick, think of a vegetable!" Predict that they have selected "carrot"—because in most cases, "carrot" (the prototype) is the vegetable they will have chosen. However, at least some concepts that are not collections of features may be stored as prototypes, such as the prototype of the concept "an odd number between 1 and 10" (Armstrong et al., 1983). Quick, think of an odd number between 1 and 10. Most people select 3, and on that basis 3 can be considered as the most typical member of this category. But such concepts are unusual in that, by definition, they require selecting a single example, and so these special cases may be represented by a single example stored individually. In fact, some researchers have made the case that not all concepts are stored as prototypes, but rather some concepts rely on storing sets of examples of the category (Medin & Schaffer, 1978; Smith & Medin, 1981). For example, your concept of a chair might correspond to representations of a collection of chairs (rocking chair, desk chair, easy chair, and so on), not a single prototype. In addition, concepts of movement or action, such as those labeled by verbs, may largely rely on functional features (for instance, whether an object can be lifted; Bird et al., 2000). At least some concepts may be stored in multiple ways or using combinations of methods, and different representations may be used in different situations (Anderson & Betz, 2001; Medin et al., 2000; Rips, 2001; Smith et al., 1998).

**PROTOTYPICAL ROLES**   Prototypes not only play a key role in how we organize objects, they also affect how we behave. Gibbons and Gerrard (1995) theorized that whether someone will engage in a health-risk behavior, such as excessive drinking of alcohol, depends on how similar the individual thinks he or she is to a prototype of the typical person who engages in that behavior. Blanton and colleagues (1997) tested this theory by studying 463 adolescents (roughly half male, half female) who lived in rural Iowa. To assess prototypes for drinking, the participants were told, "We would like you to think for a minute about the *type of person your age who drinks (alcohol)* frequently." The researchers stressed that they were not interested in anyone in particular, just "the typical teenage drinker." Following this introduction, the participants were given a set of adjectives and rated the degree to which those adjectives described their prototype.

On the basis of these ratings, Blanton and colleagues inferred the degree to which the typical teenage drinker was generally viewed by the participant as "self-assured–together (such as self-confident and independent), unattractive (unattractive and dull), or immature (immature and careless)." To the extent that an individual participant rated teenagers who drink high on the first factor and low on the other two, he or she was said to have a "positive prototype" of drinkers.

Three results are of particular interest. First, participants who had more positive prototypes of drinkers reported drinking more. Second, the more their peers tended to drink, the more the participants tended to drink. Third, adolescents who had poor relationships with their parents were more likely to associate with a drinking peer group. These results are correlational, and you already know that correlation does not imply causation—and thus the prototype could be the cause or the effect, or both the prototype and the behavior could arise for other reasons.

According to one interpretation, feeling that they are similar to the prototype shapes individuals' behavior and they develop a positive prototype of drinking on the basis of interactions with the drinking peer group; poor relationships with their parents then lead them to associate with a drinking peer group. But, according to another interpretation, people who drink more tend to develop positive prototypes of drinkers (not the other way around); heavy drinkers may select peers who are also heavy drinkers, and drinking and hanging out with others who do sours the relationships that these individuals have with their parents. Can you think of a way of sorting out which interpretation is correct?

## How Are Concepts Organized?

Many concepts can be applied to any given object. We can name an object with words that correspond to concepts at different levels of specificity: "Granny Smith apple" is very specific, "apple" is more general, and "fruit" more general still. How are different concepts organized?

Look at the objects in Figure 8.11, and name them as fast as you can. It's very likely that you name them "apple," "tree," and "dog." You probably didn't name the apple a "fruit" or a "Granny Smith" or call the tree an "oak" or the dog a "mammal" or an "an-

imal." People consistently name objects at what Rosch and her colleagues (1976) have called the **basic level**. The basic level is like the middle rung of a ladder, with more general concepts above it and more specific concepts below it. So "apple" is the basic level; "fruit" is on a rung above it, and "Granny Smith" on a rung below. Each more general concept includes a number of more specific concepts; for example, "apple" includes "Granny Smith," "Delicious," "McIntosh," and many more.

At each level of specificity, there are prototypes for the concept. For example, apple might be the prototypical fruit, and McIntosh might be the prototypical apple. The basic level indicates the level of specificity with which we are likely to apply a concept to an object. Rosch offered several ways to identify the basic level. For example, one way is based on shape: At the most specific level, if we compare individual Delicious apples with other Delicious apples, their shapes are very similar. Moving up a rung of generality, if we compare Delicious apples with McIntosh apples, Cortland apples, and so on, their shapes are pretty similar. But, moving up another rung, if we compare apples with other fruits, such as bananas, watermelons, or grapes, their shapes are not similar at all. The basic-level category is the one that is as general as possible, while still being limited to objects having similar shapes.

Some researchers theorize that sets of concepts are organized not only according to levels that vary in specificity, but also into schemas (Rumelhart, 1975; Schank & Abelson, 1977). If the basic level is like a rung on a ladder that organizes concepts in terms of specificity, a schema is like a basket that contains things that usually go together. A **schema** is a collection of concepts that specify necessary and optional aspects of a particular situation. For example, the schema for "room" indicates that it must have walls, a floor, a ceiling, and at least one door. In addition, this schema indicates that a room can also have windows, carpeting, and various types of furniture. If you know that you are looking at a room, the "room" schema is activated, the necessary concepts apply to this case, and the schema guides you to look to see which other, optional features also apply. Schemas can also organize objects into concepts based on *thematic relations*, such as that between candles and cake (Lin & Murphy, 2001). Schemas can also organize events according to scripts that unfold in time, such as the events that occur when you go to a restaurant to eat.

In addition, categories can be organized along different dimensions. Even 4-year-olds can organize categories according to scripts (such as foods eaten at breakfast), evaluations (such as junk foods) and taxonomies (such as fruits). Moreover, even 4-year-olds can assign an object (such as a banana) into multiple categories (a food eaten at breakfast and a fruit) at the same time (Nguyen & Murphy, 2003). The categories we use depend largely on the tasks at hand.

## Concepts in the Brain

Studies of how concepts are stored in the brain have shown that they are organized not only in terms of specificity and their interrelations in schemas, but also according to how they are used. For example, brain damage can impair the ability to name living things but not manufactured objects (Warrington & Shallice, 1984), or vice versa (Warrington & McCarthy, 1987). This finding suggests that the brain organizes concepts according to these two general classes. In addition, Martin and colleagues (1996) found that when the participants in their study named tools, one of the areas of the brain that was activated (as measured by PET) is used to direct movements. In contrast, this area was not activated when the participants named animals, but visual areas were activated. Characteristic actions are important for specifying the concept "tool," whereas visual properties are particularly important for specifying the concept "animal."

Basic level: A level of specificity, which is usually the most likely to be applied to an object.

Schema: A collection of concepts that specify necessary and optional aspects of a particular situation.

1. Rosch's findings with the Dani tested the linguistic relativity hypothesis. She found that the
   a. Dani's thinking about color was limited by their language.
   b. Dani's perceptions of color and their ability to learn shades of color were not limited by their language.
   c. Dani could perceive only two colors at the same time, even though their vision was otherwise normal.
   d. Dani had dozens of words for colors.
2. Research on mental imagery has found that it
   a. has no limits.
   b. is exactly the same as visual perception.
   c. seems to have many of the same properties as visual perception.
   d. is impossible since there are no eyes in the human brain and no "inner brain" to perceive the images.
3. When presented with objects to name, people will often name
   a. those that have many of their category's distinctive features more quickly.
   b. those that have fewer distinctive features more quickly.
   c. all of the objects at the same speed.
   d. those that are typical of their category more slowly but with greater accuracy.

4. If you went into a fast-food restaurant on Mars, you would be more likely to know how to order some food than how to interpret the behavior of the Martians. Why would this be the case?
   a. You have a schema for fast-food restaurants, but not for Martians.
   b. You do not have a schema for fast-food restaurants, but you do have one for Martians.
   c. You organize such situations by food rather than by social factors.
   d. Your Martian prototype would aid your processing.

## Answers

1. b 2. c 3. a 4. a

## Think It Through!

Einstein came up with many new concepts during the course of his career. How do you think a "new" concept can be formed? Is there only one way in which a new concept can be created?

Einstein claimed to think largely in images. Why might this make sense for a physicist? Would you expect the advantages of thinking in images to apply to psychologists? Would it depend on the field within psychology? Why or why not? Einstein was highly imaginative in his thinking, in the sense that he was innovative; what do you think is the relationship between the two senses of the word *imagine*—"to suppose" versus "to create a mental image"?

# PROBLEM SOLVING

Einstein never shied away from proposing radically new concepts, such as the idea that light consists of both particles and waves. But formulating concepts is only a small part of what we do while thinking. Once we form concepts, we use them in various ways, such as in solving problems. For example, Einstein used mental imagery to think about the nature of gravity. He reasoned that if you stood with some objects (such as keys and some coins) in an elevator that was falling down a long shaft, you and the objects would float within the elevator. But if the elevator started accelerating upward, you and the objects would fall to the floor—exactly like what would happen if you were in a gravity field. In fact, you couldn't tell whether you were in a gravity field or were simply accelerating. So, gravity and acceleration seemed to have something in common.

Einstein continued to use this imagery to perform a "thought experiment": Say you shined a beam of light through the left side of a glass-walled elevator. If the elevator were moving upward, the light would exit the right side a little closer to the floor than the height at which it entered on the left side, because the elevator had moved up a bit during the interval while the light was crossing through it. From the point of view of someone in the elevator, the beam of light would seem to bend as it moved across it. Einstein realized that if acceleration and gravity are comparable, then light should also bend in gravity. And this highly counterintuitive idea turned out to be correct!

Many different skills feed into your ability to solve problems—but your ability to solve problems is not simply the sum of those abilities. Solving a problem depends crucially on how you set it up. You can use language, images, or some combination of the two to specify the problem, but first you must conceptualize it—otherwise, you won't know which words and images to use. Once you set up a problem in a particular way, you can manipulate your mental images and verbal descriptions to try to solve it. In this section, we explore the differences among various kinds of problem solving.

# Solving Problems: More Than Inspiration

A **problem** is an obstacle that must be overcome to reach a goal. Problems come in many types and can often be solved in many ways. Let's consider some of the tools at your disposal for solving a diverse range of puzzles and predicaments.

## Solving the Representation Problem: It's All in How You Look at It

The first step to solving any problem is figuring out how to look at it. This fundamental challenge is called the **representation problem**. If you hit on the right way to represent a specific problem, the solution can be amazingly simple. Consider the example of the hiking monk in Figure 8.12 (based on Duncker, 1945). You have to decide whether, *at any one time of day*, the monk would be at precisely the same spot on the path, both on the day he went up and on the day he came down. At first glance, this problem may seem difficult. If the precise specifications of departure times, speed, and so on lure you into trying to use algebra, you may work on it for hours. But if you hit on the right representation, it's easy: Imagine a mountain with a monk leaving from the top at the same time that another monk leaves from the bottom. It is clear that the two monks must pass each other at a particular point on the path—and the same will be true if instead of two monks leaving at the same time on the same day, a single monk goes up on one day and goes down on another day (provided that he departs at the same time in the morning for both treks). And so the answer is simply yes.

Finding the right representation for a problem can be tricky because once you think of a problem in a certain way, you may find it difficult to drop this view and try out others (Smith & Blankenship, 1989, 1991). For example, consider the problem in Figure 8.13 on p. 358 (adapted from Duncker, 1945); after you think about it, look at its solution in Figure 8.15 (on p. 360). At first, you probably thought of the box simply as a container, and not as a potential part of the solution. Becoming stuck on one interpretation of an object or aspect of a situation is called **functional fixedness** (Behrens, 2003). Even members of the Shuar, who live in the Ecuadorian Amazon, fall into

**Problem:** An obstacle that must be overcome to reach a goal.

**Representation problem:** The challenge of how best to formulate the nature of a problem.

**Functional fixedness:** When solving a problem, getting stuck on one interpretation of an object or one part of the situation.

**FIGURE 8.12** ## The Hiking Monk Problem

A monk leaves the bottom of a mountain every Monday at 5:00 a.m. and walks up a twisty path, climbing at a rate of 1.5 miles an hour, until he reaches the top at 4:00 p.m., having taken off a half-hour for lunch. He meditates on the mountain until sundown. At 5:00 the next morning, he departs and walks down the path, going 3.5 miles an hour, until he reaches the bottom. Is there *any* point in the two journeys when he is at precisely the same location on the path at precisely the same time of day? You don't need to say what that time is, just whether there would be such a time.

**FIGURE 8.13**   **The Candle Problem**

Participants are asked to use the materials provided to mount the candle on the wall so that it can be lit. Some participants are given the materials as shown on the left; others, as shown at the right. Participants given the materials as shown at the right are more likely to solve the problem.

functional fixedness—in spite of the fact that most of their artifacts are intended to have multiple functions. German and Barrett (2005), in reporting this finding, suggest that functional fixedness may be a result of how semantic memory operates. In fact, neuroimaging studies have shown that extra brain activity is required when you need to inhibit one kind of performance and switch to another (Konishi et al., 1999).

## Algorithms and Heuristics: Getting From Here to There

To solve a problem, you need a **strategy**, an approach to solving a problem determined by the type of representation used and the processing steps to be tried. There are two types of strategies: algorithms and heuristics. Let's say you hear about a fantastic price being offered on a new music CD you covet by an independent record store, but you don't know the name of the store. You could try to find it by calling every relevant listing in the yellow pages. This process involves using an **algorithm**, a set of steps that, if followed methodically, will guarantee the right answer. But you may not have time to call every store. Instead, you might guess that the record store is in a part of town where many students live. In this case, having reduced the list of candidates to those located near the campus, you might find the store after calling only a few. This process reflects use of a **heuristic**, a strategy that does not guarantee the correct answer but offers a likely shortcut to it. One common heuristic is to divide a big problem into parts and solve them one at a time.

Another heuristic is to guess at a solution and then work backwards, looking for evidence that supports that conclusion (Norman et al., 1999). And yet another heuristic is simply to see whether you recognize one alternative solution, and assume that if you do, then it's likely to be the best (Goldstein & Gigerenzer, 2002). Heuristics don't guarantee that you'll find the correct answer, but as Einstein put it, "Anyone who has never made a mistake has never tried anything new." As shown in Figure 8.14, different algorithms or heuristics may be used for the same problem, depending on the type of answer you seek.

Heuristics are particularly useful for *ill-defined problems*, in which the goal, what you have to work with (such as the amount of money available), or the method of reaching the goal are not clearly specified. For instance, the problem of "finding some entertainment" is ill-defined. In contrast, both heuristics and algorithms are useful for *well-defined problems*, where the goal, what you have to work with, and the method of reaching the goal are clearly specified. "Finding a cheap CD in Boston" is a well-defined problem.

**Strategy:** An approach to solving a problem, determined by the type of representation used and the processing steps to be tried.

**Algorithm:** A set of steps that, if followed methodically, will guarantee the solution to a problem.

**Heuristic:** A strategy that does not guarantee the correct answer to a problem but offers a likely shortcut to it.

**FIGURE 8.14**

# Different Heuristics for the Same Problem

Depending on the precise solution that is required, problems may be solved in different ways—even when you reason purely in your head. For example, when people compute exact arithmetic they use language, and brain areas involved in word association are activated. In contrast, when people compute only approximate values, they don't use language but instead rely on a mental "number line"; in such processing, parts of the parietal lobes used in visuospatial processing are used (Dehaene et al., 1999; Zorzi et al., 2002).

## Solving Problems by Analogy: Comparing Features

Another way to solve problems requires you to compare the features of two situations, noticing what they have in common and what's different (Gentner & Gunn, 2001; Hummel & Holyoak, 1997). Let's begin with the following problem (based on Duncker, 1945): A surgeon has to remove a cancerous tumor from deep within a patient's brain. The use of a scalpel would cause permanent brain damage. An alternative is to use a beam of X rays to demolish the cancerous cells. However, the beam will also kill healthy cells in its path. Is there a way to reach only the cancerous cells and spare the healthy ones?

The solution is to split the beam into several minibeams, each aimed from a different angle but crossing at the location of the tumor. Each minibeam is so weak that it will not hurt the healthy tissue, but their combined impact will destroy the tumor. Gick and Holyoak (1980, 1983) found that most people do not realize this solution. However, if they are first presented with an analogous problem and are told to think about how it relates to the second problem, success rates skyrocket. In this case, they first read about a problem faced by a general who wants to attack a fortress. If he advances all of his troops along a single road, mines will blow them to pieces. But smaller groups could travel on various approach roads without exploding the mines. The solution is to divide the army into smaller parties and have each take a separate road to the fortress. Once people see this solution and know it is relevant, the solution to the tumor problem becomes much easier (in fact, close to 80% get the problem right). If the participants are not told that the army problem is relevant to the tumor one, however, thinking about the solution to the former does not help them much with the latter. At first glance, the two problems are unrelated. One involves soldiers and a fortress; the other, beams of radiation and a tumor. But beneath these surface differences, the problems have the same structure: Something too big is broken into parts, the parts are delivered separately, and then they are recombined. To see how a previous experience can be applied to a present case, you must recognize the similarities in the structure of the situations.

**FIGURE 8.15** **Solution to the Candle Problem**

When the box is presented as a container, functional fixedness often prevents people from imagining the box as a shelf.

Analogical thinking relies on having solutions to previous problems stored in memory, spotting similarities between a new and a previous problem, and seeing how the structure of the previous problem allows its solution to be applied to the new problem. This process is guided by your goals, which lead you to seek a particular kind of solution to the new problem (Holyoak & Thagard, 1997; Hummel & Holyoak, 1997).

## Sudden Solutions

People do not always have to work consciously through a problem, step by step. In some cases, they can "see" the solution right away; in others, the solution dawns on them after they have set the problem aside for a while.

Many researchers have suggested that people sometimes can see a solution to a problem in a flash, full-blown and complete (Guilford, 1979; Olton, 1979; Torrance, 1980). This phenomenon results from an **insight**, a new way to look at a problem that implies the solution. Insights can arise following a trial-and-error exploration in which the problem is represented in different ways. Once the problem is represented in the right way, the answer is obvious. A good example of insight is the *Wheel of Fortune* experience; once you solve the word puzzle yourself, the solution becomes so obvious that you can't imagine how the stumped contestants on the show can be so dense. *Insight learning*, discussed in Chapter 6, can follow such problem solving—making it easier to cope with similar problems in the future.

Insights may occur after a break from consciously working on a problem or performing a particular task—**incubation** is the processing that occurs when a person is not consciously working on solving a problem and that can lead to improved thinking about the solution. To study incubation, Goldman and colleagues (1992) asked participants to solve difficult anagrams (words or phrases created by rearranging the letters of other words or phrases—"dormitory" is an anagram of "dirty room"). Those who did not solve the anagrams within the allotted time were given the same problems again, either immediately, 20 minutes later, or 24 hours later. New anagrams were presented in the second set along with those previously seen but not solved. Goldman and colleagues found that the participants solved more old anagrams than new ones if they had a break, and they performed even better after a longer break. The researchers pointed out that this finding need not indicate that the a person unconsciously works on problems even when not intentionally thinking about them. For example, participants could have forgotten strategies that were not useful but that had kept them fixated during the initial session (Segal, 2004, and Smith & Blankenship, 1989, 1991, have shown such effects) or could simply have been better rested after the break.

Metcalfe (1986) tested the idea that insight involves unconscious restructuring by asking people to predict in advance whether they could solve specific problems. If people solve all problems by remembering relevant information, then they should be good at predicting their performance. In contrast, if problems can be solved by insight, a sudden shift in the way you look at a problem, success should be difficult to predict. Metcalfe found that although people could accurately predict their ability to answer questions about real-world trivia, they could not predict their performance on insight problems.

Insight: A new way to look at a problem that implies the solution.

Incubation: Processing that occurs when a person is not consciously working on solving a problem and that can lead to improved thinking about the solution.

The mechanisms underlying insight and incubation are not well understood, but it would be surprising if they turned out to be much different from the mechanisms evoked when other strategies are used in problem solving. Many insights may emerge after we try out a new way to represent a problem, or after we spot an analogy. The fact that problem-solving processes may occur unconsciously does not make them any more mysterious than the processes underlying implicit memory, discussed in Chapter 7 (Kihlstrom, 1987). Table 8.1 summarizes the various approaches to solving problems; note that either algorithms or heuristics can be used to address the representation problem and that how incubation works is yet to be explained.

**TABLE 8.1   Approaches to Problem Solving**

| Approach | Definition | Example |
|---|---|---|
| Address the representation of the problem | Change the way the problem is represented, or formulated | Use an image of two monks starting to walk the path at the same time, one from the top and the other from the bottom |
| Use an algorithm | Series of steps that is guaranteed to produce a solution | Check every music store in the phone book to find the lowest price on a CD |
| Use a heuristic | Short-cut strategy that may or may not be effective | Check music stores in the part of town where most of the students live to find the lowest price on a CD |
| Use an analogy | A type of heuristic that relies on finding points of correspondence with previously solved problems | Realizing that a particular medical problem is like a previously encountered military problem |
| Rely on incubation | Unconscious processes that can lead to a solution | "Sleeping on" the problem of how to fund a vacation, hoping you will have a better idea when you wake up |

## Cognitive Control

How do you decide how to approach solving a problem and then how to carry out your plan? Cognitive control is mental processing that manages other processing; more specifically, **cognitive control** consists of the processes that guide attention, thought, and action in the service of accomplishing a specific task. Many researchers have used the Stroop task as a simple test-bed to study cognitive control. As discussed in Chapter 4, the Stroop task requires a participant to name the color of the ink used to print words that name colors—and the words can name different colors than the ones used to print them (for example, the word "green" might be printed in red ink). To perform this task, you need to override your automatic tendency to read the word, and instead to focus your attention narrowly on the color of the ink. This feat requires considerable cognitive control.

Cognitive control: The processes that guide attention, thought, and action in the service of accomplishing a specific task.

Much of the research on cognitive control has relied on neuroimaging to observe what happens in participants' brains when they exercise cognitive control. Using this tool, researchers have hypothesized a system of distinct processes that underlie this ability (Cohen et al., in press):

1. One process formulates and maintains both an overarching goal and a set of subgoals. The prefrontal cortex (located near the front of the brain) plays a key role in these functions (O'Reilly et al., 2002).

2. Another process monitors performance and registers conflict among possible responses (such as the conflict that arises in the Stroop task when you are tempted to read the word when you should be naming the color of the ink). If performance is poor and planned responses often conflict, this is a sign that the subgoal should be changed. The anterior cingulate cortex plays a key role in this function (Kerns et al., 2004; Yeung et al., 2004).

3. Other processes must update the subgoal if the task is not being performed well. The dopamine-based systems involved in reward (see Chapter 6) act to update the representations of goals held in prefrontal cortex (Montague et al., 2004).

4. Finally, yet another set of processes controls attention to the task. If you aren't performing the task well, you either may focus harder on your current plan and try to control your actions more precisely or may abandon your current approach and explore alternative ways to accomplish the task. The processes that allocate attention rely in part on a small brain structure called the *locus coeruleus* (located on either side of the upper part of the pons, which is illustrated in Chapter 3), which operates by regulating the amount and timing of norepinephrine released.

Cognitive control is obviously not simple—nor should we expect it to be. Cognitive control lies at the very heart of voluntary action. In fact, an understanding of cognitive control should help us come to grips with long-standing puzzles about the nature of free will.

# Expertise: Why Hard Work Pays Off

Einstein had his priorities clear: Nothing, not friends, family, fame, or fortune could stand in the way of work. On visiting him in his study, a friend asked about a large meat hook that was hanging from the ceiling, ". . . bearing a thick sheaf of letters. These, Einstein explained, he had no time to answer." The friend, ". . . asking what he did when the hook was filled up, was answered by two words: 'Burn them.'" (Clark, 1971, p. 199). Einstein spent his years in the patent office thinking, studying, and working—and later credited that time as allowing him to develop expertise in his chosen field.

Expertise in any given field typically takes about 10 years to achieve, in part because it comes from encountering many examples of the types of problems in the particular area (Ericsson et al., 1993; Simon & Chase, 1973). For example, researchers have studied why you have to play chess for years to become a master. Chase and Simon (1973) tried to find out what made chess masters different from novices and very good chess players. Basing their study on the pioneering work of DeGroot (1965, 1966), Chase and Simon asked their participants to study chessboards with pieces on them for 5 seconds, and then to place the pieces properly on another board. The masters proved far superior to the novices and very good players, but only when the positions to be remembered were ones that could occur in an actual game. When the pieces were placed randomly on the board, the masters performed no better than the novices and very good players.

Chase and Simon inferred that the experts had seen so many games that they could recognize familiar positions in new games and so were able to group the pieces into single units (chunks); the novices and the very good players did not possess this information from experience. Chase and Ericsson (1981) subsequently showed that a key to enhancing problem-solving abilities is not storing larger chunks in short-term memory, but rather learning strategies (including organizing the board into chunks) for storing relevant information quickly and effectively in long-term memory, thus making an end run around the limitations of short-term memory (Ericsson & Charness, 1994, elaborate on this idea). Note that becoming an expert at chess is not merely a matter of developing a better memory for actual chess positions: Charness (1981) tested players who ranged in age from 16 to 64 and found that even the older players who had relatively poor memories could still make good decisions about which pieces to move. In fact, people who have good visual memories in general are no more likely to become good chess players than people who have poor visual memories in general (Waters et al., 2002).

An interesting aspect of expertise is that it is limited to a specific field. Being an expert in one area does not generalize to another: Chess masters are no better than anyone else at solving non-chess problems. The skills that are acquired by experience apply only to the specific area in which they were originally developed. Nevertheless, experts in any particular domain tend to approach problems related to that domain differently than nonexperts do, as summarized in Table 8.2.

**TABLE 8.2 Differences Between Expert and Nonexpert Problem-Solvers**

| Characteristic | Experts | Nonexperts |
|---|---|---|
| Organization | Organize knowledge around fundamental principles | Organize knowledge in fragmented ways |
| Type of principles used | Specific principles or concepts (such as momentum in physics) | Vaguer or more general ideas |
| Categorization of problems | Categorize based on relevant underlying principles (deep analysis) | Categorize based on observable features (superficial analysis) |
| Use of strategies | Develop an overall strategy in advance; reorganize strategy if necessary | Try to solve part of the problem without an overall strategy in mind |

Ericsson and Charness (1994) and Ericsson and colleagues (1993) reviewed a great deal of the literature on expertise and reached a surprising conclusion: Talent plays little, if any, role in determining who becomes an expert. Rather, the crucial variable is simply how much deliberate practice is invested in performing a task. **Deliberate practice** is practice motivated by the goal of improving performance. When you engage in deliberate practice, you aren't necessarily having fun, and you aren't necessarily getting any kind of imme-

Deliberate practice: Practice that is motivated by the goal of improving performance, usually by targeting specific areas of weakness and working to improve them.

The key to successful practice is to spot your weakness and target that weakness for deliberate effort toward improvement.

diate reward (Ericsson & Charness, 1994). Deliberate practice involves spotting a weakness in a given domain (such as having a poor backhand in tennis, weak breath control in singing, or difficulty integrating functions in math), and specifically targeting that weakness for practice. Einstein constantly engaged in such practice. In fact, he was an avid sailor, but always took a notebook with him when he sailed. When the wind died down, he immediately brought out his notebook and started working (Clark, 1971, p. 31). Ericsson and colleagues (1993) found that the sheer amount of time spent in deliberate practice is the primary mechanism for achieving expert levels of performance (Bloom, 1985). Moreover, and perhaps of direct personal relevance to you, Plant and colleagues (2005) found that the sheer amount of time students spend studying does not predict their grade point averages (GPAs); instead, the amount of study only matters when students engage in high-quality study (choosing an environment that allows them to concentrate and using deliberate practice). The relationship between the quality of study and GPA remained solid even when the contributions of SAT scores and high-school achievement to GPA were removed (using a statistical procedure). In fact, students who studied alone, in a quiet environment, not only had higher GPAs, but actually studied less than those who studied with friends or in environments with many distractions.

# Artificial Intelligence

In 1997, our species seemed to suffer a minor setback: A computer (with special hardware and custom software) called Deep Blue beat the world's best human chess player, Garry Kasparov. Does this mean that computers will soon be able to solve all sorts of problems better than we can? Not to worry. Deep Blue relied, basically, on a boring program. Because Deep Blue was so fast, it could work out and evaluate an enormous number of possible moves, one at a time. Deep Blue, unlike its human challengers, used a "brute force" algorithm, similar to calling every music store in the phone book alphabetically to find a particular CD. Deep Blue was an advance over earlier computer programs partly because it could "anticipate" more possible consequences of any given move, and partly because it was better at noting which moves eventually led to disaster and which put the opponent in a bad position. Moreover, it had access to information on hundreds of thousands of important previous games (including every one of its opponent's games), and thus could detect whether Kasparov was doing anything that had ever been done before.

A computer—specialized hardware plus customized software—can now beat the human world chess champion. What's next?

Another program, called Deep Fritz, has beaten every human player it has been pitted against. Unlike Deep Blue, which ran on a supercomputer and required 20 people to keep it going, Deep Fritz can run on a laptop. However, whereas Deep Blue could search about 200 million possible moves per second, Deep Fritz evaluates "only" about 2 million moves per second—but people are lucky to consider even one move a second!

Computers can now play a mean game of chess, to be sure, but the fact is that they can't figure out how to open a tin can or buy a bottle of milk. In contrast, chess-playing humans use analogical thinking, knowledge of principles, and various heuristic strategies in pursuing a checkmate. A surprisingly complex network of brain areas is involved in playing chess, tapping areas used in recognizing objects, registering spatial relations, and formulating plans (Nichelli et al., 1994).

**Artificial intelligence (AI)** is the name of the field devoted to building smart machines, machines that can "think." The existence of the human brain is the only proof that a mechanism can embody intelligence, and thus many AI researchers believe that the best way to make computers truly intelligent is to make them mimic human mental processes. AI research has led to the creation of *expert systems*, computer programs that can solve problems in ways that human experts would pursue. Although these programs sometimes are impressive, so far they have lacked the flexibility and creative flair of human thought.

An innovation in AI has been the programming of **neural networks** to imitate (roughly) the way the brain works. These computer programs have many small units that interact via connections, akin to the networks of neurons in the brain. Unlike most computer programs, these programs depend on having many processes operating at the same time (McClelland & Rumelhart, 1986; Rumelhart & McClelland, 1986). Neural networks can recognize objects remarkably well and can generalize to novel examples of a familiar category. Furthermore, such networks can mimic key aspects of human memory and conditioning (Vogel, 2005) and can learn to control movements (Carenzi et al., 2004); furthermore, when parts are disrupted, the networks often show effects similar to those of human brain damage (Kosslyn & Koenig, 1995).

# Overcoming Obstacles to Problem Solving

You can improve your ability to overcome obstacles to solving problems if you keep the following points in mind (Ellis & Hunt, 1993; Newsome, 2000):

1. A major challenge is to represent the problem effectively. One way to meet this challenge is to make sure that you really understand the problem. Explain the problem to somebody else; sometimes, the simple act of explaining leads to a representation that immediately implies a solution.

2. Keep your eye on the ball: Don't lose sight of what actually constitutes the problem. People sometimes tend to transform the problem—resist this. If the problem is "how to get to Hawaii for spring break," don't redefine the problem as "how to talk my parents into subsidizing the trip." This advice also applies to debates and arguments; you'll be surprised at how much more effective you'll be if you keep the pertinent issue in mind and don't allow yourself to be drawn off on tangents.

3. Don't get locked into viewing your resources in only one way, which is a form of functional fixedness. See whether you can come up with more than one strategy for approaching the problem. Einstein noted, "I am enough of an artist to draw freely upon my imagination. Imagination is more important than knowledge. Knowledge is limited. Imagination encircles the world" (as cited in Viereck, 1929).

4. Don't get stuck with a certain **mental set**, a fixed way of viewing the kind of solution you seek. It's okay to begin by focusing on one possible solution, but recognize that there may be more than one happy outcome. Be willing to consider alternatives. (Southern California is a great spring break destination, too.)

5. If you do get stuck, walk away from the problem for a while. A fresh look can lead to new ways of representing it or new strategies for solving it.

Artificial intelligence (AI): The field devoted to building smart machines.

Neural network: A computer program whose units interact via connections that imitate (roughly) the way the brain works.

Mental set: A fixed way of viewing the kind of solution being sought.

1. The wrong representation can hinder your ability to solve a problem, especially if you become stuck on that one interpretation. This barrier is called
   a. the representational problem.
   b. algorithm interference.
   c. a blocked solution path.
   d. functional fixedness.

2. Cooking something by following the directions in a recipe exactly is an example of the use of
   a. a heuristic.
   b. an analogy.
   c. an algorithm.
   d. a functional strategy.

3. Incubation need not involve unconscious work on solving a problem. Instead, it could operate by
   a. allowing forgetting of earlier strategies that were not effective.
   b. implicit problem solving, which relies on activating only emotionally charged memories.
   c. incubation release.
   d. unconscious restructuring of the goals and algorithms used to approach the problem.

4. Compared to novices, experts in a field
   a. are better at everything.
   b. seldom use algorithms but instead are masters at using heuristics.
   c. spend more time in deliberate practice.
   d. are more literal-minded.

## Answers

1.d 2.c 3.a 4.c

# Think It Through!

Can someone be a creative scientist if they always use algorithms? What is the most important unsolved problem you can think of (for example, poverty, crime, AIDS, the greenhouse effect)? Which approach to problem solving is most likely to be useful? In what ways might different methods of problem solving be combined to approach such a megaproblem?

Is it better to use words or images when thinking? In general, or only for certain purposes? If only for certain purposes, which kinds of thinking would best be accomplished with words? With images?

# LOGIC, REASONING, AND DECISION MAKING

Einstein did not always make good decisions. For example, when offered a job at Princeton, he was asked to tell the new Institute for Advanced Study what he would need to live and work there. His request for salary and support was so unrealistically low that it was turned down, and the administrators turned to his wife to arrive at a more reasonable arrangement. Nevertheless, this same man derived equations that explained a previously inexplicable slippage in the orbit of Mercury. When his theory produced the correct result, he was satisfied but not exuberant, noting that "I did not for one second doubt that [my calculations] would agree with observation. There was no sense in getting excited about what was self-evident" (Clark, 1971, p. 206). Self-evident? It is logic that leads someone to think that something is self-evident. How do we humans—Einstein included—reason logically? And why do we sometimes make bad decisions?

# Are People Logical?

Not all thinking consists of figuring out how to overcome obstacles; sometimes thinking is considering what follows from what, evaluating alternatives, and deciding what to do next. Decision making requires us to evaluate possible outcomes and choose one alternative or course of action over the others. Let's review the ways people reason and then consider some common errors in reasoning.

## How People Reason

**Logic** is the process of applying the principles of correct reasoning to reach a decision or to evaluate the truth of a claim. "Hector is a man; all men are human; therefore Hector is a human" is correct logic. But note that "Hector is a man; all men are Martians; therefore Hector is a Martian" is *also* correct logic. The first two statements in each case are the *premises*, and the only question in logic is whether the final statement, the *conclusion*, follows from the premises. The *content*—the actual meaning of the premises—is irrelevant to logic; only the *form*, the sequence of what-implies-what, counts in logic. If you accept the premises, then the rules of logic dictate that you must also accept the conclusion.

**DEDUCTIVE REASONING**   We have so far been discussing the process of **deductive reasoning**—that is, reasoning from the general to the particular. In deductive reasoning, the rules of logic are applied to a set of assumptions stated as premises to discover what conclusions inevitably follow from those assumptions. Much deductive reasoning appears to rely on setting up **mental models** (Johnson-Laird, 1995, 2001; Johnson-Laird et al., 2004), images or descriptions of a specific situation used as an aid to reason about abstract entities. Try this: Sam is hungrier than Susan, but Susan is less hungry than George. Is Susan the least hungry? Problems like this are very easy to solve if you imagine a line with a dot for each entity and place the dots standing for entities with more of the value (here, hunger) farther to the right (Huttenlocher, 1968; Huttenlocher et al., 1970). If you do this, when asked about the relative positions of the entities, you can simply "look" at your image and "read" the position of the dot of interest (Demarais & Cohen, 1998). Neuroimaging of people performing such reasoning shows activity in the spatial processing structures in the parietal lobes (Baker et al., 1996; Osherson et al., 1998), as expected if people are mentally manipulating spatial relations. Mental models can help us overcome some reasoning errors (Figure 8.16).

**INDUCTIVE REASONING**   Reasoning can be inductive as well as deductive. The opposite of deductive reasoning, **inductive reasoning** works toward a conclusion by moving from the particular case to a generalization. Induction uses individual examples to figure out a rule that governs them. If you ate two green apples and each was sour, you might induce that green apples in general are sour. However, your conclusion would be faulty: You ignored the evidence of Granny Smiths (which are sweet). Here's another example. What number comes next: 2, 4, 6, __ ? You probably said 8, but what if the underlying rule were simply "larger numbers"? Then 21, or 101, would also work. Or the rule might be "even numbers," and 2 would satisfy the condition; or "one-digit numbers," in which case 7 would work, and so on. The point is that every one of these additional generalizations is just as consistent with the set 2, 4, 6 as is the number 8 (Goodman, 1983). That inductive

**Logic:** The process of applying the principles of correct reasoning to reach a decision or evaluate the truth of a claim.

**Deductive reasoning:** Reasoning that applies the rules of logic to a set of assumptions (stated as premises) to discover whether certain conclusions follow from those assumptions; deduction goes from the general to the particular.

**Mental model:** An image or description of a specific situation used to reason about an abstract entity.

**Inductive reasoning:** Reasoning that uses examples to figure out a rule that governs them; induction goes from the particular (examples) to the general (a rule).

**FIGURE 8.16**   **Mental Models and Reasoning**

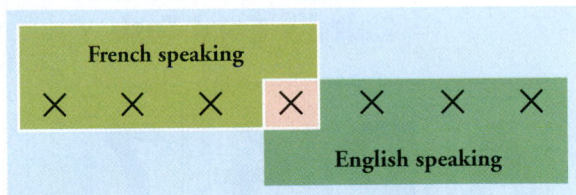

A crucial part of reasoning is to look for counterexamples. For instance, consider this problem: "More than half of the people at a meeting speak French, and more than half of the people at the meeting speak English; does it follow that more than half of the people at the meeting speak both French and English?" The mental model shown here allows you to see the answer: No.

## FIGURE 8.17 Deductive Versus Inductive Reasoning

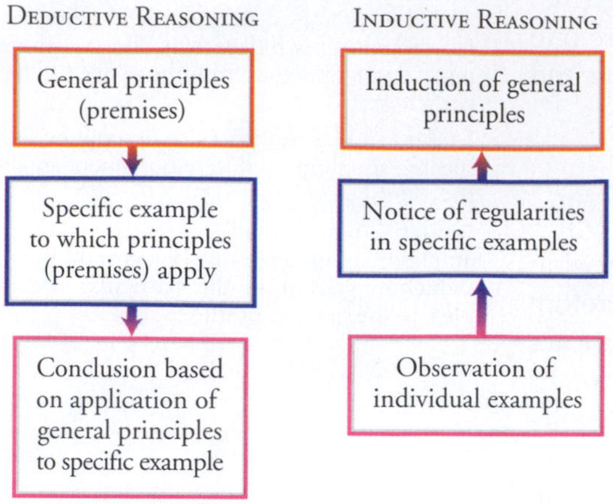

**DEDUCTIVE REASONING**

General principles (premises)

↓

Specific example to which principles (premises) apply

↓

Conclusion based on application of general principles to specific example

**INDUCTIVE REASONING**

Induction of general principles

↑

Notice of regularities in specific examples

↑

Observation of individual examples

To remember the difference between deductive and inductive reasoning, try these mnemonics: To DEduce is to move DOWN FROM something larger; to INduce is to move INTO something larger.

**Affirming the consequent:** A reasoning error that occurs because of the assumption that if a result has occurred, a specific cause must also be present.

**Confirmation bias:** A tendency to seek information that will confirm a rule, and not to seek information that is inconsistent with the rule.

## FIGURE 8.18 Wason and Johnson-Laird's Card Task

Here is the rule presented along with these cards: "If a card has a vowel on one side, then it will have an even number on the other side." How many and which of these cards must be flipped over to decide whether this rule is true?

---

reasoning works at all is something of a miracle—nevertheless, it often does (Prasada, 2000), and much of scientific discovery relies on just this kind of reasoning. Figure 8.17 schematizes the difference between deductive and inductive reasoning. Much of our reasoning involves a combination of deductive and inductive processes.

## Logical Errors

Much research has shown that humans—even extraordinary ones such as Albert Einstein—are not entirely logical.

**AFFIRMING THE CONSEQUENT** For example, people often make the error of **affirming the consequent**—that is, assuming that a specific cause is present because a particular result has occurred. Here is a cause–effect relation: "If it is sunny out, Hector wears a hat." If you see that Hector is wearing a hat, can you assume that it is sunny out? Not necessarily. Maybe Hector's on his way to a ballgame and has put on a hat with his team's logo. Maybe after checking The Weather Channel, he has put on a rain hat. Maybe he simply thinks a particular hat looks good with his outfit. Maybe—well, there might be any number of reasons, including that it is in fact sunny out. Affirming the consequent occurs because we incorrectly work backward, from result to cause. Armed with this knowledge, you can now tell what's wrong with the following reasoning:

1. Japanese do not eat much fat and have fewer heart attacks than the Americans and British.

2. The French eat a lot of fat and have fewer heart attacks than the Americans and British.

3. Japanese do not drink much red wine and have fewer heart attacks than the Americans and British.

4. Italians drink large amounts of red wine and have fewer heart attacks than the Americans and British.

5. Conclusion: Eat and drink what you like. It's speaking English that causes heart attacks.

**CONFIRMATION BIAS** Wason and Johnson-Laird (1972) devised a task that laid bare another of our reasoning frailties. Look at Figure 8.18: What would you do? The answer is that both A and 7 must be flipped. People tend to flip A, to see whether an even number is on the other side; if not, the rule would be wrong. If there is an even number on the reverse of A, most people assume the rule is confirmed. Very few think to turn over the 7: If there is a vowel on the other side, then the rule is wrong no matter what's on the reverse of A. Most people do not think about what it would take to *disconfirm* the rule. A **confirmation bias** occurs when people seek information that will confirm a rule but do not seek information that might refute it.

Now consider a variation of this task. Instead of A, D, 4, and 7, the cards say *beer, coke, 22,* and *16,* and the rule relates to drinking age: If a person is drinking beer, then he or she must be over 21 years old. Griggs and Cox (1982) found that participants in this version of the task had little problem realizing that they had to turn over both the *beer* and the *16* cards. Instead of using the rules of logic, they used their knowledge of state drinking laws.

## Framing Decisions

A key factor that determines how well we reason is how we *frame* a decision (Kahneman, 2003). A decision frame defines not only the decision to be made, but also the alternative possible outcomes and the criteria for a good decision (Bazerman, 1997; Russo & Schoemaker, 1989, 2002). Depending on how a decision is framed, the exact same outcome will seem more or less appealing to us. For example, people tend to view losses as more important than gains. Say you are a doctor faced with a new epidemic. The drug company gives you a choice between two new experimental drugs. WonderDrug-A will save 1,000 lives, whereas WonderDrug-B has a 33% chance of saving 3,000 lives but a 67% chance of saving no lives. Which would you choose? Most people go for the first alternative, even though statistically the two outcomes are the same. But now think about a decision framed this way: WonderDrug-X will lead to the loss of 2,000 lives, whereas WonderDrug-Y brings a 67% chance of losing no lives but a 33% chance of losing 6,000 lives. Again, the outcomes are the same statistically, but now the second choice is more palatable for most people. People avoid risk when it comes to thinking about possible gains, but actually prefer risk when it comes to avoiding losses (Druckman, 2001; Kahneman & Tversky, 1979, 1984; Tversky & Kahneman, 1992).

Many supermarkets provide free food samples to shoppers. But is more always better? Not according to one set of researchers. When they gave shoppers a selection of either 6 or 24 different jams to sample, the majority of shoppers surprisingly opted for the smaller selection (Iyengar & Lepper, 2000). These researchers concluded that too many choices result in too much cognitive effort, which people find aversive.

# Heuristics and Biases: Cognitive Illusions?

If the laws of logic lead to inescapable conclusions, why do people make errors in reasoning? The answer is implied in the question: because people do not always use the laws of logic, but rely instead on sets of heuristics. While often useful, these heuristics, or short-cut strategies, sometimes steer us to the wrong conclusions (Kahneman, 2003). Amos Tversky and Daniel Kahneman performed the ground-breaking studies of such errors—which earned Kahneman a Nobel Prize in 2002 (Tversky unfortunately did not live to see his work so honored).

## Representativeness

The **representativeness heuristic** assumes that the more similar something is to a prototype stored in memory, the more likely it is that the thing belongs to the category of the prototype. Tversky and Kahneman (1974) asked participants to read this passage:

> Jack is a 45-year-old man. He is married and has four children. He is generally conservative, careful, and ambitious. He shows no interest in political and social issues and spends most of his free time on his many hobbies, including home carpentry, sailing, and mathematical puzzles.

The participants were then told that Jack was selected at random from a group of 100 people, all of whom were either lawyers or engineers. Here's the trick: Half of the participants were told that 70 members of the group were lawyers and 30 were engineers; the other participants were told that 30 members of the group were lawyers and 70 engineers. Pause for a moment and imagine that there are 100 balls in a jug, 70 red and 30 black, randomly mixed up. Imagine shutting your eyes and drawing out one ball. Do you think you would be more likely to pluck out a red one than a black one? Sure.

Representativeness heuristic: The heuristic that the more similar something is to a prototype stored in memory, the more likely it is to belong to the prototype's category.

**Base-rate rule:** The rule stating that if something is chosen from a set at random, the chances that the thing will be of a particular type are directly proportional to the percentage of that type in the larger set.

Now reverse the colors, so that 70 are black and 30 red. Now you would be more likely to pull out a black one. However, when asked to decide whether Jack, who was selected at random from the group, was a lawyer or an engineer, the great majority of all participants, no matter what they had been told about the constitution of the group, said he was an engineer. The description of Jack, especially his interest in mathematical puzzles, fit the participants' ideas about the characteristics of engineers better than it fit their ideas about lawyers, and thus they labeled Jack "engineer" because he matched the prototype.

The participants in Tversky and Kahneman's study used their knowledge—or assumptions—about typical properties of people in different professions to make their decision, ignoring the **base-rate rule**. This rule states that if something is at random from a set, the chances of that thing's being a particular type are directly proportional to the percentage of that type in the larger set. Our failure to appreciate the working of this rule can be thought of as a *cognitive illusion*.

Gigerenzer, however, argues that people do not often have true cognitive illusions, but instead simply have trouble understanding descriptions of probabilities. Gigerenzer and his colleagues (1988) performed an experiment that ensured that the participants understood the information about the proportions of different professions included in the larger set under consideration. The researchers took 10 slips of paper and on each one wrote a description of a person and the person's profession. Seven slips had one profession written on it, and three had another; the slips were folded and put in an urn. Each participant drew out a single slip and read the description (but not the profession), and then guessed the profession. In this situation, the participants did well, proving themselves able to keep in mind the relative proportions of the two professions. According to Gigerenzer and colleagues, in earlier experiments, such as the one with Jack, participants did not understand the proportions of the two professions well enough to override their prior knowledge about types of people; they categorized Jack based on prior knowledge, not probability (additional support for this conclusion is provided by Goodie & Fantino, 1996).

Gigerenzer (1994, 2002) and his colleagues (Hoffrage et al., 2002) claim that people judge probabilities by thinking about how often events occur (Estes, 1976); people are very good at remembering frequencies (Hasher & Zacks, 1979, 1984). So if they have trouble understanding probabilities, they may rely on their knowledge of relative frequencies of the different choices. Gigerenzer argues that this makes perfect sense because we humans can more easily understand frequencies than probabilities. For example, consider three probabilities: .01 that a 40-year-old woman has breast cancer, .9 that she'll test positive on a mammogram if she does in fact have

Culture affects the heuristics people use to anticipate changes over time. Americans tend to think that things will continue as they have, whereas Chinese tend to think that situations regularly change over time. For example, when shown a graph that illustrated a trend (such as global economic growth over several years) and asked to extrapolate this trend into the future, Americans tended to preserve the direction and rate, whereas Chinese often changed the direction and rate (Ji et al., 2001).

the disease, .09 that she'll test positive even if she doesn't have it (a "false positive"). People can absorb this information more effectively if, instead of the probabilities, they are simply told that "only one woman in 10 who tests positive actually has breast cancer" (Gigerenzer, 2002). However, research results suggest that when people cannot use prior knowledge about how often events occur (for example, in thinking about events that only happen once, such as the destruction of the World Trade Center), people use reasoning heuristics such as representativeness. The bottom line is that people use different strategies in different situations—sometimes heuristics, sometimes relative frequencies, and sometimes other kinds of information (Ayton & Wright, 1994; Gigerenzer, 1996; Gigerenzer & Goldstein, 1996; Kahneman & Tversky, 1996; Teigen, 1994; Vranas, 2000).

## Availability

Another shortcut is the **availability heuristic**, which is the tendency to judge objects or events as more likely, common, or frequent if they are easier to bring to mind. For example, Tversky and Kahneman (1974) asked people to judge the relative proportions of English words that begin with the letter *k* and words with *k* in the third position. What do you think? Most of the participants in the study thought that *k* occurred more often as a first letter than a third letter, but in fact almost three times as many words have *k* in the third position as in the first one. Why this error? Because it is much easier to bring to mind words starting with *k* than words that have *k* in the third position. Similarly, when given a list of names of famous men and not famous women, people later will mistakenly remember that there were more men than women on the list (or vice versa, if given names of famous women and not famous men; McKelvie, 2000). The availability heuristic may also explain why people tend to think that infrequent but highly memorable events, such as murders and plane crashes, are more common than they really are, and that more frequent but mundane killers, such as stomach cancer and stroke, are less common.

The availability heuristic affects how we evaluate many sorts of information. For instance, researchers have found that the final phases of a painful experience are likely to be most available to memory, which leads to a counterintuitive prediction: In some situations, normal people will prefer more pain to less, provided that the pain tapers off at the end. In one study, participants put their hands into 14°C water, which they endured for 60 seconds. In another condition, after 60 seconds of immersion at this temperature, the water was gradually warmed to 15°C (which is still painful) over the course of 30 seconds. The participants were then asked which condition they would prefer to repeat. Most said they would prefer to have their hands in very cold water for a longer duration than a shorter duration (thus objectively suffering more total pain), provided that the final 30 seconds were less painful in the longer session (Kahneman et al., 1993).

These findings are not just a laboratory curiosity: In a subsequent study, instead of measuring responses to ice water, researchers asked patients to judge the pain of a colonoscopy, a medical procedure in which a monitoring instrument is inserted through the anus to observe the intestines (Redelmeier & Kahneman, 1996); consistent with the findings from the ice water study, the amount of pain the patients judged for the entire procedure depended largely on how they judged the final 3 minutes. As aversive as it may sound, a colonoscopy is a crucial test for those over 50 years old; it can detect colon cancer soon enough to prevent it from spreading. Knowing that patients are more likely to return for a later checkup if a procedure was less painful in the final 3 minutes, should doctors inflict a few minutes of additional (but diminished) pain after the procedure is actually complete? True, this added pain would be less severe than what came before, but it's still added pain. And is it appropriate to distort intentionally a patient's judgment of the overall amount of pain?

# Emotions and Decision Making: Having a Hunch

Einstein was once upset with himself for being "provoked into making a caustic reply." His emotions apparently got the better of him (Clark, 1971, pp. 263–264), and he vowed not to let that happen again. *Star Trek*'s Mr. Spock and Albert Einstein seemed to agree:

If you have ever budgeted time to work on a paper and then run out of hours way too soon, you may have fallen victim to the *planning fallacy*: the tendency to underestimate the time it takes to accomplish a task. This error may arise because the completion of similar tasks is more available in your memory than is their duration. The good news is that the planning fallacy can be reduced by thinking carefully about how long past projects actually took to complete (Buehler et al., 1994).

**Availability heuristic:** The tendency to judge objects or events as more likely, common, or frequent if they are easier to bring to mind.

*Star Trek*'s Mr. Spock underestimated the power of emotion, including its positive role in reasoning.

Emotion clouds reason and distorts our ability to be objective. Doesn't it? Well, not exactly. Researchers have found that sometimes emotion can actually help reasoning (Martinez-Miranda & Aldea, 2005). Bechara and colleagues (1997) found that people played a gambling game better once they had "hunches," even though they were not aware of the bases of the hunches. Evidence of a hunch was detected by the researchers as a skin-conductance response. Such a response occurred when the brain signaled the body that certain choices were risky before the participant consciously realized it. But perhaps the most interesting results concern the contrast between the normal participants and patients who had damage to the ventral medial frontal lobes (that is, the lower middle parts of the frontal lobes), parts of the brain known to play a crucial role in using emotional information to guide behavior (Damasio, 1994, 1996). These patients never showed skin-conductance responses prior to making a choice and never expressed having a hunch. By the end of the experiment, even the normal people who never consciously figured out the situation still tended to choose properly, whereas the brain-damaged patients never did. In fact, when normal people lose in a gambling game, the medial frontal cortex (an area near the damaged region in the patients tested by Bechara and colleagues) responds to each loss within a quarter of a second—well before a person could be aware of it—and responds increasingly strongly as losses build up (Gehring & Willoughby, 2002).

Such emotional responses may underlie what we mean by *intuition*. having an idea that is not easy to express. These responses appear to be based on implicit memories (see Chapter 7) and nudge conscious decision making. Without such nudges, people do not choose wisely. In real life, patients with damage to the ventral medial frontal lobes squander their money, have erratic personal lives, and may fight with coworkers. Perhaps Einstein understood this role of emotion when, contemplating politics, he commented that he hadn't realized "how much more powerful is instinct compared to intelligence" (Clark, 1971, p. 198).

However, Einstein and Mr. Spock weren't all wrong about emotion and reasoning: It is true that negative emotion can sometimes disrupt reasoning (Goel & Dolan, 2003; Gray, 1999). For example, in his second game against the chess-playing computer Deep Blue, the world champion Garry Kasparov became shaken by the unexpectedly strong performance of the computer and resigned when he still could have managed a draw (Chabris, personal communication, 1999). Schwartz and Bless (1992) summarize much evidence showing that emotions, both positive and negative, play a key role in many forms of reasoning. In fact, even reasoning about statements that describe positive emotions can be less accurate than reasoning about neutral material (Blanchette & Richards, 2004).

# LOOKING AT LEVELS

## The Ultimatum Game

On a typical day, each of us interacts with a number of other people, threading our way through competing goals and desires. Researchers who investigate how people make decisions in social interactions have found it useful to study how people play games together. One of the simplest games is called the Ultimatum Game. Here's how it works. Typically, two people play. One is the "proposer" and one is the "responder." The proposer is given an amount of money (say, $10), and instructed to tell the responder how he or she wants to divide up the money; the proposer issues a take-it-or-leave-it proposal (the "ultimatum"). If the responder accepts, the two players divide up the amount accordingly—but if the responder refuses, they each receive nothing. In either case, as soon as the responder has decided, the game ends.

Here's why the game is interesting: Logically, if you were the responder you should accept any proposal—something is better than nothing, right? Wrong. Think about this: How would you respond if someone offered to split $10 by giving you a dime, and keeping $9.90 for himself? Or what if $1000 were at stake, and you were offered $10? In such situations, most responders refuse. In fact, even when 20% of the total is offered by the proposer, about half of responders in the Western world turn down the deal (Guth et al., 1982; Thaler, 1988).

Why do responders behave as they do in the Ultimatum Game? Let's examine the results of a study by Sanfey and colleagues (2003) to better understand responders' behavior from a levels-of-analysis perspective. The investigators used fMRI to scan the brains of responders while they played against a human proposer, a computer program that made proposals, or a "roulette wheel" (which produced random offers; this was the control condition). The offers were fair (split down the middle) or unfair (biased to favor the proposer). One finding was that the responders turned down very unfair offers ($1 or $2, out of $10) more often when the offers were made by humans than when they were from the computer or via the roulette wheel. This finding shows that such decisions are not made purely on the basis of the amount of money involved.

At the level of the brain, another finding was that the anterior (front) insula cortex was more strongly activated by unfair offers from humans than those from the computer or roulette wheel. This brain area registers input from the effects of the autonomic nervous system on the body; if you have a "gut reaction" (so to speak), it is likely to activate this brain area. In fact, this brain area responded more strongly to the most unfair ($1) proposal than to even a slightly less unfair ($2) proposal. Moreover, this area was more strongly activated during unfair offers that the responder then chose to turn down than to unfair offers that were accepted. Sanfey and colleagues argue that the unfair offers elicited an emotional response, reflected by activity in this area, and that this response could prompt the responder to refuse the offer.

But this finding pushes the question back a step: Why do we have these emotional responses? Turning to the level of the person, many researchers believe that our motivation in the Ultimatum Game is rooted in a sense of fairness; we prefer to go down in flames rather than allow ourselves to be taken advantage of (Pillutla & Murnighan, 1996). But keep in mind that not everyone reacts the same way in this situation. For example, Brandstätter and Königstein (2001) found that people who had (according to the personality test they administered) emotionally unstable (that is, anxious) and extroverted (that is, outgoing) personalities or who had emotionally stable (that is, not anxious) and introverted (that is, withdrawn) personalities were most likely to reject proposals. They suggest that these rejections are "angry retaliation" to proposers who these responders feel are being unfair.

And we must also consider events at the level of the group if we are to understand why responders behave as they do. Consider again the different results Sanfey and colleagues (2003) obtained when responders played against a person versus a computer. Why did they react more strongly to the human proposer? One explanation is that people reject unfair offers in order to punish the proposer. This makes sense if you have to interact with that person again in the future, and don't want to have a reputation as a pushover. However, underscoring the power of events at the level of the group, Henrich and colleagues (2001) found that performance in this game varied dramatically in 15 different "small-scale" (rural) societies they studied, with responders in some societies accepting even very low offers and responders in others rejecting even offers over 50/50! The patterns of performance among these groups appeared to mirror key features of their real-world economic systems.

And, of course, events at the different levels interact: Depending on your personality, different proposals evoke emotional circuits in your brain, which in turn give rise to certain feelings. And those feelings may alter your goals for playing against other people (or a specific person) in the future.

We've so far discussed the Ultimatum Game only from the point of view of the responder, but we can also ask about what makes a proposer behave more or less fairly. At the level of the brain, proposers who have just seen pictures of objects that remind them of business dealings (such as a boardroom table, a man's suit, and a briefcase) offer tougher deals—even though they have no conscious awareness of having been "primed" by the objects to think competitively (Kay et al., 2004). At the level of the person, proposers who score highly on measures of "independence" and "tough-mindedness" ask for a larger share of the pie (Brandstätter & Königstein, 2001). However, Ketelaar and Au (2003) found that proposers who reported feeling guilty after playing, because they made selfish offers, were likely to be more generous when they played the game a second time. Ketelaar and Au suggest that this negative emotional state provides a kind of information to the person, alerting him or her to the costs of not being cooperative in the future. At the level of the group, theorists (using computer models) have shown that if proposers can learn how responders have behaved in the past, eventually they will alter their behavior to produce fair (50/50) proposals (Nowak et al., 2000). And, as usual, events at the three levels interact: The objects you encounter in your daily life, which in turn prime you, depend partly on where you go and what you do (which depends in part on your motivations and beliefs), and your personality affects the way you will negotiate. Moreover, Henrich and colleagues (2001) found that performance in this game varied dramatically in the different societies they studied, with proposers in two societies actually offering more than half to the responder!

At first glance, these sorts of games appear very simple (and perhaps simple-minded), and it may be surprising to see how many factors influence the way people play them. It may also be surprising to see how much can be learned by studying games such as this one. Researchers argue that these simple situations focus in like a laser beam on key aspects of human nature—and once we understand the underlying principles at work in such games, we can understand real human interactions and problem-solving processes as complex as those that underlie war and peace.

# Test Yourself

1. A common logical error that people make is to seek information that supports their ideas rather than evidence that would invalidate those ideas. This error is called
   a. deductive reasoning.
   b. affirming the consequent.
   c. the confirmation bias.
   d. affirming the antecedent.

2. Unlike deductive reasoning, inductive reasoning can, when all the premises are true,
   a. lead to more reliable conclusions.
   b. lead to false conclusions.
   c. prove a statement to be true or false.
   d. Deductive and inductive reasoning are actually the same.

3. Participants in the Tversky and Kahneman study ignored the reported percentages of professions and chose answers that fit their prototypes. This occurred because the participants
   a. used the representativeness heuristic and the base-rate rule, but chose the wrong base-rates.
   b. used only the base-rate rule.
   c. interpreted the base-rate rule too strictly.
   d. used the representativeness heuristic while ignoring the base-rate rule.

4. What does current research say about the relationship between emotion and reasoning?
   a. Emotion always hinders our reasoning.
   b. Emotion and reasoning do not interact.
   c. Emotion makes us poor problem solvers.
   d. Sometimes, emotions can enhance our reasoning.

# Answers

1. c  2. b  3. d  4. d

# Think It Through!

In what ways do the human weaknesses in logic and decision making reflect other mental processes that actually help us? Can you think of how to use any of the material you just learned to be a better debater? What is the most important aspect of the findings on the framing of decisions?

Do you think the general human weakness in using logic adversely affects world politics? Why or why not?

# REVIEW AND REMEMBER!

## Summary

### I. Language: More Than Meets the Ear

**A.** Both comprehension and production rely on four aspects of language: phonology (proper speech sounds), syntax (rules that govern how different types of words can be combined to form sentences), semantics (meanings of words, phrases, and sentences), and pragmatics (meaning that is indirect or implied).

**B.** Brain damage can disrupt language in various ways. Broca's aphasia primarily (but not exclusively) affects language production, whereas Wernicke's aphasia primarily (but not exclusively) affects language comprehension.

**C.** All meanings of words are initially activated during comprehension, but those that are irrelevant are quickly inhibited (based on the context).

**D.** Young children learn language without explicit instruction. Language is acquired gradually over time. There is probably a critical period for learning grammar and a sensitive period for learning phonology.

**E.** Although it is unlikely that a single gene is involved in the uniquely human ability to use language, it seems probable that genes do, directly or indirectly, have a great influence on this capacity.

**F.** Gestures can help you communicate, largely by freeing up brain areas for cognitive processing, but gestures themselves are not language.

**G.** Animals that are taught to use sign language (which is a true language) may not grasp key aspects of grammar, but some animals have exhibited remarkable abilities to form novel utterances, which reveal the use of simple grammar.

**H.** Adults can learn semantics and pragmatics of a new language as well as children can, but unless people learn a second language early in life, they probably will never use it as well or as "automatically" as they do their first language.

### II. Means of Thought: Words, Images, Concepts

**A.** When thinking, we use words and images as a way of keeping track of thoughts and storing them effectively, like making notations on a pad of paper. Language does not determine thought but may influence it in subtle ways.

## Your Notes

I.

A.

B.

C.

D. *Best to learn grammar & phonology as a young child*

E.

F.

G.

H.

II.

A.

**B.** Objects in visual mental images preserve many of the properties of actual objects, such as spatial extent and relative size; at least some of these properties may arise from characteristics of the brain areas that give rise to imagery.

*B.*

**C.** Thinking cannot rely solely on words or images: Both types of representations are ambiguous, and thoughts are not. If thoughts were based only on words, we would never have difficulty figuring out how to put our thoughts into words; if thoughts were based only on images, we would have trouble thinking about abstractions (such as truth and justice).

*C.*

**D.** Thoughts arise from manipulations of concepts, which specify groupings of objects or events.

*D. Concepts—groupings of objects or events*

**E.** Representations of concepts are unambiguous and can be concrete (such as "bird") or abstract (such as "justice"). Some examples of a concept category are "better" (more typical) than others.

*E.*

**F.** Concepts are organized according to how specific or general they are and according to how they are grouped to apply to a particular situation (via a schema).

*F.*

**G.** Different aspects of concepts—for example, those pertaining to characteristic appearance, movement, or function—may rely on different parts of the brain.

*G.*

## III. Problem Solving

*III.*

**A.** If a problem is not specified appropriately from the outset, it will be difficult to solve.

*A.*

**B.** People can solve problems by using heuristics (short-cut strategies that do not guarantee a correct answer) and algorithms (sets of steps that are guaranteed to produce the answer). People can also use analogies in solving problems.

*B. Heuristics: fast but unreliable*
*Algorithms: slow but sure*

**C.** Both images and words can play important roles in helping you keep track of where you are in a problem and in providing insights into how to proceed.

*C.*

**D.** Sometimes it pays to put a problem aside and let it incubate, but the emergence of insight depends on first having tried different ways to represent the problem.

*D.*

**E.** Cognitive control is required for virtually all complex activities, because such activities rely on coordination of different processes; a number of distinct parts of the brain work together to confer this ability.

*E.*

**F.** Experts develop skills in a particular area, which do not generalize beyond that area. Deliberate practice is essential as a would-be expert learns the relevant information and strategies.

*F.*

**G.** Artificial intelligence (AI) is based on the idea that human mental abilities can be duplicated in a machine, but this has not yet been achieved.

*G.*

**H.** Knowing about the obstacles to problem solving can help you to overcome them.

*H.*

## IV. Logic, Reasoning, and Decision Making

*IV.*

**A.** Reasoning involves seeing what follows from a given set of circumstances and making decisions at pivotal points. Decisions require you to evaluate possible outcomes and choose one alternative or course of action over the others.

*A.*

**B.** People are not, strictly speaking, logical; for example, we fall prey to biases, such as affirming the consequent and the confirmation bias.

**B.**

**C.** The same decision is made in different ways when it is framed differently.

*C. Framing invites different strategies.*

**D.** We often rely on heuristics, such as the availability heuristic, when making decisions. Heuristics often lead us to the correct conclusion faster than we could get there with a step-by-step algorithm; however, they also sometimes lead to errors.

*D.*

**E.** Although many people consider emotion a weakness when reasoning, in fact, emotion often helps us to develop useful hunches and useful intuitions.

*E.*

NOTE: Once you feel that you understand the material in this chapter, visit the book's Web site at www.ablongman.com/kosslyn3e to test your knowledge with additional study questions.

# Key Terms

affirming the consequent, p. 368
algorithm, p. 358
aphasia, p. 329
artificial intelligence (AI), p. 365
availability heuristic, p. 371
base-rate rule, p. 370
basic level, p. 355
Broca's aphasia, p. 329
category, p. 352
child-directed speech (CDS), p. 336
cognitive control, p. 361
concept, p. 352
confirmation bias, p. 368
critical period, p. 341
deductive reasoning, p. 367
deliberate practice, p. 363
empiricism (approach to language), p. 335
functional fixedness, p. 357
grammar, p. 339

heuristic, p. 358
incubation, p. 360
inductive reasoning, p. 367
insight, p. 360
language acquisition device (LAD), p. 335
language comprehension, p. 327
language production, p. 326
linguistic relativity hypothesis, p. 347
logic, p. 367
mental images, p. 348
mental model, p. 367
mental set, p. 365
morpheme, p. 330
nativism (approach to language), p. 335
neural network, p. 365
nonverbal communication, p. 343
overextension, p. 337
overregularization error, p. 340

phoneme, p. 327
phonology, p. 327
pragmatics, p. 332
problem, p. 357
propositional representation, p. 331
prototype, p. 352
representation problem, p. 357
representativeness heuristic, p. 369
schema, p. 355
semantics, p. 330
sensitive period, p. 341
specific language impairment, p. 342
strategy, p. 358
syntax, p. 328
telegraphic speech, p. 339
typicality, p. 352
underextension, p. 337
Wernicke's aphasia, p. 329

# CHAPTER 9

# TYPES OF INTELLIGENCE: WHAT DOES IT MEAN TO BE SMART?

J oanne (J. K.) Rowling's books about the young wizard Harry Potter have catapulted her into the role of international superstar and made her one of the world's wealthiest people. These books are chock full of clever plot twists and novel ideas. For example, the long-dead people in the portraits hanging on the walls throughout Harry's school not only talk, but develop relationships with each other. Photographs are not the inanimate tracings of remembered events, but instead are living entities, whose subjects come and go. Rowling got the idea for Harry Potter in a flash, and she knew from the start that she would write a seven-book series. She took 5 years to plan the series in detail, working out the plots for each of the novels. When she writes each book, "I know what and who's coming when, and it can feel like greeting old friends" (Fraser, 2000, p. 39). Think of it! What does it take to work out the details of seven novels in advance? Especially when you must not only attend to the usual ingredients of story-telling (the characters, the plot, and so on), but also need to create (and keep consistent) a whole new world?

At an early age, it was clear that Joanne Rowling had something special. To hear her tell it, "I was the epitome of a bookish child—short and squat, thick National Health glasses, living in a world of complete daydreams, wrote stories endlessly and occasionally came out of the fog to bully my poor sister and force her to listen to my stories and play the games I'd just invented. . . . I always felt I had to achieve, my hand always had to be the first to go up, I always had to be right" (Smith, 2001, p. 45). She proved more than adept at making up long and complex stories and was extraordinarily inventive. Foreshadowing her later interests, as a child, she made up games of wizards and witches, devising spells and concocting strange brews.

When Rowling was 9 years old, her family moved to a small town in the countryside, which pleased her greatly—except for one thing. She hated her new school, which was something out of an earlier age, with rolltop desks that actually had inkwells. And her strict, formidable new teacher, Mrs. Morgan, was also something of a throwback from another era. Mrs. Morgan inferred the level of intelligence of each child and arranged her classroom so that the bright children (in her estimation) sat on the left side, and the dull children sat on the right. She determined intelligence level in part by having the children take a test at the beginning of the year. This test required solving arithmetic problems that involved fractions. Unfortunately, Rowling had not yet learned fractions at her previous school, and so she achieved the rock-bottom score of zero—which got her a seat at the far right, at the extreme end of the "stupid row" ("I was as far right as you could get without sitting in the playground"; Rowling, 2005). However, Mrs. Morgan could not help but notice that the young Rowling did very well on examinations and asked good questions. Thus, Rowling eventually was moved to the smart side of the room. Unfortunately, in order to make this move, she had to swap seats with her best friend! And thus, "In one short walk across the room I became clever but unpopular" (Rowling, 2005).

Rowling's works attest to the fact that she's unusually bright. Could Mrs. Morgan have done a better job of assessing her students' intelligence at the outset of each year? What does it mean to be "smart," anyway? In this chapter, we discuss the nature of intelligence, intelligence testing, kinds of intelligence, how nature and nurture affect intelligence, mental retardation, giftedness, and, lastly—something at which Rowling excels—creativity.

# MEASURING INTELLIGENCE:
## What Is IQ?

J. K. Rowling wanted to go to the University of Oxford (the premier university in the United Kingdom), but was put on the waiting list and subsequently rejected. She instead attended the University of Exeter. Although she was in no danger of flunking out, she earned only average grades. Was she an underperformer? That is, did she have the ability to do much better, but—for whatever reason—was not strongly motivated? To answer such a question, we would need an objective measure of intelligence. In this section, we explore the nature of intelligence testing.

What does it mean to say that someone is or is not intelligent? Intelligence is certainly not a concrete entity that can be quantified, like the amount of water in a jug; rather, it is a concept. Psychologists have offered many definitions of intelligence, and there is considerable disagreement about what intelligence is and whether it can be accurately measured (Gardner, 2002; Gardner et al., 1996; Sternberg, 1986b, 1990; Sternberg & Detterman, 1986). What most researchers in psychology mean by "intelligence" is pretty close to the standard dictionary definition: **Intelligence** is the ability to solve problems well and to understand and learn complex material. Researchers also typically stress that a key aspect of intelligence is the ability to adapt to the environment (Sternberg, 2000). Intelligence is often associated with mental quickness, but this need not be so; sometimes, still waters do run deep. However, researchers typically assume that "solving problems well" implies "in a reasonable amount of time." There is a limit to how much time you could take when solving a problem or learning complex material and still be considered "intelligent." Virtually all tests of intelligence rely on the as-

**Intelligence:** The ability to solve problems well and to understand and learn complex material.

sumption that intelligent people can solve problems and understand and learn complex material relatively easily, and thus quickly as well.

# A Brief History of Intelligence Testing

**IQ** is short for **intelligence quotient**, a test score used in Western countries as a general measure of intelligence. To understand the meaning of IQ scores, it will be helpful to see how intelligence testing has evolved over time.

## Binet and Simon: Testing to Help

The original test from which modern IQ tests derive had a more specific and different purpose than the modern tests. Responding to a call from the French government, which had recently enacted universal elementary education, a French physician named Alfred Binet (1857–1911) and his collaborator, Theodore Simon (1873–1961), devised the first intelligence test between 1904 and 1911 (Matarazzo, 1972). Their aim was to develop an objective way to identify children in the public schools who needed extra classroom help. They started with the idea that intelligence shows itself in a wide variety of abilities, a perspective that led them to construct a test consisting of many sorts of tasks. Among other things, children were asked to copy a drawing, repeat a string of digits, recognize coins and make change, and explain why a particular statement did not make sense. Binet and Simon assumed that the children's performance on the tests reflected educational experience, and thus that special classes could help those who did poorly.

To assess performance, Binet and Simon first gave the test to a group of normal children of various ages. They noted which problems were solved by most of the 6-year-olds, by most of the 10-year-olds, and so forth; then they compared the performance of other children of the same age with those "normal" scores. So, if a child could solve all of the problems solved by most 9-year-olds, but failed those passed by most 10-year-olds, the child's *mental age (MA)* was said to be 9. Children with a mental age lower than their *chronological age (CA)* were considered relatively slow.

## Terman and Wechsler: Tests for Everyone

Binet and Simon's test was quickly adapted to suit new purposes. In 1916, Lewis Terman and his colleagues at Stanford University developed the Stanford-Binet Revision of the Binet-Simon test, which is still used to test people from age 2 to adulthood. To refine the testing further (especially for adults, by expanding the range at the "top"), to test a wider range of abilities, and to improve the method of scoring and interpreting results, David Wechsler (1958) developed another set of intelligence tests, the **Wechsler Adult Intelligence Scale (WAIS)** and the *Wechsler Intelligence Scale for Children (WISC)*. Today, the WAIS-III and the WISC-III ("III" denoting the third major versions) are the most widely used IQ tests in the United States.

Believing that Binet's test relied too much on verbal skills, Wechsler divided his test into two major parts, summarized in Table 9.1 (p. 382). The *verbal subtests* assess the ability to understand and use language by testing vocabulary, comprehension, and other aspects of verbal skill. The *performance subtests* consist of nonverbal tasks such as arranging pictures in an order that tells a story and spotting the missing element in a picture. Because the performance subtests do not focus on the ability to use and manipulate words, they probably rely less heavily than do the verbal subtests on the test-taker's education or cultural experiences.

**Intelligence quotient (IQ):** A score on an intelligence test, originally based on comparing mental age to chronological age, but later based on norms and used as a measure of general intelligence.

**Wechsler Adult Intelligence Scale (WAIS):** The most widely used intelligence test; consists of both verbal and performance subtests.

The WISC-III is administered to children individually by a trained examiner.

**TABLE 9.1** **WAIS-III Subtests With Simulated Examples of Questions**

## I. Verbal Subtests

- *Vocabulary*: Written and spoken words, which must be defined; the words are ordered in terms of increasing difficulty.
  *Example*: "What does *trek* mean?"

- *Similarities*: Questions that require explaining how the concepts named by two words are similar.
  *Example*: "How are an airplane and a car alike?"

- *Arithmetic*: Problems, all but one presented orally (one involves using blocks); the test is timed.
  *Example*: "If 2 men need 4 days to paint a house, how long would 4 men need?"

- *Digit Span*: Lists of digits, 2–9 numbers long, are presented. The test-taker repeats the digits, either in the same or reverse order.
  *Example*: "6, 1, 7, 5, 3."

- *Information*: Questions that draw on literature, history, general science, and common knowledge.
  *Example*: "Who was Martin Luther King, Jr.?"

- *Comprehension*: Questions that require understanding of social mores and conventions.
  *Example*: "Why are there taxes?"

## II. Performance Subtests

- *Picture Completion*: Drawings of common objects or scenes, each of which is missing a feature. The test-taker must point out what's missing.
  *Example*:
  What is missing?

- *Digit Symbol-Coding*: The test-taker learns a symbol for each of the numbers 1–9 and then sees numbers and must write their appropriate symbols; the test is timed.

  *Example*:

  | Shown: | | | | | Fill in: | | | |
  |---|---|---|---|---|---|---|---|---|
  | 1 | 2 | 3 | 4 | | 4 | 1 | 3 | 2 |
  | + | − | × | ÷ | | __ | __ | __ | __ |

- *Block Design*: Problems that require the test-taker to arrange blocks colored on each side—white, red, or half white and half red—to reproduce a white-and-red pattern in a fixed amount of time.
  *Example*:
  Assemble blocks to match this design:

- *Matrix Reasoning*: Items that require the test-taker to study a progression of stimuli in a sequence from which a section is missing. The test-taker must choose which of 5 given possibilities completes the sequence (for an example of a similar task, see page 398).

- *Picture Arrangement*: Sets of cards that must be arranged to tell a story.
  *Example*:
  Put the pictures in the right order.

This version is intended for people aged 16 to 89. Three additional tests are included as "spares," to be used if there are problems in administering the basic set summarized here.

# Scoring IQ Tests: Measuring the Mind

Modern IQ tests have been modified from earlier versions both in the nature of their tasks and in the way they are scored. Binet and Simon were satisfied with simply knowing whether a child was below or at par for his or her age, but later researchers wanted a more precise measure of the degree of intelligence. Early in the 20th century, William Stern, a German psychologist, developed the idea of an *intelligence quotient* (*IQ*), computed by dividing mental age (MA) by chronological age (CA) and multiplying by 100 to avoid fractional scores:

$$IQ = (MA/CA) \times 100$$

Thus, a score of 100 meant that a child's mental age exactly matched the child's chronological age. Computing IQ scores using the MA/CA ratio presents a major disadvantage, however: Because mental age does not keep developing forever, whereas chronological age marches on, test-takers cannot help but appear to become less intelligent as they age. For example, if your mental age is 25 and you are 25 years old, you would be average; but if your mental age is the same in 5 years, your IQ would drop from 100 to 83, even though you are just as smart at 30 as you were at 25. And at 40, your IQ would be about 62. But people do not actually become stupider with age. Therefore, today's IQ tests are scored not by using the MA/CA ratio but by specifying how a test-taker's performance stands relative to that of other people of the same age. A score of 100 is set as the average score.

## Interpreting IQ Scores: Standardized Samples and Norming

Although the average IQ score is set at 100, most people do not score at this precise level. How can we interpret the meaning of scores above or below this benchmark? IQ test scores are based on a large **standardized sample**, a random selection of people from the appropriate population. In this sense, a *population* is defined as a group of people who share one or more specific characteristics, such as age, sex, or any other relevant attributes. Almost always, scores are spread along a normal distribution, illustrated in Figure 9.1. When the distribution of scores follows a normal distribution, most scores fall near the middle, with gradually fewer scores toward either extreme (see Chapter 2). After the test has been given to a standardized sample of people, the developers "norm" the test to make it easy to interpret the meaning of any one test-taker's score relative to the others. **Norming** a test involves setting two measures: The first is the mean, or average; the mean of an IQ test is set at 100. The second is the standard deviation, which indicates the degree to which the individual scores deviate from the mean. The greater the number of standard deviations from the mean, the farther above or below the score is from the mean (see Chapter 2). If the scores fall into a normal distribution, a certain percentage of them occur within each standard deviation from the mean, as shown in Figure 9.1 on p. 384 (each marked unit on the bottom corresponds to one standard deviation).

For the WAIS-III IQ test, scores are adjusted so that a standard deviation is 15 points. As shown in Figure 9.1, about two thirds of all people have IQs from 85 to 115 points (that is, within one standard deviation above or below the mean), but only a bit more than a quarter have IQs either between 70 and 85 or between 115 and 130 (within the second standard deviation above or below the mean). Only 4.54% of IQ scores are above 130 or below 70.

**Standardized sample:** A random selection of people, drawn from a carefully defined population.

**Norming:** The process of setting the mean and the standard deviation of a set of test scores, based on results from a standardized sample.

## FIGURE 9.1

### The Normal Curve and WAIS-III IQ Scores

Because of its shape, the normal curve is also known as the *bell curve*. In nature, most characteristics clump around the midpoint, and progressively fewer have very high or very low measures. This diagram indicates the percentage of people who have scores on the WAIS-III IQ test that fall within different regions of the distribution.

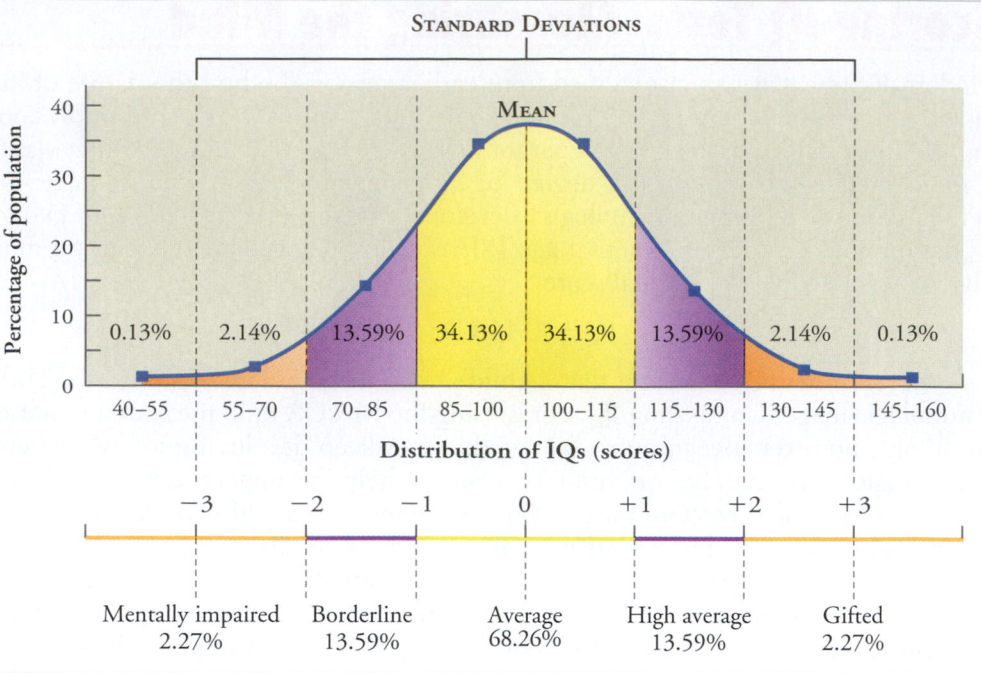

MEAN

| 0.13% | 2.14% | 13.59% | 34.13% | 34.13% | 13.59% | 2.14% | 0.13% |

| 40–55 | 55–70 | 70–85 | 85–100 | 100–115 | 115–130 | 130–145 | 145–160 |

Distribution of IQs (scores)

$-3$ $\quad$ $-2$ $\quad$ $-1$ $\quad$ $0$ $\quad$ $+1$ $\quad$ $+2$ $\quad$ $+3$

| Mentally impaired 2.27% | Borderline 13.59% | Average 68.26% | High average 13.59% | Gifted 2.27% |

## Reliability and Validity

For IQ scores to be meaningful or useful, the test must be *reliable*. A reliable test produces consistent results; that is, if you test the same group of people on two occasions, the two sets of scores will be highly positively correlated. The WAIS-III has been shown to be highly reliable. In addition, a useful test must be *valid*. A valid test measures what it is supposed to measure. Do IQ tests really measure intelligence; do they measure the ability to solve problems well and to understand and learn complex material? One way to find out whether IQ tests in fact measure intelligence is to see whether scores on these tests are related to measures of performance for other tasks that seem to require intelligence, which we consider next.

Achievement is only partly determined by intelligence; motivation is also important. Subcultures differ in the degree to which they value education, and thus the degree to which their members are strongly motivated to obtain education.

# IQ and Achievement: IQ in the Real World

More than likely, IQ scores would have ceased to interest us long ago if they did not somehow relate to performance in the real world. In the United States, people with higher IQ scores, particularly on the verbal subtests, earn higher grade point averages overall in high school and college (Cronbach, 1990; Jensen, 1980; Snow & Yalow, 1982). IQ also predicts job success to some extent (Cronbach, 1990; Wagner, 1997). People with higher IQs tend to land higher-prestige jobs and make more money; they are also more likely to enjoy stable marriages and to stay out of jail (Herrnstein & Murray, 1994). In fact, measures of intelligence taken at age 11 predict how old people will be when they die—and even whether they will succumb to heart disease or some forms of cancer (Deary et al., 2004).

Although IQ does in fact predict success on the job, this does not mean that everybody who is successful at work has a high IQ; nor are all people with high IQs necessarily successful. Correlations between IQ and job performance show that, at most, only about a quarter of the variation in job success can be predicted by IQ (Hunter, 1983; Jensen, 1980; Schmidt & Hunter, 2004; Streufert & Swezey, 1986). This means that the lion's share of that variation reflects something else. For example, the personality traits of conscientiousness and integrity also (in addition to IQ) predict success on the job (Schmidt & Hunter, 2004). Moreover, motivation, ambition, education, and other factors may figure into the mix (Lubinski, 2000, 2004), but such factors probably play less of a role than you might think (Gagné & St. Père, 2001). However, culture clearly plays a role. For example, Asian cultures, with their strong family bonds and emphasis on hard work, foster achievement (Stevenson et al., 1986), and IQ scores underpredict job success among Japanese and Chinese Americans (Flynn, 1991, 1999a, 1999b).

## Test Yourself

1. With Binet and Simon's intelligence testing, children were considered relatively slow if their
   a. chronological age was less than their mental age.
   b. chronological age was greater than their mental age.
   c. chronological age and mental age were the same.
   d. IQ was below 100.
2. Wechsler devised two intelligence tests—one for children and one for adults—which are known, respectively, as
   a. WAIS and WISC.        c. WISC and WISC-Adult.
   b. Stanford–Binet and WAIS.   d. WISC and WAIS.
3. Validity is related to the legitimacy of an intelligence test, whereas reliability is related more to the _____ of such a test.
   a. consistency        c. conciseness
   b. interpretability       d. clarity

4. A child's IQ score is a single number that
   a. indicates performance on tasks of different types.
   b. has no relationship to real-world intelligence.
   c. implies only one type of intelligence.
   d. is perfectly correlated with later job achievement in a surprisingly wide range of occupations.

## Answers

1.b  2.d  3.a  4.a

NOTE: Once you feel comfortable with the Test Yourself questions in this chapter, visit the book's Web site at www.ablongman.com/kosslyn3e for additional study questions.

## Think It Through!

Can you think of ways in which making all high school students take an IQ test would be potentially harmful? Helpful? Would it be more useful to have students tested in elementary school? Why or why not?

Based on what you learned in Chapters 6–8, what sorts of factors should influence the ability to solve problems well and to understand and learn complex material? If you were going to try to measure "intelligence," would you stress some kinds of abilities over others?

# ANALYZING INTELLIGENCE:
## One Ability or Many?

J. K. Rowling was an A-student in English and French in high school, but was—at best—only average in physics, and she confesses that to this day she has trouble understanding science (which may be why explanations for her characters' magical abilities are conspicuously absent in the Harry Potter novels). Why would she (or any of us) do well in one school subject, but poorly in another? To answer this question, we need to delve deeper into the nature of intelligence.

As noted earlier, in the United States, a high IQ score predicts, to some degree, success in school and in life. To interpret these findings, we need to know more about what, precisely, IQ tests measure. Is there some general ability, some basic intelligence, that determines IQ score? And do IQ tests tap everything meant by "intelligence"?

# Psychometric Approaches: IQ, *g*, and Specialized Abilities

How do researchers determine whether IQ scores reflect some basic, overall type of intelligence or a collection of various cognitive abilities, such as the ability to identify patterns or make use of previously learned information? Psychologists who have investigated this question have used a *psychometric approach*; they have designed tests to measure psychological characteristics and have devised ways to use correlations and other statistical techniques to analyze the results from such tests.

## Spearman's *g* Factor

Today's IQ tests include a variety of subtests, such as the picture completion, vocabulary, block design, and arithmetic subtests included in the WAIS-III. It turns out that people who do well on one subtest tend to do well on others; that is, scores on these different types of tests are positively correlated (Deary, 2000; Gottfredson, 1997; Jensen, 1998). This finding has led researchers to infer that there is a single form of intelligence that cuts across the various subtests. Early in the last century, British psychologist Charles Spearman (1927) argued that the positive correlations among scores on different types of mental tests indicate the existence of a single underlying intellectual capacity, which he labeled **g**, for "general factor." Spearman developed a new statistical tool to analyze sets of test scores, called factor analysis. **Factor analysis** is a method that uncovers the particular attributes (factors) that make scores more or less similar. A factor analysis of the correlations among different measures of performance shows, for example, that speed of processing is one important factor in many tasks, and the amount of information that can be held in working memory (see Chapter 7) is another. When he analyzed the correlations among various test scores, Spearman found that the first, and most important, factor underlying test performance was *g*. Subsequently, researchers have found that estimates of *g* taken from different sets of tests reflect the same underlying common ingredient; these separate estimates are almost perfectly correlated with each other (Johnson et al., 2004).

But if intelligence is simply *g*, then all of the scores from the different subtests should be correlated to the same degree. This is not the case: Spearman also noted a wide variation in the sizes of the correlations, which he took to reflect the influence of "specific factors," or *s*. When you perform a task, according to Spearman, you are drawing on *g* as well as on a particular type of ability, *s*, specific to that task. For example, spelling draws on a specialized ability, which is largely independent of other abilities. Some tasks, such as being able to analyze Shakespeare, rely more on *g* than on *s*; others, such as discriminating musical tones, rely more on a particular *s* than on *g*. Factor analysis documented the existence of these specific factors, and also showed that they are less important than *g* for predicting performance. In Spearman's view, IQ scores de-

*g*: "General factor," a single intellectual capacity that underlies the positive correlations among different tests of intelligence.

Factor analysis: A statistical method that uncovers the particular attributes (factors) that make scores more or less similar; the more similar the scores, the more strongly implicated are shared underlying factors.

*s*: "Specific factors," or aspects of performance that are particular to a given kind of processing—and distinct from *g*.

pend mostly on *g*; how smart you are overall depends on how much of this general intellectual capacity you have.

## Thurstone's Primary Mental Abilities

A second perspective on what IQ scores reflect came from Louis L. Thurstone (1938). Thurstone devised a battery of 56 tests and then analyzed the correlations of scores on these tests using Spearman's method of factor analysis. Thurstone found that how well you can do arithmetic has little if anything to do with how well you can notice whether a scene has changed or how well you can figure out the best way to get home when traffic is heavy (Thurstone & Thurstone, 1941). Instead of believing in a single general capacity, such as *g*, Thurstone found evidence that intelligence consists of seven separate **primary mental abilities**, fundamental abilities that are the components of intelligence and that are not outgrowths of other abilities. Verbal comprehension and spatial visualization are two of Thurstone's primary mental abilities.

In the decades since Thurstone proposed his list of primary abilities, other researchers seeking to discover the facets of intelligence have analyzed and reanalyzed similar sets of test results with varying results. Some (such as J. P. Guilford, 1967) have reported finding more than a hundred distinct factors that underlie intelligence.

## Cattell and Horn's Fluid and Crystallized Intelligences

One especially influential alternative to Thurstone's approach was proposed by Raymond B. Cattell (1971), and then developed further by his student and collaborator John Horn (1985, 1986, 1989, 1994; Horn & Cattell, 1966; Horn & Noll, 1997). These researchers suggested that instead of possessing a single general capacity, *g*, people possess two general types of intelligence: fluid and crystallized. **Fluid intelligence** is the ability to reason without relying heavily on previously learned knowledge or procedures ("a person's mental horsepower, the ability to solve cognitive problems on the spot"; Gottfredson, 2003a, p. 350). Fluid intelligence would be used to figure out novel solutions, such as how to write when a pen or pencil isn't available (one creative songsmith scribbled the lyrics to a new rock tune using the heads of burnt matches). Fluid intelligence can be measured with tests that do not rely on language, and thus some researchers have argued that it may reflect a fairer, less culturally bound measure of intelligence (Athanasiou, 2000; Braden, 2000). In contrast, **crystallized intelligence** relies on using previously learned information and procedures to reason [it is the "very general skills (e.g., language) that have been developed—crystallized—from exercising fluid *g* in the past"; Gottfredson, 2003a, p. 350]. This is the sort of intelligence that develops as you become an expert in an area. If you make good use of your college experience, you should boost your crystallized intelligence.

A variety of factors affect fluid and crystallized intelligence differently. For example, as we age, crystallized intelligence does not suffer much, if at all, whereas fluid intelligence deteriorates; we are still able to maintain our expertise in areas of strength, but the ability to shift gears quickly to solve new problems tends to decrease (Horn, 1985, 1986, 1994; Horn & Noll, 1994; Salthouse, 1996). In addition, the two forms of intelligence develop at different rates during childhood, appear to rely on different brain structures, and are not equally heritable (Horn & Masunaga, 2000; Horn & Noll, 1997); also, different facets of academic achievement are predicted by the two forms of intelligence (Evans et al., 2002). These sorts of findings provide evidence that the

**Primary mental abilities:** According to Thurstone, seven fundamental abilities that are the components of intelligence and are not outgrowths of other abilities.

**Fluid intelligence:** According to Cattell and Horn, the kind of intelligence that underlies the creation of novel solutions to problems.

**Crystallized intelligence:** According to Cattell and Horn, the kind of intelligence that relies on knowing facts and having the ability to use and combine them.

For the veteran angler, fishing consists of well-worn routines (such as putting the bait on the hook, casting the line in the water, knowing when to yank and when to wait, reeling in the fish, and so on), and thus it relies on crystallized intelligence. But what would happen if you didn't have bait, a hook, line, and sinker? You would need fluid intelligence to figure out how to catch fish.

TABLE 9.2

## Fluid Versus Crystallized Intelligence

| Fluid Intelligence | Crystallized Intelligence |
| --- | --- |
| Ability to reason about novel situations and to solve novel problems | Ability to reason using previously learned procedures |
| Ability to abstract concepts on the basis of new information or procedures | Ability to use factual knowledge acquired through education and experience |
| Ability to use reasoning that does not depend primarily on learning and acculturation | Ability to use reasoning that is based on learning and acculturation |
| Ability to manipulate abstract concepts, rules, and generalizations and to use logical relations | Ability to use language to communicate |

two types of intelligence are, in fact, distinct; if there were only a single form of intelligence, such factors should show the same effects on the two proposed sets of abilities. After the discovery of crystallized and fluid intelligences, Cattell and Horn provided evidence for a number of other "broad" factors (Jensen, 1998). Key characteristics of fluid and crystallized intelligences are summarized in Table 9.2.

## Carroll's Three-Stratum Theory of Cognitive Ability

John B. Carroll produced a landmark book in 1993, in which he reanalyzed massive amounts of test data (from over 450 high-quality studies). He found that the relations among test scores are neatly structured into a three-strata hierarchy (of the sort developed earlier by Gustafsson, 1984), shown in Figure 9.2. At the top of the hierarchy is g, and immediately under it are eight broad cognitive abilities (which include fluid and crystallized intelligences). Each of these broad abilities is infused with g, which is why they are placed under g in the diagram. And each of the broad abilities is, in turn, drawn on by narrow abilities, which are listed at the bottom of Figure 9.2.

We must stress that explaining performance in any specific task requires citing factors in all three tiers. For example, Deary (2000, drawing on the work of Carroll, 1993) discusses the ability to produce ideas. A test of this ability might require you to name as many red things as possible in a few minutes. To understand why different classmates name different numbers of red objects (that is, to understand the variation in performance), you would need to understand the roles of g (which has been shown to account for about half the variation in performance in this task), of the broad factor of general retrieval ability, and of the narrow factor of ideational fluency (which is specific to this simple task and shown at the very bottom of Figure 9.2).

This hierarchical structure of intelligence is a grand synthesis of the earlier theories, fitting them all into a single framework. For example, this structure allows us to understand fluid and crystallized intelligences by noting that they are somewhat—but not entirely—distinct. Because they have unique aspects, factors such as aging can affect them differently; but because they also both draw on g, they are highly correlated.

Many subsequent studies have supported the picture Carroll painted (Deary, 2000), and it's fair to say that almost all researchers in the field now accept a three-stratum hierarchical theory of the structure of intelligence. However, two areas of debate persist. First, Horn and his colleagues continue to maintain that fluid and crystallized intelligences sit at the apex of the hierarchy, not a single g (which would mean that there should be two nodes at the very top). They argue that the correlation between the two kinds of intelligence (which is the basis for Carroll's assuming that both fluid and crystallized intelligences include g) arises because virtually all human behavior draws on both sorts of intelligence—and thus the results of measuring such behavior cannot help but reflect both. Second, Lubinski (2004), Snow (1994, 1996), and others have argued that the middle tier can be boiled down further, namely, to quantitative, spatial, and verbal abilities. In this view, g accounts for about half the variability on a wide range of tests, and each of these three more specific abilities accounts for between 8% and 10% of the remaining variability.

FIGURE 9.2

# Carroll's Three-Stratum Theory of the Structure of Intelligence

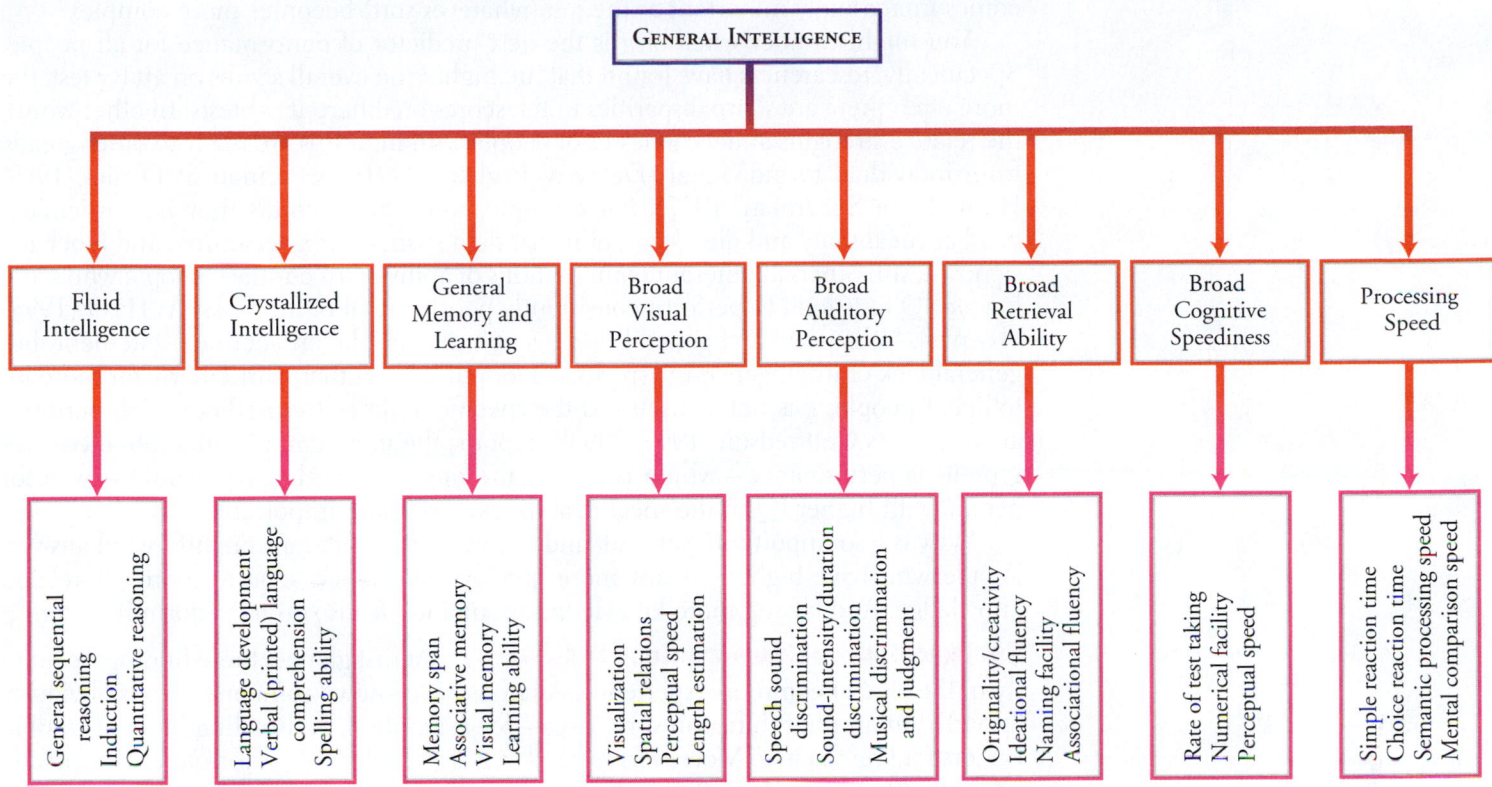

At the top of the hierarchy is *g*, a general intelligence that permeates all other mental abilities (such as general memory retrieval). The *broad abilities* capture variations on a set of highly related tests, and each of these eight abilities in turn is drawn on by the narrow *specific abilities* (such as ideational fluency, which is the ease of producing new ideas). Only selected examples of these specific abilities are included here; there are 69 in all.

## The *g* Factor and Specific Abilities in the Real World

Many researchers have attempted to predict job performance by considering both specific abilities and *g*. Although some specific abilities do predict performance to some extent (Hunter & Hunter, 1984; Lubinski, 2004; Shea et al., 2001), by and large, the heavy lifting is accomplished by *g* and—almost—by *g* alone (Gottfredson, 2003b). Perhaps counterintuitively, the measure of "general mental ability" predicts not just how well someone will do in the classroom, but also in the corporate office and even on the construction site (Kuncel et al., 2004). In fact, Schmidt and Hunter (1998, 2004) report that performance in a very wide range of occupations is predicted by *g*, and very little (if at all) by specific abilities.

At first glance, this finding is surprising, given how widely occupations differ. But think of it this way: Imagine a very easy factory job, putting a widget on a peg, over and over. Now think of a slightly more complex version, where there are three kinds of widgets, and you need to decide which peg each one goes on. Now think of an even more complex version, with 10 sorts of widgets, some of which have to be placed in specific positions relative to others. As the complexity of the job goes up, so does the extent to which performance relies on *g*. Now imagine an intellectual job, such as writing a report. Again, as the complexity goes up, so does the extent to which performance relies on g. The same g underlies performance on all sorts of jobs, and it becomes increasingly important as the job (whatever sort) becomes more complex.

You might wonder whether g is the best predictor of performance for all people. Specifically, researchers have found that the higher the overall scores on an IQ test, the more often there are sharp disparities in the scores on different subtests: In other words, the relative strengths and weaknesses of people with high IQs are likely to differ greatly from individual to individual (Deary & Pagliari, 1991; Detterman & Daniel, 1989; Hunt, 1995; Spearman, 1927). For example, some high scorers may be particularly good at vocabulary and digit span; others at digit span, matrix reasoning, and block design; and still others at different combinations of abilities. In contrast, people who score low on IQ tests tend to perform consistently poorly on all of the tasks. As Hunt (1995) observed, "It appears that general intelligence may not be an accurate statement, but general lack of intelligence is!" (p. 362). Does this mean that, particularly for more intelligent people, g is not as useful as the specific abilities for predicting job performance? No. As Gottfredson (1997, 2003b) reports, the more complex the job, the better g predicts performance—which is exactly the opposite of what you would expect for people with higher IQs if the specific abilities were more important.

Why is g so important? Schmidt and Hunter (2004) offer a straightforward answer: People who have higher g learn more quickly, and hence acquire more job-related knowledge. And having more knowledge about a job leads you to perform it better.

**THE IMPORTANCE OF HAVING A GOOD PERSONALITY**   At first glance, these findings seem to fly in the face of common experience. All of us have known someone who is obviously "smart" but an utter dunce in some area—for example, J. K. Rowling has real trouble understanding science. Moreover, as good as g is at predicting performance, it typically predicts only around 25% of the variation in performance. What's missing? Some of the missing explanation probably can be chalked up to *measurement error*, "noise" added by the imperfections of the tests. In addition, some of it may reflect personality differences. Schmidt and Hunter (2004) note that the personality traits of conscientiousness and integrity predict performance above-and-beyond g, and also note that other sets of personality traits predict certain aspects of job performance. For example, the traits of agreeableness, extraversion, and emotional stability (in addition to conscientiousness) predict how well people work together in teams (Barrick et al., 1998).

**THE IMPORTANCE OF ANALYZING THE TASKS**   There may be another reason why specific abilities have not predicted on-the-job performance. Reeve (2004) observed that enormous effort has gone into analyzing the structure of cognitive abilities (as illustrated in Figure 9.2 on p. 389), but nothing comparable has been invested in analyzing the structure of the real-world behavior to be predicted. When Reeve analyzed the structure of factual knowledge (see Chapter 7) in detail, he found that—sure enough—specific abilities did predict some specific aspects of knowledge. To be sure, g predicted general knowledge, but specific abilities also accounted for substantial hunks of the variation in how much people knew. Most notably, quantitative ability accounted for over half the variability in knowledge about science and math. However, as intriguing as these findings are, it remains to be seen whether the psychometric approach can illuminate the nature and role of specific abilities in general. In sum, it is clear that g is important for navigating through life; it predicts many outcomes, ranging from job performance to health (Gottfredson, 2004; Kuncel et al., 2004). However, g is not the entire story. We've seen that personality variables can be important, and so can specific abilities (Lubinski, 2004). But there is still more to intelligence, as we see in the following sections.

# Emotional Intelligence: Knowing Feelings

**Emotional intelligence (EI):** The ability to understand and regulate emotions effectively.

Another approach to understanding what makes us smart posits additional sorts of intelligence, which are not tapped by the standard tests. In this section, we consider one example of another sort of intelligence—emotional intelligence.

Have you ever seen someone you *know* is smart do something incredibly dumb—for instance, unintentionally or uncontrollably make a remark that infuriates a friend or boss? Salovey and Mayer (1990) believe that whether you act intelligently often depends in large part on how well you understand both your own emotions and the effects your actions have on others. Salovey and Mayer refer to the ability to understand and regulate emotions effectively as **emotional intelligence (EI)**.

EI has two major facets. One facet involves intelligence, as usually defined. This facet of EI is typically defined as having the four "branches" listed in Table 9.3, which are thought to form a hierarchy, with managing emotions being the most general dimension and perceiving emotions being the most specific. The tests for this facet of EI rely on asking test-takers to make objective decisions about emotion-laden situations, and the decisions are scored as right or wrong (Mayer et al., 2000, 2001, 2003).

The other facet of EI involves subjective experiences and inclinations. The tests for this facet of EI require test-takers to rate themselves subjectively regarding relevant characteristics, such as their degree of assertiveness, empathy, tolerance for stress, and optimism (Bar-On et al., 2000). A meta-analysis revealed that the objective measures of EI are more highly correlated with g (but nevertheless share only about 10% of the variation in performance with it) than the subjective measures (which are almost entirely distinct from g); the subjective measures are more highly correlated with measures of personality (Van Rooy et al., in press).

In recent years, EI has been the subject of intense research interest (Bar-On & Parker, 2000; Ciarrochi et al., 2001; Matthews et al., 2002; Roberts et al., 2001), and

## TABLE 9.3 The Four-Branch Model of Emotional Intelligence

The four branches of emotional intelligence are ordered here from least to most general.

| Branch | Description | Example |
|---|---|---|
| 1. Perceiving emotion | Ability to identify emotions on the basis of perceptual cues | Noticing a slight frown when a friend hears someone's name, and realizing that it signals jealousy |
| 2. Facilitating thought with emotion | Ability to harness emotional information to enhance thinking | Thinking through a planned comment to your friend, and changing the plan to avoid an anticipated rocky outcome |
| 3. Understanding emotion | Ability to comprehend emotional information about relationships, transitions from one emotion to another, and verbal information about emotion | Understanding that your friend is jealous of someone else because of your previous relationship with that person |
| 4. Managing emotion | Ability to manage emotions and emotional relationships | Noticing that you are becoming annoyed at your friend, and being able to take a deep breath, count to 10, and then respond calmly |

researchers are reporting many intriguing findings. For example, women tend to score higher than men on some dimensions of EI (Carrothers et al., 2000; Van Rooy et al., 2005), particularly those that relate to social skills (Petrides & Furnham, 2000). Nevertheless, men may (falsely) believe that they have higher EI than women do (Petrides & Furnham, 2000). In addition, members of minority groups tend to score higher than Whites, and older people tend to score higher than college students (Van Rooy et al., 2005). Moreover, people who can more accurately read variations in other people's moods tend to be better adjusted socially (Engelberg & Sjöberg, 2004).

Although the subjective measures of EI appear, in part, to assess aspects of personality (Dawda & Hart, 2000), these tests can make predictions above and beyond what is possible with personality tests (Petrides & Furnham, 2003; Van Rooy et al., in press). Recent objective tests of EI also explain behavior that is not explained by measures of personality or of verbal or fluid intelligence (Lopes et al., 2005; Lopes et al., 2003). The newest such test provides separate scores for each of the four dimensions summarized in Table 9.3 (on p. 391).

In short, this is an exciting and promising area of research, but it is still in its infancy. The research results have not yet charted the utility and limits of EI for understanding human behavior.

# Multiple Intelligences: More Than One Way to Shine?

Instead of trying to add another form of intelligence to the standard sort, some researchers have proposed sets of multiple intelligences. Although controversial, these alternative perspectives have proven attractive to many, particularly to those who work in education. Let's briefly consider the two most influential of these theories.

Linguistic intelligence is the ability to use language well, as relied on by journalists and lawyers.

**Theory of multiple intelligences:** Gardner's theory of eight distinct forms of intelligence, which can vary separately for a given individual.

## Gardner's Theory of Multiple Intelligences: Something for Everyone

Howard Gardner (1983/1993b, 1995, 1999) developed a novel view of intelligence, called the **theory of multiple intelligences**, which holds that there are eight distinct forms of intelligence and another, tentative, form, as summarized in Table 9.4.

By far the best support for Gardner's theory comes from the very findings and phenomena that inspired it in the first place. Specifically, Gardner reflected on the fact that brain damage often results in the loss of a certain ability while leaving others relatively intact. For example, language can be disrupted but the patient can still sing, or vice versa; mathematical ability can be disrupted but the patient can still speak, or vice versa; social skills can be disrupted while ordinary reasoning is unimpaired, or vice versa. Gardner reasoned that if abilities can be disrupted independently, then they arise from distinct brain systems—and hence reflect specific types of intelligence. In addition, he considered other kinds of data. He noted, for example, that although everybody learns their first language in a few years, very few people master complex mathematics so easily. If two abilities develop at different rates during childhood, he reasoned, they must rely on different underlying processes. He also observed that some abilities, such as music and mathematics, can be extraordinarily well developed in child prodigies, whereas these same children perform at average levels in other areas. This coexistence of the extraordinary and the ordinary, Gardner believes, suggests that

**TABLE 9.4**  **Gardner's Multiple Intelligences**

| Form of Intelligence | Definition | Examples of Profession in Which the Form Is Important |
|---|---|---|
| Linguistic | The ability to use language well | Journalism, law |
| Spatial | The ability to reason well about spatial relations | Architecture, surgery |
| Music | The ability to compose and understand music | Audio engineering, music |
| Logical-Mathematical | The ability to manipulate abstract symbols | Science, computer programming |
| Bodily-Kinesthetic | The ability to plan and understand sequences of movements | Dance, athletics |
| Intrapersonal | The ability to understand yourself | Ministry |
| Interpersonal | The ability to understand other people and social interactions | Politics, teaching |
| Naturalist | The ability to observe aspects of the natural environment carefully | Forest conservation |
| Existential (tentative; Gardner, 1999) | The ability to address "the big questions" about existence | Philosophy |

some intellectual capacities, such as those related to music and mathematics, may be psychologically distinct from others.

According to Gardner, most professions require combinations of different types of intelligence; to be a novelist like Rowling, for example, you need linguistic, intrapersonal, and interpersonal intelligence—but you don't need bodily-kinesthetic intelligence (in fact, Rowling admits to horrible performance at sports, once managing to break her arm playing the tame British sport of netball). Each person can be characterized by a *profile of intelligences*, with some types of intelligence being relatively strong and others relatively weak (Connell et al., 2003; Walters & Gardner, 1985).

As appealing as Gardner's theory of multiple intelligences is to many, it has not been embraced by many researchers in the field. One severe problem is that neither Gardner nor anyone else has developed a way to measure all of the separate intelligences, which makes the theory impossible to test rigorously (Hunt, 2001); however, people can rate themselves and others on each type of intelligence, which is a first step (Furnham et al., 2002). Another problem is perhaps even more fundamental: Some question whether the word *intelligence* should be applied so liberally; many of Gardner's types, they say, have more to do with talents and skills than with intelligence as most of us understand the concept.

Spatial intelligence is the ability to reason well about spatial relations, as relied on by architects and surgeons.

## Sternberg's Analytic, Practical, and Creative Intelligences

Robert Sternberg (1985, 1988b) has also developed a theory of multiple intelligences, which he calls the *Triarchic Theory of Successful Intelligence*. According to this theory, there are three types of intelligence: analytic, practical, and creative.

1. *Analytic intelligence*, the ability to learn to write clearly, do math, and understand literature, is critical for academic performance. Rowling was superb at writing and understanding literature, but not good at science or math; how could we devise a test to assess her analytic intelligence? Knowing about the distinctions among the different abilities in Figure 9.2 (p. 389), you might wonder whether this category is too broad.

2. *Practical intelligence* involves knowing how to do such things as fix a car or sew on a button, and it sometimes relies on implicit memories, learned responses and skills that guide our actions without our being aware of them (see Chapter 7); "street smarts" are a form of practical intelligence. Rowling had the following to say about metal shop, which was her least favorite subject in high school: "I was the worst in my class—just terrible, I am not a practical person. . . . It seemed to me to be all about hammering stuff until I broke it. I did try, but I just could not do it. . . . I was terrible at woodwork too" (Fraser, 2000). Does this mean that she doesn't have practical intelligence? If so, how could she work out her detailed plot lines? Again, you might ask whether this type of intelligence is too broadly defined.

3. *Creative intelligence*, which seems closely related to Cattell and Horn's fluid intelligence, is the ability to formulate novel solutions to problems. We can have no doubt about Rowling's level of this type of intelligence.

How do these three types of intelligence relate to IQ? Analytic intelligence is what IQ tests measure. However, according to Sternberg and his colleagues (Sternberg & Wagner, 1993; Sternberg et al., 1993, 2001), measures of practical intelligence are better predictors of how well someone will do on the job than are standard measures of

| TABLE 9.5 | The Nature of Intelligence: Five Views |
|---|---|
| **Theorist** | **Key Ideas** |
| **Spearman (1927)** | ■ *g* (generalized ability, contributes to all intellectual activities) |
| | ■ *s* (specialized abilities, such as spelling or distinguishing among tones) |
| | ■ IQ mostly reflects *g*. |
| **Thurstone and Thurstone (1941)** | ■ Seven primary mental abilities, such as verbal comprehension and spatial visualization |
| | ■ No *g* |
| **Cattell (1971) and Horn (1985, 1986, 1989)** | ■ Fluid intelligence (producing novel solutions to problems, such as by using burnt match heads to write) |
| | ■ Crystallized intelligence (using previously acquired knowledge appropriately, such as when doing arithmetic) |
| **Gardner (1983/1993, 1999)** | ■ At least eight multiple intelligences (including such nontraditional forms as bodily-kinesthetic and interpersonal intelligences) |
| | ■ Based on a wide variety of types of data (such as effects of brain damage, and areas in which child prodigies excel) |
| **Sternberg (1985, 1988b)** | ■ Analytic intelligence (the kind of reasoning relied upon in academic studies) |
| | ■ Practical intelligence (the kind of reasoning used to solve everyday, real-world problems) |
| | ■ Creative intelligence (the kind of reasoning needed to invent new things or to solve problems in new ways) |
| **Carroll (1993)** | ■ Three-stratum theory |
| | ■ *g* at the top, 8 broad abilities (including fluid and crystallized intelligences) in the middle tier, and 69 specific abilities (such as ideational fluency) at the bottom |

IQ, and practical intelligence is largely distinct from analytic intelligence. But these claims have proven highly controversial: Other researchers have found that IQ predicts on-the-job performance better than measures of practical intelligence do (Kuncel et al., 2004). In fact, some experts argue that even Sternberg's own data provide only weak support, if any, for his theory (Brody, 2003a, 2003b; Gottfredson, 2003a, 2003c); however, Sternberg (2003a, 2003b) maintains his views in the face of this criticism. Finally, although creative intelligence is distinct from IQ, people do need a certain level of IQ to be able to find creative solutions to problems or to create novel products that have specific uses (Guilford, 1967; Runco & Albert, 1986; Sternberg, 1985).

Table 9.5 summarizes six prominent views about the nature of intelligence.

# Test Yourself

1. Spearman looked at the correlations among scores on several intelligence subtests. If intelligence were simply the *g* factor, these sets of scores should be
   a. correlated to the same degree.
   b. not correlated at all.
   c. show a correlation of zero.
   d. correlated in groups, or factors.
2. Cattell and Horn's theory postulates two kinds of intelligence. A person who is good at using and combining familiar facts has high
   a. emotional intelligence.
   b. crystallized intelligence.
   c. fluid intelligence.
   d. primary intelligence.

3. Women score higher than men on some dimensions of emotional intelligence, especially when the
   a. women have spent a lot of time alone.
   b. men have large social networks.
   c. women are asked about personal feelings.
   d. dimensions involve social skills.
4. Sternberg's analytical intelligence is similar to Gardner's
   a. linguistic and logical-mathematical intelligences.
   b. naturalistic intelligence.
   c. fluid intelligence.
   d. intrapersonal and interpersonal intelligences.

## Answers

1. a 2. b 3. c 4. a

# Think It Through!

Given what you've read, answer the question "Is your best friend smart?" Can you do this easily? Does it make sense to classify any person as either "smart" or "stupid"?

Why do you think that performance on any given task must be understood as due to a mix of *g* and specific abilities, but performance in real-world jobs is predicted primarily by *g* alone? In most cases (we would hope!), people do not randomly select one job over another. Why would someone choose a particular kind of work, and how might this relate to both *g* and specific abilities?

# WHAT MAKES US SMART?
## Nature and Nurture

In her final year of high school, the staff and students elected J. K. Rowling to the prestigious position of Head Girl. Although neither of her parents (or any of her grandparents) had gone to a university, her father was strongly motivated and went to great lengths to attend night school. Friends commented on how bright her parents were and noted that "... it was one of their frustrations that they didn't go on to university and went through life the hard way. . . . They were a pair of very talented people" (Smith, 2001). How important was it that Rowling had bright parents? And how important was it that they read a great deal and had many books in the house?

# The Machinery of Intelligence

Intelligence is the ability to solve problems well and to understand and learn complex material. Thus, it seems reasonable to expect smart people to be good at the information processing required to solve problems, such as retrieving information from long-term memory and using information in working memory. Many researchers have examined the information processing that underlies intelligence (Anderson, 1992; Ceci, 1990; Deary, 2000; Sternberg, 1985, 1988b). But pinpointing just how the mental "machinery" of smart people differs from that of others has not been easy. Are some people smarter than others because they have bigger, faster, or more efficient brains?

## Brain Size and Intelligence: Is Bigger Always Better?

Many studies have shown that the larger a person's brain, the greater his or her intelligence as measured by IQ tests (Deary, 2000; Neisser et al., 1996; Rushton & Ankney, 1996). Larger brains do tend to contain more neurons (Haug, 1987, as cited in Rushton & Ankney, 1996). But it isn't clear whether larger brain size causes greater intelligence or whether acting intelligently causes larger brain size. As discussed earlier, interacting with the environment can change your brain, even causing it to grow. For example, as discussed in Chapter 3, rats raised in stimulating environments developed larger brains.

However, the key variable may not be overall brain size, but the size of crucial areas. For instance, the part of the brain that controls the left hand is larger in professional musicians who play stringed instruments than in other musicians, or in other people in general (Elber et al., 1995). Consider also the brain of Albert Einstein, whose name has become nearly synonymous with genius. Shortly after Einstein died, his brain was removed and preserved. When it was initially examined, researchers found that his brain had an unusually large number of glial cells (which not only help to support neurons, but are also involved in information processing; Chapter 3), particularly in the bottom portions of the left parietal lobe (Gardner et al., 1996). This part of the brain is involved in mathematical thinking (Dehaene, 1997) and spatial visualization (Kosslyn, 1994b); as discussed in Chapter 8, Einstein made extraordinarily good use of these abilities. The extra glial cells may have helped that part of his brain function more efficiently than normal. A more recent analysis of Einstein's brain showed that he actually had more neurons in this key area in both hemispheres (Witelson et al., 1999). Indeed, Einstein's parietal lobes were about 15% wider than normal. In addition, the Sylvian fissure, the major horizontal crease in the brain (above the temporal lobe) was largely missing, perhaps because extra neurons were squeezed in. However, other areas of Einstein's brain were relatively small, making the overall size of his brain only average.

From such research findings, can we conclude that the larger your brain, or the larger certain key parts, the smarter you are? No, the relation between brain size and intelligence is not so simple.

1. Females have about the same average intelligence as males, but they generally have smaller brains (Ankney, 1992; Rushton & Ankney, 1996).

2. The Neanderthals had larger brains than humans today do, but there is no evidence that they were smarter.

3. The correlation between brain size and IQ is typically small, and thus it does not necessarily apply to any particular individual.

4. Correlation does not imply causation—as usual, some third variable (perhaps related to maternal nutrition, stress, or genes) might separately affect both brain size and intelligence.

At present, the meaning of the correlation between brain size and intelligence is not clear. Moreover, skull size and brain size are only weakly correlated, so resist the temptation to measure your friends' heads before forming a study group!

## Speed: Of the Essence?

How did Rowling's teacher, Mrs. Morgan, decide how bright her students were, which then led her to assign them to desks in different parts of the classroom? Although she gave tests, she may also have used intuitions and impressions. If a student was generally slow, would that imply that he or she was therefore stupid? In this context, "slow" does not refer to voluntary speed (how effectively someone can rush to complete a task), but rather the speed of information processing. And, in fact, IQ often correlates with the time taken to respond to a stimulus, such as a light in a laboratory experiment—the higher the IQ, the faster the response tends to be (Deary, 2000; Jensen, 1980, 1987, 1991; Neubauer et al., 2000). At first glance, this correlation does not seem surprising: Many of the subtests in the WAIS-III are timed, and thus faster test-takers tend to complete more of the questions and therefore increase their chances of achieving higher scores (Wilhelm & Schulze, 2002). However, the higher a person's IQ, the more easily the person can discriminate between stimuli that are shown for very brief amounts of time; for example, people with higher IQs can judge accurately which of two lines is longer when the display is presented very briefly (Anderson, 1992; Bates & Eysenck, 1993; Deary, 2000; Kranzler & Jensen, 1989; Nettelbeck, 1987). This finding has little or nothing to do with perceptual processing itself, but rather reflects the ease of evaluating similar stimuli (Osmon & Jackson, 2002). From such evidence, many researchers conclude that IQ reflects, at least in part, the speed of mental processes (Anderson, 1992; Ceci, 1990; Deary, 1995).

Close examination, however, shows that just as the relationship between brain size and intelligence is complicated, so is the relation between speed and intelligence. IQ scores are only weakly and inconsistently related to both the speed of responding and the amount of exposure time necessary to inspect a stimulus. Much of the underlying basis of IQ has nothing to do with how quickly you can make choices (Luciano et al., 2001). Moreover, measures of neural conduction typically are only weakly related to intelligence (McRorie & Cooper, 2004; Reed et al., 2004; Vernon et al., 2000), and measures of brain function have not shown that the brain "runs faster" in people who have high IQs (Posthuma et al., 2001). Nevertheless, in some tasks, IQ is related to how quickly people can process information. Why might this be? One possibility is that speed in those tasks reflects the ease of performing some specific kind of processing—and it is that particular type of processing that is directly related to IQ. Next, we consider a current candidate for such processing.

## Working Memory: Juggling More Balls

Recent research has emphasized the relation between intelligence and working memory (WM; see Chapter 7 for a discussion of working memory).

**WORKING MEMORY AND INTELLIGENCE** The correlation between speed of processing and IQ may reflect a person's ability to focus attention and use WM effectively (Conway et al., 2002; Engle et al., 1999). Consistent with this idea, some researchers have reported that this correlation is best for tasks that are neither too easy nor too difficult (Jensen, 1993, 1998; Lindley et al., 1995). The highest correlation between IQ and speed is found when the task exercises WM as much as possible without exceeding its capacity; this correlation reflects, in part, how efficiently WM operates. When Rowling works out a surprising twist in a plot line, she needs to hold information in WM to think it through; if the situation involves many characters and draws on many past events, she may need to push her WM to its capacity.

However, researchers have now shown that g does not arise solely from WM (Ackerman et al., 2005), although the precise degree to which WM's capacity contributes to g is a topic of hot debate (Beier & Ackerman, 2005; Colom et al., 2004; Kane et al., 2005; Oberauer et al., 2005). Nevertheless, g may reflect, in part, how well the central executive component of WM can control attention and manage the flow of information representation and processing (Carpenter et al., 1990; Craik & Bialystok, 2005; Lehrl & Fischer, 1990; Unsworth & Engle, 2005). The mechanisms underlying cognitive control, as discussed in Chapter 8, may eventually provide the key to understanding such processing.

**WORKING MEMORY, INTELLIGENCE, AND THE BRAIN** Studies of the brain have also established a relationship between WM and intelligence, especially fluid intelligence. Not only can frontal lobe damage disrupt fluid intelligence (Duncan, 1995, 2005; Duncan et al., 1995, 1996), but also parts of the frontal lobes used in WM are activated in tasks that require high g (Duncan et al., 2000). Gray and colleagues (2003) reported a particularly compelling demonstration of the role of frontal cortex in WM and fluid intelligence. These researchers asked participants first to take a test that provides a good measure of g and then to take part in a very difficult WM task while their brains were scanned using fMRI. They asked the participants to note when an item was the same as one presented three places earlier in the sequence; such a task involves an enormous amount of mental juggling. For example, if the participants saw (one at a time) the words *tree, shoe, rock, tree*, they would respond "yes" only at the second presentation of *tree* because this word was presented three items earlier. As if this wasn't hard enough, the researchers added a diabolical twist to the task: The participants occasionally saw a word that had been presented two, four, or five items earlier, which had to be rejected; evaluating these "lure" stimuli (so called because they may lure people into responding incorrectly) stressed WM. When brain activation during the task that included the lure stimuli was examined, it turned out that people who had higher g were more accurate. Crucially, activation in three brain areas explained 99.9% of the relationship between g and accuracy; those areas were the left prefrontal cortex and both sides of the parietal lobes (which were probably involved in storing information about the individual stimuli).

As originally proposed by Baddeley (1986; see Chapter 7), WM is not a single structure, but instead relies on a system of processes (Mackintosh & Bennett, 2003). And neuroimaging studies have revealed that different sorts of items in reasoning tests do tap different aspects of WM. For example, Prabhakaran and colleagues (1997) used fMRI to study which brain areas are activated while participants perform **Raven's Progressive Matrices** (see Figure 9.3), which is widely used as a test of fluid intelligence (Raven, 1965, 1976). This test includes two sorts of items, which require either visual-spatial rea-

**FIGURE 9.3**

## Raven's Progressive Matrices

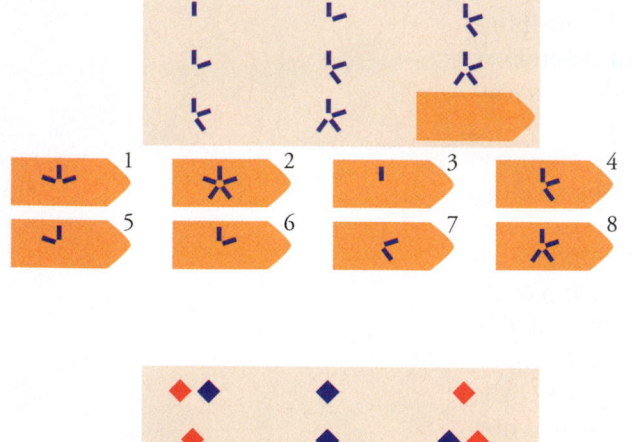

Two problems similar to those in the Raven's Progressive Matrices test, which is often taken to measure fluid intelligence and g. Which of the numbered selections fits in the empty shape in each rectangle? The top example relies on visual-spatial ability, and the bottom on analytic ability.

soning or analytical reasoning (finding an abstract rule). Prabhakaran and colleagues found that items on this test that require visual-spatial reasoning activated parts of the frontal lobes used in holding information about objects and spatial relations in WM, and items requiring analytical reasoning activated both these brain areas and parts of the frontal lobes used in holding verbal information in WM.

In short, although the nature of intelligence is still only dimly understood, some pieces are coming into focus. In response to research on the nature of intelligence, the WAIS-III, which was released in 1997, can be scored to assess four general aspects of intellectual ability: verbal comprehension, perceptual organization, working memory, and processing speed.

# Smart Genes, Smart Environment: A Single System

Intelligence must be related—in one way or the other—to the way the brain functions; it is the brain, after all, not the kidney or the big toe, that underlies reasoning and learning. But there's no reason to think that intelligence *must* be related to the genes. Could Rowling have a certain level of *g*, and high levels of some specific abilities but not others, because of the genetic deck of cards she was dealt by her parents? Or are her *g* and specific abilities mostly (or entirely) a result of her particular experiences?

## Genetic Effects: How Important Are Genes for Intelligence?

Because intelligence has many facets (see Figure 9.2 on p. 389), we would not expect it to be determined by a single gene, or even a small number of genes. And, in fact, researchers have had trouble identifying individual genes that are related to *g* (Hill et al., 1999, 2002; Plomin & Spinath, 2004). Studies (for instance, Fisher et al., 1999) have shown that multiple genes contribute to intelligence and do so in different ways. For example, a portion of DNA has been found to be associated with one type of spatial ability (Berman & Noble, 1995) but not with *g* (Petrill, Plomin, et al., 1997), and two different genes have been shown to predict performance aspects (but not verbal aspects) of IQ (Tsai et al., 2002, 2004).

### Shared Genes Versus Shared Environment: What Predicts IQ?   How can we begin to sort out the relative contributions to intelligence of the genetic component and of other factors? How strong is the genetic influence? The most common method of assessing the contribution of genes to a characteristic is to observe correlations of that characteristic among people who share different proportions of their genes (see Chapter 3).

One way that researchers have tried to sort out the effects of genes versus environment is through *adoption studies*. In these studies, the scores of adopted children are compared to those of their adoptive and their biological relatives. In some of these studies (for example, Bouchard et al., 1990), tests are given to twins who were separated soon after birth and adopted into different families. Because these twins were reared in different homes, any similarities between them are thought to reflect their common genetics. What do adoption studies find? The correlation of IQs for adult identical twins who were raised apart is higher than both that for fraternal twins and that for nontwin siblings raised together (Bouchard & McGue, 1981; Bouchard et al., 1990; Plomin, 1990). In addition, an adopted child's IQ correlates higher with the biological mother's IQ than with the adoptive mother's IQ. Moreover, although the IQs of an adopted child and the biological children in a family are positively correlated, by the time the

FIGURE 9.4

## Genetic Relatedness and Similarities in IQ

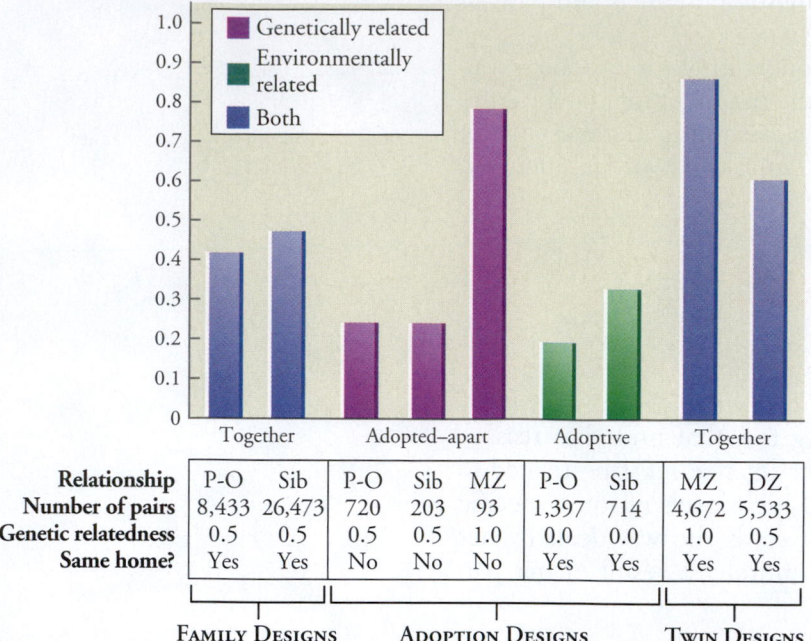

| Relationship | P-O | Sib | P-O | Sib | MZ | P-O | Sib | MZ | DZ |
|---|---|---|---|---|---|---|---|---|---|
| Number of pairs | 8,433 | 26,473 | 720 | 203 | 93 | 1,397 | 714 | 4,672 | 5,533 |
| Genetic relatedness | 0.5 | 0.5 | 0.5 | 0.5 | 1.0 | 0.0 | 0.0 | 1.0 | 0.5 |
| Same home? | Yes | Yes | No | No | No | Yes | Yes | Yes | Yes |

FAMILY DESIGNS     ADOPTION DESIGNS     TWIN DESIGNS

Correlations for pairs of parents and offspring (P-O), siblings (Sib), dizygotic twins (DZ), and monozygotic twins (MZ). The children were either raised together or apart. A "genetic relatedness" of 1.0 indicates a pair of MZ twins; 0.5, biological siblings but not identical twins; and 0.0, biologically unrelated siblings.

children grow up, virtually no correlation remains (Plomin, 1990; Plomin, Fulker, et al., 1997; Scarr & Weinberg, 1983). These findings provide clear evidence that genes affect IQ.

Other studies have tried to find out exactly how large a role genes play in determining IQ by comparing IQs of people with different numbers of genes in common. The results clearly show that the more genes in common, the higher the correlations (Figure 9.4). The usual estimate is that the heritability of IQ is around .50, which means that about half the variation in IQ can be attributed to heredity (Chipuer et al., 1990; Loehlin, 1989). (Heritability estimates indicate what proportion of observed variability in a characteristic within a population is caused by inherited factors [Bell, 1977; Lush, 1937]; see Chapter 3 for further discussion of heritability.) Keep in mind that heritability estimates have no bearing on how much of *your* personal intelligence is the result of your genes. A number that denotes heritability refers to the proportion of variation within a population, not to the proportion of the characteristic that is inherited by an individual.

Finally, we note that the Human Genome Project (International Human Genome Sequencing Consortium, 2001; Venter et al., 2001) has made feasible a very different way to study the genetic basis of intellectual abilities. Researchers can now directly compare the abilities of people who possess different genes, as identified on the chromosomes themselves. For example, Deary and colleagues (2005) found that people who have the NCSTN B haplotype (Hap B) gene score higher on a test of verbal reasoning than people who do not have this gene. One major advantage of this approach is that—in frank violation of the usual admonition that correlation does not imply causation—it is possible to use correlations to establish causal relations between genes and abilities: Different behaviors and abilities cannot change which genes people have, and thus when different genes are found to be associated with different behaviors and abilities, we can assume that the genes help to produce those differences, and not vice versa (Plomin & Spinath, 2004).

**BRAIN SIMILARITIES, GENETICS, AND INTELLIGENCE** Researchers have begun combining twin studies with neuroimaging studies to discover whether the sizes of specific brain areas are under genetic control (Gray & Thompson, 2004). As shown in Figure 9.5, Thompson and colleagues (2001) found that the amount of gray matter (neurons' cell bodies) in various portions of the frontal lobes and in Wernicke's area (which is crucial for language; see Chapter 8) is substantially more similar in identical twins than in fraternal twins—the hallmark of high heritability. In addition, the IQ scores of the twins were highly correlated with the amount of gray matter in the frontal lobes. Note, however, that the amount of gray matter need not be the *cause* of intelligence: Both the amount of gray matter and the IQ scores could *result* from other factors. For example, genes that affect the efficiency of neural transmission could also have contributed to the amount of gray matter. Or perhaps some twins tend to be peppy and others lethargic, which leads them to engage in more or less stimulating activities—and these ac-

## FIGURE 9.5  Similarities in the Brains of Two Types of Twins

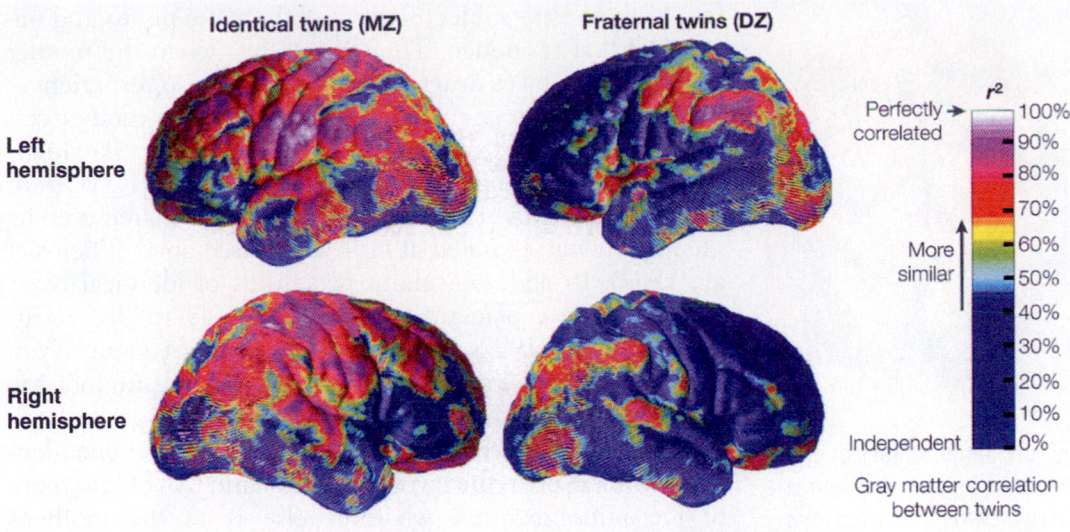

**Identical twins (MZ)**   **Fraternal twins (DZ)**

Left hemisphere

Right hemisphere

Perfectly correlated → $r^2$ 100%
90%
80%
70%
More similar 60%
50%
40%
30%
20%
10%
Independent 0%

Gray matter correlation between twins

Thompson and colleagues (2001) found that identical (MZ) twins, who share all their genes, had much more similar brains than fraternal (DZ) twins, who share half their genes. They also found that more gray matter in the frontal lobes was accompanied by a higher IQ.

---

tivities cause neuron growth in key brain areas (Chapter 3) and increase IQ. (In fact, 3-year-olds who tend to seek out stimulation score higher on IQ tests at age 11 [Raine et al., 2002], and the personality trait known as openness to experience is correlated with intelligence [McCrae & Costa, 1997a].) Such differences in temperament could themselves be genetically determined or could depend on the environment. The environment and genes engage in an intimate and intricate dance, as we consider in more detail next.

## Environmental Effects: More Real Than Apparent?

Take another look at Figure 9.4, and compare the correlations between all pairs of relatives who share half of their genes in common, such as parents and offspring (far left), nontwin siblings (second from left), and fraternal twins (at the far right). These pairs share the same amount of common genes, 50%, and thus their IQ scores should be the same, if intelligence is wholly determined by genes (Lyons & Bar, 2001). But, as you can see in the figure, the correlations of IQ scores for the different pairings vary considerably. What can account for this difference? Researchers assume that if scores are not related to genes, they must reflect effects of the environment (or, to a lesser degree, measurement error).

It is clear that the environment affects intelligence as assessed by IQ. The observed relationship between IQ and achievement, noted earlier, can also act in the opposite direction: People who achieve more can develop higher IQ scores (for example, see Kohn & Schooler, 1973; Neisser et al., 1996). Perhaps the best evidence for this comes from studies of the effects of formal schooling. For example, when poor black children moved from the rural South to Philadelphia in the 1940s, their IQs increased by a bit more than half a point for each year they spent in their new schools (Cahan & Cohen, 1989; Ceci, 1991; Ceci & Williams, 1997; Lee, 1951).

Consider some factors that make it difficult to interpret heritability estimates based on studies of twins and relatives.

## FIGURE 9.6 Fraternal and Identical Twins

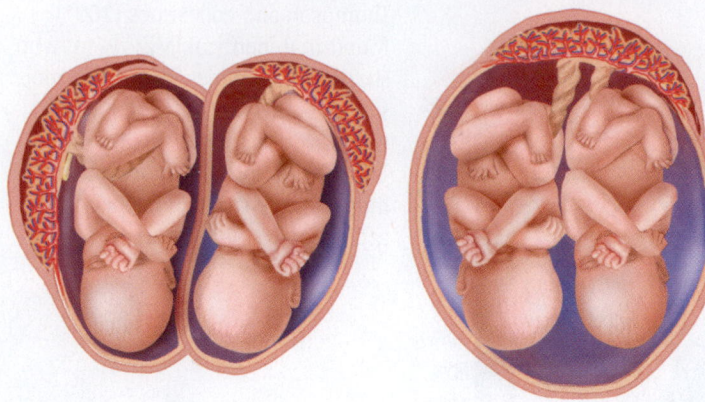

Twins can have separate placentas and separate amniotic sacs or can share a single placenta and sac; sharing results in greater environmental similarity prior to birth. Virtually all fraternal twins are in separate sacs (left), whereas about two thirds of identical twins are in the same sac (right).

### SHARED PRENATAL ENVIRONMENT: ON BEING WOMBMATES

Twins share much the same environment in the womb before birth and are subject to most of the same pluses and minuses of that residence. The fetus suffers when the mother has a bad diet, takes drugs or alcohol, smokes, or experiences a great deal of stress; the fetus profits when the mother eats well, takes vitamins, and doesn't drink, smoke, or take drugs. Aspects of this common environment affect later IQ (Devlin et al., 1997; Jacobs et al., 2001), and those are shared even by identical twins separated at birth and raised apart (Phelps et al., 1997). In addition, about two thirds of identical twins share the same placenta and amniotic sac in the uterus (Phelps et al., 1997; see Figure 9.6). At first glance, you might think that sharing the same placenta and amniotic sac would make the twins more similar, but the opposite turns out to be true: These twins compete for resources; one identical twin will be in the favored position and will obtain more of the nutrients—and whatever else is in the mother's blood—than the other. Thus, these identical twins have larger disparities in weight and length at birth than do fraternal twins, and their early environment may make them less similar than their genes would dictate.

In short, it is difficult to know how the shared prenatal environment experienced by identical twins versus that experienced by fraternal twins affects the magnitude of the correlations between their IQs.

### ADOPTIVE HOUSEHOLDS

It is not clear just how different the early environmental influences on twins raised in different homes really are. Families that seek to adopt a child share many characteristics, and these similarities are further enhanced by the fact that adoption agencies frown on placing children in deprived conditions. The households in which separated twins are placed are thus often fairly similar. When Stoolmiller (1999) mathematically corrected for the small variations among adopting families, he estimated the effects of environment on IQ to be 57%. It is not clear, however, whether this estimate applies only to the special case of twins raised apart or can be taken as a general estimate.

### MICROENVIRONMENTS: HERE, THERE, EVERYWHERE

A person's genes can help shape aspects of his or her environment. The **microenvironment** is the environment you create by your very presence. For one thing, identical twins may have more aspects of their environments in common than fraternal twins because much of the environment includes social interactions, and people respond to us in part because of the way we look and behave. So if both twins are physically appealing, they will be treated very differently than if both are homely, and ditto for twins who are sluggish and overweight versus athletic and trim. Also, to the extent that children have similar inborn tendencies, their behavior may shape their environments in similar ways. For example, children who enjoy being read to will reinforce adults for this activity, leading the adults to buy or borrow more books—thereby providing more opportunity for stimulating interactions.

In addition, depending on their personalities, people select aspects of the environment that appeal to them (perhaps, initially, for genetic reasons), and thus what appear to be different environments may in fact function pretty much the same for two people with similar inclinations. For example, two homes may differ in the number of books they contain, but a child who likes to read may seize on whatever is available and end up reading as much in a home with fewer books as a child who lives in a home with many

Microenvironment: The environment created by a person's own presence, which depends partly on appearance and behavior.

books. In short, identical twins share many characteristics that define their microenvironments, and so they live in more similar microenvironments than do other siblings. Even twins separated at birth may create similar microenvironments, and so it is not clear exactly how different the environmental influences on these twins are.

**PERCEIVED REALITY: IT'S WHAT'S INSIDE THAT COUNTS** Researchers have also observed that only about a quarter or a third of the variability in $g$ can be explained by shared environment, or aspects of the family setting that are present for all siblings in a household, such as the number of books in the house (Plomin et al., 1997). If genes account for about half the variability in intelligence and shared environment for less than half of what remains, what accounts for the rest? Some aspects of the environment don't have the same effect on all children growing up in the household; the same event can be a very different experience for different people. Watching TV can be the mindless pastime of a couch potato, but someone like Rowling could make watching TV into a stimulating experience. Even when the environment of two siblings appears to be identical, its influence depends in part on each child's predispositions and inclinations, which may be partly innate (Kagan, 1989b; Turkheimer & Waldron, 2000). A shy child, for example, will be pleased to be left alone to find solitary amusements; but the same treatment would be a punishment for an outgoing, gregarious child. The *perceived* environment, not the objective environment, is the important one.

**SELECTING THE ENVIRONMENT** In general, a shared family environment produces positive correlations among the IQ scores of all children who grow up in the same house, but these effects wear off by adulthood, and genetic influences become increasingly evident with age (McCartney et al., 1990; McGue et al., 1993; Plomin, 1990). Why? One theory is that, as people age, they are increasingly able to select their environments, and genetically determined properties, such as temperament, lead people to select certain environments over others. For example, if you are temperamentally shy, you will not take a job in sales; if you are outgoing, you might enjoy managing a hotel. Thus, as you grow older and have more choices about how to live, the effects of your environment are increasingly related to the effects of genes (Neisser et al., 1996). This does not mean, however, that the environment is not playing a crucial role in helping you function well (Cleveland et al., 2000).

Within this context, the concept of reaction range (Scarr, 1976; Scarr & McCartney, 1983) offers a framework for understanding the significance of heritability. The **reaction range** (also sometimes called the *range of reaction*) is the entire scope of possible reactions to environmental events, which is established by the genes; the environment sets your position within that range (Weinberg, 1989). In general, the greater the reaction range, the more evident the effects of the environment. Conversely, the narrower the reaction range, the more deterministic are the effects of the genes. For some genes, notably those associated with certain diseases (such as Huntington's disease; De Marchi & Mennella, 2000; Gontkovsky, 1998),

We create a part of our environments simply by the way we look and act, which influences how others treat us. This *microenvironment* is similar for twins, and their shared characteristics may in part reflect common aspects of their microenvironment, not the direct effects of the genes.

Our genes determine the range within which the environment can mold us. For example, Japanese youth are typically much taller than their parents. Why? Same genes, but different environment (especially nutrition)—which led the genes to operate differently. Similarly, genes for intelligence define a range of possible intelligences, and an individual's intelligence level embodies just one instance of what was possible given the reaction range of the genes.

Reaction range: The entire scope of possible reactions to environmental events, which is set by the genes.

simply having the gene is enough to produce an effect—these genes have very narrow reaction ranges. But most genes that affect our psychologies have broad reaction ranges; the operation of these genes is regulated by our interactions with the environment.

# Group Differences in Intelligence

How would you feel if you were told that you are a member of a group that is genetically stupid? Many groups have faced such labeling, often with far-reaching consequences. The Immigration Act of 1924 aimed to minimize immigration to the United States of "biologically weak stocks," a term that was defined to include Italians and Jews of southern and eastern Europe. During congressional testimony, supporters of the bill pointed to the results of intelligence tests, on which recent immigrants scored less well than established Americans with northern European roots. There is debate about the extent to which this testimony mattered (Snyderman & Herrnstein, 1983), but no debate over the catastrophic effects of this bill less than 20 years later, during World War II, when Jews attempting to escape Nazi Germany were severely restricted from immigrating to the United States.

Contemporary studies comparing IQ scores find that some groups have lower average scores than others; for example, Jews of European descent in Israel score about 15 points higher than Jews of North African descent. What do such findings mean?

## Within-Group Versus Between-Group Differences

If, as most experts have concluded, about 50% of the differences in IQ can be accounted for by differences in genes, is it reasonable to say that differences in IQ scores between groups are largely genetic? Absolutely not. The genetic contribution to intelligence *within* a given group cannot say anything about possible genetic differences *between* groups (N. Block, 1995; Lewontin, 1976a, 1976b; Plomin, 1988). To see why not, imagine that you have two orchards with the same kind of apple trees. You make sure that each orchard receives exactly the same amounts of sunlight, fertilizer, water, and so on. If you succeed in making the environments identical, then any differences in the sizes of apples from the two orchards should reflect genetic differences among the trees. However, say the two orchards have overall different conditions, that one gets more sunshine and water than the other (see Figure 9.7). *Within* each orchard, differences in the sizes of the apples would reflect genetic differences (assuming that the environment is exactly the same throughout the orchard). But those differences say nothing about the differences *between* the orchards. The disadvantaged environment puts the trees in one orchard in a generally lower part of the reaction range than those benefiting from the advantaged environment in the other orchard. It is even possible that the differences within the "advantaged" orchard reflect the operation of one set of genes, whereas the differences within the "disadvantaged" orchard reflect the operation of another set that allows the trees to make the most of skimpy amounts of sunshine or water. No question about it: Differences within one group cannot be used to explain differences between groups or within another group.

Researchers have shown that this analogy is not simply theoretical. For example, Eric Turkheimer and colleagues (2003) compared the IQs of monozygotic (MZ) and dizygotic (DZ) twins from both affluent and impoverished backgrounds. They found that genetics accounted for the bulk of the variations in IQ of the affluent twins (with a heritability of 72%), and that the shared environment accounted for little variation (15%). In striking contrast, the story was exactly the reverse for the impoverished twins: In this group, the shared environment accounted for the bulk of the variations in IQ (58%), and heritability accounted for little variation (10%)! This result is clear evi-

**FIGURE 9.7**

## Within-Group Differences Do Not Explain Between-Group Differences

The state of an organism is a result of interactions between genes and environment. The two groups of trees could have the same genes, but differences in the environment cause the genes to produce different characteristics. Differences among trees in the *same* environment may reflect differences in genes, but this says nothing about differences among trees in different environments.

dence that the environment plays a more important role in affecting IQ scores for impoverished children than do the genes—which makes perfect sense if we think of each pair of twins as a mini-orchard, getting different amounts of sun and water.

When you see an apple, all you have to go on is its present size, which reflects the actions of genes in a specific environment. You have no way of knowing the range of possible sizes for that type of apple. Similarly, when Mrs. Morgan, Rowling's formidable teacher, met her students, she had no way of knowing the range of their possible intelligences. Further, heritability only tells you about the effects of genes in a *certain environment*; it says nothing about their possible effects in *other environments* (Hirsch, 1971, 1997). There is no way to know how tall, or smart, Rowling would have been if she (or her mother, while pregnant) had had a different diet, experienced less stress at certain periods of her life, and so on.

### Race Differences

When you see an apple you know that it's not a tomato or an orange. But when you see a person, you cannot classify his or her race so easily. As Charles Darwin long ago pointed out, the races meld seamlessly into one another, and the very concept of race is difficult to define. In fact, some researchers believe that this concept is a social invention, not a biological reality. Today, the idea that different races exist is highly controversial; this controversy is addressed, for example, in the pages of a special issue of the journal the *American Psychologist*, edited by Anderson and Nickerson (2005).

Nevertheless, many researchers have grouped people into different races, using various criteria (including simple self-identification), and differences among these groups have been documented—and now must be explained. This section summarizes some key differences and explanations.

To begin, researchers have repeatedly shown that Asian Americans tend to score higher on IQ tests than do White Americans, who in turn tend to score higher than Black Americans (Neisser et al., 1996; Rushton, 1995; Suzuki & Valencia, 1997); Hispanic Americans tend to score between White and Black Americans. For decades, the relatively low IQ scores of Black Americans have attracted attention, and controversy has flared over the claim that their scores, and their poorer achievement, are rooted in their genes. A firestorm of debate raged when Richard Herrnstein and Charles Murray (1994) published *The Bell Curve*, in which they argued that IQ not only predicts many aspects of life and performance, but also that differences in IQ are largely genetic. However, as discussed earlier, it's not easy to disentangle effects of the environment (particularly the microenvironment) and the genes. Although we focus on White and Black Americans in the following discussion, as has most of the research literature, keep in mind that the same issues also apply to all groups that generally score relatively poorly on IQ tests.

What do we make of the finding that the average IQ score of White Americans is 10 to 15 points higher than the average among Black Americans? Does this gap necessarily imply genetic differences? Before leaping to that conclusion, we must consider numerous other accounts (N. Block, 1995; Nisbett, 1996).

**TEST BIAS?** Some have argued that the disparity in test scores simply reflects the fact that the tests were designed for a White middle-class culture, and thus are biased against Black Americans, who have a different set of common experiences. This sort of **test bias**, features of test items or design that are not appropriate for all members of the population, could apply to the verbal and general information parts of the IQ test, but what about the performance parts? The race difference in IQ scores is present even here. So a simple "biased testing" explanation is probably not correct (Glutting et al., 2000; Neisser et al., 1996; Sackett et al., 2001).

**TEST ANXIETY?** Taking IQ tests isn't simply a matter of flexing your intellectual muscles. As you no doubt know from experience, taking a test of any kind, whether an achievement test (such as the SAT) or a midterm exam or an IQ test, can be anxiety provoking. Test stress may manifest itself in distinct physical symptoms, such as a speeded-up heart rate and sweaty palms. And as you feel literally "put to the test," your thinking may become clouded by a variety of distracting thoughts. Thus, factors unrelated to intelligence may affect IQ scores and other test scores. (Something similar apparently happened to Rowling when she was writing her second Harry Potter book. Her first book was garnering attention and awards, and becoming worried that the second book wouldn't live up to people's expectations, she developed writer's block. Although she turned in the manuscript at the deadline, she then took it back to work on it more, and resubmitted it 6 months later [Chippendale, 2003].)

It is also possible that people with different backgrounds are more or less comfortable taking various sorts of tests. Indeed, Serpell (1979) found that Zambian children could reproduce patterns better using wire models (which they often used to make their own toys) than using pencil and paper, but the opposite was true for English children from the same social class (who were used to pencil and paper but not to wire models).

**BAD ENVIRONMENTS?** Others have argued that the observed IQ difference between White and Black Americans is caused by environmental differences. The people who are best off in U.S. society tend to score higher on IQ tests, and so do their children. Black Americans typically make less money than do Whites, and this factor could cause environmental differences that lead them to score lower than Whites. Some orchards get less sun and water than others, and thus the trees tend to bear smaller fruit. Flynn (1999b) points out that IQ differences between White and Black Americans can be accounted for if "the average environment for [Blacks] of 1995 matches the quality of the average environment for Whites in 1945" (p. 15). (We will discuss the reason for this shortly, when we turn to the "Flynn effect.")

**INFERIOR SCHOOLING?** Another possibility is that Black Americans tend to have inferior schooling. Fryer and Levitt (2004) found that there is no difference in intelligence among Black and White children when they begin kindergarten (provided that certain variables are controlled, such as age, birth weight, and number of children's books in

**Test bias:** Features of test items or design that lead a particular group to perform well or poorly and that thus invalidate the test.

the home). However, after 2 years of school, Blacks score notably worse than Whites. Freyer and Levitt considered a number of possible explanations for this finding, but only one received any support: Blacks tend to attend lower quality schools than do Whites.

The possibility that Blacks attend inferior schools might help to explain Lynn's (1998) report that the difference in Black and White intelligence scores has not changed over the years 1972–1996. Lynn assessed intelligence by looking at scores on a 10-item vocabulary test, and Blacks consistently fared worse than Whites. However, Fagan and Holland (2002) showed that Blacks do just as well as Whites on vocabulary tests *provided that they've had the opportunity to learn the words*. These researchers argue that Blacks simply haven't had "equal opportunity" to learn many of the words that are typically on vocabulary tests—which is consistent with the hypothesis that they tend to attend inferior schools. This is precisely the same situation faced by Rowling when she entered her new school and found herself required to work with fractions—which she had not yet been taught. And just as she was inappropriately classified as "dull" on the basis of that test, other people may be classified as being of low intelligence because they have not been previously exposed to material on the test used to assess their intelligence.

Nevertheless, the quality of schools is probably not the whole story. For example, we noted in Chapter 8 that parents on welfare talk to their children less than working-class and professional parents do—and when welfare parents do talk to their children, they use a smaller vocabulary (Hart & Risley, 1995/2002). Most of the welfare parents in this study were Black. However, as intriguing as these sorts of findings are, they cannot explain why Black children adopted into White families have lower IQ scores by the time they reach adolescence than do their White siblings (Scarr & Weinberg, 1983). These Black and White children attended the same schools, and so schooling alone—or family environment alone—cannot explain the difference in their scores.

African children who are accustomed to using wire to make their own playthings, such as this toy car, are more adept at using wire models in pattern reproduction tests.

**EFFECTS OF THE MICROENVIRONMENT?** Some have argued that the microenvironment plays a key role in IQ score differences. Black Americans have darker skin, which is part of their microenvironment; in the United States, this cue may elicit some kinds of negative treatment from the White majority. What would happen in a society in which the majority did not respond this way? Consider this example: Eyferth (1961) studied the IQs of German children who were fathered by White or Black American servicemen right after World War II. If the Black American fathers had lower IQs than the White fathers, which is not known but is likely given the group averages, and if this difference is due to genes, then the children of the Black soldiers should have had a lower average IQ. But they didn't. Both groups of children had the same average IQs. At that time, there were very few Blacks in Germany, and the majority Whites may not have had negative stereotypes about them. Thus, the children may not have experienced negative environmental influences because of their racial background.

Finally, whatever the explanation of the observed group differences in IQ scores may turn out to be, it is crucial to realize that the distributions of scores between races overlap; plenty of Black Americans have higher IQs than plenty of Whites. Group differences do not necessarily apply to any particular individual.

## Sex Differences

Group differences in intelligence are often considered only in the context of race differences, but consider another possible group difference that would affect fully half the population. Are there sex differences in IQ scores? Although some findings may suggest very small sex differences in IQ (Dai & Lynn, 1994; Held et al., 1993; Lynn & Irwing, 2004), these effects are not always found (Aluja-Fabregat et al., 2000;

Jensen, 1998). Instead, researchers typically find that males are better at some tasks than are females, and vice versa (McGillicuddy-De Lisi & De Lisi, 2002). In general, males tend to be better than females at tasks that require spatial reasoning, whereas females tend to be better than males at tasks that require verbal reasoning. Such differences have been found in at least 30 countries (Beller & Gafni, 1996; Halpern, 1992, 2000; Vogel, 1996).

Some theorists have tried to explain sex differences in spatial ability by appealing to the roles attributed to our primitive ancestors (D. M. Buss, 1995; Eals & Silverman, 1994; Geary, 1996). The men, in this view, were out hunting, which required the ability to navigate and recall where the home cave was, whereas the women stayed home, picking berries, weaving baskets, and tending children. But we really don't know much about what our male and female ancestors actually did, and even if these role descriptions are accurate, it isn't clear that women engaged in fewer spatial tasks. Gathering berries requires remembering where they are likely to grow and how to return home, and weaving baskets certainly requires spatial processing (Halpern, 1997).

**BIOLOGICAL FACTORS AND SEX DIFFERENCES**  At least some of the sex differences arise from the effects of sex hormones (Fitch & Bimonte, 2002; Hines, 2004; Kimura, 1994). One study examined women who were about to have a sex-change operation. As part of the procedure, the women received massive doses of male hormones, specifically testosterone. Within 3 months of this treatment, these people's spatial abilities increased and verbal abilities decreased (Van Goozen et al., 1995). Researchers have even found that a woman's spatial abilities shift during the course of her monthly cycle, as the balance of hormones changes (Hampson, 1990; Hampson & Kimura, 1988; Hausmann et al., 2000). Similarly, the level of male hormones shifts during the course of the day and over the seasons, and researchers have found that American males have poorer spatial abilities in the fall, when their levels of male hormones are highest, than in the spring. These hormones do not produce a more-is-better pattern, but apparently one like an upside-down U: Too little or too much is worse than intermediate amounts (Kimura, 1994). Elderly men have low levels of male hormones, and interestingly, testosterone supplements can boost their scores on spatial tests (Janowsky et al., 1994). However, these relationships between hormone levels and behavior are not always found (Halari et al., 2005; Liben et al., 2002; Wolf et al., 2000), and the effects observed probably depend on a variety of other currently unknown factors.

Additional evidence that biological factors affect sex differences comes from two sorts of studies: First, researchers have discovered differences in the structure and function of the brains of men and women. For example, it has long been known that the cerebral hemispheres are not as sharply specialized in women as in men (Jancke & Steinmetz, 1994; Springer & Deutsch, 1998), and such anatomical differences may underlie some functional differences (Gur et al., 1999; Mansour et al., 1996; Shaywitz et al., 1995). Second, sex differences in cognitive performance may be evident very early in life, even right after birth (Connellan et al., 2000; Lutchmaya & Baron-Cohen, 2002). For instance, Lutchmaya and Baron-Cohen (2002) measured the amount of time that year-old infants looked at a video clip of cars or faces and found that boys looked longer at cars than faces, but vice versa for girls. However, the video clips differed in many ways (such as speed of movement and visual complexity), and it is difficult to know exactly what produced the difference in viewing times.

**SOCIOLOGICAL FACTORS AND SEX DIFFERENCES**  Sex differences in cognitive abilities are not due solely to biological differences (Wigfield et al., 2002). To begin, some researchers argue that systematic differences in men's and women's health have muddied the waters. For example, men tend to drink more alcohol and to exercise more often than do women, and women tend to have more depressive symptoms than do men (Jorm et al., 2004). When health factors were controlled statistically, the male superiority in performance on certain cognitive tasks disappeared—and the female superiority on other tasks actually became greater. As the researchers put it, "better health and health habits in males can account for their better performance on some tests, but such factors cannot account for better female performance on other tests" (p. 16)

In addition, at least part of the sex differences may arise from how boys and girls are treated in our society. Boys and girls are encouraged to take part in "sex appropriate" activities (Lytton & Romney, 1991). This is important in part because if you do not perform activities that utilize spatial abilities, those abilities do not develop (Baenninger & Newcombe, 1989). And traditionally, girls have not been encouraged to participate in as many activities that require spatial skills, such as climbing trees and playing ball, as have boys.

Finally, keep in mind that many females are better at spatial reasoning than many males, and many males are better at verbal reasoning than many females. Here, too, differences in the group averages say nothing about differences among particular individuals.

Participating in activities that utilize spatial abilities means that the neural systems that underlie those activities are exercised. Subrahmanyam and Greenfield (1994) showed that spatial abilities could be improved by having children play certain video games, and boys and girls in these studies improved the same amount. However, sex differences in spatial abilities are evident even in early childhood, and so are unlikely to be totally the result of learning (Reinisch & Sanders, 1992; Robinson et al., 1996).

# Boosting IQ: Pumping Up the Mind's Muscle

Can experience change IQ? As you have seen in Chapter 3, even if a characteristic is heavily influenced by genetics, the environment can make a difference. So it is not surprising that varying the environment can boost general intelligence as measured by IQ score—but how, and by how much?

## The Flynn Effect: Another Reason to Appreciate Being Young

Apparently, one of the most potent ways to improve your IQ is simply to be born later! Many researchers had informally noted a trend that was documented by Flynn (1984, 1999a; Dickens & Flynn, 2001) and is now called the **Flynn effect**: In the Western world, IQ scores have generally risen about 3 points every 10 years. This means that the average IQ today would be 115 if the tests were scored the same way they were 50 years ago. (The way tests are scored is periodically adjusted, to keep the mean at 100.) Flynn (1999a) reported that the largest gains have been on tests that are probably the most free of cultural influence, such as Raven's Progressive Matrices (see Figure 9.3). The Flynn effect has been noted even with the IQ scores of people who have learning difficulties and has had the same impact on the scores of people of different races and genders (Truscott & Frank, 2001). In addition, as IQ scores have risen over time, the *g* factor has accounted for progressively less of the variability in those scores (Kane & Oakland, 2000). That is, not only has IQ in general risen, but some specific abilities have increased more than others—and the particular abilities that have gained vary for different people.

Neisser and colleagues (1996) offer three possible explanations for the Flynn effect:

- Daily life today is more challenging than it was in previous years, and the very act of coping with life's complexities may have increased IQ (Kohn & Schooler, 1973). Moreover, others have noted that school may have become more challenging, particularly in mathematics education (Blair et al., 2005).

Flynn effect: Increases in IQ in the overall population with the passage of time.

Modern toys could be contributing to the rise in IQ over generations.

- Nutrition is better. Lynn (1990) documented that height has increased along with IQ, and characteristics that improve brain functioning might also have increased along with height. Consistent with this view, Colom and colleagues (2005) report that the biggest gains have been in people of low and medium intelligence—as would be expected if low scores partly reflect bad nutrition. Sundet and colleagues (2004) also report that the gains have mainly reduced the number of people with low scores. However, Dickens and Flynn (2001) argue that nutrition must have varied across populations even as average IQ scores increased in all of them, and thus nutrition alone is not likely to explain the Flynn effect.

- Perhaps intelligence itself has not risen, but only the kind of reasoning ability that is useful in taking tests (Flynn, 1999a). One thing is clear: Today's children do not process information faster than children of earlier generations, even though they do perform better on intelligence tests (Nettelbeck & Wilson, 2004). Perhaps technology has led people to become more comfortable with the sorts of abstract thinking that are required to perform well on such tests. Indeed, TV shows such as *Sesame Street* and interactive computer software help children learn to pay attention and also expose them to tasks similar to those on IQ tests. However, this explanation fails to account for the fact that real-world indicators of "intelligent" behavior, such as the number of people playing intellectual games and the level of scientific productivity, have risen along with IQ scores (Howard, 2001).

- In addition to these possibilities, researchers have suggested that people from different groups are marrying each other more often, and their children are benefiting from "hybrid vigor" (because intermarriage among different populations tends to "weed out" recessive genes; Mingroni, 2004). Flynn (1999a), Dickens and Flynn (2001), and Williams (1998) have offered yet other possible explanations for the Flynn effect, but at present the definitive one is not known.

## Accidentally Making Kids Smarter: The Pygmalion Effect

Rowling's experiences at school clearly had an impact on her later life. Rosenthal and Jacobson (1968; Rosenthal, 1993, 1994) studied one way in which teacher-student interactions can affect intelligence. They showed that if teachers thought the children in their classes were going to become smarter, those expectations led the teachers to behave in such a way that the children actually *did* become smarter. Rosenthal and Jacobson performed a large-scale study in a public elementary school in the San Francisco area (in grades 1–6). The students first were given a nonverbal intelligence test, which was disguised as a "test of intellectual potential" (and called, nonsensically, the "Harvard Test of Inflected Acquisition"). Rosenthal and Jacobson then chose at random about 20% of the children in each of three classrooms at each of six grade levels; they told the teachers that these children had scored exceptionally well on the test and that the teachers should expect to see these children bloom intellectually over the next 8 months. The teachers did not know that the children had been assigned randomly to this group, and there was no difference in intelligence between them and the other students. At the end of the year, all the children were tested again, and lo and behold, those whom the teachers thought were going to develop intellectually actually showed larger gains in intelligence scores than did their classmates, especially in grades 1 and 2.

How could this have happened? Rosenthal and his colleagues observed the teacher-student interactions and found that the teachers treated the students they thought had greater "intellectual potential" differently. Most important, the teachers not only behaved more warmly to these students, but also put more effort into teaching them more information and more difficult material. In addition, the teachers called on these children more often and gave them more time to answer questions as well as more informative feedback about their performance, providing correct answers after wrong ones were offered. This is a *self-fulfilling prophecy*; what the teachers expected to happen, they made happen. These findings have since been repeated (Babad, 1993; Eden, 1990; Raudenbush, 1984; Rosenthal, 1993), and the effects are especially pronounced if the teachers don't know the children very well (Raudenbush, 1984).

## Intelligence Enhancement Programs: Mental Workouts

Many educational and social programs have been developed with the aim of raising intelligence. Probably the most famous is Project Head Start, which was a large-scale U.S. government initiative starting in the 1960s, designed to provide additional intellectual stimulation for disadvantaged children and to prepare them to succeed in school. Unfortunately, most such programs show only short-term gains in IQ, and the gains evaporate with time (Baumeister & Bacharach, 2000; Consortium for Longitudinal Studies, 1983; Neisser et al., 1996). However, a few studies have shown that IQ scores can be raised if children are given hours of daily supplemental schooling, beginning at a young age and continuing for years (Brody, 1997). Perhaps the best known is the Abecedarian Project (Campbell & Ramey, 1994), which was started at the University of North Carolina in 1972. It provided intensive intellectual enrichment (as well as pediatric care, nutritional supplements, and help from social workers) for children at risk of failing in school. Entering the program as young as 6 weeks of age, children were placed in a specially designed daycare setting for between 6 and 8 hours a day, 5 days a week. After 5 years, they entered a public kindergarten. By age 15, children who had been in the program still had higher IQ scores (by about 5 points) than those in a control group. Although a 5-point boost is not very large (a third of a standard deviation), the enhanced intellectual skills and abilities that underlie it may help these participants succeed at school and at work.

What determines whether enrichment programs succeed in raising intelligence? The key may be whether they help the participants reorganize how they think (Perkins & Grotzer, 1997). In particular, successful programs teach people new strategies for making decisions, organizing problems, and remembering information. People are also taught how to plan and monitor progress as they try to solve problems, and how to know when to stop and change strategies. They are taught to learn to detect situations that require particular patterns of thinking. (For example, remember problems that began like this: "A box of candy has twice as many chocolates as . . . "? The trick is often being able to figure out how to translate the situation into a specific kind of problem that you already know how to solve.) Wagner (1997) reviews ways in which people develop cognitively, many of which rely on *cognitive apprenticeship*. Cognitive apprenticeship involves, among other things, intellectual coaching—having a mentor who can show you how to think. Schellenberg (2004) suggests that such coaching might explain why music lessons can raise IQ scores for 6-year-old children (but only by an average of 2.7 points more than a control group, after 36 weeks of lessons). Table 9.6 summarizes the key ingredients of successful enrichment programs.

Rauscher and colleagues (1993) reported that listening to Mozart could briefly improve spatial reasoning. However, before changing your musical tastes or investing in a new set of CDs, note that efforts to repeat this effect have produced spotty results (Carstens et al., 1995; Chabris, 1999; Newman et al., 1995; Steele et al., 1997, 1999; Wilson & Brown, 1997), and researchers disagree about when the effect is likely to occur (for example, Chabris, 1999, versus Rauscher, 1999) if it occurs at all (McKelvie & Low, 2002). In any event, at best the effect is short-lived.

| TABLE 9.6 | Ingredients of Successful Cognitive Enrichment Programs |
|---|---|
| **Information Taught** | |
| Strategies for making decisions | |
| Strategies for organizing problems | |
| Strategies for remembering information | |
| Methods for planning and monitoring progress | |
| Knowledge about when to stop and change strategies | |
| Learning to detect situations that require particular patterns of thinking | |

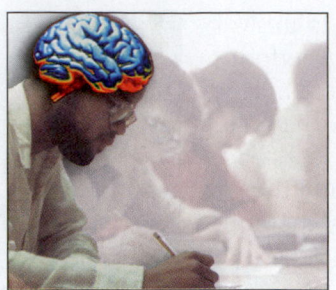

# LOOKING AT LEVELS
## Stereotype Threat

Researchers Claude Steele and Joshua Aronson (1995) conducted a study to investigate the possible effects of negative racial stereotypes on the test-taking performance of Black Americans. They asked Black and White American college students to take a test that included the most difficult items from the verbal portion of the Graduate Record Examination (GRE), a test like the SAT but used for admissions to graduate school. Some students, both Blacks and Whites, were told that the test assessed intellectual ability; another mixed group was told that it was for a study conducted by the laboratory. Blacks and Whites performed comparably when they were told that the test was simply a laboratory experiment, but Black students did much worse than Whites when they thought the test measured intelligence. In another study, Steele and Aronson (1995) asked half the participants of each race simply to list their race immediately before taking the test. The test was always described as a laboratory study, not a test of intelligence. Blacks and Whites performed the same when they did not list their races, but the simple act of being asked to list race drastically reduced the Black students' scores.

According to Steele (1997), asking Blacks about race activates information in long-term memory about negative stereotypes, such as that Blacks are not smart. If you believe that a negative stereotype addresses characteristics that are important to you, then the mere possibility that others will see you as conforming to that stereotype is threatening, even if you do not believe that you have those characteristics. Steele terms this phenomenon *stereotype threat*.

These sorts of findings have been replicated by many others (Croizet & Claire, 1998; Keller & Dauenheimer, 2003; Mayer & Hanges, 2003; Smith & White, 2002) and have been shown to apply not only to race but also to sex (women perform worse on math tests when the negative stereotype about female math ability is activated; Cadinu et al., 2003; O'Brien & Crandall, 2003; Schmader, 2002), old age (older people have poorer memories after the negative stereotype about older adults' memory is invoked; Hess et al., 2003), homosexuality (gay men have greater anxiety when interacting with preschoolers after the stereotype is activated; Bosson et al., 2004), and even athletic ability (activating the stereotype that Whites have poorer "natural athletic ability" than Blacks led Whites to practice less before a sports test; Stone, 2002).

These studies dramatically illustrate the interactions of events at the levels of the brain, the person, and the group. At the level of the brain, when you are threatened, dopamine, norepinephrine, and epinephrine are released; these neurotransmitters play a crucial role in the fight-or-flight response (see Chapters 3 and 13). When confronted by an emergency, you want to act quickly and decisively, and not be lost in thought. But what may be a good response in an emergency is not good for taking a test: These substances not only facilitate subcortical systems involved in the fight-or-flight response, but also disrupt the operation of the parts of the frontal lobes involved in working memory (Arnstein, 1998). Moreover, acute stress results in the release of a substance called *protein kinase* C, which also disrupts working memory—and may cause a person to become distractible and impulsive and to have impaired judgment (Birnbaum et al., 2004; Tan et al., 2004). Croizet and colleagues (2004) found clear evidence of such a stress response when participants took the Ravens Progressive Matrices test while experiencing stereotype threat, and Schmader and Johns (2003) found that stereotype threat does in fact disrupt working memory.

At the level of the person, stereotypes are all about the beliefs you hold. Stereotype threat disrupts performance more severely if a person strongly identifies with the negatively stereotyped group, thus allowing the threat to activate stored information about group membership (Marx et al., 2005; McFarland et al., 2003; Ployhart et al., 2003; Schmader, 2002). Moreover, the effect is larger if you feel that the stereotyped ability is important (Cadinu et al., 2003) or you feel personally stigmatized by the stereotype (Brown & Pinel, 2003). In addition, characteristics at the level of the person can reduce the effects of stereotype threat; for example, stereotype threat is less disruptive for people who use humor to cope with their anxiety (Ford et al., 2004).

At the level of the group, not only does social interaction implant stereotypes in the first place, but such interaction activates stored stereotypes. By the same token, a social interaction can alleviate the effects of stereotype threat. For example, in one study, women did much better on a challenging math test if they first read about four successful professional women (McIntyre et al., 2003). In fact, Aronson and colleagues (2002) report that coaching Black students to see intelligence as "a malleable rather than fixed capacity" helped them to earn higher grades than students in control groups who were not led to adopt this perspective.

However, researchers do not always find that activating a negative stereotype disrupts performance on relevant tasks (Cullen et al., 2004; McKay et al., 2002; Stricker & Ward, 2004). In fact, interactions among events at the various levels appear to be responsible for whether the effect occurs at all (Davies et al., 2005; Major & O'Brien, 2005; Ryan & Ryan, 2005). Some of these interactions may be subtle: Activating a negative stereotype about women's math abilities impaired performance more for women who had relatively high levels of testosterone than for women who had relatively low levels of this sex hormone (Josephs et al., 2003). Thus, a social invention—stereotypes about groups—can become part of an individual's knowledge (level of the person). And that knowledge in turn can be activated by social situations. When activated, the knowledge produces events in the brain (as well as in the body—pounding heart, sweaty palms, and so on), which in turn disrupt performance. And the disrupted performance can then reinforce the stereotypes.

# Test Yourself

1. What does current research say about the relationship between brain size and intelligence?
   a. The correlation between brain size and intelligence is large.
   b. The correlation between brain size and intelligence is typically small.
   c. Brain size is negatively correlated with intelligence.
   d. Brain size is not correlated with intelligence.
2. What is the relationship between speed of processing and intelligence?
   a. There is no relationship.
   b. Speed of processing is the same thing as intelligence.
   c. Speed of processing is negatively correlated with intelligence.
   d. Speed of processing in certain tasks is positively correlated with intelligence.
3. One reason heritability estimates may overestimate the influence of genetics on intelligence is that
   a. twins separated at birth may produce the same microenvironment.
   b. the studies fail to include twins raised together.
   c. twins don't necessarily share any genes.
   d. adopted twins could be identical.
4. What effect, if any, does genetics have on intelligence?
   a. Genes establish a range of possible intelligence levels.
   b. Genes determine IQ scores to within 1 or 2 points.
   c. Genes have little effect on intelligence unless a person experiences severe environmental deprivation.
   d. Genes completely determine intelligence.

# Answers

1.b 2.d 3.a 4.a

# Think It Through!

Say that you could measure someone's reaction ranges for particular types of intelligence (some abilities for a given person could have larger reaction ranges than others). What could you do with this information?

Do you think intelligence tests should be designed so that there are no differences between men and women or between any other two groups? What are the pros and cons of such an approach? If someone came to you feeling intellectually doomed because he thought his parents were stupid, what would you say? What concrete advice could you offer for raising intelligence?

What implications, if any, do group differences in IQ scores have for the way schools should be organized?

# DIVERSITY IN INTELLIGENCE

J. K. Rowling initially attempted to work as a bilingual secretary, but proved a miserable failure at that job. She was so disorganized that she simply could not function appropriately. Nevertheless, we would not think of her as mentally retarded. What would it take for us to have that view? And might we think of her as gifted? Few could create the startlingly imaginative world of her novels. Is that enough for her to qualify as gifted? In this section, we consider the extreme forms of intelligence, high and low, as well as the bases of creativity.

## Mental Retardation: People With Special Needs

For want of a better definition, people with an IQ score of 70 or lower (that is, who fall more than two standard deviations below the mean; see Figure 9.1 on p. 384) have traditionally been considered to be **mentally retarded**. The American Association for Mental Retardation (1992) specifies two additional criteria:

1. "significant limitations" in two or more everyday abilities, such as communication, self-care, and self-direction, and

2. the presence of the condition since childhood.

Although estimates vary widely, at least 4 million Americans are mentally retarded (Larson et al., 2001), and possibly as many as 7 million (Fryers, 1993). Mental retardation (also called *intellectual disability*) affects about 100 times more people than does total blindness (Batshaw & Perret, 1992). One out of every 10 families in the United States is directly affected by mental retardation (American Association for Mental Retardation, 1992). The good news is that just as IQ is on the rise, mild mental retardation appears to be on the decline (Howard, 2001). However, the bad news is that because of the Flynn effect, the norms for IQ tests are periodically adjusted—and thus somebody who has not been considered to be retarded one day can wake up the next day to discover that he or she has been reclassified as retarded! This renorming of IQ tests can disrupt a person's life, for instance, by having him or her fall below the bar for admission to the U.S. military (Kanaya et al., 2003).

Retardation does not imply an inability to learn. Mildly retarded people can learn to function well as normal adults, and behavioral techniques that involve explicit shaping and reinforcement (see Chapter 6) can allow even severely retarded people to master

**Mentally retarded:** People who have an IQ of 70 or less and significant limitations in at least two aspects of everyday life since childhood.

many tasks. Furthermore, many otherwise retarded children display **islands of excellence**, areas in which they perform remarkably well. *Savants* (previously called *idiot savants*), such as the main character, Raymond, in the movie *Rain Man*, have dramatic disparities in their abilities (Hermelin, 2001; Miller, 1999). For example, a savant may be able to determine the day of the week for any calendar date, including dates centuries from now or in the past (Horwitz et al., 1965) or to draw outstandingly vivid, detailed pictures (Hou et al., 2000). But the same person may be incapable of doing simple addition.

Mental retardation results when the brain fails to develop properly, which can happen in the womb or during childhood. Although hundreds of causes have now been identified, the causes of about one third of all cases are still mysteries. However, it is clear that both genetic and environmental factors can lead to retardation.

## Genetic Influences: When Good Genes Go Bad

Mutations in over 280 separate genes have been found to lead to mental retardation (Inlow & Restifo, 2004). The most common type of mental retardation (occurring in about 1 in 1,000 births) is known as **Down syndrome**, first described by British physician J. Langdon Down in 1866. Down children have an average IQ of 55, but the degree of retardation varies widely—and may disrupt everyday activities less severely than other forms of mental retardation (Chapman & Hesketh, 2000). The most frequent form of Down syndrome is not inherited, but it is caused by a genetic problem—the creation of an extra chromosome (number 21) during conception. This genetic abnormality apparently prevents neurons from developing properly, so that action potentials (neural firings) do not operate normally (Galdzicki et al., 2001). Down syndrome is more likely to occur in births to older mothers, whose eggs have been dormant for many years.

The second most common cause of mental retardation is also genetic, but in this case the child inherits a genetic quirk: A small bit of DNA on the X chromosome repeats itself many times (Eliez & Reiss, 2000). Because this defect makes the chromosome prone to breaking up when observed in the laboratory, the disorder is called **fragile X syndrome** (Madison et al., 1986; Murray et al., 1996; Sudhalter & Belser, 2001). About twice as many males as females suffer from this disorder, because males have only one X chromosome and females have two. It is rare that both of a female's X chromosomes carry the disorder; only one of the two X chromosomes is actually functional, and so even when a female has an X chromosome that carries the disorder, about half the time it is not the functioning one. The repetition of the bit of DNA is compounded over generations, and the more repeats, the more severe the symptoms (Levitas, 2000; Siomi et al., 1996). Thus, with each succeeding generation, the syndrome becomes worse.

Mental retardation also typically accompanies **autism**, a condition of intense self-involvement to the exclusion of external reality (Tager-Flusberg et al., 2001). Only about 25% of autistic people have IQs higher than 70, and thus most people with this disorder are also mentally retarded (Fombonne, 1999; Volkmar et al., 1994). Depending on the severity of the disease, people with autism are socially bizarre, are disoriented, may sometimes engage in repetitive body movements such as rocking or hand flapping, and have severe attentional difficulties; they may also be self-destructive. Although the disorder is rare (estimates range from as low as 3 out of 10,000 live births to as high as 1 out of 500), it is highly heritable: If one identical twin has it, the chances are around 60% that the other does, too. In contrast, if one fraternal twin is autistic, the chances are only 10% that the other is. Four times as many boys as girls are afflicted with autism.

**Islands of excellence:** Areas in which retarded people perform remarkably well.

**Down syndrome:** A type of mental retardation that results from the creation of an extra chromosome during conception; it is a genetic problem but not inherited.

**Fragile X syndrome:** A type of mental retardation that affects the X chromosome; it is both genetic and inherited.

**Autism:** A condition of intense self-involvement to the exclusion of external reality; about three quarters of autistic people are mentally retarded.

## Environmental Influences: Bad Luck, Bad Behavior

Drinking and driving don't mix; neither do drinking and pregnancy. If the mother drinks heavily during pregnancy, her child can be born with **fetal alcohol syndrome**. Part of this syndrome is mental retardation (Streissguth et al., 1989, 1999). Indeed, many environmental factors can lead to mental retardation. If a pregnant woman experiences malnutrition, rubella, diabetes, HIV infection, high doses of X rays, or any of a number of infections, her child may be born with mental retardation. Streissguth and colleagues (1989) found that taking antibiotics and even aspirin during pregnancy also can adversely affect the developing baby's brain. People whose retardation is due to such environmental factors tend not to have retarded children themselves.

Mental retardation can also arise if the birth is unusually difficult and the infant's brain is injured. Premature birth and low birth weight put a child at risk for retardation. In addition, some childhood diseases, such as chicken pox and measles, can sometimes cause brain damage, as can ingesting lead, mercury, or poisons. Vaccines and other medical treatments greatly reduced the incidence of mental retardation in the latter part of the 20th century(Alexander, 1991; Croen et al., 2002). Both genetic and environmental factors are summarized in Table 9.7.

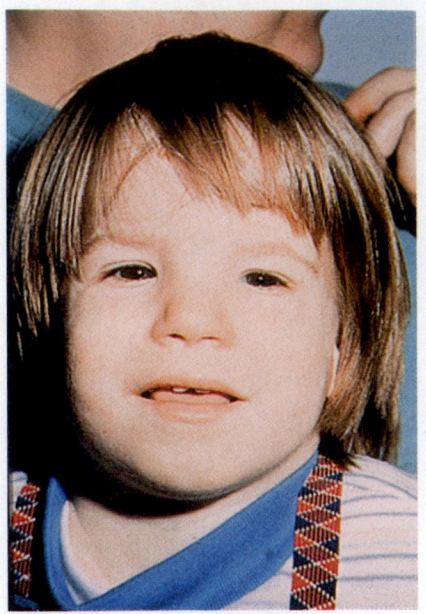

If a mother drinks alcohol heavily during pregnancy, her child can be born with fetal alcohol syndrome (FAS)—one aspect of which is mental retardation and another aspect of which is the type of facial characteristics shown here.

### TABLE 9.7 — Causes of Retardation: Common Examples

**Genetic conditions**

- Down syndrome
- Fragile X syndrome

**Problems during pregnancy**

- Use of alcohol or drugs
- Malnutrition
- Rubella
- Glandular disorders and diabetes
- Illnesses of the mother during pregnancy
- Physical malformations of the brain
- HIV infection in the fetus

**Problems at birth**

- Prematurity
- Low birth weight

**Problems after birth**

- Childhood diseases such as whooping cough, chicken pox, and measles, which may lead to meningitis and encephalitis, which can in turn damage the brain
- Accidents such as a blow to the head or near drowning
- Lead and mercury poisoning

**Poverty and cultural deprivation**

- Malnutrition
- Disease-producing conditions
- Inadequate medical care
- Environmental health hazards

# The Gifted

There is no hard-and-fast way to determine whether a person is **gifted** (Robinson et al., 2000); the term is sometimes used to refer to people who have IQs of at least 135, but more commonly denotes the 150–180 range (Winner, 1997). Much of the research on the gifted has focused on people with very high IQs, above 150, and that is the crite-

Fetal alcohol syndrome: A condition that includes mental retardation and is caused by excessive drinking of alcohol by the mother during pregnancy.

Gifted: People who have IQs between 150 and 180.

rion we apply here. It is not known how genes and the environment, including the environment in the womb, contribute to the condition. However, gifted boys tend to have lower testosterone levels than nongifted boys, whereas gifted girls may actually have higher amounts of testosterone than nongifted girls (Dohnanyiova et al., 2001; Ostatnikova et al., 2000, 2002); these findings hint at biological factors that could predispose some people to become gifted.

As expected from the idea that intelligence has different facets (as shown in the middle and bottom strata of Figure 9.2), children can be gifted in some domains while not being gifted in others (Winner, 2000a, 2000b). **Prodigies**, children with immense talent in a particular area, may be perfectly normal in other areas; for example, mathematically gifted children often are not gifted in other domains (Benbow & Minor, 1990). Achter and colleagues (1996) found that over 95% of the gifted children they tested had sharply differing mathematical and verbal abilities.

According to some researchers (such as Jackson & Butterfield, 1986) gifted children do the same kinds of processing as average children but simply do it more effectively. As Winner (1997) notes, however, some children "as young as three or four years of age have induced rules of algebra on their own (Winner, 1996), have memorized almost instantly entire musical scores (Feldman & Goldsmith, 1991), and have figured out on their own how to identify all prime numbers (Winner, 1996)" (p. 1071). Such intellectual feats suggest that the cognition of gifted children may be qualitatively different from that of other people. Specifically, Winner suggests that gifted children may be exceptionally able to intuit solutions to problems and may be driven by an extraordinary passion to master tasks.

The gifts are sometimes bestowed with a price. Gifted children are at times socially awkward and may be treated as "geeks" and "nerds" (Silverman, 1993a, 1993b; Winner, 1996). In addition, they may tend to be solitary and introverted (Silverman, 1993b). They have twice the rate of emotional and social problems as nongifted children (Winner, 1997).

If you aren't gifted as a child, does this mean you have no hope of becoming a gifted adult? Not at all. Many distinguished adults—Charles Darwin, for example—showed no signs of being gifted as children (Simonton, 1994); furthermore, most gifted children grow up to be rather ordinary adults (Richert, 1997; Winner, 2000a, 2000b).

Many eminent adults had the help of able mentors at critical phases of their lives (Bloom, 1985; Gardner, 1993a). Having an apprentice relationship with an appropriate role model can make a huge difference. That is one reason why graduate education in the sciences in the United States is based on apprenticeship: Students in PhD programs in the sciences learn at the elbows of their supervisors, not simply from reading books or listening to lectures.

Prodigies are children who have a gift in one particular area. For example, a child may be an extraordinary violinist but not so outstanding in other areas.

# Creative Smarts

Rowling had the idea for Harry Potter while she was riding on a train. "I have never felt such a huge rush of excitement. I knew immediately that this was going to be such fun to write" (Fraser, 2000, p. 37). Unfortunately, she didn't have a pencil or pen to write down what she was thinking, and so she simply thought through the story in detail. "It was a question of discovering why Harry was where he was, why his parents were dead. I was inventing it, but it felt like research" (p. 39).

Creativity lies at the heart of many forms of intelligence. **Creativity** is the ability to produce something original of high quality or to devise an effective new way of solving a problem. Creativity necessarily involves the ability to recognize and develop a novel approach, the ability to consider a problem from multiple angles and to change points

**Prodigies:** Children who demonstrate immense talent in a particular area, such as music or mathematics, but who are normal in other areas.

**Creativity:** The ability to produce something original of high quality or to devise an effective new way of solving a problem.

of view repeatedly, and the ability to develop a simple idea in different ways. Creative thought can be applied to practical problems (such as raising money), intellectual tasks (making new connections in a term paper), or artistic work (writing a novel).

## Creative Thinking: Not Just Inspiration

Creativity often comes to the fore when you face a novel problem and have to figure out a new way to solve it (Isaksen & Treffinger, 2004; Runco, 2004). As psychologists use the term, the "problem" to be solved can be very specific (such as designing a new logo for your club) or very general (such as writing a new poem). Many theorists have suggested that creativity relies on a two-stage process. In the first stage, you generate a variety of possible solutions to a problem; in the second stage, you interpret and select among them (Campbell, 1960; Martindale, 1990; Simonton, 1995, 1997).

The two-stage technique is a key aspect of an approach called *creative cognition*, in which the processes of normal cognition, such as memory and mental imagery, function to produce novel solutions to problems (Finke, 1996; Finke et al., 1992; Ward, 2001). Much research on creative cognition has grown out of the task illustrated in Figure 9.8. Finke and Slayton (1988) gave participants a set of simple shapes and asked them to combine the shapes mentally to create a recognizable form or object. In these studies, the first stage of the problem-solving process involves "mental play" with images of the forms, through rotation, size adjustment, and repositioning. To be effective in this first stage, the participants should produce many candidate creations. The right cerebral hemisphere appears to be involved in reaching for remote associations among concepts, and thus may play a special role in this stage (Seger et al., 2000). Finke and colleagues (1992) found that participants were more creative if they combined shapes without a particular goal in mind at the outset (such as creating a device that removes peach pits) and attempted an interpretation only after producing novel combinations.

The second stage of the problem-solving process in the mental combination task involves recognizing what a combination of the forms could represent. Finke and colleagues (1992) found that participants were more creative if they were asked to produce objects in a certain category, such as toys or furniture (which are not specific goals), than if they were allowed to produce objects in any category. Asking for objects in par-

---

**FIGURE 9.8**   **Creative Cognition**

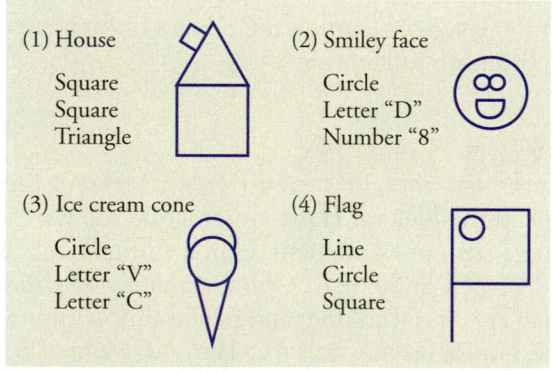

Shapes used in the Finke and Slayton (1988) experiments on a mental combination task. On a given trial, three of the shapes were selected.

The participants mentally arranged the shapes and, after 2 minutes, named and drew a picture of what they had created. Judges decided that the patterns were recognizable in 40.5% of the trials, and that 15% of those patterns were creative.

ticular categories prevented the participants from thinking about the forms in conventional ways and forced them to consider novel combinations. Each stage of this kind of problem solving often involves an interplay between two types of thinking, *divergent* and *convergent* (Guilford, 1967; Mumford, 2001). With divergent thinking, you come at a problem from a number of different angles, exploring a variety of approaches to a solution before settling on one (Mednick, 1962; Reese et al., 2001). With convergent thinking, you stay focused on one particular approach to a problem and work through a series of steps to arrive at a solution. Convergent thinking also plays a role in setting up a problem in the first place and in cutting back the lush jungle of ideas created by divergent thinking.

How many uses can you think of for a brick? Divergent thinking might lead you to consider bricks as doorstops, supports for bookshelves, or bookends.

## What Makes a Person Creative?

Some people are undoubtedly more creative than others. Why? Eysenck (1995) claims that very creative people tend to make loose associations and engage in divergent thinking. Rowling, for example, has commented on how disorganized she is, which could reflect a penchant for divergent thinking (including "going off on tangents"). However, studies of creative people suggest that they have special abilities that affect both stages of the creative process: Not only can they generate more possible solutions, but they are also able to select among them more effectively. But creativity isn't just about processing and abilities; creative people also appear to have distinctive personal characteristics.

**COGNITIVE CHARACTERISTICS OF CREATIVE PEOPLE** Creative people may tend to think differently than the rest of us. Amabile (1983, 1998) found that creative people keep options open, do not make snap decisions about the likely outcome of an effort, and are good at seeing a problem from a new vantage point. Similarly, when Guilford used factor analysis to discover which underlying abilities are tapped by various tests of creativity, he found that flexibility and the ability to reorganize information were key (similar conclusions were drawn by Aguilar-Alonso, 1996, and Eysenck, 1995). Martindale (1989, 2001) stresses that creative people tend to think in terms of analogies, tend to have high intelligence, have wide interests, don't like traditional dogmas, have high self-esteem, and like to work hard. In addition, creative people are often highly motivated and persistent, driven to create (Sulloway, 1996). Amabile (2001) emphasizes the role of hard work and strong motivation in creativity, and Heilman and colleagues (2003) underscore the importance of knowledge about the relevant domain and having the skills to be able to work with that knowledge. The qualities of creative people are summarized in Table 9.8.

Are creative people born that way? Although researchers are beginning to study and theorize about the neural bases of creativity (Ione, 2003; Dietrich, 2004; Heilman et al., 2003; Zeki, 2002), we do not yet know how the brains of creative people are special. However, we do know that—in sharp contrast to differences in IQ—differences in creativity are not strongly related to genetic differences, if at all. Furthermore, and also in contrast to IQ, shared aspects of the home (such as exposure to cultural resources, home libraries, or parents' mechanical or artistic hobbies) strongly affect creativity (Canter, 1973; Nichols, 1978; Simonton, 1988).

| TABLE 9.8 | Characteristics of Creative People |
| --- | --- |
| Make loose associations, engage in divergent thinking |
| Select among possible solutions effectively |
| Keep options open |
| Do not make snap decisions about the likely outcome of an effort |
| Good at seeing a problem from a new vantage point |
| Are flexible and able to reorganize information |
| Think in terms of analogies |
| Tend to have high intelligence |
| Have wide interests |
| Don't like traditional dogmas |
| Have high self-esteem |
| Like to work hard |
| Highly motivated and persistent |

In some ways, creativity is like pitching in baseball. Cy Young was the pitcher with the greatest number of wins in baseball history. The pitcher with the most losses? Cy Young. People who produce large numbers of creative works are also likely to produce large numbers of mundane works.

Moreover, in keeping with the overall importance of events at the different levels of analysis, creativity flourishes only when the social circumstances are right. For instance, Nakamura and Csikszentmihalyi (2001) conceive of creativity by analogy to natural selection during evolution (see Chapter 3). Just as mutations provide variations (such as longer necks for the ancestors of giraffes) that may then prove useful in the environment (where tall trees have tasty leaves), individuals provide variations in ideas, but only the ones that prove useful in the social world are selected and flourish.

**PERSONAL CHARACTERISTICS OF CREATIVE PEOPLE** Other researchers have looked for the roots of creativity by examining the personalities and backgrounds of creative people. Simonton (1984, 1988, 1990) found that in spite of romantic images of the moody Russian composer, the drunken Irish poet, and the poor Southern writer beaten as a child, the amount of stress people experience is not related to how creative they are, and social recognition of a person's accomplishments neither increases nor decreases creativity. In addition, the most creative people had intermediate amounts of formal education; either too much or too little formal education apparently stifles creativity (Simonton, 1988).

Are highly creative people mentally unstable? It has long been believed that certain mental disorders promote creativity (Kraepelin, 1921). Manic-depressive (bipolar) mental illness can result in shifts between very "high" energetic moods and very "low" depressed ones. Kay Redfield Jamison and her colleagues (Goodwin & Jamison, 1990; Jamison, 1989; Jamison et al., 1980), as well as Hershman and Lieb (1988, 1998), have argued that a "loosening" of thought that occurs during the manic phase of this disorder enhances creativity. If so, the manic phase may spur creativity by increasing the number of possible solutions a person can formulate during the first stage of the creative process (Barrantes-Vidal, 2004). Isaac Newton, Charles Dickens, and Kurt Cobain apparently suffered from this disorder, and Andreasen (1987) found that almost half the visiting faculty in the University of Iowa Writers' Workshop, an intensive course for creative writers, had experienced it. Jamison (1989) reports similar findings, particularly for poets.

In fact, various neurological disorders can alter creativity. For example, as Alzheimer's disease progresses, some patients begin to draw novel surrealistic sketches (Miller & Hou, 2004). In addition, the French composer Maurice Ravel had a brain disorder that began by affecting the left side of his brain; some of his final compositions can be understood in terms of a shift in how the cerebral hemispheres worked together as the disease progressed (Amaducci et al., 2002). And the painter Willem de Kooning may have changed his style as he developed a disease that undercut his attention span, leading him to create works that could be produced quickly (Stewart, 2002).

Although some have claimed that mental illness is associated with increased creativity, others have claimed that mental illness is independent of creativity; these claims are consistent with analyses by Dennis (1966) and Simonton (1984, 1997), who showed that the quality of a creative person's work tends to be constant over their productive years; in years when a large number of particularly good works are produced, a correspondingly large number of inferior works are also produced.

## Enhancing Creativity

Many techniques, focusing on ways to find novel solutions to problems, have been developed in an effort to enhance creativity. When designing an object, for example, Crawford (1954) suggests listing its attributes and then considering how to modify each attribute to improve the object. Say you are developing a beach chair; you would first list the essential attributes—it must support weight, recline at different angles, and so on. Then you would think about how to design different systems for supporting weight (webbing, fabric, air cushions) and for adjusting the angle (ropes, gears, air pressure), and so forth. Another useful technique is to consider how to combine attributes in new ways (Davis, 1973). For example, consider how the properties of knives, spoons, and forks could be combined to create new multipurpose eating tools. Meta-analyses suggest that training programs focusing on such techniques can be effective (Scott et al., 2004a, 2004b).

Sternberg (2001) claims that everyone can become more creative. He proposes ten ways to accomplish this: (1) *Redefine problems*. Don't accept the way a problem is characterized; think about different ways to pose it. (2) *Analyze your own ideas*. Be your own harshest critic, and change your ideas when they aren't working. (3) *Sell your ideas*. In the process of trying to persuade others, your ideas will sharpen. (4) *Knowledge is a double-edged sword*. Don't trust experts; knowing too much can be as much of a hindrance as knowing too little. (5) *Surmount obstacles*. Any truly original idea won't be embraced by everyone immediately; expect to struggle. (6) *Take sensible risks*. If an idea means a lot to you, be willing to press forward even if others resist (but take *sensible* risks—consider carefully the reasons why others are resisting). (7) *Be willing to grow*. Keep open eyes and an open mind, and be willing to change course when necessary. (8) *Believe in yourself*. If you don't, others won't either. (9) *Tolerate ambiguity*. Even very good ideas take time to work out in detail. (10) *Find what you love to do and do it*. Do your own thing—you'll be more creative if you do.

Destination Imagination (DI) is an international organization that encourages brainstorming and creativity in the context of preparing the most creative possible "solution" to a team's choice of a challenging problem. This group performed a commercial for a nutritional product that they created.

# UNDERSTANDING RESEARCH

## Constrained Creativity

**QUESTION:** Many people believe that truly creative thought requires freedom, but others have argued that creativity thrives when there is a great deal of structure. When a problem is specified precisely and the approach is made very clear, is it easier to be creative?

**ALTERNATIVES:** (1) Structure can facilitate creativity. (2) Structure can inhibit creativity. (3) Structure makes no difference.

**LOGIC:** Goldenberg and colleagues (1999) programmed a computer to engage in the most extreme form of structured thinking: following an algorithm, a step-by-step set of rules. If such structure facilitates creativity, then the computer should be able to produce creative solutions—perhaps more of them than humans who are not working within such a strict structure.

**METHOD:** The researchers first studied effective advertisements and noticed that they seemed to rely on a few simple ideas (which are involved in creativity in general; Boden, 2000). For instance, many involved replacing properties of one thing with those of another: An ad for Bally shoes, for example, suggested that the shoes gave wearers a sense of freedom by showing clouds or an inviting island in the shape of a shoe; the sense of freedom conveyed by the clouds and the island was intended to transfer to the shoes. After being armed with such rules, the computer was asked to describe ads for specific products in order to convey certain messages; its suggestions were then compared to those from humans (who were not in the ad business).

| TABLE 9.9 | Problems and Solutions: Humans Versus Computer | |
|---|---|---|
| **Problem** | **Human Idea** | **Computer Idea** |
| Convey that Apple computers are user-friendly. | An Apple computer next to a PC, with the claim: "This is the friendliest computer." | An Apple computer offers flowers. |
| Convey that Jeeps have very quiet engines. | A car alone in the country. | Two Jeeps communicating in sign language. |
| Convey that an airline has on-time performance. | A family running to an airplane, with one of the parents screaming, "Let's run, I know this airline's planes are always right on time." | A cuckoo in the shape of a jumbo jet popping out of a cuckoo clock. |

**RESULTS:** Table 9.9 presents some examples of what the computer and humans produced (as reported by Angier, 1999). Which ideas do you think are more creative? When the ads were judged by both advertising professionals and others, the computer's ideas came out on top: The judges rated its suggestions as more creative and original than those of the humans. In fact, the computer's suggestions were often judged to be as good as actual award-winning ads.

**INFERENCES:** At least in some situations, structure helps rather than hinders creativity (Perez Y Perez & Sharples, 2001). In fact, when humans were taught the rules programmed into the computer, they did as well as, and sometimes better than, the computer. However, such training is highly limited to a particular type of problem, such as writing advertisements.

## THINK CRITICALLY!

Do you think it was appropriate to compare the computer to humans who were not in the advertising business? Do you think it would have been more appropriate to compare the computer's output to the average human response or to the best human response? Why? Can you think of other situations that demand creative responses where structure might not be so useful?

# Test Yourself

1. A young girl has an IQ of 50 and functions well socially. Her mother was nearly 50 years old when the girl was born. What is the most likely cause of her mental retardation?
   a. fragile X syndrome
   b. Down syndrome
   c. autism
   d. fetal alcohol syndrome
2. A gifted individual has an IQ
   a. the same as that of a normal person.
   b. between 150 and 180, according to the most common definition.
   c. at least 2 standard deviations above the mean, 130.
   d. over 200, if the person is truly gifted, but otherwise over 180.

3. Creative people are very likely to
   a. be the offspring of noncreative people.
   b. be chronically depressed.
   c. have a low IQ.
   d. be flexible in their thinking.
4. Research on enhancing creativity has found that it
   a. can never be enhanced.
   b. is predominantly genetic.
   c. can be enhanced.
   d. cannot be studied scientifically.

# Answers

1.b 2.b 3.d 4.c

# Think It Through!

The eugenics movement seeks to improve the human species by encouraging those with extremely low IQ scores not to have children. What do you think of this idea? Do you think it is useful to define people as mentally retarded or gifted? Why or why not?

Is creativity always desirable? What would the world be like if everyone were supercreative, always trying to change things? In what circumstances might creativity be more of a drawback than a benefit? Do you think all phases of the creative process rely equally on intelligence? If not, are there ways in which people of differing intelligence might best work together to be creative?

# REVIEW AND REMEMBER!

## Summary

### I. Measuring Intelligence: What Is IQ?

**A.** The most common measure of intelligence is the score on an intelligence test, called the intelligence quotient, or IQ. IQ scores are a composite of many different underlying abilities, and the same IQ score can arise from different mixtures of relative strengths and weaknesses.

**B.** The most common IQ tests, the Wechsler Adult Intelligence Scale (WAIS) and the Wechsler Intelligence Scale for Children (WISC), consist of two sets of subtests, one that assesses verbal performance and one that assesses non-verbal performance.

**C.** When first devised, IQ was a measure of mental age compared to chronological age. Today, IQ scores are based on standardized norms for large samples, which are updated periodically so that the mean score on the WAIS or the WISC is always 100 and a standard deviation is 15.

**D.** Scores on IQ tests are positively correlated with achievement in school and on the job; they are also correlated with many aspects of success in life, such as staying out of prison or having an enduring marriage.

### II. Analyzing Intelligence: One Ability or Many?

**A.** There are many theories of intelligence, most of which posit a single overarching "general intelligence" (g) and a set of specific abilities. According to one theory, g may be broken down into fluid and crystallized intelligence. Performance in a wide range of occupations is well predicted by g, and barely—if at all—by specific abilities.

**B.** Emotional intelligence is not assessed by standard IQ tests, but it may turn out to be important in daily life.

**C.** Some researchers believe that there are many aspects of intelligence; the theory of multiple intelligences posits a number of forms of intelligence. However, this

## Your Notes

*I.*

*A.*

*B.*

*C. IQ now based on norms:*
   *100 = average;*
   *15 = each standard deviation*

*D.*

*II.*

*A.*

*B.*

*C.*

theory has yet to be tested, and many researchers question whether all of the abilities are in fact forms of intelligence.

## III. What Makes Us Smart? Nature and Nurture

**A.** Differences in intelligence among individuals may arise because key parts of people's brains vary in size or efficiency. People with larger brains tend to have higher IQ scores, but size cannot be all that is important. Although additional neurons in a larger brain area could allow the brain to process more complex information, and to do so faster, simple speed is not the crucial factor. The ability to focus, the "central executive" aspect of working memory, may be key.

**B.** Parts of the frontal lobes may allow a person to hold more information in working memory at one time.

**C.** Variations in intelligence probably reflect an intimate dance between the genes and the environment. Genes set the reaction range, the extreme upper and lower limits, of different aspects of an individual's intelligence; the environment positions the individual within this range.

**D.** Although about 50% of the variability in scores on IQ tests can be explained in terms of genetic factors, this number is an average and does not apply to individuals.

**E.** Group differences in IQ have been well documented; it is impossible to sort out the relative contributions of genes and environment to such differences. Some group differences in some abilities, such as sex differences in spatial ability, may reflect biological differences, for example, in hormone levels. However, other group differences—in IQ scores of Black and White Americans, for example— may arise in part from the ways in which environments affect individuals. Group differences may also reflect the way in which individuals' characteristics create their microenvironments and influence the reactions of others to them.

**F.** Environmental effects can also occur at the time an IQ test is administered; when this happens, test scores are not valid indicators of ability.

**G.** IQ scores in general have been rising with the passage of time, perhaps because the environment has become more complex and each new generation of children has risen to the challenge.

**H.** Intensive early training can raise IQ, but not by very much. Successful programs for boosting IQ generally teach people new strategies for making decisions, organizing problems, and remembering information, as well as for noting when it is appropriate to use a particular kind of thinking in a given situation.

**I.** All distributions of abilities within any group overlap those of other groups, and hence group differences have no applicability to particular individuals in a given group.

## IV. Diversity in Intelligence

**A.** Mental retardation is traditionally defined on the basis of overall IQ score *plus* significant difficulty with two or more everyday tasks, with both conditions existing since childhood. By this definition, someone who is retarded cannot be gifted; giftedness is defined by a very high IQ score (typically between 150 and 180).

*III.*

*A.*

*B. Frontal lobes—hold info in WM*

*C.*

*D.*

*E.*

*F.*

*G.*

*H.*

*I.*

*IV.*

*A.*

**B.** Nevertheless, even people who perform much worse than the average on many tasks can have islands of excellence, performing superbly in one or two areas.

**C.** Mental retardation can arise for many reasons, some genetic and some environmental. Not all of the genetic reasons reflect inherited defects; some reflect accidents during conception or environmental damage to genes.

**D.** Creativity leads to the production of original works or to innovative effective solution to problems. Various tests of aspects of creative thinking (such as divergent thought) have been devised, and creativity can be assessed in the laboratory by observing whether people generate novel products or solutions. At least some forms of creativity depend on specific knowledge and skills, but there may also be a general creative ability.

**E.** Creative people have many characteristics, including the tendency to make loose associations, engage in divergent thinking, keep options open, avoid snap decisions, be flexible, organize information well, and see problems from many points of view. Creativity has a very low heritability and is strongly influenced by shared environment. Brain disorders can affect creativity in various ways, at times appearing to enhance it.

NOTE: Once you feel that you understand the material in this chapter, visit the book's Web site at www.ablongman.com/kosslyn3e to test your knowledge with additional study questions.

*B.*

*C. Mental retardation: causes can be genetic (but not always inherited) or environmental.*

*D.*

*E.*

## Key Terms

autism, p. 415
creativity, p. 417
crystallized intelligence, p. 387
Down syndrome, p. 415
emotional intelligence (EI), p. 391
factor analysis, p. 386
fetal alcohol syndrome, p. 416
fluid intelligence, p. 387
Flynn effect, p. 409
fragile X syndrome, p. 415

g, p. 386
gifted, p. 416
intelligence, p. 380
intelligence quotient (IQ), p. 381
islands of excellence, p. 415
mentally retarded, p. 414
microenvironment, p. 402
norming, p. 383
primary mental abilities, p. 387
prodigies, p. 417

Raven's Progressive Matrices, p. 398
reaction range, p. 403
s, p. 386
standardized sample, p. 383
test bias, p. 406
theory of multiple intelligences, p. 392
Wechsler Adult Intelligence Scale (WAIS), p. 381

# CHAPTER 10

# EMOTION AND MOTIVATION: FEELING AND STRIVING

The people called him "Mahatma," or "great soul." As an adult, Mohandas Karamchand Gandhi was described as follows: "Quiet dark eyes. A small, weak man, with a thin face and big ears. Wearing a white cap as headgear, clothed in rough white material, barefoot. He feeds on rice and fruits, drinks only water, sleeps on the floor, rests little, works all the time. Nothing about him strikes more than an expression of great patience and great love. . . . Such is the man who has incited to revolt three hundred million men, has shaken the British Empire and launched the most powerful movement in the politics of mankind for almost two thousand years" (Rolland, 1924, cited in Markovits, 2003, p. 18). This physically slight man cast a giant shadow across the 20th century, not only changing the face of India but also inspiring Martin Luther King, Jr., and the American civil rights movement.

In spite of his saintly reputation, Gandhi was a man of flesh and blood, possessed of raw emotions and strong motivations, just like the rest of us. The personal history of Gandhi provides us with a case study of the nature of emotion and its role in motivation.

By all reports, Gandhi was a shy, ordinary child, who was perhaps a little more stubborn than his peers, but this tendency was noticeable only through the keen lens of hindsight. As a young man, he decided to become a lawyer, following in the footsteps of his father and grandfather before him. At age 19, he went to England to study law, over the objections of his mother. She relented when he promised not to touch alcohol, women, or meat, but other members of his caste (hereditary social class) were not so flexible: They viewed crossing the ocean as a form of "contamination" and excommunicated him for this act. Knowing this consequence in advance did not deter him, so determined was he to reach his goal.

When he first arrived in England, Gandhi bent over backward to adapt. He adopted English dress and manners, and even studied ballroom dancing and took French lessons so that he could have the same social skills as his British classmates. He soon realized the folly of trying to pretend to be something he was not, and he began to re-explore his roots in the Hindu faith—which provided spiritual sustenance for him in this foreign land.

Gandhi returned to India after obtaining his law degree, but was a miserable failure as a lawyer in Bombay. When rising to argue his first case in court, he was overcome with anxiety and froze, tongue-tied and speechless. Following this humiliating experience, he was happy to accept a job in South Africa, helping a group of Indian merchants with a lawsuit. This was in the waning days of the 19th century, when the social climate in South Africa was hostile to Indians, who were treated as second-class citizens—or worse, resident aliens. Gandhi's emotional and intellectual reactions to the insults—and even beatings—he experienced gave rise to an unusually strong sense of social justice, which was to stay with him the rest of his life.

Gandhi's countrymen asked him to stay in South Africa and help them fight against discrimination. He agreed, and the shy lawyer gradually evolved into a charismatic leader. As part of this evolution, he abandoned Western clothes and began to dress as an Indian peasant. He reduced his needs and simplified his life, doing his own laundry, cleaning his own chamber pots (this was before flushing toilets were available), and even learning to be a midwife so that he could deliver his fourth (and last) son. He founded a residential community based on spiritual ideals, where the residents did all the work. Every member of the community—no matter what his or her social class—had to help with even the most menial tasks, such as cleaning, and all had to learn a craft. Gandhi learned to make sandals.

Gandhi is probably most famous for developing a method of nonviolent resistance, known in India as *satyagraha* (from the Indian words *satya* and *agraha*, meaning "truth" and "hold firm to"). He stressed that this technique is not passive resistance, but instead is akin to a form of political judo, using nonviolent actions to destabilize an opponent. Unlike pacifism, satyagraha hinges on self-sacrifice and provocation. Gandhi was jailed repeatedly for leading demonstrations and civil actions.

Gandhi organized the Indian expatriates of South Africa to use his new method to resist oppressive new tax laws, as well as a Supreme Court ruling that invalidated all Hindu and Muslim marriages—which had the effect of making all Indian wives into concubines. After he prevailed, he sent a gift to his main adversary, General Jan Christian Smuts—a pair of sandals he had made in jail. Twenty-five years later, the general wrote, "I have worn these sandals for many a summer since then even though I may feel that I am not worthy to stand in the shoes of so great a man" (Nanda, 1987).

After 20 years in South Africa, Gandhi returned to India in 1915, when it was still a colony ruled by Great Britain. He became the first Indian national leader in its history (all previous leaders had been regional), spending much time with peasants and focusing on teaching them to overcome the many fears that grow from powerlessness and poverty. In disputes between management and workers, he sided with the workers and started using fasting as a political tool. He used this tool repeatedly in his career, refusing to eat until a social end was achieved (such as resolution of a dispute or an end to violence).

What emotions did Gandhi feel when confronted with the social realities of his day? How did his emotions and motivations affect him? What these two forces have in common is their power to move us. (The root of both English words—*emotion* and *motivation*—comes from the Latin *movere*, "to move.") Our motivations and emotions are intimately interwoven: We are often motivated to do something because we are feeling an emotion, as when love leads us to hug someone; or we are motivated because we look forward to changing an emotion, as when we work on an overdue project in the expectation of replacing guilt with pride. Our emotions and motivations are not always obvious; they may confuse us or compel us to do things that surprise us. In this chapter, we consider first the nature of emotion and how it affects our behavior. This analysis leads us to consider motivation—what makes us act. Finally, we focus on two of the most important motivations: hunger and sex.

# EMOTION: I Feel, Therefore I Am

Soon after his return to India, Gandhi called for nonviolent demonstrations to protest repressive laws. But the disobedience soon spun out of control, sparking arson and violence—and the British reacted by killing many Indian protestors. Gandhi admitted that he had made a "Himalayan blunder" (referring to the highest mountains in the world) because he had initiated a social movement before he understood how to lead it. The peasants had trouble grasping Gandhi's ideas about nonviolence, and they questioned whether he was serious about these ideas—or was talking about them just to confuse the British. Gandhi's views stemmed from his spiritual convictions; he believed that if people could learn to control and overcome their "internal violence" (their destructive impulses, thoughts, and goals), "external" violence would not occur. But most people did not have his self-control, and their inflamed emotions sometimes got the better of them.

What, specifically, are emotions? An **emotion** has four components: (1) a positive or negative subjective experience, (2) bodily arousal, (3) the activation of specific mental processes and stored information, and (4) characteristic behavior. Emotions not only help guide us to approach some things and withdraw from others, but they also provide visible cues that help other people know key aspects of our thoughts and desires.

## Types of Emotion: What Can You Feel?

Think of the emotions you have experienced in your life. Fear? Guilt? Guilt tinged with fear? Love? Love mixed with joy? The range of human emotions is huge. Some researchers who have studied emotions have argued that the brain produces many gradations and types of these experienced reactions by combining sets of simple signals (Plutchik & Kellerman, 1980). Just as all colors can be produced by mixtures of three primary colors, researchers have claimed that all emotions, even the most complex, arise from combinations of a simple set we all possess, which, like primary colors on an artist's palette, lie ready for us to blend, experience, and present to the world.

### Basic Emotions

Charles Darwin (1872/1965), for one, believed that many emotional behaviors—the outward acts that arise from our emotions—are inborn. He noticed that people of many races and cultures appear to use very similar facial expressions to signal similar emotional states. Moreover, blind people show those same expressions, even if they have never had the chance to observe the way others look when they have particular emotional reactions. Are we all born with a built-in set of emotions? If so, these emotions would be an essential part of what we call "human nature," constituting a defining characteristic of what it means to be human in every time and culture.

Ekman and Friesen (1971) described the results of experiments that were designed to investigate this possibility (see Figure 10.1 on p. 430). They wanted to know whether people who had never seen White faces could identify the emotions underlying facial expressions in photographs of such faces. The researchers visited a New Guinea tribe,

Emotion: A psychological state with four components: (1) a positive or negative subjective experience, (2) the activation of specific mental processes and stored information, (3) bodily arousal, and (4) characteristic overt behavior.

**FIGURE 10.1**  **Recognition of Basic Emotions**

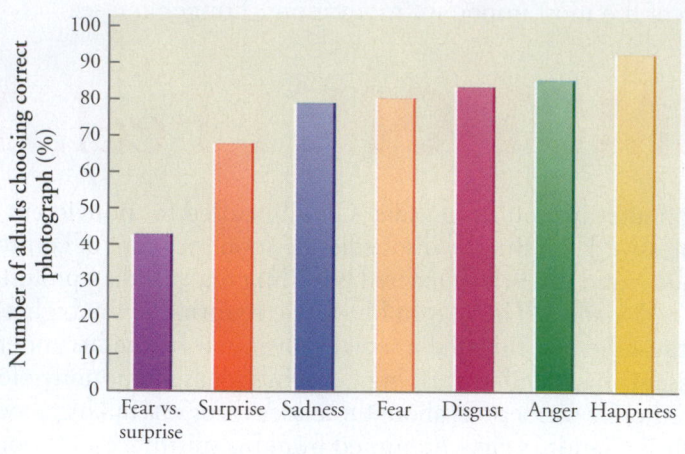

Ekman and Friesen told the participants a story, and then presented three pictures of faces displaying different emotions. The participants chose the face that showed the appropriate emotion for the story.

Participants could distinguish all of the emotions, except they tended to confuse fear and surprise. (Note that chance performance would be 33.3%.)

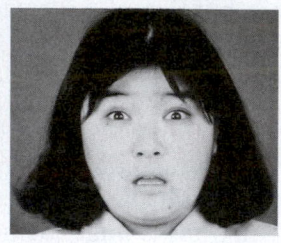

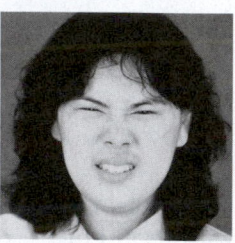

| Happy | Sad | Fear | Anger | Surprise | Disgust |

The six basic emotions that Ekman and others identified and studied. In the Ekman and Friesen study (1971), however, all the faces were Caucasian.

the Fore, who had rarely, if ever, seen White people in person or in images. Nonetheless, the Fore were able to identify expressions of happiness, anger, sadness, disgust, fear, and surprise in photos. The one difficulty they had was in distinguishing the expression of fear from that of surprise, probably because the two are very similar emotions. Also, it is possible that in Fore culture the two often go together: Most surprises in the jungle, such as the unexpected wild boar, are life-threatening, fear-inducing ones.

Ekman (1984) concluded that surprise, happiness, anger, fear, disgust, and sadness are **basic emotions**, emotions that are innate and shared by all humans. Other theorists have proposed slightly different lists of basic emotions. For example, Tomkins (1962) identified surprise, interest, joy, rage, fear, disgust, shame, and anguish. Some of the apparent disagreements may be simply a matter of word choice; *joy* and *happiness*, for example, may label the same emotion (LeDoux, 1996) or versions of it (perhaps joy is more intense than happiness, or comes and goes more quickly). Based on research with nonhuman animals, Panksepp (1998, 2005) offers a set of "emotional systems," which guide behavior (such as sexuality–lust, nurturance–care, and

**Basic emotion:** An innate emotion that is shared by all humans, such as surprise, happiness, anger, fear, disgust, or sadness.

joy–play). And other specific emotions, such as pride, have been proposed for the list of basic emotions (Tracy & Robins, 2004). But the idea that there is a fixed set of basic emotions has proven controversial. One challenge rests on the finding that some of these basic emotions are not simple. For example, Rozin and colleagues (1994) distinguish among three types of disgust, each of which is signaled by a different facial expression. A nose-wrinkling expression of disgust is associated with bad smells (and, sometimes, bad tastes); an open mouth with the tongue hanging down is associated with foods perceived as disgusting (the "yech" reaction); and a raised upper lip accompanies feelings of disgust, such as those associated with death and filth. Similarly, positive emotions can be divided at least into five types (amusement, desire, happiness, love, and interest; Keltner & Shiota, 2003).

Another challenge focuses on the role of culture in shaping emotion. Some researchers have argued that although some emotions are basic, in the sense that they have a consistent "signature" across cultures, other emotions are shaped by the social practices and norms of a culture (Keltner & Haidt, 2001). In fact, the perception of basic emotions in others turns out not to be entirely innate; learning also plays a role. Hillary Anger Elfenbein and Nalini Ambady (2002) carried out a meta-analysis of studies on the perception of emotion, looking carefully at the effects of many variables. First, they found that although people can recognize basic emotions of members of other racial groups better than you would expect by chance alone, they generally recognize emotions in their own group better than in other groups. Moreover, Elfenbein and Ambady found that some members of a minority group may actually recognize emotions on faces of members of the majority group better than they do on faces of their own group. This finding is a clear testament to the role of learning.

Thus, even with "basic" emotions, the contribution of the genes (which produce inborn tendencies) cannot be considered in isolation from events at the levels of the person (such as learning) and the group (such as whether one is a member of a specific culture).

## Separate But Equal Emotions

Have you ever watched a movie that was a four-star tear-jerker and found yourself racked with sobs *and* rolling with laughter? Or, have you ever found yourself enjoying a luscious dessert and simultaneously feeling disgusted because you are being such a glutton? There is good evidence that positive and negative emotions are not really opposite sides of the same coin. Rather, positive and negative emotions can occur at the same time, in any combination (Bradburn, 1969; Cacioppo et al., 1997; Diener & Emmons, 1984; Goldstein & Strube, 1994; Larsen et al., 2001). For example, Cacioppo and his colleagues (1997) asked students to rate on one scale how positively they felt about their roommates and on another scale how negatively they felt about their roommates. The researchers found that the degree of negative feelings students had toward their roommates was not related to the degree of positive feelings they had toward them. The students typically felt both positively and negatively toward their roommates, at the same time.

The notion that positive and negative emotions are independent is also supported by what happens in the brain when people experience emotions. Davidson and his colleagues have provided several types of evidence that there are separate systems in the brain for two general types of human emotions: *approach* emotions (such as love and happiness) and *withdrawal* emotions (such as fear and disgust; Davidson, 1992a, 1992b, 1993, 1998, 2002; Davidson et al., 2000a; Lang, 1995; Solomon & Corbit, 1974a). In general, approach emotions are positive, and withdrawal emotions are negative. EEG recordings show that the left frontal lobe tends to be more active than the right when people have approach emotions, whereas the right frontal lobe tends to be more active when people have withdrawal emotions (Simon-Thomas et al., 2005). Moreover, people who normally show more activation in the left frontal lobe tend to have a rosier outlook on life than do people who show more activation in the right frontal lobe. And brain scanning has shown that clinically depressed patients have lower activity in the left frontal lobe than do people who are not depressed (Davidson, 1993, 1994a, 1998; Davidson et al., 1999). However, these effects may be very transient; they are not reliably found in studies that use fRMI (which can only register changes over several seconds, whereas EEG can register changes that occur in a fraction of a second) (Wager et al., 2003).

# What Causes Emotions?

Distinguishing among different emotions is interesting, but it doesn't tell us what emotions are for, or why particular emotions arise when they do, any more than a theory of color perception can explain how Leonardo da Vinci painted the *Mona Lisa*. Gandhi was not a placid person; he wrote virulent critiques of Western civilization, disparaging its values and creations (for example, he detested the scale of modern cities and the ugliness of many of their buildings). Why did he feel anger? What possible good would such an emotion do him? The major theories of emotion provide insight into these questions.

## Theories of Emotion: Brain, Body, and World

It seems both obvious and logical that emotion would work like this: You are in a particular situation; that situation induces a specific emotion; that emotion leads you to behave in a certain way. The British used violence to try to trigger this process in Indian demonstrators: They would become afraid and therefore run. Although this process may seem to make sense intuitively, research has shown that it's not quite right. Each of the following theories has succeeded in capturing at least a grain of truth about how emotions actually operate.

**JAMES–LANGE THEORY** More than 100 years ago, William James (1884) argued that the intuitively plausible relation between emotion and behavior is exactly backward. James believed that you feel emotions after your body reacts (see Figure 10.2). For example, if a soldier raised his gun the moment he saw you coming, James would say that you would first run and then feel afraid, not the other way around. The emotion of fear, according to James, arises because you sense your bodily state as you are fleeing. You are aroused, and you sense your heart speeding up, your breathing increasing, and other signs that your sympathetic nervous system is being activated (see Chapter 3). According to his theory, different emotions arise from different sets of bodily reactions, and that's why emotions feel different (Reisenzein et al., 1995). Carl Lange (1887), a Danish physiologist, independently developed a similar theory, and thus the theory has come to be called the *James–Lange*

**FIGURE 10.2** **Four Theories of Emotion**

JAMES–LANGE THEORY

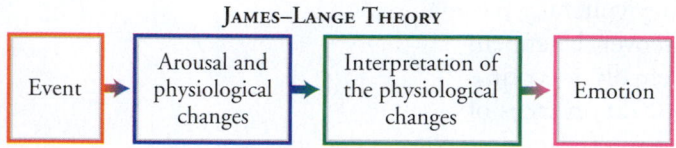

CANNON–BARD THEORY

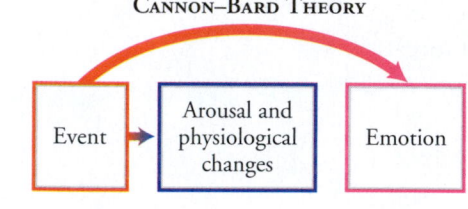

COGNITIVE THEORY

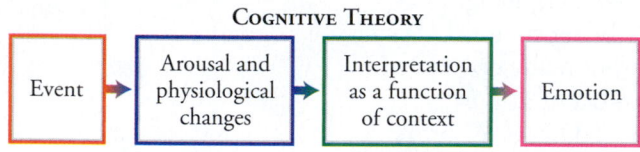

EMERGING SYNTHESIS

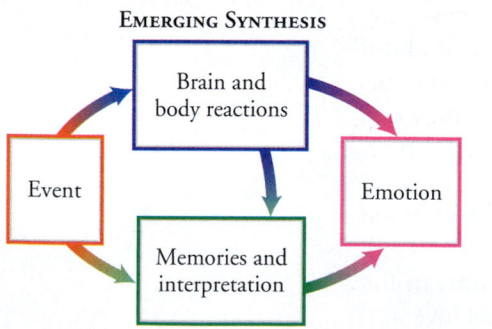

Theories of emotion differ in how they view the relationship between body reactions and interpretations of events.

*theory* (Lang, 1994). Damasio's (1994) "somatic marker hypothesis" is in many ways a contemporary version of the James–Lange theory, which hinges on the role of bodily signals (that is, somatic markers) in producing emotions.

**CANNON–BARD THEORY**   Walter Cannon (1927) claimed that the James–Lange theory focused too much on noticing bodily signals, such as heart and breathing rates. He raised a telling criticism of the James–Lange theory—that it takes many seconds for the body to become aroused and yet emotions are usually experienced before this happens. Instead, he claimed, the brain itself is all that matters. You perceive the threat of being shot, and the results of that perception marshal the body's resources for fleeing or fighting *at the same time* as they generate an emotion. According to the *Cannon–Bard theory* (see Figure 10.2), formulated by Cannon and another physiologist, Philip Bard, bodily arousal and the experience of emotion arise in tandem.

**COGNITIVE THEORY**   *Cognitive theory* holds that an emotion arises when you interpret the situation. Although some of these theorists focus solely on how people interpret the situation, without regard for bodily states, most of them consider the situation as a whole—the bodily state in the context of everything that surrounds it. According to this theory, you don't react to a stimulus and then feel an emotion after the reaction, as the James–Lange theory holds, and you don't have separate bodily and emotional reactions, as the Cannon–Bard theory has it. Rather, your reactions and the general situation together form the basis of emotions. For example, the act of running and the accompanying arousal can equally well be associated with the emotion of joy (as you rush to embrace someone you love), fear (as you flee a pursuing soldier), or excitement (as you join the crowd on the field to celebrate a football victory). The difference is not in the bodily state, but in how you interpret it at the time it occurs. Richard Lazarus, Stanley Schachter, and Magda Arnold were pioneers in developing this view. In general, the cognitive theory of emotion rests on the idea that, as Lazarus puts it, emotion "cannot be understood solely in terms of what happens in the person or in the brain, but grows out of ongoing transactions with the environment that are evaluated" (Lazarus, 1984, p. 124). This statement clearly embodies our by now familiar approach of looking at events at the levels of brain, person, and group.

**THE EMERGING SYNTHESIS**   The study of emotion is particularly exciting today because researchers are synthesizing a new theory from the best parts of what has come before. Let's briefly consider two elements of the emerging view. First, Joseph LeDoux (1996) modified the cognitive theory in an important way through his claim that there are different brain systems for different broad categories of emotions. Some of these systems operate as reflex pathways do, *independent* of thought or interpretation, whereas others *depend* on thought and interpretation. Fear, for example, relies on activation of the amygdala, a small brain structure located at the front inside part of the temporal lobes (see Chapter 3), without need for cognitive interpretation. But other emotions, such as guilt, rely on cognitive interpretation and memories of previous similar situations. Thus, the emotions we feel at any moment arise from a mixture of (1) brain and body reactions and (2) interpretations and memories pertaining to the situation. Second, other researchers are focusing on exactly how people interpret brain and body reactions. Some researchers claim that these reactions produce *core affect*, which consists of the "simplest raw feelings" that differ in the degree to which they are positive or negative and the degree to which they are strongly or weakly activated (Barrett, in press; Russell, 2003). Changes in core affect are then *categorized*, much as ambiguous stimuli are categorized (Barrett, in press). By analogy, to a farmer trying to gather his cows at dusk, a passing shadow may be seen as a cow; the farmer is categorizing the stimulus, not simply registering what is there. Similarly, context and previous experience may lead us to categorize types of core affect in ways that fit the situation, leading us to feel and express different emotions.

Which theory comes closest to the mark? To find out, let's take a closer look at the nature of emotion.

## Physiological Profiles: Are Emotions Just Bodily Responses?

Gandhi stressed the importance of inner control, which includes controlling emotions. Suppose that one of his followers was so anxious about participating in a civil action that he meditated for hours in advance—which allowed him to keep his heart from pounding and otherwise prevented his sympathetic nervous system from becoming fully activated. Would he still have felt fear after the soldiers started shooting? Yes, he probably would have. Let's see why.

Perhaps the strongest evidence against James's idea that emotions arise when people interpret their own bodily states is the finding that even people with spinal cord injuries so severe that they receive no sensations from their bodies still report having emotions (Bermond et al., 1991). However, it is possible that these patients experience emotions differently than do people with intact spinal cords. For example, one such patient described in this way what it felt like when a lit cigarette fell onto his bed: "I could have burned up right there, but the funny thing is, I didn't get all shook up about it. I just didn't feel afraid at all, like you would suppose." Speaking about another common emotion, he said, "Sometimes I act angry when I see some injustice. I yell and cuss and raise hell, because if you don't do it sometimes, I've learned people will take advantage of you, but it doesn't have the heat to it that it used to. It's a mental kind of anger" (Hohman, 1966, pp. 150–151). These quotations suggest that this man's emotions were largely rational evaluations, rather than feelings in reaction to events. Nevertheless, he did express emotions.

The James–Lange theory implies that we feel different emotions because each emotion corresponds to a largely distinct bodily state. The Indian demonstrator's heart would probably begin pounding and his palms become sweaty when he heard the guns begin to roar and his compatriots cry out in pain, and these events would probably play a key role in the emotions he felt. The lag in time for these bodily events to arise after the violence began could explain why the demonstrator would continue to feel fear even after he escaped the British soldiers. In contrast, the Cannon–Bard theory implies that our bodies are aroused similarly in different arousing situations. According to this view, arousal is arousal; it occurs not only if you are mugged, but also if you win the lottery. But physiological evidence challenges both of these theories (Barrett et al., in press).

On the one hand, the James–Lange theory has not fared well in the face of research results. For example, a meta-analysis did not reveal clear patterns of bodily responses that distinguish the different emotions (Cacioppo et al., 2000). Moreover, meta-analyses of neuroimaging data have shown a similar finding about the brain: In general, different emotions evoke overlapping patterns of brain activation, not distinct areas (Murphy et al., 2003; Phan et al., 2002, 2004; Wager et al., 2003). The James–Lange theory does not require an absolute correspondence between brain or body reactions and specific emotions, but there should be a strong correlation between them—which has not been found.

On the other hand, the Cannon–Bard theory is challenged by the finding that *some* emotions (but not all) are accompanied by distinct patterns of heart rate, body temperature, sweating, and other reactions. For example, when you feel anger, your heart rate increases and so does the temperature of your skin; and when you feel fear, your heart rate increases, but your skin temperature decreases (Levenson et al., 1990). Although James–Lange is not correct in general, distinct bodily reactions do occur in response to challenge and threat (Quigley et al., 2002; Tomaka et al., 1997) and, furthermore, in response to positive versus negative emotions (Cacioppo et al., 2000). In addition, evidence of a relationship between brain states and emotion is provided by neuroimaging data: Fear is associated with activation of the amygdala (but not uniquely, as we discuss shortly), and sadness activates part of the cingulate cortex (Phan et al., 2002).

It is also possible that a particular emotion corresponds to another bodily state, one that is not defined in terms of autonomic reactions. At least 20 muscles in your face do nothing but vary your facial expressions (Fridlund, 1994). When you move these muscles, your brain receives feedback from them. According to the **facial feedback hypothesis**, you feel emotions in part because of the way your muscles are positioned in your face (Izard, 1971; Tomkins, 1962). Presumably, reflexive neural systems and cognitive categorization systems first produce the facial expression, which then prompts the conscious experience of the emotion.

There is evidence that "putting on a happy face" is more than a phrase from a catchy song; it can actually make you feel happier. Following up on other studies (Duclos et al., 1989; Laird, 1974, 1984), Ekman and colleagues (Ekman, 1992; Ekman et al., 1990) tested this idea by leading participants to shift parts of their faces until they held specific expressions—for example, lifting the corners of the mouth until a smile and other signs of happiness were formed. The participants maintained these configurations while they rated their mood. If their faces were posed in a positive expression, they tended to rate their mood more positively than if their faces were posed in a negative expression.

However, putting on a happy face does not get our brains into exactly the same state as when we are genuinely happy (Ekman & Davidson, 1993). Thus, although facial feedback may affect emotions, our smiles, frowns, and glowers are not the only causes of our emotional experiences. Similarly, although there may be some bodily differences that accompany different emotions, there is no evidence that a distinct bodily state underlies each of our emotions.

Stick a pencil sideways (not point first) in your mouth, so that as you bite down on it, the corners of your lips turn up. Simply making this motion will actually make you feel happier (Strack et al., 1988). For more dramatic results, try to make a big smile, raising your cheeks.

## Cognitive Interpretation

Bodily factors are not enough to explain the range of feelings we have. What's missing? Our interpretations of events and the context in which events occur, both of which affect our feelings (Barrett et al., in press).

The classic experiment in this area was reported by Stanley Schachter and Jerome Singer in 1962; it is illustrated in Figure 10.3 (on p. 436). The participants, who believed that they would be taking part in a test of vision, received an injection of what they were told was a vitamin supplement. The injection was really a shot of epinephrine, which causes general arousal. Each participant then waited in a room before beginning the "vision test." Also waiting in the room was a confederate—that is, someone who is posing as a participant but is, in fact, cooperating with the investigators to set up the conditions of the experiment. The experiment consisted of having the confederate act in different ways during the "waiting period" and recording the effects of his behavior on the participant. In one condition, the confederate was manic, playing with a hula hoop, tossing paper airplanes, and generally acting silly. In another condition, the confederate was sullen and irritable; he tried to make the participant angry, and eventually stormed out of

Facial feedback hypothesis: The idea that emotions arise partly as a result of the positioning of facial muscles.

FIGURE 10.3

## The Schachter–Singer Experiment

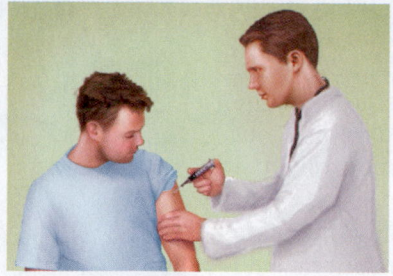

Participants received an epinephrine injection.

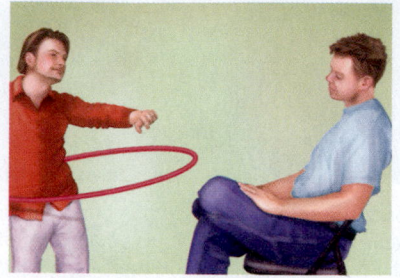
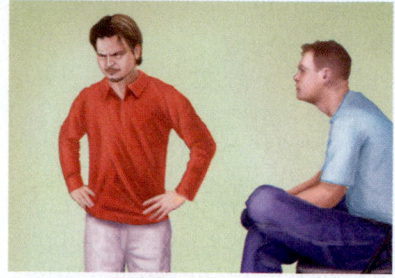

Confederates acted very differently while the participants waited.

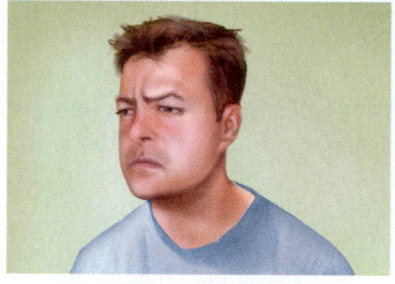

The participants reacted very differently to the drug, depending on what the confederate was doing.

Misattribution of arousal: The failure to interpret signs of bodily arousal correctly, which leads to the experience of emotions that ordinarily would not arise in the particular situation.

the room. The participants who had waited with the manic confederate reported that they felt happy, whereas the participants who had waited with the irritable confederate reported that they felt angry.

Although these participants had the same bodily arousal induced by the drug, they experienced this arousal very differently, depending on the context in which it occurred; and this difference apparently led them to attribute different explanations for the arousal. In contrast, when participants were told in advance about the drug and its effects, they did *not* feel differently in the different contexts; it was only when they interpreted the arousal as arising from the context that their feelings differed. In addition, participants in a control group, who did not receive an injection, experienced no effects of context. It is worth noting that this study took place more than 40 years ago; giving participants drugs without their knowledge is now considered unethical and impermissible.

If you interpret signs of bodily arousal incorrectly, making a cognitive error called **misattribution of arousal**, you may experience emotions that ordinarily would not arise in the particular situation. For example, in one study, male participants were given false feedback about their own internal responses (Valins, 1966). They had been asked, while looking at slides of partially nude women, to listen to what they were told was their own heart beating. The heartbeats the men heard were, in fact, not their own; they were sometimes faster and sometimes slower than the men's actual heart rates. When the participants later were asked to rate the attractiveness of each woman, their ratings were based not just on what they saw but also on what they had heard: If they had associated a rapid heartbeat with a picture, they rated the woman as more attractive. It is clear that our interpretation of bodily feedback depends on the situation—and how we interpret the situation depends at least in part on bodily feedback (Palace, 1999).

To the extent that different bodily reactions occur for different emotions, then, categorization of core affect is supplemented by less ambiguous internal stimuli; it is as if that farmer gathering his cows could hear a cowbell as well as see the passing shadow. Emotion is a complex mixture that arises when the "whispers and shouts" of the body are filtered through the expectations and interpretations of the mind.

The fact that cognitive interpretations affect how we feel does not imply that these interpretations must be conscious (Barrett et al., in press; Winkielman & Berridge, 2004). You have seen that unconscious associations can lead to hunches, which can in turn guide reasoning (Chapter 8). But more than that, emotion can be induced entirely unconsciously. For example, Winkielman and colleagues (2005) showed people happy or angry faces so briefly that they were not seen consciously. Nevertheless, thirsty people drank more of a tasty lemon-lime beverage after exposure to the happy faces—even though they were unaware of both the faces and the emotions they apparently elicited. Perceiving happiness apparently enhanced the positive value of the experience of drinking the pleasing beverage.

## Fear: The Amygdala and You

Gandhi, like most Indians of his generation, had absorbed a deep-seated fear of the ruling English. He later said that a popular jingle from his childhood had made a strong impression on him (to understand this jingle, you should know that a cubit corresponds to about 20 inches):

> Behold the mighty Englishman
> He rules the Indian small,
> Because being a meat-eater
> He is five cubits tall.

Nehru, India's first Prime Minister (in 1947), talked about the atmosphere of fear that pervaded colonial India: "fear of the army, the police, the widespread secret service; fear of the official class; fear of laws meant to suppress and of prison; fear of the landlord's agent; fear of the moneylender; fear of unemployment and starvation, which were always on the threshold" (Nehru, 1994/1946, p. 358; cited in Markovits, 2003, p. 93).

Because it is one of the best-understood emotions, fear has become a testing ground for theories of emotion. Fear causes changes in the brain, in the autonomic nervous system, in hormones, and in behavior. When people are afraid, they tend to freeze (to be "paralyzed by fear"), and they have an increased tendency to be startled, a tendency called *fear-potentiated startle* (Davis, 1992; Lang, 1995; Vrana et al., 1988). For example, as Indian demonstrators approached a line of armed soldiers, the unfolding tableau probably made them susceptible to being startled, so that they were more likely to be thrown off balance when the first gunshots rang out.

Researchers have discovered four important facts about fear from studying the brain systems that produce it:

1. After you have learned to fear an object, fear can well up later as a kind of "emotional reflex," with no thought, or cognitive interpretation, at all (LeDoux, 1996). The amygdala plays a crucial role in producing the reactions you have when you are afraid. It sends signals to other brain areas and structures, such as the hypothalamus, that cause your heart to speed up, your muscles to freeze (as Gandhi's apparently did, when he rose to plead his first case in court), and all the other autonomic reactions associated with fear. In fact, conscious awareness is not needed for a stimulus to trigger the amygdala into producing fear-related responses (Öhman, 2002).

2. There is evidence that once you learn to associate fear with an object or situation, you will always do so. Fear is a classically conditioned response, and even after its extinction, the neurons that were linked by the conditioned association still fire together (see Chapter 6). Although extinction can block whether you express the emotion, the underlying connections are still there. This is one reason why it is so easy to reinstate conditioned fear. Even though you are not aware of the association, it is never fully lost (LeDoux, 1996).

3. In spite of its reflexive nature, fear interacts with mental processes. For example, if you merely visualize yourself in a scary situation, you become susceptible to being startled (Cook et al., 1991; Lang et al., 1990; Vrana & Lang, 1990); the parts of the brain involved in cognition play a key role in "setting you up" to be easily startled.

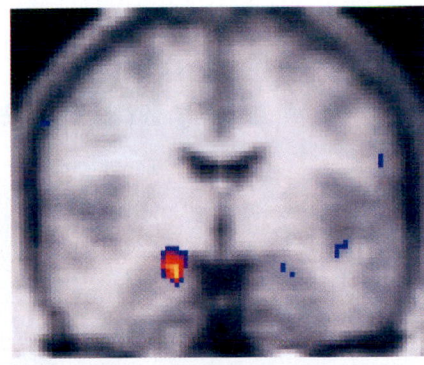

Even though participants were not aware of seeing pictures of angry faces, their amygdalae responded (Whalen et al., 1998). In addition, people who have a particular variant of a gene (SLC6A4, the human serotonin transporter gene) that affects serotonin levels show increased activation of the amygdala when they see emotional stimuli (Hariri et al., 2002).

Moreover, you can acquire fear associations merely by watching someone else be conditioned to fear a specific stimulus (Olsson & Phelps, 2004)!

4. In spite of its role in regulating fearful behaviors, the amygdala does not play a direct role in producing the emotional "feel" of fear; patients with damaged amygdalae report experiencing positive and negative emotions (such as fear) as often and as strongly as normal people do (Anderson & Phelps, 2002).

What does all this tell us about emotion in general?

- There are distinct biological events that are associated with feelings of fear, a finding that is consistent with the James–Lange theory. However, these states are not just bodily reactions; they also involve specific brain systems.

- The events that lead to fear appear to produce both the experience and the bodily reaction at the same time, which fits the Cannon–Bard theory. However, the experience and the reaction are not entirely separate; rather, the person's interpretation of the event can affect both.

- Although cognitive interpretation is not always necessary for feeling fear, it is clear that mental events do interact with emotion. Thus, aspects of cognitive theory are supported.

- In spite of the distinct events that underlie fear, particular emotions cannot be identified with the activation of a single brain area (Barrett, in press; Barrett et al., in press; Phan et al., 2002, 2004; Wager et al., 2003). For example, fear is typically the strongest emotion, and some researchers have suggested that the amygdala may be responding when we perceive or feel strong emotions in general—not just fear in particular (Davis & Whalen, 2001). In fact, researchers have found that the amygdala responds when people experience both positive and negative emotions (Aalto et al., 2002), when they read words that name positive and negative emotions (Hamann & Mao, 2002), and even when they think they've won or lost a simple game (Zalla et al., 2000). Thus, the study of fear is revealing the inner workings of emotion more generally.

In short, the three older theories of emotion all contain a grain of truth. However, the sum total of the findings is most consistent with the emerging synthesis, which includes roles for both brain-based, reflexive reactions and the categorization of bodily states in particular contexts. As illustrated in Figure 10.4, a number of brain systems

**FIGURE 10.4** **Key Brain Areas Involved in Emotion**

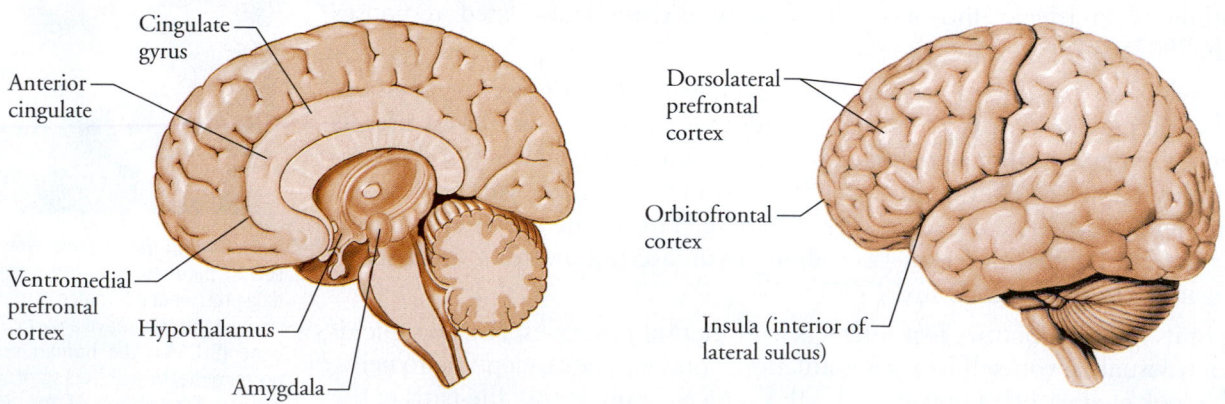

Many areas of the brain are involved in emotion, which may explain why we have such complex and rich emotional lives.

play roles in particular aspects of emotion. One specific brain area, the ventral medial frontal cortex (located in the center, lower, rear portions of the frontal lobes), is particularly interesting because it seems to play a role in emotional memory (Damasio, 1994). In addition, another part of the frontal lobes, the orbital frontal cortex (in the part of the brain immediately behind and slightly above the eyes), plays a key role in allowing us to anticipate emotional events (Roberts et al., 2004), to notice when other people feel specific emotions (such as whether they are happy, sad, or disgusted), and to experience our emotions subjectively (Beer et al., 2003; Hornak et al., 2003).

## Positive Emotions: More Than Feeling Good

Lest you think that psychologists have a morbid fascination with the dark side, we must note that much has also been learned about positive emotions (Biswas-Diener et al., 2004; Diener, 2000; Fredrickson, 2001; Lyubomirsky, 2001; Myers, 2000; Peterson, 2000; Ryan & Deci, 2000).

**HAPPINESS**   Fear and happiness differ in fundamental ways. For one, fear narrows the scope of attention and tends to restrict behavior to the small set of fight-or-flight responses; in contrast, happiness leads people to broaden the scope of attention and to be open to novel courses of action (Biswas-Diener et al., 2004). Moreover, whereas fear is a momentary state, which is easy to study in the brain, happiness is a more chronic state, bearing on the tenor of your life—this makes the brain mechanisms underlying happiness much more difficult to study. Instead, happiness has been studied largely from the levels of the person and the group.

What makes us happy? Not surprisingly, a survey of happiness in 40 countries found that money *can* sometimes buy happiness, at least to some extent: Money generally can buy happiness for those in poverty and deprivation; people tend to be happier when they are living in better economic conditions (Diener & Biswas-Diener, 2002; Schyns, 1998). However, once a person has risen above the level of poverty and deprivation, additional material resources make little—if any—difference in happiness. Although we are happier immediately after getting a big raise or winning a prize in a lottery, the blip in happiness is short-lived; before long, we are no more or less happy than we were before. This effect has been called the *hedonic treadmill* (Brickman & Campbell, 1971).

That said, it may be that the relationship between money and happiness depends on how the additional money is spent. If you use it to buy a bigger house or fancier car, you've hopped on the hedonic treadmill and can expect only a fleeting boost in happiness. But if you use it to buy "inconspicuous goods," such as freedom from having to commute through heavy traffic or longer and more relaxing or exciting vacations, then extra money can have a positive impact on your life (Frank, 2004). Immediate life circumstances, such as how we are treated by those around us and time pressure at work, clearly affect our happiness (Kahneman et al., 2004). Moreover, our attitudes have a lot to do with how happy we are: In general, happy people have adjusted their desires to be consistent with their resources and abilities (Crawford Solberg et al., 2002).

Consistent with these findings, happiness was correlated with the number of opportunities for cultural enrichment only in rich countries, which may suggest that basic needs (such as for adequate shelter and nutrition) take precedence; that is, until they are satisfied, less basic events cannot generate happiness. This notion might explain the results of surveys, taken in the United States over the period 1972–1993 which showed that Whites tended to be happier than Blacks (Aldous & Ganey, 1999). However, other factors must be at work; although White women generally make less money than White men, they generally

Researchers have found that in 16 of 17 countries they examined (the exception was Northern Ireland), marriage is linked to greater happiness than is either being single or living with someone to whom you aren't married. This increase in happiness was comparable for both men and women (Ross, 1995; Stack & Eshleman, 1998; Weerasinghe & Tepperman, 1994). Apparently, most of the effects of marriage on happiness are indirect: increasing satisfaction with household finances and improving perceived health. However, this is not all there is to it; the simple fact of being married, all by itself, contributes to happiness.

report being happier than White men. One possible additional contributor to feelings of happiness is social support, the degree to which you feel that other people are willing and able to listen and help (Myers, 2000). In China, the strongest predictor of happiness was a measure of social support (Lu, 1999; Lu et al., 1997).

But we must be cautious about generalizing from one culture to another. When asked about the sources of happiness, Chinese people focused on interpersonal interactions and external evaluations, whereas Westerners focused on the achievement of personal goals and internal evaluations (Lu & Shih, 1997a). Culture also mitigates the effects of other variables. For example, many overweight people are troubled by their weight, but this concern is particularly acute for those who live in a culture in which thinness is the norm. In addition, ethnic group plays a role; Pinhey and colleagues (1997) found that in Guam, overweight Asians and Filipinos reported being less happy than did overweight Chamorros and Micronesians, who were from groups that have larger average body mass. These results suggest that people gauge themselves relative to a reference group, and the same personal characteristics can be viewed as acceptable or unacceptable, depending on the results of comparison with that group. However, the effects of such social comparisons seem to depend on how happy you are to begin with: Researchers have found that happy people tend to pay less attention than do unhappy people to what they have or have not achieved relative to other people (Lyubomirsky, 2001; Lyubomirsky et al., 2001).

It is also clear that personality affects happiness. For example, at least in Western countries, assertive people tend to be happier than nonassertive people (Argyle & Lu, 1990). And extraverted people tend to be happier than introverted people. But more than that, happy people tend to perceive the world through rose-colored glasses; they construe situations to "maintain and even promote their happiness and positive self views" (Lyubomirsky, 2001, p. 241).

Although not much has been learned about the neural bases of happiness, some progress has been made. We have already noted that people with more activation in the left frontal lobe (not only during a particular task, but in general) tend to be happier than people with more activation in the right frontal lobe (Davidson, 1992a, 1992b, 1993, 1994a, 1998, 2002). But why do people differ in these ways? One possibility lies in their genetic make-up. At least 50% of the variability in happiness may arise from heredity (Lykken & Tellegen, 1996). Does this mean that if you are unhappy, you should just adjust because you can't change? Not at all! As we discussed in Chapter 3, genes are not destiny.

**POSITIVE PSYCHOLOGY: MORE THAN A STATE OF MIND**    Being happy is one focus of what has come to be known as *positive psychology* (Seligman & Csikszentmihalyi, 2000; Seligman & Pawelski, 2003). Researchers have shown that positive states of mind can promote *resilience*, which is the ability to bounce back from adversity, to keep an even keel (Bonanno, 2004, 2005; Tugade & Fredrickson, 2004). But more than that, maintaining a positive attitude can promote personal growth (Linley & Joseph, 2004). In fact, positive emotions can literally boost the immune system and help us cope with disease (Rosenkrantz et al., 2003; Tugade et al., 2004). Because positive emotions broaden attention and lead people to become more open and receptive, such emotions often promote effective coping strategies. And effective coping, in turn, creates more positive emotions, which produces an "upward spiral" (Fredrickson & Joiner, 2002).

# Expressing Emotions: Letting It All Hang Out?

Emotions occur in the social context of family, friends, and culture. Like Gandhi's emotions, many of our emotions arise from social interactions, both positive (Gandhi's exhilaration when he attains a victory for social justice) and negative (his fear after having been beaten by a train conductor for refusing to give up his seat to a White person). Not only do social stimuli trigger emotions, but emotions also serve social roles; these roles range from communicating to providing connections among people.

Display rule: A culture-specific rule that indicates when, to whom, and how strongly certain emotions can be shown.

## Culture and Emotional Expression: Rules of the Mode

In many ways, emotional experience is a private affair, inaccessible to others. But emotional expression is crucial for our daily interactions with other people. According to Ekman (1980), each of us learns a set of **display rules** for our culture that indicate when, to whom, and how strongly certain emotions can be shown. For example, he notes that in North America people will find it suspicious if a man's secretary seems more upset at his funeral than his wife does. In the display rules for North American culture, the closer the relation to the deceased, the more emotion may be displayed. Display rules are partly a function of habit (individuals do differ in their styles), but they largely reflect "the way things are done" in a particular region, class, or culture.

# UNDERSTANDING RESEARCH

## Culture and Emoting

Ekman (1984) describes a fascinating test of his theory that all people share the same basic emotions but that emotional expression may be different because of different display rules.

**QUESTION:** How is the experience or expression of emotion different between Westerners and Japanese people?

**ALTERNATIVES:** (1) The stereotype that Japanese people are less emotional than Westerners may be correct, and they display what they feel. (2) Japanese may experience emotions the same way as Westerners do, but display them differently. (3) Japanese may both experience and display emotions differently than Westerners do. (4) Japanese and Westerners may experience and display emotions in the same ways.

**LOGIC:** If the two groups are equally emotional but follow different display rules that regulate how they show their emotions in public (alternative 2), then both groups should show emotions when in private but behave differently when in public.

**METHOD:** Americans in Berkeley and Japanese in Tokyo were shown the same films, one positive (scenery) and one negative (a surgical procedure). Participants viewed the films either alone or in the company of a white-coated scientist. Unbeknownst to the participants, a hidden camera monitored their facial expressions as they watched the films, both when alone and with company.

**RESULTS:** Both groups showed the same range of emotional expression when they viewed the films in individual screenings, one person at a time, but the Japanese participants were notably more restrained when they were in company. Ekman analyzed slow-motion videotapes of the participants as they watched, which revealed that a Japanese participant watching alone reacted in the same way as an American. But a Japanese watching in the presence of another person would begin showing an emotional reaction, then quickly squelch it.

**INFERENCES:** According to Ekman, the initial Japanese reaction reflected the basic, innate emotions; when someone else was present, display rules came to the fore, and the participants regulated their show of emotions accordingly. Thus, Japanese experience emotions as Westerners do, but display them differently.

## THINK CRITICALLY!

If the initial emotional reaction of the Japanese participants when a second person was present was so fleeting, how certain can we be that they did in fact react the same way as the Americans? How could you check to be sure that they did not have a generalized "startle" reaction, rather than a specific emotional response?

The age of the participants is not specified, nor is the gender. Can you think of reasons why each of these variables might have affected the results?

Could the Japanese participants simply have been uncomfortable in the presence of a distant, white-coated authority figure? If so, could the results have reflected the effects of anxiety, rather than having anything to do with display rules? To test for the effects of display rules, might it have been better to vary the types of company, and predict that specific emotions would be displayed in different groups? What advantages would this research design have had?

## Body Language: Broadcasting Feelings

Nonverbal communication isn't really language (see Chapter 8), but it is a form of communication that is particularly effective at conveying emotions.

Body language is undoubtedly shaped in part by the display rules of a culture, and it plays many roles. One important role is in conveying sexual interest. For example, studies have shown that men and women hold their bodies differently in the presence of someone of the opposite sex if they are interested in that person than if they are not interested. However, interest is not conveyed in exactly the same way by men and women. Grammer (1990) found that interested men had "open postures" (with the legs relaxed and open) and watched the women, whereas interested women avoided eye contact, presented their body rotated slightly to the side (so that their breasts were seen in profile), and uncrossed their arms and legs. For both males and females, a closed posture conveyed lack of interest.

Body language also plays a role in unwanted sexual encounters. This is important for students to recognize because college women experience sexual victimization three to four times more frequently than women in general (Cummings, 1992; Hanson & Gidycz, 1993). In one study, researchers asked observers to view videotapes of ordinary people walking down the street and to rate how vulnerable they were to physical assault (Grayson & Stein, 1981). Those viewed as victims tended to move awkwardly and disjointedly, whereas "nonvictims" moved smoothly, in a coordinated, confident way. Murzynski and Degelman (1996) conducted an experiment to discover exactly which aspects of body language lead women to be perceived as vulnerable to sexual assault. They defined two victim profiles. In one, potential victims tend to walk with a long, exaggerated stride and lift their feet up rather than smoothly swinging them; in the other, they may walk with short, mincing steps. Both police officers and college students rated the women who walked in the manner of the victim profiles as more likely to be sexually assaulted than the women who walked like nonvictims.

At least some of our body language may result from innate factors. Although there has yet to be a good rigorous study of this, one anecdote is highly suggestive. In re-

Emotion is conveyed not only by facial expression, but also by tone of voice and body movements. People can sense happiness more accurately than other emotions from facial expressions—but they sense happiness least accurately from tone of voice. In contrast, of all the emotions, anger is most easily sensed from the tone of voice, and it is less well sensed from the face (Elfenbein & Ambady, 2002). Nonverbal information is not entirely conveyed by facial expression, so it's wise to pay attention to all sources of information.

viewing 30 studies of identical twins who were separated and raised apart, Faber (1981) wrote: "As with voice, the way the twins held themselves, walked, turned their heads, or flicked their wrists was more alike than any quantifiable trait the observers were able to measure. . . . If one twin had a limp, moist handshake, so did the other. If one had a spirited prance, so did the partner" (pp. 86–87).

# Emotion Regulation

Gandhi helped many ordinary people overcome fear. His techniques of collective action built on the Indian tradition of yoga, which emphasizes self-control. The very fact that display rules exist implies that we have at least some voluntary control over our emotional expressions. Researchers have shown that we also have at least some control over how our brains respond emotionally. For example, in one study, participants saw neutral or negative pictures while their brains were being scanned using fMRI. The participants were told either simply to view the pictures or to maintain their initial emotional responses to the pictures. In fact, when they maintained negative emotions, their amygdalae continued to be activated over a longer period of time. Moreover, the more strongly the participants rated their negative reaction to the picture, the more strongly their amygdalae were activated (Schaefer et al., 2002).

**REGULATING THE EMOTIONAL BRAIN**   Can people voluntarily dampen down the mechanisms that underlie emotion? Gandhi assumed that the answer is "yes," and apparently trained himself to keep his emotions in check. And his assumption was justified (Oschsner & Gross, 2005). In one neuroimaging study, researchers showed male participants erotic videos and asked them to respond normally or to try to inhibit sexual arousal (Beauregard et al., 2001). When the men were reacting normally, various brain areas involved in emotion were activated, such as the amygdala and hypothalamus. When the men were inhibiting their reactions, parts of the frontal lobe became activated—and the brain areas normally activated by those reactions no longer were. Such processing apparently is not restricted to erotic stimuli. In another study, researchers showed participants neutral and negative pictures and then measured their reactions to loud noise (by measuring eye blinks and other facial reactions; Jackson et al., 2000). The trick was that the participants were asked to maintain, suppress, or enhance their emotional reactions to the pictures. In fact, the participants were more strongly startled by the noise when they were asked to enhance their emotional reaction to a picture, and they were less strongly startled when asked to suppress this reaction. One interesting twist in the results was that people who could effectively suppress negative emotion couldn't enhance it very well, and vice versa.

Ochsner and others (2002) adapted the basic task used by Jackson and colleagues for a study using fMRI, and they reported direct evidence that suppressing emotions is correlated with changes in the activation of parts of the brain associated with emotion. In addition, Ochsner and colleagues (2004) found that asking people to think about how aversive scenes could be relevant to them boosted the activation of the amygdala (which may be one reason why Gandhi urged his followers not to dwell on slights or insults made by the British), whereas asking people to formulate alternative meanings of aversive scenes decreased the activation of the amygdala. Moreover, in both cases, the frontal lobe and anterior cingulate were activated; these regions are involved in cognitive control (see Chapter 8).

In some cases, people appear to regulate emotional reactions automatically and spontaneously (Jackson, Mueller, Dolski et al., 2003), perhaps in accord with what they consider to be socially acceptable responses. For example, in one study, White people viewed Black and White faces while their brains were scanned (Cunningham et al., 2004). When the faces were shown very briefly (30 thousandths of a second), the amygdala was more activated for Black than White faces, which suggests that the participants had a stronger emotional reaction to the Black faces. However, when the faces were shown for a longer time (a bit more than half a second), the amygdalar response was smaller, and parts of the frontal lobes that are involved in cognitive control were activated—and these regions were activated more strongly for Black than White faces. Apparently, when given more time, the participants spontaneously attempted to control their emotional reactions.

**CONSEQUENCES OF EMOTION REGULATION**  Emotion regulation is important for at least three reasons:

1. Difficulty in controlling negative emotions could be a source of violent aggression, perhaps in part because of the frustration at having to keep feelings under wraps (Davidson et al., 2000b).

2. If you try to control emotions by suppressing your overt behavior, you will impair your memory for the surrounding events (Bonanno et al., 2004; Richards & Gross, 2000), impede your ability to reason (Baumeister et al., 1998) and your ability to communicate clearly (Butler et al., 2003), and even raise your blood pressure (Butler et al., 2003). You can avoid these negative consequences if you regulate your emotions by reinterpreting the situation and your role in it (Gross, 2001, 2002; Richards, 2004; Richards et al., 2003).

3. Being able to regulate emotion is also important because emotion affects cognition (especially working memory; J. R. Gray, 2001). Positive emotions facilitate verbal tasks but interfere with spatial tasks (such as remembering an object's location or recognizing faces); negative emotions have the opposite effects. (Could these findings say something about how you might prepare to study for an English versus a geometry test?) The different effects of positive and negative emotions on cognition may arise from the fact that positive emotion activates the left frontal lobe during a verbal task, whereas negative emotion activates the right frontal lobe during a spatial task (J. R. Gray et al., 2002).

# Perceiving Emotions: A Form of Mind Reading

Emotions play a role in moving us to behave in certain ways, and they also cue others about our internal states and likely behaviors. In some cases, people may direct an emotional expression toward another person, as a deliberate form of communication; but in many cases, an emotional expression may simply be a sign, produced unconsciously, of an internal state (Russell et al., 2003); in either case, emotional expressions invite us to engage in a form of "mind reading." Just as we know that a dog is feeling hot when it pants and its tongue lolls out, we can read even unintentional expressions and draw inferences about a person's emotional state. If soldiers had lifted their guns slowly and with relaxed expressions on their faces, the Indian demonstrators probably would not have reacted by running away.

## Reading Cues

We are remarkably good at reading cues about emotion, acquiring information from even minimal cues. For instance, Dittrich and colleagues (1996) attached 13 small lights to the bodies of each of two professional dancers and had them perform dances that conveyed fear, anger, grief, joy, surprise, and disgust. Undergraduate students who later watched videotapes of the dances were able to recognize the intended emotions, even in the dark when only the lights were visible. Similarly, Bassili (1978) showed that people can recognize facial expressions of emotion in the dark from only the movements of lights attached to faces; the specific locations of the lights did not seem to matter.

The ability to read nonverbal communications is at least partly determined by experience. For example, children who watch more television tend to be better at judging emotional expressions (Feldman et al., 1996). Moreover, culture affects not only how willing you are to express emotion in specific situations, but also how sensitive you are to the emotional expressions of others (Stephan et al., 1996). When a culture makes emotions difficult to detect through more stringent display rules, it almost seems as though its members compensate by developing better abilities to detect emotions. For example, although display rules in China call for more emotional restraint than those in Australia, Chinese children can detect basic emotions more accurately than Australian children can (Markham & Wang, 1996).

In addition, the amygdala clearly plays a central role in allowing us to perceive that other people feel some particular emotions. For example, in an fMRI neuroimaging study, the amygdala responded when participants were briefly shown faces with fearful expressions—so briefly that they were not even aware of having seen the expressions (Whalen et al., 1998). Moreover, people with damage to the amygdala (but with little other brain impairment) cannot recognize fear or anger in the tone of other people's voices (Adolphs et al., 1996; Calder et al., 1996; Hamann et al., 1996; Scott et al., 1997; Young et al., 1996). But more than that, such brain-damaged patients have more difficulty identifying social emotions (such as guilt and admiration) than basic emotions (such as anger and happiness) on other people's faces. This difficulty appears to stem, at least in part, from problems in interpreting emotional expressions conveyed by the eyes (Adolphs et al., 2002).

## Perceiving by Imitating: Making the Match

"Smile and the whole world smiles along with you." Could this be more than a well-worn adage? In fact, researchers have found that when we perceive an emotional expression, we imitate it, at least somewhat (Adolphs, 2002; Niedenthal et al., 2001); such imitation can occur even when people are not consciously aware of having seen a face displaying a specific emotion (Dimberg et al., 2000). Do these findings mean that if you were totally paralyzed, you couldn't recognize emotions? Probably not. Such findings are consistent with the idea that we categorize what we see, which involves retrieving information about similar situations that occurred in the past and our responses to them (Barrett & Niedenthal, 2004).

## Individual Differences in Emotion Perception

People differ not only in their tendencies to feel certain sorts of emotions (Davidson, 1993, 1994a, 1998; Hamann & Canli, 2004; Lerner & Keltner, 2000), but also in their abilities to perceive emotions. For example, Barrett and Niedenthal (2004) assessed the relation between the degree of *valence focus* (valence is the positive/negative aspect of emotion) and the ability to perceive emotion in faces. These researchers assessed valence focus by observing the degree to which their participants used emotion words to convey pleasure versus displeasure. The participants then saw a sequence of pictures, in which a neutral face gradually morphed into one that conveyed an emotion (happy, sad, or angry). The task was to stop the sequence of photos at just the point when the emotion became evident. People who had a high valence focus could spot the onset of sad and angry expressions better than those who had a low valence focus (but not the onset of a happy expression, which may have been too intense and hence too easy to spot).

# LOOKING AT LEVELS
## Lie Detection

Gandhi was lied to often in his long and turbulent career. In South Africa, for example, General Smuts tried to lull Gandhi with agreements that he had no intention of honoring, much to the later disappointment and chagrin of the Mahatma. Gandhi no doubt would have appreciated knowing whether others were lying to him. Are there good methods for detecting lies? Lie detector tests may not be admissible evidence in court, but they are still used in various investigations. What do they really "detect"?

If distinct brain and body states accompany at least some emotions, researchers have reasoned, then there might be distinct biological "signatures" of the feelings of guilt and fear when someone is caught at some wrongdoing. This idea underlies a long history of attempts to detect deception objectively. One result has been machines called **polygraphs**, known misleadingly as "lie detectors." These machines don't "detect lies" directly; they monitor the activity of the sympathetic and parasympathetic nervous systems—in particular, changes in skin conductance, breathing, and heart rate.

The polygraph relies on asking a person questions and comparing the verbal responses to the bodily responses. But how should questions be asked? The most basic technique used with a polygraph is the *relevant/irrelevant technique* (*RIT*; Larson, 1932). Suppose you are trying to determine whether the suspect in a crime is telling the truth. When the RIT technique is used, the suspect is asked crime-related questions ("Did you break into Mr. Johnson's house last night?") and neutral questions ("Do you live at 43 Pleasant Street?"). The bodily responses accompanying the answers to the two types of questions are then compared. However, there is clearly a large difference in the emotional weight of the two types of questions. Thus, a greater bodily response to a crime-related question may reflect not guilt but simply the fact that the idea posed by the question is more arousing. To avoid this possibility, the *control question technique* (*CQT*; Reid, 1947) includes comparison questions that should have an emotional weight roughly equivalent to that of the crime-related questions. For example, in addition to the two questions above, the suspect might be asked, "Did you ever do anything you were ashamed of?"

A more recent technique is the *guilty knowledge test* (*GKT*; sometimes called the *concealed information test*), developed by Lykken (1959, 1960). In contrast to the RIT and the CQT, the GKT does not rely on asking direct questions about the crime. Instead, this test uses indirect questions that presumably only the guilty person would be in a position to answer correctly. In addition, the GKT relies on multiple-choice questions. So the suspect might be asked, "Was the color of the walls in Mr. Johnson's bedroom white? Yellow? Blue?" Someone who has never been in the room should have comparable responses to each of the choices, whereas someone who has guilty knowledge should respond selectively to the actual color. A modification of this approach is the *guilty actions test* (Bradley & Warfield, 1984; Bradley et al., 1996), which observes responses when people are given statements about actions that they may have committed.

**Polygraph:** A machine that monitors the activity of the sympathetic and parasympathetic nervous systems, particularly changes in skin conductance, breathing, and heart rate, in an attempt to detect lying.

Do these techniques work? Ben-Shakhar and Furedy (1990) report that in the laboratory the CQT on average correctly classifies 80% of the guilty and 63% of the innocent. Thus, this technique unfortunately leads too often to the classification of honest responses as lies. The GKT has a better track record; the guilty were detected 84% of the time, and the innocent 94%. However, the range of accuracy in the reviewed studies was from 64% to 100% for detecting the guilty and from 81% to 100% for detecting the innocent. Many other researchers have reported comparable results (DeClue, 2003). (You are probably getting a sense as to why polygraph evidence is not admitted in courts of law.) More recent techniques that measure electrical activity in the brain can sometimes have accuracy as high as 95%, but there is still enough variability to cast doubt on the examiner's ability to classify individual answers as untruthful (Allen & Iacono, 1997).

Polygraphs are used to detect changes in autonomic nervous system activity, which may signal that the person being interviewed is lying.

Also at the level of the brain, neuroimaging studies are beginning to illuminate just why it is so difficult to detect lies. For example, Ganis and colleagues (2003) found that unlike a rose, a lie is not a lie is not a lie. From the brain's point of view, there is more than one way to lie. Specifically, when people lied spontaneously, making up responses "on the fly," parts of the brain involved in working memory and in monitoring errors were very active; but when people lied on the basis of a well-learned "alternative reality" scenario (for example, saying that they drove to the mountains on vacation when in fact they flew to the coast), areas of the brain involved in retrieving memories were activated instead. Moreover, as other researchers have found (Kozel, Padgett, & George, 2004; Kozel, Revell, et al., 2004), the specific pattern of brain activation in each condition varied for different people, which makes interpreting the results even more complicated.

At the level of the person, we can ask whether some people are particularly gifted at detecting lies. DePaulo and her collaborators (1997) reported a meta-analysis of studies on the relation between an individual's confidence that he or she has spotted a lie and the level of the person's accuracy, and they found essentially no relation between the two (a correlation of essentially zero). Similarly, in another study, police officers viewed videotapes of an interview with a man who was lying about a murder (which he later confessed to committing); these officers correctly classified 70% of the true statements but only 57% of the lies (Vrij & Mann, 2001). Many other researchers have reported similar results (Elaad, 2003; Garrido et al., 2004; Granhag & Strömwall, 2001; Vrij, 2004). However, other evidence suggests that *some* people can distinguish truth from lies extraordinarily accurately, particularly some (but not all) of those who have been trained in law enforcement or in clinical psychology with an interest in deception (Ekman et al., 1999). A few rare people are intuitively able to pick up telltale cues of deception, but scientists have yet to isolate those cues.

At the level of the group, we can ask what cues people use to detect whether someone is lying. Researchers have discovered that we detect lies by registering *microexpressions*, flickers of expressions—such as frequent eyeblinks, quick sideways glances, or downcast eyes for as little as a tenth of a second (DePaulo et al., 2003; Ekman, 1985; Ekman & Friesen, 1975). We recognize different types of nonverbal information and can detect lies when inconsistent information arises from different sources, such as a stiff body posture combined with trusting, direct eye contact. We are also sensitive to a variety of telltale cues, summarized in Table 10.1. However, many of these cues are not highly reliable (Mann et al., 2004; Strömwall et al., 2003; Vrij & Mann, 2001).

How can we best understand lie detection? The goal of lie detection is to assess a particular social interaction in which one person is trying to mislead another person. Perhaps the greatest

**TABLE 10.1**

## Some Common (Although Not Entirely Reliable) Signs of Deception

- Frequent eye blinks
- Sideways glances
- Downcast eyes
- Stiff body posture combined with direct eye contact
- Larger pupil size
- Rising pitch of voice
- Exaggerated facial expressions
- Increased grammatical errors
- Slower and less fluent speech than normal
- Repetition of words and phrases

problem with the polygraph is that it really detects guilt or fear (the level of the person). If the person being tested lies but does not *feel* guilty or afraid, the palms won't become sweaty, heart rate won't increase, and so forth; the brain does not produce the autonomic responses associated with the feeling. And because the interviewer does not have any basis for detecting the lie, this lack of biological response in turn may alter how the person is being treated during the interview (a social interaction), and that treatment in turn can affect the person's reactions to the questions. Moreover, if the person being interviewed feels comfortable, he or she may be less likely to produce the microexpressions that some people can readily detect (without any need for the machine). Thus, in order to understand lie detection, we need to consider all three levels of analysis: The activity in the brain that produces the autonomic signals and observable behavior; the personality differences that could lead a person to feel guilty or afraid; and the rules of the society, together with the person's understanding of them, which would lead the person to feel guilty under certain circumstances.

# Test Yourself

1. The James–Lange theory and the Cannon–Bard theory differ in the relationship they assume between bodily arousal and emotion. Which of the following matches a theory and its proposed relationship correctly?
   a. James–Lange theory: Bodily arousal and emotion happen simultaneously.
   b. James–Lange theory: Bodily arousal results from emotion.
   c. Cannon–Bard theory: Bodily arousal and emotion happen simultaneously.
   d. Cannon–Bard theory: Bodily arousal precedes emotion.
2. According to the emerging synthesis of theories on emotion,
   a. some emotions are experienced independently of cognitive interpretation, whereas others depend on it.
   b. all emotions need to be labeled by the amygdala to be interpreted by the brain's executive function.
   c. emotion and bodily state of arousal are the same thing.
   d. emotion is completely independent of cognition.

3. Participants in the Schachter–Singer experiment
   a. felt the same whether or not they knew they had received a stimulant.
   b. felt differently after observing the two confederates when they knew they had received a stimulant.
   c. did not feel differently after observing the two confederates when they knew they had received a stimulant.
   d. acted in random ways in the different experimental conditions.
4. Cultures have different sets of rules about how emotion can be exhibited in public. These are called _____ rules.
   a. affection      c. emotional
   b. display        d. modal

## Answers

1. c  2. a  3. c  4. b

NOTE: Once you feel comfortable with the Test Yourself questions in this chapter, visit the book's Web site at www.ablongman.com/kosslyn3e for additional study questions.

# Think It Through!

Would the world necessarily be a better place if people could control their emotions perfectly?

Do you think children have the same emotions as adults? If cognitive interpretation plays a key role, in what ways could this limit the emotions of very young children? How might this change as development proceeded?

What would be the advantages and disadvantages of a machine that always detected lies and never mistook the truth for lying? If your school offered a course in reading "body language," would you take it? Why or why not?

# MOTIVATION AND REWARD:
## More Than Feeling Good

Gandhi eventually proved exceptionally successful as a lawyer in South Africa. Not only did he make an unusually good living, but he was also able to employ White employees—a sign of status for an Indian lawyer (Markovits, 2003). This success may have shown him the limits of what money could do and also endowed him with a measure of self-confidence, which allowed him to behave unconventionally. For example, he adopted the dress of an Indian peasant, and eventually wore only a loincloth. Why? His appearance disconcerted his upper-crust British opponents, who often had trouble reconciling his fluent English and obvious intelligence with his garb. But his motivation for dressing as he did was not simply to disconcert other people. Gandhi wanted to promote hand-spinning and hand-weaving in India, to eliminate the dependence on imported cloth that largely came from England. For him, establishing economic independence was a central part of helping India establish its dignity. But he was also motivated to help India attain political independence and develop spiritually.

## Getting Motivated: Sources and Theories of Motivation

**Motivation** is the set of requirements and desires that lead an animal (including a human) to behave in a particular way at a particular time and place. There is no single, widely accepted theory that can explain all of human motivation. There are motives based on biological needs (for example, the desire for primary reinforcers such as food to quell hunger) and motives based on learning (for example, the desire for secondary reinforcers such as a promotion); motives rooted in the internal state of a person (such as hunger) and motives sparked by the external world (such as exploration); motives based on a current situation and motives based on an expected future situation. Psychologists have analyzed, classified, and identified human motives in numerous

Motivation: The set of requirements and desires that lead an animal (including a human) to behave in a particular way at a particular time and place.

Many different goals motivate us, ranging from getting good grades, to needing to keep warm, to being the object of others' attention. What goals motivate you most strongly?

ways, developing a variety of theories of motivation. Let's look at the key concepts in these theories and find out what each has to offer as an explanation of human behavior.

## Instincts: My Genes Made Me Do It

Why do birds fly south for the winter and spiders make certain kinds of webs? Instinct. For many animals, instincts provide the main motivation for behaviors. An **instinct** is an inherited tendency to produce organized and unalterable responses to particular stimuli. For several decades at the beginning of the 20th century, some psychologists tried to explain human motivation in terms of instincts (for example, McDougall, 1908/1960); their approach is termed *instinct theory*. Much of Freud's theory, for example, hinges on ideas about how we grapple with our sexual urges, which he considered to be instinctive (these ideas are discussed in Chapter 11). But unlike many other animals, we humans are remarkably flexible in the way we can respond to any stimulus, so it is difficult to assign an important role to instincts in human motivation.

Evolutionary psychology has offered an alternative to instinct theory. Instead of proposing that a behavior itself is "hard-wired" (part of our inherited make-up), these theorists believe that goals that motivate us (such as finding attractive mates) and general cognitive strategies for achieving goals (such as deception) are inborn (Barkow et al., 1992; Buss, 1998; Cosmides & Tooby, 1996; Pinker, 1997, 2002; Plotkin, 1997). However, evolutionary theories of motivation are notoriously difficult to test because we can never know for sure what our ancestors were like and how they evolved. Moreover, some goals are unlikely to be a result of heredity. For example, Gandhi valued punctuality and was almost obsessively on time; in fact, a large gold watch was the only thing of value he owned at the time of his death. Nevertheless, evolutionary thinking can be a source of novel hypotheses that can be tested in their own right (Pinker, 1997).

## Drives and Homeostasis: Staying in Balance

Instinct theory and evolutionary theory focus on specifying particular innate behaviors or goals and strategies. In contrast, *drive theory* focuses on the mechanisms that underlie such tendencies, whether or not they are innate. A **drive** is an internal imbalance that pushes you to reach a particular goal, which in turn will reduce that imbalance. Drives differ in terms of the goals to which they direct you, but all are aimed at satisfying a requirement (decreasing an imbalance). For example, hunger is a drive that orients you toward food; thirst is a drive that impels you toward drink; being cold is a drive that nudges you toward a source of warmth. Gandhi added a woolen shawl to his loincloth when he visited Buckingham Palace, in response to the raw London weather. Some drive theories link drives with reinforcement: Something is reinforcing if it reduces an imbalance. According to this theory, if you are hungry, food is reinforcing because it reduces the imbalance experienced when you have the hunger drive; if you are not hungry, food is not reinforcing.

What is the nature of the imbalance that is quelled by reinforcement? In 1932, Walter B. Cannon published a ground-breaking book titled *The Wisdom of the Body*, in which he pointed out that for life to be sustained, certain characteristics and substances of the body must be kept within a certain range, neither rising too high nor falling too low. These characteristics and substances include body temperature and the amounts of oxygen, minerals, water, and food taken in. Bodily processes such as digestion and respiration work toward keeping the levels steady. The process of maintaining a steady state is called **homeostasis**. Homeostasis works not simply to keep the body in balance, but to keep it in balance in the range in which it functions best. The usual

**Instinct:** An inherited tendency to produce organized and unalterable responses to particular stimuli.

**Drive:** An internal imbalance that motivates animals (including humans) to reach a particular goal that will reduce the imbalance.

**Homeostasis:** The process of maintaining a steady state, in which bodily characteristics and substances are within a certain range.

analogy to homeostasis is a thermostat and furnace: The thermostat turns the furnace on when the temperature drops too low and turns it off when the temperature reaches the desired level. But Cannon pointed out that in living creatures, homeostasis often involves active behavior, not simply the passive registering of the state of the environment. To stay alive, you must nourish yourself by obtaining and taking in food and water, and you must maintain body temperature by finding shelter and wearing clothing. If the homeostatic balance goes awry, an imbalance results—and you are motivated to correct the imbalance. In fact, emotion may play a role in anticipating "homeostatic challenges before the fact" (Watt, 2005, p. 84), and thereby be a key factor in motivating us. For example, a moment's thought about how you would feel if you go outside in shirtsleeves during the dead of a Massachusetts winter would lead you to put on a coat before venturing out.

The power of homeostasis in motivation was dramatically illustrated by the classic case of a boy, referred to as D.W., who developed a craving for salt when he was a year old (Wilkins & Richter, 1940). He loved potato chips, salted crackers, pretzels, olives, and pickles. He would also eat salt directly, upending salt shakers and pouring their contents directly into his mouth. When his parents took away his salt, he would cry and carry on until they relented. When he began to talk, one of his first words was "salt." At $3^{1}/_{2}$ years of age, he was hospitalized and forced to eat standard hospital fare. Deprived of his usual salt intake, D.W. died within a few days. An autopsy revealed that he died because his adrenal glands were deficient and could not produce a hormone that is essential for the body to retain salt, which is crucial to the maintenance of homeostasis. Because D.W. needed an abnormal supply, his strong drive for salt led to behavior that caused his parents to give it to him.

## Arousal Theory: Avoiding Boredom, Avoiding Overload

People are also motivated to maintain another kind of balance, one that has nothing to do with physiological homeostasis: Simply put, we don't like stimuli that are either too boring or too arousing; instead, we seek to maintain an intermediate level of stimulation. Berlyne (1960, 1974) showed that people like random patterns, paintings, or music best when they are neither too simple nor too complex, but rather somewhere in the middle. What is classed as "simple" or "complex" depends partly on the person as well as the nature of the stimulus. For example, children find patterns complex that to adults are less so.

These findings conform to what is now known as the *Yerkes–Dodson law* (Figure 10.5), named after the researchers who first described a similar principle. This law states that we perform best when we are at an intermediate level of arousal. If we are underaroused, we are sluggish; if we are overaroused, we can't focus and sustain attention. Intermediate levels of arousal may occur when we are challenged not too much and not too little. For example, if you have to speak before a large group, you may become tongue-tied because of overarousal; if you are rehearsing the speech alone in your room, you may be understimulated and give a lackluster presentation. Indeed, people adapt to a constant set of stimuli, become bored, and then seek additional stimulation (Helson, 1964). We are apparently drawn to moderate stimulation. As intuitive as this idea may seem, not all studies have supported it (for example, Messinger, 1998), perhaps because it is difficult to define precisely levels of stimulation and how they vary.

**FIGURE 10.5** **The Yerkes–Dodson Law**

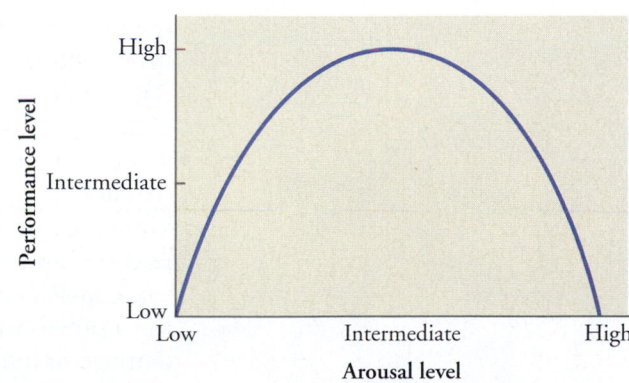

People perform best at intermediate levels of arousal.

Rewarding a child merely for performing an activity can undermine *intrinsic motivation*—it can make a child less likely to engage in that activity for its own sake (Deci et al., 1999; Lepper et al., 1973). But this need not occur. For example, praise can increase intrinsic motivation, provided that it has a number of characteristics, including being perceived as sincere, focusing on personal competence and positive traits (but not by relying on social comparisons), and helping the recipient feel autonomous (Cialdini et al., 1998; Eisenberger & Cameron, 1996; Henderlong & Lepper, 2002).

Incentive: A stimulus or event that draws animals (including humans) toward a particular goal in anticipation of a reward.

## Incentives and Reward: Happy Expectations

Homeostasis is a useful concept for understanding thirst, hunger, and certain other drives (such as those for salt, oxygen, and temperature control), and arousal theory helps explain why people select certain activities and situations and reject others. However, neither principle helps to explain other motivations, such as for sex (Beach, 1956). Your body doesn't actually need sex in the way you need food and oxygen; you can't die from celibacy. Moreover, sex is an example of an activity that invokes high arousal, not the intermediate levels we apparently prefer in other contexts. Much of what motivates us is best understood in terms of **incentives**, which are stimuli or events that draw us to achieve a particular goal in anticipation of a reward. Sex is a good example of a behavior that results from incentive-related motivation; so, too, is any money-making activity. To see the difference between a drive and an incentive, consider the fact that hunger is a drive, which is often long gone before dessert—but dessert can nevertheless still be an incentive to keep eating (as exploited by countless parents, who use dessert as an incentive to get their kids to eat their spinach).

The notion that much of motivation can best be understood in terms of incentives has led theorists to think about some aspects of motivation in terms of *expectations* of reinforcement (Wise, 2004). We tend to behave in ways that experience has shown us will produce a desirable outcome (see Chapter 6), either a positive consequence of the behavior (positive reinforcement) or the removal of a negative condition (negative reinforcement). If working 20 hours a week in a store has led to a regular paycheck, you will likely want to keep working (assuming that the check is large enough!).

Imagine that you are standing in line for a roller coaster ride or sitting in the audience waiting for the newest *Indiana Jones* movie to screen. If you are eagerly anticipating the upcoming event, a host of brain areas has become active. For one, your amygdala is probably triggering your autonomic nervous system—a tingling excitement is part and parcel of the anticipation of having a particularly good time. The amygdala—which we've just seen is a key player in emotion—is connected to the hypothalamus, which can trigger activation of the sympathetic nervous system; it also has connections to brain areas that produce the neurotransmitters dopamine and adrenaline (Cardinal et al., 2002). In addition, researchers have discovered a "cheerleader" signal in the brain, which increases as an animal nears its goal and stops right before the goal is actually reached. This signal arises in the anterior cingulate cortex, a brain area that is also involved in detecting errors and monitoring conflict between what you expect and what you get (Shidara & Richmond, 2002). Moreover, your feeling of happy anticipation also arises from neurons in other parts of the brain that are involved in emotion, notably areas of your frontal lobes and basal ganglia (O'Doherty et al., 2001; Schultz et al., 2000). In particular, areas that rely on dopamine—such as the nucleus accumbens (which is often considered part of the basal ganglia)—are activated when humans expect a reward (Wise, 2004), even with rewards as varied as money (Breiter et al., 2001) and looking at attractive faces (Aharon et al., 2001). Indeed, such brain areas are activated more strongly by an attractive face in which the eyes look right at you than by the same face when the eyes are averted (Kampe et al., 2001, 2002).

Classical conditioning may play a role in determining what is an incentive by making a previously neutral stimulus desirable (Bindra, 1968; see Chapter 6). Patients with damage to the ventral medial frontal lobe seem unable either to draw on the results of such learning or to set up new emotional associations that can guide them to make good decisions in the future (Bechara et al., 2000). In general, because we have all had different experiences, and hence learned different things, it's hard to know for sure what stimuli will serve as incentives for a given person. Consider, for example, the fact that, for Gandhi, prison was "more a luxury than a punishment. He could devote more time to prayer, study and spinning than he could outside" (Nanda, 1987).

## Learned Helplessness: Unhappy Expectations

People not only can learn new strategies for coping with problems, but they also can learn to give up trying. Martin Seligman and his colleagues first described **learned helplessness**, which occurs when an animal has an aversive experience in which nothing it does can affect what happens to it, and so it simply gives up and stops trying to change the situation or to escape (Mikulincer, 1994). As shown in Figure 10.6 (Overmeier & Seligman, 1967), when dogs were put in a cage in which they could not escape shocks, they eventually gave up responding and just huddled on the floor and endured—and they continued to do so even when they were moved to a new cage in which it was easy to escape the shocks. This condition can also afflict humans who experience a lack of control over negative events: If nothing you do seems to make an abusive spouse stop tormenting you, you may eventually just give up and stop trying. Learned helplessness can lead to depression and a range of stress-related problems.

**FIGURE 10.6**   ## The Classic "Learned Helplessness" Experiment

An animal is placed in a cage and shocked. Initially, the animal tries to escape, but it can do nothing to avoid or prevent the shocks.

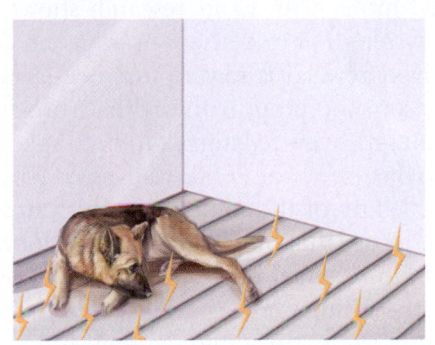

The animal eventually gives up.

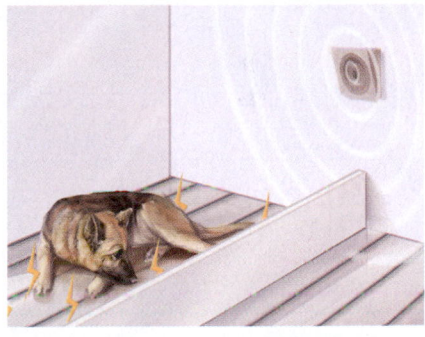

When the animal is moved into a new cage in which only a small barrier separates the side where shocks are delivered from the side where no shocks occur, it does not try to escape the shock, even when the shock is signaled by a tone.

# Needs and Wants: The Stick and the Carrot

Different things motivate different people: Gandhi was not motivated to make money; the typical entrepreneur is not motivated to give away all earthly possessions and lead a social and political revolution. Moreover, you are not motivated by the same forces day in and day out; rather, your motivations often shift over the course of the day (or year or life span). A particular motivation comes to the fore when you have a *need* or *want*. A **need** is a condition that arises from the lack of a requirement. Needs give rise to drives, which push you to reach a particular goal that will reduce the need. A low level of nutrients creates a need; hunger is a drive that will lead you to

Learned helplessness: The condition that occurs after an animal has an aversive experience in which nothing it does can affect what happens to it, and so it simply gives up and stops trying to change the situation or to escape.

Need: A condition that arises from the lack of a requirement; needs give rise to drives.

fill that need. In contrast, a **want** is a condition that arises when you have an unmet goal that will not fill a requirement. A want causes the goal to act as an incentive. You might *need* to eat, but you don't *need* a fancier car, although you might desperately *want* one—and the promise of a new car for working hard over the summer would be an incentive for you to put in long hours on the job. You are not necessarily aware of your needs or wants; **implicit motives** are needs and wants that direct your behavior unconsciously. Gandhi may not have been consciously aware of the motives that led him to imitate British dress and manners when he went to law school in London, but they affected him nonetheless.

## Is There More Than One Type of Reward?

For all needs and wants, attaining the goal reinforces the behaviors that lead to it. But what makes attaining the goal rewarding? What is "reward"? Even the strongest regulatory needs, creating drives such as hunger and thirst, arise from the brain—and those needs are satisfied not by what we do directly, but rather by the effects of our actions on the brain. To understand why something is rewarding, we must look more closely at the brain's response to events in the world. By looking at the brain mechanisms underlying reward, we find support for the distinction between needs and wants.

In Chapter 3, we discussed the idea of a "pleasure center." Olds and Milner (1954) found that rats who received electrical stimulation in certain brain areas acted as if they desired more of it. Later research showed that Olds and Milner had stumbled on a brain system that underlies reward when an animal has been deprived of the reinforcer. **Deprived reward** is reward that occurs when a biological need is met. Such reward arises from the brain pathway that runs from certain parts of the brain stem, through the (lateral) hypothalamus, on up to specific parts of the limbic system and the frontal lobes (Baxter et al., 2000; Kalivas & Nakamura, 1999; Rolls & Cooper, 1974; Wise, 1996). Many of the neurons in this circuit use, or are affected by, dopamine (Wise, 2004). Drugs that block the action of dopamine also block the rewarding effect of brain stimulation (Nader et al., 1997) and of normal reinforcers such as food or water. When given these dopamine-blockers, experimental animals (usually rats) begin to respond normally to obtain reinforcement, but then they lose interest. Because the drugs are blocking the rewarding effect of the reinforcer, the animals' response undergoes extinction (Geary & Smith, 1985; Schneider et al., 1990). Blocking dopamine can disrupt both unconditioned and conditioned positive reinforcement (Beninger, 1983, 1989; Wise, 1982). At least in some situations, the dopamine may actually signal that a reward is expected, not simply that a reward has been obtained (Cardinal et al., 2002; Garris et al., 1999; Hollerman & Schultz, 1998; Hollerman et al., 1998; Schultz, 1997; Schultz et al., 1997).

There is good evidence that the brain has a second system, which operates for **nondeprived reward**, reward that occurs when the rewarding stimulus or activity is not something that is necessary—in other words, when you had a want but not a need. For example, when ending a fast (which he often used as a political tool), even Gandhi probably felt pleasure in eating: Such pleasure is mediated by brain circuits used in deprived reward, which rely on dopamine. In contrast, if Gandhi ate one last juicy piece of fruit at the end of the meal, even though he was no longer hungry, he was eating even though he was nondeprived (it's an open question how often Gandhi actually did eat in such circumstances—but probably not often). Although dopamine plays a crucial role in producing the rewarding effects of a stimulus or activity that fills a deprivation, it does not play a role when you are not deprived. A key part of the brain involved in nondeprived reward is in the brain stem. Lesions in this area knock out the system that regis-

**Want:** A condition that arises when you have an unmet goal that will not fill a requirement; wants turn goals into incentives.

**Implicit motive:** A need or want that unconsciously directs behavior.

**Deprived reward:** Reward that occurs when a biological need is met.

**Nondeprived reward:** Reward that occurs not when a need is being met, but rather when a want is being satisfied.

ters reward when an animal is not deprived, but leave intact the system for deprived reward (Bechara & Van der Kooy, 1992; Berridge, 1996; Nader et al., 1997).

Do we usually eat dessert simply because we *like* the taste? Possibly, but *wanting* something is not the same thing as *liking* it (Berridge, 2003, 2004). For example, you can like a particular tree, bridge, or sunset very much without wanting it—and most of us can even like chocolate very much but not always want it. In fact, distinct neural circuits underlie liking something (receiving pleasure from perceiving it or thinking about it) and wanting it (Berridge, 2003, 2004; Cardinal et al., 2002; Robinson & Berridge, 2001; Wyvell & Berridge, 2000). Nevertheless, liking the taste of something can motivate you to eat it, and the nondeprived reward system will make the experience gratifying even if you aren't hungry.

The existence of different brain systems for deprived and nondeprived reward is grounds for drawing a psychological distinction between needs and wants, between motivation that arises when a requirement must be filled and motivation that arises when a goal that is not a requirement is desired. Figure 10.7 summarizes the relation between these different facets of motivation.

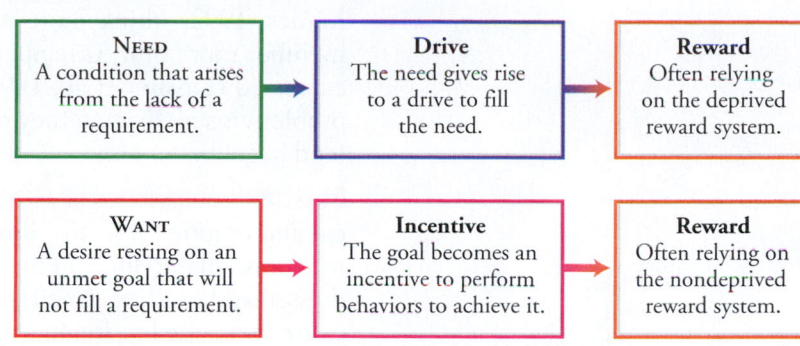

**FIGURE 10.7** **Needs and Wants**

| **NEED** A condition that arises from the lack of a requirement. | → | **Drive** The need gives rise to a drive to fill the need. | → | **Reward** Often relying on the deprived reward system. |
| **WANT** A desire resting on an unmet goal that will not fill a requirement. | → | **Incentive** The goal becomes an incentive to perform behaviors to achieve it. | → | **Reward** Often relying on the nondeprived reward system. |

Needs and wants typically trigger different sorts of events.

**Need for achievement (nAch):** The need to reach goals that require skilled performance or competence to be accomplished.

## Types of Needs: No Shortage of Shortages

There are psychological as well as bodily needs, and these needs can be organized within a hierarchy.

**PSYCHOLOGICAL NEEDS** Researchers have proposed that our psychological needs include a need to be competent, to be autonomous (Sheldon et al., 1996), to have social approval, to be dominant or in control (Kim & Kim, 1997), to be affiliated with others, to be powerful (McClelland et al., 1989), to reach closure (Kruglanski & Webster, 1996; Taris, 2000), to understand, to maintain self-esteem, and even to find the world benevolent (Stevens & Fiske, 1995). Many studies have examined individual differences in such needs. These individual differences probably arise from differences in inherited temperament (Kagan, 1994) and differences in personal experiences, such as interactions with peers (Harris, 1998) and family (Sulloway, 1997).

A classic example of a psychological need is the **need for achievement** (**nAch**; McClelland & Atkinson, 1953), which is the need to reach goals that require skilled performance or competence to be accomplished. There is a large body of research assessing the consequences of differences in this need (for example, Neel et al., 1986; Spangler, 1992). People who have a high need for achievement tend to assume that their successes are due to their personal characteristics, whereas their failures are due to environmental circumstances (Nathawat et al., 1997; Weiner & Kukla, 1970). In a meta-analysis, Spangler (1992) found that measures of "implicit" (that is, not conscious) need for achievement predict actual success better than measures of "explicit" (or conscious) need for achievement, obtained from questionnaires filled in by participants.

Another need that has attracted considerable research is the *need for cognition (NC)*, which is the need to engage in and enjoy thinking (Cacioppo & Petty, 1982; Cacioppo et al., 1996). To assess whether an individual is motivated by the need for cognition, John Cacioppo and his colleagues developed a test that includes true–false items such as "I really enjoy a task that involves coming up with new solutions to problems."

What sorts of needs do you suppose motivated President Franklin Delano Roosevelt? During FDR's entire presidency (from 1933 to 1945), he could not walk without the use of metal braces or crutches (he contracted polio in 1921 and was paralyzed thereafter). However, this did not stop him from getting around the White House on his own by using his hands to crawl from one room to another.

People whose test scores indicate that they have high NC share certain characteristics: They tend to draw more inferences when they evaluate an advertisement (Stayman & Kardes, 1992), think more about a persuasive communication and subsequently remember more of it (Cacioppo, et al., 1986), think more about attitudes they have just expressed (Lassiter et al., 1996; Leone & Ensley, 1986), are less affected by the way a problem is stated when they reason (Chatterjee et al., 2000; Smith & Levin, 1996), and tend to get better grades (Sadowski & Guelgoez, 1996).

**MASLOW'S HIERARCHY OF NEEDS**  Abraham Maslow (1970) created a hierarchy of physical and emotional needs, illustrated in Figure 10.8. Lower-level needs are considered more essential to life and must be met before needs further up the hierarchy can be addressed and satisfied. Needs toward the top of the hierarchy are considered less basic because they arise less frequently and, if not met, do not seriously impair the quality of life. You can live without understanding the world, but not without air or food. According to Maslow's theory, once a need is met, it becomes less important, and unmet, higher-level needs become more important. During a crisis (such as loss of a home due to a fire), lower-level needs take precedence, and higher-level needs are put on hold.

Maslow's hierarchy of needs has had an enormous impact on how people think about motivation, particularly in the business world (Soper et al., 1995). But is it right? There are three major difficulties with Maslow's theory. First, research has produced mixed evidence, at best, for the idea that needs are organized into a hierarchy. Results of questionnaire studies generally show that the levels are not clearly distinct from one another, as revealed by factor analysis (Wahba & Bridwell, 1976). In addition, there is no clear-cut ordering of needs (Soper et al., 1995; Wahba & Bridwell, 1976). Beer (1966), for example, found that female clerks reported strong social needs and a strong need for self-actualization but not a strong need for self-esteem. Moreover, the importance of different needs appears to vary among cultures (Diaz-Guerrero & Diaz-Loving, 2000). Second, there is no good evidence that unmet needs become more important and that met needs become less important. In fact, Hall and Nougaim (1968) found that the more consistently a need was met, the more important it became. Third, this theory fails to explain various phenomena—for example, why people voluntarily go to war and put themselves in the line of fire (Fox, 1982).

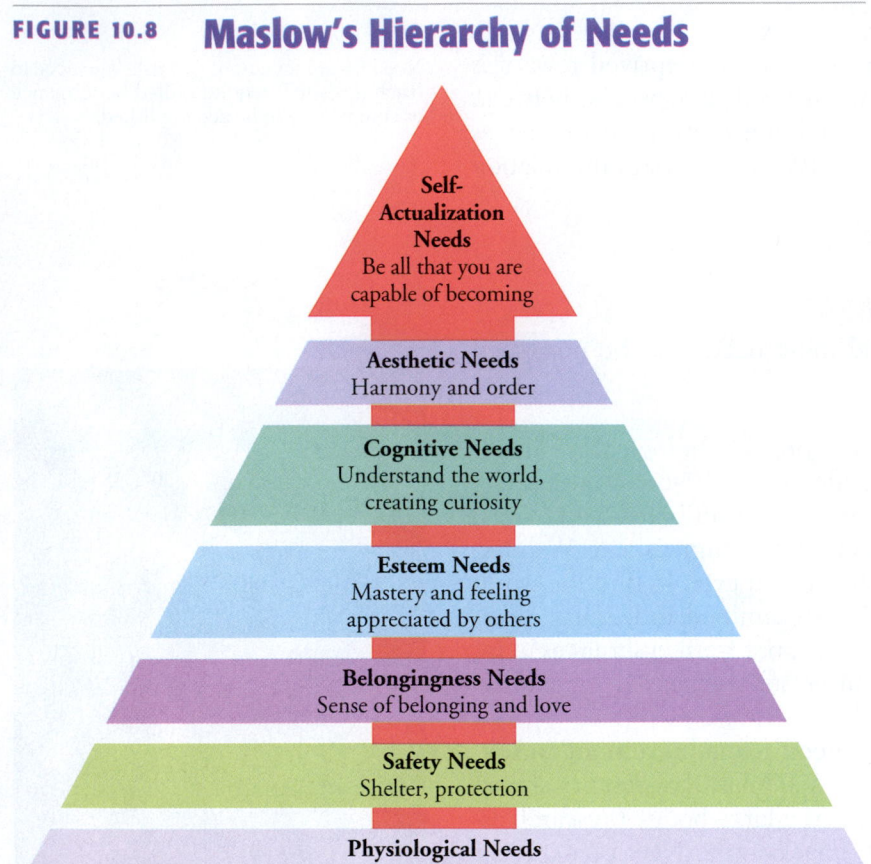

**FIGURE 10.8**  **Maslow's Hierarchy of Needs**

Self-Actualization Needs
Be all that you are capable of becoming

Aesthetic Needs
Harmony and order

Cognitive Needs
Understand the world, creating curiosity

Esteem Needs
Mastery and feeling appreciated by others

Belongingness Needs
Sense of belonging and love

Safety Needs
Shelter, protection

Physiological Needs
Water, food, air

According to Maslow's theory, needs lower in the hierarchy must be met before needs higher up become the focus of concerns.

## Regulatory Fit

Tory Higgins (2000) and his colleagues have developed a strong case for another type of motivation, which they call *regulatory fit* (Freitas & Higgins, 2002; Freitas et al., 2002; Spiegel et al., 2004). Here's the essence of the idea: Say that you are a hard-driving, high-achievement type; for you, a reminder about the likely rewards of getting good grades will motivate you to study for an exam. But now let's say that you are not oriented toward achievement, but instead toward duty and responsibility. In this case, a reminder about not letting down your parents (who are paying the tuition) will more effectively motivate you to study. Different strategies or behaviors will appeal to different people. Specifically, regulatory fit has four parts:

1. People differ in the degree to which they are *promotion-focused* or *prevention-focused*. If you have a promotion focus, you want to produce positive outcomes; if you have a prevention focus, you want to avoid negative outcomes.

2. *Eagerness-related (approach) strategies and behaviors* best fit a promotion focus, whereas *vigilance-related (avoidance) strategies and behaviors* best fit a prevention focus.

3. Regulatory fit thus occurs when promotion-focused people employ eagerness-related strategies and behaviors and when prevention-focused people employ vigilance-related strategies and behaviors.

4. Finally, people are more motivated when regulatory fit exists, and they employ the strategies and behaviors that best fit their focus.

Researchers have amassed support for this theory (Freitas & Higgins, 2002). For example, Spiegel and colleagues (2004) first had students imagine writing a report of what they would do on the upcoming Saturday and then asked the students actually to write and turn in the report after the weekend was over. Two different types of imaginal scenarios were used, eagerness-related and vigilance-related. For example, as part of the eagerness-related scenario, the students imagined themselves making the reports as vivid and interesting, whereas as part of the vigilance-related scenario, they imagined themselves not forgetting to leave anything out. Each student was given only one type of scenario, which either had or did not have regulatory fit (based on measures of each person's level of promotion or prevention focus). The results were dramatic: When regulatory fit was ensured, almost 50% more of the participants did in fact turn in the report about their Saturday than when regulatory fit was violated.

## Achievement in Individualist Versus Collectivist Cultures

Finally, we stress that many of the goals that motivate us are provided by groups, and the structure of a society determines what sorts of activities will be reinforced. Cultures can be divided into two general types that affect achievement motivation differently (although these differences may often be matters of degree and may vary for subgroups within a culture; Oyserman et al., 2002). **Individualist cultures**, such as that of the United States, emphasize the rights and responsibilities of the individual over those of the group. **Collectivist cultures**, such as that of China, emphasize the rights and responsibilities of the group over those of the individual. Such cultural differences have been shown to affect achievement goals. For example, Anglo-Australians (from an individualist culture) have been found to be focused more on personal success than on family or groups, whereas Sri Lankans (from a collectivist culture) are oriented more toward their families and groups (Niles, 1998). Similarly, Sagie and colleagues (1996) found that Americans had higher achievement motivation (as measured by scales that emphasize individual achievement) than did Japanese or Hungarians, members of collectivist cultures. Thus, growing up in one or the other type of culture influences a person's needs and wants. The effects of growing up in an individualist culture are not without a cost: Tafarodi and Swann (1996) found that Americans like themselves less than do Chinese. Why? Tafarodi and Swann believe that collectivist cultures tend to de-emphasize competition among individuals, which leads them to like each other

**Individualist culture:** A culture that emphasizes the rights and responsibilities of the individual over those of the group.

**Collectivist culture:** A culture that emphasizes the rights and responsibilities of the group over those of the individual.

more. This may lead to greater self-liking if we assume that self-liking is increased if others like us. In individualist cultures, on the other hand, members are raised to strive for freedom and independence, which tends to produce competition and conflict. In such cultures, there are more feelings of self-competence, but fewer of self-liking.

# Test Yourself

1. According to the Yerkes–Dodson law, the relationship between arousal and performance is that
   a. arousal always increases performance.
   b. arousal always decreases performance.
   c. low levels of arousal are always best for performance.
   d. intermediate levels of arousal are best for performance.
2. Needs and wants trigger different events; in general,
   a. needs trigger drives, and wants trigger incentives.
   b. needs trigger incentives, and wants trigger drives.
   c. needs trigger rewards, and wants trigger punishments.
   d. needs trigger satisfaction, and wants trigger desire.
3. Which of the following is not a weakness of Maslow's hierarchy of needs?
   a. It has affected the way businesspeople think about motivation.
   b. There is mixed evidence that needs are hierarchical.
   c. The levels in the hierarchy may not be distinct from each other.
   d. The importance of needs is affected by the cultural context.

4. In Seligman's research, the dogs' learned helplessness was demonstrated by their
   a. jumping up and down.
   b. incessant barking.
   c. failure to learn avoidance.
   d. failure to withstand the shocks.

## Answers

1.d 2.a 3.a 4.c

## Think It Through!

If you were designing a school for young children, how would you organize it so that the children were motivated as strongly as possible to learn? How can you find out what motivates a particular child?

You could argue that wants are never satisfied for very long. If this is correct, does it make sense to try to fulfill them at all? How could you tell if a motivation is a need or a want?

Do you think it might be useful to develop a drug that blocks the deprived reward system? The nondeprived reward system? Why might such a drug be dangerous? Beneficial?

# HUNGER AND EATING:
# Not Just About Fueling the Body

As a child, Gandhi was convinced that the British were able to rule India because they ate meat. Although he came from a vegetarian family, the young Gandhi began to sample meat on the sly. But he disliked having to lie to his parents and also felt sorry for the animals—and thus he abandoned his experiment. His ambivalence about food was finally settled by the happy convergence of two events during his stay in England. First, he discovered a London restaurant that prepared tasty vegetarian fare, which was fashionable in one segment of English society. And second, he chanced upon a copy of the book *Plea for Vegetarianism*, by Henry S. Salt, which led him to accept vegetarianism as part of a moral way of life. Salt related eating meat to violence, and vegetarianism to nonviolence—an idea that resonated with the young Gandhi. Later in life, Gandhi considered promoting vegetarianism to be part of his mission.

Gandhi's diet centered around fresh fruit, and the amount that he ate would have broken the budget of a typical middle-class Indian household. Reflecting on his diet, a financial backer once quipped that it cost Gandhi's friends "a great deal of money to keep him in poverty" (Markovits, 2003, p. 89). However, in spite of his love of such food, Gandhi fasted many times in his life, using the threat of his starvation to force the hands of his adversaries. What led him to want to eat and allowed him to stop eating voluntarily?

One of the drives that is best understood—and that motivates us each and every day—is hunger. Hunger is the classic drive that relies on the deprived reward system; by definition, to be hungry is to be deprived of food. However, not all eating occurs because we are hungry (Wilson, 2002). Sometimes we eat simply because it's fun, and this kind of pleasure ultimately relies on the operation of the nondeprived reward system. Hunger, and its satisfaction, affects many aspects of our lives, social and experiential as well as biological.

# Eating Behavior: The Hungry Mind in the Hungry Body

Your life is sustained by your body's **metabolism**, the sum of the chemical events in each of your cells, events that convert food molecules to the energy needed for the cells to function. Eating is necessary to maintain your metabolism. What factors determine what and when we eat?

## Is Being Hungry the Opposite of Being Full?

Although you might think of hunger as a continuum from starvation to satiety, hunger in fact arises from the action of two distinct brain systems. One system leads you to feel a need to eat; the other leads you to feel satiated (Davis & Levine, 1977; Yeomans & Gray, 1997).

The feeling of a need to eat arises when your brain senses that the level of food molecules in your blood is too low. The brain registers the quantities of two major types of food molecules: *glucose* (a type of sugar) and *fatty acids* (Friedman, 1991; Friedman et al., 1986b). In contrast, "feeling full" does not depend on the level of food molecules in the blood: You feel full well before food is digested and food molecules enter the bloodstream. If you suspect that feeling full has something to do with the state of your stomach, you're on the right track. If food is removed with a flexible tube from the stomach of a rat that has just eaten to satisfaction, the rat will eat just enough to replace the loss (Davis & Campell, 1973). But a full stomach is not enough to tell an animal to stop eating. Filling an animal's stomach with saltwater does not diminish appetite as much as filling it with milk, even if the fluids are placed directly into the stomach so that the animals cannot taste them (Deutsch et al., 1978). The stomach contains detectors that register the food value of its contents, and this information is transmitted to the brain. People know when to stop eating largely because of signals sent by sensory neurons in the stomach to the brain. Similar signals are also sent by other organs, including the upper part of the small intestine and the liver.

**Metabolism:** The sum of the chemical events in each of the body's cells, events that convert food molecules to the energy needed for the cells to function.

The brain system that regulates eating is surprisingly complex, as is revealed when it is disrupted by a stroke. For example, a person can develop what is known as *gourmand syndrome*, a neurological disorder that is characterized by an obsession with fine food. Such people do not report being hungry all of the time, and they may not overeat—but their entire lives become centered on food.

What part of the brain detects these signals? Some 50 years ago, researchers thought they had found "start" and "stop" eating centers in the brain. They had discovered that even small lesions (holes) in the lateral (side) part of the hypothalamus caused an animal to lose interest in food, even to the point of death by starvation. When this structure was electrically stimulated, the animal ate more and worked harder for food (Anand & Brobeck, 1952; Teitelbaum & Stellar, 1954). In contrast, the ventromedial (bottom, central) part of the hypothalamus was thought to be the center in the brain that told an animal it was full and should stop eating.

Other research, however, soon highlighted the difficulties in interpreting these findings. Lesions to the lateral hypothalamus suppressed the animals' interest not only in eating but also in drinking, sex, and even caring for their young; the result was often a general sluggishness. Researchers found that the lesions were disrupting not only the neurons in the lateral hypothalamus, but also connections between other brain areas. Similarly, when the ventromedial hypothalamus is damaged, animals don't just fail to stop eating, they become picky eaters (Ferguson & Keesey, 1975); indeed, they initially overeat carbohydrates (Sclafani & Aravich, 1983; Sclafani et al., 1983).

Improved methods allowed researchers to clear these muddy waters. When chemicals are used to destroy only neurons in the lateral hypothalamus and none of the connections that pass through it, hunger *is* reduced more than most other drives (Dunnett et al., 1985; Stricker et al., 1978). The ventromedial hypothalamus appears to affect other brain regions that allow stored food molecules to be released; thus, when it is damaged, the animal has no choice but to keep eating (Weingarten et al., 1985). Rather than having centers in the hypothalamus that say "eat" or "don't eat," we, and other animals, have some neurons that signal when nutrient levels are low and others that signal when stored food molecules should be released (Shiraishi et al., 2000). These neurons act not so much like buttons or switches as like sensors that provide information that guides attention and behavior. In fact, learning plays a role in how an animal interprets such signals; only after prior experience that eating reduces hunger signals and drinking reduces thirst signals do young rats intentionally seek out food or drink (as appropriate) when they are food deprived or dehydrated (Changizi et al, 2002).

## Appetite: A Moving Target

The early phases of eating depend on the taste of food. When you take the first bites of a meal or snack, you probably experience the *appetizer effect*; if those first bites taste good, your appetite is stimulated. This effect is driven in part by *opioids* in the brain; as you might suspect from their name, opioids are chemicals that behave like opium-derived drugs and cause you to experience pleasure. The opioids are released when you first eat food that tastes good (Yeomans & Gray, 1997).

As you continue to eat, your responses to food-related stimuli change. After eating some fresh-baked cookies, the smell of them doesn't seem quite as heavenly as it did before you ate them. If people have had their fill of a certain food, they rate its odor as less pleasant than they did before eating it (Duclaux et al., 1973). However, when the flavor, texture, color, or shape of a food is changed, people will eat more of the same food (Rolls et al., 1981b). After you've eaten a few chocolate chip cookies, you might find yourself not interested in more cookies, but happy to have some fresh-baked bread.

Not surprisingly, these changes in your appetite are linked to events in the hypothalamus. Neurons in the lateral hypothalamus initially fire when an animal sees or tastes a food and then reduce their firing after the animal has eaten its fill of that food (Burton et al., 1976). These neurons are selective: After they stop responding to one food, they can still be stimulated by another (Rolls et al., 1981b). But appetite, like most psychological phenomena, is governed by a complex set of brain areas. In one study, participants' brains were scanned as they ate their fill of chocolate, and then, at the request of the investigators, kept on eating and eating (Small et al., 2001). As they ate beyond the point when the candy was appetizing, activity changed in parts of the frontal lobes and the insula (which registers bodily sensations).

And appetite isn't just about the brain. To understand why you eat the amount you do, you need to consider events at the different levels of analysis. When alone, you vary the size of a meal depending on the size and length of time since your last meal—for example, by eating less for dinner if you had a late lunch (Woods et al., 2000). But this biological mechanism doesn't work so well when you eat with others (De Castro, 1990; Herman et al., 2003). When people eat in groups, they do not vary the size of their meals to reflect their degree of hunger. Moreover, the amount people eat depends on the amount others eat. In some circumstances, people not only eat more when with company, but report eating a greater amount when more people are present for a meal. Part of this effect may simply reflect the fact that when more people are present, the meal takes longer to complete. In other circumstances, people will actually eat less when eating in a group than they would when alone. You might call this the "not wanting to look like a pig" effect! It is clear that eating with other people can lead you to eat more or less than you would when alone, but the precise ways in which others exert their influence are not yet known (Herman et al., 2003).

At the level of the person, men want chocolate (and report that they enjoy it more) when they are in a good mood, for example, after they've watched films that make them happy (such as *When Harry Met Sally*; Macht et al., 2002). Moreover, anything that reminds you of good food you've eaten on a previous occasion—an event at the level of the person—can increase hunger. As usual, events at the different levels interact. For example, you get hungry when reminded of good food in part because your body responds both to perceptions of food and to thoughts of food by secreting insulin. **Insulin** is a hormone that stimulates the storage of food molecules in the form of fat. Thus, insulin reduces the level of food molecules in the blood, which may increase hunger.

## Why Does It Taste Good?

What about preferences for specific foods? Some of our tastes clearly are a consequence of beliefs that develop with experience. Some people develop disgust reactions to certain foods (Rozin & Fallon, 1986), and the very idea of that food then keeps them away from it. Such *cognitive taste aversion* is apparently long-lasting and can be formed without classical conditioning (for instance, without being nauseated after eating the food; see Batsell & Brown, 1998). Rozin and his colleagues have shown that people apparently believe that "once in contact, always in contact." If a neutral food was in contact with an aversive food, the aversive properties seem to transfer. Suppose someone dunked a sterilized, dead cockroach briefly in your glass of water. Would you want to take a sip? The answer is probably a resounding no. Similarly, if a morsel of premium chocolate fudge were molded into the shape of feces, the shape alone would make it unappealing. Rozin and his colleagues have also shown that Americans harbor exaggerated beliefs about the harmful effects of some foods; in fact, many incorrectly believe that salt and fat are harmful even at trace levels (Rozin et al., 1996).

Beliefs also play another role in determining what we want to eat: Perhaps unconsciously, people believe that "you are what you eat." Nemeroff and Rozin (1989) asked people to rate qualities of people who "ate boar" and those who "ate turtle." The boar

Insulin: A hormone that stimulates the storage of food molecules in the form of fat.

Culture plays a key role in shaping our tastes in food: The French would never give up their beloved snails or frogs; Koreans find pickled snakes delicious; Filipinos enjoy unhatched chicks in the shell; the Germans savor stuffed pig intestines; and Chileans eat a kind of sea anemone whose looks would qualify it to star in a science-fiction movie.

eaters were believed to be more likely to have boarlike qualities, such as being bearded and heavy-set.

# Overeating: When Enough Is Not Enough

We humans like the taste of fatty foods, which is bad news because eating too much fat can lead to a variety of diseases, such as diabetes, cardiovascular disease, cancer, high blood pressure, and gallbladder disease (Schiffman et al., 1999). Diet books and cookbooks are best-sellers. Does this seem ironic to you? Do we want to lose weight so that we can eat more? Or does our love of eating make us need to diet? Our culture places a premium on being thin. Nonetheless, some of us overeat, and according to the Centers for Disease Control and Prevention (2004), 31% of Americans are obese and another 34% are overweight—but why?

## Set Point: Your Normal Weight

If you lose weight, fat cells become less likely to give up their stored energy. In addition, receptors in your brain that are sensitive to low levels of fat then become active and make you hungry; you eat more, and thus you end up gaining weight. This mechanism reminded researchers of the way a thermostat turns on the heater when the room is too cold, bringing it back to a constant temperature. This analogy led to the notion that animals, including humans, settle at a particular body weight that is easiest to maintain; this weight is called the **set point**. For many years, researchers thought of the set point as relatively constant, kept that way by homeostatic mechanisms (Nisbett, 1972; Stunkard, 1982). However, more recently, some researchers have argued that the body doesn't maintain the set point the way a thermostat maintains room temperature (Berthoud, 2002; Levine & Billington, 1997). Rather, although your body weight is relatively stable, it can change if your environment changes (for example, so that you are tempted by more and fattier foods), your activities change (for example, you walk to work and thus exercise more often), or your emotional state changes (for example, you become depressed and listless).

Why would you ever eat more than your body needs? Cognitive systems in the brain are connected to, and apparently can "overpower," the hypothalamic systems that underlie hunger (Berthoud, 2002). Thus, we sometimes eat not because we're hungry, but because we're bored or lonely, or simply because we think we ought to eat (perhaps because the clock says it's lunchtime). If you eat when your body doesn't need the energy, you are "overeating"; if you overeat for a prolonged time, the number of fat cells in your body increases to store the additional energy. Thus, you gain weight. In contrast, when you lose weight, each fat cell decreases in size, but you don't lose fat cells. This may explain why it's generally easier to gain weight than to lose it. Regular, moderately vigorous exercise can speed up your metabolism, leading your cells to need more energy even when you are not exercising. This is the best method of changing your balance of energy input and output, and thereby of losing weight.

## Obesity

Set point: The particular body weight that is easiest for an animal (including a human) to maintain.

An obese person is defined as one who is more than 20% heavier than the medically ideal weight for that person's sex, height, and bone structure. By this standard, almost one third of Americans are obese. But why? Consider three theories.

**FAT PERSONALITIES?** Do obese people have weak characters that make them slaves to food? No. The personality characteristics of obese and nonobese people are similar (Nilsson et al., 1998; Poston et al., 1999). Indeed, President William Howard Taft (president from 1909 to 1913) was a grossly obese man, weighing over 300 pounds. He was so overweight that, after getting stuck in a White House bathtub, he had a new tub constructed that would hold four average-sized men. However, his size did not deter him from achieving the highest office in the land.

So, why are some people obese? Some explanations have grown out of psychodynamic theory. According to one such explanation, obese people eat when they feel stress, as a kind of defense. The evidence for this explanation is mixed: Obese people do not always overeat when they feel stress and may instead tend to overeat when aroused, positively or negatively (Andrews & Jones, 1990; McKenna, 1972). Overeating is not the same thing as an eating disorder (see Chapter 14); people don't necessarily overeat because they have a psychological problem.

**FAT GENES?** There is good reason to believe that at least some forms of obesity have a genetic basis—and may not be connected to how much a person actually eats. If one identical twin is obese, the other probably is too; variations in weight may be as much as 70% heritable (Berthoud, 2002; Ravussin & Bouchard, 2000). In fact, 58 distinct genes and portions of all chromosomes but chromosome Y (the male sex chromosome) have been related to obesity (Rankinen et al., 2002). Claude Bouchard, a researcher in this area, notes that genes may affect weight in numerous ways: "Some affect appetite, some affect satiety. Some affect metabolic rate" (quoted in Gladwell, 1998, p. 53). Thus, the genetics of obesity will not be simple to unravel, but some highlights have already been noted:

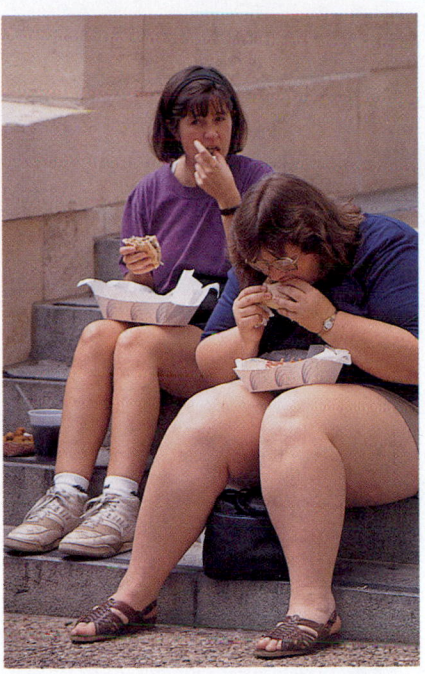

Obese people have the same "will power" to resist eating junk food as nonobese people.

1. *Feeling full.* The neurons in certain brain areas involved in registering satiety appear to rely on the neurotransmitter serotonin (Blundell, 1977, 1984, 1986; Blundell & Halford, 1998), and mutant mice that lack specific receptors for this neurotransmitter will keep eating until they become obese (Tecott et al., 1995). The notion that humans may act the same way is supported by the finding that people gain weight if they take medication that happens to block these receptors (Fitton & Heel, 1990); moreover, people who take drugs that activate these receptors report being less hungry, and they actually lose weight while on the medication (Sargent et al., 1997).

2. *Maintaining body fat.* A gene known as *ob* (short for *obese*) has been shown to play a role in governing eating and weight. This gene governs the release of a hormone called *leptin* (*leptos* is Greek for "thin"), which is released by fat cells. The more fat in the body, the more leptin is in the blood. Leptin decreases food intake and increases energy expenditure (in part by increasing heat production; Wang et al., 1999). Leptin interferes with the functioning of a neurotransmitter called *neuropeptide Y (NPY)*, which induces eating (Inui, 1999). This interference occurs in the hypothalamus, by activating or inhibiting specific neurons (Yokosuka et al., 1998); indeed, hungry rats will work hard to receive electrical stimulation of key parts of the hypothalamus, but giving them leptin decreases the rate of such responding (Fulton et al., 2000). Rosenbaum and Leibel (1999) suggest that leptin may serve to maintain a constant level of body fat by acting as a signal to the brain that the amounts of stored fat and food intake are adequate.

Genes can make a big difference. Researchers found that by altering a single gene, they could increase the production of substances that make a mouse obese.

3. *Other defective genes.* Some researchers hypothesized that obese people might have a defective *ob* gene—which, unlike the normal version of the gene, fails to decrease these people's eating after more fat has been stored. However, studies have

shown that only extremely obese people have a defect in the ob gene, and this problem is unlikely to underlie most cases of obesity (Berthoud, 2002; Mantzoros, 1999). Another candidate for the role of obesity promoter is a gene that is involved in the regulation of the stress hormone cortisol, which in turn appears to affect weight gain. Scientists altered the genes of mice so that this particular gene was turned on only in fat cells (Masuzaki et al., 2001). These mice developed a "spare tire" around their middles—much like obese humans who have an "apple shape." However, some obese humans have a "pear shape," gaining weight mostly in their thighs; these mice didn't have that problem, so this one gene cannot explain all forms of obesity.

4. *Conversion to fat versus heat.* Yet another gene has been discovered that determines whether the excess fat in food is converted to body fat or is turned into surplus body heat (Fleury et al., 1977). Animals that do not have this gene become fat when they eat amounts that normally do not increase weight. How does such a gene work? One mechanism could be the "fidget factor"; that is, the gene could affect the overall level of physical activity (Bouchard, as quoted in Gladwell, 1998, p. 53). Consider the findings reported by Levine and colleagues (1999), who asked a group of normal people to overeat a large amount each day for 8 weeks. At the end of this period, there were large differences in how much weight the volunteers gained—some people gained literally 10 times as much as others. Levine and his colleagues found that the single biggest factor that determined how much the participants gained was the number of physical movements unrelated to sports or fitness regimens—"activities of daily living, fidgeting, spontaneous muscle contraction" and the effort of maintaining posture when not reclining. Each such movement burned up some of the energy in the extra food so that it was not stored as fat. We know that temperament is partly innate (Kagan et al., 1994), and it is possible that differences in temperament lead to differences in such activity levels, which in turn affect whether extra calories are burned or stored.

**FAT ENVIRONMENT?** As we have seen, genes determine a reaction range for a particular characteristic, and the environment sets individuals within that range (Chapter 9). Some people have a propensity to become fat, but do so only in certain environments (Ravussin & Bouchard, 2000). Overeating is encouraged by many aspects of the American environment: Food is relatively cheap, fast foods are high in fat, snacking is all too easy and acceptable, and portions have grown larger in the United States (but not in many parts of Europe). At the same time, people exercise less not only because most of us drive or ride to work, but also because many of our amusements, such as watching television and surfing the Web, are sedentary. Moreover, whereas in earlier eras many people were paid for work that involved significant exercise, most now have to pay (in both cash and leisure time) to exercise (Philipson & Posner, 2003). Hill and Peters (1998) suggest three approaches to "curing the environment," which is currently the basis of a virtual epidemic in obesity:

1. Educating people to eat smaller portions,

2. Making foods that are low in fat and calories more available, and

3. Encouraging more physical activity.

Some obese people are capable of losing large amounts of weight and keeping the weight off (Tinker & Tucker, 1997). These people are able to adopt healthier eating and exercise habits. Note, however, that changes in the environment can be effective only if the reaction range for body weight is relatively large (that is, if the genes define a wide range of possible weights). If the reaction range of genes that control obesity is small, then people who have those genes may not have much choice in determining how heavy they are.

# Dieting

Even Gandhi, famous for his fasts, liked to eat. None of us especially relishes diets that require us to eat less, and we are receptive to diets that promise weight loss while allowing us to eat like we always do. Some popular diets are summarized in Table 10.2, along with the key concerns physicians have about them. A study of four popular diets found that overweight or obese people lost modest amounts of weight when following any of the diets, that the diets were equally effective, and that at least a third of people who began a diet did not stick with it (Dansinger et al., 2005). Low-carbohydrate diets (such as the Atkins) do not lead obese people to shed more pounds than standard diets, such as that advocated by Weight Watchers (Foster et al., 2003).

The science of dieting is clear: If you want to lose weight, eat fewer calories (Freedman et al., 2001) and exercise more. The most commonly recommended diet for obese people requires them to cut their normal food intake in half (Stallone &

**TABLE 10.2    Some Popular Diets and Physicians' Key Concerns About Them**

| Diet | Key Features | Key Medical Concerns |
|---|---|---|
| Dr. Atkin's New Diet Revolution (Atkins, 1992) | Diet is broken into four parts: induction, weight loss, premaintenance, and maintenance. During the induction phase, dieters eat only meats and fats. Carbohydrates are gradually reintroduced in the subsequent phases. | Diet is deficient in vitamins E, A, $B_6$, and thiamin, folate, calcium, magnesium, iron, zinc, potassium, and dietary fiber; it provides too much saturated fat, cholesterol, and animal protein. |
| Eat More, Weigh Less (Ornish, 1993) | Diet allows unlimited amounts of low-fat, plant-based foods and soy products, and moderate amounts of egg whites, nonfat dairy products, sugar, and white flour. | Diet is deficient in vitamins E, $B_{12}$, and zinc. |
| The Carbohydrate Addict's Diet (Heller & Heller, 1991) | Daily diet includes two "complementary meals," consisting of 3–4 ounces of meat and 2 cups of vegetables, and one "reward meal," consisting of 1/3 protein, 1/3 low-carbohydrate vegetables, and 1/3 high-carbohydrate foods. | Diet is deficient in calcium, iron, potassium, and fiber; it provides too much fat and cholesterol. The claim that the body produces less insulin following reward meals than it would normally is false. |
| Protein Power! (Eades & Eades, 1996) | Dieters base their caloric intake on protein requirements, determined by their Body Weight Index (body weight/body height). Carbohydrate consumption starts at 30 grams per day and progresses to 55 grams per day. | Dieters must take vitamin and mineral supplements to compensate for missing vitamins and minerals. |
| Sugar Busters! (Steward et al., 1995) | No high-glycemic foods, such as refined sugar, potatoes, corn, white rice, white bread, carrots, and beer. Protein intake and portion sizes are not regulated. | Diet is deficient in calcium, iron, and vitamin E. It is based on the false claim that eating high-glycemic foods makes you crave more high-glycemic foods, leading to insulin resistance and weight gain. |

Stunkard, 1994). But such a diet is a mixed blessing. For example, in a now classic study, Keys and his colleagues (1950) charted the effects of such a diet on a group of 36 healthy young men. After 6 months, these men weighed on average 25% less than they had at the outset. In addition, they experienced many dramatic psychological changes, resulting from events at all three levels of analysis. At the level of the brain, their perceptual processes and sleep patterns changed. They slept less, became more sensitive to light and noise, had less tolerance for cold, and showed various other physical symptoms. (Later studies have also shown that dieting disrupts the ability to focus attention; Williams et al., 2002.) At the level of the person, the content of the thoughts of the dieting young men changed. They became obsessed with food. Many began to hoard not only food, but also random junk. (This also happens with rats who are put on such diets [Fantino & Cabanac, 1980] and with people who have eating disorders and put themselves on similar diets [Crisp et al., 1980].) At the level of the group, they lost interest in sex and in interacting with other people. They also became irritable, anxious, depressed, and argumentative. Many of these symptoms persisted for months after the men began to eat normally again.

# Test Yourself

1. The _____ contains neurons that signal when levels of nutrients are low and when stored resources should be released.
   a. hypothalamus
   c. stomach
   b. amygdala
   d. small intestine
2. Eating behavior is affected by factors that can be viewed from the three levels of analysis. Which factor does *not* affect eating?
   a. levels of insulin
   c. certain genes
   b. group influences on eating
   d. height
3. One reason why diets are often ineffective is that people typically
   a. strive to eat less than the body requires to function optimally.
   b. have a set point for body weight.
   c. disrupt the functioning of insulin by exercising.
   d. eat only for pleasure.

4. What effect do genes have on obesity?
   a. Genes completely determine a person's weight.
   b. Genes set a possible range for a person's weight.
   c. Genetic effects are overshadowed by the environment.
   d. Genes are not as important as the person's choice of foods.

## Answers

1. a 2. d 3. b 4. b

# Think It Through!

In the 1930s, Coke bottles held 6.5 ounces; today, they hold a liter—more than five times the original amount. We tend to think of a bottle as a single serving or perhaps two servings. What effects do you think this sort of change has on consumption of Coke and other soft drinks? Does it make a difference that a lot of soft drink is consumed on social occasions with a lot of people? If so, how could such a difference be minimized?

# SEX: Not Just About Having Babies

Gandhi and his wife, Kasturbai, were both only 13 years old when they took their wedding vows. They had four sons together, but at age 36 Gandhi dedicated himself to chastity. And he urged everyone else to do the same. He felt that sex for pleasure was morally wrong, and that sex should only be used for procreation. He urged sexual abstention so that "sexual energy" could be preserved and channeled into social causes (Markovits, 2003, p. 94). To test his resolve in his later years, he sometimes slept with young naked women (including a grandniece, Manu); his goal was to have close physical contact but experience no sexual impulses, which would demonstrate that he had conquered his sexual urges. He may have been responding to the Hindu proverb "Conquer your passions and you conquer the world" (cited in Gross, 1998), but perhaps his attitudes about sex may also have reflected the fact that India was horribly overpopulated, which led to enormous misery and poverty. Why do people have sex?

# Sexual Behavior: A Many-Splendored Thing

People engage in sexual relations for two general reasons: to have babies (*reproductive sex*) and for pleasure (*recreational sex*). The vast majority of sexual acts, around 98% of them (Linner, 1972), are for pleasure, as opposed to procreation. Sex leads to some of the most intense of all positive emotions, and hence it is valued highly by members of our species. The earliest known attempts at contraception were developed 4,000 years ago by the Egyptians; they thought dried crocodile dung would do the job.

Alfred Kinsey began the first systematic surveys about human sexual behavior in the late 1940s. He and his colleagues interviewed thousands of Americans about their sex lives. Kinsey found that people frequently reported engaging in sexual practices then considered rare or even abnormal. However, attempts to study sexual behavior ran into some unique problems. As Freud wrote (1910, p. 41), "People in general are not candid over sexual matters, they do not show their sexuality freely, but to conceal it wear a heavy overcoat of a tissue of lies, as though the weather were bad in the world of sexuality." Psychologists have had difficulty seeing through this "tissue of lies," and even today there is debate about whether we have reliable information about many facets of human sexuality.

Most studies of sexual behavior rely on surveys. But would you volunteer to be in a study of sexual behavior? How about filling in a questionnaire about your most intimate moments? Researchers have found that not everybody is equally willing to participate in studies of sexual behavior, and thus the data are likely to come from a biased sample. Bogaert (1996), for example, found that the undergraduate males who volunteered for a study on human sexuality differed in many ways from males who volunteered for a study on personality: The former group had more sexual experience, were more interested in sexual variety, were more inclined to seek out sensation and excitement, and were less socially conforming and less likely to follow rules (Trivedi and Sabini [1998] reported similar findings). In addition, people from different cultures may respond differently when asked about their sexual and reproductive behavior: Researchers found that Hispanic American women reported less sexual activity when their interviewers were older, but Black American women did not display this bias as strongly (Ford & Norris, 1997). The researchers suspected that this bias arose because the Hispanic culture has traditionally frowned on premarital sex for women, leading the Hispanic women to underreport their sexual activity to older women who might disapprove.

In short, interview data about sex are suspect. Sampling bias as well as response bias can distort the results.

Alfred Kinsey's life and work have received renewed interest—and generated controversy—as a result of the 2004 movie about him.

## Sexual Responses: Step by Step

William Masters and Virginia Johnson (1966) were the first researchers to study systematically actual sexual behavior, not just reports or descriptions of it, with a large sample of participants. Their effort was the first that provided a look behind the "tissue of lies" about sex. Over the course of many years, Masters and Johnson brought thousands of men and women into their laboratory and devised ways to measure what the body does during sex. The outcome was a description of four stages the human body—male or female—passes through during sexual activity:

1. *Excitement* (during the initial phases, when the person becomes aroused),
2. *Plateau* (a full level of arousal),
3. *Orgasm* (accompanied by muscle contractions and, in men, ejaculation), and
4. *Resolution* (the release of sexual tension).

These stages meld into one another, with no sharp divisions separating them (Levin, 1980, 1994). The mountain of research they conducted led Masters and Johnson to reach four general conclusions, summarized in Table 10.3.

Others have built on Masters and Johnson's research and have developed a comprehensive description of the **sexual response cycle**:

*Sexual attraction* leads to *sexual desire*, *sexual excitement* (arousal), and possibly *sexual performance* (which involves becoming fully aroused, reaching orgasm, and then experiencing resolution followed by—for men—a refractory period).

Why do we have sexual responses at the times, and with the partners, we do? Not unexpectedly, events at all three levels of analysis play crucial roles in our sexual behavior.

| TABLE 10.3 | **Masters and Johnson's Conclusions** |
| --- | --- |

- Men and women are similar in their bodily reactions to sex.

- Women tend to respond more slowly than men, but stay aroused longer.

- Many women can have multiple orgasms, whereas men typically have a *refractory period*, a period of time following orgasm when they cannot become aroused again.

- Women reported that penis size is not related to sexual performance, unless the man is worried about it.

## The Role of Hormones: Do Chemicals Dictate Behavior?

In 1849, German scientist Arnold Berthold wondered why castrated roosters acted like hens. They stopped crowing, mating with hens, fighting, and engaging in other typical rooster behaviors. So, he castrated some roosters and then put the testes into their abdominal cavities. Shortly thereafter, the roosters started behaving like roosters again. Berthold reasoned that the testes produced their effects not because of nerves or other physical connections, but because they released something into the bloodstream. We now know that what the testes release is the male hormone *testosterone*.

*Hormones* are chemicals that are secreted into the bloodstream primarily by endocrine glands and that trigger receptors on neurons and other types of cells (see Chapter 3). Hormones are controlled in large part by the pituitary gland, the brain's "master gland." The pituitary gland in turn is controlled by the hypothalamus, which plays a major role in emotion and motivation and is affected by hormones produced elsewhere in the body.

**SEX HORMONES** When you are sexually aroused, hormones from the gonads (the testes and ovaries) act on the brain and genital tissue. **Androgens** are usually referred to as "male hormones" (such as testosterone), which cause many male characteristics such as beard growth and a low voice. **Estrogens**, usually referred to as "female hormones," cause many female characteristics such as breast development and the bone structure of the female pelvis. The presence of the different hormones is not all-or-none between the sexes. Both types of hormones are present in both males and females, but to different degrees. Although they exert direct effects on physical characteristics, hormones don't directly dictate behavior. Rather, they lead to a tendency to *want* to behave in certain ways in the presence of particular stimuli. That is, they modify motivation. For ex-

Sexual response cycle: The stages the body passes through during sexual activity, including sexual attraction, desire, excitement, and possibly performance (which includes full arousal, orgasm, and resolution).

Androgens: Sex hormones that cause many male characteristics such as beard growth and a low voice.

Estrogens: Sex hormones that cause many female characteristics such as breast development and the bone structure of the female pelvis.

ample, giving young women a dose of testosterone later caused their heart rates to speed up when they saw angry faces. This response could indicate that the women were more ready to "fight or defend status in face-to-face challenges" (van Honk et al., 2001, p. 241). Testosterone does more than influence sexual behavior.

**INSENSITIVITY TO SEX HORMONES**   Not everyone responds to sex hormones in a normal way. For example, people who have *androgen insensitivity syndrome* have an X and a Y chromosome and a genetic mutation that does not allow androgen receptors to develop. Thus, the lock is missing for the hormonal key, and the hormone has no effects either during development or afterward. These people, who should have been boys, grow into girls, but with testes tucked up in the belly and no uterus or ovaries. In some cases, the vagina is too shallow and must be surgically altered later in life. In spite of their genetic identities as males, the failure of male hormones to have an effect does not allow the genes to influence these individuals' sexuality. In fact, although they sometimes require appropriate female hormone supplements, people with androgen insensitivity syndrome look like women, often marry, and have normal female sex lives (which include normal orgasms during intercourse).

**OVULATION AND EROTICISM**   Sex hormones also influence our interest in sex. In fact, changes in the level of sex hormones over the course of a woman's menstrual cycle affect the degree to which she is inclined to become sexually aroused. Slob and colleagues (1996) found that erotic videos increased the temperature of the female genital area more during the days just before ovulation than during the days following ovulation, and the women who were about to ovulate generally experienced increased sexual desire and sexual fantasies for the next 24 hours. In fact, researchers have found that women who were about to ovulate tended to classify very briefly presented pictures as sexual stimuli, both when the stimuli were in fact in this category (pictures of nude men) and when they were not (pictures of babies or objects related to body care; Krug et al., 1994). And when women are ovulating, they prefer "ruggedly handsome" male faces more than when they are not ovulating (Penton-Voak & Perrett, 2000). Moreover, women are more likely to be interested in men who are not their partners while they are ovulating (Gangestad et al., 2002). However, the effects of shifting hormone levels are only tendencies, affecting different people to different degrees (Regan, 1996). For example, Van Goozen and colleagues (1997) found that only those women who had premenstrual complaints had a peak in sexual interest during the ovulatory phase of their menstrual cycle.

**TESTOSTERONE AND INTIMACY**   The relationship between hormones and motivation runs in both directions. In a famous study, a researcher who signed his paper "Anonymous" (1970) reported the effects of his building anticipation of female companionship after sustained periods of enforced celibacy. This man was a scientist who worked on a small island and only occasionally visited the mainland, where he would have brief periods of contact with the opposite sex. He apparently had time on his hands when he was alone, as he decided to measure his beard growth every day by weighing his beard clippings after shaving. He found that his beard grew thicker as his visits to the mainland approached. Just thinking about the visit apparently caused increases in his levels of androgens, which in turn caused increased beard growth. Researchers have also documented the reverse effect: Although single and married men have the same levels of testosterone in the morning, by the end of the day married men have less than unmarried men (testosterone normally decreases over the course of the day, but does so more sharply for married men; P. B. Gray et al., 2002). This was true for men who did or did not have children. Moreover, for those who did not have children, the more hours a man spent with his wife on his last day off work, the lower his testosterone levels.

But we are not simply creatures of our hormones. To study the effect of testosterone on sexual behavior and mood, Schiavi and colleagues (1997) injected men who had difficulty having erections with the hormone twice a week for 6 weeks; this course was followed by injections of a placebo for 4 weeks (the change was not known to the participants). Although the participants did ejaculate more often when they were receiving the testosterone than when they were receiving the placebo, little else changed. Testosterone did not affect the amount of sexual satisfaction, the rigidity of the penis during sex, or the participants' mood.

**OXYTOCIN AND MOTHERLY LOVE**    The so-called sex hormones aren't the only ones that affect our sex lives (Carter, 2004; Meston & Frohlich, 2000). *Oxytocin* is a hormone (produced by the pituitary gland) that increases dramatically in women immediately after they give birth, and probably helps to forge the mother–infant emotional bond (Insel, 2000). Oxytocin is also released after orgasm and may bond sex partners—perhaps even if they consciously don't like each other. Could oxytocin explain why "love is blind"? Future research will tell us.

## Sexual Stimuli

We humans are visual creatures—about half the cerebral cortex is concerned with vision. Visual stimuli play a major role in sexual attraction, particularly for men (Przybyla & Byrne, 1984). How do visual sexual stimuli affect us? Karama and colleagues (2002) scanned the brains of men and women as they watched either erotic or neutral videos. Many of the brain areas involved in reward and the anticipation of reward were activated in both sexes when watching the erotic stimuli. Critically, the hypothalamus was activated only in the male participants—and the more strongly it was activated, the more strongly the male (but not the female) participants reported being aroused. This activation suggests that the erotic material not only stimulated the men but also motivated them to want to respond accordingly. In general, men reported being more strongly aroused than did women, which could be either the cause or the effect of the differences in how their brains were activated. However, when visual stimuli do arouse women, they do so differently than for men. Women—regardless of their sexual orientation—are aroused by *both* male and female sexual stimuli, and this arousal is both reported subjectively and reflected in genital arousal (Chivers et al., 2004). In contrast, heterosexual males are aroused by sexual stimuli of women but not sexual stimuli of men (and vice versa for homosexual males). The object of sexual arousal appears to play a smaller role in women's sexual orientation than it does in men's sexual orientation.

In addition, the tendency for visual stimuli to be less important for women is modified by culture. Effa-Heap (1996) reports that Nigerian 15- to 20-year-olds of both sexes preferred adult videos over other formats of pornography. In addition, the precise nature of the video material matters. Pearson and Pollack (1997) assessed women's level of sexual arousal when they watched sexually explicit films. The researchers had groups of women watch two types of films, those designed for men and those designed specifically for women or male–female couples. The women who viewed the latter films reported greater arousal. Moreover, there are clear sex differences in the importance of other types of stimuli. Notably, women reported that body odor was the most important sensory quality that could turn them off sexually, whereas men were neutral regarding body odor (Herz & Cahill, 1997).

Sexual stimuli trigger a variety of responses because people use sex to satisfy different psychological needs. Cooper and colleagues (1998) showed that motivations for having sex can be thought of in terms of the two dimensions illustrated in

Figure 10.9, which range from avoidance to approach (the horizontal dimension) and from social connection to self-oriented independence (the vertical dimension). The importance of these dimensions varies for different people and in different contexts—for instance, for people in stable relationships, exclusive relationships, or relationships that are both stable and exclusive.

Finally, sexual responses can be triggered in many ways, affecting events at the different levels of analysis. For example, adolescents apparently model their behavior after that of their friends, and hence are more likely to have sexual relations early if their friends are having sexual relations early (DiBlasio & Benda, 1990). However, such social interactions can be mediated by biological events—including whether the adolescent has certain genes (Miller et al., 1999).

## Mating Preferences

Think about it: What sort of person would be your ideal mate? Or just a good date for tomorrow night? Evolutionary psychology has offered theories of what makes someone seem desirable as a potential mate. Some of these theories derive from Trivers's (1972) influential theory of *parental investment*. He argued that males, who typically invest less than do females in the nurturing and raising of children, should be more interested in short-term sex and less particular about mates; females, who typically are very invested in nurturing and raising children, should have opposite preferences. However, when Pedersen and colleagues (2002) tested this idea, they found that 98.9% of men and 99.2% of women hoped to have a long-term stable relationship. Very few of either gender were motivated by the prospect of continued short-term sex. In addition, the two genders spend comparable amounts of time and money in "short-term mating," such as trying to meet someone at a party (Miller et al., 2002).

Another evolutionary theory relies on the observation that because fertilization occurs in the privacy of a woman's fallopian tubes, a man can never be absolutely certain that a baby carries his genes; thus, according to this theory, men should be particularly alert to their mates' possible sexual infidelity. In contrast, because women value a man who will devote time, energy, and resources to her children, women should be particularly alert to their mates' becoming emotionally involved with someone else. When asked which would be more upsetting, their mates' falling in love with someone else or having sex with someone else, most men chose the latter and most women chose the former (Buss et al., 1992; Cramer et al., 2001–2002). However, these preferences may not be observed when participants use a continuous scale to specify their reaction to each event (DeSteno & Salovey, 1996) or when they are asked to reflect about actual experiences (Harris, 2002). Moreover, other researchers have found that men and women value remarkably similar characteristics in a potential mate (Miller et al., 2002). To avoid methodological problems (such as responding in ways that are considered socially desirable) that arise when participants are asked to make these kinds of judgments, some researchers have recorded bodily reactions to such questions (Buss et al., 1992; Grice & Seely, 2000). One particularly careful study of such reactions was conducted by Harris (2000). She asked participants to imagine

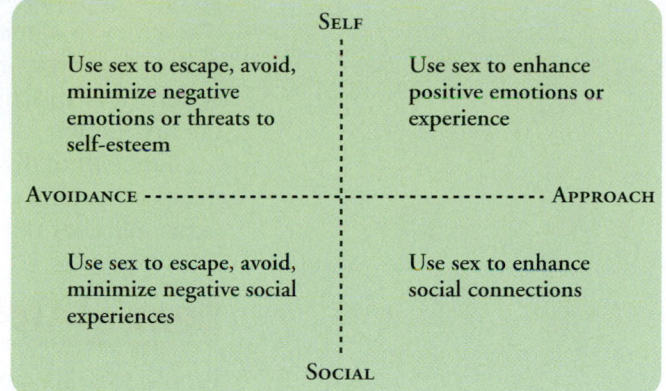

**FIGURE 10.9**  **Motives for Having Sex**

SELF

Use sex to escape, avoid, minimize negative emotions or threats to self-esteem

Use sex to enhance positive emotions or experience

AVOIDANCE — — — — — — — — — — — — APPROACH

Use sex to escape, avoid, minimize negative social experiences

Use sex to enhance social connections

SOCIAL

People engage in sex for many reasons, which Cooper and colleagues (1998) characterize as falling along two dimensions.

Certain genes that affect the brain receptors for the neurotransmitter dopamine influence the age at which people first have sexual intercourse (Miller et al., 1999).

different scenarios while she recorded their blood pressure, heart rate, and skin conductivity. Men did show greater reactions to imagining their mate having sex versus being emotionally involved with someone else. But they showed the same reactions when they imagined *themselves* having sex versus being emotionally involved with their mate. Moreover, women who had been in a committed sexual relationship showed reactions very much like those of the men—clearly counter to the predictions of evolutionary theory.

Does all of this mean that evolution had no role in shaping mate preferences? Not necessarily. However, these findings do show that mate selection, like all other human behavior, does not arise solely from events at a single level of analysis.

# Sexual Orientation: More Than a Choice

People who are sexually attracted to the opposite sex are termed **heterosexual**; people attracted to the same sex are termed **homosexual**; people attracted to both sexes are termed **bisexual**. Sexuality might best be regarded as a continuum, with most people being primarily heterosexual, and somewhere between 4% and 10% of the U.S. population being primarily homosexual in their behavior (Fay et al., 1989). Studies of bisexual men have shown that many of them tend to become more homosexually oriented over time (Stokes et al., 1997).

For many years, homosexuality was considered either a personal choice or the result of being raised a certain way (for instance, with a weak father and an overly strict mother). However, programs to train homosexuals to prefer the opposite sex have failed, even those that relied on extreme techniques such as electric shock to punish homosexual thoughts or behavior (Brown [1989] offers a personal account).

## The Biology of Homosexuality

There is now evidence that people do not choose to be homosexual or heterosexual, nor are homosexuals or heterosexuals created by the ways their parents treat them as young children. Rather, biological events appear to play a major role in determining sexual orientation.

**A GAY HYPOTHALAMUS?** LeVay (1991) studied the brains of homosexual men and found that a small part of the hypothalamus, about as large as an average-sized grain of sand, was about half the size of the same part in heterosexual men (Allen & Gorski, 1992, report related evidence). This was interesting because others had previously found that this same structure typically is smaller in women than in men. However, all of the brains LeVay studied came from men who had died of AIDS, and it is possible that the disease had something to do with the structural abnormality. But when this same structure was surgically disrupted in monkeys, they displayed atypical sexual behavior (Slimp et al., 1978). These and similar data may suggest that there is a biological predisposition for some people to become homosexual (LeVay & Hamer, 1994). However, keep in mind that correlation does not prove causation: In theory, there could be something else about being homosexual that causes these parts of the brain to change.

**OTHER BIOLOGICAL DIFFERENCES** Other differences between heterosexual and homosexual people point toward biological differences. Consider, for example, the sound that is emitted from the ears of some people in some circumstances (see the discussion in Chapter 4). In some cases the sound is a response to a heard click, although the ears

**Heterosexual**: A person who is sexually attracted to members of the opposite sex.

**Homosexual**: A person who is sexually attracted to members of the same sex.

**Bisexual**: A person who is sexually attracted to members of both sexes.

of some people emit sound even without such a trigger event. It turns out that this response to a click is less frequent and weaker for homosexual and bisexual women than for heterosexual women—and men in general have less frequent and weaker ear responses than do heterosexual women (McFadden & Pasanen, 1999). Apparently, parts of the ear are different in women with different sexual orientations. However, no such difference appears among heterosexual, bisexual, and homosexual men. Thus, these results not only show a biological difference for homosexual and bisexual women, but may also hint at different biological bases for male and female homosexuality.

**IN THE GENES?**   The findings of biological differences between homosexual and heterosexual people do not indicate whether the causes are hereditary (that is, genetic), the result of experiences in the womb, or the result of experiences during early childhood. Hamer and his colleagues (1993) studied 114 families that included a homosexual man and found that inheritance of homosexuality seemed to be passed from the mother. This result led them to examine the X chromosome, which is the sex chromosome from the mother (females have two X chromosomes, one from the mother and one from the father; males have one X chromosome, from the mother, and one Y chromosome, from the father). These researchers concluded that a small portion of the X chromosome is related to homosexual preference and behavior. However, not all studies have supported this view (McKnight & Malcolm, 2000). Moreover, although Bailey and Pillard (1991) conducted a study with twins that supported the idea that homosexuality is at least partly inherited, a later study failed to find this effect (Rice et al., 1999).

The mixed findings from genetic studies may mean that there is more than one way homosexuality can arise. One intriguing possibility is suggested by the finding that homosexual men are more likely than heterosexual men to have older brothers (Blanchard, 2001; Ellis & Blanchard, 2001). In fact, the sexual orientation of about 15% of gay men appears to arise from the fact that they had older brothers (Cantor et al., 2002). Why? It appears that the mother's body somehow "remembers" the number of boys she bore (possibly by building up specific antibodies; Ellis & Blanchard, 2001) and alters the level of testosterone accordingly. Boys with older brothers receive proportionally more testosterone during gestation, which appears to increase the likelihood that they will be homosexual. One intriguing—if preliminary—bit of evidence for this theory relies on the fact that prenatal levels of maternal testosterone regulate genes (called *Homeobox*, or *Hox*, *genes*; Kondo et al., 1997) that not only determine how the genitals develop, but also regulate testosterone levels in the fetus and dictate the relative lengths of the ring and index fingers. Some researchers have in fact found that, on average, the relative lengths of the ring and index fingers differ for homosexual and heterosexual men (Robinson & Manning, 2000). Additional research with a large number of participants suggests that this relation only occurs for gay men who have older brothers (T. J. Williams et al., 2000).

## The Environment and Homosexuality

To say that homosexuality has biological roots is not to rule out a role for the environment. Bem (1996, 1998) has argued that young boys who are not typical of their sex, in that they are not physically strong and have gentle temperaments, prefer to play with girls—and it is this socialization experience that later leads them to become homosexual. In Bem's view, "exotic becomes erotic": If young boys identify with girls and engage in girl-like behavior, it would be boys who become "dissimilar, unfamiliar and exotic" to them and thus "erotic." For girls, the reverse would apply, with "tomboy" girls choosing

FIGURE 10.10 **Major Factors That Affect Human Sexual Activity**

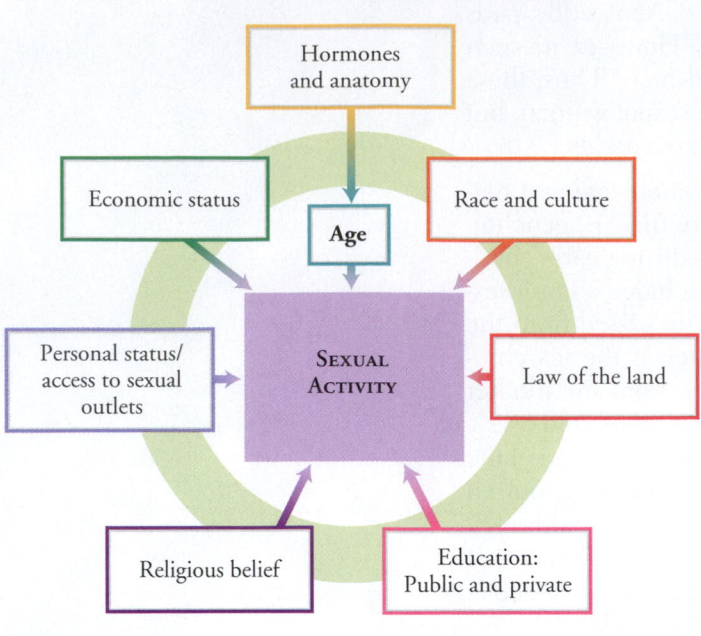

to associate with boys and engage in boy-like activities, and later finding girls exotic and hence erotic. According to this theory, biology would affect the body and temperament and only indirectly affect sexual orientation. However, to explain why it has proved so difficult to alter sexual orientation in adulthood, we would need to assume that at a certain age sexual orientation is set and thereafter difficult to modify.

# What's Normal?

For many years, the manual of the American Psychiatric Association classified homosexuality as a psychological disorder, but (after conducting a poll of its members) in 1973 this classification was deleted. What is normal sexual behavior?

## Cultural Variations: Experience Counts

Sexual behavior is partly instinctive but, like eating, it is also molded by personal tastes and by culture (see Figure 10.10). For example, among the people of the Grand Valley Dani in Indonesia, the men apparently have extraordinarily little interest in sex (Heider, 1976). They reportedly do not have intercourse with their wives for 5 years after a child is born; nor do they seem to have other sexual outlets. Nonetheless, these people do not seem unhappy. At the opposite extreme, the Mangaians, who live on an island in the South Pacific, may have sex up to the time when a woman goes into labor and may resume sex within a few days after the birth of a child, although they typically wait a few months (Marshall, 1971).

Cultural variations occur over time, even within a single group. In the 20 years that followed the decade of the 1950s, attitudes about sex changed dramatically in the United States, in large part because of the development of effective birth control. "Free sex," a motto of the 1960s, encouraged sexual liberation; people should be free, proponents said, to have sex when and where they choose (in those days, young women sometimes brought a condom and toothbrush with them on the first date). With the spread of AIDS and the resurgence of fundamentalist and evangelical religions, sexual behavior has changed, becoming more careful. But these changes in turn reduced awareness of sexually transmitted diseases (STDs), and today AIDS is again on the rise. Culture clearly affects how, when, and where sexual behavior occurs.

The male praying mantis can copulate only after its head has been ripped off, a service readily provided by the receptive female. Some lions copulate over 50 times a day. Human sexual behavior is also shaped by biological factors, but it is much more variable than that of other animals.

## Sexual Dysfunction: When Good Things Go Wrong

Despite the many variations in human sexual behavior in different times and places, psychologists do consider some sexual behaviors to be dysfunctional. Categorizing a behavior as "dysfunctional" depends in part on the individual, in part on any relationship he or she is in, and in part on the standards of the surrounding culture. *Sexual dysfunctions*, according to the 4th edition of the *Diagnostic and Statistical Manual of Mental Disorders* (American Psychiatric Association, 2000), "are characterized by a disturbance in the processes that characterize the sexual response cycle or by pain associated with sexual intercourse" (p. 535). Included in this description are disorders of sexual desire or arousal, orgasmic disorders, and sexual pain. Many problems in the sexual response cycle have psychological causes; they are not caused by physical problems with the sex organs. An example is the inability to reach the plateau stage of sexual arousal. In men, the disorder is called *male erectile dysfunction* (or *impotence*); in women, it is known as *female arousal dysfunction* (previously called *frigidity*). Masters and Johnson found that such sexual disorders often arise because of a preoccupation with personal problems, fears about the possible consequences of sexual activity, or anxiety about sexual performance.

However, at least some sexual dysfunction may have a biological cause. The drug Viagra caused quite a stir when it was first prescribed in the late 1990s because it provided a safe and effective medical treatment for impotence. Viagra (along with other drugs of its type) doesn't cause an erection. Rather, the drug operates only when a man is sexually excited, by increasing the flow of blood to the penis. Thus, Viagra is not a cure but a treatment for impotence, and it is effective only if it continues to be taken. The user of this drug who would derive the most benefit would be a middle-aged man who has difficulty maintaining an erection because of biological factors and wants to be sexually active. Some women also use Viagra now that it has been found to have a similar effect on the clitoris. However, medications for erectile dysfunction commonly have side effects, which range from headache and stomachache to changes in color vision (such as difficulty discriminating between green and blue). Furthermore, impotence is sometimes an early warning sign of a more serious health problem: The veins carrying blood to the penis can become narrowed by buildup of plaque in them; such a buildup can restrict blood flow and cause impotence, but it can also lead to heart attacks and strokes. Thus, purchasing drugs like Viagra over the Web without seeing a physician is dangerous.

## Atypical Sexual Behavior

A *paraphilia* occurs when a person can become sexually aroused or gratified when engaging in (or fantasizing about) a sexual act considered deviant. The most common paraphilias involve being sexually attracted to children (*pedophilia*) or exposing the body in public (*exhibitionism*), but many other paraphilias exist (such as a sexual interest in animals and dead people). Men have paraphilias much more often than do women.

Paraphilias include more than sexual acts; sometimes commonplace objects can become objects of sexual desire, becoming a conditioned stimuli for sexual arousal; a common example is a shoe, or even a picture of a shoe. When an object that has no inherent sexual meaning comes to be sexually arousing, it is called a *fetish*. Mental health professionals consider fetishes a problem only if they are necessary for arousal or if they are objectionable to the partner.

Another paraphilia is *transvestism* (now called *transvestic fetishism*), in which men become sexually aroused by dressing up as women. Docter and Prince (1997) asked more than 1,000 men who sometimes dressed as women to complete a survey about their lives, sexual identities, and behaviors. One finding of interest is that the vast majority (87%) claimed to be heterosexual, not homosexual. Eighty-three percent had been married at one time, and 60% were married when they filled in the survey. These men apparently enjoyed their male and female modes of behavior equally.

## Homophobia

To study one possible basis of strong negative views of homosexuals, Adams and colleagues (1996) asked two groups of male heterosexuals to watch videotapes that showed heterosexuals, lesbians, or gay men engaging in explicit sex acts. One group of men had scored high on a test of *homophobia*, which is a strong aversion to homosexuality;

the other group scored low. While both groups watched the tapes, the researchers recorded changes in penile circumference as an indication of sexual arousal. All the participants became aroused when they saw the heterosexual and lesbian videos, but only the homophobic males were aroused by the homosexual male videos. The investigators noted that psychodynamic theory might explain these results by claiming that the homophobic men had repressed homosexual impulses. Alternatively, they noted that another theory would explain the results in terms of anxiety (Barlow, 1986). In this view, the homosexual stimuli produce negative emotions, which in turn lead to anxiety, which in turn enhances arousal, which leads to erection.

# Test Yourself

1. Which of the following describes a potential source of bias that affects psychological studies of sexual behavior?
   a. Not everyone is equally willing to participate in such studies.
   b. Participants may not respond truthfully to questions about sex.
   c. There may be cultural differences that affect participants' responses.
   d. All of these are potential sources of bias.
2. What role do hormones play in human sexual behavior?
   a. They affect men's behavior more than women's.
   b. They can influence, but do not determine, our sexual behavior.
   c. They completely control our sexual behavior.
   d. They have almost no effect on our sexual behavior.

3. Studies of the responses of men and women to visual sexual stimuli have shown that
   a. women are not aroused by such stimuli.
   b. the hypothalamus is only activated when men view these stimuli.
   c. the hypothalamus is only activated when women view these stimuli.
   d. men do not respond as well as women do to visual images.
4. Studies of sexual orientation show that
   a. the environment is the sole determinant of sexual orientation.
   b. genes are the sole determinant of sexual orientation.
   c. sexual orientation is influenced by environmental and biological factors.
   d. sexual orientation is a matter of each individual's personal choice.

## Answers

# Think It Through!

Could someone feel sexual desire for a partner but have a difficult time becoming sexually aroused? Why or why not? Imagine that researchers figured out in detail the factors that lead to sexual arousal. Would it be ethical to use your knowledge of such factors to make yourself sexually attractive when you were going out on a date?

Do you think researchers should be trying to find a gene (or genes) for homosexuality? What positive uses could such knowledge have? What negative uses? Would it be ethical to try to alter such genes either before conception or in the womb?

# REVIEW AND REMEMBER!

## Summary

### I. Emotion: I Feel, Therefore I Am

**A.** Ekman identified six basic emotions: surprise, happiness, anger, fear, disgust, and sadness. Research results have shown that surprise and fear are more easily confused with each other than they are with any of the other basic emotions.

**B.** Culture and experience influence how easily emotions can be read; although humans can read emotions from any other human at better than chance levels, they do better with members of familiar cultures.

**C.** Each of several widely known theories of emotion has captured a grain of the truth. The James–Lange theory holds that you feel emotion after your body reacts to a situation. The Cannon–Bard theory holds that emotions and bodily reactions occur at the same time. Cognitive theory claims that emotions arise when you interpret your bodily reactions in the context of the specific situation. The emerging synthesis of views on emotion proposes that some emotions arise from brain responses that do not involve cognitive interpretation, whereas others depend on such interpretation.

**D.** As the James–Lange theory predicts, some emotions may arise in part from changes in bodily reactions, such as heart rate, breathing rate, and facial expression. As the Cannon–Bard theory predicts, some emotions, such as fear, are reflexes that produce the emotional experience and the bodily reaction simultaneously. As cognitive theory predicts, how you interpret the causes of your bodily reactions does in fact influence which emotion you feel. The emerging synthesis puts all of these discoveries together, recognizing that an emotion arises from a mixture of different mechanisms operating at the same time.

**E.** Fear may often be the strongest of our emotions, and the amygdala may play a role in strong emotions in general. Environmental events influence emotion; our happiness, for example, depends in part on our economic and cultural context. Emotions also arise in response to other people's emotional signals, which vary depending on their cultures. In addition, the emotions we feel depend on how we construe a situation; happy people tend to remain happy, in part because of how they view the world.

**F.** Culture shapes people's emotional reactions. It also influences how effectively they can read body language to determine another person's emotion.

**G.** We can control our emotions, both by prolonging them over time and by suppressing them; this control is directly reflected in the activation of brain mechanisms. Culture affects the display rules we use, the rules that determine when and how we express emotion.

**H.** Lies cannot be reliably detected by current methods, although some individuals are particularly adept at spotting deception.

## Your Notes

I.

A. Basic emotions: surprise, happiness, anger, fear, disgust, sadness

B.

C.

D.

E.

F.

G.

H.

## II. Motivation and Reward: Feeling Good

**A.** Some of our motivations arise from evolutionarily shaped instincts, sex being an obvious example. Other motivations are drives, such as thirst; some drives are designed to maintain homeostasis (when we are cold, we seek warmth). Still other motivations center on a preference for an intermediate level of arousal.

**B.** We are often motivated by incentives, such as the potential rewards (including money) for engaging in a behavior.

**C.** Brain systems that rely on the neurotransmitter dopamine become active in anticipation of reward.

**D.** A need is a condition that arises when you lack a requirement, which in turn gives rise to a drive to acquire specific rewards to fulfill the requirement. A want is a condition that arises when you have an unmet goal that will not fulfill a requirement, which in turn causes the goal to act as an incentive.

**E.** Needs may be related to a brain system that provides an internal reward when a deprivation is satisfied (for example, by eating when you are hungry). In contrast, many wants may be related to a system that provides a reward when you are not deprived but you achieve a desired goal.

**F.** There are many types of needs; the importance of at least some needs depends partly on your culture, particularly on whether the culture is individualist or collectivist.

**G.** Animals (including humans) can learn to be helpless if their behavior fails to reduce punishment.

**H.** Maslow proposed a hierarchy of needs, but the evidence for his highly influential theory is mixed.

**I.** Regulatory fit occurs when promotion-focused people employ eagerness-related strategies and behaviors or when prevention-focused people employ vigilance-related strategies and behaviors; people are more strongly motivated when regulatory fit exists.

## III. Hunger and Eating: Not Just About Fueling the Body

**A.** We eat for many reasons: for pleasure, for nutrition, as a social activity. The brain senses when the level of nutrients in the blood is too low and causes you to feel hungry. We often eat until signals from the stomach (and other digestive organs) indicate that we've consumed enough food.

**B.** The hypothalamus plays a particularly important role in hunger and thirst. At the beginning of a meal, taste plays an especially important role in determining whether you want to eat. As a meal progresses, changes in the type of food you are eating will keep your appetite up, and tastes (as well as thoughts) that cause insulin to be released will increase hunger.

**C.** Beliefs about the history of a food item (for example, whether it was ever in contact with something repulsive) and even associations with the shape of the food affect how appealing it is.

**D.** Overeating can cause your body weight to increase, and the increase is often difficult to lose. However, weight is determined by many factors that affect metabolism

II.

A.

B.

C.

D.

E.

*F. Needs' importance can differ in individualist vs. collectivist cultures.*

G.

H.

I.

III.

A.

B.

C.

D.

and behavior, including your set point, environment, types of activities, and emotional state. Cognitive mechanisms in the brain can override the hypothalamic mechanisms, leading us to eat when we aren't actually hungry.

**E.** Obese people do not have "weak characters" but rather may be genetically predisposed to becoming obese. Many genes are likely to affect body weight in different ways. Dieting alters cognition, emotion, and personality in obese people.

### IV. Sex: Not Just About Having Babies

**A.** Sexual attraction leads to sexual desire, sexual excitement (arousal), and possibly sexual performance (which involves becoming fully aroused, reaching orgasm, and then experiencing resolution followed, for men, by a refractory period).

**B.** Hormones play a key role in sexual development and modify motivation toward sexual behavior. Fluctuations in sex hormones affect cognition and emotion.

**C.** Sexual desire and arousal can be triggered by various cues, with visual stimuli often playing a critical role (and odors playing a particularly important role for women). Visual sexual stimuli activate the hypothalamus in men, but not in women.

**D.** Mating preferences may be influenced by evolutionary characteristics, but they are not determined by them.

**E.** There is evidence that male homosexuals differ from heterosexuals in certain brain structures and that female homosexuals and bisexuals differ from heterosexuals in the operation of certain neural systems (involved in hearing). Such biological differences, and homosexuality itself, are probably caused either by genes or by events in the womb or during childhood.

**F.** Sexual behaviors differ in different cultures, and what constitutes normal sexual behaviors even within a particular culture varies widely. Sexual variations are considered disorders only if they cause "marked distress and interpersonal difficulty."

NOTE: Once you feel that you understand the material in this chapter, visit the book's Web site at www.ablongman.com/kosslyn3e to test your knowledge with additional study questions.

*E.*

*IV.*

*A.*

*B. Hormones affect sexual development & motivation, also cognition & emotion.*

*C.*

*D.*

*E.*

*F.*

## Key Terms

androgens, p. 468
basic emotion, p. 430
bisexual, p. 472
collectivist culture, p. 457
deprived reward, p. 454
display rule, p. 441
drive, p. 450
emotion, p. 429
estrogens, p. 468
facial feedback hypothesis, p. 435

heterosexual, p. 472
homeostasis, p. 450
homosexual, p. 472
implicit motive, p. 454
incentive, p. 452
individualist culture, p. 457
instinct, p. 450
insulin, p. 461
learned helplessness, p. 453
metabolism, p. 459

misattribution of arousal, p. 436
motivation, p. 449
need, p. 453
need for achievement (nAch), p. 455
nondeprived reward, p. 454
polygraph, p. 446
set point, p. 462
sexual response cycle, p. 468
want, p. 454

# CHAPTER 11

# PERSONALITY:
## VIVE
## LA DIFFÉRENCE!

Tina and Gabe met in their introductory psychology class. They were immediately attracted to each other and started studying together. After a few conversations, they were pleased to discover that they had similar values and political views. Predictably, they began going out together. On their fourth date, though, Tina began to realize that she and Gabe weren't as much alike as she had thought; she was surprised by this because their views on so many issues were so similar. Tina sometimes had trouble "reading" Gabe because he was shy and emotionally steady, without many highs or lows—his manner was "mellow." She wondered why he wasn't more enthusiastic when she proposed activities she thought would be fun to do together, such as in-line skating, bungee-jumping, or biking. "Well, opposites attract, I guess," she thought. And although Gabe enjoyed Tina's spirit, her emotional vibrancy, and her interest in trying new things, now and then he asked her why she was so emotional and always in such a hurry. Tina began to worry that, even though they were strongly attracted to each other, a long-term relationship might reveal persistent differences between them that would be difficult to deal with.

Do these differences reveal something fundamental about Tina and Gabe as people? Do they reflect their personalities? And if so, are personalities set in stone?

The concept of personality infuses daily life. When you describe an acquaintance as "intense," wonder how a friend will handle a piece of bad news, or think about the type of partner you would like to have in life, personality is exerting its influence. What exactly is this quality, which is part and parcel of each of us? **Personality** is a set of behavioral, emotional, and cognitive tendencies that people display over time and across situations and that distinguish individuals from each other. This chapter explores the idea of personality, the perspectives of a number of different theorists who have sought to describe and explain it, and the ways in which psychologists measure it. It also considers historical views of personality, the genetic influence on personality development, the influence of learning experiences, motives, and thoughts on personality, and the effects of the social environment on personality.

# PERSONALITY: Historical Perspectives

Tina wanted to understand why Gabe was the way he was—or, put another way, why he had the personality he did. Gabe studied a lot and could do it for much longer than Tina; Tina learned a lot when she studied with him, but lately when they studied together, he'd have a big bag of pistachio nuts and sit there cracking and eating nuts while they read. It was driving Tina, well, nuts. She couldn't understand how he could just sit there hour after hour, cracking and crunching nuts while studying. And he'd leave the shells lying around on the table, creating a mess. She wanted to ask him about it—why didn't he just buy shelled nuts, and wasn't he distracted by the shelling process? But she didn't feel comfortable asking him. Why are Tina and Gabe so different? How do our personalities develop, and why do they develop differently? Among the notable theories that attempt to answer these questions are the psychodynamic theory of Sigmund Freud and the humanistic theories of Carl Rogers and Abraham Maslow.

## Freud's Theory: The Dynamic Personality

Sigmund Freud viewed personality as a bubbling cauldron, rocked by unconscious, irrational forces at war with one another, competing for expression and preventing the individual's exercise of free will. He believed in **psychological determinism**, the view that all behavior, even something as mundane as forgetting someone's name or being late for an appointment, has an underlying psychological cause. Freud proposed that two major drives, sex and aggression, are the primary motivating forces of human behavior. Tension occurs when these drives are not given opportunity for expression.

### The Structure of Personality

In order to understand Freud's view of the structure of personality, it is necessary first to understand his view of consciousness. Freud proposed that consciousness is not one thing, but rather can be thought of as divided into three levels (see Figure 11.1). The topmost level is normal awareness, or the *conscious*, which includes thoughts, feelings, and motivations of which you are aware. The second level, the *preconscious*, holds subjective material that you can easily bring into conscious awareness but are not aware of most of the time. For example, your telephone number is in your preconscious until someone asks you what it is, and at that point, it moves into your conscious awareness. The final level is the *unconscious*, which houses the thoughts, feelings, and motivations that you cannot bring into consciousness but which nevertheless influence you. A much greater proportion of your thoughts, feelings, and motivations are in the unconscious than are in the conscious.

Personality: A set of behavioral, emotional, and cognitive tendencies that people display over time and across situations and that distinguish individuals from each other.

Psychological determinism: The view that all behavior, no matter how mundane or insignificant, has an underlying psychological cause.

As part of the dynamic nature of personality (not consciousness), Freud proposed three personality structures—the id, superego, and ego (see Figure 11.1). These are not physical structures, but abstract mental entities. The **id**, which exists from birth, houses the sexual and aggressive drives, physical needs such as the need to sleep or eat, and simple psychological needs such as the need for comfort; these needs and drives constantly vie for expression. The id lives by the *pleasure principle*; wanting immediate gratification of its needs by a reduction in pain, discomfort, or tension, regardless of the consequences. Because of this insistent urge for immediate gratification, the id is sometimes compared with a demanding infant. Freud proposed that when the id's instincts threaten to erupt, anxiety can develop. When that anxiety reaches a sufficiently high level, abnormal behavior and mental illness can result.

A second personality structure, the **ego**, also develops in childhood. The ego tries to keep the id under control and ensure that rational thought governs behavior. The ego is guided by the *reality principle*, which leads it to assess what is realistically possible in the world. According to Freud's theory, the ego is also responsible for cognitive functions such as problem solving and reasoning. Although he believed that the ego develops out of the id, Freud (1937/1964) wrote fairly late in his life that the ego's characteristics may be determined by heredity (Nye, 1992).

A third personality structure, the **superego**, forms during early childhood, but after the id and ego; this entity houses the child's (and later the adult's) sense of right and wrong. The superego tries to prevent the expression of the id's inappropriate sexual and aggressive impulses. The child learns morality by internalizing—that is, taking in—the values of the parents and of the immediate culture; the superego thus isn't a Jiminy Cricket whispering in your ear, but the internalized voice of society. However, the superego's morality, because it was internalized during early childhood, remains childlike in nature. The superego is the home of the conscience, and depending on the parents' way of teaching right and wrong, it can be more or less punishing. If your superego is very harsh, you experience much anxiety and strive for perfection. The superego can cause feelings of *guilt*, an uncomfortable sensation of having done something wrong, which results in feelings of inadequacy. The superego's morality is responsible for the *ego ideal*, which provides the ultimate standard of what a person should be (Nye, 1992).

With the appearance of the superego, the ego has to work very hard to balance the demands of the id and the superego. The ego tries to give the id enough gratification to prevent it from making too much trouble, while at the same time making sure that no major moral lapses lead the superego to become too punishing. The ego must also make sure that the actions of both id and superego, as well as its own actions, don't create problems for the person in the real world.

## Personality Development: Avoiding Arrest

Freud viewed childhood as central in determining the formation of personality. He proposed five distinct phases, or stages, of development, each having an important task requiring successful resolution for healthy personality development. Four of Freud's five stages involve specific erogenous zones, areas of the body (mouth, anus, and genitals) that can provide satisfaction of instinctual drives. Freud believed that each zone demands some form of sexual gratification, with a different zone being prominent

**FIGURE 11.1**

### Freud's View of Personality Structure

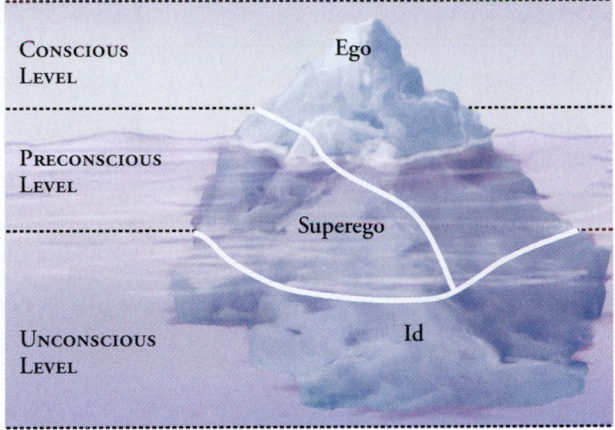

In Freud's view, only part of the mind is available for inspection and provides normal awareness (conscious); some of it is occasionally conscious (preconscious), and some is hidden, not available for observation (unconscious). Repressed thoughts, feelings, and wishes are hidden from awareness.

**Id:** A personality structure, proposed by Freud, that exists at birth and houses sexual and aggressive drives, physical needs, and simple psychological needs.

**Ego:** A personality structure, proposed by Freud, that develops in childhood and tries to balance the competing demands of the id, superego, and reality.

**Superego:** A personality structure, proposed by Freud, that is formed during early childhood and houses the sense of right and wrong, based on the internalization of parental and cultural morality.

| TABLE 11.1 | | **Freud's Psychosexual Stages** | |
|---|---|---|---|
| **Psychosexual Stage** | **Age of Stage (years)** | **Locus of Pleasure** | **Developmental Task of Stage** |
| Oral Stage | 0–1 | Mouth (sucking and biting) | Successful weaning from mother's breast or bottle |
| Anal Stage | 1–3 | Anus (retaining and expelling feces) | Successful toilet training |
| Phallic Stage | 3–6 | Clitoris or penis | Successful identification with same-sex parent |
| Latency Period | 6 to puberty | No particular locus of pleasure; sexual impulses are repressed | Successful transformation of repressed sexual urges into socially acceptable activities |
| Genital Stage | Puberty onward | Vagina or penis | 1. Successful formation of mature sexual love relationship<br>2. Successful development of interests and talents related to productive work |

during each stage. For this reason, Freud's stages are called **psychosexual stages**: oral, anal, phallic, latency, and genital (see Table 11.1).

If a child does not satisfy the needs of a given stage, he or she will develop a *fixation*, a state in which energy is still focused on an earlier stage of development even as the child moves on to the next stage. A fixation results from incomplete resolution of an earlier stage. In times of stress, Freud argued, the person will regress to the thoughts, feelings, and behaviors of the fixated stage. Such arrested development could create a **neurosis**: an abnormal behavior pattern relating to a conflict between the ego and either the id or the superego. According to Freud (1938), conflict between the ego and reality results in *psychosis*, a break from reality.

One of Freud's provocative ideas involves the phallic stage (see Table 11.1): Freud proposed that children in this stage are preoccupied with the discovery that girls don't have penises, a discovery that creates jealousy of the male's penis in girls and fear of castration in boys. Freud took inspiration from the ancient Greek story of Oedipus, who unknowingly killed his father and married his mother. Freud believed that boys in this stage jealously love their mothers and view their fathers as competitors for their mothers' love; so they both fear and hate their fathers. Freud called this dynamic the *Oedipus complex*. A boy fears that, as punishment for loving his mother and hating his father, his father will cut off his penis, the primary zone of pleasure; this concern leads to the boy's **castration anxiety**. For successful resolution, a boy must renounce his passionate love for his mother and make peace with his father, choosing to identify with him and accept his position instead of viewing him as a competitor. In doing so, the boy "introjects," or internalizes, his father's morality as part of his superego.

Girls' personality development at this stage, according to Freud, is different from that of boys; girls' version of the Oedipus complex has been labeled the *Electra complex*, after a Greek myth about a girl who avenges her father's murder, committed by her mother and her mother's lover, by persuading her brother to kill their mother. Girls at this stage experience *penis envy*, a sense of being ineffectual owing to the lack of a penis, accompanied by a desire to have a penis. Girls also struggle with feelings of anger and jealousy toward the mother: anger for neither providing a penis for her daughter nor having one herself, and jealousy because of the mother's relationship with the father. Girls ambivalently identify with their mothers. As a product of the Victorian era, Freud justified women's inferiority to men by explaining that they only partially resolved this stage. Because they do not experience castration anxiety, he wrote, they are not motivated to resolve fully this ambivalent identification with their mothers. They remain fixated at this stage and, as a result, have a less well-developed superego, less ego strength, and less ability to negotiate between reality and the id.

**Defense mechanism:** An unconscious psychological means by which a person tries to prevent unacceptable thoughts or urges from reaching conscious awareness.

**Repression:** A defense mechanism that occurs when the unconscious prevents threatening thoughts, impulses, and memories from entering consciousness.

## Defense Mechanisms: Protecting the Self

The ego's job of handling threatening material is made easier by its use of **defense mechanisms**, unconscious psychological means by which a person tries to prevent unacceptable thoughts or urges from reaching conscious awareness, thereby decreasing anxiety (see Table 11.2). Freud proposed a number of defense mechanisms; these were further developed by his daughter, Anna Freud (1895–1982), herself a noted psychoanalyst. The most important defense mechanism is **repression**, a process that occurs when the unconscious prevents threatening thoughts, impulses, and memories from entering consciousness. An example of repression might be "forgetting" to go to a dreaded dentist appointment. According to Freud, overreliance on particular defense mechanisms may lead to the development of neuroses.

---

**TABLE 11.2    Common Defense Mechanisms**

Defense mechanisms are used by the ego to prevent threatening thoughts from entering awareness.

**Denial**
Threatening thoughts are denied outright. *Example*: You have a drinking problem but deny that it is a problem (and truly believe this).

**Intellectualization**
Threatening thoughts or emotions are kept at arm's length by thinking about them rationally and logically. *Example*: While watching a frightening part of a horror movie, you focus on the special effects, make-up, camera angles, and other emotionally nonthreatening details.

**Projection**
Threatening thoughts are projected onto (attributed to) others. *Example*: You accuse your partner of wanting to have an affair rather than recognizing your own conscious or unconscious wish to have one yourself.

**Rationalization**
Creating explanations to justify threatening thoughts or actions. *Example*: In response to watching a football game instead of studying, and subsequently doing poorly on an exam, you say, "Oh, I can make up for it on the final exam."

**Reaction Formation**
Unconsciously changing an unacceptable feeling into its opposite. *Example*: You harbor aggressive impulses toward your boss, but instead you experience warm, positive feelings toward him, transforming your anger about his obnoxious behavior into an appreciation of "his fairness as a manager."

**Repression**
Anxiety-provoking thoughts, impulses, and memories are prevented from entering consciousness. *Example*: After failing an exam, you keep forgetting to tell your parents about it.

**Sublimation**
Threatening impulses are directed into more socially acceptable activities. *Example*: You sublimate your unacceptable aggressive urges to engage in physical fights by playing ice hockey.

**Undoing**
Your actions try to "undo" a threatening wish or thought. *Example*: After having the thought of eating several slices of chocolate cake, you go to the gym and work out for an hour.

---

## Freud's Followers

Freud attracted many followers, a number of whom modified his theory of personality or added ideas of their own. Among those who expanded on Freud's work, termed *neo-Freudians*, were Carl Jung, Alfred Adler, and Karen Horney.

**CARL JUNG**   Carl Jung (1875–1961) was a Swiss psychiatrist whom Freud befriended but then later severed communication with over disagreements about theory. Jung agreed with Freud's concepts of the unconscious, ego, and id but diverged from Freud over his emphasis on the centrality of sexuality in personality development. Jung developed his own theory of personality that included an entity that Jung termed the *collective unconscious*, which he added to Freud's concepts of the unconscious, the ego, and the id. According to Jung, the collective unconscious contains a rich storehouse of ideas and memories common to all humankind, which we all share on an unconscious level. The common themes in myths and stories around the world and throughout the ages, Jung claimed, spring forth from the collective unconscious in each generation. Stored in the collective unconscious are many **archetypes**, symbols that represent "aspects of the world that people have an inherited tendency to notice" (Carver & Scheier, 1996, p. 268). Among these archetypes are God, the mother, and the shadow (that is, the dark side of personality).

**ALFRED ADLER**   Whereas Freud viewed sexual and aggressive impulses as integral to personality development, Alfred Adler (1870–1937) viewed feelings of inferiority and helplessness as important in forming personality (1956). Feelings of inferiority fuel a *striving for superiority*, which Adler viewed as the source of all motivation. When severe, such inferiority feelings can hamper strivings for superiority and lead to strong feelings of inferiority—an **inferiority complex**. This complex can arise from parents' neglect or hatred. Adler viewed the Oedipus complex not as universal, but as experienced only by children who are overindulged by the opposite-sex parent (Adler, 1964).

**KAREN HORNEY**   Karen Horney (1885–1952) agreed with Freud that anxiety-inducing childhood experiences are central to later psychological problems. She disagreed, however, about the role and primacy of sexual and aggressive drives. Horney emphasized the importance of parent–child interactions in early childhood. If parents do not provide their children with consistent and real interest, warmth, and respect, Horney claimed, the children are likely to grow up with *basic anxiety*, an "all-pervading feeling of being lonely and helpless in a hostile world" (Horney, 1937, p. 89). Horney offered an alternate explanation for penis envy, which she called *privilege envy*. Rather than wanting a penis itself, Horney theorized, girls desire the privileges that go along with having a penis. Even privilege envy, however, is not a cultural universal; in some cultures, Horney proposed, men are envious of women's reproductive ability. Horney felt that Freud had disregarded the cultural and social factors that influence personality development.

## Critiquing Freudian Theory: Is It Science?

Psychoanalytic theory remains fascinating a century after Freud first conceived it, and legions of people worldwide—psychologists, writers, filmmakers, and others—have seen truth in its observations about personality. But as fascinating as Freud's theory may be, is it grounded in good science? First, as you saw in Chapter 2, a scientific theory must be testable, but many aspects of Freud's theory are difficult to test. Some key concepts were not concretely defined, some changed over time, and often the interpretation of concepts was left open. Freud believed that many actions and objects have symbolic meanings. For example, long thin objects are *phallic symbols*—they stand for

**Archetype:** A Jungian concept of a symbol that represents some basic aspect of the world and is stored in the collective unconscious.

**Inferiority complex:** The experience that occurs when inferiority feelings are so strong that they hamper striving for superiority.

a penis. However, when Freud was asked about the meaning of his sucking on a cigar, he replied, "Sometimes a cigar is only a cigar." Maybe so, but a good theory would tell us when it is and when it isn't "only a cigar."

A second criticism of Freud's theory is that it is so complicated that it can explain, or explain away, almost anything. When there is an apparent contradiction within someone's personality, it is almost always possible to appeal to a defense mechanism to explain that contradiction. If Gabe had had a difficult time with toilet training, resulting in frequent constipation, we could predict that he would have an *anal-retentive personality*. According to Freud, such people are more likely to delay gratification and to be neat, methodical, miserly, and stubborn. But, if so, then how would we explain that Gabe is often generous and so messy with the pistachios? Freud might say that Gabe's generosity and messiness are an undoing of his desire to be selfish and orderly.

Third, Freud developed his theory by analyzing patients, mostly women, and by analyzing himself. And Freud's views of women, of proper parenting, and of appropriate development were all biased by his sensibilities and surroundings, as we are biased by ours. He and his patients were upper-middle-class or upper-class products of late 19th-century Vienna; their sensibilities were not necessarily representative of other classes, times, or cultures. Applying a theory based on a particular group of people at a particular time and place to other people at another time or place raises issues of validity.

However, some aspects of Freud's theory have received support from contemporary research (see Westen, 1998, 1999). For example, the type of attachment we have to our parents predicts the type of attachment we will have to a partner and to our own children (Shaver & Hazan, 1994). Although not supporting Freud's specific psychosexual stages, such findings support the general idea that relationships with parents can affect aspects of later development. Moreover, research on defense mechanisms as coping styles has supported some aspects of Sigmund and Anna Freud's views on those mechanisms (Bond et al., 1983; Mikulincer & Horesh, 1999; Newman, Duff, et al., 1997; Silverman, 1976). More generally, research on conditioned emotional responses (see Chapter 6), implicit memory (see Chapter 7), and aspects of thinking (see Chapter 8) support the broad idea that some mental processes can be unconscious—that is, occurring without awareness. Despite the difficulty in evaluating most of Freud's theory, many aspects of it have endured because it offers a truly comprehensive, and sometimes insightful, view of people and of personality.

# Humanistic Psychology: Thinking Positively

Partly as a reaction to Freud's theory, which in many ways draws a pessimistic picture of human nature and personality formation, the humanistic psychologists have focused on people's positive aspects—their innate goodness, creativity, and free will. Rather than being driven by forces outside of their control, as the Freudians claimed, people can create solutions to their problems. A cornerstone of humanistic theories is that we all have a drive toward **self-actualization**, an innate motivation to attain our highest emotional and intellectual potential. The work of two psychologists, Abraham Maslow and Carl Rogers, represents the humanistic perspective on personality.

## Abraham Maslow

The personality theory developed by Abraham Maslow (1908–1970) is really a theory of motivation based on a hierarchy of physical and emotional needs (see Chapter 10). Lower-level needs, said Maslow, must be met before needs further up the hierarchy can

Self-actualization: An innate motivation to attain the highest possible emotional and intellectual potential.

| TABLE 11.3 | **Characteristics of Self-Actualizing People** |
|---|---|

- Perceive reality accurately and efficiently
- Accept themselves, others, and nature
- Appreciate ordinary events
- Try to solve cultural rather than personal problems
- Form deep relationships, but only with a few people
- Often experience "oceanic feelings" (a sense of oneness with nature that transcends time and space)

**Flow:** The experience of being completely absorbed with and merging smoothly into an activity and losing track of time.

**Unconditional positive regard:** Acceptance without any conditions.

Good or bad child? Rogers argues that a child may at times behave unsuitably, but that does not mean he or she is a bad child. Labeling children as "bad" may affect their developing self-concept or self-worth (Kamins & Dweck, 1999).

be satisfied; moreover, during crises, higher-level needs are put on hold while lower-level ones take priority.

Maslow proposed that the need for self-actualization is at the highest-level; this need leads people to strive to develop their full potentials, to develop all of their capacities to the greatest possible extent. Maslow studied the lives and characteristics of historical figures he considered to be at the self-actualizing level, including Albert Einstein, Mahatma Gandhi, Abraham Lincoln, and Eleanor Roosevelt. His investigation led him to propose that people who are self-actualizing have these qualities: a true perception of reality, an acceptance of themselves and their environments, an appreciation of the ordinary, a focus on cultural rather than personal problems, few but deep personal relationships, and what Maslow called "oceanic feelings" (see Table 11.3). Maslow regarded oceanic feelings as *peak experiences*, moments with intense clarity of perception (Privette & Landsman, 1983), a suspended sense of time, and a feeling of wonderment at the experience. Oceanic feelings are similar to **flow**, the experience of being completely absorbed with and merging smoothly into an activity and losing track of time (Csikszentmihalyi & Csikszentmihalyi, 1988); you may have had such an experience, becoming totally engrossed in, say, sketching, listening to music, or playing a musical instrument. Various researchers have studied Maslow's theory, particularly as it relates to motivation on the job. In the end, many of Maslow's concepts are difficult to test, and the validity of his theory remains questionable (Fox, 1982; Soper et al., 1995; Wahba & Bridwell, 1976).

## Carl Rogers

Carl Rogers (1902–1987) is noted for his formulation of client-centered therapy (see Chapter 1) and his notions of personality and its development. Like Maslow, Rogers viewed humans as possessing a need for self-actualization. But rather than viewing the satisfaction of a hierachy of needs as the driving force behind personality, he believed that the *self-concept*—our sense of ourselves and of how others see us—is central to personality development. Rogers proposed that our feelings about ourselves are in part a reflection of how others see us. Thus, we have a basic need for **unconditional positive regard**, acceptance without any conditions. Receiving unconditional positive regard, according to Rogers, is crucial for the development of a healthy self-concept. Of course, it is impossible to receive or provide unconditional positive regard all the time, and the socialization process requires that adults praise children for behaving in accordance with societal rules. This praise for specific behaviors leads children to learn *conditions of worth*, or "what it takes" to be treated as worthwhile. According to Rogers, people whose lives revolve around meeting such conditions of worth will not achieve their full human potential. In order to prevent such obstruction of potential, yet meet society's need for children to learn what is generally considered appropriate behavior, Rogers advised parents to make the distinction between a child's inappropriate *behavior* and his or her *worth* as a human being.

Humanistic theories appeal to many because of their emphasis on the uniqueness of each person and on free will. According to this view, how you live your life is determined not by unconscious forces but by using your conscious awareness and your freedom to choose your experiences. Critics of humanistic theory point out that, as with Freud's theory, many of the concepts are difficult to test and have received little research support. Moreover, the uplifting, positive view of human nature seems too idealistic to many people in light of the amount of violence and evil in the world.

# Test Yourself

1. Each of Freud's stages of personality development center around an important task that requires resolution. Failure to do this can lead to
   a. defense mechanisms.
   b. a fixation.
   c. castration anxiety.
   d. a psychosis.

2. Jung, Adler, and Horney all disagreed with Freud over his emphasis on the importance of
   a. sex and aggression.
   b. unconscious motivation.
   c. psychosexual stages.
   d. cultural influences.

3. Unlike Freud, the humanistic psychologists Rogers and Maslow focused on the innate human motivation to achieve to one's fullest potential, called _____ .
   a. self-actualization
   b. superiority complex
   c. will to strive
   d. unconditional self-concept

4. One problem with both psychoanalytic and humanistic theories is that they
   a. lack insight into human personality.
   b. are too comprehensive.
   c. are difficult to test and have little research support.
   d. assume that childhood is important in determining personality.

## Answers

NOTE: Once you feel comfortable with the Test Yourself questions in this chapter, visit the book's Web site at www.ablongman.com/kosslyn3e for additional study questions.

# Think It Through!

If you used Freudian theory to understand a historical figure's personality and motivations, do you think you could be sure about the validity of your analysis? Why or why not? Could you use a humanistic theory to understand such a person? What would you need to know about him or her?

# WHAT EXACTLY *IS* PERSONALITY?

As Tina got to know Gabe, she began to make certain assumptions about him, about who he was as a person. He studied hard and did well on psychology exams and quizzes, so Tina figured he was smart, hard-working, and conscientious. (Tina did well on her psychology exams and quizzes, too, but she didn't study much. She considered herself smart, but not particularly hard-working.) She was a bit surprised to discover that Gabe's apartment was a disaster area—she had assumed he would be as orderly and neat in his personal space as he was in his approach to schoolwork. She started to wonder whether his "personality," as she thought of it, was altogether consistent. Tina also noticed that, on dates, Gabe preferred to get together for dinner and a movie, not for lunch or an afternoon break ("Too much studying," he said). If she suggested going to a party together, Gabe invariably declined; he didn't like parties. Tina attributed this reluctance to his shyness.

The very concept of personality implies that people have enduring, stable qualities such as, say, talkativeness and curiosity. These qualities are called **personality traits**, relatively consistent characteristics exhibited across a range of situations. But notice the "relatively" in the preceding sentence. Let's see just what that means.

## Personality: Traits and Situations

Traits exist on a continuum (for example, from extremely quiet to extremely talkative). Gabe's shyness and Tina's adventurousness can be considered traits. Many personality psychologists believe that personality is built on traits. Moreover, these psychologists

**Personality trait:** A relatively consistent characteristic exhibited in different situations.

The names of Snow White's seven dwarves fit their personalities. Imagine the personalities of dwarves named Dirty, Hungry, Shifty, Flabby, Puffy, Crabby, Awful, Doleful, all of which were on Disney Studios' list of possible names (Seuling, 1976). The final choices work so well because we view their personalities as consistent with their names; but what if Grumpy were, in fact, upbeat and easy-going!

accept that each person can be placed at different locations within the same set of traits.

Gordon Allport (1897–1967) proposed that some personality traits can be grouped as *central traits*, which are traits that affect a wide range of behavior; however, the particular traits that are central will vary from individual to individual (Allport, 1937). Whether or not traits are viewed as causing behavior, they certainly aren't always accurate in *predicting* behavior (witness Gabe's domestic messiness). The situations in which we find ourselves can exert powerful influences on behaviors, thoughts, and feelings.

## The Power of the Situation

People are not necessarily consistent across situations. You may get angry in some situations, but be totally mellow in others. Someone seeing you when you're angry may infer that you're an angry person, whereas someone seeing you only in situations in which you are mellow will infer that this is your disposition. Which is the "real" you? It has been argued that if much of our behavior depends on the situation in which we find ourselves, then perhaps there aren't consistent personality traits at all. In a now-classic study that illustrates the importance of the situation on behavior, Mischel and Peake (1982) observed college students and recorded 19 different behaviors reflecting the trait of conscientiousness, defined by how regularly they attended class, how promptly they completed assignments, how neatly they made their beds, and how neatly they recorded class notes. These researchers found that the students were likely to be consistent in similar situations, but not across different types of situations.

In later research, Mischel (1984) found that inconsistency across situations is pervasive; he found this not only with the traits of honesty and conscientiousness, but also with other traits, such as aggression and dependency. Furthermore, different measures of what should be the same trait often were only weakly correlated, or not related at all. For instance, two people could score high on measures of aggression, but express their aggression differently—one through put-downs and verbal abuse, another through physical abuse (Mischel, 2004). Such findings led to the theory of *situationism*, which holds that a person's behavior is mostly governed by the particular situation, not by internal traits.

Situationism recognizes that, in part, we create our own situations, not necessarily by our actions but simply by who we are. In other words, characteristics such as age, sex, race, religion, ethnicity, and socioeconomic status can influence other people's behavior toward us, often in culturally determined ways, creating a different "situation," which can in turn lead to differences in our behavior (see the discussion of microenvironments in Chapter 9).

## Interactions Between Situation and Personality

Nineteen-year-old Tina behaves very differently with Gabe—drinking from his cup, calling him after midnight—than she does with her 52-year-old female economics professor. In each case, Tina's age, sex, and status relative to the other person might be said to influence her behavior. If you knew Tina only from economics class, you might be surprised by how different her "personality" seems when she is with Gabe. However, we can guess that Tina's way of interacting with her economics professor will be similar to how she interacts with other professors. And how she interacts with Gabe is probably similar to how she's interacted with past boyfriends. That is, there is an interaction between the person and the situation, and in situations that are psychologically similar, the person will behave in similar ways (Magnusson, 2003; Mischel, 2004; Mischel & Shoda, 1995). Specifically, when different individuals are in the same situation, they will differ in what they pay attention to, how they encode and process the stimuli they perceive, what emotions are associated with those stimuli, and then how they respond. These differences reflect an interaction between the person and the situation—*interactionism*. But what is psychologically important in a given situation will differ from person to person (Shoda & LeeTiernan, 2002). Thus, Tina's behavior is consistent in that she responds similarly to all academic authority figures, and she responds to boyfriends in a different, but consistent, way.

As predicted by interactionism, whether or not an individual enjoys a job as a park ranger (or librarian, or actor, or chemist, with the job requirements constituting some aspects of the situation) will depend in part on his or her constellation of personality traits.

In short, over long periods of time and over many similar situations, people are fairly consistent, and personality traits become reliably evident (Funder, 2001; Funder & Colvin, 1991; Kenrick & Funder, 1988; Roberts et al., 2001). Moreover, the more precisely a trait is defined, the more accurate it is in predicting behavior (Wiggins, 1992). Thus, saying that someone is sociable will not predict his or her behavior at a party nearly as well as saying that the person appears at ease in interactions with new people. This is the tradeoff: The more narrowly a trait is defined, the better it predicts behavior, but the fewer situations there are to which it can be applied. However, even when a trait is narrowly defined, there is not necessarily a one-to-one correspondence between a person's assessed level of that trait and the person's behavior. Rather, several traits may interact, along with situational factors, to influence the person's behavior (Ahadi & Diener, 1989). For example, Asian Americans tend to show lower levels of assertiveness than do White Americans on personality tests. However, Zane and colleagues (1991) found that this is true only when the people involved are strangers. Thus, it isn't accurate to describe Asian Americans as "low on the assertiveness trait"; in general, a better characterization would be the more specific "unassertive when among strangers."

Finally, although situations do influence the characteristic behaviors that people exhibit, personality also affects situations, and does so in three major ways. First, personality will influence how people perceive, encode, remember, and respond in any given situation. Second, people often can choose their situations—their jobs, their friends, their leisure activities. And, insofar as they are able, people tend to choose environments that fit their personalities. It's up to you, for instance, to decide whether to go bungee-jumping or sunbathing at the beach when you have a day off. Third, people also find opportunities to create their environments. An aggressive person, for instance, will create a tense situation by words or deeds (A. H. Buss, 1995), and others will react accordingly.

# Factors of Personality: The Big Five? Three? More?

How many personality traits are there? The answer depends on how specific you want to be about a given trait. You could be very specific, narrowing all the way down to a "shy-so-only-goes-on-dates-to-dinner-and-a-movie-but-not-to-parties" trait. Narrowing traits to this level of precision, however, poses certain problems. Each trait explains only particular patterns of thoughts, feelings, and behaviors in very specific instances. For example, you could consider sociability—which personality psychologists call "extraversion"—a trait. Or you could say that extraversion is really a combination of the

FIGURE 11.2

## Personality Profiles and Employment

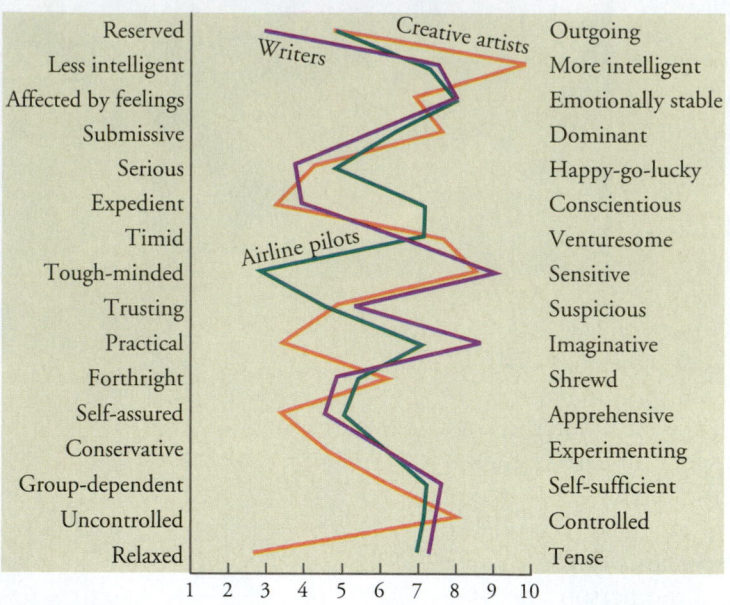

| | | |
|---|---|---|
| Reserved | | Outgoing |
| Less intelligent | | More intelligent |
| Affected by feelings | | Emotionally stable |
| Submissive | | Dominant |
| Serious | | Happy-go-lucky |
| Expedient | | Conscientious |
| Timid | | Venturesome |
| Tough-minded | | Sensitive |
| Trusting | | Suspicious |
| Practical | | Imaginative |
| Forthright | | Shrewd |
| Self-assured | | Apprehensive |
| Conservative | | Experimenting |
| Group-dependent | | Self-sufficient |
| Uncontrolled | | Controlled |
| Relaxed | | Tense |

Completed personality inventories provide personality profiles of different traits. According to Cattell's personality inventory (the 16PF for its 16 personality factors), writers, creative artists, and airline pilots show different profiles.

Big Five: The five superfactors of personality—extraversion, neuroticism, agreeableness, conscientiousness, and openness—determined by factor analysis.

more specific traits of warmth, gregariousness, and assertiveness—each of which exists on a continuum. In this case, you could say that extraversion is a *personality dimension*, a set of related personality traits. Using the statistical technique of factor analysis (see Chapter 9), some researchers have sought to discover whether specific traits are in fact associated and, together, constitute a more general personality dimension; such a personality dimension is sometimes called a *superfactor*. An early proponent of factor analysis to determine personality factors was Raymond Cattell (1905–1998); he proposed 16 personality factors (listed in Figure 11.2) (Cattell, 1943), although further factor analyses lead to fewer factors (which are in turn less predictive of specific behaviors). Personality dimensions, or superfactors, may be a useful way of conceptualizing personality, but they have a disadvantage: They predict behavior less well than do the traits on which they are built (Paunonen, 1998; Paunonen et al., 2003). Moreover, two people can score high on the same dimension, yet attain their high scores by being extreme on different traits that are part of that dimension. In such cases, they score high on the dimension for different reasons and through different mechanisms (Cervone, 2005).

Many factor analytic studies have revealed that personality traits can be reduced to five superfactors, which are listed along with their included traits in Table 11.4 (Digman, 1990; McCrae & Costa, 1987); each superfactor or trait is on a separate continuum, with the name of the superfactor or trait identifying one end of that continuum. Thus, for example, at the other end of the continuum for the superfactor neuroticism is emotional stability. These five superfactors are sometimes referred to as the *Five Factor Model*, or the **Big Five** (Goldberg, 1981): extraversion (versus introversion), neuroticism (also called *emotionality*, versus emotional stability), agreeableness (versus disagreeableness), conscientious-

| TABLE 11.4 | **The Big Five Superfactors and Their Traits** |
|---|---|
| **Superfactor** | **Traits** |
| **Extraversion** (also called *sociability*) | Warmth, gregariousness, assertiveness, activity, excitement seeking, positive emotions |
| **Neuroticism** (also called *emotionality*) | Anxiety, hostility, depression, self-consciousness, impulsiveness, vulnerability |
| **Agreeableness** | Trust, straightforwardness, altruism, compliance, modesty, tender-mindedness |
| **Conscientiousness** (also called *dependability*) | Competence, order, dutifulness, achievement striving, deliberation, self-discipline |
| **Openness** | Fantasy, aesthetics, feelings, actions, ideas, values |

ness (also called *dependability*, versus irresponsibleness), and openness to experience (versus incurious or unimaginativeness) (Costa et al., 1991). To remember these factors, which are supposed to "plumb the depths" of personality, use the mnemonic OCEAN (Openness, Conscientiousness, Extraversion, Agreeableness, and Neuroticism).

Psychologist Hans Eysenck identified not five but three superfactors, or, as he labeled them, personality dimensions: extraversion, neuroticism, and psychoticism. Eysenck's first two dimensions resemble the Big Five's superfactors of the same names, but the third—psychoticism—was originally thought to measure a propensity toward becoming psychotic, that is, toward loss of touch with reality, as occurs in schizophrenia (Eysenck, 1992). It is true that people with schizophrenia score high on this dimension; however, psychoticism as defined by Eysenck also contains traits related to social deviance (such as criminality and the inclination toward substance addiction) and to a lack of conventional socialization (such as disrespectfulness for rules and disregard for the feelings of others) (Costa & McCrae, 1995). For this reason, Eysenck's psychoticism includes some of the traits listed under the Big Five's superfactors of agreeableness and conscientiousness (or lack thereof) (Draycott & Kline, 1995; Saggino, 2000).

Instead of the term *psychoticism*, some psychologists have suggested using a broader term, such as *nonconformity* or *social deviance*, in order to highlight the traits of creativity and nonconformity that are also part of this dimension. Artists, for example, tend to score higher on this personality dimension than people who are truly psychotic (Zuckerman et al., 1988). The Big Five's superfactor of openness has no direct counterpart in Eysenck's scheme.

# Measuring Personality: Is Grumpy Really Grumpy?

Psychologists, employers, teachers, and parents—indeed, all of us—might want to be able to understand and predict the behavior of others by discovering as much as possible about their personalities. Various techniques and tests for assessing personality attempt to do just that. Most personality assessments focus on measuring overt behaviors that psychologists believe to be manifestations of a given trait, inferring the strength of a trait from an individual's behavior. The use of behavior to infer personality traits is at the heart of all methods of personality assessment discussed here.

When "meeting" in cyberspace (for example, through a dating service), people commonly try to "assess" a potential mate's personality by looking at his or her Web site or finding other information on the Internet. Such information becomes the basis for inferring personality, much as we infer personality after viewing someone's bedroom or apartment (Vazire & Gosling, 2004). However, there are standardized ways to assess person-

## Interviews

Interviews to assess personality are usually *structured*; that is, the interviewer asks all interviewees questions from predetermined sets, adding or omitting specific questions spontaneously based on the interviewees' responses. The questions often focus on specific behaviors or beliefs and do not require the person being interviewed to reflect on his or her personality. An advantage of a structured interview is that the interviewer comes away with a sense of knowing the interviewee and is able to infer different aspects of his or her personality.

An interview also has disadvantages: Unless the interviewee answers the questions honestly and accurately, the personality

assessment is not valid. In addition, from a research perspective, it is difficult to generalize about personality characteristics beyond one interviewee. An interviewer might discover that Gabe reports many conscientious behaviors, yet he confesses to keeping a messy apartment. It does not follow that all people who exhibit those same conscientious behaviors are terrible housekeepers.

## Observation

Whether we are aware of it or not, we all use observation to learn about other people's personalities; that's what Tina did to get a sense of Gabe's personality. When psychologists use observation to assess personality, they assign observers, known as "judges," to rate participants' behaviors. Each participant's personality is then inferred from the ratings.

How accurate are observations? The better the judge knows the person being rated, the more accurate the ratings (Paulhus & Bruce, 1992; Wiggins & Pincus, 1992). But strangers can also provide accurate ratings as long as their judgments are based on observations of the appropriate behaviors related to the personality trait being assessed (Ozer & Reise, 1994). For example, if you attempt to assess assertiveness by counting how often someone raises a hand in class, your conclusion may not be very accurate: Reluctance to volunteer may reflect not having read the assigned material!

## Inventories: Check This

Perhaps the most common method of personality assessment is a **personality inventory**, a paper-and-pencil test that requires those being assessed to read statements and indicate whether each is true or false about themselves (only two choices) or how much they agree or disagree with each statement along a multipoint rating scale (three or more choices). Personality inventories usually assess many different traits and contain a great number of statements, often more than 300, so as to include statements that cover different aspects of each trait. This comprehensiveness ensures the validity of the inventory.

Rather than producing a single indicator of personality (such as "friendly" or "seeks excitement"), the results of a personality inventory provide information about a number of traits in the form of a *personality profile*, a summary of the different traits that constitute someone's personality (see Figure 11.2). Personality inventories are used in a variety of settings and for a variety of purposes: by mental health professionals to assess mental illness, by research psychologists to assess how personality traits are related to other variables, and by employers to assess how personality characteristics are related to aspects of the job (Borman et al., 1997). For example, many employers use scores on the trait of conscientiousness to predict employee theft, absenteeism, termination, and "good citizenship" at work (Organ & Ryan, 1995; Sackett, 1994). But not all jobs are well served by very conscientious people; work that requires artistic ability appears to fare better in the hands of those low on conscientiousness (Hogan & Hogan, 1993).

One of the key advantages of personality inventories is that they are easy to administer; a major drawback is that responses can be biased in several ways. Some people are more likely to check off "agree" than "disagree," regardless of the content of the statement. This response style, called *acquiescence*, can be reduced by wording half the items negatively. For example, the item "I often feel shy when meeting new people" would be reworded as "I don't usually feel shy when meeting new people." Another source of bias is **social desirability**: answering questions in a way that you think makes

Personality inventory: A pencil-and-paper method for assessing personality that requires the test-takers to read statements and indicate whether each is true or false about themselves.

Social desirability: A source of bias in responding to questions on personality inventories that occurs when people try to make themselves "look good" even if it means giving untrue answers.

you "look good," even if the answer is not true. For instance, some people might not agree with the statement "It is better to be honest, even if others don't like you for it," but think that they should agree, and so respond accordingly. To compensate for this bias, many personality inventories have a scale that assesses the respondent's propensity to answer in a socially desirable manner. This scale is then used to adjust or, in the language of testing, to "correct" the scores on the part of the inventory that measures traits. Some researchers have found relatively high correlations between personality assessment by inventory and through judges' ratings (J. A. Johnson, 2000; McCrae & Costa, 1989b), lending support to the claim that the easier-to-administer personality inventories yield information similar to personality assessments by judges. However, self-reports of personality traits do not predict all types of personality-related behaviors equally well: In one study, extraversion-related behaviors were better predicted by self-report than were neuroticism-related behaviors (Spain et al., 2000).

One personality inventory is Raymond Cattell's 16PF (Cattell et al., 1970; see Figure 11.2). People's responses on this inventory are categorized into Cattell's 16 personality factors. Another, the **Minnesota Multiphasic Personality Inventory-2 (MMPI-2)**, is commonly used to assess psychopathology (Butcher & Rouse, 1996). It has 567 questions that the test-taker checks off as either true or false, it usually takes 60–90 minutes to complete. (There is a short form consisting of 370 questions.) In contrast to the MMPI-2, which primarily assesses psychopathology or maladaptive extremes of personality, the NEO Personality Inventory (NEO-PI-R) is designed to assess 30 personality traits from the Five Factor Model (*N* for Neuroticism, *E* for Extraversion, *O* for Openness—three of the Big Five superfactors—and *R* for Revised). There are both self-report and other-report (by spouse or roommate, for example) versions of this inventory. As with the MMPI-2, the NEO-PI-R has been used extensively and is considered to be both valid and reliable.

## Projective Tests: Faces in the Clouds

A **projective test** presents the respondent with an ambiguous stimulus, such as a shapeless blot of ink or a drawing of people, and asks the respondent to make sense of the stimulus. The respondent is asked to provide the story behind the stimulus: What does the inkblot look like? What are the people in the drawing doing? The theory behind projective tests is that people's personalities can be revealed by what they project onto an ambiguous stimulus as their minds impose structure on it. This is the reasoning behind the **Rorschach test** (see Figure 11.3). Developed by Herman Rorschach (1884–1922), this commonly used projective technique has 10 cards, each with a different inkblot. The ambiguous shapes of the inkblots allow people to use their imaginations as they decide what the shapes might represent or resemble (for example, a bat or a butterfly) and what features of the inkblot made them think so.

A common complaint about the use of projective tests (and the Rorschach in particular) is that their validity and reliability are questionable. For instance, an individual taking the test on different days may answer differently, leading to different assessments of the person's personality (Anastasi, 1988; Entwisle, 1972). To increase the Rorschach's reliability and validity, a comprehensive and systematic scoring method was developed (Exner, 1974), which has been extensively tested and normed

**FIGURE 11.3** **The Rorschach Test**

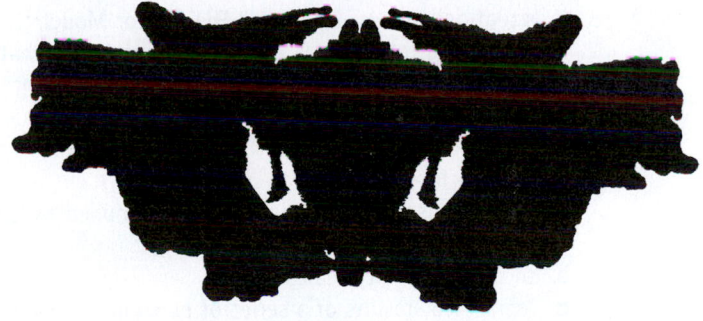

This inkblot is similar to those used in the Rorschach test, in which people are asked to decide what the inkblot resembles or represents and to tell why they think so.

People are shown a drawing like this one from the Thematic Apperception Test (TAT) and asked to explain what is happening in the picture, what led up to it, what will happen later, and what the characters are thinking and feeling.

Thematic Apperception Test (TAT): A projective test consisting of a set of detailed black-and-white drawings about which people are asked to explain various elements.

on different populations. Some (Exner, 2002; Meyer, 2002; Meyer & Archer, 2001), but not others (Lilienfeld et al., 2000; Wood, Lilienfeld, et al., 2001), view this scoring method as reliable and valid. Also controversial is how truly representative those norms are, and whether someone free of psychological disorders would appear to have psychopathology in comparison to those norms (Garb et al., 2002; Wood, Nezworski, et al., 2001).

The **Thematic Apperception Test (TAT)**, developed in the 1930s by Henry Murray, relies on the same concept as the Rorschach but uses detailed black-and-white drawings, often with people in them. Several criticisms are leveled at the TAT: (1) Although systematic scoring systems exist, only 3% of clinicians actually use a scoring system to interpret the TAT, preferring to rely on intuitive interpretations of participants' responses (Pinkerman et al., 1993). (2) From a person's response to the cards, the test administrator cannot distinguish between how the person actually thinks, feels, and would behave versus how the person *wishes* to think, feel, and behave (Lilienfeld et al., 2000). Defenders of the TAT and the Rorschach point out that the tests' abilities to predict future behavior depend not only on the test administrator's experience, but on the specific behavior(s) that the tests are being used to predict (Karon, 2000).

# Test Yourself

1. You notice that your friend seems to behave very inconsistently across a variety of situations that are only somewhat similar to each other. What view of personality best explains her behavior pattern?
   a. projectivism
   b. situationism
   c. three-trait model
   d. Five Factor Model

2. Which of the following is a Big Five superfactor that corresponds to one of Eysenck's personality dimensions?
   a. psychoticism
   b. neuroticism
   c. agreeableness
   d. conscientiousness

3. Personality inventories are
   a. lists of observed personality traits compiled by objective judges.
   b. social desirability scales.
   c. "corrected" results of a series of personal interviews.
   d. paper-and-pencil tests containing many statements about traits.

4. Unlike personality inventories, projective tests such as the Rorschach test ask people to
   a. interpret ambiguous stimuli.
   b. tell a story about a set of other people.
   c. name personalities that fit the stimuli.
   d. create images that reflect their personalities.

## Answers

1. b 2. c 3. d 4. a

# Think It Through!

Suppose you were interested in dating someone and wanted to assess his or her personality before getting too involved. Which assessment method would you choose? Why would you choose that particular method? If you could assess a prospective employer's personality, would you use the same method or a different one? Would you be able to predict your future employer's behavior if you knew his or her scores on the Big Five? Why or why not? Why might it change the accuracy of your predictions if you knew the person's scores on the specific traits that make up the five superfactors?

# BIOLOGY'S INFLUENCES ON PERSONALITY

As their relationship progressed, Tina began to notice a host of ways in which she and Gabe were different: She loved in-line skating, biking, dancing, and skiing, he liked to read outdoors (weather permitting), go on long walks, and watch movies. She liked to meet new people or hang out with her friends and generally didn't enjoy being alone; Gabe had a few close friends but was happy spending time by himself. Tina was fairly straightforward and, up to a point, flexible; Gabe seemed less direct and more rigid. Tina was spontaneous and a bit anxious; Gabe was not spontaneous and never seemed anxious, depressed, or worried. Tina could be impatient, sometimes even snappish; Gabe was always kind and gentle. When Tina was finally able to drag Gabe to a party (he kept forgetting he had agreed to go), she was surprised by his reaction: He stayed in a corner talking to one person for half an hour, then announced that he'd had enough and was ready to leave. Tina, on the other hand, felt like the party was just beginning. Taken together, the differences between them left Tina increasingly puzzled and wondering why they were attracted to each other.

Some aspects of personality are biologically based, so personalities are partly born, not entirely made. Is Gabe shy and mellow because of his biology? Is Tina outgoing and a bit anxious because of her genes or hormones? Let's explore how biology contributes to personality.

## Temperament: Waxing Hot or Cold

Psychologists use the term **temperament** to refer to innate, biologically based inclinations to engage in a certain style of behavior. Arnold Buss (1995) views temperament as having more influence on behavior than personality traits or factors, affecting not just *what* people do, think, and feel, but *how* they act, think, and feel. Such inborn tendencies can appear at an early age and persist throughout adulthood. Longitudinal studies have found that children's temperaments at age 3 are correlated with their personalities, as assessed by a personality inventory, at age 18 (Caspi, 2000; Chess & Thomas, 1996). A study of 21-year-olds also linked temperament with health-risk behaviors such as unsafe sex, alcohol dependence, violent crime, and dangerous driving (Caspi et al., 1997).

Just as psychologists have proposed different ways of classifying personality, so too with temperaments: Different personality theorists propose different sets of temperaments as fundamental. Arnold Buss and Robert Plomin (1984; A. H. Buss, 1995) propose four dimensions of temperament:

- **Sociability**: a preference for being in the company of others rather than alone (similar to the Big Five's extraversion)

- **Emotionality**: an inclination to become aroused in emotional situations, but only when the emotion of distress, fear, or anger is involved (similar to neuroticism)

- **Activity**: the general expenditure of energy, which has two components: *vigor* (the intensity of activity) and *tempo* (the speed of activity)

- **Impulsivity**: a tendency to respond to stimuli immediately, without reflection or concern for consequences

**Temperament:** Innate inclinations to engage in a certain style of behavior.

**Sociability:** A temperament dimension characterized by a preference for being in other people's company rather than alone.

**Emotionality:** A temperament dimension characterized by an inclination to become aroused in situations in which the predominant emotion is distress, fear, or anger.

**Activity:** A temperament dimension characterized by the general expenditure of energy, which has two components: vigor (intensity of the activity) and tempo (speed of the activity).

**Impulsivity:** A temperament dimension characterized by the propensity to respond to stimuli immediately, without reflection or concern for consequences.

Your temperament (such as your preferred level of vigor for activities) and personality traits will likely determine whether your idea of a good time at the beach (assuming you like beaches) will lead you to be physically active or inactive.

Studies of identical versus fraternal twins have shown that a person's degree of emotionality (neuroticism) is partly inherited. In these studies, twins answered questionnaires about their own temperaments (Eaves et al., 1989; Saudino et al., 1999) and about their cotwins' temperaments (Heath, Neale, et al., 1992), parents were asked about the temperaments of their twin children (these questionnaires also included ratings of activity and sociability, with results that also indicated genetic influence) (Buss & Plomin, 1975; Plomin & Foch, 1980). Research on twins who are raised apart has also produced evidence that activity level and sociability are partly inherited (Loehlin et al., 1985; emotionality was not assessed).

Rather than four basic temperaments, Rothbart and Derryberry (1981; Derryberry & Rothbart, 1997) propose two fundamental temperaments:

- *Reactivity* pertains to how people respond to novel or challenging events. For instance, some people consistently respond to such events with negative emotion such as fear or distress. Reactivity includes both the intensity and the time delay of the response.

- *Self-regulation* pertains to the ability to control attention and inhibit responses. Self-regulation is affected by reactivity: To the extent that someone responds to novel stimuli with negative emotion, that person will then have to manage that negative reaction. That is, he or she will have more to "regulate." Moreover, the person may become overly watchful for threatening stimuli in the future and have difficulty shifting attention away from such stimuli (Derryberry & Reed, 1994; Fox et al., 2001, 2002). Let's look at a couple of specific, well-studied temperaments in detail.

## Shyness: The Wallflower Temperament

Are you shy, or do you know someone who is? Have you ever wondered what causes one person to be shy and another outgoing? Is shyness innate? Kagan and his colleagues (1988) have found that some babies are more reactive, or sensitive, to environmental stimuli and thus are more fussy than other babies. These "high-reactive" infants are more likely than "low-reactive" babies to respond to a recording of a woman's voice or to a colored toy with crying, general distress, and increased motor activity. Such infants tend to have faster heart rates and higher levels of the stress hormone cortisol. Kagan and his colleagues have shown that babies with a fast heart rate in the womb are more likely later to become inhibited, fearful children who startle more easily; in fact, the heart activity of even 2-week-old infants can predict later inhibition (Snidman et al., 1995). These children's sympathetic nervous systems are more easily aroused, leading to a preference for situations less likely to create high arousal. As these inhibited children get older, they are usually the ones who hide behind their parents in a room full of adults.

Some of these inhibited children become shy teenagers and adults—and are often extremely self-conscious, so much so that they may painfully and ruthlessly analyze their behavior after a social interaction, an unhappy process that leads them to avoid interactions with others in the future. They become preoccupied with their shyness and its effects ("I can't stop imagining what they're thinking about me"). These preoccupying thoughts can occur in response to autonomic nervous system reactions (a pounding heart), to behavior (what to do with the hands), and to thoughts ("No one wants to talk to me"). Fear and distress in social situations are common feelings for highly inhibited people.

But not all inhibited toddlers are still inhibited at age 7, and not all inhibited children become shy adults (Kagan, 1989a). The environment can play a role either in diminishing the effects of shyness or in maintaining shyness into adulthood. Children can develop a more varied repertoire of responses to novel social situations and so may become less inhibited as they get older (Fox et al., 2005). However, children who are very inhibited or very outgoing are the least likely to change over time (Kagan et al., 1988; Zhengyan et al., 2003). Fox (cited in Azar [1995]) found that the home environment, specifically the parents, can help inhibited children by recognizing their temperament and supporting the children—by encouraging them to learn new responses to social situations and doing so in a way that promotes mastery rather than leads them to feel overwhelmed (Fox et al., 2005; Rubin et al., 2002; Wood et al., 2003). As one previously inhibited 7-year-old explained, "My parents introduced me to new things slowly" (Azar, 1995).

Having an easily aroused autonomic nervous system may produce a bias toward shyness, but the view taken by the family and culture toward such behavior will determine how a person thinks and feels about himself or herself. American culture tends to favor outgoing people, a social bias that puts shy people at a disadvantage. Their self-image as social beings is more likely to be negative, and this negative self-concept increases the likelihood of an autonomic reaction in social situations, thereby perpetuating the cycle.

## Sensation Seeking: What's New?

Another well-studied temperament is that of *sensation seeking*: the pursuit of novelty, often in high-stimulation situations, such as sky diving, fast driving, or drug and alcohol use, or occupations, such as working in a hospital emergency room (Zuckerman, 1979). High sensation seekers are more likely to send flaming e-mails (Alonzo & Akien, 2004), to surf (versus play golf, Diehm & Armatas, 2004), and to listen to punk music (Weisskirch & Murphy, 2004). High sensation seekers view a given situation as less risky than do low sensation seekers (Horvath & Zuckerman, 1993). A study of personality predictors of driving accidents found that those drivers who had had car accidents or traffic violations were more likely than those who didn't to be thrill seekers and risk takers (Trimpop & Kirkcaldy, 1997). Tina appears to have a sensation-seeking temperament, and Gabe, who actively shies away from adventurous activities, doesn't. Sensation seeking is associated with lower levels of the chemical monoamine oxidase-B (MAO-B) in the blood. MAO-B helps break down neurotransmitters for storage, affecting the amounts of those neurotransmitters that are available (Zuckerman & Kulhman, 2000), at least in males (Shekim et al., 1989).

## Biologically Based Theories of Personality

Although the Five Factor Model identifies and describes traits and superfactors, it does not take the crucial next step—it does not attempt to explain *why* these personality differences exist. For this exploration, we turn to theories of personality that involve biological

People who engage in highly stimulating hobbies such as hang gliding, downhill skiing, or snowboarding are more likely to be sensation seekers.

systems, which focus on how various aspects of biology—genes, neurotransmitters, brain areas—influence temperament and personality.

## Behavioral Activation and Inhibition Systems

Jeffrey Gray (1982, 1987, 1991) proposes two underlying biological systems that explain aspects of personality. One system, the *behavioral activation system (BAS)*, is a mechanism based on activation, or reward. The BAS can be thought of as the "go" system, working like the approach strategies and behaviors discussed in Chapter 10. This system is associated with extraversion (both the Big Five superfactor and Eysenck's dimension), and people in whom the BAS is easily activated are more sensitive to, and more easily conditioned by, reward; in contrast, introverts are more sensitive to, and more easily conditioned by, punishment. The BAS triggers positive feelings (such as elation or hope) and approach behaviors. By the same token, the BAS also underlies impulsivity, and people with an easily activated BAS tend to respond readily to even minor incentives and rewards (Meyer et al., 2005). People in whom the BAS is easily activated are also likely to have problems with substance abuse (Johnson et al., 2003).

The other system proposed by Gray, the *behavioral inhibition system (BIS)*, is a mechanism based on inhibition, or punishment. The BIS can be thought of as the "stop" system, working like the avoidance strategies and behaviors discussed in Chapter 10. This system is associated with neuroticism (again, both the Big Five's and Eysenck's). Whereas the BAS is activated by incentives and rewards, the BIS is activated by threat-related stimuli, which trigger anxiety and inhibit behavior. People with an easily activated BIS become distressed when confronted with even minor threats; in contrast, those with an insensitive BIS are not distressed by most threats and are only somewhat distressed when confronted with significant threats (Carver & White, 1994; Carver et al., 2000; Heponiemi et al., 2003; Meyer et al., 2005). Many people in whom the BIS is easily activated are also anxious and depressed (Johnson et al., 2003; Kasch et al., 2002). Table 11.5 contains questionnaire items used to assess BAS and BIS levels.

Gray and others (Davidson, 1992a, 1992b; Fox et al., 2005; Zuckerman, 2003) argue that the properties of these systems arise from characteristics of specific brain structures, neurotransmitters, and neuromodulators, and research supports this view. For example, introverts and extraverts exhibit different patterns of EEG activation while they play a card game in which money is lost (punishment) or won (reward) (Bartussek et al., 1993). Research has shown that inhibited infants—who behave in ways consistent with having a responsive BIS—have faster heart rates, both in response to stress and when at rest (Kagan et al., 1988).

Neuroimaging and EEG studies have demonstrated that the right frontal lobe is involved in withdrawal from aversive stimuli (BIS), whereas the left frontal lobe is more involved in approaching rewarding stimuli (BAS) (Davidson, 1992a, 1992b). Infants who display greater activity in their right frontal lobe exhibited more inhibited behavior at age 4 (Fox et al., 2001). Such infants focus their attention on less novel stimuli, whereas infants who have greater activity in the left frontal lobe focus on novel stimuli (Marshall et al., in preparation). Among adults, those who were inhibited as toddlers exhibit more activity in the amygdala—a brain structure involved in fear—when looking at novel faces, compared to those were not inhibited as toddlers (Schwartz et al., 2003).

People who are more sensitive to, and motivated by, reward are more likely to violate traffic rules than are people less sensitive to reward (Castellà & Pérez, 2004).

| TABLE 11.5 | **Sample Questions Used to Assess BAS and BIS** |
| --- | --- |

- Does the good prospect of obtaining money motivate you strongly to do some things?

- Do you often do things to be praised?

- Do you like being the center of attention at a party or a social meeting?

- In tasks that you are not prepared for, do you attach great importance to the possibility of failure?

- Do you often refrain from doing something because you are afraid of it being illegal?

- Are you often afraid of new or unexpected situations?

## Eysenck's Theory

Eysenck has also proposed that biological mechanisms underlie his three personality dimensions. Eysenck conceived of a hierarchy, where the personality dimensions (at the top of the hierarchy) are composed of more specific traits, which in turn are composed of automatic responses (habit responses), which are themselves based on specific, learned associations between a stimulus and response. As you will see, there is support for some aspects of Eysenck's theory (Matthews & Gilliland, 1999; Zuckerman, 2003). Let's consider Eysenck's three dimensions in more detail.

**EXTRAVERSION**   Eysenck believed that the cortex of extraverts is less easily aroused than that of introverts (Haier et al., 1984). His view was that it takes more stimulation to arouse or to overstimulate extraverts (Eysenck & Eysenck, 1967). This may at first seem an unlikely claim, but consider what it means: Because of this higher threshold, extraverts seek out activities that are more stimulating and arousing (recreational activities such as hang gliding or occupations such as espionage). Moreover, introverts and extraverts have different biological responses to caffeine, nicotine, and sedatives (Corr & Kumari, 1997; Corr et al., 1995; Stelmack, 1990), as this theory predicts. And researchers have also found differences between introverts and extraverts in skin conductance and EEG recordings (Eysenck, 1990a; Matthews & Amelang, 1993). In spite of such support, however, studies of cortical arousal—which are at the heart of Eysenck's theory—have yielded mixed results (Zuckerman, 2003).

Research suggests that extroverts are more easily conditioned by reward (such as winning money), whereas introverts are more easily conditioned by punishment (such as losing money). These differences may be related to differences in brain structure or function (Gray, 1987).

**NEUROTICISM**   Those who score high on the dimension of neuroticism are easily and intensely emotionally aroused and so are more likely to experience conditioned emotional responses—that is, emotional responses elicited by previously neutral stimuli (see Chapter 6; Eysenck, 1979). Thus, someone high on this dimension who is stuck in an elevator is more likely to develop a fear of elevators than is someone low on this dimension.

Neuroimaging data confirm that extraversion and neuroticism are associated with different types of brain activation. Canli and colleagues (2001) used fMRI to monitor brain activity while women looked at positive pictures (such as puppies playing, a happy couple) and negative pictures (such as people crying, a cemetery). The investigators then looked at the relation between the women's extraversion and neuroticism scores and their brain activity in several regions. Extraversion scores were correlated with activation in one set of brain areas when the women looked at the positive pictures (compared with negative ones); in contrast, neuroticism scores were correlated with activation in another set of brain areas when the women looked at negative pictures (compared with positive ones). These findings indicate that the two personality dimensions are not only distinct, but also related to different brain systems. However, research has not yet produced a detailed biological explanation for Eysenck's neuroticism dimension (Zuckerman, 2003).

**PSYCHOTICISM**   Eysenck views those high on psychoticism as having less control over their emotions and therefore as more likely to be aggressive or impulsive. Similarly, Zuckerman (1989, 1991, 2003) suggests that those high on psychoticism have difficulty learning not to engage in particular behaviors. Both tendencies could lead to criminal behavior. In fact, Eysenck (1990b) claimed that 50–60% of the variability in such tendencies is inherited. This does not mean that some people are born crooks, but rather that some are born with autonomic and central nervous systems whose underarousal indirectly leads them to seek risks—and some of these risks, given exposure to certain environmental influences, may be associated with criminal behavior (Eysenck, 1977).

Low arousal may occur in part because of low levels of activity of the neurotransmitter serotonin in the central nervous system, a condition that has been associated with impulsive behavior (Klinteberg et al., 1993; Linnoila et al., 1983). Indeed, Raine and colleagues (1990) showed that underarousal at age 15 (as assessed by three different measures of autonomic and central nervous system activity) predicted criminality at age 24 in 75% of cases.

Although showing an impressive link between biology and criminality, these findings do not prove that biology is destiny, in this or most other areas. By analogy, our biology leads us all to need to eat, but how, what, and when we eat are determined in large part by the way we are raised. Environmental factors play a strong role in the development of criminality (Eysenck & Gudjonsson, 1989; Henry et al., 1996). Indeed, twin studies document the influence of environmental factors in criminality (Caspi et al., 2004; McGuffin & Gottesman, 1985; Plomin et al., 1997).

## Cloninger's Theory

Cloninger and his colleagues (1993) propose that people differ on four basic personality dimensions:

- *Reward dependence* (motivated by a warm attachment to others, its opposite is pragmatism and tough-mindedness)
- *Harm avoidance* (pessimism, shyness, and a fear of uncertainty, an inhibition of approach behaviors and an increase in escape behaviors)
- *Novelty seeking* (an excited response to new situations; it is related to Gray's BAS)
- *Persistence* (the tendency to continue to seek a goal in the face of obstacles or resistance)

Cloninger further proposes that each of these dimensions corresponds to some combination of Big Five superfactors and is associated with a distinct biological system. For example, novelty seeking is similar to sensation seeking (Zuckerman & Cloninger, 1996), which in turn corresponds to a combination of a high score on extraversion and a low score on conscientiousness in the Big Five (Zuckerman, 2003). Ebstein and colleagues note that people who score higher than average on this dimension are "impulsive, exploratory, fickle, excitable, quick-tempered, and extravagant, whereas those who score lower than average tend to be reflective, rigid, loyal, stoic, slow-tempered, and frugal" (p. 78). Cloninger and his colleagues hypothesized that the novelty-seeking dimension is related to the dopamine-based reward pathway (Hansenne et al., 2002; Reif & Lesch, 2003; Wiesbeck et al., 1995; Zuckerman & Cloninger, 1996). Earlier studies with animals had shown that dopamine is involved in exploratory behavior, and a lack of dopamine in people with Parkinson's disease leads to a low level of novelty seeking (Cloninger et al., 1993). In normal people, according to Cloninger, differences in novelty seeking are caused by genetically determined differences in the regulation of dopamine. To test this hypothesis, Ebstein and colleagues (1996) examined people who have a particular gene that produces a type of dopamine receptor. They found that people who have this gene score higher on novelty seeking than do people without it. This result held true for men and women, for different age groups, and for different ethnic backgrounds. Note, however, that the genetic influence was not huge: The average difference in novelty-seeking scores between people who did and did not have the dopamine receptor gene were about half a standard deviation (this is a difference similar to that between an IQ of 110 and an IQ of 118, which is not a huge difference). Nonetheless, the behaviors associated with this gene were more effectively predicted by the score on the single personality dimension of novelty seeking than by the combination of extraversion and conscientiousness scores.

Cloninger and colleagues (1993) also propose that the dimension of harm avoidance is related to the neurotransmitter serotonin, and some research supports such a relationship (Ebstein et al., 2002; Weijers et al., 2001); however, serotonin also appears to act as a neuromodulator, ultimately influencing anxiety levels (Lesch, 2003; Reif & Lesch, 2003). The biological mechanisms of the remaining dimensions of Cloninger's theory have yet to be revealed.

## Zuckerman's Theory

Like Cloninger, Zuckerman has proposed a classification system of personality dimensions that is rooted in biological mechanisms; this system is known as the *alternative five*:

- *Sociability*, which is similar to extraversion
- *Neuroticism-anxiety*, which is similar to neuroticism
- *Impulsive sensation seeking*, which is a tendency to act impulsively. This dimension is a reconceptualization of Eysenck's psychoticism and is related to sensation seeking and Gray's BAS; it is at the opposite end of the Big Five's conscientiousness superfactor (Zuckerman, 1989; Zuckerman et al., 1999). Impulsive sensation seeking is the most studied of the alternative five; it is more typical of men than women and is associated with a diminished sensitivity to punishment or loss of reward (Zuckerman & Kuhlman, 2000). This dimension has a high heritability estimate (Fulker et al., 1980; Hur & Bouchard, 1997).
- *Activity*, which is reflected in a need for activity, a high energy level, a preference for challenges, and difficulty in relaxing
- *Aggression-hostility*, which is a tendency toward antisocial behavior, verbal aggression, and vengefulness. This dimension turns the Big Five's agreeableness on its ear (Zuckerman, 1994).

People with higher numbers of tattoos score higher on measures of sensation seeking (Roberti et al., 2004).

## Comparing the Biologically Based Theories

Although the names of the personality dimensions used in the four biologically based theories differ, there seem to be correspondences across the theories (see Table 11.6). All

| TABLE 11.6 | **Biologically Based Theories of Personality** | | |
|---|---|---|---|
| **Gray** | **Eysenck** | **Cloninger** | **Zuckerman** |
| Behavioral activation system (BAS) | Extraversion* | Reward dependence | Sociability |
| Behavioral inhibition system (BIS) | Neuroticism | Harm avoidance | Neuroticism-anxiety |
| | Psychoticism | Novelty seeking** | Impulsive sensation seeking** |
| | | Persistence | Activity |
| | | | Aggression-hostility |

*Extraversion is also inversely related to BIS levels.

**Novelty seeking and impulsive sensation seeking are also related to BAS levels.

four theories have a dimension related to sociability and a dimension related to anxiety or emotionality. The theories differ in the breadth of these dimensions and in the specific traits associated with them (Ball, 2002). In addition, Cloninger's novelty seeking and Zuckerman's impulsive sensation seeking are closely related, and Cloninger's persistence and Zuckerman's activity are moderately related (Zuckerman & Cloninger, 1996).

# Genes and Personality: Born to Be Mild?

As we noted earlier, the personality dimension of novelty seeking can be influenced by a single gene, which is a biological factor. This finding raises a question: Are all personality differences genetically determined? Behavioral geneticists seek to ascertain the influence of heredity on behavior and, in so doing, investigate a wide range of psychological phenomena, including personality. One way these researchers try to tease apart the effects of heredity and those of the environment is to compare twins separated at birth and raised apart with twins raised together (see Chapter 3). Also compared are identical and fraternal twins who share an environment but have exactly the same genes (the identical twins) or on average only half their genes in common (the fraternal twins). If the identical twins are more similar than the fraternal twins, that difference is usually attributed to effects of the genes.

# UNDERSTANDING RESEARCH

## The Minnesota Study of Twins Reared Apart

**QUESTION:** The question has two parts: First, how much of personality is genetically determined? Second, how much of personality is environmentally determined? Personality psychologists generally consider two aspects of the environment: One of these is the shared family environment; the other is the individual's unique experiences (such as winning a spelling bee or singlehandedly causing the team to lose the soccer finals). Which factor, heritability (*heritability* is the fraction of observed variability of a characteristic that arises from inherited factors; see Chapters 3 and 9) or shared environment, if either, contributes more to personality?

**ALTERNATIVES:** (1) Heritability is relatively high, and effects of shared environment small. (2) Heritability is relatively low, and effects of shared environment large. (3) Heritability and effects of shared environment are both relatively low, which would imply large effects of nonshared environment.

**LOGIC:** (1) If personality traits are highly heritable, then identical twins should be substantially more similar than fraternal twins on personality measures. (2) If personality traits are not highly heritable, then the personalities of identical twins should be no more similar than the personalities of fraternal twins. Moreover, if shared environment has a large effect, then twins reared together should be substantially more similar in their personality profiles than twins reared apart. (3) If personality traits are largely due to nonshared environment, then not only should personality profiles be comparable for identical and fraternal twins (showing low heritability), but also they should be comparable for twins raised together and twins raised apart (showing a small influence of shared environment).

**METHOD:** A group of psychologists at the University of Minnesota undertook the largest study of twins reared apart (identical and fraternal) to shed light on this issue. Called the Minnesota Study of Twins Reared Apart (MISTRA), the study involved 59 pairs of identical twins, 47 pairs of fraternal twins, and four sets of triplets adopted into different families at some point after birth (Bouchard, 1994). Once enrolled in the program, adult twins spent 6 days taking personality (including the MMPI) and intelligence (including the WAIS) tests, undergoing medical and dental exams, and answering a total of 15,000 written questions (Rosen, 1987; Segal, 1999). The researchers correlated the results within each pair in order to assess similarity.

**RESULTS:** In addition, about 24,000 pairs of twins raised together were studied to produce the correlations in Table 11.7 (Loehlin, 1992). As the results indicate, both extraversion and neuroticism have substantial heritability. In addition, both of these personality superfactors are influenced to some degree by shared environment, but this effect is more pronounced for extraversion.

**INFERENCES:** The results of MISTRA and other studies provide evidence that at least part of the variation in personality traits is caused by genetics (Bouchard, 2004; Bouchard & Loehlin, 2001). Other twin studies have shown high heritabilities for temperament (accounting for up to two thirds of the total variance), and have found comparable results among German and Polish samples. These findings suggest that shared environmental differences have much less impact than genes on temperament (Zawadzki et al., 2001). Other researchers report that Russians have similar levels of heritability for personality dimensions to those found in the West (Saudino et al., 1999). This makes sense given the additional MISTRA finding that shared environment has only a small effect on twins' personalities. However, the combined effects of genes and shared environment do not explain all the results of MISTRA and other studies—which suggests that the nonshared environment also influences personality.

**TABLE 11.7** **Correlations of Twin, Family, and Adoption Studies for Extraversion and Neuroticism**

Note that low numbers indicate little if any correlation, and higher numbers indicate a stronger correlation. Identical twins' levels of extraversion and neuroticism are more similar to each other than those of fraternal twins, and twins reared together are generally more similar than twins reared apart.

| Type of Relative | Correlation | |
| --- | --- | --- |
| | Extraversion | Neuroticism |
| Identical twins reared together | .51 | .46 |
| Fraternal twins reared together | .18 | .20 |
| Identical twins reared apart | .38 | .38 |
| Fraternal twins reared apart | .05 | .23 |
| Nonadoptive parents and offspring | .16 | .13 |
| Adoptive parents and offspring | .01 | .05 |
| Nonadoptive siblings | .20 | .09 |
| Adoptive siblings | −.07 | .11 |

## THINK CRITICALLY!

What do you think of the assumption that whatever isn't due to genes or shared environment is—by process of elimination—due to nonshared environment? Is there a way to assess nonshared environment directly? How would you measure shared environment? Is a person's environment entirely an objective reality, or does it depend on how it is perceived? What difference does this make?

## Heritability of Personality

It is worth stressing that, although personality traits—as well as work interests and social attitudes—may be partly caused by your genes, even among twins not all traits are found to be equally heritable, as shown in Figure 11.4 (Bouchard, 2004; Heath & Martin, 1990; Loehlin, 1992; Pederson et al., 1988). Even for the set of traits within a superfactor, heritability is variable. For instance, the heritability estimates for the traits within the superfactor extraversion vary from .23 for warmth to .36 for excitement seeking (Jang et al., 1998), where 1.0 would indicate complete heritability and 0 would indicate no heritability. Similar results have been found when twins rate themselves and when others rate them (Angleitner et al., 1995).

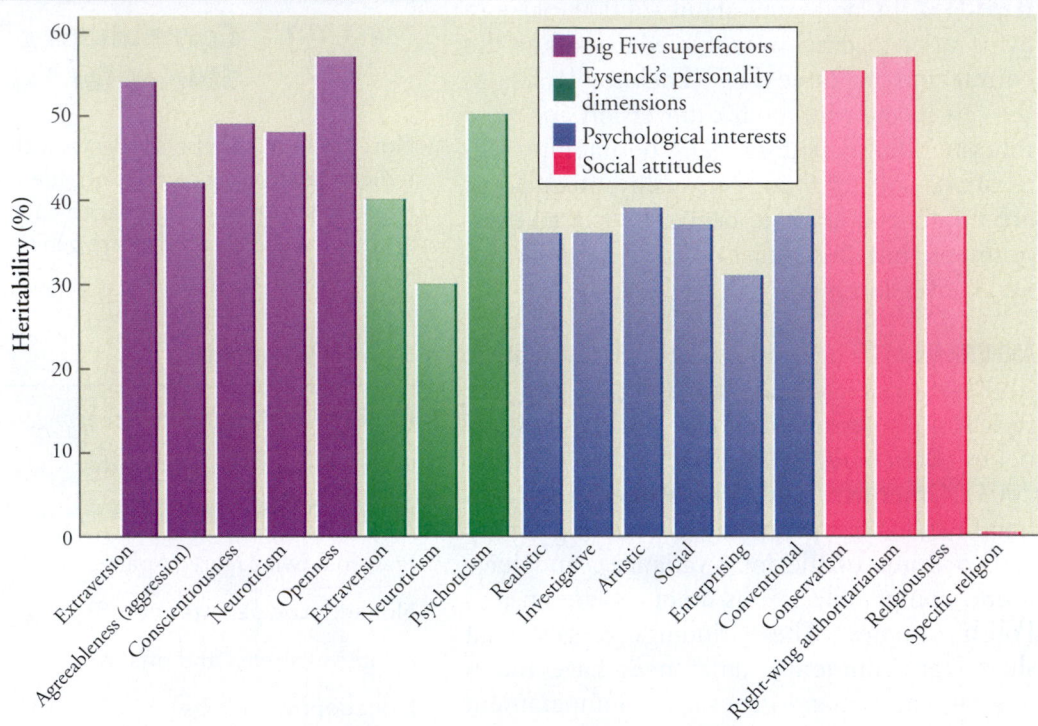

The method of using twins to obtain heritability estimates has been criticized on both statistical and methodological grounds (Joseph, 2001; Stoolmiller, 1999), and studies of adoptive families have not found such high correlations (Loehlin et al., 1981). Critics have pointed out that the adoptive homes for the twins reared apart were more similar to each other than a random selection of homes would be and that some of the twin pairs reared apart lived together through infancy or saw each other sporadically throughout childhood. Both of these factors would increase the correlations among the twin pairs, but not because of genetics.

## Heritability of Specific Behaviors

Despite such criticisms, some researchers propose a genetic origin for very specific behaviors (Bergeman et al., 1990; Kendler et al., 1992; Lyons et al., 1993): from the amount of time spent watching television (Prescott et al., 1991) and the number of childhood accidents (Phillips & Matheny, 1995) to a tendency to marry (Johnson et al., 2004) or divorce (McGue & Lykken, 1992) and even religious attitudes (Bouchard, 2004; Waller et al., 1990). Genes apparently influence the way people respond to specific situations (Lensvelt-Mulders & Hettema, 2001a). Similarly, Lykken and colleagues (1993) found a heritability estimate of .50 for work and leisure interests in a twin study, and they estimate that a subjective sense of well-being (what some might call happiness) has a heritability between .44 and .80 (Lykken & Tellegen, 1996)! Other researchers have found that the subjective sense of well-being has a higher heritability in women (.54) than in men (.46) (Roysamb et al., 2002); a particularly interesting result of this study was a suggestion that different genes may underlie variations in happiness for men and women.

Of course, nobody claims that the amount of time you spend watching television is explicitly coded in your genes. What some researchers do claim, however, is that the genes may influence characteristics such as how easily your autonomic nervous system is aroused (Lensvelt-Mulders & Hettema, 2001b; Tesser et al., 1998)—and such factors, in turn, influence personality traits. Indeed, even physical traits—such as how attractive and athletic you are—may indirectly allow your genes to influence your personality (Olson et al., 2001). If, for instance, your activity level is both "low vigor" and "low tempo" (based on Buss and Plomin's temperament) and you tend to be shy, you are more likely to spend time alone in sedentary pursuits (such as watching television) than if you are a gregarious person who likes vigorous, fast-paced activities. It is also important to note that simply because some aspects of personality have a genetic component, this does not mean that personality is fixed from birth to death. All researchers agree that other factors, such as personal experience, also shape personality. Even Eysenck (1993), who argued that much of behavior is biologically determined, conceded that the environment makes a difference in whether someone high in psychoticism will become a creative, productive researcher or artist or will be disabled by schizophrenia. As we have seen throughout this book, the environment can affect the body and the brain, in turn, leading to psychological changes (Davidson, 2001).

These identical twins were separated in infancy and adopted by different working-class families. In school, neither liked spelling, but both liked math; as adults, both worked as part-time deputy sheriffs, vacationed in Florida, had first wives named Linda, second wives named Betty, and gave their sons the same names. They both drove Chevys and liked carpentry (Holden, 1980). Moreover, their medical histories were remarkably similar, including the onset of migraine headaches at age 18. Are these similarities a result of coincidence or of the twins' shared genetics? How many similarities would any two random people have if they compared such detailed information?

## Genes and the Family Environment

As noted earlier, the MISTRA study did not generally find the family environment to be a large contributor to personality traits. The exceptions are *social closeness*, that is, the desire for intimacy with others (Tellegen et al., 1988), and *positive emotionality*, a trait "characterized by an active engagement in one's environment" (p. 1037). The relatively small influence of a shared family environment on other personality traits may simply reflect the fact that adoptive families are more similar to each other than are families in general, thereby diminishing the correlation for shared family environment (Stoolmiller, 1999). Moreover, many important aspects of the family environment are not really shared. The same family event, such as a divorce, will be experienced differently by children of different ages and cognitive abilities (Hoffman, 1991). In addition, parents do not treat each of their children exactly the same. Children create aspects of their own environments based on their temperaments at birth, leading parents to develop a different pattern of interaction with each of their children and different expectations of each child (Graziano et al., 1998; Jenkins et al., 2003; Plomin & Bergeman, 1991; Scarr & McCartney, 1983; see Chapter 9). It is also possible that there are individual differences in the susceptibility to environmental forces during personality development (Holden, 1980). Genes not only have direct effects, but indirect ones as well—and these can alter the environment, which, in turn, can alter the operation of the genes. As we discussed earlier (Chapters 3 and 9), genes and environment are best regarded as aspects of a single system.

## How Do Genes Exert Their Influence?

Unlike eye color, most aspects of personality aren't affected by a single gene. Rather, sets of genes, exerting their influence in concert, affect personality (Bouchard, 2004). Also, variations in a single gene, interacting with other genes, may affect more than one aspect of personality (Ebstein et al., 2002; Livesley et al., 2003).

Scientists are trying to identify some of the genes that affect personality. Although some studies find that a particular gene is associated with a particular trait or superfactor, variations of a single gene account for less than 10% of the genetic influence (Lesch, 2003; Reif & Lesch, 2003). Moreover, studies investigating the relationships between a particular gene and a trait or superfactor often yield inconsistent results (Livesley et al., 2003).

In addition to wanting to find the genes that influence personality, researchers want to know the mechanisms by which genes affect personality. Recent research has focused on neurotransmitters and their activities. However, the process of discovering the relationships of genes to neurotransmitters and of neurotransmitters to personality traits and superfactors has just begun. Correlational studies sometimes find relationships between levels of a neurotransmitter by-product (in the blood, urine, or saliva) and a personality trait, but subsequent studies often fail to replicate these results. The most common explanation for such inconstancies is that neurotransmitters affect personality in complex ways, both direct and indirect (Zuckerman, 2003).

## Test Yourself

1. Buss and Plomin's four dimensions of temperament include all of the following *except*
   a. impulsivity.
   b. sociability.
   c. desirability.
   d. emotionality.

2. According to Eysenck, personality differences arise mostly from
   a. environmental differences such as family characteristics.
   b. biological differences.
   c. social and cultural differences.
   d. factor analyses of personality traits.

3. What do the different biologically based theories of personality have in common?
   a. They share the idea that personality differences arise from biological differences.
   b. They all have a dimension related to sociability.
   c. They all have a dimension related to anxiety or emotionality.
   d. All of the above statements about the different theories are true.

4. A reasonable interpretation of the results of twin studies that have explored the genetic influence on personality is that they
   a. prove definitively that personality is determined more by genetic factors than by environmental ones.
   b. reveal little genetic variability in personality superfactors.
   c. demonstrate that nearly all behaviors have a specific genetic origin.
   d. suggest that at least part of the variability in personality is caused by genes.

## Answers

1.c 2.b 3.d 4.d

## Think It Through!

Imagine that you know a family in which both parents are highly extraverted, emotionally stable, not particularly creative, and very conscientious. Would you predict that their child would have the same personality features? Why or why not? If their child is very shy (one of Kagan's inhibited children), would that mean that the child will always be shy, or might he or she become like the parents? (Hint: Think about what you have learned about temperament.)

Might Gabe have been one of Kagan's inhibited children? Explain your answer.

# LEARNING AND THE COGNITIVE ELEMENTS OF PERSONALITY

Tina's and Gabe's personalities may have been shaped partly by biology, but their unique experiences also shaped their beliefs, expectations, and goals. For instance, Tina's past positive experiences with thrilling activities lead her to get excited about new stimulating activities. Similarly, Gabe may hesitate about going to parties because of previous experiences where socializing in groups was awkward and uncomfortable. How does experience build on the biological framework of our personalities, affecting our beliefs, motivations, and views of ourselves?

## Learning to Have Personality: Genes Are Not Destiny

Early learning theorists (see Chapter 6), particularly Skinner (1971) and Watson (1924), viewed personality as sets of behaviors that are acquired through experience. These theorists argued that an individual's inclination to behave in consistent ways arises from his or her conditioning history; no mental processes (or biologically based temperaments) are involved. According to this view, people may spontaneously produce a specific behavior once or twice, but they will continue to engage in the behavior only because they have been conditioned to do so. As discussed in Chapter 6, learning influences personality by creating:

- *classically conditioned behaviors*, such as a phobia (leading to a persistent avoidance of a stimulus),
- *operantly conditioned behaviors*, such as engaging in highly stimulating activities because of past reinforcement (or avoiding parties because of past "punishment" for attending), and
- *behaviors learned though observation* (such as avoiding a particular behavior after hearing about or witnessing a sibling's severe punishment for that behavior).

A behaviorist would propose that Tina, perhaps at an early age, was reinforced for engaging in stimulating physical activities, and perhaps punished for engaging in sedentary ones. Similarly, Tina may not have been appropriately reinforced for working hard at her studies. Gabe's personality, in turn, would be explained by his own history of reinforcement and punishment, and possibly some classically conditioned fear of certain social situations. Similarly, Gabe may have been reinforced for his hard work, but not for cleaning up his room.

Although a strict behaviorist view of personality is not supported by research, behavioral factors do exert an influence on personality. For example, behaviorally inhibited children tend to have poor assertiveness skills (Rubin & Borwick, 1984), and other children's reactions to them—such as laughing at them or making them the butt of pranks—will affect their social behavior (and as we discuss shortly, also their thoughts about themselves; Fox et al., 2005). And as we noted in discussing genetics and personality, personality does not develop in isolation, but through interaction with the environment (Caprara et al., 2003, 2004; Lickliter & Honeycutt, 2003a, 2003b), which reinforces and punishes various behaviors.

# The Sociocognitive View of Personality: You Are What You Expect

The sociocognitive approach to personality emphasizes that the development of personality is affected by people's thoughts, which in turn are shaped by social interactions—including those that are part and parcel of the surrounding culture. The key idea is that social interactions affect your thoughts, feelings, and behaviors—and consistent thoughts, feelings, and behaviors (consistent in a given situation at least) create personality. Thus, personality affects which stimuli are attended to or ignored, how stimuli are interpreted, and how emotions influence those interpretations. In turn, these perceptions and interpretations affect expectations, goals, and behaviors (Mischel & Shoda, 1995). For example, people high in neuroticism are more likely to search for threatening stimuli (and to remain focused on such stimuli) than those who score lower on that dimension (Derryberry & Reed, 2002; Eisenberg et al., 1995; Fox et al., 2001, 2002). Such stimuli may include body language and facial expressions.

The sociocognitive view acknowledges the influence of biological factors on personality, but emphasizes the role of the person's experiences (including social experiences), of consistent patterns of cognitive processing, of the view of self, and of behavior. Moreover, this view—as indicated by the "socio" part of its name—stresses that your society and culture contribute to your experiences, and ultimately even affect your biology (see Figure 11.5; Mischel & Shoda, 1995). For instance, levels of neuroticism among Americans have increased from 1963 to 1993 (Twenge, 2000), as cultural changes have led to an increase in crime and other dangers.

**FIGURE 11.5** How Biology, Learning, Cognition, and Culture Influence Personality

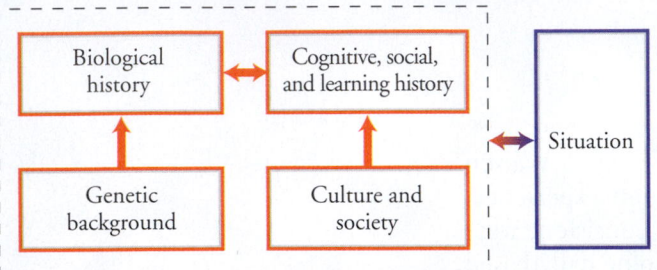

As part of their personality, people bring to any situation their genetic background and their biological, cognitive, learning, and social histories; their culture also has an influence on those elements. In turn, situations exert an influence on biology, cognition, and learning, as well as on the expression of some genes.

## Expectancies

One aspect of the sociocognitive view of personality development is the idea of **expectancies**: What you *expect* to happen has a powerful influence on your thoughts, feelings, and behaviors and, in turn, on your personality. Expectancies about the outcomes of behaviors, often based on past experiences, can explain why operant conditioning works. You learn that a certain stimulus signals a likely outcome if you behave in a certain way, so you come to expect certain outcomes from particular behaviors in certain situations. Perhaps Gabe doesn't like parties because, from his previous experience of them, he expects that he will have a miserable time and feel socially isolated (in the language of conditioning, his prior unhappy experiences constituted punishment for attending a party; see Chapter 6). Such expectancies have a powerful influence on behavior even without our awareness. Killen and his colleagues (1996) found that among 9th-grade nondrinkers, both male and female, those who had the expectancy that drinking would enhance social behavior (that is, the outcome of drinking would be more or better social behavior) were more likely to begin drinking within a year. Similar results have been found regarding expectancies about other risky behaviors (Smith et al., 2004). For example, Collins and Feeney (2004) found that how people perceive their partners' attempts to provide emotional support was influenced by their beliefs and expectancies about intimate relationships. Based on their past experiences, shy children may come to *expect* to have a bad time at parties or be teased by others. People interpret ambiguous situations according to their expectancies.

**Expectancies:** Expectations that have a powerful influence on thoughts, feelings, and behaviors and, in turn, on personality.

One type of personality difference related to expectancy focuses on **locus of control**, the source we perceive as exerting control over our life events—that is, determining the outcomes (Rotter, 1966). People who have an internal locus of control, called *internals*, are more likely to see control over events as coming from within themselves when the situation is ambiguous; that is, they feel personally responsible for what happens to them. Gabe's responsible approach to studying would indicate that he has an internal locus of control. In contrast, *externals* are people with an external locus of control; these people are more likely to see control as coming from outside forces, and they feel less personal responsibility. Because Tina does well in her classes without studying much, she chalks up her good grades to easy tests. She feels less personally responsible for her academic success than does Gabe and seems to have more of an external locus of control. Research examining locus of control among college students between 1960 and 2002 found that, over time, college students are becoming increasingly external in their locus of control; that is, they tend to feel that their lives are out of their personal control. An average college student in 2002 had a more external locus of control than did 80% of college students in the 1960s (Twenge et al., 2004).

Internals and externals have different responses to success and failure. Internals are more likely to increase their expectancies in response to success and to lower their expectancies in response to failure. Externals are likely to do the opposite, lowering their expectancies after success and raising them after failure; externals apparently reason that the present situation may change in the future—for better or worse. Thus, what you believe about a situation depends on whether you attribute the consequences you experience to your own behavior or to outside forces. As an internal, Gabe has lowered expectations about future parties because of what he sees as his failures at past ones. Tina, as an external, doesn't fully expect to maintain her high grades because she doesn't feel completely responsible for them in the first place.

**Locus of control:** The source a person perceives to be exerting control over life's events.

**Self-efficacy:** The sense of being able to follow through and produce specific desired behaviors.

## Self-Efficacy

People also differ with respect to **self-efficacy**, the sense of having the ability to follow through and produce desired behaviors (Bandura, 1977b). Those with high self-efficacy believe that they will be able to behave in a specific way if they want to do so (Ajzen, 2002). Self-efficacy is distinct from locus of control, which focuses on internal or external causes. (Note, however, that the two types of expectancies appear to have in common our self-evaluations and beliefs about our behaviors; Judge et al., 2002.) Albert Bandura (2004) hypothesized that self-efficacy helps people believe in themselves and in their ability to change or perform behaviors previously viewed as difficult or impossible. Those with high self-efficacy persist more than others when working on difficult problems (Brown & Inouye, 1978). Both Gabe and Tina have high self-efficacy, a correspondence that partly accounts for the initial sense they had of being a lot alike. Bandura (2001) also proposed another important cognitive element of personality: *self-reflectiveness*, the tendency to reflect on yourself and determine whether your behaviors are appropriate and your thoughts (such as predictions and expectations) are accurate.

An additional aspect of the cognitive view of personality is the idea of self-regulation (Bandura, 1976, 1977a). According to this concept, self-administered reinforcement or punishment allows us to regulate our own behavior. For instance, Tina might reward herself for studying all day by going in-line skating the next day. Self-regulation can occur through just thinking about your actions. When you like the way you behaved in a given situation, you praise yourself (providing reinforcement), and when you disapprove of your behavior, you blame yourself (providing punishment). Self-regulation is a powerful tool in determining behavior and feelings, both of which contribute to personality.

Although we don't know what Hillary Clinton believed about herself when she graduated from high school, it is likely that she had a high level of self-efficacy.

FIGURE 11.6

## Reciprocal Determinism

Behavior, the environment, and cognitive/personal factors all influence one another.

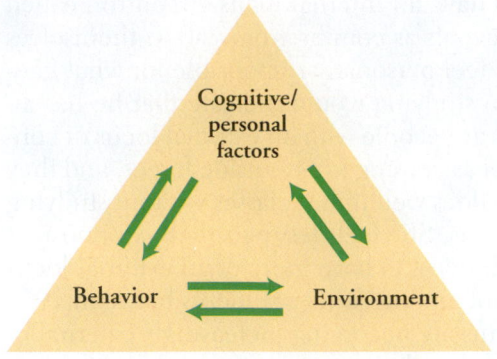

## Reciprocal Determinism

Bandura (1978, 2001) regards human behavior as part of an interactive process that involves psychological and social forces: Thoughts, expectancies, feelings, and other personal factors influence both the environment (including the social world) and behavior; in turn, the environment and personal factors influence, and are influenced by, behavior (see Figure 11.6). Bandura calls this interactive relationship **reciprocal determinism**. In essence, Bandura is acknowledging the interaction among events at different levels of analysis, as we do in this book's Looking at Levels features, except that he does not include biologically based factors. Reciprocal determinism might explain Tina's desire for highly stimulating activities (such as bungee-jumping) in this way: Because of certain aspects of her environment, such as moving a lot as a child, Tina came to *expect* a certain level of newness, excitement, even danger, from her experiences. These expectations influence her thrill-seeking behavior (bungee-jumping), but her activities also affect her expectations. Because Tina has a great time bungee-jumping, she expects to enjoy doing something similarly thrilling, and she seeks out such stimuli in her environment.

**Reciprocal determinism:** The interactive relationship between the environment, cognitive/personal factors, and behavior.

# Test Yourself

1. Which statement best expresses the sociocognitive view of personality?
   a. Hypnosis affects personality traits by changing beliefs and behavior.
   b. A society's belief and value systems create personality; people's personality differences are a function of differences in their ancestors' countries of origin.
   c. Personality is affected by social interactions, which in turn influence thoughts.
   d. All of the above statements express the sociocognitive view.

2. People with internal versus external loci of control respond to successes and failures in different ways. Which of the following is true?
   a. Externals increase their expectancies in response to success and decrease them in response to failure.
   b. Internals decrease their expectancies in response to success and increase them in response to failure.
   c. Internals increase their expectancies in response to success and decrease them in response to failure.
   d. Externals decrease their expectancies in response to both success and failure.

3. Which of the following would be the best indication that you have high self-efficacy?
   a. believing in your specific abilities and capability to follow through
   b. believing that you will usually fail, except when your locus of control is high
   c. feeling high self-esteem regardless of the outcomes of your behaviors
   d. knowing that you will fail but you are still a good person

4. Which of the following most accurately portrays Bandura's concept of reciprocal determinism?
   a. Biological, personal, and social factors interact to determine personality.
   b. Personal, environmental, and behavioral factors interact to determine personality.
   c. Behavioral and social factors are the only two influences on personality.
   d. Social factors alone determine personality.

# Answers

1. c 2. c 3. a 4. b

# Think It Through!

Imagine two people who have been together as a couple for a number of years. Whatever their personalities might have been like when they started dating each other, how would learning theorists explain their current personalities? What would be the limits or weaknesses of such an explanation? What would someone taking a sociocognitive view say about how their personalities have developed? What would be the limits of that explanation?

# SOCIOCULTURAL INFLUENCES ON PERSONALITY

Tina wondered whether some of the differences between Gabe and herself might reflect the different environments in which they had grown up. Gabe was an only child; Tina was the youngest of three, with two older brothers. Gabe grew up in a rural part of the United States and, before college, had lived in the same town his whole life. Tina, an Air Force "brat," had lived in half a dozen countries before she was 12.

Although personality is influenced by genetic and biological factors, the environment also plays a role. For example, our family environments and the ways in which we are raised contribute substantially to the personality traits of social closeness and positive emotionality (Tellegen et al., 1988). Other environmental influences on personality that psychologists have investigated include birth order, gender differences, and culture.

## Birth Order: Are You Number One?

Have you ever noticed that people who are firstborns seem more responsible and better organized, and that last-borns seem more agreeable and accommodating? If you have, you're not the first person to make a connection between personality and birth order. Alfred Adler (1964), himself a younger sibling raised in the shadow of a high-achieving brother, was one of the early personality theorists who proposed that birth order affects personality. In the past, research has not shown clear-cut evidence for the impact of birth order on personality development (Ernst & Angst, 1983), but more recent reviews of birth order research, using meta-analytic procedures, have found consistent and interesting results.

Science historian Frank Sulloway (1996) used meta-analyses to support his proposal that at least one aspect of personality, openness to experience (one of the Big Five superfactors), is shaped by birth order. But Sulloway was careful to point out that birth order acts along with other factors, such as the number of children in a family and the level of conflict between each child and his or her parents. Moreover, a person's sex (and that of his or her siblings), the number of years between siblings, temperament, social class, and loss of a parent can also affect this aspect of personality.

Sulloway developed his theory in an effort to understand why, throughout history, some people have supported scientific and political revolutions, whereas others have insisted on maintaining the status quo—and especially why such opposite views occur within the same family. From available information about the lives of historical figures, Sulloway proposed that, in general, firstborns, because of their place in the birth order, are more likely to support parental authority, see things as their parents do, and be less open to new ideas and experiences. Younger siblings, because they must find a different niche in the family and in the world around them, are more likely to be open to new ideas and experiences. In their personalities, "only" children are similar to firstborn children.

Although not all psychologists agree with his meta-analytic conclusions about birth order and personality development (Modell, 1996), and not all subsequent research has supported his views (Freese et al., 1999; Skinner, 2003), some studies have supported some aspects of Sulloway's theory (Michalski & Shakelford, 2002; Zweigenhaft, 2002); Sulloway (1999) has extended and replicated his results with over 5,000 adults and across different countries (Rohde et al., 2003). And other researchers have also contributed to this research. For example, Salmon's work (1998, 1999; Salmon & Daly, 1998) has focused on middle-born children and found that middle-borns are less close to their families than are their elder or younger siblings. For instance, when hearing political speeches, middle-borns responded more positively to the speeches when the speakers used the term *friends* than when they used the terms *brothers* and *sisters*. In contrast, firstborns and last-borns responded more positively to speeches in which family terms were used (Salmon, 1998). Further, when asked to define themselves, middle-borns were least likely to define themselves by their last names, that is, their family names (Salmon & Daly, 1998). One study found middle-borns to be more rebellious and impulsive and less conscientious than their siblings (Saroglou & Fiasse, 2003). Some research results are summarized in Table 11.8.

Findings about the importance of birth order come from more than self-report measures. When spouses were asked to complete a personality inventory about their partners, firstborn partners were described as having different personality characteristics than later-born partners (Sulloway, 1999). As rated by their partners, later-born spouses were less conscientious and more extraverted, agreeable, and open to experience than were firstborn spouses. A similar correlation between personality and birth order was found among college roommates: Firstborn roommates were perceived differently than later-born roommates. However, a study of birth order effects among families with both biological and adoptive children (where the first biological child may not have the

| TABLE 11.8 | The Effects of Birth Order on Personality | | |
| --- | --- | --- | --- |

| Firstborns and Only Children | Middle-borns | Later-borns |
| --- | --- | --- |
| ■ More responsible, ambitious, organized, academically successful, energetic, self-disciplined; conscientious | ■ More rebellious and impulsive | ■ More agreeable and warmer |
| | ■ Less closely identified with family | ■ More tender-minded, easy-going, trusting, accommodating, altruistic |
| | ■ Less conscientious | ■ More adventurous, prone to fantasy, attracted by novelty, untraditional |
| ■ More temperamental, more anxious about their status | ■ Less likely to ask for parental help in an emergency | |
| | ■ Less likely to report having been loved as a child | ■ More sociable, affectionate, excitement-seeking, fun-loving |
| ■ More assertive, dominant (Sulloway, 1996) | ■ Compared with siblings, more likely to live farther from parents and less likely to visit parents (Salmon, 1999; Salmon & Daley, 1998; Saroglou & Fiasse, 2003) | ■ More self-conscious (Saroglou & Fiasse, 2003; Sulloway, 1996) |

"firstborn" position), found that conscientiousness was the only trait common among the oldest children in those families (Beer & Horn, 2000).

In sum, birth order does appear to exert an influence on personality. However, its specific effects have not been found consistently across all studies, suggesting that other factors may temper the ways in which it shapes a given individual.

# Sex Differences in Personality: Nature and Nurture

In general, personality differences between females and males are not very great, especially when compared with the large differences among people within each sex (Costa et al., 2001). In fact, some have proposed that it is counterproductive to look for sex differences in personality, arguing that the context in which behavior takes place has a larger role in personality development (Lott, 1996). For example, there are no notable sex differences in social anxiety, locus of control, impulsiveness, or reflectiveness (Feingold, 1994).

Nonetheless, some consistent sex differences have been found (Feingold, 1994). Women tend to score higher on traits reflecting *social connectedness*, which is a focus on the importance of relationships (Gilligan, 1982). In contrast, men tend to score higher on traits reflecting *individuality* and *autonomy*, with a focus on separateness from others, achievement, and self-sufficiency. Women tend to be more empathic than men (Lennon & Eisenberg, 1987) and to report more nurturing tendencies (Feingold, 1994). In addition, as noted in Chapter 10, women assess emotion in other people better than do men (Hall, 1978, 1987; McClure, 2000). For example, women are better than men at spotting when their partners are deceiving them (McCornack & Parks, 1990).

The observed sex differences in individuality and social connectedness are somewhat evident in the ways males and females try to resolve moral dilemmas (such as whether it is acceptable to steal a very costly, rare drug in order to save a friend's life). Gilligan (1982) and others have argued that females think through moral dilemmas differently from, not less well than, males. Females are more likely to pay attention to the interpersonal context of a moral decision, to whether and how others will be hurt by the decision; males are more likely to make a moral decision based on laws or abstract principles. However, not all studies find this sex difference (Archer & Waterman, 1988). We will discuss such decision making in more detail in Chapter 12.

Males and females also differ in their degree of neuroticism, with men scoring lower, on average (Costa et al., 2001; Goodwin & Gotlib, 2004; Lynn & Martin, 1997; Zuckerman et al., 1988). However, women generally score lower on anger and aggression (Archer, 2004; Shields, 1987) and on assertiveness (Costa et al., 2001; Feingold, 1994). However, the sex difference in assertiveness is diminishing (Twenge, 2001a).

These findings are consistent with stereotypes about men and women, but the fact that sex differences exist doesn't tell us *why* they exist—what the roles of biological or cultural factors might be (sex differences caused by cultural factors are sometimes referred to as *gender differences*).

## Sociocultural Explanations

Several cultural and social theories attempt to explain personality differences between men and women. *Social role theory* proposes that boys and girls learn different skills and beliefs. For example, some computer games specifically targeted at girls emphasize

One sociocultural explanation for gender differences in personality is that as boys between the ages of 3 and 5 realize they are a different sex than their mothers, they lose their identification and connection with her and come to experience themselves as more autonomous than do girls (Choderow, 1978).

social interactions and concern for others and portray getting along as more important than winning. This emphasis is in contrast to the more typical genre, which involves killing the enemy, capturing others' territory, and defending against capture or death. These two types of computer games invite the users to cultivate different skills and lead to different moral lessons. Expectancy effects can also play a role in gender differences in personality; through direct interaction with their environments, boys and girls come to have different expectancies about likely responses when they exhibit behaviors that are seen as appropriate or inappropriate for typical gender roles (Henley, 1977).

Another cultural explanation for personality differences between men and women rests on the fact that women are most often the primary caretakers of children. Choderow (1978) proposes that between the ages of 3 and 5, boys realize that they are a different sex from their mothers, a realization that leads them to feel a loss of identification and connection with their mothers and to experience themselves as autonomous individuals. In contrast, girls do not experience this loss because they are the same sex as their mothers, and girls thus maintain a sense of connection to others. An additional cultural explanation for gender differences in assessing others' emotions is the difference in power between men and women. Traditionally, women have been less likely to hold positions of power. Being able to read the emotions of others allows women who lack power to make rapid assessments of a situation and thus confers some advantage in maintaining personal safety (Snodgrass, 1985; Tavris, 1991).

The importance of context, or situation, has raised the question of whether examining sex differences in personality is valid; in fact, different situations can produce contradictory findings (Eagly, 1987, 1995; Lott, 1996). For example, Moskowitz (1993) found differences between men and women when participants interacted with same-sex friends (males were more dominant, and females were more friendly), but those differences disappeared when the interactions were between opposite-sex strangers. Thus, although differences between men's and women's personalities have been observed, they do not necessarily hold in all situations. Moreover, a large, 26-country meta-analysis using results from the NEO-PI-R found that, in general, differences between men and women are not as large as differences within each sex. If sex (or gender) exerts a large role on personality, then more differences between men and women than the usual ones in individuality and social connectedness should have been observed. However, this was not the case (Costa et al., 2001).

## Biological Explanations

In spite of the evidence that culture and context shape gender differences, we must also note that there are biological explanations for these differences. Biological explanations for sex differences include attributing them to the effects of testosterone (see Chapters 3 and 10) (Berenbaum, 1999; Dabbs et al., 1997, 2001), as well as suggesting that men and women have evolved differently because of differences in mate selection and parenting strategies (D. Buss, 1995). According to this evolutionary view, women have a greater investment in their offspring because they cannot have as many children as men can. This greater investment, along with their caretaker role, supposedly causes women to become more strongly attached to their children, which has an evolutionary advantage: Highly attached mothers are more likely to have children who survive into adulthood and have children themselves.

From what we know of Tina and Gabe, we cannot say with certainty that any of the personality differences between them are explained by sex differences. Although he prefers to be alone more often than she does, Gabe has close friends, and we can't say whether their contrasting preferences reflect a difference in gender, in social connectedness and individuality, in temperament, or in their learning histories.

# Culture and Personality

We can see the influence of the environment on personality in two additional ways: Psychologists have found consistent differences in people's personality traits and superfactors over time and across countries.

## Personality Changes Within a Culture, Over Time: The Times They Are A-Changin'

We noted earlier that researchers have found that, over time, college students are increasingly reporting an external locus of control (Twenge et al., 2004). Similarly, the prevalence of other personality traits has also changed over time. As anxiety and neuroticism have increased significantly from 1963 to 1993, the average anxiety reported by American children in the 1980s was equivalent to the amount reported by children who were psychiatric patients in the 1950s (Twenge, 2000). In addition, the degree of extraversion has increased over time (Twenge, 2001b), and personality traits typically considered consistent with gender roles have decreased for both sexes (Twenge, 1997). Such changes are thought to reflect certain cultural shifts over the last half of the 20th century: increasing fear of crime, terrorism, and other dangers (leading to increased anxiety, neuroticism, and external locus of control), increasing valuation of traits related to extraversion, and decreasing emphasis on personality traits related to sex roles (Twenge, 1997, 2000, 2001a, 2001b, 2004).

## Consistent Personality Differences Across Cultures: Different Strokes for Different Countries

It is more difficult to compare personalities across cultures than you might think. Although it is possible to translate personality assessment measures into other languages, some concepts don't translate very well, even if the words themselves can be rendered in different languages. For example, it is possible to translate the phrase *self-esteem* into French, but the concept of self-esteem as Americans understand it has not been generally familiar in France, and so a simple translation of the words from English to French doesn't convey the meaning of the idea.

**TRANSLATING TRAITS ACROSS LANGUAGES AND CULTURES** Personality measures have been carefully translated in an effort to compensate for the problems that can arise with respect to the meaning of concepts, and such tests reveal the same Big Five personality superfactors in many, although not all, cultures (Katigbak et al., 1996, 2002; McCrae & Costa, 1997b; McCrae, Costa, et al., 1998; Paunonen & Ashton, 1998; Paunonen et al., 2000). Personality measures developed in the native language of a culture, rather than translated into it, may be more accurate for that culture, depending on the behaviors of interest (Katigbak et al., 2002). For example, Chinese college students were asked to rate other people on qualities described by Chinese adjectives (not English adjectives translated into Chinese); five personality factors were identified, but they were not the same as the Big Five found with English-language tests (Yang & Bond, 1990).

People in collectivist cultures tend to define themselves as part of a group, are very attached to the group, and see their personal goals as secondary to the group's goals. People from individualist cultures define themselves as individuals, are less attached to the group, and see their personal goals as more important than the group's goals (Triandis et al., 1988).

**INDIVIDUALIST AND COLLECTIVIST PERSONALITIES: YOURS, MINE, AND OURS** In general, personality differences have been found between collectivist and individualist cultures (see Chapter 10). Collectivist cultures often rank the needs of the group as more important than those of the individual; for instance, these cultures tend to value humility, honoring the family, and efforts to maintain the social order (Triandis et al., 1990), and people raised in them are more likely to care about others, even strangers (Hui & Triandis, 1986). Asian, African, Latin American, and Arab cultures tend to have this orientation (Buda & Elsayed-Elkhouly, 1998). In contrast, individualist cultures emphasize individual freedom, equality, and enjoyment—even at the expense of others. The United States, Great Britain, Canada, and Australia, for example, have this orientation. This distinction between cultures has been used to explain differences in crime rates, which are higher in individualist cultures: Collectivist cultures exert more social control over the individual, and criminals' actions reflect not only on themselves but also on their families. In fact, as the global economy leads collectivist cultures to shift their work habits and values to those of individualist countries, crime rates and other social ills often increase (Strom, 2000).

Are these cultural differences associated with differences in personality profiles? Bilingual Hong Kong university students were given a personality inventory based on the Five Factor Model. As you would expect from the cultural differences, the results showed that, compared with North American university students, Hong Kong students were low in extraversion in general and low in the particular traits of excitement seeking, competence, and altruism. Moreover, they were high in vulnerability, straightforwardness, and compliance (McCrae et al., 1998). Such cultural differences go beyond North America and Hong Kong: A large, 36-nation study found that people in collectivist countries tend to score higher on the Big Five superfactor of agreeableness, whereas people from individualist countries tend to score higher on extraversion and openness (Allik & McCrae, 2004; Hofstede & McCrae, 2004). As proof of the impact of culture on personality, after Chinese immigrants move to North America, their personality profiles begin to resemble those of native-born North Americans; the longer they have lived in North America, the more similar the profiles (McCrae, Costa, et al., 1998).

**WHO AM I? CROSS-CULTURAL DIFFERENCES IN SELF-CONCEPT** Not surprisingly, individualist cultures also differ from collectivist cultures in their citizens' self-concepts: People from individualist cultures characterize the "self" as a composite of traits, independent from the group; people from collectivist cultures see the "self" in relation to specific situations and contexts (Markus & Kitayama, 1991). That is, other people are incorporated into the definition of self in the latter type of culture. Perhaps for this reason, traits may be less useful for predicting behavior in collectivist cultures, such as that of the Philippines (Church & Katigbak, 2000). These cultural differences also affect individuals' behaviors and views of themselves: Americans are more likely to enhance their view of themselves through individualist-oriented behaviors, whereas Japanese are more likely to enhance their view of themselves through collectivist-oriented behaviors (Kitayama et al., 1997; Sedikides et al., 2003).

In keeping with cultural differences in self-concept and self-perception, people from collectivist cultures are more likely than those from individualist cultures to have their mood affected by the situation (Oishi et al., 2004). In addition, when asked to remember a situation where they were at the center of a scene, those from an individualist culture were more likely to report the memory using the first-person pronoun (*I*), whereas those from a collectivist culture were more likely to use a third-person pronoun (*he* or *she*) when reporting the memory (Cohen & Gunz, 2002).

**PERSONALITY BY TOPOGRAPHY AND HISTORY: INDIVIDUALISM AND COLLECTIVISM WITHIN THE UNITED STATES**    Although the United States is an individualist country, individualism varies by region (Vandello & Cohen, 1999) (see Figure 11.7). The Deep South (perhaps because of its strong self-identification as a cultural region, its history of collective farming, and the prominence of religion) is the most collectivist. The states of the Southwest are also relatively collectivist; these states have a distinctive history and an influx of immigrants from Mexico, a collectivist country. In contrast, the Great Plains and Western mountain states are particularly individualistic, perhaps because of the "vast distances, sparse population, and harsh, unpredictable weather" in that part of the country (Shortridge, 1993, p. 1011), as well as the frontier value of individuality. Thus, although people may live in a country that falls on a particular point on a collectivist–individualist continuum, there are regional, as well as individual, differences. So, to the extent that experience shapes personality, Tina's and Gabe's different geographical locations during their childhood years may have contributed to their different approaches to life.

**FIGURE 11.7**  ## Individualism Versus Collectivism, by State

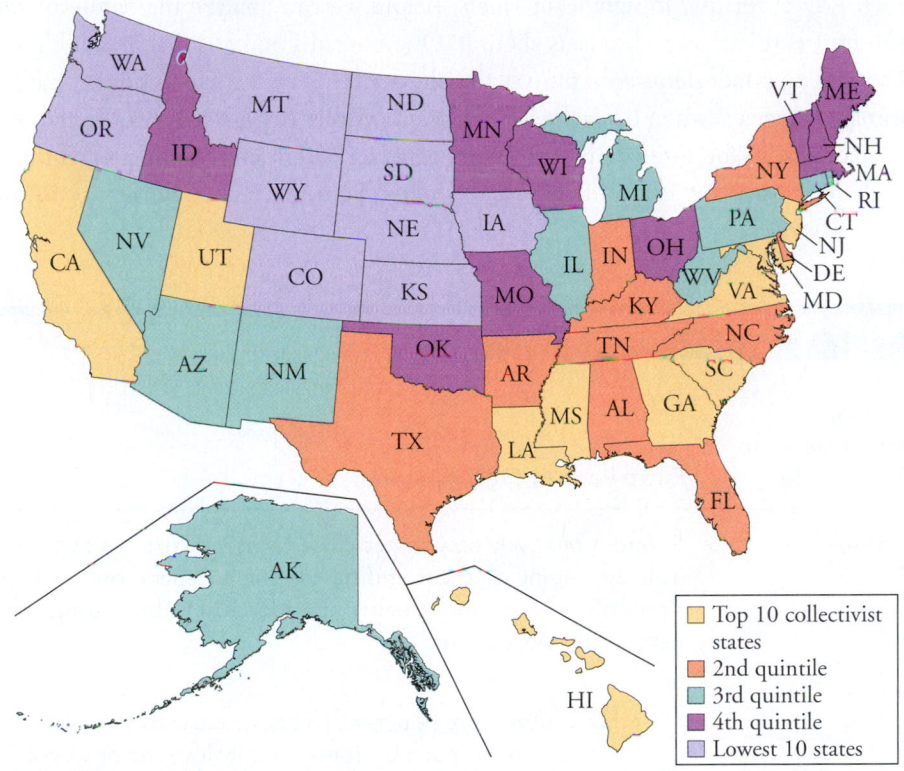

Even regions within a country differ on the individualism–collectivism dimension. Utah ranks as one of the top 10 states in collectivism, along with some states in the Deep South and the Southeast. Some of the Great Plains and Western mountain states are the most individualist, perhaps because of the "frontier" mentality and rugged geographic features.

☐ Top 10 collectivist states
☐ 2nd quintile
☐ 3rd quintile
☐ 4th quintile
☐ Lowest 10 states

# Understanding Cultural Differences in Personality: How Do Differences Arise?

How might culture produce personality differences? Hofstede and McCrae (2004) propose three possible explanations:

- The responses on personality tests reflect a social desirability bias; people fill out the tests in ways that they believe are consistent with their culture's values (but which may not necessarily be accurate representations of their personality). This explanation may also account for some of the personality changes among North Americans over time.

- Genetically influenced temperaments may differ across countries and geographic regions.

- Children in a given culture tend to be socialized according to that culture's values, and thus are more likely to exhibit personality traits valued by the culture. Note that this explanation would account for the personality changes evident among North Americans since the 1950s.

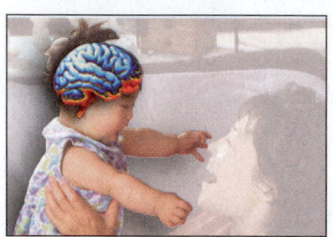

# LOOKING AT LEVELS

## Attachment

In our closest relationships, we develop deep attachments to other people. However, people differ in their *attachment style*—their way of relating to significant others. Before we can analyze the nature of attachment, we must consider some key facts about it. One crucial finding is that an adult's attachment style with a partner stems from the way that the adult interacted with his or her parent (or other primary caregiver) when he or she was an infant (Waller & Shaver, 1994). In those earliest of interactions, in the intimate choreography between parent and infant, a parent may be consistently responsive and empathic toward the infant, be neglectful or abusive, or be incon-

**TABLE 11.9   Secure, Anxious, and Avoidant Attachment Styles**

| Adult Attachment Style | Percentage of an American Sample Having This Style | First-Person Description |
|---|---|---|
| **Secure Attachment Style:** These adults seek closeness and interdependence in relationships and are not worried about the possibility of the relationship's ending. | 59% | "I find it relatively easy to get close to others and am comfortable depending on them and having them depend on me. I don't often worry about being abandoned or about someone getting too close to me." |
| **Anxious Attachment Style:** These adults want but simultaneously fear a close relationship. | 11% | "I find that others are reluctant to get as close as I would like. I often worry that my partner doesn't really love me or won't want to stay with me. I want to merge completely with another person, and this desire sometimes scares people away." |
| **Avoidant Attachment Style:** These adults are uncomfortable with intimacy and closeness, and hence structure their daily lives to avoid closeness (Tidwell et al., 1996) | 25% | "I am somewhat uncomfortable being close to others. I find it difficult to trust them completely, difficult to allow myself to depend on them. I am nervous when anyone gets too close, and often love partners want me to be more intimate than I feel comfortable being." |

sistent. According to Bowlby (1973), these interaction patterns between parent and infant mold an internal *working model* about relationships. The working model—which continues to operate throughout life—gives rise to beliefs and expectations about relationships and influences how relationship-related stimuli are perceived, remembered, and responded to. For instance, the working model leads a person to feel, react, and behave in particular ways when a romantic partner no longer seems 100% committed. The model leads a person to appraise the situation as no big deal, to ruminate about it, to become anxious, to have a "big talk" with the partner, or to pull away.

Hazan and Shaver (1987) developed three categories of adult attachment style: *secure, anxious*, and *avoidant* (see Table 11.9). Studies suggest that a majority of Americans have a secure style (Hazan & Shaver, 1987); other studies indicate that an anxious style is more common in Japan and Israel and an avoidant style in Germany (Shaver & Hazan, 1994).

The internal working models of these attachment styles are conceptualized as having two components, of which individuals can have high or low levels: *anxiety*, which is related to a *model of self*, involving beliefs that the individual is lovable and competent at relationships, and *avoidance*, which is related to a *model of other*, involving beliefs about other people's availability and responsiveness (Bartholomew & Horowitz, 1991). People differ in both components, as shown in Table 11.10, and an individual's levels of anxiety and avoidance determine which attachment style he or she will have.

Whereas those with a secure attachment have a high sense of self-worth *and* of the availability of others, those with an insecure attachment (the other three attachment styles resulting

**TABLE 11.10** **Attachment Styles That Reflect Different Levels of Anxiety (Model of Self) and Avoidance (Model of Other)**

| | | ANXIETY (and *model of self*) | |
|---|---|---|---|
| | | **Low** *(positive model of self)* | **High** *(negative model of self)* |
| **AVOIDANCE (and *model of other*)** | **Low** *(positive model of other)* | *Secure Attachment*<br>"It is easy for me to become emotionally close to others. I am comfortable depending on others and having others depend on me. I don't worry about being alone or having others not accept me." | *Preoccupied Attachment*<br>"I want to be completely emotionally intimate with others, but I often find that others are reluctant to get as close as I would like. I am uncomfortable being without close relationships, but I sometimes worry that others don't value me as much as I value them." |
| | **High** *(negative model of other)* | *Dismissive-Avoidant Attachment*<br>"I am comfortable without close emotional relationships. It is very important for me to feel independent and self-sufficient, and I prefer not to depend on others or have others depend on me." | *Fearful-Avoidant Attachment*<br>"I am uncomfortable getting close to others. I want emotionally close relationships, but I find it difficult to trust others completely or to depend on them. I worry that I will be hurt if I allow myself to become too close to others." |

from the two-component model) have a poor sense of self-worth, expect others to be unavailable, or both (Bretherton, 1991). Although the original classification of adult attachment styles included three categories (secure, anxious, and avoidant), the two-component model yields four because it divides avoidant attachment into two styles (Bartholomew, 1990; Bartholomew & Horowitz, 1991): One style is *dismissive-avoidant*, which is characterized by a positive model of self, but a negative model of other; this style is typical of people who avoid relationships because they lack a desire for them. The other style is *fearful-avoidant*, which is characterized by a negative model of both self and other and is typical of people who avoid relationships because they expect and fear rejection. Moreover, what was labeled *anxious attachment* in the three-category system is labeled *preoccupied attachment* in the two-component model.

We can best understand attachment styles—how they arise and exert their influence—from a levels-of-analysis perspective. As we noted, attachment style reflects events at the *level of the group*: It arises from interactions of caregivers and infants, and it affects adults' relationships with their partners. For example, infants who attend poor-quality day care, with few caregivers for many infants, are more likely to develop insecure attachments styles (Sagi et al., 2002). In childhood, consistent parental abuse or neglect is unlikely to engender a secure type of attachment (O'Conner et al., 2003). But our attachments styles are not fixed in stone: The relationships we have as adults can change our attachment style (Shaver & Hazan, 1994).

Moreover, just as research revealed cultural differences in attachment style using the three-category classification, so too with the two-component (four attachment styles) model. A large, 56-nation study found that secure attachment was not the most common type in all cultures (Schmitt et al., 2004): For example, in Japan, more people had preoccupied attachment than secure attachment; in Bolivia, Ethiopia, and Malaysia, more people had dismissive-avoidant attachment than secure attachment; and in Belgium and Indonesia, more people had fearful-avoidant attachment than secure attachment. In general, people from East and Southeast Asia, and from other collectivist cultures, had higher levels of preoccupied attachment than did people in individualist cultures.

At the *level of the person*, attachment style influences what you pay attention to and how you interpret what you perceive. For instance, people differ in how they process sensory information (Jerome & Liss, 2005) and how they characteristically respond to those stimuli. Paula Niedenthal and colleagues (2002) examined the effect of attachment style on adults' perception of specific types of stimuli—small changes in facial expressions: The results of their studies indicate that people with different attachment styles process such stimuli differently, although in ways consistent with each particular attachment style.

Also at the level of the person, attachment style appears to relate to how people manage their emotions. As the word implies, people with an avoidant attachment style tend to avoid emotional aspects about relationships. Consider these findings comparing avoidantly attached people to those with other attachment styles:

- They tend to require more time to remember sad and anxious occasions (Mikulincer & Orbach, 1995).
- They pay *less* attention to emotional events (Collins, 1996; Fraley & Shaver, 1997; Fraley et al., 2000).
- Although consciously denying that they feel distressed when remembering stressful family events, bodily reactions suggest that they do in fact feel anxiety and stress during the recollections (Dozier & Kobak, 1992).

- They encode less information when listening to someone speaking about relationship issues; however, they forget what they did remember at the same rate as nonavoidantly attached people (Fraley et al., 2000).

The type of attachment style also influences how people respond to the loss of a relationship: Those with an anxious attachment style are most likely to report distress, cognitive preoccupations, and anger and to use drugs or alcohol to cope; those with an avoidant style were most likely to exhibit self-reliance and distance themselves from the relationship. In contrast, those with a secure style used family and friends for support (Davis, Shaver, & Vernon, 2003).

Thus, attachment style influences a variety of events at the level of the person: sensory and perceptual processing, how emotions are managed, and how people respond to relationship-related stimuli.

At the *level of the brain*, psychologists have examined whether attachment style is related to facets of temperament. Meyer and colleagues (2005) examined the relationship between attachment style and BIS and BAS in adult women: People who had an easily activated BIS tended to have an anxious attachment style, whereas people who had an easily activated BAS tended not to have an avoidant attachment style. The women with a responsive BAS preferred to confront their partners (which is consistent with a preference for approach behaviors) when their relationship was strongly threatened, but not when the relationship was only mildly threatened. Women who had an avoidant attachment style preferred more distance—they were more likely than women with other styles to end the relationship or to become less responsive to their partner after their relationship was threatened. The association between BIS and insecure attachment has been supported by additional research (Muris & Meesters, 2002).

In addition, researchers have found that infants tend to develop an attachment style like their mother's (Siegel, 1999). For instance, if the mother has an anxious style, her child will likely have that style as well (van IJzendoorn, 1995). It could be that her own attachment style affects her moment-to-moment interactions with her infant, which leads to the development of a particular attachment style in her infant (Edelstein et al., 2004). Another possibility is that—as we saw for personality traits that have relatively high heritability—attachment styles may be (at least partly) heritable. Studies of adult twins suggest otherwise, however. A twin study of adult attachment styles found that unique environmental factors—rather than genetic factors—influence adult attachment styles the most (Brussoni et al., 2000). Another twin study confirms the minimal influence of genes: When adult twins were tested on six scales that measured different aspects of love styles in romantic relationships, little evidence of heritability of styles was found (Waller & Shaver, 1994). Twin studies with children found similar results (Bokhorst et al., 2003). As Plomin and his colleagues (1997, p. 205) put it, "Perhaps love *is* blind, at least from the DNA point of view." Even if this literally isn't true of love, at least attachment is blind from a DNA point of view.

Events at each level are not isolated from one another: It is primarily the caregiver's behavior with the infant (level of the group) that gives rise to the infant's—and with time, the adult's—internal working model of self and other (level of the person). Nevertheless, attachment style may be partly related to BAS and BIS activity (level of the brain). Furthermore, the infant's temperament (determined in part by biological factors) interacts with the caregiver's personality (and her own attachment style; Sagi et al., 1997). These factors affect each other, as well as the internal working model that the child develops and usually carries into adulthood. In turn, the adult's attachment style affects his or her relationships (level of the group). And adult relationships can change attachment style; events at the level of the group can change events at the level of the person.

To consider the interaction among events in more detail, let's examine a study by Shamir-Essakow and colleagues (2004), which focused on 103 behaviorally inhibited and uninhibited (level of the brain) preschool children who had secure or insecure attachments. They found that mothers of children who were inhibited *and* insecurely attached—in contrast to inhibited and securely attached—were less likely to be aware of their children's internal state or to validate their children's emotional experience. That is, they were not sensitive to their children (level of the group). These mothers of inhibited and insecurely attached children were more likely to be intrusive, not distinguishing their children's emotional state from their own. These mothers may be more ambivalent about their children's inhibited temperament (Rubin et al., 1995). In contrast, mothers of inhibited and securely attached children were more likely to try to put themselves in their children's shoes in order to understand their behavior, and so they were more able to identify their children's internal state and its cause. That is, they were more likely to view and accept their children as independent people, with their own minds. Underscoring the interactional nature of these events, interventions designed to train parents to become more sensitive to their infants (level of the group) lead to enhanced security of attachment in their infants (level of the person) (Bakermans-Kranenburg et al., 2003).

# Test Yourself

1. Firstborns, compared to later-borns, are usually
   a. more rebellious and impulsive.   c. more self-conscious.
   b. less open to new experiences.   d. less successful.
2. The general consensus of the results of research on social influences on personality is that
   a. social influences, such as family and friends, have little effect on personality.
   b. social influences are the most important aspect of personality development.
   c. social factors interact with biological and other factors in determining personality.
   d. personality development is genetically determined and therefore is not affected by social factors.

3. A consistent gender difference found by researchers is that
   a. females score higher on the trait of social connectedness.
   b. males score higher on the trait of social connectedness.
   c. females score higher on the trait of anger.
   d. There don't seem to be any reliable gender differences in personality.
4. The culture a person grows up in exerts a social influence on the person, but how important is this in determining his or her personality?
   a. Culture ultimately determines personality.
   b. Culture has a very small effect on personality.
   c. The type of culture, collectivist or individualist, can influence some aspects of personality.
   d. Current methods of assessing personality do not apply to more than one culture, so these types of comparisons are impossible.

# Answers

1.b  2.c  3.a  4.c

# Think It Through!

What are two possible explanations for regional personality differences between "mellow" Californians and "fast-paced" Northeasterners? (Hint: Genetic? Environmental?) How might you go about trying to determine whether either explanation is supported by research data? What type of study could you design, and what kinds of participants would you need? What would your hypothesis be—that is, what kind of results would you expect?

# REVIEW AND REMEMBER!

## Summary

### I. Personality: Historical Perspectives

**A.** People's motives, thoughts, and feelings are at the heart of Freud's psycho-dynamic theory, which focuses on three structures of personality (id, ego, and superego) and their dynamic relationships and three levels of awareness (unconscious, preconscious, and conscious), as well as sexual and aggressive drives, defense mechanisms, and psychosexual stages (oral, anal, phallic, latency, and genital).

**B.** According to Freud, when resolution of a psychosexual stage is incomplete, development is arrested, often creating a neurosis. Moreover, sexual and aggressive impulses can create anxiety, causing the use of defense mechanisms.

**C.** Neo-Freudians (such as Jung, Adler, and Horney) have added to or altered aspects of Freud's theory, generally rejecting his emphasis on sexual drives.

**D.** Maslow's and Rogers's humanistic theories also address motives, feelings, and the self, but they celebrate each person's uniqueness, stress positive qualities of human nature and free will, and emphasize self-actualization.

### II. What Exactly *Is* Personality?

**A.** Personality is a consistent set of behavioral, emotional, and cognitive tendencies that people display over time and across situations and that distinguish individuals from each other.

**B.** People do not behave in the same manner in all situations: The context, or situation, influences the way people behave, and people can influence the situation.

**C.** Some researchers have found that personality traits can be statistically grouped into five superfactors (extraversion, neuroticism, agreeableness, conscientiousness, and openness) or, according to Eysenck, three personality dimensions (extraversion, neuroticism, and psychoticism).

**D.** Personality can be measured by interviews, observation, inventories (such as Cattell's 16PF), and projective tests (such as the Rorschach test and the Thematic Apperception Test, or TAT). Inventories are the most commonly used method.

### III. Biology's Influences on Personality

**A.** Innate inclinations, often referred to as temperament, include activity, sociability, emotionality, and impulsivity. Two well-studied temperaments are shyness and sensation seeking.

## Your Notes

*I.*

*A. Structure of personality like an iceberg—parts beneath the surface*

*B.*

*C.*

*D.*

*II.*

*A.*

*B.*

*C. OCEAN = Big 5*
*PEN = Eysenck's 3 dimensions*

*D.*

*III.*

*A.*

**B.** Gray proposed two basic biological systems: the behavioral activation system (BAS) and the behavioral inhibition system (BIS). These systems underlie certain personality traits and dimensions.

*B.*

**C.** Eysenck proposed that each of his three personality dimensions (extraversion, neuroticism, and psychoticism) has a corresponding biological basis. Aspects of this theory have been supported by neuroimaging and other biological research.

*C. Extraverts have greater response to reward. Introverts have greater response to punishment.*

**D.** Cloninger proposed four biologically based personality dimensions, each with a distinct biological system: reward dependence, harm avoidance, novelty seeking, and persistence.

*D.*

**E.** According to Zuckerman, there are five biologically based personality dimensions: sociability, neuroticism-anxiety, impulsive sensation seeking, activity, and aggression-hostility.

*E.*

**F.** Some psychologists and behavioral geneticists estimate that as much as 50% of the variation in personality is inherited, although some traits appear to be more heritable than others.

*F.*

**G.** Differences in biology, such as in emotional arousability, can affect thoughts, feelings, motivations, and behaviors and can make people more or less prone to conditioned emotional responses and shyness.

*G.*

## IV. Learning and the Cognitive Elements of Personality

*IV.*

**A.** The influence of learning on personality occurs through classical and operant conditioning as well as through observational learning.

*A.*

**B.** The sociocognitive view of personality focuses on the effects of expectancies on people's thoughts, feelings, and behaviors: What we expect to happen will influence our personality development.

*B.*

**C.** Personality differences related to expectancies are exhibited in our locus of control (the source we perceive as exerting control over life events) and our self-efficacy (the sense that we have the ability to follow through and produce the behaviors we would like to perform).

*C.*

## V. Sociocultural Influences on Personality

*V.*

**A.** Birth order, along with other moderating factors, such as the number of children in a family and the level of conflict between parents and children, can influence openness to experience and other aspects of personality.

*A.*

**B.** Although there are a few broad personality differences between women and men (in social connectedness versus individuality and in high versus low neuroticism), in general, such differences tend to be small, and it is not clear whether they are due to biological or sociocultural factors. Sociocultural explanations for these differences include social role theory, identification with the primary caretaker, and differences in power. Context may predict personality better than does sex or gender.

*B.*

**C.** Personality differences have also been found between people raised in cultures that are collectivist as opposed to individualist, with people in each type of culture tending to have personality traits that are more valued in their culture.

*C. Individualist—more open & extraverted*
*Collectivist—more agreeable*

**D.** Attachment is influenced by working models of the self and of other people; these models develop dynamically through interactions with caregivers, through temperament, and through the specific ways that children and adults perceive and process the world around them.

NOTE: Once you feel that you understand the material in this chapter, visit the book's Web site at www.ablongman.com/kosslyn3e to test your knowledge with additional study questions.

## Key Terms

activity, p. 497
archetype, p. 486
Big Five, p. 492
castration anxiety, p. 484
defense mechanism, p. 485
ego, p. 483
emotionality, p. 497
expectancies, p. 510
flow, p. 488
id, p. 483
impulsivity, p. 497
inferiority complex, p. 486

locus of control, p. 511
Minnesota Multiphasic Personality Inventory-2 (MMPI-2), p. 495
neurosis, p. 484
personality, p. 482
personality inventory, p. 494
personality trait, p. 489
projective test, p. 495
psychological determinism, p. 482
psychosexual stages, p. 484
reciprocal determinism, p. 512
repression, p. 485

Rorschach test, p. 495
self-actualization, p. 487
self-efficacy, p. 511
sociability, p. 497
social desirability, p. 494
superego, p. 483
temperament, p. 497
Thematic Apperception Test (TAT), p. 496
unconditional positive regard, p. 488

# CHAPTER 12

# PSYCHOLOGY OVER THE LIFE SPAN: GROWING UP, GROWING OLDER, GROWING WISER'

ome of his classmates called him "Spielbug." Girls thought he was nerdy and unattractive. His father, Arnold, a pioneer in the use of computers in engineering, was hardly ever around and, to make matters worse, frequently uprooted his family, moving from Ohio to New Jersey, to Arizona, and finally to Northern California. Steven Spielberg was a perpetual new kid on the block. He was also, by all accounts, an unusual child, both in his appearance (he had a large head and protruding ears) and in his fearful and awkward behavior (McBride, 1999). Spielberg himself has said that he "felt like an alien" throughout his childhood. He desperately wanted to be accepted, but didn't fit in. So, at age 12, he began making films, "little 8mm things. I did it to find something that, for me, could be permanent" (quoted in R. Sullivan, 1999, p. 66). Spielberg continued to make movies as a teenager, often casting his three sisters in roles. He discovered that making movies was one way to win his peers' acceptance, as well as some small measure of power—for he sometimes induced his worst enemies to appear in his films.

When he was 16, Spielberg's parents divorced, and Spielberg blamed his father's constant traveling for the breakup. His unhappiness only deepened when his father remarried, taking for his second wife a woman Spielberg couldn't stand. At the same time that he withdrew from his father, Spielberg continued to have a close relationship with his mother, Leah, a concert pianist and artist. The split with his father lasted some 15 years.

In many ways, Spielberg's films, like the rest of his life, are shaped by his childhood. Spielberg himself has said about E.T., *The Extra-Terrestrial*, "The whole movie is really about divorce. . . . Henry's [the main character's] ambition to find a father by bringing E.T. into his life to fill some black hole—that was my struggle to find somebody to replace the dad who I felt had abandoned me" (R. Sullivan, 1999, p. 68). Many of Spielberg's other films feature children who are separated from their parents (such as the girl in *Poltergeist* and the boy in *Close Encounters of the Third Kind*). And *Back to the Future* might represent his longings to change the past, if only he could. Only when he turned 40 did he turn to adult contexts. As he matured, Spielberg's identification with oppressed people in general (not just oppressed children) led him to make movies such as *The Color Purple, Schindler's List*, and *Amistad*.

Steven Spielberg married and had a child, but eventually divorced his first wife, actress Amy Irving. His own experiences made him extremely sensitive to the effect of the divorce on his son, Max, and he made every attempt to ensure that Max did not feel abandoned. When he married again, he became deeply involved with his family (which includes seven children, some of them adopted). There was a happy development in the previous generation's father–son relationship as well: Arnold became a well-loved grandfather and a regular presence in the Spielberg household.

Spielberg's journey is one version of the universal story of human development: A skinny kid beset by fears and with few friends becomes one of the most powerful figures in the global entertainment industry; from a fragmented family life develops a man's resolve to make the best possible life for his own family; across generations, a father and a son come to like each other, now as a grandfather and a father, after 15 years of estrangement. *Developmental psychologists* study exactly these sorts of events in our lives—the fascinating and varied process of human development over the life span. In this chapter, we begin by considering prenatal development and the newborn, and we see that even here genes and environment are intimately intertwined. We next turn to infancy and childhood and observe the interplay between maturation and experience in shaping a child's physical, mental, emotional, and social development. Then we consider adolescence, a crucial time in development, bridging childhood and adulthood. And finally, we discuss adulthood and aging, gaining insights that help us understand how Arnold Spielberg could develop from a less-than-optimal father into a terrific grandfather.

# IN THE BEGINNING:
## From Conception to Birth

Steven Spielberg has been celebrated as one of the most successful moviemakers of all time. He just seemed to have a natural bent for making movies (he never attended film school). Where did his talent come from? In this section, we begin at the beginning and think about the foundations of our skills and abilities.

## Prenatal Development: Nature and Nurture From the Start

For each of us, life began with the meeting of two cells, a sperm and an egg (or *ovum*, which in Latin means "egg"). These specialized cells are sex cells, or *gametes*. The sperm penetrates the egg, and the genetic material of the sperm melds with that of the ovum. The ovum is not a passive partner in this dance of life; the sperm is drawn to the egg by chemical reactions on the surface of the egg. And when a sperm has been accepted within the egg, other reactions prevent additional sperm from penetrating. The ovum is a supercell, the largest in the human body. Even so, it is barely the size of a pinprick, and sperm are much smaller (about 1/500 of an inch). But despite their small sizes, within the ovum and sperm reside all the machinery necessary to create a new life. And, even at this earliest stage of development, *genes* (*nature*) and the *environment* (*nurture*) are intimately intertwined.

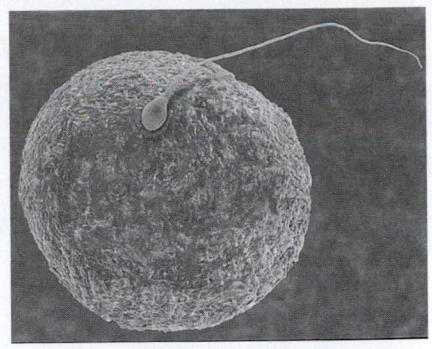

At the moment of conception, a sperm penetrates an ovum. The egg, however, is not a passive recipient; by changing its surface properties, it actively regulates the behavior of the sperm.

## From Zygote to Birth: Getting a Start in Life

The genetic heritage of every normal human being is 23 pairs of chromosomes, one member of each pair coming from an egg and the other from a sperm. A *chromosome* is a strand of DNA (*deoxyribonucleic acid*) in the nucleus of the cell. A molecule of DNA is shaped like a twisted ladder—the famous double helix—in which the "rungs" are formed by the bonds between pairs of chemicals. Each *gene* on the chromosome is a series of particular rungs (see Chapter 3). All cells in the human body except the gametes (eggs and sperm) contain all 23 pairs of chromosomes; each gamete contains only a single member of each chromosome pair. In an egg, one of these 23 is a chromosome known as X; in a sperm, the corresponding chromosome is either an X chromosome or a shorter one called a Y chromosome.

**IN THE BEGINNING**  Much of early development is determined by **maturation**, the process that produces genetically programmed changes with increasing age. But from the very start, genes and the environment interact. Although the genes in both the sperm and the egg have a major impact on the characteristics of the person who will eventually develop, the environment plays a crucial role in whether the sperm ever reaches the egg. Sperm actually "surf" on subtle muscle contractions in the uterus; these waves usually move in the correct direction in fertile women, but they either move in the wrong direction or are weak in infertile women (Kunz et al., 1997; Lyons & Levi, 1994). In addition, the fluid in the uterus must be the right consistency and must have the right chemical composition for the sperm to complete their journey (Mori et al., 1998; Shibahara et al., 1995; Singh, 1995).

The fertilization of the egg by the sperm creates a cell called a **zygote**, in which the chromosomes from the egg and from the sperm pair up so that the zygote contains the full complement of 23 pairs. If the sperm contributes an X chromosome, the offspring will be female (XX); if Y, male (XY). The Y chromosome contains a gene (the *SRY gene*, for "sex-determining region of the Y chromosome") that produces a chemical substance that ultimately causes the zygote to develop into a male; if this substance is not present, genes on the X chromosome will produce other substances that cause the baby to be female (Goodfellow & Lovell-Badge, 1993; Hawkins, 1994).

**DANCE OF THE CHROMOSOMES**  The two members of each pair of chromosomes (other than the XY pair in males) are similar—but they are not identical. For example, the gene for the shape of your earlobes is on the same spot on both chromosomes, but because of its particular chemical composition, the gene on one chromosome may code for an attached earlobe and the gene on the other for an unattached earlobe. The gametes are formed from specialized cells that, while themselves containing the full 23 pairs, in the course of division produce cells with half that number, with only one member of each pair. So, because the members of each pair are not identical, the genetic contents of the resulting gametes are not all the same. And there's another wrinkle, which further contributes to our wonderful human variety: In the course of cell division, the chromosomal decks of cards are shuffled so that pieces of the chromosomes in each pair in the parent cell are exchanged, as shown in

Maturation: The developmental process that produces genetically programmed changes with increasing age.

Zygote: A fertilized ovum (egg).

# FIGURE 12.1 The Long Road to a Zygote

The chromosomes in eggs and sperm are not simply copies of those of the parent, but rather unique combinations of the material in the two chromosomes in each pair of the parent's chromosomes. The sperm and egg combine to form the basis of a unique individual (or individuals, in the case of identical twins).

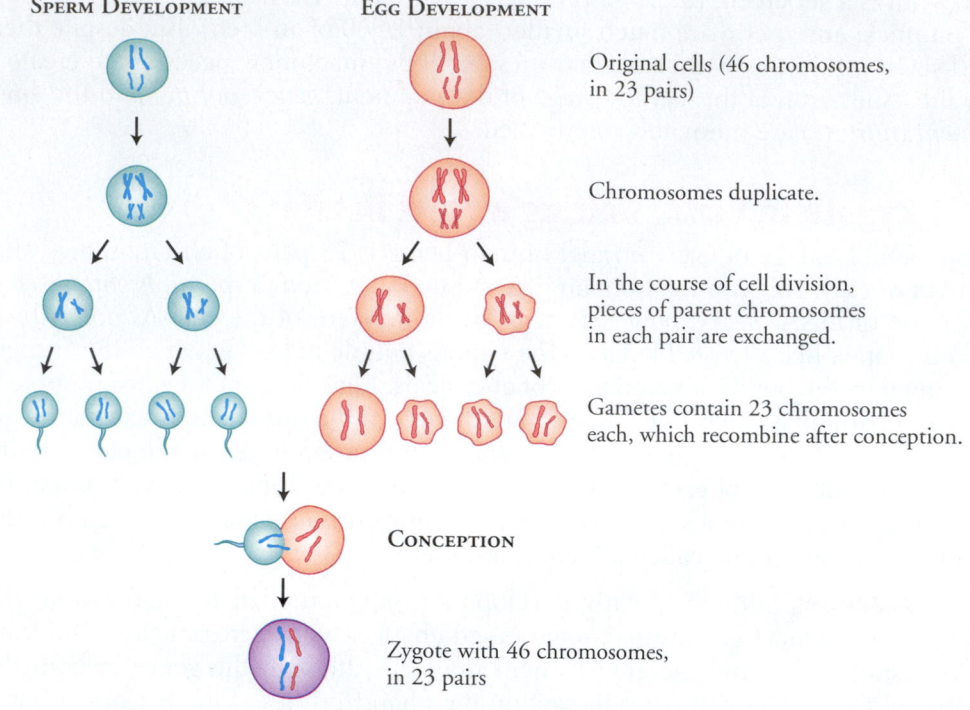

**SPERM DEVELOPMENT**      **EGG DEVELOPMENT**

Original cells (46 chromosomes, in 23 pairs)

Chromosomes duplicate.

In the course of cell division, pieces of parent chromosomes in each pair are exchanged.

Gametes contain 23 chromosomes each, which recombine after conception.

**CONCEPTION**

Zygote with 46 chromosomes, in 23 pairs

---

Figure 12.1, to form new combinations of genes. Each zygote thus consists of a unique combination of genes. In fact, in theory, each human couple can produce some 70 trillion genetically different children! The chance of your getting the particular combination of genes you received is roughly the same as the probability that a meteor will hit a particular 5-foot-by-5-foot square patch of land on the surface of the Earth!

**DIVISION AND DIFFERENTIATION**   Once formed, the zygote begins to divide. The production of certain hormones causes genes to turn on and off in a specific sequence, guiding the zygote's development (Brown, 1999; as discussed in Chapter 3, genes produce specific proteins only when they are "turned on"). Soon a cluster of cells has developed. After 3 days, about 60–70 cells have formed and organized themselves into a hollow sphere called a *blastocyst*. This sphere proceeds through an orderly progression, first forming into a tube, then developing features that in early stages look much like those of relatively primitive animals, then more complex ones.

Human development in the womb is divided into *trimesters*, three equal periods of 3 months each. The first trimester is divided into three stages: The developing baby starts off as a zygote, becomes an **embryo** when the major axis of the body is present (about 2 weeks after conception), and then becomes a **fetus** when all major body structures are present (about 8 weeks after conception; thereafter, the developing baby is called a fetus until he or she is born). At the end of the second trimester, the great bulk of the neurons each individual possesses are in place (Nowakowski, 1987; Rakic, 1975; Rodier, 1980), but they are not completely fixed; researchers have found that new neurons can be produced even in adult brains (Gould et al., 1999).

**Embryo:** A developing baby from the point where the major axis of the body is present until all major structures are present, spanning from about 2 weeks to 8 weeks after conception.

**Fetus:** A developing baby during the final phase of development in the womb, from about 8 weeks after conception until birth.

The path from zygote to birth is not always smooth. Perhaps surprisingly, about half of all fertilized eggs contain some kind of abnormality in their chromosomes. Most of these eggs are spontaneously aborted (in fact, about 30% of zygotes don't even make it to the embryo phase), and more male embryos than female embryos are aborted (Vatten & Skjaeaerven, 2004)—but even so, about 1 in 250 babies is born with an abnormality that is obvious (for example, he or she may not respond appropriately to light or loud noises), and probably more have abnormalities that are not obvious (such as subtle defects in particular brain areas, which will become evident only later in life; Plomin et al., 1997; Sadler, 1995).

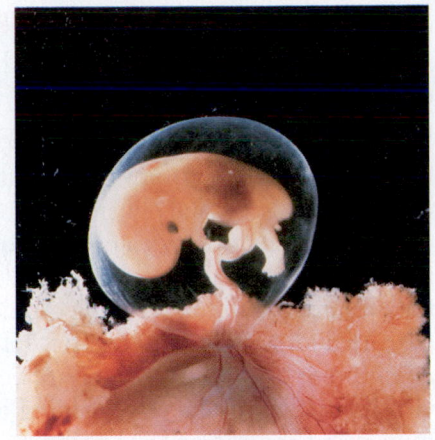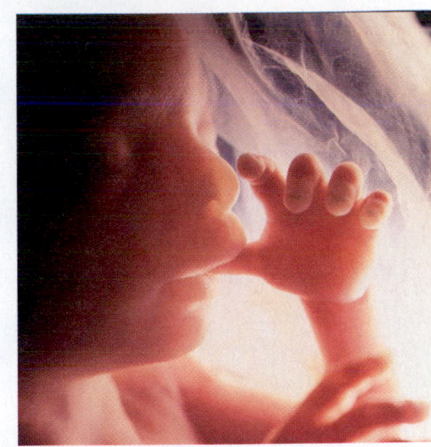

The developing fetus at 8 weeks (left) and 20 weeks (right).

## Learning and Behavior in the Womb

A popular—and misleading—image shows the fetus floating peacefully asleep in the womb. But in truth, the fetus is active nearly from the start, at first with automatic movements, such as the heart beating, and then with large-scale coordinated behaviors. As the fetus develops, the heart rate slows down (but becomes more variable), the fetus moves less often but more vigorously when it does stir, and the heart rate and movement patterns become coordinated. Some researchers have even reported sex differences in behavior in the womb, with male fetuses more active than females (Almli et al., 2001; DiPietro et al., 1996; ). After 20–25 weeks of gestation, the fetus is sensitive to both sound and light (Nilsson & Hamberger, 1990; Pujol et al., 1990). How do we know this? Because if a fetus is examined, as is sometimes medically necessary, by a special light-emitting instrument called a *fetoscope*, it will actually move its hands to shield its eyes. As the fetus develops, its movements become increasingly coordinated, and by 28 weeks, it responds to external stimulation. A bit later, its heart rate can change if the mother is startled (Kisilevsky & Low, 1998; DiPietro et al., 1996), and sometime between 25 and 34 weeks, a fetus can detect human speech (Cheour-Luhtanen et al., 1996; Zimmer et al., 1993). In fact, researchers have found that fetuses older than 33 weeks even pay attention to music (Kisilevsky et al., 2004).

In addition, there is evidence that fetuses can learn. In a classic study (DeCasper & Fifer, 1980), pregnant women read the story *The Cat in the Hat* aloud twice each day during the 6 weeks before their babies were born. A few hours after birth, the babies were tested. The researchers put earphones on the babies' little heads and a special pacifier-like device in their mouths. Sucking faster or slower on this device allowed the infants to hear either their mother's voice or another woman's voice reading the story. The infants sucked at the speed that produced their own mother's voice. Perhaps even more impressive, the researchers also gave the infants the opportunity to choose between hearing their mother read *The Cat in the Hat* or another story—and the infants preferred the story their mother had read aloud before they were born!

Moreover, characteristics of the fetus predict those of the child after birth. For example, fetuses that had more variable heart rates later developed into more linguistically able toddlers and demonstrated more sophisticated forms of symbolic play (Bornstein et al., 2002).

## Teratogens: Negative Environment Events

A **teratogen** is an external agent, such as a chemical, virus, or type of radiation, that can cause damage to the zygote, embryo, or fetus. Because of events at different stages in the course of development, different organs are vulnerable to teratogens at different times.

**MATERNAL ILLNESS** Unfortunately, the central nervous system is vulnerable at virtually every phase of prenatal development. For example, the development of the brain can be disrupted if the mother catches a virus, such as chicken pox or rubella (3-day German measles); more than half the babies born to mothers who contract rubella will be mentally retarded if the developing child is in the embryonic period at the onset of the disease. In addition, a mother who is HIV-positive can pass the virus on to the baby during gestation or birth (but only about one third of these babies contract the virus). The HIV virus causes brain damage, leading to problems in concentration, attention, memory, movement control, and the ability to reason (Clifford, 2000; Grant et al., 1999).

**ALCOHOL AND DRUGS** Another potential teratogen is alcohol, which can damage a woman's eggs before fertilization (Kaufman, 1997) as well as affect the developing baby throughout pregnancy, starting with the embryo phase. If the mother drinks enough alcohol during pregnancy, the baby may be born with *fetal alcohol syndrome*; part of this syndrome is mental retardation (Streissguth et al., 1989, 1999; see Chapter 9). If a mother consumes any alcohol during pregnancy, research suggests that she should take antioxidants, such as vitamins C and E, which may reduce the damage to the fetus (Cohen-Kerem & Koren, 2003). In addition, using heroin or cocaine during pregnancy can cause a host of problems: physical defects (Singer et al., 2002b), irritability, and sleep and attentional problems in the newborn (Fox, 1994; J. M. Miller et al., 1995; Vogel, 1997). Although prenatal exposure to cocaine may have only subtle effects in infancy (such as slowed language development; Lester et al., 1998), such exposure may have long-lasting consequences—some of which may become more marked in subsequent years (Chapman, 2000; Lester, 2000; Singer et al., 2002a). In addition, the problem is not restricted to mothers. Certain drugs (both prescription and illegal, such as cocaine) can affect the father's sperm and thereby affect the growing fetus and child (Yazigi et al., 1991).

**CAFFEINE AND SMOKING** Major diseases and strong drugs are not the only threats to healthy prenatal development. Excessive amounts of caffeine (three cups of coffee a day, according to one study) can lead to miscarriage or low birth weight, irritability, and other symptoms (Eskenazi, 1993; Eskenazi et al., 1999). Smoking during pregnancy affects both mother and fetus; it is correlated with higher rates of miscarriage, lower birth weights, smaller head size, stillbirth, and infant mortality, and it can cause attentional difficulties in the infant (Cornelius & Day, 2000; Floyd et al., 1993; Fried & Makin, 1987; Fried & Watkinson, 2000). Smoking may even damage the fetus's genes (de la Chica et al., 2005). A mother's smoking also significantly increases the chance that her baby will die from *sudden infant death syndrome* (SIDS; Pollack, 2001). Smoking during pregnancy alters the way the infant's autonomic nervous system operates, which may contribute to SIDS (Browne et al., 2000).

**DIET AND POLLUTION** A mother's poor diet can lead her infant to have fewer brain cells than normal (Morgane et al., 1993) and can increase the risk that the child will develop a host of psychological disorders—including antisocial personality disorder (Neugebauer et al., 1999) and schizophrenia (Susser et al., 1996). (Both of these disorders will be discussed in detail in Chapter 14.) In addition, the lack of even a single important vitamin or mineral can have significant effects. For example, insufficient folic acid (a type of vitamin B) can disrupt the early development of the neural tube

**Teratogen:** Any external agent, such as a chemical, virus, or type of radiation, that can cause damage to the zygote, embryo, or fetus.

that gives rise to the brain and spinal cord (Nevid et al., 1998), and thereby cause birth defects. Most important, if the mother does not have enough folic acid, the infant can be born without the top of the skull or with *spina bifida*, which occurs when the spine does not close properly. Spina bifida requires immediate surgery and can lead to problems in bladder and bowel control (and can even prove fatal). Folic acid is also essential for producing the iron-containing protein needed to form red blood cells. (However, there can be too much of a good thing: Folic acid supplements are associated with a higher incidence of fraternal twins [Källén, 2004].)

Furthermore, if the mother eats fish with high levels of methylmercury, this can cause the infant to be born deaf or to have visual problems; it may also impair auditory processing (Murata et al., 1999). Moreover, other environmental pollutants as well as ionizing radiation can have effects ranging from birth defects and cancer to behavioral difficulties (such as in paying attention). And, in other animals at least, these effects can be passed on to the third generation, to the offspring of the offspring (Friedler, 1996).

**MATERNAL STRESSORS**   The fetus is exquisitely sensitive to the mother's stress level. For example, when a pregnant woman takes a mildly stressful cognitive test (the Stroop color-word test, in which a person must ignore the colors named by words when naming the colors of the ink used to print them), the fetus stops moving, and its heart rate becomes more variable (DiPietro et al., 2003). Given this sensitivity, we should not be surprised that stressors in the mother's life can endanger the developing fetus. When the stress is severe enough, infants may subsequently experience attentional difficulties, be unusually anxious, and exhibit unusual social behavior (Weinstock, 1997). In fact, fetuses with mothers of lower socioeconomic status, who are often more stressed than those of higher socioeconomic status, move less often and less vigorously and show other differences from fetuses whose mothers are better-off (Pressman et al., 1998). There are several biological reasons for these effects: When the mother is stressed, more of her blood flows to parts of the body affected by the fight-or-flight response (such as the limbs and heart), and less flows to the uterus. She produces hormones such as cortisol, which slows down the operation of genes that guide prenatal development of the brain, suppressing brain growth (Brown, 1999). There is evidence that the babies born to stressed mothers have smaller heads than those born to unstressed mothers, which may be related to the poorer behavioral functioning scores observed for such babies (Lou et al., 1994). That said, you shouldn't despair about the fact that life often presents stress: There's evidence that *mild* stress may actually be good for the developing fetus (DiPietro, 2004).

Figure 12.2 (on p. 536) illustrates the times during gestation when particular organs are especially vulnerable.

A particularly powerful example of interactions among events at the different levels of analysis is the fact that social interactions with friends and family can lead to healthier babies being born to stressed mothers (McLean et al., 1993). Social support presumably helps to reduce the mother's stress, which in turn keeps her from the fight-or-flight state and its accompanying unfortunate consequences for the developing baby.

## Positive Environmental Events: The Earliest Head Start

The previous paragraphs might seem to suggest that our species would be better off if maturation alone controlled development. But environmental effects are not all bad, and some prenatal experiences help the fetus. For example, researchers found that mothers who ate chocolate every day during pregnancy later rated their 6-month-old babies as having more positive temperaments than did mothers who did not eat chocolate so regularly (Räikkönen et al., 2004). However, this may say more about the effects of the candy on the mother than on her infant! Other findings show more conclusively that the prenatal environment can play a positive role in development. Consider the following study by Lafuente and colleagues (1997).

FIGURE 12.2 **Vulnerability to Teratogens of Different Organs During Fetal Development**

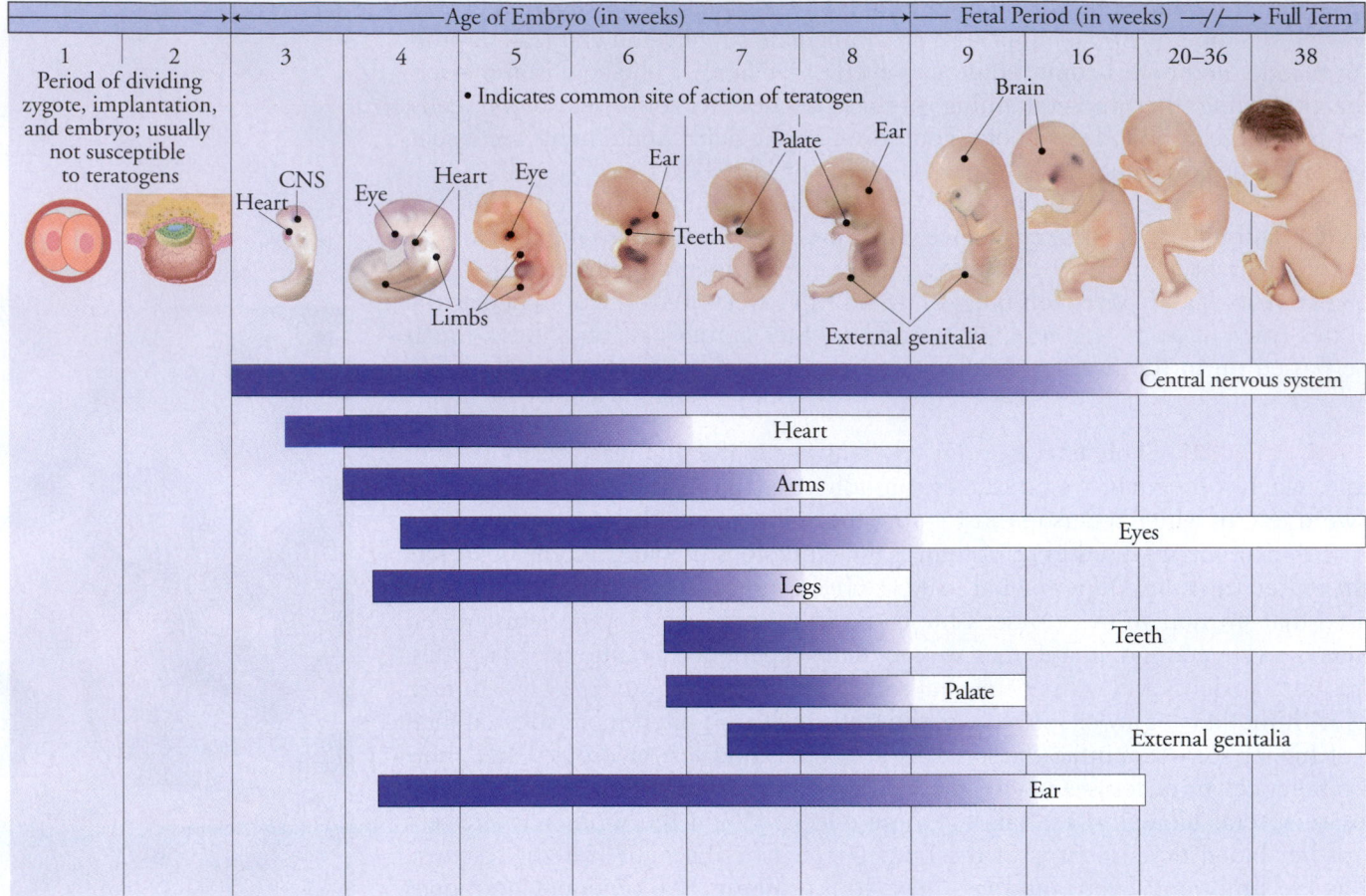

Various substances and events can disrupt development during gestation, but particular organs are especially vulnerable at different times. Dark portions of the bars indicate highly vulnerable periods; light portions indicate less vulnerable periods.

# UNDERSTANDING RESEARCH

## Stimulating the Unborn

**QUESTION:** Can playing music to an unborn child enhance development during infancy?

**ALTERNATIVES:** (1) Playing music to a fetus enhances development during infancy. (2) Playing music to a fetus impairs development during infancy. (3) Playing music to a fetus does not affect development during infancy.

**LOGIC:** If playing music to a fetus enhances subsequent development, then infants who heard music should later score higher on standard measures of cognitive and motor function than infants who did not hear music.

**METHOD:** Each of 172 pregnant women was randomly assigned to an experimental or a control group. The participants in the experimental group were given a waistband with a tape recorder and small speakers, which they used to play tapes of violin music for a total of about 70 hours (on average), starting at about 28 weeks after conception and continuing until the birth of the baby. The researchers then tracked the development of the babies during their first 6 months of life. The pregnant women in the control group did not play music to their fetuses.

**RESULTS:** The infants of mothers in the experimental group were more advanced than those of mothers in the control group; for example, they had better motor control and better vocal abilities of the sort that precede language.

**INFERENCES:** Playing music to a fetus (and perhaps providing other forms of stimulation) can enhance subsequent development. Steven Spielberg's mother played the piano frequently while she was pregnant. Could these prenatal concerts have had long-term positive effects on him? (Note that this study differs in its design and conclusion from those on the Mozart effect, mentioned in Chapter 9, in which music is played for brief periods to adults, who are then tested on aspects of IQ.)

## THINK CRITICALLY!

The mothers presumably heard the music along with their fetuses. Is it possible that the positive effects of the music on the infant arose because the mother was affected by the music? Perhaps it made her more relaxed, and thus less prone to the effects of stressors. Or perhaps the music made the mother more tolerant of the discomforts of late pregnancy, and thus more responsive to the infant—and that is what was responsible for the infant's advanced development. Can you think of a way to rule out these explanations for the effects of the music? Can you think of ways to test them directly?

# The Newborn: A Work in Progress

The human brain is not fully developed at birth, perhaps because the baby's head would not fit through the birth canal if he or she had a full-size adult brain. Much human brain development continues after birth (Johnson, 2001), and thus the newborn's abilities to think, feel, and behave differ from those of older children and adults. For example, newborns cannot be classically conditioned to associate a tone with an air puff that causes them to blink (Naito & Lipsitt, 1969; Sommer & Ling, 1970); in the rat, researchers have shown that this ability emerges only after key parts of the cerebellum have matured during infancy (Freeman & Nicholson, 2001; Rush et al., 2001).

Nevertheless, although the typical infant may seem thoroughly incompetent—capable of eating, sleeping, cooing, crying, drooling, and not much else—such an assessment is off the mark. A baby is not a blank slate, waiting for learning or maturity to descend. On the contrary, babies come equipped with a surprising range of abilities and capacities.

 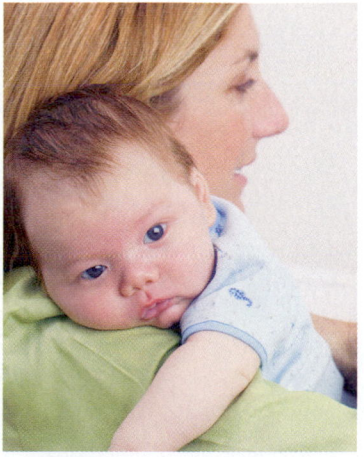

In many ways, the human infant compares unfavorably with the young of some other species. A kitten is able to walk on its own and explore its environment at only 6 weeks, an age when the human infant has no hope of even crawling.

## Sensory Capacities

Even at the earliest phases of development, babies have the beginnings of sophisticated sensory capabilities. They are born sensitive to the range of frequencies of women's voices (Hauser, 1996) and have a relatively sensitive sense of smell. Even babies who are fed by bottle prefer the odor of a woman who is breast-feeding another infant to that of a woman who is not breast-feeding (Porter et al., 1992).

Newborns also prefer to look at normal faces rather than faces with scrambled features, but this preference turns out to be part of a more general one for visual patterns that have more elements in the upper half than in the lower half (Cassia et al., 2004; Turati, 2004). Only with time do infants come to process faces like adults do (de Haan et al., 2002). Moreover, 2-day-old infants prefer to look at attractive faces (as judged by adults) than at unattractive faces (Slater et al., 2000).

In addition, 2-day-old infants can learn to pair information coming from different senses, such as vision and hearing. For example, Slater and colleagues (1997) showed such infants two visual stimuli, which differed in both color and orientation; at the same time as they presented one of the stimuli, they also presented a distinctive sound. They then switched the pairings and found that the infants paid more attention to the new combinations. These results showed that even 2-day-old infants can put visual and auditory stimuli together; if they couldn't, they wouldn't have noticed the changed pairings.

## Reflexes

Infants also come equipped with a wide range of reflexes, the most important of which are summarized in Table 12.1. As you learned in Chapter 3, a *reflex* is an automatic response to an event, an action that does not require thought. Some of the reflexes shown by infants, such as sucking, have obvious survival value, and some, such as the *Moro reflex* (in which the startled baby throws its arms wide, as if to grab hold of someone), may have had survival value for our ancestors. Other reflexes, such as the *Babinski reflex* (in which the baby's big toe flexes while the other toes fan out when the sole of his or her foot is stroked), are less obviously useful.

Some reflexes evolve with time. For example, 5- to 6-month-olds blink when they see a picture of a looming object, which appears to be moving toward them. At this age, the infants blink when the image reaches a certain size. In contrast, 6- to 7-month-old infants blink in preparation for the object's actually hitting them—which requires them to take into account not just the size of the image, but also the speed with which that size changes (Kayed & van der Meer, 2000).

Curiously, many of the reflexes that babies have at birth disappear after a while. Some of these reflexes appear to be simpler versions of later behaviors, such as walking or swimming. Should we try to preserve these reflexes? It has been shown, for example, that the stepping reflex can be retained longer if the baby's leg muscles are exercised and become stronger (the reflex appears to disappear in part because the baby gains weight and the legs can no longer support the body; Thelen, 1983, 1995). However, infants who walk earlier do not walk *better* than infants who walk later.

## Temperament: Instant Personality

A friend describing the birth of his second son expressed amazement as he realized, when handed the child immediately after birth, that the infant was *already different* from his first son, calmer and steadier. Our friend should not have been surprised. From their earliest hours, babies show the makings of individual personalities. They

TABLE 12.1 **Major Reflexes Present at Birth**

Stepping

Rooting

Moro (startle)

| Reflex | Stimulus | Response | Duration (approx.) |
|---|---|---|---|
| Withdrawal | Sharp stimulus to sole of foot | Leg flexes | Weakens after 10 days of age |
| Stepping | Held upright over flat surface | Stepping movements | Until about 2 months of age |
| Sucking | Finger in mouth | Sucking | Until about 3 months of age |
| Rooting | Stroking cheek lightly | Turns head toward stimulus, starts trying to suck | Until about 3 or 4 months of age |
| Palmar grasp | Pressing the palm | Grasps object pressing the palm | Until about 4 months of age |
| Moro (startle) | Sudden loud sound | Throws apart arms and extends legs, then brings arms together, cries | Until 5 months of age |
| Swimming | Face-down in water | Kicks and paddles in water | Until about 6 months of age |
| Tonic neck | Head turned to one side | One arm straightens while other bends, and one knee bends (resembling a "fencing" position) | Until 7 months of age |
| Plantar | Pressing the ball of the foot | All toes curl under | Until about 1 year of age |
| Babinski | Stroking sole of the foot | Big toe flexes, other toes fan out | Until about 1 year of age |
| Eye blink | Bright light in eyes | Eyes close | Life |

demonstrate differences in *temperament*, in their innate inclinations to engage in a certain style of behavior (see Chapter 11). Some babies may be inclined toward "approach," others toward "withdrawal" (Thomas & Chess, 1996). Infants who tend to show an approach response generally react positively to new situations or stimuli, such as a new food, toy, person, or place. Infants who are inclined to show a withdrawal response typically react negatively to new situations or stimuli, by crying, fussing, or otherwise indicating their discomfort (Chess & Thomas, 1987). Some babies are considered "easy" in that they do not cry often and are not demanding, whereas others are "difficult" in that they are fussy and demanding.

**BIOLOGICAL FACTORS**    That such differences are present virtually from birth suggests, at least in part, the operation of biological factors. Some of these differences may reflect events that occurred in the womb. For example, newborns who had lower levels of iron display more negative emotion and are less alert and easily soothed (Wachs et al.,

2005). In addition, as we saw in Chapter 11, babies who had a fast heart rate in the womb are more likely to become inhibited, fearful children (Kagan et al., 1988). Indeed, heart rate differences between inhibited, fearful babies and uninhibited, relaxed babies have been found at 2 weeks of age (Snidman et al., 1995). Further, at 14 and 21 months of age, inhibited babies often have narrow facial structures, whereas uninhibited babies often have broader faces. These differences may reflect the fact that facial growth at these ages can be affected by high amounts of cortisol in the blood (Kagan et al., 1998). Babies who had greater EEG activation in the right frontal lobe at 9 months of age tended to be inhibited at 14 months (Calkins et al., 1996); this is interesting because greater EEG activation in the right frontal lobe in adults has been identified with a relatively less happy mood (see Chapter 10). The influence of biological factors on temperament is also evident in the fact that at 24 months of age, identical twins have more similar temperaments than do fraternal twins (DiLalla et al., 1994). Indeed, this study of twins showed that the tendency to be inhibited has a high heritability (that is, its variability among people in general is largely accounted for by genetic differences).

For temperament, like other characteristics, the story of development over the life span reveals themes of both stability and change. Even in the first week of life, temperament varies in different settings (Wachs et al., 2004). Moreover, as you saw in Chapter 11, not all inhibited infants became shy children and adults. In fact, only children who are extremely inhibited or uninhibited are likely to stay that way; the majority of children, who fall in the middle ranges, can change dramatically (Kerr et al., 1994; Robinson et al., 1992; also Kagan et al., 1998; Schwartz et al., 1996). Nevertheless, for those infants who exhibit marked inhibited or uninhibited behavior, early temperament is likely to provide an enduring core characteristic of later personality.

**NURTURING EXPERIENCES**  Some of the stability of temperament may arise not from innate predispositions, but from early nurturing experiences. Probably the most compelling evidence of this comes from research with nonhuman animals. Meaney and his colleagues (Anisman et al., 1998; Liu et al., 1997; Meaney et al., 1991; Zaharia et al., 1996) have shown that simply handling rat pups during the first 10 days after birth has enormous effects on the way the animals later respond to stressful events. As adults, these animals don't become as nervous as other rats (as reflected by fewer feces, less "freezing" responses, and more exploration) when put in a large open field, and they have lower cortisol responses (and thus are less vulnerable to the negative effects of prolonged exposure to cortisol, as discussed in Chapter 7). They are also less prone to learned helplessness (discussed in Chapter 10; Costela et al., 1995). The effects of handling occur naturally when the mother rat licks her pups and engages in nursing with an arched back (so the pups are directly under her); offspring of mothers that behaved this way later had lower amounts of the type of RNA that produces cortisol (Liu et al., 1997) and changes in the sensitivity of the hypothalamic-pituitary-adrenal axis (Weaver et al., 2004; see Chapter 3). There is good reason to believe that similar effects extend to humans: Touching infants not only can enhance growth and development, but also can reduce the EEG activation in the right frontal lobe that is associated with depression (even in 1-month-old infants!) and can boost immune function (Field, 1998; Field et al., 1986; Jones et al., 1998). Moreover, parents who perceive their infants as having a particular sort of temperament appear to influence the development of such a temperament (Pauli-Pott et al., 2003).

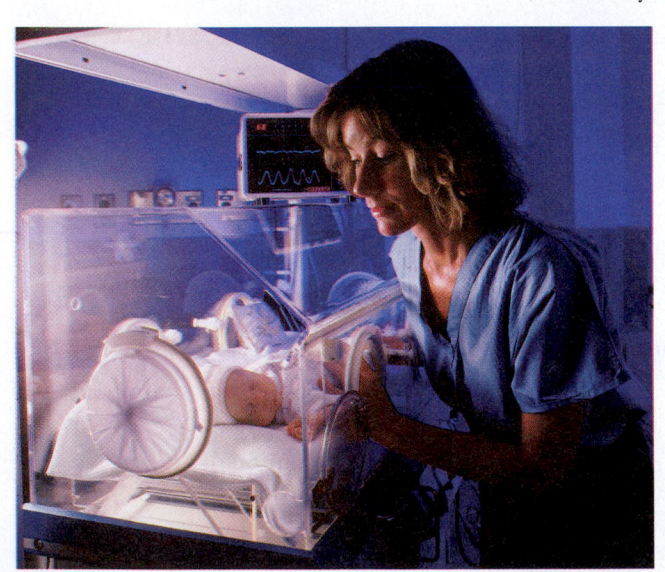

Social interactions can help babies who are born prematurely. Field and her colleagues (1986) found that premature infants who were touched three times a day (moving the babies' limbs, stroking their bodies), in 15-minute sessions, grew 50% faster, developed more quickly behaviorally, were more alert and active, and were discharged from the hospital sooner than other premature infants who were not touched three times a day.

# Test Yourself

1. How do nature and nurture control development?
   a. Nature is more important until birth, then nurture takes over.
   b. Nature is more important throughout the course of human development.
   c. Nature is important only at conception and during the prenatal period.
   d. Nature and nurture interact from conception onward to control development.
2. The proper order of prenatal development is
   a. zygote, embryo, fetus.   c. embryo, fetus, zygote.
   b. zygote, fetus, embryo.   d. fetus, embryo, zygote.
3. A teratogen is an external agent, such as a chemical, virus, or type of radiation, that can adversely affect the development of the
   a. central nervous system only.
   b. fetus only.
   c. zygote, embryo, and fetus.
   d. embryo and fetus only.

4. Research on newborns' sensory capabilities indicates that
   a. the world is a confusing jumble of sensations for newborns.
   b. newborns can do many things, including recognize voices, colors, and smells.
   c. newborns' vision is as highly developed as adults' vision.
   d. only hearing is fully functioning at birth.

## Answers

NOTE: Once you feel comfortable with the Test Yourself questions in this chapter, visit the book's Web site at www.ablongman.com/kosslyn3e for additional study questions.

## Think It Through!

Do you think that Steven Spielberg was born with the abilities that make him so successful as a filmmaker? In what ways might his abilities have been affected by a combination of biological factors, teratogens, maternal nutrition, and appropriate stimulation (perhaps even the sounds of his mother's piano playing) during his prenatal development?

If you were going to design a program to teach newly pregnant women how best to ensure the normal development of their unborn children, what would you emphasize?

# INFANCY AND CHILDHOOD:
# Taking Off

Steven Spielberg has repeatedly noted that his ability to make movies that appeal to children and to "the child inside adults" stems from the fact that he's never grown up himself. But although he may retain many childlike characteristics, the filmmaker has indeed matured. That is, his motor, perceptual, cognitive, and even social abilities have long outstripped those of even a preadolescent child. In this section, we see how this development occurs.

## Physical and Motor Development: Getting Control

If we continued to grow throughout childhood at the same rate as during infancy, we would all be giants. A newborn can look forward to being 50% longer on his or her first birthday and 75% longer on his or her second. But growth does not continue at this rate; rather, it usually occurs in a series of small spurts. Similarly, control over various parts of the body does not occur simultaneously and smoothly, but in phases. Good motor control (that is, control of the muscles) is a necessary first step for normal interaction with the world. Developmental psychologists have spent many years studying the precise ways in which babies' movements change as they grow. Two of the early pioneers, Arnold Gesell (Gesell & Thompson, 1938) and Myrtle McGraw (1943), described a series of milestones that all babies, from all races and cultures, pass in an orderly progression. In general, control progresses from the head down the trunk to the arms, and finally to the legs; at the same time, control extends out from the center of the body to the periphery (hands, fingers, toes). By the age of 2, the child has good control over all the limbs. However, fine motor control—of the sort needed to play piano or type on a keyboard—develops more slowly. And some of us do this better than others; Spielberg, for example, was notoriously clumsy and uncoordinated throughout his childhood.

In spite of the dramatic improvements with age, even young infants have remarkable control of their movements. For example, when reaching for a ball in order to toss it into a tub on the floor, 10-month-old infants reach more quickly than if they are going to drop the ball down a tube—which shows that they are planning the pair of movements in tandem (Claxton et al., 2003).

The early theorists believed that the consistent and universal order of motor development implies that this development is entirely maturational. However, later studies of motor control showed that this view cannot be correct (Thelen & Ulrich, 1991). For example, consider the unanticipated consequences of having infants sleep on their backs, in an effort to reduce the chances of SIDS (this is advocated by the "Back to Sleep" movement, which has helped to reduce SIDS in the United States by about 30% since 1994; Association of SIDS and Infant Mortality Programs, 2002). Ratliff-Schaub and colleagues (2001) found that premature infants who slept on their backs had more difficulty holding their heads up and lowering them with control than did infants who slept on their bellies. Moreover, other back-sleeping babies were slow to roll from their backs to bellies, to sit up, to creep, crawl, and to pull themselves to a standing position (B. E. Davis et al., 1998). However, the children walked at the same age, regardless of how they slept. In fact, since babies have begun sleeping on their backs, some never learn to crawl. "It was an occasional phenomenon before, and now about a third of babies skip the step of crawling and go right to walking," says Dr. Karen

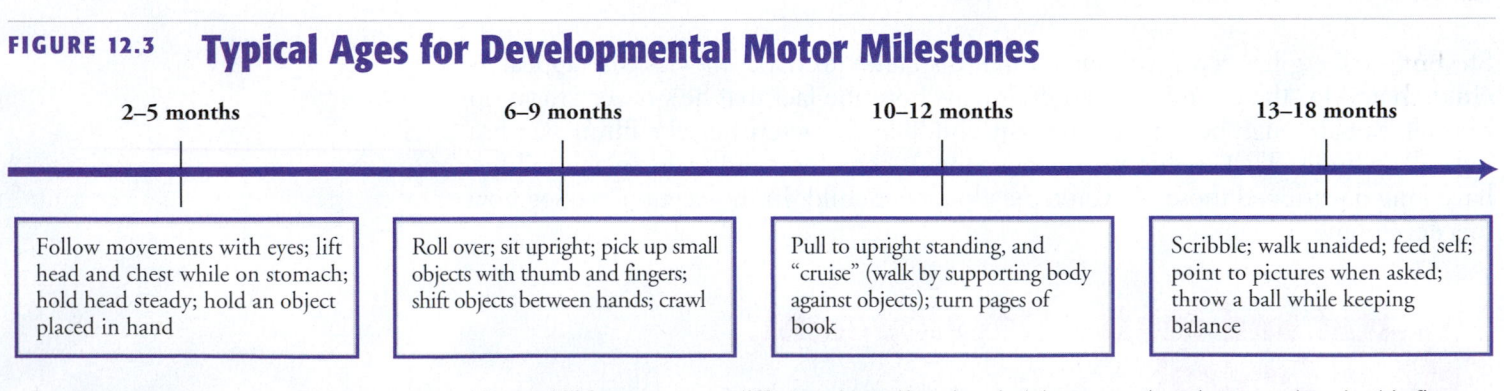

## FIGURE 12.3  Typical Ages for Developmental Motor Milestones

| 2–5 months | 6–9 months | 10–12 months | 13–18 months |
|---|---|---|---|
| Follow movements with eyes; lift head and chest while on stomach; hold head steady; hold an object placed in hand | Roll over; sit upright; pick up small objects with thumb and fingers; shift objects between hands; crawl | Pull to upright standing, and "cruise" (walk by supporting body against objects); turn pages of book | Scribble; walk unaided; feed self; point to pictures when asked; throw a ball while keeping balance |

Motor abilities emerge at different times. Keep in mind, however, that the ages given in this figure are averages and may not apply to a particular child.

Dewling (quoted by Seith, 2000). Thus, developing some aspects of motor control involves more than maturation; it also involves learning about the body and the world (Adolph, 2000; Thelen, 1995).

Developing motor control is important not simply because it allows the child to get around, but also because it helps the child develop capacities as varied as distance perception, visual search, and even using gestures to communicate. As Campos and colleagues (2000) put it, "travel broadens the mind." Figure 12.3 presents average age ranges for major motor developments (but keep in mind that various factors, such as the opportunities to use specific muscles, affect these ages).

# Perceptual and Cognitive Development: Extended Horizons

A parent probably would not tell as elaborate a story to a 3-year-old as to a 10-year-old. The reason is obvious: The younger child not only has a shorter attention span and understands fewer concepts about objects and events, but also can grasp only simple concepts about relations between objects and events (such as that one object can physically cause another to move). Where do these concepts come from? In part from perception, the organization and identification of information received through the senses; in part from cognition, or mental processes; and in part from the social environment.

## Perceptual Development: Opening Windows on the World

Along with the rest of the body, the sensory organs develop with age. For example, young infants view the world blurrily, as if through thick gauze; with age, their visual acuity increases, in part because of developments in the eye, particularly in the lens and the retina (Banks & Bennett, 1988).

**INFANT VISUAL PERCEPTION**   How do we know that infants can't see well? You obviously can't ask them, so how might you determine what babies are capable of seeing? Psychologists working in this area have developed a number of clever techniques. For example, to determine depth perception, infants are placed on a level sheet of glass that at first lies directly on a floor, but then extends over a part of the floor that has been stepped down. In this *visual cliff* experiment, researchers have found that even 6-month-old infants don't want to crawl out on the glass over the "deep end"—even when coaxed by their mothers—thus demonstrating that they can perceive depth before they can talk (Gibson & Walk, 1960).

But the visual cliff task is of no use with babies who are not yet able to crawl, so it is possible that even younger babies can see depth. How can we tell? In one study, researchers measured infants' heart rates when they were placed on the shallow or deep end of the visual cliff and found that 2-month-old babies had slower heart rates on the deep side (Campos et al., 1970); slower heart rates indicate that someone is paying closer attention, which suggests that the infants could in fact tell the difference between the two depths.

Other techniques for examining infants' visual perception measure the amount of time they spend looking at stimuli. For example, the *habituation technique* (also sometimes called the *looking time technique*), illustrated in Figure 12.4 (on p. 544), is based on the fact that all animals—including humans of all ages—*habituate* to a stimulus: If a baby looks at a particular shape long enough, he or she will no longer find it interesting—and thus will prefer to look at something new. This technique can be used to

Babies are placed on the sheet of glass over a floor that appears to be directly under the glass. A short distance ahead, the floor drops down (although the glass remains level). If the baby can perceive depth, he or she will be reluctant to crawl on the part of the glass that is over the "deep end." This is the famous visual cliff invented by Gibson and Walk (1960).

## FIGURE 12.4  The Habituation Technique

In the habituation task, the baby is first shown one stimulus and allowed to look at it until he or she is bored with it (has habituated to it).

After habituation, the baby is shown the original stimulus along with another stimulus. The baby prefers to look at something new. This technique can be used to determine what shape differences babies see and whether they see depth or other physical properties.

discover what babies can see, hear, or feel as "different." If you simply added a copy of the habituated stimulus, it would be no more interesting than the original—the infant has to perceive it as different to find it interesting. By varying how two stimuli differ (in shape, distance, color, pattern of movement, and so on) and noting the circumstances in which babies prefer a new stimulus after habituating to a previous one, it is possible to discover what differences they can detect. Habituation techniques have shown that babies can detect depth between 2 and 3 months of age. In fact, 8-week-old babies can see depth as represented by sets of points flowing on a screen, the way we do when we see a spaceship whizzing through a cloud of meteors in a movie—and these infants can even see shapes that are depicted three-dimensionally by sets of flowing points (Arterberry & Yonas, 2000).

Newborns aren't very attentive companions, but they will notice if you make direct eye contact with them; in fact, even infants 2–5 days old prefer to look at faces that look directly at them rather than faces in which the eyes are averted (Farroni et al., 2002). Thus, looking time can be used not simply to assess habituation, but as a more general reflection of what an infant notices. Such techniques have shown that newborn infants only notice isolated portions of objects; within about 2 or 3 months, they can perceive overall shapes (Spelke et al., 1993) and even organize line fragments into three-dimensional forms (Bhatt & Bertin, 2001). By about 6 months of age, they can organize sets of isolated squares into horizontal or vertical stripes (Quinn et al., 2002), can visually "chunk" groups of objects into units (Feigenson & Halberda, 2004), and can mentally fill in when their view of a moving object is briefly obstructed (Johnson et al., 2003). As they grow older, babies need less stimulus information to recognize patterns. It is tempting to speculate that their enjoyment of playing "peek-a-boo" may reflect this developing ability, in that they can use top-down processing (see Chapter 4) and their knowledge about objects to infer a whole from a part.

**UNDERSTANDING PICTURES**   Steven Spielberg is counting on the fact that you will relate emotionally to his images in a film in the same way you would relate to the events and characters if you met them in reality. Nonetheless, when watching a movie, you are in no doubt that you are seeing an image, not the thing itself. Apparently, however, 9-month-old infants aren't quite sure about which properties of objects are captured by pictures. DeLoache and her colleagues (1998) showed infants high-quality color photographs and observed the babies' reactions. The babies reached for and touched the pictures as if they were seeing the actual objects, and sometimes actually tried to pick them off the page! It wasn't as if the babies thought that the pictures *were* objects; they weren't surprised or upset when they couldn't pluck them off the page. Rather, they apparently *did not know* what pictures were and so were exploring their properties in the way that seemed most sensible. But 10 months later, at 19 months of age, the babies pointed toward the objects in the pictures and no longer tried to manipulate them. Babies apparently have to learn what pictures are, and this learning takes time. This finding transcends culture and experience: Babies from the Ivory Coast of Africa and babies from the United States acted the same way in this experimental situation—even though the children in this study from this part of Africa had never before seen pictures in books.

**INFANT AUDITORY PERCEPTION**   Compared with visual perception, auditory perception appears to be more fully developed at an earlier age. For example, researchers played consonant or dissonant versions of two sequences of tones to 4-month-olds. When the sequence was consonant, the infants looked longer at the audio speakers than when it was dissonant. Not only did they look away when the stimulus was dissonant, but they were more physically active. The researchers suggested that infants are innately tuned to find consonance more pleasing than dissonance (Zentner & Kagan, 1998). Apparently, to appreciate dissonant music, you must learn to overcome preferences that may be innate. But infant audition is unlike that of adults in a crucial way: When listening to sequences of tones that "do not conform to the rules of musical composition" (Saffran & Griepentrog, 2001, p. 74), even 8-month-old infants initially focus on absolute pitches, not relations among pitches (Saffran, 2003). Adults, in contrast, focus on relations among pitches. Thus, part of auditory development is a shift away from attending to absolute pitch to attending to relative pitch, which is more useful for music and for speech (because individual voices differ in absolute pitch).

Perceptual development continues beyond the first year of life. When, for instance, toddlers (2- and 3-year-olds) are shown an array of objects and asked whether it includes a specific object, they look haphazardly from place to place (Vurpillot, 1968). But 6- to 9-year-olds will search the array systematically, left to right, then top to bottom, as if they were reading a page. In general, by about age 11, children have perceptual abilities that are similar to (although often slower than) those of adults (Lobaugh et al., 1998; Piaget, 1969; Semenov et al., 2000), but some aspects of perceptual processing (used in organizing complex patterns) probably continue to develop until late adolescence (Sireteanu, 2000).

## Long-Term Memory Development: Living Beyond the Here and Now

As discussed in Chapter 7, we adults have both explicit and implicit long-term memories. Is the same true of infants?

**INFANT EXPLICIT MEMORY**   Many studies have documented that even 3-month-old infants can store information explicitly (Rovee-Collier, 1997). How could researchers find this out? The key idea is that recognition taps explicit memory, whereas priming taps implicit memory (priming occurs when performing a task "greases the wheels," making the same or a related task easier to perform in the future). In one study conducted to assess recognition, researchers attached one end of a ribbon to an infant's foot and the other to a mobile that hung over the crib. The mobile was decorated with plus marks of a

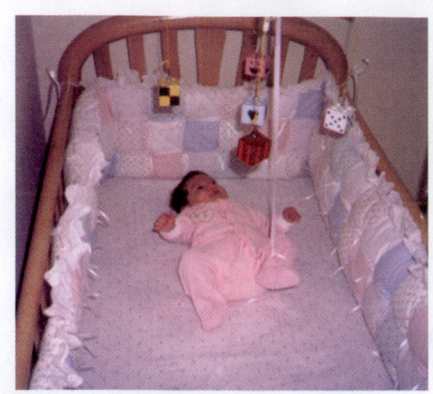

Kicking moves the mobile, which the infant finds reinforcing. Infants kick more vigorously when the marks on the mobile are the same over repeated sessions, showing that they remember what happened last time they kicked, when that stimulus was present. Gerhardstein and colleagues (2000) used this sort of apparatus to study both explicit and implicit memory.

particular size. The infants soon learned that kicking would move the mobile, which they found reinforcing—and hence they kicked at a higher rate. The researchers waited a day and then showed the infants either the identical mobile from the previous trial or one with plus marks that were either larger or smaller than on the original. The infants kicked at a higher rate only when the plus marks were the initial size. This is evidence that they recalled the original mobile explicitly (Gerhardstein et al., 2000).

**INFANT IMPLICIT MEMORY** What about implicit memory? To test whether even 3-month-old infants have such memory, the same researchers used the kicking test but now waited 2 weeks before retesting, which is a time period longer than that for which infants can recall that kicking moves the mobile (typically only up to 6–8 days after learning). They had each infant watch while the investigator held the ribbon attached to the mobile and moved it at about the same rate that the infant had moved it before. This priming event was sufficient to reactivate the memory, leading the infants to recall the relationship between kicking and moving the mobile. However, the explicit memory was not activated: Now infants increased their kicking when they saw mobiles that had all sizes of plus marks, not just when the plus marks were the original size (Gerhardstein et al., 2000). Additional studies have shown that only 7.5 seconds of priming are necessary to reactivate the memory (Sweeny & Rovee-Collier, 2001). Moreover, the priming stimulus doesn't have to be part of the to-be-remembered event; even at 6 months of age, a "forgotten" memory can be reactivated by showing the infant another event that was associated with the to-be-remembered event (Barr et al., 2001, 2002). In fact, other researchers have shown that the brain responds differently when 6-month-old infants see a novel face than when they see one that's been primed (by having been shown previously; Webb & Nelson, 2001).

**MEMORY DEVELOPMENT** You might be tempted to think that memory is like height and weight: You get more of it as you age. Not exactly. For example, in one study, researchers found that although adults recognize location better than children do, older children actually recognize color better than adults do (Gulya et al., 2002). Such findings are additional evidence that "memory" is not a single entity, but is instead comprised of multiple systems—and these systems develop at different rates.

Language-based types of memory take on increasing importance as a child gets older. For example, in one study, Simcock and Hayne (2002) asked young children to learn to operate a machine that apparently shrank the sizes of toys. Six months or a year later, the researchers tested the children's memory for this event. They found that in recalling various aspects of the event, the children used only words that they knew at the time when they initially experienced it; that is, no words learned in the intervening period were used. This finding suggested to the researchers that the "children's verbal reports of the event were frozen in time, reflecting their verbal skill at the time of encoding, rather than at the time of test" (p. 229). We noted in Chapter 7 that adults have remarkably poor memory for events that occurred during early childhood—perhaps this is one explanation.

**BRAIN DEVELOPMENT AND MEMORY** For the most part, long-term memory does improve from early childhood to adulthood. Why? Some improvement is probably due to the development of the brain (Bauer, 2002). For example, development of the hippocampus might explain why 6- to 12-month-olds show poorer recognition of an object when the context (the color of the background) is changed, whereas 18- to 24-month-olds were not affected by a context difference (Robinson & Pascalis, 2004). Changes in brain function underlie many aspects of memory development, as shown in part by the finding that an adult's brain is activated in more areas than is a 4-year-old's brain when a previously studied item is seen—and the adult's brain is activated more quickly after the item is presented (Marshall et al., 2002). In fact, even 14-year-olds differ from adults in their patterns of brain activation during memory tasks (Hepworth et al., 2001). But not all improvement in memory with age is due to brain development—events at other levels of analysis are also important. For example, adults—in particular, mothers—systematically help young children learn to label and organize to-be-remembered material (Labrell et al., 2002; Low & Durkin, 2001).

## Stages of Cognitive Development: Piaget's Theory

Thinking is more than perceiving and remembering; it also involves reasoning. It's obvious that babies don't have the mental capacity of adults; they can't even understand most problems, let alone solve them. The gradual transition from infant to adult mental capacity is known as *cognitive development*. The great Swiss psychologist Jean Piaget (1896–1980) developed a far-reaching and comprehensive theory of cognitive development. Interest in Piaget's theory helped generate other lines of research that have focused on how the gradual improvement in information processing, the maturation of the brain, and the social environment contribute to cognitive development.

Piaget was an extraordinarily sensitive observer of children's behavior.

Piaget was originally trained in biology, but early in his career, he worked in Paris with Alfred Binet's collaborator, Theodore Simon, helping to standardize Binet's newly developed intelligence tests for children (see Chapter 9). Piaget was curious about the types of reasoning mistakes children are likely to make. This new interest connected with his long-term fascination with biology and the nature of the mind, leading him to a general investigation of the reasoning processes of children at various ages. Piaget believed that babies begin with very simple, innate **schemas**, mental structures that organize perceptual input and connect it to the appropriate responses. For the youngest infant, such schemas trigger grasping and sucking at the nipple when the infant is hungry and in the presence of a bottle or breast. According to Piaget, the process of **assimilation** allows the infant to use existing schemas to take in new stimuli and respond accordingly. For example, the schema for sucking a breast can also be used for sucking a bottle or a thumb. In contrast, the process of **accommodation** results in schemas' changing as necessary to cope with a broader range of situations. As the child develops, the schemas develop in two ways: First, they become more fully *articulated*; for example, more precise motions are used to locate the nipple and suck. Second, they become *differentiated*; an original schema for sucking may give rise to two separate schemas, one for bottles and one for thumbs, which in turn may give rise to schemas for drinking with a straw, drinking from a cup, and eating solid food.

These two processes—assimilation and accommodation—together are the engine that powers cognitive development. Piaget's theory of development hinges on what results when assimilation and accommodation work in tandem, which he claimed produces a system of rules—in Piaget's terms, a "logic"—that guides the child's thought. Depending on the available schemas, different kinds of logical operations are possible. Thus, according to Piaget, the child's thinking changes systematically over time as new schemas develop.

Piaget described four major stages, or *periods*, of cognitive development, as shown in Table 12.2 (on page 548); each period is governed by a different type of logic and includes many substages, with key characteristics. The periods overlap slightly, and they may occur at different ages for different children; thus, the ages given in the table are only approximate.

**Schema:** In Piaget's theory, a mental structure that organizes perceptual input and connects it to the appropriate responses.

**Assimilation:** In Piaget's theory, the process that allows the use of existing schemas to take in new sets of stimuli and respond accordingly.

**Accommodation:** In Piaget's theory, the process that results in schemas' changing as necessary to cope with a broader range of situations.

| TABLE 12.2 | Piaget's Periods of Cognitive Development | | |
| --- | --- | --- | --- |
| **Period** | **Age** | | **Essential Characteristics** |
| **Sensorimotor** | 0–2 years | | The child acts on the world as perceived and is not capable of thinking about objects in their absence. |
| **Preoperational** | 2–7 years | | Words, images, and actions are used to represent information mentally. Language and symbolic play develop, but thought is still tied to perceived events. |
| **Concrete operations** | 7–11 years | | Reasoning is based on a logic that is tied to what can be perceived. The child is capable of organizing information systematically into categories, and can reverse mental manipulations. |
| **Formal operations** | 11 years (at the earliest) | | Reasoning is based on a logic that includes abstractions, which leads to systematic thinking about hypothetical events. |

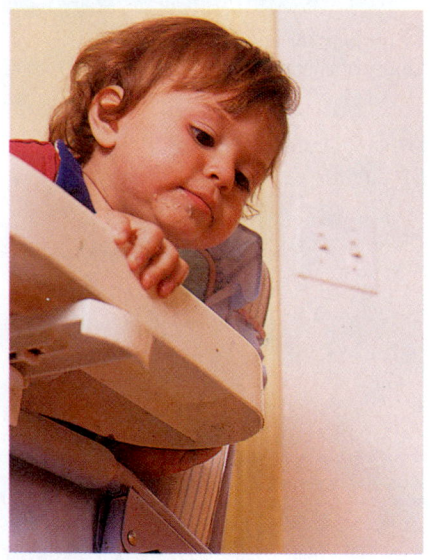

Only after an infant has object permanence does he or she understand that objects continue to exist even after they are no longer being perceived.

**Object permanence:** The understanding that objects (including people) continue to exist even when they cannot be immediately perceived.

**SENSORIMOTOR PERIOD** The infant's experience begins in the *sensorimotor period*, which extends from birth to approximately 2 years of age. According to Piaget's theory, infants initially conceive of the world solely in terms of their perceptions and actions. In this period, infants lack the ability to form mental representations that can be used to think about an object in its absence (see Chapter 8). In the early stages of the sensorimotor period, the infant does not yet have **object permanence**, the understanding that objects (including people) continue to exist even when they cannot be immediately perceived. For example, a rattle dropped by an infant over the side of the high chair is quickly forgotten—and more than forgotten: Out of sight means not just out of mind but out of existence! Piaget claimed that by the end of the sensorimotor period, by about age 2, the toddler understands that objects exist even when they are no longer perceived. In addition, Piaget claimed that a second major achievement of the sensorimotor period—at around 9 months of age—is the ability to imitate.

**PREOPERATIONAL PERIOD** Once out of the sensorimotor period, the toddler enters the *preoperational period*, from roughly age 2 until age 7. Armed with the ability to form mental representations, children in the preoperational period are able to think about objects and events that are not immediately present. As a result, they can imitate actions that occurred in the past. This newfound capacity for mental representation allows the child to engage in fantasy play. Whereas the infant might play with a bar of soap in the bath by squeezing it and watching it pop up, the preoperational child, performing the same actions, might think of the soap as a submerged submarine that is breaking the surface.

A cook asks two boys who have just ordered a large pizza, "How many slices do you want me to cut your pizza into, 8 or 12?" One boy immediately answers, "Please cut it

## FIGURE 12.5 Conservation of Liquids

In the classic conservation of liquids test, the child is first shown two identical glasses with water at the same level.

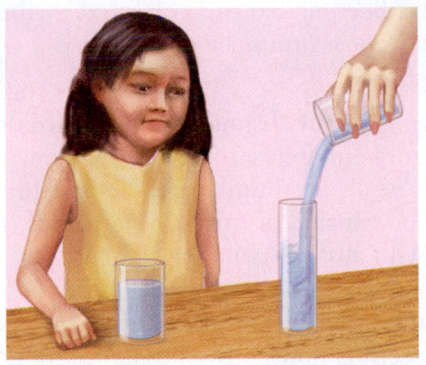

The water is poured from one of the short, wide glasses into the tall, thin one.

When asked whether the two glasses have the same amount, or if one has more, the preoperational child replies that the tall, thin glass has more. This is a failure to conserve liquids.

into 12 pieces, because I'm very hungry!" This is a joke for older children and grown-ups, but not for preoperational children, whose thoughts are limited in part because they do not yet have a "logic" for manipulating, or *operating* on, mental representations. Therefore, they often reason on the basis of appearances. One of Piaget's important discoveries is that these children do not understand **conservation**, the principle that properties such as amount or mass remain the same even when the appearance of the material or object changes, provided that nothing is added or removed. Many studies have documented that preoperational children do not conserve, and so they do not realize that cutting a pizza into 12 pieces instead of 8 does not increase the total amount of pizza. A classic example, illustrated in Figure 12.5, is that preoperational children do not understand that pouring liquid from a short wide glass into a tall thin glass does not alter the amount of liquid. Similarly, they typically think that flattening a ball of clay decreases the amount of clay and that spreading the objects in a row farther apart changes the number of objects in the row.

Both sensorimotor and preoperational children show **egocentrism**, which does not mean "selfishness" in the ordinary sense of the word, but instead the inability to take another's point of view. For example, children in this period will hold a picture they've drawn up to the telephone, to "show" it to a grandparent. They mistakenly assume that others see the same things they do.

**CONCRETE OPERATIONS PERIOD**   By the end of the preoperational period, at about age 7, children develop the ability to take another person's perspective. This ability is linked to the fact that they can now perform **concrete operations**, manipulating mental representations in much the same way as they can manipulate the corresponding objects. At this point, children are able to begin to classify objects and their properties, to grasp concepts such as length, width, volume, and time, and to understand various mental operations such as those involved in simple arithmetic. This *period of concrete operations* is Piaget's third period of cognitive development, which takes place roughly between the ages of 7 and 11. Concrete operations allow the child to reason logically, partly because this mode of conceptualizing is *reversible*; that is, it can be used to make or undo a transformation. For example, having seen the liquid

Conservation: The Piagetian principle that certain properties, such as amount or mass, remain the same even when the appearance of the material or object changes, provided that nothing is added or removed.

Egocentrism: In Piaget's theory, the inability to take another person's point of view.

Concrete operation: In Piaget's theory, a (reversible) manipulation of the mental representation of an object that corresponds to an actual physical manipulation.

being poured into a tall thin glass, the child can mentally reverse the process and imagine the liquid being poured back into the original container. Seeing that no liquid has been added or subtracted in the process, the child realizes that the amount in both glasses must be the same.

**FORMAL OPERATIONS PERIOD** By definition, concrete operations cannot be used for reasoning about abstract concepts; children in the period of concrete operations cannot figure out, for example, that whenever 1 is added to an even number, the result will always be an odd number. To be able to reason abstractly, Piaget said, requires that the child be capable of **formal operations**, reversible mental acts that can be performed even with abstract concepts. This ability emerges roughly at the age of 11 or 12, at the onset of what Piaget termed the *period of formal operations*. Rather than simply understanding the logic of "what is," as occurs with concrete operations, the emerging adolescent is now able to imagine the possibilities of "what could be." Formal operations allow children to engage in abstract thinking, to think about "what-would-happen-if" situations, to formulate and test theories, and to think systematically about the possible outcomes of an act by being able to list alternatives in advance and consider each in turn. For example, formal operations would permit a child to think about how best to spend his or her money and to weigh the benefits and drawbacks of each possible budget decision.

## The Child's Concepts: Beyond Piaget

Do children follow the stages Piaget described? When researchers use techniques different from Piaget's in order to see what children do or do not understand, they often come up with results that differ from his. Although Piaget employed very clever tasks (such as those used to assess conservation), those tasks typically assessed only easily observable aspects of behavior. When more subtle measurements are taken, evidence sometimes emerges that children can show competence well before they have reached the appropriate Piagetian stage.

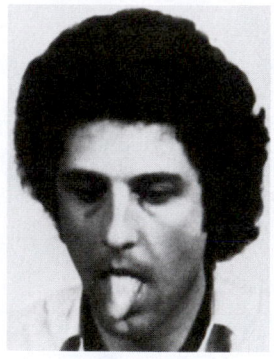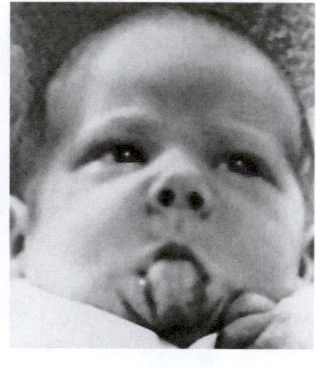

Very young infants can imitate some facial expressions, as shown in these photos from Meltzoff and Moore's study.

**EARLIER COMPETENCIES** The capacities of infants often far exceed those claimed by Piaget. For example, Andrew Meltzoff and his colleagues (notably, Meltzoff & Moore, 1977) have found that 2- to 3-week-old infants can show true imitation, and others have found that even 2-day-old infants can imitate happy and sad facial expressions (Field et al., 1982). And there's evidence that 9-month-old infants can add and subtract (McCrink & Wynn, 2004). Moreover, given what's been learned about infant memory, you won't be surprised that other researchers have shown that babies as young as 3 months old can have object permanence—they know that previously seen objects continue to exist after they are removed from sight. This refutes Piaget's idea that object permanence does not establish itself until the child is a toddler (Baillargeon, 1993, 2004; Spelke et al., 1992). Moreover, when appropriately tested, children as young as 3 years show that they understand the conservation of amount or mass (Gelman, 1972).

Piaget's theory seems to underestimate the sophistication of young children's conceptions of the world. Infants demonstrate an understanding of some physical laws even before they have developed the kinds of perceptual-motor schemas that Piaget claimed are the foundations of such knowledge. For example, even 4-month-old infants are aware of temporal intervals, showing surprise when a predictable sequence of flashing lights is interrupted (Colombo & Richman, 2002). Moreover, from experiments using looking-time methods, researchers have concluded that even young infants realize that objects need to be physically supported to remain stable

**Formal operation:** In Piaget's theory, a mental act that can be performed (and reversed) even with an abstract concept.

(Figure 12.6), that objects can't move *through* other objects, and that objects don't flit from place to place but shift along connected paths (Spelke, 1991; Spelke et al., 1992).

In contrast to Piaget's idea that formal operations are necessary to formulate and test theories, more recent research findings have suggested that in many ways the young child relates to the world as a young scientist. Faced with a bewildering set of phenomena, children try to organize stimuli and events into categories and develop theories of how those categories interact (Carey, 1985, 1988, 1995b; Keil & Silberstein, 1996; Spelke et al., 1992; Wellman, 1990). Even 1-year-old babies begin to organize categories (Waxman, 1992), and preschoolers develop sophisticated ways to determine whether an object belongs in a particular category. For example, they begin to understand that animals beget animals of the same type and that the internal biology—not the external appearance—defines the type (Keil, 1989a, 1989b).

**THEORY OF MIND**   In addition, current thinking suggests that children develop a **theory of mind**, a theory of other people's mental states—their beliefs, desires, and feelings. This theory allows them to predict what other people can understand and how they will react in a given situation (Flavell, 1999; Frye et al., 1998; S. Johnson, 2000; Lillard, 1999; Wellman, 1990). One way to assess theory of mind is to tell children a story and see whether they draw the proper inferences about the protagonist's mental state. In one story used for this purpose, a boy hides his candy in a drawer, but after he leaves the room, his mother moves the candy to a cupboard. Children are then told that the boy returns and is asked where he thinks his candy is hidden. By age 4 (which is before the age at which Piaget believed that children rise above their egocentric outlook), children believe that the boy thinks the candy is still where he put it originally, but children under 4 often believe that the boy thinks that the candy is in the cupboard. In order to get this right, the child must understand that belief does not necessarily reflect reality.

How does a theory of mind work? It is possible that children learn to "put themselves in another person's place," seeing things through another's eyes (J. R. Harris, 1995). It is also possible that children build a theory of the situations that give rise to other people's feelings (for example, seeing a child scream after being stung by a bee leads to the theory that bee stings hurt; Wellman, 1990); this approach has been called the *theory theory* (see Gopnik, 1996).

How does a theory of mind develop? The underlying process partly relies on the mother: Mothers who talk about their children's mental states more often have children who are more adept at using a theory of mind; in addition, children who have high verbal abilities also tend to develop a sophisticated theory of mind (Meins et al., 2002).

In addition, the particular theory of mind a child develops depends in part on the surrounding culture. In many African tribes, calamities such as AIDS or fires are believed to have supernatural causes (Lillard, 1999). Even within a culture, different subgroups can develop different types of theories. Lillard and colleagues (1998, as cited in Lillard, 1999) asked children to explain the behavior of a character in a story and found that children growing up in cities tended to use psychological explanations—for example, referring to the character's likes and dislikes—even at 7 years of age. In contrast, children growing up in the country rarely (only 20% of the time, compared with 60% for urban children) used such explanations; instead, rural children usually relied on aspects of the situation to explain behavior. It is not clear why this difference exists. Although researchers agree that culture plays a role in the development of a theory of

**FIGURE 12.6**   **Early Perception of Possible Events**

**POSSIBLE EVENT**

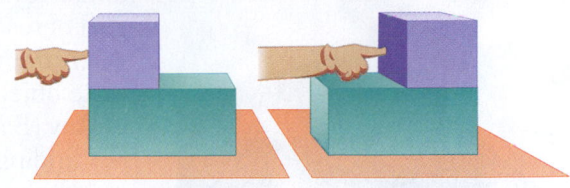

This panel shows a possible event: A box on top of another box is slid over to the edge, but it is still fully supported.

**IMPOSSIBLE EVENT**

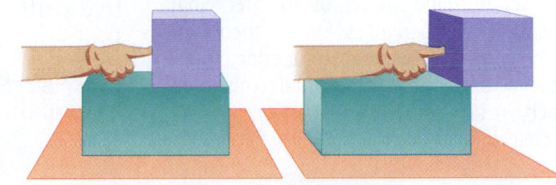

This panel shows an impossible event: The top box is slid so far over that only 15% of it is supported, and yet it does not fall. Between 3 and 6$\frac{1}{2}$ months, babies realize that one box must rest on top of the other to be supported.

Theory of mind: A theory of other people's mental states (their beliefs, desires, and feelings) that allows prediction of what other people can understand and how they will react in a given situation.

A theory of mind allows us to infer what someone else experiences. Such a theory either consists of a set of abstract principles or is based on a kind of mental simulation (which, in turn, may rely in part on abstract principles).

mind, culture cannot explain the evidence that children as young as 6 months begin to develop a theory of mind. For example, after being habituated by watching someone reach for the same toy repeatedly, infants of this age looked longer when a person reached for a new toy than when the person used a new movement to reach for the familiar toy (Woodward, 1998). Apparently the infant inferred that the person had the goal of reaching for the familiar toy and was surprised when the goal changed—but not when the motion changed. Such effects were not found when the infants saw inanimate objects (which were similar in size and shape to a human arm) touch or pick up the toy (Baldwin [2000], S. Johnson [2000], and Shimizu & Johnson [2004] report similar findings).

In short, the finding that many abilities are evident much earlier than Piaget predicted challenges his idea that all of a given child's thought reflects a single underlying logic, a logic that changes with increasing age and development. Moreover, later research has shown that many children do not enter the period of formal operations until high school, and some never enter it at all (Hooper et al., 1984; Lunzer, 1978). Nevertheless, Piaget has been proven correct in his observation that there are qualitative shifts in children's performance of specific tasks as they age. He must also be credited with discovering many counterintuitive phenomena, such as failure to conserve and egocentrism, that all subsequent theories of cognitive development must be able to explain.

## Information Processing and Neural Development

Efforts to explain the findings sparked by Piaget's theory have looked at specific changes in the way children process information and at how their brains mature. The brain develops dramatically from birth to about 3 years of age, and it continues to show substantial growth until the child is about 12 years old (Tsekhmistrenko et al., 2004). But what is this enhanced brain able to do? The *information-processing approach* is based on the idea that perception and cognition rely on a host of distinct processes in the brain, not all of which necessarily develop at the same rate.

Researchers have thus studied very specific aspects of cognitive development and have found that some mental processes do indeed develop more quickly than others. For example, even very young children are adept at using sensory memory (the very brief memory of perceptual stimulation) and at accessing information they have successfully stored in long-term memory (the relatively permanent store of information). However, anyone who has spent time with children knows that young children often perform more poorly than older children in many tasks. There are many reasons for this: Young children are not able to focus attention effectively; they are not able to formulate and follow plans effectively (Scholnick, 1995); and they do not have as much stored information that can be used in organizing and remembering input (Chi, 1978). Moreover, young children are simply slower at mental processing than older children and adults (Kail, 1988, 1991). Finally, a particularly important reason why young children may perform more poorly than older children is that their *working memory*—their ability to use information held in an active state—does not stack up well against that of older children or adults.

**DEVELOPMENT OF WORKING MEMORY**  Working memory capacity increases with age throughout childhood (Case, 1977, 1978). As working memory capacity increases, a child becomes able to perform tasks that were previously beyond reach.

The finding that working memory increases with age explains many of the phenomena documented by Piaget, such as the out-of-sight/out-of-mind behavior that he interpreted as showing a lack of object permanence (Baird et al., 2002). In this case, a *quantitative* change in capacity (the increase in its size) can lead to a *qualitative* change in performance (the transition to a new stage; Case, 1992b; Pascual-Leone, 1970). By analogy, if you have a relatively small amount of RAM memory in your computer, then you will be able to run only relatively simple programs (such as basic text editing or e-mail), but not more complicated ones (such as a complex word-processing program or large slide-show presentation). If you increase the amount of memory, you will be able not only to run more complex programs, but also to run multiple programs at the same time. A quantitative change in the amount of memory underlies qualitative changes in performance.

**WORKING MEMORY AND STRATEGIES**   Increases in working memory capacity can also affect other factors that change with age—such as the number and types of strategies a child can use. Robert Siegler's (1996) *wave model* rests on the idea that cognitive development is like a series of waves, where the waves are sets of strategies. Each wave crests at a different age, and more sophisticated strategies become possible with increasing age—but older strategies are not abandoned altogether, they are just used less often. For example, when shown a square grid that contains blocks in some of its cells and asked to report the number of blocks, children can use one of three strategies: they count clusters of blocks and add them up; they count the number of empty cells and subtract them from the total number of cells; or they guess, based on an overall impression. Younger children have difficulty using the subtraction strategy, in part, because they don't accurately calculate the total number of cells (Luwel et al., 2001). As children become older, they have more strategies to select among (Chen & Seigler, 2000; Jansen & van der Maas, 2002; Lautrey & Caroff, 1996; Siegler, 1989, 1996; Siegler & Svetina, 2002). Some strategies are automatic, and once learned will continue to be used in familiar settings; other strategies require conscious thought, and it is these that are most affected by the growth of working memory (Crowley et al., 1997, Crowley & Siegler, 1999).

**WORKING MEMORY AND BRAIN DEVELOPMENT**   What accounts for the child's improvements in working memory with age? The initial immaturity of the brain may be key. The brain undergoes rapid growth spurts (Epstein, 1980) around the ages that Piaget identified as marking transitions to new periods . Some of the increase in brain weight with age may be due to *myelinization* (the laying down of myelin, a fatty substance that serves as an insulator, on the axons), which increases the speed and efficiency of neural transmission, and some may be due to larger numbers of synapses and long-distance connections (Case, 1992c; Thatcher, 1994; Thompson et al., 2000). These changes would not only increase the speed of information processing (Demetriou et al., 2002), but also would allow more information to be activated at the same time—which, in turn, would increase working memory capacity. In fact, as more white matter matures in two different parts of the frontal lobes between the ages of 8 and 18, working memory improves (Nagy, Westerberg & Klingberg, 2004).

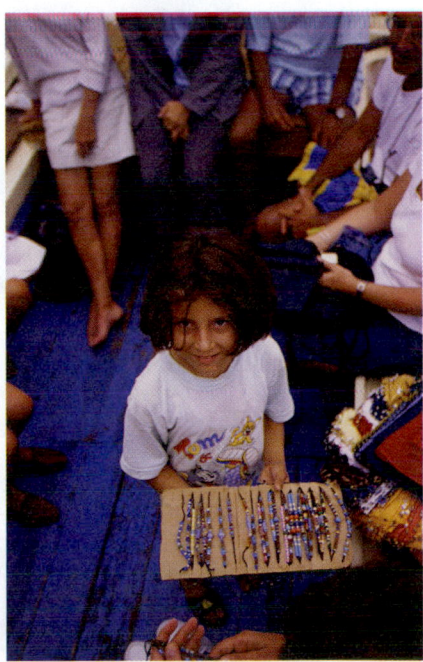

Children in different cultures master different skills; for example, middle-class North Americans often master the visual-motor skills needed to play computer games, whereas street children in Brazil may master the kinds of arithmetic needed to bargain with tourists over the prices of goods (Saxe, 1988).

## Vygotsky's Sociocultural Theory: Outside/Inside

Appreciating the importance of events at different levels of analysis leads us to look beyond any single source to explain psychological events. Thus, it isn't surprising that at least some aspects of cognitive development reflect social interactions. Russian psychologist Lev S. Vygotsky (1896–1934) emphasized the role of social interaction during development (Vygotsky, 1978, 1934/1986). Whereas Piaget believed that the child constructs representations of the world in the course of experiencing it first-hand, Vygotsky believed that the child constructs representations of the world by first

**Private speech:** The language used by a child in planning or in prompting himself or herself to behave in specific ways; also called *inner speech*.

**Attachment:** An emotional bond that leads a person to want to be with someone else and to miss him or her when separated.

absorbing his or her culture; the culture, as represented in the child's mind, then serves to guide behavior (Beilin, 1996; Kitchener, 1996). According to Vygotsky, adults promote cognitive development by guiding and explicitly instructing children, and cultural creations, particularly language, play a crucial role in development (Cole & Wertsch, 1996; Karpov & Haywood, 1998).

One of Vygotsky's key ideas is that once children learn language, they begin to use "private speech" to direct themselves (Berk, 1994a; Smolucha, 1992; Vygotsky, 1962, 1988). **Private speech** (also sometimes called *inner speech*) is language used by the child in planning or in prompting himself or herself to behave in specific ways. Children initially begin to use language in this way by actually speaking aloud to themselves, but eventually private speech becomes internalized and silent. As Vygotsky predicted, researchers have found that young children use private speech more when trying to solve a difficult task (such as folding paper in a particular way or arranging events into a story) (Berk, 1992a, 1994b; Duncan & Pratt, 1997) than when working on an easy task. They also use private speech more after they have made an error (Berk, 1992a, 1994b). Preschoolers (aged 3 to 5) also use private speech more frequently when they have to decide what to do in a free play situation than when they are put in a highly structured play situation (Krafft & Berk, 1998).

It might be tempting to think that culture is one influence on cognitive development, and the brain another. But this would be an error. The two factors interact: Culture affects the brain, and vice versa. For example, culture determines which language or languages you learn, which in turn affects how your brain processes sounds. By the same token, aspects of the brain affect culture; for example, we don't have customs that require more working memory capacity than the brain provides.

# Social and Emotional Development: The Child in the World

The psychological development of a child includes more than the improvement in mental processing and the acquisition of knowledge and beliefs. Equally impressive development occurs in the child's social interactions, such as the ability to form relationships.

## Attachment: More Than Dependency

Baby monkeys were separated from their mothers shortly after birth and were raised with two substitute "mothers." One was wire and held the baby bottle, and each young monkey needed to climb on this one to be fed. The other was covered with terry cloth and did not provide food. Baby monkeys preferred to cling to the fuzzy "mother," even though it never provided food.

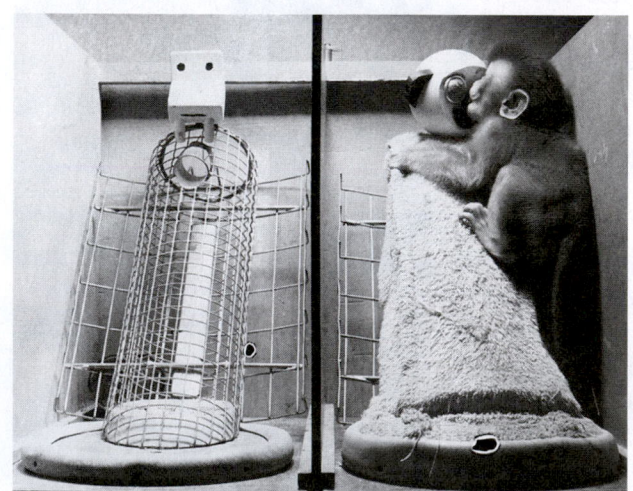

In our closest relationships, we develop deep attachments to other people. **Attachment** is an emotional bond that leads us to want to be with someone and to miss him or her when we are separated. The tendency to form such an emotional bond begins during infancy, when normal infants become attached to their primary caregivers.

**ORIGINS OF ATTACHMENT** What is the origin of the infant's attachment? Decades ago, a prominent theory—sometimes called the "cupboard theory" because it centered on food—held that infants become attached because their caregivers feed them and thus become associated with positive feelings (Sears et al., 1957). However, classic experiments by Harry Harlow and his collaborators disproved this and similar theories (for example, Harlow, 1958). These researchers found that baby monkeys became much more attached to a model "mother" that had a pleasing texture and a more realistic face than to another "mother" that lacked these characteristics, even though the latter was the only one from which they received food. The impulse to seek comfort from something soft is an innate rather than a learned characteristic of mammals.

British psychoanalyst John Bowlby (1969) developed a theory of attachment that has become widely accepted among developmental psychologists. According to Bowlby, children go through phases during the development of attachment. Just as in Piaget's stages, the order of the phases is thought to be determined biologically, but the precise ages of the transitions depend on experience. A major shift, usually occurring between 6 months and 2 years, is characterized by **separation anxiety**, which is fear of being away from the primary caregiver. This shift may arise on the heels of a transition in cognitive development—specifically, infants can now think about and remember objects (including the primary caregiver) for relatively long periods when the objects are no longer present.

**TYPES OF ATTACHMENT**   Not all babies become attached to their caregivers in the same way. Ainsworth and her colleagues (1978) developed a way to assess attachment using a scenario they called the *Strange Situation*. The setup involves a staged sequence of events designed to discover how a child reacts when left with a stranger or alone in an unfamiliar situation. If the child has developed secure attachment, he or she should show separation anxiety, becoming upset when the mother leaves, and should not be soothed equally well by a stranger as by the mother. Studies using the Strange Situation revealed four types of attachment:

- *Secure attachment* (about 60–70% of American babies) is evident if babies venture away from the mother, are upset when she leaves and not well comforted by a stranger, but calm down quickly when the mother returns.

- *Avoidant attachment* (about 15–20% of American babies) is evident if babies don't seem to care very much whether the mother is present or absent and are equally comfortable with her and a stranger; when she returns, they do not immediately gravitate to her.

- *Resistant attachment* (about 10–15% of American babies) is evident if babies do not use the mother as a base of operations but rather stay close to her and become angry when she leaves; some of these babies may go so far as to hit the mother when she returns, and they do not calm down easily thereafter.

- *Disorganized/disoriented attachment* (5–10% of American babies) is evident if the babies become depressed and have periods of unresponsiveness along with spurts of sudden emotion at the end of the procedure.

However, these differences have proven to be matters of degree, not sharply defined categories (Fraley & Spieker, 2003). Various factors influence the kind of attachment an infant will show. For example, if the mother was a heavy user of cocaine or other illicit drugs while pregnant, her infant is more likely at age 18 months to have disorganized/disoriented attachment (Swanson et al., 2000). In addition, mothers who are more sensitive to their babies' moods and behaviors had more securely attached infants (Tarabulsy et al., 2005). Moreover, the children of poor Black mothers are less securely attached than those of White mothers, which may reflect the adverse effects of poverty on a mother's ability to remain highly sensitive to her child (Bakermans-Kranenburg et al. 2004).

The type of early attachment can have long-lasting effects. Infants with secure attachment who were later studied at age 11 were found to have closer friendships and better social skills than children who had not been securely attached as infants (Shulman et al., 1994). In fact, the type of attachment determines how some genes operate: At least in monkeys, certain genes that underlie aggression and excessive

**Separation anxiety:** Fear of being away from the primary caregiver.

We know that at least some aspects of attachment are learned because infants in different cultures become attached differently. For example, American infants show less resistant attachment than do Japanese infants. In Japan, many more women are full-time caregivers for their children than in the United States, and their children are not used to being left with other adults (Takahashi, 1990).

drinking of alcohol are only activated (and thus only have their effects) when the monkey had an insecure early attachment—not when it experienced secure attachment (Suomi, 2003). Furthermore, secure attachment can lead a child to be more comfortable with exploring, which leads to better learning and can lead to more intimate love relationships later in life (Sroufe & Fleeson, 1986; Weiss, 1986).

## Is Daycare Bad for Children?

Obviously, a child will not have an opportunity to become attached to a parent who is never around. This was a major concern of Steven Spielberg, whose own father was often absent. However, according to Scarr (1998), "Exclusive maternal care of infants and young children is a cultural myth of an idealized 1950s, not a reality anywhere in the world, either now or in earlier times" (p. 95). Since 1940, less than half of all persons in the United States have lived in a "traditional" family with a full-time working father and a mother who works only in the home, and the percentage has been declining since 1950. In the United States today, over half of the mothers of babies younger than 1 year work outside the home (Behrman, 1996). Most of these children are in some form of daycare.

Is daycare bad for children? This question has been the subject of a long and sometimes intense debate; parents have felt trapped between guilt about not staying at home with their children and the necessity of supporting their families. To begin, it's worth noting that high-quality daycare (with small adult-child ratios and appropriately trained staff) enriches a child's learning experiences and improves his or her cognitive abilities (Duncan, 2003; Loeb et al., 2004). In addition, children who were securely attached to their primary caregiver before entering daycare had lower cortisol levels while they were getting used to daycare than did children who were not securely attached; this finding suggests that daycare is less stressful for securely attached children (Ahnert et al., 2004).

But—looking at the other side of the coin—what are the effects of daycare on how well children are attached to their primary caregiver? Research examining the strength of attachment of children raised at home versus those raised partly in daycare centers has found that children who entered daycare relatively early in life were as strongly attached to their mothers as those who entered relatively late (Scarr, 1998; see also NICHD Early Child Care Research Network, 1997; Roggman et al., 1994). Moreover, children were more securely attached to mothers who were strongly committed to their jobs, returned to work relatively early, and had relatively little anxiety about sending their children to daycare (Harrison & Ungerer, 2002). However, other research has shown that slightly more of the home-raised children show secure attachment in the Strange Situation (Scarr, 1998). Moreover, there is evidence that children who spend more time in "nonmaternal care" during their first $4\frac{1}{2}$ years behave more aggressively and defiantly than children who spend more time with their mothers (Belsky, 2001, 2002; NICHD Early Child Care Research Network, 2003). But these behaviors are fluid and change as the children grow older (Barry, 2002).

## Self-Concept and Identity: The Growing Self

A critical aspect of social development is the emerging sense of who you are and how you stand relative to other people. Psychologists use the term **self-concept** to refer to the beliefs, desires, values, and attributes that define a person to himself or herself. A key part of Steven Spielberg's self-concept as a child was his many fears, both large and small (McBride, 1999).

For young children, the self-concept is necessarily grounded in the level of cognitive development. Thus, preschoolers think of themselves in very concrete terms, in

Self-concept: The beliefs, desires, values, and attributes that define a person to himself or herself.

terms of behaviors and physical appearance (Keller et al., 1978). At what age do children begin to conceive of themselves as having specific characteristics? To find out, a dab of red paint was placed on babies' noses without their knowledge, and the babies then looked in a mirror. Some babies of about 15 months of age will notice the smudge and rub it off. By age 2, virtually all children have this response (Amsterdam, 1972; Lewis & Brooks-Gunn, 1979). However, this test may in fact assess understanding of temporary changes in appearance, not self-concept (Asendorpf et al., 1996). Other researchers have argued that the roots of the self-concept are present in children much younger than toddlers. Bahrick and her collaborators (1996) found that even 3-month-olds prefer to look at the face of another child of the same age rather than at their own face, which suggests that they are already familiar with the appearance of their face. Even newborns distinguish between touching themselves and being touched by someone else, a distinction that may mark the beginning of a self-concept (Rochat & Hespos, 1997).

By 3 years of age, children begin to appreciate that they have distinct psychological characteristics, such as being happy in certain situations and not in others (Eder, 1989). Children of about 8 to 11 begin to describe themselves in terms of personality traits, perhaps as "energetic" or "musical." The oldest children in this age range also describe themselves in terms of social relations (Rosenberg, 1979), such as the relationships they have with their siblings and friends. This ability to self-label depends on reasoning abilities that develop during what Piaget described as the period of formal operations.

Culture clearly affects a person's self-concept. In the collectivist cultures of Japan, China, and other Asian countries, children's self-concepts typically revolve around their relations to the group (Markus & Kitayama, 1991). In contrast, in the individualist cultures of most Western countries, children's self-concepts typically revolve around defining themselves as distinct entities that must negotiate with, and navigate through, the group.

Knowledge of your appearance is part of your self-concept.

## Gender Identity and Gender Roles

A central part of your self-concept is your identity as a member of one gender, which in turn leads you to adopt certain roles.

### GENDER IDENTITY: NOT JUST BEING RAISED WITH PINK OR BLUE
**Gender identity** is the belief that you are male or female. Part of your gender identity arises from how you are raised (Tenenbaum & Leaper, 2002), and part of it comes from the social context in which you grow up (Horowitz & Newcomb, 2001). Given the pervasive influence of events at all three levels of analysis, you might expect that biological factors also play a role—and they do. The role of such factors is vividly illustrated in the following case history (Colapinto, 2000): At 8 months of age, a boy's penis was accidentally sliced off as a split foreskin was being surgically repaired. The family and surgeons decided that it would be best to raise the boy as a girl, and so his testicles were removed and a vagina was surgically formed. The boy, previously known as "John," was now called "Joan," and her past as a boy was never discussed. Joan was treated in every way like a girl, and her friends and classmates had no reason to suspect that she was in any way extraordinary. When Joan was 9 years old, psychologist John Money (1975) wrote a famous paper in which he reported that Joan had a female gender identity, in sharp contrast to her identical twin brother, who had a strong male gender identity. This report, and others like it, led researchers to believe that gender identity was essentially neutral at birth and was formed by culture and upbringing.

However, Diamond and Sigmundson (1997) revisited John/Joan some 20 years later and recounted a very different story. They found that as a young child, she sometimes

**Gender identity:** A person's belief that he or she is male or is female.

ripped off her dresses and tried to urinate standing up. At 14, she refused to have any more vaginal surgery or to live as a girl. She was not attracted to boys and considered suicide. Even though she had been treated as a girl and even received female hormones that caused breasts to develop, she was deeply unhappy and confused. Her father finally broke down and told her about the accident. Instead of being upset on learning that she had been born a boy, she was greatly relieved. She renounced her female identity, underwent surgery to remove her breasts and reconstruct a penis, and was determined to establish a relationship with a woman. Joan became John once again. He eventually married and adopted his wife's children from a previous marriage. However, the early trauma cast a long shadow: John committed suicide in 2004, when he was just 38 years old.

What was going on here? John's brain had been exposed to high levels of androgens in the womb, which led his brain to develop in male-typical ways. These male predispositions were not something that could be arbitrarily changed simply by treating him as a female. Indeed, certain disorders result in exposure of a genetically female fetus to high levels of male hormones in the womb, and studies of such children have shown that this exposure can affect gender identity. These girls later preferred to play with boys' toys and to participate in boys' games (Berenbaum, 1999; Berenbaum & Hines, 1992). Boys can also be affected by the hormonal environment; boys who experience a relatively low amount of male sex hormones in the womb engage in less rough-and-tumble play than do boys who are exposed to the usual amount (Hines & Kaufman, 1994).

**THE DEVELOPMENT OF GENDER ROLES** **Gender roles** are the culturally determined appropriate behaviors of males versus females. It is one thing to identify yourself as male or female, but something else entirely to understand what behaviors are appropriate for your gender (Martin & Ruble, 2004). Gender roles vary in different cultures, social classes, and time periods; for example, a proper woman in Victorian England (or, perhaps, 19th-century America) would probably be very surprised to learn that a woman can be a senator or the president of a major corporation today. Conceptions about gender roles develop early. Indeed, by age 2, children have apparently learned about gender role differences (Caldera & Sciaraffa, 1998; Witt, 1997). Some preschool boys apparently believe that if they play with cross-gender toys (say, dishes instead of tools), their fathers will think that was "bad" (Raag & Rackliff, 1998).

Boys and girls play in characteristic ways, partly because of biological differences.

Freud argued that children identify with the same-sex parent, and that this is the main way in which gender roles develop (see Chapter 11). But Eleanor Maccoby believes that identification with the same-sex parent may be the *result* of gender role development, not the cause. Her account rests on events at all three levels. At the level of the group, in Maccoby's view, peer-group interactions are key to learning gender roles. It is in the peer group, she argues, that boys first learn about how to gain and maintain status in the hierarchy and that girls develop their styles of interaction (Maccoby, 1990, 1991). Maccoby and Jacklin (1987) found that 4-year-old children spent triple the amount of time playing with same-sex peers as with opposite-sex peers, and this proportion shot up to 11 times more when the children were 6 years old. According to Maccoby (1990, p. 514), "Gender segregation . . . is found in all the cultural settings in which children are in social groups large enough to permit choice."

Why does gender segregation occur? Maccoby (1988) suggests that part of the answer may lie in biological, particularly hormonal, differences. Boys play more aggres-

**Gender roles:** The culturally determined appropriate behaviors of males versus females.

sively than do girls, and their orientation toward competition and dominance may be aversive to many girls. However, shifting to the level of the person, Maccoby (1990) also notes that girls may not like playing with boys because they believe that boys are too difficult to influence; the polite manner in which girls tend to make suggestions apparently doesn't carry much weight with boys. Girls find this response (or lack of response) frustrating and retreat to the company of other girls.

## Moral Development: The Right Stuff

A key aspect of social development is the emergence of more complex ideas of morality, which center on the ability to tell right from wrong. As children grow older, their developing cognitive abilities allow them to draw more subtle inferences. The young child may feel that a girl who knocks over a lamp and breaks it is equally to blame if she smashed it intentionally, bumped it by accident while horsing around, or fell against it accidentally when the dog jumped on her. An older child is able to make clear distinctions among the three cases, seeing decreasing blame for each in turn. Piaget was a pioneer in the study of moral as well as cognitive development. His studies often involved telling children stories in which he varied the intentions of the characters and the results of their actions, and then asking the children to evaluate the characters' morality. Lawrence Kohlberg extended Piaget's approach and developed an influential theory of moral development.

**KOHLBERG'S THEORY**    Kohlberg presented boys and men with **moral dilemmas**, situations in which there are moral pros and cons for each of a set of possible actions. He asked participants to decide what the character should do and to explain why. This is the famous dilemma that confronted Heinz (Puka, 1994; see Figure 12.7):

> In Europe, a woman was near death from a special kind of cancer. There was one drug that the doctors thought might save her. It was a form of radium that a druggist in the same town had recently discovered. The drug was expensive to make, but the druggist was charging 5 times what it cost him to make the drug. He paid $400 for the radium, and charged $2,000 for a small dose of the drug. The sick woman's husband, Heinz, went to everyone he knew to borrow the money, but he could only get together about $1,000, half of what it cost. He told the druggist that his wife was dying, and asked him to sell it cheaper or let him pay later. But the druggist said, "No, I discovered the drug and I'm going to make money from it, so I won't let you have it unless you give me $2,000 now." So Heinz got desperate and broke into the man's store to steal the drug for his wife.
>
> Should Heinz have done that? Why?

Kohlberg was not so much interested in what the participants decided as in the way that they reached their decisions. What kinds of factors did they consider? Which conflicts did they identify (such as the conflict between the value of human life and the value of private property), and how did they try to resolve these conflicts? Kohlberg interviewed boys and men at length, and from their responses he identified three general levels of moral development (Kohlberg, 1969; Rest, 1979), which are ordered as follows:

- The *preconventional level* rests on the idea that good behaviors are rewarded and bad ones are punished. Correct action is what an authority figure says it is. A preconventional response to the Heinz dilemma might be, "If you let your wife die, you will get in trouble" (this and the following examples are adapted from Kohlberg, 1969, and Rest, 1979).

- The *conventional level* rests on the role of rules that maintain social order and allow people to get along. For example, a child reasoning at this level wants to be viewed as a "good person" by friends and family and tries to follow the Golden Rule

**FIGURE 12.7**    **A Moral Dilemma**

Can you imagine circumstances in which breaking into a store would not only be acceptable, but would actually be the right thing to do? If you were in a situation where you had to decide whether such an action was justified, you would be facing a moral dilemma.

**Moral dilemma:** A situation in which there are moral pros and cons for each of a set of possible actions.

("Do unto others as you would have them do unto you"). Morality is still closely tied to individual relationships ("If he lets his wife die, people would think he was some kind of heartless lizard").

- The *postconventional level* (also called the *principled level*) rests on the development of abstract principles that govern the decision to accept or reject specific rules. In the most advanced stage at this level, principles are adopted that are believed to apply to everyone. ("Human life is the highest principle, and everything else must be secondary. People have a duty to help one another to live").

**EVALUATING KOHLBERG'S THEORY** Some researchers have questioned the generality of Kohlberg's levels. For example, some have found that the levels don't apply well to people in non-Western cultures. Okonkwo (1997) studied Igbo students in Africa with Kohlberg's methods and found that in some cases the responses did not fit into any level. Although the responses clearly relied on moral reasoning, the reasoning sometimes involved factors such as family interdependence and the supreme authority of a divine being. Perhaps the strongest objection to Kohlberg's theory came from Carol Gilligan (1982), who argued that because the theory was based on studies of boys and men, it applies only to males. She believed that females tend to focus on an *ethic of care*, a concern and responsibility for the well-being of others. In contrast, Kohlberg's higher levels of moral development focus on abstract rights and justice, which Gilligan saw as a male-oriented perspective.

However, later studies have shown that differences in how males and females reason about moral issues do not reflect fundamental differences in the way their minds work. Although there is evidence that males and females do emphasize different principles in their moral reasoning (Wark & Krebs, 1996), this difference seems more a reflection of their daily activities (and the assumptions and general orientations that result from such activities) than an enduring gender difference. For example, if people are presented with dilemmas that feature concerns about raising children, men and women reason in the same ways (Clopton & Sorell, 1993). In addition, males and females score comparably on Kohlberg's tests, and both sexes reveal concerns with both caring and justice (Jadack et al., 1995; Walker, 1995). Furthermore, it is not clear that Kohlberg's levels are like traits, which characterize a person in all situations. Rather, people may use different types of moral reasoning, depending on the details of the dilemma (Trevethan & Walker, 1989).

In addition, we must distinguish between *moral reasoning* and *moral behavior*: The fact that someone reasons in a particular way doesn't guarantee that he or she will act on this reasoning. Moral behavior may be governed not simply by reasoning, but also by various aspects of your character, such as your *conscience*—which leads you to appreciate what is morally correct and feel obligated to follow this path. A conscience may develop far earlier than sophisticated moral reasoning. For example, Grazyna Kochanska and her colleagues (1994) have found that conscience typically develops at about age 3. In fact, how well an infant imitated his or her mother at ages 14 and 22 months predicted the degree to which he or she would feel guilty after transgressing at ages 33 and 45 months (Forman et al., 2004). However, having a conscience at an early age is not just about imitating adults; it has a lot to do with temperament and how a child interacts with his or her mother more generally (Kochanska, 1997). Fearful children, who are shy and anxious, learn moral standards best if their mothers gently discipline them and encourage them to do right instead of threatening them about the consequences of doing wrong. Fearless children, who are outgoing and who actively explore their surroundings, learn moral standards best when their mothers provide direct feedback, such as taking a toy away or making angry comments. But such direction has the greatest impact if these fear-

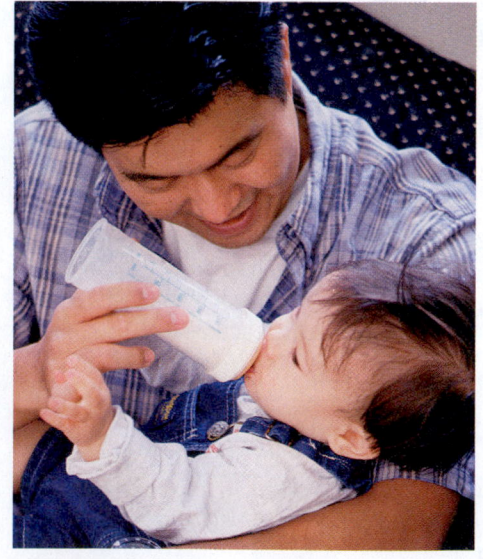
Differences in how men and women reason about moral issues may reflect the concerns that arise in their daily activities rather than inherent differences between the genders.

less children have a close, emotionally secure relationship with their mothers (Fowles & Kochanska, 2000). Fearful children may develop a conscience earlier than fearless children, in part from feeling anxious and guilty at the mere thought of doing something wrong (Kochanska et al., 2002).

And conscience is not the only aspect of character that can direct moral behavior. Another is the capacity to feel *empathy*, the ability to put yourself in another person's situation and feel what they feel. Indeed, Martin Hoffman (2000) shows that by early adolescence most children have sophisticated abilities to feel and act on empathy in a wide range of moral situations. For example, the children appreciate the unfairness of another person's not receiving a just reward for his or her efforts.

In short, many factors affect how people behave in moral situations, and some of these factors develop much earlier than does the ability to reason logically about morality. Our behavior is not just a result of how we reason, but also of who we are.

# Test Yourself

1. What is the relationship between maturation and learning in infants' development of motor control?
   a. Since development of motor control follows a universal order, maturation is entirely responsible for this aspect of development.
   b. Maturation is involved in the very early stages of motor development, but learning determines later development.
   c. Motor control develops automatically, without any input from environmental influences such as learning.
   d. Maturation and learning interact to drive motor development.

2. How would a 9-month-old and a 19-month-old child differ in their responses to a color photo of a red cube on a yellow background?
   a. The 9-month-old could not see the three-dimensional shape, but the 19-month-old could.
   b. Unlike the 19-month-old, the 9-month-old would reach for the cube and possibly try to pluck it off the page.
   c. The 9-month-old could not see the color of the cube and would have trouble picking it out, but the 19-month-old's color vision would be accurate.
   d. There would be no differences in their responses.

3. The main difference between assimilation and accommodation is that
   a. assimilation is the use of existing schemas, whereas accommodation is the creation of new schemas.
   b. accommodation is the use of existing schemas, whereas assimilation is the creation of new schemas.
   c. assimilation cannot happen without accommodation.
   d. accommodation is acquired more readily than assimilation.

4. In Harlow's work with baby monkeys, he concluded that
   a. infants associate their mother with food, and this conditioning causes attachment.
   b. infants attach to their mothers for comfort.
   c. attachment is not natural and therefore takes effort on the mother's part.
   d. all infants attach to their caregiver in the same way.

## Answers

1. d 2. b 3. a 4. b

# Think It Through!

Why would you expect variation in the ages at which stages of cognitive development are reached? Do you think schools should focus on speeding up cognitive development, so that children pass through the stages more quickly? Why or why not?

If you had a child who was born with sexual organs that were partly male and partly female, as happens on occasion, on what basis would you decide whether the child should be raised as a boy or a girl?

Can a child experience normal emotional development if he or she spends much of the day watching television? Which aspects of emotional development do you think would be affected by watching so much television?

# ADOLESCENCE: Between Two Worlds

Steven Spielberg's adolescence was different from that of many of his peers in many ways; nonetheless, the challenges he faced in those years—forming friendships, testing limits, coming to terms with a new and unfamiliar body—are essentially universal. Because his family had moved so often, none of his friends from early childhood were still with him in high school; most of his classmates, in addition, were firmly established in cliques. Spielberg craved their acceptance and used his newfound love of moviemaking and storytelling as a way of gaining it. Nevertheless, his obsession with movies and his lack of interest in the usual teenage pursuits of dating and sports continued to set him apart.

Not surprisingly, Spielberg's adolescence was not an easy time for him or, sometimes, for those around him. On one occasion, he and some friends spent 3 hours throwing rocks through plate-glass windows at a shopping mall, causing about $30,000 worth of damage (McBride, 1999, p. 88). He later said that *Poltergeist* was "all about the terrible things I did to my younger sisters" (McBride, 1999, p. 89). He fought his father's wishes for him to study math and science, declaring that someday he was going to be a famous movie director and didn't need to know those kinds of things (McBride, 1999). Extreme behavior, yes. Adolescent behavior, yes.

## Physical Development: In Puberty's Wake

Adolescence begins with **puberty**, the time when hormones cause the sex organs to mature and secondary sexual characteristics, such as breasts for women and a beard for men, to appear. These changes typically begin between ages 8–14 for girls and between ages 9–15 for boys. **Adolescence** is the period between the appearance of these sexual characteristics and, roughly, the end of the teenage years. Although girls usually experience their first period (*menarche*) about 2 years after the onset of puberty, typically between 12 and 13 years of age today (Chumlea et al., 2003), various factors influence when this occurs. In fact, in the mid-19th century, girls had their first period at about 17 years of age. In recent years, the age of puberty has declined—for both girls and boys—throughout the developed and developing world, including the United States (Finlay et al., 2002; Herman-Giddens et al., 2001), Europe (de Muinck Keizer-Schrama & Mul, 2001), China (Huen et al., 1997), and Brazil (Kac et al., 2000). This may reflect a *secular trend* in society: As children receive better health care and consistently better nutrition and lead less physically strenuous lives, puberty occurs earlier. For example, in rural Brazil, girls whose fathers were unemployed and those from low-income families had their first periods later than girls from more prosperous backgrounds (Tavares et al., 2000). Another study documented that American boys of various ethnic backgrounds are taller and heavier today than in previous generations, and these boys also develop pubic hair and mature genitalia at a younger age than was previously considered the norm (Herman-Giddens et al., 2001). Could better nutrition explain this trend? Studies have shown that overweight girls tend to experience their first periods before those who are not overweight (Kaplowitz et al., 2001), which suggests a link between diet and the age of onset of puberty. However, Black American girls tend to be overweight less often than White American girls, but are younger when they have their first periods (Herman-Giddens et al., 1997). Thus, diet alone cannot explain the secular trend. In addition, for at least some girls who have a certain gene, stress (especially caused

**Puberty:** The time when hormones cause the sex organs to mature and secondary sexual characteristics, such as breasts for women and a beard for men, to appear.

**Adolescence:** The period between the onset of puberty and, roughly, the end of the teenage years.

by having an absent father) apparently triggers early puberty (Comings, et al., 2002). Many theories have been proposed to explain the trend, ranging from the effects of additives in food (such as hormones added to animal feed and then passed on to human consumers; Teilmann et al., 2002) to various chemical pollutants in the environment (such as polybrominated biphenyls, or PBBs; Blanck et al., 2000)—but the reason or reasons underlying it are still not understood. Figure 12.8 summarizes pubertal events in girls and boys.

Physical development during adolescence also, of course, includes growth. During infancy and childhood, the body grows from the trunk outward; the upper arms grow before the lower arms, which in turn grow before the hands. At puberty, the trend is reversed: Rapid growth of the hands, feet, and legs is followed by growth of the torso (Wheeler, 1991). Do you remember when you stopped needing larger shoes but still needed larger coats? That's why. The uneven growth during adolescence can lead to an awkward, gawky look, which doesn't do wonders for a teen's sense of self-confidence.

Once the sex hormones start operating in earnest, the shoulders of young boys grow large relative to their hips, and vice versa for girls. At age 11, girls typically are taller and heavier than boys because their major growth spurt starts about 2 years before that of boys. By age 14, however, boys' heights and weights have taken off, whereas girls have stopped growing or have begun to grow more slowly. American girls typically stop growing at around age 13 (some may continue to grow until about age 16), but American boys usually continue to grow until about their 16th birthdays (and some may continue growing until they are almost 18 years old; Malina & Bouchard, 1991; Tanner, 1990).

Girls tend to mature faster than boys.

## FIGURE 12.8  **Pubertal Events in Boys and Girls**

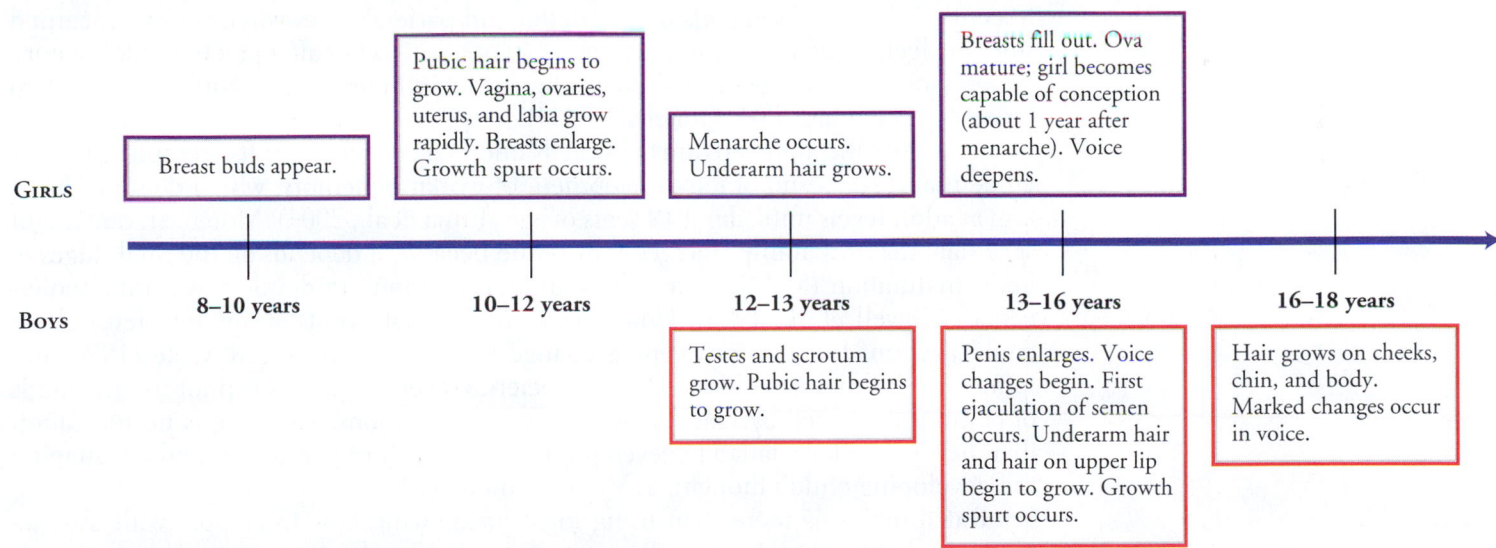

The hormones that trigger puberty cause many changes in the body, but at different ages and in different ways for boys and girls.

# Cognitive Development: Getting It All Together

The adolescent's ability to reason can become dramatically more powerful, but nevertheless be plagued with biases and distortions.

## More Reasoned Reasoning?

The major cognitive development of adolescence, achieved by some but not all adolescents, is the ability to reason abstractly. Piaget's period of formal operations covers the cognitive achievements of these adolescents. According to Piaget, formal operational thinking allows a person not only to think abstractly, but also to think systematically about abstract concepts and possible scenarios. In one of his experiments, now regarded as a classic, Piaget gave a child a set of weights, string that could be attached to the weights, and a bar to which the string could be attached, allowing the weight to swing like a pendulum. The child was asked to vary both the weight and the length of the string in order to discover what factors would make the weight swing most quickly. Adolescents in the formal operational period are not only able to figure out the possibly relevant factors (size of weight, length of string, how high the weight is raised before being dropped, force with which it is pushed), but also to understand that to discover the role of each variable, they must alter only one thing at a time. These adolescents have grasped the very essence of scientific experimentation: holding everything else constant while systematically varying one factor at a time. In short, all the cognitive machinery necessary to think scientifically can be present by about 11 or 12 years of age. But not all adolescents develop these abilities this early, and some never do.

Most adolescents in Western societies are able to grasp the rules that underlie algebra and geometry. The ability to think systematically about abstractions also allows them to think about concepts such as justice and politics, as well as about relationships and the causes of human behavior. In fact, there's evidence that the adolescent brain is better prepared to learn algebra than is the adult brain! Researchers found that adolescents and adults used parts of the frontal and parietal lobes when they first learned rules of algebra and used those rules to solve equations—but after practice, adolescents' parietal lobes stopped being activated, whereas those brain areas in adults continued to be activated (Luna, 2004; Qin et al., 2004).

How does the ability to think abstractly and logically emerge? It is tempting to conclude that it is a result of the development of working memory, which does not function at adult levels until about 19 years of age (Luna et al., 2004). Moreover, one might speculate that this ability emerges at this time because it depends on the final stages of brain maturation (and the brain does, in fact, continue to develop well into adolescence—Sowell et al., 1999). However, assuming that events at any one level alone could account for such a sweeping change would be rash indeed. Cole (1990) has found that, in many traditional African societies, even the adults cannot use the kinds of abilities described by Piaget's idea of formal operations, but there is no indication that their brains have failed to develop fully. Culture must play a role, perhaps shaping the developing child's thought, as Vygotsky theorized.

But thinking is more than using logic or knowing how to grapple with abstractions. As discussed in Chapter 8, emotion guides much of our reasoning, and such processing relies on the ventromedial (lower-center) frontal lobes. Evidence suggests that this brain area is not fully mature during adolescence, and thus emotions do not guide teenagers' thinking effectively (Hooper et al., 2004). It is tempting to speculate that this maturational lag may sometimes explain a lack of "common sense" during this stage of life.

Adolescents have sometimes been portrayed as being prone to distortions in their thinking. For example, at least some adolescents may use self-serving distortions, such as deciding that there's no need to ask because their parents really won't mind if they borrow the family car late at night (Barriga et al., 2000; Gerrard et al., 2000). In particular, they have been seen as unable to make well-reasoned judgments about themselves. This assumption contains a grain of truth, but bear in mind that adults aren't so good at making judgments about themselves either. When researchers asked adults and adolescents to assess the probability of various misfortunes happening either to them or to someone else, both age groups made remarkably similar estimates (Quadrel et al., 1993). It is sobering to note that both groups tended to *underestimate* the amount of risk they would face in various circumstances (such as having a car accident or being mugged). Both groups exhibited signs that they thought they were, to some extent, invulnerable. Both adults and adolescents sometimes use heuristics and shortcuts that can produce faulty reasoning (Jacobs & Klaczynski, 2002; see Chapter 8).

## Adolescent Egocentrism: It's All in Your Point of View

The enhanced cognitive abilities of adolescents allow them to take other points of view easily—in particular, to see themselves as they imagine others see them. Theorists have claimed that these improved abilities can lead to two kinds of distortions in adolescents' conceptions of how others view them (Greene et al., 2002).

Who is the imaginary audience?

First, the *imaginary audience* is a belief sometimes held by adolescents, in which they view themselves as actors and everyone else as an audience (Elkind, 1967; Elkind & Bowen, 1979). This view can lead teenagers to be extremely self-conscious and easily embarrassed; a pimple feels like a beacon, not unlike Rudolph's nose. Although many adolescents do not succumb to such cognitive distortions (Vartanian, 2001), those who do—perhaps because they believe others may be watching them—are less likely to engage in risky behaviors (Galanaki, 2001). However, some researchers argue that often there is nothing "imaginary" about the audience (echoing the old joke that even paranoids sometimes have enemies), and that adolescents have realistic concerns about others' opinions (Bell & Bromnick, 2003).

Second, some teenagers have a *personal fable*, which is a story in which they are the star and, as the star, have extraordinary abilities and privileges. Teenagers may have unprotected sex and drive recklessly because they believe that they are immune to the possible consequences (Lapsley, 1990; Lapsley et al., 1988). These tendencies, and other social behaviors, are clearly influenced by peers. However, adolescents are influenced primarily by their families with regard to basic values and goals (Brown et al., 1986a, 1986b).

# Social and Emotional Development: New Rules, New Roles

A bridge between childhood and adulthood, adolescence is a time of transition. The adolescent must forge a new identity, which emerges as he or she negotiates a new place in the world (Marcia, 1993). This negotiation involves not only coming to grips with changing roles in the larger society, which requires obeying new sets of rules, but also learning to live with cognitive and biological changes that affect interactions with others in many ways.

## "Storm and Stress": Raging Hormones?

The picture of adolescents as moody and troubled is nothing new. In the 18th century, German authors developed an entire genre of stories (the best known is Johann Wolfgang von Goethe's *The Sorrows of Young Werther*) about passionate, troubled young people so immersed in anguish and heartache that they committed impetuous acts of self-destruction. This body of literature came to be called *Sturm und Drang*, which translates roughly as "storm and stress." G. Stanley Hall (1904) popularized this term among psychologists when he wrote his now-classic two-volume work on adolescence.

The notion that adolescents experience a period of "storm and stress" has waxed and waned in popularity (Arnett, 1999). Anna Freud (1958) not only believed that adolescent "angst" (anguish) was inevitable but also that "normal" behavior during adolescence was in itself evidence of deep *abnormalities* in the individual. A strong reaction to this view soon followed, and only a few years ago, many psychologists were dismissing the idea as another popular misconception. However, additional studies have shown that there is in fact a tendency for normal adolescents to have three sorts of problems (Arnett, 1999):

1. Adolescents tend to have conflicts with their parents (Laursen et al., 1998). The *frequency* of the conflicts is greatest in early adolescence, whereas the *intensity* of the conflicts is greatest in midadolescence (Laursen et al., 1998). Adolescent–parent conflicts occur most often between mothers and their daughters who are just entering adolescence (Collins, 1990). These conflicts can be even worse if the parents are not getting along or become divorced. Steven Spielberg claims that *E.T.* is really about the trauma he suffered during the divorce of his parents (McBride, 1999, p. 72); he broke down sobbing at the end of its first screening (p. 333).

2. Adolescents experience extreme mood swings (Buchanan et al., 1992; Larson & Richards, 1994; Petersen et al., 1993), and by the middle of the teen years, about one third of adolescents are seriously depressed (Petersen et al., 1993)—and such depression is associated with increased levels of delinquency (Beyers & Loeber, 2003). Adolescents also often report feeling lonely and nervous.

3. Adolescents may be prone to taking risks. Anticipating Anna Freud's view, Hall (1904) went so far as to say that "a period of semicriminality is normal for all healthy [adolescent] boys" (Vol. 1, p. 404). Steven Spielberg's rock-throwing episode at the shopping mall is a perfect example of what Hall had in mind. Adolescents are relatively likely to commit crimes, drive recklessly, and have high-risk sex (Arnett, 1992; Gottfredson & Hirschi, 1990; Johnston et al., 1994). Such behaviors are related to problems in regulating emotions (Cooper et al., 2003), and they tend to peak in late adolescence.

Many adolescents don't have these problems; rather, as Arnett (1999) documents, such problems are simply "more likely to occur during adolescence than at other ages." (p. 317). But why do they occur at all? Many people assume that they are an unavoidable result of the hormonal changes that accompany puberty. The notion that the emotional turmoil of adolescence is rooted in biology was neatly captured by Greek philosopher Aristotle's remark that adolescents "are heated by Nature as drunken men by wine."

In fact, the hormonal changes that go along with puberty do make the adolescent prone to emotional swings (Brooks-Gunn et al., 1994; Buchanan et al., 1992). But hormones only predispose, they do not cause; environmental events trigger the emotional reactions (Dodge & Pettit, 2003). Moreover, the biological effects can be indirect. For example, hormonal changes can lead adolescents to want to stay up late at night and sleep late in the morning (Carskadon et al., 1993). If they are forced to wake up early to go to school, their general mood will no doubt be affected.

In sum, adolescents are more likely than people of other ages to experience "storm and stress," which arises in part from the workings of hormones. However, this is only a tendency, and the degree to which an adolescent will experience such turmoil depends on personal and cultural circumstances.

## Evolving Peer Relationships

The adolescent's relationship with his or her parents casts a long shadow. Both young men and women who have a more positive relationship with their mothers later have more positive intimate relationships with others (Robinson, 2000). Parental and peer relationships have a major impact on self-esteem (Wilkinson, 2004). However, many kinds of life experiences affect whether a young man or woman will develop intimate relationships. For example, perhaps counterintuitively, military service can enhance the ability to form intimate relationships (for example, by helping someone learn to trust and rely on others; Dar & Kimhi, 2001). Most adolescents develop predominantly same-gender networks of friends, and women's friendships tend to be stronger than men's (Roy et al., 2000). The one exception to this generalization is gay young men—who tend to have more female than male friends; moreover, gay young men tend to be less emotionally attached to their love interests than are heterosexual young men (Diamond & Dube, 2002). In addition, as portrayed in countless Hollywood "nerd films," some adolescents can be rejected by their peers. For example, girls can effectively use indirect aggression (for example, by spreading false rumors) to exclude other girls from their circle (Owens et al., 2000). Hurt pride or lowered self-esteem is not always the only result of such rejection. Many gay or bisexual students report being victimized at school, which apparently contributes to their being at risk for suicide and substance abuse and for their engaging in high-risk behaviors (Bontempo & D'Augelli, 2002).

## Teenage Pregnancy

In general, American teenage girls engage in amounts of sexual activity comparable to those of girls in other industrialized societies, but American teens do not use contra- *fail!* ception as effectively. In 2001, 33.4% of births in the United States were to unmarried mothers. However, American teens are having fewer children; in 2001, they had 25.3 births per 10,000, compared to 27.4 in 2000—an 8% decline (Wetzstein, 2002).

Which teenagers are likely to become pregnant? Those at greatest risk are poor and do not have clear career plans—and their father is likely to be absent (Ellis et al., 2003). Maynard (1996) reports that a third of the teenagers who become pregnant drop out of school even before they become pregnant. Further, over half of teenage mothers were living in poverty when they had their children. For many of these young women, particularly Black Americans, having a baby is part of "coming of age" and is in many ways equivalent to a career choice (Burton, 1990; Merrick, 1995). Unfortunately, the adult children of teen mothers are likely to leave school early, be unemployed, and be in trouble with the law for violent offences—and they themselves tend to become parents at an early age (Jaffee et al., 2001).

However, the specific consequences of having a child depend on the mother's subsequent behavior and social group: If teenage mothers do not drop out of school, they are about as likely to graduate as girls who did not give birth, and Black Americans appear to suffer the fewest economic consequences of having given birth as a teenager. Apparently, Black American teenage mothers tend to live at home, continue school, and benefit from the assistance of other members of their families (Burton, 1990, 1996; Rosenheim & Testa, 1992).

## Test Yourself

1. What is the main difference in physical development between adolescence and childhood?
   a. The trunk-outward trend of childhood growth is reversed.
   b. Unlike the young child, the adolescent grows at the same rate over the entire body.
   c. The adolescent's head starts growing, after a stable period in childhood.
   d. The same trends of physical development apply to both childhood and adolescence.

2. Adolescents may participate in risky behaviors because they
   a. underestimate the amount of risk involved in such behaviors.
   b. only care about having fun.
   c. cannot think rationally about any of their activities.
   d. tend to both underestimate risk and feel immune to consequences—but so do adults.

3. The notion that adolescents experience a period of storm and stress is
   a. true of all adolescents.
   b. true of some adolescents.
   c. false, according to most research.
   d. false, because most adolescents show little inappropriate emotion.

4. Research has shown that normal adolescents are likely to experience three kinds of problems. Which of the following is not one of them?
   a. parental conflict          c. mood swings
   b. fear of intimacy          d. risk taking

## Answers

1.a 2.d 3.b 4.b

## Think It Through!

If you were going to design a school program that takes into account the biological changes that occur during adolescence, how would it differ from your own middle school or high school experience? What kinds of classes, activities, or schedule might make the transition to adulthood easier?

Why was adolescence a particularly important period for Steven Spielberg? Do you think it played such a large role in your own life? Why or why not?

# ADULTHOOD AND AGING:
## The Continuously Changing Self

Steven Spielberg was an unhappy teenager and—in some aspects of life—a spectacularly successful young adult. But being successful in his chosen career did not mean that he was successful in all aspects of life. His first marriage ended; his relationship with his father was strained; and he was concerned that he himself would not measure up as a father (several of his movies deal with difficult relationships between fathers and sons). When he had children of his own, he realized that he needed to be an adult for them; he, and his relationships, had to change, and they did.

Famous filmmaker or not, the grown-up Steven Spielberg is in a very different phase of life than his children are; he is also in a very different phase of life than his father is. This is the human condition, and we now turn to an exploration of the stages of adult development.

## Becoming an Adult

When do you become an adult? In some cultures in Africa and elsewhere, for example, there are distinct *rites of passage*, sometimes marked with circumcision, that have a 13-year-old becoming an adult overnight; in other African cultures, a boy can become a man at any age, depending on when his father dies. In Western countries, most people aged 18–25 do not think of themselves as adults, and thus this period has been dubbed *emerging adulthood* (Arnett, 2000). Most people in Western societies follow a progression as they mature into adults, which consists of leaving their parents' home, getting a job (often after having attended college), finding a spouse, and perhaps starting their own family. However, this pattern is by no means universal; the transition from adolescent to adult need not be this patterned or direct. In fact, after an initial period of independence, some people may become more dependent on their parents—moving back in with them for extended periods and not entering into marriage or other usual adult activities (Cohen et al., 2003).

The period of emerging adulthood typically is marked by substantial positive changes in the perceptions of relationships between an individual and his or her parents; in contrast, this period is not marked by large shifts in the individual's attitudes toward religion (Lefkowitz, 2005). In addition, old conflicts with siblings tend to dampen down during this period, and people develop warmer feelings toward their brothers and sisters (Scharf et al., 2005). Moreover, people in this age range who think of themselves as adults tend to have a firmer grip on their self-identity, to have a clearer idea of the characteristics of their desired romantic partners, to be less depressed, and to engage in fewer risky behaviors than do people who do not view themselves as adults (Nelson & Barry, 2005).

Typical issues emerging in young adulthood include marriage, infertility, and parenthood. Many of these issues persist into, or can recur during, middle adulthood.

## The Changing Body: What's Inevitable, What's Not

By your early 20s, it is unlikely that you will grow taller, and your weight has typically stabilized for many years to come. For the next several decades, changes in your body should be relatively minor. True, you may come to need bifocals, and your hair may begin to gray or to thin. But the basic bodily systems continue to function well. However, after age 50 or so, noticeable changes in the body begin to occur (Lemme, 1995).

Aging has two aspects: changes that are programmed into the genes and changes that arise from environmental events (Busse, 1969; Rowe & Kahn, 1998). Many changes that come with aging arise not from inevitable processes, but rather from lack of adequate nutrition (such as fragile bones that result from osteoporosis-related calcium deficiency), lack of exercise (resulting in obesity in some elderly people and frailty in others, or just plain sluggishness and poor health; Brach et al., 2004), or lack of meaningful activities (which can lead to feelings of helplessness or apathy; Avorn & Langer, 1982; Langer & Rodin, 1976; Rodin & Langer, 1977; Rowe & Kahn, 1998). By the same token, environmental events—such as taking calcium supplements or lifting weights—can help to counter or diminish such problems.

It's not just diet that can help prevent osteoporosis; behavior can also play a role. Lifting weights helps the bones retain calcium.

## Learning to Live With Aging

A major challenge of aging is to accommodate to those changes that are inevitable and to forestall undesirable changes when you can. Many older people develop diseases or conditions that are uncomfortable or even painful, such as arthritis or collapsed vertebrae. However, in most cases, older people can cope with pain effectively, particularly if they adopt a "can-do" attitude (Melding, 1995; Rowe & Kahn, 1998). One of the inevitable age-related changes in women is *menopause*, the gradual ending of menstruation that typically occurs between the ages of 45 and 55; following menopause, eggs are no longer released and pregnancy is not possible (Wise et al., 1996). Hormonal changes that accompany menopause can lead to various bodily sensations (such as "hot flashes"); the knowledge that childbearing is no longer possible, along with the decline in youthful appearance, can adversely affect a woman's self-concept and self-esteem. On the other hand, for many women, the physical discomforts are slight, if present at all, and the idea of sexual intercourse without the threat of an unwanted pregnancy provides new pleasure. Some women feel "postmenopausal zest" and are reinvigorated by this change and the freedom it represents. For men, after about age 40, sperm production begins to fall off—but, unlike the cessation of egg production after menopause, men never fully lose the ability to produce sperm. Men do experience declining vigor (strength and energy) with age, which can affect sexual performance.

## Why Do We Age?

Why do all of us inevitably become less vigorous as we age? The combined effects of changes in the body have been likened to the effect of hitting a table with a hammer over and over (Birren, 1988). Eventually, the table will break, not because of the final blow, but because of the cumulative effects of all the blows. Some researchers believe that aging and death are programmed into the genes. An often cited piece of evidence for this idea was reported by Hayflick (1965), who found that human cells grown in the lab will divide on average only about 50 times, and then simply stop. However, all the findings that suggest programmed death can also be interpreted in other ways. For example, instead of accepting that the genes have been programmed for death, we might assume that errors accumulate over time, and finally, there are so many errors that the genes no longer function properly. If you photocopy a drawing or a page of text, and then copy the copy, and so on, you'll see how errors in reproduction multiply over repeated copying. In the case of the body, the damage may not be caused by the copying process itself, but rather by the repeated effects of bodily chemicals on each copy (Arking, 1991; Harman, 1956; Levine & Stadtman, 1992).

## Perception and Cognition in Adulthood: Taking the Good With the Bad

Cognitive abilities remain relatively stable through most of adulthood, but signs of a decline in some abilities begin to appear by age 50. The good news is that aging itself probably doesn't cause neurons to die (Long et al., 1999; Stern & Carstensen, 2000), but the bad news is that aging does impair communication among neurons, possibly by disrupting neurotransmitter functioning (S-C. Li et al., 2001) or by degrading the white matter of the brain, which provides the connections among neurons (Guttmann et al., 1998). These changes in the brain will eventually catch up with you and lead you to perform more slowly and be more prone to making errors. Indeed, by age 60, people perform most cognitive tasks more slowly than do younger people (Birren et al., 1962; Cerella, 1990; Salthouse, 1991b). The harder the task, the larger the difference in the time taken by young adults and elderly ones.

But how large is a "large" difference in time? Although even healthy elderly people require more time to carry out most tasks, the elderly are usually only a second or so slower than young people (Cerella et al., 1980), a difference that is often barely noticeable in daily life.

Shortly before death, however, many people exhibit *terminal decline* (Kleemeier, 1962). Their performance on a wide range of cognitive tasks takes a dramatic turn for the worse (Berg, 1996). This decline appears most dramatically in those who will die from cerebrovascular diseases, such as strokes and heart attacks, and it may be related to such disease states (Small & Bäckman, 2000). Thus, terminal decline is probably not an inevitable final chapter of the book of life (Bosworth & Siegler, 2002). More common is a gradual degradation in cognitive performance in the years leading up to death (Johansson et al., 2004; Small et al., 2003).

## Perception: Through a Glass Darkly?

During early and middle adulthood, worsening vision can usually be corrected with eyeglasses. Later in life, however, more severe visual difficulties emerge. More than half of the 65 and older population has *cataracts*, a clouding of the lenses of the eyes; in older people, the pupil (the opening of the eye through which light enters) also becomes smaller. Surgery can remove cataracts and result in greatly improved vision. But when such surgery has not been prescribed, moderate optical difficulties cause many older people to need greater contrast to see differences in light (Fozard, 1990). Contrasts between lit and unlit surfaces, such as shadows caused by steps, can define differences in depth, and if older people cannot perceive such definition, they are more likely to stumble over a step. Simply providing more light will not necessarily help older people to see well; because of the clouding of the lenses, more light causes more glare. Thus, the best level of illumination is a compromise between what produces the best contrast and the least glare. However, some declines in visual perception have nothing to do with the physical condition of the eyes, but rather reflect changes in how the brain functions. For instance, the elderly do not classify the identities of faces as well as younger people do—but they nevertheless classify facial expressions as well as younger people do (Kiffel et al., 2005).

Hearing is also affected by age. After age 50 or so, people have increased difficulty hearing high-frequency sounds (Botwinick, 1984; Lemme, 1995). Because consonants (such as *k*, *c*, *p*, and *t*) are produced with higher-frequency sounds than are vowels, older people often have trouble distinguishing between words that differ by a single consonant, such as *kill* and *pill*. Older people also have more difficulty shutting out background noise, a problem that may actually be worsened by hearing aids, which boost the loudness of both irrelevant background sounds and relevant sounds.

Unlike vision and hearing, the sense of taste does not decline with age (Bartoshuk et al., 1986; Ivy et al., 1992). Even in 80-year-olds, the taste buds are replaced frequently. But what we think of as the sensation of taste comes in part from smell, and the sense of smell does decline after the middle 50s (Doty et al., 1984; Ivy et al., 1992; Schiffman, 1992). As a result, as people move beyond middle age, they may prefer spicier foods; they may also have difficulty noticing if food has gone bad (Lemme, 1995).

Many herbs, vitamins, and other medicinal remedies promise to reverse the negative cognitive effects of aging. For example, the herb *Ginkgo biloba* and the drug acetyl-L-carnitine have been reported to improve blood flow to the brain (Dean et al., 1993). However, much more research is necessary before we will know for sure whether such treatments work as advertised.

## Memory: Difficulties in Digging It Out

Parts of the brain that produce the neurotransmitter acetylcholine become impaired with age (Albert & Moss, 1996; D. E. Smith et al., 1999); this neurotransmitter is crucial for the proper functioning of the hippocampus, which plays a key role in explicit memory. The less efficient processing in this part of the brain is probably one reason why older people often have trouble with some kinds of memory (Schacter, 1996); in fact, the hippocampus and related brain structures are smaller in older adults, and the sizes of these structures are correlated with recall ability (Rosen et al., 2003).

Even so, aging affects some aspects of memory more than others. *Semantic memory* (memory for facts, words, meanings, and other information that is not associated with a particular time and place) remains relatively intact into very old age (Light, 1991), and the storing of new *episodic memories* (memory for specific events) is often relatively effective. People in their 70s and 80s do fairly well if they are given a list of words and then asked to pick out these words from a longer list that also contains other words (Craik & McDowd, 1987). Moreover, the elderly have good implicit memory (Fleischman et al., 2004), and they can recall the gist of a description and its implications at least as well as younger people (Radvansky, 1999).

However, the elderly have difficulty when they must actively recall specific episodic memories: For example, they do poorly if they are given a list of common words to remember and later asked to recall them (Craik & McDowd, 1987). Tasks that require the *recall* of specific information appear to rely on the frontal lobes to dig the information out of memory, and processes accomplished there are not as efficient in the elderly as they are in younger people. Indeed, the frontal lobes—along with many other brain areas—become smaller in old age (Ivy et al., 1992; Raz et al., 1997; Resnick et al., 2003). In fact, even healthy people over age 67 or so have trouble with the same tasks that are difficult for patients with frontal lobe damage (such as sorting cards first by one rule, then switching to another rule; Schacter, 1996). Furthermore, just as patients with frontal lobe damage sometimes show *source amnesia* (forgetting the source of a learned fact), so do elderly people (Craik et al., 1990; Glisky et al., 1995; Schacter et al., 1991, 1997; Spencer & Raz, 1995). For example, Schacter and colleagues (1991) asked people to listen to novel facts (such as "Bob Hope's father was a fireman"), which were read aloud by either a man or a woman. When later asked to recall which voice read the facts, 70-year-olds were much less accurate than young people, even when they could recall the facts themselves (Schacter and his co-workers [1994] describe similar findings). Moreover, the elderly are also prone to creating false memories, which are fabricated on the basis of misleading information (Jacoby et al., 2005).

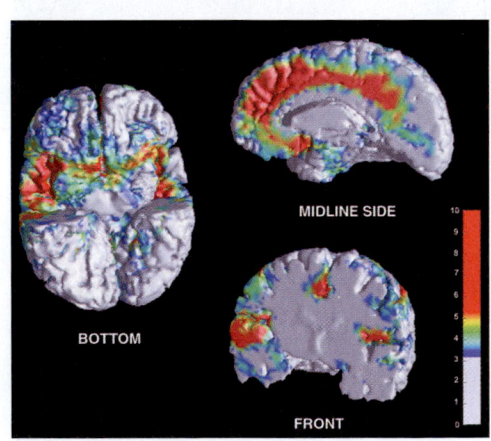

The frontal lobes are among the brain areas that lose the most gray matter in old age (Raz et al., 1997; Resnick et al., 2003), which may be one factor that affects the ability to recall information easily. In these MRI scans, the brighter the color, the more gray matter was lost with aging: *bottom,* a view from the bottom, looking up; *midline side,* a midline side view of the interior regions; *front,* a slice viewed from the front.

MIDLINE SIDE

BOTTOM

FRONT

Frontal lobe impairment is probably also responsible for difficulties the elderly have with tasks involving working memory (De Beni & Palladino, 2004). Such deficits are especially evident when elderly people must hold information in mind while doing something else at the same time (Craik et al., 1995). If strategies are needed to perform a task (such as figuring out the most efficient way to move through a store to collect different items), the frontal lobe impairments of the elderly can affect their performance (Gabrieli, 1996; S-C. Li et al., 2001). As Salthouse (1985) suggests, slowed cognitive processes may also lead the elderly to use inefficient strategies, strategies composed of many steps, each relatively simple. Ironically, there is evidence that elderly people are actually more likely than younger people to use strategies that rely more on their frontal lobes, attempting to compensate for less efficient processing in other parts of the brain (Gutchess et al., 2005).

## Intelligence and Specific Abilities: Different Strokes for Different Folks

It might seem likely that as you age, your accumulated life experience should add up to an increasingly important determinant of your intelligence. But this is not so. Researchers were surprised to discover that although overall level of intelligence is remarkably stable from age 11 to age 78 (Deary et al., 2004), genetic influences on general intelligence actually *increase* with age (Finkel et al., 1995; Plomin et al., 1994).

**CHANGES IN FLUID AND CRYSTALLIZED INTELLIGENCE**   Investigators have asked whether aging affects all types of intelligence in the same way. In particular, they have examined the effects of age on *fluid intelligence*, which involves flexibility in reasoning and the ability to figure out novel solutions, and *crystallized intelligence*, which involves using knowledge as a basis of reasoning (see Chapter 9). It might seem that crystallized intelligence, which, by definition, relies on experience, would be less influenced by age than would fluid intelligence. How could we tell? These two types of intelligence have been assessed in **longitudinal studies**, which test the same group of people repeatedly, at different ages. These findings suggest that *both* types of intelligence are stable until somewhere between the mid-50s and the early 70s, when both decline (Hertzog & Schaie, 1988). However, the very strength of longitudinal studies—the continuing use of the same group—also leads to a weakness: The participants become familiar with the type of testing, and this familiarity can influence their performance on later assessments. As shown in Figure 12.9, **cross-sectional studies** involve testing different groups of people, with each group composed of individuals of a particular age. The key here is to ensure that the groups are equated on all possible measures other than age (such as sex, educational level, and health status). Such studies have led most researchers to believe that fluid intelligence begins to decline as early as the late 20s

**Longitudinal study:** A study in which the same group of people is tested repeatedly, at different ages.

**Cross-sectional study:** A study in which different groups of people are tested, with each group composed of individuals of a particular age.

---

**FIGURE 12.9**   ## Longitudinal Versus Cross-Sectional Research Designs

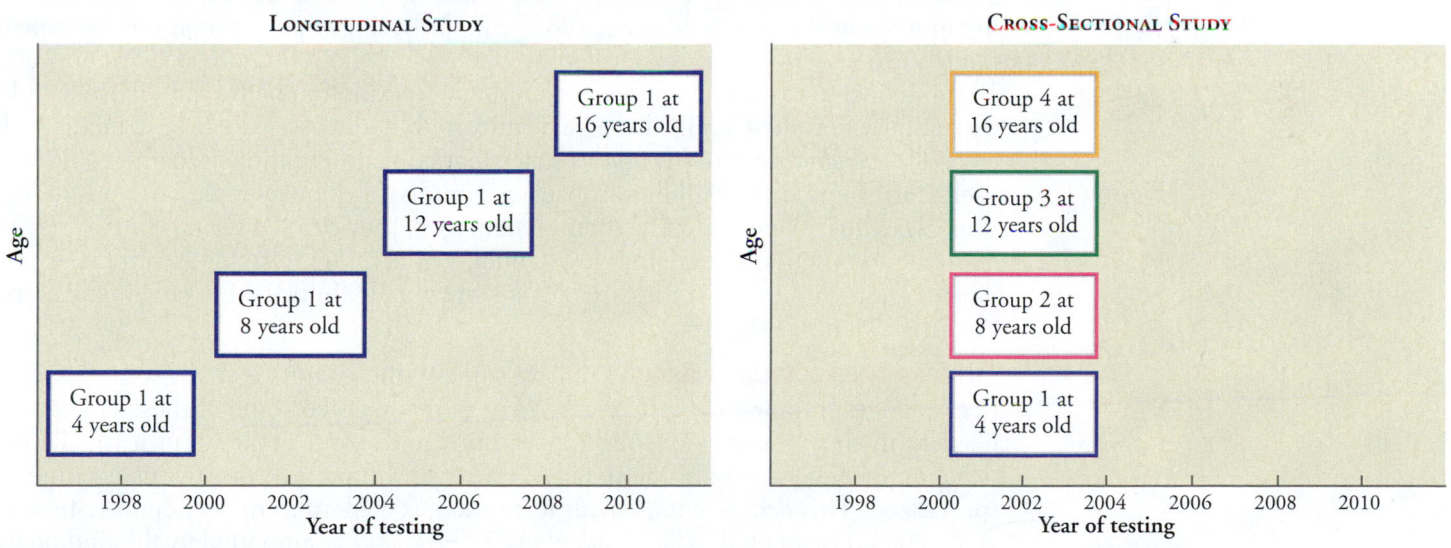

Longitudinal studies (left panel) test the same group of people repeatedly over time, whereas cross-sectional studies (right panel) test people of different ages.

Crystallized intelligence does not decline dramatically until very late in life, which allows the elderly to tell more interesting and informative stories.

(Salthouse, 1991a), whereas crystallized intelligence may actually grow with age and decline only late in life (Baltes, 1987; McArdle et al., 2002; Li et al, 2004).

**CHANGES IN SPECIFIC ABILITIES** Crystallized intelligence, rooted in experience, may be thought of as underlying much of what we mean by "wisdom." The ability to draw on such intelligence may explain why researchers found that older adults were rated as telling more interesting, higher-quality, and more informative stories than younger adults (James et al., 1998). This should be cheering news for Steven Spielberg, who plans to keep telling stories as long as he can.

Moreover, in some respects, old people actually reason better than young people. For example, in one study, researchers asked young and old participants to indicate their preferences when given either two or three alternatives—for example, chocolate or vanilla ice cream versus chocolate, vanilla, or strawberry ice cream. Young people were inconsistent, perhaps choosing vanilla when only two choices were offered, but chocolate when strawberry was included. Old people were much more consistent and "logical" in their choices (Tentori et al., 2001).

General intelligence is distinct from special abilities, such as the ability to do arithmetic or to imagine objects rotating. Not all the special abilities of a given person are affected by aging to the same degree. For example, a longitudinal study by Schaie and colleagues (Schaie, 1983, 1989, 1990b; Schaie et al., 2004) examined the effects of aging on five measures of special abilities, including the ability to recognize and understand words and the ability to rotate shapes mentally. He found that by age 60 about three fourths of the participants maintained their level of performance from the previous 7 years on at least four of the five abilities tested, and by age 81 more than half the participants maintained this level of performance. For any given person, some aspects of intelligence were affected by aging more than others (Schaie & Willis, 1993; Schaie et al., 2004). The same is true for many types of skills, which age affects in different ways for different people (Stern & Carstensen, 2000).

**COMPENSATING FOR DECLINING ABILITIES** People can often compensate for declining abilities by using abilities that are still intact (Baltes, 1987; Baltes et al., 1984). Some typists can retain their speed as they age by looking farther ahead on the page, thus taking in more as they go (Salthouse, 1984). Similarly, tennis players may compensate for reduced speed and vigor by developing better strategies (Lemme, 1995; Perlmutter, 1988). In fact, people with more education tend to function better than those with less education when their brains have been impaired by diseases, such as Alzheimer's disease. The *cerebral reserve hypothesis* states that education either strengthens the brain itself (for example, by building in backup circuits) or helps people develop multiple strategies; thus, when part of the brain is damaged, they can draw on these reserves and continue to function reasonably well (Cohen et al., 1996; Stern, 2002). In fact, simply having more leisure activities in old age may help build such cognitive reserves (Scarmeas et al., 2001).

**THE LESS-DIFFERENTIATED BRAIN** At least some of the cognitive changes in old age reflect changes in how the brain works. We've already noted some of these changes, especially in the functions of the hippocampus and frontal lobes. But a much more sweeping change must also be noted: As we age, the parts of our brains become less specialized. This *dedifferentiation*, as it is called, is evident in many neural systems (Li et al., 2004; Logan et al., 2002; Park et al., 2004)—and is supported by the finding that scores on different parts of intelligence tests are more highly correlated in the elderly than in younger people (Deary et al., 2004). In fact, even the specializations of the two cerebral hemispheres become less sharply defined with aging (Cabeza, 2002). Such a lack of specialization may give rise to slower or less efficient information processing.

# Social and Emotional Development During Adulthood

The phrase "growing up" might seem to imply that psychological development is like height: After a certain age, you reach a plateau, and that's where you stay. Not so. At least in mentally healthy people, psychological development continues throughout the life span. In discussing Steven Spielberg's 15-year split with his father, an expert on father–son relationships, James Levine, commented: "In such a split, you don't recognize that under the anger is sadness. There's denial: pretending it's not important to heal the rift. But a split in the father–child relationship always has an effect" (quoted in Sullivan, 1999, p. 67). Still, as in Spielberg's case, relationships change and evolve over time.

After a 15-year split, Steven Spielberg developed a new relationship with his dad.

## Theories of Psychosocial Stages in Adulthood

Some theorists, Freud included, believed that personality stops developing in childhood. But Erik Erikson (1921–1994) proposed three stages of adult **psychosocial development**, due to effects of maturation and learning on personality and relationships, in addition to five stages of psychosocial development through childhood and adolescence (see Table 12.3). The adult stages were defined by issues that adults are most likely to confront and need to resolve.

- The first stage, *intimacy versus isolation*, occurs in young adulthood. To navigate this stage of development successfully, the young adult must develop deep and intimate relations with others and avoid becoming socially isolated. Steven Spielberg

**Psychosocial development:** The effects of maturation and learning on personality and relationships.

---

**TABLE 12.3  Erikson's (1950) Psychosocial Stages**

| Issue to Be Resolved | Average Age | Summary |
|---|---|---|
| **Basic trust vs. mistrust** | 0–1 year | Depending on how well they are treated by caregivers, infants either develop a basic trust that the world is good or fail to develop such a basic trust. |
| **Autonomy vs. doubt** | 1–3 years | The child either is allowed to choose and make independent decisions or is made to feel ashamed and full of self-doubt for wanting to do so. |
| **Initiative vs. guilt** | 3–6 years | The child either develops a sense of purpose and direction or is overly controlled by the parents and made to feel constrained or guilty. |
| **Industry vs. inferiority** | 6–11 years | The child either develops a sense of competence and ability to work with others or becomes beset with feelings of incompetence and inferiority. |
| **Identity vs. role confusion** | Adolescence | The adolescent either successfully grapples with questions of identity and future roles as an adult or becomes confused about possible adult roles. |
| **Intimacy vs. isolation** | Young adulthood | The young adult either develops deep and intimate relations with others or is socially isolated. |
| **Generativity vs. self-absorption** | Middle adulthood | The adult in the "prime of life" must look to the future and determine what to leave behind for future generations; failing this task leads to a sense of meaninglessness in life. |
| **Integrity vs. despair** | Old age | In reflecting back on life, a person either feels that life was worthwhile as it was lived or feels despair and fears death. |

---

had serious difficulty being intimate with people, which may be one reason why his first marriage dissolved (McBride, 1999).

- The second adult stage, characterized by *generativity versus self-absorption*, occurs during the middle adult years. The challenge here is for men and women to think about the future and decide what their contributions will be for their children or for society at large. People who are highly generative agree with the African proverb "The world was not left to us by our parents. It was lent to us by our children" (which is inscribed on a wall in the UNICEF office in New York). People who fail at the task of this stage will be faced with a sense of meaninglessness in life. Steven Spielberg not only cares for his own children but also makes it a point to help young directors who are just starting out; such altruistic behavior is another type of generativity.

- The third adult stage, characterized by *integrity versus despair*, occurs during old age. The task here is to be able to reflect back on life and feel that it was worthwhile, thereby avoiding feelings of despair and fear of death.

Many theorists have picked up where Erikson left off (Gould, 1978; Havinghurst, 1953; Vaillant, 1977). Some have focused on one aspect of Erikson's theory. For example, McAdams and his colleagues developed ways to assess generativity (McAdams & de St. Aubin, 1992), and they found that adults who are concerned about providing for future generations tend to be more satisfied with their lives (McAdams et al., 1993) and to view life optimistically—believing that even bad events will eventually have a happy outcome (McAdams et al., 2001).

Many roles are open to us as we age, despite stereotypes to the contrary!

Other theorists have extended Erikson's approach by proposing additional stages. For example, Levinson (Levinson, 1977, 1978, 1986, 1990; Levinson et al., 1978), basing his work on interviews with 40 men, developed an influential theory of developmental transitions in men's lives. Perhaps the most important and interesting aspect of Levinson's theory is the *midlife transition*, which occurs when a man begins to shift from thinking of his life as marked by the time passed since birth to thinking of his life as marked by the time left until death. This transition typically occurs somewhere between the ages of 40 and 45. This change in perspective can have profound consequences, often leading a man to question the path he has chosen. According to Levinson, many men have *midlife crises*, which can lead them to end marriages and begin others, change jobs, or make other major life changes. In Steven Spielberg's case, this crisis seems to have caused him to deal with conflicting emotions about being Jewish; one result was his movie *Schindler's List*, in which he confronted his fears and ambivalence about his Jewish identity (which were particularly severe because of his strong need for acceptance; McBride, 1999).

## Continued Personality Development

We must distinguish between the changes in perspective represented by the psychosocial changes and changes in personality; evidence indicates that personality does not change substantially during adulthood (Costa et al., 2000; Johnson et al., 2005; Schaie et al., 2004). In fact, Costa and McCrae (1988) tested more than a thousand adults, both men and women, using standardized measures (not interviews) of the Big Five personality dimensions: openness to experience, conscientiousness, extraversion, agreeableness, and neuroticism (see Chapter 11). The participants ranged in age from 21 to 96 years. In addition to asking the participants to complete the measures, the researchers also asked 167 spouses to fill in the measures about the participants. Eighty-nine men and 78 women were tested twice, 6 years apart; thus, both cross-sectional and longitudinal data were collected. The results were clear: There were very few differences in any of the dimensions of personality over the years, and when such differences were found, they were very small. Moreover, Costa and McCrae found that personality was equally stable over time for men and women. They concluded that "aging itself has little effect on personality. This is true despite the fact that the normal course of aging includes disease, bereavement, divorce, unemployment, and many other significant events for substantial portions of the population" (p. 862). As a matter of fact, objective tests have shown that even when a person feels that his or her personality has changed (over the course of 6–9 years) during middle age, it really hasn't (Herbst et al., 2000).

Apparent changes in personality over time probably reflect not so much changes in the person as changes in the life challenges that he or she is confronting at the time: For many people, aging is accompanied by changes in marital status, parenting, and job-related factors. Such major life changes often become less frequent or severe as a person grows older, which could explain the finding that people become increasingly consistent in the degree to which they can be described by particular traits until around age 50, and thereafter are stable (Roberts & DelVecchio, 2000). Consistency, in this sense, refers to the relative ordering of people according to a trait—with increasing age, your ranking relative to other people will become more stable. This stability could reflect, in part, your settling into a niche in life, and thus restricting the range and variety of situations you encounter.

## Mature Emotions

The poet Robert Browning wrote, "Grow old along with me! / The best is yet to be / The last of life, for which the first is made." He may have been more right than he realized. In one study, people of different ages were prompted to report their emotions at various times over the course of a week (Carstensen et al., 2000). The researchers found that as people enter old age, they tend to experience more extended periods of highly positive emotions and less enduring spells of negative emotions than do younger people. Moreover, positive emotions were evoked as regularly for the elderly as for the young. Negative emotions, on the other hand, arose increasingly less often until about age 60 (when they leveled off).

But the news is even better than this. Older people are, well, more "mature" in their emotional responses. With age, people become better able to regulate emotions (Gross et al., 1997). In fact, elderly Americans of European and Chinese ethnic backgrounds had smaller changes in heart rate when watching emotional films than did younger people (Tsai et al., 2000). But this doesn't mean that their emotions are blunted or diminished; even when heart rate changes were smaller, older participants had subjective responses comparable to those of younger participants.

## Adult Relationships: Stable Changes

Perhaps as a result of their increased ability to grapple with emotions, older people tend to change their outlook on life. Laura Carstensen and her collaborators have developed

At one point, approximately 2,500 people well over 100 years old were reported to be living in countries comprising the former Soviet Union. One purportedly 168-year-old gentleman, who was still walking half a mile daily and gardening, attributed his longevity to the fact that he didn't marry until he was 65 (Seuling, 1986). Second marriages are common among elderly people.

the *socioemotional selectivity theory*, which rests on the idea that older people come to focus on the limited time they have left, which in turn changes their motivations (Carstensen & Charles, 1998; Lang & Carstensen, 2002). Consistent with this theory, these researchers find that as people age, they come increasingly to value emotionally fulfilling relationships. This leads older people to prefer the company of those with whom they are emotionally close. The same findings hold true both for White and Black Americans (Fung et al., 2001).

In general, as people age, they interact with fewer people, but these interactions tend to be more intimate (Carstensen, 1991, 1992)—older people don't miss the broader social networks that they had when they were young (Lansford et al., 1998). Relationships earlier in life tend to include more friends than relatives, but with age the mix reverses, with more time spent with relatives than with friends. This pattern is even more pronounced among Latinos than Americans of European descent (Levitt et al., 1993). In later life, a relationship long dormant can be picked up and reestablished with minimal effort (Carstensen,1992); after young adulthood, temperament and personality variables are relatively stable, which makes it easy to "know" someone again even after a long lapse.

During young adulthood, people are concerned that their relationships with friends and relatives are equitable—that neither party gives more than he or she receives (Lemme, 1995; Walster et al., 1978). As people age, such concerns recede into the background. In successful marriages, the members of the couple think of themselves as a team, not separate people who are in constant negotiations (Keith & Schafer, 1991). Because they are in it for the long haul, people trust that the balance of favors and repayment will even out over time. Thus, older couples resolve their differences with less negative emotion than do younger couples (Carstensen et al., 1995).

## Death and Dying

We began this chapter with the very earliest phase of development, and we close it with the last of life's experiences. The psychology of death has two faces: The effects on the person who is dying and the effects on friends and relatives.

**Grief** is the emotion of distress that follows the loss of a loved one, and **bereavement** is the experience of missing a loved one and longing for his or her company. People in the United States tend to go through the grieving process in three phases (Lemme, 1995; Lindemann, 1991):

1. Until about 3 weeks after the death, the bereaved person is in a state of shock. He or she feels empty, disoriented, and, sometimes, in a state of denial and disbelief; these feelings eventually settle into a state of deep sorrow. (This shock may be buffered by having to make funeral arrangements, deal with lawyers, and so on, but it nevertheless exists during this period.)

2. From 3 weeks to about a year following the death, the bereaved person experiences emotional upheavals, from anger to loneliness and guilt. During this time, people often review their relations with the deceased, wondering whether they should have done things differently, whether the death was inevitable. During this phase, people may think that they catch glimpses of the deceased in crowds or hear the person talking to them.

3. By the beginning of the second year, grief lessens. The bereaved person may largely stop thinking of the deceased and, in the case of a spouse's death,

**Grief:** The emotion of distress that follows the loss of a loved one.

**Bereavement:** The experience of missing a loved one and longing for his or her company.

be ready to become committed to a new intimate relationship. However, bereavement may continue indefinitely, particularly when a person is reminded of the deceased by special places or events, such as anniversaries or birthdays. Indeed, even years after an adult child has died, the parents tend to be more depressed and their health declines more rapidly, compared to parents who have not experienced such a loss. But such a tragedy may also bring the parents closer together, leading them to become more satisfied in their marriage (de Vries et al., 1997).

Wortman and Silver (1989) shook up this area of research by challenging key assumptions about the response to the death of a loved one. In particular, they challenged the idea that we must "work through" our loss, and that eventually we should expect to recover from the loss. That is, for many years, mental health clinicians urged the bereaved to "work through" their grief, which involves talking to others about their feelings and striving to finish the relationship with the dead (Lindstrom, 2002). But there is little evidence that such practices help (Davis et al., 2000). In fact, many clinicians now recommend suppressing or avoiding negative thoughts and emotions (not discussing them freely), focusing on positive emotions, and maintaining an internal relationship with the deceased.

The effects of the death of a friend or loved one depend on many factors. You might think that the death of a mate would have more severe effects if the marriage was conflicted, given the "unfinished business" at the end. But this has not turned out to be true (Carr et al., 2000). You also might think that the death would be easier to bear if you had a lot of forewarning. Again, this is not necessarily so (Carr et al., 2001). When forewarned, some people begin grieving before the death, and the accompanying depression doesn't necessarily let up afterwards; however, if women don't become depressed when forewarned that their husbands will die, this leaves them particularly vulnerable to becoming depressed after the death (Carnelley et al., 1999). In addition, a woman's reaction to her husband's death will be different if she was dependent on him (more anxiety after his death) than if she was not (less anxiety; Carr et al., 2000). And a bereaved person's reaction depends in part on the age of the deceased. Most deaths in the United States and Canada tend to occur at a relatively old age; the average age of death in some Latin American countries is much younger. The grief for someone who has had a full life is different from the grief for someone who has been cut down in his or her prime.

Concern about our own deaths apparently does not increase with age: Death anxiety either stays the same over the course of life or actually decreases near the end (Lemme, 1995). Women report fearing death more often than men do (Lonetto & Templer, 1986). However, this finding could simply mean that women are more honest or self-aware, or that men—consciously or unconsciously—avoid confronting the topic. In addition, because women tend to live longer than men, they may have had more opportunity to witness and to become concerned about death. Cultural differences clearly influence the ways in which people view and react to death (Kalish & Reynolds, 1977; Platt & Persico, 1992). Researchers who studied the Maya people of Central America found that they did not try to fight death. Elderly people announce that their time has come and then retire to a mat or hammock and wait to die. They refuse food or water, ignore attempts by others to talk to them, and soon die. Their attitude toward death is fostered by their strong belief in an afterlife in paradise (Steele, 1992). In contrast, people of the Kaliai, a tribe in Papua New Guinea, almost never die of old age, instead meeting death in battle or as a result of an accident. Thus, they do not view death as a natural occurrence; they look for someone to blame for such deaths, usually a sorcerer (Counts & Counts, 1992).

## Keeping the Aging Brain Sharp

In old age, particularly in the years just before death, many people do not function as well mentally as they did earlier in life, even if they are physically healthy (Small & Bäckman, 2000). Is this deterioration inevitable? As people age, the brain receives less blood, which means that it is sustained by fewer nutrients and less oxygen (Ivy et al., 1992). The blood supply to the brain decreases with age because the blood vessels themselves become smaller. Why does this happen? One reason may be that the brain cells are not working as hard, so they need less blood—which in turn leads the vessels to adjust (Ivy et al., 1992). This is like Catch-22: The neurons don't work as effectively because they receive fewer blood-borne nutrients and less oxygen, but the reason they don't receive as much is that they haven't been functioning as effectively as they did before.

But focusing on the brain alone is not enough. At the level of the person (at least in the United States), the elderly have absorbed societally transmitted negative conceptions about aging—and these stereotypes apparently can undermine the will to live. In one study, young and elderly people were shown positive or negative words concerning old age; the words were presented too briefly to be seen consciously—and hence functioned as unconscious "primes." The elderly participants were more likely to say that they would reject treatment for serious illness after being primed with negative words than they were after being primed with positive words; the negative words apparently activated stored negative concepts about aging. For the young participants, the type of words used as primes made no difference (Levy et al., 1999–2000).

As usual, we must also consider events at the level of the group. Social interactions clearly affect how well older people can cope with stress (Krause, 2004), which in turn affects the stress response; and older people experience cognitive degradation when they lose social support (Aartsen et al., 2004). But more than that, it is tempting to hypothesize that if you managed to engage your elderly parents, grandparents, or other family members in more challenging tasks, you could literally increase the blood supply to their brains and improve their thinking abilities. This result is plausible because "mental workouts" appear to enhance cognitive function in the elderly (Rowe & Kahn, 1998); in fact, training over the course of only 10 sessions can substantially improve memory, reasoning, and speed of processing in the elderly (Ball et al., 2002). Moreover, dendrites continue to grow normally even into old age (Coleman & Flood, 1986), and as neurons die, new connections may be formed to compensate for losses (Cotman, 1990). In one study, when elderly rats were moved from their standard cages into a rat playpen full of toys and other rats, they developed heavier brains with more extensive connections among neurons. Moreover, other researchers have found that mice that live in an enriched environment (complete with lots of attractive toys, other mice to play with, and opportunities to explore and exercise) retain more neurons as they age (Kempermann et al., 1998). Indeed, simply giving animals the chance to exercise enhances neuronal growth and improves survival rates (Cotman & Berchtold, 2002; van Praag et al., 1999). Very likely the same would be true for humans who were provided with more stimulating environments (Avorn & Langer, 1982; Langer & Rodin, 1976; Rodin & Langer, 1977; Rowe & Kahn, 1998). In fact, researchers have found that the brain generally becomes smaller with aging, but that people with more education have less severe size reductions (Coffey et al., 1999).

Research with mice suggests that it's not the pure amount of stimulation that boosts brain function, but rather the amount of novelty that's encountered (Kempermann & Gage, 1999). If this result generalizes to humans, travel may truly broaden the mind, even for the elderly!

Thus, if your otherwise healthy parents or grandparents are understimulated by their surroundings (as occurs in some nursing homes as well as in many home environments), this could affect their brains. The changes in their brains could in turn lead them to avoid mental challenge and engagement, which in turn could lead to changes in self-concept and level of self-esteem. These changes then may lead them to become lethargic and to avoid social interaction. And not interacting with others could lead to even less effective neural functioning, and so on. Clearly, there is ample opportunity for events at all three levels to interact.

However, it is unlikely that all of the functions that are impaired with age can be helped simply by getting your grandparents to use their brains more, or even by changing their conceptions of what it means to be elderly. MRI scans of more than 3,600 apparently normal elderly people (aged 65 to 97) revealed that slightly over one third had brain lesions. These were often small and usually affected subcortical structures, but some of the lesions were probably large enough to perhaps affect a specific cognitive function (Bryan et al., 1997). Damage to the white matter can also disrupt cognition in the elderly (Koga et al., 2002). Thus, possible effects of changing beliefs and of social interactions must be considered within the context of changes in the brain. As always, events at the three levels interact.

# Test Yourself

1. One biological view of aging argues that it is programmed into the genes. A different interpretation is that
   a. aging causes the copies of genes to contain more errors, until they fail to function properly.
   b. genes have on-off switches that break down during aging as a result of wear and tear.
   c. aging is due entirely to environmental factors such as stress, lack of exercise, and poor diet.
   d. genes are programmed to affect development, not aging.
2. How does intelligence change with aging?
   a. Intelligence increases until death.
   b. Fluid intelligence declines more than crystallized intelligence.
   c. Crystallized declines more than fluid intelligence.
   d. Intelligence declines dramatically after middle age.
3. How does aging affect emotions?
   a. With increasing age, people are less able to regulate their emotions.
   b. With increasing age, emotions become very dulled.
   c. With increasing age, people are better able to regulate their emotions.
   d. Emotions are not very important to the elderly because the relevant brain structures become less reactive.
4. Research about people's concern over their own death has found that it
   a. apparently does not increase with age.
   b. dramatically increases with age.
   c. tends to disappear soon after puberty.
   d. is a constant preoccupation among the very old.

## Answers

1.a 2.b 3.c 4.a

# Think It Through!

If you could choose several of your abilities to protect from decaying with age, which would they be? Why? If you could choose between becoming wise or having a perfect memory, which would you choose? Why?

As you age, what factors do you think will influence whether you will stay close to friends you made earlier in life?

# REVIEW AND REMEMBER!

## Summary

<table>
<tr><td>

### I. In the Beginning: From Conception to Birth

**A.** Your mother's and father's genes recombined when their eggs and sperm were formed and you received half of your chromosomes from your mother's egg and half from your father's sperm, leading you to have a unique combination of genes. The development of both the brain and the body relies on the activation of specific genes, which is regulated in part by environmental events.

**B.** Prenatal development progresses in order through a series of stages; in the first trimester (3 months), the zygote becomes an embryo, then a fetus.

**C.** The developing fetus is active and becomes increasingly coordinated over time. The fetus can detect human speech and prefers the mother's voice.

**D.** Maturational processes can be disrupted by teratogens or enhanced by certain environmental events, such as those that reduce the level of stress experienced by the mother.

**E.** Newborns have a relatively good sense of smell and can learn that different stimuli tend to occur together. They have the sensory capacities needed to organize sounds into words and recognize objects.

**F.** Newborns are equipped with a host of inborn reflexes, such as the sucking and Moro reflexes. These reflexes often disappear during the course of development.

**G.** Aspects of temperament that are present at birth may persist for many years to come.

### II. Infancy and Childhood: Taking Off

**A.** In general, motor development progresses from the head, down the trunk to the arms, and finally to the legs; at the same time, it proceeds out from the center of the body to the periphery (hands, fingers, and toes).

**B.** Perception develops so that the child can make finer discriminations, needs less stimulus information to recognize objects, can focus attention more deliberately, and can search more systematically.

**C.** Even 3-month-old infants have both implicit and explicit memory. Not all aspects of memory develop at the same rate. Although perceptual memory is present before verbal memory, not all aspects of perceptual memory change with age in the same way.

**D.** Piaget believed that each child moves through a series of major periods of cognitive development. However, these stages may not be fixed, and many abilities are evident at earlier ages than originally believed. Researchers have since found that children have at least the rudiments of many abilities far earlier than Piaget's theory would predict.

</td><td>

## Your Notes

*I.*

*A.*

*B.*

*C. Fetus—increasing coordination, preference for mom's voice*

*D.*

*E.*

*F.*

*G.*

*II.*

*A. Motor development: head → trunk → arms & legs; center → periphery*

*B.*

*C.*

*D.*

</td></tr>
</table>

**E.** Children develop a theory of mind at a very early age, and it becomes increasingly sophisticated.

**F.** Cognitive development arises in part from improved information processing, particularly more efficient working memory, which probably in part reflects neural development. However, as Vygotsky stressed, culture and instruction also play a role in cognitive development.

**G.** Children become attached to their caregivers through a series of stages, but may end up being attached in different ways.

**H.** Being in daycare as an infant does not necessarily lead to poorer attachment to the primary caregiver.

**I.** The self-concept begins to develop during very early infancy, and it probably affects many social interactions, including gender roles. Gender identity is part of the self-concept and is influenced by biological factors present since conception.

**J.** People may move through a series of stages in the way they tend to reason about moral decisions, and males and females may tend to reason slightly differently about such decisions—but this is most likely a function of their different concerns in daily life, not something intrinsic to their gender.

**K.** A conscience may develop early in life (at around 3 years old), but its development depends on a combination of temperament and the child's interactions with his or her mother.

## III. Adolescence: Between Two Worlds

**A.** The extremities (arms and legs) grow rapidly during adolescence, with the trunk lagging behind, a pattern that can produce a gawky appearance. During this period, the body acquires pubic hair and other secondary sexual characteristics. Puberty occurs earlier today than it did previously.

**B.** If the adolescent reaches Piaget's period of formal operations, he or she can reason about abstract concepts systematically—and thus becomes capable of true scientific thought. This enhanced reasoning ability affects all aspects of thinking, including conceptions of self and society.

**C.** Although hormonal changes can lead the adolescent to experience more conflicts with parents as well as to have mood swings and to tend to take risks, these tendencies are not universal.

**D.** Enhanced cognitive capacities during adolescence allow the teenager to think about relationships in more sophisticated ways, but adolescents are also affected by their perceptions of an imaginary audience and a personal fable.

**E.** Most adolescents develop strong same-gender friendships, but these bonds tend to be stronger among young women than young men.

## IV. Adulthood and Aging: The Continuously Changing Self

**A.** The period of emerging adulthood bridges adolescences and adulthood and is marked by major life transitions, including leaving the parents' home, getting a

| | |
|---|---|
| *E.* | |
| *F.* | |
| *G.* | |
| *H.* | |
| *I.* | |
| *J.* | |
| *K. Conscience—development depends on temperament & interactions with mom* | |
| *III.* | |
| *A.* | |
| *B.* | |
| *C.* | |
| *D.* | |
| *E.* | |
| *IV.* | |
| *A.* | |

job (often after having attended college), getting married, and starting a family. However, not everyone follows this path, and some may not do so in a direct way.

**B.** The body remains relatively stable until around age 50. At about this point, women experience menopause, and both men and women may begin to become less vigorous. Many of the changes in the body can be treated, either by dietary supplements (such as calcium for bone weakness) or with changes in activities (which can reduce obesity and strengthen bones).

*B.*

**C.** With age, the lens of the eye clouds, and the pupil doesn't open as much as it did before, leading to difficulty in seeing contrast. The elderly also have difficulty hearing higher-frequency sounds, and their sense of smell declines.

*C.*

**D.** With advancing old age, working memory operates less effectively, memory retrieval becomes more difficult, and people sometimes experience source amnesia.

*D. Elderly have problems with WM & memory retrieval, sometimes source amnesia.*

**E.** Although intelligence declines with advanced age, fluid intelligence may be more affected than crystallized intelligence, and a person's special abilities need not be affected much, if at all (but in different people, different abilities tend to be affected). In some respects, the elderly can reason more logically than younger people.

*E.*

**F.** Many theorists, including Erikson and Levinson, have proposed that people pass through psychosocial stages as they age. These stages may be a result of challenges posed by a particular culture; there is little evidence that personality changes substantially during adulthood.

*F.*

**G.** Adult relationships focus on closer involvement with fewer people (often relatives) and tend to be stable over long periods of time. The elderly tend to have greater emotional control than younger people.

*G.*

**H.** Grief for another's death may pass through stages, which may extend over 2 years following the death. The sense of bereavement may never entirely disappear. Concern about one's own death does not increase with age and, for some people, may actually decrease.

*H.*

**I.** Although many people experience terminal decline, this does not appear to be an inevitable final phase of life.

*I.*

**J.** In old age, the brain may not function as well as it did before, in part because the person is no longer being intellectually challenged; enrichment of the environment can in part reverse this decline.

*J.*

NOTE: Once you feel that you understand the material in this chapter, visit the book's Web site at www.ablongman.com/kosslyn3e to test your knowledge with additional study questions.

# Key Terms

accommodation, p. 547
adolescence, p. 562
assimilation, p. 547
attachment, p. 554
bereavement, p. 578
concrete operation, p. 549
conservation, p. 549
cross-sectional study, p. 573
egocentrism, p. 549
embryo, p. 532

fetus, p. 532
formal operation, p. 550
gender identity, p. 557
gender roles, p. 558
grief, p. 578
longitudinal study, p. 573
maturation, p. 531
moral dilemma, p. 559
object permanence, p. 548

private speech, p. 554
psychosocial development, p. 575
puberty, p. 562
self-concept, p. 556
separation anxiety, p. 555
schema, p. 547
teratogen, p. 534
theory of mind, p. 551
zygote, p. 531

# CHAPTER 13

# STRESS, HEALTH, AND COPING

Lisa, a college sophomore, was becoming worried about her father, Al. Only 54 years old, he always seemed exhausted, regardless of the time of day or the amount of work he'd been doing. Whenever Lisa asked him why he was so tired, he answered in generalities: "Oh, work's crazy. That's all, honey." He'd also been coughing a lot, and when Lisa asked about this, he'd reply, "I've been sick more than usual—it's just been a bad winter."

Lisa used to look forward to her visits home and her telephone conversations with her father, but now she dreaded talking to him because he always sounded so tired and dejected. Lisa suggested that he see his doctor, exercise, maybe learn some type of relaxation technique. Al finally told her the real reason he was so tense and tired: His company had laid off several of his colleagues, and he was afraid he'd be next. The layoffs meant that Al's department was now responsible for more work with less staff. In addition, as part of the downsizing, the company had moved to smaller premises. His new office was cramped, noisy, and generally unpleasant. He had trouble concentrating, and he knew his work was suffering, which made him even more concerned that he'd be fired. There was a possibility of a job offer from another company, but at a substantially lower salary. Lisa, listening to his story, understood that he had tried to protect her by not telling her. If he was fired or took the other job, he wouldn't be able to help with her college expenses, and she was already working 25 hours a week. If Al's fears materialized, she would probably have to leave school, at least for a while, or take out very large loans. He was worried about his own situation, and worried about his daughter; Lisa understood the burden of those worries, which she now shared. She worried, too, about his persistent cough—was it just from lots of winter colds, or was it something more?

This situation produced stress in both father and daughter. Just what is "stress"? Can it affect our health? How can we deal with it? Such questions, and the search for answers, are in the domain of **health psychology**, the field concerned with the promotion of health and the prevention and treatment of illness as it relates to psychological factors.

# WHAT IS STRESS?

Al began to hate going to work. Often, as he worked at his desk, he felt as if he'd just finished a race—heart beating, palms sweating, breath coming hard—but without any accompanying sense of relief or accomplishment. He was simply exhausted all of the time and felt as if his heart wasn't pumping his blood fast enough for his body's needs. He began to be seriously worried about his health, as well as his job.

In contrast, Maya, a colleague who so far had also survived at the company, didn't seem disturbed by the changes happening around them. Maya had two children and, like Al, needed her job, but she seemed to be taking this difficult situation in stride. Al didn't understand how Maya was able to stay so calm—didn't she understand what was going on?

And what about Lisa's response to pressures? She had been managing the demands of college and job well; but after her father explained his situation at work and the possible repercussions for both of them, she noticed physical symptoms in herself—sweaty palms, racing heart—even while studying or taking class notes. Al and Lisa were responding to stress.

## Stress: The Big Picture

Today, even third graders complain of feeling "stressed out," and adults take evening courses in "stress management." But what exactly *is* stress? **Stress** is the general term describing the psychological and physical response to a stimulus that alters the body's equilibrium (Lazarus & Folkman, 1984). The stimulus that throws the body's equilibrium out of balance is called a **stressor**; for instance, stepping on a piece of glass while walking barefoot and getting a puncture wound is a stressor. The body's response to a stressor is the **stress response**, also called the *fight-or-flight response*; this response consists of the bodily changes that occur to help you cope with the stressor. If you get a puncture wound, your body may produce chemicals called *endorphins* and *enkephalins*, its own versions of painkillers, and cause white blood cells to congregate at the site of the injury to fight off any infectious agents. These responses work to bring the body back to normal, to restore homeostasis.

The long list of potential stressors is categorized according to a number of criteria (Table 13.1). Stressors can be short-term (**acute stressor**) or long-term (**chronic stressor**); they can be physical, psychological (which affect events at the level of the person), or social (or, of course, some combination). Physical stressors, such as not eating for 2 days, generally apply to most people; psychological and social stressors, on the other hand, can be much more subjective. Going to a dance club for hours can be a party animal's idea of a great time or a shy person's nightmare. In general, it is our *perception* of a stimulus that determines whether it will elicit the stress response, not necessarily the objective nature of the stimulus itself.

Stress is not always a negative process, however. Stress, or more accurately, stressors, can lead to positive change and growth (Linley & Joseph, 2004). Consider that

**Health psychology:** The field concerned with the promotion of health and the prevention and treatment of illness as it relates to psychological factors.

**Stress:** The general term describing the psychological and physical response to a stimulus that alters the body's state of equilibrium.

**Stressor:** A stimulus that throws the body's equilibrium out of balance.

**Stress response:** The bodily changes that occur to help a person cope with a stressor; also called the *fight-or-flight response*.

**Acute stressor:** A stressor of short-term duration.

**Chronic stressor:** A stressor of long-term duration.

## TABLE 13.1 Examples of Types of Stressors

| Type of Stressor | Duration of Stressor | |
|---|---|---|
| | Acute | Chronic |
| **Physical** | Being injured in a car crash | Being underfed; having cancer |
| **Psychological (level of the person)** | Working against a deadline | Chronically feeling pressured by work |
| **Social** | Being humiliated | Chronic isolation; overcrowding |

college students reported that their most stressful experience during the previous 6 months had led to personal growth (Park & Fenster, 2004).

# The Biology of Stress

Austrian-born researcher Hans Selye (1907–1982), who pioneered the study of stress, established that the body responds to stressors in generally predictable ways (Selye, 1976). He called the overall stress response the **general adaptation syndrome (GAS)** and suggested that it has three distinct phases: alarm, resistance, and exhaustion (Figure 13.1).

## The Alarm Phase: Fight or Flight

Perception of a stressor triggers the **alarm phase**, which is characterized by the fight-or-flight response. In this response, the body mobilizes itself to fight or to flee from a threatening stimulus, which can be a physical threat, such as a knife at the throat, or a psychological one, such as working against a deadline.

When you perceive a threat, your brain, via the hypothalamic-pituitary-adrenal axis (the HPA axis), responds to the threat by activating the sympathetic nervous system and inhibiting the parasympathetic nervous system (see Figure 3.19 and the accompanying discussion). Neurotransmitters and hormonal secretions such as epinephrine and norepinephrine (also referred to as adrenaline and noradrenaline, respectively) cause breathing, heart rate, and blood pressure to increase and can alter immune system functioning (Madden, 2003). (Note that norepinephrine is considered a neurotransmitter when it is found in the brain, but a hormone when dispersed in other parts of the body.) These changes serve to bring more oxygen to the muscles as you prepare to fight or flee. In addition, these sympathetic nervous system changes cause your pupils to dilate (allowing more light to enter for greater visual acuity) and your palms to sweat slightly (for better gripping).

When the stress response is triggered, the hypothalamus secretes a substance that causes the release of **glucocorticoids**, another group of hormones. *Cortisol*, a glucocorticoid, not only increases the production of energy from glucose, but also has

## FIGURE 13.1

### Selye's Three-Stage Stress Response

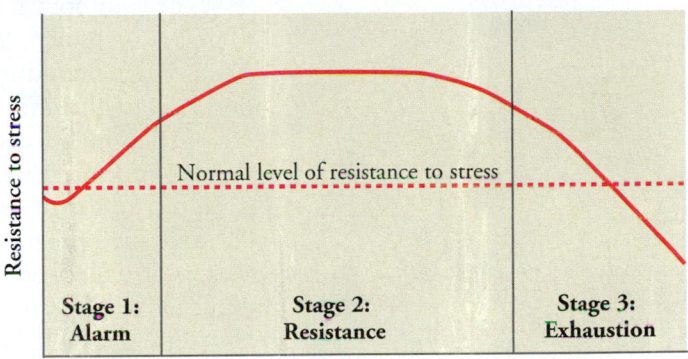

Hans Selye proposed that the body's response to prolonged stress has three stages: alarm, resistance, and exhaustion.

General adaptation syndrome (GAS): The overall stress response that has three phases: alarm, resistance, and exhaustion.

Alarm phase: The first phase of the GAS, in which a stressor is perceived and the fight-or-flight response is activated.

Glucocorticoids: A group of hormones that are released when the stress response is triggered.

an anti-inflammatory effect, which makes it effective in helping restore the body's equilibrium after physical injury. In the short run, all of these changes sharpen the senses, improve some qualities of memory (Sapolsky, 1997), and make it easier to fight or flee. Cortisol also affects neurotransmitter functioning, and thus it can affect cognition and emotion (Erikson et al., 2003); these changes in neurotransmitter functioning may account for the emotional responses and changes in thinking that can occur in extremely stressful situations.

Selye proposed that the fight-or-flight response, and the GAS more generally, is the same regardless of the nature of the stressor. Research since Selye's time indicates that this aspect of his theory was off the mark: Although the general stress response occurs with all stressors, the speed of its action and the amount of each hormone that is produced can differ, depending on the particular type of stressor (Goldstein, 1995; Henry, 1977; Pacak & Palkovits, 2001; Romero & Sapolsky, 1996).

For most of us, the threats we experience do not require the kind of *physical* response required of our distant ancestors. Taking a final exam requires sitting in a chair, not running or climbing away from an enemy. Nonetheless, your body may still react to the test-taking situation with the fight-or-flight response; it can get all revved up with nowhere to go.

## The Resistance Phase

Once your body is primed to fight or flee, you enter the **resistance phase** (also known as the *adaptation phase*), in which the body mobilizes its resources to achieve equilibrium despite the continued presence of the stressor. In other words, it *adapts* to the stressor.

Both the initial stress response and the resistance phase require energy, which comes from fat cells, muscles, and the liver. The increased blood flow (which results from increased heart and respiration rates) helps deliver the energy quickly and efficiently to the parts of the body that need it most. Digestion, growth, sex drive, and reproductive processes are slowed during times of stress. In women, menstruation may stop or may occur irregularly in response to chronic stress; in men, sperm and testosterone levels may decrease. As a matter of survival, why waste energy on these processes when it is needed elsewhere? In addition to these changes, no new energy is stored during stress; this means that chronic stress leads to a lack of any reserve of energy to repair bodily damage, producing a sense of fatigue.

Army personnel undergoing survival training had increased levels of both cortisol and *neuropeptide-Y*; the higher the neuropeptide-Y levels, the less distress they experienced (Morgan et al., 2002). Another study found that neuropeptide-Y levels were higher in combat veterans who experienced less combat trauma (Morgan et al., 2003).

During the resistance phase, cortisol helps the body return to a more normal state in the presence of a continued stressor (McEwen & Schmeck, 1994). Cortisol levels reach their peak within 20–40 minutes after the onset of the acute stressor, and they return to baseline, on average, up to 1 hour after the acute stressor has been eliminated (Dickerson & Kemeny, 2002); however, with continued stress, cortisol levels may not return to baseline. The more extreme the stressors, the more glucocorticoids are produced in an attempt to restore equilibrium, and this process decreases the functioning of the immune system. With extreme stressors, the release of cortisol also occurs with the release of *neuropeptide-Y*; a neuropeptide is a type of protein that can act as a neurotransmitter or a hormone. Neuropeptide-Y can function as a neurotransmitter that decreases the activity of the HPA axis (Antonijevic et al., 2000), thereby dampening down anxiety or fear.

## The Exhaustion Phase

If the stressor continues, the **exhaustion phase** sets in. Selye proposed that, with a continued stressor, the body becomes exhausted because its limited resources for dealing with stress are depleted. More recent research has found that rather than producing "exhaustion," the continued stress response begins to damage the body, leading to an increased risk of stress-related diseases. In addition, cortisol can damage hippocampal cells (see Chapter 7), decreasing the number of these cells as well as the amount of branching of some of their dendrites (McEwen, 2003); such changes adversely affect learning and memory (Newcomer et al., 1999; Sapolsky, 1992).

Exhaustion phase: The final stage of the GAS, in which the continued stress response itself becomes damaging to the body.

## From Stressor to Allostatic Load: Multiple Stressors and Their Time Course

Think about your past couple of weeks. You've probably endured a variety of stressors (tests, papers, financial worries, or perhaps health and family concerns). Some of the stressors (such as tests) were transient; some (such as financial worries) were longer lasting. Because people often experience multiple stressors of various types simultaneously, researchers have begun to shift how they think about the body's response to stressors. The term *allostasis* (from the Greek *allo*, meaning "other," and *stasis* meaning "stability") refers to the multiple biological changes that allow you to adapt to a stressor or a set of stressors in the short run, so your body functions within a comfortable range.

Although adaptive in the short run, maintaining equilibrium within a comfortable range through biological changes has a cost—cumulative wear and tear, referred to as the *allostatic load*. Allostatic load is the stress carried by the body to maintain equilibrium (McEwen, 1998, 2000; McEwen & Wingfield, 2003). As the number or intensity of stressors rises, so does the allostatic load. Here's an analogy: Say you have a wooden seesaw, of the sort you see in playgrounds the world over. If two 40-pound children are on it, there's relatively little load. But what if two 400-pound gorillas were to sit on the ends? Although the seesaw could still be in balance, it would be under much greater stress. And just as the probability that the seesaw will break increases when it is put under greater stress, so too with the body; greater allostatic load increases the risk of medical and psychological symptoms (Goldstein & McEwen, 2002). When you must fight or flee, more demands are made on your body than during calmer times; chronic demands (high allostatic load) will produce biological wear and tear, lessen the body's ability to respond appropriately, and possibly lead to disease or illness (Karlamangla et al., 2002; Seeman, Singer, et al., 1997). And just as the seesaw would be in greater jeopardy if those gorillas played on it for an hour instead of a minute, chronic stressors take more toll on your body than do time-limited stressors (Evans, 2003). In fact, if you often have to function with a high allostatic load, your body will switch less easily to respond to the lower demands during periods of calm, such as by lowering blood pressure (McEwen, 2000). Al clearly was trying to function under a high allostatic load, and the longer he continued in this state, the more likely it was that he would become ill.

Allostatic load isn't determined solely by environmental demands. Rather, it is affected by your past experience with the stressor, your genetic predisposition (meaning aspects of both your body and your personality that are genetically influenced), and lifestyle factors (such as amount that you exercise and your diet; McEwen, 1998; McEwen & Seeman, 1999; Seeman et al., 2002).

## When Stressed, Women May Tend and Befriend

Shelley Taylor and colleagues (2000, 2002, 2004) point out that until the last decade, much of the research on the physiology of the stress response has used male participants, mainly because women's menstrual cycles can affect measures of biological stress in complex ways. Taking an evolutionary psychology approach, these researchers propose that the fight-or-flight response does not apply to women as much as it does to men: Being pregnant and caring for children would have made fighting or fleeing difficult for our ancestors. Thus, according to Taylor and colleagues, women developed a "tend and befriend" response to stressors, designed to maximize safety and minimize distress. The "tend" element involves quieting children and trying to blend into the environment, whereas the "befriend" element involves creating and maintaining social connections so that women and their children are protected and cared for when stressors are present. However, women do show a GAS pattern of autonomic arousal similar to that observed in men, although some research suggests that men and women may differ in how responsive their HPA axes are to stressors; men may have greater increases of activity in the HPA axis, resulting in a faster heart rate, for example, in response to stressors (Taylor, Lerner, et al., 2004; Traustadóttir et al., 2003).

# It's How You Think of It: Interpreting Stimuli as Stressors

Is a new relationship stressful? How about writing a term paper? Hearing a baby cry? Being stuck in a traffic jam? The answer to all of these is maybe, maybe not. Many psychological, social, and even physical stimuli are stressors only if you *perceive* them as stressful (Lazarus & Folkman, 1984).

## Appraisal: Stressors in the Eyes of the Beholder

Physical stressors, such as a piece of glass stuck in your bare foot, are generally easy to identify, but the definition of a psychological or social stressor is more subjective. Al's colleague Maya is not bothered about the recent firings because she wants to spend more time with her children. In some respects, she wouldn't mind being out of work (and collecting unemployment) so that she could stay home for a while; between savings and her husband's paycheck, the family could get by for a few months. So, for Maya, the threat of being fired is not perceived as a stressor.

The importance of perceptions in determining whether something is a stressor was demonstrated in a classic study by Speisman and colleagues (1964). Participants were asked to watch a film of a primitive ritual involving a crude genital operation called "subincision." Participants in one group heard a "trauma" soundtrack for the film that emphasized the pain experienced by those undergoing the rite. Another group heard a "denial" soundtrack, which emphasized the positive aspects of the ritual and minimized the experience of pain. A third group heard an "intellectualization" soundtrack, which described the ceremony in a detached, clinical manner. Those in either the denial or the intellectualization group showed less of an autonomic response to the film and reported being less upset than those in the trauma group. This study demonstrated that the content of the narration about the ritual (the context, and therefore how the stimulus is perceived) affected the stress response of the participants.

Even among college students, what is considered stressful differs, depending on whether the student is traditional (went to college straight from high school) or nontraditional (took some time off between high school and college, or has multiple roles, such as student and parent or employee). Social activities have a larger impact on traditional students, whereas nontraditional students are more likely to enjoy doing homework and going to classes and to worry less about how they are doing academically (Dill & Henley, 1998).

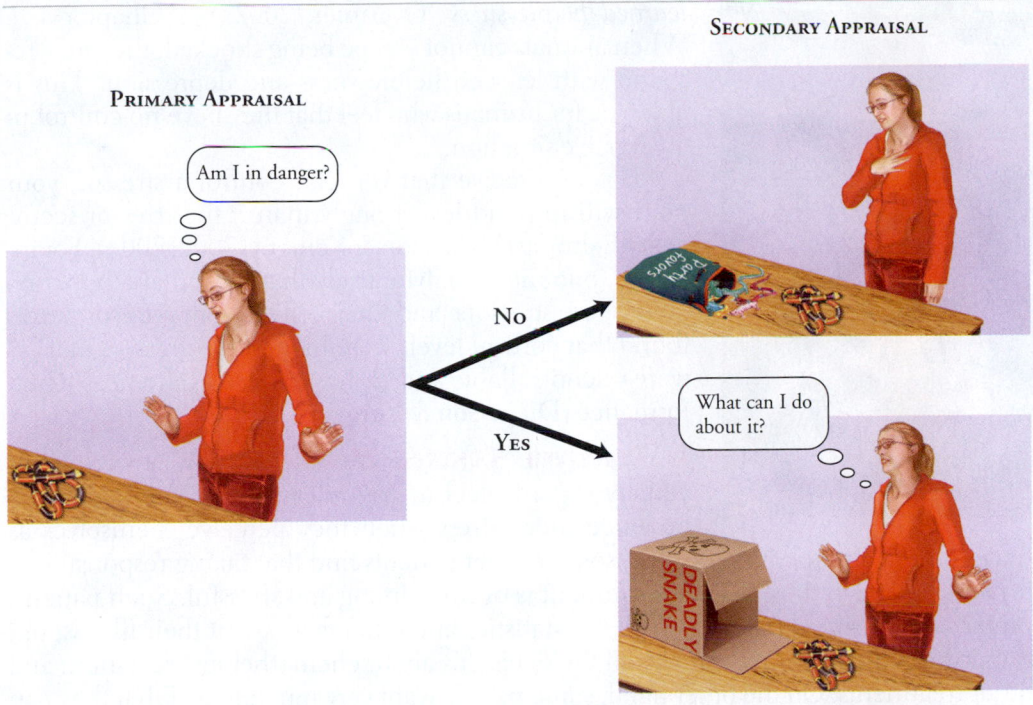

SECONDARY APPRAISAL

**FIGURE 13.2**

## Cognitive Appraisal of a Stimulus

Cognitive appraisal of a stimulus, in this case a snake, is a two-stage process: (1) determining whether a stimulus is dangerous, and, if so, (2) determining what can be done to prevent or minimize the danger.

As illustrated in Figure 13.2, this process of *cognitive appraisal* of a stimulus occurs in two phases. First, the stimulus is assessed for the likelihood of danger; this is the *primary appraisal*. This assessment is followed by the *secondary appraisal*, the determination of the resources available to deal with the stressor. In other words, the question "Am I in danger?" is followed by the question "What can I do about it?" (Bishop, 1994). (Note, however, that such appraisals can happen without conscious awareness; Smith & Kirby, 2000). After the secondary appraisal comes **coping**; that is, the person experiencing stress takes some course of action regarding the stressor, its effects, or his or her reaction to it.

Depending on how you appraise a stimulus, you will experience different emotions and your body will react in different ways (Maier et al., 2003). For instance, should you determine that you have the resources—emotional, financial, and practical—to cope with a stressor, you will likely view the stressor as a challenge, not a threat. In contrast, should you determine that you do not have the resources to cope, you probably will view the stressor as a threat (Blascovich & Tomaka, 1996). In addition, should your cognitive appraisal lead you to conclude that a stimulus is dangerous, negative emotions will be triggered—and these emotions then become a part of the problem that you must address with your coping strategies (Folkman & Moscowitz, 2004).

## Perceived Control

How do you think you would feel if your boss told you to get a project finished a day earlier than you had planned: Do you think you would experience less pressure if you had decided, all by yourself, to finish the project earlier? What if your boss had actually made the decision but gave you the impression that the final decision was yours? Research has shown that actual control is not important; what is important is whether you *perceive* a sense of control (Shapiro et al., 1996). The perception of control can affect your performance. Perceived lack of control in the face of a stressor can lead to the onset of

**Coping:** Taking some course of action regarding the stressor, its effects, or the person's reaction to it.

Cultural factors can affect people's perception of control. Western cultures, particularly that of the United States, emphasize active control of yourself and mastery of your environment. Some other cultures emphasize adaptation—accepting yourself and your circumstances (Shapiro et al., 1996), as when a train is very late.

*learned helplessness* (Overmier, 2002; see Chapter 10). When animals cannot escape being shocked, they may respond with learned helplessness and depression. This is also true for humans who feel that they have no control in an aversive situation.

If you perceive that you can control a stressor, your body will respond less strongly than if the stressor seems overwhelming (Dickerson & Kemeny, 2002, 2004). For instance, one meta-analytic study that looked at laboratory-controlled stressors and their effects on cortisol levels found that cortisol levels were highest for stressors that (1) were uncontrollable and (2) involved an evaluation of performance (Dickerson & Kemeny, 2004).

**A PERCEIVED CONTROL MISMATCH** Not everyone is equally eager to feel in control; in fact, some people experience more stress when they perceive themselves as having more control. For example, some cancer patients find that taking responsibility for and control of their medical treatment is overwhelming and stressful. Such patients prefer not to learn about and weigh the statistics and other facts about their illness, but rather want their doctors to make all the decisions about chemotherapy, radiation, and other treatments. On the other hand, some people want very much to feel that they can control a situation but may, at least after a certain point, not have much real opportunity to do so. Once a college or job application is written and an interview is over, for example, there's not much you can do to get yourself accepted or hired; nothing is left but to wait for the decision. Thus, there can be a mismatch between perceived control and the preferred level of control in a given situation (Shapiro et al., 1996).

**IF IT'S NOT CONTROLLABLE, AT LEAST LET IT BE PREDICTABLE** Even for those who prefer to have more control, perceiving a lack of control doesn't always produce stress. This apparent contradiction is resolved by another factor: Many things that are beyond our control are at least *predictable*. You have no control over whether or not you take math quizzes (at least, not if you want to pass the course), but announced quizzes are likely to be less stressful than surprise quizzes. If quizzes are announced, you can relax on the days when none are scheduled; in contrast, the possibility of surprise quizzes means that the beginning of every class can be stressful as you wait to learn your fate. However, if surprise quizzes are a frequent occurrence in a course, you will habituate to them and not view them to be as great a stressor—the quizzes, unpleasant as they might be, will no longer be so unpredictable.

Another example of the importance of control and unpredictability is seen in the administration of pain medication. When postsurgery patients are allowed to determine when and how much pain medication they receive (through an intravenous tube connected to a pump by their bed), they give themselves less medication than when it is administered by a nurse they have called. Why is this? Because a patient who must ring for a nurse has little control of the situation *and* cannot predict what will happen—what the dosage will be, when the nurse will come, even if the nurse has heard the call. The uncertainty and unpredictability as to when the pain medication will come can heighten the experience of pain. When medication is self-regulated, predictability and control are restored, and the pain becomes more manageable (Chapman, 1989).

Researchers looking at the role of social class in the perception of control and health found that, not surprisingly, people with lower incomes perceived less control in their lives *and* were in poorer health. Those who did have a greater sense of control, regardless of income, had better health (Lachman & Weaver, 1998).

**WARNING! UNCONTROLLABLE STRESSOR AHEAD!** Although warning of an upcoming stressor can reduce the sensations of stress, vague information can make the stress worse. When Al heard that there were going to be unspecified changes at work, this vague information only served to increase his general level of stress response. But even a specific warning is not helpful if it comes either too far in advance of or immediately before an event. When received too far in advance, the information serves only to increase anticipation; when the information arrives immediately before the event, there may be no time to put coping strategies into play (Sapolsky, 1997).

In general, perceived control is helpful only when you can see how much worse things could have been; then you can feel positive about what you have controlled. In the face of a catastrophic stressor, such as the diagnosis of a terminal illness, perceived control actually *increases* the stress: Things can't be much worse, and if the person given the diagnosis has perceived control, he or she may feel responsible for the catastrophic stressor (Pitman et al., 1995; Sapolsky, 1997).

# Sources of Stress

Psychologists have found that certain types of stimuli are more likely to be appraised as stressful. That is, certain events and situations are more likely to lead to a stress response.

## Internal Conflict

Stress can be caused by **internal conflict**, the emotional predicament people experience when they make difficult choices. The choices may involve competing goals, actions, impulses, or situations. Miller (1959) categorized three types of internal conflict. **Approach–approach conflict** results when competing alternatives are equally positive. Although this kind of conflict can be stressful, it is not necessarily experienced as unpleasant because both options are pleasing. For instance, if you had to choose between two very good job offers and wanted both jobs about equally, you would be facing an approach–approach conflict. The contrary case is **avoidance–avoidance conflict**, which results when competing alternatives are equally unpleasant. In such circumstances, making a choice can be very stressful. Faced with the choice of either taking a job you really don't want or being unemployed (and needing to pay back college loans), you would experience an avoidance–avoidance conflict. The third type of internal conflict, **approach–avoidance conflict**, occurs when a possible course of action has both positive and negative aspects and thus produces *both* approach *and* avoidance. If you were offered a job that you wanted but that would require you to move to a city in which you didn't want to live, you would experience approach–avoidance conflict. These three types of conflict are illustrated in Figure 13.3 (on p. 596).

## Life's Hassles

In the 1960s, researchers began to explore the stressfulness of various life experiences. These investigations led to the idea that certain events, such as divorce or job loss, were stressful for almost everyone (Holmes & Rahe, 1967). What was perhaps more surprising was the finding that positive events, such as vacations and job promotions, could also be stressors. Subsequent research, however, has not shown these kinds of events, positive or negative, to be reliable predictors of stress-related illness. Because this original line of research focused on the events themselves and not the *perception* of the events, it was not, in fact, a valid way to measure life's stressors. More recent work has focused on life's daily hassles, rather than major changes in life circumstances, as

Internal conflict: The emotional predicament people experience when making difficult choices.

Approach–approach conflict: The internal conflict that occurs when competing alternatives are equally positive.

Avoidance–avoidance conflict: The internal conflict that occurs when competing alternatives are equally unpleasant.

Approach–avoidance conflict: The internal conflict that occurs when a course of action has both positive and negative aspects.

FIGURE 13.3 **Three Types of Internal Conflict That Can Lead to Stress**

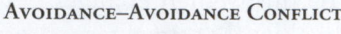

APPROACH–APPROACH CONFLICT     AVOIDANCE–AVOIDANCE CONFLICT     APPROACH–AVOIDANCE CONFLICT

better predicting distress and stress-related illnesses (Chamberlain & Zika, 1990; Tein et al., 2000).

All of the daily hassles—the "little things" (which are sometimes not so little but ongoing), such as concern about the health of someone in your family, having too many things to do, misplacing or losing things, trying to lose weight—add up to create stress. Those who report more daily hassles also report more psychological problems (D'Angelo & Wierzbicki, 2003; Kanner et al., 1981; Mroczek & Almeida, 2004) and physical symptoms (DeLongis et al., 1982), and they are more likely to experience problems with the immune system (Bosch et al., 1998; Martin & Dobbin, 1988; Peters et al., 2003) as well as higher cholesterol levels (Twisk et al., 1999).

Consider this study: Participants were asked to solve a three-dimensional puzzle within 8 minutes; the participants did not know that a full solution was impossible. They were then asked to explain to another person how to solve the puzzle. To increase the stressful nature of the task, the explanations had to be verbal only; the participants could not demonstrate with the puzzle pieces or use gestures. Those participants who had experienced a high number of daily hassles over the previous 2 months were more likely to have their immune systems suppressed after the puzzle task than those who did not report a high number of daily hassles (Brosschot et al., 1994). Thus, experiencing frequent daily hassles can cause an encounter with a mild stressor, as represented by the puzzle task, to be experienced as more distressful and more apt to provoke a change in the immune system. Think about what this means for the allostatic load—the stress level—of the many people caring for an ill relative or partner, as occurs in nearly a quarter of American households (National Alliance for Caregiving and American Association of Retired Persons, 1997). The stress of such daily, long-term caretaking creates a risk of illness for the caregiver.

Interruptions are another feature of daily life that can be a stressor. Think of how you feel when you're trying to study or write a paper and are repeatedly interrupted by phone calls or visitors. If your reaction is to feel more "stressed out," you're not alone. Interruptions during a mentally challenging task can be stressful enough to cause large increases in cortisol levels (Earle et al., 1999; Suarez et al.,

Life's daily hassles can be significant stressors, leading to psychological and physical symptoms.

1998). Note that email "interruptions" may not feel as stressful because you choose—that is, control—when to check your e-mail.

Thus, what you perceive as a stressor depends on the amount and nature of the stressors you are already experiencing. If you have four tests, quizzes, essays, or papers due each week, a week with only two of these tasks will seem less stressful. But if you've been lucky enough to take courses with only modest homework assignments, a week with two tests or quizzes can feel overwhelming. If you perceive a situation as an improvement, you will experience the stimulus as less stressful than if you perceive things as getting worse (Sapolsky, 1997).

## Work- and Economic-Related Factors

Work, like any other situation or set of tasks, can be a source of stress. Some work-related stressors are environmental: bad lighting, noise, crowding, and the demands of shift work (see Chapter 5). Other stressors relate to the job itself: the physical and mental workload, level of perceived control over the job, and time pressure. Still other work-related stressors involve personality: People bring their personal characteristics to work with them, and some of these can create stress not just for the individuals, but also for those who must interact with them.

**STRESSFUL WORKING ENVIRONMENTS: FLOOR PLANS AND NOISE** The arrangement of work spaces can cause stress. In a traditional *closed plan design*, the walls of offices extend from floor to ceiling, and employees work alone or in small groups in enclosed spaces that are entered through doors (Figure 13.4, left). In an attempt to maximize available space and increase communication efficiency, a number of other work space configurations have been tried, many of which are *open plan designs* (see Figure 13.4, right). Open plans do not provide auditory or visual privacy, and noise made by the activities of other people cannot be avoided (Proctor & Van Zandt, 1994). Al's office

**FIGURE 13.4** **Closed and Open Office Plans**

How office space is arranged can affect stress level. Traditional office layouts like the one on the left have the advantage of some privacy and less noise, but they use space inefficiently and can make communications within the organization difficult. The more modern layout on the right provides efficiency of space and communication, but neither privacy nor quiet.

changed from a closed plan to an open one. He now has no door, no window, no privacy. A study of employees whose office space changed from closed to open found that they were less satisfied with the open plan (Brennan et al., 2002). Those exposed to environmental noise for prolonged periods of time tend to perform more poorly, have higher blood pressure and other symptoms, and exhibit a lower tolerance for frustration (Cohen et al., 1986; Evans et al., 1998; Repetti, 1993; Wallenius, 2004). However, noise itself does not systematically lead to increased cortisol levels (Dickerson & Kemeny, 2004); rather, it is an inability to control your exposure to noise that is the most important predictor of its negative effects (Glass & Singer, 1972).

**JOB RESPONSIBILITIES: WHAT A STRESSFUL JOB!** The job itself, of course, can be a source of stress. It isn't surprising that jobs that entail unrealistic deadlines, time pressure, responsibility for the safety of other workers, or a demanding workload can lead to stress, insomnia, and illness (Kalimo et al., 2000). In general, stressful jobs are those that both are very demanding and allow the employee little control over how the demands of the job are met, such as a job on an assembly line. The *demand-control model* (Karasek, 1979; Karasek et al., 1981; Theorell & Karasek, 1996) emphasizes that stress arises when you are required to perform a demanding job but don't have much control over how the work is done. In fact, a study of English workers found that employees who felt that they did not have much control over their jobs had a 50% higher risk of developing coronary heart disease than those who felt such a sense of control (Marmot, 1998). Other studies find similar results (Bishop et al., 2003). Those who feel that they work hard at their jobs but receive little in the way of recognition or promotion are twice as likely to develop coronary heart disease as those who feel that they receive recognition or job advancement (Bosma et al., 1998). Another way of thinking about work-related stress is to examine the ratio of effort to reward, where much effort and little reward is associated with increased risk factors for heart disease, such as high blood pressure (Kuper & Marmot, 2003).

Particularly stressful are jobs in which workers must make decisions that affect others, must keep others busy and happy, and, most notably, are responsible for others' lives (McLean, 1980). Air traffic controller is a good example of such a job. A study of Canadian, New Zealander, and Singaporean air traffic controllers found that some elements of the job were generally most stressful: working at peak traffic conditions, a fear of causing accidents, and equipment limitations. However, the same aspects of the job were not equally stressful in the different countries. Those air traffic controllers in Western cultures were similar in viewing the general work environment as stressful, but those from a collectivist culture (Singapore) reported stress from their fear of slowing down as a controller and from their relationships with local management (Shouksmith & Taylor, 1997). These cross-cultural differences highlight the role that culture can play with regard to which specific aspects of a job are perceived as stressors.

Air traffic controllers have an extremely stressful job. They are literally controlling the lives of millions of air travelers.

Burnout: A work-related state characterized by chronic stress, accompanied by physical and mental exhaustion, a sense of little accomplishment, and cynicism about the job.

**BURNOUT: EXHAUSTED CYNIC AT WORK** Some people find that their work energizes, motivates and inspires them, that they enjoy work (Maslach et al., 2001). Others, however, are not so fortunate. Chronic stressors on the job, physical and mental exhaustion, a sense of little accomplishment, and cynicism about the job add up to **burnout** (Maslach, 2003). Employees with burnout feel tired all the time, often show symptoms of depression, and frequently feel trapped in the job. Burnout is not a switch that is thrown, but instead it creeps up over time (Hätinen et al., 2004). The risk of burnout increases when the job has specific characteristics (Green et al., 1991; Schaufeli & Enzmann, 1998; Seltzer & Numeroff, 1988):

- the work role is ambiguous;
- there is chronic work-related conflict;
- the demands of the job lead to a work overload;
- social support is chronically lacking;
- a sense of ineffectiveness or lack of appreciation prevails;
- the supervisor is inconsiderate;
- requires involvement and commitment to others (such as nursing or teaching);
- promotions are unlikely; and
- the job entails rigid rules that seem unfair.

Although work-related factors are the predominant influence leading to burnout, some personal characteristics can also contribute to this condition:

- being single and younger (Maslach, 2003);
- scoring high on the personality superfactor neuroticism (see Chapter 11);
- having low self-esteem;
- taking work more seriously or performing more conscientiously than necessary (Witt et al., 2004);
- disliking being involved with others when the job requires it; and
- having an insecure attachment style rather than a secure one (see Chapter 11 for a discussion of adult attachment styles) (Pines, 2004).

Although vacations help temporarily, burnout returns quickly when the person goes back to the same job with the same stressors (Westman & Eden, 1997). The remedy for burnout can be drastic—changing jobs or beginning a new career (Bernier, 1998)—but social support (Sand & Miyazaki, 2000) and outside interests can also help.

**WORKPLACE VIOLENCE** Sometimes conflict at work can lead to violence, as seen in far too many news reports. When workplace violence erupts, typically an employee feels that a supervisor has been unfair in assigning raises, jobs, or promotions. Moreover, a dictatorial supervisor and very stressful working conditions also contribute to the likelihood of violence (Neuman & Baron, 1998). The risk of violence can be decreased by teaching and rewarding cooperative behavior, by dealing with the causes of anger (Deffenbacher et al., 1996), and by training supervisors to be sensitive to employees' experiences on the job (Baron, 1977).

**ECONOMIC FACTORS** Economic factors are also associated with stress. Being unemployed (not by choice) is a significant stressor, affecting health and well-being (Hamilton et al., 1993). In the United States, people with lower socioeconomic status (SES) have consistently been found to have poorer health than those with higher SES, whether health status is measured objectively or subjectively (Adler et al., 2000; Gallo & Matthews, 2003) or by assessment of immune system functioning (Owen et al., 2003). Those whose jobs have less status and who are paid less tend to live in poorer neighborhoods, which tend to have fewer shops, recreational facilities, health care facilities, and higher crime—all factors that make life more difficult and stressful—increasing the allostatic load. Such people have higher risk of heart disease (Roux et al., 2001), poorer health, and higher mortality rates (Taylor et al., 1997). Stressful living situations that are related to a lack of financial resources can outstrip available coping resources and create a chronic stress response (Gallo & Matthews, 2003).

Hostile people are more likely to perceive stressors in situations in which nonhostile people do not perceive stressors (Hardy & Smith, 1988; Suarez & Williams, 1989).

## Hostility

Although some jobs and work (or home) environments may be more stressful than others, some people seem to experience stress more than others, regardless of their circumstances. Cardiologists Meyer Friedman and Ray Rosenman (1974) studied men who had coronary heart disease and discovered a common set of traits, including a sense of urgency, competitiveness, and interpersonal hostility. Friedman and Rosenman called this constellation of traits *Type A personality*. Subsequent research was unable to obtain the same clear-cut findings relating Type A personality to the incidence of coronary heart disease, but investigators were able to refine the concept of a stressed, heart disease–prone personality (Hecker et al., 1988). The most important component of the Type A personality in predicting heart disease is **hostility**, a trait characterized by mistrust, an expectation of harm and provocation by others, and a cynical attitude (Hart & Hope, 2004; Miller et al., 1996; Smith & Ruiz, 2002; Williams, Paton, et al., 2000). For instance, Barefoot and his colleagues (1983) found that medical students who scored in the top 20% on a hostility scale were more than four times as likely to develop heart disease 25 years later as were their low-hostility peers. Those same high-hostility doctors were seven times more likely than their low-hostility peers to die of any cause by age 50. Further research (Barefoot et al., 1989) found that, among lawyers, increased mortality was associated with an untrusting and cynical view of people, repeated negative emotions in personal interactions, and recurrent expressions of overt anger and aggression in the face of difficulties or frustrations. Other studies have found a similar link between hostility and risk factors for heart disease (Knox et al., 2004; Kop, 2003).

Men are generally more hostile than women (Miller et al., 1999; Räikkönen et al., 1999), and researchers found that even at the same level of hostility, men's blood pressure is more affected by their hostility than is women's (Räikkönen et al., 1999). When interrupted while concentrating on a task, highly hostile men had elevated heart rates, blood pressure, and cortisol production, as well as exhibiting other changes associated with a negative mood such as anger (Suarez et al., 1998). Regardless of their sex, people high in hostility are more likely to have a higher heart rate and blood pressure throughout the day, no matter what their mood. In contrast, people low in hostility showed cardiac changes only when they were in a negative mood (Davis et al., 2000; Räikkönen et al., 1999).

Hostility need not be a lifelong trait. Cognitive and behavioral programs (see Chapter 15) designed to help reduce anger levels can reduce not only hostility (Beck & Fernandez, 1998) and anger (DiGiuseppe & Tafrate, 2003), but also anger-related autonomic arousal and blood pressure increases (Gidron et al., 1999); these changes were generally maintained 1 year after the end of a 5-week program (Deffenbacher et al., 1996).

Hostility: The personality trait associated with heart disease and characterized by mistrust, an expectation of harm and provocation by others, and a cynical attitude.

# Test Yourself

1. The difference between the stressor and the stress response is that the
   a. stress response triggers the stressor.
   b. stressor is the stimulus and the stress response is the bodily change.
   c. stress response is purely cognitive, whereas the stressor is biological.
   d. stressor is the bodily change, and the stress response is the mental reaction.
2. Which combination accurately portrays one phase of Selye's general adaptation syndrome?
   a. resistance: internal efforts to restore homeostasis
   b. exhaustion: fight-or-flight response
   c. alarm: bodily damage
   d. alarm: mobilization of resources to achieve homeostasis
3. What is the relation between perceived control of stressors and the stress response?
   a. Uncontrollable but predictable stressors cause the most intense fight-or-flight response.
   b. Perceived control is more important than actual control in limiting a stress response.
   c. It is always stressful to have perceived control in an adverse situation.
   d. It is never stressful to have perceived control in an adverse situation.
4. A stressful work environment most likely has
   a. a closed plan office.
   b. frequent deadlines.
   c. employees who work very hard.
   d. controllable exposure to noise.

## Answers

NOTE: Once you feel comfortable with the Test Yourself questions in this chapter, visit the book's Web site at www.ablongman.com/kosslyn3e for additional study questions.

# Think It Through!

Suppose you wanted a job that wasn't very stressful. What job-related factors would you perceive as being *least* likely to produce stress—the nature of the job itself, the frequency of deadlines, the physical work environment, or other factors? What job-related factors would you perceive as being *most* likely to produce stress?

Once you started work, what bodily indicators might suggest that your new job was, in fact, fairly stressful? Why do those bodily changes occur?

# STRESS, DISEASE, AND HEALTH

Al was clearly experiencing a great deal of stress, and his being sick so often only made matters worse. He'd had to miss work some days, which didn't help his sense of control in his difficult situation. Sometimes he'd cough so much that he would have trouble sleeping, and then he'd lie awake worrying that he had lung cancer. He had started smoking again, after having quit 5 years before, so it was hard to know whether the more frequent colds and coughs were from the cigarettes or from the stress of work. He'd been having a few more drinks than usual, and he wasn't getting any exercise; he worried that if he started exercising, he'd bring on a heart attack. In short, Al wasn't doing very well, and he knew it.

The stress response is a good thing, very useful when the stressor is acute, such as a piece of glass in the foot; but there can be too much of a good thing. Too strong a stress response for too long a time—too great an allostatic load—can lead to stress-related illness.

# The Immune System: Catching Cold

No question about it: Stress can affect the immune system, which functions to defend the body against infection. Critical to the immune system are two classes of white blood cells: **B cells**, which mature in the bone marrow, and **T cells**, which mature in the thymus, an organ located in the chest. One type of T cell is the **natural killer (NK) cell**, which detects and destroys damaged or altered cells, such as precancerous cells before they become tumors. Glucocorticoids, which are released when the stress response is triggered, hinder the formation of some white blood cells (including NK cells) or kill other white blood cells (Cohen & Herbert, 1996; McEwen et al., 1997), making the body more vulnerable to infection and tumor growth. For this reason, many studies investigating the relationship between stress and the immune system measure the number of circulating white blood cells, such as NK cells. People who exhibit greater sympathetic nervous system responses to stress also show the most changes in immune system functioning (Bachen et al., 1995; Manuck et al., 1991), indicating that changes in the immune system are moderated by changes in the sympathetic nervous system. Exposure to some chronic psychological stressors can increase inflammation and the risk for autoimmune disorders (Miller, Cohen, & Ritchey, 2002).

A field called *psychoneuroimmunology* focuses on the ways in which mental and emotional states affect the immune system. For example, researchers have found that traditional elderly Chinese are more likely to die right after the Harvest Moon festival, an important event in their culture, than just before it, whereas orthodox Jews show no difference in mortality rates during this period. However, the pattern is exactly reversed around the High Holy Days, the most important days in the Jewish year; it is now the Jews who hold on until the holidays are over and the Chinese who are unaffected (Phillips & Smith, 1990; Phillips et al., 1992). What does this have to do with the immune system? People probably live longer because their bodies are fighting off whatever ailment is killing them.

But stress can harm the immune system. Because stress can impair the functioning of the white blood cells, it can play a role in the length of time it takes a wound to heal: The wounds of women who experienced a high level of stress by caring for a relative with Alzheimer's disease took 9 days longer to heal than those of women of similar age and economic status who were not engaged in such caregiving (Kiecolt-Glaser et al., 1995). In another study, dental student participants received slight mouth wounds on two different occasions (3 days before a major test and during summer vacation). The wounds given before exams, when, presumably, the students were experiencing more stressors, took 40% longer to heal (Marucha et al., 1998). Moreover, stress can increase the risk of infection after receiving a wound (Rojas et al., 2002). Major stressors such as a natural disaster (a devastating earthquake or hurricane) or victimization (being robbed or raped) can affect the immune system. Among people living in Florida neighborhoods damaged by Hurricane Andrew in 1992, the victims who perceived their losses to be most severe experienced the most changes in number of NK cells (Ironson et al., 1997).

But not everyone who is exposed to trauma responds the same way. Some survivors of traumatic events later (sometimes considerably later) experience *posttraumatic stress disorder (PTSD)*, a psychological disorder characterized by involuntary reexperiencing of the trauma through unwanted thoughts, sensations, and dreams, heightened arousal, and avoidance of anything associated with the trauma. (A further discussion of PTSD appears in Chapter 14.) In general, trauma survivors who had higher heart rates immediately after the trauma were more likely to develop PTSD (Bryant et al., 2003; Yehuda et al., 1998), as were those who had lower blood levels of the neurotransmitter GABA (Vaiva et al., 2004). Moreover, those who did develop PTSD often showed extraordinary autonomic system responsiveness to stimuli similar to those present during

The immune system's job is to fend off infectious agents such as viruses or precancerous cells. The release of glucocorticoids (as occurs during stress) suppresses the functioning of the immune system, making it more difficult for the body to fight the invaders and leaving the body more vulnerable to infection. This photo shows two natural killer (NK) cells (yellow) attacking a leukemia cell (red). The NK cells have made contact and are beginning to engulf and destroy the leukemia cell.

A study of allergic responses found that, among Japanese couples who do not habitually kiss, kissing privately for up to 30 minutes increased their immune responses (Kimata, 2003). Could this be a new stress reduction technique?

**B cell:** A type of white blood cell that matures in the bone marrow.

**T cell:** A type of white blood cell that matures in the thymus.

**Natural killer (NK) cell:** A type of T cell that detects and destroys damaged or altered cells, such as precancerous cells.

the trauma (Casada et al., 1998; Keane et al., 1998). Thus, for example, survivors of Hurricane Andrew who have PTSD are more likely to experience a large stress response on a windy day than are people who have never lived through a severe hurricane. Even when not in the presence of such stimuli, those who develop PTSD are generally more autonomically responsive (Cohen et al., 1998).

# Cancer

Although stress can't cause cancer, there is evidence that it can affect the growth of some cancerous tumors. How can this happen?

Traumatic events, such as experiencing the devastation of a hurricane, can affect the immune system, as well as produce psychological symptoms such as anxiety and depression.

- *If the immune system is suppressed, NK cells do not work as well to prevent the spread of tumor cells.* Levy and her colleagues (Levy et al., 1985, 1987, 1988) found a relationship among the perception of inadequate social support, feelings of distress and fatigue with little joy, and lower levels of NK cell activity. Such negative psychological experiences, by weakening the immune system, left people more vulnerable to the growth of cancerous tumors. Locke and colleagues (1984) found similar results.

- *Stress can facilitate the growth of capillaries feeding into the tumor.* When stress has a distinct physical cause, our bodies produce more capillaries to supply blood to that area. If the stressor is an injury or infection (such as would be caused by a puncture wound in the foot), capillary growth is beneficial because the vessels carry more white blood cells to the part of the body that needs them. However, if a tumor is already present in the body, the stress response will cause more blood to be supplied to the tumor, literally feeding it and supporting its growth. Stress does not appear to *cause* a tumor to develop, only to assist in its growth.

- *The perception of control can also play a role in the progression of some types of cancer.* Among cancer patients, those who did not perceive much control and felt helpless about their cancer were likely to have a recurrence sooner and to die earlier from the cancer (Andersen et al., 1994; Watson et al., 1991).

Although psychological factors can affect the immune system, these findings should be interpreted with caution. The type of cancer, and biological factors related to the progression of the disease, can outweigh psychological factors in tumor growth (Compas et al., 1998; Grossarth-Maticek et al., 2000), especially in the final stages of the disease (Cohen & Herbert, 1996). Moreover, some people may be genetically endowed with an immune system that is more effective at warding off illness. Data on twins reared together and apart suggest that, on average, identical twins have more key antibodies in common (7 out of a possible 9) than do fraternal twins (4 out of a possible 9) (Kohler et al., 1985).

# Heart Disease

Stress can also lead, indirectly, to heart disease. Let's examine how.

## How Stress Affects the Heart

The increased blood pressure created by chronic stress, in combination with hormonally induced narrowing of the arteries, promotes **atherosclerosis**, or the buildup of plaque (fatty deposits) on the inside walls of the arteries (Figure 13.5, p. 604). As

Atherosclerosis: A medical condition characterized by plaque buildup in the arteries.

**FIGURE 13.5**

## Stress on the Arteries

CUT SECTION THROUGH BRANCHING ARTERY

Each time a stressor causes an increase in blood pressure, the branching points of arteries are at risk for damage. The hormones released during the fight-or-flight response also cause blood vessels to constrict, which has the net effect of increasing blood pressure even more. Thus, if someone experiences frequent stressors, his or her blood vessels take a pounding. With rapidly increased blood pressure, the circulating blood can create a slight tear of the arterial wall, creating a place for plaque to attach itself to the artery wall. Once this occurs, the artery gets narrower and narrower (as plaque builds and builds). This atherosclerosis makes the work of pumping blood through the body even harder for the heart.

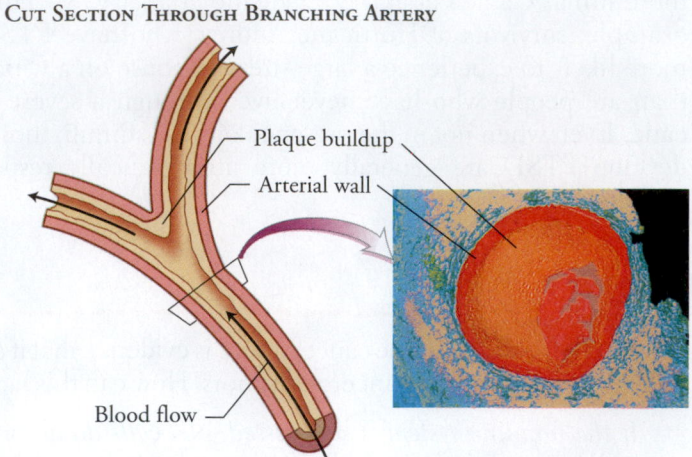

Plaque buildup

Arterial wall

Blood flow

plaque accumulates, the arteries narrow—which makes the heart work even harder to meet the body's need for nutrients and oxygen. Working harder means pumping the blood with more power, creating more damage to the arteries, and a vicious cycle is created. This chronic wear and tear on the cardiovascular system can lead to heart damage, which can lead to sudden death from inadequate blood supply to the heart muscle or from irregular electrical firing of the muscle, preventing coordinated heartbeats.

When a person experiences a strong stressor, his or her body's response may cause a piece of plaque to break off (Strike et al., 2004). The loosened plaque may then block an artery going to the heart, preventing or limiting blood flow to that organ, leading to a heart attack. For someone who already has heart disease, even extremely positive states of stress, such as joy or orgasm, can precipitate this event and cause sudden death.

Some people, perhaps because of a history of heart disease or an overly responsive HPA axis, are more vulnerable to calamitous aftereffects of stress. For these people, work stress can increase the risk of a heart attack; for example, if such a person is working under a tight deadline, this can increase the risk of heart attack soon after the deadline (Moller et al., 2005), as can being stuck in traffic (Peters et al., 2004). Such stress-related heart attacks need to be distinguished from the recently identified and potentially fatal "broken heart syndrome," which has caused people to die after becoming extremely upset; this syndrome occurs when a person has a massive amount (up to 34 times the normal level) of adrenaline in response to an acute emotional stressor, along with a temporary weakening of the heart so that it cannot pump effectively (Wittstein, 2005).

### Stress, Emotions, and Heart Disease

Stressors often elicit negative emotions such as fear, anger, sadness, and helplessness. Such emotions can produce a rise in heart rate that lasts longer than does the rise following positive emotions (Brosschot & Thayer, 2003). When the stressors are chronic, they can lead to helplessness, depression, and despair. Depression in particular appears to be associated with a greater likelihood of heart disease (Barth et al., 2004; Ferketich et al., 2000; Kiecolt-Glaser & Glaser, 2002; Rosengren et al., 2004). Consider these findings:

- Depressed people have a faster heartbeat even when at rest (Moser et al., 1998), and they tend to have high blood pressure (Carney et al., 1999).

- People who are more likely to experience negative emotions (that is, they are high in the personality dimension of neuroticism, see Chapter 11) have an increased risk of heart disease and heart attacks, perhaps from a biological hyperreactivity to stress (Habra et al., 2003).

It isn't surprising, then, that those who have had an episode of depression have a higher risk of developing heart problems, and once having had a heart attack, those who are depressed are more likely to have further health problems (Frasure-Smith et al., 1999). When the depression is treated, however, these stress-related responses subside, and heart rate and blood pressure decrease (Kolata, 1997). Anxiety is also associated with heart disease (Kubzansky & Kawachi, 2000; Kubzansky et al., 1998), possibly because it can lead to high blood pressure and changes in cardiac functioning—and also because people may attempt to cope with it by engaging in unhealthy behaviors, such as smoking or drinking.

## Lifestyle Can Make a Difference

The course of heart disease can be affected by a change in lifestyle. A study of people with severe heart disease found that intensive changes in diet, exercise, stress management (such as meditation), and social support could help to halt the narrowing of the arteries, and could even reverse the atherosclerosis and minimize further damage to the heart (Ornish et al., 1998). Other studies confirm the positive effects of such intensive lifestyle changes (Lisspers et al., 2005).

# Health-Impairing Behaviors

In general, stress can also have a less direct, though no less serious, effect on health: In attempting to cope with stressors, people may engage in self-destructive behaviors such as overeating, smoking, or having one drink too many (Steptoe et al., 1998). The term *health-impairing behaviors* generally refers to any actions that have the potential to damage health. These behaviors include smoking, substance abuse, poor nutrition, lack of exercise, and risky behaviors such as unsafe sex or unprotected suntanning.

## Why Do We Engage in Health-Impairing Behaviors?

Fifty years ago, or even 20 years ago, people may not have realized that smoking or being a couch potato could endanger their health. Now, we know. Yet some of us still don't eat right, may drink too much, or may otherwise make what we know are unhealthy choices. Why, despite our knowledge and all the health warnings, do we do this? As illustrated in Figure 13.6, research focuses on four factors, including *perceived risk* (how much we think engaging in a behavior puts us at risk to develop a health problem) and *perceived severity* (how severe we perceive that health problem to be) (Weinstein, 2000). Often, our estimates of long-term risks are not very accurate, at least not in relation to ourselves (see Chapters 8 and 12). We may see ourselves as "invulnerable" and thereby underestimate the risks of health-impairing behaviors (Weinstein, 1984, 1993). Thus, although you may know

**FIGURE 13.6** **Factors Influencing Willingness to Engage in Risky Behavior: The Example of Unprotected Sex**

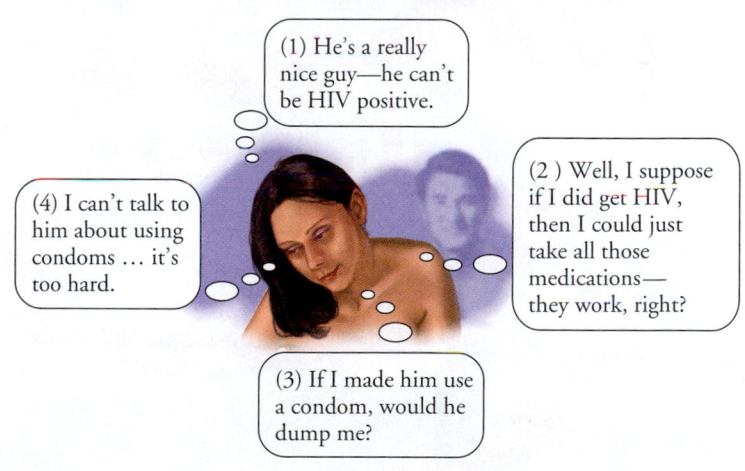

We can understand a woman's risky sexual behavior by knowing: (1) her perceptions about her risk to develop AIDS, (2) how severe she thinks the health problem could be, (3) her knowledge of alternatives, and (4) how easy such alternatives are to implement.

the statistics regarding health problems that can develop as a result of a variety of behaviors, often you don't think those problems could happen to you. Also determining your behavior is your awareness of ways to prevent the health problems and how easy it is to do so (Weinstein, 1993).

In essence, if you do not think you are at risk, you are more likely to engage in the health-impairing behaviors. You appraise the risks, and if you do not perceive yourself to be vulnerable, you do not take precautions. As we shall see, however, even perceiving yourself to be at risk doesn't guarantee that you will take precautions.

## Changing Health-Impairing Behaviors

Changing a problematic behavior pattern can be difficult, as most smokers have learned when they try to quit and have to make several attempts before they are successful.

**FIVE STEPS TOWARD CHANGE**  Some programs that promote changing unhealthy behaviors such as smoking, drinking, and overeating look at progress as either/or: Participants either change their behavior or they continue it; they either quit or they don't quit. Based on extensive research, Prochaska and his colleagues (Prochaska, Norcross, et al., 1994) have developed a different conception of change, with five stages (see Figure 13.7):

**FIGURE 13.7  Stages of Change**

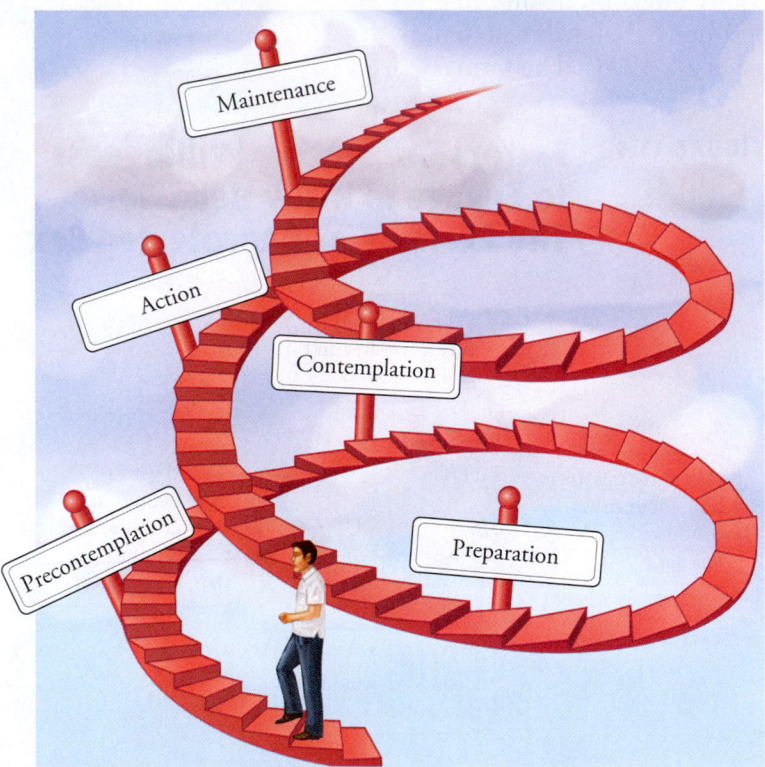

According to Prochaska's model, change occurs over five stages, but people rarely go directly from the first stage to the last without relapsing. That is why the illustration of the model resembles a spiral.

1. *Precontemplation*: The person has no intention of changing the problematic behavior and will often deny that there is a problem. He or she may change temporarily if a lot of pressure is applied by others but will relapse once that pressure is removed.

2. *Contemplation*: The person acknowledges that there is a problem and may even begin to think about doing something about it. Real action, though, is seen as far in the future, not in the present. It is easy for people to get stuck in this phase.

3. *Preparation*: The person has a plan of action to change, makes adjustments to the plan, and intends to begin changing within a month, making a specific commitment to change. However, some people in this stage still have mixed feelings about change and may not begin to change when they intended, leading to a relapse to an earlier stage. People in this stage are very aware of the problem, its causes, and possible solutions.

4. *Action*: This is the stage most obvious to others because people in this stage change their behaviors and their environments. People in this stage also receive the most support.

5. *Maintenance*: The person in this stage is consolidating the gains he or she has made and has an eye on relapse prevention. Without a strong commitment to maintenance, relapse to the first or second stage is likely. Friends and family may be less supportive because action has already been taken; however, because people in this stage are still vulnerable to relapse, support remains important.

This conception is based on the observation that, in reality, most people go through stages of change, each stage having its own tasks that must be completed in order to progress to the next stage. Moreover, progress is not necessarily constant, and people may relapse to an earlier stage before resuming forward movement. This model of change has been applied to a variety of behaviors: helping people to stop smoking, drinking, drug use, or overeating and to start using condoms, using sunscreen, exercising, or getting mammograms (Litt et al., 2002; Prochaska & Norcross, 2001; Prochaska, Velicer, et al., 1994).

If you have a behavior you'd like to change, take this test to find out which stage of change you are in:

|   |   | YES | NO |
|---|---|---|---|
| 1. | I solved my problem more than 6 months ago. | ☐ | ☐ |
| 2. | I have taken action on my problem within the past 6 months. | ☐ | ☐ |
| 3. | I intend to take action in the next month. | ☐ | ☐ |
| 4. | I intend to take action in the next 6 months. | ☐ | ☐ |

If you answered no to all four questions, you are in the precontemplation stage. If you answered yes only to question 4, you are in the contemplation stage. If you answered yes to questions 3 and 4, you are in the preparation stage. If you answered yes to question 2, but not to question 1, you are in the action stage. If you answered yes to question 1—honestly—then you are in the maintenance phase (from Prochaska, Norcross, et al., 1994).

**PROCESSES THAT ENCOURAGE CHANGE**    A number of different processes, or interventions, may help people move from one stage of change to another. An *intervention*, as the term is used by psychotherapists, is a specific technique or treatment for reducing health-impairing behaviors.

- For those in the earliest stages of change, there are two helpful processes:
  1. *Consciousness raising* involves becoming aware of both the problem and the way the person avoids addressing it. Al's view of his smoking and drinking was that they would take care of themselves when his work problems were resolved, so he didn't feel that he had to do anything about them.
  2. *Social liberation* occurs when external forces help create more alternatives to the behavior and provide both information about the problematic behavior and support. This process occurs at the level of the group. Social liberation is imposed on Al at work, where he can't smoke because the office is smoke-free. The hours he can smoke each day are limited because he has to leave the building to have a cigarette. This also makes the act of smoking less convenient, less comfortable, and less pleasurable.

- In the move from contemplation through preparation and toward action, two other processes are helpful:
  1. *Emotional arousal* consists of focused awareness and feelings directed toward change. Al experienced emotional arousal when he realized that his body was a wreck and he couldn't go on this way.
  2. *Self-reevaluation* involves taking stock, both emotionally and intellectually, and addressing the question of whether engaging in the problematic behavior is what the person really wants to be doing—whether it reflects the person he or she wants to be. Often, part of this reevaluation is weighing the pros and cons of changing or maintaining the behavior.

Public service ads like this one use social liberation to nudge people to change health-compromising behavior: The ad shows an alternative to driving drunk, namely, using a taxi, and tries to create social pressure for this alternative behavior.

## Moving Through the Stages: The Shifting Pros and Cons

The pros of changing a problematic behavior usually increase between the precontemplation and the contemplation stages, and the cons of changing the behavior usually decrease between the contemplation and the action stages. From precontemplation to preparation, the pros often go up twice as much as the cons go down; what's happening is that as the person gets ready to act, he or she realizes that there are more reasons to change the behavior. Thus, interventions for people in the precontemplation stage should focus on the pros of changing the behavior. For Al, the intervention should focus on the advantages of quitting smoking. For those in the contemplation stage, interventions should focus on decreasing the cons of changing the problematic behavior (Herzog et al., 1999; Prochaska, Velicer, et al., 1994). For Al, this would mean questioning the reasons to keep smoking—are those reasons still as strong as they had been? In terms of the types of internal conflict we discussed earlier, the approach desires begin clearly to outweigh the avoidance desires, and the scale of conflict tips toward change.

If you, or Al, wanted to make the transition from the action stage to the maintenance stage, you could make use of many operant conditioning techniques (see Chapter 6)—such as reward, stimulus control, and *countering*, the substitution of healthier behaviors for the problem behaviors. For example, as Al became more motivated to change his smoking habit, he could reward himself for not buying cigarettes or for days or hours spent without smoking with a healthier indulgence, such as buying an intriguing paperback or a music CD; he could substitute for pulling out a cigarette, lighting up, and puffing away by instead pulling out a stick of gum, unwrapping it, and savoring the first mouth-watering bite into it. Relationships can also be helpful in providing physical, emotional, and moral support throughout the effort to change the behavior.

# Test Yourself

1. Stress affects the immune system by
   a. impairing the functioning of white blood cells.
   b. increasing the blood level of natural killer cells.
   c. increasing the number of B cells.
   d. triggering production of both B cells and T cells.
2. How does stress affect cancer?
   a. Too much stress can cause cancer.
   b. Stress can affect the growth of some kinds of tumors.
   c. Stress cannot affect cancer in any way.
   d. Stress has the greatest effect in the final stages of cancer.
3. What do many health-impairing behaviors have in common?
   a. They involve violence toward others.
   b. They always involve excesses of a behavior.
   c. They are often used to cope with stressors.
   d. They inevitably lead to weight gain.
4. People stop engaging in health-impairing behaviors when
   a. the perceived severity of those behaviors is low.
   b. they contemplate taking action.
   c. they maintain the desired action.
   d. approach desires outweigh avoidance desires.

## Answers

1. a 2. b 3. c 4. d

# Think It Through!

Suppose you were caught in a thunderstorm and were soaking wet by the time you got home. Would you now be more likely to catch a cold? Why or why not? What factors might make you more or less likely to catch a cold? What if you had been out very late or instead had had a lot of sleep? Why might these factors matter, or would they not matter? Why might Al become sicker as time goes on?

# STRATEGIES FOR COPING

Once the realization that he was truly in bad shape sank in, Al finally recognized that he needed to take action. He looked around the office to see how other people were doing, how they were handling the stress of the difficult situation at work. He paid particular attention to Maya, who didn't seem ruffled by the unsettled atmosphere and the layoffs. Al was puzzled by her reaction, or apparent lack thereof, and he talked with Lisa about it. Lisa suggested that perhaps Maya had particularly effective ways of dealing with stress. She pointed out that the perception of stress depends not only on your view of a situation, but also on the conscious actions you take in response to the stressors. *Coping* is the inclusive term for the multitude of techniques that people employ to handle stress or their reactions to it. Some of these techniques may "come naturally," arising partly from temperament; others can be learned.

## Coping Strategies: Approaches and Tactics

Different people tend to use different coping strategies, and the use of a particular strategy may also depend on the situation and the emotions aroused by it (Folkman & Moscowitz, 2004). People cope in two broad ways: They rely on *reactive coping*, which involves responding to current or past stressors; and *proactive coping*, which involves responding to *potential* stressors, such as a possible upcoming medical procedure, or as is the case with Al, the possibility of a layoff (Aspinwall & Taylor, 1997; Schwarzer & Knoll, 2003). *Proactive* means "taking action before—not in response to—events."

### Problem-Focused and Emotion-Focused Coping

Another way to classify coping strategies is by considering whether they address internal or external circumstances (Carver et al., 1989). **Problem-focused coping** involves the use of strategies that alter either the environment itself or the way in which the person and the environment interact (see Table 13.2). This type of coping is more common when people believe that their actions can affect the stressor (Park et al., 2004), and it tends to be used by people with a high score on the Big Five personality superfactor conscientiousness (see Chapter 11; Watson & Hubbard, 1996). In contrast, **emotion-focused coping** involves the use of strategies that change a person's emotional response to the stressor (see Table 13.2). This type of coping usually decreases arousal. People are more likely to adopt emotion-focused coping when they do not think their actions can affect the stressor itself, and so they must alter their perception of, or response to, the stressor.

Typically, people use more than one strategy in response to a given stressor. The effectiveness of a particular strategy depends in part on a person's accuracy in assessing whether the environment can, in fact, be changed. For example, suppose Lisa assumes that if she gets straight A's in the spring term, she can probably get a scholarship to cover next year's tuition. Here she is approaching the need to pay for her education with the problem-focused coping strategy of *planning*: She is coping with a stressor by thinking about how to manage it (see Table 13.2, on p. 610). If she works hard all spring and carefully rations her social time, Lisa is using two problem-focused strategies: *active coping* and *suppression of competing activities*. What Lisa doesn't know, however, is that the financial aid office awards all of next year's scholarships before the end of the spring term, so her efforts for top grades will not help her achieve her goal of a scholarship. As this example demonstrates, although it is adaptive to try to adopt

**Problem-focused coping:** Coping focused on changing the environment itself or the way the person interacts with the environment.

**Emotion-focused coping:** Coping focused on changing the person's emotional response to the stressor.

| TABLE 13.2 | Problem-Focused and Emotion-Focused Coping Strategies |
|---|---|
| **Strategy** | **Description** |
| **Problem-Focused Strategies** | |
| Active coping | Actively tries to remove or work around stressor, or to ameliorate its effects. |
| Planning | Thinks about how to manage stressor. |
| Instrumental social support | Seeks concrete advice, assistance, information. |
| Suppression of competing activities | Puts other activities on hold in order to concentrate on and cope with stressor. |
| Restraint coping | Waits to act until the appropriate time. |
| **Emotion-Focused Strategies** | |
| Emotional social support | Seeks encouragement, moral support, sympathy, and understanding from others. |
| Venting emotions | Focuses on and talks about distressing feelings. |
| Positive reinterpretation/growth | Reinterprets the stressor or situation in a positive way or as a challenge. |
| Behavioral disengagement | Reduces efforts to deal with the stressor (as occurs with learned helplessness). |
| Mental disengagement | Turns to other activities to distract attention from the stressor. |

problem-focused coping in the face of stressors, such an approach is effective only when applied to factors that are controllable. Accurate information and appraisal are important to determine whether this is the case.

The coping strategies people use are affected by their allostatic load—the level of stressors in their lives: The more stressors they face, the more people are likely to use avoidant coping strategies such as distraction and behavioral or mental disengagement, which aim to decrease the focus on the stressor and increase the focus on other matters (Ingledew et al., 1997). In *behavioral disengagement*, people reduce their efforts to deal actively with the stressor (Table 13.2). In its extreme form, this disengagement can lead to a sense of helplessness. In *mental disengagement*, people turn to other activities to distract their attention from the stressor. So, the more stressors that Al and Lisa experience, the less likely they are to cope actively with them.

Avoidant coping strategies can be adaptive when nothing can be done to change a stressor (Folkman & Moscowitz, 2004). Studies (with male participants) have indicated that those perceiving less control over events are less likely to use problem-focused coping strategies (which involve direct action) and more likely to use emotion-focused strategies, such as distraction and emotional support (David & Suls, 1999). Moreover, adjusting their approach in such a way can help people cope more effectively (Christensen et al., 1995; Terry & Hynes, 1998). If Al doesn't think that anything he does at work will ultimately affect whether he gets laid off, he is less likely to use active coping strategies.

Coping strategies are inherently neither good nor bad, but rather their effectiveness depends on the context, the culture, and the situation (such as the degree to which you can control the stressor). Even within a situation, the specific timing of events can influence the use of coping strategies; for example, the strategy you use as you walk into an exam room (perhaps suppressing competing activities or seeking emotional support from classmates) may be different from the strategy you use once you see that the exam is harder than you thought (perhaps leading you to plan how to allocate your time so that you first fill in the answers that you know best).

# UNDERSTANDING RESEARCH
## Emotional Disclosure and Health

Another type of emotion-focused coping strategy is venting (see Table 13.2)—that is, focusing on and talking about the stressor. James Pennebaker (1989) wondered whether *writing* about a stressor has a positive effect on health.

**QUESTION:** Does writing about an upsetting experience lead to better health?

**ALTERNATIVES:** (1) Writing about an upsetting experience will cause the writer's health to decline. (2) Writing about an upsetting experience will cause the writer's health to improve. (3) Writing about an upsetting experience will not cause the writer's health to change.

**LOGIC:** (1) If writing about an upsetting experience leads to poorer health, then those who write about such experiences should fare worse than those who do not write about such experiences. (2) If writing about an upsetting experience leads to better health, then those who write about such experiences should fare better than those who do not write about such experiences. (3) If writing about an upsetting experience has no effect on health, then those who write about such experiences should fare the same as those who do not write about such experiences.

**METHOD:** Participants were college students who were randomly divided into two groups—the experimental group and the control group. Participants in the experimental group, referred to as the "emotional expressiveness" group, were asked to write for 20 minutes a day for 4 consecutive days, they were told that their writing samples would remain confidential. Pennebaker gave half of them the following instructions:

> During each of the 4 writing days, I want you to write about the most traumatic and upsetting experiences of your whole life. You can write on different topics each day or on the same topic for all 4 days. The important thing is that you write about your deepest thoughts and feelings. Ideally, whatever you write about should deal with an event or experience that you have not talked about with others in detail.

Participants in the control group were asked to write each day about superficial topics. In this study, researchers assessed "health" by the number of visits to the student health services. In addition, participants were asked to rate their moods immediately after writing and at the end of the school year.

**RESULTS:** In this study and variants of it, students who were asked to write about an emotional topic were more likely to report negative moods immediately after writing, although their overall moods were more positive by the end of the school year (Pennebaker et al., 1990). Perhaps paradoxically, those who wrote about traumatic events were less likely to get sick (as measured by visits to the student health center) in the months following the expressive writing. Similar results were reported by Pennebaker and Francis (1996) and were found even when the writing occurred via e-mail (Sheese et al., 2004).

**INFERENCES:** Writing about a traumatic event allows the writer to work through and come to terms with the experience, which in turn appears to reduce the negative effects of stress on the immune system. This interpretation is buttressed by the results of

Writing in detail about upsetting or difficult experiences can enhance immune system functioning and can lead to better moods.

other studies that assessed the relation between writing and immune function (Petrie et al., 1995, 1998), absenteeism from work (Francis & Pennebaker, 1992), and specific medical problems (Smyth et al., 1999). It appears, however, that writing only briefly—say, just a 3-minute outline of a traumatic experience—doesn't provide enough emotional expression to confer the benefits; the participants must actively process their experiences by writing about them in detail (Páez et al., 1999).

These studies suggest that focusing on and "working through" feelings about a traumatic experience have positive effects, although it may take a while for these effects to appear. *Venting* as investigated in these studies does not mean that internal "pressure" is released, as Freud believed. Rather this process could simply help a person come to terms with an emotion—to make sense of and make peace with emotional events.

## THINK CRITICALLY!

In addition to health center visits and mood ratings, what other dependent measures might you include to assess the effect of written emotional expression, and why would you include these? What if, instead of writing for 20 minutes, as in the original study, participants spoke into a tape recorder for the same amount of time? Do you think the results of such a study would differ from those of the original study?

## Thought Suppression

Purposefully trying not to think about something emotionally arousing or distressing is **thought suppression** (Wegner et al., 1987). Suppose Al and Lisa used thought suppression. They would try not to think about Al's work situation and all that depended on it. However, research has shown that trying *not* to think about something can have the paradoxical effect of causing that "suppressed" thought to pop into consciousness more than it does when you are not trying to suppress it. This phenomenon is referred to as a *rebound effect*. Research on the application of thought suppression to health and illness has shown that the act of suppressing emotional thoughts actually magnifies both the intensity of the thoughts and the autonomic reactions to those thoughts (Clark et al., 1991; Wegner et al., 1987). Attempts to suppress thoughts that are emotionally charged (either positive or negative) have also been associated with changes in the sympathetic nervous system (Gross & Levenson, 1997).

Some people use thought suppression more frequently than others. Such "high thought suppressors" have less success in suppressing thoughts related to a stressor when they are under a heavy allostatic load. Because of the rebound effect, the subsequent increase in thoughts about the stressor may lead to excessive focus on it and to depression (Beevers & Meyer, 2004; Koster et al., 2003; Wenzlaff & Luxton, 2003). Additional research suggests that current measures of thought suppression may assess only failed attempts at suppression—not the use of the strategy itself—and those failures then result in rebound (Rassin, 2003).

## Humor: Is Laughter the Best Medicine?

Although humor may not work as well as an antibiotic in curing strep throat, it can be an effective strategy for emotion-focused coping. Humor provides an opportunity to vent emotions, mentally disengage, and make a positive reinterpretation of a stressor (Martin, 2001; Robinson, 1977a, 1977b). A study looking at the effects of humor on anxiety among participants who waited for medical treatment found that those who watched a humorous silent film felt less anxious than those who watched a nonhumorous silent film and less anxious than those in a control group that did not watch any film (Nemeth, 1979). Other studies have found similar beneficial effects of humor in reduc-

**Thought suppression:** The coping strategy that involves purposefully trying not to think about something emotionally arousing or distressing.

ing anxiety (Ford et al., 2004). Berk (1989) found that participants in his study had higher levels of NK cells and other positive immune system changes while watching an hour-long funny video than on another day, when they did not watch a video. Another study found that after watching a humorous video (as compared with a nonhumorous one), participants had increased production of certain immune system secretions in their saliva (Perera et al., 1998).

In various ways, these studies illustrate the effects of humor on the immune system. But why does humor have these effects? Laughter may be one mechanism. A recent study found that laughter (while watching a funny movie) led the inner lining of blood vessels to dilate, which thereby increased blood flow. In contrast, when watching a disturbing movie, blood vessels narrowed, reducing blood flow (Miller et al., 2005). What it is about laughter that causes this change is not yet known. Laughter isn't the only aspect of humor that can be beneficial to health. Martin (2001) reviewed the various studies of the effects of humor on the immune system and concluded that humor may change your cognitive appraisal of a stressful situation—and that's why it boosts immune function.

Generally, studies of the relationship between humor and stress indicate that people who tend to exercise their sense of humor have a different appraisal of a given situation. They are more likely to view a potentially stressful situation as challenging rather than threatening, and they are more likely to develop realistic expectations of their own performance (Martin, 1996).

Is humor an effective coping strategy? Should we all try to be like Tina Fey and Amy Poehler? Thankfully for those who can't tell a joke, people who have the ability either to produce or appreciate humor benefit from its stress-buffering effects (Martin & Dobbin, 1988; Nezu et al., 1988).

## Aggression: Coping Gone Awry

For good or ill, one way to cope with stressors is through **aggression**, behavior that is intended to harm another living being who does not wish to be harmed (Baron & Richardson, 1994). Couples who were more verbally and physically aggressive with each other were more likely to report a higher number of stressful events than couples who were not as abusive (Eby, 2004; Straus, 1980). However, this is only a correlation, and thus cause and effect are unclear: It is possible that stress leads to aggression, but it is also possible that people who are abusive *create* more stressful events in their lives by their aggressive manner (see Chapters 9 and 11 for discussions of how people create their own microenvironments; McGuffin & Katz, 1993; Thapar & McGuffin, 1996; Wang et al., 2005). However, using correlational designs, which assess only whether two factors vary together, not whether one causes the other—in combination with experimental ones, which can reveal causation—investigators have found a number of specific stressors that are associated with or lead to aggression.

Some people are more aggressive than others. For example, the personality trait of aggressiveness (measured by a self-report paper-and-pencil test) predicts actual aggressive behavior. Hockey players who scored higher on aggressiveness before the hockey season spent more time in the penalty box for aggressive penalties, but not for nonaggressive penalties (Bushman & Wells, 1998).

**ENVIRONMENTAL FACTORS** External factors in the environment, such as noise and heat, can sometimes spark aggression (Berkowitz & Harmon-Jones, 2004), and the target is usually innocent people who happen to be in the line of fire. Depression and pain are also associated with increased aggression (Berkowitz, 1998). These unpleasant experiences have in common the ability to predispose people to make a negative appraisal of a stimulus, particularly if the potential for threat is ambiguous. For instance, if Al has a headache, he may be more likely than if he were pain-free to assume that a colleague's comment ("Hey Al, quitting early?" on a day he's going to pick up Lisa for a weekend visit) has hostile intent. Rather than taking the remark as office kidding, he might worry that he was viewed as a slacker and thus a good candidate to be laid off next.

**HOSTILE ATTRIBUTION BIAS** Although external stressors such as noise and pain can clearly lead to inaccurate and negative appraisals of a stimulus, some people are more

**Aggression:** Behavior that is intended to harm another living being who does not wish to be harmed.

FIGURE 13.8

## Factors Leading to Aggression

When do an unpleasant emotional state and negative mood lead to aggression? Various factors, at the levels of the brain, person, and group, and their interactions, help determine whether aggression will be the end result.

likely than others to make a negative appraisal of an ambiguous, or even neutral, stimulus, even without the presence of such stressors. The propensity to misread the intentions of others, interpreting them negatively, is referred to as the **hostile attribution bias** (Dodge & Newman, 1981; Nasby et al., 1979). Because Al doesn't have a hostile attribution bias, he would not normally interpret his colleague's comment as a threat.

**AGGRESSIVE TENDENCIES** Many stressors lead to an unpleasant internal state and increased negative mood, which in turn can lead to the fight-or-flight response. Whether a person responds to this internal state with aggression is determined by events at the three levels of analysis: in part by the person's biology (including his or her genes, hormones, arousal levels, and central nervous system traumas or abnormalities); in part by his or her thoughts, beliefs, feelings, and expectations (which arise in part from his or her history of reinforcement and observational learning); and in part by the culture's expectations of appropriate behavior. And all of these factors interact (Berkowitz, 1998).

Clearly, however, not everyone responds to an unpleasant internal state and negative mood with aggression. Some people, whose initial response to a threat is fear, will try to "flee" by escaping or avoiding whatever or whomever instigated the negative situation. Others will respond initially with irritation, annoyance, or anger (see Figure 13.8). Berkowitz proposes that this initial response is then tempered by further cognitive processing about the desired goals and expectations of punishment, reward, or harm, allowing people to make a final determination of a feeling of anger or fear (although some people fight or flee without further appraisal).

**GENDER DIFFERENCES IN AGGRESSION** If aggression is defined by physical acts, then, as children and adults, males are more aggressive than females. The results of a meta-analysis by Eagly and Steffen (1986) found that females are less likely to be aggressive if they think the aggression will physically harm another person, backfire on themselves, or cause them to feel considerable guilt or shame. However, when considering acts of aggression that do not cause physical harm, such as hurting other people's relationships (or threatening to do so), males are not necessarily more aggressive than females. Nonphysical aggression includes threatened or actual social exclusion of a friend, gossiping, or withdrawing acceptance of another person. Because of her gender (that is, the social expectations for someone of her sex), Lisa may be less likely than a male fellow student to shove someone when she feels aggressive; however, she might gossip about someone or slight that person in some way. *Relational aggression* is the term for nonphysical aggression that damages relationships or uses relationships to injure others psychologically, for example, by socially excluding them (Crick & Grotpeter, 1995); relational aggression is instigated more by females than by males.

Males and females differ with regard to the types of situations likely to elicit aggression, whether physical or verbal. For example, one meta-analytic study found that males are more likely than females to be aggressive in response to criticism of their intellectual ability (Bettencourt & Miller, 1996).

Hostile attribution bias: The propensity to misread the intentions of others as negative.

**SELF-ESTEEM AND NARCISSISM** Not surprisingly, hostile people are more likely than others to behave aggressively (Anderson & Bushman, 1997). However, determining why some people use aggression as a coping strategy is more difficult than you may think. Conventional wisdom, at least in the United States, has been that aggression is more likely to be perpetrated by people who feel bad about themselves—that is, who have low self-esteem—and that their aggression toward others is a way of bolstering their view of themselves. Is conventional wisdom right? Research results (Baumeister et al., 1996; Bushman, 1998) indicate that the answer is a resounding no! On the contrary, most aggressors are people who think exceedingly well of themselves (that is, have high self-esteem) and experience an insult as a threat to their positive self-view. Their aggression is a response to a perceived threat (Bushman, 1998). Not *all* people with high self-esteem are likely to be more aggressive; the aggressors are a subset of this group whose positive view of themselves may be either overinflated (that is, it doesn't correspond to reality) or unstable (Baumeister et al., 1996; Morf & Rhodewalt, 2001). Such people may view a threat to their positive self-image as likely to lead to a drop in self-esteem, and thus they defend against this drop (and the ensuing negative emotions) with aggressive behavior (Bushman et al., 2001; Twenge & Campbell, 2003).

On April 20, 1999, Littleton, Colorado's Columbine High School students Dylan Klebold and Eric Harris killed 15 people (including themselves). It was reported that Eric Harris would get enraged at the smallest slight (Lowe, 1999). Before the rampage, Harris had received several rejections, including a rejection for entry into the Marine Corps 5 days before the killings. Could this rejection have threatened an unrealistically high sense of self-esteem?

This subcategory of aggressive people high in self-esteem has been referred to as *narcissists*: people who think well of themselves but whose feelings of high self-esteem are not firmly grounded in reality (Bushman, 1998). That is, they have an overinflated, unjustified positive view of themselves. Other people who are high in self-esteem may have a well-founded self-assessment. The concept of narcissism (or exaggerated self-love, as originally conceived by Freud) takes its name from the Greek myth of Narcissus, who fell in love with his own reflection in the water, pined away, and died from unrequited love of his own image. Just as men are more likely to be physically aggressive, men also score higher on scales of narcissism (Bushman, 1998); they also have higher self-esteem in general.

Imagine that you agreed to participate in a psychological study and, as part of the study, wrote an essay on some topic. You get the essay back with this comment: "This is the worst essay I've ever read." Later, you are competing with the person who wrote this comment on a reaction time test, in which the winner sets the loudness and duration of a buzzer that goes off each time the other player loses. How would you respond if you won? How obnoxious would you let the sound be? Bushman (1998) hypothesized that people who score high on narcissism would be more likely to behave aggressively than those who score low, and indeed that is what he found. For these narcissists, a poor evaluation endangered their view of themselves, and was enough to elicit aggression toward the person doing the evaluating. Participants who scored low on narcissism were less likely to perceive negative evaluations of their essays as threats, and they were less aggressive. Not only was Bushman correct in his prediction, but he also found that the narcissistic participants were more likely to be aggressive *even if their essays were positively received*; a negative evaluation simply increased their aggressive behavior. For narcissists, then, it appears that *any* evaluation is a stressor that threatens their view of themselves. Further research on male narcissists reveals that they, in contrast to other men, are less likely to feel empathic toward rape victims and, when rebuffed by women, are more likely to retaliate in some way (Bushman et al., 2003).

**SUMMING UP** We are all, at one time or another, confronted by stressors that can elicit aggression; Thornton Wilder has written, "We have all murdered, in thought." Why do only some of us act on our aggressive thoughts? Baumeister and Boden (1998) propose that the answer may lie in the difficulty aggressive people have in regulating, or controlling, themselves. In turn, the ability to control ourselves and our aggressive impulses is related to a host of factors, including community standards, the perceived likelihood of punishment, our ability to monitor our behavior, our estimate of whether it will make us feel better (Bushman et al., 2001), and a conscious decision *not* to control ourselves.

# Personality and Coping

A person's coping style can be thought of as a personality trait, much as, say, messiness or curiosity or talkativeness. In other words, different people typically use different coping strategies when experiencing a stressor.

## The Healthy Personality: Control, Commitment, Challenge

Some personality characteristics are associated with health, even in the face of stress. Kobasa (1979; Kobasa et al., 1982) has found that health is associated with the combination of the following personality traits, termed a **hardy personality**:

- a strong sense of *commitment* to yourself and your work;

- a sense of *control* over what happens to you, similar to the concept of self-efficacy (see Chapter 11); and

- a view of life's ups and downs as *challenges*, as opportunities to learn, rather than as stressors.

In a study of middle- and upper-level male managers, Kobasa found that those with the traits of a hardy personality had lower rates of illness. Note, however, that although some research has supported the link between hardiness and better health (Williams & Lawler, 2003), not all studies have found such results (Funk & Houston, 1987; Hull et al., 1987; Wiebe & McCallum, 1986).

Hardy people apparently are better prepared to deal with life's stressors because they believe in themselves (Karademas & Kalantzi-Azizi, 2004). Not surprisingly, those with a high sense of self-efficacy are less likely to become ill when confronted by stressors than those with a low sense of self-efficacy (Holahan et al., 1984). Hardy people are also less likely to be depressed, regardless of their allostatic load, compared with nonhardy people (Pengilly & Dowd, 1997, 2000). During a simulation of a submarine's becoming disabled, hardy sailors reported less stress than their nonhardy comrades (Eid et al., 2004).

Attempts to teach hardiness have been somewhat successful. Ten-session hardiness training helped a group of managers to develop new ways to appraise stimuli as less stressful, to expand their repertoire of coping strategies, and to increase their sense of control and commitment. Those managers who received this hardiness training experienced more job satisfaction and social support and less illness than managers who learned relaxation techniques or who were in a support group (Maddi, 1998).

## Optimism and Pessimism: Look on the Bright Side

A personality trait that serves as a buffer against stress is *optimism*. Optimists generally have positive expectancies about the future and work hard to attain their goals even when the going is rough (see Chapter 11 for a more detailed discussion of expectancies). Optimists tend to disagree with statements such as "I hardly ever expect things to go my way" (Scheier & Carver, 1985). This personality trait is relatively stable over time. Studies have shown that optimists:

Hardy people are less likely to have physical illnesses in response to stress. Such individuals have a strong sense of commitment, control, and challenge.

**Hardy personality:** The combination of personality traits associated with health: commitment to self and work, a sense of control over what happens, and a view of stressors as challenges.

- report less stress as college students (Baldwin et al., 2003);

- had better moods, coping skills, responses to stress, and immune functioning during examination time (during their first year of law school) than their nonoptimistic counterparts (Segerstrom et al., 1998);

- report higher levels of psychological well-being during stressful periods than nonoptimists (Scheier & Carver, 1993);

- are less likely to develop symptoms of depression (Vickers & Vogeltanz, 2000);

- recover more quickly after surgery (Scheier et al., 1989; Scheier & Carver, 1993);

- experience less distress during high-risk pregnancies (Lobel et al., 2002);

- are less likely to be rehospitalized following heart bypass surgery (Scheier et al., 1999); and

- are less likely to die of heart problems than their pessimistic counterparts (Giltay et al., 2004).

The relationship between optimism and immune system functioning is complex. Although brief, controllable, and simple stressors are associated with *increased* cellular immunity in optimists, uncontrollable, persistent, or complex stressors are associated with *decreased* cellular immunity in optimists. Susan Segerstrom (in press) suggests that when encountering more challenging stressors (uncontrollable, persistent, or complex ones), optimists are more likely to "hang in there" when the going gets rough. In contrast, *pessimists*, who tend to expect negative outcomes, are more likely to give up, disengage, or avoid the stressful situation (Solberg Nes et al., in press). With a brief, controllable, or simple stressor, the optimists' response often leads to problem solving and resolution of the stressor. However, with an uncontrollable or complex stressor, such engagement and problem solving perpetuate increased contact with the stressor, which may increase the allostatic load—and thus have negative consequences. In contrast, pessimists, because of their style of coping, are likely to minimize such contact.

Pessimism is associated with anxiety, stress, depression, and poor health (Carver & Scheier, 1992; Robinson-Whelen et al., 1998). Pessimism can be further divided into two types: *true pessimism*, in which negative expectations are anchored in past experiences of failure, and *defensive pessimism*, in which a more negative outcome is expected than is warranted by the facts. Defensive pessimism can be thought of as a proactive coping strategy, in which negative or lowered expectations motivate coping behaviors; that is, negative expectations fuel anxiety about upcoming performance, which then motivates the pessimist to figure out how to avoid performing badly. In so doing, the pessimist decreases anxiety about an upcoming task that must be accomplished (Norem, 2003). For instance, suppose Al is a defensive pessimist. In preparation for an upcoming job interview, he may expect to do poorly, which makes him anxious. He may then be driven to figure out how he could improve his performance in those worrisome aspects of his interview. Defensive pessimism, then, can be adaptive because it both motivates individuals to become prepared (Yamawaki et al., 2004) and protects them from disappointment in their performance (Cantor & Norem, 1989).

Although defensive pessimists report more negative feelings before and after they must accomplish a task than do optimists, they usually perform as well as optimists on objective measures—which suggests that their coping strategy is effective for them. But those who were defensive pessimists during their first year of college had more psychological symptoms and less satisfaction by their junior years, compared to optimists (Cantor & Norem, 1989). Defensive pessimists typically perform well on the specific task about which they are pessimistic (Showers, 1992), and their style of coping helps maintain their self-esteem, although at a lower level than for optimists.

How does optimism confer its physical and psychological benefits? It appears that optimists (as compared with pessimists) are more likely to use problem-oriented coping strategies that involve direct action, and they are more focused on coping (Linley & Joseph, 2004). They are also more likely to accept the reality of a stressful situation and to try to make the best of it, to learn and grow from the experience. This response contrasts with that of true pessimists, who, when faced with a stressor, are likely to rely on denial and attempt to avoid dealing with the stressor or to give up when the stressor seems too difficult to manage (Scheier & Carver, 1993). The way optimists cope with stressors makes them more effective in managing difficult situations. However, before you assume that it would be helpful to "train" defensive pessimists to cope more like optimists, consider the observation that optimists have a lower baseline level of anxiety and depression than do defensive pessimists; hence, the fact that optimists are relatively healthy may be related to their bodies' having lower levels of wear and tear (from lower levels of anxiety and ensuing depression). It's not easy to sort out correlation from causation with regard to optimism and its health benefits.

## Avoiders Versus Nonavoiders

Another personality factor related to health is the extent to which a person habitually uses avoidant coping strategies or takes the opposite approach and focuses on the stressor. "Avoiders" are often referred to as *repressors*, and "nonavoiders" as *sensitizers*. Repressors habitually use an avoidant strategy such as a type of thought suppression, trying *not* to think about emotionally arousing, distressing matters, whereas sensitizers habitually think about these things. In contrast to high thought suppressors, when repressors employ thought suppression, they can suppress their thoughts with little effort and they tend not to experience a rebound of the suppressed thought (Barnier et al., 2004). That is, they tend not to have failed thought suppression.

Research has found that repressors, in spite of reporting fewer problems or less stress, are more likely to have higher blood pressure (Nyklicek et al., 1998) and compromised immune function. Thus, the use of avoidant strategies has possible negative effects on health (Jamner et al., 1988; Jamner & Leigh, 1999; Levy et al., 1985; Shea et al., 1993). However, the data are less than clear-cut regarding the health effects of a repressive coping style; other studies find that sensitizers report more anxiety and have a larger biological stress response than do repressors (Rohrmann et al., 2003).

## Genes and Coping

If aspects of your personality—such as whether you are an optimist or pessimist—help determine the way you cope, then a question integral to personality research comes to the fore: Are your coping strategies genetically based, are they learned, or are they the result of an interaction of these two? Research findings suggest that the answer may depend on the specific strategy. For example, you could ask, "Are optimists born or made?" Studies of Swedish twins reared together and apart found that optimism has a heritability of 25% (Plomin et al., 1992), and other studies also suggest that optimism is partly heritable (Zuckerman, 2001). Environmental factors that may influence coping strategies include learning from prior experiences, observational learning from parents and others, and direct instruction in coping skills (Scheier & Carver, 1993). In general, Busjahn and colleagues (1999) found evidence that genetics, in combination with an individual's unique life experiences, influenced 14 out of 19 coping strategies they examined, such as self-blame, rumination, minimization, and substance abuse. In contrast, the coping strategies of getting enraged and using mental distraction showed no genetic influence.

This research on the genetic aspects of coping (and, by extension, of health), as well as much of the research on personality and its relation to coping, is not necessarily as straightforward as you might think. Researchers often ask participants how they have coped or would cope in certain situations and then assess different measures of stress, well-being, immune system functioning, or other variables. But people's behavior often differs from one situation to another (see Chapter 11), and, in fact, research shows that how particular people cope differs across situations (Schwartz et al., 1999). Furthermore, simply *asking* people how they would or did cope in certain stressful situations does not necessarily lead to an accurate picture of their actual coping behavior (Schwartz et al., 1999; Smith et al., 1999; Todd et al., 2004). So, the idea that individuals have a *typical* way of coping may not be as accurate as researchers have assumed. In addition, some other factor could account for the research results. For example, people who are optimists may report coping more effectively or positively than they actually do, and because they view the glass as half-full rather than half-empty, they selectively remember using certain strategies more than others (Schwartz et al., 1999; Smith et al., 1999). Thus, their optimism influences their memory (and their reporting) of their coping, but perhaps not their actual coping. However, this very distortion of fact—that they *remember* themselves as coping well—may be an important link between their experiences of stress and their health.

# Coping and Social Support

**Social support**, the help and support gained through interacting with others, buffers the adverse effects of stress. Certain types of positive relationships, such as a good marriage, positive contact with friends and family, participation in group activities, and involvement in a religious organization, can lengthen life expectancy. Just having such connections can have as much influence on mortality as being a nonsmoker or being physically active (House et al., 1988). Consider the following findings related to social support:

- In a study of over 4,000 men and women in Alameda County, California, the death rate for socially isolated people was twice that for people with strong social ties. Deaths were due not only to heart disease, but also to cancer, infectious disease, and other causes (Berkman & Syme, 1979).

- The benefits of social support can be gained simply from holding hands or making some other kind of physical contact (Sapolsky, 1997).

- For those undergoing a painful and frightening surgical procedure, just talking with their doctor the night before surgery positively affected recovery (Egbert et al., 1964).

- In a study of people with severe coronary heart disease, half of the group without social support died within 5 years, three times the rate for those who had a close friend or spouse (Williams et al., 1992). Other researchers have reported similar results (Rutledge et al., 2004).

- Among college students experiencing high levels of stress, those reporting high levels of social support were less likely to be depressed than those reporting lower levels of social support (Pengilly & Dowd, 1997).

Social support is also related to immune system functioning (Seeman et al., 1994). Looking at the relation between social support and catching a cold, researchers found that participants who had a wide range of acquaintances (friends, neighbors, relatives, work colleagues, people from social or religious groups, and so forth) were half as likely to catch a cold as those who were socially isolated (Cohen et al., 1997). You might

There is a confounding variable influencing the association between social support and longevity among heart patients: Although couch potatoes report less social support, it may be their sedentary behavior, not the diminished social support, that accounts for their shorter life spans (Brummett et al., 2005).

Social support: The help and support gained through interacting with others.

**Perceived social support:** The subjective sense that support is available should it be needed.

**Enacted social support:** The specific supportive behaviors provided by others.

think that contacts with more people would bring a higher likelihood of exposure to cold germs, but in fact, social isolation is as strong a risk factor for colds as smoking, stress, and not getting enough vitamin C. The key is not the total number of supportive relationships, but rather their variety. Not just any relationship will do the trick: Demanding and critical relationships—but not positive and supportive ones—are associated with stress-related symptoms (Seeman, 2000). Bad marriages are associated with suppressed immune functioning (Kiecolt-Glaser & Newton, 2001), at least in men (Kiecolt-Glaser et al., 1988). For women, marital stress is associated with coronary heart disease at a later point in time (Orth-Gomér et al., 2000).

Given the positive effects of social support, it is not surprising that attempts have been made to help isolated people develop such support. Unfortunately, this has proved surprisingly difficult (Lakey & Lutz, 1996), perhaps in part because isolated people lack the motivation or social skills to develop more supportive relationships. **Perceived social support**, the subjective sense that support is available should it be needed, is distinct from the actual size and variety of your social network, and from **enacted social support**, specific support that is provided to you, such as a friend bringing you a meal when he or she knows you aren't feeling well. Research has shown that it is generally perceived support, not enacted support, that provides the buffer against stress (Cohen & Wills, 1985). Moreover, the perception of support is unrelated to actual support. For instance, researchers observed college students, some of whom perceived a high degree of social support in their lives and some of whom perceived much less, as they responded to stressors in the presence of their friends. The participants' perceptions of their friends' support was unrelated to the actual support the friends offered (Lakey & Heller, 1988).

The person dressed in yellow in the photo is receiving enacted social support. However, she may not necessarily have the sense that support is available when she needs it (perceived social support) because these two aspects of social support are not necessarily correlated. Also, what constitutes support may differ from person to person.

## Enacted Social Support

Does marriage provide enacted social support? Not necessarily. Among married couples in which one partner was receiving a kidney transplant, enacted social support from the spouse alleviated distress only when the couple's relationship was satisfying; otherwise, such support increased distress (Frazier et al., 2003). This finding is consistent with a more general one about marriage and health: Marriages that are spiked with frequent conflict and hostile and critical behaviors are likely to have an adverse affect on health (Robles & Kiecolt-Glaser, 2003). Thus, simply being married, or in a long-term relationship, does not mean that each person in the relationship derives any health benefit related to social support from it.

## Perceived Social Support

Attachment styles (see Chapters 11 and 12) influence the perception of social support: Those with an insecure attachment style are likely to perceive less support than their securely attached counterparts, even when researchers statistically control for independent ratings of actual support (Collins & Feeney, 2004). In addition, people who perceive themselves as having low social support tend to view a given social interaction more negatively (Lakey & Dickenson, 1994); if Al is such a person, that would explain his reluctance to tell his friends about what is happening to him at work.

Memory also is involved in the perception of social support. Consider the finding that people who perceive that they have a great deal of social support also have better memories for the supportive behaviors of others (Lakey et al., 1992). In sum, as with stress, the perception of support is important (Lakey & Lutz, 1996).

# Mind–Body Interventions

When you receive an injection, take a pill, have surgery, or undergo a medical procedure, it doesn't much matter what you are thinking about and focusing on, as long as your body responds in the intended way to the intervention. In contrast, *mind–body interventions* seek to engage your mind in a particular way in order to influence your body's functioning. As you can see in Table 13.3, there are a number of commonly used mind–body techniques. One survey found that almost 20% of adults questioned had employed at least one type of mind–body intervention within the previous year (Wolsko et al., 2004). Mind–body techniques are used by people from many walks of life, including medical patients, athletes (Ryska, 1998), managers, teachers (Anderson et al., 1999), and first-year law school students (Sheehy & Horan, 2004). The National Institutes of Health has a special branch, the National Center for Complementary and Alternative Medicine (NCCAM), which is dedicated to the investigation of such techniques. NCCAM provides funding to researchers who study how a wide range of mind–body interventions can be used in treating specific diseases and pain and in maintaining health (Berman & Straus, 2004).

The goal of mind–body interventions is not to change a stressful stimulus, but to allow you to adapt to the stimulus—and, in doing so, to alter bodily functioning. Mind–body interventions can alter heart and breathing rates, hormone secretion, and brain activation. Researchers have found that both progressive muscle relaxation and hypnosis effectively decrease autonomic reactivity to stress and that deep abdominal breathing is somewhat effective. Even sitting quietly with your eyes closed for a few minutes decreases pulse rate (Forbes & Pekala, 1993). Some mind–body techniques, such as meditation and hypnosis, are intended to improve well-being by altering consciousness (Barnes et al., 2004; Wickramasekera et al., 1996; see Chapter 5 for further discussion).

## The Effects of Mind–Body Interventions

Kiecolt-Glaser and colleagues (1986) studied whether different stress-reduction techniques can boost medical students' immune systems during examinations. Half of the participants were taught hypnosis and other relaxation techniques and encouraged to practice at home; the other half were taught nothing. The students in the relaxation group did in fact have better immune functioning during the exams than the students in the control group; the same benefits later were documented for highly hypnotizable medical and dental students who learned hypnotic relaxation techniques (Kiecolt-Glaser et al., 2001).

Many mind–body techniques for people who are physically ill provide specific coping strategies, relaxation training, training in meditation (to decrease arousal and increase perceived control), increased social support (Andersen, 1997), disease-related information, and a supportive environment in which to address fears about the illness. These interventions have been found to confer the following benefits:

- improved mood and immune system functioning (Fawzy et al., 1990; Zakowski et al., 1992);
- increased lung functioning in people with asthma (Hockemeyer & Smyth, 2002);

<table>
<tr><td>TABLE 13.3<br><br>Common Mind–Body Interventions</td></tr>
</table>

- Hypnosis
- Meditation
- Yoga
- Biofeedback
- Visual imagery
- Cognitive therapy
- Stress management/ relaxation induction
- Prayer
- Tai chi

Collegiate rowers were randomly assigned to either a stress management program or a control group; those in the stress management group had fewer illnesses and injuries, and fewer medical visits to the student health center, than did those in the control group (Perna et al., 2003).

- improved control of pain (NIH Technology Assessment Panel, 1996);
- decreased levels of reported stress, emotional distress, and poor coping strategies (Tacón et al., 2004; Timmerman et al., 1998); and
- fewer subsequent heart problems (Blumenthal et al., 2002).

However, mind–body techniques do not guarantee health or stave off death (Claar & Blumenthal, 2003).

## The Placebo Effect as a Mind–Body Intervention

The fact that placebos can be effective also illustrates the link between mind and body. Simply believing that you are receiving a remedy (even if it has no medicinal effects) not only can lessen your experience of pain (Wager et al., 2004), but also can affect your immune system's functioning. One neuroimaging study found that, after participants received an intensely hot stimulus, the injection of a placebo activated the same brain areas as did an injection of a fast-acting opioid painkiller. Moreover, those who were more responsive to the pain medicine were also more responsive to the placebo (Petrovic et al., 2002).

In general, properties of the placebo itself and the way it is dispensed can make it more or less effective. For example, placebo injections are more effective than placebos taken orally, capsules are more effective than pills, and more (placebo) pills work better than fewer (placebo) pills. The color of the capsule can also make a difference: Blue capsules work best as tranquilizers; yellow, pink, and red capsules work best as stimulants (Buckalew & Ross, 1981). Moreover, if the person dispensing the treatment is friendly and sympathetic and shows an interest in the patient's problems, the placebo is more likely to be effective (Shapiro & Morris, 1978). Even the clinician's own view of a placebo's effectiveness can make a difference: If the treatment provider has high expectations for the treatment, it is more likely to be effective (Shapiro, 1964). To avoid this effect, a research study with placebos often has a *double-blind design*, in which neither those dispensing the treatment nor the participants know whether a given participant is receiving a placebo or the active medication. In a review of research that reported successful results from five treatments (for three diseases) that were later proved worthless, Roberts and colleagues (1993) found that when presented enthusiastically, these placebos were 70% effective.

Research has shown the benefits of exercise for alleviating the symptoms of some major psychological disorders, such as depression, as well as for reducing pain (Tkachuk, 1999).

# Gender, Culture, and Coping

Do men and women experience the same amounts of stress? Do people in different cultures experience different amounts of stress? Do they cope with stress equally well? Psychologists have begun to pose questions such as these in an effort to learn whether stressors affect different groups of people differently.

## Gender Differences in Coping

There is some evidence that women in Western cultures experience more stress than men. A survey of 2,500 Swedes found that women, particularly younger women, reported feeling more hassled, depressed, anxious, and hostile (Scott & Melin, 1998). As women have entered the workforce, a number of studies have focused on the effects of their multiple roles: employee, wife, mother, daughter. The effects of having multiple roles can be both positive and negative: Women who are parents tend to have more to do than men who are parents and also to experience more conflict among their different roles and to be less able to unwind at home (Clay, 1995). Women generally report more stress with multiple roles than do men, and women employed outside the home generally do more work than men in their "second shift" at home: cooking, cleaning, and shopping (Hochschild, 1989; Phillips & Imhoff, 1997). However, these multiple roles can also confer advantages: increased feelings of self-esteem and control (Pietromonaco et al., 1986), financial gain, social support from colleagues (Brannon, 1996), and decreased psychological stress (Abrams & Jones, 1994). Thus, although employment outside the home can be more stressful (particularly if there are children), it is not necessarily more stressful for women than for men. Having financial and familial resources and control over the job (Taylor et al., 1997; Tingey et al., 1996), as well as a sense of mastery at work (Christensen et al., 1998), can reduce the stress of multiple roles.

Husbands and wives also differ in the benefits and stressors accrued in marriage: Women experience more stress and negative health effects from marital conflicts, but they also experience more happiness from their marital relationships (Kiecolt-Glaser & Newton, 2001). Men and women also tend to have differences in how they cope: As summarized by Shelley Taylor and colleagues (2000, 2002), when under stress, women tend to seek out social support whereas men tend to be more action-oriented, directly addressing the cause of the stress (Luckow et al., 1998).

## Cultural Differences in Coping

Culture can help determine what constitutes a stressor, as well as when and how a person asks for assistance in coping with stressors. Different cultures may not only lead their members to view different stimuli as stressors, but also lead them to believe that they have more or less control over particular stressors. For example, crowding is a culturally defined stressor. In different cultures, different levels of *density* (the number of people in a given space) produce the perception of *crowding* (the subjective experience created by density). Members of Asian cultures experience less stress than Westerners would in high-density living conditions; Asians have developed ways of creating a sense of privacy in the midst of density, thereby providing a sense of control (Werner et al., 1997).

Culture also plays a role in defining which coping strategies are socially appropriate, as well as defining the appropriate use of social support (Aranda & Knight, 1997; Morling et al., 2003; O'Connor & Shimizu, 2002; Patterson et al., 1998). For instance, Indian students prefer emotion-focused coping strategies more than do Canadian students (Sinha et al., 2000), and people from collectivist cultures are less likely to seek social support than those from individualist cultures (Taylor, Sherman, et al., 2004). In examining the effects of culture on heart disease, Marmot and Syme (1976) studied more than 3,000 Japanese American men in the San Francisco area. The men whose upbringing was more traditionally Japanese and who still maintained strong ties with Japanese culture had two and a half times less coronary heart disease than did those men whose upbringing was more assimilated. This difference held even when the researchers controlled for diet, smoking, and other risk factors. In fact, those who were most closely tied to Japanese culture were five times less likely to have heart disease than those least involved in Japanese culture. The researchers proposed that this difference arose because of the cultural and social cohesiveness found in Japanese culture and that this cohesiveness protects against heart disease. Such cohesiveness may be part of the reason why those from collectivist cultures do not seek out social support—because they know that such support is available, they feel less need to ask (Taylor, Sherman, et al., 2004).

# LOOKING AT LEVELS

## Voodoo Death

In some cultures, it has been reported that when a shaman (religious leader) puts a curse on someone, death sometimes ensues; this phenomenon is known as *voodoo death* (Cannon, 1942). Although there is some debate as to whether voodoo death actually occurs (Hahn, 1997), research has shown that expectations of sickness can, in fact, cause sickness. This is the **nocebo effect**, a variation of the placebo effect, but with the expectation of a negative outcome rather than a positive outcome. (*Placebo* in Latin means "I will please"; *nocebo* means "I will harm.") Voodoo death represents an extreme example of the nocebo effect. But you shouldn't think that the nocebo effect happens only in primitive cultures: Among American women enrolled in a study of the risk factors for heart disease, those who believed that they were more likely to die of a heart attack were, in fact, 3.7 times more likely to die of a heart attack than other women in the study, even after researchers controlled for known risk factors for heart disease (Eaker, Pinsky, & Castelli, 1992).

Further examples of nocebo effects—including fatal ones—abound. Among presurgery patients who consulted a psychiatrist before their surgeries about their fears of the procedure, expectations about the surgery affected its outcome. Weisman and Hackett (1961) report that all five patients who were convinced of their impending death did die during surgery, whereas most of those who were unusually apprehensive about the surgery, but not convinced of death, did not die. Moreover, research with people with asthma has found a powerful nocebo effect: One group of sufferers was asked to inhale what they were told was an irritant or allergen, but that was in fact a harmless saline solution. Almost half of this group experienced an asthmatic reaction. Another group of people with asthma received the same saline solution but without any such information and had no reaction (Luparello et al., 1968).

Have you ever taken a new medicine and discovered that it had unpleasant—although not dangerous—side effects? For instance, cold medications may make you feel drowsy. But some people experience side effects that do not appear to occur directly from medicinal properties; such reactions are called *nonspecific side effects*, and they can be uncomfortable enough that they lead people to stop taking the medication. The particular nonspecific side effects vary among people taking the same medication. Arthur Barsky and colleagues (2002) propose that these effects are nocebo effects and offer two accounts for them. First, expectations may play a role; people who expect negative side effects from a new medication (perhaps because they've heard of such effects from it) may then experience them. Second, some people may have nonspecific side effects because they've become classically conditioned, perhaps by their past experiences with side effects from other medicines, which then generalize.

In addition, once people take a medication, they may come to attribute any uncomfortable bodily symptoms to it. This is a problem because we all have the uncomfortable aches and twinges, from time to time. In fact, a study of healthy college students found that 81% experienced at least one physical symptom within a 3-day stretch (Gick & Thompson, 1997). People who are most likely to develop nonspecific side effects attribute these transient disturbances to the medication.

Barsky and colleagues summarize various studies that support the position that nonspecific side effects are, in fact, nocebo effects:

**Nocebo effect:** A variation of the placebo effect in which the person expects a negative outcome instead of a positive outcome.

- Patients who were told that a medicine was a stimulant (when it was, in fact, a muscle relaxant) reported more muscle tension than those who were told that the medicine was a relaxant (Flaten et al., 1999).

- Patients with food allergies received an injection (that was saline solution) and were told that it contained the substance to which they were allergic. They subsequently developed allergic symptoms (Jewett et al., 1990).

- Healthy volunteers were told that they would receive mild electric current through their heads and that such current could produce mild headaches; 70% reported headaches, even though the current was never turned on (Schweiger & Parducci, 1981).

- Approximately 20–25% (and sometimes more) of people taking placebo medications report unpleasant side effects (Dhume et al., 1975; Drid et al., 1995; Rosenzweig et al., 1993; Shepherd, 1993; Tangrea et al., 1994). Such nonspecific effects include drowsiness, nausea, fatigue, insomnia, poor concentration, and gastrointestinal problems.

How can we understand the nocebo response? At the level of the brain, classical conditioning plays a role in the development of certain nocebo—and placebo—responses. For example, Benedetti and colleagues (2003) arranged for participants to receive injections of a substance that increases cortisol. After receiving these injections for two days, on the third day they received an injection of salt water (the nocebo). Even this inert substance now elicited a cortisol increase (the injection was the CS; see Chapter 6). Another example of a conditioned nocebo effect is anticipatory nausea before chemotherapy (see Chapter 6). In addition, some people, particularly those high in the personality dimension of neuroticism, are more likely to experience conditioned emotional responses, including these nonspecific side effects (Davis et al., 1995). Neuroticism is moderately heritable, and so this effect is partly an event at the level of the brain.

At the level of the person, the *expectation* of a negative outcome leads an individual to be hypervigilant for any bodily changes and to attribute such changes to the nocebo instead of to some other stimulus (Barsky et al., 2002). As shown in Figure 13.9, expectation of a negative response can increase pain, and expectation of a positive response can diminish pain (Benedetti et al., 2003). For those people who experience frequent nonspecific side effects, events at the level of the person include their beliefs about what such symptoms mean, as well as the ways they assess whether a bodily sensation constitutes a "side effect" (Hahn, 1999).

At the level of the group, expectations about a given nocebo can arise after one person directly *tells* another about negative effects. Participants in the study of expectations and pain by Benedetti and colleagues (2003) illustrated in Figure 13.9 were told verbally by an investigator what to expect from the (nocebo) medication. Sometimes expectations are communicated through stories, warnings, or written prohibitions. For instance, beliefs about a medicine can be shaped by advertisements, information on the Internet, friends' recountings of their experiences with the medication, or a doctor's admonitions about side effects. In addition, each culture promotes somewhat different ideas and expectations about sickness and health (Hahn, 1995).

Events at these three levels of analysis interact. For example, culture and social interactions (level of the group) provided the context for the people with asthma who were told they were inhaling a noxious stimulus (Luparello et al., 1968), for those whose pain responses were affected by their expectations (Benedetti et al., 2003), and for those people who experience frequent nonspecific side effects of medications. Such group-level events, in part, led these people to have beliefs about the "medication" they were taking and to be hypervigilant (level of the person) to their physical response (level of the brain). In addition, these events, as well as the individuals' past experiences with medications and side effects and their predisposition toward conditioned emotional responses, may have led to a classically conditioned nocebo response (level of the brain). In turn, all these events led people to interpret the bodily changes in particular ways (level of the person).

## FIGURE 13.9

## Nocebos and Expectations

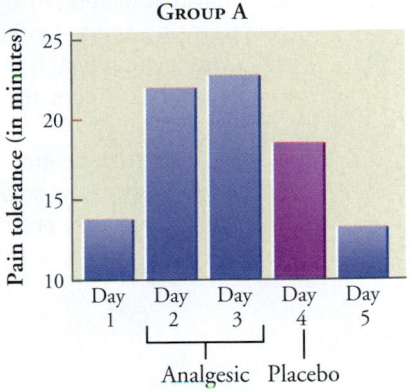

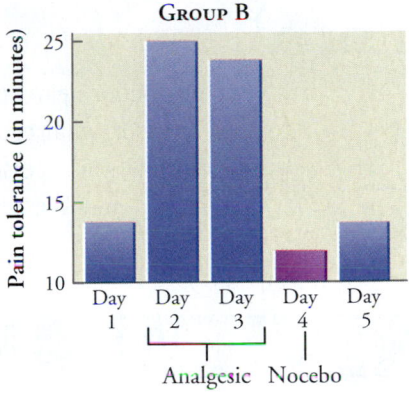

In the study by Benedetti and colleagues (2003), people in both groups, A and B, experienced a procedure that was increasingly painful; the height of each bar indicates how many minutes, on average, each group was able to tolerate the pain. On day 1 of the study, both groups received the painful procedure with no intervention; on days 2 and 3, both groups received an intravenous analgesic medication during the procedure. On day 4, both groups received an intravenous inert substance, but Group A was told that the medicine would alleviate pain (and hence the substance functioned as a placebo), whereas Group B was told that the medicine would increase pain (and hence it functioned as a nocebo).

1. Problem-focused coping strategies tend to focus on _____, whereas emotion-focused coping strategies focus more on _____.
   a. cognitive factors; behavioral factors
   b. behavioral factors; environmental factors
   c. decreasing arousal; affecting the stressor
   d. environmental factors; emotional factors
2. People who are more resistant to the negative effects of stress tend to
   a. have a sense of control and commitment.
   b. ignore the stressors around them.
   c. have appropriately pessimistic views.
   d. rely on emotion-focused coping strategies.

3. What do research results say about social support and coping?
   a. Enacted social support provides the best buffer to stress.
   b. Perceived social support provides the best buffer to stress.
   c. There is no relationship between social support and coping.
   d. Perceived social support is a reliable predictor of enacted social support.
4. How do mind–body interventions affect stress?
   a. Mind–body interventions have no effect on stress.
   b. Only mind–body interventions that involve vigorous exercise reduce stress.
   c. Mind–body interventions help reduce the physical effects of stress.
   d. Mind–body interventions increase autonomic reactivity and thus stress.

## Answers

1.d 2.a 3.b 4.c

# Think It Through!

If your next-door neighbor plays music very loudly every night when you are trying to go to sleep, and you find this to be a stressor, what could you do to lower your stress response? What type of coping strategies would work best in this situation? What personality characteristics would make you less likely to feel stressed by a noisy neighbor? If you were in a non-Western culture, could the nightly serenade be less stressful? Why or why not?

# REVIEW AND REMEMBER!

## Summary

### I. What Is Stress?

**A.** Stress is the general term describing the psychological and physical response to a stimulus that alters the body's equilibrium. The stress response of the autonomic nervous system increases heart rate and blood pressure.

**B.** Continued stressors can lead the body's response to stress to become harmful. A higher allostatic load increases the risk for medical and psychological problems.

**C.** The perception of stress helps determine what constitutes a stressor. Common sources of stress include a sense of a lack of control and predictability, internal conflicts, and daily hassles.

**D.** In the workplace, environmental factors such as noise or work-related conflict can cause stress. Work can also be a stressor because of a perceived lack of control over how the job is done or because the job entails responsibility for other people's lives or welfare. Low socioeconomic status can also cause stress.

**E.** The personality trait of hostility is associated with increased stress, heart rate, blood pressure, and cortisol production. Men are generally more hostile than women.

## Your Notes

I.

A. GAS: (1) alarm; (2) resistance; (3) exhaustion

B.

C.

D.

E.

## II. Stress, Disease, and Health

**A.** Frequent activation of the stress response can lead to changes in the immune system, which can make you vulnerable to contracting a cold or can promote the growth of existing tumors. However, stress does not cause tumors to develop.

**B.** Stress can create cardiovascular changes and can contribute to the development of heart disease through increased blood pressure.

**C.** Stress can increase the likelihood of engaging in unhealthy behaviors such as smoking, substance abuse, or poor eating habits.

**D.** Whether an individual adopts an unhealthy behavior is related to his or her perceptions of the risk of developing a health problem by engaging in the behavior and of the severity of the problem.

**E.** People often go through stages of change and typically relapse when trying to alter a health-impairing behavior.

## III. Strategies for Coping

**A.** A realistic appraisal of whether your actions can affect a stressor will help you to determine what coping strategies will be effective.

**B.** Emotion-focused coping strategies work best when the situation can't be changed, and problem-focused strategies work best when it can.

**C.** Some people have a hardy personality, meaning that they tend to have a sense of commitment and control, view stressors as challenges, and tend to be optimists.

**D.** Social support (particularly perceived social support) can help decrease the experience of stress.

**E.** Mind–body techniques, such as relaxation training, meditation, and hypnosis, can decrease the physical effects of stress.

**F.** Culture can affect both the appraisal of a stimulus as a stressor and the choice of coping strategies for managing the stressor.

**G.** Both placebo and nocebo effects illustrate the interactions between mind and body.

NOTE: Once you feel that you understand the material in this chapter, visit the book's Web site at www.ablongman.com/kosslyn3e to test your knowledge with additional study questions.

*Margin notes:*
*II.*
*A.*
*B.*
*C.*
*D.*
*E. See Fig. 13.7 for 5 stages of change.*
*III.*
*A.*
*B. Hostile attribution bias → aggression*
*C.*
*D.*
*E.*
*F.*
*G.*

# Key Terms

acute stressor, p. 588
aggression, p. 613
alarm phase, p. 589
approach–approach conflict, p. 595
approach–avoidance conflict, p. 595
atherosclerosis, p. 603
avoidance–avoidance conflict, p. 595
B cell, p. 602
burnout, p. 598
chronic stressor, p. 588
coping, p. 593

emotion-focused coping, p. 609
enacted social support, p. 620
exhaustion phase, p. 591
general adaptation syndrome (GAS), p. 589
glucocorticoids, p. 589
hardy personality, p. 616
health psychology, p. 588
hostile attribution bias, p. 614
hostility, p. 600
internal conflict, p. 595

natural killer (NK) cell, p. 602
nocebo effect, p. 624
perceived social support, p. 620
problem-focused coping, p. 609
resistance phase, p. 590
social support, p. 619
stress, p. 588
stressor, p. 588
stress response, p. 588
T cell, p. 602
thought suppression, p. 612

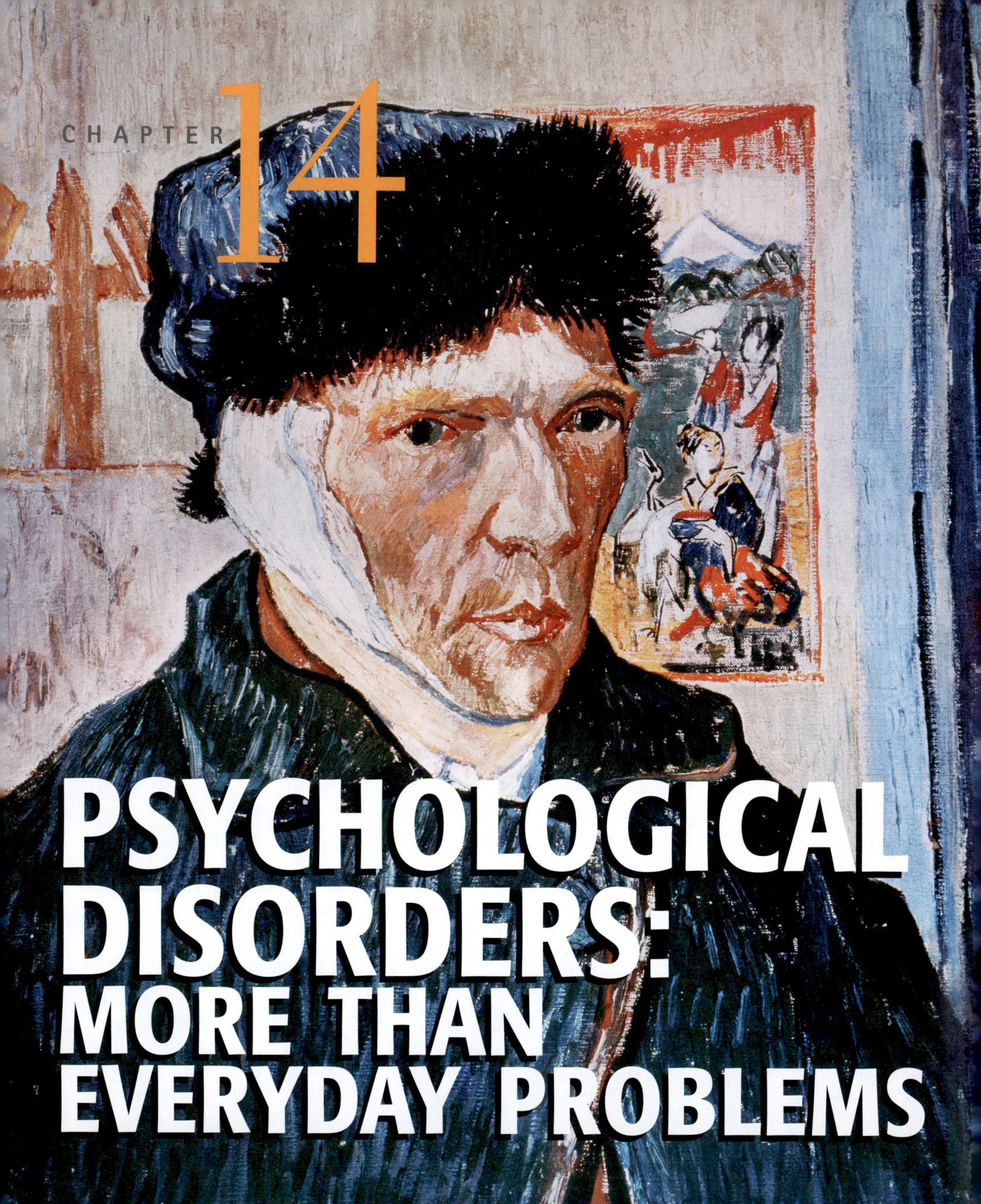

# CHAPTER 14

# PSYCHOLOGICAL DISORDERS: MORE THAN EVERYDAY PROBLEMS

Museum-goers worldwide throng to see exhibits of the works of Vincent van Gogh. Born in Holland in 1853, van Gogh created extraordinary art and took much joy in painting, but his life is a tale of misery. The son and grandson of Protestant ministers, van Gogh was the second of six children. A memoir by his sister-in-law records, "As a child he was of difficult temper, often troublesome and self-willed" (Roskill, 1963, p. 37). According to his parents, when punished, Vincent became more "difficult." As a child he showed no particular awareness of his great gifts; however, on two occasions, once when he modeled a clay elephant and again when he drew a cat, he destroyed his creations when he felt a "fuss" was being made about them (Roskill, 1963).

When van Gogh was 16, he worked as a clerk in an art gallery, but his long, moody silences and irritability isolated him from his coworkers. After 4 years, he was transferred to the gallery's office in London, where he fell in love with his landlady's daughter, Ursula. They spent many months together, until she revealed her engagement to a previous tenant and rejected van Gogh. Feeling utterly defeated, he found it difficult to concentrate at work. He frequently argued with his coworkers and was soon fired.

Van Gogh next decided on a career in the ministry but could not master the Greek and Latin necessary for the entrance exams. Instead, he became a lay pastor, preaching to miners in the Borinage, a coal-mining area in Belgium. He went without bathing and slept in a hut on bare planks, as the miners did. But the miners feared this unkempt, wild-looking man, and the church elders dismissed him. Increasingly, van Gogh found comfort in painting and drawing.

His life continued to be marked by instability. After he left the Borinage, he lived in and out of his parents' home and wandered around the country. Whereas once his interest in religion had been intense, if not obsessional, he now turned his back on religion. He developed a relationship with a pregnant prostitute, Sien, but their liaison ended after about a year and a half. Van Gogh reported that he had "attacks" during which he would hear voices; at times, he believed he was being poisoned.

When he was 35, van Gogh convinced fellow painter Paul Gauguin to share a house with him in Arles, France. As was true for all of van Gogh's relationships, he and

Gauguin frequently quarreled. According to Gauguin, after one particularly violent argument, van Gogh approached him threateningly with an open razor, but Gauguin stared him down. Van Gogh then ran to their house, where he cut off his earlobe, which he then sent to a local prostitute (not Sien). The next day he was found at home, bleeding and unconscious, and was taken to a hospital, where he remained for 2 weeks. His brother Theo spent time with him in the hospital and found Vincent in great spiritual anguish.

After his release from the hospital in January 1889, van Gogh's behavior became increasingly bizarre, so much so that within 2 months the residents of Arles petitioned that he be confined, and he again stayed for a time in the hospital. In May, van Gogh moved to the asylum at Saint-Remy, not far from Arles, where he lived on and off for the next year and a half, and where he produced many paintings. Shortly after his last release, less than 2 years after the incident with Gauguin, he purposefully ended his anguish and his life by going out into a field with a gun and shooting himself in the stomach. Yet, a few weeks before his death, he could say, "I still love art and life very much indeed" (Roskill, 1963).

Questions of art aside, van Gogh's experiences focus our attention on psychological disorders: What defines a psychological disorder? Who establishes criteria for determining what is abnormal behavior? What are the symptoms and origins of some specific disorders?

# IDENTIFYING PSYCHOLOGICAL DISORDERS: What's Abnormal?

What distinguishes unusual behaviors from behaviors that are symptoms of a psychological disorder? Before he rejected religion, van Gogh was tormented by religious ideas and believed in ghosts. Are these signs of psychological disturbance? What about his self-mutilation? What would you want to know about him before drawing any conclusions?

Mental health professionals face questions such as these every day. In this section, you will see how formulations of and findings about psychological disorders suggest answers to those questions.

## Defining Abnormality

It is difficult to give an exact definition of psychological disorders—also referred to as psychiatric disorders, mental disorders or, less systematically, mental illnesses—because they can encompass many aspects of behavioral, experiential, and bodily functioning. However, a good working definition is that a **psychological disorder** is signaled by a constellation of cognitive, emotional, and behavioral symptoms that create significant distress; impair work, school, family, relationships, or daily living; or lead to significant risk of harm. This definition takes into account three factors: distress, impairment, and danger.

Psychological disorder: The presence of a constellation of cognitive, emotional, and behavioral symptoms that create significant distress; impair work, school, family, relationships, or daily living; or lead to significant risk of harm.

### Distress

People with psychological disorders may display or experience *distress*. One example of distress that is obvious to others is repeatedly bursting into tears and expressing hopelessness about the future, for no apparent reason. However, a person's distress is not always observable to others, as when people chronically worry, feel profoundly sad for long periods of time, or hear voices that only they can hear.

## Impairment

People with psychological disorders may experience a *disability* or *impairment* in some aspect of life. Examples include a police officer who becomes so anxious that he cannot perform his job or an individual (such as van Gogh) whose emotional outbursts drive others away. An individual's impairment may not necessarily cause him or her distress but can be maladaptive nonetheless.

Psychological disorders can be very debilitating, and worldwide they rank second among diseases that lead to death and disability, a higher ranking than cancer (Murray & Lopez, 1996). The World Health Organization (2001) estimates that in the year 2000, 450 million people suffered from psychological disorders worldwide. According to some estimates, up to 48% of Americans have experienced 1 of 30 common psychological disorders at some point in their lives (Kessler et al., 1994), and 20% of Americans have a diagnosable mental disorder in any given year (Regier et al., 1993; Satcher, 1999). Psychological disorders can affect people's relationships, their ability to care for themselves, and their functioning on the job. For every 100 workers, an average of 37 work days per month are lost because of either reduced output or absences stemming from psychological disorders (Kessler & Frank, 1997).

## Danger

*Danger* can occur when symptoms of a psychological disorder cause an individual to put life (his or her own, or another's) at risk, either purposefully or accidentally. For instance, depression may lead someone to attempt suicide, extreme paranoia may provoke someone to attack other people, or a parent's disorder may be sufficiently severe that the children's safety is put at risk (as when Andrea Yates, who suffered so severely from depression that she lost touch with reality, drowned her five young children in 2001, thinking that she was rescuing them from Satan's grasp).

## Cultural and Social Influences

Picture someone hopping on one leg, thumb in mouth, trying to sing the French national anthem during a hockey game. You would probably consider this behavior abnormal; but what if the behavior was part of a fraternity initiation ritual or a new kind of performance art? A behavior that is bizarre or inappropriate in one context may be entirely appropriate in another. To be considered "disordered," it is not enough for a behavior or a set of behaviors to be deviant from the mainstream culture. Being unconventional or different in religious, political, or sexual arenas does not qualify as abnormal. What is considered deviant changes from generation to generation, and can differ across cultures.

Consider that, in 1851, Dr. Samuel Cartwright of Louisiana wrote an essay in which he declared that slaves' running away was evidence of a serious mental disorder, which he called "drapetomania" (Eakin, 2000). Also, homosexuality was officially considered a psychological disorder in the United States until 1973, and then it was removed from the *Diagnostic and Statistical Manual of Mental Disorders* (this manual is used by mental health clinicians to classify psychological disorders). And in the last decade, the determination of abnormality has been given a new twist in the United States; as health maintenance organizations (HMOs) and other types of managed care

Van Gogh's painting of the church at Auvers is unusual because of its unconventional perspective, use of color, and brushstrokes. Do these differences reflect a psychological disorder, or just a different way of seeing or conveying the structure and its surroundings?

Mathematician John Nash (left), whose life was the basis for the movie *A Beautiful Mind*, starring Oscar-winning actor Russell Crowe (right), had delusions that aliens were communicating with him. Although the movie portrayed Nash as having both hallucinations and delusions, in real life he did not have hallucinations.

organizations try to keep costs down, they have developed their own criteria for which symptoms and disorders they will pay to have treated—and have also regulated the frequency and duration of the treatment.

The line between normal and abnormal behavior is perhaps easiest to draw in the case of **psychosis**, which is an obvious impairment in the ability to perceive and comprehend events accurately, combined with a gross disorganization of behavior. People with psychoses may have **hallucinations**, mental images—in any sensory modality (but mainly visual or auditory)—so vivid that they seem real (such as hearing voices), or **delusions**, which are entrenched false beliefs that are often bizarre (such as that their thoughts are being controlled by aliens). However, such beliefs, even if false (or at least not susceptible to rational proof), should not be considered abnormal if they are an accepted part of the culture. For instance, in some religious groups, such as Pentecostals, it is not considered abnormal to hear voices, especially the voice of God (Cox, personal communication, 2000). Another example is *zar*, or spirit possession, experienced in some North African and Middle Eastern cultures. Those affected may shout, laugh, hit their heads against a wall, or exhibit other behavior that otherwise would be considered inappropriate; an experience of *zar* is not considered abnormal in the cultures in which it occurs (American Psychiatric Association, 2000).

# Explaining Abnormality

Explanations for abnormal behavior have changed with the times and reflect the thinking of each culture. In ancient Greece, abnormal behaviors, as well as medical problems, were thought to arise from imbalances of the body's four fluids, or "humors": yellow bile, phlegm, blood, and black bile. Too much phlegm, for instance, made you phlegmatic, or sluggish and slow; too much black bile made you melancholic. In 17th-century New England, abnormality was thought to be the work of the devil. In the middle of the 20th century, Sigmund Freud's work was influential, and psychodynamic theory was the instrument used to understand abnormality. Currently, in order to understand psychological disorders, many psychologists and others in the field have used the *biopsychosocial model*. This model focuses on factors at the levels of the brain, the person, and the group. In this discussion, we go one step further and show how events at those three levels are not discrete but affect one another through various interactions.

## The Brain: Genes, Neurotransmitters, and Brain Structure and Function

Van Gogh's family history points to a possible cause of his psychological problems. Van Gogh's brother Theo was often depressed and anxious, and he committed suicide within a year after Vincent's suicide; his sister Wilhelmina exhibited a long-standing psychosis; his youngest brother Cor is thought to have committed suicide. Does this history indicate that van Gogh inherited some vulnerability to a psycho-

Psychosis: An obvious impairment in the ability to perceive and comprehend events accurately, combined with a gross disorganization of behavior.

Hallucinations: Sensory images so vivid that they seem real.

Delusions: Entrenched false beliefs that are often bizarre.

logical disorder? Not necessarily, but researchers are finding increasing evidence that genetic factors frequently contribute to the development of some disorders.

Biological factors, including neurotransmitters (such as serotonin), hormones (such as adrenaline, which functions as a hormone in the body), and abnormalities in the structure of the brain, appear to play a role in the development of some psychological disorders. From a biological point of view, depression can be seen as a manifestation of an abnormal serotonin level. Similarly, the cause of an irrational fear of spiders could be the outcome of an overreactive amygdala. Although these explanations may be valid, they are only a part of the picture. *Why* are someone's serotonin levels abnormal? *Why* is someone else's amygdala overreactive to the sight of a spider? As previously noted in many contexts, our own thoughts, feelings, and behaviors, as well as our interactions with others and our environment, can affect the workings of our brains.

Thus, abnormality cannot be considered solely as a function of brain chemistry or structure. Many researchers and clinicians today believe that psychological disorders can best be explained by a **diathesis–stress model** (*diathesis* means a predisposition to a state or condition). This conceptualization, illustrated in Figure 14.1, states that "for a given disorder, there is both a predisposition to the disorder (a *diathesis*) and specific factors (*stress*) that combine with the diathesis to trigger the onset of the disorder" (Rende & Plomin, 1992, p. 177). According to the diathesis–stress model, because of certain biological factors (such as genes, abnormality of brain structures, or neurotransmitters), as well as other types of factors, some people may be more vulnerable to developing a particular disorder; however, without certain environmental stressors, the disorder is not triggered. By the same token, when experiencing a stressor, people without a biological vulnerability for a disorder may not develop that disorder. From this perspective, it's the interactions among events at the different levels of analysis that are crucial; no single event or stimulus alone can cause illness, and as noted in Chapter 13, not everyone perceives a particular event or stimulus to be a stressor. Whether because of learning or biology, or an interaction of the two, some people are more likely to perceive more stressors (and therefore to experience more stress) than others. For instance, although schizophrenia appears to have a genetic component, even if an identical twin has schizophrenia, his or her twin will not necessarily develop the disorder. The diathesis–stress model proposes that it is the *combination* of biological vulnerability and some specific other factors, such as a trauma or the death of a loved one, that elicits the disorder.

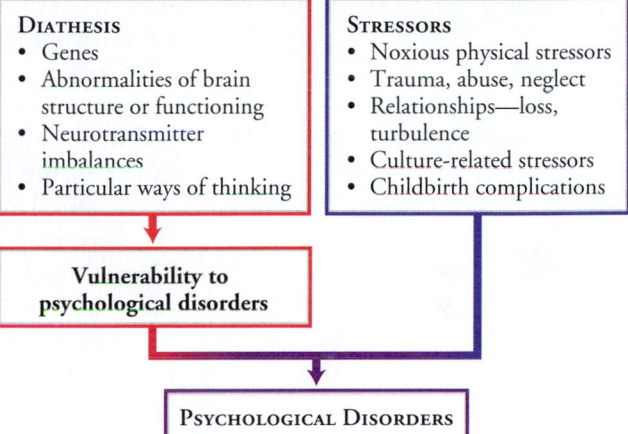

**FIGURE 14.1** **The Diathesis–Stress Model**

| DIATHESIS | STRESSORS |
|---|---|
| • Genes | • Noxious physical stressors |
| • Abnormalities of brain structure or functioning | • Trauma, abuse, neglect |
| • Neurotransmitter imbalances | • Relationships—loss, turbulence |
| • Particular ways of thinking | • Culture-related stressors |
| | • Childbirth complications |

**Vulnerability to psychological disorders**

**PSYCHOLOGICAL DISORDERS**

Most mental health researchers and professionals believe that both biological factors (diathesis) and environmental stressors (stress) together cause psychological disorders.

## The Person: Behaviors, Thoughts and Biases, and Emotions

Several factors at the level of the person also play a role in psychological disorders. One factor is classical conditioning, as in the case of Little Albert (Chapter 6), who developed a fear of white furry things based on his classical conditioning experiences with a white rat and a loud noise. Operant conditioning and observational learning can also help explain some psychological disorders. In addition, the content of mental processes, such as biases in what a person tends to pay attention to, the pattern of a person's thoughts, and the attributions that he or she makes, can also make a person vulnerable to psychological disorders. For instance, chronic negative thought patterns

Diathesis–stress model: A way of understanding the development of a psychological disorder, in which a predisposition to a given disorder (diathesis) and specific factors (stress) combine to trigger the onset of the disorder.

When something falls, do you attribute the mishap to some outside factor or to yourself? Do you ruminate about negative things or things that make you anxious, or do you tend to put them out of your mind? Some thought patterns can create a diathesis for a particular disorder.

("Nothing ever turns out right for me; what's the point in trying?") can lead to depressing feelings and can contribute to the development or maintenance of depression, as can attributing negative events to oneself rather than to circumstances ("I'm incompetent; I can't do anything right"). Learning, thoughts, and feelings may help explain why certain psychological disorders develop in some people. Furthermore, as we shall see, some disorders involve difficulties in regulating emotion—leading to feelings that seem too intense, an absence of feeling, or emotions that rapidly change.

## The Group: Social and Cultural Factors

Factors at the level of the group also play a role in triggering psychological disorders, as well as in increasing the risk of a disorder's recurrence. For example, the "stress" part of posttraumatic stress disorder is usually caused by other people (such as a terrorist or a rapist) or the physical environment (through natural disasters such as floods and earthquakes).

Culture can also influence the conception of psychological disorders. For a period during the 1960s, a number of mental health professionals argued that mental illness is a myth, merely a label applied to culturally undesirable behavior (Szasz, 1961). In this view, the label determines how people are treated and, in a self-fulfilling prophecy, may even play a role in how the "mentally ill" person behaves, once labeled.

David Rosenhan (1973) tested an aspect of this idea. In his study, people without a psychological disorder gained admittance to psychiatric hospitals by claiming that they heard voices. Once in the hospital, they behaved normally. But because they were given a psychiatric diagnosis—that is, they were labeled—their normal behavior was interpreted as pathological, and they were treated accordingly. For example, these "pseudopatients" took notes while they were in hospital; not furtively, but out in the open, in a normal manner. This behavior, interpreted by the staff through the lens of the diagnostic label, was attributed to their illness, even perceived as proof of their abnormality. Moreover, when the pseudopatients asked about eligibility for grounds privileges, the psychiatrists responded to such questions only 6% of the time; in 71% of the encounters, the doctors just moved on.

Rosenhan claimed that his study illustrated the power of labels and contexts. But does it tell us anything about the reality of mental disorders? The pseudopatients originally reported auditory hallucinations that were troubling enough to drive them to request admission to a mental hospital; people do not normally have such symptoms. How was the staff to know that the pseudopatients were lying when they described their "symptoms"? Similarly, the fact that the staff in Rosenhan's study labeled and treated the pseudopatients as if their symptoms were genuine does not indicate that psychological disorders with these symptoms do not exist, only that doctors did not recognize that the pseudopatients were "faking it" (Spitzer, 1975). In fact, the doctors *did* notice that something was amiss because, when the pseudopatients were discharged from the hospital, the diagnosis they were given was "schizophrenia, in remission," a rarely given diagnosis. Moreover, the generalizability of Rosenhan's findings are limited because he did not use any type of control or comparison group (Millon, 1975).

Diagnosing individuals involves making judgments that, like all judgments, are subject to error, and this is part of what Rosenhan felt his study illustrated. A systematic type of error in diagnosis is called a *diagnostic bias* (Meehl, 1960), and it often has the result that some people receive certain diagnoses based on nonmedical factors, such as race. For instance, studies of racial bias show that Black patients in the United States are more likely to be evaluated negatively than are White patients (Garb, 1997; Jenkins-Hall & Sacco, 1991; Strakowski et al., 1995) and are prescribed higher doses of medication (Strakowski et al., 1993). (Such biases occur at the level of the person, and thus we once again see interactions among events at the different levels of analysis.)

However, the reality of certain disorders—schizophrenia being one—is attested to by the fact that these disorders are recognized worldwide. Nevertheless, cultures differ in which behaviors they consider abnormal, and the symptoms, course, and prognosis of disorders may vary from culture to culture (Basic Behavioral Science Task Force, 1996).

Events at all three levels and the interactions among them must be examined to understand the various psychological disorders discussed in this chapter. Biological factors, emotions, learning, and thought patterns, familial, cultural, and environmental factors, *and the relationships among them* all play a role in explaining psychological disorders.

# Categorizing Disorders: Is a Rose Still a Rose by Any Other Name?

Suppose a man comes to a clinical psychologist's office complaining that he feels he is going crazy and that he has a strong sense of impending doom. How would the clinical psychologist determine the nature of this man's difficulties and figure out how best to help him? What questions should the psychologist ask? One guide to help this psychologist and other mental health clinicians is the *Diagnostic and Statistical Manual of Mental Disorders*, known to its users simply as the *DSM*.

## History of the *DSM*

In 1952, the American Psychiatric Association published the inaugural edition of the *DSM*, the first manual of mental disorders designed primarily to help clinicians diagnose and treat patients. This edition was based on psychodynamic theory. In later editions of the manual, its developers tried to avoid relying on any one theory of the causes of disorders and to base the identification of disorders on a growing body of empirical research. The fourth edition, the *DSM-IV*, published in 1994, was an attempt to refine the diagnostic criteria and make the diagnostic categories more useful to mental health researchers and practitioners.

Since the third edition, the *DSM* has described five *axes*, or types of information, that should be considered in the assessment of a patient. Clinical disorders are noted on Axis I, and personality disorders and mental retardation on Axis II. Axis III notes any general medical conditions that might be relevant to a diagnosis on Axis I or II. Psychosocial and environmental problems are identified on Axis IV, and Axis V records the patient's highest level of functioning in major areas of life within the past year. An appendix to the manual outlines aspects of the patient's cultural context that clinicians should take into account when making a diagnosis. Most of the manual, however, is devoted to describing disorders. It defines 17 major categories of psychological problems. All told, almost 300 mental disorders are specified. A revision published in 2000 and called *DSM-IV-TR* (TR stands for *Text Revision*) included more up-to-date information on incidence rates and cultural factors, but did not change the diagnostic categories nor the criteria.

## Disadvantages and Advantages of the *DSM*

The sheer number of disorders included in the *DSM-IV* has provoked criticism of the manual; the breadth of the major diagnostic categories is shown in Table 14.1. As the *DSM* has evolved, it has introduced categories that define medical problems as psychological disorders, leading to a pathologizing of mental health. For example, a new diagnosis in the *DSM-IV* was "Breathing-Related Sleep Disorder" (one cause of which

**TABLE 14.1** **DSM-IV-TR's 17 Major Categories of Disorders**

| Major Category of Disorders | Explanation |
|---|---|
| **Disorders usually first diagnosed in infancy, childhood, or adolescence** | Although disorders in this category are usually first evident early in life, some adults are newly diagnosed with one of these disorders, such as attention-deficit/hyperactivity disorder. |
| **Delirium, dementia, and amnestic and other cognitive disorders** | Disorders of consciousness and cognition. |
| **Mental disorders due to a general medical condition not elsewhere classified** | Disorders in which mental and psychological symptoms are judged to be due to a medical condition (coded on Axis III). |
| **Substance-related disorders** | Disorders of substance dependence and abuse, as well as disorders induced by a substance, such as a substance-induced psychotic disorder. |
| **Schizophrenia and other psychotic disorders** | Disorders related to psychoses. |
| **Mood disorders** | Disorders of mood or feelings. |
| **Anxiety disorders** | Disorders of anxiety. |
| **Somatoform disorders** | Disorders in which physical/medical complaints have no known medical origin (or the symptoms are not proportional to a medical condition) and so are thought to be psychological in nature. |
| **Factitious disorders** | Disorders in which the person intentionally fabricates symptoms of a medical or psychological disorder, but not for external gain (such as disability claims). |
| **Dissociative disorders** | Disorders in which there is a disruption in the usually integrated functions of consciousness, memory, or identity. |
| **Sexual and gender identity disorders** | Disorders of sexual function, the object of sexual desire, and/or of gender identity. |
| **Eating disorders** | Disorders related to eating. |
| **Sleep disorders** | Disorders related to sleep. |
| **Impulse-control disorders not elsewhere classified** | Disorders related to the ability to contain impulses (such as kleptomania). |
| **Adjustment disorders** | Disorders related to the development of distressing emotional or behavioral symptoms in response to an identifiable stressor. |
| **Personality disorders** | Disorders related to personality traits that are inflexible and maladaptive, and that cause distress or difficulty with daily functioning. |
| **Other conditions that may be a focus of clinical attention** | A problem receiving treatment for which no psychological disorder described in the manual applies or for which the symptoms do not meet the criteria for any disorder. |

is sleep apnea; see Chapter 5). Thus, the *DSM-IV* created a *psychological* or *psychiatric* disorder for a medical problem. Moreover, the *DSM-IV* does not provide a discrete boundary separating abnormality from normality (Beals et al., 2004; Double, 2002; Frances, 1998); a clinician's judgment determines whether an individual's degree of impairment is "clinically significant." Another criticism leveled at the *DSM-IV* is that some of the disorders are not clearly distinct from one another (Blais et al., 1997), although they are often presented as if they were (Tucker, 1998).

Despite these criticisms, one advantage of the *DSM-IV* is that it is theoretically neutral; that is, it makes no assumptions about why disorders arise or about the best way to treat them. Moreover, it strives to create standards that can be used to ensure reliability in diagnosis: If two people with similar symptoms and mental health histories are seen in two different cities by two different mental health clinicians who are using the *DSM-IV* to guide their diagnosis, the odds are that those people will be diagnosed with the same disorder. In fact, the *DSM-IV* is the predominant means of categorizing psychological disorders in the United States. The discussion of disorders in this chapter uses the *DSM-IV* system of categorization.

# Test Yourself

1. In defining a psychological disorder, *DSM-IV* takes into account three factors:
   a. danger, distress, and impairment.
   b. danger, dysfunction, and an ability to care for oneself.
   c. danger to others, danger to self, and hallucinations.
   d. delusions, hallucinations, and the presence of psychosis.

2. What is the difference between a delusion and a hallucination?
   a. Delusions occur more infrequently than hallucinations.
   b. Hallucinations are false beliefs, and delusions are mental images.
   c. Delusions are false beliefs, and hallucinations are mental images.
   d. Hallucinations are more bizarre than delusions, which are usually mundane.

3. According to the diathesis–stress model, the likelihood of developing depression depends on, among other factors, the person's family history of depression, which is part of the _____, and the person's current situation, which may produce the _____.
   a. stress; diathesis
   b. diathesis; stress
   c. diagnostic criteria; environmental stressors
   d. environment; disorder

4. On which axis of the *DSM-IV* would a clinician note a patient's brain tumor?
   a. I
   b. II
   c. III
   d. IV

## Answers

1.a 2.c 3.b 4.c

NOTE: Once you feel comfortable with the Test Yourself questions in this chapter, visit the book's Web site at www.ablongman.com/kosslyn3e for additional study questions.

# Think It Through!

If a classmate told you in all seriousness that someone you both know is "weird" and a "basket case," how would you respond? What would you want to know about the behavior that led your friend to this conclusion? What other questions should you ask? Why?

# MOOD DISORDERS

We cannot diagnose from a distance, but we know enough about van Gogh's life and behavior to make some educated guesses about the nature of his moods and emotional turmoil. He frequently spoke of feeling sad; still, he clung to the commonality of human feeling, saying, "I prefer feeling my sorrow to forgetting it or becoming indifferent" (Lubin, 1972, p. 22). Painting was the one thing that drove away his sadness, and sometimes he painted with a frenzy. He had bouts of irritability, had difficulty concentrating, was often miserable, and was frequently quarrelsome. People described him as odd, argumentative, very sensitive, and unpredictable. He described himself as an alcoholic. He had frequent thoughts of suicide, and in the end, at the age of 37, he died after intentionally shooting himself (Lubin, 1972).

**Mood disorders** are disorders marked by persistent or episodic disturbances in emotion that interfere with normal functioning in at least one realm of life. Among the most common mood disorders are *major depressive disorder, dysthymia* (a less intense but longer lasting form of depression), and *bipolar disorder* (formerly known as manic-depressive disorder).

## Major Depressive Disorder: Not Just Feeling Blue

When people are feeling sad or blue, they may say they are "depressed," but generally they do not mean that they are suffering from a psychological disorder. **Major depressive disorder (MDD)** is characterized by at least 2 weeks of depressed mood or loss of interest in nearly all activities, along with sleep or eating disturbances, loss of energy, and feelings of hopelessness, as described in Table 14.2 (American Psychiatric Association, 2000). Thus, major depression affects a person's "ABC's":

- *affect* (mood),
- *behavior* (actions), and
- *cognition* (thoughts).

It is estimated that up to one in five people in the United States will experience MDD in their lifetimes (American Psychiatric Association, 2000; Kessler et al., 2003; Ross, 1991), often in addition to another *DSM-IV* disorder (Kessler et al., 2003). Major depressive disorder is the most common psychological disorder in the United States (Kessler et al., 1994), and it is found among all cultural and ethnic groups (Weissman et al., 1991), as well as across the economic spectrum. In developing countries, prevalence rates are estimated to be about the same for men and for women (Culbertson, 1997), but American women are diagnosed with depression two to three times more frequently than American men (APA, 2000; Culbertson, 1997; Gater et al., 1998). Further, the overall prevalence of depression is increasing in the United States (Lewinsohn et al., 1993).

In the workplace, MDD is the leading cause of both absenteeism and "presenteeism," which occurs when a depressed person is present in body but not in mind, leading them to be less effective at work (Druss et al., 2001; Stewart et al., 2003). If current trends continue, by the year 2020, depression may well be the second most disabling disease in the United States, after heart disease (Schrof & Schultz, 1999). Some

**Mood disorders:** A category of disorders marked by persistent or episodic disturbances in emotion that interfere with normal functioning in at least one realm of life.

**Major depressive disorder (MDD):** A mood disorder characterized by at least 2 weeks of depressed mood or loss of interest in nearly all activities, along with sleep or eating disturbances, loss of energy, and feelings of hopelessness.

**TABLE 14.2**   **Diagnostic Criteria for Major Depressive Disorder**

During a period of at least 2 weeks, five or more of the following symptoms have occurred and represent a change in functioning.

- Depressed mood most of the day, almost daily (based on subjective report or observations of others).

- Markedly diminished interest or pleasure in nearly all daily activities (based on subjective or objective reports).

- Significant weight loss, not through dieting.

- Daily insomnia or hypersomnia (sleeping a lot).

- Daily psychomotor agitation (intense restlessness) or retardation (physical sluggishness).

- Daily fatigue, or loss of energy.

- Almost daily feelings of worthlessness, or inappropriate or excessive guilt.

- Almost daily diminished ability to think or concentrate, or indecisiveness (based on subjective or objective reports).

- Recurrent thoughts of death or suicide with or without a specific plan.

people with depression may experience only one episode; others experience recurrent episodes that may be frequent or separated by years; for some, depression may become more chronic (Judd et al., 1998). A 10-year study of over 300 people diagnosed with major depressive disorder found that more than one-third of the participants did not have a recurrence of depression (Solomon et al., 2000).

### MAJOR DEPRESSIVE DISORDER FROM THE INSIDE

The experience of depression is captured in words by Elizabeth Wurtzel, author of *Prozac Nation*:

In my case, I was not frightened in the least bit at the thought that I might live because I was certain, quite certain, that I was already dead. The actual dying part, the withering away of my physical body, was a mere formality. My spirit, my emotional being, whatever you want to call all that inner turmoil that has nothing to do with physical existence, were long gone, dead and gone, and only a mass of the most ... god-awful excruciating pain ... was left in its wake. (Wurtzel, 1995, p. 22)

Artist Kate Monson, who experienced depression, describes her painting as a reflection of her depression.

Elizabeth Wurtzel's description of her depression captures the essence of the painful, extremely disturbing quality of many of the symptoms. In some cases, severely depressed people also have delusions or hallucinations. Often these psychotic symptoms feature themes of guilt, deserved punishment, and personal inadequacy, such as voices asserting the individual's worthlessness.

However, members of different cultures may not experience exactly the same symptoms. Consider that people from Zimbabwe who are depressed often complain of headache and fatigue (Patel et al., 2001), as do people in Latin and Mediterranean cultures. They do not necessarily report sadness and guilt. In Asian cultures, people with major depression are likely to report weakness, tiredness, a sense of "imbalance," or other bodily symptoms (Parker et al., 2001).

# UNDERSTANDING RESEARCH

## Symptoms of Depression in China and the United States

For several decades, mental health professionals have been told that Chinese people more frequently report bodily symptoms (compared to cognitive or emotional symptoms) of depression. Such symptoms include poor appetite, tiredness, and concentration problems. Psychologists Yen, Robins, and Lin (2000) set out to compare symptoms of depression among three groups of college students: Chinese students (living in China), American students of Chinese descent, and American students of Caucasian descent.

**QUESTION:** These researchers asked: Do Chinese students report more bodily symptoms of depression than Chinese American students, who, in turn, report more bodily symptoms than Caucasian American students?

**ALTERNATIVES:** (1) Chinese students report more bodily symptoms of depression than the other two groups, and Chinese Americans, in turn, report more bodily symptoms of depression than Caucasian Americans. (2) Chinese students report more bodily symptoms than the two American groups, but the American groups report comparable numbers of such symptoms. (3) The three groups report equivalent levels of bodily symptoms of depression. (4) In some other way, the three groups differ in the number of bodily symptoms.

**LOGIC:** If their culture leads Chinese people to experience or notice bodily symptoms when depressed (to a greater extent than cognitive or emotional symptoms), then the Chinese group should score highest on questions assessing bodily symptoms, followed by the Chinese Americans (who are influenced by Chinese culture, but less so than Chinese students living in China), with the Caucasian Americans scoring lowest.

**MEASURES:** Three groups of college students participated in the study, each including both males and females: (1) Chinese, (2) Chinese Americans, and (3) Caucasian Americans. All participants completed questionnaires assessing depressive symptoms; Chinese American participants also were asked about their level of immersion in American culture.

**RESULTS:** In contrast to the expected results, the Chinese group had the *lowest* scores on the questions pertaining to bodily symptoms of depression; that is, they reported experiencing fewer such symptoms of depression than did either American group. The Chinese American and Caucasian American groups were not significantly different from each other. Moreover, among the Chinese Americans, there was no relation between how "Americanized" they were and their reported number of bodily symptoms.

**INFERENCES:** These results are inconsistent with previous studies on this topic. When a study's results differ substantially from related studies and from the study's hypotheses, researchers wonder whether methodological factors could have affected the results—that is, whether the unexpected results were obtained because of the particular research methods used. This study relied on a questionnaire that directly asked about different types of symptoms, whereas some previous studies assessed symptoms during visits to doctors or mental health professionals (where the participants were asked about their symptoms). Perhaps in these face-to-face encounters in China, participants only felt comfortable mentioning the more culturally sanctioned bodily symptoms (Nikelly, 1988) and not other symptoms, particularly in a medical setting. Moreover, in the current study, participants' answers were anonymous; perhaps this method of assessment led to differences in the reporting of symptoms. In any event, it's clear that the previous cultural stereotype is either inaccurate or applies only in restricted situations.

## THINK CRITICALLY!

If you were undertaking a study to discover whether the method of assessment—anonymous questionnaire versus face-to-face interview—accounted for this study's unexpected results, how would you assess depressive symptoms? If you decided to use both interviews and anonymous questionnaires, should you have participants complete them in a particular order? Might it matter?

Many, if not most, suicide attempts seem to be motivated by the sense of hopelessness that is often a part of depression. Approximately 30% of people with depression attempt suicide, and half of those attempters succeed. One estimate is that over 31,000 depressed people in the United States commit suicide every year, making it the 8th leading cause of death in the country (Arlas et al., 2003). Suicide prevention programs try, in part, to treat depression and alcohol use, both of which are associated with suicide (Reifman & Windle, 1995). Several common misconceptions about suicide are listed in Table 14.3. Test yourself to see whether your views of suicide are accurate.

| TABLE 14.3 | Common Misconceptions of Suicide |
| --- | --- |

- *If you talk about suicide, you won't really do it.* (False: Most people who commit suicide gave some clue or warning. Threats or statements about suicide should not be ignored.)

- *People who attempt suicide are "crazy."* (False: Suicidal people are not "crazy"; they *are* likely to be depressed or upset or to feel hopeless.)

- *Someone determined to commit suicide can't be stopped.* (False: Almost all suicidal people have mixed feelings about living and dying up until the last moment. Moreover, most suicidal people don't want to die; they want their pain to stop. And the suicidal impulse often passes.)

- *People who commit suicide weren't willing to seek help.* (False: Studies have shown that more than half of suicide victims sought medical help within the 6 months before death.)

- *Talking about suicide could give someone the idea, so you shouldn't talk or ask about it.* (False. Discussing suicide openly can be helpful to someone who is suicidal.)

Some people—approximately 6% of the American population—experience a less intense but longer-lasting type of depression called **dysthymia** (American Psychiatric Association, 2000). People who are given this diagnosis have a depressed mood for most of the day for at least 2 years and also experience two other symptoms of depression (see Table 14.2; American Psychiatric Association, 2000).

## Bipolar Disorder: Going to Extremes

In contrast to depression, **bipolar disorder** is a mood disorder marked by one or more manic episodes or by the less intense hypomania, often alternating with periods of depression. Approximately 1% of Americans have this disorder (Regier & Kaelber, 1995). A **manic episode** is a period of at least a week during which an abnormally elevated, expansive, or irritable mood persists (see Table 14.4). Being manic is not just having an "up" day. During a manic episode, the sufferer may be euphoric and enthusiastic about everything, starting conversations with strangers and making grandiose plans. People experiencing **hypomania** have less severe symptoms of mania, and their symptoms are less likely to interfere with social functioning.

### BIPOLAR DISORDER FROM THE INSIDE

Psychologist Kay Redfield Jamison describes her personal experience with mania:

There is a particular kind of pain, elation, loneliness, and terror involved in this kind of madness. When you're high, it's tremendous. The ideas and feelings are fast and frequent like shooting stars, and you follow them until you find better and brighter ones. Shyness goes, the right words and gestures are suddenly there, the power to captivate others a felt certainty. There are interests found in uninteresting people. Sensuality is pervasive and the desire to seduce and be seduced irresistible. Feelings of ease, intensity, power, well-being, financial omnipotence, and euphoria pervade one's marrow. But, somewhere, this changes. The fast ideas are far too fast, and there are far too many; overwhelming confusion replaces clarity. Memory goes. Humor and absorption on friends' faces are replaced by fear and concerns. Everything previously moving with the grain is now against—you are irritable, angry, frightened, uncontrollable, and enmeshed totally in the blackest caves of the mind. You never knew those caves were there. It will never end, for madness carves its own reality. (Jamison, 1995, p. 67)

**Dysthymia:** A mood disorder similar to major depressive disorder, but less intense and longer lasting.

**Bipolar disorder:** A mood disorder marked by one or more episodes of either mania or hypomania, often alternating with periods of depression.

**Manic episode:** A period of at least 1 week during which an abnormally elevated, expansive, or irritable mood persists.

**Hypomania:** A mood state similar to mania, but less severe, with fewer and less intrusive symptoms.

Jamison, like many people with bipolar disorder, had difficulty recognizing that she had a psychological disorder and resisted attempts at treatment for a number of years. Manic or hypomanic episodes are often preceded or followed by episodes of depression, and the cycling of the mood usually takes place over a number of years, although some people may experience rapid cycling, with four or more mood shifts in a year. If left untreated, mood swings often become more frequent over time, leading to a poorer prognosis. The early phase of an episode, before the symptoms become acute, is termed the *prodromal phase* (a *prodrome* is a warning symptom). Some people with bipolar disorder report prodromal indicators of manic or depressive symptoms that signal that an episode will occur (Keitner et al., 1996).

TABLE 14.4 **Diagnostic Criteria for a Manic Episode**

- Grandiosity or elevated sense of self-esteem.

- Less need for sleep.

- More talkative than usual, or feels pressure to keep talking, and may be difficult to interrupt.

- Racing thoughts (sometimes described as watching three different television programs simultaneously).

- Distractibility and difficulty screening out useful from extraneous material.

- Increase in goal-directed activity (this could be socially, at work, at school, or sexually) or psychomotor agitation.

- Excessive involvement in pleasurable activities that have a high potential for painful consequences (for example, unrestrained shopping sprees, sexual infidelity, unwise business investments).

# Explaining Mood Disorders

Although bipolar disorder and major depressive disorder are distinct, research has characterized them, along with dysthymia, as lying on a spectrum of mood disorders (Akiskal, 1996; Angst, 1998) that are related by biological and psychological factors. Mood disorders can best be understood by considering the interactions of events at the three levels of analysis: the brain, the person, and the group.

## Level of the Brain in Mood Disorders

Both depression and bipolar disorder arise in part from events at the level of the brain.

**BIOLOGICAL FACTORS IN DEPRESSION** Depression tends to run in families (Weissman et al., 2005), and twin studies show that if one identical twin has major depression, the co-twin is four times more likely to experience depression than is the co-twin of an affected fraternal twin (Bowman & Nurnberger, 1993; Kendler et al., 1999). This appears to be good evidence for genetic influence. However, adoption studies have not shown the same clear-cut evidence for a genetic role (Eley et al., 1998; Wender et al., 1986). More definitive evidence that biological factors play a role in depression comes from research with depressed people whose relatives also suffer from depression: The depressed people studied had unusually low activity in one area of the frontal lobe that has direct connections to many brain areas involved in emotion, such as the amygdala. This part of the frontal lobe also has connections to brain structures that produce serotonin, norepinephrine, and dopamine (Kennedy et al., 1997). Parts of this area of the frontal lobe have frequently been found to have abnormal patterns of activation in people who are depressed (Davidson et al., 2002; Liotti et al., 2002). People with depression have also been found to have smaller hippocampi, a key brain area involved in memory (Bremner

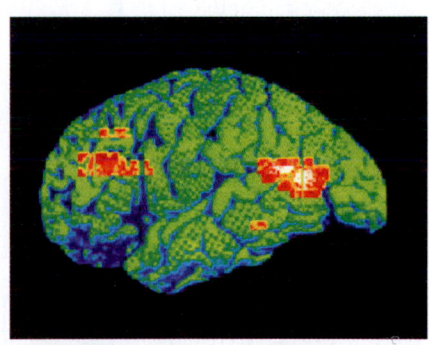

This PET scan shows brain activity of a depressed individual. Red and yellow indicate brain areas with low activity: part of the frontal lobes (at left) and the parieto-temporal area (at right). Individuals who are not depressed show higher levels of activity in these brain areas..

et al., 2000; Sheline et al., 2003). Additional studies suggest that people with depression have increased activity in the amygdala (Drevets et al., 2002), which is involved in emotional memory; the amygdala's involvement may account for the protracted thinking about emotional events that is often part of depression (Cahill et al., 2001).

Unfortunately, it is not yet clear which neurotransmitters are most involved in depression; it is not even clear whether the problem is having too much or too little of those substances (Duman et al., 1997). What *is* clear, however, is that in people with depression, some change occurs in the activity of serotonin, norepinephrine, and possibly a more recently discovered neurotransmitter, *substance P* (Kramer et al., 1998). Depression also involves a dysfunction of the HPA axis (Hasler et al., 2004; see Chapters 3 and 13 for information about the HPA axis).

**BIOLOGICAL FACTORS IN BIPOLAR DISORDER**   Among those with bipolar disorder, there is evidence that the amygdala is enlarged (Altshuler et al., 1998; Strakowski et al., 2002). The association of this disorder with some abnormality affecting the amygdala is consistent with the role of this structure in regulating mood and accessing emotional memories (LeDoux, 1996; see Chapters 7 and 10). Neuroimaging studies of people with bipolar disorder have found shifts in temporal lobe activity during manic episodes that do not occur during other mood states (Gyulai et al., 1997); these shifts may be related to activity in parts of the limbic system that are located in those lobes.

There is clear evidence for an underlying genetic relationship between bipolar and depressive mood disorders. For example, if an identical twin has bipolar disorder, the co-twin has an 80% chance of developing some kind of mood disorder (such as depression), although not necessarily bipolar disorder (Karkowski & Kendler, 1997; Vehmanen et al., 1995).

Neurotransmitters are also implicated in bipolar disorder, although the exact mechanism is unknown. There is some support for the theory that bipolar disorder involves disturbances in the functioning of serotonin (Goodwin & Jamison, 1990). Moreover, it is known that lithium, the medication usually prescribed for bipolar disorder, lowers the activity level of norepinephrine in the brain (Bunney & Garland, 1983), but just how this happens is not yet known.

## FIGURE 14.2

# Beck's Negative Triad

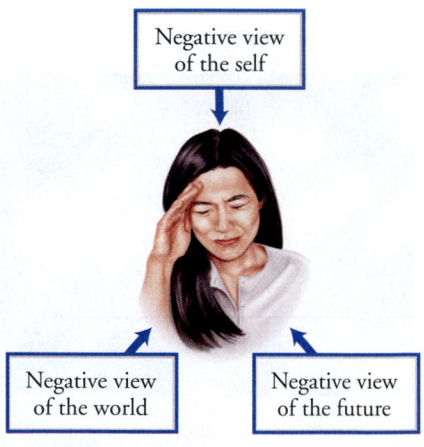

Among people who are depressed, Beck's triad of distorted, negative thinking about the world, the self, and the future add up to produce a negative view of life. However, these cognitive distortions can be corrected.

## Level of the Person in Mood Disorders

Much is known about how events at the level of the person contribute to depression, but relatively little is known about how such events contribute to bipolar disorder.

**THE PERSON AND DEPRESSION**   Compared with people who are not depressed, depressed people make more negative comments and less eye contact, are less responsive, and speak more softly and in shorter sentences (Gotlib & Robinson, 1982; Segrin & Abramson, 1994). Aaron Beck (1967) found evidence for a *negative triad of depression* in the thoughts of depressed people. This triad consists of: (1) a negative view of the world, (2) a negative view of the self, and (3) a negative view of the future (see Figure 14.2). Beck proposes that people with depression commit errors in their thinking, or *cognitive distortions*, based on these three sets of beliefs, and that these errors maintain an outlook on life that perpetuates depressing feelings and behaviors. These cognitive distortions may be based on early learning.

The phenomenon of learned helplessness (see Chapter 10) also contributes to depression; when people feel that they have no control over negative aspects of their environment, they are more likely to develop depression. Of particular interest is evidence that people's views of themselves and the world can influence their risk of developing depression. A person's characteristic way of explaining life events—his or her **attributional style**—affects the risk of depression. For people who attribute blame to themselves (versus external factors), the risk of depression rises, especially after a stressful event (Monroe & Depue, 1991). Research on attributional styles and depression finds that those people who tend to attribute unfortunate events to internal causes (their own thoughts, abilities, behaviors, and the like), and who believe that these causes are stable, are more likely to become depressed. Thus, depressing thoughts (such as "I deserved to be fired . . . I wasn't as good at my job as some other people") are more likely to lead to depressing feelings. In contrast, patterns of attributing blame to external causes ("I was laid off because I didn't have enough seniority"), even if inaccurate, are less likely to lead to depression (Abramson et al., 1978).

**THE PERSON AND BIPOLAR DISORDER**   Surprisingly little is known about how events at the level of the person contribute to bipolar disorder. About all we can say with confidence is that people with bipolar disorder have a depressive attributional style when in a depressed phase of the disorder (Lyon et al., 1999; Scott et al., 2000).

## Level of the Group in Mood Disorders

Again, although much is known about how events at the level of the group contribute to depression, relatively little is known about how such events contribute to bipolar disorder.

**THE GROUP AND DEPRESSION**   Events at the level of the group have also been tied to depression. Life stressors are associated with a subsequent first episode of depression (see Figure 14.3), and such stressors can influence how severe it becomes (Lewinsohn et al., 1999). Moreover, as would be expected according to the principles of operant conditioning (see Chapter 6), the less opportunity there is for social reinforcement because of decreased activity and contact with other people, the more likely it is that depressive symptoms will occur (MacPhillamy & Lewinsohn, 1974). Similarly, environments that not only lack positive reinforcements but also provide many "punishing" experiences (such as being regularly criticized) put people at risk for depression. For example, although not necessarily associated with the *onset* of depression, the family environment can be influential in *recovery* from a depressive episode. Living with unsupportive and critical relatives can increase the risk of a relapse of depression (Hooley & Licht, 1997; Miller et al., 1992). Some programs designed to help those with depression attempt to minimize the depressive symptoms and increase the frequency and quality of positive interactions with others (as well as help decrease the frequency and quality of punishing interactions; Teri & Lewinsohn, 1985).

Culture may also play a role in facilitating depression by influencing the type of events that are likely to lead to poor mood. For instance, among Malaysian students in a British university, depressed mood was more likely to follow negative social events, whereas, among British students, depressed mood was more likely to follow negative academic events (such as a poor grade; Tafarodi & Smith, 2001). These results are consistent with the different cultural values in collectivist versus individualist cultures (see Chapter 11).

In addition, at least some of the sex differences in the frequency of depression may be influenced by culture. For example, Nolen-Hoeksema (1987) offered a cultural explanation for the finding that women in developed countries experience depression more often than men. She and others (Nolen-Hoeksema & Morrow, 1993; Vajk et al., 1997) have found that people in developed countries who *ruminate* about (persistently ponder or

Research has found that at the beginning of a semester, college students whose attributional style led them to blame internal—as opposed to external—causes are more likely to become depressed when receiving a bad grade. These students are more likely to attribute a bad grade to their lack of ability rather than to the difficulty of the test, poor teaching, or other external factors (Peterson & Seligman, 1984).

**FIGURE 14.3**   **Stressful Life Events and Depression Among Teenagers**

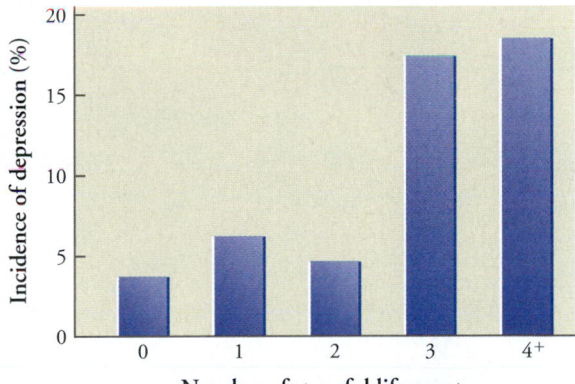

The incidence of the first episode of depression almost quadruples among those teenagers who experienced three or more stressful life events in the previous year (Lewinsohn et al., 1999). After the first depressive episode, subsequent depressive episodes are triggered more easily by fewer stressful events.

Events at the level of the group can affect the course of bipolar disorder. Social stressors that affect biological rhythms or daily schedules, such as frequent plane travel or repeated changes in work schedules, can adversely affect the course of the disease (Johnson & Roberts, 1995; Post, 1992).

dwell on) their depressed mood are more likely to have longer periods of depression. She proposes that boys and girls are taught to respond differently to stressors, and they carry these response styles with them into adulthood. Nolen-Hoeksema contends that boys are encouraged to deemphasize feelings and to use distraction and action-oriented coping strategies, whereas girls are encouraged to be introspective and not to take action. A ruminative response is known to promote depression (Nolen-Hoeksema, 2000); action and distraction can protect against depression. In fact, research has shown that depressed mood improves when college students learn to use strategies of distraction more often and learn to curtail their ruminations (Nolen-Hoeksema & Morrow, 1993). Other psychologists propose that the substantially higher rate of depression in women may also be due to biases in how the diagnosis is made and how depression is measured (Hartung & Widiger, 1998; Sprock & Yoder, 1997).

**THE GROUP AND BIPOLAR DISORDER** As with depression, there is evidence that more Americans are experiencing bipolar disorder than ever before, and at earlier ages (Goodwin & Jamison, 1990). One cause may be the unnaturally lengthened day experienced in modern society due to the pervasive use of electric lights. When a patient with rapid-cycling bipolar disorder was put in an environment without electric lights (thereby experiencing 10–14 hours of darkness a night), the cycles lengthened, bringing more stability of mood (Wehr et al., 1998).

First episodes of bipolar disorder are invariably preceded by significant stressors (Goodwin & Ghaemi, 1998). And, like people with depression, those with bipolar disorder are more likely to relapse if they live with critical families (Honig et al., 1997; Miklowitz et al., 1988). Life stressors can also impede recovery after hospitalization for bipolar disorder (Johnson & Miller, 1997). On a positive note, treatment programs designed to reduce the critical behavior of families appear to be effective in reducing relapses (Honig et al., 1997).

## Interacting Levels: Depression Is as Depression Does

As we've seen previously, events at the three levels of analysis are not independent, but rather interact in complex and subtle ways. James Coyne (1976; Coyne & Downey, 1991) proposed an influential *interactional theory of depression*. He theorizes that the depressed person, who may be biologically vulnerable to depression (level of the brain), has thoughts and impulses (level of the person) that lead him or her to do or say things that alienate others (level of the group), who might provide support (Katz & Joiner, 2001; Nolan & Mineka, 1997). Actions that alienate others include (Katz & Joiner, 2001):

- seeking excessive reassurance,
- seeking out negative feedback, and
- interpersonal aggression.

These actions may lead others to reject the depressed person (level of the group), confirming that person's negative view of himself or herself. The depressed individual may then continue to seek out feedback from others, perhaps attempting to determine whether such negative feedback was a fluke or to elicit positive feedback from others; whatever the motivation, such rejections and criticisms increase the likelihood of negative future events (Casbon et al., 2005).

But this isn't all there is to the interactions among events at the different levels: For instance, have you ever noticed that it's no fun being with a depressed person (level of the group)? A depressed mood can be contagious, and relatives and friends of a depressed individual may find themselves feeling and acting somewhat depressed, which further limits how well they can assist the depressed person (Coyne et al., 1987). Thomas Joiner (1994) found that college students who spent time with depressed roommates over a period of 3 weeks themselves became more depressed. (Indeed, anger, anxiety, and sadness have also been found to be contagious; Coyne, 1976; Hsee et al., 1990; Joiner, 1994; Katz et al., 1999; Segrin & Dillard, 1992; Sullins, 1991.) Moreover, those who develop depression are more likely to behave in ways that create stress in those around them, which in turn can trigger the onset of depression in the other people (McGuffin et al., 1988; Rende & Plomin, 1992). Thus, your roommate's or family member's depression can lead you to feel depressed, perhaps changing your brain and bodily functioning (level of the brain).

We know that van Gogh suffered from bouts of depression, at times had poor hygiene, narrowed his activities severely, and took pleasure only in painting. MDD seems like a possible diagnosis. Van Gogh's attempted assault on Gauguin, as well as the self-mutilation of his ear might be explained by MDD with psychotic features. Perhaps the auditory hallucination that told him to kill Gauguin was caused by his depression. Although a diagnosis of MDD could explain the majority of these symptoms, it is not the only possibility. Bipolar disorder is another potential diagnosis. Perhaps van Gogh's episodes of frenzied painting were manic episodes, although they could also have been an intense restlessness that can occur with depression. His attacks, which became more frequent over time, might have been episodes of mania that became psychotic; untreated episodes of mania do become more frequent.

# Test Yourself

1. Unlike people with major depressive disorder, those with dysthymia
   a. have a minimum of three depressive symptoms.
   b. do not feel depressed most of the day.
   c. recover very quickly.
   d. are more likely to be men, especially in the United States.
2. Bipolar disorder can be very similar to major depressive disorder, except for the
   a. occurrence of delusions.
   b. occurrence of hallucinations.
   c. severity of the depressive episode(s).
   d. presence of a manic episode.
3. Depression is most likely caused by
   a. genetic factors.
   b. neurotransmitter deficits.
   c. negative attitudes about the self and the world.
   d. the interaction of all these factors.

4. Depression has been related to attributional style. Specifically, the risk of depression increases for people who
   a. blame others for their problems.
   b. blame themselves for their problems.
   c. will not accept blame for anything that happens in their lives.
   d. have high scores on attribution tests.

## Answers

1. a 2. d 3. d 4. b

# Think It Through!

Suppose someone you know, someone whose sharp style of dress and confident manner you admire, starts looking unkempt and acting tired, nervous, and fidgety. Would this change suggest a psychological disorder? Why or why not? If so, what type of disorder do you have in mind and why? Would psychological impairment be the only explanation?

# ANXIETY DISORDERS

We know that van Gogh had what he called "attacks." Were these anxiety attacks? He was also considered to be nervous and had concentration problems—signs of anxiety. Can we recognize a pattern in these symptoms? Could he have had an anxiety disorder? What is an anxiety disorder?

Many people are nervous when they have to speak in public. But suppose you become *so* nervous before an in-class presentation that your mouth is dry, you feel light-headed, your heart begins to race, and you think you're having a heart attack and going crazy at the same time. These reactions are not normal "stage jitters." They are typical signs of an **anxiety disorder**, a category of disorders characterized by extreme fear (a response to an external stimulus, such as a snake) and extreme anxiety (a vague but persistent sense of foreboding or dread when not in the presence of the stimulus). Many anxiety disorders are focused on a specific object or situation. However, **generalized anxiety disorder** involves excessive anxiety and worry that is not consistently related to a specific object or situation, and approximately 3% of people have this disorder at any given point in time (American Psychiatric Association, 2000). Fear and anxiety are part of life, but people who have anxiety disorders experience *intense* or *pervasive* anxiety and/or fear or engage in *extreme* attempts to avoid these feelings. These experiences create exceptional distress that can interfere with the ability to function normally. Four major types of anxiety disorders are panic disorder, phobias, obsessive-compulsive disorder, and posttraumatic stress disorder.

Panic attacks can interfere with everyday functioning. Mob captain Tony Soprano sought professional help to keep his panic attacks under control.

## Panic Disorder

**Panic attacks** are episodes of intense fear or discomfort accompanied by symptoms such as palpitations, breathing difficulties, chest pain, nausea, sweating, dizziness, fear of going crazy or doing something uncontrollable, fear of impending doom, and a sense of unreality. These symptoms reach their peak within a few minutes of the beginning of an attack, which can last from minutes to hours. Often, these attacks are not associated with a specific situation or object and may even seem to occur randomly. One study of college students found that 12% of the participants experienced spontaneous panic attacks in college or in the years leading up to college (Telch et al., 1989). A person is said to have **panic disorder** if he or she endures frequent, unexpected panic attacks or fears additional panic attacks and thus changes aspects of his or her life in hopes of avoiding them. Internationally, approximately 3% of all people will experience panic disorder during their lifetimes (Rouillon, 1997). Some people may have episodic outbreaks of panic disorder, with years of remission; others may have more persistent symptoms.

**Anxiety disorders:** A category of disorders whose hallmark is intense or pervasive anxiety or fear, or extreme attempts to avoid these feelings.

**Generalized anxiety disorder:** An anxiety disorder whose hallmark is excessive anxiety and worry that is not consistently related to a specific object or situation.

**Panic attack:** An episode of intense fear or discomfort accompanied by physical and psychological symptoms such as palpitations, breathing difficulties, chest pain, fear of impending doom or of doing something uncontrollable, and a sense of unreality.

**Panic disorder:** An anxiety disorder whose hallmark is panic attacks or fear and avoidance of such attacks.

### PANIC DISORDER FROM THE INSIDE

Here is one person's description of a panic attack:

My breathing starts getting very shallow. I feel I'm going to stop breathing. The air feels like it gets thinner. I feel the air is not coming up through my nose. I take short rapid breaths. Then I see an image of myself gasping for air and remember what happened in the hospital. I think that I will start gasping. I get very dizzy and disoriented. I cannot sit or stand still. I start pac-

**Agoraphobia:** A condition in which people fear or avoid places that might be difficult to leave should panic symptoms occur.

People with panic disorder worry constantly about having more attacks, and in their attempts to avoid or minimize panic attacks, they may change their behavior. People may go to great lengths to try to avoid panic attacks, quitting their jobs and avoiding places (such as hot, crowded rooms or events) or activities that increase their heart rate (such as exercise, sex, or watching suspenseful movies or sporting events). Some people fear or avoid places that might be difficult to leave should a panic attack occur—for example, a plane or car; this condition is called **agoraphobia**, literally, "fear of the marketplace." Such people may completely avoid leaving home (Bouton et al., 2001) or will do so only with a close friend or relative. Agoraphobia can restrict daily life; some people have agoraphobia without panic attacks, avoiding many places because they fear either losing control of themselves in some way (such as losing bladder control) or experiencing less severe but still distressing panic symptoms.

## Level of the Brain in Panic Disorder

What causes panic attacks? A person can apparently inherit a biological vulnerability for panic, an event at the level of the brain (Crowe et al., 1983; Torgersen, 1983; van den Heuvel et al., 2000). Evidence of one possible route to such a vulnerability comes from animal studies, which suggest that panic attacks may arise from having an excessively sensitive *locus coeruleus*, a small group of cells deep in the brainstem (Gorman et al., 1989; see Figure 14.4). The locus coeruleus is the seat of an "alarm system" that triggers an increased heart rate, faster breathing, sweating, and other components of the fight-or-flight response (see Chapters 3, 10, and 13), and these bodily symptoms can lead to the experience of panic. EEG studies (Wiedemann et al., 1999) have also found unusually strong activation in the right frontal lobe relative to the left when people who suffer panic attacks see potentially panic-inducing stimuli. This suggests that the brain system involved in withdrawal emotions (as characterized by Davidson, 1992b; see Chapter 10) is relatively easily activated in people who experience panic attacks. People with panic disorder may be more sensitive than others to changes in carbon dioxide inhalation (Beck et al., 1999; Papp et al., 1993, 1997), which can come about through hyperventilation. Changes in carbon dioxide levels can elicit panic, perhaps through a "suffocation alarm" in the brain that has an abnormally low threshold for firing in some people (Coplan et al., 1998; Klein, 1993).

### FIGURE 14.4 Panic Disorder: Locus Coeruleus and the Alarm System

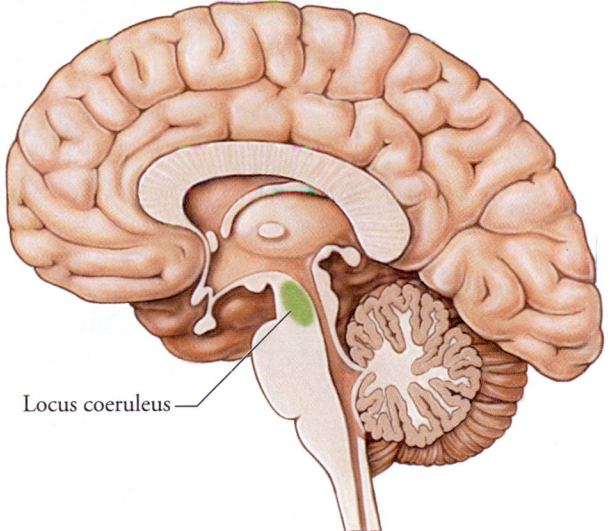

Locus coeruleus

The locus coeruleus is a group of cells in the brain stem that serves as an alarm system. When the alarm is activated, the body responds with the fight-or-flight response, including increased heart and respiration rates.

## Level of the Person in Panic Disorder

How a person interprets and responds to certain signals from the body—that is, events at the level of the person—may be critical to the development of panic disorder. For instance, people who have *anxiety sensitivity*, defined as the "belief that autonomic arousal can have harmful consequences" (Schmidt et al., 1997, p. 355), are at higher risk of experiencing spontaneous panic attacks (Plehn & Peterson, 2002; Schmidt et al., 1999). Those high in anxiety sensitivity believe that their experiences of shortness of breath necessarily indicate suffocation or that their heart palpitations must be signaling a heart attack. Studies have found that people with panic disorder are more accurate than other people at detecting changes in their heart rates when their breathing is restricted (Richards et al., 1996).

The misinterpretation of the cause of physiological events may itself increase sympathetic nervous system activity (Wilkinson et al., 1998) and lead to panic. Changes in the body can act like a *false alarm* (Beck, 1976), and after several false alarms, the sensations associated with them become *learned alarms*, which themselves trigger panic (Barlow, 1988). People can also become hypervigilant for the signals that have led to panic in the past. Thus, in a vicious cycle, these people are more likely to experience anticipatory anxiety, which increases sympathetic nervous system activity (including increased heart rate and breathing changes), which, in turn, triggers panic.

## Level of the Group in Panic Disorder

At the level of the group, although 80% of people with panic disorder reported experiencing a stressful life event before the disorder developed, the presence of such stress did not predict how severe the disorder would be, nor whether the symptoms would become chronic (Manfro et al., 1996; Rouillon, 1997). This is in contrast to other disorders, such as depression, in which the particular life stressor occurring before the illness develops is associated with the severity or course of the disorder. However, other studies have found that, compared to people without panic disorder, people with panic disorder tend to have more stressful life events during childhood and adolescence, not in the year before the onset of the disorder. In addition, there is evidence that specific types of stressors, such as those occurring in love and family relationships in adulthood, are related to the onset of panic disorder (Horesh et al., 1997). Longitudinal studies of children who go on to develop, or not develop, panic disorder may help sort out the role of stressful events in the development of panic disorder.

For people with agoraphobia, group-level events can play an important role. When a person with agoraphobia feels anxious, the presence of a close relative or friend—referred to as a "safe person"—can help decrease negative, panicky thinking. The presence of a safe person can also lower the amount of autonomic arousal experienced (Carter et al., 1995).

In addition, increasing dangers in the environment (rising crime rate) and less social connections among people have increased the baseline level of anxiety. Today's "normal" children score higher on measures of a personality trait related to anxiety than did children in the 1950s who had a psychiatric diagnosis (Twenge, 2000), suggesting that those born recently are more likely to develop anxiety disorders than those born earlier.

Culture can also influence the particular form of some panic-related symptoms. Among Khmer refugees, for example, panic attacks are associated with symptoms of *kyol goeu*, "wind overload"—a fainting syndrome that can occur when you stand up from a lying or sitting down position. Those who have experienced *kyol goeu* are more likely to be sensitive to signs of autonomic arousal in their bodies and to have negative beliefs about what the arousal means; this increased anxiety makes panic attacks more likely (Hinton et al., 2001).

Although van Gogh was anxious and irritable, we do not know enough about what happened during one of his self-reported "attacks" to know whether these episodes were panic attacks or something else. In any event, panic disorder alone would not account for his symptoms of depressed mood, irritability, and impulsiveness or for his bizarre behavior.

# Phobias: Social and Specific

A **phobia** is an exaggerated fear of an object, class of objects, or particular situations, accompanied by avoidance that is extreme enough to interfere with everyday life. Phobias can be sorted into types, based on the object or situation that is feared. **Social phobia** (or *social anxiety disorder*), is the fear of public embarrassment or humiliation and the ensuing avoidance of social situations likely to arouse this fear (Kessler, Stein, et al., 1998). People with this disorder might try to avoid eating, speaking, or performing in public or using public restrooms or dressing rooms. When unable to avoid these situations, they invariably experience anxiety or panic. This is one of the most common psychiatric diagnoses (major depressive disorder is *the* most common; American Psychiatric Association, 1994). Estimates are that approximately 13% of Americans currently experience social phobia (Fones et al., 1998).

A social phobia involves fear of public humiliation or embarrassment, whereas a specific phobia involves a fear of a particular object or situation.

A **specific phobia** is focused on a specific object or situation. Most people with a phobia about blood, for example, faint if they see blood and may, because of their phobia, avoid getting appropriate treatment for medical problems (Kleinknecht & Lenz, 1989). People may have phobias about flying, heights, spiders, or dental work (see Table 14.5). The fear may occur in the presence of the stimulus or in anticipation of it, despite an intellectual recognition that the fear is excessive or unreasonable. By avoiding the object or situation, the sufferer avoids the fear and the anxiety or panic that it might elicit.

### TABLE 14.5    Five Subtypes of Specific Phobias

| Phobia Subtype | Examples (Fear of . . . ) |
| --- | --- |
| Animal fears | Snakes, rats, insects |
| Blood–injection–injury fears | Seeing blood or receiving an injection |
| Natural environment fears | Storms, heights, the ocean |
| Situation fears | Public transportation, tunnels, bridges, elevators, dental work, flying |
| Miscellaneous fears cued by stimuli not already mentioned | Choking, vomiting, contracting an illness, falling down |

Phobia: A fear and avoidance of an object or situation extreme enough to interfere with everyday life.

Social phobia: A type of phobia involving fear of public humiliation or embarrassment and the ensuing avoidance of situations likely to arouse this fear.

Specific phobia: A type of phobia involving persistent and excessive or unreasonable fear triggered by a specific object or situation, along with attempts to avoid the feared stimulus.

## Level of the Brain in Phobias

Studies with twins suggest that phobias have a genetic component that affects events at the level of the brain (Kendler et al., 1992, 2001, 2002; D. Li et al., 2001). The genetic vulnerability may cause the amygdala, as well as other fear-related brain structures (see Chapter 10), to react too strongly in certain situations (LeDoux, 1996). However, not all identical twins are phobic if their co-twin is phobic, so nongenetic factors must play a role. Humans seem biologically *prepared* to develop phobias about certain stimuli and not others (see Chapter 6). Moreover, as we saw in the discussion of personality (Chapter 11), some people may be biologically predisposed to develop a classically conditioned fear more readily than others (Lissek et al., in press).

## Level of the Person in Phobias

Some people who have social phobias may have distorted thoughts about how other people might evaluate them. They worry about an upcoming social event, often making negative predictions about its outcome; they focus too much on their own behavior during a social interaction, and afterward they make negative interpretations about what transpired and ruminate about it (Abbott & Rapee, 2004; Amir et al., 1998; Hartman, 1983; Kocovski et al., in press; Wells, 1997; Wenzel et al., in press). This distorted thinking about social situations maintains the social phobia (Coupland, 2001; Rapee & Heimberg, 1997).

Learning may play a role in the development of specific phobias. Classical and operant conditioning, in particular, could be involved in producing some phobias (Mowrer, 1939; see Chapter 6). If a stimulus such as a thunderstorm (the *conditioned stimulus*) is paired with a traumatic event (the *unconditioned stimulus*), anxiety and fear may become *conditioned responses* to thunderstorms. Furthermore, because fear and anxiety are reduced by avoiding the feared stimulus, the avoidant behavior is operantly reinforced.

## Level of the Group in Phobias

Some researchers have suggested that classical conditioning can play a role in producing a phobia, even if indirectly. When a person observes the behavior of other people who fear particular objects or situations, observational learning can lead to the development of a phobia, by indicating what should be feared (Mineka et al., 1984). However, other researchers question the importance of classical conditioning in the origins of social phobias. These researchers note that studies of people with phobias of spiders, heights, and water have not found evidence that such conditioning played the predicted role in the majority of cases (Jones & Menzies, 1995; Menzies & Clarke, 1993, 1995a, 1995b; Poulton et al., 1999).

In addition, some researchers propose that specific phobias may reflect a genetic predisposition to fear naturally occurring situations or objects that were a danger to the human species (such as heights or water) and to which some people never habituate (Poulton & Menzies, 2002). Observational learning may also help explain why males and females tend to have different specific fears—boys are encouraged to interact more with potentially fearful objects and situations (such as playing with spiders or climbing into high places) and in the process may naturally be exposed to such stimuli (Antony & Barlow, 2002).

Finally, many people with social phobias may have been extremely shy as children (see Chapters 11 and 12; Biederman et al., 2001; Kagan, 1989b); thus, they do not *develop* a social phobia, but rather they never lost their discomfort in certain situations.

# Obsessive-Compulsive Disorder (OCD)

**Obsessive-compulsive disorder (OCD)** is marked by the presence of obsessions, either alone or in combination with compulsions. **Obsessions** are recurrent and persistent thoughts, impulses, or images that feel intrusive and inappropriate and that are difficult to suppress or ignore. Obsessions are more than excessive worries about real problems, and they may cause significant anxiety and distress. Common obsessions involve:

- thoughts of *contamination* ("Will I become contaminated by shaking her hand?"),
- repeated *doubts* ("Did I lock the door? Did I turn off the stove?"),
- the need to have things in a certain *order* (a perfect alignment of cans of food in a cupboard), or
- aggressive or horrific *impulses* (such as the urge to shout an obscenity in church).

**Compulsions** are repetitive behaviors or mental acts that some individuals feel compelled to perform in response to an obsession. Examples of compulsive behaviors are:

- *washing* in response to thoughts of contamination (washing the hands repeatedly until they are raw),
- *checking* (checking again and again that the stove is turned off or the windows closed so that it can take hours to leave the house),
- *ordering* (putting objects in a certain order or in precise symmetry, a task that may take hours until perfection is attained), and
- *counting* (counting to 100 after each obsessive thought, such as thinking about hitting one's child or shouting an obscenity).

Some people with OCD believe that a dreaded event will occur if they do not perform their ritual of checking, ordering, and so on, but the particular compulsion is not realistically connected to what they are trying to ward off, at least not in the frequency and duration with which the compulsion occurs. Approximately 2–3% of Americans suffer from OCD at some point in their lives (Robins & Regier, 1991).

### OBSESSIVE-COMPULSIVE DISORDER FROM THE INSIDE

One woman with OCD describes the ordeal of grocery shopping:

Once I have attained control of the car, I have the burden of getting into it and getting it going. This can be a big project some days, locking and unlocking the doors, rolling up and down the power windows, putting on and off the seat belts, sometimes countlessly. . . . Sometimes while driving I must do overtly good deeds, like letting cars out of streets in front of me, or stopping to let people cross. These are things everyone probably should do, but things I *must* do. . . . My trip in the car may take us to the grocery store. Inside I have certain rituals I must perform. I am relatively subtle about how I do them to avoid drawing attention to myself. Certain foods must have their packages read several times before I am allowed to purchase them. Some things need to be touched repetitively, certain tiles on the floor must be stepped on by myself and my family. I'll find myself having to go from one end of an aisle to the other and back again, just to make everything all right. I fear being accused of shoplifting sometimes because of the way I behave and the way I am always looking around to see if people have noticed my actions. (Steketee & White, 1990, pp. 12–13)

OCD can be understood by looking at events at the three levels and their interactions.

Obsessive-compulsive disorder (OCD): An anxiety disorder marked by the presence of obsessions, and sometimes compulsions.

Obsession: A recurrent and persistent thought, impulse, or image that feels intrusive and inappropriate and is difficult to suppress or ignore.

Compulsion: A repetitive behavior or mental act that an individual feels compelled to perform in response to an obsession.

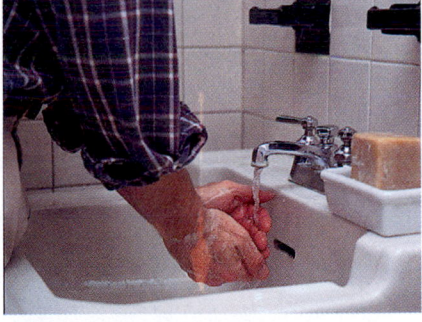

People with a hand-washing compulsion may spend hours washing their hands until they are raw.

## Level of the Brain in OCD

At the level of the brain, studies of families have produced evidence for a genetic contribution, although not a straightforward link: If one member of a family has OCD, others are more likely to have some type of anxiety disorder, but not necessarily OCD itself (Black et al., 1992; Pato et al., 2002; Torgersen, 1983). Brain structures have been implicated: Obsessions and compulsions have been related to a loop of neural activity that occurs in the caudate nucleus of the basal ganglia (Breiter et al., 1996; Jenike, 1984; Rauch et al., 1994). Obsessions may occur when the caudate nucleus does not do its normal job of "turning off" recurrent thoughts about an object or situation before they become obsessional; carrying out a compulsion may temporarily end the obsessional thoughts (Insel, 1992; Jenike, 1984; Modell et al., 1989; Saxena & Rauch, 2000). In addition, the neurotransmitter serotonin appears to play a role in OCD symptoms; serotonin-based medications such as Prozac reduce the symptoms, although the exact mechanism of this effect is unknown (Greenberg et al., 1997; Micallef & Blin, 2001).

## Level of the Person in OCD

As with other anxiety disorders, operant conditioning may play a role in OCD's emergence in an individual. Because compulsive behavior may momentarily relieve the anxiety created by obsessions, the compulsion is reinforced and thus more likely to recur. Research has found that obsessions themselves are not all that uncommon (Weissman et al., 1994)—many people experience obsessive thoughts during their lives, including thoughts about a partner during the early stages of a relationship, without developing a disorder. Salkovskis (1985; Salkovskis et al., 2000) proposes that such obsessive thoughts develop into a disorder when the person having them determines that the thoughts are about an unacceptable action (such as kill-ing a newborn child) or interprets the thoughts as conveying something fundamentally negative about himself or herself (Ferrier & Brewin, in press; Rachman, 1997). Some people may also have *thought-action fusion*, where they believe that having such "dangerous" thoughts is somehow the moral equivalent of carrying out such acts or that it increases the risk of their becoming reality (Rachman, 1993, 1997; Shafran et al., 1996). Such beliefs can lead to even more distress than the obsessive thoughts themselves.

Obsessive thoughts of this nature may imply danger to the person with the obsession or to someone else. As a result, extremely uncomfortable feelings arise, and mental rituals are created and invoked in an effort to reduce these feelings. Paradoxically, these attempts to alleviate the uncomfortable feelings associated with the obsession perpetuate its ability to induce uncomfortable feelings, and, through negative reinforcement, strengthen the mental rituals.

Research suggests that people with OCD whose predominant compulsion is checking may be more self-aware than previously believed: Participants were given pairs of words to study and asked about their confidence in their future ability to recognize the word pairs. Those with checking-related OCD did not feel confident about their future ability to remember the word pairs (in contrast to those without OCD), and their lack of certainty was well-founded: On both recognition and recall tests, they remembered fewer pairs than other participants. However, they were not accurate in *which* particular word pairs they would have difficulty recognizing (Tuna et al., 2005). Thus, their compulsion to go back and check whether they locked the door or turned off the stove may, in part, arise both because they have more difficulty remembering whether they actually performed those behaviors previously and because they have less confidence in their ability to remember things in general.

## Level of the Group in OCD

Although similar percentages of people in different countries experience OCD (Horwath & Weissman, 2000), culture plays a role in the particular symptoms displayed (Weissman et al., 1994); for example, religious obsessions and praying compulsions are more common among Turkish men with OCD than among French men with OCD (Millet et al., 2000).

In addition, research studies have shown that people with more severe OCD tended to have families who were more rejecting of them and to have experienced more kinds of family stress (Calvocoressi et al., 1995). However, the direction of causation is unclear: Were families more rejecting because their OCD relatives were more symptomatic, and therefore more difficult to live with? Or did the strong rejection by the families produce stronger symptoms of OCD in the affected relatives? Perhaps future research will be able to discover more about causation.

# Posttraumatic Stress Disorder (PTSD)

Some soldiers develop posttraumatic stress disorder.

Psychological symptoms can occur as a consequence of a traumatic event such as war, physical or sexual abuse, terrorism, or natural disasters. Victims of rape, for example, may be afraid to be alone, especially shortly after the attack. Women who have been raped may become afraid of and angry at all men, or they may experience more general feelings of anger, helplessness, guilt, pain, embarrassment, or anxiety. They may have sexual difficulties because the sexual act has been linked with such negative experiences and feelings. They may also develop physical symptoms of stress, such as stomachaches, headaches, back problems, inability to sleep, or diminished appetite. Depression may come and go over a long period. Long after the rape, they may remain afraid to trust anyone.

The diagnosis of **posttraumatic stress disorder (PTSD)** is made when three conditions are met:

1. The person experiences or witnesses an event that involves actual or threatened serious injury or death.
2. The traumatized person responds to the situation with fear and helplessness.
3. The traumatized individual then experiences three sets of symptoms:
   a. persistent re-experiencing of the traumatic event, which may take the form of intrusive, unwanted, and distressing recollections, dreams, or nightmares of the event or may involve flashbacks that can include illusions, hallucinations, and a sense of reliving the experience;
   b. persistent avoidance of anything associated with the trauma and a general emotional numbing; and
   c. heightened arousal, which can cause people with PTSD to startle easily (Shalev et al., 2000), have difficulty sleeping, or be in a constant state of hypervigilance.

**Posttraumatic stress disorder (PTSD):** An anxiety disorder experienced by some people after a traumatic event and whose symptoms include persistent re-experiencing of the trauma, avoidance of anything associated with the trauma, and heightened arousal.

These symptoms do not always appear immediately after the traumatic event, but once they start, they can persist for months or even for years.

## POSTTRAUMATIC STRESS DISORDER FROM THE INSIDE

Mr. E, age 65, complained that ever since World War II he experienced extreme nervousness that was somewhat alleviated by chewing tobacco. . . . After this wartime nervousness—consisting of subjective feelings of anxiety, itching, and shaking—developed [it got to the point where he experienced] eight such episodes in the month before he came to the hospital.

During the war Mr. E manned a landing craft that transported soldiers to the beaches. He was particularly distraught about an experience in which he felt something underfoot on a sandy beach and discovered that he was stepping on the face of a dead GI. He also described an incident in which his ship had been torpedoed and several crewmen killed. He experienced intense survivor guilt about this incident. (Hierholzer et al., 1992, p. 819)

As shown in Table 14.6, the majority of people who experience trauma do not go on to develop PTSD (Breslau et al., 1998; Koren et al., 2005; Resnick et al., 1993; Shalev et al., 1998; Yehuda, 2002a), and the type of trauma makes a difference in the outcome for a given person. For example, one study found that women were more likely to develop PTSD when their traumas resulted from crimes rather than from nat-

**TABLE 14.6    Prevalence of Traumatic Events and Rates of PTSD in Response to Such Events**

| Traumatic Event | Prevalence of Event (%) | | Rate of PTSD in Response to Event (%) | |
|---|---|---|---|---|
| | Men | Women | Men | Women |
| Rape | 0.7 | 9.2 | 65.0 | 45.9 |
| Molestation | 2.8 | 12.3 | 12.2 | 26.5 |
| Physical assault | 11.1 | 6.9 | 1.8 | 21.3 |
| Accident | 25.0 | 13.8 | 6.3 | 8.8 |
| Natural disaster | 18.9 | 15.2 | 3.7 | 5.4 |
| Combat | 6.4 | 0.0 | 38.8 | — |
| Witnessed death or injury | 40.1 | 18.6 | 9.1 | 2.8 |
| Learned about a traumatic event | 63.1 | 61.8 | 1.4 | 3.2 |
| Sudden death of loved one | 61.1 | 59.0 | 12.6 | 16.2 |
| Any traumatic event (study 1) | 60.7 | 51.2 | 8.1 | 20.4 |
| Any traumatic event (study 2) | 92.2 | 87.1 | 6.2 | 13.0 |

ural disasters (Resnick et al., 1993), and other studies corroborate this finding (Breslau et al., 1998). Other factors that affect whether PTSD will arise can be found in the interactions of events at each level of analysis: the brain, the person, and the group.

## Level of the Brain in PTSD

Some people may be biologically at risk for developing symptoms of PTSD after a trauma. Consider the result of one study: Firefighter-trainees were asked to listen to loud bursts of noise, and their tendency to be startled (indicated by blinking of the eyes) was assessed. The researchers measured this tendency before the trainees experienced any fire-related trauma in their work. The researchers later reassessed this tendency within 4 weeks after the trainees experienced such trauma. The trainees who were more reactive before a trauma were more likely to develop PTSD symptoms after a trauma (Guthrie & Bryant, 2005). Perhaps such a biological vulnerability occurs because of a genetic predisposition (Shalev et al., 1998; True et al., 1993) or some trauma experienced in childhood (Vermetten & Bremner, 2002). This predisposition could arise from having an overly reactive locus coeruleus, as occurs with panic disorder. In addition, the limbic system (including the amygdala) of people with PTSD appears to be more easily activated by mental imagery of traumatic events than that of nontraumatic events, possibly because part of the frontal lobe doesn't do as good a job of inhibiting the amygdala (Rauch et al., 1996, 2000; Shin et al., 1997, 2004).

Researchers have found that people with PTSD often have unusually small hippocampi, which may help to explain why they have intrusive memories (Bremner et al., 2003; Yehuda, 2002a). Some researchers wonder whether the biological changes that occur in response to trauma (such as the ensuing increase of the stress response, which can damage neurons in the hippocampus; see Chapter 13) lead to the smaller hippocampal size. In order to tease out biological elements that create a *vulnerability* for PTSD from those that are a result of PTSD, Mark Gilbertson and colleagues (May et al., 2004; Orr et al., 2003) have investigated specific sets of male monozygotic twins, in which one twin was exposed to combat in Vietnam and the other twin was not. Both twins had smaller hippocampi than normal, which suggests that smaller hippocampal size is not caused by exposure to trauma, but rather may represent a biological vulnerability—a diathesis—for PTSD (Gilbertson et al., 2002).

In addition, people with PTSD appear to have lower baseline levels of cortisol and, when stressed, may not produce the high levels of cortisol that typically occur with the fight-or-flight response; this difference may exist before exposure to the trauma that produces the disorder (Yehuda, 2002b). Research findings further suggest that people who develop PTSD may have more glucocorticoid receptors (Yehuda et al., 2004). This would indicate that when they are stressed, any increase in cortisol level will have an amplified effect compared to those with fewer glucocorticoid receptors (Yehuda, 2003). In other words, people who develop PTSD after a traumatic experience may have a qualitatively different response to the trauma and its aftermath (Yehuda, 2002b), which leads to the unique symptoms of PTSD.

## Level of the Person in PTSD

PTSD is not simply a biological response to trauma. Events at the level of the person also influence whether a person will develop this disorder. Such events include the traumatized person's psychological characteristics before, during, and after a trauma (Ehlers et al., 1998; Ozer et al., 2003). A history of social withdrawal, depression, or a sense of not being able to control stressors increases the risk of developing PTSD after a trauma (Joseph et al., 1995). The perception that your life is at risk during the traumatic event or that you have no control over your situation can also facilitate development of PTSD, regardless of the actual threat (Foa et al., 1989). Risk of suffering the disorder rises, too, if you believe the world is a dangerous place (Keane et al., 1985; Kushner et al., 1992). Furthermore, people who have a lower IQ are more likely to develop symptoms of PTSD in the aftermath of a trauma (Macklin et al., 1998; McNally & Shin, 1995), perhaps because they have fewer cognitive resources for coping with the trauma.

In addition, the quality of thoughts differs between those who develop PTSD and those who do not. Trauma survivors who later developed PTSD were more likely to report that their intrusive thoughts of the trauma arose spontaneously and had a vivid, "here and now" quality than were trauma survivors who did not develop PTSD. Not surprisingly, such memories were more distressing (Michael et al., in press). As in the case of phobias, classical and operant conditioning may help to explain the avoidance symptoms of PTSD. In addition, operant conditioning may be why people with PTSD are at a higher risk of developing drug abuse or dependence than those who experienced trauma but did not develop PTSD (Chilcoat & Breslau, 1998; Jacobsen et al., 2001): Substance use can lead to negative reinforcement because the symptoms of PTSD temporarily subside when the substance is taken.

## Level of the Group in PTSD

Whether trauma will lead to PTSD also depends, in part, on events at the level of the group. Support from friends, family members, or counselors immediately after a trauma may help decrease the likelihood that PTSD will develop (Kaniasty & Norris, 1992; Kaniasty et al., 1990). In the case of those exposed to trauma as part of military service, social support after coming back home can reduce the risk of PTSD (King, King, et al., 1998). Group factors play an integral role in creating the "trauma" part of the disorder, since traumatic events involving other people (violent crimes) are more likely to lead to PTSD.

## Interacting Levels: Individual Differences in Responses to Trauma

Because of differences in biological and psychological characteristics, different people are likely to experience and respond to a traumatic event differently (Bowman, 1999) and to have different experiences with social support. Consider that among male Vietnam veterans who are identical or fraternal twins, a willingness to volunteer for combat or to accept more risky assignments is partly heritable (Lyons et al., 1993). This heritability (level of the brain) may be reflected in certain temperaments such as sensation seeking (see Chapter 11): *High sensation seekers* may be more likely to volunteer for combat and thus be more at risk for certain kinds of trauma. People's personality traits and ways of viewing the world (level of the person) may also influence the amount of social support available to them (level of the group): *Extraverts* are likely to have more social support available to them than are introverts. Such traits and ways of thinking also influence how people use, or don't use, social support. In turn, the use of social support moderates the effects of the trauma. However, the more severe the trauma, the less important are events at the levels of the brain and the person in moderating its effects (Keane & Barlow, 2002).

# Test Yourself

1. The major symptom of panic disorder is
   a. constant feelings of panic and fear.
   b. episodes of intense fear and discomfort.
   c. extreme anxiety over hygiene.
   d. severe hallucinations and delusions.

2. Which of the following is *not* likely to be one of the factors leading to a specific phobia?
   a. classical and operant conditioning
   b. genetic predisposition
   c. observational learning
   d. unconscious motivation

3. In obsessive-compulsive disorder (OCD), the obsessions are _____, and the compulsions are _____.
   a. bizarre behaviors; bizarre thoughts
   b. intrusive thoughts; compelled behaviors
   c. usually of a sexual nature; usually related to hygiene
   d. coveted objects; things that must be touched

4. A diagnosis of posttraumatic stress disorder (PTSD) requires three sets of symptoms that can be summarized as re-experiencing the traumatic event, avoiding anything associated with the event, and having _____.
   a. flashbacks.
   b. hallucinations and delusions.
   c. nightmares and episodes of sleepwalking.
   d. heightened arousal.

## Answers

1. b 2. d 3. b 4. d

## Think It Through!

If a relative refused to fly because of a fear of flying, would you think that he or she has an anxiety disorder (based on what you have read)? If no, why not; if yes, which disorder and why?

Suppose that a classmate confided to you that he's been very anxious lately and that he has been going back to check that he's locked his door or his bike. What other questions might you want to ask before concluding that he might have symptoms of an anxiety disorder? What disorder and why (or why not)?

# SCHIZOPHRENIA

In the last years of his life, van Gogh apparently had increasing difficulty distinguishing between his internal experiences and external reality. He would become disoriented and not know who he was. He had delusions of being poisoned and attacked. Gauguin claimed that van Gogh referred to himself as a ghost before cutting off part of his ear. During a period of mental clarity, when van Gogh was asked about the assault on Gauguin, he said that he was given to hearing voices, that he had heard voices telling him to kill Gauguin. Then he remembered the biblical injunction "If thine own eye offend thee, pluck it out." His ear had offended him by "hearing" the voice that suggested he kill Gauguin, so he cut part of it off as penance for his sin against Gauguin (Lubin, 1972).

These aspects of van Gogh's life and behavior suggest the possibility of schizophrenia. The word *schizophrenia* is derived from two Greek words, *schizo*, meaning "to split" or "to cut," and *phren*, meaning "mind" or "reason." Books and movies sometimes portray schizophrenia as if it meant having a split personality, but schizophrenia is characterized by a split from reality, not a split between different aspects of oneself. **Schizophrenia** is a psychotic disorder that profoundly alters affect, behavior, and cognition, particularly the pattern or form of thought.

Schizophrenia: A psychotic disorder in which the patient's affect, behavior, and thoughts are profoundly altered.

# Symptoms: What Schizophrenia Looks Like

*DSM-IV* divides the symptoms of schizophrenia into two groups (see Table 14.7). **Positive symptoms** involve an excess or distortion of normal functions; an example is hallucinations. They are called positive not because they indicate something desirable, but because they mark the *presence* of certain unusual behaviors. **Negative symptoms**, on the other hand, involve a *diminution* or *loss* of normal functions; an example is a restriction in speech or movement.

## Positive Symptoms

Positive symptoms include *delusions* (distortions of thought) and *hallucinations*. Positive symptoms are usually more responsive than negative symptoms to antipsychotic medication (discussed in Chapter 15). Delusions can be complex, centering on a particular theme, such as the belief that someone, or some group, is out to "get" you. Hallucinations in schizophrenia are typically auditory; hearing voices is a common symptom. *Disorganized behavior* can consist of inappropriate, childlike silliness or unpredictable agitation. People with disorganized behavior may have difficulty with everyday tasks such as organizing meals, maintaining hygiene, and selecting their clothes (they might wear two overcoats in the summer). Another positive symptom is *disorganized speech*, as in the following example: "I may be a 'Blue Baby' but 'Social Baby' not, but yet a blue heart baby could be in the Blue Book published before the war" (Maher, 1966, p. 413).

## Negative Symptoms

Negative symptoms include flat affect, alogia, and avolition (see Table 14.7). *Flat affect* is a general failure to express or respond to emotion. There may be occasional smiles or warmth of manner, but usually the facial expression is constant; eye contact is rare and body language minimal. *Alogia*, or "poverty of speech," is characterized by brief, slow, empty replies to questions. Alogia is not an unwillingness to speak; rather, the thoughts behind the words seem slowed down. Someone with alogia speaks less

| TABLE 14.7 | Positive and Negative Symptoms of Schizophrenia | |
|---|---|
| **Positive Symptoms** | **Negative Symptoms** |
| ■ Delusions | ■ Flat affect (appears to be without emotion) |
| of *persecution* (beliefs that others are out to "get" you) | |
| of *grandeur* (beliefs that you are an important person) | ■ Alogia (brief, slow, empty replies to questions) |
| of *reference* (beliefs that normal events have special meaning directed toward you) | ■ Avolition (inability to initiate goal-directed behavior) |
| of *control* (beliefs that your feelings, behaviors, or thoughts are controlled by others) | |
| ■ Hallucinations | |
| ■ Disordered behavior | |
| ■ Disorganized speech | |

Positive symptom: An excess or distortion of normal functions, such as a hallucination.

Negative symptom: A diminution or loss of normal functions, such as a restriction in speech.

than others and doesn't use words as freely. *Avolition* is an inability to initiate or persist in goal-directed activities. Someone exhibiting avolition may sit for long periods without engaging in any behavior or social interaction.

## Diagnosing Schizophrenia

Not all of the positive or negative symptoms are present in everyone affected with schizophrenia. According to the *DSM-IV*, a diagnosis of schizophrenia requires that two or more of these symptoms are displayed for at least a week and that other signs of socially inappropriate behavior are exhibited for at least 6 months. The average age of onset of schizophrenia is the 20s, although in some people (particularly women) onset does not occur until later in life. Symptoms often develop gradually, with a prodromal phase characterized by slow deterioration in functioning, including withdrawal from other people, poor hygiene, and outbursts of anger (Heinssen et al., 2001). Eventually, the disorder reaches an active phase, in which full-blown positive and negative symptoms arise.

Approximately 1% of people worldwide will develop schizophrenia in their lifetimes (Keith et al., 1991; Kulhara & Chakrabarti, 2001). The course of schizophrenia is variable: 25% of schizophrenics have only one psychotic episode and recover relatively completely, 25% improve enough to live independently, 25% improve, but not enough to live independently, 15% do not improve and are the "chronic" cases, and 10% commit suicide (Torrey, 1988).

Did van Gogh appear to exhibit symptoms of schizophrenia? We know that he had auditory hallucinations and that he exhibited inappropriate social behavior (including poor hygiene and outbursts of anger), but he does not appear to have had negative symptoms of schizophrenia (at least not between his "attacks"). Not enough is known about his behavior during his attacks to determine whether additional symptoms accompanied them.

## Subtypes of Schizophrenia

People with schizophrenia, as mentioned earlier, tend to suffer from only some of the full range of possible symptoms. The symptoms of schizophrenia tend to cluster into groupings, from which mental health professionals and researchers have identified subtypes of schizophrenia. The *DSM-IV* specifies four subtypes of schizophrenia (see Table 14.8): paranoid, disorganized, catatonic, and undifferentiated.

*Paranoid schizophrenia* typically is characterized by specific delusional beliefs, which are limited to particular topics. If someone with this disorder isn't talking about these topics, he or she may seem perfectly normal, which sometime makes diagnosis difficult. People with this variety of schizophrenia are more likely to exhibit aggressive behavior (either toward themselves or others) and also have the highest suicide rate (13%; American Psychiatric Association, 2000; Fenton & McGlashan, 1991). Nevertheless, this subtype has the best prognosis, or prospect of recovery (Fenton & McGlashan, 1991).

*Disorganized schizophrenia* is marked by disorganized behavior and speech: Behaviors can be childish, including giggling and a strange style of dress, or may consist of public urination, defecation, and obscene and babbling speech. This subtype has the worst prognosis (Walker et al., 2004).

*Catatonic schizophrenia* involves bizarre movements; catatonic and disorganized schizophrenics may require constant care.

*Undifferentiated schizophrenia* is the diagnosis given to those whose symptoms do not meet the criteria for the other subtypes.

**TABLE 14.8**

## Four Subtypes of Schizophrenia, According to *DSM-IV-TR*

**Paranoid**

Delusions of persecution are prominent; intellectual functioning and affect are relatively intact, but auditory hallucinations are common.

**Disorganized**

Disorganized speech and behavior and flat or inappropriate affect are prominent.

**Catatonic**

Catatonic (bizarre, immobile, or relentless) motor behaviors are prominent.

**Undifferentiated**

Symptoms do not clearly fall into any of the above three subtypes.

### PARANOID SCHIZOPHRENIA FROM THE INSIDE

Jeffrey DeMann describes his first hospitalization for schizophrenia at the age of 27:

I recall vividly the delusion of believing my mother was to take my place in the shock treatments. Then I was to be quietly murdered and placed in an acid bath grave, which would dissolve any physical evidence of my existence. At this time, auditory hallucinations also were present. I could actually hear the slamming of my mother's body on the table while being administered the deadly shock. I truly believed my mother was now dead in my place. I also recall curling up on an old wooden bench and repeatedly chanting the words "Die quickly now." (DeMann, 1994, p. 580)

If van Gogh did indeed suffer from schizophrenia, a diagnosis of the paranoid subtype would seem to fit him best, because his intellectual functioning and affect remained relatively intact between "attacks." But he apparently did not have extended periods of paranoid delusions, and schizophrenia would not account for his lengthy bouts of depression.

# Why Does This Happen to Some People, But Not Others?

With few exceptions, schizophrenia occurs at about the same rate worldwide, with about 1 in 100 people developing the disorder (Gottesman, 1991). The reason some people and not others suffer from schizophrenia involves events at the three levels of analysis and their interactions.

## Level of the Brain in Schizophrenia

Biological events related to schizophrenia include genetics, abnormal brain structure and function, and hormonal and neurotransmitter activity.

**GENETIC FACTORS IN SCHIZOPHRENIA**   Twin, family, and adoption studies point to the influence of genetic factors in the development of schizophrenia (Gottesman, 1991; Kendler & Diehl, 1993; Tiernari, 1991). People who have relatives with schizophrenia have an increased risk of developing the disorder; the closer the relative, the greater the risk. However, it is important to note that even for those who have a close relative with schizophrenia, the actual incidence is still quite low. More than 80% of people who have a parent or sibling diagnosed with schizophrenia do *not* have the disorder themselves (Gottesman & Moldin, 1998). Even when there is the highest level of genetic resemblance, in pairs of identical twins, the co-twin of a schizophrenic twin has only a 48% chance of developing schizophrenia. If the disease were entirely genetic, there should be a 100% correspondence in its incidence in pairs of identical twins. And a fraternal co-twin of a person with schizophrenia has only a 17% likelihood of developing the disorder (Gottesman, 1991). Research suggests that there may be genetic overlap between schizophrenia and bipolar disorder (Cardno et al., 2002). Although genes do play a role in the etiology (underlying causation) of schizophrenia, they are clearly not the only factor.

**STRUCTURAL BRAIN ABNORMALITIES IN SCHIZOPHRENIA**   Evidence from autopsies and neuroimaging studies suggests that schizophrenia may involve abnormalities in brain structures. Someone with schizophrenia is more likely than others to have enlarged *ventricles*, cavities in the center of the brain filled with cerebrospinal fluid. Increased ventricle size means a reduction in size of the parts of the brain that contain gray matter and white matter, including the frontal cortex (Goldstein et al., 1999), which plays a central role in abstract thinking and planning. Impaired frontal lobe functioning has been the focus of a substantial amount of the research on schizophrenia.

Some research findings suggest that decreases in brain volume may occur, in part, because of using a particular medication for psychotic symptoms (Lieberman et al., 2005). However, such findings cannot fully explain the reduced brain size, because other studies have found that brain abnormalities exist even before psychotic symptoms appear and medication use has begun (Pantelis et al., 2003). One explanation is that at least some deficits in functioning may occur because of excessive pruning of neural connections in the frontal lobe during adolescence (Keshavan et al., 1994). This explanation is supported by neuroimaging studies that have revealed abnormally low numbers of dopamine receptors in the frontal lobes of people with schizophrenia (Okubo et al., 1997).

Other brain abnormalities associated with schizophrenia include a relatively small thalamus and hippocampus, which might account for the memory problems commonly encountered by people with the disorder (Schmajuk, 2001). Studies of pairs of identical twins in which only one twin has schizophrenia find that it is only the affected twin who has the smaller brain structures (Baare et al., 2001), which suggests that such brain abnormalities arise from the disorder itself, and not from the genes. These brain changes may begin during adolescence (Pantelis et al., 2003; Walker et al., 2004), and they apparently reflect a basic miswiring of brain circuits, so brain areas are connected to each other in abnormal ways. As a result of this faulty brain circuitry, neural activity doesn't occur in the way it is supposed to (Andreasen et al., 1999; Walker et al., 2004).

Researchers looking at different ways in which these brain abnormalities might arise have found several possible causes. One focus has been on the fetus's developing brain, specifically how normal brain development might go awry during pregnancy. Possibilities include:

- maternal malnourishment during pregnancy (Brown, van Os, et al., 1999; Wahlbeck et al., 2001),

- maternal illness (Buka et al., 1999; Brown et al., 2001; Gilmore et al., 1997; Mednick et al., 1998),

- maternal stress (and higher levels of glucocorticoids; see Chapter 13) during pregnancy (Weinstock, 1997; Welberg & Seckl, 2001), and

- prenatal or birth-related medical complications that lead to fetal oxygen deprivation (Cannon, 1997; Geddes & Lawrie, 1995; McNeil et al., 2000; Zornberg et al., 2000).

Because researchers have found a higher incidence of prenatal and birth complications for babies born to mothers with schizophrenia, some have argued that fetuses with a genetic predisposition to schizophrenia have an increased likelihood of abnormal development, which, in turn, leads to the higher rate of prenatal and birth complications (Goodman, 1988). However, other researchers suggest that such

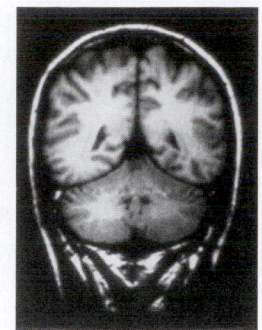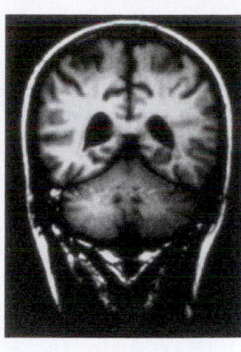

Well  Affected

28-year-old males

Those with schizophrenia have larger ventricles, smaller amounts of frontal and temporal lobe cortex, and a smaller thalamus. This decreased cortical volume probably accounts for some of the cognitive deficits found in people with this disorder (Andreasen et al., 1986, 1992).

Despite odds of one in a billion, all four of these identical quadruplets—from oldest to youngest, Nora, Iris, Myra, and Hester—went on to develop schizophrenia. The physical stressors experienced by the quads in their mother's uterus may have contributed to their developing the disorder. However, their symptoms and the onset and course of the illness differed. Hester and Iris were more disabled than were their sisters.

complications in and of themselves do not create a risk for schizophrenia in the absence of genetic vulnerability (Buka et al., 1999). Rather, according to this view, it is the combination of the genetic vulnerability and the physical complications during gestation and birth that together heighten the risk for the alteration in brain development and the later development of schizophrenia (Baaré et al., 2001).

**ELEVATED LEVELS OF STRESS-RELATED HORMONES** Children who are at risk for schizophrenia show an extreme discomfort with close relationships and exhibit relatively high levels of quirky or odd behavior. These children are also more reactive to stress and have higher baseline levels of the stress-related hormone cortisol (Walker et al., 1999; see Chapter 13). Moreover, higher levels of cortisol are associated with the severity of symptoms (Walder et al., 2000). Some researchers suggest that the increased biological changes and stressors of adolescence lead to higher levels of stress-related hormones. Prodromal symptoms of schizophrenia often begin to emerge during adolescence.

Similarly, Elaine Walker and her colleagues carefully analyzed home movies taken during the childhoods of people who were later diagnosed with schizophrenia and found that those children were different from their siblings (Grimes & Walker, 1994; Walker et al., 1993). They noted that, from infancy through adolescence, these people exhibited more involuntary movements, such as writhing or excessive movements of the tongue, lips, or arms (Walker et al., 1994). The more severe the involuntary movements, the more severe the schizophrenic symptoms in adulthood (Neumann & Walker, 1996).

**NEUROTRANSMITTERS** High levels of stress-related hormones are thought to affect activity of the neurotransmitter dopamine, and abnormalities in the functioning of this neurotransmitter have been implicated in schizophrenia (Walker & Diforio, 1997). It was once thought that an overproduction of dopamine, or an increased number or sensitivity of dopamine receptors, was responsible for schizophrenia. This *dopamine hypothesis* received support from research findings that medications that decrease the amount of dopamine reduce the positive symptoms of schizophrenia. Moreover, when people who do not have schizophrenia are given drugs that increase dopamine activity, they experience symptoms similar to those of schizophrenia (Syvalathi, 1994). Perhaps, it was thought, excess dopamine triggers a flood of unrelated thoughts, feelings, and perceptions, and the delusions are attempts to organize these disconnected events into a coherent, understandable experience (Gottesman, 1991). However, research soon indicated that the dopamine hypothesis is too simple. Although dopamine clearly plays a role in schizophrenia, other neurotransmitters, such as glutamate, and other neural processes are also involved (Goff & Coyle, 2001; Laruelle et al., 2003; Nestler, 1997; Syvalathi, 1994; Tsai & Coyle, 2002; Walker et al., 2004; Walker & Diforio, 1997; Weinberger & Lipska, 1995). In sum, researchers now agree that prenatal and birth complications may play a role in the development of schizophrenia, and some individuals are genetically vulnerable to the disorder. These factors may create abnormalities in brain structure, particularly in the frontal lobe, and in brain function, especially that of neurotransmitter systems.

## Level of the Person in Schizophrenia

Although not part of the *DSM-IV* diagnostic criteria, people with schizophrenia may have problems in processing and responding to sensory stimuli (Green et al., 1999, 2000; Krieger et al., 2001), and these problems may lead to unusual sensory experiences (such as seeing inanimate objects move of their own accord). The individuals may feel bombarded by the myriad of stimuli around them and have trouble focusing on and making sense of those stimuli, leading to additional problems in organizing what they are perceiving and experiencing.

In addition, people with schizophrenia are likely to have difficulties with interpreting and using information in various contexts (Green et al., 2000; Kuperberg & Heckers, 2000; Walker et al., 2004). They may:

- not be able to determine the importance or relevance of new information or stimuli (Hemsley, 1994) or to distinguish relevant from irrelevant stimuli (Cornblatt et al., 1997; Nuechterlein, 1991);
- lose the "big picture," or be unable to keep track of the overall goal in a multistep task;
- have difficulty understanding social cues and therefore respond inappropriately (Penn et al., 1997); or
- not realize that they are having problems (referred to as a *lack of insight*).

These deficits also affect what these people experience, which affects their beliefs and goals.

The home movies study mentioned earlier also found that those children who went on to develop schizophrenia exhibited fewer expressions of joy than their unaffected siblings (Walker et al., 1993). (This emotional dampening may also cause other people to respond less positively to the affected person.)

## Level of the Group in Schizophrenia

For someone who has been diagnosed with schizophrenia but whose symptoms have subsequently subsided, a stressful life event may act as a trigger, leading to a recurrence of symptoms (Gottesman, 1991; Ventura et al., 1989). Events at the level of the group can produce such stress. For example, almost two thirds of people hospitalized with schizophrenia live with their families after leaving the hospital, and the way members of a family express emotion can affect the likelihood of a recurrence of acute schizophrenia symptoms, although it does not *cause* schizophrenia. Families that are critical, hostile, and overinvolved are said to have **high expressed emotion**; they are more likely than families with low expressed emotion to include a member with chronic schizophrenia (Butzlaff & Hooley, 1998; Kavanagh, 1992; Vaughn & Leff, 1976). However, it is possible that the direction of causality runs the other way: Perhaps high expressed emotion families are responding to a relative with schizophrenia whose behavior is more bizarre or disruptive, and low expressed emotion families include someone whose schizophrenic symptoms are less extreme. Casting the social net wider, a longitudinal study of people with schizophrenia found that those who had larger numbers of nonrelated people in their social support networks before their first psychotic episode had the best rate of recovery 5 years after that episode (Erikson et al., 1998).

A higher rate of schizophrenia is found in urban areas and in lower socioeconomic classes (Freeman, 1994; Mortensen et al., 1999). Why might this be? Two factors appear to play a role: *social selection* and *social causation* (Dauncey et al., 1993). **Social selection**, also called *social drift*, refers to the "drifting" to lower socioeconomic classes of those who have become mentally disabled (Mulvany et al., 2001). This often happens to those who are no longer able to work and who lack family support or care (Dohrenwend et al., 1992). **Social causation** refers to the chronic psychological and

High expressed emotion: An emotional style in families that are critical, hostile, and over-involved.

Social selection: The tendency of the mentally disabled to drift to the lower economic classes; also called *social drift*.

Social causation: The chronic psychological and social stresses of living in an urban environment that may lead to an increase in the rate of schizophrenia (especially among the poor).

Why might there be a higher percentage of people with schizophrenia living in poor urban neighborhoods? According to *social selection*, people with schizophrenia drift into poorer neighborhoods because of their illness; according to *social causation*, the stress of living in such neighborhoods can trigger the disorder in those with a diathesis.

social stressors in an urban environment, particularly for the poor. The stress from these living conditions may trigger the disorder in persons who are biologically vulnerable (Freeman, 1994).

Culture may influence the percentage of patients who recover from schizophrenia. Industrialized countries generally have lower recovery rates than do developing nations (American Psychiatric Association, 2000; Kulhara & Chakrabarti, 2001), although not all studies support this finding (Edgerton & Cohen, 1994; von Zerssen et al., 1990). If this finding is further substantiated, possible explanations for it include a more tolerant attitude among people in developing countries and lower expressed emotion in extended families in such countries (El-Islam, 1991). Moreover, developing countries also tend to have collectivist cultures, which place more emphasis on the community than on the individual (see Chapters 10 and 11). People in developing countries who have schizophrenia thus may have more social support available to them.

## Interacting Levels in Schizophrenia

Events at the three levels of analysis interact: As suggested by the finding that 48% of identical co-twins develop schizophrenia if their twin has schizophrenia, biological factors play a role in the development of the disorder, leading a person to be vulnerable to it. Such a biological vulnerability, in combination with environmental and social factors and with the individual's learning history, help determine whether the disorder manifests itself. Walker and Diforio (1997) propose a specific diathesis–stress model to explain how stress can worsen schizophrenic symptoms. They note that people who develop schizophrenia do not experience more life stressors overall than people who do not develop the disorder; however, among individuals with schizophrenia, those who experience more of such stressors are likely to have more severe schizophrenic symptoms and experience more relapses (Hultman et al., 1997). And, in fact, people with schizophrenia have higher baseline levels of cortisol, an indicator of the stress response. This relationship is even more extended, since not only people with schizophrenia but also those at risk for the disorder (because of family history or evidence of some symptoms of schizophrenia) are more likely to have higher levels of cortisol. And antipsychotic medications decrease cortisol levels in people with schizophrenia.

Walker and Diforio further propose that this heightened susceptibility to stress comes about because of cortisol's effect on dopamine activity, which is to produce an overactivation of dopamine systems, which, in turn, can worsen symptoms of schizophrenia. They suggest that the negative symptoms of schizophrenia, such as social withdrawal, are attempts to reduce stress. Thus, genetic, prenatal, or birth factors increase a susceptibility to stress, and stress aggravates schizophrenic symptoms.

Van Gogh had a family history of schizophrenia, implicating a possible genetic factor, and some biographical material suggests that van Gogh's extremely strict father could be regarded as a high expressed emotion parent. And before becoming an artist, van Gogh repeatedly returned to live with his parents after leaving his various jobs. Moreover, after becoming an artist, he generally lived off money sent by his brother Theo. He was so poor that he often experienced enormous stress; for example, he often had to choose whether to spend Theo's gift of money on painting supplies or on food, and frequently chose the former (Auden, 1989).

1. The *DSM-IV* divides symptoms of schizophrenia into two groups. Positive symptoms are _____, and negative symptoms are _____.
   a. excesses of normal functioning; deficits of normal functioning
   b. deficits of normal functioning; excesses of normal functioning
   c. generally not stressful for the patient; very stressful for the patient
   d. beneficial for the person's prognosis; detrimental to the person's prognosis

2. An individual who exhibits bizarre behavior such as immobility or inappropriate karate-like movements most likely has the _____ subtype of schizophrenia.
   a. paranoid          c. catatonic
   b. disorganized      d. undifferentiated

3. Schizophrenia is most likely caused primarily by
   a. genetics and family dynamics.
   b. abnormal brain structures and functions.
   c. fetal brain development.
   d. several factors, including expressed emotion.

4. A higher rate of schizophrenia is found among poor people. One explanation for this, called _____, is that the mentally disabled drift downward into lower-class status.
   a. social causation       c. diathesis drop
   b. social selection       d. cultural accretion

## Answers

1.a 2.c 3.b 4.b

# Think It Through!

Would someone who has exhibited positive and negative symptoms of schizophrenia (at some point in their past) ever be able to function relatively normally again?

Does having a parent with schizophrenia guarantee the development of the disorder? Can the environment of an individual with schizophrenia affect his or her symptoms? If so, in what way?

What is the best evidence that van Gogh did not have schizophrenia?

# OTHER AXIS I DISORDERS:
## Dissociative and Eating Disorders

Perhaps van Gogh, like many people, suffered from more than one psychological disorder. Consider that, at the age of 24, he spoke of an "evil self" that caused him to become a disgrace and bring misery to others. He sometimes had trouble with his memory. He wrote to Theo that his frail memory "also seems to me to prove that there is quite definitely something or other deranged in my brain, it is astounding to be afraid . . . , and to be unable to remember things" (Auden, 1989, p. 363).

At times, van Gogh ate only breakfast and a dinner of coffee and bread. And while in the hospital during the last year of his life, he would eat only meager dinners of half-cooked chick-peas or alcohol or bread and a little soup (Auden, 1989). Were van Gogh to be seen by mental health professionals now, they would undoubtedly ask more about his restricted and bizarre eating habits. Particularly if van Gogh were female, mental health professionals might wonder whether his eating habits were symptoms of an eating disorder.

In addition to the disorders in the major diagnostic categories already discussed, there are several less common Axis I disorders; some of these unfortunately are becoming more common. In this section, we consider the categories of dissociative and eating disorders.

# Dissociative Disorders

The hallmark of **dissociative disorders** is a disruption in one or more of the usually integrated functions of consciousness, memory, and identity, often caused by a traumatic or very stressful event. The disruptions may be fleeting or chronic; they may come on suddenly or gradually. They can lead to several symptoms (Steinberg, 1994):

- *identity confusion*, a state of uncertainty about one's identity;
- *identity alteration*, the adoption of a new identity;
- *derealization*, the sense that familiar objects have changed or seem "unreal";
- *depersonalization*, the experience of observing oneself as if from the outside; and
- *amnesia*, the loss of memory.

These symptoms are not necessarily signs of pathology; people often have dissociative experiences in the course of ordinary life. For example, it is common to experience derealization on returning home after a long absence: The ceiling may seem lower, the furniture smaller, and so on. Even identity alteration need not signify abnormality. Possession trance (discussed in Chapter 5), which is not uncommon in some cultures, can lead to dissociation of identity, but the dissociation is not considered pathological in those cultures. In dissociative disorders, as defined by the *DSM-IV*, the dissociative experiences are severe enough to cause distress or to impair functioning. It is unclear how many people suffer from these disorders, although they are more frequently diagnosed now than in the past. In fact, some researchers and clinicians believe that several of these disorders are being overdiagnosed: One estimate is that 10% of Americans have been diagnosed with a dissociative disorder (Loewenstein, 1994).

Renee Zellweger's character in the movie *Nurse Betty* has some symptoms of a dissociative fugue: After witnessing the brutal death of her husband, she abruptly leaves her job and has some difficulty remembering aspects of her past. She thinks she is the ex-fiancée of a character in a soap opera, but doesn't realize that he is from a television show.

## Dissociative Amnesia and Dissociative Fugue

One type of dissociative disorder is **dissociative amnesia**, marked by an inability to remember important personal information, usually about a traumatic or extremely stressful event; this inability to remember is often experienced as "gaps" in memory. A soldier who has seen several days of intense and brutal combat but then cannot remember much about the battlefield experience might be suffering from dissociative amnesia. In time, some people are able to recall the terrible memories; others may never remember, developing instead a chronic form of amnesia.

**Dissociative fugue** is another dissociative disorder, marked by an inability to remember some or all of the past, combined with abrupt, unexpected disappearances from home or work. The disturbed state of consciousness may last hours, days, or months; during this time, there are no obvious signs of a disorder, nor does the sufferer otherwise attract attention. People in a dissociative fugue may ultimately come to the attention of health care or law enforcement officials because of their loss of awareness of their identities. People suffering from this disorder do not usually create new identities for themselves. At any given point in time, only 0.2% of the American population experiences this disorder, but this rate may increase during times of war or large-scale natural disasters (American Psychiatric Association, 2000).

# Dissociative Identity Disorder

The most controversial dissociative disorder, estimated to affect 1% of the American population (Loewenstein, 1994), is **dissociative identity disorder (DID)**, a condition in which two or more distinct personalities take control of the individual's behavior. This disorder was formerly known as *multiple personality disorder* and attracted immense interest after it was portrayed in the movies *The Three Faces of Eve* (1958) and *Sybil* (1976). Each personality, or *alter*, may be experienced as if it had a distinct personal history, self-image, and identity, including a separate name, mannerisms, and way of talking. Not all alters know of the existence of the other alters, a circumstance that can lead to amnesia; however, research suggests that alters may be able to access certain memories (such as implicit memories) of other alters (Elzinga et al., 2003; Huntjens et al., 2005). The gaps in memory are substantial enough that they cannot be considered ordinary forgetfulness. People with dissociative identity disorder have been reported to have from 2 to 100 alters, although 10 or fewer are more commonly reported. Stress can trigger a transition to a different alter; this switch often occurs within seconds, although it can be more gradual.

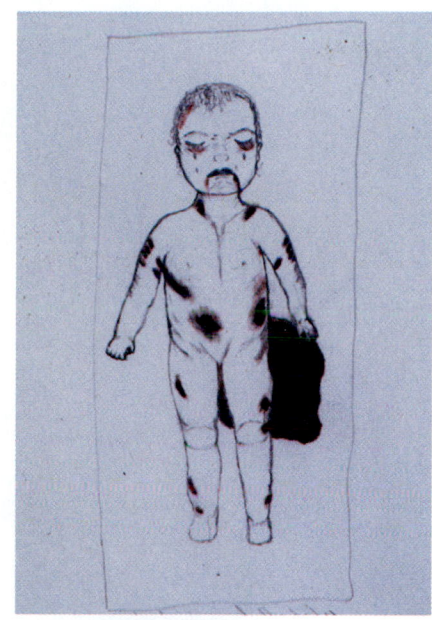

Wendy illustrates her experience with her trauma and dissociative identity disorder through her artwork. The drawing symbolizes a memory of being raped and severely beaten by her mother.

## DISSOCIATIVE IDENTITY DISORDER FROM THE INSIDE

Wendy's story captures the essence of DID:

> As a child, Wendy . . . had been physically and sexually abused as far back as she could remember . . . and there were hospital records of severe physical abuse . . . that occurred before Wendy was 2 years old. Wendy's mother was extremely sadistic and had tortured her regularly with extreme and violent means. For example, without any provocation, Wendy's mother would burn and cut her on various parts of her body. . . . Wendy had learned to rely on her hypnotic abilities to psychologically distance herself from her distressing memories and emotions. . . . Since childhood, Wendy had developed more than 20 distinct personalities! . . . Each of Wendy's personalities had its own distinct pattern of behaviors (e.g., speech, posture, mannerisms), perceived ages, sex, and appearance . . . each of Wendy's personalities possessed different physical reactions or different physical abilities. . . . By dividing things up this way, Wendy was able to have parts of herself that could contain the feelings and knowledge about the tortures and abuse that were going on at home and thereby still be able to have other parts of herself that could handle going to . . . work. (Brown & Barlow, 1997, pp. 102–108)

What might cause dissociative identity disorder? According to some researchers, most people who suffer from this disorder share two characteristics: They experienced severe and usually repeated physical abuse as young children (Ross et al., 1991), and they are very hypnotizable and can dissociate easily (Bliss, 1984; Frischholz, 1985). These two factors are related: Children who experience extreme abuse later report that they felt as though their minds temporarily left their bodies in order that they might endure the abuse. In other words, because of the severity of the situation, they dissociate. With continued abuse, and continued use of dissociation, the dissociated state develops its own memories, feelings, and thoughts, and becomes an alter (Putnam, 1989). This view is supported by work by Perry and his colleagues (1995), who found that young children who have been severely traumatized have a tendency to dissociate or to become hyperaroused in response to an aversive stimulus.

**Dissociative identity disorder (DID):** A disorder in which a person has two or more distinct personalities that take control of the individual's behavior.

There are reports that different alters have dissimilar EEG patterns, visual acuity, pain tolerance, symptoms of asthma, sensitivity to allergens, and response to insulin (American Psychiatric Association, 2000). However, such studies did not usually have an appropriate control group, which leaves open the question of whether alters have distinct biological abilities and responses (Merckelbach et al., 2002).

Some researchers and clinicians question whether dissociative identity disorder is a verifiably distinct diagnosis, because similar physiological differences occur when researchers ask participants who do *not* have symptoms of the disorder to role-play the condition (Coons et al., 1982). In fact, some researchers (Lilienfeld et al., 1999; Sarbin, 1995; Spanos, 1994) propose that DID is a form of role playing, which is the product of the beliefs and expectations of the therapist, who, without realizing it, induces patients to behave in ways consistent with the condition. Most people who are diagnosed with DID were not aware of their alters prior to being in therapy (Lilienfeld et al., 1999). However, researchers have found independent evidence of severe abuse histories in people diagnosed with DID (Lewis et al., 1997; Putnam, 1989; Swica et al., 1996). These same people had either amnesia for or scant memories of the abuse (Lewis et al., 1997; Swica et al., 1996) and evidenced signs of dissociation in childhood (Lewis et al., 1997), as would be expected from the theory of how DID develops. But there is some disagreement about how valid these studies are: The presence of abuse histories in patients does not rule out the possibility that their DID symptoms are shaped by cultural expectations and the therapist's behavior. Another question about the diagnosis of DID is whether, because of an overlap in symptoms, it should be considered a subtype of PTSD (Dell, 1998). Furthermore, other researchers note that a substantial percentage of people who are diagnosed with DID have symptoms that also meet the criteria for a particular personality disorder (Lilienfeld et al., 1999). Despite the debate about the origins and causes of dissociative identity disorder, we do know that severe trauma can lead to disruptions in consciousness and to other dissociative disorders and can have other adverse effects (Putnam, 1989; Putnam et al., 1995).

DID thus results from interacting events at the three levels: Severe trauma, cultural information about dissociative symptoms, and therapists' questions and responses (all events at the level of the group) lead to changes in bodily reactions such as hyperarousal (level of the brain) and the increased use of dissociation (level of the person). These various types of changes are likely to become chronic responses to stressors. Repeated and lengthy dissociations can become the building blocks for DID.

Could van Gogh's "attacks" have been episodes of dissociation? He once referred to his "evil self," but there is no evidence that he had any alters; and although he may have suffered some memory loss during his attacks, he could very well have been psychotic, not dissociative, at those times. Amnesia alone is not an indication of a dissociative disorder.

# Eating Disorders: You Are How You Eat?

Do you have a friend who's on a diet? If you do, the chances are that friend is a woman. Is her mood determined by the numbers on the scale? Does she want to lose more weight, even if she stops menstruating and others tell her she is too thin? If she eats more than she wants, does she feel that she must exercise, even if she's tired or sick? Is her view of herself on a given day dependent on whether she exercises that day? Does she eat as little as possible during the day, and then find herself "losing control" with food in the afternoon or evening? A "yes" response to these questions does not necessarily indicate the presence of a disorder, but it does indicate a preoccupation with food, body image, and weight. These preoccupations are typical of people with **eating disorders**, disorders involving severe disturbances in eating behavior. And although more than 90% of those diagnosed with eating disorders are females, males are increasingly suffering from these disorders, too.

## Anorexia Nervosa: You Can Be Too Thin

**Anorexia nervosa** is a potentially fatal eating disorder characterized by a refusal to maintain even a low normal weight. Someone with anorexia nervosa pursues thinness regardless of the physical consequences. Of those hospitalized with anorexia nervosa, 10% will eventually die of causes related to the disorder (American Psychiatric Association, 1994).

---

### ANOREXIA NERVOSA FROM THE INSIDE

People with anorexia nervosa develop irrational and unhealthy beliefs about food, as recounted by one woman:

> Yesterday . . . I had a grapefruit and black coffee for breakfast, and for dinner I had the . . . salad I eat every night. I always skip lunch. I had promised myself that I would only eat three-quarters of the salad since I've been feeling stuffed after it lately—but I think I ate more than the three-quarters. I know it was just lettuce and broccoli but I can't believe I did that. I was up all night worrying about getting fat. (Siegel et al., 1988, p. 17)

---

Included in the list of symptoms required for a diagnosis of anorexia nervosa are:

- distortions of how such people see their bodies ("body image"; see Figure 14.5),
- an intense fear of gaining weight or becoming fat,
- a refusal to maintain a healthy weight, and
- among females, *amenorrhea* (the cessation of menstruation).

It is common for extremely anorexic women to "know" that they are underweight, yet when they look in the mirror, they "see" fat that is not there, or generally overesti-

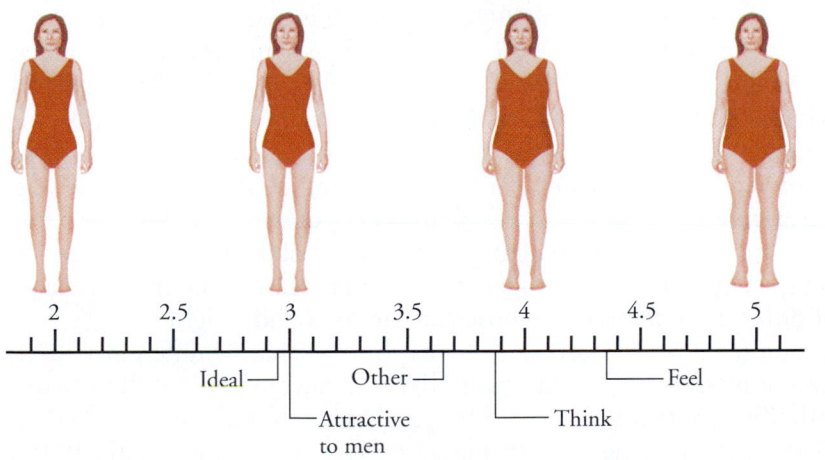

**FIGURE 14.5**

## Body Image Distortion

Many women, not only those with anorexia nervosa, have distorted body images. "Ideal" is the average of women's ratings of the ideal figure. "Attractive to men" is the average rating of the figure women believe is most attractive to men. "Other" is the average actual selection of the female figure that men find most attractive. "Think" is the average figure women think best matches their figure. "Feel" is the average figure women feel best matches their figure.

Cultural pressure on women to be thin and to attain an "ideal" body shape can contribute to eating disorders. Such pressure explains why there is a higher incidence of eating disorders now than 50 years ago, as the ideal figure has changed from the generous proportions of Marilyn Monroe to the rail-thin silhouette of today's runway models (Andersen & DiDomenico, 1992; Field et al., 1999; Nemeroff et al., 1994).

Bulimia nervosa: An eating disorder characterized by recurrent episodes of binge eating, followed by some attempt to prevent weight gain.

mate their body size (Smeets et al., 1997). They are often obsessed by thoughts of food, and these thoughts are usually based on irrational or illogical thinking (such as what are "good" and "bad" foods). They often deny that their low weight is a problem, or even that they have a problem. Some symptoms of anorexia nervosa differ from culture to culture. For example, half of young Chinese women with this disorder do not have the fear of being fat common among North Americans, but explain their restricted diet as a distaste for food or bodily discomfort when eating (Lee, 1996).

Some, but not all, people with anorexia nervosa periodically engage in *binge eating* (eating substantially more food within a certain time period than most people would eat in similar circumstances) or *purging* (getting rid of unwanted calories through vomiting or the misuse of laxatives, diuretics, or enemas), or both. Thus, there are two types of anorexia nervosa: the *binge-eating/purging type* and the classic *restricting type*, in which weight loss is achieved primarily by undereating, without purging.

## Bulimia Nervosa

People with bulimia nervosa, like those with anorexia nervosa, are usually women, but they may be of normal weight or even overweight, and thus they continue to menstruate. **Bulimia nervosa** is marked by recurrent episodes of binge eating, followed by an attempt to prevent weight gain. When that attempt is made through purging (by vomiting or with the use of laxatives), the diagnosis of bulimia nervosa is further specified as *purging type*. Attempts to restrict weight gain may also occur through other methods, such as fasting or excessive exercise, and when this is the case, the disorder is the *non-purging type*.

Some people with bulimia purge even when their eating does not constitute a binge: "If I had *one* bite of bread, just one, I felt as though I blew it! I'd stop listening to whomever was talking to me at the table. I'd start thinking, *How can I get rid of this?* I'd worry about how fat I'd look, how I couldn't fit into my clothes. My head would be flooded with thoughts of what to do now. . . . I had to undo what I'd done. The night was blown. I was a mess" (Siegel et al., 1988, p. 18). Although most people with bulimia do not realize it, in the long run, purging does not usually eliminate all the calories ingested and is, in fact, a poor method for losing weight (Garner, 1997).

## Explaining Eating Disorders

Why do people, most often women, develop eating disorders?

**LEVEL OF THE BRAIN IN EATING DISORDERS**   There is evidence of a genetic predisposition for anorexia. In one study, 56% of identical co-twins were likely to have anorexia if their twins did, compared to 5% of co-twins of affected fraternal twins (Holland et al., 1988). Moreover, another study found that relatives of those with anorexia nervosa had a higher incidence of obsessive-compulsive symptoms than did relatives of people with bulimia nervosa or control participants. This finding suggests that obsessive personality traits in a family may increase the risk for anorexia nervosa (Lilenfeld et al., 1998). However, learning (resulting in changes at the level of the person) can also account for this finding: People with obsessional relatives may learn to be obsessional; those with eating disorders have focused the obsession on food and weight.

The data for bulimia nervosa in twins shows a sharply different pattern: Twenty-three percent of identical co-twins were likely to have bulimia if their twins did, compared with 9% of co-twins of affected fraternal twins (Kendler et al., 1991). In bulimia, the environment, not genes, clearly plays the larger role (Wade et al., 1998).

As was shown by the study by Keys and colleagues (1950; see the section on dieting in Chapter 10), decreased caloric intake leads to pathological behaviors, and symptoms of eating disorders. The malnutrition and weight loss that occur with anorexia nervosa lead to changes in neurotransmitters, particularly serotonin. This neurotransmitter is also involved in obsessive-compulsive disorder, and the obsessional thinking about food and pathological eating behavior of anorexia are hypothesized to be related to alterations in serotonergic functioning (Barbarich, 2002; Kaye, 1995). Because one effect of serotonin is to create a feeling of satiety (Halmi, 1996), lower levels of serotonin may be a predisposing factor for bulimia nervosa (Pirke, 1995). The biological effects of dieting may also make women vulnerable to developing bulimia nervosa: Some, though not all, studies indicate that dieting sometimes precedes the onset of bulimia in some people (Garner, 1997). Although the research points to abnormalities or dysregulation of neurotransmitters as being involved in eating disorders, it is as yet unclear how the changes in different neurotransmitters are related; nor is it known whether these changes *precede* the development of an eating disorder, and thus may create a susceptibility to it, or instead are *consequences* of an eating disorder (Halmi, 1995).

**LEVEL OF THE PERSON IN EATING DISORDERS**   Numerous personal characteristics have been linked with eating disorders. An increased risk of developing anorexia occurs among women who are perfectionists and have a negative evaluation of themselves (Bulik et al., 2003; Fairburn et al., 1999; Tyrka et al., 2002). More generally, people with eating disorders often exhibit irrational beliefs and inappropriate expectations about their bodies, jobs, relationships, and themselves (Fairburn et al., 2003; Garfinkel et al., 1992; Striegel-Moore, 1993). They tend to engage in dichotomous, black-or-white thinking: Fruit is "good"; pizza is "bad." Moreover, as shown in Figure 14.6, when examining photographs of themselves, these women spend more time looking at their "ugly" body parts than at their "beautiful" parts; in contrast, when they look at photos of other women, they spend more time looking at those women's "beautiful" body parts than at their "ugly" parts. Women who do not have an eating disorder devote equal time to looking at their own "beautiful" and "ugly" parts, and when looking at photos of other women, spend more time looking at their "ugly" parts than at their "beautiful" parts (Jansen et al., 2005).

Perhaps people with these personality characteristics, irrational beliefs, and inappropriate expectations are especially likely to find rewards in the behaviors associated with eating disorders. Preoccupations with food can provide distractions from work, family conflicts, or social problems. By restricting their eating, people may gain a sense of increased control—over food and over life in general—although such feelings of mastery are often short-lived as the disease takes over (Garner, 1997). By purging, people with an eating disorder may relieve the anxiety created by overeating.

**LEVEL OF THE GROUP IN EATING DISORDERS**   The family and the larger culture also play important roles in the development of eating disorders. They may contribute to these disorders by encouraging a preoccupation with weight and appearance (Crowther et al., 2002; Thompson & Stice, 2001). Children have an increased risk of developing eating disorders if their families are overly concerned about appearance and weight (Strober, 1995). Symptoms of eating disorders increase among immigrants from less weight-conscious cultures (such as the Chinese and the Egyptian) as they assimilate to American culture (Bilukha & Utermohlen, 2002; Dolan, 1991; Lee & Lee, 1996), although not all studies find this (Abdollahi & Mann, 2001). One prospective study in Fiji found that, with the advent of television (and Western television shows) in that country in 1995, Fijian girls' feelings about their bodies began to shift: Whereas before watching Western television shows, they felt comfortable having a large body—the

### FIGURE 14.6

## Gazing at Body Parts: Women With and Without Eating Disorders

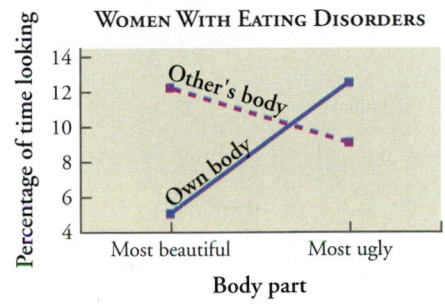

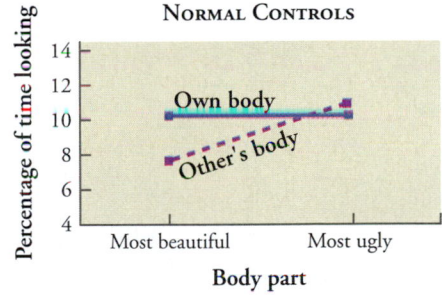

Women with eating disorders spend more time looking at their "most ugly" body parts than at their "most beautiful" parts; women without eating disorders spend equal amounts of time looking at both types of their own body parts. When looking at photos of other women, those with eating disorders look at the "most beautiful" parts more than the "most ugly" parts, and this pattern is reversed for women who do not have eating disorders (Jansen et al., 2005).

ideal body shape in their culture—after viewing such shows, 75% of girls felt too fat or big at least some of the time (Becker et al., 2002). It is not only females who are susceptible: Eating disorders are increasing among men who regularly take part in appearance- or weight-conscious activities, such as modeling and wrestling (Brownell & Rodin, 1992).

Among U.S. women, the focus on appearance and weight may derive from a desire to meet the culture's ideal of femininity (Striegel-Moore, 1993). Westernization (or modernization) increases dieting (Gunewardene et al., 2001; Lee & Lee, 2000), a risk factor for developing eating disorders. Culture also plays a role by promoting the idea that body shape can be changed and by determining the rationales people offer for their symptoms (Becker & Hamburg, 1996).

# LOOKING AT LEVELS
## Binge Eating

You have learned what eating disorders are and explanations of why they might occur. Let's consider in detail a core aspect of bulimia nervosa—binge eating. Why do some people chronically binge eat?

At the level of the brain, food restriction is a contributor to binge eating (Nakai et al., 2001; Polivy & Herman, 1993; Stice et al., 2002). In their efforts to be "in control" of food, people with bulimia generally consume fewer calories at nonbinge meals than do nonbulimics, thus setting the stage for later binge eating because they are hungry and have food cravings (Walsh, 1993); the bingeing is thus reinforced. A binge/purge episode may be followed by an endorphin rush (and the ensuing positive feelings that it creates), further reinforcing the binge/purge cycle. As one woman with bulimia reported, "I go to never-never land. Once I start bingeing, it's like being in a stupor, like being drunk . . . I'm like a different person. It's very humiliating—but not then, not while I'm eating. While I'm eating, nothing else matters" (Siegel et al., 1988, p. 20).

At the level of the person, the dichotomous thinking typical of people with eating disorders leads them to view themselves as either "good" (when dieting or restricting food intake) or "bad" (eating "forbidden foods" or feeling out of control while eating). This thinking sets the stage for bingeing if any small amount of forbidden food is eaten; a bite of a candy bar is followed by a thought like this: "Well, I shouldn't have eaten *any* of the candy bar, but since I did, I might as well eat the whole thing, especially since I really shouldn't have a candy bar again." This line of reasoning is part of the *abstinence violation effect* (Polivy & Herman, 1993; Urbszat et al., 2002), the sense of letting go of self-restraint after transgressing a self-imposed rule about food: Once you violate the rule, why not go all the way? In addition, purging is negatively reinforcing (remember, negative reinforcement is reinforcement, not punishment; see Chapter 6): Eating too much, or eating forbidden foods, can cause anxiety, which is then relieved by purging. This reinforcement then increases the likelihood of purging in the future.

At the level of the group, if social interactions are stressful, then bingeing and purging, which are usually done alone, are reinforced by the isolation they provide. Such behaviors further serve to increase the affected person's sense of isolation and decrease his or her social interactions.

Events at the different levels interact: Cultural pressure to be thin or to eat small meals leads vulnerable individuals to try to curb their food intake. The hunger caused by this undereating may trigger a binge. The binge may also be triggered by stress, social interactions, negative affect, or viewing one's appearance as very important (Polivy & Herman, 1993; Stice et al.,

2002; Vanderlinden et al., 2001); bingeing can then create positive changes (such as decreased hunger, distraction from an uncomfortable feeling or thought, and removal from difficult social interactions). This immediate reinforcement often outweighs the negative consequences that are experienced later.

Van Gogh had abnormal eating habits; could he have had an eating disorder? It is unlikely; although van Gogh often ate sparingly and peculiarly, he did not appear to be preoccupied with weight gain or body image, and no information suggests that he purged in any way.

# Test Yourself

1. Dissociative disorders involve the disruption of some aspect of integrated functioning. Dissociative fugue usually involves
   a. creation of a new identity.
   b. severe depression.
   c. hallucinations.
   d. travel to a new area.
2. Which characteristic do people who suffer from dissociative identity disorder tend to share?
   a. They have experimented with drugs.
   b. They have a family history of the disorder.
   c. They suffered severe abuse as children.
   d. They are likely to be a twin.
3. What symptom do females with anorexia nervosa experience that males with the disorder do not?
   a. intense fear of becoming fat
   b. amenorrhea
   c. refusal to maintain a normal weight
   d. distortion of body image

4. Why do people with bulimia continue to binge eat when they know that it is unhealthy?
   a. Their hypothalamus does not function normally, and consequently they do not ever feel full.
   b. The immediate reinforcement overshadows the negative consequences that they are likely to experience later.
   c. They are intentionally trying to hurt themselves.
   d. Their unconscious motivation to eat is too strong to be overcome more than once a day.

## Answers

1. d 2. c 3. b 4. b

# Think It Through!

If a friend began eating less and lost weight, what else would you want to know before concluding that she might have an eating disorder? If she confessed to you that she sometimes didn't "feel like herself" anymore, that she wasn't sure who she "really was," might you suspect she had a dissociative disorder? Why or why not?

# PERSONALITY DISORDERS

By now, it should come as no surprise to know that van Gogh was more than just unconventional; his difficulties in life went beyond his attacks, his hallucinations, and his periods of depression. Van Gogh's relationships with other people were troubled, and they often followed a pattern: Initial positive feelings and excitement about someone new in his life (such as happened with Gauguin and Sien) were invariably followed by a turbulent phase and an eventual falling out. Throughout his life, he had emotional outbursts that sooner or later caused others to withdraw their friendship. His relationship with his brother Theo is the only one that endured. Does such a pattern suggest that he may have had a personality disorder?

# Axis II Personality Disorders

Axis II of the *DSM-IV* allows the possibility of a **personality disorder**, which is a set of relatively stable personality traits that are inflexible and maladaptive, causing distress or difficulty with daily functioning. A personality disorder may occur alone, or it may be accompanied by an Axis I disorder.

Whereas Axis I symptoms—those discussed up to this point in the chapter—feel as if they are inflicted from the outside, the maladaptive traits of Axis II are often experienced as parts of the person's personality. The maladaptive traits of personality disorders cause distress or difficulty with daily functioning in school, work, social life, or relationships. They can be so subtle as to be unnoticeable in a brief encounter. It is only after getting to know the person over time that a personality disorder may become evident.

As shown in Table 14.9, *DSM-IV* organizes personality disorders into three clusters, with each grouping based on common symptoms:

- Cluster A—odd, eccentric behaviors
- Cluster B—emotional or dramatic behaviors
- Cluster C—anxious or fearful behaviors or symptoms

## TABLE 14.9  Axis II Personality Disorders

| Disorder | Description |
| --- | --- |
| **Cluster A** | |
| **Paranoid personality disorder** | A pattern of suspiciousness and distrust of others to the extent that other people's motives are interpreted as ill-intentioned. However, unlike the paranoid subtype of schizophrenia, there are no delusions or hallucinations. |
| **Schizoid personality disorder** | A pattern of detachment from social relationships and a narrow range of displayed emotion. |
| **Schizotypal personality disorder** | A pattern of extreme discomfort in close relationships, odd or quirky behavior, and cognitive or perceptual distortions (such as sensing the presence of another person or spirit). |
| **Cluster B** | |
| **Antisocial personality disorder** | A pattern of disregard or violation of the rights of others. |
| **Borderline personality disorder** | A pattern of instability in relationships, self-image, and feelings, and pronounced impulsivity (such as in spending, substance abuse, sex, reckless driving, or binge eating). Relationships are often characterized by rapid swings from idealizing another person to devaluing him or her. Recurrent suicidal gestures, threats, or self-mutilation, such as nonlethal cuts on the arm are common, as are chronic feelings of emptiness. |
| **Histrionic personality disorder** | A pattern of excessive attention seeking and expression of emotion. |
| **Narcissistic personality disorder** | A pattern of an exaggerated sense of self-importance, need for admiration, and lack of empathy. |
| **Cluster C** | |
| **Avoidant personality disorder** | A pattern of social discomfort, feelings of inadequacy, and hypersensitivity to negative evaluation. |
| **Dependent personality disorder** | A pattern of clingy, submissive behavior due to an extreme need to be taken care of. |
| **Obsessive-compulsive personality disorder** | A pattern of preoccupation with perfectionism, orderliness, and control (but no obsessions or compulsions, as occur with obsessive-compulsive disorder). |

However, these clusters were not derived from research, but rather because personality disorders within a cluster appeared to have common elements (Livesley, 2001).

Some researchers argue that the combinations of traits now defined as personality disorders should not be called "disorders" at all. Doing so, they contend, either treats normal variations in personality as pathological or creates separate Axis II categories for conditions that could be part of an Axis I clinical disorder (Hyman, personal communication, 1998; Livesley, 1998). For example, the clinging, submissive behavior that *DSM-IV* categorizes as part of the dependent personality disorder of Axis II might also characterize a personality that is within the normal range. And the symptoms of avoidant personality disorder overlap those of Axis I's social phobia—only the greater severity of the anxiety and the presence of depressive symptoms in avoidant personality disorder distinguish it from social phobia (Johnson & Lydiard, 1995); the two disorders are quantitatively, not qualitatively, different. Thus, some personality disorders can be thought of as less severe versions of Axis I disorders.

Other researchers argue that each personality disorder is not a research-validated disorder distinct from all others (Atre-Vaidya & Hussain, 1999; Horowitz, 1998). Furthermore, the criteria for the various personality disorders do not all require the same level of dysfunction. Thus, a lesser—and, in some cases, quite mild—degree of impairment is required for a diagnosis of obsessive-compulsive, antisocial, or paranoid personality disorders (Funtowicz & Widiger, 1999).

From what is known about his life, it is not impossible that van Gogh had a personality disorder; but we have no way of knowing if he, in fact, met all of the criteria.

**Antisocial personality disorder (ASPD):** A personality disorder characterized by a long-standing pattern of disregard for other people to the point of violating their rights.

# Antisocial Personality Disorder

The most intensively studied personality disorder is **antisocial personality disorder (ASPD)**, evidenced by a long-standing pattern of disregard for others to the point of violating their rights (American Psychiatric Association, 2000). Symptoms include a superficial charm; egocentrism; impulsive, reckless, and deceitful behavior without regard for others' safety; a tendency to blame others for any adversity that comes their way; and a lack of conscience, empathy, and remorse. People with this disorder talk a good line and know how to manipulate others, but they don't have the capacity to know or care how another person feels.

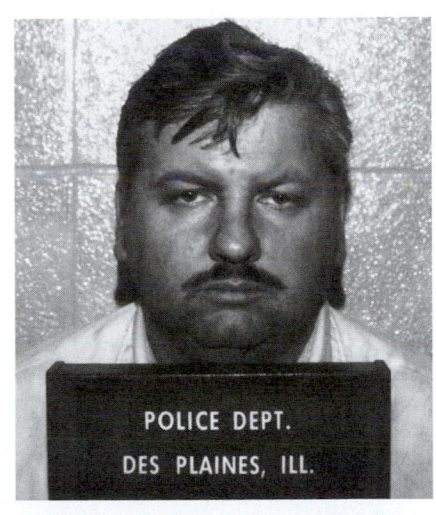

John Wayne Gacy, convicted serial killer, saw himself as a victim; he shared this feature with other people who have antisocial personality disorder.

> ### ANTISOCIAL PERSONALITY DISORDER FROM THE INSIDE
>
> A common feature among people with ASPD is that they see *themselves* as the real victims. While discussing the many and horrible murders he had committed, John Wayne Gacy portrayed himself as the 34th victim:
>
> I was made an asshole and a scapegoat . . . when I look back, I see myself more as a victim than a perpetrator. . . . I was the victim; I was cheated out of my childhood. . . . [He wondered whether] there would be someone, somewhere who would understand how badly it had hurt to be John Wayne Gacy. (Hare, 1993, p. 43)

Antisocial personality disorder occurs three times more frequently in men than in women, and although only 1–2% of Americans are diagnosed with this disorder, 60% of males in U.S. prisons are estimated to have it (Moran, 1999). Cross-cultural studies have found a similar pattern of symptoms in both Western and non-Western cultures

(Zoccolillo et al., 1999). Many people diagnosed with antisocial personality disorder also abuse alcohol and other drugs (Nigg & Goldsmith, 1994).

# Understanding Antisocial Personality Disorder

What causes antisocial personality disorder? As you've seen for other psychological disorders, this one is best understood by examining events at the three levels of analysis and their interactions.

## Level of the Brain in Antisocial Personality Disorder

Evidence for the contribution of biological factors (level of the brain) arises from a number of sources. Some of the data on antisocial personality disorder come from studies of certain types of criminal behavior patterns, which are related to some of the symptoms of antisocial personality disorder. These data show that the disorder runs in families (Nigg & Goldsmith, 1994). Moreover, adoption studies show that environment matters only if a child's biological parents were criminals; if they were, there was a slight increase in criminal behavior for boys adopted into a family of law-abiding people, but there was a whopping increase in criminal behavior if they were adopted into a family of criminals. If the biological parents were not criminals, the adopted child's later criminal behavior was the same whether he or she grew up in a law-abiding or criminal family (Mednick et al., 1984). Criminal behavior provides a clear example of how genes and environment can interact: The genes predispose; the environment triggers.

Genes may produce a relatively underresponsive central and autonomic nervous system. In turn, this might lead people with such genes to seek out highly arousing, thrilling activities (Quay, 1965).

## Level of the Person in Antisocial Personality Disorder

Research suggests that people with antisocial personality disorder have difficulty controlling their impulses and modulating their anger (Zlotnick, 1999). In addition, they have difficulty understanding how others feel, which engenders a lack of empathy (Kagan & Reid, 1986).

## Level of the Group in Antisocial Personality Disorder

People with this personality disorder may not bond appropriately with their parents. Perhaps it is because, as children, they often experienced or witnessed abuse, deviant behavior, or lack of concern for the welfare of others by peers, parents, or others (Gabbard, 1990; Patterson, 1986; Patterson et al., 1989; Pollock et al., 1990). The behaviors of models who lack basic regard for others may later be imitated (Elliott et al., 1985).

## Interacting Levels in Antisocial Personality Disorder

How might events at these levels of analysis interact? To begin with, a depressed central and autonomic nervous system (level of the brain) might leave people who develop antisocial personality disorder relatively unaffected by social rejection or mild punishment. In other words, when people have an underresponsive nervous system, the normal social and legal consequences of inappropriate behavior might not make them feel anxious (level of the person). However, a moderate level of arousal is optimal for performance (see Chapter 10). Together, these consequences of an underresponsive nervous system might produce another important result—difficulty in learning to control impulses (level of the person). In fact, Schachter and Latané (1964) found that such people have difficulty learning to avoid shocks. But when they are injected with adrenaline so that their level of arousal is increased, they learn to avoid shocks at the same rate as other people. This underresponsiveness of the nervous system may also be related to poor parental bonding, since normal stimulation provided by parents may not be enough to engage these infants. Moreover, as these individuals grow up, learning antisocial behavior from others in the immediate environment may be arousing enough to hold their interest and increase their learning (level of the person), which creates a vicious cycle. In addition, their underresponsiveness may have *caused* their caregivers to treat them differently (level of the group).

# Test Yourself

1. People with personality disorders have personality traits that are
   a. extremely bizarre.
   b. inflexible.
   c. always changing.
   d. stressful to them.

2. Personality disorders are sometimes difficult to diagnose because
   a. the problematic traits may only be revealed over time and not in the context of a diagnostic interview.
   b. the patients' personalities keep changing, leading to different diagnoses.
   c. people with personality disorders fake many other types of personality traits.
   d. Axis II of the *DSM-IV* is difficult to interpret.

3. Individuals with antisocial personality disorder are often very charming. Why then is the disorder called antisocial?
   a. These individuals often kill others, but then feel terrible remorse.
   b. These individuals have no personal conscience, but they do have a social conscience.
   c. These individuals generally are recluses and avoid social contacts.
   d. These individuals often violate the social rights of others.

4. Are antisocial personality disorder and criminality biological or environmentally determined?
   a. The way someone is raised completely determines whether they will engage in criminal behavior.
   b. The environment has very little to do with criminal behavior.
   c. People choose to commit crimes and become antisocial, so neither influence is important.
   d. For those with a biological vulnerability, the environment can influence whether they develop criminal behavior.

## Answers

1. b  2. a  3. d  4. d

# Think It Through!

At first, your new neighbor seemed like a really nice guy—then you got to know him better. Weeks ago he borrowed money because of an "emergency," but he never repaid you. When you ask for your money back, he always has an excuse. Whenever friends come by to see you, he seems to make a point of sticking his head out the door and charming your visitors. You become increasingly frustrated because your friends can't understand why you keep complaining about him. Would you suspect that antisocial personality disorder might be in the picture? Why? If you knew that a mental health clinician had diagnosed him as having antisocial personality disorder, what could you infer about his family history? What should you *not* infer?

# A CAUTIONARY NOTE ABOUT DIAGNOSIS

The events of van Gogh's life present an opportunity to explore the ways in which the human psyche can be troubled and the ways in which the mental health field presently classifies disorders. But that is not the same as proposing a diagnosis of someone who, while in art is very close to us, is in his person very distant in time.

No mental health clinician can really know with certainty from what, if any, specific disorder van Gogh suffered. Major depressive disorder and schizophrenia are possibilities, as is bipolar disorder (Jamison, 1993). Alternatively, his "attacks" and hallucinations might have been due to delirium tremens (DTs), caused by withdrawal from alcohol (see Chapter 5); but such a diagnosis would not explain why van Gogh had attacks even during lengthy periods of sobriety (Lubin, 1972). Possibly he suffered from a form of epilepsy, and his attacks were seizures; before epileptic seizures, victims are sometimes overcome with religious feelings and delusions. The possibility of epilepsy, a neurological disorder not a psychological one, points to the importance of ensuring that a patient does not have a medical disorder that can cause psychological symptoms. Only after ruling out medical illnesses can the mental health clinician or researcher have confidence in a diagnosis of a psychological disorder.

Similarly, it may be tempting to use the knowledge you acquired in this chapter to diagnose friends, family members, or yourself, However, the information in this chapter is only a brief introduction to the topic of psychological disorders. The ability to diagnose accurately requires detailed knowledge and extensive training. You would undoubtedly not consider yourself qualified to diagnose a neuropsychological problem after reading about the brain in Chapter 3 or to diagnose a memory problem after reading Chapter 8. If you suspect that you or someone close to you may have a psychological disorder, consult with a mental health clinician. Information about finding a mental health clinician, and about treatments for psychological disorders, is discussed in the following chapter.

# REVIEW AND REMEMBER!

## Summary

### I. Identifying Psychological Disorders: What's Abnormal?

**A.** A psychological disorder is signaled by a constellation of cognitive, emotional, and behavioral symptoms that create significant distress, impairment, and danger.

**B.** Behaviors that are merely deviant from the mainstream culture are not considered to be "disordered."

**C.** Psychological disorders are best understood as arising from the interactions of events at the levels of the brain, the person, and the group.

## Your Notes

I.

A.

B.

C.

**D.** The catalog of psychiatric disorders in the *DSM-IV* distinguishes among disorders on the basis of the symptoms exhibited or reported and the reported history of the symptoms. The *DSM-IV* includes both clinical and personality disorders.

*D. Axis I = clinical disorders*
*Axis II = personality disorders*

## II. Mood Disorders

**A.** Major depressive disorder (MDD) is characterized by depressed mood and loss of interest or pleasure, along with sleep or eating disturbances, loss of energy, and feelings of hopelessness.

**B.** Dysthymia is a less intense, but longer-lasting type of depression.

**C.** Bipolar disorder involves episodes of mania or hypomania, which may or may not alternate with depression.

**D.** Some people are biologically vulnerable to developing these disorders; further, neurotransmitters are implicated in both major depressive disorder and bipolar disorder, although the exact mechanisms of their influence are not yet understood.

**E.** People's worldviews, thought patterns, and attributional styles, such as the negative triad of depression, also play a role in the development of major depressive disorder. Learned helplessness can also contribute to depression.

**F.** Operant conditioning and the available rewards or punishments in the environment also may be related to the development of depression, and life stressors are associated with the first episode of depression and with the severity of the disorder.

**G.** Women in developed countries experience depression more often than do men. This difference may occur because, as children, girls are taught to be introspective and not to take action. As women, such rumination may promote depression.

**H.** Depressed people, through their actions, may inadvertently alienate others, who then reject those depressed people, who, in turn, view the rejection as confirmation of their negative views.

**I.** The rate of occurrence of bipolar disorder is increasing, and it is affecting people at earlier ages.

## III. Anxiety Disorders

**A.** Anxiety disorders include panic disorder, specific and social phobias, obsessive-compulsive disorder (OCD), and posttraumatic stress disorder (PTSD).

**B.** People with panic disorder may avoid places or activities in order to minimize the possibility of additional panic attacks; when such avoidance restricts daily life, it is referred to as agoraphobia.

**C.** People can inherit a biological vulnerability for panic. Moreover, an anxiety sensitivity can increase the risk for panic disorder, as can a misinterpretation of certain bodily sensations.

**D.** People can be biologically vulnerable to developing both social and specific phobias. Although learning can also contribute, it is unclear to what extent it does so.

*II.*
*A.*
*B.*
*C.*
*D.*
*E.*
*F.*
*G.*
*H.*
*I.*
*III.*
*A.*
*B.*
*C.*
*D.*

**E.** Neutral activity in the caudate nucleus is related to OCD. Compulsions may momentarily relieve the anxiety that obsessions cause, operantly reinforcing the compulsions.

**F.** Not everyone who experiences a traumatic event goes on to develop PTSD. The type of trauma, the response to it, and other factors can increase or decease the risk of developing PTSD.

## IV. Schizophrenia

**A.** Schizophrenia involves a markedly restricted range of affect, odd or disorganized thoughts, delusions or hallucinations, and behaviors; it is characterized by positive and negative symptoms.

**B.** The *DSM-IV* specifies four subtypes of schizophrenia: paranoid, disorganized, catatonic, and undifferentiated, each with a different set of symptoms and prognosis.

**C.** Research findings on schizophrenia point to genetic and biological abnormalities in those affected. These abnormalities include enlarged ventricles and a decrease in the frontal cortex. Such abnormalities may arise during fetal development and may arise from maternal illness or malnutrition during pregnancy and prenatal or birth-related complications.

**D.** Children at risk for schizophrenia show extreme discomfort with close relationships, exhibit high levels of odd or quirky behavior, are more reactive to stress, and have higher baseline levels of cortisol.

**E.** Those with schizophrenia who have high expressed emotion families are more likely to suffer a recurrence. However, this finding is only a correlation.

**F.** Social selection and social causation are factors that may account for the higher rates of schizophrenia in urban areas and in lower socioeconomic classes.

## V. Other Axis I Disorders: Dissociative and Eating Disorders

**A.** Dissociative disorders are characterized by identity confusion, derealization, depersonalization, and amnesia.

**B.** Trauma or severe stress influences the development of these disorders.

**C.** Types of dissociative disorders are dissociative amnesia, dissociative fugue, and dissociative identity disorder (DID).

**D.** People with DID experienced severe (and usually repeated) physical abuse as young children. They are also very hypnotizable and can dissociate easily.

**E.** DID symptoms may be shaped by cultural expectations and therapists' behavior.

**F.** Eating disorders (anorexia nervosa and bulimia nervosa) are characterized by preoccupations with weight and body image, as well as abnormal eating (such as restriction, binges, and purges).

**G.** Symptoms of anorexia nervosa include a refusal to maintain a healthy weight, a fear of becoming fat, a disturbed body image, and amenorrhea (in women).

**H.** Symptoms of bulimia include recurrent binge eating episodes, followed by an attempt to prevent weight gain.

| Notes |
|---|
| *E.* |
| *F. PTSD: With severe trauma, other factors don't matter as much.* |
| *IV.* |
| *A.* |
| *B. Paranoid subtype—best prognosis* |
| *C.* |
| *D.* |
| *E.* |
| *F.* |
| *V.* |
| *A.* |
| *B.* |
| *C.* |
| *D.* |
| *E.* |
| *F.* |
| *G.* |
| *H.* |

**I.** Genetic factors are more influential in the development of anorexia nervosa than of bulimia nervosa, and environmental factors, specifically the cultural emphasis on thinness, affect the development of both eating disorders.

*I.*

**J.** Biological factors related to dieting (food restriction) and binge eating can also lead to the development of an eating disorder.

*J. Abstinence violation effect → bingeing*

## VI. Personality Disorders

*VI.*

**A.** Personality disorders are sets of inflexible and maladaptive personality traits that cause distress or difficulty in work, school, or in other social spheres.

*A.*

**B.** Such traits may be unnoticeable in a brief encounter and may only reveal themselves over time.

*B.*

**C.** In contrast to Axis I disorders, which seem to the sufferer to be inflicted from the outside, personality disorders, which are on Axis II, are experienced as part of the personality itself.

*C.*

**D.** Antisocial personality disorder is the most intensively studied personality disorder; the key symptom is a long-standing pattern of disregard for others to the point of violating their rights.

*D.*

**E.** Antisocial personality has a biological basis, perhaps an underresponsive central and autonomic nervous system.

*E.*

**F.** For those who are biologically vulnerable, the environment in which they are raised can influence whether they later develop criminal behavior.

*F.*

NOTE: Once you feel that you understand the material in this chapter, visit the book's Web site at www.ablongman.com/kosslyn3e to test your knowledge with additional study questions.

## Key Terms

agoraphobia, p. 649
anorexia nervosa, p. 671
antisocial personality disorder (ASPD), p. 677
anxiety disorders, p. 648
attributional style, p. 644
bipolar disorder, p. 642
bulimia nervosa, p. 672
compulsion, p. 653
delusions, p. 632
diathesis–stress model, p. 633
dissociative amnesia, p. 668
dissociative disorders, p. 668
dissociative fugue, p. 668
dissociative identity disorder (DID), p. 669

dysthymia, p. 642
eating disorders, p. 671
generalized anxiety disorder, p. 648
hallucinations, p. 632
high expressed emotion, p. 665
hypomania, p. 642
manic episode, p. 642
major depressive disorder (MDD), p. 638
mood disorders, p. 638
negative symptom, p. 660
obsession, p. 653
obsessive-compulsive disorder (OCD), p. 653

panic attack, p. 648
panic disorder, p. 648
personality disorders, p. 676
phobia, p. 651
positive symptom, p. 660
posttraumatic stress disorder (PTSD), p. 655
psychological disorder, p. 630
psychosis, p. 632
schizophrenia, p. 659
social causation, p. 665
social phobia, p. 651
social selection, p. 665
specific phobia, p. 651

# CHAPTER 15

# TREATMENT: HEALING ACTIONS, HEALING WORDS

At 2 a.m., Beth sat hunched over her textbook and notes, studying for her midterm. Concentration was difficult; she had to struggle to make sense of the words before her eyes. She'd read the same page four times and still couldn't remember what it said. She tried to give herself a pep talk ("Okay, Beth, read it one more time, and then you'll understand it"), but her upbeat words would be drowned out by a different, negative internal monologue (*"Well, Beth, you've really screwed yourself, and there's no way out of it now. You're going to fail, get kicked out of school, never be employed, end up destitute, homeless, hopeless, talking to yourself on the street"*).

Beth was 21 years old, a junior in college. She'd already had to walk out of two exams because she couldn't answer most of the questions, although she had understood the material earlier. Her thoughts had been jumbled, and she'd had a hard time organizing her answers to the questions. She'd always been nervous before a test or class presentation, but this year her anxiety had spun out of control. Taking the first quiz of the semester, she simply drew a blank when she tried to answer the questions.

Since then, she'd become more anxious, and depressed as well. With each quiz she couldn't finish, with each paper that required more concentration than she could summon, she felt herself spiraling downward, helpless. She had no hope that the situation would change by itself, and no amount of good intentions or resolutions or even effort made a difference. She began cutting classes and spent much of her time in bed; she had no interest in doing anything with her friends because she felt she didn't deserve to have fun. She'd put off saying anything to her professors; at first she figured things would get better, and then she was too embarrassed to face them. But she knew that eventually she'd have to talk to them or else she'd definitely fail her courses.

She finally did talk to her professors. Several of them suggested that she seek treatment, or at least go to the campus counseling center, but she didn't want to do that. Taking that step, she felt, would be admitting to herself and to the world not only that something was wrong with her, but also that she was too weak to deal with it herself.

Beth was reluctant to seek help partly because when she was growing up, her mother had experienced bouts of depression severe enough to require hospitalization several times. Beth recognized that she, too, was becoming depressed, and she was afraid that if she went to see a therapist, she'd end up in the hospital.

Finally, Beth confided in a family friend, Nina, who had been the school nurse at Beth's elementary school. Nina told Beth that people with problems like hers often felt much better after psychotherapy and that her problems were not severe enough to warrant hospitalization. She also pointed out that there were many forms of therapy available to Beth that were not as readily available to her mother 20 years earlier. Modern treatments, Nina said, ranged from psychologically based approaches, such as cognitive and behavioral therapies, to biologically based treatments such as medication. Research has revealed that, for a given problem, some treatments may be more effective than others, and for Beth's problems, there were a number of potentially helpful treatments. Beth agreed to see a therapist, but didn't know where to begin to find one. The campus counseling center could be useful, Nina said, but Beth might also explore other ways to find a therapist who would be right for her needs, such as the Internet and referral organizations.

Let's make a similar exploration in this chapter, examining the different types of therapy, how they work, and what research has to say about their effectiveness. Many of the therapies discussed in this chapter rest on principles or theories discussed in previous chapters of this book. Here, we apply these principles and theories to treatment of psychological disorders (see Chapter 14). First, though, let's examine historical influences on psychotherapy.

# HISTORICAL INFLUENCES ON PSYCHOTHERAPY:
## Insight-Oriented Therapies

Beth didn't know much about psychotherapy, and she made an appointment with a psychotherapist she picked from the phone book. If Beth had called an insight-oriented therapist, chances are that the therapist would ask Beth about her past, her relationships with family members, how she felt about her family, and about her feelings in general and would ask surprisingly little about her current anxiety or her depression.

Therapies that aim to remove distressing symptoms by leading someone to understand their causes through deeply felt personal insights are called **insight-oriented therapies**. The key idea underlying this approach is that once someone truly understands the causes of distressing symptoms (which often arise from past relationships), the symptoms themselves will diminish. Psychoanalysis is the original insight-oriented therapy; client-centered therapy is also considered an insight-oriented therapy because it rests on the belief that therapeutic change follows from the experience of insight.

**Insight-oriented therapy:** A type of therapy that aims to remove distressing symptoms by leading people to understand their causes through deeply felt personal insights.

**Psychoanalysis:** An intensive form of therapy, originally developed by Freud, based on the idea that people's psychological difficulties are caused by conflicts among the id, the ego, and the superego.

## Psychodynamic Therapy: Origins in Psychoanalysis

Developed by Sigmund Freud, **psychoanalysis** is a type of therapy directly connected to Freud's theory of personality, which holds that people's psychological difficulties are caused by conflicts among the three psychic structures of the mind: the id, the ego, and the superego. According to Freud, the id strives for immediate gratification of its needs, the superego tries to impose its version of morality, and the ego attempts to balance the demands of id, superego, and external reality. These unconscious competing demands can create anxiety and other symptoms (see Chapter 11). The goal of psychoanalysis is to help patients understand the unconscious motivations that lead them to behave in specific ways; if the motivations and feelings remain unconscious, those forces are more likely to shape patients' behavior, without their awareness. According to this theory, only after true understanding—that is, insight—is attained can patients choose more adaptive, satisfying, and productive behaviors.

In psychoanalysis, patients talk about their problems, and the analyst tries to infer the root causes. At its beginnings, this method was revolutionary because, before Freud, most European patients were treated medically for psychological problems. Freud started out using hypnosis but, over time, developed the method of **free association**, in which the patient says whatever comes into his or her mind. The resulting train of thought reveals the issues that concern the patient, as well as the way he or she is handling them. Because Freud (1900/1958) viewed dreams as the "royal road to the unconscious," another important feature of psychoanalysis is the use of **dream analysis**, the examination of the content of dreams to gain access to the unconscious. Freud did not believe that psychoanalysis was a cure, but rather that it could transform abject misery into ordinary unhappiness.

Psychoanalysis has declined in popularity over the last several decades for a number of reasons; one is the outlay of time and money required for the four to five sessions per week. The average patient engages in 835 sessions before completing psychoanalysis (Voth & Orth, 1973), which usually lasts at least 4 years. Some patients who begin psychoanalysis never complete it. Psychoanalysis is rarely paid for by health insurance. A second reason for the decline of psychoanalysis is that studies have not generally found this type of treatment to be effective in treating various disorders, such as those discussed in Chapter 14.

A less intensive form of psychoanalysis, and one that is more common today, is **psychodynamic therapy**. Although based on psychoanalytic theory, its techniques differ in some important ways, including less frequent sessions and a decreased emphasis on sexual and aggressive drives. Recent trends in psychodynamic therapy include the development of short-term versions of psychotherapy (Bloom, 1997; Crits-Christoph, 1992; Malan, 1976; Sifneos, 1992), which might involve therapy lasting 12 to 20 sessions. However, short-term psychodynamic therapy differs somewhat in goals and focus from its longer-term counterpart, often focusing on current rather than past relationships (Greenberg & Mitchell, 1983; Kohut, 1977; Sullivan, 1953; Winnicot, 1958/1992). At least one study found that when psychiatrists refer people for psychological treatment, they do not refer all prospective patients to psychodynamic therapy, only those who are healthier and who do not have a personality disorder (Svanborg et al., 1999). Such people, who are often seeking help for relationship difficulties, may benefit from the insight that can be attained through short-term therapy (Kivlighan et al., 2000).

Psychoanalysis usually takes place 4 or 5 days a week for a number of years. Psychodynamic therapy can take place anywhere from several times a month to twice a week. The patient lies on a couch in psychoanalysis, and the analyst sits in a chair behind the couch, out of the patient's range of sight so that the patient can better free associate without seeing the analyst's reactions to his or her thoughts. In psychodynamic therapy, the client and therapist sit in chairs facing each other.

## Theory of Psychodynamic Therapy

The goal of psychodynamic therapy, like that of psychoanalysis, is to bring unconscious impulses and conflicts into awareness. Doing so leads to intellectual and emotional insights, which are supposed to give the patient more control over these impulses. With this control, the patient can actively and consciously choose behaviors instead of acting

**Free association:** A technique used in psychoanalysis and psychodynamic therapies in which the patient says whatever comes to mind and the train of thought reveals the patient's issues and ways of dealing with them.

**Dream analysis:** A technique used in psychoanalysis and psychodynamic therapy in which the therapist examines the content of dreams to gain access to the unconscious.

**Psychodynamic therapy:** A less intensive form of psychoanalysis.

on unconscious impulses. Both psychoanalysis and psychodynamic therapy try to link the patient's current difficulties with past experiences, and both forms of treatment view the patient's relationship with the therapist as an integral part of treatment. Given the importance of relationships, the therapy relationship can provide a "corrective emotional experience"—that is, a new, positive experience of relationships, which can lead to changes in symptoms, behavior, and personality (Alexander & French, 1946).

From a psychodynamic perspective, Beth's anxiety and depression might reflect two competing desires. On the one hand, Beth wants to be different from her mother. Doing well in school and going on to graduate school represent a path different from that taken by her mother, who, although she did well in college, elected not to pursue a graduate degree. Although her plan was not necessarily logically thought out, Beth hoped that by making different choices in her own life, she could avoid the intermittent depressions that had plagued her mother. On the other hand, Beth loves her mother, and the idea of academically passing a parent by, in essence, abandoning her, causes Beth to feel guilty about her accomplishments. Although Beth's anxiety and depression are upsetting and debilitating, part of her may feel relief that those symptoms prevent her from leaving her mother behind. Psychodynamic theory would say that, by gaining insight into these issues, Beth will not have to "act out" her ambivalent feelings (that is, impulsively or compulsively behave in a maladaptive way) and will have more control over her anxiety and depression.

## Techniques of Psychodynamic Therapy

Along with dream analysis and free association, psychodynamic therapists rely on **interpretation**, deciphering the patient's words and behaviors and assigning unconscious motivations to them. Through the therapist's interpretations, the patient becomes aware of his or her motives and potential conflicts within the unconscious. The patient's own interpretations are not considered as accurate as those of the therapist because they are biased by the patient's conflicts. Slips of the tongue—or *Freudian slips*—are interpreted as having unconscious meanings. For example, should Beth tell her therapist that her mother recommended that she come to therapy (instead of her mother's friend, which was the case, and what she meant to say), the therapist might interpret this as Beth's wish that her mother would take care of her by suggesting that she seek therapy.

Through interpretation, patients also become aware of their *defense mechanisms*, unconscious mechanisms used to handle conflictual and distressing thoughts and feelings (see Chapter 11). At some point in the course of psychodynamic therapy, patients are likely to experience **resistance**, a reluctance or refusal to cooperate with the therapist. Resistance can range from unconscious forgetting to outright refusal to comply with a therapist's request. Resistance can occur as the patient explores or remembers painful feelings or experiences in the past. Thus, if Beth comes late to a therapy session, a psychodynamic therapist might interpret this behavior as resistance: Perhaps Beth does not want to work on the issues currently being explored or is concerned about something that she doesn't want to share with her therapist.

Over the course of therapy, patients may come to relate to their therapist as they did to someone who was important in their lives, perhaps a parent. This phenomenon is called **transference**. If Beth began asking how the therapist is feeling, or if she began to talk less about her own distressing feelings because she worried that the therapist might become upset, Beth would be "transferring" onto her therapist her usual style of relating with her mother, in which she views her mother as fragile and needing protection. The therapeutic value of transference is that patients can talk about what they are experiencing (which they may very well have been unable to do with the parent)

Interpretation: A technique used in psychodynamic therapies in which the therapist deciphers the patient's words and behaviors, assigning unconscious motivations to them.

Resistance: A reluctance or refusal to cooperate with the therapist, which can range from unconscious forgetting to outright refusal to comply with a therapist's request.

Transference: The process by which patients may relate to their therapists as they did to some important person in their lives.

to heighten understanding. Moreover, the therapist's acceptance of uncomfortable or shameful feelings helps patients accept those feelings in order to choose whether to act on them. A psychodynamic therapist would likely interpret Beth's questions about the therapist's well-being as transference. Beth and her therapist would then talk about what it was like for Beth to feel so protective toward, and careful with, her mother.

# Humanistic Therapy: Client-Centered Therapy

Like the humanistic approach to personality (see Chapter 11), humanistic therapy emphasizes free will, personal growth, self-esteem, and mastery. This approach is in contrast to psychodynamic therapy, which emphasizes the past, mental mechanisms, and the working through of conflictual impulses and feelings. One of the early proponents of humanistic psychology was Carl Rogers, who developed a therapeutic approach that came to be called **client-centered therapy** and that focuses on people's potential for growth and the importance of an empathic therapist. Instead of using the term "patient," which suggests treating a person with an illness (a medical term), Rogers used the term "client."

## Theory of Client-Centered Therapy

Rogers believed that a person's distressing symptoms grow out of a blocked potential for personal growth. The goal of client-centered therapy is to dismantle that block so that clients can reach their full potential. Within Rogers's framework, problems arise because of a lack of a coherent, unified sense of self. An example is a mismatch, or **incongruence**, between the real self (who you actually are) and the ideal self (who you would like to be). By helping clients to become more like their ideal selves, client-centered therapy lessens the incongruence, and the clients feel better. Within the framework of client-centered therapy, Beth's problems may stem from incongruence between her real self (a self that has to work hard for good grades and feels shame and guilt about the imperfections that remind her of her mother's depression) and her ideal self (a self that always does the "right thing" and never experiences sadness, hopelessness, or anxiety). The tension between her real and ideal selves creates a fragmented sense of self, which drains Beth's time and energy; these different parts of herself are in conflict with each other and prevent her from reaching her full potential.

## Techniques of Client-Centered Therapy

The client-centered therapist should be warm, able to see the world as the client does, and able to empathize with the client. The therapist does not offer analyses to the client; instead, the therapist reflects back the thrust of what the client has said. However, the therapist must not simply parrot the client's words or phrases but show accurate and genuine empathy. Such empathy lets the client know that he or she is really understood. If the therapist does not accurately reflect what the client says or is not genuinely empathic, the intervention will fail. The therapist must also provide *unconditional positive regard*; that is, he or she must convey positive feelings for the client regardless of the client's thoughts, feelings, or actions. The therapist does this by continually showing the client that he or she is inherently worthy as a human being. According to the theory, genuine empathy and unconditional positive regard allow the client to decrease the incongruence between the real and ideal selves. Although Beth was not able to take some of her exams (real self), a client-centered therapist's empathy and unconditional positive regard would allow Beth to see that she is still smart (ideal self) and that everyone sometimes has

**Client-centered therapy:** A type of insight-oriented therapy that focuses on people's potential for growth and the importance of an empathic therapist.

**Incongruence:** According to client-centered therapy, a mismatch between a person's real self and his or her ideal self.

Being rejected by a partner can leave a person feeling bad about himself or herself. Client-centered therapy makes a distinction between the person's actions in the relationship and the fact he or she is still a worthwhile, good person.

negative, uncomfortable feelings. This therapeutic approach could help Beth see her real and ideal selves in a different light and allow her to think of herself more positively.

The client-centered therapist provides both genuine empathy and unconditional positive regard by making a distinction between the client as a person and the client's behaviors. The therapist could dislike a client's behavior but still view the client as a good person. If Beth were seeing a client-centered therapist, the topic of a therapy session might be what it was like for Beth during her mother's bouts of depression. A session might include this exchange:

BETH: I was so disappointed and ashamed when I'd come home from school and she'd still be in bed, wearing her bathrobe.

THERAPIST: Yes, it must have caused you to feel ashamed, anxious, and worried when you came home and found your mother still in bed.

BETH: And I felt that it was my fault, that I wasn't doing enough to make her feel better.

THERAPIST: Although you felt that it was your fault, you did all that you possibly could. You were concerned about her. You were, and still are, a good, worthwhile person.

BETH: And now I spend most of the day in bed and don't bother to get dressed . . . am I becoming like my mother?

THERAPIST: You and your mother are two separate individuals. Although you may have some things in common, and right now that may include depression, that doesn't mean that your path in life is identical to hers.

The therapist repeatedly emphasizes the worthiness of the client until the client comes to accept this valuation and is able to reach his or her potential by making different, healthier choices and decisions. When successful, client-centered therapy can achieve its objective in a few months rather than years.

## Evaluating Insight-Oriented Therapies

Psychodynamic therapies are difficult to evaluate, for several reasons. One is that there isn't much research to evaluate. Consider that for every research article on transference, there are 500 related to psychodynamic theories. Most research on psychodynamically oriented treatment has been case studies, which limits the reliability and generalizability of the findings (Roth & Fonagy, 2005). Moreover, the interpretations the therapists made in these cases have not tested, and they may not be correct. For instance, research shows that interpretations of transference during therapy are rarely—if ever—helpful to the treatment (Henry et al., 1994). Psychodynamic therapists have tended to view treatment failures as the patient's responsibility rather than the therapist's. It is possible that this view is correct—lack of behavioral change may result from insufficient insight—but insight is not objectively measurable, at least not yet.

Psychodynamic therapy appears to work best with patients who are able to articulate their feelings and want to understand their unconscious mental processes (and who have the time and money for lengthy treatment). Some meta-analyses find that short-term psychodynamic therapy is as effective as, but not superior to, other short-term treatments (Crits-Christoph, 1992; Leichsenring, 2001; Leichsenring et al., 2004). However, some studies contradict this conclusion (Svartberg & Stiles, 1991), particularly studies with a 1-year follow-up (Barkham et al., 1999). Moreover, researchers have not extensively investigated whether short-term psychodynamic therapy can help those with specific disorders.

Although Rogers proposed the first real insight-oriented alternative to psychodynamic therapy and made the treatment amenable to research by tape-recording therapy sessions, research has not been as supportive as he might have wished. Nevertheless, almost all forms of therapy incorporate Rogers's view that the therapist's warmth, empathy, and positive regard for the client are fundamental for a working relationship between client and therapist (Lambert, 1983; Roth & Fonagy, 2005). However, most other therapies do not rest on the idea that these factors are enough to bring about change. Moreover, although client-centered therapy was the first major school of therapy to focus on assessing the effectiveness of the treatment, it can be difficult to measure which clients have achieved their potentials.

In sum, although there are differences between the insight-oriented therapies, the people most likely to benefit from these treatments are similar in that they are relatively healthy, articulate individuals who are interested in knowing more about their own motivations rather than seeking to address specific symptoms, such as those related to anxiety. Moreover, little research indicates that insight-oriented treatments are likely to be successful for most disorders. We now turn to examine treatments that have received greater support from research.

# Test Yourself

1. What purpose do free association and dream analysis play in psychoanalysis?
   a. They help reveal the patient's irrational thoughts.
   b. They help the patient gain access to unconscious motivations.
   c. They provide ideas and images that become tools for role-playing.
   d. They allow the analyst to tap into the patient's superego.
2. Resistance occurs when a patient refuses to cooperate with a therapist, for example, by
   a. unconsciously forgetting to mention important details.
   b. taking on the role of the therapist.
   c. offering false interpretations of dreams.
   d. refusing to transfer feelings to the therapist.
3. In client-centered therapy, the therapist looks for incongruence, or a(n)_____, in the client.
   a. mismatch between the needs of the id and the rules of the superego
   b. inconsistency among basic beliefs
   c. irrational and maladaptive thought pattern
   d. mismatch between the ideal and true selves

4. What is one of the major differences between psychodynamic therapy and client-centered therapy?
   a. Client-centered therapy, unlike psychodynamic therapy, is an insight-oriented therapy.
   b. Psychodynamic therapy, unlike client-centered therapy, is an insight-oriented therapy.
   c. Client-centered therapy is based on a more positive view of human nature than is psychodynamic therapy.
   d. Client-centered therapy uses hypnosis, and psychodynamic therapy relies on medication.

## Answers

1 b 2 a 3 d 4 c

NOTE: Once you feel comfortable with the Test Yourself questions in this chapter, visit the book's Web site at www.ablongman.com/kosslyn3e for additional study questions.

# Think It Through!

Imagine two people, one of whom is the ideal candidate for insight-oriented therapy and one of whom is the worst possible candidate. How would you describe these two people? If a friend tells you that he or she is in insight-oriented therapy, what can you assume about his therapy? What can't you assume?

# COGNITIVE–BEHAVIOR THERAPY

Suppose Beth's therapist (chosen from listings in the phone book) starts asking questions not about her family and her relationships, but about what she currently believes about herself and her abilities. Suppose the therapist also inquires about her behaviors: What does she do before sits down to study or take an exam? What, in detail, does she do during the day? Has she ever tried any relaxation techniques? These are questions about thoughts and behaviors. Odds are that Beth has contacted a cognitive–behavior therapist.

**Cognitive–behavior therapy (CBT)** seeks both to change problematic behaviors and irrational thoughts and to provide new, more adaptive behaviors and beliefs to replace the old, maladaptive ones. CBT utilizes techniques from both behavior therapy and cognitive therapy; behavior therapy itself rests on learning principles discussed in Chapter 6. Let's begin by discussing behavior and cognitive therapies separately so that you can understand the unique focus of each approach.

## Behavior Therapy and Its Techniques

Traditionally, **behavior therapy** focused on changing observable, measurable behavior. Joseph Wolpe (1915–1997) profoundly altered the practice of psychotherapy in 1958 when he published *Psychotherapy by Reciprocal Inhibition*. He was a psychiatrist, but his concern with behavior created a new form of treatment that particularly appealed to psychologists because of its emphasis on quantifiable results. In general, behavior therapy rests on well-researched principles of learning (see Chapter 6; Wolpe, 1997). Whereas Wolpe focused on applications of classical conditioning, B. F. Skinner focused on applications of operant conditioning. As noted in Chapter 6, applications of both sorts of learning can be employed more broadly: in education, marketing, sports, military training, medicine, and business. Here we consider ways in which these techniques are used to treat many of the psychological disorders discussed in Chapter 14.

### Theory of Behavior Therapy

In behavior therapy, distressing symptoms are seen as the result of learning. Through the use of social learning—that is, modeling—as well as through classical and operant conditioning, clients can change unwanted behaviors by learning new ones; it is easiest to change a problematic behavior by replacing it with a new, more adaptive one. The behavior therapist is interested in the ABCs of the behavior:

- its *antecedents* (what is the stimulus that triggers the problematic behavior?),
- the problematic *behavior* itself, and
- its *consequences* (what is reinforcing the behavior?).

Behavior therapy's lack of interest or belief in an unconscious "root cause" was revolutionary. Behaviors and performance are emphasized, the therapist takes an active, directive role in treatment, and "homework"—between-session tasks for the client to work on—is an important component of the treatment. Therapists took a new look at treatment results: Did the client experience less frequent or less intense symptoms after therapy? The ABCs of Beth's anxiety are noted in Table 15.1.

### Techniques of Behavior Therapy

Behavioral techniques rest on classical conditioning, operant conditioning, and social learning principles.

Cognitive–behavior therapy (CBT): A type of therapy that aims to change problematic behaviors and irrational thoughts and provide new, more adaptive behaviors and beliefs to replace old, maladaptive ones.

Behavior therapy: A type of therapy, based on well-researched learning principles, that focuses on changing observable, measurable behaviors.

TABLE 15.1

# The ABCs of Beth's Anxiety

The possible antecedents and consequences of Beth's problematic behavior.

| Antecedents | (Problematic) Behavior | Consequences |
|---|---|---|
| The antecedent for Beth's anxiety might be the act of sitting down to study for an exam or waiting in class to receive her exam booklet. | The behavior is the conditioned emotional response of fear and anxiety, evidenced by her sweating hands and racing heart rate and her inability to do her schoolwork. | The consequences might include negative reinforcement (the uncomfortable symptoms go away) when skipping an exam, reinforcement of related nonacademic avoidant behaviors (such as sleeping through an exam), and subsequent social isolation, leading to a loss of pleasant activities and opportunities for social reinforcement, which, in turn, can lead to depression. |

**TECHNIQUES BASED ON CLASSICAL CONDITIONING**    One classical conditioning technique commonly used to treat anxiety disorders is **exposure**. It is based on the principle of habituation (see Chapter 6). Patients are asked to *expose* themselves to feared stimuli in a planned and (usually) gradual way (see Figure 15.1, on p. 694, for an example of a planned, gradual exposure to feared situations). In general, exposure and habituation do not occur naturally because people with an anxiety disorder avoid the feared stimulus. People can be exposed to the feared stimulus in any of three ways:

- *imaginal exposure*, where they imagine the feared stimulus;
- *in vivo exposure*, where they expose themselves to the actual stimulus; or
- *virtual reality exposure*, where they use virtual reality techniques to expose themselves to the stimulus.

Exposure, like all other behavioral and cognitive therapy techniques, is primarily directed at the levels of person and group; however, such techniques also affect events at the level of the brain. Consider a neuroimaging study of people with a spider phobia who had exposure treatment (Paquette et al., 2003). Before treatment, fMRI scans indicated that when these people saw pictures of spiders, part of the prefrontal cortex and the parahippocampal gyrus were activated; in contrast, when people who did not have such a phobia saw these pictures, these brain areas were not activated. After successful exposure therapy, another round of fMRI scans was done. The results were dramatically different: Now, when the people who used to have phobias saw the pictures of spiders, the key brain areas were no longer activated. Exposure had "rewired" neural circuits that apparently had been involved in the phobia.

A related technique, *exposure with response prevention*, is a planned, programmatic procedure that exposes the client to the anxiety-provoking object or situation but prevents the usual maladaptive response. For instance, clients with an obsessive-compulsive disorder (OCD) that compels them to wash their hands repeatedly would, using exposure with response prevention, intentionally get their hands dirty during a therapy session and then stop themselves from washing their hands immediately afterward. In this way, they would habituate to the anxiety. Researchers have found that exposure with response prevention is as effective as medication for OCD; moreover, such behavioral treatment can have longer-lasting benefits (Foa et al., 2005; Marks, 1997). However, not all people who have OCD are willing to use this behavioral technique (Stanley & Turner, 1995).

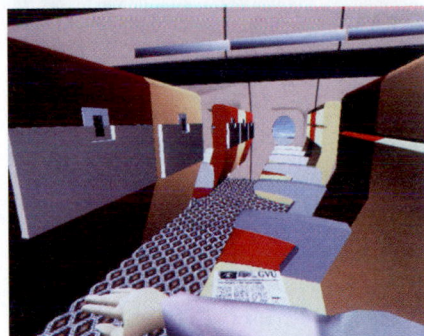

Virtual reality exposure appears to work as well as in vivo (actual) exposure for fears of flying and heights (Emmelkamp et al., 2001, 2002; Rothbaum et al., 2001, 2002).

**Exposure:** A therapeutic technique based on classical conditioning that rests on the principle of habituation.

FIGURE 15.1

## Planning for Exposure: Hierarchy of Agoraphobic Fear and Avoidance

This is one person's hierarchy of feared and avoided situations. Exposure treatment for this person's agoraphobia would begin with the least feared situation (a 5-block walk to the park alone), continuing over time to the most feared.

### AGORAPHOBIA HIERARCHY

List the situations that cause you anxiety. Then, using the scale from 0 to 8, rate each situation according to the fear it provokes and how often you try to avoid it.

| 0 | 1 | 2 | 3 | 4 | 5 | 6 | 7 | 8 |
|---|---|---|---|---|---|---|---|---|
| No Fear | | Mild Fear | | Moderate Fear | | Strong Fear | | Extreme Fear |
| Never Avoid | Occasionally Avoid | | Sometimes Avoid | | | Often Avoid | | Always Avoid |

| SITUATION | Fear/ Avoidance |
|---|---|
| Walk to the park, alone (5 blocks) | 2 |
| Walk to the store alone (10 blocks) | 3 |
| Shop in mall with family member, 15 minutes | 4 |
| Shop in mall with family member, one hour | 5 |
| Shop in mall alone, 15 minutes | 5 |
| Shop in mall alone, one hour | 6 |
| Drive to sister's place with family member (20 minutes) | 6 |
| Drive to sister's place alone (20 minutes) | 7 |
| Drive to brother's place with family member (one hour) | 8 |
| Drive to brother's place alone (one hour) | 8 |
| Drive to brother's place alone in peak hour (two hours) | 8 |
| | |

If an alcoholic drank to excess only when in a bar, limiting or eliminating the occasions of going to a bar would be an example of stimulus control.

**Stimulus control:** A behavior therapy technique that involves controlling the exposure to a stimulus that elicits a conditioned response, so as to decrease or increase the frequency of the response.

The technique of exposure with response prevention has also been used to treat people with bulimia nervosa. In this case, rather than induce vomiting after eating a "forbidden food," the person does not throw up (or delays it as long as possible). Before the exposure to forbidden foods, client and therapist develop strategies that the client can use while trying not to engage in the maladaptive behavior, such as taking a walk around the block or watching a movie.

Another technique, called **stimulus control**, involves controlling exposure to a stimulus that elicits a conditioned response, so as to decrease or increase the frequency of the response. For instance, a woman with bulimia who binges on donuts would exert stimulus control by buying only a single donut rather than a dozen.

An additional technique based on classical conditioning is **systematic desensitization**, a procedure that teaches people to be relaxed in the presence of a feared object or situation. This technique, developed by Wolpe for treating phobias, grew out of the idea that someone cannot be fearful (and hence anxious) and relaxed at the same time. Systematic desensitization uses **progressive muscle relaxation**, a relaxation technique whereby the muscles are sequentially relaxed from one end of the body to the other, usually from feet to head. Although progressive muscle relaxation is used in systematic desensitization, it can be used by itself to induce relaxation (visit www.ablongman.com/kosslyn3e for instructions on progressive muscle relaxation).

FIGURE 15.2

## Systematic Desensitization of an Elevator Phobia

With systematic desensitization, a man with an elevator phobia would list a hierarchy of activities related to using an elevator. Next, he would successfully learn to make himself relax, using techniques such as progressive muscle relaxation.

He then starts out imagining items at the low end of the hierarchy, such as pressing an elevator button. When he becomes anxious, he stops imagining that scene and uses relaxation techniques to become fully relaxed again.

When he can imagine the elevator-related situations on the lower end of the hierarchy without anxiety, he progresses to situations that make him more anxious, stopping to do the relaxation technique when he becomes anxious.

Systematic desensitization continues in this fashion until the man can imagine being fully immersed in the most feared situation (a stuck elevator) without anxiety. He would then follow the same procedure in a real elevator.

When using systematic desensitization to overcome a phobia, therapist and client begin by constructing a hierarchy of real or imagined activities related to the feared object or situation—such as a fear of elevators (see Figure 15.2). This hierarchy begins with the least fearful activity, such as pressing an elevator call button, progressing to the most fearful, being stuck in a stopped elevator. Over the course of a number of sessions, clients work on becoming relaxed when imagining increasingly anxiety-provoking activities.

**TECHNIQUES BASED ON OPERANT CONDITIONING** Techniques based on operant conditioning make use of the principles of reinforcement, punishment, and extinction, with the goal of **behavior modification**—that is, changing the behavior, not focusing on thoughts or feelings. Setting the appropriate *response contingencies*, or behaviors that

Systematic desensitization: A behavior therapy technique that teaches people to be relaxed in the presence of a feared object or situation.

Progressive muscle relaxation: A relaxation technique whereby the person relaxes muscles sequentially from one end of the body to the other.

Behavior modification: A category of therapeutic techniques for changing behavior based on operant conditioning principles.

**Token economy:** A treatment program that uses secondary reinforcers (tokens) to bring about behavior modification.

**Self-monitoring techniques:** Behavioral techniques that help the client identify the antecedents and consequences of a problematic behavior.

will earn reinforcement, is crucial. *Extinction*, eliminating a behavior by not reinforcing it, is another important tool of the behavioral therapist.

Therapists also use behavior modification techniques in group settings, such as inpatient psychiatric units. In these facilities, it is possible to change the response contingencies for an undesired behavior as well as for a desired behavior. Behavior modification can be used to change even severely maladaptive behaviors. *Secondary reinforcers*, those that are learned and don't inherently satisfy a biological need, are used in treatment programs not only with psychiatric patients but also with mentally retarded children and adults, and even in prisons. Patients or others must earn "tokens" by behaving appropriately; these tokens then can be traded for small items such as cigarettes or candy at a "token store" or for privileges such as going out for a walk or watching a particular TV show.

These **token economies**—treatment programs that use secondary reinforcers to change behavior—can be used to mold social behavior directly by modifying what patients say to one another and to nonpatients. For instance, using a token economy, hospitalized patients with schizophrenia can learn to talk to others, answer questions, or eat more normally. Operant conditioning can also modify how patients perceive specific stimuli, such as when someone with schizophrenia begins to interpret a question as something that requires an answer. Although token economies can be effective, their use is declining because of ethical and moral questions about depriving patients and clients of secondary reinforcers (such as television, cigarettes, and walks on the grounds) if they do not earn them through behavior change (Glynn, 1990).

In addition, operant conditioning principles have led to **self-monitoring techniques**, such as keeping a daily log about instances of a problematic behavior. Such self-monitoring can help identify the antecedents and consequences of the problematic behavior (see Figure 15.3), which can clarify how behavior modification may be best achieved. Daily logs are used for a variety of problems, including poor mood, anxiety, overeating, smoking, sleep problems, and compulsive gambling.

**FIGURE 15.3**

## Daily Self-Monitoring Log

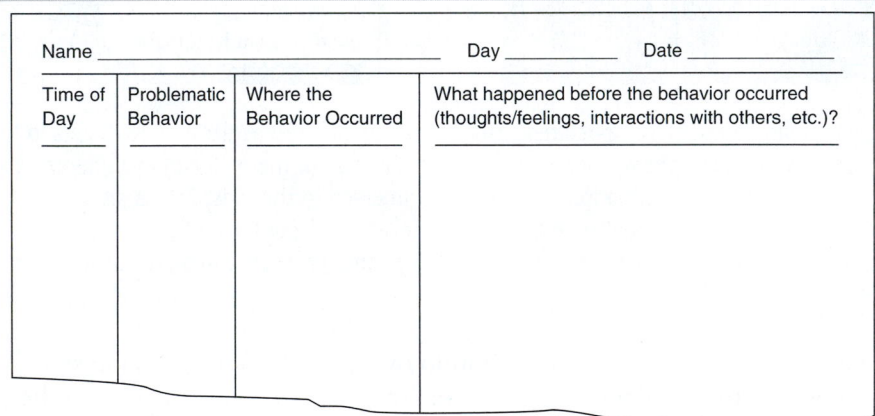

This daily self-monitoring log helps clients become aware of the antecedents, or "triggers," to their problematic behaviors. The column for time of day helps determine whether there is a daily or weekly pattern. Noting where the behavior occurred helps establish whether certain environments play a role in the behavior, perhaps serving as conditioned stimuli. Writing down thoughts, feelings, interactions with others, or other factors (such as level of hunger) that preceded the problematic behavior helps identify irrational thought patterns, distressing feelings, states, or situations that lead to the behavior. With knowledge of the factors, the client and therapist can develop appropriate targets of change for the therapy.

If Beth used behavior modification techniques, she would seek to establish response contingencies for behaving in desired new ways: She might reward herself with a movie or a dinner out after taking an exam, or allow herself an hour's conversation with a friend after studying for 2 hours.

**TECHNIQUES BASED ON OBSERVATIONAL LEARNING** Observational learning also plays a role in behavior therapy, particularly with children and with people who have phobias, especially animal phobias (Goetestam & Berntzen, 1997). Patients observe other people interacting with the feared stimulus in a relaxed way and learn to do the same.

# Cognitive Therapy and Techniques: It's the Thought That Counts

The ripples of the cognitive revolution in psychology (see Chapter 1) were felt in therapy as well as in research. Therapists began to examine the mental processes that contribute to behavior, not simply the physical stimuli that trigger it. It became clear that people's thoughts (cognitions), not just their learning histories, influence their feelings and behavior, and do so in myriad ways. Just thinking about a past positive experience with love can put you in a good mood, and thinking about an unhappy love experience can have the opposite effect (Clark & Collins, 1993). A cognitive therapist would focus on Beth's thoughts and the way in which one thought leads to another, contributing to her emotional experience of anxiety and depression.

## Theory of Cognitive Therapy

The way people interpret events can affect their well-being (Chapter 13); such interpretation (involving conscious and unconscious processes) imparts meaning to what we perceive. **Cognitive therapy** aims to help clients think rationally in order to reinterpret events that otherwise lead to distressing feelings and behaviors: It is the interpretation of any experience that determines the response to that experience. Two particularly important contributors to cognitive therapy were Albert Ellis and Aaron Beck. Although both were pioneers of cognitive therapy, their treatments also rely in part on aspects of behavioral theory and therapy.

Albert Ellis (b. 1913) is a clinical psychologist who in the 1950s developed a treatment called *rational-emotive behavior therapy (REBT)*. REBT emphasizes rational, logical thinking and assumes that distressing feelings or symptoms are caused by faulty or illogical thoughts. Researchers have supported this idea, for example by showing that such faulty thinking is associated with higher scores on a measure of daily hassles (Ziegler & Leslie, 2003.) People may develop illogical or irrational thoughts as a result of their experiences and never assess whether these thoughts are valid. They elevate irrational thoughts to "godlike absolutist musts, shoulds, demands, and commands" (Ellis, 1994a, p. 103). According to REBT, Beth's thought that she needs to do well in school is based on a dysfunctional, irrational belief that in order to be a lovable, deserving human being, she must earn good grades; if she does not, she believes that she will be unlovable and worthless.

Ellis (1994a) proposed three processes that interfere with healthy functioning:

1. *self-downing*, or being critical of oneself for performing poorly or being rejected;

2. *hostility and rage*, or being unkind to or critical of others for performing poorly; and

3. *low frustration tolerance*, or blaming everyone and everything for "poor, dislikable conditions."

Cognitive therapy: A type of therapy that focuses on the client's thoughts rather than his or her feelings or behaviors.

REBT focuses on creating more rational thoughts. In Beth's case, these might be, "I might be disappointed or disappoint others if I don't do well this semester, but they will still love and care about me." This more rational thinking should then dampen down the problematic behavior, allowing her to choose more rational courses of action. Part of the goal of REBT is educational, and clients should be able to use the techniques on their own once they have mastered them. Like behavior therapy, REBT is oriented toward *solving* problems as opposed to exploring them psychologically. The REBT therapist encourages self-acceptance and a new way of thinking; self-blame is viewed as counterproductive because it involves faulty beliefs. Shortcomings or failures are viewed as simply part of life, not as crimes or signs of moral weakness.

Psychiatrist Aaron Beck (b. 1921) developed a form of cognitive therapy that, like REBT, rests on the premise that irrational thoughts are the root cause of psychological problems, and that recognition of their irrationality and adoption of more realistic, rational thoughts cause psychological problems to improve. According to his theory, irrational thoughts that arise from a systematic bias, such as the belief that if you tell your friend you are mad at her she will reject you, are considered **cognitive distortions** of reality; several common distortions are presented in Table 15.2. Such cognitive distortions (or faulty thoughts, in the vocabulary of REBT) are learned and maintained through reinforcement.

Unlike REBT, which relies on the therapist's attempts to persuade the client that his or her beliefs are irrational, Beck's version of cognitive therapy encourages the client to view beliefs as hypotheses to be tested. Thus, interactions with the world provide opportunities to perform "experiments" to ascertain the accuracy of the client's be-

**TABLE 15.2**  **Five Common Cognitive Distortions**

| Distortion | Description | Example |
|---|---|---|
| **Dichotomous thinking** | Also known as black-and-white thinking, which allows for nothing in between the extremes; you are either perfect or a piece of garbage. | Beth thinks that if she doesn't get an A on a test, she has failed in life. |
| **Mental filter** | Magnifying the negative aspects of something while filtering out the positive. | Beth remembers only the things she did that were below her expectations but doesn't pay attention to (or remember) the things she did well. |
| **Mind reading** | Thinking you know exactly what other people are thinking, particularly as it relates to you. | Beth believes that she *knows* her professors think less of her because of what happened on the exams (when in fact they don't think less of her, but are concerned about her). |
| **Catastrophic exaggeration** | Thinking that your worst nightmare will come true and that it will be intolerable. | Beth's fear is that she'll be kicked out of school and end up homeless; a more likely reality is that she may have to take some courses over again. |
| **Control beliefs** | Believing either that you are helpless and totally subject to forces beyond your control, or that you must tightly control your life for fear that, if you don't, you will never be able to regain control. | Until talking to her family friend, Nina, Beth thought there was nothing she could do to change the downward spiral of events, and that she was either totally in control of her studying or else not in control at all. |

liefs (Hollon & Beck, 1994). Beck and his colleagues have approached treatment empirically, developing measures to assess depression, anxiety, and other problems and to evaluate the effectiveness of treatment.

## Techniques of Cognitive Therapy

Some of the same techniques are used in REBT and Beck's cognitive therapy, but each approach also relies on its own distinctive techniques.

**REBT TECHNIQUES** The REBT therapist helps the client identify his or her irrational beliefs, relying on verbal persuasion (Hollon & Beck, 1994) and then works through a sequence of techniques with the client. These techniques can be remembered by the alphabetical sequence ABCDEF: Distressing feelings exist because an *activating event* (A) along with the person's *beliefs* (B) lead to a *highly charged emotional consequence* (C). It is not the event itself that created the problem, but rather the beliefs attached to the event led to a problematic consequence. Thus, changing the beliefs will lead to a different consequence. This is done by helping the client *dispute* (D) the irrational beliefs and perceive their illogical and self-defeating nature. Such disputes lead to an *effect* (E; also called an *effective new philosophy*), a new way of feeling and acting. Finally, clients may have to take *further action* (F) to solidify the change in beliefs. Each session is devoted to a specific aspect of the client's problem. Often, at the outset of a session, client and therapist will determine what effect the client wants from the intervention. Beth and a REBT therapist might agree on what the effect should be when she studies—namely, less anxiety—and go through the ABCDEF procedure to achieve that effect. Figure 15.4 illustrates the ABCDEF techniques applied to Beth's anxiety.

**FIGURE 15.4** **The ABCDEF Technique Applied to Beth's Anxiety**

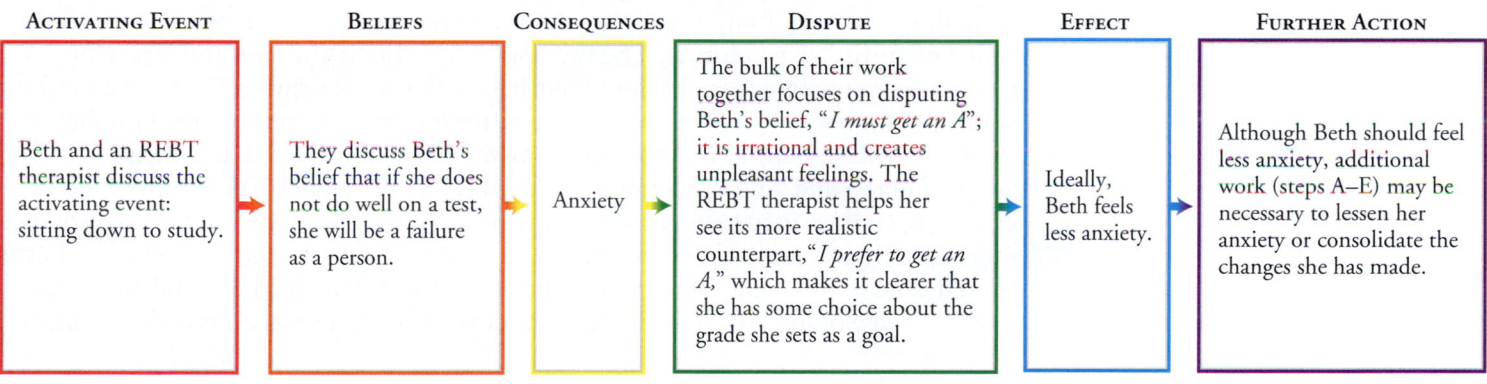

| ACTIVATING EVENT | BELIEFS | CONSEQUENCES | DISPUTE | EFFECT | FURTHER ACTION |
|---|---|---|---|---|---|
| Beth and an REBT therapist discuss the activating event: sitting down to study. | They discuss Beth's belief that if she does not do well on a test, she will be a failure as a person. | Anxiety | The bulk of their work together focuses on disputing Beth's belief, "*I must get an A*"; it is irrational and creates unpleasant feelings. The REBT therapist helps her see its more realistic counterpart, "*I prefer to get an A*," which makes it clearer that she has some choice about the grade she sets as a goal. | Ideally, Beth feels less anxiety. | Although Beth should feel less anxiety, additional work (steps A–E) may be necessary to lessen her anxiety or consolidate the changes she has made. |

The REBT therapist sometimes argues with the client to help him or her confront (and dispute) the faulty cognitions that contribute to his or her distress. The therapist may also use role-playing to help the client practice new ways of thinking and behaving (Ellis, 1994b). REBT can be helpful with anxiety, unassertiveness (Haaga & Davison, 1989), and unrealistic expectations; it is generally not successful with psychotic disorders.

**BECK'S COGNITIVE THERAPY TECHNIQUES** Beck's cognitive therapy often makes use of a daily record of dysfunctional thoughts (see Figure 15.5, on p. 700). Clients are asked to identify the situation in which the automatic negative thoughts (comparable to irrational beliefs) occurred, rate their emotional state, write down the automatic negative thoughts and their rational response to those thoughts (comparable to the REBT "dispute"), and

FIGURE 15.5

## Daily Record of Dysfunctional Beliefs

| Situation | Emotion(s) | Automatic Thought(s) | Rational Response | Outcome |
|---|---|---|---|---|
| Actual event or stream of thoughts | Rate (1–100%) | ATs that preceded emotion Rate belief in ATs (1–100%) | Write rational response to ATs Rate belief in rational response (1–100%) | Rerate AT (1–100%) |
| 1. Sit down to study | Anxious 70% | I won't be able to do as well on the test as I would like. —100% (Dichotomous thinking) | I might not be able to do as well as I want, but that doesn't mean that I will necessarily fail. —50% | Anxious 50% |
| 2. In bed in the morning | Sad 80% | There's no point in getting out of bed—the day will be awful. I fail at everything I try. —90% (Mental filter) | Although I may not "succeed" in the goals I set for myself, it is possible that my expectations are too high, that I have too many expectations, or that I only notice the goals I don't attain, and don't notice the ones I do. —70% | Sad 6% |

In a daily record of dysfunctional beliefs, clients like Beth are asked to identify the situation in which their automatic negative thoughts occurred, rate their emotional state (Emotions column), write down the automatic thought, their rational response to the automatic negative thoughts, and then rerate their emotional state (Outcome column).

then rerate their emotional state. Clients should rate their emotional state as improved after going through this process. Although this technique appears straightforward, it can be hard to use because the client has believed the "truth" of the automatic thought for so long that it doesn't seem to be distorted or irrational. The process of helping clients shift their thinking away from automatic, dysfunctional thoughts to more realistic ones is called **cognitive restructuring**. The therapist helps clients examine and assess the accuracy of the automatic thoughts and their habitual ways of viewing themselves and the world and then helps them search for alternative interpretations for those thoughts.

Cognitive therapy also makes use of **psychoeducation**—that is, educating clients about therapy and research findings pertaining to their disorders or problems. This knowledge is then used to help clients develop a more realistic, undistorted view of their problems. Beth was afraid to seek treatment because she was afraid she would be hospitalized; a cognitive therapist might explain to her the criteria for a hospital admission so that this fear wouldn't become the basis for developing irrational automatic thoughts.

## Cognitive–Behavior Therapy

In some sense, the distinction between behavior therapy and cognitive therapy is really a matter of emphasis; they are not categorically distinct. We've already noted that cognitive therapy implicitly involves behavior change. Similarly, behavior therapy involves changing cognitions: For instance, during exposure treatment, clients get to see that their negative automatic thoughts do not, in fact, come to pass. That is, through exposure, they learn that catastrophic events don't transpire when using an elevator or that touching dirt (for someone with OCD) won't lead to a catastrophe or fatal illness (Emmelkamp, 2004).

In the last quarter of the 20th century, therapists began to use both cognitive and behavioral techniques within the same treatment. This merging of therapies grew out of the recognition that cognitions and behaviors affect each other, and both affect feel-

**Cognitive restructuring:** The process of helping clients shift their thinking away from the focus on automatic, dysfunctional thoughts to more realistic ones.

**Psychoeducation:** The process of educating clients about therapy and research findings pertaining to their disorders or problems.

TABLE 15.3

## TABLE 15.3 The Focus, Goals, and Techniques of Cognitive–Behavior Therapy

Although cognitive–behavior therapy addresses clients' symptoms and focuses on symptom relief as a goal in and of itself, cognitive and behavioral techniques have different foci and goals.

| Type of Techniques | Focus | Goal | Specific Technique |
|---|---|---|---|
| Behavioral techniques | Maladaptive behavior | Change the behavior, its antecedents, or its consequences | Relaxation techniques, systematic desensitization, exposure with response prevention, stimulus control, behavior modification, observational learning |
| Cognitive techniques | Automatic, irrational thoughts | Change dysfunctional, unrealistic thoughts to more realistic ones / Recognize the relationships among thoughts, feelings, and behaviors | Cognitive restructuring (or Ellis's ABCDEF technique), psycho-education, role playing |

ings—and that alterations in cognitions, behaviors, and feelings are often a part of most psychological disorders. CBT combines the goals and techniques of both behavior and cognitive therapies (Table 15.3). The two sets of techniques can work together to promote therapeutic change: Cognitive techniques change thoughts, which then affect feelings and behaviors; behavioral techniques change behaviors, which, in turn, lead to new experiences, feelings, and ways of relating, which then change how people think about themselves and the world. These techniques may also be used to treat stress-related problems (see Chapter 13). CBT is appropriate for a wide range of clients and disorders and provides the opportunity for clients to learn new coping strategies and master new tasks.

# Test Yourself

1. When systematic desensitization is used to overcome a phobia, the desensitizing activities
   a. become increasingly more intense as the treatment progresses.
   b. become less intense as the treatment progresses.
   c. are presented in a random, but counterbalanced order.
   d. are not directly related to the phobia.
2. Behavior modification is based on
   a. the principles of classical conditioning.
   b. the principles of operant conditioning.
   c. changing the thoughts of the client.
   d. imagining fearful situations.

3. The cognitive therapy developed by Ellis focuses on identifying
   a. illogical or irrational thoughts.
   b. behaviors that lead to self-destruction.
   c. drugs that regulate neurotransmitter functioning.
   d. patterns of reinforced behavior.
4. Which of the following is a shared characteristic of behavior and cognitive techniques?
   a. They rely on clients' active participation.
   b. They mainly seek to understand clients' underlying motivations.
   c. They require clients to meet with a therapist twice each week.
   d. They rely on clients' completion of a daily log regarding the problematic behavior.

## Answers

1.a 2.b 3.a 4.a

# Think It Through!

If you read about a study that claimed that CBT treatment effectively reduces kleptomania (compulsive stealing not done for material need), what questions would you ask about how the study was conducted? Suppose that each therapist in the study treated some clients with CBT and some with client-centered therapy. What would you need to know before agreeing with the conclusions about the superiority of CBT? Why? Would CBT be effective if a client was not motivated or had a poor memory? From what you know about her, would you recommend CBT to Beth? Explain your answers.

# BIOMEDICAL THERAPIES

Thinking about her mother's depression led Beth to wonder whether medication might help her own anxiety and depression. Five years earlier, Beth's mother had participated in a research study in the hospital to which she had been admitted, where she was treated successfully with antidepressant medication and cognitive–behavior therapy. Although Beth's mother had tried medication many years before, it hadn't helped. Yet the new medication seemed to help a great deal. Might there be medications or other biomedical treatments that would help Beth feel better? With recent advances in knowledge about the brain have come advances in biomedical treatments of many disorders.

## Psychopharmacology

The use of medication to treat psychological disorders and problems is known as **psychopharmacology**. In the last two decades, the number and types of medications for the treatment of psychological disorders have multiplied. As scientists learn more about the brain and its neurotransmitters, researchers are able to develop new medications to target symptoms more effectively and with fewer side effects. Thus, for any given disorder, there are more medication options.

### Schizophrenia and Other Psychotic Disorders

The most common type of medication for the treatment of schizophrenia and other psychotic disorders is **antipsychotic medication** (also called *neuroleptic medication*), which generally reduces psychotic symptoms but does not cure the disorder. Antipsychotic drugs have long been known to have an effect on the positive symptoms of schizophrenia (see Chapter 14), such as hallucinations. Traditional antipsychotic medications include Thorazine and Haldol. However, long-term use of these medications can cause **tardive dyskinesia**, an irreversible movement disorder in which the affected person involuntarily smacks his or her lips, displays facial grimaces, and exhibits other symptoms. *Atypical antipsychotics* are a newer group of antipsychotic drugs that affect the neurotransmitter dopamine (as does traditional antipsychotic medication), as well as other neurotransmitters. For instance, the atypical antipsychotic medication Risperdal cuts down on the amount of free serotonin and dopamine available in the brain, which affects the ease with which signals cross synapses. In addition to decreasing positive symptoms, such as hallucinations, these newer drugs also counteract negative symptoms, such as apathy, lack of interest, and withdrawal, and are effective in improving cognitive functioning (Keefe et al., 1999); all of which can have the effect of allowing psychological therapies to be more effective (Ballus, 1997). These drugs also appear to have fewer side effects than traditional antipsychotic medications, and they are associated with very little de-

**Psychopharmacology:** The use of medication to treat psychological disorders and problems.

**Antipsychotic medication:** Medication that reduces psychotic symptoms.

**Tardive dyskinesia:** An irreversible movement disorder in which the person involuntarily smacks his or her lips, displays facial grimaces, and exhibits other symptoms; caused by traditional antipsychotic medication.

crease in gray brain matter compared to the traditional antipsychotic Haldol (Lieberman et al., 2005). Increasing amounts of data suggest that pharmacological treatment administered soon after the first psychotic episode is associated with a better long-term prognosis, compared to treatment begun later (see Chapter 14; Wyatt et al., 1997).

## Mood Disorders

The number of medications to treat mood disorders continues to grow.

**MEDICATIONS FOR DEPRESSION** Effective pharmacological treatment for depression began in earnest in the 1950s with the discovery of **tricyclic antidepressants (TCAs)**, named for the three rings in their chemical structure. Elavil is an example of this class of drug. For decades, TCAs were the only effective antidepressant medication readily available, although their common side effects include constipation, dry mouth, blurred vision, and low blood pressure. These medications affect serotonin levels, and they can take weeks to work. Although another type of medication, **monoamine oxidase inhibitors (MAOIs)**, was the first antidepressant medication discovered, MAOIs have never been as widely prescribed as TCAs, for two major reasons. First, MAOIs require users not to eat or drink anything that contains the substance *tyramine* (such as cheese and wine) because of potentially fatal changes in blood pressure. Second, they are particularly effective with atypical depression involving increased appetite and hypersomnia (increased need for sleep; Prien & Kocsis, 1995) but less effective with typical symptoms of depression.

**Selective serotonin reuptake inhibitors (SSRIs)**, such as Prozac, Zoloft, and Paxil, were developed in the 1980s. They generally have fewer side effects (they only work on *selective* serotonin receptors), and thus, people are less likely to stop taking them (Anderson, 2000); however, by 2004, researchers were finding that SSRI use among children and adolescents was associated with an increased risk of suicide (Martinez et al., 2005). This increased risk with SSRIs (compared to other antidepressants) has not been found among adults (Fergusson et al., 2005; Gunnell et al., 2005).

A common side effect of SSRIs is decreased sexual interest. In addition, many people experience a "Prozac poop-out" after a while, no longer attaining the same benefit from what had previously been an effective dose. A meta-analysis of the use of Prozac in treating depression found it to be as effective as, but not more so than, TCAs (Agency for Health Care Policy and Research, 1999; Geddes et al., 2000). Researchers continue to discover ways to alleviate symptoms of depression without as many side effects and to discover additional biological mechanisms so that those who do not respond to existing antidepressants can obtain relief from medication. Some newer antidepressants (such as Serzone, Effexor, and Remeron) don't fall into the existing categories; these drugs, which affect both the serotonin and norepinephrine systems, are sometimes referred to as **serotonin/norepinephrine reuptake inhibitors (SNRIs)**. Antidepressant medications are also given to people experiencing dysthymia.

In addition, studies of an extract from the flowering plant **St. John's wort**, *Hypericum perforatum*, suggest that it may be effective as a short-term treatment of mild to moderately severe depression (Agency for Health Care Policy and Research, 1999; Gaster & Holroyd, 2000), although not without minor side effects. One study found that St. John's wort is actually more beneficial than the SSRI Paxil in treating moderate to severe depression (Szegedi et al., 2005). Moreover, medications that block substance P, a neurotransmitter, have been used successfully to treat depression (Kramer et al., 1998, 2004; Rupniak, 2002), although further study will ultimately determine their effectiveness. Substance P blockers do not operate by altering norepinephrine or serotonin directly, as do other antidepressants, but rather these medications work by another mechanism that involves other types of receptors in the brain (Bender, 1998; Santarelli & Saxe, 2003).

**Tricyclic antidepressant (TCA):** A type of antidepressant medication named for the three rings in the chemical structure.

**Monoamine oxidase inhibitor (MAOI):** A type of antidepressant medication that requires strict adherence to a diet free of tyramine.

**Selective serotonin reuptake inhibitor (SSRI):** A type of antidepressant medication that affects only selective serotonin receptors, with relatively few side effects.

**Serotonin/norepinephrine reuptake inhibitor (SNRI):** A newer type of antidepressant that affects both serotonin and norepinephrine neurotransmitter systems.

**St. John's wort:** An herbal remedy for mild to moderate depression.

Studies so far show that the herbal remedy St. John's wort can be effective in treating mild to moderately severe depression.

**ANTIDEPRESSANT EFFECT AS PLACEBO EFFECT?** As we saw in Chapter 13, a person's beliefs and expectations about medication can affect the individual's symptoms through the *placebo effect*, the healing effect that occurs after taking a medically inactive substance that nevertheless has medicinal effects. Consider that a meta-analysis of the effectiveness of antidepressants found that about 75–80% of the effect of antidepressants can be achieved with a placebo. Only about 25% of the response to an antidepressant arises from the active ingredients in the medication. Thus, among those helped by an antidepressant, much—if not most—of the positive response arises from expectations that symptoms will get better (Kirsch & Lynn, 1999; Kirsch et al., 2002a; Kirsch & Sapirstein, 1998; Walach & Maidhof, 1999). In addition, more than half of the antidepressant studies funded by drug companies have found that medication and placebo were equally effective (Kirsch et al., 2002a; Kirsch et al., 2002b).

When the placebo has ingredients that mimic the side effects of antidepressants (so that patients think they are taking the medication and not a placebo), the difference in effectiveness between a true antidepressant and the placebo is even smaller (Greenberg & Fisher, 1989). Moreover, depressed people taking either an SSRI or a placebo medication had similar changes in brain functioning (Leuchter et al., 2002). Thus, someone's *beliefs* about what will happen after taking antidepressant medication (level of the person) affect what happens (level of the brain), which, in turn, affects the person's interactions with others (level of the group).

Note that this does *not* mean that people taking antidepressants should necessarily go off their medication. Taking a placebo is *not* the same as not taking a medication. Rather, it appears that the act of taking a placebo promotes biological changes that would not otherwise occur.

**MEDICATIONS FOR BIPOLAR DISORDER** For bipolar disorder, mood stabilizers such as *lithium* can prevent a recurrence of both manic and depressive phases, although up to half of those with this disorder either will show no significant improvement or will be unable to tolerate the side effects, which include gastrointestinal problems, increased thirst, and trembling. These individuals can instead take a mood stabilizer such as Depakote or Tegretol to minimize the recurrence of manic episodes. During a manic episode, doctors often prescribe antipsychotic drugs or antianxiety drugs. The usual treatment regimen for schizophrenia and bipolar disorder may involve lifelong use of medication.

## Anxiety Disorders

For most anxiety disorders (including panic disorder, the panic symptoms of phobias, and PTSD), **benzodiazepines** are often the medication prescribed. Xanax and Valium are types of benzodiazepines, which affect the target symptoms within 36 hours and do not need to be taken for 10 days or more to build up to an effective level, as is the case with antidepressants. However, they can cause drowsiness and are potentially lethal when taken with alcohol. In addition, a person using benzodiazepines can develop tolerance and dependence (see Chapter 5) and can experience withdrawal reactions. For these reasons, drugs of this class are often prescribed only for short periods of time, such as during a particularly stressful period. Antidepressants (TCAs, SSRIs, or SNRIs) may be prescribed for long-term treatment of anxiety disorders, although the dosage may be lower or higher than that used in the treatment of depression, depending on the anxiety disorder (Gorman & Kent, 1999; Kasper & Resinger, 2001; Rivas-Vazques, 2001). Obsessive-compulsive disorder can be treated effectively with SSRI antidepressants such as clomiprimine, although at a higher dose than that prescribed for depression or other anxiety disorders.

Table 15.4 provides a summary of medications and their effects.

Benzodiazepine: A type of antianxiety medication that affects the target symptoms within 36 hours and does not need to be taken for more than a week to be effective.

## TABLE 15.4  Summary of Medications and Their Effects

| Type of Disorder | Type of Medication | Desired Effects | Side Effects |
|---|---|---|---|
| **Schizophrenia and other psychotic disorders** | Traditional antipsychotics | Decreases positive symptoms | Long-term use can cause tardive dyskinesia. |
| | Atypical antipsychotics | Decreases positive and negative symptoms | |
| **Depression** | Tricyclics | More effective with typical depressive symptoms | Tricyclics: Constipation, dry mouth, blurred vision, low blood pressure. |
| | SSRIs/SNRIs | | SSRIs: Decreased sex drive. |
| | St. John's wort | | |
| | MAOIs | More effective with atypical depressive symptoms | MAOIs: Potentially lethal in combination with tyramine-related foods. |
| **Bipolar disorder** | Lithium | Decreases mood swings | Kidney or gastrointestinal problems; dry mouth. |
| **Anxiety disorders** | Tricyclics, SSRIs/SNRIs | Decreases panic symptoms with regular use | See "Depression" side effects above. |
| | Benzodiazepines | Short term use: Decreases panic symptoms | Drowsiness; tolerance and withdrawal with continued use; potentially lethal if combined with alcohol. |

# Electroconvulsive Therapy

Essentially a controlled brain seizure, **electroconvulsive therapy (ECT)** was developed in the 1930s as a treatment for schizophrenia. It was based on the idea that schizophrenia and epilepsy are incompatible, and thus ECT-induced epilepsy should relieve the symptoms of schizophrenia. Although it does not cure schizophrenia, it is still a recommended treatment when medication does not work (Lehman & Steinwachs, 1998). ECT has been particularly helpful in treating certain mood disorders, such as psychotic depression and manic episodes of bipolar disorder (Maletzky, 2004). In fact, over 80% of those receiving ECT suffer from depression (Eranti & McLoughlin, 2003; Sackeim et al., 1995), often, those with severe depression who have not received much benefit from psychotherapy or medication (Lam et al., 1999) or those for whom drugs are inadvisable for medical reasons. Although the treatment can be effective, the reasons are not well understood. The patient is given a muscle relaxant before each ECT treatment and is under anesthesia during the procedure; because of the anesthesia, ECT is administered in a hospital and generally requires a hospital stay. Patients may experience temporary memory loss for events right before, during, or after each treatment. After a course of 6–12 sessions, usually administered two or three times a week over several weeks (Husain et al., 2004; Shapira et al., 1998; Vieweg & Shawcross, 1998), depression often lifts; relief may come sooner for the depressed elderly (Tew et al., 1999).

ECT was considered a major biomedical treatment in the 1940s and 1950s, but the ready availability of medications in subsequent decades led to a decline in its use. Another reason for its decreased use was that some patients seemed to experience significant cognitive impairment, including memory loss. And, as it became known that it was sometimes used in understaffed institutions to produce a docile patient population (as immortalized in the book and movie *One Flew Over the Cuckoo's Nest*), ECT became politically unpopular. However, improvements in the way ECT is administered have significantly reduced the cognitive deficits and undesirable side effects, and since

**Electroconvulsive therapy (ECT):** Use of an electric current to induce a controlled brain seizure in people with certain psychological disorders such as psychotic depression or those for whom medication has not been effective or recommended.

the 1980s, the use of ECT has increased (Glass, 2001). However, severely depressed patients helped by ECT are at risk for relapse, particularly if they do not take medication after the ECT treatments end (Birkenhäger et al., 2004; Sackeim et al., 2001). The increase in ECT's use reflects a new appreciation of its effectiveness, as well as a recognition that not all people with depression, mania, or schizophrenia can either take medication or find it helpful. In recent years, ECT is more frequently administered to affluent patients than to those in publicly funded hospitals (Sackeim et al., 1995).

## Transcranial Magnetic Stimulation

A new treatment currently being researched is *transcranial magnetic stimulation (TMS)* (see Chapter 3), a procedure in which an electromagnetic coil on the scalp transmits pulses of high-intensity magnetism to the brain in short bursts lasting 100–200 microseconds. Although it is not yet known exactly how this magnetic field changes brain neurophysiology and neurochemistry, TMS has varying effects, depending on the exact location of the coil on the head and the frequency of the pulses. Placebo studies of TMS (in which the procedure of TMS is administered, but at an angle that does not affect the brain) have found that actual TMS is more effective than the placebo (George et al., 1999; Klein et al., 1999). Studies of people with depression who have not responded to medication have yielded positive results, with depressive symptoms decreasing after TMS (Epstein et al., 1998; Figiel et al., 1998; Klein et al., 1999). Some studies have found that severely depressed people receiving TMS respond as well as those receiving ECT (Dannon et al., 2002; Janicak et al., 2002). Should additional studies confirm these early positive results, TMS offers a number of advantages over ECT, including easier administration (it requires neither anesthesia nor hospitalization) and minimal side effects. The most common short-term side effect, experienced by 5–20% of patients, is a slight headache.

TMS has been administered to people with depression, bipolar disorder (Grisaru, Chudakov, et al., 1998), schizophrenia (Hoffman et al., 2003; Poulet et al., 2005), OCD (Alonso et al., 2001), and PTSD (Grisaru, Amir, et al., 1998). But more research, particularly on the coil's location and the stimulation's frequency, is needed before TMS can be declared a treatment of choice rather than an experimental one (Kauffmann et al,. 2004; Schlaepfer et al., 2003).

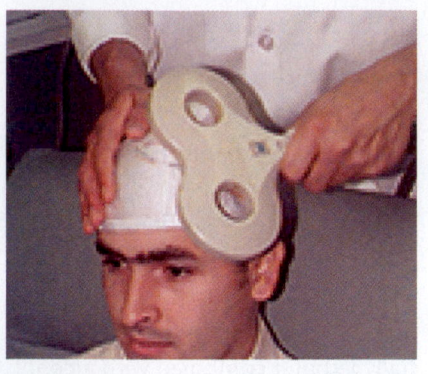
Unlike someone undergoing ECT, the person receiving transcranial magnetic stimulation is awake and does not need anesthesia.

# Test Yourself

1. What do MAOIs, SSRIs, and SNRIs have in common?
   a. They all have potentially fatal side effects.
   b. They all restrict blood flow to the brain.
   c. They all depress activity in the brain's prefrontal cortex.
   d. They all affect neurotransmitter functioning.
2. Both SSRIs and SNRIs work by
   a. preventing the reuptake of certain neurotransmitters.
   b. adding more of certain neurotransmitters to the bloodstream.
   c. metabolizing almost all of certain neurotransmitters produced by the brain.
   d. preventing certain neurotransmitters from inhibiting reuptake.

3. What is the current perspective on the use of ECT?
   a. It is an outdated technique that is of no benefit to anyone with a psychological disorder.
   b. The undesirable side effects have been reduced, making it useful in some cases.
   c. It can replace most drugs for treating schizophrenia.
   d. It is largely ineffective for treating severe depression.
4. Based on experimental research, an advantage of TMS over ECT is that TMS
   a. is much more effective than ECT.
   b. has no side effects at all.
   c. is much easier to administer than ECT.
   d. No advantages have yet been found for TMS.

## Answers

1.d 2.a 3.b 4.c

## Think It Through!

Suppose your best friend's mother has bipolar disorder. What treatment would likely be given to her? Why? Suppose instead that your friend's father has schizophrenia; what treatment might he receive?

Under what circumstances might you consider ECT to be a reasonable treatment for someone?

# OTHER FORMS OF TREATMENT

During the course of her therapy, Beth talked about her vivid memories of her mother's episodes of depression, about the times when her mother would lie in bed most of the day. However, her mother had not had an episode of severe depression in the last 5 years. Beth was surprised when her therapist raised the possibility of having her mother come in for a few sessions; the idea had not occurred to her.

Beth's questions about treatment continued. Cost-related forces were changing the way health care was delivered. How might these changes affect her mother and the course of her own therapy? As health insurance companies and health care professionals seek ways to provide effective treatment in a time- and cost-efficient manner, some psychological therapies have changed; today, increasing emphasis is placed on considering a wider array of treatments that might be helpful and on intervening as early as possible.

## Modalities: When Two or More Isn't a Crowd

Each therapy approach mentioned so far can be implemented in a variety of **modalities**, or forms. **Individual therapy**—therapy in which one client is treated by one therapist—is a modality. Other modalities have one or more therapists working with a family or with a group of people who share some commonality, such as a diagnosis of agoraphobia. Each theoretical orientation discussed earlier can be brought to bear in these various modalities: individual, group, or family.

**Modality:** A form of therapy.

**Individual therapy:** A therapy modality in which an individual client is treated by a single therapist.

**Group therapy:** A therapy modality in which a number of clients with compatible needs meet together with one or two therapists.

### Group Therapy

Clients with compatible needs who meet together with one or two therapists are engaging in **group therapy**. This modality became offered more frequently after World War II, when there were many more veterans seeking treatment than there were therapists available to treat them individually. The course of treatment in group therapy can range from a single occasion (usually an educational session) to ongoing treatment lasting for years. Some groups are for members who have a particular problem or disorder, focusing on, for instance, recent divorce or post-traumatic stress disorder. These groups may offer emotional support, psychoeducation, and concrete strategies for managing the problem or disorder. Other groups have members who do not share any specific problem or disorder, but rather who want to learn more about maladaptive or inappropriate ways in which they are interacting with people; the therapy group provides an opportunity to learn about themselves and change their undesired patterns of behavior.

Group therapy can help reduce shame and isolation and can provide support and an opportunity to interact in new ways with other people.

In addition to offering information, support, and (if the group has a cognitive–behavioral orientation) between-session homework assignments, group therapy provides something that individual therapy cannot: interaction with other people who are experiencing similar difficulties. The group experience can decrease the sense of isolation and shame that clients sometimes feel. In revealing their own experiences and being moved by others', clients often come to see their own lives and difficulties in a new light. Also, because some clients' problems relate to their interpersonal interactions, the group provides a safe opportunity for clients to try out new behaviors.

## Family Therapy

In **family therapy**, a family as a whole, or a subset of some of its members, such as a couple, is treated. A "family" is often defined as consisting of those who think of themselves or function as a family; thus, blended families created by marriage are seen in family therapy, as are other nontraditional families. The most common theoretical orientation among those providing family therapy is **systems therapy**, which starts from the premise that no client is an island: A client's symptoms occur in a larger context, or system (the family and subculture), and any change in one part of the system will affect the rest of the system. Thus, the client is referred to as the "identified patient," although the system (the couple or the family) is considered the "patient" that is to be treated. Systems therapy was originally used exclusively with families; in fact, some of the pioneers in systems therapy would refuse to see individuals without their families. For this reason, systems therapy is sometimes referred to as "family therapy," although this is a misnomer. Some therapists treat entire families, but not necessarily from a systems approach. They may use a psychodynamic or behavioral approach. Similarly, some systems therapists see individuals without their families, but the therapy makes use of systems theory. Systems therapy can also be the theoretical framework used to treat couples in therapy.

Systems therapy focuses on a family's communication, structure, and power relationships. The theory views the identified patient's symptoms as attempts to convey a message. Initially, a systems therapist takes a family history to discover which members of the family are close to one another or angry with one another and to ascertain more generally how anger, sadness, and other feelings or issues are handled within the family. Systems therapists often illustrate these relationships graphically (see Figure 15.6). In some cases, one parent may be underinvolved and the other overinvolved; treatment would be directed to encourage the underinvolved parent to be more involved, and the overinvolved parent to be less involved. Or, the parents' relationship with each other may need strengthening, with consequences for other family members, because conflict between parents affects their children's behavior (Kitzmann, 2000).

Systems therapy techniques include (Minuchin, 1974; Minuchin & Fishman, 1981):

- **paradoxical intention**, which encourages a behavior that seems contradictory to the desired goal (Stanton, 1981)—this technique has also been called "prescribing the symptom" and is useful in treating families who appear resistant or unable to change or who aren't able to implement suggestions from the therapist;

- **reframing**, in which the therapist offers a new way of conceptualizing, or "framing," the problem; and,

- **validation**, in which the therapist conveys his or her understanding of clients' feelings and wishes.

### FIGURE 15.6

## Systems Therapy: Family Interaction

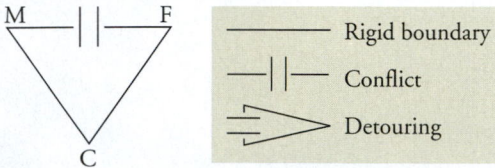

This triangle graphically represents the following type of family interaction: The mother and father criticize each other and then reroute their conflict by both attacking their child. Systems therapy would focus on decreasing the conflict between the parents and strengthening their relationship.

**Family therapy:** A therapy modality in which a family (or certain members of a family) is treated.

**Systems therapy:** A type of therapy that views a client's symptoms as occurring in a larger context, or system (the family and subculture), and holds that a change in one part of the system affects the rest of the system.

**Paradoxical intention:** A systems therapy technique that encourages a behavior that seems contradictory to the desired goal.

**Reframing:** A therapy technique in which the therapist offers a new way of conceptualizing, or "framing," the problem.

**Validation:** A therapy technique in which the therapist conveys his or her understanding of the client's feelings and wishes.

For instance, in a family in which the parents fight a lot, an adolescent boy's rebelliousness may serve to unite his parents in their anger and frustration at him. The systems therapist might explain to the family that their son is intentionally being rebellious to keep his parents united (validation), for fear of what could happen to the parents' relationship if he wasn't causing them problems (reframing). The family therapist might praise the son for his efforts at keeping his parents together, and even urge him not to stop rebelling yet, because his parents haven't yet practiced how to relate to each other without fighting (paradoxical intention).

A therapist with a systems orientation treating Beth might, after taking a family history, reframe the problem. The therapist might propose that Beth is sacrificing herself: Beth's difficulties allow her mother to be a "good mother" to Beth in ways she had not been when Beth was younger, such as frequently checking how Beth is doing. Thus, Beth's illness serves the function of allowing her mother to feel good about herself as a mother. The therapist might also validate Beth's offering of herself in this way—suggesting that her concern for her mother is so great that she would sacrifice her own current opportunities in order to provide this opportunity for her mother. The therapist might even give Beth a paradoxical intention: Beth should not get better until her mother becomes a "nervous wreck" from worrying about Beth. This paradoxical intention would serve the purpose of indirectly pointing out how Beth's behavior may in fact have the opposite effect of the one she desires.

Self-help group: A group whose members focus on a specific disorder or event and do not usually have a clinically trained leader; also called a *support group*.

Bibliotherapy: The use of self-help books and tapes for therapeutic purposes.

## Self-Help Therapies

Self-help therapies are available both in groups and individually.

**HELPING GROUPS** Self-help groups (sometimes referred to as *support groups*) can be used on their own or as a supplement to psychotherapy and are focused on a specific disorder or event. They do not usually have a clinically trained leader, although a mental health professional may be involved in some capacity (Shepherd et al., 1999). Alcoholics Anonymous (AA), the first self-help program, is based on 12 steps toward recovery. Most 12-step programs view a belief in a Higher Power (for most people, God) as crucial to recovery, and meta-analytic results show that weekly attendance in group meetings is associated with drug or alcohol abstinence, whereas less than weekly attendance is not (Fiorentine, 1999). People who are not religious can also benefit from attending AA meetings (Winzelberg & Humphreys, 1999) or meetings of Smart Recovery, an organization for overcoming drug or alcohol abuse that does not use a 12-step approach but is based on cognitive behavioral principles. Another self-help group that does not use the 12-step approach is the National Depressive and Manic Depressive Association, which helps those suffering from bipolar disorder or depression and their families and friends. Self-help groups not only are valuable sources of information and support, but also can provide referrals to therapists who are knowledgeable about the particular disorder or problem. Relatives of those with a psychological disorder report that such groups are helpful in providing support and promoting self-understanding (Citron et al., 1999). As is true in group therapy, self-help groups can be invaluable in decreasing feelings of isolation and shame.

**HELPING YOURSELF** Self help is not limited to groups. The last two decades have witnessed a proliferation of self-help books and tapes dealing with a wide range of problems; the use of such materials is sometimes referred to as **bibliotherapy**. Many of these materials incorporate philosophies and techniques of the therapies discussed in this chapter, and therapists often suggest that clients read particular books (Adams & Pitre, 2000; Starker, 1988). Researchers have found that such material can help with depression and

Meta-analyses revealed that self-help materials help primarily people with depression (Cuijpers, 1997), headache, sleep disturbances, and fears (Gould & Clum, 1993), and such materials can also reduce anxiety (Finch et al., 2000; Scogin et al., 1990). For many people, self-administered treatment programs available through books and audiotapes appear to be more effective than no treatment at all (Scogin et al., 1990).

anxiety (Febbraro, in press; Floyd et al., 2004; Gregory et al., 2004), but are not as effective for helping people to eliminate habits such as smoking, drinking, and overeating. Not surprisingly, those who complied with the materials' recommendations fared better than those who did not (Gould & Clum, 1993).

Another vehicle for self-help is the Internet, where there are "support groups" in chat rooms and psychoeducation on Web sites. However, user beware: Information on a Web site may not be accurate, and people in an online support group may not be who they claim to be (Finn & Banach, 2000; Waldron et al., 2000). Other self-help tools are available in CD-ROM form or are downloadable. Such tools include self-monitoring logs and information and instructions on using exposure or cognitive restructuring.

Some of the Web-based self-help cognitive–behavioral programs are better than no treatment. Perhaps because of the interactive nature of the technology, some research indicates that Web-based programs may be more effective than traditional self-help therapies—at least for some disorders (Richards et al., 2003) and compared to no treatment (Carlbring et al., 2001). Although such tools can be effective (Berström et al., 2003; Proudfoot et al., 2003; van den Berg et al., 2004), there are few rigorous studies comparing them to face-to-face therapy (Kaltenthaler et al., 2004; Luce et al., 2003; Ritterband et al., 2003). Moreover, such programs may not address the needs, concerns, or questions of all users, possibly leading some who could benefit to stop the program (Clarke et al., 2002; Tate & Zabinski, 2004).

# Innovations in Psychotherapy

As psychologists learn more about effective treatments, treatment changes. Changes also occur as a result of technological and economic realities.

## Psychotherapy Integration: Mixing and Matching

In the last quarter century, many therapists have moved away from a single theoretical orientation, such as psychodynamic or behavioral. Surveys found that between 68% (Jensen et al., 1990) and 98% (Smith, 1982) of mental health professionals identify themselves as *eclectic* in orientation. A therapist using **psychotherapy integration** uses techniques from different theoretical orientations, with an overarching theory of how the integrated techniques will achieve the goals of treatment. A therapist's integrating of specific techniques *without* regard for an overarching theory is referred to as **technical eclecticism** (Beutler & Hodgson, 1993). This integrative approach involves the incorporation of new techniques based on research findings and the clinical needs of a particular client at a specific point in the treatment (Stricker, 1993). Such an approach provides the aspects of therapy that are common to all theoretical orientations (such as offering hope, a caring listener, and a new way of thinking about problems) and employs specific techniques for a given disorder, such as exposure with response prevention for people with OCD (Weinberger, 1995). Two clients with the same diagnosis may receive different integrative treatments from the same therapist, based on factors other than the diagnosis—such as family issues, a client's preference for directive versus nondirective treatment, and other concerns.

## Managed Care and Psychotherapy

The cost of health care in general became extremely expensive in the last two decades of the 20th century, and the system of health care administration known as *managed care* was developed as a way to contain costs. Managed care seeks to limit the cost of health care while providing services deemed medically necessary by health care admin-

Psychotherapy integration: The use of techniques from different theoretical orientations with an overarching theory of how the integrated techniques will be used to achieve the goals of treatment.

Technical eclecticism: The use of specific techniques that may benefit a particular client, without regard for an overarching theory.

istrators. However, when managed care organizations alone determine what services are necessary for mental health, they alone come to define mental health. As shown in Figure 15.7, however, some suggest that mental health should be defined by society, the individual client, and the mental health professional (Strupp, 1997; Strupp & Hadley, 1977).

Like it or not, today's standard of what constitutes good health care is being driven not by clinicians, but by the financial bottom line. In mental health, one way to reduce costs has been to limit the amount of inpatient and outpatient services. Thus, psychotherapy providers, regardless of theoretical orientation or modality, have tried to meet the challenge of attaining the same level of effectiveness in a reduced number of sessions. There is some support for the idea that a time limit on psychotherapy can accelerate the rate of therapeutic change (Reynolds et al., 1996).

Although therapists have become adept at helping clients get better in fewer sessions, it is unclear whether brief therapy provides long-term positive change or protection against relapse. There is a dose–effect relationship between therapy and outcome: the more therapy, the greater its positive effect, up to a point. Many of the studies examining the effectiveness of time-limited psychotherapy were based on treatments of approximately 20 sessions, more than is currently allowed by some health insurance companies, except in cases of chronic mental illness such as schizophrenia. Note, however, that for many specific phobias, brief—even one session—treatments can be very effective (Hellström & Öst, 1995; Öst et al., 1997; Öst et al., 2001).

**FIGURE 15.7** **Who Should Decide How Mental Health Is Defined?**

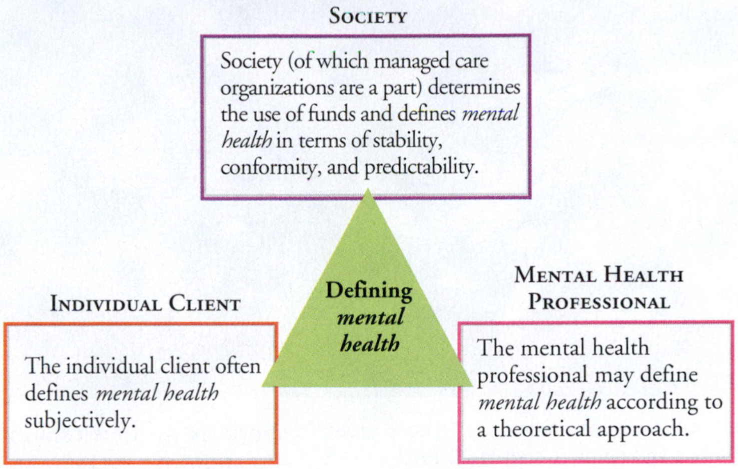

Strupp (1997; Strupp & Hadley, 1977) suggests that three groups should determine how mental health is defined: society, the individual client, and the mental health professional.

## Time and Therapy: Therapy Protocols and Brief Therapy

The last 25 years has seen a rise in the use of *therapy protocols*, detailed session-by-session manuals specifying how therapy should proceed for a specific disorder from a certain theoretical orientation (such as behavior therapy for panic disorder or cognitive therapy for depression). These manual-based treatments were created, in part, to ensure that when a research study was testing the effectiveness of a given therapy (for example, CBT), all the therapists were using the same techniques in the same way. This meant, of course, that the results of the study were relevant to the treatment's effectiveness because the conditions were comparable. Some clinicians advocate the use of therapy performed without deviation from treatment manuals (Addis, 1997). However, a large study of the manual-based treatment of panic disorder found that, even when therapists adhere to the manual, each therapist, as an individual, makes his or her own unique contribution to the treatment (Huppert et al., 2001; Malik et al., 2003). Many of the protocols for manual-based therapy were developed for treatment lasting 15–20 sessions. Today, many managed care organizations in different parts of the United States will approve 3–10 sessions, and the therapist must request additional sessions, precluding the systematic use of sessions as is done in manual-based therapy. Research indicates that those with recent, focused problems in one sphere of life (such as work) receive more benefit from brief psychotherapy than those who have difficulties in multiple spheres or who have long-standing problems (Barkham & Shapiro, 1990; Klosko et al., 1990; Roth & Fonagy, 2005; Strupp & Binder, 1984).

Manual-based treatments usually focus on specific disorders, and they tend to utilize behavioral or cognitive–behavioral techniques. For instance, there are research-based

IPT for depression was adapted to a group format and administered in 30 rural villages in Uganda (which were randomly selected). Compared to depressed people in control villages, who received no treatment, those who received group IPT had a significant reduction of their depressive symptoms and were able to function better in their daily lives (Bolton et al., 2003).

High-tech gadgets such as this palmtop computer are at the cutting edge of brief CBT; they are often preprogrammed with tasks to help participants self-monitor their thoughts.

**Interpersonal therapy (IPT):** A type of researched, manual-based treatment that focuses on how issues that arise in the client's current relationships can affect mood.

**Cybertherapy:** Therapy over the Internet.

treatment manuals for behavior therapy for various anxiety disorders and for CBT for depression, anxiety disorders, and eating disorders. (Elkin et al., 1989; Linden et al., 2005; Wilson & Fairburn, 2002).

Another type of researched, manual-based treatment is **interpersonal therapy (IPT)**, which focuses on how issues that arise in the client's current relationships can affect mood. This type of therapy arose from theory about the importance of interpersonal relationships (Sullivan, 1953) and was developed in the late 1970s for a research study examining various treatments of depression. The goal of IPT is to help the client's relationships work better and become more satisfying. IPT for depression rests on the assumption that if the relationships are functioning better, the depression will lessen. Therapeutic techniques include helping clients explore the consequences of their actions in their relationships and facilitating better personal communication, perhaps by encouraging clients to tell others how they feel. IPT protocols have been adapted to treat people with bulimia nervosa (Mitchell et al., 2002) and PTSD (Bleiberg & Markowitz, 2005).

## Technology and Therapy: High-Tech Treatment

Technological advances have been incorporated into therapies; such technological tools include PDAs, CD-ROM or downloadable software, and communication via the Internet.

**HIGH-TECH TREATMENT EXTENDERS: TOOLS OF THE TRADE**   Computer technology is now used to facilitate brief treatment (Gega et al., 2004) through the use of PDAs (or palmtop devices) and software. The goal of using these technologies is to reduce symptoms through increased access to (computerized) treatment, lessening the amount of time spent with the therapist. Palmtop devices can be used for portable self-monitoring. For instance, a PDA may have an alarm that goes off at set or random times during the day, signaling the client to assess mood, hunger, anxiety, or some other relevant variable or to employ a previously learned technique such as muscle relaxation. Consider that research on the use of a palmtop device that was preprogrammed with cognitive–behavioral tasks found that 4 weeks of such assisted treatment (plus 8 weeks of practice with the device) was—as determined at follow-up—as effective as 12 weeks of regular CBT (Newman, Kenardy, et al., 1997). Subsequent studies have found similar results (Przeworski & Newman, 2004).

Another form of high-tech treatment extender is software that facilitates behavioral techniques such as exposure (sometimes through virtual reality programs) or cognitive techniques such as cognitive restructuring; this type of software is used in conjunction with therapy. These kinds of materials contrast with computer programs that are used exclusively as self-help treatments (Christensen et al., 2004).

**THERAPY OVER THE INTERNET: DOCTOR ONLINE**   The advent of the Internet has also led to a form of treatment sometimes referred to as **cybertherapy**, or therapy over the Internet. This sort of therapy may be helpful for those who have no ready access to mental health services (Tate & Zabinski, 2004), such as rural residents, as well as for people who have severe medical problems in addition to psychological ones and people with agoraphobia. Several types of cybertherapeutic interactions are possible. One is an Internet version of individual therapy, in the form of a "pay-for-each-response" e-mail exchange with a therapist. Some therapists have voiced concern about such types of interactions, considering the treatment less effective than face-to-face sessions and ethically questionable (Ragusea & VandeCreek, 2003), for the following reasons:

1. The anonymity offered via the Internet cuts two ways, and the "therapist" offering the treatment may not be professionally trained or licensed.

2. Confidentiality and privacy cannot be guaranteed on the Internet.

3. The multitude of nonverbal cues (facial expressions, body language, emotional responsiveness, tone of voice) that pass between client and therapist are absent during most forms of cybertherapy (Bloom, 1998; Ragusea & VandeCreek, 2003); although some people are using webcams to provide nonverbal cues, the video quality still leaves something to be desired. On the plus side, it has been argued that simply putting thoughts and feelings on paper (or rather, on screen) can be therapeutic, as can having a complete transcript of the treatment for later reading and reflection (Murphy & Mitchell, 1998).

Other types of cybertherapy include "live" two-person chat rooms and therapist-led online support groups (Taylor & Luce, 2003) as well as listserv-type support groups that allow people to interact via e-mail. Such support groups can be helpful (Houston et al., 2002; Miller & Gergen, 1998), but more research is needed. Although studies generally find that cybertherapy is more effective than no treatment (Lange et al., 2001, 2003), there is little research as to whether cybertherapy—particularly simultaneous interactions (as in chat rooms)—is as effective as face-to-face therapy (Tate & Zabinski, 2004). E-mail has also been used in family therapy in cases when some family members live too far away to attend sessions (King et al., 1998), but researchers have yet to test whether this tool is an effective addition to family therapy.

# Prevention: Sometimes Worth More Than a Pound of Cure

Programs intended to prevent mental illness aim to halt the development or progression of psychological disorders by using social or cultural interventions. As shown in Figure 15.8, such interventions typically fall into one of three categories:

- *Universal preventive interventions* target all members of a general group, some of whom may be at higher risk to develop a given disorder (Mrazek & Haggerty, 1994). Examples of universal prevention programs include school programs on preventing suicide or drug abuse.

- *Selective preventive interventions* target subgroups that have a higher risk of developing a given disorder than the general population (Mrazek & Haggerty, 1994). For instance, research suggests that children with a depressed parent are at higher risk than those without a depressed parent to develop psychological disorders such as depression, anxiety disorders, and alcohol dependence (Weissman et al., 1997). Those at risk in this way might receive cognitive therapy to help modify irrational automatic thoughts that could lead to depression; a study that provided CBT to such at-risk adolescents helped minimize the later development of depression (Clarke et al., 2001). Another example is a program for people who are

**FIGURE 15.8**

## Three Types of Preventive Interventions

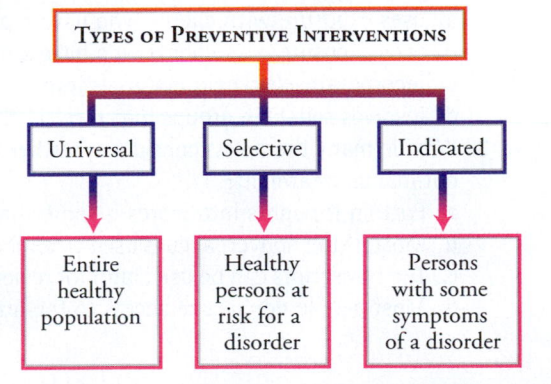

TYPES OF PREVENTIVE INTERVENTIONS

Universal — Entire healthy population

Selective — Healthy persons at risk for a disorder

Indicated — Persons with some symptoms of a disorder

Historical Influences / Cognitive–Behavior Therapy / Biomedical Therapies / Other Forms / Which Therapy Works Best? / Review and Remember    713

Employee stress management programs are an example of universal preventive interventions.

sensitive to anxiety, in which participants were taught exposure techniques; the goal of the program was to prevent the development of anxiety disorders among those at risk (Schmidt & Vasey, 2002). Programs in selective prevention may be administered by a community mental health center, a hospital, or another facility providing mental health services.

■ *Indicated preventive interventions* target those at higher risk who have some symptoms of a disorder, but not the full-blown disorder (Mrazek & Haggerty, 1994). An example is experimental treatment for adolescents at extremely high risk for developing schizophrenia: Some of these young people are given a low dose of an antipsychotic medication at the first signs of symptoms (but before psychosis develops) and others are given a placebo. The hope is that such an intervention will minimize the frequency and duration of episodes of schizophrenia, and early results indicate that these intervention efforts can be effective (Cannon et al., 2002; McGorry & Edwards, 1998), as can CBT for those at heightened risk (Morrison et al., 2004). Community mental health centers and hospitals offer indicated interventions.

Some prevention programs are available through publicly funded services such as community rape crisis centers or Head Start preschool programs. Others may be offered through private sources, such as health insurance companies or employers. For example, these organizations may offer stress management programs or support groups for relatives of those diagnosed with Alzheimer's disease (these relatives experience significant amounts of stress and are at risk for developing disorders such as anxiety and depression).

The Internet has also become a vehicle for preventive interventions (of all three types), with psychoeducation, CBT tools, and online discussion groups targeted to appropriate individuals, such as a program for college-aged women who had significant body-image concerns (Zabinski et al., 2004).

# Test Yourself

1. Systems therapy utilizes techniques such as reframing, validation, and _____.
   a. self-help groups
   b. paradoxical intention
   c. integration
   d. eclecticism
2. Bibliotherapy
   a. uses exposure with clients who have a phobia of libraries.
   b. uses exposure with clients who have a phobia of books.
   c. incorporates self-help materials into treatment.
   d. involves self-help groups that meet in the local library.
3. Why do many therapists consider cybertherapy to be less than optimal as treatment?
   a. Putting thoughts into words is somewhat therapeutic.
   b. Most of the nonverbal cues used by a therapist are missing.
   c. The transcripts can be used later for reviewing the sessions.
   d. Most people don't have access to the Internet or e-mail.

4. What is the difference between selective and indicated preventive interventions?
   a. The selective interventions are for people with a disorder, and the indicated interventions are for those at risk of developing a disorder.
   b. The selective interventions are for people with severe symptoms of a disorder, and the indicated interventions are for those with mild symptoms.
   c. The selective interventions are for people with personal problems, and the indicated interventions are for those with symptoms of some disorder.
   d. The selective interventions are for people with a risk of developing a disorder, and the indicated interventions are for those with some symptoms of a disorder.

## Answers

1. b 2. c 3. b 4. d

# Think It Through!

Suppose a friend decides to seek help for a problem. He tells you that his therapist is "eclectic"—what does that mean? He also tells you that he's agreed to participate in a study of manual-based treatment. What can you infer about his treatment, and what should you not infer?

Suppose a different friend shows no sign of any disorder, but is involved in a prevention program: What type of preventive intervention would that program likely be?

# WHICH THERAPY WORKS BEST?

After a number of therapy sessions, Beth began to feel better. She was going to class more often, and felt better able to handle studying and preparing for tests. She wanted to know what it was about the therapy that was helping her, and why her therapist used specific techniques at certain times. Her treatment had not included medication, and she still wondered whether she would be feeling even better—or worse—if she had taken medication. She also wondered whether her therapy would be as effective for other people in her situation. If her best friend went to see Beth's therapist for anxiety and depression, would her friend fare as well as Beth?

## Issues in Psychotherapy Research

Hundreds of types of psychotherapy are currently available (Garfield & Bergin, 1994), but many of them do not rest on well-constructed and replicated research. Research is crucial for determining how well a new or old type of therapy treats a particular problem. It is easy to claim that a new therapy is a wonder cure, but harder to back up that claim with solid data. There are many issues to consider when evaluating findings about psychotherapy.

Research that asks whether clients feel better, function better, live more independently, or have fewer symptoms after treatment is called **outcome research**. These questions are trickier to answer than it would seem because they depend on how you define "outcome"; in research lingo, the answers to the questions depend on what you designate as the therapy's dependent variable. For example, you could have clients rate their thoughts, feelings, *or* behaviors, which are not necessarily highly correlated and might yield different outcomes (Kazdin, 1994). You must also decide how long after the end of treatment to assess outcome (Roth & Fonagy, 2005): Immediately afterward? A month later? A year later? And even if you find that clients are better after treatment, how can you know that this occurred because of the treatment itself and not simply because their symptoms improved with time? Suppose you do find that the group that received treatment fared better than a group that did not receive treatment but rather is on a waiting list for it—a *wait-list control group*. Can you attribute the improvement to the treatment itself? How can you know which elements of the treatment were the ones that led to clients' improvement? These questions get at the heart of some the challenges of conducting outcome research. Let's examine some of the key issues.

## Positive Change in Therapy: The Healing Powers

Although therapy does not always reduce the frequency or intensity of the troublesome symptoms that bring people to treatment, it often works (Garfield & Bergin, 1994;

Outcome research: Research that asks whether, after psychotherapy, clients are feeling better, functioning better, living more independently, and experiencing fewer symptoms.

Lambert & Ogles, 2004; Matt & Navarro, 1997). As psychologists have attempted to understand why psychotherapy works, they have categorized two types of beneficial factors—*common factors* and *specific factors*. **Common factors** are curative aspects of therapy common to all types of treatment. For instance, just going to and being in therapy provides hope, a chance of emotional expression, support and advice, an explanation and understanding of one's difficulties, and an opportunity to experiment with new behaviors and thoughts (Garfield & Bergin, 1994). Table 15.5 lists some common factors. Research points to the importance of the therapy relationship, and common factors are at least as important in determining positive outcomes as specific factors (Ackerman et al., 2001; Lambert & Barley, 2001; Norcross, 2001).

Carl Rogers appears to have been at least partly correct: A supportive and warm therapy relationship facilitates the success of the therapy (Beutler et al., 1994; Roth & Fonagy, 2005).

**A COMMON FACTOR: EXPRESSING EMOTIONS** One common aspect of therapies is that clients spend time focusing on and talking about their emotions—fear, worry, anxiety, disappointment, sadness, despair. Does the expression of emotion have a therapeutic effect? The answer appears to be yes. In studies where some participants were asked to write about their feelings concerning a stressful event, these participants made fewer doctor visits, showed improved immune functioning, and had a greater sense of well-being than those in the control group (these studies are discussed in greater detail in Chapter 13; Pennebaker, 2004; Pennebaker et al., 1990). When participants were asked about their writing experiences, 76% described the writing as helping them attain insight; one said, "It made me think things out and really realize what my problem is" (Pennebaker et al., 1990). In fact, studies comparing the benefits of this particular form of expressive writing with the benefits of a few sessions of psychotherapy have found that both interventions have similarly positive effects in the long run (Murray et al., 1989). It is as if the act of deliberately processing the emotional experience, whether in writing or with a therapist, transforms the experience into a less upsetting event. However, participants seeing a psychotherapist had more positive moods immediately after therapy sessions, and those using expressive writing had more negative moods immediately after writing.

The psychotherapy sessions and the writing exercises focused on feelings surrounding a traumatic event that occurred in the past, often an event about which the participants had not told anyone. Thus, the therapy and the writing provided opportunities for participants to think about issues that they had not previously explored and constituted a type of exposure treatment, focusing on thoughts about the traumatic event. Moreover, such emotional expression created a cognitive structure for thinking about the issues (Pennebaker, 2004; Sloan & Marx, 2004). It should be noted, however, that most studies on emotional expression through writing have used relatively healthy college undergraduates as participants. It remains to be seen whether the therapeutic results will be the same with participants who have been diagnosed with psychological disorders.

**SPECIFIC FACTORS** In contrast to common factors are **specific factors**—those aspects that relate to the particular type of therapy employed. With the advent of cognitive and behavioral treatments, researchers shifted from asking the general question of whether therapy is helpful (the answer is yes; Lambert & Ogles, 2004) to asking whether one type of therapy is better than another for treating particular problems or disorders. That is, are specific factors related to a type of therapy or a particular technique uniquely helpful for treating a given disorder? For people with OCD, exposure with response prevention is a specific factor, and this is the most important factor in improvement (Abramowitz, 1997).

**Common factor:** In psychotherapy, a curative aspect that is common to all types of treatment.

**Specific factor:** In psychotherapy, a curative aspect that is related to the specific type of therapy being employed.

**TABLE 15.5** **Common Factors**

All effective therapies have certain factors in common: They provide support and opportunities for learning, and they help people behave in new ways.

| Factors Related to Support Provided by the Therapy | Factors Related to Therapy's Opportunities for Learning | Factors Related to New Behaviors Resulting from Therapy |
|---|---|---|
| Therapist's warmth, respect, empathy, genuineness, acceptance | Advice | Behavioral regulation |
| The bond between therapist and client | Cognitive learning | Cognitive mastery |
| Reassurance | Corrective emotional experience | Facing and dealing with fears |
| Decreased isolation | Feedback | Taking risks |
| Identification with therapist | Insight | Attempts at mastery |
| Positive relationship with therapist | Changing expectations of personal effectiveness | Modeling |
| Structure provided by therapy sessions | | Practice |
| | | Experience with success |

## Comparing Therapy Approaches and the Allegiance Effect

In reviewing research comparing different types of therapy, Lester Luborsky and colleagues (1975, 1977, 1999) noticed an allegiance effect: Researchers of a particular orientation tended to find evidence supporting that orientation. However, this effect appears to have decreased more recently, perhaps because, knowing about the allegiance effect, researchers have taken steps to ensure that all comparison therapies are carried out equally competently (Emmelkamp, 2004).

## What's an Appropriate Control Group?

When researchers are testing whether a medication is effective, participants in a study are usually assigned either to a group that receives the medication or to a group that receives a placebo. The effects of the medication are compared to those of the placebo to determine whether the drug is effective. Applying this approach to gauging whether psychotherapy is effective is more complex: What is a "placebo therapy"? Suppose that the therapist providing the "placebo" treatment is warm and supportive, but refrains from using specific therapeutic techniques? The common factors of therapist warmth and support are real, and thus such a "placebo" treatment (called an *attention placebo*; Kendall et al., 2004) shares common factors with the treatment to which it is compared, but it does not provide the specific techniques of that treatment (Lambert & Ogles, 2004).

Another possibility is to compare treatment to no treatment. For ethical and other reasons, this usually means putting one group of participants on a waiting list for treatment while another group receives the treatment. Both groups are compared before and after the time interval of treatment. Utilizing a control group reduces the possibility that any improvement in the treatment group occurred simply because the symptoms got better with time. However, long-term follow-up comparisons between the two groups become impossible once the wait-list control group receives the treatment.

*Treatment as usual* describes another type of control group: Participants in this group receive whatever treatment is currently practiced for the particular disorder while another group receives a new treatment (Kendall et al., 2004), and researchers ask whether the new treatment works better than the usual one.

When a treatment group is compared to a wait-list control group, there is usually a bigger difference between the two groups than when a group receiving a treatment is compared to a group receiving an attention placebo (Grissom, 1996; Lipsey & Wilson, 1993), which suggests that common factors (such as attention and therapist warmth) are an important ingredient of change, at least in the treatment of some disorders (Lambert & Ogles, 2004).

## Reducing Confounds

In the last several decades, research on specific factors has become increasingly sophisticated and increasingly focused. The general goal has been to reduce the number of possible confounds that might account for client differences after treatment, which makes it possible to attribute any positive (or negative) change to the therapy itself. When two treatment groups are to be compared in a study, what if—before treatment begins—the groups differ on any of the confounding factors listed in Table 15.6?

Among possible client factors, for instance, what if clients receiving one type of treatment rather than another happen to have more supportive friends and relatives available? That group might fare better after treatment, but not necessarily because of the specific treatment. Or in another study with a wait-list control group, a treatment group may not fare as well because those clients happened to have more severe symptoms, compared to the clients in the control group.

Among therapist factors, what if two treatments were compared, and one group of clients had greater symptom relief, but the therapist providing that treatment happened

| **TABLE 15.6** **Possible Confounding Factors** | | |
| --- | --- | --- |
| **Client Factors** | **Therapist Factors** | **Treatment Factors** |
| Clients may differ in: | Therapists may differ in: | The treatment may differ in: |
| ■ Severity and chronicity of symptoms | ■ Type of treatment performed | ■ How client and therapist see the problem and its solution |
| ■ Age | ■ Experience level | |
| ■ Personality | ■ How much supervision they receive | ■ The fit of client's and therapist's personalities |
| ■ Motivation and readiness to change | ■ General competence (such as sensitivity) | ■ The client's and therapist's ethnic heritage |
| ■ Presence of additional disorders | ■ Ability to implement specific techniques | ■ Overall therapist's caseload and severity of clients' problems |
| ■ Level of social support | | ■ The type of treatment used to treat a given disorder |
| ■ Level of stressors | | |
| ■ Number of treatment sessions received | | |

to be more experienced? And regarding treatment factors, what if one treatment group happened to have clients who didn't see eye to eye with the therapist about the nature of their problem and its solution? It wouldn't be a surprise if such a group didn't fare as well after treatment.

Thus, one issue in therapy research is how to minimize the number of possible confounding variables.

## Randomized Controlled Trials

To reduce the likelihood of confounds, many large studies that compare two or more treatments assign clients randomly to one or another treatment group (or to a control group). Such studies are referred to as *randomized controlled trials (RCTs)*.

**RANDOM ASSIGNMENT**   A critical element of RCTs is the random assignment of participants to groups. Let's examine this more closely. What would it mean if participants were not randomly assigned to their treatment group? Suppose those who were more depressed were put in one of the medication groups, but that all the therapy groups turned out to be more improved than the medication groups; we couldn't then conclude that therapy was more effective than medication because the participants in the medication groups were in worse shape to begin with. Random assignment is crucial if we want to be able to infer anything about the effectiveness of one treatment over another. However, there are many confounding variables that are not solved by RCTs (Roth & Fonagy, 2005). For instance, it may not be possible to randomize participants with respect to everything that may be important.

**SPECIFIC DISORDERS AND EXCLUSION CRITERIA**   To minimize further the likelihood of confounds, researchers may exclude from the study people whose symptoms do not meet the exact criteria for a disorder or people who have more than one diagnosis, such as depression *and* panic disorder or an anxiety disorder *and* substance abuse (Stirman et al., 2005). How do such exclusions reduce the probability of confounding variables? Suppose you are studying the effects of a treatment for depression. Further suppose that some clients in the treatment group also have substance abuse problems, other clients are depressed and have an anxiety disorder but not substance abuse problems, and other clients are depressed but do not have another disorder. What if the treatment is helpful for clients with certain types of *comorbid disorders* (that is, two disorders that exist at the same time) but not others? The conclusions that can be drawn from the study are limited by the specific variety of comorbid disorders that clients in the study have.

However, excluding clients with comorbid disorders has a drawback: Even if an RCT finds that a particular treatment is helpful for those diagnosed with only one disorder, that same treatment may not be helpful for those with that disorder plus another disorder (Seligman, 1995; Westen & Morrison, 2001). So, treatment that is helpful for depressed people who are only depressed (and not also anxious or abusing substances, for example) may not be helpful for those with depression and some other disorder. Although the exclusion criterion makes research findings more clear-cut, it limits their generalizability because most clients arriving at a therapist's office have more than one type of disorder. For example, more than half of those diagnosed with an anxiety disorder have at least one additional disorder, and 30–40% of those with a diagnosis of depression also have a diagnosis of a personality disorder (Sleek, 1997).

Moreover, even when studies exclude people with comorbid disorders, not everyone with the same disorder has the exact same symptoms to the same degree. And people with a different mix of symptoms may—due to the luck of the draw—end up in different groups, which may, in turn, affect the study's results because a treatment may be effective for some symptoms but not others. The RCT design doesn't address this issue of heterogeneity among clients with the same disorder.

**REDUCING THERAPIST AND TREATMENT CONFOUNDS** In addition to minimizing confounds related to the clients in a study, research also seeks to minimize confounds related to the therapists and the treatment they employ (see Table 15.6) For instance, studies may employ a treatment manual and require therapists to be supervised to ensure that they are following the manual. Other confounding therapist factors noted in Table 15.6 are less frequently addressed.

Some of the possible confounding treatment factors, such as the fit of the client's and therapist's personalities, are complex and extraordinarily difficult to assess. In some cases, factors may not be specifically addressed in the study's design, but rather are examined statistically after its completion, such as by investigating whether gender-related factors are at play (Beutler et al., 2003). Meta-analysis may be able to sort out some confounding therapist and treatment factors, but a meta-analysis is only as good as the studies that go into it. If such an analysis is based on studies that aren't similar in fundamental aspects (such as the specific type of therapy, the length of treatment, and the exact diagnosis of participants), it isn't clear what the results mean (Lambert & Ogles, 2004). For instance, a small but growing number of studies have examined various forms of time-limited psychodynamically oriented therapy, and a number of meta-analyses have looked at the overall effect of such treatment, finding evidence to support its effectiveness (Crits-Christoph, 1992; Leichsenring, 2001). However, some studies that have been included in the meta-analyses are arguably not focused on psychodynamic therapy but on what could even be considered CBT (Roth & Fonagy, 2005), calling into to question what, exactly, is being evaluated in the meta-analyses.

**GENERALIZABILITY: THE EFFICACY VERSUS EFFECTIVENESS TRADE-OFF** Even with all the efforts to minimize possible confounds, psychologists are left with a more fundamental question about what, exactly, is being studied and what are the broad implications of the results? Assessing the effects of therapy through RCTs is referred to as testing its *efficacy*. This contrasts with assessing therapy's *effectiveness*—the effects of therapy as it is normally conducted, with patients who may have more than one disorder or whose symptoms may not meet the exact criteria for a given disorder, with therapists who may not be using a manual or may use one flexibly, and with a number of sessions that may exceed the number specified by the average health insurance company. Whereas RCTs strive to document whether treatments' outcomes are *reliable*—that is, they can be replicated—research that does not rely on RCTs strives to document whether treatments' outcomes are *valid*—that is, whether the treatments are effective as they are actually conducted by most clinicians most of the time (Roth & Fonagy, 2005). Although therapy in RCT studies generally leads to better outcomes than therapy in general practice (Shadish et al., 2000), this finding may reflect several factors (Morrison et al., 2003; Roth & Fonagy, 2005):

- Therapists in RCTs receive more supervision than otherwise occurs.

- Therapists in RCTs may have had more training than would a random set of therapists.

- Clients in RCTs may be more motivated for treatment (and ready for change) than are a random set of clients.

- Clients with multiple diagnoses (and more problems) are excluded from RCTs.

**OUTCOME MEASURES** A crucial part of a study is the outcome measures themselves, those variables that the researchers actually assess. Measures can focus on behaviors, thoughts, or feelings in relation to specific symptoms or on more general patterns of functioning. Different types of therapy might be differentially effective with each of these possible outcome measures. For instance, medication might be more effective than cognitive therapy for some symptoms of depression, such as tiredness and poor appetite, but be less effective for other symptoms, such as poor relationships or negative thinking (Segal et al., 1999). The type of outcome measures used can bias the results in favor of one form of therapy over another. In order to avoid this pitfall, some studies collect data with multiple types of outcome measures (Blatt et al., 2000; Imber et al., 1991).

**DROP-OUTS**   A methodological problem encountered in any research on treatment is how to handle the phenomenon of people dropping out of the study before treatment is completed. Consider that 50% or more of those who begin treatment in a research study may drop out (Kazdin, 1994). And if more participants drop out of one group than another, you can draw only limited conclusions about the treatments. For example, more people may drop out of a medication group because of unpleasant side effects, or more people may drop out of a placebo group because they don't feel any better. Thus, it's not always clear how to calculate a treatment's effect: Should you include only those who finished the treatment or also those who dropped out before completion? Psychologists have developed statistical methods to address this issue (Kendall et al., 2004).

**FOLLOW-UP**   Finally, it is important for outcome research to determine what happens after treatment ends, and whether the results change with the passage of time. How much time should pass before obtaining follow-up results? The longer the period of time, the harder it will be to track down participants, leading to attrition. In addition, some disorders, such as major depression, often recur; thus, symptoms are likely to increase after long enough periods of time (Roth & Fonagy, 2005).

# UNDERSTANDING RESEARCH

## For OCD: CBT Plus Medication, Without Exclusion

Researchers have found that exposure with response prevention is helpful for OCD. However, that research excluded people with an additional diagnosis. Franklin and colleagues (2002) set out to investigate whether similar results would occur when patients with both OCD and another disorder are not excluded.

**QUESTION:** When people who have OCD *and* another psychological disorder are not excluded from participating in research on treatment, is CBT based on exposure with response prevention *plus* medication more effective for treating the OCD than CBT alone?

**ALTERNATIVES:** For this broader sample, (1) the combined treatment is as effective as CBT alone; (2) the combined treatment is *more* effective than CBT alone; or (3) the combined treatment is *less* effective than CBT alone.

**LOGIC:** If CBT *plus* medication increases the overall effectiveness of treatment, such combined treatment should lead to fewer OCD symptoms than CBT alone.

**METHOD:** Fifty-six people with OCD participated in this study; approximately half of the participants were taking medication at the time the study began (referred to as the "CBT + medication group"), and half were not (referred to as the "CBT-alone group").

Participants were not randomly assigned to these treatment groups; their membership in one or the other group was based on whether they happened to be taking medication at the time the study began. The members of the two groups had comparable symptoms before CBT began. CBT was based on a manual intended as a flexible guide rather than an exact blueprint. Treatment took place in 18 sessions, typically lasting 2 hours each.

**RESULTS:** CBT substantially reduced symptoms in both groups, and to the same extent.

**INFERENCES:** Medication neither interfered with nor enhanced the benefits of CBT. One drawback of the study, however, is that those who were taking medication prior to CBT could have had more symptoms before taking medication than they had at the time the study began. If they had had more symptoms before taking medication, the two treatment groups (CBT + medication and CBT alone) cannot be considered to have been equivalent before CBT began. An advantage of this study's design, however, is that it more closely resembles treatment that isn't part of a research project—where some people who seek CBT may have other disorders and may already be taking medication.

## THINK CRITICALLY!

How could a research study determine whether people with OCD who take medication and also receive CBT have, at the outset of the study, similar severity of symptoms to those with OCD who do not take medication but only receive CBT? What would be the drawback(s) of conducting such a study? Suppose that participants in the medication group agreed to stop their medication before the study began, and their symptoms did not reduce to the same level as those who were not taking medication. What could you conclude about the two groups, and what should you not conclude?

## Which Treatment Works Best for Which Disorder?

In looking for specific factors that can alleviate symptoms—and do so efficiently—much research has tried to answer this question: Which treatment works best for a given disorder? Some organizations have created lists of *empirically supported treatments* (ESTs, also referred to as *empirically validated treatments* or *evidence-based treatments*), which are treatments that clearly or probably are efficacious for a particular disorder (Chambless et al., 1996; Chambless & Hollon, 1998). Table 15.7 notes the specific criteria for considering a treatment to be empirically supported.

Not all mental health researchers and clinicians agree that such EST lists guarantee the best outcome (Ablon & Marci, 2004; Garfield, 1996, 1998; Goldfried & Eubanks-Carter, 2004; Lambert & Barley, 2001; Westen et al., 2004a, 2004b). Criticisms of EST lists include the following:

- It may not be valid to apply RCT results to therapy not part of a research study.

- Such lists do not recognize that common factors can be at least as important as specific factors in influencing outcome.

- The lists do not recognize the effects of therapist- and client-related factors.

---

**TABLE 15.7** **Criteria for Empirically Supported Treatments (ESTs)**

- The treatment group is compared to a control group or to a group receiving another type of treatment. An EST is significantly superior, or of comparable efficacy to a treatment already considered efficacious.

- Studies assessing the treatment must:

  • use a treatment manual,

  • include participants in the study in a reliable and valid way,

  • have the treatment focus on a specific disorder, and

  • use methodologically sound outcome assessment measures.

---

- They do not recognize the importance of being flexible regarding clients' needs and any comorbid problems that might require deviation from a therapy manual.

In fact, the National Institute for Health and Clinical Excellence in the United Kingdom deliberately does not use EST lists because of these issues.

Most treatments on an EST list utilize CBT techniques because that is the type of therapy most frequently studied. However, the CBT label may be too broad; in some cases, only very specific techniques may be helpful for a given disorder. For example, exposure with response prevention—but not other CBT techniques—is most helpful for OCD. IPT is another treatment cited as an EST for some disorders. Although some studies may find short-term psychodynamic therapy helpful (Sandahl et al., 2004; Svartberg et al., 2004), the small number of these studies precludes evaluating its effectiveness in general (and so it is usually not considered an EST).

Another problem with ESTs is that many people do not respond to the first treatment they receive. For instance, even among those who receive one of the ESTs for depression, up to half may continue to have significant symptoms at the end of treatment (Hollon et al., 1992). Thus, these people may subsequently receive another type of treatment, and some treatments may work better as a "second line of defense" for some people.

## Therapy, Medication, or Both?

We've noted that therapy—specifically behavior therapy—can work as well as medication to alleviate OCD. Is this general result true for other disorders? The answer to this global question is no, but the specific treatment or treatments that is most effective varies from disorder to disorder (Gloaguen et al., 1998; Reynolds et al., 1999; Thase et al., 1997). As we discuss specific treatments for particular disorders below, we will also note relevant comparisons with medication.

**DEPRESSION** As noted in Table 15.8 (on p. 725), CBT and IPT have repeatedly been shown to provide relief from depression (Blatt et al., 2000). However, depression has one of the highest relapse rates among psychological disorders, and it appears that common factors—common at least among different forms of CBT and IPT—rather than specific techniques, may be key to therapeutic change with depression (Emmelkamp, 2004).

In a neuroimaging study of CBT's effects, 17 depressed adults had PET scans taken before and after 15–20 CBT sessions (Goldapple et al., 2004). As expected, symptom reduction was associated with changes in brain function. However, some brain areas were more active after treatment (such as the hippocampus and part of the cingulate cortex), whereas other areas were less active (such as regions of the frontal lobe). Thus, depression is not caused simply because some brain areas are not activated enough; at least some areas may be too active. In addition, the researchers compared these findings with those from patients who improved after they took the SSRI Paxil. This treatment produced strikingly different brain changes (see Figure 15.9): Following this drug treatment, portions of the frontal lobe became more active (not less active, as was found following CBT), and the hippocampus became less active, not more active. Thus, the two types of treatment for depression affect the brain differently. The bottom line is that depression arises from a set of brain areas working in abnormal ways, and several changes in how those

**FIGURE 15.9**

## Brain Changes After Successful CBT for Depression Versus Medication

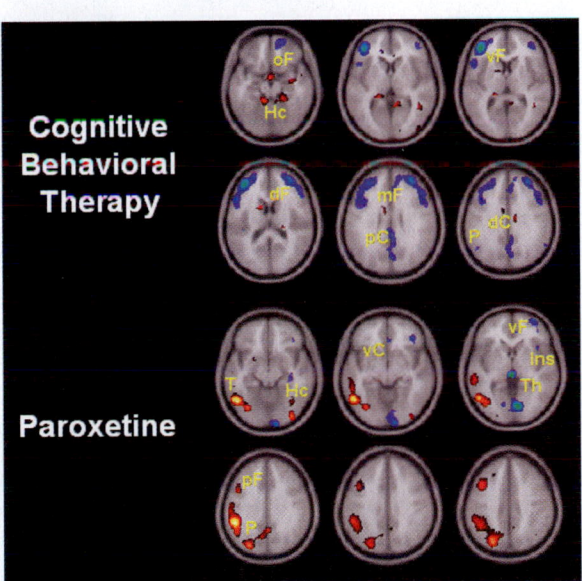

CBT and medication for depression produce different changes in brain activity, which suggests that the different therapies rely on different mechanisms. Increased activity is shown in orange and decreased activity is shown in blue.

areas function can be associated with improvement. However, it is likely that the different brain changes produce different patterns of symptom change, but this has yet to be established.

Medication does alleviate depression for many people; why, therefore, might someone choose psychotherapy over medication? The main drawback of medication becomes apparent when you look at how people with depression fare over the long haul. When medication is discontinued, the relapse rate is high, a fact that has led some doctors to recommend continued use of medication for those at risk for additional depressive episodes (American Psychiatric Association, 2000b). Cognitive–behavioral treatment provides an equivalent benefit without the side effects of drugs (Antonuccio et al., 1995; DeRubeis et al., 2005), and it may help prevent relapse (Hollon & Shelton, 2001; Hollon et al., 2005). The skills and tools learned during psychological treatment are likely to remain after treatment stops.

CBT may also help treat residual symptoms of depression following treatment with antidepressant medication (Paykel et al., 2005). This supplemental use of CBT lowers the relapse rate when medication is discontinued (Fava et al., 1998a; Otto et al., 2005). At a 6-year follow-up, those who had supplemental CBT were less likely to have had another episode of depression than those without CBT (Fava et al., 1998b). Similarly, a number of studies have found that medication and cognitive therapy combined may be more helpful than medication alone, even with severely depressed people (Macaskill & Macaskill, 1996; Thase et al., 1997), although not all studies have found an additional benefit of adding medication to CBT or IPT (Browne et al., 2002; Oei & Yeoh, 1999; Otto et al., 2005).

**ANXIETY DISORDERS** For a number of anxiety disorders, exposure appears to be particularly helpful (see Table 15.8). In comparison to medication, researchers have shown that particular types of psychotherapy (CBT and IPT) provide as much, if not more, long-term relief of symptoms (Gould et al., 1995; Otto et al., 2005). In the treatment of panic disorder, for instance, although medication and CBT work about equally well, CBT does a better job of preventing symptom relapse (Chambless & Gillis, 1993; Otto et al., 1994). And as we saw, for OCD, one behavior therapy technique—exposure with response prevention—is as helpful as medication, and possibly more helpful over the long term (Foa et al., 2005). Moreover, combining the exposure treatment with medication wasn't more beneficial than just using exposure. However, some researchers question whether these findings generalize to clients diagnosed with more than OCD alone (Kozak et al., 2000). In the treatment of social phobias, research shows that SSRIs and group CBT are equally helpful (Davidson et al., 2004; Heimberg et al., 1998). However, when medication is discontinued, the symptoms usually return; in contrast, the beneficial effects of CBT continue after treatment ends.

**OTHER DISORDERS** For the treatment of bulimia nervosa, CBT and IPT have been shown to have efficacy in RCTs (see Table 15.8); the results are less conclusive for the treatment of anorexia nervosa. Meta-analytic studies of medication versus CBT for treating participants with bulimia nervosa have found CBT to be more effective (Whittal et al., 1999).

For the treatment of schizophrenia, family interventions are efficacious, but research results are not yet available to indicate whether cognitive therapy has efficacy or effectiveness in treating delusions (Gaudiano, 2005). Unlike treatment of most of the disorders listed in

Although medication can work in treating social phobia, such as a fear of public speaking, it is not necessarily superior to CBT because symptoms often return after medication is stopped. CBT's benefits usually last after treatment ends.

Table 15.8, medication for schizophrenia and bipolar disorder is clearly superior to therapy, although CBT can help decrease psychotic symptoms (Gould et al., 2001; Rector & Beck, 2001; Thase & Jindal, 2004). For people with these disorders, therapy can play a role in helping them to accept the need to take medication on a lifelong or long-term basis (Colom et al., 1998; Tohen & Grundy, 1999) and can provide an opportunity to learn new relationship skills after the medication has helped them to be more stable. Moreover, psychological treatment in conjunction with medication can help patients to identify any triggers of the psychotic, manic, or depressive episodes and can help prevent relapses (Buchkremer et al., 1997; Goldstein, 1992). Recent guidelines for the treatment of schizophrenia advocate behavioral and cognitive skills training to encourage compliance with the medication regimen and social skills training to help improve functioning (Lehman & Steinwachs, 1998). CBT can also be effective in helping to reduce positive symptoms in schizophrenic patients who are not helped by medication (Kuipers et al., 1997, 1998; Sensky et al., 2000; Tarrier et al., 1998). A meta-analysis of nonmedication treatments for schizophrenia found that those patients with more chronic symptoms were more responsive to psychotherapy than those whose symptoms were more transient (Mojtabai et al., 1998).

**CAVEAT**  We need to end this section with a caveat: As with all research that examines groups of people, the results of research on the efficacy or effectiveness of various treatments do not necessarily apply to a particular individual. Thus, for any particular person with a given disorder, one type of therapy may be more effective than another, which in turn may be more effective than medication. The opposite may be true for someone else with apparently identical symptoms. Moreover, a number of disorders have a moderately high rate of relapse. For instance, in some studies, as many as half of those who receive a psychological treatment for depression later have a relapse (Gortner et al., 1998; Westen & Morrison, 2001). For such individuals, a combination of therapy and medication may be most helpful (Thase & Jindal, 2004).

| TABLE 15.8 | Which Treatment for Which Disorder? |
|---|---|

Listed here are particular treatments that are considered ESTs for some of the disorders discussed in Chapter 14. Note that all the disadvantages of ESTs apply to the treatments in this table, which primarily lists treatments based on their efficacy (in RCTs), not necessarily their effectiveness with clients used outside the confines of a research study.

**Mood Disorders**

| Depression | **CBT** |
|---|---|
| | **IPT** |
| | *Short-term psychodynamic therapy* |
| Bipolar Disorder | *CBT focused on depressive symptoms, creating a stable lifestyle, and relapse prevention* |
| | *Family interventions* |

**Anxiety Disorders**

| Panic Disorder | **CBT, particularly exposure** |
|---|---|
| Specific Phobia | **Exposure therapy (in vivo)** |
| Social Phobia | **CBT, particularly exposure** |
| OCD | **Exposure with response prevention** |
| PTSD | **CBT** |

**Eating Disorders**

| Anorexia Nervosa | *CBT* |
|---|---|
| | *Family therapy* |
| | *Focused psychodynamic therapy* |
| Bulimia Nervosa | **CBT** |
| | **IPT** |

| Schizophrenia | **Family interventions** |
|---|---|
| | *Cognitive therapy for delusions* |

Note: Treatments in boldface have clear evidence of efficacy in RCTs; treatments in italics have some, but limited evidence of efficacy.

## Treatment for an Ethnically Diverse Population

According to the 2000 census, 30% of the population of the United States are members of an ethnic minority, and this number continues to grow (Zane et al., 2004). As the composition of the American population changes, so too does the composition of

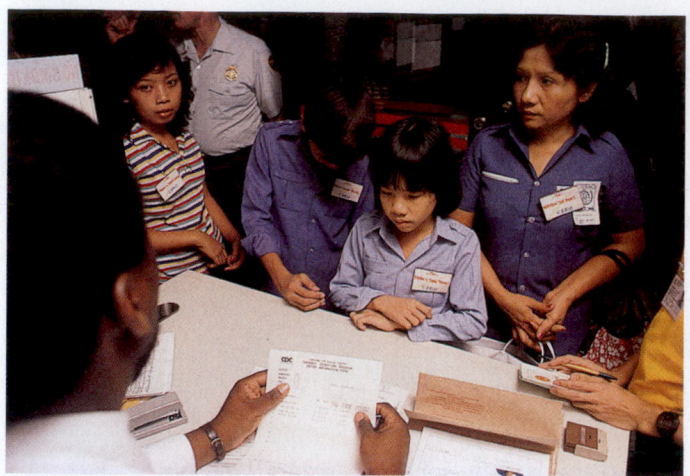

Therapists try to be aware of unique ethnic and cultural factors that can play a role in treatment, such as the stressors related to being an immigrant, a refugee, or a member of a minority group.

the population seeking mental health services. At least until the early 1990s, most psychotherapy research did not include information about race, education, or economic status. However, these factors may influence the effectiveness of a given treatment for a particular client (Francis & Aronson, 1990). Psychotherapists are now more aware of the need to consider a client's background, cultural values, and attitudes about psychotherapy (McGoldrick et al., 1996; Ramirez, 1999). For instance, a client's immigrant or refugee experience creates a stressor that can affect mental health. And members of minority groups who are born and raised in the United States may experience prejudice and other hardships that can affect mental health.

An example of the importance of understanding a symptom's cultural context can be found in *ataques de nervios* (Spanish for "attack of nerves"), which some Puerto Rican women experience. This condition is a physical expression of strong emotions and includes trembling, heart palpitations, numbness, difficulty breathing, loss of consciousness, and a hyperkinetic (overactive) state (Rivera-Arzola & Ramos-Grenier, 1997). The context for this illness is a culture in which women are likely to endure great hardships, have little real power, and are actively discouraged from expressing anger. *Ataque de nervios* provides a culturally sanctioned way for them to express an inability to cope with a current situation, and the community responds (Rivera-Arzola & Ramos-Grenier, 1997).

It is clear that the most effective therapist is one who is aware of both the cultural and familial contexts of a client's disorder. It is part of a therapist's responsibility to be aware of cultural or racial issues that can affect all aspects of treatment—diagnosis, the process of the therapy, and its goals (Helms & Cook, 1999; Ramirez, 1999). The therapist should inquire about the client's understanding of the meaning of the problem, so that therapist and client can discuss and come to agreement on the nature of the problem, the interventions to be used, and the expected goals (Higgenbotham et al., 1988; Kleinman, 1978).

Although age, sex, and ethnicity do not appear to play a systematic role in therapy outcomes generally (Beutler et al., 1994; Lam & Sue, 2001), research suggests that some people (such as some Asian Americans) prefer a therapist from their own ethnic group, and such matching leads to better outcomes for them (Sue et al., 1994). In general, however, there is yet no clear-cut evidence that matching client and therapist by ethnicity results in better outcomes for clients of most ethnic groups (Garfield, 1994). Some attempts have been made to develop particular therapies for certain ethnic groups, with varying success; for example, *cuento therapy* (from the Spanish word for "fable"), which uses folktales or stories, has proved helpful with some Latino/Latina children (Sue et al., 1994).

# How to Pick a Therapist and a Type of Therapy

Suppose you, like Beth, decide to seek psychotherapy. How do you pick a therapist? Keep several factors in mind when trying to find someone who could most effectively help you. If your problem is identifiable (such as depression or anxiety), it's a good idea to see someone who has experience in treating people with that problem.

There are many state and national referral agencies and professional associations, such as the American Psychological Association, the National Association of Social Workers, and the American Psychiatric Association (see Chapter 1 for a discussion regarding different types of mental health practitioners). Regional organizations, such as the Massachusetts Eating Disorders Association or the Manic-Depressive and Depressive Association of Boston (MDDA-Boston), can also provide referrals for specific problems. These organizations all have national associations that can also supply the names of therapists with expertise in treating specific problems.

If a certain type of therapy seems as if it may be a good fit with your problem, you might want to obtain referrals for a therapist who is experienced at providing that type of treatment. National organizations such as those listed in Table 15.9 may be able to refer you to therapists in your local area.

It can be helpful to get the names of several therapists because any one therapist may not have compatible office hours, location, or available times. You can also ask friends, family members, teachers, and religious leaders for recommendations, as well as the counseling center at your college or university. Many insurance companies will authorize or reimburse treatment only if the provider is on their list. Thus, it's best to tell the therapists you are considering what insurance coverage you have and ask whether their services are reimbursed by that company; if they don't know, call the company and check. Alternatively, call your insurance company and ask for referrals to a therapist who is experienced in helping people with your problem or in a particular type of therapy.

It is important that you feel comfortable with your therapist. If you don't, you may be less likely to talk about what's on your mind or about how you are really doing. And if you aren't able to talk about these things, the therapy can't be as helpful. It's also important to feel that the therapist is trustworthy—if the therapist doesn't have your trust, you will find it easy to discount what he or she says if it is something that you don't want to hear. If after one or two sessions, you realize that you just don't feel comfortable, make an appointment with someone else and see whether the situation feels different. Therapists are used to this initial "try out" period, and you shouldn't worry about possibly hurting their feelings by switching to someone else.

| TABLE 15.9 | National Organizations for Specific Types of Therapy |
|---|---|

- American Association for the Advancement of Behavior Therapy
- Beck Institute for Cognitive Therapy and Research
- Albert Ellis Institute
- American Institute for Cognitive Therapy
- International Society for Interpersonal Psychotherapy
- American Psychoanalytic Association

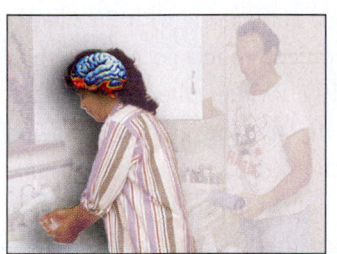

# LOOKING AT LEVELS

## Treating Obsessive-Compulsive Disorder

We know that both behavior therapy and medication can help those with obsessive-compulsive disorder (OCD). But do the two types of treatments exert their beneficial effects in a similar way? And can we fully understand why these treatments work by considering only the level of the brain?

OCD is marked by intrusive, illogical thoughts and overpowering compulsions to repeat certain acts, such as hand-washing to get rid of germs (see Chapter 14). In some cases, OCD can be disabling. To study the effects of behavior therapy on this disorder, the brain activity of nine people with OCD was examined by PET scanning before and after behavior therapy

FIGURE 15.10 **Brain PET Scans Before and After Behavior Therapy**

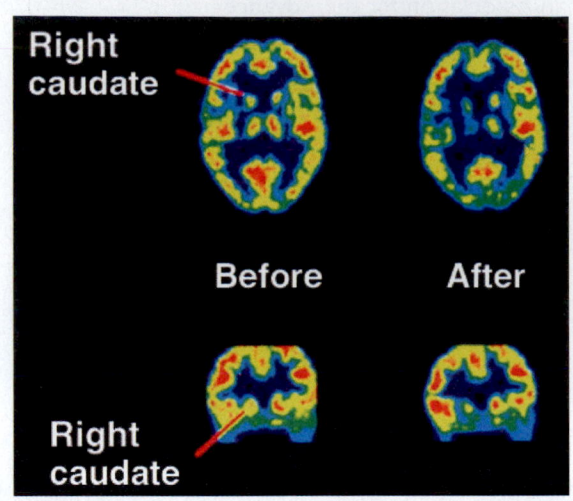

These PET scans show someone with OCD before (left) and after (right) 2 months of behavior therapy. Note the changes in the right caudate after successful treatment.

(which included exposure with response prevention) (Baxter et al., 1992). In addition, to compare such therapy to medication, the brains of nine other people with OCD were also scanned, before and after they received the SSRI fluoxetine (Prozac), which suppresses some of the symptoms of OCD. The scans revealed that behavior therapy and Prozac both decrease activity in the right caudate (part of the basal ganglia involved in automatic behaviors). The drug also affected the anterior cingulate and thalamus, both of which are involved in attention. The effects of behavior therapy on the brain were replicated by Schwartz and colleagues (1996; see Figure 15.10) and Nakatani and colleagues (2003).

But, as usual, considering the brain in isolation will not tell us the complete story. At the level of the person, researchers have also shown that trying new behaviors (not washing dirty hands or not rechecking a locked door) and testing the truth of automatic negative thoughts (that nothing catastrophic happened after leaving the hands dirty or not checking that the door was locked) encourage people to replace old, maladaptive thoughts and behaviors with more adaptive ones and provide a sense of mastery and hope (Emmelkamp, 2004). These events at the level of the person, in turn, lead the individuals to persist in engaging in the new behaviors. These events, in turn, affect events at the level of the brain: the functioning of specific brain circuits.

Events at the level of the group are also involved. It is interactions with another person—the therapist—that help to change the thoughts, feelings, and behaviors of the individual with OCD. And just like people with schizophrenia (see Chapter 14), people with OCD whose family members are high in expressed emotion—particularly in expressing hostile criticism—are more likely to relapse (Chambless & Steketee, 1999; Emmelkamp et al., 1992). People with OCD who were receiving behavior therapy were six times more likely to drop out of treatment if relatives provided hostile criticism (versus constructive criticism or support; Chambless & Steketee, 1999). Thus, although exposure with response prevention can be very helpful, events at the level of the group can influence whether clients relapse after the treatment or even stick with it.

Given that family members can sometimes play such an important role, treatment for OCD may also specifically target group-level events, changing family members' responses to the client's symptoms and to his or her newly learned strategies (Van Noppen & Steketee, 2003). For instance, prior to treatment, family members may have gone along with the client's wishes, for example, by not touching certain "contaminated" objects; such accommodation can inadvertently reinforce the client's maladaptive beliefs and behaviors. Alternatively, family members may become (understandably) angry and frustrated by the client's behavior, which leads them to be hostile; however, such a response usually increases the patient's anxiety and symptom severity. In such cases, psychoeducation or behavior therapy for the family members focuses on helping them not to accommodate to the client's symptoms and instructs them in how to support the client's efforts at exposure with response prevention. Such family participation can help reduce the OCD symptoms (Grunes et al., 2001; Van Noppen & Steketee, 2003).

Moreover, as symptoms subside, the client's personal relationships often change. For example, some of the time and energy that was devoted to OCD rituals can now be spent on relationships. Thus, events at the three levels of analysis and their interactions are helpful in understanding different aspects of treatment for this disorder.

# Test Yourself

1. Some researchers want to know whether clients have fewer symptoms and feel better after participating in therapy. This type of research is known as
   a. experimental psychology.
   b. psychoanalytic review.
   c. in-home monitoring research.
   d. outcome research.
2. What is the general consensus on the effectiveness of drugs versus psychotherapy for treating depression?
   a. Drugs are always the more effective treatment for depression.
   b. Psychotherapy is vastly superior to drugs for treating depression.
   c. Psychotherapy can work as well as drugs for treating depression.
   d. Neither drugs nor psychotherapy has any lasting effect on the symptoms of depression.

3. For the treatment of anxiety disorders, should we conclude that therapy and medication are equally effective?
   a. No, medication is superior to therapy.
   b. No, therapy is superior to medication.
   c. Medication is superior to therapy, but it has no long-lasting benefit after people stop taking it.
   d. Although the two are equally effective, therapy is likely to have a longer-lasting benefit after treatment ends.
4. What does research say about the influence of clients' sex, age, and ethnicity on the outcomes of therapy?
   a. Clients benefit more from a therapist who is of the same sex, age, and ethnicity.
   b. Clients benefit more from a therapist who differs from them in sex, age, and ethnicity.
   c. In general, these three factors do not systematically affect the outcomes of therapy.
   d. The matching of the client's and therapist's age and sex does not seem to matter, but the ethnicity of the therapist can influence the outcome of therapy.

## Answers

# Think It Through!

Suppose you were designing a treatment program for an ethnically diverse set of depressed clients. What would you want to know about these clients? How would you use that information? How would you design a study to test the effectiveness of your new program? Why would you do it that way?

# REVIEW AND REMEMBER!

## Summary

### I. Historical Influences on Psychotherapy: Insight-Oriented Therapies

**A.** Insight-oriented therapies rest on the belief that psychological problems are caused by emotional forces.

**B.** Such treatments focus on helping people gain insight into their problems and propose that such insight will lead to changes in thoughts, feelings, and behavior.

**C.** Examples of insight-oriented therapies are psychodynamic therapy and client-centered therapy.

**D.** Psychodynamic therapy focuses on unconscious conflicts and sexual and aggressive drives. The goal of the therapy is to make unconscious conflict conscious.

**E.** Psychodynamic techniques include free association, dream analysis, interpretation, and the use of transference.

## Your Notes

I.

A.

B.

C.

D.

E.

**F.** Client-centered therapy focuses on each client's unique experiences and potential for growth. The goal of the therapy is to unblock the client's potential for growth by decreasing incongruence.

**G.** Client-centered techniques include showing empathy and unconditional positive regard toward the client.

## II. Cognitive–Behavior Therapy

**A.** Behavior therapy is grounded in the idea that psychological problems are a product of a client's learning history. Treatment seeks to help the client develop more adaptive behaviors.

**B.** Behavioral techniques based on classical conditioning include systematic desensitization, progressive muscle relaxation, exposure, and stimulus control.

**C.** Behavioral techniques based on operant conditioning include behavior modification and self-monitoring.

**D.** Cognitive therapy is grounded in the idea that psychological problems are caused by faulty perceptions or interpretations. Treatments seek to help the client develop more realistic thoughts.

**E.** The REBT sequence of techniques (ABCDEF) may be used by a therapist in trying to persuade the client to give up his or her irrational beliefs.

**F.** Beck's cognitive therapy involves the identification of dysfunctional automatic thoughts and cognitive distortions and replacing them with more rational responses.

**G.** Both types of cognitive therapy generally focus on current problems and often assign between-session homework.

## III. Biomedical Therapies

**A.** Medication is one type of biomedical therapy. Medications are used to treat schizophrenia and mood and anxiety disorders, as well as other disorders.

**B.** For schizophrenia and other psychotic disorders, traditional antipsychotic medications reduce positive symptoms but can cause serious side effects. Atypical antipsychotic medications can also reduce negative symptoms and have less serious side effects.

**C.** TCAs, MAOIs, SSRIs, SNRIs, and St. John's wort can be used to treat depression. Mood stabilizers such as lithium can help alleviate symptoms of bipolar disorder.

**D.** Benzodiazepines may be used as a short-term treatment for anxiety disorders. For longer-term treatment, antidepressants can be helpful.

**E.** Electroconvulsive therapy is used with severely depressed people when other treatments have failed.

**F.** Treatment by transcranial magnetic stimulation is still considered experimental.

## IV. Other Forms of Treatment

**A.** Psychological treatment can be provided in a variety of forms, including individual, family, and group therapy; self-help resources include books and tapes, as well as groups such as AA.

**B.** Systems therapy views a client's symptoms in a family context; it seeks to reduce the symptoms by changing the family system. Techniques include reframing, validation, and paradoxical intention.

---

| Notes |
|-------|
| F. |
| G. |
| II. |
| A. |
| B. |
| C. |
| D. |
| E. |
| F. See Table 15.2. |
| G. |
| III. |
| A. |
| B. |
| C. |
| D. |
| E. ECT—best for psychotic depression when medications don't work |
| F. |
| IV. |
| A. |
| B. |

**C.** Therapy protocols and brief therapy have been more widely used in recent years, partly because of the growth of managed care.

**D.** Cybertherapy refers to therapy over the Internet, through e-mail, chat rooms, or therapist-led online support groups. Such treatment is considered less than optimal.

**E.** Prevention programs offer universal, selective, and indicated interventions.

## V. Which Therapy Works Best?

**A.** The answers to various questions about psychotherapy research determine what conclusions can be drawn from the results of a given study and how far the results generalize to other circumstances.

**B.** Research on psychotherapy shows that, overall, those who receive some type of psychotherapy fare better than those who don't receive any treatment.

**C.** An effective therapy has both common and specific factors that contribute toward its success.

**D.** For some disorders, symptoms can worsen when clients stop taking medication that had been helpful. Beneficial psychotherapies can continue to exert their positive influence after treatment ends.

**E.** Research shows that certain types of psychotherapy are more effective with certain disorders than with others; for example, exposure with response prevention is a particularly effective treatment for OCD.

**F.** It is also important to understand the ethnic and cultural factors related to a client's problems and goals.

NOTE: Once you feel that you understand the material in this chapter, visit the book's Web site at www.ablongman.com/kosslyn3e to test your knowledge with additional study questions.

*C. Brief therapy = 20 sessions or less*

*D.*

*E.*

*V.*

*A.*

*B.*

*C. Minimize confounds when assessing therapy's effectiveness*

*D.*

*E.*

*F.*

## Key Terms

antipsychotic medication, p. 702
behavior modification, p. 695
behavior therapy, p. 692
benzodiazepine, p. 704
bibliotherapy, p. 709
client-centered therapy, p. 689
cognitive–behavior therapy (CBT), p. 692
cognitive distortions, p. 698
cognitive restructuring, p. 700
cognitive therapy, p. 697
common factor, p. 716
cybertherapy, p. 712
dream analysis, p. 687
electroconvulsive therapy (ECT), p. 705
exposure, p. 693
family therapy, p. 708
free association, p. 687

group therapy, p. 707
incongruence, p. 689
individual therapy, p. 707
insight-oriented therapy, p. 686
interpersonal therapy (IPT), p. 712
interpretation, p. 688
modality, p. 707
monoamine oxidase inhibitor (MAOI), p. 703
outcome research, p. 715
paradoxical intention, p. 708
progressive muscle relaxation, p. 694
psychoanalysis, p. 686
psychodynamic therapy, p. 687
psychoeducation, p. 700
psychopharmacology, p. 702
psychotherapy integration, p. 710
reframing, p. 708

resistance, p. 688
selective serotonin reuptake inhibitor (SSRI), p. 703
self-help group, p. 709
self-monitoring techniques, p. 696
serotonin/norepinephrine reuptake inhibitor (SNRI), p. 703
specific factor, p. 716
stimulus control, p. 694
St. John's wort, p. 703
systematic desensitization, p. 694
systems therapy, p. 708
tardive dyskinesia, p. 702
technical eclecticism, p. 710
token economy, p. 696
transference, p. 688
tricyclic antidepressant (TCA), p. 703
validation, p. 708

CHAPTER 16

# SOCIAL PSYCHOLOGY: MEETING OF THE MINDS

In 1993, Sarah Delany, known as Sadie, and her younger sister Elizabeth, called Bessie, published their first book, *Having Our Say* (Delany et al., 1993). What's remarkable about these authors is that they were 104 and 102 at the time of publication. Their book recounts the story of their lives, their experiences as Black children and then as Black women during a century of American history. It was during their childhood that the South's Jim Crow laws came into effect, legalizing separate facilities—separate schools, separate water fountains, separate seats on the bus, separate toilets—for Blacks and Whites; it was during their adulthood that these laws were struck down.

Sadie and Bessie had 8 brothers and sisters. Their father, Henry, had been born a slave but was freed by emancipation. He became vice principal of St. Augustine's School (now St. Augustine's College), a Black college in Raleigh, North Carolina. Their mother, Nanny James, who had both Black and White grandparents, was light-skinned. In addition to managing her 10 children, she was the matron of the college, overseeing many of its daily functions. The Delany children were educated at "St. Aug's," where their father also taught. All 10 children became college-educated professional men and women—a remarkable feat for anyone of that era, regardless of race or sex. Sadie earned both a bachelor's and a master's degree from Columbia University and became a teacher. In 1926, she became the first Black woman appointed to teach home economics at the high school level in New York City. Bessie went to dental school at Columbia in 1923, where she was the only Black woman, and she was the second Black woman licensed to practice dentistry in New York City.

The Delany family, well known in Black society in North Carolina and in New York City's Harlem neighborhood, was considered to be part of an elite group of educated Blacks. But the road was not easy for the sisters. People, Black and White, developed attitudes toward and stereotypes about the sisters, and some discriminated against them—because they were Black, because they were women, or simply because they were Delanys.

Like the Delanys, we are all targets of other people's attitudes and stereotypes, and we have attitudes and stereotypes of our own about other people. And like the Delanys, we all feel pressure from others to behave in certain ways, and we exert pressure on others to behave in certain ways. How we think about other people and interact in relationships and groups is the focus of the subfield of psychology called **social psychology**.

Many of the phenomena psychology seeks to understand—sensation, learning, and memory, to name just a few—take place primarily at the levels of the brain and the person, but are influenced, as shown in the Looking at Levels features in this book, by the environment and the social world. In this chapter, the central emphasis is the level of the group. By definition, social psychology is about our relationships with other people. It focuses on two general topics: the way we think about others (*social cognition*) and the way we act toward them, individually and in groups (*social behavior*). And these interactions affect our thoughts, feelings, behaviors, even our brains. Are there psychological principles that underlie the ways we think about and behave toward other people? If so, what are they?

# SOCIAL COGNITION:
## Thinking About People

The Delany sisters' parents worked hard to protect their children as much as possible from prejudice, discrimination, and intimidation. They also tried to instill in their children a sense of dignity, self-respect, and respect for and support of others. They encouraged their children to think about the world and their places in it, in specific ways. For example, their parents called each other Mr. and Mrs. Delany in front of others, including their children. This was a conscious decision. It was common for Whites to call Blacks by their first names in instances in which they would use surnames for other Whites; therefore, Mr. and Mrs. Delany deliberately chose to use formal titles to convey respect for each other and the expectation of respect from others.

In this chapter, we focus largely on the ways people think about other people, in other words, on social cognition—*cognition* because it is about how we think, and *social* because the thoughts involve other people and the social world in general. **Social cognition** does not focus on the "objective" social world, but instead on how individuals perceive their social worlds and how they attend to, store, remember, and use information about other people and the social world.

## Making an Impression

The Delany children, like many other children, were always told to "make a good impression." Have you ever been told, even long after childhood, essentially the same thing—to comb your hair or dress up a bit before meeting someone for the first time? You may have wondered, "I know what kind of person I am. Why do I need to appear a particular way for other people?" An obvious answer is, of course, that other people *don't* know what kind of person you are, and they make inferences about you from things they notice at that initial meeting. Social psychologists have found that first impressions can make a difference (Schlenker, 1980), we tend to give earlier information more weight than later information. Even the position you assume when sitting shapes other people's impression of you: When females sit with their legs open and their arms

**Social psychology:** The subfield of psychology that focuses on how people think about other people and interact in relationships and groups.

**Social cognition:** The area of social psychology that focuses on how people perceive their social worlds and how they attend to, store, remember, and use information about other people and the social world.

held away from their upper bodies (more common among males), they are seen as less feminine; when males sit with their thighs against each other and their arms touching their upper bodies (more common among females), they are seen as less masculine (Vrugt & Luyerink, 2000).

The name that psychologists use for the process by which we develop such initial views of others is **impression formation**. The creating and receiving of impressions is a two-way street, and the term **impression management** refers to our efforts to control how others will view us.

People use two common strategies to make a good impression. *Self-enhancement strategies* involve making yourself look good, perhaps by appearing particularly well groomed or knowledgeable about particular topics. *Other-enhancement strategies* involve eliciting a positive mood or reaction from the other person by asking for advice (Morrison & Bies, 1991) or by being particularly attentive to convey the impression that you like him or her (Wayne & Ferris, 1990).

## Thin Slices Are Enough

In the process of forming impressions of others, we take in large amounts of information (verbal and nonverbal) quickly and, sometimes without conscious awareness, mold our impressions into judgments. If you were observing a job applicant who was interviewing for a job, how much time do you think it would take you to form your impression of the candidate? Suppose you observed a video clip of the interview and the sound was off—how long should the clip be for you to assess the candidate? Most of the time, our observations from "thin slices" of less than 5 minutes of behavior are remarkably accurate (Ambady et al., 2000). In fact, often just 10 seconds is enough. Consider that during mock "initial screening" job interviews, observers' ratings of 10-second video clips of interviewees walking in the door, greeting the interviewer, and sitting down predicted the interviewers' evaluations of the candidates (Prickett et al., in preparation; cited in Gladwell, 2000). Similarly, after listening to 20 seconds of recordings of physicians speaking during routine office visits, participants were able to predict from the tone of voice which physicians were most likely to have been sued in the past for malpractice (Ambady et al., 2002). Another study found that participants who observed 10-second video clips of teachers both interacting with students and talking about them could accurately gauge the teachers' expectations of their students (Babad et al., 1989). Other studies have yielded similar results (Borkenau et al., 2004).

From such nonverbal and verbal communications, we infer other people's personality traits (see Chapter 11), particularly traits that we view as important. If you are at a party with many strangers and are interested in finding someone with whom you later can go bungee jumping, you probably will focus on verbal and nonverbal behavior that you think represents the temperament of sensation seeking or the personality trait of adventurousness. In contrast, if you were looking for a good study partner among new classmates (or party guests), you would focus on other traits—and might even form a negative impression of someone who seemed to be a sensation-seeker. Clearly, the context affects the impression you form of other people.

After watching a 15-second video clip of a man and woman interacting, observers were able to identify accurately the type of relationship between the two—whether they were strangers, platonic friends, or lovers (Ambady et al., 2001).

## Halo and Primacy Effects

When forming impressions, you are also likely to respond to a *halo effect*: If you think someone has a positive and important trait (at least in one context), you are

**Impression formation:** The process of developing initial views of others.

**Impression management:** A person's efforts to control how others will view him or her.

Due to the halo effect, because this individual has won the lottery, we may assume that she's very competent—or lucky—in general. Such an association is not necessarily accurate.

likely to infer that he or she has other positive and important traits. In North America, for instance, if you think someone is physically attractive, you will probably think that he or she has other attributes you consider to be positive (Eagly et al., 1991; Feingold, 1992). However, not all positive traits contribute equally to your impression of another person.

Whether positive, neutral, or negative, the information you notice early on is more likely to bias your impression than the information you pick up subsequently, a tendency that is referred to as the *primacy effect* (Anderson & Barrios, 1961). It is because of the primacy effect that it behooves you to dress and groom yourself so that you look your best for an interview or a blind date and to take care in writing your ad for a dating Web site or your blurb for your school's facebook: What people notice about you initially will shape their later view of you.

## Self-Fulfilling Prophecy

The process of impression formation involves *perceiving* another person. This process requires you to direct your attention to particular behaviors and to interpret them. As we saw in Chapter 4, one process that guides our perceptions is *top-down processing*. Similarly, impression formation also can involve top-down processing: We often "see" what we expect to see and, in doing so, create a *self-fulfilling prophecy* (Darley & Gross, 1983). In a classic study, psychologists went into an elementary school classroom and administered a test to students. Teachers were then told which particular students would have extremely positive performance over the year, supposedly based on their test results. In fact, these particular students were chosen at random. At the end of the school year, those who had been noted as destined for great performance did in fact show this pattern relative to their classmates who were not so marked. Thus, the teachers' impressions and expectations of the students shaped the way they treated the students, which in turn shaped the students' performance (Rosenthal & Jacobson, 1968; see Chapter 9). Even when we are motivated to perceive another person's behavior accurately and not use top-down processing, we are accurate only when we pay careful attention; when distracted, we fall victim to the self-fulfilling prophecy (Biesanz et al., 2001).

Another classic example of the self-fulfilling prophecy was shown in a study by Snyder and colleagues (1977; see Figure 16.1). They created 51 pairs of men and women, each member of the pair unknown to and unseen by the other. Each member was placed in a separate room. Before they began speaking on the phone, the men received photographs of a woman they were told was their partner. Half of the men received a photo of an attractive woman; the other half received a photo of an unattractive woman. Each pair then spoke on the phone, and the woman's side of the conversation was taped. Independent judges (who did not know the women, nor did they know about the photographs) listened to the tapes. The judges rated as more warm and friendly the women whose partners had been given the "attractive" photo, whereas women who were rated less warm and friendly had partners who had received the "unattractive" photo. Thus, it appears that the men who thought they were speaking to an attractive woman asked questions of her, and responded to what she said, in ways that led her to be friendlier, on average, than the women in the "unattractive" group. The men's expectations led to a self-fulfilling prophecy that shaped the women's behavior: The "attractive" women behaved in a friendlier way—more attractively—toward their partners.

**FIGURE 16.1**

# Self-Fulfilling Prophecy

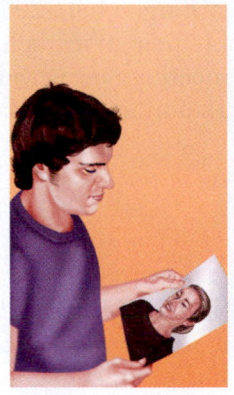    

Male and female participants who have never met are placed in separate rooms. Before they speak to each other on the phone, the men are shown a photograph of either an attractive or an unattractive woman. They are told the woman in the photo is their "partner," with whom they will speak on the phone.

The partners speak to each other. The woman's side of the conversation is taped separately.

Judges later listened to the woman's side of each conversation, and they rated the women whose partners were given an attractive photo as more warm, likeable, and flirtatious than those whose partners had been given an unattractive photo. Men's beliefs about their partners became a self-fulfilling prophecy; they asked questions and responded to the "attractive" women in ways that elicited more attractive responses.

Not all "prophecies" are equally self-fulfilling, however. Stephanie Madon and colleagues (2004) examined a different type of self-fulfilling prophecy: Parents' beliefs about their 7th-grade children's alcohol use. On the one hand, 7th graders whose parents overestimated their drinking were likely to drink more 1 year later, which is consistent with a self-fulfilling prophecy. On the other hand, however, such a prophecy did not exist for 7th graders whose parents underestimated their drinking.

## Impression Management

Do you remember times when you've been on your "best behavior" on meeting someone? You may have tried to monitor yourself, making sure that you weren't too talkative—or that you talked enough—or seemed confident without appearing conceited. It turns out that when you work hard to create an impression that is different than your normal one—and thus regulating yourself considerably—you are subsequently likely to exhibit a *rebound effect*, where you don't regulate your behavior very well (Vohs et al., 2005). The harder you work to present an image of yourself that is different from your normal one, the more rebound you will have afterward. Getting to know others—and their getting to know you—through

Some people unconsciously mimic the nonverbal behavior of others (Cheng & Chartrand, 2003; van Baaren et al., 2004), and both parties are often unaware of the mimicry. Nonetheless, such mimicry can build rapport and liking between the two people (Chartrand & Bargh, 1999). People who strive to get along with a new person they meet are more likely to engage in mimicry than people who do not have such a goal (Lakin & Chartrand, 2003).

e-mail and chat rooms may have minimized such a rebound effect because nonverbal behaviors are absent. Chat room users report that they are better able to express their true selves in this medium than in face-to-face interactions (Bargh et al., 2002), perhaps because they can focus on what their words—but not their other behaviors—convey. As video chats become more common, initial meetings using video chats may end up requiring the same efforts at behavioral regulation as face-to-face initial meetings.

## Attitudes and Behavior: Feeling and Doing

When you read or hear the news, your attitudes affect your interpretation of the events being reported. In a smaller arena, your attitudes about people from a particular ethnic group will determine how you feel about them. For instance, your attitude about Blacks will determine how you *feel* about Blacks, which will, in turn, affect how you feel when you read about the Delanys. And in your own circle, if a friend tells you that she's had an abortion, your attitude toward abortion will influence your feelings about your friend. An **attitude** is an overall evaluation about some aspect of the world—people, issues, or objects (Petty & Wegener, 1998). This evaluation has three components: affective, behavioral, and cognitive, summarized by the acronym ABC (Breckler, 1984):

- *Affective* refers to your feelings about the object or issue.
- *Behavioral* refers to your predisposition to act in a particular way toward the object or issue (note that this component does not refer to an actual behavior, but an inclination to behave in a certain way).
- *Cognitive* refers to what you believe or know about the object or issue.

Your attitudes can affect your behavior. The opportunity for the interplay of attitude and behavior can be seen in Sadie's father's comment to her: "Daughter, you are college material. You owe it to your nation, your race, and yourself to go. And if you don't go, then shame on you" (Delany et al., 1993, p. 91). His remarks reflected the components of his attitude toward higher education for Blacks: He was passionately positive about it (affective); his inclination to promote higher education was reflected in his comment to Sadie (behavioral); he had no doubt about the power of education to elevate the position of Blacks in American society (cognitive).

Attitudes can be positive (such as being in favor of energy conservation), negative (such as disliking speed limits on highways), or neutral (such as not being moved one way or the other by a political candidate). The same issue—for instance, whether American troops should intervene in a foreign war—can evoke strong negative (NO!) or positive (YES!) attitudes. These different evaluations are accompanied by different changes in facial muscles (Cacioppo et al., 1986) and in brain activation (Davidson, 1992a). We can also have ambivalent attitudes, with simultaneous negative and positive reactions being equally strong.

### Attitudes and Cognitions

Just as attention can play an important role in how we process and remember perceptual information in the physical world (see Chapters 4 and 7), attitudes play an important role in how we process information and remember events in our social world (Eagly & Chaiken, 1998). Particularly in ambiguous social situations, our attitudes help organize events and thus determine what information is attended to, processed,

**Attitude:** An overall evaluation about some aspect of the world.

encoded, and remembered. This is one reason why people in the same social situation can come away with different versions of what occurred.

Our attitudes also affect how we shape our goals and expectations and how we interpret obstacles we encounter while trying to achieve our goals, perhaps inducing stress in ourselves through our interpretations. (As a general rule, it is not an event itself, but how it is perceived that determines whether it induces stress; see Chapter 13.) Our attitudes guide us as we selectively evaluate information; generally, we find information that is contrary to our attitudes to be unconvincing, and we may even try to disprove it (Eagly & Chaiken, 1998). As an example, consider the effect of socioeconomic class in the workplace (Gerteis & Savage, 1998). If you think that someone from a lower socioeconomic class will make a bad colleague, you will look for any evidence of shoddy work. You may not notice your colleague's well-performed tasks, and if you do notice them, you make up reasons that discount or discredit your colleague's abilities—perhaps, you say, those are easy tasks.

When an event is ambiguous, our attitudes can influence our cognitive processing of the event. A study of Princeton and Dartmouth students who watched a motion picture of a controversial Princeton–Dartmouth football game found that, although all students saw the same motion picture of the game, students from the different schools described different events (Hastorf & Cantril, 1954), such as which team started rough play.

Attitudes are shaped by individual experiences as well as personality and temperament. If you are a sensation seeker, you will be more likely to have a positive attitude toward risky professions, such as being a war correspondent. However, learning (see Chapter 6) can also affect your attitudes. Suppose a friend's relative was a war correspondent who was murdered while on assignment. Observing how this death affected your friend (observational learning) will influence your attitudes. Similarly, operant conditioning can shape your attitudes: For example, imagine that you attended a local rally that became violent, and you were almost arrested (a consequence of your attending this event). This learning experience could affect your attitude toward high-risk journalism. Moreover, even classical conditioning can affect your attitudes (called *evaluative conditioning*; see Chapter 6): Did you acquire a conditioned fear response while attending the violent rally? If so, this fear might generalize to similar events in the future—which would impede your being an effective war correspondent.

## Predicting Behavior

Suppose, after all of your experiences, you still have a positive attitude toward high-risk journalism. Does that mean that you'll actually become a war correspondent? More generally, if you know someone's attitudes, can you predict his or her behavior? Consider the experience of psychologist Richard La Piere (1934), described in Chapter 1: He traveled the country in the 1930s with a young Chinese couple. They stayed in 67 paid lodgings and ate in 184 restaurants and cafés. Six months after each visit, La Piere sent a questionnaire to those establishments inquiring whether they would accept Chinese people as customers. More than 90% of the lodgings and restaurants said no. Yet on their trip, La Piere and his colleagues were refused only once. Attitudes influence behavior, but they do not always lead to behavior that is consistent with them.

Several factors determine how likely it is that an attitude toward a behavior will lead to the behavior's occurrence. An attitude is more likely to affect behavior when it is (Eagly & Chaiken, 1998):

- strong,
- relatively stable,
- directly relevant to the behavior,
- important, or
- easily accessed from memory.

For instance, suppose you strongly dislike eating Moroccan food—an attitude. Against your better judgment, you went to a Moroccan restaurant recently and only picked at the food. If a friend invites you today to a meal at a Moroccan restaurant, you are likely to suggest another place to go: Your attitude about Moroccan food is strong, stable, directly relevant to your behavior, and easily accessed from memory. But if you haven't eaten this type of food in years, don't feel that strongly about it now, and have almost forgotten why you ever disliked it, you would be less likely to object to your friend's choice of a Moroccan restaurant (Sanbonmatsu & Fazio, 1990). Attitudes based on indirect experience, such as hearsay, have less influence on behavior than those based on direct experience (Regan & Fazio, 1977).

## Behavior Affects Attitudes

If a professor assigned an essay on a topic about which you didn't have very strong feelings (say, supporting curbside recycling versus recycling at a local center), do you think writing the essay would influence your subsequent views? Research has shown that it can: When people are asked repeatedly to assert an attitude on a given topic, thus priming that attitude and making it easier to access, they are more likely to behave in ways consistent with that attitude, compared with those who did not repeatedly express the attitude (Fazio et al., 1982; Powell & Fazio, 1984). In fact, repeatedly asserting an attitude can make the attitude more extreme (Downing et al., 1992). Many self-help or self-improvement programs capitalize on this finding, encouraging participants to express frequent "affirmations," positive statements about themselves, their intentions, and their abilities. Such repeated affirmations can strengthen people's positive attitudes about themselves.

## Assessing Attitudes Directly and Indirectly

Suppose a journalist for your campus newspaper is doing a survey of students' attitudes toward affirmative action in college admissions. The reporter randomly goes up to people and asks them, "What's your view of affirmative action in college admissions?" The question explicitly and directly asks for people's attitudes on that issue. However, do you think the answers would necessarily accurately reflect everyone's attitudes? Why might people not respond with their "real" attitudes? One potential reason is the *social desirability bias* (see Chapter 11), the tendency of people's responses to reflect their desire to be seen by others in a positive light—which leads them to answer in a way that they think is socially desirable (Rudman, 2004).

Because such explicit measures may not always be accurate—particularly when the topic of interest is seen as controversial—psychologists have endeavored to assess people's attitudes without asking them directly, using various techniques borrowed from cognitive psychology (Fazio & Olson, 2003). Indirect measures that implicitly, but not explicitly, assess attitudes include those using priming procedures (as discussed in Chapter 7) and those measuring response times. Such indirect measures can assess attitudes that are outside of conscious awareness, as they do with memories. For example, the *implicit association test (IAT)* measures the strength of association between an evaluation, such as "good" or "bad," and a concept, category, or group of people (such as "fat people"). In a typical version of the IAT, the task is to classify words (such as "marvelous" and "treacherous") as good or bad *and*, mixed in with good/bad judgments, to indicate when a target stimulus is in one of two categories (such as "thin" versus "fat"). Here's the crucial variable: The key on the keyboard you use to indicate that a target word (such as "marvelous") is "good" is *also* the key you use to respond to one of the categories (such as "fat"), and the key you use to indicate that a target word (such as "awful") is "bad" is also the key you use to respond to the other category ("thin"). The trick is in which category is paired with "good" and which is paired with "bad." For example, fat-related stimuli (such as photographs of heavy people) might be paired with "good" and thin-related stimuli might be paired with "bad," or vice versa. If you have a strong association between "thin" and your evaluation of thinness (let's say "good"), then you will have interference when you need to press the same key to indicate "thin" and "bad"—and thus will take longer than when the key is assigned to the compatible (to you) judgments "thin" and "good." Thus, by comparing the response time differences in the two conditions, when the responses are associated in different ways, researchers can discover the degree to which you associate a concept, category or group of people with an evaluation.

The correlation between implicit and explicit measures of attitudes may be low when the topic is potentially divisive or when social desirability is exerting an influence (Devine et al., 2002; Dovidio et al., 2002). The more sensitive the topic, the more the explicit responses may be distorted (Fazio & Olson, 2003). In contrast, when the topic being asked about isn't a "hot button" issue, attitudes assessed indirectly and directly usually have a relatively high correlation (Nosek et al., 2002; Rudman, 2004).

However, don't assume that indirectly assessed attitudes are a measure of "real" attitudes. Attitudes assessed through indirect methods can be subject to transient or enduring emotions, such as fear or anger (DeSteno et al., 2004; Rudman, 2004), or to aspects of the context (Blair, 2002). Perhaps for this reason, attitudes assessed indirectly do not necessarily predict behavior better than attitudes assessed directly (Fazio & Alson, 2003; Lambert et al., 2005). Whether implicit or explicit measures are better in predicting that an attitude will lead to behavior depends on the situation and the person's motivation for acting in a particular way, which raises the question—as yet unanswered—of what constitutes a "real" attitude (Fazio & Olson, 2003).

## Cognitive Dissonance

Attitudes and behavior don't always go hand in hand, as dramatically demonstrated by La Piere's study. But most people prefer that their attitudes and behavior are consistent (Snyder & Ickes, 1985). When an attitude and behavior—or two attitudes—are inconsistent, an uncomfortable state that psychologists refer to as **cognitive dissonance** arises. Cognitive dissonance is accompanied by heightened arousal (Losch & Cacioppo, 1990).

**CREATING DISSONANCE** Festinger and Carlsmith's (1959) classic study on cognitive dissonance found that, counterintuitively, participants who were paid less to tell someone that a boring task was enjoyable reported afterward that they enjoyed the task more than those who were paid a greater amount (Figure 16.2, p. 742). How can we understand this? By the effects of cognitive dissonance reduction. The participants who were paid less, only $1, could not have justified reporting that they enjoyed the task for that amount. To reduce the "dissonance" between what they did and what they received, they appear to have convinced themselves, unconsciously, that they really *did* enjoy the task, so much that they were willing to say that they enjoyed it even though they received little reimbursement. The participants who were paid more felt no such compulsion; the money they received, they apparently felt, adequately compensated them for telling someone that they liked the task. For these participants, there was no dissonance to be resolved. In general, research has shown that the less reason there is to

Cognitive dissonance: The uncomfortable state that arises because of a discrepancy between an attitude and behavior or between two attitudes.

**FIGURE 16.2** **Cognitive Dissonance**

In Festinger and Carlsmith's classic 1959 study, participants were asked to perform a very boring, repetitive task: putting spools on a tray, then dumping them out, and starting all over again.

Participants were given either $1 or $20 (a lot of money in those days) and were then asked to tell another person that the task was, in fact, quite interesting.

After telling the other person about the task, the participants were asked to rate how much they liked the task. Those who were paid $1 to tell the other person that they liked the task reported actually liking the task more than those paid $20 to do so!

engage in a behavior that is counter to an attitude, the stronger the dissonance. Cognitive dissonance does not occur with every inconsistency; it is experienced only by people who believe that they have a choice and that they are responsible for their course of action, and thus for any negative consequences (Cooper, 1998; Goethals et al., 1979).

Ask yourself these questions: Do you think that giving to charity (either money or time) is a good thing? Do you think that homeless people should be helped? If you answered "yes" to these questions, when was the last time you donated time or money to help a homeless person? Do you ignore homeless people on the street? You may feel uncomfortable after answering these questions. These feelings arise from the contradiction—the dissonance—between your attitudes about helping the homeless and your behavior related to this issue.

Another explanation for these findings on cognitive dissonance comes from **self-perception theory**, which states that people come to understand themselves by making inferences from their behavior and the events surrounding their behavior—much as they draw inferences from observing other people's behavior (Bem, 1972). The influence of such self-perception is especially clear when we do not have strong feelings or motivations that help us understand our behavior. This theory would say that participants in Festinger and Carlsmith's study tried to understand why they would tell someone they liked a boring task when they were paid only $1. They explained it to themselves the same way they would explain the behavior in someone else: They must have actually liked the task. However, this explanation doesn't rule out the possibility that the participants experienced cognitive dissonance.

**REDUCING DISSONANCE** Because cognitive dissonance creates an uncomfortable state, we try to decrease it. How do we minimize cognitive dissonance once it has occurred? We can use *indirect strategies*, such as trying to feel good about ourselves in other areas of life, or *direct strategies*, which involve actually changing our attitudes or behavior.

Self-perception theory: The theory that people come to understand themselves by making inferences from their behavior and the events surrounding their behavior.

Cognitive dissonance can occur when our attitudes and our behavior are inconsistent, even though we have a choice about how to behave.

Direct strategies also include attempts to obtain additional information supporting our attitude or behavior. Alternatively, we can trivialize an inconsistency between two conflicting attitudes (or between an attitude and a behavior) as being unimportant, and therefore less likely to cause cognitive dissonance (Simon et al., 1995). For example, suppose you really believe in, and talk about, the issue of homelessness and of the need to help homeless people. Then a friend points out that you talk about this issue repeatedly but don't do anything about it. This observation would probably induce cognitive dissonance in you. To lessen it, you could use an indirect strategy by telling yourself what a good person you are, or by finding information about how hard it is for one individual to do anything about homelessness, or by simply saying, "Well, my heart's in the right place." Or, you could implement a direct strategy that has an impact on homelessness, such as volunteering to work in a shelter.

Attempts to reduce dissonance can also explain why people who are not generally immoral may act immorally (Tsang, 2002). These individuals can:

1. *change how they understand their immoral act*, in order to see it as having a higher moral purpose or as being less immoral than what some other people do;
2. *minimize their responsibility for it*;
3. *disregard the negative consequences* (by avoiding knowledge of the results or minimizing the harm); or
4. *blame and dehumanize the victims* (Bandura, 1999; Tsang, 2002).

For instance, those otherwise upstanding citizens who cheat on their taxes may tell themselves that it's not really cheating because they:

1. view their lessened tax payment as a protest against a government policy;
2. argue that it's not really their fault, they need the money because the cost of living is so high;
3. claim that the government collects so much money that the small amount they don't pay is totally inconsequential; or
4. blame the President or members of Congress for imposing "such a high income tax" while giving themselves high salaries, lots of perks, and even tax breaks.

Cognitive dissonance has been used to increase behaviors that promote health. Stone and his colleagues (1997) set up a situation in which participants were induced to feel that they were being hypocritical. Sexually active college students were asked to write and videotape a talk on AIDS prevention for high school students. Participants who were asked to write speeches based on reasons they *personally* had not always used condoms were then more likely to purchase condoms offered for sale than those participants who were asked to include in their speech reasons why *other* people might not use condoms.

## Attitude Change: Persuasion

Walking to class, have you ever been approached by someone offering you a leaflet about an upcoming event, a political candidate, or a new product? If so, someone (or some company) was trying to encourage you to do something: go to the event, vote for the candidate, or buy the product. We are bombarded by attempts to change our attitudes about things, through advertisements, editorials, and conversations with friends. These efforts to change our attitudes are called **persuasion**.

**ROUTES TO PERSUASION** Petty and Cacioppo (1986), in their *elaboration likelihood model* of attitude change, propose two routes to persuasion: central and peripheral. You are being affected by the *central route* when you pay close attention to the content of the argument—when you carefully read the leaflet to decide whether to attend the event, vote for the candidate, or buy the product. If you already hold the opposite view from that expressed in the leaflet, you will likely only be persuaded by strong arguments. But people who try to persuade us know that we don't always have the time, energy, or expertise to use the central route. Therefore, they may rely instead on the *peripheral route* to persuade us. This route consists of attempts to sway us based not on the content of an argument, but rather on the attractiveness and expertise of the source (as in celebrity endorsements; Hovland & Weiss, 1951; Kiesler & Kiesler, 1969), the number of arguments presented (although not necessarily how "strong" we think they are), or information about how other people respond to the message. Furthermore, the **mere exposure effect** can change attitudes through the peripheral route: Simply becoming familiar with something (being exposed to it) can change your attitude toward it—generally, in a favorable way. And this attitude can generalize to similar objects or people (Zajonc, 2001).

After Katie Couric's colonoscopy was televised live into millions of homes, there was a 20% increase in the number of colonoscopy screenings performed (Dobson, 2002). This televised event undoubtedly persuaded more people to have the same procedure, using both central and peripheral routes. Can you describe how?

**PERSUASIVE PEOPLE** Various characteristics of the person who tries to persuade us affect the peripheral route. Fast speakers are generally more persuasive than slow speakers (Miller et al., 1976). Not surprisingly, people who are perceived as honest are more persuasive (Priester & Petty, 1995).

If you've ever heard a Republican speaking to a group of Democrats (or vice versa), you may have noticed a persuasion technique used to convince people who hold the opposite view, whatever that view is: The would-be persuader uses a two-sided approach. That is, he or she presents both sides of an argument rather than only one side (as is common if the audience already agrees with the speaker).

**PERSUASIVE MESSAGE** If an attempt at persuasion arouses strong emotions in you, particularly fear, it is more likely to work, especially if it includes specific advice about what you can do to bring about a more positive outcome (Leventhal et al., 1965). This technique is used in public service messages that try to scare people into behaving differently, such as ads that graphically describe how someone contracted AIDS by not using a condom and then strongly recommend condom use. And when a message does not appear to be *trying* to persuade you to change your attitude, it is often more effective than one that is obviously trying to persuade you. In addition, culture can influence what makes a persuasive case (Lehman et al., 2004): East Asians—compared to European North Americans—are more likely to be persuaded by an advertisement that highlights group harmony and family integrity (Han & Shavitt, 1994).

Persuasion: Attempts to change people's attitudes.

Mere exposure effect: The change—generally favorable—in attitude that can result from simply becoming familiar with something.

**WHEN SIMPLISTIC ARGUMENTS WORK** If you are not paying full attention to an attempt at persuasion, you are less likely to be persuaded by a rational argument that requires you to think deeply, but more likely to be persuaded by a simplistic argument; this comes about at least in part because your inattention makes you less able to develop a counterargument (Allyn & Festinger, 1961; Romero et al., 1996). So, if you are watching a TV commercial while sorting the laundry, you are more likely to be persuaded by it than if you're focused on it.

**THWARTING PERSUASION ATTEMPTS** Attempts at persuasion are often foiled by four common obstacles:

1. *Strong attitude.* If we, as listeners, already have a strong attitude about an issue, as opposed to a weak one, we are less likely to be persuaded to change our current attitude (Petty & Krosnick, 1996). Indeed, among identical twins reared apart, certain attitudes appear to be heritable, strong, and resistant to change. For instance, the attitude toward the death penalty has a high heritability; whatever is responsible for this attitude is, at least in part, affected by the genes (Tesser, 1993).

2. *Reactance.* Reactance is the development of a negative reaction to someone who is seen as trying too hard or too often to change our opinion. In this case, we may very well change our minds in the *opposite* direction from that intended by the persuader, even if we would not otherwise take that position; this response is called *negative attitude change* (Brehm, 1966).

3. *Forewarning.* If we know in advance that someone is going to try to persuade us of something, we are less likely to be persuaded (Cialdini & Petty, 1979; Petty & Cacioppo, 1981), although this is not always the case (Romero et al., 1996).

4. *Selective avoidance.* We may simply bypass someone's attempt to persuade us by deliberate use of selective avoidance, such as changing the channel during TV commercials.

In an effort to persuade smokers to quit, this ad uses persuasion techniques. Which techniques are at work here?

## Social Cognitive Neuroscience

Attitudes are often unconscious, and therefore can be difficult to measure. As we've seen, one way to approach this thorny problem is to tap into unconscious processes by observing telltale behavioral signs (such as those measured by indirect measures). Another way to tap into unconscious processes is to examine the brain itself. **Social cognitive neuroscience** attempts to understand social cognition not only by specifying the cognitive mechanisms (such as those involved in memory, attention, and perception) that underlie it, but also by discovering how those mechanisms are rooted in the brain (Blakemore et al., 2004; D. T. Gilbert, 2002; Heatherton, 2004; Ochsner & Lieberman, 2001). Social cognitive neuroscience bridges cognitive neuroscience and social psychology. On the one hand, as we saw in Chapter 1, cognitive neuroscience rests on the idea that "the mind is what the brain does"—and thus focuses on how mental processes can be related to brain structure and function. On the other hand, the field of social cognition addresses how social events are related to cognitive function. Social cognitive neuroscience ties together the two fields, attempting to fathom how social cognition arises from cognitive processes that, in turn, arise from the brain. This approach allows researchers to use the methods of neuroscience to grapple with questions that cannot easily be answered in other ways.

Here's an example: Do you think that reduction of your cognitive dissonance depends on your consciously noticing the dissonance? The traditional view implies that you reason about the causes of cognitive dissonance in order to reduce this

Social cognitive neuroscience: The subfield of psychology that attempts to understand social cognition not only by specifying the cognitive mechanisms that underlie it, but also by discovering how those mechanisms are rooted in the brain.

uncomfortable feeling. Lieberman and colleagues (2001) set out to test this idea. They studied patients with brain damage that produced amnesia; these patients could not consciously recall anything they had recently experienced. If you met the most severely affected of these patients, talked to him for 3 hours, and then left the room for 10 minutes, he would have no idea who you were when you returned (Schacter, 1996). Lieberman and colleagues realized that if cognitive dissonance reduction depends on recalling the events that led to the dissonance, then these patients should not experience such reduction. These researchers used a classic way to induce cognitive dissonance: If a researcher gives you two sets of stimuli that you like almost to the same degree and requires you to decide which one you like better, you will end up liking the set you choose even more than you did at first (and disliking the rejected set; Brehm, 1956). Because the two sets are in fact so similar, you can find reasons for liking either one—but when forced to choose, you need to reduce the dissonance that arises from rejecting one that you do in fact like (but a hair less than the other) by exaggerating the differences between them. The question was, would amnesic patients behave the same way? The answer was yes: Even amnesic patients become more positive about the chosen set and more negative about the rejected one. Their attitudes toward the sets shifted even though these patients had no conscious memory of ever having chosen between the two almost equivalent sets! Thus, the traditional view is wrong: You don't need to be conscious of the causes of dissonance in order to try to reduce it.

The social cognitive neuroscience approach has been used to study a wide range of topics related to social cognition, such as the nature of moral disgust (Moll et al., 2005), empathy (Decety & Jackson, 2004; Ruby & Decety, 2003), and the self (Heatherton et al., 2004; Macrae et al., 2004), and it has even been used to investigate why people rack up credit card debt (Spinella et al., 2004). The examples go on and on.

Some of the most intriguing findings of studies in social cognitive neuroscience relate to the nature of attitudes. For example, have you ever wondered how people can harbor contradictory attitudes at the same time? Wood and colleagues (2005) found that the left frontal lobe plays a key role in representing and expressing positive attitudes, whereas the right frontal lobe plays a key role in representing and expressing negative attitudes; this finding suggests that the two sorts of information are processed—at least in part—independently. The social cognitive neuroscience approach is playing an especially important role in illuminating the nature of attitudes about race. For instance, in another study, researchers used fMRI to monitor how strongly the amygdala was activated while White participants viewed unfamiliar Black and White faces (Phelps et al., 2000). The amygdala is a part of the brain that is activated when people encode aversive stimuli (see Chapter 10). The amygdala was more strongly activated by Black faces, compared to White faces, for those White participants whose indirectly measured scores indicated negative attitudes about Blacks. (Consistent findings were also reported by Hart and colleagues [2000].) But the researchers did not find this relationship between amygdala activation and indirectly measured scores when the White participants viewed the faces of *familiar* Black celebrities, such as Michael Jordan. Clearly, it was not just the race of individual faces that triggered the amygdala, but the participants' feelings about race more generally. To see why this effect occurs, we need to find out about stereotypes.

## Stereotypes: Seen One, Seen 'Em All

In the social world we inhabit, we could easily be overwhelmed by the torrent of information conveyed by other people—their words, postures, gestures, and facial expressions—to say nothing of what we can infer about their attitudes and goals, and even what other people have said about them. The world is full of information and stimuli, and if we had no way of organizing this input flying at us from all directions, assaulting our senses, we would live in chaos. In the physical realm, we organize all of this information by principles such as Gestalt groupings of visual stimuli (see Chapter 4). To avoid drowning in this sea of social information, we create stereotypes, a type of *schema* (see Chapter 8) that provides cognitive shortcuts for processing all of this information about the social world (Allport, 1954; Gilbert & Hixon, 1991; Macrae et al., 1994). A **stereotype** is a belief (or set of beliefs) about people in a particular category; the category can be defined by race, sex, social class, religion, ethnic background, hair color, sport, hobby, and myriad other characteristics. A stereotype may be positive (such as "women are nurturing"), neutral (such as "Mexicans eat spicy food"), or negative (such as "soccer fans drink too much").

When lawyers select a jury, they try to have certain potential jurors excluded because of stereotypes about how people of a certain race, sex, age, or profession are likely to view the case. But one study found that lawyers' stereotype-based expectations of whether jurors would be likely to convict were often incorrect (Olczak et al., 1991).

## Stereotypes Affect Attention, Cognition, and Behavior

Not only can stereotypes affect how we feel about other people, but our expectations of others based on our stereotypes—and our behavior with them—can lead *them* to behave in certain ways. (See Chapter 11 for an example of how expectations of others can change their behavior.) As with other types of classification, stereotypes can be useful shortcuts. But stereotypes are caricatures, not reasoned formulations, and they are often incorrect. The effect of errors we make when using stereotypes is anything but trivial. Perhaps because we often strive for cognitive efficiency, we prefer to read information consistent with our stereotypes, and we process such information more quickly (Hugenberg & Bodenhausen, 2004; Smith, 1998). As with attitudes, we are less likely to attend to, and therefore encode or remember, information inconsistent with our stereotypes (Johnston & Macrae, 1994), and, in fact, we may deny the truth of such information (O'Sullivan & Durso, 1984). Such stereotype-preserving actions are particularly likely if we believe that people's behavior is best explained by their traits, rather than the situation (see Chapter 11; Plaks et al., 2001).

Once a stereotype is activated, we respond to a person's membership in the particular category, not to the characteristics of the individual person. Here's how this works. Suppose that you have a positive stereotype of New Englanders, believing them to be punctual and hard-working. When you meet someone from Maine, your "New Englander" stereotype is activated. You will then be more likely to notice aspects of her behavior that are consistent with your stereotype, and in thinking about her, you will be more likely to remember those aspects. You may not notice when she comes in late, or you will come up with plausible excuses for her tardiness and see it as the exception to the rule. The stereotype thus lives on and may shape your future thinking. One way this influence on thinking occurs is that information relevant to the stereotype is recalled faster than unrelated information (Dovidio et al., 1986). However, if you are motivated to be accurate and do *not* assume that a stereotype applies to a particular individual, you can minimize the impact of stereotypes (Wyer et al., 2000).

Sometimes the conflict between a stereotype and the actual behavior of someone from the stereotyped group is too great to be ignored—but rather than change the stereotype, we are more likely to create a new subtype within it (Anderson, 1983; Anderson et al., 1980). So, for example, if your New England acquaintance's chronic lateness and laziness are too great to ignore, you might create a subtype—"New Englander having a hard time coping." This allows you to preserve your stereotype of

**Stereotype:** A belief (or set of beliefs) about people in a particular category.

New Englanders as punctual and hard-working. Because of this psychological phenomenon—creating subtypes in order to preserve a stereotype—stereotypes can be extremely difficult to change or eliminate. However, under certain circumstances, stereotypes *can* change: when the exception is made to appear typical of its group and when we are encouraged to think that the person's behavior results from his or her characteristics, *not* the situation (Wilder et al., 1996).

## Cognition and Prejudice

Stereotyping can lead to **prejudice**, which is an attitude, generally negative, toward members of a group (Arkes & Tetlock, 2004). Prejudice includes not only beliefs and expectations about the group but also an emotional component: Simply thinking about members of a disliked group can produce strong feelings about them (Bodenhausen et al., 1994). As is the case with attitudes and stereotypes, information inconsistent with a prejudice is less likely to be attended to and remembered accurately than is information consistent with a prejudice, making prejudice self-perpetuating.

Prejudice may be conscious and intentional; it may also be conscious and unintentional, or even unconscious and unintentional (Carter & Rice, 1997; Fazio et al., 1995; Greenwald & Banaji, 1995). And emotions can influence prejudice in two ways: The *presence of negative feelings* may account for conscious prejudice, whether intentional or unintentional. But even if someone does not have negative feelings toward a group, prejudice can also arise from the *absence of positive feelings* (Pettigrew & Meertens, 1995); in this case, the prejudice is unconscious (Banaji et al., 2004). Thus, someone can be prejudiced against a group with whom he or she has no experience; for instance, someone from an Asian country might have a prejudice against people with red hair that is engendered by the absence of any positive feelings toward or experiences with such people.

# UNDERSTANDING RESEARCH

## How Stereotypes Can Prime Behavior

The case of Amadou Diallo may illustrate unconscious prejudice. In February 1999, four New York City undercover police officers were driving down a Bronx street in an unmarked car. At 12:40 in the morning, they noticed a Black man acting suspiciously on the stoop of a building, peering out, then "slinking" back into the doorway. A serial rapist was still at large, and from what the police could see, the man on the stoop resembled the general description of the rapist. The plainclothes officers approached the man, Amidou Diallo, identified themselves as police, showed their badges, and ordered him to put his hands up. It is not known why Mr. Diallo pulled out his wallet in response, but the police officers reported that they thought it was a gun, and they shot him 41 times. Mr. Diallo died.

Psychologist Keith Payne (2001) wanted to understand more about the psychological processes that would lead the officers to see a wallet as a gun, and so he conducted the following study.

**QUESTION:** Can group stereotypes affect behavior without conscious awareness?

**ALTERNATIVES:** (1) Yes, group stereotypes can affect behavior without conscious awareness. (2) No, group stereotypes do not affect behavior outside of conscious awareness.

Prejudice: An attitude (generally negative) toward members of a group.

**LOGIC:** If group stereotypes affect behavior outside of conscious awareness, then photos that prime racial stereotypes should automatically facilitate associations between the stereotype and objects consistent with it (see Chapter 7 for a discussion of priming).

**METHOD:** Thirty-one participants who were not Black saw the face of a White or a Black man (shown in the photos), which then disappeared. The face was followed by a picture of either a gun or a tool (see photos), and the participants were to press one key if they saw a gun or another key if they saw a tool. They could take their time, and they were asked to be as accurate as possible.

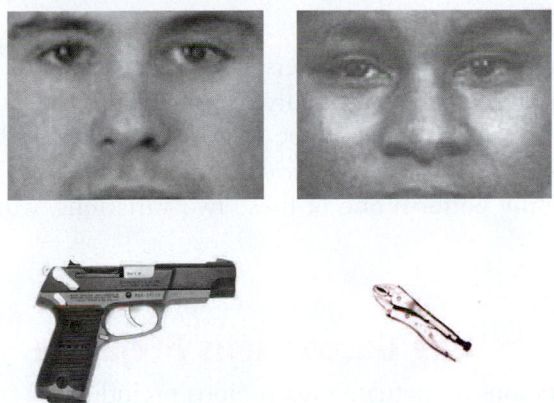

**RESULTS:** The participants made very few errors (such as pressing a key for a gun when a tool was shown). However, when they saw the Black face followed by the gun, they pressed the appropriate key more quickly than they did when they saw the White face followed by the gun. In addition, when they saw the White face followed by the tool, they pressed the appropriate key more quickly than they did when they saw the Black face followed by the tool.

**INFERENCES:** The photos served to prime racial stereotypes, facilitating associations between the stereotype and objects consistent with it. A common stereotype about Blacks includes traits of hostility, aggression, and criminality (Devine & Elliot, 1995; Dovidio et al., 1986). Thus, guns are consistent with this stereotype. Similar results have been found with stereotype-consistent and -inconsistent words primed by gender (Banaji & Hardin, 1996).

A follow-up study by the same researcher (Payne, 2001) gave participants who were not Black only half a second to respond to each face–object pair, which pushed the participants to make more errors; thus, rather than focusing on response times, this study focused on the number of errors participants made after the different primes. White participants were more likely to identify a tool incorrectly as a gun when primed by a Black face than by a White one.

These results were buttressed by those from another study, by Correll and colleagues (2002). Using a videogame, they instructed participants to shoot only at armed "people" in the videogame. Some of the videogame people were Black and some White; some were holding guns, and some were holding nonthreatening objects. Participants correctly and more quickly decided to shoot at armed Blacks than at armed Whites, and they decided not to shoot at unarmed Whites more quickly than at unarmed Blacks. Being strongly aware of a cultural stereotype of Blacks as violent, aggressive, and dangerous (even if participants themselves didn't hold this stereotype) was associated with deciding to shoot at Black people in the videogame, even when the participants were not certain about the object in the Black people's hands.

Applying these results to the Diallo murder, we can understand how the police officers were primed to see an ambiguous shape (Mr. Diallo's wallet in the dim light) as a gun. Such stereotype-consistent prejudice is often unconscious and depends on the context; had these police officers been off duty and attending a movie when a Black man took his wallet out of his pocket, they probably would not have reached for their guns.

## THINK CRITICALLY!

Why might Payne have conducted two versions of the study, one in which the participants were encouraged to be maximally accurate (and take their time) and another in which they were encouraged to be as fast as possible? What information did the second study provide that the first study did not? If you wanted to replicate Payne's research, but could only perform one of these two variations, which one would you choose, and why?

## Processes Perpetuating Unconscious Prejudice

Some cognitive operations perpetuate unconscious prejudice:

- *Social categorization* leads people to divide the world automatically into categories of "us" and "them," both consciously and unconsciously. According to *social identity theory* (Tajfal, 1982), in an effort to enhance self-esteem, people usually think of their own group—the **ingroup**—favorably. The other group, the **outgroup**, is usually disliked and assumed to possess more undesirable traits (Brewer & Brown, 1998; Fiske, 1998; Judd et al., 1991; Lambert, 1995; Linville & Fischer, 1993; Rustemli et al., 2000; Vonk & van Knippenberg, 1995). When we identify with an ingroup, we are more inclined to like, trust, help, and cooperate with other ingroup members than we are to like, trust, help, and cooperate with outgroup members (Brewer & Brown, 1998). Our views of the ingroup and the outgroup can lead to unconscious prejudice (DeSteno et al., 2004; Fiske, 2002).

- *Illusory correlation* is a tendency to overestimate the strength of a relationship between two things (Mullen & Johnson, 1990). This cognitive operation may explain why White people overestimate the number of crimes committed by Black men, and hence maintain their prejudice (Hamilton & Sherman, 1989).

- *Illusion of outgroup homogeneity* is an inclination to view an outgroup as being more homogeneous (that is, having members who are more similar to one another) than the ingroup.

- The corollary, *ingroup differentiation*, is the inclination to view members of an ingroup (that is, your own group) as more heterogeneous (more diverse) than those of another group. For example, a research study found that non-Hispanic Americans were less likely to distinguish among different types of Latinos (a perceived outgroup from the point of view of the non-Hispanics) than were Latinos themselves. However, the Latinos differentiated their own subgroup from all other Latino groups; for example, Mexican Americans were more likely to categorize themselves as a particular group—the ingroup—and to lump Cuban Americans and Puerto Ricans together as other Latinos—the outgroup (Huddy & Virtanen, 1995).

Ingroup: An individual's own group.
Outgroup: A group other than an individual's own.

According to social identity theory, members from both of these high school groups view their own group as superior to the other, and these views (conscious or not) may lead to prejudicial behavior against those in the other group.

## Discrimination

When Bessie Delany was in dental school, a White professor failed her on some work that she knew was good. A White girlfriend, also a dental student, offered to hand in Bessie's work as her own to see what grade the work would be given this time. Bessie's friend passed with the same work that had earned Bessie a failing grade.

Bessie's experience was one of *discrimination*; specifically, she suffered the effect of prejudiced behavior. Her professor's behavior was influenced by his prejudice against Bessie because of her race, her membership in a particular social category. As with stereotypes, people discriminate on the basis of just about anything that distinguishes groups: gender, race, social class, hair color, religion, college attended, height, and on and on. As with prejudice, discrimination may be subtle, and sometimes even unconscious.

Most Americans believe that discrimination is wrong; when their own discriminatory behavior is pointed out to them, they are uncomfortable (Devine & Monteith, 1993), and they may subsequently reduce such behavior (Monteith, 1996). This phenomenon provides another example of the way we act to reduce cognitive dissonance: Becoming aware of the discrepancy between attitudes and behavior leads to the discomfort of cognitive dissonance, which can be reduced through changing future behaviors.

## Why Does Prejudice Exist?

The effects of prejudice are limiting, damaging, and painful. Why then does prejudice exist?

**REALISTIC CONFLICT THEORY** The *realistic conflict theory* (Bobo, 1983) suggests a reason—competition for scarce resources such as good housing, jobs, and schools. As groups compete for these resources, increasingly negative views of the other groups take form, eventually becoming prejudice.

A classic experiment, the Robber's Cave study, showed how easily prejudice can be created from competition (see Figure 16.3 on p. 752; Sherif et al., 1961). A set of 11-year-old boys was divided into two groups, Eagles and Rattlers, at a special overnight

FIGURE 16.3

# The Creation and Dissolution of Prejudice: The Robber's Cave Study

Eleven-year-old boys at a special overnight summer camp (called the Robber's Cave) were the participants in this study. In the initial phase of the study, the boys were randomly divided into two groups and separated from each other for a week. During this time, activities fostered a sense of cohesion in each group.

During the 2-week-long second phase, the two groups competed for highly desired prizes such as pocket knives and medals. Conflict between the two groups quickly escalated from name calling to direct acts (destroying personal property). Negative attitudes as well as negative behavior developed, with each group labeling members of the other with pejorative terms such as "coward."

In the third phase, the two groups were brought together to work on a number of superordinate goals, such as restoring the camp's water supply. Tensions between the groups dissolved by the 6th day of this phase.

camp called the Robber's Cave. The two groups competed for valued prizes. Conflict between the two groups quickly escalated into prejudice and discrimination, with boys from competing groups sometimes calling each other names and even destroying each other's property. However, such attitudes and behavior stopped when the two groups no longer competed for resources but cooperated for larger, mutually beneficial goals such as restoring the camp's water supply. Although the study has several limitations (it is unclear if the findings generalize to girls, non-White boys, or adults), it does illustrate how prejudice can both develop and dissipate (Sherif et al., 1961).

**SOCIAL CATEGORIZATION AND SOCIAL LEARNING THEORY** The Robber's Cave study supports the view of realistic conflict theory that competition between groups for scarce resources can produce prejudice. But are scarcity and competition necessary to produce prejudice? Apparently not. *Social categorization theory* provides one explanation for prejudice in the absence of scarcity or competition: In this view, the psychological forces leading to ingroup favoritism are so powerful that creating even an *arbitrary* "us" and "them" can lead to unconscious favoritism and discriminatory behavior (Feather, 1996; Perdue et al., 1990). This social categorization can lead to discrimination in two distinct ways: (1) The ingroup is actively favored, and (2) the outgroup is actively disfavored.

Although social categorization can perpetuate a skewed picture of other people, it is efficient because once we've made an "us" versus "them" distinction, we can then use our stereotypes about "us" and "them" to understand behavior, saving us the effort of paying close attention to other people and actively processing our observations of their behavior. Because we expect certain behaviors from outgroup members, just being in their presence can activate our stereotypes about them (Bargh et al., 1996). We may then behave in ways that elicit behavior from an outgroup member that is consistent with that stereotype, even if he or she wouldn't otherwise behave that way (Major & O'Brien, 2005; Snyder, 1984, 1992). This process thus becomes a self-fulfilling prophecy: The elicited behavior confirms our stereotype, and we regard the outgroup member's behavior as "proof" of the validity of our prejudices (Fiske, 1998). However, our goals in a given situation or interaction can lessen the use of these cognitive shortcuts: If it is important to be accurate in our view of an outgroup member, we are more motivated to think actively, and perhaps accurately, about that person (Fiske, 1998).

Once a prejudicial attitude is in place, *social learning theory* (see Chapter 6) explains how it can be spread and passed through generations as a learned stereotype. Parents, peers, television, movies, and other aspects of the culture provide models of prejudice (Pettigrew, 1969). When prejudice is translated into words and actions, it may be reinforced. Scarce resources, competition, natural cognitive mechanisms, and learning may all contribute to the development and maintenance of prejudice.

## Changing Prejudice: Easier Said Than Done

Psychology has shown us how prejudice develops and deepens. Equally important, can psychology show us how to arrest the development of prejudice? The answer is yes, but the task is not easily accomplished.

**INCREASED CONTACT** One method of decreasing prejudice is described by the *contact hypothesis*, which holds that increased contact between different groups will decrease prejudice between them (Pettigrew, 1981). Increased contact serves several purposes:

1. Both groups are more likely to become aware of similarities between the groups, which can enhance mutual attraction.

2. Even though stereotypes resist change, when stereotypic views are met with enough inconsistent information or exceptions, those views *can* change (Kunda & Oleson, 1995).

3. Increased contact can shatter the illusion that the outgroup is homogeneous (Baron & Byrne, 1997).

Increased contact does reduce prejudice (Emerson et al., 2002), particularly under certain conditions, as when people are working toward a shared goal and all of those involved are deemed to be equal. For example, politically influential members of Israeli and Palestinian groups met informally and unofficially for sessions of intensive interactive problem solving. The increased contact that occurred while working on the larger goal of resolving obstacles to peace talks was partly successful in lowering the barriers between the two sides. After the Oslo Peace Accord in 1993, many of those involved viewed these informal group meetings as directly and indirectly laying the foundation for the beginning steps toward peace (Kelman, 1997). The meetings, although not designed to reduce prejudice, nonetheless fulfilled one of the steps in that direction: coming together to work toward a shared goal. Other conditions, however, were not met: The participants from the two sides were *not* equal (Brewer & Brown, 1998), nor did they view each other as typical of their respective populations. Although they were able to work together toward the one goal of beginning peace discussions, the larger task of hammering out an agreement and sticking to it did not progress smoothly.

**RECATEGORIZATION** Another way to decrease prejudice is through **recategorization**—that is, shifting the categories of "us" and "them" so that the two groups are no longer distinct entities. Examples of recategorization are familiar in everyday life. An assembly-line worker who is promoted to management experiences recategorization: The identity of "us" and "them" changes. When distinctions between groups are minimized so that

What are children in Bosnia being taught about Gavrilo Princip, the man who started World War I by assassinating Archduke Franz Ferdinand D'Este of Austria-Hungary in 1914? Textbooks in the Serb-controlled part of Bosnia call the act "heroic"; a Croatian textbook refers to Princip as an "assassin trained and instructed by the Serbs to commit this act of terrorism"; and a Muslim textbook refers to him as "a nationalist" and says the resulting anti-Serbian rioting "was only stopped by police from all three ethnic groups" (Hedges, 1997). Social learning theory explains how such different perspectives can lead to prejudice toward other ethnic groups.

Recategorization: A means of reducing prejudice by shifting the categories of "us" and "them" so that the two groups are no longer distinct entities.

Many science fiction stories rely on recategorization to shift the animosity from country against country to a united Earth defending against a common enemy—aliens. Recategorization may decrease prejudice toward the new members of the ingroup, but some outgroup will undoubtedly still be thought of negatively (Tajfel, 1982). In the movie *Men In Black*, humans are allied with some aliens—a new definition of "us"—against a different type of alien.

different groups can be thought of as a single entity, recategorization can decrease prejudice. Working together toward a common goal facilitates recategorization, as occurred in the Robber's Cave study when, instead of being Eagles or Rattlers, all boys became simply campers who had no running water.

**MUTUAL INTERDEPENDENCE** Social psychologist Eliot Aronson and his colleagues devised another way to decrease prejudice, which has been used in many American classrooms. This technique, called the *jigsaw classroom*, is a cooperative learning technique (Aronson & Osherow, 1980; Aronson & Patnoe, 1997). Integrated groups of five or six students from different backgrounds are formed and given an assignment, such as learning about the American War of Independence (see Figure 16.4). Each member of a jigsaw group researches a different aspect of the project (such as military strategy, George Washington's actions, women's roles); after doing their separate research, the students researching the same topic form a new group—an expert group—composed of one member from each jigsaw group. For instance, all students researching George Washington will meet together after doing their research; this is the "George Washington" expert group. These expert groups meet to share information and rehearse presentations. The expert groups then disband, and each member writes a report and reads it to his or her original jigsaw group. The only way that jigsaw group members can learn about all of the topics is to pay close attention to everyone's reports; as with a jigsaw puzzle, each member's contribution is a piece of the whole, and each person depends on the others. The jigsaw classroom decreases prejudice (Aronson & Osherow, 1980; Walker & Crogan, 1998) in ways

**FIGURE 16.4** ## The Jigsaw Classroom

The classroom is divided into groups of 5 or 6 children from different backgrounds (jigsaw groups), and each group studies the same general subject. The general subject has 5 or 6 separate research topics, and each group member is assigned a different topic to research.

After each student does his or her research, they reconfigure into expert groups, where one member from each jigsaw group meets with his or her counterparts from the other groups. Expert groups discuss the results of their research and practice their presentations. This is the "George Washington" expert group.

Each member of the jigsaw group presents his or her research to the rest of the group. Every student is tested on all of the information, so students must listen closely to every presentation. This method fosters interdependence and mutual respect and reduces prejudice.

similar to other techniques: by increasing contact between individuals from different "groups" and creating new, integrated groups that require mutual interdependence in order to achieve a superordinate goal.

# Attributions: Making Sense of Events

When you read about the Delany sisters' successes, how did you explain them? Did you say to yourself, "The sisters worked hard and persevered?" or "They were lucky"? Whatever your reaction, it reflects not only your attitudes, stereotypes, and prejudices, but the attributions you make. **Attributions** are our explanations for the causes of events or behaviors.

## What Is the Cause?

Usually, events and actions have many possible causes. An unreturned telephone call to a friend might be an indication that your friend is very busy, is annoyed at you, or is simply having problems with voice-mail. If a politician you admire changes position on an issue, do you explain the behavior as a sincere change of heart, a cave-in to heavy campaign contributors, or a calculated attempt to appeal to new supporters?

The particular attributions people make are of two broad types: internal and external. **Internal attributions** (also called *dispositional attributions*) explain a person's behavior in terms of that person's preferences, beliefs, goals, or other characteristics. For instance, if a friend leaves a math lecture very confused, you could attribute his confusion to internal factors: "I guess he's not very good at math." **External attributions** (also called *situational attributions*) explain a person's behavior in terms of the situation (Kelley, 1972; Kelley & Michela, 1980). If you make an external attribution for your friend's confusion, you might say, "The professor gave a really bad lecture today."

The attributions you make about events affect both you and other people (see Table 16.1): Blaming yourself for negative events (internal attribution) can suppress your immune system (Segerstrom et al., 1996; see Chapter 13). Blaming yourself or others affects behavior: Mothers who view their children's misbehavior as the children's fault are likely to discipline their children more harshly than mothers who attribute such misbehavior to other causes, such as their own parenting practices (Slep & O'Leary, 1998).

How do you decide whether to attribute someone's behavior to internal or external causes? Take the following situation: When Sadie Delany wanted a job teaching at a high school, there were no Black high school teachers in New York. At Bessie's urging, Sadie applied for the job. After her application was received, school administrators asked Sadie to come in for a meeting, she simply didn't go. (She later apologized, explaining she had "forgotten.") She subsequently received a letter that offered her the job. When she appeared on the first day of school, the school administrators were very surprised to find out she was Black—but did not deny her the job. Did Sadie's decision to miss the face-to-face interview reflect an enduring "doesn't play by the rules" trait, or was it based on the realities of that particular situation? How do we decide? Harold

### TABLE 16.1 — Examples of Types of Attributions

| | Internal Attributions | External Attributions |
|---|---|---|
| **Attributions About Oneself** | *Positive*: I did a good job because I'm smart.<br><br>*Negative*: I did a bad job because I'm inept. | *Positive*: I did a good job because the task was easy.<br><br>*Negative*: I did a bad job because the time allotted for the task was too short. |
| **Attributions About Others** | *Positive*: She did a good job because she's smart.<br><br>*Negative*: She did a bad job because she's inept. | *Positive*: She did a good job because the task was easy.<br><br>*Negative*: She did a bad job because the time allotted for the task was too short. |

**Attribution:** An explanation for the cause of an event or behavior.

**Internal attribution:** An explanation of someone's behavior that focuses on the person's preferences, beliefs, goals, or other characteristics; also called *dispositional attribution*.

**External attribution:** An explanation of someone's behavior that focuses on the situation; also called *situational attribution*.

Kelley's **theory of causal attribution** identifies rules for deciding whether to attribute a behavior to a person's enduring traits or to the situation. In this view, when people try to understand the behavior of others, they automatically, without conscious awareness, take into account three dimensions: consensus, consistency, and distinctiveness.

- *Consensus.* Would other people react similarly in the situation? If so, greater weight should be given to the situation than to personal traits. For example, would other Black women applying for the high school teaching job that Sadie eventually obtained not show up for the face-to-face interview? If so, the behavior has high consensus.

- *Consistency.* Has the person responded in the same way in similar situations? If so, the cause of the behavior is likely to be stable (either internal or external). For example, if Sadie avoided personal interviews when applying for similar jobs, her behavior would have high consistency.

- *Distinctiveness.* Has the person responded differently in situations that are not similar? If so, the cause may be situational. For example, if Sadie didn't usually miss meetings or appointments on purpose, her behavior in this case had high distinctiveness.

According to Kelley's theory, you attribute someone's behavior to internal causes if consensus and distinctiveness are low and consistency is high. In contrast, if consensus, consistency, and distinctiveness are all high, you attribute the behavior to external causes. You attribute behavior to both internal and external causes if consensus is low and consistency and distinctiveness are high. If we knew that Sadie's behavior during the application process had high consensus, consistency, and distinctiveness, we would be able to attribute her behavior to external causes.

Do people really think this way? If you follow Kelley's rules, making causal attributions involves a lot of cognitive work. Nonetheless, people apparently do use all of the factors proposed by Kelley if an event or behavior is either unexpected or has a negative outcome. In other cases, however, people usually take shortcuts, letting their general beliefs and biases guide their attributions.

## Taking Shortcuts: Attributional Biases

Like stereotypes, **attributional biases** are cognitive shortcuts for determining attributions that generally occur outside our awareness. They help lessen the cognitive load required to make sense of the world, but they can lead to errors. These errors have implications for social relationships, the legal system, and social policy.

When you see a homeless person, to what do you attribute his or her homelessness? Chances are that the correspondence bias is at work if you assume that his or her plight is due to an internal trait such as laziness rather than to external factors such as a run of bad luck, a high unemployment rate, and a lack of affordable housing.

**THE CORRESPONDENCE BIAS** Suppose, for example, you are a member of a jury and hear that the defendant confessed to the crime. It turns out that the confession was extracted after many hours of tough, coercive questioning by police. The judge then throws out the confession, striking it from the record, and tells you, the jury, to ignore it. Would you? Could you? Researchers using mock juries found that jurors in this situation assume that the confession was heartfelt and vote guilty more often than jurors who do not hear about a confession (Kassin & Wrightsman, 1981). The "jurors" are demonstrating the **correspondence bias** (also called the *fundamental attribution error*; Ross et al., 1977), the strong tendency to interpret other people's behavior as caused by internal causes rather than external ones. In the courtroom example, jurors would thus be more likely to view the confession as evidence of guilt (an internal attribute) than coercion (an external attribute). You are even likely to assume that other people fall prey to the correspondence bias more than you do, at least if you are from an individualist culture (Van Boven et al., 2003).

The correspondence bias is one of the most common attributional biases and a frequent source of error. This bias is at work, for example, when the sight of a homeless man on a bench leads us to assume his plight is due to an internal trait such as laziness rather than external factors such as a run of bad luck, a high unemployment rate, and a lack of affordable housing, or when a driver cuts in front of you on the road, and you attribute his lack of road etiquette to his despicable personality traits rather than situational factors (J. S. Baxter et al., 1990). The correspondence bias helps perpetuate discrimination because fault is attributed to the person, not to the circumstances. Once the correspondence bias shapes how you understand a particular person's behavior, you are likely to ignore the context of future behavior (that is, the surrounding situation), and thus the effect of the initial error is multiplied.

**SELF-SERVING BIAS**   Related to the correspondence bias is the **self-serving bias** (Brown & Rogers, 1991; Miller & Ross, 1975), the inclination to attribute your failures to external causes and your successes to internal ones, but to attribute other people's failures to internal causes and their successes to external causes. As a result, you consider the negative actions of others as arbitrary and unjustified, but perceive your own negative actions as understandable and justifiable (Baumeister et al., 1990). You are angry and slam things around because you've had a terrible day; your roommate throws tantrums because he or she has an awful temper. A culture, ethnic group, or nation as a whole may engage in this type of bias, attributing positive values and traits to its own group and negative values and traits to other groups, thereby sustaining ethnic or cultural conflict (Rouhana & Bar-Tal, 1998).

Not all cultures exhibit these various biases to the same degree. Just as different cultures promote different personality traits (see Chapter 11), they also lead people to use attributional biases somewhat differently. For example, accounts of crimes in Chinese-language newspapers are more likely to give external explanations for the criminals' behavior, whereas for the same offense, English-language newspapers are more likely to emphasize internal factors (Morris & Peng, 1994).

Because of the self-serving bias, you are likely to believe that you are kinder, more generous, and more selfless than other people. Research suggests that you probably overestimate your own generosity, rather than underestimating that of other people (Epley & Dunning, 2000).

**BELIEF IN A JUST WORLD**   Attributions can also be distorted by a **belief in a just world** (Lerner, 1980), the assumption that people get what they deserve; this contrasts with the assumption that untoward events can happen randomly and "justice" may not always prevail. Because most Americans are richer than most Egyptians, Colombians, or Bulgarians, they must, according to this bias, also be smarter or work harder. According to the belief in a just world, if you get what you deserve, you must have done something to deserve what you get—notice the circular reasoning here!

The belief in a just world can shape reactions to violent crime (particularly rape; Karuza & Carey, 1984), and it contributes to the practice of blaming the victim. For example, those who strongly believe in a just world are more likely than others to view AIDS as a deserved punishment for homosexual behavior (Glennon & Joseph, 1993) and to view the plight of a disadvantaged group, such as immigrants, as deserved (Dalbert & Yamauchi, 1994). The belief in a just world can maintain discriminatory behaviors (Lipkus & Siegler, 1993). However, when individuals identify with victims, as occurred for many Americans in the weeks and months after September 11, 2001, rather than blame the victims, the belief in a just world was associated with a desire for

**Self-serving bias:** A person's inclination to attribute his or her own failures to external causes and own successes to internal causes, but to attribute other people's failures to internal causes and their successes to external causes.

**Belief in a just world:** An attributional bias that assumes that people get what they deserve.

revenge 2 months after the attacks (Kaiser et al., 2004). People may make an attribution based on the belief in a just world when their sense of justice has been violated; in order restore a sense of order and justice, they seek to see the people hurt by the untoward event as somehow undeserving of their plight (Hafer & Bègue, 2005).

# Test Yourself

1. One reason why impression formation is subject to self-fulfilling prophecies is that
   a. the observer's attention is directed to particular behaviors that correspond to his or her impressions of the other person.
   b. the observer is being influenced by the recency effect and the halo effect.
   c. impression formation uses "bottom-up" processing.
   d. positive traits are more important than negative ones in the formation of impressions.

2. An attitude is most likely to lead to a related behavior when the attitude is
   a. unstable.
   b. accepted as fact.
   c. difficult to access from memory.
   d. strong.

3. What happens when a stereotype is activated?
   a. Our thinking but not our behavior is affected by the content of the stereotype.
   b. We see only positive qualities of the individual being stereotyped.
   c. We see only negative qualities of the individual being stereotyped.
   d. We react to a person's membership in a category rather than his or her individual characteristics.

4. Which of the following attributions best demonstrates the correspondence bias?
   a. She did well on that test because it was easy.
   b. She did poorly on that test because it was too hard.
   c. She failed that test because she is incompetent.
   d. She succeeded because her mother is famous.

## Answers

1.a 2.d 3.d 4.c

NOTE: Once you feel comfortable with the Test Yourself questions in this chapter, visit the book's Web site at www.ablongman.com/kosslyn3e for additional study questions.

# Think It Through!

If you were to design an antismoking campaign based on your knowledge of persuasion and stereotypes, what strategies might you include?

What psychological factors might explain the ways in which people attribute their success in quitting or their failure to quit smoking?

If you wanted to help people resist the pull of advertisements or political campaigns, what information would be particularly important to convey? Explain.

# SOCIAL BEHAVIOR: Interacting With People

The Delanys had very definite ideas about how they were supposed to behave with people. Based on their ideas about marriage, both Sadie and Bessie decided early on not to marry. They both wanted careers, and women of that era often had to choose between a career and marriage. Moreover, their father instilled in them a sense of self-reliance, as evidenced in his advice to Sadie about going to Columbia University: He advised her not to take a scholarship because she might then feel indebted to the people who offered it. He encouraged her to pay for her own education.

The Delanys also had definite ideas about how other people should be treated. They were taught to help others, regardless of skin color; the family motto was "Your job is to help someone." The Delanys stuck by their beliefs, even when others did not agree. Bessie recounted a time she vacationed in Jamaica with a darker-skinned Jamaican-born friend. There, Bessie learned that there were two official classes of Jamaican Negroes: "White Negroes," who had more privileges in society, and "Black Negroes," who were considered to be in a lower social class. The young women stayed with the family of Bessie's friend, who was a "Black Negro." "White Negroes" extended invitations to Bessie (a lighter-skinned Black woman) and ignored her friend. Bessie refused all invitations until her friend was invited as well.

Whereas social cognition pertains to individuals' perceptions of the social world, social behavior pertains to diverse types of behavior—from intimate relationships to obedience—that occur in and are affected by social situations.

# Relationships: Having a Date, Having a Partner

Sadie and Bessie's White maternal great-great-grandmother had a liaison with a slave while her husband was away fighting in the War of 1812. This relationship produced two daughters, half-sisters to the seven children she had already had with her husband. When her husband returned home, he adopted the two girls as his own. No one knew exactly what happened to her lover, although it was rumored that he ran away on the husband's return. The relationship between the Delanys' great-great-grandmother and biological great-great-grandfather would appear to have been based on more than a passing interest, given that the relationship spanned a number of years. Why were they attracted to each other? Why are we attracted to certain people? Why do we like particular people, and love others?

As the Delany children's ancestors undoubtedly experienced almost 2 centuries ago, and you may be experiencing now, relationships are strong stuff. They can lead to our most positive emotions and, as you saw in Chapter 13, can help us cope with events outside the relationship (Berscheid & Reis, 1998). They can also be the source of negative emotions: When asked about the "last bad thing that happened to you," almost half the respondents reported conflict in a significant relationship (Cupach & Spitzberg, 1994).

## Liking: To Like or Not to Like

Even though Sadie and Bessie decided not to marry, they did have boyfriends. Why were they attracted to certain men—why are you attracted to some people and not others?

**REPEATED CONTACT**   First impressions play an initial role, as does *repeated contact*, which usually leads to a more positive evaluation of someone (Moreland & Zajonc, 1982; Zajonc, 1968). The Delany sisters recount that a lot of "racial mixing, especially after slavery days, was just attraction between people, plain and simple, just like happened in our family, on Mama's side. You know, when people live in close proximity, they can't help but get attracted to each other" (Delaney et al., 1993, p. 76).

**SIMILARITY**   *Similarity* is a second factor in the development of liking, the more similar a stranger's attitudes are to your own, the more likely you are to be attracted (Montoya & Horton, 2004; Tesser, 1993). The adage "Opposites attract" has *not* been borne out by

Recent research recognizes that physical distance may no longer be as important as it once was for defining "repeated contact": Internet chatrooms and interest groups make it possible for a couple to "meet" and have a relationship without any physical contact (Bargh et al., 2002; McKenna et al., 2002; Parks & Roberts, 1998).

Passionate love: An intense feeling that involves sexual attraction, a desire for mutual love and physical closeness, arousal, and a fear that the relationship will end.

Companionate love: A type of love marked by very close friendship, mutual caring, liking, respect, and attraction.

Triangular model of love: The theory that love has three dimensions: passion (including sexual desire), intimacy (closeness), and commitment.

research. Similarity of preferred activities (Lydon et al., 1988), even similar ways of communicating, can lead to increased attraction and liking. For instance, we are more likely to be attracted to someone whose nonverbal cues are the same as those used in our own culture (Dew & Ward, 1993). In general, the greater the similarity, the more probable it is that our liking for another person will endure (Byrne, 1971).

**ATTRACTION** A third, and major, factor is *physical attraction* (Collins & Zebrowitz, 1995; Hatfield & Sprecher, 1986). In part, the role of physical attraction in liking may be influenced by our stereotypes about attractive people—such as that they are smarter and happier. Although the stereotype that people who are physically more attractive possess more desirable attributes is found in various cultures, what constitutes "more desirable" differs across cultures. For instance, in Korea, attractive people are thought to have greater integrity and concern for others—qualities more valued in that collectivist culture than in individualist Western ones (Wheeler & Kim, 1997; see Chapters 10 and 11 for discussion of collectivist versus individualist cultures).

## Loving: How Do I Love Thee?

Despite all the poems and plays, novels and movies, that chronicle, celebrate, and analyze love, its mystery endures. Its variations, components, styles, and fate over time have all been examined by psychologists. Loving appears to be a qualitatively different feeling from liking, not simply very strong liking (Rubin, 1970). Moreover, attitudes about and experiences with love appear to be similar across cultures as diverse as those of Russia, Japan, and the United States (Sprecher, Aron, et al., 1994).

**TYPES OF LOVE** People talk about "loving" all sorts of things in all sorts of ways. You might say you love a pet, a friend, a parent, a mate, and pizza with anchovies; obviously you don't mean quite the same thing in each case. Love is usually studied in the context of relationships. **Passionate love**—the intense, often sudden feeling of being "in love"—involves sexual attraction, a desire for mutual love and physical closeness, arousal, and a fear that the relationship will end. **Companionate love** is marked by very close friendship, mutual caring, liking, respect, and attraction (Caspi & Herbener, 1990).

**FIGURE 16.5 Sternberg's Triangular Model of Love**

According to Sternberg's triangular theory of love, passion, intimacy, and commitment form three points of a triangle. Any given relationship may have only one component (at a point), two components (one of the sides of the triangle), or all three components (the center of the triangle).

**DIMENSIONS OF LOVE** What do the various sorts of love have in common, and how can we understand their differences? Robert Sternberg has proposed a **triangular model of love** (1986a, 1988a). Love, he says, has three dimensions:

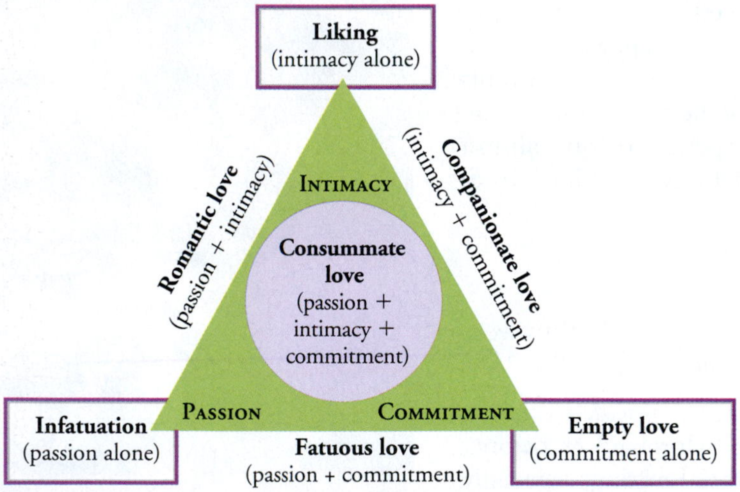

1. *passion* (including sexual desire),
2. *intimacy* (emotional closeness and sharing), and
3. *commitment* (the conscious decision to be in the relationship).

Particular relationships reflect different proportions of each dimension, in amounts that are likely to vary over time (see Figure 16.5). According to Sternberg's theory, most types of love relationships involve two of the three components; only "consummate love" has passion, intimacy, *and* commitment.

**LOVE: ATTACHMENT STYLES** Attachment style is another way of thinking about different kinds of love relationships. As dis-

cussed in Chapter 11, the attachment style shown with a partner stems from the interaction pattern developed between parent and child (Waller & Shaver, 1994). For instance, adults who seek closeness and interdependence in relationships and are not worried about the possibility of the loss of the relationship, about 59% of an American sample, are said to have a *secure* style of attachment (Mickelson et al., 1997). Those who are uncomfortable with intimacy and closeness, about 25% of an American sample, have an *avoidant* style and structure their daily lives so as to avoid closeness (Tidwell et al., 1996). Those who want but simultaneously fear a relationship have an *anxious–ambivalent* style (Hazan & Shaver, 1990); about 11% of Americans have this style. Although these studies indicate that a majority of Americans have a secure attachment style (Hazan & Shaver, 1987), an anxious–ambivalent style is more common in Japan and Israel, and an avoidant style more common in Germany (Shaver & Hazan, 1994).

**LOVE IS IN THE GENES—NOT!**   Are our love relationships in part genetically determined? Apparently not. When twins were tested on six scales that measured different aspects of romantic relationships, little evidence of heritability was found (Waller & Shaver, 1994). As Plomin and his colleagues (1997) put it, "Perhaps love *is* blind, at least from the DNA point of view" (p. 205). If our attachment style isn't genetically influenced, are we doomed to repeat the style of our childhood interactions with our parents? Although these early interactions affect attachment style, the outcome is not set in stone at childhood's end. The relationships we have as adults can change our attachment style (Shaver & Hazan, 1994).

**GROWING LOVE**   As you may have experienced in your relationships, a sense of intimacy usually progresses in stages (Honeycutt et al., 1998), and how we feel in a relationship influences the relationship itself. A growing feeling of intimacy comes from three factors:

1.  feeling understood by your partner,
2.  feeling "validated," that is, feeling that your emotions and point of view are respected, and
3.  feeling that the other person cares for you (Reis & Shaver, 1988).

As a relationship progresses, love seems to deepen over time (Sprecher, 1999). And just as mood can influence other aspects of our lives, such as memory, it influences us in this area as well: We are more likely to think our relationships are good when we're in a positive mood. Moreover, our attributions for serious conflicts in our relationships shift in response to our moods: In a bad mood, we are more likely to attribute relationship problems to vague, stable, internal factors; in a good mood, we are more likely to attribute the causes of conflict to specific, unstable, external factors (Forgas et al., 1994).

## Making Love Last

As noted, the way we think about people, things, and events can have a powerful effect on our feelings, behaviors, and subsequent thoughts. This is also true of relationships. If you are asked to think about the external reasons and pressures to stay in a relationship (having something to do on Saturday nights, your parents' approval, and so on), you will view commitment to the relationship as less likely, and will report less love for your partner, than if you think about the enjoyment you experience in the relationship and other intrinsic motivational factors (Seligman et al., 1980).

Research results indicate that sex is only one facet of lasting love. Myers (1993) summarizes four factors that determine whether love will be sustained:

1. "Similarity breeds content" (p. 170): You are more likely to stay involved with someone who is similar to you (Byrne, 1971).

2. Successful couples have sex more often than they argue, and people in successful marriages have sex more often than those in less successful marriages.

3. Successful couples are intimate: They share their innermost thoughts and feelings.

4. People in successful marriages share in decision making and in the daily burdens of maintaining a house and home.

Reciprocity also has a part in close relationships: If you want to sustain close relationships, you should help people who help you, and not hurt them (Gouldner, 1960; Kinnunen & Pulkkinen, 2004). If someone does you a favor, you have an obligation to return the favor sometime in the future, although this obligation does not necessarily extend indefinitely (Burger et al., 1997). However, in successful long-term relationships, members do not keep track of debts, assuming that they will average out over time.

## Mating Preferences: Your Cave or Mine?

Is love the reason people settle down and have children? According to evolutionary theory, those couples among our ancestors who were more closely bonded to each other and to their children were more likely to have offspring who survived. Thus, evolutionary theorists propose, humans today are genetically predisposed not only to search for sex but also to fall in love and to tend to their children (Trivers, 1972).

**EVOLUTIONARY REASONS FOR MATE SELECTION**  Finding someone attractive and liking, or even loving, that person is different from choosing him or her as a mate; we may date people we wouldn't necessarily want to marry. Why do we view certain people as potential mates, and not others? Evolutionary theorists propose that a reason why men are attracted by a well-proportioned body and symmetrical features is that these characteristics, along with other features, signal fertility and health (Thornhill & Gangestad, 1993). This view is supported by research with identical female twins; the twin whose face was more symmetrical was rated as more attractive (Mealey et al., 1999). In contrast, women find men attractive who appear to be able to protect and nourish them and their children; in modern society, researchers translate this characteristic as having good earning potential (D. M. Buss, 1989, 1999; Sprecher, Sullivan, et al., 1994).

Evolutionary theorists propose that women are attracted to men who will be good providers, and men are attracted to women who have physical attributes associated with fertility. However, not all research supports this view: As women gain more economic power, they become more interested in a man's attractiveness.

Evolutionary psychologists have argued that characteristics associated with reproduction are particularly likely to have been shaped by natural selection. David Buss (1989) asked people in 37 countries to rank 18 different characteristics in order of how important those are in ideal mates. In most respects, men and women valued the characteristics similarly; everybody agreed, for example, that kindness and intelligence are of paramount importance, and that emotional stability, dependability, and a good disposition are important (similar findings are reported by Cramer et al., 1996; Li et al., 2002). Respondents also valued mutual attraction and love. However, men and women did not have identical desires: Men tended to focus on physical attractiveness, whereas women tended to focus on wealth and power. Basing his view on evolutionary theory (Trivers, 1972, 1985), Buss (1994) has argued that women seek characteristics in men that would direct resources to their children, whereas men seek characteristics in women that indicate high fertility.

**MATE SELECTION: NOT JUST FOR EVOLUTIONARY REASONS** Ann Speed and Steven Gangestad (1997) found slightly different results when they collected less subjective ratings. In their study, they asked members of a sorority and a fraternity to nominate other members whom they felt scored high on specific qualities such as physical attractiveness and likelihood of financial success. The investigators then examined which of these characteristics predicted the frequency with which those nominated were asked out on dates. Perhaps the most interesting results concerned the men. As expected, romantically popular men were seen by their peers as confident, outgoing, and "trend-setting." However, they were not seen as likely to succeed financially or as being the best leaders, both characteristics that would seem to reflect the qualities that evolution is supposed to favor in males. Mate selection is not just about evolutionarily relevant characteristics.

Other studies have shown that as women come to have more economic power, their preference in mates becomes more similar to men's—that is, physical attractiveness becomes more important (Eagly & Wood, 1999; Gangestad, 1993). Women's preference for men who make good providers may reflect women's historic economic dependence on men rather than a true biological preference. In general, then, the sex differences are more pronounced in studies that use self-reports than in ones that measure actual behavior (Feingold, 1990) and in situations in which women have less economic power.

However, evolution is more than natural selection (see Chapters 1 and 3); we have inherited some characteristics not because they are adaptive in themselves but rather because they are associated with other characteristics that are adaptive. Nor are the brain's circuits all dictated from birth: Learning changes the brain's neural connections, and development itself allows the environment to shape the way the brain works. Moreover, culture obviously plays an important role in shaping mate preferences: What is deemed an attractive body type changes with time (Wolf, 1991). Also, the characteristics that make a man a good provider depend in part on the culture and the individual's role in it; the traits that make a man a good rancher are not necessarily those of a good stockbroker. In short, it would be a serious error to assume that what people find attractive or unattractive in a potential mate can be entirely explained by analyses of what might have been useful for mating among our distant ancestors.

What constitutes an "attractive" body type differs over time and across cultures. Women who today would be considered overweight or even obese in the United States have a body type that has been and continues to be attractive in some other cultures.

**RELATIONSHIPS: A SOCIAL EXCHANGE** How else, then, do psychologists explain why we get into and stay in relationships? Another approach looks for explanations in the immediate situation. **Social exchange theory** offers a rather unromantic view, holding that individuals are like accountants, trying to maximize the gains and minimize the losses in their relationships. If the losses outweigh the gains, the relationship is likely to end. In order for a relationship to continue, it must be profitable enough for both parties (Kelley, 1979; Sprecher, 1998; Thibaut & Kelley, 1959). But what is "enough"? The profits and losses in a relationship are compared with expectations based on past relationships, or the *comparison level*. Thus, if you have just left an abusive relationship, your comparison level is likely to be low, and a relationship without abuse might be seen as one providing a big profit.

In short, we enter, maintain, and leave relationships for a multitude of reasons. Unless a relationship is arranged for us by others, as it is in some cultures, attractiveness and similarity are two key factors that influence whom we like and whom we love.

**Social exchange theory:** The theory that proposes that individuals act to maximize the gains and minimize the losses in their relationships.

# Social Organization: Group Rules, Group Roles

The military tries to instill a sense of "groupness" in new recruits: The group's goal, such as a successful military action, is supposed to become more important than an individual's goal, such as staying alive.

If you live with other people, in the same apartment or on the same dorm floor, you might agree that the people in your living unit constitute a group, even if you don't get along. But if you live in a building with a number of apartments, or a residence hall with many floors, would everyone living there be considered part of a group, even if they don't all know one another? What, exactly, constitutes a group? Social psychologists have long wrestled with such questions and have come up with a number of definitions. There are some commonalities, though, in the use of the term **group**: regular interaction among members, some type of social or emotional connection with one another, a common frame of reference, and some type of interdependence (Levine & Moreland, 1998). In a group, each of us may feel, think, and act less from the point of view of an individual and more from the point of view of a group member. Military training, such as boot camp, is a dramatic example of a situation that promotes the shift from feeling like an individual to feeling like a group member: Loyalties and actions are no longer driven by individual goals but by group goals.

Disappointed fans riot at a European soccer game. Are they violent because they've become deindividuated? Probably not. In this case, they engage in situation-specific behaviors that are inconsistent with general expectations of appropriate behavior.

At the other extreme of group experience is **deindividuation**, traditionally defined as the loss of sense of self that occurs when people in a group are literally *anonymous*—their identities are unknown to others in the group. This is often the situation in crowds. With deindividuation, attention is focused on external events, and a high level of arousal is experienced (Diener, 1977). When this occurs, people respond to external cues and immediate feelings and act on them without monitoring the appropriateness of their behaviors. Violence by fans at European soccer matches has usually been explained as arising from deindividuation. However, a meta-analytic study on deindividuation suggests that loss of self is not the precipitating cause of the behaviors attributed to deindividuation, as has traditionally been thought. Rather, the behaviors result from the sense, shared by members of the crowd, that certain behaviors are permissible in the particular circumstances that would not be acceptable otherwise (Postmes & Spears, 1998).

## Norms: The Rules of the Group

The Delany sisters recount that in their hometown of Raleigh, North Carolina, even strangers passing on the street would nod and say good morning or good evening. But when Sadie and Bessie moved to New York City, they discovered that courteous behavior toward strangers did not always bring about a pleasant exchange, and they had to learn a new way of behaving in their new social context. Perhaps you, like them on their arrival in New York, have at one time or another been the "new kid on the block"—in school or college, in a new neighborhood, in an already established group of people. Chances are you didn't know the "rules"—how people were supposed to behave toward one another, and especially how you, a new member, were supposed to behave. Once you figured things out by watching other people (Gilbert, 1995)—an ob-

Group: A social entity characterized by regular interaction among members, some emotional connection, a common frame of reference, and a degree of interdependence.

Deindividuation: The loss of sense of self that occurs when people in a group are anonymous.

vious case of observational learning—you probably felt more comfortable in the group. And, in fact, groups create such rules and structures to help the group function.

The rules that implicitly or explicitly govern members of a group are called **norms**. They are, in essence, shared beliefs that are enforced through the group's use of *sanctions*, or penalties (Cialdini & Trost, 1998). Just as individuals have attitudes, groups have norms (Wellen et al., 1998). Norms pervade our everyday experience, defining the behaviors that make us good family members, friends, neighbors, partners, employees, employers, students, teachers, and so on. Norms guide us in what we say—and don't say—in chat rooms and e-mail exchanges (Bargh & McKenna, 2004). Psychologists categorize norms into two types: *Injunctive norms* refer to behavior that is typically approved or disapproved of, whereas *descriptive norms* refer to behavior that people typically engage in (Cialdini & Goldstein, 2004). For instance, people may typically feel that eating a lot of high-fat foods will meet with disapproval (injunctive norm), but nonetheless eat large quantities of that type of food (descriptive norm).

**DIFFERENT NORMS FOR DIFFERENT FOLKS** Norms may vary from group to group, or by age, sex, race, social class, or geographic region. For example, in the culture of the American South, honor is very important. Southern men are more likely than Northern men to think that their reputation is threatened when others swear at them in public, and thus they respond with more aggressive behavior (Cohen et al., 1996). Moreover, Cohen and his colleagues found that Southerners in general were more likely than Northerners to view such aggressive responses as appropriate. Southern norms for appropriate reactions to an insult are reflected in the more lenient judicial sentences given to certain types of violent offenders (Nisbett & Cohen, 1996).

Although norms can endure over time, even if the members of the group change (Jacobs & Campbell, 1961), norms can also change. This is the case for the use of "Ms." When this form of address was introduced, it was seen as one that would be used only by radical feminists. Now, however, it is much more widely used and positively viewed (Crawford et al., 1998). Another example of changing norms is found among adolescents in India who watch Western TV shows (and derive from them what they perceive of as Western norms). Their attitudes about drugs, alcohol, and sex change, and they reject the social norms of Indian society and become more Western (Varma, 2000).

**PERCEIVING NORMS** How we *perceive* norms is important. Even if those perceptions are not necessarily accurate, we still behave in accordance with them. For instance, some anti-drug programs emphasize both *why* people should say no to drugs and *how* to say no. But it appears that training students *how* to say no leads them to think that offers of drugs, and drug use in general, are more common than they really are, thereby creating the impression of a pro–drug-use social norm and leading to an increase in drug use. This is particularly true for alcohol use among college students (see Table 16.2, on p. 766; Berkowitz, 1997). Programs that focus only on *why* you should say no appear to be more successful (Botvin, 1995; Cialdini & Trost, 1998; Donaldson, 1995; Hansen et al., 1988). Programs aimed at emphasizing a drug-abstinent norm or a moderate-drinking norm also appear to be effective (Barnett et al., 1996; Berkowitz, 1997). Perceived norms can also affect how willing you are to become involved in social causes: If you perceive that becoming involved would violate an implicit group norm and make you "deviant" from others, you are less likely to work for social action (Ratner & Miller, 2001).

Hearing gossip provides an opportunity to learn about a group's norms—and what happens when those norms are violated (Baumeister et al., 2004).

Norms can affect all kinds of behavior, including a cold sufferer's willingness to wear a surgical mask when out in public. This Japanese woman is behaving according to one of her culture's norms: It is frowned on for a cold sufferer to go outside without a mask and spread cold germs to others.

**Norm:** A shared belief that is enforced through a group's use of penalties.

TABLE 16.2 **Personal Attitudes and Perceived Norms**

What college students *think* are the norms for alcohol use are not necessarily accurate. Most students in a 1986 study had a more conservative view of alcohol use than they thought their peers did, but their peers were similarly conservative. This table shows the percentage of students personally agreeing with each item and the percentage of students who thought that an item was the "norm" on campus. As you can see, the only time students' personal attitudes were near the perceived norm was in the lack of enthusiasm for total abstinence.

| Item | Personal Attitudes (% of students agreeing) | Perceived Norm |
|---|---|---|
| Drinking is never a good thing to do. | 1.4 | 0.1 |
| Drinking is all right, but a student should never get "smashed." | 12.7 | 0.8 |
| An occasional "drunk" is okay as long as it doesn't interfere with grades or responsibilities. | 66.0 | 35.4 |
| An occasional "drunk" is okay even if it does occasionally interfere with grades or responsibilities. | 9.3 | 33.2 |
| A frequent "drunk" is okay if that's what the individual wants to do. | 9.5 | 29.5 |

The false perception of a norm may explain why eating disorder prevention programs that feature speakers who have recovered from an eating disorder may inadvertently lead students to develop symptoms of such a disorder (Carter et al., 1997; Mann et al., 1997): Students inflate the perceived norm of eating disorders on campus after hearing and seeing the speaker and are thus led to change their behavior in the direction of the perceived norm.

## Roles and Status

In contrast to norms, **roles** are the behaviors that members in different positions in a group are expected to perform. Groups often create different roles to fulfill different group functions. Sometimes roles are assigned officially, as when a group votes for a leader; sometimes roles are filled informally, without a specific election or appointment. Roles help a group delineate both responsibility *within* the group and responsibility *to* the group.

In a **status hierarchy**, different roles reflect the distribution of power in a group. The Delany sisters described the status hierarchy of the South during and after Jim Crow laws: "White men were the most powerful, followed by White women. Colored people were absolutely below them and if you think it was hard for colored men, honey, colored women were on the bottom" (Delany et al., 1993, pp. 75–76). You can

Role: The behaviors that a member in a given position in a group is expected to perform.

Status hierarchy: The positioning of roles that reflects who has power over whom within a group.

often tell who has a high-status position in a group from nonverbal cues: High-status members are more likely to maintain eye contact, be physically intrusive (somewhat "in your face"), and stand up straight (Leffler et al., 1982). You can also identify high-status members from what they say and how they say it: They are usually the ones who criticize or interrupt others or tell them what to do. In addition, other members direct their comments to the high-status member (Skvoretz, 1988). Perhaps because of the absence of nonverbal cues, social status differences have been found to be less prominent in groups communicating by e-mail rather than face to face (Dubrovsky et al., 1991).

## When Roles Become Reality: The Stanford Prison Experiment

In the summer of 1971, nine Stanford University students were apparently arrested in Palo Alto, some searched spread-eagle style against a city police car. They were read their Miranda rights, and thrown into prison. Despite the fact that all nine knew that they were innocent of the crime they were accused of—armed robbery and burglary—the group soon adopted a prisoner-like mentality. In fact, the nine prisoners, like the nine guards who watched over them, were all participants in a psychological study.

This study later became famous, and it is now known as the *Stanford Prison Experiment* (Haney et al., 1973, 1976; Zimbardo et al., 2000). Earlier that August, Professor Philip Zimbardo had placed the following ad in the local newspaper, the Palo Alto Times: "Male college students needed for psychological study of prison life. $15 per day for 1–2 weeks. . . . " Some 70 people applied, and the 24 judged to be most healthy and "normal" (having no history of psychological problems or past problems with the police or drugs) were selected. Half of these students were randomly assigned (by flipping a coin) to be guards and half to be prisoners. Of these, 9 students actually played guards, and 9 played prisoners; the others were back-ups, in case they later were needed.

Student prisoners received prison uniforms, stayed in cells, and were referred to only by a number—all of which served as regular reminders of their new status. The guards, on the other hand, were given uniforms, handcuffs, keys, whistles, and billy clubs. The guards had offices, which—unlike the prisoners' cells—they were free to enter and leave as they pleased. The guards habitually wore mirrored sunglasses, which were intended to disorient the prisoners by cutting them off from many common social cues. These students were not given any specific training or instructions, other than to maintain "law and order" and to behave in a way that would command the respect of the prisoners.

The purpose of the experiment was to observe how the relationships between prisoners and guards developed over time. In remarkably short order, prisoners behaved passively, as if they realized that since they had no control over what happened to them, they should stop trying. In contrast, the guards began to act as if they had genuine power over the prisoners and to explore the limits of that power. Some, but not all, of the guards taunted the prisoners and harassed them (such as by sliding their billy clubs across the bars, causing a click-clacking repetitive slapping sound).

The prisoners did not adjust to their new status easily, and after one day, they staged a rebellion. They ripped off their numbers, screamed at the guards, and jammed their cots against their cell doors. The guards responded by spraying the prisoners with fire extinguishers, and then forcing them to take off their clothing. The guards also took away the prisoners' beds. Moreover, to set an example, the guards treated the leaders of the rebellion particularly harshly, putting them in solitary confinement. In addition, the guards cleverly set up a special "privilege

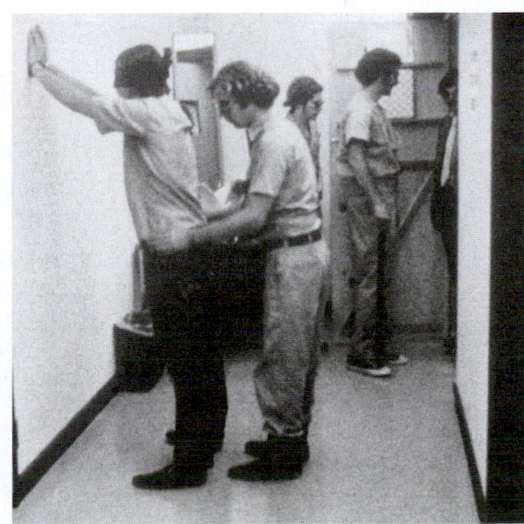

In the Stanford Prison Experiment, student guards fell into their new roles easily, exploring their power. Student prisoners, in turn, reacted to their new status by staging a rebellion.

cell." The prisoners who had the smallest role in the rebellion were put in this cell, where they had beds, could wash, and eat—and the other prisoners watched this, but themselves did not have beds or the privileges granted to the favored inmates. But soon even "bad" prisoners were allowed into this cell, and "good" ones moved out—which greatly confused and disoriented the prisoners. The net effect of this was to drive a wedge into the group, breaking up feelings of solidarity among the prisoners.

After their failed attempt to assert their dignity, the prisoners apparently slipped more fully into their roles, as did the guards. According to Zimbardo, they lost their identities as students. The prisoners became like sheep, motivated merely to survive and avoid the attention of the guards. In so doing, the prisoners largely stopped interacting with each other, and apparently not only lost their self-respect, but also respect for the other prisoners. To all appearances, the prisoners had become depressed.

Later, rumors (which turned out to be unfounded) that the prisoners planned to escape served to make the guards increasingly sadistic. For example, some forced prisoners to clean toilets using their bare hands. And some guards prevented the prisoners from using the toilet, and instead made them urinate and defecate into buckets in their cells—and then forced them to keep the filled buckets in their cells. When the guards became bored, they forced the prisoners to do jumping jacks, pushups, or engage in other unwarranted punishments.

Zimbardo later reported that he was shocked at how quickly and deeply the prisoners and guards slipped into opposing roles. He was so disturbed by the turn of events that he terminated the experiment early; the expected 2-week duration of the study shrank to only 6 days.

The participants in this study were ordinary, middle-class healthy students, who were randomly assigned to the different roles. The situation alone seems to have transformed not only their perceptions and behavior, but even aspects of their characters.

Zimbardo (2004) attributes the atrocities at Abu Ghraib prison in 2004 to the same situational factors that were at work during his Stanford study—roles, norms, and the status hierarchy. Others, however, point out that personality factors were likely at work at Abu Ghraib, but did not play a role in the Stanford Prison Experiment: Zimbardo's participants had been carefully screened to exclude those with a history of legal, substance, or psychological problems. Abu Ghraib's guards had no such screening, and one guard, at least, had several restraining orders against him by his ex-wife because of his history of violence (Saletan, 2004).

# Yielding to Others: Going Along With the Group

In Raleigh when the Jim Crow laws were in effect, Black customers in a White-owned shoe store were supposed to sit in the back of the store to try on shoes. On one occasion when Sadie Delany shopped for shoes, she was asked by the White owner, Mr. Heller, to sit in the back. She asked, "Where, Mr. Heller?" And he gestured to the back saying, " 'Back there.' And I would say, 'Back *where*?' . . . Finally, he'd say, 'Just sit anywhere, Miss Delany.' And so I would sit myself down in the White section, and smile" (Delany et al., 1993, p. 84). What made Sadie able to resist Mr. Heller's request—or his order, backed by law? What made Mr. Heller give up his attempt to have Sadie comply with the law and social convention? What made him call her "Miss Delany" and not "Sadie"? What would you have done if you were Sadie? In what circumstances do we go along with the group, do what someone asks of us, obey orders? When do we resist?

# Conformity and Independence: Doing What's Expected

Social norms tell us how we ought to behave, and sometimes we change our beliefs or behavior in order to follow these norms. This change in beliefs or behavior because of pressure from others is known as **conformity**. For example, immigrants must decide how much to conform to the norms of their new country and how much to retain the ways of their homeland (Lorenzo-Hernandez, 1998). Two types of social influence—informational and normative—can lead to conformity.

**INFORMATIONAL SOCIAL INFLUENCE** One type of social influence is *informational social influence*, which occurs when we conform to others' views or behavior because we want to be right and we believe that they are correct (Cialdini & Goldstein, 2004). This type of conformity is most likely to occur when the situation is ambiguous, when there is a crisis, or when other people are experts. Suppose you are working in a study group that is trying to solve a complex engineering problem, or that you are part of a medical team trying to agree on a diagnosis of a particularly perplexing case. The majority agree on an answer that doesn't seem right to you. What would make you more likely to go along with the majority view? Research indicates that *task difficulty* increases conformity: The harder the task, the more you are likely to conform—at least in part because you are less sure of yourself. *Social comparison theory* (Festinger, 1950) is consistent with this explanation: All people are driven to evaluate their abilities and opinions. When their abilities or views cannot be measured objectively, they seek out others, particularly people similar to themselves, to serve as a basis of comparison (Morris et al., 1976). Thus, even when we are initially certain, the disagreement of other members of our group can make us doubt (Orive, 1988).

**NORMATIVE SOCIAL INFLUENCE** Informational social influence, however, cannot be the only explanation for conformity. Conformity can also arise from *normative social influence*, which occurs when we conform because we want to be liked or thought of positively, as demonstrated in pioneering research by Solomon Asch (1951, 1955). If you had been a participant in Asch's original study, you would have found yourself in a group with five to seven others and been asked to perform a task of visual perception. You are all shown a target line and asked to say which of three other lines matches the length of the target line. Each person gives an answer aloud; you are next to last. This sounds like an easy task, as you can see in Figure 16.6 (on p. 770), but it soon becomes perplexing. For 12 of the 18 times you are shown the lines, everyone else gives the wrong answer! Will you agree with the answer everyone else is giving?

In fact, in Asch's experiment, only one person in the group was the true participant; the others were confederates playing a role. Seventy-six percent of participants went along with the confederates at least once, and approximately one third of participants' total responses conformed with the obviously wrong majority.

Why would these people conform with the norm established by the group? Variations on Asch's original experiment showed that characteristics of the situation are part of the answer. When participants *wrote* their answers instead of announcing them to the group, they gave the correct response 98% of the time, reflecting the fact that participants accurately perceived the lines.

**SOCIAL SUPPORT** *Social support* also influences conformity. If another group member openly disagrees with the group consensus, conformity is less likely (Morris & Miller, 1975). When Asch had one confederate disagree—that is, give the correct answer—91% of the real participants did not conform with the group answer. Furthermore, the more *cohesive* a group—the more attraction and commitment members have toward it—the more likely members are to conform, as are members who identify more strongly with a group's norms (Prapavessis & Carron, 1997; Schofield et al., 2001; Terry

**Conformity:** A change in beliefs or behavior in order to follow a group's norms.

## FIGURE 16.6

## Asch's Conformity Study

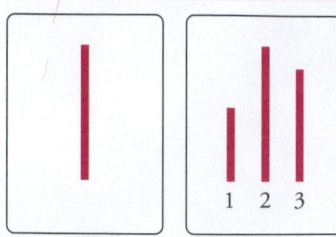

Participants in Asch's classic study on conformity were shown lines similar to these and asked the following type of question: Here are three lines of different lengths and a fourth target line. Which of the three lines matches the target line?

Only two people have yet to give their opinions, but everyone else appears to have given the same incorrect answer. Which would you say was the correct line if you were next in line? Asch (1951, 1955) created this situation with the use of confederates, and the true participant was the next-to-last person. Although 76% of participants conformed to the incorrect group response at least once, over the entire experiment, approximately two thirds of responses were independent of the majority.

& Hogg, 1996). And when a member of a less powerful group, such as a social or political minority, is in a group with more powerful members, the minority member may be more likely to conform (Roll et al., 1996). In general, despite the pressure to conform to group norms, not everyone is equally affected (Trafimow & Finlay, 1996).

One person not given to conformity for its own sake was Sadie and Bessie Delany's maternal grandfather, James Millam. A White man, he fell in love with a free woman, Martha Logan, who was one-quarter Black; marriage between them was, at the time, illegal. In such situations, it was usual for the man to marry a White woman and establish the Black woman as his mistress. Millam refused to conform to this convention; he lived openly with Martha Logan without benefit of marriage. Why would he not conform? Because to go along with the group, to conform, against one's beliefs or better judgment, leads to a loss of choice, of independence. The desire to retain a sense of individuality (Maslach et al., 1987) or control (Burger, 1992; Burger & Cooper, 1979) also provides reasons for not conforming. Thus, to understand someone's choice to conform, you need to look not only at the situation and the group but also at that person's characteristics—such as his or her commitment to the group or desire for individuality.

Were the people in Asch's study typical? All were men, but the results of later studies with women as participants were similar (Eagly & Carli, 1981). However, Asch's original participants may have been influenced by their culture. His experiment has been repeated by many researchers in many countries, and studies in countries with a more collectivist orientation, such as China, found higher levels of conformity than did those in individualistic countries (Bond & Smith, 1996). Furthermore, the findings of conformity studies over the years suggest that conformity has decreased since Asch's original work was done (Bond & Smith, 1996). Thus, characteristics of the individual, his or her relationship to the group, characteristics of the group, and the larger culture can all affect conformity and independence.

# Compliance: Doing What You're Asked

Even if you don't want to go along with a group's norms, you may be willing to comply with a direct request, as occurs when someone asks, "Could you please tell me how to get to the library?" **Compliance** is a change in behavior brought about through a direct request rather than by social norms. When the driver of the car in the next lane gestures to you, asking to be let into your lane in front of you, you will either comply or not.

**PRINCIPLES OF COMPLIANCE**   Without realizing it, you are a target of multiple requests for compliance each day, from TV commercials, in conversations with friends, or through questions on a survey form. Skill at getting people to comply is key to success in many occupations, from sales and advertising to lobbying, politics, and health prevention programs. Psychologist Robert Cialdini decided to find out from "compliance professionals"—people in jobs such as advertising, fund-raising, and door-to-door sales—exactly what they know about the subject. He inferred that the essence of effective compliance technique lies in six principles (Cialdini, 1994; Cialdini & Goldstein, 2004):

1. *Friendship/liking.* People are more likely to comply with a request from a friend than from a stranger.

2. *Commitment/consistency.* People tend to be more likely to comply when the request is consistent with a previous commitment.

3. *Scarcity.* People are more likely to comply with requests related to limited, short-term, rather than open-ended, opportunities.

4. *Reciprocity.* People tend to comply with a request that comes from someone who has provided a favor.

5. *Social validation.* People are more likely to comply if they think that others similar to themselves would comply.

6. *Authority.* People tend to comply with a request if it comes from someone who appears to be in authority.

**COMPLIANCE TECHNIQUES**   To see these principles at work, let's examine a few of the techniques most often used to win compliance. The commitment/consistency principle explains why a classic compliance technique, the **foot-in-the-door technique**, works so often. In this method, first you make an insignificant request, if you meet with compliance, you follow up with a larger request. Consider the study by Freedman and Fraser (1966), who had a male investigator phone housewives, asking what brand of soap they used. Three days later, the same man telephoned and asked if five or six people could perform a 2-hour inventory of everything in the housewife's cupboards, drawers, and closets. Fifty-three percent of the housewives who had agreed to the simple first request agreed to this much larger second request. In contrast, when housewives did not receive the first request but were asked to allow the inventory, only 22% complied.

The foot-in-the-door technique appears to work, at least in part, because people want to seem consistent (Guadagno et al., 2001). If you agree to the first request, you are being a nice person; declining the second request would call this self-perception into question. The commitment/consistency principle also explains the success of an unethical sales technique, the **lowball technique**, which consists of first getting someone to make an agreement and then increasing the cost of that agreement. Suppose

Compliance: A change in behavior prompted by a direct request rather than by social norms.

Foot-in-the-door technique: A technique that achieves compliance by beginning with an insignificant request, which is then followed by a larger request.

Lowball technique: A compliance technique that consists of getting someone to make an agreement and then increasing the cost of that agreement.

Car salespeople are notorious for using the lowball technique; however, some car makers have changed to a nonnegotiable pricing policy so that there is less opportunity for the lowball technique.

you see an advertisement for some shoes you've been eyeing—for a very low price. You go the store and are told that the shoes are no longer available at that price, but you can get them for a somewhat higher (although still discounted) price. What do you do? Many people would comply with the request to buy the shoes at the higher price.

Reversing the foot-in-the-door procedure also works; this is the **door-in-the-face technique**. You begin by making a very large request; when it is denied, as expected, you make a smaller request—for what you actually wanted in the first place. For instance, in one study (Cialdini et al., 1975), college students were stopped on campus and asked to serve as unpaid counselors to a group of juvenile delinquents for 2 hours a week for 2 years. Not surprisingly, no one agreed. Then the same students were asked to take the group on a 2-hour field trip. Fifty percent agreed. In contrast, when students were asked only to make the field trip without the larger, first request, only 17% agreed.

The door-in-the-face technique is a staple of diplomacy and labor–management negotiations. Why does it work? The reciprocity principle may hold the answer. If your first request is denied and you then make a smaller one, you appear to be making concessions, and the other party tries to reciprocate.

People sometimes go to surprising lengths to comply with a request. Kassin and Kiechel (1996) provided one example in a study that involved the *appearance* that participants had destroyed some data after being explicitly warned not to touch the ALT key on a keyboard. Sixty-nine percent of the participants agreed with a request to sign a confession that they had destroyed data—even though they had done no such thing. Nine percent made up details to support their (false) admission of guilt. You might suspect that something about the laboratory situation created an unnatural, unrealistic result. But Kassin and Kiechel were reproducing a result found in life: Innocent suspects sometimes comply with requests for a (false) confession to having committed a crime, even one as serious as murder (Kassin, 1997). Even more surprising, some of those who falsely confessed to a crime came to believe they actually committed it (see Chapter 7 for a discussion of how this can occur).

## Obedience: Doing as You're Told

If people can be so obliging in response to a polite request, what happens when they receive an order? Compliance with an order is called **obedience**. The nature of obedience attracted intense study in the United States after World War II, when the world heard about atrocities apparently committed in the name of obedience.

**THE MILGRAM STUDY**   The most famous study of obedience was carried out by Stanley Milgram (1963). Milgram expected that Americans would not follow orders to inflict pain on innocent people. In testing this hypothesis, his challenge was to design a study that gave the appearance of inflicting pain without actually doing so. He hit on the following procedure: Suppose you volunteered to participate in a study of memory. You are asked to act the part of "teacher" (see Figure 16.7). You are paired with a "learner" (a confederate), who, you are told, was asked to memorize a list of pairs of common words. You, the teacher, are to present one word from each pair and keep track of how well the learner does in correctly remembering the other word. If the learner makes a mistake, you are to administer a shock, increasing the voltage with each successive mistake. Although the shock generator is a phony and no shock at all is administered, you do not know this.

This is precisely what Milgram did; by prearrangement, at 120 volts, the learner shouted that the shocks were becoming too painful. At 150 volts, the learner asked to stop. At 180, he screamed that he couldn't stand the pain. At 300, he pounded on the wall and demanded to be set free. At 330 volts, there was only silence—an "incorrect response" according to the directions of the experimenter, who stood beside the teacher.

Door-in-the-face technique: A compliance technique in which someone makes a very large request and then, when it is denied, as expected, makes a smaller request (for what is actually desired).

Obedience: Compliance with an order.

How far would you go in obeying the experimenter's instructions? If you were like the participants in Milgram's study, when the learner cried out in pain or refused to go on, you would turn to the experimenter for instructions, who would reply that the experiment had to proceed and that he would take full responsibility. Would you obey? When Milgram described the experiment to a group of psychiatrists, they predicted that only a "pathological fringe" of at most 2% of the population would go to the maximum shock level. In fact, much to Milgram's surprise, 65% of the participants went to the highest level. Some of the participants, but apparently not all, felt terrible about what they were doing. But they still continued to administer the shocks.

**UNDERSTANDING MILGRAM'S RESULTS** The willingness of so many of Milgram's participants to obey orders to hurt others disturbed many people. Was there something distinctive about Milgram's participants that could explain the results? In the original studies, the participants were men. Later studies, however, found similar results with women (Milgram, 1965, 1974), as well as with people in Jordan, Germany, and Australia, and with children (Kilham & Mann, 1974; Shanab & Yahya, 1977).

Why did so many participants obey orders to hurt someone else? Were there particular characteristics of the situation that fostered obedience? Compliance research suggests two ways in which the study's design increased the likelihood of obedience. First, Milgram's experiment applied something like the foot-in-the-door-technique: Participants were first ordered to give a trivial amount of shock before going on to give apparently harmful ones. When participants were allowed to set the punishment voltage themselves, none ever went past 45 volts. Second, additional research indicated that people become more likely to comply with a request if it comes from someone in authority; the same holds true for obedience (Bushman, 1984, 1988). In a variant of the study (Milgram, 1974), when a college student was the one who gave a fellow student the order to shock, instead of an older, white-coated experimenter, obedience fell to only 20%. When the experimenters were two authority figures who disagreed with each other, no participants administered further shocks. It appears that the more authoritative the person who gives the order, the more likely it is to be obeyed; when someone in authority gives an order, the person obeying can deny responsibility for his or her actions.

Later variations of Milgram's original study point to other characteristics of the situation that have an important influence on obedience. *Proximity* to the learner is one. When teachers saw the learners while they were being shocked, and even held an electrode directly on the accomplice's skin (with a "special insulating glove"), 30% progressed to the maximum voltage, compared with 65% in the original design. Proximity to the experimenter also matters: When the experimenter telephoned his commands to the teacher instead of giving face-to-face instructions, obedience dropped to 21%.

**FIGURE 16.7** **The Milgram Obedience Study**

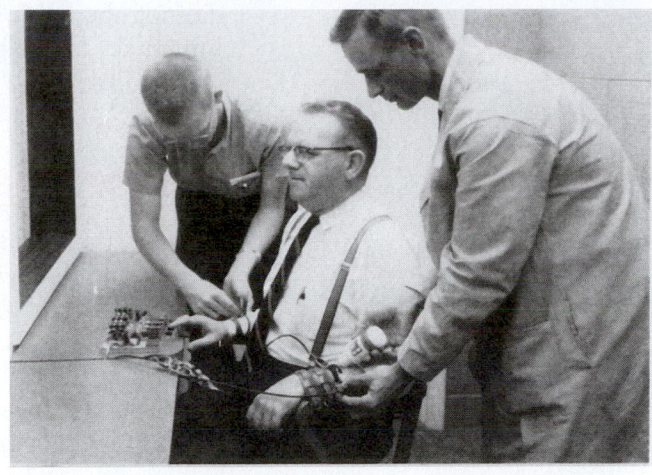

Each participant was paired with another man, having drawn lots to decide who would be the "teacher" and the "learner." In fact, the participant was always the teacher. The learner was always the same 47-year-old accountant who was a confederate in the study. The man who introduced himself as the experimenter was an actor. The learner was asked to memorize a list of pairs of common words; the teacher was to present the words, keep track of how well the learner did, and punish the learner for incorrect responses. The teacher watched as the learner was brought to a cubicle where the experimenter asked him to sit down and strapped him in a chair to "prevent excess movement." The experimenter attached shock electrodes to his wrist. Throughout the remainder of the study, the teacher could not see the learner, and all communication took place via an intercom.

The teacher was seated in front of the shock generator. The generator had 30 switches labeled in 15-volt increments from 15 to 450 volts. A description below each switch ranged from "Slight Shock" to "Danger: Severe Shock." The labels under the last two switches were ominous: "XXX." At the outset, the teacher was given a sample shock of 45 volts so that he could know what it felt like.

As disturbing as Milgram's results were, it is important to remember that not all participants obeyed the experimenter, and in some conditions the great majority did not obey; it is the specifics of the situation (such as proximity to the learner) that influences an individual's willingness to obey an order to hurt someone else (Blass, 1999, Gibson, 1991, A. G. Miller et al., 1995).

# Performance in Groups: Working Together

When Sadie and Bessie went to New York City, they moved into their brother Hubert's apartment, along with another brother and sister. Now there were five Delanys living in a three-room apartment. In such tight quarters, it helped to be very organized and to have clear rules and clear roles. Even though the apartment was Hubert's, and they all participated in making decisions, Sadie would have the final say because she was the oldest. How do groups make decisions? What are the advantages and disadvantages of working as a group?

## Decision Making in Groups: Paths to a Decision

After living in Hubert's apartment for a while, Sadie and Bessie got a place of their own in New York, and their mother came to live with them. However, at some point, their mother's health began to fade, and it was no longer safe for her to be home alone all day while her daughters were at work. The situation required that one of the sisters leave her job to stay home with Mrs. Delany (it never occurred to them to hire someone to stay at home with their mother while they were out at work). How did they decide who would stay home? This question faces many families today, and the path to a solution often involves group decision making. Such decision making also occurs in other contexts: Political parties, military planners, and athletic teams must decide on strategies; clinical groups must decide who receives what medical treatment and for how long; college admissions officers decide who is accepted and who is not. How are decisions made in groups?

In general, if a group is not initially unanimous in favor of a particular decision, it is likely that the view favored by the majority will prevail (Levine & Moreland, 1998). The larger the majority, the more likely it is that their choice will "win." This path is known as the *majority-win rule*, and it works well when the decision involves judgments or opinions (Hastie & Kameda, 2005). But there are times—you may have been present at some—when what began as the minority position eventually "wins." When there is an objectively correct answer, the *truth-win rule* works well because its inherent worthiness is recognized by the group (Kirchler & Davis, 1986). In general, groups reach a better decision when one solution can be shown to be correct (Hastie, 1986; Hastie & Kameda, 2005; Laughlin & Ellis, 1986).

**GROUP POLARIZATION** Group decision making does not always lead to the best decision. The opinion of a powerful member can shift others' opinions by might rather than right. Group decisions can also be marred by **group polarization**, the tendency of members of the group to take more extreme positions (with the same orientation as their initial opinions) after discussion (Isenberg, 1986; Levine & Moreland, 1998). This polarization of attitude can last well beyond the initial discussion (Liu & Latané, 1998).

One reason group polarization develops is that some members of the group may give very compelling reasons for their initial views, and more of them. In listening to these reasons, members who are in general agreement may become more convinced of the correctness of that initial assessment and more extreme in their views (Burnstein, 1982). This route to group polarization is more likely to be a factor when an intellec-

Group polarization: The tendency of group members' opinions to become more extreme (in the same direction as their initial opinions) after group discussion.

tual issue is at stake or when the group's goal is to make a "correct" or task-oriented decision (Kaplan, 1987). Another reason behind group polarization is that, through discussion, members can figure out the group's consensus on the issue and may be tempted to increase their standing in the group (and improve their view of themselves) by taking a more extreme position in accordance with the group norm (Goethals & Zanna, 1979). This route to group polarization is likely to occur when the issue requires judgments and when the group is more focused on group harmony than on correctness (Kaplan, 1987).

**GROUPTHINK**   Groupthink is another means by which decision making can go awry. **Groupthink** refers to the tendency of people who try to solve problems together to accept one another's information and ideas without subjecting them to critical analysis. According to Janis (1982), members of a group are most likely to fall into groupthink when they are especially close. In such instances, rather than realistically thinking through a problem, members are more concerned with agreeing with one another. This tendency has been used to explain many real-life disasters, such as why NASA launched the space shuttle *Challenger* despite widespread concerns about its booster rockets. (The failure of the booster rockets ended up causing the shuttle to crash.) Although the evidence that groupthink leads to bad decisions is mixed (Aldag & Fuller, 1993), a meta-analysis revealed that cohesive groups tend to make poorer decisions if the cohesiveness grew out of "interpersonal attraction"—the members' feelings about one another (Mullen et al., 1994). In such groups, the members want to seem cooperative, and so refrain from asking questions or making comments that they otherwise would, potentially leading to a different outcome than would result if they did question or comment. Groups that have a norm of coming to consensus are more vulnerable to groupthink than those that have a norm of minority dissent (Postmes et al., 2001).

**DECISION MAKING IN HETEROGENEOUS VERSUS HOMOGENEOUS GROUPS**   The variety of people in a group may also affect its decision-making process and performance (Kerr & Tindale, 2004). In general, as a group becomes more heterogeneous, it communicates less effectively (Maznevski, 1994; Zenger & Lawrence, 1989), and subgroups of similar members may form, causing nonsimilar members to feel alienated (Jackson et al., 1991). Some of the negative effects of heterogeneous groups can be minimized in the following ways:

- educating members about their similarities and differences, leading to recategorization by increasing a sense of the group as a team (creating an "us");
- increasing social skills among members; and
- teaching members conflict resolution skills (Caudron, 1994).

Paradoxically, although heterogeneity can create some group conflict, it can also have a positive effect on the group's performance (McLeod & Lobel, 1992) because of the increased innovation and flexibility that diversity brings to a group (Levine & Moreland, 1998).

## Social Loafing and Social Compensation

When responsibility for an outcome is spread among the members of a group, some members may be likely to let other members work harder (Latané et al., 1979), a phenomenon that has been called **social loafing**. One way to prevent social loafing is to instill a sense of importance and responsibility in each person, even if the work is boring or if the member's contribution is anonymous (Harkins & Petty, 1982; Rynes et al., 2005). Making the task attractive also reduces social loafing, as does knowing that individual as well as group performance will be evaluated (Harkins & Szymanski, 1989;

Groupthink: The tendency of people who try to solve problems together to accept one another's information and ideas without subjecting them to critical analysis.

Social loafing: The tendency to work less hard when responsibility for an outcome is spread over a group's members.

When a group as a whole is responsible for a task, some members may work less hard than they would if they were individually responsible for the task. This tendency toward social loafing can be countered by evaluating everyone's performance separately or by making the task attractive.

Hoeksema-van Orden et al., 1998; Karau & Williams, 1993). If you have lived with other people, you may have experienced the effects of social loafing: When dishes pile up in the sink or the bathroom goes uncleaned for weeks, each member of the household is doing some social loafing, waiting for somebody else to do the work.

Although working in groups may lead some people to indulge in social loafing, it may lead others to engage in *social compensation*, working harder in a group than they do when alone. Social compensation usually occurs when some members of the group see the task to be done as important but don't expect that other members will pull their weight (Williams & Karau, 1991). Social compensation occurs when someone finally washes the dishes or cleans the bathroom: The mess bothers someone enough that he or she cleans it all up. But the person who tackles the task is doing more than his or her share.

## Social Facilitation: Everybody Loves an Audience

Sometimes being part of a group, or just being in the presence of other people, can increase performance, this effect is called **social facilitation**. However, usually the presence of others enhances performance only on well-learned, simple tasks; on complicated, less well-learned tasks, the presence of others can hinder performance (Guerin, 1993). The presence of others appears to increase arousal, which then facilitates the *dominant* response in that situation (Schmitt et al., 1986; Seta & Seta, 1992). Thus, well-learned responses are likely to come to the fore when you are aroused, and you will be less likely to execute complicated or recently learned behaviors. Hence, at a concert, a musician may perform an old song better than a new one, whereas when practicing at home that same day, she probably could play them both equally well.

# Helping Behavior: Helping Others

When Bessie Delany began her dentistry practice in 1923, both cleanings and extractions were $2 each, and a silver filling cost $5. When she retired in 1950, she charged the same rates and was proud of it. In fact, she treated people regardless of their ability to pay. The Delany family ethic was to help others. This quality is called **altruism**, which has been defined as "the motivation to increase another person's welfare" (Batson, 1998, p. 282). What made Bessie so willing to help others? Why do we help other people? What circumstances encourage altruism?

## Prosocial Behavior

Acting to benefit others, called **prosocial behavior**, includes sharing, cooperating, comforting, and helping (Batson, 1998). Whether or not we help someone depends on factors about us, about the situation, and about the person we could help.

**CHARACTERISTICS OF THE HELPER**   We are more likely to help others if we have certain personality traits, such as a high need for approval, a predisposition to feeling personal and social responsibility, and an empathic concern for others (Batson et al., 1986; Eisenberg et al., 1989, 2002), or we are generally high on the personality dimension agreeableness (see Chapter 11; Carlo et al., in press; Graziano et al., 2004). People who tend to be helpers also have a belief in a just world, an internal locus of control, and

Social facilitation: The increase in performance that can occur simply as a result of being part of a group or in the presence of other people.

Altruism: The motivation to increase another person's welfare.

Prosocial behavior: Acting to benefit others.

less concern for their own welfare (Bierhoff et al., 1991). Bessie Delany seemed to feel a sense of personal and social responsibility toward others and could empathize with their plights. She also appeared to have less concern for her own welfare; when she was in dental school, a White girl born with syphilis came to the dental clinic—only Bessie volunteered to help her.

Group identity also plays a role in prosocial behavior. We are more likely to help and cooperate with other members of our group (Hewstone et al., 2002; Stürmer et al., 2005). Principles of learning (see Chapter 6) are also influential. Through our learning history, we may have been reinforced for helping or punished for not helping (Grusec et al., 2002). Moreover, parents, teachers, and others are models for observational learning. Thus, in time, we come to reward ourselves for helping, feel good after helping, and punish ourselves or feel guilty when we don't (Batson, 1998). Being in a positive mood may also make us more likely to help others (Guéguen & De Gail, 2003).

Prosocial behavior also appears to have an effect at the level of the brain: Choosing to act for mutual benefit, rather than individual benefit, increases activation in the "reward" areas of the brain (Rilling et al., 2002). When we choose not to act for mutual benefit but for our own, our distressing feelings—often resulting from cognitive dissonance—may be assuaged in a number of ways. Some people perform a prosocial act other than the one facing them (McMillen & Austin, 1971); others minimize the impact they would have made had they chosen to cooperate—"I probably couldn't have made a difference anyway" (Kerr & Kaufman-Gilliland, 1997).

**CHARACTERISTICS OF THE PERSON BEING HELPED AND THE SITUATION**   Some people in need of assistance are more likely to be helped than others. Who are they? First, we are more likely to help people we view as similar to ourselves (Park & Schaller, 2005). Consider an experiment in which Americans in three foreign cities asked for directions: Residents of those cities who were similar in age to the Americans requesting help were more likely to give directions (Rabinowitz et al., 1997). Second, we are more likely to help friends or people we like (remember, similarity facilitates liking). Third, we are more likely to help people we believe are not responsible for their predicaments, or those who give a socially acceptable justification for their plight (Weiner, 1980). In fact, the more justification the requester gives, the more likely he or she is to receive help (Bohm & Hendricks, 1997).

How the act of helping is framed can also influence our prosocial behavior. We are more likely to help when:

- the "cost" of helping seems to decline, as when helping others is framed as an opportunity for personal development (Perlow & Weeks, 2002);
- the "rewards" of helping appear to increase (Guéguen & De Gail, 2003); and
- there appears to be an increased "cost" of *not* helping (Dovidio et al. 1991), such as a heightened sense of shame and guilt (Penner et al., 2005).

## Bystander Intervention

A great deal has been learned about a specific type of prosocial behavior—bystander intervention—as a result of research inspired by one dreadful incident. At about 3 a.m. on March 13, 1964, a 28-year-old woman named Catherine Genovese—known to her neighbors as Kitty—was brutally murdered in Queens, a borough of New York City, only minutes from her own apartment building. She was coming home from her job as a manager of a bar. When her attacker first caught and stabbed her, she screamed for help. The lights came on in several apartments overlooking the scene of the crime, and a man

New York City's firefighters displayed their altruism in September 2001, both when going into the burning World Trade Center towers to rescue people inside and when searching through the burning rubble for survivors.

**FIGURE 16.8**

# Bystander Intervention

Participants thought they were involved in a study of campus life but instead were exposed to an "emergency" with a varying number of bystanders. Participants went into a private cubicle and were told that they could all hear one another, but only one student would be able to speak during any 2-minute period; when all had spoken, the cycle would start again. They were also told that the experimenter would not be listening. Participants were led to believe that either four, one, or no other students ("bystanders") were listening. In fact, there was only one true participant at a time; the rest of the voices on the intercom were prerecorded tapes.

Study on campus life

The crisis came after one (prerecorded) voice confessed to having seizures in stressful situations. This person subsequently seemed to be having a seizure, and asked for help.

I er think I need er … help because I er I'm er h-h-having a a a real problem … (choking sounds) … I'm gonna die er … seizure (chokes, then is quiet)

Would participants leave their cubicles to get help? Their responses depended greatly on the perceived number of bystanders. The great majority of participants went to get help when they thought they were the only ones aware of the problem, but they helped less often the more bystanders they thought were aware of the problem.

What should I do?

**Bystander effect:** The decrease in offers of assistance that occurs as the number of bystanders increases.

yelled down to her attacker to leave her alone. Her attacker briefly stopped and walked away. The apartment lights went out. The attacker returned and stabbed her again, she screamed again, to no avail, although lights again came on in the surrounding apartments. The attacker left in a car, and Kitty Genovese dragged herself to the lobby of an apartment building near her own. The attacker returned again, and this time he kept stabbing her until she died. The gruesome ordeal took some 35 minutes and at least part of it was heard by no less than 38 neighbors. Only one person called the police (Rosenthal, 1964).

Darley and Latané (1968) hypothesized that if only a few of those 38 neighbors had heard the attack, those few would have been more likely to help Kitty Genovese. This relationship is known as the **bystander effect**: As the number of bystanders increases, offers of assistance decrease. To test this relationship, Darley and Latané, with the aid of confederates, created the following situation. Imagine yourself as a participant in a study, taking part in a telephone conference about campus life with a number of others. Each participant speaks without interruption, and when everyone has spoken, the first person gets to speak again, and so on. Suppose another participant mentions that when stressed he gets seizures; then you hear that person stutter, start to choke, and ask for help. Would you get help? If you were like most participants in Darley and Latané's study (1968) (see Figure 16.8), and you believed that there were only two people in the telephone conference—you and the person with seizures—you would very likely seek help. But if you had been told that there were three participants, you would be less likely to seek help, and even less likely with a total of six participants. In short, attempts to help rose as the number of apparent bystanders dropped: When participants thought that they were the only one aware of the "emergency," 85% of them left the cubicle and got the experimenter within the first minute. When they thought there was one other bystander, 65% helped within the first minute. When participants thought there were four other bystanders, only 25% helped within the first minute. At the end of 4 minutes, all in the smallest group helped, as did 85% of those in the mid-sized group, but only 60% in the largest group.

From this and other studies, Darley and Latané (1970) described five steps, or "choice points," in bystander intervention (see Figure 16.9). At each step, various factors, such as the number of bystanders and characteristics of the bystanders, shape the likelihood that someone will help. For example, consider Step 2, perceiving the event as an emergency. If a situation is ambiguous, leaving you uncertain about whether the emergency is real, you may hesitate to offer help. If other bystanders are present, your hesitancy may be increased by *evaluation apprehension*—a fear that you might be

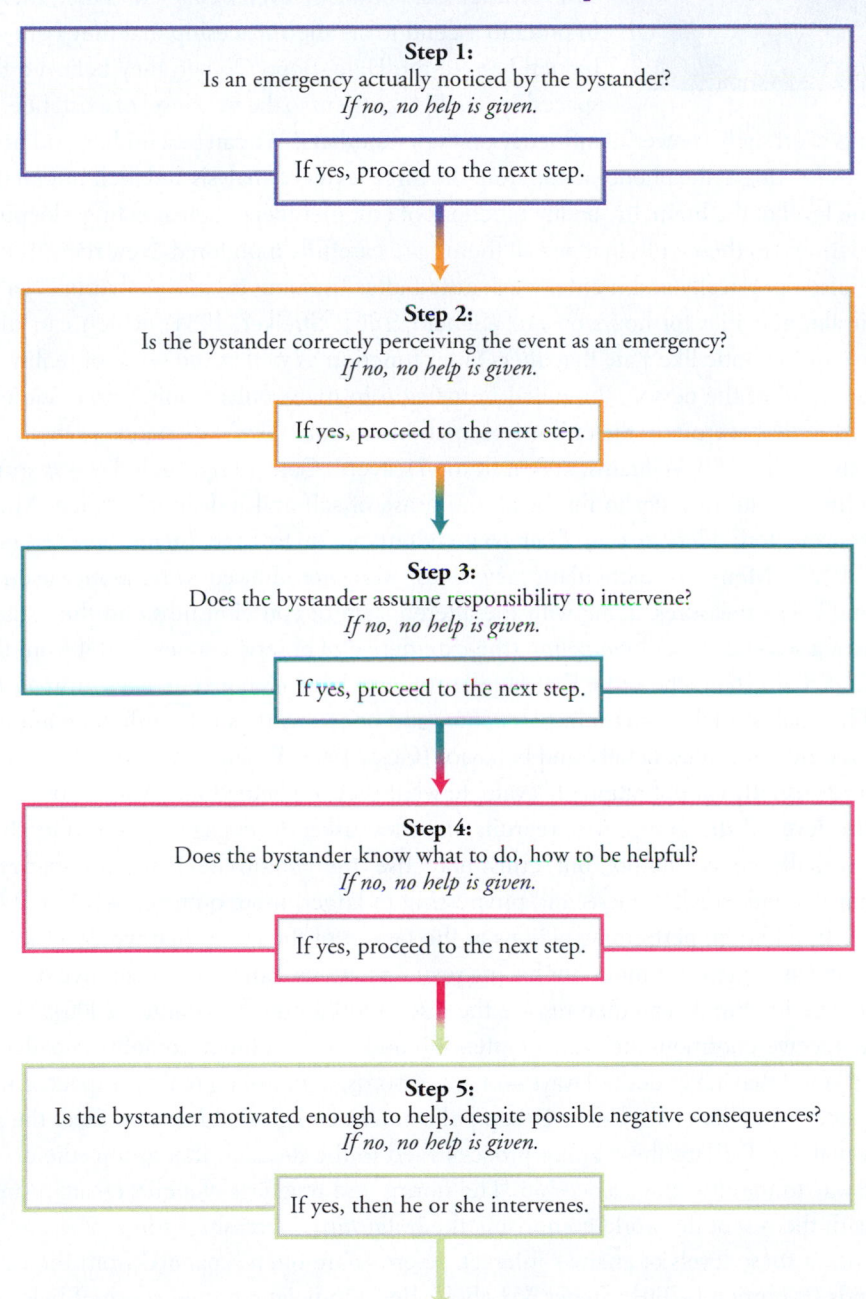

**FIGURE 16.9** **The Five Choice Points of Bystander Intervention**

**Step 1:**
Is an emergency actually noticed by the bystander?
*If no, no help is given.*

If yes, proceed to the next step.

**Step 2:**
Is the bystander correctly perceiving the event as an emergency?
*If no, no help is given.*

If yes, proceed to the next step.

**Step 3:**
Does the bystander assume responsibility to intervene?
*If no, no help is given.*

If yes, proceed to the next step.

**Step 4:**
Does the bystander know what to do, how to be helpful?
*If no, no help is given.*

If yes, proceed to the next step.

**Step 5:**
Is the bystander motivated enough to help, despite possible negative consequences?
*If no, no help is given.*

If yes, then he or she intervenes.

embarrassed or ridiculed if you try to intervene because there may be no emergency after all. The number of bystanders also influences Step 3, assuming responsibility. The more bystanders there are, the less responsible each one feels for offering help, creating a **diffusion of responsibility**. Fortunately, once people have learned about the bystander effect, they are subsequently more likely to intervene (Beaman et al., 1978).

# LOOKING AT LEVELS
## Cults

In 1997, members of the Heaven's Gate cult killed themselves in order to ascend to an alien spaceship that they believed was hidden behind the Hale–Bopp Comet; they believed that the spaceship would take them to the next level of existence. How is it that cults exert such a powerful influence on their members? We can best understand how cults function by looking at the phenomenon from the three levels of analysis and their interactions.

At the level of the brain, the bodily functions of cult members, such as eating, sleeping, and sexual relations (in those cults that permit them), are carefully monitored. New recruits in many cults are often physically and mentally exhausted after listening to music, chanting, or engaging in similar activities for hours on end (Schein, 1961; Streiker, 1984), which can induce a meditative or hypnotic-like state that alters brain function as well as the sense of reality.

At the level of the person, the initial immersion in many cults requires dramatic changes on the part of new recruits as the cult strives to eliminate members' experience of themselves as individuals (West, 1980; Williams, 2003). In the Heaven's Gate group, each day was structured down to the minute in order to minimize the sense of self and individual choice. Moreover, members were forbidden to trust their own judgments or to have "inappropriate" curiosity (Bearak, 1997). Members, particularly new ones, were not allowed to be alone, even in the bathroom. These measures, along with the altered state of consciousness and the exhaustion, can induce a sense of *depersonalization* (the experience of observing oneself as if from the outside) and *derealization* (the sense that familiar objects have changed or seem unreal; Singer, 1995). The goal of such changes in perception and consciousness is to influence and control the new recruit's attitudes, beliefs, and behavior (Gesy, 1993; Richmond, 2004). In such states, new recruits usually cannot rationally evaluate what they are being told (Walsh, 2001).

At the level of the group, new recruits are often asked to engage in behaviors that they would normally refuse to do, but cults may use the foot-in-the-door compliance technique, starting with small requests and progressing to larger, more outrageous, ones (Miller et al., 1999). In addition, performing actions at the behest of the group that would otherwise be refused, such as begging for money or having sexual relations, can induce cognitive dissonance; only a change in attitude can then resolve the discomfort aroused (Galanter, 2000). Moreover, members receive enormous amounts of attention and reinforcement, sometimes called "love-bombing," for behaving in desired ways—in other words, conforming to their expected role and to group norms (Miller et al., 1999). Group polarization and groupthink may affect the group's decision making. Perhaps these group processes led to the decision that group suicide was an effective way to join the alien spaceship. The norms and practices of a cult create a strong in-group (with the rest of the world comprising the outgroup), increasing group cohesion.

Events at these levels of analysis interact: Recruits are often separated from their families and friends (Richmond, 2004; Singer & Lalich, 1995) to heighten their sense of belonging to the cult (level of the group). Moreover, the arousal and the unpleasant changes in perception and consciousness (levels of brain and person) are calmed by the positive response of group members after a recruit complies with the cult members' requests—or obeys their orders (level of the group). Such negative reinforcement (level of the person) leads to changes in self-concept and heightens the importance of, and dependence on, the group (Galanter, 2000).

# Test Yourself

1. When Buss asked people from different cultures to rank the characteristics of an ideal mate, in general, the responses of men and women were
   a. highly variable from culture to culture.
   b. very similar, even across cultures.
   c. not overlapping at all.
   d. exactly the same.

2. Milgram demonstrated that people often obey authority figures to a disturbing degree. In follow-up studies, when would a participant be *least* likely to shock the confederate (the learner)?
   a. when the experimenter was older
   b. when the confederate was in close proximity
   c. when the confederate was far away
   d. when the experimenter was in close proximity

3. Being in a group can increase or decrease the probability of a behavior. For example, people often perform well-learned tasks better when they are in a social situation, as a result of _____, yet they will not work as hard when they share responsibility, as a result of _____.
   a. social loafing; social facilitation
   b. social facilitation; social loafing
   c. social loafing; groupthink
   d. groupthink; social facilitation

4. According to research on prosocial behavior, when are you most likely to help someone else?
   a. when the person is very different from you
   b. when you have negative thoughts about the person that you want to change
   c. when you believe that the person's predicament is not his or her fault
   d. when the person refuses to ask for help

## Answers

1.b 2.b 3.b 4.c

# Think It Through!

When Sadie Delany began her job as a New York high school teacher, how might she have learned the school's norms and students' and teachers' roles?

Imagine that you have started a new job working in a large corporation. Based on what you have learned, what colleagues are you likely to be attracted to and why? If your boss wants employees to do something "slightly illegal," what factors may make employees less likely to go along with this request (or order)? Will working as a group change the way the work is performed? Why or why not? If an employee is injured at work, what factors may make the employees who witness the incident more likely to help?

# A FINAL WORD:
# Ethics and Social Psychology

The researchers who conducted many of the studies described in this chapter did not tell participants about the true nature of the experiments at the outset, and several used confederates. Many of the classic social psychology studies were carried out before the discipline established rigorous ethical guidelines (see Chapter 1). In fact, some of the guidelines were formulated *because* these studies raised serious ethical concerns. Keep in mind, however, several issues related to the use of deception in psychology. First, many of the pioneering researchers did not expect to cause psychological distress. For example, Milgram initially did not expect participants to be willing to shock learners at higher "voltage" levels, although he did continue to perform variants of his study after he knew the results of his first study. Second, some psychological phenomena are extremely difficult, if not impossible, to study if the participant knows the true nature of the experiment. For example, could you think of a way to design a study on conformity *without* using deception? Third, at present, in order to receive approval for a study that uses deception, researchers must show that the deception is absolutely necessary (that the information could not be ascertained without deception), that the information is valuable and the deception minimal, and that at the conclusion of the study, the investigators will fully explain to the participants the nature of the study and the reasons for deception. (In fact, participants in Milgram's study were the first to be systematically and fully informed about the purposes and predictions of the study immediately after their participation; Blass, 2004.) In short, deception is now permitted in research only if it is crystal clear that the participants will not be harmed and that important knowledge will be gained.

# REVIEW AND REMEMBER!

## Summary

### I. Social Cognition: Thinking About People

**A.** We can form impressions of others quickly, in as little as 10 seconds. The halo and primacy effects can influence the impressions we form, and these impressions can become self-fulfilling prophecies.

**B.** Attitudes and stereotypes help reduce the cognitive effort required to understand the social world. Our impressions, attitudes, stereotypes, and attributions affect how we process, encode, and remember information.

**C.** Our attitudes can affect our behavior and are especially likely to do so when they are strong, stable, relevant, important, and easily accessible.

**D.** Conflict between an attitude and our behavior (or between two attitudes) can lead to cognitive dissonance, which we are then driven to reduce.

**E.** Efforts to change attitudes are attempts at persuasion. Central routes to persuasion require more time, energy, or expertise than peripheral routes.

**F.** Persuasion attempts can be thwarted by strong attitudes, reactance, forewarning, and selective avoidance.

**G.** Social cognitive neuroscience has helped reveal that cognitive dissonance and other social cognitive phenomena can occur outside conscious awareness.

**H.** The human process of categorizing objects (including people) leads to stereotypes, and our stereotypes of others affect our behavior toward them and the ways others behave toward us and can lead to prejudice and discrimination.

**I.** Because our stereotypes create biases in the way we process information, they often seem more accurate than they really are and thus are difficult to change.

**J.** Although we are driven to make attributions to understand events or behavior, our reasoning about the causes of these phenomena may rely on attributional biases, such as the correspondence bias, the self-serving bias, and the belief in a just world. Such biases can lead us to understand people's behavior inaccurately.

## Your Notes

I.

A.

B.

C.

D.

E.

F.

G.

H. Jigsaw classroom can decrease prejudice through interdependence.

I.

J.

## II. Social Behavior: Interacting With People

**A.** In our intimate relationships, we are more likely to be attracted to, and to like, people we view as similar to ourselves or with whom we have repeated contact.

**B.** Love can be understood by examining different types of love, by using Sternberg's triangular model of love's three dimensions, or by looking at different attachment styles.

**C.** All groups have norms and roles and assign status to members; these factors guide members' behaviors in a group. Zimbardo's prison study provides an example of the power of group norms and roles and status within a group.

**D.** Conformity is affected by informational and normative social influences, depending on the situation. Asch's conformity experiment illustrates normative social influence.

**E.** The foot-in-the-door, lowball, and door-in-the-face techniques are used to increase compliance.

**F.** Obedience to an order can be affected by various factors, including the status and proximity of the person giving the order.

**G.** The style of a group's decision making depends on the group's goals and composition and on the ways in which members articulate their views before the group.

**H.** Being in a group can help or harm a given individual's performance.

**I.** Prosocial behavior is affected by characteristics of the helper, the person being helped, and the situation. Psychological principles, such as the bystander effect and diffusion of responsibility, also determine when and whom we help.

NOTE: Once you feel that you understand the material in this chapter, visit the book's Web site at www.ablongman.com/kosslyn3e to test your knowledge with additional study questions.

*II.*

*A.*

*B.*

*C. Perception of norms (even if inaccurate) can influence behavior.*

*D.*

*E. See p. 771 for compliance principles.*

*F.*

*G.*

*H.*

*I.*

# Key Terms

altruism, p. 776
attitude, p. 738
attribution, p. 755
attributional bias, p. 756
belief in a just world, p. 757
bystander effect, p. 778
cognitive dissonance, p. 741
companionate love, p. 760
compliance, p. 771
conformity, p. 769
correspondence bias, p. 756
deindividuation, p. 764
diffusion of responsibility, p. 780
door-in-the-face technique, p. 772
external attribution, p. 755
foot-in-the-door technique, p. 771

group, p. 764
group polarization, p. 774
groupthink, p. 775
impression formation, p. 735
impression management, p. 735
ingroup, p. 750
internal attribution, p. 755
lowball technique, p. 771
mere exposure effect, p. 744
norm, p. 765
obedience, p. 772
outgroup, p. 750
passionate love, p. 760
persuasion, p. 744
prejudice, p. 748

prosocial behavior, p. 776
recategorization, p. 753
role, p. 766
self-perception theory, p. 742
self-serving bias, p. 757
social cognition, p. 734
social cognitive neuroscience, p. 745
social exchange theory, p. 763
social facilitation, p. 776
social loafing, p. 775
social psychology, p. 734
status hierarchy, p. 766
stereotype, p. 747
theory of causal attribution, p. 756
triangular model of love, p. 760

# REFERENCES

Aalto, S., Naatanen, P., Wallius, E., Metsahonkala, L., Stenman, H., Niem, P. M., & Karlsson, H. (2002). Neuroanatomical substrata of amusement and sadness: A PET activation study using film stimuli. *Neuroreport: For Rapid Communication of Neuroscience Research, 13*, 67–73.

Aartsen, M. J., van Tilburg, T., Smits, C. H. M., & Knipscheer, K. C. P. M. (2004). A longitudinal study of the impact of physical and cognitive decline on the personal network in old age. *Journal of Social & Personal Relationships, 21*, 249–266.

Abbott, M. J., & Rapee, R. M. (2004). Post-event rumination and negative self-appraisal in social phobia before and after treatment. *Journal of Abnormal Psychology, 113*, 136–144.

Abdollahi, P., & Mann, T. (2001). Eating disorder symptoms and body image concerns in Iran: Comparisons between Iranian women in Iran and in America. *International Journal of Eating Disorders, 30*, 259–268.

Abel, T., Martin, K. C., Bartsch, D., & Kandel, E. R. (1998). Memory suppressor genes: Inhibitory constraints on the storage of long-term memory. *Science, 279*, 338–341.

Ablon, J. S., & Marci, C. (2004). Psychotherapy process: The missing link. Comment on Westen, Novotny, and Thompson-Brenner (2004). *Psychological Bulletin, 130*, 664–668.

Abraham, H. D. (1983). Visual phenomenology of the LSD flashback. *Archives of General Psychiatry, 40*, 884–889.

Abramowitz, J. S. (1997). Effectiveness of psychological and pharmacological treatments for obsessive-compulsive disorder: A quantitative review. *Journal of Consulting and Clinical Psychology, 65*, 44–52.

Abrams, L. R., & Jones, R. W. (1994, August). *The contribution of social roles to psychological distress in businesswomen.* Paper presented at the 102nd annual convention of the American Psychological Association, Los Angeles, CA.

Abramson, L. Y., Seligman, M. E., & Teasedale, J. D. (1978). Learned helplessness in humans: Critique and reformulation. *Journal of Abnormal Psychology, 87*, 49–74.

Achter, J., Lubinski, D., & Benbow, C. P. (1996). Multipotentiality among the intellectually gifted: "It was never there and already it's vanishing." *Journal of Counseling Psychology, 43*, 65–76.

Ackerman, P. L., Beier, M. E., & Boyle, M. O. (2005). Working memory and intelligence: The same or different constructs? *Psychological Bulletin, 131*, 30–60.

Ackerman, S. J., Benjamin, L. S., Beutler, L. E., Gelso, C. J., Goldfried, M. R., Hill, C., Lambert, M. J., Norcross, J. C., Orlinsky, D. E., & Rainer, J. (2001). Empirically supported therapy relationships: Conclusions and recommendations of the Division 29 Task Force. *Psychotherapy: Theory, Research, Practice, Training, 38*, 495–497.

Adams, H. E., Wright, W. L., & Lohr, B. A. (1996). Is homophobia associated with homosexual arousal? *Journal of Abnormal Psychology, 105*, 440–445.

Adams, J. (1967). *Human memory.* New York: McGraw-Hill.

Adams, R. B., Jr., & Kleck, R. E. (2003). Perceived gaze direction and the processing of facial displays of emotion. *Psychological Science, 14*, 644–647.

Adams, S. J., & Pitre, N. (2000). Who uses bibliotherapy and why? A survey from an underserviced area. *Canadian Journal of Psychiatry, 45*, 645–649.

Adcock, I. M. (2000). Molecular mechanisms of glucocorticosteroid actions. *Pulmonary Pharmacology and Therapeutics, 13*, 115–126.

Addis, D. R., & Tippett, L. J. (2004). Memory of myself: Autobiographical memory and identity in Alzheimer's disease. *Memory, 12*, 56–74.

Addis, M. E. (1997). Evaluating the treatment manual as a means of disseminating empirically validated psychotherapies. *Clinical Psychology: Science & Practice, 4*, 1–11.

Ader, R. (1976). Conditioned adrenocortical steroid elevations in the rat. *Journal of Comparative and Physiological Psychology, 90*, 1156–1163.

Ader, R., & Cohen, N. (1975). Behaviorally conditioned immunosuppression. *Psychosomatic Medicine, 37*, 333–340.

Adler, A. (1956). *The individual psychology of Alfred Adler: A systematic presentation of selections from his writings* (H. L. Ansbacher & R. R. Ansbacher, Eds.). New York: Basic Books.

Adler, A. (1964). *Social interest: A challenge to mankind.* New York: Capricorn Books. (Original work published 1933)

Adler, N. E., Epel, E. S., Castellazzo, G., & Ickovics, J. R. (2000). Relationship of subjective and objective social status with psychological and physiological functioning: Preliminary data in healthy white women. *Health Psychology, 19*, 586–592.

Adolph, K. E. (2000). Specificity of learning: Why infants fall over a veritable cliff. *Psychological Science, 11*, 290–295.

Adolphs, R. (2002). Neural systems for recognizing emotion. *Current Opinion in Neurobiology, 12*, 169–177.

Adolphs, R., Baron-Cohen, S., & Tranel, D. (2002). Impaired recognition of social emotions following amygdala damage. *Journal of Cognitive Neuroscience, 14*, 1264–1274.

Adolphs, R., Damasio, H., Tranel, D., & Damasio, A. R. (1996). Cortical systems for the recognition of emotion in facial expressions. *Journal of Neuroscience, 16*, 7678–7687.

Agency for Health Care Policy and Research. (1999). Newer antidepressant drugs are equally as effective as older-generation drug treatments, research shows. AHCPR Pub. No. 99-E013. Rockville, MD: Author.

Aglioti, S., Smania, N., Manfred, M., & Berlucchi, G. (1996). Disownership of left hand and objects related to it in a patient with right brain damage. *Neuroreport, 8*, 293–296.

Aguilar-Alonso, A. (1996). Personality and creativity. *Personality and Individual Differences, 21*, 959–969.

Ahadi, S., & Diener, E. (1989). Multiple determinants and effect size. *Journal of Personality and Social Psychology, 56*, 398–406.

Aharon, I., Etcoff, N., Ariely, D., Chabris, C. F., O'Connor, E., & Brieter, H. C. (2001). Beautiful faces have variable reward value: fMRI and behavioral evidence. *Neuron, 32*, 537–551.

Ahmed, S. T., Lombardino, L. J., & Leonard, C. M. (2001a) Specific language impairment: Definitions, causal mechanisms and neurobiological factors. *Journal of Medical Speech-Language Pathology, 9*, 1–15.

Ahmed, S. T., Lombardino, L. J., & Leonard, C. M. (2001b). "Specific language impairment: Definitions, causal mechanisms, and neurobiological factors": Erratum. *Journal of Medical Speech-Language Pathology, 9*, 211.

Ahnert, L., Gunnar, M. R., Lamb, M. E., & Barthel, M. (2004). Transition to child care: Associations with infant-mother attachment, infant negative emotion, and cortisol elevations. *Child Development, 75*, 639–650.

Ainsworth, M. D. S., Blehar, M. C., Waters, E., & Wahl, S. (1978). *Patterns of attachment: A psychological study of the Strange Situation.* Hillsdale, NJ: Erlbaum.

Ajzen, I. (2002). Perceived behavioral control, self-efficacy, locus of control, and the theory of planned behavior. *Journal of Applied Social Psychology, 32*, 665–683.

Akhtar, N., & Tomasello, M. (1996). Two-year-olds learn words for absent objects and actions. *British Journal of Developmental Psychology, 14*, 79–93.

Akiskal, H. S. (1996). The prevalent clinical spectrum of bipolar disorders: Beyond DSM–IV. *Journal of Clinical Psychopharmacology, 16*(Suppl. 1), 4S–14S.

Alberini, C. (2004) Mechanisms of memory destabilization: Are consolidation and reconsolidation similar or distinct processes? *Trends in Neuroscience, 28*, 51–56.

Albert, M., & Ayres, J. J. B. (1997). One-trial simultaneous and backward excitatory fear conditioning in rats: Lick suppression, freezing, and rearing to CS compounds and their elements. *Animal Learning & Behavior, 25*, 210–220.

Albert, M. S., Duffy, F. H., & McAnulty, G. B. (1990). Electrophysiologic comparisons between two groups of patients with Alzheimer's disease. *Archives of Neurology, 47*, 857–863.

Albert, M. S., & Moss, M. B. (1996). Neuropsychology of aging: Findings in humans and monkeys. In E. L. Schneider, J. W. Rowe, T. E. Johnson, N. J. Holbrook, & J. H. Morrison (Eds.), *Handbook of the biology of aging* (4th ed.). San Diego, CA: Academic Press.

Alcock, J. E. (1987). Parapsychology: Science of the anomalous of search for the soul? *Behavioral and Brain Sciences, 10*, 553–565.

Aldag, R. J., & Fuller, S. R. (1993). Beyond fiasco: A reappraisal of the groupthink phenomenon and a new model of group decision processes. *Psychological Bulletin, 113*, 533–552.

Aldous, J., & Ganey, R. F. (1999). Family life and the pursuit of happiness: The influence of gender and race. *Journal of Family Issues, 20*, 155–180.

Alexander, C. N., Robinson, P., Orme-Johnson, D. W., Schneider, R. H., & Walton, K. G. (1994a). The effects of transcendental meditation compared to other methods of relaxation and meditation in reducing risk factors, morbidity, and mortality. *Homeostasis, 35*, 243–264.

Alexander, C. N., Robinson, P., & Rainforth, M. (1994b). Treating and preventing alcohol, nicotine, and drug abuse through transcendental meditation: A review and statistical meta-analysis of 19 studies. *Alcoholism Treatment Quarterly, Vol. II*, 13–87.

Alexander, D. (1991). Keynote address. In *President's Committee on Mental Retardation, Summit on the National Effort to Prevent Mental Retardation and Related Disabilities.*

Alexander, F., & French, T. (1946). *Psychoanalytic theory.* New York: Ronald.

Alibali, M. W., Bassok, M., Solomon, K. O., Syc, S. E., & Goldin-Meadow, S. (1999). Illuminating mental representations through speech and gesture. *Psychological Science, 10*, 327–333.

Alkire, M. T., Haier, R. J., & James, H. F. (1998). Toward the neurobiology of consciousness: Using brain imaging and anesthesia to investigate the anatomy of consciousness. In S. Hameroff, A. Kaszniak, & A. Scott (Eds.), *Toward a science of consciousness II.* Cambridge, MA: MIT Press.

Allen, J. J. B., & Iacono, W. G. (1997). A comparison of methods for the analysis of event-related potentials in deception detection. *Psychophysiology, 34*, 234–240.

Allen, L. S., & Gorski, R. A. (1992). Sexual orientation and the size of the anterior commissure in the human brain. *Proceedings of the National Academy of Sciences of the United States of America, 89*, 7199–7202.

Allik, J., & McCrae, R. R. (2004). Toward a geography of personality traits: Patterns of profiles across 36 cultures. *Journal of Cross-Cultural Psychology, 35*, 13–28.

Allison, J. (1970). Respiratory changes during transcendental meditation. *Lancet, 1(7651)*, 833–834.

Allport, G. (1954). *The nature of prejudice.* Oxford, England: Addison-Wesley.

Allport, G. W. (1937). *Personality: A psychological interpretation.* New York: Holt.

Allyn, J., & Festinger, L. (1961). The effectiveness of unanticipated persuasive communications. *Journal of Abnormal and Social Psychology, 62*, 35–40.

Almli, C. R., Ball, R. H., & Wheeler, M. E. (2001). Human fetal and neonatal movement patterns: Gender differences and fetal-to-neonatal continuity. *Developmental Psychobiology, 38*, 252–273.

Alonso, P., Pujol, J., Cardoner, N., Benlloch, L., Deus, J., Menchon, J. M., et al. (2001). Right prefrontal repetitive transcranial magnetic stimulation in obsessive-compulsive disorder: A double-blind, placebo-controlled study. *American Journal of Psychiatry, 158*, 1143–1145.

Alonzo, M., & Aiken, M. (2004). Flaming in electronic communication. *Decision Support Systems, 36*, 205–221.

Altshuler, L. L., Bartzokis, G., Grieder, T., Curran, J., & Mintz, J. (1998). Amygdala enlargement in bipolar disorder and hippocampal reduction in schizophrenia: An MRI study demonstrating neuroanatomic specificity. *Archives of General Psychiatry, 55*, 663–664.

Aluja-Fabregat, A., Colom, R., Abad, F., & Juan-Espinosa, M. (2000). Sex differences in general intelligence defined as g among young adolescents. *Personality & Individual Differences, 28*, 813–820.

Amabile, T. M. (1983). *The social psychology of creativity.* New York: Springer-Verlag.

Amabile, T. M. (1998, September–October). How to kill creativity. *Harvard Business Review*, pp. 76–87.

Amabile, T. M. (2001). Beyond talent: John Irving and the passionate craft of creativity. *American Psychologist, 56*, 333–336.

Amaducci, L., Grassi, E., & Boller, F. (2002). Maurice Ravel and right-hemisphere musical creativity: Influence of disease on his last musical works? *European Journal of Neurology, 9*, 75–82.

Ambady, M., Bernieri, F. J., & Richeson, J. A. (2000). Toward a histology of social behavior: Judgmental accuracy from thin slices of the behavioral stream. In M. P. Zanna (Ed.), *Advances in experimental social psychology* (Vol. 32, pp. 201–271). New York: Academic Press.

Ambady, N., Conroy, M., Tobia, A., & Mullins, J. (2001). Friends, lovers, and strangers: Judging dyadic relationships from thin slices. Manuscript submitted for publication.

Ambady, N., Laplante, D., Nguyen, T., Rosenthal, R., Chaumeton, N., & Levinson, W. (2002). Surgeons' tone of voice: A clue to malpractice history. *Surgery. 132*, 5–9.

Ambady, N., & Rosenthal, R. (1992). Thin slices of expressive behavior as predictors of interpersonal consequences: A meta analysis. *Psychological Bulletin, 111*, 256–274.

Ambady, N., & Rosenthal, R. (1993). Half a minute: Predicting teacher evaluations from thin slices of behavior and physical attractiveness. *Journal of Personality and Social Psychology, 64*, 431–441.

Ambrose, N. G., Yairi, E., & Cox, N. (1993). Genetic aspects of early childhood stuttering. *Journal of Speech & Hearing Research, 36*, 521–528.

American Association for Mental Retardation (1992). *Mental retardation: Definition, classification, and systems of supports* (9th ed.). Washington, DC: Author.

American Psychiatric Association. (1994). *Diagnostic and statistical manual of mental disorders* (4th ed.). Washington, DC: Author.

American Psychiatric Association. (2000a). *Diagnostic and statistical manual of mental disorders* (5th ed.). Washington, DC: Author.

American Psychiatric Association. (2000b). Practice guideline for the treatment of patients with major depressive disorder (revision). *American Journal of Psychiatry, 157*(Suppl.), 1–45.

Amir, N., Foa, E. B., & Coles, M. E. (1998). Automatic activation and strategic avoidance of threat-relevant information in social phobia. *Journal of Abnormal Psychology, 107*, 285–290.

Amsterdam, B. (1972). Mirror self-image reactions before age two. *Developmental Psychology, 5*, 297–305.

Anand, B. K., & Brobeck, J. R. (1952). Food intake and spontaneous activity of rats with lesions in the amygdaloid nuclei. *Journal of Neurophysiology, 15*, 421–430.

Anastasi, A. (1988). *Psychological testing* (6th ed.). New York: Macmillan.

Anch, A. M., Bowman, C. P., Mitler, M. M., & Walsh, J. K. (1988). *Sleep: A scientific perspective.* Englewood Cliffs, NJ: Prentice-Hall.

Andersen, A. E., & DiDomenico, L. (1992). Diet vs. shape content of popular male and female magazines: A dose response relationship to the incidence of eating disorders? *International Journal of Eating Disorders, 11*, 283–287.

Andersen, B. (1997, July). Psychological interventions for individuals with cancer. *Clinician's Research Digest, 16*(Suppl.), 1–2.

Andersen, B. L., Kiecolt-Glaser, K. K., & Glaser, R. (1994). A biobehavioral model of cancer stress and disease course. *American Psychologist, 49*, 389–404.

Anderson, A. K., & Phelps, E. A. (2002). Is the human amygdala critical for the subjective experience of emotion? Evidence of intact dispositional affect in patients with amygdala lesions. *Journal of Cognitive Neuroscience, 14*, 709–720.

Anderson, C. A. (1983). Abstract and concrete data in the perseverance of social theories: When weak data lead to unshakable beliefs. *Journal of Experimental Social Psychology, 19*, 930–1108.

Anderson, C. A., Berkowitz, L., Donnerstein, E., Huesmann, L. R., Johnson, J. D., Linz, D., Malamuth, N. M., & Martella, E. (2003). The influence of media violence on youth. *Psychological Science in the Public Interest, 4*, 81–110.

Anderson, C. A., & Bushman, B. J. (1997). External validity of "trivial" experiments: The case of laboratory aggression. *Review of General Psychology, 1*, 19–41.

Anderson, C. A., Lepper, M. R., & Ross, L. (1980). Perseverance of social theories: This role of explanation in the persistence of discredited information. *Journal of Personality and Social Psychology, 39*, 1037–1049.

Anderson, I. M. (2000). Selective serotonin reuptake inhibitors versus tricyclic antidepressants: A meta-analysis of efficacy and tolerability. *Journal of Affective Disorders, 58*, 19–36.

Anderson, J. R. (2000). *Cognitive psychology and its implications* (5th ed.). New York: Worth.

Anderson, J. R., & Betz, J. (2001). A hybrid model of categorization. *Psychonomic Bulletin & Review, 8*, 629–647.

Anderson, M. (1992). *Intelligence and development: A cognitive theory.* Oxford, England: Blackwell.

Anderson, M. C., Ochsner, K. N., Kuhl, B., Cooper, J., Robertson, E., Gabrieli, S. W., Glover, G. H., and Gabrieli, J. D. E. (2004). Neural systems underlying the suppression of unwanted memories. *Science, 303*, 232–235.

Anderson, N. B. (1998). Levels of analysis in health science: A framework for integrating sociobehavioral and biomedical research. In S. M. McCann, J. M. Lipton, et al. (Eds.), *Annals of the New York Academy of Sciences: Vol. 840, Neuroimmunomodulation: Molecular aspects, integrative systems, and clinical advances* (pp. 563–576). New York: New York Academy of Sciences.

Anderson, N. B., & Nickerson, K. J. (2005). Genes, race, and psychology in the genome era. *American Psychologist, 60*, 5–8.

Anderson, N. H., & Barrios, A. A. (1961). Primacy effects in personality impression formation. *Journal of Abnormal and Social Psychology, 63*, 346–350.

Anderson, V. L., Levinson, E. M., Barker, W., & Kiewra, K. R. (1999). The effects of meditation on teacher perceived occupational stress, state and trait anxiety, and burnout. *School Psychology Quarterly, 14*, 3–25.

Ando, J., Ono, Y., & Wright, M. J. (2001). Genetic structure of spatial and verbal working memory. *Behavior Genetics, 31*, 615–624.

Andreasen, N. C. (1987). Creativity and mental illness: Prevalence rates in writers and their first-degree relatives. *American Journal of Psychiatry, 144*, 1288–1292.

Andreasen, N. C., Nasrullah, H., Dunn, V., Olson, S., Grove, W., Erhardt, J., et al. (1986). Structural abnormalities in the fronal system in schizophrenia. *Archives of General Psychiatry, 43,* 136–144.

Andreasen, N. C., Nopoulos, P., O'Leary, D. S., Miller, D. D., Wassink, T., & Flaum, M. (1999). Defining the phenotype of schizophrenia: Cognitive dysmetria and its neural mechanisms. *Biological Psychiatry, 46,* 908–920.

Andreasen, N. C., Rezai, K., Alliger, R., Swayze, V., Flaum, M., Kirchner, P., et al. (1992). Hypofrontality in neuroleptic-naïve patients and in patients with chronic schizophrenia: Assessment with xenon-133 single proton emission computed tomography and the Tower of London. *Archives of General Psychiatry, 49,* 943–958.

Andrews, H. B., & Jones, S. (1990). Eating behaviour in obese women: A test of two hypotheses. *Australian Psychologist, 25,* 351–357.

Angier, N. (1999, September 7). Route to creativity: Following bliss or dots? *New York Times,* F3 (col. 1).

Angleitner, A., Riemann, R., & Strelau, J. (1995). A study of twins using the self-report and peer-report NEO-FFI sclaes. Paper presented at the seventh meeting of the International Society for the Study of Individual Differences, July 15–19, Warsaw, Poland.

Anglin, J. M. (1993). Vocabulary development: A morphological analysis. *Monographs of the Society for Research in Child Development, 58*(10, Serial No. 238).

Angst, J. (1998). The emerging epidemiology of hypomania and bipolar II disorder. *Journal of Affective Disorders, 50,* 143–151.

Anisman, H., Zaharia, M. D., Meaney, M. J., & Merali, Z. (1998). Do early-life events permanently alter behavioral and hormonal responses to stressors? *International Journal of Developmental Neuroscience, 16,* 149–164.

Ankney, C. D. (1992). Sex differences in relative brain size: The mismeasure of women, too? *Intelligence, 16,* 329–336.

Anonymous. (1970). Effects of sexual activity on beard growth in man. *Nature, 226,* 867–870.

Antoch, M. P., Song, E. J., Chang, A. M., Vitaterna, M. H., Zhao, Y., Wilsbacher, L. D., et al. (1997, May 16). Functional identification of the mouse circadian Clock gene by transgenic BAC rescue. *Cell, 89*(4), 655–667.

Antonijevic, I. A., Murck, H., Bohlhalter, S., Frieboes, R., Holsboer, F., & Steiger, A. (2000). Neuropeptide Y promotes sleep and inhibits ACTH and cortisol release in young men. *Neuropharmacology, 39,* 1474–1481.

Antonuccio, D. O., Danton, W. G., & DeNelsky, G. Y. (1995). Psychotherapy versus medication for depression: Challenging the conventional wisdom with data. *Professional Psychology: Research & Practice, 26,* 574–585.

Antony, M. M., & Barlow, D. H. (2002). Specific phobias. In D. H. Barlow (Ed.), *Anxiety and its disorders* (2nd ed., pp. 380–417). New York: Guilford Press.

Aram, D. M., Morris, R., & Hall, N. E. (1992). The validity of discrepancy criteria for identifying children with developmental language disorders. *Journal of Learning Disabilities, 25,* 549–554.

Arana, G. W., & Rosenbaum, J. F. (2000). *Handbook of Psychiataric Drug Therapy.* Philadelphia: Lippincott Williams & Wilkins.

Aranda, M. P., & Knight, B. G. (1997). The influence of ethnicity and culture on the caregiver stress and coping process: A socio-cultural review and analysis. *Gerontologist, 37,* 342–354.

Archer, J. (2004). Sex differences in aggression in real-world settings: A meta-analytic review. *Review of General Psychology, 8,* 291–232.

Archer, S. L., & Waterman, A. S. (1988). Psychological individualism: Gender differences or gender neutrality? *Human Development, 31,* 65–81.

Arguin, M., Cavanagh, P., & Joanette, Y. (1994). Visual feature integration with an attention deficit. *Brain and Cognition, 24,* 44–56.

Argyle, M. L., & Lu, L. (1990). Happiness and social skills. *Personality & Individual Differences, 11,* 1255–1261.

Arkes, H. R., & Tetlock, P. E. (2004). Attributions of implicit prejudice, or "Would Jesse Jackson 'fail' the Implicit Association Test?" *Psychological Inquiry, 15,* 257–278.

Arking, R. (1991). *Biology of aging: Observations and principles.* Englewood Cliffs, NJ: Prentice Hall.

Arlas, E., Anderson, R. S., Kung, H.-C., Murphy, S. L., & Kochanek, K. D. (2003). Deaths: Final data for 2001. National Vital Statistics Reports. National Center for Health Statistics, Centers for Disease Control and Prevention, U.S. Dept. of Health and Human Services. DHHS Publication Number (PHS) 2001-1120 PRS 03-0436. Retrieved from: http://www.cdc.gov/nchs/about/major/dvs/mortdata.htm; pdf file nvsr52_09p9.pdf

Armstrong, S. L., Gleitman, L. R., & Gleitman, H. (1983). What some concepts might not be. *Cognition, 13,* 263–308.

Arnell, K. M., & Jolicoeur, P. (1999). The attentional blink across stimulus modalities: Evidence for central processing limitations. *Journal of Experimental Psychology: Human Perception and Performance, 25,* 630–648.

Arnett, J. (1992). Reckless behavior in adolescence: A developmental perspective. *Developmental Review, 12,* 339–373.

Arnett, J. J. (1999). Adolescent storm and stress, reconsidered. *American Psychologist, 54,* 317–326.

Arnett, J. J. (2000). Emerging adulthood: A theory of development from the late teens through the twenties. *American Psychologist, 55,* 469–480.

Arnsten, A. F. T. (1998) The biology of being frazzled. *Science, 280,* 1711–1712.

Aronson, E., & Osherow, N. (1980). Cooperation, prosocial behavior, and academic performance: Experiments in the desegregated classroom. *Applied Social Psychology Annual, 1,* 163–196.

Aronson, E., & Patnoe, S. (1997). *The jigsaw classroom: Building cooperation in the classroom* (2nd ed.). New York: Addison Wesley Longman.

Aronson, J., Fried, C. B., & Good, C. (2002). Reducing the effects of stereotype threat on African American college students by shaping theories of intelligence. *Journal of Experimental Social Psychology, 38,* 113–125.

Arterberry, M. E., & Yonas, A. (2000). Perception of three-dimensional shape specified by optic flow by 8-week-old infants. *Perception & Psychophysics, 62,* 550–556.

Asch, S. E. (1951). Effects of group pressure upon the modification and distortion of judgment. In H. Guetzkow (Ed.), *Groups, leadership, and men* (pp. 177–190). Pittsburgh: Carnegie.

Asch, S. E. (1955). Opinions and social pressure. *Scientific American, 193,* 31–35.

Asendorpf, J. B., Warkentin, V., & Baudonniere, P.-M. (1996). Self-awareness and other-awareness: II. Mirror self-recognition, social contingency awareness, and synchronic imitation. *Developmental Psychology, 32,* 313–321.

Ashbridge, E., Walsh, V., & Cowley, A. (1997). Temporal aspects of visual search studied by transcranial magnetic stimulation. *Neuropsychologia, 35,* 1121–1131.

Ashton, C. H. (2001). Pharmacology and effects of cannabis: A brief review. *British Journal of Psychiatry, 178,* 101–106.

Aslin, R. N., Saffran, J. R., & Newport, E. L. (1999). Statistical learning in linguistic and nonlinguistic domains. In B. MacWhinney (Ed.), *The emergence of language* (pp. 359–380). Mahwah, NJ: Erlbaum.

Aspinwall, L. G., & Taylor, S. E. (1997). A stitch in time: Self-regulation and proactive coping. *Psychological Bulletin, 121,* 417–436.

Associated Press. (2001, August 9). Man's best friend finally understood: A bark deciphered. *Wall Street Journal Europe,* p. 18.

Association of SIDS and Infant Mortality Programs (2002). Infant sleep positioning and SIDS. Retrieved from http://www.asip1.org/isp.html

Athanasiou, M. S. (2000). Current nonverbal assessment instruments: A comparison of psychometric integrity and test fairness. *Journal of Psychoeducational Assessment, 18,* 211–229.

Atienza, M., Cantero, J. L., & Stickgold, R. (2004). Posttraining sleep enhances automaticity in perceptual discrimination. *Journal of Cognitive Neuroscience, 16,* 53–64.

Atkinson, R. C., & Shiffrin, R. M. (1968). Human memory: A proposed system and its control processes. In K. W. Spence & J. T. Spence (Eds.), *The psychology of learning and motivation: Advances in research and theory* (Vol. 2, pp. 89–195). New York: Academic Press.

Atkinson, R. C., & Shiffrin, R. M. (1971). The control of short-term memory. *Scientific American, 225,* 82–90.

Atre-Vaidya, N., & Hussain, S. M. (1999). Borderline personality disorder and bipolar mood disorder: Two distinct disorders or a continuum? *Journal of Mental and Nervous Disorders, 187,* 313–315.

Auden, W. H. (1989). *Van Gogh: A self-portrait.* New York: Marlowe.

Avorn, J., & Langer, E. (1982). Induced disability in nursing home patients: A controlled trial. *Journal of the American Geriatrics Society, 30,* 397–400.

Azar, B. (1995). Timidity can develop in the first days of life. *APA Monitor, 26*(11), 23.

Azrin, N. H., Sisson, R. W., Meyers, R., & Godley, M. (1982). Alcoholism treatment by disulfiram and community reinforcement therapy. *Journal of Behavior Therapy and Experimental Psychiatry, 13,* 105–112.

Baare, W. F., van Oel, C. J., Pol, H., Schnack, H. G., Durston, S., Sitskoorn, M. M., & Kahn, R. S. (2001). Volumes of brain structures in twins discordant for schizophrenia. *Archives of General Psychiatry, 58,* 33–40.

Baars, B. J. (2002). The conscious access hypothesis: Origins and recent evidence. *Trends in Cognitive Sciences, 6,* 47–52.

Babad, E. (1993). Pygmalion—25 years after interpersonal expectations in classroom. In P. D. Blanck (Ed.), *Interpersonal expectations: Theory, research, and applications* (pp. 125–153). Cambridge, England: Cambridge University Press.

Babad, E., Bernieri, F., & Rosenthal, R. (1989). Nonverbal communication and leakage in the behavior of biased and unbiased teachers. *Journal of Personality & Social Psychology, 56,* 89–94.

Baccus, J. R., Baldwin, M. W., & Packer, D. J. (2004). Increasing implicit self-esteem through classical conditioning. *Psychological Science, 15*, 498–502.

Bachen, E. A., Manuck, S. B., Cohen, S., Muldoon, M. F., Raible, R., Herbert, T. B., & Rabin, B. S. (1995). Adrenergic blockage ameliorates cellular immune responses to mental stress in humans. *Psychosomatic Medicine, 57*, 366–372.

Baddeley, A. (1986). *Working memory*. Oxford, England: Clarendon Press.

Baddeley, A. (1992). Working memory: The interface between memory and cognition. *Journal of Cognitive Neuroscience, 4*, 281–288.

Baddeley, A. (1994). The magical number seven: Still magic after all these years? *Psychological Review, 101*, 353–356.

Baeck, E. (2002). The neural networks of music. *European Journal of Neurology, 9*, 449–456.

Baenninger, M., & Newcombe, N. (1989). The role of experience in spatial test performance: A meta-analysis. *Sex Roles, 20*, 327–344.

Baer, L., Ackerman, R., Surman, O., Correia, J., Griffith, J., Alpert, N., & Hackett, T. (1990). PET studies during hypnosis and hypnotic suggestion. In P. Berner (Ed.), *Psychiatry: The state of the art, biological psychiatry, higher nervous activity* (pp. 293–298). New York: Plenum Press.

Bahrick, H. P., & Phelps, E. (1987). Retention of Spanish vocabulary over eight years, *Journal of Experimental Psychology: Learning, Memory and Cognition, 13*, 344–349.

Bahrick, L. E., Moss, L., & Fadil, C. (1996). Development of visual self-recognition in infancy. *Ecological Psychology, 8*, 189–208.

Bailey, J. M., & Pillard, R. C. (1991). A genetic study of male sexual orientation. *Archives of General Psychiatry, 48*, 1089–1096.

Bailey, M., Engler, H., Hunzeker, J., & Sheridan, J. F. (2003). The hypothalamic-pituitary-adrenal axis and viral infection. *Viral Immunology, 16*, 141–157.

Baillargeon, R. (1993). The object concept revisited: New directions in the investigation of infants' physical knowledge. In C. E. Granrud (Ed.), *Visual perception and cognition in infancy* (pp. 265–315). Hillsdale, NJ: Erlbaum.

Baillargeon, R. (2004). Infants' physical world. *Current Directions in Psychological Science, 13*, 89–94.

Baily, C. H., & Chen, M. (1989). Time course of structural changes at identified sensory neuron synapses during long-term sensitization in *Aplysia*. *Journal of Neuroscience, 9*, 1774–1781.

Baird, A., Kagan, J., Gaudette, T., Walz, K., Hershlag, N., & Boas, D. (2002). Frontal lobe activation during object permanence: Data from near-infrared spectroscopy. *NeuroImage, 16*, 1120–1126.

Baker, F. (2001). The effects of live, taped, and no music on people experiencing posttraumatic amnesia. *Journal of Music Therapy, 38*, 170–192.

Baker, R. R. (1980). Goal orientation by blindfolded humans after long-distance displacement: Possible involvement of a magnetic sense. *Science, 210*, 555–557.

Baker, S. C., Dolan, R. J., & Frith, C. D. (1996). The functional anatomy of logic: A PET study of inferential reasoning. *NeuroImage, 3*, S218.

Bakermans-Kranenburg, M. J., van IJzendoorn, M. H., & Juffer, F. (2003). Less is more: Meta-analyses of sensitivity and attachment interventions in early childhood. *Psychological Bulletin, 129*, 195–215.

Bakermans-Kranenburg, M. J., van IJzendoorn, M. H., & Kroonenberg, P. M. (2004). Differences in attachment security between African-American and white children: Ethnicity or socio-economic status? *Infant Behavior & Development, 27*, 417–433.

Baldwin, D. A. (2000). Interpersonal understanding fuels knowledge acquisition. *Current Directions in Psychological Science, 9*, 40–45.

Baldwin, D. R., Chambliss, L. N., & Towler, K. (2003). Optimism and stress: An African-American college student perspective. *College Student Journal, 37*, 276–285.

Ball, K., Berch, D. B., Helmers, K. F., Jobe, J. B., Leveck, M. D., Marsiske, M., et al. (2002). Effects of cognitive training interventions with older adults: A randomized controlled trial. JAMA: *Journal of the American Medical Association, 288*, 2271–2281.

Ball, S. A. (2002). Big Five, alternative five, and seven personality dimensions: Validity in substance-dependent patients. In P. T. Costa, Jr., & T. A. Widiger (Eds.), *Personality disorders and the five-factor model of personality* (2nd ed., pp. 177–201). Washington, DC: American Psychological Association.

Ball, T. S. (1971). *Itard, Seguin, and Kephart: Sensory education—A learning interpretation*. Columbus, OH: Merrill.

Ballus, C. (1997). Effects of antipsychotics on the clinical and psychosocial behavior of patients with schizophrenia. *Schizophrenia Research, 28*, 247–255.

Baltes, P. B. (1987). Theoretical propositions of life-span developmental psychology: On the dynamics between growth and decline. *Developmental Psychology, 23*, 611–626.

Baltes, P. B., Dittmann-Kohli, F., & Dixon, R. A. (1984). New perspectives on the development of intelligence in adulthood: Toward a dual-process conception and a model of selective optimization with compensation. In P. B. Baltes & O. G. Brim, Jr. (Eds.), *Life-span development and behavior* (Vol. 6, pp. 33–76). San Diego, CA: Academic Press.

Banaji, M. R., Nosek, B. A., & Greenwald, A. G. (2004). No place for nostalgia in science: A response to Arkes and Tetlock. *Psychological Inquiry, 15*, 279–310.

Bandura, A. (1976). Self-reinforcement: Theoretical and methodological considerations. *Behaviorism, 4*, 135–155.

Bandura, A. (1977a). *Social learning theory*. Englewood Cliffs, NJ: Prentice-Hall.

Bandura, A. (1977b). Self-efficacy: Toward a unifying theory of behavior change. *Psychological Review, 84*, 191–215.

Bandura, A. (1978). The self-system in reciprocal determinism. *American Psychologist, 33*, 344–358.

Bandura, A. (1986). *Social foundations of thought and action: A social-cognitive theory*. Englewood Cliffs, NJ: Prentice-Hall.

Bandura, A. (1999). Moral disengagement in the perpetration of inhumanities. *Personality & Social Psychology Review, 3*, 193–209.

Bandura, A. (2001). Social cognitive theory: An agentic perspective. *Annual Review of Psychology, 52*, 1–26.

Bandura, A. (2004). Health promotion by social cognitive means. *Health Education & Behavior, 31*, 143–164.

Bandura, A., Grusec, J. E., & Menlove, F. L. (1967). Vicarious extinction of avoidance behavior. *Journal of Personality & Social Psychology, 5*, 16–23.

Bandura, A., Ross, D., & Ross, S. A. (1961). Transmission of aggression through imitation of aggressive models. *Journal of Abnormal and Social Psychology, 63*, 575–582.

Bandura, A., Ross, D., & Ross, S. A. (1963). Imitation of film-mediated aggressive models. *Journal of Abnormal & Social Psychology, 66*, 3–11.

Banich, M. T., & Federmeier, K. D. (1999). Categorical and metric spatial processing distinguished by task demands and practice. *Journal of Cognitive Neuroscience, 11*, 153–166.

Banks, M. S., & Bennett, P. J. (1988). Optical and photoreceptor immaturities limit the spatial and chromatic vision of human neonates. *Journal of the Optical Society of America, 5*, 2059–2079.

Bao, S., Chen, L., & Thompson, R. F. (2000). Learning- and cerebellum-dependent neuronal activity in the lateral pontine nucleus. *Behavioral Neuroscience, 114*, 254–261.

Bar, M., & Biederman, I. (1998). Subliminal visual priming. *Psychological Science, 9*, 464–469.

Bar, M., Tootell, R. B., Schacter, D. L., Greve, D. N., Fischl, B., Mendola, J. D., et al. (2001). Cortical mechanisms specific to explicit visual object recognition. *Neuron, 29*, 529–535.

Barabasz, A. F., & Lonsdale, C. (1983). Effects of hypnosis on P300 olfactory-evoked potential amplitudes. *Journal of Abnormal Psychology, 92*, 520–523.

Barañano, D. E., Ferris, C. D., & Snyder, S. H. (2001). Atypical neural messengers. *Trends in Neurosciences, 24*, 99–106.

Barbarich, N. (2002). Is there a common mechanism of serotonin dysregulation in anorexia nervosa and obsessive compulsive disorder? *Eating & Weight Disorders, 7*, 221–231.

Barber, J. (1997). Hypnosis and memory: A cautionary chapter. In G. A. Fraser (Ed.), *The dilemma of ritual abuse: Cautions and guides for therapists* (pp. 17–29). Washington, DC: American Psychiatric Press.

Barber, J., & Adrian, C. (1982). *Psychological approaches to the management of pain*. New York: Brunner/Mazel.

Barber, T. X. (1969). An empirically based formulation of hypnotism. *American Journal of Clinical Hypnosis, 12*, 100–130.

Barber, T. X., Spanos, N. P., & Chaves, J. F. (1974) *Hypnosis, imagination, and human potentialities*. New York: Pergamon.

Barbur, J. L., Watson, J. D. G., Frackowiak, R. D. G., & Zeki, S. (1993). Conscious visual perception without V1. *Brain, 116*, 1293–1302.

Barclay, J. R., Bransford, J. D., Franks, J. J., McCarrell, N. S., & Nitsch, K. (1974). Comprehension and semantic flexibility. *Journal of Verbal Learning and Verbal Behavior, 13*, 471–481.

Barefoot, J. C., Dahlstrom, W. G., & Williams, R. B. (1983). Hostility, CHD incidence, and total mortality: A 25-year follow-up study of 255 physicians. *Psychosomatic Medicine, 45*, 59–63.

Barefoot, J., Dodge, K., Peterson, B., Dahlstrom, W., & Williams, R. (1989). The Cook-Medley Hostility Scale: Item content and ability to predict survival. *Psychosomatic Medicine, 51*, 46–57.

Barger, L. K., Cade, B. E., Ayas, N. T., Cronin, J. W., Rosner, B., Speizer, F. E., & Czeisler, C. A. (Harvard Work Hours, Health, and Safety Group). (2005). Extended work shifts and the risk of motor vehicle crashes among interns. *New England Journal of Medicine, 352*, 125–134.

Bargh, J. A., Chen, M., & Burrows, L. (1996). Automaticity of social behavior: Direct effects of trait construct and stereotype activation on action. *Journal of Personality and Social Psychology, 71*, 230–244.

Bargh, J. A., & McKenna, K. Y. A. (2004). The Internet and social life. *Annual Review of Psychology, 55*, 573–590.

Bargh, J. A., McKenna, K. Y. A., & Fitzsimons, G. M. (2002). Can you see the real me? Activation and expression of the "true self" on the Internet. *Journal of Social Issues, 58*, 33–48.

Barinaga, M. (2001). How cannabinoids work in the brain. *Science, 291*, 2530–2531.

Barkham, M., & Shapiro, D. A. (1990). Brief psychotherapeutic interventions for job-related distress: A pilot study of prescriptive and exploratory therapy. *Counseling Psychology Quarterly, 3*, 133–147.

Barkham, M., Shapiro, D. A., Hardy, G. E., & Rees, A. (1999). Psychotherapy in two-plus-one sessions: Outcomes of a randomized controlled trial of cognitive-behavioral and psychodynamic-interpersonal therapy for subsyndromal depression. *Journal of Consulting and Clinical Psychology, 67*, 201–211.

Barkow, J. H., Cosmides, L., & Tooby, J. (Eds.). (1992). *The adapted mind: Evolutionary psychology and the generation of culture.* New York: Oxford University Press.

Barlow, D. H. (1986). Causes of sexual dysfunction: The role of anxiety and cognitive interference. *Journal of Consulting and Clinical Psychology, 54*, 140–148.

Barlow, D. H. (1988). *Anxiety and its disorders.* New York: Guilford Press.

Barlow, D. H., & Craske, M. G. (2000). *Mastery of your anxiety and panic,* 3rd ed. (MAP 3) (client workbook and client workbook for agoraphobia). Boulder, CO: Graywind Publications.

Barnes, V. A., Davis, H. C., Murzynowski, J. B., & Treiber, F. A. (2004). Impact of meditation on resting and ambulatory blood pressure and heart rate in youth. *Psychosomatic Medicine, 66*, 909–914.

Barnes, V. A., Treiber, F., & Davis, H. (2001). Impact of transcendental meditation on cardiovascular function at rest and during acute stress in adolescents with high normal blood pressure. *Journal of Psychosomatic Research, 51*, 597–605.

Barnet, R. C., Arnold, H. M., & Miller, R. R. (1991). Simultaneous conditioning demonstrated in second-order conditioning: Evidence for similar associative structure in forward and simultaneous conditioning. *Learning & Motivation, 22*, 253–268.

Barnett, L. A., Far, J. M., Mauss, A. L., & Miller, J. A. (1996). Changing perceptions of peer norms as a drinking reduction program for college students. *Journal of Alcohol & Drug Education, 41*, 39–62.

Barnier, A. J., Levin, K., & Maher, A. (2004). Suppressing thoughts of past events: Are repressive copers good suppressors? *Cognition & Emotion, 18*, 513–531.

Bar-On, R., Brown, J. M., Kirkcaldy, B. D., & Thome, E. P. (2000). Emotional expression and implications for occupational stress: An application of the emotional quotient inventory (EQ-i). *Personality and Individual Differences, 28*, 1107–1118.

Baron, R., & Byrne, D. (1997). *Social psychology* (8th ed.). Needham Heights, MA: Allyn & Bacon.

Baron, R. A. (1977). *Human aggression.* New York: Plenum.

Baron, R. A., & Richardson, D. (1994). *Human aggression* (2nd ed.). New York: Plenum.

Barone, P. (2003). Clinical strategies to prevent and delay motor complications. *Neurology, 61*, S12–S16.

Barr, R., Vieira, A., & Rovee-Collier, C. (2001). Mediated imitation in 6-month-olds: Remembering by association. *Journal of Experimental Child Psychology, 79*, 229–252.

Barr, R., Vieira, A., & Rovee-Collier, C. (2002). Bidirectional priming in infants. *Memory & Cognition, 30*, 246–255.

Barrantes-Vidal, N. (2004). Creativity & madness revisited from current psychological perspectives. *Journal of Consciousness Studies, 11*, 58–78.

Barrett, L. F. (in press). Solving the emotion paradox: Categorization and the experience of emotion. *Personality and Social Psychology Review.*

Barrett, L. F., & Niedenthal, P. M. (2004). Valence focus and the perception of facial affect. *Emotion, 4*, 266–274.

Barrett, L. F., Ochsner, K. N., & Gross, J. J. (in press). Automaticity and emotion. In J. Bargh (Ed.), *Automatic processes in social thinking and behavior.* New York: Psychology Press.

Barrick, M. R., Stewart, G. L., Neubert, M. J., & Mount, M. K. (1998). Relating member ability and personality to work-team process and team effectiveness. *Journal of Applied Psychology, 83*, 377–391.

Barriga, A. Q., Landau, J. R., Stinson, B. L., Liau, A. K., & Gibbs, J. C. (2000). Cognitive distortion and problem behaviors in adolescents. *Criminal Justice & Behavior, 27*, 36–56.

Barry, E. (2002, September 3). After day care controversy, psychologists play nice. *Boston Globe,* E1–E3.

Barsky, A. J., Saintfort, R., Rogers, M. P., & Borus, J. F. (2002). Nonspecific medication side effects and the nocebo phenomenon. *JAMA: Journal of the American Medical Association, 287*, 622–627.

Barth, J., Schumacher, M., & Herrmann-Lingen, C. (2004). Depression as a risk factor for mortality in patients with coronary heart disease: A meta-analysis. *Psychosomatic Medicine, 66*, 802–813.

Bartholomew, K. (1990). Avoidance of intimacy: An attachment perspective. *Journal of Social & Personal Relationships, 7*, 147–178.

Bartholomew, K., & Horowitz, L. M. (1991). Attachment styles among young adults: A test of a four-category model. *Journal of Personality & Social Psychology, 61*, 226–244.

Barton, J. J. S., Cherkasova, M. V., Press, D. Z., Intriligator, J. M., & O'Connor, M. (2004). Perceptual functions in prosopagnosia. *Perception, 33*, 939–356.

Bartoshuk, L. M., & Beauchamp, G. K. (1994). Chemical senses. *Annual Review of Psychology, 45*, 419–449.

Bartoshuk, L. M., Duffy, V. B., Lucchina, L. A., Prutkin, J., & Fast, K. (1998). PROP (6-n-propylthiouracil) supertasters and the saltiness of NaCl. *Annals of the New York Academy of Science, 855*, 793–796.

Bartoshuk, L. M., Rifkin, B., Marks, L. E., & Bars, P. (1986). Taste and aging. *Journal of Gerontology, 41*, 51–57.

Bartussek, D., Diedrich, O., Naumann, E., & Collet, W. (1993). Introversion-extraversion and event-related potential (ERP): A test of J. A. Gray's theory. *Personality and Individual Differences, 14*, 565–574.

Baruch, D. E., Swain, R. A., & Helmstetter, F. J. (2004). Effects of exercise on Pavlovian fear conditioning. *Behavioral Neuroscience, 118*, 1123–1127.

Basic Behavioral Science Task Force of the National Advisory Mental Health Council (1996). Basic behavioral science research for mental health. *American Psychologist, 51*, 722–731.

Bassili, J. N. (1978). Facial motion in the perception of faces and of emotional expression. *Journal of Experimental Psychology: Human Perception & Performance, 4*, 373–379.

Bast, T., Zhang, W., & Feldon, J. (2003). Dorsal hippocampus and classical fear conditioning to tone and context in rats: Effects of local NMDA-receptor blockade and stimulation. *Hippocampus, 13*, 657–675.

Bastien, C. H., Morin, C. M., Ouellet, M., Blais, F. C., & Bouchard, S. (2004). Cognitive-behavioral therapy for insomnia: Comparison of individual therapy, group therapy, and telephone consultations. *Journal of Consulting & Clinical Psychology, 72*, 653–659.

Bastien, C. H., Vallières, A., & Morin, C. M. (2004). Precipitating factors of insomnia. *Behavioral Sleep Medicine, 2*, 50–62.

Bates, E., Thal, D., Trauner, D., Fenson, J., Aram, D., Eisele, J., & Nass, R. (1997). From first words to grammar in children with focal brain injury. *Developmental Neuropsychology, 13*, 275–343.

Bates, T. C., & Eysenck, H. J. (1993). Intelligence, inspection time, and decision time. *Intelligence, 17*, 523–531.

Batsell, W. R., Jr., & Brown, A. S. (1998). Human flavor-aversion learning: A comparison of traditional aversions and cognitive aversions. *Learning & Motivation, 29*, 383–396.

Batshaw, M., & Perret, Y. (1992). *Children with disabilities: A medical primer.* Baltimore: Brookes.

Batson, C. D. (1998). Altruism and prosocial behavior. In D. T. Gilbert, S. T. Fiske, & G. Lindzey (Eds.), *The handbook of social psychology* (4th ed., pp. 282–316). New York: McGraw-Hill.

Batson, C. D., Bolen, M. H., Cross, J. A., & Neuringer-Benefiel, H. E. (1986). Where is the altruism in the altruistic personality? *Journal of Personality & Social Psychology, 50*, 212–220.

Baudry, M., & Lynch, G. (2001). Remembrance of arguments past: How well is the glutamate receptor hypothesis of LTP holding up after 20 years? *Neurobiology of Learning & Memory, 76*, 284–297.

Baumeister, A. A., & Bacharach, V. R. (2000). Early generic educational intervention has no enduring effect on intelligence and does not prevent mental retardation: The Infant Health and Development Program. *Intelligence, 28*, 161–192.

Baumeister, R. F., & Boden, J. M. (1998). Aggression and the self: High self-esteem, low self-control, and ego threat. In R. G. Geen & E. Donnerstein (Eds.), *Human aggression: Theories, research, and implications for social policy* (pp. 111–137). San Diego, CA: Academic Press.

Baumeister, R. F., Smart, L., & Boden, J. M. (1996). Relation of threatened egotism to violence and aggression: The dark side of high self-esteem. *Psychological Review, 103*, 5–33.

Baumeister, R. F., Stillwell, A., & Wotman, S. R. (1990). Victim and perpetrator accounts of interpersonal conflict: Autobiographical narratives about anger. *Journal of Personality and Social Psychology, 59,* 994–1003.

Baumeister, R. F., Zhang, L., & Vohs, K. D. (2004). Gossip as cultural learning. *Review of General Psychology, 8,* 111–121.

Bavelier, D., & Neville, H. J. (2002). Cross-modal plasticity: Where and how? *Nature Reviews Neuroscience, 3,* 443–452.

Baxendale, S. (2004). Memories aren't made of this: Amnesia at the movies. *British Medical Journal, 329,* 1480–1483.

Baxter, J. S., Macrae, C. N., Manstead, A. S. R., Stradling, S. G., & Parker, D. (1990). Attributional biases and driver behavior. *Social Behaviour, 5,* 185–192.

Baxter, L. R., Schwartz, J. M., Bergman, K. S., Szuba, M. P., Guze, B. H., Mazziota, J. C., et al. (1992). Caudate glucose metabolic rate changes with both drug and behavior therapy for obsessive-compulsive disorder. *Archives of General Psychiatry, 49,* 681–689.

Baxter, M. G., Parker, A., Lindner, C. C. C., Izquierdo, A. D., & Murray, E. A. (2000). Control of response selection by reinforcer value requires interaction of amygdala and orbital prefrontal cortex. *Journal of Neuroscience, 20,* 4311–4319.

Bayley, P. J., Hopkins, R. O., & Squire, L. R. (2003). Successful recollection of remote autobiographical memories by amnesic patients with medial temporal lobe lesions. *Neuron, 38,* 135–144.

Bazerman, M. (1997). *Judgment in managerial decision making* (4th ed.). New York: Wiley.

Beach, F. A. (1956). Characteristics of masculine "sex drive." In M. Jones (Ed.), *Nebraska Symposium on Motivation* (pp. 1–32). Lincoln: University of Nebraska Press.

Beals, J., Novins, D. K., Spicer, P., Orton, H. D., Mitchell, C. M., Barón, A. E., et al. (2004). Challenges in operationalizing the DSM-IV clinical significance criterion. *Archives of General Psychiatry, 61,* 1197–1207.

Beaman, A., Barnes, P., Kletz, B., & McQuirk, B. (1978). Increasing helping rates through information dissemination: Teaching pays. *Personality and Social Psychology Bulletin, 4,* 406–411.

Bearak, B. (1997, March 29). Time of puzzles heartbreak binds relatives left behind. *New York Times,* 1.

Beatty, J. (1995). *Principles of behavioral neuroscience.* Dubuque, IA: Brown & Benchmark.

Beaumont, M., Batejat, D., Pierard, C., Van Beers, P., Denis, J. B., Coste, O., Doireau, P., Chauffard, F., French, J., & Lagarde D. (2004). Caffeine or melatonin effects on sleep and sleepiness after rapid eastward transmeridian travel. *Journal of Applied Physiology, 96,* 50–58.

Beauregard, M., Levesque, J., & Bourgouin, P. (2001). Neural correlates of conscious self-regulation of emotion. *Journal of Neuroscience, 21,* 6993–7000.

Bechara, A., Damasio, H., Tranel, D., & Damasio, A. R. (1997). Deciding advantageously before knowing the advantageous strategy. *Science, 275,* 1293–1294.

Bechara, A., Tranel, D., & Damasio, H. (2000). Characterization of the decision-making deficit of patients with ventromedial prefrontal cortex lesions. *Brain, 123,* 2189–2202.

Bechara, A. & Van der Kooy, D. (1992). A single brain stem substrate mediates the motivational effects of both opiates and food in nondeprived rats but not in deprived rats. *Behavioral Neuroscience, 106,* 351–363.

Beck, A. T. (1967). *Depression: Causes and treatment.* Philadelphia: University of Pennsylvania Press.

Beck, A. T., Emery, G., & Greenberg, R. L. (1985). *Anxiety disorders and phobias: A cognitive perspective.* New York: Basic Books.

Beck, A. T., Rush, A. J., Shaw, B. F., & Emery, G. (1979). *Cognitive therapy of depression: A treatment manual.* New York: Guilford Press.

Beck, H. (1976). Neuropsychological servosystems, consciousness, and the problem of embodiment. *Behavioral Sciences, 21,* 139–160.

Beck, J. G., Ohtake, P. J., & Shipherd, J. C. (1999). Exaggerated anxiety is not unique to CO2 in panic disorder: A comparison of hypercapnic and hypoxic challenges. *Journal of Abnormal Psychology, 108,* 473–482.

Beck, R., & Fernandez, E. (1998). Cognitive-behavioral therapy in the treatment of anger: A meta-analysis. *Cognitive Therapy & Research, 22,* 63–74.

Becker, A., & Hamburg, P. (1996). Culture, the media, and eating disorders. *Cross-Cultural Psychiatry, 4,* 163–167.

Becker, A. E., Burwell, R. A., Herzog, D. B., Hamburg, P., & Gilman, S. E. (2002). Eating behaviours and attitudes following prolonged exposure to television among ethnic Fijian adolescent girls. *British Journal of Psychiatry, 180,* 509–514.

Beer, J. M., & Horn, J. M. (2000). The influence of rearing order on personality development within two adoption cohorts. *Journal of Personality, 68,* 789–819.

Beer, J. S., Heerey, E. A., Keltner, D., Scabini, D., & Knight, R. T. (2003). The regulatory function of self-conscious emotion: Insights from patients with orbitofrontal damage. *Journal of Personality & Social Psychology, 85,* 594–604.

Beer, M. (1966). *Leadership, employee needs, and motivation* (Monograph No. 129). Columbus: Ohio State University, Bureau of Business Research, College of Commerce.

Beevers, C. G., & Meyer, B. (2004). Thought suppression and depression risk. *Cognition & Emotion, 18,* 859–867.

Behrens, R. R. (2003). Thinking outside of the box: On Karl Duncker, functional fixedness, and the adaptive value of engaging in purposely deviant acts. *Gestalt Theory, 25,* 63–70.

Behrman, R. E. (Ed.). (1996). *The future of children: Financing child care* (Vol. 6, No. 2). Los Altos, CA: Center for the Future of Children, The David and Lucile Packard Foundation.

Behrmann, M. (2000). The mind's eye mapped onto the brain's matter. *Current Directions in Psychological Science, 9,* 50–54.

Beier, M. E., & Ackerman, P. L. (2005). Working memory and intelligence: Different constructs. Reply to Oberauer et al. (2005) & Kane et al. (2005). *Psychological Bulletin, 131,* 72–75.

Beilin, H. (1996). Mind and meaning: Piaget and Vygotsky on causal explanation. *Human Development, 39,* 277–286.

Beilock, S. L., Carr, T. H., MacMahon, C., & Starkes, J. L. (2002). When paying attention becomes counterproductive: Impact of divided versus skill-focused attention on novice and experienced performance of sensorimotor skills. *Journal of Experimental Psychology: Applied, 8,* 6–16.

Belkin, M. & Rosner, M. (1987). Intelligence, education, and myopia in males, *Archives of Opthamology, 105,* 1508–1511.

Bell, A. E. (1977). Heritability in retrospect. *Journal of Heredity, 68,* 297–300.

Bell, J. H., & Bromnick, R. D. (2003). The social reality of the imaginary audience: A ground theory approach. *Adolescence, 38,* 205–219.

Beller, M., & Gafni, N. (1996). The 1991 international assessment of educational progress in mathematics and sciences: The gender differences perspective. *Journal of Educational Psychology, 88,* 365–377.

Bellugi, U., Poizner, H., & Klima, E. S. (1993). Language, modality, and the brain. In M. Johnson (Ed.), *Brain development and cognition* (pp. 380–388). Cambridge, MA: Blackwell.

Belsky, J. (2001). Emanuel Miller Lecture: Developmental risks (still) associated with early child care. *Journal of Child Psychology & Psychiatry & Allied Disciplines, 42,* 845–859.

Belsky, J. (2002). Quantity counts: Amount of child care and children's socioemotional development. *Journal of Developmental & Behavioral Pediatrics, 23,* 167–170.

Bem, D. J. (1972). Self-perception theory. In L. Berkowitz (Ed.), *Advances in experimental social psychology* (Vol. 6, pp. 1–62). San Diego: Academic Press.

Bem, D. J. (1996). Exotic becomes erotic: A developmental theory of sexual orientation. *Psychological Review, 103,* 320–335.

Bem, D. J. (1998). Is EBE theory supported by the evidence? Is it androcentric? A reply to Peplau et al. *Psychological Review, 108,* 395–398.

Bem, D. J., & Honorton, C. (1994). Does psi exist? Replicable evidence for an anomalous process of information transfer. *Psychological Bulletin, 115,* 4–18.

Benbow, C. P., & Minor, L. L. (1990). Cognitive profiles of verbally and mathematically precocious students: Implications for identification of the gifted. *Gifted Child Quarterly, 34,* 21–26.

Bender, K. J. (1998). "Substance P" antagonist relieves depression. *Psychiatric Times, 15*(11).

Benedetti, F., Pollo, A., Lopiano, L., Lanotte, M., Vighetti, S., & Rainero, I. (2003). Conscious expectation and unconscious conditioning in analgesic, motor, and hormonal placebo/nocebo responses. *Journal of Neuroscience, 23,* 4315–4323.

Beninger, R. J. (1983). The role of dopamine in locomotor activity and learning. *Brain Research Reviews, 6,* 173–196.

Beninger, R. J. (1989). Dissociating the effects of altered dopaminergic function on performance and learning. *Brain Research Bulletin, 23,* 365–371.

Bensafi, M., Tsutsui, T., Khan, R., Levenson, R. W., & Sobel, N. (2004). Sniffing a human sex-steroid derived compound affects mood and autonomic arousal in a dose-dependent manner. *Psychoneuroendocrinology, 29,* 1290–1299.

Ben-Shakhar, G., & Furedy, J. J. (1990). *Theories and applications in the detection of deception: A psychophysiological and international perspective.* New York: Springer-Verlag.

Benson, D. F., & Greenberg, J. P. (1969). Visual form agnosia: A specific deficit in visual recognition. *Archives of Neurology, 20,* 82–89.

Berenbaum, S. A. (1999). Effects of early androgens on sex-typed activities and interests in adolescents with congenital adrenal hyperplasia. *Hormones & Behavior, 35*, 102–110.

Berenbaum, S. A., & Hines, M. (1992). Early androgens are related to childhood sex-typed toy preferences. *Psychological Science, 3*, 203–206.

Berg, S. (1996). Aging, behavior, and terminal decline. In J. E. Birren & K. W. Schaie (Eds.), *Handbook of the psychology of aging* (4th ed., pp. 323–337). New York: Academic Press.

Bergeman, C. S., Plomin, R., Pederson, N. L., McClearn, G. E., & Nesselroad, J. R. (1990). Genetic and environmental influences on social support: The Swedish Adoption/Twin Study of Aging (SATSA). *Journal of Gerontology: Psychological Sciences, 45*, P101–P106.

Berk, L. (1989). Eustress of mirthful laughter modifies natural killer cell activity. *Clinical Research, 37*, 115.

Berk, L. E. (1992a). Children's private speech: An overview of theory and the status of research. In R. M. Diaz & L. E. Berk (Eds.), *Private speech: From social interaction to self-regulation* (pp. 17–53). Hillsdale, NJ: Erlbaum.

Berk, L. E. (1994a). Vygotsky's theory: The importance of make-believe play. *Young Children, 50*, 30–39.

Berk, L. E. (1994b). Why children talk to themselves. *Scientific American, 271*(5), 78–83.

Berkman, L. F., & Syme, S. L. (1979). Social networks, host resistance, and mortality: A nine year follow-up study of Alameda Country residents. *American Journal of Epidemiology, 109*, 186–204.

Berko, J. (1958). The child's learning of English morphology. *Word, 14*, 150–177.

Berkowitz, L. (1997). Some thoughts extending Bargh's argument. In R. S. Wyer, Jr. (Ed.), *The automaticity of everyday life* (pp. 83–94). Mahwah, NJ: Lawrence Erlbaum.

Berkowitz, L. (1998). Affective aggression: The role of stress, pain, and negative affect. In R. G. Geen & E. Donnerstein (Eds.), *Human aggression: Theories, research, and implications for social policy* (pp. 49–72). San Diego, CA.: Academic Press.

Berkowitz, L., & Harmon-Jones, E. (2004). Toward an understanding of the determinants of anger. *Emotion, 4*, 107–130.

Berlyne, D. E. (1960). *Conflict, arousal, and curiosity*. New York: McGraw-Hill.

Berlyne, D. E. (Ed.). (1974). *Studies in the new experimental aesthetics: Steps toward an objective psychology of aesthetic appreciation*. Washington, DC: Hemisphere.

Berman, J. D., & Straus, S. E. (2004). Implementing a research agenda for complementary and alternative medicine. *Annual Review of Medicine, 55*, 239–254.

Berman, S. M., & Noble, E. P. (1995). Reduced visuospatial performance in children with the D2 dopamine receptor A1 allele. *Behavior Genetics, 25*, 45–58.

Bermond, B. N., Fasotti, L., & Schuerman, J. (1991). Spinal cord lesions, peripheral feedback, and intensities of emotional feelings. *Cognition & Emotion, 5*, 201–220.

Bernier, D. (1998). A study of coping: Successful recovery from severe burnout and other reactions to severe work-related stress. *Work & Stress, 12*, 50–65.

Berridge, K. C. (1996). Food reward: Brain substrates of wanting and liking. *Neuroscience and Biobehavioral Reviews, 20*, 1–20.

Berridge, K. C. (2003). Pleasures of the brain. *Brain and Cognition, 52*, 106–128.

Berridge, K. C. (2004). Motivation concepts in behavioral neuroscience. *Physiology and Behavior, 81*, 179–209.

Berridge, K. C., & Robinson, T. E. (1998) What is the role of dopamine in reward: Hedonic impact, reward learning, or incentive salience? *Brain Research Review, 28*, 309–369.

Berscheid, E., & Reis, H. T. (1998). Attraction and close relationships. In D. T. Gilbert, S. T. Fiske, & G. Lindzey (Eds.), *The handbook of social psychology* (4th ed., pp. 193–281). New York: McGraw-Hill.

Berscheid, E., & Walster, E. (1978). *Interpersonal attraction* (2nd ed.). Reading, MA: Addison-Wesley.

Berson, D. M., Dunn, F. A., & Takao, M. (2002). Phototransduction by retinal ganglion cells that set the circadian clock. *Science, 295*, 1070–1073.

Berström, J., Holländare, F., Carlbring, P., Kaldo-Sandström, V., Ekselius, L., & Andersson, G. (2003). Treatment of depression via the Internet: A randomized trial of a self-help programme. *Journal of Telemedicine & Telecare, 9*, 85.

Best, J. (2001). *Damned lies and statistics: Untangling the numbers from the media, politicians, and activists*. Berkeley: University of California Press.

Best, P. J., White, A. M., & Minai. A. (2001). Spatial processing in the brain: The activity of hippocampal place cells. *Annual Review of Neuroscience, 24*, 459–486.

Bettencourt, B. A., & Miller, N. (1996). Sex differences in aggression as a function of provocation: A meta-analysis. *Psycholoigical Bulletin, 119*, 422–447.

Beutler, L. E., & Hodgson, A. B. (1993). Prescriptive psychotherapy. In G. Stricker & J. R. Gold (Eds.), *Comprehensive handbook of psychotherapy integration* (pp. 151–164). New York: Plenum Press.

Beutler, L. E., Machado, P. P., & Neufeldt, S. A. (1994). Therapist variables. In A. E. Bergin & S. L. Garfield (Eds.), *Handbook of psychotherapy and behavior change* (4th ed., pp. 229–269). New York: Wiley.

Beutler, L. E., Moleiro, C., Malik, M., Harwood, T. M., Romanelli, R., Gallagher-Thompson, D., & Thompson, L. (2003). A comparison of the dodo, EST, and ATI factors among comorbid stimulant-dependent, depressed patients. *Clinical Psychology & Psychotherapy, 10*, 69–85.

Beyers, J. M., & Loeber, R. (2003). Untangling developmental relations between depressed mood and delinquency in male adolescents. *Journal of Abnormal Child Psychology, 31*, 247–266.

Bhatt, R. S., & Bertin, E. (2001). Pictorial cues and three-dimensional information processing in early infancy. *Journal of Experimental Child Psychology, 80*, 315–332.

Biedenkapp, J. C., & Rudy, J. W. (2004). Context memories and reactivation: Constraints on the reconsolidation hypothesis. *Behavioral Neuroscience, 118*, 956–964.

Biederman, I. (1987). Recognition-by-components: A theory of human image understanding. *Psychological Review, 94*, 115–147.

Biederman, J., Hirshfeld-Becker, D. R., Rosenbaum, J. F., Hérot, C., Friedman, D., Snidman, N., et al. (2001). Further evidence of association between behavioral inhibition and social anxiety in children. *American Journal of Psychiatry, 158*, 1673–1679.

Bierhoff, H. W., Klein, R., & Kramp, P. (1991). Evidence for the altruistic personality from data on accident research. *Journal of Personality, 59*, 263–280.

Biesanz, J. C., Neuberg, S. L., Smith, D. M., Asher, T., & Judice, T. N. (2001). When accuracy-motivated perceivers fail: Limited attentional resources and the reemerging self-fulfilling prophecy. *Personality & Social Psychology Bulletin, 27*, 621–629.

Bihrle, A. M., Brownell, H. H., Powelson, J. A., & Gardner, H. (1986). Comprehension of humorous and non-humorous materials by left and right brain-damaged patients. *Brain and Cognition, 5*, 399–411.

Bindra, D. (1968). Neuropsychological interpretation of the effects of drive and incentive motivation on general activity and instrumental behavior. *Psychological Review, 75*, 1–22.

Bird, H., Howard, D., & Franklin, S. (2000). Why is a verb like an inanimate object? Grammatical category and semantic category deficits. *Brain & Language, 72*, 246–309.

Birkenhäger, T. K., Renes, J. W., & Pluijms, E. M. (2004). One-year follow-up after successful ECT: A naturalistic study in depressed inpatients. *Journal of Clinical Psychiatry, 65*, 87–91.

Birnbaum, S. G., Yuan, P. X., Wang, M., Vijayraghavan, S., Bloom, A. K., Davis, D. J., et al. (2004). Protein kinase C overactivity impairs prefrontal cortical regulation of working memory. *Science 306*, 882–884.

Birren, J. E. (1988). Behavior as a cause and a consequence of health and aging. In J. J. F. Schroots, J. E. Birren, & A. Svanborg (Eds.), *Health and aging* (pp. 25–41). New York: Springer.

Birren, J. E., Riegel, K. F., & Morrison, D. F. (1962). Age differences in response speed as a function of controlled variations of stimulus conditions: Evidence of a general speed factor. *Gerontologia, 6*, 1–18.

Bishop, D. V. M. (1983). Linguistic impairment after left hemidecortication for infantile hemiplegia? A reappraisal. *Quarterly Journal of Experimental Psychology, 35A*, 199–207.

Bishop, D. V. M., North, T., & Donlan, C. (1995). Genetic basis of specific language impairment: Evidence from a twin study. *Developmental Medicine and Child Neurology, 37*, 56–71.

Bishop, G. D. (1994). *Health psychology: Integrating mind and body*. Boston, MA: Allyn & Bacon.

Bishop, G. D., Enkelmann, H. C., Tong, E. M. W., Why, Y. P., Diong, S. M., Ang, J., & Khader, M. (2003). Job demands, decisional control, and cardiovascular responses. *Journal of Occupational Health Psychology, 8*, 146–156.

Bisiach, E., & Luzzatti, C. (1978). Unilateral neglect of representational space. *Cortex, 14*, 129–133.

Biswas-Diener, R., Diener, E., & Tamir, M. (2004). The psychology of subjective well-being. *Daedalus, 133*, 18–24.

Bjork, E. L., & Bjork, R. A. (2003). Intentional forgetting can decrease, residual influences of to-be-forgotten information. *Journal of Experimental Psychology: Learning, Memory, & Cognition, 29*, 524–531.

Bjork, R. A. (1972). Theoretical implications of directed forgetting. In A. W. Melton & E. Martin (Eds.), *Coding processes in human memory* (pp. 217–235). Washington, DC: Winston.

Bjork, R. A. (1994). Memory and metamemory considerations in the training of human bings. In J. Metcalfe & A. Shimamura (Eds.), *Metacognition: Knowing about knowing* (pp. 185–205). Cambridge, MA: MIT Press.

Black, D. W., Noyes, R., Goldstein, R. B., & Blum, N. (1992). A family study of obsessive-compulsive disorder. *Archives of General Psychiatry, 49*, 362–368.

Black, J. E., Jones, T. A., Nelson, C. A., & Greenough, W. T. (1998). Neuronal plasticity and the developing brain. In N. E. Alessi, J. T. Coyle, S. I. Harrison, & S. Eth (Eds.), *Handbook of child and adolescent psychiatry: Vol 6. Basic psychiatric science and treatment* (pp. 31–53). New York: Wiley.

Blair, C., Gamson, D., Thorne, S., & Baker, D. (2005). Rising mean IQ: Cognitive demand of mathematics education for young children, population exposure to formal schooling, and the neurobiology of the prefrontal cortex. *Intelligence, 33*, 93–106.

Blair, H. T., Schafe, G. E., Bauer, E. P., Rodrigues, S. M., & LeDoux, J. E. (2001). Synaptic plasticity in the lateral amygdala: A cellular hypothesis of fear conditioning. *Learning & Memory, 8*, 229–242.

Blair, I. V. (2002). The malleability of automatic stereotypes and prejudice. *Personality & Social Psychology Review, 6*, 242–261.

Blais, M. A., Hilsenroth, M. J., & Castlebury, F. D. (1997). Psychometric characteristics of the Cluster B personality disorders under DSM-III–R and DSM-IV. *Journal of Personality Disorders, 11*, 270–278.

Blakemore, S., Winston, J., & Frith, U. (2004). Social cognitive neuroscience: Where are we heading? *Trends in Cognitive Sciences, 8*, 216–222.

Blalock, E. M., Chen, K, Sharrow, K., Herman, J. P., Porter, N. M., Foster, T. C., & Landfield, P. W. (2003). Gene microarrays in hippocampal aging: Statistical profiling identifies novel processes correlated with cognitive impairment. *Journal of Neuroscience, 23*, 3807–3819.

Blamey, P., Barry, J., Bow, C., Sarant, J., Paatsch, L., & Wales, R. (2001). The development of speech production following cochlear implantation. *Clinical Linguistics & Phonetics, 15*, 363–382.

Blanchard, R. (2001). Fraternal birth order and the maternal immune hypothesis of male homosexuality. *Hormones & Behavior, 40*, 105–114.

Blanchette, I., & Richards, A. (2004). Reasoning about emotional and neutral materials. *Psychological Science, 15*, 745–752.

Blanck, H. M., Marcus, M., Tolbert, P. E., Rubin, C., Henderson, A. K., Hertzberg, V. S., et al. (2000). Age at menarche and Tanner stage in girls exposed *in utero* and postnatally to polybrominated biphenyl. *Epidemiology, 11*, 641–647.

Blanton, H., Gibbons, F. X., Gerrard, M., Conger, K. J., & Smith, G. E. (1997). Role of family and peers in the development of prototypes associated with substance abuse. *Journal of Family Psychology, 11*, 271–288.

Blascovich, J., & Tomaka, J. (1996). The biopsychosocial model of arousal regulation. *Advances in Experimental Social Psychology, 28*, 1–51.

Blass, T. (1999). The Milgram Paradigm after 35 years: Some things we now know about obedience to authority. *Journal of Applied Social Psychology, 29*, 955–978.

Blass, T. (2004). *The man who shocked the world: The life and legacy of Stanley Milgram.* New York: Basic Books.

Blatt, S. J., Zuroff, D. C., Bondi, C. M., & Sanislow, C. A., III. (2000). Short- and long-term effects of medication and psychotherapy in the brief treatment of depression: Further analyses of data from the NIMH TDCRP. *Psychotherapy Research, 10*, 215–234.

Bleiberg, K. L., & Markowitz, J. C. (2005). A pilot study of interpersonal psychotherapy for posttraumatic stress disorder. *American Journal of Psychiatry, 162*, 181–183.

Bliss, E. L. (1984). Spontaneous self-hypnosis in multiple personality disorder. *Psychiatric Clinics of North America, 7*, 135–148.

Block, N. (1995). How heritability misleads about race. *Cognition, 56*, 99–128.

Bloom, B. L. (1997). *Planned short-term psychotherapy: A clinical handbook* (2nd ed.). Boston, MA: Allyn & Bacon.

Bloom, B. S. (1985). Generalizations about talent development. In B. S. Bloom (Ed.), *Developing talent in young people* (pp. 507–549). New York: Ballantine Books.

Bloom, F. E., & Lazerson, A. (1988). *Brain, mind, behavior* (2nd ed.). New York: Freeman.

Bloom, J. W. (1998). The ethical practice of WebCounseling. *British Journal of Guidance & Counselling, 26*, 53–59.

Blumenthal, J. A., Babyak, M., Wei, J., O'Connor, C., Waugh, R., Eisenstein, E., et al. (2002). Usefulness of psychosocial treatment of mental stress-induced myocardial ischemia in men. *American Journal of Cardiology, 89*, 164–168.

Blundell, J. E. (1977). Is there a role for 5-hydroxytryptamine in feeding? *International Journal of Obesity, 1*, 15–42.

Blundell, J. E. (1986). Serotonin manipulations and the structure of feeding behaviour. *Appetite, 7*, 39–56.

Blundell, J. E., & Halford, J. C. G. (1998). Serotonin and appetite regulation: Implications for the pharmacological treatment of obesity. *CNS Drugs, 9*, 473–495.

Bly, B. M., & Kosslyn, S. M. (1997). Functional anatomy of object recognition in humans: Evidence from PET and fMRI. *Current Opinion in Neurology, 10*, 5–9.

Bobo, L. (1983). Whites' opposition to busing: Symbolic racism or realistic group conflict? *Journal of Personality and Social Psychology, 45*, 1196–1210.

Bochner, S., & Jones, J. (2003). *Child language development: Learning to talk.* London: Whurr.

Boddy, J. (1992). Comment on the proposed DSM-IV criteria for trance and possession disorder. *Transcultural Psychiatric Research Review, 29*, 323–330.

Boden, M. A. (2000). State of the art: Computer models of creativity. *Psychologist, 13*, 72–76.

Bodenhausen, G. V., Kramer, G. P., & Susser, K. (1994). Happiness and stereotypic thinking in social judgment. *Journal of Personality and Social Psychology, 66*, 621–632.

Bogaert, A. F. (1996). Volunteer bias in human sexuality research: Evidence for both sexuality and personality differences in males. *Archives of Sexual Behavior, 25*, 125–140.

Bohannon, J. N., III, & Bonvillian, J. D. (2001). Theoretical approaches to language acquisition. In J. B. Gleason (Ed.), *The development of language* (5th ed., pp. 254–314). Boston: Allyn & Bacon.

Bohm, J. K., & Hendricks, B. (1997). Effects of interpersonal touch, degree of justification, and sex of participant on compliance with a request. *Journal of Social Psychology, 137*, 460–469.

Boivin, D. B., Czeisler, C. A., Dijk, D., Duffy, J. F., Folkard, S., Minors, D. S., et al. (1997). Complex interaction of the sleep-wake cycle and circadian phase modulates mood in healthy subjects. *Archives of General Psychiatry, 54*, 145–152.

Boivin, D. B., & James, F. O. (2002a). Circadian adjustment to night-shift work by judicious light and darkness exposure. *Journal of Biological Rhythms, 17*, 556–567.

Boivin, D. B., & James, F. O. (2002b). Phase-dependent effect of room light exposure in a 5-h advance of the sleep-wake cycle: Implications for jet lag. *Journal of Biological Rhythms, 17*, 266–276.

Bokert, E. (1968). The effects of thirst and a related verbal stimulus on dream reports. *Dissertation Abstracts, Vol. 28*(11-B), 4753. (18192)

Bokhorst, C. L., Bakermans-Kranenburg, M. J., Fearon, R. M. P., van IJzendoorn, M. H., Fonagy, P., & Schuengel, C. (2003). The importance of shared environment in mother-infant attachment security: A behavioral genetic study. *Child Development, 74*, 1769–1782.

Bolton, P., Bass, J., Neugebauer, R., Verdeli, H., Clougherty, K. F., Wickramaratne, P., Speelman, L., Ndogoni, L., & Weissman, M. (2003). Group interpersonal psychotherapy for depression in rural Uganda: A randomized controlled trial. *Journal of the American Medical Association, 289*, 3117–3124.

Bonanno, G. A. (2004). Loss, trauma, and human resilience: Have we underestimated the human capacity to thrive after extremely aversive events? *American Psychologist, 59*, 20–28.

Bonanno, G. A. (2005). Clarifying and extending the construct of adult resilience. *American Psychologist, 60*, 265–267.

Bonanno, G. A., Papa, A., Lalande, K., Westphal, M., & Coifman, K. (2004). The importance of being flexible: The ability to both enhance and suppress emotional expression predicts long-term adjustment. *Psychological Science, 15*, 482–487.

Bond, M., Gardiner, S. T., Christian, H., & Sigel, J. J. (1983). Empirical study of self-rated defense styles. *Archives of General Psychiatry, 40*, 333–338.

Bond, R., & Smith, P. B. (1996). Culture and conformity: A meta-analysis of studies using Asch's (1952b, 1956) line judgment task. *Psychological Bulletin, 119*, 111–137.

Bonnefond, A., Muzet, A., Winter-Dill, A., Bailloeuil, C., Bitouze, F., & Bonneau, A. (2001). Innovative working schedule: Introducing one short nap during the night shift. *Ergonomics, 44*, 937–945.

Bonnel, A.-M., Faita, F., Peretz, I., & Besson, M. (2001). Divided attention between lyrics and tunes of operatic songs: Evidence for independent processing. *Perception & Psychphysics, 63*, 1201–1213.

Bontempo, D. E., & D'Augelli, A. R. (2002). Effects of at-school victimization and sexual orientation on lesbian, gay, or bisexual youths' health risk behavior. *Journal of Adolescent Health, 30*, 364–374.

Borg, E., & Counter, S. A. (1989). The middle ear muscles. *Scientific American, 261*, 74–80.

Boring, E. G. (1950). *A history of experimental psychology* (2nd ed.). New York: Appleton-Century-Crofts.

Borkenau, P., Mauer, N., Riemann, R., Spinath, F. M., & Angleitner, A. (2004). Thin slices of behavior as cues of personality and intelligence. *Journal of Personality & Social Psychology, 86,* 599–614.

Borman, W. C., Hanson, M. A., & Hedge, J. W. (1997). Personnel selection. *Annual Review of Psychology, 48,* 299–337.

Bornstein, M. H., DiPietro, J. A., Hahn, C. S., Painter, K., Haynes, O. M., & Costigan, K. A. (2002). Prenatal cardiac function and postnatal cognitive development: An exploratory study. *Infancy, 3,* 475–494.

Bornstein, M. H., Tal, J., Rahn, C., Galperin, C. Z., et al. (1992). Functional analysis of the contents of maternal speech to infants of 5 and 13 months in four cultures: Argentina, France, Japan, and the United States. *Developmental Psychology, 28,* 593–603.

Bornstein, S. R., & Chrousos, G. P. (1999) Clinical review 104. Adrenocorticotropin (ACTH)- and non-ACTH-mediated regulation of the adrenal cortex: Neural and immune inputs. *Journal of Clinical Endocrinology and Metabolism, 84,* 1729–1736.

Boroditsky, L. (2001). Does language shape thought? Mandarin and English speakers' conceptions of time. *Cognitive Psychology, 43,* 1–22.

Borroni, A. M., Fichtenholtz, H., Woodside, B. L., & Teyler, T. J. (2000). Role of voltage-dependent calcium channel long-term potentiation (LTP) and NMDA LTP in spatial memory. *Journal of Neuroscience, 20,* 9272–9276.

Bosch, J. A., Brand, H. S., Ligtenberg, A. J. M., Bermond, B., Hoogstraten, J., & Nieuw Amgerongen, A. V. (1998). The response of salivary protein levels and S-IgA to an academic examination are associated with daily stress. *Journal of Psychophysiology, 12,* 384–391.

Bosma, H., Stansfelt, S. A., & Marmot, M. G. (1998). Job control, personal characteristics, and heart disease. *Journal of Occupational Health Psychology, 3,* 402–409.

Bosson, J. K., Haymovitz, E. L., & Pinel, E. C. (2004). When saying and doing diverge: The effects of stereotype threat on self-reported versus non-verbal anxiety. *Journal of Experimental Social Psychology, 40,* 247–255.

Bosworth, H. B., & Siegler, I. C. (2002). Terminal change in cognitive function: An updated review of longitudinal studies. *Experimental Aging Research, 28,* 299–315.

Botting, N., & Conti-Ramsden, G. (2001). Non-word repetition and language development in children with specific language impairment (SLI). *International Journal of Language & Communication Disorders, 36,* 421–432.

Bottini, G., Corcoran, R., Sterzi, R., Paulesu, E., Schenone, P., Scarpa, P., et al. (1994). The role of the right hemisphere in the interpretation of figurative aspects of language: A positron emission tomography activation study. *Brain, 117,* 1241–1253.

Bottini, G., Paulesu, E., Sterzl, R., Warburton, E., Wise, R. J. S., Vallar, G., et al. (1995). Modulation of conscious experience by peripheral sensory stimuli. *Nature, 376,* 778–781.

Botvin, G. J. (1995). Drug abuse prevention in school settings. In G. J. Botvin, S. Schinke, & M. A. Orlandi (Eds.), *Drug abuse prevention with multiethnic youth* (pp. 169–192). Newbury Park, CA: Sage.

Botwinick, J. (1984). *Aging and behavior: A comprehensive integration of research findings.* New York: Springer.

Bouchard, T. J., Jr. (1994). Genes, environment, and personality. *Science, 264,* 1700–1701.

Bouchard, T. J., Jr. (2004). Genetic influence on human psychological traits: A survey. *Current Directions in Psychological Science, 13,* 148–151.

Bouchard, T. J., Jr., & Loehlin, J. C. (2001). Genes, evolution, and personality. *Behavior Genetics, 31,* 243–273.

Bouchard, T. J., Jr., Lykken, D. T., McGue, M., Segal, N. L., & Tellegen, A. (1990). Sources of human psychological differences: The Minnesota Study of Twins Reared Apart. *Science, 250,* 223–228.

Bouchard, T. J., & McGue, M. (1981). Familial studies of intelligence: A review. *Science, 212,* 1055–1059.

Bourguignon, E. (1973). *Altered states of consciousness and social change.* Columbus: Ohio State University Press.

Bousfield, W. A. (1953). The occurrence of clustering in the recall of randomly arranged associates. *Journal of General Psychology, 49,* 229–240.

Bouton, M. (1993). Context, time and memory retrieval in the interference paradigms of Pavlovian conditioning. *Psychological Bulletin, 114,* 80–99.

Bouton, M. (1994). Context, ambiguity and classical conditioning. *Current Directions in Psychological Science, 3,* 49–52.

Bouton, M. E. (2000). A learning theory perspective on lapse, relapse, and the maintenance of behavior change. *Health Psychology, 19,* 57–63.

Bouton, M. E. (2002). Context, ambiguity, and unlearning: Sources of relapse after behavioral extinction. *Biological Psychiatry, 52,* 976–979.

Bouton, M. E., Mineka, S., & Barlow, D. H. (2001). A modern learning theory perspective on the etiology of panic disorder. *Psychological Review, 108,* 4–32.

Bowdle, B. F., & Gentner, D. (2005). The career of metaphor. *Psychological Review, 112,* 193–216.

Bower, G. H. (1972). Mental imagery and associative learning. In L. Gregg (Ed.), *Cognition and learning and memory* (pp. 51–88). New York: Wiley.

Bower, G. H. (1981). Mood and memory. *American Psychologist, 36,* 129–148.

Bower, G. H. (1992). How might emotions effect learning? In S.-Å. Christianson (Ed.), *The handbook of emotion and memory: Research and theory* (pp. 3–31). Hillsdale, NJ: Erlbaum.

Bower, G. H., Clark, M. C., Lesgold, A. M., & Winzenz, D. (1969). Hierarchical retrieval schemes in recall of categorized word lists. *Journal of Verbal Learning and Verbal Behavior, 8,* 323–343.

Bowlby, J. (1969). *Attachment and loss: Vol. 1, Attachment.* New York: Basic Books.

Bowlby, J. (1973). *Separation: Anxiety & anger.* Vol. 2 of *Attachment and loss.* London: Hogarth Press.

Bowman, E. S., & Nurnberger, J. I. (1993). Genetics of psychiatry diagnosis and treatment. In D. L. Dunner (Ed.), *Current psychiatric therapy* (pp. 46–56). Philadelphia: Saunders.

Bowman, M. L. (1999). Individual differences in posttraumatic distress: Problems with the DSM-IV model. *Canadian Journal of Psychiatry, 44,* 21–33.

Brach, J. S., Simonsick, E. M., Kritchevsky, S., Yaffe, K., & Newman, A. B. (2004). The association between physical function and lifestyle activity and exercise in the health, aging and body composition study. *Journal of the American Geriatrics Society, 52,* 502–509.

Bradburn, N. M. (1969). *The structure of psychological well-being.* Chicago: Aldine.

Braden, J. P. (2000). Editor's introduction: Perspectives on nonverbal assessment of intelligence. *Journal of Psychoeducational Assessment, 18,* 204–220.

Bradley, M. M., Greenwald, M. K., Petry, M. C., & Lang, P. J. (1992). Remembering pictures: Pleasure and arousal in memory. *Journal of Experimental Psychology: Learning, Memory, and Cognition, 18,* 379–390.

Bradley, M. T., MacLaren, V. V., & Carle, S. B. (1996). Deception and nondeception in Guilty Knowledge and Guilty Actions Polygraph Tests. *Journal of Applied Psychology, 81,* 153–160.

Bradley, M. T., & Warfield, J. F. (1984). Innocence, information, and the Guilty Knowledge Test in the detection of deception. *Psychophysiology, 21,* 683–689.

Bradshaw, G. L., & Anderson, J. R. (1982). Elaborative encoding as an explanation of levels of processing. *Journal of Verbal Learning & Verbal Behavior, 21,* 165–174.

Brainard, G. C., Hanifin, J. P., Greeson, J. M., Byrne, B., Glickman, G., Gerner, E., & Rollag, M. D. (2001). Action spectrum for melatonin regulation in humans: Evidence for a novel circadian photoreceptor. *Journal of Neuroscience, 21,* 6405–6412.

Braksiek, R. J., & Roberts, D. J. (2002). Amusement park injuries and deaths. *Annals of Emergency Medicine, 39,* 65–72.

Brandstätter, H., & Königstein, M. (2001). Personality influences on ultimatum bargaining decisions. *European Journal of Personality, 15,* S53–S70.

Brannon, L. (1996). *Gender: Psychological perspectives.* Needham Heights, MA: Simon & Schuster.

Bransford, J. D., & Franks, J. J. (1971). The abstraction of linguistic ideas. *Cognitive Psychology, 2,* 331–350.

Brashers-Krug, T., Shadmehr, R., & Bizzi, E. (1996). Consolidation in human motor memory. *Nature, 382,* 252–254.

Braun, K. A., Ellis, R., & Loftus, E. F. (2002). Make my memory: How advertising can change our memories of the past. *Psychology & Marketing, 19,* 1–23.

Braver, T. S., & Cohen, J. D. (2000). On the control of control: The role of dopamine in regulating prefrontal function and working memory. In S. Monsell & J. Driver (Eds.), *Attention and performance XVIII: Control of cognitive processes* (pp. 713–737). Cambridge, MA: MIT Press.

Breckler, S. J. (1984). Empirical validation of affect, behavior, and cognition as distinct components of attitude. *Journal of Personality and Social Psychology, 47,* 1191–1205.

Bregman, A. S. (1990). *Auditory scene analysis: The perceptual organization of sound.* Cambridge, MA: MIT Press.

Bregman, A. S. (1993). Auditory scene analysis: Hearing in complex environments. In S. McAdams & E. Bigand (Eds.), *Thinking in sound: The cognitive psychology of human audition* (pp. 10–36). New York: Oxford University Press.

Bregman, E. O. (1934). An attempt to modify the emotional attitudes of infants by the conditioned response technique. *Journal of Genetic Psychology, 45,* 169.

Brehm, J. W. (1956). Post-decision changes in the desirability of alternatives. *Journal of Abnormal and Social Psychology, 52,* 384–389.

Brehm, J. W. (1966). *A theory of psychological reactance.* New York: Academic Press.

Breiter, H. C., Aharon, I., Kahneman, D., Dale, A., & Shizgal, P. (2001). Functional imaging of neural responses to expectancy and experience of monetary gains and losses. *Neuron, 30*, 619–639.

Breiter, H. C., Rauch, S. L., Kwong, K. K., Baker, J. R., Weisskoff, R. M., Kennedy, D. N., et al, (1996). Functional magnetic resonance imaging of symptom provocation in obsessive-compulsive disorder. *Archives of General Psychiatry, 53*, 595–606.

Bremner, J. D., Narayan, M., Anderson, E. R., Staib, L. H., Miller, H. L., & Charney, D. S. (2000). Hippocampal volume reduction in major depression. *American Journal of Psychiatry, 157*, 115–117.

Bremner, J. D., Stienberg, M., Southwick, S. M., Johnson, D. R., & Charney, D. S. (1993). Use of the structured clinical interview for DSM-IV dissociative disorders for systemic assessment of dissociative symptoms in posttraumatic stress disorder. *American Journal of Psychiatry, 150*, 1011–1014.

Bremner, J. D., Vythilingam, M., Vermetten, E., Southwick, S. M., McGlashan, T., Nazeer, A., Khan, S., Vaccarino, L. V., Soufer, R., Garg, P. K., Ng, C. K., Staib, L. H., Duncan, J. S., & Charney, D. S. (2003). MRI and PET study of deficits in hippocampal structure and function in women with childhood sexual abuse and posttraumatic stress disorder. *American Journal of Psychiatry, 160*, 924–932.

Brennan, A., Chugh, J. S., & Kline, T. (2002). Traditional versus open office design: A longitudinal study. *Environment & Behavior, 34*, 279–299.

Breslau, N., Chilcoat, H. D., Kessler, R. C., Peterson, E. L., & Lucia, V. C. (1999). Vulnerability to assaultive violence: Further specification of the sex difference in post-traumatic stress disorder. *Psychological Medicine, 29*, 813–821.

Breslau, N., Kessler, R. C., Chilcoat, H. D. Schultz, L. R., Davis, G. C., & Andreski, P. (1998). Trauma and posttraumatic stress disorder in the community: The 1996 Detroit Area Survey of Trauma. *Archives of General Psychiatry, 55*, 626–632.

Brewer, A. A., Press, W. A., Logothetis, N. K., & Wandell, B. A. (2002). Visual areas in Macaque cortex measured using functional magnetic resonance imaging. *Journal of Neuroscience, 22*, 10416–10426.

Brewer, C., Meyers, R. J., & Johnsen, J. (2000). Does disulfiram help to prevent relapse in alcohol abuse? *CNS Drugs, 14*, 329–341.

Brewer, J. B., Zhao, Z., Desmod, J. E., Glover, G. H., & Gabrielli, J. D. E. (1998). Making memories: Brain activity that predicts how well visual experience will be remembered. *Science, 281*, 1185–1187.

Brewer, K. R., & Wann, D. L. (1998). Observational learning effectiveness as a function of model characteristics: Investigating the importance of social power. *Social Behavior & Personality, 26*,1–10.

Brewer, M. B., & Brown, R. J. (1998). Intergroup relations. In D. T. Gilbert, S. T. Fiske, & G. Lindzey (Eds.), *The handbook of social psychology* (4th ed., pp. 554–594). New York: McGraw-Hill.

Brewer, W. F. (1988). Qualitative analysis of the recalls of randomly sampled autobiographical events. In M. M. Gruneberg & P. E. Morris (Eds.), *Practical aspects of memory: Current research and issues, Vol. 1: Memory in everyday life* (pp. 263–268). New York: John Wiley & Sons.

Brickman, P., & Campbell, D. T. (1971). Hedonic relativism and the good society. In M. H. Appley (Ed.), *Adaptation-level theory: A symposium* (pp. 215–231). New York: Academic Press.

Broadbent, D. E. (1971). The magic number seven after fifteen years. In A. Kennedy & A. Wilkes (Eds.), *Studies in long-term memory* (pp. 2–18). New York: Wiley.

Brochard, R., Dufour, A., & Després, O. (2004). Effect of musical expertise on visuospatial abilities: Evidence from reaction times and mental imagery. *Brain & Cognition, 54*, 103–109.

Brody, J. (1998, April 6). Dealing with sleep deprivation. *International Herald Tribune*, 9.

Brody, N. (1997). Intelligence, schooling, and society. *American Psychologist, 52*, 1046–1050.

Brody, N. (2003a). Construct validation of the Sternberg triarchic abilities test: Comment and reanalysis. *Intelligence, 31*, 319–329.

Brody, N. (2003b). What Sternberg should have concluded. *Intelligence, 31*, 339–342.

Brooks-Gunn, J., Graber, J. A., & Paikoff, R. L. (1994). Studying links between hormones and negative affect: Models and measures. *Journal of Research on Adolescence, 4*, 469–486.

Brosschot, J. F., Benschop, R. J., Godaert, G. L. R., Olff, M., de Smet, M. Heijnen, C. J., & Ballieux, R. E. (1994). Influence of life stress on immunological reactivity to mild psychological stress. *Psychosomatic Medicine, 56*, 216–224.

Brosschot, J. F., & Thayer, J. F. (2003). Heart rate response is longer after negative emotions than after positive emotions. *International Journal of Psychophysiology, 50*, 181–187.

Brown, A. S., Cohen, P., Harkavy-Friedman, J., & Babulas, V. (2001). Prenatal rubella, premorbid abnormalities, and adult schizophrenia. *Biological Psychiatry, 49*, 473–486.

Brown, A. S., van Os, J., Driessens, C., Hoek, S. W., & Susser, E. S. (1999). Prenatal famine and the spectrum of psychosis. *Psychiatric Annals, 29*, 145–150.

Brown, B. (1999). Optimizing expression of the common human genome for child development. *Current Directions in Psychological Science, 8*, 37–41.

Brown, B. B., Clasen, D., & Eicher, S. (1986a). Perceptions of peer pressure, peer conformity dispositions, and self-reported behavior among adolescents. *Developmental Psychology, 22*, 521–530.

Brown, B. B., Lohr, M. J., & McClenahan, E. L. (1986b). Early adolescents' perceptions of peer pressure. *Journal of Early Adolescence, 6*, 139–154.

Brown, I., Jr., & Inouye, D. K. (1978). Learned helplessness through modeling: The role of perceived similarity in competence. *Journal of Personality and Social Psychology, 36*, 900–908.

Brown, J. D., & Rogers, R. J. (1991). Self-serving attributions: The role of physiological arousal. *Personality and Social Psychology Bulletin, 17*, 501–506.

Brown, P. L., & Jenkins, H. M. (1968). Auto-shaping of the pigeon's key peck. *Journal of the Experimental Analysis of Behavior, 68*, 503–507.

Brown, R. (1989). Roger Brown. In G. Lindzey (Ed.), *A history of psychology in autobiography* (Vol. 8, pp. 37–60). Stanford, CA: Stanford University Press.

Brown, R., & Kulik, J. (1977). Flashbulb memories. *Cognition, 5*, 73–99.

Brown, R., & McNeill, D. (1966). The "tip of the tongue" phenomenon. *Journal of Verbal Learning and Verbal Behavior, 5*, 325–337.

Brown, R. P., & Pinel, E. C. (2003). Stigma on my mind: Individual differences in the experience of stereotype threat. *Journal of Experimental Social Psychology, 39*, 626–633.

Browne, C. A., Colditz, P. B., & Dunster, K. R. (2000). Infant autonomic function is altered by maternal smoking during pregnancy. *Early Human Development, 59*, 209–218.

Browne, G., Steiner, M., Roberts, J., Gafni, A., Byrne, C., Dunn, E., et al. (2002). Sertraline and/or interpersonal psychotherapy for patients with dysthymic disorder in primary care: 6-month comparison with longitudinal 2-year follow-up of effectiveness and costs. *Journal of Affective Disorders, 68*, 317–320.

Brownell, H., Gardner, H., Prather, P., & Martino, G. (1995). Language, communication, and the right hemisphere. In H. S. Kirshner (Ed.), *Handbook of neurological speech and language disorders* (pp. 325–349). New York: Dekker.

Brownell, H. H., Michelow, D., Powelson, J., & Gardner, H. (1983). Surprise but not coherence: Sensitivity to verbal humor in right hemisphere patients. *Brain and Language, 18*, 20–27.

Brownell, H. H., Potter, H. H., Michelow, D., & Gardner, H. (1984). Sensitivity to lexical denotation and connotation in brain-damaged patients: A double dissociation. *Brain and Language, 22*, 253–265.

Brownell, H. H., Simpson, T. L., Bihrle, A. M., Potter, H. H., & Gardner, H. (1990). Appreciation of metaphoric alternative word meanings by left and right brain-damaged patients. *Neuropsychologia, 28*, 375–383.

Brownell, K. D., & Rodin, J. (1992). *Medical, metabolic, and psychological effects of weight cycling*. Unpublished manuscript, Yale University.

Brozinsky, C. J., & Bavelier, D. (2004). Motion velocity thresholds in deaf signers: Changes in lateralization but not in overall sensitivity. *Cognitive Brain Research, 21*, 1–10.

Brugger, P., Landis, T., & Regard, M. (1990). A "sheep-goat effect" in repetition avoidance: Extrasensory perception as an effect of subjective probability? *British Journal of Psychology, 81*, 455–468.

Brummett, B. H., Mark, D. B., Siegler, I. C., Williams, R. B., Babyak, M. A., Clapp-Channing, N. E., & Barefoot, J. C. (2005). Perceived social support as a predictor of mortality in coronary patients: Effects of smoking, sedentary behavior, and deperssive symptoms. *Psychosomatic Medicine, 67*, 40–45.

Brunner, D. P., Dijk, D. J., Tobler, I., & Borbely, A. A. (1990). Effect of partial sleep deprivation on sleep stages and EEG power spectra: Evidence for non-REM and REM sleep homeostasis. *Electroencephalogr. Clin. Neurophysiol., 75*, 492–499.

Brussoni, M. J., Jang, K. L., Livesley, W. J., & MacBeth, T. M. (2000). Genetic and environmental influences on adult attachment styles. *Personal Relationships, 7*, 283–289.

Bryan, R. N., Wells, S. W., Miller, T. J., Elster, A. D., Jungreis, C. A., Poirier, V. C., et al. (1997). Infarctlike lesions in the brain: Prevalence and anatomic characterisitcs at MR imaging of the elderly—data from the Cardiovascular Health Study. *Radiology, 202*, 47–54.

Bryant, R. A., Harvey, A. G., Guthrie, R. M., & Moulds, M. L. (2003). Acute Psychophysiological arousal and posttraumatic stress disorder: A two-year prospective study. *Journal of Traumatic Stress, 16*, 439–443.

BSCS & Videodiscovery. (2000). *The brain: Understanding neurobiology through the study of addiction.* Colorado Springs, CO: BSCS & Videodiscovery.

Buchanan, C. M., Eccles, J., & Becker, J. (1992). Are adolescents the victims of raging hormones? Evidence for activational effects of hormones on moods and behavior at adolescence. *Psychological Bulletin, 111,* 62–107.

Buchkremer, G., Klingberg, S., Holle, R., Schulze-Moenking, H., & Hornung, W. P. (1997). Psychoeducational psychotherapy for schizophrenic patients and their key relatives or care-givers: Results of a 2-year follow-up. *Acta Psychiatrica Scandinavica, 96,* 483–491.

Buckalew, L. W., & Ross, S. (1981). Relationship of perceptual characteristics to efficacy of placebos. *Psychological Reports, 49,* 955–961.

Buckner, R. L., Kelley, W. M., & Petersen, S. E. (1999). Frontal cortex contributes to human memory formation. *Nature Neuroscience, 2,* 311–314.

Buda, R., & Elsayed-Elkhouly, S. M. (1998). Cultural differences between Arabs and Americans: Individualism-collectivism revisited. *Journal of Cross-Cultural Psychology, 29,* 487–492.

Buehler, R., Griffin, D., & Ross, M. (1994). Exploring the "planning fallacy": Why people underestimate their task completion times. *Journal of Personality & Social Psychology, 67,* 366–381.

Buka, S. L., Goldstein, J. M., Seidman, L. J., Zornberg, G. L., Donatelli, J. A., Denny, L. R., & Tsuang, M. T. (1999). Prenatal complications, genetic vulnerability, and schizophrenia: The New England Longitudinal Studies of Schizophrenia. *Psychiatric Annals, 29,* 151–156.

Bulik, C. M., Tozzi, F., Anderson, C., Mazzeo, S. E., Aggen, S., & Sullivan, P. F. (2003). The relation between eating disorders and components of perfectionism. *American Journal of Psychiatry, 160,* 366–368.

Buller, K. M. (2003). Neuroimmune stress responses: Reciprocal connections between the hypothalamus and the brainstem. *Stress: The International Journal on the Biology of Stress, 6,* 11–17.

Bunce, S. C., Bernat, E., Wong, P. S., & Shevrin, H. (1999). Further evidence for unconscious learning: Preliminary support for the conditioning of facial EMG to subliminal stimuli. *Journal of Psychiatric Research, 33,* 341–347.

Bunney, W. E., & Garland, B. L. (1983). Possible receptor effects of chronic lithium administration. *Neuropharmacology, 22,* 367–372.

Burger, J. M. (1992). *Desire for control: Personality, social, and clinical perspectives.* New York: Plenum.

Burger, J. M., & Cooper, H. M. (1979). The desirability of control. *Motivation and Emotion, 3,* 381–393.

Burger, J. M., Horita, M., Kinoshita, L., Roberts, K., & Vera, C. (1997). Effects of time on the norm of reciprocity. *Basic & Applied Social Psychology, 19,* 91–100.

Burish, T. G., & Carey, M. P. (1986). Conditioned aversive responses in cancer chemotherapy patients: Theoretical and developmental analysis. *Journal of Counseling and Clinical Psychology, 54,* 593–600.

Burnstein, E. (1982). Persuasion as argument processing. In H. Brandstatter, J. H. Davis, & G. Stocker-Krechgauer (Eds.), *Group decision making* (pp. 103–124). London: Academic Press.

Burton, L. M. (1990). Teenage childbearing as an alternative life-course strategy in multigeneration Black families. *Human Nature, 1,* 123–143.

Burton, L. M. (1996). Age norms, the timing of family role transitions, and intergenerational caregiving among aging African American women. *Gerontologist, 36,* 199–208.

Burton, M. J., Rolls, E. T., & Mora, F. (1976). Effects of hunger on the responses of neurons in the lateral hypothalamus to the sight and taste of food. *Experimental Neurology, 51,* 668–677.

Busemeyer, J. R. (2004, in press). So, whatever happened to signal detection theory? *PsycCRITIQUES.*

Bushman, B. J. (1984). Perceived symbols of authority and their influence on compliance. *Journal of Applied Social Psychology, 14,* 501–508.

Bushman, B. J. (1988). The effects of apparel on compliance: A field experiment with a female authority figure. *Personality and Social Psychology Bulletin, 14,* 459–467.

Bushman, B. J. (1998). Threatened egotism, narcissism, self-esteem, and direct and displaced aggression: Does self-love or self-hate lead to violence? *Journal of Personality and Social Psychology, 75,* 219–229.

Bushman, B. J., Baumeister, R. F., & Phillips, C. M. (2001). Do people aggress to improve their mood? Catharsis beliefs, affect regulation opportunity, and aggressive responding. *Journal of Personality and Social Psychology, 81,* 17–32.

Bushman, B. J., Bonacci, A. M., van Dijk, M., & Baumeister, R. F. (2003). Narcissism, sexual refusal, and aggression: Testing a narcissistic reactance model of sexual coercion. *Journal of Personality & Social Psychology, 84,* 1027–1040.

Bushman, B. J., & Cooper, H. M. (1990). Effects of alcohol on human aggression: An integrative research review. *Psychological Bulletin, 107,* 1–14.

Bushman, B. J., & Wells, G. L. (1998). Trait aggressiveness and hockey penalties: Predicting hot tempers on the ice. *Journal of Applied Psychology, 83,* 969–974.

Busjahn, A., Faulhaber, H. D., Freier, K., & Luft, F. C. (1999). Genetic and environmental influences on coping styles: A twin study. *Psychosomatic Medicine, 61,* 469–475.

Buss, A. H. (1995). *Personality: Temperament, social behavior, and the self.* Needham Heights, MA: Allyn & Bacon.

Buss, A. H., & Plomin, R. (1975). *A temperament theory of personality development.* New York: Wiley Interscience.

Buss, A. H., & Plomin, R. (1984). *Temperament: Early developing personality traits.* Hillsdale, NJ: Erlbaum.

Buss, D. M. (1994). *The evolution of desire: Strategies of human mating.* New York: Basic Books.

Buss, D. M. (1995). Psychological sex differences: Origins through sexual selection. *American Psychologist, 50,* 164–168.

Buss, D. M. (1998). The psychology of human mate selection: Exploring the complexity of the strategic repetoire. In C. B. Crawford & D. L. Krebs (Eds.), *Handbook of evolutionary psychology: Ideas, issues, and applications* (pp. 405–429). Mahwah, NJ: Erlbaum.

Buss, D. M. (1999). *Evolutionary psychology: The new science of the mind.* Boston: Allyn & Bacon.

Buss, D. M., Larsen, R. J., Western, D., & Semmelroth, J. (1992). Sex differences in jealousy: Evolution, physiology, and psychology. *Psychological Science, 3,* 251–255.

Busse, E. W. (1969). Theories of aging. In E. W. Busse & E. Pfeiffer (Eds.), *Behavior and adaptation in later life* (pp. 11–32). Boston: Little, Brown.

Butcher, J. N., & Rouse, S. V. (1996). Personality: Individual difference and clinical assessment. *Annual Review of Psychology, 47,* 87–111.

Butler, E. A., Egloff, B., Wilhelm, F. H., Smith, N. C., Erickson, E. A., & Gross, J. J. (2003). The social consequences of expressive suppression. *Emotion, 3,* 48–67.

Butters, N., Heindel, W. C., & Salmon, D. P. (1990). Dissociation of implicit memory in dementia: Neurological implications. *Bulletin of the Psychonomic Society, 28,* 359–366.

Butzlaff, R. L., & Hooley, J. M. (1998). Expressed emotion and psychiatric relapse: A meta-analysis. *Archives of General Psychiatry, 55,* 547–552.

Byrne, D. (1971). *The attraction paradigm.* New York: Academic Press.

Cabeza, R. (2002). Hemispheric asymmetry reduction in older adults: The HAROLD model. *Psychology & Aging, 17,* 85–100.

Cabeza, R., & Nyberg, L. (1997). Imaging cognition: An empirical review of PET studies with normal subjects. *Journal of Cognitive Neuroscience, 9,* 1–26.

Cabeza, R., & Nyberg, L. (2000). Imaging cognition II: An empirical review of 275 PET and fMRI studies. *Journal of Cognitive Neuroscience, 12,* 1–47.

Cabeza, R., Prince, S. E., Daselaar, S. M., Greenberg, D. L., Budde, M., Dolcos, F., LaBar, K. S., & Rubin, D. C. (2004). Brain activity during episodic retrieval of autobiographical and laboratory events: An fMRI study using a novel photo paradigm. *Journal of Cognitive Neuroscience, 16,* 1583–1594.

Cacioppo, J. T., Berntson, G. G., Larsen, J. T., Poehlmann, K. M., & Ito, T. A. (2000). The psychophysiology of emotion. In R. Lewis & J. M. Haviland-Jones (Eds.), *The handbook of emotion* (2nd ed., pp. 173–191). New York: Guilford Press.

Cacioppo, J. T., Gardner, J. T., & Berntson, W. L. (1997). Beyond bipolar conceptualizations and measures: The case of attitudes and evaluative space. *Personality & Social Psychology Review, 1,* 3–25.

Cacioppo, J. T., & Petty, R. E. (1982). The need for cognition. *Journal of Personality & Social Psychology, 42,* 116–131.

Cacioppo, J. T., Petty, R. E., Feinstein, J. A., & Jarvis, W. B. G. (1996). Disposition differences in cognition motivation: The life and times of individuals varying in need for cognition. *Psychological Bulletin, 119,* 197-253.

Cacioppo, J. T., Petty, R. E., Kao, C. F., & Rodriguez, R. (1986). Central and peripheral routes to persuasion: An individual difference perspective. *Journal of Personality & Social Psychology, 51,* 1032–1043.

Cacioppo, J. T., Petty, R. E., Losch, M. E., & Kim, H. S. (1986). Electromyographic activity over facial muscle regions can differentiate the valence and intensity of affective reactions. *Journal of Personality and Social Psychology, 50,* 260–268.

Cadinu, M., Maass, A., Frigerio, S., Impagliazzo, L., & Latinotti, S. (2003). Stereotype threat: The effect of expectancy on performance. *European Journal of Social Psychology, 33,* 267–285.

Cahan, S., & Cohen, N. (1989). Age versus schooling effects on intelligence development. *Child Development, 60,* 1239–1249.

Cahill, L., Haier, R. J., Fallon, J., Alkire, M. T., Tang, C., Keator, D., et al. (1996). Amygdala activity at encoding correlated with long-term free recall of emotional information. *Proceedings of the National Academy of Sciences, USA, 93,* 8016–8021.

Cahill, L., Haier, R. J., White, N. S., Fallon, J., Kilpatrick, L., Lawrence, C., et al. (2001). Sex-related differences in amygdala activity during emotionally influenced memory storage. *Neurobiology of Learning & Memory, 75,* 1–9.

Cahill, L., Prins, B., Weber, M., & McGaugh, J. L. (1994). Adrenergic activation and memory for emotional events. *Nature, 371,* 702–704.

Cailliet, R. (1993). *Pain: Mechanisms and management.* Philadelphia: Davis.

Cain, W. S. (1973). Spatial discrimination of cutaneous warmth. *American Journal of Psychology, 86,* 169–181.

Cain, W. S. (1979). To know with the nose: Keys to odor identification. *Science, 203,* 467–470.

Cain, W. S. (1982). Odor identification by males and females: Predictions and performance. *Chemical Senses, 7,* 129–141.

Cain, W. S., & Gent, J. F. (1991). Olfactory sensitivity: Reliability, generality, and association with aging. *Journal of Experimental Psychology: Human Perception and Performance, 17,* 382–391.

Cajochen, C., Knoblauch, V., Wirz-Justice, A., Kräuchi, K., Graw, P., & Wallach, D. (2004). Circadian modulation of sequence learning under high and low sleep pressure conditions. *Behavioural Brain Research, 151,* 167–176.

Calder, A. J., Young, A. W., Rowland, D., Perrett, D. I., Hodges, J. R., & Etcoff, N. L. (1996). Face perception after bilateral amygdala damage: Differentially severe impairment of fear. *Cognitive Neuropsychology, 13,* 699–745.

Caldera, Y. M., & Sciaraffa, M. A. (1998). Parent-toddler play with feminine toys: Are all dolls the same? *Sex Roles, 39,* 657–668.

Calkins, S. D. (1994). Individual differences in the biological aspects of temperament. In J. E. Bates & T. D. (Eds.), *Temperament: Individual differences at the interface of biology and behavior* (pp. 199–217). Washington, DC: American Psychological Association.

Calkins, S. D., Fox, N. A., & Marshall, T. R. (1996). Behavioral and physiological antecedents of inhibited and uninhibited behavior. *Child Development, 67,* 523–540.

Calvocoressi, L., Lewis, B., Harris, M., Trufan, S. J., et al. (1995). Family accommodation in obsessive-compulsive disorder. *American Journal of Psychiatry, 152,* 441–443.

Cameron-Faulkner, T., Lieven, E., & Tomasello, M. (2003). A construction based analysis of child directed speech. *Cognitive Science, 27,* 843–873.

Cammarota, M., Bevilaqua, L. R. M., Medina, J. H., & Izquierdo, I. (2004). Retrieval does not induce reconsolidation of inhibitory avoidance memory. *Learning & Memory, 11,* 572–578.

Campbell, D. T. (1960). Blind variation and selective retention in creative thought as in other knowledge processes. *Psychological Review, 67,* 380–400.

Campbell, F. A., & Ramey, C. T. (1994). Effects of early intervention on intellectual and academic achievement: A follow-up study of children from low-income families. *Child Development, 65,* 684–698.

Campos, J. J., Anderson, D. I., Barbu-Roth, M. A., Hubbard, E. M., Hertenstein, M. J., & Witherington, D. (2000). Travel broadens the mind. *Infancy, 1,* 149–219.

Campos, J. J., Langer, A., & Krowitz, A. (1970). Cardiac responses on the visual cliff in prelocomotor human infants. *Science, 170,* 196–197.

Canli, T., Zhao, Z., Desmond, J. E., Kang, E., Gross, J., & Gabrieli, J. D. E. (2001). An fMRI study of personality influences on brain reactivity to emotional stimuli. *Behavioral Neuroscience.*

Cannon, C. M., & Bseikri, M. R. (2004). Is dopamine required for natural reward? *Physiology & Behavior, 81,* 741–748.

Cannon, T. D. (1997). On the nature and mechanisms of obstetric influences in schizophrenia: A review and synthesis of epidemiologic studies. *International Review of Psychiatry, 9,* 387–397.

Cannon, T. D., Huttunen, M. O., Dahlstroem, M., Larmo, I., Raesaenen, P., & Juriloo, A. (2002). Antipsychotic drug treatment in the prodromal phase of schizophrenia. *American Journal of Psychiatry, 159,* 1230–1232.

Cannon, W. B. (1927). The James-Lange theory of emotions: A critical examination and an alternative theory. *American Journal of Psychology, 39,* 106–124.

Cannon, W. B. (1932). *The wisdom of the body.* New York: Norton.

Cannon, W. B. (1942). Voodoo death. *American Anthropologist, 44,* 169–181.

Cansino, S., Ducorps, A., & Ragot, R. (2003). Tonotopic cortical representation of complex sounds. *Human Brain Mapping, 20,* 71–81.

Cantalupo, C., & Hopkins, W. D. (2001). Asymmetric Broca's area in great apes: A region of the ape brain is uncannily similar to one linked with speech in humans. *Nature, 414,* 505.

Cantor, J. M., Blanchard, R., Paterson, A. D., & Bogaert, A. F. (2002). How many gay men owe their sexual orientation to fraternal birth order? *Archives of Sexual Behavior, 31,* 63–71.

Cantor, N., & Norem, J. K. (1989). Defensive pessimism and stress and coping. *Social Cognition, 7,* 92–112.

Cappa, S. F., & Grafman, J. (2004). Neuroimaging of higher cognitive function. *Cortex, 40,* 591–592.

Caprara, G. V., Barbaranelli, C., Pastorelli, C., & Cervone, D. (2004). The contribution of self-efficacy beliefs to psychosocial outcomes in adolescence: Predicting beyond past behavior and global dispositional tendencies. *Personality and Individual Differences, 37,* 751–763.

Caprara, G. V., Steca, P., Cervone, D., & Artistico, D. (2003). The contribution of self-efficacy beliefs to dispositional shyness: On socialcognitive systems and the development of personality dispositions. *Journal of Personality, 71,* 943–970.

Caramazza, A., & Zurif, E. B. (1976). Dissociation of algorithmic and heuristic processes in language comprehension: Evidence from aphasia. *Brain & Language, 3,* 572–582.

Cardinal, R. N., Parkinson, J. A., Hall, J., & Everitt, B. (2002). Emotion and motivation: The role of the amygdala, ventral striatum, and prefrontal cortex. *Neuroscience and Biobehavioral Reviews, 26,* 321–352.

Cardinal, R. N., Parkinson, J. A., Marbini, H. D., Toner, A. J, Bussey, T. J., Robbins, T. W., & Everitt, B. J. (2003). The role of the anterior cingulate cortex in the control over behavior by Pavlovian conditioned stimuli in rats.*Behavioral Neuroscience, 117,* 566–587.

Cardno, A. G., Rijsdijk, F. V., Sham, P. C., Murray, R. M., & McGuffin, P. (2002). A twin study of genetic relationships between psychotic symptoms. *American Journal of Psychiatry 159,* 539–545.

Carenzi, F., Bendahan, P., Roschin, V. Y., Frolov, A. A., Gorce, P., & Maier, M. A. (2004). A generic neural network for multi-modal sensorimotor learning. *Neurocomputing: An International Journal, 58,* 525–533.

Carey, M. P., & Burish, T. G. (1988). Etiology and treatment of the psychological side effects associated with cancer chemotherapy: A critical review and discussion. *Psychological Bulletin, 104,* 307–325.

Carey, S. (1978). The child as word learner. In J. Bresnan, G. Miller, & M. Halle (Eds.), *Linguistic theory and psychological reality* (pp. 264–293). Cambridge, MA: MIT Press.

Carey, S. (1985). *Conceptual change in childhood.* Cambridge, MA: Bradford/MIT Press.

Carey, S. (1988). Conceptual differences between children and adults. *Mind and Language 3,* 67–82.

Carey, S. (1995b). On the origin of causal understanding. In D. Sperber, D. Premack, & A. J. Premack (Eds.), *Causal cognition: A multidisciplinary debate* (pp. 268–302). Oxford: Clarendon Press.

Carlbring, P., Westling, B. E., Ljungstrand, P., Ekselius, L., & Andersson, G. (2001). Treatment of panic disorder via the Internet: A randomized trial of a self-help program. *Behavior Therapy, 32,* 751–764.

Carlo, G., Okun, M. A., Knight, G. P., & de Guzman, M. T. (in press). The interplay of traits and motives on volunteering: Agreeableness, extraversion and prosocial value motivation. *Personality and Individual Differences.*

Carlson, N. R. (1994). *Physiology of behavior.* Needham Heights, MA: Allyn & Bacon.

Carlsson, C. P. O., & Sjoelund, B. H. (2001). Acupuncture for chronic low back pain: A randomized placebo-controlled study with long-term follow-up. *Clinical Journal of Pain, 17,* 296–305.

Carlyon, R. P. (2004). How the brain separates sounds. *Trends in Cognitive Sciences, 8,* 465–471.

Carmines, E. G., & Zeller, R. A. (1979). *Reliability and validity assessment.* Beverly Hills, CA: Sage.

Carnelley, K. B., Wortman, C. B., & Kessler, R. C. (1999). The impact of widowhood on depression: Findings from a prospective survey. *Psychological Medicine, 29,* 1111–1123.

Carney, R. M., Freeland, K. E., Veith, R. C., Cryer, P. E., Skala, J. A., Lynch, T., & Jaffe, A. S. (1999). Major depression, heart rate, and plasma norepinephrine in patients with coronary heart disease. *Biological Psychiatry, 45,* 458–463.

Carpenter, P. A., Just, M. A., & Shell, P. (1990). What one intelligence test measures: A theoretical account of the processing in the Raven Progressive Matrices test. *Psychological Review, 97,* 404–431.

Carr, D., House, J. S., Kessler, R. C., Nesse, R. M., Sonnega, J., & Wortman, C. (2000). Marital quality and psychological adjustment to widowhood among older adults: A longitudinal analysis. *Journals of Gerontology: Series B: Psychological Sciences & Social Sciences, 55B,* S197–S207.

Carr, D., House, J. S., Wortman, C., Neese, R., & Kessler, R. C. (2001). Psychological adjustment to sudden and anticipated spousal loss among older widowed persons. *Journals of Gerontology: Series B: Psychological Sciences & Social Sciences, 56B,* S237-S248.

Carr, J. L., & VanDeusen, K. M. (2004). Risk factors for male sexual aggression on college campuses. *Journal of Family Violence, 19,* 279–289.

Carrington, P. (1977). *Freedom in meditation.* Garden City, NY: Anchor Press/Doubleday.

Carroll, J. (1993). *Human cognitive abilities: A survey of factor-analytic studies.* New York: Cambridge University Press.

Carroll, L. (1992). Alice in wonderland. Authoritative texts of Alice's adventures in wonderland, Through the looking-glass, The hunting of the snark. Backgrounds. In D. J. Gray (Ed.), *Essays in criticism* (2nd ed.). New York: Norton.

Carrothers, R. M., Gregory, S. W., Jr., & Gallagher, T. J. (2000). Measuring emotional intelligence of medical school applicants. *Academic Medicine, 75,* 456–463.

Carskadon, M., Vieria, C., & Acebo, C. (1993). Association between puberty and delayed phase preference. *Sleep, 16,* 258–262.

Carstens, C. B., Huskins, E., & Hounshell, G. W. (1995). Listening to Mozart may not enhance performance on the revised Minnesota Paper Form Board Test. *Psychological Reports, 77,* 111–114.

Carstensen, L. L. (1991). Socioemotional selectivity theory: Social activity in life-span context. In K. W. Schaie & M. P. Lawton (Eds.), *Annual review of gerontology and geriatrics* (Vol. 11, pp. 195–217). New York: Springer.

Carstensen, L. L. (1992). Social and emotion patterns in adulthood: Support for socioemotional selectivity theory. *Psychology & Aging, 7,* 331–338.

Carstensen, L. L., & Charles, S. T. (1998). Emotion in the second half of life. *Current Directions in Psychological Science, 7,* 144–149.

Carstensen, L. L., Gottman, J. M., & Levenson, R. W. (1995). Emotional behavior in long-term marriage. *Psychology & Aging, 10,* 140–149.

Carstensen, L. L., Pasupathi, M., Mayr, U., & Nesselroade, J. R. (2000). Emotional experience in everyday life across the adult life span. *Journal of Personality & Social Psychology, 79,* 644–655.

Carter, C., & Rice, C. L. (1997). Acquisition and manifestation of prejudice in children. *Journal of Multicultural Counseling and Development, 25,* 185–194.

Carter, C. S. (2004). Oxytocin and the prairie vole: A love story. In J. T. Cacioppo & G. G. Berntson (Eds.), *Essays in social neuroscience* (pp. 53–63). Cambridge, MA: MIT Press.

Carter, J. C., Stewart, D. A., Dunn, V. J., and Fairburn, C. G. (1997). Primary prevention of eating disorders: Might it do more harm than good? *International Journal of Eating Disorders, 22,* 167–172.

Carter, M. M., Hollon, S. D., Carson, R., & Shelton, R. C. (1995). Effects of a safe person on induced distress following a biological challenge in panic disorder with agoraphobia. *Journal of Abnormal Psychology, 104,* 156–163.

Cartford, M. C., Gemma, C., & Bickford, P. C. (2002). Eighteen-month-old Fischer 344 rats fed a spinach-enriched diet show improved delay classical eye-blink conditioning and reduced expression of tumor necrosis factor a (TNF ()) and TNF β in the cerebellum. *Journal of Neuroscience, 22,* 5813–5816.

Carver, C. S., Meyer, B., & Antoni, M. H. (2000). Responsiveness to threats and incentives expectancy of recurrence and distress and disengagement: Moderator effects in early-stage breast cancer patients. *Journal of Consulting and Clinical Psychology, 68,* 965–975.

Carver, C. S., & Scheier, M. F. (1992). Confidence, doubt, and coping with anxiety. In D. G. Forgays, T. Sosnowski, & K. Wrzesniewski (Eds.), *Anxiety: Recent developments in cognitive, psychophysiological, and health research* (pp. 13–22). Washington, DC: Hemisphere Publishing.

Carver, C. S., & Scheier, M. F. (1996). *Perspectives on personality.* Boston: Allyn & Bacon.

Carver, C. S., Scheier, M. F., & Weintraub, J. K. (1989). Assessing coping strategies: A theoretically based approach. *Journal of Personality and Social Psychology, 56,* 267–83.

Carver, C. S., & White, T. L. (1994). Behavioral inhibition, behavioral activation, and affective responses to impending reward and punishment: The BIS/BAS scales. *Journal of Personality and Social Psychology, 67,* 319–333.

Casada, J. H., Amdur, R., Larsen, R., & Liberzon, I. (1998). Psychophysiologic responsivity in posttraumatic stress disorder: Generalized hyperresponsiveness versus trauma specificity. *Biological Psychiatry, 44,* 1037–1044.

Casbon, T. S., Burns, A. B., Bradbury, T. N., & Joiner, T. E., Jr. (2005). Receipt of negative feedback is related to increased negative feedback seeking among individuals with depressive symptoms. *Behaviour Research and Therapy, 43,* 485–504.

Case, R. (1977). Responsiveness to conservation training as a function of induced subjective uncertainty, M-space, and cognitive style. *Canadian Journal of Behavioral Sciences, 9,* 12–25.

Case, R. (1978). Intellectual development from birth to adulthood: A neo-Piagetian approach. In R. S. Siegler (Ed.), *Children's thinking: What develops?* (pp. 37–71). Hillsdale, NJ: Erlbaum.

Case, R. (1992b). *The mind's staircase.* Hillsdale, NJ: Erlbaum.

Case, R. (1992c). The role of the frontal lobes in the regulation of cognitive development. *Brain and Cognition, 20,* 51–73.

Caspi, A. (2000). The child is father of the man: Personality continuities from childhood to adulthood. *Journal of Personality and Social Psychology, 78,* 158–172.

Caspi, A., Begg, D., Dickson, N., Harrington, H., Langley, J., Moffitt, T. E., & Silva, P. A. (1997). Personality differences predict health-risk behaviors in young adulthood: Evidence from a longitudinal study. *Journal of Personality and Social Psychology, 73,* 1052–1063.

Caspi, A., & Herbener, E. S. (1990). Continuity and change: Assortative marriage and the consistency of personality in adulthood. *Journal of Personality and Social Psychology, 58,* 250–258.

Caspi, A., Moffitt, T. E., Morgan, J., Rutter, M., Taylor, A., Arseneault, L., et al. (2004). Maternal expressed emotion predicts children's antisocial behavior problems: Using monozygotic-twin differences to identify environmental effects on behavioral development. *Developmental Psychology, 40,* 149–161.

Cassia, V. M., Turati, C., & Simion, F. (2004). Can a nonspecific bias toward top-heavy patterns explain newborns' face preference? *Psychological Science, 15,* 379–383.

Cassone, V. M., Warren, W. S., Brooks, D. S., & Lu, J. (1993). Melatonin, the pineal gland and circadian rhythms. *Journal of Biological Rhythms, 8*(Suppl.), S73–S81.

Castellà, J., & Pérez, J. (2004). Sensitivity to punishment and sensitivity to reward and traffic violations. *Accident Analysis & Prevention, 36,* 947–952.

Catalan-Ahumeda, M., Dewggouj, N., De Volder, A., Melin, J., Michel, C., & Veraart, C. (1993). High metabolic activity demonstrated by positron emission tomography in human auditory cortex in case of deafness of early onset. *Brain Research, 623,* 287–292.

Cattell, R. B. (1943). The description of personality: Basic traits resolved into clusters. *Journal of Abnormal and Social Psychology, 38,* 476–506.

Cattell, R. B. (1971). *Abilities: Their structure, growth, and action.* Boston: Houghton Mifflin.

Cattell, R. B., Eber, H. W., & Tatsuoka, M. M. (1970). *Handbook for the Sixteen Personality Factor Questionnaire (16PF).* Champaign, IL: Institute for Personality and Ability Testing.

Caudron, S. (1994). Diversity ignites effective work teams. *Personnel Journal, 73,* 54–63.

Cavallaro, S., Schreurs, B. G., Zhao, W., D'Agata, V., & Alkon, D. L. (2001). Gene expression profiles during long-term memory consolidation. *European Journal of Neuroscience, 13,* 1809–1815.

Cave, C. B. (1997). Very long-lasting priming in picture naming. *American Psychological Society, 8,* 322–325.

Cave, C. B., & Kosslyn, S. M. (1993). The role of parts and spatial relations in object identification. *Perception, 22,* 229–248.

Cave, C. B., & Squire, L. R. (1992). Intact and long-lasting repetition priming in amnesia. *Journal of Experimental Psychology: Learning, Memory, and Cognition, 18,* 509–520.

Ceci, S. J. (1990). *On intelligence . . . more or less: A bio-ecological treatise on intellectual development.* Englewood Cliffs, NJ: Prentice-Hall.

Ceci, S. J. (1991). How much does schooling influence general intelligence and its cognitive components? A reassessment of the evidence. *Developmental Psychology, 27,* 703–722.

Ceci, S. J., & Williams, W. M. (1997). Schooling, intelligence, and income. *American Psychologist, 52,* 1051–1058.

Center for Addiction and Substance Abuse at Columbia University (2002). *Substance use and risky sexual activity.* Retrieved from http://www.casacolumbia.org/newsletter1457/newsletter_show.htm?doc_id=95635

Center for the Advancement of Health (1998). Facts of life: An issue briefing for health reporters, 3(3), 2.

Centers for Disease Control and Prevention (2003). National Center for Health Statistics, National Health Interview Survey, family core and sample adult questionnaires. Table 65.

Centers for Disease Control and Prevention. (2004). *Health, United States, 2004: With chartbook on trends in the health of Americans.* Washington, DC: U.S. Department of Health and Human Services.

Cerella, J. (1990). Aging and information-processing rate. In J. E. Birren & K. W. Schaie (Eds.), *Handbook of the psychology of aging* (3rd ed., pp. 201–221). San Diego, CA: Academic Press.

Cerella, J., Poon, L., & Williams, D. (1980). Age and the complexity hypothesis. In L. W. Poon (Ed.), *Aging in the 1980s* (pp. 332–340). Washington, DC: American Psychological Association.

Cervone, D. (2005). Personality architecture: Within-person structures and processes. *Annual Review of Psychology, 56,* 423–452.

Chabris, C. F. (1999). Prelude or requiem for the "Mozart effect"? *Nature, 400*, 826–827.

Chabris, C. F., & Kosslyn, S. M. (1998). How do the cerebral hemispheres contribute to encoding spatial relations? *Current Directions in Psychological Science, 7*, 8–14.

Chalmers, D. J. (1996). *The conscious mind.* New York: Oxford University Press.

Chamberlain, K., & Zika, S. (1990). The minor events approach to stress: Support for the use of daily hassles. *British Journal of Psychology, 81*, 469–481.

Chambers, J. M., Cleveland, W. S., Kleiner, B., & Turkey, P. A. (1983). *Graphical methods for data analysis.* Belmont, CA: Wadsworth.

Chambless, D. L. (1996). In defense of dissemination of empirically supported psychological interventions. *Clinical Psychology: Science & Practice, 3*, 230–235.

Chambless, D. L., & Gillis, M. M. (1993). Cognitive therapy of anxiety disorders. *Journal of Consulting and Clinical Psychology, 61*, 248–260.

Chambless, D. L., & Hollon, S. D. (1998). Defining empirically supported therapies. *Journal of Consulting & Clinical Psychology, 66*, 7–18.

Chambless, D. L., & Steketee, G. (1999). Expressed emotion and behavior therapy outcome: A prospective study with obsessive-compulsive and agoraphobic outpatients. *Journal of Consulting & Clinical Psychology, 67*, 658–665.

Chan, J., & Yang, J. (1999). *I am Jackie Chan.* New York: Ballantine Books.

Chang, R. C., Blaisdell, A. P., & Miller, R. R. (2003). Backward conditioning: Mediation by the context. *Journal of Experimental Psychology: Animal Behavior Processes, 29*, 171–183.

Changizi, M. A., McGehee, R. M. F., & Hall, W. G. (2002). Evidence that appetitive responses for dehydration and food-deprivation are learned. *Physiology & Behavior, 75*, 295–304.

Chao, L. L., & Martin, A. (1999). Cortical regions associated with perceiving, naming, and knowing about colors. *Journal of Cognitive Neuroscience, 11*, 25–35.

Chapman, C. (1989). Giving the patient control of opioid analgesic administration. In C. Hill & W. Fields (Eds.), *Advances in pain research and therapy* (Vol. 11). New York: Raven Press.

Chapman, C. R., & Nakamura, Y. (1999). A passion of the soul: An introduction to pain for consciousness researchers. *Consciousness and Cognition, 8*, 391–422.

Chapman, J. K. (2000). Developmental outcomes in two groups of young children: Prenatally cocaine exposed and noncocaine exposed: Part 2. *Infant-Toddler Intervention, 10*, 81–96.

Chapman, R. S. (2000). Children's language learning: An interactionist perspective. *Journal of Child Psychology and Psychiatry, 41*, 33–54.

Chapman, R. S., & Hesketh, L. J. (2000). Behavioral phenotype of individuals with Down syndrome. *Mental Retardation & Developmental Disabilities Research Reviews, 6*, 84–95.

Charness, N. (1981). Aging and skilled problem solving. *Journal of Experimental Psychology: General, 110*, 21–38.

Chartrand, T. L., & Bargh, J. A. (1999). The chameleon effect: The perception-behavior link and social interaction. *Journal of Personality & Social Psychology, 76*, 893–910.

Chase, W. G., & Ericsson, K. A. (1981). Skilled memory. In J. R. Anderson (Ed.), *Cognitive skills and their acquisition.* Hillsdale, NJ: Erlbaum.

Chase, W. G., & Simon, H. A. (1973). The mind's eye in chess. In W. G. Chase (Ed.), *Visual information processing* (pp. 215–281). New York: Academic Press.

Chatterjee, S., & Callaway, E. M. (2003). Parallel colour-opponent pathways to primary visual cortex. *Nature, 426*, 668–671.

Chatterjee, S., Heath, T. B., Milberg, S. J., & France, K. R. (2000). The differential processing of price in gains and losses: The effects of frame and need for cognition. *Journal of Behavioral Decision Making, 13*, 61–75.

Chaudhari, N., Landin, A. M., & Roper, S. D. (2000). A metabotropic glutamate receptor variant functions as a taste receptor. *Nature Neuroscience, 3*, 113–119.

Chaves, J. F. (1989). Hypnotic control of clinical pain. In N. P. Spanos & J. F. Chaves (Eds.), *Hypnosis: The cognitive-behavioral perspective* (pp. 242–272). Buffalo, NY: Prometheus Books.

Chen, Z., & Siegler, R. S. (2000). Across the great divide: Bridging the gap between understanding of toddlers' and older children's thinking. *Monographs of the Society for Research in Child Development, 65*, v-96.

Cheng, C. M., & Chartrand, T. L. (2003). Self-monitoring without awareness: Using mimicry as a nonconscious affiliation strategy. *Journal of Personality & Social Psychology, 85*, 1170–1179.

Cheng, D. T., Knight, D. C., Smith, C. N., Stein, E. A., & Helmstetter, F. J. (2003). Functional MRI of human amygdala activity during Pavlovian fear conditioning: Stimulus processing versus response expression. *Behavioral Neuroscience, 117*, 3–10.

Cheour-Luhtanen, M., Alho, K., Sainio, K., Rinne, T., & Reinikainen, K. (1996). The ontogenetically earliest discriminative response of the human brain. *Psychophysiology, 33*, 478–481.

Cherry, E. C. (1953). Some experiments on the recognition of speech with one and two ears. *Journal of the Acoustical Society of America, 25*, 975–979.

Chess, S., & Thomas, A. (1987). *Know your child.* New York: Basic Books.

Chess, S., & Thomas, A. (1996). *Temperament: Theory and practice.* New York: Brunner/Mazel.

Chi, M. T. H. (1978). Knowledge structures and memory development. In R. S. Siegler (Ed.), *Children's thinking: What develops?* (pp. 73–96). Hillsdale, NJ: Erlbaum.

Chick, J., Gough, K., Falkowski, W., Kershaw, P., Hore, B., Mehta, B., et al. (1992). Disulfiram treatment of alcoholism. *British Journal of Psychiatry, 161*, 84–89.

Chilcoat, H. D., & Breslau, N. (1998). Posttraumatic stress disorder and drug disorders testing causal pathways. *Archives of General Psychiatry, 55*, 913–917.

Child, I. L. (1985). Psychology and anomalous observations: The question of ESP in dreams. *American Psychologist, 40*, 1219–1230.

Chippendale, L. A. (2003). *Triumph of the imagination: The story of writer J. K. Rowling.* Philadelphia: Chelsea House.

Chipuer, H. M., Rovine, M. J., & Plomin, R. (1990). LISREL modeling: Genetic and environmental influences on IQ revisited. *Intelligence, 14*, 11–29.

Chivers, M. L., Rieger, G., Latty, E., & Bailey, J. M. (2004). A sex difference in the specificity of sexual arousal. *Psychological Science, 15*, 736–744.

Choderow, N. (1978). *The reproduction of mothering.* Berkeley: University of California Press.

Chomsky, C. (1969). *The acquisition of syntax in children from 5 to 10.* Cambridge, MA: MIT Press.

Chomsky, N. (1957). *Syntactic structures.* Mouton: The Hague.

Chomsky, N. (1972). *Language and mind.* New York: Harcourt Brace.

Chorpita, B. F., & Barlow, D. H. (1998). The development of anxiety: The role of control in the early environment. *Psychological Bulletin, 124*, 3–21.

Christensen, A. J., Benotsch, E. G., Wiebe, J. S., & Lawton, W. J. (1995). Coping with treatment-related stress: Effects on patient adherence in hemodialysis. *Journal of Consulting & Clinical Psychology, 63*, 454–459.

Christensen, H., Griffiths, K. M., & Jorm, A. F. (2004). Delivering interventions for depression by using the internet: Randomised controlled trial. *British Medical Journal, 328*, 265–269.

Christensen, K. A., Stephens, M. A. P., & Townsend, A. L. (1998). Mastery in women's multiple roles and well-being: Adult daughters providing care to impaired parents. *Health Psychology, 17*, 163–171.

Christian, K. M., & Thompson, R. F. (2003). Neural substrates of eyeblink conditioning: Acquisition and retention. *Learning & Memory, 10*, 427–455.

Christman, S. D. (2002). Hemispheric asymmetries in categorical judgments of directions versus coordinate judgments of velocity of motion. *Psychonomic Bulletin and Review, 9*, 298–305.

Christmann, C., & Leuthold, H. (2004). The attentional blink is susceptible to concurrent perceptual processing demands. *Quarterly Journal of Experimental Psychology: Human Experimental Psychology, 57*, 357–377.

Chun, M. M. (1997). Types and tokens in visual processing: A double dissociation between the attentional blink and repetition blindness. *Journal of Experimental Psychology: Human Perception and Performance, 23*, 738–755.

Chun, M. M. (2000). Contextual cueing of visual attention. *Trends in Cognitive Sciences, 4*, 170–177.

Church, T. A., & Katigbak, M. S. (2000). Trait psychology in the Philippines. *American Behavioral Scientist, 44*, 73–94.

Cialdini, R. B. (1994). Interpersonal influence. In N. S. Shavitt & T. C. Brock (Eds.), *Persuasion: Psychological insights and perspectives* (pp. 195–218). Boston: Allyn & Bacon.

Cialdini, R. B., Eisenberg, N., Green, B. L., Rhoads, K., & Bator, R. (1998). Undermining the undermining effect of reward on sustained interest. *Journal of Applied Social Psychology, 28*, 249–263.

Cialdini, R. B., & Goldstein, N. J. (2004). Social influence: Compliance and conformity. *Annual Review of Psychology, 55*, 591–621.

Cialdini, R. B., & Petty, R. (1979). Anticipatory opinion effects. In B. Petty, T. Ostrom, & T. Brock (Eds.), *Cognitive responses in persuasion.* Hillsdale, NJ: Erlbaum.

Cialdini, R. B., & Trost, M. R. (1998). Social influence: Social norms, conformity, and compliance. In D. T. Gilbert, S. T. Fiske, & G. Lindzey (Eds.), *The handbook of social psychology* (4th ed., pp. 151–192). New York: McGraw-Hill.

Cialdini, R. B., Vincent, J. A., Lewis, S. K., Catalan, J., Wheeler, D., & Darby, B. L. (1975). Reciprocal concessions procedure for inducing compliance: The door-in-the-face technique. *Journal of Personality and Social Psychology, 31,* 206–215.

Ciarrochi, J., Forgas, J. P., & Mayer, J. D. (2001). Emotional intelligence in everyday life. Philadelphia: Psychology Press.

Cicero, T. J. (1978). Tolerance to and physiological dependence on alcohol: Behavioral and neurobiological mechanisms. In M. A. Lipton, A. DiMascio, & K. F. Killman (Eds.), *Psychopharmacology.* New York: Raven.

Citron, M., Solomon, P., & Draine, J. (1999). Self-help groups for families of persons with mental illness: Perceived benefits of helpfulness. *Community Mental Health Journal, 35,* 15–30.

Claar, R. L., & Blumenthal, J. A. (2003). The value of stress-management interventions in life-threatening medical conditions. *Current Directions in Psychological Science, 12,* 133–137.

Clancy, S. A., McNally, R. J., Schacter, D. L., Lenzenweger, M. F., & Pitman, R. K. (2002). Memory distortion in people reporting abduction by aliens. *Journal of Abnormal Psychology, 111,* 455–461.

Clancy, S. A., Schacter, D. L., McNally, R. J., & Pitman, R. K. (2000). False recognition in women reporting recovered memories of sexual abuse. *Psychological Science, 11,* 26–31.

Claparède, E. (1911/1951). Recognition and "me-ness." Originally published in *Archives de Psychologie, 11,* 79–90. Reprinted in D. Rappaport (Ed.), (1951). *Organization and pathology of thought* (pp. 58–75). New York: Columbia University Press.

Clapp, G. (1988). *Child study research: Current perspectives and applications.* Lexington, MA: Lexington Books/D.C. Heath.

Clarey, J. C., Barone, P., & Imig, T. J. (1992). Physiology of thalmus and cortex. In A. N. Popper & R. R. Fay (Eds.), *The mammalian auditory pathway: Neurophysiology* (pp. 232–334). New York: Springer-Verlag.

Clark, D. M., Ball, S., & Pape, D. (1991). An experimental investigation of thought suppression. *Behaviour Research and Therapy, 29,* 253–257.

Clark, E. V. (1983). Meanings and concepts. In P. H. Mussen (Ed.), *Handbook of child psychology: Vol. 3, Cognitive development* (pp. 787–840). New York: Wiley.

Clark, E. V. (1993). *The lexicon in acquisition.* Cambridge: Cambridge University Press.

Clark, L. F., & Collins, J. E. (1993). Remembering old flames: How the past affects assessments of the present. *Personality & Social Psychology Bulletin, 19,* 399–408.

Clark, R. E., Manns, J. R., & Squire, L. R. (2002). Classical conditioning, awareness, and brain systems. *Trends in Cognitive Sciences, 6,* 524–531.

Clark, R. W. (1971). *Einstein: The life and times.* New York: World Publishing.

Clarke, G., Reid, E., Eubanks, D., O'Connor, E., DeBar, L. L., Kelleher, C., Lynch, F., & Nunley, S. (2002). Overcoming depression on the Internet (ODIN): A randomized controlled trial of an Internet depression skills intervention program. *Journal of Medical Internet Research, 4,* e14.

Clarke, G. N., Hornbrook, M., Lynch, F., Polen, M., Gale, J., Beardslee, W., et al. (2001). A randomized trial of a group cognitive intervention for preventing depression in adolescent offspring of depressed parents. *Archives of General Psychiatry, 58,* 1127–1134.

Claxton, L. J., Keen, R., & McCarty, M. E. (2003). Evidence of motor planning in infant reaching behavior. *Psychological Science, 14,* 354–356.

Clay, R. (1995). Working mothers: Happy or haggard? *The APA Monitor, 26*(11), 1, 37.

Cleary, A. M., & Greene, R. L. (2002). Paradoxical effects of presentation modality on false memory. *Memory, 10,* 55–61.

Cleveland, H. H., Jacobson, K. C., Lipinski, J. J., & Rowe, D. C. (2000). Genetic and shared environmental contributions to the relationship between the HOME environment and child and adolescent achievement. *Intelligence, 28,* 69–86.

Clifford, D. B. (2000). Human immunodeficiency virus-associated dementia. *Archives of Neurology, 57,* 321–324.

Cloninger, R., Svarkic, D. M., & Prysbeck, T. R. (1993). Psychobiological model of temperament and character. *Archives of General Psychiatry, 50,* 975–990.

Clopton, N. A., & Sorell, G. T. (1993). Gender differences in moral reasoning: Stable or situational? *Psychology of Women Quarterly, 17,* 85–101.

Coats, E. J., & Feldman, R. S. (1996). Gender differences in nonverbal correlates of social status. *Personality & Social Psychology Bulletin, 22,* 1014–1022.

Coe, W. C. (1978). The credibility of posthypnotic amnesia: A contextualists' view. *International Journal of Clinical & Experimental Hypnosis, 26,* 218–245.

Coffey, C. E., Saxton, J. A., Ratcliff, G., Bryan, R. N., & Lucke, J. F. (1999). Relation of education to brain size in normal aging: Implications for the reserve hypothesis. *Neurology, 53,* 189–196.

Cohen, C. I., Strashun, A., Ortega, C., & Horn, L. (1996). The effects of poverty and education on temporoparietal perfusion in Alzheimer's disease: A reconsideration of the cerebral reserve hypothesis. *International Journal of Geriatric Psychiatry, 11,* 1105–1110.

Cohen, D., & Gunz, A. (2002). As seen by the other . . . perspectives on the self in the memories and emotional perceptions of Easterners and Westerners. *Psychological Science, 13,* 55–59.

Cohen, D., Nisbett, R. E., Bowdle, B. F., & Schwarz, N. (1996). Insult, aggression, and the southern culture of honor: An "experimental ethnography." *Journal of Personality and Social Psychology, 70,* 945–960.

Cohen, J. D., Aston-Jones, G., & Gilzenrat, M. S. (in press). A systems level theory of attention and cognitive control. In M. I. Posner (Ed.), *Cognitive neuroscience of attention.* New York: Guilford Press.

Cohen, J. D., Peristein, W. M., Braver, T. S., Nystrom, L. E., Noll, D. C., Jonides, J., & Smith, E. E. (1997). Temporal dynamics of brain activation during a working memory task. *Nature, 386,* 604–608.

Cohen, M. R., & Newsome, W. T. (2004). What electrical microstimulation has revealed about the neural basis of cognition. *Current Opinion in Neurobiology, 14,* 169–177.

Cohen, P., Kasen, S., Chen, H., Hartmark, C., & Gordon, K. (2003). Variations in patterns of developmental transitions in the emerging adulthood period. *Developmental Psychology, 39,* 657–669.

Cohen, S., Doyle, W. J., Skoner, D. P., Rabin, B. S., & Gwaltney, J. M., Jr. (1997). Social ties and susceptibility to the common cold. *Journal of the American Medical Association, 277,* 1940–1944.

Cohen, S., Evans, F. W., Krantz, D. S., & Stokols, D. S. (1986). *Behavior, health, and environmental stress.* New York: Plenum Press.

Cohen, S., & Herbert, T. B. (1996). Health Psychology: Psychological factors and physical disease from the perspective of human psychoneuroimmunology. *Annual Review of Psychology, 47,* 113–142.

Cohen, S., & Wills, T. (1985). Stress, social support and the buffering hypothesis. *Psychological Bulletin, 98,* 310–357.

Cohen-Kerem, R., & Koren, G. (2003). Antioxidants and fetal protection against ethanol teratogenicity I. Review of the experimental data and implications to humans. *Neurotoxicology & Teratology, 25,* 1–9.

Colado, M. I., O'Shea, E., & Green, A. R. (2004). Acute and long-term effects of MDMA on cerebral dopamine biochemistry and function. *Psychopharmacology, 173,* 249–263.

Colapinto, J. (2000). *As nature made him: The boy who was raised as a girl.* New York: HarperCollins.

Cole, G. G., Heywood, C., Kentridge, R., Fairholm, I., & Cowey, A. (2003). Attentional capture by colour and motion in cerebral achromatopsia. *Neuropsychologia, 41,* 1837–1846.

Cole, M. (1990). Cognitive development and formal schooling: The evidence from cross-cultural research. In L. C. Moll (Ed.), *Vygotsky and education* (pp. 89–110). New York: Cambridge University Press.

Cole, M. (1996). *Cultural psychology: A once and future discipline.* Cambridge, MA: Harvard University Press.

Cole, M., & Wertsch, J. V. (1996). Beyond the individual-social antinomy in discussions of Piaget and Vygotsky. *Human Development, 39,* 250–256.

Coleman, P., & Flood, D. (1986). Dendritic proliferation in the aging brain as a compensatory repair mechanism. *Progress in Brain Research, 70,* 227–236.

Collins, A. M., & Loftus, E. F. (1975). A spreading activation theory of semantic memory. *Psychological Review, 82,* 407–428.

Collins, M. A., & Zebrowitz, L. A. (1995). The contributions of appearance to occupational outcomes in civilian and military settings. *Journal of Applied Social Psychology, 25,* 129–163.

Collins, N. L. (1996). Working models of attachment: Implications for explanation, emotion, and behavior. *Journal of Personality & Social Psychology, 71,* 810–832.

Collins, N. L., & Feeney, B. C. (2004). Working models of attachment shape perceptions of social support: Evidence from experimental and observational studies. *Journal of Personality & Social Psychology, 87,* 363–383.

Collins, W. A. (1990). Parent-child relationships in the transition to adolescence: Continuity and change in interaction, affect, and cognition. In R. Montemayor, G. R. Adams, & T. P. Gullota (Eds.), *From childhood to adolescence: A transitional period?* (pp. 85–106). Newbury Park, CA: Sage.

Colmenero, J. M., Catena, A., Fuentes, L. J., & Ramos, M. M. (2004). Mechanisms of visuospatial orienting in deafness. *European Journal of Cognitive Psychology, 16,* 791–805.

Colom, F., Vieta, E., Martinez, A., Jorquera, A., & Gasto, C. (1998). What is the role of psychotherapy in the treatment of bipolar disorder? *Psychotherapy & Psychosomatics, 67,* 3–9.

Colom, R., Lluis-Font, J. M., & Andrés-Pueyo, A. (2005). The generational intelligence gains are caused by decreasing variance in the lower half of the distribution: Supporting evidence for the nutrition hypothesis. *Intelligence, 33*, 83–91.

Colom, R., Rebollo, I., Palacios, A., Juan-Espinosa, M., & Kyllonen, P. C. (2004). Working memory is (almost) perfectly predicted by g. *Intelligence, 32*, 277–296.

Colombo, J., & Richman, W. A. (2002). Infant timekeeping: Attention and temporal estimating in 4-month-olds. *Psychological Science, 13*, 475–479.

Colome, A. (2001). Lexical activation in bilinguals' speech production: Language-specific or language-independent? *Journal of Memory & Language, 45*, 721–736.

Comery, T. A., Shah, R., & Greenough, W. T. (1995). Differential rearing alters spine density on medium-sized spiny neurons in the rat corpus striatum: Evidence for association of morphological plasticity with early response gene expression. *Neurobiology of Learning & Memory, 63*, 217–219.

Comings, D. E., Muhleman, D., Johnson, J. P., & MacMurray, J. P. (2002). Parent-daughter transmission of the androgen receptor gene as an explanation of the effect of father absence on age of menarche. *Child Development, 73*, 1046–1051.

Compas, B. E., Haaga, D. A. F., Keefe, F. J., Leitenberg, H., & Williams, D. A. (1998). Sampling of empirically supported psychological treatments from health psychology, *Journal of Consulting and Clinical Psychology, 66*, 89–112.

Comstock, G., & Paik, H. (1991). *Television and the American child*. San Diego, CA: Academic Press.

Cone, E. J. (1995). Pharmacokinetics and pharmacodynamics of cocaine. *Journal of Analytical Toxicology, 19*, 459–477.

Congdon, N. G., Friedman, D. S., & Lietman, T. (2003). Important causes of visual impairment in the world today. *JAMA: Journal of the American Medical Association, 290*, 2057–2060.

Conger, R. D., Neppl, T., Kim, K. J., & Scaramella, L. (2003). Angry and aggressive behavior across three generations: A prospective, longitudinal study of parents and children. *Journal of Abnormal Child Psychology, 31*, 143–160.

Conn, J. H., & Conn, R. N. (1967). Discussion of T. X. Barber's "Hypnosis as a causal variable in present day psychology: A critical analysis." *International Journal of Clinical & Experimental Hypnosis, 15*, 106–110.

Connell, M. W., Sheridan, K., Gardner, H., & Sternberg, R. J. (Eds.). (2003). *The psychology of abilities, competencies, and expertise*. New York: Cambridge University Press.

Connellan, J., Baron-Cohen, S., Wheelwright, S., Batki, A., & Ahluwalia, J. (2000). Sex differences in human neonatal social perception. *Infant Behavior & Development, 23*, 113–118.

Connor, C. E. (2002). Reconstructing a 3D world. *Science, 298*, 376–377.

Consortium for Longitudinal Studies (Ed.). (1983). *As the twig is bent . . . Lasting effects of preschool programs*. Hillsdale, NJ: Erlbaum.

Conway, A. R. A., Cowan, N., & Bunting, M. F. (2001). The cocktail party phenomenon revisited: The importance of working memory capacity. *Psychonomic Bulletin & Review, 8*, 331–335.

Conway, A. R. A., Cowan, N., Bunting, M. F., Therriault, D. J., & Minkoff, S. R. B. (2002). A latent variable analysis of working memory capacity, short-term memory capacity, processing speed, and general fluid intelligence. *Intelligence, 30*, 163–183.

Conway, M. A., & Rubin, D. C. (1993). The structure of autobiographical memory. In A. F. Collins, S. E. Gathercole, M. A. Conway, & P. E. Morris (Eds.), *Theories of memory* (pp. 103–137). Hillsdale, NJ: Erlbaum.

Conyers, C., Miltenberger, R., Romaniuk, C., Kopp, B., & Himle, M. (2003). Evaluation of DRO schedules to reduce disruptive behavior in a preschool classroom. *Child & Family Behavior Therapy, 25*, 1–6.

Cook, E. W., III, Hawk, L. W., Davis, T. L., Stevenson, V. E. (1991). Affective individual differences and startle reflex modulation. *Journal of Abnormal Psychology, 100*, 5–13.

Coons, P. M., Milstein, V., & Marley, C. (1982). EEG studies of two multiple personalities and a control. *Archives of General Psychiatry, 39*, 823–825.

Cooper, J. (1998). Unlearning cognitive dissonance: Toward an understanding of the development of dissonance. *Journal of Experimental Social Psychology, 34*, 562–575.

Cooper, M. L., Shapiro, C. M., & Powers, A. M. (1998). Motivations for sex and risky sexual behavior among adolescents and young adults: A functional perspective. *Journal of Personality and Social Psychology, 75*, 1528–1558.

Cooper, M. L., Wood, P. K., Orcutt, H. K., & Albino, A. (2003). Personality and the predisposition to engage in risky or problem behaviors during adolescence. *Journal of Personality and Social Psychology, 84*, 390–410.

Cooper, R. P., Abraham, J., Berman, S., & Staska, M. (1997). The development of infants' preference for motherese. *Infant Behavior & Development, 20*, 477–488.

Coplan, J. D., Goetz, R., Klein, D. F., Papp, L. A., Fyer, A. J., Liebowitz, M. R., et al. (1998). Plasma cortisol concentrations preceding lactate-induced panic: Psychological, biochemical, and physiological correlates. *Archives of General Psychiatry, 55*, 130–136.

Corbetta, M., & Shulman, G. L. (2002). Control of goal-directed and stimulus-driven attention in the brain. *Nature Reviews Neuroscience, 3*, 201–215.

Coren, S. (1996). *Sleep thieves: An eye-opening exploration into the science and mysteries of sleep*. New York: Free Press.

Corkin, S. (2002). What's new with the amnestic patient H. M.? *Nature Reviews Neuroscience, 3*, 153–160.

Cornblatt, B., & Obuchowski, M. (1997). Update of high-risk research: 1987–1997. *International Review of Psychiatry, 9*, 437–447.

Cornblatt, B., Obuchowski, M., Schnur, D. B., & O'Brien, J. (1997). Attention and clinical symptoms in schizophrenia. *Psychiatric Quarterly, 68*, 343–359.

Cornelius, M. D., & Day, N. L. (2000). The effects of tobacco use during and after pregnancy on exposed children. *Alcohol Research & Health, 24*, 242–249.

Corr, P. J., & Kumari, V. (1997). Sociability/impulsivity and attenuated-dopaminergic arousal: Critical flicker/fusion frequency and procedural learning. *Personality and Individual Differences, 22*, 805–815.

Corr, P. J., Pickering, A. D., & Gray, J. A. (1995). Sociability/impulsivity and caffeine-induced arousal: Critical flicker/fusion frequency and procedural learning. *Personality and Individual Differences, 18*, 713–730.

Correll, J., Park, B., Judd, C. M., & Wittenbrink, B. (2002). The police officer's dilemma: Using ethnicity to disambiguate potentially threatening individuals. *Journal of Personality & Social Psychology, 83*, 1314–1329

Cosmides, L., & Tooby, J. (1996). Are humans good intuitive statisticians after all? Rethinking some conclusions from the literature on judgment under uncertainty. *Cognition, 58*, 1–73.

Costa, P. T., Jr., Herbst, J. H., McCrae, R. R., & Siegler, I. C. (2000). Personality at midlife: Stability, intrinsic maturation, and response to life events. *Assessment, 7*, 365–378.

Costa, P. T., & McCrae, R. R. (1988). Personality in adulthood: A six-year longitudinal study of self-reports and spouse ratings on the NEO personality inventory. *Journal of Personality and Social Psychology, 54*, 853–863.

Costa, P. T., & McCrae, R. R. (1995). Primary traits of Eysenck's P-E-N System: Three- and five-factor solutions. *Journal of Personality and Social Psychology, 69*, 308–317.

Costa, P. T., Jr., & McCrae, R. R. (1997). Longitudinal stability of adult personality. In R. Hogan, J. A. Johnson, & S. R. Briggs (Eds.), *Handbook of personality psychology* (pp. 269–290). San Diego: Academic Press.

Costa, P. T., McCrae, R. R., & Dye, D. A. (1991). Facet scales for agreeableness and conscientiousness: A revision of the NEO Personality Inventory. *Personality and Individual Differences, 12*, 887–898.

Costa, P. T., Terracciano, A., & McCrae, R. R. (2001). Gender differences in personality traits across cultures: Robust and surprising findings. *Journal of Personality and Social Psychology, 81*, 322–331.

Costela, C., Tejedor-Real, P., Mico, J. A., & Gilbert-Rahola, J. (1995). Effect of neonatal handling on learned helplessness model of depression. *Physiology and Behavior, 57*, 407–410.

Cotman, C. (1990). The brain: New plasticity/new possibility. In R. N. Butler, M. R. Oberlink, & M. Schechter (Eds.), *The promise of productive aging: From biology to social policy* (pp. 70–84). New York: Springer.

Cotman, C. W., & Berchtold, N. C. (2002). Exercise: A behavioral intervention to enhance brain health and plasticity. *Trends in Neurosciences, 25*, 295–301.

Cotter, D. R., Pariante, C. M., &Everall, I. P. (2001). Glial cell abnormalities in major psychiatric disorders: The evidence and implications. *Brain Research Bulletin, 55*, 585–595.

Council, J. R., Kirsch, I., & Grant, D. L. (1996). Imagination, expectancy and hypnotic responding. In R. G. Kunzendorf, N. P. Spanos, & B. J. Wallace (Eds.), *Hypnosis and imagination* (pp. 41–65). Amityville, NY: Baywood.

Counts, D. A., & Counts, D. R. (1992). "I'm not dead yet!" Aging and death: Process and experience in Kaliai. In L. A. Platt & V. R. Persico, Jr. (Eds.), *Grief in cross-cultural perspective: A casebook* (pp. 307–343). New York: Garland.

Coupland, N. J. (2001). Social phobia: Etiology, neurobiology, and treatment. *Journal of Clinical Psychiatry, 62*, 25–35.

Coupland, N. J., Singh, A. J.. Sustrik, R. A., Ting, P., & Blair, R. J. (2003). Effects of diazepam on facial emotion recognition. *Journal of Psychiatry & Neuroscience, 28*, 452–463.

Cowan, N. (2001). The magical number 4 in short-term memory: A reconsideration of mental storage capacity. *Behavioral and Brain Sciences, 24*, 87–114.

Cowan, W. M., Fawcett, J. W., O'Leary, D. D. M., & Stanfield, B. B. (1984). Regressive events in neurogenesis. *Science, 225*, 1258–1265.

Cowey, A., & Stoerig, P. (1995). Blindsight in monkeys. *Nature, 373,* 247–249.

Coyne, J. C., & Downey, G. (1991). Social factors in psychopathology: Stress, social support, and coping processes. *Annual Review of Psychology, 42,* 401–425.

Coyne, J. C., Kessler, R. C., Tal, M., Turnbull, J., Wortman, C., & Greden, J. (1987). Living with a depressed person: Burden and psychological distress. *Journal of Clinical and Consulting Psychology, 55,* 347–352.

Crago, M., & Crago, H. (1983). *Prelude to literacy.* Carbondale: Southern Illinois University Press.

Craik, F., & Bialystok, E. (2005). Intelligence and executive control: Evidence from aging and bilingualism. *Cortex, 41,* 222–224.

Craik, F. I., & McDowd, J. M. (1987). Age differences in recall and recognition. *Journal of Experimental Psychology: Learning, Memory, & Cognition, 13,* 474–479.

Craik, F. I. M., Anderson, N. D., Kerr, S. A., & Li, K. Z. H. (1995). Memory changes in normal aging. In A. D. Baddeley, B. A. Wilson, & F. N. Watts (Eds.), *Handbook of memory disorders* (pp. 211–241). New York: Wiley.

Craik, F. I. M., & Lockhart, R. S. (1972). Levels of processing: A framework for memory research. *Journal of Verbal Learning and Verbal Behavior, 11,* 671–684.

Craik, F. I. M., & Tulving, E. (1975). Depth of processing and the retention of words in episodic memory. *Journal of Experimental Psychology: General, 104,* 268–294.

Cramer, R. E., Abraham, W. T., Johnson, L. M., & Manning-Ryan, B. (2001–2002). Gender differences in subjective distress to emotional and sexual infidelity: Evolutionary or logical inference explanation? *Current Psychology: Developmental, Learning, Personality, Social, 20,* 327–336.

Cramer, R. E., Schaefer, J. T., & Reid, S. (1996). Identifying the ideal mate: More evidence for male–female convergence. *Current Psychology: Developmental, Learning, Personality, Social, 16,* 157–166.

Crawford, H. J. (1994). Brain dynamics and hypnosis: Attentional and disattentional processes. *International Journal of Clinical and Experimental Hypnosis 42,* 204–232.

Crawford, H. J., Gur, R. C., Skolnick, B., Gur, R. E., & Benson, D. (1993). Effects of hypnosis on regional cerebral blood flow during ischemic pain with and without suggested hypnotic analgesia. *International Journal of Psychophysiology, 15,* 181–195.

Crawford, M., Stark, A. C., & Renner, C. H. (1998). The meaning of Ms.: Social assimilation of a gender concept. *Psychology of Women Quarterly, 22,* 197–208.

Crawford, R. P. (1954). *The technique of creative thinking: How to use your ideas to achieve success.* New York: Hawthorn Books.

Crawford Solberg, E., Diener, E., Wirtz, D., Lucas, R. E., & Oishi, S. (2002). Wanting, having, and satisfaction: Examining the role of desire discrepancies in satisfaction with income. *Journal of Personality & Social Psychology, 83,* 725–734.

Crick, F. (1994). *The astonishing hypothesis: The scientific search for the soul.* New York: Scribners.

Crick, F., & Koch, C. (1995). Are we aware of neural activity in primary visual cortex? *Nature, 375,* 121–123.

Crick, F., & Koch, C. (1998). Consciousness and neuroscience. *Cerebral Cortex, 8,* 97–107.

Crick, F., & Mitchison, F. (1983). The function of dream sleep. *Nature, 304,* 111–114.

Crick, F., & Mitchison, G. (1986). REM sleep and neural nets. *Journal of Mind and Behavior, 7,* 229–250.

Crick, N. R., & Grotpeter, J. K. (1995). Relational aggression, gender, and social-psychological adjustment. *Child Development, 66,* 710–722.

Crisp, A. H., Hsu, L. K., & Harding, B. (1980). The starving hoarder and voracious spender: Stealing in anorexia nervosa. *Journal of Psychosomatic Research, 24,* 225–231.

Crist, R. E., Li, Wu, & Gilbert, C. D. (2001). Learning to see: Experience and attention in primary visual cortex. *Nature Neuroscience, 4,* 519–525.

Crits-Christoph, P. (1992). The efficacy of brief dynamic psychotherapy: A meta-analysis. *American Journal of Psychiatry, 149,* 151–158.

Croen, L. A., Grether, J. K., Hoogstrate, J., & Selving, S. (2002). The changing prevalence of autism in California. *Journal of Autism & Developmental Disorders, 32,* 207–215.

Croizet, J., Després, G., Gauzins, M., Huguet, P., Leyens, J., & Méot, A. (2004). Stereotype threat undermines intellectual performance by triggering a disruptive mental load. *Personality & Social Psychology Bulletin, 30,* 721–731.

Croizet, J.-C., & Claire, T. (1998) Extending the concept of stereotype and threat to social class: The intellectual underperformance of students from low socio-econimic backgrounds. *Personality & Social Psychology Bulletin, 24,* 588–594.

Cronbach, L. J. (1990). *Essentials of psychology testing* (5th ed.). New York: HarperCollins.

Crowe, R., Noyes, R., Pauls, D., & Slyman, D. (1983). A family study of panic disorder. *Archives of General Psychiatry, 40,* 1065–1069.

Crowley, K., Shrager, J., & Siegler, R. S. (1997). Strategy discovery as a competitive negotiation between metacognitive and associative mechanisms. *Developmental Review, 17,* 462–489.

Crowley, K., & Siegler, R. S. (1999). Explanation and generalization in young children's strategy learning. *Child Development, 70(2),* 304–316.

Crowley, S. J., Lee, C., Tseng, C. Y., Fogg, L. F., & Eastman, C. I. (2003). Combinations of bright light, scheduled dark, sunglasses, and melatonin to facilitate circadian entrainment to night shift work. *Journal of Biological Rhythms, 18,* 513–523.

Crowther, J. H., Kichler, J. C., Shewood, N. E., & Kuhnert, M. E. (2002). The role of familial factors in bulimia nervosa. *Eating Disorders: The Journal of Treatment & Prevention, 10,* 141–151.

Cruz, A., & Green, B. G. (2000). Thermal stimulation of taste. *Nature, 403,* 889–892.

Cruz, C., Detwiler, C., Nesthus, T., & Boquet, A. (2003). Clockwise and counter-clockwise rotating shifts: Effects on sleep duration, timing, and quality. *Aviation, Space, & Environmental Medicine, 74,* 597–605.

Csikszentmihalyi, M., & Csikszentmihalyi, I. S. (Eds.). (1988). *Optimal experience: Psychological studies of flow in consciousness.* New York: Cambridge University Press.

Cuijpers, P. (1997). Bibliotherapy in unipolar depression: A meta-analysis. *Journal of Behavior Therapy & Experimental Psychiatry, 28,* 139–147.

Culbertson, F. M. (1997). Depression and gender: An international review. *American Psychologist, 52,* 25–31.

Cullen, M. J., Hardison, C. M., & Sackett, P. R. (2004). Using SAT–grade and ability–job performance relationships to test predictions derived from stereotype threat theory. *Journal of Applied Psychology, 89,* 220–230.

Cummings, N. (1992). Self-defense training for college women. *Journal of American College Health, 40,* 183–188.

Cunningham, W. A., Johnson, M. K., Raye, C. L., Gatenby, J. C., Gore, J. C., & Banaji, M. R. (2004). Separable neural components in the processing of Black and White faces. *Psychological Science, 15,* 806–813.

Cupach, W. P., & Spitzberg, B. H. (1994). *The dark side of interpersonal communication.* Hillsdale, NJ: Erlbaum.

Cupchik, G. C., Phillips, K., & Hill, D. S. (2001). Shared processes in spatial rotation and musical permutation. *Brain & Cognition, 46,* 373–382.

Curtiss, S. (1977). *Genie: A psycholinguistic study of a modern-day "wild child."* New York: Academic Press.

Curtiss, S. (1989). The independence and task-specificity of language. In M. H. Bornstein & J. S. Bruner (Eds.), *Interaction in human development* (pp. 105–137). Hillsdale, NJ: Erlbaum.

Curtius, M. (1996, July 3). Man won't be retried in repressed memory case murder: Prosecutor says there is not enough evidence to re-convict him of crime daughter recalled years later. *Los Angeles Times,* pg. 1.

Czeisler, C. A., Duffy, J. F., Shanahan, T. L., Brown, E. N., Mitchell, J. F., Rimmer, D. W., et al. (1999). Stability, precision, and near-24-hour period of the human circadian pacemaker. *Science, 284,* 2101–2103.

Dabbs, J. M., Jr., Riad, J. K., & Chance, S. E. (2001). Testosterone and ruthless homicide. *Personality & Individual Differences, 31,* 599–603.

Dabbs, J. M., Jr., Strong, R., & Milun, R. (1997). Exploring the mind of testosterone: A beeper study. *Journal of Research in Personality, 31,* 577–587.

Dackis, C. A., & O'Brien, C. P. (2001). Cocaine dependence: A disease of the brain's reward centers. *Journal of Substance Abuse Treatment, 21,* 111–117.

Dadds, M. R., Bovberg, D. H., Redd, W. H., & Cutmore, T. R. H. (1997). Imagery in human classical conditioning. *Psychological Bulletin, 122,* 89–103.

Dafters, R. I., Hoshi, R., & Talbot, A. C. (2004). Contribution of cannabis and MDMA ("ecstasy") to cognitive changes in long-term polydrug users. *Psychopharmacology, 173,* 405–410.

Dahloef, P., Norlin-Bagge, E., Hedner, J., Ejnell, H., Hetta, J., & Haellstroem, T. (2002). Improvement in neuropsychological performance following surgical treatment for obstructive sleep apnea syndrome. *Acta Oto-Laryngologica, 122,* 86–91.

Dai, X. Y., & Lynn, R. (1994). Gender differences in intelligence among Chinese children. *The Journal of Social Psychology, 134,* 123–125.

Dalbert, C., & Yamauchi, L. (1994). Belief in a just world and attitudes toward immigrants and foreign workers: A cultural comparison between Hawaii and Germany. *Journal of Applied Social Psychology, 24,* 1612–1626.

Damasio, A. R. (1994). *Descartes' error: Emotion, reason, and the human brain.* New York: Grosset/Putnam.

Damasio, A. R. (1996). The somatic marker hypothesis and the possible functions of the prefrontal cortex. *Philosophical Transactions of the Royal Society London Series B, 351,* 1413–1420.

Damasio, H., Grabowski, T. J., Tranel, D., Hichwa, R. D., & Damasio, A. R. (1996). A neural basis for lexical retrieval. *Nature, 380,* 499–505.

D'Angelo, B., & Wierzbicki, M. (2003). Relations of daily hassles with both anxious and depressed mood in students. *Psychological Reports, 92,* 416–418.

Dannon, P. N., Dolberg, O. T., Schreiber, S., & Grunhaus, L. (2002). Three and six-month outcome following courses of either ECT or rTMS in a population of severely depressed individuals—Preliminary report. *Biological Psychiatry, 51,* 687–690.

Dannon, P. N., Lowengrub, K., Amiaz, R., Grunhaus, L., & Kotler, M. (2004). Comorbid cannabis use and panic disorder: Short term and long term follow-up study. *Human Psychopharmacology, 19*(2), 97–101.

Dansinger, M. L., Gleason, J. A., Griffith, J. L., Selker, H. P., & Schaefer, E. J. (2005). Comparison of the Atkins, Ornish, Weight Watchers, and Zone diets for weight loss and heart disease risk reduction: A randomized trial. *Journal of the American Medical Association, 293,* 43–53.

Dar, Y., & Kimhi, S. (2001). Military service and self-perceived maturation among Israeli youth. *Journal of Youth & Adolescence, 30,* 427–448.

D'Arcy, R. C. N., Connolly, J. F., Service, E., Hawco, C. S., & Houlihan, M. E. (2004). Separating phonological and semantic processing in auditory sentence processing: A high-resolution event-related brain potential study. *Human Brain Mapping, 22,* 40–51.

Darley, J. M., & Gross, P. H. (1983). A hypothesis-confirming bias in labeling effects. *Journal of Personality & Social Psychology, 44,* 20–33.

Darley, J. M., & Latané, B. (1968). Bystander intervention in emergencies: Diffusion of responsibility. *Journal of Personality and Social Psychology, 10,* 202–214.

Darley, J. M., & Latané, B. (1970). Norms and normative behavior: Field studies of social interdependence. In J. Macauley & L. Berkowitz (Eds.), *Altruism and helping behavior* (pp. 83–101). New York: Academic Press.

Das, A., & Gilbert, C. D. (1995). Long-range horizontal connections and their role in cortical reorganization revealed by optical recording of cat primary visual cortex. *Nature, 375,* 780–784.

Daumann, J., Hensen, G., Thimm, B., Rezk, M., Till, B., & Gouzoulis-Mayfrank, E. (2004). Self-reported psychopathological symptoms in recreational ecstasy (MDMA) users are mainly associated with regular cannabis use: Further evidence from a combined cross-sectional/longitudinal investigation. *Psychopharmacology, 173,* 398–404.

Dauncey, K., Giggs, J., Baker, K., & Harrison, K. (1993). Schizophrenia in Nottingham: Lifelong residential mobility of a cohort. *British Journal of Psychiatry, 163,* 613–619.

Davelaar, E. J., Goshen-Gottstein, Y., Ashkenazi, A., Haarmann, H. J., & Usher, M. (2005). The demise of short-term memory revisited: Empirical and computational investigations of recency effects. *Psychological Review, 112,* 3–42.

Davey, G. C. L. (1992). Classical conditioning and the acquisition of human fears and phobias: A review of synthesis of the literature. *Advances in Behavior Research and Therapy, 14,* 29–66.

David, J. P., & Suls, J. (1999). Coping efforts in daily life: Role of Big Five traits and problem appraisals. *Journal of Personality, 67,* 265–294.

Davidson, J. R. T., Foa, E. B., Huppert, J. D., Keefe, F. J., Franklin, M. E., Compton, J. S., Zhao, N., Connor, K. M., Lynch, T. R., & Gadde, K. M. (2004). Fluoxetine, comprehensive cognitive behavioral therapy, and placebo in generalized social phobia. *Archives of General Psychiatry, 61,* 1005–1013.

Davidson, R. J. (1992a). Emotion and affective style: Hemispheric substrates. *Psychological Science, 3,* 39–43.

Davidson, R. J. (1992b). A prolegomenon to the structure of emotion: Gleanings from neuropsychology. *Cognition and Emotion, 6,* 245–268.

Davidson, R. J. (1993). Parsing affective space: Perspectives from neuropsychology and psychophysiology. *Neuropsychology, 7,* 464–475.

Davidson, R. J. (1994a). Honoring biology in the study of affective style. In P. Ekman & R. J. Davidson (Eds.), *The nature of emotion: Fundamental questions* (pp. 321–328). New York: Oxford University Press.

Davidson, R. J. (1998). Affective style and affective disorders: Perspectives from affective neuroscience. *Cognition and Emotion, 12,* 307–330.

Davidson, R. J. (2001). Toward a biology of personality and emotion. *Annals of the New York Academy of Sciences, 935,* 191–207.

Davidson, R. J. (2002). Anxiety and affective style: Role of prefrontal cortex and amygdala. *Biological Psychiatry, 51,* 68–80.

Davidson, R. J. (2004). What does the prefrontal cortex "do" in affect: Perspectives on frontal EEG asymmetry research. *Biological Psychology, 67,* 219–233.

Davidson, R. J., Abercrombie, H., Nitschke, J. B., & Putnam, K. (1999). Regional brain function, emotion and disorders of emotion. *Current Opinion in Neurobiology, 9,* 228–234.

Davidson, R. J., Jackson, D. C., & Kalin, N. H. (2000a). Emotion, plasticity, context, and regulation: Perspectives from affective neuroscience. *Psychological Bulletin, 126,* 890–909.

Davidson, R. J., Kabat-Zinn, J., Schumacher, J., Rosenkranz, M., Muller, D., Santorelli, S. F., Urbanowski, F., Harrington, A., Bonus, K., & Sheridan, J. F. (2003). Alterations in brain and immune function produced by mindfulness meditation. *Psychosomatic Medicine, 65,* 564–570.

Davidson, R. J., Pizzagalli, D., Nitschke, J. B., & Putnam, K. M. (2002). Depression: Perspectives from affective neuroscience. *Annual Review of Psychology, 53,* 545–574.

Davidson, R. J., Putnam, K. M., & Larson, C. L. (2000b). Dysfunction in the neural circuitry of emotion regulation—A possible prelude to violence. *Science, 289,* 591–594.

Davies, P. G., Spencer, S. J., & Steele, C. M. (2005). Clearing the air: Identity safety moderates the effects of stereotype threat on women's leadership aspirations. *Journal of Personality & Social Psychology, 88,* 276–287.

Davis, B. E., Moon, R. Y., Sachs, H. C., & Ottolini, M. C. (1998). Effects of sleep position on infant motor development. *Pediatrics, 102,* 1135–1140.

Davis, C., Ralevski, E., Kennedy, S. H., & Neitzert, C. S. (1995). The role of personality factors in the reporting of side effect complaints to moclobemide and placebo. *Journal of Clinical Psychopharmacology, 15,* 347–352.

Davis, D., Shaver, P. R., & Vernon, M. L. (2003). Physical, emotional, and behavioral reactions to breaking up: The roles of gender, age, emotional involvement, and attachment style. *Personality & Social Psychology Bulletin, 29,* 871–884.

Davis, G. A. (1973). *Psychology of problem solving. Theory and practice.* New York: Basic Books.

Davis, J. D., & Campbell, C. S. (1973). Peripheral control of meal size in the rat: Effects of sham feeding on meal size and drinking rate. *Journal of Comparative & Physiological Psychology, 83,* 379–387.

Davis, J. D., & Levine, M. W. (1977). A model for the control of ingestion. *Psychological Review, 84,* 379–412.

Davis, K. D., Kiss, Z. H., Luo, L., Tasker, R. R., Lozano, A. M., & Dostrovsky, J. O. (1998). Phantom sensations generated by thalamic microstimulation. *Nature, 391,* 385–387.

Davis, M. (1992). The role of the amygdala in conditioned fear. In J. P. Aggleton (Ed.), *The amygdala: Neurobiological aspects of emotion, memory, and mental dysfunction* (pp. 255– 306). New York: Wiley-Liss.

Davis, M., & Whalen, P. J. (2001). The amygdala: Vigilance and emotion. *Molecular Psychiatry, 6,* 13–34.

Davis, M. C., Matthews, K. A., & McGrath, C. E. (2000). Hostile attitudes predict elevated vascular resistance during interpersonal stress in men and women. *Psychosomatic Medicine, 62,* 17–25.

Dawda, D., & Hart, S. D. (2000). Assessing emotional intelligence: Reliability and validity of the Bar-On Emotional Quotient Inventory (EQ-i) in university students. *Personality and Individual Differences, 28,* 797–812.

Deary, I. J. (1995). Auditory inspection time and intelligence: What is the direction of causation? *Developmental Psychology, 31,* 237–250.

Deary, I. J. (2000). *Looking down on human intelligence: From psychometrics to the brain.* Oxford, UK: Oxford University Press.

Deary, I. J., Hamilton, G., Hayward, C., Whalley, L. J., Powell, J., Starr, J. M., & Lovestone, S. (2005). Nicastrin gene polymorphisms, cognitive ability level and cognitive ageing. *Neuroscience Letters, 373,* 110–114.

Deary, I. J., & Pagliari, C. (1991). The strength of g at different levels of ability: Have Detterman & Daniel rediscovered Spearman's "law of diminishing returns"? *Intelligence 15,* 247–250.

Deary, I. J., Whiteman, M. C., Starr, J. M., Whalley, L. J., & Fox, H. C. (2004). The impact of childhood intelligence on later life: Following up the Scottish mental surveys of 1932 and 1947. *Journal of Personality & Social Psychology, 86,* 130–147.

De Benedittis, G. (2003). Understanding the multidimensional mechanisms of hypnotic analgesia. *Contemporary Hypnosis, 20,* 59–80.

De Beni, R., & Palladino, P. (2004). Decline in working memory updating through ageing: Intrusion error analyses. *Memory, 12,* 75–89.

DeBlack, S. S. (2003). Cigarette smoking as a risk factor for cataract and age-related macular degeneration: A review of the literature. *Optometry: Journal of the American Optometric Association, 74,* 99–110.

DeCasper, A. J., & Fifer, W. P. (1980). On human bonding: Newborns prefer their mothers' voices. *Science, 208,* 1174–1176.

De Castro, J. M. (1990). Social facilitation of duration and size but not rate of the spontaneous meal intake of humans. *Physiology & Behavior, 47,* 1129–1135.

Decety, J., & Jackson, P. L. (2004). The functional architecture of human empathy. *Behavioral and Cognitive Neuroscience Reviews, 3*, 406–412.

Deci, E. L., Koestner, R., & Ryan, R. M. (1999). The undermining effect is a reality after all—Extrinsic rewards, task interest, and self-determination: Reply to Eisenberger, Pierce, and Cameron (1999) and Lepper, Henderlong, and Gingras (1999). *Psychological Bulletin, 125*, 692–700.

DeClue, G. (2003). The polygraph and lie detection. *Journal of Psychiatry and Law, 31*, 361–368.

Deese, J. (1959). On the prediction of occurrence of particular verbal intrusions in immediate recall. *Journal of Experimental Psychology, 58*, 17–22.

Deffenbacher, J. L., Oetting, E. R., Huff, M. E., Cornell, G. R., & Dalleger, C. J. (1996). Evaluation of two cognitive-behavioral approaches to general anger reduction. *Cognitive Therapy & Research, 20*, 551–573.

DeGroot, A. D. (1965). *Thought and choice in chess.* The Hague: Mouton.

DeGroot, A. D. (1966). Perception and memory versus thought. In B. Kleinmuntz (Ed.), *Problem solving* (pp. 19–50). New York: Wiley.

de Haan, M., Pascalis, O., & Johnson, M. H. (2002). Specialization of neural mechanisms underlying face recognition in human infants. *Journal of Cognitive Neuroscience, 14*, 199–209.

Dehaene, S. (1997). *The number sense: How the mind creates mathematics.* New York: Oxford University Press.

Dehaene, S., Spelke, E., Pinel, P., Stanescu, R., & Tsivkin, S. (1999). Sources of mathematical thinking: Behavioral and brain-imaging evidence. *Science, 284*, 970–974.

Dehaene-Lambertz, G., & Dehaene, S. (1994). Speed and cerebral correlates of syllable discrimination in infants. *Nature, 370*, 292–295.

Dehaene-Lambertz, G., & Pena, M. (2001). Electrophysiological evidence for automatic phonetic processing in neonates. *Neuroreport, 12*, 3155–3158.

De Houwer, J., Thomas, S., & Baeyens, F. (2001). Associative learning of likes and dislikes: A review of 25 years of research on human evaluative conditioning. *Psychological Bulletin, 127*, 853–869.

de la Chica, R. A., Ribas, I., Giraldo, J., Egozcue, J., & Fuster, C. (2005). Chromosomal instability in amniocytes from fetuses of mothers who smoke. *JAMA: Journal of the American Medical Association, 293*, 1212–1222.

Delany, S. L., Delany, A. E., & Hearth, A. H. (1993). *Having our say: The Delany sisters' first 100 years.* New York: Delta.

Delk, J. L., & Fillenbaum, S., (1965). Difference in perceived color as a function of characteristic color. *American Journal of Psychology, 78*, 290–293.

Dell, P. F. (1998). Axis II pathology in outpatients with dissociative identity disorder. *Journal of Nervous & Mental Disease, 186*, 352–356.

DeLoache, J. S., Pierroutsakos, S. L., Uttal, D. H., Rosengren, K. S., & Gottlieb, A. (1998). Grasping the nature of pictures. *Psychological Science, 9*, 205–210.

DeLongis, A., Coyne, J. C., Dakof, G., Folkman, S., & Lazrus, R. S. (1982). Relationship of daily hassles, uplifts, and major life events to health status. *Health Psychology, 1*, 119–136.

DeMann, J. A. (1994). First person account: The evolution of a person with schizophrenia. *Schizophrenia Bulletin, 20*, 579–582.

Demarais, A. M., & Cohen, B. H. (1998). Evidence for image–scanning eye movement during transitive inference. *Biological Psychology, 49*, 229–247.

De Marchi, N., & Mennella, R. (2000). Huntington's disease and its association with psychopathology. *Harvard Review of Psychiatry, 7*, 278–89.

Dement, W. C. (1974). *Some must watch while some must sleep.* San Francisco: W. H. Freeman.

Dement, W. C., & Vaughan, C. (1999). *The promise of sleep: A pioneer in sleep medicine explores the vital connection between health, happiness, and a good night's sleep.* New York: Dell.

Demetriou, A., Christou, C., Spanoudis, G., & Platsidou, M. (2002). The development of mental processing: Efficiency, working memory, and thinking. *Monographs of the Society for Research in Child Development, 67*, vii-154.

Denis, M., & Kosslyn, S. M. (1999). Scanning visual images: A window on the mind. *Current Psychology of Cognition, 18*, 409–465.

Dennett, D. C. (1991). *Consciousness explained.* Boston: Little, Brown.

Dennis, W. (1966). Goodenough scores, art experience, and modernization. *Journal of Social Psychology, 68*, 211–228.

DePaulo, B. M., Charlton, K., Cooper, H., Lindsay, J. J., & Muhlenbruck, L. (1997). The accuracy-confidence correlation in the detection of deception. *Personality & Social Psychology Review, 1*, 346–357.

DePaulo, B. M., Lindsay, J. J., Malone, B. E., Muhlenbruck, L., Charlton, K., & Cooper, H. (2003). Cues to deception. *Psychological Bulletin, 129*, 74–118.

DePaulo, B. M., Stone, J. I., & Lassiter, G. D. (1985). Telling ingratiating lies: Effects of target sex and target attractiveness on verbal and nonverbal deceptive success. *Journal of Personality & Social Psychology, 48*, 1191–1203.

De Renzi, E. (1982). *Disorders of space exploration and cognition.* New York: Wiley.

De Renzi, E., Liotti, M., & Nichelli, P. (1987). Semantic amnesia with preservation of autobiographic memory. A case report. *Cortex, 23*, 575–597.

Derryberry, D., & Reed, M. A. (1994). Temperament and the self-organization of personality. *Development & Psychopathology, 6*, 653–676.

Derryberry, D., & Rothbart, M. K. (1997). Reactive and effortful processes in the organization of temperament. *Development & Psychopathology, 9*, 633–652.

DeRubeis, R. J., Hollon, S. D., Amsterdam, J. D., Shelton, R. C., Young, P. R., Salomon, R. M., O'Reardon, J. P., Lovett, M. L., Gladis, M. M. Brown, L. L., & Gallop, R. (2005). Cognitive therapy vs. medications in the treatment of moderate to severe depression. *Archives of General Psychiatry, 62*, 409–416.

D'Esposito, M., Detre, J. A., Alsop, D. C., Shin, R. K., Atlas, S., & Grossman, M. (1995). The neural basis of the central executive system of working memory. *Nature, 378*, 279–281.

DeSteno, D., Dasgupta, N., Bartlett, M. Y., Cajdric, A. (2004). Prejudice from thin air: The effect of emotion on automatic intergroup attitudes. *Psychological Science, 15*, 319–324.

DeSteno, D. A., & Salovey, P. (1996). Evolutionary origins of sex differences in jealousy? Questioning the "fitness" of the model. *Psychological Science, 7*, 367–372.

Detterman, D. K., & Daniel, M. H. (1989). Correlates of mental tests with each other and with cognitive variables are highest for low IQ groups. *Intelligence, 13*, 349–359.

Deutsch, J. A., Young, W. G., & Kalogeris, T. J. (1978). The stomach signals satiety. *Science, 201*, 165–167.

De Valois, R. L., & De Valois, K. K. (1975). Neural coding of color. In E. C. Carterette & M. P. Friedman (Eds.), *Handbook of perception* (pp. 117–166). New York: Academic Press.

De Valois, R. L., & De Valois, K. K. (1993). A multi-stage color model. *Vision Research, 33*, 1053–1065.

de Villiers, P. A., & de Villiers, J. G. (1992). Language development. In M. H. Bornstein & M. E. Lamb (Eds.), *Developmental psychology: An advanced textbook* (3rd ed., pp. 337–418). Hillsdale, NJ: Erlbaum.

Devine, P. G., & Elliot, A. J. (1995). Are racial stereotypes really fading? The Princeton trilogy revisted. *Personality & Social Psychology Bulletin, 21*, 1139–1150.

Devine, P. G., & Monteith, M. J. (1993). The role of discrepancy-associated affect in prejudice reduction. In D. M. Mackie & D. L. Hamilton, et al. (Eds.), *Affect, cognition, and stereotyping: Interactive processes in group perception* (pp. 317–344). San Diego, CA: Academic Press.

Devine, P. G., Plant, E. A., Amodio, D. M., Harmon-Jones, E., & Vance, S. L. (2002). The regulation of explicit and implicit race bias: The role of motivations to respond without prejudice. *Journal of Personality & Social Psychology, 82*, 835–848.

Devlin, B., Daniels, M., & Roeder, K. (1997). The heritability of IQ. *Nature, 388*, 468–471.

Devlin, J. T., Matthews, P. M., & Rushworth, M. F. S. (2003). Semantic processing in the left inferior prefrontal cortex: A combined functional magnetic resonance imaging and transcranial magnetic stimulation study. *Journal of Cognitive Neuroscience, 15*, 71–84.

de Vries, B., Davis, C. G., Wortman, C. B., & Lehman, D. R. (1997). Long-term psychological and somatic consequences of later life parental bereavement. *Omega: Journal of Death & Dying, 35*, 97–117.

Dew, A. M., & Ward, C. (1993). The effects of ethnicity and culturally congruent and incongruent nonverbal behaviors on interpersonal attraction. *Journal of Applied Social Psychology, 23*, 1376–1389.

Dewhurst, S. A., & Conway, M. A. (1994). Pictures, images, and recollective experience. *Journal of Experimental Psychology: Learning, Memory, and Cognition, 20*, 1088–1098.

de Wijk, R. A., & Cain, W. S. (1994). Odor identification by name and by edibility: Life-span development and safety. *Human Factors, 36*, 182–187.

de Wijk, R. A., Schab, F. R., & Cain, W. S. (1995). Odor identification. In F. R. Schab & R. G. Crowder (Eds.), *Memory for odors* (pp. 21–37). Mahwah, NJ: Erlbaum.

Dhume, V. G., Agshikar, N. V., & Diniz, R. S. (1975). Placebo-induced side effects in healthy volunteers. *Clinician, 39*, 289–290.

Diamond, L. M., & Dube, E. M. (2002). Friendship and attachment among heterosexual and sexual-minority youths: Does the gender of your friend matter? *Journal of Youth & Adolescence, 31*, 155–166.

Diamond, M., & Sigmundson H. K. (1997). Sex reassignment at birth. Long-term review and clinical implications. *Archives of Pediatrics & Adolescent Medicine, 151*, 298–304.

Diamond, M. C., Rosenzweig, M. R., Bennett, E. L., Lindner, B., & Lyon, L. (1972). Effects of environmental enrichment and impoverishment on rat cerebral cortex. *Journal of Neural Biology, 3*, 47–64.

Diaz-Guerrero, R., & Diaz-Loving, R. (2000). Needs and values in three cultures: Controversy and a dilemma. *Interdisciplinaria, 17*, 137–151.

DiBlasio, F. A., & Benda, B. B. (1990). Adolescent sexual behavior: Multivariate analysis of a social learning model. *Journal of Adolescent Research, 5*, 449–466.

Dick, F., Bates, E., Wulfeck, B., Utman, J. A., Dronkers, N., & Gernsbacher, M. A. (2001). Language deficits, localization, and grammar: Evidence for a distributive model of language breakdown in aphasic patients and neurologically intact individuals. *Psychological Review, 108*, 759–788.

Dickens, W. T., & Flynn, J. R. (2001). Heritability estimates versus large environmental effects: The IQ paradox resolved. *Psychological Review, 108*, 346–369.

Dickerson, S. S., & Kemeny, M. E. (2002). Acute stressors and cortisol responses: A theoretical integration and synthesis of laboratory research. *Psychological Bulletin, 130*, 355–391.

Dickerson, S. S., & Kemeny, M. E. (2004). Acute stressors and cortisol responses: A theoretical integration and synthesis of laboratory research. *Psychological Bulletin, 130*, 355–391.

Diehm, R., & Armatas, C. (2004). Surfing: An avenue for socially acceptable risk-taking, satisfying needs for sensation seeking and experience seeking. *Personality & Individual Differences, 36*, 663–677.

Diener, E. (1977). Deindividualtion: Causes and consequences. *Social Behavior and Personality, 5*, 143–155.

Diener, E. (2000). Subjective well-being: The science of happiness and a proposal for a national index. *American Psychologist, 55*, 34–43.

Diener, E., & Biswas-Diener, R. (2002). Will money increase subjective well-being? *Social Indicators Research, 57*, 119–169.

Diener, E., & Emmons, R. A. (1984). The independence of positive and negative affect. *Journal of Personality and Social Psychology, 47*, 1105–1117.

Dienstfrey, H. (1991). *Where the mind meets the body.* New York: HarperCollins.

Dietrich, A. (2004). The cognitive neuroscience of creativity. *Psychonomic Bulletin & Review, 11*, 1011–1026.

DiGiuseppe, R., & Tafrate, R. C. (2003). Anger treatment for adults: A meta-analytic review. *Clinical Psychology: Science and Practice, 10*, 70–84.

Digman, J. M. (1990). Personality structure: Emergence of the five-factor model. *Annual Review of Psychology, 41*, 417–440.

DiLalla, L. F., Kagan, J., Reznick, J. S. (1994). Genetic etiology of behavioral inhibition among 2-year-old children. *Infant Behavior & Development, 17*, 405–412.

Dill, P. L., & Henley, T. B. (1998). Stressors of college: A comparison of traditional and nontraditional students. *Journal of Psychology, 132*, 25–32.

Dillbeck, M. C., & Orme-Johnson, D. W. (1987). Physiological differences between transcendental meditation and rest. *American Psychologist*, 879–881.

Dimberg, J., Thunberg, M., & Elmehed, K. (2000). Unconscious facial reactions to emotional facial expressions. *Psychological Science, 11*, 86–89.

Dinges, D., Pack, F., Williams, K., Gillen, K., Powell, J., Ott, G., et al. (1997). Cumulative sleepiness, mood disturbance, and psychomotor vigilance performance decrements during a week of sleep restricted to 4–5 hours per night. *Sleep, 20*, 267–277.

Dion, K., Berscheid, E., & Walster, E. (1972). What is beautiful is good. *Journal of Personality & Social Psychology, 24*, 285–290.

DiPietro, J. A. (2004). The role of prenatal maternal stress in child development. *Current Directions in Psychological Science, 13*, 71–74.

DiPietro, J. A., Costigan, K. A., & Gurewitsch, E. D. (2003). Fetal response to induced maternal stress. *Early Human Development, 74*, 125–138.

DiPietro, J. A., Hodgson, D. M., Costigan, K. A., Hilton, S. C., & Johnson, T. R. B. (1996). Fetal neurobehavioral development. *Child Development, 67*, 2553–2567.

Di Pietro, M., Laganaro, M., Leemann, B., & Schnider, A. (2004). Receptive amusia: Temporal auditory processing deficit in a professional musician following a left temporo-parietal lesion. *Neuropsychologia, 42*, 868–877.

Dixon, M. R., Rehfeldt, R. A., & Randich, L. (2003). Enhancing tolerance to delayed reinforcers: The role of intervening activities. *Journal of Applied Behavior Analysis, 36*, 263–266.

Dobson, M., & Markham, R. (1993). Imagery ability and source monitoring: Implications for eyewitness memory. *British Journal of Psychology, 32*, 111–118.

Dobson, R. (2002, May 11). Broadcast of star's colonoscopy puts up screening by 20%. *British Medical Journal, 324*, 1118.

Docter, R. F., & Prince, V. (1997). Transvestism: A survey of 1032 cross-dressers. *Archives of Sexual Behavior, 26*, 589–605.

Dodge, K. A., & Newman, J. P. (1981). Biased decision-making processes in aggressive boys. *Journal of Abnormal Psychology, 90*.

Dodge, K. A., & Pettit, G. S. (2003). A biopsychosocial model of the development of chronic conduct problems in adolescence. *Developmental Psychology, 39*, 349–371.

Doheny, M. (1993). Effects of mental practice on performance of a psychomotor skill. *Journal of Mental Imagery, 17*(3–4), 111–118.

Dohnanyiova, M., Ostatnikova, D., & Laznibatova, J. (2001). Spatial imagery, testosterone and anthropometric characteristics in intellectually gifted and control children. *Homeostasis in Health & Disease, 41*, 53–55.

Dohrenwend, B. P., Levav, I., Shrout, P. E., Schwartz, S., Naveh, G., Link. B. G., Skodol, A. E., & Stueve, A. (1992). Socioeconomic status and psychiatric disorders: The causation-selection issue. *Science, 255*, 946–952.

Dohrmann, R. J., & Laskin, D. M. (1978). An evaluation of electromyographic biofeedback in the treatment of myofascial pain-dysfunction syndrome. *J. Am. Dent. Assoc., 96*, 656–662.

Dolan, B. (1991). Cross-cultural aspects of anorexia nervosa and bulimia: A review. *International Journal of Eating Disorders, 10*, 67–79.

Dolan, R. J., & Fletcher, P. C. (1997). Dissociating prefrontal and hippocampal function in episodic memory encoding. *Nature, 388*, 582–585.

Domar, A. D., Noe, J. M., & Benson, H. (1987). The preoperative use of the relaxation response with ambulatory surgery patients. *Journal of Human Stress, 13*, 101–107.

Dominey, P. F., & Dodane, C. (2004). Indeterminacy in language acquisition: The role of child directed speech and joint attention. *Journal of Neurolinguistics, 17*, 121–145.

Domjan, M., Cusato, B., & Krause, M. (2004). Learning with arbitrary versus ecologically conditioned stimuli: Evidence from sexual conditioning. *Psychonomic Bulletin and Review, 11*, 232–246.

Donaldson, S. O. (1995). Peer influence on adolescent drug use: A perspective rom the trench of experimental evaluation research. *American Psychologist, 50*, 801–802.

Doty, R. L., Bartoshuk, L. M., & Snow, J. B., Jr. (1991). Causes of olfactory and gustatory disorders. In T. V. Getchell, R. L. Doty, L. M. Bartoshuk, & J. B. Snow, Jr. (Eds.), *Smell and taste in health and disease* (pp. 449–462). New York: Raven.

Doty, R. L., Shaman, P., Applebaum, M. S. L., Gilberson, R., Siksorski, L., & Rosenberg, L. (1984). Smell identification ability: Changes with age. *Science, 226*, 1441–1443.

Double, D. (2002). The limits of psychiatry. *British Medical Journal, 324*, 900–904.

Dovidio, J. F., Evans, N., & Tyler, R. B. (1986). Racial stereotypes: The contents of their cognitive representations. *Journal of Experimental Social Psychology, 22*, 22–37.

Dovidio, J. F., Kawakami, K., & Gaertner, S. L. (2002). Implicit and explicit prejudice and interracial interaction. *Journal of Personality & Social Psychology, 82*, 62–68.

Dovidio, J. F., Piliavin, J. A., Gaertner, S. L., Schroeder, D. A., & Clark, R. D., III. (1991). The arousal: Cost-reward model and the process of intervention: A review of the evidence. In M. S. Clark (Ed.), *Prosocial behavior* (pp. 86–118). Thousand Oaks, CA: Sage Publications.

Dowdall, G. W., Crawford, M., & Wechsler, H. (1998). Binge drinking among American college women: A comparison of single-sex and coeducational institutions. *Psychology of Women Quarterly, 22*, 705–715.

Dowling, J. E. (1992). *Neurons and networks: An introduction to neuroscience.* Cambridge, MA: Harvard University Press.

Downing, J. W., Judd, C. M., & Brauer, M. (1992). Effects of repeated expressions on attitude extremity. *Journal of Personality and Social Psychology, 63*, 17–29.

Dozier, M., & Kobak, R. R. (1992). Psychophysiology in attachment interviews: Converging evidence for deactivating strategies. *Child Development, 63*, 1473–1480.

Drake, C. L., Roehrs, T. A., Burduvali, E., Bonahoom, A., Rosekind, M., & Roth, T. (2001). Effects of rapid versus slow accumulation of 8 hours of sleep loss. *Psychophysiology, 38*, 979–987.

Draycott, S. G., & Kline, P. (1995). The Big Three or the Big Five—the EPQ-R vs the NEO-PI: A research note, replication and elaboration. *Personality & Individual Differences, 18*, 801–804.

Drayna, D., Manichaikul, A., de Lange, M., Snieder, H., & Spector, T. (2001). Genetic correlates of musical pitch recognition in humans. *Science, 291*, 1969–1972.

Drevets, W. C., Price, J. L., Bardgett, M. E., Reich, T., Todd, R. D., & Raichle, M. E. (2002). Glucose metabolism in the amygdala in depression: Relationship to diagnostic subtype and plasma cortisol levels. *Pharmacology, Biochemistry & Behavior, 71*, 431–447.

Drewnowski, A., Henderson, S. A., & Barratt-Fornell, A. (2001). Genetic taste markers and food preferences. *Drug Metabolism and Disposition, 4*, 535–538.

Drid, M. D., Raybaud, F., De Lunardo, C., Iacono, P., & Gustovic, P. (1995). Influence of the behavior pattern on the nocebo response of healthy volunteers. *British Journal of Clinical Pharmacology, 39*, 204–206.

Driskell, J., Copper, C., & Moran, A. (1994). Does mental practice enhance performance? *Journal of Applied Psychology, 79*(4), 481–492.

Druckman, D. & Bjork, R. A. (1994). *Learning, remembering, believing: Enhancing human performance.* Washington, DC: National Academy Press.

Druckman, D., & Swets, J. A. (Eds.). (1988). *Enhancing human performance: Issues, theories, and techniques.* Washington, DC: National Academy Press.

Druckman, J. N. (2001). Evaluating framing effects. *Journal of Economic Psychology, 22*, 91–101.

Drummond, S. P. A., Brown, G. G., Gillin, J. C., Stricker, J. L., Wong, E. C., & Buxton, R. B. (2000). *Nature, 403*, 655–657.

Druss, B. G., Schlesinger, M., & Allen, H. M. Jr. (2001). Depressive symptoms, satisfaction with health care, and 2-year work outcomes in an employed population. *American Journal of Psychiatry, 158*, 731–734.

Dubrovsky, V. J., Kiesler, S., & Sethna, B. N. (1991). The equalization phenomenon: Status effects in computer-mediated and face-to-face decision-making groups. *Hum. Comput. Interact., 6*, 119–146.

Duclaux, R., Feisthauer, J., & Cabanac, M. (1973). The effects of eating on the pleasantness of food and nonfood odors in man. *Physiology & Behavior, 10*, 1029–1033.

Duclos, S. E., Laird, J. D., Schneider, E., Sexter, M., Stern, L., & Van Lighten, O. (1989). Emotion-specific effects of facial expressions and postures on emotional experience. *Journal of Personality and Social Psychology, 57*, 100–108.

Duman, R. S., Heninger, G. R., & Nestler, E. J. (1997). A molecular and cellular theory of depression. *Archives of General Psychiatry, 54*, 597–606.

Duncan, G. J., & National Institute of Child Health & Human Development Early Child Care. (2003). Modeling the impacts of child care quality on children's preschool cognitive development. *Child Development, 74*, 1454–1475.

Duncan, H. F., Gourlay, N., & Hudson, W. (1973). *A study of pictorial perception among Bantu and White primary school children in South Africa.* Johannesburg, South Africa: Witwatersrand University Press.

Duncan, J. (1995). Attention, intelligence, and the frontal lobes. In M. S. Gazzaniga (Ed.), *The cognitive neurosciences* (pp. 721–733). Cambridge, MA: MIT Press.

Duncan, J. (2005). Frontal lobe function and general intelligence: Why it matters. *Cortex, 41*, 215–217.

Duncan, J., Burgess, P., & Emslie, H. (1995). Fluid intelligence after frontal lobe lesions. *Neuropsychologia, 33*, 261–268.

Duncan, J., Emslie, H., Williams, P., Johnson, R., & Freer, C. (1996). Intelligence and the frontal lobe: The organization of goal-directed behavior. *Cognitive Psychology, 30*, 257–303.

Duncan, J., Seitz, R. J., Kolodny, J., Bor, D., Herzog, H., Ahmed, A., et al. (2000). A neural basis for general intelligence. *Science, 289*, 457–460.

Duncan, R. M., & Pratt, M. W. (1997). Microgenetic change in the quantity and quality of preschoolers' private speech. *International Journal of Behavioral Development, 20*, 367–383.

Duncker, K. (1945). On problem solving. *Psychological monographs, 58* (No. 270).

Dunnett, S. B., Lane, D. M., & Winn, P. (1985). Ibotenic acid lesions of the lateral hypothalamus: Comparison with 6-hydroxydopamine-induced sensorimotor deficits. *Neuroscience, 14*, 509–518.

Dupuy, B., & Krashen, S. D. (1993). Incidental vocabulary acquisition in French as a foreign language. *Applied Language Learning, 4*, 55–63.

Durrheim, K., and Dixon, J. (2004). Attitudes in the fiber of everyday life: The discourse of racial evaluation and the lived experience of desegregation. *American Psychologist, 59*, 626–636.

Dusek, D., & Girdano, D. A. (1980). *Drugs: A factual account.* Reading, MA: Addison Wesley.

Eacott, M. J., & Crawley, R. A. (1999). Childhood amnesia: On answering questions about very early life events. *Memory, 7*, 279–292.

Eagly, A. (1987). *Sex differences in social behavior: A social-role interpretation.* Hillsdale, NJ: Erlbaum.

Eagly, A. H. (1995). The science and politics of comparing women and men. *American Psychologist, 50* 145–158.

Eagly, A. H., Ashmore, R. D., Makhijani, M. G., & Longo, L. C. (1991). What is beautiful is good, but . . . : A meta-analytic review of research on the physical attractiveness stereotype. *Psychological Bulletin, 110*, 109–128.

Eagly, A. H., & Carli, L. (1981). Sex of researchers and sex-typed communications as determinants of sex differences in influence-ability: A meta-analysis of social influence studies. *Psychological Bulletin, 90*, 1–20.

Eagly, A. H., & Chaiken, S. (1998). Attitude structure and function. In D. T. Gilbert, S. T. Fiske, & G. Lindzey (Eds.), *The handbook of social psychology* (4th ed., pp. 269–322). New York: McGraw-Hill.

Eagly, A. H., & Steffen, V. J. (1986). Gender and aggressive behavior: A meta-analytic review of the social psycholgical literature. *Psychological Bulletin, 100*, 309–330.

Eagly, A. H., & Wood, W. (1999). The origins of sex differences in human behavior: Evolved dispositions versus social roles. *American Psychologist, 54*, 408–423.

Eaker, E. D., Pinsky, J., & Castelli, W. P. (1992). Myocardial infarction and coronary death among women: psychosocial predictors from a 20-year follow-up of women in the Framingham Study. *American Journal of Epidemiology, 135*, 854–864.

Eakin, E. (2000, January 15). Bigotry as mental illness or just another norm. *New York Times*, p. A21.

Eals, M., & Silverman, I. (1994). The hunter-gatherer theory of spatial sex differences: Proximate factors mediating the female advantage on recall of object arrays. *Ethology and Sociobiology, 15*, 95–105.

Earle, T. L., Linden, W., & Weinberg, J. (1999). Differential effects of harassment on cardiovascular and salivary cortisol stress reactivity and recovery in women and men. *Journal of Psychosomatic Research, 46*, 125–141.

Eaves, L. J., Eysenck, H. J., & Martin, N. G. (1989). *Genes, culture and personality: An empirical approach.* London: Academic Press.

Ebbinghaus, H. (1885/1964). *Memory: A contribution to experimental psychology.* New York: Dover.

Eberman, C., & McKelvie, S. J. (2002). Vividness of visual imagery and source memory for audio and text. *Applied Cognitive Psychology, 16*, 87–95.

Ebstein, R. P., Benjamin, J., & Belmaker, R. H. (2002). Behavioral genetics, genomics, and personality. In R. Plomin, J. C. DeFries, I. W. Craig, & P. McGuffin (Eds.), *Behavioral genetics in the postgenomic era* (pp. 365–388). Washington, DC: American Psychological Association.

Ebstein, R. P., Novick, O., Umansky, R., Priel, B., Osher,Y., Blaine, D., et al. (1996). Dopamine D4 receptor (D4DR) exon III polymorphism associated with the human personality trait of Novelty Seeking. *Nature Genetics, 12*, 78–80.

Eby, K. K. (2004). Exploring the stressors of low-income women with abusive partners: Understanding their needs and developing effective community responses. *Journal of Family Violence, 19*, 221–232.

Edelman, G. M., & Tononi, G. (2000). A *universe of consciousness: How matter becomes imagination.* New York: Basic Books.

Edelstein, R. S., Alexander, K. W., Shaver, P. R., Schaaf, J. M., Quas, J. A., Lovas, G. S., & Goodman, G. S. (2004). Adult attachment style and parental responsiveness during a stressful event. *Attachment & Human Development, 6*, 31–52.

Eden, D. (1990). Pygmalion without interpersonal contrast effects: Whole groups gain from raising manager expectations. *Journal of Applied Psychology, 75*, 394–398.

Eder, R. A. (1989). The emergent personologist: The structure and content of 3-, 5-, and 7-year-olds' concepts of themselves and other persons. *Child Development, 60*, 1218–1228.

Edgerton, R. B., & Cohen, A. (1994). Culture and schizophrenia: The DOSMD challenge. *British Journal of Psychiatry, 164*, 222–231.

Effa-Heap, G. (1996). The influence of media pornography on adolescents. *IFE Psychologia: An International Journal, 4*, 80–90

Egbert, L. D., Battit, G. E., Welch, C. E., & Barlett, M. K. (1964). Reduction of postoperative pain by encouragement and instruction of patients. *New England Journal of Medicine, 270*, 825–827.

Ehlers, A., Mayou, R. A., & Bryant, B. (1998). Psychological predictors of chronic posttraumatic stress disorder after motor vehicle accidents. *Journal of Abnormal Psychology, 107*, 508–519.

Eich, E. (1989). Theoretical issues in state dependent memory. In H. L. Roediger, III, & F. I. M. Craik (Eds.), *Varieties of memory and consciousness: Essays in honour of Endel Tulving* (pp. 331–354). Hillsdale, NJ: Erlbaum.

Eich, E. (1995). Searching for mood dependent memory. *Psychological Science, 6*, 67–75.

Eid, J., Johnsen, B. H., Saus, E., & Risberg, J. (2004). Stress and coping in a week-long disabled submarine exercise. *Aviation, Space, & Environmental Medicine, 75*, 616–621.

Eimas, P. D., & Corbit, J. D. (1973). Selective adaptation of linguistic feature detectors. *Cognitive Psychology, 4*, 99–109.

Einstein, A. (1945). A testimonial from Professor Einstein (Appendix II). In J. Hadamard, *An essay on the psychology of invention in the mathematical field* (pp. 142–143). Princeton, NJ: Princeton University Press.

Eisenberg, M., Kobilo, T., Berman, D. E., & Dudai, Y. (2003). Stability of retrieved memory: Inverse correlation with trace dominance. *Science, 301*, 1102–1104.

Eisenberg, N., Fabes, R. A., & Murphy, B. (1995). The relations of shyness and low sociability to regulation and emotionality. *Journal of Personality & Social Psychology, 68*, 505–517.

Eisenberg, N., Guthrie, I. K., Cumberland, A., Murphy, B. C., Shepard, S. A., Zhou, Q., & Carlo, G. (2002). Prosocial development in early adulthood: A longitudinal study. *Journal of Personality & Social Psychology, 82*, 993–1006.

Eisenberg, N., Miller, P. A., Schaller, M., Fabes, R. A., Fultz, J., Shell, R., & Shea, C. L. (1989). The role of sympathy and altruistic personality traits in helping: A reexamination. *Journal of Personality, 57*, 41–67.

Eisenberger, R., & Cameron, J. (1996). Detrimental effects of reward: Reality or myth? *American Psychologist, 51*, 1153–1166.

Ekman, P. (1980). Biological and cultural contributions to body and facial movement in the expression of emotion. In A. O. Rorty (Ed.), *Explaining emotions*. Berkeley: University of California Press.

Ekman, P. (1984). Expression and the nature of emotion. In K. R. Scherer & P. Ekman (Eds.), *Approaches to emotion* (pp. 319–343). Hillsdale, NJ: Erlbaum.

Ekman, P. (1985). *Telling lies: Clues to deceit in the marketplace, marriage, and politics*. New York: Norton.

Ekman, P. (1992). Facial expressions of emotion: New findings, new questions. *Psychological Science, 3*, 34–38.

Ekman, P., & Davidson, R. J. (1993). Voluntary smiling changes regional brain activity. *Psychological Science, 4*, 342–345.

Ekman, P., Davidson, R. J., & Friesen, W. V. (1990). The Duchenne smile: Emotional expression and brain psychology II. *Journal of Personality & Social Psychology, 58*, 342–353.

Ekman, P., & Friesen, W. (1971). Constants across cultures in the face and emotion. *Journal of Personality & Social Psychology, 17*, 124–129.

Ekman, P., & Friesen, W. V. (1975). *Unmasking the face*. Englewood Cliffs, NJ: Prentice-Hall.

Ekman, P., O'Sullivan, M., & Frank, M. G. (1999). A few can catch a liar. *Psychological Science, 10*, 263–266.

Elaad, E. (2003). Effects of feedback on the overestimated capacity to detect lies and the underestimated ability to tell lies. *Applied Cognitive Psychology, 17*, 349–363.

Elber, T., Pantev, C., Wienbruch, C., Rockstroh, B., & Taub, E. (1995). Increased cortical representation of the fingers of the left hand in string players. *Science, 270*, 305–307.

Elenkov, I. J., Wilder, R. L., Chrousos, G. P., & Vizi, E. S. (2000). The sympathetic nerve—an integrative interface between two supersystems: The brain and the immune system. *Pharmacological Reviews, 52*, 595–638.

Eley, T. C., Deater-Deckard, K., Fombone, E., Fulker, D. W., & Plomin, R. (1998). An adoption study of depressive symptoms in middle childhood. *Journal of Child Psychology & Psychiatry & Allied Disciplines, 39*, 337–345.

Elfenbein, H. A., & Ambady, N. (2002). On the universality and cultural specificity of emotion recognition: A meta-analysis. *Psychological Bulletin, 128*, 203–235.

Eliez, S., & Reiss, A. L. (2000). Genetics of childhood disorders: XI. Fragile X syndrome. *Journal of the American Academy of Child & Adolescent Psychiatry, 39*, 264–266.

El-Islam, M. F. (1991). Transcultural aspects of schizophrenia and ICD-10. *Psychiatria Danubina, 3*, 485–494.

Elkin, I., Shea, M. T., Watkins, J. T., Imber, S. D., Sotsky, S. M., Collins, J. F., Glass, D. R., Pilkonis, P. A., Leber, W. R., Docherty, J. P., Fiester, S. J., & Parloff, M. B. (1989). National Institute of Mental Health Treatment of Depression Collaborative Research Program: General effectiveness of treatments. *Archives of General Psychiatry, 46*, 971–982.

Elkind, D. (1967). Egocentrism in adolescence. *Child Development, 38*, 1025–1034.

Elkind, D., & Bowen, R. (1979). Imaginary audience behavior in children and adolescence. *Developmental Psychology, 15*, 33–44.

Elliott, D., Huizinga, D., & Ageton, S. S. (1985). *Multiple problem youth: Delinquency, substance use, and mental health problems*. New York: Springer-Verlag.

Ellis, A. (1994a). The treatment of borderline personalities with rational emotive behavior therapy. *Journal of Rational-Emotive & Cognitive Behavior Therapy, 12*, 101–119.

Ellis, A. (1994b). Rational emotive behavior therapy approaches to obsessive-compulsive disorder (OCD). *Journal of Rational-Emotive & Cognitive Behavior Therapy, 12*, 121–141.

Ellis, A. W., & Young, A. W. (1987). *Human cognitive neuropsychology*. Hillsdale, NJ: Lawrence Erlbaum.

Ellis, B. J., Bates, J. E., Dodge, K. A., Fergusson, D. M., Horwood, L. J., Pettit, G. S., & Woodward, L. (2003). Does father absence place daughters at special risk for early sexual activity and teenage pregnancy? *Child Development, 74*, 801–821.

Ellis, H. C. (1973). Stimulus encoding processes in human learning and memory. In G. H. Bower (Ed.), *The psychology of learning and motivation* (Vol. 7, pp. 124–182). New York: Academic Press.

Ellis, H. C., & Hunt, R. R. (1993). *Fundamentals of cognitive psychology* (5th ed.). Dubuque, IA: Brown Communications.

Ellis, L., & Blanchard, R. (2001). Birth order, sibling sex ratio, and maternal miscarriages in homosexual and heterosexual men and women. *Personality & Individual Differences, 30*, 543–552.

Elman, J. L., Bates, E. A., Johnson, M. H., Karmiloff-Smith, A., et al. (1996). *Rethinking innateness: A connectionist perspective on development*. Cambridge: MIT Press.

Elzinga, B. M., Phaf, R. H., Ardon, A. M., & van Dyck, R. (2003). Directed forgetting between, but not within, dissociative personality states. *Journal of Abnormal Psychology, 112*, 237–243.

Emerson, M. O., Kimbro, R. T., & Yancey, G. (2002). Contact theory extended: The effects of prior racial contact on current social ties. *Social Science Quarterly, 83*, 745–761.

Emmelkamp, P. M. G. (2004). Behavior therapy with adults. In M. J. Lambert (Ed.), *Bergin and Garfield's handbook of psychotherapy and behavior change*, 5th ed. (pp. 393–446). New York: Wiley and Sons.

Emmelkamp, P. M. G., Bruynzeel, M., Drost, L., & Van Der Mast, C. A. P. G. (2001). Virtual reality treatment in acrophobia: A comparison with exposure in vivo. *CyberPsychology & Behavior, 4*, 335–339.

Emmelkamp, P. M. G., Kloek, J., & Blaauw, E. (1992). Obsessive-compulsive disorders. In P. H. Wilson (Ed.), *Principles and practice of relapse prevention* (pp. 213–234). New York: Guilford Press.

Emmelkamp, P. M. G., Krijn, M., Hulsbosch, A. M., de Vries, S., Schuemie, M. J., & van der Mast, C. A. P. G. (2002). Virtual reality treatment versus exposure in vivo: A comparative evaluation in acrophobia. *Behaviour Research & Therapy, 40*, 509–516.

Emmorey, K. (1993). Processing a dynamic visual-spatial language: Psycholinguistic studies of American Sign Language. *Journal of Psycholinguistic Research, 22*, 153–187.

Engel, S. A., Glover, G. H., & Wandell, B. A. (1997). Retinotopic organization in human visual cortex and the spatial precision of functional MRI. *Cerebral Cortex, 7*, 181–192.

Engelberg, E., & Sjöberg, L. (2004). Emotional intelligence, affect intensity, and social adjustment. *Personality and Individual Differences, 37*, 533–542.

Engle, R. W., Tuholski, S. W., Laughlin, J. E., & Conway, A. R. A. (1999). working memory, short-term memory and general fluid intelligence: A latent variable approach. *Journal of Experimental Psychology: General, 128*, 309–331.

Entwisle, D. R. (1972). To dispel fantasies about fantasy-based measures of achievement motivation. *Psychological Bulletin, 77*, 377–391.

Epley, N., & Dunning, D. (2000). Feeling "holier than thou": Are self-serving assessments produced by errors in self- or social prediction? *Journal of Personality & Social Psychology, 79*, 861–875.

Epstein, C. M., Figiel, G. S., McDonald, W. M., Amazon-Leece, J., & Figiel, L. (1998). Rapid rate transcranial magnetic stimulation in young and middle-aged refractory depressed patients. *Psychiatric Annals, 28*, 36–39.

Epstein, H. T. (1980). EEG developmental stages. *Developmental Psychobiology, 13*, 629–631.

Eranti, S. V., & McLoughlin, D. M. (2003). Changing use of ECT: Author's reply. *British Journal of Psychiatry, 183*, 173.

Erdelyi, M. H. (1984). The recovery of unconcious (inaccessible) memories: Laboratory studies of hypermnesia. In G. H. Bower (Ed.), *The psychology of learning and motivation: Advances in research and theory* (Vol. 18, pp. 95–127). New York: Academic Press.

Erickson, K., Drevets, W., & Schulkin, J. (2003). Glucocorticoid regulation of diverse cognitive functions in normal and pathological emotional states. *Neuroscience & Biobehavioral Reviews, 27*, 233–246.

Ericsson, K. A., & Charness, N. (1994). Expert performance. *American Psychologist, 49*, 725–747.

Ericsson, K. A., Krampe, R. Th., & Tesch-Ràmer, C. (1993). The role of deliberate practice in the acquisition of expert performance. *Psychological Review, 100*, 363–406.

Erikson, D. H., Beiser, M., & Iacono, W. G. (1998). Social support predicts 5-year outcome in first-episode schizophrenia. *Journal of Abnormal Psychology, 107*, 681–685.

Ernst, C., & Angst, J. (1983). *Birth order: Its influence on personality*. Berlin: Springer-Verlag.

Ernst, M. O., & Bülthoff, H. H. (2004). Merging the senses into a robust percept. *Trends in Cognitive Sciences, 8*, 162–169.

Eskenazi, B. (1993). Caffeine during pregnancy: Grounds for concern? *Journal of the American Medical Association, 270*, 2973–2974.

Eskenazi, B., Stapleton, A. L., Kharrazi, M., & Chee, W. Y. (1999). Associations between maternal decaffeinated and caffeinated coffee consumption and fetal growth and gestational duration. *Epidemiology, 10*, 242–249.

Esterling, B. A., L'Abate, L., Murray, E. J., & Pennebaker, J. W. (1999). Empirical foundations for writing in prevention and psychotherapy: Mental and phsycial health outcomes. *Clinical Psychology Review, 19*, 79–96.

Estes, W. (1976). The cognitive side of probability learning. *Psychological Review, 83*, 37–64.

Etcoff, N. L., Ekman, P., Magee, J. J., & Frank, M. G. (2000). Lie detection and language comprehension. *Nature, 405*, 139.

Evans, G. W. (2003). A multimethodological analysis of cumulative risk and allostatic load among rural children. *Developmental Psychology, 39*, 924–933.

Evans, G. W., Bullinger, M., & Hygge, S. (1998). Chronic noise exposure and physiological response: A prospective study of children living under environmental stress. *Psychological Science, 9*, 75–77.

Evans, J. J., Floyd, R. G., McGrew, K. S., & Leforgee, M. H. (2002). The relations between measures of Cattell-Horn-Carroll (CHC) cognitive abilities and reading achievement during childhood and adolescence. *School Psychology Review, 31*, 246–262.

Exner, J. E. (1974). *The Rorschach: A comprehensive system.* Oxford, UK: John Wiley.

Exner, J. E., Jr. (2002). A new nonpatient sample for the Rorschach Comprehensive System: A progress report. *Journal of Personality Assessment, 78*, 391–404.

Eyferth, K. (1961). Ein Vergleich der Beurteilung projektiver Tests durch verschiedene Berteiler [A comparison of judging projective tests by different judges]. *Zeitschrift fuer Experimentelle und Angewandte Psychologie, 8*, 329–338.

Eysenck, H. J. (1977). *Crime and personality,* St. Albans, England: Paladin Frogmore.

Eysenck, H. J. (1979). The conditioning model of neurosis. *Behavioral and Brain Sciences, 2*, 155–199.

Eysenck, H. J. (1990a). Genetic and environmental contributions to individual differences: The three major dimensions of personality. *Journal of Personality, 58*, 245–261.

Eysenck, H. J. (1990b). Biological dimensions of personality. In L. A. Pervin (Ed.), *Handbook of personality: Theory and research* (pp. 244–276). New York: Guilford.

Eysenck, H. J. (1992). Four ways five factors are *not* basic. *Personality and Individual Differences, 13*, 667–673.

Eysenck, H. J. (1993). The structure of phenotypic personality traits: Comment. *American Psychologist, 48*, 1299–1300.

Eysenck, H. J. (1995). *Genius: The natural history of creativity.* Cambridge, England: Cambridge University Press.

Eysenck, H. J., & Gudjonsson, G. (1989). *The causes and cures of criminality.* New York: Plenum Press.

Eysenck, S. B. G., & Eysenck, H. J. (1967). Salivary response to lemon juice as a measure of introversion. *Perceptional and motor skills, 24*, 1047–1053.

Fabbro, F. (2001). The bilingual brain: Bilingual aphasia. *Brain & Language, 79*, 201–210.

Faber, S. (1981). *Identical twins reared apart.* London: Blackwell.

Fagan, J. L., & Holland, C. R. (2002). Equal opportunity and racial differences in IQ. *Intelligence, 30*, 361–387.

Fairburn, C. G., Cooper, Z., Doll, H. A., & Welch, S. L. (1999). Risk factors for anorexia nervosa: Three integrated case-control comparisons. *Archives of General Psychiatry, 56*, 468–476.

Fairburn, C. G., Stice, E., Cooper, Z., Doll, H. A., Norman, P. A., & O'Connor, M. E. (2003). Understanding persistence in bulimia nervosa: A 5-year naturalistic study. *Journal of Consulting & Clinical Psychology, 71*, 103–109.

Fantino, M., & Cabanac, M. (1980). Body weight regulation with a proportional hoarding response in the rat. *Physiology & Behavior, 24*, 939–942.

Farhi, P. (1996, February 26). Study finds real harm in TV violence. *Washington Post*, A1.

Farrar, W. T., IV, Van Orden, G. C., & Hamouz, V. (2001). When SOFA primes TOUCH: Interdependence of spelling, sound, and meaning in "semantically mediated" phonological priming. *Memory & Cognition, 29*, 530–539.

Farroni, T., Csibra, G., Simion, F., & Johnson, M. H. (2002). Eye contact detection in humans from birth. *Proceedings of the National Academy of Sciences USA, 99*, 9602–9605.

Farthing, G. (1992) *The psychology of consciousness.* Englewood Cliffs, NJ: Prentice-Hall.

Fast, K., & Fujiwara, E. (2001). Isolated retrograde amnesia. *Neurocase, 7*, 269–272.

Fatt, I., & Weissman, B. A. (1992). *Physiology of the eye: An introduction to the vegetative functions* (2nd ed.). Boston: Butterworth-Heinemann.

Fava, G. A. Rafanelli, C., Grandi, S., Conti, S., & Belluardo, P. (1998a). Prevention of recurrent depression with cognitive behavioral therapy: Preliminary findings. *Archives of General Psychiatry, 55*, 816–820.

Fava, G. A., Rafanelli, C., Grandi, S., Canestrari, R., & Morphy, M. A. (1998b). Six-year outcome for cognitive behavioral treatment of residual symptoms in major depression. *American Journal of Psychiatry, 155*, 1443–1445.

Fawzy, F. I., Kemeny, M. E., Fawzy, N. W., Elashoff, R., Morton, D., Cousins, N., & Fahey, J. L. (1990). A structured psychiatric intervention for cancer patients: II. Changes over time in immunological measures. *Archives of General Psychiatry, 47*, 729–735.

Fay, R. E., Turner, C. F., Klassen, A. D., & Gagnon, J. H. (1989). Prevalence and patterns of same-gender sexual contact among men. *Science, 243*, 338–348.

Fazio, R. H., Chen, J., McDonel, E. C., & Sherman, S. J. (1982). Attitude accessibility and the strength of the object-evaluation association. *Journal of Experimental Psychology, 18*, 339–357.

Fazio, R. H., Jackson, J. R., Dunton, B. C., & Williams, C. J. (1995). Variability in automatic activation as an unobstrusive measure of racial attitudes: A bona fide pipeline? *Journal of Personality and Social Psychology, 69*, 1013–1027.

Fazio, R. H., & Olson, M. A. (2003). Implicit measures in social cognition research: Their meaning and use. *Annual Review of Psychology, 54*, 297–327.

Feather, N. T. (1996). Social comparisons across nations: Variables relating to the subjective evaluation of national achievement and to personal and collective. *Australian Journal of Psychology, 48*, 53–63.

Febbraro, G. A. R. (in press). Investigation into the effectiveness of bibliotherapy and minimal contact interventions in the treatment of panic attacks. *Journal of Clinical Psychology.*

Feigenson, L., & Halberda, J. (2004). Infants chunk object arrays into sets of individuals. *Cognition, 91*, 173–190.

Feingold, A. (1990). Gender differences in effects of physical attractiveness on romantic attraction: A comparison across five research paradigms. *Journal of Personality and Social Psychology, 59*, 981–993.

Feingold, A. (1992). In A. Manstead & M. Hewstone (Eds.), *The Blackwell encyclopedia of social psychology* (p. 313). New York: McGraw-Hill.

Feingold, A. (1994). Gender differences in personality: A meta-analysis. *Psychological Bulletin, 116*, 429–456.

Feldman, D. H., & Goldsmith, L. T. (1991). *Nature's gambit: Child prodigies and the development of human potential.* New York: Teachers College Press.

Feldman, J. B. (2004). The neurobiology of pain, affect and hypnosis. *American Journal of Clinical Hypnosis, 46*, 187–200.

Feldman, R. S., Coats, E. J., & Spielman, D. A. (1996). Television exposure and children's decoding of nonverbal behavior. *Journal of Applied Social Psychology, 26*, 1718–1733.

Fell, J., Klaver, P., Elger, C. E., & Guillén, F. (2002). Suppression of EEG Gamma activity may cause the attentional blink. *Consciousness and Cognition, 11*, 114–122.

Felleman, D. J., & Van Essen, D. C. (1991). Distributed hierarchical processing in the primate cerebral cortex. *Cerebral Cortex, 1*, 1–47.

Fenton, W., & McGlashan, T. (1991). Natural history of schizophrenia subtypes: I. Longitudinal study of paranoid, hebephrenic, and undifferentiated schizophrenia. *Archives of General Psychiatry, 48*, 969–977.

Ferguson, N. B., & Keesey, R. E. (1975). Effect of a quinine-adulterated diet upon body weight maintenance in male rats with ventromedial hypothalamic lesions. *Journal of Comparative & Physiological Psychology, 89*, 478–488.

Fergusson, D., Doucette, S., Glass, K. C., Shapiro, S., Healy, D., Hebert, P., & Hutton, B. (2005). Association between suicide attempts and selective serotonin reuptake inhibitors: Systematic review of randomised controlled trials. *British Medical Journal, 330*, 396–369.

Ferketich, A. K., Schwartzbaum, J. A., Frid, D. J., & Moeschberger, M. L. (2000). Depression as an antecedent to heart disease among women and men in the NHANES I study. National Health and Nutrition Examination Survey. *Archives Internal Medicine, 160*, 1261–1268.

Fernald, A., Taeschner, T., Dunn, J., Papousek, M., Boysson-Bardies, B., & Fukui, I. (1989). A cross-language study of prosodic modifications in mothers' and fathers' speech to infants. *Child Development, 64*, 637–656.

Ferrier, S., & Brewin, C. R. (in press). Feared identity and obsessive-compulsive disorder. *Behaviour Research and Therapy.*

Ferveur, J.-F., Stoertkuhl, K. F., Stocker, R. F., & Greenspan, R. J. (1995). Genetic feminization of brain structures and changed sexual orientation in male *Drosophila. Science, 267*, 902–905.

Festinger, L. (1950). Informed social communication. *Psychological Review, 57*, 271–282.

Festinger, L., & Carlsmith, J. M. (1959). Cognitive consequences of forced compliance. *Journal of Abnormal and Social Psychology, 58*, 203–210.

Ficca, G., Lombardo, P., Rossi, L., & Salzarulo, P. (2000). Morning recall of verbal material depends on prior sleep organization. *Behavioural Brain Research, 112*, 159–163.

Ficker, J. H. I., Wiest, G. H., Lehnert, G., Meyer, M., & Hahn, E. G. (1999). Are snoring medical students at risk of failing their exams? *Sleep, 22*, 205–209.

Field, A. E., Camargo, C. A., Jr., Taylor, B., Berkey, C. S., & Colditz, G. A. (1999). Relation of peer and media influences to the development of purging behaviors among preadolescent and adolescent girls. *Archives of Pediatric Adolescent Medicine, 153*, 1184–1189.

Field, A. P., Psychol, C., & Morgan, J. (2004). Post-event processing and the retrieval of autobiographical memories in socially anxious individuals. *Journal of Anxiety Disorders, 18*, 647–663.

Field, T., Schanberg, S., Scarfidi, F., Bauer, C., Vega-Lahr, N., Garcia, R., et al. (1986). Tactile/kinesthetic stimulation effects on preterm neonates. *Pediatrics, 77*, 654–658.

Field, T. M. (1998). Touch therapy effects on development. *International Journal of Behavioral Development, 22*, 779–797.

Field, T. M., Woodson, R., Greenberg, R., & Cohen, D. (1982). Discrimination and imitation of facial expressions by neonates. *Science, 218*, 179–181.

Fields, R. D., & Stevens-Graham, B. (2002). New insights into neuron-glia communication. *Science, 298*, 556–562.

Figiel, G. S., Epstein, C., McDonald, W. M., Amazon-Leece, J., Figiel, L., Saldivia, A., & Glover, S. (1998). The use of rapid-rate transcranial magnetic stimulation (rTMS) in refractory depressed patients. *Journal of Neuropsychiatry & Clinical Neurosciences, 10*, 20–25.

Finch, A. E., Lambert, M. J., & Brown, G. (2000). Attacking anxiety: A naturalistic study of a multimedia self-help program. *Journal of Clinical Psychology, 56*, 11–21.

Fink, B., Grammer, K., & Thornhill, R. (2001). Human (*Homo sapiens*) facial attractiveness in relation to skin texture and color. *Journal of Comparative Psychology, 115*, 92–99.

Finke, R. A. (1996). Imagery, creativity, and emergent structure. *Consciousness & Cognition, 5*, 381–393.

Finke, R. A., & Slayton, K. (1988). Explorations of creative visual synthesis in mental imagery. *Memory & Cognition, 16*, 252–257.

Finke, R. A., Ward, T. B., & Smith, S. M. (1992). *Creative cognition: Theory, research, and applications.* Cambridge, MA: MIT Press.

Finkel, D., Pedersen, N. L., McGue, M., & McClearn, G. E. (1995). Heritability of cognitive abilities in adult twins: Comparison of Minnesota and Swedish data. *Behavioral Genetics, 25*, 421–432.

Finlay, F. O., Jones, R., & Coleman, J. (2002). Is puberty getting earlier? The views of doctors and teachers. *Child: Care, Health & Development, 28*, 205–209.

Finn, J., & Banach, M. (2000). Victimization online: The down side of seeking services for women on the Internet. *CyberPsychology & Behavior, 3*, 243–254.

Fiorentine, R. (1999). After drug treatment: Are 12-step programs effective in maintaining abstinence? *American Journal of Drug and Alcohol Abuse, 25*, 93–116.

Fiorillo, C. D. (2004). The uncertain nature of dopamine. *Molecular Psychiatry, 9*, 122–123.

Fischer, C., Hatzidimitriou, G., Wlos, J., Katz, J., & Ricaurte, G. (1995). Reorganization of ascending 5-HT axon projections in animals previously exposed to recreational drug 3,4-methelenedioxymetham-phetamine (MDMA, "Ecstasy"). *Journal of Neuroscience, 15*, 5476–5485.

Fisher, P. J., Turic, D., Williams, N. M., McGuffin, P., Asherson, P., Ball, D., et al. (1999). DNA pooling identifies QTLs on Chromosome 4 for general cognitive ability in children. *Human Molecular Genetics, 8*, 915–922.

Fisher, R. P., & Craik, F. I. M. (1977). The interaction between encoding and retrieval operations in cued recall. *Journal of Experimental Psychology: Human learning and Perception, 3*, 153–171.

Fisher, R. P., & Geiselman, R. E. (1992). *Memory enhancing techniques for investigative interviewing: The cognitive interview.* Springfield: Charles C. Thomas.

Fisher, R. P., Geiselman, R. E., & Amador, M. (1989). Field test of the cognitive interview: Enhancing the recollection of actual victims and witnesses of crime. *Journal of Applied Psychology, 74*, 722–727.

Fiske, S. (1998). Stereotyping, prejudice, and discrimination. In D. T. Gilbert, S. T. Fiske, & G. Lindzey (Eds.). *The handbook of social psychology* (4th ed., pp. 357–411). New York: McGraw-Hill.

Fiske, S. T. (2002). What we know about bias and intergroup conflict, the problem of the century. *Current Directions in Psychological Science, 11*, 123–128.

Fitch, R. H., & Bimonte, H. A. (2002). Hormones, brain, and behavior: Putative biological contributions to cognitive sex differences. In A. McGillicuddy-De Lisi & R. De Lisi (Eds), *Biology, society, and behavior: The development of sex differences in cognition* (pp. 55–91). Westport, CT: Ablex.

Fitton, A., & Heel, R. C. (1990). Clozapine: A review of its pharacological properties and therapeutic use schizophrenia. *Drugs, 40*, 722–747.

Fivush, R., & Edwards, V. J. (2004). Remembering and forgetting childhood sexual abuse. *Journal of Child Sexual Abuse, 13*, 1–19.

Fivush, R., & Vasudeva, A. (2002). Remembering to relate: Socioemotional correlates of mother-child reminiscing. *Journal of Cognition & Development, 3*, 73–90.

Flas, W., Dupont, P., Reynvoet, B., & Orban, G. A. (2002). The quantitative nature of a visual task differentiates between ventral and dorsal steam. *Journal of Cognitive Neuroscience, 14*, 646–658.

Flaten, M. A., Simonsen, T., & Olsen, H. (1999). Drug-related information generates placebo and nocebo responses that modify the drug response. *Psychosomatic Medicine, 61*, 250–255.

Flavell, J. H. (1999). Cognitive development: Children's knowledge about the mind. *Annual Review of Psychology, 50*, 21–45.

Fleischman, D. A., Wilson, R. S., Gabrieli, J. D. E., Bienias, J. L., & Bennett, D. A. (2004). A longitudinal study of implicit and explicit memory in old persons. *Psychology and Aging, 19*, 617–625.

Fletcher, A. C., Elder, G. H. Jr., & Mekos, D. (2000). Parental influences on adolescent involvement in community activities. *Journal of Research on Adolescence, 10*, 29–48.

Fleury, C., Neverova, M., Collins, S., Raimbault, S., Champign, O., Levi-Meyrueis, C., et al. (1977). Uncoupling protein-2: A novel candidate thermogenic protein linked to obesity and insulin resistance. *Nature Genetics, 15*, 269–272.

Flexser, A., & Tulving, E. (1978) Retrieved independence in recognition and recall. *Psychological Review, 85*, 153–171.

Floyd, M., Scogin, F., McKendree-Smith, N. L., Floyd, D. L., & Rokke, P. D. (2004). Cognitive therapy for depression: A comparison of individual psychotherapy and bibliotherapy for depressed older adults. *Behavior Modification, 28*, 297–318.

Floyd, R. L., Rimer, B. K., Giovino, G. A., Mullen, P. D., & Sullivan, S. E. (1993). A review of smoking in pregnancy: Effects on pregnancy outcomes and cessation efforts. *Annual Review of Public Health, 14*, 379–411.

Flynn, J. R. (1984). The mean IQ of Americans: Massive gains 1932 to 1978. *Psychological Bulletin, 95*, 29–51.

Flynn, J. R. (1991). *Asian Americans: Achievement beyond IQ.* Hillsdale, NJ: Erlbaum.

Flynn, J. R. (1999a). Massive IQ gains in fourteen nations: What IQ tests really measure. *Psychological Bulletin, 101*, 171–191.

Flynn, J. R. (1999b). Searching for justice: The discovery of IQ gains over time. *American Psychologist, 54*, 5–20.

Foa, E. B., Liebowitz, M. R., Kozak, M. J., Davies, S., Campeas, R., Franklin, M. E., Huppert, J. D., Kjernisted, K., Rowan, V., Schmidt, A. B., Simpson, H. B., & Tu, X. (2005). Randomized, placebo-controlled trial of exposure and ritual prevention, clomipramine, and their combination in the treatment of obsessive-compulsive disorder. *American Journal of Psychiatry, 162*, 151–161.

Foa, E. B., Steketee, G., & Olasov-Rothbaum, B. O. (1989). Behavioral/cognitive conceptualization of post-traumatic stress disorder. *Behavior Therapy, 20*, 155–176.

Fodor, J. A. (1968). *Psychological explanation: An introduction to the philosophy of psychology.* New York: Random House.

Fodor, J. A. (1983). *The modularity of mind.* Cambridge, MA: MIT Press.

Folkman, S., & Moskowitz, J. T. (2000). Positive affect and the other side of coping. *American Psychologist, 55*, 647–654.

Folkman, S., & Moskowitz, J. T. (2004). Coping: Pitfalls and promise. *Annual Review of Psychology, 55*, 745–774.

Fombonne, E. (1999). The epidemiology of autism: A review. *Psychological Medicine, 29*, 769–786.

Fones, C. S. L., Manfro, G. G., & Pollack, M. H. (1998). Social phobia: An update. *Harvard Review of Psychiatry, 5*, 247–259.

Forbes, E. J., & Pekala, R. J. (1993). Psychophysiological effects of several stress management techniques. *Psychological Reports, 72*, 19–27.

Ford, C. S., & Beach, F. (1951). *Patterns of sexual behavior.* New York: Harper & Row.

Ford, K., & Norris, A. E. (1997). Effects of interviewer age on reporting of sexual and reproductive behavior of Hispanic and African American youth. *Hispanic Journal of Behavioral Sciences, 19*, 369–376.

Ford, T. E., Ferguson, M. A., Brooks, J. L., & Hagadone, K. M. (2004). Coping sense of humor reduces effects of stereotype threat on women's math performance. *Personality & Social Psychology Bulletin, 30*, 643–653.

Forgas, J. P., Levinger, G., & Moylan, S. (1994). Feeling good and feeling close: Mood effects on the perception of intimate relationships. *Personal Relationships, 2*, 165–184.

Forge, K. L., & Phemister, S. (1987). The effect of prosocial cartoons on preschool children. *Child Study Journal, 17*, 83–88.

Forgione A. G. (1988). Hypnosis in the treatment of dental fear and phobia. *Dental Clinics of North America, 32*, 745–761.

Forman, D. R., Aksan, N., & Kochanska, G. (2004). Toddlers' responsive imitation predicts preschool-age conscience. *Psychological Science, 15*, 699–704.

Foster, G. D., Wyatt, H. R., Hill, J. O., McGuckin, B. G., Brill, C., Mohammed, B. S., et al. (2003). A randomized trial of a low-carbohydrate diet for obesity. *New England Journal of Medicine, 348*, 2082–2090.

Fouts, G., & Burggraf, K. (2000). Television situation comedies: Female weight, male negative comments, and audience reactions. *Sex Roles, 42*, 925–932.

Fouts, R., & Mills, S. (1997). *Next of kin.* New York: William Morrow.

Fowles, D. C., & Kochanska, G. (2000). Temperament as a moderator of pathways to conscience in children: The contribution of electrodermal activity. *Psychophysiology, 37*, 788–795.

Fox, C. H. (1994). Cocaine use in pregnancy. *Journal of the American Board of Family Practice, 7*, 225–228.

Fox, E., Russo, R., Bowles, R., & Dutton, K. (2001). Do threatening stimuli draw or hold attention in subclinical anxiety? *Journal of Experimental Psychology General, 130*, 681–700.

Fox, E., Russo, R., & Dutton K. (2002). Attentional bias for threat: Evidence for delayed disengagement from emotional faces. *Cognition & Emotion, 16*, 355–379.

Fox, N. A., Henderson, H. A., Marshall, P. J., Nichols, K. E., & Ghera, M. M. (2005). Behavioral Inhibition: Linking biology and behavior within a developmental framework. *Annual Review of Psychology, 56*, n.p.

Fox, W. M. (1982). Why we should abandon Maslow's Need Hierarchy Theory. *Journal of Humanistic Education and Development, 21*, 29–32.

Fozard, J. (1990). Vision and hearing in aging. In J. E. Birren & K. W. Schaie (Eds.), *Handbook of the psychology of aging* (3rd ed., pp. 150–170). San Diego: Academic Press.

Fraley, R. C., Garner, J. P., & Shaver, P. R. (2000). Adult attachment and the defensive regulation of attention and memory: Examining the role of preemptive and postemptive defensive processes. *Journal of Personality & Social Psychology, 79*, 816–826.

Fraley, R. C., & Shaver, P. R. (1997). Adult attachment and the suppression of unwanted thoughts. *Journal of Personality & Social Psychology, 73*, 1080–1091.

Fraley, R. C., & Spieker, S. J. (2003). Are infant attachment patterns continuously or categorically distributed? A taxometric analysis of strange situation behavior. *Developmental Psychology, 39*, 387–404.

Frances, A. (1998). Problems in defining clinical significance in epidemiological studies. *Archives of General Psychiatry, 55*, 119.

Francis, J. R., & Aronson, H. (1990). Communicative efficacy of psychotherapy research. *Journal of Consulting and Clinical Psychology, 58*, 368–370.

Francis, M. E., & Pennebaker, J. W. (1992). Putting stress into words: The impact of writing on physiological, absentee, and self-reported emotional well-being measures. *American Journal of Health Promotion, 6*, 280–286.

Frank, R. H. (2004). How not to buy happiness. *Daedalus, 133*, 69–79.

Franklin, M. E., Abramowitz, J. S., Bux, D. A. Jr., Zoellner, L. A., & Feeny, N. C. (2002). Cognitive-behavioral therapy with and without medication in the treatment of obsessive-compulsive disorder. *Professional Psychology: Research & Practice, 33*, 162–168.

Fraser, L. (2000). *Conversations with J. K. Rowling.* New York: Scholastic.

Frasure-Smith, N., Lesperance, F., Juneau, M., Talajic, M., & Bourassa, M. G. (1999). Gender, depression, and one-year prognosis after myocardial infarction. *Psychosomatic Medicine, 61*, 26–37.

Frazier, P. A., Tix, A. P., & Barnett, C. L. (2003). The relational context of social support: Relationship satisfaction moderates the relations between enacted support and distress. *Personality & Social Psychology Bulletin, 29*, 1133–1146.

Fredrickson, B. L. (2001). The role of positive emotions in positive psychology: The broaden-and-build theory of positive emotions. *American Psychologist, 56*, 218–226.

Fredrickson, B. L., & Joiner, T. (2002). Positive emotions trigger upward spirals toward emotional well-being. *Psychological Science, 13*, 172–175.

Freedman, J. L., & Fraser, S. C. (1966). Compliance without pressure: The foot-in-the-door technique. *Journal of Personality and Social Psychology, 4*, 195–202.

Freedman, M. R., King, J., & Kennedy, E. (2001). Popular diets: A scientific review. *Obesity Research, 9*, 1S–40S.

Freedman, M. S., Lucas, R. J., Soni, B., von Schantz, M., Muñoz, M., David-Gray, Z., & Foster, R. (1999). Regulation of mammalian circadian behavior by non-rod, non-cone, ocular photoreceptors. *Science, 284*, 502–504.

Freeman, H. (1994). Schizophrenia and city residence. *British Journal of Psychiatry, 164*(Suppl. 23), 39–50.

Freeman, J. H., Jr., & Nicholson, D. A. (2001). Ontogenetic changes in the neural mechanisms of eyeblink conditioning. *Integrative Physiological & Behavioral Science, 36*, 15–35.

Freeman, W. J. (1991). The psychology of perception. *Scientific American, 264*, 78–85.

Freese, J., Powell, B., & Steelman, L. C. (1999). Rebel without a cause or effect: Birth order and social attitudes. *American Sociological Review, 64*, 207–231.

Freitas, A. L., & Higgins, E. T. (2002). Enjoying goal-directed action: The role of regulatory fit. *Psychological Science, 13*, 1–6.

Freitas, A. L., Liberman, N., & Higgins, E. T. (2002). Regulatory fit and resisting temptation during goal pursuit. *Journal of Experimental Social Psychology, 38*, 291–298.

Freud, A. (1958). Adolescence. *Psychoanalytic Study of the Child, 15*, 255–278.

Freud, S. (1900/1958). *The interpretation of dreams.* New York: Basic Books.

Freud, S. (1910). The origin & development of psychoanalysis. *American Journal of Psychology, 21*, 181–218.

Freud, S. (1937/1964). Analysis terminable and interminable. In J. Strachey (Ed. and Trans.), *The standard edition of the complete psychological works of Sigmund Freud* (Vol. 23, pp. 209–253).

Freud, S. (1938). *The basic writings of Sigmund Freud.* New York: Modern Library (Random House).

Fridlund, A. J. (1994). *Human facial expression: An evolutionary view.* San Diego, CA: Academic Press.

Fried, P. A., & Makin, J. E. (1987). Neonatal behavioral correlates of prenatal exposure to marijuana, cigarettes, and alcohol in a low risk population. *Neurobehavioral Toxicology and Teratology, 9*, 1–7.

Fried, P. A., & Watkinson, B. (2000). Visuoperceptual functioning differs in 9- to 12-year-olds prenatally exposed to cigarettes and marihuana. *Neurotoxicology & Teratology, 22*, 11–20.

Friedler, G. (1996). Paternal exposures: Impact on reproductive and developmental outcome: An overview. *Pharmacology, Biochemistry & Behavior, 55*, 691–700.

Friedman, M., & Rosenman, R. (1974). *Type A behavior and your heart.* New York: Knopf.

Friedman, M. I. (1991). Metabolic control of calorie intake. In M. T. Friedman, M. G. Tordoff, & M. R. Kare (Eds.), *Chemical senses.* New York: Marcel Dekker.

Friedman, M. I., Tordoff, M. G., & Ramirez, I. (1986b). Integrated metabolic control of food intake. *Brain Research Bulletin, 17*, 855–859.

Friedrich, R. W. (2004). Odorant receptors make scents. *Nature, 430*, 511–512.

Friesen, C. K., & Kingstone, A. (1998). The eyes have it! Reflexive orienting is triggered by nonpredictive gaze. *Psychonomic Bulletin & Review, 5*, 490–495.

Frischholz, E. J. (1985). The relationship among dissociation, hypnosis, and child abuse in the development of multiple personality. In R. P. Kluft (Ed.), *Childhood antecedents of multiple personality* (pp. 99–120). Washington, DC: American Psychiatric Press.

Fryer, R. G., & Levitt, S. D. (2004). Understanding the Black-White test score gap in the first two years of school. *The Review of Economics and Statistics, 86*, 447–464.

Fryers, T. (1993). Epidemiological thinking in mental retardation: Issues in taxonomy and population frequency. In N. W. Bray (Ed.), *International review of research in mental retardation* (Vol. 19). Novato, CA: Academic Therapy Publications.

Fulker, D. W., Eysenck, S. B., & Zuckerman, M. (1980). A genetic and environmental analysis of sensation seeking. *Journal of Research in Personality, 14*, 261–281.

Fuller, R. K., Branchey, L., Brightwell, D. R., Derman, R. M., Emrick, C. D., Iber, F. L., et al. (1986). Disulfiram treatment of alcoholism: A Veterans Administration cooperative study. *Journal of the American Medical Association 256*(11):1449–1455.

Fulton, S., Woodside, B., & Shizgal, P. (2000). Modulation of brain reward circuitry by leptin. *Science, 287*, 125–128.

Funder, D. C., & Colvin, C. R. (1991). Explorations in behavioral consistency: Properties of persons, situations, and behaviors. *Journal of Personality and Social Psychology, 60*, 773–794.

Fung, H. H., Carstensen, L. L., & Lang, F. R. (2001). Age-related patterns in social networks among European Americans and African Americans: Implications for socioemotional selectivity across the life span. *International Journal of Aging & Human Development, 52*, 185–206.

Funk, S. C., & Houston, B. K. (1987). A critical analysis of the hardiness sale's validity and utility. *Journal of Personality and Social Psychology, 53*, 572–578.

Funtowicz, M. N., & Widiger, T. A. (1999). Sex bias in the diagnosis of personality disorders: An evaluation of the *DSM-IV* criteria. *Journal of Abnormal Psychology, 108*, 195–201.

Furnham, A., Shahidi, S., & Baluch, B. (2002). Sex and culture differences in perceptions of estimated multiple intelligence for self and family: A British-Iranian comparison. *Journal of Cross-Cultural Psychology, 33*, 270–285.

Fuster, J. M. (1997). Network memory. *Trends in Neuroscience, 20*, 451–459.

Gabbard, G. O. (1990). *Psychodynamic psychiatry in clinical practice.* Washington, DC: American Psychiatric Press.

Gabrieli, J. D. E. (1996). Memory systems analyses of mnemonic disorders in aging and age-related diseases. *Proceedings of the National Academy of Sciences, USA, 93*, 13534–13540.

Gabrieli, J. D. E., Desmond, J. E., Demb, J. B. Wagner, A. D., Stone, M. V., Vaidya, C. J., & Glover, G. H. (1996). Functional magnetic resonance imaging of semantic memory processes in the frontal lobes. *Psychological Science, 7*, 278–283.

Gabrieli, J. D. E., Fleischman, D. A., Keane, M. M., Reminger, S. L., & Morrell, F. (1995). Double dissociation between memory systems underlying explicit and implicit memory in the human brain. *American Psychological Society, 6*, 76–82.

Gagliese, L., & Katz, J. (2000). Medically unexplained pain is not caused by psychopathology. *Pain Research & Management, 5*, 251–257.

Gagné, F., & St Père, F. (2001). When IQ is controlled, does motivation still predict achievement? *Intelligence, 30*, 71–100.

Galanaki, E. (2001). The "imaginary audience" and the "personal fable" in relation to risk behavior and risk perception during adolescence. *Psychology: The Journal of the Hellenic Psychological Society, 8*, 411–430.

Galanter, M. (2000). Cults. In A. E. Kazdin (Ed.), *Encyclopedia of psychology* (Vol. 2, pp. 380–382). Washington, DC: American Psychological Association.

Galdzicki, Z., Siarey, R., Pearce, R., Stoll, J., & Rapoport, S. I. (2001). On the cause of mental retardation in Down syndrome: Extrapolation from full and segmental tirsomy 16 mouse models. *Brain Research Reviews, 35*, 115–145.

Gale, G. D., Anagnostaras, S. G., & Fanselow, M. S. (2001). Cholinergic modulation of Pavlovian fear conditioning: Effects of intrahippocampal scopolamine infusion. *Hippocampus, 11*, 371–376.

Gallagher, M., McMahan, R. W., & Schoenbaum, G. (1999). Orbitofrontal cortex and representation of incentive value in associative learning. *Journal of Neuroscience, 19*, 6610–6614.

Gallaher, P. E. (1992). Individual differences in nonverbal behavior. Dimensions of style. *Journal of Personality and Social Psychology, 63*, 133–145.

Gallo, L. C., & Matthews, K. A. (2003). Understanding the association between socioeconomic status and physical health: Do negative emotions play a role? *Psychological Bulletin, 129*, 10–51.

Gandour, J., & Baum, S. R. (2001). Production of stress retraction by left- and right-hemisphere-damaged patients. *Brain & Language, 79*, 482–494.

Gangestad, S. W. (1993). Sexual selection and physical attractiveness: Implications for mating dynamics. *Human Nature, 4*, 205–235.

Gangestad, S. W., Thornhill, R., & Garver, C. E. (2002). Changes in women's sexual interests and their partners' mate-retention tactics across the menstrual cycle: Evidence for shifting conflicts of interest. *Proceedings of the Royal Society of London: B, Biological Sciences, 269*, 975–982.

Ganis, G., Kosslyn, S. M., Stose, S., Thompson, W. L., & Yurgelun-Todd, D. (2003). Neural correlates of different types of deception: An fMRI investigation. *Cerebral Cortex, 13*, 830–836.

Ganis, G., Thompson, W. L., & Kosslyn, S. M. (2004). Brain areas underlying visual imagery and visual perception: An fMRI study. *Cognitive Brain Research, 20*, 226–241.

Garb, H. N. (1997). Race bias, social class bias, and gender bias in clinical judgment. *Clinical Psychology: Science & Practice, 4*, 99–120.

Garb, H. N., Wood, J. M., Lilienfeld, S. O., & Nezworski, M. T. (2002). Effective use of projective techniques in clinical practice: Let the data help with selection and interpretation. *Professional Psychology: Research & Practice, 33*, 454–463.

Garbarino, S., Beelke, M., Costa, G., Violani, C., Lucidi, F., Ferrillo, F., & Sannita, W. G. (2002). Brain function and effects of shift work: Implications for clinical neuropharmacology. *Neuropsychobiology, 45*, 50–56.

Garcia, J., Ervin, F. R., & Koelling, R. A. (1966). Learning with prolonged delay of reinforcement. *Psychonomic Science, 5*, 121–122.

Garcia, J., & Koelling, R. (1966). Relation of cue to consequence in avoidance learning. *Psychonomic Science, 4*, 123–124.

Garcia-Arraras, J. E., & Pappenheimer, J. R. (1983). Site of action of sleep-inducing muramyl peptide isolated from human urine: Microinjection studies in rabbit brains. *Journal of Neurophysiology, 49*, 528–533.

Garden, S., Cornoldi, C., & Logie, R. H. (2002). Visuo-spatial working memory in navigation. *Applied Cognitive Psychology, 16*, 35–50.

Gardner, H. (1985). *The mind's new science: A history of the cognitive revolution.* New York: Basic Books.

Gardner, H. (1993a). *Creating minds: An anatomy of creativity as seen through the lives of Freud, Einstein, Picasso, Stravinsky, Eliot, Graham, and Gandhi.* New York: Basic Books.

Gardner, H. (1993b). *Frames of mind: The theory of multiple intelligences.* New York: Basic Books. (Original work published 1983)

Gardner, H. (1995, November). Reflections on multiple intelligences: Myths and messages. *Phi Delta Kappan*, pp. 200–209.

Gardner, H. (1999). *Intelligence reframed: Multiple intelligences for the 21st century.* New York: Basic Books.

Gardner, H. (2002). Three distinct meanings of intelligence. In R. J. Sternberg, J. Lautrey, & T. I. Lubart (Eds.), *Models of intelligence: International perspectives* (pp. 43–45). Washington, DC: American Psychological Association.

Gardner, H., Kornhaber, M. L., & Wake, W. K. (1996). *Intelligence: Multiple perspectives.* Ft. Worth, TX: Harcourt Brace.

Gardner, R. A., & Gardner, B. T. (1969). Teaching sign language to a chimpanzee. *Science, 165*, 664–672.

Garfield, S. L. (1994). Research on client variables in psychotherapy. In A. E. Bergin & S. L. Garfield (Eds.), *Handbook of psychotherapy and behavior change* (4th edition, pp. 190–228). New York: John Wiley & Sons.

Garfield, S. L. (1996). Some problems associated with "validated" forms of psychotherapy. *Clinical Psychology: Science & Practice, 3*, 218–229.

Garfield, S. L. (1998). Some comments on empirically supported treatments. *Journal of Consulting & Clinical Psychology, 66*, 121–125.

Garfield, S. L., & Bergin, A. E. (1994). Introduction and historical overview. In A. E. Bergin & S. L. Garfield (Eds.), *Handbook of psychotherapy and behavior change* (4th edition, pp. 3–18). New York: John Wiley & Sons.

Garfinkel, P. E., Goldbloom, D., David, R., Olmsted, M. P., Garner, D. M., & Halmi, K. A. (1992). Body dissatisfaction in Bulimia Nervosa: Relationship to weight and shape concerns and psychological functioning. *International Journal of Eating Disorders, 11*, 151–161.

Garner, D. M. (1997). Psychoeducational principles in treatment. In D. M. Garner & P. E. Garfinkel (Eds.), *Handbook of treatment for eating disorders* (2nd ed.). New York: Guilford Press.

Garrard, P., Lambon, R. M. A., Hodges, J. R., & Patterson, K. (2001). Prototypicality, distinctiveness, and intercorrelation: Analyses of the semantic attributes of living and nonliving concepts. *Cognitive Neuropsychology, 18*, 125–174.

Garrido, E., Masip, J., & Herrero, C. (2004). Police officers' credibility judgments: Accuracy and estimated ability. *International Journal of Psychology, 39*, 254–275.

Garrigue, S., Bordier, P., Jais, P., Shah D. C., Hocini M., Raherison C., Tunon De Lara, M., Haïssaguerre, M., & Clementy, J. (2002). Benefit of atrial pacing in sleep apnea syndrome. *New England Journal of Medicine, 346*, 404–412.

Garris, P. A., Kilpatrick, M., Bunin, M. A., Michael, D., Walker, Q. D., & Wightman, R. M. (1999). Dissociation of dopamine release in the nucleus accumbens from intracranial self-stimulation. *Nature, 398*, 67–69.

Garry, M., & Polaschek, D. L. L. (2000). Imagination and memory. *Current Directions in Psychological Science, 9*, 6–10.

Garvey, C. (1974). Requests and responses in children's speech. *Journal of Child Language, 2*, 41–60.

Gaser, C., & Schlaug, G. (2003). Brain structures differ between musicians and non-musicians. *Journal of Neuroscience, 23*, 9240–9245.

Gaster, B., & Holroyd, J. (2000). St. John's Wort for depression: A systematic review. *Archives of Internal Medicine, 160*, 152–156.

Gater, R., Tansella, M., Korten, A., Tiemens, B. G., Mavreas, V. G., & Olatawura, M. O. (1998). Report from the World Health Organization collaborative study on psychological problems in general health care. *Archives of General Psychiatry, 55*, 405–413.

Gaudiano, B. A. (2005). Cognitive behavior therapies for psychotic disorders: Current empirical status and future directions. *Clinical Psychology: Science & Practice, 12*, 33–50.

Gauthier, I., Skudkarski, P., Gore, J. C., & Anderson, A. W. (2000). Expertise for cars and birds recruits brain areas involved in face recognition. *Nature Neuroscience, 3*, 191–197.

Gauthier, I., & Tarr, M. J. (2002). Unraveling mechanisms for expert object recognition: Bridging brain activity and behavior. *Journal of Experimental Psychology: Human Perception & Performance, 28*, 431–446.

Gauthier, I., Tarr, M. J., Anderson, A. W., Skudlarski, P., & Gore, J. C. (1999). Activation of the middle fusiform "face area" increases with expertise in recognizing novel objects. *Nature Neuroscience, 2*, 568–573.

Gazzaniga, M. S. (1995). Consciousness and the cerebral hemispheres. In M. S. Gazzaniga (Ed.), *The cognitive neurosciences* (pp. 1391–1400). Cambridge, MA: MIT Press.

Gazzaniga, M. S., (Ed.). (2004). *The cognitive neurosciences III*. Cambridge, MA: MIT Press.

Gazzaniga, M. S., & LeDoux, J. E. (1979). *The integrated mind*. New York: Plenum.

Geary, D. C. (1996). Sexual selection and sex differences in mathematical abilities. *Behavioral and Brain Sciences, 19*, 229–284.

Geary, N., & Smith, G. P. (1985). Pimozide decreases the positive reinforcing effects of sham fed sucrose in the rat. *Pharmacology, Biochemistry, & Behavior, 22*, 787–790.

Geddes, J. R., Freemantle, N., Mason, J., Eccles, M., & Boynton, J. (2000). SSRIs versus alternative antidepressants in depressive disorder. *Cochrane Database System Review (2)*: CD001851.

Geddes, J. R., & Lawrie, S. M. (1995). Obstetric complications and schizophrenia: A meta-analysis. *British Journal of Psychiatry, 67*, 786–793.

Gega, L., Marks, I., & Mataix-Cols, D. (2004). Computer-aided CBT self-help for anxiety and depressive disorders: Experience of a London clinic and future directions. *Journal of Clinical Psychology, 60*, 147–157.

Gegenfurtner, K. R., & Kiper, D. C. (2003). Color vision. *Annual Review of Neuroscience, 26*, 181–206.

Geinisman, Y. (2000). Structural synaptic modifications associated with hippocampal LTP and behavioral learning. *Cerebral Cortex, 10*, 952–962.

Geiselman, R. E., Fisher, R. P., MacKinnon, D. P., & Holland, H. L. (1985). Eyewitness memory enhancement in the police interview. *Cognitive Journal of Applied Psychology, 70*, 401–412.

Gelfand, S. A. (1981). *Hearing*. New York: Marcel Dekker.

Gelman, R. (1972). Logical capacity of very young children: Number invariance rules. *Child Development, 43*, 75–90.

Gentile, D. A., Walsh, D. A. Ellison, P. R., Fox, M., & Cameron, J. (2004). Media violence as a risk factor for children: A longitudinal study. *Paper presented at the American Psychological Society 16th Annual Convention*, Chicago, Illinois (May, 2004).

Gentner, D., & Bowdle, B. F. (2001). Convention, form, and figurative language processing. *Metaphor & Symbol, 16*, 223–247.

Gentner, D., & Gunn, V. (2001). Structural alignment facilitates the noticing of differences. *Memory & Cognition, 29*, 565–577.

George, M. S., Lisanby, S. H., & Sackheim, H. A. (1999). Transcranial magnetic stimulation: Applications in neuropsychiatry. *Archives in General Psychiatry, 56*, 300–311.

Gerhardstein, P., Adler, S. A., & Rovee-Collier, C. (2000). A dissociation in infants' memory for stimulus size: Evidence for the early development of multiple memory systems. *Developmental Psychobiology, 36*, 123–135.

Gerlai, R. (1996). Gene-targeting studies of mammalian behavior: Is it the mutation of the background genotype? *Trends in Neuroscience, 19*, 177–181.

German, D. C., & Bowden, D. M. (1974). Catecholamine systems as the neural substrate for intracranial self-stimulation: A hypothesis. *Brain Research, 73*, 381–419.

German, T. P., & Barrett, H. C. (2005). Functional fixedness in a technologically sparse culture. *Psychological Science, 16*, 1–5.

Gerrard, M., Gibbons, F. X., Reis-Bergan, M., & Russell, D. W. (2000). Self-esteem, self-serving cognitions, and health risk behavior. *Journal of Personality, 68*, 1177–1201.

Gerstmann, J. (1942). Problem of imperception of disease and of impaired body territories with organic lesions. *Archives of Neurology and Psychiatry, 48*, 890–913.

Gerteis, J., & Savage, M. (1998). The salience of class in Britain and America: A comparative analysis. *British Journal of Sociology, 49*, 252–274.

Gerwig, M., Dimitrova, A., Kolb, F. P., Maschke, M., Brol, B., Kunnel, A., Böring, D., Thilmann, A. F., Forsting, M., Diener, H. C., & Timmann, D. (2003). Comparison of eyeblink conditioning in patients with superior and posterior inferior cerebellar lesions. *Brain, 126*, 71–94.

Gesell, A., & Thompson, H. (1938). *The psychology of early growth including norms of infant behavior and a method of genetic analysis*. New York: Macmillan.

Gesy, L. J. (Ed.). (1993). *Today's destructive cults and movements*. Huntington, IN: Our Sunday Visitor Publications.

Gibbons, F. X., & Gerrard, M. (1995). Predicting young adults' health-risk behavior. *Journal of Personality and Social Psychology, 69*, 505–517.

Gibson, J. J. (1966). *The senses considered as perceptual systems*. Boston: Houghton Mifflin.

Gibson, J. J., & Walk, R. D. (1960). The "visual cliff." *Scientific American, 202*, 64–71.

Gibson, J. T. (1991). Training people to inflict pain: State terror and social learning. *Journal of Humanistic Psychology, 31*, 72–87.

Gick, M. L., & Holyoak, K. J. (1980). Analogical problem solving. *Cognitive Psychology, 12*, 306–355.

Gick, M. L., & Holyoak, K. J. (1983). Schema induction and analogical transfer. *Cognitive Psychology, 15*, 1–38.

Gick, M. L., & Thompson, W. G. (1997). Negative affect and the seeking of medical care in university students with irritable bowel syndrome. *Journal of Psychosomatic Research, 43*, 535–540.

Gidron, Y., Davidson, K., & Bata, I. (1999). The short-term effects of a hostility-reduction intervention on male coronary heart disease patients. *Health Psychology, 18*, 416–420.

Giesbrecht, B., & Kingstone, A. (2004). Right hemisphere involvement in the attentional blink: Evidence from a split-brain patient. *Brain & Cognition, 55*, 303–306.

Gigerenzer, G. (1994). Why the distinction between single-event probabilities and frequencies is relevant for psychology and vice versa. In G. Wright & P. Ayton (Eds.), *Subjective probability* (pp. 129–162). New York: Wiley.

Gigerenzer, G. (1996). On narrow norms and vague heuristics: A reply to Kahneman & Tversky (1996). *Psychological Review, 103*, 592–596.

Gigerenzer, G. (2002). *Calculated risks: How to know when numbers deceive you*. New York: Simon & Schuster.

Gigerenzer, G., & Goldstein, D. G. (1996). Reasoning the fast and frugal way: Models of bounded rationality. *Psychological Review, 103*, 650–669.

Gigerenzer, G., Hell, W., & Blank, H. (1988). Presentation and content: The use of base rates as a continuous variable. *Journal of Experimental Psychology: Human Perception and Performance, 14*, 513–525.

Gilbert, D. T. (1995). Attribution and interpersonal perception. In A. Tesser (Ed.), *Advanced social psychology* (pp. 99–147). New York: McGraw-Hill.

Gilbert, D. T. (2002). Are psychology's tribes ready to form a nation? *Trends in Cognitive Sciences, 6*, 3.

Gilbert, D. T., & Hixon, J. G. (1991). The trouble of thinking: Activation and application of stereotypic beliefs. *Journal of Personality and Social Psychology, 60*, 509–517.

Gilbert, S. (2002, June 25). When brain trauma is at the other end of the thrill ride. *New York Times*, D5.

Gilbertson, M. W., Shenton, M. E., Ciszewski, A., Kasai, K., Lasko, N. B., Orr, S. P., & Pitman, R. K. (2002). Smaller hippocampal volume predicts pathologic vulnerability to psychological trauma. *Nature Neuroscience, 5*, 1242–1247.

Gilger, J. W. (1995). Behavioral genetics: Concepts for research and practice in language development and disorders. *Journal of Speech and Hearing Research, 38*, 1126–1142.

Gilligan, C. (1982). *In a different voice*. Cambridge, MA: Harvard University Press.

Gilmore, J. H., Sikich, L., & Lieberman, J. A. (1997). Neuroimaging, neurodevelopment, and schizophrenia. *Child & Adolescent Psychiatric Clinics of North America, 6*(2), 325–341.

Giltay, E. J., Geleijnse, J. M., Zitman, F. G., Hoekstra, T., & Schouten, E. G. (2004). Dispositional optimism and all-cause and cardiovascular mortality in a prospective cohort of elderly dutch men and women. *Archives of General Psychiatry, 61*, 1126–1135.

Ginandes, C., Brooks, P., Sando, W., Jones, C., & Aker, J. (2003). Can medical hypnosis accelerate post-surgical wound healing? Results of a clinical trial. *American Journal of Clinical Hypnosis, 45*, 333–351.

Gladwell, M. (1998, February 2). The Pima paradox. *New Yorker*, pp. 44–57.

Gladwell, M. (2000, May 29). The new-boy network: What do job interviews really tell us? *New Yorker*, 68–72, 84, 86.

Glanzer, M., & Cunitz, A. R. (1966). Two storage mechanisms in free recall. *Journal of Verbal Learning and Verbal Behavior, 6*, 351–360.

Glaser, R., & Kiecolt-Glaser, J. K. (1998). Stress-associated immune modulation: Relevance to viral infections and chronic fatigue syndrome. *American Journal of Medicine, 105*, 35S–42S.

Glass, D., & Singer, J. (1972). *Urban stress: Experiments on noise and social stressors*. New York: Academic Press.

Glass, R. M. (2001). Electroconvulsive therapy: Time to bring it out of the shadows. *Journal of the American Medical Association, 285*, n.p.

Glennon, F., & Joseph, S. (1993). Just world belief, self-esteem, and attitudes towards homosexuals with AIDS. *Psychological Reports, 72*, 584–586.

Gloaguen, V., Cottraux, J., Cucherat, M., & Blackburn, I. (1998). A meta-analysis of the effects of cognitive therapy in depressed patients. *Journal of Affective Disorders, 49*, 59–72.

Gluck, M., & Myers, C. (2000). *Gateway to memory: An introduction to neural network modeling of the hippocampus and learning.* Cambridge, MA: MIT Press.

Glucksberg, S., Newsome, M. R., & Goldvarg, Y. (2001). Inhibition of the literal: Filtering metaphor-irrelevant information during metaphor comprehension. *Metaphor & Symbol, 16,* 277–293.

Glutting, J. J., Oh, H-J., Ward, T., & Ward, S. (2000). Possible criterion-related bias of the WISC-III with a referral sample. *Journal of Psychoeducational Assessment, 18,* 17–26.

Glynn, S. M. (1990). Token economy approaches for psychiatric patients: Progress and pitfalls over 25 years. *Behavior Modification, 14,* 383–407.

Godden, D. R., & Baddeley, A. D. (1975). Context-dependent memory in two natural environments: On land and underwater. *British Journal of Psychology, 66,* 325–331.

Godemann, F., Ahrens, B., Behrens, S., Berthold, R., Gandor, C., Lampe, F., & Linden, M. (2001). Classic conditioning and dysfunctional cognitions in patients with panic disorder and agoraphobia treated with an implantable cardioverter/defibrillator. *Psychosomatic Medicine, 63,* 231–238.

Goedde, H. W., & Agarwal, D. P. (1987). Aldehyde hydrogenase polymorphism: Molecular basis and phenotypic relationship to alcohol sensitivity. *Alcohol & Alcoholism* (Suppl. 1), 47–54.

Goel, V., & Dolan, R. J. (2003). Explaining modulation of reasoning by belief. *Cognition, 87,* B11–B22.

Goetestam, K. G., & Berntzen, D. (1997). Use of the modelling effect in one-session exposure. *Scandinavian Journal of Behaviour Therapy, 26,* 97–101.

Goethals, G. R., Cooper, J., & Naficy, A. (1979). Role of foreseen, foreseeable, and unforeseeable behavioral consequences in the arousal of cognitive dissonance. *Journal of Personality and Social Psychology, 37,* 1179–1185.

Goethals, G. R., & Zanna, M. P. (1979). The role of social comparison in choice shifts. *Journal of Personality and Social Psychology, 37,* 1469–1185.

Goff, D. C., & Coyle, J. T. (2001). The emerging role of glutamate in the pathophysiology and treatment of schizophrenia. *American Journal of Psychiatry, 158,* 1367–1377.

Goldapple, K., Segal, Z., Garson, C., Lau, M., Bieling, P., Kennedy, S., & Mayberg, H. (2004). Modulation of cortical-limbic pathways in major depression. *Archives of General Psychiatry, 61,* 34–41.

Goldberg, E. (2001). *The executive brain: Frontal lobes and the civilized mind.* New York: Oxford University Press.

Goldberg, L. R. (1981). Language and individual differences: The search for universals in personality lexicons. In L. Wheeler (Ed.), *Review of personality and social psychology* (Vol. 2, pp. 141–165). Beverly Hills, CA: Sage.

Goldenberg, J., Mazursky, D., & Solomon, S. (1999). Essays on science and society: Creative sparks. *Science, 285,* 1495–1496.

Goldfried, M. R., & Eubanks-Carter, C. (2004). On the need for a new psychotherapy research paradigm: Comment on Westen, Novotny, and Thompson-Brenner (2004). *Psychological Bulletin, 130,* 669–673.

Goldin-Meadow, S., & Mylander, C. (1998). Spontaneous sign systems created by deaf children in two cultures. *Nature, 391,* 279–281.

Goldin-Meadow, S., Nusbaum, H., Kelly, S. D., & Wagner, S. (2001). Explaining math: Gesturing lightens the load. *Psychological Science, 12,* 516–522.

Goldman, W. P., Wolters, N. C. W., & Winograd, E. (1992). A demonstration of incubation in anagram problem solving. *Bulletin of the Psychonomic Society, 30,* 36–38.

Goldstein, A. (1994). *Addiction: From biology to drug policy.* New York: Freeman.

Goldstein, D. G., & Gigerenzer, G. (2002). Models of ecological rationality: The recognition heuristic. *Psychological Review, 109,* 75–90.

Goldstein, D. S. (1995). *Stress, catecholamines, and cardiovascular disease.* New York: Oxford University Press.

Goldstein, D. S. (2000). *The autonomic nervous system in health and disease.* New York: Marcel Dekker.

Goldstein, D. S., & McEwen, B. (2002). Allostasis, homeostats, and the nature of stress. *Stress: International Journal on the Biology of Stress, 5,* 55–58.

Goldstein, J. M., Goodman, J. M., Seidman, L. J., Kennedy, D. N., Makris, N., Lee, H., et al. (1999). Cortical abnormalities in schizophrenia identified by structural magnetic resonance imaging. *Archives of General Psychiatry, 56,* 537–547.

Goldstein, M. D., & Strube, M. J. (1994). Independence revisited: The relation between positive and negative affect in a naturalistic setting. *Personality & Social Psychology Bulletin, 20,* 57–64.

Goldstein, M. J. (1992). Psychosocial strategies for maximizing the effects of psychotropic medications for schizophrenia and mood disorder. *Psychopharmacology Bulletin, 28,* 237–240.

Goldstone, R. L., Steyvers, M., & Rogosky, B. J. (2003). Conceptual interrelatedness and caricatures. *Memory & Cognition, 31,* 169–180.

Gomez, R., & Gomez, A. (2005). Convergent, discriminant and concurrent validities of measures of the behavioural approach and behavioural inhibition systems: Confirmatory factor analytic approach. *Personality & Individual Differences, 38,* 87–102.

Gontkovsky, S. T. (1998). Huntington's disease: A neuropsychological overview. *Journal of Cognitive Rehabilitation, 16,* 6–9.

Goodale, M. A., & Milner, A. D. (1992). Separate visual pathways for perception and action. *Trends in Neurosciences, 15,* 20–25.

Goode, E. (1999, November 2). New clues to why we dream. *New York Times,* p. D1.

Goodfellow, P. N., & Lovell-Badge, R. (1993). SRY and sex determination in mammals. *Annual Review of Genetics, 27,* 71–92.

Goodglass, H. (1976). Agrammatism. In H. Whitaker & H. A. Whitaker (Eds.), *Studies of neurolinguistics.* New York: Academic Press.

Goodie, A. S., & Fantino, E. (1996). Learning to commit or avoid the base-rate error. *Nature, 380,* 247–249.

Goodman, N. (1983). *Fact, fiction, and forecast* (4th ed.). Cambridge: Harvard University Press.

Goodman, R. (1988). Are complications of pregnancy and birth causes of schizophrenia? *Developmental Medical Child Neurology, 30,* 391–395.

Goodwin, F. K., & Ghaemi, S. N. (1998). Understanding manic–depressive illness. *Archives of General Psychiatry, 55,* 23–25.

Goodwin, F. K., & Jamison, K. R. (1990). *Manic-depressive illness.* New York: Oxford University Press.

Goodwin, R. D., & Gotlib, I. H. (2004). Gender differences in depression: The role of personality factors. *Psychiatry Research, 126,* 135–142.

Gopnik, A. (1996). The post-Piaget era. *Psychological Science, 7,* 221–225.

Gopnik, M. (1990). Dysphasia in an extended family. *Nature, 344,* 715.

Gopnik, M. (1997). Language deficits and genetic factors. *Trends in Cognitive Sciences, 1,* 5–9.

Gopnik, M. (1999). Familial language impairment: More English evidence. *Folia Phoniatrica et Logopaedica, 51,* 5–19.

Gopnik, M., & Crago, M. (1991). Familial aggregation of a developmental language disorder. *Cognition, 39,* 1–50.

Gordon, N. (2004). The neurology of sign language. *Brain & Development, 26,* 146–150.

Gorman, J. M., & Kent, J. M. (1999). SSRIs and SNRIs: Broad spectrum of efficacy beyond major depression. *Journal of Clinical Psychiatry, 60*(Suppl. 4), 33–39.

Gorman, J. M., Liebowitz, M. R., Fyer, A. J., & Stein, J. (1989). A neuroanatomical hypothesis for panic disorder. *American Journal of Psychiatry, 146,* 148–161.

Gortner, E. T., Gollan, J. K., Dobson, K. S., & Jacobson, N. S. (1998). Cognitive-behavioral treatment for depression: Relapse prevention. *Journal of Consulting & Clinical Psychology, 66,* 377–384.

Gotlib, I. H., & Robinson, L. A. (1982). Responses to depressed individuals: Discrepancies between self-report and observer rated behavior. *Journal of Abnormal Psychology, 91,* 231–240.

Gottesman, I. I. (1991). *Schizophrenia genesis: The origins of madness.* New York: Freeman.

Gottesman, I. I., & Moldin, S. O. (1998). Genotypes, genes, genesis, and pathogenesis in schizophrenia. In M. F. Lenzenweger & R. H. Dworkin (Eds.), *Origins and development of schizophrenia: Advances in experimental psychopathology* (pp. 5–26). Washington, DC: American Psychological Association.

Gottfredson, L. (1997). Why "g" matters: The complexity of everyday life. *Intelligence, 24,* 79–132.

Gottfredson, L. S. (2003a). Dissecting practical intelligence theory: Its claims and evidence. *Intelligence, 31,* 343–397.

Gottfredson, L. S. (2003b). g, jobs and life. In H. Nyborg (Ed.), *The scientific study of general intelligence: Tribute to Arthur R. Jensen.* Oxford, UK: Elsevier Science.

Gottfredson, L. S. (2003c). Discussion: On Sternberg's "Reply to Gottfredson." *Intelligence, 31,* 415–424.

Gottfredson, L. S. (2004). Intelligence: Is it the epidemiologists' elusive "fundamental cause" of social class inequities in health? *Journal of Personality and Social Psychology, 86,* 174–199.

Gottfredson, M. R., & Hirschi, T. (1990). *A general theory of crime.* Stanford, CA: Stanford University Press.

Gottfried, J. A., & Dolan, R.J. (2003). The nose smells what the eye sees—crossmodal visual facilitation of human olfactory perception. *Neuron, 39,* 375–386.

Gottlieb, G. (1998). Normally occurring environmental and behavioral influences on gene activity: From central dogma to probabilistic epigenesis. *Psychological Review, 105,* 792–802.

Gould, E., Tanapat, P., Hastings, N. B., & Shors, T. J. (1999). Neurogenesis in adulthood: A possible role in learning. *Trends in Cognitive Sciences, 3,* 186–192.

Gould, J. L. (1998). Sensory bases of navigation. *Current Biology, 8,* R731–R738.

Gould, R. (1978). *Transformations.* New York: Simon & Schuster.

Gould, R. A., & Clum, G. A. (1993). A meta-analysis of self-help treatment approaches. *Clinical Psychology Review, 13,* 169–186.

Gould, R. A., Mueser, K. T., Bolton, E., Mays, V., & Goff, D. (2001). Cognitive therapy for psychosis in schizophrenia: An effect size analysis. *Schizophrenia Research, 48,* 335–342.

Gould, R. A., Otto, M. W., & Pollack, M. H. (1995). A meta-analysis of treatment outcome for panic disorder. *Clinical Psychology Review, 15,* 819–844.

Gould, S. J., & Lewontin, R. C. (1979). The spandrels of San Marco and the Panglossian paradigm: A critique of the adaptationist programme. *Proceedings of the Royal Society of London, Series B, 205,* 581–598.

Gouldner, A. W. (1960). The norm of reciprocity: A preliminary statement. *American Sociological Review, 25,* 161–179.

Grafen, A. (2002). A state-free optimization model for sequences of behaviour. *Animal Behaviour, 63,* 183–191.

Grammer, K. (1990). Strangers meet: Laughter and nonverbal signs of interest in opposite-sex encounters. *Journal of Nonverbal Behavior, 14,* 209–236.

Granhag, P. A., & Strömwall, L. A. (2001). Deception detection: Interrogators' and observers' decoding of consecutive statements. *Journal of Psychology: Interdisciplinary & Applied, 135,* 603–620.

Grant, B. F., & Dawson, D. A. (1997). Age at onset of alcohol use and its association with DSM-IV alcohol abuse and dependence: Results from the National Longitudinal Alcohol Epidemiologic Survey. *Journal of Substance Abuse, 9,* 103–110.

Grant, B. F., Stinson, F. S., Dawson, D. A., Chou, S. P., Dufour, M. C., Compton, W., Pickering, R. P., & Kaplan, K. (2004). Prevalence and co-occurrence of substance use disorders and independent mood and anxiety disorders: Results from the National Epidemiologic Survey on Alcohol and Related Conditions. *Archives of General Psychiatry, 61,* 807–816.

Grant, I., Marcotle, T. D., Heaton, R. K., & HNRC Group, San Diego, CA, USA. (1999). Neurocognitive complications of HIV disease. *Psychological Science, 10,* 191–195.

Gratton, G., & Fabiani, M. (2001a). The event-related optical signal: A new tool for studying brain function. *International Journal of Psychophysiology, 42,* 109–121.

Gratton, G., & Fabiani, M. (2001b). Shedding light on brain function: The event-related optical signal. *Trends in Cognitive Sciences, 5,* 357–363.

Graves, L., Pack, A., & Abel, T. (2001). Sleep and memory: A molecular perspective. *Trends in Neurosciences, 24,* 237–243.

Gray, J. A. (1982). Précis of the neuropsychology of anxiety: An enquiry into the functions of the septo-hippocampal system. *Behavioral & Brain Sciences, 5,* 469–534.

Gray, J. A. (1987). Perspectives on anxiety and impulsiveness: A commentary. *Journal of Research in Personality, 21,* 493–509.

Gray, J. A. (1991). The neuropsychology of temperament. In J. Strelau & A. Angleitner (Eds.), *Explorations in temperament: International perspectives on theory and measurement* (pp. 105–128). New York: Plenum Press.

Gray, J. R. (1999). A bias toward short-term thinking in threat-related negative emotional states. *Personality and Social Psychology Bulletin, 25,* 65–75.

Gray, J. R. (2001). Emotional modulation of cognitive control: Approach-withdrawal states double-dissociate spatial from verbal two-back task performance. *Journal of Experimental Psychology: General, 130,* 436–452.

Gray, J. R., Braver, T. S., & Raichle, M. E. (2002). Integration of emotion and cognition in the lateral prefrontal cortex. *Proceedings of the National Academy of Sciences USA, 99,* 4115–4120.

Gray, J. R., Chabris, C. F., & Braver, T. S. (2003). Neural mechanisms of general fluid intelligence. *Nature Neuroscience, 6,* 316–322.

Gray, J. R., & Thompson, P. M. (2004). Neurobiology of intelligence: Science and ethics. *Nature Reviews Neuroscience, 5,* 471–482.

Gray, P. B., Kahlenberg, S. M., Barrett, E. S., Lipson, S. F., & Ellison, P. T. (2002). Marriage and fatherhood are associated with lower testosterone in males. *Evolution & Human Behavior, 23,* 193–201.

Grayson, B. and Stein, M. I. (1981) Attracting assault: Victims' nonverbal cues. *Journal of Communication 31,* 68–75.

Graziano, W. G., Habashi, M., Sheese, B. E., & Tobin, R. (2004). Feeling compassion and helping the unfortunate: A social motivational analysis. Manuscript submitted for publication.

Graziano, W. G., Jensen-Campbell, L. A., & Sullivan-Logan, G. M. (1998). Temperament, activity, and expectations for later personality development, *Journal of Personality and Social Psychology, 74,* 1266–1277.

Green, A. R. (2004). MDMA: Fact and fallacy, and the need to increase knowledge in both the scientific and popular press. *Psychopharmacology, 173,* 231–233.

Green, A. R., Cross, A. J., & Goodwin, G. M. (1995) Review of the pharmacology and clinical pharmacology of 3,4-methylenedioxymethamphetamine (MDMA or "Ecstasy"). *Psychopharmacology, 119,* 247–260.

Green, D. E., Walkey, F. H., & Taylor, A. J. W. (1991). The three-factor structure of the Maslach Burnout Inventory: A multicultural, multinational confirmatory study. *Journal of Social Behavior & Personality, 6,* 453–472.

Green, D. M. (1976). *An introduction to hearing.* Hillsdale, NJ: Erlbaum.

Green, D. M., & Swets, J. A. (1966). *Signal detection theory and psychophysics.* New York: Wiley.

Green, J. P., Lynn, S. J., & Malinoski, P. (1998). Hypnotic pseudomemories, pre-hypnotic warnings, and malleability of suggested memories. *Applied Cognitive Psychology, 12,* 431–444.

Green, M. F. (2001). *Schizophrenia revealed: From neurons to social interactions.* New York: W.W. Norton.

Green, M. F., Kern, R. S., Braff, D. L., & Mintz, J. (2000). Neurocognitive deficits and functional outcome in schizophrenia: Are we measuring the "right stuff"? *Schizophrenia Bulletin, 26,* 119–136.

Green, M. F., Nuechterlein, K. H., Breitmeyer, B., & Mintz, J. (1999). Backward masking in unmedicated schizophrenic patients in psychotic remission: possible reflection of aberrant cortical oscillation. *American Journal of Psychiatry, 156,* 1367–1373.

Greenberg, B. D., Altemus, M., & Murphy, D. L. (1997). The role of neurotransmitters and neurohormones in obsessive-compulsive disorder. *International Review of Psychiatry, 9,* 31–44.

Greenberg, D. L., & Rubin, D. C. (2003). The neuropsychology of autobiographical memory. *Cortex, 39,* 687–728.

Greenberg, J. R., & Mitchell, S. A. (1983). *Object relations in psychoanalytic theory.* Cambridge, MA: Harvard University Press.

Greenberg, R. P., & Fisher, S. (1989). Examining antidepressant effectiveness: Findings, ambiguities and some vexing puzzles. In S. Fisher & R. P. Greenberg (Eds.), *The limits of biological treatments for psychological distress* (pp. 1–37). Hillsdale, NJ: Erlbaum.

Greene, K., Krcmar, M., Rubin, D. L., Walters, L. H., & Hale, J. L. (2002). Elaboration in processing adolescent health messages: The impact of egocentrism and sensation seeking on message processing. *Journal of Communication, 52,* 812–831.

Greenfield, P. M., & Savage-Rumbaugh, S. (1990). Grammatical combination in *Pan paniscus:* Processes of learning and invention in the evolution and development of language. In S. Parker & K. Gibson (Eds.), *"Language" and intelligence in monkeys and apes: Comparative developmental perspectives* (pp. 540–578). New York: Cambridge University Press.

Greenough, W. T., Black, J. E., & Wallace, C. S. (1987). Experience and brain development. *Child Development, 58,* 539–559.

Greenough, W. T., & Chang, F.-L. F. (1985). Synaptic structural correlates of information storage in mammalian nervous systems. In C. W. Cotman (Ed.), *Synaptic plasticity* (pp. 335–372). New York: Guilford.

Greenwald, A. G., & Banaji, M. R. (1995). Implicit social cognition: Attitudes, self-esteem, and stereotypes. *Psychological Review, 102,* 4–27.

Greenwald, A. G., Spangenberg, E. R., Pratkanis, A. R., & Eskenazi, J. (1991). Double-blind tests of subliminal self-help audiotapes. *Psychological Science, 2,* 119–122.

Gregg, V. R., Winer, G. A., Cottrell, J. E., Hedman, K. E., & Fournier, J. S. (2001). The persistence of a misconception about vision after educational interventions. *Psychonomic Bulletin and Review, 8,* 622–626.

Gregory, R. L. (1974). *Concepts and mechanisms of perception.* New York: Scribner's.

Gregory, R. L., & Harris, J. P. (1984). Real and apparent movement nulled. *Nature, 307,* 729–730.

Gregory, R. J., Schwer Canning, S., Lee, T. W., & Wise, J. C. (2004). Cognitive bibliotherapy for depression: A meta-analysis. *Professional Psychology: Research & Practice, 35,* 275–280.

Grézes, J., & Decety, J. (2001). Functional anatomy of execution, mental simulation, observation, and verb generation of actions: A meta-analysis. *Human Brain Mapping, 12,* 1–19.

Grice, H. P. (1975). Logic and conversation. In P. Cole & J. L. Morgan (Eds.), *Syntax and semantics: Vol. 3, Speech acts* (pp. 41–58). New York: Seminar Press.

Grice, J. W., & Seely, E. (2000). The evolution of sex differences in jealousy: Failure to replicate previous results. *Journal of Research in Personality, 34*, 348–356.

Griffiths, T. D., Warren, J. D., Dean, J. L., & Howard, D. (2004). "When the feeling's gone": A selective loss of musical emotion. *Journal of Neurology, Neurosurgery & Psychiatry, 75*, 344–345.

Griggs, R. A., & Cox, J. R. (1982). The elusive thematic-materials effect in Wason's selection task. *British Journal of Psychology, 73*, 407–420.

Grigorenko, E. L. (2003). Epistasis and the genetics of complex traits. In R. Plomin, J. C. DeFries, et al. (Eds.), *Behavioral genetics in the postgenomic era* (pp. 247–266). Washington, DC: American Psychological Association.

Grillo, C., La Mantia, I., Triolo, C., Scollo, A., La Boria, A., Intelisano, G., & Caruso, S. (2001). Rhinomanometric and olfactometric variations throughout the menstrual cycle. *Annals of Otology, Rhinology & Laryngology, 110*, 785–789.

Grill-Spector, K. (2003). The neural basis of object perception. *Current Opinion in Neurobiology, 13*, 159-166.

Grill-Spector, K., Kushnir, T., Hendler, T., Edelman, S., Itzchak, Y., & Malach, R. (1998). A sequence of object-processing stages revealed by fMRI in the human occipital lobe. *Human Brain Mapping, 6*, 316–328.

Grilly, D. (1994). *Drugs and human behavior* (2nd ed.). Boston: Allyn & Bacon.

Grimes, K., & Walker, E. F. (1994). Childhood emotional expressions, educational attainments, and age at onset of illness in schizophrenia. *Journal of Abnormal Psychology, 103*, 784–790.

Grimshaw, G. M., Adelstein, A., Bryden, M. P., & MacKinnon, G. E. (1998). First-language acquisition in adolescence: Evidence for a critical period for verbal language development. *Brain & Language, 63*, 237–255.

Grisaru, N., Amir, M., Cohen, H., & Kaplan, Z. (1998). Effect of transcranial magnetic stimulation in posttraumatic stress disorder: A preliminary study. *Biological Psychiatry, 44*, 52–55.

Grisaru, N., Chudakov, B., Yaroslavsky, Y., & Belmaker, R. H. (1998). Transcranial magnetic stimulation in mania: A controlled study. *American Journal of Psychiatry, 155*, 1608–1610.

Grissom, R. J. (1996). The magical number .7 ± .2: Meta-meta-analysis of the probability of superior outcome in comparisons involving therapy, placebo, and control. *Journal of Consulting & Clinical Psychology, 64*, 973–982.

Grodzinsky, Y. (1986). Language deficits and the theory of syntax. *Brain and Language, 27*, 135–159.

Gross, C. R., Kreitzer, M. J., Russas, V., Treesak, C., Frazier, P.A., & Hertz, M. I. (2004). Mindfulness meditation to reduce symptoms after organ transplant: A pilot study. *Advances in Mind Body Medicine, 20*, 20–29.

Gross, J., & Levenson, R. W. (1997). Hiding feelings: The acute effects of inhibiting negative and positive emotion. *Journal of Abnormal Psychology, 106*, 95–103.

Gross, J. J. (1998). The emerging field of emotion regulation: An integrative review. *Review of General Psychology, 2*, 271–299.

Gross, J. J. (2001). Emotion regulation in adulthood: Timing is everything. *Current Directions in Psychological Science, 10*, 214–219.

Gross, J. J. (2002). Emotion regulation: Affective, cognitive, and social consequences. *Psychophysiology, 39*, 281–291.

Gross, J. J., Carstensen, L. L., Pasupathi, M., Tsai, J., Goetestam Skorpen, C., & Hsu, A. Y. C. (1997). Emotion and aging: Experience, expression, and control. *Psychology & Aging, 12*, 590–599.

Grossarth-Maticek, R., Eysenck, H. J., Boyle, G. J., Heeb, J., Costa, C. D., & Diel, I. J. (2000). Interaction of psychosocial and physical risk factors in the causation of mammary cancer, and its prevention through psychological methods of treatment. *Journal of Clinical Psychology, 56*, 33–50.

Grossberg, S., Mingolla, E., & Ross, W. D. (1997). Visual brain and visual perception: How does the cortex do perceptual grouping? *Trends in Neuroscience, 20*, 106–111.

Grossman, P., Niemann, L., Schmidt, S., & Walach, H. (2004). Mindfulness-based stress reduction and health benefits. A meta-analysis. *Journal of Psychosomatic Research, 57*, 35–43.

Grossman, R. P., & Till, B. D. (1998). The persistence of classically conditioned brand attitudes. *Journal of Advertising, 27*, 23–31.

Gruber, A. J., Pope, H. G., Hudson, H. I., & Yurgelun-Todd, D. (2003). Attributes of long-term heavy cannabis users: A case control study. *Psychological Medicine, 33*, 1415–1422.

Grunes, M. S., Neziroglu, F., & McKay, D. (2001). Family involvement in the behavioral treatment of obsessive-compulsive disorder: A preliminary investigation. *Behavior Therapy, 32*, 803–820.

Grusec, J. E., Davidov, M., & Lundell, L. (2002). Prosocial and helping behavior. In P. K. Smith & C. H. Hart (Eds.), *Blackwell handbook of childhood social development* (pp. 457–474). Malden, MA: Blackwell Publishers.

Guadagno, R. W., Asher, T., Demaine, L. H., & Cialdini, R. B. (2001). When saying yes leads to saying no: Preference for consistency and the reverse foot-in-the-door effect. *Personality & Social Psychology Bulletin, 27*, 859–867.

Guéguen, N., & De Gail, M. (2003). The effect of smiling on helping behavior: Smiling and Good Samaritan behavior. *Communication Reports, 16*, 133–140.

Guerin, B. (1993). *Social facilitation.* Paris: Cambridge University Press.

Guilford, J. P. (1967). *The nature of human intelligence.* New York: McGraw-Hill.

Guilford, J. P. (1979). Some incubated thoughts on incubation. *Journal of Creative Behavior, 13*, 1–8.

Guillery, B., Desgranges, B., Katis, S., de la Sayette, V., Viader, F., & Eustache, F. (2001). Semantic acquisition without memories: Evidence from transient global amnesia. *Neuroreport, 12*, 3865–3869.

Gulick, W. L., Gescheider, G. A., & Frisina, R. D. (1989). *Hearing: Physiological acoustics, neural coding, and psychoacoustics.* New York: Oxford University Press.

Gulya, M., Rossi-George, A., Hartshorn, K., Vieira, A., Rovee Collier, C., Johnson, M. K., & Chalfonte, B. L. (2002). The development of explicit memory for basic perceptual features. *Journal of Experimental Child Psychology, 81*, 276–297.

Gunewardene, A., Huon, G. F., & Zheng, R. (2001). Exposure to westernization and dieting: A cross-cultural study. *International Journal of Eating Disorders, 29*, 289–293.

Gunnell, D., Saperia, J., Ashby, D. (2005). Selective serotonin reuptake inhibitors (SSRIs) and suicide in adults: meta-analysis of drug company data from placebo controlled, randomised controlled trials submitted to the MHRA's safety review. *British Medical Journal, 330*, 385–388.

Gur, R. C., Turetsky, B. I., Matsui, M., Yan, M., Bilker, W., Hughett, P., & Gur, R. E. (1999). Sex differences in brain gray and white matter in healthy young adults: Correlations with cognitive performance. *Journal of Neuroscience, 19*, 4065–4072.

Gureje, O., Mavreas, V., Vazquez-Barquero, J. L., & Janca, A. (1997). Problems related to alcohol use: A cross-cultural perspective. *Culture, Medicine, and Psychiatry, 21*, 199–211.

Gustafsson, J.-E. (1984). A unifying model for the structure of mental abilities. *Intelligence, 8*, 179–203.

Gutchess, A. H., Welsh, R. C., Hedden, T., Bangert, A., Minear, M., Liu, L. L., & Park, D. C. (2005). Aging and the neural correlates of successful picture encoding: Frontal activations compensate for decreased medial-temporal activity. *Journal of Cognitive Neuroscience, 17*, 84–96.

Guth, W., Schmittberger, R., & Schwarze, B. (1982). An experimental analysis of ultimatum bargaining. *Journal of Economic Behavior and Organization, 3*, 367–388.

Guthrie, G. M., Guthrie, H. A., Fernandez, T. L., & Esterea, N. O. (1982). Cultural influences and reinforcement stratifies. *Behavior Therapy, 13*, 624–637.

Guthrie, R. M., & Bryant, R. A. (2005). Auditory startle response in firefighters before and after trauma exposure. *American Journal of Psychiatry, 162*, 283–290.

Guttmann, C. R. G., Jolesz, F. A., Kikinis, R., Killiany, R. J., Moss, M. B., Sandor, T., & Albert, M. S. (1998). White matter changes with normal aging, *Neurology, 50*, 972–978.

Gyulai, L., Abass, A., Broich, K., & Reilley, J. (1997). I-123 lofetamine single-photon computer emission tomography in rapid cycling bipolar disorder: A clinical study. *Biological Psychiatry, 41*, 152–161.

Haaga, D. A., & Davison, G. C. (1989). Slow progress in rational-emotive therapy outcome research: Etiology and treatment. *Cognitive Therapy & Research, 13*, 493–450.

Haapasalo, J., & Pokela, E. (1999). Child-rearing and child abuse antecedents of criminality. *Aggression & Violent Behavior, 4*, 107–127.

Habra, M. E., Linden, W., Anderson, J. C., & Weinberg, J. (2003). Type D personality is related to cardiovascular and neuroendocrine reactivity to acute stress. *Journal of Psychosomatic Research, 55*, 235–245.

Hacker, A. (1992). *Two nations: Black and white, separate, hostile, unequal.* New York: Scribner's.

Hafer, C. L., & Bègue, L. (2005). Experimental research on just-world theory: Problems, developments, and future challenges. *Psychological Bulletin, 131*, 128–167.

Hahn, R. A. (1995). *Sickness and healing: An anthropological perspective.* New Haven, CT: Yale University Press.

Hahn, R. A. (1997). The nocebo phenomenon: Scope and foundations. In A. Harrington (Ed.), *The placebo effect: An interdisciplinary exploration.* Cambridge, MA: Harvard University Press.

Hahn, R. A. (1999). Expectations of sickness: Concept and evidence of the no-cebo phenomenon. In I. Kirsch (Ed.), *How expectancies shape experience* (pp. 333–356). Washington, DC: American Psychological Association.

Haier, R. J., et al. (1984) Evoked potential augmenting-reducing and personality differences. *Personality & Indiv. Differences 5*, 293–301.

Hakuta, K., Bialystok, E., & Wiley, E. (2003). Critical evidence: A test of the critical-period hypothesis for second-language learning. *Psychological Science, 14*, 31–38.

Halari, R., Hines, M., Kumari, V., Mehrotra, R., Wheeler, M., Ng, V., & Sharma, T. (2005). Sex differences and individual differences in cognitive performance and their relationship to endogenous gonadal hormones and gonadotropins. *Behavioral Neuroscience, 119*, 104–117.

Hall, D. T., & Nougaim, K. E. (1968). An examination of Maslow's need hierarchy in an organizational setting. *Organizational Behavior and Human Performance, 3*, 12–35.

Hall, G. S. (1904). *Adolescence: Its psychology and its relation to physiology, anthropology, sociology, sex, crime, religion, and education* (Vols. I & II). Englewood Cliffs, NJ: Prentice-Hall.

Hall, J., Thomas, K. L., & Everitt, B. J. (2001). Cellular imaging of *zif268* expression in the hippocampus and amygdala during contextual and cued fear memory retrieval: Selective activation of hippocampal CA1 neurons during the recall of contextual memories. *Journal of Neuroscience, 21*, 2186–2193.

Hall, J. A. (1978). Gender effects in decoding nonverbal cues. *Psychological Bulletin, 85*, 845–857.

Hall, J. A. (1987). On explaining gender differences: The case of nonverbal communication. In P. Shaver & C. Hendrick (Eds.), *Sex and gender.* Newbury Park, CA: Sage.

Hall, J. A., & Matsumoto, D. (2004). Gender differences in judgments of multiple emotions from facial expressions. *Emotion, 4*, 201–206.

Hall, J. F. (1984). Backward conditioning in Pavlovian type studies: Reevaluation and present status. *Pavlovian Journal of Biological Science, 19*, 163–168.

Halle, M. (1990). Phonology. In D. N. Osherson & H. Lasnik (Ed.), *An invitation to cognitive science: Vol. 1, Language* (pp. 43–68). Cambridge, MA: MIT Press.

Hallem, E. A., Ho, M. G., & Carlson, J. R. (2004) The molecular basis of odor coding in the *Drosophila* antenna. *Cell, 117*, 965–979.

Halmi, K. (1995). Basic biological overview of eating disorders. In F. E. Bloom & D. J. Kupfer (Eds.), *Psychopharmacology: The fourth generation of progress.* New York: Raven Press.

Halmi, K. (1996). The psychobiology of eating behavior in anorexia nervosa. *Psychiatry Research, 62*, 23–29.

Halpern, A. R. (1988). Mental scanning in auditory imagery for songs. *Journal of Experimental Psychology: Learning, Memory and Cognition, 14*, 434–443.

Halpern, A. R., & Zatorre, R. J. (1999). When that tune runs through your head: A PET investigation of auditory imagery for familiar melodies. *Cerebral Cortex, 9*, 697–704.

Halpern, D. F. (1992). *Sex differences in cognitive ability.* Hillsdale, NJ: Erlbaum.

Halpern, D. F. (1997). Sex differences in intelligence: Implications for education. *American Psychologist, 52*, 1091–1102.

Halpern, D. F. (2000). *Sex differences in cognitive abilities* (3rd ed.). London: LEA.

Hamann, S., & Canli, T. (2004). Individual differences in emotion processing. *Current Opinion in Neurobiology, 14*, 233–238.

Hamann, S., & Mao, H. (2002). Positive and negative emotional verbal stimuli elicit activity in the left amygdala. *Neuroreport: For Rapid Communication of Neuroscience Research, 13*, 15–19.

Hamann, S. B., Stefanacci, L., Squire, L. R., Adolphs, R., Tranel, D., Damasio, H., & Damasio, A. (1996). Recognizing facial emotion. *Nature, 379*, 497.

Hamer, D. H., Hu, S., Magnuson, V. L., Hu, N., & Pattatucci, A. M. (1993). A linkage between DNA markers on the X chromosome and male sexual orientation. *Science, 261*, 321–327.

Hamilton, D. L., & Sherman, S. J. (1989). Illusory correlations: Implications for stereotype theory and research. In D. Bar-Tal, C. F. Graumann, A. W. Kruglanski, & W. Stroebe (Eds.), *Stereotyping and prejudice: Changing conceptions* (pp. 59–82). New York: Springer-Verlag.

Hamilton, M. E., Voris, J. C., Sebastian, P. S., Singha, A. K., Krejci, L. P., Elder, I. R., et al. (1998). Money as a tool to extinguish conditioned responses to cocaine in addicts. *Journal of Clinical Psychology, 54*, 211–218.

Hamilton, V. L., Hoffman, W. S., Broman, C. L., & Rauma, D. (1993). Unemployment, distress, and coping: A panel study of autoworkers. *Journal of Personality and Social Psychology, 65*, 234–247.

Hampson, E. (1990). Estrogen-related variations in human spatial and articulatory motor skills. *Psychoneuroendocrinology, 15*, 97–111.

Hampson, E., & Kimura, D. (1988). Reciprocal effects of hormonal fluctuations on human motor and perceptual-spatial skills. *Behavioral Neuroscience, 102*, 456–459.

Han, S., & Humphreys, G. W. (2002). Segmentation and selection contribute to local processing in hierarchical analysis. *Quarterly Journal of Experimental Psychology: Human Experimental Psychology, 55A*, 5–21.

Han, S., & Kim, M. (2004). Visual search does not remain efficient when executive working memory is working. *Psychological Science, 15*, 623–628.

Han, S., & Shavitt, S. (1994). Persuasion and culture: Advertising appeals in individualistic and collectivistic societies. *Journal of Experimental Social Psychology, 30*, 326–350.

Haney, C., Banks, W. C., & Zimbardo, P. G. (1973). Interpersonal dynamics in a simulated prison. *International Journal of Criminology and Penology, 1*, 69–97.

Haney, C., & Zimbardo, P. G. (1976). Social roles and role-playing: Observations from the Stanford prison study. In E. P. Hollander & R. G. Hunt (Eds.), *Current perspectives in social psychology* (4th ed., pp. 266–274). New York: Oxford University Press.

Haney, M., Ward, A. S., Comer, S. D., Foltin, R. W., & Fischman, M. W. (1999). Abstinence symptoms following smoked marijuana in humans. *Psychopharmacology, 141*, 395–404.

Hann, M., Humphreys, K., & Johnson, M. H. (2002). Developing a brain specialized for face perception: A converging methods approach. *Developmental Psychobiology, 40*, 200–212.

Hansen, W. B., Graham, J. W., Wolkenstein, B. H., Lundy, B. Z., Pearson, J., Flay, B. R., & Joshnson, C. A. (1988). Differential impact of three alcohol prevention curricula on hypothesized mediating variables. *Journal of Drug Education, 18*, 143–153.

Hansenne, M., Pinto, E., Pitchot, W., Reggers, J., Scantamburlo, G., Moor, M., & Ansseau, M. (2002). Further evidence on the relationship between dopamine and novelty seeking: A neuroendocrine study. *Personality & Individual Differences, 33*, 967–977.

Hanson, K. A., & Gidycz, C. A. (1993). Evaluation of a sexual assault prevention program. *Journal of Consulting & Clinical Psychology, 61*, 1046–1052.

Hapidou, E. G., & De Catanzaro, D. (1988). Sensitivity to cold pressor pain in dysmenorrheic and non-dysmenorrheic women as a function of menstrual cycle phase. *Pain, 34*, 277–283.

Haraldsson, E., & Gissurarson, L. R. (1987). Does geomagnetic activity affect extrasensory perception? *Personality and Individual Differences, 8*, 745–747.

Haraldsson, E., & Houtkooper, J. M. (1992). Effects of perceptual defensiveness, personality and belief on extrasensory perception tasks. *Personality and Individual Differences, 13*, 1085–1096.

Harandi, A. A., Esfandani, A., & Shakibaei, F. (2004). The effect of hypnotherapy on procedural pain and state anxiety related to physiotherapy in women hospitalized in a burn unit. *Contemporary Hypnosis, 21*, 28–34.

Hardy, J. D., & Smith, T. W. (1988). Cynical hostility and vulnerability to disease: Social support, life stress, and physiological response to conflict. *Health Psychology, 7*, 447–459.

Hare, R. D. (1993). *Without conscience: The disturbing world of the psychopaths among us.* New York: Pocket Books.

Harinath, K., Malhotra, A. S., Pal, K., Prasad, R., Kumar, R., Kain, T. C., Rai, L., & Sawhney, R. C. (2004). Effects of Hatha yoga and Omkar meditation on cardiorespiratory performance, psychologic profile, and melatonin secretion. *Journal of Alternative and Complementary Medicine, 10*, 261–268.

Hariri, A. R., Mattay, V. S., Tessitore, A., Kolachana, B., Fera, F., Goldman, D., et al. (2002). Serotonin transporter genetic variation and the response of the human amygdala. *Science, 297*, 400–403.

Harkins, S., & Szymanski, K. (1989). Social loafing and group evaluation. *Journal of Personality and Social Psychology, 56*, 934–941.

Harkins, S. G., & Petty, R. E. (1982). Effects of task difficulty and task uniqueness on social loafing. *Journal of Personality & Social Psychology, 43*, 1214–1229.

Harlow, H. F. (1958). The nature of love. *American Psychologist, 13*, 573–685.

Harman, D. (1956). Aging: A theory based on free radical and radiation chemistry. *Journal of Gerontology, 11*, 298–300.

Harris, C. R. (2000). Psychophysiological responses to imagined infidelity: The specific innate modular view of jealousy reconsidered. *Journal of Personality & Social Psychology, 78*, 1082–1091.

Harris, C. R. (2002). Sexual and romantic jealousy in heterosexual and homosexual adults. *Psychological Science, 13*, 7–12.

Harris, J. R. (1995). Where is the child's environment? A group socialization theory of development. *Psychological Review, 102*, 458–489.

Harris, J. R. (1998). *The nurture assumption: Why children turn out the way they do.* New York: Free Press.

Harris, R. J., Schoen, L. M., & Hensley, D. L. (1992). A cross-cultural study of story memory. *Journal of Cross-Cultural Psychology, 23*, 133–147.

Harrison, L. J., & Ungerer, J. A. (2002). Maternal employment and infant-mother attachment security at 12 months postpartum. *Developmental Psychology, 38,* 758–773.

Harrison, P. J. (2002). The neuropathology of primary mood disorder. *Brain, 125,* 1428–1449.

Hart, A. J., Whalen, P. J., Shin, L. M., McInerney, S. C., Fischer, H., & Rauch, S. L. (2000). Differential response in the human amygdala to racial outgroup vs. ingroup face stimuli. *Neuroreport, 11,* 2351–2355.

Hart, B., & Risley, T. R. (1995/2002) *Meaningful differences in everyday parenting and intellectual development in young American children.* Baltimore: Paul H. Brookes.

Hart, B., & Risley, T. R. (1999). *The social world of children learning to talk.* Baltimore: Paul H. Brookes.

Hart, H. C., Palmer, A. R., & Hall, D. A. (2003). Amplitude and frequency-modulated stimuli activate common regions of human auditory cortex. *Cerebral Cortex, 13,* 773–781.

Hart, J., Berndt, R. S., & Caramazza, A. (1985). Category-specific naming deficit following cerebral infarction. *Nature, 316,* 439–440.

Hart, K. E., & Hope, C. W. (2004). Cynical hostility and the psychosocial vulnerability model of disease risk: Confounding effects of neuroticism (negative affectivity) bias. *Personality & Individual Differences, 36,* 1571–1582.

Hartman, L. M. (1983). A metacognitive model of social anxiety: Implications for treatment. *Clinical Psychology Review, 3,* 435–456.

Hartung, C. M., & Widiger, T. A. (1998). Gender differences in the diagnosis of mental disorders: Conclusions and controversies of the DSM-IV. *Psychological Bulletin, 123,* 260–278.

Hasegawa, I., Fukushima, T., Ihara, T., & Miyashita, Y. (1998). Callosal window between prefrontal cortices: Cognitive interaction to retrieve long-term memory. *Science, 281,* 814–818.

Hasher, L., & Zacks, R. T. (1979). Automatic and effortful processes in memory. *Journal of Experimental Psychology: General, 108,* 356–388.

Hasher, L., & Zacks, R. T. (1984). Automatic processing of fundamental information. The case of frequency of occurrence. *American Psychologist, 39,* 1327–1388.

Hasler, G., Drevets, W. C., Manji, H. K., & Charney, D. S. (2004). Discovering endophenotypes for major depression. *Neuropsychopharmacology, 29,* 1765–1781.

Hastie, R. (1986). Review essay: Experimental evidence on group accuracy. In B. Grofman & G. Guillermo (Eds.), *Information pooling and group decision making* (Vol. 2, pp. 129–157). Greenwich, CT: JAI Press.

Hastie, R., & Kameda, T. (2005). The robust beauty of majority rules in group decisions. *Psychological Review, 112,* 494–508.

Hastorf, A. H., & Cantril, H. (1954). They saw a game; a case study. *Journal of Abnormal and Social Psychology, 49,* 129–134.

Hatano, G., & Osawa, K. (1983). Digit memory of grand experts in abacus-derived mental calculation. *Cognition, 15,* 95–110.

Hatfield, E., & Sprecher, S. (1986). Men's and women's preferences in marital partners in the United States, Russia, and Japan. *Journal of Cross-Cultural Psychology. 26,* 728–750.

Hätinen, M., Kinnunen, U., Pekkonen, M., & Aro, A. (2004). Burnout patterns in rehabilitation: Short-term changes in job conditions, personal resources, and health. *Journal of Occupational Health Psychology, 9,* 220–237.

Haug, H. (1987). Brain sizes, surfaces, and neuronal sizes of the cortex cerebri: A stereological investigation of man and his variability and a comparison with some mammals (primates, whales, marsupials, insectivores, and one elephant). *American Journal of Anatomy, 180,* 126–42.

Hauri, P. (1970). Evening activity, sleep mentation, and subjective sleep quality. *Journal of Abnormal Psychology, 76,* 270–275.

Hauser, M. (1996). *The evolution of communication.* Cambridge, MA: MIT Press.

Hausmann, M., Slabbekoorn, D., Van Goozen, S. H. M., Cohen-Kettenis, P. T., & Guenteurkuen, O. (2000). Sex hormones affect spatial abilities during the menstrual cycle. *Behavioral Neuroscience, 114,* 1245–1250.

Havinghurst, R. (1953). *Human development and education.* New York: Longmans, Green.

Hawkins, J. R. (1994). Sex determination. *Human Molecular Genetics, 3,* 1463–1467.

Haxby, J. V., Gobbini, M. I., Furey, M. L., Ishai, A., Schouten, J. L., & Pietrini, P. (2001). Distributed and overlapping representations of faces and objects in ventral temporal cortex. *Science, 293,* 2425–2430.

Haxby, J. V., Grady, C. L., Horowitz, B., Ungerleider, L. G., Mischkin, M., Carson, R. E., et al. (1991). Dissociation of object and spatial visual processing pathways in human extrastriate cortex. *Proceedings of the National Academy of Sciences, USA, 88,* 1621–1625.

Haxby, J. V., Horowitz, B., Ungerleider, L. G., Maisog, J. M., Pietrini, P., & Grady, C. L. (1994). The functional organization of human extrastriate cortex: A PET-rCBF study of selective attention to faces and locations. *Journal of Neuroscience, 14,* 6336–6353.

Hayashi, T., Yamaguchi, T., Kitahara, K., Sharpe, L. T., Jägle, H., Yamade, S., Ueyama, H., Motulsky, A. G., & Deeb, S. S. (2001). The importance of gene order in expression of the red and green visual pigment genes and in color vision. *Color Research & Application, 26,* S79–S83.

Hayflick, L. (1965). The limited in vitro lifetime of human diploid cell strains. *Experimental Cell Research, 37,* 614–636.

Hazan, C., & Shaver, P. R. (1987). Romantic love conceptualized as an attachment process. *Journal of Personality and Social Psychology, 52,* 511–524.

Hazan, C., & Shaver, P. R. (1990). Love and work: An attachment-theoretical perspective. *Journal of Personality and Social Psychology, 59,* 270–280.

Heath, A. C., & Martin, N. G. (1990) Psychoticism as a dimension of personality: A multivariate genetic test of Eysenck and Eysenck's Psychoticism construct. *Journal of Personality and Social Psychology, 58,* 11–121.

Heath, A. C., Neale, M. C., Kessler, R. C., Eaves, L. H., & Kendler, K. S. (1992). Evidence for genetic influences on personality from self-reports and informant ratings. *Journal of Personality and Social Psychology, 63,* 85–96.

Heatherton, T. F. (2004). Introduction to special issue on social cognitive neuroscience. *Journal of Cognitive Neuroscience, 16,* 1681–1682.

Heatherton, T. F., Macrae, C. N., & Kelley, W. M. (2004). What the social brain sciences can tell us about the self. *Current Directions in Psychological Science, 13,* 190–193.

Hebert, L. E., Scherr, P. A., Bienias, J. L., Bennett, D. A., & Evans, D. A. (2003). Alzheimer disease in the US population: Prevalence estimates using the 2000 census. *Archives of Neurology, 60,* 1119–1122.

Hebert, R., & Tan, G. (2004). Quantitative EEG phase evaluation of transcendental meditation. *Journal of Neurotherapy, 8,* 120–121.

Hecker, M., Chesney, M. N., Black, G., & Frautsch, N. (1988). Coronary-prone behaviors in the Western Collaborative Group Study. *Psychosomatic Medicine, 50,* 153–164.

Hedges, C. (1997, November 26). Bosnia's factions push their versions of war into the history books. *International Herald Tribune,* 5.

Heeger, D. J., & Ress, D. (2002). What does fMRI tell us about neuronal activity? *Nature Reviews Neuroscience, 3,* 142–151.

Hefco, V., Olariu, A., Hefco, A., & Nabeshima, T. (2004). The modulator role of the hypothalamic paraventricular nucleus on immune responsiveness. *Brain, Behavior & Immunity, 18,* 158–165.

Heilman, K. M., Nadeau, S. E., & Beversdorf, D. O. (2003). Creative innovation: Possible brain mechanisms. *Neurocase, 9,* 369–379.

Heisel, M. J., & Mongrain, M. (2004). Facial expressions and ambivalence: Looking for conflict in all the right faces. *Journal of Nonverbal Behavior, 28,* 35–52.

Heit, G., Smith, M. E., & Halgren, E. (1988). Neural encoding of individual words and faces by the human hippocampus and amygdala. *Nature, 333,* 773–775.

Hekkanen, S. T., & McEvoy, C. (2002). False memories and source-monitoring problems: Criterion differences. *Applied Cognitive Psychology, 16,* 73–85.

Held, J. D., Alderton, D. L., Foley, P. P., & Segall, D. O. (1993). Arithmetic reasoning gender differences: Explanations found in the Armed Services Vocational Aptitude Battery. *Learning and Individual Differences, 5,* 171–186.

Hellige, J. B. (1993). *Hemispheric asymmetry: What's right and what's left.* Cambridge, MA: Harvard University Press.

Hellige, J. B., & Sergent, J. (1986). Role of task factors in visual field asymmetries. *Brain and Cognition, 5,* 200–222.

Hellström, K., & Öst, L.-G. (1995). One-session therapist directed exposure vs. two forms of manual directed self-exposure in the treatment of spider phobia. *Behaviour Research and Therapy, 33,* 959–965.

Helms, J. E., & Cook, D. A. (1999). *Using race and culture in counseling and psychotherapy: Theory and process.* Needham Heights, MA: Allyn & Bacon.

Helson, H. (1964). *Adaptation-level theory: An experimental and systematic approach to behavior.* New York: Harper & Row.

Hemsley, D. R. (1994). Perceptual and cognitive abnormalities as the bases for schizophrenic symptoms. In A. S. David & J. C. Cutting (Eds.), *The neuropsychology of schizophrenia* (pp. 97–116). Hillsdale, NJ: Lawrence Erlbaum Associates.

Hemsley, D. R. (1998). The disruption of the "sense of self" in schizophrenia: Potential links with disturbances of information processing. *British Journal of Medical Psychology, 71,* 115–124.

Henderlong, J., & Lepper, M. R. (2002). The effects of praise on children's intrinsic motivation: A review and synthesis. *Psychological Bulletin, 128,* 774–795.

Henley, N. M. (1977). *Body politics: Power, sex, and non-verbal communication.* Englewood Cliffs, NJ: Prentice-Hall.

Henrich, J., Boyd, R. Bowles, S., Camerer, C., Fehr, E., Gintis, H., & McElreath, R. (2001). In search of *Homo economicus*: Behavioral experiments in 15 small-scale societies. *American Economic Review (AEA Papers and Proceedings), 91,* 73–78.

Henry, B., Caspi, A., Moffitt, T. E., & Silva, P. A. (1996). Temperamental and familial predictors of violent and nonviolent criminal convictions: Age 3 to Age 18. *Developmental Psychology, 32,* 614–623.

Henry, J. P. (1977). *Stress, health, and the environment.* New York: Springer-Verlag.

Henry, W. P., Strupp, H. H., Schacht, T. E., & Gaston, L. (1994). Psychodynamic approaches. In A. E. Bergin & S. L. Garfield (Eds.), *Handbook of psychotherapy and behavior change* (4th ed., pp. 467–508). New York: John Wiley & Sons.

Hensel, H. (1982). *Thermal sensations and thermoreceptors in man.* Springfield, IL: Thomas.

Henson, R., Shallice, T., & Dolan, R. (2000). Neuroimaging evidence for dissociable forms of repetition priming. *Science, 287,* 1269–1272.

Heponiemi, T., Keltikangas-Järvinen, L., Puttonen, S., & Ravaja, N. (2003). BIS/BAS sensitivity and self-rated affects during experimentally induced stress. *Personality & Individual Differences, 34,* 943–957.

Hepworth, S. L., Rovet, J. F., & Taylor, Margot J. (2001). Neurophysiological correlates of verbal and nonverbal short-term memory in children: Repetition of words and faces. *Psychophysiology, 38,* 594–600.

Herman, C. P., Roth, D. A., & Polivy, J. (2003). Effects of the presence of others on food intake: A normative interpretation. *Psychological Bulletin, 129,* 873–886.

Herman-Giddens, M. E., Slora, E. J., Wasserman, R. C., Bourdony, C. J., Bhapkar, M. V., Koch, G. G., & Hasemeier, C. M. (1997). Secondary sexual characteristics and menses in young girls seen in office practice: A study from the Pediatric Research in Office Settings Network. *Pediatrics, 99,* 505–512.

Herman-Giddens, M. E., Wang, L., & Koch, G. (2001). Secondary sexual characteristics in boys: Estimates from the National Health and Nutrition Examination Survey III, 1988–1994. *Archives of Pediatric Adolescent Medicine, 155,* 1022–1028.

Hermann, J. A., deMontes, A. I., Dominguez, B., Montes, F., & Hopkins, B. L. (1973). Effects of bonuses for punctuality on the tardiness of industrial workers. *Journal of Applied Behavior Analysis, 4,* 267–272.

Hermelin, B. (2001). *Bright splinters of the mind: A personal story of research with autistic savants.* London: Jessica Kingsley.

Hernandez, P. J., & Kelley, A. E. (2004). Long-term memory for instrumental responses does not undergo protein synthesis-dependent reconsolidation upon retrieval. *Learning & Memory, 11,* 748–754.

Herrera, H. (1983). *Frida: Biography of Frida Kahlo.* New York: Harper and Row.

Herrnstein, R. J. (1990). Behavior, reinforcement and utility. *Psychological Science, 1,* 217–224.

Herrnstein, R. J., & Murray, C. (1994). *The bell curve: Intelligence and class structure in American life.* New York: Free Press.

Hershman, D. J., & Lieb, J. (1988). *The key to genius/manic-depression and the creative life.* New York: Prometheus Books.

Hershman, D. J., & Lieb, J. (1998). *Manic depression and creativity.* New York: Prometheus Books.

Hertzog, C., & Schaie, K. W. (1988). Stability and change in adult intelligence: 2. Simultaneous analysis of longitudinal means and covariance structures. *Psychology and Aging, 3,* 122–130.

Herxheimer, A., & Petrie, K. J. (2002). Melatonin for the prevention and treatment of jet lag. Cochrane Library, disk issue 4: CD001520.

Herxheimer, A., & Waterhouse, J. (2003). The prevention and treatment of jet lag. *British Medical Journal, 326,* 296–297.

Herz, R. S., & Cahill, E. D. (1997). Differential use of sensory information in sexual behavior as a function of gender. *Human Nature, 8,* 275–286.

Herz, R. S., & Schooler, J. W. (2002). A naturalistic study of autobiographical memories evoked by olfactory and visual cues: Testing the Proustian hypothesis. *American Journal of Psychology, 115,* 21–32.

Herzog, T. A., Abrams, D. B., Emmons, K. M., Linnan, L. A., & Shadel, W. G. (1999). Do processes of change predict smoking stage movements? A prospective analysis of the transtheoretical model. *Health Psychology, 18,* 369–375.

Hess, T. M., Auman, C., Colcombe, S. J., & Rahhal, T. A. (2003). The impact of stereotype threat on age differences in memory performance. *Journals of Gerontology: Series B: Psychological Sciences & Social Sciences, 58,* P3–P11.

Hewstone, M., Rubin, M., & Willis, H. (2002). Intergroup bias. *Annual Review of Psychology, 51,* 575–604.

Hierholzer, R., Munson, J., Peabody, C., & Rosenberg, J. (1992). Clinical presentation of PTSD in World War II combat veterans. *Hospital and Community Psychiatry, 43,* 816–820.

Higgenbotham, H. N., West, S., & Forsyth, D. (1988). *Psychotherapy and behavior change: Social, cultural and methodological perspectives.* New York: Pergamon.

Higgens, S. T., & Morris, E. K. (1984). Generality of free-operant avoidance conditioning to human behavior. *Psychological Bulletin, 96,* 247–272.

Higgins, E. T. (2000). Making a good decision: Value from fit. *American Psychologist, 55,* 1217–1230.

Hilgard, E. R. (1965). *Hypnotic susceptibility.* New York: Harcourt, Brace & World.

Hilgard, E. R. (1992). Dissociation and theories of hypnosis. In E. Fromm & M. R. Nash (Eds.), *Contemporary hypnosis research* (pp. 69–101). New York: Guilford Press.

Hilgard, E. R., & Hilgard, J. R. (1994). *Hypnosis in the relief of pain.* New York: Brunner/Mazel.

Hilgard, E. R., Hilgard, J. R., Macdonald, J., Morgan, A. H., & Johnson, L. S. (1978). Covert pain in hypnotic analgesia: Its reality as tested by the real-simulator design. *Journal of Abnormal Psychology, 87,* 239–246.

Hill, J. O., & Peters, J. C. (1998). Environmental contributions to the obesity epidemic. *Science, 280,* 1371–1374.

Hill, L., Chorney, M. J., Jubinski, D., Thompson, L. A., & Plomin, R. (2002). A quantitative trait locus not associated with cognitive ability in children: A failure to replicate. *Psychological Science, 13,* 561–562.

Hill, L., Craig, I. W., Asherson, P., Ball, D., Eley, T., Ninomiya, T., et al. (1999). DNA pooling and dense marker maps: A systematic search for genes for cognitive ability. *Neuroreport, 10,* 843–848.

Hillis, A. E., Wityk, R. J., Tuffiash, E., Beauchamp, N. J., Jacobs, M. A., Barker, P. B., & Selnes, O. A. (2001). Hypoperfusion of Wernicke's area predicts severity of semantic deficit in acute stroke. *Annals of Neurology, 50,* 561–566.

Hines, M. (2004). *Brain gender.* New York: Oxford University Press.

Hines, M., & Kaufman, F. R. (1994). Androgen and the development of human sex-typical behavior: Rough-and-tumble play and sex of preferred playmates in children with congenital adrenal hyperplasia (CAH). *Child Development, 65,* 1042–1053.

Hinton, D., Um, K., & Ba, P. (2001). Kyol goeu ("wind overload") Part I: A cultural syndrome of orthostatic panic among Khmer refugees. *Transcultural Psychiatry, 38,* 403–432.

Hirokawa, E. (2004). Effects of music listening and relaxation instructions on arousal changes and the working memory task in older adults. *Journal of Music Therapy, 41,* 107–127.

Hirsch, J. (1971). Behavior-genetic analysis and its biosocial consequences. In R. Cancro (Ed.), *Intelligence: Genetic and environmental influences* (pp. 88–106). New York: Grune & Stratton.

Hirsch, J. (1997). The triumph of wishful thinking over genetic irrelevance. *Cahiers de Psychologie Cognitive/Current Psychology of Cognition, 16,* 711–720.

Hobson, J. A. (1989). *Sleep.* New York: Scientific American Library.

Hobson, J. A. (1995). *Sleep.* New York: Scientific American Library.

Hobson, J. A., & McCarley, R. W. (1977). The brain as a dream state generator: An activation-synthesis hypothesis of the dream process. *American Journal of Psychiatry, 134,* 1335–1348.

Hobson, J. A., Pace-Schott, E., & Stickgold, R. (2000). Dreaming and the brain: Toward a cognitive neuroscience of conscious states. *Behavioral and Brain Sciences, 23.*

Hochman, D. W. (2000). Optical monitoring of neuronal activity: Brain-mapping on a shoestring. *Brain & Cognition, 42,* 56–59.

Hochschild, A. (1989). *The second shift: Working parents and the revolution at home.* New York: Viking.

Hockemeyer, J., & Smyth, J. (2002). Evaluating the feasibility and efficacy of the self-administered manual-based stress management intervention for individuals with asthma: Results from a controlled study. *Behavioral Medicine, 27,* 161–172.

Hoeks, J. C., Vonk, W., & Schriefers, H. (2002). Processing coordinated structures in context: The effect of topic-structure on ambiguity resolution. *Journal of Memory & Language, 46,* 99–119.

Hoeksema-van Orden, C. Y. D., Gaillard, A. W. K., & Buunk, B. P. (1998). Social loafing under fatigue. *Journal of Personality and Social Psychology, 75,* 1179–1190.

Hoffman, D. D., & Richards, W. A. (1984). Parts of recognition. *Cognition, 18,* 65–96.

Hoffman, L. W. (1991). The influence of the family environment on personality: Accounting for sibling differences. *Psychological Bulletin, 110,* 187–203.

Hoffman, M. L. (2000). *Empathy and moral development: Implications for caring and justice.* New York: Cambridge University Press.

Hoffman, R. E., Hawkins, K. A., Gueorguieva, R., Boutros, N. N., Rachid, F., Carroll, K., & Krystal, J. H. (2003). Transcranial magnetic stimulation of left temporal cortex and medication-resistent auditory hallucinations. *Archives of General Psychiatry, 60,* 49–56.

Hoffrage, U., Gigerenzer, G., Krauss, S., & Martignon, L. (2002). Representation facilitates reasoning: What natural frequencies are and what they are not. *Cognition, 84,* 343–352.

Hofstede, G., & McCrae, R. R. (2004). Personality and culture revisited: Linking traits and dimensions of culture. *Cross-Cultural Research: The Journal of Comparative Social Science, 38,* 52–88.

Hogan, J., & Hogan, R. T. (1993). Ambiguities of conscientiousness. Presented at 10th Annual Meeting of Society Industrial and Organizational Psychology, Orlando, FL.

Hohlstein, L. A., Smith, G. T., & Atlas, J. G. (1998). An application of expectancy theory to eating disorders: Development and validation of measures of eating and dieting expectancies. *Psychological Assessment, 10,* 49–58.

Hohman, G. W. (1966). Some effects of spinal cord lesions on experienced emotional feelings. *Psychophysiology, 3,* 143–156.

Holahan, C. K., Holahan, C. J., & Belk, S. S. (1984). Adjustment in aging: The roles of life stress, hassles, and self-efficacy. *Health Psychology, 3,* 3315–328.

Holcombe, A. O., & Cavanagh, P. (2001). Early binding of feature pairs for visual perception. *Nature Neuroscience, 4,* 127–128.

Holden, C. (1980). Identical twins reared apart. *Science, 207,* 1323–1328.

Holland, J., Sicotte, N., & Treasure, J. (1988). Anorexia nervosa: Evidence for a genetic basis. *Journal of Psychosomatic Research, 32,* 561–571.

Hollerman, J. R., & Schultz, W. (1998). Dopamine neurons report an error in the temporal prediction of reward during learning. *Nature Neuroscience, 1,* 304–309.

Hollerman, J. R., Tremblay, L., & Schultz, W. (1998). Influence of reward expectation on behavior-related neuronal activity in primate striatum. *Journal of Neurophysiology, 80,* 947–963.

Hollis, K. L. (1997). Compenorary research on Pavlovian conditioning: A "new" functional analysis. *American Psychologist, 52,* 956–965.

Hollon, S. D., & Beck, A. T. (1994). Cognitive and cognitive-behavioral therapies. In A. E. Bergin & S. L. Garfield (Eds.), *Handbook of psychotherapy and behavior change* (4th ed., pp. 428–466). New York: John Wiley & Sons.

Hollon, S. D., DeRubeis, R. J., Evans, M. D., Wiemer, M. J., Garvey, M. J., Grove, W. M., & Tuason, V. B., (1992). Cognitive therapy and pharmacotherapy for depression: Singly and in combination. *Archives of General Psychiatry, 49,* 774–781.

Hollon, S. D., DeRubeis, R. J., Shelton, R. C., Amsterdam, J. D., Salomon, R. M., O'Reardon, J. P., Lovett, M. L., Young, P. R., Haman, K. L., Freeman, B. B., & Gallop, R. (2005). Prevention of relapse following cognitive therapy vs. medications in moderate to severe depression. *Archives of General Psychiatry, 62,* 417–422.

Hollon, S. D., & Shelton, R. C. (2001). Treatment guidelines for major depressive disorder. *Behavior Therapy, 32,* 235–258.

Holmes, D. S. (1984). Meditation and somatic arousal reduction. A review of the experimental evidence. *American Psychologist, 39,* 1–10.

Holmes, T. H., & Rahe, R. H. (1967). The social readjustment rating scale. *Journal of Psychosomatic Research, 11,* 213–218.

Holyoak, K. J., & Thagard, P. (1997). The analogical mind. *American Psychologist, 52,* 35–44.

Honeycutt, J. M., Cantrill, J. G., Kelly, P., & Lambkin, D. (1998). How do I love thee? Let me consider my options: Cognition, verbal strategies, and the escalation of intimacy. *Human Communication Research, 25,* 39–63.

Honig, A., Hofman, A., Rozendaal, N., & Dingemans, P. (1997). Psycho-education in bipolar disorder: Effect on expressed emotion. *Psychiatry Research, 72,* 17–22.

Honorton, C. (1997). The Ganzfeld novice: Four predictors of initial ESP performance. *Journal of Parapsychology, 61,* 143–158.

Hooley, J. M., & Licht, D. M. (1997). Expressed emotional and causal attributions in the spouses of depressed patients. *Journal of Abnormal Psychology, 106,* 298–306.

Hooper, C. J., Luciana, M., Conklin, H. M., & Yarger, R. S. (2004). Adolescents' performance on the Iowa gambling task: implications for the development of decision making and ventromedial prefrontal cortex. *Developmental Psychology, 40,* 1148–1158.

Hooper, F. H., Hooper, J. O., & Colbert, K. K. (1984). *Personality and memory correlates of intellectual functioning: Young adulthood to old age.* Basel, Switzerland: Karger.

Hopf, J.-M., & Mangun, G. R. (2000). Shifting visual attention in space: An electrophysiological analysis using high spatial resolution mapping. *Clinical Neurophysiology, 111,* 1241–1257.

Horesh, N., Amir, M., Kedem, P., Goldberger, Y., & Kotler, M. (1997). Life events in childhood, adolescence and adulthood and the relationship to panic disorder. *Acta Psychiatrica Scandinavica, 96,* 373–378.

Horn, J. (1985). Remodeling old models of intelligence. In B. B. Wolman (Ed.), *Handbook of intelligence* (pp. 267–300). New York: Wiley.

Horn, J. (1989). Models of intelligence. In R. L. Linn (Ed.), *Intelligence: Measurement, theory, and public policy* (pp. 29–73). Urbana: University of Illinois Press.

Horn, J., & Cattell, R. B. (1966). Refinement and test of the theory of fluid and crystallized general intelligences. *Journal of Educational Psychology, 57,* 253–270.

Horn, J. L. (1986). Intellectual ability concepts. In R. J. Sternberg (Ed.), *Advances in the psychology of human intelligence* (Vol. 3, pp. 35–77). Hillsdale, NJ: Erlbaum.

Horn, J. L. (1994). Theory of fluid and crystallized intelligence. In R. J. Sternberg (Ed.), *The encyclopedia of human intelligence* (Vol. 1, pp. 443–451). New York: Macmillan.

Horn, J. L., & Masunaga, H. (2000). New directions for research into aging and intelligence: The development of expertise. In T. J. Perfect & E. A. Maylor (Eds.), *Models of cognitive aging* (pp. 125–159). Oxford, UK: Oxford University Press.

Horn, J. L., & Noll, J. (1994). A system for understanding cognitive capabilities: A theory and the evidence on which it is based. In D. K. Detterman (Ed.), *Current topics in human intelligence, Vol. 4: Theories of intelligence.* Norwood, NJ: Ablex.

Horn, J. L., & Noll, J. (1997). Human cognitive capabilities: Gf-Gc theory. In D. P. Flanagan, J. L. Genshaft, & P. L. Harrison (Eds.), *Contemporary intellectual assessment: Theories, tests and issues* (pp. 53–91). New York: Guilford.

Hornak, J., Bramham, J., Rolls, E. T., Morris, R. G., O'Doherty, J., Bullock, P. R., & Polkey, C. E. (2003). Changes in emotion after circumscribed surgical lesions of the orbitofrontal and cingulate cortices. *Brain, 126,* 1691–1712.

Horney, K. (1937). *Neurotic personality of our times.* New York: Norton.

Horowitz, J. L., & Newcomb, M. D. (2001). A multidimensional approach to homosexual identity. *Journal of Homosexuality, 42,* 1–19.

Horowitz, M. J. (1998). Personality disorder diagnoses. *American Journal of Psychiatry, 155,* 1464.

Horvath, P., & Zuckerman, M. (1993). Sensation seeking, risk appraisal and risky behavior. *Personality & Individual Differences, 14,* 41–52.

Horwath, E., & Weissman, M. M. (2000). The epidemiology and cross-national presentation of obsessive-compulsive disorder. *Psychiatric Clinics of North America, 23,* 493–507.

Horwitz, W. A., Kestenbaum, C., Person, E., & Jarvik, L. (1965). Identical twin— "idiot savants"—calendar calculators. *American Journal of Psychiatry, 121,* 1075–1079.

Hoshi, Y., Oda, I., Wada, Y., Ito, Y., Yamashita, Y., Oda, M., et al. (2000). Visuospatial imagery is a fruitful strategy for the digit span backward task: A study with near-infrared optical tomography. *Cognitive Brain Research, 9,* 339–342.

Hou, C., Miller, B. L., Cummings, J. L., Goldberg, M., Mychack, P., Bottino, V., & Benson, D. F. (2000). Artistic savants. *Neuropsychiatry, Neuropsychology, & Behavioral Neurology, 13,* 29–38.

House, J., Landis, K., & Umberson, D. (1988). Social relationships and health. *Science, 241,* 540–545.

Houston, T. K., Cooper, L. A., & Ford, D. E. (2002). Internet support groups for depression: A 1-year prospective cohort study. *American Journal of Psychiatry, 159,* 2062–2068.

Hovland, C. I., & Weiss, W. (1951). The influence of source credibility on communication effectiveness. *Public Opinion Quarterly, 15,* 635–650.

Howard, R. W. (2001). Searching the real world for signs of rising population intelligence. *Personality & Individual Differences, 30,* 1039–1058.

Hsee, C. K., Elaine, H., Carlson, J. G., & Chemtob, C. (1990). The effect of power on susceptibility to emotional contagion. *Cognition & Emotion, 4*(4), 327–340.

Hsieh, L., Gandour, J., Wong, D., & Hutchins, G. D. (2001). Functional heterogeneity of inferior frontal gyrus is shaped by linguistic experience. *Brain & Language, 76,* 227–252.

Hu, K., Ivanov, P., Hilton, M. F., Chen, Z., Ayers, R. T., Stanley, H. E., & Shea, S. A. (2004). Endogenous circadian rhythm in an index of cardiac vulnerability independent of changes in behavior. *Proceedings of the National Academy of Science, 101,* 18223–18227

Hu, W. (1990, Nov. 2–3). *The pragmatic motivation behind the use of the inverted sentence in the Beijing dialect.* Paper presented at Midwest Conference on Asian Affairs, Bloomington, IN.

Hu, W. (1995). Verbal semantics of presentative sentences. *Yuyan Yanjiu (Linguistic Studies), 29,* 100–112.

Hubacek, J. A., Pitha, J., Skodova, Z., Adamkova, V., Lanska, V., & Poledne, R. (2001). A possible role of apolipoprotein E polymorphism in predisposition to higher education. *Neuropsychobiology, 43,* 200–203.

Huddy, L., & Virtanen, S. (1995). Subgroup differentiation and subgroup bias among Latinos as a function of familiarity and positive distinctiveness. *Journal of Personality and Social Psychology, 68,* 97–108.

Huen, K. F., Leung, S. S., Lau, J. T., Cheung, A. Y., Leung, N. K., & Chiu, M. C. (1997). Secular trend in the sexual maturation of southern Chinese girls. *Acta Paediatrica, 86,* 1121–1124.

Huerta, P. T., Scearce, K. A., Farris, S. M., Empson, R. M., & Prusky, G. T. (1996). Preservation of spatial learning in fyn tyrosine kinase knockout mice. *Neuroreport, 7,* 1685–1689.

Huesmann, L. R., & Eron, L. D. (1986). *Television and the aggressive child: A cross-national comparison.* Hillsdale, NJ: Erlbaum.

Huesmann, L. R., Moise-Titus, J., Podolski, C., & Eron, L. D. (2003). Longitudinal relations between children's exposure to TV violence and their aggressive and violent behavior in young adulthood: 1977–1992. *Developmental Psychology, 39,* 201–221.

Huff, D. (1954). *How to lie with statistics.* New York: Norton.

Huff, N. C., & Rudy, J. W. (2004). The amygdala modulates hippocampus-dependent context memory formation and stores cue-shock associations. *Behavioral Neuroscience, 118,* 53–62.

Hugdahl, K. (1995a). Classical conditioning and implicit learning: The right hemisphere hypothesis. In R. J. Davidson & K. Hugdahl (Eds.), *Brain asymmetry* (pp. 235–267). Cambridge, MA: MIT Press.

Hugdahl, K. (1995b). *Psychophysiology: The mind-body perspective.* Cambridge, MA: Harvard University Press.

Hugdahl, K. (2001). *Psychophysiology: The mind-body perspective* (2nd ed.). Cambridge, MA: Harvard University Press.

Hugdahl, K., & Davidson, R. J. (Eds.) (2003). *The asymmetrical brain.* Cambridge, MA: MIT Press.

Hugenberg, K., & Bodenhausen, G. V. (2003). Facing prejudice: Implicit prejudice and the perception of facial threat. *Psychological Science, 14,* 640–643.

Hugenberg, K., & Bodenhausen, G. V. (2004). Ambiguity in social categorization: The role of prejudice and facial affect in race categorization. *Psychological Science, 15,* 342–345.

Hui, C. H., & Triandis, H. C. (1986). Individualism-collectivism: A study of cross-cultural researchers. *Journal of Cross-cultural psychology, 17,* 225–248.

Hull, J. G., Van Treuren, R. R., & Virnelli, S. (1987). Hardiness and health: A critique and alternative approach. *Journal of Personality & Social Psychology, 53,* 518–530.

Hultman, C. M., Wieselgren, I., & Oehman, A. (1997). Relationships between social support, social coping and life events in the relapse of schizophrenic patients. *Scandinavian Journal of Psychology, 38,* 3–13.

Hummel, J. E., & Biederman, I. (1992). Dynamic binding in a neural network for shape recognition. *Psychological Review, 99,* 480–517.

Hummel, J. E., & Holyoak, K. J. (1997). Distributed representations of structure: A theory of analogical access and mapping. *Psychological Review, 104,* 427–466.

Humphreys, G. W., Riddoch, M. J., & Price, C. J. (1997). Top-down processes in object identification: Evidence from experimental psychology, neuropsychology and functional anatomy. *Philosophical Transactions of the Royal Society, London, 352,* 1275–1282.

Hunt, E. (1995). *Will we be smart enough? A cognitive analysis of the coming workforce.* New York: Russell Sage.

Hunt, E. (2001). Multiple views of multiple intelligence. *Contemporary Psychology, 46,* 5–7.

Hunter, J. E. (1983). A casual analysis of cognitive ability, job knowledge, job performance, and supervisor ratings. In F. Landy, S. Zedeck, & J. Cleveland (Eds.), *Performance measurement and theory* (pp. 257–266). Hillsdale, NJ: Erlbaum.

Hunter, J. E., & Hunter, R. F. (1984). Validity and utility of alternative predictors of job performance. *Psychological Bulletin, 96,* 72–98.

Huntjens, R. J. C., Peters, M. L., Postma, A., Woertman, L., Effting, M., & van der Hart, O. (2005). Transfer of newly acquired stimulus valence between identities in dissociative identity disorder (DID). *Behaviour Research and Therapy, 43,* 243–255.

Huppert, J. D., Bufka, L. F., Barlow, D. H., Gorman, J. M., Shear, M. K., & Woods, S. W. (2001). Therapists, therapist variables and cognitive-behavioral therapy outcome in a multicenter trial for panic disorder. *Journal of Consulting and Clinical Psychology, 69,* 747–755.

Hur, Y., & Bouchard, T. J., Jr. (1997). The genetic correlation between impulsivity and sensation seeking traits. *Behavior Genetics, 27,* 455–463.

Husain, M., & Jackson, S. R. (2001). Vision: Visual space is not what it appears to be. *Current Biology, 11,* R753–R755.

Husain, M. M., Rush, A. J., Fink, M., Knapp, R., Petrides, G., Rummans, T., Biggs, M. M., O'Connor, K., Rasmussen, K., Litle, M., Zhao, W., Bernstein, H. J., Smith, G., Mueller, M., McClintock, S. M., Bailine, S. H., & Kellner, C. H. (2004). Speed of response and remission in major depressive disorder with acute electroconvulsive therapy (ECT): A consortium for research in ECT (CORE) report. *Journal of Clinical Psychiatry, 65,* 485–491.

Huttenlocher, J. (1968). Constructing spatial images: A strategy in reasoning. *Psychological Review, 75*(6), 550–560.

Huttenlocher, J., Higgins, E. T., Milligan, L., & Kaufman, B. (1970). The mystery of the "negative equative" construction. *Journal of Verbal Learning and Verbal Behavior, 9,* 334–341.

Huttenlocher, P. (2002). *Neural plasticity.* Cambridge, MA: Harvard University Press.

Hyde, K. L., & Peretz, I. (2004). Brains that are out of tune but in time. *Psychological Science, 15,* 356–360.

Hyde, T. S., & Jenkins, J. J. (1973). Recall for words as a function of semantic, graphic, and syntactic orientation tasks. *Journal of Verbal Learning and Verbal Behavior, 12,* 471–480.

Hyman, A., Mentzer, T., & Calderone, L. (1979). The contribution of olfaction to taste discrimination. *Bulletin of Psychonomic Society, 13,* 359–362.

Iansek, R., & Porter, R. C. (1980). The monkey globus pallidus: Neuronal discharge properties in relation to movement. *Journal of Physiology, 301,* 439–455.

Ikemoto, S., & Panksepp, J. (1996). Dissociations between appetitive and consummatory responses by pharmacological manipulations of reward-relevant brain regions. *Behavioral Neuroscience, 110,* 331–345.

Imber, S. D., Pilkonis, P. A., Sotsky, S. M., Elkin, I., Watkins, J. T., Collins, J. F., et al. (1991). Mode-specific effects among three treatments for depression. *Journal of Consulting and Clinical Psychology, 58,* 352–359.

Ingledew, D. K., Hardy, L., & Cooper, C. L. (1997). Do resources bolster coping and does coping buffer stress? An organizational study with longitudinal aspect and control for negative affectivity. *Journal of Occupational Health Psychology, 2,* 118–133.

Inlow, J. K., & Restifo, L. L. (2004). Molecular and comparative genetics of mental retardation. *Genetics, 166,* 835–881.

Inman, D. J., Silver, S. M., & Doghramji, K. (1990). Sleep disturbance in post-traumatic stress disorder: A comparison with non-PTSD insomnia. *Journal of Traumatic Stress, 3,* 429–437.

Insel, T. R. (1992). Toward a neuroanatomy of obsessive-compulsive disorder. *Archives of General Psychiatry, 49,* 739–744.

Insel, T. R. (2000). Toward a neurobiology of attachment. *Review of General Psychology, 4,* 176–185.

International Human Genome Sequencing Consortium (2001). Initial sequencing and analysis of the human genome. *Nature, 409,* 860–921.

Intriligator, J., & Cavanagh, P. (2001). The spatial resolution of visual attention. *Cognitive Psychology, 43,* 171–216.

Inui, A. (1999). Feeding and body-weight regulation by hypothalamic neuropeptides—mediation of the actions of leptin. *Trends in Neurosciences, 22,* 62–67.

Ione, A. (2003). Examining Semir Zeki's "Neural concept formation and art: Dante, Michelangelo, Wagner." *Journal of Consciousness Studies, 10,* 58–66.

Ironson, G., Wynings, C., Schneiderman, N., Baum, A., Rodriguez, M., Greenwood, D., et al. (1997). Posttraumatic stress symptoms, intrusive thoughts, loss, and immune function after Hurricane Andrew. *Psychosomatic Medicine, 59,* 128–141.

Isaksen, S. G., & Treffinger, D. J. (2004). Celebrating 50 years of reflective practice: Versions of creative problem solving. *Journal of Creative Behavior, 38,* 75–101.

Isenberg, D. J. (1986). Group polarization: A critical review and meta-analysis. *Journal of Personality & Social Psychology, 50,* 1141–1151.

Itkowitz, N. I., Kerns, R. D., & Otis, J. D. (2003). Support and coronary heart disease: The importance of significant other responses. *Journal of Behavioral Medicine, 26,* 19–30.

Iverson, J. M., & Goldin-Meadow, S. (1998). Why people gesture when they speak. *Nature, 396,* 228.

Iverson, J. M., & Goldin-Meadow, S. (2001). The resilience of gesture in talk: Gesture in blind speakers and listeners. *Developmental Science, 4,* 416–422.

Ivry, R. B., & Robertson, L. C. (1998). *The two sides of perception.* Cambridge, MA: The MIT Press.

Ivry, R. B., & Spencer, R. M. C. (2004). The neural representation of time. *Current Opinion in Neurobiology, 14,* 225–232.

Ivy, G., MacLeod, C., Petit, T., & Markus, E. (1992). A physiological framework for perceptual and cognitive changes in aging. In F. I. M. Craik & T. A.

Salthouse (Eds.), *The handbook of aging and cognition* (pp. 273–314). Hillsdale, NJ: Erlbaum.

Iyengar, S. S., & Lepper, M. R. (2000). When choice is demotivating: Can one desire too much of a good thing? *Journal of Personality & Social Psychology, 79*, 995–1006.

Izard, C. E. (1971). *The face of emotion*. New York: Appleton-Century-Crofts.

Jackson, D. C., Malmstadt, J. R., Larson, C. L., & Davidson, R. J. (2000). Suppression and enhancement of emotional responses to unpleasant pictures. *Psychophysiology, 37*, 515–522.

Jackson, D. C., Mueller, C. J., Dolski, I., Dalton, K. M., Nitschke, J. B., Urry, H. L., Rosenkranz, M. A., et al. (2003). Now you feel it, now you don't: Frontal brain electrical asymmetry and individual differences in emotion regulation. *Psychological Science, 14*, 612–617.

Jackson, N., & Butterfield, E. (1986). A conception of giftedness designed to promote research. In R. J. Sternberg & J. E. Davidson (Eds.), *Conceptions of giftedness* (pp. 151–181). New York: Cambridge University Press.

Jackson, S. E., Brett, J. F., Sessa, V. I., Cooper, D. M., Julin, J. A., & Peyronnin, K. (1991). Some differences make a difference: Individual dissimilarity and group heterogeneity as correlates of recruitment, promotion, and turnover. *Journal of Applied Psychology, 76*, 675–689.

Jacobs, G. D., Pace-Schott, E. F., Stickgold, R., & Otto, M. W. (2004). Cognitive behavior therapy and pharmacotherapy for insomnia: A randomized controlled trial and direct comparison. *Archives of Internal Medicine, 164*, 1888–1896.

Jacobs, J. E., & Klaczynski, P. A. (2002). The development of judgment and decision making during childhood and adolescence. *Current Directions in Psychological Science, 11*, 145–149.

Jacobs, N., Van Gestel, S., Derom, C., Thiery, E., Vernon, P., Derom, R., & Vlietinck, R. (2001). Heritability estimates of intelligence in twins: Effect of chorion type. *Behavior Genetics, 31*, 209–217.

Jacobs, R. C., & Campbell, D. T. (1961). The perpetuation of an arbitrary tradition through several generations of a laboratory microculture. *Journal of Abnormal and Social Psychology, 62*, 649–648.

Jacobsen, L. K., Mencl, W. E., Pugh, K. R., Skudlarski, P., & Krystal, J. H. (2004). Preliminary evidence of hippocampal dysfunction in adolescent MDMA ("ecstasy") users: Possible relationship to neurotoxic effects. *Psychopharmacology, 173*, 383–390.

Jacobsen, L. K., Southwick, S. M., & Kosten, T. R. (2001). Substance use disorders in patients with posttraumatic stress disorder: A review of the literature. *American Journal of Psychiatry, 158*, 1184–1190.

Jacobsen, T., Schröger, E., & Alter, K. (2004). Pre-attentive perception of vowel phonemes from variable speech stimuli. *Psychophysiology, 41*, 654–659.

Jacoby, L. L., Bishara, A. J., Hessels, S., & Toth, J. P. (2005). Aging, subjective experience, and cognitive control: Dramatic false remembering by older adults. *Journal of Experimental Psychology: General, 134*, 131–148.

Jadack, R. A., Hyde, J. S., Moore, C. F., & Keller, M. L. (1995). Moral reasoning about sexually transmitted diseases. *Child Development, 66*, 167–177.

Jaffee, S., Caspi, A., Moffitt, T. E., Belsky, J., & Silva, P. (2001). Why are children born to teen mothers at risk for adverse outcomes in young adulthood? Results from a 20-year longitudinal study. *Development & Psychopathology, 13*, 377–397.

Jakobson, R., & Halle, M. (1956). *Fundamentals of language*. The Hague: Mouton.

James, L. E., Burke, D. M., Austin, A., & Hulme, E. (1998). Production and perception of "verbosity" in younger and older adults. *Psychology and Aging, 13*, 355–367.

James, T. W., Culham, J., Humphrey, G. K., Milner, A. D., & Goodale, M. A. (2003). Ventral occipital lesions impair object recognition but not object-directed grasping: An fMRI study. *Brain, 126*, 2463–2475.

James, W. (1884). What is emotion? *Mind, 9*, 188–205.

James, W. (1890/1950). *Principles of psychology*. New York: Dover.

Jameson, K. A., Highnote, S. M., & Wasserman, L. M. (2001). Richer color experience in observers with multiple photopigment opsin genes. *Psychonomic Bulletin & Review, 8*, 244–261.

Jamison, K. R. (1989). Mood disorders and patterns of creativity in British writers and artists. *Psychiatry, 52*, 125–134.

Jamison, K. R. (1993). *Touched with fire: Manic-depressive illness and the artistic temperament*. New York: Free Press.

Jamison, K. R. (1995). *An unquiet mind: A memoir of moods and madness*. New York: Vintage Books, p. 67.

Jamison, K. R., Gerner, R. H., Hammen, C., & Padesky, C. (1980). Clouds and silver linings: Positive experiences associated with primary affective disorders. *American Journal of Psychiatry, 137*, 198–202.

Jamner, L. D., & Leigh, H. (1999). Repressive/defensive coping, endogenous opioids and health: How a life so perfect can make you sick. *Psychiatry Research, 85*, 17–31.

Jamner, L. D., Schwartz, G. E., & Leigh, H. (1988). The relationship between repressive and defensive coping styles and monocyte, eosinophile, and serum glucose levels: Support for the opioid peptide hypothesis of repression. *Psychosomatic Medicine, 50*, 567–575.

Janata, P., Tillman, B., & Bharucha, J. J. (2002). Listening to polyphonic music recruits domain-general attention and working memory circuits. *Cognitive, Affective & Behavioral Neuroscience, 2*, 121–140.

Jancke, L., & Steinmetz, H. (1994). Interhemispheric-transfer time and corpus callosum size. *Neuroreport, 5*, 2385–2388.

Jang, K. L., McCrae, R. R., Angleitner, A., Riemann, R., & Livesley, W. J. (1998). Heritability of facet-level traits in a cross-cultural twin sample: Support for a hierarchical model of personality. *Journal of Personality and Social Psychology, 74*, 1556–1565.

Janicak, P. G., Dowd, S. M., Martis, B., Alam, D., Beedle, D., Krasuski, J., et al. (2002). Repetitive transcranial magnetic stimulation versus electroconvulsive therapy for major depression: Preliminary results of a randomized trial. *Biological Psychiatry, 51*, 659–667.

Janis, I. L. (1982). *Victims of groupthink* (2nd ed.). Boston: Houghton Mifflin.

Janowiak, J. J. (1994). Meditation and college students' self-actualization and rated stress. *Psychological Reports, 75*, 1007–1010.

Janowsky, J. S., Oviatt, S. K., & Orwoll, E. S. (1994). Testosterone influences spatial cognition in older men. *Behavioral Neuroscience, 108*, 325–332.

Jansen, A., Nederkoorn, C., & Mulkens, S. (2005). Selective visual attention for ugly and beautiful body parts in eating disorders. *Behaviour Research and Therapy, 43*, 183–196.

Jansen, B. R. J., & van der Maas, H. L. J. (2002). The development of children's rule use on the balance scale task. *Journal of Experimental Child Psychology, 81*, 383–416.

Jason, L. A., & Fries, M. (2004). Helping parents reduce children's television viewing. *Research on Social Work Practice, 14*, 121–131.

Jeannerod, M., & Frak, V. (1999). Mental imaging of motor activity in humans. *Current Opinion in Neurobiology, 9*, 735–739.

Jenike, M. (1984). Obsessive-compulsive disorder: A question of a neurologic lesion. *Compr. Psychiatry, 25*, 298–304.

Jenkins, J. M., Rasbash, J., & O'Connor, T. G. (2003). The role of the shared family context in differential parenting. *Developmental Psychology, 39*, 99–113.

Jenkins-Hall, K., & Sacco, W. P. (1991). Effects of client race and depression on evaluations by white therapists. *Journal of Social Clinical Psychology, 10*, 322–333.

Jenner, P. (2002). Pharmacology of dopamine agonists in the treatment of Parkinson's disease. *Neurology, 58*, S1–S8.

Jensen, A. R. (1980). *Bias in mental testing*. New York: Free Press.

Jensen, A. R. (1987). Psychometric g as a focus of concerted research effort. *Intelligence, 11*, 193–198.

Jensen, A. R. (1991). *General mental ability: From psychometrics to biology*. Paper presented at the Annual Meeting of the American Association for the Advancement of Science, Washington, DC.

Jensen, A. R. (1998). *The g factor: The science of mental ability*. Westport, CT: Praeger.

Jensen, J. P., Bergin, A. E., & Greaves, D. W. (1990). The meaning of eclecticism: New survey and analysis of components. *Professional Psychology: Research and Practice, 21*, 124–130.

Jerome, E. M., & Liss, M. (2005). Relationships between sensory processing style, adult attachment, and coping. *Personality & Individual Differences, 38*, 1341–1352.

Jevning, R., Wallace, R. K., & Beidebach, M. (1992). The physiology of meditation: A review. A wadeful hypnometabolic integrated response. *Neuroscience and Biobehavioral Reviews, 16*, 415–424.

Jewett, D. L., Fein, G., & Greenberg, M. H. (1990). A double-blind study of symptom provocation to determine food sensitivity. *New England Journal of Medicine, 323*, 429–433.

Ji, L-J., Nisbett, R. E., & Su, Y. (2001). Culture, change, and prediction. *Psychological Science, 12*, 450–456.

Johansson, B., Hofer, S. M., Allaire, J. C., Maldonado-Molina, M. M., Piccinin, A. M., Berg, S., et al. (2004). Change in cognitive capabilities in the oldest old: The effects of proximity to death in genetically related individuals over a 6-year period. *Psychology and Aging, 19*, 145–156.

Johnson, J. A. (2000). Predicting observers' ratings of the Big Five from the CPI, HPI, and NEO-PI-R: A comparative validity study. *European Journal of Personality, 4*, 1–19.

Johnson, J. D., Noel, N. E., & Sutter, J. (2000). Alcohol and male sexual aggression: A cognitive disruption analysis. *Journal of Applied Social Psychology.*

Johnson, K. E., & Eilers, A. T. (1998). Effects of knowledge and development on subordinate level categorization. *Cognitive Development, 13,* 515–545.

Johnson, M. H. (2001). Functional brain development in humans. *Nature Reviews Neuroscience, 2,* 475–483.

Johnson, M. K., Hashtroudi, S., & Lindsy, D. S. (1993). Source monitoring. *Psychological Bulletin, 114,* 3–28.

Johnson, M. K., Nolde, S. F., Mather, M., Kounios, J., Schacter, D. L., & Curran, T. (1997). The similarity of brain activity associated with true and false recognition memory depends on test format. *Psychological Science, 8,* 250–257.

Johnson, M. K., & Raye, C. L. (1981). Reality monitoring. *Psychological Review, 88,* 67–85.

Johnson, M. R., & Lydiard, B. (1995). Personality disorders in social phobia. *Psychiatric Annals, 25,* 554–563.

Johnson, S. (2000). The recognition of mentalistic agents in infancy. *Trends in Cognitive Sciences, 4,* 22–28.

Johnson, S. C., Leslie, C., Baxter, L. C., Lana S., Wilder, L. S., Pipe, J. G., Heiserman, J. E., & Prigatano, G. P. (2002). Neural correlates of self-reflection. *Brain, 125,* 1808–1814.

Johnson, S. L., & Miller, I. (1997). Negative life events and time to recovery from episodes of bipolar disorder. *Journal of Abnormal Psychology, 106,* 449–457.

Johnson, S. L., Turner, R. J., & Iwata, N. (2003). BIS/BAS levels and psychiatric disorder: An epidemiological study. *Journal of Psychopathology & Behavioral Assessment, 25,* 25–36.

Johnson, S. M., & Roberts, J. E. (1995). Life events and bipolar disorder: Implications from biological theories. *Psychological Bulletin, 117,* 434–449.

Johnson, S. P., Bremner, J. G., Slater, A., Mason, U., Foster, K., & Cheshire, A. (2003). Infants' perception of object trajectories. *Child Development, 74,* 94-108.

Johnson, W., Bouchard, T. J. Jr., Krueger, R. F., McGue, M., & Gottesman, I. I. (2004). Just one g: Consistent results from three test batteries. *Intelligence, 32,* 95–107.

Johnson, W., McGue, M., & Krueger, R. F. (2005). Personality stability in late adulthood: A behavioral genetic analysis. *Journal of Personality, 73,* 523–551.

Johnson, W., McGue, M., Krueger, R. F., & Bouchard, T. J., Jr. (2004). Marriage and personality: A genetic analysis. *Journal of Personality & Social Psychology, 86,* 285–294.

Johnson-Laird, P. N. (1995). Mental models, deductive reasoning, and the brain. In M. S. Gazzaniga (Ed.), *The cognitive neurosciences* (pp. 999–1008). Cambridge, MIT Press.

Johnson-Laird, P. N. (2001). Mental models and deduction. *Trends in Cognitive Science, 5,* 434–443.

Johnson-Laird, P. N., Legrenzi, P., & Girotto, V. (2004). How we detect logical inconsistencies. *Current Directions in Psychological Science, 13,* 41–45.

Johnston, L. C., & Macrae, C. N. (1994). Changing social stereotypes: The case of the information seeker. *European Journal of Social Psychology, 24,* 581–592.

Johnston, L. D., O'Malley, P. M., & Bachman, J. G. (1994). *National survey results on drug use from the Monitoring the Future study, 1975–1993* (NIH Publication No. 94–3810). Washington, DC: U.S. Government Printing Office.

Joiner, T. E. (1994). Contagious depression: Existence, specificity to depressed symptoms, and the role of reassurance seeking. *Journal of Personality and Social Psychology, 67,* 287–296.

Jolicoeur, P. (1998). Modulation of the attentional blink by on-line response selection: Evidence from speeded and unspeeded Task 1 decisions. *Memory & Cognition, 26,* 1014–1032.

Jones, D. (1996). *Physical attractiveness and the theory of sexual selection: Results from five populations.* Museum of Anthropology: University of Michigan.

Jones, M. K., & Menzies, R. G. (1995). The etiology of fear of spiders. *Anxiety, Stress & Coping: An International Journal, 8,* 227–234.

Jones, N. A., Field, T., & Davalos, M. (1998). Massage therapy attenuates right frontal EEG asymmetry in one-month-old infants of depressed mothers. *Infant Behavior & Development, 21,* 527–530.

Jones, T. A., & Greenough, W. T. (1996). Ultrastructural evidence for increased contact between astrocytes and synapses in rats reared in a complex environment. *Neurobiology of Learning and Memory, 65,* 48–56.

Jonides, J., Lacey, S. C., & Nee, D. E. (2005). Processes of working memory in mind and brain. *Current Directions in Psychological Science, 14,* 2–5.

Jorm, A. F., Anstey, K. J., Christensen, H., & Rodgers, B. (2004). Gender differences in cognitive abilities: The mediating role of health state and health habits. *Intelligence, 32,* 7–23.

Joseph, J. (2001). Separated twins and the genetics of personality differences: A critique. *American Journal of Psychology, 114,* 1–30.

Joseph, S., Williams, R., & Yule, W. (1995). Psychosocial perspectives on post-traumatic stress disorder. *Clinical Psychology Review, 15,* 515–544.

Josephs, R. A., Newman, M. L., Brown, R. P., & Beer, J. M. (2003). Status, testosterone, and human intellectual performance: Stereotype threat as status concern. *Psychological Science, 14,* 158–163.

Joubert, S., Barbeau, E., Walter, N., Ceccaldi, M., & Poncet, M. (2003). Preservation of autobiographical memory in a case of pure progressive amnesia. *Brain & Cognition, 53,* 235–238.

Judd, C. M., Ryan, C. S., & Parke, B. (1991). Accuracy in the judgment of in-group and out-group variability. *Journal of Personality and Social Psychology, 61,* 366–379.

Judd, L. L., Akiskal, H. S., Maser, J. D., Zeller, P. J., Endicott, J., Coryell, W., et al. (1998). A prospective 12-year study of subsyndromal and syndromal depressive: Symptoms in unipolar major depressive disorders. *Archives of General Psychiatry, 55,* 694–700.

Judge, T. A., Erez, A., Bono, J. E., & Thoresen, C. J. (2002). Are measures of self-esteem, neuroticism, locus of control, and generalized self-efficacy indicators of a common core construct? *Journal of Personality and Social Psychology, 83,* 693–710.

Julesz, B. (1971). *Foundations of cyclopean perception.* Oxford, UK: University of Chicago Press.

Jusczyk, P. W. (1995). Language acquisition: Speech sounds and phonological development. In J. L. Miller & P. D. Eimas (Eds.), *Handbook of perception and cognition: Vol. 11. Speech, language, and communication* (pp. 263–301). Orlando, FL: Academic Press.

Kabat-Zinn, J., Wheeler, E., Light, T., Skillings, A., Scharf, M. J., Copley, T. G., et al. (1998). Influence of a mindfulness meditation-based stress reduction intervention on rates of skin clearing in patients with moderate to severe psoriasis undergoing phototherapy (UVB) and photochemotherapy (PUVA). *Psychosomatic Medicine, 60,* 625–632.

Kac, G., Auxiliadora de Santa Cruz Coel, & Velasquez-Melendez, G. (2000). Secular trend in age at menarche for women born between 1920 and 1979 in Rio de Janeiro, Brazil. *Annals of Human Biology, 27,* 423–428.

Kagan, J. (1989a). Temperamental contributions to social behavior. *American Psychologist, 44,* 668–674.

Kagan, J. (1989b). *Unstable ideas: Temperament, cognition, and self.* Cambridge, MA: Cambridge University Press.

Kagan, J. (1994). On the nature of emotion. *Monographs of the Society for Research in Child Development, 59,* 7–24, 250–283.

Kagan, J., Reznick, J. S., & Snidman, N. (1988). Biological bases of childhood shyness. *Science, 240,* 167–171.

Kagan, J., Snidman, N., & Arcus, D. (1998). Childhood derivatives of high and low reactivity in infancy. *Child Development, 69,* 1483–1493.

Kagan, J., Snidman, N., Arcus, D., & Reznick, J. S. (1994). *Galen's prophecy: Temperament in human nature.* New York: Basic Books.

Kagan, R. M., & Reid, W. J. (1986). Critical factors in the adoption of emotionally disturbed youths. *Child Welfare, 65,* 63–73.

Kahneman, D. (2003). A perspective on judgment and choice. *American Psychologist, 58,* 697–720.

Kahneman, D., Fredrickson, B. L., Schreiber, C. A., & Redelmeier, D. A. (1993). When more pain is preferred to less: Adding a better end. *Psychological Science, 4,* 401–405.

Kahneman, D., Krueger, A. B., Schkade, D. A., Schwarz, N., & Stone, A. A. (2004). A survey method for characterizing daily life experience: The day reconstruction method. *Science. 306,* 1776–1780.

Kahneman, D., & Tversky, A. (1979). Prospect theory: An analysis of decision under risk. *Econometrica, 47,* 263–291.

Kahneman, D., & Tversky, A. (1984). Choices, values, and frames. *American Psychologist, 39,* 341–350.

Kahneman, D., & Tversky, A. (1996). On the reality of cognitive illusions: A reply to Gigerenzer's critique. *Psychological Review, 103,* 582–591.

Kail, R. (1988). Developmental functions speeds of cognitive processes. *Journal of Experimental Child Psychology, 45,* 339–364.

Kail, R. (1991). Processing time declines exponentially during childhood and adolescence. *Developmental Psychology, 27,* 259–266.

Kaiser, C. R., Vick, S. B., & Major, B. (2004). A prospective investigation of the relationship between just-world beliefs and the desire for revenge after September 11, 2001. *Psychological Science, 15,* 503–506.

Kalimo, R., Tenkanen, L., Haermae, M., Poppius, E., & Heinsalmi, P. (2000). Job stress and sleep disorders: Findings from the Helsinki Heart Study. *Stress Medicine, 16,* 65–75.

Kalish, R. A., & Reynolds, D. K. (1977). The role of age in death attitudes. *Death Education, 1*, 205–230.

Kalivas, P. W., & Nakamura, M. (1999). Neural systems for behavioral activation and reward. *Current Opinion in Neurobiology, 9*, 223–227.

Källén, B. (2004). Use of folic acid supplementation and risk for dizygotic twinning. *Early Human Development, 80*, 143–151.

Kallio, S., & Revonsuo, A. (2003). Hypnotic phenomena and altered states of consciousness: A multilevel framework of description and explanation. *Contemporary Hypnosis, 20*, 111–164.

Kaltenthaler, E., Parry, G., & Beverley, C. (2004). Computerized cognitive behaviour therapy: A systematic review. *Behavioural & Cognitive Psychotherapy, 32*, 31–55.

Kamin, L. (1969). Predictability, surprise, attention and conditioning. In B. A. Campbell and R. M. Church (Eds.), *Punishment and aversive behavior.* New York: Appleton-Century-Crofts.

Kamins, M. L., & Dweck, C. S. (1999). Person versus process praise and criticism: Implications for contingent self-worth and coping. *Developmental Psychology, 35*, 835–847.

Kampe, K. K. W., Frith, C. D., Dolan, R. J., & Frith, U. (2001). Reward value of attractiveness and gaze. *Nature, 413*, 589–590.

Kampe, K. K. W., Frith, C. D., Dolan, R. J., & Frith, U. (2002). Reward value of attractiveness and gaze: Correction. *Nature, 416*, 602.

Kanaya, T., Scullin, M. H., & Ceci, S. J. (2003). The Flynn effect and U.S. policies: The impact of rising IQ scores on American society via mental retardation diagnoses. *American Psychologist, 58*, 778–790.

Kandel, E. R., Schwartz, J. H., & Jessell, T. M. (2000). *Principles of neural science.* New York: McGraw-Hill/Appleton & Lange.

Kane, H., & Oakland, T. D. (2000). Secular declines in Spearman's g: Some evidence from the United States. *Journal of Genetic Psychology, 161*, 337–345.

Kane, M. J., Hambrick, D. Z., & Conway, A. R. A. (2005). Working memory capacity and fluid intelligence are strongly related constructs: Comment on Ackerman, Beier, & Boyle (2005). *Psychological Bulletin, 131*, 66–71.

Kaniasty, K., & Norris, F. H. (1992). Social support and victims of crime: Matching event, support, and outcome. *American Journal of Community Psychology, 20*, 211–241.

Kaniasty, K. Z., Norris, F. H., & Murrell, S. A. (1990). Received and perceived social support following natural disaster. *Journal of Applied Psychology, 20*, 85–114.

Kanner, A. D., Coyne, J. C., Schaefer, C., & Lazarus, R. S. (1981). Comparison of two modes of stress management: Daily hassles and uplifts versus major life events. *Journal of Behavioral Medicine, 4*, 1–39.

Kanwisher, N. (1991). Repetition blindness and illusory conjunctions: Errors in binding visual types with visual tokens. *Journal of Experimental Psychology: Human Perception and Performance, 17*, 404–421.

Kanwisher, N., McDermott, J., & Chun, M. M. (1997). The fusiform face area: A module in human extrastriate cortex specialized for face perception. *Journal of Neuroscience, 17*, 4302–4311.

Kanwisher, N., Tong, F., & Nakayama, K. (1998). The effect of face inversion on the human fusiform face area. *Cognition, 68*, B1–B11.

Kanwisher, N. G. (1987). Repetition blindness: Type recognition without token individuation. *Cognition, 27*, 117–143.

Kaplan, M. F. (1987). The influencing process in group decision making. In C. Hendrick (Ed.), *Review of personality and social psychology* (Vol. 8, pp. 189–212). Newbury Park, CA: Sage.

Kaplowitz, P. B., Slora, E. J., Wasserman, R. C., Pedlow, S. E., & Herman-Giddens, M. E. (2001). Earlier onset of puberty in girls: Relation to increased body mass index and race. *Pediatrics, 108*, 347–353.

Karacan, I., Goodenough, D. R., Shapiro, A., & Starker, S. (1966). Erection cycle during sleep in relation to dream anxiety. *Archives of General Psychiatry, 15*, 183–189.

Karademas, E. C., & Kalantzi-Azizi, A. (2004). The stress process, self-efficacy expectations, and psychological health. *Personality & Individual Differences, 37*, 1033–1043.

Karama, S., Lecours, A. R., Leroux, J-M., Bourgouin, P., Beaudoin, G., Joubert, S., & Beauregard, M. (2002). Areas of brain activation in males and females during viewing of erotic film excerpts. *Human Brain Mapping, 16*, 1–13.

Karasek, R. A. (1979). Job demands, job decision latitude, and mental strain: Implications for job redesign. *Administration Science Quarterly, 24*, 285–307.

Karasek, R. A., Baker, D., Marxer, F., Ahlbom, A. & Theorell, T. (1981). Job decision latitude, job demands, and cardiovascular disease: A prospective study of Swedish men. *American Journal of Public Health, 71*, 694–705.

Karau, S. J., & Williams, K. D. (1993). Social loafing: A meta-analytic review and theoretical integration. *Journal of Personality and Social Psychology, 65*, 681–706.

Karkowski, L. M., & Kendler, K. S. (1997). An examination of the genetic relationship between bipolar and unipolar illness in an epidemiological sample. *Psychiatric Genetics, 7*, 159–163.

Karlamangla, A. S., Singer, B. H., McEwen, B. S., Rowe, J. W., & Seeman, T. E. (2002). Allostatic load as a predictor of functional decline. MacArthur studies of successful aging. *Journal of Clinical Epidemiology, 55*, 696–710.

Karni, A., & Sagi, D. (1993). The time course of learning a visual skill. *Nature, 365*, 250–252.

Karni, A., Tanne, D., Rubenstein, B. S., Askenasi, J. J. M., & Sagi, D. (1994). Dependence on REM sleep of overnight improvement of a perceptual skill. *Science, 265*, 679–682.

Karon, B. J. (2000). The clinical interpretation of the Thematic Apperception Test, Rorschach, and other clinical data: A reexamination of statistical versus clinical prediction. *Professional Psychology: Research and Practice, 31*, 230–233.

Karpov, Y. V., & Haywood, H. C. (1998). Two ways to elaborate Vygotsky's concept of mediation. *American Psychologist, 53*, 27–36.

Karuza, J., & Carey, T. O. (1984). Relevance preference and adaptiveness of behavioral blame for observers of rape victims. *Journal of Personality, 52* 249–262.

Kasch, K. L., Rottenberg, J., Arnow, B. A., & Gotlib, I. H. (2002). Behavioral activation and inhibition systems and the severity and course of depression. *Journal of Abnormal Psychology, 111*, 589–597.

Kasper, S., & Resinger, E. (2001). Panic disorder: The place of benzodiazpines and selective serotonin reuptake inhibitors. *European Neuropsychopharmacology, 11*, 307–321.

Kassin, S. M. (1997). The psychology of confession evidence. *American Psychologist, 52*, 221–233.

Kassin, S. M., & Kiechel, K. L. (1996). The social psychology of false confessions: Compliance, internalization, and confabulation. *Psychological Science, 7*, 125–128.

Kassin, S. M., & Wrightsman, L. S. (1981). Coerced confessions, judicial instruction, and mock juror verdicts. *Journal of Applied Social Psychology, 11*, 489–506.

Katigbak, M. S., Church, A. T., & Akamine, T. X. (1996). Cross-cultural generalizability of personality dimensions: Relating indigenous and imported dimensions in two cultures. *Journal of Personality and Social Psychology, 70*, 99–114.

Katigbak, M. S., Church, A. T., Guanzon-Lapena, M., Angleles, C., Annadaisy, J., & del Pilar, G. H. (2002). Are indigenous personality dimensions culture specific? Philippine inventories and the five-factor model. *Journal of Personality & Social Psychology, 82*, 89–101.

Katona, I., Rancz, E. A., Acsady, L., Ledent, C., Mackie, K., Hajos, N., & Freund, T. F. (2001). Distribution of CB1 cannabinoid receptors in the amygdala and their role in the control of GABAergic transmission. *Journal of Neuroscience, 21*, 9506–9518.

Katona, I., Sperlagh, B., Magloczky, Z., Santha, E., Kofalvi, A., Czirjak, S., et al. (2000). GABAergic interneurons are the targets of cannabinoid actions in the human hippocampus. *Neuroscience, 100*, 797–804.

Katz, J., Beach, S. R. H., & Joiner, T. E. (1999). Contagious depression in dating couples. *Journal of Social & Clinical Psychology, 18*(1), 1–13.

Katz, J., & Joiner, T. E., Jr. (2001). The aversive interpersonal context of depression: Emerging perspectives on depressotypic behavior. In R. M. Kowalski (Ed.), *Behaving badly: Aversive behaviors in interpersonal relationships* (pp. 117–147). Washington, DC: American Psychological Association.

Kauffmann, C. D., Cheema, M. A., & Miller, B. E. (2004). Slow right prefrontal transcranial magnetic stimulation as a treatment for medication-resistant depression: A double-blind, placebo-controlled study. *Depression & Anxiety, 19*, 59–62.

Kaufman, M. H. (1997). The teratogenic effects of alcohol following exposure during pregnancy, and its influence on the chromosome constitution of the pre-ovulatory egg. *Alcohol & Alcoholism, 32*, 113–128.

Kavanagh, D. J. (1992). Recent developments in expressed emotion in schizophrenia. *British Journal of Psychiatry, 148*, 601–620.

Kawai, N., Honda, M., Nakamura, S., Samatra, P., Sukardika, K., Nakatani, Y., Shimojo, N., & Oohashi, T. (2001). Catecholamines and opioid peptides increase in plasma in humans during possession trances. *Neuroreport, 12*, 3419–3423.

Kay, A. C., Wheeler, S. C., Bargh, J. A., & Ross, L. (2004). Material priming: The influence of mundane physical objects on situational construal and competitive behavioral choice. *Organizational Behavior & Human Decision Processes, 95*, 83–96.

Kay, D. A., & Anglin, J. M. (1982). Overextension and underextension in the child's expressive and receptive speech. *Journal of Child Language, 9*, 83–98.

Kaye, W. H. (1995). Neurotransmitters and anorexia nervosa. In K. D. Brownell & C. G. Fairburn (Eds.), *Eating disorders and obesity: A comprehensive handbook* (pp. 255–260). New York: Guilford Press.

Kayed, N. S., & van der Meer, A. (2000). Timing strategies used in defensive blinking to optical collisions in 5- to 7-month-old infants. *Infant Behavior & Development, 23,* 253–270.

Kazdin, A. E. (1994). Methodology, design, and evaluation in psychotherapy research. In A. E. Bergin & S. L. Garfield (Eds.), *Handbook of psychotherapy and behavior change* (4th ed., pp. 19–71). New York: John Wiley & Sons.

Keane, R. M., Kolb, L. C., Kaloupek, D. G., Orr, S. P., Blanchard, E. B., Thomas, et al. (1998). Utility of psychophysiology measurement in the diagnosis of post-traumatic stress disorder: Results from a Department of Veterans' Affairs cooperative study. *Journal of Consulting and Clinical Psychology,* 914–923.

Keane, T. M., & Barlow, D. H. (2002). Posttraumatic stress disorder. In D. H. Barlow (Ed.), *Anxiety and its disorders* (2nd ed., pp. 418–453). New York: Guilford.

Keane, T. M., Zimering, R. T., & Caddell, J. M. (1985). A behavioral formulation of post-traumatic stress disorder in Vietnam veterans. *Behavior Therapist, 8,* 9–12.

Keefe, R. S. E., Silva, S. G., Perkins, D. O., & Lieberman, J. A. (1999). The effects of atypical antipsychotic drugs on neurocognitive impairment in schizophrenia: A review and meta-analysis. *Schizophrenia Bulletin, 25,* 201–222.

Keenan, J. P., Nelson, A., O'Connor, M., & Pascual-Leone, A. (2001). Self-recognition and the right hemisphere. *Nature, 409,* 305.

Keil, F. C. (1989a). *Concepts, kind, and cognitive development.* Cambridge, MA: MIT Press.

Keil, F. C. (1989b). The origins of an autonomous biology. In M. R. Gunnar & M. Marstsos (Eds.), *The Minnesota symposium on child psychology: Vol. 25, Modularity and constraints in language and cognition* (pp. 103–137). Hillsdale, NJ: Erlbaum.

Keil, F. C., & Silberstein, C. S. (1996). Schooling and the acquisition of theoretical knowledge. In D. R. Olson & N. Torrance (Eds.), *Handbook of education and human development: New models of learning, teaching and schooling.* Cambridge, MA: Blackwell.

Keith, P. M., & Schafer, R. B. (1991). *Relationships and well-being over the life stages.* New York: Praeger.

Keith, S. J., Regier, D. A., & Rae, D. S. (1991). Schizophrenic disorders. In L. N. Robins & D. A. Regier (Eds.), *Psychiatric disorders in America: The Epidemiologic Catchment Area Study* (pp. 33–52). New York: Free Press.

Keitner, G. I., Solomon, D. A., Ryan, C. E., Miller, I. W., & Mallinger, A. (1996). Prodromal and residual symptoms in bipolar I disorder. *Comprehensive Psychiatry, 37,* 362–367.

Keller, A., Ford, L. H., & Meacham, J. A. (1978). Dimensions of self-concept in preschool children. *Developmental Psychology, 14,* 483–489.

Keller, J., & Dauenheimer, D. (2003). Stereotype threat in the classroom: Dejection mediates the disrupting threat effect on women's math performance. *Personality & Social Psychology Bulletin, 29,* 371–381.

Kelley, H. H. (1972). Attribution in social interaction. In E. E. Jones, D. E. Kanouse, H. H. Kelley, R. E. Nisbett, S. Vahns, & B. Weiner (Eds.), *Attribution: Perceiving the causes of behavior.* Morristown, NJ: General Learning Press.

Kelley, H. H. (1979). *Personal relationships: Their structures and processes.* Hillsdale, NJ: Erlbaum.

Kelley, H. H., & Michela, J. L. (1980). Attribution theory and research. *Annual Review of Psychology, 31,* 57–501.

Kelley, W. M., Macrae, C. N., Wyland, C. L., Caglar, S., Inati, S., & Heatherton, T. F. (2002). Finding the self? An event-related fMRI study. *Journal of Cognitive Neuroscience, 14,* 785–794.

Kelley, W. M., Miezin, F. M., McDermott, K. B., Buckner, R. L., Raichle, M. E., Cohen, N. J., et al. (1998). Hemispheric specialization in human dorsal frontal cortex and medial temporal lobe for verbal and nonverbal memory encoding. *Neuron, 20,* 927–936.

Kellogg, R. T. (2001). Presentation modality and mode of recall in verbal false memory. *Journal of Experimental Psychology: Learning, Memory, & Cognition, 27,* 913–919.

Kellogg, W. N., & Kellogg, L. A. (1933). *The ape and the child.* New York: McGraw-Hill.

Kelly, S. P., Thornton, J., Lyratzopoulos, G., Edwards, R., & Mitchell, P. (2004). Smoking and blindness: Strong evidence for the link, but public awareness lags. *BMJ: British Medical Journal, 328,* 537–538.

Kelman, H. (1997). Group processes in the resolution of international conflicts. *American Psychologist, 52,* 212–220.

Keltner, D., & Haidt, J. (2001). Social functions of emotions. In T. J. Mayne & G. A. Bonanno (Eds.), *Emotions: Current issues and future directions* (pp. 192–213). New York: Guilford Press.

Keltner, D., & Shiota, M. N. (2003). New displays and new emotions: A commentary on Rozin and Cohen (2003). *Emotion, 3,* 86–91.

Kemp, D. T. (1978). Stimulated acoustic emissions from within the human auditory system. *Journal of the Acoustical Society of America, 64,* 1386–1391.

Kemp, D. T. (1979). Evidence of mechanical nonlinearity and frequency selective wave amplification in the cochlea. *Archives of Otology, Rhinology, and Laryngology, 224,* 37–45.

Kempermann, G., Kuhn, H. G., & Gage, F. H. (1998). Experience-induced neurogenesis in the senescent dentate gyrus. *Journal of Neuroscience, 18,* 3206–3212.

Kempermann, G., Wiscott, L., & Gage, F. H. (2004). Functional significance of adult neurogenesis. *Current Opinion in Neurobiology, 14,* 186–191.

Kendall, P. C., Holmbeck, G. N., & Verduin, T. (2004). Methodology, design, and evaluation in psychotherapy research. In M. J. Lambert (Ed.), *Handbook of psychotherapy and behavior change,* 5th ed. (pp. 16–43). New York: Wiley.

Kendler, K. S., & Diehl, S. R. (1993). The genetics of schizophrenia: A current genetic-epidemiologic perspective. *Schizophrenia Bulletin, 19,* 87–112.

Kendler, K. S., Gardner, C. O., & Prescott, C. A. (1999). Clinical characteristics of major depression that predict risk of depression in relatives. *Archives of General Psychiatry, 56,* 322–327.

Kendler, K. S., Jacobsen, K. C., Myers, J., & Prescott, C. A. (2002). Sex differences in genetic and environmental risk factors for irrational fears and phobias. *Psychological Medicine, 32,* 209–217.

Kendler, K. S., MacLean, C., Neale, M., Kessler, R. C., Heath, A. C., & Eaves, L. J. (1991). The genetic epidemiology of bulimia nervosa. *American Journal of Psychiatry, 148,* 1627–1637.

Kendler, K. S., Neale, M. C., Kessler, R. C., Heath, A. C., & Eaves, L. J. (1992). The genetic epidemiology of phobias in women: The interrelationship of agoraphobia, social phobia, situational phobia and simple phobia. *Archives of General Psychiatry, 49,* 273–281.

Kendrick, K. M., da Costa, A. P., Leigh, A. E., Hinton, M. R., & Peirce, J. W. (2001). Sheep don't forget a face. *Nature, 414,* 165–166.

Kennedy, M. M. (1979). *The mystery of hypnosis.* New York: Contemporary Perspectives.

Kennedy, S. H., Javanmard, M., Franco, J., & Vaccarino, F. J. (1997). A review of functional neuroimaging in mood disorders: Positron emission tomography and depression. *Canadian Journal of Psychiatry, 42,* 467–475.

Kenrick, D. T., & Funder, D. C. (1988). Profiting from the controversy: Lessons from the person-situation debate. *American Psychologist, 43,* 23–34.

Kerns, J. G., Cohen, J. D., MacDonald, A. W., III, Cho, R. Y., Stenger, V. A., & Carter, C. S. (2004). Anterior cingulate conflict monitoring and adjustments in control. *Science, 303,* 1023–1026.

Kerr, M., Lambert, W. W., Stattin, H., & Klackenberg-Larsson, I. (1994). Stability of inhibition in a Swedish longitudinal sample. *Child Development, 65,* 138–146.

Kerr, N. L., & Kaufman-Gilliland, C. M. (1997). " . . . and besides, I probably couldn't have made a difference anyway": Justification of social dilemma defection via perceived self-inefficacy. *Journal of Experimental Social Psychology, 33,* 211–230.

Kerr, N. L., & Tindale, R. S. (2004). Group performance and decision making. *Annual Review of Psychology, 55,* 623–655.

Kertesz, A. (1981). Anatomy of jargon. In J. Brown (Ed.), *Jargonaphasia* (pp. 63–112). New York: Academic Press.

Keshavan, M. S., Anderson, S., & Pettigrew, J. W. (1994). Is schizophrenia due to excessive synaptic pruning in the prefrontal cortex? The Feinberg hypothesis revisited. *Journal of Psychiatry Research, 28,* 239–265.

Kessler, R. C., Berglund, P., Demler, O., Jin, R., Koretz, D., Merikangas, K. R., et al. (2003). The epidemiology of major depressive disorder: Results from the National Comorbidity Survey Replication (NCS-R). *JAMA: Journal of the American Medical Association, 289,* 3095–3105.

Kessler, R. C., & Frank, R. G. (1997). The impact of psychiatric disorders on work loss days. *Psychological Medicine, 27,* 861–873.

Kessler, R. C., McGonagle, K. A., Zhao, S., Nelson, C. B., Hughes, M., Eshelman, S., et al. (1994). Lifetime and 12-month prevalence of DSM-III–R psychiatric disorders in the United States: Results from the National Comorbidity Study. *Archives of General Psychiatry, 51,* 8–19.

Kessler, R. C., Sonnega, A., Bromet, E., Hughes, M., et al. (1995). Posttraumatic stress disorder in the National Comorbidity Survey. *Archives of General Psychiatry, 52,* 1048–1060.

Kessler, R. C., Stein, M. B., & Berglund, P. (1998). Social phobia subtypes in the National Comorbidity Survey. *American Journal of Psychiatry, 155,* 613–619.

Ketelaar, T., & Au, W. T. (2003). The effects of feelings of guilt on the behaviour of uncooperative individuals in repeated social bargaining games: An affect-as-information interpretation of the role of emotion in social interaction. *Cognition & Emotion, 17,* 429–453.

Keys, A., Brozek, J., Henschel, A., Mickelsen, O., & Taylor, H. L. (1950). *The biology of human starvation*. Minneapolis: University of Minnesota Press.

Kidd, K. K. (1993). Associations of disease with genetic markers: Déjà vu all over again. *Neuropsychiatric Genetics, 48*, 71–73.

Kiecolt-Glaser, J., Glaser, R., Strain, E., Stout, J., Tarr, K., Holliday, J., & Speicher, C. (1986). Modulation of cellular immunity in medical students. *Journal of Behavioral Medicine, 9*, 5+.

Kiecolt-Glaser, J. K., & Glaser, R. (2002). Depression and immune function: Central pathways to morbidity and mortality. *Journal of Psychosomatic Research, 53*, 873–876.

Kiecolt-Glaser, J. K., Marucha, P. T., Atkinson, C., & Glaser, R. (2001). Hypnosis as a modulator of cellular immune dysregulation during acute stress. *Journal of Consulting and Clinical Psychology, 69*, 674–682.

Kiecolt-Glaser, J. K., Marucha, P. T., Malarky, W. B., Mercado, A. M., & Glaser, R. (1995). Slowing of wound healing by psychological stress. *Lancet, 346*, 1194–1196.

Kiecolt-Glaser, J. K., & Newton, T. L. (2001). Marriage and health: His and hers. *Psychological Bulletin, 127*, 472–503.

Kiecolt-Glaser, J. K., Page, G. G., Marucha, P. T., MacCallum, R. C., & Glaser, R. (1998). Psychological influences on surgical recovery perspectives from psychoneuroimmunology. *American Psychologist, 53*, 1209–1218.

Kiesler, C. A., & Kiesler, S. B. (1969). *Conformity*. Reading, MA: Addison-Wesley.

Kiffel, C., Campanella, S., & Bruyer, R. (2005). Categorical perception of faces and facial expressions: The age factor. *Experimental Aging Research, 31*, 119–147.

Kihlstrom, J. F. (1985). Hypnosis. *Annual Review of Psychology, 36*, 385–418.

Kihlstrom, J. F. (1987). The cognitive unconscious. *Science, 273*, 1445–1452.

Kilham, W., & Mann, L. (1974). Level of destructive obedience as a function of transmitter and executant roles in the Milgram obedience paradigm. *Journal of Personality and Social Psychology, 29*, 696–702.

Killen, J. D., Hayward, C., Wilson, D. M., Haydel, K. F., Robinson, T. N., Taylor, C. B., et al. (1996). Predicting onset drinking in a community sample of adolescents: The role of expectancy and temperament. *Addictive Behaviors, 21*, 473–480.

Kim, J., Lim, J., & Bhargava, M. (1998). The role of affect in attitude formation: A classical conditioning. *Journal of the Academy of Marketing Science, 26*, 143–152.

Kim, K. H. S., Relkin, N. R., Lee, K., & Hirsch, J. (1997). Distinct cortical areas associated with native and second languages. *Nature, 388*, 171–174.

Kim, M., & Kim, H. (1997). Communication goals: Individual differences between Korean and American speakers. *Personality & Individual Differences, 23*, 509–517.

Kimata, H. (2003). Kissing reduces allergic skin wheal responses and plasma neurotrophin levels. *Physiology & Behavior, 80*, 395–398.

Kimble, G. A. (1981). Biological and cognitive constraints of learning. In L. T. Benjamin, Jr. (Ed.), *The G. Stanley Hall Lecture Series* (Vol. 1). Washington, DC: American Psychological Association.

Kimchi, R., & Razpurker-Apfeld, I. (2004). Perceptual grouping and attention: Not all groupings are equal. *Psychonomic Bulletin & Review, 11*, 687–696.

Kimura, D. (1994). Body asymmetry and intellectual pattern. *Personality and Individual Differences, 17*, 53–60.

King, A. C., Oman, R. F., Brassington, G. S., Bliwise, D. L., & Haskell, W. L. (1997). Moderate-intensity exercise and self-rated quality of sleep in older adults: A randomized controlled trial. *Journal of the American Medical Association, 277*, 32–37.

King, L. A., King, D. W., Fairbank, J. A., Keane, T. M., & Adams, G. A. (1998). Resilience-recovery factors in post-traumatic stress disorder among female and male Vietnam veterans: Hardiness, postwar social support, and additional stressful life events. *Journal of Personality and Social Psychology, 74*, 420–434.

King, S. A., Engi, S., & Poulos, S. T. (1998). Using the internet to assist family therapy. *British Journal of Guidance and Counselling, 26*, 43–52.

Kingdom, F. A. A., Beauce, C., & Hunter, L. (2004). Colour vision brings clarity to shadows. *Perception, 33*, 907–914.

Kingstone, A., Friesen, C. K., & Gazzaniga, M. S. (2000). Reflexive joint attention depends on lateralized cortical connections. *Psychological Science, 11*, 159–166.

Kinnunen, U., & Pulkkinen, L. (2003). Childhood socio-emotional characteristics as antecedents of marital stability and quality. *European Psychologist, 8*, 223–237.

Kintsch, W. (1998). *Comprehension: A paradigm for cognition*. New York: Cambridge University Press.

Kirchler, E., & Davis, J. H. (1986). The influence of member status differences and task type on group consensus and member position change. *Journal of Personality & Social Psychology, 51*, 83–91.

Kirkmeyer, S. V., & Tepper, B. J. (2003). Understanding creaminess perception of dairy products using free-choice profiling and genetic responsivity to 6-n-propylthiouracil. *Chemical Senses, 28*, 527–536.

Kirsch, I. (1999). Clinical hypnosis as a nondeceptive placebo. In I. Kirsch, A. Capafons, E. Cardeña-Buelna, & S. Amigó (Eds.), *Clinical hypnosis and self-regulation: Cognitive-behavioral perspectives* (pp. 211–225). Washington, DC: American Psychological Association.

Kirsch, I. (2004). Conditioning, expectancy, and the placebo effect: Comment on Stewart-Williams and Podd (2004). *Psychological Bulletin, 130*, 341–343.

Kirsch, I., & Council, J. R. (1992). Situational and personality correlates of hypnotic responsiveness. In E. Fromm & M. R. Nash (Eds.), *Contemporary hypnosis research* (pp. 267–291). New York: Guilford.

Kirsch, I., & Lynn, S. J. (1999). Automaticity in clinical psychology. *American Psychologist, 54*, 504–515.

Kirsch, I., Lynn, S. J., Vigorito, M., & Miller, R. R. (2004). The role of cognition in classical and operant conditioning. *Journal of Clinical Psychology, 60*, 369–392.

Kirsch, I., Moore, T. J., Scoboria, A., & Nicholls, S. S. (2002a). The emperor's new drugs: An analysis of antidepressant medication data submitted to the U.S. Food and Drug Administration. *Prevention and Treatment, 5*, n.p.

Kirsch, I., & Sapirstein, G. (1998). Listening to Prozac but hearing placebo: A meta-analysis of antidepressant medication. *Prevention & Treatment, 1*, Article 0002a.

Kirsch, I., Scoboria, A., & Moore, T. J. (2002b). Antidepressants and placebos: Secrets, revelations, and unanswered questions. *Prevention & Treatment, 5*, n.p.

Kirschvink, J. L., Walker, M. M., & Diebel, C. E. (2001). Magnetite-based magnetoreception. *Current Opinion in Neurobiology, 11*, 462–467.

Kisilevsky, B. S., Hains, S. M. J., Jacquet, A. Y., Granier-Deferre, C., & Lecanuet, J. P. (2004). Maturation of fetal responses to music. *Developmental Science, 7*, 550–559.

Kisilevsky, B. S., & Low, J. A. (1998). Human fetal behavior: 100 years of study. *Developmental Review, 18*, 1–29.

Kitayama, S., Markus, H. R., Matsumoto, H., & Norasakkunkit, V. (1997). Individual and collective processes in the construction of the self: Self-enhancement in the United States and self-criticism in Japan. *Journal of Personality & Social Psychology, 72*, 1245–1267.

Kitchener, R. F. (1996). The nature of the social for Piaget and Vygotsky. *Human Development, 39*, 243–249.

Kitzmann, K. M. (2000). Effects of marital conflict on subsequent triadic family interactions and parenting. *Developmental Psychology, 36*, 3–13.

Kivlighan, D. M., Jr., Multon, K. D., & Patton, M. J. (2000). Insight and symptom reduction in time-limited psychoanalytic counseling. *Journal of Counseling Psychology, 47*, 50–58.

Kleemeier, R. W. (1962). Intellectual changes in the senium. *Proceedings of the American Statistical Association, 1*, 290–295.

Klein, D. F. (1993). False suffocation alarms, spontaneous panics, and related conditions: An integrative hypothesis. *Archives of General Psychiatry, 50*, 306–317.

Klein, E., Kreinin, I., Chistyakov, A., Koren, D., Mecz, L., Marmur, S., et al. (1999). Therapeutic efficacy of right prefrontal slow repetitive transcranial magnetic stimulation in major depression: A double-blind controlled study. *Archives of General Psychiatry, 56*, 315–320.

Kleinknecht, R. A., & Lenz, J. (1989). Blood/injury fear, fainting and avoidance of medical treatment: A family correspondence study. *Behaviour Research and Therapy, 27*, 537–547.

Kleinman, A. (1978). Clinical relevance of anthropological and cross-cultural research: Concepts and strategies. *American Journal of Psychiatry, 135*, 427–431.

Klerman, E. B., Davis, J. B., Duffy, J. F., Dijk, D., & Kronauer, R. E. (2004). Older people awaken more frequently but fall back asleep at the same rate as younger people. *Sleep: Journal of Sleep & Sleep Disorders Research, 27*, 793–798.

Klima, E. S., & Bellugi, U. (1979). *The signs of language*. Cambridge, MA: Harvard University Press.

Klinkenborg, V. (1997, January 5). Awakening to sleep. *New York Times Magazine*, 26.

Klinteberg, B., Andersson, T., Magnusson, D., & Stattin, H. (1993). Hyperactive behavior in childhood as related to subsequent alcohol problems and violent offending: A longitudinal study of male subjects. *Personality and Individual Differences, 15*, 381–388.

Klosko, J. S., Barlow, D. H., Tassinari, R., & Cerny, J. A. (1990). A comparison of alprazolam and behavior therapy in treatment of panic disorder. *Journal of Consulting and Clinical Psychology, 58*, 77–84.

Knauth, P. (1997). Changing schedules: Shiftwork. *Chronobiology International, 14*, 159–171.

Knox, S. S., Weidner, G., Adelman, A., Stoney, C. M., & Ellison, R. C. (2004). Hostility and physiological risk in the National Heart, Lung, and Blood Institute Family Heart Study. *Archives of Internal Medicine, 1642,* 2442–2448.

Knudsen, E. I. (2004). Sensitive periods in the development of the brain and behavior. *Journal of Cognitive Neuroscience, 16,* 1412–1425.

Knutson, B., Adams, C. M., Fong, G. W., & Hommer, D. (2001). Anticipation of increasing monetary reward selectively recruits nucleus accumbens. *Journal of Neuroscience, 21:RC159,* 1–5.

Kobasa, S. C. (1979). Stressful life events, personality and health: An inquiry into hardiness. *Journal of Personality and Social Psychology, 37* 1–11.

Kobasa, S. C., Maddit, S. R., & Kuhn, S. (1982). Hardiness and health: A prospective study. *Journal of Personality and Social Psychology, 42,* 168–177.

Kochanska, G. (1997). Multiple pathways to conscience for children with different temperaments: From toddlerhood to age 5. *Development Psychology, 33,* 228–240.

Kochanska, G., DeVet, K., Goldman, M., Murray, K., & Putman, S. P. (1994). Maternal reports of conscience development and temperament in young children. *Child Development, 65,* 852–868.

Kochanska, G., Gross, J. N., Lin, M-H., & Nichols, K. E. (2002). Guilt in young children: Development, determinants, and relations with a broader system of standards. *Child Development, 73,* 461–482.

Kocovski, N. L., Endler, N. S., Rector, N. A., & Flett, G. L. (in press). Ruminative coping and post-event processing in social anxiety. *Behaviour Research and Therapy.*

Koffka, K. (1935). *Principles of Gestalt psychology.* New York: Harcourt Brace.

Koga, H., Yuzuriha, T., Yao, H., Endo, K., Hiejima, S., Takashima, Y., et al. (2002). Quantitative MRI findings and cognitive impairment among community dwelling elderly subjects. *Journal of Neurology, Neurosurgery & Psychiatry, 72,* 737–741.

Kohlberg, L. (1969). Stage and sequence: The cognitive-developmental approach to socialization. In D. S. Goslin (Ed.), *Handbook of socialization theory and research* (pp. 347–480). Chicago: Rand McNally.

Kohler, P. F., Rivera, V. J., Eckert, E. D., Bouchard, T. J., Jr., & Heston, L. L. (1985). Genetic regulation of immunoglobulin and specific antibody levels in twins reared apart. *Journal of Clinical Investigation, 75,* 883–888.

Kohler, S., Kapur, S., Moscovitch, M., Winocur, G., & Houle, S. (1995). Dissociation of pathways for object and spatial vision: A PET study in humans. *Neuroreport, 6,* 1865–1868.

Köhler, W. (1925/1956). *The mentality of apes.* New York: Vintage.

Kohn, M. L., & Schooler, C. (1973). Occupational experience and psychological functioning: An assessment of reciprocal effects. *American Sociological Review, 38,* 97–118.

Kohut, H. (1977). *The restoration of self.* New York: International Universities Press.

Kolata, G. (1997, January 14). Which comes first: Depression or heart disease? *New York Times,* C1.

Kolata, G., & Peterson, I. (2001, July 21). New photo method may aid witnesses in saying, "It's him." *New York Times,* A1, A13.

Kolb, F. C., & Braun, J. (1995). Blindsight in normal observers. *Nature, 377,* 336–338.

Kondo, T., Zakany, J., Innis, J. W., & Duboule, D. (1997). Of fingers, toes and penises. *Nature, 390,* 185–198.

Konishi, M. (1993). Listening with two ears. *Scientific American, 268,* 66–73.

Konishi, S., Nakajima, K., Uchida, I., Kikyo, H., Kameyama, M., & Miyashita, Y. (1999). Common inhibitory mechanism in human inferior prefrontal cortex revealed by event-related functional MRI. *Brain, 122,* 981–991.

Koob, G. F. (1999). Drug reward and addiction. In M. J. Zigmond, F. E. Bloom, S. C. Landis, J. L. Roberts, & L. R. Squire (Eds.), *Fundamental neuroscience* (pp. 1261–1279). San Diego: Academic Press.

Kop, W. J. (2003). The integration of cardiovascular behavioral medicine and psychoneuroimmunology: New developments based on converging research fields. *Brain, Behavior & Immunity, 17,* 233–237.

Koren, D., Norman, D., Cohen, A., Berman, J., & Klein, E. M. (2005). Increased PTSD risk with combat-related injury: A matched comparison study of injured and uninjured soldiers experiencing the same combat events. *American Journal of Psychiatry, 162,* 276–282.

Kosslyn, S. M. (1975). On retrieving information from visual images. In R. Schank & B. Nash-Webber (Eds.), *Theoretical issues in natural language processing.* Arlington, VA: Association for Computational Linguistics.

Kosslyn, S. M. (1976). Can imagery be distinguished from other forms of internal representation? Evidence from studies of information retrieval times. *Memory and Cognition, 4,* 291–297.

Kosslyn, S. M. (1978). Measuring the visual angle of the mind's eye. *Cognitive Psychology, 10,* 356–389.

Kosslyn, S. M. (1980). *Image and mind.* Cambridge, MA.: Harvard University Press.

Kosslyn, S. M. (1987). Seeing and imagining in the cerebral hemispheres: A computational approach. *Psychological Review, 94,* 148–175.

Kosslyn, S. M. (1992). Cognitive neuroscience and the human self. In A. Harrington (Ed.), *So human a brain.* New York: Pergamon.

Kosslyn, S. M. (1994a). *Elements of graph design.* New York: Freeman.

Kosslyn, S. M. (in press). *Graph design for the eye and mind.* New York: Oxford University Press.

Kosslyn, S. M., Digirolamo, G. J., Thompson, W. L., & Alpert, N. M. (1998). Mental rotation of objects versus hands: Neural mechanisms revealed by positron emission tomography. *Psychophysiology, 35,* 151–161.

Kosslyn, S. M., Ganis, G., & Thompson, W. L. (2001). Neural foundations of imagery. *Nature Reviews Neuroscience, 2,* 635 –642.

Kosslyn, S. M., & Koenig, O. (1995). *Wet mind: The new cognitive neuroscience.* New York: Free Press.

Kosslyn, S. M., Koenig, O., Barrett, A., Cave, C. B., Tang, J., & Gabrieli, J. D. E. (1989). Evidence for two types of spatial representations: Hemispheric specialization for categorical and coordinate relations. *Journal of Experimental Psychology: Human Perception and Performance, 15,* 723–735.

Kosslyn, S. M., Pascual-Leone, A., Felician, O., Camposano, S., Keenan, J. P., Thompson, W. L., et al. (1999). The role of area 17 in visual imagery: Convergent evidence from PET and rTMS. *Science, 284,* 167–170.

Kosslyn, S. M., Segar, C., Pani, J., & Hillger, L. A. (1990). When is imagery used in everyday life? A diary study. *Journal of Mental Imagery. 14,* 131–152.

Kosslyn, S. M., & Thompson, W. L. (2003). When is early visual cortex activated during visual mental imagery? *Psychological Bulletin, 129,* 723–746.

Kosslyn, S. M., Thompson, W. L., Costantini-Ferrando, M. F., Alpert, N. M., & Spiegel, D. (2000). Hypnotic visual illusion alters brain color processing. *American Journal of Psychiatry.*

Kosslyn, S. M., Thompson, W. L., & Ganis, G. (in press). *The case for mental imagery.* New York: Oxford University Press.

Kosslyn, S. M., Thompson, W. L., Kim, I. J., & Alpert, N. M. (1995). Topographical representations of mental images in primary visual cortex. *Nature, 378,* 496–498.

Koster, E. H. W., Rassin, E., Crombez, G., & Näring, G. W. B. (2003). The paradoxical effects of suppressing anxious thoughts during imminent threat. *Behaviour Research & Therapy, 41,* 1113–1120.

Koutstaal, W., & Schacter, D. L. (1997). Inaccuracy and inaccessibility in memory retrieval: Contributions from cognitive psychology and cognitive neuropsychology. In P. S. Appelbaum, L. Uyehara, & M. Elin (Eds.), *Trauma and memory: Clinical and legal controversies* (pp. 93–137). New York: Oxford University Press.

Kovacs, I. (1996). Gestalten of today: Early processing of visual contours and surfaces. *Behavioural Brain Research, 82,* 1–11.

Kozak, M. J., Liebowitz, M. R., & Foa, E. B. (2000). Cognitive behavior therapy and pharmacotherapy for obsessive-compulsive disorder: The NIMH-sponsored collaborative study. In W. K. Goodman, M. V. Rudorfer, & J. D. Masur (Eds.). *Obsessive-compulsive disorder: Contemporary issues in treatment* (pp. 501–530). Mahwah, NJ: Erlbaum.

Kozel, F. A., Padgett, T. M., & George, M. S. (2004). A replication study of the neural correlates of deception. *Behavioral Neuroscience, 118,* 852–856.

Kozel, F. A., Revell, L. J., Lorberbaum, J. P., Shastri, A., Elhai, J. D., Horner, M. D., et al. (2004). A pilot study of functional magnetic resonance imaging brain correlates of deception in healthy young men. *Journal of Neuropsychiatry and Clinical Neurosciences, 16,* 295–305.

Kozhevnikov, M., Kosslyn, S. M., & Shephard, J. M. (in press). Spatial versus object visualizers: A new characterization of visual cognitive style. *Memory and Cognition*

Kraepelin, E. (1921). Ueber Entwurtzelung [Depression]. *Zietschrift fuer die Gasamte Neurologie und Psychiatrie, 63,* 1–8.

Krafft, K. C., & Berk, L. E. (1998). Private speech in two preschools: Significance of open-ended activities and make-believe play for verbal self-regulation. *Early Childhood Research Quarterly, 13,* 637–658.

Kramer, M. S., Cutler, N., Feighner, J., Shrivastava, R., Carman, J., Sramek, J. J., et al. (1998). Distinct mechanism for antidepressant activity by blockade of central substance P receptors. *Science, 281,* 1640–1645.

Kramer, M. S., Winokur, A., Kelsey, J., Preskorn, S. H., Rothschild, A. J., Snavely, D., Ghosh, K., Ball, W. A., Reines, S. A., Munjack, D., Apter, J. T., Cunningham, L., Kling, M., Bari, M., Getson, A., & Lee, Y. (2004). Demonstration of the efficacy and safety of a novel substance P (NK-sub-1) receptor antagonist in major depression. *Neuropsychopharmacology, 29,* 385–392.

Kranzler, J. H., & Jensen, A. R. (1989). Inspection time and intelligence: A meta-analysis. *Intelligence, 13,* 329–347.

Krause, N. (2004). Stressors arising in highly valued roles, meaning in life, and the physical health status of older adults. *Journals of Gerontology: Series B: Psychological Sciences and Social Sciences, 59B,* S287–S291.

Kreitzer, A. C., Carter, A. G., & Regehr, W. G. (2002). Inhibition of interneuron firing extends the spread of endocannabinoid signaling in the cerebellum. *Neuron, 34,* 787–796.

Kreitzer, A. C., & Regehr, W. G. (2001a). Retrograde inhibition of presynaptic calcium influx by endogenous cannabinoids at excitatory synapses onto Purkinje cells. *Neuron, 29,* 717–727.

Krieger, S., Lis, S., & Gallhofer, B. (2001). Cognitive subprocesses and schizophrenia: A reaction time decomposition. *Acta Psychiatrica Scandanavia Supplement, 104,* 18–27.

Kringelbach, M. L., Araujo, I., & Rolls, E. T. (2001). Face expression as a reinforcer activates the orbitofrontal cortex in an emotion-related reversal task. *Neuroimage 13(6),* S433.

Kritchevsky, M., Chang, J., & Squire, L. R. (2004). Functional amnesia: Clinical description and neuropsychological profile of 10 cases. *Learning and Memory, 11,* 213–226.

Krug, R., Pietrowsky, R., Fehm, H. L., & Born, J. (1994). Selective influence of menstrual cycle on perception of stimuli with reproductive significance. *Psychosomatic Medicine, 56,* 410–417.

Kruglanski, A. W., & Webster, D. M. (1996). Motivated closing of the mind: "Seizing" and "freezing." *Psychological Review, 103,* 263–283.

Krumhansl, C. L., (1991). Music perception: Tonal structures in perception and memory. *Annual Review of Psychology, 42,* 277–303.

Krumhansl, C. L. (2000). Rhythm and pitch in music cognition. *Psychological Bulletin, 126,* 159–179.

Krummenacher, J., Müller, H. J., & Heller, D. (2002). Visual search for dimensionally redundant pop-out targets: Parallel-coactive processing of dimensions is location specific. *Journal of Experimental Psychology: Human Perception & Performance, 28,* 1303–1322.

Kubzansky, L. D., & Kawachi, I. (2000). Going to the heart of the matter: Do negative emotions cause coronary heart disease? *Journal of Psychosomatic Research, 48,* 323–337.

Kubzansky, L. D., Kawachi, I., Weiss, S. T., & Sparrow, D. (1998). Anxiety and coronary heart disease: A synthesis of epidemiological, psychological, and experimental evidence. *Annals of Behavioral Medicine, 20,* 47–58.

Kuhl, P. K. (1989). On babies, birds, modules, and mechanisms: A comparative approach to the acquisition of vocal communication. In R. J. Dooling & S. H. Husle (Eds.), *The comparative psychology of audition: Perceiving complex sounds* (pp. 379–419). Hillsdale, NJ: Erlbaum.

Kuhl, P. K., Williams, K. A., Lacerda, F., Stevens, K. N., et al. (1992). Linguistic experience alters phonetic perception in infants by 6 months of age. *Science, 255,* 606–608.

Kuipers, E., Fowler, D., Garety, P. Chisholm, D., Freeman, D., Dunn, G., et al. (1998). London–East Anglia randomised controlled trial of cognitive-behavioural therapy for psychosis. III: Followup and economic evaluation at 18 months. *British Journal of Psychiatry, 173,* 61–68.

Kuipers, E., Garety, P., Fowler, D., Dunne, G., Bebbington, P., Freeman, D., & Hadley, C. (1997). London–East Anglia randomised controlled trial of cognitive-behavioural therapy for psychosis. I: Effects of the treatment phase. *British Journal of Psychiatry, 171,* 319–327.

Kulhara, P., & Chakrabarti, S. (2001). Culture and schizophrenia and other psychotic disorders. *Psychiatric Clinics of North American, 24,* 449–464.

Kuncel, N. R., Hezlett, S. A., & Ones, D. S. (2004). Academic performance, career potential, creativity, and job performance: Can one construct predict them all? *Journal of Personality and Social Psychology, 86,* 148–161.

Kunda, Z., & Oleson, K. C. (1995). Maintaining stereotypes in the face of disconfirmation: Constructing grounds for subtyping deviants. *Journal of Personality and Social Psychology, 68,* 565–579.

Kunde, W. (2004). Response priming by supraliminal and subliminal action effects. *Psychological Research/Psychologische Forschung, 68,* 91–96.

Kung, J., Su, N., Fan, R., Chai, S., & Shyu, B. (2003). Contribution of the anterior cingulate cortex to laser-pain conditioning in rats. *Brain Research, 970,* 58–72.

Kuntze, M. F., Stoermer, R., Mager, R., Roessler, A., Mueller-Spahn, F., & Bullinger, A. H. (2001). Immersive virtual environments in cue exposure. *CyberPsychology & Behavior, 4,* 497–501.

Kunz, G., Beil, D., Deiniger, H., Einspanier, A., Mall, G., & Leyendecker, G. (1997). The uterine peristaltic pump. Normal and impeded sperm transport within the female genital tract. *Advances in Experimental Medicine and ...gy, 424,* 267–277.

Kuper, H., & Marmot, M. (2003). Job strain, job demands, decision latitude, and risk of coronary heart disease within the Whitehall II study. *Journal of Epidemiology & Community Health, 57,* 147–153.

Kuperberg, G., & Heckers, S. (2000). Schizophrenia and cognitive function. *Current Opinion in Neurobiology, 10,* 205–210.

Kushner, M., Riggs, D., Foa, E., & Miller, S. (1992). Perceived controllability and the development of posttraumatic stress disorder (PTSD) in crime victims. *Behaviour Research and Therapy, 31,* 105–110.

Kvale, G., & Hugdahl, K. (1994). Cardiovascular conditioning and anticipatory nausea and vomiting in cancer patients. *Behavioral Medicine, 20,* 78–83.

Kwong, M. J., Bartholomew, K., Henderson, A. J. Z., & Trinke, S. J. (2003). The intergenerational transmission of relationship violence. *Journal of Family Psychology, 17,* 288–301.

Labrell, F., Pecheux, M.-G., & Le Metayer, F. (2002). Effect of parental input and effect of children's competence on the recall of object in preschool children. *Cahiers de Psychologie Cognitive/Current Psychology of Cognition, 21,* 91–111.

Lachman, M. E., & Weaver, S. L. (1998). The sense of control as a moderator of social class differences in health and well-being. *Journal of Personality and Social Psychology, 74,* 763–773.

Lacks, P., & Morin, C. M. (1992). Recent advances in the assessment and t reatment of insomnia. *Journal of Consulting & Clinical Psychology, 60,* 586–594.

Laeng, B., Chabris, C. F., & Kosslyn, S. M. (2003). Asymmetries in encoding spatial relations. In K. Hugdahl & R. J. Davidson (Eds.), *The asymmetrical brain* (pp. 303–339). Cambridge, MA: MIT Press.

Lafuente, M. J., Grifol, R., Segarra, J., Soriano, J., Gorba, M. A., & Montesinos, A. (1997). Effects of the Firstart method of prenatal stimulation on psychomotor development: The first six months. *Pre- & Peri-Natal Psychology Journal, 11,* 151–162.

La Guardia, J. G., Ryan, R. M., Couchman, C. E., & Deci, E. L. (2000). Within-person variation in security of attachment: A self-determination theory perspective on attachment, need fulfillment, and well-being. *Journal of Personality & Social Psychology, 79,* 367–384.

Lai, C. S. L., Fisher, S. E., Hurst, J. A., Vargha-Khadem, F., & Monaco, A. P. (2001). A forkhead-domain gene is mutated in a severe speech and language disorder. *Nature, 413,* 519–523.

Laird, J. D. (1974). Self-attribution of emotion: The effects of expressive behavior on the quality of emotional experience. *Journal of Personality & Social Psychology, 29,* 475–486.

Laird, J. D. (1984). The real role of facial response in the experience of emotion: A reply to Tourangeau and Ellsworth, and others. *Journal of Personality & Social Psychology, 47,* 909–917.

Lakey, B., & Dickenson, L. G. (1994). Antecedents of perceived support: Is perceived family environment generalized to new social relationships? *Cognitive Therapy and Research, 18,* 39–53.

Lakey, B., & Heller, K. (1988). Social support from a friend, perceived support, and social problem solving. *American Journal of Community Psychology, 16,* 811–824.

Lakey, B., & Lutz, C. J. (1996). Social support and preventative and therapeutic interventions. In G. R. Pierce, B. R. Sarason, & I. G. Sarason (Eds.), *Handbook of social support and the family.* New York: Plenum Press.

Lakey, B., Moineau, S., & Drew, J. B. (1992). Perceived social support and individual differences in the interpretation and recall of support behavior. *Journal of Social and Clinical Psychology, 11,* 336–348.

Lakin, J. L., & Chartrand, T. L. (2003). Using nonconscious behavioral mimicry to create affiliation and rapport. *Psychological Science, 14,* 334–339.

Lalumiere, M. L., & Quinsey, L. (1998). Pavlovian conditioning of sexual interests in human males. *Archives of Sexual Behavior, 27,* 241–252.

Lam, A. G., & Sue, S. (2001). Client diversity. *Psychotherapy: Theory, Research, Practice, Training, 38,* 479–486.

Lam, D. H., Hayward, P., Watkins, E. R., Wright, K., & Sham, P. (2005). Relapse prevention in patients with bipolar disorder: Cognitive therapy outcome after 2 years. *American Journal of Psychiatry, 162,* 324–329.

Lam, R. W., Bartley, S., Yatham, L. N., Tam, E. M., & Zis, A. P. (1999). Clinical predictors of short-term outcome in electroconvulsive therapy. *Canadian Journal of Psychiatry, 44,* 158–163.

Lambert, A. J. (1995). Stereotypes and social judgment: The consequences of group variability. *Journal of Personality and Social Psychology, 68,* 388–403.

Lambert, A. J., Payne, B. K., Ramsey, S., & Shaffer, L. M. (2005). On the predictive validity of implicit attitude measures: The moderating effect of perceived group variability. *Journal of Experimental Social Psychology, 41,* 114–128.

Lambert, M. J. (1983). Introduction to assessment of psychotherapy outcome: Historical perspective and current issues. In M. J. Lambert, E. R. Christensen, & S. S. De-Julio (Eds.), *The assessment of psychotherapy outcome* (pp. 3–32). New York: Wiley-Interscience.

Lambert, M. J. (Ed.). (2004). *Bergin & Garfield's handbook of psychotherapy and behavior change* (5th ed.). New York: Wiley & Sons.

Lambert, M. J., & Barley, D. E. (2001). Research summary on the therapeutic relationship and psychotherapy outcome. *Psychotherapy: Theory, Research, Practice, Training, 38,* 357–361.

Lambert, M. J., & Ogles, B. M. (2004). The efficacy and effectiveness of psychotherapy. In M. J. Lambert (Ed.), *Bergin and Garfield's handbook of psychotherapy and behavior change,* 5th ed. (pp. 139–193). New York: Wiley and Sons.

Lamm, C., Windischberger, C., Leodolter, U., Moser, E., & Bauer, H. (2001). Evidence for premotor cortex activity during dynamic visuospatial imagery from single-trial functional magnetic resonance imaging and event-related slow cortical potentials. *NeuroImage, 14,* 268–283.

Land, E. H. (1959). Experiments in color vision. *Scientific American, 200,* 84–99.

Land, E. H. (1983). Recent advances in retinex theory and some implications for cortical computations: Color vision and the natural image. *Proceedings of the National Academy of Sciences, USA, 80,* 5163–5169.

Landrigan, C. P., Rothschild, J. M., Cronin, J. W., Kaushal, R., Burdick, E., Katz, J. T., Lilly, C. M., Stone, C. M., Lockley, S. W., Bates, D. W., & Czeisler, C. A. (Harvard Work Hours, Health and Safety Group). (2004). Effect of reducing interns' work hours on serious medical errors in intensive care units. *New England Journal of Medicine, 351,* 1838–1848.

Lane, H. (1976). *The wild boy of Aveyron.* Cambridge, MA: Harvard University Press.

Lang, E. V., Benotsch, E. G., Fick, L. J., Lutgendorf, S., Berbaum, M. L., Berbaum, K. S., Logan, H., & Spiegel, D. (2000). Adjunctive non-pharmacological analgesia for invasive medical procedures: A randomised trial. *Lancet, 355,* 1486–1490.

Lang, F. R., & Carstensen, L. L. (2002). Time counts: Future time perspective, goals, and social relationships. *Psychology & Aging, 17,* 125–139.

Lang, P. J. (1994). The varieties of emotional experience: A meditation on the James-Lange theory. *Psychological Review (Special Issue: The Centennial Issue), 101,* 211–221.

Lang, P. J. (1995). The emotion probe: Studies of motivation and attention. *American Psychologist, 50,* 372–385.

Lang, P. J., Bradley, M. M., Cuthbert, B. N. (1990). Emotion, attention, and the startle reflex. *Psychological Review, 97,* 377–395.

Lange, A., van de Ven, J., & Schricken, B. (2003). Interapy: Treatment of post-traumatic stress via the Internet. *Cognitive Behaviour Therapy, 32,* 110–124.

Lange, A., van de Ven, J.-P., Schrieken, B., & Emmelkamp, P. M. G. (2001). Interapy. Treatment of posttraumatic stress through the Internet: A controlled trial. *Journal of Behavior Therapy & Experimental Psychiatry, 32,* 73–90.

Lange, C. (1887). *Uber gemuthsbewegungen.* Leipzig: Theodor Thomas.

Langer, E. J., & Rodin, J. (1976). The effects of choice and enhanced personal responsibility for the aged: A field experiment in an institutional setting. *Journal of Personality & Social Psychology, 34,* 191–198.

Lansford, J. E., Sherman, A. M., & Antonucci, T. C. (1998). Satisfaction with social networks: An examination of socioemotional selectivity theory across cohorts. *Psychology & Aging, 13,* 544–552.

La Piere, R. T. (1934). Attitude and actions. *Social Forces, 13,* 230–237.

Lapsley, D. K. (1990). Egocentrism theory and the "new look" at the imaginary audience and personal fable in adolescence. In R. M. Lerner, A. C. Petersen, & J. Brooks-Gunn (Eds.), *The encyclopedia of adolescence* (pp. 281–286). New York: Garland.

Lapsley, D. K., Jackson, S., Rice, K., & Shadid, G. (1988). Self-monitoring and the "new look" at the imaginary audience and personal fable: An ego-developmental analysis. *Journal of Adolescent Research, 3,* 17–31.

LaRossa, M. M. (2000). Developmental milestones. Retrieved from http://www.emory.edu/Peds/neonatology/mileston.htm

Larsen, J. T., McGraw, A. P., & Cacioppo, J. T. (2001). Can people feel happy and sad at the same time? *Journal of Personality & Social Psychology, 81,* 684–696.

Larson, J. A. (1932). *Lying and its detection: A study of deception and deception tests.* Chicago: University of Chicago Press.

Larson, R., & Richards, M. H. (1994). *Divergent realities: The emotional lives of mothers, fathers, and adolescents.* New York: Basic Books.

Larson, S. A., Lakin, K. C., Anderson, L., Kwak, N., Lee, J., & Anderson, D. (2001). Prevalence of mental retardation and developmental disabilities: Estimates from the 1994/1995 National Health Interview Survey Disability Supplements. *American Journal on Mental Retardation, 106,* 231–252.

Laruelle, M., Kegeles, L. S., & Abi-Dargham A. (2003). Glutamate, dopamine, and schizophrenia: from pathophysiology to treatment. *Annals of the New York Academy of Sciences, 1003,* 138–158.

Lassiter, G. D., Apple, K. J., & Slaw, R. D. (1996). Need for cognition and thought-induced attitude polarization: Another look. *Journal of Social Behavior & Personality, 11,* 647–665.

Latané, B., Williams, K., & Harkins, S. (1979). Many hands make light the work: The causes and consequences of social loafing. *Journal of Personality and Social Psychology, 37,* 822–832.

Laughlin, P. R., & Ellis, A. L. (1986). Demonstrability and social combination processes in mathematical intellective tasks. *Journal of Experimental Social Psychology, 22,* 177–189.

Laursen, B., Coy, K. C., & Collins, W. A. (1998). Reconsidering changes in parent-child conflict across adolescence: A meta-analysis. *Child Development, 69,* 817–832.

Lautrey, J., & Caroff, X. (1996). Variability and cognitive development. *Polish Quarterly of Developmental Psychology, 2,* 71–89.

Lawless, H. T. (1984). Oral chemical irritation: Psychophysical properties. *Chemical Senses, 9,* 143–155.

Lazarus, R. S., & Folkman, S. (1984). *Stress, appraisal, and coping.* New York: Springer.

Lazev, A. B., Herzog, T. A., & Brandon, T. H. (1999). Classical conditioning of environmental cues to cigarette smoking. *Experimental and Clinical Psychopharmacology, 7,* 56–63.

Leak, G. K., Gardner, L. E., & Parsons, C. J. (1998). Jealousy and romantic attachment: A replication and extension. *Representative Research in Social Psychology, 22,* 21–27.

Leavitt, F. (1997). False attribution of suggestibility to explain recovered memory of childhood sexual abuse following extended amnesia. *Child Abuse & Neglect, 21,* 265–272.

LeBihan, D., Jezzard, P., Turner, R., Cuenod, C. A., Pannier, L., & Prinster, A. (1993). Practical problems and limitations in using Z-maps for processing of brain function MR images. *Abstracts of the 12th Meeting of the Society of Magnetic Resonance in Medicine, 1,* 11.

Leccese, A. P. (1991). *Drugs and society: Behavioral medicines and abusable drugs.* Englewood Cliffs, NJ: Prentice-Hall.

LeDoux, J. E. (1995). Emotion: Clues from the brain. *Annual Review of Psychology, 46,* 209–235.

LeDoux, J. E. (1996). *The emotional brain: The mysterious underpinnings of emotional life.* New York: Simon & Schuster.

Lee, A. M., & Lee, S. (1996). Disordered eating and its psychosocial correlates among Chinese adolescent females in Hong Kong. *International Journal of Eating Disorders, 20,* 177–183.

Lee, E. S. (1951). Negro intelligence and selective migration: A Philadelphia test of the Klineberg hypothesis. *American Sociological Review, 16,* 227–233.

Lee, J. L. C., Everitt, B. J., & Thomas, K. L. (2004). Independent cellular processes for hippocampal memory consolidation and reconsolidation. *Science, 304,* 339–343.

Lee, S. (1996). Clinical lessons from the cross-cultural study of anorexia nervosa. *Eating Disorders Review, 7(3),* 1

Lee, S., & Lee, A. M. (2000). Disordered eating in three communities of China: A comparative study of female high school students in Hong Kong, Shenzhen, and rural Hunan. *International Journal of Eating Disorders, 27,* 317–327.

Lee, W., & Hotopf, M. (in press). Personality variation and age: Trait instability or measurement unreliability? *Personality and Individual Differences.*

Leffler, A., Gillespie, D. L., & Conaty, J. C. (1982). The effects of status differentiation on non-verbal behavior. *Social Psychology Quarterly, 45,* 153–151.

Lefkowitz, E. S. (2005). "Things have gotten better": Developmental changes among emerging adults after the transition to university. *Journal of Adolescent Research, 20,* 40–63.

Lehman, A. F., & Steinwachs, D. M. (1998). Translating research into practice: The Schizophrenia Patients Outcome Research Team (PORT) Treatment Recommendations. *Schizophrenia Bulletin, 24,* 1–10.

Lehman, D. R., Chiu, C., & Schaller, M. (2004). Psychology and culture. *Annual Review of Psychology, 55,* 689–714.

Lehrl, S., & Fischer, B. (1990) A basic information psychological parameter (BIP) for the reconstruction of concepts of intelligence. *European Journal of Personality, 4,* 259–286.

Leibowitz, H. W. (1971). Sensory, learned and cognitive mechanisms of size perception. *Annals of the New York Academy of Sciences, 188,* 47–62.

Leichsenring, F. (2001). Comparative effects of short-term psychodynamic psychotherapy and cognitive-behavioral therapy in depression: A meta-analytic approach. *Clinical Psychology Review, 21,* 401–419.

Leichsenring, F. (2004). Randomized controlled versus naturalistic studies: A new research agenda. *Bulletin of the Menninger Clinic, 68,* 137–151.

Leichsenring, F., & Leibing, E. (2003). The effectiveness of psychodynamic therapy and cognitive behavior therapy in the treatment of personality disorders: A meta-analysis. *American Journal of Psychiatry*, 160, 1223–1232.

Leichsenring, F., Rabung, S., & Leibing, E. (2004). The efficacy of short-term psychodynamic psychotherapy in specific psychiatric disorders: A meta-analysis. *Archives of General Psychiatry*, 61, 1208–1216.

Lemme, B. H. (1995). *Development in adulthood*. Needham Heights, MA: Allyn & Bacon.

Lennenberg, E. H. (1967). *Biological foundations of language*. New York: Wiley.

Lennon, R., & Eisenberg, N. (1987). Gender and age differences in empathy and sympathy. In N. Eisenberg & J. Strayer (Eds.), *Empathy and its development* (pp. 195–217). New York: Cambridge University Press.

Lensvelt-Mulders, G., & Hettema, J. (2001a). Analysis of genetic influences on the consistency and variability of the Big Five across different stressful situations. *European Journal of Personality*, 15, 355–371.

Lensvelt-Mulders, G., & Hettema, J. (2001b). Genetic analysis of autonomic reactivity to psychologically stressful situations. *Biological Psychology*, 58, 25–40.

Leone, C., & Ensley, E. (1986). Self-generated attitude change: A person by situation analysis of attitude polarization and attenuation. *Journal of Research in Personality*, 20, 434–446.

Leopold, D. A., & Logothetis, N. K. (1996). Activity changes in early visual cortex reflect monkeys' percepts during binocular rivalry. *Nature*, 379, 549–553.

Lepper, M. R., Greene, D., & Nisbett, R. E. (1973). Undermining children's intrinsic interest with extrinsic reward: A test of the "overjustification" hypothesis. *Journal of Personality and Social Psychology*, 28, 129–137.

Leproult, R., Colecchia, E. F., Berardi, A. M., Stickgold, R., Kosslyn, S. M., & Van Cauter, E. (2003). Individual differences in subjective and objective alertness during sleep deprivation are stable and unrelated. *American Journal of Physiology-Regulatory Integrative and Comparative Physiology*, 284, R280–R290.

Leproult, R., Copinschi, G., Buxton, O., & Van Cauter, E. (1997). Sleep loss results in an elevation of cortisol levels the next evening. *Sleep*, 20, 865–870.

Leproult, R., Van Reeth, O., Byrne, M. M., Sturis, J., & Van Cauter, E. (1997). Sleepiness, performance, and neuroendocrine function during sleep deprivation: Effects of exposure to bright light or exercise. *Journal of Biological Rhythms*, 12, 245–258.

Lerner, J. S., & Keltner, D. (2000). Beyond valence: Toward a model of emotion-specific influences on judgement and choice. *Cognition and Emotion*, 14, 473–493.

Lerner, M. J. (1980). *The belief in a just world: A fundamental illusion*. New York: Plenum Press.

Lesch, K. P. (2003). Neuroticism and serotonin: A developmental genetic perspective. In R. Plomin, J. C. DeFries, et al. (Eds.), *Behavioral genetics in the postgenomic era* (pp. 389–423). Washington, DC: American Psychological Association.

Lester, B. M. (2000). Prenatal cocaine exposure and child outcome: A model for the study of the infant at risk. *Israel Journal of Psychiatry & Related Sciences*, 37, 223–235.

Lester, B. M., LaGasse, L. L., & Seifer, R. (1998). Cocaine exposure and children: The meaning of subtle effects. *Science*, 282, 633–634.

Leuchter, A. F., Cook, I. A., Witte, E. A., Morgan, M., & Abrams, M. (2002). Changes in brain function of depressed subjects during treatment with placebo. *American Journal of Psychiatry*, 159, 122–129.

LeVay, S. (1991). A difference in hypothalamic structure between heterosexual and homosexual men. *Science*, 253, 1034–1037.

LeVay, S., & Hamer, D. (1994). Evidence for a biological influence in male homosexuality. *Scientific American*, 270, 44–49. Levenson, R. W. (1992). Autonomic nervous system differences among emotions. *Psychological Science*, 3, 23–27.

Levenson, R. W, Ekman, P., & Friesen, W. V. (1990). Voluntary facial action generates emotion-specific autonomic nervous system activity. *Psychophysiology*, 27, 363–384.

Leventhal, G. S., Singer, R., & Jones, S. (1965). The effects of fear and specificity of recommendation upon attitudes and behavior. *Journal of Personality and Social Psychology*, 2, 20–29.

Levie, W. H., & Lentz, R. (1982). Effects of text illustrations: A review of research. *Educational Communication and Technology Journal*, 30, 195–232.

Levin, J. R., Anglin, G. J., & Carney, R. N. (1987). On empirically validating functions of pictures in prose. In D. M. Willows & H. A. Houghton (Eds.), *The psychology of illustration: I. Basic research* (pp. 51–85). New York: Springer-Verlag.

Levin, R. J. (1994). Human male sexuality: Appetite and arousal, desire and drive. In C. R. Legg & D. Booth (Eds.), *Appetite: Neural and behavioral bases* (pp. 127–164). New York: Oxford University Press.

Levin, R. S. (1980). The physiology of sexual function in women. *Clinics in Obstetrics and Gynaecology*, 7, 213–252.

Levine, A. S., & Billington, C. J. (1997). Why do we eat? A neural systems approach. *Annual Review of Nutrition*, 17, 597–619.

Levine, B. (2004). Autobiographical memory and the self in time: Brain lesion effects, functional neuroanatomy, and lifespan development. *Brain & Cognition*, 55(1), 54–68.

Levine, B., Turner, G. R., Tisserand, D., Hevenor, S. J., Graham, S. J., & McIntosh, A. R. (2004). The functional neuroanatomy of episodic and semantic autobiographical remembering: A prospective functional MRI study. *Journal of Cognitive Neuroscience*, 16, 1633–1646.

Levine, J. A., Eberhardt, N. L., & Jensen, M. D. (1999). The role of nonexercise activity thermogenesis in resistance to fat gain in humans. *Science*, 283, 212–214.

Levine, J. M., & Moreland, R. L. (1998). Small groups. In D. T. Gilbert, S. T. Fiske, & G. Lindzey (Eds.), *The handbook of social psychology* (4th ed., pp. 415–469). New York: McGraw-Hill.

Levine, L. J., & Bluck, S. (2004). Painting with broad strokes: Happiness and the malleability of event memory. *Cognition & Emotion*, 18, 559–574.

Levine, R. L., & Bluni, T. D. (1994). Magnetic field effects on spatial discrimination learning in mice. *Physiology and Behavior*, 55, 465–467.

Levine, R. L., & Stadtman, E. R. (1992). Oxidation of proteins during aging. *Generations*, 16(4), 39–42.

Levinson, D. J. (1977). The mid-life transition: A period in adult psychosocial development. *Psychiatry: Journal for the Study of Interpersonal Processes*, 40, 99–112.

Levinson, D. J. (1978). Eras: The anatomy of the life cycle. *Psychiatric Opinion*, 15, 10–11, 39–48.

Levinson, D. J. (1986). A conception of adult development. *American Psychologist*, 41, 3–13.

Levinson, D. J. (1990). A theory of life structure development in adulthood. In C. N. Alexander & E. J. Langer (Eds.), *Higher stages of human development: Perspectives on adult growth* (pp. 35–53). New York: Oxford University Press.

Levinson, D., Darrow, C., Klein, E. Levinson, M., & Braxton, M. (1978). *The seasons of a man's life*. New York: Ballantine.

Levitas, A. (2000). Fragile X syndrome. *Journal of the American Academy of Child and Adolescent Psychiatry*, 39, 398–399.

Levitt, A. G., & Wang, Q. (1991). Evidence for language-specific rhythmic influences in the reduplicative babbling of French- and English-learning infants. *Language and Speech*, 34, 235–249.

Levitt, M. J., Weber, R. A., & Guacci, N. (1993). Convoys of social support: An intergenerational analysis. *Psychology and Aging*, 8, 323–326.

Levy, B., Ashman, O., & Dror, I. (1999–2000). To be or not to be: The effects of aging stereotypes on the will to live. *Omega: Journal of Death & Dying*, 40, 409–420.

Levy, S. M., Herberman, R. B., Lippman, M. N., & d'Angelo, T. (1987). Correlation of stress factors with sustained depression of natural killer cell activity and predicted prognosis in patients with breast cancer. *Journal of Clinical Oncology*, 5, 348–353.

Levy, S. M., Herberman, R. B., Maluish, A. M., Schlien, B., & Lippman, M. (1985). Prognostic risk assessment in primary breast cancer by behavioral and immunological parameters. *Health Psychology*, 4, 99–113.

Levy, S. M., Lee, J., Bagley, C., & Lippman, M. (1988). Survival hazards analysis in first year recurrent breast cancer patients: Seven-year follow-up. *Psychosomatic Medicine*, 50, 520–528.

Lewinsohn, P. M., Allen, N. B., Seeley, J. R., & Gotlib, I. H. (1999). First onset versus recurrence of depression: Differential processes of psychosocial risk. *Journal of Abnormal Psychology*, 108, 483–489.

Lewinsohn, P. M., Rohde, P., Seeley, J. R., & Fischer, S. A. (1993). Age-cohort changes in the lifetime occurrence of depression and other mental disorders. *Journal of Abnormal Psychology*, 102, 110–120.

Lewis, B., & Thompson, L. A. (1992). A study of developmental speech and language disorders in twins. *Journal of Speech and Hearing Research*, 35, 1086–1094.

Lewis, D. O., Yeager, C. A., Swica, Y., Pincus, J. H., & Lewis, M. (1997). Objective documentation of child abuse and dissociation in 12 murderers with dissociative identity disorder. *American Journal of Psychiatry*, 154, 1703–1710.

Lewis, M., & Brooks-Gunn, J. (1979). *Social cognition and the acquisition of self*. New York: Plenum.

Lewontin, R. C. (1976a). Further remarks on race and the genetics of intelligence. In N. J. Block & G. Dworkin (Eds.), *The IQ controversy* (pp. 107–112). New York: Pantheon Books.

Lewontin, R. C. (1976b). Race and intelligence. In N. J. Block & G. Dworkin (Eds.), *The IQ controversy* (pp. 78–92). New York: Pantheon Books.

Li, D., Chokka, P., & Tibbo, P. (2001). Toward an integrative understanding of social phobia. *Journal of Psychiatry & Neuroscience, 26,* 190–202.

Li, N. P., Bailey, J. M., Kenrick, D. T., & Linsenmeier, J. A. W. (2002). The necessities and luxuries of mate preferences: Testing the tradeoffs. *Journal of Personality & Social Psychology, 82,* 947–955.

Lê, S., Cardebat, D., Boulanouar, K., Hénaff, M., Michel, F., Milner, D., Dijkerman, C., Puel, M., & Démonet, J. (2002). Seeing, since childhood, without ventral stream: A behavioural study. *Brain, 125,* 58–74.

Li, S-C., Lindenberger, U., & Sikström, S. (2001). Aging cognition: From neuromodulation to representation. *Trends in Cognitive Science, 5,* 479–486.

Li, S-C., Lindenberger, U., Hommel, B., Aschersleben, G., Prinz, W., & Baltes, P. B. (2004). Transformations in the couplings among intellectual abilities and constituent cognitive processes across the life span. *Psychological Science, 15,* 155–163.

Libby, L. K., Eibach, R. P., & Gilovich, T. (2005). Here's looking at me: The effect of memory perspective on assessments of personal change. *Journal of Personality & Social Psychology, 88,* 50–62.

Liben, L. S., Susman, E. J., Finkelstein, J. W., Chinchilli, V. M., Kunselman, S., Schwab, J., et al. (2002). The effects of sex steroids on spatial performance: A review and an experimental clinical investigation. *Developmental Psychology, 38,* 236–253.

Lichtenberg, P., Bachner-Melman, R., Ebstein, R. P., & Crawford, H. J. (2004). Hypnotic susceptibility: Multidimensional relationships with Cloninger's tridimensional personality questionnaire, COMT polymorphisms, absorption, and attentional characteristics. *International Journal of Clinical & Experimental Hypnosis, 52,* 47–72.

Lickliter, R., & Honeycutt, H. (2003a). Developmental dynamics: toward a biologically plausible evolutionary psychology. *Psychological Bulletin, 129,* 819–835.

Lickliter, R., & Honeycutt, H. (2003b). Developmental dynamics and contemporary evolutionary psychology: Status quo or irreconcilable views? Reply to Bjorklund (2003), Krebs (2003), Buss and Reeve (2003), Crawford (2003), and Tooby et al. (2003). *Psychological Bulletin, 129,* 866–872

Liddell, C. (1997). Every picture tells a story—or does it? Young South African children interpreting pictures. *Journal of Cross-Cultural Psychology, 28,* 266–282.

Lieberman, D. Z. (2003). An automated treatment for jet lag delivered through the Internet. *Psychiatric Services, 54,* 394–396.

Lieberman, J. A. Tollefson, G. D., Charles, C., Zipursky, R., Sharma, T., Kahn, R. S., Keefe, R. S. E., Green, A. I., Gur, R. E., McEvoy, J., Perkins, D, Hamer, R. M., Gu, H., & Tohen, M., for the HGDH Study Group (2005). Antipsychotic drug effects on brain morphology in first-episode psychosis. *Archives of General Psychiatry, 62,* 361–370.

Lieberman, M. D., Ochsner, K. N., Gilbert, D. T., & Schacter, D. L. (2001). Attitude change in amnesia and under cognitive load. *Psychological Science, 12,* 135–140.

Light, L. (1991). Memory and aging: Four hypotheses in search of data. *Annual Review of Psychology, 42,* 333–376.

Lilenfeld, L. R., Kaye, W. H., Greeno, C. G., Merikangas, K. R., Plotnicov, K., Pollice, C., et al. (1998). A controlled family study of anorexia nervosa and bulimia nervosa: Psychiatric disorders in first-degree relatives and effects of proband comorbidity. *Archives of General Psychiatry, 55,* 603–610.

Lilienfeld, S. O., Lynn, S. J., Kirsch, I., Chaves, J. F., Sarbin, T. R., Ganaway, G. K., & Powell, R. A. (1999). Dissociative identity disorder and the sociocognitive model: Recalling the lessons of the past. *Psychological Bulletin, 125,* 507–523.

Lilienfeld, S. O., Wood, J. M., & Garb, H. N. (2000). The scientific status of projective techniques. *Psychological Science in the Public Interest, 1,* 27–66.

Lillard, A. S. (1999). Developing a cultural theory of mind: The CIAO approach. *Current Directions in Psychological Science, 8,* 57–61.

Lin, E. L., & Murphy, G. L. (2001). Thematic relations in adults' concepts. *Journal of Experimental Psychology: General, 130,* 3–28.

Lindblom, K. (2001). Cooperating with Grice: A cross-disciplinary metaperspective on uses of Grice's cooperative principle. *Journal of Pragmatics, 33,* 1601–1623.

Lindemann, E. (1991). The symptomatology and management of acute grief. *American Journal of Psychiatry, 144,* 141–148.

Linden, M., Zubraegel, D., Baer, T., Franke, U., & Schlattmann, P. (2005). Efficacy of cognitive behaviour therapy in generalized anxiety disorders. *Psychotherapy & Psychosomatics, 74,* 36–42.

Lindley, R. H., Wilson, S. M., Smith, W. R., & Bathurst, K., (1995). Reaction time (RT) and IQ: Shape of the task complexity function. *Personality and Individual Differences, 18,* 339–345.

Lindsay, D. S., & Johnson, M. K. (1989). The eyewitness suggestibility effect and memory for source. *Memory & Cognition, 17,* 349–358.

Lindsay, P. H., & Norman, D. A (1977). *Human information processing: An introduction to psychology* (2nd ed.). New York: Academic Press.

Lindsay, R. C., & Wells, G. L. (1985). Improving eyewitness identifications from lineups: Simultaneous versus sequential lineup presentation. *Journal of Applied Psychology, 70,* 556–564.

Lindsay, S., Hagen, L., Read, J. D., Wade, K. A., & Garry, M. (2004). True photographs and false memories. *Psychological Science, 15,* 149–154.

Lindstrom, T. C. (2002). "It ain't necessarily so" . . . Challenging mainstream thinking about bereavement. *Family & Community Health, 25,* 11–21.

Linley, P. A., & Joseph, S. (2004). Positive change following trauma and adversity: A review. *Journal of Traumatic Stress, 17,* 11–21.

Linner, B. (1972). *Sex and society in Sweden.* New York: Harper Colophon.

Linnoila, M., Virkkunen, M., Scheinin, M., Nuutila, A., Romin, R., & Goodwin, F. K. (1983). Low cerebrospinal fluid 5-hydroxindoleacetic acid concentration differentiates impulsive from non-impulsive violent behavior. *Life Sciences, 33,* 2609–2614.

Linville, P. W., & Fischer, G. W. (1993). Exemplar and abstraction models of perceived group variability and stereotypicality. *Social Cognition, 11,* 92–125.

Liotti, M., Mayberg, H. S., McGinnis, S., Brannan, S. L., & Jerabek, P. (2002). Unmasking disease-specific cerebral blood flow abnormalities: Mood challenge in patients with remitted unipolar depression. *American Journal of Psychiatry, 159,* 1830–1840.

Lipkus, I. M., & Siegler, I. C. (1993). The belief in a just world and perceptions of discrimination. *Journal of Psychology, 127,* 465–474.

Lipsey, M. W., & Wilson, D. B. (1993). The efficacy of psychological, educational, and behavioral treatment: Confirmation from meta-analysis. *American Psychologist, 48,* 1181–1209.

Lissek, S., Powers, A. S., McClure, E. B., Phelps, E. A., Woldehawariat, G., Grillon, C., & Pine, D. S. (in press). Classical fear conditioning in the anxiety disorders: A meta-analysis. *Behaviour Research and Therapy.*

Lisspers, J., Sundin, Ö., Öhman, A., Hofman-Bang, C., Rydén, L., & Nygren, A. (2005). Long-term effects of lifestyle behavior change in coronary artery disease: Effects on recurrent coronary events after percutaneous coronary intervention. *Health Psychology, 24,* 41–48.

Litt, M. D., Kleppinger, A., & Judge, J. O. (2002). Initiation and maintenance of exercise behavior in older women: Predictors from the social learning model. *Journal of Behavioral Medicine, 25,* 83–97.

Liu, D., Diorio, J., Tannenbaum, B., Caldji, C., Francis, D., Freedman, A., et al. (1997). Maternal care, hippocampal glucocorticoid receptors, and hypothalamic-pituitary-adrenal responses to stress. *Science, 277,* 1659–1662.

Liu, J. H., & Latané, B. (1998). Extremitization of attitudes: Does thought- and discussion-induced polarization cumulate? *Basic & Applied Social Psychology, 20,* 103–110.

Livesley, W. J. (1998). Suggestions for a framework for an empirically based classification of personality disorder. *Canadian Journal of Psychiatry 43,* 137–147.

Livesley, W. J. (Ed.). (2001). *Handbook of personality disorders: Theory, research, and treatment.* New York: Guilford Press.

Livesley, W. J., Jang, K. L., & Vernon, P. A. (2003). Genetic basis of personality structure. In T. Millon & M. J. Lerner (Eds.), *Handbook of psychology: Personality and social psychology* (Vol. 5, pp. 59–83). New York: John Wiley.

Lobaugh, N. J., Cole, S., & Rovet, J. F. (1998). Visual search for features and conjunctions in development. *Canadian Journal of Experimental Psychology, 52,* 201–212.

Lobel, M., Marie Yali, A., Zhu, W., DeVincent, C. J., & Meyer, B. A. (2002). Beneficial associations between optimistic disposition and emotional distress in high-risk pregnancy. *Psychology & Health, 17,* 77–96.

Locke, A., & Ginsborg, J. (2003). Spoken language in the early years: The cognitive and linguistic development of three- to five-year-old children from socioeconomically deprived backgrounds. *Educational & Child Psychology, 20,* 68–79.

Locke, S. E., Kraus, L., Leserman, J., Hurst, M. W., Heisel, J. S., & Williams, R. M. (1984). Life change stress, psychiatric symptoms, and natural killer-cell activity. *Psychosomatic Medicine, 46,* 441–453.

Lockley, S. W., Cronin, J. W., Evans, E. E., Cade, B. E., Lee, C. J., Landrigan, C. P., Rothschild, J. M., Katz, J. T., Lilly, C. M., Stone, P. H., Aeschbach, D., & Czeisler, C. A. (2004). Effect of reducing interns' weekly work hours on sleep and attentional failures. *New England Journal of Medicine, 351,* 1829–1837.

Loeb, S., Fuller, B., Kagan, S. L., & Carrol, B. (2004). Child care in poor communities: Early learning effects of type, quality, and stability. *Child Development, 75,* 47–65.

Loehlin, J. C. (1989). Partitioning environmental and genetic contributions to behavioral development. *American Psychologist, 44,* 1285–1292.

Loehlin, J. C. (1992). *Genes and environment in personality development.* Newbury Park, CA: Sage.

Loehlin, J. C., Horn, J. M., & Willerman, L. (1981). Personality resemblance in adoptive families. *Behavior Genetics, 11,* 309–330.

Loehlin, J. C., Willerman, L., & Horn, J. M. (1985). Personality resemblances in adoptive families when the children are late-adolescent or adult. *Journal of Personality and Social Psychology, 48,* 376–392.

Loewenstein, R. J. (1994). Diagnosis, epidemiology, clinical course, treatment, and cost effectiveness of treatment for dissociative disorders and MPD: Report submitted to the Clinton Administration Task Force on Health Care Financing Reform. *Dissociation: Progress in the Dissociative Disorders, 7,* 3–11.

Loftus, E. F. (1993). The reality of repressed memories. *American Psychologist, 48,* 518–537.

Loftus, E. F. (2004). Memories of things unseen. *Current Directions in Psychological Science, 13,* 145–147.

Loftus, E. F., Miller, D. G., & Burns, H. J. (1978). Semantic integration of verbal information into a visual memory. *Journal of Experimental Psychology: Human Learning and Memory, 4,* 19–31.

Loftus, E. F., & Pickrell, J. E. (1995). The formation of false memories. *Psychiatric Annals, 25,* 720–725.

Logan, J. M., Sanders, A. L., Snyder, A. Z., Morris, J. C., & Buckner, R. L. (2002). Under-recruitment and nonselective recruitment: Dissociable neural mechanisms associated with aging. *Neuron, 33,* 827–840.

Logie, R. H. (1986). Visuo-spatial processing in working memory. *Quarterly Journal of Experimental Psychology, 80,* 229–247.

Logie, R. H., & Baddeley, A. D. (1990). Imagery and working memory. In P. J. Hampson & D. F. Marks (Eds.), *Imagery: Current developments* (pp. 103–128). London: Routledge.

Logie, R. H., & Marchetti, C. (1991). Visuo-spatial working memory: Visual, spatial or central executive? In R. H. Logie & M. Denis (Eds.), *Mental images in human cognition* (pp. 105–115). Amsterdam: North-Holland.

Loke, W., & Song, S. (1991). Central and peripheral visual processing in hearing and non-hearing individuals. *Bulletin of Psychonomic Society, 29,* 437–440.

Lonetto, R., & Templer, D. (1986). *Death anxiety.* New York: Hemisphere.

Long, J. M., Mouton, P. R., Jucker, M., & Ingram, D. K. (1999). What counts in brain aging? Design-based stereological analysis of cell number. *Journals of Gerontology: Series A: Biological Sciences & Medical Sciences, 54A,* B407–B417.

Lonky, M. L. (2003). Human consciousness: A systems approach to the mind/brain interaction. *Journal of Mind & Behavior, 24,* 91–118.

Loori, A. A. (2005). Multiple intelligences: A comparative study between the preferences of males and females. *Social Behavior & Personality, 33,* 77–88.

Lopes, P. N., Salovey, P., Côté, S., & Beers, M. (2005). Emotion regulation abilities and the quality of social interaction. *Emotion, 5,* 113–118.

Lopes, P. N., Salovey, P., & Straus, R. (2003). Emotional intelligence, personality, and the perceived quality of social relationships. *Personality and Individual Differences, 35,* 641–658.

Lopez, F. G. (2003). The assessment of adult attachment security. In S. J. Lopez & C. R. Snyder (Eds.), *Positive psychological assessment: A handbook of models and measures* (pp. 285–299). Washington, DC: American Psychological Association.

Lorenzo-Hernandez, J. (1998). How social categorization may inform the study of Hispanic immigration. *Hispanic Journal of Behavioral Sciences, 20,* 39–59.

Losch, M., & Cacioppo, J. (1990). Cognitive dissonance may enhance sympathetic tonis, but attitudes are changed to reduce negative effect rather than arousal. *Journal of Experimental Social Psychology, 26,* 289–304.

Lott, B. (1996) Politics or science? The question of gender sameness/difference. *American Psychologist, 51,* 153–154.

Lou, H. C., Hansen, D., Nordentoft, M., Pryds, O., et al. (1994). Prenatal stressors of human life affect fetal brain development. *Developmental Medicine & Child Neurology, 36,* 826–832.

Low, J., & Durkin, K. (2001). Individual differences and consistency in maternal talk style during joint story encoding and retrospection: Associations with children's long-term recall. *International Journal of Behavioral Development, 25,* 27–36.

Lowe, C. F. (1979). Determinants of human operant behaviour. In M. D. Zeiler & P. Harzem (Eds.), *Advances in analysis of behavior (Vol. 1): Reinforcement and the organization of behavior.* New York: Wiley.

Lowe, P. (1999, May 2). Alike and different. *Denver Post.*

Lowe, S. M. (1995). Essay. In F. Kahlo, *The diary of Frida Kahlo: An intimate self-portrait* (pp. 25–29). New York: Abradale Press.

Lu, L. (1999). Personal or environmental causes of happiness: A longitudinal analysis. *Journal of Social Psychology, 139,* 79–90.

Lu, L., & Shih, J. B. (1997a). Sources of happiness: A qualitative approach. *Journal of Social Psychology, 137,* 181–188.

Lu, L., Shih, J. B., Lin, Y. Y., & Ju, L. S. (1997). Personal and environmental correlates of happiness. *Personality & Individual Differences, 23,* 453–462.

Lubin, A. J. (1972). *Stranger on the earth: Vincent van Gogh.* New York: Da Capo Press.

Lubinski, D. (2000). Scientific and social significance of assessing individual differences: Sinking shafts at a few critical points. *Annual Review of Psychology, 51,* 405–444.

Lubinski, D. (2004). Introduction to the special section on cognitive abilities: 100 years after Spearman's (1904) "'General intelligence,' objectively determined and measured." *Journal of Personality and Social Psychology, 86,* 96–111.

Luborsky, L., Diguer, L., Seligman, D. A., Rosenthal, R., Krause, E. D., Johnson, S., et al. (1999). The researcher's own therapy allegiances: A "wild card" in comparisons of treatment efficacy. *Clinical Psychology: Science & Practice 6,* 95–106.

Luborsky, L., Singer, B., & Luborsky, L. (1975). Comparative studies of psychotherapies: Is it true that "everyone has won and all must have prizes"? *Archives of General Psychiatry, 32,* 995–1008.

Lucas, R. J., Freedman, M. S., Muñoz, M., Garcia-Fernandez, J-M., & Foster, R. G. (1999). Regulation of the mammalian pineal by non-rod, non-cone, ocular photoreceptors. *Science, 284,* 505–507.

Luce, G. G. (1971). *Biological rhythms in human and animal physiology.* New York: Dover.

Luce, K. H., Winzelberg, A. J., Zabinski, M. F., & Osborne, M. I. (2003). Internet-delivered psychological interventions for body image dissatisfaction and disordered eating. *Psychotherapy: Theory, Research, Practice, Training, 40,* 148–154.

Luciano, M., Wright, M. J., Smith, G. A., Geffen, G. M., Geffen, L. B., & Martin, N. G. (2001). Genetic covariance among measures of information processing speed, working memory, and IQ. *Behavior Genetics, 31,* 581–592.

Luck, S. J., Vogel, E. K., & Shapiro, K. L. (1996). Word meanings can be accessed but not reported during the attentional blink. *Nature, 383,* 616–618.

Luckow, A., Reifman, A., & McIntosh, D. N. (1998, August). *Gender differences in coping: A meta-analysis.* Poster session presented at the 106th Annual Convention of the American Psychological Association, San Francisco, CA.

Lueck, C. J., Zeki, S., Friston, K. J., Deiber, M. P., Cope, P., Cunningham ,V. J., Lammertsma, A. A., Kennard, C.. & Frackowiak, R. S. (1989). The colour centre of the cerebral cortex in man. *Nature, 340,* 386–389.

Luna, B. (2004). Algebra and the adolescent brain. *Trends in Cognitive Sciences, 8,* 437–439.

Luna, B., Garver, K. E., Urban, T. A., Lazar, N. A., & Sweeney, J. A. (2004). Maturation of cognitive processes from late childhood to adulthood. *Child Development, 75,* 1357–1372.

Lunzer, E. A. (1978). Formal reasoning: A reappraisal. In B. Z. Presseisen, D. Goldstein, & M. H. Appel (Eds.), *Topics in cognitive development: Vol. 2. Language and operational thought* (pp. 47–76). New York: Plenum.

Luparello, T. J., Lyons, H. A., Bleecker, E. R., & McFadden, E. R. (1968). Influences of suggestion on airway reactivity in asthmatic subjects. *Psychosomatic Medicine, 30,* 819–825.

Luria, A. R. (1968). *The mind of a mnemonist: A little book about a vast memory* (L. Solotaroff, Trans.). Cambridge, MA: Harvard University Press. (Original work published 1887)

Lush, J. L. (1937). *Animal breeding plans.* Ames, IA: Collegiate Press.

Lutchmaya, S., & Baron-Cohen, S. (2002). Human sex differences in social and non-social looking preferences, at 12 months of age. *Infant Behavior & Development, 25,* 319–325.

Lutz, A., Greischar, L. L., Rawlings, N. B., Ricard, M., & Davidson, R. J. (2004). Long-term mediators self-induce high-amplitude gamma synchrony during mental practice. *Proceedings of the National Academy of Sciences, 101,* 16369–16373.

Luwel, K., Verschaffel, L., Onghena, P., & De Corte, E. (2001). Strategic aspects of children's numerosity judgement. *European Journal of Psychology of Education, 16,* 233–255.

Lydon, J. E., Jamieson, D. W., & Zanna, M. P. (1988). Interpersonal similarity and the social and intellectual dimensions of first impressions. *Social Cognition, 6,* 269–286.

Lykken, D., & Tellegen, A. (1996). Happiness is a stochastic phenomenon. *Psychological Science, 7,* 186–189.

Lykken, D., Bouchard, T. J., Jr., McGue, M., & Tellegen, A. (1993). Heritability of interests: A twin study. *Journal of Applied Psychology, 78,* 649–661.

Lynch, E. D., Lee, M. K., Morrow, J. E., Welcsh, P. L., Leon, P. E., & King, M. C. (1997). Nonsyndromic deafness DFNA1 associated with mutation of human homolog of the *Drosophila* gene diaphanous. *Science, 278,* 1315–1318.

Lynn, R. (1990). The role of nutrition in secular increases in intelligence. *Personality & Individual Differences, 11,* 273–285.

Lynn, R. (1998). Has the black-white intelligence difference in the United States been narrowing over time? *Personality and Individual Differences, 25,* 999–1002.

Lynn, R., & Irwing, P. (2004). Sex differences on the progressive matrices: A meta-analysis. *Intelligence, 32,* 481–498.

Lynn, R., & Martin, T. (1997). Gender differences in extraversion, neuroticism, and psychoticism in 37 nations. *Journal of Social Psychology, 137,* 369–373.

Lyon, H. M., Startup, M., & Bentall, R. P. (1999). Social cognition and the manic defense: Attributions, selective attention, and self-schema in bipolar affective disorder. *Journal of Abnormal Psychology, 108,* 273–282.

Lyons, E. A., & Levi, C. S. (1994). Sperm are not like salmon: Altered myometrial contractility is significant in unexplained infertility rates. *Radiology, 193[P],* 144.

Lyons, L. C., & Crawford, H. J. (1997) Sustained attentional and disattentional abilities and arousability: Factor analysis and relationship to hypnotic susceptibility. *Personality and Individual Differences 26,* 1071–1084.

Lyons, M. J., & Bar, J. L. (2001). Is there a role for twin studies in the molecular genetics era? *Harvard Review of Psychiatry, 9,* 318–332.

Lyons, M. J., Goldberg, J., Eisen, S. A., True, W., Tsuang, M. T., Meyer, J. M., & Henderson, W. G. (1993). Do genes influence exposure to trauma: A twin study of combat. *American Journal of Medical Genetics (Neuropsychiatric Genetics), 48,* 22–27.

Lytton, H., & Romney, D. M. (1991). Parents' differential socialization of boys and girls: A meta-analysis. *Psychological Bulletin, 109,* 267–296.

Lyubomirsky, S. (2001). Why are some people happier than others? The role of cognitive and motivational processes in well-being. *American Psychologist, 56,* 239–249.

Lyubomirsky, S., Tucker, K. I., & Kasri, F. (2001). Responses to hedonically conflicting social comparisons: Comparing happy and unhappy people. *European Journal of Social Psychology, 31,* 511–535.

Maas, J. B. (1998). *Power sleep.* New York: Harper Perennial.

Macaskill, N. D., & Macaskill, A. (1996). Rational-emotive therapy plus pharmacotherapy versus pharmacotherapy alone in the treatment of high cognitive dysfunction depression. *Cognitive Therapy & Research, 20,* 575–592.

Macchi, M. M., Boulos, Z., Ranney, T., Simmons, L., & Campbell, S. S. (2002). Effects of an afternoon nap on nighttime alertness and performance in long-haul drivers. *Accident Analysis & Prevention, 34,* 825–834.

Maccoby, E. E. (1988). Gender as a social category. *Developmental Psychology, 26,* 755–765.

Maccoby, E. E. (1990). Gender and relationships: A developmental account. *American Psychologist, 45,* 513–520.

Maccoby, E. E. (1991). Gender and relationships: A reprise. *American Psychologist, 46,* 538–539.

Maccoby, E. E., & Jacklin, C. N. (1987). Gender segregation in childhood. In H. W. Reese (Ed.), *Advances in child development and behavior* (Vol. 20, pp. 239–288). New York: Academic Press.

MacDonald, J. A., & Balakrishnan, J. D. (in press). Signal detection theory. *Encyclopedia of Cognitive Science.*

MacGregor, A. J., Griffiths, G. O., Baker, J., & Spector, T. D. (1997). Determinants of pressure pain threshold in adult twins: Evidence that shared environmental influences predominate. *Pain, 73,* 253–257.

Macht, M., Roth, S., & Ellgring, H. (2002). Chocolate eating in healthy men during experimentally induced sadness and joy. *Appetite, 39,* 147–158.

Mackintosh, N. J., & Bennett, E. S. (2003). The fractionation of working memory maps onto different components of intelligence. *Intelligence, 31,* 519–531.

Macklin, M. L., Metzger, L. J., Litz, B. T., McNally, R. J., Lasko, N. B., Orr, S. P., & Pitman, R. K. (1998). Lower precombat intelligence is a risk factor for posttraumatic stress disorder. *Journal of Consulting & Clinical Psychology, 66,* 323–326.

MacLean, C. R. K., Walton, K. G., Winneberg, S. R., Levitsky, D. K., Manderino, J. V., Waziri, R., et al. (1997). Effects of the Transcendental Meditation program on adaptive mechanisms: Changes in hormone levels and responses to stress after 4 months of practice. *Psychoneuroendocrinology, 22,* 277–295.

Macmillan, M. (1992). Inhibition and the control of behavior: From Gall to Freud via Phineas Gage and the frontal lobes. *Brain & Cognition, 19,* 72–104.

Macmillan, M. B. (1986). A wonderful journey through skull and brains: The travels of Mr. Gage's tamping iron. *Brain & Cognition, 5,* 67–107.

MacPhillamy, D. J., & Lewinsohn, P. M. (1974). Depression as a function of levels of desired and obtained pleasure. *Journal of Abnormal Psychology, 83,* 651–657.

Macrae, C. N., Bodenhausen, G. V., Milne, A. B., & Jetten, J. (1994). Out of mind but back in sight: Stereotypes on the rebound. *Journal of Personality and Social Psychology, 67,* 808–817.

Macrae, C. N., Moran, J. M., Heatherton, T. F., Banfield, J. F., & Kelley, W. M. (2004). Medial prefrontal activity predicts memory for self. *Cerebral Cortex, 14,* 647–654.

Madden, K. S. (2003). Catecholamines, sympathetic innervation, and immunity. *Brain, Behavior & Immunity, 17,* S5–S10.

Maddi, S. R. (1998). The effectiveness of hardiness training. *Consulting Psychology Journal: Practice and Research, 50,* 78–86.

Madill, A., & Holch, P. (2004). A range of memory possibilities: The challenge of the false memory debate for clinicians and researchers. *Clinical Psychology & Psychotherapy, 11,* 299–310.

Madison, L. S., George, C., & Moeschler, J. B. (1986). Cognitive functioning in the fragile-X syndrome: A study of intellectual, memory and communication skills. *Journal of Mental Deficiency Research, 30,* 129–148.

Madon, S., Guyll, M., Spoth, R., & Willard, J. (2004). Self-fulfilling prophecies: The synergistic accumulative effect of parents' beliefs on children's drinking behavior. *Psychological Science, 15,* 837–845.

Magee, W. L., & Davidson, J. W. (2002). The effect of music therapy on mood states in neurological patients: A pilot study. *Journal of Music Therapy, 39,* 20–29.

Magnusson, D. (2003). The person approach: Concepts, measurement models, and research strategy. *New Directions in Child Adolescent Development, 101,* 3–23.

Maher, B. A. (1966). *Principles of psychopathology: An experimental approach.* New York: McGraw-Hill.

Maier, K. J., Waldstein, S. R., & Synowski, S. J. (2003). Relation of cognitive appraisal to cardiovascular reactivity, affect, and task engagement. *Annals of Behavioral Medicine, 26,* 32–41.

Major, B., & O'Brien, L. T. (2005). The social psychology of stigma. *Annual Review of Psychology, 56,* 393–421.

Malan, D. H. (1976). *The frontier of brief psychotherapy: An example of the convergence of research and clinical practice.* New York: Plenum Medical.

Maletzky, B. M. (2004). The first-line use of electroconvulsive therapy in major affective disorders. *Journal of ECT, 20,* 112–117.

Malik, M. L., Beutler, L. E., Alimohamed, S., Gallagher-Thompson, D., & Thompson, L. (2003). Are all cognitive therapies alike? A comparison of cognitive and noncognitive therapy process and implications for the application of empirically supported treatment. *Journal of Consulting & Clinical Psychology, 71,* 150–158.

Malina, R. M., & Bouchard, C. (1991). *Growth, maturation, and physical activity.* Champaign, IL: Human Kinetics.

Mandler, G. (1967). Organization in memory. In K. W. Spence & J. T. Spence (Eds.), *The psychology of learning and motivation* (Vol. 1, pp. 327–372). San Diego, CA: Academic Press.

Manfro, G. G., Otto, M. W., McArdle, E. T., Worthington, J. J., III, Rosenbaum, J. F., & Pollack, M. H. (1996). Relationship of antecedent stressful life events to childhood and family history of anxiety and the course of panic disorder. *Journal of Affective Disorders, 41,* 135–139.

Mangan, B. (2001, October). Sensation's ghost: The non-sensory "fringe" of consciousness. *Psyche: An Interdisciplinary Journal of Research on Consciousness, 7(18).* Retrieved from http://psyche.cs.monash.edu.au/v7/psyche-7-18-mangan.html

Mann, S., Vrij, A., & Bull, R. (2004). Detecting true lies: Police officers' ability to detect suspects' lies. *Journal of Applied Psychology, 89,* 137–149.

Mann, T., Nolen-Hoeksema, S., Huang, K., Burgard, D., Wright, A., & Hanson, K. (1997). Are two interventions worse than none? Joint primary and secondary prevention of eating disorders in college females. *Health Psychology, 16,* 3.

Manning, B. H., Merin, N. M., Meng, I. D., & Amaral, D. G. (2001). Reduction in opioid- and cannabinoid-induced antinociception in rhesus monkeys after bilateral lesions of the amygdaloid complex. *Journal of Neuroscience, 21,* 8238–8246.

Manns, J. R., Hopkins, R. O., & Squire, L. R. (2003). Semantic memory and the human hippocampus. *Neuron, 38,* 127–133.

Mansour, C. S., Haier, R. J., & Buchsbaum, M. S. (1996). Gender comparisons of cerebral glucose metabolic rate in healthy adults during a cognitive task. *Personality and Individual Differences, 20,* 183–191.

Manto, M., & Pandolfo, M. (Eds.) (2001). *Cerebellum and its disorders*. New York: Cambridge University Press.

Mantzoros, C. S. (1999). The role of leptin in human obesity and disease: A review of current evidence. *Annals of Internal Medicine, 130*, 651–657.

Manuck, S. B., Cohen, S., Rabin, B. S., Muldoon, M. F., & Bachen, E. A. (1991). Individual differences in cellular immune response to stress. *Psychological Science, 2*, 111–115.

Maquet, P., Laureys, S., Peigneux, P., Fuchs, S., Petiau, C., Phillips, C., et al. (2000). Experience-dependent changes in cerebral activation during human REM sleep. *Nature Neuroscience, 3*, 831–836.

Marcel, A. J. (1983). Conscious and unconscious perceptions: Experiments on visual masking and word recognition. *Cognitive Psychology, 15*, 197–237.

Marcus, G. F., Vijayan, S., Rao, S. B., & Vishton, P. M. (1999). Rule learning by 7-month-old infants. *Science, 283*, 77–80.

Mareschal, D., & Johnson, M. H. (2003). The "what" and "where" of object representations in infancy. *Cognition, 88*, 259–276.

Marica, James E. (1993). The status of the statuses: Research review. In J. E. Marica, A. S. Waterman, D. R. Matteson, S. L. Archer, & J. L. Orlofsky (Eds.), *Ego identity: A handbook for psychosocial research* (pp. 22–41). New York: Springer.

Marini, P., Ramat, S., Ginestroni, A., & Paganini, M. (2003). Deficit of short-term memory in newly diagnosed untreated parkinsonian patients: Reversal after L-dopa therapy. *Neurological Sciences, 24*, 184–185.

Marinova-Todd, S., Marshall, D., & Snow, C. (2000). Three misconceptions about age and L2 learning. *TESOL Quarterly, 34*, 9–34.

Markham, R., & Wang, L. (1996). Recognition of emotion by Chinese and Australian children. *Journal of Cross-Cultural Psychology, 27*, 616–643.

Markovits, C. (2003). *The un-Gandhian Gandhi: The life and afterlife of the Mahatma*. London: Anthem Press.

Marks, I. (1997). Behaviour therapy for obsessive-compulsive disorder: A decade of progress. *Canadian Journal of Psychiatry, 42*, 1021–1027.

Marks, I. M. (1969). *Fears and phobias*. New York: Academic Press.

Markson, L., & Bloom, P. (1997). Evidence against a dedicated system for word learning in children. *Nature, 385*, 813–815.

Markus, H. R., & Kitayama, S. (1991). Culture and the self: Implications for cognition, emotion, and motivation. *Psychological Review, 98*, 224–253.

Markus, S. J. (2002). *Neuroethics: Mapping the field*. New York: Dana Press.

Marmot, M. G. (1998). Improvement of social environment to improve health. *Lancet, 331*, 57–60.

Marmot, M. G., & Syme, S. L. (1976). Acculturation and coronary heart disease in Japanese-Americans. *American Journal of Epidemiology, 104*, 225–247.

Maroun, M., & Richter-Levin, G. (2003). Exposure to acute stress blocks the induction of long-term potentiation of the amygdala-prefrontal cortex pathway in vivo. *Journal of Neuroscience, 23*, 4406–4409.

Marr, D. (1982). *Vision: A computational investigation into the human representation and processing of visual information*. New York: Freeman.

Marsh, R. L., Landau, J. D., & Hicks, J. L. (1997). Contributions of inadequate source monitoring to unconscious plagiarism during idea generation. *Journal of Experimental Psychology: Learning, Memory, and Cognition, 23*, 886–897.

Marshall, D. H., Drummey, A. B., Fox, N. A., & Newcombe, N. S. (2002). An event-related potential study of item recognition memory in children and adults. *Journal of Cognition & Development, 3*, 201–224.

Marshall, D. S. (1971). Sexual behavior on Mangaia. In D. S. Marshall & R. C. Suggs (Eds.), *Human sexual behavior* (pp. 103–162). New York: Basic Books.

Marshall, P. J., Hardin, M. G., & Fox, N. A. (in press). Electrophysiological responses to auditory novelty in temperamentally different 9-month-old infants.

Martin, C. L., & Ruble, D. (2004). Children's search for gender cues: Cognitive perspectives on gender development. *Current Directions in Psychological Science, 13*, 67–70.

Martin, R. A. (1996). The Situational Humor Response Questionnaire (SHRQ) and Coping Humor Scale (CHS): A decade of research findings. *Humor: International Journal of Humor Research, 9*, 251–272.

Martin, R. A. (2001). Humor, laughter, and physical health: Methodological issues and research findings. *Psychological Bulletin, 127*, 504–519.

Martin, R. A., & Dobbin, J. P. (1988). Sense of humor, hassles, and immunoglobulin A: Evidence for a stress-moderating effect of humor. *International Journal of Psychiatry in Medicine, 18*, 93–105.

Martindale, C. (1989). Personality, situation, and creativity. In J. A. Glover, R. R. Ronning, & C. R. Reynolds (Eds.), *Handbook of creativity* (pp. 211–228). New York: Plenum.

Martindale, C. (1990). *The clockwork muse: The predictability of artistic styles*. New York: Basic Books.

Martindale, C. (2001). Oscillations and analogies: Thomas Young, M.D., F.R.S., genius. *American Psychologist, 56*, 342–345.

Martinez, C., Rietbrock, S., Wise, L., Ashby, D., Chick, J., Moseley, J., Evans, S., & Gennell, D. (2005). Antidepressant treatment and the risk of fatal and non-fatal self harm in first episode depression: Nested case-control study. *British Medical Journal, 330*, 389–393.

Martínez-Miranda, J., & Aldea, A. (2005). Emotions in human and artificial intelligence. *Computers in Human Behavior, 21*, 323–341.

Marucha, P. T., Kiecolt-Glaser, J. K., & Favagehi, M. (1998). Mucosal wound healing is impaired by examination stress. *Psychosomatic Medicine, 60*, 362–365.

Marx, D. M., Stapel, D. A., & Muller, D. (2005). We can do it: The interplay of construal orientation and social comparisons under threat. *Journal of Personality & Social Psychology, 88*, 432–446.

Masataka, N. (1996). Perception of motherese in a signed language by 6-month-old deaf infants. *Developmental Psychology, 32*, 874–879.

Maschke, M., Schugens, M., Kindsvater, K., Drepper, J., Kolb, F. P., Diener, H., Daum, I., & Timmann, D. (2002). Fear conditioned changes of heart rate in patients with medial cerebellar lesions. *Journal of Neurology, Neurosurgery & Psychiatry, 72*, 116–118.

Maslach, C. (2003). Job burnout: New directions in research and intervention. *Current Directions in Psychological Science, 12*, 189–192.

Maslach, C., Santee, R. T., & Wade, C. (1987). Individuation, gender role, and dissent: Personality mediators of situational forces. *Journal of Personality and Social Psychology, 53*, 1088–1194.

Maslach, C., Schaufeli, W. B., & Leiter, M. P. (2001). Job burnout. *Annual Review of Psychology, 52*, 397–422.

Maslow, A. H. (1970). *Motivation and personality* (2nd ed.). New York: Harper & Row.

Mason, M. F., Hood, B. M., & Macrae, C. N. (2004). Look into my eyes: Gaze direction and person memory. *Memory, 12*, 637–643.

Masters, W. H., & Johnson, V. E. (1966). *Human sexual response*. Boston: Little, Brown.

Matarazzo, J. D. (1972). *Wechsler's measurement and appraisal of adult intelligence*. Baltimore: Williams & Wilkins.

Mather, M., Henkel, L. A., & Johnson, M. K. (1997). Evaluating characteristics of false memories: Remember/know judgments and memory characteristics questionnaire compares. *Memory & Cognition, 25*, 826–837.

Matthews, B. A., Shimoff, E., Catania, A. C., & Sagvolden, T. (1977). Uninstructed human responding: Sensitivity to ratio and interval contingencies. *Journal of the Experimental Analysis of Behavior, 27*, 453–467.

Matthews, G., & Amelang, M. (1993). Extraversion, arousal theory and performance: A study of individual differences in the EEG. *Personality and Individual Differences, 14*, 347–363.

Matthews, G., & Gilliland, K. (1999). The personality theories of H. J. Eysenck and J. A. Gray: A comparative review. *Personality and Individual Differences, 26*, 583–626.

Matthews, G., Zeidner, M., & Roberts, R. D. (2002). *Emotional intelligence: Science and myth*. Cambridge, MA: MIT Press.

Mauch, D. H., Nägler, K., Schumacher, S., Göritz, C., Müller, E. C., Otto, A., & Pfrieger, F. W. (2001). CNS synaptogenesis promoted by glia-derived cholesterol. *Science, 294*, 1354–1357.

May, F. S., Chen, Q. C., Gilbertson, M. W., Shenton, M. E., & Pitman, R. K. (2004). Cavum septum pellucidum in monozygotic twins discordant for combat exposure: Relationship to posttraumatic stress disorder. *Biological Psychiatry, 55*, 656–658.

Mayer, D. M., & Hanges, P. J. (2003). Understanding the stereotype threat effect with "culture-free" tests: An examination of its mediators and measurement. *Human Performance, 16*, 207–230.

Mayer, J. D., Caruso, D. R., & Salovey, P. (2000). Emotional intelligence meets traditional standards for an intelligence. *Intelligence, 27*, 267–298.

Mayer, J. D., Salovey, P., & Caruso, D. (2001). *The Mayer-Salovey-Caruso Emotional Intelligence Test* (MSCEIT). Toronto: Multi-Health Systems.

Mayer, J. D., Salovey, P., Caruso, D. R., & Sitarenios, G. (2001). Emotional intelligence as a standard intelligence. *Emotion, 1*, 232–242.

Mayer, J. D., Salovey, P., Caruso, D. R., & Sitarenios, G. (2003). Measuring emotional intelligence with the MSCEIT V2.0. *Emotion, 3*, 97–105.

Mayer, R. E. (1997). *Thinking, problem solving, cognition*. New York: Freeman.

Mayes, A. R., & Downes, J. J. (Eds.). (1997). *Theories of organic amnesia*. Hove, England: Psychology Press/Erlbaum (UK) Taylor & Francis.

Maynard, R. A. (Ed.). (1996). *Kids having kids: A Robin Hood Foundation special report on the costs of adolescent childbearing*. New York: Robin Hood Foundation.

Maznevski, M. L. (1994). Understanding our differences: Performance in decision-making groups with diverse members. *Human Relations, 47*, 531–552.

McAdams, D. P., & de St. Aubin, E. (1992). A theory of generativity and its assessment through self-report, behavioral acts, and narrative themes in autobiography. *Journal of Personality & Social Psychology, 62*, 1003–1015.

McAdams, D. P., de St. Aubin, E., & Logan, R. L. (1993). Generativity among young, midlife, and older adults. *Psychology & Aging, 8*, 221–230.

McAdams, D. P., Reynolds, J., Lewis, M., Patten, A. H., & Bowman, P. J. (2001). When bad things turn good and good things turn bad: Sequences of redemption and contamination in life narrative and their relation to psychosocial adaptation in midlife adults and in students. *Personality & Social Psychology Bulletin, 27*, 474–485.

McArdle, J. J., Ferrer-Caja, E., Hamagami, F., & Woodcock, R. W. (2002). Comparative longitudinal structural analyses of the growth and decline of multiple intellectual abilities over the life span. *Developmental Psychology, 38*, 115–142.

McBride, J. (1999). *Steven Spielberg: A biography.* New York: Da Capo.

McCarley, R. W., & Hobson, J. A. (1975). Neuronal excitability modulation over the sleep cycle: A structural and mathematical model. *Science, 189*, 58–60.

McCartney, K., Harris, M. J., & Bernieri, F. (1990). Growing up and growing apart: A developmental meta-analysis of twin studies. *Psychological Bulletin, 107*, 226–237.

McClelland, D. C., & Atkinson, J. W. (1953). *The achievement motive.* New York: Appleton-Century-Crofts.

McClelland, J. L., & Rumelhart, D. E. (1986). *Parallel distributed processing: Explorations in the microstructure of cognition.* Cambridge: MIT Press.

McClintock, M. K. (1971). Menstrual synchrony and suppression. *Nature, 229*, 244–245.

McCloskey, M., & Zaragoza, M. (1985). Misleading postevent information and memory for events: Arguments and evidence against memory impairment hypotheses. *Journal of Experimental Psychology: General, 114*, 1–16.

McClure, E. B. (2000). A meta-analytic review of sex differences in facial expression processing and their development in infants, children, and adolescents. *Psychological Bulletin, 126*, 424–453.

McCornack, S. A., & Parks, M. R. (1990). What women know that men don't: Sex differences in determining the truth behind deceptive messages. *Journal of Social and Personal Relationships, 7*, 107–118.

McCrae, R. H., & Costa, P. T., Jr. (1987). Validation of the five-factor model of personality across instruments and observers. *Journal of Personality and Social Psychology, 52*, 81–90.

McCrae, R. H., & Costa, P. T., Jr. (1989b). Different points of view: Self-reports and ratings in the assessment of personality. In J. P. Forgas & J. M. Innes (Eds.), *Recent advance in social psychology: An international perspective* (pp. 429–439). Amsterdam: Elsevier North-Holland.

McCrae, R. H., & Costa, P. T., Jr. (1997a). Conceptions and correlates of Openness to Experience. In R. Hogan, J. Johnson, & S. Briggs (Eds.), *Handbook of personality psychology* (pp. 825–847). San Diego, CA: Academic Press.

McCrae, R. H., & Costa, P. T., Jr. (1997b). Personality trait structure as a human universal. *American Psychologist, 52*, 509–516.

McCrae, R. H., Costa, P. T., Jr., DelPilar, G. H. Rolland, J. P., & Parker, W. D. (1998). Cross-cultural assessment of the five-factor model: The revised NEO personality inventory. *Journal of Cross-Cultural Psychology, 29*, 171–188.

McCrae, R. H., Stone, S. V., Fagan, P. J., & Costa, Jr., P. T. (1998). Identifying causes of disagreement between self-reports and spouse ratings of personality. *Journal of Personality, 66*, 285–313.

McCrink, K., & Wynn, K. (2004). Large-number addition and subtraction by 9-month-old infants. *Psychological Science, 15*, 776–781.

McDaniel, M. A., & Einstein, G. O. (1986). Bizarre imagery as an effective memory aid: The importance of distinctiveness. *Journal of Experimental Psychology: Learning, Memory, & Cognition, 12*, 54–65.

McDaniel, M. A., & Einstein, G. O. (2005). Material appropriate difficulty: A framework for determining when difficulty is desirable for improving learning. In A. F. Healy (Ed.), *Experimental cognitive psychology and its applications* (pp. 73–85). Washington, DC: American Psychological Association.

McDaniel, M. A., Einstein, G. O., DeLosh, E. L., & May, C. P. (1995). The bizarreness effect: It's not surprising, it's complex. *Journal of Experimental Psychology: Learning, Memory, & Cognition, 21*, 422–435.

McDermott, K. B., & Roediger, H. L., III. (1998). Attempting to avoid illusory memories: Robust false recognition of associates persists under conditions of explicit warnings and immediate testing. *Journal of Memory and Language, 39*, 508–520.

McDougall, W. (1908/1960). *Introduction to social psychology.* New York: Barnes & Noble.

McEwen, B. S. (1997). Possible mechanisms for atrophy of the human hippocampus. *Molecular Psychiatry, 2*, 255–262.

McEwen, B. S. (1998). Stress, adaptation, and disease: Allostasis and allostatic load. In S. M. McCann, J. M. Lipton, E. M. Sternberg, et al. (Eds.), *Annals of the New York Academy of Sciences: Neuroimmunomodulation: Molecular aspects, integrative systems, and clinical advances* (Vol. 840, pp. 33–44). New York: New York Academy of Sciences.

McEwen, B. S. (2000). Allostasis and allostatic load: Implications for neuropsychopharmacology. *Neuropsychopharmacology, 22*, 108–124.

McEwen, B. S. (2003). Mood disorders and medical illness: Mood disorders and allostatic load. *Biological Psychiatry, 54*, 200–207.

McEwen, B. S., Biron, C. A., Brunson, K. W., Bulloch, K., Chambers, W. H., Dhabhar, F. S., et al. (1997). The role of adrenocorticoids as modulators of immune function in health and disease: Neural, endocrine and immune interactions. *Brain Research Review, 23*, 79–133.

McEwen, B. S., & Schmeck, H. M., Jr. (1994). *The hostage brain.* New York: Rockefeller University Press.

McEwen, B. S., & Seeman, T. (1999). Protective and damaging effects of mediators of stress: Elaborating and testing the concepts of allostasis and allostatic load. In N. E. Adler, M. Marmot, B. S. McEwen, & J. Stewart, (Eds.), *Socioeconomic status and health in industrial nations: Social, psychological, and biological pathways* (pp. 30–47). New York: New York Academy of Sciences.

McEwen, B. S., & Wingfield, J. C. (2003). Response to commentaries on the concept of allostasis. *Hormones & Behavior, 43*, 28–30.

McFadden, D. (1982). *Tinnitus: Facts, theories and treatments.* Washington, DC: National Academy Press.

McFadden, D., & Pasanen, E. G. (1999). Spontaneous otoacoustic emissions in heterosexuals, homosexuals, and bisexuals. *Journal of the Acoustical Society of America, 105*, 2403–2413.

McFadden, D., & Plattsmier, H. S. (1983). Aspirin can potentiate the temporary hearing loss induced by intense sounds. *Hearing Research, 9*, 295–316.

McFarland, L. A., Lev-Arey, D. M., & Ziegert, J. C. (2003). An examination of stereotype threat in a motivational context. *Human Performance, 16*, 181–205.

McGaugh, J. L. (2000). Memory—a century of consolidation. *Science, 287*, 248–251.

McGaugh, J. L., & Herz, M. J. (1972). *Memory consolidation.* San Francisco: Albion.

McGillicuddy-De Lisi, A., & De Lisi, R. (Eds.). (2002). *Biology, society, and behavior: The development of sex differences in cognition.* Westport, CT: Ablex.

McGoldrick, M., Giordano, J., & Pearce, J. K. (Eds.). (1996). *Ethnicity and family therapy* (2nd ed.). New York: Guilford Press.

McGorry, P. D., & Edwards, J. (1998). The feasibility and effectiveness of early intervention in psychotic disorders: The Australian experience. *International Clinical Psychopharmacology, 13*(Suppl 1), S47–S52.

McGraw, K., Hoffman, R. I., Harker, C., & Herman, J. H. (1999). The development of circadian rhythms in a human infant. *Sleep, 22*, 303–310.

McGraw, M. B. (1943). *The neuromuscular maturation of the human infant.* New York: Columbia University Press.

McGue, M., Bouchard, T. J., Jr., Iacono, W. G., & Lykken, D. T. (1993). Behavioral genetics of cognitive ability: A life-span perspective. In R. Plomin & G. E. McClearn (Eds.), *Nature, nurture & psychology* (pp. 59–76). Washington, DC: American Psychological Association.

McGue, M., & Lykken, D. T. (1992). Genetic influence on the risk of divorce. *Psychological Science, 3*, 368–373.

McGuffin, P., & Gottesman, I. I. (1985). Genetic influences on normal and abnormal development. In M. Rutter & L. Hersov (Eds.), *Child and adolescent psychiatry: Modern approaches* (2nd ed., pp. 17–33). Oxford, England: Blackwell Scientific.

McGuffin, P., & Katz, R. (1993). Genes, adversity and depression. In R. Plomim & G. E. McClearn (Eds.), *Nature, nurture, and psychology* (pp. 217–230). Washington, DC: American Psychological Association.

McGuffin, P., Katz, R., Aldrich, J., & Bebbington, P. (1988). The Camberwell Collaborative Depression Study. II. Investigation of family members. *British Journal of Psychiatry, 152*, 766–774.

McHugh, T. J., Blum, K. I., Tsien, J., Tonegawa, S., & Wilson, M. (1996). Impaired hippocampal representation of space in CA1-specific NMDAR1 knockout mice. *Cell, 87*, 1339–1349.

McIntyre, R. B., Paulson, R. M., & Lord, C. G. (2003). Alleviating women's mathematics stereotype threat through salience of group achievements. *Journal of Experimental Social Psychology, 39*, 83–90.

McKay, P. F., Doverspike, D., Bowen-Hilton, D., & Martin, Q. D. (2002). Stereotype threat effects on the Raven Advanced Progressive Matrices scores of African-Americans. *Journal of Applied Social Psychology, 32,* 767–787.

McKellar, P. (1965). The investigation of mental images. In S. A. Bartnet & A. McLaren (Eds.), *Penguin science survey B (biological sciences)* (pp. 79–94). New York: Penguin.

McKelvie, P., & Low, J. (2002). Listening to Mozart does not improve children's spatial ability: Final curtains for the Mozart effect. *British Journal of Developmental Psychology, 20,* 241–258.

McKelvie, S. J. (2000). Quantifying the availability heuristic with famous names. *North American Journal of Psychology, 2,* 347–356.

McKenna, K. Y. A., Green, A. S., & Gleason, M. E. J. (2002). Relationship formation on the Internet: What's the big attraction? *Journal of Social Issues, 58,* 9–31.

McKenna, R. J. (1972). Some effects of anxiety level and food cues on the eating behavior of obese and normal subjects: A comparison of the Schachterian and psychosomatic conceptions. *Journal of Personality and Social Psychology, 22,* 311–319.

McKnight, J., & Malcolm, J. (2000). Is male homosexuality maternally linked? *Psychology, Evolution & Gender, 2,* 229–239.

McLaughlin, S., & Margolskee, R. F. (1994). The sense of taste. *American Scientist, 82,* 538–545.

McLean, A. A. (1980). *Work stress.* Reading, MA: Addison-Wesley.

McLeod, P. L., & Lobel, S. A. (1992). The effects of ethinic diversity on idea generation in small groups. *Academy of Management Best Paper Proceedings, 22,* 227–231.

McMillen, D. L., & Austin, J. B. (1971). Effect of positive feedback on compliance following transgression. *Psychonomic Science, 24,* 59–61.

McNally, R. J. (2003). *Remembering trauma.* Cambridge, MA: Harvard University Press.

McNally, R. J. (2004). Is traumatic amnesia nothing but psychiatric folklore? *Cognitive Behaviour Therapy, 33,* 97–101.

McNally, R. J., & Clancy, S. A. (in press). Sleep paralysis, sexual abuse, and space alien abduction. *Transcultural Psychiatry.*

McNally, R. J., Lasko, N. B., Clancy, S. A., Macklin, M. L., Pitman, R. K., & Orr, S. P. (2004). Psychophysiological responding during script-driven imagery in people reporting abduction by space aliens. *Psychological Science, 15,* 493–497.

McNally, R. J., & Shin, L. M. (1995). Association of intelligence with severity of posttraumatic stress disorder symptoms in Vietnam combat veterans. *American Journal of Psychiatry, 152,* 936–938.

McNeil, T. F., Cantor-Graae, E., & Weinberger, D. R. (2000). Relationship of obstetric complications and differences in size of brain structures in monozygotic twin pairs discordant for schizophrenia. *American Journal of Psychiatry, 157,* 203–212.

McRorie, M., & Cooper, C. (2004). Synaptic transmission correlates of general mental ability. *Intelligence, 32,* 263–275.

Mealey, L., Bridgestock, R., & Townsend, G. C. (1999). Symmetry and perceived facial attractiveness: A monozygotic co-twin comparison. *Journal of Personality and Social Psychology, 76,* 151–158.

Meaney, M. J., Mitchell, J. B., Aitken, D. H., Bhatnagar, S., Bodnoff, S. R., Iny, L. J., & Sarrieau, A. (1991). The effects of neonatal handling on the development of the adrenocortical response to stress: Implications for neuropathology and cognitive deficits in later life. *Psychoneuroendocrinology, 16,* 85–103.

Medin, D. L., Lynch, E. B., & Solomon, K. O. (2000). Are there kinds of concepts? *Annual Review of Psychology, 51,* 121–147.

Medin, D. L., & Schaffer, M. M. (1978). A context theory of classification learning. *Psychological Review, 85,* 207–238.

Mednick, S. (1962). The associative basis of the creative process. *Psychological Review, 69,* 220–232.

Mednick, S. A., Gabrielli, W. F., & Hutchings, B. (1984). Genetic factors in criminal behavior: Evidence from an adoption cohort. *Science, 224,* 891–893.

Mednick, S. A., Watson, J. B., Huttunen, M., Cannon, T. D., Katila, H., Machon, R., et al. (1998). A two-hit working model of the etiology of schizophrenia. In M. F. Lenzenweger & R. H. Dworkin (Eds.), *Origins and development of schizophrenia: Advances in experimental psychopathology* (pp. 27–66). Washington, DC: American Psychological Association.

Mednick, S., Nakayama, K., & Stickgold, R. (2003). Sleep-dependent learning: A nap is as good as a night. *Nature Neuroscience, 6,* 697–698.

Meehl, P. (1960). The cognitive activity of the clinician. *American Psychologist, 15,* 19–27.

Meeter, M., & Murre, J. M. J. (2004). Consolidation of long-term memory: Evidence and alternatives. *Psychological Bulletin, 130,* 843–857.

Mehl, L. E. (1994). Hypnosis and conversion of the breech to the vertex position. *Archives of Family Medicine, 3,* 881–887l.

Mehl-Madrona, L. E. (2004). Hypnosis to facilitate uncomplicated birth. *American Journal of Clinical Hypnosis, 46,* 299–312.

Meins, E., Fernyhough, C., Wainwright, R., Gupta, M. D., Fradley, E., & Tuckey, M. (2002). Maternal mind-mindedness and attachment security as predictors of theory of mind understanding. *Child Development, 73,* 1715–1726.

Meister, I. G., Krings, T., Foltys, H., Boroojerdi, B., Müller, M., Töpper, R., & Thron, A. (2004). Playing piano in the mind—an fMRI study on music imagery and performance in pianists. *Cognitive Brain Research, 19,* 219–228.

Melding, P. S. (1995). How do older people respond to chronic pain? A review of coping with pain and illness in elders. *Pain Review, 2,* 65–75.

Mellet, E., Petit, L., Mazoyer, B., Denis, M., & Tzourio, N. (1998). Reopening the mental imagery debate: Lessons from functional neuroanatomy. *NeuroImage, 8,* 129–139.

Mello, C. V., Vicario, D. S., & Clayton, D. F. (1992). Song presentation induces gene expression in the songbird forebrain. *Proceedings of the National Academy of Science, USA, 89,* 6818–6822.

Meltzoff, A. N., & Moore, M. K. (1977). Imitation of facial and manual gestures by human neonates. *Science, 198,* 75–78.

Melzack, R., & Wall, P. D. (1982). *The challenge of pain.* New York: Basic Books.

Menyuk, P., Liebergott, J. W., & Schultz, M. C. (1995). *Early language development in full-term and premature infants.* Hillsdale, NJ: Erlbaum.

Menzies, R. G., & Clarke, J. C. (1993). The etiology of childhood water phobia. *Behaviour Research & Therapy, 31,* 499–501.

Menzies, R. G., & Clarke, J. C. (1995a). The etiology of acrophobia and its relationship to severity and individual response patterns. *Behaviour Research & Therapy, 33,* 795–803.

Menzies R. G., & Clarke, J. C. (1995b). The etiology of phobias: A nonassociative account. *Clinical Psychology Review, 15,* 23–48.

Merchant, H., Battaglia-Mayer, A., & Georgopoulos, A. P. (2003). Functional organization of parietal neuronal responses to optic-flow stimuli. *Journal of Neurophysiology, 90,* 675–682.

Merckelbach, H., Devilly, G. J., & Rassin, E. (2002). Alters in dissociative identity disorder. Metaphors or genuine entities? *Clinical Psychology Review, 22,* 481–497.

Merlo, A., & Schotter, A. (2003). Learning by not doing: An experimental investigation of observational learning. *Games & Economic Behavior, 42,* 116–136.

Merrick, E. N. (1995). Adolescent childbearing as career "choice": Perspective from an ecological context. *Journal of Counseling & Development, 73,* 288–295.

Merzenich, M. M., Jenkins, W. M., Johnston, P., Shreiner, C., Miller, S. L., & Tallal, P. (1996). Temporal processing deficits of language-learning impaired children ameliorated by training. *Science, 271,* 77–81.

Merzenich, M. M., Kaas, J. H., Wall, J. T., Sur, M., Nelson, R. J., & Felleman, D. J. (1983a). Progression of change following median nerve section in the cortical representation of the hand in areas 3b and 1 in adult owl and squirrel monkeys. *Neuroscience, 10(3),* 639–665.

Merzenich, M. M., Kaas, J. H., Wall, J., Nelson, R. J., & Sur, M. (1983b). Topographic reorganization of somatosensory cortical areas 3b and 1 in adult monkeys following restricted deafferentation. *Neuroscience, 8,* 33–55.

Messinger, S. M. (1998). Pleasure and complexity: Berlyne revisited. *Journal of Psychology, 132,* 558–560.

Meston, C. M., & Frohlich, P. F. (2000). The neurobiology of sexual function. *Archives of General Psychiatry, 57,* 1012–1030.

Metcalfe, J. (1986). Premonitions of insight predict impending error. *Journal of Experimental Psychology: Learning, Memory, and Cognition, 12,* 623–634.

Meyer, B., Olivier, L., & Roth, D. A., (2005). Please don't leave me! BIS/BAS, attachment styles, and responses to a relationship threat. *Personality and Individual Differences, 38,* 151–162.

Meyer, D. E., & Schvaneveldt, R. W. (1971). Facilitation in recognizing pairs of words: Evidence of a dependence between retrieval operations. *Journal of Experimental Psychology, 90,* 227–234.

Meyer, G. J. (2002). Exploring possible ethnic differences and bias in the Rorschach Comprehensive System. *Journal of Personality Assessment, 78,* 104–129.

Meyer, G. J., & Archer, R. P. (2001). The hard science of Rorschach research: What do we know and where do we go? *Psychological Assessment, 13,* 486–502.

Michael, T., Ehlers, A., Halligan, S. L., & Clark, D. M. (in press). Unwanted memories of assault: What intrusion characteristics are associated with PTSD? *Behaviour Research and Therapy.*

Michalski, R. L., & Shackelford, T. K. (2002). An attempted replication of the relationships between birth order and personality. *Journal of Research in Personality, 36,* 182–188.

Mickelson, K. D., Kessler, R. C., & Shaver, P. R. (1997). Adult attachment in a nationally representative sample. *Journal of Personality & Social Psychology, 73,* 1092–1106.

Mignot, E. (2001). A commentary on the neurobiology of the hypocretin/orexin system. *Neuropsychopharmacology, 25,* S5-S13.

Miklowitz, D. J., Goldstein, M. J., Nuechterlein, K. H., Snyder, K. S., & Mintz, J. (1988). Family factors and the course of bipolar affective disorder. *Archives of General Psychiatry, 45,* 225–231.

Mikulincer, M. (1994). *Human learned helplessness: A coping perspective.* New York: Plenum.

Mikulincer, M., & Horesh, N. (1999). Adult attachment style and the perception of others: The role of projective mechanisms. *Journal of Personality and Social Psychology, 76,* 1022–1034.

Mikulincer, M., & Orbach, I. (1995). Attachment styles and repressive defensiveness: The accessibility and architecture of affective memories. *Journal of Personality & Social Psychology, 68,* 917–925.

Miles, L. E. M., Raynal, D. M., & Wilson, M. A. (1977). Blind man living in normal society has circadian rhythms of 24.9 hours. *Science, 198,* 421–423.

Milgram, S. (1963). Behavioral study of obedience. *Journal of Abnormal and Social Psychology, 67,* 371–378.

Milgram, S. (1965). Some conditions of obedience and disobedience to authority. *Human Relations, 18,* 57–76.

Milgram, S. (1974). *Obedience to authority: An experimental view.* New York: Harper & Row.

Miller, A. G., Collins, B. E., & Brief, D. E. (1995). Perspectives on obedience to authority: The legacy of the Milgram experiments. *Journal of Social Issues, 51,* 1–19.

Miller, B. L., & Hou, C. E. (2004). Portraits of artists: Emergence of visual creativity in dementia. *Archives of Neurology, 61,* 842–844.

Miller, E. M. (1992). On the correlation of myopia and intelligence. *Genetic, Social and General Psychology Monographs 118,* 361–383.

Miller, G. A. (1956). The magical number seven, plus or minus two: Some limits on our capacity for processing information. *Psychological Review, 63,* 81–97.

Miller, G. E., Cohen, S., & Ritchey, A. K. (2002). Chronic psychological stress and the regulation of pro-inflammatory cytokines: A glucocorticoid resistance model. *Health Psychology, 21,* 531–541.

Miller, G. E., Dopp, J. M., Stevens, S. Y., & Fahey, J. L. (1999). Psychosocial predictors of natural killer cell mobilzation during marital conflict. *Health Psychology, 18,* 262–271.

Miller, I. W., Keitner, G. E., Whisman, M. A., Ryan, C. E., Epstein, N. B., & Bishop, D. S. (1992). Depressed patients with dysfunctional families: Description and course of illness. *Journal of Abnormal Psychology, 101,* 637–646.

Miller, J. K., & Gergen, K. J. (1998). Life on the line: The therapeutic potentials of computer mediated conversation. *Journal of Marital and Family Therapy, 24,* 189–202.

Miller, J. M., Boudreaux, M. C., & Regan, F. A. (1995). A case-control study of cocaine use in pregnancy. *American Journal of Obstetrics and Gynecology, 172,* 180–185.

Miller, L. C., Putcha-Bhagavatula, A., & Pedersen, W. C. (2002). Men's and women's mating preferences: Distinct evolutionary mechanisms? *Current Directions in Psychological Science, 11,* 88–93.

Miller, M. G., & Ross, M. (1975). Self-serving biases in attribution of causality: Fact or fiction? *Psychological Bulletin, 82,* 313–325.

Miller, M., Mangano, C., Park, Y., Goel, R., Plotnick, G., & Vogel, R. A. (2005, March 7). Divergent effects of laughter and mental stress on endothelial function: Potential impact of entertainment. Scientific session of the American College of Cardiology, Orlando, FL.

Miller, N. E. (1959). Liberalization of basic S-R concepts: Extensions to conflict behavior, motivation, and social learning. In S. Koch (Ed.), *Psychology: A study of science* (Vol. 2). New York: McGraw-Hill.

Miller, N., Maruayama, G., Beaber, R. J., & Valone, K. (1976). Speed of speech and persuasion. *Journal of Personality and Social Psychology, 34,* 615–624.

Miller, T. Q., Smith, T. W., Turner, C. W., Guijarro, M. L., & Hallet, A. J. (1996). A meta-analytic review of research on hostility and physical health. *Psychological Bulletin, 119,* 322–348.

Miller, T. W., Veltkamp, L. J., Kraus, R. F., Lane, T., & Heister, T. (1999). An adolescent vampire cult in rural America: Clinical issues and case study. *Child Psychiatry & Human Development, 29,* 209–219.

Miller, W. B., Pasta, D. J., MacMurray, J., Chiu, C., Wu, H., & Comings, D. E. (1999). Dopamine receptor genes are associated with age at first sexual intercourse. *Journal of Biosocial Science, 31,* 43–54.

Millet, B., Leclaire, M., Bourdel, M. C., Loo, H., Tezcan, E., & Kuloglu, M. (2000). Comparison of sociodemographic, clinical and phenomenological characteristics of Turkish and French patients suffering from obsessive-compulsive disorder. *Canadian Journal of Psychiatry, 45,* 848.

Millon, T. (1975). Reflections on Rosenhan's "On being sane in insane places." *Journal of Abnormal Psychology, 84,* 456–461.

Mills, D. L., Coffey-Corina, S., & Neville, H. J. (1997). Language comprehension and cerebral specialization from 13 to 20 months. *Developmental Neuropsychology, 13,* 397–445.

Milner, A. D., & Goodale, M. A. (1995). *The visual brain in action.* New York: Oxford University Press.

Milner, B., Corkin, S., & Teuber, H. L. (1968). Further analysis of the hippocampal amnesic syndrome: 14-year followup study of H. M. *Neuropsychologia, 6,* 215–234.

Milton, J., & Weisman, R. (1999a). Does psi exist? Lack of replication of an anomalous process of information transfer. *Psychological Bulletin, 125,* 387–391.

Milton, J., & Weisman, R. (1999b). A meta-analysis of mass-media tests of extrasensory perception. *British Journal of Psychology, 90,* 235–240.

Mineka, S., Davison, M., Cook, M., & Keir, R. (1984). Observational conditioning of snake fear in Rhesus monkeys. *Journal of Abnormal Psychology, 93,* 355–372.

Mingroni, M. A. (2004). The secular rise in IQ: Giving heterosis a closer look. *Intelligence, 32,* 65–83.

Minuchin, S. (1974). *Families and family therapy.* Cambridge, MA: Harvard University Press.

Minuchin, S., & Fishman, H. C. (1981). *Family therapy techniques.* Cambridge, MA: Harvard University Press.

Miscallef, J., & Blin, O. (2001). Neurobiology and clinical pharmacology of obsessive-compulsive disorder. *Clinical Neuropharmacology, 24,* 191–207.

Mischel, W. (1984). Convergences and challenges in the search for consistency. *American Psychologist, 39,* 351–364.

Mischel, W. (2004). Toward an integrative science of the person. *Annual Review of Psychology, 55,* 1–22.

Mischel, W., & Peake, P. K. (1982). Beyond déjà vu in the search for cross-situational consistency. *Psychological Review, 90,* 394–402.

Mischel, W., & Shoda, Y. (1995). A cognitive-affective system theory of personality: Reconceptualizing situations, dispositions, dynamics, and invariance in personality structure. *Psychological Review, 102,* 246–268.

Mischel, W., Shoda, Y., & Rodriguez, M. L. (1989). Delay of gratification in children. *Science, 244,* 933–938.

Mishkin, M. (1982). A memory system in the monkey. *Philosophical Transactions of the Royal Society of London Series B, 298,* 85–95.

Mishkin, M., & Appenzeller, T. (1987). The anatomy of memory. *Scientific American, 256,* 80–89.

Mitchell, J. E., Halmi, K., Wilson, G. T., Agras, W. S., Kraemer, H., & Crow, S. (2002). A randomized secondary treatment study of women with bulimia nervosa who fail to respond to CBT. *International Journal of Eating Disorders, 32,* 271–281.

Miyazaki, K. (1993). Absolute pitch as an inability: Identification of musical intervals in a tonal context. *Music Perception, 11,* 55–71.

Modell, J. (1996). Family niche and intellectual bent. [Review of *Born to Rebel* by F. J. Sulloway]. *Science, 275,* 624.

Modell, J., Mountz, J., Curtis, G., & Greden, J. (1989). Neurophysiologic dysfunction in basal ganglia/limbic striatal and thalamocortical circuits as a pathogenetic mechanisms of obsessive-compulsive disorder. *Journal of Neuropsychiatry, 1,* 27–36.

Mogilner, A., Grossman, J. A., Ribary, U., Joliot, M., Volkman, J., Rapaport, D., et al. (1993). Somatosensory cortical plasticity in adult humans revealed by magnetoencephalography. *Proceedings of the National Academy of Sciences, USA, 90*(8), 3593–3597.

Mojtabai, R., Nicholson, R. A., & Carpenter, B. N. (1998). Role of psychosocial treatments in management of schizophrenia: A meta-analytic review of controlled outcome studies. *Schizophrenia Bulletin, 24,* 569–587.

Moll, J., de Oliveira-Souza, R., Moll, F. T., Ignácio, F. A., Bramati, I. E., Caparelli-Dáquer, E. M., & Eslinger, P. J. (2005). The moral affiliations of disgust: A functional MRI study. *Cognitive & Behavioral Neurology, 18,* 68–78.

Moller, J., Theorell, T., de Faire, U., Ahlbom, A., & Hallqvist, J. (2005). Work related stressful life events and the risk of myocardial infarction. Case-control and case-crossover analyses within the Stockholm Heart Epidemiology Programme (SHEEP). *Journal of Epidemiological Community Health, 59,* 23–30.

Money, J. (1975). Ablatio penis: normal male infant sex-reassigned as a girl. *Archives of Sexual Behavior, 4,* 65–71.

Monk, T. H., Buysse, D. J., Reynolds, C. F., Berga, S. L., Jarrett, D. B., Begley, A. E., & Kupfer, D. J. (1997). Circadian rhythms in human performance and mood under constant conditions. *Journal of Sleep Research, 6,* 9–18.

Monnier, P. (2003). Redundant coding assessed in a visual search task. *Displays, 24*, 49–55.

Monroe, S. M., & Depue, R. A. (1991). Life stress and depression. In J. Becker & A. Kleinman (Eds.), *Psychosocial aspects of depression* (pp. 101–130). Hillsdale, NJ: Erlbaum.

Montague, P. R., Hyman, S. E., & Cohen, J. D. (2004). Computational roles for dopamine in behavioural control. *Nature, 431*, 760–767.

Montoya, R. M., & Horton, R. S. (2004). On the importance of cognitive evaluation as a determinant of interpersonal attraction. *Journal of Personality & Social Psychology, 86*, 696–712.

Moody, D. B., Stebbins, W. C., & May, B. J. (1990). Auditory perception of communication signals by Japanese monkeys. In W. C. Stebbins & M. A. Berkley (Eds.), *Comparative perception: Complex signals* (pp. 311–343). New York: Wiley.

Moore, A. B., & Conway, T. (2004). Speaking clearly: Reviewing aphasia from assessment to treatment. *Journal of the International Neuropsychological Society, 10*, 1022–1024.

Moore, B. C. J. (1982). *Introduction to the psychology of hearing* (2nd ed.). New York: Academic Press.

Moore, K. L. (1998). *The developing human: Clinically oriented embryology* (6th ed.). Philadelphia: Saunders.

Moore-Ede, M. (1982). *The clocks that time us: Physiology of the circadian timing system.* Cambridge, MA: Harvard University Press.

Moran, P. (1999). The epidemiology of antisocial personality disorder. *Social Psychiatry & Psychiatric Epidemiology, 34*, 231–242.

Moreland, R. L., & Zajonc, R. B. (1982). Exposure effects in person perception: Familiarity, similarity, and attraction. *Journal of Experimental Social Psychology, 18*, 395–415.

Morf, C. C., & Rhodewalt, F. (2001). Unraveling the paradoxes of narcissism: A dynamic self-regulatory processing model. *Psychological Inquiry, 12*, 177–196.

Morgan, C. A., III, Rasmusson, A. M., Winters, B., Hauger, R. L., Morgan, J., Hazlett, G., & Southwick, S. (2003). Trauma exposure rather than posttraumatic stress disorder is associated with reduced baseline plasma neuropeptide-Y levels. *Biological Psychiatry, 54*, 1087–1091.

Morgan, J. L., & Demuth, K. D. (1996). *Signal to syntax: Bootstrapping from speech to grammar in early acquisition.* Hillsdale, NJ: Erlbaum.

Morgan, M. A., Schulkin, J., & LeDoux, J. E. (2003). Ventral medial prefrontal cortex and emotional perseveration: The memory for prior extinction training. *Behavioural Brain Research, 146*, 121–130.

Morgan, M. J., McFie, L., Fleetwood, L. H., & Robinson, J. A. (2002). Ecstasy (MDMA): Are the psychological problems associated with its use reversed by prolonged abstinence? *Psychopharmacology, 159*, 294–303.

Morgane, P. J., Austin-LaFrance, R., Bronzino, J., Tonkiss, J., Diaz-Cintra, S., Cintra, L., et al. (1993). Prenatal malnutrition and development of the brain. *Neuroscience and Biobehavioral Reviews, 17*, 91–128.

Mori, H., Kamada, M., Maegawa, M., Yamamoto, S., Aono, T., Futaki, S., et al. (1998). Enzymatic activation of immunoglobulin binding factor in female reproductive tract. *Biochemical and Biophysical Research Communications, 246*, 409–413.

Morling, B., Kitayama, S., & Miyamoto, Y. (2003). American and Japanese women use different coping strategies during normal pregnancy. *Personality & Social Psychology Bulletin, 29*, 1533–1546.

Morris, A. L., & Harris, C. L. (2004). Repetition blindness: Out of sight or out of mind? *Journal of Experimental Psychology: Human Perception & Performance, 30*, 913–922.

Morris, C. D., Bransford, J. D., & Franks, J. J. (1977). Levels of processing versus transfer-appropriate processing. *Journal of Verbal Learning and Verbal Behavior, 16*, 519–533.

Morris, J., & Dolan, R. (2002). The amygdala and unconscious fear processing. In B. de Gelder, E. de Haan, E., & C. Heywood (Eds.), *Out of mind: Varieties of unconscious processes* (pp. 185–204). London: Oxford University Press.

Morris, M. W., & Peng, K. (1994). Culture and cause: American and Chinese attributions for social and physical events. *Journal of Personality and Social Psychology, 67*, 949–971.

Morris, R. (1984). Developments of a water-maze procedure for studying spatial learning in the rat. *Journal of Neuroscience Methods, 11*, 47–60.

Morris, S. (1979) *The book of strange facts and useless information.* Garden City, NY: Doubleday.

Morris, W. N., Worchel, S., Bois, J. L., Pearson, J. A., Rountree, C. A., Samaha, G. M., et al. (1976). Collective coping with stress: Group reactions to fear, anxiety, and ambiguity. *Journal of Personality and Social Psychology, 33*, 674–679.

Morris, W., & Miller, R. (1975). The effects of consensus-breaking and consensus preempting partner onreduction in conformity. *Journal of Experimental Social Psychology, 11*, 215–223.

Morrison, A. P., French, P., Walford, L., Lewis, S. W., Kilcommons, A., Green, J., Parker, S., & Bentall, R. P. (2004). Cognitive therapy for the prevention of psychosis in people at ultra-high risk: Randomised controlled trial. *British Journal of Psychiatry, 185*, 291–297.

Morrison, E. W., & Bies, R. J. (1991). Impression management in the feedback-seeking process: A literature review and research agenda. *Academy of Management Review, 16*, 322–341.

Morrison, K. H., Bradley, R., & Westen, D. (2003). The external validity of controlled clinical trials of psychotherapy for depression and anxiety: A naturalistic study. *Psychology & Psychotherapy: Theory, Research & Practice, 76*, 109–132.

Morse, D. R., Martin, J. S., Furst, M. L., & Dubin, L. L. (1977). A physiological and subjective evaluation of meditation, hypnosis, and relaxation. *Psychosomatic Medicine, 39*, 304–324.

Mortensen, P. B., Pedersen, C. B., Westergaard, T., Wohlfahrt, J., Ewald, H., Mors, O., et al. (1999). Effects of family history and place and season of birth on the risk of schizophrenia. *New England Journal of Medicine, 340*, 603–608.

Moscovitch, M., & Craik, F. I. M. (1976). Depth of processing, retrieval cues, and uniqueness of encoding as factors in recall. *Journal of Verbal Learning and Verbal Behavior, 15*, 447–458.

Moser, M., Lehofer, M., Hoehn-Saric, R., McLeod, D. R., Hildebrandt, G., Steinbrenner, B., et al. (1998). Increased heart rate in depressed subjects in spite of unchanged autonomic balance. *Journal of Affective Disorders, 48*, 115–124.

Moskowitz, D. S. (1993). Dominance and friendliness: On the interaction of gender and situation. *Journal of Personality, 61*, 387–409.

Mowrer, O. H. (1939). A stimulus-response analysis of anxiety and its role as a reinforcing agent. *Psychological Review, 46*, 553–565.

Mrazek, P., & Haggerty, R. (1994). *Reducing risks for mental disorders: Frontiers for preventive intervention research.* Washington, DC: National Academy Press.

Mroczek, D. K., & Almeida, D. M. (2004). The effect of daily stress, personality, and age on daily negative affect. *Journal of Personality, 72*, 355–378.

Muehlenhard, C. L., & Linton, M. A. (1987). Date rape and sexual aggression in dating situations: Incidence and risk factors. *Journal of Counseling Psychology, 34*, 186–196.

Mullen, B., Anthony, T., Salas, E., & Driskell, J. E. (1994). Group cohesiveness and quality of decision making: An integration of tests of the groupthink hypothesis. *Small Group Research, 25*, 189–204.

Mullen, B., & Johnson, C. (1990). Distinctiveness-based illusory correlations and stereotyping: A meta-analytic integration. *British Journal of Social Psychology, 29*, 11–28.

Mulvany, F., O'Callaghan, E., Takei, N., Byrne, M., Fearson, P., & Larkin, C. (2001). Effect of social class at birth on risk and presentation of schizophrenia: Case control study. *British Medical Journal, 323*, 1398–1401.

Mumford, M. D. (2001). Something old, something new: Revisiting Guilford's conception of creative problem solving. *Creativity Research Journal, 13*, 267–276.

Münte, T. F., Altenmüller, E., & Jäncke, L. (2002). The musician's brain as a model of neuroplasticity. *Nature Reviews Neuroscience, 3*, 473–478.

Münte, T. F., Kohlmetz, C., Nager, W., & Altenmüller, E. (2001). Superior auditory spatial tuning in conductors. *Nature, 409*, 580.

Murata, K., Weihe, P., Renzoni, A., Debes, F., Vasconcelos, R., Zino, F., et al. (1999). Delayed evoked potentials in children exposed to methylmercury from seafood. *Neurotoxicology & Teratology, 21*, 343–348.

Muris, P., & Meesters, C. (2002). Attachment, behavioral inhibition, and anxiety disorder symptoms in normal adolescents. *Journal of Psychopathology & Behavioral Assessment, 24*, 97–106.

Murphy, C. (1986). Taste and smell in the elderly. In H. L. Meiselman & R. S. Rivlin (Eds.), *Clinical measurement of taste and smell* (pp. 343–371). New York: Macmillan.

Murphy, F. C., Nimmo-Smith, I., & Lawrence, A. D. (2003). Functional neuroanatomy of emotions: A meta-analysis. *Cognitive, Affective & Behavioral Neuroscience, 3*, 207–233.

Murphy, L. J., & Mitchell, D. L. (1998). When writing helps to heal: E-mail as therapy. *British Journal of Guidance and Counseling, 26*, 21–32.

Murray, C. J. L., & Lopez, A. D. (Eds.). (1996). *The global burden of disease. A comprehensive assessment of mortality and disability from diseases, injuries, and risk factors in 1990 and projected to 2020.* Cambridge, MA: Harvard School of Public Health.

Murray, E. J., Lamnin, A., & Carver, C. (1989). Emotional expression in written essays and psychotherapy. *Journal of Social and Clinical Psychology, 8*, 414–429.

Murray, I. R., Arnott, J. L., & Rohwer, E. A. (1996). Emotional stress in synthetic speech: Progress and future directions. *Speech Communication, 20,* 85–91.

Murzynski, J. & Degelman, D. (1996). Body language of women and judgments of vulnerability to sexual assault. *Journal of Applied Social Psychology 26,* 1617–1626.

Myers, C. E., McGlinchey-Berroth, R., Warren, S., Monti, L., Brawn, C. M., & Gluck, M. A. (2000). Latent learning in medial temporal amnesia: Evidence for disrupted representational but preserved attentional processes. *Neuropsychology, 14,* 3–15.

Myers, D. G. (2000). The funds, friends, and faith of happy people. *American Psychologist, 55,* 56–67.

Nadel, L., & Hardt, O. (2004). The spatial brain. *Neuropsychology, 18,* 473–476.

Nader, K., Bechara, A., & van der Kooy, D. (1997). Neurobiological constraints on behavioral models of motivation. *Annual Review of Psychology, 48,* 85–114.

Nader, K., Schafe, G. E., & LeDoux, J. E. (2000). Fear memories require protein synthesis in the amygdala for reconsolidation after retrieval. *Nature, 406,* 722–726.

Nadler, J., Thompson, L., & van Boven, L. (2003). Learning negotiation skills: Four models of knowledge creation and transfer. *Management Science, 49,* 529–540.

Nagahama, Y., Okada, T., Katsumi, Y., Hayashi, T., Yamauchi, H., Oyanagi, C., et al. (2001). Dissociable mechanisms of attentional control within the human prefrontal cortex. *Cerebral Cortex, 11,* 85–92.

Nagel, E. (1979). *The structure of science: Problems in the logic of scientific explanation* (2nd ed.). Indianapolis, IN: Hackett.

Nagy, Z., Westerberg, H., & Klingberg, T. (2004). Maturation of white matter is associated with the development of cognitive functions during childhood. *Journal of Cognitive Neuroscience, 16,* 1227–1233.

Naito, T., & Lipsitt, L. P. (1969). Two attempts to condition eyelid responses in human infants. *Journal of Experimental Child Psychology, 8,* 263–270.

Nakai, Y., Fujita, T., Kuboki, T., Nozoe, S., Kubo, C., Yoshimasa, Y., et al. (2001). Nationwide survey of eating disorders in Japan. *Seishin Igaku (Clinical Psychiatry), 43,* 1373–1378.

Nakamura, J., & Csikszentmihalyi, M. (2001). Catalytic creativity: The case of Linus Pauling. *American Psychologist, 56,* 337–341.

Nakatani, E., Nakgawa, A., Ohara, Y., Goto, S., Uozumi, N., Iwakiri, M., Yamamotob, Y., Motomura, K., Iikura, Y., & Yamagami, T. (2003). Effects of behavior therapy on regional cerebral blood flow in obsessive-compulsive disorder. *Psychiatry Research: Neuroimaging, 124,* 113–120.

Nakayama, K., He, Z. J., & Shimojo, S. (1995). Visual surface representation: A critical link between lower-level and higher-level vision. In S. M. Kosslyn & D. N. Osherson (Eds.), *Visual cognition: An invitation to cognitive science, Vol. 2* (2nd ed., pp. 1–70). Cambridge, MA: MIT Press.

Nakayama, K., & Mackeben, M. (1989). Sustained and transient components of focal visual attention. *Vision Research, 29,* 1631–1647.

Nanda, S. B. R. (1987). *Mahatma Gandhi: His life in pictures.* [Online edition]. Delhi, India: Central Electric Press. Retrieved June, 2005 from http://www.mkgandhi.org/bio5000/birth.htm

Nasby, W., Hayden, B., & DePaulo, B. M. (1979). Attributional bias among aggressive boys to interpret unambiguous social stimuli as displays of hostility. *Journal of Abnormal Psychology 89,* 459–468.

Nathawat, S. S., Singh, R., & Singh, B. (1997). The effect of need for achievement on attributional style. *Journal of Social Psychology, 137,* 55–62.

National Admissions to Substance Abuse Treatment Services, November 2001, funded by the Substance Abuse and Mental Health Service Administration, DHHS. The latest data are available at 1-800-729-6686 or online at www.samhsa.gov

National Alliance for Caregiving & American Association of Retired Persons. (1997). *Family Caregiving in the U.S.: Findings from a National Study.* Bethesda, MD: Author.

National Heart, Lung, and Blood Institute. (2003). Who gets obstructive sleep apnea? Retrieved August 13, 2005, from http://www.nhlbi.nih.gov/health/dci/Diseases/SleepApnea/SleepApnea_WhoIsAtRisk.html

National Institute for Occupational Safety and Health. (1998). *Criteria for a recommended standard: Occupational noise exposure.* Cincinnati, OH: Author.

National Institute of Child Health and Human Development Early Child Care Research Network (2003). Does amount of time spent in child care predict socioemotional adjustment during the transition to kindergarten? *Child Development, 74,* 976–1005.

National Institute on Drug Abuse (1998). Slide Teaching Packet I, For Health Practitioners, Teachers and Neuroscientists. Section III: Introduction to Drugs of Abuse: Cocaine, Opiates (Heroin) and Marijuana (THC).

National Institute on Drug Abuse, (2003). InfoFax: Drug Addiction treatment methods. Retrieved from http://www.drugabuse.gov/infofax/treatmeth.html

National Institute on Drug Abuse. (2004, September). NIDA InfoFacts: Crack and cocaine. Retrieved August, 2005, from http://www.drugabuse.gov/DrugPages/Cocaine.html

National Science Foundation (2001). National survey of recent college graduates. Washington, DC: National Science Foundation, Division of Science Resources Statistics.

National Sleep Foundation. (1998). Omnibus sleep in America poll. Retrieved 2002, from http://www.sleepfoundation.org/publications

National Sleep Foundation. (2002). "Sleep in America" poll. Retrieved from www.sleepfoundation.org/2002poll.html

National Sleep Foundation. (2004). Sleep in America poll. Retrieved August 13, 2005, from http://www.sleepfoundation.org/hottopics/index.php?secid=16&id=143

Natsoulas, T. (2001). On the intrinsic nature of states of consciousness: Attempted inroads from the first-person perspective. *Journal of Mind & Behavior, 22,* 219–248.

Nawrot, M., Nordenstrom, B., & Olson, A. (2004). Disruption of eye movements by ethanol intoxication affects perception of depth from motion parallax. *Psychological Science, 15,* 858–865.

Nayatani, Y. (2001). Some modifications to Hering's opponent-colors theory. *Color Research & Application, 26,* 290–304.

Nayatani, Y. (2003). A modified opponent-colors theory considering chromatic strengths of various hues. *Color Research & Application, 28,* 284–297.

Neel, R. G., Tzeng, O. C., & Baysal, C. (1986). Need achievement in a cross-cultural contact study. *International Review of Applied Psychology, 35,* 225–229.

Neisser, U. (1967). *Cognitive psychology.* New York: Appleton-Century-Crofts.

Neisser, U., Boodoo, G., Bouchard, T. J., Jr., Boykin, A. W., Brody, N., Ceci, S. J., et al. (1996). Intelligence: Knowns and unknowns. *American Psychologist, 51,* 77–101.

Neisser, U., & Harsch, N. (1992). Phantom flashbulbs: False recollections of hearing news about *Challenger.* In E. Winograd & U. Neisser (Eds.), *Affect and accuracy in recall: Studies of "flashbulb memories"* (pp. 9–31). Cambridge, UK: Cambridge University Press.

Neitz, J., Neitz, M., & Kainz, P. M. (1996). Visual pigment gene structure and the severity of color vision defects. *Science, 274,* 801–804.

Nelson, C. A. (1999). Human plasticity and human development. *Current Directions in Psychological Science, 8,* 42–45.

Nelson, C. B., Heath, A. C., & Kessler, R. C. (1998). Temporal progression of alcohol dependence symptoms in the U.S. household population: Results from the National Comorbidity Survey. *Journal of Consulting & Clinical Psychology, 66,* 3, 474–483.

Nelson, K. (1981). Individual differences in language development: Implications for development and language. *Developmental Psychology, 17,* 170–187.

Nelson, L. J., & Barry, C. M. (2005). Distinguishing features of emerging adulthood: The role of self-classification as an adult. *Journal of Adolescent Research, 20,* 242–262.

Nemec, P., Altmann, J., Marhold, S., Burda, H., & Oelschläger, H. H. A. (2001). Neuroanatomy of magnetoreception: The superior colliculus involved in magnetic orientation in a mammal. *Science, 294,* 366–368.

Nemeroff, C. J., Stein, R., Diehl, N. S., & Smilach, K. M. (1994). From the Cleavers to the Clintons: Role choices and body orientation as reflected in magazine article content. *International Journal of Eating Disorders, 16,* 167–176.

Nemeroff, C., & Rozin, P. (1989). "You are what you eat": Applying the demand-free "impressions" technique to an unacknowledged belief. *Ethos, 17,* 50–69.

Nemeth, P. (1979). *An investigation into the relationship between humor and anxiety.* Unpublished doctoral dissertation. University of Maryland, College Park.

Nestler, E. J. (1997). Schizophrenia: An emerging pathophysiology. *Nature, 385,* 578–579.

Nestler, E. J., DiLeone, R., & Monteggia, L. M. (2001). Inducible, cell-targeted mutations in mice: New tools for genetically dissecting behavior. *International Journal of Comparative Psychology, 14,* 111–122.

Nettelbeck, T. (1987). Inspection time and intelligence. In P. A. Vernon (Ed.), *Speed of information processing and intelligence.* Norwood, NJ: Ablex.

Nettelbeck, T., & Wilson, C. (2004). The Flynn effect: Smarter not faster. *Intelligence, 32,* 85–93.

Neubauer, A. C., Spinath, F. M., Riemann, R., Borkenau, P., & Angleitner, A. (2000). Genetic and environmental influences on two measures of speed of information processing and their relation to psychometric intelligence: Evidence from the German Observational Study of Adult Twins. *Intelligence, 28,* 267–289.

Neugebauer, R., Hoek, H. W., & Susser, E. (1999). Prenatal exposure to wartime famine and development of antisocial personality disorder in early adulthood. *JAMA: Journal of the American Medical Association, 282,* 455–462.

Neuman, J. H., & Baron, R. A. (1998). Workplace violence and workplace aggression: Evidence concerning specific forms, potential causes, and preferred targets. *Journal of Management, 3,* 391–419.

Neumann, C., & Walker, E. F. (1996). Childhood neuromotor soft signs, behavior problems, and adult psychopathology. In T. Ollendick & R. Prinz (Eds.), *Advances in clinical child psychology.* New York: Plenum Press.

Nevid, J., Rathus, S., & Rubenstein, H. (1998). *Health in the new millennium.* New York: Worth.

Neville, H. J. (1988). Cerebral organization for spatial attention. In J. Stiles-Davis, M. Kritchevsky, & U. Bellugi (Eds.), *Spatial cognition: Brain bases and development.* Hillsdale, NJ: Erlbaum.

Neville, H. J. (1990). Intermodal competition and compensation in development. *Annals of the New York Academy of Sciences, 608,* 71–91.

Neville, H. J., & Lawson, D. (1987). Attention to central and peripheral visual space in movement detection tasks: An event-related and behavioral study: II. Congenitally deaf adults. *Brain Research, 405,* 268–283.

Neville, H. J., Schmidt, A., & Kutas, M. (1983). Altered visual-evoked potentials in congenitally deaf adults. *Brain Research, 266,* 127–132.

Newby, R. W., & Davis, J. B. (2004). Relationships between locus of control and paranormal beliefs. *Psychological Reports, 94,* 1261–1266.

Newcombe, N. S., Drummey, A. B., Fox, N. A., Lie, E., & Ottinger-Alberts, W. (2000). Remembering early childhood: How much, how, and why (or why not). *Current Directions in Psychological Science, 9,* 55–58.

Newcomer, J. W., Selke, G., Melson, A. K., Hershey, T., Craft, S., Richards, K., & Alderson, A. L. (1999). Decreased memory performance in healthy humans induced by stress-level cortisol treatment. *Archives of General Psychiatry, 56,* 527–533.

Newman, A. J., Bavelier, D., Corina, D., Jezzard, P., & Neville, H. J. (2002). A critical period for right hemisphere recruitment in American Sign Language processing. *Nature Neuroscience, 5,* 76–80.

Newman, J., Rosenbach, J. H., Burns, K. L., Latimer, B. C. Matocha, H. R. & Vogt, E. R. (1995). An experimental test of "The Mozart effect": Does listening to his music improve spatial ability? *Perceptual and Motor Skills, 81,* 1379–1387.

Newman, L. S., Duff, K. J., & Baumeister, R. F. (1997). A new look at defensive projection: Thought suppression, accessibility, and biased person perception. *Journal of Personality and Social Psychology, 72,* 980–1001.

Newman, M. G., Kenardy, J., Herman, S., & Taylor, C. B. (1997). Comparison of palmtop-computer-assisted brief cognitive-behavioral treatment to cognitive-behavioral treatment for panic disorder. *Journal of Consulting and Clinical Psychology, 65,* 178–183.

Newsome, G. L., III. (2000). A review of some promising approaches to understanding and improving thinking skills. *Journal of Research & Development in Education, 33,* 199–222.

Newton, P. M. (1970). Recalled dream content and the maintenance of body image. *Journal of Abnormal Psychology, 76,* 134–139.

Nezu, A. M., Nezu., C. M., & Blissett, S. E. (1988). Sense of humor as a moderator of the relationship between stressful events and psychological distress: A prospective study. *Journal of Personality and Social Psychology, 54,* 520–525.

Ng, V. W. K., Bullmore, E. T., de Zubicaray, G. I., Cooper, A., Suckling, J., & Williams, S. C. R. (2001). Identifying rate-limiting nodes in large-scale cortical networks for visuospatial processing: An illustration using fMRI. *Journal of Cognitive Neuroscience, 13,* 537–545.

Nguyen, S. P., & Murphy, G. L. (2003). An apple is more than just a fruit: Cross-classification in children's concepts. *Child Development, 74,* 1783–1806.

NICHD Early Child Care Research Network. (1997). The effects of infant child care on infant-mother attachment security: Results of the NICHD study of early child care. *Child Development, 68,* 860–879.

Nichelli, P., Grafman, J., Pietrini, P., Alway, D., Carton, J. J., & Miletich, R. (1994). Brain activity in chess playing. *Nature, 369,* 191.

Nichols, R. C. (1978). Twin studies of ability, personality, and interests. *Homo, 29,* 158–173.

Niedenthal, P. M., Brauer, M., Halberstadt, J. B., & Innes-Ker, A. H. (2001). When did her smile drop? Facial mimicry and the influences of emotional state on the detection of change in emotional expression. *Cognition & Emotion, 15,* 853–864.

Niedenthal, P. M., Brauer, M., Robin, L., & Innes-Ker, &. H. (2002). Adult attachment and the perception of facial expression of emotion. *Journal of Personality & Social Psychology, 82,* 419–433.

Nielsen, T. A. (2000). A review of mentation in REM and NREM sleep: "Covert" REM sleep as a possible reconciliation of two opposing models. *Behavioral Brain Science, 23*(6), 851–866.

Nigg, J. T., & Goldsmith, H. H. (1994). Genetics of personality disorders: Perspectives from personality and psychopathology research. *Psychological Bulletin, 115,* 346–380.

NIH Technology Assessment Panel. (1996). Integration of behavioral and relaxation approaches into the treatment of chronic pain and insomnia. *Journal of the American Medical Association, 276,* 313–318.

Nikelly, A. G. (1988). Does *DSM-III-R* diagnose depression in non-Western patients? *International Journal of Social Psychiatry, 34,* 316–320.

Niles, S. (1998). Achievement goals and means: A cultural comparison. *Journal of Cross-Cultural Psychology, 29,* 656–667.

Nilsson, L., & Hamberger, L. (1990). *A child is born.* New York: Delacorte.

Nilsson, T., Ericsson, M., Poston, W. S. C., Linder, J., Goodrick, G. K., & Foreyt, J. P. (1998). Is the assessment of coping capacity useful in the treatment of obesity? *Eating Disorders: The Journal of Treatment & Prevention, 6,* 241–251.

Niparko, J. K., & Blankenhorn, R. (2003). Cochlear implants in young children. *Mental Retardation & Developmental Disabilities Research Reviews, 9,* 267–275.

Nisbett, R. E. (1972). Hunger, obesity, and the ventromedial hypothalamus. *Psychological Review, 79,* 433–453.

Nisbett, R. E. (1996). Race, genetics, and IQ. In C. Jencks & M. Phillips (Eds.), *The black-white test score gap* (pp. 86–102). Washington, DC: Brookings Institution.

Nisbett, R. E., & Cohen, D. (1996). *Culture of honor: The psychology of violence in the South.* Boulder, CO: Westview.

Nodelmann, P. (1988). *Words about pictures.* Athens: University of Georgia Press.

Nolan, S. A., & Mineka, S. (1997, November). Verbal, nonverbal, and gender-related factors in the interpersonal consequences of depression and anxiety. Presented at the annual meeting of the Association for the Advancement of Behavior Therapy, Miami Beach, FL.

Nolen-Hoeksema, S. (1987). Sex differences in unipolar depression: Evidence and theory. *Psychological Bulletin, 101,* 259–282.

Nolen-Hoeksema, S. (2000). The role of rumination in depressive disorders and mixed anxiety/depressive symptoms. *Journal of Abnormal Psychology, 109,* 504–511.

Nolen-Hoeksema, S., & Morrow, J. (1993). Effects of rumination and distraction on naturally occurring depressed mood. *Cognition & Emotion, 7,* 561–570.

Norcross, J. C. (2001). Purposes, processes and products of the task force on empirically supported therapy relationships. *Psychotherapy: Theory, Research, Practice, Training, 38,* 345–356.

Norem, J. N. (2003). Pessimism: Accentuating the positive possibilities. In E. C. Chang & L. J. Sanna (Eds.), *Virtue, vice, and personality: The complexity of behavior* (pp. 91–104). Washington, DC: American Psychological Association.

Norman, G. R., Brooks, L. R., Colle, C. L., & Hatala, R. M. (1999). The benefit of diagnostic hypotheses in clinical reasoning: Experimental study of an instructional intervention for forward and backward reasoning. *Cognition & Instruction, 17,* 433–448.

Norman, K. A., & Schacter, D. L. (1997). False recognition in younger and older adults: Exploring the characteristics of illusory memories. *Memory & Cognition, 25,* 838–848.

Nosek, B. A., Banaji, M. R., & Greenwald, A. G. (2002). Harvesting implicit group attitudes and beliefs from a demonstration Web site. *Group Dynamics: Theory, Research, & Practice, 6,* 101–115.

Nosek, B. A., Banaji, M., & Greenwald, A. G. (2002b). Harvesting implicit group attitudes and beliefs from a demonstration web site. *Group Dynamics, 6,* 101–115.

Nowak, M. A., Page, K. M., & Sigmund, K. (2000). Fairness versus reason in the ultimatum game. *Science, 289,* 1773–1775.

Nowakowski, R. S. (1987). Basic concepts of CNS development. *Child Development, 58,* 568–595.

Nuechterlein, K. H. (1991). Vigilance in schizophrenia and related disorders. In S. R. Steinhauer, J. H. Gruzelier, & J. Zubin (Eds.), *Neuropsychology, psychophysiology, and information processing* (pp. 397–433). New York: Elsevier Science.

Núñez, J. P., & de Vincente, F. (2004). Unconscious learning. Conditioning to subliminal visual stimuli. *Spanish Journal of Psychology, 7,* 13–28.

Nyberg, L., McIntosh, A. R., Houle, S., Nilsson, L. G., & Tulving, E. (1996). Activation of medial temporal structures during episodic memory retrieval. *Nature, 380,* 715–717.

Nye, R. D. (1992). *Three psychologies: Perspectives from Freud, Skinner, and Rogers.* Pacific Grove, CA: Brooks-Cole.

Nyklicek, I., Vingerhoets, A. J. J. M., Van Heck, G. L., & Van Limpt, M. C. A. M. (1998). Defensive coping in relation to casual blood pressure and self-reported daily hassles and life events. *Journal of Behavioral Medicine, 21,* 145–161.

Oberauer, K., Schulze, R., Wilhelm, O., & Süß, H.-M. (2005). Working memory and intelligence—their correlation and their relation: Comment on Ackerman, Beier, & Boyle (2005). *Psychological Bulletin, 131,* 61–65.

O'Brien, L. T., & Crandall, C. S. (2003). Stereotype threat and arousal: Effects on women's math performance. *Personality & Social Psychology Bulletin, 29,* 782–789.

Ochsner, K. N., & Gross, J. J. (2005). The cognitive control of emotion. *Trends in Cognitive Sciences, 9,* 242–249.

Ochsner, K. N., & Lieberman, M. D. (2001). The emergence of social cognitive neuroscience. *American Psychologist, 56,* 717–734.

Ochsner, K. N., Bunge, S. A., Gross, J. J., & Gabrieli, J. D. E. (2002). Rethinking feelings: An fMRI study of the cognitive regulation of emotion. *Journal of Cognitive Neuroscience, 14,* 1215–1229.

Ochsner, K. N., Ray, R. D., Cooper, J. C., Robertson, E. R., Chopra, S., Gabrieli, J. D. E., & Gross, J. J. (2004). For better or for worse: Neural systems supporting the cognitive down- and up-regulation of negative emotion. *NeuroImage, 23,* 483–499.

O'Conner, T. G., Marvin, R. S., Rutter, M., Olrick, J. T., & Britner, P. A. (2003). Child-parent attachment following early institutional deprivation. *Development & Psychopathology, 15,* 19–38.

O'Connor, D. B., & Shimizu, M. (2002). Sense of personal control, stress and coping style: A cross-cultural study. *Stress & Health: Journal of the International Society for the Investigation of Stress, 18,* 173–183.

O'Doherty, J., Dayan, P., Schultz, J., Deichmann, R., Friston, K., & Dolan, R. J. (2004). Dissociable roles of ventral and dorsal striatum in instrumental conditioning. *Science, 304,* 452–454.

O'Doherty, J., Kringelbach, M. L., Rolls, E. T., Hornak, J., & Andrews, C. (2001). Abstract reward and punishment representations in the human orbitofrontal cortex. *Nature Neuroscience, 4,* 95–102.

O'Doherty, J., Winston, J., Critchley, H., Perrett, D., Burt, D. M., & Dolan, R. J. (2003). Beauty in a smile: The role of medial orbitofrontal cortex in facial attractiveness. *Neuropsychologia, 41,* 147–155.

Oei, T. P. S., & Yeoh, A. E. O. (1999). Pre-existing antidepressant medication and the outcome of group cognitive-behavioural therapy. *Australian & New Zealand Journal of Psychiatry, 33,* 70–76.

O'Grady, W., & Lee, M. (2005). A mapping theory of agrammatic comprehension deficits. *Brain & Language, 92,* 91–100.

Ohayon, M. M., Lemoine, P., Arnaud-Briant, V., & Dreyfus, M. (2002). Prevalence and consequences of sleep disorders in a shift worker population. *Journal of Psychosomatic Research, 53,* 577–583.

Öhman, A. (2002). Automaticity and the amygdala: Nonconscious responses to emotional faces. *Current Directions in Psychological Science, 11,* 62–66.

Ohman, A., Fredrikson, M., Hugdahl, K., & Rimmo, P.-A. (1976). The premise of equipotentiality in human classical conditioning: Conditioned electrodermal responses to potentially phobic stimuli. *Journal of Experimental Psychology: General, 105,* 313–337.

Oishi, S., Diener, E., Napa Scollon, C., & Biswas-Diener, R. (2004). Cross-situational consistency of affective experiences across cultures. *Journal of Personality & Social Psychology, 86,* 460–472.

Ojemann, G. A. (1983). Brain organization for language from the perspective of electrical stimulation mapping. *Behavioral and Brain Sciences, 6,* 189–230.

Ojemann, G. A., Ojemann, J., Lettich, E., & Berger, M. (1989). Cortical language localization in left, dominant hemisphere. *Journal of Neurosurgery, 71,* 316–326.

O'Keefe, J., & Nadel, L. (1978). *The hippocampus as a cognitive map.* Oxford, UK: Clarendon.

Okello, E. J., Savelev, S. U., & Perry, E. K. (2004). In vitro anti-beta-secretase and dual anti-cholinesterase activities of *Camellia sinensis L.* (tea) relevant to treatment of dementia. *Phytotherapy Research, 18,* 624– 627.

Okonkwo, R. U. N. (1997). Moral development and culture in Kohlberg's theory: A Nigerian (Igbo) evidence. *IFE Psychologia: An International Journal, 5,* 117–128.

Okubo, M., & Michimata, C. (2002). Hemispheric processing of categorical and coordinate relations in the absence of low spatial frequencies. *Journal of Cognitive Neuroscience, 14,* 291–297.

Okubo, M., & Michimata, C. (2004). The role of high spatial frequencies in hemispheric processing of categorical and coordinate spatial relations. *Journal of Cognitive Neuroscience, 16,* 1576–1582.

Okubo, Y., Suhara, T., & Suzuki, K., Kobayashi, K., Inoue, O., Teraski, O., et al. (1997). Decreased prefrontal dopamine D1 receptors in schizophrenia revealed by PET. *Nature, 385,* 634–636.

Olczak, P. V., Kaplan, M. F., & Penrod, S. (1991). Attorneys' lay psychology and its effectiveness in selecting jurors: Three empirical studies. *Journal of Social Behavior and Personality, 6,* 431–452.

Olds, J., & Milner, P. (1954). Positive reinforcement produced by electrical stimulation of septal area and other regions of rat brain. *Journal of Comparative & Physiological Psychology, 47,* 419–427.

Olson, C. R. (2001). Object-based vision and attention in primates. *Current Opinion in Neurobiology, 11,* 171–179.

Olson, I. R., & Chun, M. M. (2002). Perceptual constraints on implicit learning of spatial context. *Visual Cognition, 9,* 273–302.

Olson, J. M., Vernon, P. A., Harris, J. A., & Jang, K. L. (2001). The heritability of attitudes: A study of twins. *Journal of Personality & Social Psychology, 80,* 845–860.

Olsson, A., & Phelps, E. A. (2004). Learned fear of "unseen" faces after Pavlovian, observational, and instructed fear. *Psychological Science, 15,* 822–828.

Olton, R. M. (1979). Experimental studies of incubation: Searching for the elusive. *Journal of Creative Behavior, 13,* 9–22.

O'Reilly, R. C., Noelle, D. C., Braver, T. S., & Cohen, J. D. (2002). Prefrontal cortex and dynamic categorization tasks: Representational organization and neuromodulatory control. *Cerebral Cortex, 12,* 246–257.

O'Reilly, R. C., & Rudy, J. W. (2000). Computational principles of learning in the neocortex and hippocampus. *Hippocampus, 10,* 389–397.

O'Reilly, R. C., & Rudy, J. W. (2001). Conjunctive representations in learning and memory: Principles of cortical and hippocampal function. *Psychological Review, 108,* 311–345.

Organ, D. W., & Ryan, K. (1995). A meta-analytic review of attitudinal and dispositional predictors of organizational citizenship behavior. *Personnel Psychology, 48,* 775–802.

Orive, R. (1988). Social projection and social comparison of opinions. *Journal of Personality and Social Psychology, 54,* 953–964.

Ornish, D., Scherwitz, L. W., Billings, J. H., Gould, K. L., Merritt, T. A., Sparler, S., et al. (1998). Intensive lifestyle changes for reversal of coronary heart disease. *Journal of the American Medical Association, 280,* 2001–2007.

Ornstein, R. (1986). *Multimind: A new way of looking at human behavior.* Boston: Houghton Mifflin.

Orr, S. P., Metzger, L. J., Lasko, N. B., Macklin, M. L., Hu, F. B., Shalev, A. Y., et al. (2003). Physiologic responses to sudden, loud tones in monozygotic twins discordant for combat exposure: Association with posttraumatic stress disorder. *Archives of General Psychiatry, 60,* 283–288.

Orth-Gomér, K., Wamala, S. P., Horsten, M., Schenck-Gustafsso, K., Schneiderman, N., & Mittleman, M. A. (2000). Marital stress worsens prognosis in women with coronary heart disease: The Stockholm female coronary risk study. *Journal of the American Medical Association, 284,* 3008–3014.

Osborn, D. R. (1996). Beauty is as beauty does? Makeup and posture effects on physical attractiveness judgments. *Journal of Applied Social Psychology, 26,* 31–51.

Osherson, D., Perani, D., Cappa, S., Schnur, T., Grassi, F., & Fazio, F. (1998). Distinct brain loci in deductive versus probabilistic reasoning. *Neuropsychologia, 36,* 369–376.

Osmon, D. C., & Jackson, R. (2002). Inspection time and IQ: Fluid or perceptual aspects of intelligence? *Intelligence, 30,* 119–127.

Ost, J. (2003). Seeking the middle ground in the "memory wars." *British Journal of Psychology, 94,* 125–139.

Öst, L.-G., Alm, T., Brandberg, M. & Breitholtz, E. (2001). One vs. five sessions of exposure and five sessions of cognitive therapy in the treatment of claustrophobia. *Behaviour Research and Therapy, 39,* 167–183.

Öst, L.-G., Brandberg, M., & Alm, T. (1997). One vs. five sessions of exposure in the treatment of flying phobia. *Behaviour Research and Therapy, 35,* 987–996.

Ostatnikova, D., Laznibatova, J., Putz, Z., Mataseje, A., Dohnanyiova, M., & Pastor, K. (2000). Salivary testosterone levels in intellectually gifted and non-intellectually gifted preadolescents: An exploratory study. *High Ability Studies, 11,* 41–54.

Ostatnikova, D., Laznibatova, J., Putz, Z., Mataseje, A., Dohnanyiova, M., & Pastor, K. (2002). Biological aspects of intellectual giftedness. *Studia Psychologica, 44,* 3–13.

O'Sullivan, C. S., & Durso, F. T. (1984). Effects of schema-incongruent information on memory for stereotypical attributes. *Journal of Personality and Social Psychology, 47,* 55–70.

Otto, M. W., Gould, R. A., & Pollack, M. H. (1994). Cognitive-behavioral treatment of panic disorder: Considerations for the treatment of patients over the long term. *Psychiatric Annals, 24,* 307–315.

Otto, M. W., Smits, J. A. J., & Reese, H. E. (2005). Combined psychotherapy and pharmacotherapy for mood and anxiety disorders in adults: Review and analysis. *Clinical Psychology: Science & Practice, 12,* 72–86.

Ouimette, P. C. (1997). Psychopathology and sexual aggression in nonincarcerated men. *Violence & Victims, 12,* 389–395.

Overmeier, J. B., & Seligman, M. E. P. (1967). Effects of inescapable shock upon subsequent escape and avoidance responding. *Journal of Comparative and Physiological Psychology, 63,* 28–33.

Overmier, J. B. (2002). On learned helplessness. *Integrative Physiological & Behavioral Science, 37,* 4–8.

Owen, N., Poulton, T., Hay, F. C., Mohamed-Ali, V., & Steptoe, A. (2003). Socioeconomic status, C-reactive protein, immune factors, and responses to acute mental stress. *Brain, Behavior & Immunity, 17,* 286–295.

Owens, L., Shute, R., & Slee, P. (2000). "I'm in and you're out . . . " Explanations for teenage girls' indirect aggression. *Psychology, Evolution & Gender, 2,* 19–46.

Oyserman, D., Coon, H. M., & Kemmelmeier, M. (2002). Rethinking individualism and collectivism: Evaluation of theoretical assumptions and meta-analyses. *Psychological Bulletin, 128,* 3–72.

Ozer, D. J., Best, S. R., Lipsey, T. L., & Weiss, D. S. (2003). Predictors of posttraumatic stress disorder and symptoms in adults: A meta-analysis. *Psychological Bulletin, 129,* 52–73.

Ozer, D. J., & Reise, S. P. (1994). Personality assessment. *Annual Review of Psychology, 45,* 357–88.

Pacak, K., & Palkovits, M. (2001). Stressor specificity of central neuroendocrine responses: Implications for stress-related disorders. *Endocrine Review, 22,* 502–548.

Páez, D., Velasco, C., & González, J. L. (1999). Expressive writing and the role of alexythimia as a dispositional deficit in self-disclosure and psychological health. *Journal of Personality and Social Psychology, 77,* 630–641.

Pagano, R. R., Rose, R. M., Stivers, R. M., & Warrenburg, S. (1976). Sleep during transcendental meditation. *Science, 191,* 308–309.

Pagnoni, G., Zink, C. F., Montague, P. R., & Berns, G. S. (2002). Activity in human ventral striatum locked to errors of reward prediction. *Nature Neuroscience, 5,* 97–98.

Paivio, A. (1971). *Imagery and verbal processes.* New York: Holt, Rinehart & Winston.

Palace, E. M. (1999). Response expectancy and sexual dysfunction. In I. Kirsch (Ed.), *How expectancies shape experience* (pp. 173–196). Washington, DC: American Psychological Association.

Palmer, S. E. (1992a). Modern theories of Gestalt perception. In G. W. Humphreys (Ed.), *Understanding vision: An interdisciplinary perspective* (pp. 39–70). Oxford, England: Blackwell.

Panagopoulos, A., Von Grünau, M. W., & Galera, C. (2004). Attentive mechanisms in visual search. *Spatial Vision, 17,* 353–371.

Panksepp, J. (1998). *Affective neuroscience: The foundations of human an animal emotions.* London: Oxford University Press.

Panksepp, J. (2005). Affective consciousness: Core emotional feelings in animals and humans. *Consciousness and Cognition: An International Journal, 14,* 30–80.

Pantelis, C., Velakoulis, D., McGorry, P. D., Wood, S. J., Suckling, J., Phillips, L. J., et al. (2003). Neuroanatomical abnormalities before and after onset of psychosis: a cross-sectional and longitudinal MRI comparison. *Lancet, 361,* 281–288.

Pantev, C., Roberts, L. E., Schulz, M., Engelien, A., & Ross, B. (2001). Timbre-specific enhancement of auditory cortical representations in musicians. *Neuroreport: For Rapid Communication of Neuroscience Research, 12,* 169–174.

Papp, L. A., Klein, D. F., & Gorman, J. M. (1993). Carbon dioxide hypersensitivity, hyperventilation, and panic disorder. *American Journal of Psychiatry, 150,* 1149–1157.

Papp, L. A., Martinez, J. M., Klein, D. F., Coplan, J. D., Norman, R. G., Cole, R., et al. (1997). Respiratory psychophysiology of panic disorder: Three respiratory challenges in 98 subjects. *American Journal of Psychiatry, 154,* 1557–1565.

Paquette, V., Lévesque, J., Mensour, B., Leroux, J. M., Beaudoin, G., Bourgouin, P., & Beauregard, M. (2003). "Change the mind and you change the brain": Effects of cognitive-behavioral therapy on the neural correlates of spider phobia. *Neuroimage, 18,* 401–409.

Paradis M. (1990). Language lateralization in bilinguals: Enough already! *Brain and Language, 39,* 576–586.

Paradis M. (1992). The Loch Ness monster approach to bilingual language lateralization: A response to Berquier and Ashton. *Brain and Language, 43,* 534–537.

Paradis, M. (2001). The need for awareness of aphasia symptoms in different languages. *Journal of Neurolinguistics, 14,* 85–91.

Paradis M., & Goldblum, M. C. (1989). Selective crossed aphasia in a trilingual aphasic patient followed by reciprocal antagonism. *Brain and Language, 36,* 62–75.

Park, C. L., Armeli, S., & Tennen, H. (2004). Appraisal-coping goodness of fit: A daily Internet study. *Personality & Social Psychology Bulletin, 30,* 558–569.

Park, C. L., & Fenster, J. R. (2004). Stress-related growth: Predictors of occurrence and correlates with psychological adjustment. *Journal of Social & Clinical Psychology, 23,* 195–215.

Park, D. C., Polk, T. A., Park, R., Minear, M., Savage, A., & Smith, M. R. (2004). Aging reduces neural specialization in ventral visual cortex. *Proceedings of the National Academy of Sciences U S A, 101,* 13091–13095.

Park, J. H., & Schaller, M. (2005). Does attitude similarity serve as a heuristic cue for kinship? Evidence of an implicit cognitive association. *Evolution & Human Behavior, 26,* 158–170.

Parker, A., & Gellatly, A. (1997). Movable cues: A practical method for reducing context-dependent forgetting. *Applied Cognitive Psychology, 11,* 163–173.

Parker, G., Cheah, Y.-C., & Roy, K. (2001). Do the Chinese somatize depression? A cross-cultural study. *Social Psychiatry & Psychiatric Epidemiology, 36,* 287–293.

Parkin, A. J. (1987). *Memory and amnesia: An introduction.* Oxford, England: Blackwell.

Parks, K. A., & Fals-Stewart, W. (2004). The temporal relationship between college women's alcohol consumption and victimization experiences. *Alcoholism: Clinical & Experimental Research, 28,* 625–629.

Parks, M. R., & Roberts, L. D. (1998). "Making MOOsic": The development of personal relationships on line and a comparison to their off-line counterparts. *Journal of Social & Personal Relationships, 15,* 517–537.

Parpura, V., & Haydon, P. G.(2000) Physiological astrocytic calcium levels stimulate glutamate release to modulate adjacent neurons. *Proceedings of the National Academy of Sciences USA, 97,* 8629–8634.

Pascual-Leone, A., Grafman, J., Cohen, L. G., Roth, B. J., & Hallett, M. (1997). Transcranial magnetic stimulation. A new tool for the study of higher cognitive functions in humans. In J. Grafman & F. Boller (Eds.), *Handbook of neuropsychology* (Vol. 11). Amsterdam: Elsevier.

Pascual-Leone, A., Tormos, J. M., Keenan, J., Tarazona, F., Cañete, C., & Catalá, M. D. (1998). Study and modulation of human cortical excitability with transcranial magnetic stimulation. *Journal of Clinical Neurophysiology, 15,* 333–343.

Passingham, D., & Sakai, K. (2004). The prefrontal cortex and working memory: Physiology and brain imaging. *Current Opinion in Neurobiology, 14,* 163–168.

Pasupathi, M. (2003). Emotion regulation during social remembering: Differences between emotions elicited during an event and emotions elicited when talking about it. *Memory, 11,* 151–163.

Patel, S., Cravatt, B. F., & Hillard, C. J. (in press). Synergistic interactions between cannabinoids and environmental stress in the activation of the central amygdala. *Neuropsychopharmacology.*

Patel, V., Abas, M., Broadhead, J., Todd, C., & Reeler, A. (2001). Depression in developing countries: Lessons from Zimbabwe. *British Medical Journal, 322,*482–484.

Pato, M. T., Pato, C. N., & Pauls, D. L. (2002). Recent findings in the genetics of OCD. *Journal of Clinical Psychiatry, 63,* 30–33.

Patterson, G. R. (1986). Performance models for antisocial boys. *American Psychologist, 41,* 432–444.

Patterson, G. R., DeBaryshe, B. D., & Ramsey, E. (1989). A developmental perspective on antisocial behavior. *American Psychologist, 44,* 329–335.

Patterson, T. L., Semple, S. J., Shaw, W. S., Yu, E., He, Y., Zhang, M. Y., et al. (1998). The cultural context of caregiving: A comparison of Alzheimer's caregivers in Shanghai, China and San Diego, California. *Psychological Medicine, 28,* 1071–1084.

Paulhus, D. L., & Bruce, M. N. (1992). The effect of acquaintanceship on the validity of personality impressions: A longitudinal study. *Journal of Personality and Social Psychology, 63,* 816–824.

Pauli-Pott, U., Mertesacker, B., Bade, U., Haverkock, A., & Beckmann, D. (2003). Parental perceptions and infant temperament development. *Infant Behavior & Development, 26,* 27–48.

Paunonen, S. V. (1998). Hierarchical organization of personality and prediction of behavior. *Journal of Personality and Social Psychology, 74,* 538–556.

Paunonen, S. V., & Ashton, M. C. (1998). The structured assessment of personality across cultures. *Journal of Cross-Cultural Psychology, 29,* 150–170.

Paunonen, S. V., Haddock, G., Forsterling, F., & Keinonen, M. (2003). Broad versus narrow personality measures and the prediction of behaviour across cultures. *European Journal of Personality, 17,* 413–433.

Paunonen, S. V., Zeidner, M., Engvik, H. A., Oosterveld, P., & Maliphant, R. (2000). The nonverbal assessment of personality in five cultures. *Journal of Cross-Cultural Psychology, 31,* 220–239.

Paus, T. (1996). Location and function of the human frontal eye-field: A selective review. *Neuropsychologia, 34,* 475–483.

Pavlov, I. P. (1927). *Conditioned reflexes* (G. V. Anrep, Trans.). London: Oxford University Press.

Paykel, E. S., Scott, J., Cornwall, P. L., Abbott, R., Crane, C., Pope, M., & Johnson, A. L. (2005). Duration of relapse prevention after cognitive therapy in residual depression: Follow-up of controlled trial. *Psychological Medicine, 35,* 59–68.

Payne, B. K. (2001). Prejudice and perception: The role of automatic and controlled processes in misperceiving a weapon. *Journal of Personality & Social Psychology, 81,* 181–192.

Payne, B. R., & Lomber, S. G. (2001). Reconstructing functional systems after lesions of cerebral cortex. *Nature Reviews Neuroscience, 2,* 911–919.

Payne, D. G. (1987). Hypermnesia and reminiscence in recall: A historical and empirical review. *Psychological Bulletin, 101,* 5–27.

Payne, D. L. (1992). *Pragmatics of word order flexibility.* Amsterdam: John Benjamins.

Pearson, S. E., & Pollack, R. H. (1997). Female response to sexually explicit films. *Journal of Psychology & Human Sexuality, 9,* 73–88.

Pecher, D. (2001). Perception is a two-way junction: Feedback semantics in word recognition. *Psychonomic Bulletin & Review, 8,* 545–551.

Pedersen, W. C., Miller, L. C., Putcha-Bhagavatula, A. D., & Yang, Y. (2002). Evolved sex differences in the number of partners desired? The long and short of it. *Psychological Science, 13,* 157–161.

Pederson, C. L., Maurer, S. H., Kaminski, P. L., Zander, K. A., Peters, C. M., Stokes-Crowe, L. A., & Osborn, R. E. (2004). Hippocampal volume and memory performance in a community-based sample of women with posttraumatic stress disorder secondary to child abuse. *Journal of Traumatic Stress, 17,* 37–40.

Pederson, N. L., Plomin, R., McClearn, G. E., & Friberg, L. (1988) Neuroticism, extraversion and related traits in adult twins reared apart and reared together. *Journal of Personality and Social Psychology, 55,* 950–957.

Pedreira, M. E., Perez-Cuesta, L. M., & Maldonado, H. (2004) Mismatch between what is expected and what actually occurs triggers memory reconsolidation or extinction. *Learning and Memory, 11,* 579–585.

Pelletier, C. L. (2004). The effect of music on decreasing arousal due to stress: A meta-analysis. *Journal of Music Therapy, 41,* 192-214.

Penfield, W. (1955). The permanent record of the stream of consciousness. *Acta Psychologica, 11,* 47–69.

Penfield, W., & Rasmussen, T. (1950). *The cerebral cortex of man: A clinical study of localization of function.* New York: Macmillan.

Pengilly, J. W., & Dowd, E. T. (1997). Hardiness and social support as moderator of stress in college students. Paper presented at the annual convention of the Association for the Advancement of Behavior Therapy, Miami Beach, FL.

Pengilly, J. W., & Dowd, E. T. (2000). Hardiness and social support as moderators of stress. *Journal of Clinical Psychology, 56,* 813–820.

Penn, D. L., Corrigan, P. W., Bentall, R. P., Racenstein, J. M., & Newman L. (1997). Social cognition in schizophrenia. *Psychological Bulletin, 121,* 114–132.

Pennebaker, J. W. (1989). Confession, inhibition and disease. In L. Berkowitz (Ed.), *Advances in experimental social psychology* (Vol. 22, pp. 211–244). New York: Academic Press.

Pennebaker, J. W. (2004). Theories, therapies, and taxpayers: On the complexities of the expressive writing paradigm. *Clinical Psychology: Science & Practice, 11,* 138–142.

Pennebaker, J. W., Colder, M., & Sharp, L. K. (1990). Accelerating the coping process. *Journal of Personality and Social Psychology, 58,* 528–537.

Pennebaker, J. W., & Francis, M. E. (1996). Cognitive, emotional, and language processes in disclosure. *Cognition & Emotion, 10,* 601–626.

Penner, L. A. Dovidio, J. F., Piliavin, J. A., & Schroeder, D. A. (2005). Prosocial behavior: Multilevel perspectives. *Annual Review of Psychology, 56,* np

Penton-Voak, I. S., & Perrett, D. I. (2000). Female preference for male faces changes cyclically: Further evidence. *Evolution & Human Behavior, 21,* 39–48.

Perdue, C. W., Dovidio, J. F., Gurtman, M. B., & Tyler, R. B. (1990). Us and them: Social categorization and the process of intergroup bias. *Journal of Personality and Social Psychology, 59,* 475–486.

Perera, S., Sabin, E., Nelson, P., & Lowe, D. (1998). Increases in salivary lysozyme and IgA concentrations and secretory rates independent of salivary flow rates following viewing of a humorous videotape. *International Journal of Behavioral Medicine, 5,* 118–128.

Peretz, I., Blood, A. J., Penhune, V., & Zatorre, R. (2001). Cortical deafness to dissonance. *Brain, 124,* 928–940.

Peretz, I., & Hyde, K. L. (2003). What is specific to music processing? Insights from congenital amusia. *Trends in Cognitive Sciences, 7,* 362–367.

Perez Y Perez, R., & Sharples, M. (2001). MEXICA: A computer model of a cognitive account of creative writing. *Journal of Experimental & Theoretical Artificial Intelligence, 13,* 119–139.

Perkins, D. N., & Grotzer, T. A. (1997). Teaching intelligence. *American Psychologist, 52,* 1125–1133.

Perkins, H. W., & Berkowitz, A. D. (1986). Perceiving the community norms of alcohol use among students: Some research implications for campus alcohol education programming. *International Journal of the Addictions, 21,* 961–976.

Perlmutter, M. (1988). Cognitive potential throughout life. In J. E. Birren & V. L. Bengtson (Eds.), *Emergent theories of aging* (pp. 247–267). New York: Springer.

Perlow, L., & Weeks, J. (2002). Who's helping whom? Layers of culture and workplace behavior. *Journal of Organizational Behavior, 23,* 345–361.

Perna, F. M., Antoni, M. H., Baum, A., Gordon, P., & Schneiderman, N. (2003). Cognitive behavioral stress management effects on injury and illness among competitive athletes: A randomized clinical trial. *Annals of Behavioral Medicine, 25,* 66–73.

Perrett, D. I., Lee, K. J, Penton-Voak, I., Rowland, D., Yoshikawa, S., Burt, D. M., et al. (1998). Effects of sexual dimorphism on facial attractiveness. *Nature, 394,* 884–887.

Perry, B. D., Pollard, R. A., Blakley, T. L., Baker, W. L., & Vigilante, D. (1995). Childhood trauma, the neurobiology of adaptation, and "use-dependent" development of the brain: How "states" become "traits." *Infant Mental Health Journal, 16,* 271–291.

Peter, R., Alfredsson, L., Hammar, N., Siegrist, J., Theorell, T., & Westerholm, P. (1998). High effort, low reward and cardiovascular risk factors in employed Swedish men and women—baseline results from the WOLF study. *Journal of Epidemiology and Community Health, 52,* 540–547.

Peters, A., Von Klot, S., Heier, M., Trentinaglia, I., Hörmann, A., Wichmann, H. E., & Löwel, H. (Cooperative Health Research in the Region of Augsburg Study Group). (2004). Exposure to traffic and the onset of myocardial infarction. *New England Journal of Medicine, 351,* 1721–1730.

Peters, M. L., Godaert, G. L. R., Ballieux, R. E., & Heijnen, C. J. (2003). Moderation of physiological stress responses by personality traits and daily hassles: Less flexibility of immune system responses. *Biological Psychology, 65,* 21–48.

Petersen, A. C., Compas, B. E., Brooks-Gunn, J., Stemmler, M., Ey, S., & Grant, K. E. (1993). Depression in adolescence. *American Psychologist, 48,* 155–168.

Petersen, R. C. (1977, July). Marihuana research findings: 1976. Summary. *NIDA Research Monograph, 14,* 1–37.

Petersen, R. C. (1979). Importance of inhalation patterns in determining effects of marihuana use. *Lancet, 31,* 727–728.

Peterson, C. (2000). The future of optimism. *American Psychologist, 55,* 44–55.

Peterson, C., & Seligman, M. E. (1984). Causal explanations as a risk factor for depression: Theory and evidence. *Psychological Review, 91,* 347–374.

Petitto, L. A., & Marentette, P. F. (1991). Babbling in the manual mode: Evidence for the ontogeny of language. *Science, 251,* 1493–1496.

Petrides, K. V., & Furnham, A. (2000). Gender differences in measured and self-estimated trait emotional intelligence. *Sex Roles, 42,* 449–461.

Petrides, K. V., & Furnham, A. (2003). Trait emotional intelligence: Behavioural validation in two studies of emotion recognition and reactivity of mood induction. *European Journal of Personality, 17,* 39–57.

Petrie, K. J., Booth, R. J., & Pennebaker, J. W. (1998). The immunological effects of thought suppression. *Journal of Personality and Social Psychology, 75,* 1264–1272.

Petrie, K. J., Booth, R. J., Pennebaker, J. W., Davison, K. P., & Thomas, M. G. (1995). Disclosure of trauma and immune response to a hepatitis B vaccination program. *Journal of Consulting and Clinical Psychology, 63,* 787–792.

Petrill, S. A., Plomin, R., McClearn, G. E., Smith, D. L., Vignetti, S., Chorney, M. J., et al. (1997). No association between general cognitive ability and the A1 allele of the D2 dopamine receptor gene. *Behavior Genetics, 27,* 29–31.

Petrovic, P., Kalso, E., Petersson, K. M., & Ingvar, M. (2002). Placebo and opioid analgesia—imaging a shared neuronal network. *Science, 295,* 1737–1740.

Pettigrew, T. F. (1969). Racially separate or together? *Journal of Social Issues, 24,* 43–69.

Pettigrew, T. F. (1981). Extending the stereotype concept. In D. L. Hamilton (Ed.), *Cognitive processes in stereotyping and intergroup behavior* (pp. 303–331). Hillsdale, NJ: Erlbaum.

Pettigrew, T. F., & Meertens, R. W. (1995). Subtle and blatant prejudice in western Europe. *European Journal of Social Psychology, 25,* 57–75.

Petty, R. E., & Cacioppo, J. T. (1981). *Attitudes and persuasion: Classic and contemporary approaches.* Dubuque, IA: Wm. C. Brown.

Petty, R. E., & Cacioppo, J. T. (1986). The elaboration likelihood model of persuasion. In L. Berkowitz (Ed.), *Advances in experimental social psychology* (Vol. 19, pp. 123–205). New York: Academic Press.

Petty, R. E., & Krosnick, J. A. (1996). *Attitude strength: Antecedents and consequences*. Hillsdale, NJ: Erlbaum.

Peyron, C., Faraco, J., Rogers, W., Ripley, B., Overeem, S., Charnay, Y., Nevsimalova, S., Aldrich, M., Reynolds, D., Albin, R., Li, R., Hungs, M., Pedrazzoli, M., Padigaru, M., Kucherlapati, M., Fan, J., Maki, R., Lammers, G. J., Bouras, C., Kucherlapati, R., Nishino, S., & Mignot, E. (2000). A mutation in a case of early onset narcolepsy and a generalized absence of hypocretin peptides in human narcoleptic brains. *National Medicine, 6,* 991–997.

Pezdek, K., Finger, K., & Hodge, D. (1997). Planting false childhood memories: The role of event plausibility. *Psychological Science, 8,* 437–441.

Pfaffmann, C. (1978). The vertebrate phylogeny, neural code, and integrative processes of taste. In E. C. Carterette & M. P. Friedman (Eds.), *Handbook of perception* (pp. 51–123). New York: Academic Press.

Pfrieger, F. W. (2002). Role of glia in synapse development. *Current Opinion in Neurobiology, 12,* 486–490.

Phan, K. L., Wager, T., Taylor, S. F., & Liberzon, I. (2002). Functional neuroanatomy of emotion: A meta-analysis of emotion activation studies in PET and fMRI. *Neuro-Image, 16,* 331–348.

Phan, K. L., Wager, T., Taylor, S. F., & Liberzon, I. (2004). Functional neuroimaging studies of human emotions. *CNS Spectrums, 9,* 258–266.

Phelps, E. A., O'Connor, K. J., Cunningham, W. A., Funayama, E. S., Gatenby, J. C., Gore, J. C., & Banaji, M. R. (2000). Performance on indirect measures of race evaluation predicts amygdala activation. *Journal of Cognitive Neuroscience, 12,* 729–738.

Phelps, J. A., Davis, J. O., & Schartz, K. M. (1997). Nature, nurture, and twin research strategies. *Current Directions in Psychological Science, 6,* 117–121.

Philipson, T. J., & Posner, R. A. (2003). The long-run growth in obesity as a function of technological change. *Perspectives in Biology and Medicine, 46,* S87–S107.

Phillips, C., Pellathy, T., Marantz, A., Yellin, E., Wexler, K., Poeppel, D., et al. (2000). Auditory cortex accesses phonological categories: An MEG mismatch study. *Journal of Cognitive Neuroscience, 12,* 1038–1055.

Phillips, D. P., & Smith, D. G. (1990). Postponement of death until symbolically meaningful occasions. *Journal of the American Medical Association, 263,* 1947–1951.

Phillips, D. P., Van Voorhees, C. A., & Ruth, T. E. (1992). The birthday: Lifeline or deadline. *Psychosomatic Medicine, 54,* 532–542.

Phillips, K., & Matheny, A. P., Jr. (1995). Quantitative genetic analysis of injury liability in infants and toddlers. *American Journal of Medical Genetics (Neuropsychiatric Genetics), 60,* 64–71.

Phillips, S. D., & Imhoff, A. R. (1997). Women and career development: A decade of research. *Annual Review of Psychology, 48,* 31–59.

Piaget, J. (1962). *Play, dreams, and imitation in childhood.* New York: W. W. Norton.

Piaget, J. (1969). *The mechanisms of perception* (G. N. Seagrim, Trans.). New York: Basic Books.

Pickles, J. O. (1988). *An introduction to the physiology of hearing* (2nd ed.). London: Academic Press.

Pietromonaco, P. R., Manis, J., & Frohardt-Lane, K. (1986). Psychological consequences of multiple social roles. *Psychology of Women Quarterly, 10,* 373–381.

Pihl, R. O., Paylan, S. S., Gentes-Hawn, A., & Hoaken, P. N. S. (2003). Alcohol affects executive cognitive functioning differentially on the ascending versus descending limb of the blood alcohol concentration curve. *Alcoholism: Clinical & Experimental Research, 27,* 773–779.

Pillutla, M. M., & Murnigham, J. K. (1996), Unfairness, anger and spite: Emotional rejections of ultimatum offers. *Organizational Behavior and Human Decision Processes, 68,* 208–224.

Pine, D. S., Cohen, P., & Brook, J. (2001). Adolescent fears as predictors of depression. *Biological Psychiatry, 50,* 721–724.

Pinel, J. P. J. (1993). *Biopsychology* (2nd ed.). Boston: Allyn & Bacon.

Pines, A. M. (2004). Adult attachment styles and their relationship to burnout: A preliminary, cross-cultural investigation. *Work & Stress, 18,* 66–80.

Pinhey, T. K., Rubinstein, D. H., & Colfax, R. S. (1997). Overweight and happiness: The reflected self-appraisal hypothesis reconsidered. *Social Science Quarterly, 78,* 747–755.

Pinker, S. (1994). *The language instinct: How the mind creates language.* New York: Morrow.

Pinker, S. (1997). *How the mind works.* New York: Norton.

Pinker, S. (1999). *Words and rules: The ingredients of language.* New York: Basic Books, Inc.

Pinker, S. (2002). *The blank slate: The modern denial of human nature.* New York: Viking Press.

Pinker, S., & Jackendoff, R. (2005). The faculty of language: What's special about it? *Cognition, 95,* 201–236.

Pinkerman, J. E., Haynes, J. P., & Keiser, T. (1993). Characteristics of psychological practice in juvenile court clinics. *American Journal of Forensic Psychology, 11,* 3–12.

Pirke, K. M. (1995). Physiology of bulimia nervosa. In K. D. Brownell & C. G. Fairburn (Eds.), *Eating disorders and obesity: A comprehensive handbook* (pp. 261–265). New York: Guilford Press.

Pitman, D. L., Natelson, B. H., Ottenmiller, J. E., McCarty, R., Pritzel, T., & Tapp, W. N. (1995). Effects of exposure to stressors of varying predictability on adrenal function in rats. *Behavioral Neuroscience, 109,* 767–776.

Pizzagalli, D. A., Greischar, L. L., & Davidson, R. J. (2003). Spatio-temporal dynamics of brain mechanisms in aversive classical conditioning: High-density event-related potential and brain electrical tomography analyses. *Neuropsychologia, 41,* 184–194.

Plaks, J. E., Stroessner, S. J., Dweck, C. S., & Sherman, J. W. (2001). Person theories and attention allocation: Preferences for stereotypic versus counterstereotypic information. *Journal of Personality and Social Psychology, 80,* 876–893.

Plant, E. A., Ericsson, K. A., Hill, L., & Asberg, K. (2005). Why study time does not predict grade point average across college students: Implications of deliberate practice for academic performance. *Contemporary Educational Psychology, 30,* 96–116

Platt, L. A., & Persico, V. R., Jr. (Eds.). (1992). *Grief in cross-cultural perspective: A casebook.* New York: Garland.

Plaut, D. C., McClelland, J. L., Seidenberg, M. S., & Patterson, K. E. (1996). Understanding normal and impaired word reading: Computational principles in quasi-regular domains. *Psychological Review, 103,* 56–115.

Plehn, K., & Peterson, R. A. (2002). Anxiety sensitivity as a predictor of the development of panic symptoms, panic attacks, and panic disorder: A prospective study. *Journal of Anxiety Disorders, 16,* 455–474.

Ploghaus, A., Tracey, I., Gati, J. S., Clare, S., Menon, R. S., Matthews, P. M., & Rawlins, J. N. P. (1999). Dissociating pain from its anticipation in the human brain. *Science, 284,* 1979–1981.

Plomin, R. (1988). The nature and nurture of cognitive abilities. In R. J. Sternberg (Ed.), *Advances in the psychology of human intelligence* (Vol. 4, pp. 1–33). Hillsdale, NJ: Erlbaum.

Plomin, R. (1990). *Nature and nurture: An introduction to human behavioral genetics.* Pacific Grove, CA: Brooks/Cole.

Plomin, R. (1995). Genetics and children's experiences in the family. *Journal of Child Psychology and Psychiatry, 36,* 33–68.

Plomin, R., & Bergeman, C. S. (1991). The nature of nurture: Genetic influences on "environmental" measures. *Behavioral and Brain Sciences, 14,* 373–427.

Plomin, R., & DeFries, J. C. (1998). The genetics of cognitive abilities and disabilities: Investigations of specific cognitive skills can help clarify how genes shape the components of intellect. *Scientific American, 278,* 40–47.

Plomin, R., DeFries, J. C., Craig, I. W., & McGuffin, P. (Eds.). (2003). *Behavioral genetics in the postgenomic era.* Washington, DC: APA Books.

Plomin, R., DeFries, J. C., McClearn, G. E., & Rutter, M. (1997). *Behavioral genetics* (3rd ed.). New York: Freeman.

Plomin, R., & Foch, T. T. (1980). A twin study of objectively assessed personality in childhood. *Journal of Personality and Social Psychology, 39,* 680–688.

Plomin, R., Fulker, D. W., Corley, R., & DeFries, J. C. (1997). Nature, nurture, and cognitive development from 1 to 16 years: A parent-offspring adoption study. *Psychological Science, 8,* 442–447.

Plomin, R., & Kosslyn, S. M. (2001). Genes, brain and cognition. *Nature Neuroscience, 4,* 1153–1155.

Plomin, R., Pedersen, N. L., Lichtenstein, P., & McClearn, G. E. (1994). Variability and stability in cognitive abilities are largely genetic later in life. *Behavior Genetics, 24*(3), 207–215.

Plomin, R., Scheier, M. F., Bergeman, C. S., Pederson, N. L., Nesselroade, J. R., & McClearn, G. E. (1992). Optimism, pessimism and mental health: A twin/adoption analysis. *Personality and Individual Differences, 13,* 921–930.

Plomin, R., & Spinath, F. M. (2004). Intelligence: Genetics, genes and genomics. *Journal of Personality and Social Psychology, 86,* 112–129.

Plotkin, H. (1994). *The nature of knowledge: Concerning adaptations, instinct and the evolution of intelligence.* New York: Allen Lane/Viking Penguin.

Plotkin, H. (1997). *Evolution in mind: An introduction to evolutionary psychology.* Cambridge, MA: Harvard University Press.

Ployhart, R. E., Ziegert, J. C., & McFarland, L. A. (2003). Understanding racial differences on cognitive ability tests in selection contexts: An integration of stereotype threat and applicant reactions research. *Human Performance, 16,* 231–259.

Plutchik, R., & Kellerman, I. (Eds.). (1980). *Emotion: Theory, research, and experience. Vol. 1. Theories of emotion*. New York: Academic Press.

Poizner, H., & Kegl, J. (1992). Neural basis of language and motor behavior: Perspectives from American Sign Language. *Aphasiology, 6*, 219–256.

Poizner, H., Klima, E. S., & Bellugi, U. (1987). *What the hands reveal about the brain*. Cambridge, MA: MIT Press.

Poldrack, R. A., Clark, J., Paré-Blagoev, E. J., Shohamy, D., Creso Moyano, J., Myers, C., & Gluck, M. A. (2001). Interactive memory systems in the human brain. *Nature, 414*, 546–550.

Poldrack, R. A., & Wagner, A. D. (2004). What can neuroimaging tell us about the mind? Insights from prefrontal cortex. *Current Directions in Psychological Science, 13*, 177–181.

Polivy, J., & Herman, C. P. (1993). Etiology of binge eating: Psychological mechanisms. In C. G. Fairburn & G. T. Wilson (Eds.), *Binge eating: Nature, assessment, and treatment* (pp. 173–205). New York: Guilford Press.

Pollack, H. A. (2001). Sudden infant death syndrome, maternal smoking during pregnancy, and the cost-effectiveness of smoking cessation intervention. *American Journal of Public Health, 91*, 432–436.

Pollock, V. E., Briere, J., Schneider, L., Knop, J., Mednick, S. A., & Goodwin, D. H. (1990). Childhood antecedents of antisocial behavior: Parental alcoholism and physical abusiveness. *American Journal of Psychiatry, 147*, 1290–1293.

Pope, K. S. (1996). Memory, abuse, and science: Questioning claims about the false memory syndrome epidemic. *American Psychologist, 51*, 957–974.

Porter, R. H., Makin, J. W., Davis, L. B., & Christensen, K. M. (1992). An assessment of the salient olfactory environment of formula-fed infants. *Physiology & Behavior, 50*, 907–911.

Posner, M. I., & Raichle, M. (1994). *Images of mind*. New York: Freeman.

Post, R. M. (1992). Transdirection of psychosocial stress into the neurobiology of recurrent affective disorder. *American Journal of Psychiatry, 149*, 999–1010.

Posthuma, D., Neale, M. C., Boomsma, D. I., & de Geus, E. J. C. (2001). Are smarter brains running faster? Heritability of alpha peak frequency, IQ, and their interrelation. *Behavior Genetics, 31*, 567–579.

Postmes, T., & Spears, R. (1998). Deindividuation and antinormative behavior: A meta-analysis. *Psychological Bulletin, 123*, 238–259.

Postmes, T., Spears, R., & Cihangir, S. (2001). Quality of decision making and group norms. *Journal of Personality & Social Psychology, 80*, 918–930.

Poston, W. S. C., Ericsson, M., Linder, J., Nilsson, T., Goodrick, G. K., & Foreyt, J. P. (1999). Personality and the prediction of weight loss and relapse in the treatment of obesity. *International Journal of Eating Disorders, 25*, 301–309.

Poulet, E., Brunelin, J., Bediou, B., Bation, R., Forgeard, L., Dalery, J., D'Amato, T., & Saoud, M. (2005). Slow transcranial magnetic stimulation can rapidly reduce resistant auditory hallucinations in schizophrenia. *Biological Psychiatry, 57*, 188–191.

Poulton, R., & Menzies, R. G. (2002). Non-associative fear acquisition: A review of the evidence from retrospective and longitudinal research. *Behaviour Research & Therapy, 40*, 1227–1249.

Poulton, R., Menzies, R. G., Craske, M. G., Langley, J. D., & Silva, P. A. (1999). Water trauma and swimming experiences up to age 9 and fear of water at age 18: A longitudinal study. *Behaviour Research & Therapy, 37*, 39–48.

Powell, M. C., & Fazio, R. H. (1984). Attitude accessibility as a function of repeated attitudinal expression. *Personality and Social Psychology Bulletin, 10*, 139–148.

Prabhakaran, V., Smith, J. A. L., Desmond, J. E., Glover, G. H., & Gabrieli, J. E. (1997). Neural substrates of fluid reasoning: An fMRI study of the neocortical activation during performance of the Raven's Progressive Matrices Test. *Cognitive Psychology, 33*, 43–63.

Prapavessis, H., & Carron, A. V. (1997). Sacrifice, cohesion, and conformity to norms in sport teams. *Group Dynamics: Theory, Research, and Practice, 1*, 231–240.

Prasada, S. (2000). Acquiring generic knowledge. *Trends in Cognitive Science, 4*, 66–72.

Prather, D. C. (1973). Prompted mental practice as a flight simulator. *Journal of Applied Psychology, 57*, 353–355.

Prescott, C. A., Johnson, R. C., & McArdle, J. J. (1991). Genetic contributions to television viewing. *Psychological Science, 2*, 430–431.

Prescott, J., Soo, J., Campbell, H., & Roberts, C. (2004). Responses of PROP taster groups to variations in sensory qualities within foods and beverages. *Physiology & Behavior, 82*, 459–469.

Pressley, M., Brown, R. El-Dinary, P. B., & Allferbach, P. (1995). The comprehension instruction that students need: Instruction fostering constructively responsive reading. *Learning Disabilities Research & Practice, 10*, 215–224.

Pressman, E. K., DiPietro, J. A., Costigan, K. A., Shupe, A. K., & Johnson, T. R. B. (1998). Fetal neurobehavioral development: Associations with socioeconomic class and fetal sex. *Developmental Psychobiology, 33*, 79–91.

Prickett, T., Gada-Jain, N., & Bernieri, F. J. (in preparation). First impression formation in a job interview: The first 20 seconds. Cited in Ambady (2000); cited in Gladwell, M. (2000, May 29), *The New Yorker*.

Prien, R. F., & Kocsis, J. H. (1995). Long term treatment of mood disorders. In F. E. Bloom & D. J. Kupfer (Eds.), *Psychopharmacology: The fourth generation of progress* (pp. 1067–1080). New York: Raven Press.

Priester, J. R., & Petty, R. E. (1995). Source attributions and persuasion: Perceived honesty as a determinant of message scrutiny. *Personality and Social Psychology Bulletin, 21*, 637–654.

Privette, G., & Landsman, T. (1983). Factor analysis of peak performance: The full use of potential. *Journal of Personality and Social Psychology, 44*, 195–200.

Prochaska, J. O., & Norcross, J. C. (2001). Stages of change. *Psychotherapy: Theory, Research, Practice, Training, 38*, 443–448.

Prochaska, J. O., Norcross, J. C., & DiClemente, C. C. (1994). *Changing for good*. New York: William Morrow.

Prochaska, J. O., Velicer, W. F., Rossi, J. S., Goldstein, M. G., Marcus, B. H., Rakowski, W., et al. (1994). Stages of change and decisional balance for 12 problem behaviors. *Health Psychology, 13*, 39–46.

Proctor, R. W., & Van Zandt, T. (1994). *Human factors in simple and complex systems*. Boston: Allyn & Bacon.

Proksch, J., & Bavelier, D. (2002). Changes in the spatial distributions of visual attention after early deafness. *Journal of Cognitive Neuroscience, 14*, 687–701.

Proudfoot, J., Goldberg, D., Mann, A., Everitt, B., Marks, I., & Gray, J. A. (2003). Computerized, interactive, multimedia cognitive-behavioural program for anxiety and depression in general practice. *Psychological Medicine, 33*, 217–227.

Przeworski, A., & Newman, M. G. (2004). Palmtop computer-assisted group therapy for social phobia. *Journal of Clinical Psychology, 60*, 179–188.

Przybyla, D. P., & Byrne, D. (1984). The mediating role of cognitive processes in self-reported sexual arousal. *Journal of Research in Personality, 18*, 54–63.

Pujol, R., Lavigne-Rebillard, M., & Uziel, A. (1990). Physiological correlates of development of the human cochlea. *Seminars in Perinatology, 14*, 275–280.

Puka, B. (Ed.). (1994). *Kohlberg's original study of moral development*. New York: Garland.

Putnam, F. W. (1989). *Diagnosis and treatment of multiple personality disorder*. New York: Guilford Press.

Putnam, F. W., Helmers, K., Horowitz, L. A., & Trickett, P. K. (1995). Hypnotizability and dissociativity in sexually abused girls. *Child Abuse and Neglect, 19*, 645–655.

Putnam, H. (1973). Reductionism and the nature of psychology. *Cognition, 2*, 131–146.

Qin, Y., Carter, C. S., Silk, E. M., Stenger, V. A., Fissell, K., Goode, A., & Anderson, J. R. (2004). The change of the brain activation patterns as children learn algebra equation solving. *Proceedings of the National Academy of Sciences U S A, 101*, 5686–5691.

Quadrel, M. J., Fischhoff, B., & Davis, W. (1993). Adolescent (in)vulnerability. *American Psychologist, 48*, 102–116.

Quay, H. C. (1965). Psychopathic personality as pathological stimulus-seeking. *American Journal of Psychiatry, 122*, 180–183.

Quigley, K. S., Barrett, L. F., & Weinstein, S. (2002). Cardiovascular patterns associated with threat and challenge appraisals: A within-subjects analysis. *Psychophysiology, 39*, 292–302.

Quinn, J. G. (1991). Encoding and maintenance of information in visual working memory. In R. H. Logie & M. Denis (Eds.), *Mental images in human cognition* (pp. 95–104). Amsterdam: North-Holland.

Quinn, P. C., Bhatt, R. S., Brush, D., Grimes, A., & Sharpnack, H. (2002). Development of form similarity as a Gestalt grouping principle in infancy. *Psychological Science, 13*, 320–328.

Raag, T., & Rackliff, C. L. (1998). Preschoolers' awareness of social expectations of gender: Relationships to toy choices. *Sex Roles, 38*, 685–700.

Rabin, M. D., & Cain, W. S. (1986). Determinants of measured olfactory sensitivity. *Perception & Psychophysics, 39*, 281–286.

Rabinowitz, F. E., Sutton, L., Schutter, T., Brow, A., Krizo, C., Larsen, J., et al. (1997). Helpfulness to lost tourists. *Journal of Social Psychology, 137*, 502–509.

Rachman, S. (1993). Obsessions, responsibility and guilt. *Behaviour Research and Therapy, 31*, 149–154.

Rachman, S. (1997). A cognitive theory of obsessions. *Behaviour Research & Therapy, 35*, 793–802.

Radvansky, G. A. (1999). Aging, memory, and comprehension. *Current Directions in Psychological Science, 8*, 49–53.

Raemae, P., Sala, J. B., Gillen, J. S., Pekar, J. J., & Courtney, S. M. (2001). Dissociation of the neural systems for working memory maintenance of verbal and nonspatial visual information. *Cognitive, Affective & Behavioral Neuroscience, 1*, 161–171.

Ragusea, A. S., & VandeCreek, L. (2003). Suggestions for the ethical practice of online psychotherapy. *Psychotherapy: Theory, Research, Practice, Training, 40*, 94–102.

Rahman, Q., Wilson, G. D., & Abrahams, S. (2004). Sex, sexual orientation, and identification of postivie and negative facial affect. *Brain & Cognition, 54*, 179–185.

Räikkönen, K., Matthews, K. A., Flory, J. D., & Owens, J. F. (1999). Effects of hostility on ambulatory blood pressure and mood during daily living in healthy adults. *Health Psychology, 18*, 44–53.

Räikkönen, K., Pesonen, A. K., Järvenpää, A. L., & Strandberg, T. E. (2004). Sweet babies: Chocolate consumption during pregnancy and infant temperament at six months. *Early Human Development, 76*, 139–145.

Raine, A., Reynolds, C., Venables, P. H., & Mednick, S. A. (2002). Stimulation seeking and intelligence: A prospective longitudinal study. *Journal of Personality & Social Psychology, 82*, 663–674.

Raine, A., Venables, P. H., & Wiliams, M. (1990). Relationships between central and autonomic measures of arousal at age 15 years and criminality at age 24 years. *Archives of General Psychiatry, 47*, 1003–1007.

Rainville, P., Duncan, G. H., Price, D. D., Carrier, B., & Bushnell, M. C. (1997). Pain affect encoded in human anterior cingulate but not somatosensory cortex. *Science, 277*, 968–971.

Rajaram, S., Srinivas, K., & Roediger, H. L., III. (1998). A transfer-appropriate processing account of context effects in word fragment completion. *Journal of Experimental Psychology: Learning, Memory, & Cognition, 24*, 993–1004.

Rakic, P. (1975). Timing of major ontogenetic events in the visual cortex of the rhesus monkey. In N. Buchwald & M. Brazier (Eds.), *Brain mechanisms in mental retardation* (pp. 3–40). New York: Academic Press.

Ramachandran, V. S. (1993). Behavioral and magnetoencephalographic correlates of plasticity in the adult human brain. *Proceedings of the National Academy of Sciences, 90*, 10413–10420.

Ramachandran, V. S., Rogers-Ramachandran, D., & Stewart, M. (1992). Perceptual correlates of massive cortical reorganization. *Science, 258*, 1159–1160.

Ramamoorthy, Y., Yu, A. M., Suh, N., Haining, R.L., Tyndale, R. F., & Sellers, E.M. (2002) Reduced (+/–)-3,4-methylenedioxymethamphetamine ("ecstasy") metabolism with cytochrome P450 2D6 inhibitors and pharmacogenetic variants in vitro. *Biochemical Pharmacology, 63*, 2111–2119.

Ramel, W., Goldin, P. R., Carmona, P. E., & McQuaid, J. R. (2004). The effects of mindfulness meditation on cognitive processes and affect in patients with past depression. *Cognitive Therapy & Research, 28*, 433–455.

Ramirez, M., III. (1999). *Multicultural psychotherapy: An approach to individual and cultural differences* (2nd ed.). Needham Heights, MA: Allyn & Bacon.

Rankinen, T., Pérusse, L., Weisnagel, S. J., Snyder, E. E. Chagnon, Y. C., & Bouchard, C. (2002). The human obesity gene map: The 2001 update. *Obesity Research, 10*, 196–243.

Rao, H., Zhou, T., Zhuo, Y., Fan, S., & Chen, L. (2003). Spatiotemporal activation of the two visual pathways in form discrimination and spatial location: A brain mapping study. *Human Brain Mapping, 18*, 78–89.

Rao, S. C., Rainer, G., & Miller, E. K. (1997). Integration of what and where in the primate prefrontal cortex. *Science, 276*, 821–834.

Rapee, R. M., & Heimberg, R. G. (1997). A cognitive-behavioral model of anxiety in social phobia. *Behaviour Research & Therapy, 35*, 741–756.

Rassin, E. (2003). The White Bear Suppression Inventory (WBSI) focuses on failing suppression attempts. *European Journal of Personality, 17*, 285–298.

Ratliff-Schaub, K., Hunt, C. E., Crowell, D., Golub, H., Smok-Pearsall, S., Palmer, P., et al. (2001). Relationship between infant sleep position and motor development in preterm infants. *Journal of Developmental & Behavioral Pediatrics, 22*, 293–299.

Rauch, S. L., Jenike, M. A., Alpert, N. M., Baer, L., Breiter, H. C. R., Savage, C. R., & Fischman, A. J. (1994). Regional cerebral blood flow measured during symptom provocation in obsessive-compulsive disorder using oxygen 15–labeled carbon dioxide and positron emission tomography. *Archives of General Psychiatry, 51*, 62–70.

Rauch, S. L., van der Kolk, B. A., Risler, R. E., Alpert, N. M., Orr, S. P., Savage, C. R., et al. (1996). A symptom provocation study of posttraumatic stress disorder using positron emission tomography and script-driven imagery. *Archives of General Psychiatry, 53*, 380–387.

Rauch, S. L., Whalen, P. J., Shin, L. M., McInerney, S. C., Macklin, M. L., Lasko, N. B., et al. (2000). Exaggerated amygdala response to masked facial stimuli in posttraumatic stress disorder: A functional MRI study. *Biological Psychiatry, 47*, 769–776.

Raudenbush, S. W. (1984). Magnitude of teacher expectancy effects on pupil IQ as a function of the credibility of expectancy induction: A synthesis of findings from 18 experiments. *Journal of Educational Psychology, 76*, 85–97.

Rauscher, F. H. (1999). Prelude or requiem for the "Mozart effect"? *Nature, 400*, 827–828.

Rauscher, F. H., Shaw, G. L., & Ky, K. N. (1993). Music and spatial task performance. *Nature, 365*, 611.

Raven, J. C. (1965). *Advanced progressive matrices: Sets I and II.* London: Lewis.

Raven, J. C. (1976). *Standard progressive matrices: Sets A, B, C, D & E.* Oxford, England: Oxford Psychologists Press.

Ravussin, E., & Bouchard, C. (2000). Human genomics and obesity: Finding appropriate target drugs. *European Journal of Pharmacology, 410*, 131–145.

Ray, W. J., Sabsevitz, D., DePascalis, V., Quigley, K., Aikens, D., & Tubbs, M. (2000). Cardiovascular reactivity during hypnosis and hypnotic susceptibility: Three studies of heart rate variability. *International Journal of Clinical & Experimental Hypnosis, 48*, 22–31.

Raymond, J. E., Shapiro, K. L., & Arnell, K. M. (1992). Temporary suppression of visual processing in an RSVP task: An attentional blink? *Journal of Experimental Psychology: Human Perception and Performance, 18*, 849–860.

Raz, A., Shapiro, T., Fan, J., & Posner, M. (2002). Hypnotic suggestion and the modulation of the Stroop effect. *Archives of General Psychiatry, 59*, 1155–1161.

Raz, N., Gunning, F. M., Head, D., Dupuis, J. H., McQuain, J. M., Briggs, S. D., et al. (1997). Selective aging of human cerebral cortex observed in vivo: Differential vulnerability of the prefrontal gray matter. *Cerebral Cortex, 7*, 268–282.

Razran, G. H. S. (1940). Conditioned response changes in rating and appraising sociopolitical solutions. *Psychological Bulletin, 37*, 481.

Reber, P. J., Siwiec, R. M., Gitleman, D. R., Parrish, T. B., Mesulam, M.-M., & Paller, K. A. (2002). Neural correlates of successful encoding identified using functional magnetic resonance imaging. *Journal of Neuroscience, 22*, 9541–9548.

Rechtschaffen, A., Gilliland, M. A., Bergmann, B. M., & Winter, J. B. (1983). Physiological correlates of prolonged sleep deprivation in rats. *Science, 221*, 182–184.

Rector, N. A., & Beck, A. T. (2001). Cognitive behavioral therapy for schizophrenia: An empirical review. *Journal of Nervous & Mental Disease, 189*, 278–287.

Redd, W. H., Dadds, M. R., Futterman, A. D., Taylor, K. L., & Bovbjerg, D. J. (1993). Nausea induced by mental images of chemotherapy. *Cancer, 72*, 629–636.

Redelmeier, D. A., & Kahneman, D. (1996). Patients' memories of painful medical treatments: Real-time and retrospective evaluations of two minimally invasive procedures. *Pain, 66*, 3–8.

Reed, T. E., Vernon, P. A., & Johnson, A. M. (2004). Confirmation of correlation between brain nerve conduction velocity and intelligence level in normal adults. *Intelligence, 32*, 563–572.

Reese, E. (2002). Social factors in the development of autobiographical memory: The state of the art. *Social Development, 11*, 124–142.

Reese, H. W., Lee, L.-J., Cohen, S. H., & Puckett, J. M., Jr. (2001). Effects of intellectual variables, age, and gender on divergent thinking in adulthood. *International Journal of Behavioral Development, 25*, 491–500.

Reeve, C. L. (2004). Differential ability antecedents of general and specific dimensions of declarative knowledge: More than g. *Intelligence, 32*, 621–652.

Regan, D. T., & Fazio, R. H. (1977). On the consistency between attitudes and behavior: Look to the method of attitude formation. *Journal of Experimental Psychology, 13*, 38–45.

Regan, P. C. (1996). Rhythms of desire: The association between menstrual cycle phases and female sexual desire. *Canadian Journal of Human Sexuality, 5*, 145–156.

Regier D. A., & Kaelber, C. T. (1995). The Epidemiologic Catchment Area (ECA) program: Studying the prevalence and incidence of psychopathology. In M. T. Tsuang, M. Tohen, & G. E. P. Zahner (Eds.), *Textbook in psychiatric epidemiology* (pp. 133–157). New York: John Wiley & Sons.

Regier, D. A., Narrow, W. E., Rae, D. S., Manderscheid, R. W., Locke, B. Z., & Goodwin, F. K. (1993). The de facto US mental and addictive disorders service system. Epidemiologic Catchment Area prospective 1-year prevalence rates of disorders and services. *Archives of General Psychiatry, 50*, 85–94.

Reid, J. E. (1947). A revised questioning technique in lie-detection tests. *Journal of Criminal Law & Criminology, 37*, 542–547.

Reid, R. C. (1999). Vision. In M. J. Zigmond, F. E. Bloom, S. C. Landis, J. L. Roberts, & L. R. Squire (Eds.), *Fundamental neuroscience* (pp. 821–851). New York: Academic Press.

Reif, A., & Lesch, K. (2003). Toward a molecular architecture of personality. *Behavioural Brain Research, 139,* 1–20.

Reifman, A., & Windle, M. (1995). Adolescent suicidal behaviors as a function of depression, hopelessness, alcohol use, and social support: A longitudinal investigation. *American Journal of Community Psychology, 23,* 329–354.

Reinberg, A., Vieux, N., Andlauer, P., & Smolensky, M. (1983). Tolerance to shift work: A chronobiological approach. In J. Mendlewicz & H. M. van Praag (Eds.), *Biological rhythms and behavior advances in biological psychiatry* (Vol. 2, pp. 20–34). Basel, Switzerland: Karger.

Reinisch, J. M., & Sanders, S. A. (1992). Prenatal hormonal contributions to sex differences in human cognitive and personality development. In A. A. Gerall, H. Moltz, & I. I. Ward (Eds.), *Sexual differentiation: Vol. II. Handbook of behavioral neurobiology* (pp. 221–243). New York: Plenum.

Reis, H. T., & Shaver, P. (1988). Intimacy as an interpersonal process. In S. W. Duck (Ed.), *Handbook of basic principles* (pp. 367–389). Chichester, England: Wiley.

Reis, V. A.; Zaidel, D. W. (2001). Brain and face: Communicating signals of health in the left and right sides of the face. *Brain & Cognition, 46,* 240–244.

Reisenzein, R., Meyer, W., & Schützwohl, A. (1995). James and the physical basis of emotion: A comment on Ellsworth. *Psychological Review, 102,* 757–761.

Rende, R., & Plomin, R. (1992). Diathesis-stress models of psychopathology: A quantitative genetic perspective. *Applied & Preventative Psychology. 1,* 177–182.

Rensink, R. A., O'Regan, J. K., & Clark, J. J. (1997). To see or not to see: The need for attention to perceive changes in scenes. *Psychological Science, 8,* 368–373.

Repetti, R. L. (1993). Short-term effects of occupational stressors on daily mood and health complaints. *Health Psychology, 12,* 125–131.

Rescorla, R. A. (1967). Pavlovian conditioning and its proper control procedures. *Psychological Review, 74,* 71–80.

Resnick, H. S., Kilpatrick, D. G., Dansky, B. S., Saunders, B., & Best, C. L. (1993). Prevalence of civilian trauma and posttraumatic stress disorder in a representative national sample of women. *Journal of Consulting and Clinical Psychology, 61,* 984–991.

Resnick, S. M., Pham, D. L., Kraut, M. A., Zonderman, A. B., & Davatzikos, C. (2003). Longitudinal magnetic resonance imaging studies of older adults: A shrinking brain. *Journal of Neuroscience, 23,* 3295–3301.

Rest, J. R. (1979). *Development in judging moral issues.* Minneapolis: University of Minnesota Press.

Reynolds, C. F., III., Frank, E., Perel, J. M., Imber, S. D., Cornes, C., Miller, M. D., et al. (1999). Nortriptyline and interpersonal psychotherapy as maintenance therapies for recurrent major depression: A randomized controlled trial in patients older than 59 years. *Journal of the American Medical Association, 281,* 39–45.

Reynolds, S., Stiles, W. B., Barkham, M., Shapiro, D. A., Hardy, G. E., & Rees, A. (1996). Acceleration of changes in session impact during contrasting time-limited psychotherapies. *Journal of Consulting & Clinical Psychology, 64,* 577–586.

Rhodes, G., Byatt, G., Michie, P. T., & Puce, A. (2004). Is the fusiform face area specialized for faces, individuation, or expert individuation? *Journal of Cognitive Neuroscience, 16,* 189–203.

Rice, G., Anderson, C., Risch, N., & Ebers, G. (1999). Male homosexuality: Absence of linkage to microsatellite markers at Xq28. *Science, 284,* 665–667.

Rice, M. E., & Grusec, J. E. (1975). Saying and doing: Effects on observer performance. *Journal of Personality and Social Psychology, 32,* 584–593.

Rich, A. N., & Mattingley, J. B. (2002). Anomalous perception in synaesthesia: A cognitive neuroscience perspective. *Nature Reviews Neuroscience, 3,* 43–52.

Richards, J. C., Edgar, L. V., & Gibbons, P. (1996). Cardiac acuity in panic disorder. *Cognitive Therapy and Research, 20,* 361–376.

Richards, J., Klein, B., & Carlbring, P. (2003). Internet-based treatment for panic disorder. *Cognitive Behaviour Therapy, 32,* 125–135.

Richards, J. M. (2004). The cognitive consequences of concealing feelings. *Current Directions in Psychological Science, 13,* 131–134.

Richards, J. M., Butler, E. A., & Gross, J. J. (2003). Emotion regulation in romantic relationships: The cognitive consequences of concealing feelings. *Journal of Social & Personal Relationships, 20,* 599–620.

Richards, J. M., & Gross, J. J. (2000). Emotion regulation and memory: The cognitive costs of keeping one's cool. *Journal of Personality & Social Psychology, 79,* 410–424.

Richert, E. S. (1997). Excellence with equity in identification and programming. In N. Colangelo & G. A. Davis (Eds.), *Handbook of gifted education* (2nd ed., pp. 75–88). Boston: Allyn & Bacon.

Richmond, L. J. (2004). When spirituality goes awry: Students in cults. *Professional School Counseling, 7,* 367–375.

Riddoch, M. J., Humphreys, G. W., Jacobson, S., Pluck, G., Bateman, A., & Edwards, M. (2004). Impaired orientation discrimination and localisation following parietal damage: On the interplay between dorsal and ventral processes in visual perception. *Cognitive Neuropsychology, 21,* 597–623.

Rilling, J. K., Gutman, D. A., Zeh, T. R., Pagnoni, G., Berns, G. S., & Kilts, C. D. (2002). A neural basis for social cooperation. *Neuron, 35,* 395–405.

Rinaldi, M. C., Marangolo, P., & Baldassarri, F. (2004). Metaphor comprehension in right brain-damaged patients with visuo-verbal and verbal material: A dissociation (re)considered. *Cortex, 40,* 479–490.

Riordan-Eva, P. (1992). Blindness. In D. Vaugh, T. Ashbury, & P. Riordan-Eva (Eds.), *General opthalmology* (pp. 404–409). Norwalk, CT: Appleton & Lange.

Rips, L. (2001). Necessity and natural categories. *Psychological Bulletin, 127,* 827–852.

Rips, L. J., Shoben, E. J., & Smith, E. E. (1973). Semantic distance and the verification of semantic relations. *Journal of Verbal Learning and Verbal Behavior, 12,* 1–20.

Ritterband, L. M., Gonder-Frederick, L. A., Cox, D. J., Clifton, A. D., West, R. W., & Borowitz, S. M. (2003). Internet interventions: In review, in use, and into the future. *Professional Psychology: Research & Practice, 34,* 527–534.

Rivas-Vazques, R. A. (2001). Antidepressants as first-line agents in the current pharmacotherapy of anxiety disorders. *Professional Psychology: Research and Practice, 32,* 101–104.

Rivera, G., & Colle, M.-P. (1994). *Frida's fiesta's: Recipes and reminiscences of life with Frida Kahlo* (K. Krabbenhoft, Trans.). New York: Clarkson N. Potter.

Rivera-Arzola, M., & Ramos-Grenier, J. (1997). Anger, ataques de nervios, and la mujer puertorriquena: Sociocultural considerations and treatment implications. In J. G. Garcia & M. C. Zea (Eds.), *Psychological interventions and research with Latino populations.* Boston, MA: Allyn & Bacon.

Robbins, T. W., & Everitt, B. J. (1998). Motivation and reward. In M. J. Zigmond, F. E. Bloom, S. C. Landis, J. L. Roberts, & L. R. Squire (Eds.), *Fundamental neuroscience* (pp. 1245–1260). New York: Academic Press.

Robbins, T. W., & Everitt, B. J. (1999). Interaction of the dopaminergic system with mechanisms of associative learning and cognition: Implications for drug abuse. *Psychological Science, 10,* 199–202.

Roberson, D., Davidoff, J., Davies, I. R. L., & Shapiro, L. R. (2004). The development of color categories in two languages: A longitudinal study. *Journal of Experimental Psychology: General, 133,* 554–571.

Roberti, J. W., Storch, E. A., & Bravata, E. A. (2004). Sensation seeking, exposure to psychosocial stressors, and body modifications in a college population. *Personality & Individual Differences, 37,* 1167–1177.

Roberts, A. H., Kewman, D. G., Mercier, L., & Hovell, M. (1993). The power of nonspecific effects in healing: Implications for psychosocial and biological treatments. *Clinical Psychology Review, 13,* 375–391.

Roberts, B. W., Caspi, A., & Moffitt, T. E. (2001). The kids are alright: Growth and stability in personality development from adolescence to adulthood. *Journal of Personality & Social Psychology, 81,* 670–683.

Roberts, B. W., & DelVecchio, W. F. (2000). The rank-order consistency of personality traits from childhood to old age: A quantitative review of longitudinal studies. *Psychological Bulletin, 126,* 3–25.

Roberts, N. A., Beer, J. S., Werner, K. H., Scabini, D., Levens, S. M., Knight, R. T., & Levenson, R. W. (2004). The impact of orbital prefrontal cortex damage on emotional activation to unanticipated and anticipated acoustic startle stimuli. *Cognitive, Affective & Behavioral Neuroscience, 4,* 307–316.

Roberts, R. D., Zeidner, M., & Matthews, G. (2001). Does emotinal intelligence meet traditional standards for an intelligence? Some new data and conclusions. *Emotion, 1,* 196–231.

Robins, L. N., & Regier, D. A. (1991). *Psychiatric disorders in America: The epidemiological catchment area study.* New York: Free Press.

Robinson, A. J., & Pascalis, O. (2004). Development of flexible visual recognition memory in human infants. *Developmental Science, 7,* 527–533.

Robinson, J. L., Kagan, J., Reznick, J. S., & Corley, R. (1992). The heritability of inhibited and uninhibited behavior: A twin study. *Developmental Psychology, 28,* 1030–1037.

Robinson, L. C. (2000). Interpersonal relationship quality in young adulthood: A gender analysis. *Adolescence, 35,* 775–784.

Robinson, N. M., Abbott, R. D., Berninger, V. W., & Busse, J. (1996). The structure of abilities in math-precocious young children: Gender similarities and differences. *Journal of Educational Psychology, 88,* 341–352.

Robinson, N. M., Zigler, Z., & Gallagher, J. J. (2000). Two tails of the normal curve: Similarities and differences in the study of mental retardation and giftedness. *American Psychologist, 55*, 1413–1424.

Robinson, S. J., & Manning, J. T. (2000). The ratio of the 2nd to 4th digit length and male homosexuality. *Evolution and Human Behaviour, 21*, 333–345.

Robinson, T. E., & Berridge, K. C. (2001). Incentive-sensitization and addiction. *Addiction, 96*, 103–114.

Robinson, T. N., Wilde, M. L., Navracruz, L. C., Haydel, K. F., & Varady, A. (2001). Effects of reducing children's television and video game use on aggressive behavior: A randomized controlled trial. *Archives of Pediatric Adolescent Medicine, 155*, 17–23.

Robinson, V. (1977a). *Humor and the health professions.* Thorofare, NJ: Slack.

Robinson, V. (1977b). Humor in nursing. In C. Carlson & B. Blackwell (Eds.), *Behavioral concepts and nursing interventions.* Philadelphia: Lippincott.

Robinson-Whelen, S., Kim, C., MacCallum, R. C., & Kiecolt-Glaser, J. K. (1998). Distinguishing optimism from pessimism in older adults: Is it more important to be optimistic or not to be pessimistic? *Journal of Personality and Social Psychology, 73*, 1345–1353.

Robles, T. F., & Kiecolt-Glaser, J. K. (2003). The physiology of marriage: Pathways to health. *Physiology & Behavior, 79*, 409–416.

Rochat, P., & Hespos, S. J. (1997). Differential rooting response by neonates: Evidence for an early sense of self. *Early Development & Parenting, 6*, 105–112.

Rodier, P. (1980). Chronology of neuron development. *Developmental Medicine and Child Neurology, 22*, 525–545.

Rodin, J., & Langer, E. J. (1977). Long-term effects of a control-relevant intervention with the institutionalized aged. *Journal of Personality & Social Psychology, 35*, 897–902.

Rodriguez, V., Valdes-Sosa, M., & Freiwald, W. (2002). Dividing attention between form and motion during transparent surface perception. *Cognitive Brain Research, 13*, 187–193.

Roediger, H. L., III (1980). Memory metaphors in cognitive psychology. *Memory & Cognition, 8*, 231–246.

Roediger, H. L., III, & McDermott, K. B. (1993). Implicit memory in normal human subjects. In F. Bohler & J. Grafman (Eds.), *Handbook of neuropsychology* (Vol. 8, pp. 63–131). Amsterdam: Elsevier.

Roediger, H. L., III, & McDermott, K. B. (1995). Creating false memories: Remembering words not presented in lists. *Journal of Experimental Psychology: Learning, Memory, and Cognition, 21*, 803–814.

Roediger, H. L., III, Meade, M. L., & Bergman, E. T. (2001). Social contagion of memory. *Psychonomic Bulletin & Review, 8*, 365–371.

Roediger, H. L., III, & Thorpe, L. A. (1978). The role of recall time in producing hypermnesia. *Memory & Cognition, 6*, 296–305.

Roggman, L. A., Langlois, J. H., Hubbs-Tait, L., & Rieser-Danner, L. A. (1994). Infant day-care, attachment, and the "file drawer problem." *Child Development, 65*, 1429–1443.

Rohde, P. A., Atzwanger, K., Butovskayad, M., Lampert, A., Mysterud, I., Sanchez-Andres, A., & Sulloway, F. J. (2003). Perceived parental favoritism, closeness to kin, and the rebel of the family: The effects of birth order and sex. *Evolution & Human Behavior, 24*, 261–276.

Rohrmann, S., Netter, P., Hennig, J., & Hodapp, V. (2003). Repression-sensitization, gender, and discrepancies in psychobiological reactions to examination stress. *Anxiety, Stress & Coping: An International Journal, 16*, 321–329.

Rojas, I. G., Padgett, D. A., Sheridan, J. F., & Marucha, P. T. (2002). Stress-induced susceptibility to bacterial infection during cutaneous wound healing. *Brain, Behavior and Immunity, 16*, 74–84.

Roll, S., McClelland, G., & Abel, T. (1996). Differences in susceptibility to influence in Mexican American and Anglo females. *Hispanic Journal of Behavioral Sciences, 18*, 13–20.

Rollman, G. B. (1991). Pain responsiveness. In M. A. Heller & W. Schiff (Eds.), *The psychology of touch* (pp. 91–114). Hillsdale, NJ: Erlbaum.

Rollman, G. B., & Harris, G. (1987). The detectability, discriminability, and perceived magnitude of painful electrical shock. *Perception & Psychophysics, 42*, 257–268.

Rolls, B. J., Rowe, E. A., Rolls, E. T., Kingston, B., Megson, A., & Gunary, R. (1981). Variety in a meal enhances food intake in man. *Physiology & Behavior, 26*, 215–221.

Rolls, E. T., & Cooper, S. J. (1974). Connection between the prefrontal cortex and pontine brain-stimulation reward sites in the rat. *Experimental Neurology, 42*, 687–699.

Romach, M. K., & Sellers, E. M. (1991). Management of the alcohol withdrawal syndrome. *Annual Review of Medicine, 42*, 323–340.

Romani, G. L., Williamson, S. J., & Kaufman, L. (1982). Tonotopic organization of the human auditory cortex. *Science, 216*, 1339–1340.

Romero, A. A., Agnew, C. R., & Insko, C. A. (1996). The cognitive mediation hypothesis revisited: An empirical response to methodological and theoretical criticism. *Personality & Social Psychology Bulletin, 22*, 651–665.

Romero, L., & Sapolsky, R. (1996). Patterns of ACTH secretagog secretion in response to psychological stimuli. *Journal of Neuroendocrinology, 8*, 243–258.

Roozendaal, B. (2003). Systems mediating acute glucocorticoid effects on memory consolidation and retrieval. *Progress in Neuro-Psychopharmacology & Biological Psychiatry, 27*, 1213–1223.

Rosch, E. (1973). Natural categories. *Cognitive Psychology, 4*, 328–350.

Rosch, E. (1975). The nature of mental codes for color categories. *Journal of Experimental Psychology: Human Perception and Performance, 1*, 303–322.

Rosch, E. (1978). Principles of categorization. In E. Rosch, & B. B. Lloyd (Eds.), *Cognition and categorization* (pp. 27–48). Hillsdale, NJ: Erlbaum.

Rosch, E., Mervis, C. B., Gray, W. D., Johnson, D. M., & Boyes-Braem, P. (1976). Basic objects in natural categories. *Cognitive Psychology, 8*, 382–439.

Rosen, A. C., Prull, M. W., Gabrieli, J. D. E., Stoub, T., O'Hara, R., Friedman, L., et al. (2003). Differential associations between entorhinal and hippocampal volumes and memory performance in older adults. *Behavioral Neuroscience, 117*, 1150–1160.

Rosen, A. C., Rao, S. M., Caffarra, P., Scaglioni, A., Bobholz, J. A., Woodley, S. J., et al. (1999). Neural basis of endogenous and exogenous spatial orienting: A functional MRI study. *Journal of Cognitive Neuroscience, 11*, 135–152.

Rosen, C. M. (1987). The eerie world of reunited twins. *Discover, 8*, 36–46.

Rosenbaum, M., & Leibel, R. L. (1999). The role of leptin in human physiology. *New England Journal of Medicine, 341*, 913–915.

Rosenberg, M. (1979). *Conceiving the self.* New York: Basic Books.

Rosengren, A., Hawken, S., Ôunpuu, S., Sliwa, K., Zubaid, M., Almahmeed, W. A., et al. (2004). Association of psychosocial risk factors with risk of acute myocardial infarction in 11119 cases and 13648 controls from 52 countries (the INTERHEART study): Case-control study. *Lancet, 364*, 953–962.

Rosenhan, D. L. (1973). On being sane in insane places. *Science, 179*, 250–258.

Rosenheim, M. K., & Testa, M. F. (Eds.). (1992). *Early parenthood and coming of age in the 1990s.* New Brunswick, NJ: Rutgers University Press.

Rosenkranz, M. A., Jackson, D. C., Dalton, K. M., Dolski, I., Ryff, C. D., Singer, B. H., et al. (2003). Affective style and in vivo immune response: Neurobehavioral mechanisms. *Proceedings of the National Academy of Sciences, USA, 100*, 11148–11152.

Rosenthal, A. M. (1964). *Thirty-eight witnesses.* New York: McGraw-Hill.

Rosenthal, R. (1976). *Experimenter effects in behavioral research.* New York: Irvington.

Rosenthal, R. (1986). Meta-analytic procedure and the nature of replication: The Ganzfeld debate. *Journal of Parapsychology, 50*, 316–336.

Rosenthal, R. (1991). *Meta-analytic procedures for social research.* Beverly Hills, CA: Sage.

Rosenthal, R. (1993) Interpersonal expectations: Some antecedents and some consequences. In P. D. Blanck (Ed.), *Interpersonal expectations: Theory, research, and applications* (pp. 3–24). Cambridge, England: Cambridge University Press.

Rosenthal, R. (1994). Interpersonal expectancy effects: A 30-year perspective. *Current Directions in Psychological Sciences, 3*, 176–179.

Rosenthal, R., & Jacobson, L. (1968). *Pygmalion in the classroom.* New York: Holt, Rinehart & Winston.

Rosenzweig, P., Brohler, S., & Zipfel, A. (1993). The placebo effect in healthy volunteers: Influence of experimental conditions on the adverse events profile during phase I studies. *Clinical Pharmacological Therapy, 54*, 579–583.

Rosip, J. C., & Hall, J. A. (2004). Knowledge of nonverbal cues, gender, and nonverbal decoding accuracy. *Journal of Nonverbal Behavior, 28*, 267–286.

Roskill, M. (1963). *The letters of Vincent van Gogh.* London: William Collins.

Ross, C. A. (1991). Epidemiology of multiple personality disorder and dissociation. *Psychiatric Clinics of North America, 14*, 503–517.

Ross, C. A., Miller, S. D., Bjornson, L., Reagor, P., & Fraser, G. A. (1991). Abuse histories in 102 cases of multiple personality disorder. *Canadian Journal of Psychiatry, 36*, 97–101.

Ross, C. E. (1995). Reconceptualizing marital status as a continuum of social attachment. *Journal of Marriage & the Family, 57*, 129–140.

Ross, L., Greene, D., & House, P. (1977). The false consensus effect: An egocentric bias in social perception and attribution processes. *Journal of Experimental Social Psychology, 13*, 279–301.

Rossi, E. L., & Cheek, D. B. (1988). *Mind-body therapy,* New York: Norton.

Roth, A., & Fonagy, P. (2005). *What works for whom: A critical review of psychotherapy research* (2nd ed.). New York: Guilford.

Rothbart, M. K., & Derryberry, D. (1981). Development of individual differences in temperament. In M. E. Lamb & A. L. Brown (Eds.), *Advances in developmental psychology* (Vol. I, pp. 37–86). Hillsdale, NJ: Erlbaum.

Rothbart, M. K., Derryberry, D., & Posner, M. I. (1994). A psychobiological approach to the development of temperament. In J. E. Bates & T. D. Wachs (Eds.), *Temperament: Individual differences at the interface of biology and behavior* (pp. 83–116). Washington, DC: American Psychological Association.

Rothbaum, B. O., Hodges, L., Anderson, P. L., Price, L., & Smith, S. (2002). Twelvemonth follow-up of virtual reality and standard exposure therapies for the fear of flying. *Journal of Consulting & Clinical Psychology, 70,* 428–432.

Rothbaum, B. O., Hodges, L., Smith, S., Lee, J. H., & Price, L. (2001). A controlled study of virtual reality exposure therapy for the fear of flying. *Journal of Consulting & Clinical Psychology, 68,* 1020–1026.

Rotter, J. B. (1966). Generalized expectancies for internal versus external control of reinforcement. *Psychological Monographs, 80*(1, Whole No. 609).

Rouhana, N. N., & Bar-Tal, D. (1998). Psychological dynamics of intractable ethnonational conflicts: The Israeli-Palestinian case. *American Psychologist, 53,* 761–770.

Rouillon, F. (1997). Epidemiology of panic disorder. *Human Psychopharmacology Clinical & Experimental, 12*(Suppl. 1), S7–S12.

Roux, A. V. D., Merkin, S. S., Arnett, D., Chambless, L. D., Massing, M., Nieto, F. J., et al. (2001). Neighborhood of residence and incidence of coronary heart disease. *New England Journal of Medicine, 345,* 99–106.

Rovee-Collier, C. (1997). Dissociations in infant memory: Rethinking the development of implicit and explicit memory. *Psychological Review, 104,* 467–498.

Rowe, J. W., & Kahn, R. L. (1998). *Successful aging.* New York: Pantheon.

Rowling, J. K. (2005). My life so far. Part of interview with Amazon.co.uk. Retrieved October 30, 2005 from http://www.cliphoto.com/potter/interview.htm#lifesofar

Roy, R., Benenson, J. F., & Lilly, F. (2000). Beyond intimacy: Conceptualizing sex differences in same-sex relationships. *Journal of Psychology, 134,* 93–101.

Royet, J., & Plailly, J. (2004). Lateralization of olfactory processes. *Chemical Senses, 29,* 731–745.

Roysamb, E., Harris, J. R., Magnus, P., Vitterso, J., & Tambs, K. (2002). Subjective well-being: Sex-specific effects of genetic and environmental factors. *Personality & Individual Differences, 32,* 211–223.

Rozin, P. (1982). "Taste-smell confusions" and the duality of the olfactory sense. *Perception and Psychophysics, 31,* 397–401.

Rozin, P., Ashmore, M., & Markwith, M. (1996). Lay American conceptions of nutrition: Dose insensitivity, categorical thinking, contagion, and the monotonic mind. *Health Psychology, 15,* 438–447.

Rozin, P., & Fallon, A. (1986). The acquisition of likes and dislikes for foods. In National Research Council et al. (Eds.), *What is America eating? Proceedings of a symposium.* Washington, DC: National Academy Press.

Rozin, P., & Jonides, J. (1977). Mass reaction time: Measurement of the speed of the nerve impulse and the duration of mental processes in class. *Teaching of Psychology, 4,* 91–94.

Rozin, P., Lowery, L., & Ebert, R. (1994). Varieties of disgust faces and the structure of disgust. *Journal of Personality & Social Psychology, 66,* 870–881.

Rubin, K., & Borwick, D. (1984). The communication skills of children who vary with regard to sociability. In H. Sypher & J. Applegate (Eds.), *Social cognition and communication.* Hillsdale, NJ: Erlbaum.

Rubin, K. H., Burgess, K. B., & Coplan, R. J. (2002). Social withdrawal and shyness. In P. K. Smith & C. H. Hart (Eds.), *Blackwell handbook of childhood social development* (pp. 330–352). Malden, MA: Blackwell Publishers.

Rubin, K. H., Stewart, S. L., & Coplan, R. J. (1995). Social withdrawal in childhood: Conceptual and empirical perspectives. *Advances in Clinical Child Psychology, 17,* 157–196.

Rubin, L. J. (1996). Childhood sexual abuse: False accusations of "false memory"? *Professional Psychology Research and Practice, 27,* 447–451.

Rubin, Z. (1970). Measurement of romantic love. *Journal of Personality and Social Psychology, 16,* 265–273.

Ruby, P., & Decety, J. (2003). What you believe versus what you think they believe: A neuroimaging study of conceptual perspective-taking. *European Journal of Neuroscience, 17,* 2475–2480.

Rudman, L. A. (2004). Sources of implicit attitudes. *Current Directions in Psychological Science, 13,* 79–82.

Ruiz, C. J., Wray, K., Delay, E. R., Margolskee, R. F., & Kinnamon, S. C. (2003). Behavioral evidence for a role of α-gustducin in glutamate taste. *Chemical Senses, 28,* 573–579.

Rumelhart, D. E. (1975). Notes on schema for stories. In D. G. Bobrow & A. M. Collins (Eds.), *Representations and understanding: Studies in cognitive science* (pp. 211–236). New York: Academic Press.

Rumelhart, D. E., & McClelland, J. L. (1986). *Parallel distributed processing: Explorations in the microstructure of cognition: Volume 1, Foundations* (2nd ed.), Cambridge, MA: MIT Press.

Runco, M. A. (2004). Creativity. *Annual Review of Psychology, 55,* 657–687.

Runco, M. A., & Albert, R. S. (1986). The threshold theory regarding creativity and intelligence: An empirical test with gifted and nongifted children. *Creative Child & Adult Quarterly, 11,* 212–218.

Rupniak, N. M. (2002, February). Elucidating the antidepressant actions of substance P (NK1 receptor) antagonists. *Current Opinion in Investigational Drugs, 3*(2), 257–261.

Rush, A. N., Robinette, B. L., & Stanton, M. E. (2001). Ontogenetic differences in the effects of unpaired stimulus preexposure on eyeblink conditioning in the rat. *Developmental Psychobiology, 39,* 8–18.

Rushton, J. P. (1975). Generosity in children: Immediate and long-term effects of modeling, preaching, and moral judgement. *Journal of Personality and Social Psychology, 31,* 459–466.

Rushton, J. P. (1995). *Race, evolution and behavior: A life-history perspective.* New Brunswick, NJ: Transaction.

Rushton, J. P., & Ankney, C. D. (1996). Brain size and cognitive ability: Correlations with age, sex, social class, and race. *Psychonomic Bulletin & Review, 3,* 21–36.

Russell, J. A. (2003). Core affect and the psychological construction of emotion. *Psychological Review, 110,* 145–172.

Russell, J. A., Bachorowski, J.-A., & Fernández-Dols, J.-M. (2003). Facial and vocal expressions of emotion. *Annual Review of Psychology, 54,* 329–349.

Russell, M. J., Switz, D. M., & Thompson, K. (1980). Olfactory influences on the human menstrual cycle. *Pharmacology, Biochemistry, & Behavior, 13,* 737–8.

Russell, R. (2003). Sex, beauty, and the relative luminance of facial features. *Perception, 32,* 1093–1107.

Russo, J. E., & Schoemaker, P. J. H. (1989). *Decision traps.* New York: Doubleday.

Russo, J. E., & Schoemaker, P. J. H. (2002). *Winning decisions: Getting it right the first time.* New York: Doubleday.

Rustemli, A., Mertan, B., & Ciftci, O. (2000). In-group favoritism among native and immigrant Turkish cypriots: Trait evaluations of in-group and out-group targets. *Journal of Social Psychology, 140,* 26–34.

Rutledge, T., Reis, S. E., Olson, M., Owens, J., Kelsey, S. F., Pepine, C. J., et al. (2004). Social networks are associated with lower mortality rates among women with suspected coronary disease: The National Heart, Lung, and Blood Institute-Sponsored Women's Ischemia Syndrome Evaluation Study. *Psychosomatic Medicine, 66,* 882–888.

Ryan, K. E., & Ryan, A. M. (2005). Psychological processes underlying stereotype threat and standardized math test performance. *Educational Psychologist, 40,* 53–63.

Ryan, L., Nadel, L., Keil, K., Putnam, K., Schnyer, D., Trouard, T., & Moscovitch, M. (2001). Hippocampal complex and retrieval of recent and very remote autobiographical memories: Evidence from functional magnetic resonance imaging in neurologically intact people. *Hippocampus, 11,* 707–714.

Ryan, R. M., & Deci, E. L. (2000). Self-determination theory and the facilitation of intrinsic motivation, social development, and well-being. *American Psychologist, 55,* 68–78.

Rymer, R. (1993). *Genie: An abused child's flight from silence.* New York: HarperCollins.

Ryner, L. C., Goodwin, S. F., Castrillon, D. H., Anand, A., Villella, A., Baker, B. S., et al. (1996). Control of male sexual behavior and sexual orientation in *Drosophila* by the fruitless gene. *Cell, 87,* 1079–1089.

Rynes, S. L., Gerhart, B., & Parks, L. (2005). Personnel psychology: Performance evaluation and pay-for-performance. *Annual Review of Psychology, 56,* 561–600.

Ryska, T. A. (1998). Cognitive-behavioral strategies and precompetitive anxiety among recreational athletes. *Psychological Record, 48,* 697–708.

Sabourin, M. E., Cutcomb, S. D., Crawford, H. J., & Pribram, K. (1990–1991). EEG correlates of hypnotic susceptibility and hypnotic trance: Spectral analysis and coherence. *International Journal of Psychophysiology, 10,* 125–142.

Sachs, J. S. (1967). Recognition memory for syntactic and semantic aspects of connected discourse. *Perception and Psychophysics, 2,* 437–442.

Sackeim, H. A., Devanand, D. P., & Nobler, M. S. (1995). Electroconvulsive therapy. In F. E. Bloom & D. J. Kupfer (Eds.), *Psychopharmacology: The fourth generation of progress* (pp. 1123–1141). New York: Raven Press.

Sackeim, H. A., Haskett, R. F., Mulsant, B. H., Thase, M. E., Mann, J. J., Pettinati, H. M., et al. (2001). Continuation pharmacotherapy in the prevention of relapse following electroconvulsive therapy: A randomized controlled trial. *Journal of the American Medical Association, 285,* 1299–1307.

Sackett, P. R. (1994). Integrity testing for personnel selection. *Current Directions in Psychological Science, 3,* 73–76.

Sackett, P. R., Schmitt, N., Ellingson, J. E., & Kabin, M. B. (2001). High-stakes testing in employment, credentialing, and higher education: Prospects in a post-affirmative-action world. *American Psychologist, 56,* 302–318.

Sacks, O. (1995). *An anthropologist on Mars: Seven paradoxical tales*. New York: Knopf.

Sadler, T. W. (1995). *Langman's medical embryology* (7th ed.). Baltimore: Williams & Wilkins.

Sadowski, C. J., & Guelgoez, S. (1996). Elaborative processing mediates the relationship between need for cognition and academic performance. *Journal of Psychology, 130*, 303–307.

Sadr, J., Jarudi, I., & Sinha, P. (2003). The role of eyebrows in face recognition. *Perception, 32*, 285–293.

Saffran, J. R. (2001). Words in a sea of sounds: The output of infant statistical learning. *Cognition, 81*, 149–169.

Saffran, J. R. (2003). Absolute pitch in infancy and adulthood: The role of tonal structure. *Developmental Science, 6*, 35–43.

Saffran, J. R., & Griepentrog, G. J. (2001). Absolute pitch in infant auditory learning: Evidence for developmental reorganization. *Developmental Psychology, 37*, 74–85.

Saggino, A. (2000). The Big Three or the Big Five? A replication study. *Personality & Individual Differences, 28*, 879–886.

Sagi, A., Koren-Karie, N., Gini, M., Ziv, Y., & Joels, T. (2002). Shedding further light on the effects of various types and quality of early child care on infant-mother attachment relationship: The Haifa Study of Early Child Care. *Child Development, 73*, 1166–1186.

Sagi, A., van IJzendoorn, M. H., Scharf, M., Joels, T., Mayseless, O., & Aviezer, O. (1997). Ecological constraints for intergenerational transmission of attachment. *International Journal of Behavioral Development, 20*, 287–299.

Sagie, A., Elizur, S., & Hirotsugu, Y. (1996). The structure and strength of achievement motivation: A cross-cultural comparison. *Journal of Organization Behavior, 17*, 431–444.

Saha, L. J. (Ed.). (2004). Levels of analysis in the social psychology of education [Editorial]. *Social Psychology of Education, 7*, 253–255.

Sakai, N., Kobayakawa, T., Gotow, N., Saito, S., & Imada, S. (2001). Enhancement of sweetness ratings of aspartame by a vanilla odor presented either by orthonasal or retronasal routes. *Perceptual & Motor Skills, 92*, 1002–1008.

Saldana, H. N., & Rosenblum, L. D. (1993). Visual influences on auditory pluck and bow judgments. *Perception & Psychophysics, 54*, 406–416.

Saletan, 2. (2004, May 12). Situationist ethics: The Stanford Prison Experiment doesn't explain Abu Ghraib. *Slate Magazine*. Retrieved from http://slate.msn.com/id/2100419/

Salkovskis, P. M. (1985). Obsessional-compulsive problems: A cognitive-behavioral analysis. *Behaviour Research and Therapy, 23*, 571–583.

Salkovskis, P. M., Wroe, A. L., Gledhill, A., Morrison, N., Forrester, E., Richards, C., et al. (2000). Responsibility attitudes and interpretations are characteristic of obsessive–compulsive disorder. *Behaviour Research and Therapy, 38*, 347–372.

Salmon, C. A. (1998). The evocative nature of kin terminology in political rhetoric. *Politics and the Life Sciences 17*, 51–57.

Salmon, C. A. (1999). On the impact of sex and birth order on contact with kin. *Human Nature, 10*, 183–197.

Salmon, C. A., & Daly, M. (1998). Birth order and familial sentiment: Middleborns are different. *Evolution and Behavior, 19*, 299–312.

Salmon, D. P., & Butters, N. (1995). Neurobiology of skill and habit learning. *Current Opinion in Neurobiology, 5*, 184–190.

Salovey, P., & Mayer, J. D. (1990). Emotional intelligence. *Imagination, Cognition, and Personality, 9*, 185–211.

Salthouse, T. A. (1984). Effects of age and skill in typing. *Journal of Experimental Psychology: General, 113*, 345–371.

Salthouse, T. A. (1985). Speed of behavior and its implications for cognition. In J. E. Birren & K. W. Schaie (Eds.), *Handbook of the psychology of aging* (2nd ed., pp. 400–426). New York: Van Nostrand Reinhold.

Salthouse, T. A. (1991a). Cognitive facets of aging well. *Generations, 15*(1), 35–38.

Salthouse, T. A. (1991b). *Theoretical perspectives on cognitive aging*. Hillsdale, NJ: Erlbaum.

Salthouse, T. A. (1996). The processing-speed theory of adult age differences in cognition. *Psychological Review, 103*, 403–428.

Samoluk, S. B., & Stewart, S. H. (1998). Anxiety sensitivity and situation-specific drinking. *Journal of Anxiety Disorders, 12*, 407–419.

Sampaio, E., Maris, S., & Bach-y-Rita, P. (2001). Brain plasticity: "Visual" acuity of blind persons via the tongue. *Brain Research, 908*, 204–207.

Sanbonmatsu, D. M., & Fazio, R. H. (1990). The role of attitudes in memory-based decision making. *Journal of Personality and Social Psychology, 59*, 614–622.

Sand, G., & Miyazaki, A. D. (2000). The impact of social support on salesperson burnout and burnout components. *Psychology & Marketing, 17*, 13–26.

Sandahl, C., Gerge, A., & Herlitz, K. (2004). Does treatment focus on self-efficacy result in better coping? Paradoxical findings from psychodynamic and cognitive-behavioral group treatment of moderately alcohol-dependent patients. *Psychotherapy Research, 14*, 388–397.

Sanfey, A. G., Rilling, J. K., Aronson, J. A., Nystrom, L. E., & Cohen, J. D. (2003). The neural basis of economic decision-making in the Ultimatum Game. *Science, 300*, 1755–1758.

Santarelli, L., & Saxe, M. D. (2003). Substance P antagonists: Meet the new drugs, same as the old drugs? Insights from transgenic animal models. *CNS Spectrums, 8*, 589–596.

Sanudo-Pena, M., Tsou, K., Romero, J., Mackie, K., & Walker, J. M. (2000). Role of the superior colliculus in the motor effects of cannabinoids and dopamine. *Brain Research, 853*, 207–214.

Sapolsky, R. M. (1992). *Stress, the aging brain, and the mechanisms of neuron death*. Cambridge, MA: MIT Press.

Sapolsky, R. M. (1996). Why stress is bad for your brain. *Science, 273*, 749–750.

Sapolsky, R. M. (1997). *Why zebras don't get ulcers*. New York: Freeman.

Sarbin, T. R. (1995). On the belief that one body may be host to two or more personalities. *International Journal of Clinical & Experimental Hypnosis, 43*, 163–183.

Sarbin, T. R., & Coe, W. C. (1972). *Hypnosis: A social psychological analysis of influence communication*. New York: Holt, Rinehart, & Winston.

Sargent, J. D., Beach, M. L., Dalton, M. A., Mott, L. A., Tickle, J. J., Ahrens, M. B., & Heatherton, T. L. (2001). Effect of seeing tobacco use in films on trying smoking among adolescents: Cross sectional study. *British Medical Journal, 323*, 1394–1397.

Sargent, P. A., Sharpley, A. L., Williams, C., Goodall, E. M., & Cowen, P. J. (1997). 5-HT-sub(2C) receptor activation decreases appetite and body weight in obese subjects. *Psychopharmacology, 133*, 309–312.

Saroglou, V., & Fiasse, L. (2003). Birth order, personality, and religion: A study among young adults from a three-sibling family. *Personality & Individual Differences, 35*, 19–29.

Satcher, D. (1999). *Mental health: A report of the Surgeon General*. Washington, DC: Department of Health and Human Services.

Saudino, K. J., Gagne, J. R., Grant, J., Ibatoulina, A., Marytuina, T., Ravich-Scherbo, I., & Whitfield, K. (1999). Genetic and environmental influences on personality in adult Russian twins. *International Journal of Behavioral Development, 23*, 375–389.

Savage-Rumbaugh, S., McDonald, K., Sevcik, R. A., Hopkins, W. D., & Rubert, E. (1986). Spontaneous symbol acquisition and communicative use by pygmy chimpanzees (*Pan paniscus*). *Journal of Experimental Psychology: General, 112*, 211–235.

Savazzi, S., & Marzi, C. A. (2002). Speeding up reaction time with invisible stimuli. *Current Biology, 12*, 403–407.

Saxena, S., & Rauch, S. L., (2000). Functional neuroimaging and the neuroanatomy of obsessive-compulsive disorder. *Psychiatric Clinics of North America, 23*, 563–586.

Scarmeas, N., Levy, G., Tang, M.-X., Manly, J., & Stern, Y. (2001). Influence of leisure activity on the incidence of Alzheimer's disease. *Neurology, 57*, 2236–2242.

Scarr, S. (1976). An evolutionary perspective on infant intelligence: Species patterns and individual variations. In M. Lewis (Ed.), *Origins of intelligence* (pp. 165–197). New York: Plenum.

Scarr, S. (1998). American child care today. *American Psychologist, 53*(2), 95–108.

Scarr, S., & McCartney, K. (1983). How people make their own environments: A theory of genotype-environment effects. *Child Development, 54*, 424–435.

Scarr, S., & Weinberg, R. A. (1983). The Minnesota Adoption Studies: Genetic differences and malleability. *Child Development, 54*, 260–267.

Schachter, S., & Latané, B. (1964). Crime, cognition, and the autonomic nervous system. In D. Levine (Ed.), *Nebraska Symposium on Motivation* (Vol. 12, pp. 221–273). Lincoln: University of Nebraska Press.

Schachter, S., & Singer, J. (1962). Cognitive, social and physiological determinants of emotional state. *Psychological Review, 69*, 379–399.

Schacter, D. L. (1987). Implicit memory: History and current status. *Journal of Experimental Psychology: Learning, Memory, and Cognition, 13*, 501–518.

Schacter, D. L. (1996). *Searching for memory: The brain, the mind, and the past*. New York: Basic Books.

Schacter, D. L. (1999). The seven sins of memory: Insights from psychology and cognitive neuroscience. *American Psychologist, 54*, 182–203.

Schacter, D. L., & Badgaiyan, R. D. (2001). Neuroimaging of priming: New perspectives on implicit and explicit memory. *Current Directions in Psychological Science, 10*, 1–4.

Schacter, D. L., Cendan, D. L., Dodson, C. S., & Clifford, E. R. (2001). Retrieval conditions and false recognition: Testing the distinctiveness heuristic. *Psychonomic Bulletin & Review, 8*, 827–833.

Schacter, D. L., Kaszniak, A. K., Kihlstrom, J. F., & Valdiserri, M. (1991). The relation between source memory and aging. *Psychology and Aging, 6*, 559–568.

Schacter, D. L., Koutstaal, W., & Norman, K. A. (1997). False memories and aging. *Trends in Cognitive Sciences, 1*, 229–236.

Schacter, D. L., Osowiecki, D., Kaszniak, A. W., Kihlstrom, J. F., & Valdiserri, M. (1994). Source memory: Extending the boundaries of age-related deficits. *Psychology and Aging, 9*, 81–89.

Schacter, D. L., Reiman, E., Curran, T., Yun, L. S., Bandy, D., McDermott, K. B., & Roediger, H. L., III (1996). Neuroanatomical correlates of veridical and illusory recognition memory: Evidence from positron emission tomography. *Neuron, 2*, 267–274.

Schacter, D. L., & Wagner, A. D. (1999). Medial temporal lobe activations in fMRI and PET studies of episodic encoding and retrieval. *Hippocampus, 9*, 7–24.

Schaefer, S. M., Jackson, D. C., Davidson, R. J., Aguirre, G. K., Kimberg, D. Y., & Thompson-Schill, S. L. (2002). Modulation of amygdalar activity by the conscious regulation of negative emotion. *Journal of Cognitive Neuroscience, 14*, 913–921.

Schaffner, K. F. (1967). Approaches to reduction. *Philosophy of Science, 34*, 137–147.

Schaie, K. W. (1983). The Seattle longitudinal study: A 21-year exploration of psychometric intelligence in adulthood. In K. W. Schaie (Ed.), *Longitudinal studies of adult psychological development* (pp. 64–135). New York: Guilford.

Schaie, K. W. (1989). Individual differences in rate of cognitive change in adulthood. In V. L. Bengtson & K. W. Schaie (Eds.), *The course of later life: Research and reflections* (pp. 65–85). New York: Springer.

Schaie, K. W. (1990b). The optimization of cognitive functioning in old age: Predictions based on cohort-sequential and longitudinal data. In P. B. Baltes & M. M. Baltes (Eds.), *Successful aging: Perspectives from the behavioral sciences* (pp. 94–117). Cambridge, England: Cambridge University Press.

Schaie, K. W., & Willis, S. L. (1993). Age difference patterns of psychometric intelligence in adulthood: Generalizability within and across ability domains. *Psychology and Aging, 8*, 44–55.

Schaie, K. W., Willis, S. L., & Caskie, G. I. L. (2004). The Seattle longitudinal study: Relationship between personality and cognition. *Aging, Neuropsychology, & Cognition, 11*, 304–324.

Schank, R. C., & Abelson, R. P. (1977). *Scripts, plans, goals, and understanding.* Hillsdale, NJ: Erlbaum.

Scharf, M., Shulman, S., & Avigad-Spitz, L. (2005). Sibling relationships in emerging adulthood and in adolescence. *Journal of Adolescent Research, 20*, 64–90.

Schaufeli, W. B., & Enzmann, D. (1998). *The burnout companion to study and practice: A critical analysis.* London: Taylor & Francis.

Scheflin, A., & Brown, D. (1996). Repressed memory or dissociative amnesia: What science says. *Journal of Psychiatry and Law, 24*, 143–188.

Scheier, M. F., & Carver, C. S. (1985). Optimism, coping, and health: Assessment and implications of generalized outcome expectancies. *Health Psychology, 4*, 219–247.

Scheier, M. F., & Carver, C. S. (1993). On the power of positive thinking: The benefits of being optimistic. *Current Directions in Psychological Science, 2*, 26–30.

Scheier, M. F., Matthews, K. A., Owens, J. F., Magovern, G. J., Lefebvre, R. C., Abbott, R. A., & Carver, C. S. (1989). Dispositional optimism and recovery from coronary artery bypass surgery: The beneficial effects on physical and psychological well-being. *Journal of Personality and Social Psychology, 57*, 1024–1040.

Scheier, M. F., Matthews, K. A., Owens, J. F., Schulz, R., Bridges, M. W., Magovern, G. J., & Carver, C. S. (1999). Optimism and rehospitalization after coronary artery bypass graft surgery. *Archives of Internal Medicine, 159*, 829–835.

Schein, E. H. (1961). *Coercive persuasion.* New York: W.W. Norton.

Schellenberg, E. G. (2004). Music lessons enhance IQ. *Psychological Science, 15*, 511–514.

Schiavi, R. C., White, D., Mandeli, J., & Levine, A. C. (1997). Effect of testosterone administration on sexual behavior and mood in men with erectile dysfunction. *Archives of Sexual Behavior, 26*, 231–241.

Schifano, F. (2004). A bitter pill. Overview of ecstasy (MDMA, MDA) related fatalities. *Psychopharmacology, 173*, 242–248.

Schiffman, S. S. (1992). Aging and the sense of smell: Potential benefits of fragrance enhancement. In S. Van Toller & G. H. Dodd (Eds.), *Fragrance: The psychology and biology of perfum* (pp. 51–62). London: Elsevier.

Schiffman, S. S., Graham, B. G., Sattely-Miller, E. A., & Warwick, Z. S. (1999). Orosensory perception of dietary fat. *Current Directions in Psychological Science, 7*, 137–143.

Schilder, P. (1938). Psychoanalytic remarks on *Alice in Wonderland* and Lewis Carroll. *Journal of Nervous & Mental Disease, 87*, 159–168.

Schlaepfer, T. E., Kosel, M., & Nemeroff, C. B. (2003). Efficacy of repetitive transcranial magnetic stimulation (rTMS) in the treatment of affective disorders. *Neuropsychopharmacology, 28*, 201–205.

Schlaug, G., Jancke, L., Huang, Y., & Steinmetz, H. (1995). In vivo evidence of structural brain asymmetry in musicians. *Science, 267*, 699–701.

Schlenker, B. R. (1980). *Impression management: The self-concept, social identity, and interpersonal relations.* Belmont, CA: Brooks/Cole.

Schmader, T. (2002). Gender identification moderates stereotype threat effects on women's math performance. *Journal of Experimental Social Psychology, 38*, 194–201.

Schmader, T., & Johns, M. (2003). Converging evidence that stereotype threat reduces working memory capacity. *Journal of Personality & Social Psychology, 85*, 440–452.

Schmajuk, N. A. (2001). Hippocampal dysfunction in schizophrenia. *Hippocampus, 11*, 599–613.

Schmid, W., & Aldridge, D. (2004). Active music therapy in the treatment of multiple sclerosis patients: A matched control study. *Journal of Music Therapy, 41*, 225–240.

Schmidt, F. L., & Hunter, J. (1998). The validity and utility of selection methods in personnel psychology: Practical and theoretical implications of 85 years of research findings. *Psychological Bulletin, 124*, 262–274.

Schmidt, F. L., & Hunter, J. (2004). General mental ability in the world of work: Occupational attainment and job performance. *Journal of Personality and Social Psychology, 86*, 162–173.

Schmidt, N. B., Lerew, D. R., & Jackson, R. J. (1997). The role of anxiety sensitivity in the pathogenesis of panic: Prospective evaluation of spontaneous panic attacks during acute stress. *Journal of Abnormal Psychology, 106*, 355–364.

Schmidt, N. B., Lerew, D. R., & Jackson, R. J. (1999). Prospective evaluation of anxiety sensitivity in the pathogenesis of panic: Replication and extension. *Journal of Abnormal Psychology, 108*, 532–537.

Schmidt, N. B, & Vasey, M. (2002). Primary prevention of psychopathology in a high risk youth population. In D. Roth (Ed.), *New Research in Mental Health, 15* (pp. 203–209). Columbus: Ohio Department of Mental Health.

Schmidt, S. R. (2002). Outstanding memories: The positive and negative effects of nudes on memory. *Journal of Experimental Psychology: Learning, Memory, & Cognition, 28*, 353–361.

Schmitt, B. H., Gilovich, T., Goore, N., & Joseph, L. (1986). Mere presence and social facilitation: One more time. *Journal of Experimental Social Psychology, 22*, 242–248.

Schmitt, D. P. (2002). How shall I compare thee? Evolutionary psychology viewed as a psychological science. *Psychology, Evolution & Gender, 4*, 219–230.

Schmitt, D. P., Alcalay, L., Allensworth, M., Allik, J., Ault, L., Austers, I., et al. (2004). Patterns and universals of adult romantic attachment across 62 cultural regions: Are models of self and of other pancultural constructs? *Journal of Cross-Cultural Psychology, 35*, 367–402.

Schmolck, H., Buffalo, E. A., & Squire, L. R. (2000). Memory distortions develop over time: Recollections from the O. J. Simpson trial verdict after 15 and 32 months. *Psychological Science, 11*, 39–45.

Schneider, L. H., Davis, J. D., Watson, C. A., & Smith, G. P. (1990). Similar effect of raclopride and reduced sucrose concentration on the micro-structure of sucrose sham feeding. *European Journal of Pharmacology, 186*, 61–70.

Schneider, M., & Koch, M. (2002). The cannabinoid agonist WIN 55,212-2 reduces sensorimotor gating and recognition memory in rats. *Behavioural Pharmacology, 13*, 29–37.

Schofield, P. E., Pattison, P. E., Hill, D. J., & Borland, R. (2001). The influence of group identification on the adoption of peer group smoking norms. *Psychology & Health, 16*, 1–16.

Scholnick, E. K. (1995, Fall). Knowing and constructing plans. *SRCD Newsletter*, pp. 1–2, 17.

Schön, D., Magne, C., & Besson, M. (2004). The music of speech: Music training facilitates pitch processing in both music and language. *Psychophysiology, 41*, 341–349.

Schrof, J. M., & Schultz, S. (1999, March 8). Melancholy nation. *U.S. News and World Report*, pp. 56–63.

Schul, R., Slotnick, B. M., & Dudai, Y. (1996). Flavor and the frontal cortex. *Behavioral Neuroscience, 110*, 760–765.

Schultz, W. (1997). Dopamine neurons and their role in reward mechanisms. *Current Opinion in Neurobiology, 7*, 191–197.

Schultz, W., Dayan, P., & Montague, P. R. (1997). A neural substrate of prediction and reward. *Science, 275*, 1593–1599.

Schultz, W., Tremblay, W., & Hollerman, J. R. (2000). Reward processing in primate orbitofrontal cortex and basal ganglia. *Cerebral Cortex, 10*, 272–283.

Schwartz, C. E., Wright, C. I., Shin, L. M., Kagan, J., & Rauch, S. L. (2003). Inhibited and uninhibited infants "grown up": Adult amygdalar response to novelty. *Science, 300*, 1952–1953.

Schwartz, J. E., Neale, J., Marco, C., Shiffman, S. S., & Stone, A. A. (1999). Does trait coping exist? A momentary assessment approach to the evaluation of traits. *Journal of Personality and Social Psychology, 77*, 360–369.

Schwartz, J. M., Stoessel, P. W., Baxter, L. R., Martin, K. M., & Phelps, M. E. (1996). Systematic changes in cerebral glucose metabolic rate after successful behavior modification treatment of obsessive-compulsive disorder. *Archives of General Psychiatry, 53*, 109–113.

Schwartz, N., & Bless, H. (1992). Constructing reality and its alternatives: An inclusion/exclusion model of assimilation and contrast effects in social judgment. In L. L. Martin & A. Tesser (Eds.), *The construction of social judgments* (pp. 217–245). Hillsdale, NJ: Erlbaum.

Schwarz, N. (1999). Self-reports: How the questions shape the answers. *American Psychologist, 54*, 93–105.

Schwarzer, R., & Knoll, N. (2003). Positive coping: Mastering demands and searching for meaning. In S. J. Lopez & C. R. Snyder (Eds.), *Positive psychological assessment: A handbook of models and measures* (pp. 393–409). Washington, DC: American Psychological Association.

Schweiger, A., & Parducci, A. (1981). Nocebo: The psychologic induction of pain. *Pavlovian Journal of Biological Science, 16*, 140–143.

Schyns, P. (1998). Crossnational differences in happiness: Economic and cultural factors explored. *Social Indicators Research, 43*, 3–26.

Scicli, A. P., Petrovich, G. D., Swanson, L. W., & Thompson, R. F. (2004). Contextual fear conditioning is associated with lateralized expression of the immediate early gene c-fos in the central and basolateral amygdalar nuclei. *Behavioral Neuroscience, 118*, 5–14.

Sclafani, A., & Aravich, P. F. (1983). Macronutrient self-selection in three forms of hypothalamic obesity. *American Journal of Physiology, 244*, R686–R694.

Sclafani, A., Aravich, P. F., & Xenakis, S. (1983). Macronutrient preferences in hypothalamic hyperphagic rats. *Nutrition & Behavior, 1*, 233–251.

Scogin, F., Bynum, J., Stephens, G., & Calhoon, S. (1990). Efficacy of self-administered treatment programs: Meta-analytic review. *Professional Psychology: Research & Practice, 21*, 42–47.

Scott, B., & Melin, L. (1998). Psychometric properties and standardised data for questionnaires measuring negative affect, dispositional style and daily hassles: A nationwide sample. *Scandinavian Journal of Psychology, 39*, 301–307.

Scott, G., Leritz, L. E., & Mumford, M. D. (2004a). The effectiveness of creativity training: A quantitative review. *Creativity Research Journal, 16*, 361–388.

Scott, G., Leritz, L. E., & Mumford, M. D. (2004b). Types of creativity training: Approaches and their effectiveness. *Journal of Creative Behavior, 38*, 149–179.

Scott, J., Stanton, B., Garland, A., & Ferrier, I. N. (2000). Cognitive vulnerability in patients with bipolar disorder. *Psychological Medicine, 30*, 467–472.

Scott, S. K., Young, A. W., Calder, A. J., Hellawell, D. J., Aggleton, J. P. & Johnson, M., (1997) Impaired auditory recognition of fear and anger following bilateral amygdala lesions. *Nature, 385*, 254–257.

Scott, T. R., & Plata-Salaman, C. R. (1991). Coding of taste quality. In T. V. Getchell, R. L. Doty, L. M. Bartoshuk, & J. B. Snow, Jr. (Eds.), *Smell and taste in health and disease* (pp. 345–368). New York: Raven.

Searle, J. R. (2000). Consciousness. *Annual Review of Neuroscience, 23*, 557–578.

Sears, R., Maccoby, E., & Levin, H. (1957). *Patterns of child rearing.* New York: Harper & Row.

Sedikides, C., Gaertner, L., & Toguchi, Y. (2003). Pancultural self-enhancement. *Journal of Personality & Social Psychology, 84*, 60–79.

Seeman, R. E., Berkman, L. F., Blazer, D., & Rowe, J. W. (1994). Social ties and support and neuroendocrine function: The MacArthur studies of successful aging. *Annals of Behavioral Medicine, 16*, 95–106.

Seeman, T. E. (2000). Health promoting effects of friends and family on health outcomes in older adults. *American Journal of Health Promotion, 14*, 362–370.

Seeman, T. E., Singer, B. H., Rowe, J. W., Horwitz, R. I., & McEwen, B. S. (1997). Price of adaptation—allostatic load and its health consequences: MacArthur studies of successful aging. *Archives of Internal Medicine, 157*, 2259–2268.

Seeman, T. E., Singer, B. H., Ryff, C. D., Dienberg Love, G., & Levy-Storms, L. (2002). Social relationships, gender, and allostatic load across two age cohorts. *Psychosomatic Medicine, 64*, 395–406.

Segal, E. (2004). Incubation in insight problem solving. *Creativity Research Journal, 16*, 141–148.

Segal, N. L. (1999). *Entwined lives: Twins and what they tell us about human behavior.* New York: Dutton/Penguin.

Segal, Z. V., Gemar, M., & Williams, S. (1999). Differential cognitive response to a mood challenge following successful cognitive therapy or pharmacotherapy for unipolar depression. *Journal of Abnormal Psychology, 108*, 3–10.

Seger, C. A., Desmond, J. E., Glover, G. H., & Gabrieli, J. D. E. (2000). Functional magnetic resonance imaging evidence for right-hemisphere involvement in processing unusual semantic relationships. *Neuropsychology, 14*, 361–369.

Segerstrom, S. C. (in press). Optimism and immunity: Do positive thoughts always lead to positive effects? *Brain, Behavior, and Immunity.*

Segerstrom, S. C., Taylor, S. E., Kemeny, M. E., & Fahey, J. L. (1998). Optimism is associated with mood, coping, and immune change in response to stress. *Journal of Personality and Social Psychology, 74*, 1646–1655.

Segerstrom, S. C., Taylor, S. E., Kemeny, M. E., Reed, G. M., & Visscher, B. R. (1996). Causal attributions predict rate of immune decline in HIV-seropositive gay men. *Health Psychology, 15*, 485–493.

Segrin, C., & Abramson, L. Y. (1994). Negative reactions to depressive behaviors: A communication theory analysis. *Journal of Abnormal Psychology, 103*, 655–668.

Segrin, C., & Dillard, J. P. (1992). The interactional theory of depression: A meta-analysis of the research literature. *Journal of Social & Clinical Psychology, 11*(1), 43–70.

Seith, R. (2000). Back sleeping may delay infant crawling. CWK Network. Retrieved from http://www.kidsmd.com/Tipsheets/21_may2301/crawling.html

Sekiyama, K., Kanno, I., Miura, S., & Sugita, Y. (2003). Auditory-visual speech perception examined by fMRI and PET. *Neuroscience Research, 47*, 277–287.

Seligman, M. E., & Csikszentmihalyi, M. (2000). Positive psychology: An introduction. *American Psychologist, 55*, 5–14.

Seligman, M. E. P. (1971). Phobias and preparedness. *Behavior Therapy, 2*, 307–320.

Seligman, M. E. P. (1995). The effectiveness of psychotherapy: The *Consumer Reports* study. *American Psychologist, 50*, 965–974.

Seligman, M. E. P., & Pawelski, J. O. (2003). Positive psychology: FAQs. *Psychological Inquiry, 14*, 159–163.

Seltzer, J., & Numeroff, R. E. (1988). Supervisory leadership and subordinate burnout. *Academy of Management Journal, 31*, 439–446.

Selye, H. (1976). *The stress of life.* New York: McGraw-Hill.

Semenov, L. A., Chernova, N. D., & Bondarko, V. M. (2000). Measurement of visual acuity and crowding effect in 3–9-year-old children. *Human Physiology, 26*, 16–20.

Sensky, T., Turkington, D., Kingdon, D., Scott, J. L., Scott, J., Siddle, R., et al. (2000). A randomized controlled trial of cognitive-behavioral therapy for persistent symptoms in schizophrenia resistant to medication. *Archives of General Psychiatry, 57*, 165–172.

Sereny, G., Sharma, V., Holt, J., & Gordis, E. (1986). Mandatory supervised Antabuse therapy in an outpatient alcoholism program: A pilot study. *Alcoholism (NY), 10*, 290–292.

Serpell, R. (1979). How specific are perceptual skills? A cross-cultural study of pattern reproduction. *British Journal of Psychology, 70*, 365–380.

Seta, J. J., & Seta, C. E. (1992). Increments and decrements in mean arterial pressure as a function of audience composition: An averaging and summation analysis. *Personality and Social Psychology Bulletin, 18*, 173–181.

Setliff, A. E., & Marmurek, H. H. C. (2002). The mood regulatory function of autobiographical recall is moderated by self-esteem. *Personality and Individual Differences, 32*, 761–771.

Seuling, B. (1975). *You can't eat peanuts in church and other little-known laws.* New York: Doubleday.

Seuling, B. (1976). *The loudest screen kiss and other little-known facts about the movies.* New York: Doubleday.

Seuling, B. (1978). *The last cow on the White House lawn and other little-known facts about the presidency.* New York: Doubleday.

Seuling, B. (1986). *You can't sneeze with your eyes open and other freaky facts about the human body.* New York: Ballantine.

Seuling, B. (1988). *It is illegal to quack like a duck and other freaky laws.* New York: Dutton.

Shadish, W. R., Navarro, A. M., Matt, G. E., & Phillips, G. (2000). The effects of psychological therapies under clinically representative conditions: A meta-analysis. *Psychological Bulletin, 126*, 512–529.

Shafran, R., Thordarson, D. S., & Rachman, S. (1996). Thought-action fusion in obsessive compulsive disorder. *Journal of Anxiety Disorders, 10*, 379–391.

Shalev, A. Y., Peri, T., Brandes, D., Freedman, S., Orr, S. P., & Pitman, R. K. (2000). Auditory startle response in trauma survivors with posttraumatic stress disorder: A prospective study. *American Journal of Psychiatry, 157,* 255–261.

Shalev, A. Y., Sahar, T., Freedman, S., Peri, T., Glick, N., Brandes, D., et al. (1998). A prospective study of heart rate response following trauma and the subsequent development of posttraumatic stress disorder. *Archives of General Psychiatry, 55,* 553–559.

Shallenberger, R. S. (1993). *Taste chemistry.* New York: Blackie Academic.

Shallice, T., Fletcher, P., Frith, C. D., Grasby, P., Frackowiak, R. S. J., & Dolan, R. J. (1994). Brain regions associated with acquisition and retrieval of verbal episodic memory. *Nature, 368,* 633–635.

Shamir-Essakow, G., Ungerer, J. A., Rapee, R. M., & Safier, R. (2004). Caregiving representations of mothers of behaviorally inhibited and uninhibited preschool children. *Developmental Psychology, 40,* 899–910.

Shanab, M. E., & Yahya, K. A. (1977). A behavioral study of obedience in children. *Journal of Personality and Social Psychology, 35,* 530–536.

Shapira, B., Tubi, N., Drexler, H., Lidsky, D., Calev, A., & Lerer, B. (1998). Cost and benefit in the choice of ECT schedule: Twice versus three times weekly ECT. *British Journal of Psychiatry, 172,* 44–48.

Shapiro, A. K. (1964). Factors contributing to the placebo effect: Their significance for psychotherapy. *American Journal of Psychotherapy, 18,* 73–88.

Shapiro, A. K., & Morris, L. A. (1978). The placebo effect in medical and psychological therapies. In S. L. Garfield & A. E. Bergin (Eds.), *Handbook of psychotherapy and behavior change: An empirical analysis* (2nd ed.). New York: Wiley.

Shapiro, D. H. (1982). Overview: Clinical and physiological comparison of meditation with other self-control strategies. *American Journal of Psychiatry, 139,* 267–274.

Shapiro, D. H. Jr., Schwartz, C. E., & Astin, J. A. (1996). Controlling ourselves, controlling our world: Psychology's role in understanding positive and negative consequences of seeking and gaining control. *American Psychologist, 51,* 1213–1230.

Sharpsteen, D. J., & Kirkpatrick, L. A. (1997). Romantic jealousy and adult romantic attachment. *Journal of Personality & Social Psychology, 72,* 627–640.

Shaver, P. R., & Hazan, C. (1994). Attachment. In A. L. Weber & J. H. Harvey (Eds.), *Perspectives on close relationships.* Boston: Allyn & Bacon.

Shaw, P. J., Bergmann, B. M., & Rechtschaffen, A. (1998). Effects of paradoxical sleep deprivation on thermoregulation in the rat. *Sleep, 21,* p. 7–17.

Shaywitz, B. A., Shaywitz, S. E., Pugh, K. R., Constable, R. T., Skudlarski, P., Fulbright, R. K., et al. (1995). Sex differences in the functional organization of the brain for language. *Nature, 373,* 607–611.

Shea, D. L., Lubinski, D., & Benbow, C. P. (2001). Importance of assessing spatial ability in intellectually talented young adolescents: A 20-year longitudinal study. *Journal of Educational Psychology, 93,* 604–614.

Shea, J. D., Burton, R., & Girgis, A. (1993). Negative affect, absorption, and immunity. *Physiological Behavior, 53,* 449–457.

Sheehan, P. W. (1988). Memory distortion in hypnosis. *International Journal of Clinical Experimental Hypnosis, 36,* 296–311.

Sheehan, T. P., Chambers, R. A., & Russell, D. S. (2004). Regulation of affect by the lateral septum: Implications for neuropsychiatry. *Brain Research Reviews, 46,* 71–117.

Sheehy, R., & Horan, J. J. (2004). Effects of stress inoculation training for 1st-year law students. *International Journal of Stress Management, 11,* 41–55.

Sheen, M., Kemp, S., & Rubin, D. (2001). Twins dispute memory ownership: A new false memory phenomenon. *Memory & Cognition, 29,* 779–788.

Sheese, B. E., Brown, E. L., & Graziano, W. G. (2004). Emotional expression in cyberspace: Searching for moderators of the Pennebaker disclosure effect via e-mail. *Health Psychology, 23,* 457–464.

Sheinberg, D. L., & Logothetis, N. K. (2001). Noticing familiar objects in real world scenes: The role of temporal cortical neurons in natural vision. *Journal of Neuroscience, 21,* 1340–1350.

Shekim, W. O., Bylund, D. B., Frankel, F., Alexson, J., Jones S. B., Blue, L. D., et al. (1989). Platelet MAO activity and personality variations in normals. *Psychiatry Research, 27,* 81–88.

Sheldon, K. M., Ryan, R., & Reis, H. T. (1996). What makes for a good day? Competence and autonomy in the day and in the person. *Personality & Social Psychology Bulletin, 22,* 1270–1279.

Sheline, Y. I., Gado, M. H., & Kraemer, H. C. (2003). Untreated depression and hippocampal volume loss. *American Journal of Psychiatry, 160,* 1516–1518.

Shelton, J. R., & Caramazza, A. (1999). Deficits in lexical and semantic processing: Implications for models of normal language. *Psychonomic Bulletin & Review, 6,* 5–27.

Shen, J., & Rothman, D. L. (2002). Magnetic resonance spectroscopic approaches to study neuronal: Glial interactions. *Biological Psychiatry, 52,* 694–700.

Shepard, R. N. (1967). Recognition memory for words, sentences and pictures. *Journal of Verbal learning and Verbal Behavior, 6,* 156–163.

Shepard, R. N., & Metzler, J. (1971). Mental rotation of three-dimensional objects. *Science, 171,* 701–703.

Shepherd, G. M. (1999). Information processing in dendrites. In M. J. Zigmond, F. E. Bloom, S. C. Landis, J. L. Roberts, & L. R. Squire (Eds.), *Fundamental neuroscience* (pp. 363–388). New York: Academic Press.

Shepherd, M. (1993). The placebo: From specificity to the non-specific and back. *Psychological Medicine, 23,* 569–578.

Shepherd, M. D., Schoenberg, M., Slavich, S., Wituk, S., Warren, M., & Meissen, G. (1999). Continuum of professional involvement in self-help groups. *Journal of Community Psychology, 27,* 39–53.

Sherif, M., Harvey, O. J., White, B. J., Hood, W. R., & Sherif, C. W. (1961). *Intergroup conflict and cooperation: The robber's cave experiment.* Norman, OK: University Book Exchange.

Shi, C., & Davis, M. (2001). Visual pathways involved in fear conditioning measured with fear-potentiated startle: Behavioral and anatomic studies. *Journal of Neuroscience, 21,* 9844–9855.

Shibahara, H., Shigeta, M., Toji, H., & Koyama, K. (1995). Sperm immobilizing antibodies interfere with sperm migration from the uterine cavity through the fallopian tubes. *American Journal of Reproductive Immunology, 34,* 120–124.

Shidara, M., & Richmond, B. J. (2002). Anterior cingulate: Single neuronal signals related to degree of reward expectancy. *Science, 296,* 1709–1711.

Shields, S. A. (1987). Women, men, and the dilemma of emotion. In P. Shaver & C. Hendrick (Eds.), *Sex and gender* (pp. 229–250). Newbury Park, CA: Sage.

Shiffrin, R. M. (1999). 30 years of memory. In C. Izawa (Ed.), *On human memory: Evolution, progress, and reflections on the 30th anniversary of the Atkinson-Shiffrin model* (pp. 17–33). Hillsdale, NJ: Erlbaum.

Shigenobu, K. (2001). Psychoneuroimmunology: A dialogue between the brain and the immune system. *Journal of International Society of Life Information Science, 19,* 141–143.

Shimizu, Y. A., & Johnson, S. C. (2004). Infants' attribution of a goal to a morphologically unfamiliar agent. *Developmental Science, 7,* 425–430.

Shin, L. M., Kosslyn, S. M., McNally, R. J., Alpert, N. M., Thompson, W. L., Raush, S. L., et al. (1997). Visual imagery and perception in posttraumatic stress disorder: A positron emission tomographic investigation. *Archives of General Psychiatry, 54,* 233–241.

Shin, L. M., Orr, S. P., Carson, M. A., Rauch, S. L., Macklin, M. L., Lasko, N. B., et al. (2004). Regional cerebral blood flow in the amygdala and medial prefrontal cortex during traumatic imagery in male and female Vietnam veterans with PTSD. *Archives of General Psychiatry, 61,* 168–176.

Shioiri, S., Cavanagh, P., Miyamoto, T., & Yaguchi, H. (2000). Tracking the apparent location of targets in interpolated motion. *Vision Research, 40,* 1365–1376.

Shiraishi, T., Oomura, Y., Sasaki, K., & Wayner, M. J. (2000). Effects of leptin and orexin-A on food intake and feeding related hypothalamic neurons. *Physiology & Behavior, 71,* 251–261.

Shneider, W., & Chein, J. M. (2003). Controlled and automatic processing: Behavior, theory, and biological mechanisms. *Cognitive Science, 27,* 525–559.

Shoda, Y., & LeeTiernan, S. (2002). What remains invariant? Finding order within a person's thoughts, feelings, and behaviors across situations. In D. Cervone & W. Mischel (Eds.), *Advances in personality science* (pp. 241–270). New York: Guilford Press.

Shoda, Y., LeeTiernan, S. J., & Mischel, W. (2002). Personality as a dynamical system: emergence of stability and consistency in intra- and interpersonal interactions. *Personality and Social Psychology Review, 6,* 316–325.

Shoda, Y., Mischel, W. & Wright, J. C. (1994). Intraindividual stability in the organization and patterning of behavior: Incorporating psychological situations into the idiographic analysis of personality. *Journal of Personality and Social Psychology, 67,* 674–687.

Shortridge, J. R. (1993). The Great Plains. In M. K. Cayton, E. J. Gorn, & P. W. Williams (Eds.), *Encyclopedia of American social history* (Vol. 2, pp. 1001–1015). New York: Scribner's.

Shouksmith, G., & Taylor, J. E. (1997). The interaction of culture with general job stressors in air traffic controllers. *International Journal of Aviation Psychology, 7,* 343–352.

Showers, C. (1992). The motivational and emotional consequences of considering positive or negative possibilities for an upcoming event. *Journal of Personality and Social Psychology, 63,* 474–484.

Shulman, G. L., McAvoy, M. P., Cowan, M. C., Astafiev, S. V., Tansy, A. P., d'Avossa, G., & Corbetta, M. (2003). Quantitative analysis of attention and detection signals during visual search. *Journal of Neurophysiology, 90,* 3384–3397.

Shulman, S., Elicker, J., & Sroufe, L. A. (1994). Stages of friendship growth in preadolescence as related to attachment history. *Journal of Social & Personal Relationships, 11,* 341–361.

Sidorenko, V. N. (2000). Effects of Medical Resonance Therapy Music in the complex treatment of epileptic patients. *Integrative Physiological & Behavioral Science, 35,* 212–217.

Siegel, A. M., Andersen, R. A., Freund, H., & Spencer, D. D. (Eds.). (2003). The parietal lobes. Philadelphia: Lippincott Williams & Wilkins.

Siegel, D. J. (1999). *The developing mind: Toward a neurobiology of interpersonal experience.* New York: Guilford Press.

Siegel, J. L., & Longo, D. L. (1981). The control of chemotherapy induced emesis. *Annals of Internal Medicine, 95,* 352–359.

Siegel, J. M. (2004). Hypocretin (orexin): Role in normal behaviour and neuropathy. *Annual Review of Psychology, 55,* 125–148.

Siegel, M., Brisman, J., & Weinshel, M. (1988). *Surviving an eating disorder: Strategies for family and friends.* New York: Harper and Row.

Siegel, S. (1988). State dependent learning and morphine tolerance. *Behavioral Neuroscience, 102,* 228–232.

Siegel, S., Baptista, M. A. S., Kim, J. A., McDonald, R. V., & Weise-Kelly, L. (2000). Pavlovian psychopharmacology: The associative basis of tolerance. *Experimental & Clinical Psychopharmacology, 8,* 276–293.

Siegel, S., & Ramos, B. M. C. (2002). Applying laboratory research: Drug anticipation and the treatment of drug addiction. *Experimental & Clinical Psychopharmacology, 10,* 162–183.

Siegler, R. S. (1989). Mechanisms of cognitive development. *Annual Review of Psychology, 40,* 353–379.

Siegler, R. S. (1996). *Emerging minds. The process of change in children's thinking.* New York: Oxford University Press.

Siegler, R. S., & Svetina, M. (2002). A microgenetic/cross-sectional study of matrix completion: Comparing short-term and long-term change. *Child Development, 73,* 793–809.

Sifneos, P. E. (1992). *Short-term anxiety-provoking psychotherapy: A treatment manual.* New York: Basic Books.

Silverman, L. (1976). Psychoanalytic theory: The reports of my death are greatly exaggerated. *American Psychologist, 31,* 621–637.

Silverman, L. K. (1993b). A developmental model for counseling the gifted. In L. K. Silverman (Ed.), *Counseling the gifted and talented* (pp. 51–78). Denver, CO: Love.

Simcock, G., & Hayne, H. (2002). Breaking the barrier? Children fail to translate their preverbal memories into language. *Psychological Science, 13,* 225–231.

Simmons, J. A., & Chen, L. (1989). The acoustic basis for target discrimination by FM echo-locating bats. *Journal of the Acoustical Society of America, 86,* 1333–1350.

Simon, H. A., & Chase, W. G. (1973). Skill in chess. *American Scientist, 61,* 394–403.

Simon, L., Greenberg, J., & Brehm, J. (1995). Trivialization: The forgotten mode of dissonance reduction. *Journal of Personality and Social Psychology, 68,* 247–260.

Simons, D. J. (2000). Current approaches to change blindness. *Visual Cognition, 7,* 1–15.

Simons, D. J., & Ambinder, M. S. (2005). Change blindness. *Current Directions in Psychological Science, 14,* 44–48.

Simons, D. J., & Levin, D. T. (1997). Change blindness. *Trends in Cognitive Sciences, 1,* 261–267.

Simon-Thomas, E. R., Role, K. O., & Knight, R. T. (2005). Behavioral and electrophysiological evidence of a right hemisphere bias for the influence of negative emotion on higher cognition. *Journal of Cognitive Neuroscience, 17,* 518–529.

Simonton, D. K. (1984). *Genius, creativity, and leadership: Historiometric inquiries.* Cambridge, MA: Harvard University Press.

Simonton, D. K. (1988). Creativity, leadership, and chance. In R. J. Sternberg (Ed.), *The nature of creativity* (pp. 386–436). New York: Cambridge University Press.

Simonton, D. K. (1990). Political pathology and societal creativity. *Creativity Research Journal, 3,* 85–99.

Simonton, D. K. (1994). *Greatness: Who makes history and why.* New York: Guilford.

Simonton, D. K. (1995). Foresight in insight? A Darwinian answer. In R. J. Sternberg & J. E. Davidson (Eds.), *The nature of insight* (pp. 465–494). Cambridge, MA: MIT Press.

Simonton, D. K. (1997). Creative productivity: A predictive and explanatory model of career trajectories and landmarks. *Psychological Review, 104,* 66–89.

Simos, P. G. (2001). *Vision in the brain.* The Netherlands: Swets & Zeitlinger.

Singer, L. T., Arendt, R., Minnes, S., Farkas, K., Salvator, A., Kirchner, H. L., & Kliegman, R. (2002a). Cognitive and motor outcomes of cocaine-exposed infants. *Journal of the American Medical Association, 287,* 1952–1960.

Singer, L. T., Salvator, A., Arendt, R., Minnes, S., Farkas, K., & Kliegman, R. (2002b). Effects of cocaine/polydrug exposure and maternal psychological distress on infant birth outcomes. *Neurotoxicology & Teratology, 24,* 127–135.

Singer, M. A., & Goldin-Meadow, S. (2005). Children learn when their teacher's gestures and speech differ. *Psychological Science, 16,* 85–89.

Singer, M. T. (1995). Cults: Implications for family therapists. In R. H. Mikesell et al. (Eds.), *Integrating family therapy: Handbook of family psychology and systems theory* (pp. 519–527). Washington, DC: American Psychological Association.

Singer, M. T., & Lalich, J. (1995). *Cults in our midst.* San Francisco: Jossey-Bass.

Singer, W. (1998). Consciousness and the structure of neuronal representation. *Philosophical Transactions of the Royal Society B, 353,* 1829–1840.

Singh, V. N. (1995). Human uterine amylase in relation to infertility. *Hormone and Metabolic Research, 27,* 35–36.

Sinha, B. K., Willson, L. R., & Watson, D. C. (2000). Stress and coping among students in India and Canada. *Canadian Journal of Behavioral Sciences, 32,* 218–225.

Siomi, M. C., Zhang, Y., Siomi, H., & Dreyfuss, G. (1996). Specific sequences in the fragile X syndrome protein FMR1 and the FXR proteins mediate their binding to 60S ribosomal subunits and the interactions among them. *Molecular and Cellular Biology, 16,* 3825–3832.

Sireteanu, R. (2000). Texture segmentation, "pop-out," and feature binding in infants and children. In C. Rovee-Collier & L. P. Lipsitt (Eds.), *Progress in infancy research* (Vol. 1, pp. 183–249). Mahwah, NJ: Erlbaum.

Skinner, B. F. (1953). *Science and human behavior.* New York: Macmillan.

Skinner, B. F. (1956). A case history in scientific method. *American Psychologist, 11,* 221–233.

Skinner, B. F. (1971). *Beyond freedom and dignity.* New York: Knopf.

Skinner, N. F. (2003). Birth order effects in dominance: Failure to support Sulloway's view. *Psychological Reports, 92,* 387–388.

Skowronski, J. J., Gibbons, J. A., Vogl, R. J., & Walker, W. R. (2004). The effect of social disclosure on the intensity of affect provoked by autobiographical memories. *Self & Identity, 3,* 285–309.

Skowronski, J. J., & Walker, W. R. (2004). How describing autobiographical events can affect autobiographical memories. *Social Cognition, 22,* 555–590.

Skvoretz, J. (1988). Models of participation in status-differentiated groups,. *Social Psychology Quarterly, 51,* 43–57.

Slater, A., Brown, E., & Badenoch, M. (1997). Intermodal perception at birth: Newborn infants' memory for arbitrary auditory-visual pairings. *Early Development & Parenting, 6,* 99–104.

Slater, A., Quinn, P. C., Hayes, R., & Brown, E. (2000). The role of facial orientation in newborn infants' preference for attractive faces. *Developmental Science, 3,* 181–185.

Sleek, S. (1997, November). Online therapy services raise ethical questions. *APA Monitor,* p. 1, 38.

Slep, A. M. S., & O'Leary, S. G. (1998). The effects of maternal attributions on parenting: An experimental analysis. *Journal of Family Psychology, 12,* 234–243.

Slimp, J. C., Hart, B. L., & Goy, R. W. (1978). Heterosexual, autosexual and social behavior of adult male rhesus monkeys with medial preoptic-anterior hypothalamic lesions. *Brain Research, 142,* 105–122.

Sloan, D. M., & Marx, B. P. (2004). Taking pen to hand: Evaluating theories underlying the written disclosure paradigm. *Clinical Psychology: Science & Practice, 11,* 121–137.

Slob, A. K., Bax, C. M., Hop, W. C. J., Rowland, D. L., & van der Werff ten Bosch, J. J. (1996). Sexual arousability and the menstrual cycle. *Psychoneuroendocrinology, 21,* 545–558.

Slotnick, S. D., Moo, L. R., Tesoro, M. A., & Hart, J. (2001). Hemispheric asymmetry in categorical versus coordinate spatial processing revealed by temporary cortical deactivation. *Journal of Cognitive Neuroscience, 13,* 1088–1096.

Small, B. J., & Bäckman, L. (2000). Time to death and cognitive performance. *Current Directions in Psychological Science, 6,* 168–172.

Small, B. J., Fratiglioni, L., von Strauss, E., & Backman, L. (2003). Terminal decline and cognitive performance in very old age: Does cause of death matter? *Psychology and Aging, 18,* 193–202.

Small, D. M., Zatorre, R. J., Dagher, A., Evans, A. C., & Jones-Gotman, M. (2001). Changes in brain activity related to eating chocolate: From pleasure to aversion. *Brain, 124,* 1720–1733.

Smeets, M. A. M., Smit, F., Panhuysen, G. E. M., & Ingleby, J. D. (1997). The influence of methodological differences on the outcome of body size estimation studies in anorexia nervosa. *British Journal of Clinical Psychology, 36*, 263–277.

Smith, C. A., & Kirby, L. D. (2000). Consequences require antecedents: Toward a process model of emotion elicitation. In J. P. Forgas (Ed.), *Feeling and thinking: The role of affect in social cognition* (pp. 83–106). New York: Cambridge University Press.

Smith, D. (1982). Trends in counseling and psychotherapy. *American Psychologist, 37*, 802–809.

Smith, D. E., Roberts, J., Gage, F. H., & Tuszynski, M. H. (1999). Age-associated neuronal atrophy occurs in the primate brain and is reversible by growth factor gene therapy. *Proceedings of the National Academy of Sciences U.S.A., 96*, 10893–10898.

Smith, D. V., & Frank, M. E. (1993). Sensory coding by peripheral taste fibers. In S. A. Simon & S. D. Roper (Eds.), *Mechanisms of taste transduction* (pp. 295–338). Boca Raton, FL: CRC Press.

Smith, D. W., Davis, J. L., & Fricker-Elhai, A. E. (2004). How does trauma beget trauma?: Cognitions about risk in women with abuse histories. *Child Maltreatment, 9*, 292–303.

Smith, E. E. (1988). Concepts and thought. In R. J. Sternberg & E. E. Smith (Eds.), *The psychology of human thought* (pp. 19–49). New York: Cambridge University Press.

Smith, E. E. (2000). Neural bases of human working memory. *Current Directions in Psychological Science, 9*, 45–49.

Smith, E. E., & Jonides, J. (1999). Storage and executive processes in the frontal lobes. *Science, 283*, 1657–1661.

Smith, E. E., & Medin, D. L. (1981). *Categories and concepts.* Cambridge, MA: Harvard University Press.

Smith, E. E., Patalano, A. L., & Jonides, J. (1998). Alternative strategies of categorization. *Cognition, 65*, 167–196.

Smith, E. R. (1998). Mental Representation and memory. In D. T. Gilbert, S. T. Fiske, & G. Lindzey (Eds.), *The handbook of social psychology* (4th ed., Vol. 1, pp. 391–445). New York: McGraw-Hill.

Smith, J. C. (2004). Alterations in brain any immune function produced by mindfulness meditation: Three caveats. *Psychosomatic Medicine, 66*, 148–149.

Smith, J. C., & Joyce, C. A. (2004). Mozart versus New Age music: Relaxation states, stress, and ABC Relaxation Theory. *Journal of Music Therapy, 41*, 215–224.

Smith, J. L., & White, P. H. (2002). An examination of implicitly activated, explicitly activated, and nullified stereotypes on mathematical performance: It's not just a woman's issue. *Sex Roles, 47*, 179–191.

Smith, M. E. (1993). Television violence and behavior: a research summary. ERIC Digest. Syracuse, NY: Educational Resources Information Center Clearinghouse on Information and Technology (ED 366 329).

Smith, R. E., Leffingwell, T. R., & Ptacek, J. T. (1999). Can people remember how they coped? Factors associated with discordance between same-day and retrospective reports. *Journal of Personality and Social Psychology, 76*, 1050–1061.

Smith, S. (2001). *J. K. Rowling: A biography.* London: Michael O'Mara Books.

Smith, S. M., & Blankenship, S. E. (1989). Incubation effects. *Bulletin of the Psychonomic Society, 27*, 311–314.

Smith, S. M., & Blankenship, S. E. (1991). Incubation and the persistence of fixation in problem solving. *American Journal of Psychology, 104*, 61–87.

Smith, S. M., & Levin, I. P. (1996). Need for cognition and choice framing effects. *Journal of Behavioral Decision Making, 9*, 283–290.

Smith, S. M., & Vela, E. (2001). Environmental context-dependent memory: A review and meta-analysis. *Psychonomic Bulletin & Review, 8*, 203–220.

Smith, T. W., & Ruiz, J. M. (2002). Psychosocial influences on the development and course of coronary heart disease: Current status and implications for research and practice. *Journal of Consulting & Clinical Psychology, 70*, 548–568.

Smolucha, F. C. (1992). A reconstruction of Vygotsky's theory of creativity. *Creativity Research Journal, 5*, 49–67.

Smyth, J. M., Stone, A. A., Hurewitz, A., & Kaell, A. (1999). Effects of writing about stressful experiences on symptom reduction in patients with asthma or rheumatoid arthritis. *Journal of the American Medical Association, 281*, 1304–1329.

Snidman, N., Kagan, J., Riordan, L., & Shannon, D. C. (1995). Cardiac function and behavioral reactivity during infancy. *Psychophysiology, 32*, 199–207.

Snodgrass, S. E. (1985). Women's intuition: The effect of subordinate role on interpersonal sensitivity. *Journal of Personality and Social Psychology, 49*, 146–155.

Snow, C. E. (1991). The language of the mother–child relationship. In M. Woodhead & R. Carr (Eds.), *Becoming a person* (pp. 195–210). London: Routledge.

Snow, C. E. (1999). Social perspectives on the emergence of language. In B. MacWhinney (Ed.), *The emergence of language* (pp. 257–276). Mahwah, NJ: Erlbaum.

Snow, C. E. (2002). Second language learners' contributions to our understanding of languages of the brain. In A. M. Galaburda, S. M. Kosslyn, & Y. Christen (Eds.), *Languages of the brain* (pp. 151–165) Cambridge, MA: Harvard University Press.

Snow, C. E., Burns, M. S., & Griffin, P. (Eds.). (1998). *Preventing reading difficulties in young children.* Washington, DC: National Academy Press.

Snow, C. E., Tabors, P. O., & Dickinson, D. K. (2001). Language development in the preschool years. In D. K. Dickinson & P. O. Tabors (Eds.), *Beginning literacy with language: Young children learning at home and school* (pp. 1–25). Baltimore: Paul H. Brookes.

Snow, R. E. (1994). A person-situation interaction theory of intelligence in outline. In A. Demetriou & A. Efklides (Eds.), *Intelligence, mind, and reasoning: Structure and development* (pp. 11–28). Amsterdam: Elsevier.

Snow, R. E. (1996). Aptitude development and education. *Psychology, Public Policy, and Law, 3/4*, 536–560.

Snow, R., & Yalow, R. (1982). Education and intelligence. In R. J. Sternberg (Ed.), *Handbook of human intelligence* (pp. 493–585). New York: Cambridge University Press.

Snowdon, D. A., Greiner, L. H., & Markesbery, W. R. (2000). Linguistic ability in early life and the neuropathology of Alzheimer's disease and cerebrovascular disease: Findings from the nun study. *Annals of the New York Academy of Sciences, 903*, 34–38.

Snyder, L. H., Batista, A. P., & Andersen, R. A. (2000). Intention-related activity in the posterior parietal cortex: A review. *Vision Research, 40*, 1433–1441.

Snyder, M. (1984). When belief creates reality. In L. Berkowitz (Ed.), *Advances in experimental social psychology* (Vol. 25, pp. 67–114). San Diego, CA: Academic Press.

Snyder, M. (1992). Motivational foundations of behavioral confirmation. In M. P. Zanna (Ed.), *Advances in experimental social psychology* (Vol. 18, pp. 248–306). New York: Academic Press.

Snyder, M., & Ickes, W. (1985). Personality and social behavior. In G. Lindzey & E. Aronson (Eds.), *Handbook of social psychology* (3rd ed., Vol. 2, pp. 883–947). New York: Random House.

Snyder, M., Tanke, E. D., & Berscheid, E. (1977). Social perception and interpersonal behavior: On the self-fulfilling nature of social stereotypes. *Journal of Personality and Social Psychology, 35*, 656–666.

Snyderman, M., & Herrnstein, R. J. (1983). Intelligence tests and the Immigration Act of 1924. *American Psychologist, 38*, 986–995.

Sohal, R. S., & Weindruch, R. (1996). Oxidative stress, caloric restriction, and aging. *Science, 273*, 59–63.

Solberg, E. E., Ekeberg, O., Holen, A., Ingjer, F., Sandvik, L., Standal, P. A., & Vikman, A. (2004). Hemodynamic changes during long meditation. *Applied Psychophysiology & Biofeedback, 29*, 213–221.

Solberg, E. E., Holen, A., Ekeberg, Å., Osterud, B., Halvorsen, R., & Sandvik, L. (2004). The effects of long meditation on plasma melatonin and blood serotonin. *Medical Science Monitor, 10*, CR96–101.

Solberg Nes, L., Segerstrom, S. C., & Sephton, S. E. (in press). Engagement and arousal: optimism's effects during a brief stressor. *Personality Social Psychology Bulletin.*

Soli, S. D. (1994). Hearing aids: Today and tomorrow. *Echoes: The newsletter of the Acoustical Society of America, 4*, 1–5.

Solms, M. (1997). *The neuropsychology of dreams: A clinico-anatomical study.* Mahwah, NJ: Erlbaum.

Solomon, D. A., Keller, M. B., Leon, A. C., Mueller, T. I., Lavori, P. W., Shea, M. T., et al. (2000). Multiple recurrences of major depressive disorder. *American Journal of Psychiatry, 157*, 229–233.

Solomon, R. L., & Corbit, J. D. (1974a). An opponent-process theory of motivation: I. Temporal dynamics of affect. *Psychological Review, 78*, 3–43.

Sommer, F. G., & Ling, D. (1970). Auditory testing of newborns using eyeblink conditioning. *Journal of Auditory Research, 10*, 292–295.

Soper, B., Milford, G. E., & Rosenthal, G. T. (1995). Belief when evidence does not support the theory. *Psychology & Marketing, 12*, 415–422.

Soto-Faraco, S., & Spence, C. (2001). Spatial modulation of repetition blindness and repetition deafness. *Quarterly Journal of Experimental Psychology: Human Experimental Psychology, 54*, 1181–1202.

Sowell, E. R., Thompson, P. M., Holmes, C. J., Jernigan, T. L., & Toga, A. W. (1999). In vivo evidence for post-adolescent brain maturation in frontal and striatal regions. *Nature Neuroscience, 2*, 859–61.

Spangler, W. D. (1992). Validity of questionnaire and TAT measures of need for achievement: Two meta-analyses. *Psychological Bulletin, 112*, 140–154.

Spanos, N. P. (1994). Multiple identity enactments and multiple personality disorder: A sociocognitive perspective. *Psychological Bulletin, 116,* 143–165.

Spearman, C. (1927). *The abilities of man.* New York: Macmillan.

Speisman, J. C., Lazarus, R. S., Mordkoff, A., & Davison, L. (1964). Experimental reduction of stress based on ego-defense theory. *Journal of Abnormal and Social Psychology, 68,* 367–380.

Spelke, E. S. (1991). Physical knowledge in infancy: Reflections on Piaget's theory. In S. Carey & R. Gelman (Eds.), *The epigenesis of mind: Essays on biology and cognition* (pp. 133–169). Hillsdale, NJ: Erlbaum.

Spelke, E. S., Breinlinger, K., Jacobson, K., & Phillips, A. (1993). Gestalt relations and object perception: A developmental study. *Perception, 22,* 1483–1501.

Spelke, E. S., Breinlinger, K., Macomber, J., & Jacobson, K. (1992). Origins of knowledge. *Psychological Review, 99,* 605–632.

Spencer, W. D., & Raz, N. (1995). Differential age effects on memory for content and context: A meta-analysis. *Psychology and Aging, 10,* 527–539.

Sperling, G. (1960). The information available in brief visual presentations. *Psychological Monographs, 74,* 1–29.

Sperling, R. (2001). The volumes of memory. *Journal of Neurology, Neurosurgery & Psychiatry, 71,* 5–6.

Spiegel, D., Bierre, P., & Rootenberg, J. (1989). Hypnotic alteration of somatosensory perception. *American Journal of Psychiatry, 146,* 749–754.

Spiegel, D., & Cardeña, E. (1991). Disintegrated experience: The dissociated disorders revisited. *Journal of Abnormal Psychology, 100,* 366–378.

Spiegel, D., Cutcomb, S., Ren, C., & Pribram, K. (1985). Hypnotic hallucination alters evoked potentials. *Journal of Abnormal Psychology, 94,* 249–255.

Spiegel, S., Grant-Pillow, H., & Higgins, E. T. (2004). How regulatory fit enhances motivational strength during goal pursuit. *European Journal of Social Psychology, 34,* 39–54.

Spiers, H. J., Maguire, E. A., & Burgess, N. (2001). Hippocampal amnesia. *Neurocase, 7,* 357–382.

Spinella, M., Yang, B., & Lester, D. (2004). Prefrontal system dysfunction and credit card debt. *International Journal of Neuroscience, 114,* 1323–1332.

Spitzer, R. L. (1975). On pseudoscience in science, logic in remission, and psychiatric diagnosis: A critique of Rosenhan's "On being sane in insane places." *Journal of Abnormal Psychology, 84,* 442–452.

Sprecher, S. (1998). The effect of exchange orientation on close relationships. *Social Psychology Quarterly, 61,* 220–231.

Sprecher, S. (1999). "I love you more today than yesterday": Romantic partners' perceptions of changes in love and related affect over time. *Journal of Personality and Social Psychology, 76,* 46–53.

Sprecher, S., Aron, A., Hatfield, E., Cortese, A., Potapova, E., & Levitskaya, A. (1994). Love: American style, Russian style and Japanese style. *Personal Relationships, 1,* 349–369.

Sprecher, S., Sullivan, Q., & Hatfield, E. (1994). Mate selection preferences: Gender differences examined in a national sample. *Journal of Personality and Social Psychology, 66,* 1074–1080.

Springer, S. P., & Deutsch, G. (1994). *Left brain, right brain.* New York: Freeman.

Springer, S. P., & Deutsch, G. (1998). *Left brain, right brain: Perspectives from cognitive neuroscience* (5th ed.). New York: Freeman.

Sprock, J., & Yoder, C. Y. (1997). Women and depression: An update on the report of the APA Task Force. *Sex Roles, 36,* 269–303.

Squire, L. R. (1987). *Memory and the brain.* New York: Oxford University Press.

Squire, L. R. (1992). Memory and the hippocampus: A synthesis from findings with rats, monkeys, and humans. *Psychological Review, 99,* 195–231.

Squire, L. R. (2004). Memory systems of the brain: A brief history and current perspective. *Neurobiology of Learning and Memory, 82,* 171–177.

Squire, L. R., Clark, R. E., & Knowlton, B. J. (2001). Retrograde amnesia. *Hippocampus, 11,* 50–55.

Squire, L. R., & Kandel, E. R. (1999). *Memory: From mind and molecules.* New York: Scientific American Books.

Squire, L. R., Ojemann, J. G., Miezin, F. M., Petersen, S. E., Videen, T. O., & Raichle, M. E. (1992). Activation of the hippocampus in normal humans: A functional anatomical study of memory. *Proceedings of the National Academy of Sciences, USA, 89,* 1837–1841.

Squire, L. R., & Schacter, D. L. (Eds.). (2002). *Neuropsychology of memory* (3rd ed.). New York: Guilford Press.

Sroufe, L. A., & Fleeson, J. (1986). Attachment and the construction of relationships. In W. W. Hartup & Z. Rubin (Eds.), *Relationships and development* (pp. 51–71). Hillsdale, NJ: Erlbaum.

Stack, S., & Eshleman, J. R. (1998). Marital status and happiness. *Journal of Marriage and the Family, 60,* 527–536.

Staddon, J. E. R., & Cerutti, D. T. (2003). Operant conditioning. *Annual Review of Psychology, 54,* 115–144.

Stager, C. L., & Werker, J. F. (1997). Infants listen for more phonetic detail in speech perception than in word-learning tasks. *Nature, 388,* 381–382.

Stallone, D. D., & Stunkard, A. J. (1994). Obesity. In A. Frazer & P. B. Molinoff (Eds.), *Biological bases of brain function and disease* (pp. 385–403). New York: Raven Press.

Standing, L., Conezio, J., & Haber, R. N. (1970). Perception and memory for pictures: Single-trial learning of 2500 visual stimuli. *Psychonomic Science, 19,* 73–74.

Stanley, M. A., & Turner, S. M. (1995). Current status of pharmacological and behavioral treatment of obsessive-compulsive disorder. *Behavior Therapy, 25,* 153–186.

Stanton, M. D. (1981). Strategic approaches to family therapy. In A. S. Gurman & D. P. Kniskern (Eds.), *Handbook of family therapy* (pp. 361–402). New York: Brunner/Mazel.

Starker, S. (1988). Psychologists and self-help books: Attitudes and prescriptive practices of clinicians. *American Journal of Psychotherapy, 42,* 448–455.

Stayman, D. M., & Kardes, F. R. (1992). Spontaneous inference processes in advertising: Effects of need for cognition and self-monitoring on inference generation and utilization. *Journal of Consumer Psychology, 1,* 125–142.

Steblay, N., Dysart, J., Fulero, S., & Lindsay, R. C. L. (2001). Eyewitness accuracy rates in sequential and simultaneous lineup presentations: A meta-analytic comparison. *Law & Human Behavior, 25,* 459–473.

Steele, C., & Josephs, R. A. (1990). Alcohol myopia: Its prized and dangerous effects. *American Psychologist, 45,* 921–933.

Steele, C. M. (1997). A threat in the air: How stereotypes shape intellectual identity and performance. *American Psychologist, 52,* 613–629.

Steele, C. M., & Aronson, J. (1995). Stereotype threat and the intellectual test performance of African Americans. *Journal of Personality & Social Personality, 69,* 797–811.

Steele, C. M., Critchlow, B., & Liu, T. J. (1985). Alcohol and social behavior II: The helpful drunkard. *Journal of Personality and Social Psychology, 48,* 35–46.

Steele, C. M., & Southwick, L. (1985). Alcohol and social behavior I: The psychology of drunken excess. *Journal of Personality and Social Psychology, 48,* 18–34.

Steele, K. M., Ball, T. N., & Runk, R. (1997). Listening to Mozart does not enhance backwards digit span performance. *Perceptual and Motor Skills, 84,* 1179–1184.

Steele, K. M., Bella, S. D., Peretz, I., Dunlop, T., Dawe, L. A., Humphrey, G. K., et al. (1999). Prelude or requiem for the "Mozart effect"? *Nature, 400,* 827–828.

Steele, R. L. (1992). Dying, death, and bereavement among the Maya Indians of Mesoamerica: A study in anthropological psychology. In L. A. Platt & V. R. Persico, Jr. (Eds.), *Grief in cross-cultural perspective: A casebook* (pp. 399–424). New York: Garland.

Steinberg, M. (1994). Systematizing dissociation: Symptomatology and diagnostic assessment. In D. Spiegel (Ed.), *Dissociation: Culture, mind, and body* (pp. 59–90). Washington, DC: American Psychiatric Press.

Steketee, G., & White, K. (1990). When once is not enough: Help for obsessive-compulsives. Oakland, CA: New Harbinger.

Stelmack, R. M. (1990). Biological bases of extraversion: Psychophysiological evidence. *Journal of Personality, 58,* 293–311.

Stephan, W. G., Stephan, C. W., & de Vargas, M. C. (1996). Emotional expression in Costa Rica and the United States. *Journal of Cross-Cultural Psychology, 27,* 147–160.

Steptoe, A., Lipsey, Z., & Wardle, J. (1998). Stress, hassles and variations in alcohol consumption, food choice and physical exercise: A diary study. *British Journal of Health Psychology, 3,* 51–63.

Steptoe, A., Wardle, J., Bages, N., Sallis, J. F., Sanabria-Ferrand, P., & Sanchez, M. (2004). Drinking and driving in university students: An international study of 23 countries. *Psychology & Health, 19,* 527–540.

Sterling-Smith, R. S. (1976). A special study of drivers most responsible in fatal accidents. Summary for Management Report, Contract DOT HS 310-3-595. Washington, DC: Department of Transportation.

Stern, K., & McClintock, M. K. (1998). Regulation of ovulation by human pheromones. *Nature, 392,* 177–179.

Stern, P. C., & Carstensen, L. L. (Eds.). (2000). *The aging mind: Opportunities in cognitive research.* Washington, DC: National Academy Press.

Stern, Y. (2002). What is cognitive reserve? Theory and research application of the reserve concept. *Journal of the International Neuropsychological Society, 8,* 448–460.

Sternbach, R. A. (1978). Psychological dimensions and perceptual analyses, including pathologies of pain. In E. C. Carterette & M. P. Friedman (Eds.), *Handbook of perception* (pp. 231–261). New York: Academic Press.

Sternberg, R. J. (1985). *Beyond IQ: A triarchic theory of human intelligence*. Cambridge, England: Cambridge University Press.

Sternberg, R. J. (1986a). A triangular theory of love. *Psychological Review, 93*, 119–135.

Sternberg, R. J. (1988a). *The triangle of love*. New York: Basic Books.

Sternberg, R. J. (1988b). *The triarchic mind: A new theory of human intelligence*. New York: Viking.

Sternberg, R. J. (1990). *Metaphors of mind: Conceptions of the nature of intelligence*. New York: Cambridge University Press.

Sternberg, R. J. (2001). Teaching psychology students that creativity is a decision. *General Psychologist, 36*, 8–11.

Sternberg, R. J. (2003a). Issues in the theory and measurement of successful intelligence: A reply to Brody. *Intelligence, 31*, 331–337.

Sternberg, R. J. (2003b). Our research program validating the triarchic theory of successful intelligence: Reply to Gottfredson. *Intelligence, 31*, 399–413.

Sternberg, R. J. (Ed.). (2000). *Handbook of intelligence*. New York: Cambridge University Press.

Sternberg, R. J., & Detterman, D. K. (Eds.). (1986). *What is intelligence? Contemporary viewpoints on its nature and definition*. Norwood, NJ: Ablex.

Sternberg, R. J., Nokes, C., Geissler, P. W., Prince, R., Okatcha, F., Bundy, D. A., & Grigorenko, E. L. (2001). The relationship between academic and practical intelligence: A case study in Kenya. *Intelligence, 29*, 1–18.

Sternberg, R. J., & Wagner, R. K. (1993). The g-ocentric view of intelligence and job performance is wrong. *Current Directions in Psychological Science, 2*, 1–5.

Sternberg, R. J., Wagner, R. K., & Okagaki, L. (1993). Practical intelligence: The nature and role of tacit knowledge in work. In J. M. Puckett, H. W. Reese, et al. (Eds.), *Mechanisms of everyday cognition*. Hillsdale, NJ: Erlbaum.

Stevens, L. E., & Fiske, S. T. (1995). Motivation and cognition in social life: A social survival perspective. *Social Cognition, 13*, 189–214.

Stevenson, H., Lee, S., & Stigler, J. (1986). Mathematics achievement of Chinese, Japanese, and American children. *Science, 231*, 693–699.

Stewart, E. G. (2002). de Kooning's dementia. *American Journal of Alzheimer's Disease & Other Dementias, 17*, 313–317.

Stewart, W. F., Ricci, J. A., Chee, E., Hahn, S. R., & Morganstein, D. (2003). Cost of lost productive work time among US workers with depression. *JAMA: Journal of the American Medical Association, 289*, 3135–3144.

Stewart-Williams, S., & Podd, J. (2004). The placebo effect: Dissolving the expectancy versus conditioning debate. *Psychological Bulletin, 130*, 324–340.

Stice, E., Presnell, K., & Spangler, D. (2002). Risk factors for binge eating onset in adolescent girls: A 2-year prospective investigation. *Health Psychology, 21*, 131–138.

Stickgold, R. (1998). Sleep: Off-line memory reprocessing. *Trends in Cognitive Science, 2*, 484–492.

Stickgold, R., Fosse, R., & Walker, M. P. (2002). Linking brain and behavior in sleep-dependent learning and memory consolidation. *Proceedings of the National Academy of Science, 99*, 16519–16521.

Stickgold, R., James, L., & Hobson, J. A. (2000). Visual discrimination learning requires sleep after training. *Nature Neuroscience, 3*, 1237–1238.

Stickgold, R., Malia, A., Maguire, D., Roddenberry, D., & O'Connor, M. (2000). Replaying the game: Hypnagogic images in normals and amnesics. *Science, 290*, 350–353.

Stickgold, R., Rittenhouse, C. D., & Hobson, J. A. (1994). Dream splicing: A new technique for assessing thematic coherence in subjective reports of mental activity. *Consciousness & Cognition: An International Journal, 3*, 114–128.

Stickgold, R., Whidbee, D., Schirmer, B., Paqtel, V., & Hobson, J. A. (2000). Visual discrimination task improvement: A multi-step process occurring during sleep. *Journal of Cognitive Neuroscience, 12*, 246–254.

Stirman, S. W., DeRubeis, R. J., Crits-Christoph, P., & Rothman, A. (2005). Can the randomized controlled trial literature generalize to nonrandomized patients? *Journal of Consulting & Clinical Psychology, 73*, 127–135.

Stoel-Gammon, C., & Otomo, K. (1986). Babbling development of hearing-impaired and normally hearing subjects. *Journal of Speech and Hearing Disorders, 51*, 33–41.

Stokes, J. P., Damon, W., & McKirnan, D. J. (1997). Predictors of movement toward homosexuality: A longitudinal study of bisexual men. *Journal of Sex Research, 34*, 304–312.

Stone, J. (2002). Battling doubt by avoiding practice: The effects of stereotype threat on self-handicapping in white athletes. *Personality & Social Psychology Bulletin, 28*, 1667–1678.

Stone, J., Cooper, J., Wiegand, A. W., & Aronson, E. (1997). When exemplification fails: Hypocrisy and the motive for self-integrity. *Journal of Personality and Social Psychology, 72*, 54–65.

Stoolmiller, M. (1999). Implications of the restricted range of family environments for estimates of heritability and nonshared environment in behavior-genetic adoption studies. *Psychological Bulletin, 125*, 392–409.

Strakowski, S. M., Adler, C. M., & DelBello, M. P. (2002). Volumetric MRI studies of mood disorders: Do they distinguish unipolar and bipolar disorder? *Bipolar Disorders, 4*, 80–88.

Strakowski, S. M., Lonczak, H. S., Sax, K. W., West, S. A., Crist, R. M., & Thienhaus, O. J. (1995). The effects of race on diagnosis and disposition from a psychiatric emergency service. *Journal of Clinical Psychiatry, 56*, 101–107.

Strakowski, S. M., Shelton, R. C., & Kolbrener, M. L. (1993). The effects of race and comorbidity on clinical diagnosis in patients with psychosis. *Journal of Clinical Psychiatry, 54*, 96–102.

Strasburger, V. C., & Wilson, B. J. (2002). *Children, adolescents and the media*. Thousand Oaks, CA: Sage Publications.

Straus, M. A. (1980). Social stress and marital violence in a national sample of American families. *Annals of the New York Academy of Sciences, 347*, 229–250.

Straus, M. A. (2000). Corporal punishment and primary prevention of physical abuse. *Child Abuse & Neglect, 24*, 1109–1114.

Straus, M. A., & Gelles, R. J. (1980). *Behind closed doors: Violence in the American family*. New York: Anchor/Doubleday.

Straus, M. A., & McCord, J. (1998). Do physically punished children become violent adults? In S. Nolen-Hoeksema (Ed.), *Clashing views on abnormal psychology: A Taking Sides custom reader* (pp. 130–155). Guilford, CT: Dushkin/McGraw-Hill (1998).

Straus, M. A., Sugarman, D. B., & Giles-Sims, J. (1997). Spanking by parents and subsequent antisocial behavior of children. *Archives of Pediatrics & Adolescent Medicine, 151*, 761–767.

Streiker, L. D. (1984). *Mind-bending: Brainwashing, cults, and deprogramming in the '80s*. Garden City, NY: Doubleday.

Streissguth, A. P., Barr, H. M., Bookstein, F. L., Sampson, P. D., & Olson, H. C. (1999). The long-term neurocognitive consequences of prenatal alcohol exposure: A 14-year study. *Psychological Science, 10*, 186–190.

Streissguth, A. P., Barr, H. M., Sampson, P. D., Darby, B. L., & Martin, D. C. (1989). IQ at age 4 in relation to maternal alcohol use and smoking during pregnancy. *Developmental Psychology, 25*, 3–11.

Streufert, S., & Swezey, R. W. (1986). *Complexity, managers, and organizations*. Orlando, FL: Academic Press.

Stricker, E. M., Swerdloff, A. F., & Zigmond, M. J. (1978). Intrahypothalamic injections of kainic acid produce feeding and drinking deficits in rats. *Brain Research, 158*, 470–473.

Stricker, G. (1993). The current status of psychotherapy integration. In G. Stricker & J. R. Gold (Eds.), *Comprehensive handbook of psychotherapy integration* (pp. 533–545). New York: Plenum Press.

Stricker, L. J., & Ward, W. C. (2004). Stereotype threat, inquiring about test takers' ethnicity and gender, and standardized test performance. *Journal of Applied Social Psychology, 34*, 665–693.

Striegel-Moore, R. H. (1993). Etiology of binge eating: A developmental perspective. In C. G. Fairburn & G. T. Wilson (Eds.), *Binge eating: Nature, assessment, and treatment* (pp. 144–172). New York: Guilford Press.

Strike, P. C., Magid, K., Brydon, L., Edwards, S., McEwan, J. R., & Steptoe, A. (2004). Exaggerated platelet and hemodynamic reactivity to mental stress in men with coronary artery disease. *Psychosomatic Medicine, 66*, 492–500.

Strober, M. (1995). Family-genetic perspective on anorexia nervosa and bulimia nervosa. In C. G. Fairburn & K. Brownell (Eds.), *Comprehensive textbook of eating disorders and obesity* (pp. 212–218). New York: Guilford Press.

Strom, S. (2000, January 4). Tradition of equality fading in new Japan. *New York Times*.

Stromswold, K., Caplan, D., Alpert, N., & Rauch, S. (1996). Localization of syntactic comprehension by positron emission tomography. *Brain and Language, 52*, 452–473.

Strömwall, L. A., Granhag, P. A., & Jonsson, A. (2003). Deception among pairs: "Let's say we had lunch and hope they will swallow it!" *Psychology, Crime and Law, 9*, 109–124.

Strupp, H. H. (1997). Research, practice, and managed care. *Psychotherapy, 34*, 91–94.

Strupp, H. H., & Hadley, S. W. (1977). A tripartite model of mental health and therapeutic outcomes: With special reference to negative effects in psychotherapy. *American Psychologist. 32*, 187–19.

Strupp, J. J., & Binder, J. L. (1984). *Psychotherapy in a new key: A guide to time-limited dynamic psychotherapy*. New York: Basic Books.

Stunkard, A. J. (1982). Anorectic agents lower a body weight set point. *Life Science, 30*, 2043–2055.

Stürmer, S., Snyder, M., & Omoto, A. M. (2005). Prosocial emotions and helping: The moderating role of group membership. *Journal of Personality & Social Psychology, 88*, 532–546.

Stutts, J. C., Wilkins, J. W., Osberg, J. S., & Vaughn, B. V. (2003). Driver risk factors for sleep-related crashes. *Accident Analysis & Prevention, 35*, 321–333.

Suarez, E. C., Kuhn, C. M., Schanberg, S. M., Williams, R. B., Jr., & Zimmermann, E. A. (1998). Neuroendocrine, cardiovascular, and emotional responses of hostile men: The role of interpersonal challenge. *Psychosomatic Medicine, 60*, 78–88.

Suarez, E., & Williams, R. (1989). Situational determinants of cardiovascular and emotional reactivity in high and low hostile men. *Psychosomatic Medicine, 51*, 404–418.

Subrahmanyam, K., & Greenfield, P. M. (1994). Effect of video game practice on spatial skills in girls and boys. *Journal of Applied Developmental Psychology, 15*(special issue), 13–32.

Sudhalter, V., & Belser, R. C. (2001). Conversational characteristics of children with Fragile X syndrome: Tangential language. *American Journal on Mental Retardation, 106*, 389–400.

Sue, S., Zane, N., & Young, K. (1994). Research on psychotherapy with culturally diverse populations. In A. E. Bergin & S. L. Garfield (Eds.), *Handbook of psychotherapy and behavior change* (4th ed., pp. 783–820). New York: John Wiley & Sons.

Suga, N. (1990). Biosonar and neural computation in bats. *Scientific American, 262*, 60–68.

Sugita, Y. (2004). Experience in early infancy is indispensable for color perception. *Current Biology, 14*, 1267–1271.

Sullins, E. S. (1991). Emotional contagion revisited: Effects of social comparison and expressive style on mood convergence. *Personality & Social Psychology Bulletin, 17*(2), 166–174.

Sullivan, H. S. (1953). *The interpersonal theory of psychiatry.* Oxford, England: Norton.

Sullivan, L. (1999). Looking at vision: Reflections on the role of religious vision in the project of visual truth. In M. Zyniewicz (Ed.), *The papers of the Henry Luce III fellows in theology* (Vol. 3, pp. 115–140). Atlanta, GA: Scholars Press.

Sullivan, R. (1999, June). Dad again. *Life*, pp. 66–68.

Sulloway, F. J. (1996). *Born to rebel: Birth order, family dynamics, and creative lives.* New York: Vintage.

Sundet, J. M., Barlaug, D. G., & Torjussen, T. M. (2004). The end of the Flynn effect? A study of secular trends in mean intelligence test scores of Norwegian conscripts during half a century. *Intelligence, 32*, 349–362.

Suomi, S. J. (2003). Gene-environment interactions and the neurobiology of social conflict. *Annals of the New York Academy of Sciences, 1008*, 132–139.

Surguladze, S. A., Young, A. W., Senior, C., Brébion, G., Travis, M. J., & Phillips, M. L. (2004). Recognition accuracy and response bias to happy and sad facial expressions in patients with major depression. *Neuropsychology, 18*, 212–218.

Susser, E., Neugebauer, R., Hoek, H. W., Brown, A. S., Lin, S., Lanbovitz, D., & Gorman, J. M. (1996). Schizophrenia after prenatal famine: Further evidence. *Archives of General Psychiatry, 53*, 25–31.

Sutton, R. S., & Barto, A. G. (1998). *Reinforcement learning.* Cambridge, MA: MIT Press.

Suzuki, L. A., & Valencia, R. R. (1997). Race-ethnicity and measured intelligence: Educational implications. *American Psychologist, 52*, 1103–1114.

Svanborg, P., Gustavsson, J. P., & Weinryb, R. M. (1999). What patient characteristics make therapists recommend psychodynamic psychotherapy or other treatment forms? *Acta Psychiatrica Scandinavica, 99*, 87–94.

Svartberg, M., & Stiles, T. C. (1991). Comparative effects of short-term psychodynamic psychotherapy: A meta-analysis. *Journal of Consulting & Clinical Psychology, 59*, 704–714.

Svartberg, M., Stiles, T. C., & Seltzer, M. H. (2004). Randomized, controlled trial of the effectiveness of short-term dynamic psychotherapy and cognitive therapy for cluster C personality disorders. *American Journal of Psychiatry, 161*, 810–817.

Swaab, D. F. (2003). *The human hypothalamus: Basic and clinical aspects. Part 1: Nuclei of the human hypothalamus.* Amsterdam: Elsevier.

Swanson, K., Beckwith, L., & Howard, J. (2000). Intrusive caregiving and quality of attachment in prenatally drug-exposed toddlers and their primary caregivers. *Attachment & Human Development, 2*, 130–148.

Sweeney, B., & Rovee-Collier, C. (2001). The minimum duration of reactivation at 6 months: Latency of retrieval and reforgetting. *Infant Behavior & Development, 24*, 259–280.

Swica, Y., Lewis, D. O., & Lewis, M. (1996). Child abuse and dissociative identity disorder/multiple personality disorder: The documentation of childhood maltreatment and the corroboration of symptoms. *Child & Adolescent Psychiatric Clinics of North America, 5*, 431–447.

Swinney, D. A. (1979). Lexical access during sentence comprehension: (Re)consideration of context effects. *Journal of Verbal Learning and Verbal Behavior, 18*, 645–659.

Syvalathi, E. K. G. (1994). Biological factors in schizophrenia: Structural and functional aspects. *British Journal of Psychiatry, 164* (Suppl. 23), 9–14.

Szasz, T. S. (1961). *The myth of mental illness: Foundations of a theory of personal conduct.* New York: Hoeber-Harper.

Szegedi, A., Kohnen, R., Dienel, A. , & Kieser, M. (2005). Acute treatment of moderate to severe depression with hypericum extract WS 5570 (St John's wort): Randomised controlled double blind non-inferiority trial versus paroxetine. *British Medical Journal, 330*, 503.

Tacón, A. M., Caldera, Y. M., & Ronaghan, C. (2004). Mindfulness-based stress reduction in women with breast cancer. *Families, Systems & Health, 22*, 193–203.

Tafarodi, R. W., & Smith, A. J. (2001). Individualism-collectivism and depressive sensitivity to life events: The case of Malaysian sojourners. *International Journal of Intercultural Relations, 25*, 73–88.

Tafarodi, R. W., & Swann, W. B., Jr. (1996). Individualism-collectivism and global self-esteem: Evidence for a cultural trade-off. *Journal of Cross-Cultural Psychology, 27*, 651–672.

Tager-Flusberg, H. (2001). Putting words together: Morphology and syntax in the preschool years. In J. B. Gleason (Ed.), *The development of language* (4th ed., pp. 159–209). Boston: Allyn & Bacon.

Tager-Flusberg, H., Joseph, R., & Folstein, S. (2001). Current directions in research on autism. *Mental Retardation & Developmental Disabilities Research Reviews, 7*, 21–29.

Tajfel, H. (1982). *Social identity and intergroup relations.* Cambridge, England: Cambridge University Press.

Takahashi, T., Sasaki, M., Itoh, H., Yamadera, W., Ozone, M., Obuchi, K., Hayashida, K., Matsunaga, N., & Sano, H. (2002). Melatonin alleviates jet lag symptoms caused by an 11-hour eastward flight. *Psychiatry & Clinical Neurosciences, 56*, 301–302.

Takeuchi, A. H., & Hulse, S. H. (1993). Absolute pitch. *Psychological Bulletin, 113*, 345–361.

Talarico, J. M., Rubin, D. C. (2003). Confidence, not consistency, characterizes flashbulb memories. *Psychological Science, 14*, 455–461.

Tallal, P., Miller, S. L., Bedi, G., Byma, G., Wang, X., Nagarajan, S. S., et al. (1996). Language comprehension in language-learning impaired children improved with acoustically modified speech. *Science, 271*, 81–84.

Tan, H., Zhong, P., & Yan, Z. (2004). Corticotropin-releasing factor and acute stress prolongs serotonergic regulation of GABA transmission in prefrontal cortical pyramidal neurons. *Journal of Neuroscience, 24*, 5000–5008.

Tanabe, S., Ichikawa, K., Hukami, K., & Nakashima, S. (2001). A family with protanomaly and deuteranomaly. *Color Research & Application, 26*, S93–S95.

Tangrea, J. A., Adrianza, M. E., & Helzer, W. E. (1994). Risk factors for the development of the placebo adverse reactions in a multicenter clinical trial. *Annals of Epidemiology, 4*, 327–331.

Tanner, J. M. (1990). *Foetus into man* (2nd ed.). Cambridge, MA: Harvard University Press.

Tarabulsy, G. M., Bernier, A., Provost, M. A., Maranda, J., Larose, S., Moss, E., et al. (2005). Another look inside the gap: Ecological contributions to the transmission of attachment in a sample of adolescent mother-infant dyads. *Developmental Psychology, 41*, 212–224.

Taris, T. W. (2000). Dispositional need for cognitive closure and self-enhancing beliefs. *Journal of Social Psychology, 140*, 35–50.

Tarr, M. J., & Gauthier, I. (2000). FFA: A flexible fusiform area for subordinate-level visual processing automatized by expertise. *Nature Neuroscience, 3*, 764–769.

Tarrier, N., Yusupoff, L., Kinney, C., McCarthy, E., Gledhill, A., Haddock, G., & Morris, J. (1998). Randomised controlled trial of intensive cognitive behaviour therapy for patients with chronic schizophrenia. *British Medical Journal, 317*, 303–307.

Tarter, R. E., Jones, B. M., Simpson, C. D., & Vega, A. (1971). Effects of task complexity and practice on performance during acute alcohol intoxication. *Perceptual & Motor Skills, 33*, 307–318.

Tate, D. F., & Zabinski, M. F. (2004). Computer and Internet applications for psychological treatment: Update for clinicians. *Journal of Clinical Psychology, 60*, 209–220.

Tavares, C. H., Haeffner, L. S., Barbieri, M. A., Bettiol, H., Barbieri, M. R., & Souza, L. (2000). Age at menarche among schoolgirls from a rural community in Southeast Brazil. *Cad Saude Publica, 16*, 709–715.

Tavris, C. (1991). The mismeasure of woman: Paradoxes and perspective in the study of gender. In J. D. Goodchilds (Ed.), *Psychological perspectives on human diversity in America* (pp. 89–136). Washington, DC: American Psychological Association.

Taylor, C. B., & Luce, K. H. (2003). Computer- and Internet-based psychotherapy interventions. *Current Directions in Psychological Science, 12,* 18–22.

Taylor, S. E., Klein, L. C., Lewis, B. P., Gruenewald, T. L., Gurung, R. A. R., & Updegraff, J. A. (2000). Biobehavioral responses to stress in females: Tend-and-befriend, not fight-or-flight. *Psychological Review, 107,* 411–429.

Taylor, S. E., Lerner, J. S., Sage, R. M., Lehman, B. J., & Seeman, T. E. (2004). Early environment, emotions, responses to stress, and health. *Journal of Personality, 72,* 1365–1393.

Taylor, S. E., Lewis, B. P., Gruenewald, T. L., Gurung, R. A. R., Updegraff, J. A., & Klein, L. C. (2002). Sex differences in biobehavioral responses to threat: Reply to Geary and Flinn (2002). *Psychological Review, 109,* 751–753.

Taylor, S. E., Sherman, D. K., Kim, H. S., Jarcho, J., Takagi, K., & Dunagan, M. S. (2004). Culture and social support: Who seeks it and why? *Journal of Personality & Social Psychology, 87,* 354–362.

Taylor, S. W., Repetti, R. L., & Seeman, T. (1997). Health psychology: What is an unhealthy environment and how does it get under the skin? *Annual Review of Psychology, 48,* 411–447.

Tecott, L. H., Sun, L. M., Akana, S. F., Strack, A. M., Lowenstein, D. H., Dallman, M. F., & Julius, D. (1995). Eating disorder and epilepsy in mice lacking 5-HT2C serotonin receptors. *Nature, 374,* 542–546.

Tedlock, B. (1992). The role of dreams and visionary narratives in Mayan cultural survival. *Ethos, 20,* 453–476.

Teigen, K. H. (1994). Variants of subjective probabilities: Concepts, norms, and biases. In G. Wright & P. Ayton (Eds.), *Subjective probability.* New York: Wiley.

Teilmann, G., Juul, A., Skakkeback, N. E., & Toppari, J. (2002). Putative effects of endocrine disrupters on pubertal development in the human. *Best Practice & Research Clinical Endocrinology & Metabolism, 16,* 105–121.

Tein, J. Y., Sandler, I. N., & Zautra, A. J. (2000). Stressful life events, psychological distress, coping, and parenting of divorced mothers: A longitudinal study. *Journal of Family Psychology, 14,* 27–41.

Teitelbaum, P., & Stellar, E. (1954). Recovery from the failure to eat produced by hypothalamic lesions. *Science, 120,* 894–895.

Telch, M. J., Lucas, J. A., & Nelson, P. (1989). Nonclinical panic in college students: An investigation of prevalence and symptomatology. *Journal of Abnormal Psychology, 98,* 300–306.

Tellegen, A., & Atkinson, G. (1974). Openness to absorbing and self-altering experiences ("absorption"), a trait related to hypnotic susceptibility. *Journal of Abnormal Psychology, 83,* 268–277.

Tellegen, A., Lykken, D. T., Bouchard, T. J., Wilcox, K. J., Segal, N. L., & Rich, S. (1988). Personality similarity in twins reared apart and together. *Journal of Personality and Social Psychology, 54,* 1031–1039.

Tenenbaum, H. R., & Leaper, C. (2002). Are parents' gender schemas related to their children's gender-related cognitions? A meta-analysis. *Developmental Psychology, 38,* 615–630.

Tentori, K., Osherson, D., Hasher, L., & May, C. (2001). Wisdom and aging: Irrational preferences in college students but not older adults. *Cognition, 81,* B87-B96.

Teri, L., & Lewinsohn, P. M. (1985). Group intervention for unipolar depression. *Behavior Therapist, 8,* 109–111, 123.

Terrace, H. S. (1979, November). How Nim Chimpsky changed my mind. *Psychology Today,* 23–28.

Terrace, H. S., Pettito, L. A., & Bever, T. G. (1976). *Project Nim, progress report I.* New York: Columbia University Press.

Terry, D. J., & Hogg, M. A. (1996). Group norms and the attitude-behavior relationship: A role for group identification. *Personality & Social Psychology Bulletin, 22,* 776–793.

Terry, D. J., & Hynes, G. J. (1998). Adjustment to a low-control situation: Reexamining the role of coping responses. *Journal of Personality and Social Psychology, 74,* 1078–1092.

Tesser, A. (1993). The importance of heritability of psychological research: The case of attitudes. *Psychological Review, 100,* 129–142.

Tesser, A., Whitaker, D., Martin, L., & Ward, D. (1998). Attitude heritability, attitude change and physiological responsivity. *Personality & Individual Differences, 24,* 89–96.

Tew, J. D., Jr., Mulsant, B. H., Haskett, R. F., Prudic, J., Thase, M. E., Crowe, R. R., et al. (1999). Acute efficacy of ECT in the treatment of major depression in the old-old. *American Journal of Psychiatry, 156,* 1865–1870.

Thalbourne, M. A. (1989). Psychics and ESP: A reply to Grimmer and White. *Australian Psychologist, 24,* 307–310.

Thaler, R. H. (1988). The ultimatum game. *Journal of Economic Perspectives, 2,* 195–206.

Thannickal, T. C., Siegel, J. M., Nienhuis, R., & Moore, R. Y. (2003). Pattern of hypocretin (orexin) soma and axon loss, and gliosis, in human narcolepsy. *Brain Pathology, 13,* 340–351.

Thapar, A., & McGuffin, P. (1996). Genetic influences on life events in childhood. *Psychological Medicine, 26,* 813–820.

Thase, M. E., Greenhouse, J. B., Frank, E., Reynolds, C. F., III, Pilkonis, P. A., Hurley, K., et al. (1997). Treatment of major depression with psychotherapy or psychotherapy-pharmacotherapy combinations. *Archives of General Psychiatry, 54,* 1009–1015.

Thase, M. E., & Jindal, R. D. (2004). Combining psychotherapy and psychopharmacology for treatment of mental disorders. In M. J. Lambert (Ed.), *Bergin and Garfield's handbook of psychotherapy and behavior change,* 5th ed. (pp. 743–766). New York: Wiley and Sons.

Thatcher, R. W. (1994). Cyclic cortical reorganization: Origins of human cognitive development. In G. Dawson & K. W. Fischer (Eds.), *Human behavior and the developing brain* (pp. 232–266). New York: Guilford.

Thelen, E. (1983). Learning to walk is still an "old" problem: A reply to Zelazo. *Journal of Motor Behavior, 15,* 139–161.

Thelen, E. (1995). Motor development: A new synthesis. *American Psychologist, 50,* 79–95.

Thelen, E., & Ulrich, B. D. (1991). Hidden skills: A dynamic systems analysis of treadmill stepping during the first year. *Monographs of the Society for Research in Child Development, 56*(1, Serial No. 223).

Theorell, T., & Karasek, R. A. (1996). Current issues relating to psychosocial job strain and cardiovascular disease research. *Journal of Occupational Health Psychology, 1,* 9–26.

Thesen, T., Vibell, J. F., Calvert, G. A., & Österbauer, R. A. (2004). Neuroimaging of multisensory processing in vision, audition, touch, and olfaction. *Cognitive Processing, 5,* 84–93.

Thibaut, J. W., & Kelley, H. H. (1959). *The social psychology of groups.* New York: Wiley.

Thomas, A., & Chess, S. (1996). *Temperament: Theory and practice.* New York: Brunner/Mazel.

Thompson, J. K. (1990). *Body image disturbance: Assessment and treatment.* New York: Pergamon Press.

Thompson, J. K., & Stice, E. (2001). Thin-ideal internalization: Mounting evidence for a new risk factor for body-image disturbance and eating pathology. *Current Directions in Psychological Science, 10,* 181–183.

Thompson, P. M., Cannon, T. D., Narr, K. L., van Erp, T., Poutanen, V. P., Huttunen, M., et al. (2001). Genetic influences on brain structure. *Nature Neuroscience, 12,* 1253–1258.

Thompson, P. M., Giedd, J. N., Woods, R. P., MacDonald, D., Evans, A. C., & Toga, A. W. (2000). Growth patterns in the developing brain detected by using continuum mechanical tensor maps. *Nature, 404,* 190–193.

Thompson, R. F. (1993). *The brain, a neuroscience primer* (2nd ed.). New York: Freeman.

Thompson, R. F., Bao, S., Chen, L., Cipriano, B. D., Grethe, J. S., Kim, J. J., Thompson, J. K., Tracy, J. A., Weninger, M. S., & Krupa, D. J. (1997). Associative learning. *International Review of Neurobiology, 41,* 151–189.

Thompson, W. L., & Kosslyn, S. M. (2000). Neural systems activated during visual mental imagery: A review and meta-analyses. In A. W. Toga & J. C. Mazziotta (Eds.), *Brain mapping: The systems.* San Diego, CA: Academic Press.

Thorn, B. L., & Gilbert, L. A. (1998). Antecedents of work and family role expectations of college men. *Journal of Family Psychology, 12,* 259–267.

Thorndike, E. L. (1927). The law of effect. *American Journal of Psychology, 39,* 212–222.

Thorndike, E. L. (1949). The law of effect. In *Selected writings from a connectionist's psychology* (pp. 13–26). New York: Appleton-Century-Crofts. (Original work published 1933)

Thornhill, R., & Gangestad, S. W. (1993). Human facial beauty: Averageness, symmetry, and parasite resistance. *Human Nature, 4,* 237–269.

Thornhill, R., & Gangestad, S. W. (1999). Facial attractiveness. *Trends in Cognitive Sciences, 3,* 452–460.

Thurstone, L. L. (1938). *Primary mental abilities.* Chicago: University of Chicago Press.

Thurstone, L. L., & Thurstone, T. G. (1941). *Factorial studies of intelligence.* Chicago: University of Chicago Press.

Tidwell, M. O., Reis, H. T., Shaver, P. R. (1996). Attachment, attractiveness, and social interaction: A diary study. *Journal of Personality & Social Psychology, 71,* 729–745.

Tiernari, P. (1991). Interaction between genetic vulnerability and family environment: The Finnish adoptive family study of schizophrenia. *Acta Psychiatrica Scandinavica, 84,* 460–465.

Till, B. D., & Priluck, R. L. (2000). Stimulus generalization in classical conditioning: An initial investigation and extension. *Psychology & Marketing, 17,* 55–72.

Timmerman, I. G. H., Emmelkamp, P. M. G., & Sanderman, R. (1998). The effects of a stress-management training program in individuals at risk in the community at large. *Behaviour Research & Therapy, 36,* 863–875.

Tingey, H., Kiger, G., & Riley, P. J. (1996). Juggling multiple roles: Perceptions of working mothers. *Social Science Journal, 33,* 183–191.

Tinker, J. E., & Tucker, J. A. (1997). Motivations for weight loss and behavior change strategies associated with natural recovery from obesity. *Psychology of Addictive Behaviors, 11,* 98–106.

Tkachuk, G. A. (1999). Exercise therapy for patients with psychiatric disorders: Research and clinical implications. *Professional Psychology: Research and Practice, 30,* 275–282.

Todd, M., Tennen, H., Carney, M. A., Armeli, S., & Affleck, G. (2004). Do we know how we cope? Relating daily coping reports to global and time-limited retrospective assessments. *Journal of Personality & Social Psychology, 86,* 310–319.

Tohen, M., & Grundy, S. (1999). Management of acute mania. *Journal of Clinical Psychology, 60*(Suppl. 5), 31–34.

Tolman, E. C., & Honzik, C. H. (1930a). Degrees of hunger, reward and nonreward, and maze learning in rats. *University of California Publications in Psychology, 4,* 241–256.

Tolman, E. C., & Honzik, C. H. (1930b). Introduction and removal of reward, and maze performance in rats. *University of California Publications in Psychology, 4,* 257–275.

Tomaka, J., Blascovich, J., Kibler, J., & Ernst, J. M. (1997). Cognitive and physiological antecedents of threat and challenge appraisal. *Journal of Personality & Social Psychology, 73,* 63–72.

Tomasello, M. (2004). Les aspects pragmatiques de la communication chez les primates. *Psychologie Francaise, 49,* 209–218.

Tomkins, S. S. (1962). *Affect, imagery, consciousness, Vol I. The positive affects.* New York: Springer-Verlag.

Tong, F., Nakayama, K., Moscovitch, M., Weinrib, O., & Kanwisher, N. (2000). Response properties of the human fusiform face area. *Cognitive Neuropsychology, 17,* 257–279.

Tootell, R. B. H., Mendola, J. D., Hadjikhani, N. K., Ledden, P. J., Liu, A. K., Reppas, J. B., et al. (1997). Functional analysis of V3A and related areas in human visual cortex. *Journal of Neuroscience, 17,* 7060–7078.

Tootell, R. B., Silverman, M. S., Switkes, E., & de Valois, R. L. (1982). Deoxyglucose analysis of retinotopic organization in primate striate cortex. *Science, 218,* 902–904.

Torgersen, S. G. (1983). Genetic factors in anxiety disorders. *Archives of General Psychiatry, 40,* 1085–1089.

Torrance, E. P. (1980). Creativity and style of learning and thinking characteristics of adaptors and innovators. *Creative Child and Adult Quarterly, 5,* 80–85.

Torrey, E. F. (1988). *Nowhere to go: The tragic odyssey of the homeless mentally ill.* New York: Harper & Row.

Torrubia, R., ¡vila, C., Moltó, J., & Caseras, X. (2001). The sensitivity to punishment and sensitivity to reward questionnaire (SPSRQ) as a measure of Gray's anxiety and impulsivity dimensions. *Personality & Individual Differences, 31,* 837–862.

Tovée, M. J., & Cornelissen, P. L. (2001). Female and male perceptions of female physical attractiveness in front-view and profile. *British Journal of Psychology, 92,* 391–402.

Tractinsky, N., & Meyer, J. (1999). Chartjunk or goldgraph? Effects of presentation objectives and content desirability on information presentation. *MIS Quarterly, 23,* 397–420.

Tracy, J. L., & Robins, R. W. (2004). Show your pride: Evidence for a discrete emotion expression. *Psychological Science, 15,* 194–197.

Trafimow, D., & Finlay, K. (1996). The importance of subjective norms for a minority of people: Between-subjects and within-subjects analyses. *Personality and Social Psychology Bulletin, 22,* 820–828.

Traustadóttir, T., Bosch, P. R., & Matt, K. S. (2003). Gender differences in cardiovascular and hypothalamic-pituitary-adrenal axis responses to psychological stress in healthy older adult men and women. *Stress: The International Journal on the Biology of Stress, 6,* 133–140.

Treisman, A. M. (1964a). Monitoring and storage of irrelevant messages in selective attention. *Journal of Verbal Learning and Verbal Behavior, 3,* 449–459.

Treisman, A. M. (1964b). Selective attention in man. *British Medical Bulletin, 20,* 12–16.

Treisman, A. M., & Gormican, S. (1988). Feature analysis in early vision: Evidence from search asymmetries. *Psychological Review, 95,* 15–48.

Treisman, A. M., & Schmidt, H. (1982). Illusory conjunctions in the perception of objects. *Cognitive Psychology, 14,* 107–141.

Treisman, A. M., & Souther, J. (1985). Search asymmetry: A diagnostic for preattentive processing of separable features. *Journal of Experimental Psychology: General, 114,* 285–310.

Treue, S. (2003). Climbing the cortical ladder from sensation to perception. *Trends in Cognitive Sciences, 7,* 469–471.

Trevethan, S. D., & Walker, L. J. (1989). Hypothetical versus real-life moral reasoning among psychopathic and delinquent youth. *Development and Psychopathology, 1,* 91–103.

Triandis, H. C., Bontempo, R. Villareal, M. J., Asai, M., & Lucca, N. (1988). Individualism and collectivism: Cross-cultural perspectives on self-ingroup relationships. *Journal of Personality and Social Psychology, 54,* 323–338.

Triandis, H. C., McCusker, C., & Hui, C. H. (1990). Multimethod probes of individualism and collectivism. *Journal of Personality and Social Psychology, 59,* 1006–1020.

Trimpop, R., & Kirkcaldy, B. (1997). Personality predictors of driving accidents. *Personality & Individual Differences, 23,* 147–152.

Trivedi, M. A., & Coover, G. D. (2004). Lesions of the ventral hippocampus, but not the dorsal hippocampus, impair conditioned fear expression and inhibitory avoidance on the elevated T-maze. *Neurobiology of Learning & Memory, 81,* 172–184.

Trivedi, N., & Sabini, J. (1998). Volunteer bias, sexuality, and personality. *Archives of Sexual Behavior, 27,* 181–195.

Trivers, R. (1972). Parental investment and sexual selection. In B. Campbell (Ed.), *Sexual selection and the descent of man, 1871–1971* (pp. 136–179). Chicago: Aldine.

Trivers, R. (1985). *Social evolution.* Menlo Park, CA: Benjamin/Cummings.

True, W. R., Rice, J., Eisen, S. A., Heath, A. C., Phil, D., Goldberg, J., et al. (1993). A twin study of genetic and environmental contributions to liability for posttraumatic stress symptoms. *Archives of General Psychiatry, 50,* 257–264.

Truscott, S. D., & Frank, A. J. (2001). Does the Flynn effect affect IQ scores of students classified as LD? *Journal of School Psychology, 39,* 319–334.

Tsai, G., & Coyle, J. T. (2002). Glutamatergic mechanisms in schizophrenia. *Annual Review of Pharmacology and Toxicology, 42,* 165–179.

Tsai, J. L., Levenson, R. W., & Carstensen, L. L. (2000). Autonomic, subjective, and expressive responses to emotional films in older and younger Chinese Americans and European Americans. *Psychology & Aging, 15,* 684–693.

Tsai, S.-J., Hong, C.-H., Yu, W-Y. Y., & Chen, T.-J. (2004). Association study of a brain-derived neurotrophic factor (BDNF) Val66Met polymorphism and personality trait and intelligence in healthy young females. *Neuropsychobiology, 49,* 13–16.

Tsai, S-J., Yu, Y. W.-Y., Lin, C-H., Chen, T-J., Chen, S-P., & Hong, C-J. (2002). Dopamine D2 receptor and N-methyl-D-aspartate receptor 2B subunit genetic variants and intelligence. *Neuropsychobiology, 45,* 128–130.

Tsang, J. (2002). Moral rationalization and the integration of situational factors and psychological processes in immoral behavior. *Review of General Psychology, 6,* 25–50.

Tsao, D. Y., Freiwald, W. A., Knutsen, T. A., Mandeville, J. B., & Tootell, R. B. H. (2003). Faces and objects in macaque cerebral cortex. *Nature Neuroscience, 6,* 989–995.

Tsekhmistrenko, T. A., Vasil'eva, V. A., Shumeiko, N. S., & Vologirov, A. S. (2004). Quantitative changes in the fibroarchitectonics of the human cortex from birth to the age of 12 years. *Neuroscience and Behavioral Physiology, 34,* 983–988.

Tsien, J. Z., Chen, D. F., Gerber, D., Tom, C., Mercer, E. H., Anderson, D. J., et al. (1996). Subregion- and cell type–restricted gene knockout in mouse brain. *Cell, 87,* 1317–1326.

Tucker, G. J. (1998). Putting DSM-IV in perspective. *American Journal of Psychiatry 155*(2), 159–161

Tucker, P. (2003). The impact of rest breaks upon accident risk, fatigue and performance: A review. *Work & Stress, 17,* 123–137.

Tugade, M. M., & Fredrickson, B. L. (2004). Resilient individuals use positive emotions to bounce back From negative emotional experiences. *Journal of Personality and Social Psychology, 86,* 320–333.

Tugade, M. M., Fredrickson, B. L., & Barrett, L. F. (2004). Psychological resilience and positive emotional granularity: Examining the benefits of positive emotions on coping and health. *Journal of Personality, 72,* 1161–1190.

Tuller, D. (2003, January 8). A quiet revolution for those prone to nodding off. *New York Times.*

Tulving, E. (1983). *Elements of episodic memory.* New York: Oxford University Press.

Tulving, E., & Thomson, D. M. (1973). Encoding specificity and retrieval processes in episodic memory. *Psychological Review, 80,* 359–380.

Tuna, S., Tekcan, I., & TopÁuoglu, V. (2005). Memory and metamemory in obsessive-compulsive disorder. *Behaviour Research and Therapy, 43,* 15–27.

Turati, C. (2004). Why faces are not special to newborns: An alternative account of the face preference. *Current Directions in Psychological Science, 13,* 5–8.

Turkheimer, E., Haley, A., Waldron, M., D'Onofrio, B., & Gottesman, I. I. (2003). Socioeconomic status modifies heritability of IQ in young children. *Psychological Science, 14,* 623–628.

Turkheimer, E., & Waldron, M. (2000). Nonshared environment: A theoretical, methodological, and quantitative review. *Psychological Bulletin, 126,* 78–108.

Turner, A. M., & Greenough, W. T. (1985). Differential rearing effects on rat visual cortex synapses. I. Synaptic and neuronal density and synapses per neuron. *Brain Research, 329,* 195–203.

Tversky, A., & Kahneman, D. (1974). Judgment under uncertainty: Heuristics and biases. *Science, 185,* 1124–1131.

Tversky, A., & Kahneman, D. (1992). Advances in prospect theory: Cumulative representation of uncertainty. *Journal of Risk and Uncertainty, 5,* 297–323.

Twenge, J. M. (1997). Changes in masculine and feminine traits over time: A meta-analysis. *Sex Roles, 36,* 305–325.

Twenge, J. M. (2000). The age of anxiety? Birth cohort change in anxiety and neuroticism, 1952–1993. *Journal of Personality and Social Psychology, 79,* 1007–1021.

Twenge, J. M. (2001a). Changes in women's assertiveness in response to status and roles: A cross-temporal meta-analysis, 1931–1993. *Journal of Personality & Social Psychology, 81,* 133–145.

Twenge, J. M. (2001b). Birth cohort changes in extraversion: A cross-temporal meta-analysis, 1966–1993. *Personality & Individual Differences, 30,* 735–748.

Twenge, J. M., & Campbell, W. K. (2003). "Isn't it fun to get the respect that we're going to deserve?" Narcissism, social rejection, and aggression. *Personality & Social Psychology Bulletin, 29,* 261–272.

Twenge, J. M., Zhang, L., & Im, C. (2004). It's beyond my control: A cross-temporal meta-analysis of increasing externality in locus of control, 1960–2002. *Personality & Social Psychology Review, 8,* 308–319.

Twisk, J. W. R., Snel, J., Kemper, H. C. G., & van Mechelen, W. (1999). Changes in daily hassles and life events and the relationship with coronary heart disease risk factors: A 2-year longitudinal study in 27–29-yr-old males and females. *Journal of Psychosomatic Research, 46,* 229–240.

Tyrka, A. R., Waldron, I., Graber, J. A., & Brooks-Gunn, J. (2002). Prospective predictors of the onset of anorexic and bulimic syndromes. *International Journal of Eating Disorders, 32,* 282–290.

Ubell, E. (1995, January 15). New devices can help you hear. *Parade Magazine,* pp. 14–15.

Ullian, E. M., Sapperstein, S. K., Christopherson, K. S., & Barres, B. A. (2001). Control of synapse number by glia. *Science, 291,* 657–661.

Ullman, M. T. (2001). The neural basis of lexicon and grammar in first and second language: The declarative/procedural model. *Bilingualism: Language & Cognition, 4,* 105–122.

Ungerleider, L. G. (1995). Functional brain imaging studies of cortical mechanisms for memory. *Science, 270,* 769–775.

Ungerleider, L. G., & Haxby, J. V. (1994). "What" and "where" in the human brain. *Current Opinion in Neurology, 4,* 157–165.

Ungerleider, L. G., & Mishkin, M. (1982). Two cortical visual systems. In D. J. Ingle, M. A. Goodale, & R. J. W. Mansfield (Eds.), *Analysis of visual behavior* (pp. 549–586). Cambridge, MA: MIT Press.

Unsworth, N., & Engle, R. W. (2005). Working memory capacity and fluid abilities: Examining the correlation between Operation Span and Raven. *Intelligence, 32,* 67–81.

Urbszat, D., Herman, C. P., & Polivy, J. (2002). Eat, drink, and be merry, for tomorrow we diet: Effects of anticipated deprivation on food intake in restrained and unrestrained eaters. *Journal of Abnormal Psychology, 111,* 396–401.

Vaillant, G. (1977). *Adaptation to life.* Boston: Little, Brown.

Vaiva, G., Thomas, P., Ducrocq, F., Fontaine, M., Boss, V., Devos, P., et al. (2004). Low posttrauma GABA plasma levels as a predictive factor in the development of acute Posttraumatic Stress Disorder. *Biological Psychiatry, 55,* 250–254.

Vajk, F. C., Craighead, W. E., Craighead, L. W., & Holley, C. (1997, November). Risk of major depression as a function of response styles to depressed mood. Poster presented at the annual meeting of the Association for the Advancement of Behavior Therapy, Miami Beach, FL.

Valdez, P., Ramírez, C., & García, A. (2003). Adjustment of the sleep-wake cycle to small (1–2 h) changes in schedule. *Biological Rhythm Research, 34,* 145–155

Valenstein, E. T. (1973). *Brain control.* New York: Wiley.

Valins, S. (1966). Cognitive effects of false heart-rate feedback. *Journal of Personality & Social Psychology, 4,* 400–408.

van Baaren, R. B., Holland, R. W., Kawakami, K., & van Knippenberg, A. (2004). Mimicry and prosocial behavior. *Psychological Science, 15,* 71–74.

van Boven, L., White, K., Kamada, A., & Gilovich, T. (2003). Intuitions about situational correction in self and others. *Journal of Personality & Social Psychology, 85,* 249–258.

Van Cauter, E., Leproult, R., & Plat, L. (2000). Age-related changes in slow wave sleep and REM sleep and relationship with growth hormone and cortisol levels in healthy men. *Journal of the American Medical Association, 284,* 861–868.

Van Cauter, E., & Turek, F. W. (2000). Roles of sleep-wake and dark-light cycles in the control of endocrine, metabolic, cardiovascular and cognitive function. In B. S. McEwen (Ed.), *Coping with the environment: Handbook of physiology series. Part 2: Environmental regulation of states and functions of the organism.*

Vandello, J. A., & Cohen, D. (1999). Patterns of individualism and collectivism across the United States. *Journal of Personality and Social Psychology, 77,* 279–292.

van den Berg, S., Shapiro, D. A., Bickerstaffe, D., & Cavanagh, K. (2004). Computerized cognitive-behaviour therapy for anxiety and depression: A practical solution to the shortage of trained therapists. *Journal of Psychiatric & Mental Health Nursing, 11,* 508–513.

van den Heuval, O. A., van de Wetering, B. J., Veltman, D. J., & Pauls, D. L. (2000). Genetic studies of panic disorder: A review. *Journal of Clinical Psychiatry, 61,* 756–766.

Vanderlinden, J., Grave, R. D., Vandereycken, W., & Noorduin, C. (2001). Which factors do provoke binge-eating? An exploratory study in female students. *Eating Behaviors, 2,* 79–83.

Van Essen, D. C. (1997). A tension-based theory of morphogenesis and compact wiring in the central nervous system. *Nature, 385,* 313–318.

Van Goozen, S. H. M, Cohen-Kettenis, P. T., Gooren, J. J. G., Frijda, N. H., & Van De Poll, N. E. (1995). Gender differences in behaviour: Activating effects of cross-sex hormones. *Psychoneuroendocrinology, 20,* 343–363.

Van Goozen, S. H., Wiegant, V. M., Endert, E., Helmond, F. A., & Van de Poll, N. E. (1997). Psychoendocrinological assessment of the menstrual cycle: The relationship between hormones, sexuality, and mood. *Archives of Sexual Behavior, 26,* 359–382.

van Honk, J., Tuiten, A., Hermans, E., Putnam, P., Koppeschaar, H., Thijssen, J., Verbaten, R., & van Doornen, L. (2001). A single administration of testosterone induces cardiac accelerative responses to angry faces in healthy young women. *Behavioral Neuroscience, 115,* 238–242.

van Honk, J., Tuiten, A., van den Hout, M., Koppeschaar, H., Thijssen, J., de Haan, E., & Verbaten, R. (2000). Conscious and preconscious selective attention to social threat: Different neuroendocrine response patterns. *Psychoneuroendocrinology, 25,* 577–591.

van IJzendoorn, M. (1995). Adult attachment representations, parental responsiveness, and infant attachment: A meta-analysis on the predictive validity of the Adult Attachment Interview. *Psychological Bulletin, 117,* 387–403.

Vanni, S., Revonsuo, A., Saarinen, J., & Hari, R. (1996). Visual awareness of objects correlates with activity of right occipital cortex. *Neuroreport, 8,* 183–186.

Van Noppen, B., & Steketee, G. (2003). Family responses and multifamily behavioral treatment for obsessive-compulsive disorder. *Brief Treatment & Crisis Intervention, 3,* 231–247.

van Praag, H., Kempermann, G., & Gage, F. H. (1999). Running increases cell proliferation and neurogenesis in the adult mouse dentate gyrus. *Nature Neuroscience, 2,* 266–270.

Van Rooy, D. L., Alonso, A., & Viswesvaran, C. (2005). Group differences in emotional intelligence scores: theoretical and practical implications. *Personality and Individual Differences, 38,* 689–700.

Van Rooy, D. L., Viswesvaran, C., & Pluta, P. (in press). A meta-analytic evaluation of construct validity: What is this thing called emotional intelligence? *Human Performance.*

van Zoest, W., & Donk, M. (2004). Bottom-up and top-down control in visual search. *Perception, 33,* 927–937.

Varela, F., & Shear, J. (Eds.). (1999). *The view from within: First-person methodologies.* London: Imprint Academic.

Vargha-Khadem, F., Isaacs, E. B., Papaleloudi, H., Polkey, C. E., & Wilson, J. (1991). Development of language in 6 hemispherectomized patients. *Brain, 114,* 473–495.

Vargha-Khadem, F., Watkins, K., Alcock, K., Fletcher, P., & Passingham, R. (1995). Praxic and nonverbal cognitive deficits in a large family with a genetically transmitted speech and language disorder. *Proceedings of the National Academy of Sciences, USA, 92,* 930–933.

Varma, A. (2000). Impact of watching international television programs on adolescents in India. *Journal of Comparative Family Studies, 31*, 117–126.

Vartanian, L. R. (2001). Adolescents' reactions to hypothetical peer group conversations: Evidence for an imaginary audience? *Adolescence, 36*, 347–380.

Vasterling, J., Jenkins, R. A., Tope, D. M., & Burish, T. G. (1993). Cognitive distraction and relaxation training for the control of side effects due to cancer chemotherapy. *Journal of Behavioral Medicine, 16*, 65–80.

Vatten, L. J., & SkjaeÊrven, R. (2004). Offspring sex and pregnancy outcome by length of gestation. *Early Human Development, 76*, 47–54.

Vaughn, C., & Leff, J. (1976). Measurement of expressed emotion in the families of psychiatric patients. *British Journal of Social and Clinical Psychology, 15*, 1069–1177.

Vazire, S., & Gosling, S. D. (2004). e-Perceptions: Personality impressions based on personal Websites. *Journal of Personality & Social Psychology, 87*, 123–132.

Vecera, S. P., & Rizzo, M. (2004). What are you looking at? Impaired "social attention" following frontal-lobe damage. *Neuropsychologia, 42*, 1657–1665.

Vehmanen, L., Kaprio, J., & Loennqvist, J. (1995). Twin studies on concordance for bipolar disorder. *Psychiatria Fennica, 26*, 107–116.

Venter, J. C., Adams, M. D., Myers, E. W., Li, P. W., Mural, R. J., Sutton, G. G., et al. (2001). The sequence of the human genome. *Science, 291*, 1304–1351.

Ventura, J., Nuechterlein, K. H., Lukoff, D., & Hardesty, J. P. (1989). A prospective study of stressful life events and schizophrenic relapse. *Journal of Abnormal Psychology, 98*, 407–411.

Verfaellie, M., Keane, M. M., & Cook, S. P. (2001). The role of explicit memory processes in cross-modal priming: An investigation of stem completion priming in amnesia. *Cognitive, Affective & Behavioral Neuroscience, 1*, 222–228.

Vermetten, E., & Brenner, J. D. (2002). Circuits and systems in stress. I. Preclinical studies. *Depression & Anxiety, 15*, 126–147.

Vernon, P. A., Wickett, J. C., Bazana, P. G., & Stelmack, R. M. (2000). The neuropsychology and psychophysiology of human intelligence. In R. J. Sternberg (Ed.), *Handbook of intelligence* (pp. 245–264). Cambridge, UK: Cambridge University Press.

Verstraten, F. A. J., Cavanagh, P., & Labianca, A. T. (2000). Limits of attentive tracking reveal temporal properties of attention. *Vision Research, 40*, 3651–3664.

Vickers, K. S., & Vogeltanz, N. D. (2000). Dispositional optimism as a predictor of depressive symptoms over time. *Personality and Individual Differences, 28*, 259–272.

Vieilledent, S., Kosslyn, S. M., Berthoz, A., & Giraudo, M. D. (2003). Does mental simulation of following a path improve navigation performance without vision? *Cognitive Brain Research, 16*, 238–249.

Vieilledent, S., Kosslyn, S. M., Berthoz, A., & Giraudo, M. D. (in press). Does mental simulation of following a path improve navigation performance without vision? *Behavioral Brain Review.*

Viereck, G. S. (1929, October 26). What life means to Einstein: An interview by George Sylvester Viereck. *Saturday Evening Post.*

Vieweg, R., & Shawcross, C. R. (1998). A trial to determine any difference between two and three times a week ECT in the rate of recovery from depression. *Journal of Mental Health (UK), 7*, 403–409.

Villarreal, D. M., Do, V., Haddad, E., & Derrick, B. E. (2002). NMDA receptor antagonists sustain LTP and spatial memory: Active processes mediate LTP decay. *Nature Neuroscience, 5*, 48–52.

Villringer, A., & Chance, B. (1997). Non-invasive optical spectroscopy and imaging of human brain function. *Trends in Neurosciences, 20*, 435–442.

Vinar, O. (2001). Neurobiology of drug dependence. *Homeostasis in Health & Disease, 41*, 20–34.

Viney, W. (1993). *A history of psychology: Ideas and context.* Needham Heights, MA: Allyn & Bacon.

Vogel, D. D. (2005). A neural network model of memory and higher cognitive functions. *International Journal of Psychophysiology, 55*, 3–21.

Vogel, E. K., & Luck, S. J. (2002). Delayed working memory consolidation during the attentional blink. *Psychonomic Bulletin & Review, 9*, 739–743.

Vogel, G. (1996). School achievement: Asia and Europe top in the world, but reasons are hard to find. *Science, 274*, 1296.

Vogel, G. (1997). Cocaine wreaks subtle damage on developing brains. *Science, 278*, 38–39.

Vohs, K. D., Baumeister, R. F., & Ciarocco, N. J. (2005). Self-regulation and self-presentation: Regulatory resource depletion impairs impression management and effortful self-presentation depletes regulatory resources. *Journal of Personality & Social Psychology, 88*, 632–657.

Volkmar, F. R., Klin, A., Siegel, B., et al. (1994). Field trial for autistic disorder in DSM-IV. *American Journal of Psychiatry, 151*, 1361–1367.

Volkow, N. D., Chang, L., Wang, G., Fowler, J. S., Franceschi, D., Sedler, M. J., et al. (2001). Higher cortical and lower subcortical metabolism in detoxified methamphetamine abusers. *American Journal of Psychiatry, 158*, 383–389.

von der Heydt, R., & Peterhans, E. (1989). Mechanisms of contour perception in monkey visual cortex. I. Lines of pattern discontinuity. *Journal of Neuroscience, 9*, 1731–1748.

von der Malsburg, C. (2002). How are neural signals related to each other and to the world? *Journal of Consciousness Studies, 9*, 47–60.

Vonk, R., & van Knippenberg, A. (1995). Processing attitude statements from ingroup and out-group members: Effects of within-group and within-person inconsistencies on reading times. *Journal of Personality and Social Psychology, 68*, 215–227.

von Zerssen, D., Leon, C. A. Moller, H., Wittchen, H., Pfister, H., & Sartorius, N. (1990). Care strategies for schizophrenic patients in a transcultural comparison. *Comprehensive Psychiatry, 31*, 398–408.

Voth, H. M., & Orth, M. H. (1973). *Psychotherapy and the role of the environment.* New York: Behavioral Press.

Voudouris, N. J., Peck, C. L., & Coleman, G. (1985). Conditioned placebo responses. *Journal of Personality and Social Psychology, 48*, 47–53.

Vrana, S. R. & Lang, P. J. (1990). Fear imagery and the startle-probe reflex. *Journal of Abnormal Psychology, 99*, 181–189.

Vrana, S. R., Spence, E. L., & Lang, P. J. (1988). The startle probe response: A new measure of emotion? *Journal of Abnormal Psychology, 97*, 487–491.

Vranas, P. B. M. (2000). Gigerenzer's normative critique of Kahneman and Tversky. *Cognition, 76*, 179–193.

Vrij, A. (2004). Why professionals fail to catch liars and how they can improve. *Legal and Criminological Psychology, 9*, 159–181.

Vrij, A., & Mann, S. (2001). Telling and detecting lies in a high-stake situation: The case of a convicted murderer. *Applied Cognitive Psychology, 15*, 187–203.

Vrugt, A., & Luyerink, M. (2000). The contribution of bodily posture to gender stereotypical impressions. *Social Behavior & Personality, 28*, 91–104.

Vuilleumier, P., & Sagiv, N. (2001). Two eyes make a pair: Facial organization and perceptual learning reduce visual extinction. *Neuropsychologia, 39*, 1144–1149.

Vurpillot, E. (1968). The development of scanning strategies and their relation to visual differentiation. *Journal of Experimental Child Psychology, 6*, 632–650.

Vygotsky, L. S. (1962). On inner speech. In E. Hanfman & G. Vakar (Eds. and Trans.), *Thought and language* (pp. 130–138). Cambridge, MA: MIT Press.

Vygotsky, L. S. (1978). *Mind in society: The development of higher mental processes.* Cambridge, MA: Harvard University Press. (Original works published 1930, 1933, 1935)

Vygotsky, L. S. (1986). *Thought and language* (A. Kozulin, Trans.). Cambridge, MA: MIT Press. (Original work published 1934)

Vygotsky, L. S. (1988). On inner speech. In M. B. Franklin & S. S. Barten (Eds.), *Child language: A reader* (pp. 181–187). New York: Oxford University Press.

Vythilingam, M., Vermetten, E., Anderson, G. M., Luckenbaugh, D., Anderson, E. R., Snow, J., Staib, L. H., Charney, D. S., & Bremner, J. D. (2004). Hippocampal volume, memory, and cortisol status in Major Depressive Disorder: Effects of treatment. *Biological Psychiatry, 56*, 101–112.

Wachs, T. D., Pollitt, E., Cueto, S., & Jacoby, E. (2004). Structure and cross-contextual stability of neonatal temperament. *Infant Behavior & Development, 27*, 382–396.

Wachs, T. D., Pollitt, E., Cueto, S., Jacoby, E., & Creed-Kanashiro, H. (2005). Relation of neonatal iron status to individual variability in neonatal temperament. *Developmental Psychobiology, 46*, 141–153.

Wade, N. (2002, June 18). A genomic treasure hunt may be striking gold. *New York Times*, D1–D4.

Wade, T., Martin, N. G., & Tiggemann, M. (1998). Genetic and environmental risk factors for the weight and shape concerns characteristic of bulimia nervosa. *Psychological Medicine, 28*, 761–771.

Waelti, P., Dickinson, A., & Schultz, W. (2001). Dopamine responses comply with basic assumptions of formal learning theory. *Nature, 412*, 43–48.

Wager, T. D., Phan, K. L., Liberzon, I., & Taylor, S. F. (2003). Valence, gender, and lateralization of functional brain anatomy in emotion: A meta-analysis of findings from neuroimaging. *NeuroImage. 19*, 513–531.

Wager, T. D., Rilling, J. K., Smith, E. E., Sokolik, A., Casey, K. L., Davidson, R. J., et al. (2004). Placebo-induced changes in fMRI in the anticipation and experience of pain, *Science, 303*, 1162–1167.

Wagner, A. D., Schacter, D. L., Rotte, M., Koutstaal, W., Maril, A., Dale, A. M., et al. (1998). Building memories: Remembering and forgetting of verbal experiences as predicted by brain activity. *Science, 281*, 1188–1191.

Wagner, J. A. (1995). Studies of individualism-collectivism: Effects on cooperation in groups. *Academy of Management Review, 38*, 152–172.

Wagner, R. K. (1997). Intelligence, training, and employment. *American Psychologist, 52*, 1059–1069.

Wagstaff, G. F. (1999). Hypnosis and forensic psychology. In Kirsch, I. Capafons, A., Cardeña-Buelna E., & Amigó, S. Clinical hypnosis and self-regulation: Cognitive-behavioral perspectives (pp. 277–308). Washington, DC: American Psychological Association.

Wahba, M. A., & Bridwell, L. G. (1976). Maslow reconsidered: A review of research on the need hierarchy theory. Organizational Behavior & Human Decision Processes, 15, 212–240.

Wahlbeck, K., Forsén, T., Osmond, C., Barker, D. J. P., & Eriksson, J. G. (2001). Association of schizophrenia with low maternal body mass index, small size at birth, and thinness during childhood. Archives of General Psychiatry, 58, 48–52.

Walach, H., & Maidhof, C. (1999). Is the placebo effect dependent on time? A meta-analysis. In I. Kirsch (Ed.), How expectancies shape experience (pp. 321–332). Washington, DC: American Psychological Association.

Walder, D., Walker, E., & Lewine, R. J. (2000). The relations among cortisol release, cognitive function and symptom severity in psychotic patients. Biological Psychiatry, 48, 1121–1132.

Waldron, V. R., Lavitt, M., & Kelley, D. (2000). The nature and prevention of harm in technology-mediated self-help settings: Three exemplars. Journal of Technology in Human Services, 17, 267–293.

Walker, E. F., & Diforio, D. (1997). Schizophrenia: A neural diathesis-stress model. Psychological Review, 104, 667–685.

Walker, E. F., Grimes, K. E., Davis, D., & Smith, A. (1993). Childhood precursors of schizophrenia: Facial expressions of emotion. American Journal of Psychiatry, 150, 1654–1660.

Walker, E. F., Logan, C. B., & Walder, D. (1999). Indicators of neurdevelopmental abnormality in schizotypal personality disorder. Psychiatric Annals, 29, 132–136.

Walker, E. F., Savoie, T., Davis, D. (1994). Neuromotor precursors of schizophrenia. Schizophrenia Bulletin, 148, 661–666.

Walker, E., Kestler, L., Bollini, A., & Hochman, K. M. (2004). Schizophrenia: Etiology and course. Annual Review of Psychology, 55, 401–430.

Walker, I., & Crogan, M. (1998). Academic performance, prejudice, and the Jigsaw Classroom: New pieces of the puzzle. Journal of Community & Applied Social Psychology, 8, 381–393.

Walker, L. J. (1995). Sexism in Kohlberg's moral psychology? In W. M. Kurtines & J. L. Gewirtz (Eds.), Moral development: An introduction (pp. 83–107). Boston: Allyn & Bacon.

Walker, M. P., Brakefield, T., Hobson, J. A., & Stickgold, R. (2003). Dissociable stages of human memory consolidation and reconsolidation. Nature, 425, 616–620.

Walker, M. P., Brakefield, T., Seidman, J., Morgan, A., Hobson, J. A., & Stickgold, R. (2003). Sleep and the time course of motor skill learning. Learning & Memory, 10, 275–284.

Walker, M. P., Liston, C., Hobson, J. A., & Stickgold, R. (2002). Cognitive flexibility across the sleep-wake cycle: REM-sleep enhancement of anagram problem solving. Cognitive Brain Research, 14, 317–324.

Walker, M. P., & Stickgold, R. (2004). Sleep-dependent learning and memory consolidation. Neuron, 44, 121–133.

Walker, W. R., Skowronski, J. J., Gibbons, J. A., Vogl, R. J., & Thompson, C. P. (2003). On the emotions that accompany autobiographical memories: Dysphoria disrupts the fading affect bias. Cognition & Emotion, 17, 703–723.

Walker, W. R., Skowronski, J. J., & Thompson, C. P. (2003). Life is pleasant—and memory helps to keep it that way! Review of General Psychology, 7, 203–210.

Wallace, R. K. (1970). Physiological effects of transcendental meditation. Science, 167, 1751–1754.

Wallace, R. K., Benson, H., & Wilson, A. F. (1971). A wakeful hypometabolic physiologic state. American Journal of Physiology, 221, 795–799.

Wallenius, M. A. (2004). The interaction of noise stress and personal project stress on subjective health. Journal of Environmental Psychology, 24, 167–177.

Waller, N. G., Kojetin, B. A., Bouchard, T. J., Jr, Lykken, D. T., & Tellegen, A. (1990). Genetic and environmental influences on religious interests, attitudes, and values: A study of twins reared apart and together. Psychological Science, 1, 138–142.

Waller, N. G., & Shaver, P. R. (1994). The importance of non-genetic influences on romantic love styles: A twin family study. Psychological Science, 5, 268–274.

Walsh, B. T. (1993). Binge eating in bulimia nervosa. In C. G. Fairburn & G. T. Wilson (Eds.), Binge eating: Nature, assessment, and treatment (pp. 37–49). New York: Guilford Press.

Walsh, Y. (2001). Deconstructing "brainwashing" within cults as an aid to counselling psychologists. Counselling Psychology Quarterly, 14, 119–128.

Walster, E., Walster, G. W., & Berscheid, E. (1978). Equity: Theory and research. Needham Heights, MA: Allyn & Bacon.

Walters, J., & Gardner, H. (1985). The development and education of intelligences. In F. Link (Ed.), Essays on the intellect (pp. 1–21). Washington, DC:

Curriculum Development Association/Association for Supervision and Curriculum Development.

Wang, Q., & Conway, M. A. (2004). The stories we keep: Autobiographical memory in American and Chinese middle-aged adults. Journal of Personality, 72, 911–938.

Wang, T., Hartzell, D. L., Rose, B. S., Flatt, W. P., Hulsey, M. G., Menon, N. K., et al. (1999). Metabolic responses to intracerebroventricular leptin and restricted feeding. Physiology & Behavior, 65, 839–848.

Wang, X., Merzenich, M. M., Sameshima, K., & Jenkins, W. (1995). Remodelling of hand representation in adult cortex determined by timing of tactile stimulation. Nature, 378, 71–75.

Wang, X., Trivedi, R., Trieber, F., & Snieder, H. (2005). Genetic and environmental influences on anger expression, John Henryism, and stressful life events: The Georgia cardiovascular twin study. Psychosomatic Medicine, 67, 16–23.

Wanska, S. K., & Bedrosian, J. L. (1985). Conversational structure and topic performance in mother–child interaction. Journal of Speech and Hearing Research, 28, 579–584.

Wanska, S. K., & Bedrosian, J. L. (1986). Topic and communicative intent in mother–child discourse. Journal of Child Language, 13, 523–535.

Ward, C. (1994). Culture and altered states of consciousness. In W. J. Lonner & R. S. Malpass (Eds.), Psychology and culture. Boston: Allyn & Bacon.

Ward, T. B. (2001). Creative cognition, conceptual combination, and the creative writing of Stephen R. Donaldson. American Psychologist, 56, 350–354.

Wareing, M., Murphy, P. N., & Fisk, J. E. (2004). Visuospatial memory impairments in users of MDMA ("ectasy"). Psychopharmacology, 173, 391–397.

Wark, G. R., & Krebs, D. L. (1996). Gender and dilemma differences in real-life moral judgment. Developmental Psychology, 32, 220–230.

Warren, J. D., Warren, J. E., Fox, N. C., & Warrington, E. K. (2003). Nothing to say, something to sing: Primary progressive dynamic aphasia. Neurocase, 9, 140–153.

Warren, R. M., & Warren, R. P. (1970). Auditory illusions and confusions. Scientific American, 223, 30–36.

Warrington, E. K., & McCarthy, R. (1987). Categories of knowledge: Further fractionation and an attempted integration. Brain, 110, 1273–1296.

Warrington, E. K., & McCarthy, R. A. (1988). The fractionation of retrograde amnesia. Brain and Cognition, 7, 184–200.

Warrington, E. K., & Shallice, T. (1984). Category-specific semantic impairments. Brain, 107, 829–854.

Wartenburger, I., Heekeren, H. R., Burchert, F., Heinemann, S., De Bleser, R., & Villringer, A. (2004). Neural correlates of syntactic transformations. Human Brain Mapping, 22, 72–81.

Washburne, C. (1956). Alcohol, self and the group. Quarterly Journal of Studies on Alcohol, 17, 108–123.

Wason, P. C., & Johnson-Laird, P. N. (1972). Psychology of reasoning: Structure and content. Cambridge, MA: Harvard University Press.

Wässle, H. (2004). Parallel processing in the mammalian retina. Nature Reviews Neuroscience, 5, 747–757.

Waters, A. J., Gobet, F., & Leyden, G. (2002). Visuospatial abilities of chess players. British Journal of Psychology, 93, 557–565.

Watkins, L. R., Milligan, E. D., & Maier, S. F. (2001). Glial activation: A driving force for pathological pain. Trends in Neuroscience, 24, 450–455.

Watkins, P. C., Grimm, D. L., & Kolts, R. (2004). Counting your blessings: Positive memories among grateful persons. Current Psychology: Developmental, Learning, Personality, Social, 23, 52–67.

Watson, D., & Hubbard, B. (1996). Adaptation style and dispositional structure: Coping in the context of the five-factor model. Journal of Personality, 64, 737–774.

Watson, J. B. (1913). Psychology as a behaviorist views it. Psychological Review, 20, 158–177.

Watson, J. B. (1924). The unverbalized in human behavior. Psychological Review, 4, 273–280.

Watson, J. M., Bunting, M. F., Poole, B. J., & Conway, A. R. A. (2005). Individual differences in susceptibility to false memory in the Deese-Roediger-McDermott paradigm. Journal of Experimental Psychology: Learning, Memory, & Cognition, 31, 76–85.

Watson, J., & Rayner, R. (1920). Conditioned emotional reactions. Journal of Experimental Psychology, 3, 1–14.

Watson, M., Greer, S., Rowden, L., Gorman, C., Robertson, B., Bliss, J. M., & Tunmore, R. (1991). Relationships between emotional control, adjustment to cancer, and depression and anxiety in breast cancer patients. Psychological Medicine, 21, 51–57.

Watt, C. A., & Morris, R. L. (1995). The relationship among performance on a prototype indicator of perceptual defence/vigilance, personality, and extrasensory perception. Personality and Individual Differences, 19, 635–648.

Watt, D. F. (2005). Panksepp's common sense view of affective neuroscience is not the commonsense view in large areas of neuroscience. *Consciousness and Cognition: An International Journal, 14,* 81–88.

Waugh, N. C., & Norman, D. A. (1965). Primary memory. *Psychological Review, 72,* 89–104.

Waxman, S. R. (1992). Linguistic and conceptual organization. *Lingua, 92,* 229–257.

Wayne, S. J., & Ferris, G. R. (1990). Influence tactics and exchange quality in supervisor-subordinate interactions: A laboratory experiment and field study. *Journal of Applied Psychology, 75,* 487–499.

Weaver, I. C. G., Cervoni, N., Champagne, F. A., D'Alessio, A. C., Sharma, S., Seckl, J. R., et al. (2004). Epigenetic programming by maternal behavior. *Nature Neuroscience, 7,* 847–854.

Webb, S. J., & Nelson, C. A. (2001). Perceptual priming for upright and inverted faces in infants and adults. *Journal of Experimental Child Psychology, 79,* 1–22.

Webster, J. I., & Sternberg, E. M. (2004). Role of the hypothalamic-pituitary-adrenal axis, glucocorticoids and glucocorticoid receptors in toxic sequelae of exposure to bacterial and viral products. *Journal of Endocrinology, 181,* 207–221.

Webster, J.I., Tonelli, L., & Sternberg, E. M. (2002). Neuroendocrine regulation of immunity. *Annual Review of Immunology, 20,* 125–163.

Wechsler, D. (1958). *The measurement and appraisal of adult intelligence* (5th ed.). Baltimore: Williams & Wilkins.

Wechsler, H., Dowdall, G. W., Maenner, G., Gledhill-Hoyt, J., & Lee, H. (1998). Changes in binge drinking and related problems among American college students between 1993 and 1997. *Journal of American College Health, 47,* 57–68.

Wechsler, H., Fulop, M., Padilla, A., Lee, H., & Patrick, K. (1997). Binge drinking among college students: A comparison of California with other states. *Journal of American College Health, 45,* 273–277.

Weerasinghe, J., & Tepperman, L. (1994). Suicide and happiness: Seven tests of the connection. *Social Indicators Research, 32,* 199–233.

Wegner, D. M., Schneider, D. J., Carter, S. R., & White, T. L. (1987). Paradoxical effects of thought suppression. *Journal of Personality & Social Psychology, 53,* 5–13.

Wegner, D. M., Wenzlaff, R. M., & Kozak, M. (2004). Dream rebound: The return of suppressed thoughts in dreams. *Psychological Science, 15,* 232–236.

Wehr, T. A., Turner, E. H., Shimada, J. M., Clark, C. H., Barker, C., & Liebenluft, E. (1998). Treatment of a rapidly cycling bipolar patient by using extended bedrest and darkness to stabilize the timing and duration of sleep. *Biological Psychiatry, 43,* 822–828.

Weijers, H. G., Wiesbeck, G. A., Jakob, F., & Boning, J. (2001). Neuroendocrine responses to fenfluramine and its relationship to personality in alcoholism. *Journal of Neural Transmission, 108,* 1093–1105.

Weinberg, R. A. (1989). Intelligence and IQ: Landmark issues and great debates. *American Psychologist, 44,* 98–104.

Weinberger, D. R., & Lipska, B. K. (1995). Cortical maldevelopment, antipsychotic drugs, and schizophrenia: A search for common ground. *Schizophrenia Research, 16,* 87–110.

Weinberger, J. (1995). Common factors aren't so common: The common factors dilemma. *Clinical Psychology: Science and Practice, 2,* 45–69.

Weiner, B. (1980). A cognitive (attribution) emotion-action model of motivated behavior: An analysis of judgments of help-giving. *Journal of Personality and Social Psychology, 39,* 186–200.

Weiner, B., & Kukla, A. (1970). An attributional analysis of achievement motivation. *Journal of Personality & Social Psychology, 15,* 1–20.

Weingarten, H. P., Chang, P., & McDonald, T. J. (1985). Comparison of the metabolic and behavioral disturbances following paraventricular- and ventromedial-hypothalamic lesions. *Brain Research Bulletin, 14,* 551–559.

Weinstein, N. D. (1984). Why it won't happen to me: Perceptions of risk factors and susceptibility. *Health Psychology, 3,* 431–457.

Weinstein, N. D. (1993). Testing four competing theories of health-protective behavior. *Health Psychology, 12,* 324–333.

Weinstein, N. D. (2000). Perceived probability, perceived severity, and health-protective behavior. *Health Psychology, 19,* 65–74.

Weinstein, S. (1968). Intensive and extensive aspects of tactile sensitivity as a function of body part, sex, and laterality. In D. R. Kenshalo (Ed.), *The skin senses* (pp. 195–218). Springfield, IL: Thomas.

Weinstock, M. (1997). Does prenatal stress impair coping and regulation of hypothalamic-pituitary-adrenal axis? *Neuroscience & Biobehavioral Reviews, 21,* 1–10.

Weiskrantz, L. (1986). *Blindsight: A case study and implications.* New York: Oxford University Press.

Weisman, A. D., & Hackett, T. P. (1961). Predilection to death: Death and dying as a psychiatric problem. *Psychosomatic Medicine, 23,* 232–256.

Weiss, R. S. (1986). Continuities and transformations in social relationships from childhood to adulthood. In W. W. Hartup & Z. Rubin (Eds.), *Relationships and development* (pp. 95–110). Hillsdale, NJ: Erlbaum.

Weisskirch, R. S., & Murphy, L. C. (2004). Friends, porn, and punk: Sensation seeking in personal relationships, Internet activities and music preference among college students. *Adolescence, 39,* 189–201.

Weissman, D. E., Griffie, J., Gordon, D. B., & Dahl, J. L. (1997). A role model program to promote institutional changes for management of acute and cancer pain. *Journal of Pain & Symptom Management, 14,* 274–279.

Weissman, M. M., Bruce, M. L., Leaf, P. J., Florio, L., & Holzer, C. (1991). Affective disorders. In L. N. Robins & D. A. Regier (Eds.), *Psychiatric disorders in America* (pp. 53–80). New York: Free Press.

Weissman, M. M., Wickramaratne, P., Nomura, Y., Warner, V., Verdeli, H., Pilowsky, D. J., et al. (2005). Families at high and low risk for depression: A 3-generation study. *Archives of General Psychiatry, 62,* 29–36.

Welberg, L. A., & Seckl, J. R. (2001). Prenatal stress, glucocorticoids and the programming of the brain. *Journal of Neuroendocrinology, 2,* 113–128.

Wellman, H. M. (1990). *The child's theory of mind.* Cambridge, MA: Bradford/MIT Press.

Wells, A. (1997). *Cognitive therapy of anxiety disorders: A practice manual and conceptual guide.* Chichester, UK: Wiley.

Wells, G. L., Malpass, R. S., Lindsay, R. C. L., Fisher, R. P., Turtle, J. W., & Fulero, S. M. (2000). From the lab to the police station: A successful application of eyewitness research. *American Psychologist, 55,* 581–598.

Wender, P. H., Kety, S. S., Rosenthal, D., Schulsinger, F., Ortmann, J., & Luhde, I. (1986). Psychiatric disorders in the biological and adoptive families of adopted individuals with affective disorders. *Archives of General Psychiatry, 43,* 923–929.

Wenzel, A., Finstrom, N., Jordan, J., & Brendle, J. R. (in press). Memory and interpretation of visual representations of threat in socially anxious and nonanxious individuals. *Behaviour Research and Therapy.*

Wenzlaff, R. M., & Luxton, D. D. (2003). The role of thought suppression in depressive rumination. *Cognitive Therapy & Research, 27,* 293–308.

Werner, C., Brown, B., & Altman, I. (1997). Environmental psychology. In J. W. Berry, M. H. Segall, & C. KagitÁibasi (Eds.), *Handbook of cross-cultural psychology, Vol. 3: Social behavior and applications* (pp. 255–290). Needham Heights, MA: Allyn & Bacon.

Wertheimer, M. (1912). Experimentelle Studien über das Sehen Bewegung. *Zeitschrift für Psychologie, 61,* 247–250.

Wertheimer, M. (1923). Untersuchungen zur Lehre von der Gestalt, II (Laws of organization in perceptual forms, II). In W. D. Ellis (Ed.), *A source book of Gestalt psychology* (pp. 71–88). London: Routledge & Kegan Paul.

Wessel, I., & Wright, D. B. (2004). Emotional memory failures: On forgetting and reconstructing emotional experiences. *Cognition & Emotion, 18,* 449–455.

West, L. J. (1980). Persuasive techniques in contemporary cults. In M. Galanter (Ed.), *Cults and new religious movements* (pp. 165–192). Washington, DC: American Psychiatric Press.

Westen, D. (1998). The scientific legacy of Sigmund Freud. Toward a psychodynamically informed psychological science. *Psychological Bulletin, 124,* 333–371.

Westen, D. (1999). The scientific status of unconscious processes: Is Freud really dead? *Journal of the American Psychoanalytic Association, 47*(Suppl.), 1–45.

Westen, D. & Morrison, K. (2001). A multidimensional metaanalysis of treatments for depression, panic, and generalized anxiety disorder: An empirical examination of the status of empirically supported therapies. *Journal of Consulting and Clinical Psychology, 60,* 875–899.

Westen, D., Novotny, C. M., & Thompson-Brenner, H. (2004a). The empirical status of empirically supported psychotherapies: Assumptions, findings, and reporting in controlled clinical trials. *Psychological Bulletin, 130,* 631–663.

Westen, D., Novotny, C. M., & Thompson-Brenner, H. (2004b). The next generation of psychotherapy research: Reply to Ablon and Marci (2004), Goldfried and Eubanks-Carter (2004), and Haaga (2004). *Psychological Bulletin, 130,* 677–683.

Westman, M., & Eden, D. (1997). Effects of a respite from work on burnout: Vacation relief and fade-out. *Journal of Applied Psychology, 82,* 516–527.

Wetsman, A., & Marlowe, F. (1999). How universal are preferences for female waist-to-hip ratios? Evidence from the Hadza of Tanzania. *Evolution and Human Behavior, 20,* 219–228.

Wetzstein, C. (2002, June 7). U.S. teens' birthrate lowest in 6 decades. *Washington Times.*

Whalen, P. J., Rauch, S. L., Etcoff, N. L., McInerney, S. C., Lee, M. B., & Jenike, M. A. (1998). Masked presentations of emotional facial expressions modulate amygdala activity without explicit knowledge. *Journal of Neuroscience, 18,* 411–418.

Wheeler, B. L., Shiflett, S. C., & Nayak, S. (2003). Effects of number of sessions and group or individual music therapy on the mood and behavior of people who have had strokes or traumatic brain injuries. *Nordic Journal of Music Therapy, 12,* 139–151.

Wheeler, L., & Kim, Y. (1997). What is beautiful is culturally good: The physical attractiveness stereotype has different content in collectivistic cultures. *Personality and Social Psychology Bulletin, 23,* 795–800.

Wheeler, M. D. (1991). Physical changes of puberty. *Endocrinology and Metabolism Clinics of North America, 20,* 1–14.

White, A., & Hardy, L. (1995). Use of different imagery perspectives on the learning and performance of different motor skills. *British Journal of Psychology, 86*(2), 169–180.

White, G. L., & Taytroe, L. (2003). Personal problem-solving using dream incubation: Dreaming, relaxation, or waking cognition? *Dreaming, 13,* 193–209.

White, J. M., & Ryan, C. F. (1996). Pharmacological properties of ketamine. *Drug & Alcohol Review, 15,* 145–155.

White, T. G. (1982). Naming practices, typicality, and underextension in child language. *Journal of Experimental Child Psychology, 33,* 324–346.

Whittal, M. L., Agras, W. S., & Gould, R. A. (1999). Bulimia nervosa: A meta-analysis of psychosocial and pharmacological treatments. *Behavior Therapy, 30,* 117–135.

Whorf, B. (1956). *Language, thought, and reality.* Cambridge, MA: MIT Press.

Wickramasekera, I., Davies, T. E., & Davies, S. M. (1996). Applied psychophysiology: A bridge between the biomedical model and the biopsychosocial model in family medicine. *Professional Psychology: Research & Practice, 27,* 221–233.

Wiebe, D. J., & McCallum, D. M. (1986). Health practices and hardiness as mediators in the stress-illness relationship. *Health Psychology, 5,* 425–438.

Wiedemann, G., Pauli, P., Dengler, W., Lutzenberger, W., Birbaumer, N., & Buchkremer, G. (1999). Frontal brain asymmetry as a biological substrate of emotions in patients with panic disorders. *Archives of General Psychiatry, 56,* 78–84.

Wiesbeck, G. A., Mauerer, C., Thome, J., Jakob, F., & Boening, J. (1995). Neuroendocrine support for a relationship between "novelty seeking" and dopaminergic function in alcohol-dependent men. *Psychoneuroendocrinology, 20,* 755–761.

Wigfield, A., Battle, A., Keller, L. B., & Eccles, J. S. (2002). Sex differences in motivation, self-concept, career aspiration, and career choice: Implications for cognitive development. (pp. 93–124) In A. McGillicuddy-De Lisi & R. De Lisi (Eds.), *Biology, society, and behavior: The development of sex differences in cognition.* Westport, CT: Ablex.

Wiggins, J. S., & Pincus, A. L. (1992). Conceptions of personality disorders and dimensions of personality. *Psychological Assessment: Journal of Consulting and Clinical Psychology, 1,* 305–316.

Wiggins, J. S., & Pincus, A. L. (1994). Personality structure and the structure of personality disorders. In P. T. Costa & T. A. Widiger (Eds.), *Personality disorders and the five-factor model of personality.* Washington, D.C.: American Psychological Association.

Wigram, T., Pedersen, I. N., & Bonde, L. O. (2002). *A comprehensive guide to music therapy: Theory, clinical practice, research and training.* London, UK: Jessica Kingsley Publishers.

Wilder, D. A., Simon, A. F., & Faith, M. (1996). Enhancing the impact of counter-stereotypic information: Dispositional attributions for deviance. *Journal of Personality and Social Psychology, 71* 276–287.

Wildman, D. E., Grossman, L. I., and Goodman, M. (2002). Functional DNA in humans and chimpanzees shows they are more similar to each other than either is to other apes. In M. Goodman & A. S. Moffat (Eds.), *Probing human origins* (pp. 1–10). Cambridge, MA: American Academy of Arts and Sciences.

Wilhelm, O., & Schulze, R. (2002). The relation of speeded and unspeeded reasoning with mental speed. *Intelligence, 30,* 537–554.

Wilkins, L. & Richter, C. P. (1940). A great craving for salt by a child with corticoadrenal insufficiency. *Journal of the American Medical Association, 114,* 866–868.

Wilkinson, D. J. C., Thompson, J. M., Lambert, G. W., Jennings, G. L., Schwarz, R. G., Jefferys, D., et al. (1998). Sympathetic activity in patients with panic disorder at rest, under laboratory mental stress, and during panic attacks. *Archives of General Psychiatry, 55,* 511–520.

Wilkinson, R. B. (2004). The role of parental and peer attachment in the psychological health and self-esteem of adolescents. *Journal of Youth and Adolescence, 33,* 479–493.

Willer, J. C., Le, B. D., & De, B. T. (1990). Diffuse noxious inhibitory controls in man: Involvement of an opioidergic link. *European Journal of Pharmacology, 182,* 347–355.

Williams, C. N. (2003). America's opposition to new religious movements: Limiting the freedom of religion. *Law & Psychology Review, 27,* 171–182.

Williams, D. M., & Lawler, K. A. (2003). Importance of macro social structures and personality hardiness to the stress-illness relationship in low-income women. *Journal of Human Behavior in the Social Environment, 7,* 121–140.

Williams, J. E., Paton, C. C., Eigenbrodt, M. L., Nieto, F. J., & Tyroler, H. A. (2000). Anger proneness predicts coronary heart disease risk: Prospective analysis from the atherosclerosis risk in communities (ARIC) study. *Circulation, 101,* 2034–2039.

Williams, J. M. G., Healy, H., Eade, J., Windle, G., Cowen, P. J., Green, M. W., & Durlach, P. (2002). Mood, eating behaviour and attention. *Psychological Medicine, 32,* 469–481.

Williams, K. D., & Karau, S. J. (1991). Social loafing and social compensation: The effects of expectations of coworker performance. *Journal of Personality and Social Psychology, 61,* 570–581.

Williams, L. M. (1994). Recall of childhood trauma: A prospective study of women's memories of child sexual abuse. *Journal of Consulting and Clinical Psychology, 62,* 1167–1176.

Williams, R., Barefoot, J., Califf, R., Haney, T., Saunders, E., Pryor, D., et al. (1992). Prognostic importance of social and economic resources among patients with angiographically documented coronary artery disease. *Journal of the American Medical Association, 267,* 520+.

Williams, S. M., Sanderson, G. F., Share, D. L., & Silva, P. A. (1988). Refractive error, IQ and reading ability: A longitudinal study from age seven to 11. *Developmental Medicine & Child Neurology, 30,* 735–742.

Williams, T. J., Pepitone, M. E., Christensen, S. E., Cooke, B. M., Huberman, A. D., Breedlove, N. J., et al. (2000). Finger length patterns and human sexual orientation. *Nature, 404,* 455–456.

Williams, W. (1998). Are we raising smarter kids today? School-and-home-related influences on IQ. In U. Neisser (Ed.), *The rising curve: Long-terms gains in IQ and related measures* (pp. 125–154). Washington, DC: American Psychological Association.

Wilson, C. S. (2002). Reasons for eating: Personal experiences in nutrition and anthropology. *Appetite, 38,* 63–67.

Wilson, G. T., & Fairburn, C. G. (2002). Treatments for eating disorders. In P. E. Nathan & J. M. Gorman (Eds.), *A guide to treatments that work* (2nd ed., pp. 559–592). London: Oxford University Press.

Wilson, R. I., Kunos, G., & Nicoll, R. A. (2001). Presynaptic specificity of endocannabinoid signaling in the hippocampus. *Neuron, 31,* 453–462.

Wilson, R. I., & Nicoll, R. A. (2001). Endogenous cannabinoids mediate retrograde signalling at hippocampal synapses. *Nature, 410,* 588–592.

Wilson, R. I., & Nicoll, R. A. (2002). Endocannabinoid signaling in the brain. *Science, 296,* 678–682.

Wilson, T. L., & Brown, T. L. (1997). Reexamination of the effect of Mozart's music on spatial-task performance. *Journal of Psychology, 131,* 365–370.

Winer, G. A., & Cottrell, J. E. (1996). Does anything leave the eye when we see? Extramission beliefs of children and adults. *Current Directions in Psychological Science, 5,* 137–142.

Winer, G. A., Cottrell, J. E., Gregg, V., Fournier, J. S., & Bica, L. A. (2002). Fundamentally misunderstanding visual perception: Adults' belief in visual emissions. *American Psychologist, 57,* 417–424.

Winer, G. A., Cottrell, J. E., Gregg, V., Fournier, J. S., & Bica, L. A. (2003). Do adults believe in visual emissions? *American Psychologist, 58,* 495–496.

Winer, G. A., Cottrell, J. E., Karefilaki, K. D., & Gregg, V. R. (1996). Images, words and questions: Variables that influence beliefs about vision in children and adults. *Journal of Experimental Child Psychology, 63,* 499–525.

Winkelman, M. (2003). Complementary therapy for addiction: "drumming out drugs". *American Journal of Public Health, 93,* 647–651.

Winkielman, P., & Berridge, K. C. (2004). Unconscious emotion. *Current Directions in Psychological Science, 13,* 120–123.

Winkielman, P., Berridge, K. C., & Wilbarger, J. L. (2005). Unconscious affective reactions to masked happy versus angry faces influence consumption behavior and judgments of value. *Personality & Social Psychology Bulletin, 31,* 121–135.

Winner, E. (1996). *Gifted children: Myths and realities.* New York: Basic Books.

Winner, E. (1997). Exceptionally high intelligence and schooling. *American Psychologist, 52,* 1070–1081.

Winner, E. (2000a). Giftedness: Current theory and research. *Current Directions in Psychological Science, 9,* 153–156.

Winner, E. (2000b). The origins and ends of giftedness. *American Psychologist, 55,* 159–169.

Winnicott, D. W. (1958). *Collected papers: Through paediatrics to psychoanalysis*. London: Tavistock.

Winter, A. (1998). *Mesmerized: Powers of mind in Victorian Britain*. Chicago: University of Chicago Press.

Winzelberg, A., & Humphreys, K. (1999). Should patients' religiosity influence clinicians' referral to 12-step self-help groups? Evidence from a study of 3,018 male substance abuse patients. *Journal of Consulting and Clinical Psychology, 67*, 790–794.

Wise, P. M., Krajnak, K. M., & Kashon, M. L. (1996). Menopause: The aging of multiple pacemakers. *Science, 273*, 67–70.

Wise, R. A. (1996). Addictive drugs and brain stimulation reward. *Annual Review of Neuroscience, 19*, 319–340.

Wise, R. A. (2004). Dopamine, learning and motivation. *Nature Reviews Neuroscience, 5*, 483–494.

Witelson, S. F., Kigar, D. L., & Harvey, T. (1999). The exceptional brain of Albert Einstein. *Lancet, 353*, 2149–2153.

Witt, L. A., Andrews, M. C., Carlson, D. S. (2004). When conscientiousness isn't enough: Emotional exhaustion and performance among call center customer service representatives. *Journal of Management, 30*, 149–160.

Witt, S. D. (1997). Parental influence on children's socialization to gender roles. *Adolescence, 32*, 253–259.

Witter, M. P., Wouterlood, F., & Witter, M. (2002). *The parahippocampal region: Organization and role in cognitive functions*. New York: Oxford University Press.

Wittstein, I. S., Thiemann, D. R., Lima, J. A. C., Baughman, K. L., Schulman, S. P., Gerstenblith, G., et al. (2005). Neurohumoral features of myocardial stunning due to sudden emotional stress. *New England Journal of Medicine, 352*, 539–548.

Wixted, J. T., & Ebbesen, E. B. (1991). On the form of forgetting. *Psychological Science, 2*, 409–415.

Wixted, J. T., & Ebbesen, E. B. (1997). Genuine power curves in forgetting: A quantitative analysis of individual subject forgetting functions. *Memory & Cognition, 25*, 731–739.

Wolf, A., & Thatcher, R. (1990). Cortical reorganization in deaf children. *Journal of Clinical and Experimental Neuropsychology, 12*, 209–221.

Wolf, N. (1991). *The beauty myth*. New York: Anchor/Doubleday.

Wolf, O. T., Preut, R., Hellhammer, D. H., Kudielka, B. M., Schuermeyer, T. H., & Kirschbaum, C. (2000). Testosterone and cognitive in elderly men: A single testoterone injection blocks the practice effect in verbal fluency, but has no effect on spatial or verbal memory. *Biological Psychiatry, 47*, 650–654.

Wolpe, J. (1958). *Psychotherapy by reciprocal inhibition*. Stanford, CA: Stanford University Press.

Wolpe, J. (1997). Thirty years of behavior therapy. *Behavior Therapy, 28*, 633–635.

Wolsko, P. M., Eisenberg, D. M., Davis, R. B., & Phillips, R. S. (2004). Use of mind-body medical therapies: Results of a national survey. *Journal of General Internal Medicine, 19*, 43–50.

Wood, J. J., McLeod, B. D., Sigman, M., Hwang, W., & Chu, B. C. (2003). Parenting and childhood anxiety: Theory, empirical findings, and future directions. *Journal of Child Psychology & Psychiatry, 44*, 134–151.

Wood, J. M., Lilienfeld, S. O., Nezworski, M. T., & Garb, H. N. (2001). Coming to grips with negative evidence for the comprehensive system for the Rorschach: A comment on Gacono, Loving, and Bodholdt; Ganellen; and Bornstein. *Journal of Personality Assessment, 77*, 48–70.

Wood, J. M., Nezworski, M. T., Garb, H. N., & Lilienfeld, S. O. (2001). Problems with the norms of the comprehensive system for the Rorschach: Methodological and conceptual considerations. *Clinical Psychology: Science & Practice, 8*, 397–402.

Wood, J. N., Romero, S. G., Knutson, K. M., & Grafman, J. (2005). Representation of attitudinal knowledge: Role of prefrontal cortex, amygdala and parahippocampal gyrus. *Neuropsychologia, 43*, 249–259.

Wood, P. (1963). Dreaming and social isolation. *Dissertation Abstracts, 23*(9609), 4749–4750.

Woods, S. C., Schwartz, M. W., Baskin, D. G., & Seeley, R. J. (2000). Food intake and the regulation of body weight. *Annual Review of Psychology, 51*, 255–277.

Woodward, A. L. (1998). Infants selectively encode the goal object of an actor's reach. *Cognition, 69*, 1–34.

Woody, E. Z., & Bowers, K. S. (1994). A frontal assault on dissociated control. In S. J. Lynn & J. W. Rhue (Eds.), *Dissociation: Clinical and theoretical perspectives* (pp. 52–79). New York: Guilford Press.

Woolfolk, R. L., Parrish, M. W., & Murphy, S. M. (1985). The effects of positive and negative imagery on motor skill performance. *Cognitive Therapy and Research, 9*, 335–341.

World Health Organization (2001). The world health report 2001. Mental health: New understanding, new hope. Geneva, Switzerland: Author.

Worthington, T. S. (1979). The use in court of hypnotically enhanced testimony. *International Journal of Clinical & Experimental Hypnosis, 27*, 402–416.

Wortman, C. B., & Silver, R. C. (1989). The myths of coping with loss. *Journal of Consulting & Clinical Psychology, 57*, 349–357.

Wraga, M. J., Thompson, W. L., Alpert, N. M., & Kosslyn, S. M. (2003). Implicit transfer of motor strategies in mental rotation. *Brain and Cognition, 52*, 135–143.

Wurtzel, E. (1995). *Prozac nation: A memoir*. New York: Riverhead.

Wyatt, R. J., Green, M. F., & Tuma, A. H. (1997). Long-term morbidity associated with delayed treatment of first admission schizophrenic patients: A re-analysis of the Camarillo State Hospital data. *Psychological Medicine, 27*, 261–268.

Wyer, N. A., Sherman, J. W., & Stroessner, S. J. (2000). The roles of motivation and ability in controlling the consequences of stereotype suppression. *Personality & Social Psychology Bulletin, 26*, 13–25.

Wyvell, C. L., & Berridge, K. C. (2000). Intra-accumbens amphetamine increases the conditioned incentive salience of sucrose reward: Enhancement of reward "wanting" without enhanced "liking" or response reinforcement. *Journal of Neuroscience, 20*, 8122–8130.

Xerri, C., Merzenich, M. M., Jenkins, W., & Santucci, S. (1999). Representational plasticity in cortical area 3b paralleling tactual motor skill acquisition in adult monkeys. *Cerebral Cortex, 9*, 264–276.

Yamadori, A. (1997). Body awareness and its disorders. In M. Ito & Y. Miyashita (Eds.), *Cognition, computation, and consciousness* (pp. 169–176). Oxford, England: Oxford University Press.

Yamawaki, N., Tschanz, B. T., & Feick, D. L. (2004). Defensive pessimism, self-esteem instability, and goal strivings. *Cognition & Emotion, 18*, 233–249.

Yang, K., & Bond, M. H. (1990). Exploring implicit personality theories with indigenous or imported constructs: The Chinese case. *Journal of Personality and Social Psychology, 58*, 1087–1095.

Yazigi, R. A., Odem, R. R., & Polakoski, K. L. (1991). Demonstration of specific binding of cocaine to human spermatozoa. *Journal of the American Medical Association, 266*, 1956–1959.

Yehuda, R. (2002a). Post-traumatic stress disorder. *New England Journal of Medicine, 346*, 108–114.

Yehuda, R. (2002b). Clinical relevance of biologic findings in PTSD. *Psychiatric Quarterly, 73*, 123–133.

Yehuda, R. (2003). Adult neuroendocrine aspects of PTSD. *Psychiatric Annals, 33*, 30–36.

Yehuda, R., Golier, J. A., Yang, R., & Tischler, L. (2004). Enhanced sensitivity to glucocorticoids in peripheral mononuclear leukocytes in posttraumatic stress disorder. *Biological Psychiatry, 55*, 1110–1116.

Yehuda, R., McFarlane, A. C., & Shalev, A. Y. (1998). Predicting the development of posttraumatic stress disorder from the acute response to a traumatic event. *Biological Psychiatry, 44*, 1305–1313.

Yen, S., Robins, C. J., & Lin, N. (2000). A cross-cultural comparison of depressive symptom manifestation in China and the United States. *Journal of Consulting and Clinical Psychology, 68*, 993–999.

Yeomans, M. R., & Gray, R. W. (1997). Effects of naltrexone on food intake and changes in subjective appetite during eating: evidence for opioid involvement in the appetizer effect. *Physiology & Behavior, 62*, 15–21.

Yeshurun, Y., & Carrasco, M. (1998). Attention improves or impairs visual performance by enhancing spatial resolution. *Nature, 396*, 72–75.

Yeshurun, Y., & Carrasco, M. (1999). Spatial attention improves performance in spatial resolution tasks. *Vision Research, 39*, 293–306.

Yeung, N., Botvinick, M. M., & Cohen, J. D. (2004). The neural basis of error detection: Conflict monitoring and the error-related negativity. *Psychological Review, 111*, 931–959.

Yokosuka, M., Xu, B., Pu, S., Kalra, P. S., & Kalra, S. P. (1998). Neural substrates for leptin and neuropeptide Y (NPY) interaction: Hypothalamic sites associated with inhibition of NPY-induced food intake. *Physiology & Behavior, 64*, 331–338.

Yost, W. A., & Dye, R. H. (1991). Properties of sound localization by humans. In R. A. Altschuler, R. P. Bobbin, B. M. Clopton, & D. W. Hoffman (Eds.), *Neurobiology of hearing: The central auditory system* (pp. 389–410). New York: Raven.

Young, A. W., Hellawell, D. J., Van De Wal, C., & Johnson, M. (1996). Facial expression processing after amygdalotomy. *Neuropsychologia, 34*, 31–39.

Young, F. A. (1981). Primate myopia. *American Journal of Optometry and Physiological Optics, 58*, 560–566.

Young, L. R., Oman, C. M., Merfeld, D., Watt, D., Roy, S., DeLuca, C., et al. (1993). Spatial orientation and posture during and following weightlessness: Human experiments on Spacelab Life Sciences 1. *Journal of Vestibular Research: Equilibrium & Orientation, 3*, 231–239.

Yu, D. W., & Shepard, G. H. (1998). Is beauty in the eye of the beholder? *Nature, 396,* 321–322.

Zabinski, M. F., Wilfley, D. E., Calfas, K. J., Winzelberg, A. J., & Taylor, C. B. (2004). An interactive psychoeducational intervention for women at risk of developing an eating disorder. *Journal of Consulting & Clinical Psychology, 72,* 914–919.

Zacks, J., & Tversky, B. (1999). Bars and lines: A study of graphic communication. *Memory & Cognition, 27,* 1073–1079.

Zaharia, M. D., Kulczycki, J., Shanks, N., Meaney, M. J., & Anisman, H. (1996). The effects of early postnatal stimulation on Morris water-maze acquisition in adult mice: Genetic and maternal factors. *Psychopharmacology, 128,* 227–239.

Zaidel, E., & Iacoboni, M. (2003). *The parallel brain: The cognitive neuroscience of the corpus callosum.* Cambridge, MA: MIT Press

Zajicek, J. (2004). Primary progressive multiple sclerosis. *Cognitive Neuropsychology, 21,* 2784–2785.

Zajonc, R. B. (1968). Attitudinal effects of mere exposure. *Journal of Personality & Social Psychology, 9*(2, Pt. 2), 1–27.

Zajonc, R. B. (2001). Mere exposure: A gateway to the subliminal. *Current Directions in Psychological Science, 10,* 224–228.

Zakowski, S., Hall, M. H., & Baum, A. (1992). Stress, stress management, and the immune system. *Applied and Preventative Psychology, 1,* 1–13.

Zalla, T., Koechlin, E., Pietrini, P., Basso, G., Aquino, P., Sirigu, A., & Grafman, J. (2000). Differential amygdala responses to winning and losing: A functional magnetic resonance imaging study in humans. *European Journal of Neuroscience, 12,* 1764–1770.

Zamora, M. (1990). *Frida Kahlo: The brush of anguish.* San Francisco, CA: Chronicle.

Zane, N., Hall, G. C. N., Sue, S., Young, K., & Nunez, J. (2004). Research on psychotherapy with culturally diverse populations. In M. J. Lambert (Ed.), *Bergin and Garfield's handbook of psychotherapy and behavior change,* 5th ed. (pp. 805–821). New York: Wiley and Sons.

Zane, N. W. S., Sue, S., Hu, L., & Kwon, J. H. (1991). Asian-American assertion: A social learning anyalysis of cultural differences. *Journal of Counseling Psychology, 38,* 63–70.

Zatorre, R. J., & Halpern, A. R. (1993). Effect of unilateral temporal-lobe excision on perception and imagery of songs. *Neuropsychologia, 31,* 221–232.

Zawadzki, B., Strelau, J., Oniszcenko, W., Riemann, R., & Angleitner, A. (2001). Genetic and environmental influences on temperament. *European Psychologist, 6,* 272–286.

Zeki, S. (2002). Neural concept formation and art: Dante, Michelangelo, Wagner. *Journal of Consciousness Studies, 9,* 53–76.

Zeki, S. M. (1978). Functional specialisation in the visual cortex of the rhesus monkey. *Nature, 274,* 423–428.

Zeki, S. M. (1993). *Vision of the brain.* London: Blackwell.

Zenger, T. R., & Lawrence, B. S. (1989). Organizational demography: The differential effect of age and tenure distributions on technical communication. *Academy of Management Journal, 32,* 353–376.

Zentner, M. R., & Kagan, J. (1998). Infants' perception of consonance and dissonance in music. *Infant Behavior & Development, 21,* 483–492.

Zhang, L. I., Bao, S., & Merzenich, M. M. (2001). Persistent and specific influences of early acoustic environments on primary auditory cortex. *Nature Neuroscience, 4,* 1123–1130.

Zhang, Q., & Zhu, Y. (2001). The relationship between individual differences in working memory and linear reasoning. *Journal of Psychology in Chinese Societies, 2,* 261–282.

Zhdanova, I., & Wurtman, R. (1996, June). "How does melatonin affect sleep? *Harvard Mental Health Newsletter,* p. 8

Zhengyan, W., Huichang, C., & Xinyin, C. (2003). The stability of children's behavioral inhibition: A longitudinal study from two to four years of age. *Acta Psychologica Sinica, 35,* 93–100.

Zhu, H., Guo, Q., & Mattson, M. P. (1999). Dietary restriction protects hippocampal neurons against the death-promoting action of a presenilin-1 mutation. *Brain Research, 842,* 224–229.

Ziegler, D. J., & Leslie, Y. M. (2003). A test of the ABC model underlying rational emotive behavior therapy. *Psychological Reports, 92,* 235–240.

Zihl, J., von Cramon, D., & Mai, N. (1983). Selective disturbance of movement vision after bilateral brain damage. *Brain, 106,* 313–340.

Zimbardo, P. G., Maslach, C., & Haney, C. (2000). Reflections on the Stanford Prison Experiment: Genesis, transformations, consequences. In T. Blass (Ed.), *Obedience to authority: Current perspectives on the Milgram paradigm* (pp. 193–237). Mahwah, NJ: Erlbaum.

Zimmer, E. Z., Fifter, W. P., Young-Ihl, K., Rey, H. R., Chao, C. R., & Myers, M. M. (1993). Response of the premature fetus to stimulation by speech sounds. *Early Human Development, 33,* 207–215.

Zlotnick, C. (1999). Antisocial personality disorder, affect dysregulation and childhood abuse among incarcerated women. *Journal of Personality Disorders, 13,* 90–95.

Zoccolillo, M., Price, R., Ji, T., & Hwu, H. (1999). Antisocial personality disorder: Comparisons of prevalence, symptoms, and correlates in four countries. In P. Cohen, C. Slomkowski, et al. (Eds.), *Historical and geographical influences on psychopathology* (pp. 249–277). Mahwah, NJ: Erlbaum.

Zola, S. M., Squire, L. R., Teng, E., Stefanacci, L., Buffalo, E. A., & Clark, R. E. (2000). Impaired recognition memory in monkeys after damage limited to the hippocampal region. *Journal of Neuroscience, 20,* 451–463.

Zornberg, G. L., Buka, S. L., & Tsuang, M. T. (2000). Hypoxic-ischemia-related fetal/neonatal complications and risk of schizophrenia and other nonaffective psychoses: A 19-year longitudinal study. *American Journal of Psychiatry 157,* 196–202.

Zorzi, M., Priftis, K., & Umiltà, C. (2002). Neglect disrupts the mental number line. *Nature, 417,* 138–139.

Zuckerman, M. (1979). *Sensation seeking: Beyond the optimal level of arousal.* Hillsdale, NJ: Erlbaum.

Zuckerman, M. (1989). Personality as a third dimensions: A psychobiological approach. *Personality & Individual Differences, 10,* 391–418.

Zuckerman, M. (1991). *Psychobiology of personality.* Cambridge, England: Cambridge University Press.

Zuckerman, M. (1994). *Behavioral expressions and biosocial bases of sensation seeking.* New York: Cambridge University Press.

Zuckerman, M. (1995). Good and bad humors: Biochemical bases of personality and its disorders. *Psychological Science, 6,* 325–332.

Zuckerman, M. (2001). Optimism and pessimism: Biological foundations. In E. C. Chang (Ed.), *Optimism and pessimism: Implications for theory, research and practice* (pp. 169–188). Washington, DC: American Psychological Association.

Zuckerman, M. (2003). Biological bases of personality. In T. Millon & M. J. Lerner (Eds.), *Handbook of psychology: Personality and social psychology* (Vol. 5, pp. 85–116). New York: John Wiley.

Zuckerman, M., & Cloninger, C. R. (1996). Relationships between Cloninger's, Zuckerman's, and Eysenck's dimensions of personality. *Personality & Individual Differences, 21,* 283–285.

Zuckerman, M., DePaulo, B. M., & Rosenthal, R. (1981). Verbal and nonverbal communication of deception. In L. Berkowitz (Ed.), *Advances in experimental social psychology* (Vol. 14, pp. 1–59). New York: Academic Press.

Zuckerman, M., Joireman, J., Kraft, M., & Kuhlman, D. M. (1999). Where do motivational and emotional traits fit within three factor models of personality? *Personality & Individual Differences, 26,* 487–504.

Zuckerman, M., & Kuhlman, D. M. (2000). Personality and risk-taking: Common biosocial factors. *Journal of Personality, 68,* 999–1029.

Zuckerman, M., Kuhlman, D. M., & Camac, C. (1988). What lies beyond E and N? Factor analyses of scales believed to measure basic dimensions of personality. *Journal of Personality and Social Psychology, 54,* 96–107.

Zurek, P. M. (1981). Spontaneous narrowband acoustic signal emitted by human ears. *Journal of Acoustical Society of America, 69,* 514–523.

Zurek, P. M. (1985). Acoustic emissions from the ear: A summary of results from humans and animals. *Journal of the Acoustical Society of America, 78,* 340–344.

Zurif, E. B. (1995). Brain regions of relevance to syntactic processing. In L. Gleitman & M. Lieberman (Eds.), *An invitation to cognitive science* (2nd ed., Vol. 1). Cambridge, MA: MIT Press.

Zurif, E. B. (2000). Syntactic and semantic composition. *Brain and Language, 71,* 261–263.

Zurif, E. B., Caramazza, A., & Myerson, R. (1972). Grammatical judgments of agrammatic aphasics. *Neuropsychologia, 10,* 405–417.

Zweigenhaft, R. L. (2002). Birth order effects and rebelliousness: Political activism and involvement with marijuana. *Political Psychology, 23,* 219–233.

Zwicker, E., & Schloth, E. (1984). Interrelation of different oto-acoustic emissions. *Journal of Acoustical Society of America, 75,* 1148–1154.

# GLOSSARY

**Absolute pitch:** The ability to identify a particular note by itself, not simply in relation to other notes.

**Absolute threshold:** The smallest amount of a stimulus needed in order to detect that the stimulus is present.

**Absorption:** The capacity to concentrate totally on external material.

**Academic psychologist:** The type of psychologist who focuses on teaching and conducting research.

**Accommodation (in eye):** The phenomenon that occurs when muscles adjust the shape of the lens so that it focuses light on the retina from objects at different distances.

**Accommodation (in Piaget's theory):** The process that results in schemas' changing as necessary to cope with a broader range of situations.

**Acquisition:** In classical conditioning, the initial learning of the conditioned response (CR).

**Action potential:** The shifting change in charge that moves down the axon.

**Activation–synthesis hypothesis:** The theory that dreams arise from random bursts of nerve cell activity, which may affect brain cells involved in hearing and seeing; the brain attempts to make sense of this hodgepodge of stimuli, resulting in the experience of dreams.

**Active interaction:** Occurs when people choose, partly based on genetic tendencies, to put themselves in specific situations and to avoid others.

**Activity:** A temperament dimension characterized by the general expenditure of energy, which has two components: vigor (intensity of the activity) and tempo (speed of the activity).

**Acute stressor:** A stressor of short-term duration.

**Adaptation:** A characteristic that increases an organism's fitness for an environment.

**Adolescence:** The period between the onset of puberty and, roughly, the end of the teenage years.

**Adoption study:** A study in which characteristics of children adopted at birth are compared to those of their adoptive parents or siblings versus their biological parents or siblings (often twins). These studies often focus on comparisons of twins who were raised in the same versus different households.

**Affirming the consequent:** A reasoning error that occurs because of the assumption that if a result has occurred, a specific cause must also be present.

**Afterimage:** The image left behind by a previous perception.

**Aggression:** Behavior that is intended to harm another living being who does not wish to be harmed.

**Agonist:** A chemical that mimics the effects of a neurotransmitter by activating a type of receptor.

**Agoraphobia:** A condition in which people fear or avoid places that might be difficult to leave should panic symptoms occur.

**Alarm phase:** The first phase of the GAS, in which a stressor is perceived and the fight-or-flight response is activated.

**Alcohol myopia:** The disproportionate influence of immediate experience on behavior and emotion due to the effects of alcohol use.

**Algorithm:** A set of steps that, if followed methodically, will guarantee the solution to a problem.

**All-or-none law:** States that if the neuron is sufficiently stimulated, it fires, sending the action potential all the way down the axon and releasing chemicals from the terminal buttons; either the action potential occurs or it doesn't.

**Altered state of consciousness (ASC):** State of awareness that is other than the normal waking state.

**Altruism:** The motivation to increase another person's welfare.

**Amnesia:** A loss of memory over an entire time span, resulting from brain damage caused by accident, infection, or stroke.

**Amphetamines:** Synthetic stimulants.

**Amplitude:** The height of the peaks in a light wave.

**Amygdala:** A subcortical structure that plays a special role in fear and is involved in other sorts of emotions, such as anger.

**Androgens:** Sex hormones that cause many male characteristics such as beard growth and a low voice.

**Anorexia nervosa:** An eating disorder characterized by the refusal to maintain even a low normal weight, and an intense fear of gaining weight.

**Antagonist:** A chemical that interferes with the effect of a neurotransmitter (often by blocking a receptor).

**Anterograde amnesia:** Amnesia that leaves consolidated memories intact but prevents new learning.

**Antipsychotic medication:** Medication that reduces psychotic symptoms.

**Antisocial personality disorder (ASPD):** A personality disorder characterized by a long-standing pattern of disregard for other people to the point of violating their rights.

**Anxiety disorders:** A category of disorders whose hallmark is intense or pervasive anxiety or fear, or extreme attempts to avoid these feelings.

**Aphasia:** A disruption of language caused by brain damage.

**Applied psychologist:** The type of psychologist who studies how to improve products and procedures and conducts research to help solve specific practical problems.

**Approach–approach conflict:** The internal conflict that occurs when competing alternatives are equally positive.

**Approach–avoidance conflict:** The internal conflict that occurs when a course of action has both positive and negative aspects.

**Archetype:** A Jungian concept of a symbol that represents some basic aspect of the world and is stored in the collective unconscious.

**Artificial intelligence (AI):** The field devoted to building smart machines.

**Assimilation:** In Piaget's theory, the process that allows the use of existing schemas to take in new sets of stimuli and respond accordingly.

**Atherosclerosis:** A medical condition characterized by plaque buildup in the arteries.

**Attachment:** An emotional bond that leads a person to want to be with someone else and to miss him or her when separated.

**Attention:** The act of focusing on particular information, which allows it to be processed more fully than what is not attended to.

**Attentional blink:** A rebound period in which a person cannot pay attention to one thing after having just paid attention to another.

**Attitude:** An overall evaluation about some aspect of the world.

**Attribution:** An explanation for the cause of an event or behavior.

**Attributional bias:** A cognitive shortcut for determining attribution that generally occurs outside of conscious awareness.

**Attributional style:** A person's characteristic way of explaining life events.

**Autism:** A condition of intense self-involvement to the exclusion of external reality; about three quarters of autistic people are mentally retarded.

**Automatic processing:** Processing that allows you to carry out a sequence of steps without having to pay attention to each one or to the relations between the steps.

**Autonomic nervous system (ANS):** Controls the smooth muscles in the body, some glandular functions, and many of the body's self-regulating activities, such as digestion and circulation.

**Availability heuristic:** The tendency to judge objects or events as more likely, common, or frequent if they are easier to bring to mind.

**Avoidance–avoidance conflict:** The internal conflict that occurs when competing alternatives are equally unpleasant.

**Avoidance learning:** In classical conditioning, learning that occurs when a CS is paired with an unpleasant US that leads the organism to try to avoid the CS.

**Axon:** The sending end of the neuron; the long cablelike structure extending from the cell body.

**B cell:** A type of white blood cell that matures in the bone marrow.

**Basal ganglia:** Subcortical structures that play a role in planning and producing movement.

**Base-rate rule:** The rule stating that if something is chosen from a set at random, the chances that the thing will be of a particular type are directly proportional to the percentage of that type in the larger set.

**Basic emotion:** An innate emotion that is shared by all humans, such as surprise, happiness, anger, fear, disgust, or sadness.

**Basic level:** A level of specificity, which is usually the most likely to be applied to an object.

**Behavior:** The outwardly observable acts of an individual, alone or in a group.

**Behavior modification:** Any technique that brings about therapeutic change in behavior through the application of operant conditioning principles and the use of secondary reinforcers.

**Behavior therapy:** A type of therapy, based on well-researched learning principles, that focuses on changing observable, measurable behaviors.

**Behavioral genetics:** The field in which researchers attempt to determine the extent to which the differences among people are due to their genes or to the environment.

**Behaviorism:** The school of psychology that focuses on how a specific stimulus (object, person, or event) evokes a specific response (behavior in reaction to the stimulus).

**Belief in a just world:** An attributional bias that assumes that people get what they deserve.

**Benzodiazepine:** A type of antianxiety medication that affects the target symptoms within 36 hours and does not need to be taken for more than a week to be effective.

**Bereavement:** The experience of missing a loved one and longing for his or her company.

**Bias (in experimental research):** An effect that occurs when beliefs, expectations, or habits alter how participants in a study respond or affect how a researcher sets up or conducts a study, thereby influencing its outcome.

**Bias (in signal detection theory):** A person's willingness to report noticing a stimulus.

**Bibliotherapy:** The use of self-help books and tapes for therapeutic purposes.

**Big Five:** The five superfactors of personality—extraversion, neuroticism, agreeableness, conscientiousness, and openness—determined by factor analysis.

**Binocular cues:** Cues to the distance of an object that arise from both eyes working together.

**Biological preparedness:** A built-in readiness for certain conditioned stimuli to elicit particular conditioned responses, so less conditioning (training) is necessary to produce learning.

**Bipolar disorder:** A mood disorder marked by one or more episodes of either mania or hypomania, often alternating with periods of depression.

**Bisexual:** A person who is sexually attracted to members of both sexes.

**Blackout:** A period of time for which an alcoholic has no memory of events that transpired while he or she was intoxicated.

**Bottom-up processing:** Processing that is initiated by stimulus input.

**Brain circuit:** A set of neurons that affect one another.

**Brainstem:** The set of neural structures at the base of the brain, including the medulla and pons.

**Breadth of processing:** Processing that organizes and integrates information into previously stored information, often by making associations.

**Broca's aphasia:** Problems with producing language following brain damage (typically to the left frontal lobe).

**Bulimia nervosa:** An eating disorder characterized by recurrent episodes of binge eating, followed by some attempt to prevent weight gain.

**Burnout:** A work-related state characterized by chronic stress, accompanied by physical and mental exhaustion, a sense of little accomplishment, and cynicism about the job.

**Bystander effect:** The decrease in offers of assistance that occurs as the number of bystanders increases.

**Case study:** A scientific study that focuses on a single instance of a situation, examining it in detail.

**Castration anxiety:** A boy's anxiety-laden fear that, as punishment for loving mother and hating father, his father will cut off his penis (the primary zone of pleasure).

**Categorical perception:** Identifying sounds as belonging to distinct categories that correspond to the basic units of speech.

**Category:** A grouping in which the members are specific cases of a more general type.

**Cell body:** The central part of a neuron (or other cell), which contains the nucleus.

**Cell membrane:** The skin of a cell.

**Central executive:** The set of processes that operates on information in one or another of two specialized STMs; part of working memory.

**Central nervous system (CNS):** The spinal cord and the brain.

**Central tendency:** The clustering of the most characteristic values, or scores, for a particular group.

**Cerebellum:** A large structure at the base of the brain that is concerned in part with physical coordination, estimating time, and paying attention.

**Cerebral cortex:** The convoluted pinkish-gray outer layer of the brain, where most mental processes take place.

**Cerebral hemisphere:** A left or right half-brain, shaped roughly like half a sphere.

**Chemical senses:** Taste and smell, which rely on sensing the presence of specific chemicals.

**Child-directed speech (CDS):** Speech by caregivers to babies that relies on short sentences with clear pauses, careful enunciation, exaggerated intonation, and a high-pitched voice.

**Chronic stressor:** A stressor of long-term duration.

**Chunk:** A unit of information, such as a digit, letter, or word.

**Circadian rhythms:** The body's daily fluctuations in response to the cycle of dark and light, which occur with blood pressure, pulse rate, body temperature, blood sugar level, hormone levels, and metabolism.

**Classical conditioning:** A type of learning that occurs when a neutral stimulus becomes paired (associated) with a stimulus that causes a reflexive behavior and, in time, is sufficient to produce that behavior.

**Client-centered therapy:** A type of insight-oriented therapy that focuses on people's potential for growth and the importance of an empathic therapist.

**Clinical psychologist:** The type of psychologist who provides psychotherapy and is trained to administer and interpret psychological tests.

**Cocktail party phenomenon:** The effect of not being aware of other people's conversations until your name is mentioned, and then suddenly hearing it.

**Code:** A type of mental representation, an internal "re-presentation" (such as in words or images) of a stimulus or event.

**Cognitive–behavior therapy (CBT):** A type of therapy that aims to change problematic behaviors and irrational thoughts and provide new, more adaptive behaviors and beliefs to replace old, maladaptive ones.

**Cognitive control:** The processes that guide attention, thought, and action in the service of accomplishing a specific task.

**Cognitive dissonance:** The uncomfortable state that arises because of a discrepancy between an attitude and behavior or between two attitudes.

**Cognitive distortions:** Irrational thoughts that arise from a systematic bias in the way a person thinks about reality.

**Cognitive learning:** The acquisition of information that often is not immediately acted on but is stored for later use.

**Cognitive neuroscience:** A blending of cognitive psychology and neuroscience (the study of the brain) that aims to specify how the brain stores and processes information.

**Cognitive psychology:** The approach in psychology that attempts to characterize how information is stored and operated on internally.

**Cognitive restructuring:** The process of helping clients shift their thinking away from the focus on automatic, dysfunctional thoughts to more realistic ones.

**Cognitive therapy:** A type of therapy that focuses on the client's thoughts rather than his or her feelings or behaviors.

**Collectivist culture:** A culture that emphasizes the rights and responsibilities of the group over those of the individual.

**Color blindness:** An inability, either acquired (by brain damage) or inherited, to perceive certain hues.

**Color constancy:** Seeing objects as having the same color in different viewing situations.

**Common factor:** In psychotherapy, a curative aspect that is common to all types of treatment.

**Companionate love:** A type of love marked by very close friendship, mutual caring, liking, respect, and attraction.

**Complex inheritance:** The joint action of combinations of genes working together.

**Compliance:** A change in behavior prompted by a direct request rather than by social norms.

**Compulsion:** A repetitive behavior or mental act that an individual feels compelled to perform in response to an obsession.

**Computer-assisted tomography (CT,** formerly **CAT):** A neuroimaging technique that produces a three-dimensional image of brain structures using X rays.

**Concentrative meditation:** A form of meditation in which the meditator restricts attention and concentrates on one stimulus while disregarding everything else.

**Concept:** An unambiguous, sometimes abstract, internal representation that defines a grouping of a set of objects (including living things) or events (including relationships).

**Concrete operation:** In Piaget's theory, a (reversible) manipulation of the mental representation of an object that corresponds to an actual physical manipulation.

**Conditioned emotional response (CER):** An emotional response elicited by a previously neutral stimulus.

**Conditioned response (CR):** A response that depends, or is conditional, on pairings of the conditioned stimulus with an unconditioned stimulus; once learned, the conditioned response occurs when the conditioned stimulus is presented alone.

**Conditioned stimulus (CS):** An originally neutral stimulus that acquires significance through pairings with an unconditioned stimulus (US).

**Conduction deafness:** A type of deafness caused by a physical impairment of the external or middle ear.

**Cones:** Cone-shaped retinal cells that respond most strongly to one of three wavelengths of light; the combined outputs from cones that are most sensitive to different wavelengths play a key role in producing color vision.

**Confirmation bias:** A tendency to seek information that will confirm a rule, and not to seek information that is inconsistent with the rule.

**Conformity:** A change in beliefs or behavior in order to follow a group's norms.

**Confound (or confounding variable):** An independent variable that varies along with the ones of interest, and could be the actual basis for what you are measuring.

**Consciousness:** A person's awareness of his or her own existence, sensations, and cognitions.

**Conservation:** The Piagetian principle that certain properties, such as amount or mass, remain the same even when the appearance of the material or object changes, provided that nothing is added or removed.

**Consolidation:** The process of converting information stored dynamically in LTM into a structural change in the brain.

**Continuous reinforcement:** Reinforcement given for each desired response.

**Contrapreparedness:** A built-in disinclination (or even an inability) for certain conditioned stimuli to elicit particular conditioned responses.

**Control condition:** A condition administered to the same participants who receive the experimental condition; this effectively makes the participants both the experimental and the control group.

**Control group:** A group that is treated exactly the same way as the experimental group, except that the one aspect of the situation being studied is not manipulated for this group. The control group holds constant— "controls"—all of the variables in the experimental group except the one of interest.

**Controlled processing:** Processing that requires paying attention to each step of an action and using working memory (WM) to coordinate the steps.

**Convergence:** The degree to which the eyes are crossed when a person fixates on an object.

**Coping:** Taking some course of action regarding the stressor, its effects, or the person's reaction to it.

**Cornea:** The transparent covering over the eye, which serves partly to focus the light onto the back of the eye.

**Corpus callosum:** The large band of nerve fibers that connects the two halves of the brain.

**Correlation coefficient** (or *correlation*): An index of how closely interrelated two sets of measured variables are, which ranges from −1.0 to +1.0. The higher the correlation (in either direction), the better we can predict the value of one type of measurement when given the value of the other.

**Correspondence bias:** The strong tendency to interpret other people's behavior as due to internal (dispositional) causes rather than external (situational) ones.

**Cortisol:** A hormone produced by the outer layer of the adrenal glands that helps the body cope with the extra energy demands of stress by breaking down and converting protein and fat to sugar.

**Counseling psychologist:** The type of psychologist who is trained to help people with issues that naturally arise during the course of life.

**Crack:** Cocaine in crystalline form, usually smoked in a pipe (free-basing) or rolled into a cigarette.

**Creativity:** The ability to produce something original of high quality or to devise an effective new way of solving a problem.

**Critical period:** A narrow window of time when a certain type of learning is possible.

**Cross-sectional study:** A study in which different groups of people are tested, with each group composed of individuals of a particular age.

**Crystallized intelligence:** According to Cattell and Horn, the kind of intelligence that relies on knowing facts and having the ability to use and combine them.

**Cues:** Stimuli that trigger or enhance remembering; reminders.

**Cybertherapy:** Therapy over the Internet.

**Dark adaptation:** The process whereby exposure to darkness causes the eyes to become more sensitive, allowing for better vision in the dark.

**Data:** Objective observations.

**Debriefing:** An interview after a study to ensure that the participant has no negative reactions as a result of participation and understands why the study was conducted.

**Decay:** The fading away of memories with time because the relevant connections between neurons are lost.

**Decibel (dB):** A measure of loudness on a base-10 logarithmic scale; the threshold for hearing is set at 0 dB.

**Deductive reasoning:** Reasoning that applies the rules of logic to a set of assumptions (stated as premises) to discover whether certain conclusions follow from those assumptions; deduction goes from the general to the particular.

**Defense mechanism:** An unconscious psychological means by which a person tries to prevent unacceptable thoughts or urges from reaching conscious awareness.

**Deindividuation:** The loss of sense of self that occurs when people in a group are anonymous.

**Delayed reinforcement:** Reinforcement given some period of time after the desired behavior is exhibited.

**Deliberate practice:** Practice that is motivated by the goal of improving performance, usually by targeting specific areas of weakness and working to improve them.

**Delusions:** Entrenched false beliefs that are often bizarre.

**Dendrite:** The treelike part of a neuron that receives messages from the axons of other neurons.

**Deoxyribonucleic acid, or DNA:** The molecule that contains genes.

**Dependent variable:** The aspect of the situation that is measured as an independent variable is changed; the value of the dependent variable depends on the independent variable.

**Depressants:** A class of substances, including barbiturates, alcohol, and antianxiety drugs, that depress the central nervous system, decreasing the user's behavioral activity and level of awareness; also called *sedative-hypnotic drugs.*

**Deprived reward:** Reward that occurs when a biological need is met.

**Depth of processing:** The number and complexity of the operations involved in processing information, expressed in a continuum from shallow to deep.

**Descriptive statistics:** Concise ways of summarizing properties of sets of numbers.

**Diathesis–stress model:** A way of understanding the development of a psychological disorder, in which a predisposition to a given disorder (diathesis) and specific factors (stress) combine to trigger the onset of the disorder.

**Dichotic listening:** A procedure in which participants hear stimuli presented separately to the two ears (through headphones) and are instructed to listen only to sounds presented to one ear.

**Diffusion of responsibility:** The diminished sense of responsibility to help that each person feels as the number of bystanders grows.

**Discrimination:** The ability to engage in a learned behavior in response to a particular stimulus but not in response to a similar one.

**Discriminative stimulus:** The cue that tells the organism whether a specific response will lead to the expected reinforcement.

**Disinhibition:** The inhibition of inhibitory neurons, which makes other neurons (the ones that are usually inhibited) more likely to fire and which usually occurs as a result of depressant use.

**Display rule:** A culture-specific rule that indicates when, to whom, and how strongly certain emotions can be shown.

**Dissociative amnesia:** An inability to remember important personal information, often experienced as memory "gaps."

**Dissociative disorders:** A category of disorders involving a disruption in the usually integrated functions of consciousness, memory, and/or identity.

**Dissociative fugue:** An inability to remember some or all of the past, combined with abrupt, unexpected departures from home or work.

**Dissociative identity disorder (DID):** A disorder in which a person has two or more distinct personalities that take control of the individual's behavior.

**Divided attention:** The process of shifting focus back and forth between different stimuli or tasks.

**Dizygotic:** From different eggs and sharing only as many genes as any pair of brothers or sisters—on average, half.

**Door-in-the-face technique:** A compliance technique in which someone makes a very large request and then, when it is denied, as expected, makes a smaller request (for what is actually desired).

**Double-blind design:** The participant is "blind" to (unaware of) the predictions of the study (and so cannot consciously or unconsciously produce the predicted results), and the experimenter is "blind" to the condition assigned to the participant (and so experimenter expectancy effects cannot produce the predicted results).

**Double pain:** The sensation that occurs when an injury first causes a sharp pain, and later a dull pain; the two kinds of pain arise from different fibers sending their messages at different speeds.

**Down syndrome:** A type of mental retardation that results from the creation of an extra chromosome during conception; it is a genetic problem but not inherited.

**Dream analysis:** A technique used in psychoanalysis and psychodynamic therapy in which the therapist examines the content of dreams to gain access to the unconscious.

**Drive:** An internal imbalance that motivates animals (including humans) to reach a particular goal that will reduce the imbalance.

**Dysthymia:** A mood disorder similar to major depressive disorder, but less intense and longer lasting.

**Eating disorders:** A category of disorders involving a severe disturbance in eating behavior.

**Effect:** The difference in the dependent variable that is due to the changes in the independent variable.

**Ego:** A personality structure, proposed by Freud, that develops in childhood and tries to balance the competing demands of the id, superego, and reality.

**Egocentrism:** In Piaget's theory, the inability to take another person's point of view.

**Elaborative encoding:** Encoding that involves great breadth of processing.

**Electroconvulsive therapy (ECT):** Use of an electric current to induce a controlled brain seizure in people with certain psychological disorders such as psychotic depression or those for whom medication has not been effective or recommended.

**Electroencephalogram:** A recording from the scalp of electrical activity in the brain over time, which produces a tracing of pulses at different frequencies.

**Electroencephalograph (EEG):** A machine that records electrical current produced by the brain.

**Embryo:** A developing baby from the point where the major axis of the body is present until all major structures are present, spanning from about 2 weeks to 8 weeks after conception.

**Emotion:** A psychological state with four components: (1) a positive or negative subjective experience, (2) the activation of specific mental processes and stored information, (3) bodily arousal, and (4) characteristic overt behavior.

**Emotion-focused coping:** Coping focused on changing the person's emotional response to the stressor.

**Emotional intelligence (EI):** The ability to understand and regulate emotions effectively.

**Emotionality:** A temperament dimension characterized by an inclination to become aroused in situations in which the predominant emotion is distress, fear, or anger.

**Empiricism (approach to language):** The approach that views language as entirely the result of learning.

**Enacted social support:** The specific supportive behaviors provided by others.

**Encoding:** The process of organizing and transforming incoming information so that it can be entered into memory, either to be stored or to be compared with previously stored information.

**Encoding failure:** A failure to process to-be-remembered information well enough to begin consolidation.

**Endogenous cannabinoids:** Neuromodulators released by the receiving neuron that then influence the activity of the sending neuron.

**Endorphins:** Painkilling chemicals produced naturally in the brain.

**Episodic memories:** Memories of events that are associated with a particular context—a time, place, and circumstance.

**Estrogen:** The hormone that causes breasts to develop and is involved in the menstrual cycle.

**Estrogens:** Sex hormones that cause many female characteristics such as breast development and the bone structure of the female pelvis.

**Evocative (or reactive) interaction:** Occurs when genetically influenced characteristics draw out behaviors from other people.

**Evolution:** Gene-based changes in the characteristics of members of a species over successive generations.

**Evolutionary psychology:** The approach in psychology that assumes that certain cognitive strategies and goals are so important that natural selection has built them into our brains.

**Exhaustion phase:** The final stage of the GAS, in which the continued stress response itself becomes damaging to the body.

**Expectancies:** Expectations that have a powerful influence on thoughts, feelings, and behaviors and, in turn, on personality.

**Experimental condition:** A part of a study in which the participant receives the complete procedure that defines the experiment. Usually this is accompanied by a control condition, with the same participants receiving both experimental and control conditions.

**Experimental group:** A group that receives the complete procedure that defines the experiment.

**Experimenter expectancy effects:** Effects that occur when an investigator's expectations lead him or her (consciously or unconsciously) to treat participants in a way that encourages them to produce the expected results.

**Explicit (or declarative) memories:** Memories that can be retrieved at will and represented in STM; verbal and visual memories are explicit if they can be called to mind as words or images.

**Exposure:** A therapeutic technique based on classical conditioning that rests on the principle of habituation.

**External attribution:** An explanation of someone's behavior that focuses on the situation; also called *situational attribution*.

**Extinction (in classical conditioning):** The process by which a CR comes to be eliminated through repeated presentations of the CS without the presence of the US.

**Extinction (in operant conditioning):** The fading out of a response following an initial burst of that behavior after the withdrawal of reinforcement.

**Extrasensory perception (ESP):** The ability to perceive and know things without using the ordinary senses.

**Facial feedback hypothesis:** The idea that emotions arise partly as a result of the positioning of facial muscles.

**Factor analysis:** A statistical method that uncovers the particular attributes (factors) that make scores more or less similar; the more similar the scores, the more strongly implicated are shared underlying factors.

**False memories:** Memories of events or situations that did not, in fact, occur.

**Family therapy:** A therapy modality in which a family (or certain members of a family) is treated.

**Fetal alcohol syndrome:** A condition that includes mental retardation and is caused by excessive drinking of alcohol by the mother during pregnancy.

**Fetus:** A developing baby during the final phase of development in the womb, from about 8 weeks after conception until birth.

**Figure:** In perception, a set of characteristics (such as shape, color, texture) that corresponds to an object.

**Fixed interval schedule:** Reinforcement schedule in which reinforcement is given for a response emitted after a fixed interval of time.

**Fixed ratio schedule:** Reinforcement schedule in which reinforcement is given after a fixed number of responses.

**Flashback:** A hallucination that recurs without the use of a drug.

**Flashbulb memory:** An unusually vivid and accurate memory of a dramatic event.

**Flow:** The experience of being completely absorbed with and merging smoothly into an activity and losing track of time.

**Fluid intelligence:** According to Cattell and Horn, the kind of intelligence that underlies the creation of novel solutions to problems.

**Flynn effect:** Increases in IQ in the overall population with the passage of time.

**Food aversion (taste aversion):** A classically conditioned avoidance of a certain food or taste.

**Foot-in-the-door technique:** A technique that achieves compliance by beginning with an insignificant request, which is then followed by a larger request.

**Forebrain:** The cortex, thalamus, limbic system, and basal ganglia.

**Forgetting curve:** A graphic representation of the rate at which information is forgotten over time: Recent events are recalled better than more distant ones, but most forgetting occurs soon after learning.

**Formal operation:** In Piaget's theory, a mental act that can be performed (and reversed) even with an abstract concept.

**Fovea:** The small, central region of the retina with the highest density of cones and the highest resolution.

**Fragile X syndrome:** A type of mental retardation that affects the X chromosome; it is both genetic and inherited.

**Free association:** A technique used in psychoanalysis and psychodynamic therapies in which the patient says whatever comes to mind and the train of thought reveals the patient's issues and ways of dealing with them.

**Frequency:** The number of waves per second that move past a given point.

**Frequency theory:** The theory that higher frequencies produce higher rates of neural firing.

**Frontal lobe:** The brain lobe located behind the forehead; the seat of planning, memory search, motor control, and reasoning, as well as numerous other functions.

**Functional fixedness:** When solving a problem, getting stuck on one interpretation of an object or one part of the situation.

**Functional magnetic resonance imaging (fMRI):** A type of MRI that usually detects the amount of oxygen being brought to a particular place in the brain while a task is performed.

**Functionalism:** The school of psychology that sought to understand how the mind helps individuals *function*, or adapt to the world.

**g:** "General factor," a single intellectual capacity that underlies the positive correlations among different tests of intelligence.

**Gate control (of pain):** The top-down inhibition of interneurons that regulate the input of pain signals to the brain.

**Gender identity:** A person's belief that he or she is male or is female.

**Gender roles:** The culturally determined appropriate behaviors of males versus females.

**Gene:** A stretch of DNA that produces a specific protein.

**General adaptation syndrome (GAS):** The overall stress response that has three phases: alarm, resistance, and exhaustion.

**Generalization:** The ability to emit a learned behavior in response to a similar stimulus.

**Generalized anxiety disorder:** An anxiety disorder whose hallmark is excessive anxiety and worry that is not consistently related to a specific object or situation.

**Generalized reality orientation fading:** A tuning out of external reality during hypnosis.

**Genotype:** The genetic code within an organism.

**Gestalt laws of organization:** A set of rules describing the circumstances—such as proximity, good continuation, similarity, closure, and good form—under which marks will be grouped into perceptual units.

**Gestalt psychology:** An approach to understanding mental processes that focuses on the idea that the whole is more than the sum of its parts.

**Gifted:** People who have IQs between 150 and 180.

**Glial cell:** A type of cell that surrounds neurons, influences the communication among neurons, and generally helps in the "care and feeding" of neurons.

**Glove anesthesia:** Hypnotically induced lack of feeling in the hand.

**Glucocorticoids:** A group of hormones that are released when the stress response is triggered.

**Grammar:** The set of rules that determines how words can be organized into an infinite number of acceptable sentences in a language.

**Grief:** The emotion of distress that follows the loss of a loved one.

**Ground:** In perception, the background, which must be distinguished in order to pick out figures.

**Group:** A social entity characterized by regular interaction among members, some emotional connection, a common frame of reference, and a degree of interdependence.

**Group polarization:** The tendency of group members' opinions to become more extreme (in the same direction as their initial opinions) after group discussion.

**Group therapy:** A therapy modality in which a number of clients with compatible needs meet together with one or two therapists.

**Groupthink:** The tendency of people who try to solve problems together to accept one another's information and ideas without subjecting them to critical analysis.

**Gyrus:** A bulge between sulci in the cerebral cortex.

**Habit:** A well-learned response that is carried out automatically (without conscious thought) when the appropriate stimulus is present.

**Habituation:** The learning that occurs when repeated exposure to a stimulus decreases an organism's responsiveness to the stimulus.

**Hair cells:** The cells with stiff hairs along the basilar membrane of the inner ear that, when moved, produce nerve impulses that are sent to the brain; these cells are the auditory equivalent of rods and cones.

**Hallucinations:** Sensory images so vivid that they seem real.

**Hallucinogen:** A substance that induces hallucinations.

**Hardy personality:** The combination of personality traits associated with health: commitment to self and work, a sense of control over what happens, and a view of stressors as challenges.

**Health psychology:** The field concerned with the promotion of health and the prevention and treatment of illness as it relates to psychological factors.

**Heritability:** The degree to which variability in a characteristic is due to genetics.

**Heterosexual:** A person who is sexually attracted to members of the opposite sex.

**Heuristic:** A strategy that does not guarantee the correct answer to a problem but offers a likely shortcut to it.

**Hidden observer:** A part of the self that experiences (and can record) what the part of the self involved in a hypnotic trance does not consciously experience.

**High expressed emotion:** An emotional style in families that are critical, hostile, and overinvolved.

**Hindbrain:** The medulla, pons, cerebellum, and parts of the reticular formation.

**Hippocampus:** A subcortical structure that plays a key role in allowing new information to be stored in the brain's memory banks.

**Homeostasis:** The process of maintaining a steady state, in which bodily characteristics and substances are within a certain range.

**Homosexual:** A person who is sexually attracted to members of the same sex.

**Hormone:** A chemical that is produced by a gland and can act as a neuromodulator.

**Hostile attribution bias:** The propensity to misread the intentions of others as negative.

**Hostility:** The personality trait associated with heart disease and characterized by mistrust, an expectation of harm and provocation by others, and a cynical attitude.

**Humanistic psychology:** The school of psychology that assumes people have positive values, free will, and deep inner creativity, the combination of which leads them to choose life-fulfilling paths to personal growth.

**Hypermnesia:** Memory that improves over time without feedback, particularly with repeated attempts to recall.

**Hypnogogic sleep:** The initial stage of sleep, which lasts about 5 minutes and can include the sensation of gentle falling or floating or a sudden jerking of the body.

**Hypnosis:** A state of mind characterized by a focused awareness on vivid, imagined experiences and decreased awareness of the external environment.

**Hypnotic induction:** The procedure used to attain a hypnotic trance state.

**Hypomania:** A mood state similar to mania, but less severe, with fewer and less intrusive symptoms.

**Hypothalamic-pituitary-adrenal (HPA) axis:** The hypothalamus, pituitary gland, and adrenal glands, which work together to fight off infection.

**Hypothalamus:** A brain structure that sits under the thalamus and plays a central role in controlling eating and drinking and in regulating the body's temperature, blood pressure, and heart rate.

**Hypothesis:** A tentative idea that might explain a set of observations.

**Id:** A personality structure, proposed by Freud, that exists at birth and houses sexual and aggressive drives, physical needs, and simple psychological needs.

**Immediate reinforcement:** Reinforcement given immediately after the desired behavior is exhibited.

**Implicit (or nondeclarative) memories:** Memories that cannot be voluntarily called to mind, but nevertheless influence behavior or thinking.

**Implicit motive:** A need or want that unconsciously directs behavior.

**Impression formation:** The process of developing initial views of others.

**Impression management:** A person's efforts to control how others will view him or her.

**Impulsivity:** A temperament dimension characterized by the propensity to respond to stimuli immediately, without reflection or concern for consequences.

**Incentive:** A stimulus or event that draws animals (including humans) toward a particular goal in anticipation of a reward.

**Incidental learning:** Learning that occurs without intention.

**Incongruence:** According to client-centered therapy, a mismatch between a person's real self and his or her ideal self.

**Incubation:** Processing that occurs when a person is not consciously working on solving a problem and that can lead to improved thinking about the solution.

**Independent variable:** The aspect of the situation that is intentionally varied while another aspect is measured.

**Individual therapy:** A therapy modality in which an individual client is treated by a single therapist.

**Individualist culture:** A culture that emphasizes the rights and responsibilities of the individual over those of the group.

**Inductive reasoning:** Reasoning that uses examples to figure out a rule that governs them; induction goes from the particular (examples) to the general (a rule).

**Inferential statistics:** The results of tests that reveal whether differences or patterns in measurements reflect true differences or patterns versus just chance variations.

**Inferiority complex:** The experience that occurs when inferiority feelings are so strong that they hamper striving for superiority.

**Informed consent:** The requirement that a potential participant in a study be told what he or she will be asked to do and be advised of possible risks and benefits of the study before agreeing to take part.

**Ingroup:** An individual's own group.

**Inhibitory conflict:** An internal response when a behavior is both strongly instigated and inhibited.

**Insight:** A new way to look at a problem that implies the solution.

**Insight learning:** Learning that occurs when a person or animal suddenly grasps what something means and incorporates that new knowledge into old knowledge.

**Insight-oriented therapy:** A type of therapy that aims to remove distressing symptoms by leading people to understand their causes through deeply felt personal insights.

**Insomnia:** Repeated difficulty falling asleep, difficulty staying asleep, or waking up too early.

**Instinct:** An inherited tendency to produce organized and unalterable responses to particular stimuli.

**Insulin:** A hormone that stimulates the storage of food molecules in the form of fat.

**Intelligence:** The ability to solve problems well and to understand and learn complex material.

**Intelligence quotient (IQ):** A score on an intelligence test, originally based on comparing mental age to chronological age, but later based on norms and used as a measure of general intelligence.

**Intentional learning:** Learning that occurs as a result of trying to learn.

**Interference:** The disruption of the ability to remember one piece of information by the presence of other information.

**Internal attribution:** An explanation of someone's behavior that focuses on the person's preferences, beliefs, goals, or other characteristics; also called *dispositional attribution.*

**Internal conflict:** The emotional predicament people experience when making difficult choices.

**Interneuron:** A neuron that is connected to other neurons, not to sense organs or muscles.

**Interpersonal therapy (IPT):** A type of researched, manual-based treatment that focuses on how issues that arise in the client's current relationships can affect mood.

**Interpretation:** A technique used in psychodynamic therapies in which the therapist deciphers the patient's words and behaviors, assigning unconscious motivations to them.

**Interval schedule:** Partial reinforcement schedule based on time.

**Introspection:** The process of "looking within."

**Ion:** An atom that has a positive or negative charge.

**Iris:** The circular muscle that adjusts the size of the pupil.

**Islands of excellence:** Areas in which retarded people perform remarkably well.

**Just-noticeable difference (JND):** The size of the difference in a stimulus property needed for the observer to notice that a change has occurred.

**Kinesthetic sense:** The sense that registers the movement and position of the limbs.

**Knockin mice:** Mice in which a new gene has been added or substituted for one already there.

**Knockout mice:** Mice in which part of the genetic code has been snipped away, deleting all (or crucial parts) of a gene so that it is disabled.

**Language acquisition device (LAD):** An innate mechanism, hypothesized by Chomsky, that contains the grammatical rules common to all languages and allows language acquisition.

**Language comprehension:** The ability to understand the message conveyed by words, phrases, and sentences.

**Language production:** The ability to speak or otherwise use words, phrases, and sentences to convey information.

**Latent content:** The symbolic content and meaning of a dream.

**Latent learning:** Learning that occurs without behavioral signs.

**Law of Effect:** Actions that subsequently lead to a "satisfying state of affairs" are more likely to be repeated.

**Learned helplessness:** The condition that occurs after an animal has an aversive experience in which nothing it does can affect what happens to it, and so it simply gives up and stops trying to change the situation or to escape.

**Learning:** A relatively permanent change in behavior that results from experience.

**Lesion:** A region of impaired tissue.

**Level of the brain:** Events that involve the structure and properties of the organ itself—brain cells and their connections, the chemical soup in which they exist, and the genes.

**Level of the group:** Events that involve relationships between people (such as love, competition, and cooperation), relationships among groups, and culture. Events at the level of the group are one aspect of the environment; the other aspect is the physical environment itself (the time, temperature, and other physical stimuli).

**Level of the person:** Events that involve the nature of beliefs, desires, and feelings—the *content* of the mind, not just its internal mechanics.

**Limbic system:** A set of brain areas, including the hippocampus, amygdala, and other areas, that have long been thought of as being involved in fighting, fleeing, feeding, and sex.

**Linguistic relativity hypothesis:** The idea that perceptions and thoughts are shaped by language, and thus people who speak different languages think differently.

**Lobes:** The four major parts of each cerebral hemisphere—occipital, temporal, parietal, and frontal.

**Locus of control:** The source a person perceives to be exerting control over life's events.

**Logic:** The process of applying the principles of correct reasoning to reach a decision or evaluate the truth of a claim.

**Longitudinal study:** A study in which the same group of people is tested repeatedly, at different ages.

**Long-term memory (LTM):** A memory store that holds a huge amount of information for a long time (from hours to years).

**Long-term potentiation (LTP):** A receiving neuron's increased sensitivity to input from a sending neuron, resulting from previous activation.

**Loudness:** The strength of a sound; pressure waves with greater amplitude produce the experience of louder sound.

**Lowball technique:** A compliance technique that consists of getting someone to make an agreement and then increasing the cost of that agreement.

**Magnetic resonance imaging (MRI):** A technique that uses magnetic properties of atoms to take sharp pictures of the structures of the brain.

**Magnetoencephalography (MEG):** A technique for assessing brain activity that relies on recording magnetic waves from the outside of the head.

**Major depressive disorder (MDD):** A mood disorder characterized by at least 2 weeks of depressed mood or loss of interest in nearly all activities, along with sleep or eating disturbances, loss of energy, and feelings of hopelessness.

**Manic episode:** A period of at least 1 week during which an abnormally elevated, expansive, or irritable mood persists.

**Manifest content:** The obvious, memorable content of a dream.

**Maturation:** The developmental process that produces genetically programmed changes with increasing age.

**Mean:** The arithmetic average.

**Median:** The score that is the midpoint of the set of values; half the values fall above the median, and half fall below the median.

**Meditation:** An altered state of consciousness characterized by a sense of deep relaxation and loss of self-awareness.

**Medulla:** The lowest part of the lower brainstem, which plays a central role in automatic control of breathing, swallowing, and blood circulation.

**Memory store:** A set of neurons that serves to retain information over time.

**Mendelian inheritance:** The transmission of characteristics by individual elements of inheritance (genes), each acting separately.

**Meninges:** Membranes that cover the brain.

**Mental images:** Representations like those that arise during perception, but based on stored information rather than on immediate sensory input.

**Mental model:** An image or description of a specific situation used to reason about an abstract entity.

**Mental processes:** What the brain does when a person stores, recalls, or uses information or has specific feelings.

**Mental set:** A fixed way of viewing the kind of solution being sought.

**Mentally retarded:** People who have an IQ of 70 or less and significant limitations in at least two aspects of everyday life since childhood.

**Mere exposure effect:** The change—generally favorable—in attitude that can result from simply becoming familiar with something.

**Meta-analysis:** A statistical technique that allows researchers to combine results from different studies, which can determine whether there is a relationship among variables that transcends any one study.

**Metabolism:** The sum of the chemical events in each of the body's cells, events that convert food molecules to the energy needed for the cells to function.

**Microelectrode:** A tiny probe inserted into the brain to record the electrical activity of individual neurons.

**Microenvironment:** The environment created by a person's own presence, which depends partly on appearance and behavior.

**Midbrain:** Brainstem structures that lie between forebrain and hindbrain, including parts of the reticular formation.

**Mindfulness meditation:** A combination of concentrative and opening-up meditation in which the meditator focuses on whatever is most prominent at the moment; also known as *awareness meditation.*

**Minnesota Multiphasic Personality Inventory-2 (MMPI-2):** A personality inventory primarily used to assess psychopathology.

**Misattribution of arousal:** The failure to interpret signs of bodily arousal correctly, which leads to the experience of emotions that ordinarily would not arise in the particular situation.

**Mnemonic devices:** Strategies that improve memory, typically by using effective organization and integration.

**Modality:** A form of therapy.

**Modality-specific memory stores:** Memory stores that retain input from a single sense, such as vision or audition, or from a specific processing system, such as language.

**Mode:** The value that appears most frequently in the set of data.

**Monoamine oxidase inhibitor (MAOI):** A type of antidepressant medication that requires strict adherence to a diet free of tyramine.

**Monocular static cues:** Information that specifies the distance of an object that can be picked up with one eye without movement of the object or eye.

**Monozygotic:** From the same egg and having identical genes.

**Mood disorders:** A category of disorders marked by persistent or episodic disturbances in emotion that interfere with normal functioning in at least one realm of life.

**Moral dilemma:** A situation in which there are moral pros and cons for each of a set of possible actions.

**Morpheme:** The smallest unit of meaning in a language.

**Motion cues:** Information that specifies the distance of an object on the basis of its movement.

**Motivation:** The set of requirements and desires that lead an animal (including a human) to behave in a particular way at a particular time and place.

**Motor neuron:** A neuron that sends signals to muscles to control movement.

**Motor strip:** The brain area, located immediately in front of the central sulcus, that controls fine movements and is organized by body part; also called *primary motor cortex.*

**Mutation:** A physical change in a gene.

**Myelin:** A fatty substance that helps impulses travel down the axon more efficiently.

**Narcolepsy:** Sudden attacks of extreme drowsiness.

**Narcotic analgesics:** A class of strongly addictive drugs, such as heroin, that relieve pain.

**Nativism (approach to language):** The view that people are born with some knowledge.

**Natural killer (NK) cell:** A type of T cell that detects and destroys damaged or altered cells, such as precancerous cells.

**Natural selection:** Changes in the frequency of genes in a population that arise because genes allow an organism to have more offspring that survive.

**Need:** A condition that arises from the lack of a requirement; needs give rise to drives.

**Need for achievement (nAch):** The need to reach goals that require skilled performance or competence to be accomplished.

**Negative punishment:** Occurs when a behavior leads to the removal of a pleasant event or circumstance, thereby decreasing the likelihood of a recurrence of the behavior.

**Negative reinforcement:** Occurs when an unpleasant event or circumstance that follows a behavior is removed, thereby increasing the likelihood of a recurrence of the behavior.

**Negative symptom:** A diminution or loss of normal functions, such as a restriction in speech.

**Nerve deafness:** A type of deafness that typically occurs when the hair cells are destroyed by loud sounds.

**Neural network:** A computer program whose units interact via connections that imitate (roughly) the way the brain works.

**Neuroendocrine system:** The system, regulated by the CNS, that makes hormones that affect many bodily functions and that also provides the CNS with information.

**Neuroimaging:** Brain-scanning techniques that produce a picture of the structure or functioning of neurons.

**Neuromodulator:** A chemical that alters the effect of a neurotransmitter.

**Neuron:** A cell that receives signals from other neurons or sense organs, processes these signals, and sends the signals to other neurons, muscles, or organs; the basic unit of the nervous system.

**Neurosis:** An abnormal behavior pattern relating to a conflict between the ego and either the id or the superego.

**Neurotransmitter:** A chemical that carries a signal from the terminal button on one neuron to the dendrite or cell body of another.

**Night terrors:** Vivid and frightening experiences while sleeping; the sleeper may appear to be awake during the experience but has no memory of it the following day.

**Nightmare:** A dream with strong negative emotion.

**Nocebo effect:** A variation of the placebo effect in which the person expects a negative outcome instead of a positive outcome.

**Nondeprived reward:** Reward that occurs not when a need is being met, but rather when a want is being satisfied.

**Nonverbal communication:** Facial expressions and body language that allow others to infer an individual's internal mental state.

**Norm:** A shared belief that is enforced through a group's use of penalties.

**Normal consciousness:** State of awareness that occurs during the usual waking state; also called *waking consciousness*.

**Normal distribution:** The familiar bell-shaped curve, in which most values fall in the midrange of the scale and scores are increasingly less frequent as they taper off symmetrically toward the extremes.

**Norming:** The process of setting the mean and the standard deviation of a set of test scores, based on results from a standardized sample.

**Obedience:** Compliance with an order.

**Object permanence:** The understanding that objects (including people) continue to exist even when they cannot be immediately perceived.

**Observational learning:** Learning that occurs through watching others, not through reinforcement.

**Obsession:** A recurrent and persistent thought, impulse, or image that feels intrusive and inappropriate and is difficult to suppress or ignore.

**Obsessive-compulsive disorder (OCD):** An anxiety disorder marked by the presence of obsessions, and sometimes compulsions.

**Occipital lobe:** The brain lobe at the back of the head; concerned entirely with different aspects of vision.

**Opening-up meditation:** A form of meditation in which the meditator focuses on a stimulus but also broadens that focus to encompass the whole of his or her surroundings.

**Operant conditioning:** The process by which a behavior becomes associated with its consequences.

**Operational definition:** A definition of a variable that specifies how it is measured or manipulated.

**Opiate:** A narcotic, such as morphine, derived from the opium poppy.

**Opponent cells:** Cells that pit the colors in a pair, most notably blue/yellow or red/green, against each other.

**Opponent process theory of color vision:** The theory that if a color is present, it causes cells that register it to inhibit the perception of the complementary color (such as red versus green).

**Optic nerve:** The large bundle of nerve fibers carrying impulses from the retina into the brain.

**Outcome research:** Research that asks whether, after psychotherapy, clients are feeling better, functioning better, living more independently, and experiencing fewer symptoms.

**Outgroup:** A group other than an individual's own.

**Overextension:** An overly broad use of a word to refer to a new object or situation.

**Overregularization error:** A mistake that occurs in speech because the child applies a newly learned rule even to cases where it does not apply.

**Panic attack:** An episode of intense fear or discomfort accompanied by physical and psychological symptoms such as palpitations, breathing difficulties, chest pain, fear of impending doom or of doing something uncontrollable, and a sense of unreality.

**Panic disorder:** An anxiety disorder whose hallmark is panic attacks or fear and avoidance of such attacks.

**Paradoxical cold:** The sensation of cold that occurs when certain nerves in the skin are stimulated by something hot.

**Paradoxical intention:** A systems therapy technique that encourages a behavior that seems contradictory to the desired goal.

**Parasympathetic nervous system:** Part of the ANS that is "next to" the sympathetic system and that tends to counteract its effects.

**Parietal lobe:** The brain lobe across the top part of the brain behind the ears, which is involved in registering spatial location, attention, and motor control.

**Partial reinforcement:** Reinforcement given only intermittently.

**Passionate love:** An intense feeling that involves sexual attraction, a desire for mutual love and physical closeness, arousal, and a fear that the relationship will end.

**Passive interaction:** Occurs when genetically shaped tendencies of parents or siblings produce an environment that is passively received by the child.

**Perceived social support:** The subjective sense that support is available should it be needed.

**Percentile rank:** The percentage of data that have values at or below a particular value.

**Perception:** The act of organizing and interpreting sensory input as signaling a particular object or event.

**Perceptual constancy:** The perception of characteristics that occurs when an object or quality (such as shape or color) looks the same even though the sensory information striking the eyes changes.

**Perceptual set:** The sum of your assumptions and beliefs that lead you to expect to perceive certain objects or characteristics in particular contexts.

**Peripheral nervous system (PNS):** The autonomic nervous system and the sensory-somatic nervous system.

**Personality:** A set of behavioral, emotional, and cognitive tendencies that people display over time and across situations and that distinguish individuals from each other.

**Personality disorders:** A category of disorders in which relatively stable personality traits are inflexible and maladaptive, causing distress or difficulty with daily functioning.

**Personality inventory:** A pencil-and-paper method for assessing personality that requires the test-takers to read statements and indicate whether each is true or false about themselves.

**Personality trait:** A relatively consistent characteristic exhibited in different situations.

**Persuasion:** Attempts to change people's attitudes.

**Phenotype:** The observable structure and behavior of an organism.

**Pheromones:** Chemicals that function like hormones but are released outside the body (in urine and sweat).

**Phobia:** A fear and avoidance of an object or situation extreme enough to interfere with everyday life.

**Phoneme:** The basic building block of speech sounds.

**Phonology:** The structure of the sounds that can be used to produce words in a language.

**Pitch:** How high or low a sound seems; higher frequencies of pressure waves produce the experience of higher pitches.

**Pituitary gland:** The "master gland" that regulates other glands but is itself controlled by the brain, primarily via connections from the hypothalamus.

**Place theory:** The theory that different frequencies activate different places along the basilar membrane.

**Placebo:** A medically inactive substance that is presented as though it has medicinal effects.

**Plasticity:** The brain's ability to be molded by experience.

**Polygraph:** A machine that monitors the activity of the sympathetic and parasympathetic nervous systems, particularly changes in skin conductance, breathing, and heart rate, in an attempt to detect lying.

**Pons:** A bridge between the brainstem and the cerebellum that plays a role in functions ranging from sleep to control of facial muscles.

**Pop-out:** Phenomenon that occurs when a stimulus is sufficiently different from the ones around it that it is immediately evident.

**Population:** The entire set of relevant people or animals.

**Positive punishment:** Occurs when a behavior leads to an undesired consequence, thereby decreasing the likelihood of a recurrence of that behavior.

**Positive reinforcement:** Occurs when a desired reinforcer is presented after a behavior, thereby increasing the likelihood of a recurrence of that behavior.

**Positive symptom:** An excess or distortion of normal functions, such as a hallucination.

**Positron emission tomography (PET):** A neuroimaging technique that uses small amounts of radiation to track blood flow or energy consumption in the brain.

**Posthypnotic suggestion:** A suggestion regarding a change in perception, mood, or behavior that will occur *after* leaving the hypnotic state.

**Posttraumatic stress disorder (PTSD):** An anxiety disorder experienced by some people after a traumatic event and whose symptoms include persistent re-experiencing of the trauma, avoidance of anything associated with the trauma, and heightened arousal.

**Pragmatics:** The way in which words and sentences in a language convey meaning indirectly, by implying rather than asserting.

**Prediction:** An expectation about specific events that should occur in particular circumstances if the theory or hypothesis is correct.

**Prejudice:** An attitude (generally negative) toward members of a group.

**Primacy effect:** Increased memory for the first few stimuli in a set.

**Primary mental abilities:** According to Thurstone, seven fundamental abilities that are the components of intelligence and are not outgrowths of other abilities.

**Primary reinforcer:** An event or object, such as food, water, or relief from pain, that is inherently reinforcing.

**Priming:** The result of having just performed a task that facilitates repeating the same or an associated task.

**Private speech:** The language used by a child in planning or in prompting himself or herself to behave in specific ways; also called *inner speech*.

**Proactive interference:** Interference that occurs when previous knowledge makes it difficult to learn something new.

**Problem:** An obstacle that must be overcome to reach a goal.

**Problem-focused coping:** Coping focused on changing the environment itself or the way the person interacts with the environment.

**Prodigies:** Children who demonstrate immense talent in a particular area, such as music or mathematics, but who are normal in other areas.

**Progressive muscle relaxation:** A relaxation technique whereby the person relaxes muscles sequentially from one end of the body to the other.

**Projective test:** A method used to assess personality and psychopathology that involves asking the test-taker to make sense of an ambiguous stimulus.

**Propositional representation:** A mental sentence that expresses the unambiguous meaning of an assertion.

**Prosocial behavior:** Acting to benefit others.

**Prototype:** The most typical example of a concept category.

**Pruning:** A process whereby certain connections among neurons are eliminated.

**Pseudopsychology:** Theories or statements that at first glance look like psychology, but are in fact superstition or unsupported opinion pretending to be science.

**Psychiatric nurse:** A nurse with a master's degree and a clinical specialization in psychiatric nursing who provides psychotherapy and works with medical doctors to monitor and administer medications.

**Psychiatrist:** A physician who focuses on mental disorders; unlike psychologists, psychiatrists can prescribe drugs, but they are not trained to administer and interpret psychological tests, nor are they trained to interpret and understand psychological research.

**Psychoanalysis:** An intensive form of therapy, originally developed by Freud, based on the idea that people's psychological difficulties are caused by conflicts among the id, the ego, and the superego.

**Psychodynamic theory:** A theory of how thoughts and feelings affect behavior; refers to the continual push-and-pull interaction among conscious and unconscious forces.

**Psychodynamic therapy:** A less intensive form of psychoanalysis.

**Psychoeducation:** The process of educating clients about therapy and research findings pertaining to their disorders or problems.

**Psychological determinism:** The view that all behavior, no matter how mundane or insignificant, has an underlying psychological cause.

**Psychological disorder:** The presence of a constellation of cognitive, emotional, and behavioral symptoms that create significant distress; impair work, school, family, relationships, or daily living; or lead to significant risk of harm.

**Psychology:** The science of mental processes and behavior.

**Psychopharmacology:** The use of medication to treat psychological disorders and problems.

**Psychophysics:** The study of the relation between physical events and the corresponding experience of those events.

**Psychosexual stages:** Freud's developmental stages based on erogenous zones; the specific needs of each stage must be met for its successful resolution.

**Psychosis:** An obvious impairment in the ability to perceive and comprehend events accurately, combined with a gross disorganization of behavior.

**Psychosocial development:** The effects of maturation and learning on personality and relationships.

**Psychotherapy:** The process of helping clients learn to change so they can cope with troublesome thoughts, feelings, and behaviors.

**Psychotherapy integration:** The use of techniques from different theoretical orientations with an overarching theory of how the integrated techniques will be used to achieve the goals of treatment.

**Puberty:** The time when hormones cause the sex organs to mature and secondary sexual characteristics, such as breasts for women and a beard for men, to appear.

**Pupil:** The opening in the eye through which light passes.

**Random assignment:** The technique of assigning participants randomly, that is, by chance, to the experimental and the control groups, so that no biases can sneak into the composition of the groups.

**Range:** The difference obtained when you subtract the smallest score from the largest, the simplest measure of variability.

**Ratio schedule:** Partial reinforcement schedule based on a specified number of emitted responses.

**Raven's Progressive Matrices:** A nonverbal test that assesses fluid intelligence and *g*.

**Raw data:** Individual measurements, taken directly from the situation being studied.

**Reaction range:** The entire scope of possible reactions to environmental events, which is set by the genes.

**Reality monitoring:** An ongoing awareness of the perceptual and other properties that distinguish real from imagined stimuli.

**Recall:** The act of intentionally bringing explicit information to awareness, which requires transferring the information from LTM to STM.

**Recategorization:** A means of reducing prejudice by shifting the categories of "us" and "them" so that the two groups are no longer distinct entities.

**Recency effect:** Increased memory for the last few stimuli in a set.

**Receptor:** A site on a dendrite or cell body where a messenger molecule attaches itself; like a lock that is opened by one key, a receptor receives only one type of neurotransmitter or neuromodulator.

**Reciprocal determinism:** The interactive relationship between the environment, cognitive/personal factors, and behavior.

**Recognition:** The act of encoding an input and matching it to a stored representation.

**Reflex:** An automatic response to an event.

**Reframing:** A therapy technique in which the therapist offers a new way of conceptualizing, or "framing," the problem.

**Rehearsal:** The process of repeating information over and over to retain it in STM.

**Reinforcement:** The process by which consequences lead to an increase in the likelihood that the response will occur again.

**Reinforcer:** An object or event that comes after a response and that changes the likelihood of its recurrence.

**Reliability:** Data are reliable if the same results are obtained when the measurements are repeated.

**REM rebound:** The higher percentage of REM sleep that occurs following a night lacking the normal amount of REM.

**REM sleep:** Stage of sleep characterized by rapid eye movements and marked brain activity.

**Repetition blindness:** The inability to see the second occurrence of a stimulus that appears twice in succession.

**Repetition priming:** Priming that makes the same information more easily accessed in the future.

**Replication:** Collecting the same observations or measurements and finding the same results as were found previously.

**Representation problem:** The challenge of how best to formulate the nature of a problem.

**Representativeness heuristic:** The heuristic that the more similar something is to a prototype stored in memory, the more likely it is to belong to the prototype's category.

**Repressed memories:** Real memories that have been pushed out of consciousness because they are emotionally threatening.

**Repression:** A defense mechanism that occurs when the unconscious prevents threatening thoughts, impulses, and memories from entering consciousness.

**Resistance:** A reluctance or refusal to cooperate with the therapist, which can range from unconscious forgetting to outright refusal to comply with a therapist's request.

**Resistance phase:** The second phase of the GAS, in which the body mobilizes its resources to achieve equilibrium, despite the continued presence of the stressor; also called the *adaptation phase*.

**Response bias:** A tendency to respond in a particular way regardless of respondents' actual knowledge or beliefs.

**Response contingency:** The relationship that occurs when a consequence is dependent on the organism's emitting the desired behavior.

**Resting potential:** The negative charge within a neuron when it is at rest.

**Reticular formation:** Two-part structure in the brainstem; the "ascending" part plays a key role in keeping a person awake and alert; the "descending" part is important in producing autonomic nervous system reactions.

**Retina:** A sheet of tissue at the back of the eye containing cells that convert light to neural impulses.

**Retinal disparity** (also called *binocular disparity*): The difference between the images striking the retinas of the two eyes.

**Retrieval:** The process of accessing information stored in memory.

**Retroactive interference:** Interference that occurs when new learning impairs memory for something learned earlier.

**Retrograde amnesia:** Amnesia that disrupts previous memories.

**Reuptake:** The process by which surplus neurotransmitter is reabsorbed back into the sending neuron so that the neuron can effectively fire again.

**Rods:** Rod-shaped retinal cells that are very sensitive to light but register only shades of gray.

**Role:** The behaviors that a member in a given position in a group is expected to perform.

**Rorschach test:** A projective test consisting of a set of inkblots that people are asked to interpret.

***s*:** "Specific factors," or aspects of performance that are particular to a given kind of processing—and distinct from *g*.

**Sample:** A group that is drawn from a larger population and measured or observed.

**Sampling bias:** A bias that occurs when the participants or items are not chosen at random, but instead are chosen so that one attribute is over- or underrepresented.

**Sampling error:** Any difference that arises from the luck of the draw, due to nonrandom sampling from a population, not because two samples are in fact representative of different populations.

**Schema (in cognition):** A collection of concepts that specify necessary and optional aspects of a particular situation.

**Schema (in Piaget's theory):** A mental structure that organizes perceptual input and connects it to the appropriate responses.

**Schizophrenia:** A psychotic disorder in which the patient's affect, behavior, and thoughts are profoundly altered.

**Scientific method:** The scientific method involves specifying a problem, systematically observing events, forming a hypothesis of the relation between variables, collecting new observations to test the hypothesis, using such evidence to formulate and support a theory, and finally testing the theory.

**Secondary reinforcer:** An event or object, such as attention, praise, money, a good grade, or a promotion, that is reinforcing but that does not inherently satisfy a physical need.

**Selective attention:** The process of picking out a particular quality, object, or event for relatively detailed analysis.

**Selective serotonin reuptake inhibitor (SSRI):** A type of antidepressant medication that has relatively few side effects and that acts by blocking the reuptake of the neurotransmitter serotonin at selective serotonin receptors.

**Self-actualization:** An innate motivation to attain the highest possible emotional and intellectual potential.

**Self-concept:** The beliefs, desires, values, and attributes that define a person to himself or herself.

**Self-efficacy:** The sense of being able to follow through and produce specific desired behaviors.

**Self-help group:** A group whose members focus on a specific disorder or event and do not usually have a clinically trained leader; also called a *support group*.

**Self-monitoring techniques:** Behavioral techniques that help the client identify the antecedents and consequences of a problematic behavior.

**Self-perception theory:** The theory that people come to understand themselves by making inferences from their behavior and the events surrounding their behavior.

**Self-serving bias:** A person's inclination to attribute his or her own failures to external causes and own successes to internal causes, but to attribute other people's failures to internal causes and their successes to external causes.

**Semantic memories:** Memories of the meanings of words, concepts, and general facts about the world.

**Semantics:** The meaning of a word or sentence.

**Sensation:** The awareness of properties of an object or event that occurs when a type of receptor (such as those at the back of the eye, in the ear, on the skin) is stimulated.

**Sensitive period:** A window of time when a particular type of learning is *easiest*, but not the only time it can occur.

**Sensitivity:** In signal detection theory, the threshold level for distinguishing between a stimulus and noise; the lower the threshold, the greater the sensitivity.

**Sensory memory (SM):** A memory store that holds a large amount of perceptual input for a very brief time, typically less than 1 second.

**Sensory neuron:** A neuron that responds to input from sense organs.

**Sensory-somatic nervous system (SSNS):** Part of the PNS that consists of neurons in the sensory organs (such as the eyes and ears) that convey information to the brain, as well as neurons that actually trigger muscles and glands.

**Separation anxiety:** Fear of being away from the primary caregiver.

**Serial position effect:** Having superior memory for the items at the beginning and at the end of a list ("serial position" refers to the order of the items in the sequence).

**Serotonin/norepinephrine reuptake inhibitor (SNRI):** A newer type of antidepressant that affects both serotonin and norepinephrine neurotransmitter systems.

**Set point:** The particular body weight that is easiest for an animal (including a human) to maintain.

**Sexual response cycle:** The stages the body passes through during sexual activity, including sexual attraction, desire, excitement, and possibly performance (which includes full arousal, orgasm, and resolution).

**Shape constancy:** Seeing objects as having the same shape even when the image on the retina changes.

**Shaping:** The gradual process of reinforcing an organism for behavior that gets closer to the desired behavior.

**Short-term memory (STM)** (also called *immediate memory*): A memory store that holds relatively little information (typically 5 to 9 items) for only a few seconds (but perhaps as long as 30 seconds).

**Signal detection theory:** A theory explaining why people detect signals independently of bias; the theory is based on the idea that signals are always embedded in noise, and thus the challenge is to distinguish signal from noise.

**Size constancy:** Seeing an object as being the same size when viewed at different distances.

**Skeletal system:** Consists of nerves that are attached to striated muscles.

**Sleep:** The naturally recurrent experience during which normal consciousness is suspended.

**Sleep apnea:** A disorder characterized by a temporary cessation of breathing during sleep, usually preceded by a period of difficult breathing accompanied by loud snoring.

**Sociability:** A temperament dimension characterized by a preference for being in other people's company rather than alone.

**Social causation:** The chronic psychological and social stresses of living in an urban environment that may lead to an increase in the rate of schizophrenia (especially among the poor).

**Social cognition:** The area of social psychology that focuses on how people perceive their social worlds and how they attend to, store, remember, and use information about other people and the social world.

**Social cognitive neuroscience:** The subfield of psychology that attempts to understand social cognition not only by specifying the cognitive mechanisms that underlie it, but also by discovering how those mechanisms are rooted in the brain.

**Social desirability:** A source of bias in responding to questions on personality inventories that occurs when people try to make themselves "look good" even if it means giving untrue answers.

**Social exchange theory:** The theory that proposes that individuals act to maximize the gains and minimize the losses in their relationships.

**Social facilitation:** The increase in performance that can occur simply as a result of being part of a group or in the presence of other people.

**Social loafing:** The tendency to work less hard when responsibility for an outcome is spread over a group's members.

**Social phobia:** A type of phobia involving fear of public humiliation or embarrassment and the ensuing avoidance of situations likely to arouse this fear.

**Social psychology:** The subfield of psychology that focuses on how people think about other people and interact in relationships and groups.

**Social selection:** The tendency of the mentally disabled to drift to the lower economic classes; also called *social drift*.

**Social support:** The help and support gained through interacting with others.

**Social worker:** A mental health professional who uses psychotherapy to help families (and individuals) and teaches clients to use the social service systems in their communities.

**Sociocognitive theory (of hypnosis):** The view that a person in a trance voluntarily enacts the role of a hypnotized person as he or she understands it, which leads to behaviors and experiences believed to be produced by hypnosis.

**Somasthetic senses:** Senses that have to do with perceiving the body and its position in space—specifically, kinesthetic sense, vestibular sense, touch, temperature sensitivity, pain sense, and possibly magnetic sense.

**Somatosensory strip:** The brain area, located immediately behind the central sulcus, that registers sensation on the body and is organized by body part.

**Source amnesia:** A failure to remember the source of information.

**Specific factor:** In psychotherapy, a curative aspect that is related to the specific type of therapy being employed.

**Specific language impairment:** A specific problem in understanding grammar and complex words that is not related to more general cognitive deficits.

**Specific phobia:** A type of phobia involving persistent and excessive or unreasonable fear triggered by a specific object or situation, along with attempts to avoid the feared stimulus.

**Speech-segmentation problem:** The problem of organizing a continuous stream of speech into separate parts that correspond to individual words.

**Spinal cord:** The flexible rope of nerves that runs inside the backbone, or spinal column.

**Split-brain patient:** A person whose corpus callosum has been severed for medical reasons, so that neuronal impulses no longer pass from one hemisphere to the other.

**Spontaneous recovery (in classical conditioning):** The event that occurs when the CS again elicits the CR after extinction has occurred.

**Spontaneous recovery (in operant conditioning):** The process by which an old response reappears if there is a period of time after extinction.

**St. John's wort:** An herbal remedy for mild to moderate depression.

**Standard deviation:** A kind of "average variability" in a set of measurements.

**Standardized sample:** A random selection of people, drawn from a carefully defined population.

**State-dependent retrieval:** Recall that is better if it occurs in the same psychological state that was present when the information was first encoded.

**Statistical significance:** The conclusion that the measured relationship is not simply due to chance.

**Statistics:** Numbers that summarize or indicate differences or patterns of differences in measurements.

**Status hierarchy:** The positioning of roles that reflects who has power over whom within a group.

**Stereotype:** A belief (or set of beliefs) about people in a particular category.

**Stimulants:** A class of substances that excite the central nervous system, leading to increases in behavioral activity and heightened arousal.

**Stimulus control:** A behavior therapy technique that involves controlling the exposure to a stimulus that elicits a conditioned response, so as to decrease or increase the frequency of the response.

**Stimulus discrimination:** The ability to distinguish among stimuli similar to the CS and to respond only to the actual CS.

**Stimulus generalization:** A tendency for the CR to be elicited by neutral stimuli that are like, but not identical to, the CS; in other words, the response generalizes to similar stimuli.

**Storage:** The process of retaining information in memory.

**Strategy:** An approach to solving a problem, determined by the type of representation used and the processing steps to be tried.

**Stress:** The general term describing the psychological and physical response to a stimulus that alters the body's state of equilibrium.

**Stress response:** The bodily changes that occur to help a person cope with a stressor; also called the *fight-or-flight response*.

**Stressor:** A stimulus that throws the body's equilibrium out of balance.

**Stroke:** A source of brain damage that occurs when blood (with its life-giving nutrients and oxygen) fails to reach part of the brain, causing neurons in that area to die.

**Structuralism:** The school of psychology that sought to identify the basic elements of experience and to describe the rules and circumstances under which these elements combine to form mental *structures*.

**Subcortical structures:** Parts of the brain located under the cerebral cortex and beneath the ventricles.

**Substance abuse:** Drug or alcohol use that causes distress or trouble with functioning in major areas of life, occurs in dangerous situations, or leads to legal difficulties.

**Substance dependence:** Chronic substance abuse that is characterized by seven symptoms, the two most important being tolerance and withdrawal.

**Successive approximations:** The series of smaller behaviors involved in shaping a complex behavior.

**Sulcus:** A crease in the cerebral cortex.

**Superego:** A personality structure, proposed by Freud, that is formed during early childhood and houses the sense of right and wrong, based on the internalization of parental and cultural morality.

**Suprachiasmatic nucleus (SCN):** A small part of the hypothalamus just above the optic chiasm that registers changes in light, leading to production of hormones that regulate various bodily functions.

**Survey:** A set of questions, typically about beliefs, attitudes, preferences, or activities.

**Sympathetic nervous system:** Part of the ANS that readies an animal to fight or to flee by speeding up the heart, increasing breathing rate to deliver more oxygen, dilating the pupils, producing sweat, increasing salivation, inhibiting activity in the stomach, and relaxing the bladder.

**Synapse:** The place where an axon of one neuron can send signals to the membrane (on a dendrite or cell body) of another neuron.

**Synaptic cleft:** The gap between the axon of one neuron and the membrane of another, across which communication occurs.

**Syntax:** The internal structure of a sentence, determined by a set of rules (grammar) for combining different parts of speech into acceptable arrangements.

**Systematic desensitization:** A behavior therapy technique that teaches people to be relaxed in the presence of a feared object or situation.

**Systems therapy:** A type of therapy that views a client's symptoms as occurring in a larger context, or system (the family and subculture), and holds that a change in one part of the system affects the rest of the system.

**T cell:** A type of white blood cell that matures in the thymus.

**Tardive dyskinesia:** An irreversible movement disorder in which the person involuntarily smacks his or her lips, displays facial grimaces, and exhibits other symptoms; caused by traditional antipsychotic medication.

**Taste buds:** Microscopic structures on the bumps on the tongue surface, at the back of the throat, and inside the cheeks; the four types of taste buds are sensitive to sweet, sour, salty, and bitter tastes.

**Technical eclecticism:** The use of specific techniques that may benefit a particular client, without regard for an overarching theory.

**Telegraphic speech:** Speech that packs a lot of information into a few words, typically omitting words such as *the*, *a*, and *of*.

**Temperament:** Innate inclinations to engage in a certain style of behavior.

**Temporal lobe:** The brain lobe under the temples, in front of the ears, where sideburns begin to grow down; among its many functions are visual memory and hearing.

**Teratogen:** Any external agent, such as a chemical, virus, or type of radiation, that can cause damage to the zygote, embryo, or fetus.

**Terminal button:** A structure at the end of a branch of an axon that, when the neuron is triggered, releases chemicals into the space between neurons.

**Test bias:** Features of test items or design that lead a particular group to perform well or poorly and that thus invalidate the test.

**Testosterone:** The hormone that causes males to develop facial hair and other sex characteristics and to build up muscle volume.

**Texture gradient:** Progressive change in texture that signals distance.

**Thalamus:** A subcortical structure that receives inputs from sensory and motor systems and plays a crucial role in attention; often thought of as a switching center.

**Thematic Apperception Test (TAT):** A projective test consisting of a set of detailed black-and-white drawings about which people are asked to explain various elements.

**Theory:** An interlocking set of concepts or principles that explain a set of observations.

**Theory of causal attribution:** The theory that people decide whether to attribute a given behavior to a person's enduring traits or to the situation based on whether the behavior shows consensus, consistency, and distinctiveness.

**Theory of mind:** A theory of other people's mental states (their beliefs, desires, and feelings) that allows prediction of what other people can understand and how they will react in a given situation.

**Theory of multiple intelligences:** Gardner's theory of eight distinct forms of intelligence, which can vary separately for a given individual.

**Thought suppression:** The coping strategy that involves purposefully trying not to think about something emotionally arousing or distressing.

**Threshold:** The point at which stimulation is strong enough to be noticed.

**Tinnitus:** A form of hearing impairment signaled by a constant ringing or noise in the ears.

**Token economy:** A treatment program that uses secondary reinforcers (tokens) to bring about behavior modification.

**Tolerance:** The condition of requiring more of a substance to achieve the same effect (because the usual amount provides a diminished response).

**Tonotopic organization:** The use of distance along a strip of cortex to represent differences in pitch.

**Top-down processing:** Processing that is guided by knowledge, expectation, or belief.

**Trace conditioning:** A type of forward classical conditioning where the presentation of the conditioned stimulus (CS) ends before the presentation of the unconditioned stimulus (US) begins.

**Trance logic:** An uncritical acceptance of incongruous, illogical events during a hypnotic trance.

**Trance state:** A hypnotically induced altered state of consciousness in which awareness of the external environment is diminished.

**Trance theory:** The view that a person in a trance experiences an altered, dissociated state of consciousness characterized by increasing susceptibility and responsiveness to suggestions.

**Transcranial magnetic stimulation (TMS):** A technique where the brain is stimulated from outside by putting a wire coil on a person's head and delivering a magnetic pulse. The magnetic fields are so strong that they make neurons under the coil fire.

**Transduction:** The process whereby physical energy is converted by a sensory neuron into neural impulses.

**Transfer appropriate processing:** Processing used to retrieve material that is the same type as was used when it was originally studied, which improves memory retrieval.

**Transference:** The process by which patients may relate to their therapists as they did to some important person in their lives.

**Triangular model of love:** The theory that love has three dimensions: passion (including sexual desire), intimacy (closeness), and commitment.

**Trichromatic theory of color vision:** The theory that color vision arises from the combinations of neural impulses from three different kinds of sensors, each of which responds maximally to a different wavelength.

**Tricyclic antidepressant (TCA):** A type of antidepressant medication named for the three rings in the chemical structure.

**Twin study:** A study that compares identical and fraternal twins to determine the relative contribution of genes to variability in a behavior or characteristic.

**Typicality:** The degree to which an entity is representative of its concept category.

**Unconditional positive regard:** Acceptance without any conditions.

**Unconditioned response (UR):** The reflexive response elicited by a particular stimulus.

**Unconditioned stimulus (US):** A stimulus that elicits an automatic response (UR), without requiring prior learning.

**Unconscious:** Outside conscious awareness and not able to be brought to consciousness at will.

**Underextension:** An overly narrow use of a word to refer to a new object or situation.

**Validation:** A therapy technique in which the therapist conveys his or her understanding of the client's feelings and wishes.

**Validity:** A measure is valid if it does in fact measure what it is supposed to measure.

**Variable:** An aspect of a situation that can vary, or change; specifically, a characteristic of a substance, quantity, or entity that is measurable.

**Variable interval schedule:** Reinforcement schedule in which reinforcement is given for a response emitted after a variable interval of time.

**Variable ratio schedule:** Reinforcement schedule in which reinforcement is given after a variable number of responses.

**Ventricle:** A hollow area in the center of the brain that stores fluid.

**Vestibular sense:** The sense that provides information about the body's orientation relative to gravity.

**Want:** A condition that arises when you have an unmet goal that will not fill a requirement; wants turn goals into incentives.

**Wavelength:** The distance between the arrival of peaks of a light wave (measured in nanometers); shorter wavelengths correspond to higher frequencies.

**Weber's law:** The rule that a constant percentage of a magnitude change is necessary to detect a difference.

**Wechsler Adult Intelligence Scale (WAIS):** The most widely used intelligence test; consists of both verbal and performance subtests.

**Wernicke's aphasia:** Problems with comprehending language following brain damage (typically to the left posterior temporal lobe).

**Withdrawal symptoms:** The onset of uncomfortable or life-threatening effects when the use of a substance is stopped.

**Working memory (WM):** The system that includes two specialized STMs (auditory loop and visuospatial sketchpad) and a central executive that operates on information in them to plan, reason, or solve a problem.

**Zygote:** A fertilized ovum (egg).

# NAME INDEX

Aalto, S., 438
Aarkes, H. R., 748
Aartsen, M. J., 580
Abas, M., 227
Abbott, M. J., 652
Abdollahi, P., 673
Abel, T.,311
Abelson, R. P., 355
Abraham, H. D., 227
Abramowitz, J. S., 716
Abrams, L. R., 623
Abramson, L. Y., 644, 645
Achter, J., 417
Ackerman, P. L., 398
Ackerman, S. J., 716
Adams, H. E., 475
Adams, J., 311
Adams, R. B., Jr., 157
Adams, S. J., 709
Adcock, I. M., 105
Addis, D. R., 300
Addis, M. E., 711
Ader, R., 249
Adler, A., 486, 513
Adler, N. E., 599
Adolph, K. E., 543
Adolphs, R., 102
Adrian, C., 213
Agarwal, D. P., 122
Agency for Health Care Policy
    and Research, 703
Aglioti, S., 96
Aguilar-Alonso, A., 419
Ahadi, S., 491
Aharon, I., 452
Ahmed, S. T., 342
Ahnert, L. 556
Aiken, M., 499
Ainsworth, M. D. S., 555
Ajzen, I., 511
Akhtar, N., 337
Akiskal, H. S., 643
Alberini, C., 285, 286
Albert, M., 237
Albert, M. S., 313, 572
Albert, R. S., 395
Albon, J. S., 722
Alcock, J. E., 182
Aldag, R. J., 775
Aldea, A., 372
Aldous, J., 439
Aldridge, D., 107
Alexander, C. N., 216
Alexander, D., 416
Alexander. F., 688
Alibali, M. W., 344
Alkire, M. T., 191
Allen, J. J. B., 447
Allen, L. S., 472
Allik, J., 522
Allison, J., 216
Allport, G., 747
Allport, G. W., 490

Allyn, J., 745
Almeida, D. M., 596
Almli, C. R., 533
Alonso, P., 706
Alonzo, M., 499
Altshuler, L. L., 644
Aluja-Fabregat, A., 407
Alzheimer's Association, 314
Amabile, T. M., 419
Amaducci, L., 420
Ambady, M., 735
Ambady, N., 343, 431, 442, 735
Ambinder, M. S., 161
Ambrose, N. G., 342
Amelang, M., 501
American Association for
    Mental Retardation,
    414
American Psychiatric
    Association, 206, 219, 474,
    632, 635, 638, 642, 647,
    651, 661, 666, 668, 670,
    671, 677, 724
Amir, M., 706
Amir, N., 652
Amsterdam, B., 557
Anand, B. K., 460
Anastasi, A., 495
Anch, A. M., 193
Andersen, A. E., 672
Andersen, B., 621
Andersen, B. L., 603
Anderson, A. K., 438
Anderson, C. A., 272, 615, 747
Anderson, I. M., 703
Anderson, J. R., 287, 288, 353
Anderson, M., 396, 397
Anderson, M. C., 21, 312
Anderson, N. B., 8, 405
Anderson, N. H., 736
Anderson, V. L., 621
Ando, J., 281
Andreasen, N. C., 420
Andrews, H. B., 463
Angier, N., 422
Angleitner, A., 506
Anglin, J. M., 337
Angst, J., 643
Anisman, H., 540
Ankney, C. D., 396
Anonymous, 469
Antoch, M. P., 203
Antonijevic, I. J., 590
Antonuccio, D. O., 724
Appenzeller, T., 264, 296
Aram, D. M., 341
Arana, G. W., 224
Aranda, M. P., 623
Archer, J., 515
Archer, R. P., 496
Archer, S. L., 515
Arguin, M., 152
Argyle, M. L., 440

Arking, R., 570
Arlas, E., 641
Armatas, C., 499
Armstrong, S. L., 353
Arnett, J., 566
Arnett, J. J., 566, 569
Arnow, B. A., 500
Aron, A., 760
Aronson, E., 754
Aronson, H., 726
Aronson, J., 412, 413
Arquin, M., 152
Arterberry, M. E., 544
Asai, M., 518
Asch, S. E., 769, 770
Asendorpf, J. B., 557
Ashbridge, E., 159
Ashton, C. H., 84
Ashton, M. C., 517
Aslin, R. N., 336
Aspinwall, L. G., 609
Associated Press, 327
Association of SIDS and Infant
    Mortality Programs, 542
Athanasiou, M. S., 387
Atienza, M., 200
Atkinson, G., 212
Atkinson, J. W., 455
Atkinson, R. C., 279
Atre-Vaidya, N., 677
Au, W. T., 374
Auden, W. H., 666, 667
Austin, J. B., 777
Avorn, J., 569, 580
Ayres, J. J. B., 237
Ayton, P., 370
Azar, B., 499
Azrin, N, H., 248

Baare, W. F. C., 663, 664
Baars, B. J., 191
Babad, E., 411, 735
Baccus, J. R., 244
Bacharach, V. R., 411
Bachen, E. A., 602
Bäckman, L., 571, 580
Baddeley, A., 280, 281, 398
Baddeley, A. D., 281, 304, 305
Badgaiyan, R. D., 295
Baeck, E., 106
Baenninger, M., 409
Baer, L., 213
Bahrick, H. P., 287
Bahrick, L. E., 557
Baile, C. A., 463
Bailey, J. M., 473
Bailey, M., 105
Baillargeon, R., 550
Baily, C. H., 310
Baird, A., 552
Baker, F., 107
Baker, R. R., 181
Baker, S. C., 367

Bakermans-Kranenburg, M.
    J.,524, 555
Balakrishnan, J. D., 136
Baldwin, D. A., 552
Baldwin, D. R., 616
Balkwill, D., 44
Ball, K., 580
Ball, S. A., 504
Ball, T. S., 341
Ballus, C., 702
Baltes, P. B., 574
Banach, M., 710
Banaji, M. R., 748, 749
Bandura, A., 270, 271, 511,
    512, 743
Banich, M. T., 154
Banks, M. S., 543
Bao, S., 244
Bar, J. L., 401
Bar, M., 151, 160
Barabasz, A. F., 213
Barañano, D. E., 82
Barbarich, N., 673
Barber, J., 213, 306
Barber, T. X., 212
Barbur, J. L., 191
Barclay, J. R., 304
Barefoot, J. C., 600
Barger, L. K., 197
Bargh, J. A., 737, 738 ,751, 759,
    765
Barinaga, M., 84
Barkham, M., 690, 711
Barkow, J. H., 19., 450
Barley, D. E., 716., 722
Barlow, D. H., 476, 650, 652,
    658, 669
Barnes, V. A., 216, 621
Barnet, R. C., 237
Barnett, L. A., 765
Barnier, A. J., 306, 618
Baron, R., 753
Baron, R. A., 599, 613
Bar-On, R., 391
Barone, P., 86
Barr, R., 546
Barrantes-Vidal, N., 420
Barrett, H. C., 358
Barrett, L. F., 433, 434, 435,
    436, 438, 440, 445
Barrick, M. L., 390
Barriga, A. Q., 565
Barrios, A. A., 736
Barry, C. M., 569
Barry, E., 556
Barsky, A. J., 525, 624
Bar-Tal, D., 757
Barth, J., 604
Bartholomew, K., 521, 522
Barto, A. G., 263
Barton, J. J. S., 156
Bartoshuk, L. M., 178, 571
Baruch, D. E., 243

Bartussek, D., 500
Basic Behavioral Science Task
    Force of the National
    Advisory Mental Health
    Council, 635
Bassili, J. N., 445
Bast, T., 242
Bastien, C. H., 206
Bates, E., 341
Bates, T. C., 397
Batsell, W. R., Jr., 461
Batshaw, M., 414
Batson, C. D., 776, 777
Baudry, M., 297
Baum, S. R., 333
Baumeister, A. A., 411
Baumeister, R. F., 444, 487,
    615, 757, 765
Bavelier, D., 169
Baxendale, S., 312
Baxter, J. S., 757
Baxter, L. R., 728
Baxter, M. G., 454
Bayley, P. J., 312
Bazerman, M., 369
Beach, F., 164
Beach, F. A., 452
Beals, J., 637
Bearak, B., 780
Beatty, J., 139
Beauchamp, G. K., 178
Beaumont, M., 203
Beauregard, M., 443
Bechara, A., 372, 452
Beck, A., 644, 650
Beck, A. T., 648, 649, 699, 725
Beck, R., 600
Becker, A. E., 674
Bedrosian, J. L., 340
Beer, J. M., 515
Beer, J. S., 439
Beer, M., 456
Beevers, C. G., 612
Bègue, L., 758
Behrens, R. R., 357
Behrman, R. E., 556
Behrmann, M., 351
Beier, M. E., 398
Beilin, H., 554
Beilock, S. L., 159
Bell, A. E., 400
Bell, J. H., 565
Beller, M., 408
Bellugi, U., 343
Belser, R. C., 415
Belsky, J., 556
Bem, D. J., 182, 473, 742
Benda, B. B., 471
Bender, K. J., 703
Benedetti, F., 625
Beninger, R. J., 454
Bennett, E. S., 398
Bennett, P. J., 543

Bensafi, M., 177
Ben-Shakhar, G., 447
Benson, D., 213
Berchtold, N. C., 580
Berenbaum, S. A., 516, 558
Berg, S., 571
Bergeman, C. S., 506, 507
Berger, M., 114
Bergin, A. E., 715, 716
Berk, L., 613
Berk, L. E., 554
Berkman, L. F., 619
Berko, J., 339
Berkowitz, L., 272, 613, 614, 765
Berlyne, D. E., 451
Berman, J. D., 621
Berman, S., 336
Bermond, B. N., 434
Bernier, D., 599
Berntzen, D., 697
Berridge, K. C., 263, 455
Berscheid, E., 759
Berson, D. M., 140, 203
Berström, J., 710
Berthoud, H-R., 462, 463, 464
Bertin, E., 544
Best, J., 54, 61
Best, P. J., 296
Bettencourt, B. A., 614
Betz, J., 353
Beutler, L. E., 710, 716, 720, 726
Beyers, J. M., 566
Bhatt, R. S., 544
Bialystok, E., 398
Biedenkapp, J. C., 285
Biederman, I., 146, 151, 160
Biederman, J., 652
Bierhoff, H. W., 777
Biesanz, J. C., 736
Bihrle, A. M., 99
Billington, C. J., 462
Bilukha, O. O., 673
Bimonte, H. A., 408
Binder, J. L., 711
Bindra, D., 452
Bird, H., 353
Birkenhäger, T. K., 706
Birnbaum, S. G., 412
Birren, J. E., 570, 571
Bishop, D. V. M., 341, 342
Bishop, G. D., 593, 598
Bisiach, E., 191
Biswas-Diener, R., 439
Bjork, E. L., 312
Bjork, R. A., 214, 287, 312
Black, D. W., 654
Blair, C., 409
Blair, H. T., 297
Blair, I. V., 741
Blais, M. A., 637
Blakemore, S., 21, 745
Blalock, E. M., 87
Blamey, P., 328
Blanchette, I., 372
Blanck, H. M., 563

Blankenhorn, R., 169
Blankenship, S. E., 357, 360
Blanton, H., 353, 354
Blascovich, J., 593
Blass, T., 774, 782
Blatt, S. J., 721, 723
Bleiberg, K. L., 712
Bless, H., 372
Blin, O., 654
Bliss, F. L., 669
Block, N., 404, 406
Bloom, B. L., 687
Bloom, B. S., 364, 417
Bloom, F. E., 208
Bloom, J. W., 713
Bloom, P., 337
Bluck, S., 300
Blumenthal, J. A., 622
Blundell, J. E., 463
Bluni, T. D., 181
Bly, B. M., 151
Bobo, L., 751
Bochner, S., 339
Boddy, J., 214
Boden, J. M., 444, 615
Boden, M. A., 421
Bodenhausen, G. V., 266, 747, 748
Bogaert, A. F., 467
Bohannon, J. N., III, 335
Bohm, J. K., 777
Boivin, D. B., 204, 205
Bokert, E., 200
Bokhorst, C. L., 523
Bonanno, G. A., 440, 444
Bond, M., 487
Bond, M. H., 517
Bond, R., 770
Boning, J., 503
Bonnefond, A., 205
Bonnel, A. M., 159
Bontempo, D. E., 567
Bonvillian, J. D., 335
Borg, E., 167
Boring, E. G., 12
Borkenau, P., 735
Borman, W. C., 494
Bornstein, M. H., 336, 533
Bornstein, S. R., 105
Boroditsky, L., 348
Borroni, A. M., 297
Borwick, D., 509
Bosch, J. A., 596
Bosma, H., 598
Bosson, J. K., 412
Bosworth, H. B., 571
Botting, N., 342
Bottini, G., 191, 332
Botvin, G. J., 765
Botwinick, J., 571
Bouchard, C., 463, 464, 563
Bouchard, T. J., 399, 507
Bouchard, T. J., Jr., 399, 503, 505, 506, 508
Bourguignon, E., 192, 214, 218
Bousfield, W. A., 288
Bouton, M. E., 240, 649

Bovbjerg. D. J., 248
Bowden, D. M., 101
Bowdle, B. F., 332
Bowen, R., 565
Bower, G. H., 288, 305, 316, 317
Bowers, K. S., 212
Bowlby, J., 521, 555
Bowman, E. S., 643, 658
Brach, J. S., 569
Bradburn, N. M., 431
Braden, J. P., 387
Bradley, M. M., 288
Bradley, M. T., 446
Bradshaw, G. L., 287
Brainard, G. C., 203
Brakefield, T., 285
Branchey, L., 248
Brandstätter, H., 373, 374
Brannon, L., 623
Bransford, J. D., 331
Brashers-Krug, T., 285
Brasiek, R. J., 109
Braun, J., 160
Braun, K. A., 309
Braver, T. S., 281
Breckler, S. J., 738
Bregman, A. S., 170
Bregman, E. O., 239
Brehm, J. W., 745, 746
Breiter, H. C., 654
Bremner, J. D., 643, 657
Brennan, A., 598
Breslau, N., 656, 657, 658
Brewer, A. A., 94
Brewer, C., 248
Brewer, J. B., 284, 296
Brewer, K. R., 271
Brewer, M. B., 750, 753
Brewer, W. F., 291
Brewin, C.R., 654
Brickman, P., 439
Bridwell, L. G., 456, 488
Brightwell, D. R., 248
Broadbent, D. E., 280
Broadhead, J., 227
Brobeck, J. R., 460
Brochard, R., 107
Brody, J., 196
Brody, N., 395
Bromnick, R. D., 565
Brooks-Gunn, J., 557, 567
Brosschot, J. F., 596, 604
Brown, A. S., 461, 663, 669
Brown, B., 532, 535
Brown, B. B., 565
Brown, D., 314
Brown, I., Jr., 511
Brown, J. D., 19, 757
Brown, P. L., 265
Brown, R., 289, 302, 316, 472
Brown, R. J., 750, 753
Brown, R. P., 413
Brown, T. L., 411
Browne, C. A., 534
Browne, G., 724
Brownell, H. H., 332, 674

Brozinsky, C. J., 169
Bruce, M. N., 494
Brugger, P., 182
Brummett, B. H., 619
Brunner, D. P., 196
Brussoni, M. J., 523
Bryan, R. N., 581
Bryant, R. A., 306, 602, 657
Bseikri, M. R., 263
Buchanan, C. M., 566, 567
Buchkremer, G., 725
Buckalew, L. W., 622
Buda, R., 518
Buehler, R., 371
Buka, S. L., 663, 664
Bulik, C.M., 673
Buller, K, M., 105
Bülthoff, H. H., 152
Bunce, S. C., 244
Burger, J. M., 762, 770
Burggraf, K., 273
Burish, T. G., 248, 249
Burnstein, E., 774
Burton, L. M., 567, 568
Burton, M. J., 460
Busemeyer, J. R., 136
Bushman, B. J., 222, 613, 615, 616, 773
Busjahn, A., 618
Buss, A. H., 491, 497, 498
Buss, D. M., 19, 408, 450, 471, 516, 762
Busse, E. W., 569
Butcher, J. N., 495
Butterfield, E., 417
Butters, N., 295
Butzlaff, R. L., 665
Byrne, D., 470, 753, 760, 762

Cabanac, M., 466
Cabeza, R., 110, 292, 299, 574
Cacioppo, J. T., 431, 434, 435, 455, 456, 738, 741, 744, 745
Cadinu, M., 412, 413
Cahan, S., 401
Cahill, E. D., 470, 644
Cailliet, R., 181
Cain, W. S., 175, 180
Cajochen, C., 197
Calder, A. J., 445
Caldera, Y. M., 558
Calkins, S. D., 540
Callaway, E. M., 142
Calvcoressi, L., 655
Cameron, J., 452
Cameron-Faulkner, T., 336
Cammarota, M., 285
Campbell, C. S., 459
Campbell, D. T., 418, 439, 765
Campbell, F. A., 411
Campbell, W. K., 615
Campos, J. J., 534, 543
Canli, T., 289, 445, 501
Cannon, C. M., 263
Cannon, T. D., 714
Cannon, W. B., 433, 624

Cansino, S.,168
Cantalupo, C., 330
Canter, S., 419
Cantor, J. M., 473
Cantor, N., 617
Cantril, H., 739
Cappa, S. F., 110
Caramazza, A., 329
Caprara, G. V., 509
Cardeña, E., 212
Cardinal, R. N., 242, 243, 244, 263, 452, 454, 455
Cardno, A. G., 662
Carenzi, F., 365
Carey, M. P., 248
Carey, S., 337, 551
Carey, T. O., 757
Carlbring, P., 710
Carli, L., 770
Carlo, G., 776
Carlsmith, J. M., 741
Carlson, N. R., 329
Carlsson, C. P. O., 181
Carlyon, R. P., 170
Carmines, E, G., 49
Carnelley, K. B., 579
Carney, R. M., 604
Caroff, X., 553
Carpenter, P. A., 398
Carr, D., 579
Carr, J. L., 223
Carrasco, M., 157
Carrington, P., 216
Carroll, J., 388, 394
Carroll, L., 189, 193, 215, 218, 227
Carron, A. V., 769
Carrothers, R. M., 392
Carskadon, M., 567
Carstens, C. B., 411
Carstensen, L. L., 570, 574, 577, 578
Carter, C., 748
Carter, C. S., 470
Carter, J. C., 766
Carter, M. M., 650
Cartford, M. C., 244
Carver, C. S., 486, 500, 609, 616, 617, 618
Casada, J. H., 603
Casbon, T. S., 646
Case, R., 552, 553
Caspi, A., 497, 502, 760
Cassia, V. M., 538
Cassone, V. M., 208
Castellà, J., 500
Castelli, W. P., 624
Catalan-Ahumeda, M., 169
Cattell, R. B., 387, 388, 394, 492, 495
Cavallaro, S., 298
Caudron, S., 775
Cavanagh, P., 158
Cave, C. B., 152, 294, 295
Ceci, S. J., 397
Cendan, D. L., 309

Center for Addiction and Substance Abuse at Columbia University, 220
Center for the Advancement of Health, 195, 208
Centers for Disease Control and Prevention, 220, 462
Cerella, J., 571
Ceruti, D. T., 260
Cervone, D., 492
Chabris, C. F., 154, 372, 411
Chaiken, S., 738, 739
Chakrabarti, S., 661, 666
Chalmers, D. J., 190
Chamberlain, K., 596
Chambless, D. L., 722, 724, 728
Chan, J., 233, 235, 253, 267, 268, 271
Chance, B., 113
Chang, F. L. F., 120
Chang, J., 312
Chang, R. C., 237
Changizi, M. A., 460
Chao, L. L., 143, 284
Chapman, C., 594
Chapman, C. R., 181
Chapman, J. K., 534
Chapman, R. S., 336, 415
Charles, S. T., 578
Charness, N., 364
Chartrand, T. L., 737
Chase, W. G., 287, 362, 363
Chatterjee, S., 142, 456
Chaudhari, N., 178
Chaves, J. F., 214
Cheek, D. B., 211, 213
Chein, J. M., 294
Chen, L., 171
Chen, M., 310
Chen, Z., 553
Cheng, C. M., 737
Cheng, D. T., 242
Cheour-Luhtanen, M., 533
Cherry, E. C., 172, 280
Chess, S., 497, 539
Chi, M. T. H., 552
Chick, J., 248
Chilcoat, H, D., 658
Chippendale, L. A., 406
Chipuer, H. M., 400
Chivers, M. L., 470
Choderow, N., 516
Chomsky, C., 340
Chomsky, N., 330, 335
Chorney, M. J., 712
Christensen, A. J., 610
Christensen, K. A., 623
Christian, K. M., 243, 265
Christie, J., 44
Christman, C., 162
Christman, S. D., 154
Chudakov, B., 706
Chun, M. M., 147, 153, 162
Church, T. A., 518
Cialdini, R. B., 452, 745, 765, 769, 771, 772

Ciarrochi, J., 391
Cicero, T. J., 223
Citron, M., 709
Claar, R. L., 622
Claire, T., 412
Clancy, S. A., 314
Clapp, G., 272
Clarey, J. C., 168
Clark, D. M., 612
Clark, E. V., 337
Clark, J., 296, 364
Clark, L. F., 697
Clark, R. E., 243
Clark, R. W., 325, 326, 332, 362, 363, 366, 371, 372
Clark, S. A., 120
Clarke, G., 710
Clarke, G. N., 713
Clarke, J. C., 652
Claxton, L. J., 542
Clay, R., 623
Cleary, A. M., 309
Cleveland, H. H., 403
Clifford, D. B., 534
Cloninger, C. R., 502, 504
Cloninger, R., 502, 503
Clopton, N. A., 560
Clum, G. A., 709, 710
Coats, E. J., 342
Coe, W. C., 212
Coffey, C. E., 580
Cohen, A., 666
Cohen, B. H., 367
Cohen, C. I., 765
Cohen, D., 519, 574, 765
Cohen, H., 603
Cohen, J. D., 281, 362, 619
Cohen, L. G., 114
Cohen, M. R., 114
Cohen, N., 249, 401
Cohen, P., 569
Cohen, S., 598, 602, 603, 620
Cohen-Kerem, R., 534
Colado, M. I., 225
Colapinto, J., 557
Cole, G. G., 143
Cole, M., 18, 554, 564
Coleman, P., 580
Colle, M. P., 165
Collins, A. M., 291
Collins, J. E., 697
Collins, M. A., 760
Collins, N. L., 510, 522, 620
Collins, W. A., 566
Colom, F., 725
Colom, R., 398, 410
Colombo, J., 550
Colome, A., 334
Colomenero, J. M., 169
Colvin, C. R., 491
Comery, T. A., 120
Comings, D. E., 563
Compas, B. E., 603
Cone, E. J., 225
Congdon, N. G., 144
Conger, R. D., 256
Conn, J. H., 212

Conn, R. N., 212
Connell, M. W., 393
Connellan, J., 408
Connor, C. E., 145
Consortium for Longitudinal Studies, 411
Conti-Ramsden, G., 342
Conway, A. R. A., 172, 397
Conway, M. A., 291, 299, 300
Conway, T., 329
Conyers, C. 257
Cook, D. A., 726
Cook, E. W., III, 437
Cooke, A., 319
Coons, P. M., 670
Cooper, C., 397
Cooper, H. M., 220, 770
Cooper, J., 742
Cooper, M. L., 470, 471, 566
Cooper, R. P., 336
Cooper, S. J., 454
Coover, G. D., 243
Copinschi, G., 196
Coplan, J. D., 649
Copper, C., 71
Corbetta, M., 152, 153, 158
Corbit, J. D., 170, 431
Corchoran, C., 499
Coren, S., 197, 203
Corkin, S., 285, 293
Corley, R., 403
Cornblatt, B., 665
Cornelissen, P. L., 164
Cornelius, M. D., 534
Corr, P. J., 501
Correll, J., 749
Costa, P. T., 493, 515, 516, 576
Costa, P. T., Jr., 401, 492, 495, 517, 518
Costela, C., 540
Cotman, C., 580
Cotman, C. W., 580
Cotter, D. R., 87
Council, J. R., 212
Counter, S. A., 167
Counts, D. A., 579
Counts, D. R., 579
Coupland, N. J., 265, 652
Cowan, M. W., 119
Cowan, N., 280
Cowley, A., 160
Cox, H., 632
Cox, J. R., 368
Coyle, J. T., 664
Coyne, J., 646, 647
Crago, H., 149
Crago, M., 149, 342
Craig, I., 399
Craig, I. W., 113
Craik, F., 398
Craik, F. I., 572
Craik, F. I. M., 51, 286, 287
Cramer, R. E., 471, 762
Crandall, C. S., 412
Crawford Solberg, E., 439
Crawford, H. J., 212, 213
Crawford, M., 220, 765

Crawford, R. P., 420
Crawley, R. A., 313
Crick, F., 190, 191, 201, 229
Crick, N. R., 614
Crisp, A. H., 466
Crist, R. E., 147
Crits-Christoph, P., 687, 690, 720
Croen, L. A., 416
Crogan, M., 745
Croizet, J., 412
Croizet, J. -C., 412
Cronbach, L. J., 384
Crowe, R., 649
Crowley, K., 553
Crowley, S. J., 205
Crowther, J. H., 673
Cruz, A., 179
Cruz, C., 205
Csikszentmihalyi, I. S., 488
Csikszentmihalyi, M., 420, 440, 488
Cuijpers, P, 709
Culbertson, F. M., 638
Cullen, M. J., 413
Cummings, N., 442
Cunitz, A. R., 283
Cunningham, W. A., 444
Cupach, W. P., 759
Cupchik, G. C., 107
Curtiss, S., 341
Curtius, M., 314
Cutcomb, S. D., 213
Czirjak, S., 83

Dabbs, J. M., Jr., 516
Dackis, C. A., 103
Dadds, M. R., 242, 248
Dafters, R. I., 226
Dahloef, P., 208
Dai, X. Y., 407
Dalbert, C., 757
Daly, M., 514
Damasio, A., 445
Damasio, A. R., 372, 433, 439
Damasio, H., 331
D'Angelo, B., 596
Daniel, M. H., 390
Dannon, P. N., 227, 706
Dansinger, M. L., 465
Dar, Y., 567
D'Arcy, R. C. N., 331
Darley, J. M., 736, 778, 779
Darwin, C., 124, 429
Das, A., 120
Dauenheimer, D., 412
D'Augelli, A. R., 567
Daumann, J., 226
Davelaar, E. J., 283
Davey, G. C. L., 248
David, J. P., 610
Davidson, J. R. T., 724
Davidson, J. W., 107
Davidson, R. J., 7, 99, 216, 217, 431, 432, 435, 440, 444, 445, 500, 507, 643, 649, 738

Davies, P. G., 413
Davis, B. E., 542
Davis, C., 625
Davis, C. G., 600
Davis, D., 523
Davis, G. A., 421
Davis, H., 216
Davis, J. D., 459
Davis, J. H., 774
Davis, K. D. 100
Davis, M., 242, 437, 438
Davis, M. C., 579
Davison, G. C., 699
Dawda, D., 392
Dawson, D. A., 220
Day, N. L., 534
Deary, I. J., 384, 386, 388, 390, 396, 397, 400
De Benedittis, G., 213
De Beni, R., 572
DeBlack, S. S., 144
DeCasper, A. J., 533
De Castro, J. M., 461
De Catanzaro, D., 181
Decety, J., 351, 746
Deci, E. L., 439, 452
DeClue, G., 447
Deese, J., 307
Deffenbacher, J. L., 599, 600
De Gail, M., 777
Degarrod, L. N., 202
Degelman, D., 442
DeGroot, A. D., 362
de Haan, M., 538
Dehaene, S., 336, 359, 396
Dehaene-Lambertz, G., 170, 336
De Houwer, J., 245
de la Chica, R. A., 534
Delaney, S. L., 733, 738, 759, 766, 767
De Lisi, R., 408
Delk, J. L., 153
Dell, P. F., 670
DeLoache, J. S., 545
DeLongis, A., 596
DeLuca, C., 44
DelVecchio, W. F., 577
DeMann, J. A., 662
Demarais, A. M., 367
De Marchi, N., 403
Demb, J. B., 295
Dement, W. C., 196, 200
Demetriou, A., 553
de Muinck Keizer-Schrama, S. M. P. F., 562
Demuth, K. D., 42
Denis, M., 349
Dennett, D. C., 191
Dennis, W., 420
DePaulo, B. M., 447
DePietro, J. A., 535
Depue, R. A., 645
De Renzi, E., 154, 313
Derman, R. M., 248
Derryberry, D., 498
DeRubeis, R. J., 724

D'Esposito, M., 281
de St. Aubin, E., 576
DeSteno, D., 741, 750
DeSteno, D. A., 471
Detterman, D. K., 380, 390
Deutsch, G., 99, 408
Deutsch, J. A., 459
De Valois, K. K., 141
De Valois, R. L., 141
de Villiers, J. G., 339
de Villiers, P. A., 339
De Vincente, F., 244
Devine, P. G., 741, 749, 751
Devlin, J. T., 331
de Vries, B., 579
Dew, A. M., 760
Dewhurst, S. A., 291
de Wijk, R. A., 175
Dhume, V. G., 625
Di Pietro, M., 106
Diamond, L. M., 567
Diamond, M., 557
Diamond, M. C., 120
Diaz-Guerrero, R., 456
Diaz-Loving, R., 456
DiBlasio, F. A., 471
Dick, F., 336
Dickens, W. T., 409, 410
Dickenson, L. G., 620
Dickerson, S. S., 590, 594, 598
DiDomencio, L., 672
Diehl, S. R., 662
Diehm, R., 499
Diener, E., 431, 439, 491, 764
Dienstfrey, H., 249
Dietrich, A., 419
Diforio, D., 664, 666
DiGiuseppe, R., 600
Digman, J. M., 492
DiLalla, L. F. 540
Dill, P. L. 592
Dillard, J. P., 647
Dillbeck, M. C., 216
Dimberg, J., 445
Dinges, D., 196
Dion, K., 164
DiPietro, J. A., 533
Dittrich, W. H., 444
Dixon, J., 8
Dixon, M. R., 260
Dobbin, J. P., 596, 613
Dobson, M., 309
Dobson, R., 744
Docter, R. F., 475
Dodane, C., 336
Dodge, K. A., 567, 614
Doheny, M., 71
Dohnanyiova, M., 417
Dohrenwend, B. P., 665
Dohrmann, R. J., 265
Dolan, B., 673
Dolan, R., 102
Dolan, R. J., 291, 296, 372
Dolski, I., 443
Domar, A. D., 216
Dominey, P. F., 336
Domjan, M., 238

Donaldson, S. O., 765
Donk, M., 152
Doty, R. L., 176, 571
Double, D., 637
Dovidio, J. F., 8, 741, 747, 749, 777
Dowd, E. T., 616, 619
Dowling, J. E., 84, 139
Downes, J. J., 313
Downey, G., 646
Downing, J. W., 740
Dozier, M., 522
Drake, C. L., 197
Draycott, S. G., 493
Drayna, D., 173
Drevets, W. C., 644
Drewnowski, A. 178
Drid, M. D., 625
Driskell, J., 71
Druckman, D., 71, 214
Druckman, J. N., 369
Drummond, S. P. A., 197
Druss, B. G., 638
Duancey, K., 665
Dube, E. M., 567
Dubrovsky, V. J., 767
Duclaux, R., 460
Duclos, S. E., 435
Dudai, Y., 179, 285
Duff, K. J., 487
Duman, R. S., 644
Duncan, G. J., 556
Duncan, H. F., 149
Duncan, J., 398
Duncan, R. M., 554
Duncker, K., 357, 359
Dunnett, S. B., 460
Dunning, D., 757
Dupuy, B., 345
Durkin, K., 547
Durrheim, K., 8
Durso, F. T., 747
Dusek, D., 227
Dweck, C. S., 488
Dye, D. A., 492
Dye, R. H., 170

Eacott, M. J., 313
Eagly, A., 516
Eagly, A. H., 516, 614, 736, 738, 739, 763, 770
Eaker, E. D., 624
Eakin, E., 631
Eals, M., 408
Earle, T. L., 596
Eaves, L. J., 498
Ebbesen, E. B., 310
Ebbinghaus, H., 282, 310
Eberman, C., 309
Ebstein, R. P., 502, 503, 508
Eby, K. K., 613
Edelman, G. M., 191
Edelstein, R. S., 523
Eden, D., 411, 599
Eder, R. A., 557
Edgerton, R. B., 666
Edleman, G. M., 191

Edwards, J., 714
Edwards, V. J., 314
Effa-Heap, G., 470
Egbert, L. D., 619
Ehkers, A., 657
Eich, E., 305
Eid, J., 616
Eilers, A. T., 337
Eimas, P. D., 170
Einstein, A., 95, 347
Einstein, G. O., 287
Eisenberg, M., 285
Eisenberg, N., 510, 515, 776
Eisenberger, R., 452
Ekeberg, O., 216
Ekman, P., 429, 430, 435, 441, 447
Elaad, E., 447
Elber, T., 107, 396
Elenkov, I. J., 105
Eley, T. C., 643
Elfenbein, H. A., 431, 442
Eliez, S., 415
El-Islam, M. F., 666
Elkin, I., 712
Elkind, D., 565
Elliot, A. J., 749
Elliott, D., 678
Ellis, A., 697, 699
Ellis, A. L., 774
Ellis, A. W., 99
Ellis, B. J., 567
Ellis, H. C., 348, 365
Ellis, L., 473
Elman, J. L., 336
Elsayed-Elkhouly, S. M., 518
Elzinga, B. M., 669
Emerson, M. O., 753
Emmelkamp, P. M. G., 693, 700, 717, 723, 728
Emmons, R. A., 431
Emmorey, K., 343
Emrick, C. D., 248
Engel, S. A., 145
Engelberg, E., 392
Engle, R. W., 397, 398
Engvik, H. A., 517
Ensley, E., 456
Entwisle, D. R., 495
Enzmann, D., 599
Epley, N., 757
Epstein, C. M., 204, 706
Epstein, H. T., 553
Eranti, S. V., 205
Erdelyi, M. H., 305
Ericsson, K. A., 287, 362, 364
Erikson, D. H., 665
Erikson, K., 590
Ernst, M. O., 152
Eron, L. D., 272
Eshleman, J. R., 439
Eskenazi, B., 534
Estes, W., 370
Etcoff, N., 452
Etcoff, N. L., 333
Eubanks-Carter, C., 722
Evans, G. W., 591, 598

Evans, J. J., 387
Everitt, B., 452, 454, 455
Everitt, B. J., 101
Exner, J. E., 495
Exner, J. E., Jr., 496
Eyferth, K., 407
Eysenck, H. J., 397, 419, 493, 498, 501, 502, 507
Eysenck, S. B. G., 501

Fabbro, F., 344
Faber, S., 443
Fabiani, M., 113
Fagan, J. L., 407
Fairburn, C. G., 673, 712
Falkowski, W., 248
Fallon, A., 461
Fals-Stewart, W., 223
Fantino, E., 370
Fantino, M., 466
Farhi, P., 272
Farrar, W. T., IV, 328
Farroni, T., 544
Farthing, G., 200
Fast, K., 313
Fatt, I., 138
Fava, G. A., 724
Fawzy, F. I., 621
Fay, R. E., 472
Fazio, R. H., 740, 741, 748
Feather, N. T., 752
Febbraro, G. A. R., 710
Federmeier, K. D., 154
Feeney, B. C., 510, 620
Feigenson, L., 544
Feingold, A., 515, 736, 763
Feldman, D. H., 417
Feldman, J. B., 214
Feldman, R. S., 342, 445
Fell, J., 162
Felleman, D. J., 160, 166
Fenster, J. R., 589
Fenton, W., 661
Ferguson, N. B., 460
Fergusson, D., 703
Ferketich, A. K., 604
Fernald, A., 336
Fernandez, E., 600
Ferrier, S., 654
Ferris, G. R., 735
Ferveur, J. F., 118
Festinger, L. 741, 745, 769
Fiasse, L., 514
Ficca, G., 39
Ficker, J. H. I., 207
Field, A. E., 642
Field, A. P., 300
Field, T., 540
Field, T. M., 540, 550
Fields, R. D., 87
Fifer, W. P., 533
Figiel, G. S., 706
Fillenbaum, S., 153
Finch, A. E., 709
Fink, B., 163
Finke, R. A., 418

Finkel, D., 573
Finkelstein, J. W., 408
Finlay, F. O., 562
Finlay, K., 770
Finn, J., 710
Fiorentine, R., 709
Fiorillo, C. D., 263
Fischer, B., 398
Fischer, C., 225
Fischer, G. W., 750
Fisher, R. P., 287, 319
Fisher, S., 704
Fishman, H. C., 708
Fiske, S., 750, 753
Fiske, S. T., 455, 750
Fitch, R. H., 408
Fitton, A., 463
Fivush, R., 314
Flas, W., 151
Flaten, M. A., 624
Flavell, J. H., 551
Fleeson, J., 556
Fleischman, D. A., 572
Fletcher, A. C., 271
Fletcher, P. C., 296
Fleury, C., 464
Flexser, A., 305
Flood, D., 580
Floyd, M., 710
Floyd, R. L., 534
Flynn, J. R., 385, 406, 409, 410
Foa, E. B., 658, 693, 724
Foch, T. T., 498
Fodor, J. A., 8
Folkman, S., 588, 592, 593, 609, 610
Fombonne, E., 415
Fonagy, P., 690, 691, 711, 715, 716, 719, 720, 721
Fones, C. S. L., 651
Forbes, E. J., 621
Ford, C. S., 164
Ford, K., 467
Ford, T. E., 413, 613
Forgas, J. P., 761
Forge, K. L., 273
Forgione, A. G., 214
Forman, D. R., 560
Foster, G. D., 465
Fouts, G., 273
Fouts, R., 344
Fowles, D. C., 561
Fox, C. H., 534
Fox, E., 498, 500, 510
Fox, N. A., 499, 500, 509
Fox, W. M., 456, 488
Fozard, J., 571
Frackowiak, R. S. J., 191
Frak, V., 351
Fraley, R. C., 522, 523, 555
Frances, A., 637
Francis, J. R., 726
Francis, M. E., 611, 612
Frank, A. J., 409
Frank, M. E., 177
Frank, R. G., 631
Frank, R. H., 439

Franks, J. J., 331
Frant, D. L., 212
Fraser, L., 379, 394, 417
Fraser, S. C., 771
Frasure-Smith, N., 605
Frazier, P. A., 620
Fredrickson, B. L., 439, 440
Freedman, J. L., 771
Freedman, M. R., 465
Freedman, M. S., 140
Freeman, H., 665, 666
Freeman, J. H., Jr., 537
Freeman, W. J., 175
Freese, J., 514
Freitas, A. L., 456, 457
French, T., 688
Freud, A., 566
Freud, S., 200, 229, 467, 483, 484, 687
Fridlund, A. J., 435
Fried, P. A., 534
Friedler, G., 535
Friedman, M., 600
Friedman, M. I., 459
Friedrich, R. W., 175
Fries, M., 257
Friesen, C. K., 157
Friesen, W., 429, 430
Friesen, W. V., 447
Frischholz, E. J., 669
Frohlich, P. F., 470
Frye, D., 551
Fryer, R. G., 406, 407
Fryers, T., 414
Fujiwara, E., 313
Fulker, D. W., 400, 403, 503
Fuller, R. K., 248
Fuller, S. R., 775
Fulton, S., 463
Funder, D. C., 491
Fung, H. H., 578
Funk, S. C., 616
Funtowicz, M. N., 677
Furedy, J. J., 447
Furnham, A., 392, 393
Fuster, J. M., 291
Futterman, A. D., 248

Gabbard, G. O., 678
Gabrieli, J. D. E., 295, 572
Gaertner, S. L., 8
Gafni, N., 408
Gage, F. H., 580
Gagliese, L., 181
Gagné, F., 385
Galanski, E., 565
Galanter, M., 780, 781
Galdzicki, Z., 415
Gale, G. D., 243
Gallagher, M., 264
Gallaher, P. E., 343
Gallo, L. C., 599, 600
Gandour, J., 333
Ganey, R. F., 439
Gangestad, S., 763
Gangestad, S. W., 163, 469, 762
Ganis, G., 18, 351, 447

Garabino, S., 204
Garb, H. N., 496, 635
Garbarino, S., 204
Garcia, J., 246, 248
Garcia-Arraras, J. E., 202
Garcia-Fernandez, J-M., 139
Garden, S., 281
Gardner, B. T., 344
Gardner, H., 17, 296, 380, 382, 392, 393, 394, 396, 417
Gardner, R. A., 344
Garfield, S. L., 715, 716, 722, 726
Garfinkle, P. E., 673
Garg, P. K., 298
Garner, D. M., 672, 673
Garrard, P., 352
Garrido, E., 447
Garrigue, S., 207
Garris, P. A., 454
Garry, M., 309
Garvey, C., 340
Gaser, C., 107
Gaster, B., 703
Gater, R., 638
Gaudiano, B. A., 724
Gauthier, I., 156
Gazzaniga, M. S., 18, 98, 191
Geary, D. C., 408
Geary, N., 454
Geddes, J. R., 703
Gega, L., 712
Gegenfurtner, K. R., 142
Gehring, W. J., 372
Geinisman, Y., 297
Geiselman, R. E., 306, 319
Gellatly, A., 305
Gelles, R. J., 256
Gelman, R., 550
Gent, J. F., 175
Gentile, D. A., 272
Gentner, D., 332, 359
George, M. S., 447, 706
Gerstmann, J., 96
Gerteis, J., 739
Gerwig, M., 243
Gescheider, G. A., 170
Gesell, A., 542
Gesy, L. J., 780
Ghaemi, S. N., 646
Gibbons, J. A., 300
Gibson, J. J., 148, 543
Gibson, J. T., 774
Gick, M. L., 359, 624
Gidron, Y., 600
Gidycz, C. A., 442
Giesbrecht, B., 162
Gigerenzer, G., 358, 37, 147
Gilbert, D. T., 745, 747, 764
Gilbert, L. A., 269
Gilbert, S., 109

Gilbertson, M. W., 657
Gilger, J. W., 342
Gilligan, C., 515, 560
Gilliland, K., 501
Gillis, M. M., 724
Gilmore, J. H., 663
Giltay, E. J., 617
Ginandes, C., 214
Ginsborg, J., 339
Girdano, D. A., 227
Gissurarson, L. R., 182
Gladwell, M., 463, 464, 735
Glanzer, M., 283
Glaser, R., 105, 197, 604
Glass, D., 598
Glass, R. M., 706
Glennon, F., 757
Glisky, E. L., 572
Gloaguen, V., 723
Gluck, M., 102
Glucksberg, S., 332
Glutting, J. J., 406
Glynn, S. M., 696
Godden, D. R., 304, 305
Godemann, F., 238
Goedde, H. W., 122
Goel, V., 372
Goetestam, K. G., 697
Goethals, G. R., 742, 775
Goff, D. C., 664
Goldapple, K., 723
Goldberg, E., 96
Goldberg, L. R., 492
Goldblum, M. C., 345
Goldenberg, J., 421, 422
Goldfried, M. R., 722
Goldin-Meadow, S., 343, 344
Goldman, W. P., 360
Goldsmith, H. H., 678
Goldsmith, L. T., 417
Goldstein, A. 220
Goldstein, D. G., 358, 370
Goldstein, D. S., 89, 590, 591
Goldstein, M. D., 431
Goldstein, M. J., 725
Goldstein, N. J., 765, 769, 771
Goldstien, J. M., 663
Goldstone, R. L., 353
Gontkovsky, S. T., 403
Goodale, M. A., 153
Goodall, E. M., 463
Goode, E., 201, 202
Goodfellow, P. N., 531
Goodglass, H., 329
Goodie, A. S., 370
Goodman, N., 367
Goodman, R., 663
Goodwin, F. K., 420, 644, 646
Goodwin, R. D., 515
Gopnik, M., 342, 551
Gorcynski, R., 249
Gordon, A. H., 343
Gordon, N., 343
Gorman, J. M., 704
Gormican, S., 158
Gorski, R. A., 472
Gortner, E. T., 725

Gosling, S. D., 493
Gotlib, I. H., 500, 515, 644
Gottesman, I. I., 502, 662, 664, 665
Gottfredson, L., 386, 390
Gottfredson, L. S., 387, 389, 390, 395
Gottfredson, M. R., 566
Gottfried, J. A., 291
Gottlieb, G., 121
Gough, K., 248
Gould, E., 120, 532
Gould, J. L., 181
Gould, R., 576
Gould, R. A., 709, 710, 724, 725
Gould, S. J., 20, 126
Gouldner, A. W., 762
Grafen, A., 16, 364
Grammer, K., 442
Grant, B. F., 220
Grant, I., 534
Gratton, G., 113
Graves, L., 39
Gray, J. A., 500, 501
Gray, J. R., 372, 398, 400, 444
Gray, P. B., 469
Gray, R. W., 459, 460
Grayson, B., 442
Graziano, W. G., 507, 776
Green, A. R., 226
Green, B. G., 179
Green, D. E., 599
Green, D. M., 136, 167
Green, J. P., 306, 664, 665
Green, M. W., 225
Greenberg, B. D., 654
Greenberg, D. L., 299
Greenberg, J. R., 687
Greenberg, R. P., 704
Greene, K., 565
Greene, R. L., 309
Greenfield, P. M., 344, 408
Greenwald, A. G., 172, 748
Gregory, R. J., 710
Gregory, R. L., 150, 165
Grèzes, J., 351
Grice, H. P., 332
Grice, J. W., 471
Griepentrog, G. J., 545
Griffiths, T. D., 106
Griggs, R. A., 368
Grill-Spector, K., 145, 151
Grilly, D., 220
Grimshaw, G. M., 341
Grisaru, N., 706
Grissom, R. J., 718
Grodzinsky, Y., 329
Groleau, N., 44
Groman, J, M, 649
Gross, C. R., 216
Gross, J., 2612
Gross, J. J., 467, 577
Gross, P. H., 736
Grossarth-Maticek, R., 603
Grossberg, S., 146
Grossman, P., 216

Grossman, R. P., 245
Grotpeter, J. K., 614
Grotzer, T. A., 411
Gruber, A. J., 227
Grundy, S., 725
Grunes, M. S., 728
Grusec, J. E., 777
Guadagno, R. W., 771
Gudjonsson, G., 502
Guéguen, N., 777
Guelgoez, S., 456
Guerin, B., 776
Guilford, J. P., 360, 387, 395, 419
Guilleminault, C., 206
Guillery, B., 295
Guinn, J. G., 281
Gulick, W. L., 170
Gulya, M., 546
Gunewardene, A., 674
Gunn, V., 359
Gunnell, D., 703
Gunz, A., 519
Gureje, O., 223
Gustafsson, J.-E., 388
Gutchess, A. H., 572
Guth, W., 373
Guthrie, G. M., 258
Guthrie, R. M., 657
Guttmann, C. R. G., 570
Gyulai, L., 644

Haaga, D. A., 699
Haapasalo, J., 256
Habra, M. E., 605
Hackett, T. P., 624
Hadley, S. W., 711
Hafer, C. L., 758
Haggerty, R., 713, 714
Hahn, R. A., 624, 625
Haidt, J., 431, 501
Hakuta, K., 345
Halari, R., 408
Halberda, J., 544
Halford, J. C. G., 463
Hall, C. S., 237
Hall, D. T., 456
Hall, G. S., 566
Hall, J., 103, 243
Hall, J. A., 266, 343, 515
Halle, M., 327
Hallem, E. A., 175
Hallett, M., 114
Halmi, K., 673
Halpern, A. R., 173, 296
Halpern, D. F., 328, 408
Hamann, S., 438, 445
Hamann, S. B., 445
Hamberger, L. 533
Hamburg, P., 674
Hamer, D., 472
Hamer, D. H., 473
Hamilton, D. L., 750
Hamilton, M. E., 244
Hamilton, V. L., 599
Hampson, E., 408
Han, E. G., 207

Han, S., 159, 744
Haney, C., 767
Haney, M., 228
Hanges, P. J., 412
Hann, M., 156
Hansen, W. B., 765
Hansenne, M., 502
Hanson, K. A., 442
Hanson, M. A., 494
Hapidou, E. G., 181
Haraldsson, E., 182
Harandi, A. A., 214
Hardin, C. D., 749
Hardt, O., 296
Hardy, J. D., 600
Hardy, L., 71
Hare, R. D., 677
Harinath, K., 217
Hariri, A. R., 437
Harkins, S., 775
Harkins, S. G., 775
Harman, D., 570
Harmon-Jones, E., 613
Harris, C. L., 162
Harris, C. R., 471
Harris, G., 181
Harris, J. P., 150
Harris, J. R., 455, 551
Harris, R. J., 287
Harrison, L. J., 556
Harrison, P. J., 87
Harsch, N., 289
Hart, A. J., 746
Hart, B., 338, 339
Hart, H. C., 95
Hart, J., 43
Hart, K. E., 600
Hart, S. D., 392
Hartman, B. J., 169, 652
Hartung, C. M., 646
Hasegawa, I., 292
Hasher, L., 370
Hasler, G. 644
Hastie, R., 774
Hastorf, A. H., 739
Hatano, G., 287
Hatfield, E., 760
Hätinen, M., 599
Haug, H., 396
Hauri, P., 200
Hauser, M., 19, 538
Hausmann, M., 408
Havinghurst, R., 576
Hawkins, J. R., 531
Haxby, J. V., 151
Hayashi, T., 143
Haydon, P. G., 86
Hayflick, L., 570
Hayne, H., 546
Haywood, H. C., 554
Hazan, C., 487, 521, 522, 761
Heath, A. C., 498
Heatherton, T. F., 745, 746
Hebert, R., 313
Hecker, M., 600
Heckers, L. S., 665

Hedge, J. W., 494
Hedges, C., 753
Heeger, D. J., 113
Heel, R. C., 463
Hefco, V., 105
Heider, K. G., 474
Heilman, K. M., 419
Heimberg, R. G., 652, 724
Heinssen, R. K., 661
Heisel, M. J., 266
Heit, G., 110
Hekkanen, S. T., 308
Held, J. D., 407
Heller, K., 620
Hellige, J. B., 99, 154
Hellström, K, 711
Helms, J. E., 726
Hemsley, D. R., 665
Henderlong, J., 452
Hendricks, B., 777
Henley, N. M., 516
Henley, T. B., 592
Henrich, J., 373, 374
Henry, B., 502
Henry, J. P., 590
Henry, W. P., 690
Hensel, H., 180
Henslin, J. M., 7
Henson, R., 295
Heponiemi, T., 500
Hepworth, S. L., 547
Herbener, E. S., 760
Herbert, T. B., 602, 603
Herbst, J. H., 577
Herman, C. P., 461, 674
Herman-Giddens, M. E., 562
Hermann, J. A., 257
Hermelin, B., 415
Hernandez, P. J., 285
Herrera, H., 134,140, 147, 171
Herrnstein, R. J., 16, 384, 404, 406
Hertzog, C., 573
Herxheimer, A., 203, 208
Herz, M. J., 285
Herz, R. S., 305, 470
Herzog, T. A., 608
Hesketh, L. J., 415
Hespos, S. J., 557
Hess, T. M., 412
Hettema, J., 507
Hewstone, M., 777
Hierholzer, R., 656
Higgenbotham, H. N., 726
Higgens, S. T., 262
Higgins, E. T., 456, 457
Highnote, S. M., 140
Hilgard, E. R., 210, 212, 213, 214
Hilgard, J. R., 213, 214
Hill, J. O., 465
Hill, L., 399
Hillis, A. E., 329
Hillis, S. L., 216
Hines, M., 558
Hinton, D., 650

Hirokawa, E., 107
Hirsch, J., 405
Hirschi, T., 566
Hixon, J. G., 747
Hobson, J. A., 193, 195, 199, 200, 202, 206, 229
Hochman, D. W., 113
Hochschild, A., 623
Hockemeyer, J., 621
Hodgson, A. B., 710
Hoeks, J. C., 329
Hoeksama-van Orden, C. Y. D., 776
Hoffman, D. D., 152
Hoffman, L. W., 507
Hoffman, M. L. 561
Hoffman, R. E., 706
Hoffrage, U., 370
Hofstede, G., 518, 519
Hogan, J., 494
Hogan, R. T., 494
Hogg, M. A., 770
Hohlstein, L. A., 255
Hohman, G. W., 434
Holahan, C. K., 616
Holch, P., 314
Holcombe, A. O., 150, 152
Holden, C., 507
Holen, A., 217
Holland, A. L., 672
Holland, C. R., 407
Hollerman, J. R., 263, 452
Hollis, K. L., 241
Hollon, S. D., 699, 722, 723, 724
Holmes, D. S., 216
Holmes, T. H., 595
Holroyd, J., 703
Holyoak, K. J., 360
Hommer, D., 103, 263
Honeycutt, H., 509
Honeycutt, J. M., 761
Honig, A., 646
Honorton, C., 182
Honzik, C. H., 267
Hooley, J. M., 645, 665
Hooper, F. H., 552, 564
Hope, C. W., 600
Hopf, J. M., 158
Hopkins, W. D., 330
Horan, J. J., 621
Hore, B., 248
Horesh, N., 487, 650
Horn, J., 387, 388, 394
Horn, J. L., 387, 394
Horn, J. M., 515
Hornak, J., 439
Horney, K., 486
Horowitz, J. L., 557
Horowitz, L. M., 521, 522
Horowitz, M. J., 677
Horowitz, W. A., 415
Horton, R. S., 759
Horvath, P., 499
Horwath, E., 655
Hoshi, Y., 113

Hou, C., 415
Hou, C. E., 420
House, J., 619
Houston, B. K., 616
Houston, T. K., 713
Houtkooper, J. M., 182
Hovland, C. I., 744
Howard, R. W., 410, 414
Hsee, C. K., 647
Hsieh, L., 328
Hu, K., 203
Hu, W., 339
Hubacek, J. A., 298
Hubbard, B., 609
Hubel, D. H., 145
Huddy, L., 750
Huen, K. F., 562
Huerta, P. T., 297
Huff, D., 61
Huff, N. C., 242
Hugdahl, K., 99, 172, 249, 293
Hugenberg, K., 266, 747
Huichang, C., 499
Hull, J. G., 616
Hulse, S. H., 173
Hultman, C. M., 666
Hummel, J. E., 151, 360
Humphreys, G. W., 152, 153, 156, 159
Humphreys, K., 709
Hunt, E., 390, 393
Hunt, R. R., 365
Hunter, J., 385, 389, 390
Hunter, J. E., 385, 389
Hunter, R. F., 389
Huntjens, R. J. C., 669
Huppert, J. D., 711
Hur, Y., 503
Hurvich, L. M., 142
Husain, M., 145
Husain, M. M., 705
Hussain, S. M., 677
Huttenlocher, J., 367
Huttenlocher, P., 119
Huttunen, M., 400, 401
Hyde, K. L., 107
Hyde, T. S., 288
Hyman, A., 179
Hyman, S., 677
Hynes, G. J., 610

Iacoboni, M., 97
Iacono, W. G., 447
Iansek, R., 103
Ickes, W., 741
Ikemoto, S., 263
Imhoff, A, R., 623
Ingledew, D. K., 610
Inlow, J. K., 415
Inman, D. J., 196
Inouye, D. K., 511
Insel, T. R., 470, 654
International Human Genome Sequencing Consortium, 400
Intriligator, J., 158, 160

Inui, A., 463
Ione, A., 419
Ironson, G., 602
Irwing, P., 407
Isaacs, E. B., 341
Isaksen, S. G., 418
Isenberg, D. J., 774
Itkowitz, N. I., 253
Iver, F. L., 248
Iverson, J. M., 344
Ivry, R. B., 99, 104
Ivy, G., 571, 572, 580
Iyengar, S. S., 369
Izard, C. E., 435

Jackendoff, R., 327, 330
Jacklin, C. N., 558
Jackson, D. K., 44
Jackson, N., 417
Jackson, P. L., 746
Jackson, R., 397
Jackson, S. E., 775
Jackson, S. R., 145
Jacobs, G. D., 207
Jacobs, J. E., 565
Jacobs, N., 402
Jacobs, R. C., 765
Jacobsen, L. K., 225, 658
Jacobsen, T. W., 151
Jacobson, L., 410, 736
Jacoby, L. L., 572
Jadack, R. A., 560
Jaffee, S., 568
Jakobson, R., 327
James, F. O., 205
James, K. E., 151
James, L., 39, 200
James, L. E., 574
James, T. W., 151
James, W., 190, 432
Jameson, D., 142
Jameson, K. A., 140
Jamison, K. R., 420, 642, 644, 646, 680
Jamner, L. D., 618
Janata, P., 107
Jancke, L., 408
Jang, K. L., 507, 508
Janicak, P. G., 706
Janis, I. L., 775
Janowiak, J. J., 216
Janowsky, J. S., 408
Jansen, B. R. J., 553, 673
Jason, L. A., 257
Jeannerod, M., 351
Jenike, M., 654
Jenkins, H. M., 265
Jenkins, J. J., 288
Jenkins, J. M., 507
Jenkins, R. A., 249
Jenkins-Hall, K. 635
Jenner, P., 86
Jensen, A. R., 384, 385, 386, 388, 397, 398, 408, 710
Jerome, E. M., 522
Jevning, R., 215, 217

Jewett, D. L., 625
Ji, L-J., 370
Jindal, R. D., 725
Johansson, B., 571
Johns, M., 412
Johnsen, J., 248
Johnson, C., 750
Johnson, J. A., 495
Johnson, J. D., 222
Johnson, K. E., 337
Johnson, M. H., 151, 537
Johnson, M. R., 677
Johnson, S., 551, 552
Johnson, S. C., 299, 552
Johnson, S. L., 500, 646
Johnson, S. P., 544
Johnson, V. E., 467
Johnson, W., 386, 506, 576
Johnson-Laird, P. N., 367, 368
Johnston, L. C., 566, 747
Joiner, T., 440
Joiner, T. E., 646, 647
Jolicoeur, P., 162
Jones, D., 163
Jones, J., 339
Jones, M. K., 652
Jones, N. A., 540
Jones, R. W., 623
Jones, S., 463
Jonides, J., 80
Jordan, C. I., 473
Jorm, A. F., 409
Joseph, J., 506
Joseph, S., 440, 588, 618, 658, 757
Josephs, R. A., 222, 413
Joubert, S., 299
Joyce, C. A., 107
Jubinski, D., 399
Judd, C. M., 750
Judd, L. L., 639
Julesz, B., 148
Julius, D., 463
Jusczyk, P. W., 336

Kabat-Zinn, J., 216
Kac, G., 562
Kaelber, C. T., 642
Kagan, J., 403, 455, 464, 499, 500, 540, 545, 652
Kagan, R. M., 678
Kahn, R. L., 569, 570, 580
Kahneman, D., 369, 370, 371, 439
Kail, R., 552
Kaiser, C. R., 758
Kalantzi-Azizi, A., 616
Kalimo, R., 598
Kalish, R. A., 579
Kalivas, P. W., 454
Källén, B., 535
Kallio, S., 213
Kaltenthaler, , E., 710
Kameda, T., 774
Kamin, L., 241
Kamins, M. L., 488

Kampe, K. K. W., 452
Kanaya, T., 414
Kandel, E. R., 291, 295, 296, 311
Kane, H., 409
Kane, M. J., 398
Kaniasty, K. Z., 658
Kanner, A. D., 596
Kanwisher, N., 156
Kanwisher, N. G., 162
Kaplan, M. F., 775
Kaplowitz, P. B., 562
Karacan, I., 194
Karademas, E. C., 616
Karama, S., 470
Karasek, R. A., 598
Karau, S. J., 776
Kardes, F. R., 456
Karkowski, L. M., 644
Karlamangla, A. S., 591
Karni, A., 201, 229, 291
Karon, B. J., 496
Karpov, Y. V., 554
Karuza, J., 757
Kasch, K. L., 500
Kasper, S., 704
Kassin, S. M., 756, 772
Katigbak, M. S., 517, 518
Katona, I., 83
Katz, J., 181, 646
Katz, R., 613
Kauffmann, C. D., 706
Kaufman, F. R., 558
Kaufman, M. H., 534
Kaufman-Gilliland, C. M., 777
Kavanagh, D. J., 665
Kawachi, I., 605
Kawai, N., 214
Kawakami, K., 8
Kay, A. C., 374
Kay, D. A., 337
Kayed, N. S., 538
Kazdin, A. E., 715, 721
Keane, R. M., 603
Keane, T. M., 658
Keefe, R. S., 702
Keenan, J. P., 191
Keesey, R. E., 460
Kegl, J., 343
Keil, F. C., 551
Keith, P. M., 578, 661
Keitner, G. I., 642
Keller, A., 557
Keller, J., 412
Kellerman, I., 429
Kelley, A. E., 285
Kelley, H. H., 755, 763
Kelley, S. P., 144
Kelley, W. M., 284, 299
Kellogg, L. A., 344
Kellogg, W. N., 344
Kelman, H., 753
Keltner, D., 439, 445
Kemeny, M. E., 590, 594, 598
Kemp, D. T., 166
Kempermann, G., 120, 580

Kenardy, J., 712
Kendall, P. C., 717, 718, 721
Kendler, K. S., 506, 643, 644, 651, 662, 672
Kendrick, K. M., 155
Kennedy, M. M., 211
Kennedy, S. H., 643
Kenrick, D. T., 491
Kent, J. R., 704
Kerns, J. G., 362
Kerr, M., 540
Kerr, N. L., 775, 777
Kershaw, P., 248
Kertesz, A., 329
Keshavan, M. S., 663
Kessler, R. C., 631, 638, 650
Ketelaar, T., 374
Keys, A., 466, 673
Kidd, K. K., 342
Kiechel, K. L., 772
Kiecolt-Glaser, J. K., 105, 197, 602, 604, 620, 621, 623
Kiesler, C. A., 744
Kiesler, S. B., 744
Kiffel, C., 571
Kihlstrom, J. F., 181, 361
Kilham, W., 773
Killen, J. D., 510
Kim, H., 455
Kim, I. J., 350
Kim, J., 245
Kim, K. H. S., 344
Kim, M., 455
Kim, Y., 760
Kimata, H., 602
Kimble, G. A., 238
Kimhi, S., 567
Kimichi, R., 146
Kimura, D., 408
Kinde, W., 161
King, A. C., 207
King, D. P., 203
King, L. A., 713
King, S. A., 658
Kingdom, F. A. A., 140
Kingstone, A., 157, 162
Kinnuen, U., 762
Kintsch, W., 332
Kiper, D. C., 142
Kirby, L. D., 593
Kirchler, E., 774
Kirkcaldy, B., 499
Kirkmeyer, S. V., 178
Kirsch, I., 210, 212, 220, 241, 253, 704
Kirschvink, J. L., 181
Kisilvesky, B. S., 533
Kitayama, S., 518, 557
Kitchener, R. F., 554
Kitzmann, K. M., 708
Kivlighan, D. M., Jr., 687
Klaczynski, P. A., 565
Kleck, R. E., 157
Kleemeier, R. W., 571
Klein, D. F., 649
Klein, E., 706

Kleinman, A., 726
Klerman, E. B., 195
Klienknecht, R. A., 651
Kline, P., 493
Klingberg, T., 553
Klinkenborg, V., 195, 204
Klinteberg, B., 502
Klosko, J. S., 711
Knauth, P., 205
Knight, B. G., 623
Knoll, N., 609
Knox, S. S., 600
Knudsen, E. I., 341
Knutson, B., 103, 263
Kobak, R. R., 522
Kobasa, S. C., 616
Koch, C., 190, 191
Koch, M., 84
Kochanska, G., 560, 561
Kocovski, N. L., 651
Kocsis, J. H., 703
Koelling, R. A., 246, 248
Koenig, O., 8, 18, 152, 158, 365
Koestner, R., 452,
Kofalvi, A., 83
Koffka, K., 146
Koga, H., 581
Kohlberg, L., 559
Kohler, P. F., 603
Kohler, S., 151
Köhler, W., 268
Kohn, M. L., 401, 409
Kohut, H., 687
Kolata, G., 304, 605
Kolb, F. C., 160
Kondo, T., 473
Königstein, M., 373, 374
Konishi, S., 171, 358
Koob, G. F., 101
Kop, W. J., 600
Koren, D., 656
Koren, G., 534
Kosslyn, S. M., 8, 61, 65, 99, 115, 151, 152, 153, 154, 158, 191, 213, 296, 348, 349, 350, 351, 352, 365, 396
Koster, E. H. W., 612
Koutstaal, W., 305
Kovacs, I., 146
Kozak, M. J., 724
Kozel, F. A., 447
Kozhevnikov, M., 21
Kraepelin, E., 420
Krafft, K. C., 554
Kramer, M. S., 644, 703
Kranzler, J. H., 397
Krashen, S. D., 345
Krause, N., 580
Krebs, D. L., 560
Kreitzer, A. C., 83
Krieger, S., 664
Kring, A. M., 343
Kringelbach, M. L., 265
Kritchevsky, M., 312
Krosnick, J. A., 745

Krug, R., 469
Kruglanski, A. W., 455
Krumhansl, C. L., 107, 172, 173
Krummenacher, J., 158
Kubzansky, L. D., 605
Kuhl, P. K., 170, 336
Kuhlman, D. M., 499
Kuipers, E., 725
Kukla, A., 455
Kulhara, P., 661, 666
Kulik, J., 289
Kumari, V., 501
Kuncel, N. R., 389, 390, 395
Kunda, Z., 753
Kunde, W., 160
Kung, J., 244
Kuntze, M. F., 245
Kunz, G., 531
Kuper, H., 598
Kuperberg, G., 665
Kushner, M., 658
Kvale, G., 249
Kwong, M. J., 256

Labrell, F., 547
Lachman, M. E., 594
Lacks, P., 206
Laeng, B., 99, 153, 154
Lafuente, M. J., 535
Lai, C. S. L., 342
Laird, J. D., 435
Lakey, B., 620, 621
Lakin, J. L., 737
Lalich, J., 780
Lalumiere, M. L., 244
Lam, A. G., 726
Lam, R. W., 705
Lambert, A. J., 741, 750
Lambert, M. J., 691, 716, 717, 718, 720, 722
Lamm, C., 351
Land, E. H., 147
Landrigan, C. P., 197
Landsman, T., 488
Lane, H., 341
Lang, E. V., 213, 214
Lang, F. R., 578
Lang, P. J., 431, 433
Lange, A., 713
Lange, C., 432
Langer, E., 569, 580
Langer, E. J., 580
Lansford, J. E., 578
La Piere, R. T., 8, 43, 739
Lapsley, D. K., 565
Larson, J. A., 446
Larson, R., 566
Larson, S. A., 414, 431
Larurelle, M., 664
Laskin, D. M., 265
Lassiter, G. D., 456
Latané, B., 679, 774, 775, 778, 779
Laughlin, P. R., 774
Laursen, B., 566

Lautrey, J., 553
Law, G., 44
Lawler, K. A., 616
Lawless, H. T., 178
Lawrence, B. S., 775
Lawson, D., 169
Lazarus, R. S., 433, 588, 592
Lazerson, A., 208
Lazev, A. B., 244
Lê, S., 151
Leaper, C., 557
Leavitt, F., 314
LeBihan, D., 351
Leccese, A. P., 225
LeDoux, J. E., 98, 102, 103, 243, 265, 430, 433, 437, 644, 652
Lee, A. M., 673, 674
Lee, E. S., 401
Lee, J. L. C., 285
Lee, K. K., 248
Lee, M., 330
Lee, S., 672, 673, 674
LeeTiernan, S., 491
Leff, J., 665
Leffler, A., 767
Lefkowitz, E. S., 569
Legrenzi, P., 367, 725
Lehman, D. R., 744
Lehrl, S., 398
Leibowitz, H. W., 148
Leichsenring, F., 690, 720
Leigh, H., 618
Lemme, B. H., 569, 571, 574, 578, 579
Lennenberg, E. H., 341
Lennon, R., 515
Lensveldt-Mulders, G., 507
Lentz, R., 284
Lenz, J., 651
Leone, C., 456
Leopold, D. A., 191
Lepper, M. R., 369, 452
Leproult, R., 197
Lerner, J. S., 445, 592
Lerner, M. J., 757
Lesch, K., 502, 503, 508
Lesch, K. P., 503, 508
Leslie, Y. M., 697
Lester, B. M., 534
Lettich, E., 114
Leuchter, A. F., 704
Leuthold, H., 162
LeVay, S., 472
Levenson, R. W., 435, 612
Leventhal, G. S., 744
Levie, W. H., 284
Levin, D. T., 161
Levin, I. P., 456
Levin, J. R., 284
Levin, R. J., 468
Levin, R. S., 468
Levine, A. S., 462
Levine, B., 299
Levine, D. N., 151
Levine, J. A., 464
Levine, J. M., 764, 774, 775

Levine, L. J., 300
Levine, M. W., 459
Levine, R. L., 181, 570
Levinson, D. J., 576
Levitas, A., 415
Levitsky, D.K., 216
Levitt, A. G., 337
Levitt, M. J., 578
Levitt, S. D., 406, 407
Levy, B., 580
Levy, C. S., 531
Levy, S. M., 603, 618
Lewinsohn, P. M., 638, 645
Lewis, B., 342
Lewis, D. O., 670
Lewis, M., 557
Lewontin, R. C., 20, 126, 404
Li, D., 652
Li, N. P., 762
Li, S-C., 570, 572, 574
Libby, L. K., 300
Liben, L. S., 408
Licht, D. M., 645
Lichtenberg, P., 212
Lichtenberg, P. A., 212
Lickliter, R., 509
Liddell, C., 149
Lieberman, D. Z., 208
Lieberman, J. A., 663, 703
Lieberman, M. D., 745, 746
Light, L., 572
Lijam, N., 118
Lilienfeld, S. O., 496, 670
Lillard, A. S., 551
Lilnfeld, L. R., 672
Lin, E. L., 355
Lin, N., 640
Lindblom, K., 332
Lindemann, E., 578
Linden, M., 712
Lindley, R. H., 398
Lindsay, D. S., 309
Lindsay, P. H., 291
Lindsay, R. C., 303
Lindsay, S., 308
Lindstrom, T. C., 579
Lindsy, D. S., 309
Ling, D, 537
Linley, P. A., 440, 588, 618
Linner, B., 467
Linnoila, M., 502
Linton, M. A., 222
Linville, P. W., 750
Liotti, M., 643
Lipkus, I. M., 757
Lipsey, M. W., 718
Lipsitt, 537
Lipska, B. K., 664
Lipson, S. F., 469
Liss, M., 522
Lissek, S., 652
Lisspers, J., 605
Litt, M. D., 607
Liu, D., 540
Liu, J. H., 774
Livesley, W. J., 508, 677
Llinas, R. R., 191
Lobaugh, N. J., 545

Lobel, M., 617
Lobel, S. A., 775
Locke, A., 339
Locke, S. E., 603
Lockhart, R. S., 286
Lockley, S. W., 197
Loeb, S., 556
Loeber, R., 566
Loehlin, J. C., 498, 505, 506
Loewenstein, R. J., 668, 669
Loftus, E. F., 291, 307, 308, 309
Logan, J. M., 574
Logothetis, N. K., 145, 191
Loke, W., 169
Lomber, S. G., 120
Lonetto, R., 579
Long, J. M., 570
Longo, D. L., 249
Lonky, M. L., 87
Lonnqvist, J., 123, 400, 401
Lonsdale, C., 213
Looren de Jong, H., 8
Loori, A. A., 345
Lopes, P. N., 392
Lopez, A. D., 631
Lorenzo-Hernandez, J., 769
Losch, M., 741
Lott, B., 515, 516
Lou, H. C., 535
Lovell-Badge, R., 531
Low, J., 411, 547
Low, J. A., 533
Lowe, C. F., 262
Lowe, P., 615
Lowe, S. M., 133
Lowenstaum, I., 248
Lu, L., 440
Lubin, A. J., 638, 659, 680
Lubinski, D., 385, 388, 390
Luborsky, L., 717
Lucas, R. E., 439
Lucas, R. J., 140
Lucca, N., 518
Luce, G. G., 204
Luce, K. H., 710, 713
Luciano, M., 397
Luck, S. J., 160, 162
Luckow, A., 623
Lueck, C. J., 143
Luna, B., 564
Lunzer, E. A., 552
Luparello, T. J., 624, 625
Luria, A. R., 277, 278, 291, 304, 307, 309, 317
Lush, J. L., 400
Lutchmaya, S., 408
Lutz, A., 217
Lutz, C. J., 620, 621
Luwel, K., 553
Luxton, D. D., 612
Luyerink, M., 735
Luzzatti, C., 191
Lydiard, B., 677
Lydon, J. E., 760
Lykken, D., 440, 507
Lykken, D. T., 446, 507
Lynch, E. B., 353

Lynch, E. D., 168
Lynch, G., 297
Lynn, R., 407, 408, 410, 515
Lynn, S. J., 210, 220, 241, 253, 704
Lyon, H. M., 645
Lyons, E. A., 531
Lyons, L. C., 212
Lyons, M. J., 401, 506, 658
Lytton, H., 409
Lyubomirsky, S., 439, 440

Maany, I., 248
Maas, J. B., 206
Macaskill, N. D., 724
Macchi, M. M., 205
Maccoby, E. E., 558, 559
MacDonald, J. A., 136
MacGregor, A. J., 181
Macht, M., 461
Mackeben, M., 157
MacKinnon, D. P., 306
Mackintosh, N. J., 398
MacLaren, V. V., 446
MacLean, C. R. K., 216
Macmillan, M. B., 97
MacPhilamy, D. J., 645
Macrae, C. N., 299, 746, 747
Madden, K. S., 589
Maddi, S. R., 616
Madill, A., 314
Madison, L. S., 415
Madon, S., 737
Magee, W. L., 107
Magloczky, Z., 83
Magnusson, D., 491
Maher, B. A., 660
Maidhof, C., 704
Maier, K. J., 593
Major, B., 413
Major, B. N., 753
Makin, J. E., 534
Malan, D. H., 687
Malarky, W. B., 197
Malcolm, J., 473
Maletzky, B. M., 705
Malia, A., 200
Malik, M. L., 711
Malina, R. M., 563
Maliphant, R., 517
Manderino, J. V., 216
Mandler, G., 280
Manfro, G. G., 650
Mangan, B., 191
Mangun, G. R., 158
Mann, L., 773
Mann, S., 447
Mann, T., 673, 766
Manning, B. H., 83
Manning, J. T., 473
Manns, J. R., 285, 313
Mansour, C. S., 408
Manto, M., 104
Mantzoros, C. S., 464
Manuck, S. B., 602
Mao, H., 438
Maquet, P. 41

Marcel, A. J., 160
Marchetti, C., 281
Marci, C., 722
Marcia, J. E., 565
Marcus, G. F., 339
Marentette, P. F., 337
Mareschal, D., 151
Margolskee, R. F., 177
Marini, P., 86
Marinova-Todd, S., 345
Markham, R., 309, 445
Markovits, C., 427, 437, 449, 459, 467
Markowitz, J. C., 712
Marks, I., 693
Marks, I. M., 239
Markson, L., 337
Markus, H. R., 557
Markus, S. J., 32
Marlowe, F., 164
Marmot, M. G., 598, 623
Marmurek, H. H. C., 306
Maroun, M., 298
Marr, D., 8, 135, 145
Marrow, J., 644, 645
Marsh, R. L., 310
Marshall, D. H., 547
Marshall, D. S., 474
Martin A., 143, 284, 355
Martin, C. L., 558
Martin, L. L., 435
Martin, N. G., 506
Martin, R. A., 596, 612, 613
Martin, T., 515
Martindale, C., 418, 419
Martinez, C., 703
Martínez-Miranda, J., 372
Marucha, P. T., 197, 602
Marx, B. P., 716
Marx, D. M., 413
Marzi, C. A., 159
Masataka, N., 336
Maslach, C., 598, 599, 770
Maslow, A. H., 456
Mason, M. F., 157
Masters, W. H., 467
Masunaga, H., 387
Masuzaki, H., 464
Matarazzo, J. D., 381
Matheny, A. P., Jr., 506
Mather, M., 309
Matsumoto, D., 266
Matt, G. E., 716
Matthews, B. A., 262
Matthews, G., 391, 501
Matthews, K. A., 599, 600
Mattingly, J. B., 152
Mauch, D. H., 86
May, F. S., 657
Mayer, D. M., 412
Mayer, J. D., 391
Mayer, W., 44
Mayes, A. R., 313
Maynard, R. A., 567
Maznevski, M. L., 775
McAdams, D. P., 576
McArdle, J. J., 574

McBride, J., 529, 556, 562, 566, 576
McCallum, D. M., 616
McCarley, R. W., 201 202, 229
McCarrell, N. S., 304
McCarthy, R. A., 312, 355
McCartney, K., 121, 403, 507
McClearn, G. E., 117, 121, 124
McClelland, D. C., 455
McClelland, J. L., 365
McClintock, M. K., 176
McCloskey, M., 308
McClure, E. B., 515
McCord, J., 256
McCornack, S. A., 515
McCoy, N. L., 176, 177
McCrae, R. H., 401, 492, 495, 518, 519, 576
McCrink, K., 550
McDaniel, M. A., 287, 318
McDermott, K. B., 292, 307, 309
McDougall, W., 450
McDowd, J. M., 572
McEvoy, C., 308
McEwen, B. S., 298, 590, 591, 602
McFadden, D., 168,169, 473
McFarland, L. A., 413
McGaugh, J. L., 285, 288
McGillicuddy-De Lisi, A., 408
McGlashan, T., 661
McGoldrick, M., 726
McGorry, P. D., 714
McGraw, K., 203
McGraw, M. B., 542
McGue, M., 403
McGuffin, P., 502, 613, 647
McHugh, T. J., 297
McIntosh, A. R., 292, 299
McIntyre, R. B., 413
McKay, P. F., 413
McKellar, P., 348, 351
McKelvie, P., 411
McKelvie, S. J., 309, 370
McKenna, K. Y. A., 759, 765
McKenna, R. J., 463
McKnight, J., 473
McLaughlin, S., 177
McLean, A. A., 598
McLean, D. E., 535
McLeod, P. L., 775
McLoughlin, D. M., 705
McMillen, D. L., 777
McNally, R. J., 307, 314, 658
McNeill, D., 302
McRorie, M., 397
Mealey, L., 762
Meany, M. J., 540
Medin, D. L., 352, 353
Mednick, S., 197, 419
Mednick, S. A., 663, 678
Meehl, P., 634
Meertens, R. W., 748
Meesters, C., 523
Meeter, M., 285
Mehl, L. E., 213

Mehl-Madrona, L. E., 214
Mehta, B., 248
Meins, E., 551
Meister, I. G., 106, 173
Melding, P. S., 570
Melin, J., 169
Melin, L., 622
Mellet, E., 296, 351
Mello, C., 120
Meltzoff, A. N., 550
Melzack, R., 181
Mennella, R., 403
Menyuk, P., 337
Menzies, R. G., 652
Mercado, A. M., 197
Merchant, H., 21
Merckelbach, H., 670
Merfeld, D., 44
Merlo, A., 272
Merrick, E. N., 567
Merzenich, M. M., 120, 339
Messinger, S. M., 451
Meston, C. M., 470
Metcalfe, J., 360
Meyer, B., 500, 523, 612
Meyer, D. E., 333
Meyer, G. J., 496
Meyer, J., 65
Micallef, J., 654
Michael, T., 658
Michalski, R. L., 514
Michela, J. L., 755
Michimata, C., 99, 154
Mickelson, K. D., 761
Mignot, E., 206
Mikulincer, M., 453, 487, 522
Miles, L. E. M., 203
Milgram, S., 772, 773
Miller, A. G., 774
Miller, B. L., 415, 420
Miller, D. T., 765
Miller, E. M., 44, 645
Miller, G. A., 280
Miller, G. E., 602
Miller, I., 646
Miller, J. K., 713
Miller, J. M., 534
Miller, L. C., 471
Miller, L. K., 415
Miller, M., 613
Miller, M. G., 757
Miller, N., 614, 744
Miller, N. E., 595
Miller, R, 769
Miller, T. Q., 600
Miller, T. W., 780
Miller, W. B., 471, 600
Millet, B., 655
Millon, T. 634
Mills, D. L., 337
Mills, S., 344
Milner, A. D., 153
Milner, B., 102
Milner, P., 101, 454
Milton, J., 182
Mineka, S., 646, 652
Mingroni, M. A., 410

Minor, L. L., 417
Minors, D. S., 204
Minuchin, S., 708
Mischel, W., 258, 490, 491, 510
Mishkin, M., 151, 264, 296
Mitchell, D. L., 713
Mitchell, J. E., 712
Mitchell, J. F., 203
Mitchell, S. A., 687
Mitchison, G., 201, 229
Miyazaki, A. D., 599
Miyazaki, K., 173
Modell, J., 514, 654
Modestino, S., 44
Mogilner, A., 120
Mojtabai, R., 725
Moldin, S. O., 662
Moll, J., 746
Moller, J., 604
Money, J., 557
Mongrain, M., 266
Monk, T. H., 196
Monnier, P., 158
Monroe, S. M., 455, 645
Montague, P. R., 263, 265, 362
Monteith, M. J., 751
Montoya, R. M., 759
Moody, D. B., 170
Moore, A. B., 329
Moore, B. C. J., 171
Moore, M. K., 550
Moore-Ede, M., 204
Moran, P., 677
Moreland, R. L., 759, 764, 774, 775
Morf, C. C., 615
Morgan, A., 71
Morgan, C. A., III, 590
Morgan, J. L., 42
Morgan, M. A., 243
Morgan, M. J., 281, 590
Morgane, P. J., 534
Mori, H., 531
Morin, C. M., 206, 207
Morling, B., 623
Morris, A. L., 162
Morris, C. D., 287
Morris, E. K., 262
Morris, J., 102
Morris, L. A., 622
Morris, M. W., 757
Morris, R., 297
Morris, R. L., 182
Morris, S., 320
Morris, W., 769
Morris, W. N., 769
Morrison, A. P., 714
Morrison, K., 719, 726
Morrison, K. H., 720
Morse, D. R., 216
Mortensen, P. B., 665
Moscovitch, M., 287
Moscowitz, J. T., 593
Moser, M., 604
Moskowitz, D. S., 516
Moskowitz, J. T., 609, 610

Moss, M. B., 572
Mowrer, O. H., 652
Mrazek, P., 713, 714
Mroczek, D. K., 596
Muehlenhard, C. L., 222
Mueller, C. J., 443
Mul, D., 562
Mullen, B., 750, 775
Mulvany, F., 665
Mumford, M. D., 421
Münte, T. F., 107, 108
Murata, K., 535
Muris, P., 523
Murnigham, J. K., 373
Murphy, C., 175
Murphy, F. C., 434
Murphy, G. L., 355
Murphy, L. C., 499
Murphy, L. J., 713
Murphy, S. M., 70, 71
Murray, C., 384, 406
Murrary, C. J. L., 631
Murray, E. J., 716
Murray, I. R., 415
Murre, J. M. J., 285
Murzynski, J., 442
Myers, C., 102
Myers, C. E., 268
Myers, D. G., 439, 440, 761
Mylander, C., 343

Nadel, L., 296
Nader, K., 285, 454, 455
Nadler, J., 272
Nagahama, Y., 159
Nagel, E., 8
Nagy, Z., 553
Naito, T., 537
Nakai, Y., 674
Nakamura, J., 420
Nakamura, M., 454
Nakamura, Y., 181
Nakatani, E., 728
Nakayama, K., 135, 145, 157
Nanda, S. B. R., 428, 453
Napa Scollon, C., 400, 401
Nasby, W., 614
Nathawat, S. S., 455
National Admissions to Substance Abuse Treatment Services, 228
National Alliance for Caregiving and American Association of Retired Persons, 596
National Heart, Lung, & Blood Institute, 207
National Institute on Drug Abuse, 219, 225, 227
National Sleep Foundation, 196
Natsoulas, T., 190
Navarro, A. M., 716
Nawrot, M., 150
Nayatani, Y., 143
Neale, M. C., 498,
Neel, R. G., 455

Neiderhiser, D., 248
Neisser, U., 289, 302, 396, 401, 403, 405, 406, 409, 411
Neitz, J., 142
Nelson, A., 546
Nelson, C. B., 223
Nelson, K., 337
Nelson, L. J., 569
Nemec, P., 181
Nemeroff, C., 461
Nemeroff, C. J., 672
Nemeth, P., 612
Nestler, E. J., 119 ,644
Nettelbeck, T., 397, 410
Neubauer, A. C., 397
Neugebauer, R., 534
Neuman, J. H., 599
Neumann, C., 664
Nevid, J., 534
Neville, H. J., 169
Newcomb, M. D., 557
Newcombe, N., 409
Newcombe, N. S., 313
Newcomer, J. W., 591
Newman, A. J., 344
Newman, J., 411
Newman, J. P., 614
Newman, L. S., 487
Newman, M. G., 712
Newman, M. L., 413
Newsome, G. L., III, 365
Newsome, W. T., 114
Newton, P. M., 200
Newton, T. L., 620, 623
Nezu, A. M., 613
Nezworski, M. T., 496
Ng, V. W. K., 151
Nguyen, S. P., 355
NICHD Early Child Care Research Network, 556
Nichelli, P., 365
Nichols, R. C., 315, 419
Nicholson, D. A., 537
Nickerson, K. J., 405
Nicoll, R. A., 84, 227
Niedenthal, P. M., 445, 522
Nielsen, T. A., 200
Nigg, J.T., 678
NIH Technology Assessment Panel, 622
Niles, S., 457
Nilsson, L., 533
Niparko, J. K., 169
Nisbett, R. E., 406, 462, 765
Noble, E. P., 399
Nocks, J. J., 248
Nodelmann, P., 149
Nolan, S. A., 646
Nolen-Hoeksema, S., 644, 645
Noll, J., 387
Norcross, J. C., 606, 607, 716
Norem, J. K., 617
Norem, J. N., 617
Norman, D. A., 279, 291
Norman, G. R., 358
Norris, A. E., 467
Norris, F. H., 658

Nosek, B. A., 741
Nougaim, K. E., 456
Nowak, M. A., 374
Nowakowski, R. S., 532
Nuechterlein, K. H., 665
Numeroff, R. E., 599
Núñez, J. P., 244
Nurnberger, J. I., 643
Nyberg, L., 110, 292
Nye, R. D., 483
Nyklicek, I., 618

Oakland, T. D., 409
Oberauer, K., 398
O'Brien, C. P., 103
O'Brien, L. T., 412, 413, 753
Ochsner, K. N., 443, 745
O'Conner, T. G., 522
O'Connor, D. B., 623
O'Doherty, J., 163, 263, 452
Oei, T. P. S., 724
Ogles, B. M., 716, 717, 718, 720
O'Grady, W., 330
Ohayon, M. M., 204
Öhman, A., 238, 437
Oishi, S., 439, 518
Ojemann, G. A., 114
Ojemann, J., 114
O'Keefe, J., 296
Okello, E. J., 313
Okonkwo, R. U. N., 560
Okubo, M., 154
Okubo, Y., 663
Olczak, P. V., 747
Olds, J., 101, 454
O'Leary, S. G., 755
Oleson, K. C., 753
Olson, C. R., 145
Olson, I. R., 147
Olson, J. M., 507
Olson, M. A., 740, 741
Olsson, A., 438
Olton, R. M., 360
Oman, C. M., 44
Oosterveld, P., 517
Orbach, I., 522
O'Reilly, R. C., 243, 263, 362
Organ, D. W., 494
Orive, R., 769
Ornish, D., 605
Ornstein, R., 215
Orr, S. P., 657
Orth, M. H., 687
Orth-Gomér, K., 620
Osawa, K., 287
Osborn, D. R., 163, 164
Osherow, N., 754
Osherson, D., 367
Osmon, D. C., 397
Ost, J., 314
Öst, L.-G., 711
O'Sullivan, C. S., 747
Otomo, K., 337
Otto, M. W., 724
Ouimette, P. C., 222
Overmeier, J. B., 453, 593

Owen, M., 399
Owen, N., 599
Owens, L., 567
Oyserman, D., 457
Ozer, D. J., 494, 657

Pacak, K., 590
Padgett, T. M., 447
Páez, D., 612
Pagano, R. R., 217
Pagliari, 390
Pagnoni, G., 103
Paivio, A., 284, 317
Palace, E. M., 436
Palkovits, M., 590
Palladino, P., 572
Palmer, S. E., 146, 153
Panagopoulos, A., 160
Pandolfo, M., 104
Panksepp, J., 263, 430
Pantelis, C.,663
Pantev, C., 108, 396
Pantelis, C., 663
Papaleloudi, H., 341
Papp, L. A., 649
Pappenheimer, J. R., 202
Paquette, V., 693
Paradis, M., 345
Parducci, A., 625
Park, C. L., 589, 609
Park, D. C., 574
Park, J. H., 777
Parker, A., 305
Parker, D. J., 244
Parkin, A. J., 313
Parks, K. A., 223
Parks, M. R., 515, 759
Parpura, V., 86
Parrish, M. W., 70, 71
Pasanen, E. G., 473
Pascalis, O., 546
Pascual-Leone, A., 114
Pascual-Leone, J., 553
Passingham, D., 281
Pasupathi, M., 300
Patel, S., 227
Patel, V., 640
Patnoe, S., 754
Pato, M. T., 654
Paton, C. C., 600
Patterson, T. L., 623
Patterson, G. R., 678
Paulhus, D. L., 494
Pauli-Pott, U., 540
Paunonen, S. V., 492, 517
Paus, T., 158
Pavlov, I. P., 236
Pawelski, J. O., 440
Paykel, E. S., 724
Payne, B. K. 748, 749
Payne, B. R., 120
Payne, D. G., 305
Payne, D. L., 339
Peake, P. K., 490
Pearson, S. E., 470
Pecher, D., 328
Pedersen, W. C., 471

Pederson, C. L., 298
Pederson, W. C., 471
Pedreira, M. E., 286
Pekala, R. J., 621
Pelletier, C. L., 107
Pena, M., 170
Penfield, W., 114, 311
Peng, K., 757
Pengilly, J. W., 616, 619
Pennebaker, J. W., 611, 612, 716
Penner, L. A., 777
Penton-Voak, I. S., 469
Perdue, C. W., 752
Perera, S., 613
Peretz, I., 106, 107
Perez Y Perez, R., 422
Pérez, J., 500
Perez-Cuesta, L. M., 286
Peristein, W. M., 281
Perkins, D. N., 411
Perlmutter, M., 574
Perlow, L., 777
Perna, F. M., 621
Perot, P., 114
Perret, Y., 414
Perrett, D. I., 163, 469
Perry, B. D., 669
Persico, V, R., Jr., 579
Peterhans, E., 146
Peters, A., 604
Peters, J. C., 464
Peters. M. L., 596
Petersen, A. C., 566
Petersen, R. C., 228
Peterson, C., 645
Peterson, I., 304
Peterson, R. A., 650
Petit, L., 296, 351
Petitto, L. A., 344
Petrides, K. V., 392
Petrie, K. J., 203, 208, 612
Petrill, S. A., 399
Petrovic, P., 181, 622
Pettigrew, T. F., 748, 753
Pettit, G. S., 567, 738, 744, 745, 775
Petty, R., 745
Peyron, C., 206
Pezdek, K., 308
Pfaffmann, C., 177
Phan, K. L., 435
Phelps, E., 287
Phelps, E. A., 9, 438, 746
Phelps, J. A., 402
Phemister, S., 273
Philipson, T. J., 464
Phillips, C., 328
Phillips, D. P., 602
Phillips, K., 506
Phillips, S. D., 623
Piaget, J., 269, 545
Pickering, A. D., 501
Pickles, J. O., 166
Pickrell, J. E., 307
Pietromonaco, P. R., 623
Pihl, R. O., 222

Pillard, R. C., 473
Pillutla, M. M., 373
Pincus, A. L., 494
Pine, D. S., 257
Pinel, E. C., 413
Pinel, J. P. J., 179
Pinel, P., 360
Pines, A. M., 599
Pinhey, T. K., 440
Pinker, S., 19, 148, 325, 327, 330, 335, 339, 340, 341, 342, 343, 344, 352, 450
Pinkerman, J. E., 496
Pinsky, J., 624
Pinto, L. H., 203
Pirke, K. M., 673
Pitino, L., 176, 177
Pitman, D. L., 595
Pitre, N., 709
Pizzagalli, D. A., 242
Plailly, J., 175
Plaks, J. E., 747
Plant, E. A., 364
Plata-Salaman, C. R., 178
Platt, L. A., 579
Plattsmier, H. S., 168
Plaut, D. C., 334
Plehn, K., 650
Ploghaus, A., 181
Plomin, R., 117, 121, 123, 124, 342, 399, 400, 404, 497, 498, 502, 507, 523, 533, 573, 618, 633, 647, 761
Plotkin, H., 19, 450
Ployhart, R. E., 413
Podd, J., 241
Pokela, E., 256
Polaschek, D. L. L., 309
Poldrack, R. A., 296
Poldrak, R. A., 110
Polivy, J., 674
Polkey, C. E., 341
Pollack, H. A., 534
Pollack, R. H., 470
Pollock, V. E., 678
Pope, K. S., 314
Porter, R. C., 103
Porter, R. H., 538
Posner, M. I., 110, 112
Posner, R. A., 464
Posthuma, D., 397
Postmes, T., 764, 775
Poston, W. S. C., 463
Poulet, E., 706
Poulton, R., 652
Powell, M. C., 740
Prabhakaran, V., 398, 399
Prapavessis, H., 769
Prasada, S., 368
Prather, D. C., 71
Pratt, M. W., 554
Prescott, C. A., 506
Prescott, J., 178
Pressley, M., 316
Pressman, E. K., 535
Preut, R., 408
Prickett, T., 735

Prien, R. F., 703
Priester, J. R., 744
Priluck, R. L., 245
Prince, V., 475
Privette, G., 488
Prochaska, J. O., 606, 607, 608
Proctor, R. W., 262, 597
Proksch, J., 169
Proudfoot, J., 710
Przeworski, A., 712
Przybyla, D. P., 470
Pujol, R., 533
Puka, B., 559
Pulkkinen, L., 762
Putnam, F. W., 669, 670
Putnam, H., 8

Qin, Y., 564
Quadrel, M. J., 565
Quay, H.C., 678
Quigley, K. S., 435
Quinn, P. C., 544
Quinsey, L., 244

Raag, T., 558
Rabin, M. D., 175
Rabinowitz, F. E., 777
Rachman, S., 654
Rackliff, C. L., 558
Radvansky, G. A., 572
Raemae, P., 281
Ragusea, A. S., 713
Rahe, R. H., 595
Rahman, Q., 266
Raichle, M., 110, 112
Räikkönen, K., 535, 600
Raine, A., 401, 502
Rainville, P., 181
Rajaram, S., 287
Rakic, P., 532
Ramachandran, V. S., 120
Ramamoorthy, Y., 226
Ramel, W., 216
Ramey, C. T., 411
Ramirez, M., III, 726
Ramos, B. M. C., 244
Ramos-Grenier, J., 726
Rankinen, T., 463
Rao, H., 151
Rao, S. C., 151
Rapee, R. M., 652
Rasmussen, T., 114
Rassin, E., 612
Ratliff-Schaub, K., 542
Ratner, R. K., 765
Rauch, S. L., 654, 657
Raudenbush, S. W., 411
Rauscher, F. H., 411
Raven, J. C., 398
Ravussin, E., 463, 464
Ray, W. J., 212
Raye, C. L., 309
Raymond, J. E., 162
Rayner, R., 238, 239
Raz, A., 210
Raz, N., 572
Razpurker-Apfeld, I., 146

Razran, G. H. S., 245
Reber, P. J., 312
Rector, N. A., 725
Redd, W. H., 248
Reed, M. A., 498
Reed, T. E., 397
Reeler, A., 227
Reese, H. W., 419
Reeve, C. L., 390
Regan, D. T., 740
Regan, P. C., 469
Regehr, W. G., 83
Regier, D. A., 631, 642, 653
Reid, J. E., 446
Reid, R. C., 141,142
Reid, W. J., 678
Reif, A., 502, 503, 508
Reifman, A., 641
Reinberg, A., 205
Reinisch, J. M., 409
Reis, H. T., 759, 761
Reis, V. A., 163
Reise, S. P., 494
Reisenzein, R., 432
Reiss, A. L., 415
Rende, R., 633, 647
Rensink, R. A., 162
Repetti, R. L., 598
Rescorla, R. A., 241
Resinger, E., 704
Resnick, H. S., 656, 657
Resnick, S. M., 572
Ress, D., 113
Rest, J. R., 559
Restifo, L. L., 415
Revell, L. J., 447
Revonsuo, A., 213
Reynolds, C. F., 196
Reynolds, C. F., III, 711, 723
Reynolds, D. K., 579
Reznick, J. S., 498
Rhine, J. B., 182
Rhine, L. E., 182
Rhodes, G., 156
Rhodewalt, F., 615
Rice, C. L., 748
Rice, G., 473
Rice, M. E., 271
Rich, A. N., 152
Richards, A., 372
Richards, J., 710
Richards, J. C., 65
Richards, J. M., 444
Richards, M. H., 566
Richards, W. A., 152
Richardson, D., 613
Richert, E. S., 417
Richman, W. A., 550
Richmond, B. J., 452
Richmond, L. J., 780
Richter, C. P., 451
Richter-Levin, G., 298
Riddoch, M. J., 151
Rilling, J. K., 777
Rinaldi, M. C., 333
Riordan-Eva, P., 144
Rips, L., 353

Rips, L. J., 352
Risley, T. R., 338, 339
Ritchey, A. K., 602
Ritson, B., 248
Ritterband, L. M., 710
Rivas-Vazques, R. A., 704
Rivera, G., 165
Rivera-Arzola, M., 726
Rizzo, M., 157
Robbins, T. W., 101, 103, 265
Roberson, D., 348
Roberti, J. W., 503
Roberts, A. H., 622
Roberts, B. W., 491, 577
Roberts, D. J., 109
Roberts, L. D., 759
Roberts, N. A., 439
Roberts, R. D., 391
Robertson, L. C., 99
Robins, C. J., 640
Robins, L. N., 653
Robins, R. W., 431
Robinson, A. J., 546
Robinson, J. L., 540
Robinson, L. A., 644
Robinson, L. C., 567
Robinson, N. M., 409, 416
Robinson, S. J., 473
Robinson, T. E., 263, 455
Robinson, T. N., 272
Robinson, V., 612
Robinson-Whelen, S., 617
Robles, T. F., 620
Rochat, P., 557
Rodier, P., 152
Rodin, J., 569, 580, 674
Rodriguez, V., 159
Roediger, H. L., III, 292, 307, 308, 309, 318, 319
Roehrs, T. A., 197
Rogers, P. J., 757
Roggman, L. A., 556
Rohde, P. A., 514
Rohrmann, S., 618
Rojas, I. G., 602
Roll, S., 770
Rollman, G. B., 181
Rolls, B. J., 460, 461
Rolls, E. T., 452
Romach, M. K., 223
Romani, G. L., 168
Romero, A. A., 745
Romero, L., 590
Romin, R., 502
Romney, D. M., 409
Roozendaal, B., 298
Ropner, R., 248
Rosch, E., 347, 352, 355
Rosen, A. C., 158, 572
Rosen, C. M., 505
Rosenbaum, J. F., 224
Rosenberg, M., 557
Rosenblum, L. D., 171
Rosengren, A., 604
Rosenhan, D. L., 634
Rosenheim, M. K., 568
Rosenkranz, M. A., 440

Rosenman, R., 600
Rosenthal, A. M., 778
Rosenthal, R., 52, 61, 182, 343, 410, 411, 736
Rosenzweig, P., 625
Rosip, J. C., 343
Roskill, M., 629, 630
Rosner, M., 44
Ross, C. A., 669
Ross, C. E., 439
Ross, L., 756
Ross, M., 757
Ross, S., 622
Rossi, E. L., 211, 213
Roth, A., 690, 691, 711, 715, 716, 719, 720, 721
Roth, B. J., 114
Rothbart, M. K., 498
Rothbaum, B. O., 693
Rotter, J. B., 511
Rouhana, N. N., 757
Rouillon, F., 648, 650
Rouse, S. V., 495
Roux, A. V. D., 600
Rovee-Collier, C., 545, 546
Rowe, J. W., 569, 570, 580
Rowling, J. K., 380
Roy, R., 567
Roy, S., 44
Royet, J., 175
Roysamb, E., 507
Rozin, P., 80, 179, 431, 461
Rubin, D. C., 289, 299
Rubin, K., 509
Rubin, K. H., 499, 524
Rubin, L. J., 314
Rubin, Z., 760
Ruble, D., 558
Ruby, P., 746
Rudman, L. A., 740, 741
Rudy, J. W., 242, 243, 263, 285
Ruiz, C. J., 178
Ruiz, J. M., 600
Rumelhart, D. E., 355, 365
Runco, M. A., 395, 418
Rupniak, N. M., 703
Rush, A. N., 537
Rushton, J. P., 271, 396, 405
Russell, J. A., 433, 444
Russell, M. J., 176
Russell, R., 163
Russo, J. E., 369
Rustemli, A., 750
Rutledge, T., 619
Rutter, M., 117, 121, 124
Ryan, A. M., 413
Ryan, C. F., 228
Ryan, K., 494
Ryan, K. E., 413
Ryan, R. M., 439
Rymer, R., 341
Ryner, L. C., 118
Rynes, S. L., 254, 775
Ryska, T. A., 621

Sabini, J., 467
Sabourin, M. E., 213

Sacco, W. P., 635
Sachs, J. S., 331
Sackeim, H. A., 705, 706
Sackett, P. R., 406, 494
Sacks, O. 165
Sadler, T. W., 533
Sadowski, C. J., 456
Sadr, J., 156
Saffran, J. R., 336, 545
Saggino, A., 493
Sagi, A., 522, 523
Sagi, D., 291
Sagie, A., 457
Saha, L. J., 8
Sakai, K., 281
Sakai, N., 179
Saldana, H. N., 171
Saletan, W., 768
Salmon, C. A., 514
Salovey, P., 391, 471
Salthouse, T. A., 387, 571, 572, 574
Sameshima, K., 120
Samoluk, S. B., 255
Sampaio, E., 179
Sanbonmatsu, D. M., 740
Sand, G., 599
Sanders, S. A., 409
Sandhal, C., 723
Sanfrey, A. G., 373
Sangoram, A. M., 203
Santarelli, L., 703
Santha, E., 83
Sanudo-Pena, M., 83
Sapirstein, G., 704
Sapolsky, R., 590, 591
Sapolsky, R. M., 197, 298, 590, 595, 597, 619
Sarbin, T. R., 212
Sargent, J. D., 272
Sargent, P. A., 463
Saroglou, V., 514
Saudino, K. J., 498, 505
Savage, M., 739
Savage-Rumbaugh, S., 344
Savazzi, S., 159
Saxe, G. B., 553
Saxe, M. D., 703
Saxena, S., 654
Scarmeas, N., 574
Scarr, S., 121, 400, 403, 407, 507, 556
Schab, F. R., 175
Schachter, S., 435, 679
Schacter, D. L., 102, 268, 292, 294, 295, 296, 305, 309, 310, 314, 572, 746
Schaefer, S. M., 443
Schafer, R. B., 578
Schaffer, M. M., 353
Schaffner, K. F., 8
Schaie, K. W., 573, 574, 576
Schaller, M., 777
Schank, R. C., 355
Scharf, M., 569
Schaufeli, W. B., 599
Scheflin, A., 314

Scheier, M. F., 486, 616, 617, 618
Schein, E. H., 780
Schellenberg, E. G., 411
Schiavi, R. C., 470
Schifano, F., 226
Schiffman, S. S., 462
Schilder, P., 201
Schlaepfer, T. E., 706
Schlaug, G., 107, 173
Schlenker, B. R., 734
Schloth, E., 166
Schmader, T., 412, 413
Schmajuk, N. A., 663
Schmeck, H. M., Jr., 590
Schmid, W., 107
Schmidt, F. L., 385, 389, 390
Schmidt, H., 150, 152
Schmidt, N. B., 650, 714
Schmidt, S. R., 290
Schmidt, W. J., 103
Schmitt, B. H., 776
Schmitt, D. P., 19, 522
Schmolck, H., 289
Schneider, L. H., 454
Schneider, M., 84
Schneider, W., 294
Schoemaker, P. J. H., 369
Schofield, P. E., 769
Scholnick, E. K., 552
Schön, D., 107
Schooler, C., 401, 409
Schooler, J. W., 305
Schotter, A., 272
Schrof, J. M., 638
Schul, R., 179
Schulenberg, J., 220
Schultz, W., 638
Schulze, R., 397
Schvaneveldt, R. W., 333
Schwartz, C. E., 500
Schwartz, J. E., 619, 728
Schwartz, N., 372, 439
Schwarz, N., 44
Schwarzer, R., 609
Schweiger, A., 625
Schyns, P., 439
Sciaraffa, M. A., 558
Scicli, A. P., 242
Sclafani, A., 460
Scogin, F., 709
Scott, B., 622
Scott, G., 421
Scott, J., 645
Scott, S. K., 445
Scott, T. R., 178
Searle, J. R., 190
Sears, R., 554
Sedikides, C., 518
Seely, E., 471
Seeman, R. E., 619
Seeman, T. E., 591, 620
Segal, E., 360
Segal, N. L., 505, 507
Segal, Z. V., 721
Seger, C. A., 418
Segerstrom, S. C., 617, 755

Segrin, C., 644, 647
Seith, R., 543
Sekiyama, K., 95
Seldin, M. F., 239
Seligman, C., 761
Seligman, M. E., 440, 645
Seligman, M. E. P., 440, 453, 719
Sellers, E. M., 223
Seltzer, J., 599
Selye, H., 589, 590
Semenov, L. A., 545
Sensky, T. 725
Sereny, G., 248
Sergent, J., 99
Serpell, R., 406
Seta, C. E., 776
Seta, J. J., 776
Setliff, A. E., 306
Seuling, B., 150, 172, 179, 200, 206, 248, 271, 342, 578
Shackelford, T. K., 514
Shafran, R., 654
Shalev, A. Y., 655, 656, 657
Shallenberger, R. S., 178
Shallice, T., 295, 355
Shamir-Essakow, G., 524
Shanab, M. E., 773
Shapira, B., 705
Shapiro, A. K., 622
Shapiro, D. A., 711
Shapiro, D. H., 216
Shapiro, D. H., Jr., 593, 594
Sharples, M., 422
Sharrow, K., 87
Shastri, A., 447
Shaver, P., 761
Shaver, P. R., 487, 521, 522, 523, 761
Shavitt, S., 744
Shaw, P. J., 197
Shaw, S., 248
Shawcross, C. R., 705
Shaywitz, B. A., 328, 408
Shea, D. L., 389
Shea, J. D., 618
Shear, J., 190
Sheehan, P. W., 306
Sheehan, T. P., 7
Sheehy, R., 621
Sheen, M., 308
Sheese, B. E., 611
Sheinberg, D. L., 145
Shekim, W. O., 499
Sheldon, K. M., 455
Sheline, Y. L., 644
Shelton, J. R., 329
Shelton, R. C., 724
Shepard, G. H., 164
Shepard, R. N., 282
Shepherd, G. M., 82
Shepherd, M., 625
Shepherd, M. D., 709
Sherif, M., 751, 752
Sherman, D. K., 623
Sherman, S. J., 750
Shi, C., 242

Shibahara, H., 531
Shidara, M., 452
Shields, S. A., 515
Shiffrar, M. M., 146
Shiffrin, R. M., 279
Shigenobu, K., 105
Shimizu, M., 623
Shimizu, Y. A., 552
Shin, L. M., 657, 658
Shioiri, S., 150
Shiota, M. N., 431
Shiraishi, T., 460
Shoda, Y., 491, 510
Shortridge, J. R., 519
Shouksmith, G., 598
Showers, C., 617
Shreiner, C., 339
Shulman, G. L., 152, 153, 158
Shulman, S., 555
Sidorenko, V. N., 107
Siegel, A. M., 95
Siegel, D. J., 523
Siegel, J. L., 249
Siegel, M., 671, 672, 674
Siegel, S., 244
Siegler, I. C., 571, 757
Siegler, R. S., 553
Sifneos, P. E., 687
Sigel, J. M., 206
Sigmundson, H. K., 557
Silberstein, C. S., 551
Silver, R. C., 579
Silverman, I., 408
Silverman, L., 487
Silvia, P. J., 191
Simmons, J. A., 171
Simock, G., 546
Simon, H. A., 362, 363
Simon, L., 743
Simons, A. D., 455
Simons, D. J., 161
Simon-Thomas, E. R., 432
Simonton, D. K., 417, 418, 419, 420
Simos, P. G., 94
Singer, B. H., 591
Singer, J., 435, 598
Singer, L. T., 534
Singer, M. A., 344
Singer, M. T., 780
Singer, W., 191
Singh, V. N., 531
Sinha, B. K., 623
Siomi, M. C., 415
Sireteanu, R., 545
Sjöberg, L., 392
Sjoelund, B. H., 181
Skinner, B. F., 249, 252, 262, 509
Skinner, N. F., 514
Skjaeaerven, R., 533
Skowronski, J. J., 300
Skvoretz, J., 767
Slakovskis, P. M., 654
Slater, A., 538
Slayton, K., 418
Sleek, S., 719

Slep, A. M. S., 755
Slimp, J. C., 472
Sloan, D. M., 716
Slob, A. K., 469
Slotnick, S. D., 154
Small, B. J., 571, 580
Small, D. M., 461
Smeets, M. A. M., 672
Smith, A. J., 645
Smith, C. A., 593
Smith, D., 710
Smith, D. E., 572
Smith, D. G., 602
Smith, D. V., 177
Smith, D. W., 510
Smith, E. E., 281, 305, 353
Smith, E. R., 747
Smith, J. A. L., 398, 399
Smith, J. C., 107, 215
Smith, J. L., 412
Smith, M. E., 272
Smith, P. B., 770
Smith, R. E., 619
Smith, S., 379, 396
Smith, S. M., 305, 357, 360, 456
Smith, T. W., 600
Smyth, J., 621
Smyth, J. M., 612
Snidman, N., 498, 540
Snodgrass, S. E., 516
Snow, C., 345
Snow, C. E., 42, 339, 345
Snow, R., 384
Snow, R. E., 388
Snowdon, D. A., 313
Snyder, L. H., 158
Snyder, M., 736, 741, 753
Snyderman, M., 404
Sohal, R. S., 119
Solberg Nes, L., 617
Solberg, E. E., 216, 217
Soli, S. D., 168
Solms, M., 201, 202, 229
Solomon, D. A., 639
Solomon, R. L., 431
Sommer, F. G., 537
Song, S., 169
Soper, B., 456, 488
Sorell, G. T., 560
Soto-Faraco, S., 162
Souther, J., 158
Southwick, L., 221
Sowell, E. R., 564
Spain, J. A., 495
Spangler, D. L., 455
Spearman, C., 386, 387, 390, 394
Spears, R., 764
Speed, A., 763
Speisman, J. C., 592
Spelke, E. S., 544, 550, 551
Spence, C., 162
Spencer, R. M. C., 104
Spencer, W. D., 572
Sperlagh, B., 83
Sperling, G., 279

Sperling, R., 296
Spiegel, D., 212
Spiegel, S., 456, 457
Spieker, S. J., 555
Spiers, H. J., 296, 313
Spinath, F. M., 399, 400
Spinella, M., 746
Spitzberg, B. H., 759
Spitzer, R. L., 634
Sprecher, S., 760, 761, 762, 763
Springer, S. P., 99, 408
Sprock, J., 646
Squire, L. R., 102, 291, 292, 295, 311, 312,
Sroufe, L. A., 556
Stack, S., 439
Staddon, J. E. R., 260
Stadtman, E. R., 570
Stager, C. L., 336
Stallone, D. D., 466
Standing, L., 282
Stanley, M. A., 693
Stanton, M. D., 708
Starker, S., 709
Stayman, D. M., 456
Steblay, N., 303
Steele, C. M., 221, 222, 412
Steele, K. M., 411
Steele, R. L., 579
Steffen, V. J., 614
Stein, E. A., 242
Stein, M. B., 651
Stein, M. I., 442
Steinmetz, H., 408
Steinwachs, D. M., 705, 725
Steketee, G., 653, 728
Stellar, E., 460
Stelmack, R. M., 501
Stenberg, R. J., 760
Stephan, W. G., 445
Stepper, S., 435
Steptoe, A., 220, 605
Sterling-Smith, R. S., 228
Stern, K., 176
Stern, P. C., 570, 574
Stern, Y., 574
Sternbach, R. A., 180
Sternberg, E. M., 105
Sternberg, R. J., 380, 393, 394, 395, 396, 421
Stevens, L. E., 455
Stevens-Graham, B., 87
Stevenson, H., 385
Stewart, E. G., 420
Stewart, S. H., 255
Stewart, W. F., 638
Stewart-Williams, S., 241
Stice, E., 673, 674
Stickgold, R., 39, 197, 199, 200, 201
Stiegel-Moore, R. H., 673, 674
Stiles, T. C., 690
Stirman, S. W., 719
Stoel-Gammon, C., 337
Stoerig, P., 160
Stokes, J. P., 472
Stone, J., 412, 743

Stone, M. V., 295
Stoolmiller, M., 402, 506, 507
St. Père, F., 385
Strack, F., 435
Strakowski, S. M., 635, 644
Straus, M. A., 256, 613
Straus, S. E., 621
Streiker, L. D., 780
Streissguth, A. P., 416, 534
Stricker, E. M., 460
Stricker, G., 710
Stricker, L. J., 413
Strike, P. C., 604
Strober, M., 673
Strom, S., 518
Stromswold, K., 329
Strömwall, L. A., 447
Strube, M. J., 431
Strupp, H. H., 711
Strupp, J. J., 711
Stunkard, A. J., 462, 466
Stürmer, S., 777
Stutts, J. C., 205
Suarez, E., 600
Suarez, E. C., 596, 600
Subrahmanyam, K., 408
Sudhalter, V., 415
Sue, S., 726
Sueling, B., 143
Suga, N., 171
Sugita, Y., 147
Sullins, E. S., 647
Sullivan, H. S., 687, 712
Sullivan, Q., 762
Sullivan, R., 161, 529, 530, 575
Sulloway, F. J., 455, 513, 514
Suls, J., 610
Sundet, J. M., 410
Suomi, S. J., 556
Surguladze, S. A., 266
Susser, E., 534
Sutton, R. S., 263
Suzuki, L. A., 405
Svanborg, P., 687
Svartberg, M., 690, 723
Svetina, M., 553
Swann, W. B., Jr., 457
Swanson, K., 555
Sweeny, B., 546
Swets, J. A., 71, 136
Swezey, R. W., 385
Swica, Y., 670
Swinney, D. A., 333
Syme, S. L., 619, 623
Syvalathi, E. K. G., 664
Szasa, T. S., 634
Szegedi, A., 703
Szymanski, K., 775

Tacón, A. M., 622
Tafarodi, R. W., 457, 645
Tafrate, R. C., 600
Tager-Flusberg, H., 336, 415
Tajfel, H., 745, 750
Takahashi, J. S., 203
Takahashi, Y., 555

Takeuchi, A. H., 173
Talarico, J. M., 289
Tallal, P., 339
Tan, G., 217
Tan, H., 412
Tanabe, S., 143
Tangrea, J. A., 625
Tanner, J. M., 563
Tarabulsy, G. M., 555
Taris, T. W., 455
Tarr, M. J., 156
Tarrier, N., 725
Tarter, R. E., 222
Tate, D. F., 710, 712, 713
Tavares, C. H., 562
Tavris, C., 516
Taylor, C. B., 713
Taylor, J. E., 598
Taylor, K. L., 248
Taylor, S. E., 592, 609, 623
Taylor, S. W., 600, 623
Taytroe, L., 200
Tecott, L. H., 463
Tedlock, B., 202
Teigen, K. H., 370
Teilmann, G., 563
Tein, J. Y., 596
Teitelbaum, P., 460
Telch, M. J., 648, 399, 440, 506,
    507, 513
Templer, D., 579
Tenebaum, H. R., 557
Tentori, K., 574
Tepper, B. J., 178
Tepperman, L., 439
Teri, L., 645
Terrace, H. S., 344
Terry, D. J., 610, 769
Tesser, A., 507, 745, 759
Testa, M. F., 568
Tetlock, P. E., 748
Tew, J. D., Jr., 705
Thagard, P., 360
Thaler, R. H., 373
Thannickal, T. C., 206
Thapar, A., 613
Thase, M. E., 455, 723, 724,
    725
Thatcher, R., 169
Thatcher, R. W., 553
Thayer, J. F., 604
Thelen, E., 538, 542, 543
Theorell, T., 598
Thesen, T., 171
Thibaut, J. W., 763
Thomas, A., 497, 539
Thompson, D. M., 305
Thompson, H., 542
Thompson, J. K., 673
Thompson, L. A., 342
Thompson, P. M., 123, 400,
    401, 553
Thompson, R. F., 82, 243, 265
Thompson, W. G., 624
Thompson, W. L., 296, 351
Thorn, B. L., 269
Thorndike, E. L., 249

Thornhill, R., 163, 762
Thorpe, L. A., 319
Thurstone, L. L., 387, 394
Thurstone, T. G., 387, 394
Tidwell, M. O., 520, 761
Tiernari, P., 662
Till, B. D., 245
Timmerman, I. G. H., 622
Tindale, R. S., 775
Tingey, H., 623
Tinker, J. E., 464
Tippett, L. J., 300
Tkachuk, G. A., 622
Todd, C., 227
Todd, M., 619
Tohen, M., 725
Tolman, E. C., 267
Tom, C., 297
Tomaka, J., 435, 593
Tomasello, M., 337, 344
Tomkins, S. S., 430, 435
Tong, F., 156
Tononi, G., 191
Tootell, R. B., 145, 151
Tope, D. M., 249
Torgersen, S. G., 654
Torley, D., 248
Torrance, E. P., 360
Torrey, E. F., 661
Tovée, M. J., 164
Tracey, I., 181
Tractinsky, N., 65
Tracy, J. L., 431
Trafimow, D, 770
Traustadóttir, T., 592
Treffinger, D. J., 418
Treisman, A. M., 150, 152, 158,
    172
Tremblay, W., 452
Treue, S., 145
Trevethan, S. D., 560
Triandis, H. C., 518
Trimpop, R., 499
Trivedi, M. A., 242
Trivedi, N., 467
Trivers, R., 471, 762
Trogersen, S. G., 649
Trost, M. R., 765
True, W. R., 657
Truscott, S. D., 409
Tsai, G., 644
Tsai, S-J., 399, 577
Tsang, J., 743
Tsao, D. Y., 151
Tsekhmistrenko, T. A., 552
Tsien, T. J., 297
Tucker, G. J., 637
Tucker, J. A., 464
Tucker, P., 204
Tugade, M. M., 440
Tuller, D., 206
Tulving, E., 51, 286, 287, 305
Tuna, S., 654
Turati, C., 538
Turek, F. W., 195, 208
Turkheimer, E., 403, 404
Turner, A. M., 120

Turner, S. M., 693
Tversky, A., 369, 370, 371
Tversky, B., 65
Twenge, J. M., 510, 511, 515,
    517, 615, 650
Twisk, J. W. R., 596
Tyrka, A. R., 673
Tzschentke, T. M., 103

Ubell, E., 169
Ullian, E. M., 86
Ullman, M. T., 345
Ullman, S., 151
Ulrich, B. D., 542
Ungerer, J. A., 556
Ungerleider, L. G., 151, 291
Unsworth, N., 398
Utermohlen, V., 673

Vaidya, C. J., 295
Vaillant, G., 576
Vaiva, G., 602
Vajk, F. C., 645
Valdez, P., 205, 208
Valencia, R. R., 405
Valenstein, E. T., 101
Valins, S., 436
Valois, R. L., 145
van Baaren, R. B., 737
Van Boven, L., 756
Van Cauter, E., 195, 208
VandeCreek, L., 713
Vandello, J. A., 519
van den Berg, S., 710
van den Heuvel, O. A., 649
Vanderlinden, J., 675
van der Maas, H. L. J., 553
van der Meer, A., 538
VanDeusen, K. M., 223
Van Essen, D. C., 93, 160,
    166
Van Goozen, S. H., 469
Van Goozen, S. H. M., 408
van Honk, J., 469
van IJzendoorn, M., 523
van Knippenberg, A., 750
Vanni, S., 191
Van Noppen, B., 728
Van Os, J., 663
van Praag, H., 580
Van Reeth, O., 197
Van Rooy, D. L., 391, 392
Van Zandt, T., 262, 597
van Zoest, W., 152
Varela, F., 190
Vargha-Khadem, F., 341, 342
Varma, A., 767
Vartanian, L. R., 565
Vasey, M., 714
Vasterling, J., 249
Vatten, L. J., 533
Vaughn, C., 665
Vazire, S., 493
Vecera, S. P., 157
Vela, E., 2005
Velicer, W. F., 607, 608
Venter, J. C., 400

Ventura, J., 665
Verfaellie, M., 295
Vermetten, E., 657
Vernon, M. L., 523
Vernon, P. A., 397, 508
Verstraten, F. A. J., 160
Vickers, K. S., 617
Vieilledent, S., 71
Viereck, G. S., 365
Vieweg, R., 705
Villarreal, D. M., 297
Villringer, A., 113
Vinar, O., 103
Viney, W., 238
Virtanen, S., 750
Vizi, E. S., 83
Vogel, D. D., 365
Vogel, G., 408, 534
Vogeltanz, N. D., 617
Vohs, K. D., 737
Volkmar, F. R., 415
Volkow, N. D., 225
von der Heydt, R. 146
von der Malsburg, C., 191
Vonk, R., 750
Von Zerssen, D., 666
Voth, H. M., 687
Voudouris, N. J., 249
Vrana, S. R., 437
Vranas, P. B. M., 370
Vrij, A., 447
Vrugt, A., 735
Vuilleumier, P., 147
Vurpillot, E., 545
Vygotsky, L.S., 553
Vythilingam, M., 298

Wachs, T. D., 539
Wade, C., 672
Wade, N., 117
Waelti, P., 263
Wager, T., 434
Wager, T. D., 432, 434, 438,
    622
Wagner, A. D., 110, 284, 295,
    296
Wagner, R. K., 384, 394, 411
Wagstaff, G. F., 212
Wahba, M. A., 456, 488
Wakler, E., 663
Walach, H., 704
Waldron, M., 403
Waldron, V. R., 710
Walk, R. D., 543
Walker, E. F., 664, 665, 666
Walker, I., 745
Walker, L. J., 560
Walker, M. P., 200, 285
Walker, N. G., 661
Walker, W. R., 300
Wall, P. D., 181
Wallace, A. R., 124
Wallenius, M. A., 598
Waller, N. G., 506, 520, 523,
    761
Walsh, B. T., 674
Walsh, V., 114

Walsh, Y., 780
Walster, E., 578
Walters, J., 393
Wang, L., 445
Wang, Q., 300, 337
Wang, T., 463
Wang, X., 120, 613
Wann, D. L., 271
Wanska, S. K., 340
Ward, C., 192, 211, 214, 760
Ward, W. C., 413
Wareing, M., 225
Warfield, J. F., 446
Wark, G. R., 560
Warren, J. D., 106, 107
Warren, R. M., 171
Warren, R. P., 171
Warrington, E. K., 312, 355
Wartenburger, I., 329
Washburne, C., 222
Wason, P. C., 368
Wasserman, L. M., 140
Wässle, H., 138
Waterhouse, J., 208
Waterman, A. S., 515
Waters, A. J., 363
Watkins, L. R., 87
Watkins, P. C., 300
Watkinson, B., 534
Watson, D., 609
Watson, J., 238, 239
Watson, J. B., 347, 509
Watson, J. M., 309
Watson, M., 603
Watt, C. A., 182
Watt, D., 44
Watt, D. F., 451
Waugh, N. C., 279
Waxman, S. R., 551
Wayne, S. J., 735
Wayner, M. J., 460
Waziri, R., 216
Weaver, I. C. G., 540
Weaver, S. L., 594
Webb, S. J., 546
Webster, D. M., 455
Webster, J. I., 105
Wechsler, D., 381
Wechsler, H., 220
Weeks, J., 777
Weerasinghe, J., 439
Wegener, D. T., 738
Wegner, D. M., 201, 612
Wehr, T. A., 646
Weijer, H. G., 503
Weinberg, R. A., 400, 403, 407
Weinberger, D. R., 664, 710
Weindruch, R., 119
Weiner, B., 455, 777
Weingarten, H. P., 460
Weinstein, N. D., 605, 606
Weinstein, S., 180
Weinstock, M., 535
Weiskrantz, L., 160
Weisman, A., D., 624
Weiss, R. S., 556
Weiss, W., 744

Weisskirch, R. S., 499
Weissman, B. A., 138
Weissman, D. E., 713
Weissman, M. M., 638, 643, 654
Wellman, H. M., 551
Wells, G. L., 303, 613, 652
Wender, P. H., 643
Wenzel, A., 652
Wenzlaff, R. M., 612
Werker, J. F., 336
Werner, C., 623
Wertheimer, M., 146, 150
Wertsch, J. V., 554
Wessel, I., 314
West, L. J. 780
Westen, D., 487, 719, 722, 725
Westerberg, H., 553
Westman, M., 599
Wetsman, A., 164
Wetzstein, C., 567
Whalen, P. J., 437, 438, 445
Wheeler, B. L., 107
Wheeler, L., 760
Wheeler, M. D., 563
Whidbee, D., 200, 201
White, A., 71
White, G. L., 200
White, J. M., 228
White, K., 653
White, P. H., 412
White, T. G., 337
White, T. L., 500
Whittal, M. L., 724
Whorf, B., 347
Wickramasekera, I., 621
Widiger, T. A., 646, 677
Wiebe, D. J., 616

Wiedemann, G., 649
Wierzbicki, M., 596
Wiesel, T. N., 145
Wigfield, A., 408
Wiggins, J. S., 491, 494
Wigram, T., 107
Wilder, D. A., 748
Wildman, D. E., 118
Wilhelm, O., 397, 398
Wilkins, L., 451
Wilkinson, D. J. C., 567, 650
Willer, J. C., 181
Williams, C., 463
Williams, C. N., 780
Williams, D. M., 616
Williams, J. E., 600
Williams, J. M. G., 466
Williams, K. D., 776
Williams, L. M., 314
Williams, R., 600, 619
Williams, S. M., 44
Williams, T. J., 473
Williams, W., 410
Williams, W. M., 401
Willis, S. L., 574
Willoughby, A. R., 372
Wills, T., 620
Wilson, C., 410
Wilson, C. S., 459
Wilson, D. B., 718
Wilson, D. M., 510
Wilson, G. T., 712
Wilson, J., 341
Wilson, R. I., 83, 84, 227
Wilson, T. L., 411
Windle, G., 466
Winer, G. A., 137
Wingfield, J. C., 591
Winkelman, M., 107

Winkielman, P., 436
Winneberg, S. R., 216
Winner, E., 416, 417
Winnicot, D. W., 687
Winter, A., 210, 213
Winzelberg, A., 709
Wirtz, D., 439
Wise, P. M., 570
Wise, R. A., 452, 454
Wiseman, R., 182
Witelson, S. F., 95, 396
Witt, S. D., 558
Witter, M., 95
Wittstein, I. S., 604
Witt, L. A., 599
Wixted, J. T., 310
Wolf, A., 169
Wolf, N., 763
Wolf, O. T., 408
Wolpe, J., 692
Wolsko, P. M., 621
Wood, J. J., 499
Wood, J. M., 496
Wood, J. N., 746
Wood, P., 200
Wood, W., 763
Woods, S. C., 461
Woodside, B., 463
Woody, E. Z., 212
Woolfolk, R. L., 70, 71
World Health Organization, 631
Worthington, T. S., 306
Wortman, C. B., 579
Wraga, M. J., 351
Wright, D. B., 314
Wright, G., 370
Wrightsman, L. S., 756
Wurtman, R., 203

Wyatt, R. J., 703
Wyer, N. A., 747
Wynn, K., 550
Wyvell, C. L., 455

Xerri, C., 120
Xinyin, C., 499

Yahya, K. A., 773
Yalow, R., 384
Yamadori, A., 96
Yamauchi, L., 757
Yamawaki, N., 617
Yang, J., 233, 235, 253, 267, 268, 271
Yang, K., 517
Yazigi, R. A., 535
Yehuda, R., 602, 656, 657
Yen, S., 640
Yeoh, A. E. O., 724
Yeomans, M. R., 459, 460
Yeshurun, Y., 157
Yeung, N., 264, 294, 362
Yoder, C. Y., 646
Yokosuka, M., 463
Yonas, A., 544
Yost, W. A., 170
Young, A. W., 99
Young, L. R., 44
Yu, D. W., 164

Zabinski, M. F., 710, 712, 713, 714
Zacks, J., 65
Zacks, R. T., 370
Zaharia, M. D., 540
Zaidel, D. W., 163
Zaidel, E., 97
Zajicek, J., 80

Zajonc, R. B., 744, 759
Zakowski, S., 621
Zalla, T., 438
Zamira, M., 134
Zane, N., 725
Zane, N. W. S., 491
Zanna, M. P., 775
Zaragoza, M., 308
Zatorre, R. J., 173, 296
Zawadzki, B., 505
Zebrowitz, L. A., 760
Zeidner, M., 517
Zeki, S., 419
Zeki, S. M., 143, 150, 160
Zeller, R. A., 49
Zenger, T. R., 775
Zentner, M. R., 545
Zhang, Q., 168, 281
Zhdanova, I., 203
Zhengyan, W., 499
Zhu, H., 119
Zhu, Y., 168, 281
Ziegler, D. J., 697
Zihl, J., 150
Zika, S., 596
Zimbardo, P. G., 767, 768
Zimmer, E. Z., 533
Zlotnick, C., 678
Zoccolillo, M., 678
Zola, S. M., 296
Zornberg, G. L. 663
Zorzi, M., 359
Zuckerman, M., 44, 493, 499, 500, 501, 502, 503, 504, 508, 515, 618
Zurek, P. M., 166
Zurif, E. B., 329
Zweigenhaft, R. L., 514
Zwicker, E., 166

# SUBJECT INDEX

*Note:* Page numbers followed by f indicate figures; page numbers followed by t indicate tables; **boldface** type indicates key terms and the page numbers where they are defined.

AA, 709
ABCDEF technique, 699, 699f
ABCs, of problematic behavior, 692, 693t
Abecedarian Project, 411
**Absolute pitch**, 107, **173**
**Absolute threshold, 136**
**Absorption, 212**
Abstinence violation effect, 674
Abu Ghraib prison, 768
**Academic psychologists, 24–25**
**Accommodation, 138**, 547
Acetylcholine (ACh), 83t, 84, 313, 572
Acetyl-L-carnitine, 571
ACh, 83t, 84
Achievement, need for (nAch), 455
**Acquisition, 236**, 240f
Acronyms, 318
ACTH, 105
**Action potential** 80, 81f
**Activation-synthesis hypothesis, 201**
**Active interaction, 122**
**Activity, 497**
Acupuncture, 181
Acute phase response, 105
**Acute stressor, 588**–589
**Adaptation, 13, 124**
Adaptation phase, 590
Adler, Alfred, 15, 486
**Adolescence, 562**–568
    depression during, 645f
**Adoption studies, 123**, 399–400, 402
Adrenal glands, 104, 105
Adrenaline, 83t
Adrenocorticotropin hormone (ACTH), 105
Adulthood, 568–581
Advertising, 245
Affect, 300, 660
**Affirming the consequent, 368**
**Afterimage, 142**
    demonstration of, 142f
**Aggression, 613**
    factors leading to, 614f
    modeling of, 270, 272t, 272–273
    sexual, 221, 222–223
    stress and, 613–616
**Agonists, 85**, 86
**Agoraphobia, 649**, 650, 694, 694f
Agreeableness, 492
AI, 364–365
**Alarm phase, 589**–590
Alarm system, and panic disorder, 649
Alcohol
    abuse of, 218–219, 223–224, 248
    biological effects of, 220–221
    cocaine and, 225
    prenatal development and, 416, 534

psychological effects of, 221–223, 223t
    sexual aggression and, 222f
**Alcohol myopia, 222**
Alcoholics Anonymous (AA), 709
**Algorithm, 358**
Ali, Muhammed, 214
*Alice's Adventures in Wonderland*, 189, 190, 193, 206, 209, 214–215
Alien abduction, memories of, 307f
Allegiance effect, 717
Alleles, 116
All-nighters, 197–199
**All-or-none law, 80**
Allostasis, 591
Allostatic load, 591
Alogia, 660–661
Alter, 669–670
**Altered states of consciousness (ASC), 191**–192. *See also* Hypnosis; Meditation
Alternative five, 503, 504
**Altruism, 776**
Alzheimer's disease, 119, 298, 300, 313, 420, 714
Ambiguity, resolving, 333–335
Ambiguous figures, 146f, 146–147
Amenorrhea, 671
American Psychiatric Association, 635, 727
American Psychological Association, 727
*American Psychologist*, 405
American Sign Language (ASL), 343–344
Ames room, 149
*Amistad*, 530
**Amnesia, 310, 312**–313, 572, 668, 746
Amphetamine psychosis, 225
**Amphetamines, 219, 225**
**Amplitude, 137**
Amusia, 107
Amygdala, 102–103
    fear and, 242, 243, 437–439, 445, 500
    memory and, 289
    music processing and, 106
    racial prejudice and, 9
Analgesia, 213, 219, 226
Analogies, 359–360
Anal-retentive personality, 487
Analysis, levels of. *See* Levels of analysis
Analytic intelligence, 393, 395
Androgen insensitivity syndrome, 469
**Androgens, 468**–469
4,16-Androstadien-3-one (AND), 177

Animal research, 30, 118, 235–238, 246–248, 251–252, 260, 261, 268–269, 344, 463–464
Anions, 80
Anomalous cognition (psi), 182
**Anorexia nervosa**, 22, **671**–672, 725
Anosognosia, 96
ANS, 88–90, 104
Antabase, 248
**Antagonists, 85**
Antecedents, 692, 693
**Anterograde amnesia, 313**
*Anthropologist on Mars, An*, 143
Anticipatory nausea, 248–249
Antidepressants, 703–704
**Antipsychotic medication, 702**–703, 705
**Antisocial personality disorder (ASPD), 677**–679
Anvil, 167
Anxiety
    basic, 486
    castration, 484–485
    separation, 555
    test, 406
**Anxiety disorders, 648**–658, 704, 705, 725
Anxiety sensitivity, 649–650
Anxious attachment style, 520t, 520–524, 761
Aphasia, 329
Apolipoprotein E (apoE), 298
Appetizer effect, 460
**Applied psychologist, 25**–26
**Approach-approach conflict, 595**, 596f
**Approach-avoidance conflict, 595**, 596f
Approach emotions, 431–432
**Archetype, 486**
Aristotle, 348, 352, 566
Arousal theory, 451, 452
Arteries, stress on, 604f
Articulatory loop, 281
**Artificial intelligence (AI), 364**–365
Asch's conformity study, 769–770, 770f
ASL, 343–344
Aspartame (NutraSweet), 179
**Assimilation, 547**
Associative learning, 235
Astigmatism, 143
Astrocytes, 86
Astronauts, 37, 38, 39, 54, 65
*Ataques de nervios*, 726
**Atherosclerosis, 603**–604
Atmospheric perspective, 148
**Attachment, 554**–556
Attachment styles, 520t, 520–524, 555, 760–761

**Attention, 157**–162
Attention placebo, 717
**Attentional blink, 162**
Attitude, 738–745, 766
Attractiveness, features of, 163–164
**Attribution(s), 755**–758
    types of, 755t
**Attributional bias, 756**–758
**Attributional style, 644**–645
Atypical antipsychotics, 702, 705
Auditory perception, 169–173, 545
Auditory scene analysis, 170
Auditory sensation, 165–169
**Autism, 415**
Autobiographical memories, 299–300
**Automatic processing, 294**, 295t
Autonomic nervous system (ANS), 88–90, 104
**Availability heuristic, 371**
**Avoidance–avoidance conflict, 595**, 596f
**Avoidance learning, 238**
Avoidant attachment style, 520t, 520–524, 555, 618, 761
Avoiders, 618
Avolition, 661
Awareness meditation, 215
Axel, Richard, 175
Axes, 635
Axis I symptoms, 635, 676
Axis II symptoms, 635, 676–677
**Axon, 79**, 80

B cell, 602
Babinski reflex, 538, 539t
"Back to Sleep" movement, 542
*Back to the Future*, 530
Backward pairing, 236–237
Bandura, Albert, 269–270
    study on observational learning of, 270f
Barbiturates, 206, 208, 224
Bard, Philip, 433
Barn owls, hearing of, 171
Barrymore, Drew, 312
BAS, 500t, 500, 503
**Basal ganglia, 103**, 294f
**Base-rate rule, 370**
Basic anxiety, 486
**Basic emotion(s), 429, 430**–431
    recognition of, 430f
**Basic level, 354, 355**
Basic-level names, 354f
Basilar membrane, 167–168
Bats, hearing of, 171
*Beautiful Mind, A*, 632
Bechterev, Vladimir, 237–238
Beck, Aaron, 18, 697

Beck's cognitive therapy, 698–699
Beck's negative triad of depression, 644f, 644–645
Beethoven, Ludwig van, 173
**Behavior(s), 4, 5**
  abnormal, 632–635. *See also* Psychological disorders
  aggressive. *See* Aggression
  attitudes and, 738–745
  disorganized, 660
  of fetus, 533
  health-impairing, 605–608
  hypnosis and, 211
  modifying, 257–258, 695–697
  prosocial, 776–777
  sexual, 118, 176–177, 442, 466–476
**Behavior modification, 257–258, 695–697**
**Behavior therapy, 692–697, 701, 728f**
Behavioral activation system (BAS), 500t, 500, 503
**Behavioral genetics, 122–126**
Behavioral inhibition system (BIS), 500t, 500, 503
Behavioral techniques, 701t
**Behaviorism, 15–16, 20t, 21, 251–252, 335, 509**
Belief, and perception, 161f
**Belief in a just world, 757–758**
Bell curve, 384
*Bell Curve, The*, 406
Bellugi, Ursula, 27
**Benzodiazepine(s), 224, 704, 705**
**Bereavement, 578–579**
Berthold, Arnold, 468
Beta-endorphin, 83t
Between-group differences, versus within-group differences, 405f
Bias, 51–52, **136**
  attributional, 756–758
  confirmation, 368
  correspondence, 756–757
  diagnostic, 634–635
  hostile attribution, 613–614
  sampling, 51–52
  self-serving, 757
  social desirability, 740
  test, 406
**Bibliotherapy, 709–710**
**Big Five, 492–493, 495**
  traits in, 492t
Bilingualism, 344–345
Binding, 84
Binet, Alfred, 381, 383
Binge drinking, 220
Binge eating, 672, 674–675
**Binocular cues, 148–150**
Binocular disparity, 148
**Biological preparedness, 238–239**
Biologically based theory of personality, 503t
Biomedical therapies, 702–706
Biopsychosocial model, of abnormal behavior, 632–635
**Bipolar disorder, 420, 638, 642–643, 644, 645, 646, 704, 705, 725**
Birdsong, 120

Birth order, 513–515
  personality and, 514t
BIS, 500t, 500, 503
**Bisexual, 472–474**
**Blackout, 223**
Blastocyst, 532
Blind spot, 139
  finding, 139f
Blindness, 142–143, 161–162
Blindsight, 160
Bobo doll, 270
Bodily-kinesthetic intelligence, 393
Body image, distortion of, 671f
Body language, 442–443, 444–445
Body weight, 462–466
**Bottom-up processing, 152–153, 158, 181**
Brain(s). *See also specific parts*
  aging, 580–581
  auditory imagery and, 173
  bodily functions and, 101, 103
  changes after treatments for depression, 723f
  circuits in, 78–87
  concepts and, 355
  emotions and, 97, 100–104, 242–244, 437–439, 438f
  hormones and, 101
  hunger and, 459–460, 463
  language and, 99, 329, 332–333, 340–342, 343
  language areas of, 329f
  memory and, 97, 102, 296–300, 546–547, 553
  mental images and, 350–351
  in operant conditioning, 262–266
  pain and, 100
  physical coordination and, 103–104
  recording techniques and, 109–114, 213
  sensation and, 95–96
  similarities of, in twins, 400–401, 401f
  size of, intelligence and, 396–397
  sleep and, 202–205
  stroke in, 109, 117, 201–202
  vision and, 94–95, 96, 97–98, 138–140, 151–153
Brain, level of the. *See* Level of the brain
**Brain circuit, 78**
Brain waves, during sleep, 194f
**Brainstem, 103**
**Breadth of processing, 287–288, 316**
Brightness, 140
British Sign Language (BSL), 343
Broad mental abilities, 388–389
Broca, Paul, 329
**Broca's aphasia, 329**
Broca's area, 329, 345
"Broken heart syndrome," 604
Buchanan, James, 143
Buck, Linda, 175
**Bulimia nervosa, 22, 672–673, 674–675, 724, 725**
**Burnout, 598–599**
Bush, George W., 51–52

Buss, David, 19
**Bystander effect, 777, 778–780**
Bystander intervention, 778f, 779f

Caffeine, 226, 534
Calkins, Mary Whiton, 27, 28
Cancer, and stress, 603
Candle problem, 357, 358f, 360f
Cannabinoids, endogenous, 82–84, 83t, 227
Cannon, Walter, 433, 450–451
Cannon-Bard theory, 433, 434–435, 438
Carbohydrate Addict's Diet, 465
Carbon monoxide, 77, 78, 82, 88, 94–95
Card task (Wason and Johnson-Laird), 368f
Carey, Susan, 27
Carroll, Lewis, 189
Carroll's three-stratum theory of intelligence, 388–389, 389f, 394t
Cartwright, Dr. Samuel, 631
Cascio, Veronica, 314
**Case study, 43**, 48t
**Castration anxiety, 484–485**
CAT, 111
Cataract, 144, 572
Catastrophic exaggeration, 698t
Catatonic schizophrenia, 661
**Categorical perception, 170**
Categorical spatial relations, 153–154
**Category, 352**
*Cat in the Hat, The*, 533
Cations, 79
Cattell and Horn's fluid and crystallized intelligences, 387–388, 388t, 394t
Cattell's personality factors, 492, 492f, 494
Causal attribution, theory of, 755–756
CBT, 692–701, 723–725
  brain changes with, 723f
**Cell body, 78**, 80
**Cell membrane, 78**, 80
Center for Cognitive Liberty and Ethics, 32
**Central executive, 281**
**Central nervous system (CNS), 89, 90, 91–93, 104**
Central nucleus, 243
**Central tendency, 56–58**
Central traits, 490
**Cerebellum, 103**–104, 294f
**Cerebral cortex, 92**, 94–97, 123
**Cerebral hemisphere(s), 91**, 97–99
  eyes and, 98f
  language and, 328, 332–333
  smell and, 175
  spatial relations and, 154–155
  specialization of, 99
Cerebral reserve hypothesis, 574
*Challenger*, 775
Chan, Jackie, 233–234, 235, 250, 252, 253–254, 255–256, 257, 258, 259–260, 267, 268, 269, 271
Change, Prochaska's stages of, 606

Change blindness, 161–162
Channels, 80, 81
**Chemical senses, 174.** *See also* Smell; Taste
Chemotherapy, 248–249
**Child-directed speech (CDS), 42, 336**
Childhood amnesia, 313
Chimpanzees, and language, 344
Chinese Drama Academy, 233–234, 235, 257
Cholesterol, 86
Chomsky, Noam, 17, 335
Chromosome, 531–532
**Chronic stressor, 588–589, 604–605**
Chronological age (CA), 381, 383
**Chunk, 280,** 316
Chunking, 280f
**Circadian rhythms, 140, 203f, 203–205**
Civil rights movement, 427
Clairvoyance, 182
**Classical conditioning, 235–249**
  incentives and, 452–453
  versus operant conditioning, 264t, 264–265
  phases of, 237f
  of a phobia, 239f
  psychological disorders and, 33, 693
  substance abuse and, 244–245
  of taste aversion, 246f
  variations of procedure for, 237f
Clever Hans, 52
**Client-centered therapy, 16–17, 488, 689–691**
Clinical neuropsychologist, 23, 26, 43
**Clinical psychologist, 22–23, 26, 30–31**
Clinton, Hillary, 511
Clomipramine, 704
Cloninger's theory of personality, 502–503, 504
Closed plan office design, 597
*Close Encounters of the Third Kind*, 530
Closure, 146
Clusters, of Axis II personality disorders, 676t
CNS, 89, 90, 91–93, 104
Cobain, Kurt, 420
Cocaethylene, 225
Cocaine, 219, 224–225
Cochlea, 167, 328
Cochlear implants, 328
**Cocktail party phenomenon, 172**
**Code, 284**
Code of conduct, for psychologists, 31t
Coding space, 153f
Cognition
  anomalous, 182
  attitudes and, 738–739
  conditioned stimulus and, 241–244
  creative, 418f, 418–419
  need for, 455–456
  social, 510–512, 734–758
Cognitive appraisal, 592–593, 593f
Cognitive apprenticeship, 411
**Cognitive-behavior therapy (CBT), 692–701, 701t, 723f, 723–725**

Cognitive control, 361–362
Cognitive development, 547–554, 564–565, 570–574
　Piaget's periods of, 548t
Cognitive dissonance, 741–744, 742f
Cognitive distortions, 644, 698, 698t
Cognitive enrichment programs, 411t
Cognitive illusion, 370
Cognitive learning, 267–268
Cognitive map, 268
Cognitive neuroscience, 18, 20t, 21
Cognitive psychologist, 24, 26, 43
Cognitive psychology, 17–18, 20t, 21
Cognitive restructuring, 700
Cognitive taste aversion, 461
Cognitive techniques, 701t
Cognitive theory of emotion, 433, 435–437
Cognitive therapy, 697–700, 701
Coin, choosing correct image of, 283f
Collective unconscious, 486
Collectivism, in United States, 519f
Collectivist culture(s), 457–458, 518, 519
Colombine High School, 615
Color blindness, 142–143
Color constancy, 147
Color Purple, The, 530
Color vision, 140–143
Color mixing, 141f
Columbus, Christopher, 137
Common factor(s), 716, 717t
Comorbid disorders, 719
Companionate love, 760
Comparison level, 763
Compensatory systems, 119f
Complex inheritance, 117
Compliance, 771–772
Compulsion(s), 653–655
Computer-assisted tomography (CT), 111
Concealed information test, 446
Concentrative meditation, 215
Concept, 352–355. See also Self-concept
Concrete operation(s), 548, 549–550
Conditioned compensatory response, 244–245
Conditioned emotional response (CER), 238
Conditioned response (CR), 236, 240, 243, 245, 246, 249, 293
Conditioned stimulus (CS), 236–237, 238–241, 249
　cognition and, 241–244
　taste aversion and, 245–248
Conditioning. See Classical conditioning; Operant conditioning
Conditions of worth, 488
Conduction deafness, 169
Cones, 138–139, 139f, 141–142
Confidence interval, 58
Confirmation bias, 368
Conflict, 221, 595, 596
Conformity, 769–770

Confounds (or confounding variables or factors), 46–47, 47f, 718t
　reducing, 718–719
Conscience, 560
Conscientiousness, 492, 493, 494
Conscious, 482–483
Consciousness, 190–192
　raising, 607
　in structuralism, 11
Conservation, 549
　of liquids, 549f
Consolidation, 284–285
Construct validity, 50t
Contact hypothesis, 753
Content, 6–7. See also Level of the person
Content validity, 50t
Continuity, 146
Continuous Positive Airway Pressure (CPAP), 207
Continuous reinforcement, 260–261
Contrapreparedness, 239
Control
　cognitive, 361–362
　gate, 181
　locus of, 511
　perception of, 593–595, 603
　stimulus, 694
Control beliefs, 698t
Control condition, 47
Control group, 46–47, 715, 717–718
Control question technique (CQT), 446, 447
Control sequence, for genes, 297
Controlled processing, 294, 295t
Convergence, 148
Convergent thinking, 419
Cooke, Alistair, 319–320
Coordinate spatial relations, 153–154
Coping, 593
　emotion-focused, 609–616
　gender differences in, 622–623
　immune system and, 617–621
　problem-focused, 609–611
　reactive, 609
　strategies for, 609–625
Cornea, 138
Corpus callosum, 91–92
Correlation, 44, 45f, 59, 750
Correlation coefficient, 44, 59
Correlational research, 44–45, 48t
Correspondence bias, 756–757
Corticotropin-releasing hormone (CRH), 105
Cortisol, 104–105, 589–590
　obesity and, 464
　sleep deprivation and, 197
Cosmides, Lida, 19
Counseling psychologist, 23, 26
Countering, 608
Counter-irritant, 181
Couric, Katie, 744
CPAP, 207
Crack, 225
Cramming, 287
Cranial nerves, 90
Creative cognition, 418f, 418–419

Creative intelligence, 394–395
Creative people, characteristics of, 418–419, 419t
Creative solutions, of humans versus computers, 422t
Creativity, 417–422
Crick, Francis, 190, 201
Crime witnesses, 319
Criterion validity, 50t
Critical period, 341
Cross-sectional study, 573–574
　versus longitudinal study, 573f
Crowe, Russell, 632
Crystallized intelligence, 387–388, 389, 573–574
CT scan, 111
Cuento therapy, 726
Cues, 148–150, 304f, 304–306
　about emotion, 444–445
　unintentional, 52, 53
Cults, 780–781
Cultural universality, 19–20
Culture, 7. See also Level of the group
　attachment and, 555
　cognitive development and, 553–554
　collectivist, 457–458, 518, 519
　coping and, 623
　emotions and, 441–442, 445
　food tastes and, 461
　hearing and, 172–173
　heuristics and, 370
　individualist, 457–458, 518, 519
　memory and, 300
　personality and, 517–520
　psychological disorders and, 634–635, 640–641, 645–646, 650, 666, 673–674
　self-concept and, 557
　sexual behaviors and, 474
　treatment and, 725–726
Cumulative recorder, 252f
Cupboard theory, 554
Cybertherapy, 712–713
Cycle, of sound waves, 166
Cytokines, 105

DA. See Dopamine
Daily self-monitoring log, 696f
Dani, the, 347–348
Dark adaptation, 139
Darwin, Charles, 12–13, 19, 124, 405, 417
Data, 38–39, 55–56, 61–64
Date rape, 221, 222–223
Daycare, 556
dB, 166
Deafness, 162, 168–169
Death, 578–579, 624–625
Debriefing, 30
Decay, 310–311
Deception, signs of, 447t
Decibel (dB), 166
Decibel levels, 166f
Declarative memories, 292–293, 296, 545–546
Dedifferentiation, 574
Deductive reasoning, 367, 368f

Deep Blue, 364, 372
Deep Fritz, 364
Defense mechanisms, 485t, 485, 487, 688
Defensive pessimism, 617
Defibrillator, 238
Deindividuation, 764
de Kooning, Willem, 420
Delany, Bessie, 733, 734, 751, 755, 758–759, 764, 766, 774, 776, 777
Delany, Henry, 733, 734, 738, 758–759
Delany, Sadie, 733, 734, 738, 755, 756, 758–759, 764, 766, 768, 774
Delayed conditioning, 236
Delayed reinforcement, 258
Deliberate practice, 363–364
Delta waves, 194
Delusions, 632, 660
Demand-control model, 598
Dendrite, 79, 80
Deoxyribonucleic acid (DNA), 116, 116f, 531
Depakote, 704
Dependability, 492, 493
Dependent variable, 45–46, 46f, 55–56
Depersonalization, 780
Depressants, 219, 220–224
Depression, 685–686. See also Bipolar disorder; Dysthymia; Major depressive disorder
　environment and, 645
　interactional theory of, 646–647
　negative triad of, 644f, 644–645
　placebo effect and, 704
　research on, 640–641
　stress and, 604–605
　treatments for, 703–704, 705, 712, 722, 725
　twin studies on, 643–644
Deprived reward, 454–455
Depth cues, 148–150
　types of, 150f
Depth of processing, 286f, 286–287, 316
Derealization, 668, 780
Descartes, René, 11
Descriptive norms, 765
Descriptive research, 42–44, 48
Descriptive statistics, 55–58
D'Este, Archduke Franz Ferdinand, 753
Destination Imagination (DI), 421
Determinism, reciprocal, 512
Developmental motor milestones, 542f
Developmental psychologist, 24, 25, 26, 530, 542
Diagnostic and Statistical Manual of Mental Disorders (DSM), 631, 635–637, 676
　major categories in, 636t
　subtypes of schizophrenia in, 661t
Diagnostic bias, 634–635
Diagnostic criteria
　for manic episodes, 643t
　for major depressive disorder, 639t
Diallo, Amadou, 748–750
Diathesis-stress model, 633, 633f

Dichotic listening, **172**, 172f
Dichotomous thinking, 698t
Dickens, Charles, 420
DID, 669–670
Diet, and prenatal development, 534–535
Dieting, 465–466
Diets, physicians' concerns about, 465t
Diffuse optical tomography (DOT), 113
**Diffusion of responsibility, 780**
Direct strategies, 742–743
**Discrimination, 241, 259**, 751
**Discriminative stimulus, 259**
**Disinhibition, 220**–221
Dismissive-avoidant attachment, 521–522
Disorganized behavior, 660
Disorganized/disoriented attachment, 555
Disorganized schizophrenia, 661
Disorganized speech, 660
**Display rule, 441**
Dispositional attributions, 755–756
**Dissociative amnesia, 668**
**Dissociative disorders, 668**–670
**Dissociative fugue, 668**
**Dissociative identity disorder (DID), 669**, 670
Dissonance, cognitive, 741–744, 742f
Distance, visual, 147–150
Distortion, cognitive, 644, 698
Distributed practice, 287, 316–317
Divergent thinking, 419
**Divided attention, 159**
**Dizygotic, 123.** *See also* Fraternal twins
DNA, 116, 116f, 531
Dog, prototype of, 353f
Dolphins, and shaping, 260f, 261
Donne, John, 7
**Door-in-the-face technique, 772**
Dopamine (DA), 83t, 84, 86, 103
  antipsychotic medication and, 702
  novelty seeking and, 502
  in operant conditioning, 263
  reward and, 452, 454
  sexual behavior and, 471
Dopamine hypothesis, 664
DOT, 113
**Double-blind design, 52**, 622
**Double pain, 180**
Down, J. Langdon, 415
**Down syndrome, 415**
Dr. Atkin's New Diet Revolution, 465t
Drapetomania, 631
**Dream analysis, 687**
Dream diaries, 200
Dreaming, 200–202
  purpose of, 202t
**Drive, 450**–451
Drive theory, 450–451
Drugs. *See also specific drugs*
  abuse of, 218–219
  actions and effects of, 219t
  classical conditioning and, 244–245
  prenatal development and, 534, 535

*DSM. See Diagnostic and Statistical Manual of Mental Disorders*
Dual codes, 284
D.W., case of, 451
Dynamic memory, 284–285
Dysfunctional beliefs, daily record of, 700f
**Dysthymia, 638, 642**

e, 219, 225–226
Eagerness-related approach strategies, 457
Ear, 167–168
  anatomy of, 167f
Eardrum, 167
**Eating disorders, 22, 670, 671**–675, 724, 725
  gazing at body parts and, 673f
Eat More, Weigh Less diet, 465t
Ebbinghaus, Hermann, 282–283, 310
  forgetting curve of, 310f
Echoic memory, 280
Economic-related stressors, 599–600
Ecstasy, 219, 225–226
ECT, 705–706
Edges, perception of, 145f
Educational psychologist, 26
EEG, 109–110, 110f
**Effect, 45**–46, 59
Effexor, 703
**Ego, 483**, 686–687
**Egocentrism, 549**
Ego ideal, 483
Einstein, Albert, 325–326, 327, 331–332, 346–347, 356–357, 358, 362–363, 364, 366, 371–372, 396, 488
Elaboration likelihood, 744
**Elaborative encoding, 287**–288
Elavil, 703
Electra complex, 484–485
**Electroconvulsive therapy (ECT), 705**–706
**Electroencephalogram, 110**
**Electroencephalograph (EEG), 109**–110, 110f
  meditation and, 217
  sleep and, 193–195
Electromagnetic radiation, 137–138
  range of, 137f
Ellis, Albert, 18
Ellis's cognitive therapy, 697–698
**Embryo, 532**–537
Emerging adulthood, 569
**Emotion(s), 428, 429**–448
  in adolescents, 566–568
  brain and, 97, 100–104, 242–244, 437–439, 438f
  decision making and, 371–374
  expressing, 440–444, 716, 717
  hearing and, 172–173
  mature, 577
  memory and, 288–290
  perceiving, 444–448
  sleep deprivation and, 196
  smell and, 175
  theories of, 432f, 432–434

types of, 354, 355, 429–432, 439–440, 665
**Emotion-focused coping, 609**–616
  strategies for, 610t
Emotion regulation, 443–444
Emotional arousal, 607
**Emotional intelligence (EI), 391**–392
  four-branch model of, 391t
**Emotionality, 492, 497**
Empathy, 561
Empirically supported treatments (ESTs), 722–723
  criteria for, 722t
  efficacy of, 725t
Empirically validated treatments, 722
**Empiricism, 335**
**Enacted social support, 620**
Encoding, 278–290, 315–319
**Encoding failure, 310**
Encoding specificity principle, 304–305, 317
Endocrine glands, 104–105
  major, 105f
**Endogenous cannabinoids, 82**–84, 83t, 227
**Endorphins, 181**, 588
Enkephalins, 588
Environment, 7
  aging brain and, 580
  depression and, 645
  fetus and, 534–537
  genes and, 119–122
  homosexuality and, 473–474
  intelligence and, 401–404, 406
  language and, 338–339
  mental retardation and, 416
  overeating and, 464–465
  personality and, 507, 517–520
  prenatal development and, 534–537
  stress and, 597–599, 613
  temperament and, 540
Epilepsy, 97, 107
Epinephrine, 83t, 435–436
**Episodic memories, 291**–292, 299–300, 301, 572
Erikson's psychosocial stages in adulthood, 575t, 575–576
Error
  margin of, 58
  measurement, 390
  overregulation, 340
  sampling, 60
Escher, Maurits, 146
ESP, 53, 182
**Estrogen(s), 104, 468**–469
ESTs, 722t, 722–723, 725t
*E.T., The Extra-Terrestrial*, 529–530
Ethic of care, 560
Ethical principles, for psychologists, 31t
Ethics, 29–32, 781–782
Evaluation apprehension, 779–780
Evaluative conditioning, 245, 739
Event-related optical signal (EROS), 113–114
Events, possible versus impossible, 551f
Evidence-based treatments, 722
**Evocative interaction, 121**

Evolution, 123–124, 125
**Evolutionary psychology, 18, 19, 20t**, 762–763
Evolutionary theory of sleep, 199
Excitatory neurotransmitter substance, 84
Excitotoxic injury, 119
**Exhaustion phase, 591**
Exhibitionism, 475
Existential intelligence, 393
**Expectancies, 153, 510**–511, 516
Expectations, and nocebos, 625f
**Experimental condition, 47**
Experimental design, 48t
**Experimental group, 46**–47
Experimental research, 45–48
**Experimenter expectancy effects, 52**
Experiments, 45–48
Expert systems, 365
Expert versus nonexpert approaches to problem solving, 363t
Expertise, 362–364
**Explicit memory, 292**–293, 296, 545–546
**Exposure, 693**–694, 724
Exposure with response prevention, 693–694
**External attribution, 755**–756
Externals, 511
**Extinction, 240, 240f, 259**, 696
**Extrasensory perception (ESP), 53, 182**
Extraversion, 492, 501, 505, 505t, 658
Eye
  anatomy of, 138
  and cerebral hemispheres, 98f
Eye-blink conditioning, 243–244, 298
Eye blink reflex, 539t
Eyewitnesses, 319
Eysenck's personality dimensions, 493, 501–502, 503t

Face validity, 50t
Facial expressions, 265–266, 435
**Facial feedback hypothesis, 435**
Factor analysis, 386–387
False alarm, 650
**False memories, 307f, 307**–310
Falsifiable theory, 41
Family interaction, 708f
**Family therapy, 708**–709
Farsightedness, 143
FAS, 416
Fatty acids, 459
Fear, 242–244, 439–440, 445, 500
Fear conditioning, 242–243
Fear-potentiated startle, 437
Fearful-avoidant attachment, 521–522
Fechner, Gustav Theodor, 135
Female arousal dysfunction, 475
**Fetal alcohol syndrome, 416**, 534
Fetal development, and vulnerability to teratogens, 536f
Fetish, 475
Fetoscope, 533
**Fetus, 532**–537
Fidget factor, 464

*50 First Dates*, 312
**Figure**, 145–147, 170
Filtering, 160
*Finding Nemo*, 312
Five Factor Model, 492–493, 495
Fixation, 484
**Fixed interval schedule, 261**
**Fixed ratio schedule, 261–262**
**Flashback, 227**
**Flashbulb memory, 289**
Flat affect, 660
Flight-or-fight response, 89, 94, 412, 588–590
**Flow, 488**
**Fluid intelligence, 387–388, 389**
aging and, 573
working memory and, 398–399
Fluoxetine, 703, 728
**Flynn effect, 409–411**
fMRI, 113
**Food aversion, 245–248, 249, 461**
**Foot-in-the-door technique, 771–772, 780**
Ford, Gerald, 200
Fore, the, 430
**Forebrain, 100**
Foreshortening, 148
Forgetting, 310–313
**Forgetting curve, 310**, 310f
**Formal operation(s), 548, 550**
Forward conditioning, 236
**Fovea, 138**
**Fragile X syndrome, 415**
Franklin-Lipsker, Eileen, 314
Fraternal twins, 123, 402f, 404–405, 415. *See also* Twin studies
**Free association, 687**
**Frequency, 137**
place coding of, 168f
Frequency distributions, 56
**Frequency theory, 168**
Freud, Anna, 485, 566
Freud, Sigmund, 14–15
Freud's theory of dreaming, 200–201
Freud's theory of personality, 482–485
defense mechanisms in, 485t
psychosexual stages in, 484t
structures of, 483f
Freudian slips, 688
Frigidity, 475
**Frontal lobe(s), 91, 92, 96–97**
behavioral activation and, 500
coding and, 284
emotion regulation and, 443–444
memory and, 281, 292
Fruit flies, sexual behavior of, 118
Fugue, dissociative, 668
Fulton, John, 112
Functional amnesia, 312
**Functional fixedness, 357–358**
**Functional magnetic resonance imaging (fMRI), 113**
**Functionalism, 12–13, 20t, 21**
Fundamental attributional error, 756–757
Fusiform face area (FFA), 156

*g*, 386–390
GABA, 83t
Gacy, John Wayne, 677
Gage, Phineas, 97
Gall, Franz Joseph, 92
Gambling, 262
Gametes, 530–532
Gamma-amino butyric acid (GABA), 83t
Gandhi, Mohandas Karamchand, 427–428, 432, 443, 446, 449, 458–459, 466–467, 488
Ganglion cells, 140
Ganzfeld procedure, 182
Gardner's theory of multiple intelligences, 392–393, 393t, 394t
GAS, 589–591
**Gate control (of pain), 181**
Gauguin, Paul, 629–630, 647
Gazzaniga and LeDoux experiment, 98, 99f
Gender differences
in aggression, 614
in coping, 622–623
in personality, 515–517
**Gender identity, 557–558**
**Gender roles, 558**
**Gene(s), 115, 116–126, 531**
coping and, 618–619
homosexuality and, 473
intelligence and, 399–401
language and, 341–342
memory and, 297–298, 311
mental retardation and, 415
ob, 463–464
personality and, 504–508
Gene mapping, 118
**General adaptation syndrome (GAS), 589–591**
General factor (*g*), 386–390
**Generalization, 258–259**
Generalization gradient, 241
**Generalized anxiety disorder, 648**
**Generalized reality orientation fading, 210**
Genetic relatedness, and IQ, 400f
Genetics, behavioral, 122–126
Genie, 341
**Genotype, 116**, 117f
Genovese, Kitty, 777–778
**Gestalt laws of organization, 146**, 170
**Gestalt psychology, 13–14**, 20
Gestures, 344
**Gifted, 416–417**
Ginkgo biloba, 571
Glands. *See* Endocrine glands
**Glial cell(s), 86–87**
**Glove anesthesia, 213–214**
**Glucocorticoids, 589–590**, 602
Glucose, 459
Glutamate, 83t, 86, 119, 178
Good continuation, 146
Good form, 146
Gore, Albert, 51–52
Gourmand syndrome, 460
Graduate Record Examination (GRE), 412

Grain, of image, 350, 351
**Grammar, 339–342**
Grant, Ulysses S., 248
Graphs, 62–66
Gray matter. *See* Cerebral cortex
Greebles, 156
**Grief, 578–579**
**Ground, 145**
in hearing, 170
**Group, 764–768**
control, 46–47, 715, 717, 718
experimental, 46–47
performance in, 774–776
self-help, 709–710
yielding to, 768–774
Group, level of the. *See* Level of the group
**Group polarization, 775–776**
**Group therapy, 707–708**
**Groupthink, 775**
Guilty actions test, 446
Guilty knowledge test (GKT), 446, 447
**Gyrus, 92**, 93

**Habit, 293–294**, 296
**Habituation, 234–235**, 543–544, 544f, 693
**Hair cells, 167–168**
Haldol, 702, 703
**Hallucinations, 632**, 660
**Hallucinogen(s), 219, 227–228**
Halo effect, 735–736
Hammer, 167
Hap B gene, 400
Happiness, 439–440, 442
**Hardy personality, 616**
Harm avoidance, 502, 503
Harris, Eric, 615
Harvard Test of Inflected Acquisition, 410
Hassles and stress, 595–597
*Having Our Say*, 733
Health-impairing behaviors, 605–608
**Health psychology, 588**
Hearing, 165–173
Heart disease, 603–605
Heart rate, 243
Heaven's Gate cult, 780–781
Hedonic treadmill, 439
Hemisphere, cerebral. *See* Cerebral hemisphere(s)
Hering, Ewald, 141–142
**Heritability, 122**, 123. *See also* Adoption studies; Twin studies
of attachment style, 523
of autism, 415
of intelligence, 399–401
of personality, 504–506, 506f
of psychoticism, 501–502
of specific behaviors, 506–507
of temperament, 498
Heroin, 219, 226
**Heterosexual, 472–474**, 475
Heterozygous genes, 116, 117f
**Heuristic(s), 358–359**
availability, 371
culture and, 370

different, for same problem, 359f
representativeness, 369–370
**Hidden observer, 212**
Hierarchical organization, 288f, 316
Hierarchy
of intelligence, 388–389
of needs, 456f, 456, 487–488
status, 766–768
**High expressed emotion, 665**
Higher order conditioning, 241, 241f
Hiking monk problem, 357
Himba language, 348
**Hindbrain, 104**
Hippocampus, 102
fear conditioning and, 242–243
operant conditioning and, 263–264
HIV virus, and prenatal development, 534
H.M., case of, 102, 293–294, 313
Homeobox genes, 473
**Homeostasis, 450–451**, 452
Homophobia, 475–476
**Homosexual, 472–474**, 631
Homozygous genes, 116, 117f
**Hormone(s), 104–105**
brain and, 101
in puberty, 566–567
sex, 408, 468–469
stress-related, 664
Horney, Karen, 486
Hospital of St. Mary of Bethlehem, 330
**Hostile attribution bias, 613–614**
**Hostility, 600**, 615, 697
*How to Lie with Statistics*, 61
Hox genes, 473
HPA axis, 105, 106f
Hue, 140
Hull, Clark L., 15
Human factors psychologist, 25
Human Genome Project, 118, 400
**Humanistic psychology, 16–17, 20t**, 487–488
Humanistic therapy, 689–690
Humor
comprehension of, 332
and stress, 612–613
Hunger, 458–466
Hurricane Andrew, 602–603
Hybrid vigor, 410
5-Hydroxytryptamine (5HT), 83t
Hypercolumn, 145
*Hypericum perforatum*, 703
Hypermetropia, 143, 144f
**Hypermnesia, 305–306**
Hypnic jerk, 193
**Hypnogogic sleep, 193**
**Hypnosis, 181, 208, 210–214**
induced alterations with, 211f
**Hypnotic induction, 210**
Hypnotizability, distribution of, 212f
Hypocretin, 206
**Hypomania, 642**
**Hypothalamic-pituitary-adrenal (HPA) axis, 105**, 106f
**Hypothalamus, 101–102**, 105
eating and, 460–461
homosexuality and, 472

Hypothesis, 39–40. *See also specific hypotheses*

*I Am Jackie Chan*, 233
Iconic memory, 279–280
**Id, 483,** 686–687
Identical twins, 123, 402f, 402–405. *See also* Twin studies
Identification, visual, 151–157
Identity alteration, 668
Identity confusion, 668
Illusions
  cognitive, 370
  of outgroup homogeneity, 750
  visual, 135f
Illusory correlation, 750
Images
  interactive, 317
  manipulating objects in, 350f
  scanning of visual mental, 349f
Imaginal exposure, 693
Imaginary audience, 565
Immediate memory, 280–281
**Immediate reinforcement, 258**
Immigration Act of 1924, 404
Immune responses, 104, 105–106
Immune system
  conditioning, 249
  coping strategies and, 617–621
  stress and, 105, 600–603
Implicit association test (IAT), 740–741
**Implicit memories, 292–295,** 546
**Implicit motive, 454**
Impotence, 475
**Impression formation, 735**
**Impression management, 735,** 737–738
**Impulsivity, 497**
**Incentive(s), 452–453**
**Incidental learning, 288**
**Incongruence, 689**
**Incubation, 360–361**
**Independent variable, 45–46,** 46f
Indicated preventive interventions, 714
Indirect strategies, 742
**Individual therapy, 707,** 712–713
Individualism, in United States, 519f
**Individualist culture(s), 457–458,** 518, 519
Inducible knockouts, 119, 297
**Inductive reasoning, 367–368,** 368f
Industrial/organizational (I/O) psychologist, 25, 26
Infantile amnesia, 313
**Inferential statistics, 58–61**
**Inferiority complex, 486**
Information-processing approach, 17, 552–553
Informational social influence, 769
**Informed consent, 29**
**Ingroup, 750**
Ingroup differentiation, 750
Inheritance, 116–117
**Inhibitory conflict, 221**
Inhibitory neurotransmitter substance, 84
Initialisms, 318

Injunctive norms, 765
**Insight, 360–361**
**Insight learning, 268–269,** 360–361
**Insight-oriented therapy, 686–691**
**Insomnia, 205t, 206–207**
**Instinct, 450**
Instinct theory, 450
Institute for Advanced Study, 366
Institutional review board (IRB), 30
Instrumental conditioning, 251
Insula, 106
**Insulin, 461**
Intellectual disability, 414–416
**Intelligence, 380–381.** *See also* Crystallized intelligence; Fluid intelligence
  analyzing, 385–395
  brain size and, 396–397
  diversity in, 414–422
  emotional, 391–392
  environment and, 401–404, 406
  genes and, 399–401
  group differences in, 404–409
  intrapersonal, 393
  linguistic, 392, 393
  logical-mathematical, 393
  measuring, 380–385
  multiple, 392–393
  music, 393
  practical, 394–395
  psychometric approaches to, 386–390
  race differences in, 405–407
  sex differences in, 407–409
  spatial, 393, 409
  stereotyping, 412–413
  three-stratum theory of, 388, 389f
  working memory and, 397–399
**Intelligence quotient (IQ), 381–385**
  genetic relatedness and, 400f
  heritability of, 399–401, 404–405
  improving, 409–413
  microenvironment and, 407
  processing speech and, 397
  schooling and, 406–407
**Intentional learning, 288**
Interactional theory of depression, 646–647
Interactionism, 490–491
Interactionist theories of language, 336
Interactive images, 317
**Interference, 311**
**Internal attribution(s), 755–756**
**Internal conflict, 595,** 596f
Internals, 511
International Space Station (ISS), 37, 38, 39, 42, 54, 70
**Interneuron(s), 78,** 91
**Interpersonal therapy (IPT), 712,** 723–725
**Interpretation, 688,** 690
**Interval schedule, 261**
Intervention, 607–608, 714
Interviews, structured, 493–494
Intrapersonal intelligence, 393
Intrinsic motivation, 452
**Introspection, 12**
Introversion, 501

Intuition, 372
In vivo exposure, 693
I/O psycholgist, 25, 26
**Ion(s), 79,** 81f
IPT, 712, 723–725
IQ. *See* Intelligence quotient
IRB, 30
**Iris, 138**
**Islands of excellence, 415**

James, Nanny, 733, 734
James, William, 13
James–Lange theory, 432–433, 434–435, 438
Jamison, Kay Redfield, 642
Jefferson Airplane, 227
Jet lag, 208–209
  minimizing, 208t
Jigsaw classroom, 754f, 754–755
Jim Crow laws, 733, 766, 768
JND, 136
Johnson, Dwayne, 121
Jordan, David Starr, 311
Jordan, Michael, 746
Jung, Carl, 486
**Just-noticeable difference (JND), 136**

Kahlo, Frida, 133–134, 147, 155, 165, 171, 174–175
Kahlo, Guillermo, 134
Kaliai tribe, 579
Kasparov, Garry, 364, 372
Kelley's theory of causal attribution, 755–756
Ketamine, 228
**Kinesthetic sense, 179,** 180
King, Martin Luther, Jr., 427
Kinsey, Alfred, 467
Klebold, Dylan, 615
**Knockin mice, 119**
**Knockout mice, 118,** 297–298
Kohlberg's theory of moral development, 559–561
Külpe, Oswald, 12
*Kyol goeu*, 650

Language, 326–335
  acquisition of, 340f
  body, 442–443, 444–445
  brain and, 99, 329, 329f, 332–333, 340–342, 343
  development of, 335–342
  environment and, 338–339
  four aspects of, 327f
  sign, 169, 343–344
**Language acquisition device (LAD), 335**
**Language comprehension, 327,** 337f
**Language production, 326–327**
La Piere, Richard, 8, 43, 739
**Latent content, 200–201**
**Latent learning, 268**
  discovery of, 268f
Law of common fate, 13
**Law of Effect, 251**
Law of proximity, 13
L-dopa, 86

Learned alarm, 650
**Learned helplessness, 453,** 593–594, 644
  experiment on, 453f
**Learning, 234.** *See also* Classical conditioning; Operant conditioning
  avoidance, 238
  cognitive, 267–268
  of fetus, 533
  incidental, 288
  insight, 268–269, 360–361
  intentional, 288
  latent, 268
  nonassociative, 234, 293
  observational, 269–273, 697
  personality and, 509–512
  sleep and, 197, 199–200
  specific phobias and, 652
  trial-and-error, 251
Leptin, 463
**Lesion, 109**
Lesioning studies, 109
**Level of the brain, 6,** 7–8, 9. *See also* Levels of analysis
  in antisocial personality disorder, 678–679
  in eating disorders, 672–673
  in mood disorders, 643–644
  in OCD, 654
  in panic disorder, 649
  in phobias, 652
  in PTSD, 657
  in schizophrenia, 662–664
**Level of the group, 7,** 8. *See also* Levels of analysis
  in antisocial personality disorder, 678–679
  in eating disorders, 673–674
  in mood disorders, 645–646
  in OCD, 655
  in panic disorder, 650–651
  in phobias, 652
  in PTSD, 658
  in schizophrenia, 665–666
**Level of the person, 6–8.** *See also* Levels of analysis
  in antisocial personality disorder, 678–679
  in eating disorders, 673
  in mood disorders, 644–645
  in OCD, 654–655
  in panic disorder, 649–650
  in phobias, 652
  in PTSD, 657–658
  in schizophrenia, 664–665
Levels of analysis, 5–9
  abnormal behavior and, 632–636
  aging brain and, 580–581
  attachment styles and, 520–524
  attractiveness and, 163–164
  autobiographical memory and, 299–300
  behaviorism and, 15
  binge eating and, 674–675
  cults and, 780–781
  in depression, 646–647
  diet and, 466

evolutionary psychology and, 19
facial expressions and, 265–266
functionalism and, 12
Gestalt psychology and, 13
graph design and, 65–66
humanistic psychology and, 16
on jet lag, 208–209
lie detection and, 446–448
music and, 106–108
OCD treatment and, 727–728
psychodynamic theory and, 14–15
social interactions and, 535
stereotyping intelligence and, 412–413
structuralism and, 12
ultimatum game and, 372–374
voodoo death and, 624–625
Lie detection, 446–448
Lightness, 140
**Limbic system,** 101f, **102**–103
Lincoln, Abraham, 488
Linear perspective, 148
Lineups, police, 303–304
Linguistic intelligence, 392, 393
**Linguistic relativity hypothesis, 347**–348
Liquids, conservation of, 549f
Listening, dichotic, 172
Lithium, 704, 705
Little Albert, 238, 239f, 240–241
**Lobes, 91,** 92f
Lock-and-key mechanism of smell, 175f
Locke, John, 11, 348
Locus coeruleus, 362, 649f
**Locus of control, 511**
Logic, 210, 367–369
Logical-mathematical intelligence, 393
**Longitudinal study, 573**
versus cross-sectional study, 573f
**Long-term memory (LTM), 281**–283
**Long-term potentiation (LTP), 297**
Looking time technique, 543
**Loudness, 166, 170**–171
Love
triangular model of, 760f
types of, 760
"Love-bombing," 780
Low frustration tolerance, 697
**Lowball technique, 771**–772
LSD, 219
LTM, 281–283
LTP, 297
Luria, Alexander, 277

Macular degeneration, 144
**Magnetic resonance imaging (MRI), 111**–112
Magnetic resonance spectroscopy (MRS), 113
Magnetic sense, 181
**Magnetoencephalography (MEG), 110**
Magritte, René, 146
**Major depressive disorder (MDD), 638**–642, 643–647
diagnostic criteria for, 639t
Majority-win rule, 774

Male erectile dysfunction, 475
Malingering, 312
Managed care, 710–711
Mandala, 215
Mandarin Chinese language, 348
Manic-Depressive and Depressive Association of Boston (MMDA-Boston), 727
**Manic episode, 420, 642,** 643t
**Manifest content, 200**–201
MAO, 44
MAO-B, 499
MAOI(s), 703, 705
Marijuana, 84, 219, 227–228
Margin of error, 58
Maslow, Abraham, 16–17, 487–488
Maslow's hierarchy of needs, 456, 456f
Massachusetts Eating Disorders Association, 727
Massed practice, 287
Master gland, 105
Masters and Johnson's research on sexual behavior, 467–468, 468t, 475
Mating preferences, 471–472, 762–763
**Maturation, 531**
Mayans, 202, 579
Mayes, Larry, 309
McKinley, William, 271
MDD, 638–642, 643–647
MDMA, 219, 225–226, 281
**Mean, 56**–57
Measurement error, 390
Mechanism, 5–6, 7
Medial orbital frontal cortex, 163
**Median, 56**–57
Medications, 723–725
effects of, 705t
**Meditation, 214, 215**–217
**Medulla, 103**
MEG, 110
Melatonin, 140
meditation and, 217
sleep and, 203, 208
Memory. *See also specific types*
accuracy of, 307–314
in adulthood, 572
brain and, 97, 102, 296–300, 546–547, 553
development of, 545–547
dreams and, 201
emotions and, 288–290
encoding information into, 278–290
genes and, 297–298
hypnosis and, 211
improving, 315–320
major types of long-term, 295f
smell and, 175
storage of, 290–300
stress and, 298, 412
three-stage model of, 279, 279f
**Memory store, 279**
Memory suppressor genes, 311
*Men in Black,* 754
Menarche, 562
Mendel, Gregor, 115
**Mendelian inheritance, 116**
**Meninges, 91**

Meningitis, 91
Menopause, 570
Menstrual cycles, and pheromones, 175
Mental age (MA), 381
Mental filter, 698t
Mental health, definition of, 711f
**Mental images, 348**–351
**Mental model, 367**
reasoning and, 367f
Mental practice, and performance, 70–72, 71f
**Mental processes, 4, 5**
Mental retardation, 414–416
causes of, 416t
**Mental set, 365**
Mental space, 348–350
**Mentally retarded, 414**
Menu model of natural selection, 125f
**Mere exposure effect, 744**
**Meta-analysis, 60**–61
**Metabolism, 459**
Metaphors, comprehension of, 332, 333
Method of loci, 317
**Microelectrode, 110**–111
**Microenvironment, 402**–403, 407
Microexpressions, 447
Microstimulation, 114
**Midbrain, 104**
Midlife transition, 576
Milgram's obedience study, 772–774, 773f, 782
Mind–body interventions, 621t, 621–622
*Mind of a Mnemonist: A Little Book About a Vast Memory, The,* 277
Mind reading, 698t
**Mindfulness meditation, 215**
**Minnesota Multiphasic Personality Inventory-2 (MMPI-2), 495**
Minnesota Study of Twins Reared Apart (MISTRA), 504–505
*Mir,* 37
**Misattribution of arousal, 436**
MISTRA, 504–505
MMPI-2, 495
**Mnemonic devices, 317**–319
**Modality, 707**–710
**Modality-specific memory stores, 291, 296**
**Mode, 57**
Model
of abnormal behavior, 632–635
Five Factor, 492–493, 495
of memory, 279
mental, 367
Modeling, 270, 271–273
of aggressive behavior, 272t
*Momento,* 312
Monet, Claude, 135
Monoamine oxidase (MAO), 44
Monoamine oxidase-B (MAO-B), 499
**Monoamine oxidase inhibitor (MAOI), 703, 705**
**Monocular static cues, 148**–150
**Monozygotic, 123.** *See also* Identical twins

Monroe, Marilyn, 674
Monson, Kate, 639
**Mood disorders, 638**–647, 703–704, 705–706, 725. *See also* Bipolar disorder; Depression
**Moral dilemma,** 559f, **559**–561
Moro reflex, 538, 539t
**Morpheme, 330**
Morphine, 181
**Motion cues, 149**–150
Motion parallax, 149–150
**Motivation, 428**–429, **449**–453, 454, 470–471
Motives, for sex, 471f
Motor development, 541–543
milestones in, 542f
**Motor neuron, 78**
**Motor strip, 97**
Mozart, Wolfgang Amadeus, 411
MRI, 111–112
MRS, 113
MS, 80
Multiple intelligences, Gardner's theory of, 392–393
Multiple personality disorder, 669–670
Multiple sclerosis (MS), 80, 107
Murray, Henry, 496
Music, 172–173
brain and, 106–108
prenatal development and, 536–537
Music intelligence, 393
Music therapy, 107
**Mutation, 118**
Muybridge, Eadweard, 161
**Myelin, 80, 87,** 92, 553
Myelinization, 553
Myopia, 143, 144f

nAch, 455
Narcissists, aggression in, 615
**Narcolepsy,** 205t, **206**
**Narcotic analgesics, 219, 226**
Nash, John, 632
National Association of Social Workers, 727
National Center for Complementary and Alternative Medicine (NCCAM), 621
National Depressive and Manic Depressive Association, 709
National Institute for Health and Clinical Excellence, 723
National Institutes of Health, 621
National organizations, for types of therapy, 727t
**Nativism, 335**
Natural experiments, 109
**Natural killer (NK) cell(s), 602,** 603
**Natural selection, 124**–125
menu model of, 125f
Naturalist intelligence, 393
Naturalistic observation, 42–43, 48t
NCSTN B Haplotype (Hap B) gene, 400
Near infrared spectroscopy (NIRS), 113
Nearsightedness, 143

Need(s), **453**–454, **455**–456, **487**–488
  Maslow's hierarchy of, 456, 456f
  versus wants, 455f
**Need for achievement (nAch), 455**
Need for cognition (NC), 455–456
Negative affect, 300
Negative attitude change, 745
Negative correlation, 45
**Negative punishment, 254f, 255**
**Negative reinforcement, 254f, 255,**
  **255f, 256f**
**Negative symptom(s), 660t, 660–661**
Negative triad of depression, 644, 644f
Nehru, Jawaharlal, 437
Neo-Freudians, 486
NEO Personality Inventory (NEO-PI-
  R), 495, 516
**Nerve deafness, 169**
Nervous system, 88–93
  major parts of, 89f
Network, 6, 7, 365. See also Level of
  the group
Neural conduction time, 81f
Neural impulses, 79–80
**Neural network, 365**
**Neuroendocrine system, 104**–105
Neuroethics, 32
**Neuroimaging, 111**–114, 213
Neuroleptic medication. See
  Antipsychotic medication
**Neuromodulator(s), 82**–86
  major, 83t
**Neuron(s), 78**–81
  linking of, 243
  parts of, 80f
  stimulating, 114–115
  types of, 79f
Neuropeptide Y (NPY), 463, 590
Neuropsychologist, clinical, 23, 26, 43
Neuroscience, cognitive, 18, 20, 21
**Neurosis, 484**
Neuroticism, 492, 501, 505, 505t, 625
**Neurotransmitter(s), 82**–86, 85f
  major, 83t
  schizophrenia and, 664
  sleep and, 202–205
  stimulants, 225f
Neutral stimulus, 238
Newborn development, 537–540
Newell, Alan, 17
Newton, Isaac, 420
Nicotine, 226
**Night terrors, 205**, 205t
**Nightmare(s), 205**, 205t
NIRS, 113
Nitric oxide, 82
NK cell(s), 602, 603
NMDA receptor, 297
**Nocebo effect, 624**–625
Nocebos, and expectations, 625f
Nonassociative learning, 234, 293
Nonavoiders, 618
Nonconformity, 493, 501–502
Nondeclarative memories, 292–295
**Nondeprived reward, 454**–455
Nonpurging type, of bulimia nervosa,
  672

Nonsense syllables, 282–283
Nonspecific side effects, 624, 625
Nontasters, 178
**Nonverbal communication, 8**–9,
  342–**343**. See also Body language;
  Facial expressions
Nonviolent resistance, 428
Noradrenaline (NA), 83t
Norepinephrine (NE), 83t
**Norm(s), 765**–766
  perceived, and personal attitudes,
  766t
**Normal consciousness, 191**
Normal curve, 384f
**Normal distribution, 57**–58, 57f
Normative social influence, 769, 770
**Norming, 383**
Norton, Ken, 214
Novelty seeking, 502
Nucleus accumbens, 103
Null hypothesis, 58–59
*Nurse Betty*, 668
NutraSweet, 179
Nutrition, and IQ, 410

**Obedience, 772**–774
Obesity, 462–465
Ob gene, 463–464
**Object permanence, 548**
Observation, 38–39
  naturalistic, 42–43, 48
  of personality, 494, 509
**Observational learning, 269**–273,
  270f, 697
**Obsession(s), 653**–655
**Obsessive-compulsive disorder**
  **(OCD), 653**–655, 693, 704, 716,
  721–722, 725, 727–728
**Occipital lobe, 91**, 92, **94**–95
Occlusion cue, 148
Occupations, and personality profiles,
  492f
OCD. See Obsessive-compulsive disor-
  der
Oceanic feelings, 488
Octave, 172
Oedipus complex, 484–485
OFC, 163
Office plans, 597f
Olfaction, 174–177, 179
Olfactory system, 176f
*One Flew Over the Cuckoo's Nest*, 705
Onset difference, 171
Open plan office designs, 597–598
**Opening-up meditation, 215**
Openness to experience, 401, 492, 493
**Operant conditioning, 250**–266
  versus classical conditioning, 264t
  personality and, 509
  phases of, 251f
  psychological disorders and, 695–697
**Operational definition, 39**–40
**Opiate, 219, 226**
Opioids, 460
**Opponent cells, 142**
**Opponent process theory of color vi-
  sion, 142**

Optical imaging, 113–114
Optic chiasm, 204f
**Optic nerve, 98f, 139**
Optimism, 616–618, 619
Orbitofrontal cortex, 265
Orexin, 206
Organic amnesia, 312–313
Organization
  Gestalt laws of, 146, 170
  tonotopic, 168
Oslo Peace Accord, 753
**Outcome research, 715**
**Outgroup, 750**
**Overextension, 337**–338, 338f
**Overregulation error, 340**
Ovulation, 469
Ovum, 530–532
Oxytocin, 470

Pain, 100, 180–181
Palmar grasp reflex, 539t
**Panic attacks, 648**–651
**Panic disorder, 648**–651, 725
Papillae, 177
**Paradoxical cold, 180**
**Paradoxical intention, 708**
Paranoid scizophrenia, 661, 662
Paraphilia, 475
**Parasympathetic nervous system, 89,**
  **90**
Paraventricular nucleus, 105
Parental investment, theory of, 472
**Parietal lobe, 91**, 92, **95**–96
Parkinson, James, 86
Parkinson's disease, 85–86, 103
**Partial reinforcement, 260**–261
**Passionate love, 760**
**Passive interaction, 121**
Pavlov, Ivan, 235
Pavlovian conditioning, 235–237. See
  *also* Classical conditioning
Pavlov's apparatus, 236f
Paxil, 703, 723
PDAs, and therapy, 712
Pedophilia, 475
Pegword system, 318
Penis envy, 484–485
Penny, choosing correct image of, 283f
Pentecostal religion, 632
**Perceived social support, 620**–621
**Percentile rank, 58**
**Perception, 134**–135. See *also* Auditory
  perception; Visual perception
  in adulthood, 570–574
  belief and, 161f
  categorical, 170
  development of, 543–545
  of emotions, 444–448
  hypnosis and, 211
  of norms, 765–766
  of possible events, 551f
  self-, 742
  subliminal, 160–161
**Perceptual constancy, 147**
Perceptual expectancies, 153
**Perceptual set, 153**
Perceptual unit, 13–14

Perfect pitch, 107
**Peripheral nervous system (PNS),**
  88–90
Persistence, 502
Person, level of the. See Level of the
  person
Personal fable, 565
**Personality, 482**
  biological influences on, 497–508
  biologically based theories of, 503t
  birth order and, 514t
  coping and, 616–619
  environment and, 506, 517–520
  heritability of, 504–506, 506f
  sociocognitive approach to, 510f,
  510–512
  sociocultural influences on, 513–524
  structure of (Freud), 483f
  theories of, 482–488, 499–504
  traits in, 489–496
Personality dimensions, 492–493
**Personality disorders, 669**–670, 675,
  **676–677**
  Axis II, 676t
**Personality inventory, 494**–495
Personality profiles, 492f, 494–495
Personality psychologist, 24, 25, 26, 43
**Personality trait(s), 489**–496
**Persuasion, 744**–745
Pessimism, 617–618
PET, 112, 112f, 115, 728f
Phallic symbols, 486–487
Phantom limb, 100
Phase, difference in, 170–171
**Phenotype, 116**
**Pheromones, 176**–177
  increased sexual behavior and, 177f
Phi phenomenon, 150
**Phobia, 238**, 239f, **651**–652
  subtypes of, 651t
  systematic desensitization of, 695f
**Phonemes, 327**–328
Phonemic restoration effect, 171
**Phonology, 327**–328, 331
Phrenologists, 92–93
Physical abuse, and DID, 669–670
Physical attraction, 760
Physical coordination, and brain,
  103–104
Physical environment, 7
Physiological psychologist, 25, 26
Piaget's theory of cognitive develop-
  ment, 547–550, 564
  periods in, 548t
Pinker, Steven, 19
**Pitch, 107, 166**, 173
**Pituitary gland, 105**
Place coding, of sound frequency, 168f
**Place theory, 168**
**Placebo, 55**–56, 717
Placebo effect, 622, 704
Planning fallacy, 371
Plantar reflex, 539t
Planum temporale, 173
**Plasticity, 120**
Plato, 137, 348
*Plea for Vegetarianism*, 459

Pleasure center, 101–102, 454
Pleasure principle, 483
PNS, 88–90
Pollution, and prenatal development, 534–535
*Poltergeist*, 530, 562
**Polygraph, 446–448**
**Pons, 103**
**Pop-out, 157**–158, 158f, 159
**Population, 59**–60, 383
Positive affect, 300
Positive correlation, 45
Positive emotions, 439–440
Positive psychology, 440
**Positive punishment,** 254f, **255**
**Positive reinforcement, 253**–254, 254f, 255f
**Positive symptom(s), 660,** 660t
**Positron emission tomography (PET), 112,** 112f, 115, 728f
Possession trance, 214
Possible events, perception of, 551f
**Posthypnotic suggestion, 210**
Postmenopausal zest, 570
**Posttraumatic stress disorder (PTSD),** 602–603, **655**–658, 725
  rates of, in response to traumatic events, 656t
Potter, Harry, 379, 417
Practical intelligence, 394–395
Practice
  deliberate, 363–364
  distributed, 287, 316–317
  massed, 287
  mental, 70–72
**Pragmatics,** 331, **332**–333
Praying mantis, 474
Precognition, 182
Preconscious, 482–483
**Prediction,** 40–41
**Prejudice,** 9, **748**–755
  creation and dissolution of, 752f
Prenatal development, 530–540
Preoccupied attachment, 521–522
Preoperational period, 548–549
Prevention focus, 457
Preventive interventions, 713f, 713–714
**Primacy effect, 283,** 736
Primary appraisal, 593
Primary auditory cortex, 168
**Primary mental abilities, 387**
Primary motor cortex. *See* Motor strip
**Primary reinforcer(s), 257**–258
Primary visual cortex, 145
**Priming, 160,** 294–295
Princeton University, 366
Princip, Gavrilo, 753
**Private speech, 554**
Privilege envy, 486
Proactive coping, 609
**Proactive interference, 311**
**Problem,** 356, **357**–365
**Problem-focused coping, 609**–611
  strategies for, 610t
Problem solving, 356–365
  approaches to, 361t
  by experts versus nonexperts, 363t

Procedural memory, 293–294, 296
Processing
  bottom-up, 152–153, 158, 181
  breadth of, 287–288, 316
  controlled, 294, 295
  depth of, 286–287, 316
  information, 17, 552–553
  speed of, 397
  top-down, 152–153, 158, 181, 736–737
Prochaska's model of change, 606
**Prodigies, 417**
Prodromal phase, 642
Profile of intelligences, 393
**Progressive muscle relaxation, 694**
Project A, 267
Project Head Start, 411, 714
**Projective test, 495**–496
Promotion focus, 457
**Propositional representations, 331,** 331f
6-n-Propylthiouracil (PROP), 178
**Prosocial behavior, 776**–777
Prosopagnosia, 155–157
Protein Power! diet, 465
**Prototype, 352**–354
  of dog, 353f
Proximity, 146
Prozac, 703, 728
*Prozac Nation*, 639
**Pruning, 119**–120
**Pseudopsychology, 52**–53
Psi, 182
**Psychiatric nurse, 23**
**Psychiatrist, 23**
Psychoactive substances, actions and effects of, 219t
**Psychoanalysis,** 15, **686**–689
**Psychodynamic theory, 14**–15, 20t, 21
**Psychodynamic therapy, 687**–689, 690–691
**Psychoeducation, 700**
Psychokinesis (PK), 182
**Psychological determinism, 482**–487
**Psychological disorder(s), 630**–632.
  *See also specific disorders*
  categorizing, 635–637, 693
  culture and, 634–635, 640–641, 645–646, 650, 666, 673–674
  DSM categories of, 636t
  observational learning and, 697
Psychological needs, 455–456
Psychological thought, schools of, 20t
Psychologists. *See also specific types*
  clinical principles and code of conduct for, 31t
  job satisfaction of, 27t
  occupations of, 26t, 27f
**Psychology,** 4–5, 10–21. *See also specific subfields*
  women in, 27–28
Psychometric approaches, to intelligence, 386–390
Psychoneuroimmunology, 602
**Psychopharmacology, 702**–705
**Psychophysics, 135**–136
**Psychosexual stages,** 484t, 484–485

**Psychosis,** 225, 484, **632**
**Psychosocial development, 575**–576
Psychosocial stages (Erikson), 575t, 575–576
**Psychotherapy, 23,** 715–726
*Psychotherapy by Reciprocal Inhibition,* 692
**Psychotherapy integration, 710**
Psychoticism, 493, 501–502
PTSD, 602–603, 655–658
**Puberty, 562**–563, 563f, 566–567
Punch-drunk, 103–104
Punishment, 255–257
  facial expressions as, 265–266
  personality and, 500, 501
  versus punishment, 256f
**Pupil, 138**
Purging, 672, 674–675
Purging type, of bulimia nervosa, 672
Puzzle box, Thorndike's, 251
Pygmalion effect, on intelligence, 410–411

QALMRI method, 67–70
Quantitative data, 39
Quasi-experimental design, 47–48, 48t

Race, and intelligence, 405–407
Racial prejudice, 8–9, 748–750
*Rain Man*, 415
**Random assignment, 46**–47
Randomized controlled trials (RCTs), 719–721
**Range, 58**
Range of reaction, 403–404
Rapid eye movement (REM), 194. *See also* REM sleep
RAS, 103
**Ratio schedule, 261**–262
Rational-emotive behavior therapy (REBT), 697–699
Ravel, Maurice, 420
**Raven's Progressive Matrices,** 398f, 398–399, 409, 412
**Raw data, 56**
RCTs, 719–721
Reactance, 745
**Reaction range, 403**–404
Reactive coping, 609
Reactive interaction, 121–122
Reactivity, 498
Reagan, Ronald, 37
Realistic conflict theory, 751–752
**Reality monitoring, 309**–310
Reality principle, 483
Reasoning, 97, 367–368
  deductive versus inductive, 368f
Rebound effect, 207, 612, 737
REBT, 697–699
**Recall, 302**–306, 572
**Recategorization, 753**–754
**Recency effect, 283**
**Receptor(s), 84**
  in memory, 297
  in vision, 134. *See also* Cones; Rods
**Reciprocal determinism, 512,** 512f
**Recognition, 302**–306

Reconsolidation, 285–286
Recovered memory, 314
Redundant signal effect, 159
**Reflex(es), 91,** 91f, 538, 539t
**Reframing, 708**
Regulatory fit, 456–457
**Rehearsal, 280**
**Reinforcement,** 16, **252**–255, 256
  drives and, 450–451
  expectations of, 452
  facial expressions as, 265–266
  immediate, 258
  reward and, 454–455
  schedules of, 260–262, 262f
**Reinforcer(s), 252**–255, 257–258, 696
Relational aggression, 614
Relationships, 759–763
Relaxation training, 216–217
Relevant/irrelevant technique (RIT), 446
**Reliability, 49,** 384
**REM rebound, 196**
**REM sleep, 194,** 195f
  dreams and, 200
  narcolepsy and 206
Remeron, 703
Remus, 341
Repeated contact, 759
**Repetition blindness, 162**
Repetition deafness, 162
**Repetition priming, 294**–295
**Replication, 38**–39
**Representation problem, 357**
**Representativeness heuristic,** 369–370
**Repressed memories, 313**–314
Repression, 485
Repressors, 618
Research
  correlational, 44–45, 48
  on creativity, 421–422
  on depression, 640–641
  descriptive, 42–44, 48
  on emotional expression, 441–442
  ethics in, 29–32
  experimental, 45–48
  on fetus stimulation, 536–537
  on mental practice and performance, 70–72
  observational, 42–43, 48
  on OCD therapy, 721–722
  outcome, 715
  on police lineups, 303–304
  psychotherapy, 715–726
  on racial stereotypes, 748–750
  on resolving ambiguity, 333–335
  on sleep deprivation, 197–198
  on spatial relations, 154–155
  on split-brain patient, 98
  on taste aversion, 246–248
  on venting, 611–612
Research methods, 48t
**Resistance, 688**
**Resistance phase, 590**
Resistant attachment, 555

Response
  conditioned, 236, 240, 243, 245, 246, 249, 293
  conditioned compensatory, 244–245
  conditioned emotional, 238
  immune, 104, 105–106
  unconditioned, 236, 243, 245, 246, 249
**Response bias, 51,** 467
**Response contingency, 252,** 695–696
**Resting potential, 79**
Restorative theory of sleep, 199
Restricting type, of anorexia nervosa, 672
Restructuring, cognitive, 700
Reticular activating system (RAS), 103
**Reticular formation, 103**
**Retina, 138–139**
**Retinal disparity, 148,** 148f
**Retrieval, 278,** 301–306, 319–320. *See also* Recall; Recognition
**Retroactive interference, 311**
**Retrograde amnesia, 313**
**Reuptake, 84**
Reward, 452, 454–455, 500, 501
Reward dependence, 502
Rhodopsin, 139
Rhyming words, 318
Risperdal, 702
Rites of passage, 569
Rivera, Diego, 133, 134, 165, 171, 174–175
Robber's Cave study, 751–752, 752f, 754
Rock, The, 121
**Rods, 138**–139, 139f
Rogers, Carl, 16–17, 488, 689, 691, 716
**Roles, 558–559,** 766–768. *See also* Social role theory
Romulus, 341
Roosevelt, Eleanor, 488
Roosevelt, Franklin Delano, 455
Rooting reflex, 539t
Rorschach, Herman, 495
**Rorschach test, 495,** 495f
Rowling, J. K., 379, 380, 385, 390, 393, 395, 398, 406, 414, 417, 419
Rubella, and prenatal development, 534
*Rush Hour,* 253

*s,* 386
S. *See* Shereshevskii, S. K.
Sacks, Oliver, 143
Salivation, measuring, 235–237, 240, 241, 242
Salt, Henry S., 459
**Sample, 59**–60
  standardized, 383
**Sampling bias, 51**–52, 467
**Sampling error, 60**
Sanctions, 764
Saturation, 140
*Satyagraha,* 428
Savants, 415
Schachter-Singer experiment, 435–436, 436f

**Schema, 355,** 547
*Schindler's List,* 530, 576
**Schizophrenia, 659**–666, 696, 702–703, 705–706, 714, 724–725
  subtypes of, 661t
School psychologist, 26
Schwann cells, 86, 87f
**Scientific method, 38**–41, 40f
SCN, 203, 204f, 208
Searching, 158–159
Secondary appraisal, 593
**Secondary reinforcer(s), 257,** 258, 696
Secure attachment style, 520t, 520–524, 555, 761
Sedative-hypnotic drugs, 219, 220–224
**Selective attention, 157**
Selective avoidance, 745
Selective preventive interventions, 713–714
**Selective serotonin reuptake inhibitor (SSRI),** 85, **703,** 704, 705
**Self-actualization, 17,** 487–488
**Self-concept,** 488, 518–519, **556**–557
Self-downing, 697
**Self-efficacy, 511**
Self-esteem, and aggression, 615
Self-fulfilling prophecy, 736–737, 737f
**Self-help group(s), 709**–710
  daily log as, 696f
**Self-monitoring techniques, 696**
**Self-perception theory, 742**
*Self-Portrait with Cropped Hair,* 147
Self-reevaluation, 607
Self-reflectiveness, 511
Self-regulation, 498
**Self-serving bias, 757**
Selye's stress response, 589f, 589–591
**Semantic memories, 291**–292, 312–313, 572
  networks of, 292f
**Semantics, 330**–331
Semicircular canals, 180
**Sensation,** 95–96, **134.** *See also* Auditory sensation; Visual sensation
Sensation seeking, 44, 499, 658
**Sensitive period, 341**
**Sensitivity, 136,** 649–650
Sensitization, 235
Sensitizers, 618
Sensorimotor gating, 118
Sensorimotor period, 548
**Sensory memory (SM), 279**–280
**Sensory neuron, 78**
**Sensory-somatic nervous system (SSNS),** 89, 90
Sentence, syntactic analysis of, 328f
**Separation anxiety, 555**
**Serial position effect, 283,** 283f
Serotonin, 83t
  harm avoidance and, 503
  MDMA and, 225–226
  obesity and, 463
**Serotonin/norepinephrine reuptake inhibitor (SNRI), 703,** 704, 705
Serzone, 703
*Sesame Street,* 410

Set point, 462
Seven Little Fortunes, 250, 257
Sex, motives for, 471f
Sex cells, 530–532
Sexual activity, factors affecting, 474f
Sexual aggression, 221, 222–223
  alcohol and, 222f
Sexual behavior, 118, 442, 466–476
  pheromones and, 176–177
  risky, 605f
Sexual dysfunctions, 474–475
Sexual orientation, 472–474
**Sexual response cycle, 468**
S.F., case of, 287
**Shape constancy, 147**
**Shaping, 259**–260, 260f, 261
Shereshevskii, S. V., 277–278, 280–281, 288, 290–291, 301, 304, 306, 307, 317, 319
Shift work, 204–205
**Short-term memory (STM), 280**–281
Shuar, the, 357–358
Shyness, 498–499
Sickle-cell anemia, 126
SIDS, 542
Signal detection outcomes, 136f
**Signal detection theory, 136,** 137
Sign language, 168, 343–344
Similarity, 146, 759–760
Simon, Herbert A., 17
Simon, Theodore, 381, 383, 547
Simonides, 317
Simultaneous conditioning, 237
Single-cell recording, 110–111
Situational attributions, 755–756
Situationism, 490
**Size constancy,** 63, **147,** 149f
**Skeletal system, 90,** 140
Skewed distribution, 57
Skills, 294, 295
Skinner, B. F., 15, 692
Skinner box, 251–252, 252f
**Sleep, 193**
  brain and, 202–205
  brain waves during, 194f
  deprivation of, 196–199, 199f
  dreaming and, 200–202
  function of, 199–200
  stages of, 193–195, 195f
**Sleep apnea,** 205, **207**–208
Sleep cycles, 194–195
Sleep disorders, 205–208
  symptoms of, 205t
Sleep spindles, 193–194
Slow-wave sleep (SWS), 194, 195
SM, 279–280
Smart Recovery, 709
Smell, 174–177, 179
  lock-and-key mechanism of, 175f
Smoking, and prenatal development, 534
Smuts, Jan Christian, 428, 446
Snoring, and sleep apnea, 207
SNRIs, 703, 704, 705
**Sociability, 493, 497**
Social anxiety disorder, 651–652

Social behavior, 734, 758–759
  altruism as, 776–781
  in groups, 764–768
  in relationships, 759–763
Social categorization theory, 750, 752–753
**Social causation, 665**–666
**Social cognition,** 510–512, **734**–758
**Social cognitive neuroscience, 745**–746
Social comparison theory, 769
Social compensation, 776
**Social desirability, 494**–495, 740
Social desirability bias, 740
Social deviance, 493, 501–506
Social drift, 665–666
Social environments, 7
**Social exchange theory, 763**
**Social facilitation, 776**
Social identity theory, 750, 751
Social learning theory, 269–270, 753
Social liberation, 607
**Social loafing, 775**–776
Social organization, 764–768
**Social phobia, 651**–652, 724, 725
Social psychologist, 24, 25, 26
**Social psychology, 734,** 781–782
Social role theory, 515–516
**Social selection, 665**–666
**Social support, 619**–621, 769–770
**Social worker, 23**
**Sociocognitive theory, 212,** 510–512
Sociocultural theory, 553–554
Socioemotional selectivity theory, 578
**Somasthetic senses, 179**–181
Somatic marker hypothesis, 433
**Somatosensory strip, 95**–96, 96f
Soprano, Tony, 648
*Sorrows of Young Werther, The,* 566
Sound waves, 166–167
Sounds, 170–173
  place coding and, 168f
**Source amnesia, 310,** 572
Space, 153–154, 159–160
Spatial extent, 349, 351
Spatial intelligence, 393, 409
Spatial relations, 153f, 153–155
Spearman's g factor, 386–387, 394t
Spears, Britney, 152
Special Theory of Relativity, 326, 347
**Specific factor, 716**
Specific factor (*s*), 386
**Specific language impairment, 342**
Specific mental abilities, 388–390, 574
**Specific phobia, 651**–652, 725
  subtypes of, 651t
Speech
  brain and, 97, 98–99
  child-directed, 42, 336
  disorganized, 660
  private, 554
**Speech-segmentation problem, 170**
Spelke, Elizabeth, 27
Sperm, 530–532
Spielberg, Arnold, 529–530
Spielberg, Steven, 529–530, 537, 541, 542, 556, 562, 568–569, 575, 576

Spina bifida, 535
Spinal column, 90–91
**Spinal cord, 90–91**
Spirit possession, 632
**Split-brain patient, 97–99,** 99f
Spock (Mr.), 371–372
**Spontaneous recovery, 240,** 240f, **259**
Sport psychologist, 25–26
Spurzheim, J. G., 92
SSNS, 89, 90
SSRIs, 85, 703, 704, 705
**St. John's wort, 703,** 705
**Standard deviation, 58**
**Standardized sample, 383**
Stanford Prison Experiment, 767–768
Stanford-Binet Revision of Binet-Simon Test, 381
**State-dependent retrieval, 305**
Static cues, 148–149
**Statistical significance, 59**
Statistics, 54–66
    descriptive, 55–58
    inferential, 58–61
**Status hierarchy, 766–768**
Stepping reflex, 539t
**Stereotype, 746, 747–750**
Stern, Robert, 760
Stern, William, 383
Sternberg's triangular model of love, 760, 760f
Sternberg's triarchic theory of intelligence, 393–395, 394t
**Stimulants, 219, 224–226,** 470–472
    reuptake of neurotransmitters and, 225f
Stimulus
    cognitive appraisal of, 593f
    conditioned, 236–237, 238–239
    discriminative, 259
    neutral, 238
**Stimulus control, 694**
**Stimulus discrimination, 241**
**Stimulus generalization, 240–241**
Stirrup, 167
STM, 280–281, 282–283
**Storage, 278,** 281–283, 290–300
Strange Situation, 555–556
**Strategy, 358,** 742–743
Stream of consciousness, 190
Stress, 588–589
    arteries and, 604f
    biology of, 589–592
    coping with, 609–615
    depression in teenagers and, 645f
    disease and, 601–608
    hormones and, 664
    memories and, 298, 412
    neuroendocrine system and, 104–105
    neuroimmune system and, 105
    prenatal development and, 535
    sources of, 595–600, 613
**Stress response, 588–589**
**Stressor(s), 588–589**
    acute, 588–589
    chronic, 588–589, 604–605
    perception of, 592–595

types of, 589t
    work-related, 597–599
**Stroke, 109,** 117, 201–202
Stroop color naming task, 160, 210, 361, 362
Stroop effect, 160
**Structuralism, 11–12,** 20t
Structural memory, 284–285
*Sturm und Drang,* 566–567
**Subcortical structures,** 92, 100f, 100–104. *See also specific structures*
Subincision, 592
Subliminal perception, 160–161
    demonstration of, 161f
**Substance abuse, 218–219,** 244–245
**Substance dependence, 219**
    symptoms of, 218t
Substance P, 644, 703
**Successive approximations, 260**
Sucking reflex, 539t
Sugar Busters! diet, 465t
Suicide, 641, 703
    misconceptions about, 641t
**Sulcus,** 92, 93
Sultan the chimp, 268–269
**Superego, 483,** 687
Superfactors, 492t, 492–493
Superior colliculus, 181
Supertasters, 178
Support groups, 709–710
**Suprachiasmatic nucleus (SCN), 203,** 204f, 208
Surrealist painting, 133
**Survey, 43–44,** 48t
Survival of the fittest, 124
"Sweet" test, 307f, 308f
Swimming reflex, 539t
SWS, 194, 195
*Sybil,* 43, 669
**Sympathetic nervous system, 89–90**
**Synapse,** 82, 82f
**Synaptic cleft, 82**
Synesthesia, 152f
Syntactic analysis, 328f
**Syntax, 328–329,** 330
**Systematic desensitization, 245,** 694–695
    of elevator phobia, 695f
**Systems therapy, 708–709**

T cell, 602
Taft, William Howard, 463
Takara Company, 327
**Tardive dyskinesia, 702**
Tarzan, 341
Task analysis, 390
Taste, 177–179
Taste aversion, 245–248, 249, 461
    conditioning of, 246f
**Taste buds, 177**
    location of, 177f
TAT, 496
TCAs, 703, 704, 705
Tea, and memory, 313
**Technical eclecticism, 710**
Teenagers. *See* Adolescence; Puberty

Tegretol, 704
**Telegraphic speech, 339**
Telepathy, 53, 182
Television, and modeling, 272–273
**Temperament, 497–499,** 538–540
**Temporal lobe,** 91, 92, **95**
"Tend and befriend" response, 592
**Teratogen(s), 534–536**
    vulnerability of different organs to, 536f
Terman, Lewis, 381
**Terminal button(s), 79,** 80
Terminal decline, 571
Terminals, 79
Test anxiety, 406
**Test bias, 406**
**Testosterone, 104,** 468–470, 473
Tetrahydrocannibinol (THC), 227
*Tetris,* 200
**Texture gradient, 148**
**Thalamus, 100–101**
**Thematic Apperception Test (TAT), 496**
Thematic relations, 355
**Theory, 40–41**
**Theory of causal attribution, 756**
**Theory of mind, 551–552**
**Theory of multiple intelligences, 392–393**
Theory theory, 551
Therapy protocols, 711–712
Thorazine, 702
Thorndike, Edward Lee, 15
Thorndike's puzzle box, 251, 251f
Thought-action fusion, 654
**Thought suppression, 612**
*Three Faces of Eve, The,* 43, 669
Three Mile Island, 204
Three-stratum theory of intelligence, 388–389
**Threshold, 136,** 166
**Tinnitus, 169**
Tip-of-the-tongue phenomenon, 302
Titchener, Edward, 11
TMS, 114, 115, 706
**Token economy, 696**
Tokens, 257
**Tolerance, 219**
Tolman and Honzik's discovery of latent learning, 268f
Tonic neck reflex, 539t
**Tonotopic organization, 168**
Tooby, John, 19
**Top-down processing, 152–153,** 158, 181, 736–737
Topographically organized areas, 351
Touch, 180
**Trace conditioning, 236,** 243
**Trance logic, 210**
Trance state, 210
Trance theory, 212
Transcranial magnetic stimulation (TMS), 114, 115, 706
Transduction, 138
Transfer appropriate processing, 287
Transference, 688, 690
Transvestic fetishism, 475

Transvestism, 475
Traumatic events, and rates of PTSD, 656t
Treatment as usual control group, 718
Treisman, Anne, 27
Trial-and-error learning, 251
**Triangular model of love, 760**
Triarchic Theory of Successful Intelligence, 393–395
**Trichromatic theory of color vision, 141**
**Tricyclic antidepressant (TCA), 703,** 704, 705
Trimesters, 532
True pessimism, 617
Truth-win rule, 774
Twain, Mark, 54
**Twin studies, 122–123**
    on attachment styles, 523
    on body language, 443
    on brain similarity, 401f
    on cerebral cortex, 123
    on depression, 643–644
    on eating disorders, 672
    on intelligence, 399–401, 402–403
    on pain thresholds, 181
    on personality, 504–507
    on phobias, 652
    on romantic relationships, 761
    on temperament, 498, 540
Twins, 123, 402f. *See also* Fraternal twins; Identical twins
*Two Fridas, The,* 133
Tympanic membrane, 167
Type A personality, 600
**Typicality, 352**
Tyramine, 703

Ultimatum game, 372–374
Umami, 178
**Unconditional positive regard, 488,** 689–690
**Unconditioned response (UR), 236,** 243, 245, 246, 249
**Unconditioned stimulus (US), 236–237,** 238–240, 241–242, 243, 245, 246, 248, 249
**Unconscious, 14,** 482–483
**Underextension, 337–338,** 338f
Undifferentiated schizophrenia, 661
Unilateral visual neglect, 96
Universal preventive interventions, 713
User expectations, 220, 227

Valence focus, 445–446
**Validation, 708**
**Validity, 49–51,** 50t, 384
Valium, 704
van Gogh, Vincent, 629–630, 631, 632, 638, 647, 648, 650–651, 659, 661, 662, 666, 667, 670, 675, 680
Variability, 58, 122, 123
**Variable(s), 39,** 45–46, 46f, 55–56
    confounding, 46, 47f, 718–719
**Variable interval schedules, 261**
**Variable ratio schedules, 262**
Venting, 611–612

Ventricles, 92
Verbal codes, 284
Vesicles, 84
**Vestibular sense, 180**
Viagra, 475
Victor, the Wild Boy of Aveyron, 341
Vigilance, 158
Vigilance-related avoidance strategies, 457
Violence
    modeling of, 270, 272t, 272–273
    workplace, 599
Virtual reality exposure, 693
Vision. *See also* Visual perception; Visual sensation
    brain and, 94–95, 96, 97–98, 138–140, 151–153
    color, 140–143
    difficulties with, 95f, 143–144, 144f
    receptors in, 134. *See also* Cones; Rods
Visual cliff experiment, 543
Visual codes, 284
Visual illusions, 135f
Visual mental images, 349f
Visual-motor tasks, 196
Visual neglect, unilateral, 96
Visual perception, 134, 144–155, 543–545

Visual pathways, 151f
Visual sensation, 134, 135–137
Visuospatial sketchpad, 281
von Goethe, Johann Wolfgang, 566
von Helmholtz, Hermann, 140–141
von Restorf effect, 289–290
Voodoo death, 624–625
Vygotsky's sociocultural theory, 553–554

WAIS. *See* Wechsler Adult Intelligence Scale
Wait-list control group, 715, 717–718
Waking consciousness, 191
Walker, Wesley, 149
Walter, K., 112
**Want(s), 454,** 455
    versus needs, 455f
Washburn, Margaret Floy, 11, 27
Washington, George, and sleep, 206
Wason and Johnson-Laird's card task, 368f
Watson, John B., 15, 245
**Wavelength, 137**
Wave model, 553
**Weber's law, 136**
**Wechsler Adult Intelligence Scale (WAIS), 381**–382, 383–384, 386, 399

normal curve and scores on, 384f
    subtests of, 382t
Wechsler Intelligence Scale for Children (WISC), 381
Weight Watchers, 465t
**Wernicke's aphasia, 329**
Wernicke's area, 329, 345
Wertheimer, Max, 13
What pathway, 151–153, 156
*Wheel of Fortune* experience, 360
*When Harry Met Sally,* 461
Where pathway, 151, 153–154, 156, 157
White matter, 92
"White Rabbit," 227
*Who Am I?,* 233
Wilder, Thornton, 615
"Wind overload," 650
WISC, 381
*Wisdom of the Body, The,* 450–451
Wish fulfillment, 200–201
Withdrawal emotions, 431–432
Withdrawal reflex, 539t
**Withdrawal symptoms, 219**
Within-group differences, versus between group differences, 405f
Witnesses, to crimes, 319
WM, 280–281

Women in psychology, 27–28
Woods, Tiger, 3, 4, 10, 16, 26
Words, use of, 318, 347–348
**Working memory (WM), 280–281**
    development of, 552–553
    intelligence and, 397–399
    parts of, 281f
Working model, of relationships, 521
Work-related stressors, 597–599
Worth, conditions of, 488
Wundt, Wilhelm, 11, 12
Wurtzel, Elizabeth, 639

Xanax, 704

Yates, Andrea, 631
Yerkes-Dodson law, 451
Yoda, 330
Young, Cy, 420
Young, Thomas, 140–141

*Zar,* 632
Zeitgebers, 208
Zellweger, Renee, 668
Zoloft, 703
**Zygote, 531**–537

# CREDITS

## Source Notes

**Figure 1.2, p. 27:** National Science Foundation (2001).

**Figure 1.3, p. 27:** National Science Foundation (2001).

**Table 1.3, p. 31:** APA (2002).

**Figure 2.7, p. 62:** From Kosslyn, 1994a, pp. 209 and 211. Data for illustration on left from Natural Resources Defense Council.

**Figure 2.8, p. 63:** From Kosslyn, 1994a, pp. 209 and 211. Data for illustration on left from Natural Resources Defense Council.

**Figure 2.9, p. 63:** From Kosslyn, 1994a, p. 227. Data from Hacker, 1992, p. 98, cited in *Newsweek*, 23 March 1992, p. 61.

**Figure 2.10, p. 64:** From Kosslyn, 1994a, p. 219. Data from Morgan Stanley Capital International, cited in *The Economist World Atlas and Almanac*, 1989, p. 90.

**Figure 2.11, p. 64:** From Kosslyn, 1994a, p. 225. Data from Weisberg, 1980, cited in Chambers et al., 1983, p. 371.

**Figure 3.1, p. 79:** From Dowling, 1992.

**Figure 3.6, p. 85:** Adapted from *Psychology: Themes and Variations* (with InfoTrac), 5th edition, by Weiten. © 2001. Reprinted with permission from Wadsworth, a division of Thomson Learning: www.thomsonrights.com.

**Figure 3.13, p. 96:** From Bisiach et al., 1981.

**Figure 4.22, p. 160:** From *Psychology* by Peter Gray. © 1991, 1994, 2002 by Worth Publishers. Used with permission.

**Figure 5.2, p. 195:** Walker & Stickgold, 2004, Figure 1A

**Figure 5.3, p. 195:** Reprinted with permission from H. P. Roffwarg, J. N. Muzio, and W. C. Dement, "Ontogenic development of human sleep–dream cycle," *Science*, 152, 604–619. Copyright 1966 American Association for the Advancement of Science.

**Figure 5.5, p. 203:** hprct.dom.com/2001/presentations/hursh/sld009.htm

**Table 5.3, p. 208:** Herxheimer & Waterhouse, 2003; Van Cauter & Turek, 2000.

**Table 5.4, p. 218:** American Psychiatric Association (2000). Reprinted with permission from the *Diagnostic and Statistical Manual of Mental Disorders*, Fourth Edition, Text Revision. Copyright © 2000 American Psychiatric Association.

**Figure 6.3, p. 237:** (Delayed, Trace, and Simultaneous) From *Psychology: Themes and Variations* (with InfoTrac), 5th edition, by Weiten. © 2001. Reprinted with permission from Wadsworth, a division of Thomson Learning: www.thomsonrights.com. Fax: 800 730-2215. (Backward) From *Psychology*, 3rd edition, by Saul Kassin © 2000. Adapted by permission of Pearson Education, Inc., Upper Saddle River, NJ.

**Figure 7.4, p. 281:** Adapted from *Working Memory* by Alan Baddeley, Clarendon Press (1986). Reprinted by permission of Oxford University Press.

**Figure 7.9, p. 292:** Adapted from Lindsay & Norman, 1977.

**Figure 7.11, p. 295:** Reprinted with permission from L. R. Squire and S. Zola-Morgan, "The medial temporal lobe memory system," in *Science*, 253, 1380–1386. Copyright 1992 American Association for the Advancement of Science.

**Figure 7.12, p. 304:** Adapted from Barclay et al., 1974.

**Table 7.1, p. 295:** Based on Schneider and Chein (2003)

**Figure 8.9, p. 350:** Reprinted with permission from R. N. Shephard and J. Metzler, "Mental rotation of three dimensional objects," *Science*, 171, 701–703. Copyright 1971 American Association for the Advancement of Science.

**Figure 8.16, p. 367:** Adapted from Johnson-Laird, 2001, p. 441.

**Table 8.2, p. 363:** Based on Mayer (1997).

**Figure 9.2, p. 389:** From Deary (2000), p. 15.

**Figure 9.4, p. 400:** From Plomin and Spinath (2004).

**Table 9.1, p. 382:** Actual WAIS test items cannot be published; part of the table was adapted from Gardner et al., 1996, pp. 80–81.

**Table 9.2, p. 388:** Adapted from information on the website of the Institute for Applied Psychometrics at www.iapsych.com

**Table 9.3, p. 391:** Adapted from Mayer, Salovey, Caruso, & Sitarenios (2001, Table 2, p. 235).

**Table 9.7, p. 416:** From http://thearc.org/faqs/mrqa.html

**Table 9.9, p. 422:** Computer programmed by Goldenberg and colleagues (1999); examples from Angier (1999).

**Figure 10.2, p. 432:** From Lester A. Lefton, *Psychology*, 7th edition. Published by Allyn and Bacon, Boston, MA. © 2000 by Pearson Education. Reprinted by permission of the publisher.

**Figure 10.10, p. 474:** From "Human male sexuality: Appetite, arousal, desire and drive" by R. J. Levin, in *Appetite, Neural and Behavioral Bases* edited by Charles R. Legg and David Booth (1994). Reprinted by permission of Oxford University Press.

**Table 10.1, p. 447:** Based on DePaulo, Stone and Lassiter, 1985; DePaulo et al. (2003); Ekman (1985); Zuckerman et al. (1981).

**Table 10.2, p. 465:** Adapted from Freedman, King & Kennedy (2001).

**Figure 11.4, p. 506:** Data for Big Five superfactors, psychological interests and social attitudes from Bouchard, 2004. Data for Eysenck's three dimensions of personality—extraversion and neuroticism from Pederson et al., 1988; psychoticism from Heath & Martin, 1990.

**Figure 11.5, p. 510:** Adapted from Mischel & Shoda, 1995, p. 262.

**Figure 11.7, p. 519:** Data from Vandello & Cohen, 1999.

**Table 11.2, p. 485:** From Freud (1933/1965), p. 70.

**Table 11.3, p. 488:** From Maslow (1968).

**Table 11.4, p. 492:** Adapted from Costa, McCrae, & Dye (1991).

**Table 11.5, p. 500:** From Torrubia, 2001.

**Table 11.6, p. 503:** Cloninger & Zuckerman, 1996; Ebstein et al., 2002; Gomez & Gomez, 2005; Zuckerman, Joireman, et al., 1999; Zuckerman & Kuhlman, 2000.

**Table 11.7, p. 505:** Adapted from Loehlin (1992).

**Table 11.9, p. 520:** Percentages of three attachment styles in second column from Michelson et al. (1997); first-person descriptions in third column from Lopez (2003, p. 288).

**Table 11.10, p. 521:** First-person descriptions from Bartholomew & Horowitz (1991).

**Figure 12.2, p. 536:** Adapted from Moore (1998).

**Figure 12.3, p. 542:** Based on LaRossa (2000).

**Figure 13.1, p. 589:** From Selye, Hans (1978). *The Stress of Life*, Second Edition. Copyright 1976. Reprinted by permission of The McGraw-Hill Companies.

**Figure 13.7, p. 606:** Adapted from Prochaska, Norcross, et al., 1994, p. 49.

**Figure 13.8, p. 614:** Adapted from Berkowitz, 1998, p. 50.

**Figure 13.9, p. 625:** Benedetti et al., 2003.

**Table 13.2, p. 610:** Adapted from Carver et al. (1989).

**Figure 14.3, p. 645:** Lewinsohn et al., 1999, Table 1.

**Figure 14.5, p. 671:** Adapted from Thompson (1990, p. 11). From Thompson, J. K. (1990). *Body Image Disturbance: Assessment and Treatment*. Copyright 1990 by Pergamon Press. Reprinted by permission of The McGraw-Hill Companies.

**Figure 14.6, p. 673:** Jansen et al., 2005, p. 190.

**Table 14.1, p. 636:** Adapted from American Psychiatric Association (2000). Reprinted with permission from the *Diagnostic and Statistical Manual of Mental Disorders*, Fourth Edition, Text Revision. Copyright 2000 American Psychiatric Association.

**Table 14.2, p. 639:** Adapted from American Psychiatric Association (2000). Reprinted with permission from the *Diagnostic and Statistical Manual of Mental Disorders*, Fourth Edition, Text Revision. Copyright 2000 American Psychiatric Association.

**Table 14.3, p. 641:** Adapted from Suicide Awareness\Voices of Education (SA\VE), PO Box 24507, Minneapolis, MN 55424; Phone: (612) 946-7998; Internet: http://www.save.org; E-mail: save@winternet.com.

**Table 14.4, p. 643:** Adapted from American Psychiatric Association (2000). Reprinted with permission from the *Diagnostic and Statistical Manual of Mental Disorders*, Fourth Edition, Text Revision. Copyright 2000 American Psychiatric Association.

**Table 14.5, p. 651:** Adapted from American Psychiatric Association (2000). Reprinted with permission from the *Diagnostic and Statistical Manual of Mental Disorders*, Fourth Edition, Text Revision. Copyright 2000 American Psychiatric Association.

**Table 14.6, p. 656:** Data on rape, molestation, physical assault, accident, natural disaster, combat, and any traumatic event (upper row) from Kessler et al. (1995); data on witnessed death or injury, learned about traumatic event, sudden death of loved one, and any traumatic event from Breslau et al. (1998, 1999).

**Table 14.8, p. 661:** Adapted from American Psychiatric Association (2000). Reprinted with permission from the *Diagnostic and Statistical Manual of Mental Disorders*, Fourth Edition, Text Revision. Copyright 2000 American Psychiatric Association.

**Table 14.9, p. 676:** Adapted from American Psychiatric Association (2000). Reprinted with permission from the *Diagnostic and Statistical Manual of Mental Disorders*, Fourth Edition, Text Revision. Copyright 2000 American Psychiatric Association.

**Figure 15.1, p. 694:** From Barlow & Craske (2000), *Mastery of anxiety and panic* (3rd ed.), p. 151.

**Figure 15.5, p. 700:** Format adapted from Beck et al., 1979.

**Figure 15.6, p. 708:** From Minuchin, 1974, pp. 53, 61. Adapted and reprinted by permission of the publisher from *Families and Family Therapy* by Salvador Minuchin. Cambridge, Mass.: Harvard University Press, Copyright © 1974 by the President and Fellows of Harvard College.

**Figure 15.8, p. 713:** Adapted from Feldner et al., 2004, p. 407.

**Figure 15.10, p. 728:** Schwartz, *Archives of General Psychiatry*, Volume 53(2), February 1996. 109–113.

**Table 15.2, p. 698:** Adapted from Beck (1967).

Table 15.5, p. 717: Lambert & Ogles, 2004, p. 173.

Table 15.7, p. 722: Kendall et al., 2004, p. 18.

Table 15.8, p. 725: Roth & Fonagy, 2005, pp. 481–484.

Figure 16.2, p. 742: Festinger & Carlsmith, 1959.

Figure 16.9, p. 779: Darley and Latané (1970).

Table 16.2, p. 766: Reprinted from Perkins and Berkowitz, "Perceiving the community norms of alcohol use among students," *International Journal of the Addictions*, 21, Sept/Oct 1986, pp. 961–974, by courtesy of Marcel Dekker, Inc.

## Text and Illustration Credits

Table 1.3, p. 31: Direct quotes with portions abridged; a complete description can be found at http://www.apa.org/ethics/code2002.html. Copyright © 2002 by the American Psychological Association. Adapted with permission.

Figure 2.2, p. 45: From *Introduction to the Practice of Statistics* by David S. Moore and George P. McCabe. © 1989, 1993, 1999 by W. H. Freeman and Company. Used with permission.

Figure 3.1, p. 79: Figure from Dowling, J. E. (1992). *Neurons and Networks: An Introduction to Neuroscience*. Reprinted by permission of Cajal Institute, CSIC, Madrid, Spain.

Figure 3.6, p. 85: Adapted from *Psychology: Themes and Variations* (with InfoTrac), 5th edition, by Weiten. © 2001. Reprinted with permission from Wadsworth, a division of Thomson Learning: www.thomsonrights.com. Fax: 800 730-2215.

Figure 3.13, p. 96: From Bisiach et al., "Brain and conscious representations of outside reality," *Neuropsychologica*, Vol. 19. Copyright 1981, with permission from Elsevier Science.

Figure 3.15, p. 99: From Gazzaniga, M. S., and LeDoux, J. E., *The Integrated Mind*. New York: Plenum Press, 1978. Reprinted with permission.

Figure 3.23, p. 117: Adapted from *Introduction to Psychology*, 3rd edition, by Kalat. © 1993. Reprinted with permission from Wadsworth, a division of Thomson Learning: www.thomsonrights.com. Fax: 800 730-2215.

Figure 4.5, p. 139: From Dowling, J. E., and Boycott, B. B., "Organization of the primate retina: Electron microscopy" (1966). *Proceedings of the Royal Society* (London), B166, 80–111, Figure 7. Reprinted by permission.

Figure 4.22, p. 160: From *Psychology* by Peter Gray. © 1991, 1994, 2002 by Worth Publishers. Used with permission.

Figure 5.2, p. 195: From *Sleep* by J. Allan Hobson. Copyright 1989 by J. Allan Hobson, M.D. Reprinted by permission of Henry Holt and Company, LLC.

Figure 5.3, p. 195: Reprinted with permission from H. P. Roffwarg, J. N. Muzio, and W. C. Dement, "Ontogenic development of human sleep-dream cycle," *Science*, 152, 604–619. Copyright 1966 American Association for the Advancement of Science.

Table 5.4, p. 218: Reprinted with permission from the *Diagnostic and Statistical Manual of Mental Disorders*, Fourth Edition, Text Revision. Copyright © 2000 American Psychiatric Association.

Figure 6.3 (Delayed, Trace, and Simultaneous), p. 237: From *Psychology: Themes and Variations* (with InfoTrac), 5th edition, by Weiten. © 2001. Reprinted with permission from Wadsworth, a division of Thomson Learning: www.thomsonrights.com. Fax: 800 730-2215.

Figure 6.3 (Backward), p. 237: From *Psychology*, 3/e, by Kassin, Saul, © 2000. Adapted by permission of Pearson Education, Inc., Upper Saddle River, NJ.

Figure 6.15, p. 262: Figure from "Teaching machines" by B. F. Skinner, *Scientific American*, 1961. Reprinted by permission of the estate of Mary E. and Dan Todd.

Figure 7.4, p. 281: From *Working Memory* by Alan Baddeley, Clarendon Press (1986). Reprinted by permission of Oxford University Press.

Figure 7.5, p. 283: Figure adapted by Glanzer, M., and Cunitz, A. R., "Two storage mechanisms in free recall," *Journal of Verbal Learning and Verbal Behavior*, 5, 351–360, 1996. Reprinted by permission of the author.

Figure 7.8, p. 288: From G. H. Bower et al., "Hierarchical retrieval schemes in recall of categorized word lists," *Journal of Verbal Learning and Behavior*, Vol. 8, 323–343. Copyright 1969, with permission from Elsevier Science.

Figure 7.9, p. 292: From Peter H. Lindsay and Donald A. Norman, *Human Information Processing: An Introduction to Psychology*, 2/e. Academic Press, 1977. Reprinted by permission of Donald A. Norman.

Figure 7.11, p. 295: Reprinted with permission from L. R. Squire and S. Zola-Morgan, "The medical temporal lobe memory system," in *Science*, 253, 1380–1386. Copyright 1992 American Association for the Advancement of Science.

Figure 8.5, p. 337: Figure from Reznick, J. S., and Goldfield, B. A., "Rapid change in lexical development in comprehension and production," *Developmental Psychology*, 28, 406–413. Copyright © 1992 by the American Psychological Association. Reprinted with permission.

Figure 8.8, p. 349: From Kosslyn, S. M., Ball, T. M., and Reiser, B. J., "Visual images preserved metric spatial information: Evidence from studies of image scanning," *Journal of Experimental Psychology: Human Perception and Performance, 4*, 47–60. Copyright © 1978 by the American Psychological Association. Reprinted with permission.

Figure 8.9, p. 350: Reprinted with permission from R. N. Shephard and J. Metzler, "Mental rotation of three-dimensional objects," *Science, 171*, 701–703. Copyright 1971 American Association for the Advancement of Science.

Figure 8.15, p. 360: From *Cognition: Exploring the Science of the Mind* by Daniel Reisberg. Copyright © 1997 by W. W. Norton & Company, Inc. Used by permission of W. W. Norton & Company, Inc.

Figure 8.16, p. 367: From P. N. Johnson-Laird, "Mental models and deduction," *Trends in Cognitive Sciences*, Vol. 5, 434–443. Copyright 2001, with permission from Elsevier Science.

Figure 9.3, p. 398: From V. Prabhakaran et al., "Neural substrates of fluid reasoning: An fMRI study of the neocortical activation during performance of the Raven's Progressive Matrices Test," *Cognitive Psychology*, Vol. 33, 43–63. Copyright 1997, with permission from Elsevier Science.

Figure 9.4, p. 400: Adapted from *Behavioral Genetics* by R. Plomin, J. C. DeFries, G. E. McClearn, and M. Rutter. © 1980, 1990, 1997, 2001 by Worth Publishers. Used with permission.

Figure 9.8, p. 418: From Finke, R. A., and Slayton, K. (1988), "Explorations of creative visual synthesis in mental imagery," *Memory and Cognition, 16*, 252–257. Reprinted by permission.

Figure 10.2, p. 432: From Lester A. Lefton, *Psychology*, 7/e. Published by Allyn and Bacon, Boston, MA. © 2000 by Pearson Education. Reprinted by permission of the publisher.

Figure 10.9, p. 471: Figure from Cooper, M. L., Shapiro, C. M., and Powers, A. M., "Motivations for sex and risky behavior among adolescents and young adults: A functional perspective," *Journal of Personality and Social Psychology*, 75, 1528–1558. Copyright © 1998 by the American Psychological Association. Reprinted with permission.

Figure 10.10, p. 474: From "Human male sexuality: Appetite, arousal, desire and drive" by R. J. Levin, in *Appetite: Neural and Behavioral Bases* edited by Charles R. Legg and David Booth (1994). Reprinted by permission of Oxford University Press.

Figure 11.1, p. 483: From Lester A. Lefton, *Psychology*, 8/e. Published by Allyn and Bacon, Boston, MA. © 2003 by Pearson Education. Reprinted by permission of the publisher.

Figure 11.2, p. 492: Adapted from Cattell, Eber, and Tatsuoka. Copyright © 1970 by the Institute for Personality and Ability Testing, Inc. Reproduced by permission. "16PF" is a trademark belonging to IPAT, Inc.

Figure 11.7, p. 519: Figure from Vandello, J. A., and Cohen, D. (1999), "Patterns of individualism and collectivism across the United States," *Journal of Personality and Social Psychology*, 77, 279–292. Copyright © 1999 by the American Psychological Association. Reprinted with permission.

Figure 12.6, p. 551: Figure from Baillargeon, Renee (1994), "How do infants learn about the physical world?" *Current Directions in Psychological Science*, 3(5), 133–140. Reprinted by permission of Blackwell Publishers.

Figure 13.1, p. 589: From Selye, Hans (1978). *The Stress of Life*, Second Edition. Copyright 1976. Reprinted by permission of The McGraw-Hill Companies.

Figure 13.7, p. 606: Figure from *Changing for Good* by James O. Prochaska, John C. Norcross, and Carlo C. Diclemente. Copyright © 1994 by James O. Prochaska, John C. Norcross, and Carlo C. Diclemente. Reprinted with permission of HarperCollins Publishers, Inc.

Table 14.1, p. 636; Table 14.2, p. 639; Table 14.4, p. 643; Table 14.5, p. 651; Table 14.8, p. 661; Table 14.9, p. 676: Reprinted with permission from the *Diagnostic and Statistical Manual of Mental Disorders*, Fourth Edition, Text Revision. Copyright 2000 American Psychiatric Association.

Figure 14.5, p. 67: From Thompson, J. K. (1990). *Body Image Disturbance: Assessment and Treatment*. Copyright 1990 by Pergamon Press. Reprinted by permission of The McGraw-Hill Companies.

Figure 15.6, p. 708: Adapted and reprinted by permission of the publisher from *Families and Family Therapy* by Salvador Minuchin, pp. 53, 61, Cambridge, Mass.: Harvard University Press, Copyright © 1974 by the President and Fellows of Harvard College.

Figure 16.5, p. 760: Sternberg's Triangular Theory of Love. Reprinted by permission of Robert Sternberg.

Table 16.2, p. 766: Reprinted from Perkins and Berkowitz, "Perceiving the community norms of alcohol use among students," *International Journal of the Addictions*, 21, Sept/Oct 1986, pp. 961–974, by courtesy of Marcel Dekker, Inc.

# Photo and Cartoon Credits